# Oxford Dictionary of
# National Biography

*Volume 13*

# Oxford Dictionary of National Biography

IN ASSOCIATION WITH
## The British Academy

*From the earliest times to the year* 2000

*Edited by*
H. C. G. Matthew
*and*
Brian Harrison

*Volume 13*
Constable–Crane

**OXFORD**
UNIVERSITY PRESS

# OXFORD
## UNIVERSITY PRESS

Great Clarendon Street, Oxford OX2 6DP

Oxford University Press is a department of the University of Oxford.
It furthers the University's objective of excellence in research, scholarship,
and education by publishing worldwide in

Oxford New York

Auckland Bangkok Buenos Aires Cape Town
Chennai Dar es Salaam Delhi Hong Kong Istanbul Karachi
Kolkata Kuala Lumpur Madrid Melbourne Mexico City Mumbai Nairobi
São Paulo Shanghai Taipei Tokyo Toronto

Oxford is a registered trade mark of Oxford University Press
in the UK and in certain other countries

Published in the United States
by Oxford University Press Inc., New York

British Library Cataloguing in Publication Data
Data available

Library of Congress Cataloging in Publication Data
Data available: for details see volume 1, p. iv

ISBN 0-19-861363-6 (this volume)
ISBN 0-19-861411-X (set of sixty volumes)

Text captured by Alliance Phototypesetters, Pondicherry
Illustrations reproduced and archived by
Alliance Graphics Ltd, UK
Typeset in OUP Swift by Interactive Sciences Limited, Gloucester
Printed in Great Britain on acid-free paper by
Butler and Tanner Ltd,
Frome, Somerset

# LIST OF ABBREVIATIONS

## 1 *General abbreviations*

| | |
|---|---|
| AB | bachelor of arts |
| ABC | Australian Broadcasting Corporation |
| ABC TV | ABC Television |
| *act.* | active |
| A$ | Australian dollar |
| AD | *anno domini* |
| AFC | Air Force Cross |
| AIDS | acquired immune deficiency syndrome |
| AK | Alaska |
| AL | Alabama |
| A level | advanced level [examination] |
| ALS | associate of the Linnean Society |
| AM | master of arts |
| AMICE | associate member of the Institution of Civil Engineers |
| ANZAC | Australian and New Zealand Army Corps |
| appx *pl.* appxs | appendix(es) |
| AR | Arkansas |
| ARA | associate of the Royal Academy |
| ARCA | associate of the Royal College of Art |
| ARCM | associate of the Royal College of Music |
| ARCO | associate of the Royal College of Organists |
| ARIBA | associate of the Royal Institute of British Architects |
| ARP | air-raid precautions |
| ARRC | associate of the Royal Red Cross |
| ARSA | associate of the Royal Scottish Academy |
| art. | article / item |
| ASC | Army Service Corps |
| Asch | Austrian Schilling |
| ASDIC | Antisubmarine Detection Investigation Committee |
| ATS | Auxiliary Territorial Service |
| ATV | Associated Television |
| Aug | August |
| AZ | Arizona |
| *b.* | born |
| BA | bachelor of arts |
| BA (Admin.) | bachelor of arts (administration) |
| BAFTA | British Academy of Film and Television Arts |
| BAO | bachelor of arts in obstetrics |
| *bap.* | baptized |
| BBC | British Broadcasting Corporation / Company |
| BC | before Christ |
| BCE | before the common (*or* Christian) era |
| BCE | bachelor of civil engineering |
| BCG | bacillus of Calmette and Guérin [inoculation against tuberculosis] |
| BCh | bachelor of surgery |
| BChir | bachelor of surgery |
| BCL | bachelor of civil law |
| BCnL | bachelor of canon law |
| BCom | bachelor of commerce |
| BD | bachelor of divinity |
| BEd | bachelor of education |
| BEng | bachelor of engineering |
| bk *pl.* bks | book(s) |
| BL | bachelor of law / letters / literature |
| BLitt | bachelor of letters |
| BM | bachelor of medicine |
| BMus | bachelor of music |
| BP | before present |
| BP | British Petroleum |
| Bros. | Brothers |
| BS | (1) bachelor of science; (2) bachelor of surgery; (3) British standard |
| BSc | bachelor of science |
| BSc (Econ.) | bachelor of science (economics) |
| BSc (Eng.) | bachelor of science (engineering) |
| bt | baronet |
| BTh | bachelor of theology |
| *bur.* | buried |
| C. | command [identifier for published parliamentary papers] |
| *c.* | *circa* |
| c. | *capitulum pl. capitula*: chapter(s) |
| CA | California |
| Cantab. | Cantabrigiensis |
| cap. | *capitulum pl. capitula*: chapter(s) |
| CB | companion of the Bath |
| CBE | commander of the Order of the British Empire |
| CBS | Columbia Broadcasting System |
| cc | cubic centimetres |
| C$ | Canadian dollar |
| CD | compact disc |
| Cd | command [identifier for published parliamentary papers] |
| CE | Common (*or* Christian) Era |
| cent. | century |
| cf. | compare |
| CH | Companion of Honour |
| chap. | chapter |
| ChB | bachelor of surgery |
| CI | Imperial Order of the Crown of India |
| CIA | Central Intelligence Agency |
| CID | Criminal Investigation Department |
| CIE | companion of the Order of the Indian Empire |
| Cie | Compagnie |
| CLit | companion of literature |
| CM | master of surgery |
| cm | centimetre(s) |

| | |
|---|---|
| Cmd | command [identifier for published parliamentary papers] |
| CMG | companion of the Order of St Michael and St George |
| Cmnd | command [identifier for published parliamentary papers] |
| CO | Colorado |
| Co. | company |
| co. | county |
| col. *pl.* cols. | column(s) |
| Corp. | corporation |
| CSE | certificate of secondary education |
| CSI | companion of the Order of the Star of India |
| CT | Connecticut |
| CVO | commander of the Royal Victorian Order |
| cwt | hundredweight |
| $ | (American) dollar |
| *d.* | (1) penny (pence); (2) died |
| DBE | dame commander of the Order of the British Empire |
| DCH | diploma in child health |
| DCh | doctor of surgery |
| DCL | doctor of civil law |
| DCnL | doctor of canon law |
| DCVO | dame commander of the Royal Victorian Order |
| DD | doctor of divinity |
| DE | Delaware |
| Dec | December |
| dem. | demolished |
| DEng | doctor of engineering |
| des. | destroyed |
| DFC | Distinguished Flying Cross |
| DipEd | diploma in education |
| DipPsych | diploma in psychiatry |
| diss. | dissertation |
| DL | deputy lieutenant |
| DLitt | doctor of letters |
| DLittCelt | doctor of Celtic letters |
| DM | (1) Deutschmark; (2) doctor of medicine; (3) doctor of musical arts |
| DMus | doctor of music |
| DNA | dioxyribonucleic acid |
| doc. | document |
| DOL | doctor of oriental learning |
| DPH | diploma in public health |
| DPhil | doctor of philosophy |
| DPM | diploma in psychological medicine |
| DSC | Distinguished Service Cross |
| DSc | doctor of science |
| DSc (Econ.) | doctor of science (economics) |
| DSc (Eng.) | doctor of science (engineering) |
| DSM | Distinguished Service Medal |
| DSO | companion of the Distinguished Service Order |
| DSocSc | doctor of social science |
| DTech | doctor of technology |
| DTh | doctor of theology |
| DTM | diploma in tropical medicine |
| DTMH | diploma in tropical medicine and hygiene |
| DU | doctor of the university |
| DUniv | doctor of the university |
| dwt | pennyweight |
| EC | European Community |
| ed. *pl.* eds. | edited / edited by / editor(s) |
| Edin. | Edinburgh |
| edn | edition |
| EEC | European Economic Community |
| EFTA | European Free Trade Association |
| EICS | East India Company Service |
| EMI | Electrical and Musical Industries (Ltd) |
| Eng. | English |
| enl. | enlarged |
| ENSA | Entertainments National Service Association |
| ep. *pl.* epp. | *epistola(e)* |
| ESP | extra-sensory perception |
| esp. | especially |
| esq. | esquire |
| est. | estimate / estimated |
| EU | European Union |
| ex | sold by (*lit.* out of) |
| excl. | excludes / excluding |
| exh. | exhibited |
| exh. cat. | exhibition catalogue |
| f. *pl.* ff. | following [pages] |
| FA | Football Association |
| FACP | fellow of the American College of Physicians |
| facs. | facsimile |
| FANY | First Aid Nursing Yeomanry |
| FBA | fellow of the British Academy |
| FBI | Federation of British Industries |
| FCS | fellow of the Chemical Society |
| Feb | February |
| FEng | fellow of the Fellowship of Engineering |
| FFCM | fellow of the Faculty of Community Medicine |
| FGS | fellow of the Geological Society |
| fig. | figure |
| FIMechE | fellow of the Institution of Mechanical Engineers |
| FL | Florida |
| *fl.* | *floruit* |
| FLS | fellow of the Linnean Society |
| FM | frequency modulation |
| fol. *pl.* fols. | folio(s) |
| Fr | French francs |
| Fr. | French |
| FRAeS | fellow of the Royal Aeronautical Society |
| FRAI | fellow of the Royal Anthropological Institute |
| FRAM | fellow of the Royal Academy of Music |
| FRAS | (1) fellow of the Royal Asiatic Society; (2) fellow of the Royal Astronomical Society |
| FRCM | fellow of the Royal College of Music |
| FRCO | fellow of the Royal College of Organists |
| FRCOG | fellow of the Royal College of Obstetricians and Gynaecologists |
| FRCP(C) | fellow of the Royal College of Physicians of Canada |
| FRCP (Edin.) | fellow of the Royal College of Physicians of Edinburgh |
| FRCP (Lond.) | fellow of the Royal College of Physicians of London |
| FRCPath | fellow of the Royal College of Pathologists |
| FRCPsych | fellow of the Royal College of Psychiatrists |
| FRCS | fellow of the Royal College of Surgeons |
| FRGS | fellow of the Royal Geographical Society |
| FRIBA | fellow of the Royal Institute of British Architects |
| FRICS | fellow of the Royal Institute of Chartered Surveyors |
| FRS | fellow of the Royal Society |
| FRSA | fellow of the Royal Society of Arts |

| | | | | |
|---|---|---|---|---|
| FRSCM | fellow of the Royal School of Church Music | | ISO | companion of the Imperial Service Order |
| FRSE | fellow of the Royal Society of Edinburgh | | It. | Italian |
| FRSL | fellow of the Royal Society of Literature | | ITA | Independent Television Authority |
| FSA | fellow of the Society of Antiquaries | | ITV | Independent Television |
| ft | foot *pl.* feet | | Jan | January |
| FTCL | fellow of Trinity College of Music, London | | JP | justice of the peace |
| ft-lb per min. | foot-pounds per minute [unit of horsepower] | | jun. | junior |
| FZS | fellow of the Zoological Society | | KB | knight of the Order of the Bath |
| GA | Georgia | | KBE | knight commander of the Order of the British Empire |
| GBE | knight or dame grand cross of the Order of the British Empire | | KC | king's counsel |
| GCB | knight grand cross of the Order of the Bath | | kcal | kilocalorie |
| GCE | general certificate of education | | KCB | knight commander of the Order of the Bath |
| GCH | knight grand cross of the Royal Guelphic Order | | KCH | knight commander of the Royal Guelphic Order |
| GCHQ | government communications headquarters | | KCIE | knight commander of the Order of the Indian Empire |
| GCIE | knight grand commander of the Order of the Indian Empire | | KCMG | knight commander of the Order of St Michael and St George |
| GCMG | knight or dame grand cross of the Order of St Michael and St George | | KCSI | knight commander of the Order of the Star of India |
| GCSE | general certificate of secondary education | | KCVO | knight commander of the Royal Victorian Order |
| GCSI | knight grand commander of the Order of the Star of India | | keV | kilo-electron-volt |
| GCStJ | bailiff or dame grand cross of the order of St John of Jerusalem | | KG | knight of the Order of the Garter |
| GCVO | knight or dame grand cross of the Royal Victorian Order | | KGB | [Soviet committee of state security] |
| | | | KH | knight of the Royal Guelphic Order |
| GEC | General Electric Company | | KLM | Koninklijke Luchtvaart Maatschappij (Royal Dutch Air Lines) |
| Ger. | German | | km | kilometre(s) |
| GI | government (*or* general) issue | | KP | knight of the Order of St Patrick |
| GMT | Greenwich mean time | | KS | Kansas |
| GP | general practitioner | | KT | knight of the Order of the Thistle |
| GPU | [Soviet special police unit] | | kt | knight |
| GSO | general staff officer | | KY | Kentucky |
| Heb. | Hebrew | | £ | pound(s) sterling |
| HEICS | Honourable East India Company Service | | £E | Egyptian pound |
| HI | Hawaii | | L | lira *pl.* lire |
| HIV | human immunodeficiency virus | | l. *pl.* ll. | line(s) |
| HK$ | Hong Kong dollar | | LA | Lousiana |
| HM | his / her majesty('s) | | LAA | light anti-aircraft |
| HMAS | his / her majesty's Australian ship | | LAH | licentiate of the Apothecaries' Hall, Dublin |
| HMNZS | his / her majesty's New Zealand ship | | Lat. | Latin |
| HMS | his / her majesty's ship | | lb | pound(s), unit of weight |
| HMSO | His / Her Majesty's Stationery Office | | LDS | licence in dental surgery |
| HMV | His Master's Voice | | *lit.* | literally |
| Hon. | Honourable | | LittB | bachelor of letters |
| hp | horsepower | | LittD | doctor of letters |
| hr | hour(s) | | LKQCPI | licentiate of the King and Queen's College of Physicians, Ireland |
| HRH | his / her royal highness | | LLA | lady literate in arts |
| HTV | Harlech Television | | LLB | bachelor of laws |
| IA | Iowa | | LLD | doctor of laws |
| ibid. | *ibidem*: in the same place | | LLM | master of laws |
| ICI | Imperial Chemical Industries (Ltd) | | LM | licentiate in midwifery |
| ID | Idaho | | LP | long-playing record |
| IL | Illinois | | LRAM | licentiate of the Royal Academy of Music |
| illus. | illustration | | LRCP | licentiate of the Royal College of Physicians |
| illustr. | illustrated | | LRCPS (Glasgow) | licentiate of the Royal College of Physicians and Surgeons of Glasgow |
| IN | Indiana | | LRCS | licentiate of the Royal College of Surgeons |
| in. | inch(es) | | LSA | licentiate of the Society of Apothecaries |
| Inc. | Incorporated | | LSD | lysergic acid diethylamide |
| incl. | includes / including | | LVO | lieutenant of the Royal Victorian Order |
| IOU | I owe you | | M. *pl.* MM. | Monsieur *pl.* Messieurs |
| IQ | intelligence quotient | | m | metre(s) |
| Ir£ | Irish pound | | | |
| IRA | Irish Republican Army | | | |

| | |
|---|---|
| m. *pl.* mm. | membrane(s) |
| MA | (1) Massachusetts; (2) master of arts |
| MAI | master of engineering |
| MB | bachelor of medicine |
| MBA | master of business administration |
| MBE | member of the Order of the British Empire |
| MC | Military Cross |
| MCC | Marylebone Cricket Club |
| MCh | master of surgery |
| MChir | master of surgery |
| MCom | master of commerce |
| MD | (1) doctor of medicine; (2) Maryland |
| MDMA | methylenedioxymethamphetamine |
| ME | Maine |
| MEd | master of education |
| MEng | master of engineering |
| MEP | member of the European parliament |
| MG | Morris Garages |
| MGM | Metro-Goldwyn-Mayer |
| Mgr | Monsignor |
| MI | (1) Michigan; (2) military intelligence |
| MI1c | [secret intelligence department] |
| MI5 | [military intelligence department] |
| MI6 | [secret intelligence department] |
| MI9 | [secret escape service] |
| MICE | member of the Institution of Civil Engineers |
| MIEE | member of the Institution of Electrical Engineers |
| min. | minute(s) |
| Mk | mark |
| ML | (1) licentiate of medicine; (2) master of laws |
| MLitt | master of letters |
| Mlle | Mademoiselle |
| mm | millimetre(s) |
| Mme | Madame |
| MN | Minnesota |
| MO | Missouri |
| MOH | medical officer of health |
| MP | member of parliament |
| m.p.h. | miles per hour |
| MPhil | master of philosophy |
| MRCP | member of the Royal College of Physicians |
| MRCS | member of the Royal College of Surgeons |
| MRCVS | member of the Royal College of Veterinary Surgeons |
| MRIA | member of the Royal Irish Academy |
| MS | (1) master of science; (2) Mississippi |
| MS *pl.* MSS | manuscript(s) |
| MSc | master of science |
| MSc (Econ.) | master of science (economics) |
| MT | Montana |
| MusB | bachelor of music |
| MusBac | bachelor of music |
| MusD | doctor of music |
| MV | motor vessel |
| MVO | member of the Royal Victorian Order |
| n. *pl.* nn. | note(s) |
| NAAFI | Navy, Army, and Air Force Institutes |
| NASA | National Aeronautics and Space Administration |
| NATO | North Atlantic Treaty Organization |
| NBC | National Broadcasting Corporation |
| NC | North Carolina |
| NCO | non-commissioned officer |
| ND | North Dakota |
| n.d. | no date |
| NE | Nebraska |
| *nem. con.* | *nemine contradicente*: unanimously |
| new ser. | new series |
| NH | New Hampshire |
| NHS | National Health Service |
| NJ | New Jersey |
| NKVD | [Soviet people's commissariat for internal affairs] |
| NM | New Mexico |
| nm | nanometre(s) |
| no. *pl.* nos. | number(s) |
| Nov | November |
| n.p. | no place [of publication] |
| NS | new style |
| NV | Nevada |
| NY | New York |
| NZBS | New Zealand Broadcasting Service |
| OBE | officer of the Order of the British Empire |
| obit. | obituary |
| Oct | October |
| OCTU | officer cadets training unit |
| OECD | Organization for Economic Co-operation and Development |
| OEEC | Organization for European Economic Co-operation |
| OFM | order of Friars Minor [Franciscans] |
| OFMCap | Ordine Frati Minori Cappucini: member of the Capuchin order |
| OH | Ohio |
| OK | Oklahoma |
| O level | ordinary level [examination] |
| OM | Order of Merit |
| OP | order of Preachers [Dominicans] |
| op. *pl.* opp. | opus *pl.* opera |
| OPEC | Organization of Petroleum Exporting Countries |
| OR | Oregon |
| orig. | original |
| OS | old style |
| OSB | Order of St Benedict |
| OTC | Officers' Training Corps |
| OWS | Old Watercolour Society |
| Oxon. | Oxoniensis |
| p. *pl.* pp. | page(s) |
| PA | Pennsylvania |
| p.a. | per annum |
| para. | paragraph |
| PAYE | pay as you earn |
| pbk *pl.* pbks | paperback(s) |
| *per.* | [during the] period |
| PhD | doctor of philosophy |
| pl. | (1) plate(s); (2) plural |
| priv. coll. | private collection |
| pt *pl.* pts | part(s) |
| pubd | published |
| PVC | polyvinyl chloride |
| q. *pl.* qq. | (1) question(s); (2) quire(s) |
| QC | queen's counsel |
| R | rand |
| R. | Rex / Regina |
| *r* | recto |
| r. | reigned / ruled |
| RA | Royal Academy / Royal Academician |

| | |
|---|---|
| RAC | Royal Automobile Club |
| RAF | Royal Air Force |
| RAFVR | Royal Air Force Volunteer Reserve |
| RAM | [member of the] Royal Academy of Music |
| RAMC | Royal Army Medical Corps |
| RCA | Royal College of Art |
| RCNC | Royal Corps of Naval Constructors |
| RCOG | Royal College of Obstetricians and Gynaecologists |
| RDI | royal designer for industry |
| RE | Royal Engineers |
| repr. *pl.* reprs. | reprint(s) / reprinted |
| repro. | reproduced |
| rev. | revised / revised by / reviser / revision |
| Revd | Reverend |
| RHA | Royal Hibernian Academy |
| RI | (1) Rhode Island; (2) Royal Institute of Painters in Water-Colours |
| RIBA | Royal Institute of British Architects |
| RIN | Royal Indian Navy |
| RM | Reichsmark |
| RMS | Royal Mail steamer |
| RN | Royal Navy |
| RNA | ribonucleic acid |
| RNAS | Royal Naval Air Service |
| RNR | Royal Naval Reserve |
| RNVR | Royal Naval Volunteer Reserve |
| RO | Record Office |
| r.p.m. | revolutions per minute |
| RRS | royal research ship |
| Rs | rupees |
| RSA | (1) Royal Scottish Academician; (2) Royal Society of Arts |
| RSPCA | Royal Society for the Prevention of Cruelty to Animals |
| Rt Hon. | Right Honourable |
| Rt Revd | Right Reverend |
| RUC | Royal Ulster Constabulary |
| Russ. | Russian |
| RWS | Royal Watercolour Society |
| S4C | Sianel Pedwar Cymru |
| s. | shilling(s) |
| s.a. | *sub anno*: under the year |
| SABC | South African Broadcasting Corporation |
| SAS | Special Air Service |
| SC | South Carolina |
| ScD | doctor of science |
| S$ | Singapore dollar |
| SD | South Dakota |
| sec. | second(s) |
| sel. | selected |
| sen. | senior |
| Sept | September |
| ser. | series |
| SHAPE | supreme headquarters allied powers, Europe |
| SIDRO | Société Internationale d'Énergie Hydro-Électrique |
| sig. *pl.* sigs. | signature(s) |
| sing. | singular |
| SIS | Secret Intelligence Service |
| SJ | Society of Jesus |

| | |
|---|---|
| Skr | Swedish krona |
| Span. | Spanish |
| SPCK | Society for Promoting Christian Knowledge |
| SS | (1) Santissimi; (2) Schutzstaffel; (3) steam ship |
| STB | bachelor of theology |
| STD | doctor of theology |
| STM | master of theology |
| STP | doctor of theology |
| *supp.* | supposedly |
| suppl. *pl.* suppls. | supplement(s) |
| s.v. | *sub verbo / sub voce*: under the word / heading |
| SY | steam yacht |
| TA | Territorial Army |
| TASS | [Soviet news agency] |
| TB | tuberculosis (*lit.* tubercle bacillus) |
| TD | (1) *teachtaí dála* (member of the Dáil); (2) territorial decoration |
| TN | Tennessee |
| TNT | trinitrotoluene |
| trans. | translated / translated by / translation / translator |
| TT | tourist trophy |
| TUC | Trades Union Congress |
| TX | Texas |
| U-boat | *Unterseeboot*: submarine |
| Ufa | Universum-Film AG |
| UMIST | University of Manchester Institute of Science and Technology |
| UN | United Nations |
| UNESCO | United Nations Educational, Scientific, and Cultural Organization |
| UNICEF | United Nations International Children's Emergency Fund |
| unpubd | unpublished |
| USS | United States ship |
| UT | Utah |
| *v* | verso |
| v. | versus |
| VA | Virginia |
| VAD | Voluntary Aid Detachment |
| VC | Victoria Cross |
| VE-day | victory in Europe day |
| Ven. | Venerable |
| VJ-day | victory over Japan day |
| vol. *pl.* vols. | volume(s) |
| VT | Vermont |
| WA | Washington [state] |
| WAAC | Women's Auxiliary Army Corps |
| WAAF | Women's Auxiliary Air Force |
| WEA | Workers' Educational Association |
| WHO | World Health Organization |
| WI | Wisconsin |
| WRAF | Women's Royal Air Force |
| WRNS | Women's Royal Naval Service |
| WV | West Virginia |
| WVS | Women's Voluntary Service |
| WY | Wyoming |
| ¥ | yen |
| YMCA | Young Men's Christian Association |
| YWCA | Young Women's Christian Association |

## 2 Institution abbreviations

| | |
|---|---|
| All Souls Oxf. | All Souls College, Oxford |
| AM Oxf. | Ashmolean Museum, Oxford |
| Balliol Oxf. | Balliol College, Oxford |
| BBC WAC | BBC Written Archives Centre, Reading |
| Beds. & Luton ARS | Bedfordshire and Luton Archives and Record Service, Bedford |
| Berks. RO | Berkshire Record Office, Reading |
| BFI | British Film Institute, London |
| BFI NFTVA | British Film Institute, London, National Film and Television Archive |
| BGS | British Geological Survey, Keyworth, Nottingham |
| Birm. CA | Birmingham Central Library, Birmingham City Archives |
| Birm. CL | Birmingham Central Library |
| BL | British Library, London |
| BL NSA | British Library, London, National Sound Archive |
| BL OIOC | British Library, London, Oriental and India Office Collections |
| BLPES | London School of Economics and Political Science, British Library of Political and Economic Science |
| BM | British Museum, London |
| Bodl. Oxf. | Bodleian Library, Oxford |
| Bodl. RH | Bodleian Library of Commonwealth and African Studies at Rhodes House, Oxford |
| Borth. Inst. | Borthwick Institute of Historical Research, University of York |
| Boston PL | Boston Public Library, Massachusetts |
| Bristol RO | Bristol Record Office |
| Bucks. RLSS | Buckinghamshire Records and Local Studies Service, Aylesbury |
| CAC Cam. | Churchill College, Cambridge, Churchill Archives Centre |
| Cambs. AS | Cambridgeshire Archive Service |
| CCC Cam. | Corpus Christi College, Cambridge |
| CCC Oxf. | Corpus Christi College, Oxford |
| Ches. & Chester ALSS | Cheshire and Chester Archives and Local Studies Service |
| Christ Church Oxf. | Christ Church, Oxford |
| Christies | Christies, London |
| City Westm. AC | City of Westminster Archives Centre, London |
| CKS | Centre for Kentish Studies, Maidstone |
| CLRO | Corporation of London Records Office |
| Coll. Arms | College of Arms, London |
| Col. U. | Columbia University, New York |
| Cornwall RO | Cornwall Record Office, Truro |
| Courtauld Inst. | Courtauld Institute of Art, London |
| CUL | Cambridge University Library |
| Cumbria AS | Cumbria Archive Service |
| Derbys. RO | Derbyshire Record Office, Matlock |
| Devon RO | Devon Record Office, Exeter |
| Dorset RO | Dorset Record Office, Dorchester |
| Duke U. | Duke University, Durham, North Carolina |
| Duke U., Perkins L. | Duke University, Durham, North Carolina, William R. Perkins Library |
| Durham Cath. CL | Durham Cathedral, chapter library |
| Durham RO | Durham Record Office |
| DWL | Dr Williams's Library, London |
| Essex RO | Essex Record Office |
| E. Sussex RO | East Sussex Record Office, Lewes |
| Eton | Eton College, Berkshire |
| FM Cam. | Fitzwilliam Museum, Cambridge |
| Folger | Folger Shakespeare Library, Washington, DC |
| Garr. Club | Garrick Club, London |
| Girton Cam. | Girton College, Cambridge |
| GL | Guildhall Library, London |
| Glos. RO | Gloucestershire Record Office, Gloucester |
| Gon. & Caius Cam. | Gonville and Caius College, Cambridge |
| Gov. Art Coll. | Government Art Collection |
| GS Lond. | Geological Society of London |
| Hants. RO | Hampshire Record Office, Winchester |
| Harris Man. Oxf. | Harris Manchester College, Oxford |
| Harvard TC | Harvard Theatre Collection, Harvard University, Cambridge, Massachusetts, Nathan Marsh Pusey Library |
| Harvard U. | Harvard University, Cambridge, Massachusetts |
| Harvard U., Houghton L. | Harvard University, Cambridge, Massachusetts, Houghton Library |
| Herefs. RO | Herefordshire Record Office, Hereford |
| Herts. ALS | Hertfordshire Archives and Local Studies, Hertford |
| Hist. Soc. Penn. | Historical Society of Pennsylvania, Philadelphia |
| HLRO | House of Lords Record Office, London |
| Hult. Arch. | Hulton Archive, London and New York |
| Hunt. L. | Huntington Library, San Marino, California |
| ICL | Imperial College, London |
| Inst. CE | Institution of Civil Engineers, London |
| Inst. EE | Institution of Electrical Engineers, London |
| IWM | Imperial War Museum, London |
| IWM FVA | Imperial War Museum, London, Film and Video Archive |
| IWM SA | Imperial War Museum, London, Sound Archive |
| JRL | John Rylands University Library of Manchester |
| King's AC Cam. | King's College Archives Centre, Cambridge |
| King's Cam. | King's College, Cambridge |
| King's Lond. | King's College, London |
| King's Lond., Liddell Hart C. | King's College, London, Liddell Hart Centre for Military Archives |
| Lancs. RO | Lancashire Record Office, Preston |
| L. Cong. | Library of Congress, Washington, DC |
| Leics. RO | Leicestershire, Leicester, and Rutland Record Office, Leicester |
| Lincs. Arch. | Lincolnshire Archives, Lincoln |
| Linn. Soc. | Linnean Society of London |
| LMA | London Metropolitan Archives |
| LPL | Lambeth Palace, London |
| Lpool RO | Liverpool Record Office and Local Studies Service |
| LUL | London University Library |
| Magd. Cam. | Magdalene College, Cambridge |
| Magd. Oxf. | Magdalen College, Oxford |
| Man. City Gall. | Manchester City Galleries |
| Man. CL | Manchester Central Library |
| Mass. Hist. Soc. | Massachusetts Historical Society, Boston |
| Merton Oxf. | Merton College, Oxford |
| MHS Oxf. | Museum of the History of Science, Oxford |
| Mitchell L., Glas. | Mitchell Library, Glasgow |
| Mitchell L., NSW | State Library of New South Wales, Sydney, Mitchell Library |
| Morgan L. | Pierpont Morgan Library, New York |
| NA Canada | National Archives of Canada, Ottawa |
| NA Ire. | National Archives of Ireland, Dublin |
| NAM | National Army Museum, London |
| NA Scot. | National Archives of Scotland, Edinburgh |
| News Int. RO | News International Record Office, London |
| NG Ire. | National Gallery of Ireland, Dublin |

| | |
|---|---|
| NG Scot. | National Gallery of Scotland, Edinburgh |
| NHM | Natural History Museum, London |
| NL Aus. | National Library of Australia, Canberra |
| NL Ire. | National Library of Ireland, Dublin |
| NL NZ | National Library of New Zealand, Wellington |
| NL NZ, Turnbull L. | National Library of New Zealand, Wellington, Alexander Turnbull Library |
| NL Scot. | National Library of Scotland, Edinburgh |
| NL Wales | National Library of Wales, Aberystwyth |
| NMG Wales | National Museum and Gallery of Wales, Cardiff |
| NMM | National Maritime Museum, London |
| Norfolk RO | Norfolk Record Office, Norwich |
| Northants. RO | Northamptonshire Record Office, Northampton |
| Northumbd RO | Northumberland Record Office |
| Notts. Arch. | Nottinghamshire Archives, Nottingham |
| NPG | National Portrait Gallery, London |
| NRA | National Archives, London, Historical Manuscripts Commission, National Register of Archives |
| Nuffield Oxf. | Nuffield College, Oxford |
| N. Yorks. CRO | North Yorkshire County Record Office, Northallerton |
| NYPL | New York Public Library |
| Oxf. UA | Oxford University Archives |
| Oxf. U. Mus. NH | Oxford University Museum of Natural History |
| Oxon. RO | Oxfordshire Record Office, Oxford |
| Pembroke Cam. | Pembroke College, Cambridge |
| PRO | National Archives, London, Public Record Office |
| PRO NIre. | Public Record Office for Northern Ireland, Belfast |
| Pusey Oxf. | Pusey House, Oxford |
| RA | Royal Academy of Arts, London |
| Ransom HRC | Harry Ransom Humanities Research Center, University of Texas, Austin |
| RAS | Royal Astronomical Society, London |
| RBG Kew | Royal Botanic Gardens, Kew, London |
| RCP Lond. | Royal College of Physicians of London |
| RCS Eng. | Royal College of Surgeons of England, London |
| RGS | Royal Geographical Society, London |
| RIBA | Royal Institute of British Architects, London |
| RIBA BAL | Royal Institute of British Architects, London, British Architectural Library |
| Royal Arch. | Royal Archives, Windsor Castle, Berkshire [by gracious permission of her majesty the queen] |
| Royal Irish Acad. | Royal Irish Academy, Dublin |
| Royal Scot. Acad. | Royal Scottish Academy, Edinburgh |
| RS | Royal Society, London |
| RSA | Royal Society of Arts, London |
| RS Friends, Lond. | Religious Society of Friends, London |
| St Ant. Oxf. | St Antony's College, Oxford |
| St John Cam. | St John's College, Cambridge |
| S. Antiquaries, Lond. | Society of Antiquaries of London |
| Sci. Mus. | Science Museum, London |
| Scot. NPG | Scottish National Portrait Gallery, Edinburgh |
| Scott Polar RI | University of Cambridge, Scott Polar Research Institute |
| Sheff. Arch. | Sheffield Archives |
| Shrops. RRC | Shropshire Records and Research Centre, Shrewsbury |
| SOAS | School of Oriental and African Studies, London |
| Som. ARS | Somerset Archive and Record Service, Taunton |
| Staffs. RO | Staffordshire Record Office, Stafford |
| Suffolk RO | Suffolk Record Office |
| Surrey HC | Surrey History Centre, Woking |
| TCD | Trinity College, Dublin |
| Trinity Cam. | Trinity College, Cambridge |
| U. Aberdeen | University of Aberdeen |
| U. Birm. | University of Birmingham |
| U. Birm. L. | University of Birmingham Library |
| U. Cal. | University of California |
| U. Cam. | University of Cambridge |
| UCL | University College, London |
| U. Durham | University of Durham |
| U. Durham L. | University of Durham Library |
| U. Edin. | University of Edinburgh |
| U. Edin., New Coll. | University of Edinburgh, New College |
| U. Edin., New Coll. L. | University of Edinburgh, New College Library |
| U. Edin. L. | University of Edinburgh Library |
| U. Glas. | University of Glasgow |
| U. Glas. L. | University of Glasgow Library |
| U. Hull | University of Hull |
| U. Hull, Brynmor Jones L. | University of Hull, Brynmor Jones Library |
| U. Leeds | University of Leeds |
| U. Leeds, Brotherton L. | University of Leeds, Brotherton Library |
| U. Lond. | University of London |
| U. Lpool | University of Liverpool |
| U. Lpool L. | University of Liverpool Library |
| U. Mich. | University of Michigan, Ann Arbor |
| U. Mich., Clements L. | University of Michigan, Ann Arbor, William L. Clements Library |
| U. Newcastle | University of Newcastle upon Tyne |
| U. Newcastle, Robinson L. | University of Newcastle upon Tyne, Robinson Library |
| U. Nott. | University of Nottingham |
| U. Nott. L. | University of Nottingham Library |
| U. Oxf. | University of Oxford |
| U. Reading | University of Reading |
| U. Reading L. | University of Reading Library |
| U. St Andr. | University of St Andrews |
| U. St Andr. L. | University of St Andrews Library |
| U. Southampton | University of Southampton |
| U. Southampton L. | University of Southampton Library |
| U. Sussex | University of Sussex, Brighton |
| U. Texas | University of Texas, Austin |
| U. Wales | University of Wales |
| U. Warwick Mod. RC | University of Warwick, Coventry, Modern Records Centre |
| V&A | Victoria and Albert Museum, London |
| V&A NAL | Victoria and Albert Museum, London, National Art Library |
| Warks. CRO | Warwickshire County Record Office, Warwick |
| Wellcome L. | Wellcome Library for the History and Understanding of Medicine, London |
| Westm. DA | Westminster Diocesan Archives, London |
| Wilts. & Swindon RO | Wiltshire and Swindon Record Office, Trowbridge |
| Worcs. RO | Worcestershire Record Office, Worcester |
| W. Sussex RO | West Sussex Record Office, Chichester |
| W. Yorks. AS | West Yorkshire Archive Service |
| Yale U. | Yale University, New Haven, Connecticut |
| Yale U., Beinecke L. | Yale University, New Haven, Connecticut, Beinecke Rare Book and Manuscript Library |
| Yale U. CBA | Yale University, New Haven, Connecticut, Yale Center for British Art |

# 3 Bibliographic abbreviations

Adams, *Drama* — W. D. Adams, *A dictionary of the drama*, 1: *A–G* (1904); 2: *H–Z* (1956) [vol. 2 microfilm only]

*AFM* — J O'Donovan, ed. and trans., *Annala rioghachta Eireann / Annals of the kingdom of Ireland by the four masters*, 7 vols. (1848–51); 2nd edn (1856); 3rd edn (1990)

Allibone, *Dict.* — S. A. Allibone, *A critical dictionary of English literature and British and American authors*, 3 vols. (1859–71); suppl. by J. F. Kirk, 2 vols. (1891)

*ANB* — J. A. Garraty and M. C. Carnes, eds., *American national biography*, 24 vols. (1999)

Anderson, *Scot. nat.* — W. Anderson, *The Scottish nation, or, The surnames, families, literature, honours, and biographical history of the people of Scotland*, 3 vols. (1859–63)

*Ann. mon.* — H. R. Luard, ed., *Annales monastici*, 5 vols., Rolls Series, 36 (1864–9)

*Ann. Ulster* — S. Mac Airt and G. Mac Niocaill, eds., *Annals of Ulster (to AD 1131)* (1983)

*APC* — *Acts of the privy council of England*, new ser., 46 vols. (1890–1964)

*APS* — *The acts of the parliaments of Scotland*, 12 vols. in 13 (1814–75)

Arber, *Regs. Stationers* — F. Arber, ed., *A transcript of the registers of the Company of Stationers of London, 1554–1640 AD*, 5 vols. (1875–94)

*ArchR* — *Architectural Review*

*ASC* — D. Whitelock, D. C. Douglas, and S. I. Tucker, ed. and trans., *The Anglo-Saxon Chronicle: a revised translation* (1961)

*AS chart.* — P. H. Sawyer, *Anglo-Saxon charters: an annotated list and bibliography*, Royal Historical Society Guides and Handbooks (1968)

*AusDB* — D. Pike and others, eds., *Australian dictionary of biography*, 16 vols. (1966–2002)

Baker, *Serjeants* — J. H. Baker, *The order of serjeants at law*, SeldS, suppl. ser., 5 (1984)

Bale, *Cat.* — J. Bale, *Scriptorum illustrium Maioris Brytannie, quam nunc Angliam et Scotiam vocant: catalogus*, 2 vols. in 1 (Basel, 1557–9); facs. edn (1971)

Bale, *Index* — J. Bale, *Index Britanniae scriptorum*, ed. R. L. Poole and M. Bateson (1902); facs. edn (1990)

*BBCS* — *Bulletin of the Board of Celtic Studies*

*BDMBR* — J. O. Baylen and N. J. Gossman, eds., *Biographical dictionary of modern British radicals*, 3 vols. in 4 (1979–88)

Bede, *Hist. eccl.* — *Bede's Ecclesiastical history of the English people*, ed. and trans. B. Colgrave and R. A. B. Mynors, OMT (1969); repr. (1991)

Bénézit, *Dict.* — E. Bénézit, *Dictionnaire critique et documentaire des peintres, sculpteurs, dessinateurs et graveurs*, 3 vols. (Paris, 1911–23); new edn, 8 vols. (1948–66), repr. (1966); 3rd edn, rev. and enl., 10 vols. (1976); 4th edn, 14 vols. (1999)

*BIHR* — *Bulletin of the Institute of Historical Research*

Birch, *Seals* — W. de Birch, *Catalogue of seals in the department of manuscripts in the British Museum*, 6 vols. (1887–1900)

*Bishop Burnet's History* — *Bishop Burnet's History of his own time*, ed. M. J. Routh, 2nd edn, 6 vols. (1833)

*Blackwood* — *Blackwood's [Edinburgh] Magazine*, 328 vols. (1817–1980)

Blain, Clements & Grundy, *Feminist comp.* — V. Blain, P. Clements, and I. Grundy, eds., *The feminist companion to literature in English* (1990)

*BL cat.* — *The British Library general catalogue of printed books* [in 360 vols. with suppls., also CD-ROM and online]

*BMJ* — *British Medical Journal*

Boase & Courtney, *Bibl. Corn.* — G. C. Boase and W. P. Courtney, *Bibliotheca Cornubiensis: a catalogue of the writings … of Cornishmen*, 3 vols. (1874–82)

Boase, *Mod. Eng. biog.* — F. Boase, *Modern English biography: containing many thousand concise memoirs of persons who have died since the year 1850*, 6 vols. (privately printed, Truro, 1892–1921); repr. (1965)

Boswell, *Life* — *Boswell's Life of Johnson: together with Journal of a tour to the Hebrides and Johnson's Diary of a journey into north Wales*, ed. G. B. Hill, enl. edn, rev. L. F. Powell, 6 vols. (1934–50); 2nd edn (1964); repr. (1971)

Brown & Stratton, *Brit. mus.* — J. D. Brown and S. S. Stratton, *British musical biography* (1897)

Bryan, *Painters* — M. Bryan, *A biographical and critical dictionary of painters and engravers*, 2 vols. (1816); new edn, ed. G. Stanley (1849); new edn, ed. R. E. Graves and W. Armstrong, 2 vols. (1886–9); [4th edn], ed. G. C. Williamson, 5 vols. (1903–5) [various reprs.]

Burke, *Gen. GB* — J. Burke, *A genealogical and heraldic history of the commoners of Great Britain and Ireland*, 4 vols. (1833–8); new edn as *A genealogical and heraldic dictionary of the landed gentry of Great Britain and Ireland*, 3 vols. [1843–9] [many later edns]

Burke, *Gen. Ire.* — J. B. Burke, *A genealogical and heraldic history of the landed gentry of Ireland* (1899); 2nd edn (1904); 3rd edn (1912); 4th edn (1958); 5th edn as *Burke's Irish family records* (1976)

Burke, *Peerage* — J. Burke, *A general [later edns A genealogical] and heraldic dictionary of the peerage and baronetage of the United Kingdom* [later edns *the British empire*] (1829–)

Burney, *Hist. mus.* — C. Burney, *A general history of music, from the earliest ages to the present period*, 4 vols. (1776–89)

Burtchaell & Sadleir, *Alum. Dubl.* — G. D. Burtchaell and T. U. Sadleir, *Alumni Dublinenses: a register of the students, graduates, and provosts of Trinity College* (1924); [2nd edn], with suppl., in 2 pts (1935)

*Calamy rev.* — A. G. Matthews, *Calamy revised* (1934); repr. (1988)

*CCI* — *Calendar of confirmations and inventories granted and given up in the several commissariots of Scotland* (1876–)

*CCIR* — *Calendar of the close rolls preserved in the Public Record Office*, 47 vols. (1892–1963)

*CDS* — J. Bain, ed., *Calendar of documents relating to Scotland*, 4 vols., PRO (1881–8); suppl. vol. 5, ed. G. G. Simpson and J. D. Galbraith [1986]

*CEPR letters* — W. H. Bliss, C. Johnson, and J. Twemlow, eds., *Calendar of entries in the papal registers relating to Great Britain and Ireland: papal letters* (1893–)

*CGPLA* — *Calendars of the grants of probate and letters of administration* [in 4 ser.: *England & Wales, Northern Ireland, Ireland*, and *Éire*]

Chambers, *Scots.* — R. Chambers, ed., *A biographical dictionary of eminent Scotsmen*, 4 vols. (1832–5)

*Chancery records* — chancery records pubd by the PRO

*Chancery records* (RC) — chancery records pubd by the Record Commissions

CIPM — *Calendar of inquisitions post mortem*, [20 vols.], PRO (1904–); also *Henry VII*, 3 vols. (1898–1955)

Clarendon, *Hist. rebellion* — E. Hyde, earl of Clarendon, *The history of the rebellion and civil wars in England*, 6 vols. (1888); repr. (1958) and (1992)

Cobbett, *Parl. hist.* — W. Cobbett and J. Wright, eds., *Cobbett's Parliamentary history of England*, 36 vols. (1806–1820)

Colvin, *Archs.* — H. Colvin, *A biographical dictionary of British architects, 1600–1840*, 3rd edn (1995)

Cooper, *Ath. Cantab.* — C. H. Cooper and T. Cooper, *Athenae Cantabrigienses*, 3 vols. (1858–1913); repr. (1967)

CPR — *Calendar of the patent rolls preserved in the Public Record Office* (1891–)

Crockford — *Crockford's Clerical Directory*

CS — Camden Society

CSP — *Calendar of state papers* [in 11 ser.: *domestic*, *Scotland*, *Scottish series*, *Ireland*, *colonial*, *Commonwealth*, *foreign*, *Spain* [at Simancas], *Rome*, *Milan*, and *Venice*]

CYS — Canterbury and York Society

DAB — *Dictionary of American biography*, 21 vols. (1928–36), repr. in 11 vols. (1964); 10 suppls. (1944–96)

DBB — D. J. Jeremy, ed., *Dictionary of business biography*, 5 vols. (1984–6)

DCB — G. W. Brown and others, *Dictionary of Canadian biography*, [14 vols.] (1966–)

*Debrett's Peerage* — *Debrett's Peerage* (1803–) [sometimes *Debrett's Illustrated peerage*]

Desmond, *Botanists* — R. Desmond, *Dictionary of British and Irish botanists and horticulturists* (1977); rev. edn (1994)

*Dir. Brit. archs.* — A. Felstead, J. Franklin, and L. Pinfield, eds., *Directory of British architects, 1834–1900* (1993); 2nd edn, ed. A. Brodie and others, 2 vols. (2001)

DLB — J. M. Bellamy and J. Saville, eds., *Dictionary of labour biography*, [10 vols.] (1972–)

DLitB — Dictionary of Literary Biography

DNB — *Dictionary of national biography*, 63 vols. (1885–1900), suppl., 3 vols. (1901); repr. in 22 vols. (1908–9); 10 further suppls. (1912–96); *Missing persons* (1993)

DNZB — W. H. Oliver and C. Orange, eds., *The dictionary of New Zealand biography*, 5 vols. (1990–2000)

DSAB — W. J. de Kock and others, eds., *Dictionary of South African biography*, 5 vols. (1968–87)

DSB — C. C. Gillispie and F. L. Holmes, eds., *Dictionary of scientific biography*, 16 vols. (1970–80); repr. in 8 vols. (1981); 2 vol. suppl. (1990)

DSBB — A. Slaven and S. Checkland, eds., *Dictionary of Scottish business biography, 1860–1960*, 2 vols. (1986–90)

DSCHT — N. M. de S. Cameron and others, eds., *Dictionary of Scottish church history and theology* (1993)

Dugdale, *Monasticon* — W. Dugdale, *Monasticon Anglicanum*, 3 vols. (1655–72); 2nd edn, 3 vols. (1661–82); new edn, ed. J. Caley, J. Ellis, and B. Bandinel, 6 vols. in 8 pts (1817–30); repr. (1846) and (1970)

DWB — J. E. Lloyd and others, eds., *Dictionary of Welsh biography down to 1940* (1959) [Eng. trans. of *Y bywgraffiadur Cymreig hyd 1940*, 2nd edn (1954)]

EdinR — *Edinburgh Review, or, Critical Journal*

EETS — Early English Text Society

Emden, *Cam.* — A. B. Emden, *A biographical register of the University of Cambridge to 1500* (1963)

Emden, *Oxf.* — A. B. Emden, *A biographical register of the University of Oxford to AD 1500*, 3 vols. (1957–9); also *A biographical register of the University of Oxford, AD 1501 to 1540* (1974)

EngHR — *English Historical Review*

Engraved Brit. ports. — F. M. O'Donoghue and H. M. Hake, *Catalogue of engraved British portraits preserved in the department of prints and drawings in the British Museum*, 6 vols. (1908–25)

ER — The English Reports, 178 vols. (1900–32)

ESTC — *English short title catalogue, 1475–1800* [CD-ROM and online]

Evelyn, *Diary* — *The diary of John Evelyn*, ed. E. S. De Beer, 6 vols. (1955); repr. (2000)

Farington, *Diary* — *The diary of Joseph Farington*, ed. K. Garlick and others, 17 vols. (1978–98)

*Fasti Angl.* (Hardy) — J. Le Neve, *Fasti ecclesiae Anglicanae*, ed. T. D. Hardy, 3 vols. (1854)

*Fasti Angl., 1066–1300* — [J. Le Neve], *Fasti ecclesiae Anglicanae, 1066–1300*, ed. D. E. Greenway and J. S. Barrow, [8 vols.] (1968–)

*Fasti Angl., 1300–1541* — [J. Le Neve], *Fasti ecclesiae Anglicanae, 1300–1541*, 12 vols. (1962–7)

*Fasti Angl., 1541–1857* — [J. Le Neve], *Fasti ecclesiae Anglicanae, 1541–1857*, ed. J. M. Horn, D. M. Smith, and D. S. Bailey, [9 vols.] (1969–)

*Fasti Scot.* — H. Scott, *Fasti ecclesiae Scoticanae*, 3 vols. in 6 (1871); new edn, [11 vols.] (1915–)

FO List — *Foreign Office List*

Fortescue, *Brit. army* — J. W. Fortescue, *A history of the British army*, 13 vols. (1899–1930)

Foss, *Judges* — E. Foss, *The judges of England*, 9 vols. (1848–64); repr. (1966)

Foster, *Alum. Oxon.* — J. Foster, ed., *Alumni Oxonienses: the members of the University of Oxford, 1715–1886*, 4 vols. (1887–8); later edn (1891); also *Alumni Oxonienses … 1500–1714*, 4 vols. (1891–2); 8 vol. repr. (1968) and (2000)

Fuller, *Worthies* — T. Fuller, *The history of the worthies of England*, 4 pts (1662); new edn, 2 vols., ed. J. Nichols (1811); new edn, 3 vols., ed. P. A. Nuttall (1840); repr. (1965)

GEC, *Baronetage* — G. E. Cokayne, *Complete baronetage*, 6 vols. (1900–09); repr. (1983) [microprint]

GEC, *Peerage* — G. E. C. [G. E. Cokayne], *The complete peerage of England, Scotland, Ireland, Great Britain, and the United Kingdom*, 8 vols. (1887–98); new edn, ed. V. Gibbs and others, 14 vols. in 15 (1910–98); microprint repr. (1982) and (1987)

Genest, *Eng. stage* — J. Genest, *Some account of the English stage from the Restoration in 1660 to 1830*, 10 vols. (1832); repr. [New York, 1965]

Gillow, *Lit. biog. hist.* — J. Gillow, *A literary and biographical history or bibliographical dictionary of the English Catholics, from the breach with Rome, in 1534, to the present time*, 5 vols. [1885–1902]; repr. (1961); repr. with preface by C. Gillow (1999)

*Gir. Camb. opera* — *Giraldi Cambrensis opera*, ed. J. S. Brewer, J. F. Dimock, and G. F. Warner, 8 vols., Rolls Series, 21 (1861–91)

GJ — *Geographical Journal*

Gladstone, *Diaries* — *The Gladstone diaries: with cabinet minutes and prime-ministerial correspondence*, ed. M. R. D. Foot and H. C. G. Matthew, 14 vols. (1968–94)

*GM* — *Gentleman's Magazine*

Graves, *Artists* — A. Graves, ed., *A dictionary of artists who have exhibited works in the principal London exhibitions of oil paintings from 1760 to 1880* (1884); new edn (1895); 3rd edn (1901); facs. edn (1969); repr. [1970], (1973), and (1984)

Graves, *Brit. Inst.* — A. Graves, *The British Institution, 1806–1867: a complete dictionary of contributors and their work from the foundation of the institution* (1875); facs. edn (1908); repr. (1969)

Graves, *RA exhibitors* — A. Graves, *The Royal Academy of Arts: a complete dictionary of contributors and their work from its foundation in 1769 to 1904*, 8 vols. (1905–6); repr. in 4 vols. (1970) and (1972)

Graves, *Soc. Artists* — A. Graves, *The Society of Artists of Great Britain, 1760–1791, the Free Society of Artists, 1761–1783: a complete dictionary* (1907); facs. edn (1969)

Greaves & Zaller, *BDBR* — R. L. Greaves and R. Zaller, eds., *Biographical dictionary of British radicals in the seventeenth century*, 3 vols. (1982–4)

Grove, *Dict. mus.* — G. Grove, ed., *A dictionary of music and musicians*, 5 vols. (1878–90); 2nd edn, ed. J. A. Fuller Maitland (1904–10); 3rd edn, ed. H. C. Colles (1927); 4th edn with suppl. (1940); 5th edn, ed. E. Blom, 9 vols. (1954); suppl. (1961) [see also *New Grove*]

Hall, *Dramatic ports.* — L. A. Hall, *Catalogue of dramatic portraits in the theatre collection of the Harvard College library*, 4 vols. (1930–34)

*Hansard* — *Hansard's parliamentary debates*, ser. 1–5 (1803–)

Highfill, Burnim & Langhans, *BDA* — P. H. Highfill, K. A. Burnim, and E. A. Langhans, *A biographical dictionary of actors, actresses, musicians, dancers, managers, and other stage personnel in London, 1660–1800*, 16 vols. (1973–93)

*Hist. U. Oxf.* — T. H. Aston, ed., *The history of the University of Oxford*, 8 vols. (1984–2000) [1: *The early Oxford schools*, ed. J. I. Catto (1984); 2: *Late medieval Oxford*, ed. J. I. Catto and R. Evans (1992); 3: *The collegiate university*, ed. J. McConica (1986); 4: *Seventeenth-century Oxford*, ed. N. Tyacke (1997); 5: *The eighteenth century*, ed. L. S. Sutherland and L. G. Mitchell (1986); 6–7: *Nineteenth-century Oxford*, ed. M. G. Brock and M. C. Curthoys (1997–2000); 8: *The twentieth century*, ed. B. Harrison (2000)]

*HJ* — *Historical Journal*

HMC — Historical Manuscripts Commission

Holdsworth, *Eng. law* — W. S. Holdsworth, *A history of English law*, ed. A. L. Goodhart and H. L. Hanbury, 17 vols. (1903–72)

HoP, *Commons* — *The history of parliament: the House of Commons* [1386–1421, ed. J. S. Roskell, L. Clark, and C. Rawcliffe, 4 vols. (1992); 1509–1558, ed. S. T. Bindoff, 3 vols. (1982); 1558–1603, ed. P. W. Hasler, 3 vols. (1981); 1660–1690, ed. B. D. Henning, 3 vols. (1983); 1690–1715, ed. D. W. Hayton, E. Cruickshanks, and S. Handley, 5 vols. (2002); 1715–1754, ed. R. Sedgwick, 2 vols. (1970); 1754–1790, ed. L. Namier and J. Brooke, 3 vols. (1964), repr. (1985); 1790–1820, ed. R. G. Thorne, 5 vols. (1986); in draft (used with permission): 1422–1504, 1604–1629, 1640–1660, and 1820–1832]

*IGI* — *International Genealogical Index*, Church of Jesus Christ of the Latterday Saints

*ILN* — *Illustrated London News*

IMC — Irish Manuscripts Commission

Irving, *Scots.* — J. Irving, ed., *The book of Scotsmen eminent for achievements in arms and arts, church and state, law, legislation and literature, commerce, science, travel and philanthropy* (1881)

*JCS* — *Journal of the Chemical Society*

*JHC* — *Journals of the House of Commons*

*JHL* — *Journals of the House of Lords*

John of Worcester, *Chron.* — *The chronicle of John of Worcester*, ed. R. R. Darlington and P. McGurk, trans. J. Bray and P. McGurk, 3 vols., OMT (1995–) [vol. 1 forthcoming]

Keeler, *Long Parliament* — M. F. Keeler, *The Long Parliament, 1640–1641: a biographical study of its members* (1954)

Kelly, *Handbk* — *The upper ten thousand: an alphabetical list of all members of noble families*, 3 vols. (1875–7); continued as *Kelly's handbook of the upper ten thousand for 1878* [1879], 2 vols. (1878–9); continued as *Kelly's handbook to the titled, landed and official classes*, 94 vols. (1880–1973)

*LondG* — *London Gazette*

*LP Henry VIII* — J. S. Brewer, J. Gairdner, and R. H. Brodie, eds., *Letters and papers, foreign and domestic, of the reign of Henry VIII*, 23 vols. in 38 (1862–1932); repr. (1965)

Mallalieu, *Watercolour artists* — H. L. Mallalieu, *The dictionary of British watercolour artists up to 1820*, 3 vols. (1976–90); vol. 1, 2nd edn (1986)

*Memoirs FRS* — *Biographical Memoirs of Fellows of the Royal Society*

MGH — Monumenta Germaniae Historica

*MT* — *Musical Times*

Munk, *Roll* — W. Munk, *The roll of the Royal College of Physicians of London*, 2 vols. (1861); 2nd edn, 3 vols. (1878)

*N&Q* — *Notes and Queries*

*New Grove* — S. Sadie, ed., *The new Grove dictionary of music and musicians*, 20 vols. (1980); 2nd edn, 29 vols. (2001) [also online edn; see also Grove, *Dict. mus.*]

Nichols, *Illustrations* — J. Nichols and J. B. Nichols, *Illustrations of the literary history of the eighteenth century*, 8 vols. (1817–58)

Nichols, *Lit. anecdotes* — J. Nichols, *Literary anecdotes of the eighteenth century*, 9 vols. (1812–16); facs. edn (1966)

*Obits. FRS* — *Obituary Notices of Fellows of the Royal Society*

O'Byrne, *Naval biog. dict.* — W. R. O'Byrne, *A naval biographical dictionary* (1849); repr. (1990); [2nd edn], 2 vols. (1861)

OHS — Oxford Historical Society

*Old Westminsters* — *The record of Old Westminsters*, 1–2, ed. G. F. R. Barker and A. H. Stenning (1928); suppl. 1, ed. J. B. Whitmore and G. R. Y. Radcliffe [1938]; 3, ed. J. B. Whitmore, G. R. Y. Radcliffe, and D. C. Simpson (1963); suppl. 2, ed. F. E. Pagan (1978); 4, ed. F. E. Pagan and H. E. Pagan (1992)

OMT — Oxford Medieval Texts

Ordericus Vitalis, *Eccl. hist.* — *The ecclesiastical history of Orderic Vitalis*, ed. and trans. M. Chibnall, 6 vols., OMT (1969–80); repr. (1990)

Paris, *Chron.* — *Matthaei Parisiensis, monachi sancti Albani, chronica majora*, ed. H. R. Luard, Rolls Series, 7 vols. (1872–83)

*Parl. papers* — *Parliamentary papers* (1801–)

*PBA* — *Proceedings of the British Academy*

| | |
|---|---|
| Pepys, *Diary* | *The diary of Samuel Pepys*, ed. R. Latham and W. Matthews, 11 vols. (1970–83); repr. (1995) and (2000) |
| Pevsner | N. Pevsner and others, Buildings of England series |
| *PICE* | *Proceedings of the Institution of Civil Engineers* |
| Pipe rolls | *The great roll of the pipe for . . .*, PRSoc. (1884–) |
| PRO | Public Record Office |
| *PRS* | *Proceedings of the Royal Society of London* |
| PRSoc. | Pipe Roll Society |
| *PTRS* | *Philosophical Transactions of the Royal Society* |
| *QR* | *Quarterly Review* |
| RC | Record Commissions |
| Redgrave, *Artists* | S. Redgrave, *A dictionary of artists of the English school* (1874); rev. edn (1878); repr. (1970) |
| *Reg. Oxf.* | C. W. Boase and A. Clark, eds., *Register of the University of Oxford*, 5 vols., OHS, 1, 10–12, 14 (1885–9) |
| *Reg. PCS* | J. H. Burton and others, eds., *The register of the privy council of Scotland*, 1st ser., 14 vols. (1877–98); 2nd ser., 8 vols. (1899–1908); 3rd ser., [16 vols.] (1908–70) |
| *Reg. RAN* | H. W. C. Davis and others, eds., *Regesta regum Anglo-Normannorum, 1066–1154*, 4 vols. (1913–69) |
| *RIBA Journal* | *Journal of the Royal Institute of British Architects* [later *RIBA Journal*] |
| *RotP* | J. Strachey, ed., *Rotuli parliamentorum ut et petitiones, et placita in parliamento*, 6 vols. (1767–77) |
| *RotS* | D. Macpherson, J. Caley, and W. Illingworth, eds., *Rotuli Scotiae in Turri Londinensi et in domo capitulari Westmonasteriensi asservati*, 2 vols., RC, 14 (1814–19) |
| RS | Record(s) Society |
| Rymer, *Foedera* | T. Rymer and R. Sanderson, eds., *Foedera, conventiones, literae et cuiuscunque generis acta publica inter reges Angliae et alios quosvis imperatores, reges, pontifices, principes, vel communitates*, 20 vols. (1704–35); 2nd edn, 20 vols. (1726–35); 3rd edn, 10 vols. (1739–45); facs. edn (1967); new edn, ed. A. Clarke, J. Caley, and F. Holbrooke, 4 vols., RC, 50 (1816–30) |
| Sainty, *Judges* | J. Sainty, ed., *The judges of England, 1272–1990*, SeldS, suppl. ser., 10 (1993) |
| Sainty, *King's counsel* | J. Sainty, ed., *A list of English law officers and king's counsel*, SeldS, suppl. ser., 7 (1987) |
| SCH | Studies in Church History |
| Scots peerage | J. B. Paul, ed. *The Scots peerage, founded on Wood's edition of Sir Robert Douglas's Peerage of Scotland, containing an historical and genealogical account of the nobility of that kingdom*, 9 vols. (1904–14) |
| SeldS | Selden Society |
| *SHR* | *Scottish Historical Review* |
| *State trials* | T. B. Howell and T. J. Howell, eds., *Cobbett's Complete collection of state trials*, 34 vols. (1809–28) |
| *STC, 1475–1640* | A. W. Pollard, G. R. Redgrave, and others, eds., *A short-title catalogue of ... English books ... 1475–1640* (1926); 2nd edn, ed. W. A. Jackson, F. S. Ferguson, and K. F. Pantzer, 3 vols. (1976–91) [see also Wing, *STC*] |
| STS | Scottish Text Society |
| SurtS | Surtees Society |

| | |
|---|---|
| Symeon of Durham, *Opera* | *Symeonis monachi opera omnia*, ed. T. Arnold, 2 vols., Rolls Series, 75 (1882–5); repr. (1965) |
| Tanner, *Bibl. Brit.-Hib.* | T. Tanner, *Bibliotheca Britannico-Hibernica*, ed. D. Wilkins (1748); repr. (1963) |
| Thieme & Becker, *Allgemeines Lexikon* | U. Thieme, F. Becker, and H. Vollmer, eds., *Allgemeines Lexikon der bildenden Künstler von der Antike bis zur Gegenwart*, 37 vols. (Leipzig, 1907–50); repr. (1961–5), (1983), and (1992) |
| Thurloe, *State papers* | *A collection of the state papers of John Thurloe*, ed. T. Birch, 7 vols. (1742) |
| *TLS* | *Times Literary Supplement* |
| Tout, *Admin. hist.* | T. F. Tout, *Chapters in the administrative history of mediaeval England: the wardrobe, the chamber, and the small seals*, 6 vols. (1920–33); repr. (1967) |
| *TRHS* | *Transactions of the Royal Historical Society* |
| *VCH* | H. A. Doubleday and others, eds., *The Victoria history of the counties of England*, [88 vols.] (1900–) |
| Venn, *Alum. Cant.* | J. Venn and J. A. Venn, *Alumni Cantabrigienses: a biographical list of all known students, graduates, and holders of office at the University of Cambridge, from the earliest times to 1900*, 10 vols. (1922–54); repr. in 2 vols. (1974–8) |
| Vertue, *Note books* | [G. Vertue], *Note books*, ed. K. Esdaile, earl of Ilchester, and H. M. Hake, 6 vols., Walpole Society, 18, 20, 22, 24, 26, 30 (1930–55) |
| *VF* | *Vanity Fair* |
| Walford, *County families* | E. Walford, *The county families of the United Kingdom, or, Royal manual of the titled and untitled aristocracy of Great Britain and Ireland* (1860) |
| Walker rev. | A. G. Matthews, *Walker revised: being a revision of John Walker's Sufferings of the clergy during the grand rebellion, 1642–60* (1948); repr. (1988) |
| Walpole, *Corr.* | *The Yale edition of Horace Walpole's correspondence*, ed. W. S. Lewis, 48 vols. (1937–83) |
| Ward, *Men of the reign* | T. H. Ward, ed., *Men of the reign: a biographical dictionary of eminent persons of British and colonial birth who have died during the reign of Queen Victoria* (1885); repr. (Graz, 1968) |
| Waterhouse, *18c painters* | E. Waterhouse, *The dictionary of 18th century painters in oils and crayons* (1981); repr. as *British 18th century painters in oils and crayons* (1991), vol. 2 of *Dictionary of British art* |
| Watt, *Bibl. Brit.* | R. Watt, *Bibliotheca Britannica, or, A general index to British and foreign literature*, 4 vols. (1824) [many reprs.] |
| *Wellesley index* | W. E. Houghton, ed., *The Wellesley index to Victorian periodicals, 1824–1900*, 5 vols. (1966–89); new edn (1999) [CD-ROM] |
| Wing, *STC* | D. Wing, ed., *Short-title catalogue of ... English books ... 1641–1700*, 3 vols. (1945–51); 2nd edn (1972–88); rev. and enl. edn, ed. J. J. Morrison, C. W. Nelson, and M. Seccombe, 4 vols. (1994–8) [see also *STC, 1475–1640*] |
| *Wisden* | *John Wisden's Cricketer's Almanack* |
| Wood, *Ath. Oxon.* | A. Wood, *Athenae Oxonienses ... to which are added the Fasti*, 2 vols. (1691–2); 2nd edn (1721); new edn, 4 vols., ed. P. Bliss (1813–20); repr. (1967) and (1969) |
| Wood, *Vic. painters* | C. Wood, *Dictionary of Victorian painters* (1971); 2nd edn (1978); 3rd edn as *Victorian painters*, 2 vols. (1995), vol. 4 of *Dictionary of British art* |
| *WW* | *Who's who* (1849–) |
| *WWBMP* | M. Stenton and S. Lees, eds., *Who's who of British members of parliament*, 4 vols. (1976–81) |
| *WWW* | *Who was who* (1929–) |

**Constable family** (*per. c.*1300–1488), gentry, of Flamborough, owed both their surname and their Yorkshire base to service with Hugh d'Avranches, earl of Chester, who held an estate in Flamborough in 1086. The direct male line came to an end in 1139 and it was almost certainly an illegitimate son who inherited Flamborough and Holme-on-Spalding Moor, which were to remain in the hands of his descendants for the rest of the middle ages. The family was distinct from the Constables of Halsham, and the existence of two knightly families of the same name in the East Riding offers considerable scope for confusion.

For much of their history the Constables of Flamborough seem to have been of little importance outside their immediate area. A rare example of political involvement occurred at the beginning of the fourteenth century, when **Sir Robert** [i] **Constable** (*fl.* 1313–1338/9), the eldest son of **Sir William** [i] **Constable** (*d.* 1319), allied himself with Thomas, earl of Lancaster. In 1313 Robert was among those pardoned for his involvement in the death of the king's favourite Piers Gaveston in the previous year and he was again associated with the earl in May 1321, when the local Bridlington chronicler noted him among the northern gentry present at the earl's 'parliament' at Pontefract. Like many northerners, however, he later dissociated himself from the earl. He was not present at the Sherburn meeting in the following month, and in 1322 was given powers of array by the king. After that he appears to have withdrawn from public affairs, and in October 1331 secured exemption from office, although he was made an arrayer again early in 1333.

A partial explanation for Robert's withdrawal may have been his chronic indebtedness. From 1317 until the mid-1330s he acknowledged debts to a wide range of local merchants and clerics, as well as to more influential figures. His financial position may have eased by 1338–9, when he bought a mill and pasture in Flamborough, but in terms of public office the family remained eclipsed for a further decade. Robert is not recorded after his purchase of the mill, but it is unclear when he died or who succeeded him. His eldest son was probably the Sir William [ii] Constable associated with him in the mid-1330s, but there is no reference to the latter as head of the family, and he was certainly dead by 1346 when **Sir Marmaduke** [i] **Constable** (*d.* 1378), presumably William [ii]'s younger brother, was lord of Flamborough. By 1351 Marmaduke had the resources to undertake rebuilding at Flamborough and obtained licence to crenellate the manor. Alongside this suggestion of growing prosperity Marmaduke was taking on a larger public role. In 1349 he was appointed an executor of Archbishop Zouche, he was added to the commission of the peace in 1351, and was sheriff of Yorkshire in 1360–62 and 1366–7. He was discharged as commissioner in May 1370, which seems to mark the end of his public career, although he did not die until 21 May 1378. His last months were overshadowed by the murder of his kinsman John at Holme-on-Spalding Moor in June 1377 by two men identified as the cousins of the parson. There had been trouble there in 1365, when a commission

of oyer and terminer had been appointed to investigate Marmaduke's complaint that the residents had attacked his manor house, and John's death was perhaps linked with continuing local unrest.

Marmaduke was succeeded by his son **Sir Robert** [ii] **Constable** (*c.*1353–1400/01), who continued the family's slow rise into a more than purely local prominence. During his father's lifetime he had begun a military career, campaigning in Brittany in 1373 with John of Gaunt, duke of Lancaster. This was the family's first known association with the house of Lancaster since 1321, and it is unclear whether the connection had been maintained in the intervening generations. It may have been for his service on that campaign that Robert was knighted. His military activity continued as head of the family (he served in Brittany under Thomas of Woodstock in 1380 and in Scotland under Gaunt in 1383) alongside involvement in local government. He was a justice of the peace for the East Riding and sheriff of Yorkshire in 1385–6 and 1394–5, and was returned to parliament in 1388. He acquired land in Butterwick in Ryedale, Yorkshire, in 1395, and it may also have been Robert who forged the links with the Percy family that were to be of such importance to the family in the next century. By 1405 (but not in 1378) the Constables held land of the earl of Northumberland in Nafferton, Yorkshire, and elsewhere.

Robert was unmarried at his father's death, but within three years had married Margaret Skipwith, the widow of Alexander Surtees (*d.* 1380) of North Gosforth, Northumberland. They were pardoned for marrying without licence in January 1384, but the marriage must have taken place earlier, since Robert's heir was old enough to inherit at his father's death, which occurred in late 1400 or early 1401. It is indicative of the family's growing importance that Robert [ii] is the first Constable whose wife can be securely identified. Of the heads of family discussed so far, William [i]'s wife is completely unknown. Katherine, the first wife of his son Robert [i], was probably a Thwing, to judge by the inclusion of Robert and Katherine and their children among the kinsfolk remembered in the chantry of Thomas Thwing. Robert's second wife, Joan, cannot be identified beyond the fact that she was a widow with dower lands in Hook. Marmaduke [i] was married twice, to Joan and Elizabeth, but the surname of neither is known. There is no evidence that any of the marriages brought the family significant land.

It was the marriage arranged by Robert [ii] for his son and heir, **Sir Marmaduke** [ii] **Constable** (*d.* 1404), that was ultimately to secure for the Constables their first major territorial gains, although this could not have been foreseen at the time. **Katherine Constable** (*d. c.*1404), Marmaduke's wife, the daughter of Robert Cumberworth of Somerby, Lincolnshire, was not an heiress at the time of the marriage, but her brother Thomas died childless in 1451, and Katherine's grandson was his heir. Marmaduke died in summer 1404, when his heir, Robert [iii], was a minor, and at least part of the family's lands passed into the keeping of the king's esquire Thomas Strickland.

When **Sir Robert** [iii] **Constable** (*d.* 1441) regained possession is unknown. He had married Agnes (*d.* in or after 1467), daughter of Sir William Gascoigne, by 1422, for his heir, Robert [iv], was born on Easter day 1423. It was a marriage that brought links to an important duchy of Lancaster dynasty, but it does not seem to have contributed much to the Constables' standing in local affairs. It was Robert [iii]'s kinsman and namesake of Barnby by Bossall (*d.* 1454) who was to hold office in the duchy in the 1430s and 1440s. Robert of Flamborough made his will in May 1441 and was dead by the middle of June, leaving two sons (his heir, Robert [iv], and William [iii], who was to end his career as subdean of York) and two daughters.

**Sir Robert** [iv] **Constable** (1423–1488) was still under age at his father's death and did not take possession of his lands until July 1444. By 1448 he had married Agnes, daughter of Sir Roger Wentworth of North Elmsall, Yorkshire, and Margery, dowager Lady Ros. The marriage drew Robert into the schemes of his brother-in-law, Philip, to secure possession of the wardship of Thomas Fastolf against the opposition of Sir John Fastolf. Philip Wentworth was rising fast in the king's service in this period, although there is no evidence that Robert benefited directly. A more tangible boost to Robert's standing came in 1451 when he inherited the Cumberworth estates of his great-uncle Thomas, which gave him a role in Lincolnshire as well as Yorkshire: he was to be sheriff of the latter in 1461–2 and 1478–9, and of the former in 1466–7.

As these appointments suggest, Robert [iv] Constable weathered the defeat of Lancaster in 1461, in spite of the family's connections with the Percys. As early as August 1461 Edward IV had granted him the stewardship of the Yorkshire lands of the earl of Northumberland and Thomas, Lord Ros, at £40 p.a., and land grants, including some of the Ros lands, followed. Such royal favour helped to ensure that Robert and his son Sir Marmaduke *Constable (*d.* 1518) were far wealthier and more influential than their predecessors. Although Marmaduke's gains in the service of Richard III were transient, by the time of Robert [iv]'s death in May 1488 the family fortunes had been put on a sound footing. One measure of their new affluence is the fact that Robert [iv] was able to make landed provision for all his younger sons: Robert [v], Philip, William [iv], and Roger. Marmaduke was able to do the same for his three younger sons, and in addition bequeathed each of them 100 marks in plate. A generation later the family's prosperity was to be revealed, and lost, in the forfeitures that followed the involvement of Marmaduke's son and heir, Sir Robert *Constable, in the Pilgrimage of Grace. The Constable arms were quarterly gules and vair, over all a bend or.　　ROSEMARY HORROX

**Sources** Chancery records · [J. Raine and J. Raine], eds., *Testamenta Eboracensia*, 1–4, SurtS, 4, 30, 45, 53 (1836–69) · W. Farrer and others, eds., *Early Yorkshire charters*, 12 vols. (1914–65), vol. 12 · HoP, *Commons, 1386–1421* · J. R. Maddicott, *Thomas of Lancaster, 1307–1322: a study in the reign of Edward II* (1970) · A. Smith, 'Litigation and politics: Sir John Fastolf's defence of his English property', *Property and politics*, ed. A. J. Pollard (1984), 59–75
**Wealth at death** over £300 p.a.—Robert Constable; partial evaluation: *CIPM, Henry VII*, 1, nos. 363, 366

**Constable, Archibald** (1774–1827), publisher, was born in the parish of Carnbee near Anstruther in Fife on 24 February 1774, one of the seven children of Thomas Constable (1736–1791) and Elizabeth Myles (1733–1819). Thomas Constable was a farmer who became noted for his interest in agricultural improvement and who came to manage the estates of the earl of Kellie.

**Education and training** Constable was educated in the parish school of Carnbee, which he attended for about eight years. In his memoir Constable says that his interest in publishing began with the pleasure he took in a bookshop and stationer's which opened in nearby Pittenweem in 1786, and which led to his being apprenticed for six years from February 1788 to Peter Hill of Edinburgh, who had recently set up as a publisher. Hill's shop was initially in Parliament Close but about 1790 he moved to the High Street, at the Cross. The business was thus not just in the centre of Edinburgh, but at the centre of Edinburgh life, and through his work Constable became accustomed to meeting the literary figures who frequented the city, including Robert Burns.

During Constable's time as an apprentice Hill began to sell old books as well as new. When part of the library of the earl of Moray was offered for sale, Constable proposed a catalogue; he was entrusted with the task, which involved pricing as well as listing. Thereafter he regularly produced catalogues of books for sale, and expanded his activities into cataloguing private libraries for their owners. These activities laid the foundation of Constable's knowledge of books as objects, and fostered his contacts with many private collectors.

**Early years as publisher** After the completion of his apprenticeship Constable stayed with Hill as his clerk for a further year, and on 16 January 1795, just before that year elapsed, he married Mary Willison (*d.* 1814), the daughter of an Edinburgh printer. At twenty-one Constable was determined to establish his own business. He spent a month in February or March 1795 in London learning about London publishing, and met the pre-eminent London publishers Cadell and Longman. Using a loan of £150 from two friends and £300 worth of books from his father-in-law to exchange for others, he got a basic stock. He then undertook a tour of Fife and Perthshire visiting big houses in search of old books to purchase, and on his return to Edinburgh he opened his own shop on the north side of the High Street, erecting the notice 'Scarce Old Books' over the door. He published his first catalogue in May 1795, and this won him many customers. These included Thomas Thomson, who in 1806 became deputy clerk register; David Herd, the song collector; George Chalmers, the Scottish antiquary who was chief clerk to the Board of Trade in London; Richard Gough, the English antiquary; Andrew Plummer, sheriff of Selkirkshire; John Pinkerton; and Walter Scott, although the exact year when Scott began to buy from Constable is not known. A supplement to his first catalogue attracted John, third duke of Roxburghe, the celebrated book collector, who became one of Constable's most regular customers. In the following year, on the advice of Professor John Leslie, he began to import foreign books, and this extended his connections with the Scottish academic establishment. 'My great ambition', wrote Constable, 'was to pick up curious and valuable works relative to the history and literature of Scotland', and he considered himself to be the first in the book trade to take 'a deep interest in securing and preserving all books relating to Scottish literature' (T. Constable, 1.22). Constable was an antiquarian bookseller until 1815, when he retired from that line of business in order to concentrate on publishing.

Constable's first works as a publisher, in the autumn of 1795, were religious and political pamphlets on current subjects such as the slave trade, but as the expenses were borne by the authors, he was able to learn about what did and did not sell without any risk to himself. The first publication commissioned by Constable was *Fragments of Scottish History* (1798), which included Robert Birrel's diary of 1532–1605, and William Patten's account of Hertford's invasion of Scotland in 1544 and Somerset's in 1547; Constable paid the editor, John Graham Dalyell, between £20 and £30. Soon afterwards Dalyell became curator of the Advocates' Library, and bought many books and manuscripts from Constable. Constable's first copyright purchase was the *Discourses* of the Revd Dr John Erskine, minister at Old Greyfriars, and at that time perhaps the best-known and best-loved inhabitant of Edinburgh.

The basis for Constable's later success as a publisher was established in these early years: he was forming good connections with London publishers who would accept large quantities of stock at wholesale prices, and also with the retail booksellers who sold the books to individual buyers; he was cultivating wealthy collectors and purchasers of books; and he was looking for good authors.

In his work as a book publisher Constable's staple output consisted largely of works of historical scholarship and modern editions of the kind of literature and history he sold as an antiquarian bookseller. In 1801, for instance, he published Dalyell's edition of *Scottish Poems of the Sixteenth Century* in two volumes, and John Leyden's edition of *The Complaynt of Scotland*; in 1802 he took a quarter-share in the first edition of Walter Scott's two-volume *Minstrelsy of the Scottish Border*, for which Cadell and Davies in London were the lead publishers; in 1804 he published Scott's edition of *Sir Tristrem* and Alexander Murray's edition of James Bruce's *Travels to Discover the Source of the Nile* (7 volumes), and had a fifth-share in the four volumes of Malcolm Laing's *History of Scotland*; in 1806 he was lead publisher in Robert Jamieson's *Popular Ballads and Songs* (2 volumes), and in 1814 of Scott's edition *The Works of Jonathan Swift* (19 volumes). These are but some examples of a great output that continued over all the years that Constable was a publisher.

Constable entered journal publishing in 1800 in setting up the *Farmer's Magazine*, and in 1801 he purchased the *Scots Magazine*, founded in 1739. He must soon have recognized that well-conducted journals would ensure a steady cash-flow, and so the list of journals under Constable's management is not surprising: in 1803 he became the publisher of the *Edinburgh Medical and Surgical Journal*; he later added the *Edinburgh Philosophical Journal* and the publications of the Royal Society of Edinburgh, the Highland Society, the Caledonian Horticultural Society, and the Wernerian Society; in 1813 he became the publisher of the *Edinburgh Annual Register*.

**The *Edinburgh Review*** Had Constable merely published works of scholarship and the journals of learned societies, he would have been a significant but not a great publisher. It was the establishment of the *Edinburgh Review* in 1802 that made him a publisher who mattered. The original idea came from Sidney Smith, who put it to Francis Horner and Francis Jeffrey. Although Jeffrey later said that he could not remember when the project was first discussed, by January 1802 the 'founding fathers' of the *Review* had chosen their publisher, Archibald Constable. Initially the *Review* operated as a collective: most of the twenty-nine articles of the first number were written by the editorial team; there was no individual editor, the group discussing all contributions in Jeffrey's flat in Buccleuch Place or on the premises of the printer, Constable's father-in-law, David Willison. The first number of the *Edinburgh Review* appeared on 10 October 1802. Early in 1803 Smith proposed to Constable that the *Review* should be put on a permanent footing, with a salaried editor, and with all contributors being paid. From the fourth number Constable paid Jeffrey to be editor, and fixed contributors' rates at 'sixteen guineas per sheet' (T. Constable, 1.49)— but according to Jeffrey many contributors received at least 20 or 25 guineas a sheet for their contributions. High fees attracted good contributors of a class who would not otherwise have been writing for reviews, but they also ensured the dominance of the editor.

Constable had a good product, but the success of the *Review* was dependent on sales. The book-buying public was concentrated in south-east England, and it was essential to have a London partner to push Constable's publications in the south: a normal division of responsibilities gave Scotland, the north of England, and all Ireland to Constable, and the rest of England (south of Leeds) and Wales to the London partner. The southern management of the *Review* was regularly moved. The first number was handled in London by Joseph Mawman, but subsequent numbers were entrusted to Longmans, who in 1803 bought a half-share in the *Review*. After issue 21 Constable bought back the half-share, and the London sales were then handled by John Murray, and from 1809 by Constable's own London 'branch', Constable, Hunter, Park, and Hunter. However, within a year Park died, necessitating the closure of Constable's London business in 1810. Sales of the *Edinburgh Review* were next handled by White, Cochrane & Co. Longmans purchased a half-share in the publication in 1814, and purchased it outright following Constable's bankruptcy in 1826. The variety of partners in the one venture was unusual, but as Constable had no capital, a London partner was essential. The lead publisher in any venture was responsible for the manufacture of the books, but by having London partners Constable was assured of an initial bulk sale which brought immediate money back into his own business.

In 1803 Constable took on a partner, Alexander Hunter, son of the owner of the large estate of Blackness in Forfarshire. The business was valued at £5000, and so Hunter put £2500 into what now became Archibald Constable & Co. Hunter had no publishing expertise. Nominally he was to act as the firm's accountant, but his real significance lay in his paying £2500 to Constable for a half-share in the business. It was the first time that Constable had had any money.

**Scott as a Constable author** The extant records do not show that Constable had a long-term strategy for growth, and yet when looking at his actions one must conclude that he had a very keen awareness of that goal and what could attain it. If the *Review* changed Constable into one of the most important publishers of the age, his association with Scott was intended to make him the most successful. Walter Scott was already established as the best-selling author of the day. Longmans purchased the copyright of Scott's *Minstrelsy* in 1802 for £500, and of *The Lay of the Last Minstrel* in November 1805 for a further £500. Constable had a share in both, and knew the *Lay* had gone through six editions and sold 6700 copies by the end of 1806. Constable offered Scott 1000 guineas for the copyright of his next poem, *Marmion*, an unprecedented offer for a work of imaginative literature, and one which Scott accepted on 31 January 1807. Constable retained a half-share in the work, and sold quarter-shares to John Murray and to William Miller in London. It was a bold stroke, intended to secure Scott for the Constable stable. As an investment *Marmion* was overwhelmingly successful: the first edition of 2000 copies sold at £1 11s. 6d., and the 6000 copies of the third and fourth editions, published within eleven months of the first, sold at the cheaper price of 12s. But the strategic aim failed, not because of Constable, but because of his associates. In April 1808 Jeffrey published his hostile review of *Marmion* in the *Edinburgh Review*; he properly identified many issues for critical debate, but Scott found its manner and tone offensive, particularly when coming from a friend. In the October issue Jeffrey published an article against continuing the Peninsular War; Scott (like many others) cancelled his subscription. Then Hunter offended Scott who in January 1809 wrote 'Constable & I are quite broken owing to Mr. Hunters extreme incivility to which I will certainly never subject myself more' (*Letters of Sir Walter Scott*, 2.146).

Scott's break with Constable was disastrous for both parties. Indeed it can be argued that the seeds of their financial failure in 1826 were sown here, for Scott now established his own publishing company: on 19 July 1809 Scott and James and John Ballantyne signed a deed of co-partnery which set up the publishing business of John Ballantyne & Co. However, by 1812 John Ballantyne & Co. was in serious financial difficulties, in part because of a national financial crisis, and in part because Scott and the Ballantynes did not have Constable's instinct for marketable products. Their solution was to sell out to Constable.

What Scott did not know was that Archibald Constable

& Co. was itself in financial difficulties. Hunter left the partnership in 1811, and Constable later noted: 'Hunter advanced originally in 1804, £2500; in 1811 he had drawn that sum and about £4000 besides—consequently, with the £17,000 paid to him, he gained fully £21,000 by being A. C.'s partner' (T. Constable, 1.160). On 1 May 1811 the business was valued at £35,930 and the incoming partners, Robert Cathcart and Cathcart's brother-in-law Robert Cadell, paid Hunter £17,000 for his share of the business. Cathcart did not put new money into the business: he bought out Hunter. In the following year, 1812, the firm purchased the copyright and stock of the *Encyclopaedia Britannica* for a price in excess of £13,000. However, Cathcart died unexpectedly in November 1812, and the remaining partners, Archibald Constable and Robert Cadell, were required by the terms of the agreement to purchase Cathcart's three-eighths share in the business. And when Thomson Bonar, who held a third-share in *Britannica*, died in 1813 Constable and Cadell had to repay his advances of £6000 and to purchase his share in the copyright, which the complicated terms of their agreement valued at £11,000; in all another £10,000 was taken out of the business.

Between 1803 and 1811 Archibald Constable & Co. achieved a phenomenal rate of growth, and the profits of £1350 paid to Cathcart in 1812 imply a prosperous company. But Constable's lack of working capital made him totally reliant on bank borrowing, and in the national financial crisis of 1812–14 Constable found it difficult to raise new loans to meet his obligations to buy Cathcart's and Bonar's shares in the business. In these circumstances Constable's negotiations with Scott were difficult and protracted. Eventually on 18 May 1813 Constable bought John Ballantyne stock valued at £1467 for £900, a discount of nearly 40 per cent, a quarter-share in Scott's poem *Rokeby* for £700, and volumes of the *Edinburgh Annual Register* valued at £2400 for £400, in all £2000 in bills payable in six, twelve, and eighteen months. A condition of the sale was that John Ballantyne & Co. ceased to be an active publisher.

Constable had regained Scott, but at a cost, and the firm's financial problems continued into 1814. So severe were they that Constable spent October 1814 in London, although his wife was dying (and indeed did die on 28 October), while he was away trying to reduce the firm's indebtedness to the banks by selling a half-share in the *Edinburgh Review* to Longmans, and stocks of books at discounted prices to whoever would buy.

What saved them all was Scott's *Waverley*. Constable offered £700 for the copyright of *Waverley*, but Scott refused, and instead granted what was effectively a licence to publish an edition of 1000 copies of *Waverley* in return for receiving 'half profits'. These 'profits' were not profits in the modern sense of the term, but the publisher's receipts, less the cost of manufacturing and advertising. From this the publisher took half (and had to meet the costs of distribution and overheads from it), and paid the author half. By 1819 11,500 three-volume sets of *Waverley* had been sold, and the positive contribution to the publisher's income must have approached £3000 from that novel alone. Longer print runs on later novels, and higher prices (*Waverley*, 1814, was priced at £1 1s.; *The Antiquary*, 1816, at £1 4s.; and *Kenilworth*, 1821, at £1 11s. 6d.) increased their profitability. The first seven Waverley novels must have brought Archibald Constable & Co. over £20,000 by 1820.

Scott well knew the value of his literary property, and he knew the power given to him by the wealth his novels generated. But he did not use this power to increase his share of the income. Robert Cadell, Constable's partner, admitted that Scott might well have got better terms for himself, but Scott, through his agent John Ballantyne, offered titles to other publishers on the same or similar terms to ensure that he got money when he wanted it, and not when the publisher deigned to pay him. Thus his second novel, *Guy Mannering*, went to Longmans because, as a result of the precarious position of Constable & Co., Cadell delayed making an agreement in October 1814. The third, *The Antiquary*, came back to Constable. The fourth novel went to William Blackwood and his London partner John Murray to test their ability to sell fiction. But Scott came back to Constable, because he considered him to have a greater capacity to sell books than any other publisher.

The letters between Constable and Cadell in 1814 show that they hated Scott's business practices, and considered John Ballantyne thoroughly dishonest. But although Cadell wanted to have no more to do with Scott and the Ballantynes, Constable and Scott needed each other. Constable needed Scott because Scott was the most successful writer of the age. He had to pay to retain Scott as a Constable author, and even in 1818 was not sure of him. To secure Scott he purchased Scott's existing copyrights in 1819, and in the 1820s signed contracts for as yet unwritten and unnamed works of fiction. In 1822, for instance, he agreed contracts for three new novels on 11 March, 3 May, and 8 October, and felt it safe to do this because he had, in 1818, taken out insurance on Scott's life. Constable promoted Scott by advertising heavily, and by keeping him in the public eye; away back in February 1814 Constable had remarked to Longman 'the necessity of keeping up Mr Scott's name by the greatest attention to the sale of his works increases every day' (NL Scot., MS 789, 22). He was rewarded with an unparalleled flow of literary work, but the letters between them show that the publisher was repeatedly trying to control the flow, by getting Scott to speed up or slow down, to suit his sense of the market and his own financial exigencies. Scott needed Constable because Constable was better at selling books than anyone else, and thus facilitated Scott's lavish expenditure on Abbotsford.

**Encyclopaedia Britannica** The third of Constable's major projects was the *Encyclopaedia Britannica*, which Constable purchased in 1812. When Constable commented on 8 May 1812 that it was 'the greatest speculation we ever made' (T. Constable, 2.302) he was right in both senses of the phrase, for he paid in excess of £13,000 for the copyright

and remaining stock of the fifth edition, and proceeded to turn the work into the most distinguished compendium of knowledge of its day. The contents of the fifteen volumes of the fifth edition had already been determined before Constable made his purchase, but he at once commissioned Leslie and Dalyell to advise him on the defects of the fifth edition and what would be required to rectify them. On receiving their report Constable decided to publish a supplement. He commissioned new articles from eminent writers and scholars including Dugald Stewart the philosopher (whom he paid £1600), John Playfair the mathematician, and Walter Scott. He appointed Macvey Napier as editor of the supplement, paying him a fee of £1575, with an extra £735 if more than 7000 copies were sold, as well as expenses of £300. In 1819 Napier was employed as editor of the sixth edition, which was to extend to twenty-five volumes.

Constable claimed that sales of the *Encyclopaedia* between 1812 and 1821 brought in £60,000, that the profits to date could not have been less than £20,000 (T. Constable, 2.329) with £10,000 to come, and that the copyright was worth £12,000. But it is not the monetary value which most impresses the reader of Constable's (almost illegible) letters, nor even the immense generosity of his payments to contributors (by any standards so huge as to make the world of letters buzz with amazement), but the excitement he shows in planning the work, in commissioning articles, and in discussing the progress of the supplement with the editor. After the early numbers Constable left Jeffrey to get on with the *Review*; he interfered with Scott's work only occasionally and with considerable caution; but the supplement to the *Encyclopaedia* was his creation.

**The 1820s** If the three great projects of Constable's first twenty years as a publisher were the *Edinburgh Review*, the *Encyclopaedia Britannica*, and Walter Scott, his ambition in the 1820s was to revolutionize publishing. On 17 January 1819 he offered Scott £12,000 for the purchase of all his copyrights, in fiction, in poetry, and in prose; Scott was initially reluctant, but was talked into agreement. Part of the objective was, as argued above, to secure Scott as a Constable author; another was, no doubt, to escape the necessity of having to deal with the Ballantynes (that was certainly a prospect relished by Cadell, although he was only allowed to enjoy the prospect: the aim was not realized). But Constable had a longer-term strategy: he immediately ordered collected editions of Scott's fiction and poetry. *Novels and Tales of the Author of Waverley* appeared in twelve volumes in 1819, and the set was republished four times between 1821 and 1825, in three different formats. The collected poems, also in twelve volumes, appeared in 1820; by 1825 the set had been republished five times in five separate formats. Constable purchased further copyrights in 1821 and 1823, and the collections *Historical Romances* and *Novels and Romances* followed in 1822 and 1824. Working with his new partner in London, Hurst, Robinson & Co., Constable was realizing the value of literary property in a way no previous publisher had attempted. As before, marketing was the key. The product was designed for different market sectors: the octavo version of *Novels and Tales* sold at £7 4s., the duodecimo at £6, and the 18mo at £4 4s. Novels did not fit precisely into volumes, thus necessitating the purchase of complete sets. Advertising was again heavy, but the product was of higher value than sets of the individual novels, and so the unit costs were lower. The different formats were sold in different parts of the country: Hurst, Robinson & Co. was particularly adept at selling the cheaper 18mo, disposing of 5000 copies of *Novels and Tales*.

In 1823 Scott presented Constable with the manuscripts of all the novels, and this further raised Constable's ambitions, for on 25 March he proposed a new complete edition of the novels, in a handsome format, annotated by Scott himself: 'in my opinion', he wrote, 'it is the Author only who could do anything at all acceptable in the way of genuine illustration' (*Letters of Sir Walter Scott*, 7.354). Constable's estimate of the profit was £20,000, which he was prepared to share with Scott. Scott initially demurred, but by late 1825 had accepted Constable's proposals, and was working on *Waverley*, when the crash took place in January 1826.

Even bolder were Constable's plans for his *Miscellany*, and the mass publication of fiction and works of popular history. He laid his plans out to Scott at a meeting in Abbotsford in May 1825, which J. G. Lockhart reported in an exuberant and ample passage in his *Memoirs of the Life of Sir Walter Scott, bart.*:

> I have now settled my outline of operations—a three shilling or half-crown volume every month, which must and shall sell, not by thousands, or tens of thousands, but by hundreds of thousands—ay, by millions! Twelve volumes in the year … so good that millions will wish to have them, and so cheap that every butcher's callant may have them.   (Lockhart, 6.31)

Constable was planning 'nothing less than a total revolution in the art and traffic of bookselling' (ibid., 6.28). Scott recognized that the plan was both daring and visionary, and told Constable that he would be known as 'the grand Napoleon of the realms of *print*' (ibid., 6.31). The list was to include Scott's novels, but Hurst Robinson objected lest cheap reprints should harm sales of existing stock, and so on 30 August Constable told Scott that the series would consist of miscellaneous non-fiction works, some reprints of standard works, and other new titles commissioned for the series. The series was dedicated to the king, a privilege obtained by Scott, who wrote to George IV's secretary explaining:

> Our great publisher in Scotland has formed a plan which, though intended for his profit in the first instance, cannot, I think, but have the best possible effect in supplying this new and extended demand for literature among the lower classes, by reprinting at a moderate rate, and selling at a low profit, a great number of the most standard English works both in history, in the belles lettres, as well as in science, and in the department of voyages and travels, natural history, and so forth.   (*Letters of Sir Walter Scott*, 9.262–3)

**The bankruptcy**   The grand Napoleon of the realms of print did not see the fulfilment of his greatest scheme because of his bankruptcy in January 1826 (although a modified version began publication on 6 January 1827). According to Lockhart in his *Memoirs of the Life of Sir Walter Scott, bart.* (1837–8) the failure of Archibald Constable & Co. and James Ballantyne & Co., and of Constable, Cadell, Ballantyne, and Scott as individuals (there was then no limited liability and the personal assets of partners in a business were at risk), was due to a complete failure in accounting, exacerbated by a 'maddening period of panic' (Lockhart, 6.118) in the last weeks of 1825. It is not now possible to review the financial position of Archibald Constable & Co., as the accounts of Constable's trustees are lost; one list of Constable's liabilities indicates debts of about £150,000 and another about £200,000, but neither gives usable information about when and for what purpose the debts were incurred. Even so, the accusations of financial incompetence made by Lockhart against them all (ibid., 6.113–20) are incompatible with the fact that Constable as publisher and Ballantyne as printer had conducted two extraordinarily successful businesses for twenty-five years. They also take no account of economic conditions in the winter of 1825–6: there was a national financial crisis. Depositors fearing that banks would fail withdrew their money; the banks called in loans as they became due in order to meet their own liabilities. The result was that Constable was unable to recycle his firm's borrowings. In January 1826 the firm and its partners were bankrupt. Their property was sequestrated, and was sold over the next few years for the benefit of the creditors, who, in the end, were paid a dividend of only 2s. 9d. in the pound. In his *Journal* Scott commented: 'Constable's business seems unintelligible. No man thought the house worth less than £150,000—Constable told me when he was making his will that he was worth £80,000 … No doubt trading almost entirely on accomodation [*sic*] is dreadfully expensive' (p. 71). Trading on accommodation, in other words relying on bank borrowings to finance the business, was expensive, but although it must have reduced the available profit it does not explain the enormous gap between assets and liabilities. It is probable that the firm overestimated the value of the stock; normally the value was reckoned to be what it would fetch if sold at advertised prices. More importantly, those responsible for selling the assets of Archibald Constable & Co. did not understand the value of copyrights: the Waverley copyrights were sold at auction on 19 December 1827 to Scott's trustees for £8400, but sales of the novels in the 1830s suggest that the copyrights were worth ten times what Scott's trustees paid for them. Of course had Scott's trustees not got a bargain Scott's own edition of the Waverley novels would never have proceeded, and would not have generated the enormous sums it did. None the less Constable knew the value of copyrights while his trustees did not, and his valuation of them may explain how he came to estimate his personal fortune at £80,000. In 1838 his eldest son, David, wrote:

> But had the bankers of London understood the value of an assignment of copyright by an author to his publisher, and of *such* copyrights as those of the writings of the Author of

Waverley or the Encyclopædia Britannica, as well as they understand the value of a bill of lading of a cargo of hides or tallow from St. Petersburg, I feel perfectly assured that no loss would have been sustained in any quarter, so far as literature and the publications of Constable and Co. were concerned.    (T. Constable, 3.469)

**Death**  Soon after the failure of the business Constable and Cadell quarrelled, and parted company. Constable lost his fine house, and he and his family went to live in rented accommodation. He tried to re-create his life as a publisher but was deserted by Scott, who chose to work with Cadell. (The latter had seriously misrepresented Constable's negotiations with bankers in London in the weeks preceding the crash.) Constable's health had been in decline for some years: he suffered from 'dropsy', fluid retention possibly indicating partial heart failure. He died on 21 July 1827.

By his first marriage to Mary Willison, Constable had at least eight children, including Elizabeth, who married Constable's partner Robert Cadell on 14 October 1817 but who died on 16 July the following year. He married Charlotte Neale on 12 February 1818 and had a second family. At death he was destitute, and was able to leave nothing to his first family, but his second was supported by the proceeds of an annuity.

Constable's eldest son, David Constable (1795–1867), became a book collector, travelling on the continent in 1817 in search of old and valuable books, and assisting Scott and scholars such as Sir James Mackintosh (T. Constable, 2.521–7). He qualified as an advocate in 1819 and appears to have earned a modest income from the law. He inherited his grandfather's printing business, but his involvement with his father's financial affairs led to the sale of his collection and the loss of the printing business's most significant customer. This and his father's death in 1827 led to a breakdown. He married in 1828 and went to live in Brussels, had two sons and a daughter (who died in infancy), and became a widower in 1835. He had another serious breakdown, and retired to Ayrshire, before returning to Edinburgh and the protection of his brother Thomas [see below] and his family. He died on 4 January 1867.

**Thomas Constable** (1812–1881), printer, was born in Edinburgh on 29 June 1812. He learned the trade of printer with C. Richards of St Martin's Lane in London, and took over the Willison printing business owned by his brother David in 1833. He moved the business from Craig's Close, off the High Street in Edinburgh, to 11 Thistle Street in the New Town, and traded under his own name, Thomas Constable. By 1834 he had won contracts from Robert Cadell and Adam and Charles Black, the present and the future publishers of Scott's works. In 1835 he had four presses; by 1852 he had sixteen, as well as a cylinder and three platen machines. In 1835 he had a Greek fount; by 1852 he had added Arabic, Hebrew, Coptic, Sanskrit, German, and music.

On 14 October 1837 Constable married Lucia Anna Cowan, daughter of the Penicuik papermaker Alexander Cowan, who had been his father's trustee. In 1839 he was appointed her majesty's printer and publisher in Edinburgh, and in 1853 the firm began to print for London publishers. In 1859 he was appointed printer to the University of Edinburgh. By 1861 Constable employed fifty compositors, making his firm the biggest in Edinburgh. He assumed his son Archibald as a partner in 1865, the firm changing its name to T. and A. Constable, the name under which it traded as the foremost Edinburgh printer until its demise in the 1980s.

About 1847 Thomas Constable branched out into publishing under the name Thomas Constable & Co. when he purchased for £10,000 the copyright of the works of Thomas Chalmers, the economist and theologian who more than any other person had been responsible for the Disruption of 1843 and the establishment of the Free Church of Scotland. In 1854 he began the series of schoolbooks known as Constable's Educational Series, and he also published the first of the ten volumes of the complete works of Dugald Stewart edited by Sir William Hamilton. Constable gave up publishing in 1860 when he sold the business to Edmonston and Douglas.

In his later years Thomas Constable wrote a few minor biographies and one major book, the three volumes of *Archibald Constable and his Literary Correspondents* (1873). In this work Constable ably transforms into narrative the records of Archibald Constable & Co., which now constitute one of the great manuscript collections of the National Library of Scotland, comes to a wise and understated view of his father's career and achievement, and makes a fairer and better informed assessment of the financial disaster of 1826 than any that had previously been published. Thomas Constable died on 26 May 1881.

DAVID HEWITT

**Sources**  T. Constable, *Archibald Constable and his literary correspondents*, 3 vols. (1873) • NL Scot., Constable MSS 319–332, 668–683, 789–803, 23230–23234, 23618–23621 • T. and A. Constable, Printers, Edinburgh, NL Scot., MSS 23237–23617 • *DNB* • *Brief notes on the origins of T. & A. Constable Ltd* (1936) • *The letters of Sir Walter Scott*, ed. H. J. C. Grierson and others, centenary edn, 12 vols. (1932–79) • J. G. Lockhart, *Memoirs of the life of Sir Walter Scott*, 7 vols. (1837–8) • *The journal of Sir Walter Scott*, ed. W. E. K. Anderson (1972) • *IGI*
**Archives**  NL Scot., corresp. and business papers, MSS 319–332, 668–683, 789–803, 7200, 8991 • NL Scot., papers [Thomas Constable] • NL Scot., corresp. [Thomas Constable] | Bodl. Oxf., letters to C. K. Sharpe • NL Scot., MSS 23230–23234; 23618–23621 • NL Scot., MSS 23237–23617 [Archibald Constable; Thomas Constable] • NL Scot., corresp. with John Lee • NL Scot., corresp. with Sir Walter Scott • NRA, priv. coll., corresp. with William Creech
**Likenesses**  H. Raeburn, oils, *c*.1808, repro. in Constable, *Archibald Constable*; priv. coll. • A. Geddes, oils, *c*.1813, Scot. NPG • J. Northcote, portrait, oils, *c*.1818, priv. coll. • etching, 1823 (after J. Kay), NPG • T. Faed, group portrait, oils, 1849 (*Sir William Scott and his friends at Abbotsford*), Scot. NPG • G. T. Payne, mezzotint (after H. Raeburn), BM

**Constable** [*formerly* Tunstall]**, Cuthbert** (*c*.1680–1747), antiquary, was the second son of Francis Tunstall (1638–1713), landowner, of Wycliffe Hall and Scargill Castle, and Cecily Constable (*c*.1657–1712), daughter of John Constable, second Viscount Dunbar, of Burton Constable. A

Catholic, he was educated in the English college at Douai in France, which he entered in 1700, and afterwards took the degree of MD in the University of Montpellier. In 1718 he inherited from his uncle William Constable, fourth and last Viscount Dunbar, the estate of Burton Constable, near Hull, in the East Riding of Yorkshire, on condition that he assume the name of Constable. On 20 June 1719 he married Amey Clifford (1705–1731), the fifth daughter of Hugh, second Baron Clifford of Chudleigh (1663–1730), and Anne Preston (d. 1734). In 1731 Amey died of smallpox when pregnant with their fifth child; she was buried at St Pancras in London. On 12 August 1735 he married Elizabeth Heneage (1709–1765), the daughter of George Heneage of Hainton in Lincolnshire, and from this marriage was born Marmaduke *Tunstall, formerly Constable, later a distinguished naturalist.

An accomplished scholar, Constable planned but did not complete a biography of the Catholic controversialist Abraham Woodhead (1609–1678). He did, however, compose the biographical account for his publication of Woodhead's *Ancient Church Government, Part 3*, in 1736. In addition, Constable, styled the 'Catholic Maecenas of his age' (Gillow, *Lit. biog. hist.*, 1.548), supported the scholarship of others. He provided Richard Challoner with the manuscript 'Suffering of the Catholics', by John Knaresborough, chaplain at Burton Constable, for the *Memoirs of Missionary Priests* (1741–2), and he contributed to the cost of publishing Charles Dodd's *Church History* (1737–42). He formed an extensive library at Burton Constable, enriched with valuable manuscripts, including the Woodhead manuscripts, obtained from Lisbon in 1728 from Francis Nicholson (1650–1731), a Catholic convert, formerly of University College, Oxford; Nicholson's biography of Woodhead; and his own correspondence with Nicholson and Thomas Hearne. Constable died at home at Burton Constable Hall on 14 March 1747; the cause of his death was not recorded. He was buried at Halsham on 20 March 1747. In 1802 his remains were deposited in the family mausoleum at Halsham.                THEODOR HARMSEN

**Sources** East Yorkshire RO, Beverley, Yorkshire, Constable MSS · W. Yorks. AS, Leeds, Yorkshire Archaeological Society, Woodhead MSS · M. J. Boyd, '"The Catholic Maecenas of his age": Cuthbert Constable (c.1680–1747) of Burton Constable', *East Yorkshire Local History Series*, 51 (1998), 28–37 · *Remarks and collections of Thomas Hearne*, ed. C. E. Doble and others, 11 vols., OHS, 2, 7, 13, 34, 42–3, 48, 50, 65, 67, 72 (1885–1921) · *Catalogue of the important Burton Constable manuscripts* (1889) · *Catalogue of the Burton Constable library of printed books* (1889) [sale catalogue, Sotheby, Wilkinson, and Hodge, London, 27–29 June 1889] · E. W. Crossley, *Catalogue of manuscripts and deeds in the library of the Yorkshire Archaeological Society*, 2nd edn (1931); repr. (1986) · G. Poulson, *The history and antiquities of the seigniory of Holderness*, 2 (1841), 224–49 · Nichols, *Illustrations*, 5.506–14 · J. Foster, ed., *Pedigrees of the county families of Yorkshire*, 3 (1874) · M. Slusser, 'Abraham Woodhead (1608–78): some research notes, chiefly about his writings', *Recusant History*, 15 (1979–81), 406–22 · *Principal family and estate collections: family names A–K*, HMC (1996), 33–4 · Gillow, *Lit. biog. hist.* · parish register (burial), Halsham and Swine, 20 March 1747 · will, proved York, 30 May 1713, W. Yorks. AS, Leeds, 1/114/144 [Francis Tunstall, copy]
**Archives** BL, corresp., Sloane MS 4034, fol. 358 · Bodl. Oxf. · Bodl. Oxf., corresp., MS Don. c.79 | Bodl. Oxf., MSS Rawl. K. (Hearne-Smith), letters 4, 27b, 27c · U. Hull, Brynmor Jones L., Knaresborough MSS · W. Yorks. AS, Leeds, Yorkshire Archaeological Society, corresp. and papers relating to Abraham Woodhead
**Likenesses** P. van Bleeck, oils, c.1735 (with his second wife, Elizabeth Heneage), Burton Constable Hall, Burton Constable, Yorkshire
**Wealth at death** Burton Constable estate; seigniory of Holderness: HMC, *Principal family and estate collections*; Constable estate papers, esp. DDCC 130/211, 134/22; Borth. Inst., Beverley probate records

**Constable, Henry** (1562–1613), polemicist and poet, was born in Newark-on-Trent, the only child of Sir Robert Constable (d. 1591) and Christiana, daughter of John Dabridgecourt of Langdon Hall, Warwickshire, and widow of Anthony Forster. His family was distinguished: his grandfather Robert Constable married Katherine Manners, sister of Thomas, earl of Rutland; their second son, Henry's father, Robert, made a judicious marriage whose connections opened up a career of military service and public office—he was knighted on the field of battle by Thomas, earl of Sussex, while serving in Scotland, acted as marshal of Berwick between 1576 and 1578, and became master of the queen's ordnance some time before 23 July 1588. Sir Robert died on 12 November 1591.

Henry Constable matriculated as fellow-commoner at St John's College, Cambridge, at Easter 1578, and took his BA on 29 January 1580 by special grace, nominated first in the *ordo senioritatis* (possibly because of his social standing). He is mentioned in the registers of Lincoln's Inn on 21 February 1583, but by 12 September was at St Johnston's (Perth), reporting to his father on the cool reception given to Walsingham by the Scottish court. The latter recommended him to the English ambassador in Paris, Sir Edward Stafford. Constable acted as gentleman-spokesman for the protestant cause in Paris between 14 December 1583 and April 1585; he impressed the ambassador, who told Walsingham on 30 May 1584 that he might be used to bolster the protestant fervour of Henri of Navarre. There are reports from this period of plans to journey to meet Beza in Geneva, and to Italy. In May 1585 Constable was at Heidelberg, where he answered an attack on the queen by a Roman Catholic exile, Thomas Throckmorton. There may have been other journeys, given a sonnet to the queen which mentioned his recent travels in Poland and a phrase in his funeral oration which talked of his having been a soldier in his youth. A commonplace book copy survives of Constable's answer to Cardinal William Allen's justification of Sir William Stanley's surrender of Deventer to Spanish troops, printed in 1587.

Constable was probably at court during 1588–9: he attended the earl of Rutland's funeral in March 1588, wrote a sonnet to Penelope Rich on the birth of her daughter in that year, was described as familiar with Arabella Stuart by 1589, and was said by the secretary of the apostolic delegate to France to be a favourite of the queen. He was at Edinburgh in 1589, ostensibly to bring greetings from members of the English court on James VI's marriage; a coded report of the visit to Burghley, dated 20 October, indicates that members of the Essex circle were using Constable to assure James of their loyalty to him above Arabella. Constable was reported to show himself a protestant at the time, an impression confirmed by a text he published in September 1589, *Examen pacifique de la doctrine des Huguenots* (London, with false Paris imprint; a second edition appeared in 1590). This answered Cardinal Bellarmine's *Responsio ad praecipua capita apologiae*. Constable wrote as though a Roman Catholic, arguing that the divisions between the Reformed and Roman churches were so recent as must inspire moderation in claims for absolute truth; French Roman Catholics were urged to support the newly crowned Henri IV. The tract was translated by 'W. W.' as *The Catholike Moderator, or, A Moderate Examination of the Doctrine of the Protestants* (1623) and answered by Lawrence Anderton and William Smith.

Poetry also engaged Constable's attention at this time. There are three major extant collections of his works. A sequence of twenty-three sonnets, *Diana*, was published in London by Richard Smith in 1592 (Constable left with the Essex expedition to assist Henri IV in August 1591, and the preface describes the poems as 'by misfortune left as Orphans'). Elizabeth I, his cousin Mary, countess of Shrewsbury, and Penelope, Lady Rich, have been named as his 'mistress'. A second edition, with five new sonnets by Constable, eight from Sir Philip Sidney's *Certaine Sonets*, and a further unassigned forty-one sonnets, came out under Constable's name, probably in 1594, though it is likely that this was Smith's project. The Todd manuscript contains nine groups of seven Italian-form sonnets by Constable on the theme of love. Seventeen 'Spirituall sonnettes, to the honour of God: and hys saintes', in British Library, Harleian MS 7553, fols. 32–40, were not published in Constable's lifetime. His editor, Joan Grundy, speculates that the secular sonnets were written before Constable's conversion (*Poems*, 59–60, 84–5); the date of the spiritual sonnets is in dispute.

Between Constable's arrival in France and the death of his father he declared himself a Roman Catholic. Living on a small pension from Henri IV, he made Paris his base (at some time he lived at Mignon College), but was also at Rome before August 1595 and in 1600, Rouen on 8 January 1596, Scotland in 1599, Antwerp, and Brussels. However, his connections with the Essex circle continued until 1597, shown in a series of letters to Essex and Anthony Bacon which protested his loyalty to Elizabeth. As a corollary, he declared his support for James's claim to the English throne over that of the infanta, and acted to frustrate Jesuit actions in France (he was a friend of Christopher Bagshaw, the chief protagonist in the archpriest controversy, and in 1598 handed over to the French government letters from English Jesuits). His plans for securing the welfare of English Roman Catholics used his acquaintance with those in power: a college was to be set up in Paris, Henri was to lean on Elizabeth to tolerate recusants, and the conversions of Anne of Denmark, or even of James himself, were to be attempted. On 1 March 1599 Constable landed at Leith; James initially refused him an audience, and though he spoke with Anne, he was ordered by the sessions of the kirk to subscribe to the articles of religion or leave the country. Having regained the

king's favour, hunting and conversing on poetry and divinity with him, Constable stayed until September, though he accounted the visit a failure on his return to Paris. Yet he continued to nurse hopes of a conversion, going to Rome in 1600 to ask the pope to support another mission to James.

During this period Constable continued to write on theology: he sent to Bacon in January 1596 an unpublished manuscript on an encounter between French divines, and wrote another on English affairs before 1597 (neither extant). He answered a tract by R. Doleman (Robert Persons), *A Conference about the Next Succession* of 1595, which put forward the claims of the infanta. Constable's *Discoverye of a Counterfecte Conference … for Thadvancement of a Counterfecte Tytle* (Paris, 1600, under the false imprint of Cologne) was among a number of tracts which supported James's title. At this time, Constable was described as 'a litle man redd face pumpled gray heair and a smale beard' (*CSP dom.*, Elizabeth, addenda, 34.41).

On James's accession Constable cautiously wrote to certain Scottish friends, and then, on 11 June 1603, to the earl of Rutland and Robert Cecil asking them to intercede for permission for him to return to England. By December he was at court, apparently well received. A warrant of 8 February 1604 allowed him to take possession of his father's lands. He maintained contact with the papal nuncio in Paris, Del Bufalo, as he planned further ways to influence James on the issue of toleration, including an international conference of theologians to dispute differences between the faiths. Cecil was alerted to his schemes: Constable was imprisoned in the Tower from 14 April to 9 July 1604, then confined to his own house, deprived of his inheritance, and imprisoned at least twice (he was in the Fleet on 9 February 1608). He was allowed to leave England on 31 July 1610 and returned to Paris, where he was present at a theological disputation on 4 September 1612. He was sent to Liège by his friend, Cardinal Jacques Davy du Perron, to try to convert Dr Benjamin Carier, a protestant divine, and died there on 9 October 1613.

Constable was highly regarded in his own time as a poet and polemicist; only since the 1950s has his latter role been reacknowledged. He was a notable Roman Catholic convert, who abandoned his home and inheritance to use his family's high standing and his own popularity at court to promote in tracts, disputations, and personal contact the controversial position that devout Roman Catholics could be loyal subjects of the English crown. He was also at the forefront of the development of the sonnet in English literature: the second English poet after Sidney to publish a sonnet sequence and the initiator of a Tridentine aesthetic in his 'Spirituall sonnettes'. His 'Ambrosiack Muse' was linked to Sidney's in Ben Jonson's praise (*Underwoods*, 27, ll. 25–8), Sir John Harington claimed him as his 'very good friend' (*Orlando Furioso*, 1591, sig. Bbiiiv), *The Return from Parnassus* and Gabriel Harvey put him with Edmund Spenser, and he was imitated by poets such as Michael Drayton, Sir William Alexander, and Barnabe Barnes. His most extended contemporary assessment was in Edmund Bolton's *Hypercritica* (1618): 'a great Master in the English Tongue, nor had any Gentleman of our Nation a more pure, quick, or higher Delivery of Conceit' (J. Haslewood, *Ancient Critical Essays upon English Poets and Poesy*, 1815, 2.250). CERI SULLIVAN

Sources The poems of Henry Constable, ed. J. Grundy (1960) · G. Wickes, 'Henry Constable, poet and courtier, 1562–1613', *Biographical Studies*, 2 (1953–4), 272–300 · A. F. Allison and D. M. Rogers, eds., *The contemporary printed literature of the English Counter-Reformation between 1558 and 1640*, 2 vols. (1989–94) · F. Salmon, 'Praedatrix praeda fit ipsa suae': Mary Magdalen, Frederico Borromeo, and Henry Constable's *Spirituall Sonnettes*', *Recusant History*, 18 (1986–7), 227–36 · T. W. N. Parker, *Proportional form in the sonnets of the Sidney circle* (1998) · A. Shell, *Catholicism, controversy, and the English literary imagination, 1558–1660* (1999)
Archives BL, Harleian MS 7553, fols. 32–40 · NL Ire., Marsh MS (Z.3.5.21) · V&A, MS Dyce 44, fols. 12–43
Wealth at death nugatory: Wickes, 'Henry Constable', 292–4

**Constable, Henry**, first Viscount Dunbar (1588–1645), landowner and royalist army officer, was the eldest son of Sir Henry Constable (*c*.1559–1608) of Burton Constable and Halsham in Holderness, and Margaret Dormer (*d*. 1637), daughter of Sir William Dormer of Wing, Buckinghamshire. Sir Henry Constable was elected MP for Hedon in 1584, 1586, and 1604, and for the county of Yorkshire in 1589, and was sheriff there in 1586–7. Although the Constables had become one of the richest families in the East Riding as a result of their acquisition of many former monastic properties, Henry Constable's mother and uncle Joseph Constable were two of the most obstinate recusants in Yorkshire; his father conformed outwardly but left legacies to students in foreign seminaries. Accompanied by his private tutor he entered Trinity College, Oxford, at the age of eight and spent three years there. He succeeded to the considerable family estate at the age of twenty.

Constable was knighted on 14 March 1615 and created Baron Constable and Viscount Dunbar in the Scottish peerage on 14 November 1620. He was deputy justice in eyre for Galtres forest and deputy lieutenant in the East Riding, but was best-known as a hard-drinking, heavy-gambling papist. At one session alone he was said to have lost £3000. In 1630 he compounded for his recusancy and later received a letter from King Charles excusing him from church attendance.

In 1639 Dunbar helped the king raise money for his Scottish war and in 1642 he was denounced in the Commons as 'a powerful papist' who had supplied Charles with 'great store of arms' (Coates, Young, and Snow, 240). Early in 1644 he subscribed to the Yorkshire engagement and took a colonel's commission in Newcastle's royalist army. All three of his sons fought on the king's side: John (1615–1668), the eldest, was eventually exiled to Amsterdam, and Matthew and Henry joined their father when he took refuge with Sir Hugh Cholmley at Scarborough. On 28 June 1645 Dunbar died of wounds received in the siege of the castle, where both his younger sons were injured. Burton Constable Hall was plundered, the estate sequestered by parliament, and John inherited debts of £17,550.

On account of her recusancy John's widowed mother, Mary (*d*. 1659), daughter of Sir John Tufton of Hothfield, Kent, lost all but one third of her portion of £200 a year. JACK BINNS

Sources East Riding of Yorkshire Archives Service, Beverley, Burton Constable MSS, DDCC · U. Hull, Brynmor Jones L., Burton Constable papers, DHO · B. English, *The great landowners of East Yorkshire, 1530–1910* (1990) · DNB · *Dugdale's visitation of Yorkshire, with additions*, ed. J. W. Clay, 2 (1907) · CSP dom., 1591–7; 1603–10; 1623–6; 1628–9; 1635–6; 1644 · J. W. Clay, ed., *Yorkshire royalist composition papers*, 3, Yorkshire Archaeological Society, 20 (1896), 113–15 · G. Poulson, *The history and antiquities of the seigniory of Holderness*, 2 vols. in 4 (1840–41) · J. T. Cliffe, *The Yorkshire gentry from the Reformation to the civil war* (1969) · *Calendar of the manuscripts of the most hon. the marquis of Salisbury*, 5, HMC, 9 (1894); 7 (1899); 12 (1910); 14 (1923); 18 (1940) · J. Rushworth, *Historical collections*, new edn, 1–2 (1721) · W. H. Coates, A. Steele Young, and V. F. Snow, eds., *The private journals of the Long Parliament*, 1: *3 January to 5 March 1642* (1982) · J. W. Clay, *The extinct and dormant peerages of the northern counties of England* (1913), 30 · H. E. D. Blakiston, *Trinity College* (1898), 84 · J. W. Clay, ed., *Abstracts of Yorkshire wills in the time of the Commonwealth*, Yorkshire Archaeological Society, 9 (1890), 140 · private information (2004)
Archives East Riding of Yorkshire Archives Service, Beverley, letters to John Kyrton · U. Hull, Brynmor Jones L., MSS, DHO
Likenesses British school, oils, 1634 (aged forty-six), Burton Constable Hall, Yorkshire
Wealth at death £17,550 in debt—estate in trust, paying him £700 p.a., his heir £300, and his wife £200: East Riding of Yorkshire Archives Service, Beverley, DDCC, 139/129; 145/12; *Yorkshire royalist composition papers*, 3.113–15; *Committee for compounding*, 3.2146–56; English, *Great landowners of East Yorkshire*, 82, 105, 117, 138

**Constable, John** (*fl.* 1511–1520), Latin poet, son of Roger and Isabel Constable of London, studied under William Lily (presumably before he became master of St Paul's), and at Beam Hall, Oxford, proceeding BA in November 1511 and MA in July 1515; in June 1515 he was ordained priest. His later career is unknown. He describes himself as 'Londinensis et artium professor' ('a Londoner and master of arts') in his *Epigrammata*, printed by Pynson in November 1520, and pride in his native city and its varied trade shines in his epigram 'In Londinium'. This volume, containing twenty-six pages of mostly elegiac verse, appears to be the sole survivor of a reasonable literary output, including a work entitled 'Querela veritatis'. His contemporary reputation as rhetorician and poet was high (Wood, *Ath. Oxon.*, 1.27–9); later critics are unkind, Charles Trice Martin calling the epigrams 'dull and pointless' (*DNB*), though admitting the versification to be correct, a judgement echoed by Leicester Bradner in 1940: 'a medieval type of mind … he has nothing to say as a poet. The volume merely serves to establish him as one who wished to be regarded as a humanist' (Bradner, 18).

Constable's humanistic aspirations are indeed significant, and perhaps deserve a more sympathetic assessment. He was in the vanguard of the British Latin Renaissance; a letter from another printer, Berthelet, at the end of Constable's *Epigrammata* praises him as a 'praestans vir' ('a distinguished man'), helping to drive out barbarous Latinity alongside William Horman. Constable has an epigram 'In Bossum Liliomastigem' (a year before Lily and Horman's *Antibossicon*). He defends himself against the charge of levity. Many epigrams show genuine religious feeling, and occasional elegance. Oxford is praised, with 'aula Boemia' (Beam Hall), its master John Plaisted, and other notables; idle young noblemen are sharply castigated. Henry VIII is a Caesar, Solomon, and Maecenas; Katherine of Aragon a star of virtue, and Constable's longest poem, thirty-six lines to Thomas More, neatly turns some complimentary puns ('Morus conspicuus moribus est suis'). There are epitaphs for his parents, brother Richard, and sister Martha (apparently a precocious Minerva). He himself is neither genius nor buffoon, but a worthy precursor of the mid-century flowering of academic Latin verse.                                          D. K. MONEY

**Sources** Wood, *Ath. Oxon.*, new edn, 1.27 • Wood, *Ath. Oxon.: Fasti* (1820), 2 • Foster, *Alum. Oxon.* • Emden, *Oxf.*, vol. 4 • M. McDonnell, ed., *The registers of St Paul's School, 1509–1748* (privately printed, London, 1977) • *Hist. U. Oxf.* 2: *Late med. Oxf.* • J. Constable, *Epigrammata* (1520) • L. Bradner, *Musae Anglicanae: a history of Anglo-Latin poetry, 1500–1925* (1940) • J. W. Binns, *Intellectual culture in Elizabethan and Jacobean England: the Latin writings of the age* (1990)

**Constable** [*alias* Lacey], **John** [*pseud.* Clerophilus Alethes] (1676/1678–1743), Jesuit, was born in Lincolnshire on 10 November 1676 or 1678. The names of his parents have not been found, but as he used the alias of Lacey that may have been his mother's family name; Lacy was also the name of a remote Constable ancestor. In 1690 he joined his elder brother, Joseph (or Marmaduke), at the English College at St Omer, and in 1695 followed him into the Society of Jesus. After his noviciate at Watten in Flanders and studies for the priesthood at Liège, he was ordained about 1704. From 1705 to 1711 he lectured in philosophy, scripture, and theology and taught Hebrew to the Jesuit students at Liège. After a few years on the staff of St Omer College and assisting in the training of Jesuit novices he crossed to England about 1723 and became chaplain to the Fitzherbert family at Swynnerton in Staffordshire.

During the years he was at Swynnerton Constable wrote several works that were published and others that remained in manuscript. He always wrote under the pseudonym Clerophilus Alethes. In Oliver's opinion, 'unquestionably F. Constable is entitled to rank amongst the ablest and best informed men in the English [Jesuit] province' (Oliver, 57). His first published work was *Remarks upon F. Le Courayer's Book in Defence of the English Ordinations &c* (n.d.). This was an answer to Le Courayer's dissertation on the validity of Anglican orders and of the succession of the bishops of the Church of England published in Brussels in 1723. In 1726 Le Courayer published a defence of his dissertation, and Constable replied with *The stratagem discovered, or, An essay of an apology for F. Le Courayer's late work in 4 vols. entitled 'Défense de la dissertation &c' wherein strong instances are produced to show that he writes 'booty' and is only a sham defender of these ordinations, while he very much confirms the judgment of their invalidity* (1727).

On 16 July 1735 Constable was made rector of the Jesuit 'district' of St Chad, the Jesuit priests working in Staffordshire. He continued to engage in controversy. Further publications included a justification of the antiquity of the eucharist and repudiations of deism and latitudinarianism. In 1741, in a vigorous reply to an attack on the Jesuits by Charles Dodd (H. Tootell), a Catholic priest who had published a three-volume history of the English church, he published *A specimen of amendments candidly proposed to the compiler of the work which he calls 'The church history of England from the year 1500 to the year 1688'*. Dodd replied with *An Apology for the 'Church History of England'* (1742), a work 'angry, coarse and abusive' (Oliver, 58). Constable's answer, 'Advice to the author of the *Church History of England*', was described as 'searching, smart and acute' (ibid.), but was never published because the author 'was not solicitous enough to keep the unity of the spirit in the bond of peace' (ibid.). It remains in manuscript at Stonyhurst with other unpublished works.

Among Constable's other publications were *Reflections upon Accuracy of Style. In Five Dialogues* (1734) and *The Conversation of Gentlemen Considered. In Six Dialogues* (1738). He died at Swynnerton, Staffordshire, on 27 March 1743, and was buried the next day in the parish church.

                                          GEOFFREY HOLT

**Sources** H. Foley, ed., *Records of the English province of the Society of Jesus*, 3 (1878), 207; 7 (1882–3), 159 • G. Oliver, *Collections towards illustrating the biography of the Scotch, English and Irish members, SJ* (1838), 57–8 • Gillow, *Lit. biog. hist.*, 1.552–4 • A. de Backer and others, *Bibliothèque de la Compagnie de Jésus*, new edn, 2, ed. C. Sommervogel (Brussels, 1891), 1374; 9 (Brussels, 1900), 102 • R. Trappes-Lomax, ed., 'Addresses of the stations in England served by the Jesuits fathers, 1727–1734', *Miscellanea, VIII*, Catholic RS, 13 (1913), 160–89, esp. 176 • *The letter book of Lewis Sabran*, ed. G. Holt, Catholic RS, 62 (1971), 82 • *DNB* • G. Holt, *The English Jesuits, 1650–1829: a biographical dictionary*, Catholic RS, 70 (1984), 67 • *The memoirs of Gregorio Panzani*, ed. and trans. J. Berington (1793), preface x, xi • *N&Q*, 3rd ser., 9 (1866), 38 • T. Jones, ed., *A catalogue of the collection of tracts for and against popery*, 1, Chetham Society, 48 (1859), 215 • W. T. Lowndes, *The bibliographer's manual of English literature*, ed. H. G. Bohn, [new edn], 2 (1864), 654–5 • F. Blom and others, *English Catholic books, 1701–1800: a bibliography* (1996), 82–3 • J. Kirk, *Biographies of English Catholics in the eighteenth century*, ed. J. H. Pollen and E. Burton (1909), 54

**Archives** Archives of the British Province of the Society of Jesus, London, document, 58/2/8 • Stonyhurst College, Lancashire, MSS

**Constable, John** (1776–1837), landscape painter and draughtsman, was born on 11 June 1776 at East Bergholt House, Church Street, East Bergholt, Suffolk, the fourth of six children of Golding Constable (1739–1816), merchant, mill owner, and gentleman farmer, and Ann (1748–1815), daughter of William Watts (c.1717–1773), cooper, and Jane Brickbeck (d. 1771) of London. Golding was the sixth of ten children of John Constable (1705–1777), farmer and landowner in Bures St Mary, Suffolk, and Judith Garrad; in 1764 he inherited from a paternal uncle money, stocks, and substantial property including the copyhold of a watermill in Flatford on the River Stour where it divides the counties of Suffolk and Essex. His marriage in 1767, followed by the birth of three children, necessitated a move in 1774 from the house at Flatford mill to nearby East Bergholt, where he built an imposing residence with stables and coachhouse. It was here that John Constable was born two years later. The house and its grounds, indeed the entire village and surrounding landscape with views of

John Constable (1776–1837), self-portrait, *c*.1804

the Stour valley in all directions, formed a principal feature of his art throughout his life. As he explained to a friend in 1821, 'I associate my "careless boyhood" to all that lies on the banks of the *Stour*. They made me a painter … I had often thought of pictures of them before I had ever touched a pencil' (*Correspondence*, 6.78). Constable's highly original approach to landscape painting, fuelled by his desire to elevate the genre and shaped by his emotional and economic attachment to that part of East Anglia already known before his death as 'Constable's country', has ensured that his contribution to the development of landscape art in nineteenth-century Britain is rivalled only by that of his contemporary J. M. W. Turner.

**The Suffolk years, 1776–1799** A frail infant hastily baptized on the night of his birth by the Revd W. W. Driffield, Constable nevertheless enjoyed a hearty childhood and *c*.1783 was sent to boarding-school in Fordstreet, Essex, and then to Lavenham, Suffolk. Mistreated there by a brutal usher, Constable returned home and continued his education as a day boy at nearby Dedham grammar school whose headmaster, the Revd Thomas Grimwood, treated him with kindness and indulged his early interest in painting. Captivated by the possibility of becoming an artist and reputedly disinclined to scholarly pursuit, Constable resisted family pressure to prepare for a career in the church. When it became apparent, however, that the disabilities of his elder brother Golding would prevent his taking over from their father, Constable reluctantly began training in the family business at the age of sixteen. Although he would ultimately have had a managerial role

in the diverse and substantial corn and coal trade established by Golding senior, Constable was exposed to the practical side of the milling business as well, working in his father's windmill on East Bergholt Heath, gauging the evanescent meteorological conditions, and familiarizing himself with the navigable River Stour, with its watermills, locks, barges, towpaths, and adjacent fields, all of which were crucial to the family's prosperity. The knowledge he gained in these years, coupled with what he later characterized as 'his over-weaning affection for these scenes' (*Discourses*, 13), would subsequently inform the impassioned naturalism of his landscape art even when the scenery depicted was not East Anglian.

While thus employed, Constable continued to paint and draw, not professionally, but as a gentlemanly pursuit. Practical advice concerning materials and technique was provided by an amateur landscape painter, the local plumber and glazier John Dunthorne, who was Constable's frequent painting companion. Access to tuition of a different sort, as well as entrée into the higher echelons of the art world, were fortuitously managed by Constable's mother in 1795 when she arranged an introduction to Sir George Beaumont, then visiting his own mother in Dedham. A distinguished painter and patron, Beaumont encouraged the young artist, commending his copies of engravings after Raphael and perhaps giving him practical advice about drawing techniques. More relevant to Constable's future career, however, was the opportunity to examine closely Claude's *Hagar and the Angel* (1646; National Gallery), a small landscape owned and highly valued by Beaumont. Constable would later look back on his first sight of this painting 'as an important epoch in his life' (Leslie, 1845, 6), triggering as it did a lifelong devotion to an artist thought to have painted directly from nature. Constable's youthful infatuation with painting was strengthened most significantly in 1796 when, engaged on family business outside London, he was introduced to two professional artists, John Cranch and J. T. (Antiquity) Smith, whose practical instruction improved his drawing skills and enriched his knowledge of the theoretical foundations of academic art; with their guidance he began to assemble what would become in the next forty years an impressive library and print collection (*Further Documents and Correspondence*, 25–52).

With an unwavering enthusiasm for art, Constable nevertheless dejectedly informed Smith in 1797 that he must 'attend to my Father's business … I certainly see it will be my lot to walk through life in a path contrary to that which my inclination would lead me' (*Correspondence*, 2.10). In 1799, however, freed from family obligation when his younger brother Abram, now aged sixteen, was able to take his place, Constable left home with a sufficient allowance and parental consent to study art in London.

**Early years in London, 1799–1809** In February 1799, armed with a letter of introduction from the author and philanthropist Priscilla Wakefield, Constable presented himself to Joseph Farington, an influential royal academician whose friendly intervention facilitated his entry into the London art world. In March he was admitted to the Royal

Academy Schools as a probationer, restricted to drawing in the antique academy until February 1800 when he was enrolled as a student in the life academy. Constable's transition from life in East Bergholt to London was eased by the presence in the city of several family members, including his elder sister Martha Whalley and his maternal uncle David Pike Watts, a wealthy connoisseur and collector who took an active interest in his nephew's career. Constable's 'kind monitor' Dr John Fisher, the rector of Langham and canon of Windsor when they first met in 1798, proved an influential friend in London, particularly after he became bishop of Salisbury and chaplain to the Royal Academy in 1807. While fellow students increased Constable's circle of friends, he continued to cultivate his connections with mentors such as Beaumont and Farington who gave him not only practical advice, but access to old master paintings, drawings, and prints which he was permitted to copy. Such copying, as Constable reported in a letter to Dunthorne in 1800, enabled him to 'acquire execution. The more facility of practice I get, the more pleasure I shall find in my art; without the power of execution I should be continually embarrassed' (*Correspondence*, 2.24). Although his life was now essentially London-based, Constable returned to Suffolk frequently, maintaining close contact with family and friends there, but more importantly indulging his need to paint and draw from nature. Evidence that he was already beginning to formulate his personal vision of landscape art appears in a letter of May 1802 to Dunthorne:

> For these two years past I have been running after pictures and seeking the truth at second hand ... I shall shortly return to Bergholt where I shall make some laborious studies from nature—and I shall endeavour to get a pure and unaffected representation of the scenes that may employ me ... There is room enough for a natural painture.    (ibid., 2.32)

Several small oil sketches painted during his lengthy visit to Bergholt that year, including *Dedham Vale* and *Dedham Vale: Evening* (V&A), mark what is widely recognized as the starting point of a commitment to outdoor study that was to be the foundation of his art. This commitment, however, would always be tempered by his understanding of the theoretical precepts of Sir Joshua Reynolds and by his continued willingness to incorporate what he could learn from past artists, particularly Claude, Rembrandt, Rubens, Ruisdael, Wilson, and Gainsborough.

Stimulated by parental pressure to achieve some degree of financial independence, Constable found it necessary to resort to portraiture, finding many of his sitters through family and friends. East Anglian connections also led to a few commissions for altarpieces, but *Christ Blessing the Elements* (1810; St James's Church, Nayland), a rather saccharine, passionless painting, suggests that religious art did not engage Constable's creative capabilities; and an unwelcome offer of employment as a drawing instructor at a military school in 1802 was wisely turned down. As he confided to Dunthorne, 'it would have been a death blow to all my prospects of perfection in the Art I love' (*Correspondence*, 2.31). Although he continued to attend the life academy as a student until at least 1808—

producing competent, sensitively drawn nude studies—he showed no inclination to pursue large-scale figural painting, thereby forfeiting what his parents would have seen as a more lucrative and prestigious career. The training he received in anatomy lectures and life classes, however, no doubt improved his understanding of the human form and augmented the early advice about figure placement which he attributed to J. T. Smith and frequently repeated in later life:

> Do not set about inventing figures for a landscape taken from nature; for you cannot remain an hour in any spot, however solitary, without the appearance of some living thing that will in all probability accord better with the scene and time of day than will any invention of your own. (Leslie, 1845, 7)

Constable's parents were justified in their concern for his future. By 1809 they were still supplementing his meagre income and worried about his continued devotion to landscape painting. Even the three tours he made to expand his repertoire of picturesque scenery—the Peak District in 1801, a month-long voyage down the Thames and along the Kentish coast in 1803, and the Lake District in 1806—had been subsidized by family or friends. After ten years in London, however bleak his prospects may have looked and however small his impact in the public arena, he was none the less making progress: he had exhibited works at the Royal Academy and British Institution; he was beginning to explore promising techniques in watercolour and oil sketching that would lead to significant developments; and he was producing a remarkable number of drawings (two to three hundred in 1806 alone) that tested his compositional skills and kindled a lifelong experimental approach to graphic techniques and media. Bold enough to consider putting his name forward as an associate of the academy in 1807 (though he decided against it), he remained convinced that a career was possible. His perseverance intensified in 1809 when a friendship of several years blossomed into serious courtship and, realizing that marriage was impossible without financial security and professional recognition, he renewed his efforts with fervour.

**Early courtship and career, 1809–1811** Constable probably first encountered Maria Elizabeth Bicknell (1788–1828) when, as a twelve-year-old child, she came to visit her maternal grandfather, Durand Rhudde, the wealthy rector of East Bergholt, chaplain-in-ordinary to George III, and one of the most influential residents of the village. She was the eldest of five children of Charles Bicknell, solicitor to the Admiralty and the prince regent, and his second wife, Maria Elizabeth Rhudde. Miss Bicknell may have aroused Constable's interest in 1806 during a visit to Bergholt when she was eighteen and he thirty. It was not until she came of age in 1809, however, that they declared their mutual affection, only to be met with family resistance led by the implacable Dr Rhudde, but dutifully implemented by her parents. Why Rhudde objected remains a mystery, but his threat to disinherit not only his granddaughter but all her siblings suggests a dislike of Constable that stemmed from something more personal than the struggling artist's precarious financial situation or his family's connections to trade. Some past offence, real or imagined (and possibly committed by Constable's father rather than himself), may have triggered Rhudde's absolute refusal to sanction the alliance; but whatever the cause, his relentless intervention plagued the couple's seven-year courtship which was marked by clandestine meetings and secret correspondence. The letters they exchanged throughout these years, as they move from polite decorum to heartfelt devotion, are a poignant chronicle of their relationship, but they also provide the emotional background for Constable's vigorous and anxious campaign to prove himself.

Constable's mother, astute about the vagaries of village life, interceded with maternal shrewdness when she could. She intercepted gossip from the rectory and encouraged her son to present Rhudde with a watercolour drawing of his church, complete with respectful inscription (1811; Lady Lever Art Gallery, Port Sunlight). Her letters, displaying what has been perceptively characterized as 'a consistent mercantile protestantism' (Rosenthal, 10), urged him to pursue his goals with Christian fortitude, patience, and diligence since only by these would he reap the benefits of his industry and earn the money without which he could never contemplate marriage. Bolstered by her support, and by a conviction that he was destined to inaugurate a genre of landscape that was not only original but 'moral', he redoubled his efforts to make his mark and his living.

Constable had painted few outdoor oil sketches since his intensive period of activity in 1802; and those, such as *The Rectory, East Bergholt* (1808; FM Cam.) or *View at Epsom* (1809; Tate collection) are, though marked by a fresh spontaneity, subdued both in handling and colour. From 1810, however, a greater boldness in his palette and urgency in his brushwork appear. Two dated sketches from that year, *The Rectory from East Bergholt House* and *View on the Stour* (Philadelphia Museum of Art), and several undated ones of Dedham Vale looking west from the Suffolk side of the Stour reveal a renewed desire to capture the varied look of the natural landscape in a form that, in conjunction with numerous drawings, might be used in his London studio to construct paintings for exhibition. This working method produced the panoramic *Dedham Vale: Morning* (priv. coll.), shown at the academy in 1811. Arcadian in mood, but utterly faithful to the local topography, its originality confirms the progress Constable had made since his first academy exhibit of 1802, *The Edge of a Wood* (Art Gallery of Ontario), with its heavy reliance on Gainsborough. Having sought election as an associate for the first time in 1810 without receiving a single vote, Constable was especially keen that *Dedham Vale: Morning*, the most ambitious painting he had yet produced, should prove his worth both to the academicians and to Maria's family. He later told his engraver David Lucas that no painting ever caused him more anxiety and that 'he had even said his prayers before it' (*Further Documents and Correspondence*, 55).

**Courtship and career, 1811–1816** For the next five years Constable continued to divide his time between London and Bergholt painting portraits for money but, for fame, devoting himself to the landscape. Despite worrying weight loss and depression, he filled his sketchbooks with hundreds of drawings and further explored the possibilities of outdoor sketching in oil. Working on canvas, board, and specially prepared papers, he experimented with even more innovative handling, making rapid and vibrant notations of the scenery and the changing weather. By painting the same sites from many different viewpoints, he tested the compositional variations that he hoped would, when amalgamated in his studio, contribute to the natural effect and verisimilitude of his finished works. By 1816 his studio—and his memory—would be stocked with images of Dedham Vale from both sides of the Stour. Although there was special emphasis on Flatford mill and lock, Willy Lott's house (later to be immortalized in 'The Hay Wain', 1821; National Gallery), and views of and from East Bergholt, he had amassed an almost encyclopaedic visual record of whatever caught his eye: animals and humans as they moved down lanes, through fields, or along the river; domestic buildings and churches as they nestled in the valley or rose on the horizon; and, of course, the sky.

In 1812 Constable exhibited *A Water-Mill* (priv. coll.) at the Royal Academy, a work whose genesis can be traced, like so many of his paintings, from a salmagundi of drawings, sketches, and studies. It features Flatford mill and lock, a site arguably associated in his mind at this time with Maria and one that had so fully absorbed him since 1810 that the mill 'had become as much Constable's business as his father's' (Bermingham, 105). Local scenery continued to provide the subject matter for his exhibited works during these years, but he was still unsettled about the process by which he could achieve the desired effect. As he told his uncle in 1814, in response to one of Watts's kindly but critical letters, 'I know I have great deficiencies and that I have not yet, in a single instance, realised my ideas of art' (*Correspondence*, 4.38). At least one of his works exhibited in 1815, *Boat-Building* (V&A), and perhaps a second, *View of Dedham* (Boston Museum of Fine Arts), were painted entirely in the open air during his visits to Bergholt the previous year, the former occupying his afternoons, the latter his mornings. Yet despite these various efforts to find an original manner of painting his native scenery—that 'natural painture' he had been pursuing since 1802—Constable was still struggling to gain a foothold. Encouraged by the voiced support of some academicians, he had put his name forward for an associateship several more times, but the votes were not forthcoming. Farington, who continued to offer advice as though Constable were still a student, suggested that he study Claude more closely to overcome the sketchy, unfinished handling that was seen by the academy to be his greatest fault. Those few reviewers in the popular press who were beginning to notice Constable with some regularity now, particularly Robert Hunt in *The Examiner*, also expressed reservations about his supposedly careless execution, but they were none the less struck by qualities they characterized as 'natural', 'fresh', and 'truthful'. Indeed, the first known review of Constable had in 1807 singled out with apparent prescience several salient features that would engage both his supporters and detractors throughout his life: his boldness, his colouring, and his 'attention to Nature' (*St. James's Chronicle*, 7–9 May).

Constable's ties to East Bergholt, though still strong in 1816, were about to change radically. The sudden death of his mother in 1815 and the death of his father after months of ill health the following year were emotionally traumatic for him, but his share of the inheritance eased his financial worries and removed at least one of the barriers to his marriage. The frustrations of a seven-year courtship had taken their toll on his art but not lessened his feelings for Maria. When further difficulties with Dr Rhudde erupted in 1816, Constable persuaded her that they had waited long enough. Aged forty, he was about to achieve a private happiness without which, as his friends and family all suspected, he would never advance professionally: 'all my hopes and prospects in life', he had written to her in 1814, 'are included in my attachment to you' (*Correspondence*, 2.119).

**Marriage, family, and the academy, 1816–1819** On 2 October 1816 Constable and Maria were married at St Martin-in-the-Fields, London, by Bishop Fisher's nephew, John Fisher (1788–1832), who since their first meeting in Salisbury in 1811 had become the artist's closest friend. Fisher, himself only recently married, invited the Constables to his vicarage in Osmington, Dorset, where they spent six weeks of their honeymoon, returning to London in December. Constable, who had lived in bachelor's lodgings in at least six different locations in London since 1799, brought Maria to his rooms at 63 Charlotte Street where he had been living for five years. Within six months they moved to 1 Keppel Street, Bloomsbury, by which time he had already suffered a miscarriage and was pregnant again. A son, the first of seven children, was born in December 1817; his arrival may have softened the heart of Dr Rhudde, who ultimately bequeathed to Maria the same portion as her siblings when he died in 1819. The child, as Constable's first biographer, the artist C. R. Leslie, recalled, was seen almost as often in his father's arms as in his mother's: 'His fondness for children exceeded, indeed, that of any man I ever knew' (Leslie, 1845, 77).

To supplement the interest he was receiving from his father's bequest, plus his annual share of the family business and Maria's small annuity from her father, Constable calculated that he would need to earn an additional £100–150 per year to cover their expenses. He still relied heavily for his income on portraiture (*Mrs Jane Andrew*, 1818; Tate collection; *Mrs James Pulham, Sr*, 1818; Metropolitan Museum of Art, New York) and on occasional paintings of specific sites, such as *Wivenhoe Park, Essex*, commissioned by General Slater-Rebow in 1816 (National Gallery of Art, Washington). Only a few of his landscapes shown at the Royal Academy or British Institution since 1802 had found buyers, and those for the most part had been purchased by family or acquaintances. In 1818, however, he sold two paintings at the British Institution and a third there the following year. The report of these sales in the press served as useful advertising, alerting other buyers in the market place to his potential, but that service was also being performed by the reviewers who had begun to notice him with increasing frequency and with greater appreciation for the vivacity and spirit of his landscapes.

Maria, pregnant again by late 1818, gave birth to a daughter the following summer. His wife's health, delicate even before their marriage, was to be a constant source of concern to Constable; and in August 1819 he rented a cottage in Hampstead where Maria and the children would be spared the bad air of London for at least a few months. This retreat to a suburban (indeed, almost rural) setting would become an annual event, benefiting not only Maria's lungs but introducing Constable to a landscape that delighted him, engaging both his affections and his artistic creativity. As subject matter, Hampstead would never dislodge the pre-eminence of the Stour valley; with its glorious skies, however, it now began to attract his attention as Salisbury had done since his first visit there in 1811.

Although settled and calm in his private life at last, Constable still faced professional frustration. He had failed yet again to become an associate member of the academy in the elections of 1817 and 1818; but with the same tenacity that had brought him to London in 1799 and sustained him in his difficult courtship, he renewed his efforts to discover an original, innovative style that would gain academic approval, public recognition, and patronage. He exhibited only one painting at the academy in 1819, *A Scene on the River Stour* ('The White Horse', Frick Collection, New York), but it achieved much that had so far eluded him. Measuring 6 feet by 4 (the first of what came to be known as his 'six-footers'), it was the largest canvas he had submitted and represents an unprecedented development in his working method. Constable had by this time spent almost two decades experimenting with various procedures by which direct work from nature could be transformed into paintings deemed suitable for exhibition. To paint anything so large as 'The White Horse', a Stour Canal scene, direct from the motif was certainly impractical; the lengthy stays in East Anglia where such outdoor work could be done were now precluded by the sale of the parental home in East Bergholt and by his reluctance to be separated so long from his family in London. His solution was to comb through his extensive store of drawings and oil sketches as before, but to use them in conjunction with an intermediary, full-scale (that is, 6 foot) oil sketch on which he could test the effects of composition as well as of the chiaroscuro, that crucial balance of light and shadow so important to his perception of 'natural' landscape painting. Although much is still unknown about his precise working methods, Constable's experimentation unleashed a new power, enabling him to paint fresh and vibrant large-scale works in his Keppel Street studio without direct access to the actual scene. 'The White Horse', well received by the reviewers, was purchased by Constable's friend Fisher for 100 guineas; and in November

1819 the artist was finally elected an associate of the academy.

**Salisbury and Hampstead, the early 1820s** The continued centrality of the Stour valley in Constable's life and art cannot be overstated, but from now until his death his visits there were infrequent and of short duration. No longer under pressure to stock his studio or his memory with East Anglian views, he drew or sketched when there, it would seem, simply because he could not restrain himself if he had materials with him and a site or an effect caught his eye. Never forsaking his commitment to the fundamental importance of outdoor study, however, he merely focused his attention—and his affections—on other locales.

After exhibiting his second 'six-footer' in 1820, another canal scene bought this time by Fisher as a gift for his solicitor (*Stratford Mill*; National Gallery), Constable took Maria and the children to Salisbury for a long and idyllic summer visit. They stayed with Fisher, now a canon living in a spacious house in the close from which Constable had ample opportunity to deepen his intimacy with the cathedral and its environs. His outdoor oil sketches and drawings, which included views of Stonehenge and Old Sarum, reveal a wide range of handling, from the closely detailed to the exuberantly free, and, in keeping with his standard procedure, would be consulted in subsequent years for works executed in his London studio (*Salisbury Cathedral from the Bishop's Grounds*, 1823, and *Stonehenge*, 1836; V&A). This long visit intensified the already well-established friendship between Constable and Fisher. Their shared passion for landscape (Fisher was an amateur artist) and for their young families is fully revealed in their lengthy correspondence which, though ending with Fisher's early death in 1832, provides a poignant record of the joys and disappointments of Constable's private and professional life. Both men enjoyed a ribald sense of humour and indulged in satiric jibes at their colleagues, particularly those who brought their professions into disrepute. Only Constable's friendship with Leslie approached the closeness of his attachment to Fisher, and it is in his correspondence with these two men that his deeply held views about life and art are most fully articulated.

Immediately upon their return to London, Maria (pregnant again) was settled with the children in a house in Hampstead. Although he needed to work in his Keppel Street studio, Constable stayed with them when he could and, invigorated by the surrounding landscape, began a new campaign of open-air sketching that once again transformed his painting. Concentrating on views from Hampstead Heath, which served as a virtual meteorological observatory, he embarked on a series of sky studies that throughout the early 1820s would enhance his understanding of the natural phenomena so crucial to his vision of landscape art. Already very knowledgeable about weather and its effects from his practical experience in the family business, he pursued both theoretical and empirical confirmation of what he had learned. Certainly aware of the contemporary scientific work of Luke Howard and Thomas Forster, he treated the heath as a laboratory for his own experiments, painting between October 1820 and October 1822 over one hundred studies in which the sky is the chief feature. Many are annotated with the date and time, wind speed and direction, the preceding weather conditions and those that followed. 'His accurate studies match almost perfectly the contemporary weather records'; despite the challenge of rapid, open-air oil sketching, 'he was able to capture those momentary glimpses of shape, process, colour and meteorological truth' (Thornes, 200).

Constable informed Fisher in October 1821 that he had 'done a good deal of skying', writing at great length about his attempts to conquer 'that most arduous' difficulty faced by a landscape painter:

> if the Sky is *obtrusive*—(as mine are) it is bad, but if they are *evaded* (as mine are not) it is worse … It will be difficult to name a class of Landscape, in which the sky is not the '*key note*', the *standard of 'Scale'*, and chief '*Organ of sentiment*' … The sky is the '*source of light*' in nature—and governs every thing. (*Correspondence*, 6.76–7; see also Thornes, 278–82, for Fleming-Williams's sensitive decipherment of this exceptionally telling letter to savour the orthographic and punctuation complexities typical of Constable's prose.)

The conjunction of art and science in his landscapes is perhaps most fully revealed in the effect Constable's 'skying' had on his studio work at this time. What he learned at Hampstead enabled him to unite the sky and land to an unprecedented degree and illustrates a maxim he later expressed in one of his lectures: '*We see nothing till we truly understand it*' (*Discourses*, 64).

Although Hampstead provided an occasional second home where Maria could recuperate, the birth of their third child in 1821 and the imminent arrival of another the following summer necessitated a larger London house for the family, prompting a move in June 1822 from Keppel Street to 35 Charlotte Street, Fitzroy Square. The residence (now demolished) of the recently deceased Joseph Farington, it was a house Constable knew well and would remain his London home until his own death in 1837. Although it was preferable in many ways, Constable regretted leaving the house where he had painted four of his important 'six-footers': 'The 5 happiest & most interesting years of my life', he told Fisher, 'were passed in Keppel St. I got my children and my fame in that house, neither of which would I exchange with any other man' (*Correspondence*, 6.99).

**Brighton, the mid-1820s** Charlotte Street, though more agreeable in general, did little to restore Maria's health. Advised to 'try the sea' in 1824, Constable took lodgings for the family in Brighton, the first of several extended stays there. Travelling down from London to be with them whenever he could, Constable loosed his creative energy on the sea shore with its bustling activity and windswept skies. Drawings and oil sketches, frequently annotated with temporal and meteorological details, record Constable's fascination with his new surroundings (*Brighton Beach, with Colliers*, V&A). Not having had such sustained access to the coast since his honeymoon trip to Dorset in 1816, he was struck by the magnificence of the sea, though its 'everlasting voice', he told Fisher, was drowned by the din of the beach which was like 'Piccadilly by the sea-side' (*Correspondence*, 6.171). Undeterred, however, he drew and painted what passed before him in all its variety: the people, the boats, and the evanescent effects of sky and waves. In typical fashion, the stock of images produced here resurfaced in small studio works which were then used by Constable to construct the large-scale *Chain Pier, Brighton* (Tate collection), shown at the 1827 academy exhibition. Some reviewers, surprised by a 'six-footer' devoted to a seaside resort rather than an inland canal, none the less praised Constable for its adherence to nature and freshness of colour. *The Times* thought it one of his best works and declared him 'unquestionably the first landscape painter of the day' (11 May 1827). The *Morning Post*, however, found its colouring defective and thought it looked as if there were '*streaks of ink* dashed across it' (20 June 1827).

**Constable and France**  By the mid-1820s Constable's reputation in England was already marked by this troubling contradiction. Credited with originality, he was praised for not painting in the 'manner' of any other artist. Yet his own 'mannerisms'—loose handling, bold impasto, and a certain 'spottiness' that would come to be known as 'Constable's snow' or whitewash—were a cause of concern to reviewers, academicians, and potential patrons. What was perceived as his 'naturalism' was hailed as his greatest strength, enabling him to capture the peculiarities of English landscape; but paradoxically his persistent concentration on the rural was thought to be repetitive, preventing his mastery of the more imaginative or 'poetic' aspects of the landscape tradition.

While the English public dithered over Constable's strengths and weaknesses, the more radical factions of the French art world, in a flurry of enthusiastic support, revelled in his freshness and apparent rejection of staid landscape conventions. The first Frenchman to take notice was Charles Nodier who, having seen the third 'six-footer', *Landscape: Noon* ('The Hay Wain'), at the 1821 academy exhibition, published a rhapsodic report in his *Promenade de Dieppe aux montagnes d'Écosse* (1821; Eng. trans., 1822, 49). Equally impressed, Amédée Pichot and Théodore Géricault also sent word back to France that year. As news of their keen interest spread, it sparked the curiosity of two Parisian dealers, John Arrowsmith and Claude Schroth, who were responsible for a remarkable interlude in Constable's career. Arrowsmith, having seen 'The Hay Wain' at the 1822 British Institution exhibition, purchased it in 1824 with a small Yarmouth scene and the fourth 'six-footer', *View on the Stour near Dedham* (1822; Huntington Gallery, San Marino, California). Both he and Schroth visited Constable's studio and commissioned several other paintings, and Arrowsmith then arranged for the two large canvases plus a small Hampstead view to be shown at the 1824 Paris Salon. Although conservative French critics were shocked by Constable's unorthodox handling and colour, the response was otherwise very positive and he was awarded a gold medal by Charles X at the close of the exhibition. Eugène Delacroix and Paul Huet, both directly influenced by Constable, credited him

accordingly; and as his fame spread, he heard reports that his paintings had become something of a *cause célèbre*. Artists, he told Fisher in December 1824, showed:

> much desire to purchase them & deposit them in a place in which they can have access to them … they have made a decided stir, and have set all the students in landscape thinking—they say on going to begin a landscape, Oh! this shall be—*a la Constable*!!! (*Correspondence*, 6.185–6)

A year later Constable reported to Fisher that Arrowsmith had 'a room in his house called Mr. Constable's room … He says my landscapes have made an epoch there' (ibid., 6. 209).

Unfortunately, events conspired to halt the flow of Constable's paintings to the continent. Offended one afternoon by Arrowsmith's impertinence, the artist severed relations in a fit of pique (instantly regretting the loss of income). Although both dealers ceased trading within a few years anyway, Constable continued to hear reports of his influence abroad. Having sent two paintings to an exhibition in Lille, he was notified in 1826 that he had been awarded another gold medal; and in 1827 he sent *The Cornfield* (1826; National Gallery) to the Paris Salon. That same year, Arrowsmith's *View on the Stour near Dedham* was shown in Douai; in 1833 Constable exhibited a version of *A Barge Passing a Lock* in Brussels and in 1834 he was invited to exhibit again in Lille. In 1835 Thomas Uwins reported that there was 'no English painter's name known so well' in France as Constable's (*Correspondence*, 5.179). There is still much to be discovered about Constable's impact on nineteenth-century French art. Historians, responding to Delacroix's enthusiastic comments in his journals, may have on occasion overestimated Constable's influence on subsequent developments in French landscape painting; but that he generated during his own lifetime a greater frisson among the artists in France than those in England, that he showed them effects of light and atmosphere they had never yet seen, is incontrovertible.

**The late 1820s**  An associate of the academy since 1819, Constable sought full membership on several occasions, and failed. He had, none the less, made substantial progress in his profession; and, if there were few people who understood precisely what he was trying to achieve, there were several who spoke of his 'genius' and originality. Sales were increasing; unfortunately so were his expenses. A fifth child had been born in 1825, a sixth in 1826. Maria's consumption, compounded by so many pregnancies, was worsening; and in 1827, with Maria pregnant yet again, Constable transferred the family permanently to Hampstead where he leased 6 Well Walk, keeping only his studio and a few rooms in Charlotte Street for his own use. 'Our little drawing room commands a view unequalled in Europe', he told Fisher, pleading in the same letter for a loan of £100 (*Correspondence*, 6.231). His financial worries were alleviated in 1828, however, by an inheritance of £20,000 from Maria's father, but she had little time to enjoy it. She died on 23 November, leaving Constable with seven children under the age of eleven. 'The face of the World is totally changed to me', he told his brother (*Further Documents and Correspondence*, 81). Three months later, aged fifty-two, he was finally elected a full member of the academy. 'It has been delayed until I am solitary, and cannot impart it' (Leslie, 1845, 186).

Throughout this decade Constable had confined his exhibited studio works to those places he knew best, but he was becoming less tied to the topographical accuracy of the previous decade and intensifying the expressive robustness of his handling, particularly in his use of the palette knife to create surface texture. In *The Leaping Horse* (1825; RA) Constable had come close to 'an abstracted art, and part of the brilliance of his effect is in the tension created through his efforts to force this into a figurative one' (Rosenthal, 164–6). This tension is particularly evident in *Hadleigh Castle* (Yale Center for British Art, New Haven), exhibited at the 1829 academy within months of Maria's death. Simultaneously expressive and descriptive, Constable's brushwork combines with the palette knife to create an ode to melancholy and ruin. Reviewers, stunned by its power, were none the less perplexed by its surface texture which was likened to chopped hay and whitewash. Abuse of a personal nature began this year when the critic Edward Dubois credited Constable's academy membership to his recent acquisition of wealth. His attacks on Constable's merit and integrity continued in the following decade; and he, with several other reviewers, intensified their light-hearted (and occasionally mean-spirited) ridicule of Constable's increasingly rough and broken handling (Ivy, *Constable and the Critics*, 14–56).

**The mezzotints** Constable, unlike many contemporary landscape painters, had very little contact with the print publishing industry or the burgeoning illustrated-book trade; and when he decided shortly after Maria's death to have several of his paintings and sketches engraved, he retained absolute control over the entire publishing venture. Choosing mezzotint as the process most suited to translate his bold handling and to convey his thoughts about the importance of chiaroscuro in landscape art, he engaged David Lucas to engrave *Various Subjects of Landscape, Characteristic of English Scenery* (generally known as *English Landscape*). Initially published between 1830 and 1832 in five separate parts and reissued in 1833 with several pages of letterpress text, it contained twenty-two mezzotints, all of which progressed from first proof to published state amid much dithering and petulance on Constable's part and infinite patience on Lucas's. Several more plates were planned as an appendix, six of which were issued just after Constable's death. Throughout their collaboration, which is chronicled in a remarkable series of letters (Shirley, 16–151, and *Correspondence*, 4.314–463), Constable interfered constantly, never actually working on the steel himself but doing everything he could to shape the gradually emerging black and white images as they developed from proof to proof. The autobiographical visual imagery, particularly in the *Frontispiece* (his birthplace) and the *Vignette* (Hampstead Heath), represents a genre of self-referential landscape that might be called 'egotistical topography'; coupled with the plates, the letterpress in *English Landscape* (his 'book' as he called it) virtually serves as Constable's apologia and manifesto. As he

explained to Leslie, 'many can read print & cannot read mezzotint' (*Correspondence*, 3.108). Lucas also engraved six large plates after Constable, but only *Hadleigh Castle* and *Salisbury Cathedral from the Meadows* were fully collaborative, though not published until after his death.

**The last years, 1830–1837** Concern for his children, grief for the loss of his wife, bouts of ill health caused by rheumatism and anxiety about the perceived threats to both state and church (as someone so politically conservative and anti-reform as Constable would have viewed the impending changes) plagued the last years of his life. Much of his time was taken up with duties at the academy (serving on the council and exhibition hanging committees and as visitor in the life academy) and as a director of the Artists' General Benevolent Institution with which he had been actively involved since 1818. Between 1833 and 1836 he delivered several lectures on the history of landscape painting at the Literary and Scientific Society of Hampstead, the Worcester Literary and Scientific Institution, and the Royal Institution in London, the last drawing eminent scientists and literary figures including Faraday and Wordsworth. In 1836 he was elected a member of both the Royal Institution and the Graphic Society. His outdoor work was severely limited during the 1830s, but he sketched or drew when the opportunity arose: at Hampstead, Worcester, Petworth (where he had been invited by Lord Egremont), Folkestone (where his two eldest sons were in school), and Arundel on the Sussex coast. His large exhibited works did not sell, but he had lately cultivated a reputation as someone reluctant to part with his paintings, preferring to retain them for his studio gallery and as future property for his children. Critics, bothered and bewildered by his increasingly unorthodox, rough, and 'frittered' handling, were none the less bewitched by his effects. Apparently unconvinced that the handling was necessary for the effects, they assumed that underneath late paintings like *Salisbury Cathedral from the Meadows* (1831; National Gallery), *The Opening of Waterloo Bridge* (1832; Tate collection), and *The Valley Farm* (1835; Tate collection) there lurked a *real* naturalism wilfully spoiled by Constable's final layer of scumbling and highly textured impasto.

Seriously depressed by the deaths in 1832 of Fisher and John Dunthorne junior, who had served as his studio assistant for several years, Constable still derived great pleasure from his children and his art, although his correspondence reveals an underlying disquietude. On the evening of 31 March 1837, after returning to Charlotte Street from a charitable errand, he became ill, suffering from giddiness and sickness during the night. He died in the early hours of 1 April; despite a post-mortem the cause of death was not determined. His death mask preserves the strong features of a man known in his youth as 'the handsome miller'. Constable was buried with his wife in the churchyard of St John's, Hampstead, and left an estate valued at £25,000 to his seven children, all of whom were still minors. In the absence of a will, Constable's elder brother Golding and a cousin by marriage, Lancelot Archer-Burton, were with the consent of the family elected to administer the estate and act as guardians for the children, one of whom (Charles Golding) had gone to sea in 1835 at the age of fourteen and at the time of his father's death was on an East Indiaman bound for Bombay. When Constable's eldest son, John Charles, came of age in December 1838, he assumed responsibility for the estate and at his early death in 1841 his eldest sister, Maria Louisa, took his place. Several of Constable's children possessed artistic ability, particularly the youngest, Lionel Bicknell, whose works were for many years misattributed to his father. Subsequent generations descending from Charles Golding, Constable's only child to have children of his own, have produced both amateur and professional artists.

**The posthumous reputation and critical heritage: the discovery of Constable** Constable's children may have inherited their grandfather's wealth, but more important for the future of their father's reputation, they inherited his life's work. During his career he sold relatively little of what he produced, and his house was filled with not only the finished paintings, but all the preparatory sketches and drawings and the usual studio detritus surrounding an extremely active artistic life of almost forty years. An auction in 1838 dispersed some of the paintings, but the vast majority stayed with the family. Fleming-Williams and Parris's exhaustive study *The Discovery of Constable* exposes the copies, forgeries, and misattributions that have complicated Constable studies and traces the crucial sales, exhibitions, and bequests to the national collections that account for the growing public consciousness of his art up to the 1930s. Throughout that period he was either praised or denigrated because of his painting style, valued or vilified according to prevailing tastes. Ruskin compared him unfavourably with Turner; Delacroix declared him the 'father' of modern French landscape. Leslie's *Memoirs of the Life of John Constable*, first published in 1843 in a limited edition (and illustrated with impressions from *English Landscape*), was republished in a cheaper, smaller format in 1845 and has since been reissued numerous times. Drawn primarily from the artist's letters, Leslie's hagiographic biography established a private and professional persona for Constable with which subsequent biographers and historians have had to contend. Leslie virtually created a Constable whose development was a personal journey of self-discovery and whose art was purely and simply 'natural' in its devotion to an unmediated experience of English landscape. At the turn of the twentieth century, historians shifted their interest to his sketches and studies, but continued to view him as an 'innocent eye', a Wordsworth of landscape painting; but just as literary criticism increasingly unearthed layers of meaning in Wordsworth's poetry, so art historians began a reassessment of Constable's art, placing it within a wider cultural context. By the middle of the twentieth century it became obvious that landscape art (even when 'unpeopled') signifies more than the land depicted. Literary, geographical, agricultural, scientific, political, religious, and psychosocial perspectives are all now regularly applied to the 'reading' of Constable's *œuvre*, aided by the eight volumes of correspondence and related documents published between 1962 and 1975 by the Suffolk Records Society. Inspired by John Barrell's 1980 seminal study, *The Dark Side of the Landscape*, many Constable scholars have sought to reinterpret the 'naturalism' of his art, rejecting the idea that any landscape painter in eighteenth- or nineteenth-century Britain could have approached a rural setting in a pure, simple, or unmediated manner. Their conclusions have not lessened the perceived importance of Constable to the development of landscape painting, nor the public's fondness for his art; but they have shown that an art created for the public arena and for posterity, as Constable's was, inevitably signifies something beyond the artist's private journey toward self-discovery, toward that 'natural painture' he had sought since 1802.

Although historiographical interpretations of Constable have changed enormously since his death, the works themselves have for the most part suffered only those changes attributable to 'the mellowing hand of Time', incompetent and misguided restoration, or later overpainting. He frequently reworked his paintings (even after their sale on occasion) and, especially in the early years, reused canvases; but, as Sarah Cove's research has shown (Cove, 493–516), Constable was acutely knowledgeable about his materials, their limitations and potential. He was experimental in his handling, but not careless in his working methods nor unaware of the dangers of ignoring traditional wisdom. His library contained theoretical treatises and practical manuals, and his friendship with the colourman George Field ensured that he kept up with the latest developments in materials and techniques. Consequently, his works are in remarkably good condition and have consistently increased in value. When they come onto the market, paintings that sold for hundreds of pounds or less during his lifetime now sell for millions, drawings for tens of thousands. Constable only occasionally signed his finished works; sketches and drawings are frequently inscribed with notes, though not necessarily with his signature or initials.

**Public and private collections** The complete range of Constable's work can be seen in the Victoria and Albert Museum, which received an incomparable and sensitively selected bequest in 1888 from his last surviving child, Isobel Constable. She had also arranged gifts to supplement the holdings of the National Gallery, the Royal Academy, and the British Museum (department of prints and drawings), which already owned a choice selection of the mezzotints. Prime examples of his work are to be found in many other institutions including: the Tate collection; the National Gallery, Washington; the Yale Center for British Art, New Haven; the Frick Collection, New York; the Huntington Gallery, San Marino, California; the Art Institute of Chicago; the Philadelphia Museum of Art. In addition to paintings, the Boston Museum of Fine Arts, the Metropolitan Museum, New York, the Ashmolean Museum, Oxford, and the Fitzwilliam Museum, Cambridge, all have extensive collections of the mezzotints, particularly the last which owns much of what remained in Lucas's studio, the prints as well as the correspondence from Constable.

Many works are still in private collections, both in Britain and abroad.

In 1923 the London county council marked Constable's house in Well Walk (now numbered 40) with a blue plaque. His birthplace was demolished long ago, but 'Constable country', particularly East Bergholt, Flatford, and Dedham, has been part of the heritage industry since at least the 1890s when Thomas Cook Ltd first arranged tours there.                                           JUDY CROSBY IVY

**Sources** John Constable's correspondence, ed. R. B. Beckett, 6 vols., Suffolk RS, 4, 6, 8, 10–12 (1962–8) · John Constable's discourses, ed. R. B. Beckett (1970) · John Constable: further documents and correspondence, ed. L. Parris, C. Shields, and I. Fleming-Williams, Suffolk RS, 18 (1975) · C. R. Leslie, Memoirs of the life of John Constable (1843); 2nd edn (1845) · G. Reynolds, The early paintings and drawings of John Constable, 2 vols. (1996) · G. Reynolds, The later paintings and drawings of John Constable, 2 vols. (1984) · L. Parris and I. Fleming-Williams, Constable (1991) [exhibition catalogue, Tate Gallery, London, 13 June – 15 Sept 1991] · I. Fleming-Williams and L. Parris, The discovery of Constable (1984) · A. Shirley, The published mezzotints of David Lucas after John Constable (1930) · M. Rosenthal, Constable: the painter and his landscape (1983) · A. Bermingham, 'Mapping the self: Constable/country', Landscape and ideology: the English rustic tradition, 1740–1860, British edn (1987), 87–155 · J. C. Ivy, Constable and the critics, 1802–1837 (1991) · J. E. Thornes, John Constable's skies: a fusion of art and science (1999) · S. Cove, 'Constable's oil painting materials and techniques', in L. Parris and I. Fleming-Williams, Constable (1991), 493–529 [exhibition catalogue, Tate Gallery, London, 13 June – 15 Sept 1991] · I. Fleming-Williams, Constable and his drawings (1990) · S. Daniels, 'John Constable and the making of Constable country', Fields of vision: landscape imagery and national identity in England and the United States (1993), 200–42 · J. Barrell, The dark side of the landscape: the rural poor in English painting, 1730–1840 (1980) · J. C. Ivy, 'Reading mezzotints: Mr Constable's English landscape', Journal of the Printing Historical Society, 25 (1996), 47–68 · J. Gage, George Field and his circle (1989) [exhibition catalogue, Fitzwilliam Museum, Cambridge, 27 June – 3 Sept 1989] · G. Reynolds, Constable: the natural painter (1965) · I. Fleming-Williams, Constable: a master draughtsman (1994) [exhibition catalogue, Dulwich Picture Gallery, London] · G. Reynolds, Catalogue of the Constable collection, Victoria and Albert Museum, 2nd edn (1973) · L. Parris, I. Fleming-Williams, and C. Shields, Constable: paintings, watercolours, and drawings (1976); 2nd edn (1976) [exhibition catalogue, Tate Gallery, London, 18 Feb – 25 April 1976] · Morning Herald (3 April 1837) · Morning Post (4 April 1837) · Ipswich Journal (8 April 1837) · GM, 2nd ser., 7 (1837), 664 · blue plaque file, English Heritage · administration, 1 June 1837, PRO, PROB 6/213, fols. 239r–239v · PRO, PROB 31/1368/1081 [2 proxies, 1 affidavit, and declaration of the estate of Constable] · PRO, IR 26/245, fols. 224v–225r [death duties of Constable] · administration, 20 Dec 1838, PRO, PROB 6/214, fol. 298v · administration, 7 April 1841, PRO, PROB 6/217, fol. 246v · C. S. Rhyne, 'Changes in the appearance of paintings by John Constable', Appearance, opinion, change: evaluating the look of paintings (1990), 72–84 [conference papers] · C. J. Holmes, Constable and his influence on landscape painting (1902) · C. S. Rhyne, John Constable: toward a complete chronology (1990)
**Archives** BL, corresp. and papers, Egerton MS 3253 · Exeter Central Library, west country studies library, sketchbook · FM Cam., MSS · priv. coll., MSS and artefacts · priv. coll. · V&A, letters | BL, corresp. with C. R. Leslie, Egerton MS 3255 · FM Cam., corresp., mainly with David Lucas
**Likenesses** D. Gardner, oils, 1796, V&A · H. Howard, oils, 1797, priv. coll. · R. R. Reinagle, oils, c.1799, NPG · J. Constable, self-portrait, pencil and watercolour, c.1804, NPG [see illus.] · J. Constable, self-portrait, pencil, 1806, Tate collection · J. Harden, pencil, 1806, BM · C. R. Leslie, oils, c.1830, RA · C. R. Leslie, pencil, c.1830–1839, BM · D. Lucas, mezzotint, 1830?–1839 (after C. R. Leslie), repro. in Leslie, Memoirs (1843) · D. Maclise, pencil, 1831?, NPG · S. Joseph, death mask, 1837, priv. coll. · R. J. Lane, lithograph, 1845 (after pencil drawing by C. R. Leslie), BM, NPG · J. Harden, two group portraits, drawings, BM · T. H. Maguire, lithograph (after D. Gardner, 1796), repro. in Leslie, Memoirs (1845) · bronze cast of death mask (after S. Joseph), NPG
**Wealth at death** £25,000: administration, PRO, PROB 6/213, fols. 239r–239v; inventory, PRO, PROB 31/1368/1081; PRO, death duty registers, IR 26/245, fols. 224v–225r

**Constable, Katherine** (d. c.1404). See under Constable family (per. c.1300–1488).

**Constable, Sir Marmaduke** (d. 1378). See under Constable family (per. c.1300–1488).

**Constable, Sir Marmaduke** (d. 1404). See under Constable family (per. c.1300–1488).

**Constable, Sir Marmaduke** (1456/7?–1518), soldier and administrator, was the son of Sir Robert *Constable (1423–1488) of Flamborough, Yorkshire [see under Constable family (per. c.1300–1488)], and Agnes, daughter of Sir Roger Wentworth of North Elmsall, Yorkshire, and Margery, dowager Lady Ros. Marmaduke is described as aged thirty-one and more at his father's death in May 1488, which would give a birth date of 1456 or 1457. This fits the circumstances of his career better than the claim in his epitaph in Flamborough church that he was aged seventy when he fought at Flodden (1513), which would push his birth date back by over a decade. Unlike their kinsmen of Barnby by Bossall, who were Neville associates, the Flamborough Constables followed the Percys. Sir Robert transferred readily to the service of Edward IV in 1461, but father and son were both retained by Henry Percy, fourth earl of Northumberland, after his restoration in 1470 and shared the stewardship of his lands in the East Riding. Marmaduke served under the earl in the Scottish campaigns of the early 1480s and was knighted by him beside Berwick in August 1481. According to his epitaph he had earlier gone with Edward IV into France, presumably in Northumberland's contingent.

Constable then entered the service of Richard III. He was a knight of the body by December 1483, when he was one of the king's associates given forfeited land and office in Kent in the aftermath of Buckingham's rebellion. Constable's Kentish base was to be the Stafford honour of Tonbridge, where he was made steward in December 1483 and where the inhabitants were informed in January that the king had deputed him 'to make his abode among you' (BL, Harl. MS 4332, fol. 81). However, the king had second thoughts about where Constable would be most useful and on 28 March granted him all the major duchy of Lancaster offices in the north midlands, including the constableship of Tutbury, which became his base. Unlike his predecessor in the offices, William, Lord Hastings, Constable was explicitly forbidden to retain the local gentry and was evidently intended to act under stricter royal control than Hastings, to whom Edward had allowed great independence of action.

It is not clear whether Constable fought at Bosworth. Perhaps, like Northumberland, he was present without fighting. He certainly escaped attainder, and was pardoned on 18 November. By May 1486, when he was granted the stewardships of Bawtry and Hotham, Yorkshire, he was again a knight of the body. He succeeded his father in May 1488, having formerly held Holme on Spalding moor, Yorkshire, and Somerby, Lincolnshire, which his father had settled on him. In November 1488 he became sheriff of Yorkshire and thus played a major role in dealing with the unrest of 1489 in which the earl of Northumberland was killed. In 1492 he accompanied the king to France and was involved in the ensuing negotiations which led to the treaty of Étaples. It seems that after Northumberland's death Constable became associated with Thomas Howard, earl of Surrey, who was taking an increasing role in northern affairs. In 1509 Surrey nominated him as a knight of the Garter, although he was not elected. In 1513 Constable served under Howard at Flodden, where he commanded the left wing; he received a letter of thanks from the king.

Constable died on 20 November 1518. His will, made the previous May, requested that he be buried as soon as his body was cold, 'without calling of friends or any other solemnity' (Raine, 91). He had married twice. With his first wife, Margery, daughter of William, Lord Fitzhugh, Constable had no children. With his second wife, Joyce, the daughter of Humphrey Stafford of Grafton, he had four sons (Robert, who succeeded him, Marmaduke, William, and John) and two daughters. His second son, **Sir Marmaduke Constable** (c.1480–1545), soldier, married Barbara, daughter of Sir John Sotehill of Everingham, by November 1502, the year in which the Sotehill lands were divided between her and her sister Mary, the wife of John Normanville, after the death of their imbecile brother, George. Constable fought under his father at Flodden and was knighted on the battlefield. He fought in several later Scottish campaigns, accompanied Henry VIII to the Field of Cloth of Gold and was a knight of the body by 1533. Unlike his elder brother Robert he did not support the Pilgrimage of Grace and his share of the spoils of the dissolution was Drax Priory, founded by his wife's ancestors. He died on 14 September 1545; his wife had died on 4 October 1540.                                                            ROSEMARY HORROX

**Sources** Chancery records · R. Horrox, *Richard III, a study of service*, Cambridge Studies in Medieval Life and Thought, 4th ser., 11 (1989) · K. Dockray, 'Sir Marmaduke Constable of Flamborough', *Richard III: crown and people*, ed. J. Petre (1985), 218–23 · [J. Raine], ed., *Testamenta Eboracensia*, 5, SurtS, 79 (1884) · *N&Q*, 3rd ser., 2 (1862), 208 · HoP, *Commons* · J. Foster, ed., *Pedigrees of the county families of Yorkshire*, 3 (1874)

**Archives** BL, Harley MS 4332, fol. 81

**Constable, Sir Marmaduke** (c.1480–1545). *See under* Constable, Sir Marmaduke (1456/7?–1518).

**Constable, Sir Robert** (*fl.* 1313–1338/9). *See under* Constable family (*per.* c.1300–1488).

**Constable, Sir Robert** (c.1353–1400/01). *See under* Constable family (*per.* c.1300–1488).

**Constable, Sir Robert** (d. 1441). *See under* Constable family (*per.* c.1300–1488).

**Constable, Sir Robert** (1423–1488). *See under* Constable family (*per.* c.1300–1488).

**Constable, Robert** (late 1450s–1501), lawyer, was the second son of Sir Robert Constable (d. 1488) of Flamborough, Yorkshire, and Gray's Inn, and the younger brother of Sir Marmaduke *Constable (d. 1518), who inherited the Flamborough estate and whom he followed to Lincoln's Inn in 1477. Unlike his brothers, he persevered with the law, and in 1489 became a bencher of his inn. His 1489 reading was given on the first two chapters of Westminster I and includes an account of the law concerning entails, which, though full of precise and ingenious learning, was sufficiently traditional to omit all mention of the recently invented common recovery. In 1494 he delivered his second reading, probably on the Statute of *Quo warranto*. Soon afterwards he received his writ to become a serjeant-at-law and, since it was the custom for the junior serjeant-elect to deliver a reading, he gave a third course of lectures in Lincoln's Inn in 1495. Like Thomas Frowyk (d. 1506), his brother graduand in the Inner Temple, he chose the pseudo-statute *Prerogativa regis*, which he expounded in copious detail. This reading was printed in 1949, but only as far as the seventh chapter of the statute; more remains in manuscript. Constable seems to have avoided major royal office, though he was a justice of the peace and served as a member of the council of Lord Scrope of Upsale. In 1501 he was commissioned as a justice of assize and rode the western circuit. Doubtless he could have expected a permanent justiceship in the near future, but he died a relatively young man on 22 November of that year.

In 1490, Constable married Beatrice, widow of Ralph, Lord Greystoke (d. 1487), whose maiden name was Hawtcliff. The marriage is alluded to in his serjeant's reading, where he mentions his wife's suit for dower against Lord Dacre of Gilsland as committee of the lands of Lord Greystoke's heir. Besides enjoying the dower lands, his professional income enabled him to make substantial purchases in south-east Yorkshire. In 1497 and 1498 he paid 800 marks to Sir Thomas Lovell for the manors of Newsham and Broughton. He was also, according to his will, a parishioner of Holme on Spalding Moor. But his principal seat was established at North Cliffe, in the parish of Sancton, where his descendants remained until 1695.

Constable's widow, Beatrice, took the veil in 1502 and died in 1505; she was buried at Sancton. They left two sons, Marmaduke and Robert, and two daughters, Elizabeth and Jane. The elder son, Marmaduke (d. 1525), is not be confused with a contemporary Marmaduke Constable (d. 1545), the son of the serjeant's brother Marmaduke, nor yet with a fourth person of the same name (d. 1560), who was the son of Sir Robert Constable (d. 1537). Marmaduke, not quite twelve years of age in 1501, was left £20 by his father for his exhibition at Cambridge for three years from the age of fifteen, and £24 for a further three years at inn of chancery. His mother left him another 10 marks to support him at Cambridge, and £10 for five years 'in the courtt and chancery'. In the event, he took up a military career, and fought against the Scots. He died in his thirties and left his law books to his younger brother, Robert. One of the Constable law books is now in the Bodleian Library, an important manuscript containing fifteenth-century year-books.                                    J. H. BAKER

**Sources** R. Constable, *Prerogativa regis: tertia lectura Roberti Constable …*, ed. S. E. Thorne (1949) • S. E. Thorne and J. H. Baker, eds., *Readings and moots at the inns of court in the fifteenth century*, 1, SeldS, 71 (1954) • [J. Raine], ed., *Testamenta Eboracensia*, 3–5, SurtS, 45, 53, 79 (1865–84); [J. W. Clay], ed., 6, SurtS, 106 (1902) • W. P. Baildon, ed., *The records of the Honorable Society of Lincoln's Inn: the black books*, 1 (1897) • GEC, *Peerage* • E. W. Ives, *The common lawyers of pre-Reformation England* (1983) • Baker, *Serjeants* • BL, Lansdowne MS 1119, fols. 67v–73r • University College, Oxford, MS 162, fols. 110r–185r • Bodl. Oxf., MS Lat. misc. C.55 • R. Dodsworth, *Yorkshire church notes*, ed. J. W. Clay, Yorkshire Archaeological Society, Record Series, 34 (1904) • J. S. Purvis, ed., *Monastic chancery proceedings (Yorkshire)*, Yorkshire Archaeological Society, Record Series, 88 (1934) • will, PRO, PROB 11/13, sig. 5 • *CIPM, Henry VII*, 2, no. 567
**Archives** Hovingham Hall, Yorkshire, North Cliffe deeds

**Constable, Sir Robert** (1478?–1537), rebel, of Flamborough, in the East Riding of Yorkshire, was probably born in 1478, the eldest of four sons and two daughters of Sir Marmaduke *Constable (1456/7?–1518), soldier and administrator, and his wife, Joyce, the daughter of Sir Humphrey Stafford of Grafton, Cheshire. Sir Marmaduke *Constable the younger [*see under* Constable, Sir Marmaduke (1456/7?–1518)] was his brother. By his marriage to Jane, daughter of Sir William Ingleby of Ripley, Yorkshire, Constable had three sons and four (or possibly five) daughters.

Little is known of Constable's early life and education. From his early career, however, it seems likely that he was trained as a soldier and retained a preference for the traditional militaristic pursuits of his class. He was in the royal army which defeated the Cornish rebels at Blackheath and was knighted on the battlefield on 17 June 1497. In 1511 he took part in the short-lived military expedition against the Moors led by Thomas Darcy, Baron Darcy, undertaken at the request of Ferdinand of Spain. Two years later he participated in the battle of Flodden, alongside his father, brothers, and other kinsmen. Constable forged increasingly close connections with the court at this time, where, by 1517, he had been appointed knight of the body.

Upon the death of his father in 1518, Constable succeeded to the considerable estates centred on the principal family seat of Flamborough. Thereafter he continued to participate in the administration of his locality. He was JP and commissioner of array for the East Riding from the early 1500s until the outbreak of the Pilgrimage of Grace in 1536. In the early 1530s he was also sworn of the king's council of the north, which had been newly reconstituted following the downfall of Cardinal Thomas Wolsey, archbishop of York. His influence in the region was augmented by his appointment to a number of stewardships, including those of the crown lordships of Sheriff Hutton (which he was required to relinquish in 1532) and Hotham and the Percy lordships of Leconfield and Pocklington, all

in Yorkshire. He was also steward of the Yorkshire liberty of Howden for Cuthbert Tunstall, bishop of Durham.

By nature Constable was volatile and noted for his 'dangerous disposition' (Dodds and Dodds, 1.46). In the early 1520s his feuds were among those which, within Yorkshire, created much dissension and he was called to account for his behaviour before Thomas Howard, earl of Surrey, Henry VIII's lieutenant in the north. In 1525 he obtained a royal pardon for his 'riotous' abduction of a royal ward (*LP Henry VIII*, 4/1, no. 1115). In the early 1530s, as a result of his involvement in further disputes, he made several appearances before the court of Star Chamber. In 1534 Constable's unseemly behaviour led to calls for his dismissal from the commission of the peace.

The precise motivation behind Constable's rebellious participation in the Pilgrimage of Grace is not clear. His family had long been tenants and clients of the earls of Northumberland, who had extensive landed interests in the East Riding and Constable was a member of the council of Henry Percy, sixth earl of Northumberland. Percy affinities undoubtedly played a part in the rebellion and this, to some extent, may have accounted for Constable's stance. Other factors, such as his increasing dissatisfaction with the aims of royal government, may also have played a part. In religious matters, too, he, along with his old friends Darcy and John Hussey, Baron Hussey, maintained a traditional stance. In 1534 all three men had agreed upon their aversion towards heresy and their determination to die as 'Christian men'.

Whatever his ultimate motivation—and despite his initial reluctance and claims that he was coerced—Constable was quickly drawn into the pilgrimage and soon became one of its leaders. He adopted, in the first instance, a resolutely rebellious stance but subsequently went on to accept a royal pardon under the terms of the agreement reached at Doncaster in early December 1536. During Sir Francis Bigod's revolt in January 1537, Constable strove to stay the commons and maintain order, in accordance with the December agreement. Nevertheless, the resurgence of the rebellion provided the crown with the opportunity to take reprisals against the rebel leaders. Constable, together with other leading pilgrims, was summoned to London where he was imprisoned in the Tower of London and subsequently indicted, not for his activities in the main phase of the rebellion, but for offences allegedly committed after his pardon. Following his trial and condemnation, Constable was taken to Hull for execution. On 6 July 1537, he was taken to the town's Beverley Gate and there hanged in chains.                    CHRISTINE M. NEWMAN

**Sources** *LP Henry VIII* • M. H. Dodds and R. Dodds, *The Pilgrimage of Grace, 1536–1537, and the Exeter conspiracy, 1538*, 2 vols. (1915) • R. R. Reid, *The king's council in the north* (1921) • M. Bush, *The Pilgrimage of Grace: a study of the rebel armies of October 1536* (1996) • M. Bush and D. Bownes, *The defeat of the Pilgrimage of Grace* (1999) • A. Fletcher, *Tudor rebellions*, 3rd edn (1983) • W. A. Shaw, *The knights of England*, 2 vols. (1906), vol. 2 • HoP, *Commons, 1509–58* • [F. W. Dendy and C. H. Hunter Blair], eds., *Visitations of the north*, 4 pts, SurtS, 122, 133, 144, 146 (1912–32) • B. English, *The great landowners of east Yorkshire, 1530–1910* (1990) • W. Brown, ed., *Yorkshire Star Chamber proceedings*, 1, Yorkshire Archaeological Society, 41 (1909) • J. A. Froude, *History of*

*England*, 2nd edn, 12 vols. (1858–66), vol. 3 · R. W. Hoyle, *The Pilgrimage of Grace and the politics of the 1530s* (2001)
**Archives** BL, family and estate papers, Add. MSS 40132–40137
**Wealth at death** held fifty-one manors which were forfeited upon attainder: U. Hull, manuscripts and archives database (catalogue of Constable, Maxwell, and Sherburne family papers)

**Constable, Thomas** (1812–1881). *See under* Constable, Archibald (1774–1827).

**Constable, Thomas Hugh**. *See* Clifford, Sir Thomas Hugh, first baronet (1762–1823).

**Constable, Sir William** (*d.* 1319). *See under* Constable family (*per. c.*1300–1488).

**Constable, Sir William**, baronet (*bap.* 1590, *d.* 1655), parliamentarian army officer and regicide, was baptized on 4 March 1590, the only son of Sir Robert Constable (*d.* 1600) of Flamborough and Holme, Yorkshire, and his wife, Anne, daughter of John Hussey of Duffield in the same county. William belonged to an ancient Yorkshire family of several branches, and is often confused with an elder kinsman and namesake who was involved in Essex's plot of 1601. On 15 February 1608 he married Dorothy (*bap.* 1590, *d.* 1656), the daughter of Sir Thomas *Fairfax of Denton (later first Baron Fairfax of Cameron), but their union produced no surviving children. He was created a baronet on 29 June 1611.

Constable rose to prominence in the 1620s when he emerged as one of Yorkshire's leading figures in the 'country' interest. He was an ally of Sir Thomas Wentworth (the future earl of Strafford) in his struggle with Sir John Savile, and in 1626 he successfully contested the county election against the Saviles after Wentworth had been pricked as sheriff. The following year he was summoned before the privy council and imprisoned as a loan refuser. In 1628 he was returned for Scarborough with the backing of his friend Edmund Sheffield, Lord Mulgrave. He and another friend, Sir Matthew Boynton, were made deputy lieutenants for the East Riding by Wentworth in 1629 after Sir John Hotham had recommended them as 'the ablest and best affected to do his Majesty service in respect of their undoubted affection in religion' (Hotham to Wentworth, 7 Jan 1629, Sheffield Central Library, Wentworth Woodhouse Muniments, Strafford Papers., 12(50)). Constable was summoned before the privy council again in 1630 for refusing to compound for distraint of knighthood.

Although a man of godly convictions, Constable led a spendthrift existence, and was forced to sell most of his estate—worth over £1000 a year—to cover his debts. He parted with the manor of Holme in 1634 (to Sir Marmaduke Langdale for £6500) and the manor of Flamborough two years later. It was probably his ailing fortunes as much as his dislike of Laudian 'new ceremonies' that made him consider emigrating to America during Charles I's personal rule. In 1635 he and Boynton made secret preparations to settle in Connecticut, where Viscount Saye and Sele and Lord Brooke had obtained a grant of land, but the difficulties involved forced them to abandon the venture. In April 1637 Constable obtained a pass for himself and his

wife to travel on the continent, and in June they crossed over to the Netherlands where they were joined by Boynton and his family. By 1640 they were leading members of the gathered church established at Arnhem by Philip Nye and Thomas Goodwin.

Constable had returned to England by March 1641, and with the support of his brother-in-law, Ferdinando *Fairfax, second Lord Fairfax, stood for election at Knaresborough in November, only to lose on a poll to one of the townsmen, William Dearlove. Constable petitioned the Commons against the result, and as the royalist interest (with which Dearlove was associated) dwindled at Westminster during 1642 so Constable's stock improved, until on 17 August his election was declared good. Despite his debts he raised a regiment of parliamentarian foot in 1642, which he commanded with distinction at Edgehill. In July 1643 he was given command of the forces of the East Riding under Ferdinando, Lord Fairfax, and during the spring of 1644 he won a series of engagements against the royalists in Yorkshire. On 23 March 1645 the Commons acknowledged his 'faithful Services' as well as his 'great Losses' with a grant of £1000 (*JHC*, 4, 1644–6, 88). Deprived of his command by the self-denying ordinance, he became a mainstay of the northern association committee, and emerged as a minor figure in the Independent interest at Westminster. After Sir Thomas Fairfax (later third baron) wrote to the speaker in February 1647 commending his uncle's services to parliament, the Commons awarded Constable £1984 for his arrears. He was among those MPs who fled to the army in August, and his loyalty to the Independents' cause was further rewarded in December, when he was given command of John Lambert's regiment of foot. The following month he was commissioned to assist Colonel Robert Hammond in guarding the king at Carisbrooke.

Constable was made governor of Gloucester in 1648, his regiment having been sent to the town to quell unrest. During November and December he played a leading role in the council of officers as it moved towards confrontation with parliament. He supported the army's remonstrance to the Commons of 20 November, and was a member of various committees for deciding army policy, including the joint committee of officers, Levellers, and radical MPs for drawing up the *Agreement of the People*. He may also have been one of the subcommittee to organize Pride's Purge. Appointed to the commission for trying the king, he attended the trial proceedings regularly and was a signatory to the death warrant [*see also* Regicides]. In February 1649 he was elected to the first council of state, and he was subsequently a member of the second and fourth councils, serving twice as president of the latter. He was one of the more active councillors, attending over 400 meetings and sitting on numerous conciliar committees, mostly concerning military affairs. In May 1650 the Rump passed a bill for transferring Holme from the sequestered Sir Marmaduke Langdale back to Constable.

Constable was largely inactive in national politics after the dissolution of the Rump, though he was warmly recommended by the Gloucestershire Independent churches during canvassing for membership of the nominated assembly. He died on 15 June 1655, and despite requesting in his will to be buried 'without ostentation' (*Abstracts of Yorkshire Wills in the Time of the Commonwealth*, ed. W. J. Clay, Yorkshire Archaeological Society record ser. 9, 1890, 82), was given an elaborate state funeral and interred in Westminster Abbey on 21 June. At the Restoration his estate was confiscated and his remains were dug up and thrown into a common pit. DAVID SCOTT

**Sources** 'Constable, Sir William', HoP, *Commons, 1640–60* [draft] · 'Constable, Sir William', HoP, *Commons, 1604–29* [draft] · *JHC*, 2–7 (1640–59) · J. T. Cliffe, *The Yorkshire gentry from the Reformation to the civil war* (1969) · G. W. Johnson, ed., *The Fairfax correspondence: memoirs of the reign of Charles the First*, 2 (1848) · C. H. Firth and G. Davies, *The regimental history of Cromwell's army*, 2 vols. (1940) · *CSP dom.*, 1640–55 · J. Rushworth, *Historical collections*, new edn, 7 (1721) · *The Clarke papers*, ed. C. H. Firth, 1–2, CS, new ser., 49, 54 (1891–4) · R. Bell, ed., *Memorials of the civil war … forming the concluding volumes of the Fairfax correspondence*, 1 (1849) · D. Underdown, *Pride's Purge: politics in the puritan revolution* (1971) · *Dugdale's visitation of Yorkshire, with additions*, ed. J. W. Clay, 2 (1907) · IGI

**Archives** BL, family papers, Add. MSS 40132–40137 | BL, Add. MS 40135, fol. 24v · BL, muster roll, Add. Ch 66608 · Bodl. Oxf., Fairfax MS 32, fols. 35, 37

**Constable, William** (1783–1861), traveller and photographer, was born on 5 April 1783 at Tedhams, Horley Mill, Horley, Surrey, the fifth child in the family of seven sons and two daughters of James Constable (1749–1838), miller and country shopkeeper of Horley, and his wife, Susanna Jordan (1748–1826). He had virtually no formal education. In 1797 he entered the drapery business of Henry Browne, a high constable of Lewes, Sussex, a keen scientist with a private laboratory and a printing press, who encouraged his assistant's artistic and scientific interests. In 1802 he joined his elder brother Daniel in founding a drapery business at 3 North Street, Brighton, where he drew and published *A New and Correct Plan of Brighthelmstone*. In 1806 the two brothers embarked on a journey of exploration to the United States. They travelled from New York to New Orleans and back, by boat, by mule, or on foot. Constable kept a detailed record and made watercolour studies which are important early topographical documents. He was engaged to plan a new town in Big Beaver Creek, Pennsylvania, which he called New Brighton.

On his return to England in 1808 Constable rebuilt and operated the family watermill at Horley and pursued a career as an engineer. He was appointed surveyor to the turnpike trustees of the London to Brighton roads (1818) and was responsible for the construction of a tunnel (1823) and suspension bridge in Reigate. In 1837 he was appointed engineer and surveyor of a proposed railway in Jamaica, but the project fell through.

In 1841 Constable embarked on the most important phase of his career, as a pioneer photographer, opening a daguerreotype portrait studio at 57 Marine Parade, Brighton, on 8 November. He built 'a room … in front of the house … of which the roof and front consisted of plate glass' ('Photographic portraits', *Brighton Gazette*, 11 Nov 1841). He called this daylight studio 'the Photographic

William Constable (1783–1861), self-portrait, *c*.1845

Institution' in promotional announcements, extolling the virtues of the exceptional light provided by his south-facing marine location. He exchanged ideas and information with other early practitioners and invested much thought in the technical and artistic refinement of his chosen medium. His correspondence reveals a close awareness of technical developments being pursued in London and elsewhere. He undertook a journey to Paris, for example, to visit 'two principal makers of lenses … Chevalier and Lerebours' (W. Constable to L. Glukman, 1 June 1846, priv. coll.) and enjoyed the visits to Marine Parade of several photographers, including Richard Dykes Alexander from Ipswich, Antoine Claudet from London, and Leone Glukman from Dublin.

Constable was the first to photograph Prince Albert, in March 1842 (Royal Archives, Windsor Castle), and by 1848 was able to boast of 'many sitters from the ranks that are called noble' (W. Constable to L. Glukman, 13 Feb 1848, priv. coll.), with a client list which included William Cavendish, sixth duke of Devonshire, Ferdinand, duke of Saxe-Coburg and Gotha, the earl of Belfast, the earl of Morton, the marquess of Lorne, the marchioness of Donegal, and the grand duchess of Parma. His daguerreotypes are among the finest relics of photography's first decade. Rejecting the easy convention of the stiff and formal head and shoulders, he made fine full-length portraits, setting his subjects against a simple draped curtain or broadly painted landscape backdrop on a carpeted dais which could be revolved to find the optimum fall of light. His more overtly artistic endeavours included posed allegorical subjects or such set pieces as a chess game or a conversation over a lunch table. His business declined through the 1850s in the face of increasing competition, though his scientific interests continued undiminished. He was a founder member of the Brighton and Sussex Natural History Society in 1855.

Surviving daguerreotype self-portraits reveal a slim figure with strongly chiselled features. Constable's letters confirm a highly inquisitive mind regarding natural and scientific phenomena and suggest a phlegmatic temperament and a dry humour. He displayed an exceptional breadth of curiosity and his career was marked by an evident spirit of adventure and an impressive range of achievements. He had married Jemima Mott (1780–1829) on 11 January 1816 but lived as a childless widower after her death in 1829. He died on 22 December 1861 at his home, 16 Egremont Place, Brighton, and was buried in Horley churchyard. His correspondence, watercolours, and some daguerreotypes are in private collections; other daguerreotypes are in the Smithsonian Institution, Washington, DC.                                    PHILIPPE GARNER

Sources *Brighton Herald* (6 Nov 1841) · *Brighton Herald* (22 Dec 1861) · Susanna Grece, MS journal, Smithsonian Institution, Washington, DC · Susanna Grece, MS journal, priv. coll. · Constable correspondence, priv. coll.
Archives priv. coll. | priv. coll., MS journal of Susanna Grece · Smithsonian Institution, Washington, DC, MS journal of Susanna Grece
Likenesses W. Constable, self-portrait, daguerreotype, *c.*1845, priv. coll. [*see illus.*] · W. Constable, two self-portraits in group portraits, daguerreotype, priv. coll. · W. Constable, two self-portraits, daguerreotypes, priv. coll.
Wealth at death under £1500: probate, 28 March 1862, *CGPLA Eng. & Wales*

**Constable, William George** (1887–1976), art historian and gallery director, was born at 17 Gerard Street, Derby, on 27 October 1887, the elder child and only son of William George Samuel Constable and his wife, Remeliah Isabella Webb. The celebrated painter John Constable belonged to the same family although the relationship, never precisely established, was not very close; however, the fact that William possessed a fairly exact facsimile of the painter's prominent and somewhat bird-like nose was frequently commented upon.

Constable attended Derby School, of which his father was headmaster, before going up to St John's College, Cambridge, where he was the MacMahon law student and Whewell scholar of the university. He obtained a first class in part 2 of the economics tripos in 1910. From Cambridge he went to London and, joining the Inner Temple, read for the bar, to which he was called in 1914. But the direction of his career was entirely changed after a horrific experience in 1916: while serving as an officer in the Sherwood Foresters, he was buried alive by the explosion of a shell near him in the trenches. His batman dug him out, but he was subsequently invalided out of the army.

It was during his long convalescence that Constable decided to give up law and to look to the arts for a living.

He enrolled as a student at the Slade School of Fine Art and came under the influence of Henry Tonks and Philip Wilson Steer, with whom he came to share a weekly supper, the fourth member of the party being George Moore. During his Slade years, he met a wide range of artists, including J. S. Sargent, Jacob Epstein, Wyndham Lewis, Degas, and Roger Fry. He became a competent but never a very interesting painter, as he himself recognized, so in 1922 he began to work as a tour guide at the Wallace Collection, and soon afterwards started to write art criticism for the *New Statesman* and the *Saturday Review*. The keeper, D. S. MacColl, took a kindly interest in him, associating him with the work he himself was doing on artworks in the collection and suggesting Canaletto and his works as subjects for research. Constable was secretary of the committee for the important British primitives exhibition at the Royal Academy, and through his involvement cemented a friendship with S. C. Cockerell; this led to his cataloguing of the Marlay collection in the Fitzwilliam Museum, Cambridge.

Late in 1923 Constable moved to the National Gallery, where he was to remain for eight years, the last two as assistant director. Through visits on behalf of the estates duty office, he built up an impressive knowledge of British private collections, which he supplemented with a systematic examination of provincial art galleries and museums. Soon after the First World War he had established a friendship with Bernard Berenson; he now built up contacts with continental art historians and curators, such as Wilhelm Bode, and British collectors, such as George Eumorfopolous. He would probably have succeeded Augustus Daniel as director of the gallery, but in 1931 he was persuaded to become the first director of the newly formed Courtauld Institute of Art in the University of London, which opened in the following year. Here he embarked on an ambitious academic programme. At this date, no British university offered a degree course in art history, and Constable decided to introduce a comprehensive and wide-ranging course to remedy this omission. The British ignorance of art appalled him, and, with W. E. Williams, he was involved in the 'Art for the People' project, which aimed to send exhibitions to previously unused venues. He recruited an impressive body of lecturers for the institute, including Roger Fry, Kenneth Clark, and E. K. Waterhouse, and travelled widely to act as an ambassador for the Courtauld. In 1933 the Warburg Institute became attached to the Courtauld—bringing in such experts as Rudolf Wittkower—and in 1934 a scientific department and laboratory was set up. By that date Constable was experiencing difficulties with the governing body, whom he believed to be more concerned with the maintenance of numbers than of the highest academic standards. Constable was not prepared to compromise, and early in 1937, to the consternation of his friends and many of the students, he resigned.

From 1935 to 1937 Constable was Slade professor of fine arts at Cambridge in succession to Fry; he was then offered the curatorship of painting at the Museum of Fine Arts at Boston. Thus in March 1938 the Constables set sail for 'the other Cambridge', in Massachusetts. Although he never renounced his British citizenship, it was to remain their home for the rest of his life. On 29 May 1926 he had married Olivia (b. 1901/2), daughter of Arthur Carson Roberts, of Chelsea, legal adviser to the Ministry of Health; they had two sons, John and Giles.

Constable held the curatorship of paintings at Boston until October 1957: almost twenty years. He rehung the main galleries, made some notable acquisitions, and was responsible for many important exhibitions. He fostered a taste for modern British art in Boston, and during his curatorship significant gifts of works by Henry Tonks, W. R. Sickert, and William Orpen were added to the collection. Constable was an excellent administrator, but his work as an art historian proved more memorable. He wrote two major books: *Richard Wilson*, which appeared in 1953, has remained the standard work on this painter; *Canaletto*, published in two volumes in 1962, was described as 'perhaps the most exhaustive handling a prolific artist has ever received' (Links, 311) and it remains the basis of all scholarship on Canaletto. Constable was always an indefatigable traveller, and in 1937, after he had left the Courtauld Institute, a Leverhulme fellowship enabled him to spend some months in Venice, vital for this work. He took the trouble to see personally almost all the 500 paintings and 300 drawings described, in addition to sketchbooks, engravings, and etchings. Constable's other books include *The Painter's Workshop* (1954), *John Flaxman* (1927), *Art History and Connoisseurship* (1938), and *Art Collecting in the United States* (1964). He also compiled or edited, with punctilious accuracy, a long series of exhibition and other catalogues.

In his personal relations 'W. G.', as he was universally known, even to his wife, was unfailingly kind, generous, and approachable. Yet at heart he was a shy and private man, not easy to know, for all his outward geniality and friendliness. He received many honours. They included fellowships of the Society of Antiquaries and of the American Academy of Arts and Sciences, an honorary fellowship of St John's College, Cambridge (1956), and honorary doctorates of three universities; he was also made a chevalier of the Légion d'honneur, and commendatore of the Crown of Italy. He died at Cambridge, Massachusetts, on 3 February 1976.

ALEC CLIFTON-TAYLOR, rev. ROSEMARY MITCHELL

**Sources** J. G. Links, 'W. G. Constable', *Burlington Magazine*, 118/878 (April 1976), 311–12 • W. G. Constable, 'Some notes for an obituary', *Apollo*, 77 (Jan 1963), 28–31 • W. G. Constable, 'Some notes for an obituary', *Apollo*, 77 (Feb 1963), 116–19 • T. Pignatti, 'In memoriam: William George Constable', *Arte Veneta*, 30 (1976), 277–8 • H. Hall, 'Early twentieth-century British paintings in the Museum of Fine Arts, Boston', *Apollo*, 120/271 (Sept 1984), 195–200 • personal knowledge (1986) • private information (1986) • b. cert. • m. cert.
**Archives** St John's College, London, papers | BL, corresp. with Albert Monsbridge, Add. MS 65257B • Harvard University, near Florence, Italy, Center for Italian Renaissance Studies, letters to B. Berenson • U. Glas. L., letters to D. S. MacColl
**Likenesses** E. Polunin, oils, c.1936, NPG • photograph, repro. in *Apollo*, 77 (Jan 1963), 28

**Constance, duchess of Brittany** (c.1161–1201), was the only daughter and sole heir of *Conan (IV), duke of Brittany (c.1135–1171), and Margaret, daughter of Henry, earl of Huntingdon (d. 1152), and *Ada de Warenne (d. 1178), and sister to *Malcolm IV (r. 1153–65) and *William I (r. 1165–1214), kings of Scotland. Her parents married in 1160 and Constance is first mentioned in 1166 as a young child, when Conan was persuaded by *Henry II to betroth her to *Geoffrey, the fourth son of his marriage to *Eleanor of Aquitaine. The subordination of the native Breton ruling dynasty to their powerful Plantagenet neighbours, symbolized by this act, provides the background to Constance's own life: it shaped her personal destiny and that of her children, and radically affected the political history of Brittany and the Angevin empire as a whole.

After Conan (IV)'s death in 1171 Henry II further tightened his hold on Brittany. Conan's widow married Humphrey (III) de Bohun, hereditary constable of England. It is likely that Constance accompanied her mother to England, where Margaret had dower lands, and Constance's claims as countess of Richmond were eventually acknowledged by the king. After the constable's death (1185) mother and daughter remained close; Margaret is found on at least one occasion with Constance in Brittany, where she died early in 1201; she was buried, according to her wishes, at Sawtry Abbey, Huntingdonshire. But little is definitely known of Constance's movements or whereabouts before her marriage to Geoffrey was finally celebrated in 1181; during their betrothal, although Geoffrey was occasionally to be found in Brittany, usually after being dispatched by Henry II, the duchy was administered almost entirely by men nominated by the English king, with only the barest reference to the young duchess or her rights.

Matters changed when Constance and Geoffrey married. Until Geoffrey's premature death in August 1186 Constance was frequently at her husband's side, both within and outside the duchy. She was actively associated in his government of Brittany at a critical moment in the duchy's institutional and legal development. Together they also made benefactions to several Breton abbeys (among them Beaulieu, Boquen, and Bonrepos), as well as a grant to Rouen Cathedral in memory of Geoffrey's eldest brother, Henry, the Young King (d. 1183). Constance also patronized Ste Croix de Quimperlé. Two daughters were born during Geoffrey's lifetime: *Eleanor (d. 1241) and Matilda (d. before 1189), while at Easter 1187 (29 March) Constance gave birth to a posthumous son, *Arthur, for whom high hopes were entertained by Bretons chafing at Angevin domination.

On Geoffrey's death, although Constance assumed control of the duchy, it was under the continuing supervision of Henry II, at whose command in February 1189 she married *Ranulf (III), sixth earl of Chester (d. 1232). In contrast to her first marriage, this appears to have been an unhappy and loveless affair; Constance and Ranulf seldom kept each other's company, no children were born, and the major incident in the marriage was Ranulf's seizure of his wife at Pontorson in 1196, while on her way to

Normandy for an interview with Richard I, and her subsequent imprisonment in his castle at St James de Beuvron. His part in this ploy can be surmised since, as king, Richard had also been very anxious to continue the tradition of Plantagenet control of Brittany. In 1190 he acknowledged his nephew, Arthur, as his own heir in the treaty of Messina negotiated with Tancred of Sicily, and he tried to smother dissension among Breton nobles anxious to shake off his authority. Some, appointed by Constance to high positions in the Breton administration or as members of her council, also served Richard in a similar capacity. But disputes continued and tension remained high; soon after returning from captivity in Austria (1194), Richard invaded Brittany in force, further alienating many Bretons by his aggression. Ranulf's capture of Constance exacerbated matters still more, while her subsequent escape from confinement gave rise to many legends.

By 1198 peaceful relations with Richard I had once again been restored, following complex negotiations which can only be traced with great difficulty through not entirely trustworthy later sources, which apparently paraphrase contemporary records. But both Constance and Ranulf were anxious to end their marriage and it was annulled (probably in 1199). The death of Richard I, on 6 April 1199, the claims of Arthur to the Angevin succession, and his rivalry with John, opened a final dramatic chapter in Constance's life. Initially she was closely involved in the military and diplomatic moves of Arthur and his supporters to implement his claims to the Angevin succession. She was with him at Angers in April 1199 after an invasion of Anjou, and accompanied him to Le Mans shortly afterwards to seek the support of the barons of Maine. Her role as Arthur's 'councillor' is acknowledged in several charters from this period.

In the autumn of 1199 Constance married Gui de Thouars, younger brother of Aimery, vicomte de Thouars, a move probably designed to widen her political contacts, but which also brought her considerable personal happiness. She also sought help for Arthur at Tours from Philip Augustus, king of France. However, domestic matters increasingly claimed her attention: three more daughters were born in quick succession—Alix (later duchess of Brittany), Marguerite, and Catherine—and Constance gradually withdrew from active politics. The treaty of Le Goulet (22 May 1200), by which Philip reserved Arthur's wardship, while stipulating that he must perform homage for Brittany to King John, represented a severe setback for the policies Constance and her supporters had been pursuing. Moreover, by summer 1201, Constance was ailing; some contemporary sources claim she had contracted leprosy, though it is more probable that recent pregnancies had undermined her constitution. She died in early September 1201, and was buried in the Cistercian abbey of Villeneuve (diocese of Nantes) which had been refounded in 1200 through her generous endowment.

MICHAEL JONES

**Sources** GEC, *Peerage* · P. le Baud, *Histoire de Bretagne avec les chroniques des maisons de Vitré et de Laval*, ed. le sieur d'Hozier (Paris, 1638) · Y. Hillion, 'La Bretagne et la rivalité Capétiens–Plantagenets. Un exemple: la duchesse Constance, 1186–1202', *Annales de Bretagne et des Pays de l'Ouest*, 92 (1985), 111–44 · M. Jones, 'La vie familiale de la duchesse Constance: le témoignage des chartes', *Bretagne et pays celtiques, langues, histoire, civilisation: mélanges offerts à la mémoire de Léon Fleuriot, 1923-1987*, ed. G. le Menn and J.-Y. le Moing (Rennes, 1992), 349–60 · M. Jones, 'The Capetians and Brittany', *Historical Research*, 63 (1990), 1–16 · J. Le Patourel, 'Henri II Plantagenêt et la Bretagne', *Mémoires de la Société d'Histoire et d'Archéologie de la Bretagne*, 58 (1981), 99–116; repr. in J. Le Patourel, *Feudal empires: Norman and Plantagenet* (1984) · M. Craig, 'A second daughter of Geoffrey of Brittany', *BIHR*, 50 (1977), 112–15 · J. Everard and M. Jones, eds., *The charters of Duchess Constance of Brittany and her family, 1171–1221* (1999) · J. Everard, *Brittany and the Angevins: province and empire, 1158–1203* (2000)

**Constanduros** [*née* Tilling], **Mabel** (1880–1957), comedienne and writer, was born on 29 March 1880 at Devonshire House, Peckham Road, Camberwell, London, one of the seven children of Richard Stephen Tilling, managing director of the Thomas Tilling & Son bus company, and his wife, Sophie Thorn. She was educated at various establishments, including the Mary Datchelor School in Camberwell and a boarding-school on the south coast, and then worked as her father's private secretary. She was married during the 1900s to Athanasius Constanduros, an insurance broker, who died in 1937. They had three children, of whom only a son, Michael, survived into adulthood. The marriage clearly failed long before 1937; Mabel's autobiography mentions her husband hardly at all and never favourably or by name. She moved in the late 1920s or early 1930s to the village of Bury in Sussex, where she took responsibility for bringing up her son. Her active membership of an amateur dramatic society from about 1910 to 1920 led to a period of training at the Central School of Speech Training. Here she discovered a facility for writing short stories and 'cockney sketches', and was encouraged to approach the BBC for employment. She joined the Radio Repertory Company in February 1925 and made her first broadcast on 23 March that year.

Mabel Constanduros is remembered above all for her creation of the Buggins family, the first radio family, which made its initial appearance on 1 September 1925 in the sketch 'The Buggins Family out for a Day', with regular broadcasts beginning in 1928. Between 1928 and 1948, when the family made its final broadcasts during BBC's *Children's Hour*, Constanduros wrote and performed in over 250 Buggins radio scripts. Initially she played all six speaking parts: Grandma Buggins, Mrs Buggins, her three children (Emma, Alfie, and Baby Buggins), and Aunt Maria. For some years the father of the Buggins household was an unspeaking presence, but in the early 1930s the part was created by Michael Hogan, with whom Mabel had written a number of radio plays and sketches. He was followed by John Rorke, who co-wrote many of the later scripts. Grandma, a crusty, cantankerous old biddy described by Constanduros as 'one of the tiresomest and cussedest creatures I could imagine' (Gifford, 37–8), lay at the heart of the programme, which became extremely popular with audiences as a result of its skilful characterization and gentle humour combined with sheer appreciation of Constanduros's acting skills. The popularity of the family was such that the Ministry of Food used Mrs Buggins to broadcast recipes during the Second World War. Constanduros made a well-received variety début at the Coliseum in September 1929, and the family seemed destined for a highly successful live career, but their creator never enjoyed this work and abandoned it quite swiftly. She continued to act, however, appearing successfully as Mrs Bones in A. P. Herbert's operetta *Derby Day* in 1932 and undertaking a certain amount of film work. Her last live stage performance was at the Palace Theatre, Watford, in 1953. The Buggins family was not the only radio family she created: the English family Robinson, which she created with her nephew Denis Constanduros, first appeared in a radio play in 1939 and continued through 1940 as an occasional feature.

Given Mabel's remarkable success with the Buggins family, it is interesting that in her autobiography she claimed to 'think of myself first as a writer and secondly as a straight actress' (Constanduros, 64). She was certainly a prolific playwright, credited with having written over 100 plays by herself and many more in collaboration with others (notably Howard Agg and Denis Constanduros). Her most successful—written with her nephew—was *Acacia Avenue*, which ran for over 200 performances at the Vaudeville Theatre in 1943. Perhaps her family situation explains why, when reading the correspondence between Constanduros and the BBC, one is struck by the constant arguments about fees. Nevertheless she blended happily into local Sussex life, and Mrs Buggins made one of her last appearances when she opened Aldingbourne church fête in 1956. Constanduros died of a heart attack in the Royal West Sussex Hospital, Chichester, on 8 February 1957. Although today her reputation has faded, she was a popular cultural figure between the wars, helping to establish the style and flavour of British radio comedy.

BARRY TOOK

**Sources** M. Constanduros, *Shreds & patches* (1946) · *The Stage* (14 Feb 1957) · *Chichester & Southern Post* (16 Feb 1957) · D. Gifford, *The golden age of radio* (1985) · b. cert. · d. cert. · *CGPLA Eng. & Wales* (1957)
**Archives** BL, corresp. with Society of Authors, Add. MS 63225 | FILM BFI NFTVA, performance footage
**Likenesses** photograph, repro. in Gifford, *Golden age of radio*
**Wealth at death** £12,168: probate, 30 April 1957, *CGPLA Eng. & Wales*

**Constant, Hayne** (1904–1968), mechanical and aeronautical engineer, was born at Gravesend, Kent, on 26 September 1904, the second son of the family of six children of Frederick Charles Constant, dental surgeon, of Gravesend and later Folkestone, and his wife, (Mary) Theresa Hayne, of Northfleet, Kent. Educated at King's College choir school, Cambridge, King's School, Canterbury, the Technical Institute in Folkestone, and Sir Roger Manwood's School in Sandwich, he entered Queens' College, Cambridge, in 1924 as an open exhibitioner where he took a second class in part one of the mathematical tripos (1925) followed by a first class in the mechanical sciences tripos (1927). He was awarded a college scholarship. After taking his degree in 1927 Constant stayed in Cambridge for a postgraduate year to work on the torsional vibration of crankshafts which he reported in his first publication. For the next six years he was a member of the engine department of the Royal Aircraft Establishment (RAE), Farnborough, working on carburettors, dynamometers, and the effects of vibration on aircraft. A paper to the Royal Aeronautical Society describing and analysing tests on a biplane suspended upside down and vibrated by rotating masses mounted on the aircraft won him the Busk memorial prize in 1932.

From 1934 to 1936 Constant held the post of lecturer at Imperial College, but found it not to his liking and returned to RAE where, in July 1936, he was put in charge of the supercharger section under Dr A. A. Griffith, head of the engine department. After a few months, in March 1937, Constant presented a case to the Aeronautical Research Council for the development of the aircraft gas turbine engine. Working almost alone he had designed a small axial flow compressor and various gas turbine engine schemes which were described in his report. The report was well received and authority was given to start a programme, mainly in collaboration with Metropolitan-Vickers, for the development of gas turbine engines, involving the design, building, and testing of some six axial flow compressors and several parts of gas turbine engines.

Meanwhile a prototype of Frank Whittle's turbojet engine, made by Power Jets Ltd, was tested in 1937 and from then on its further development was supported by the Air Ministry. Constant saw the Whittle scheme as applicable only to short-range high altitude fighter aircraft, but with the outbreak of war in 1939 he suggested to Power Jets that a jet engine with the flow passing straight through an axial compressor, an annular combustion chamber, and axial flow turbine should be jointly developed. In the event Constant's scheme was developed and built by Metropolitan-Vickers. It was flight-tested in 1943 and became the prototype of the modern jet engine. It was Constant's most important individual contribution to aircraft propulsion. His other contributions ranged from his rule for determining the flow angle leaving a cascade of compressor blades, the specification and layout of other axial flow jet engines, and his leadership of the research and development programme which continued at RAE after he became head of the engine department in 1941, and then later at Pyestock near Farnborough after the end of the war.

From 1941 the team in the turbine division of the RAE engine department grew in numbers and facilities, but in 1944, much to Constant's dismay, the division was transferred from RAE to merge with Power Jets Ltd as a nationalized company: Power Jets (Research and Development) Ltd. Two years later this became the National Gas Turbine Establishment based at Pyestock with Constant as deputy, then director. In 1948 Constant was elected fellow of the Royal Society and won the James Clayton prize of the Institution of Mechanical Engineers. In 1951 he was appointed CBE and in 1958 CB. In 1963 he was awarded the gold medal of the Royal Aeronautical Society. He published twenty-three papers, ten patent specifications, and an unpretentious book, *Gas Turbines and their Problems* (1948), revised and enlarged in 1953.

In 1960 Constant reluctantly left Pyestock to become scientific adviser to the Air Ministry and then chief scientist (RAF), Ministry of Defence (1964). His friends thought he was not very happy in Whitehall and that he obviously would have preferred to remain in research and inventive activities.

Constant was a man of austere habit and thought with a self-contained reserve, but with a keen mind delighting in logical argument about technical matters. He would question the facts and objectives, almost arrogantly, behind any proposed design or development, sharpening each point of decision by arguments based on facts and fundamental physical principles, an approach which did not always endear him to his superiors, but greatly encouraged the younger engineers on his staff. In committee his speech was precise and economical. He was not only concerned about the professional development and rewards of his staff, but also their housing and sports. He was unmarried and his relaxations included tennis, skiing, amateur dramatics, motor cycles, sailing and boat building, and light music. It was typical of him to tackle each of them with zest and enjoy them with others and then to proceed to the next interest. He retired in 1962 to live in the bungalow of his own design, Ripelhyrst, Kiln Way, Grayshott, Hindhead, Surrey, where he died on 12 January 1968.                                    WILLIAM HAWTHORNE, *rev.*

**Sources**  W. R. Hawthorne, H. Cohen, and A. R. Howell, *Memoirs FRS*, 19 (1973), 269–79 • F. Whittle, *Jet: the story of a pioneer* (1953) • W. R. Hawthorne, 'Aircraft propulsion from the back room', *Aeronautical Journal*, 82 (1978), 93–108 • private information (1981) • personal knowledge (1981) • *Register of King's School, Canterbury* (1932), 263 • *CGPLA Eng. & Wales* (1968)

**Likenesses**  photograph, repro. in Hawthorne, Cohen, and Howell, *Memoirs FRS*

**Wealth at death**  £19,214: probate, 19 March 1968, *CGPLA Eng. & Wales*

**Constantine**, earl of Fife (*d.* in or after **1128**). *See under* Macduff family, earls of Fife (*per. c.*1095–1371).

**Constantine I** [Flavius Valerius Constantinus; *known as* Constantine the Great] (**272/3–337**), Roman emperor, was born at Naissus (modern Niš in Serbia) on 22 February 272 or 273. The year of his birth remains uncertain for lack of epigraphic evidence and calculations of the date are based on passing references in contemporary, or near contemporary, writers. These vary widely, suggesting that his age at death in 337 was between sixty and sixty-five years. A study of his career points to the latter age as best fitting the known facts about his various military appointments before his elevation to the throne. It has been noted that Constantine obscured his real age in order to dissociate himself, retrospectively, from the persecution of the Christian church which took place under his patrons the emperors Diocletian and Galerius, persecutions which his position might have required him to endorse or act upon. His claim to have been 'a mere child' in 303 when the great

Constantine I (272/3–337), head

persecution began seems to be a disingenuous attempt to distance himself from these events.

**Parentage and early career**  Constantine's father, Flavius Valerius Constantius, was the future emperor *Constantius I (250?–306). Before elevation to imperial status Constantius served as an officer in the army of Aurelian in the east, probably in 271 or 272; by 284–5 he was governor of the Adriatic province of Dalmatia, and probably praetorian prefect of Maximian, the western emperor, in 288–93. In 293 he was raised to the rank of Caesar and became emperor (Augustus) on the retirement of Diocletian and Maximian in 305. Constantine's mother, Flavia Julia *Helena (c.248–328/9), was of low social status, possibly the daughter of the manager of an imperial posting station. Drepanum, her birthplace in Bithynia (a province on the Black Sea coast of present-day Turkey), was renamed by her son Helenopolis. Later stories connecting her birth with Camulodunum (Colchester) in Britain can be discounted. Helena's relationship with Constantius is uncertain; opinion veers towards identifying her as his mistress, rather than legal wife. In any event her presence at Naissus in the province of Moesia Superior indicates that she accompanied Constantius on his military postings. The relationship ended when Constantius made a dynastic marriage with Theodora, the daughter of the emperor Maximian, at a date possibly before 289 or as late as 293. His father's second marriage provided Constantine with a family of three half-brothers and three half-sisters.

Few details of Constantine's career before he became emperor have survived, indeed they may have been deliberately suppressed. Allusive statements by contemporaries suggest that after his father's promotion to Caesar,

Constantine served in various military capacities in the east, perhaps also standing as hostage for his father's good behaviour in the west. While attached to the staff of the Caesar Galerius, Constantine served in Syria, Mesopotamia, and on the Danubian frontier between *c*.293 and 299. The following years, 301–5, were spent in the entourage of Diocletian, both at the court in Nicomedia and on imperial tours to Egypt and Rome.

Events following the abdication of Diocletian and Maximian in 305 saw Constantius as emperor in the west and Galerius in the east. Whereas a nephew of Galerius, Maximinus Daia, was elevated to be Caesar in the east, Constantine was passed over in favour of Severus II, a Pannonian army officer. Probably anxious for Constantine's future safety, Constantius persuaded Galerius to allow his son to join him. Fearing retraction of this concession, Constantine hastened west by forced marches. It is claimed in pro-Constantinian sources that, crossing the territory of Severus, he disabled the horses of the imperial posting stations on his route to prevent pursuit by the forces of the hostile western Caesar. The story may be an invention designed to denigrate Severus, whose territory Constantine later occupied.

**From multiple rulers to sole emperor, 305–324** Constantine arrived at Gesoriacum (Boulogne) in the summer of 305 and joined his father who was preparing an expedition against the Picts. This tribe may have been menacing the northern frontier of Britain; on the other hand the campaign may have been designed to reinforce the start of the new reign with an easy victory in an unimportant province. Constantine's part in the actual campaign is not recorded; his earlier military career suggests that participation would have been very active, especially in the light of his father's declining health. Constantius died on 25 July 306 at Eburacum (York) and Constantine was immediately proclaimed emperor by the army. The only detailed account of this event is given by Eutropius (*d.* 340), whose laconic comment is that 'all those about pressed him, especially Crocus, the king of the Alemanni, an ally of Constantius and a member of his entourage' (Eutropius, chap. 41, in *Liber de caesaribus*, ed. Bird). Nothing further is known about Crocus; a number of suggestions have been advanced as to his status. Possibly he was serving in the British expeditionary force as commander of an auxiliary force made up of his German followers; if so this body may have been decisive in securing the election. On the other hand Crocus may have been accompanying Constantius in a personal capacity, even as a hostage. That being so, he may have been in a position to guarantee Germanic assistance on the continent should Constantine be persuaded to cross the channel to occupy his father's territories.

Constantine's elevation was unconstitutional and Galerius, as senior emperor, recognized Severus, the western Caesar, as his new imperial colleague in the west. None the less, though technically a usurper, Constantine effectively controlled the army of Britain, as well as his father's expeditionary force, and extended his *de facto* rule over Constantius' territories of Gallia, Hispania, and Germania, where he set up his administrative capital at Trier. His position was reluctantly recognized by Galerius, who made him Caesar of the west. Encouraged by these events, Maxentius, the son of the emperor Maximian who came out of retirement, seized power in Italy. Severus surrendered to Maximian in 307 and committed suicide. In the same year Constantine allied himself with Maximian by marriage with his daughter Flavia Maxima Fausta, at the same time repudiating his mistress Minervina, the mother of his oldest son, Crispus. Fausta bore him three sons and two daughters before her execution in 326, shortly after Constantine had ordered the death of Crispus. The discovery of a relationship between the son and step-mother is usually advanced as an explanation of these events.

A constitutional conference at Carnuntum, on the Danube east of Vienna, in 308 failed to meet the expectations of the individuals contending for power and recognition. Maximian again retired, a new emperor, Licinius, was appointed, and Maxentius condemned as a usurper. In 310 Constantine assumed the imperial title himself as did his fellow junior ruler, Maximinus Daia. There were now four emperors, and a usurper ruling in Italy. Maximian again attempted to emerge from retirement; but, defeated by Constantine at Massalia (Marseilles), the colleague of Diocletian either committed suicide or was executed by his son-in-law.

Between his accession and 312, Constantine dealt with a number of internal and external crises. In particular he campaigned on, and fortified, the Rhine frontier as a preliminary to advancing further south and east into the domains of his imperial rivals. These preparations bore fruit when in 312 he attacked Italy, routing Maxentius at the battle of the Milvian Bridge on the northern outskirts of Rome. The defeat of Maxentius (312) and the elimination of Maximian (310), Maximinus Daia (313), Severus II (307), and, by natural causes, Galerius (311), left Constantine master of the west. A series of conflicts with Licinius, his eastern colleague, left him sole ruler in 324.

**Visits to Britain, 307–314** Numismatic evidence points to three occasions when Constantine returned to Britain. In each case coins were issued by the London mint which played a part in the ritual associated with a formal imperial *adventus*, or state visit. The symbolism of the three coin issues associated with these visits originates in the third century and shows the emperor riding to the left, his hand raised in salutation; a captive may be crouched below the raised hoof of the horse. The iconography of the emperor's portrait also points to the coins being a special issue, since, in contrast to the normal portrait where the emperor faces to the right, the ruler's bust faces to the left and is often shown with elaborate body armour, shield, spear, and helmet or some combination of these elements.

The first issue of the London mint probably occurred in the summer of 307. Constantine is correctly styled Caesar, though the reverse proclaims ADVENTVS AVGG (that is, 'Augustorum'), thus proclaiming that the Caesar's visit partakes of the actions of all of the rulers. The date of the issue is circumscribed by the fact that Constantine did not adopt the style AVGVSTVS on his coinage until either late July or December 307. Nothing is known about this visit; possibly a connection should be sought in the celebration of marriage to Fausta in the spring of 307 or to the defeat of German tribesmen, settled by Constantius on the west bank of the Rhine, who had pillaged parts of Gallia and Germania. Constantine's biographer Eusebius noted that when established in power the emperor visited the provinces formerly ruled by his father: a tour of Britain might have been part of this programme.

The second issue of Adventus coins, which to judge by surviving specimens was very large, dates to a period shortly before the invasion of Italy in 312. Zosimus records that troops from Britain made up part of the Constantinian army and Eusebius records what may be a second visit. The examination of coin deposits in forts in Britain suggests that the garrisons of the outpost forts of Hadrian's Wall, and a number of other forts in northern Britain, were withdrawn as contributions to Constantine's new mobile force. These troops from Britain probably served in all of the campaigns down to the overthrow of Licinius, Constantine's last rival for undivided imperial power, in 324. A third Adventus series dates to 314. Constantine was in residence in Trier between August 313 and March 314. By the autumn he was in the Balkans campaigning against Licinius. A visit to Britain in the spring or summer of 314 is entirely feasible. Either at this time, or during previous visits, changes in the administration of Britain may have been initiated. That this was the occasion of warfare cannot be ruled out, since Constantine bore the title *Britannicus Maximus* from 314.

**First Christian emperor** Constantine's victory in Italy is intimately associated with his conversion to Christianity. Two versions of events by contemporaries are extant. The earliest, recounted by Lactantius, tutor to Crispus, says that Constantine had a dream on the eve of the battle of the Milvian Bridge in which he was commanded to put the chi–rho monogram of Christ on the shields of his soldiers. A version given by the emperor to Eusebius a quarter of a century later claims that on his march to Rome he and the army saw, in broad daylight, a cross of light in the sky and the words 'hoc signo victor eris' ('by this sign you will conquer'). Constantine had already shown a predilection towards Christianity in that he had restored property to victims of the persecutions and was accompanied on his Italian campaign by Hosius, a Spanish bishop. On the other hand his adherence to traditional paganism, even while ostensibly Christian, should not be overlooked. While doubt has been cast on the story that Constantine experienced a vision of Apollo promising victory in 310, shortly before the overthrow of Maximian, support for this episode may be found in the fact that Constantine's principal coinage bore a figure of Sol and the legend 'Soli invicto comiti' ('the unconquered sun my companion') for a number of years after his experience of miraculous Christianity. Further, Constantine continued to hold the

office of *pontifex maximus*, the chief priest of the state cult of Jupiter, Juno, and Minerva.

That the emperor's conversion was sincere, if not precipitous, is attested by the benefactions bestowed on the clergy, the construction of churches in Italy and Palestine, and the foundation in 326 of Constantinopolis (Istanbul) as an alternative Christian capital, far removed from the traditional paganism of Rome itself. Constantine's religious policy did not force conversion on the pagan majority, although he sequestered the accumulated treasures of pagan temples (perhaps more to augment his financial resources than to make a religious gesture) and instituted antisemitic legislation. Sacrifice was prohibited, as was divination. There is little doubt that the emperor's change of religion acted as a stimulus to conversion among members of the administrative classes and the higher ranks of the army. The adoption by the church of the administrative structure of the empire for its own regional organization ensured that governments and ecclesiastical institutions were soon inextricably intertwined and the attempt by the emperor Julian (r. 360–63) to undo the results of Constantine's conversion met with little success.

Active in theological matters, Constantine convened a number of councils of the church and participated very directly in the proceedings of the Council of Nicaea (May 325) which laid down the basis of modern orthodox Christianity in the Nicene creed. As was normal for many converts at the period, Constantine delayed baptism until on his deathbed at Nicomedia on 22 May 337. His burial place in the newly erected church of the Holy Apostles in Constantinopolis signified his status as the thirteenth apostle, though in normal Roman style he was deified by his Christian sons and successors.

**Administrative and military reform** That Constantine had to contend with co-rulers and rivals for more than half of his reign profoundly affected his administration. Heir to the least prosperous part of the empire, he adapted his financial and military policies to accommodate the situation. Reform of the gold coinage *c*.310, by the issue of lightweight coins, led, inadvertently, to a stabilization of the currency since military success enforced circulation over an ever widening sphere of authority and the recovery of the more valuable currency of defeated rivals. The absolute necessity of protecting the frontiers of the provinces which constituted his power base in the west while he was warring against rivals in the east led to profound changes in the structure of the army. Faced with the prospect of warfare on more than one front, Constantine built upon the experience of Gallienus (r. 253–68) and split his forces into sedentary frontier garrisons and an élite mobile force. This division into *comitatenses* (mobile forces) and *limitanei* (frontier forces) characterized Roman military strategy throughout the fourth to sixth centuries. With these tactical changes came changes in pay scales between the troops, the frontier forces suffering thereby. Élite forces flourished at the expense of the frontiers, which had to be massively reinforced in the reign of Valentinian I (r. 364–75). As a tactical innovation the mobile army served Constantine well but put into the hands of subsequent usurpers a ready-made weapon with which to weaken fundamentally the fabric of the empire. The reign also saw an increased use of officers of German origin in both the middle and higher ranks of the army, at the same time as German troops were incorporated into tactical formations.

**Assessment** While he is often characterized as a revolutionary, closer study of Constantine's reign suggests a marked degree of conservatism. Even the conversion to Christianity may be seen in a political light were it to be preparatory to the eventual conquest of the east, with its possibly majority Christian population. Constantine adhered to the reforms of Diocletian (r. 284–305), implementing the changes which led to the creation of a large, professional civil service and an efficient tax recovery system. He enhanced a system of military and civil ranks and honours which bypassed the influence of the pagan senatorial class, but caused distress in the cities of the empire by sequestrating their funds.

After operating within the tetrarchic system for most of his reign, the emperor sought to re-establish its principles in his plans for the succession. His intention to divide the provinces between his relatives was thwarted after his death by the enmity between the families of Helena and Theodora, his father's two wives. An interregnum, lasting from May to September 337, saw the triumph of Constantine's sons and the elimination of his half-brothers and nephews, with the exception of the still infant Gallus (Caesar, 351–4) and Julian (Augustus, 360–63). The empire was then divided between Constantine II (r. 337–40), who took the north-western provinces, Constans (r. 337–50), who took Italy, Africa, and the Balkans, and Constantius II (r. 337–61), whose portion was the east.

Constantine's historic eminence was guaranteed by the Christian church, whose early historians constructed the image of an ideal ruler—as he came to be known, Constantine the Great. Few hostile contemporary accounts survived the winnowing of a millennium and a half of Christian historiography but such as do suggest that piety, superstition, ruthlessness, and opportunism combined in a personality of huge energy and unquenchable self-confidence. P. J. CASEY

**Sources** Liber de caesaribus of Sextus Aurelius Victor, ed. and trans. H. W. Bird (1994) • T. D. Barnes, The new empire of Diocletian and Constantine (1982) • T. D. Barnes, Constantine and Eusebius (1981) • P. J. Casey, 'Constantine the Great in Britain: the evidence of the coinage of the London mint, 312–14', Collectanea Londiniensia: studies … presented to Ralph Merrifield, ed. J. Bird and others (1978), 181–94 • S. Lieu and D. Monserrat, From Constantine to Julian: pagan and Byzantine views (1996) • R. Macmullen, Constantine (1969) • H. A. Pohlsander, The emperor Constantine (1996) • 'Epitome de caesaribus', Sexti Aurelii Victoris liber de caesaribus, ed. F. Pichlmayr, rev. edn, rev. R. Gruendel (Leipzig, 1966), 133–76; another edn (1970)
**Likenesses** silver medallion, 315, Staatliche Münzsammlung, Munich • head, Palazzo dei Conservatori, Rome [see illus.]
**Wealth at death** enormous wealth

**Constantine I** [Causantín mac Cinaeda] (d. **876**), king in Scotland, was the son of *Kenneth I (d. 858). It has been suggested that his mother may have belonged to the Pictish royal matriline (perhaps a daughter of Uurad, king of Picts from 839 to 842), but this is incapable of proof. He was probably Kenneth I's eldest surviving son, and had at least one brother, King Aed (d. 878), and two sisters, one of whom married Rhun, son of Arthgal, king of Dumbarton, and had a son, Eochaid, who challenged for the kingship in the confused period following Constantine I's death.

Constantine succeeded his uncle *Donald I [see under Kenneth I] to the kingship on the latter's death on 13 April 862. During his reign his kingdom's heartland in east-central Scotland suffered from intense Scandinavian pressure. In 866 Olaf, the Norwegian king of Dublin, 'wasted Pictland' and wintered there. In 870–71 Olaf returned to Britain and took 'a very great spoil of people', including Picts, as captives. Olaf had taken Dumbarton in 870, and this may have allowed Constantine to gain the upper hand over the kings there: in 872 he arranged for the assassination of Arthgal, king of Dumbarton. In 875 Constantine was attacked by Hálfdan, the Danish king of York, and suffered a crushing defeat at Dollar, in what is now Clackmannanshire. His forces were driven back to the highlands in Atholl and the east-central lowlands were occupied by the invaders for a year. And in the following year Constantine was killed by the Danes at the battle known as *inber dub fáta*, 'long dark river-mouth' (unidentified). He was succeeded by his brother Aed (perhaps after an interregnum of a year) and is said to have been buried on Iona. He had a son, *Donald II (d. 900) [see under Constantine II], whose mother is unknown. DAUVIT BROUN

**Sources** A. O. Anderson, ed. and trans., Early sources of Scottish history, AD 500 to 1286, 1 (1922), 296–304, 350–55 • M. O. Anderson, Kings and kingship in early Scotland, rev. edn (1980), 249–53, 265–89 • A. O. Anderson, ed., Scottish annals from English chroniclers, AD 500 to 1286 (1908), 62 • B. Hudson, 'Elech and the Scots in Strathclyde', Scottish Gaelic Studies, 15 (1988), 145–9 • A. P. Smyth, Warlords and holy men: Scotland, AD 80–1000 (1984), 191–5 • M. Miller, 'The last century of Pictish succession', Scottish Studies, 23 (1979), 39–67 • M. O. Anderson, 'Dalriada and the creation of the kingdom of the Scots', Ireland in early mediaeval Europe, ed. D. Whitelock, R. McKitterick, and D. Dumville (1982), 106–32

**Constantine II** [Causantín mac Aeda] (d. **952**), king in Scotland, was the son of King Aed (d. 878). It has been suggested that a King Dyfnwal of Strathclyde was his brother, but this is simply a misreading of an Irish source's obit of Domnall mac Áeda, king of the northern Uí Néill. Constantine succeeded as king to his cousin **Donald II** [Domnall mac Causantín] (d. 900), who was the son of *Constantine I (d. 876) and the first ruler to be described as 'king of Scotland' (ri Alban) in contemporary record. Alba referred to the region over which Donald and his successors established their rule, and was probably only the area bounded approximately by the River Spey to the north, the Forth to the south, and the central highlands to the west. The title 'king of Scotland' replaced the earlier 'king of Picts', and the people of the kingdom ceased to be known as Picts, and became simply 'inhabitants of Scotland' (fir Alban or Albanaig). Since Alba had hitherto denoted 'Britain' in Gaelic, this represents an extraordinary change in terminology, suggesting that the adoption of *Alba* as the kingdom's name represented the coining of a radically new identity, and perhaps signifying an attempt, following a period of disruption and uncertainty between 875 and 889, to establish a new political order based on dynastic kingship. During the reign of Donald II (889–900) 'the Northmen wasted Pictland' (Anderson, *Early Sources*, 1.395), but Donald defeated the Danes in a battle on some unidentified islands, before being killed by Scandinavians at Dunnottar, Kincardineshire. He was later reported to have been buried on Iona.

The long reign of Constantine II was probably crucial for the new kingdom's survival, allowing the new political order to be consolidated. It is now that mormaers (literally 'chief steward', the ruler of a province) are first heard of, and the first reference is found to one of a number of post-Pictish regional names associated with earls. It is possible, moreover, that Constantine was responsible for establishing St Andrews as the chief bishopric of his kingdom. If this is so, and the creation of earls and earldoms was in some sense his initiative, then it could be claimed not only that Constantine was the first king to be inaugurated as 'king of Scotland', but that he laid the foundations of the kingdom's political and ecclesiastical structure for the next five centuries.

Constantine's reign also represented a turning point in the kingdom's fortunes in its struggle for survival against Danish incursions. In 903 the grandsons of Ívarr plundered Dunkeld and 'all Scotland', but in 904 Constantine met them in battle at an unknown location in Strathearn, in modern Perthshire, and comprehensively defeated them; there are no more recorded Scandinavian invasions for half a century. In 905–6 he made an agreement at Scone with Bishop Cellach, probably the first chief bishop of 'Scotland', which may represent Constantine's backing for the church in an attempt to restore social order—of which the creation of earldoms may have formed a part—in the wake of more than sixty years of repeated invasion and worsening political instability. In the 910s Constantine went on the offensive and backed the Bernicians against Rognvald, Danish king of York, culminating in a titanic but indecisive battle in 918 (probably) on the River Tyne in Lothian.

The rise of the kings of Wessex changed the balance of power in Britain, however. In 920 along with other northern kings Constantine made a peace with Edward of Wessex, but he allied himself with the kings of Norse Dublin, marrying his daughter to King Guthfrith's son *Olaf. After Edward of Wessex died, Constantine made his peace with Edward's successor, Æthelstan, in 927; and Æthelstan may have stood as godfather for one of Constantine's sons, possibly *Indulf (d. 962). In 934, however, he renewed his alliance with Dublin against Æthelstan, causing Æthelstan to make a fruitless invasion in retaliation. When Olaf, Constantine's son-in-law, became king of Dublin, he joined forces with Constantine and the king of Dumbarton and invaded England in 937, only to suffer a crushing defeat at the battle of 'Brunanburh'. This may have weakened Constantine's hold on the kingship itself, for some time between 940 and 945 he relinquished it to his cousin,

*Malcolm I, the son of Donald II, and 'in his old age, being decrepit', retired to St Andrews, where he may have become abbot of the Céli Dé. He died at St Andrews in 952 and was buried there. In addition to his son Indulf and his daughter who married Olaf Guthfrithson, Constantine had at least one other son who, unnamed, died at 'Brunanburh'.                    DAUVIT BROUN

**Sources** A. O. Anderson, ed. and trans., *Early sources of Scottish history, AD 500 to 1286*, 1 (1922), 395–451 · M. O. Anderson, *Kings and kingship in early Scotland*, rev. edn (1980), 249–53, 265–89 · A. P. Smyth, *Warlords and holy men: Scotland, AD 80–1000* (1984), 197–209 · A. O. Anderson, ed., *Scottish annals from English chroniclers, AD 500 to 1286* (1908), 64–73 · B. Hudson, '*Elech* and the Scots in Strathclyde', *Scottish Gaelic Studies*, 15 (1988), 145–9 · M. Miller, 'The last century of Pictish succession', *Scottish Studies*, 23 (1979), 39–67 · M. O. Anderson, 'Dalriada and the creation of the kingdom of the Scots', *Ireland in early mediaeval Europe*, ed. D. Whitelock, R. McKitterick, and D. Dumville (1982), 106–32

**Constantine III** [Flavius Claudius Constantinus] (*d.* 411), Roman emperor proclaimed in Britain, competed during his short reign (407–11) with the legitimate emperor Honorius to be the western Roman emperor. The pressure he exerted on Honorius's government increased its difficulty in controlling Alaric and the Goths, and thus contributed to the sack of Rome in 410. By withdrawing troops from Britain in 407, he also indirectly brought Roman rule in the province to an end, since his officials were unable to maintain their authority. The sequence of events is complex, however, and surviving narratives are incomplete and inconsistent, although they can be reconciled and supplemented by conjecture. The principal narratives are by two early-Byzantine historians, Sozomen *c.*443 and Zosimus *c.*500, both of whom used an excellent contemporary account, now lost, written by the Egyptian Greek Olympiodorus.

On 31 December 406, a host of Vandals, Alans, and Sueves crossed the Rhine and poured into Gaul. In Britain the Roman garrison proclaimed Gratianus, a British civilian, as emperor; four months later it deposed him in favour of Constantine, who is said by the contemporary historian Orosius to have been only a common soldier with nothing but his name to recommend him. As a usurper he is conventionally said to have been 'gluttonous' (Gregory of Tours, ii.9) and 'unreliable' (*Sidonius*, 5.9.1), but he was more energetic and decisive than the legitimate emperor Honorius. Nothing is known of his previous career or connections, except the names of his sons Constans and Julianus, both of them named, like their father, after fourth-century emperors who had been active in Gaul and Britain. It is not stated that these names were assumed only in 407. At his father's accession, Constans was actually a monk; Constantine himself was a Christian. It is quite possible that he was a Briton like Gratianus and his own general Gerontius, but there is no explicit testimony. Nor are the Roman garrison's motives clear. It contained nine mobile units, according to the *Notitia dignitatum* (a contemporary list of civil and military appointments throughout the empire), and these nine units may have been largely recruited from Germans and other outsiders; but there were also many frontier units

Constantine III (*d.* 411), coin

(the *Notitia* names forty-six) of varying but inferior quality which were recruited locally. According to Zosimus, the British army feared an attack by the invaders of Gaul, but Constantine's strategy was not to defend Britain alone: in summer 407 he took an army to Gaul, with which he defeated the invaders inconclusively before reinstating the Rhine frontier. However, this initiative was also a threat to the central government, and Constantine's joint commanders-in-chief were defeated and killed by the Goth Sarus, an officer dispatched by Stilicho, the general who dominated Honorius's court in north Italy; but their successors Gerontius and Edobichus (a Frank) forced Sarus to retreat across the Alps. By May 408, even though the invaders were still at large, Constantine ruled Gaul and Britain from his capital at Arelate (Arles).

Stilicho now concentrated an army at Ticinum (Pavia) to recover Gaul with the help of the Gothic king Alaric, but it mutinied and lynched many of his allies in the government; then Stilicho himself was arrested by his rivals and executed on 22 August 408 for appeasing the Goths. Constantine meanwhile had appointed Constans as his deputy (Caesar) and sent him with Gerontius and an army to Spain, where they soon crushed the local resistance led by kinsmen of Honorius. The new regime in Italy, distracted by the problem of controlling Alaric, proved more amenable than Stilicho's. It received an embassy from Constantine, who (like Magnus Maximus) excused his usurpation by saying that it had been forced upon him by the soldiers, and Honorius gave him a purple robe in recognition. In January 409 they shared the consulship, at least in the reckoning of the provinces controlled by Constantine. This was the high tide of his fortunes.

In Spain, Constans replaced the native garrisons of the Pyrenees with German units of his own, the *Honoriaci*, whose title indicates that they had been raised before the usurpation but it is not known whether it was for service in Britain or in Gaul. Leaving his new wife at Caesaraugusta (Saragossa), Constans returned to Arelate

on a visit to his father. Gerontius seized the opportunity to rebel and proclaim an emperor of his own, Maximus, for reasons which are not clear. His rebellion should probably be connected with the disaster of October 409, when the Vandals, Alans, and Sueves forced their way into Spain through the Pyrenees, the new garrisons proving ineffective. According to Orosius, a Spaniard, they actually joined the invaders. Gerontius may have feared supersession when Constans returned with a general called Justus, or he may have simply usurped authority in a crisis, like Constantine himself in Britain. Constantine now sent reinforcements to Spain and promoted Constans to full emperor (Augustus) to command them, but the soldiers went over to Gerontius, and Constans was forced to take refuge in Vienna (Vienne on the River Rhône). Constantine meanwhile had tried to secure his eastern front by invading Italy; ostensibly he was aiding Honorius against Alaric, and he was probably responding to an invitation from Honorius's general Allobichus, but when Allobichus fell from power and was executed, Constantine was forced to retreat to Arelate.

By 411, therefore, Constantine's position was desperate. Gerontius had invaded Gaul and, after killing Constans at Vienne, was besieging Arelate in the east; Honorius's new and efficient commander-in-chief, the future emperor Constantius III, had crossed the Alps with an army. Constantine's only hope was his other general Edobichus, whom he had sent across the Rhine to collect German allies. First Gerontius was forced to retreat when most of his army deserted him for Constantius, then Constantius besieged Arelate himself. Edobichus attempted to rescue Constantine, but his army fell into an ambush; and when Constantine heard that he was dead, he tried to forestall his own death by abdicating and having himself consecrated as a Christian priest. Arelate now surrendered to Constantius, who sent Constantine and his younger son Iulianus back to Italy under a promise of safe conduct, but the party was intercepted by order of Honorius; the two prisoners were executed 30 miles from Ravenna; Constantine's head was stuck onto a pole and arrived (at Ravenna presumably) on 18 September 411.

Constantine was the last Roman emperor to rule Britain. Gerontius had incited 'the barbarians in Gaul' against him when he rebelled, probably in autumn 409, and the resulting loss of Spain and most of his army made Constantine unable to resist 'the barbarians from across the Rhine'. Both terms are used by Zosimus, and it is not clear whether he means the same tribes by both; nor is it clear whether they were the Vandals, Alans, and Sueves *before* they crossed the Pyrenees, or such of them as did not invade Spain, or other tribes which invaded Gaul in their wake (notably the Franks, Alamanni, and Burgundians), or even Saxons who invaded Britain. Zosimus adds that these attacks now:

> forced the inhabitants of Britain and some of the tribes in Gaul to secede from Roman rule and to be independent, obeying Roman laws no longer. And so the Britons took up arms, and risked their lives to free their own cities from the barbarians who were attacking them; and the whole of

Armorica [Brittany] and other Gallic provinces copied the Britons by freeing themselves in this way, expelling the Roman officials and establishing whatever government they wished.　(Zosimus, vi.5.2)

What this all meant has been much debated by modern scholars, but since Constantine's is the last Roman imperial coinage to reach Britain, it follows that the inhabitants of Roman Britain, by shaking off the usurper for themselves, did not pass once more under the control of the central government. This in any case had more pressing problems of its own in Gaul and Italy, as Honorius admitted c.410 by his famous advice to the cities of Britain that they defend themselves.　　　　　　　　　　R. S. O. TOMLIN

**Sources** C. E. Stevens, 'Marcus, Gratian and Constantine', *The Athenaeum* [Pavia], 36 (1958), 316–47 • E. A. Thompson, 'Britain, AD 406–410', *Britannia*, 8 (1977), 303–18 • Sozomen, *Kirchengeschichte*, ed. J. Bidez and G. C. Hansen, 9 (Berlin, 1960), 11–15 • Zosimus, *Historia nova: the decline of Rome*, ed. and trans. J. J. Buchanan and H. T. Davis (1967), vi.1–5, 13; v. 27, 31–2, 43 • Olympiodorus, 'Fragments', *The fragmentary classicising historians of the later Roman empire*, ed. and trans. R. C. Blockley, 2 (1983), 152–210 • Orosius, 'Historiarum libri septem', *Patrologia Latina*, 31 (1846), col. 740 • Gregory of Tours, *The history of the Franks*, ed. and trans. L. Thorpe (1974), bk 9 • *Sidonius: poems and letters*, ed. and trans. W. B. Anderson, 2 vols (1936–65) • O. Seeck, ed., *Notitia dignitatum* (1876) • T. Mommsen, ed., 'Consularia constantinopolitana', *Chronica minora saec. IV. V. VI. VII.*, 1, MGH Auctores Antiquissimi, 9 (Berlin, 1892), 411 • S. S. Frere, *Britannia: a history of Roman Britain*, 3rd edn (1987), 353–77 • P. Salway, *Roman Britain* (1981), 415–44 • A. S. Esmonde Cleary, *The ending of Roman Britain* (1989), 131–61 • J. R. Martindale, *The prosopography of the later Roman empire*, 2: AD 395–527 (1980), 310, 316, 508 • J. Matthews, *Western aristocracies and imperial court, AD 364–425* (1975), 308–13
**Likenesses** coin, BM [*see illus.*] • coin portrait on gold solidus, AM Oxf.

**Constantine III** (d. 997). *See under* Culen (d. 971).

**Constantine mac Fergus** (d. 820). *See under* Picts, kings of the (act. c.300–c.900).

**Constantine, George** (b. c.1500, d. in or before 1561), evangelical reformer, was born near the Cheshire–Shropshire border and educated at a local school before going on to Trinity College, Cambridge, in 1517–18. He became BCL in 1523–4. He took minor orders in 1521, and was subsequently ordained to the priesthood. He became vicar of Sedgley, Staffordshire, about 1526. It was almost certainly at Cambridge that Constantine became an enthusiast for the Reformation. In early 1527 he was in London, where he associated with the lawyer and pamphleteer Simon Fish and recruited Robert Necton to act as an agent for Tyndale's English New Testament.

In 1528 Constantine was engaged in spreading reformation ideas back in Shropshire, and later that year he was in Antwerp, having abandoned clerical dress. He was now actively being sought by the English authorities for his heterodoxy. At about this time he married, being one of the first English priests of the Reformation period to do so. As a protection against extradition he took out Antwerp citizenship, giving his profession as physician. He probably assisted William Tyndale in the publication and distribution of 'The examination of William Thorpe' early in 1530. Later in the year he returned to England. He was

arrested in 1531 and personally examined and imprisoned by Lord Chancellor Sir Thomas More in More's own house in Chelsea. Under heavy pressure Constantine co-operated with More, providing the chancellor with evidence which led to the interception of one consignment of books and the arrest of Necton for a second time. However, when the book agent Richard Bayfield, whom More had also been interrogating, was executed, Constantine decided that he would be safer out of More's reach. He escaped and fled back to rejoin his wife in Antwerp on 6 December 1531.

Constantine probably returned to England some time after More's resignation in 1532. He had custody of some of Thomas Poyntz's children when Poyntz was arrested in the Low Countries while attempting to secure the release of William Tyndale. Constantine was closely touched by the arrest and execution of Queen Anne Boleyn and those accused of adulterous relations with her: he admired Anne for her religious convictions and had links with some of those executed with her, having been in the service of Henry Norris and at school with William Brereton. He later expressed as much scepticism as was politic while Henry was still on the throne about the charges under which they died.

Constantine had some minor role as a go-between for Cromwell and the printers in the publication of the first approved English bibles in the later 1530s. He was arrested for treason in 1539 on the evidence of John Barlow after a long journey in Barlow's company full of conversational indiscretions. Constantine wrote what he claimed was a full account of these for Cromwell. It provides his views on a range of topics including the true authorship of Henry's book on the seven sacraments, Anne Boleyn and her lovers, the two current candidates for Henry's hand from Milan and Cleves, clerical marriage, the young earl of Surrey, and the proper treatment for Henry's ulcerous leg. He was imprisoned in the Tower, but released at an unknown date.

In the late 1540s Constantine's interests shifted to south Wales, where Bishop William Barlow of St David's made him vicar of Llawhaden and then, in 1546, appointed him his registrar. When a general visitation in six circuits was organized to implement religious reform in the following year, Constantine was a member of the circuit embracing Wales and the Welsh marches. In 1549 he became archdeacon of Carmarthen. He played a vigorous part in the enforcement of the Edwardian reformation in the diocese, for instance pulling down the high altar of St Peter's Church in Carmarthen, but became embroiled in the unedifying and highly personal conflicts which erupted between Robert Ferrar, Barlow's successor as bishop, and the cathedral chapter. Ferrar tried to deprive him of his registrarship, and eventually Constantine emerged as one of the bishop's leading opponents. His daughter had married Thomas Young, another of Ferrar's adversaries. Under Mary he adapted sufficiently at first to be able to retain his position as registrar, and in 1555 he took part in Ferrar's trial and condemnation for heresy. According to an unconfirmed report which reached John Foxe, Constantine and Young sought and obtained Ferrar's forgiveness before his execution.

Constantine subsequently took refuge on the continent, being enrolled as a citizen of Emden on 6 May 1556. Having returned to England after the accession of Elizabeth, he became archdeacon of Brecon in 1559, and was also appointed to that year's royal visitation, on a circuit identical to that of 1547. But he seems to have played little part in its proceedings and was dead by 3 February 1561, when a successor was instituted in his archdeaconry. His son-in-law Thomas Young became Elizabeth's first archbishop of York.                                         ANDREW HOPE

**Sources** J. Foxe, *Acts and monuments*, 7 (1858) · T. Amyot, 'Transcript of an original manuscript, containing a memorial from George Constantyne to Thomas, Lord Cromwell', *Archaeologia*, 23 (1831), 50–78 · St Thomas More, *The confutation of Tyndale's answer*, ed. L. A. Schuster and others, 3 vols. (1973), vol. 8 of *The Yale edition of the complete works of St Thomas More* · St Thomas More, *The apology*, ed. J. B. Trapp (1979), vol. 9 of *The Yale edition of the complete works of St Thomas More* · J. Strype, *Ecclesiastical memorials*, 3 vols. (1822) · A. J. Brown, *Robert Ferrar: Yorkshire monk, Reformation bishop and martyr in Wales, c.1500–1555* (1997) · A. Pettegree, *Marian protestantism: six studies* (1996) · *LP Henry VIII*, vols. 4–5, 9–10, 14, addenda · *Letters of Sir John Hackett*, ed. E. F. Rogers (1971) · G. Williams, *Wales and the Reformation* (1997) · G. Williams, *The Welsh and their religion* (1991) · G. Williams, *Welsh Reformation essays* (1967) · *DWB*, 114–15

**Constantine, Learie Nicholas**, Baron Constantine (1901–1971), cricketer and politician, was born on 21 September 1901 at Petit Valley, Diego Martin, near Maraval, Trinidad, the second child and eldest son of Lebrun Samuel Constantine (1874–1942), cricketer and cocoa estate overseer, and his wife, Anaise Pascall. His mother and father were, respectively, the child and grandchild of slaves. His upbringing was happy, if patriarchal, and he played cricket with the family from a very early age on their cocoa estate. He enjoyed an economic security that he would later (but in private) compare favourably with what he saw in the Lancashire of the 1930s. He left school at the age of fifteen, never a remote contender for the island scholarships to secondary education which were the passports to a career. But as a cricketer he captained St Ann's School, Port of Spain, in 1916 and 1917.

**Cricket: Nelson and the West Indies**  Constantine's father, who had toured England twice with the West Indies (1900, 1906), and whose estate had prospered during the cocoa boom of the First World War, secured him a clerkship in a firm of solicitors. Lebrun captained Victoria at cricket, yet he would not allow his son to play for three seasons until he had established himself as chief clerk. But Lebrun stood down from the Trinidad trials in 1921 to give his son his first opportunity for colonial selection after a successful season with Shannon (which the Victoria club had become). A first-class début against Barbados at Port of Spain was followed, in 1922, with the only appearance together, at that level, of father and son: again against Barbados in the triangular tournament in British Guiana.

It was Constantine's fielding, rather than any outstanding performance with bat or ball, which won him selection for the tour to England in 1923. And so it proved: *Wisden* called him 'an amazingly good cover-point' (Wisden, 1924, 423) and Pelham Warner—with an empathy for the Trinidadian whose birthplace he shared—thought he was 'the finest fielder in the world' (P. Warner, *Lord's 1787–1945*, 188). Some mild taunts from undergraduates led him to score 77 in an hour against Oxford University, responding in the only way open to him. By now cricket had replaced work. He was briefly unemployed until the firm of Trinidad Leaseholds, with whom he would resume links later,

Learie Nicholas Constantine, Baron Constantine (1901–1971), by Godfrey Argent, 1968

offered him a clerkship (1926). The post enabled Constantine to marry, on 25 July 1927, Norma Agatha Cox (1903–1971), daughter of Faustin Cox of Port of Spain, a chemist. She would give him the stability he needed, urge him to look beyond his cricket, and be his consolation when circumstances and attitudes upset him. Their only child, Gloria, was born in 1928. Trinidad Leaseholds, for whom he played on Saturdays, gave him the time off for colonial cricket and leave of absence to tour England in 1928.

A match in June 1928 had long-term implications both for West Indies' cricket and for Constantine himself. The tourists had been doing badly and gates were low. Constantine, against medical advice, agreed to play against Middlesex at Lord's and, on the second day, his side faced defeat by an innings. By scoring 86 runs in an hour, taking seven Middlesex wickets for 57 in 14 overs, and then hitting 103 for the West Indies in another hour, he enabled his team to win by three wickets. When the Australian C. A. Macartney, who was watching, persuaded his own country to invite the West Indies to tour, as a test-playing country, they were established for the future. As for Constantine, he was approached by Nelson, the Lancashire league club, to become their professional. He played for them for eight seasons (1929–37) and lived in the town until 1949. His influence on the town stretched far beyond the horizons of cricket. As a player, he contributed both to the club's own success and to the overall benefit of clubs in the league. Attendances rose by thousands when he played. Among his outstanding performances were all ten wickets for 10 runs in thirty-seven balls against Accrington in 1933 and 192 not out against East Lancashire in 1937. He became one of the best-paid sportsmen in Britain. In 1934 another club offered him a much higher fee than had been offered to Donald Bradman, then at the height of his fame. Constantine moved in a middle-class milieu in the largely working-class and nonconformist community of Nelson in the years of the depression. He was accepted because of his tact, his moral standing, his friendliness to children, and his commitment; he ultimately received the freedom of the borough.

Between joining Nelson in 1929 and the outbreak of war in 1939, Constantine—save for one game in 1945—played out the remainder of his first-class cricket. He was available for the West Indies in the majority of their tests. His career figures, as a batsman and as a bowler, do not reflect his true worth. In eighteen test matches he averaged 19.24 with the bat and 30.10 with the ball. In all first-class games (1922–45) he made 4475 runs (24.05), including five centuries, and took 439 wickets (20.48). He secured 133 catches. At the highest levels he was a bowler rather than a batsman, achieving considerable pace, with a high, smooth action. His batting, better suited to the one-day game he played in league cricket, was aggressive, powerful, unorthodox, and magnetic. To cut a ball off the middle stump requires a fine eye. But it was as a fielder that he shone. His close catching was feline in its anticipation and from the deep he could throw with disconcerting accuracy. His cricket was that of the romantic. He would have

been entombed, had he played in the classical tradition of other great players.

**Racial issues** During the Second World War Constantine was employed by the Ministry of Labour, in conjunction with the Colonial Office, as a welfare officer. He was responsible for the welfare of West Indians arriving to work in munitions factories in Liverpool and held a watching brief on the needs of west African seamen. His work involved him in race relations at various levels—with government departments, employers, trade unions, the League of Coloured Peoples (of which he was briefly president), the churches, and, to some extent, the United States forces. The contribution to the war effort, for which he was uniquely qualified, was matched by broadcasts for the BBC to the Caribbean and to listeners in Britain, by lecturing to the forces, by hospital visits, and by playing in charity cricket matches. A game at Colwyn Bay in 1943 raised nearly £4000 for the Red Cross prisoner of war fund. But in that same year, while playing for the dominions against England at Lord's, there was an incident which highlighted racial attitudes. Cheered by the crowds by day, Constantine and his family were refused accommodation at night. In *Constantine* v. *Imperial Hotel, London, Ltd* (1944) Mr Justice Birkett awarded him nominal damages against the hotel for 'failing to receive and lodge him'. The decision to retain Sir Patrick Hastings, an eminent advocate, as his counsel, was taken at the highest levels. The case was seen as of utmost importance in assuring the goodwill of non-white peoples in the empire to the war cause. It also explains why Constantine continued to take up the causes of ordinary fellow countrymen whose unofficial ambassador he felt he was. Constantine's war work ended symbolically when he led the dominions, the only non-white man in the side, to an exciting victory against England at Lord's in August 1945, playing a major role in the field himself. In the new year honours in 1946 he was appointed MBE.

'My own future is obscure' (Howat, 142), Constantine declared in a BBC broadcast in 1946. Yet he himself challenged this uncertainty by confirming his reputation as a broadcaster, especially on cricket. 'He was a producer's dream with an excellent voice, sincere and unaffected', recorded a BBC internal minute, though fluency prevailed over accuracy, especially when he reminisced. Broadcasting, with occasional professional appearances as a cricketer or coach, helped him financially while he strove, for eight years, to qualify as a barrister. The year 1954 was a major landmark. Constantine was called to the bar by the Middle Temple, accepted an appointment in the legal department of his old employers, Trinidad Leaseholds, and published *Colour Bar*. The book was received with some surprise for its bitterness, but it endorsed his concern for the thousands whose social and economic prospects were blighted by prejudice.

**Trinidadian politics and diplomacy** The return to live in Trinidad, after twenty-five years, was not undertaken without misgivings, though the in-house paper *Regent News* reported that 'seldom has public acclaim been given so ungrudgingly to a son of the soil' (*Regent News*, January 1955). Constantine's stay with Trinidad Leaseholds proved short-lived (1954–6) and, with the blessing of his employers, he accepted the first chairmanship of the People's National Movement Party. He won a seat in the legislative council and was appointed (1956) minister for communications, works, and utilities in the administration of Eric Williams. The measure of his achievements lay in securing new inter-island shipping, a road- and bridge-building policy, and new schools. As a minister, he produced concrete results and coped with problems. He was less successful as a debater in the legislative council and he incurred some hostility by accusing members of a 'bankruptcy of thoughts' (*Official Report of Debates*, 9, October 1959) and making invidious comparisons with political behaviour in Britain. Nevertheless, to a political opponent, 'he was of inestimable service at a crucial time in Trinidad's history' (Howat, 178).

It was, however, with few regrets, that Constantine left politics to become Trinidad's first high commissioner in London (1961) and a knighthood followed in the 1962 new year's honours list. His period of office (1961–4) coincided with the increased immigration of West Indians into Britain and he would admit that he saw his concern for them as his major responsibility. That concern led him to intervene in the allegations that the Bristol Bus Company had refused employment to a West Indian bus conductor. With a personal visit to Bristol, comments to reporters, and an article in the press, he was seen to have acted impetuously, although *The Times* supported, in principle, his recognition of the moral responsibilities owed to new peoples coming into Britain. But he himself thought that even his own government felt he had exceeded his duties and that view contributed to his decision not to seek a second term of office. His resignation also marked an end to his relationship with Williams—in which there was always a tinge of jealousy on the latter's part at Constantine's popularity—and influenced him in deciding to stay in Britain. To his high commissionership Constantine had brought certain known qualities which served him well but had added nothing to his reputation.

**The bar, broadcasting, and peerage** Now in his sixties and not in the best of health, Constantine at last fulfilled an ambition when he entered (1964) the chambers of Sir Dingle Foot. On his first appearance in court, as junior counsel, he was sent for by the judge. Wondering what procedural misdemeanour he had committed, he was greeted with 'My dear Sir Learie, what an honour to have you in my court' (Howat, 211). Although a very junior barrister, Constantine had been elected (1963) an honorary member of the Middle Temple. He also played, in 1964, his last match, appearing for a BBC eleven. Broadcasting, indeed, had continued to provide him with some employment, though he was less successful as a cricket commentator in the medium of television. In 1968 he became a governor of the BBC; his contributions won praise, while the chairman, Lord Hill, regretted the appointment had not been made much earlier.

Constantine also served on two newly created bodies,

the Sports Council (1965) and the Race Relations Board (1966), and was elected rector of St Andrews University in 1967. A life peerage came in 1969, allegedly blocked in earlier years by the independent Trinidad. The earl marshal of England, unusually, attended the introduction into the House of Lords of the first black peer. 'Baron Constantine played a marathon, heraldic innings' reported *The Times* (27 March 1969). In a speech in March 1971 Constantine successfully urged the protection of the Commonwealth sugar agreement if Britain entered the European Economic Community. Four months later he died in Brondesbury, Hampstead, London, on 1 July 1971; his widow survived him by only two months.

A state funeral took place on 8 July at Aroica cemetery in Trinidad. Constantine was posthumously awarded the Trinidad cross, and there was a memorial service in Westminster Abbey. Cricket apart—and he was identified as the man who led 'the emancipation of West Indies cricket' (*Trinidad Guardian*, 2 July 1971)—Constantine's reputation must rest on his contribution to racial tolerance, his benevolent view of empire and Commonwealth, and his personal acceptance within the British 'establishment'. In the end he was more English than Trinidadian and he needed that wider platform.

GERALD M. D. HOWAT

**Sources** G. Howat, *Learie Constantine* (1975) · L. N. Constantine, *Cricket and I* (1933) · L. N. Constantine, *Cricket crackers* (1949) · L. N. Constantine, *Cricketers' carnival* (1950) · L. N. Constantine, *Cricket in the sun* (1946) · *Wisden*, esp. 1970, 1972 · P. Bailey, P. Thorn, and P. Wynne-Thomas, *Who's who of cricketers* (1984) · *The Times* (2 July 1971) · *Daily Telegraph* (2 July 1971) · C. L. R. James, *Beyond a boundary* (1963) · N. Cardus, *The Playfair Cardus* (1963) · L. N. Constantine, 'Race in the world', rectorial address, U. St Andr., 1968 · S. Morris, 'Learie Constantine', *New Community* (Jan 1971) · *CGPLA Eng. & Wales* (1971)

**Archives** BBC WAC, microfilm of broadcasts | FILM BFI NFTVA, 'Learie Constantine', 1946 · BFI NFTVA, *Black firsts*, 19 July 1998 · BFI NFTVA, propaganda film footage (MoI) · BFI NFTVA, sports footage

**Likenesses** photographs, 1928–69, Hult. Arch. · photograph, 1929–1939?, repro. in Constantine, *Cricket and I* · G. Argent, photograph, 1968, NPG [*see illus.*]

**Wealth at death** £5143: resealed probate, 14 Feb 1972, *CGPLA Eng. & Wales* (1971)

**Constantinidis** [*née* Connell], **Joanna** (1927–2000), potter, was born on 12 December 1927 at Purey Court Nursing Home, York, the second daughter and second of the three children of James Connell (1897–1957), factory manager, and his wife, Clara Peterson (1886–1977).

Connell showed artistic flair at an early age. Though art was not taught at Ecclesfield grammar school, which she attended from 1939 to 1945, she was an energetic draughtsman at home and determined to study painting, and from 1946 to 1949 she attended Sheffield College of Art. Here she enthusiastically discovered pottery, instructed in its rudiments by H. R. Stone, a persuasive teacher with a particular interest in slipware. Connell found information on ceramics sparse, but pored over the few texts then available, such as Bernard Leach's *A Potter's Book*, which encouraged her experiments with clays and

**Joanna Constantinidis** (1927–2000), by Tim Macpherson

glazes. In 1951 she became ceramics lecturer at Chelmsford Technical College, teaching pottery to adults—a post she held until retirement in 1989. She proved a sensitive and inspiring tutor, but was also able to develop here her own technical abilities and artistic direction. She looked for ideas in early Staffordshire slipware, seventeenth-century saltglaze, and industrial products. Drawing remained an essential springboard for her work at the wheel. It was Eric Jones, her art instructor at Sheffield, who had emphasized how much can be achieved in a single line, an aesthetic lesson she never forgot. It instilled in her an increasingly pronounced economy of language. In the mid-fifties her pots were clearly indebted to the Anglo-oriental vision of Bernard Leach, with their rich ash glazes and resist decoration. She exhibited at the Red Rose Guild, the British Crafts Centre, and the influential 'Pictures for Schools' exhibitions at the Whitechapel Art Gallery, London. Yet, in only a short time, she became dissatisfied with the shapes of her pots and their glazes, which she felt were a distraction from the intrinsic qualities of form and the clay's expressive potential.

Highly impressed by several exhibitions of work by the leading potters Lucie Rie and Hans Coper, put on at London's Berkeley Galleries through the 1950s, Connell began to change her approach. Since 1959 she had been established in a new studio in Great Baddow, near Chelmsford, where she remained until her death. Here she began to produce—like Rie and Coper—cleaner and simpler pots. Decoration was confined to broad fluting and incising, and she employed matt glazing, to better emphasize body and form. The result was more urban and modernist

in quality, seeming to coalesce with much of the new architecture and art being produced at this time. By the early 1970s her work had become more sculptural and convoluted, altered after leaving the wheel by cutting, folding, and reassembling. None the less these objects still preserved the rhythms of the turning wheel, what she came to describe as the pots' 'latent energy'. By finally eliminating glazes and concentrating on lustres, she could now define and accentuate the 'bone' of the pot more effectively. On 30 September 1961 she had married the Greek film-maker and writer Photis Georges Constantinidis (*b*. 1936), a relationship which intensified her interest in ancient Mediterranean pots, in the austerity of classical art and architecture, and in the clarifying light of the Greek region. Her austere eye looked not only to the language of modern abstraction, but to that of contemporary cinema, where maximum expression was often achieved through the simplest of means.

Constantinidis's technical command and artistic originality was recognized by the medal of honour at the 1978 'International exhibition of ceramic art' in Faenza. Her work was also being acquired by public collections such as the Victoria and Albert Museum, London, and the National Museum of Modern Art in Kyoto. Through the eighties and nineties her work was pared down as she concentrated on bowls and tall cylinders. Large open leaning pots and tapering vessels explored and defined space with a new authority. In her final years Constantinidis, now living separately from her husband (who had returned to Greece), spent most of her time in her studio, producing not only fine individual pots, but an elegant range of well-designed porcelain tableware. Ascetic and reserved, Constantinidis was passionately dedicated to ceramics, but was also a deeply affectionate woman with a highly developed sense of humour as well as formidable intellect. In 1995 she was honoured with a touring retrospective of her work organized by the University of Derby. In the spring of 2000 she suffered her first stroke, but was able to complete work for a solo exhibition at the Victoria and Albert Museum in May. She died at Broomfield Hospital, Chelmsford, on 1 August 2000 and was cremated at Chelmsford on 9 August.

Joanna Constantinidis was a radical potter who helped to reinvent the wheel-formed vessel through her innovative methods of clay manipulation. She strove for a structural and material essence, producing a honed-down and disciplined ceramic architecture which was also highly sensual and expressive. DAVID WHITING

**Sources** L. Shaw-Miller, *Joanna Constantinidis: ceramics from twenty five years* (1995) [exhibition catalogue, University of Derby] · D. Whiting, 'Sources of inspiration: Joanna Constantinidis', *Crafts*, 149 (1997), 46–9 · *The Times* (5 Aug 2000) · *The Guardian* (3 Aug 2000) · *The Independent* (4 Aug 2000) · private information (2004) [John Connell, brother] · b. cert. · d. cert.
**Likenesses** T. Macpherson, photograph, Ceramic Review collection, London [*see illus.*] · photographs, repro. in Whiting, 'Sources of inspiration: Joanna Constantinidis' · photographs, repro. in *Ceramic Review*

**Constantius I** [Flavius Valerius Constantius; *called* Constantius Chlorus] (**250?–306**), Roman emperor, was born in the

Constantius I (250?-306), medallion

Balkan province of Illyricum on 31 March, probably in
250. It is alleged that he was related to the emperor Claudius Gothicus (Claudius II) (r. 268–70), though this may be a
later invention to enhance the imperial family's antecedents. His parentage is unknown but the subsequent use
of names in the family suggest that his father may have
been a Flavius Delmatius and his mother possibly Julia
Constantia. His nickname Chlorus ('the Pale') is not
recorded before the sixth century but is likely to be a contemporary reference to his personal appearance. He
embarked on a military career the nature of which suggests that he had powerful patronage, serving successively as a *protector* (that is, a member of the immediate
military entourage of the emperor, probably Aurelian),
unit commander, and a governor of the Adriatic province
of Dalmatia, probably in 284 or 285. Less reliable sources
suggest that he served as a general under the emperor
Probus (r. 276–82). His military ability drew him to the
attention of the joint emperors Diocletian and Maximian
and he served as praetorian prefect to Maximian from 288
to 293, presumably campaigning in northern Gaul where
a peasants' revolt had erupted.

In 293 new constitutional arrangements were implemented by which the emperors made preparation for
their planned eventual retirement by creating two designated successors; Constantius was promoted to imperial
rank as Caesar and heir apparent to the western ruler,
Maximian. His immediate task was to recover parts of
Gaul and Britain which had been wrested from imperial
control by the usurper Carausius (r. c.286–293). An attempt
to recover Britain by Maximian had failed and, as a consequence, hostile forces were well established on the continental mainland. Gesoriacum (Boulogne), the principal
stronghold of Carausius in Gaul, was besieged. Denied
relief by a fleet from Britain by a mole which blocked
access to the River Liane, the city fell. Carausius was assassinated by Allectus, his principal minister, who succeeded

him and maintained hostilities. Following further campaigning, Gaul was cleared of hostile garrisons. In 296 an
invasion force comprising two separate armies descended
on southern Britain. One army, led by the praetorian prefect Asclepiodotus, landed in the area of modern Hampshire and defeated the army led by Allectus in person. The
usurper fell in the conflict. The other force, led by Constantius, failed to make a landfall owing to adverse weather conditions, being delayed by contrary winds and fog
and only arriving, via the Thames, in time to prevent the
looting of London by fleeing remnants of the usurper's
forces. None the less, a triumphant entry into London, the
provincial capital, is recorded both by contemporary historians and by commemorative medals struck for issue to
participants in the campaign. A copy now in the British
Museum of a medal found at Arras in northern France
bears depictions of Constantius and of his rescue of London. After the recovery of the island, widespread administrative changes were introduced which were probably
overseen by the Caesar. Later events suggest that, possibly
after an initially poor reception, Constantius's conduct
immediately after the suppression of the revolt gave him
a degree of popular support from the people of Britain
which was reflected in the reign of Constantine.

Marriage, or a less formal liaison, with Flavia Julia *Helena produced one son, later to be the emperor *Constantine I (the Great). On elevation to imperial rank, Constantius divorced Helena and entered a dynastic marriage
with Theodora, the step-daughter of the emperor Maximian, with whom he had six children. Helena, later converted to Christianity by her son, embarked on a life of pilgrimage and church building; she was later canonized.
Enmity between the two branches of Constantius's family
culminated in the massacre of Theodora's kin following
the death of Constantine the Great in 337.

After the campaign in Britain, Constantius was occupied for four years in warfare on the Rhine frontier. In the
persecution of Christianity which was inaugurated by
Diocletian and Maximian in 303, Constantius is credited
with not having implemented the full rigour of the law in
territory under his control. The story may owe more to the
subsequent career of Constantine than to a coherent
administrative decision by Constantius prompted by religious sympathy.

In May 305 the emperors Diocletian and Maximian
retired from office, handing the succession to Constantius
in the west and Galerius in the east. Shortly after his accession events in Britain needed imperial intervention. A
campaign in northern Britain was called for against the
Picts, a generic name for the tribes of the highlands of
Scotland. According to contemporary sources, possibly
echoing accounts of campaigns in the region conducted
in the first century AD by the governor Gnaeus Julius
Agricola and by the emperor Septimius Severus in the first
decade of the third century, Constantius is credited with
having penetrated to the extreme north of Scotland. Victory was achieved in 305 since in that year Constantius
took the additional names Britannicus Maximus for the

second time, the first having been after the defeat of Allectus.

Constantius died at Eburacum (York) on 25 July 306, sufficiently long after the assumption of Britannicus Maximus to suggest that his last illness was prolonged and prevented him from returning to London, much less to the imperial capital at Trier. Constitutional arrangements, made at the resignation of Diocletian and Maximian, designated Severus II as successor to Constantius, but the presence of Constantine with his father in Britain ensured, probably with paternal connivance, that Constantine should be proclaimed emperor on the death of his father. Based on the power of the army of Britain, Constantine forced his constitutional recognition on the legitimate emperors, eventually achieving sole imperial power in 324.    P. J. CASEY

**Sources** R. A. B. Mynors, ed., *XII panegyrici Latini* (1964), vi(vii), viii(v) · D. Kienast, *Römische Kaisertabelle: Grundzüge einer römischen Kaiserchronologie* (Darmstadt, 1990)
**Likenesses** medallion, BM [*see illus.*]

**Conti, Italia Emily Stella** (1873–1946), actress and founder of the Italia Conti academy of theatre arts, was born on 9 September 1873 at 265 Vauxhall Bridge Road, London, the eldest child of Luigi Conti (*d*. 1884), lyric singer, and his wife, Emily Mary (1844–1914), daughter of Henry James Castle (1809–1891), professor of civil engineering at King's College, London. Luigi Conti was born in Italy and had sung in opera there before going to Paris. When the Germans invaded France in 1870, he made his way to England, where he gave singing lessons to earn his living. After Italia's birth the family moved to Duncannon House, Brighton. Five more children were born there: Ferdinand (*b*. 1875), Arthur Catalani (*b*. 1876), Evelyn Martheze (1877–1931), Adèle Bianca (*b*. 1879), and Guy Benevuto (1881–1906).

Following their father's death in 1884, Italia Conti became a boarder at Kensington Academy; the boys, through their father's masonic lodge, received scholarships to Emmanuel School and Clapham grammar school, while Evelyn went to the Royal Masonic School. Their mother, needing a source of income, acquired a private school, Eversley, in Clapham Park Road, where she took in a dozen or so pupils as boarders. Her own children returned for the holidays and here Italia, aged fifteen, recruited her siblings and other children as actors, and their parents as audience, for her first stage performance—of Shakespearian tableaux, followed by a children's play.

Now determined to become an actress, Italia Conti frequented the theatres and she became so enthralled with the productions of Ellen Terry and Henry Irving at the Lyceum Theatre that she wrote to Terry, and to her great delight was invited to call on the star in her dressing-room. Terry was impressed by Italia's enthusiasm and arranged for her to have lessons with Macklin, a former member of the Lyceum company. When the Lyceum was taken over by Augustin Daly and his American company, Italia secured a small walk-on part in *The Last Word*. It was her first paid role. She also learned about voice production from the comedian Adah Rehan. After a part in *Diplomacy* on tour, she spent the next few years appearing at venues around the country with various companies.

In 1911 the actor–manager Charles Hawtrey, impressed by Italia's handling of children in the fairy scenes of *The Two Hunchbacks*, invited her to train children for the first production of *Where the Rainbow Ends*, a Christmas play for children, set to Roger Quilter's incidental music. The play was a great success, and after its run the children begged Italia to continue their training. She gave up most of her own acting, and recruited her sister Bianca to help her. Thus, informally, the Conti stage school came into being, its first studio being in a basement room under a public house. The children thrived on her teaching, and she found them employment. A second *Rainbow* season was equally successful, and the school moved to a gymnasium at the Passmore Edwards settlement in Tavistock Square. Overwork and pleurisy drove her into a nursing home in 1918, but she was able to sit on a government advisory committee dealing with regulations affecting children on the stage. At her urging, under the act of 1921 licensing was transferred from the magistrates to the local authority, and this enabled travelling licences to be granted to children working in touring companies.

Between the wars the Conti school expanded. Bianca was joined by the ballet teacher Thérèse Heyman and Grace Seppings, a former pupil; other friends and relatives joined the staff, while Italia dealt with auditions, contracts, rights, and arrangements for care of her charges while they were on tour. An operation for breast cancer in 1921 slowed her down only briefly. When Hawtrey died penniless in 1923 she bought his rights in *Rainbow*, which brought her a continuing income. She moved it to the Holborn Empire, installing her brother Ferdinand in a small office there as her business manager. Bertie Murray, husband of her sister Bianca, was stage manager. Bianca took classes at a studio in Paddington Street; Evelyn kept the accounts at Great Ormond Street.

In 1925 the Conti school moved to 15 Lamb's Conduit Street, where it occupied several rooms under the meeting place of the Ancient Order of Druids. Ruby, a young dancer who had been at the school since the age of nine, moved in as a companion to Italia and ran the household. In 1931, after Ruby left to get married, Italia moved to a modern house, named Evelyn Cottage after her recently deceased sister, on the clifftop at Southbourne, near Bournemouth. During the summer months her child pupils came down from London to enjoy the house and garden and her private beach. To replace Ruby, Arthur Conti's daughter Ruth, who was keen to take singing lessons, lived with her. Italia enjoyed an extremely busy social life, invited to every theatrical occasion: birthdays, presentations, first nights, and other celebrations. In 1937 she took a flat at 6 Russell Mansions, in Southampton Row. But with the outbreak of war and the mass evacuation of children, her world fell apart. The school closed, though a few of the children were taken to Bournemouth. Ruth and some of her other younger assistants were called up. In May 1940 bombs fell on Lamb's Conduit Street, destroying the studio; a few weeks later the Holborn Empire suffered a similar fate. With no income from pupils or rights, Italia faced financial ruin.

Within months, however, matters improved. Rooms were taken at Tavistock Little Theatre. Children began to return, classes restarted. Italia managed to keep *Rainbow* on the provincial road from 1941. In 1943 Ruby, whose daughter Hilary was now at school, was enticed back, to share teaching with Bianca. It was Ruby's idea to start an educational side, to harmonize all the teaching and the-atre work, although Italia was not in favour of this. Tour-ing the thirty-fifth production of *Rainbow* during the win-ter of 1945–6, Italia caught a cold, which failed to respond to nursing. It progressed to pneumonia and she died, unmarried, at Evelyn Cottage a few days later, on 8 Febru-ary 1946. She was cremated, and her ashes were scattered at Southbourne.

Italia Conti was a lady of immensely strong character, passionately fond of children, and able to discern and develop their nascent abilities. Her pupils included Noël Coward, Gertrude Lawrence, Anton Dolin, Jack Hawkins, Hermione Gingold, Richard Todd, and Roger Livesey. The school continued to prosper after her death, in the hands of Bianca (who inherited the *Rainbow* rights), Ruth, and Hilary. Now the Italia Conti academy of theatre arts, it includes a school as well as performing arts studios and has links with the South Bank University.

ANITA McCONNELL

**Sources** J. Selby-Lowndes, *The Conti story* (1954) • *The Times* (6–7 Feb 1925) [legal case of *Grenfell* v. *Conti*] • *The Times* (9 Feb 1946) • *WWW* • BL, Add. MS 56682, fols. 168–200; Add. MS 63370, fols. 46–103 • b. cert. • d. cert.
**Archives** BL, corresp., Add. MS 56682, fols. 168–200 | BL, corresp. with League of Dramatists, Add. MS 63370, fols. 46–103
**Likenesses** S. Grayson, portrait, 1961 • photograph, repro. in *The Times* (9 Feb 1946), 7e
**Wealth at death** £13,219 0s. 11d.—save and except settled land: probate, 22 June 1946, *CGPLA Eng. & Wales*

**Conversus, Claudius**. *See* Coventry, William (*fl.* *c.*1340/1360).

**Conway** [*née* Finch]**, Anne**, Viscountess Conway and Killultagh (**1631–1679**), philosopher, was born on 14 December 1631, the posthumous and second surviving daughter of Heneage *Finch (1580–1631), former speaker of the House of Commons, who predeceased her birth by a week, and of his second wife, Elizabeth, daughter of Wil-liam Cradock and widow of Richard Bennett, and was the half-sister of Heneage *Finch (1621–1682) and John *Finch (1626–1682). Little is known about Anne's upbringing and education. A good part of it was spent at home in the house that is now Kensington Palace. Anne's aptitude for learning must have been obvious, and her desire to study philosophy resulted in arrangements being made through her brother, John Finch, for her to receive instruction from his Cambridge tutor, the Cambridge Pla-tonist Henry More. Since, as a woman, she was not able to attend the university, More instructed her by letter. This early tutorial relationship, which commenced in 1650, subsequently blossomed into a lifelong friendship which

afforded Anne intellectual companionship unmatched for a woman of her generation. On 11 February 1651 Anne married at Kensington Edward *Conway (*c.*1623–1683), the eldest son of the second Viscount Conway and Killul-tagh, who owned estates in Warwickshire and Ulster, at Portmore. Her husband's efforts in opposing the Irish uprising had helped to secure his family's fortunes in the immediate aftermath of the English civil war, and on the death of his father on 26 June 1655, he became third Vis-count Conway. After the Restoration he played an active part in English and in Irish politics. The couple had only one child, a son, Heneage, who was born on 6 February 1658 but died of smallpox on 14 October 1660.

The first part of Anne's married life was spent in London (where Lord Conway owned a house in Queen Street) and at Ragley Hall in Warwickshire (the Conway family seat). From 1661 to 1664 she visited Ireland. Chronic illness, however, took its toll, increasingly curtailing her move-ments. Her illness took the form of repeated bouts of chronic pain which grew more severe and more frequent as she got older. The main symptom was a headache, but her whole body was affected during these episodes, which first occurred when she was only twelve. She sought the advice of the leading medical practitioners of her time, including Sir Theodore Turquet de Mayerne, William Har-vey, and Thomas Willis. An account of her symptoms is given, anonymously, by Willis in his *De anima brutorum* (1672). In 1656 she travelled to Paris in the hope that tre-panning might bring relief, but she was dissuaded from going through with the operation. In 1666 her husband persuaded the healer Valentine Greatrakes, known as the 'Irish stroker', to visit her, but he had no more success than the other physicians she consulted. The increasing severity of her illness meant that, for the last years of her life, she was confined to her home, Ragley Hall.

Her semi-retired way of life notwithstanding, Lady Con-way was able to pursue her interest in philosophy. Her husband appears to have encouraged her in her intellec-tual pursuits. At all events, marrying into the Conway fam-ily made her the mistress of one of the largest private libraries in England. In spite of the disabling effects of her illness, she was at the centre of a lively intellectual circle. The most significant figure in this group was Henry More, with whom she kept up a correspondence when he could not visit her in person. Through More, Lady Conway had contact with others of the Cambridge Platonists, includ-ing Ralph Cudworth and John Worthington. From 1666 to 1672, Elizabeth Foxcroft, the sister of Benjamin Which-cote, lived with her as her companion. In Ireland she enjoyed the company of Jeremy Taylor, of whom Lord Conway was chief patron, and of George Rust.

It was Lady Conway's search for a cure for her illness that brought her into contact with Francis Mercury Van Helmont, son of the Flemish biologist and natural philo-sopher, who first met her in 1670 when he was visiting England on a mission on behalf of Princess Elizabeth of Bohemia. Van Helmont returned to become a member of Lady Conway's household for the last years of her life. He awakened her interest in studying Jewish cabbala, bringing her into contact with the German cabbalist scholar Christian Knorr von Rosenroth. Van Helmont also had a profound influence on her religious life. Through him she encountered Quakerism. During her last years she was visited by the Quaker leaders George Fox, Robert Barclay, George Keith, and William Penn. She used her influence to help imprisoned members of their following. She converted to Quakerism just before her death, despite opposition from Henry More and her own family. When she died on 23 February 1679, Van Helmont preserved her body in a glass coffin. Contrary to her express wish not to be given a Church of England funeral, she was buried in the family vault at Arrow church, Warwickshire, according to the Anglican rite.

For a woman of her time, Anne Conway had unusual opportunities to pursue her interest in philosophy, but she treated it as very much a private activity and never wrote for publication. After her death a manuscript treatise was discovered among her effects. This was published anonymously in a Latin translation with the title, *Principia philosophiae antiquissimae et recentissimae* in Amsterdam in 1690 under the auspices of Van Helmont who wrote a short preface for it. An English translation by J. C. was published, also anonymously, in London in 1692, with the title, *The Principles of the most Ancient and Modern Philosophy*. This treatise clearly shows her acquaintance with contemporary philosophy as well as the impact of her cabbalistic studies. Her *Principia* outlines an original metaphysical system according to which all created things are constituted of monads of spiritual substance deriving from God. She proposes a tripartite hierarchy of being where the infinite monads of created substance express the infinity of the divine creator, and where causality is mediated through an intermediate level of being that participates in both the divine and created being. Since God is essentially good, so too is his creation. Conway denies the eternity of hell, arguing for a perfective order of things. In the course of her discussion she attacks the dualism of Descartes and Henry More, and the materialism of Hobbes and Spinoza. As a theodicy and monadology, her system anticipates the philosophy of Gottfried Wilhelm Leibniz. It is certain that Leibniz knew of the work, and indeed possessed a copy (probably the gift of their mutual friend, Van Helmont). SARAH HUTTON

**Sources** The Conway letters: the correspondence of Anne, Viscountess Conway, Henry More, and their friends, 1642–1684, ed. M. H. Nicolson, rev. edn, ed. S. Hutton (1992) • Principia philosophiae antiquissimae et recentissimae de Deo, Christo & Creatura id est de Spiritu & materia in genere (1690) • J. C., trans., The principles of the most ancient and modern philosophy: concerning God, Christ, and the creature; that is, concerning spirit and matter in general (1692) • R. Ward, The life of the learned and pious Dr Henry More (1710) • S. Hutton, 'Of physic and philosophy', Religio medici: medicine and religion in seventeenth-century England, ed. A. Cunningham and O. Grell (1996), 228–46 • S. Hutton, 'Ancient wisdom and modern philosophy: Anne Conway, F. M. van Helmont, and the seventeenth-century Dutch interchange of ideas', Quaestiones Infinitae, 4 (1994), 1–16 • S. Hutton, 'Anne Conway, critique de Henry More: l'esprit et la matière', Archives de Philosophie, 58 (1995), 371–84 • T. Willis, De anima brutorum quae hominis vitalis ac sensitiva est exercitationes duae (1672) • F. N. Macnamara and A. Story-

Maskelyne, eds., The parish register of Kensington, co. Middlesex, from AD 1539 to AD 1675 (1890)
**Archives** BL, corresp., Add. MSS 23213–23217 • Christ's College, Cambridge • PRO, state papers, domestic | Hunt. L., Hastings MSS
**Likenesses** S. van Hoogstraten, oils (Anne Conway?), Mauritshuis, The Hague • oils, Ragley Hall, Warwickshire
**Wealth at death** £1700, plus estate inherited from mother: will

**Conway, Edward**, first Viscount Conway and first Viscount Killultagh (c.1564–1631), politician, was the son and heir of Sir John *Conway (d. 1603), of Arrow, Warwickshire, and Ellen or Eleanor, daughter of Sir Fulke Greville (d. 1560) of Beauchamp's Court, Warwickshire. His family were substantial Warwickshire landowners by the late sixteenth century. About 1593 Conway married Dorothy (d. 1612), widow of Edward Bray of Great Barrington, Gloucestershire, and daughter of Sir John Tracy of Toddington, in the same county.

Edward pursued a military career, and was knighted by the earl of Essex at the sacking of Cadiz (1596), where he commanded a regiment of foot. Afterwards he served in the Netherlands as governor of the Brill. His time there may help account for the enthusiasm of his protestant convictions, as also the Christian name of his most famous daughter, Brilliana, baptized there in 1598 [see Harley, Brilliana, Lady Harley]. His convictions were shared by his fellow officer Sir Horace Vere, who in 1607 married Dorothy Conway's sister Mary.

In the first parliament held in the reign of James I, Conway sat as member for Penryn. When Brill was delivered up to the states of Holland (1616), he received a pension of £500 per annum. Before 30 December 1619 he married Katherine (d. 1639), widow of John West, grocer and citizen of London, and daughter of Giles Hueriblock or Hambler of Ghent in the Spanish Netherlands. In 1620 he was an ambassador at Brussels and at Prague, and on 28 June 1622 he was sworn of the privy council. On 30 January 1623, under the patronage of the marquess of Buckingham, he was made secretary of state. His admission to Gray's Inn in 1624 was honorary, and there is no evidence to suggest that his lack of formal education had hindered him in his role as secretary, though his first royal master was apt to jest that his secretary of state was illiterate. Conway was returned for Evesham to the parliament which assembled on 19 February 1624. Like his cousin Fulke Greville (1554–1628) he had up until this point shown himself a staunch supporter of a 'protestant' foreign policy, and in the Commons he was a keen advocate of Buckingham's policy of war with Spain.

After Charles I's accession continued royal favour kept him in office as secretary, and on 24 March 1625 he was created Baron Conway of Ragley in the county of Warwick; on 8 December he was appointed captain of the Isle of Wight. In the House of Lords he took a hand in co-ordinating the defence of Buckingham in the Commons in 1626. Its proceedings proved a turning point for Conway; not only did he follow Buckingham in abandoning the anti-Spanish policy, but he expressed himself in a letter to the earl of Carlisle on 5 June greatly disillusioned with parliament itself. On 15 March 1627 he was created

Viscount Killultagh of Killultagh, co. Antrim, Ireland, and on 26 June Viscount Conway of Conway Castle in Caernarvonshire. In the early stages of collecting the forced loan that year he showed sensitivity to local sentiment, but later he advised a harder line against Gloucestershire refusers. By late 1627 he was arguing for war, mainly against France, and for extra parliamentary supply to fund it. Conway became lord president of the council in December 1628. He died in St Martin's Lane, London, on 3 January 1631, and was buried at Arrow on 12 January.

Notwithstanding his prominence in the affairs of state, Conway's papers reveal the assiduity with which he performed 'the role of linking the county gentry with the government', performing many favours at court for his Warwickshire friends, neighbours, and kinsmen (Hughes, 25–6). He was 'part of the last manifestation of the Elizabethan style of central government which ensured that relatively broad strands of opinion, particularly religious opinion, were represented in the Privy Council' (ibid., 88–9). Their passing marked the end of an era in relations between Warwickshire and the court, and the beginning of a fatal division between court and country. Conway's eldest son, Edward *Conway (*bap.* 1594, *d.* 1655), who succeeded as second viscount, was much less interested in local affairs.                                          SEAN KELSEY

Sources G. E. Aylmer, *The king's servants: the civil service of Charles I, 1625–1642* (1961) · R. Lockyer, *Buckingham: the life and political career of George Villiers, first duke of Buckingham, 1592–1628* (1981) · A. Hughes, *Politics, society and civil war in Warwickshire, 1620–1660* (1987) · J. Eales, *Puritans and roundheads: the Harleys of Brampton Bryan and the outbreak of the English civil war* (1990) · R. P. Cust, *The forced loan and English politics, 1626–1628* (1987) · GEC, *Peerage* · DNB · J. Foster, *The register of admissions to Gray's Inn, 1521–1889, together with the register of marriages in Gray's Inn chapel, 1695–1754* (privately printed, London, 1889) · PRO, PROB 11/160, fols. 409r–410v

Archives BL, letters to Walter Aston, Add. MSS 36446–36447 · BL, corresp. with Lord Carlisle, Egerton MSS 2593, 2596 · CKS, letters to Lionel Cranfield, U269/1/OE172, 208

Wealth at death estate at Ragley valued at £900 p.a.; pension from crown valued at £2000 p.a.; disposed of extensive real estate in Warwickshire and Ulster; made bequests worth several hundred pounds: will, PRO, PROB 11/160, fols. 409r–410v; Hughes, *Politics, society and civil war*, 26n.

**Conway, Edward**, second Viscount Conway and second Viscount Killultagh (*bap.* 1594, *d.* 1655), politician and book collector, was baptized at Arrow, Warwickshire, on 10 August 1594, the eldest son of Edward *Conway, first Viscount Conway and first Viscount Killultagh (*c.*1564–1631), of Ragley and his first wife, Dorothy (*d.* 1612), widow of Edward Bray and daughter of Sir John Tracy of Toddington, Gloucestershire. He matriculated from Queen's College, Oxford, on 3 May 1611, aged sixteen, but may not have stayed long at university: the earl of Clarendon suggests that he may have learned military strategy under his uncle by marriage, Sir Horace Vere, while living at Brill in the Netherlands, where his father was posted. Knighted on 25 March 1618, about October 1621 he married Frances (1596/7–1671), daughter of Sir Francis *Popham (1572/3–1644) and his wife, Anne Dudley. In 1624 and 1625 Conway was nominated by Fulke Greville, Lord Brooke, as MP for Warwick, but this proved to be his only public service for

the locality. In 1626 he sat as MP for Yarmouth in the Isle of Wight and in 1628, his father having become in the interim Viscount Killultagh (co. Antrim) and Viscount Conway of Conway, he was summoned to parliament in the right of the Conway barony.

Following the death of his father on 3 January 1631, Conway succeeded as second Viscount Conway. Within a few months he had leased out Ragley Hall and, turning his back on his native county and its government, he spent most of the 1630s either in London or in Ireland. He was a man who, according to Clarendon, 'reserved so much of his time for books and study that he was well-versed in the parts of learning', and Georg Rudolph Weckherlin regarded him as a 'very learned man … curious for all manner of rarities' (Raylor, 95). His early literary connections included Sir John Beaumont and Michael Drayton and, over a longer period, Ben Jonson, John Donne the younger, and Sir John Suckling, whose work he especially prized. The separates associated with him and his family, held in the British Library (MS 23229), contain pieces by many of these writers and by Thomas Carew, as well as a large selection of political verse. Conway had a particular interest in burlesque and satire and was an intelligent literary critic, neatly differentiating English plays from classical models, boasting later to his daughter-in-law Anne *Conway that 'if the English language were understood by other nations, they would certainly imitate them' (*Conway Letters*, 30–32).

Conway's extensive correspondence with booksellers, agents, and other collectors reveals a serious bibliophile with a network of connections in Brussels, Florence, and Paris. Like his father he had a particular interest in English literature and collected 350 English play texts and more than 340 romances. His library was massive. The 1637 list of his London books runs to over 500 volumes; a sequestration list of 1643 catalogues 5000 or more volumes. His Irish library at Lisnegarvey, co. Antrim, on the estates that had come to the family from his father's brother, appeared to have contained somewhere between 8000 and 9900 books and manuscripts. The surviving volumes (many of which can be identified in Armagh Public Library by their armorial bindings) encompass an enormous range of subjects and indicate a substantial interest in science and mathematics, and several languages (Latin, French, Italian, Portuguese, and Spanish).

Conway was also a prolific and gossipy letter writer. An extensive correspondence with his secretary and agent in Ireland, George *Rawdon, based mainly at Brookhill, near Lisburn, co. Antrim, survives. In 1639 Conway was able to use his long-standing connection with the lord deputy, Thomas Wentworth, Viscount Wentworth, to ensure that his brother-in-law Sir Robert Harley escaped the burden of the sheriffdom of Hertfordshire. Other correspondents included George Garrard, Sir Kenelm Digby, Theodore Turquet de Mayerne, and John Selden.

In 1639 Conway served as a general of horse against the Scots, but the following year was defeated at Newburn; his account of and explanation for the debacle survives among the Lansdowne manuscripts in the British Library.

In 1642–3 he was both a privy councillor and marshal of the army in Ireland. As the civil war unfolded he had family members on both sides, and his own position was not straightforward. Although described by the earl of Clarendon as 'a voluptuous man in eating and drinking' (Clarendon, *Hist. rebellion*, 1.186), and clearly a gourmand who summoned delicacies from all over Europe, he was nominated in 1643 to the Westminster assembly of divines. That spring, however, he was implicated in the plot of Edmund Waller and others to seize London for the king, and briefly imprisoned. On his release he joined the king at Oxford for a period, and one substantial manuscript of royalist verse (Hunt., HM 16522) can be associated with him; most of its contents were subsequently published in *Rump Songs* (1662). Yet he kept in close touch with his sister, Brilliana, besieged by royalists at her home in Herefordshire until her death on 31 October [*see* Harley, Brilliana, Lady Harley]. He was sequestered as a delinquent, but by 1644 had begun to compound for his estates. As a result of diminishing income from his estates as rents proved difficult to collect, by 1646–7 he was heavily in debt. In the early 1650s he retired to Petworth, Sussex, to the house of Algernon Percy, earl of Northumberland, but later he travelled abroad. He died at Lyons in France on 26 June 1655; his body was subsequently brought back to England and buried at Arrow. He was succeeded as third Viscount Conway by his son, Edward *Conway (c.1623–1683).

JAMES KNOWLES

**Sources** GEC, *Peerage* · A. Hughes, *Politics, society and civil war in Warwickshire, 1620–1660* (1987) · J. Eales, *Puritans and roundheads: the Harleys of Brampton Bryan and the outbreak of the English civil war* (1990) · Clarendon, *Hist. rebellion* · I. Roy, 'The libraries of Edward, second Viscount Conway, and others: an inventory and valuation of 1643', *BIHR*, 41 (1968), 35–46 · 1637 book list, PRO, SP16/372/111 · H. R. Plomer, 'A cavalier's library', *The Library*, new ser., 5 (1904), 158–72 · *The Conway letters: the correspondence of Anne, Viscountess Conway, Henry More, and their friends, 1642–1684*, ed. M. H. Nicolson, rev. edn, ed. S. Hutton (1992) · T. Raylor, *Cavaliers, clubs and literary culture* (Delaware, 1994) · T. Birrell, 'Reading as pastime: the place of light literature in some gentlemen's libraries of the seventeenth century', *Property of a gentleman: the formation, organisation and dispersal of the private library, 1620–1920*, ed. R. Myers and M. Harris, St Paul's Bibliographies (1991), 113–31 · private information (2004) [J. Morris] · BL, Lansdowne MS 493, item 45

**Archives** BL, corresp., index of MSS, III, 1984 | Hunt. L., Hastings MSS, Irish papers

**Conway, Edward**, earl of Conway (c.1623–1683), politician, was the first surviving son and heir of Edward *Conway, second Viscount Conway and second Viscount Killultagh (bap. 1594, d. 1655), politician and bibliophile, and his wife, Frances (1596/7–1671), daughter of Sir Francis *Popham. Apparently not enjoying any formal education the young Conway spent time in Paris, however, where he had some instruction in military arts in 1640. In 1649 his father signed over to him his justly famous library in consideration of debts for which Edward had stood surety, and evidently he was able to obtain some little learning thereby. He was a fellow of the Royal Society from 2 January 1668, and the author of a book called *Opuscula philosophica*.

On 11 February 1651 Conway married Anne (1631–1679) [*see* Conway, Anne], daughter of Sir Heneage Finch, recorder of London, and half-sister of Heneage Finch, first earl of Nottingham. Four years later, in 1655, he succeeded to his father's titles. The third viscount's stance towards the public authorities of the Commonwealth era is uncertain. However, in 1656 his wife's uncle wrote to the lord protector's councillors imploring their assistance in the liberation of the viscount who had been kidnapped, robbed, and imprisoned by Ostenders *en route* for France. Conway had 'no hope of release but through you, by reason of his bearing arms for and his known affection to the present Government' (*CSP dom.*, 1656–7, 16.59–60). Within a short space of time the viscount was ransomed. In 1657 he was certainly appointed to the Warwickshire assessment committee as part of the policy of healing and settling in local government. In 1660 Conway was at the head of the local gentry coup in Warwickshire, repeated across the country and vital to the momentum of Restoration, which saw the return of the reins of power, and principally the command of the local militia, into the hands of social élites.

At the outset of his public career, after Charles II assumed his English throne, Conway's principal sphere of influence was in Ireland. In 1660 he was a member of the Irish privy council. A confidant of the duke of Ormond and closely associated with the increasingly beleaguered court interest of Lord Chancellor Clarendon, in November 1666 he counselled the lord lieutenant that 10,000 Irish troops be sent into England as a defence against invasion or rebellion, amid growing signs of the imminent collapse of the Clarendon regime—a suggestion with a startlingly Straffordian ring, which seems to have sparked rumours of an intention to impose arbitrary government. Conway was subsequently named in the lord chancellor's compromise proposal for a commission to examine the royal finances, offered to deflect demands in parliament for the establishment of a committee of accounts. Conway's support for the court and the prerogative were strengthened further by his personal interest in the defeat of the Irish Cattle Bill, under which he stood to lose a considerable source of income from the rearing of Irish cows for English markets. By mid-January 1667 the Cavalier Parliament had reached crisis point. Looking on, Conway wrote that 'either the kingdom will be reduced to a commonwealth or the king must dissolve this present [parliament] and govern by some other medium' (Seaward, 289). When Clarendon fell Conway lamented the sorry state to which government descended. Writing to his brother-in-law, Sir John Finch, in February 1668 shortly before the latter's return from Italy, he told him that 'you will have the advantage of coming into a Court where there is not one man of ability' (*CSP dom.*, 1667–8, 258). However, he managed the transition reasonably well, successfully ingratiating himself with Arlington.

Conway was much occupied with the administration of Ireland, where he spent a considerable portion of his time, having a fine estate at Lisburn, co. Antrim. He was made governor of Charlemont Fort in 1671, and extended his authority over the counties of Armagh, Tyrone, Monaghan, and part of Down from 1672. He was joint commissioner of the Irish customs, 1673–5, and held a commission as lieutenant-general of horse in the Irish army from 1674. Tory in his politics, Conway was enlisted by Danby in 1675 to persuade members of the English House of Lords resident in Ireland to attend and support the court. Later Danby and his wife would urgently solicit Conway's personal assistance in repelling the bill of attainder brought in against the first minister in the spring of 1679. It is unclear whether or not Conway made any effort to assist, but whatever he did it did not impede his appointment as master of the ordnance in Ireland early in summer that year. His wife, whose religious convictions he had on occasion indulged by securing the release of Quakers from prison, died on 23 February 1679, and her body was preserved in a glass case until her husband could return from Ireland to attend her funeral which did not take place for over two months.

On 3 December 1679 the third viscount was created first earl of Conway and was introduced to the House of Lords by his new title on 21 October 1680. It was rumoured that he paid £10,000 to the duchess of Portsmouth for the honour. Conway steadfastly opposed exclusion. On 2 February 1681 he joined the English privy council at Whitehall and was also appointed lord lieutenant of Warwickshire during the minority of the earl of Northampton. He acted as secretary of state for the north of England from then until January 1683, when he resigned amid allegations that he was complicit in 'crimes and misdemeanours … either in relation to the King's person or his public negotiations or transactions with foreign ambassadors, or in not rightly pursuing the King's instructions to ambassadors abroad' (*CSP dom.*, *Jan–June 1687*, 32). He retired, with a generous pension, to Ragley Hall, his family's Warwickshire seat, where he set about disarming dissenters and rooting out all local evidence of subversion and disaffection to the crown. His second wife, Elizabeth (*d.* 1681), daughter of George Booth, first Baron Delamere, whom he married at an unknown date, brought him a dowry of £13,000. She died in July 1681, and by 30 August following Conway had married Ursula (*d.* 1697), daughter of George Stawell of Cothelstone, Somerset, this time netting himself £30,000. In July 1683 he was advised that his return to court would be very welcome, and that he might expect a warm enough reception there. However, he died on 11 August following and was buried on 25 August at Arrow, Warwickshire. Advantageous as his matches had been, he left no heir, and all his honours became extinct at his death. His wife survived him and married John Sheffield, later duke of Buckingham.                              SEAN KELSEY

**Sources** CSP dom., *1640*; *1649–50*; *1656–7*; *1660–83*; *1687* • GEC, *Peerage*, 3.401–2 • I. Roy, 'The libraries of Edward, second Viscount Conway, and others: an inventory and valuation of 1643', *BIHR*, 41 (1968), 35–46 • A. Hughes, *Politics, society and civil war in Warwickshire, 1620–1660* (1987) • P. Seaward, *The Cavalier Parliament and the reconstruction of the old regime, 1661–1667* (1989) • A. Swatland, *The House of Lords in the reign of Charles II* (1996) • IGI • PRO, PROB 11/374, fols. 357r–358r • PRO, PROB 11/374, fols. 413v–414r • The Conway letters: the correspondence of Anne, Viscountess Conway, Henry More, and their friends, 1642–1684, ed. M. H. Nicolson, rev. edn, ed. S. Hutton (1992)
**Archives** BL, letter-book, Add. MS 35104 | BL, corresp. and papers, Add. MSS 23213–23214, 37979–37990, 41809, 41824, 41834 • BL, corresp. with Lord Danby, Add. MSS 28049, 28053; Egerton MSS 3329–3334 • BL, letters to Sir Edward Dering, Stowe MSS 744–745 • BL, letters to Lord Essex, Stowe MSS 200–208, *passim* • Hunt. L., papers and letters to Sir George Rawdon
**Wealth at death** as well as disposing of extensive real and personal estate in England and Ireland, also made cash bequests totalling £4300: will, PRO, PROB 11/374, fols. 357r–358r, 413v–414r

**Conway, Essie Ruth** (1862–1934), headmistress and educationist, was born on 24 September 1862 at Upper Swinford, Worcestershire, the second of the four daughters of Thomas Conway (1832/3–1913), a railway clerk and later a corn merchant's clerk, and his wife, Catherine Colvin (1835–1900). Educated at Congreave School, Worcestershire, she moved with her family to Liverpool in 1875, where she became a pupil teacher at Upper Park board school. Aged twenty, she went to Lincoln Training College for two years, returning to Upper Park board school as an assistant mistress in 1884. In 1887 she became head of Ashfield Street board school, Liverpool, moving two years later to a larger board school at Clint Road. Her last appointment, in 1904, was as principal of Tiber Street School, a new experiment in Liverpool of an all-age mixed school intended to accommodate 1000–2000 pupils. She remained there until her retirement in 1926, the management structure of the school permitting her to take frequent absences to carry out her local, regional, and national public duties.

A loyal supporter and powerful advocate of the importance of union membership, Essie Conway was involved with the Liverpool and District National Union of Teachers (NUT), becoming its first ever woman president in 1909, and with the Lancashire County NUT, where she was president of the County Teachers' Association from 1920 until her death. She represented Liverpool at national level from 1899, becoming a member of the NUT executive in 1910 and its second woman president in 1918. Although a strong supporter of the women's cause, becoming chair of the Liverpool Women Citizens Association in 1920, she did not join the National Union of Women Teachers when it was founded in 1920. Her way to achieve equality was to work with the main union and to educate public opinion. A strong advocate of equal pay, she made frequent speeches championing this issue during her time on the Burnham committee set up in 1919 to determine a national pay scale for teachers. She was also deeply concerned with other issues, such as the education of primary school children, the training and useful employment of young people, superannuation, and, particularly, the professional status of teachers, being from 1912 an enthusiastic member of the Teachers' Registration Council.

An opportunity to focus on these areas came through Conway's role as one of the few women members of the consultative committee of the Board of Education, representing elementary schoolteachers and the NUT from 1920 until her death in 1934. She was involved in all seven reports produced during this time: on the curriculum for boys and girls in secondary schools; on psychological tests; on the education of the adolescent; on books in public elementary schools; on the primary school; on infant and nursery schools; and on secondary education. She was not afraid to be outspoken, and in the 1925 departmental report on the training of teachers for public elementary schools was one of four to sign a memorandum of dissent, emphasizing raising professional status and the provision of more rigorous academic training.

Essie Conway was a persuasive and effective speaker, noted for her sharp (although never caustic) wit and admired for her ability to persuade her audience. A committed Anglican, she believed in caring for and helping others, but also adhered firmly to the ethic of self-help. Her politics were Conservative and her guiding principles were duty, service, and patriotism. A woman with strong high-minded principles, candid but compassionate, incredibly hard-working, ambitious, and successful, she was widely recognized and applauded by her contemporaries. In 1918 she was awarded an honorary MA from Liverpool University and in 1925 made a CBE for her services to education. Her achievements have, however, been largely ignored by later generations. Her lower-middle-class origins, her traditional Conservative approach, and her belief that women had a key role in the home caring for the family perhaps help to explain this neglect. Furthermore, rather than devoting herself to a single cause or issue her involvement in a wide range of other educational bodies, political work, and church organizations diffused her talents. After suffering poor health for a number of years she died at her home, 57 Hartington Road, Sefton Park, Liverpool, on 19 December 1934, and was buried two days later at Smithdown Road cemetery in Liverpool.     SYLVIA HARROP and CHRISTINE WILLIAMS

**Sources** C. E. Williams, 'The life, work and achievements of Essie Ruth Conway CBE, MA, JP, 1862–1934', MEd diss., U. Lpool, 1997 · *Schoolmaster and Woman Teacher's Chronicle* (April 1918) · *Schoolmaster and Woman Teacher's Chronicle* (May 1919) · *Schoolmaster and Woman Teacher's Chronicle* (Jan 1920) · *Schoolmaster and Woman Teacher's Chronicle* (July 1920) · *Schoolmaster and Woman Teacher's Chronicle* (Oct 1925) · *Schoolmaster and Woman Teacher's Chronicle* (March 1926) · *Schoolmaster and Woman Teacher's Chronicle* (Jan–Dec 1928) · *Schoolmaster and Woman Teacher's Chronicle* (Dec 1934) · *Schoolmaster and Woman Teacher's Chronicle* (Jan 1935) · *Schoolmaster and Woman Teacher's Chronicle* (Feb 1935) · *Journal of Education*, 66 (Dec 1934) · *Liverpool Daily Post and Mercury* (Dec 1934) · *Liverpool Echo* (Dec 1934) · log books, Upper Park board school, Lpool RO · log books, managers' minute books, Tiber Street board school, 1904–22, Lpool RO · Consultative Committee Reports, 1924–33, PRO, HMSO reports · b. cert. [baptism] · d. cert. · parish register, Upper Swinford, Worcestershire, 1862

**Likenesses** F. T. Copnall, oils, 1934; at Walker Art Gallery, Liverpool, in 1934

**Wealth at death** £12,038 13s. 7d.: probate, 1 March 1935, *CGPLA Eng. & Wales* (1934)

**Conway, Francis Charles Seymour-**, third marquess of Hertford (1777–1842). *See under* Conway, Francis Ingram-Seymour-, second marquess of Hertford (1743–1822).

**Conway, Francis Ingram-Seymour-**, second marquess of Hertford (1743–1822), politician, was born Francis Seymour-Conway on 12 February 1743 in London, the eldest son of Francis Seymour-*Conway, first marquess of Hertford (1718–1794), courtier, and Lady Isabella Fitzroy (1726–1782), youngest daughter of Charles Fitzroy, second duke of Grafton. Known by the courtesy title of Viscount Beauchamp, he was educated at Eton College (1754–9), before he matriculated at Christ Church, Oxford, on 2 February 1760; he took his MA on 15 June 1762. Beauchamp then travelled on the grand tour with his tutor, the antiquary Walter Bowman, during 1764 and 1765. The early stages of his political career were determined by his father's ability to obtain preferments through government service which were then passed on to his children. While his father was lord lieutenant of Ireland Beauchamp was made a privy councillor for Ireland (1765) and he acted as chief secretary to his father (1765–6) before his appointment as constable of Dublin Castle (1766–1822). He also represented Lisburn in the Irish House of Commons from 1761 to 1768.

Beauchamp entered the British House of Commons in 1766 as member for Lostwithiel and during the Chatham government he followed the political line set by his uncle General Henry Seymour *Conway. He was considered to be primarily interested in politics as a means of augmenting his family's parliamentary power base and income, and his success in taking over the borough of Orford, which he represented from 1768 until his inheritance of his father's title in 1794, was a move towards the achievement of these aims; for Orford, despite its proximity to the family's estate at Sudbourne, had previously been a Treasury borough. Beauchamp spoke regularly in the House of Commons between 1774 and 1788 and he was credited 'if not with eloquence, at least with knowledge of the subject' (*Memoirs of … Wraxall*, 4.137). During the American War of Independence he was a reliable supporter of Lord North's administration and he held minor ministerial office as a lord of the Treasury (1774–80), a cofferer of the household (1780–82), and a privy councillor for Great Britain from 1780. However he never attained the post of secretary at war to which he aspired. His chief parliamentary enthusiasms and causes were focused on Ireland, where he expressed consistent and strong support for the repeal of the penal laws against Roman Catholics, and upheld religious toleration. While a strong supporter of the political links between Britain and Ireland, he argued against the formal political and commercial union of the two countries and any act of compulsion directed against the Irish parliament. His views are best summarized in a pamphlet, *A Letter to the First Company of Belfast Volunteers*, published in 1782. In the later part of his career in the Commons he was generally associated with the Foxite opposition against Pitt, but in 1793 he spoke in favour of the Aliens Bill and seconded Pitt's address to the king, which paved the way for the abandonment of neutrality in favour of war with revolutionary France. Later in the same year he was employed as an informal roving ambassador to the king of Prussia and to other German courts, and he was given a minor military mission in the same area of Europe in the following year. In the course of these missions he clashed with Lord Malmesbury, the official emissary to Prussia, and no permanent position was forthcoming; but in 1794 he in any case succeeded to the marquessate and an income of over £70,000 per annum, drawn largely from his Irish estates. He subsequently acquired the lease of Manchester (later Hertford) House in 1797, which became his principal London residence, and it remained within the Hertford family until the establishment of the Wallace Collection. On taking his seat in the House of Lords he took no part in debates on political subjects.

On 4 February 1768 Hertford had married Alicia Elizabeth Windsor (1749–1772), second daughter and coheir of Herbert Windsor, first Viscount Windsor, and Alice Clavering. His second wife, whom he married on 20 May 1776, was Isabella Anne Ingram Shepheard (1760–1834), eldest daughter and coheir of Charles Ingram, ninth and last Viscount Irwin or Irvine (d. 1778), and his wife, Frances [see Ingram, Frances, Viscountess Irwin (1734?–1807)]. On the death of his mother-in-law on 20 November 1807, Hertford and his wife inserted the name Ingram before Seymour in recognition of the large fortune that they had simultaneously inherited. At about the same time the marchioness became an intimate friend (but not mistress) of the prince of Wales, the future prince regent and George IV, a role she continued to play until 1820, and in which she exercised some influence, not merely in securing patronage for her husband and son, but also in promoting tory and anti-Catholic measures.

On Pitt's return to government in 1804 Hertford was appointed master of the horse (1804–6) and he was compensated with the Order of the Garter when he was displaced in the Grenville administration. His wife's influence at court helped to secure him the position of lord chamberlain of the household (1812–21), but his career did not culminate in elevation to the much coveted dukedom, which was refused by Lord Liverpool in 1822, just before Hertford's death. Hertford's aspirations for the advancement of himself and his family followed closely the pattern set by his father, but although he was well informed on most political subjects, he displayed no pronounced political talents and relied on his wealth, connections, and parliamentary influence to gain access to the corridors of power. His taste in English portraitists is still visible in some items by Downman, Romney, and Reynolds, now in the Wallace Collection. He died on 17 June 1822 at Hertford House, Manchester Square, London, and was buried in the family vault in Ragley, Warwickshire, on 28 June.

Hertford's only surviving son from his second marriage was **Francis Charles Seymour-Conway**, third marquess of Hertford (1777–1842), courtier, who was born on 11 March 1777, and was educated at Christ Church, Oxford, and also at St Mary Hall there, from which he graduated in 1796. Between 1797 and his accession to the title—until when he was known as Lord Yarmouth—he represented Orford, Lisburn, co. Antrim, and Camelford, all seats controlled by the Hertford interest. On 18 May 1798 he married, in defiance of his parents, Maria Emily Fagnani

[**Maria Emily Seymour-Conway**, marchioness of Hertford (1770/71–1856), society hostess]. She was the daughter of the Marchesa Fagnani (d. 1804), and a great heiress on account of the rival claims to her paternity by George *Selwyn (1719–1791) and William *Douglas, fourth duke of Queensberry (1725–1810), who both left their fortunes to her. Their first two children were a daughter, Frances Maria, later marquise de Chévigné (1799–1822), and a son, Richard Seymour-Conway (1800–1870), who succeeded as fourth marquess of Hertford. The couple were detainees of Napoleon in France (1802–5), and during that period a third child, Lord Henry *Seymour (1805–1859), was born to Maria; his father was probably Count Casimir de Montrond (1768–1843). After this period the marriage had effectively ended and the future third marchioness never returned to England, dividing her time between Paris and Boulogne. She played an important part in the upbringing of her elder son's illegitimate son, the future collector and benefactor Sir Richard Wallace. Lord Yarmouth was involved in a series of minor diplomatic missions after his return from France and he became an intimate of the prince of Wales who appointed him vice-chamberlain in 1812. He was appointed knight of the Garter on his accession to the marquessate in 1822 so as to secure to the government interest the eight pocket boroughs that he controlled. However, despite charm and obvious intellectual ability, his interests in politics were diverted substantially in later years by the gambling and debauchery that earned him sufficient notoriety to be satirized by Disraeli as Lord Monmouth in *Coningsby* (1844) and by Thackeray as the marquess of Steyne in *Vanity Fair* (1847–8). He was the first major art collector in his family and also commissioned Decimus Burton to build St Dunstan's Villa in Regent's Park. His taste was similar to that of his friend the future George IV, and some of the miniatures, paintings, and French furniture and sculpture held today in the Wallace Collection derive from his acquisitions. Hertford died at Dorchester House, Park Lane, London, on 1 March 1842 and was buried at Arrow on 19 March. His wife died in rue Taitebout, Paris, on 2 March 1856, where she was buried in what became a family vault in the cemetery at Père Lachaise.                                    T. J. HOCHSTRASSER

**Sources** J. Brooke, 'Seymour Conway, Francis', HoP, *Commons, 1754–90* · W. Stokes and R. G. Thorne, 'Seymour Conway, Francis', HoP, *Commons, 1790–1820* · B. Falk, *'Old Q's' daughter: the history of a strange family* (1951) · P. Hughes, *The founders of the Wallace collection* (1981) · *The historical and the posthumous memoirs of Sir Nathaniel William Wraxall, 1772–1784*, ed. H. B. Wheatley, 5 vols. (1884) · J. Ingamells, ed., *A dictionary of British and Irish travellers in Italy, 1701–1800* (1997), 63 · GEC, *Peerage*

**Archives** BL, corresp. and papers, Egerton MSS 3257–3265 · Warks. CRO, accounts and papers | BL, letters to G. W. Croker, Add. MSS 60286–60289 · BL, letters to C. J. Fox, Add. MS 51458 · BL, letters to Lord Grenville, Add. MS 59016 · BL, letters to Lord Harwicke, Add. MSS 35644–35763 · BL, corresp. with first and second earls of Liverpool, Add. MSS 38213–38309 · BL, letters to Sir Robert Peel, Add. MSS 40222–40401 · BL, letters to Sir Robert Wilson, Add. MS 30112 · Warks. CRO, letters to earl of Denbigh

**Likenesses** T. Kettle, oils, c.1775; formerly at Ragley Hall, Warwickshire · J. Downman, drawing, 1783, Ragley Hall, Warwickshire · F. Chantrey, bust, AM Oxf. · F. Chantrey, sculpture, AM

Oxf. • F. Chantrey, statue, AM Oxf. • attrib. J. Reynolds, oils, Ragley Hall, Warwickshire

## Conway, Francis Seymour-, first marquess of Hertford

**(1718–1794)**, courtier and politician, was born on 5 July 1718 in Lindsey House, Chelsea, Middlesex, the son and heir of Francis Seymour-Conway, first Baron Conway of Ragley (1679–1732), politician, and his third wife, Charlotte (d. 1734), the daughter of John and Elizabeth Shorter of Bybrook, Kent. His mother was the granddaughter of Sir John Shorter, lord mayor of London, and the sister of Catherine Shorter, the first wife of Sir Robert Walpole. From 1732 he attended Eton College, and in the same year he succeeded his father as second Baron Conway. On 29 May 1741 he married Isabella (1726–1782), the fourth and youngest daughter of Charles Fitzroy, second duke of Grafton, and his wife, Henrietta Somerset. They had seven sons, including Lord Hugh *Seymour, naval officer, and six daughters. On 3 August 1750 he was created Viscount Beauchamp and earl of Hertford, titles recently extinct by the death of Algernon Seymour, seventh duke of Somerset. Described by his cousin Horace Walpole as 'a perfect courtier' (Walpole, *Memoirs*, 1.269), Hertford held a succession of posts. He became a lord of the bedchamber and KG in 1757 and was sworn of the privy council in 1763. He served as ambassador to France in 1763–5, lord lieutenant of Ireland in 1765–6, and lord chamberlain from 1766 to 1782 and again from April to December 1783. He was also lord lieutenant of Warwickshire from 1757 until his death.

Hertford was the head of a sizeable family interest. His brother Henry Seymour *Conway (1719–1795), army officer and politician, was a political and military figure of importance, and his six sons were all members of parliament. He exerted control over the parliamentary borough of Orford from the 1760s and also influenced elections in Coventry. His ability to provide for himself and his family was the object of envy. The earl of Bristol once described him as 'an excellent sollicitor, [who] has a constant appetite for all preferments for himself and family, with the quickest digestion and the shortest memory of past favours of any of the present noblemen of this modest and reasonable age' (Brooke, 71).

Hertford was at the peak of his importance from 1766 to 1782, when he was at the centre of court life as lord chamberlain and acted as friend and confidant to George III. With the king's blessing, he was active in negotiations in 1767 that sought to strengthen the Chatham administration. At one point he was mentioned as a possible first minister. Although he was tempted by the prospect of a promotion in the peerage (a personal ambition), he declined, citing his disinclination to speak in parliament. With the aid of Walpole he influenced his brother to remain part of the Chatham administration. After the latter resigned in 1768, Hertford worked with some success to prevent him from drawing too close to the opposition, at least until the outbreak of the war with the American colonies in 1775. Hertford himself continued to support Lord North's administration and the war in America, in which three of his sons served. His correspondence with Walpole, however, shows him to have doubted the prospects of its success. In 1779 he again acted as an intermediary in negotiations designed to shore up an embattled ministry, unsuccessfully approaching members of the opposition through the duke of Grafton, his wife's nephew.

Following Lord North into opposition in 1782, Hertford became more of a party politician. He voted by proxy against Shelburne's peace preliminaries in February 1783. He then briefly returned to office with the Fox–North coalition and resumed his old post as lord chamberlain. After being dismissed with the coalition at the end of the year, he again followed North into opposition, reportedly spurning the younger Pitt's offer of a marquessate. He opposed Pitt's Regency Bill in 1788. In the realignment that followed the outbreak of war with revolutionary France he finally went over to Pitt, and on 3 July 1793 was created marquess of Hertford and earl of Yarmouth. The owner of extensive estates in co. Antrim, he also exerted influence in Irish politics. He served a relatively uneventful term as lord lieutenant in 1765–6 and had a decisive influence on elections in the borough of Lisburn, which was briefly shaken by the Volunteer movement in 1783.

Hertford died on 14 June 1794 from complications resulting from a riding accident at the home of his daughter, the countess of Lincoln, in Putney. He was buried on 23 June at Arrow, Warwickshire, where his wife had been buried twelve years earlier. His eldest son, Francis Ingram-Seymour-*Conway (1743–1822), politician, succeeded to the titles.     WILLIAM C. LOWE

**Sources** H. Walpole, *Memoirs of the reign of King George the Third*, ed. G. F. R. Barker, 4 vols. (1894) • Walpole, *Corr.*, vols. 37–9 • *The correspondence of King George the Third from 1760 to December 1783*, ed. J. Fortescue, 6 vols. (1927–8) • J. Brooke, *The Chatham administration, 1766–1768* (1956) • *GM*, 1st ser., 64 (1794), 581 • GEC, *Peerage* • *The later correspondence of George III*, ed. A. Aspinall, 5 vols. (1962–70) • A. A. Locke, *The Seymour family* (1914) • E. M. Johnston, *Great Britain and Ireland, 1760–1800* (1963)

**Archives** BL, Add. MSS 23218–23219 • BL, corresp. and papers, Egerton MSS 3257–3265 | BL, corresp. with George Grenville, Add. MS 57811 • BL, Hertford MSS, Egerton MSS 3060–3062 • BL, corresp. with Charles Jenkinson, Add. MSS 38203, 38304–38308, 38570 • BL, corresp. with duke of Newcastle, Add. MSS 32861–32974 • Sheff. Arch., letters to Lord Rockingham

**Likenesses** J. Reynolds, oils, exh. RA 1785, Ragley Hall, Warwickshire • J. Astley, oils, Ragley Hall, Warwickshire • J. Dixon, mezzotint (after unknown artist), BM, NPG • G. Morland, oils, Ragley Hall, Warwickshire • C. Warren, line engraving (after W. H. Brown, 1791), BM, NPG; repro. in *The Senator* (1791)

## Conway, Henry Seymour

**(1719–1795)**, army officer and politician, was born on 21 July 1719, probably at Lindsey House, Chelsea, Middlesex, the second son of Francis Seymour Conway, first Baron Conway of Ragley (1679–1732), and his third wife, Charlotte (c.1683–1734), the younger daughter of John and Elizabeth Shorter of Bybrook, Kent. His mother's sister Catherine was the wife of Sir Robert Walpole.

**Early career** Conway entered Eton College in 1732. His cousins Edward and Horace Walpole also attended Eton at this time, and with the latter he maintained a lifelong friendship and correspondence. Their letters reveal a

**Henry Seymour Conway** (1719–1795), by Thomas Gainsborough, exh. RA 1780

strong emotional interdependence: Walpole was Conway's chief or only confidant in his youth. His confession in 1737 that a vulgar expression by Lady Caroline Fitzroy, with whom he was in love, provoked 'a strong garrison of anti-venerial thoughts' (Walpole, *Corr.*, 37.3), followed by an account of his attending a masquerade dressed as a woman, has been interpreted as evidence of Conway's sexual ambiguity, supporting the proposition that his relationship with Walpole had a sexual element—something insinuated by contemporaries later in Conway's career.

On 27 June 1737 Conway was commissioned lieutenant in the 5th dragoons. His military duties were not yet so arduous as to prevent his joining Walpole and Thomas Gray on their tour of Europe between May and October 1739, though he remained in Geneva while they proceeded to Italy. He found Geneva society tedious and by February 1740 had returned to Paris, where he related to Walpole his promotion to captain-lieutenant in the 8th dragoons: 'I am a-going over to fight like a *tigre*' (Walpole, *Corr.*, 37.45). Nevertheless, that year his attention was taken by a visit to the Conway family estates in co. Antrim, in preparation for his unopposed election as member for

that county in the Irish parliament, which formally took place on 19 October 1741. In May 1741 (formally dated 14 February 1741) he joined the 1st foot guards as captain-lieutenant, a rank equivalent to lieutenant-colonel in the army, and that summer he studied drawing and mathematics under private tutors.

On 28 December 1741 Conway's long parliamentary career began when he was returned as MP for Higham Ferrers, Northamptonshire, by Thomas Watson-Wentworth, first earl of Malton, on the recommendation of Sir Robert Walpole. Horace Walpole later wrote that Conway, 'having set out upon a plan of fashionable virtue' (Walpole, *Memoirs of … George II*, 1.27), had voted against the government in 1742 on army supply and alienated George II and William Augustus, duke of Cumberland, but there seems to be no other evidence for this. In July 1742 Conway joined his brigade of guards as part of the so-called pragmatic army assembled for the defence of the Netherlands. The nearest his regiment came to action was in the battle of Dettingen on 27 June 1743, but here the guards formed the rearguard and missed the fighting. Writing to his elder brother, Francis Seymour-*Conway, second Baron Conway and later earl and marquess of Hertford, he complained: 'You can't imagine how terrible it was not to be engaged … and been put always upon what is called the post of honour' (Walpole, *Corr.*, 37.138).

Conway attended the parliamentary sessions during the autumn and winter. Along with other army officers who were also members of parliament he returned to campaign in the Netherlands in May 1744. In that year he served as aide-de-camp to the commander-in-chief, Field Marshal George Wade. His romantic attachment to Lady Caroline Fitzroy had been renewed about 1741, but in 1744 he concluded that his lack of means made a marriage impossible. Walpole, who had in any case strongly opposed the match, was willing to bestow a large portion of his own income, mostly from government offices, on his friend. He reasoned: 'If I ever felt much for anything … it was certainly for my mother. I look upon you as my nearest relation to her, and I think I can never do enough to show my gratitude and affection to her' (Walpole, *Corr.*, 37.170). Conway felt unable to accept this too generous offer. During the following year's campaigning Conway (who was now aide-de-camp to Prince William Augustus, duke of Cumberland, the new commander-in-chief) returned to Flanders just in time to take part in the battle of Fontenoy on 30 April 1745. He distinguished himself in the battle where only twenty-four of his company survived, and reportedly engaged single-handedly with two French grenadiers.

Conway left Flanders in October 1745, when he was recalled as part of the force intended to combat the Jacobite rising. He spent the winter of 1745 and spring of the following year in pursuit of Charles Edward Stuart's forces in northern England and Scotland. On 15 April 1746 he was gazetted colonel of the 48th foot, and on 16 April he fought in the battle of Culloden. Conway remained in Scotland, gathering intelligence reports and writing verses, until he returned to Westminster in November for the parliamentary session.

In spring 1747 Conway returned to the Netherlands. On 1 July, while on active service, he was re-elected to the Commons, this time for Penryn in Cornwall, in the interest of Hugh Boscawen, second Viscount Falmouth, a supporter of the Pelham ministry. He fought at Laffeldt on 2 July, where he narrowly escaped death, and was taken prisoner by the French, but was released on parole after three days. Conway was able to return to England in November, and on 19 December, at Somerset House chapel, Westminster, he married Caroline Bruce, countess of Ailesbury (1721–1803), the daughter of Lieutenant-General John Campbell, later fourth duke of Argyll, and the widow of Charles Bruce, third earl of Ailesbury. Lady Ailesbury (as she continued to be known) had one daughter from her first marriage, Lady Mary Bruce (1740–1796), who married Charles *Lennox, third duke of Richmond. Conway and his wife had one child, Anne (1749–1828) [see Damer, Anne Seymour]. The summer following his marriage Conway leased Latimers, in Chesham, Buckinghamshire, a sixteenth-century house owned by the Cavendish family but disliked by Horace Walpole: 'Old but of a bad age' (Walpole, Corr., 9.102).

Conway had been transferred from the 48th foot to the 34th foot in 1749 and in July 1751 went to join his regiment on Minorca, which failed to impress him: 'The country is one entire heap of rock and sand; not a tree for shelter nor a brook for refreshment in the whole island' (Walpole, Corr., 37.310). He was anxious to escape and lobbied Cumberland for a new regiment, eventually receiving the 13th dragoons on 21 December 1751.

After visiting Florence, where he met Horace Walpole's correspondent Horace Mann, he travelled to Rome, then returned to England in February or March 1752, when he purchased Park Place, at Remenham, near Henley-on-Thames, from Augusta, princess dowager of Wales. Shortly afterwards Conway and his wife followed his regiment to co. Sligo, leaving their daughter to be cared for by Walpole. They also spent part of 1753 in Sligo, when Walpole kept his friend informed of the Marriage Bill passing through parliament. Conway, who professed a 'philosophical' indifference to politics, and seems at the time to have been happy with his family cultivating Park Place, on returning home in June 1753 claimed puzzlement at the heat generated in the passage of the legislation:

> I don't clearly understand but I must own myself and very honestly do a miserable politician … and it's so much the nature of Englishness to divide and subdivide that if there were but two left in the world I believe they'd form two parties and if there was but one he'd quarrel with himself. (Walpole, Corr., 37.367)

He again visited his regiment in Ireland, now at Athlone, co. Westmeath, in May 1754.

Conway regarded his Irish connections as burdensome, but it was Ireland that would invigorate his political career. The 1754 election saw him returned for St Mawes, Cornwall, again by Lord Falmouth. In May 1755 he was unexpectedly named as chief secretary for Ireland by the new lord lieutenant, William Cavendish, marquess of Hartington (fourth duke of Devonshire from December 1755), probably at Cumberland's suggestion. He finally took his seat in the Irish House of Commons as MP for co. Antrim on 17 October 1755. Conway's relaxed temperament was expected to assist Hartington settle the political dispute between the speaker of the Irish Commons, Henry Boyle, on one hand, and George Stone, archbishop of Armagh, and the Ponsonby family, on the other. This had bedevilled Irish politics for several years, and had reached a crisis when in 1753 Boyle and many of his leading supporters had voted with the opposition against the government over the issue of the principle of royal consent being required for a bill apportioning a surplus in the Treasury to the payment of the national debt. Boyle and his allies had been removed from their offices and replaced by allies of Stone and the Ponsonbys. Hartington was a relative of the Ponsonbys but was also closely associated with James Fitzgerald, twentieth earl of Kildare, one of Boyle's most vociferous allies. Conway conducted negotiations on Devonshire's behalf and reported their progress to the government in Westminster. In a letter to the prime minister, Thomas Pelham-Holles, duke of Newcastle, Conway carefully expressed the settlement agreed between the parties on the question of the address to the king at the opening of the 1755 parliamentary session, and probably helped make it acceptable to the ministry. Newcastle wrote that he entirely depended upon Conway's 'good sense and integrity' (Walpole, Corr., 37.404). Negotiations continued into early 1756, when Boyle was bought off with an earldom, Stone excluded from the list of lords justices, and Ponsonby made speaker of the Commons. Conway declared 'that the government was once more vested in the hands of the governor' (McCracken, 178), but the undertaker system survived until the Townshend lieutenancy of 1767–72. Conway was promoted major-general on 30 January and returned to England in May. He remained an Irish MP until 1761.

**The Rochefort expedition and its aftermath** Conway was appointed in April 1757 a groom of the bedchamber, a position he had long sought. He spent much of his time after his return from Ireland in semi-retirement at Park Place, but in June he was returned to active service. Initially stationed at Bradford Peverell, near Blandford, Dorset, in July he was appointed deputy military commander of the proposed expedition to raid the French fort of Rochefort. Conway, like his superior Sir John Mordaunt, expressed doubts about the operation and probably remained sceptical of a successful outcome.

The naval force and troop transports after some delay set sail from the Isle of Wight on 6 September and reached the Basque Roads on 21 September. Here after further delays only the small Isle d'Aix was captured. A council of war was called on 25 September, where the senior officers of both the army and the navy decided that a direct attack on Rochefort could not succeed. Conway repeatedly advocated an attack on Fort Fouras, but his colleagues would only support a night attack, and when this was cancelled he was unwilling to take sole responsibility for a day assault. No further incursions were proposed and the fleet sailed for home on 1 October, arriving at Portsmouth on 6 October. In a letter to his brother, Conway wrote, 'These strange resolutions and irresolutions are endless and impossible and improper to relate' (Walpole, *Corr.*, 37.508), and later, 'I expect my share of blame; and for the only time of my life dread to come back to England' (ibid.). Conway gave evidence at Mordaunt's court martial; Mordaunt was eventually acquitted, but the affair badly damaged the reputations of both men, and Conway was made to feel the king's displeasure at court. When George II was presented with a list of the proposed staff officers for the 1758 campaign, the king struck out the names of Mordaunt, Conway, and the third in command at Rochefort, Edward Cornwallis. When the commander-in-chief, Jean Louis Ligonier, pointed out that Conway had tried to take action the king replied, 'Yes … après dîner la moutarde' (Walpole, *Memoirs of … George II*, 3.5), and said he would think of Conway, but not then. In spite of this, Conway's efforts to join the expedition to St Malo or that to the West Indies in November 1758 were unsuccessful. He remained militarily inactive (although he continued to attend the Commons) until sent, at Ligonier's behest, to sign a cartel for an exchange of prisoners at Sluys on 6 February 1759.

Soon after the accession of George III in October 1760, Conway twice wrote to John Stuart, third earl of Bute, the king's mentor, to remind the new king of his 'desire for military employment'. He wrote to Bute again in February 1761 asking him to intercede so that he could 'throw himself at His Majesty's feet if he has given any intentional offence' (Walpole, *Memoirs of … George III*, 1.xxxvi). At last, at the end of March 1761, Conway was sent to Germany as deputy to John Manners, marquess of Granby, commander of the British forces in the allied army led by Prince Ferdinand of Brunswick. At the battle of Vellinghausen on 15–16 July, Conway's corps, entrusted to him by Ferdinand, were placed in the centre of the allied line but were not attacked. During Granby's absence Conway became acting commander of the British forces in winter 1761–2. He was present at the battle of Wilhelmstal on 24 June 1762 and in the following month captured the castle at Waldeck, which surrendered on 11 July, Conway exclaiming: 'it cost me two days but the French don't shine at these defences … they let me frighten them out by marching up with scaling ladders when my ammunition was out' (Walpole, *Corr.*, 38.163).

Following the signing of the peace preliminaries at Fontainebleau in November 1762, Conway was responsible for the embarkation of British forces in Europe. Some weeks before returning to England on 31 March he learned from his brother that Bute had apologized to the French concerning his management of the embarkation. Conway believed that Bute had acted thus because some of his army friends had voted in parliament against the peace, and he became convinced that Bute saw no role for him on the peacetime establishment. As a result Conway had informed Hertford that he did not intend to deserve favour by his own parliamentary conduct. This could be considered predictable: Conway's friends Walpole and

Augustus Fitzroy, third duke of Grafton, were in opposition, as were most of his other connections. Grafton was the nephew of Lady Caroline Fitzroy and of Conway's sister-in-law Isabella Hertford, and returned Conway for Thetford at the 1761 election. When the parliamentary session opened Conway voted (on 15 and 23 November) against the new prime minister, George Grenville, to hear a complaint by John Wilkes that his arrest by general warrant breached his privilege as an MP. Then on 16 and 18 February Conway spoke and voted against the use of general warrants. The king insisted that as a consequence of his actions Conway should be deprived of his posts of groom of the bedchamber and colonel of the 1st dragoons. Attempts were made by Grenville himself and Walpole to mitigate the punishment. Conway thought he would lose only the civil post. The bedchamber, although prestigious, carried a relatively small salary, and the colonelcy constituted his principal income. In April 1764, following the prorogation of parliament, his dismissal was made public. Walpole at once wrote offering him £6000, and there was also an offer of £1000 from the duke of Devonshire. Although his income was now reduced from some £6000 per annum to £2000, Conway decided that retrenchment was preferable and declined the offers. When Devonshire died later that year Conway was left £5000 'as a testimony of my friendship for him and of my sense of his honourable conduct and friendship for me' (*London Chronicle*, 16 Oct 1764, 363).

Conway's dismissal became a *cause célèbre*. The government, stung by Walpole's remark at an opposition dinner that Conway's case indicated that ministers intended a purge of the army, published an anonymous pamphlet on 24 May 1764, *An Address to the Public on the Late Dismission of a General Officer*, written by the historian and propagandist William Guthrie. The address, although not mentioning Walpole by name, tried to force a retraction. Walpole replied with *A Counter-Address to the Public on the Late Dismission of a General Officer*. On 30 August Guthrie retaliated with *A Reply to the Counter Address*, which insinuated that Walpole was suffering from sexual frustration at being unable to consummate his passion for Conway. Walpole never enlarged upon the background to this allegation, and most of his correspondence with Conway from the early 1760s onwards seems to have been destroyed. This was probably to protect both their reputations, although Walpole was more concerned with their roles in political history than with sexual impropriety. Walpole never denied his affection for his cousin or his desire to advance his political career. The allegation was intended rather to discredit Walpole by exposing his supposed 'effeminacy' than to suggest sexual motives on Conway's part.

Conway was seriously alarmed by this crisis and wrote to his brother saying he was now finished with politics but would tell him 'how disagreeably I have myself been the object of them'. He added, 'I trust their efforts to hurt my reputation have only shown their malice' (Walpole, *Memoirs of … George III*, 1.xli). However, Conway remained a martyr in the eyes of Grenville's opponents and was envisaged as a prominent component of any ministry they might form. The involvement of Cumberland and Devonshire's brother Lord John Cavendish in negotiations to replace Grenville in late 1764 and early 1765 can have done Conway no harm. Despite the confidence of his friends in his political abilities, Conway still saw the military as his principal career, and it was with great reluctance that he accepted Cumberland's proposal and joined the Rockingham administration in July 1765 as secretary of state for the southern department. The new ministry had hoped to include prominent members of the Commons who could direct government business there, including Charles Yorke, Charles Townshend, and, most importantly of all, William Pitt, but only Yorke joined the administration, as attorney-general. Well before parliament met in December, it was clear that Conway, well-meaning but irresolute under pressure, would be the leader of the Commons.

**Secretary of state under Rockingham** The administration was concerned initially with matters close to Conway's own circumstances, including the restoration of dismissed army officers and a declaration that general warrants were illegal. They had also committed themselves to Pitt's scheme for a triple alliance between Britain, Russia, and Prussia, and Conway achieved some success in negotiating with the French over their outstanding debts in Canada and the fortifications at Dunkirk. There was no mention of the issue that was to dominate parliamentary affairs for the foreseeable future: the crisis engendered by Grenville's recent Stamp Act. As southern secretary, Conway was responsible for American compliance with the act, a potential source of personal conflict, as he had spoken and voted against the Stamp Act in the Commons in February. The act was to come into force on 1 November. American opposition was first thought by ministers to be the work of a small minority. Conway's response to the letters from Governor Bernard of Massachusetts and General Thomas Gage, received in October, mentioned his military background and expressed the government's reluctance to use excessive force against what they still thought was a temporary disturbance: he ordered Bernard to 'inforce a due Obedience to the Laws' with 'such a timely Exertion of Force as the Occasion may require', but endorsed 'lenient and persuasive Methods' (Langford, 80) if possible. Similarly, he told General Gage to use force if other measures were insufficient, but added that Gage should observe 'the utmost exertion of your prudence' (Cobbett, *Parl. hist.*, 16.113). By December Conway and his colleagues knew that the situation had deteriorated to a stage where the Stamp Act was unenforceable without the involvement of an impractically large armed force, and he may have been one of the ministers who argued for the repeal of the Stamp Act at the cabinet of 27 December. If so, his position was close to that eventually taken up by the Rockingham government.

Policy formulation was complicated by the growing pressure to restructure the ministry in order to include William Pitt, and negotiations took place in early January 1766. Conway and Grafton at first favoured including Pitt, even though he would not reveal his position on

American policy to his potential colleagues without having told the king and parliament first. This was unacceptable to Rockingham, as were Pitt's other demands, which would have seen Newcastle leave the ministry and Rockingham himself give way to Earl Temple, and Conway backed down. Pitt's support for repeal of the Stamp Act was a mixed blessing for Conway, as he followed it with a denial of parliament's right to impose taxes on the colonies; Pitt's personal authority over the house left Conway in shadow, and it was in this unenviable position that he prepared to introduce the government's resolutions.

As decided by the end of January 1766, repeal was to be preceded by the Declaratory Act, affirming British sovereignty in the colonies. Conway told the Massachusetts agent, Dennys De Berdt, that the ministry were for repeal of the Stamp Act but could secure a majority only by including a measure that asserted parliamentary sovereignty against colonial defiance. His wish that the Americans would petition against the Stamp Act to ease the government's way perhaps shows his continued yearning for consensus; his hopes were dashed, for most of the petitions from America directly challenged parliament's authority, in particular that from the congress of colonial representatives which had met in New York in October 1765 to co-ordinate the campaign for repeal. He failed to stop the petition being presented, but it was not received by the house and thus could not be debated, as it was signed by an association and not by individuals. Conway was anxious to assure the Americans that their opinions were not being disregarded, but his main priority was to prevent a Commons debate that could have fired anti-American passions and polarized opinion between Pitt's contention that, as a result of the Stamp Act, 'the Original Compact with the Americans was Broke' (*Correspondence of George III*, 1.246) and Grenville's determination that the act should remain in force.

Conway introduced the government's five resolutions, including the clause that would become the Declaratory Act, in the Commons on 3 February. The ministry won the day and defeated a resolution by Grenville opposed to repeal, but Conway's contribution to the debate, that repeal was the only way to avoid a war with America and Britain's continental enemies, was overshadowed by speeches from Pitt, Townshend, and Yorke, generally regarded as more effective orators. When repeal itself was debated in the Commons on 21 February, Conway's case, that parliament had a right to tax the colonies but should not actually exercise that power, held the day, although a speech in support of the government by Edmund Burke was considered more decisive.

Horace Walpole later wrote of Conway as the hero of the hour: fellow members of parliament 'huzzaed him thrice, stopped him to thank and compliment him, and made a lane for his passage' (Walpole, *Memoirs of … George III*, 3.29). Yet to many contemporaries his management of the Commons appeared uncertain. Walpole acknowledged that he 'could not be induced to traffic with Members, though offended that none of them paid court to him' (ibid., 3.97). In May 1766, following Grafton's resignation,

Conway moved to the northern department and his stepson Richmond succeeded him as southern secretary. This relieved Conway of American problems but underlined the problem that no more senior politician would join an administration seen as fatally crippled.

**Secretary of state under Chatham** Conway was content with the new administration formed in July 1766; Pitt, at the head of the ministry and ennobled as earl of Chatham, told him the administration would consist 'of the best and ablest men, without any regard to parties, distinctions and connections' (Brooke, *Chatham Administration*, 12). He remained at the northern department and sought to maintain what appeared to have been Chatham's original plan, to lead a reinforced Rockingham ministry. This foundered on issues of personality and Chatham's determination to break up the party loyalties that had grown up during the 1760s. Conway's mediation between Rockingham and Chatham foundered, and by 25 November most of the Rockingham group had gone into opposition rather than renounce those of their friends whom Chatham felt unsuitable for office. For Conway, for whom the Rockingham ministry had always been an interim administration until a stronger ministry could be formed including Pitt, this was an embarrassment. He chose not to resign, but his estrangement from Chatham and his wish to keep faith both with his old friends and with George III led him to concentrate on routine administration in his department. In March 1767 he appointed David Hume as his under-secretary; Hume had been his brother's secretary as ambassador to France, and the previous year the two had negotiated over a pension for Jean-Jacques Rousseau, then living in Derbyshire.

Conway, and the new southern secretary William Petty, second earl of Shelburne, were expected to put into effect Chatham's 'northern system' of diplomacy, which saw Britain as the ally of Prussia and Russia. Conway was more sympathetic to an Austrian alliance and was probably not disappointed when negotiations with Prussia and Russia proved unfruitful. Unlike Chatham, Conway and Shelburne perceived no immediate threat from France and Spain and concentrated on colonial issues and the strengthening of the fragile ministry. A Swedish proposal for a treaty remained unanswered by Conway for eighteen months, causing the ambassador, Baron Gustaf Adolf Nolken, to exclaim: 'The Secretaries of State are so busy in Parliament that they conduct their offices like a secondary business' (Scott, 113).

Conway's instinct for conciliation frequently conflicted with Chatham's more combative approach. Like Charles Townshend, now chancellor of the exchequer, he opposed Chatham's desire to acquire the East India Company's territories for the crown, but was forced by Grafton and George III to acquiesce in the scheme. Even so, during the first debate on the motion to establish a parliamentary inquiry into the company's lands and revenues, he described himself as a passenger in administration. On 26 May 1767 he voted against the ministry's bill to restrain the company's dividends, although the measure passed.

The plan to seize the East India Company's revenues had been intended to meet a perceived gap in government revenues, which Townshend intended to meet by taxing the import of tea and some other household goods into America. Conway was astonished that the plan was never discussed in cabinet. He refused to introduce the plan in the Commons and twice voted against the ministry, on 13 and 15 May. None the less, Townshend's American Revenue Bill received the royal assent by 29 June with scarcely any effective opposition.

Conway had entered office following his defence of American interests, and, with these interests now threatened by his own government, he told George III and Rockingham in May that he would resign at the end of the session. Rockingham trusted that his secession would lead to a comprehensive administration that encompassed his own followers plus the Grenvilles and Bedfords. Conway hoped to use the ensuing negotiations to bring Rockingham and his friends into the Chatham ministry, believing that Rockingham should be prepared to come in 'on his own bottom' (*Autobiography … of Grafton*, 1.321), in Grafton's words, and not as leader of a new coalition.

As Conway's date for resignation (22 July) approached, Grafton told the king that, without Conway, he must also resign. The king wrote a desperate letter to Lord Hertford: 'Indeed your brother has it now in his power to extricate me out of all my difficulties by lending himself to my civil service' (*Correspondence of George III*, 1.499). Conway also found himself a prisoner of the now divided opposition. Rockingham insisted upon his remaining in office, the Bedfords on his returning to the army. Contemporaries and later commentators have thought that these were two incompatible reactions to Grenville's requirement for a stronger American policy, but Bedford's main reservation had been his lack of confidence in Conway as a parliamentarian.

Negotiations failed, and on 31 July Grafton asked Lady Chatham to tell her husband 'that General Conway has given him authority to say, that, though the particular situation is not fixed on, he is determined to stand forward in the House of Commons to carry on the king's business' (*Correspondence of William Pitt*, 3.281–2). Conway's rupture with the Rockinghams was complete. Edmund Burke wrote to Rockingham that 'Conway is fairly gone to the devil' (*Correspondence*, 1.321), but he continued to seek a middle way, attempting to distance himself from his colleagues while remaining loyal to the king.

In August 1767 Conway was made lieutenant-general of the ordnance, and he continued, at Horace Walpole's suggestion, as secretary of state without salary. However, this gesture failed to appease the anger of the Rockinghams. At the end of the year negotiations between Grafton and the Bedfords at last allowed Conway an honourable escape, and in January 1768 he resigned the northern department to Thomas Thynne, third Viscount Weymouth, and North became leader of the Commons. Conway remained in the cabinet at the king's desire, and was appointed colonel of the 4th dragoons.

**Drift into opposition** During the new parliament elected in March 1768 Conway, who remained member for Thetford, concentrated on his own work at the ordnance. He was not present at the cabinet meeting on 20 April which decided on Wilkes's expulsion, although he soon afterwards expressed his opposition and successfully postponed action until the subsequent session of parliament. He remained useful as a peacemaker, negotiating compensation with Jeffrey Amherst in July and August 1768 following the latter's dismissal as governor of Virginia. He maintained his interest in American policy and in November and December 1768 objected to the proposals of Wills Hill, earl of Hillsborough, now secretary of state for America, to coerce opposition in Massachusetts, and he even voted against the milder resolution agreed by the rest of the cabinet that condemned the votes of the Massachusetts assembly, which challenged parliamentary supremacy. The cabinet's olive branch to the Americans, decided at a meeting on 1 May 1769, was the repeal of all Townshend's duties except those on tea; Conway, in the minority, sought the repeal of all duties. He had proposed in the Commons on 19 April that the government promise not to levy further taxes against the Americans, and this promise was made.

The Wilkes affair had also returned to plague the cabinet. Conway remained opposed to the expulsion of Wilkes, which offended some cabinet members and George III. He avoided the vote on expulsion in February but then spoke in favour of parliamentary supremacy on 17 March, as the issue had become a matter of 'the liberty of the people against the liberty of parliament' (Brooke, 'Conway, Hon. Henry Seymour', 245). Later he voted for the seating of Henry Luttrell, Wilkes's opponent.

The withdrawal of the Chathamites from the Grafton ministry led to Conway's being offered the position of master-general of the ordnance in January 1770. Conway declined, according to Walpole because he did not want to offend his friend Granby and because he sought to distance himself from the duke of Bedford's party, whose power in the ministry was rising. Instead, he offered to do the work of the master-general without taking the salary. George III is said to have told Conway 'he was a phenomenon; that there was no satisfying other people, but he would not take even what was offered to him' (Walpole, *Memoirs of … George III*, 4.132). As Conway pointed out to Walpole, he did not need the extra £400 in his salary that the promotion would bring. Soon afterwards Lord North became prime minister, and although George III advised him that Conway could be managed through 'little marks of attention' (*Correspondence of George III*, 2.126–7), by October Conway had become sufficiently estranged from his colleagues to resign from the cabinet. That month he was made colonel of the Royal Horse Guards (the Blues). He was at first friendly to the ministry, but in March 1772 he offended George III by opposing the Royal Marriages Bill. Although he said he supported the principle of the bill, he was unable to vote a compliment—that the king's family should ask the sovereign's permission to marry—into a royal right of veto. Despite a reproving letter from his

brother Hertford, the lord chamberlain, Conway vigorously opposed the bill in committee. Conway was promoted general on 26 May 1772, but when it became clear that the king intended to appoint George, fourth Viscount Townshend, an officer junior to Conway, as master-general of the ordnance, he resigned from the ordnance on 23 October. 'At the earnest solicitation of Lord North' (Brooke, 'Conway, Hon. Henry Seymour', 246) he was compensated with the governorship of Jersey.

American affairs continued to engross Conway's parliamentary activity, and his wish to preserve his integrity drove further the wedge between him and the North ministry. After the Boston Tea Party in December 1773 he supported the punitive Boston Port Bill of March 1774 in the hope that support for this measure might allow the repeal of the tax on tea, for which he voted in April. In May he opposed the third reading of North's bill to enhance the powers of the crown in Massachusetts Bay. He defended British authority over America, but expressed his concern that actions since the Stamp Act had turned the British government into aggressors against the crown's American subjects.

Without political or meaningful military office Conway was able to devote more time to his private affairs. On 8 June 1774 he left London on a tour of the continent, visiting battlefields in the Netherlands and Germany, dining with his former commanding officer Prince Ferdinand in Brunswick, and proceeding to Potsdam, where he was entertained by Frederick the Great. After a visit to the Saxon court in Dresden he went to Vienna, where he stayed with his friend the British ambassador, Sir Robert Murray Keith. There he was received by Emperor Joseph II and his mother Maria Theresa. He spent a week with the emperor's army near Buda in Hungary before moving to rejoin Frederick the Great with his camp at Breslau in Silesia, then returned to Austrian territory, where he joined Joseph II at a military review in Prague. The tour ended in Paris, where he was joined by his wife and daughter. The *London Chronicle* (6 August 1774) was wrong to assume that Conway was engaged in formal diplomatic negotiations on the part of the government; rather, he was reinforcing his personal connections with British diplomats abroad and foreign princes and officials, in anticipation of a full-scale war against the colonies—which to Conway must have seemed certain.

Conway's absence during the general election of 1774 had deprived him of his seat at Thetford. He returned to parliament in March 1775 as MP for Bury St Edmunds, still as a nominee of Grafton. He renewed his criticisms of government policy and on 5 April opposed the third reading of the Prohibitory Bill, leading Richard Rigby to say he should emigrate to Philadelphia and join the rebels.

**The American war** Conway from the first strongly opposed the war with the colonies. In the Commons in October 1775 he condemned 'the butchery of his fellow-subjects' (Thomas, *Tea Party to Independence*, 278) as 'cruel, unnecessary and unnatural' (Cobbett, *Parl. hist.*, 18.761). The speech was considered his best by many parliamentarians. He continued to harry the administration on America and in

1776 brought forward a motion requiring to know General William Howe's instructions for seeking peace. He defended the administration where he agreed with their measures, and was often proposed as commander-in-chief, but in the context of the war and the opinions of North and George III this possibility could be little more than mischief-making.

The alliance between the colonies and France in February 1778 led Conway to take an active interest in his position as governor of Jersey, and in June that year he toured the forts and garrisons on the island and on Guernsey. On 1 May 1779 Jersey repulsed a French attack. Conway set sail on hearing the news but reached the island only on 3 May. However, a second partially successful invasion was made on 6 January 1781, during which the lieutenant-governor was briefly captured. Strong weather prevented Conway reaching Jersey, and he later received news that the French attack had been defeated. Greatly unwell, he decided to return to Park Place. While convalescing he received letters from Hillsborough, the secretary of state, which implied dereliction of duty but allowed him further leave of absence, even though the governorship was not a residential one. The matter was smoothed over by a further letter which assured him that his conduct was approved by the king.

Conway continued to oppose the war, often more stridently than the indecisive opposition factions. In 1780 he had introduced an unsuccessful bill to address American grievances once peace was achieved. Respect for his integrity was widespread in the Commons. Once the opposition saw, at the beginning of 1782, that the Commons was in a state where it might vote to end the war and so bring down the North ministry, Conway was identified as the person most likely to succeed in carrying a motion against the further prosecution of an offensive war in North America. The first, on 22 February 1782, was defeated by 194 votes to 193, but on 27 February the motion was repeated and carried by 234 votes to 215.

**Commander-in-chief** North resigned on 20 March; in the Rockingham–Shelburne ministry that followed, Conway became commander-in-chief and a member of the cabinet. His opinions were thought decisive at the cabinet meeting on 30 June which agreed to make American independence conditional on successfully negotiating a general peace treaty. Conway remained in the government following Rockingham's death and the installation of Shelburne as prime minister, and was later attacked in the Commons by both Fox and Burke as politically naïve. Shelburne himself had commented on his innocence. Conway said he 'looked to measures only, and not to men' (Brooke, 'Conway, Hon. Henry Seymour', 246). He believed American independence must be a precondition of any negotiation, and would not be deflected by the antagonism between Fox and Shelburne. During the autumn Fox's attacks on the Shelburne ministry revealed splits in the cabinet over the terms for peace with America. Conway agreed with William Pitt the younger, now chancellor of the exchequer, that the provisional articles made with the Americans in November 1782 made independence unconditional. Although by early 1783 Conway had moved closer to the opposition, he supported the government in the vote on 18 February which brought down the Shelburne ministry. He remained as commander-in-chief under the Fox–North coalition but withdrew from the cabinet, and he resigned on the defeat of the coalition in December 1783.

**Final years** Conway strongly deprecated Pitt's minority administration, writing to Grafton on 4 January 1784 that he considered an administration supported solely by the crown as impracticable. In parliament he inveighed against Pitt's 'sulky silence' (Cannon, 172) after defeat on the East India Bill. At what turned out to be his last parliamentary speech, on 24 March 1784, Conway told Pitt that 'he had hitherto been fool enough to consider the House of Commons as of consequence to the country, and weight in the constitution; but the Right Hon. gentleman had undeceived him … and proved it to be a cypher' (Cobbett, *Parl. hist.*, 24, 1784, 773). Conway expected to be returned at Bury St Edmunds, but the loss of the American colonies and widespread hostility to the Bourbon powers had made his high whig principles unpalatable to electors, and Grafton, finding his influence threatened, replaced him with another candidate.

Conway retired to Park Place, where he immersed himself in arboreal cultivation, a longstanding passion (in 1778 he had given the poet George Crabbe a work on botany), and pursued literary interests. He adapted Louis de Boissy's play *Les dehors trompeurs* as *False Appearances*, which was performed first at the duke of Richmond's private theatre in May 1788 and in 1789 enjoyed several performances at the Theatre Royal, Drury Lane. He was also involved in designing the bridge over the Thames at Henley, near Park Place, built between 1785 and 1787, including sculptures of the river gods Thame and Isis by his daughter Anne Damer.

Conway was appointed field marshal on 12 October 1793. He continued to entertain: in 1818 Hannah More remembered 'the brilliant society of Field-Marshal Conway's house' (Walpole, *Corr.*, 37.xiv). He died suddenly, of a cramp in the stomach, at Park Place on 9 July 1795, and was buried on 20 July in the Ragley old vault, Arrow church, Warwickshire.

Nineteenth-century historians could be dismissive of Conway. Lord John Russell, later first Earl Russell, in *The Life and Times of Charles James Fox* (1853–7), and Philip, fifth Earl Stanhope, in *The Life of William Pitt* (1861–2), both paid little attention to Conway, portraying him as a parliamentary pawn set amid the Chathams, Bedfords, and Grenvilles. William Hunt, in the *Dictionary of National Biography*, remarked on the attention paid him by Horace Walpole, but said 'He was by no means so remarkable a man as Walpole makes him out' although admitting 'he was conspicuous for integrity and a delicate sense of honour'. Twentieth-century research on the American War of Independence in British politics has not entirely overturned the picture of Conway as lacking decision or leadership, but has still presented a more impressive picture of him, as a far-sighted and influential figure whose opinions were widely appreciated in Great Britain and America. The towns of Conway, New Hampshire, and Conway, Massachusetts, are testimony to his efforts to avert the conflict between Great Britain and her North American colonies. CLIVE TOWSE

**Sources** Walpole, *Corr.* · H. Walpole, *Memoirs of the reign of King George II*, ed. J. Brooke, 3 vols. (1985) · H. Walpole, *Memoirs of the reign of King George III*, ed. D. Jarrett, 4 vols. (2000) · R. Savony, *His Britannic Majesty's army in Germany* (1966) · P. Langford, *The first Rockingham administration, 1765–1766* (1973) · *Autobiography and political correspondence of Augustus Henry, third duke of Grafton*, ed. W. R. Anson (1898) · J. Brooke, *The Chatham administration, 1766–1768* (1956) · P. D. G. Thomas, *British politics and the Stamp Act crisis: the first phase of the American revolution, 1763–1767* (1975) · P. D. G. Thomas, *The Townshend duties crisis* (1987) · P. D. G. Thomas, *Tea party to independence: the third phase of the American revolution, 1773–1776* (1991) · P. D. G. Thomas, *John Wilkes: a friend of liberty* (1996) · *The correspondence of Edmund Burke*, 1, ed. T. W. Copeland (1958) · *The Grenville papers: being the correspondence of Richard Grenville … and … George Grenville*, ed. W. J. Smith, 4 vols. (1852–3) · *Additional Grenville papers, 1763–1765*, ed. J. R. G. Tomlinson (1962) · *Correspondence of John, fourth duke of Bedford*, ed. J. Russell, 3 vols. (1842–6) · *DNB* · *The letters of David Hume*, ed. J. Y. T. Greig, 2 vols. (1932) · L. G. Mitchell, *Charles James Fox and the disintegration of the whig party, 1782–1794* (1971) · R. J. S. Hoffman, *The marquis* (1973) · R. Pares, *King George III and the politicians* (1953) · M. A. Thomson, *The secretaries of state, 1681–1782* (1932) · H. M. Scott, *British foreign policy in the age of the American Revolution* (1997) · Cobbett, *Parl. hist.*, vols. 16, 18, 24 · J. Norris, *Shelburne and reform* (1963) · J. Cannon, *The Fox–North coalition* (1969) · *The correspondence of King George the Third from 1760 to December 1783*, ed. J. Fortescue, 6 vols. (1927–8) · G. Thomas, earl of Albemarle [G. T. Keppel], *Memoirs of the marquis of Rockingham and his contemporaries*, 2 vols. (1852) · R. R. Sedgwick, 'Conway, Hon. Henry Seymour', HoP, *Commons, 1715–54* · J. L. McCracken, 'The conflict between the Irish administration and parliament, 1753–6', *Irish Historical Studies*, 3 (1942–3), 159–79 · *The last journals of Horace Walpole*, ed. Dr Doran, rev. A. F. Steuart, 2 vols. (1910) · R. Whitworth, *William Augustus, duke of Cumberland: a life* (1992) · J. L. Bullion, 'British ministers and American resistance to the Stamp Act, October–December 1765', *William and Mary Quarterly*, 3rd ser., 49 (1992), 89–107 · G. G. Waterhouse, 'A military tour of Europe in 1774', *Army Quarterly*, 52 (1946), 92–100, 268–73; 53 (1947), 121–31 · *Correspondence of William Pitt, earl of Chatham*, ed. W. S. Taylor and J. H. Pringle, 4 vols. (1838–40)

**Archives** BL, letter-books, Add. MSS 17497–17498, 21501–21503 · Derbys. RO, corresp. relating to Ireland · Yale U., Lewis Walpole Library, corresp. and letter-books | BL, corresp. with R. Gunning, Egerton MSS 2696–2697 · BL, letters to Sir R. M. Keith, Add. MSS 35505–35542 · BL, corresp. with Lord Liverpool, Add. MSS 38210–38217, 38306–38310, 38463, 38570 · BL, corresp. with Sir Andrew Mitchell, Add. MS 6810 · BL, corresp. with duke of Newcastle, Add. MSS 32858–33070, *passim* · Chatsworth House, Derbyshire, letters to duke of Devonshire · NL Ire., letters to Charles O'Hara · priv. coll., letters to Lord Shelburne · Sheff. Arch., corresp. with Lord Rockingham · Suffolk RO, Bury St Edmunds, letters to duke of Grafton · U. Mich., Clements L., corresp. with Thomas Gage

**Likenesses** I. Gossett, wax medallion, 1760, NPG · J. Berwick, 1767, Yale U., Lewis Walpole Library · T. Gainsborough, oils, exh. RA 1780, Inveraray Castle, Argyll & Bute [*see illus.*] · Mrs Damer, marble bust, 1785 · Walker & Boutall, engraving, 1790–99 (after J. Reynolds) · W. Angus, line engraving (after T. Stothard), BM, NPG; repro. in *European Magazine* (1782) · R. Cosway, miniature, V&A · B. Dandridge, portrait, Houghton Hall, Norfolk · J. G. Eccardt, group portrait; formerly at Strawberry Hill, Twickenham · W. Greatbach, stipple and line engraving (after J. G. Eckardt), NPG · Heath, stipple and line engraving, NPG · C. Tomkins, mezzotint (after J. Reynolds), BM, NPG · portraits, repro. in Walpole, *Corr.*

**Wealth at death** approx. £10,000–£15,000; Park Place estate worth less than £400 p.a.; raised £10,000 for daughter's marriage settlement; at death estate at twenty-seven years' purchase would have been valued at *c*.£10,000: Walpole, *Corr.*, 22.499; 37.575 n. 8

**Conway, Hugh**. *See* Fargus, Frederick John (1847–1885).

**Conway, Sir John** (d. 1603), writer and soldier, was the son and heir of Sir John Conway of Arrow, Warwickshire, landowner, and Katherine, daughter of Sir Ralph Verney and his wife, Elizabeth. Little is known of his youth or education but he was well read. He was knighted in 1559, on the accession of Elizabeth I. On 26 July 1573 the queen granted him a two-year licence to 'pass beyond the seas, about the Queens affairs: and protection during that time' (*CPR, 1572–5*, 56). He seems to have been hot-headed. In 1578 he was attacked in London by Ludovic Grevil, and would probably have been killed if his servant had not warded off the sword blows. The incident caused outrage at the time as Robert Rich, second Baron Rich, had also been attacked on the same day. In December 1583 he seems to have been imprisoned in connection with the Somerville–Arden case, and during his incarceration he probably wrote his 'Meditations and Praiers'. He also wrote commendatory verses prefixed to Geoffrey Fenton's *Certaine Tragicall Discourses* (1567) and *Poesie of Floured Praiers* (1611). Conway was connected with Robert Dudley, earl of Leicester, because of the proximity of their landholdings in Warwickshire, a centre of Dudley power and influence. He was among Leicester's protestant clients and neighbours recruited for the expedition to the Netherlands in 1585. In 1586 he was the English commander in Middelburg, on Walcheren Island, close to the port and cautionary town of Flushing. He was master of Leicester's artillery from about June. He was well connected at court through membership of the Dudley clientele but became disillusioned with Leicester's lacklustre military leadership, and wrote on 28 January 1587 to Sir William Cecil, Lord Burghley, lord treasurer, and Sir Francis Walsingham, principal secretary, with an account of the betrayal of Zutphen and Deventer only two days earlier. His letters reveal his strong protestant leanings, and he laid much of the blame for the losses on Leicester. He noted sourly in his letter to Burghley that although Sir William Stanley had allegedly opened the gates of Deventer 'for the discharge of his conscience', the payment was 'said to be 13,000 pounds' (*CSP for.*, 12.340–41). Despite his views, Leicester had made Conway governor of the important and isolated garrison of Ostend on 29 December 1586, where he was to serve until 1590. During this period he was involved in a number of major incidents. In 1587 Alessandro Farnese, duke of Parma, threatened Ostend as part of his preparations to prepare the way for the arrival of the Spanish Armada. Reinforcements under Sir Roger Williams, *en route* for Ostend, were diverted into Sluys. Their heroic but unsuccessful defence of the town removed the threat to Ostend during 1587. In the following year the impending arrival of the Armada disrupted supplies of food to Ostend, and in late August the garrison broke out into a 'wonderful dangerous mutiny'. They complained of victuals that were 'neither wholesome, savoury, nor man's meat'. The victualler was thrown into the harbour by the irate troops, and Conway and his officers were imprisoned in the common gaol, after ten of the mutineers had discharged their muskets at them (*CSP for.*, 22.xxxvi–xxxix). The queen took the complaints of the troops seriously, and Peregrine Bertie, Lord Willoughby de Eresby, Leicester's replacement, restored calm in late September by promising to rectify the grievances, and by removing the ringleaders to assist in the defence of Bergen op Zoom.

In the wake of the Armada, a counter-attack was planned against Spain by raiding Portugal, and Conway was caught up in the controversy between Willoughby and Sir John Norris over the provision of troops from the English garrisons in the Netherlands for the expedition. Conway was reluctant to reduce the size of his garrison, or lose his veterans, due to the dilapidated state of the town defences and the continuing threat from the Spaniards. He was grateful for the insistence of the states general, who commissioned him as an officer and contributed to his salary, that he should maintain the integrity of his garrison. Conway co-operated with them. Willoughby regarded the affair as interference from the privy council.

Conway was in a difficult position because he had upset his officers during the mutiny, Norris during the recruitment for the Portugal expedition, and Willoughby during the inspection of the town defences. His captains demanded his recall. He was licensed to leave in July 1590. However, in August—taking advantage of the reduction of the Spanish forces, who had been drawn off to France— he launched a series of aggressive raids in the surrounding area. His most successful nearly ended in disaster when his force of 600 was cut off by the tide at east Dunkirk on 28 August 1590. He was attacked by the Spanish garrisons from Nieuwpoort and Dunkirk in force, and lost most of the booty that had been collected, although he did bring his force and 750 cattle safely back to Ostend. He claimed to have inflicted great damage on the enemy. Under pressure from Willoughby he announced that he was willing to resign. He was replaced by Sir Edward Norris, Norris's brother, and does not appear to have served in the Netherlands again.

Conway died on 4 October 1603, and was buried in Arrow church, where a monument was erected in his memory by his wife, Ellen, daughter of Sir Fulke Greville of Beauchamp's Court, Warwickshire, and his wife, Anne. They had four sons, including Fulke, John, and Thomas, and four daughters, Elizabeth, Katherine, Mary, and Frances. Edward *Conway (*d.* 1631), the eldest son, was created Viscount Conway and Viscount Killultagh in 1627.

M. A. STEVENS

**Sources** DNB · *CSP for.*, *1588–90* · E. M. Tennison, *Reign of Elizabeth I*, vol. 1586 · *CPR*, *1580–82* · S. Adams, 'The Dudley clientèle, 1553–1563', *The Tudor nobility*, ed. G. W. Bernard (1992), 241–65 · S. Adams, 'Baronial contexts? Conformity and change in the noble affinity, 1500–1600', *The end of the middle ages? England in the fifteenth and sixteenth centuries*, ed. J. L. Watts, The Fifteenth Century Series, 6 (1998), 155–97
**Archives** PRO, calendars of state papers · PRO, calendar of patent rolls
**Likenesses** monument, Arrow church, Warwickshire

**Conway, Katharine St John**. *See* Glasier, Katharine St John Bruce (1867–1950).

**Conway, Maria Emily Seymour-**, marchioness of Hertford (1770/71–1856). *See under* Conway, Francis Ingram-Seymour-, second marquess of Hertford (1743–1822).

**Conway, (William) Martin**, Baron Conway of Allington (1856–1937), art historian and mountaineer, was born on 12 April 1856 at Rochester, Kent, the only son of William Conway, a low-church evangelical vicar of St Nicholas's Church, Rochester, afterwards rector of St Margaret's Church, Westminster, and his wife, Elizabeth, daughter of Adam Martin MD of Rochester. He had two sisters. Martin Conway was educated at Repton School and from 1875 at Trinity College, Cambridge, where he studied history, graduating BA in 1879 and MA in 1882. He was a Cambridge University extension lecturer from 1882 to 1885. Conway climbed extensively in the Alps as an undergraduate, and was elected to the Alpine Club in 1877. In 1881 he published the *Zermatt Pocketbook*, the model for a series of Conway and Coolidge's Climbers' Guides, edited with W. A. B. Coolidge. Conway was responsible for many beautiful mountain names, such as Wellenkuppe, Windjoch, and Dent du Requin.

Another of Conway's interests was woodcuts and early printed books. This was encouraged by the university librarian, Henry Bradshaw, who financed the journeys on which Conway collected the material for *Woodcutters of the Netherlands in the Fifteenth Century* (1884), the most learned of his thirty books. While touring art galleries in Italy in 1883, Conway met Katrina, the only child of Charles Lambard, of Augusta, Maine, builder of the Chesapeake and Ohio Railway, and stepdaughter of Manton Marble, an investor and former editor and owner of the *New York World*. Conway was already engaged to Rose Shakespear, but he broke this engagement, ostensibly on religious grounds, and married Katrina at Marble's home, 532 Fifth Avenue, New York, on 10 June 1884. Supported by Katrina's family, the couple moved to Park Street, London, where their only child, Agnes, was born on 2 May 1885.

Conway became Roscoe professor of art at University College, Liverpool, in 1885. He published books on Reynolds, Gainsborough, early Flemish artists, and Albrecht Dürer, and organized congresses in Liverpool, Edinburgh, and Birmingham on the relationship between art and industry. Conway resigned from his Liverpool position in 1888 and moved to London, where he frequented the Savile Club, gave lectures, and published a book on the art of the ancient world, which was the result of nine months' travel with his family in the Near East. Conway and his wife bought paintings as her income increased, and Conway later recounted his experiences in this area in *The Sport of Collecting* (1914).

(William) **Martin Conway, Baron Conway of Allington** (1856–1937), by Bassano, 1895

In 1892 Conway led a large-scale mountaineering expedition to the Karakoram Himalayas with the financial support of scientific societies and his father-in-law, Manton Marble. Marble was not sure about Conway's motives: 'Tis not quite relevant to your art-career to be climbing mountains, but I perceive that Alpine, Caucasian, or Himalayan supereminence may be the corner-stone of artistic eminence' (Evans, 134). Conway's large party surveyed the Baltoro glacier and the region around K2, and ascended Pioneer Peak on Baltoro Kangri, which at 6890 metres may have constituted an altitude record at the time.

Conway returned to acclaim in England, but he did not rest on his laurels. After publishing a book about the Karakoram in 1894, he walked the length of the Alps with two Gurkha soldiers in a gruelling publicity stunt that formed the basis of a popular book, *The Alps from End to End* (1895). He received a knighthood in 1895 and shortly afterwards made an unsuccessful bid to win a seat in parliament as a Liberal. In 1896 Conway surveyed in Spitsbergen, an island in the Arctic circle about which he wrote several books. According to Arnold Lunn, Conway's experiments with skis while crossing Spitsbergen made him one of the pioneers of British skiing. In 1898 Conway travelled south to climb Illimani in Bolivia and Aconcagua in Argentina with two alpine guides. Before leaving Bolivia, Conway accepted an unsolicited offer from the Bolivian president

of a mining concession for the Acre territory, a vast region at the headwaters of the Amazon. In 1902 Conway sold his original South American syndicate at a profit of $20,000, although he remained a director of other ventures and, for the next thirty years, actively invested in South American rubber, railroad, and gold companies.

Conway also enjoyed the non-pecuniary rewards of his fame. Marble's prediction that Conway's climbing would add to his reputation as an art historian was ultimately vindicated. In 1901 he was offered a term as the Slade professor of fine arts at Cambridge. He resumed writing art history, including works on Tuscan art, the great masters, the Van Eycks, and Giorgione. After he resigned the Slade professorship in 1904, he and his wife bought and restored Allington Castle, near Maidstone. He served as president of the Alpine Club from 1902 to 1904 and was first president of the Alpine Ski Club in 1908. He was awarded the Founders Medal of the Royal Geographical Society in 1905. As a celebrity, Conway later received free passes to Swiss resorts in winter and summer from Henry Lunn and other travel agents and hoteliers.

The First World War rekindled Conway's interest in politics. His conservative political views were expressed in *The Crowd in Peace and War* (1915), which he considered his best book. In 1917 Conway was appointed director-general of the Imperial War Museum, an honorary post which he retained until his death. In 1917–18 he toured the Western Front for the museum; his daughter, Agnes, played a central role in collecting material on women's war work. Conway was almost non-partisan in his politics. On 14 August 1918 he asked the Conservative central office for a constituency; the next day he asked the Liberal whip for their nomination. He was later nominated and duly elected as a Unionist, representing the combined English universities from 1918 to 1931, when he was raised to the peerage as Baron Conway of Allington. He received an honorary LittD from both Durham and Manchester in 1919. After the war he undertook two important journeys, one to Morocco and Palestine and the other to Soviet Russia, researching material for lectures on Zionism which he gave in Britain and the United States. These two journeys formed the basis of two further books: *Palestine and Morocco: Lands of the Overlap* (1923) and *Art Treasures in Soviet Russia* (1925). The first allowed him to compare the effects of French and British rule, while for the second he was granted access to the art collections confiscated by the Bolsheviks.

Conway served as a trustee of the Wallace Collection and the National Portrait Gallery and was active in the Society of Authors and the Society of Antiquaries. He was one of the first to realize the value of the systematic and comprehensive collection of photographic records of architecture and art and he presented his own collection of 100,000 photographs to the Courtauld Institute of Art. In later years he published several autobiographical works: *Mountain Memories* (1920), *Episodes of a Varied Life* (1932), and *A Pilgrim's Quest for the Divine* (1936). Satirical cartoons emphasized his bushy eyebrows, wire glasses, plump jowls, and pug nose. A portrait executed in 1934 by Augustus John shows him with long, flowing white hair.

In 1924 Conway began a love affair with Mrs Monica Hadow, a divorcee forty-four years his junior with whom he worked, but this ended when she remarried in 1930. When his wife, Katrina, died on 22 November 1933, she left her estate, including Allington Castle, to their daughter, although Conway continued to live there and at Westminster. On 17 November 1934, he married Iva, daughter of Daniel Christian and widow of Reginald Lawson, of Saltwood Castle, Kent. He died at the Empire Nursing Home, Vincent Square, London, on 19 April 1937, and a memorial service was held on 23 April at St Margaret's, Westminster.                      PETER H. HANSEN

**Sources** J. Evans, *The Conways: a history of three generations* (1966) · CUL, Conway MSS · A. L. Mumm, *The Alpine Club register*, 3 (1928), 74–83 · C. W. and others, 'In memoriam: Lord Conway of Allington, 1856–1937', *Alpine Journal*, 49 (1937), 248–59 · *The Times* (20 April 1937) · P. H. Hansen, 'British mountaineering, 1850–1914', PhD diss., Harvard U., 1991 · P. Stansky, 'Art, industry, and the aspirations of William Martin Conway', *Victorian Studies*, 19 (1975–6), 465–84 · Venn, *Alum. Cant.* · W. W. Rouse Ball and J. A. Venn, eds., *Admissions to Trinity College, Cambridge*, 5 (1913), 508 · P. H. Hansen, 'Vertical boundaries, national identities: British mountaineering on the frontiers of Europe and the empire, 1868–1914', *Journal of Imperial and Commonwealth History*, 24 (1996), 48–71
**Archives** Bodl. Oxf. · CUL, corresp., diaries, and papers, Add. 7676 · Hunt. L., letters · IWM, London, war diary · NL Wales, letters · RGS, notes for history of Spitzbergen | BL, Blakeney collection, Add. MS 63123, fols. 48–54 · CUL, letters to Oscar Browning · CUL, corresp. with Lord Hardinge · NL Scot., letters from Lord Rosebery; corresp. incl. Lord Rosebery · RGS, corresp. with Royal Geographical Society · Zentralbibliothek, Zürich, Coolidge MSS
**Likenesses** E. O. Ford, medallion, 1893, NPG · Bassano, negatives, 1895, NPG [*see illus.*] · cartoons, 1920–29, IWM · photograph, *c.*1930, CUL · A. John, 1934, priv. coll. · W. & D. Downey, woodburytype photograph, NPG; repro. in W. Downey and D. Downey, *The cabinet portrait gallery*, 4 (1893) · E. Edis, photograph, NPG · A. Melnikoff, bronze head, IWM · photographs, repro. in Evans, *The Conways*
**Wealth at death** £761 7s. 8d.: probate, 17 July 1937, *CGPLA Eng. & Wales*

**Conway, Moncure Daniel** (1832–1907), social reformer and ethical preacher, was born on 17 March 1832 at Middleton plantation, Stafford county, Virginia, the second of the six children of Walker Peyton Conway (1805–1884), a slave-owning planter, attorney, and judge, and his wife, Margaret (1807–1891), self-taught homoeopathic doctor, daughter of John Moncure Daniel, a United States army surgeon, and his wife, Margaret. His pious Methodist parents were both Virginia born, from distinguished Chesapeake families of English and (on his mother's side) French Huguenot descent. As a youth Conway knew he was expected to emulate his politically and socially prominent male relatives. He took seriously their values—responsibility, honour, leadership, attention to duty—and always admired these Virginians even after breaking with them decisively. The only home he had built for himself, in London's Bedford Park, he named Inglewood, after the Virginia home of his earliest memories.

Nevertheless, Conway early displayed unusual predilections, more compatible with those of his female relatives. He loved music and literature, incurring a flogging by his

Moncure Daniel Conway (1832–1907), by Debenham & Gabell

Fredericksburg Academy instructor for absconding at midday to glimpse Charles Dickens during a brief visit in 1842. Compassionate, emotionally open, and convinced of the value of conciliation, he was more comfortable witnessing his mother soothe the sick than his father chastise criminals. His mother's vocal criticisms of slavery—shared by other influential female relatives—affected him profoundly.

After attending the Fredericksburg classical and mathematical academy (1841–7) and receiving a BA in 1849 from Dickinson College in Carlisle, Pennsylvania, Conway briefly studied law, but abandoned it for the Methodist ministry, which he entered on his nineteenth birthday. This career proved short-lived. Disturbed by what he saw as a dogmatic repression of free thought, he resigned late in 1852; the following February, forfeiting his paternal inheritance, he entered Harvard Divinity School to train for the Unitarian ministry. While in Massachusetts he began a friendship with Ralph Waldo Emerson, whose writing had inspired him to assert his individuality and break with Methodism. At an anti-slavery rally near Boston on 4 July 1854 Conway's distance from his roots lengthened, as he declared himself an abolitionist and denounced Virginia's entanglement with slavery.

Soon after receiving his BD in July 1854 Conway gained the Unitarian pulpit in Washington, DC. He was dismissed in October 1856 for anti-slavery sermons, but immediately hired by Unitarians in Cincinnati, Ohio. When in 1858 he debunked New Testament miracles, one-third of his congregation defected. Conway compensated by attracting newcomers intrigued by his growing religious eclecticism and legitimation of spiritual uncertainty. In Cincinnati Conway began seriously studying Asian religions, and became known nationally as a vigorous exponent of liberal religion. His personal life became more settled after his marriage to Ellen Dana (1833–1897), daughter of a Cincinnati businessman, on 1 June 1858. They would have three sons and one daughter.

Conway's ministerial career was interrupted by the American Civil War, which found his pro-Union mother and sister in the north, his father in the south, and his brothers in the Southern army. Conway supported the South's subjugation, but only if union were synonymous with emancipation: President Lincoln's slowness in effecting full emancipation depressed him, as did Virginia's ongoing ordeal. He coped by writing two anti-slavery books, *The Rejected Stone* (1861) and *The Golden Hour* (1862), and by co-editing a Boston anti-slavery newspaper, *The Commonwealth*, launched in September 1862. He was buoyed up temporarily by his August 1862 move from Cincinnati to Concord, Massachusetts, where he lived near Emerson and other congenial friends, and by his service that summer to thirty-three of his father's escaped slaves, whom he resettled in Ohio. But the war always tormented him. Finally, in April 1863 he escaped through expatriation, his pretext being an anti-slavery speaking tour in England. Shortly after arrival he sent for his family, never really expecting to return.

Conway had no plan when he began his European exile, but a remarkable stroke of timing rewarded his gamble. His first speech in England (6 May 1863) was at South Place Chapel, London's noted free-religious institution, at that moment reeling internally because of the unexpected orthodoxy of its minister. In August South Place hired Conway. It was a perfect match: the congregation applauded Conway's intellectual boldness, encouraging his attacks on sabbatarianism, sexual prudery, blasphemy laws, patriarchy, monarchy, and other apparent restraints on liberty, conscience, and expression. Led by Conway, South Place exceeded even its level of prestige during the long (1817–53) ministry of W. J. Fox.

With full congregational support Conway substituted 'meditations' for prayers in 1869 and ordinary seats for pews in 1872. He ceased to call himself minister; sermons became 'discourses'. Beginning in 1873 he read from his own *Sacred Anthology*, a pioneering compilation of excerpts from the sacred books of the world's religions. In essence, Conway intellectually became agnostic, though he shunned the term, maintaining an emotional reverence for religious feeling, for the individual's critically minded but devoted quest for spiritual meaning and truth. Berated by the orthodox, Conway was credited by many spiritually restless individuals with salvaging their waning faith in religion's relevance. This ability to connect with thoughtful individuals, combined with his logic, learning, and graceful phraseology, compensated for his oratorical limitations and kept audiences entranced. A journalist who visited one Sunday in 1880 described Conway as 'the least orthodox preacher in London', whose words bore 'an oracular impress' (Davidson, 241–2).

Conway published not only many South Place discourses but also a torrent of articles for both British and American periodicals: breezy travel pieces, gossipy accounts of celebrities, weighty ruminations on politics and religion. In 1870 he was a war correspondent in France for the New York *World* and the London *Daily News*. He was English agent for American writers, including Louisa May Alcott, Mark Twain, and Walt Whitman, writing a highly influential article on Whitman for the *Fortnightly* (15 October 1866). He developed as a scholar, though his scholarship remained partly polemical. Particularly noteworthy was *Demonology and Devil-Lore* (1879), a work of comparative mythology probing the origins of beliefs in demons and devils, now largely superseded but full of insight and lively speculation.

Conway's interest in comparative religion led him to India in 1883–4, after speaking in Australia. He was disillusioned: he had known Hindu and Muslim intellectuals in London, but displays of popular religious fervour and uncritical 'superstition' frightened and repelled him. He sailed to England with enthusiasm for his work shaken. This influenced his decision to return to America, as did his father's death in 1884 and his realization that his two younger children, born in London, had no attachment to the United States. Conway's affection for his native country had persisted along with his American accent. In 1885 the Conways settled in New York. Several books followed: two horrible novels, several works of history, and biography of widely varying quality. The best was an enduring two-volume biography of Thomas Paine (1892), followed by a skilfully edited four-volume collection of Paine's writings. Paine had fascinated Conway for forty years; life in London had cemented a sense of kinship with this earlier transatlantic radical.

After pleas to return Conway served again at South Place from 1893 to 1897, making his final mark on an institution that would survive through the twentieth century as the South Place Ethical Society, with headquarters after 1929 at Conway Hall (named after him), Red Lion Square. His wife's terminal illness prompted a final resignation; she died in New York on Christmas day 1897. Early in 1898 the Spanish-American War deepened Conway's darkening mood. He denounced this conflict and America's ensuing imperialist adventures. That summer, for the second time, war caused expatriation. He settled in Paris and began work on his memoirs. His *Autobiography, Memories and Experiences* (2 vols., 1904) was followed by *My Pilgrimage to the Wise Men of the East* (1906), a mellowed account of his Indian sojourn coupled with additional reminiscence. Both were moving, humane reflections by a septuagenarian who had lived a stunningly varied and engaged life. Both reflected Conway's rejection of his long-standing faith in progress, and evidenced his renewed belief in the independent reality of evil. His autobiography stands as an enduring account of the nineteenth century, as well as an apt foreshadowing of the darker attitudes of the twentieth. Conway died at 5 rue Villedo, Paris, of natural causes on 15 November 1907, and was cremated in Père Lachaise cemetery.

Conway was tall and robust, idiosyncratically handsome when younger, resembling a weathered, white-bearded Jehovah in later life. His dread of intellectual submissiveness, born of boyhood pressures, manifested itself in a confrontational style that alienated some people, especially before and after his London years. But he was at bottom a warm, sociable man, who loved the theatre, good food and wine, billiards, cigars, and company, both male and female. An enthusiastic and knowledgeable art collector, he developed close and enduring friendships with key Pre-Raphaelites, becoming perhaps the closest thing to a spiritual adviser many in that Bohemian group would know. An ardent feminist, he was eulogist at the 1902 funeral of his friend the American woman's rights pioneer Elizabeth Cady Stanton. He also admired feminine beauty, unselfconsciously patronizing Parisian dance halls and revelling in the allure of Isadora Duncan. For much of his life he attracted young enthusiasts of both sexes, including the distinguished American photographer Edward Steichen, a fellow Paris expatriate who supervised Conway's cremation (his ashes were laid in Kensico cemetery in Valhalla, New York). But Conway encouraged not disciples but independent individuals who followed the motto inscribed on a wall at South Place: 'To Thine Own Self Be True'. They were, as he often told them, and repeated in his memoirs, 'Those who think at all think freely' (Conway, *Autobiography*, 2.445).

JOHN D'ENTREMONT

**Sources** Col. U., M. D. Conway MSS · M. D. Conway, *Autobiography: memories and experiences*, 2 vols. (1904) · Dickinson College, Carlisle, Pennsylvania, M. D. Conway MSS · J. d'Entremont, *Southern emancipator: Moncure Conway, the American years, 1832–1865* (1987) · J. d'Entremont, *Moncure Conway, 1832–1907: American abolitionist, spiritual architect of South Place, author of the life of Thomas Paine* (1977) · J. M. Davidson, *Eminent English liberals, in and out of parliament* (1880), 241–52 · C. M. Davies, *Unorthodox London, or, Phases of religious life in the metropolis*, 3rd edn (1875), 2–19 · W. S. Smith, *The London heretics, 1870–1914* (New York, 1968), 106–24 · S. Budd, *Varieties of unbelief: atheists and agnostics in English society, 1850–1960* (1977), 220–4

**Archives** Col. U. · Dickinson College, Carlisle, Pennsylvania | Cincinnati Historical Society, Ohio, Unitarian church records · Harvard U., William Dean Howells MSS · Harvard U., Charles Sumner MSS

**Likenesses** T. Spicer-Simson, bust, *c.*1900, Dickinson College, Carlisle, Pennsylvania · E. Steichen, colour photographs, 1907, Dickinson College, Carlisle, Pennsylvania · Debenham & Gabell, photogravure, repro. in Conway, *Autobiography*, vol. 1, frontispiece [*see illus.*] · oils, South Place Ethical Society, Conway Hall, Red Lion Square, London · photographs, Col. U. · photographs, Dickinson College, Carlisle, Pennsylvania

**Conway, Richard** (1573–1626), Jesuit, was born in New Ross, co. Wexford, to Patrick Conway (*d.* 1587), a member of a prominent New Ross family, and his wife (*née* White). There were at least two children: Richard and a brother, George. Richard left Ireland for Portugal when about sixteen or seventeen years of age, as education was prohibited to Catholics in his own country. He entered the Irish College at Lisbon in the winter of 1589–90. For some eighteen months he took a course in humanities in the college, and on 22 July 1592 entered the Jesuit novitiate at Coimbra.

After his religious profession two years later, Conway was sent to Spain for his ecclesiastical studies: philosophy at Monterey (1595–8) and theology at the Royal College, Salamanca (1598–1602). He was ordained priest in 1600. He was stationed at the Irish Seminary College, Salamanca, as preacher and confessor, and often acted as vice-rector, at first under Thomas White (1600–05) and then for a troubled period under three Spanish rectors (1605–8). He had full charge of the Irish seminary at Salamanca as rector from 1608 to 1613, then of that of Santiago during 1613–18. In 1619 he became rector of the newly founded Irish College of Seville, serving until 1622, to which position he was again appointed in 1625. He continued in this position until his death the following year.

Conway guided the different colleges through many troubles, and was involved in all the detailed negotiations with the royal court, bishops, and local authorities which were required in the setting up and maintenance of new colleges. In addition to these offices, he acted as prefect of all the Irish colleges in Spain and Portugal, and as procurator of the Irish mission, in which capacity he was called on to attend to the financial and other affairs of the Irish mission in areas as far apart as Rome, Germany, Flanders, France, and Ireland, as well as Spain and Portugal. He became, as a result, one of the best-known and respected Irish churchmen in the early years of the seventeenth century. He spoke the Irish language fluently and had a deep interest in the history of his country. It was through him, it seems, that the Codex Salmanticensis, from which John Colgan OFM and the Bollandists derived much of their knowledge of the early Irish saints, came into the possession of the Irish College at Salamanca and was thus preserved. He himself compiled a history of English rule in Ireland, the publication of which was prohibited by the Jesuit general lest it cause irritation to the English king and further endanger lives in Ireland.

Under Conway's aegis, the pattern was firmly established of the colleges sending back to the Irish mission numerous well-trained priests, prepared with knowledge and endowed with zeal, who were to play a major part in preserving Catholicism in the country. Contemporaries spoke of Conway as a man of prayer and mortification, and a lover of learning. And one contemporary account records that by his zeal, pleasant manners, and exemplary life he succeeded in obtaining large contributions from the royal court, prelates, and other sources for the relief not only of the seminaries but for other students, ecclesiastic and lay, who could not be accommodated in the seminaries, and, also, for a considerable number of Irish girls who fled Ireland for religion's sake. Some of these entered convents, while for others he begged dowries to enable them to marry well. He died at the Irish College in Seville on 1 December 1626, after an illness of four months, aged fifty-three, and was buried in Seville.

THOMAS J. MORRISSEY

**Sources** Irish Jesuit Archives, Dublin, MacErlean transcripts · J. MacErlean, 'Life of Richard Conway, S. J. (1573–1626)', *Irish Monthly*, 51 (1923), 88–94, 148–55, 191–5, 251–4, 306–9, 362–5, 415–19, 462–5, 525–8, 581–5, 628–32; 52 (1924), 46–9, 91–4 · T. J. Morrissey, 'Some Jesuit contributions to Irish education', PhD diss., 2 vols., National University of Ireland, 1975, vol. 1 · T. J. Morrissey, *James Archer of Kilkenny* (1979)

**Conway, Robert Seymour** (1864–1933), classical scholar and philologist, was born at Stoke Newington, London, on 20 September 1864, the eldest son of Samuel Conway, Congregational minister, and his wife, Amy Curling. He was educated at the City of London School under Edwin Abbott, from whom he learned accuracy in detail, an interest in comparative philology, and a broad outlook on literature. After proceeding to Cambridge as a scholar of Gonville and Caius College, he obtained first classes in both parts of the classical tripos (1885, 1887). He was distinguished in part two for an essay, later published as *Verner's Law in Italy* (1887).

In 1887 Conway was appointed classical lecturer at Newnham College, Cambridge, where he met Margaret Mary, daughter of William Hall, an ironmaster in the midlands, whom he married in 1891. They had one son and four daughters. Shortly after this appointment he was elected a fellow of Gonville and Caius. In 1893 he became professor of Latin at University College, Cardiff, and in 1903 Hulme professor of Latin in the University of Manchester, where he remained until his resignation in 1929. He improved the teaching of Latin and established a final honours examination in Latin alone.

In 1897 Conway published *The Italic Dialects* (2 vols.), which was followed after many years by *The Prae-Italic Dialects of Italy* (with Joshua Whatmough and Elizabeth Johnson, 3 vols., 1933). While at Manchester he undertook an edition of Livy. He set about his task with enthusiasm and examined many manuscripts, especially in Italy. Three successive volumes were published (books i–v, 1914; vi–x, 1919; xxi–xxv, 1929) in collaboration with William Charles Flamstead Walters, after whose death he produced a fourth volume (books xxvi–xxx, published posthumously, 1935), with the help of Stephen Keymer Johnson. The work is very thorough, providing copious information about variant readings in the manuscripts.

Conway's other great interest was in Virgil: or, as he always insisted on spelling it, 'Vergil'. In 1907 he published in collaboration with J. B. Mayor and William Warde Fowler a small but important book, *The Messianic Eclogue*; and many papers on Virgilian subjects followed, including an attempt to find a new site for Virgil's farm (*Where was Vergil's Farm?*, 1923). The edition of the *Aeneid*, book i, published in 1935 after his death by his son Geoffrey Seymour Conway is perhaps his happiest piece of work, for it combines all his main interests.

Conway was an accurate scholar in his own fields, but they were somewhat limited. He never lectured or wrote on a Greek author, and outside Livy, Virgil, and Cicero his acquaintance with Latin authors was not comprehensive. But he had great enthusiasms and a power of instigating his pupils to research on their own account. His frequent visits to Italy gave him a deep love of the country, and it was a high pleasure to him when in 1929 he was made commander of the order of the Crown of Italy. Among other distinctions he received honorary degrees from the universities of Dublin (1921), Padua (1922), and Oxford (1928); and he was elected an honorary fellow of Gonville and Caius College in 1920 and a fellow of the British Academy in 1918. He was a founder of the Classical Association, and its president in 1927. He died at 4 Dorset Square, London, on 28 September 1933.

CYRIL BAILEY, *rev.* J. H. W. PENNEY

**Sources** C. Bailey, 'Robert Seymour Conway, 1864–1933', *PBA*, 22 (1936), 434–44 · *WWW* · *The Times* (29 Sept 1933) · *CGPLA Eng. & Wales* (1934)
**Archives** Bodl. Oxf., letters to Gilbert Murray
**Likenesses** W. Stoneman, photograph, 1921, NPG · portrait, University of Manchester, classics department
**Wealth at death** £4149 7s. 8d.: probate, 24 April 1934, *CGPLA Eng. & Wales*

**Conway, Roger** (d. *c*.1360), Franciscan friar and theologian, was a native of Conwy in north Wales, who probably entered the order in Chester, and was a member of the custody of Worcester. He studied at Oxford and was DTh by 10 February 1355, when—as guardian of the Franciscan convent in Worcester—he received papal permission to live in the London Greyfriars, 'for the spiritual recreation of himself and of the nobles of England, who are said to frequent the friary in great numbers' (*CEPR letters*, 3.563). He received the royal alms on behalf of the London Greyfriars on 4 February 1356 and became lector in theology at this convent, subsequently acting (*c*.1357–8) as provincial of the Friars Minor in England. In London he preached on the poverty of Christ, and was the most prominent, and frequently quoted, defender of mendicant poverty against the attacks of Richard *Fitzralph, archbishop of Armagh (d. 1360). He is probably identical with the Franciscan who in 1356 took up the challenge, when Fitzralph wagered his Bible that no friar could find a scriptural text that would prove their claims concerning Christ's mendicancy. With the provincial of the English Dominicans, John Tatenhall, Conway in 1358 led a delegation of friars to Avignon, where they petitioned the pope to compel the English bishops to punish those who led the faithful astray by slandering the friars and by attacking papal powers to grant them pastoral privileges.

Conway's *Defensio religionis mendicantium*, a treatise on the hearing of confessions by the friars, was previously regarded as a reply to Fitzralph's *Defensio curatorum*, but is now recognized as a refutation of the latter's *De audientia confessionum*, a treatise on the papal bull *Vas electionis* (1321), composed during the hearing in Avignon *c*.1358. Incorporating material written before 6 December 1352, since in chapter 7 Clement VI is mentioned as the present pope, whereas in chapter 5 the pope is named as Innocent VI (*r.* 1352–62), it consists primarily of a defence of the mendicant privilege of hearing confessions, though it also examines the question of dominion.

Conway further composed a *Tractatus de regalia Christi*, also known as *Quaestiones tres de Christi paupertate et de dominio temporali* ('Three questions on Christ's poverty and on the nature of the dominion he enjoyed in this life'). The work is of interest as suggesting modifications in earlier, primarily Franciscan, concepts of mendicant poverty—presumably because Conway was now arguing on behalf of all four orders of friars—while strenuously resisting Fitzralph's attack on the entire mendicant state.

A further work on mendicant pastoral privileges attributed to Conway, *Intellectus fratrum de constitutione Vas electionis quoad negativam ibidem definitam*, is largely identical with the second part of the *Defensio mendicantium*. In his writings Conway shifted the emphasis away from poverty and mendicancy, and back to pastoral issues. He procured on 14 July 1359 from Innocent VI a bull reaffirming the papal confirmation of the privileges contained in *Vas electionis*. According to John Bale, who gives no source, Conway died in London in 1360 and was buried in the choir of the Franciscan church there. He gave at least three, possibly four, manuscripts containing patristic, homiletic, canonistic, and exegetical works to his native convent in Chester (three are now in the library of Gray's Inn, London), but sold a copy of Thomas Aquinas's commentary on part of the *Sentences* of Peter Lombard to Lewis Charlton (d. 1369), a fellow theologian who was later bishop of Hereford. KATHERINE WALSH

**Sources** *CEPR letters*, 3.563 · Bale, *Cat.*, 1.459–60 · R. Conway, *Defensio religionis medicantium, Monarchia sancti Romani imperii*, ed. M. Goldast, 2 (Frankfurt, 1611–14), 1419–44 · A. G. Little, *The Grey friars in Oxford*, OHS, 20 (1892), 239–41 · A. G. Little, *Franciscan papers, lists, and documents* (1943) · C. L. Kingsford, *The Grey friars of London*, British Society of Franciscan Studies, 6 (1915), 18, 22, 65, 72, 125, 193 · Emden, *Oxf.*, 1.479 · *Hist. U. Oxf.* 2: *Late med. Oxf.*, 182, 438 · P. Lavery, 'De Fr Rogerii Conway, OFM vita et operibus deque eiusdem controversiis cum Ricardo Radulpho, archiepiscopo Armachano', diss., lectorate in theology, St Antony's College, Rome, 1930 · A. Gwynn, *The English Austin friars in the time of Wyclif* (1940), 88–90 · G. Williams, *The Welsh church from conquest to Reformation*, rev. edn (1976), 83 · K. Walsh, 'Archbishop FitzRalph and the friars at the papal court in Avignon, 1357–60', *Traditio*, 31 (1975), 223–45, esp. 239–43 · K. Walsh, *A fourteenth century scholar and primate: Richard FitzRalph in Oxford, Avignon, and Armagh* (1981), esp. 341–4 and ad indicem

**Archives** Österreichische Nationalbibliothek, Vienna, CVP 4127 · Bibliothèque Nationale, Paris, Cod. Lat. 3222 · Bodl. Oxf., MS Rawl. G.40

**Conway, Russ** [*real name* Trevor Herbert Stanford] (1925–2000), pianist and composer, was born at 71 Coronation Road, Bedminster, Bristol, on 2 September 1925, the son of Herbert Stanford, a commercial traveller in the confectionery trade, and his wife, Patranella, *née* Green (d. 1939/40), a pianist. He became a scholar at Bristol Cathedral school where he sang treble and showed a natural ability as a pianist, although he claimed to have had only one piano lesson in his life, having spent the money for his lessons on visits to the cinema. At the age of ten he played the organ at a local church in Bristol and at twelve gave an organ recital at Colston Hall. In 1940, having been involved in some acts of petty theft, he was sentenced to three months at the borstal establishment on HMS *Akbar* in Heswall. In 1942 he was conscripted into the Royal Navy and served in the Mediterranean and the Aegean. He was awarded a Distinguished Service Medal for his 'services while minesweeping' during the invasion of Greece. About this time he lost the tip of one of his fingers, not in action, but while using a bread slicer. During periods of

leave, he would play piano in a nightclub, but, being still unsure of his future career, he joined the merchant navy on his discharge from the Royal Navy, and only finally left the sea in 1955 because of a recurring stomach complaint.

By then Stanford's mother had died and his father had remarried, so he went to London where he was a relief pianist in a club. He was offered a job as a rehearsal pianist and asked to write a piece for the 'Radio show' at Earls Court. This, his first composition, titled 'Primera', was conducted on television by Eric Robinson. Subsequently he worked for Columbia record producer Norman Newell, firstly as an audition pianist and later as the co-writer of many successful songs recorded by Joan Regan, Dennis Lotis, Lita Roza, and Gracie Fields. He also worked as an accompanist for these artists and others, including Dorothy Squires and Adelaide Hall. He gained more experience by working as a song-plugger for Chappell's and eventually got the chance to make his own solo piano recordings, the first being 'Roll up the Carpet' in 1957. The name Trevor Stanford being considered unsuited to go with the vivacious music that he played, he took the performing name of Russ Conway—the Russ filched from Russ Henderson (of the Russ Henderson Trinidad Steel Band) and the Conway from a singer named Steve Conway. He generally used his real name for his composing activities. By November 1957 he had achieved best-selling status when his medley 'Party Pops' reached number twenty-four in the charts and by May 1959 he had fully developed his own commercial ragtime style in the Winifred Atwell mode. Between 1957 and 1967 he had thirty-two recordings on the market and had sold over 250,000 LPs by 1961. By the end of his career the total sales were over 30 million. He wrote the score for a musical starring Frankie Howerd, *Mister Venus*, in 1958, but it was not a great success.

Conway became one of the most popular recording pianists of all time when he started playing and recording his own compositions. 'Side Saddle' and 'Roulette' both became number one hits in 1959, followed by the top-ten hits 'Snow Coach' and 'China Tea' in 1960, and many others. There was also a popular recording of the theme from the 'Warsaw' concerto with the Geoff Love Orchestra; and recordings with traditional jazz musicians including Jack Parnell, Kenny Baker, George Chisholm, and Don Lusher. The appeal of his bright and propulsively swinging style was enhanced by his own good looks and charm, the famous friendly Russ Conway smile and wink being effectively deployed at well-timed moments during his stage and television performances. After making guest appearances on many television shows, appearing in several royal command performances, and topping the bill at the London Palladium, he became a regular feature of *Billy Cotton's Band Box* in 1962 and he and Cotton were very effective foils for one another. At the same time he was appearing in *The Black and White Minstrel Show*. At the peak of his success he lived near Addlestone, Surrey, and later settled in Eastbourne, Sussex.

In 1965 Conway suffered a nervous breakdown as the

result of overwork. For a while he concentrated on song-writing and presented a BBC Radio 2 series, *The Russ Conway Hour*. He had a mild stroke in 1968 and had to give up performing, helping for a while at his brother's factory in Somerset. But he returned to the stage in 1971, working in a less demanding way, and retained a considerable band of admirers, which was said to include the queen mother and Elton John. His health began to deteriorate more seriously in the 1990s, not helped by an addiction to alcohol, heavy smoking, and lavish spending habits which led almost to bankruptcy. From 1989 he suffered from stomach cancer but refused to give in to his illness and worked tirelessly for the Russ Conway Cancer Fund, which he founded in 1990 to raise money for research into the illness. He was awarded the lord mayor of Bristol's medal in 1996 for the work he had done in promoting gala concerts for the fund.

Conway never married; he was guarded about his private life, but admitted in a 1995 interview to being unsure of his sexuality (*Daily Telegraph*, 17 Nov 2001). At one time he had planned to marry the secretary of his fan club, Carol Wayne, but in an example of the ill luck that seemed to dog him, she died suddenly in 1974. He played his last concert in Eastbourne in September 2000, and died in hospital there on 16 November 2000. His funeral was held at St Mary Redcliffe Church in Bristol on 6 December, and he was afterwards cremated at South Bristol crematorium.

Peter Gammond

**Sources** P. Gammond, *The Oxford companion to popular music* (1991) · W. Gurden, R. Gunn, and C. White, 'Russ Conway', home. wanadoo.nl/rock_and_roll/russ.htm, Nov 2001 · 'Russ Conway', www.onlineweb.com/theones/conway/russ_conway.htm, Nov 2001 · A. Steven, *The Scotsman* (17 Nov 2000) · *The Times* (17 Nov 2000) · *Daily Telegraph* (17 Nov 2000) · D. Barker, *The Guardian* (17 Nov 2000) · S. Leigh, *Independent Weekend Review* (18 Nov 2000) · b. cert. · *The Stage* (23 Nov 2000); (30 Nov 2000) · CGPLA Eng. & Wales (2001)
**Likenesses** photographs, 1960–70, Hult. Arch.
**Wealth at death** £220,472—gross; £211,648—net: probate, 30 May 2001, *CGPLA Eng. & Wales*

**Conway, William Augustus** [*real name* William Augustus Rugg] (**1789–1828**), actor, was born in Henrietta Street, Cavendish Square, London, and was educated under a clergyman named Payne in Barbados, where he had been sent to live with friends of his mother. He returned to England in weak health at the age of eighteen. In Bath he saw a play for the first time and developed a longing for the stage strong enough to triumph over his family's objections. Accordingly he appeared at Chester as Zanga in Edward Young's tragedy *The Revenge*, with such success that the manager, Macready, offered him an engagement. After playing varied roles in many northern and midland towns, from Macbeth to Glen Alvon in John Home's *Douglas*, he appeared in 1812 at the Crow Street Theatre, Dublin, in the parts vacated by J. G. Holman, who had gone to America. There, it is said, he formed a violent but unavailing passion for Eliza O'Neill, with whom he acted. He also met Charles Mathews, who recommended him to Covent Garden, where he made his London début on 4 October 1813, as Alexander the Great in a piece of that name altered from Lee's *Rival Queens*. During the season he played various Shakespearian characters, including Petruchio, Orlando, Othello, Romeo, Coriolanus, Henry V, and Antony in *Julius Caesar*. Jaffier in *Venice Preserv'd*, Alonzo in *The Revenge*, Rolla in *Pizarro*, and other parts of importance were assigned him, though, as the company at Covent Garden included Charles Young and Charles Kemble, he had occasionally to take secondary roles. The season of 1815–16 added to his list of characters Macbeth, Theseus in *A Midsummer Night's Dream*, Beverley in Edward Moore's *The Gamester*, Posthumus in *Cymbeline*, and Henry V in Garrick's *Jubilee*, acted on 23 April 1816 for the Shakespeare bicentenary. Conway then disappeared from Covent Garden, and was next heard of in Bath, where he performed in March 1817 Joseph Surface in *The School for Scandal*. He stayed in Bath until 1820, playing a range of characters in tragedy and comedy, and in July 1821 appeared at the Haymarket as Lord Townly in John Vanbrugh's 'The Provoked Husband'. Here he remained during the season, at the end of which he withdrew from the English stage. A malignant attack upon him, said to be by the dramatist Theodore Hook, was the cause of his retirement.

A curious circumstance in Conway's life was the infatuation for him shown, on his appearance in London, by the friend of Dr Johnson Hester Lynch Piozzi, then almost eighty years of age. It was rumoured that Conway showed Charles Mathews a letter from her offering him marriage. In the sale of Conway's effects in New York after his death, there figured a copy of Young's *Night Thoughts*, on which was written, 'Presented to me by my dearly attached friend, the celebrated Mrs Piozzi'. More sensible conduct is, however, generally assigned her, and the authenticity of *The Love Letters of Mrs Piozzi, Written when she was Eighty, to Aug. W. Conway* (London 1843) is disputed. Conway's conduct, at least, appears to have been honourable. There are records of his having been sent a cheque by Mrs Piozzi for £500, a few days before her death in May 1821, which he returned to the executors of her will, declining to take advantage of what he considered a posthumous grant, even though at the time he was in need of money.

At the close of 1823 Conway started for America, and appeared on 12 January 1824 at the Park Theatre in New York, where he played Coriolanus, Lord Townly, Beverley, Petruchio, and other parts with great success. Later he delivered in New York some religious discourses. Early in 1828 he took a passage to Charleston. When the vessel arrived off Charleston bar, Conway threw himself overboard, and was drowned. He was a good actor and might well have been on the threshold of a brilliant career. He was, however, self-conscious, ill at ease, and morbidly sensitive to criticism, which could have been a reason for his suicide.

In 1863, Conway's son Frederick Bartlett Conway (1819–1874), with his wife, Sarah Crocker (1834–1875), opened the first theatre in Brooklyn, the Park Theatre. They also opened the Brooklyn Theatre in 1871.

Joseph Knight, *rev.* Nilanjana Banerji

**Sources** Adams, *Drama* • P. Hartnoll, ed., *The concise Oxford companion to the theatre* (1972) • *Autobiography, letters and literary remains of Mrs Piozzi*, ed. A. Hayward, 2 vols. (1861) • Hall, *Dramatic ports.* • T. A. Brown, *History of the American stage* (1870) • Genest, *Eng. stage* • J. N. Ireland, *Records of the New York stage, from 1750 to 1860*, 1 (1866) • *Theatrical Inquisitor, and Monthly Mirror*, 2–4 (1813–14)
**Archives** JRL, letters to Hester Piozzi
**Likenesses** De Wilde, drawing, 1810, Garr. Club, Mathews collection • W. Say, mezzotint, pubd 1815 (after G. H. Harlow), BM, NPG • G. H. Harlow, group portrait, oils, exh. RA 1817 (*Court for the trial of Queen Catherine*), Royal Shakespeare Theatre Museum, Stratford-upon-Avon • G. H. Harlow, oils, Royal Shakespeare Theatre Museum, Stratford-upon-Avon

**Conway, William John** (1913–1977), cardinal, was born on 22 January 1913 at 108 Dover Street, Belfast, the eldest of the nine children of William Conway (1880–1955), owner of a paint shop, and his wife, Anne Donnelly (1890–1982), daughter of William Donnelly of Carlingford, co. Louth. A brother died young, the two other brothers became priests in the diocese of Down and Connor, two sisters became teachers, one a nurse and two civil servants. Two of the sisters married and had families.

Educated at St Mary's Christian Brothers' School in Belfast, where he won various prizes and finally a university scholarship, Conway entered the Queen's University of Belfast, in 1930. There he read honours English, which he combined with courses in scholastic philosophy as part of his preparation for the priesthood. In 1933 he began his theological studies at St Patrick's College, Maynooth. Ordained to the priesthood on 20 June 1937, he returned to Maynooth to complete a doctorate in theology. On receipt of his DD in 1938 he enrolled at the Pontifical Gregorian University in Rome for the doctorate in canon law, which he obtained in 1941. Because of the wartime restrictions on travel on the continent, Conway and other priests coming back to Ireland from Rome made their way to Lisbon and thence by seaplane to Shannon.

On his return to his native diocese Conway was appointed to teach English and Latin in St Malachy's College, Belfast, in 1941. A year later he was chosen by the bishops of Ireland to fill the vacant chair of moral theology and canon law in Maynooth. He held that post for sixteen years, during the last of which he combined it with the office of vice-president. In that capacity he replied for many years to queries on problems relating to canon law in the *Irish Ecclesiastical Record* and occasionally contributed articles to it, as also to the *Irish Theological Quarterly*.

In 1958 Conway became titular bishop of Neve and auxiliary (or assistant) bishop to Cardinal D'Alton, archbishop of Armagh. His episcopal ordination took place in St Patrick's Cathedral, Armagh, on 27 July 1958. As auxiliary bishop he resided in Dundalk and took charge of that parish, as well as sharing in the episcopal burdens of the aged and ailing D'Alton. On the latter's death in 1963 he was chosen by Pope Paul VI as his successor and installed as archbishop in St Patrick's Cathedral on 25 September 1963. He was created a cardinal on 22 February 1965.

The Second Vatican Council had opened in October 1962. As auxiliary bishop, Conway had attended the first session; as primate, he presided over the deliberations of the Irish bishops for the other three sessions. He himself spoke on various topics, pleading that the council concern itself with the rights, duties, and responsibilities of priests, as well as of bishops, and commenting on the role of the laity, and on mixed marriages. Cautious and conservative both in manner and in theological approach, his contributions to the conciliar debates were not frequent or spectacular, and he did not rate as one of the major figures of the council.

None the less, Conway's reputation for a measured and moderate response to the decrees of the council won him a place on the committee of three cardinals which presided over the first international synod of bishops, representing all the episcopal conferences in the world, which emerged from the council. He had been elected president of the Irish episcopal conference and in that capacity guided his colleagues in the establishment of the various commissions which had been recommended by the council to co-ordinate the work of the laity and deal with issues such as ecumenism, catechetics, the renewal of the liturgy, justice, and peace. He played a leading part in the establishment of Trocaire (an Irish word meaning mercy), as a national agency for world development, which quickly provided generous financial and personal help to countries of the 'third world'. In accordance with a conciliar suggestion that seminarians should follow, when suitable, some courses at universities, he oversaw the opening of St Patrick's College, Maynooth, to lay students. The arts and science departments of the college already formed a recognized college of the National University of Ireland; once opened to lay students they quickly expanded and soon the seminarians were dwarfed numerically by the lay students.

During the greater part of his episcopate Conway was preoccupied with the political problems of Northern Ireland, within which his cathedral city and about half of his diocese lay. The demand for civil rights and for an end to discrimination against Roman Catholics in the state, which had been growing more clamorous for a few years, burst on to the British, and indeed the wider political world, in October 1968, when a march in Derry was blocked by over-vigorous police measures. The civil rights activists demanded equality of opportunity in employment and in the allocation of public housing, an end to the multiple franchise for local government, and a restructured police system with the abolition of the B specials or auxiliary part-time constabulary. Conway advocated equality of citizenship as a necessary foundation for harmonious relations between protestant and Catholic. When, in the wake of the civil rights campaign, the resistance of extreme Unionists to political accommodation ultimately led to serious violence on the streets of Belfast and Derry, culminating in the destruction of rows of Catholic-occupied houses, he called for the protection of the British army, and in August 1969 the army arrived to protect the Catholic community. Within two years the Irish Republican Army regrouped and began a guerrilla campaign against the army and the police forces of Northern Ireland to achieve its aim of establishing a united Ireland.

Conway and his fellow bishops in Northern Ireland deplored this development, rejected the actions of 'a handful of men without any mandate' and asked 'who in his sane senses wants to bomb a million Protestants into a united Ireland?' (*Belfast Telegraph*, 13 Sept 1971). When, in August 1971, the government of Northern Ireland introduced internment without trial and imprisoned many people whose connection with republicanism was tenuous, Conway and his colleagues repeated their denunciation of those whose violent deeds were bringing shame and disgrace on noble and just causes, and also condemned the methods used by the police including 'interrogation in depth', which they described as immoral and inhuman, and unworthy of the British people (*Belfast Telegraph*, 22 Nov 1971). On several occasions the cardinal joined with the heads of the other three main churches in repudiating violence, and in December 1974 they placed an advertisement in the local papers begging their members to pray for peace at Christmas and afterwards, and to speak of peace to their families, neighbours, and strangers (*Belfast Telegraph*, 12 Dec 1974). His pleas went unheeded, however, and at his death the IRA campaign was still in full swing.

The political antagonisms between protestant and Catholic hindered but did not prevent the development of ecumenical relations. Conway enjoyed a close friendship with Archbishop Simms, the primate of the Church of Ireland, and with many Anglican, Presbyterian, and Methodist clergy. Under his co-chairmanship various ecumenical conferences were held at Dundalk.

In 1975 Cardinal Conway suffered a heart attack but recovered and resumed his normal activity. He died at Ara Coeli, Armagh, from gall bladder disease on 17 April 1977, and on 22 April was interred in the grounds of his cathedral at Armagh beside the grave of his predecessor.

AMBROSE MACAULAY

**Sources** P. Mulligan, T. McDonnell, and others, *Seanchas Ardmhacha*, 9 (1978–9), 155–75 · B. J. Canning, *Bishops of Ireland, 1870–1987* (1987), 50–56 · *Irish Independent* (19 April 1977) · *Irish Independent* (20 April 1977) · *Irish Independent* (23 April 1977) · *Irish Press* (18 April 1977) · *Irish Press* (19 April 1977) · *Irish Press* (23 April 1977) · *Irish Times* (18 April 1977) · *Irish Times* (19 April 1977) · *Irish Times* (22 April 1977) · *Irish Times* (23 April 1977) · *Annuario Pontificio* (1966)
**Archives** Armagh Roman Catholic diocesan archives, Armagh, papers | FILM BFI NFTVA, news footage
**Likenesses** portrait, Ara Coeli, co. Armagh · portrait, St Patrick's College, Maynooth
**Wealth at death** £6527: probate, 6 Dec 1977, *CGPLA NIre.*

**Cony, William** (*d.* 1707), naval officer, was one of four children of unknown parentage, possibly born in Sutton, Oxfordshire. He was appointed second lieutenant of the *Torbay* on 3 October 1696 and transferred twenty-three days later to the *Humber*. In May 1699 he was appointed third lieutenant of the *Kent* and moved in March 1701 to the *Boyne*. In September, still a third lieutenant, he was appointed to the *Sorlings* (32 guns). Four months later, having been promoted to first lieutenant, he moved to the *Boyne* before moving to the *Chichester* in March 1702. He was appointed commander of the *Maidstone* in January 1703 and in April 1704 was appointed captain of the *Sorlings*.

Cony was married to Catherine Pleydell (*d.* 1715) by the time he made out his will while at sea on 13 June 1704. He bequeathed gold mourning rings 'of a Guinea value' to his brother-in-law Edmund Pleydell and other members of the Pleydell family. He gave a shilling to his brother Edward and 50 guineas to his sister Elizabeth, and appointed his wife his sole executor.

In October 1705 Cony was sent to the Baltic with the *Pendennis* (50 guns) and the *Blackwall*. On 20 October the three ships escorted a homeward-bound Baltic convoy and met four French men-of-war and five merchant ships commanded by the Chevalier St-Pol. In the ensuing battle, St-Pol and two of the English captains died and Cony twice repelled boarders. He was badly wounded but declared later that 'I struck not the Queen's colours but defended the ship to the last moment, and was taken sword in hand being overpowered by numbers'. After Cony was captured he suffered 'barbarous usage … I was stripped naked and left cold with my wounds bleeding' until a French officer arrived (PRO, ADM 1/5266, Cony to [Josiah Burchett], Dunkirk, 20 Nov [1705]). Learning that Cony was the captain the Frenchman expressed concern at this treatment and had his wounds dressed—'My being alive I look on as a wonderful Providence' (ibid.). Cony was imprisoned at Dunkirk, where he was well treated by the governor until his release. In his absence a court martial held on 29 January 1706 investigated the capture of the *Sorlings* and resolved that Cony 'did particularly distinguish himself … and having been several times boarded and repulsing the enemy and received several dangerous wounds' and recommended him to 'his Royal Highnesses Favour' (PRO, ADM 1/5266, CM 29 Jan 1706).

As a result Cony was appointed to the *Romney* (52 guns) and joined Sir Cloudesley Shovell in the Mediterranean before taking part in the reduction of Ostend. In December 1706 Cony, cruising with the *Milford* and the *Fowey*, learned about a French ship, which they sighted on 17 December in Malaga Bay. The French privateer of sixteen guns, which had bronze cannon from the French flagship *Magnamine* on board, lay close to the mole under the town's cannon, but Cony 'resolved to go in with his own ship and fetch her off'. He sailed in 'under French colours' and anchored 'within pistol shot' next to the Frenchman, who sent a boat to greet him. Cony captured the crew, 'put out the English colours and fired a whole broadside into the ship', and continued to fire until he 'drove the men out of her'. Then he sent his boat, cut the privateer's cables, and sailed out of the bay with his prize, 'notwithstanding a very warm fire from all the works of Malaga upon him', without losing a man (*LondG*, 4298; PRO, ADM 51/4261/7, *Milford*).

On 3 January 1707 Cony burnt the fifty-gun French ship *Content*. Two days later he challenged another ship. After it ignored him for the third time, he declared: 'I am The Queen of England's Man of War. If he were a Algereene he should bring to under my stern else I would fire at him'. Cony fired a gun at the ship:

> which in an instance was returned with a general fire of small arms and then a broadside. I was ready for him and I thought myself obliged to defend Her Majesty's Honour and my own Reputation and not to suffer Her Majesty's Colours to be affronted with powder and ball.

The chase eventually put out Algerine colours, but as the two ships were very near the shore and the Algerine 'got so close in among the rocks' Cony stood off (PRO, ADM 1/1593, Cony to [Josiah Burchett], 27 March 1707). On 8 January Cony and the other ships burnt the forty-gun French privateer *La Mercuré*.

Cony wrote to Burchett from Lisbon in March 1707:

> I Return His Royal Highness Thanks for the Honour he is pleased to do me in taking notice of the great success I have had in my cruise. I beg you to assure his Royal Highness that I will endeavour to do everything in my power to preserve his opinion of me.   (PRO, ADM 1/1593, Cony to [Josiah Burchett], 27 March 1707)

Cony took part in Shovell's attack on Toulon and was in Sir Thomas Dilkes's flagship at the bombardment of Toulon. He returned to England with Shovell and died on 22 October 1707 when the *Romney*, inshore of Shovell's flagship, ran on the rocks in the Isles of Scilly and was lost with all hands.                                          PETER LE FEVRE

**Sources** captains' letters 'C', 1704–, PRO, Admiralty MSS, ADM 1/1593 · courts martial records, 1705–7, PRO, ADM 1/5266 · *LondG* (16–20 Jan 1706) · captain's log, *Milford*, 26 Nov 1706–13 Jan 1707, PRO, ADM 51/4261/7 · J. H. Owen, *War at sea under Queen Anne, 1702–1708* (1938) · J. Hutchins, *The history and antiquities of the county of Dorset*, 3rd edn, ed. W. Shipp and J. W. Hodson, 1 (1861), 199 · will of William Cony, 1707, PRO, PROB 11/498, fols. 55v–56 · will of Catherine Cony, 1715, PRO, PROB 11/558, fols. 335v–336r

**Conybeare, Frederick Cornwallis** (1856–1924), biblical and Armenian scholar, was born at Coulsdon, Surrey, on 14 September 1856, the third son of John Charles Conybeare, barrister, of Coulsdon, and his wife, Mary Catharine, *née* Vansittart. He was educated at Tonbridge School from 1868 to 1876 (his father having moved to Tonbridge), and in January 1876 he proceeded with a scholarship to University College, Oxford; he obtained a first class in classical moderations (1877), and in *literae humaniores* (1879), and graduated BA (1880) and MA (1882). He was elected fellow of his college in 1880 and was made praelector in philosophy and, for one year only, in ancient history.

Possessing a private income Conybeare was able to resign his college appointments in 1887 and to devote himself to research, studying, at the suggestion of a friend, the Armenian language (and later also Georgian). At first he gathered material for the textual criticism of Greek classics from ancient Armenian versions, and he published *Collation with the Ancient Armenian Versions of the Greek Text of Aristotle's Categories* (1892) along with various articles, mainly in the American *Journal of Philology* (1889–1924), dealing with the text of Plato. He also produced comments on and translations of other Greek authors. Conybeare also travelled to various places where there

were collections of Armenian manuscripts, and this literature being mainly religious he became interested in church history and in the textual criticism of the Septuagint and New Testament. The former study was one in which members of his family—notably Bishop John Conybeare and William John Conybeare—had previously won distinction. He made numerous discoveries, of which the most notable was the ascription to the 'Presbyter Aristion' of the last twelve verses of St Mark's gospel in a manuscript in the monastery library at Echmiadzin, Transcaucasia. In a Viennese manuscript he discovered a translation of textual importance of the commentary of Ephrem of Syria on Acts. In the library of the holy synod in Moscow he unearthed *The Key of Truth*, the sole surviving monument of the Eastern Paulicians, in whose doctrines he became interested. He also brought to light from Armenian and Georgian printed books and manuscripts numerous documents bearing on the history of early Christianity and its sects, and on general biblical and patristic literature. He was employed to catalogue the Armenian manuscripts in the British Museum (the catalogue was published in 1913) and the Bodleian Library, Oxford (catalogue published in 1918). He became FBA (1903) and honorary LLD of St Andrews (1913).

The frankness with which Conybeare expressed his opinions endeared him to his friends but involved him in controversies. Having obtained private information about the Dreyfus affair Conybeare published in 1898 his much noticed pro-Dreyfus book, *The Dreyfus Case*. In 1904 he joined the Rationalist Press Association, which published his *Myth, Magic, and Morals, a Study of Christian Origins* (1909); its somewhat cynical scepticism elicited a rejoinder from William Sanday in *A New Marcion* (1909). But Conybeare also attacked the rationalist school, which denied the historicity of Jesus Christ, in *The Historical Christ*, published by the same association in 1914. John MacKinnon Robertson, a leading writer of that school, was also a prominent member of the association, which Conybeare left in 1915, presumably because of the controversy evoked by his book.

Soon after the outbreak of war in 1914 Conybeare, against the advice of friends, wrote a letter in reply to Professor Kuno Meyer in which he blamed the outbreak of war on Sir Edward Grey and H. H. Asquith. Meyer, then in New York, published it, despite a request from Conybeare not to do so. The affair brought on Conybeare criticism from the British press and alienated many of his friends. In 1917 he sold his Oxford house, and in 1921 he took one at Folkestone, though still spending much time overseas. In 1919 he visited the United States to deliver the Lowell lectures at Harvard.

Conybeare was twice married: first, in 1883 to Mary Emily (*d*. 1886), second daughter of Friedrich Max Müller, the philologist; she accompanied him on his travels and assisted him in translating R. H. Lotze's *Outlines of a Philosophy of Religion* (1892); secondly, in 1888 to Jane Macdowell, with whom he had one son and one daughter. Conybeare died at his home, 21 Trinity Gardens, Folkestone, Kent, on

9 January 1924, and was buried four days later at Golders Green. His valuable collection of Armenian books was given after his death to the London Library.

D. S. MARGOLIOUTH, rev. ROGER T. STEARN

Sources A. C. Clarke, 'F. C. Conybeare', *PBA*, 11 (1924–5), 469–74 • *The Times* (10 Jan 1924), 12 • Foster, *Alum. Oxon.* • *WWW, 1916–28* • *Revue des études Arméniennes*, 6, fasc. 2 (1926) • *CGPLA Eng. & Wales* (1924)
**Wealth at death** £26,734 2s. 6d.: probate, 27 Aug 1924, *CGPLA Eng. & Wales*

**Conybeare, John** (1692–1755), bishop of Bristol, was born on 31 January 1692 at Pinhoe, near Exeter. He was educated at the Exeter Free School. His father, the vicar of Pinhoe, whose vicarage was wrecked by the famous storm of 1703, died about 1706 'of a disorder caught on that occasion'. Friends helped Conybeare to continue his education, and he was admitted at Exeter College, Oxford, on 22 March 1708. He was elected a probationary fellow of his college in June 1710, and full fellow on 14 July 1711. He was a member of the strongly whig Constitutional Club. Conybeare graduated BA on 17 July 1713, and on 30 June 1714 was appointed praelector in philosophy by his college. On 19 December 1714 he was ordained deacon, and on 27 May 1716 priest.

After holding a curacy for a short time at Fetcham, Surrey, Conybeare returned to Oxford, became tutor of his college, and soon obtained a reputation as a staunchly orthodox Anglican. The university church of St Mary's was crowded when he was in the pulpit. In 1719 he was one of those in the forefront of the move to prosecute Thomas Warton for heterodoxy. A sermon of his on miracles published in 1722 went through four editions, and was followed by another on the mysteries in 1724. Bishop Gibson appointed him one of the newly founded king's preachers at Whitehall; and in May 1724 Lord Chancellor Macclesfield presented him to the small rectory of St Clement's, Oxford. He was proctor in 1725, and proceeded BD in June 1728, and DD in January 1729. Among his pupils were Thomas Secker and the two sons of Charles Talbot, then solicitor-general. Conybeare dedicated two sermons to the solicitor-general and his father, William Talbot, bishop of Durham. His chances of preferment were injured by the death of the bishop in 1730. In the same year, however, he was elected rector of Exeter College. In 1732 he published *A Defence of Reveal'd Religion* in reply to Tindal's controversial *Christianity as Old as the Creation*; Conybeare's work was praised as one of the four ablest books produced on the occasion. Warburton called it 'one of the best-reasoned books in the world'. Conybeare was a temperate and able writer, and his lucid arguments attracted support from as far afield as Germany.

The Exeter rectorship was a poor one, and soon afterwards Bishop Gibson successfully procured Conybeare's appointment to the deanery of Christ Church. He was installed in January 1733, and on 6 June 1733 married Jemima (*bap.* 1703, *d.* 1747), daughter of William and Elizabeth Juckes of Hoxton Square, London. The Conybeares had five children.

At Exeter College Conybeare effected many reforms,

putting a stop to the sale of servants' places and opposing absenteeism and pluralism among the fellows; he instituted tutorial fees and restored lectures. In 1734 he entertained the prince of Orange at the deanery. Conybeare seems to have been energetic at Christ Church. In 1735 he published *Calumny Refuted, or, An Answer to the Personal Slander of Dr Richard Newton*, this time when Newton was endeavouring to obtain a charter for Hart Hall, a plan opposed by Conybeare. He subsequently led the whig interest in the parliamentary election of 1737 against Newton and the tory interest, and he thereafter remained a staunch whig, publishing a sermon on *True Patriotism* in 1749. His hopes of a bishopric were lowered by the death of Charles Talbot, while lord chancellor, in 1737, and by Bishop Gibson's loss of influence at court. In 1750, however, after Archbishop Herring interceded with Newcastle on his behalf, he was appointed to the see of Bristol, in succession to Joseph Butler. With the bishopric he continued to hold the Christ Church deanery. Conybeare was by now a widower, following the death of Jemima on 29 October 1747; his health was broken by gout and he was disabled for most of his episcopate. He died in Bristol on 13 July 1755, and was buried in Bristol Cathedral. Two of his children survived him, Jemima (*d.* 1785) and William, who was to become DD and rector of St Botolph without Bishopsgate. They were left without much provision, and Archbishop Secker arranged for two volumes of sermons to be published by subscription for their benefit in 1757. As there were 4600 subscribers, many of whom took more than one copy, the results must have been satisfactory. Nevertheless Secker was obliged to solicit a pension of £140 for Conybeare's dependants.

LESLIE STEPHEN, rev. WILLIAM GIBSON

Sources *The autobiography of Thomas Secker, archbishop of Canterbury*, ed. J. S. Macauley and R. W. Greaves (1988) • W. R. Ward, *Georgian Oxford: university politics in the eighteenth century* (1958) • BL, Add. MS 32719, fols. 210, 337, 345 • C. W. Boase, ed., *Registrum Collegii Exoniensis*, new edn, OHS, 27 (1894) • *IGI* • W. K. Stride, *Exeter College* (1900) • *Hist. U. Oxf. 5: 18th-cent. Oxf.*
**Archives** Bodl. Oxf., sermons
**Likenesses** portrait, Exeter College, Oxford; version, Christ Church Oxf.
**Wealth at death** estate very small; Archbishop of Canterbury obtained pension for dependants

**Conybeare, John Josias** (1779–1824), geologist, antiquary, and Church of England clergyman, was born on 10 June 1779 at St Botolph's rectory, Bishopsgate, London, elder son of the then rector, William Conybeare (1739–1815), and his wife, Margaret Hester Olivier (1764–1806). William Daniel *Conybeare (1787–1857) was his younger brother. He attended Westminster School (where he was captain of school) before going up to Christ Church, Oxford. There he won the chancellor's prize in 1800, graduating BA in 1801 and MA in 1804. From 1808 until 1812 he was professor of Anglo-Saxon at Oxford, and from 1812 until 1821 professor of poetry.

Conybeare was ordained on 13 June 1802, prebendary of York from 1803, and in 1812 became vicar of Batheaston, in Somerset. He resided there from 1814 and much improved the parish, erecting a national school in the churchyard

(1818) and a chemical laboratory at the front of his vicarage. He married Mary (1790–1848), only daughter of the Revd Charles Davies (1742–1810), on 21 February 1814.

Conybeare was an early enthusiast for both chemistry and geology. He set up his own laboratory in Oxford in 1804, and published fourteen scientific papers—the most significant of his geology papers concerning Devon and Cornwall. He was one of the original honorary members of the Geological Society of London and, between 1807 and 1812, visited many English counties, probably with his brother, gathering geological data with which he constructed rudimentary geological maps. He was a member of the Revd Richard Warner's Bath Literary Breakfasts, and was also, according to the surveyor R. C. Taylor (1789–1851), one of a triumvirate of local clerics who there supported the geologist William Smith and helped disseminate his results.

Conybeare died suddenly of apoplexy, on 11 June 1824 at the house of Stephen Groombridge at Blackheath, having just delivered the Bampton lectures for 1824 at Oxford. He was buried at Batheaston on 20 June. News of his sudden death confused many, including Robert Bakewell (1768–1843) in England and Benjamin Silliman (1779–1864) in America. They both assumed this death was that of his brother W. D. Conybeare, who thus has the melancholy distinction of having had his death announced prematurely twice. The Society of Antiquaries, which had published 'endless Anglo Saxon texts' (Evans, 235) for Conybeare from 1811 to 1823, still felt able to encourage the posthumous publication in 1826 of his *Illustrations of Anglo-Saxon Poetry*, edited by his brother. The early death of Conybeare, who 'was considered one of the most learned men of his day' (Mitchell, 332), was widely mourned.

H. S. TORRENS

**Sources** H. C. A. Conybeare, *Conybeare wills and administrations: part 4, 1824–1857* (1914) · E. W. B. [E. W. Brayley], *Annals of Philosophy*, 8 (1824), 161–9 · W. S. Mitchell, 'Rev. J. J. Conybeare', *Proceedings of the Bath Natural History and Antiquarian Field Club*, 2 (1872), 329–32 · R. C. Taylor, 'Note', in J. W. Morris, *Handbook to Bath* (1888), 117 · J. J. Conybeare, geological maps of English counties, BGS · B. M. W. Dobbie, *An English rural community* (1969) · E. W. Brayley, *GM*, 1st ser., 94/2 (1824), 187, 376–8, 482 · *Bath Chronicle* (24 June 1824), 2 · J. Evans, *A history of the Society of Antiquaries* (1956) · F. C. Conybeare, ed., *Letters and exercises of the Elizabethan schoolmaster John Conybeare* (1905), 114–57 · R. Warner, *Literary recollections*, 2 (1830), 113

**Archives** BGS, notes and maps · Ches. & Chester ALSS, corresp. and notes

**Likenesses** T. Uwins, watercolour and pencil drawing, BM

**Wealth at death** under £16,000—unsettled personalty only: H. C. A. Conybeare, *Conybeare wills and administrations*

**Conybeare, William Daniel** (1787–1857), geologist and dean of Llandaff, was born at St Botolph's rectory, Bishopsgate, London, on 7 June 1787, younger son of the rector, William Conybeare (1739–1815), and his wife, Margaret Hester Olivier (1764–1806). His elder brother was John Josias *Conybeare (1779–1824). From 1802 to 1803 he attended Westminster School and he entered Christ Church, Oxford, in 1805, graduating BA in 1808 (first class in classics, second in mathematics), and MA in 1811.

Conybeare had been introduced to fossil hunting at his parents' Bexley summer home, and Stukeley's *Itinerarium*

*curiosum* (1776) was another early inspiration. By 1809 he 'was prepared at once to seize the general fact of the successive distribution' of fossils in rocks 'when first laid down as an admitted fact in … geology' (W. D. Conybeare, 137). He visited many southern English counties between 1807 and 1812 to compile geological maps, was elected member of the Geological Society of London in 1811, and was much involved with the new Oxford Geology Club—also established in 1811. In 1813 he studied Northern Ireland with William Buckland; they convinced themselves, and soon others, that basalt here was volcanic in origin. Conybeare was also much involved with the Geological Society's map, published in 1820.

Conybeare had been ordained deacon in 1813 and on 23 August 1814 married Sarah Anne (1790/91–1864), daughter of Captain Charles Ranken or Rankin of the East India Company, of co. Down, Ireland; the Conybeares had six children, the eldest of whom was William John *Conybeare, Church of England clergyman and author. Once married he had to leave Oxford; he settled as curate in Suffolk. In 1815 Conybeare's father died. His father had 'received, for thirty to forty years, an annual income of not less than £3500 from ecclesiastical preferments alone' (H. C. A. Conybeare, pt 3, 47), so his death meant that Conybeare was to have few financial worries for the remainder of his life. The following year he went on an important continental tour, with Buckland and Greenough, to gain 'a general view of the Formations of the Continent … to identify them with those of England and to ascertain to what extent the science had been cultivated abroad' (Torrens, 'Geology') during the Napoleonic Wars.

In 1817 Conybeare took up a new curacy at Chalcombe near Banbury, but the following year moved as a priest to Cropredy. In August 1819 he was appointed lecturer to St Luke's, Brislington, Bristol, and he was elected FRS that December. With Henry De la Beche, whom he had met at the Oxford club's Clifton meeting in 1818, he started work on the extinct marine reptiles *Ichthyosaurus* and *Plesiosaurus* (Conybeare's newly recognized genus). The two men helped inaugurate the Bristol Literary and Philosophical Institution in 1820 and also its associated society. Conybeare was encouraged by now living next to one of the earliest collectors of liassic reptiles, G. W. Braikenridge (1775–1856). This work culminated in three important papers by Conybeare, published between 1821 and 1824. About this time he also undertook a detailed survey of south-west coalfields with William Buckland—work published in 1824. During the survey, in 1820, he gave field tuition to Adam Sedgwick.

Conybeare's most important work, with William Phillips, was *Outlines of the Geology of England and Wales, Part One* (ultimately the only part published), which appeared in June 1822. Conybeare extended and vastly improved Phillips's earlier attempts of 1816–18. The book stratigraphically surveyed all rocks down to the Old Red Sandstone. It also contained full catalogues of the fossils found in each formation, and first named the Carboniferous. It became Roderick Murchison's 'scientific bible' (Geikie, 1.126) and Whewell called it 'an event far more important than it might at first appear', because of 'the vast impulse which it gave to the study of sound descriptive geology … felt and acknowledged in other countries as well as in Britain' (Whewell, 429). This book and the geological maps of Smith (1815) and Greenough (1820) inspired French visitors to England in 1823 to learn how to prepare an equivalent map and memoir for France. The German Karl von Zittel called the book 'classic' and confirmed how the methods it had adopted 'signified the scientific recognition and marked success of William Smith's reform' (Zittel, 426).

In January 1823 Conybeare started publication of a 'Memoir illustrative of a general geological map of the principal mountain chains of Europe', with a coloured map in the *Annals of Philosophy*. Only six parts appeared, the last in September 1823, because this work had caused a serious breach with G. B. Greenough, president of the Geological Society of London (1807–13, 1818–20, and 1833–5), by June 1823. Greenough felt his plans for a similar map should have had priority. As a result, both projects were abandoned, Conybeare's half-finished. The death of Conybeare's only brother in June 1824 also affected him deeply and he published nothing further on geology between 1824 and 1829.

In 1822 Conybeare had been appointed rector of Sully, Glamorgan, and in 1827 he left Brislington to live there. Late in that year he was elected corresponding member of the Institut de France, for his reptilian studies and stratigraphic work. William Phillips died in April 1828 and Conybeare now hoped to complete his *Outlines*, by collaborating with Adam Sedgwick of Cambridge. However, a serious carriage accident in October 1829, which resulted in Conybeare's being badly concussed, helped put paid to this. Conybeare was elected an honorary MA of Cambridge University in 1831 and at the Oxford meeting of the British Association for the Advancement of Science in 1832 he read an important 'Report on the progress … of geology' to the first geology section. Conybeare was by now the leading diluvialist theoretician in England and led opposition to Lyell's *Principles of Geology* in the 1830s, although Lyell could now note with justice that Conybeare 'promises but does not perform' (Wilson, 273).

In April 1836 Conybeare presented himself to the family rectory of Axminster and moved to Devon. He was thus on hand in 1839 and 1840 to make his last significant geological observations, on the Lyme Regis landslip. With William Dawson and Professor and Mrs Buckland he issued *Ten Plates* describing the landslip in 1840, but the 1830s had seen him busiest on theological matters, preaching the Oxford Bampton lectures in 1839. In the 1840s Conybeare abandoned his geology. He remained at Axminster until a final move to Llandaff in 1848, where, having become dean in 1845, he was much involved in restoring the cathedral. He died on 12 August 1857 at the rectory, Itchenstoke, Hampshire. Conybeare had been the 'most impressive intellectually' (Rupke, 10) of the early Oxford school of geologists, but his reputation has since suffered because of the loss of his archives.

H. S. TORRENS

**Sources** W. D. Conybeare, 'Fragment of autobiography', *Letters and exercises of the Elizabethan schoolmaster John Conybeare*, ed. F. C. Conybeare (1905) • J. E. Portlock, *Quarterly Journal of the Geological Society*, 14 (1858), xxiv–xxxii • F. J. North, 'Dean Conybeare, geologist', *Transactions of the Cardiff Naturalists' Society*, 66 (1935), 15–68 • H. C. A. Conybeare, *Conybeare wills and administrations: part 3, 1706–1815* (1913–14) • H. C. A. Conybeare, *Conybeare wills and administrations: part 4, 1824–1857* (1913–14) • H. S. Torrens, 'Geology in peace time: an English visit to study German mineralogy and geology (and visit Goethe, Werner and Raumer) in 1816', *Algorismus: Studien zur Geschichte der Mathematick und der Naturwissenschaften*, 23 (1998), 147–75 • N. Rupke, *The great chain of history* (1983) • M. J. S. Rudwick, 'A critique of uniformitarian geology: a letter from W. D. Conybeare to Charles Lyell, 1841', *Proceedings of the American Philosophical Society*, 111 (1967), 272–87 • L. Wilson, *Charles Lyell: the years to 1841* (1972) • K. A. von Zittel, *History of geology and palaeontology* (1901) • H. S. Torrens, 'The scientific ancestry and historiography of *The Silurian System*', *Journal of the Geological Society*, 147 (1990), 657–62 • A. Geikie, *Life of Sir Roderick I. Murchison*, 2 vols. (1875) • W. Whewell, *History of the inductive sciences*, 3rd edn, 3 (1857)

**Archives** Ches. & Chester ALSS, corresp. and papers • U. Edin. L., corresp. | GS Lond., letters to R. I. Murchison • NMG Wales, letters to Sir Henry de la Beche

**Likenesses** photograph, *c.*1850, NMG Wales, Geology department • engraving (after unknown portrait), repro. in H. B. Woodward, *History of the Geological Society of London* (1907), facing p. 40 • etching (after photograph), repro. in Geikie, *Life of Sir Roderick I. Murchison*, vol. 1, opposite p. 115 • print, NPG; repro. in *ILN* (1857)

**Wealth at death** approx. £70,000: H. C. A. Conybeare, *Conybeare wills and administrations: part 4, 1824–1857* (1913–14), 45–9

**Conybeare, William John** (1815–1857), Church of England clergyman and author, was born on 1 August 1815 at Eliot Place, Lewisham, the eldest of six children of William Daniel *Conybeare (1787–1857), geologist and dean of Llandaff, and his wife, Sarah Anne, daughter of Captain Charles Rankin. The infant Conybeare enjoyed a peripatetic life determined by his father's geological interests, until in 1819 the family settled at Brislington, Bristol, moving to Sully, Glamorgan, in 1827. The following year Conybeare was sent to Westminster School, where his friends included George Lynch Cotton. While at the school he permanently damaged one eye, and in 1829 experienced the first serious bout of the ill health that dogged him throughout his life, obliging him to spend much time at home. In 1833 he went up to Trinity College, Cambridge, as a pensioner, where he won the college Greek Testament prize in 1834 and a scholarship in 1835. He graduated BA in 1837 as third classic and thirty-fifth wrangler; he was elected a minor fellow of Trinity in 1839, and on taking his MA in 1840 proceeded to a major fellowship. He served the college as third sub-lecturer and steward before being appointed mathematical lecturer in 1842.

Although he had joined Lincoln's Inn in 1840, Conybeare was then ordained deacon, and travelled in Italy and Greece before being ordained priest in 1841. He was subsequently appointed Whitehall preacher, serving until 1844. In 1842 Conybeare left Cambridge to become first principal of the Liverpool Collegiate Institution, a school 'for two social grades which lie between the higher ranks of English society on the one hand and those who send their children to National Schools on the other' (H. C. A. Conybeare, 36). On 22 December of the same year he married Eliza (1820–1903), daughter of the Revd Joseph Rose of

Rothley, Leicestershire, and first cousin once removed of Thomas Babington Macaulay. There were three children: John William Edward (1843–1931), later vicar of Barrington, Cambridgeshire, historian of the county and convert to Roman Catholicism; Bruce Dicey (1846–1850); and Grace (b. 1855).

When illness prompted Conybeare to resign his Liverpool post in 1848 his father presented him to the family living of Axminster, Devon, worth some £1000 per annum. Here he co-operated with his college friend and successor at Liverpool, John Saul Howson, on *The Life and Epistles* (originally, in best Victorian fashion, *Life and Letters*) *of St Paul* (1852). His health worsened. In 1852 a supposedly therapeutic visit to the house in Funchal, Madeira, taken by his father for Conybeare's fatally consumptive brother, John Crawford William, probably caused his own tuberculosis. The next three years passed in further recuperative travel, Conybeare resigning Axminster in 1854. In 1856 he finally settled at Warren Cottage, Weybridge, Surrey, where he died from tuberculosis on 23 July 1857. He was buried in Weybridge; his father, taken ill travelling to visit him, succumbed three weeks after his son's death.

Conybeare's modern reputation rests on his activity as a reviewer and novelist during his last years (although *St Paul* enjoyed currency into the twentieth century, especially in the United States). The articles he wrote on religious subjects for the *Quarterly Review* (1847–56) and the *Edinburgh Review* (1852–4) exhibit a witty but occasionally brutally combative style: *The Record* dubbed him the 'BRUMMAGEN Sydney Smith' (3 Nov 1853). His character assassination of 'Bishop Phillpotts' (*Edinburgh Review*, 95, 1852) and his insightful study 'The church in the mountains' (ibid., 97, 1853) are often cited, but his most important and controversial article, published in the *Edinburgh Review* (98, 1853) and in several subsequent revised editions, was 'Church parties'. Containing numerical estimates of the strength of different factions of the mid-nineteenth-century Church of England and lively accounts of their clerical cultures, this remains the starting point for investigations into the subject, and popularized the term 'broad church' as a description of liberal Anglicanism.

Conybeare's last major publication was the novel *Perversion, or, The Causes and Consequences of Infidelity* (1856), which drew on his articles and his own and friends' lives for a melodramatic account of the sources of scepticism in the extremes of contemporary religious culture (including—unexpectedly through the character of an otherwise Flashmanesque villain—Mormonism). If Conybeare's deficiencies as a novelist account in part for *Perversion*'s lukewarm reception, passages which suggested a *roman-à-clef* caused scandal, especially its blunt portrayal of homoeroticism in an Anglo-Catholic Oxford tutor (possibly modelled on Frederick William Faber). Others bemoaned *Perversion*'s lack of charity to scepticism: Richard Holt Hutton described it as a 'hard church novel' and its author as a man of 'vigorous and somewhat menacing understanding' (Hutton, 127–8). More recently *Perversion*

has received attention as a significant example of the literature of the Victorian crisis of faith, one commentator characterizing it as 'a long and convincing argument by case history, rather than by sermonizing, for the liberal theological and practical views of Coleridge and Thomas Arnold' (Wolff, 283–4). Taken together with the article literature and sermons, the novel identifies Conybeare's own theological position as what he dubbed 'normal broad church', with more sympathy for Thomas Arnold and Julius Charles Hare than Benjamin Jowett and Rowland Williams. ARTHUR BURNS

**Sources** H. C. A. Conybeare, *Conybeare wills and administrations: part 4, 1563–1864* [1914] • W. J. Conybeare, 'W. J. Conybeare: "Church parties"', ed. R. A. Burns, *From Cranmer to Davidson: a Church of England miscellany*, ed. S. Taylor (1999) • R. L. Wolff, *Gains and losses: novels of faith and doubt in Victorian England* (1977) • *The Record* (3 Nov 1853) • *EdinR*, 104 (1856), 518–31 • R. H. Hutton, 'The hard church novel', *National Review*, 5 (July 1856), 127–46 • *The Guardian* (11 June 1856)
**Archives** NL Wales, Harpton Court MSS
**Wealth at death** £16,000; all left to widow: will, Conybeare, *Conybeare wills*

**Conyers family** (*per. c.*1375–*c.*1525), gentry, became the dominant family in Wensleydale in the fifteenth century, with their main residence at Hornby in the North Riding of Yorkshire; they eclipsed the other branches of the northern family of which they were a junior branch. Their success was partly due to genetics—the family was unusually fertile—but it was primarily due to a series of extremely good marriages. This was not just a matter of finding a wealthy heiress for the heir in each generation, but of establishing younger sons on the lands of more modest heiresses, so that by the early sixteenth century, when the heir was elevated to a barony, his success was underpinned by the establishment of junior members of the family throughout the north-east.

The founder of the Hornby line was **John Conyers** (*d.* in or before 1412), a lawyer in the service of John of Gaunt, duke of Lancaster, who married Margaret, the heir of Anthony St Quintin of Hornby, in the reign of Richard II. John's exact place in the wider Conyers pedigree remains uncertain. He was the younger brother of Sir Robert Conyers, who shared with him a grant of the custody of Skelton Castle in August 1403 and was later to be one of John's executors. Their father was also called Robert, and it is probably the three of them who are accused of an attack on the prior of Guisborough's estates, including Ormesby, in 1376. Robert Conyers *le filz* and John his brother were also involved, at about the same time, in a dispute with Philip Darcy, although this was evidently later resolved, and John acted as Darcy's attorney in 1398. Robert the father may have been a younger brother of John Conyers of Sockburn (*d.* 1395), whose heir was also, confusingly, called Robert but was never knighted—which distinguishes him from John of Hornby's father and brother. John of Hornby's mother is unknown. It was probably his father who, *c.*1373, was married to Alice, but this seems to have been a second marriage, with the sons of the first marriage already adult. The elder Robert married a third time, if he can be identified with the Sir Robert Conyers and Joan, his wife, who received papal letters of plenary remission in 1394. Sir Robert the son married Alina, who can probably be identified with the heir of William Percy of Kildale, who brought Ormesby into the family; their son was John Conyers of Ormesby (d. 1438). A third brother, William, was also the father of a son called John.

John Conyers of Hornby died in or just before 1412. He had acquired at least one further manor, that of Solberge-on-Wiske, which he had been granted by Michael de la Pole, earl of Suffolk, and which he used to make provision for his younger sons, Richard and Thomas. His heir was his son **Christopher Conyers** (d. 1461x5), who married Ellen, the daughter and coheir of Thomas Rolleston and his wife, Beatrice Haulay. The Rolleston inheritance in Yorkshire and Lincolnshire was divided between Ellen and her sister Margaret (the wife of John Tirwhit) in November 1415. Ellen died in 1433 and Christopher subsequently married Margaret, daughter of Robert Waddesley. With his two wives Christopher fathered twenty-five children, including twelve sons and, unusually, he made landed provision for a high proportion of the younger sons. To some extent he could afford to do this because his eldest son and heir, John [see below], had married an heiress—Margery (d. 1469), the younger coheir of Philip, Lord Darcy—but the endowment of the younger sons did not all come out of Christopher's own estate; he was also purchasing land extensively.

Other children were provided for by their marriages to heiresses—again testimony to Christopher's purchasing power, but also to his local standing, although he was never knighted (which allows him to be distinguished from his namesake who headed the Sockburn branch of the family from 1431) and was never sheriff. His influence presumably derived from his service to the junior Nevilles, who held Middleham in Wensleydale, an association that also helps to explain Christopher's appointment as bailiff of Richmondshire in June 1436, initiating a family connection with the administration of the shire that was to endure for the rest of the century. In March 1436 he was one of the feoffees to the use of the will of Richard Neville, earl of Salisbury, although his relatively lowly social status is reflected by his placing in the list.

Christopher's son and heir **Sir John Conyers** (d. 1490) had a considerably higher profile, even during his father's lifetime. He received his wife's share of the Darcy inheritance in May 1433, although the lands of the two Darcy dowagers did not come into his possession until the 1450s. In March 1442 John joined his father as bailiff of Richmondshire, by May 1447 had been knighted, and in November 1448 began his first term as sheriff of Yorkshire. Like his father, John was a Salisbury retainer, but, unlike the now elderly Christopher, John was drawn into the conflicts of the 1450s. He was with the duke of York and the Nevilles at the rout of Ludlow in 1459, and was attainted at the Coventry parliament. He escaped the worst consequences of attainder, however, by having put his wife's inheritance into the hands of trustees who included men acceptable to the Lancastrian regime—a

tactic adopted by Thomas Harrington at the same time. Christopher, meanwhile, first safeguarded himself by securing a pardon in December 1459 and then early the following year made an elaborate settlement to protect his land should he die while his heir was under attainder—a real risk since he must have turned seventy (having been old enough to act as one of his father's executors in 1412).

Christopher's anxieties proved groundless and he lived long enough to see the Yorkists triumph at Towton in 1461. He was dead by 1465, when an extant Middleham account shows John retained at £20 p.a. by Salisbury's heir, the earl of Warwick, but does not mention Christopher. For the rest of John's life he was to be the linchpin of the Middleham retinue—a role that in 1471 allowed him to move smoothly into the service of the new lord of Middleham, Richard, duke of Gloucester, after the defeat and death of the earl of Warwick, in whose earlier rebellions the Conyers family had been deeply implicated. The family thus retained its claim on the patronage and favour of the greatest northern nobleman—an important consideration when John was looking to advance not only the twelve children he had fathered, but also his younger siblings, such as Brian, his eldest half-brother, for whom he acquired Pinchingthorpe from the Sockburn branch of the family.

From a national perspective Sir John's career reached its climax in 1483, when the lord of Middleham became king. John was made a knight of the body and a knight of the Garter, but his importance to the new king (and, perhaps, his own inclinations) kept him in the north, and unlike many of Richard's other northern allies he did not move south to enjoy the spoils of royal patronage. His kinsmen, too, tended to remain based within Richmondshire—creating a slight sense of distance from the king's inner circle which perhaps stood them in good stead when Richard was defeated by Henry Tudor in 1485. As in 1471 the interests of the Conyers family and the new lord of Middleham coincided: one wanting lordship, the other needing to win over the Middleham connection. Barely a month after Bosworth, on 25 September, Sir John was among those commissioned to administer the oath of loyalty to the new king. In February 1486, when he was already a knight of the body again, John and his grandson and heir, **William Conyers** (1467/8–1524), whose father, another John, had died in 1469, were made bailiff, steward, and constable of Richmond, and constable of Middleham. Henry almost immediately had second thoughts about the constableship of Middleham, and granted it in May to Robert Carre, but the alliance of the Conyers and the crown was not seriously compromised. Although the disaffected continued to see Richmondshire as a potential source of support against Henry VII, the Conyers gave them no encouragement; indeed William helped to suppress the revolt of 1489.

When John died on 14 March 1490, William Conyers was the heir to two half-baronies. He inherited the Darcy lands from his grandfather, and in 1491 finally received his share of the Fauconberg lands after the death in December 1490 of his grandmother Joan Neville, widow of William Neville, earl of Kent, whose youngest daughter, Alice, had married John Conyers junior (d. 1469). William's own marriages reflect the contemporary awareness that he was heir to a great estate. His first wife, Mary, whom he married in 1479, was a daughter of John *Scrope, fifth Baron Scrope of Bolton; his second wife, Anne Neville, was a daughter of Ralph Neville, third earl of Westmorland (d. 1499). By 1505 William was being informally referred to as Lord Conyers, and he received a personal summons to the first parliament of Henry VIII in 1509. The elevation was a tribute to his personal standing, since his share of the two baronies was in each case that of the younger daughter, and the Strangways family, who had married the senior daughter in both cases, was not similarly promoted. The Conyers arms were azure, a maunch or; differenced.            ROSEMARY HORROX

**Sources** Chancery records · PRO · Report of the Deputy Keeper of the Public Records, 31–3 (1870–72) · CEPR letters · [J. Raine, J. Raine, and J. W. Clay], eds., Testamenta Eboracensia, 6 vols., SurtS, 4, 30, 45, 53, 79, 106 (1836–1902) · A. J. Pollard, North-eastern England during the Wars of the Roses: lay society, war and politics, 1450–1500 (1990) · A. J. Pollard, 'The Richmondshire community of gentry during the Wars of the Roses', Patronage, pedigree and power in later medieval England, ed. C. D. Ross (1979), 37–59 · R. Surtees, The history and antiquities of the county palatine of Durham, 4 vols. (1816–40) · R. Horrox, Richard III, a study of service, Cambridge Studies in Medieval Life and Thought, 4th ser., 11 (1989) · R. Somerville, History of the duchy of Lancaster, 1265–1603 (1953) · W. Brown, ed., Yorkshire deeds, 1, Yorkshire Archaeological Society, 39 (1909)

**Conyers, Christopher** (d. 1461×5). See under Conyers family (per. c.1375–c.1525).

**Conyers, John** (d. in or before 1412). See under Conyers family (per. c.1375–c.1525).

**Conyers, Sir John** (d. 1490). See under Conyers family (per. c.1375–c.1525).

**Conyers, Sir John** (c.1587–1664), royalist army officer, was the son and heir of Christopher Conyers, esquire, of Horden, in the parish of Easington, co. Durham, and his second wife, Anne, daughter of John Hedworth, esquire, of Harraton, co. Durham, and his wife, Jane. About 1603 John Conyers travelled to the Netherlands to pursue a military career, and about 1606 he married Frances, daughter of Thomas Groves, citizen of York. The marriage was acknowledged at Easington on 7 April 1608. His principal estates were at Horden, where his sons Richard and Christopher were baptized in 1617 and 1621. During the 1620s he returned to the wars in the Dutch service, and subsequently as lieutenant-colonel to Sir John Borlase in the Danish forces. He was created a baronet on 14 July 1628 and granted a pension of £100 per annum. In 1629 he was at Delft and in 1635 at Nijmegen, where he advised Edward Conway, second Viscount Conway, of Dutch current affairs, signing himself as Lord Conway's poor cousin.

By 1639 Conyers was settled at Breda, and was approached by Secretary Windebank and Viscount Conway to serve against the Scots covenanters. He was offered £5 a day as lieutenant-general of horse and governor of Berwick upon Tweed's garrison. Abandoning the Dutch service with great reluctance (he was still at The Hague on 10 March 1640), he did not arrive at Berwick until 25 June 1640 and by 1 August he was already lamenting his garrison's lack of pay. After the defeat at Newburn he skirmished with the Scots and prepared Berwick to withstand a siege, building a fort on the town's Northumberland side. In November the earl of Strafford commanded Conyers to return to York where he watched the army's discipline collapse and heard complaints of the conduct of his unpaid troopers. He confided to Viscount Conway on 13 February 1641: 'I would I had stayed at Breda' (CSP dom., 1640–41, 459).

In April 1641 Conyers discovered the first army plot, communicating his suspicions to the earl of Northumberland and Viscount Conway. Falsely believing the bishops to be instigators of the plot, he briefly supported root and branch abolition of the episcopacy. Although Russell describes him as a 'crusty old anti-Puritan' (Russell, 'The first army plot of 1641', 105), Conyers wrote to Viscount Conway on 28 May 1641: 'I fear so long as the Bishops have any power the Church of England will hang towards that of Rome, and will never be aright settled to the true service of God' (CSP dom., 1640–41, 588).

Conyers won the trust of the parliamentary opposition and it was rumoured that he would command the horse sent against the Irish rebels. On 11 February 1642, after sustained pressure from both houses, the king assented to Conyers's replacing Sir John Byron as lieutenant of the Tower of London. Clarendon believed him 'a soldier of very good estimation … having the reputation of one of the best officers of horse at that time' (Clarendon, Hist. rebellion, 3.168). Conyers declined service in parliament's armies, and on 17 July 1643 successfully petitioned for leave to attend his affairs in the Netherlands where he held estates through his wife. He surrendered custody of the Tower to Sir Robert Harley on 11 August 1643. In April 1645 he remained in the Netherlands and the House of Lords informed him that they intended no disrespect by appointing Colonel West in his place.

In September 1645 the Scots army was quartered on his estates, and he claimed to have lost goods worth £1500 to the soldiery. On 21 September parliament sequestered his estate. He offered parliament £100 as a pledge of goodwill, which was accepted only after he promised to lend a further £200. In August 1648 his composition fine was set at £651, and on 8 September following he was cleared of delinquency.

In 1656 Conyers's old friend's son Edward, now third Viscount Conway, was captured at sea by Ostenders and in August Conyers signed a bond for the payment of his ransom of 2400 gulden. After the Restoration, in November 1661, he began service as a deputy lieutenant for co. Durham. He died, probably in Easington, on 4 December 1664 and was buried two days later at Easington.

ANDREW J. HOPPER

**Sources** GEC, Baronetage, vol. 2 · CSP dom., 1628–31; 1635; 1639–47; 1656–7 · JHL, 4–7 (1628–45) · [R. Welford], ed., Records of the committee *for compounding, etc., with delinquent royalists in Durham and Northumberland during the civil war*, SurtS, 111 (1905) • C. Russell, *The fall of the British monarchies, 1637–1642* (1991) • C. Russell, 'The first army plot of 1641', *TRHS*, 5th ser., 38 (1988), 85–106 • R. Surtees, *The history and antiquities of the county palatine of Durham*, 1 (1816) • Clarendon, *Hist. rebellion* • *Seventh report*, HMC, 6 (1879) • *The correspondence of John Cosin D.D., lord bishop of Durham*, ed. [G. Ornsby], 2, SurtS, 55 (1872) • Venn, *Alum. Cant.*, 1/1 • *Durham monuments, or, The shields of arms, effigies and inscriptions in the churches, castles and halls of the county of Durham*, Newcastle upon Tyne records committee, 5 (1925) • J. Foster, ed., *Pedigrees recorded at the visitations of the county palatine of Durham* (1887)

**Archives** BL, Add. MS 5497, fol. 69 • PRO, State Papers 16/477/26, 12, 54; 16/480/73 • PRO, State Papers 77/29/544

**Wealth at death** allegedly had £477 p.a. before war (1642?); £1500 in goods and stock claimed lost to armies requisitioning: Welford, ed., *Records*, 176–7

**Conyers, John** (c.1633–1694), apothecary and archaeologist, was the eldest son of Edward Conyers (*b.* 1590) and his wife, Jane Clarke. The parents had married in London in January 1632 at the church of St Faith, the ruins of which lie under St Paul's Cathedral; however, by the time John Conyers was bound apprentice in August 1649 for eight years to Robert Phelps, citizen and apothecary of London, his parents were living at Little Bowden in Leicestershire. In February 1658 Conyers was examined and found proficient in his trade, and he gained his freedom of the London Society of Apothecaries. He never rose to great eminence in the society, but nevertheless paid his £15 livery fine in December 1667. On 13 February 1666 at the church of St Clement Danes he married Mary Glisson, niece of the eminent physician Francis *Glisson. They had eight daughters and two sons, but only two daughters survived childhood.

Conyers was one of the many apothecaries who stayed in London during the plague period of 1665 to 1666. He had his own specific remedies for the infection and he advertised them in his booklet, *Direction for the Prevention and Cure of the Plague, Fitted for the Poorer Sort* [n.d.]. After the great fire of 1666 Conyers was to be found at the White Lyon, Fleet Street. There he was innovative enough to prepare an artificial mineral water, 'an essence made of the mineral which giveth the virtue to Tunbridge waters' (memoranda book). Conyers's pharmaceutical work was of great interest to him and was often used in his attempts to explain the phenomena of magnetism, electricity, fermentation, and fossilization. He experimented with the recently discovered phosphorus made by the chemist Godfrey Hanckwitz, and he was a frequent guest at the meetings of the Royal Society. He numbered among his friends such eminent people as Robert Hooke and Thomas Tompion, and he was on excellent terms with Jonathan Goddard, lecturer in physic at Gresham College. Goddard was a determined antagonist of apothecaries who practised medicine, which suggests that Conyers confined himself to running his pharmacy, making most of his own medicines and dispensing physicians' prescriptions.

Conyers participated eagerly in contemporary intellectual activities, offering solutions to mathematical problems, such as how to trisect an angle. He was keenly interested in meteorology and made observations with his thermoscopes, irrespective of the time of day. A practical man, he devised a number of inventions, details of which were published in the *Transactions* of the Royal Society: a hygroscope, which the royal astronomer John Flamsteed borrowed in order to copy; an ear trumpet; and a pump, which Conyers claimed and Glisson and Goddard confirmed was used with great success on the new channel of the Fleet River.

However, Conyers is best remembered for his work in archaeology. The rebuilding of London after the great fire gave him the opportunity to gather 'antiquities', but he was a discerning and well-intentioned collector. His treasures were described in detail and compared with those in other collections, such as that of Elias Ashmole. Conyers understood the importance of the association of finds and he was the first person to suggest that the flint hand-axe was a weapon fashioned by humans. Even more importantly he realized the value of stratigraphy. He noted that small fragments of coloured stones were found at the east end of St Paul's Cathedral at a depth of 15 feet, and that there remained some Roman pottery even lower,

> which tells me this laying so low & the Roman pott 6 or 8 or 10 foot deeper that as tyme passed awaye I might see the epochs or beginnings of things & in these various heights of ground poynt & show with my finger the Romans concernes lay deepest, then higher those of more recent or fresher concerne. (memoranda book, fol. 109*b*)

The *Athenian Mercury* of 21 November 1691 relates that his 'curiosities' could be viewed by the public, and it praised the range of materials to be seen.

By 1693 Conyers's health was failing and the Society of Apothecaries noted that he had 'left off trade'. He died survived by his wife, and was buried on 8 April 1694 at St Bride's, Fleet Street. His will was not found but it is known from the 1695 edition of Camden's *Britannia* that Dr John Woodward was already in possession of most of his collection.      JUANITA BURNBY

**Sources** memoranda book, BL, Sloane MS 958, fols. 105*r*–142*r* • medicines and prescriptions, BL, Sloane MS 1650 • archaeological, BL, Sloane MSS 61, 816, 839, 852, 916, 937, 919, 2031 • archaeological, BL, Harley MS 5953 • *Phil. Trans. Roy. Soc.*, 12 (1677–8), 888–90, 1027–9; no. 129 [pump; ear trumpet; hygroscope] • Society of Apothecaries minutes, GL, MSS 8200/1, 8200/2 • 'Inhabitants in St Bride's, 1666', GL, MS 14819 • R. G. [R. Gough], *British topography*, [new edn], 1 (1780), 718–20 • *Athenian Mercury* (21 Nov 1691) • T. D. Whittet, *The apothecaries in the Great Plague of London, 1665* (1970), 17 [advert for plague medicine] • G. E. Cokayne and E. A. Fry, eds., *Calendar of marriage licences issued by the faculty office, 1632–1714*, British RS, 33 (1905) • J. Burnby, 'John Conyers, London's first archaeologist', *Trans. L. & M. A. S.*, 35 (1984), 63–80 • parish register (burial), London, St Bride's, 8 April 1694

**Archives** GL, Society of Apothecaries minutes | BL, Sloane MSS, Harley MSS

**Conyers, Richard** (1725–1786), Church of England clergyman, was born at Lastingham, Yorkshire, in February 1725. He was educated at the free grammar school, Coxwold, and was admitted as a pensioner to Jesus College, Cambridge, on 2 July 1742. He graduated BA in 1745, MA in 1749, and LLD in 1767. He was ordained deacon and served as curate of Kirby Misperton in Yorkshire from 1745 to 1750; he was ordained priest by the archbishop of York on

21 September 1755. He was rector of Helmsley from 1756 to 1775 and curate of Kirkdale from 1756 to 1762. He was converted to evangelicalism not through personal contacts but by reading. Despairing about the meaning of the 'unsearchable riches of Christ' (Ephesians 3: 8) he found salvation on Christmas day 1758 by juxtaposing 'without shedding of blood there is no remission' (Hebrews 9: 20) with 'the blood of Jesus Christ cleanseth us from all sin' (I John 2: 7). It may have been his evangelicalism that inspired him to take a chaplaincy to the navy in 1761 but his ties with Yorkshire were reinforced by his reappointment to Kirby Misperton as rector, alongside his living at Helmsley, in 1763.

In 1767 Conyers was one of the three clergymen consulted by William Cowper and Mrs Mary Unwin about where they should settle after her husband's death. In his poem 'Truth' Cowper wrote:

'Tis open, and ye cannot enter,—why?
Because ye will not, Conyers would reply—
And he says much that many may dispute,
And cavil at it with ease, but none refute.
(ll.357–60)

In 1767 Conyers joined two campaigns of open-air field preaching with, first, Selina Hastings, countess of Huntingdon, and, later, George Whitefield; both were prominent Calvinists, whom he supported. John Wesley wished Conyers to maintain the movement's unity, saying that he was 'a deeply serious man who would fain reconcile Arminians and Calvinists' (Jago, 169), and Conyers seemed conciliatory, telling Wesley in 1763 that 'As far as the doctrine you teach has come to my knowledge I know not one part to which I could not subscribe, both with hand and heart' (ibid.). The following year, however, when Wesley visited him, his housekeeper told him briefly that her master was not available.

Though his preaching was hampered by a perpetual idiosyncratic, nervous delivery a hearer described Conyers's sermons as 'aweful, earnest, and movingly pathetic, directing men to repentance and pleading the mercies of God' (Walsh, chap. 4) but Robert Hay Drummond, archbishop of York, who opposed Calvinism, differed. Having heard a sermon by Conyers during his visitation of the diocese in 1764 he thought that it was 'compounded of gloom and absurdity' (Walsh, 10) and told him: 'If you go on preaching such stuff, you will drive all your parish mad. Were you to inculcate the morality of Socrates, you would do more good than canting about the new birth' (Seymour, 2.280).

Conyers described his work in a letter to the archbishop after the visitation. He held only one Sunday service at Kirby Misperton but a service every weekday for the larger parish of Helmsley, as well as one on Sunday, and he followed George Herbert's example in urging his people to pray in the fields when they heard the church bell. He concentrated his pastoral efforts on this parish. Since its scattered hamlets were over 2 miles from the church he acted like his contemporary William Grimshaw, in the similar Yorkshire parish of Haworth, by holding prayer meetings and scriptural expositions for the parishioners, who welcomed him 'readily and cheerfully' (Jago, 104) and, avoiding 'repetitions and plainness' (ibid., 103), by catechizing the children and young people on Saturday and Sunday evenings. He had a monthly communion service with about 450 communicants, and in 1767 he encouraged congregational singing by compiling a hymn book to replace the metrical psalms and paraphrases in worship.

In 1765 Conyers married Jane (bap. 1718), sister of John Thornton and widow of Nathaniel Knipe; she died in 1774. The following year Thornton appointed Conyers rector of St Paul's Church, Deptford. Conyers accepted the position but was so upset that he could not deliver his farewell sermon in Helmsley church, and he departed at midnight, perhaps because his weeping Yorkshire parishioners had declared 'that they would lay themselves along the road, and if he was determined to leave them, his carriage should drive over them' (Dews, 226).

At Deptford Conyers converted the rectory's coach house and stables into a meeting-place where, four times a week, he gave well-attended lectures, mainly on scriptural exposition; he also preached every Sunday in the church, despite an evening lecturer who contradicted what he had said in the morning. He was now respected as a spiritual adviser and was visited by William Romaine, Henry Venn, George Pattrick, and other evangelical clergymen.

On the morning of Sunday 23 April 1786 Conyers had an apoplectic fit while preaching. As he was being taken away he said, 'I am going to my master', and he died that afternoon. He was buried at his church; his funeral sermon was preached by Thomas Scott and subsequently published.                                   LEONARD W. COWIE

Sources  G. R. Balleine, *A history of the evangelical party in the Church of England* (1908) · J. Jago, *Aspects of the Georgian church* (1997) · J. D. Walsh, 'The Yorkshire evangelicals in the eighteenth century', PhD diss., U. Cam., 1956 · Venn, *Alum. Cant.* · J. Walsh and S. Taylor, 'Introduction: the church and Anglicanism in the "long" eighteenth century', *The Church of England, c.1689–c.1833*, ed. J. Walsh, C. Haydon, and S. Taylor (1993), 1–64 · A. Pollard, 'Conyers, Richard', *The Blackwell dictionary of evangelical biography, 1730–1860*, ed. D. M. Lewis (1995) · N. Dews, *The history of Deptford*, 2nd edn (1884) · [A. C. H. Seymour], *The life and times of Selina, countess of Huntingdon* (1841) · L. E. Elliott-Binns, *The early evangelicals* (1953) · A. J. Dunkin, *History of the county of Kent* (1855) · will, PRO, PROB 11/1142, sig. 269
**Wealth at death**  estate bequeathed to sister; annuities of £15 p.a. to Martin Hawkins, £7 p.a. to Anne, wife of Robert Hudson of Walworth, £40 p.a. to son-in-law: will, PRO, PROB 11/1142, sig. 269

**Conyers, William**, first Baron Conyers (1467/8–1524). *See under* Conyers family (*per. c.*1375–*c.*1525).

**Conyngham, Albert**. *See* Denison, Albert, first Baron Londesborough (1805–1860).

**Conyngham** [*née* Denison], **Elizabeth**, Marchioness Conyngham (1769–1861), royal mistress, was born in London, the eldest of the three known children of Joseph *Denison (*c.*1726–1806), cloth merchant and banker, and his wife, Elizabeth Butler. Little is known of her early life, but her father made a fortune in banking, and in 1787 purchased an estate in Surrey and another near Scarborough.

independence, Conyngham took little further active interest in politics, although he generally supported the tory and ministerial party in the Lords. He is said to have owed his elevation to the marquessate in 1816 to his wife's relationship with the prince regent.

The Conynghams were neither particularly wealthy nor particularly well connected in the early years of their marriage. In the exclusive, not to say snobbish, circles of the aristocracy, Elizabeth's mercantile origins were always held against her, and she was generally considered rather vulgar. According to Creevey, Lady Conyngham 'owed her first introduction to Dublin high life exclusively to Lady Glengall' (Maxwell, 371). She was, however, accounted a beauty, and acquired lovers and admirers including Lord Ponsonby and Tsar Nicholas I. (She was on the continent during the peace talks of 1814–15.) She had five children who survived to adulthood, the second son becoming second Marquess Conyngham and the third, Albert *Denison, succeeding to her brother's fortune and being created Baron Londesborough.

According to the duke of Wellington, Elizabeth Conyngham had decided as early as 1806 to become the mistress of George, prince of Wales (Oman, 191). There were rumours that she was becoming his favourite by 1819, but she did not become *maîtresse en titre* until the summer of 1820, when, according to Lady Jerningham, she finally ousted her predecessor: 'Lady Hertford's day is closed and Lady Conyngham is now the meteor' (Melville, 277). She was the latest (and, it proved, the last) of the series of women with whom *George IV fell in love. His passion and devotion are undisputed, although even contemporaries doubted whether the relationship was physically consummated. Caricaturists and wits found the idea of the fat, ageing king and his large, ageing mistress hilarious, and the king's behaviour in public fed their humour. He was besotted with his new companion, and 'sits kissing her hand with a look of the most devoted submission' (Surtees, 155). During his attempt to divorce Queen Caroline in 1820 he could not keep company with Lady Conyngham, and was in consequence 'bored and lonely' (Lady Cowper, 17 Oct 1820, quoted in Smith, *Queen on Trial*, 122). His determination to exclude his wife from the coronation was matched by his desire to have Lady Conyngham close at hand, and throughout the ceremony he 'was continually nodding & winking at Ly. Conyngham & sighing & making eyes at her', compounding his behaviour at one point by taking off a diamond brooch and kissing it at her. Some, like Mrs Arbuthnot, found his behaviour disgusting, but the more charitable Lady Cowper, writing on 20 July 1821, thought that the king had struggled to get through the service, and that 'a cheering draught in the shape of a look from Ly. C. … revived him like Magic or Ether' (Smith, 185). A peculiarity of the affair was that Lady Conyngham pined for the respectability her situation as a mistress fundamentally denied her, and affected great piety. She 'seemed to think that by the forms of religion she could atone for everything else', said the duke of Wellington (Oman, 204).

Lady Conyngham, who quickly earned the nicknames

**Elizabeth Conyngham, Marchioness Conyngham (1769–1861),** by Sir Thomas Lawrence, 1802

Her brother, William Joseph *Denison, went into the family banking business, and her sister, Anna Maria, married in 1793 Sir Robert Wenlock, later created Baron Wenlock. The following year, on 5 July, Elizabeth married Henry Conyngham.

**Henry Conyngham**, first Marquess Conyngham (1766–1832), was born on 26 December 1766, the elder of the twin sons of Francis Pierrepoint Burton, second Baron Conyngham (*d.* 1787) (who took the surname Conyngham in 1781 on succeeding to the title), and his wife, Elizabeth Clements (*d.* 1814/1816), sister of the first earl of Leitrim. He succeeded his father as the third Baron Conyngham in 1787, and was created Viscount Conyngham in the Irish peerage in 1789. In 1794 he raised the Londonderry regiment, and was made lieutenant-colonel that August; for this action, and for his influence as a magistrate during the upheavals in Ireland in the 1790s, he was created Viscount Mountcharles and Earl Conyngham, again in the Irish peerage, on 5 November 1797. In the Irish House of Lords he was a vigorous supporter of the Act of Union between Britain and Ireland; when it was passed in 1801 he was elected one of the first Irish representative peers, was made a knight of St Patrick, and received £15,000 in cash for his close borough of Killybegs in the Irish House of Commons. Having thus benefited considerably from the sale of his country's

La Regnante and the Vice Queen, wielded great influence over the king. Although thought to be whiggishly inclined she had no political ambition, and her power was wielded exclusively to further the personal and financial ambitions of herself and her family. Lord Conyngham was given a United Kingdom peerage in 1821, was sworn of the privy council, and appointed lord steward of the household, and captain, constable, and lieutenant of Windsor Castle, while their second son was appointed first groom of the chamber and master of the robes. The entire family lived with the king (although not directly under his roof) and at his expense, and Lady Conyngham was the recipient of constant gifts of jewels, including some sapphires from the crown jewels. Lady Granville was shown her Christmas presents in 1823:

> A magnificent cross, seized from the expiring body of a murdered bishop in the island of Scio. An almanack, gold with flowers embossed on it of precious stones. A gold melon, which upon being touched by a spring falls into compartments like the quarters of an orange, each containing different perfumes.   (Surtees, 178)

But although she had no real political ambition, Lady Conyngham's feelings and actions had political repercussions. In May 1821 her attempt to have her sons' tutor, Charles Sumner, appointed a canon of Windsor almost caused a ministerial crisis, with the prime minister, Lord Liverpool, threatening to resign if the king went ahead with the appointment. The refusal of the wives of the king's ministers to receive Lady Conyngham worsened the relationship between king and government; in particular, her feud with Lady Castlereagh (wife of the foreign secretary) caused constant political difficulties, especially concerning projected royal visits abroad. She also disliked the keeper of the privy purse, Sir Benjamin Bloomfield, and was instrumental in his removal. With his successor, Sir William Knighton, she struck up a mutually beneficial alliance.

Having achieved her ambition, Lady Conyngham was frequently dissatisfied with her lot. The company of the querulous, over-dependent king, who was frequently unwell, grew wearisome, and she was kept in her place only by renewed gifts of jewels. The king too grew bored, but he disliked change and with Lady Conyngham he had the comfort of a habit, and rumours of the favourite's fall from grace were always premature. George IV's death early in the morning of 26 June 1830 brought her reign to a rapid conclusion. She spent the remainder of the night packing, and by the following morning had left Windsor for her brother's house, *en route* for Paris. Society believed that she was accompanied by 'wagonloads' of plunder; but although the king had bequeathed her all his plate and jewels (some of which, as family heirlooms, were not his to give) she refused the entire legacy.

Lord Conyngham, who was made a general in 1830, broke his staff of office at the king's funeral and held no further royal office. He died at his house in Hamilton Place, Piccadilly, on 28 December 1832 and was buried in the family vault at St Mary's Church, Patrixbourne, Kent.

Following the death of the king, Lady Conyngham virtually disappears from the historical record. Lady Granville notes that Paris was agog to see her in August 1831, and found her to be 'still beautiful' (Surtees, 246). The duke of Wellington was still speaking darkly of her to his friends in the later 1830s, but thereafter the tongues that had wagged for so long fell silent. Lady Conyngham herself lived for another thirty years, enjoying the sometimes bitter fruits of her labours, dying at the age of ninety-two at her home, Bifrons, Patrixbourne, near Canterbury, Kent, on 11 October 1861. She had outlived all but one of her children. Her estate was proved at under £200,000: she left her real estate to her only surviving son, Francis Nathaniel, along with her diamonds, pearls, and emeralds, which she desired should become family heirlooms. She made provision for her granddaughters out of the £30,000 left to her by her banker brother, and left them her other jewels. Although Lady Conyngham was *persona non grata* at Queen Victoria's court, her son, the second marquess, had been lord chamberlain to William IV, and as such brought news of her accession to the young queen and retained his post until 1839. His daughter, Jane, Lady Churchill, was one of the queen's ladies of the bedchamber and among her closest friends.                                      K. D. REYNOLDS

**Sources**  E. A. Smith, *George IV* (1999) · J. Prebble, *The king's jaunt: George IV in Scotland, August 1822* (1988) · *The Greville memoirs, 1814–1860*, ed. L. Strachey and R. Fulford, 8 vols. (1938) · L. Melville, *Regency ladies*, 2nd edn (New York, [n.d., 1927?]) · B. Pool, ed., *The Croker papers, 1808–1857*, new edn (1967) · E. A. Smith, *A queen on trial* (1993) · *The Creevey papers*, ed. H. Maxwell, 3rd edn (1905) · V. Surtees, *A second self* (1990) · C. Oman, *The Gascoyne heiress* (1968) · *The private letters of Princess Lieven to Prince Metternich, 1820–1826*, ed. P. Quennell (1937) · *The letters of Lady Palmerston*, ed. T. Lever (1957) · E. Longford [E. H. Pakenham, countess of Longford], *Wellington*, 2: *Pillar of state* (1972) · *Wellington and his friends: letters of the first duke of Wellington*, ed. seventh duke of Wellington [G. Wellesley] (1965) · *The Lieven–Palmerston correspondence, 1828–1856*, ed. and trans. Lord Sudley [A. P. J. C. J. Gore] (1943) · Burke, *Peerage* (1901) · will · d. cert. · *CGPLA Eng. & Wales* (1861) · IGI

**Archives**  NL Ire., corresp. [Henry Conyngham] · NRA, priv. coll., corresp. and papers [Henry Conyngham] | BL, corresp. with R. Peel, Add. MSS 40221–40400 [Henry Conyngham] · BL, letters to Prince Lieven, Add. MS 47258 [Henry Conyngham] · RA, letters to T. Lawrence [Henry Conyngham]

**Likenesses**  T. Lawrence, oils, 1802, Birmingham Museums and Art Gallery [*see illus.*] · T. Lawrence, oils, repro. in Prebble, *The king's jaunt*; priv. coll.

**Wealth at death**  under £200,000: probate, 10 Dec 1861, *CGPLA Eng. & Wales*

**Conyngham, Sir Gerald Ponsonby Lenox-** (1866–1956), geodesist, was born on 21 August 1866 at Springhill, Moneymore, Ireland, the seventh of eleven children of Sir William Fitzwilliam Lenox-Conyngham (1824–1906) and his wife, Laura Calvert (*d.* 1917), fourth daughter of George Arbuthnot, of Elderslie, Surrey, founder of the firm of Arbuthnot & Co. of Madras, India. When Lenox-Conyngham was ten years old the family moved to Edinburgh, where he attended the Edinburgh Academy. At seventeen he entered the Royal Military Academy at Woolwich, and in 1885 passed out first in his batch with the sword of honour and the Pollock medal. As a lieutenant in the Royal Engineers he spent two years at the School of

Military Engineering at Chatham before being posted to India. In 1889 he applied for a transfer to the survey of India and joined the trigonometrical branch, where he began his career as a surveyor and geodesist.

The observations of the survey included an extensive series of measurements of longitude along parallels of latitude intended to determine the curvature of the geoid in a direction perpendicular to that given by the older observations of latitude. These longitudes though determined with great care showed puzzling discrepancies. In 1889 Sidney Burrard set out to find the cause of the discrepancies. Lenox-Conyngham was appointed his assistant, so beginning the long collaboration and friendship which was one of the main influences of Lenox-Conyngham's scientific interests. An explanation was found for the discrepancies, and satisfactory measurements obtained. On 15 November 1890 he married Elsie Margaret (d. 1918), daughter of Surgeon-General Sir Alexander Frederick Bradshaw who became head of the Army Medical Services in India. They had one daughter.

In 1894 Burrard and Lenox-Conyngham undertook a redetermination of the longitude of Karachi relative to Greenwich by using the land telegraph line across Europe and Persia. The results were most satisfactory: a redetermination thirty years later using wireless signals gave a longitude differing by only 0.02 seconds from that which Burrard and Lenox-Conyngham had found.

Burrard next examined the observations of latitude acquired by the survey since the beginning of the century, and concluded that the anomalies in north India in zones parallel to the mountains could be ascribed to a dense subterranean mass to the south of the Gangetic plain. The most direct method of locating such a hidden mass is by measuring the acceleration due to gravity, using pendulum apparatus. Burrard and Lenox-Conyngham purchased and modified a recently designed apparatus with four half-second pendulums. From 1903 to 1908 Lenox-Conyngham undertook a series of gravity measurements in India which was perhaps his most important contribution to science.

By 1931 Lenox-Conyngham had discovered that, far from a great excess of mass where the hidden range was supposed to be, there was instead a defect of mass along the foot of the Himalayas and for some distance from them. This strip of negative gravity anomalies and deficient density was the first identification of a phenomenon which was subsequently found to occur widely, particularly on the outer edges of island arcs. The work of Burrard and Lenox-Conyngham on the gravity anomalies in India revived interest in this branch of geodesy by showing that its results have a wider interest than the mere study and reduction of errors in surveying.

In 1912 Lenox-Conyngham became superintendent of the trigonometrical survey and in 1914 a colonel. In 1918 he was elected FRS and in 1919 he was made a knight bachelor. His wife was made OBE in 1918.

Lenox-Conyngham left India in 1920 and a few months after his return to England was asked to join the committee for promoting the study of geodesy in Cambridge. The university could provide no funds, but Trinity College offered a praelectorship in geodesy. This was offered to Lenox-Conyngham who took up residence in Cambridge and in 1921 was made a fellow of Trinity. In the following year the university created a readership in geodesy for him. With almost no financial support from the university he started to teach the basics of geodesy to a small group of undergraduates and later also to officers sent to Cambridge from many colonial survey departments. Assisted by Sir Horace Darwin he designed a set of pendulum apparatus which was constructed by Darwin's Cambridge Instrument Company as an improvement on the one used in India. It employed two invar pendulums swinging in opposite phase within an airtight chamber. Lenox-Conyngham's one-man school of geodesy, eventually the department of geodesy and geophysics, then extended its work to include seismology and geothermal measurements where Lenox-Conyngham had little previous knowledge. But his interest was keen and his encouragement indefatigable. He used his influence extensively in procuring funds and apparatus. He also travelled widely, visiting scientific conferences all over the world. In 1925 he took the opportunity of a visit to Queensland to tour the Great Barrier Reef and consider the evolution of Pacific islands and reefs in relation to isostasy.

During the Second World War Lenox-Conyngham continued his lectures to rather depleted audiences although the experimental work in the department ceased. After the war when the department reopened great advantage was taken of the new techniques, in which Lenox-Conyngham took a keen interest even after his retirement in 1947.

Lenox-Conyngham had two complete and successful careers, one in India, the other in Cambridge. The master of Trinity, G. M. Trevelyan, said: 'He is a scholar, a soldier, and a great public servant, and he looks all three' (The Times, 29 Oct 1956, 14a). As he grew older, Lenox-Conyngham's commanding presence became even more dignified and impressive. He had a rigid attitude to matters of the conventions in which he had been brought up, combined with an extraordinary openness of mind in matters of science. He was always delighted to see new methods of physics and engineering applied to the problems on which he had worked earlier. His genuine interest, friendliness, and lack of pretence, made him remarkably successful as head of a department in which most of the staff were forty years his junior. Lenox-Conyngham died at Addenbrooke's Hospital, Cambridge, on 27 October 1956, not long after his ninetieth birthday. His funeral took place in Trinity College chapel.

MARY MUNRO, rev. ANITA McCONNELL

Sources E. Bullard, Memoirs FRS, 3 (1957), 129–40 · The Times (29 Oct 1956), 14a · The Times (1 Nov 1956), 12c · The Times (5 Nov 1956), 12g · 'Electro-telegraph longitude operations, Chapter 5: selection of stations and … narrative', Great trigonometrical survey of India, 19 vols. (1870–1910), vol. 17 (1901) · J. de Graaff-Hunter, Nature, 178 (1956), 1211–12 · G. Lenox-Conyngham, 'The Cambridge pendulum apparatus', GJ, 73 (1929), 326–41, esp. 334–41 [discussion] · Burke, Gen. Ire. · CGPLA Eng. & Wales (1957)

**Archives** CUL, diaries and papers | Bodl. Oxf., corresp. with Sir Aurel Stein · CAC Cam., corresp. with Sir Edward Bullard, etc. · CAC Cam., corresp. with A. V. Hill · PRO NIre., letters to Janet Hearle, D1598
**Likenesses** W. Stoneman, photograph, 1921, NPG · W. Stoneman, photograph, 1932, NPG · H. Lamb, charcoal and chalk drawing, 1947, Trinity Cam.
**Wealth at death** £34,965 12s. 6d.: probate, 18 March 1957, CGPLA Eng. & Wales

**Conyngham, Henry**, first Marquess Conyngham (1766–1832). *See under* Conyngham, Elizabeth, Marchioness Conyngham (1769–1861).

**Conyngham, William Burton** (1733–1796), politician and improver, was born William Burton in 1733, the second son of Francis Burton (1696–1743), politician and landowner, of Buncraggy, co. Clare, Ireland, and Mary Conyngham (d. 1737), the only surviving daughter of Major-General Henry Conyngham and the sister of Henry, first Earl Conyngham (1705–1781). His early years are obscure, but the close relationship he enjoyed with Earl Conyngham as an adult suggests that his uncle became his guardian following the death of his father on 20 March 1743. He was educated at Queens' College, Cambridge, from 1750 and at Lincoln's Inn (1753), but he entered the army in preference to the law. He was commissioned captain in 1759, and, following promotion to the rank of lieutenant-colonel in 1766, demonstrated his organizational skill by devising and overseeing a scheme to transform the 12th regiment of dragoons into light cavalry. This was his main achievement as a soldier as not long afterwards differences with the Irish administration over the allocation of his regiment's 'non-effective fund' contributed to his decision in 1769 to seek permission to sell his commission (Bartlett, 7). The other contributory factor was political.

Burton had entered the Irish House of Commons in 1761 as MP for Lord Conyngham's borough of Newtownlimavady. Since his uncle spent most of his time abroad, Burton looked after his interest in the constituency and his extensive properties in counties Meath and Donegal. However, the rejection by the lord lieutenant, Lord Townshend, of his uncle's 'insatiable' demands for preferment, which Lord Conyngham justified on account of 'the great services of his family', so discommoded the self-important peer that he directed his nephew 'to throw up his commission' and to go into opposition (Bartlett, 15, 29, 105). Burton was not averse to taking the 'patriot' stand his uncle advised because of his own differences with Townshend, but he was not able to dispose of his commission until 1774, by which time his standing with the Irish administration had greatly improved. Described by one Dublin Castle insider in 1773 as 'a sensible man' and 'a friend to government in all reasonable measures', his appointment as aide-de-camp to Lord Harcourt and his zealous support of the administration in the House of Commons paved the way for his appointment as commissioner and comptroller of the barrack board and subsequently as teller of the exchequer (Bodkin, 204). Government office provided Burton with a substantial income, and since he had displaced his elder brother, Francis

Pierpoint Burton, in his uncle's affections the anticipation was that he would be the primary beneficiary from Lord Conyngham's will. William Burton certainly acted as if this was so during the 1770s. In the continuing absence of his uncle he made the Conyngham seat at Slane his home, and, expanding on the partnership he reached with the local landowner Blayney Townley Balfour in 1763, which resulted in the construction of the largest flour mill in the country, he conceived plans for further development. Arthur Young, who reported approvingly in his tour of Ireland on the substantial sums Burton expended on the improvement of Slane and its environs, indicated that he had a considerable impact. In common with many of a similar outlook, Burton was convinced that Ireland had the potential to become a wealthy and flourishing economy if it made the most of its resources.

Although instinctively an economic patriot, Burton was less enamoured of the political agenda of the patriots in the Irish House of Commons in the late 1770s and early 1780s. None the less, he was so far persuaded of the merits of 'free trade' that he broke with the Irish administration to support the Commons' call for the removal of the restrictions on Ireland's freedom to trade in October 1779. His decision was significant because of his high public standing arising out of the perception of him as 'a very honorable and pleasing man and a great promoter of public improvements' (Sayles, 238). His reputation in this respect was dramatically enhanced following Earl Conyngham's bequest to him of a life interest in the extensive Conyngham estates in counties Meath and Donegal on his death in April 1781 with the proviso that Burton and his brother Francis, who became by special remainder Baron Conyngham of Mountcharles and the heir to properties in Limerick and England, changed their name to Conyngham. William Conyngham, as Burton was known thereafter, was now at liberty to set his ambitious plans in train to improve the Slane residence and estate. The challenge facing him in co. Donegal was greater, but he had already determined that 'if I should be in possession of any of that property, I would dedicate part of it to the improvement of that coast and raise if possible a commercial spirit in its inhabitants' (BL, Add. MS 40180, fol. 38). The key, he concluded, lay in the rich shoals of fish that were then to be found on the Donegal coast, and with their exploitation in mind he ensured that fisheries legislation enacted in 1781 included specific provisions to promote the construction of 'stores and buildings for … curing and preserving … fish and houses for accommodating the people employed in the said business' (21 Geo. III, c.37), and shortly afterwards he 'began building a town' for this purpose. He also sought to tempt 'intelligent farmers' to move from England with the promise of land 'at a very trifling rent' so that 'the land in the neighbourhood [should] be rendered capable of furnishing subsistence to the inhabitants' (BL, Add. MS 35126, fol. 246). His efforts were interrupted by illness, which caused him to spend much of 1783 and 1784 in Iberia, but on his return he expanded his plans for the development of his Donegal estate and he secured parliamentary approval in 1785 for a scheme to build a fishing town on Inismacadurn Island and a road network through the remote Rosses region that would be funded equally by himself and the exchequer. This inaugurated a phase of intense regional development, as dockyards, quays, salt and rope works, and other buildings were constructed on Inismacadurn, which was renamed Rutland Island in honour of the then lord lieutenant. Conyngham's schemes did not meet with unanimous approval, but his doughty defence of his plan against the criticisms of local rivals and powerful Cork mercantile interests overcame all opposition, until disappointing herring shoals in the late 1780s undermined the economic basis of the undertaking. Conyngham sought to protect his initiative by seeking additional official backing, and by devising a scheme for a further major infusion of capital, but nothing came of either, and by the early 1790s he had to reconcile himself to the fact that the £20,000 provided by parliament and the more than £30,000 raised on the Conyngham estates had not produced the improvement in the north-west he had aspired to bring about.

Conyngham complemented his schemes for improvement with the promotion of antiquarian endeavour. Through his membership of the antiquities committee of the Dublin Society, his presidency of the Hibernian Antiquarian Society, and his founding membership of the Royal Irish Academy he played an important facilitative role in the advancement of antiquarian scholarship. He made the impressive personal collection of drawings of ruined historic buildings and antiquities that he commissioned from such figures as Gabriel Berenger, Angelo Bigari, John James Barralet, and Austin Cooper available to scholars such as Francis Grose, Edward Ledwich, and Charles Vallancey to illustrate their publications. He wrote a number of antiquarian papers himself based upon his observations and excavations in Iberia. He also contributed significantly to the development of Dublin. He was a patron of the architect James Gandon and an active member of the Wide Streets commission, as a result of which the new road linking Park Gate and Island Bridge put in place in the mid-1780s was named after him. He died, unmarried, at home in Harcourt Place, Dublin, on 31 May 1796, following which the lands he had had for life passed to his nephew, Viscount Conyngham. He was buried in Slane. Though politically inclined towards conservatism (significantly, he spoke against Catholic enfranchisement in 1793), William Burton Conyngham, as he is now known, was otherwise a man of such energy and vision that he was deserving of the accolade of 'superior patriot' bestowed on him by Charles O'Conor (*Letters*, 2.232). JAMES KELLY

**Sources** T. Bartlett, ed., *Macartney in Ireland, 1768–72* (1978) · C. E. F. Trench, 'William Burton Conyngham, 1733–96', *Journal of the Royal Society of Antiquaries of Ireland*, 115 (1985), 40–63 · C. E. F. Trench, 'William Burton Conyngham, "profound scholar and antiquary", 1733–96', *Ríocht na Midhe*, 8 (1987), 113–28 · J. Kelly, 'William Burton Conyngham and the north-west fishery of the 18th century', *Journal of the Royal Society of Antiquaries of Ireland*, 115 (1985), 64–85 · NL Ire., Sydney MSS, MS 52 · BL, Buckingham MSS, Add. MS 40180 · BL, Young MSS, Add. MS 35126 · H. Grattan, *Memoirs of the life and times of the Rt Hon. Henry Grattan*, 5 vols. (1839–46) · J. Porter, P. Byrne, and W. Porter, eds., *The parliamentary register, or, History of the proceedings and debates of the House of Commons of Ireland, 1781–1797*, 17 vols. (1784–1801) · M. Bodkin, ed., 'Notes on the Irish parliament in 1773', *Proceedings of the Royal Irish Academy*, 48C (1942–3), 145–232 · G. O. Sayles, ed., 'Contemporary sketches of the members of the Irish parliament in 1782', *Proceedings of the Royal Irish Academy*, 56C (1953–4), 227–86 · *The letters of Charles O'Conor of Belanagare*, ed. C. C. Ward and R. E. Ward, 2 vols. (1980) · E. Lodge, *Peerage, baronetage, knightage and companionage of the British empire*, 81st edn, 3 vols. (1912) · Venn, *Alum. Cant.*

**Archives** PRO, War Office MSS, WO 27/11 | BL, Buckingham MSS, Add. MSS 40179–40180, 40733 · BL, Young MSS, Add. MS 35126 · NL Ire., Sydney MSS, MS 52 · PRO NIre., corresp. with first marquess of Abercorn · TCD, Conolly MSS, MS 3984

**Likenesses** H. D. Hamilton, pastel drawing, 1780, NG Ire. · mezzotint, 1780, NG Ire. · L. Schiavonetti, engraving, 1790–99 (after G. Stuart), NL Ire. · C. H. Hodges, engraving, 1792 (after G. Stuart), NL Ire. · G. Stuart, oils, 1792, NG Ire. · G. Stuart, oils, 1792, Slane Castle, Meath · V. Green, engraving (after H. D. Hamilton), NL Ire.

**Conyngton, Richard**. *See* Conington, Richard (d. 1330).

**Conzen, (Michael Robert) Günter** (1907–2000), geographer, was born on 21 January 1907 in Reinickendorf, Berlin, the only child of (Otto) Michael Conzen (1879–1945), sculptor, and his wife, Martha Etlich (1883–1963). He was educated at the Treitschke-Schule in Berlin (1917–26), at the Friedrich-Wilhelms-Universität, Berlin (1926–33), where he studied geography, history, and philosophy, and at the Victoria University of Manchester (1934–6), where he was one of the first two students to take the diploma course in town and country planning.

In 1933, shortly before he was due to complete his university studies in Berlin, Conzen learned that he was one of the Social Democratic sympathizers wanted by the SS. He managed to reach Hamburg and board a Russian cargo ship bound for London. There Frieda (Freda) Marie Klara Siebenhüner (1911–1995), whom he had known for several years in Berlin, was waiting for him, having moved to England as an au pair. They were married on 20 July 1935 at the Manchester South register office, Conzen signing the certificate 'Günther Conzen', though to English colleagues he became known as Con.

Opportunities in geography in Great Britain at this time were minimal for a German refugee, and after training as a town planner Conzen worked as junior and then senior assistant to W. Dobson Chapman, consultant in regional and town planning in Macclesfield, Cheshire, between 1936 and 1940. This experience, in the context of his training in Berlin, led him to publish 'Towards a systematic approach in planning science: geoproscopy' (*Town Planning Review*, 18, 1938, 1–26).

At the beginning of the Second World War Conzen still had German nationality: the papers confirming his naturalization as a British citizen arrived literally while he was at the police station going through the initial proceedings of internment. During the war he was assistant lecturer in geography at the University of Manchester, from where he graduated MA in historical geography under the supervision of H. J. Fleure and where he became a member of the research group on rural planning set up by R. A. Cordingley. His only child, Michael Peter, who became professor of geography in the University of Chicago, was born in 1944.

After the Second World War Conzen was very content to stay in Britain, which he found congenial if rather insular. He worked on a British government initiative to re-establish professional relations between British and German geographers. He moved to a lectureship in the geography department at King's College, Newcastle (later the University of Newcastle upon Tyne), and north-east England became the laboratory for his path-breaking contributions to urban morphology. Sensitivity to historical layering in the landscape, conceptualization of historico-geographical processes, rigorous terminology, and carefully designed visual representations were hallmarks of his work. Human geographers in the English-speaking world gave his work a muted reception, being by the 1960s more concerned with quantitative analysis and the functional aspect of cities. Conzen none the less persisted in his approach.

It was not until 1960 that Conzen's most important piece of research, *Alnwick, Northumberland: a Study in Town-Plan Analysis*, was published. It was intended as the first part of a trilogy analysing the town plan, building fabric, and land use of an urban area. So exacting were the standards of its author that it took about eight years to complete, and the two companion volumes were never completed. A second edition, including a glossary of technical terms, was published in 1969. The first edition was quickly followed by Conzen's application of its techniques and concepts to the city centre of Newcastle upon Tyne. For the study of Alnwick and a collection of papers on related topics he was awarded the degree of Dr.Phil. *magna cum laude* by the University of Giessen.

Conzen had set urban morphology on a new footing, conceptualizing it as an enquiry into the historical and geographical composition of townscapes based on their ground plan, building fabric, and land use. He had demonstrated the significance of the individual plot of land as the basic unit of analysis, and uncovered some of the myriad ways in which such plots were juxtaposed at different scales. He had developed, in many cases pioneered, such ideas as the burgage cycle, market concretion, the urban fringe belt, fixation lines, and townscape cells and their grouping into urban morphological regions.

The approach that had led to these ideas also provided the basis for proposals for townscape management. In the 1950s, well before the urban conservation movement had gathered momentum, Conzen had worked on the conservation of the historical townscape of Whitby: but his ideas on townscape management rested on German-influenced ideas on geographical regions which were poorly understood, if known at all, by English-speaking geographers and planners. In Whitby he was aware of the gulf between his scholarly ideas and the town councillors' ability to make use of them, and he left conservation campaigns to others.

Conzen held a personal chair in the University of Newcastle upon Tyne from 1965 until his retirement in 1972. It was only after his retirement that his reputation spread beyond the disciplines of geography and planning and beyond his countries of birth and adoption, and that he became acknowledged as the founder of the Conzenian school of urban morphology which sought to understand the built environment by analysing its elemental physical dimensions and conceptualizing their relationships in a cultural world.

In the 1980s Conzen's work achieved wider prominence through the publication by the Institute of British Geographers of a 'special publication' on his work, the commissioning by the French government of a multidisciplinary report on urban morphology, and the increasing adoption of his ideas by other researchers, in particular by those working within the interdisciplinary urban morphology research group at Birmingham University. The foundation in the 1990s of the International Seminar on Urban Form further increased the recognition of Conzen's work by urban morphologists. The continued momentum of Conzen's own research well into his nineties was remarkable. Just before retiring he had begun to investigate Japanese castle towns as the basis for a cross-cultural comparison with European towns. His undiminished perfectionism allowed publication of only one paper on this topic, although sequels were in preparation.

In the 1990s Conzen was absorbed in writing a monograph on the nature and development of urban morphology as a field of knowledge, but at the time of his death only an outline was complete. It was prepared for publication posthumously as an appendix to a volume of his papers, many previously unpublished, written between 1932 and 1998.

Conzen died on 4 February 2000 at Moorfield House Nursing Home, Gosforth, Newcastle upon Tyne, and was cremated a week later at West End crematorium, Newcastle. A memorial to him and his wife, Freda, stands in St Andrew's and West Jesmond cemetery, Newcastle upon Tyne, where his ashes were buried. Below the dedication has been symbolized the meeting of the three roads in the triangular market place at Alnwick, the core of the historic town that was the subject of Conzen's monograph that transformed geographical urban morphology.

J. W. R. WHITEHAND

**Sources** personal knowledge (2004) · private information (2004) [Michael P. Conzen, son] · www.bham.ac.uk/geography/umrg/ [urban morphology research group web site, U. Birm.], 22 Oct 2001 · J. W. R. Whitehand, *Journal of Historical Geography*, 27 (2001), 93–7 · J. W. R. Whitehand, *The Independent, Wednesday Review* (8 March 2000), 6 · J. W. R. Whitehand, 'An intellectual legacy for ISUF', *Urban Morphology*, 4 (2000), 45–7 · m. cert. · d. cert.
**Archives** U. Birm. | FILM U. Birm., department of geography, video interview, 1988
**Likenesses** photograph, repro. in Whitehand, *Journal of Historical Geography*, 93 · photograph, repro. in *Transactions of the Institute of British Geographers*, new ser., 25 (2000), 521 · photograph, repro. in *The Independent, Wednesday Review*, 6 · photographs, repro. in *Urban Morphology*, 90, 93
**Wealth at death** £412,062—gross; £409,904—net: probate, 17 Oct 2000, *CGPLA Eng. & Wales*

**Coode, John** (*c*.1648–1709), planter and politician in America, was born in Penryn, Cornwall, the second of three sons of John Coode (1622–1713), lawyer, and his wife, Grace (*d.* 1694), daughter of Thomas Robins of Glasney College. Coode briefly attended Exeter College, Oxford, from 1664 to 1666, and took orders as a Church of England priest about 1669. Coode emigrated to Maryland after being 'turned out' of his Penryn parish in 1672. The precise cause of his dismissal remains a mystery, but may have stemmed either from the rebelliousness or the lack of personal discipline that marked his later career.

'Deformed and club-footed, with a "face resembling that of a baboon or monkey"', Coode was 'defiant, quick to anger, impious, argumentative, boastful, theatrical, and given to a weakness for alcohol' (Jordan, 'John Coode', 2). Despite his deficiencies of appearance and personality, within two years of his arrival in Maryland Coode married Susannah (*d.* before 1684), widow of Robert Slye (*c.*1628–1671), a prominent planter and merchant, and daughter of Thomas Gerard (1608–1673), a large landowner. The couple had two sons before Susannah's death.

Coode's marriage brought both wealth and political power. By 1676 he received commissions as justice of the peace and militia captain, and was elected to the House of Delegates. Suspected of involvement in a conspiracy by former governor Josias Fendall to overthrow the rule of the proprietor Charles Calvert, third Baron Baltimore, in 1681, Coode lost his county offices but retained his seat in the lower house until 1682 and was eventually cleared of the treason charge.

Coode became coroner of St Mary's county in 1678 but held no other major office until the late 1680s. In the interim, following Susannah's death, Coode was married some time before 1685 to Elizabeth Hook. They had four children, a son and three daughters. Elizabeth Coode survived her husband and remarried in the year following his death.

As relations between Lord Baltimore and the Maryland colonists became more contentious towards the end of the 1680s, St Mary's voters in 1688 again elected Coode to the lower house. Once in office, Coode became one of the leaders of a successful effort, led largely by disaffected protestants, to overthrow proprietary rule. Taking advantage of the revolution of 1688 spirit, he gathered a sizeable armed force that marched on the capital in July 1689. The Protestant Associators secured the surrender of the smaller body of Lord Baltimore's supporters without bloodshed on 27 July. The associators pledged their allegiance to William and Mary and asked to be designated a royal, rather than a proprietary, colony. While awaiting a response from England, a special convention met in late August to form an interim government. Coode was the acknowledged military leader, being named commander-in-chief of the militia, as well as naval officer for the Potomac district and quorum justice for St Mary's county. Coode's second rebellion not only restored the offices to him that he had lost in the first but also brought additional power as one of the leading figures within the government.

To strengthen their hand, the associators appointed Coode, his brother-in-law, and a third delegate to act as agents in England for the incumbent government. The three appeared before the lords of trade in November 1690 to present fifty-two 'Articles against the Lord Baltimore' and to defend the associators against charges submitted by proprietary witnesses. Coode made a highly negative impression upon the board's secretary, William Blathwayt, and others during his months in England. Although Lionel Copley, the first royal governor, listed Coode among his nominees for the governor's council, the crown did not include him in the commission. He returned to Maryland in 1692 deprived of the position of prominence he had held when he left for England. With the arrival of Francis Nicholson as governor in 1694, following the death of Copley, Coode received a commission as St Mary's militia officer and sheriff. Within two years he was at odds with Nicholson and confronting charges that he had embezzled public money while head of the association government and owed the crown over £400 in naval office revenues. Nicholson used Coode's admission that he had been ordained as a Church of England priest to force his disqualification as delegate. Stripped of office and facing suits for embezzlement and blasphemy, Coode fled to Virginia. By 1698 he was thoroughly implicated by the other conspirators in a campaign to discredit Nicholson. Although eventually captured, tried, and convicted, he was pardoned by Nicholson's successor.

Coode was elected as a delegate to the colony's legislature for the final time in 1708, but the assembly refused to seat him. He died between 27 February and 28 March 1709, and was survived by his wife. He left personal property valued at £259 13*s*. 8*d*. and more than 1000 acres of land. Unable to sustain a cooperative working relationship with any representative of proprietary or royal authority, Coode left his children only a material legacy. None of his sons ever achieved political prominence and his own name is tarnished with the epithet 'perennial malcontent', used by all who write of him and his role in Maryland history.                                                                    JEAN B. RUSSO

**Sources** E. C. Papenfuse, A. F. Day, D. W. Jordan, and G. A. Stiverson, eds., *A biographical dictionary of the Maryland legislature, 1635–1789*, 1 (1979) • D. W. Jordan, 'John Coode, perennial rebel', *Maryland Historical Magazine*, 70 (1975), 1–28 • L. G. Carr and D. W. Jordan, *Maryland's revolution of government* (1974) • D. W. Jordan, *Foundations of representative government in Maryland, 1632–1715* (1987) • R. J. Brugger, *Maryland: a middle temperament* (1988) • D. M. Owings, *His lordship's patronage: offices of profit in colonial Maryland* (1953)

**Wealth at death** £259 13*s*. 8*d*. in personal estate, incl. seven slaves; over 1000 acres of land: Papenfuse, Day, Jordan, and Stiverson, eds., *Biographical dictionary*, 234

**Coode, Sir John** (1816–1892), civil engineer, was born at Bodmin on 11 November 1816, the son of Charles Coode, solicitor, and Ann, daughter of Joseph Bennett, rector of Great Wigborough, Essex. He was educated at Bodmin grammar school and after leaving school entered his father's office. His natural tastes, however, were not for law but for engineering, and he was therefore articled to the civil engineer James Meadows Rendel of Plymouth. On completion of his pupillage he worked briefly with Rendel and subsequently on the new Great Western Railway line between Bristol and Exeter. Coode married, on 5 October 1842, Jane Dod, daughter of William Price of Weston-super-Mare; they had at least one son.

Between 1844 and 1847 Coode had his own practice in Westminster as a consulting engineer, working predominantly on the proposed Santander to Madrid Railway. In 1847 he was appointed resident engineer in charge of the construction of the works at Portland harbour, which had been designed by Rendel. On the death of the latter in 1856 Coode was appointed engineer-in-chief, a post he retained until the completion of the work in 1872. This harbour provided the largest area of deep water of any artificial harbour in Great Britain, and was a work of major national importance at the time, constructed partly by the use of convict labour. The first stone of the great breakwater was laid by the prince consort on 25 July 1849, and the work was completed in 1872. Coode was knighted in 1872 for his services in connection with this undertaking. In 1856, Coode had established his firm of consulting engineers which survived, with amalgamations, through three generations of his direct descendants. From 1858 he served as a member of the royal commission on harbours of refuge around Britain and Ireland. He also began to develop his overseas work.

Coode was consulted by several of the most important British colonial governments, notably by those of the South African and Australian colonies, in reference to proposed harbour works, and he made several journeys to South Africa, Australia, and India in connection with the schemes upon which his advice was sought. Following his appointment as engineer-in-chief for Table Bay harbour, work proceeded from 1859 to 1870, with the subsequent addition of a graving dock in 1882. For many years, Coode served as consulting engineer for harbours to the crown agents, leading to many appointments in the British colonies. In 1873, he reported on the harbour for Colombo; construction of this major harbour started in 1874, and the works, extended with increasing trade, were completed in 1885. In 1877 he designed the works for Port Natal, Durban; the previous year he had advised on harbour works for Mossel Bay, Knysna, and Plattenberg Bay in Cape Colony. In 1878 he recommended harbour improvements for Port Phillip, Melbourne, where 'Coode island' results from realignment of the River Yarra. He also advised the state of Victoria on several other harbour proposals and river improvements. He inspected major and minor harbours in New Zealand, leading to recommendations for works undertaken at Dunedin.

In 1885 Coode inspected sites for port works at Trincomali, Bombay, and Singapore, selecting the latter for a new graving dock. In the same year he gave comprehensive advice for port developments for New South Wales. He also advised on harbour proposals for St Lucia, Trinidad, Accra, Lagos, Kyrenia, Penang, Sierra Leone, Heligoland (a British colony), Newfoundland, Pondoland, Fremantle and Port Adelaide. Among the great number of other harbour works for which Coode was responsible

may be mentioned Waterford harbour, and plans for the Dover commercial harbour, work for which was proceeding at the time of his death. He was a member of the royal commission on metropolitan sewage discharge (1882–4), and of the international commission of the Suez Canal; on the latter he served from 1884 until his death in 1892. He was made KCMG in 1886.

Coode was probably the most distinguished harbour engineer of the nineteenth century. He was elected a member of the Institution of Civil Engineers in 1849, served for many years on the council, and was president from May 1889 to May 1891. He was also an active member of the Royal Colonial Institute, and sat on its council from 1881 until his death. Coode contributed a paper to the Institution of Civil Engineers in 1852 on the Chesil Bank (*Proc. Inst. Civil Eng.*, 12.520), providing a cogent explanation for the physical characteristics of this long shingle feature. He also wrote many professional reports about the harbour projects he was engaged upon, and these were often published. Coode died at Brighton on 2 March 1892 following a severe operation in Italy the previous year. T. H. BEARE, *rev.* ALAN MUIR WOOD

**Sources** PICE, 113 (1892–3), 334–43 · private information (1901) · *CGPLA Eng. & Wales* (1892) · m. cert. · *The Times* (3 March 1892)
**Archives** priv. coll., reprints, papers, and other archives
**Likenesses** C. Wilkinson, oils, priv. coll. · bust; formerly in the possession of Mrs Lillington, vicarage, Havering-atte-Bower, near Romford, 1901 · oils · wood-engraving (after photograph), NPG; repro. in *ILN* (27 April 1872)
**Wealth at death** £57,409 1s. 3d.: probate, 21 April 1892, *CGPLA Eng. & Wales*

**Cook**. *See also* Coke, Cooke.

**Cook, Captain**. *See* Cook, James (1728–1779).

**Cook, Sir Albert Ruskin** (1870–1951), physician and missionary, was born on 2 March 1870 in the London suburb of Hampstead, the twelfth of thirteen children of William Henry Cook (1825–1882), a family physician who practised in Tunbridge Wells and then in London, and his wife, Harriet Bickersteth (1830–1918), daughter of Edward *Bickersteth, rector of Watton in Hertfordshire and sister of Edward Henry *Bickersteth, bishop of Exeter. Both Cook's grandfather and uncle had strong connections with the Church Missionary Society (CMS). The classical scholar Arthur Bernard *Cook was his brother.

As a youth Cook—who had grey-blue eyes and reddish hair—lived in London. Two years after his father's death the family moved from their home in Abbey Road to a leased house in Carlingford Street, near Hampstead Heath. After a few years at preparatory school he won a scholarship to St Paul's School, London, in 1881; initially he followed the arts curriculum, but later he turned his efforts towards science. From 1889 to 1893 Cook attended Trinity College, Cambridge (BA, 1893). During these years he established a reputation as an excellent student, and supported himself by tutoring fellow students and by selling antiquarian books. On 13 July 1893 he received a Shuter scholarship from St Bartholomew's Hospital, where he underwent his clinical training. He qualified MB in 1895 and MD in 1901. Nine days after qualifying in 1895 he submitted an application to join the CMS, which eventually accepted him as a medical missionary for service in Uganda, then a British protectorate.

On 3 September 1896 Cook and a party of eleven other CMS missionaries, including his future wife, Katherine Timpson (d. 1938), whom he married in 1900, left England on the SS *Khedive*, bound for Aden, where they changed to the SS *Canara* for the journey to east Africa. On 1 October 1896 Cook and his colleagues landed at Mombasa. After an 84-day, 850-mile overland journey, during which Cook attended to 2230 patients, the CMS party arrived in Mengo, near Kampala, on 19 February 1897. Two days later Cook started seeing patients in a shed which originally had been a smithy. Within a month he was examining fifty to eighty patients daily. On 14 May 1897 Cook opened Mengo Hospital, which consisted of two houses with reed walls, thatched roofs, and mud floors, and had beds for twelve patients. By the mid-1930s, Mengo Hospital had become the cornerstone of one of the best medical infrastructures in sub-Saharan Africa. Apart from providing accommodation for 132 Africans, twelve Europeans, and twenty-four Indian patients, Mengo Hospital maintained a training school for African medical assistants and a radiological department with the country's only complete X-ray apparatus. Additionally Mengo Hospital was associated with the Lady Coryndon Maternity Training School, which opened in June 1921. Cook received a medal with two clasps for his services during the Nubian uprising of 1897–8.

During his years in Uganda Cook also performed some significant scientific work, often in conjunction with his brother John (1871–1946), who also worked as a physician in Uganda between 1899 and 1920. In February 1901, for example, the brothers Cook diagnosed the first cases of sleeping sickness, a disease which eventually claimed the lives of at least 200,000 Ugandans who lived beside Lake Victoria or on the Buvuma Islands. During the following years, Cook identified the treponema of relapsing fever and published his findings in the *Journal of Tropical Medicine*.

Apart from his regular duties at Mengo Hospital and his scientific work, Cook also engaged in missionary work. On 8 March 1904 he started on a ten-week, 642-mile safari by bicycle, with his wife and Bishop Alfred Tucker of the CMS, to Acholi, where the party established a mission station. The following year he went on a similar journey, which lasted more than six months, to southern Sudan, where he helped to organize a mission station at Bor, a small settlement north of Juba on the River Nile. To support future missionary activities among the Dinka people at this remote location, Cook wrote several manuals in the Dinka language.

After the First World War Cook strove to improve the quality of maternity and child welfare throughout Uganda. To achieve this goal he performed work for the government-sponsored Social Purity Campaign, which sought to reduce the number of cases of venereal disease in the country. Cook and his wife also sought donations for the construction of the Lady Coryndon Maternity

Training School which, by 1929, was serving more than 10,000 patients annually. In 1923 he published *Amagezi agokuzalisa*, a textbook in Luganda for midwifery students, and about the same time he helped to create a network of twenty-two country health stations staffed by trained midwives. Cook's *Handbook of Midwifery for Teaching Native Midwives* was published in 1931.

By the early 1930s Cook's medical career was drawing to an end. In 1932 he was knighted in recognition of his many contributions to the establishment and development of western medicine in Uganda. Although he retired on 2 March 1934 Cook continued to work as a consultant to Mengo Hospital. He also served as president, and later as honorary vice-president, of the Uganda Literary and Scientific Society, which published the prestigious *Uganda Journal*, to which Cook contributed several articles. In 1937 Cook and his wife, Katherine, represented Uganda at the coronation of King George VI. On 17 May 1938 she died as a result of complications associated with a severe bout of malaria. In 1945 the Uganda Literary and Scientific Society published Cook's *Uganda Memories, 1897–1940*, a classic book which is essential for understanding not only his medical work but also the history of the early British colonial period in Uganda.

Cook remained active until the end of his life, primarily working on his diaries or writing scientific and historical articles. During the last years of his life he became addicted to morphine, reportedly because he suffered from chronic insomnia and missed his late wife. On 23 April 1951 he died at his home at Makindye Hill, near Kampala, Uganda. After receiving the only royal funeral to have been granted to a European, he was buried next to his wife at the cathedral of St Paul, Namirembe Hill, Kampala. The marble cross that marks his grave is inscribed, on the orders of the king (*kabaka*) of Buganda, 'to a true friend of Uganda'. Cook was survived by an only daughter, Margaret, who also was a physician. Cook and his wife also had an adopted son, David, who lived primarily with a missionary colleague, Sister Emily Watney; he was killed on active service during the Second World War.

As befitted his professional and religious callings, Cook was a gentle, quiet, dedicated, and humble man, with simple tastes. He was well liked by everyone who knew him. His pioneering work in establishing an adequate healthcare system for the Ugandan people remains his greatest legacy.

THOMAS PAUL OFCANSKY

**Sources** W. R. Billington, 'Albert Cook: a biographical note', *East African Medical Journal*, 28 (1951), 397–401 • A. R. Cook, *Uganda memories, 1897–1940* (1945) • A. R. Cook, 'Further memories of Uganda', *Uganda Journal*, 2 (1934), 97 • A. R. Cook, 'The journey to Uganda in 1896', *Uganda Journal*, 1 (1934), 83 • A. R. Cook, 'An early newspaper in Uganda and comments on the news contained therein', *Uganda Journal*, 4 (1936–7), 27–40 • W. D. Foster, *Sir Albert Cook: a missionary doctor in Uganda* (1978) • W. D. Foster, *The early history of scientific medicine in Uganda* (1970) • B. O'Brien, *That good physician* (1962) • T. P. Ofcansky, 'The life and times of Sir Albert Ruskin Cook', *Journal of the History of Medicine and Allied Sciences*, 37 (1982), 225–8 • *Medical Directory* (1940) • Venn, *Alum. Cant.* • WWW

**Archives** RCP Lond. • Wellcome L., corresp., and papers | Bodl. RH, Davies MSS • Bodl. RH, Matson MSS • Makerere University,

Uganda, Sir Albert Cook Library, Mengo MSS · U. Birm., G3/A7, MC/1

**Likenesses** A. R. Cook, self-portrait, photograph, repro. in Cook, *Uganda memories* · A. T. Schofield, photograph, repro. in Cook, *Uganda memories* · photograph, repro. in *East African Medical Journal* · photograph (with general staff of Mengo Hospital), repro. in Foster, *Early history of scientific medicine in Uganda* · photographs, repro. in O'Brien, *That good physician* · photographs, repro. in Foster, *Sir Albert Cook*

**Wealth at death** £1389 7s. 11d. in England: Ugandan administration with will sealed in England, 24 May 1952, *CGPLA Eng. & Wales*

**Cook, Ann** (*fl. c.*1725–*c.*1760), cookery writer, was born probably in the late 1690s, perhaps in co. Durham. Little is known of her except what appears in the autobiographical 'Plan of house-keeping' included in the second and third editions of her cookery book; her narrative is an account of her feud with Esquire Flash, who was in fact Lancelot Allgood (1711–1782), the half-brother of Hannah Glasse (1708–1770), author of the best-selling *The Art of Cookery, Made Plain and Easy* (1747). According to Ann Cook's own account she was in service as a cook-housekeeper before her marriage to John Cook, master of the Black Bull inn in Hexham, Northumberland, probably about 1727. There were several children of the marriage, including three sons—John (*bap.* 1733), William (*bap.* 1735), and Robert (*bap.* 1737)—and at least two daughters, one of whom was born about 1728. The feud with Allgood seems to have begun in 1740, when a misunderstanding arose over some wine that Allgood accused John Cook of having stolen. Ann's vigorous defence of her husband inflamed the quarrel, which lasted for years; although Cook was finally exonerated Allgood apparently continued to do his utmost to ruin the Cooks' trade. Late in 1745 they moved to the Queen's Head inn in Morpeth, Northumberland, but their landlord, Thomas Pye, turned out to be Allgood's cousin. The feud continued, with Allgood publicly denouncing Cook in July 1746 as a rogue and a Jacobite, and by 1749 Pye had triggered a rumour that John Cook was insolvent. The Cooks now moved to Newcastle upon Tyne, intending to set up a pastry-cook's shop, but within a month John Cook was seized for debt.

Ann Cook's autobiography ends at this point, probably in 1750. Apparently she decided to try to make money by writing a cookery book. *The New System of Cookery* was advertised in the *Newcastle Journal* in February 1753 but when the book appeared in 1754, by which time she was living in Groat Market, Newcastle, its title was *Professed Cookery*, the change being part of Ann Cook's revenge on the Allgoods. The book contains recipes and two virulent attacks on Hannah Glasse, in a poem and in 'An essay on the lady's art of cookery'. Glasse's book had appeared anonymously ('By a Lady') but her authorship was revealed in the fourth edition of 1751; Ann Cook's essay is a lengthy denunciation of Glasse's recipes, with page-by-page comments on the 1751 edition. Cook ridicules the idea that a lady could teach servants cookery; throughout Glasse is referred to as the 'Lady Teacher' and her recipes are condemned as 'stupid' and 'expensive' (Cook, 1754, 11). The poem, a piece of appalling doggerel, contains similar comments but it also, correctly, accuses Glasse of plagiarism and shows that Ann Cook knew about Hannah Glasse's illegitimacy. Cook's own recipes are somewhat old-fashioned compared to those of her rival but suggest familiarity with Glasse's French sources. In 1755 the autobiographical 'Plan' was added to the second edition of *Professed Cookery*, and an undated third edition came out in London, perhaps after 1760, in which the author is described as lodging in Fuller's Rents, Holborn, with Mr Moor, a cabinet-maker. Nothing more is known of Ann Cook after her move to London. GILLY LEHMANN

**Sources** A. Cook, *Professed cookery*, 3rd edn [n.d., 1760?] · A. Cook, *Professed cookery* (1754) · M. H. Dodds, 'The rival cooks: Hannah Glasse and Ann Cook', *Archaeologia Aeliana*, 4th ser., 15 (1938), 43–68 · parish registers, Hexham, Northumberland, 18 Nov 1733, 21 Aug 1735, 10 Aug 1737 [baptism] · A. Cook and R. Burnet, *Ann Cook and friend* (1936) · V. Maclean, *A short-title catalogue of household and cookery books published in the English tongue, 1701–1800* (1981)

**Cook, Arthur Bernard** (1868–1952), classical scholar and archaeologist, was born in Hampstead, London, on 22 October 1868, the son of William Henry Cook MD (1825–1882) and his wife, Harriet Bickersteth (1830–1918), of a family which produced several noted evangelical figures, including her brother, Edward Henry Bickersteth, who became bishop of Exeter. Cook was a scholar of St Paul's School in a brilliant period. He matriculated in 1887, holding a major scholarship at Trinity College, Cambridge. He obtained first classes in both parts of the classical tripos (1889, 1891), won the Craven scholarship (1889), the chancellor's medal for English verse (1889), the chancellor's first medal for classics (1891), and the members' prize for Latin essay (1892). His older brother, Edward Bickersteth Cook, had died in 1881, but his younger brother Albert Ruskin *Cook (1870–1951) followed him to Trinity, also holding a major scholarship, to read natural sciences before becoming a physician and medical missionary.

Henry Jackson, praelector in ancient philosophy and later regius professor of Greek, exercised a remarkable and richly merited influence on men reading classics at Trinity in Cook's time, and it was no accident that Cook's first book was *The Metaphysical Basis of Plato's 'Ethics'* (1895). But there were other forces to influence him in his formative years. In his inaugural lecture Cook paid tribute to John Henry Middleton, the Slade professor of art, and Charles Waldstein (later Sir Charles Walston), the first reader in classical archaeology and director of the Fitzwilliam Museum. The former he recalled as 'a realist with a grasp of facts' but the latter as 'prolix, polysyllabic, on occasion plethoric, but always persuasive and not seldom convincing' (A. B. Cook, *The Rise and Progress of Classical Archaeology*, 1931, 51–2). Comparative philology as part of the classical tripos had been an important influence on Cook. James Frazer was also a Cambridge presence, not teaching but working in the full enthusiasm of the movement of thought to which E. B. Tylor and William Robertson Smith had given so powerful an impulse. In England as elsewhere the history of religion then excited interest and 'The bee in Greek mythology' (1895), both in the *Journal of Hellenic Studies*, and the noteworthy 'Greek votive offerings' in *Folk-Lore* (1903). The *Classical Review* contains his highly original and stimulating papers 'Associated reminiscences' (1901) and 'Unconscious iterations' (1902). He also started work on an edition of Theocritus. Cook was to supply the commentary on the historical and archaeological material, and Peter Giles, master of Emmanuel College in Cambridge from 1911 to 1935, the compilation of a critical text. The study was never published, though the manuscript was presented, after Cook's death, to the Cambridge University Library.

Following the expiry of his fellowship at Trinity, Cook was elected lecturer in classics at Queens' College in 1900, and a fellow in 1903. In 1907 he resigned the chair at Bedford College and became reader in classical archaeology at Cambridge. This was the period when his focus started to turn to Zeus. A series of papers in the *Classical Review* between 1902 and 1906, and another in *Folk-Lore* between 1903 and 1907, were the forerunners of his monumental *Zeus: a Study in Ancient Religion* (3 vols. in 5, 1914, 1925, and 1940), which the Revd C. T. Wood, the senior fellow of Queens' College, described as 'an incredibly rich mine of information on most forms of religion' (Wood, *Queens' College Record*, 5). This study shows a fabulous command of every kind of material which could be brought to bear on the subject—ancient literature, monumental evidence, the Near Eastern background, and folklore and folk-ways from all parts, all presented with supreme accuracy and so indexed as to be instantly available. *Zeus* would be indispensable to students in many fields, even if every single conclusion of its author were rejected. Perhaps no one has equalled Cook in his ability to present the views of others with generous fairness and to state objections to his own; no one has surpassed him in awareness of the fact that the ancients took their gods seriously. He constantly brought forth new data and parallels and suggestive ideas, and his sheer knowledge of the works of ancient art was so wide and thorough that his lack of aesthetic taste hardly affected his powers of interpreting and illustrating them. His sense of historical criticism and chronological stratification was weak: he drew confident inferences for early times from very late writers, and he never appreciated Wissowa's fundamental discovery of the contrast between the religious heritages of Rome and Greece. Nevertheless, recognition of Cook's research came in 1941 with his election as a fellow of the British Academy, following the publication of the third volume of *Zeus* (1940). Cook was also a foreign member of the American Philosophical Society and the German Archaeological Institute, as well as a member of the Folklore Society.

In Cambridge Cook's responsibilities included the curatorship of the Museum of Classical Archaeology in Little St Mary's Lane, which housed the cast collection. He also brought order to the library. Women were permitted to attend his lectures on Greek sculpture, although in 1920 Cook voted against awarding degrees to women, much to the annoyance of his friend Jane Harrison. He proceeded LittD in 1926. In 1928 he became general editor for

Arthur Bernard Cook (1868–1952), by unknown photographer

as perhaps never before or since. Cook's deep and continuing evangelical convictions predisposed him towards thought on these things, without alienating him from those who shared his interest but not his beliefs.

Cook applied for the chair of Greek at University College, London, in 1892 at the time that A. E. Housman was elected to the chair of Latin. Although the application failed, perhaps because of Cook's youth and inexperience, he was appointed professor of Greek at Bedford College, London, in 1893, a post he held until 1907. At the same time he was elected to a fellowship at Trinity, which he held until 1899. He led a dual life, commuting by train to London, where he taught, and returning to Cambridge for research and writing. London also gave him access to the riches of the collections in the British Museum which were to stimulate his writing. In 1894 he married Emily (*d.* 1943), daughter of George Thomas Maddox, of Hampstead. They had one daughter, Phyllis, and a son who died in infancy.

Cook was influenced by other students of Greek religion in Cambridge, notably by Jane Harrison, Gilbert Murray, and Francis Cornford. Some have seen Cook as a marginal member of this group, and Murray recalled that Cook 'was a great help to us, but not one of us' (letter to Jessie Stewart, 26 Oct 1953: Beard, 116). At one point he formed part of a select class with Frazer, Jane Harrison, and Francis Cornford, learning Hebrew at the feet of Robert Hatch Kennett, the regius professor of Hebrew. Cook's interest in Greek religion was developed in a series of articles—for example, 'Animal worship in the Mycenaean age' (1894)

Methuen's Handbooks of Archaeology, a role he retained until 1949. Former pupils wrote volumes for the series, such as Winifred Lamb of the Fitzwilliam Museum with *Greek and Roman Bronzes* (1929), and Charles T. Seltman with *Greek Coins* (1933). In 1931 Cook became the first holder of the Laurence chair of classical archaeology, from which he retired in 1934 to be succeeded by Alan J. B. Wace. In the following year Cook was elected vice-president of Queens' College.

Cook travelled widely in the Mediterranean to pursue his research—to Italy, Sicily, Greece, and Turkey. He formed his own collection of antiquities, including Greek and Roman coins, to support his studies; most were dispersed before his death. For example, some items were presented to the Liverpool Museum, which had been badly damaged during the Second World War. A head of Aphrodite, allegedly collected on the Athenian acropolis in 1890, was presented to Queens' College and was placed in the library. A twelfth-century manuscript of the Pauline epistles and a thirteenth-century manuscript of the Bible were presented to Ridley Hall in 1947. A small selection of items was bequeathed to the Fitzwilliam Museum by his daughter. A further selection of antiquities was purchased by the Otago Museum in Dunedin, New Zealand, after Cook's death, in part through the good offices of A. D. Trendall.

Unlike his friend Frazer, Cook could not live a life of pure research, and he probably would not have wished to do so. He was an admirable lecturer, always clear, thorough, and entertaining; he was supremely helpful to younger men, whether undergraduates or colleagues. Anyone who came to consult him was sure to go away with 'a pocket of references' and a sense of encouragement. His weight of learning was never oppressive and was accompanied by a warm friendliness, a joy in living, and a puckish humour which went with the twinkle of his keen eyes. His natural instinct for collecting extended to the maintenance of a scrapbook, entitled 'Explicanda', for first-hand accounts of the unexplained and of extrasensory perception. He never seemed pressed for time and knew how to relax in talk or tennis or travel; his spare, wiry physique appeared to sustain his long labours with ease. Cook's favourite poet was Robert Browning, and he also composed poetry. His satirical 'Criticism criticised' was published in the *Cambridge Review* (1892). In later years he avoided academic reviewing, quoting 'judge not that ye be not judged'. Cook retained his evangelical faith, serving on the council of Ridley Hall, the evangelical Anglican theological college in Cambridge, from 1906. He also served as a Sunday school teacher. He regularly attended evensong at Queens' College, his position next to the preacher enabling him to insert *sotto voce* comments during the delivery, such as 'Come to the point', or 'You have said that already', or even 'Bravo, that's got them'.

In 1943 Cook's wife, Emily, died. One of Cook's last public appearances was in 1948 at the quincentenary celebrations of Queens' College during the visit of the then Queen Elizabeth. Cook bore ill health in his closing years

with serene courage and without losing his old gaiety. There are two accounts of deathbed conversations that reflect his continuing mischievous sense of humour. His niece, on a final visit, was talking to a comatose Cook and mentioned that she had just visited the British Museum with her son. Cook opened one eye and asked, 'What did you go to see?', and received the reply, 'Well, we had two hours to spare, so we did the lot!' With the words 'May you be forgiven', Cook sank back on his pillow. In another instance the Revd Henry Chadwick, then dean of Queens' College, was reading the opening verses of the 121st psalm to Cook, only to receive the comment, 'that is a mistranslation' (Seltman, 300–01). Cook died at his home, 19 Cranmer Road, Cambridge, on 26 April 1952 and was buried on 2 May following a funeral at Queens' College, Cambridge.

A. D. NOCK, rev. DAVID GILL

**Sources** *The Times* (28 April 1952) · C. Seltman, 'Arthur Bernard Cook, 1868–1952', *PBA*, 38 (1952), 296–302 · personal knowledge (1971) · C. T. W. [C. T. Wood], 'Arthur Bernard Cook', *Queens' College Record* (1951–2), 4–6 · C. T. Wood, *The Dial* [Queen's College, Cambridge], 105 (1952), 3–4 [incl. photograph] · H. J. Rose, 'A. B. Cook, 1868–1952', *Folklore*, 64 (1953), 491–2 · S. Arlen, *The Cambridge ritualists: an annotated bibliography of the works by and about Jane Ellen Harrison, Gilbert Murray, Francis M. Cornford, and Arthur Bernard Cook* (1990) · R. V. Nicholls, 'Tryphosa and her toy', *Cambridge*, 9 (1981), 41–5 · F. W. B. Bullock, *The history of Ridley Hall, Cambridge*, 2: AD 1908–1951 (1953) · P. G. Naiditch, *A. E. Housman at University College, London: the election of 1892* (1988) · J. Stewart, *Jane Ellen Harrison: a portrait from letters* (1959) · M. Beard, *The invention of Jane Harrison* (2000) · A. Robinson, *The life and work of Jane Ellen Harrison* (2002) · private information (2004) [H. Chadwick; E. Bridger and P. Bewes, family]

**Archives** CUL, collection | FM Cam., antiquities · National Museum and Galleries on Merseyside, antiquities · Otago Museum, Dunedin, New Zealand, antiquities · Ridley Hall, Cambridge

**Likenesses** T. Haddon, oils, 1933, Queens' College, Cambridge · photograph, repro. in Seltman, 'Arthur Bernard Cook' · photograph, British Academy [see illus.]

**Wealth at death** £14,249 9s. 8d.: probate, 16 June 1952, CGPLA Eng. & Wales

**Cook, Arthur James** (1883–1931), trade unionist, was born on 22 November 1883 in Wookey, Somerset, the oldest of ten children of Thomas Cook, a soldier, and his wife, Selina. Selina's religious convictions were a formative influence on Cook's early life. At the age of twelve he began work near Cheddar as a labourer on the farm of Caleb Durbin, whose radical politics also influenced his development. Cook became a boy preacher, and was offered a place at Baptist college to train for the ministry. Instead, in 1901, he joined the exodus of agricultural workers from the west country attracted by high wages in the south Wales coalfield.

Moving to Porth, in the Rhondda, Cook began work in the Trefor colliery in Trehafod. On his first day underground, a miner working nearby was killed in a roof fall, and Cook helped carry him home to his family, experiences which left a lasting impression. As a Baptist preacher he was active in the religious revival of 1904–5, but shortly afterwards began to take an interest in trade

Arthur James Cook (1883–1931), by unknown photographer

union and political matters. Apparently around late 1905 or early 1906 he came into contact with the Independent Labour Party (ILP), which he joined. His politics were ill-received by his chapel, from which he had to resign, along with his wife Annie (née Edwards), whom he married in 1906. He became active in the union at the Coedcae colliery, where he now worked, and quickly became a lodge official. He claimed that he had held every official lodge position before 1914.

The south Wales coalfield was experiencing explosive growth, and the Rhondda, the heart of the coalfield, grew by over a third between 1901 and 1911. In this frontier society, signs of a new militancy appeared, especially around the Cambrian combine dispute of 1910–11. In its aftermath some younger miners formed the Unofficial Reform Committee, with which Cook was associated, and produced the famous pamphlet entitled *The Miners' Next Step* (1912). Its central themes of a class struggle, an industrial union, and the need for rank-and-file control reflected Cook's own beliefs, and shaped his actions for the next decade.

Cook was awarded a two-year scholarship by the Pontypridd and Rhondda district of the South Wales Miners' Federation (SWMF) to the Central Labour College (CLC) in 1911, where he absorbed the college's Marxist teachings. He did not return for his second year, instead becoming actively involved once more in the labour movement. Elected as chairman of Coedcae lodge in 1913 and of the Lewis Merthyr joint committee of lodges in January 1914, he was also influential in establishing the Industrial Democracy League and agitated for independent working-class education.

Cook openly opposed the First World War in April 1916, after which time he was under persistent police surveillance. Arrested and charged with sedition in March 1918 under the Defence of the Realm Act, he was sentenced to three months' imprisonment, of which he served two.

After his release from prison, he became increasingly seen as a leader of the left in the Rhondda.

Against a background of industrial turmoil, Cook, a committed revolutionary, was elected in November 1919 as miners' agent for the Rhondda no. 1 district, a full-time post through which he automatically became a member of the SWMF executive. In January 1921 his meteoric rise continued when he became a member of the executive of the Miners' Federation of Great Britain (MFGB). A month later the decontrol of the mining industry was announced, with a consequent end to a national wages agreement and wage reductions. A three-month lock-out from April 1921 ended in defeat for the miners; at its end Cook was again jailed for two months' hard labour for incitement and unlawful assembly.

Cook was a member of the South Wales Socialist Society, and a foundation member of the Communist Party, from which he resigned in 1921, although he remained close to it. In 1923 Cook and others launched the miners' minority movement in south Wales, which gave him important backing the following year when he won the south Wales nomination in his bid for general secretaryship of the MFGB. He won the national ballot and assumed office on 14 April 1924. Committed to ending private ownership in the coal industry, and the overthrow of capitalism, in office Cook also displayed a capacity for innovation. He worked to build the 'triple alliance' with rail and transport unions, and, through regular campaigning visits to the coalfields, stayed close to his membership.

When further wage cuts were demanded in 1925, Cook mobilized the MFGB to resist and, with the support of the Trades Union Congress (TUC), won a nine-month subsidy from the Baldwin government. When the subsidy ended in 1926 conflict was inevitable, although Cook, sensing the weakness in the union's situation, sought to avoid it. The TUC called a general strike in support of the locked out miners, but after nine days it was called off. When negotiations failed, Cook threw himself into the dispute, touring coalfields. He was a magnetic orator with an emotional style. He was revered by the miners for his unstinting commitment to their cause and for his public defence of 'Not a Penny off the Pay, Not a Second on the Day.' Such public obduracy masked a desire to negotiate a settlement which would stop the suffering in the coalfield and the undermining of the union through a drift back to work. The strain of his work as the only full-time national official and his tireless efforts during the lock-out led to his physical and mental exhaustion. After seven months the miners were completely defeated, membership fell markedly, and rival unions were set up in various coalfields.

Cook was vilified in the press and in sections of the labour movement for what was perceived as poor leadership (a criticism which has been effectively rebutted by his biographer Paul Davies). He became isolated within the MFGB and the TUC, where he opposed the trend towards 'Mondism' and reaffirmed his belief in class struggle. In 1929 Cook broke with his erstwhile allies in the Communist Party as they adopted the policy of 'class against class', including the formation of a breakaway United Mineworkers of Scotland. In his last years Cook, realizing the weakness of the MFGB, followed a pragmatic line within the industry. Although he gave general support to the second Labour government, his concern at high unemployment in the coalfields led to his signing the 'Mosley manifesto' in December 1930 which made radical recommendations for economic recovery, involving state intervention and a public works programme. He never publicly supported Sir Oswald Mosley's New Party when it was launched in March 1931, although he may have made supportive comments privately before its fascist nature became apparent.

Cook's health had been a concern since the 1926 lockout. Ignoring all advice he refused to reduce his workload, and continuously drove himself to the point of breakdown. His failure to seek medical attention for an injury to his leg, aggravated by a kick from a demonstrator in 1926, resulted in its amputation in January 1931. He suffered further ill health, and was then found to have cancer. He died on 2 November 1931 at Manor House Hospital in Golders Green and was cremated at the Golders Green crematorium. He was survived by his wife, a son, and two daughters. Cook retained the loyalty and affection of the miners long after his death. A levy of a halfpenny per miner raised £1032 for his dependants.                    HYWEL FRANCIS

**Sources**  P. Davies, *A. J. Cook* (1987) · R. H. Desmarais and J. Saville, 'Cook, Arthur James', *DLB*, vol. 3 · D. Smith, 'Tonypandy, 1910: definitions of community', *Past and Present*, 87 (1980) · D. Smith, ed., *A people and a proletariat: essays in the history of Wales, 1780–1980* (1980) · *CGPLA Eng. & Wales* (1931)
**Archives**  JRL, Labour History Archive and Study Centre, corresp. and papers | NL Wales, Mainwaring MSS · PRO, Home Office MSS, HO 45/10743 · U. Wales, Swansea, Horner MSS · U. Warwick Mod. RC, corresp. with International Transport Workers' Federation
**Likenesses**  photographs, 1925–6, Hult. Arch. · Quiz [P. Evans], caricature, mechanical reproduction, NPG; repro. in *Saturday Review* (25 Aug 1925) · photograph, Sci. Mus., Science and Society Picture Library [*see illus.*] · photographs, Trades Union Congress, London
**Wealth at death**  £2965 2s. 6d.: probate, 28 Dec 1931, *CGPLA Eng. & Wales*

**Cook, Sir Basil Alfred Kemball-** (1876–1949), civil servant, was born at 23 Montpelier Crescent, Brighton, Sussex, on 21 May 1876, the second son of Herbert Kemball Cook, headmaster of a preparatory school at Stanmore, and his wife, Marion, daughter of Henry Davies. He was a nephew of Sir Edward Tyas Cook, and two other uncles were distinguished schoolmasters, at Winchester and St Paul's, while another, Arthur Francis Leach, became chief charity commissioner.

Kemball-Cook was educated at Temple Grove, where he won scholarships for Westminster and Eton, choosing the latter. He went to Cambridge in 1895, having been elected to a scholarship at King's College, and in 1898 was placed in the first division of the second class of part one of the classical tripos. He did not distinguish himself on the playing fields—he had a severe illness when about thirteen—but he rowed in the King's College trial eights in 1895, was a keen cyclist and hill walker in his earlier years, and later

became and remained an enthusiastic motorist. He was always a skilful photographer. At Cambridge he belonged to a group that included men such as John Evelyn Shuckburgh and Hugh Fletcher Moulton, and the friendships that were formed continued after they left university.

Kemball-Cook passed into the first class of the civil service by open competition and was appointed to the transport department of the Admiralty in 1900. This department was responsible for providing the merchant shipping to carry all the requirements of the fighting forces of the empire, work that required close and daily contact and negotiation with the British shipping industry. In 1906 he married Nancy Annie, daughter of Henry Pavitt, superintendent of a sugar works; they had four sons and one daughter.

The outbreak of war with Germany in 1914 threw great responsibilities on the transport department and led to rapid increases in staff. Kemball-Cook had been promoted to principal and when the department became part of the newly created Ministry of Shipping, effectively taking control of all British navigation, he became director of naval sea transport (1917). He distinguished himself in this post and in 1918 was appointed CB. To ability and energy he joined the capacity for working harmoniously with the representatives of the United States, France, and other countries whose shipping interests were large, and whose goodwill and help were necessary. This led in 1920 to his being seconded for service with the reparation commission in Paris, where he became chairman of the managing board of the maritime service. In 1921 he was appointed assistant British delegate on the reparation commission, a post that he held until 1926, and which necessitated long residence in Paris. In 1925 he was appointed KCMG. When his work with the reparation commission ended he retired from the civil service.

In 1927 Kemball-Cook became managing director of the British Tanker Company Ltd, a post in which he was responsible for the efficiency of the shipping fleet of the Anglo-Persian Oil Company. He held this position until 1935. In 1930 his first marriage ended in divorce, and the following year he married Cécile Protopopesco, a widow, and daughter of Paul Olenitch, a former general in the imperial Russian army. From 1936 to 1938 he was director of the British Guiana Consolidated Goldfields Ltd, a business syndicate that held exclusive rights to search for gold in that country. The failure of this venture, and of others, broke Kemball-Cook financially: in 1929–35 he had added a director's salary of £10,000 per annum to his civil service pension, but in July 1937 this income virtually ceased; a year later he was declared bankrupt with debts of over £17,000 and assets of less than £20. He subsequently blamed his insolvency on the high cost of alimony payments to his former wife, on high levels of income tax, and on a heavy loss on the stock exchange in 1931. In the opinion of the official receiver, though, the true cause was 'unjustifiable extravagance, coupled with a tendency to speculation' (*The Times*, 3 Feb 1939). During the Second World War he served as an air-raid warden and from 1942 to 1948 he acted first as deputy and then as divisional food officer for London.

Kemball-Cook was a man of high intellectual qualities, quick in comprehension, lucid and crisp in discussion. He was always ready to accept a new or different point of view and was quick to assess its validity; but he was also firm in maintaining his position if not convinced by arguments. He was a first-rate organizer and a rapid worker. His personality was pleasant and friendly and he quickly gained the confidence of those with whom he worked, including many members of foreign governments and organizations. He received a number of foreign decorations, including commander of the Légion d'honneur. He had a keen sense of humour and read much, and in his Admiralty days was a great admirer of Pepys, whom he quoted to good purpose. He died suddenly at his home, 9 Queen's Gate, London, on 28 November 1949.

E. J. FOLEY, *rev.* MARK POTTLE

**Sources** *The Times* (5 Aug 1938) · *The Times* (4 Nov 1938) · *The Times* (3 Feb 1939) · *The Times* (29 Nov 1949) · personal knowledge (1959) · private information (1959) · Venn, *Alum. Cant.*
**Archives** NRA, priv. coll., memoirs
**Likenesses** W. Stoneman, photograph, 1919, NPG

**Cook** [*née* Graves], **Cecily Mary** (1889/90–1962), trade unionist and suffrage campaigner, daughter of Alfred Graves, was probably born in London, but little else is known about her early life. She married Herbert G. N. Cook, a secretary, on 6 November 1909. The couple's only child, a son, died at about the age of nineteen. Following Herbert Cook's early death, Cecily lived for many years with Arthur Thomas Hagg, a professional artist.

Active in the labour and women's movements for around half a century, in her early years Cecily Cook was an ardent trade unionist and prominent suffrage campaigner. She later joined the information and research department of the Independent Labour Party (ILP), where she prepared weekly notes for speakers and memoranda for the use of MPs, as well as articles and pamphlets. Cecily Cook was also active in constituency politics, serving as Clement Attlee's chief woman worker when he contested Limehouse for Labour in 1922 and 1923, and standing herself as a Co-operative Women's Guild nominee for a seat on the London county council at Wandsworth in 1925.

Cecily Cook joined the Earlsfield branch (London) of the Co-operative Women's Guild in 1920. She later moved to the Marylebone branch where she held the offices of president and secretary. Following the break with Labour, Mrs Cook left the ILP, and from 1933 to 1938 worked as member of the guild head office staff. After one unsuccessful attempt, she was elected guild secretary in 1940, a position she retained until her retirement thirteen years later. Cecily Cook was strongly internationalist in outlook and in 1951 was made president of the International Co-operative Women's Guild. She was honoured for her co-operative work when she was appointed OBE in 1948.

The guild's most successful period as a radical organization campaigning for women's rights was over before Cecily Cook was elected to a position of national leadership. Nevertheless, she was an important voice in emphasizing the guild's traditional role in educating for citizenship, and became a significant promoter of the benefits of peace and reconstruction. Guild membership fell during wartime but by 1950 had recovered some of its losses, an achievement in part explained by Cecily Cook's enthusiasm and devotion to duty. Her work with the guild was characterized by her belief in the centrality of the spirit of co-operation to the democratic ideal.

Cecily Cook had many recreational interests, including gardening, poetry, and archaeology. She was said to be an indomitable and inspiring figure, although essentially modest in character. She died on 28 June 1962 at the Whittington Hospital, Archway, London, and was cremated at Golders Green crematorium on 3 July 1962. Mrs Cook left little money, and probate of her will was granted to Arthur Hagg.

DAVID THOMS

**Sources** J. Bellamy and H. F. Bing, 'Cook, Cecily Mary', *DLB*, vol. 2 · *Co-operative News* (18 May 1940) · *Woman's Outlook* (8 July 1940) · *Co-operative Review* (July 1962) · *Manchester Guardian* (9 May 1947) · J. Gaffin and D. Thoms, *Caring and sharing: the centenary history of the Co-operative Women's Guild* (1983) · *The Times* (13 July 1962) · d. cert. · *CGPLA Eng. & Wales* (1962)
**Wealth at death** £503 1s. 3d.: probate, 29 Aug 1962, *CGPLA Eng. & Wales*

**Cook, Ebenezer** (*b. c.*1667, *d.* in or after **1732**), poet, was the son of Andrew Cook (*d.* 1712), a planter and merchant, of Dorchester county, Maryland, and Anne Bowyer, who married in London on 1 August 1665. In 1694 Ebenezer Cook was an adult living in St Mary's City, Maryland (then capital of the colony). He was in London on 26 September 1700, when Edward Ebbitts of Dorchester county delegated his power of attorney to Cook. His earliest extant poem was a hudibrastic satire of Maryland as a frontier environment with illiterate lawyers and magistrates living among savage American Indians, wolves, and rattlesnakes. Or so it seemed to the greenhorn narrator of Cook's *The Sot-Weed Factor, or, A Voyage to Maryland: a Satyr* (1708). 'Sot-weed', or the weed that makes one drunk, was an idiom for tobacco. Actually Cook, an old Maryland hand, imitated and burlesqued the English anti-promotion literature, closely following the structure of a popular seventeenth-century song, 'A West Country Man's Voyage to New England'. To the English audience Cook's *Sot-Weed Factor* satirized Maryland and America; but to the American audience it satirized the common preconceptions about America. For example, the timorous narrator believes he hears the hissing of a rattlesnake, but it is really the buzzing of a mosquito, though neither the greenhorn speaker nor the uninitiated audience realize this.

Cook's father died in London on 1 January 1712; he left Cook's Point, in Dorchester county, to Ebenezer and his sister, Anna. By 1717 the poet had returned to Maryland where he sold his share of Cook's Point. He moved to Baltimore county by 1721 and became the deputy receiver-general for Charles Calvert, third Baron Baltimore. After a printing press was established in Annapolis in 1726, Ebenezer Cook had an outlet for his poetry. From 1727 to 1732 he wrote a series of elegies, the first being his *Elogy on the Death of Thomas Bordley, Esq.* (1727), which was signed 'Ebenezer Cook, Poet-Laureat, of Maryland'. Why he assumed this title is not clear: it was perhaps a private joke.

Cook turned to Maryland's trade and economy in his poem *Sotweed redivivus, or, The Planters Looking-Glass, by E. C. Gent.* (1730). After calling for tobacco legislation and for a paper currency, the author recommended that the planters should diversify their crops, not just raise tobacco.

Cook's *The Maryland muse, containing I. The history of Colonel Nathaniel Bacon's rebellion in Virginia, done into hudibrastick verse, from an old MS. II. The sotweed factor* (1731) contained a hudibrastic poem based upon John Cotton's history of Nathaniel Bacon's rebellion in Virginia (1676), as well as the 'third edition' of *The Sot-Weed Factor* (no copy of the second edition is known). The *History of Nathaniel Bacon's Rebellion* is the first of a number of fictional versions of the tragic history, though its burlesque deprives the story of its seriousness and importance. The poem is without the double vision that gives *The Sot-Weed Factor* distinction. Cook's last two known poems, both elegies, were written in 1732, one on Governor Benedict Leonard Calvert and the other on William Lock, a justice of the Maryland court. Cook probably wrote other poems, for all his poetry published in Maryland survives in unique copies (except *Sotweed redivivus* which has two extant copies). The poet and local historian who sent him a copy of Cotton's manuscript history of Bacon's rebellion in 1730 or 1731 addressed Cook as 'Old Poet', echoing Cook's characterization of himself in *Sotweed redivivus*. Cook is not known to have married, and no reference to him is known after 1732.                                    J. A. Leo Lemay

**Sources** J. A. L. Lemay, 'Ebenezer Cook', *Men of letters in colonial Maryland* (Knoxville, Tenn., 1972), 77–110 · L. C. Wroth, 'The Maryland muse' by Ebenezer Cooke (1935) · E. H. Cohen, 'The elegies of Ebenezer Cooke', *Early American Literature*, 4 (1969), 49–72 · R. D. Arner, 'Ebenezer Cook's *Sot-weed factor*: the structure of satire', *Southern Literary Journal*, 4 (1971), 33–47 · R. D. Arner, 'Ebenezer Cook: satire in the colonial South', *Southern Literary Journal*, 8 (1975), 153–64

**Cook, Edward Dutton** (1831–1883), theatre critic and author, born at 9 Grenville Street, Brunswick Square, London, on 30 January 1831, was the second son of George Simon Cook (*d.* 1852) of Grantham, Lincolnshire, a solicitor of the firm of Le Blanc and Cook of Blackfriars, London, who had nine children. At the age of six he went to a school kept by a Miss Boswell at Haverstock Hill. He moved to another school at Bradmore House, Chiswick, and finally, about 1843, entered King's College School. Having completed his education he was articled to his father, and remained in his office for about four years, after which he found work in the Madras Railway Company's office in New Broad Street in the City. In his spare time he followed his artistic and literary tastes, and as soon as he was able he left the railway company and devoted himself entirely to literature as a profession. Having studied painting under Rolt, and learned engraving,

he at one time sought employment on *Punch* as a draughtsman on wood. In 1859 he became a member of the Artists' rifle corps and of the Ramblers' Club, which met every night from November to May at Dick's Tavern, Fleet Street. About this period, in conjunction with Leopold Lewis, he wrote a melodrama entitled *The Dove and the Serpent*, which was produced with much success, under Nelson Lee's management, at the City of London Theatre.

From 1867 to October 1875 Cook was the theatre critic for the *Pall Mall Gazette*, while simultaneously acting as the assistant editor of the *Cornhill Magazine* (1868–71). In 1875 he resigned from the *Pall Mall Gazette* when some of his articles were tampered with, and was asked by Edmund Yates to become theatre critic for *The World* newspaper, a post he held until his death. Meanwhile, on 20 August 1874, he married Linda Scates, the second daughter of Joseph Scates, whom he had met at Gad Hill, at the house of Charles Dickens. She was a pupil of the Royal Academy of Music and a well-known pianist. Soon they had a daughter, whom they named Sylvia after the heroine of Cook's first novel.

Cook was a writer of numerous articles on art topics in various reviews, newspapers, and periodicals, and the author of many works of fiction. Of the latter, *Paul Foster's Daughter*, his first work, served to establish his reputation in 1861. Although he remained a prolific writer, with *Hobson's Choice*, *Young Mr Nightingale*, and many other novels being published regularly, his later novels did not maintain the popularity which his earlier works achieved: his style was not sufficiently sensational to suit the fashion of the period. He was one of the contributors to the *Dictionary of National Biography*, and furnished the dramatic and theatrical lives in letter A to the first and second volumes. Most successful were his writings on the theatre, which include *A Book of the Play* (1876), *Hours with the Players* (two vols., 1881), *Nights at the Play*, and *On the Stage* (both 1883, the former containing selected articles from his contributions to the *Pall Mall Gazette* and *The World*, including his notices of early London appearances of Henry Irving and Ellen Terry). Cook died suddenly of syncope, following heart disease, at his home, 69 Gloucester Crescent, on 11 September 1883, and was buried in Highgate cemetery on 15 September.                        G. C. Boase, *rev.* Nilanjana Banerji

**Sources** *The Times* (13 Sept 1883) · *The Times* (14 Sept 1883) · *The Graphic* (29 Sept 1883) · *Longman's Magazine* (Dec 1883) · P. Hartnoll, ed., *The Oxford companion to the theatre*, 3rd edn (1967) · P. Hartnoll, ed., *The concise Oxford companion to the theatre* (1972) · Adams, *Drama* · *The life and reminiscences of E. L. Blanchard, with notes from the diary of Wm. Blanchard*, ed. C. W. Scott and C. Howard, 2 vols. (1891) · *The Theatre*, 4th ser., 2 (1883), 212–14

**Likenesses** portrait, repro. in *The Graphic*, 321

**Wealth at death** £1975 16s. 6d.: probate, 23 Oct 1883, *CGPLA Eng. & Wales*

**Cook, Sir Edward Tyas** (1857–1919), journalist, born on 12 May 1857, at Brighton, was the youngest son of Silas Kemball Cook, secretary of the Royal Naval Hospital, Greenwich, and his wife, Emily Archer, proprietor of a preparatory school. He was educated at Winchester, of which college he was elected a fellow in 1903, and New College, Oxford. He was president of the Oxford Union (1879), and

Sir Edward Tyas Cook (1857–1919), by James Russell & Sons

graduated with a double first in 1880. In 1881 he joined the Inner Temple, but he never took his bar finals. University contemporaries admired Cook's abilities and character and it was assumed that he would enjoy a brilliant career in politics. Immediately upon leaving Oxford he acted as secretary of the London Society for Extension of University Teaching (1882–5). He unsuccessfully applied for a number of appointments but turned down an offer to enter the civil service. His long-held ambition was to become a journalist, and he made occasional contributions to a variety of journals, including *Truth*, the *Oxford Chronicle*, and the *Pall Mall Gazette*. In August 1888 Cook accepted a part-time editorial post on the *Pall Mall Gazette*, later succeeding Alfred Milner, a lifelong friend, as W. T. Stead's assistant editor. Cook always acknowledged the debt he owed to Stead, and in his turn as editor applied some of Stead's ideas. But as a writer his methods were the opposite of Stead's; he relied upon quiet, incisive argument, not emphatic assertion and remonstrance. Cook was always a copious writer. His approach to any subject was cool, methodical, and cautious; his style, crisp and analytical. Those who engaged him in controversy rapidly discovered the rich variety of polemical weapons he effortlessly commanded, and the deadly accuracy of his tenacious memory for recondite facts.

In 1889, when Stead resigned as editor of the *Pall Mall Gazette*, Cook was appointed his successor. Although his rule was to last scarcely twenty-one months, Cook made his mark as a conscientious editor. In Henry Massingham's informed opinion, Cook made the *Gazette* a 'young man's paper' (Massingham, 188); certainly most of the leading contributors were under the age of forty. On social issues the paper took a more advanced line than the *Daily News*, but Cook maintained Stead's enthusiastic support for a 'big' navy and Liberal Imperialist measures. W. W. Astor's purchase of the *Pall Mall Gazette* in the tory interest obliged Cook and his political staff to resign. With the financial backing of George Newnes, they were able to launch the *Westminster Gazette* in January 1893. It was intended to carry on the journalistic and political traditions of the *Pall Mall Gazette*. Again Cook's tenancy as editor was short-lived, for in 1895 he was offered and accepted the editorship of the *Daily News*, a newspaper that earlier, in conversation with Newnes, he had disdained as a mere party mouthpiece. The veteran manager and effective political editor of the *Daily News*, Sir John Robinson, was amazed by Cook's appointment and acquiesced in it only grudgingly. Under Cook's stewardship, sales of the *Daily News* continued to fall. Cook declared that as editor it was his duty to keep 'steadily in view the larger interests and duties of the country', and to ignore 'mere party considerations in the face of national emergency' (Koss, 1.399). By this he meant that, despite war in South Africa, he would continue to express his strong imperialist sympathies. This brought him into direct conflict with the radical, Little Englander wing of the Liberal Party. The consequence was inevitable. In January 1901, when the *Daily News* was sold to new proprietors, including George Cadbury, the Quaker, Cook was abruptly dismissed. Effectively he was banished to the political wilderness for remaining attached to a philosophy—imperialism—that had become thoroughly discredited. Cook was unrepentant and remained an unreformed Roseberyite Liberal. Nor did he make any secret of his continued admiration for Alfred Milner. When he departed from the *Daily News*, he was offered refuge as a leader writer by the *Daily Chronicle*, an undistinguished, halfpenny newspaper. He stayed there until 1910, but his heart was never in the task. He gave the best of himself in those years before the outbreak of the First World War to the editing of Ruskin's writings. Cook's admiration for Ruskin had begun in boyhood and never wavered; he was assisted in his monumental enterprise by Alexander Wedderburn. The *Works* (1903–11), in thirty-nine substantial volumes, remain the definitive edition of Ruskin's writings. As J. A. Spender noted, it was Ruskin's 'great good fortune' that he, 'the most copious and unrestrained of English writers', should enjoy as his editor and biographer 'the coolest, most cautious, most critical of writers' (*Westminster Gazette*, 2 Oct 1919). Cook's *Ruskin* (1911) was followed by other successful biographies, *Florence Nightingale* (1913) and *Delane of The Times* (1915).

Soon after the outbreak of the First World War, Cook was recruited to play a part in Britain's propaganda campaign. To the Oxford series he contributed a pamphlet, *How Britain Strove for Peace* (1914), designed to demonstrate Germany's war guilt. On 6 August 1914, Winston Churchill announced the setting up of a press bureau, a hasty improvisation. In 1915, with Sir Frank Swettenham, Cook was appointed joint director. It was no sinecure. The original aim of the bureau had been to guide rather than restrict newspaper coverage of the war, but the Admiralty and War Office proved stubborn and recalcitrant partners in an enterprise that, in Cook's own words, 'was never constituted at all—"it growed"—left to work out its scope and methods as experience might suggest' (Cook, introduction). The respect in which Cook was held by fellow journalists, his wisdom, and his untiring energy allowed a difficult task to be performed with the minimum of friction. The unremitting industry of the war years undoubtedly undermined his health. He left a dispassionate and balanced essay, *The Press in War-Time: with some Account of the Official Press Bureau* (1920), which was published posthumously.

In 1884 Cook married Emily Constance Baird; theirs was a happy marriage, but there were no children. Emily died in 1903. Cook was knighted in 1912, and made a KBE in 1917. In 1918 he suffered a stroke. The following year he developed pleurisy and then pneumonia. He died at his much-loved country home, Rose Cottage in South Stoke, Oxfordshire, on 30 September 1919.

In late Victorian and Edwardian London, Cook was one of the most influential journalists. He took a high view of journalism as a profession, although his claim to exercise complete independence as an editor was exaggerated. Though a convinced Liberal he was never afraid to criticize his party. A reserved, shy, silent man, he was a most generous and loyal friend.                    A. J. A. MORRIS

**Sources** J. Saxon Mills, *Sir Edward Cook KBE: a biography* (1921) · *Westminster Gazette* (2 Oct 1919) · J. W. Robertson Scott, *The life and death of a newspaper* (1952) [chaps. 21–32] · E. T. Cook, *The press in wartime* (1920) · H. W. Massingham, *The London daily press* (1892) · S. E. Koss, *The rise and fall of the political press in Britain*, 1 (1981)

**Archives** BL, corresp. and papers, Add. MS 39927 · Bodl. Oxf., diaries | BL, corresp. with W. E. Gladstone, Add. MSS 44461–44789 · BL, corresp. with Macmillans, Add. MS 55046 · CAC Cam., letters to W. T. Stead · King's AC Cam., letters to Oscar Browning · NL Scot., corresp. mainly with Lord Rosebery · Richmond Local Studies Library, London, Slader MSS · U. Newcastle, Robinson L., corresp. with W. T. Stead

**Likenesses** J. Russell & Sons, photograph, NPG [*see illus.*] · Spy [L. Ward], cartoon, chromolithograph, NPG; repro. in *VF* (24 Aug 1899) · photograph, repro. in Robertson Scott, *Life and death of a newspaper*

**Wealth at death** £11,168 18s. 10d.: probate, 19 Nov 1919, CGPLA Eng. & Wales

**Cook, Eliza** (1812–1889), poet and journalist, was born on 24 December 1812 in London Road, Southwark, the youngest of eleven children of Joseph Cook, a tinman and brazier. Her poem 'The Streets' recalls her London childhood. Her father retired from business when she was about nine years old, and the family moved to a farm in St Leonard's Forest, near Horsham, Sussex. Cook was probably largely self-educated, but with her mother's encouragement she began to write poetry before the age of fifteen. In a preface to her collected *Poems* (1845), she described this as a period in which 'rhyme was probably faster than reason'. Her mother died when she was fifteen, and poems such as 'The

**Eliza Cook** (1812–1889), by unknown photographer

Old Arm-Chair' and 'I miss thee, my mother' testify to her loss.

Cook's first volume of poetry, *Lays of a Wild Harp*, was published in 1835. Shortly thereafter she began submitting poems under her initials to the *Weekly Dispatch*, *Metropolitan Magazine*, and *New Monthly Magazine*. Her work was praised by William Jerdan in the *Literary Gazette*, and the popular response to her poems prompted her to reveal her name to the public. She was then living in St George's Road, Walworth. Her second volume of poetry, *Melaia and other Poems*, was published in 1838 and reissued in 1840 and 1845; it met with popular success in both England and America. Her last volume, *New Echoes and other Poems*, was published in 1864.

The appeal of Cook's poems lay in their simple forms and subjects and in the sentiment which infused them, which has aptly been described as 'consistently humane' (Taylor, 190). Her work was compared to that of Robert Burns, whom she admired. Cook wrote with great sympathy of marginal figures, including labourers, poor children, homesick seafarers, and American Indians. In A. H. Miles's *Poets and Poetry of the Nineteenth Century*, J. H. Ingram wrote that Cook 'sang for the people, and was comprehended of the people'. Cook's treatment of the disfranchised was informed by strong democratic beliefs, forcefully expressed in her poem 'Nature's Gentleman':

> Nature with a matchless hand, sends forth *her* nobly born,
> And laughs the paltry attributes of wealth and rank to
>    scorn.

Some of her poems, such as 'A Song, to "The People" of England', were overtly revolutionary. As a testament to their widespread popularity, a number of her poems (including 'The Old Arm-Chair', 'The Old Water Mill', 'The Indian Hunter', and 'O come to the ingle side') were set to music by various composers in the 1840s and 1850s. In addition, her poem on Thomas Hood ('Poor Hood') led to the erection of a memorial to him in Kensal Green cemetery.

In 1849 Cook began publishing a weekly miscellany, *Eliza Cook's Journal*. In her first issue Cook punned on her surname, describing her editorial role as that of preparing 'a plain feast, where the viands will be all of my own choosing, and some of my own dressing'. The goal of her *Journal* was to assist in the 'stirring development of progressive mind in "the mass"' by providing materials that would provide a 'steady and free communion with Truth'. While her *Journal* was certainly directed towards women readers and contained many of the staples of women's magazines—including poetry, tips on housekeeping and childcare, and juvenile fiction—it was also directed to members of the working classes. The *Journal* thus supported and extended the democratic ideals expressed in Cook's poetry. During its five-year run the *Journal* regularly featured strongly worded essays (many of them written by Cook) advocating increased educational and employment opportunities for women and for working-class people. Its pages supported public libraries, mechanics' institutions, extended Sunday hours for museums and exhibitions, and expanded career opportunities for women (such as interior and fashion design, engraving, typesetting, and watchmaking). *Eliza Cook's Journal* also supported emigration and looked to America for models of social reform. In addition to her own work, Cook published essays, poetry, and fiction by Samuel Smiles, Eliza Meteyard (Silverpen), Frances Deane, and Charles Hardwick. Cook's journalistic endeavours met with success: the *Journal* achieved a first-year circulation of between 50,000 and 60,000 copies (Altick, 394). Forced by ill health to cease publication in 1854, Cook used her final 'Word to my readers' to thank readers for supporting her 'efforts in the cause of simple Poetry and popular Progression', and to reiterate that she had undertaken the *Journal* 'less with the desire of gaining my daily bread than with the wish to be of use to my fellow creatures'. Many of her essays were reissued in 1860 as *Jottings from my Journal*, and in 1865 sayings and aphorisms from the *Journal* were collected, supplemented by new material, and published as *Diamond Dust*.

The sentiments expressed in Cook's poetry and prose reflect her efforts to break free from the societal limitations imposed on her class and gender. A woman who prided herself on her tiny hands and feet, Cook dressed in unconventionally masculine attire and wore her hair short. J. Leach notes that Cook's dress 'proclaimed a determination to be herself' and relates how an 1851 story in the *New York Times* describes her as 'Tilting back in her chair, planting both feet on the fender', and 'bluffly order[ing] a glass of beer' (Leach, 157). Cook was also most probably a lesbian. She never married, and from 1845 to 1849 she was closely linked with the American actress Charlotte Cushman (1816–1876), to whom she wrote passionate poetic tributes ('To Charlotte Cushman').

Although collected editions of her works appeared in the 1870s and 1880s, Cook's public life ended in the 1860s. In 1863 she was granted a civil-list pension of £100 per annum. She appears to have lived in relative seclusion and semi-invalidism until her death at her home, Beech House, 23 Thornton Hill, Wimbledon, on 23 September 1889.                                                                    SOLVEIG C. ROBINSON

**Sources** *DNB* · B. Taylor, 'Eliza Cook', *Victorian Britain: an encyclopedia*, ed. S. Mitchell (1988), 190 · J. Leach, *Bright particular star: the life and times of Charlotte Cushman* (1970), 157–66, 188 · *Eliza Cook's journal*, 12 vols. (1849–54) · *The Times* (26 Sept 1889) · *ILN* (5 Oct 1889) · *Englishwoman's Review*, 20 (1889), 539–40 · E. Cook, *The poetical works: complete edition with explanatory notes etc.* [n.d., 1882?] · F. Warne, preface, in E. Cook, *The poetical works* [1869] · E. Cook, *The poems of Eliza Cook: comprising 'Melaia'; together with her miscellaneous pieces* (1845) · S. C. Robinson, 'Defining the nature of good literature: Victorian women of letters, 1850–1900', PhD diss., University of Chicago, 1994 [esp. chap. 4, 'A press of their own: women editors and women's periodicals', pp. 184–203] · W. T. Price, *A life of Charlotte Cushman* (1894) · L. Faderman, *Surpassing the love of men: romantic friendship and love between women from the Renaissance to the present* (1981), 222–3 · Blain, Clements & Grundy, *Feminist comp.*, 23–31 · P. Schlueter and J. Schlueter, eds., *An encyclopedia of British women writers* (1988) · J. H. Ingram, 'Eliza Cook', *The Victorian poets: the bio-critical introductions to the Victorian poets from A. H. Miles's 'The poets and poetry of the nineteenth century'*, ed. W. E. Fredeman, 1 (New York, 1986), 269–72 · K. Hickok, 'Cook, Eliza', *Dictionary of British women writers*, ed. J. Todd (1989) · K. Hickok, *Representations of women: nineteenth-century British women's poetry* (1984) · B. Kreissman, *Minor British poets, 1789–1918*, 3 vols. (1983), 2.28 · *The new Cambridge bibliography of English literature*, [2nd edn], 3, ed. G. Watson (1969), 516 · R. D. Altick, *The English common reader: a social history of the mass reading public, 1800–1900* (1957) · *CGPLA Eng. & Wales* (1889) · L. Merrill, *When Romeo was a woman: Charlotte Cushman and her circle of female spectators* (1999), 138–67 · K. Gleadle, *The early feminists: radical Unitarians and the emergence of the women's rights movement, 1831–51* (1995) · *Notable women of our own times* [1883] · d. cert.

**Likenesses** H. Watkins, photograph, *c.*1856–1859, NPG · H. Adlard, stipple (after T. Smart), NPG · H. Adlard, stipple (after W. Trautschuld), BM, NPG · F. W. Evans, carte-de-visite, NPG · F. Holl, engraving (after photograph by J. Watkins), repro. in E. Cook, *The poetical works* (1869), facing title page · A. Miles, group portrait, black and white, repro. in *Reynolds's Miscellany*, 2 (1847) · D. J. Pound, stipple and line print (after photograph by J. Watkins), NPG; repro. in D. J. Pound, ed., *Drawing room portrait gallery of eminent personages*, 8 vols. (1859–62) · H. B. Willis, lithograph (after J. Watkins), BM, NPG · etching (after unknown artist), NPG · photograph, NPG [*see illus.*] · portrait (after photograph. by London Stereoscopic Co.), repro. in *ILN* (5 Oct 1889) · portrait, repro. in *Notable women of our own times* (1883)

**Wealth at death** £5957 9s.: probate, 12 Dec 1889, *CGPLA Eng. & Wales*

**Cook, Ernest Edward** (1865–1955), art collector and preservationist, was born at Camberwell, London, on 4 September 1865, the second of the three sons of John Mason *Cook (1834–1899), travel agent [*see under* Cook, Thomas], and Emma, daughter of Thomas William Hodges of Knighton, Leicestershire. He was the grandson of Thomas *Cook (1808–1892), the founder of Thomas Cook & Sons, the travel agents. A Methodist and teetotaller, and a bachelor, he lived most of his working life in London; in retirement he also lived at 1 Sion Hill Place, Lansdown, Bath.

Educated at Mill Hill School in north London, and at a private college in Germany, Ernest Cook entered the family business at an early age, and went on to play a leading role in the development of its banking operations. He and his elder brother, Frank Henry Cook (1862–1931), successfully carried on the family business after their father's death. But they had grown up in the shadow of their father, 'an uncompromising paternalist if ever there was one' (Brandon, 243), and they possessed neither the creative imagination of Thomas, nor the executive drive of John Mason Cook. The firm continued to prosper, nevertheless, until the brothers sold it to the Compagnie Internationale des Wagons-Lits of Belgium for £3.5 million in February 1928. 'It is not known whether the sale was prompted by shrewd intimations of the coming slump or whether the brothers simply wanted to retire from the business' (ibid., 266).

Following the sale, Cook retired from business, moved to Bath, and devoted his remaining years to cultural and related pursuits. He formed an impressive collection of fine and decorative art, mainly eighteenth-century, which he bequeathed to the National Arts Collection Fund. The largest bequest ever left the fund, it comprised 237 oils, watercolours, and prints. English artists included Bonington, Constable, Crome, Gainsborough, Morland, Reynolds, Romney, Turner, and Zoffany; the continental schools were represented by Claude, Hobbema, van Ruisdael, Tiepolo, and DeWint. In addition the collection contained important Chippendale, Sheraton, and Adam furniture; Beauvais and Mortlake tapestries; and English, continental, and Chinese export porcelain. The collection was dispersed after Cook's death among nearly a hundred public institutions, ranging from major national museums to small local foundations.

It was once said of Cook that he collected country estates as some people collected rare silver and antique furniture. Why he did so is not entirely clear. Although a keen shot and follower of hounds, in contrast to his brothers (both of whom had invested heavily in country estates) he had little zest for country living nor interest in farming. Rather his passion is believed to have derived from a deep and sentimental love of old England, particularly during the Georgian period, with its grand country houses, old landed families, coaching, and traditional sports. He regarded the estate and the estate community as a vanishing heritage which, together with the old paternalistic relationship between landowners and their tenants and workers, he sought to preserve.

Cook's interest in historic buildings was sparked by his purchase in 1928 of a Georgian terrace in Bath. In 1931 he purchased Montacute House, in Somerset, and the assembly rooms at Bath, on behalf of the Society for the Preservation of Ancient Buildings. By 1933 he had conceived the idea of forming a collection of landed estates to be preserved for the nation. His chosen vehicle was the National Trust, which at the time seemed best placed to further his objectives: to preserve his properties intact for the benefit of posterity, for him to be able to enjoy them during his lifetime, and, on his death, to be exempt from estate and inheritance duties.

Cook's relationship with the National Trust was crucial to the trust's long-term development. Concerned in the early years mainly with the protection of landscapes and open spaces, by the 1920s the trust had lost much of its original momentum and, beset by financial worries, was rudderless. Cook had assigned to it a half-share in his holdings of Wagon-Lits stock, worth about £100,000, in 1933. He and his agent, John Burrow Hill (1886–1962), convinced the trust of the need to preserve country houses and, to provide for their upkeep, also their estates. The 1937 National Trust Act empowered the trust to hold land for the express purpose of maintaining and conserving property. The Country Houses Scheme, launched by the National Trust later that year, signalled the commencement of a major new phase in the work of that body.

During the period 1931–1955 over £1.2 million was expended by Cook in the purchase of seventeen landed estates, totalling about 37,000 acres, located mainly in the south of England and ranging in size from about 900 to more than 4000 acres. Coleshill, Great Maytham, Hartwell, and Montacute possessed houses of architectural distinction, and Slimbridge and Little Dalby were famous hunting estates. Of the seventeen, six were disposed of and seven were vested in the Ernest Cook Trust. Only three—Bradenham, Buscot, and Coleshill, plus Boarstall Tower, and the original gifts of Montacute and the Bath assembly rooms—passed to the National Trust. Until the late 1940s Cook had fully intended to bequeath all his properties to that body, including his Bath house. This was on the understanding that the trust would, as a matter of course, declare them 'inalienable'; that is, it would undertake never to sell or dispose of all or any part of them. This it was unprepared to do. From 1945 relations deteriorated, until in 1951 Cook decided to vest the estates in his own landowning trust, leaving the National Trust with just the three estates already covenanted to it by agreements with their previous owners.

The Ernest Cook Trust came formally into being on 9 January 1952; it was endowed with 12,322 acres of land and a further 2940 acres was added between 1953 and 1961. It was set up as an educational trust, Cook having been advised that property thus vested would be exempt from death duties, provided the income was used solely for educational purposes. The trustees were empowered to establish or support any educational institution or initiative, except agricultural colleges. They were enjoined in the preamble to the trust deed to preserve the estates, but in fact they had the power to dispose of them if necessary. From modest beginnings, the Ernest Cook Trust grew to the position where its educational donations put it well within the top 100 charitable trusts, and by the early 1990s it was the country's leading rural and agricultural educational foundation.

While he lived Ernest Cook remained a remote and shadowy figure, with his contribution to the preservation of the national heritage in the fields of art, environment, and education scarcely recognized. By nature desperately shy and retiring, he had few family ties and communicated mainly through intermediaries, principally John Burrow Hill, his friend and agent. He shunned publicity, so that even royalty had difficulty in discovering his connection with the District Nurses Fund, which he had founded with a donation of £100,000 in 1930. Kind and gracious in his personal dealings, he took a keen interest in his tenants and staff, helping them whenever he could. He was not a conservationist in the modern sense, but a preservationist and extreme conservative, whose greatest fear was that his properties might one day be nationalized and overrun by vulgar hordes.

Ernest Cook died of chronic myocardial degeneration on 14 March 1955 at his Bath home and was cremated at a private ceremony at the Arnos crematorium, Bristol, on 18 March 1955.                                                    E. J. T. COLLINS

**Sources** E. J. T. Collins and others, eds., *Innovation and conservation: Ernest Edward Cook and his country estates* (1988) · *A gift to the nation: the fine and decorative art collections of Ernest E. Cook* (1991) [exhibition catalogue, Holburne Museum and Crafts Study Centre, Bath, 16 May–1 Sept 1991] · *A guide to the location of the fine and decorative art collections of Ernest E. Cook bequeathed through the National Art Collections Fund in 1995* (1991) · 'The Ernest Cook bequest to the National Art Collections fund', *The Connoisseur*, 136 (1955), 20–21 · *The Times* (16 March 1955) · *Bucks Free Press* (14 Sept 1962) [obit. of J. B. Hill] · P. Brandon, *Thomas Cook: 150 years of popular tourism* (1991) · J. Lees-Milne, *Ancestral voices* (1975) · J. Lees-Milne, *Prophesying peace* (1977) · M. Waterson, *The National Trust: the first hundred years* (1994) · *CGPLA Eng. & Wales* (1955)
**Archives** Archive of the Ernest Cook Trust, Fairford Park, Fairford, Gloucestershire | Archive of the National Trust, Queen Anne's Gate, London [esp. B/T/4, 532, 645]
**Likenesses** photograph, Ernest Cook Trust, Fairford Park, Fairford, Gloucestershire
**Wealth at death** £875,331 14s. 1d.: probate, 2 June 1955, *CGPLA Eng. & Wales*

**Cook, Florence Eliza** (1856–1904), spiritualist and medium, was born on 3 June 1856 at Cobham, Kent, the eldest of the four children of Henry Cook (d. 1879), a compositor, and his wife, Emma Till. The Cook family moved from Kent to London about 1859, and took up residence at 6 Bruce Villas, Eleanor Road, Dalston, in the London suburb of Hackney. It was here that many of Florence Cook's most important séances took place. She began to develop her mediumship at the age of fourteen, and by 1871 her séances were being reported in the spiritualist press. In the spring of 1873 she succeeded in producing Katie King, the first full-form spirit materialization seen in Britain. The medium—petite, pretty, and dark—and spirit—similar in features but auburn-haired—attracted a devoted and influential following.

Florence Cook's first patron was a wealthy Manchester spiritualist, Charles Blackburn, and the second was William Crookes, a scientist and future president of the Royal Society. Although controversial, allegations that she and Crookes had an affair during 1873–4 throw serious doubt on Crookes's avowal of the medium's genuineness. Cook was several times accused of fraud, most notably by George Sitwell and Carl von Buch in 1880.

On 29 April 1874 Florence Cook married Edward Elgie Corner (d. 1928), a master mariner from Dalston, and temporarily withdrew from giving séances. Two daughters, Kate and Edith, were born to the marriage, which was said

to have been unhappy. Florence Cook later undertook a European tour in 1899 in an unsuccessful attempt to revive her mediumistic career. Her younger sister, Kate Selina, also became a medium, and both she and her mother inherited a substantial amount of money from Charles Blackburn in 1891. Florence, who received nothing, died in reduced circumstances of pneumonia at 20 Battersea Rise, London, on 22 April 1904.

ALEX OWEN

**Sources** *The Spiritualist* (1871–4) · *Medium and Daybreak* (1873–4) · 'The mysteries of mediumship', *Light*, 14 (1894), 607–8 · 'The mysteries of mediumship [pt 2]', *Light*, 15 (1895), 7–9 · T. H. Hall, *The spiritualists: the story of Florence Cook and William Crookes* (1962) · A. Owen, *The darkened room: women, power and spiritualism in late Victorian England*, pbk edn (1989) · J. Oppenheim, *The other world: spiritualism and psychical research in England, 1850–1914* (1985) · R. G. Medhurst and K. M. Goldney, 'William Crookes and the physical phenomena of mediumship', *Proceedings of the Society for Psychical Research*, 54 (1963–6), 25–157 · *Crookes and the spirit world*, ed. M. R. Barrington and others (1972) · E. J. Dingwall, *The critics' dilemma: further comments on some nineteenth century investigations* (1966) · F. Podmore, *Modern spiritualism: a history and a criticism* (1902) · b. cert. · m. cert. · d. cert.
**Likenesses** photograph, 1874, London, Harry Price collection · photograph, c.1874 (Katie King), London, Harry Price collection · photograph, c.1874 (Katie King with a male sitter), London, Harry Price collection · photograph, c.1898, repro. in Hall, *The spiritualists*
**Wealth at death** apparently no possessions: Hall, *Spiritualists*, 160

**Cook, Sir Francis**, first baronet (1817–1901), merchant and art collector, was born at Clapham, Surrey, on 3 January 1817, the second son of the seven children of William Cook (1784–1869) of Roydon Hall, Kent, and his wife, Mary Ann (d. 1862), the daughter of John Lainson. William Cook, whose family came from Wymondham in Norfolk, had established a business as a retail linen draper in Clerkenwell which was later moved to Fish Street Hill. By 1819 he had opened a wholesale warehouse at 89 Cheapside, taking into partnership his brother James in 1822 and a Mr Gladstones in 1825. In 1834 the firm moved to 21–3 St Paul's Churchyard, becoming Cook, Son, and Gladstones, and, in 1843, Cook & Son. The concern became one of the largest of its kind in the country, both as a manufacturing and distributing house, conducting a large trade in Great Britain and the colonies in all kinds of silk, linen, woollen, and cotton goods. When William Cook died in 1869 he left a fortune of over £2 million.

Francis Cook was educated at Totteridge and at Frankfurt and started work in the print department of his father's firm in 1833, becoming a partner in 1843. On the death of Francis's eldest brother, William, in 1852, the firm assumed the style of Cook, Son & Co. On his father's death Francis Cook became its head. Despite other interests, he actively superintended his business and when in England continued his almost daily attendance in the City until within ten days of his death. He encouraged the employment of commercial representatives who travelled to the localities with samples of the firm's goods, using the extended railway networks. The firm became essentially a distributing, rather than a manufacturing house, and imported increasing quantities of ready-made garments from Germany.

In 1841 Cook made his first visit to Portugal, where Robert Lucas, the father of his first wife, Emily Martha (d. 1884), lived in Lisbon; he married Emily on 1 August 1841. He subsequently spent parts of each spring and autumn in Portugal, and in 1856 bought the palace of Monserrate at Cintra, a place redolent with romantic associations. He had the building completely restored and embarked on the development of its magnificent gardens. He gradually acquired vast areas of land near Cintra and renewed the prosperity of the district. In recognition of his services to the area and his benevolence to the poor, in 1864 Cook was created visconde de Monserrate by the king of Portugal.

About 1860 Cook acquired Doughty House in Richmond Hill, Surrey, and began to assemble one of the most important collections of pictures formed in England during this period. Although he had acquired some pictures prior to this, the 100 paintings which formed the nucleus of his collection were purchased in 1860 from John Charles Robinson, who continued to advise him on his collection, and who provided him with many of his further acquisitions. Cook purchased works of all the major schools of European painting. He and Robinson shared an enthusiasm for Spanish art, and one of the pictures Cook received in 1860 was *Christ Driving the Money-Changers from the Temple* by El Greco (National Gallery of Art, Washington), which was followed in 1863 by *The Old Woman Cooking Eggs* (National Gallery of Scotland, Edinburgh). The collection included the *Madonna and Child* by Lorenzo Monaco (Toledo Museum, Ohio), works by Filippo Lippi, Sodoma, Parmigianino, Sebastiano del Piombo, and Titian, the *Three Maries at the Sepulchre* by Jan van Eyck (Museum Boymans-van Beuningen, Rotterdam), and works by Dürer, Rogier van der Weyden, Berckheyde, Rubens, Rembrandt, and Metsu. The French pictures at Doughty House included the *Landscape with Lightning* by Francisque Millet (National Gallery, London) and the *Portrait of Diane of Poitiers* by Clouet. Although there were not many English paintings, Cook owned works by Gainsborough, Hogarth, and Turner. Italian maiolica, bronzes, ivories, tapestries, and antique statuary also formed part of the collection, which was vast in its scope.

Cook tried to make his private collection accessible to students. On 16 January 1873 he was elected FSA. His first wife died on 12 August 1884, and on 1 October 1885 he married Tennessee, daughter of Robert Buckman Claflin of New York, who had established her own career as a writer and banker and was a prominent advocate of women's rights. In 1885 he established Alexandra House as a home for women students of music and other branches of the arts and as a tribute to the Princess of Wales (later Queen Alexandra), at a cost of £80,000. He was created a baronet on 10 March 1886. Sir Francis died at Doughty House, Richmond Hill, on 17 February 1901, and was buried at Norwood cemetery. He had two sons and a daughter, all children of his first marriage. The main portion of his estate went to his elder son, Frederick Lucas, who succeeded to the baronetcy, part of his collection of works of art going to his younger son, Wyndham Francis.

CHARLES WELCH, rev. HELEN DAVIES

**Sources** *The Times* (19 Feb 1901) • *The Times* (13 March 1901) • *Daily Telegraph* (19 Feb 1901) • *Thames Valley Times* (20 Feb 1901) • *Richmond and Twickenham Times* (23 Feb 1901) • *Daily News* (19 Feb 1901) • *Daily Graphic* (19 Feb 1901) • *The Standard* (19 Feb 1901) • *Whitehall Review* (21 Feb 1901) • *Country Life*, 9 (1901), 227–8 • *Reynold's Weekly Advertiser* (24 Feb 1901) • *Freelance* (2 March 1901) • Burke, *Gen. GB* (1906) • C. Sebag-Montefiore, 'Three lost collectors of London', *NACF Magazine*, 38 (1988), 50–56 • T. Borenius, J. O. Kronig, and M. W. Brockwell, *A catalogue of the paintings at Doughty House, Richmond and elsewhere in the collection of Sir Frederick Cook*, ed. H. Cook, 3 vols. (1913) • J. C. Robinson, *Memoranda on fifty pictures* (1868) • J. C. Robinson, 'The gallery of pictures by the old masters formed by Francis Cook of Richmond', *Art Journal*, new ser., 5 (1885), 133–7 • H. E. Davies, 'Sir John Charles Robinson (1824–1913): his role as a connoisseur and creator of public and private collections', DPhil diss., U. Oxf., 1992 • private information (1912) • private information (2004)
**Archives** NRA, priv. coll.
**Likenesses** bust, Queen Alexandra's House, South Kensington, London • bust, Doughty House, Richmond, Surrey • bust, Montserrate, Sintra, Portugal • wood-engraving, repro. in *ILN* (19 March 1887)
**Wealth at death** £1,600,000: probate, 9 March 1901, *CGPLA Eng. & Wales*

**Cook, Frederick Charles** (1804–1889), clergyman and biblical scholar, was born on 1 December 1804 at Millbrook, near Southampton, Hampshire, the son of William Cook. He was admitted as a sizar at St John's College, Cambridge, on 8 July 1824, and as a foundress scholar on 8 November 1825. In 1828 he took a first-class award in the classical tripos, and he graduated BA in 1831 and MA in 1844. He also studied under B. G. Niebuhr at Bonn, and became involved in a financially unsuccessful attempt at running a school near Paris. He then returned to England, where he was ordained deacon in the established church on 22 December 1839 and priest on 20 December 1840.

In 1841 Cook became secretary to the London diocesan board and an inspector of schools in London and Middlesex; on 31 January 1844 he became one of her majesty's inspectors of church schools. On 2 June 1846, at Brighton, he married Janet Barbara Sophia (Jessie) MacKenzie (1810–1889), daughter of Alexander Douglas MacKenzie of Bursledon, Hampshire, and his wife, Sophia; they had no children. Cook was then living at St Michael, Highgate, in London. In 1849 he edited two poetry anthologies for schools, and in the following year his commentary on the book of Acts was published. On 30 June 1855 he was installed prebendary of Ealdstreet, in St Paul's Cathedral.

While in London Cook participated in an attempt at dialogue with representatives of the Eastern Orthodox church. On 30 March 1857 he was appointed chaplain-in-ordinary to Queen Victoria and on 14 September 1861 he became prebendary of Carlton-cum-Thurlby, in Lincoln Cathedral. On 13 February 1862 he was elected preacher at Lincoln's Inn: according to the obituary of Cook in *Notes and Gleanings*, E. B. Denison described him as the best preacher in England.

By 1863, following the unease caused by *Essays and Reviews* (1860) and by J. W. Colenso's ideas, it had occurred

Frederick Charles Cook (1804–1889), by Camille Silvy, 1861

to J. E. Denison, speaker of the House of Commons, that the biblical questions raised should be answered by an authoritative commentary incorporating the church's traditional beliefs. This idea was eventually realized as *The Holy Bible … with … Commentary* (or Speaker's Commentary, 10 vols., 1871–81). In view of his knowledge of Hebrew and of the archaeology of the Holy Land, Cook was appointed general editor, 'the great work of his life' (*Notes and Gleanings*), and wrote all or part of the commentary on Job, Mark, and six other books. Many felt that the learning displayed in the work was neutralized by its apologetic aim, and the Pentateuch section was severely criticized by Colenso and others.

In April 1864 Cook had been installed prebendary and canon residentiary of Exeter Cathedral, and in 1867, the better to tackle his work on the commentary, he was beginning to study Egyptian hieroglyphics. He was made precentor of Exeter Cathedral on 11 May 1872 and resigned the preachership at Lincoln's Inn in 1880 because of ill health. From then on Cook devoted himself largely to linguistic studies, but his deep misgivings about the Revised Version of the Bible led to four publications on the subject between 1881 and 1885. In *The Origins of Religion and Language* (1884) he propounded a primeval unity of language and belief among humanity.

Cook was a complete invalid during the last four years of his life, but he continued adding to his remarkable book collection, which he bequeathed to the Exeter chapter and which remains part of Exeter Cathedral Library. The collection contains works in many more than the fifty-two

languages with which Cook was reportedly acquainted. Cook was also the author of several sermons, and he contributed to various books and periodicals on religious and linguistic subjects. A photograph, apparently taken when Cook was in his eighties, shows him with a generous growth of white hair and beard. Cook died at his house in Exeter Cathedral close on 22 June 1889 and was buried at the cemetery in St Thomas, near Exeter, Devon, on 26 June. His wife died three months later, on 5 October.

A conservative scholar of international repute, Cook was philanthropic, hospitable, and well liked, a Christian gentleman who used his gifts in the service of his faith and who came to represent a bygone age. One of the tributes to him claimed that he 'had done the work of at least a dozen men' (*Western Morning News*, 24 June 1889).

PETER W. THOMAS

**Sources** *Notes and Gleanings*, 2/20 (15 Aug 1889), 114–20 [obituarist J. D. Montgomery] · biographical archive, St John Cam., no. 3088 · *Western Morning News* (24 June 1889) · Black Book, 13 Feb 1862, Lincoln's Inn, London, 29, 354–5 · Black Book, 3 June 1880, Lincoln's Inn, London, 35, 73–4 · census returns for The Close, Exeter, 1871, PRO, RG 10/2063; 1881, RG 11/2151 · *Western Times* (25 June 1889) · H. R. Luard, ed., *Graduati Cantabrigienses*, 7th edn (1884), 117 [for the years 1800–1884] · *Fasti Angl., 1541–1857*, [St Paul's, London], 34 · Exeter Cathedral chapter acts, 1864–89, Exeter Cathedral, dean and chapter archives, 3590–93 · Lincoln Cathedral chapter acts, Lincoln Cathedral, A/3/18, 113 [14/9/1861] · G. W. Kitchin, *Edward Harold Browne* (1895), 200–23 · parish register (burials), St Thomas, Devon [26/6/1889] · biographical archive, St John Cam.
**Archives** BL, Add. MS 56285 · Exeter Cathedral · St John Cam. | BL, Dawson MSS · BL, Add. MS 56273 · Durham Cath. CL, letters to Joseph Barber Lightfoot · LPL, letters to Lady Burdett-Coutts · LPL, letters to A. C. Tait · U. Durham, Auckland Castle episcopal records, Lightfoot MSS · U. Nott. L., department of manuscripts and special collections, corresp. with John Evelyn Denison
**Likenesses** C. Silvy, photograph, 1861, NPG [*see illus.*] · O. Angel, photograph, *c*.1888, Exeter Cathedral Library · O. Angel, photograph, *c*.1888, repro. in *Notes and Gleanings*
**Wealth at death** £11,934 16s. 5d.: resworn probate, July 1890, CGPLA Eng. & Wales

**Cook, Sir Frederick Charles** (1875–1947), highway engineer and advocate of motorways, was born at Switzerland House, Kingston Crescent, Portsea, Hampshire, on 22 April 1875, the second child of Charles Christopher Cook (*bap.* 1840), contractor, and his wife, Fanny, *née* Bailey (*b.* 1839). His parents soon moved to Worthing, where his sister had been born in 1868. He was educated at New College, Worthing, and at Brighton Technical School. His civil-engineering skills were honed from 1891 by tutelage under Miles Aspinall, borough engineer of Worthing. From 1894 Cook worked under H. H. Scot, borough surveyor of Hove, as an engineering assistant, registering then as a student member of the Institution of Civil Engineers (ICE). At St Cuthbert's, Kilburn, on 3 September 1898 he married Amelia May (*b.* 1872), daughter of George Frederick Bult, gentleman. They had three sons and a daughter (the latter predeceased him). That working experience and courtship allowed him to appreciate the case for a London–Brighton motorway, put to parliament in 1906.

In 1897 Cook became chief assistant at Nuneaton and Chilvers Coton urban district council; he then undertook a three-year spell as town surveyor and water engineer of

Hinckley. He returned to Nuneaton's service as its engineer and surveyor in 1903 and stayed until 1915, successfully proposing the Thornton reservoir and associated pumping plant (a large scheme costing £170,000) soon after qualifying as an associate member of the ICE in 1909. In 1914–15 he raised and commanded 216 army troop, Royal Engineers, in France, before commanding 209 field company, and 24 chequer division of the Royal Engineers. He was several times mentioned in dispatches, winning the MC, the DSO, and the Croix de Guerre, and reaching the rank of major. In 1919 he was appointed city engineer of Oxford.

Cook was elected a full member of the ICE in mid-1920 and in November 1920 became an engineering inspector at the new Ministry of Transport. He rose rapidly to divisional road engineer, Midland division, in 1921, and deputy chief engineer, roads, in 1929, finally succeeding Sir Charles Bressey as chief highway engineer in 1935. He attended an important conference of the Canadian Roads Convention at Quebec and the Permanent International Association of Road Congresses conference at Washington, USA, in 1930, where his diary and report to the minister record how its business in forwarding the construction of concrete motor roads was achieved. In 1935 he drove to a conference in Budapest held from 10 to 14 September on the proposed trans-continental motor route from London to Istanbul promoted by Sir Stenson Cooke, secretary of the Automobile Association. In 1937 Cook was appointed CB. Later that year he attended the twenty-third annual convention of the Canadian Good Roads Association, and then addressed a conference of the American Association of State Highway Officials in Washington. Thereafter he toured several American cities, freeways, and parkways, investigating urban road design and long-distance road traffic engineering issues. In 1936 his close knowledge of North American practice informed a paper he gave to the ICE entitled 'Road design and road safety'. Motorways were not yet part of departmental policy in Britain, for their tolled format built with private capital had been rejected in private parliamentary bills in 1906, 1911, 1924, and 1928. However, the highways and bridges committee of Lancashire county council in July 1937 adopted a proposal to build one from Carnforth to Warrington. Cook's reports to the minister of transport, (Edward) Leslie Burgin, helped shape the climate of concern to reduce the rising trend of road accidents so that in 1938 a delegation from Lancashire persuaded Burgin to accept the principle and route of a motorway while offering it no government funding.

Cook's paper for the meeting of the British Association for the Advancement of Science in Cambridge in 1938 looked forward cautiously to the impact of motorways. These issues also played a central role in his official work with the Roads Research Laboratory—founded in 1933—notably as chairman of the departmental committee on the design and layout of roads in built-up areas. He chaired a conference at the ICE on that subject for the Institution of Municipal and County Engineers on 20 October 1943. He was a member of the council of the ICE from 1935, chairing its new road engineering division from the outset, before becoming the ICE's vice-president in 1944, during Herbert Manzoni's presidency.

Cook's most important report on the value of motorways was written just after he had retired in April 1942, when it was agreed that he should remain at the Ministry of Transport in an advisory capacity, concentrating on general highway and development planning issues. His memorandum 'Post-war planning and motorways' persuaded the cabinet to build motorways for fast-moving traffic. It was prepared between April and August 1942, though it was not until July 1943 that Frederick Leathers, minister of war transport, released it for scrutiny by the war cabinet's reconstruction policy committee. Cook's ideas found support from among the county surveyors, while the ICE's panel on roads, road bridges, and tunnels had reported in favour of motorways in February 1942. He also utilized advice from the Institution of Municipal and County Engineers and from Herbert Manzoni, city engineer of Birmingham. He was backed by Sir Cyril Hurcomb, director-general of the Ministry of War Transport. Leathers commented that Cook's conclusions 'strike a right balance between providing progressively for our reasonable needs and launching out on the scale advocated by some enthusiasts who are perhaps unduly influenced by continental analogies' (20 July 1943, PRO, CAB 117/266). Alfred Barnes, minister of transport in the post-war Attlee ministry, announced on 6 May 1946 government approval in principle for motorway planning. It was not until 1956 that the cabinet could approve funds for constructing the first motorway, the Preston bypass on the route of 1937. Completed in December 1958 it was opened by the prime minister, Harold Macmillan.

Cook also contributed to highways policy between 1942 and 1944 on such matters as road safety, accommodation for heavy lorries, tolls, reorganization of powers available to highway authorities, and schemes to complete Waterloo Bridge, maintain design effort on a tunnel at Dartford, and build a bridge over the Severn at Aust. He chaired many of the key meetings on policy during this period. He was knighted early in 1942 for his contributions to highway policy.

After the war Cook became a director of the firm of consulting engineers Howard Humphreys, working on road construction, water supply, and sewerage schemes in the dominions. He also served on the special roads committee of the Royal Automobile Association from 1944, helping to define the design features and exclusions that informed the Ministry of Transport's specification for motorways issued in 1948 and the Special Roads Act of 1949. He was a nominee for the presidency of the ICE at the time of his death, which occurred at his home, The Mount, Ashtead Park, Ashtead, Surrey, on 15 May 1947. He was buried in Ashtead. R. C. D. BALDWIN

**Sources** *Journal of the Institution of Civil Engineers*, 28 (1946–7), 419–20 • *WWW*, 1941–50 • b. cert. • m. cert. • P. Baldwin and R. C. D. Baldwin, eds., *The motorway achievement*, 1: *Visualisation of the system* [forthcoming] • C. H. W. Biggs, *Notes on Nuneaton in connection with the Institution of Municipal and County Engineers* (11 May 1912) [incl. a photograph and biography; copy, Inst. CE] · J. Charlesworth, *History of British motorways* (1984), 16 · highways policy, motorways, tools, and estuarial crossings, and detailed notes on three major conferences, Inst. CE, Sir Frederick Cook papers · various files in the MT and CAB series, PRO, esp. CAB 117/266 · *CGPLA Eng. & Wales* (1947)

**Archives**  Inst. CE, diary of trip to North America · Inst. CE, MS on post-war planning of highways

**Wealth at death**  £1580 11s. 4d.: probate, 28 Aug 1947, *CGPLA Eng. & Wales*

**Cook, George** (1772–1845), Church of Scotland minister and ecclesiastical historian, was born in December 1772 in St Andrews, the second son of the Revd John Cook, professor of moral philosophy in the University of St Andrews, and Janet, daughter of the Revd John Hill, minister of St Andrews. John *Cook (1771–1824) was his elder brother. Educated at the United College at the University of St Andrews (1786–90), he was awarded an MA in 1790 and spent the next four years studying divinity at St Mary's College at St Andrews. Cook was licensed a preacher in the Church of Scotland by St Andrews presbytery in April 1795 and the following June was presented by the principal and masters of St Mary's College to the living of Laurencekirk. On 23 February 1801 Cook married Diana, daughter of Alexander Shank, minister of St Cyrus, with whom he had seven children.

In 1808 Cook published his first major work, *An Illustration of the General Evidence Establishing the Reality of Christ's Resurrection*, and the same year received the degree of DD from St Andrews University. Subsequently he devoted himself to the study of the constitution and history of the Church of Scotland. In 1811 he published the *History of the Reformation in Scotland*, which was followed in 1815 by the *History of the Church of Scotland*. In 1820 he published *The Life of George Hill*, a biography of the long-time leader of the moderate party in the Church of Scotland, who was also his maternal uncle, and in 1822 a *General and Historical View of Christianity*. His work was characterized by lucidity and accuracy, although his narrative style was cold and formal.

From an early period Cook took a prominent part in the general assembly, and on the death of George Hill in 1819 he endeavoured to succeed him as leader of the moderate party. Cook had, however, in opposition to the general views of the party, taken a decided stand against pluralities and non-residence—publishing a pamphlet on the importance of a resident parish clergy in 1816. Many moderates therefore distrusted him as a reformer with popular sympathies, and when he was proposed as moderator of the general assembly in 1821 and 1822 he was defeated on both occasions by large majorities. His temperate views, however, won over the party and he was unanimously elected moderator in 1825: from this time he was generally recognized as leader of the moderate party. In 1829 he was appointed professor of moral philosophy at St Andrews University, and demitted his charge at Laurencekirk, though this made no change in his relation to the Church of Scotland.

In 1834 the evangelical party, under the leadership of Thomas Chalmers, gained control of the general assembly

George Cook (1772–1845), by David Octavius Hill and Robert Adamson, 1843–5

and sought to modify the civil law of patronage by passing the Veto Act. This gave male communicants in a parish the right to veto the presentation of an unacceptable patron's candidate to the ministry of that parish. Cook strenuously opposed the passing of the Veto Act, claiming that it was an illegal infringement on the civil rights of patrons and presentees, and would involve the church in conflict with the civil courts. It would be more effective and constitutional, he argued, to leave it to presbyteries to judge the fitness of presentees and to refuse to ordain or translate unacceptable ones. When, as he predicted, the Veto Act did lead to conflict between church and state, Cook maintained that an established church had to accept the decisions of the civil courts with respect to the civil law of patronage, and repeal its Veto Act. He rejected the evangelical argument that this would compromise the church's 'spiritual independence'. Though unable to compete with Chalmers as a popular orator, Cook possessed great readiness of reply, while clear and logical exposition and accurate knowledge of the laws and constitution of the church enabled him to hold his own in technical arguments.

In 1843 the patronage conflict culminated in the Disruption of the Church of Scotland. Cook became leader of the majority, who remained in the established church, and he sought to rebuild trust between the church and state. However, he did not long survive the Disruption. Shortly after the assembly of 1844 he was attacked by heart disease, and he died suddenly at St Andrews on 13 May 1845. Four sons and one daughter survived him, including his eldest son, John *Cook (1807–1874), minister at Haddington.

T. F. HENDERSON, rev. STEWART J. BROWN

**Sources** *Fasti Scot.*, new edn, 5.477–8 · J. Bryce, *Ten years of the Church of Scotland*, 2 vols. (1850) · R. Buchanan, *The ten years' conflict*, 2 vols. (1849) · A. Turner, *The Scottish secession* (1859)
**Archives** U. St Andr. | NL Scot., corresp. with Archibald Constable · NRA, priv. coll., letters to the earl of Haddingdon · U. Edin., New Coll. L., letters to Thomas Chalmers
**Likenesses** D. O. Hill, four calotype photographs, 1843, Scot. NPG · D. O. Hill and R. Adamson, calotype, 1843–5, NPG [*see illus.*] · Hodgetts, mezzotint (in dean of Thistle robes; after J. Caw), Scot. NPG
**Wealth at death** £8392 18*s.* 6*d.*: inventory, 1845, Scotland

**Cook, Henry** (1642?–1700), decorative painter, has been described as the son of a portraitist of the same name employed by the Ironmongers' Company in 1640; it is impossible, however, to reconcile this with the accounts of the company, which record payments to an Edward Cocke, painter. According to Bernard Buckeridge, Henry Cook was well educated and accomplished; he may have attended Cambridge University. It is possible that he travelled to Italy to study painting and that he spent some time working in Salvator Rosa's studio, although accounts of this journey are confused.

Cook did not enjoy a great deal of success in the early stages of his career and seems to have lived in obscurity until he obtained an introduction to Sir Gordon Copley from Edward Lutterel which led to his decorating the former's new house in Yorkshire for £150. He subsequently spent five years living with the painter Theodore Russel (nephew of the artist Cornelius Johnson and pupil of Van Dyck); during this period he killed a man in a brawl over a woman—whom he was eventually to marry—and fled abroad, spending at least seven years in Italy until his crime was forgotten. He then went into partnership with a house painter in Knaves Acre, off Wardour Street, London.

Cook was employed by William III to reintegrate Raphael's cartoons (they had been cut up and kept as strips since being sent to the tapestry works at Mortlake). This took place about 1697, with the help of Parry Walton, the surveyor of paintings. The adhesion of the strips on to canvas and the restoration of the cartoons was devised in conjunction with Sir Christopher Wren's remodelling of the king's gallery at Hampton Court, which was designed to display the repaired works. Cook was also responsible for making at least one set of copies of the cartoons, using turpentine and distemper, a new technique which he pioneered. This set was presumably made for William III, who sent it to Holland. He also seems to have restored other paintings in the Royal Collection and to have made copies of them for the king.

Most of Cook's painting was on a large scale and of a decorative nature. He completed a wall-painting at Chelsea Hospital which had been begun by Antonio Verrio in 1687 (Verrio was paid £210 15*s.* for the work in 1688), signing the work in the lower right-hand corner 'H. Cooke Pinxit'. He was paid £295 for the work about 1690. The central area of the painting contains a life-size equestrian portrait of Charles II attended by marine deities, with the hospital in the background. According to George Vertue, the painting was a gift from the earl of Ranelagh whose house in Chelsea Cook had decorated.

Cook's other decorative schemes included the ceiling of the board room of the New River Company in Islington, London, which survives. This oval compartment, which depicts William III supported by winged allegorical figures, was painted between 1688 and 1697. He also painted the east end of New College chapel, Oxford, with a *Salutation* within a false apse; this was destroyed in 1788.

Apart from being a restorer and decorative painter, Cook was also an easel painter, his picture of *A Listening Faun* having been commemorated in an epigram by John Elsum, while George Vertue records a picture of *Charity* with life-size figures. He amassed a significant collection of books, paintings, and drawings which were sold after his death. He died on 18 November 1700 at his house in Bloomsbury Square, London; he was buried on 22 November at St Giles-in-the-Fields. His executors were the portraitist John Closterman and the banker and goldsmith James Seamer. The latter owned his self-portrait 'in his own hair' which was passed from George Vertue to Horace Walpole. It appeared in the Strawberry Hill sale of 18 May 1842, and was engraved by Bannerman for Walpole's *Anecdotes of Painting* (1862).

KATHRYN BARRON

**Sources** E. Croft-Murray, *Decorative painting in England, 1537–1837*, 1 (1962), 66, 245–6 · Vertue, *Note books*, 1.30, 40, 42, 88, 93, 94; 2.24, 134–5; 4.27–8, 29, 65 · J. Shearman, *Raphael's cartoons in the collection of Her Majesty the Queen* (1972), 148–9 · [B. Buckeridge], 'An essay towards an English school of painting', in R. de Piles, *The art of painting, with the lives and characters of above 300 of the most eminent painters*, 3rd edn (1754), 354–439, esp. 363
**Likenesses** Bannerman, engraving (after self-portrait by H. Cook), repro. in H. Walpole, *Anecdotes of painting in England: with some account of the principal artists*, ed. R. N. Wornum, new edn, 2 (1862), pp. 602–4

**Cook, Henry Caldwell** (1886–1939), schoolteacher and educationist, was born on 20 May 1886 at 1 The Elms, Toxteth Park, Liverpool, the fourth son of William Cook, merchant, and his wife, Jessie Euphrasia (formerly Caldwell). His father had considerable business interests in Argentina, and following the family's move to London Cook was educated at a preparatory school in St John's Wood, then as a boarder at Highgate School before entering Lincoln College, Oxford, in 1905. He took second-class honours in English language and literature in 1909, followed by the Oxford diploma in education, with distinction, in 1911. That year he approached Dr W. H. D. Rouse, headmaster of the Perse School, Cambridge, for employment (without salary), as the school's innovative methods interested him. There he remained as a form master and teacher of English for the whole of his teaching career. From 1915 he saw active service in the Artists' Rifles in France, and Rouse later noted that the war left its mark on him (Beacock, *Play Way English*, v).

In his early years at the Perse School, Cook encouraged

boys in acting, public speaking, and writing their own plays. These were published as the Perse playbooks (nos. 1–5, 1912–15; no. 6, 1921). His teaching methods attracted national attention at a time when similar innovations entailing spontaneous creative work by pupils and a renunciation of the teacher's traditional authoritarianism were being promoted by a number of prominent educationists. Largely at his own expense he established the 'Mummery', a permanent theatrical space in the school, and his curriculum centred on creative performance of Shakespeare. In 1917 he published *The Play Way, an Essay in Educational Method*, widely read and reprinted many times, in which he gave colourful descriptions, embellished by drawings and photographs, of his young secondary-school pupils indulging their imaginations, making plays, writing ballads, and lecturing on their interests and hobbies. Its challenge to traditional formality was sharpened by disillusionment with world war on his own part and on the part of many of his readers. Its title, much misunderstood, became mistakenly synonymous with progressive education in general. The distinctive and sometimes idiosyncratic details of his approach were principally applied, however, in the teaching of English language and literature, and it is in this area of the curriculum that his writings have had long-lasting impact.

Broadly, Cook's educational principles were that effective learning comes not from reading and listening but from action and experience, and that good work is more often the result of spontaneous effort and free interest than of compulsion. Play was observed to be the natural means of study for children: 'By Play I mean the *doing* of anything one *knows* with one's heart in it' (*Play Way*, 17). He hoped to persuade his pupils that their education was a journey of their choice, on which they travelled at their own pace. Only by their own efforts could they attain that perfection of inherent ability which is the true end of education. His belief in the value for civilization of artistic practice was influential and corresponded with the ideas of other contemporary innovators. His emphasis on play and creativity may be related to earlier psychological investigations by Karl Groos and G. Stanley Hall, and to artist educators such as Franz Cižek and Emil Jacques-Dalcroze, who recognized the seriousness of children's creative activity and the quality of their art. He encouraged folk-dancing at school, with the support of his friend Cecil Sharp. His engagement in open-air activities such as swimming, camping, and scouting was shared by other innovative colleagues at the Perse School.

Following the publication of *The Play Way* Cook's work was celebrated and the school was much visited. Notable pupils were Humphrey Jennings, Spike Hughes, F. R. Leavis, and Marius Goring. Jennings and Hughes each published several poems in *Perse Playbook* no. 6 (1921), and both Hughes and Goring publicly recorded their debt to Cook. His teaching methods were resurrected at the Perse School from 1941, to the influence of which the director Sir Peter Hall testified, and the school was prominent in the revival of education through drama in the 1960s.

Cook was remembered as immensely tall, always clad in a Norfolk jacket and light-coloured knickerbockers, made of home spun. Their clean and wholesome smell was lightened with a whiff of scent, quite in keeping with the fastidious neatness of his wavy greying hair. One former pupil thought that he 'might have been drawn by Aubrey Beardsley'. Some saw him 'impeccably dressed and civilized in speech and behaviour, as the epitome of the gentleman we aspired to become', though others reacted more negatively to 'his mode of dress and rather precious manner' (Perse School Archive MSS). He remained a bachelor, always quiet, retiring, and somewhat hard to know. The evidently homosexual aspects of his personality have been considered only by later commentators, and must be understood in the context of public school life and contemporary cults of sensibility. During his career at the Perse he had rooms in the house of a teacher colleague, R. B. Appleton, and they lie in adjacent unmarked graves. After Rouse's retirement a new regime at the school was hostile to Cook's methods. Consequent stress led in 1931 to a nervous breakdown, and in 1933 he retired. He lived an increasingly reclusive life in Cambridge, where he died at the Devonshire Nursing Home, 97 Tenison Road, of pneumonia, heart failure, and acute alcohol poisoning on 21 May 1939. He was buried on 24 May in the borough cemetery, Newmarket Road, Cambridge. The contribution of alcohol to his death was disputed by Rouse, who insisted that he had died of a broken heart (Mitchell, 166).                    PETER CUNNINGHAM

**Sources** D. A. Beacock, *Play way English for today: the methods and influence of H. Caldwell Cook* (1943) • S. J. D. Mitchell, *Perse: a history of the Perse School, 1615–1976* (1976) • *WWW, 1929–40* • *Cambridge Daily News* (22 May 1939) • b. cert. • d. cert. • R. J. W. Selleck, *English primary education and the progressives, 1914–1939* (1972) • J. Adams, *Modern developments in educational practice*, 2nd edn (1928), 205–26 • Spike Hughes [P. C. Hughes], *Opening bars* (1946), 56–64 • R. W. Allen, 'Shakespeare: "someone with a relevant message". Issues arising from … some traditions of Shakespeare teaching in schools', MEd diss., University of Sheffield, 1994 • D. A. Beacock, 'Henry Caldwell Cook', Perse School Archive • 'The Perse players, 1920–28', Perse School Archive • MSS, Perse School Archive [reminiscences of old Perseans] • *The Times* (20 June 1912), 9d • P. Hall, *Making an exhibition of myself* (1993), 37, 48 • *Cambridge Daily News* (25 May 1939), 5
**Archives** Christ's College, Cambridge, letter to W. H. D. Rouse
**Likenesses** photograph, repro. in Beacock, *Play way English for today*, frontispiece
**Wealth at death** £574 16s. 0d.: probate, 21 June 1939, CGPLA Eng. & Wales

**Cook** [*name in religion* Faringdon], **Hugh** (d. **1539**), abbot of Reading, was probably professed as a Benedictine monk before 1500. Born Hugh Cook, he subsequently adopted the arms of the Cook family of Kent, though his monastic surname suggests that he originated from Faringdon in Berkshire. He seems to have received his education entirely within the abbey, and, having previously served as sub-chamberlain, was elected abbot on the death of Thomas Worcester in September 1520. Almost at once he assumed the temporal duties expected of a mitred abbot, being placed alongside temporal landowners on commissions of the peace and other governmental commissions for Berkshire from 1526 to 1538.

During Faringdon's rule the grammar school attached to the abbey flourished greatly, attracting sons of the nobility and gentry who in 1534 included James Bassett, the son of Lady Lisle from an earlier marriage and stepson of Lord Lisle, the governor of Calais. About 1524 Edward Cox, the school's humanist master, published a treatise, *The Arte or Crafte of Rhethoryke*, which he dedicated to the abbot. In his last months of freedom in 1539 the abbot concluded a new teaching agreement between the abbey and Cox.

Midway between London and Oxford, and not far from Windsor, the abbey frequently received royal and academic visitors. Faringdon first entertained Henry VIII in January 1521, when the king made an oblation to the image of 'the Child of Grace' at the monastery; by 1532 the abbot had been appointed one of the royal chaplains and in the autumn of 1537 he both sang a requiem mass for Queen Jane Seymour at Hampton Court and participated in her burial at Windsor.

In 1528 Thomas Garret stopped at Reading Abbey on route to Oxford, and sold a number of heretical books to the prior, John Shirbourne, who was subsequently imprisoned for a time in the Tower. Faringdon took firm action against his errant monk, refusing in 1532 to permit him to return to the abbey. He similarly showed little sympathy with three monks who later in the decade appealed to the bishop of Salisbury against Roger London, the abbey's anti-Lutheran divinity reader, and successfully withstood the bishop's attempt to impose Richard Cobbe, a married man and former priest, as divinity lecturer upon the house.

Faringdon appears always to have been conservative in his religions opinions, and was among the minority in convocation in April 1533 who believed the pope could dispense from the impediment of affinity with a brother's widow, even when the marriage had been consummated. Nevertheless, he still managed to retain the government's favour almost to the end. A frequent attender of the House of Lords, in 1530 he had signed the petition to the pope against the delay in the divorce proceedings, offering the king the use of his abbey's library to find arguments for the annulment of his marriage. He took the oath recognizing the royal supremacy, and in 1536 he acquiesced in the act authorizing the dissolution of the lesser monasteries, though this may have been in the hope that the greater houses might yet be spared. From at least 1534 the abbot had been paying an annuity of 20 marks to Cromwell. In 1537 Cromwell heard that the abbot had been associating with favourers of the bishop of Rome, but took no action against him. Early in 1538 the abbot and convent of Abingdon yielded their house to the crown, and when Cromwell's officials came to Reading to suppress the grey friars in the following September, they took the opportunity to draw up an inventory of the abbey's relics, at the same time commenting approvingly that there was a daily scripture lecture in the chapter house in Latin and English. On this visit Faringdon put himself at the king's command, but still took no steps to surrender his abbey.

In mid-August 1539, however, Cromwell received a report that Faringdon was selling the abbey's sheep, corn, and woods to the king's disadvantage. This seems to have precipitated his removal to the Tower on a charge of treason, and on 19 September, in his absence, crown officials suppressed the house.

Much speculation has arisen over the precise nature of Faringdon's sedition. The French ambassador believed the abbot had some complicity in the Exeter conspiracy, and certainly John Rugge, one of his associates, a former prebendary of Salisbury who had retired to the abbey, was closely connected with the Pole circle. The charges in Faringdon's indictment, however, relate exclusively to his religious opinions, alleging that on no fewer than three occasions he had upheld the papal supremacy. Together with Rugge and John Eynon, priest of St Giles, Reading, he was found guilty of treason and hanged before the abbey gatehouse on 14 November 1539. Since no members of the community were involved in Faringdon's treason the government allowed the monks of Reading their pensions at the dissolution.                    CLAIRE CROSS

**Sources** *LP Henry VIII*, vols. 3–15 · J. E. Paul, 'The last abbots of Reading and Colchester', *BIHR*, 33 (1960), 115–21 · *VCH Berkshire*, vol. 2 · D. Knowles [M. C. Knowles], *The religious orders in England*, 3 (1959) · G. Baskerville, *English monks and the suppression of the monasteries* (1937) · G. W. O. Woodward, *The dissolution of the monasteries* (1966)

**Cook, Ida** [*pseud.* Mary Burchell] (**1904–1986**), author and campaigner for Jewish refugees, was born on 24 August 1904 at 37 Croft Avenue, Sunderland, the second of four children of William James Cook (1865–1959), surveyor of customs and excise, and his wife, Mary, *née* Brown (1872–1961). Together with her elder sister **(Mary) Louise Cook** (1901–1991), Ida Cook courageously rescued Jews from the Nazis during the 1930s. In 1965 the sisters were honoured for their rescue work and named among the 'Righteous Gentiles' by Yad Vashem Martyrs and Heroes' Remembrance Authority in Jerusalem.

The Cook sisters came to their rescue work through an unusual route: opera. After leaving the Duchess' School, Alnwick, they took civil service jobs in London and developed a passionate interest in opera. Despite their meagre salaries they were regulars in the gallery queue at Covent Garden and became known to many of the stars who passed on their way to the stage door. Acquaintances grew to friendships with some of the greatest singers of the century including Amelita Galli-Curci, Rosa Ponselle, Tito Gobbi, and Maria Callas. Among the luminaries they came to know were the Austrian conductor Clemens Krauss and his future wife, the soprano Viorica Ursuleac. In 1934 Ursuleac asked the sisters to help a Jewish friend, the musicologist Mitia Mayer-Lismann, make her way out of Germany.

Once the Mayer-Lismann family was safe in England the Cooks continued their efforts to help other Jews escape the Nazis. Under cover of their international reputation as eccentric spinster-sister opera fanatics willing to go anywhere to hear a favourite singer, and in collaboration with Krauss (who even arranged to perform in cities the sisters needed to visit and briefed them on the production's particulars, with which they regaled German border guards), the Cooks made repeated trips to Germany from the mid-1930s until the outbreak of war between Britain and Germany in 1939. Under the pretext of going to the opera the sisters would arrive in Germany, interview Jews desperate to emigrate, attend a performance, and return to Britain with jewellery and other valuables hidden on their persons or in their luggage. The valuables, property of the would-be emigrés, served as immigration guarantees for the British government, which accepted few immigrants who could not guarantee their financial security—a virtual impossibility for German Jews, forbidden by law to leave Germany with their money. Unlikely smugglers, the mild-mannered sisters were endlessly inventive in their strategies of evasion. Once, entrusted with a diamond brooch, they pinned it to a cheap jumper and walked through customs unmolested. Before smuggling out furs they replaced the German labels with labels from London stores. With these precautions, and by themselves engaging in a little theatricality, putting on their nervous British spinster act, the sisters managed, despite great risk to themselves, to help twenty-nine persons escape from almost certain death.

The success of the Cook sisters' smuggling operation depended, in part, on the sisters' remaining quiet and unobtrusive, but they became quite vocal in Britain. When their smuggling operation and refugee work became increasingly expensive—the Cooks themselves put up guarantees for refugees, as did their family—Ida Cook shook off her shyness and spoke, eventually with enormous and effective eloquence, in churches across Britain. She pleaded for funds, for sponsors for refugees who had no money, and for increased awareness and concern for European Jews. Meanwhile Louise, who had a great facility for languages, quickly perfected her German in order to ease their way in Nazi territory. The financial needs growing ever more urgent, Ida left the civil service and became a prolific writer of romance fiction under the pseudonym Mary Burchell. Her sudden earnings helped finance their urgent project. Moreover, her great popularity contributed to the success of the publishers Mills and Boon and brought the sisters, after the war, a substantial income, money that they used in later decades for the further support of refugees and displaced persons and for generous gifts to friends and family in need, as well as for opera performances, travel, and financial support of young singers.

Over the course of her long life Ida Cook wrote more than 110 romance novels, many of which were translated for readers on the continent and in Asia. She helped to found, and for many years served as president of, the Romantic Novelists' Association. She also wrote a memoir, *We Followed our Stars* (1950), ghosted the autobiography of the singer Tito Gobbi, *My Life* (1979), and published many articles on musical subjects. A lively, witty, and popular lecturer, she spoke to numerous and varied audiences, from women's clubs to music groups to hospital patients, about music, performers, and romance writing.

Louise remained with the civil service until her retirement, but her job did not seem greatly to affect their extensive schedule of travel, usually to hear music or visit musical friends on the continent or in the US (Ida dubbed some of these trips 'Cook's tours').

The Cook sisters kept a flat in Dolphin Square, London, where they housed refugees during the war and later fêted such opera stars as Callas and Gobbi. The Cooks were famous for their Dolphin Square parties, which brought together music lovers rich and poor, celebrated and unknown. Ida and Louise themselves, neither of whom married, lived together all their lives in their family home near Wandsworth Common, London. In a radio interview Ida called Louise 'the perfect lifelong companion', and persons who knew them report that the sisters seemed always to be together and never to argue. A close friend called them 'a unit'. The sisters maintained a wide circle of friends, persons from many different social realms and ranks, many of whom affectionately testify to the sisters' kindness, generosity, and conservative political views.

Ida Cook died of cancer in Parkside Hospital, Wimbledon, on 22 December 1986. Louise Cook died in Westminster Hospital of septicaemia on 27 March 1991. Both were cremated at Putney Vale crematorium, London. Having lived all their lives with the belief that money was to be enjoyed on the one hand and shared with those who needed it on the other, the sisters left relatively little for their heirs.          Rebecca A. Pope and Susan J. Leonardi

**Sources** I. Cook, *We followed our stars*, rev. edn (1976) · private information (2004) [family, friends, and colleagues] · BBC Radio 4 *Woman's Hour* interview with S. McGregor, 1979 · BBC Radio 4, *Conversation Piece* interview with S. McGregor, 20 June 1981 · audiotape of memorial programme for Ida Cook, 23 June 1987, Recorded Vocal Arts Society, London · b. cert. · b. cert. [Mary Louise Cook] · d. cert. · d. cert. [Mary Louise Cook]

**Archives** Theatre Museum, London, collection |SOUND BL NSA, documentary recordings · Recorded Vocal Arts Society, London

**Wealth at death** £91,012: probate, 16 June 1987, *CGPLA Eng. & Wales* · £150,567—Mary Louise Cook: probate, 1991, *CGPLA Eng. & Wales*

**Cook, James** (1571/2–1610), Church of England clergyman, was born at Chale on the Isle of Wight and went to Winchester College in 1585, aged thirteen. In 1592 he matriculated (as a *plebeius*) at New College, Oxford, where he became a fellow in January 1593. On 29 October 1597 he was admitted BCL at Oxford; he was incorporated as such at Cambridge in 1607. He was created DCL at Oxford on 16 April 1608. By 1609 he was rector of Houghton, Hampshire. Cook enjoyed the patronage of Bishop Thomas Bilson of Winchester, whose chaplain he is said to have been. It was to Bilson that in 1608 Cook dedicated his *Juridica trium quaestionum*. Influenced by the ideas of the French jurist Jean Bodin, Cook's treatise is a defence of the king's sovereignty, especially in matters of religion, and above all against the Jesuits—it was intended to answer a recent attack on Sir Edward Coke by Robert Persons, and also to uphold the rightfulness of proceedings against Henry Garnett, executed for treason in 1606. According to Wood, Cook was renowned for his expertise in Greek, and left a collection of poems, under the title *Poemata varia*, which does not appear to have survived. He died on 2 October 1610.

STEPHEN WRIGHT

**Sources** Cooper, *Ath. Cantab.*, vol. 2 · Wood, *Ath. Oxon.*, new edn, 2.95–6 · B. P. Levack, *The civil lawyers in England, 1603–1641* (1973) · J. Cooke, *Juridica trium quaestionum … (1608)* · T. F. Kirby, *Winchester scholars: a list of the wardens, fellows, and scholars of … Winchester College* (1888) · Wood, *Ath. Oxon.: Fasti* (1815), 275, 326

**Cook, James** (1728–1779), explorer, was born on 27 October 1728 in the village of Marton in Cleveland, North Riding of Yorkshire, the son of James Cook (1694–1779), a day labourer, and his wife, Grace Pace (1701/2–1765).

**Education and early years in the navy** Cook spent most of his childhood in the nearby village of Great Ayton where his father had found employment as a farm foreman and where he attended Postgate School. At the age of seventeen he went to work in a shop in the fishing village of Staithes on the north Yorkshire coast. He remained there for eighteen months before signing an apprenticeship agreement with John Walker, a highly respected Quaker shipowner, whose ships were employed in the North Sea coal trade. Cook spent eleven years in these highly dangerous waters, which were subject to violent storms, shifting sandbanks, and uncharted shoals—a valuable lesson in seamanship and navigation that was to serve him well later in his career. In 1755 Cook was offered the command of one of Walker's ships, but instead, on 17 June 1755, he enlisted in the Royal Navy as an able seaman as he was determined 'to take his future fortune' that way (Kippis, 4).

Cook's abilities were soon recognized and within a month he was rated master's mate. On 29 June 1757 he passed the examination for master and thus became responsible for the navigation and handling of ships of the Royal Navy. Cook spent most of the Seven Years' War in North American waters. As master of the 60 gun *Pembroke* under Captain John Simcoe, he was present at the surrender of Louisburg on 26 July 1758. The day after the surrender Cook went ashore, where he met Major Samuel Holland, an army officer who was making a plan of the fortress with a plane table. Cook invited Holland on board the *Pembroke* to meet Simcoe, an officer with a scientific bent, to explain the use of this instrument. From this moment Cook took an active interest in hydrographic surveying and a few months later, during a raid on French settlements in the Gulf of St Lawrence, surveyed the Bay of Gaspé; the chart was published by Mount and Page the following year. During the winter of 1758–9, spent in Halifax, Cook and Holland compiled a chart of the gulf and St Lawrence River from plans in the possession of Admiral Durrell, which was published in London by Thomas Jeffreys in 1760. During the following spring Cook was one of several masters of the fleet that surveyed and marked the Traverse, the principal hazard in the St Lawrence River, and their work enabled the entire British fleet to pass safely through and attack Quebec. After the fall of Quebec, Cook was appointed master of the 70 gun *Northumberland* under Captain Alexander, Lord Colville. During the

James Cook (1728–1779), by Nathaniel Dance, 1776

next three and a half years Cook surveyed Halifax harbour, compiled sailing directions of the Gulf of St Lawrence, and studied the theory of navigation. In July 1762 the *Northumberland* played a prominent part in the brief campaign leading to the recapture of St John's, Newfoundland, from the French, enabling Cook to carry out a number of surveys which so impressed Colville that he informed their lordships 'that from my Experience of Mr Cook's Genius and Capacity, I think him well qualified for the Work he has performed, and for greater Undertakings of the same kind' (Colville to Clevland, 30 Dec 1762, PRO, ADM 1/482, quoted in Beaglehole, 59). Thomas Graves, the governor of Newfoundland, was equally impressed and when he asked for a marine surveyor to chart the north and west coasts of Newfoundland he specifically asked for Cook. After the French capitulation Colville returned to England where Cook was discharged on 11 November. After a brief courtship Cook married Elizabeth (1740/41–1835), daughter of Samuel Batts, landlord of The Bell inn, Execution Dock, Wapping, on 21 December 1762, at St Margaret's, Barking, Essex.

**Surveying in Newfoundland, 1763–1767** On 19 April 1763 Cook took passage for Newfoundland in Graves's ship the *Antelope*. Immediately on arrival Graves sent Cook to survey the islands of St Pierre and Miquelon which were to be restored to France. At the end of July Cook sailed for the northern end of Newfoundland in the specially purchased 68 ton schooner the *Grenville*, and in her surveyed Croque, Quirpon, and Noddy harbours, before returning to St John's at the end of September. He then returned in the *Tweed* to England, where he spent the winter working on his charts in his house in Mile End, in east London, returning to St John's the following spring. In 1764, now in command of the *Grenville*, Cook sailed once again for the north of the island to resume his surveys under the orders of the new governor and his former captain, Commodore Sir Hugh Palliser. On 14 July Cook 'went into the Bay Sacre, Measured a base Line and fix'd Flaggs on the Different Islands, &c' (PRO, ADM 52/1263). The base was extended to the west by triangulation, while Cook established the latitudes of salient points by meridian altitudes of the sun. At the same time the *Grenville*'s boats obtained soundings off the coast. Over the next four years Cook surveyed the whole of the west and south coasts of the island in a similar manner, returning to England each autumn in the *Grenville* to draw his charts and refit the schooner. One of the difficulties facing Cook during his survey was his inability to observe for longitude, with the result that his charts of the island were graduated only for latitude. However, on 5 August 1766 he observed an eclipse of the sun on the Burgeo Islands off the south coast of Newfoundland, from which Dr John Bevis computed the longitude of the islands, which he published in 1767 in the *Philosophical Transactions* (57.215–16). This enabled Cook to calculate the longitude of a number of other places on the south coast of Newfoundland for inclusion in his sailing directions. In 1766, with permission from the Admiralty, Cook began publishing his surveys and sailing directions. Subsequently his surveys were published in 1769 in a folio atlas by Thomas Jeffreys, who republished Cook's sailing directions in the same year in *The Newfoundland Pilot*. These were incorporated in the famous *North American Pilot* published by Sayer and Bennett in 1775, which remained in use for many years.

**The transit of Venus and the voyage of the *Endeavour*, 1768–1771**  Cook returned to England on 15 November 1767. At the time the Royal Society was planning an expedition to the south Pacific to observe the transit of Venus across the face of the sun, which would enable the distance between the earth and the sun to be calculated. The Royal Society's first choice to lead this expedition was Alexander Dalrymple, but the Admiralty, who were to provide the ship, insisted that it should be commanded by a naval officer, and so Cook was appointed instead. The Whitby-built *Earl of Pembroke* of 336 tons was bought by the Admiralty and renamed *Endeavour*. Having passed for lieutenant on 13 May, Cook was appointed in command of her on 25 May 1768 and joined her two days later. The astronomer Charles Green was appointed by the Royal Society to observe the transit of Venus, with Cook as the second observer. Joseph Banks, a wealthy amateur botanist, also joined the expedition, bringing with him as his assistants Daniel Solander and Diedrich Spöring together with the landscape artist Alexander Buchan and the botanical artist Sydney Parkinson. The island of Tahiti, whose longitude had recently been determined astronomically by Samuel Wallis, was chosen for the observation.

The *Endeavour* sailed from Plymouth on 25 August 1768 and, after calling at Madeira and Rio de Janeiro and rounding Cape Horn, anchored in Matavai Bay on the north

coast of Tahiti on 13 April 1769. After successfully observing the transit on 3 June Cook, in accordance with his secret instructions, then sailed due south as far as 40°S to search for the great southern continent that geographers considered must exist in the Southern Ocean. Failing to sight land Cook then altered course to the west to investigate the land seen by Abel Tasman in 1642. The east coast of New Zealand was sighted on 6 October and Cook spent the next six months carrying out a running survey of New Zealand's North and South islands in which he established that Tasman's Staeten Landt was not part of the supposed southern continent. During this survey Cook was able to determine his longitude with considerable accuracy by means of the newly established method of lunar distances.

Cook next carried out a running survey of the unknown east coast of Australia in which his discovery of Botany Bay was to have a significant effect on the history of that continent. During the survey Cook was forced to spend over six weeks in Endeavour River making temporary repairs after running aground on an isolated coral reef, now known as Endeavour Reef. He then made for Batavia (Jakarta) in the Dutch East Indies for more permanent repairs. In sailing through Endeavour Strait Cook confirmed the discovery of Luis Vaez de Torres in 1606 that Australia was not joined to New Guinea as shown on most maps. Before his final departure from Australia Cook took possession of the whole of the east coast of Australia in the name of George III, naming it New South Wales. After further calls at Table Bay and St Helena, Cook finally anchored in the Downs on 12 June 1771. Although thirty members of the ship's company and Banks's party, including both artists, died during the voyage, mainly as a result of illnesses contracted in Batavia, the voyage was judged a success and Cook was promoted to commander on 29 August 1771.

**The first voyage of the *Resolution*, 1772–1775**  In spite of the achievements of Cook's first voyage it was clear that there were vast areas in the Southern Ocean where a great land mass might yet be found. Cook therefore proposed that a search for it should be made by circumnavigating the globe from west to east in a high southern latitude, thereby taking advantage of the strong prevailing westerly winds to be found there. Cook's plan was accepted and two further Whitby-built vessels were purchased and named *Resolution* and *Adventure*, Cook being given command of the former and Tobias Furneaux command of the latter. As a result of disagreements Banks, who was to accompany the expedition, withdrew and his place was taken by the German-born scientist Johann Reinhold Forster and his son George, while William Hodges was engaged as the expedition's artist. An important secondary aim of the expedition was to give extended trials to a copy of John Harrison's prize-winning chronometer H4 made by Larcum Kendall, known as K1, and three others made to the design of John Arnold. To supervise these trials the board of longitude appointed two astronomers, William Wales to the *Resolution* to take charge of K1 and

Arnold no. 3 and William Bayly to the *Adventure* to take charge of Arnold nos. 1 and 2.

Cook sailed from Plymouth on 13 July 1772. After calling at Table Bay, where the Swedish botanist Anders Sparrman joined the expedition, he set a course to the south, and on encountering numerous tabular bergs, altered course to the east to begin his first ice-edge cruise. On 17 January 1773 he became the first person to cross the Antarctic circle. On 9 February, during an unsuccessful search in lower latitudes for land discovered by Kerguelen in 1772, the two ships became separated in a fog. When contact was not regained Cook decided to continue his sweep to the south before the onset of the southern winter, reaching Dusky Sound, in New Zealand's South Island on 27 March 1773, after a passage lasting four months without sighting land. He remained there for six weeks refreshing his crew and surveying this extensive inlet before joining Furneaux at the agreed rendezvous in Queen Charlotte Sound.

On 7 June, with Furneaux in company, Cook got under way and after an uneventful passage anchored on 26 August in Matavai Bay. He then spent the next two months working his way back to Queen Charlotte Sound through the Society Islands and Tonga. Off the east coast of New Zealand's North Island the two ships were struck by a severe gale and on 30 October became separated for a second time. After waiting in vain for three weeks for Furneaux in Queen Charlotte Sound, Cook sailed on his second ice-edge cruise. On 26 January 1774 he crossed into the Antarctic circle for the third time (having done so a second time the previous month) and four days later, at 71°10′ S, 106°54′ W, achieved his farthest south. Cook now decided to spend one more winter in the south Pacific so that he could explore the south Atlantic the following summer. Making his way back to Tahiti, Cook anchored briefly off Easter Island, the first land to be sighted for 104 days. He next called at the Marquesas Islands before anchoring once more in Matavai Bay on 22 April. After spending a few weeks in the Society Islands Cook set off once again for Queen Charlotte Sound, visiting Tonga for a second time and carrying out running surveys of the New Hebrides (Vanuatu) and the north-eastern side of New Caledonia. In Queen Charlotte Sound he learned that Furneaux had arrived a few days after his departure and had sailed some days later. On 11 November Cook set off on the long voyage home, spending Christmas at anchor in the appropriately named Christmas Sound in Tierra del Fuego. After examining the north coast of Staten Island, Cook began his third ice-edge cruise, during which he rediscovered South Georgia on 14 January 1775 and discovered the South Sandwich Islands a few days later. Following an unsuccessful search for Bouvet's Cape Circumcision, Cook anchored in Table Bay on 21 March. After calling at St Helena, Ascension, and Fayal in the Azores, Cook dropped anchor in Spithead on 30 July after an absence of three years and eighteen days, during which four men had died, but only one from sickness and none from scurvy—a remarkable achievement.

**The second voyage of the *Resolution*, 1776–1779** On his return to England Cook was promoted to post captain on 9 August 1775 and appointed fourth captain of Greenwich Hospital, an appointment he accepted with the proviso that it would not preclude him from being considered for further service. At first he was occupied with the publication of his journal under the general editorship of John Douglas, canon of Windsor, since the account of his first voyage by John Hawkesworth had been highly criticized. In March 1776 Cook was elected a fellow of the Royal Society and at the same time awarded the society's Copley medal for his work on the prevention of scurvy. Early in 1776 Cook came out of retirement to command a further expedition to the Pacific with the purpose 'that an attempt should be made to find out a Northern Passage by Sea from the Pacific to the Atlantic Ocean' (BL, Egerton MS 2177B). Once again he was appointed to the *Resolution* with the newly purchased *Discovery*, commanded by Charles Clerke, as consort. Cook and Lieutenant James King were to act as astronomers on board the *Resolution*, while William Bayly was appointed once more as the *Discovery*'s astronomer. The artist John Webber, appointed to the *Resolution*, completed the scientific staff.

Cook sailed from Plymouth on 12 July 1776, anchoring on 18 October in Table Bay, where he was joined by the *Discovery*. On crossing the Indian Ocean, Cook fixed the position of Prince Edward and Marion islands. He next carried out a running survey of the north coast of Kerguelen, establishing the island's longitude accurately with the aid of K1, which was once again carried on board the *Resolution*. After brief stops in Adventure Bay in Van Diemen's Land and his old anchorage in Queen Charlotte Sound, adverse winds forced Cook to call at Tonga instead of making directly for Tahiti. On eventually reaching the Society Islands, Omai, the Society Islander Furneaux had brought back to England, was landed at Raiatea. Cook then continued across the Pacific, making his first major 'discovery' on this voyage when Oahu and Kauai, at the western end of the Hawaiian Islands, were sighted on 18 January 1778. Next the north-west coast of North America was sighted on 7 March and for the next six and a half months Cook carried out a running survey of some 4000 miles of its coast from Cape Blanco on the coast of Oregon to Icy Cape on the north coast of Alaska, where he was forced to turn back by an impenetrable wall of ice. A search for a route back to Europe north of Siberia also proved fruitless. During this cruise Cook became the first European to enter Nootka Sound on the north-west coast of Vancouver Island, where he remained for a month taking astronomical observations and cutting spars for use as spare masts and yardarms. Trade was carried out with the native Mowachaht for furs, mostly of the sea otter, which when sold later in China drew attention to the commercial potential of this trade.

**Cook's death and legacy** Cook decided to winter in the Hawaiian Islands, which he had named after his patron the earl of Sandwich, before making a further attempt to find a north-west passage the following year. After carrying out a running survey of the easternmost of the Hawaiian Islands, Cook anchored in Kealakekua Bay on the island of Hawaii on 17 January 1779. At first he was well received and by some accounts was considered by the Hawaiians as the embodiment of their god Lono. On 4 February 1779 Cook got under way to continue his survey of the islands but was forced to return to Kealakekua Bay for repairs after the *Resolution*'s foremast was damaged in a violent storm. It soon became clear that his return was not welcome, and bad relations culminated in the theft of the *Discovery*'s cutter. On the morning of 14 February Cook, with less than his usual judgement, landed with an escort of marines in an attempt to persuade the local chief to return on board where he intended to hold him as a hostage against the return of the cutter. The chief readily agreed to accompany Cook, but at the landing place they were met by a hostile crowd and in the altercation that followed Cook and four of the marines were killed. Cook's body and those of the marines were carried away by the Hawaiians and, according to custom, were cut up and the flesh scraped from the bones and ceremonially burnt, the bones being distributed among the various chiefs. Clerke, who now took command of the expedition, eventually managed to persuade the Hawaiians to return the majority of Cook's bones. These were put into a coffin and, on the afternoon of 21 February, were committed to the waters of Kealakekua Bay. On 23 February the two ships put to sea to complete the survey of the Hawaiian Islands. Clerke then set a course for Petropavlovsk Bay in Kamchatka, from where he sailed once more for the Arctic in an unsuccessful attempt to complete Cook's instructions, in spite of the fact that he was dying of tuberculosis. Clerke died in sight of Kamchatka as the expedition was returning to Petropavlovsk and it was left to John Gore, who succeeded to the command, to bring the expedition safely back to England.

Cook was survived by his wife but of their six children only three survived to young adulthood and none married so he left no descendants. His legacy lies in his contributions to exploration and science. In his three voyages to the Pacific, Cook disproved the existence of a great southern continent, completed the outlines of Australia and New Zealand, charted the Society Islands, the New Hebrides, New Caledonia, and the Hawaiian Islands, and depicted accurately for the first time the north-west coast of America, leaving no major discoveries for his successors. In addition the scientific discoveries in the fields of natural history and ethnology were considerable and the drawings made by the artists were of great significance.

There are numerous statues and monuments to Cook in many parts of the world, but the monument erected by Palliser in the grounds of The Vache, his country house in Chalfont St Giles, is perhaps the most significant. It consists of a square plinth, within a square tower, open on all sides, with a lengthy eulogy to Cook inscribed on the four sides of the plinth, beginning with the words 'To the Memory of Captain James Cook The ablest and most renowned Navigator this or any country hath produced'. In 1874 an obelisk to Cook's memory was erected near the spot where he fell, but the best memorial to him is the present-day map of the Pacific, which he did so much to shape.

ANDREW C. F. DAVID

**Sources** *The journals of Captain James Cook*, ed. J. C. Beaglehole, 4 vols. in 5, Hakluyt Society, extra ser., 34a, 35, 36a–b, 37 (1955–74) [incl. *The life of Captain James Cook*, vol. 4] • R. A. Skelton and R. V. Tooley, *The marine surveys of James Cook in North America, 1758–1768*, Map Collector's Circle, 37 (1967) • R. A. Skelton, *James Cook, surveyor of Newfoundland* (1965) • A. Kippis, *The life of Captain James Cook* (1788) • A. David, 'James Cook's 1762 survey of St John's harbour and adjacent parts of Newfoundland', *Terrae Incognitae*, 40 (1998), 63–71 • J. Rae, *Captain James Cook Endeavours* (1997) • PRO, MS ADM 52/1263 • BL, Egerton MS 2177B

**Archives** BL, drawings, charts, maps, and papers relating to his voyages, Add. MSS 8959–8960, 11803, 15500, 15507–15508, 15513–15514, 15331, 17693, 21593, 23920–23921, 31360, 37327, 37528, 38530, 42714 • BL, fragment of logbook, Add. MS 71094 • BL, journal and papers, Egerton MSS 2177 (A–B)–2179, 2591 • BL, logbooks and papers, Add. MSS 27885–27890, 27955–27956, 27958 • BL, transcripts of journal and logbooks, M/754 [copies] • Captain Cook Memorial Museum, Whitby, Yorkshire, fragment of journal; letters • Harvard U., Houghton L., fragment of directions for sailing from Louisburg to Quebec • Hunt. L., fragment of journal relating to discovery of Botany Bay • Hydrographic Office, Taunton, Chart Archives • Mitchell L., NSW • NA Canada, directions for sailing from the island of Scaterie to Quebec • NL Aus., journal, letter-book, notebook, and papers • NL Ire., journal • NL NZ, Turnbull L., logbook • NMM, drafts of narrative of second voyage • Peabody Essex Museum, Salem, Massachusetts, corresp. • PRO, Admiralty MSS • State Library of New South Wales, Sydney, Dixson wing • UCL, directions for sailing to Quebec | BL, letters to John Douglas, Egerton MS 2180

**Likenesses** W. Hodges, oils, *c.*1772–1775, NMM • N. Dance, oils, 1776, NMM [*see illus.*] • J. Webber, oils, 1776, National Museum of New Zealand, Wellington • J. Webber, oils, 1776, NPG • J. Webber, oils, 1782, priv. coll.; Sotheby's Australia, 23 March 1983 • F. Bartolozzi, stipple, pubd 1784 (after J. Webber), NPG • J. Flaxman junior, Wedgwood medallion, 1784, Castle Museum and Art Gallery, Nottingham • J. K. Sherwin, line engraving, pubd 1784 (after N. Dance), NPG • A. Birrell, line print, pubd 1785 (after D. Dodd), BM, NPG • Thornton, line engraving, pubd 1785 (after unknown artist), NPG • L. Le Vieux, marble bust, 1790, NPG • J. Zoffany, group portrait, oils, *c.*1795 (*The Death, Captain James Cook at Hawaii, 14/2/1779*), NMM • T. Woolner, statue, *c.*1879, Sydney, Australia • J. Basire, line print (after W. Hodges), BM, NPG; repro. in J. Cook, *A voyage towards the south pole and round the world*, 2nd edn, 2 vols. (1777) • Pigeot, line engraving (after N. Dance), NPG

**Wealth at death** £10 each to two sisters and two friends; house and furniture to Mrs Cook; one third of residue of estate to Mrs Cook; remaining two-thirds to be invested for benefit of children: will, 24 Jan 1780, PRO, PROB 11/1060; Beaglehole, *Life of Captain James Cook*, 690–91

**Cook, Sir James Wilfred** (1900–1975), organic chemist and educationist, was born in South Kensington, London, on 10 December 1900, the younger son (there was also a daughter) of Charles William Cook, coachman, of Hitchin, and his wife, Frances, daughter of Aaron Wall of Herefordshire. He attended Sloane School, Chelsea, and entered University College, London, in 1917, where he became Tuffnell scholar and gained second-class honours at the end of his second year. London subsequently awarded him his MSc (1921), PhD (1923), and DSc (1925).

Cook's first appointment, in 1920, was as lecturer at the Sir John Cass Technical Institute, where he worked with Dr E. de Barry Barnett, publishing some thirty papers on derivatives of the organic compound anthracene. He collaborated with Sir Ernest Kennaway and this led to his appointment in 1929 to the research institute of the Royal Cancer Hospital. Over the next ten years:

> he made his outstanding contribution to cancer research, first demonstrating the carcinogenicity of polycyclic benzenoid hydrocarbons and then isolating from coal tar its main carcinogenic component, which he showed to be the pentacyclic hydrocarbon, 3,4-benzpyrene. This work … showed for the first time that cancer could be induced by minute quantities of a pure chemical compound.
> (Rydon, 9)

The findings began to explain the high incidence of skin cancers among chimney sweeps and workers in the coal-tar industry.

In 1930 Cook married Elsie Winifred, *née* Griffiths (*d.* 1966). The couple had three sons. London University appointed him reader in pathological chemistry in 1932, and, in 1935, professor of chemistry. The following year he was awarded, with Kennaway, the prize of the International Union Against Cancer, and in 1938 he was elected a fellow of the Royal Society.

In 1939 Cook was appointed to the regius chair of chemistry in Glasgow, which he held until 1954. He continued his research on polycyclic aromatic hydrocarbons, while his work on colchicine, an alkaloid with the potential to inhibit tumour growth by arresting cell division, established its later accepted formula and led to new work on the tropolones. While at Glasgow Cook served as president of the Royal Institute of Chemistry, 1949–51, and was a member of the University Grants Committee (1950–54).

In 1954 Cook was appointed principal of the University College of the South West, a college which had been seeking university status for some thirty years and teetering on the brink of it for five. Under Cook's leadership, the University of Exeter received its charter in 1955, and he became its first vice-chancellor. Between 1955 and 1963 he presided over an expansion of the university which established its academic standards, and saw the erection of many new buildings. Indeed, Exeter soon began to be recognized in students' eyes as one of the most attractive universities in the country. This period of growth ensured the university a secure future.

Cook was also concerned with higher education in developing countries and on his retirement from Exeter in 1966 he accepted the vice-chancellorship of the federal University of East Africa, consisting of the colleges at Kampala, Nairobi, and Dar es Salaam. It was not an easy time for an Englishman to head a federal university with the newly independent Kenya, Uganda, and Tanzania keen to establish their own universities. Cook negotiated a formal dissolution date for the federal university, and guided the three colleges towards autonomy, winning the respect of all parties. Soon after he left in 1970 all three were established as national universities. Following his first wife's death, in 1967 he married Vera Elizabeth, *née* Ford, a biologist whom he had first met when she was recorder of Section X of the British Association and he was president-elect of the section. She was the daughter of William John Ford, surveyor in the London customs and excise.

On his return from Africa Cook renewed an association with the New University of Ulster, where he had been chairman of its academic planning board, and became chairman of its academic advisory committee. Cook's contributions as scientist and administrator were widely recognized, by his knighthood in 1963, by honorary degrees from the universities of Dublin (1948), Rennes (1960), Nigeria (1961), Exeter (1967), and Ulster (1970), and his many research prizes, including the Davy medal of the Royal Society in 1954.

Many of Cook's contemporaries mentioned his reserve and his sardonic sense of humour, contributing to an appearance of strength and some aloofness. Those who knew him well, and especially in later life, found him more relaxed and entertaining. Cook's home was at The Burn, 15A Knowle Road, Budleigh Salterton, when he died at Exeter on 21 October 1975. HARRY KAY, *rev.*

**Sources** J. M. Robertson, *Memoirs FRS*, 22 (1976), 71–103 · H. N. Rydon, 'Sir James Cook, DSc, LLD, FRS (1900–1975)', *University of Exeter Gazette*, 80 (1976), 8–10 · *The Times* (25 Oct 1975) · private information (1986) · personal knowledge (1986) · B. W. Clapp, *The University of Exeter: a history* (1982)
**Archives** RS, letters to Sir Robert Robinson
**Likenesses** W. Stoneman, photograph, 1938, NPG · W. Bird, photograph, 1962, NPG · W. Stoneman, photograph, RS · portraits, repro. in Clapp, *The University of Exeter*
**Wealth at death** £36,485: probate, 31 Dec 1975, *CGPLA Eng. & Wales*

**Cook, John** (*bap.* 1608, *d.* 1660), judge and regicide, was the eldest son of the landowner Isaac Cook (*d. c.*1658) and his wife, Elizabeth Twigden, of Burbage and Husbands Bosworth, Leicestershire; he was baptized on 18 September 1608 at Husbands Bosworth. Cook matriculated as a commoner from Wadham College, Oxford, in January 1623, although he was apparently in residence as early as March 1621, and left without a degree in June 1624. His father is styled esquire in the record of John's admission to Gray's Inn on 1 November 1623, where he came under the influence of the puritan preacher Richard Sibbes. Cook also benefited from the advice of an older barrister, Thomas Brickenden, in his early struggles with the *Tenures* of Littleton, 'undoubtedly the most crabbed Author to begin with any Science in the world' (J. Cook, *Vindication of the Professors and Profession of the Law*, 1646, 94), and later advocated the appointment of two law professors at each inn of court. He was nevertheless called to the bar in November 1631, and even hostile witnesses later expressed respect 'for his profession-sake, being learned therein' (*State trials*, 5.1082).

The difficulty of building a practice in Westminster Hall may well explain Cook's next career move, signalled by his admission to King's Inns, Dublin, in November 1634. During this first stay in Dublin of 'almost two years' (Firth, 15) he attracted the patronage of Lord Deputy Wentworth, who may have commissioned him to prepare a printed edition of the Irish statutes. If so, the project seemingly failed; Cook later refers obliquely to his own personal shortcomings as having obliged him to leave Ireland, but no other evidence corroborates the suggestion of a royalist journalist that he had embezzled moneys provided by Wentworth. Whatever his reasons, Cook certainly travelled widely on the continent during the later 1630s. Visits to France and Italy gave him a fund of useful knowledge about the history and institutions of Counter-Reformation Europe, as well as the experience of dining at the English College, Rome, in April 1638 (Chaney, 276). In Geneva he lodged with the eminent liberal Calvinist theologian Giovanni Diodati, signing the 'Album amicorum' of the Neapolitan protestant noble Camillo Cerdogni in August 1638. While staying with some English congregational exiles, probably in the Netherlands, he began to read the works of Henry Ainsworth and other separatists, and to question the validity of the Church of England's episcopal administration.

Cook next appears in 1641 in the persona of a young lawyer, addressing his former patron Strafford, now imprisoned in the Tower. In a document transcribed by William Knowler and printed by Charles Firth, the original of which seems to have disappeared, Cook paid his respects in elaborately obsequious terms, while offering Strafford a series of legal arguments for his defence. Thereafter he vanishes from view, until his assignment by the House of Lords on 12 February 1646 as counsel for John Lilburne at the rehearing of the latter's conviction in Star Chamber nearly ten years before. Cook at his own trial in 1660 would claim to be 'no swordsman' (*State trials*, 5.1094), and in 1646 referred to 'us that have been London Residentes' during the civil war (*Vindication*, 76). As for what had prompted him 'to adhere so cordially and constantly to the Parliament against the late Oxford party', he himself asserted that 'Scripture grounds and reasons of state', as distinct from legal points or precedents, were the 'Arguments and motives which swayed me' (Cook, *Redintegratio amoris*, 17).

Early in 1646 Cook also launched his career as a public commentator on current issues. *The Vindication of the Professors and Profession of the Law* was written in response to an anonymous pamphlet of the previous year which had urged the rejection of common lawyers as recruiter MPs. Defending his occupation against various conventional charges, Cook maintained that England's laws were 'either actually, or potentially, the best in the world' (*Vindication*, 35), even if changes were needed to ensure that existing legal institutions contradicted neither God's word nor the dictates of reason. In detailing numerous desirable innovations and reforms, such as a national land registry, Cook naïvely assumed that acceptance in principle would more or less guarantee legislative implementation. His far-sighted and original proposals for reconstituting legal education similarly foundered on the indifference or hostility of the rulers of the inns of court. Cook married on 12 September 1646 Frances Cutler, who probably died in or before 1659.

Over the next four years Cook published a further five tracts, and wrote others which remained unprinted. Addressing the political crisis arising from the army's occupation of London, *Redintegratio amoris, or, A Union of Hearts* and *What the Independents would Have* both appeared in the autumn of 1647. The former argued that the army alone could secure liberty of conscience and reform the courts of justice, both preconditions of a peaceful settlement, while the latter provides a succinct apologia for limited religious toleration. In February 1648 his *Unum necessarium, or, The Poore Mans Case* advocated numerous measures to relieve social distress, including diversion of grain from beer to bread by suppressing alehouses, and the provision of subsidized loans and medical services to the poor (the latter an issue arising from the College of Physicians' prosecution of the empiric Dr William Trigg, who had retained Cook as counsel).

Whatever notice Cook's writings had already attracted was overshadowed in January 1649 when he took on the invidious task of prosecuting Charles I. The king's refusal to plead largely confined Cook's public role as solicitor-general for the Commonwealth to reading the indictment which he had drafted. A version of his intended speech for the prosecution, published shortly after the king's execution as *King Charls his Case, or, An Appeal to All Rational Men*, characterized the trial as 'the most comprehensive, impartial, and glorious piece of justice that ever was acted' and claimed 'I went as cheerfully about it, as to a Wedding' (p. 39) [*see also* Regicides]. Yet Cook's zeal earned him little material reward other than the mastership of St Cross Hospital, Winchester, and then appointment as chief justice of Munster. Having accompanied Oliver Cromwell to Ireland in the summer of 1649, he took up the latter post in March 1650, after prosecuting his former client Lilburne and other Leveller leaders, and serving on the court which convicted the royalist duke of Hamilton. Cook's visionary experience during a sea passage from Wexford to Kinsale forms the centrepiece of his *A True Relation*, and also figures in his wife's shorter account ([F. Cook], *Mris Cookes Meditations*), both appearing in the spring of 1650.

Cook sought with some success to provide cheap, accessible, and summary justice in Munster by reducing fees, office-holders, and professional lawyers, amalgamating law and equity, and proceeding on circuit through the province. These initiatives were understandably more popular with tenants than landlords, against whom he may have consciously discriminated. Cook's judicial role in Munster became increasingly circumscribed as he antagonized powerful political and religious interests, and in 1655 he was offered a judgeship in Dublin. A letter of refusal addressed to Lord Deputy Henry Cromwell eloquently expresses his conscientious scruples, deprecating at some length the 'Grand Cheat and Abominable Idoll Call'd the Course of the Courts' (Maclysaght, 443–4). But after returning to England in 1657, Cook was again offered an Irish judge's place, which he accepted early in 1659, possibly for financial reasons. Besides a defence of the civilian republican Edmund Ludlow, he may have published later that year a broadsheet propounding a series of measures designed to restore 'these poor shaken and shattered Nations' (Ludlow, 87; J. C., *Magna Charta*, 1659). He married again about this time; his second wife was Mary, daughter of Henry Chawner of Barwell, Leicestershire, and their daughter, Free-love, was an infant at the time of his execution.

As the prospects of a Stuart restoration strengthened, Monck's Irish ally Sir Charles Coote seized Cook in February 1660. Sent a prisoner to the Tower of London, in early June Cook was exempted by name from the proposed parliamentary act of indemnity and oblivion. While its outcome was inevitable, his trial for treason at the Old Bailey lasted longer than that of any other indicted regicide, thanks to both his skilful self-defence, and the legally anomalous nature of the crown's case. After conviction and sentencing Cook abandoned any attempt to mitigate his role in the king's trial. Protesting in a letter to his infant daughter that 'thou art the Child of one whom God counted worthy to suffer for his sake', his confident avowals of spiritual assurance may also have helped comfort his wife, to whose tearful last farewell on the morning of 16 October he reportedly responded 'My dear Lamb, let us not part in a showre, God hath wiped away all tears' (*Speeches and Prayers*, 81, 82). Cook's scaffold speech at Tyburn asserted that 'I am not convinced of any thing I have done amisse, as to that I have been charged with' (ibid., 31). However, in a series of articles in *Notes and Queries* (1913) J. B. Williams questioned the authenticity of *Speeches and Prayers* ('The forged "Speeches and prayers" of the regicides', *N&Q*, 11th ser. 7, 301–2, and 8, 22–3). As G. E. Aylmer has noted, 'John Cook, that epitome of honest Independency and frustrated reforming zeal, remains *sui generis*' (G. E. Aylmer, *The State's Servants*, 1973, 276). Samuel Pepys saw Cook's head in Westminster Hall on 21 October; it is unclear when or if his remains were buried.

WILFRID PREST

**Sources** T. C. Barnard, *Cromwellian Ireland: English government and reform in Ireland, 1649–1660* (1975) · *DNB* · Greaves & Zaller, *BDBR*, 166–7 · *State trials*, vol. 5 · C. H. Firth, ed., 'Papers relating to Thomas Wentworth … from the mss of Dr William Knowler', *Camden miscellany, IX*, ed. C. H. Firth, CS, new ser., 53 (1890), 14–20 · J. Cook, *Redintegratio amoris, or, A union of hearts* (1647) · E. Ludlow, *A voyce from the watch tower*, ed. A. B. Worden, CS, 4th ser., 21 (1978) · *The speeches and prayers of some of the late king's judges* (1660) · Thurloe, *State papers*, vols. 4, 6–7 · R. B. Gardiner, ed., *The registers of Wadham College, Oxford*, 1 (1889) · J. Nichols, *The history and antiquities of the county of Leicester*, 4 (1807–11), 468 · E. Chaney, *The grand tour and the great rebellion* (1985) · *Mercurius Elenticus*, 56 (6–13 Feb 1649) · Black Book, 1607–1730, fol. 20, Library of the King's Inns, Dublin, MS B1/1 · E. Maclysaght, *Irish life in the seventeenth century* (1950), 417–46 · *IGI* · Foster, *Alum. Oxon., 1500–1714*, vol. 1 · J. Foster, *The register of admissions to Gray's Inn, 1521–1889, together with the register of marriages in Gray's Inn chapel, 1695–1754* (privately printed, London, 1889), 171 · J. Cook, *What the Independents would have* (1647), 1
**Archives** Bodl. Oxf., letter to H. Cromwell, Rawl. MS A.189
**Likenesses** T. Simon, silver medal, BM · group portrait, line engraving (*The regicides executed in 1660*), BM · line engraving, BM · line engraving, NPG
**Wealth at death** seems never to have enjoyed financial security; practice as a barrister was not large: J. Cook, *Vindication of the professors and profession of the law* (1646), 40 · mastership of Cross Hospital was worth £800 p. a.; not clear that he continued to hold this position after moving to Ireland: V. Rowe, *Sir Henry Vane*, 55, n. 5 · as attainted felon, property passed to the Crown at his death, although he believed that sequestration of his Irish estates would require a separate act of parliament: *Speeches and prayers*, 23 · Irish holdings incl. estate at Barnahely, co. Cork, other property at Waterford, and possibly Dublin: *CSP Ire., 1660–62*; *Egmont*, HMC, 1.611 · English lands in Bedfordshire and Hampshire: *Calendar of treasury books, 1660–1667*, 1.92

**Cook, John** (1771–1824), Church of Scotland minister and Hebrew scholar, eldest son of the Revd John Cook, professor of moral philosophy at the University of St Andrews, and his wife, Janet, daughter of the Revd John Hill, was born on 24 November 1771. He graduated at St Andrews in 1788. He was licensed for the ministry of the Church of Scotland on 19 September 1792, and was ordained minister of Kilmany, Fife, on 9 May 1793. He held this charge until 12 October 1802; his immediate successor was Thomas Chalmers. Cook left Kilmany to fill the chair of Hebrew and divinity at St Mary's College, St Andrews, a position which he held until his death. On 2 July 1803 he married Elizabeth (d. 1848), daughter of George *Hill (1750–1819), principal of St Mary's College. They had three daughters and five sons, among whom was the ecclesiastical historian John *Cook (1807–1869). On 16 May 1816 Cook became moderator of the general assembly. He published *Inquiry into the Authenticity of the Books of the New Testament* (1821). He died on 28 November 1824.

ALEXANDER GORDON, rev. ROSEMARY MITCHELL

**Sources** *Fasti Scot.* · Anderson, *Scot. nat.* · Allibone, *Dict.*

**Cook, John** (1807–1869), Church of Scotland minister, was born at St Andrews on 1 September 1807, the eldest son of John *Cook (1771–1824), Church of Scotland minister, and his wife, Elizabeth Hill (d. 1848). He graduated AM at St Andrews in 1823, and in 1824 he was factor to St Mary's College. He was licensed for the ministry of the Church of Scotland on 13 August 1828, and ordained minister of Laurencekirk, in Kincardineshire, on 3 September 1829. On 9 May 1837 he married Rachel Susan, *née* Farquhar; they had five daughters, the youngest of whom was Rachel Susan *Scott, educationist and journalist. From Laurencekirk he was translated to St Leonard's at St Andrews, on 11 September 1845. On 9 December 1848 he was made DD at St Andrews; and on 19 June 1860 he was appointed to the chair of divinity and ecclesiastical history in that university. He held this post until 30 July 1868, having resigned his pastoral charge on 30 September 1863, on becoming one of the deans of the Chapel Royal.

Cook was an efficient ecclesiastical administrator and an able pamphleteer on church affairs, publishing such topical pieces as *Evidence on Church Patronage* (1838). The general assembly (of which he was elected moderator on 19 May 1859) appointed him convener of many of its important committees, including those on education (1849), the improvement of the conditions of parish schoolmasters (1850), aids to devotion (1857), and army and navy chaplains (1859). In 1859 he was chosen an assessor to the university court of St Andrews, under the new constitution of the Scottish universities. He died on 17 April 1869 at St Andrews; his wife survived him. A painted window to his memory was placed in the college church at St Andrews.

ALEXANDER GORDON, rev. ROSEMARY MITCHELL

**Sources** *Fasti Scot.* • Boase, *Mod. Eng. biog.*
**Archives** U. St Andr. L., corresp. with James Forbes
**Wealth at death** £4711 16s. 4d.: confirmation, 24 May 1869, NA Scot., SC 20/50/41/820–825

**Cook, John** (1807–1874), Church of Scotland minister, was born on 12 September 1807, the eldest son of George *Cook (1772–1845), also a Church of Scotland minister, and his wife, Diana, eldest daughter of Revd Alexander Shank. In 1823 he graduated AM at the University of St Andrews. He was licensed for the ministry of the Church of Scotland by the presbytery of Fordoun on 17 September 1828, and ordained minister of Cults, Fife, on 1 June 1832. He was translated to the second charge at Haddington on 26 November 1833. On 14 July 1840 he married Helen, the daughter of Henry Davidson, sheriff clerk of East Lothian. They had five daughters before her death in January 1860.

In common with other members of his family Cook was a strong supporter of the moderate party in the Church of Scotland. In May 1842 he was suspended from judicial functions for nine months by the general assembly, as a result of his support for the ministers of Strathbogie, who had complied with a decree from the court of sessions in a patronage case. Cook's promotion to the first charge at Haddington naturally followed on the Disruption of 1843; in the same year the degree of DD was conferred on him by his university.

A strong and persuasive speaker, Cook commanded much respect as a leading figure in the church courts; he was the author of *Styles of Writs and Forms of Procedure in the Church Courts of Scotland* (1850), which was praised in the *Edinburgh Advertiser*. In 1854 the general assembly made him convener of its committee for improving education and religious instruction in Scotland. He was elected subclerk of assembly on 25 May 1859, principal clerk on 22 May 1862, and became moderator on 24 May 1866. Cook's position as a leader of the moderates in ecclesiastical politics was unattended by any latitudinarian tendencies in the area of doctrine. He died on 11 September 1874 at the manse, Haddington.

ALEXANDER GORDON, rev. ROSEMARY MITCHELL

**Sources** *Fasti Scot.*, 1.370–71 • Boase, *Mod. Eng. biog.* • Allibone, *Dict.* • Irving, *Scots.*
**Wealth at death** £357 1s. 1d.: confirmation, 29 Feb 1876, *CCI* • under £20 in England: probate, 29 Sept 1875, *CGPLA Eng. & Wales* • £8950 7s. 8d.: additional inventory, *CCI*

**Cook, John Douglas** (1808?–1868), newspaper editor, was born at Banchory-Ternan in Aberdeenshire, probably in 1808, although he favoured 1811. An unsubstantiated rumour suggested he was the illegitimate son of Thomas *Hope (1769–1831), author, and thus half-brother to the Rt Hon. A. J. B. Beresford *Hope, Conservative politician, who affirmed the earlier date (Bevington, 10–11). Cook may have attended the University of Aberdeen (Escott, 231). At an early age he obtained an appointment as a clerk in India, probably through an uncle, Sir George Rose. After a quarrel with his employers Cook returned, on foot for a great part of the way. Destitute in London, he tried literature, possibly including hack work. After an anonymous article was accepted by *The Times*, he became a reporter,

leader writer, and friend of John Walter, the proprietor. Cook also indexed the early volumes of the *Quarterly Review*. When Walter was elected for Nottingham as a tory in 1841, Cook served as his canvassing agent and became acquainted with Lord Lincoln (later fifth duke of Newcastle), who appointed Cook as secretary to his newly established commission inquiring into the revenues of the duchy of Cornwall.

About 1848 some Peelites, including Lincoln, bought the *Morning Chronicle* and appointed Cook the editor. As Lincoln's *protégé* Cook took close instruction from him on the line that the paper was to take, and its stance became determinedly Peelite. He had close relations, too, with Gladstone, who as well as taking Cook's advice regarded him as a useful publicist and intermediary. Cook showed great resourcefulness, originality, and imagination, but spent money lavishly. He hired Philip Harwood as co-editor; they worked together until Cook's death. One contributor, Henry Maine, recruited his Cambridge pupils Vernon Harcourt and James Fitzjames Stephen. The paper, though a literary success with such works as Henry Mayhew's series 'Labour and the poor', was a political and financial failure. It was sold in 1854 and Cook was replaced as editor.

Cook planned a new journalistic venture with a contributor, Beresford Hope, which was to be the joint property of the two with the power of purchase secured to the survivor. The new weekly paper, the *Saturday Review of Politics, Literature, Science and Art*, first appeared on 3 November 1855 and became an organ of moderate conservatism, policing the world of letters and politics. Business relations between Cook and Beresford Hope were frequently strained by Cook's tendency to overrule his partner's political and religious stances despite Beresford Hope's greater financial contribution. Cook kept the paper as much as possible out of theological controversy and made it a rule to have 'the Liberals to write on matters where they were most conservative, and the Conservatives on topics which they could treat liberally' (Griffiths, 168). As circulation increased, due to the excellent editing and lively writing, so did the size and scope of the paper. Because Cook valued scholarly, politically minded young men who could address an educated readership, nearly all his contributors were graduates of Oxford or Cambridge and loyal writers from the *Morning Chronicle*. Over the years contributors left to become eminent in various directions; however controversy over *Essays and Reviews* caused several regulars to depart, eventually won over by Cook's tact. The *Saturday Review* became the leading critical weekly at least partially as a result of the addition of John Morley from 1863 until 1867, who attributed his journalistic success to his patron John Douglas Cook, 'the queer, intemperate, and almost illiterate, but wonderfully successful editor-manager' (Hirst, 38). At Cook's instigation Morley wrote the slashing review of Swinburne's *Poems and Ballads*. Leslie Stephen joined his brother on the staff in 1865. To keep harmonious unity, these three were among those restricted to writing middles and reviews and kept away from the leaders. Although Cook paid less generously than on the *Morning Chronicle*, he did provide Morley and Leslie Stephen with an annual retainer fee. An annual dinner for male contributors inspired Cook's staff with the sense of honour and privilege gained through writing for the *Saturday Review*. Eliza Lynn Linton, formerly with the *Morning Chronicle* until an angry disagreement with Cook, contributed 'The girl of the period' (14 March 1868), perhaps the most sensational middle article of Cook's editorship.

Cook's instinct for recognizing ability in others and his judgement in directing them made him one of the most efficient editors of his day. Each Tuesday he presented writers with their assignments in his rooms at The Albany, Piccadilly, London; Harwood remained in charge of the office at Southampton Street. Cook was an exacting editor and reader, unstinting of himself and his health. He spent only brief vacations at his house in Tintagel, Cornwall—purchased with profits from the weekly—at which he annually entertained the Beresford Hopes. He died, unmarried, of chronic liver disease in his rooms in The Albany on 10 August 1868, and was buried at Tintagel. No notice appeared in the *Saturday Review* at Beresford Hope's request; however a memorial tribute in the *Pall Mall Gazette* was reprinted in *The Times*.

BARBARA QUINN SCHMIDT

**Sources** M. M. Bevington, *The Saturday Review, 1855–1868: representative educated opinion in Victorian England* (1941); repr. (1966) • H. W. Law and I. Law, *The book of the Beresford Hopes* (1925) • *The Times* (18 Aug 1868), 5 • T. H. S. Escott, *Masters of English journalism* (1911), 231–2 • G. S. Layard, *Mrs Lynn Linton: her life, letters and opinions* (1901), 56–61, 136–9 • K. Powell, 'The Saturday Review', *British literary magazines*, ed. A. Sullivan, [3]: *The Victorian and Edwardian age, 1837–1913* (1984), 379–83 • J. W. Robertson Scott, *The story of the Pall Mall Gazette* (1950), 26–8 • J. A. Cassidy, *Algernon C. Swinburne* (1964), 115 • F. W. Hirst, *Early life and letters of John Morley* (1927), 38–47 • H. R. Fox Bourne, *English newspapers: chapters in the history of journalism*, 2 (1887), 232–51 • D. Skilton, *Anthony Trollope and his contemporaries* (1972), 53–7 • J. Gross, *The rise and fall of the man of letters: aspects of English literary life since 1800* (1969), 62–103 • J. Grant, *The Saturday Review: its origin and progress, its contributors and its character* (1873) • D. Griffiths, ed., *The encyclopedia of the British press, 1422–1992* (1992) • S. E. Koss, *The rise and fall of the political press in Britain*, 1 (1981) • d. cert. • *DNB* • P. T. Srebrnik, *Alexander Strahan: Victorian publisher* (1986), 10

**Archives** BL, letters to W. E. Gladstone, Add. MSS 44372–44380 • U. Nott. L., department of manuscripts and special collections, letters to the fifth duke of Newcastle

**Wealth at death** under £50,000: probate, 2 Sept 1868, *CGPLA Eng. & Wales*

**Cook, John Manuel** (1910–1994), classical archaeologist, was born on 11 December 1910 at 28 Wilkinson Street, Sheffield, the elder son of the Revd Charles Robert Cook, vicar of Fence in Pendle, Lancashire, and Mary Manuel Arnold, daughter of a furniture manufacturer in Sheffield, both of whom were still alive in 1939. He had an elder brother, Robert Manuel *Cook (1909–2000), who also became a classical archaeologist, and a younger sister, Margaret. He was educated at home with Robert, then at a boarding-school at Newton-le-Willows, and then at Marlborough College. He went to King's College, Cambridge (1929–32), where he took a first and won the Sir William Browne medal for a Greek ode and the members' Latin essay prize. He was always as much at home with classical languages as with the archaeology to which he devoted his career.

A studentship took Cook to the British School at Athens (1934–6), where he followed the then-fashionable research subject: analysis of archaic Greek pottery. His area was the pottery of Athens; his study was published in the annual of the British School in 1938, and remains fundamental. In 1936 he was appointed assistant in humanity, and in 1938 lecturer in classics at Edinburgh University, where he helped to establish his subject. On 28 June 1939 he married Enid May (1912/13–1976), daughter of William Allan Robertson, chief inspector of schools for Scotland; she was a distinguished classicist and a key figure in Cook's career, offering efficiency and good counsel to a man who could sometimes seem indecisive in all but scholarly matters. Their two sons both followed distinguished academic careers, in Islamic studies and in music.

During the Second World War Cook's knowledge of modern Greek and of Greece led him from the Royal Scots into the intelligence corps, as a lieutenant-colonel. In 1943 he was parachuted into western Greece, to serve as liaison officer with the resistance; this was followed by staff work in Athens compiling *Works of Art in Greece … Losses and Survivals in the War* (HMSO, 1946).

Cook had barely returned to Edinburgh in 1946 when he was appointed director of the British School at Athens, where he served until 1954. During the war the school had housed the Red Cross, and its hostel and library were in the hands of the British embassy until 1947. Only in 1950–51 were its fortunes made the responsibility of the British Academy, and it was then necessary to hand over to the Greek authorities property in Knossos, including Sir Arthur Evans's Villa Ariadne. Cook had to deal with the complex administrative problems of this difficult period of transition but was able at the same time to relaunch the school as the base for British archaeological research in Greece, with a growing number of graduate students. He was also instrumental in the reopening of the German Institute and in the birth of the Swedish Institute in Athens.

In his research Cook began to turn from pottery studies to the field. Excavation in Greece was not yet possible, so an excavation at Old Smyrna (Bayrakli) was begun in collaboration with Ankara University (1948–51). This proved of prime importance for the pre-classical period, and Cook was diligent in seeing that publication of the material assigned to the British team was properly and quickly conducted (in the school annual), although he had to return to the subject much later—in the posthumous *Temples of Athena* (with R. V. Nicholls, 1998)—to correct some misapprehensions.

Interest in Turkey led Cook into an ambitious programme of survey along its western shores, much of it in collaboration with George E. Bean. He was well suited to such gruelling work, and his expertise with inscriptions and texts meant that it was far more comprehensive than most. It led to major articles in the school annual.

Cook left the school in 1954, in good order and with a healthy future in prospect, and was appointed lecturer, then reader (1955), then professor of ancient history and classical archaeology (1958) at the University of Bristol; as a result Bristol became a major and expanding centre for classical archaeological studies: Cook was also much involved in university affairs, as dean of faculty and as pro-vice-chancellor. His academic work was devoted largely to distilling what he had already accomplished, in the semi-popular *Greeks in Ionia and the East* (1962), in important chapters for the *Cambridge Ancient History* (vol. 2, chap. 2, 1975; vol. 3, chaps. 1 and 3, 1982), and in regular reports on Asia Minor for *Archaeological Reports*, for which he had to write the lengthy Greek sections while director in Athens. But he returned often to Turkey and to the work of survey that was crowned by his book *The Troad* (1973), a study that is a classic of the genre.

Cook's interest in the East led him to begin in 1969, with his wife, a series of journeys into Iran and beyond, encouraged by a chapter commissioned for the *Cambridge History of Iran*, which appeared in 1985. There his energy and topographic skills, combined with an excellent command of sources, placed him in a better position than many, whose experience was more text-bound and eastern, to judge the achievements of the Achaemenid empire. His wife died in 1976, and the loss seemed to destroy his interest in further study, but on 3 August 1977 he married a close friend of his and Enid's, Agnes (Nancy) Easton Law, *née* Murphy (*b.* 1916), a schoolteacher who was herself recently widowed. She restored his devotion to study, and he retired to live in Edinburgh. A result was the completion and publication of *The Persian Empire* (1983), a work that established his authority over a subject far from the Greek world.

Cook's honest scholarship and hardy pursuit of knowledge in the field, combined with his work in the Athens school and then in Bristol, made him one of the most important figures in classical archaeology in post-war Britain. He was elected fellow of the Society of Antiquaries (1948), of the German Archaeological Institute, and of the British Academy (1974). He died, aged eighty-three, in the Royal Infirmary, Stirling, on 2 January 1994, of an illness aggravated by the emphysema from which he had suffered in later years.                    JOHN BOARDMAN

**Sources** J. Boardman, *PBA*, 87 (1995), 265–73 • J. M. Cook, 'Greece in the 1930s', priv. coll. [MS memoir] • J. M. Cook, 'In the mountains of Greece, 1943–4', priv. coll. [manuscript memoir] • J. M. Cook, 'A fifteen-day visit to Athos, Sept 1945', priv. coll. [MS memoir] • *The Times* (11 Jan 1994) • *The Independent* (7 Jan 1994) • b. cert. • m. certs. [E. M. Robertson; A. E. Law] • d. cert.
**Wealth at death** £221,641.67: confirmation, Scotland, 1994, *CCI*

**Cook, John Mason** (1834–1899). *See under* Cook, Thomas (1808–1892).

**Cook, Sir Joseph** (1860–1947), prime minister of Australia, was born on 7 December 1860 at Silverdale, near Stoke-on-Trent, Staffordshire, the eldest son of William Cooke, coalminer, and his wife, Margaret Fletcher. His childhood was spent in poverty and hard work. He first worked as a pit boy at the age of nine, and after his father died in 1873, he became the principal wage-earner of the family.

Devoted to self-improvement, he studied during his lunch breaks and at night, developing the discipline, self-confidence, and endurance that were to last throughout his life. He became a lay preacher in the Primitive Methodist church and only his family obligations prevented his training for the ministry. Cook dropped the 'e' from his surname and rejected gambling, alcohol, and tobacco, preferring to read the Bible and the works of Ralph Waldo Emerson.

Cook was soon a passionate trade unionist, holding all the principal positions in his local miners' lodge by the age of twenty-three. He was an uncompromising advocate of his cause, and remained all his life a ruthless political debater with few skills in negotiation. On 8 August 1885 at the Wolstanton Primitive Methodist Chapel he married Mary, the schoolteacher daughter of George Turner, of Chesterton, Staffordshire. Her brother was one of several Silverdale miners who had migrated to the New South Wales coal town of Lithgow, west of Sydney. In December 1885 Cook departed for Lithgow, to be joined in January 1887 by his wife and baby son, the first of the six sons and three daughters of the marriage. He was soon involved in preaching and trade union activity, becoming a leading spokesman for the Lithgow miners. In June 1891 he entered the New South Wales legislative assembly representing the newly formed Labor Party and in October 1893 was elected leader of the Parliamentary Labor Party. The party was deeply divided, however, both over the tariff issue and over the willingness of the parliamentarians to accept the 'pledge', the commitment to vote together to follow policies determined by the party's extra-parliamentary conference. Although a protectionist in Silverdale and at first in Lithgow, Cook had been converted by the single-tax arguments of Henry George to free trade. He rejected the pledge and his rigidity in negotiation contributed to a disastrous split in the Labor Party. Cook was re-elected in 1894 as an independent Labor candidate, but soon afterwards accepted the offer of the post of postmaster-general in the Free Trade government led by George Reid, with an annual salary of £1500. For decades afterwards, this decision led Cook to be seen by the Labor Party as the first of a long line of 'rats', who gained political and personal advantage by betraying Labor principles and the people who had put them into parliament. For his part, Cook was beginning his lifelong change from Labor to conservative, from working class to middle class, from republican to imperialist, from free trade back to protectionism, always with complete confidence in the correctness of his current position.

As postmaster-general and later as minister for mines and agriculture, Cook was energetic, adopting ideas such as putting postmen on bicycles and extending the telephone network. He appointed William Farrer to the position of government wheat experimentalist. His early views were reflected in his unsuccessful attempts to introduce local option for public house licences and to prevent lottery tickets being sent through the mail, but his support of retrenchment in the public service and balanced budgets reflected his new political alliance rather than his working-class upbringing. Above all, he loyally supported the more colourful Reid, under whose influence his abhorrence of tobacco was replaced by a taste for cigars.

A man of limited vision, Cook was initially reluctant to enter the new commonwealth parliament, but was persuaded to contest the seat of Parramatta, which included Lithgow and his former New South Wales electorate, for Reid's Free Trade Party in the first federal election in March 1901. He won easily, but spent most of the next several years in opposition, savagely attacking the Protectionist governments of Edmund Barton and Alfred Deakin. In the unstable politics of three-party competition, Cook became Reid's principal supporter in the move to unite the Protectionists and Free-Traders in an antisocialist alliance. He was now uncompromisingly committed to defending the interests of the rich and successful. Having moved from Lithgow to the middle-class Sydney suburb of Marrickville in 1901, he moved again in 1908 to Baulkham Hills, the most exclusive part of his electorate. Cook had left the Primitive Methodists for the mainstream Methodists in 1902.

In 1905 Cook became deputy leader of the Free Trade Party and in 1908 succeeded Reid as leader. In 1909, despite Cook's rigidity in negotiations, a 'Fusion' ministry united the non-Labor parties, with Deakin as prime minister and Cook as his loyal deputy and minister for defence. The government lasted less than a year, but saw Cook's most significant ministerial achievements. Closely following British advice, especially that given by Lord Kitchener, he laid down the basis for compulsory military training, established the Royal Military College, and agreed that the new Australian navy would be constituted to act as part of the empire's Pacific Fleet, rather than comprising coastal vessels as Labor preferred. He took firm decisions to start or to expedite munitions factories (including the small arms factory at Lithgow), initiated contracts for military supplies, and even offered a prize for the design of a fighter plane.

In 1910 Labor defeated the Fusion ministry in a landslide. As Deakin's deputy in the leadership of what was now called the Liberal Party, Cook vehemently denounced the Labor Party and its works. In January 1913 Deakin unexpectedly resigned and Cook was elected leader by twenty votes to nineteen over Sir John Forrest. In elections in May, the Liberals won a narrow majority in the house of representatives, while Labor retained control of the senate. Cook thus became prime minister, in office but not in power. His principal achievement was tactical, creating the circumstances to permit a double dissolution to resolve the conflict between the two houses. To widespread surprise, Labor won the subsequent election in September 1914, with majorities in both houses.

The European crisis and outbreak of the First World War came during the election campaign. Cook, always more concerned with domestic than imperial or international politics, was slow to respond, and the governor-general, Sir Ronald Munro Ferguson, had to initiate Australian

mobilization. Cook pledged full support for Britain, transferring control of the Royal Australian Navy to the Admiralty and offering a contingent of 20,000 troops. In opposition once more, he supported the Labor government's war policies, but soon felt the need to introduce conscription. This view was supported by the new Labor prime minister, W. M. Hughes, but only a minority of his party. After defeat in a national referendum in 1916, Hughes and his followers left the Labor Party to form a minority government. In 1917 they formed a coalition with the Liberals. Outmanoeuvred in negotiation, Cook was relegated to minister for the navy while Hughes remained prime minister, although his former Labor supporters were outnumbered by the Liberals. After the 1917 election, the two elements merged to form the Nationalist Party. Once more, Cook served as loyal deputy to a more skilful and quick-witted leader.

In 1918 Cook accompanied Hughes to London for the Imperial Conference, but only attended the powerless war conference while Hughes represented Australia in the more significant war cabinet. Cook's self-esteem was assuaged by the award of the GCMG and a busy social round. The following year Cook supported Hughes at Versailles, but again he was usually relegated to relatively unimportant discussions, apart from sitting on the commission which drew the boundaries for Czechoslovakia, where he dutifully followed Foreign Office advice. In 1920–21 Cook was treasurer in the Nationalist government, applying strictly conservative approaches to the difficult problems of inflation, unemployment, and low wages. He was rewarded with a five-year term as high commissioner in London, a position he thoroughly enjoyed. He promoted migration to and investment in Australia and established good relations with the higher strata of London society, including the king, to whom, with his sharply pointed beard, he bore a passing resemblance; but the prime minister, S. M. Bruce, created a separate channel for Anglo-Australian communications on important political matters. Cook's wife was appointed DBE in 1925 for her services to the Red Cross Society. After his return to Australia in 1927, Cook was chairman of a royal commission into the finances of South Australia, but otherwise left public life. He built a large block of flats in the exclusive Sydney suburb of Bellevue Hill, at Trahlee Road, living in one, Silchester, until his death there on 30 July 1947. He was survived by his wife, five sons, and three daughters. He was cremated in Sydney after a state funeral.

PETER EDWARDS

**Sources** J. Murdoch, *Sir Joe: a political biography of Sir Joseph Cook* (1996) · J. Murdoch, *Sir Joe: a biographical sketch of Sir Joseph Cook* (1979) · G. Bebbington, *Pit boy to prime minister* (1986) · F. K. Crowley, 'Cook, Sir Joseph', *AusDB*, vol. 8 · P. G. Edwards, *Prime ministers and diplomats* (1983)

**Archives** NL Aus., MS 762 and MS 2212 | NL Aus., corresp. with Viscount Novar, MS 696 · NL Aus., corresp. with Alfred Deakin | FILM BFI NFTVA, news footage

**Likenesses** J. Guthrie, sketch, c.1919–1921 (for *Statesmen of World War I*), Scot. NPG · J. Guthrie, group portrait, oils, c.1924–1930 (*Statesmen of World War I*), NPG · N. Carter, portrait, Parliament House, Canberra, Australia

**Cook, (Mary) Louise** (1901–1991). *See under* Cook, Ida (1904–1986).

**Cook, Peter Edward** (1937–1995), humorist and entertainer, was born on 17 November 1937 at Shearbridge, Middle Warberry Road, Torquay, Devon, the only son and eldest of the three children of Alexander Edward (Alec) Cook (*d.* 1984), colonial civil servant, and his wife, (Ethel Catherine) Margaret, *née* Mayo (*d.* 1994). His father had a distinguished career in the colonial service as a district officer in Nigeria, later permanent secretary of its eastern region, and as financial secretary to the crown colony of Gibraltar; despite his numerous absences abroad it was a close and sustaining family to which Cook remained devoted throughout his life.

Cook was educated at Radley College and Pembroke College, Cambridge, at both of which institutions he gave evidence of a precocious talent for comedy, both as writer and performer, offstage and on. His characteristic style developed early: a contemporary at Radley described his ability to 'spin a whole fantastic web of absurdity from the merest thread of an idea or phrase' (Cook, 6). In particular he hit upon an *alter ego*—based on a Mr Boylett, the school's high-table butler—who would deliver obsessional monologues, in a droning, strangled voice, on various mundane subjects, often the nature and activities of insects. This creation, later metamorphosing into Mr Grole and E. L. Wisty, was central to Cook's comedy for the whole of his career.

Although Cook went up to Cambridge with the idea of joining the Foreign Office, his talents as a comedian and his charismatic personality pointed in a different direction. By the end of his second year, in summer 1959, his reputation had gone beyond the bounds of the university. His starring role performing his own material in that year's Footlights revue led to his being commissioned by the theatrical impresario Michael Codron to write the major part of a West End revue, *Pieces of Eight*, with Kenneth Williams in the cast and some additional material by the then little-known Harold Pinter, which opened at the Apollo Theatre in September. This was a more-or-less traditional revue (as was its successor, *One Over the Eight*, to which he was also the chief contributor), but that tradition was comprehensively scuppered by the project Cook became involved in the following year, immediately he left Cambridge.

*Beyond the Fringe* was originally conceived by John Bassett as a late-night filler at the Edinburgh Festival to follow a production of *The Seagull* at the Lyceum Theatre. It featured Cook, Jonathan Miller, Alan Bennett, and Dudley Moore, all recent Oxbridge graduates, performing their own material. There were no sets, plain costumes, no musical numbers, no dancing girls. Among its topics were capital punishment, Shakespeare, the nuclear threat, and the British nostalgia for war. Cook's principal solo pieces involved a Grole–Wisty figure lamenting his failure to

Peter Edward Cook (1937–1995), by Sir Cecil Beaton, 1962

become a judge, and an impersonation of the prime minister, Harold Macmillan. The show, which opened in London in May 1961, was an instant triumph, not least because it caught—indeed partially initiated—a new mood in the country: an impatience with outmoded convention and a rejection of the deference accorded to public figures and institutions. It was, wrote Kenneth Tynan, 'the moment when English comedy took its first decisive step into the second half of the twentieth century' (*The Observer*, 14 May 1961).

While still at Cambridge, Cook had been planning a cabaret theatre on the lines of the pre-war German satirical nightclubs 'which had done so much', as he put it, 'to prevent the rise of Adolf Hitler' (*The Independent*). Incorporated as a members-only club to avoid the stage censorship then exercised by the lord chamberlain, The Establishment opened in London in October 1961. In the summer of the following year he extended his influence in the so-called satire boom by buying a majority shareholding in *Private Eye* magazine. In October 1962 *Beyond the Fringe* went to Broadway, where it enjoyed another huge success, and Cook lost no time in developing a New York branch of The Establishment. He followed this up in 1964 by opening a straight theatre on the same premises. Its initial production, the American première of Ann Jellico's *The Knack*, starred George Segal and was directed by Mike Nichols. In October 1963 he married Wendy Snowden, whom he had known since his Cambridge days; their two daughters, Lucy and Daisy, were born in 1964 and 1965 respectively.

Owing to financial difficulties, encountered while Cook was 3000 miles away, the London Establishment collapsed, and while its New York base continued to prosper for a time, this was the end of his career as an impresario. This was a pity, because he was an imaginative and resourceful producer with a gift for bringing the best out of his collaborators. On the other hand it freed him to concentrate on the thing he did better than anyone else—

being funny. In his case the public manifestation of his comedy—on stage or television—was the tip of a colossal iceberg: there were innumerable recollections of him in private embarking on vertiginous spirals of invention, spectacular connections, subversions of language and logic, through which fabulous worlds of ideas were created, flourished, and vanished, like the birth and death of little universes. It could be exhausting to everybody—except him, because these weren't comic routines, this was just Cook's mind working.

Surprisingly enough for such an apparently solipsistic creative method, Cook's talent found its perfect expression, professionally speaking, in his partnership with Dudley Moore. In two series of *Not Only But Also*, made for the BBC between 1965 and 1967, they produced what many regarded as the finest sustained comedy ever to appear on British television. In particular, their Pete and Dud characters—two lugubrious down-at-heels in flat caps, incessantly rambling on about the tedium of having famous female film stars invading their bedrooms and flaunting their 'busty substances' at them—became iconic figures, their south London whine imitated by half the population. The series were immensely popular, with John Lennon, Peter Sellers, and many others pleading to make guest appearances.

Cook, however, had ambitions beyond television, and was determined to break into feature films. He had already starred, with Moore and a big-name cast including Sellers, Tony Hancock, and Ralph Richardson, in *The Wrong Box* (1964), but had been constrained by a poor script (not his own). So in 1967, after the first two series of *Not Only*, he took a year off to write, on his own, an original screenplay. This was *Bedazzled* (1967), directed by Stanley Donen, a reworking of the Faust legend with Cook as the Devil and Moore as the downtrodden little failure whom he tempts with seven wishes in exchange for eternal damnation. His script was inventive and, unusually for someone whose normal approach to writing was so spontaneous, carefully crafted, but the result was muted in effect and proved commercially disappointing—though not in continental Europe, where it was a big hit. It did, however, expose his limitations as a leading man for the movies, although he continued to harbour ambitions as a romantic lead and—still less plausibly—a rock singer. There followed a clutch of feature films, *A Dandy in Aspic* (1968), *Monte Carlo or Bust*, and *The Bed-Sitting Room* (1969), and *The Rise and Rise of Michael Rimmer* (1970), all of which failed to enhance his reputation in that field.

Cook's television partnership with Moore resumed in 1970, with a third series of *Not Only* for the BBC, where his unique talents triumphantly reasserted themselves. In the autumn of the following year they took a stage show, *Behind the Fridge*, on a tour of Australia, then brought it first to London (1971) and subsequently, under the title *Good Evening*, to New York, where it ran for thirteen months, breaking the Broadway record for a two-man show. However, Cook's personal life had by then come under increasing strain: his marriage had broken up in

1970 and divorce followed the next year, Wendy Cook being given custody of their two daughters.

Although Cook immediately got engaged to the actress Judy Huxtable (she had been cited in the divorce case; they married in February 1974) the loss, as he saw it, of his daughters caused him immense distress. He developed an addiction to drugs and, especially, drink which dominated much of the rest of his life. It began to affect his work and in particular his relationship with Dudley Moore, who resented his increasingly erratic behaviour. Cook for his part vented some of his inner despair in occasionally vituperative behaviour towards Moore, some of which was painfully evident in the series of recordings issued under the rubric of *Derek and Clive*. The origin of these was a tape made privately in 1973 of improvised duologues, wildly if erratically funny and predominantly scatological, which became bootleg classics and were commercially released in 1976. The two succeeding albums, *Derek and Clive Come Again* (1977) and *Derek and Clive ad nauseam* (1979), were much blacker in tone, sometimes violently misogynist and scarcely funny at all—though some would disagree. Cook's hatred of hypocrisy had become generalized rage, expressing itself in obscenity after obscenity. From now on the poise and elegance which had characterized his comedy emerged only fitfully, as in a piece he performed for the 1979 Amnesty International charity show *The Secret Policeman's Ball*, a devastating parody of the judge's summing up in the Jeremy Thorpe trial.

One constant in Cook's life was *Private Eye*. He was still sole proprietor (although he never paid himself a penny) and over the years an inspiring, if erratic, contributor. He was credited with the idea of a speech bubble attached to a photograph of a famous person, which thereafter became *Private Eye*'s trademark front cover. He also thought up the features 'Mrs Wilson's Diary', which ran throughout Harold Wilson's governments, and 'True Stories'. Whenever somebody sued the magazine for libel—James Goldsmith and Robert Maxwell being conspicuous examples—he relished the opportunity to take a leading part in the trials and the invariably consequent fund-raising.

There were periods in which Cook fought his drink problem and much of his creative drive returned: 1980 saw a television special, *Peter Cook & Co.*, where he teamed up with John Cleese and Rowan Atkinson among others, and he co-wrote and starred in the movie *Yellowbeard* (1982). The intervening year was spent in Los Angeles starring in a sitcom for CBS called *The Two of Us*. But much of the last decade of his life, by his own testimony, was passed in watching bad television, gambling, charity golf, and drinking. There were cameo appearances on television and in some largely forgettable films, probably the best of which was *Whoops Apocalypse!* (1985), a satire on the Falklands War, with Cook as a deranged prime minister in the Anthony Eden mould. His state of mind, to say nothing of his attempts to come off drink, were undermined by a series of personal blows. In 1984 his father died; his marriage to Judy Huxtable, passionate and turbulent as it had always been, came to an end in 1989.

Yet astonishingly, in the face of what seemed like determined self-destruction, Cook produced work which ranked beside the best of his achievements of the 1960s and 1970s. First, he took to ringing up a late-night radio phone-in show in the guise of Sven, a Norwegian fisherman deserted by his wife Jutte, anxious and confused, constantly falling back on the only subject he felt qualified to discuss, namely fish. Unpaid and unrecognized (it took Clive Bull, the show's host, some months before he realized to whom he was talking), this was Cook creating for creation's sake. More conventionally, he drew on an old character, Sir Arthur Streeb-Greebling, for a series of twelve five-minute television interviews shown at Christmas 1990 under the title *A Life in Pieces*, reminiscing about his life in a manner which wove surreal fantasy with elements of Cook's own life. An extended version, now called *Why Bother?*, with Chris Morris as interviewer instead of Ludovic Kennedy, and with many more improvised flights of fancy, was broadcast on BBC Radio 3 in 1994.

A few months earlier Cook had recorded a special edition of the chat show *Clive Anderson Talks Back*, in which he was interviewed in four separate guises: a football manager, a rock star, a judge, and a man abducted by aliens. This was Cook once more in full command of his material, his characters, and himself, and seemed to herald a personal renaissance. Much of the credit for this was due to his third wife, Chiew Lin Chong, property consultant and daughter of Swee Loke Chung, businessman. They had met in 1982 and were married on 18 November 1989, immediately after his second divorce; Lin devoted herself to caring for him, trying to bring some calm and order into his life. But the renaissance was short-lived. In June 1994 he was devastated by the death of his mother, and on 9 January of the following year, in the Royal Free Hospital, Camden, London, he himself died from liver failure. A memorial service held at St John's parish church, Hampstead, in May 1995 was attended by innumerable friends and colleagues; it was a testament to the affection and admiration in which the most original comic talent of his generation had been held.                    JOHN BIRD

**Sources** H. Thompson, *Peter Cook: a biography* (1997) · L. Cook, ed., *Something like fire: Peter Cook remembered* (1996) · H. Carpenter, *That was satire that was* (2000) · R. Wilmut, *From fringe to flying circus* (1980) · *The Times* (10 Jan 1995) · *The Guardian* (10 Jan 1995) · *The Independent* (10 Jan 1995) · *Daily Telegraph* (10 Jan 1995) · S. Seymour, 'Peter, my beautiful brother', *The Guardian* (15 Oct 1996) · *WWW*, 1991–5 · private information (2004) · personal knowledge (2004) · b. cert. · m. cert. [Chiew Lin Chong] · d. cert.
**Likenesses** C. Beaton, photograph, 1962, NPG [*see illus.*] · photograph, repro. in *The Times* · photograph, repro. in *The Guardian* · photograph, repro. in *The Independent* · photograph, repro. in *Daily Telegraph* · photographs, repro. in Thompson, *Peter Cook* · photographs, Hult. Arch.
**Wealth at death** £1,095,900: probate, 10 May 1996, *CGPLA Eng. & Wales*

**Cook, Richard** (1784–1857), history painter, was born in London and was baptized on 17 October 1784 at St Giles Cripplegate, London, the son of Richard Cook (*fl.* 1785–1804), painter, and Jane, *née* Tuck whom he married at St Leonard, Shoreditch, on 22 July 1784. Farington recorded in his *Diary* for 18 November 1816 that, according to the sculptor John Rossi, 'Cooke [*sic*] the new Associate, is a native of Gloucestershire. His father, who was a farmer, has retired from business, having sufficient to live upon' would appear to be inaccurate (Farington, *Diary* 14, 4926). The work of both Cooks has been 'inextricably confused' (Stewart and Cutten, 142). He obtained admission into the schools of the Royal Academy when sixteen years of age, and received the Society of Arts gold medal in 1832. He first exhibited at the Royal Academy *A Landscape*, in 1808. At that period he resided at 41 North Audley Street, Grosvenor Square; in the same year he sent to the British Institution *The Agony of Christ* and *Hector Reproving Paris*. In 1814 he exhibited at the Royal Academy a portrait of G. F. Cooke, and *Acis and Galatea*, afterwards engraved by W. Taylor. He then lived at 12 Greek Street, Soho Square. In 1816, being elected an associate of the Royal Academy, he sent from 50 Upper Marylebone Street five pictures: four derived from Scott's *Lady of the Lake*, and *Ceres, disconsolate for the loss of Proserpine, rejects the solicitation of Iris, sent to her by Jupiter*. In 1822 Cook was elected Royal Academician, and from that time forward he almost seems to have relinquished his profession. He married a lady of fortune, which enabled him to entertain liberally his brother artists. He died in Cumberland Place, Hyde Park, London, on 11 March 1857. A sale of his pictures, sketches, and prints at Christie and Manson and Woods on 1 June 1857 included Thomas Stothard's *George III and Queen, Sitting, Surrounded by a Family of Boys and Girls*. The British Museum preserves several of Cook's drawings, chiefly studies for book illustrations, executed in 1806; a large study for the *Lady of the Lake*; a tinted pencil portrait of Mrs Cook, and a folio volume containing numerous carefully drawn figures, furniture, and arms, from the eighth to the fifteenth century. In addition to illustrating several classics published by John Sharpe, Cook provided illustrations to works by Fénelon, Shakespeare, Homer, Goldsmith, Ovid, Dryden, and Tasso. Further examples of Cook's work are in Swansea Art Gallery; one of his sketchbooks is in the Mitchell Library, Glasgow.                    L. A. FAGAN, *rev.* ANNETTE PEACH

**Sources** IGI · B. Stewart and M. Cutten, *The dictionary of portrait painters in Britain up to 1920* (1997) · S. C. Hutchison, 'The Royal Academy Schools, 1768–1830', *Walpole Society*, 38 (1960–62), 123–91, esp. 159 · Farington, *Diary* · G. Popp and H. Valentine, *Royal Academy of Arts directory of membership: from the foundation in 1768 to 1995, including honorary members* (1996) · Mallalieu, *Watercolour artists*
**Archives** Mitchell L., Glas., sketchbook · RA, general assembly minutes

**Cook, Robert**. *See* Cooke, Robert (*d.* 1593).

**Cook, Robert Manuel** (1909–2000), classical archaeologist, was born on 4 July 1909 at 28 Wilkinson Street, Eccleshall, Sheffield, Yorkshire, the elder son and eldest of the three children of Charles Robert Cook, vicar of Fence in Pendle, Lancashire, and his wife, Mary Manuel, *née* Arnold, daughter of a furniture manufacturer in Sheffield. He had a younger brother, John Manuel *Cook (1910–1994), who also became a classical archaeologist, and a younger sister, Margaret. He was educated at home, together with John, then at a boarding-school at Newton-le-Willows, then at Marlborough College. He went to Clare College, Cambridge (1929–32), where he took firsts in the classical tripos, with distinction in classical archaeology. As Walston student of the university Cook spent two years at the British School at Athens (1932–4) working on the archaic *Fikellura* pottery of Rhodes, the subject of a major article he wrote for the *Annual* of the British School in 1936. This line of research, encouraged by the director of the school, Humfry Payne, who pioneered such studies in wares other than the Athenian, determined much of his work in later years.

In 1934 Cook was appointed assistant lecturer, then lecturer in classics at Manchester University, where he was warden of St Anselm's Hall (1936–8). On 11 July 1938 he married Kathleen (1915/16–1979), daughter of James Frank Porter, a poor-law official, and his wife, Eileen Hardman. There were no children of the marriage. Cook and his wife later collaborated on *Southern Greece: an Archaeological Guide*, published by Faber in 1968.

During the Second World War, Cook worked in the civil service, where 'he much enjoyed matching his ingenuity against any industrialist who hoped to evade some irksome regulation' (*The Times*, 20 Sept 2000). In 1945 he returned to Cambridge as Laurence reader in classical archaeology, becoming professor in 1962. He retired in 1976. At Cambridge he broadened his pottery studies to embrace most of the eastern Greek world, publishing results in a series of articles, mainly in the British School's *Annual*, but culminating in a major monograph on a cognate subject, *Clazomenian Sarcophagi* (1981), and a general work, *East Greek Pottery* (with P. Dupont, 1998). He regarded the classification of pottery as a major resource for the study of Greek history and art, and his *Greek Painted Pottery* (1960; 3rd edn, 1992) long remained the principal, comprehensive, modern source for the subject. His method was scrupulous and all-embracing, subjecting every aspect of the material, physical as well as economic, to close scrutiny, not distracted by broader art-historical considerations or the iconographic studies which became increasingly popular in such scholarship in his later years. These he regarded as purely speculative. His more openly 'scientific' research led him into study of archaeomagnetism for dating and of the construction of ancient kilns.

Cook applied his archaeological and pottery expertise to many other literary and historical matters, demonstrating how the physical evidence, properly regarded, might contribute to other classical studies. Articles in the British School *Annual* and the *Journal of Hellenic Studies* covered such diverse subjects as Hesiod's poems, the origins of sculpture, of the alphabet, and of coinage, the relevance of pottery studies to understanding ancient trade, motives for colonization, the relationship of art and Homer, and the pitfalls of absolute chronologies. He several times targeted particular new theories and subjected them to the rigour he expected and often found wanting. The attitudes he adopted were widely influential among the post-war generation of scholars. An essential element was reasoned scepticism in the face of inadequately based

theory, however well established it had become in academic literature. The approach might seem negative, but it was salutary and proved most productive; he was scathing about many of the more 'modern' approaches which he judged ill-founded and even irresponsible in their handling of the primary evidence.

Cook could also write for a broader public, as in the *Guide* he published with his wife. His *Greek Art* (1972) was very much in the no-nonsense vein of his other studies, and survived well (being reprinted by Penguin in 1976), as did *The Greeks till Alexander* (1961). *Greek Art* attested his other major archaeological interest, Greek architecture, which was awarded the longest chapter.

Cook was elected a fellow of the German Archaeological Institute (Berlin) in 1953, and of the British Academy in 1974. In Cambridge he was never a 'college man' and was averse to all forms of ceremonial. He was a devoted curator of the university cast collection, having the casts repainted to make them look more like stone than plaster, and writing a *Guide* to them in 1986. He had to fight, successfully, for the independence of his subject in the university when there was a strong move to demote it and to abandon the chair. He was a fiercely effective chairman—for the faculty, and for the British School at Athens (1983–7)—properly intolerant of members who had not read their papers or who wasted time. He made some enemies, but many more friends, especially among his pupils and the young in general, since all his work, scholarly and public, was conducted with a certain irreverent wit and essential kindliness.

Cook died in Cambridge on 10 August 2000, just after his ninety-first birthday, and was buried there on 23 August. His wife predeceased him. JOHN BOARDMAN

**Sources** J. Boardman, 'Robert Manuel Cook', *PBA*, 115 (2002) · *The Times* (20 Sept 2000) · *Daily Telegraph* (21 Sept 2000) · *The Independent* (31 Oct 2000) · *WWW* · personal knowledge (2004) · private information (2004) · b. cert. · m. cert.
**Archives** U. Cam., Museum of Classical Archaeology
**Likenesses** photograph, repro. in *The Times* · photograph, repro. in *Daily Telegraph* · photograph, repro. in *The Independent*
**Wealth at death** £1,466,144—gross; £1,462,966—net: probate, 20 Dec 2000, *CGPLA Eng. & Wales*

**Cook, Robert Percival** (1906–1989), biochemist, was born on 14 April 1906 in Melbourne, Australia, the fourth in the family of three sons and two daughters of Francis Percival Cook (1867–1933), stationer and printer, and his wife, Alice May Margaret, *née* Robertson (1870–1950). His grandfather John Cook had emigrated to Australia from Appledore, Devon. He was educated at Trinity grammar school (1912–14) and then (1914–22) at Scotch College, Melbourne, which, in his words, 'gave a good didactic education in the old Scots tradition'. During studies for his BSc (1925) at the University of Melbourne his interest in biochemistry was encouraged by William J. Young, who with A. Harden had discovered the important role of phosphates in alcoholic fermentation.

In April 1926, Cook travelled to London to work with A. J. Clark in the department of pharmacology at University

College. Three months' work resulted in his first published paper, in the *Journal of Physiology*—a token of future productivity. In the same year he enrolled at Gonville and Caius College, Cambridge, and gained his PhD in 1930 for work on bacterial metabolism; he was also a member of the renowned research school led by Sir Frederick Gowland Hopkins. In 1928–9 Cook spent six months' study leave at the Pasteur Institute in Paris, where he met Milada Anastasia Novakova (*b*. 1903/4). They were married in Cambridge on 8 November 1929, and had two sons and one daughter. Robert and Milada published a translation of Claude Bernard's *Leçons sur les phénomènes de la vie: communs aux animaux et végétaux*. The award of a Beit memorial fellowship supported Cook's further research, including collaboration with J. B. S. Haldane, which demonstrated the multiplicity of oxygenases concerned in bacterial cell respiration. Between 1932 and 1935 Cook was engaged in the citric acid industry, returning to Cambridge, again as a Beit fellow, in 1935.

With characteristic enterprise, Cook began medical studies in 1938, qualifying as MB, BChir (Cambridge) in 1943. In 1940 he was appointed lecturer in biochemistry in the physiology department, University College, Dundee. His expertise was utilized in wartime studies of topics such as the nutritional value of school meals. In 1942, he was awarded a DSc by the University of Melbourne. Much of his subsequent career was enthusiastically dedicated to research and teaching in biochemistry. After years of determined effort, in 1965 he achieved designation of the biochemistry laboratories as a separate department, and when the University of Dundee came into being, a chair of biochemistry was inaugurated (1967). Cook, who had been a senior lecturer since 1945, recommended that a younger biochemist should be appointed. He was given a personal chair (1971), and retired as emeritus professor in 1973. He had been elected fellow of the Royal Society of Edinburgh in 1946.

Cook's most influential and wide-ranging scientific contributions were concerned with the biochemistry and metabolism of cholesterol. A series of papers initiated in 1938, entitled 'Cholesterol metabolism', explored the effects of dietary cholesterol on tissues and organs of various animals. Metabolites of cholesterol were also isolated and analysed. These extensive studies indicated, for example, marked differences in the susceptibility of rats and rabbits to high levels of cholesterol: the rabbits readily developed the severe lesions of the aortal intima (that is, inner wall) that constitute atheroma—broadly, the result of deposits such as fats, cholesterol, and calcified matter. Atheroma is a significant factor in human heart disease, and Cook's work helped to stimulate the subsequent expansion of research in this field. He skilfully applied chromatographic techniques to the analysis of sterols that are minor constituents of commercial cholesterol (from wool wax). The possible participation of such 'companions' of cholesterol in atheroma was also being investigated by the distinguished chemist Louis Fieser, in whose Harvard laboratory Cook spent a fruitful period in 1952. Publication of the book *Cholesterol* in 1958 established Cook's international reputation. In addition to devising and editing the work, with chapters by world authorities, he was the author of several chapters. The book has retained its unique value: the massive proliferation of research now precludes the compilation of a comparable survey in a single volume. Great attention is now devoted to the role of 'minor' sterols, present at low levels but potentially of high potency, both in physiology, and in the pathology of human arterial disease.

Cook's tall, animated figure and attractively outgoing character—warm, humorous, knowledgeable, and strongly opinionated—enlivened many scientific meetings. He was active in the Biochemical Society, the Scottish Society for Experimental Medicine, and the Nutrition Society. Cook died at Dundee on 26 August 1989, and was survived by his wife. C. J. W. BROOKS

**Sources** personal records of fellows, Royal Society of Edinburgh · private information (2004) · *Daily Telegraph* (31 Aug 1989) · personal knowledge (2004) · m. cert.
**Archives** University of Dundee, archives, corresp. and papers; further corresp. and papers; personal papers and papers relating to department of biochemistry, University of Dundee; further biochemistry papers
**Wealth at death** £99,819.33: confirmation, 16 Oct 1989, *CCI*

**Cook, Robert William Arthur** [Robin; *pseud.* Derek Raymond] **(1931–1994)**, writer, was born on 12 June 1931 at 8 Montague Place, London, the elder of two sons of Arthur Cook (*d. c.*1973), a company director, and Pamela Florence Pollock, of American-Jewish extraction (she was previously married to an Anglo-German with whom she had three sons). Cook's paternal great-grandfather took part in the charge of the light brigade, of which he was a survivor. Cook had an unhappy childhood, hating his mother and despising his father. His uncle John, seemingly the only adult who showed him any affection, was killed in the engine room of a torpedoed ship in April 1941 when Cook was nine.

Cook attended St Peter's Court before going to Eton College in 1944. He disliked Eton, though he later conceded it was 'an excellent preparation for vice of any kind' (*The Times*), and at sixteen he refused to stay any longer. He was subsequently sent to Turret Court, an establishment for difficult public-school boys. In 1949–51 he did two years' national service with the 7th Royal Tank regiment, and became a lance-corporal. On 15 September 1959 he married Dora Sherwood. He thereafter spent time in Italy, Spain, and America, but in 1960 was back in London and involved with organized crime. His Etonian manner was a useful asset to the Charles da Silva gang, who practised 'long-firming', the running of a bogus, fraudulent company to obtain goods on credit before disappearing. They also sold non-existent property.

Throughout the early sixties Cook lived between a fast Chelsea set and the underworld, a crossover which gave rise to his first novel, *The Crust on its Uppers* (1962). Eric Partridge is said to have recognized this as the greatest source of slang for a quarter of a century (Meades, 440). Its terminology includes Cook's division of the world into 'morries' (sharp operators, people in the know, one's friends) and 'slag' (the rest). Cook's examination of upper-middle-class decay proceeded further with subsequent novels such as *The Legacy of the Stiff Upper Lip* (1965). He lived hard in the early sixties, and was remembered by one wit ness as the man who 'behaved badly before anyone else did' (quoted ibid., 441). Divorced from Dora Sherwood, Cook married Eugene Eva Marie Grossman on 12 October 1963.

Cook was in rural Italy during the late 1960s and spent a couple of years working as a London minicab driver at the start of the 1970s. By 1971 his marriage to his second wife was over, and he became involved with Sandra Valerie Haggerty. The breakup of this relationship in 1973 precipitated a new stage of his life. He moved to France and settled in Le Puech, where he spent the next eighteen years. Meanwhile the success of the American mass-market novelist Robin Cook meant that Cook needed a pseudonym: he adopted the name Derek Raymond, taken from two men he particularly respected, Derek Head and John Raymond, the latter the book reviewer and critic.

In 1983 Cook published under his pseudonym *He Died with his Eyes Open*, the first of his infamous 'Factory' novels ('factory' being slang for a police station). Narrated by an unnamed policeman with a penchant for soliloquy, the Derek Raymond books were far darker, more Gothic explorations of evil and violence than the Robin Cook titles. *I was Dora Suarez* (1990), about a murdered prostitute, was widely reported to have caused a publishing editor to be physically sick while reading it.

The sensibility of the Factory series is essentially poetic in its saturated, Jacobean treatment of psychic dereliction. The Factory novels have at least as much to do with Cook's personal demons as with life on the street, and they feature a synthetic argot, the language of an underworld which has never quite existed. They attracted comparisons with Donne and Beckett, and were variously described as 'the best British crime novels of the 1980s' and 'the naffest pieces of crime fiction ever written' (quoted in *The Times*). Nevertheless, their sheer extremity and excess gave them a certain cachet.

In 1992 Cook published his autobiography, *The Hidden Files*. This was reticent about his criminal career but dwelt on his childhood, on 'metaphysics', and on the rationale of the 'black novel': an arresting phrase in English, though relatively familiar in French as *roman noir*. Cook was an atheist, but he described his probes into abjection and despair with almost religious intensity. 'I am often terrified by the work I do on the lost,' he writes in *The Hidden Files*: 'I do not mean the dead, so much as those whose misery, as formless as it is profound, is so great that they wish they were dead' (Raymond, *The Hidden Files*, 67). Writing of why the detective in *Suarez* picks up a murdered woman's head and kisses it, he suggested, 'What is remarkable about *I was Dora Suarez* has nothing to do with literature at all; what is remarkable about it is that in its own way … it struggles after the same message as Christ' (ibid., 98).

Cook was well respected in France, where his work was filmed; *He Died with his Eyes Open* was filmed as *On ne meurt*

*que deux fois* (1985), and *The Devil's Home on Leave* as *Les mois d'avril sont meurtriers* (1987). He became a cult celebrity during the early nineties and moved back to London, where he lived in a small flat in West Hampstead. Towards the end of his life he read with a literary circus of writers including Iain Sinclair, Christopher Petit, and Kathy Acker. He made a record with a band called Gallon Drunk, and featured with Iain Sinclair and others in Christopher Petit's 1992 Channel 4 film *The Cardinal and the Corpse*. A tall, thin, cadaverous man with a patrician accent and a trademark beret, Cook became a Soho character. He was a heavy drinker with a taste for premium-strength lagers, and died from liver failure at his home, 106A Bathurst Gardens, Kensal Rise, London, on 30 July 1994. He was cremated at the north London crematorium, near Harlesden. PHIL BAKER

**Sources** D. Raymond [R. Cook], *The hidden files: an autobiography* (1992) • *The Times* (1 Aug 1994) • J. Meades, 'Robin Cook: reprobate', *Peter knows what Dick likes* (1989) • *Catalogue 53: the cardinal and the corpse*, Iain Sinclair Books (1992) [book-dealing catalogue featuring items relevant to film: digressions and sidelights on Cook] • R. Cook, *The crust on its uppers* (1962) • D. Raymond, *I was Dora Suarez* (1990) • P. Baker, 'Taxi rides to nowhere', *TLS* (1992) • P. Parker and F. Kermode, eds., *The reader's companion to twentieth-century writers* (1995) • *Contemporary authors*, 25–28R, pp. 157–8 • A. Calcutt and R. Shephard, *Cult fiction: a reader's guide* (1998) • personal knowledge (2004) • private information (2004) [M. Jakubowski, agent] • d. cert.

**Wealth at death** £57,619: probate, 15 Dec 1994, *CGPLA Eng. & Wales*

**Cook, Samuel** (1786–1861), Chartist, was born on 15 July 1786 at Trowbridge, Wiltshire, the son of Samuel Cook, a cloth manufacturer, and his wife, Amy. After his apprenticeship with a draper at Poole, Cook sought work in London, Birmingham, and Manchester. In 1810 he married Maria (1787/8–1827), the daughter of George Jones, a builder from Edgbaston, and they had six children. In partnership with his brother Joseph, Cook established a business in Liverpool, but it quickly ran into difficulties, and in 1818 the business was declared bankrupt. On 8 May 1819, following his release from debtors' prison, he moved to Gibraltar House, Dudley, where he established a draper's shop. The business was successful until 1843, when he was again declared bankrupt. In this shop Cook displayed a number of posters outlining political events, and the business became the focal point of radicalism in the Black Country. He was 'the radical conscience of middle-class Dudley, a dissident whose integrity was recognised by many who did not share his views' (Rowley and Taylor, 64). As a nonconformist Cook advocated the religious, social, and political rights of many fellow dissenters. He opposed church rates at Dudley from 1823 onwards, called for Catholic emancipation in 1829, and sought 'genuine democracy' in parochial administration and better working and living conditions in the town.

In 1826, in his defence of the nailers' strike at Dudley and Lye, Cook accused the government of starving the local populace, and subsequently the Home Office arraigned him for seditious libel. He declined bail and was imprisoned at Worcester gaol. On 1 August 1827, in spite of the valiant efforts of his barrister, Sir John Campbell, Cook was convicted, forced to pay a £100 fine, and bound over to keep the peace. His release was greeted with great enthusiasm by a crowd reputed to be over 40,000 strong at Dudley. Tragedy, however, struck his family on 7 September 1827, when his wife died, aged thirty-nine, allegedly as a direct consequence of her last pregnancy.

During the demand for parliamentary reform in the early 1830s, Cook expressed his middle-class radical sentiments with a series of reform posters and became the chairman of Dudley Political Union. In April 1832 he was accused of sedition, but the local magistrates found in favour of the defence, as there was insufficient evidence to convict him. In March 1836 Cook was not so successful, as he was accused and convicted of libel by Thomas Badger, an ardent tory magistrate, whom he blamed for corrupting the judicial process.

After the passing of the Reform Bill in 1832 Cook assisted the parliamentary career of Sir John Campbell, as well as expressing his views that the whig reforms had not gone far enough. In March 1834 he published *Some of the Principles of Dudley Radicalism*—a series of public statements which foreshadowed the Chartist demands of the late 1830s. Other publications from this period include *To the Magistrates of the County of Worcester* (1830) and *To All Genuine Reformers* (1835). On 19 July 1839, because of his association with the Chartist movement, Cook was arrested for holding an unlawful assembly at Dudley and was remanded on £300 bail. At his trial witnesses noted that Cook had encouraged a tumultuous crowd to take action against the Metropolitan Police, and had called for the abolition of the monarchy and the House of Lords. The jury convicted him, and Cook was imprisoned for six months.

Released from prison in April 1840, Cook was 'quite unrepentant and vociferous in his criticisms of the conduct of the visiting magistrate in impounding letters he had written to his children' (Rowley and Taylor, 65). In January 1841 he was appointed as sub-treasurer of the Dudley National Charter Association and greatly assisted in the recruitment of new members. In support of the miners' strike of July and August 1842 Cook posted a number of purportedly inflammatory posters, and on 20 August he was arrested for advertising a Chartist rally in Birmingham. There is no evidence of any subsequent prosecution.

In 1844 after his business had been declared bankrupt, Cook entered into a partnership with his son, Samuel Quartus Cook. From 1846 Cook became involved in the Chartist Land Company and in the following year contested the general election at Wolverhampton. Between 1845 and 1848 he supplied statistical information on mining accidents in south Staffordshire, helped promote the Dudley Mechanics' Institute from February 1848, and in the 1850s promoted the cause of trade unionism in the Black Country. Although Chartism had rapidly declined after 1848, Cook tried to revive its fortunes—notably in August 1855, when he promoted the Staffordshire Chartist and Complete Suffrage Association. He continued to promote radical reform, helped to organize a miners' strike in May 1858, and petitioned for almshouses in 1859. He sponsored a number of self-help and discussion groups, particularly the Dudley Mutual Improvement Society, the Temple of Investigation, the Manhood Suffrage Association, and the Working Men's Institute, and remained committed to radicalism until his death on 8 December 1861. He was buried shortly afterwards at King Street Independent Chapel, Dudley, where his funeral was attended by a small number of mourners. It has been observed that Cook could have:

> lived a comfortable and prosperous life if he had, like most middle class people of the time, ignored the injustices and desperate poverty of the mass of the people. Instead he threw in his lot with the working class of Dudley, never flinching from the consequences. Tough, uncompromising … he is one of the local leaders entitled to a place of high honour in the annals of the British working class movement. (Barnsby, 61)

RICHARD C. ALLEN

**Sources** *A full report of the trial of Samuel Cook, draper, Dudley, for an alleged seditious libel, tried at Worcester, August 1 1827, before Mr Justice Littledale*, 2nd edn (1827) · *Birmingham Daily Post* (10 Dec 1861) · *Worcestershire Chronicle* (11 Dec 1861) · *Staffordshire Advertiser* (14 Dec 1861) · *Wolverhampton Journal* (14 Dec 1861) · *Worcester Herald* (14 Dec 1861) · *National Reformer* (18 Jan 1862) · J. Rowley and E. Taylor, 'Cook, Samuel', *DLB*, vol. 6 · *IGI* · census returns for Dudley, St Thomas, 1851, 1861 · G. Chandler and I. C. Hannah, *Dudley as it was and as it is today* (1949) · G. J. Barnsby, *The Dudley working class movement, 1750–1860* (1986) · C. F. G. Clark, ed., *The curiosities of Dudley and the Black Country, from 1800 to 1860* (1881) · C. F. G. Clark, 'Dudley in the nineteenth century', in E. Blocksidge, *Dudley almanack* (1892) · C. F. G. Clark, *1819–1897: an illustrated souvenir of F. W. Cook's drapery warehouses…* (1897) · H. M. Atkins and others, *Dudley* (1988)
**Archives** Dudley Public Library, Samuel Cook poster collection
**Likenesses** portrait, repro. in Clark, *1819–1897*
**Wealth at death** under £20: Rowley and Taylor, 'Cook, Samuel'

**Cook, Samuel** (1806–1859), watercolour painter, was born at Camelford in Cornwall. His mother kept a bakehouse, and under the same roof was a small school where Cook learned to read and write. This was, however, the extent of his formal education. At the age of nine he was apprenticed to a firm of woollen manufacturers at Camelford, where he was said to have amused himself by making chalk drawings on the workshop floor, much to the annoyance of the foreman, who disparaged his talent. He nevertheless found additional employment in sign-painting, and his work adorned public houses and other local businesses. He also painted stage scenery for itinerant showmen, and grained wood. On the termination of his apprenticeship he became assistant to a painter and glazier in Plymouth. Cook later established his own painting and glazing business in the city, but continued to devote every spare hour to sketching. His favourite locations were on the nearby quays and along the stretches of coast around Plymouth and Clovelly. Most of his works were coastal scenes, but he also executed several inland views.

Cook's sketches attracted the attention of local art enthusiasts, and he found generous and wealthy patrons, including the duke of Devonshire, Lady Morley, and the family of Earl Mount Edgcumbe. Encouraged by them, he sent some drawings to the committee of the New Society of Painters in Water Colours on its foundation in 1831. He applied for membership in 1843 but was rejected, though he was eventually elected an associate in 1849 and a member in 1854. He was a regular contributor to the gallery in Pall Mall until his death and also exhibited once at Suffolk Street. In 1858 his painting *A Fisherman's Cottage, by the Mewstone, at the Entrance to Plymouth Sound* was displayed at the Liverpool Society of Fine Arts.

Cook was always a weak colourist, and his pictures tended to be overlooked when hung next to the deepertoned works of contemporaries. But his paintings also exhibited 'such quiet, simple truth, and so much real artistic feeling' that he came to be highly regarded by his peers (*Art Journal*, 23, 1861, 212). Even when his painting had attained a degree of excellence, though, he preferred not to depend solely upon his art, and because he never relinquished his trade the number of his works was relatively small. He died on 7 June 1859 at his home, North Prospect, Stoke Damerel, Devon, survived by his wife, Elizabeth. L. H. CUST, *rev.* MARK POTTLE

**Sources** *Art Journal*, 23 (1861), 212 · Redgrave, *Artists* · E. Morris and E. Roberts, *The Liverpool Academy and other exhibitions of contemporary art in Liverpool, 1774–1867* (1998) · Bryan, *Painters* (1886–9) · Wood, *Vic. painters*, 2nd edn · d. cert.
**Likenesses** F. Talfourd, chalk drawing, BM
**Wealth at death** under £2000: probate, 18 July 1859, CGPLA Eng. & Wales

**Cook, Stanley Arthur** (1873–1949), biblical scholar and Semitist, was born on 12 April 1873 at St John's Terrace, King's Lynn, Norfolk, the son of John Thomas Cook, coal merchant, and his wife, Frances Sarah Else. He was educated at Wyggeston School, Leicester, and at Gonville and Caius College, Cambridge, where he was a scholar. He was placed in the first class of the Semitic languages tripos in 1894, was Tyrwhitt Hebrew scholar and Mason Hebrew prizeman in 1895, and in 1896 won the Jeremie Septuagint prize. Cook married on 16 April 1898 Annette (1873/4–1942), daughter of William Thomas Bell, lithographic printer's manager; they had no children. From 1904 to 1932 he was lecturer in Hebrew at his old college of which he became a fellow in 1900, and from 1912 to 1920 was also lecturer in comparative religion. In 1931 he was appointed university lecturer in Aramaic, and in 1932 he was the first layman to be elected to the regius professorship of Hebrew, a post he held until his retirement in 1938.

Cook grew up in the days of William Robertson Smith, T. K. Cheyne, A. B. Davidson, S. R. Driver, and other pioneers in Old Testament research, and he belongs with them to the history of biblical scholarship. His association as a young man (1896–1903) with the *Encyclopaedia Biblica* was the beginning of a long period of editorial work, which included the editorship for thirty years (1902–32) of the *Quarterly Statement* of the Palestine Exploration Fund. He was on the editorial staff of the eleventh and fourteenth editions of the *Encyclopaedia Britannica*. For more than fifty years he produced original work which in extent and variety was astonishing. Up to 1910 his interest was centred

on Semitic languages, inscriptions, history, Old Testament analysis, and archaeology. After 1910 he was drawn to the study of psychology, philosophy, sociology, and religion in all its aspects. The publication of *The Study of Religions* (1914) marks the transition from his earlier to his later interests. Henceforward his life's work was directed towards the relating of his vast knowledge of Semitic antiquity to all problems of human existence. In the views he held he was bold but not rash, and his writings, although difficult to read, were always stimulating and often challenging. Some of his work was soon superseded, but his more solid contributions, such as his fine chapters in the *Cambridge Ancient History*, of which he was a joint editor, and his monumental Schweich lectures (1925, published 1930) had more lasting value. Cook was elected president of the Society for Old Testament Study in 1925, an honorary member of the Society of Biblical Literature (USA) in 1931, and FBA in 1933. He took the degree of LittD at Cambridge in 1920 and received the honorary degrees of DD from the University of Aberdeen (1937) and DLitt from Oxford (1938). In 1948, on the occasion of his seventy-fifth birthday, he was presented with a volume entitled *Essays and Studies* which contained a select bibliography of his writings. Cook died after a short illness at the Evelyn Nursing Home, Cambridge, on 26 September 1949.

D. W. THOMAS, *rev.*

**Sources** *The Times* (28 Sept 1949) · *The Times* (4 Oct 1949) · *Cambridge Review* (28 Jan 1950) · D. Winton Thomas, 'Stanley Arthur Cook, 1873–1949', *PBA*, 36 (1950), 261–76 · personal knowledge (1959) · CGPLA Eng. & Wales (1950) · b. cert. · m. cert.
**Archives** Palestine Exploration Fund, London, corresp. and papers relating to his contributions to quarterly statement of Palestine Exploration Fund
**Likenesses** W. Stoneman, photograph, 1934, NPG
**Wealth at death** £32,338 15s.: probate, 11 Feb 1950, CGPLA Eng. & Wales (1949)

**Cook, Sir Theodore Andrea** (1867–1928), journalist and sportsman, was born on 28 March 1867 at Exmouth, Devon, the second son of Henry Cook (d. 1884), an assistant master at a preparatory school in Exmouth, and his second wife, Jane Elizabeth Robins, an artist who had exhibited at the Royal Academy. When his father was appointed headmaster of King Alfred's Grammar School, Wantage, Cook followed as a pupil but was then sent to the preparatory school in Exmouth where his father had taught. There he was strongly influenced by the muscular Christianity of the headmaster, Charles Ridley Carr. In 1881 he won a scholarship to Radley College, where he met with many scholastic and athletic successes: he was head of the school, captain of football, and captain of boats. As a classical scholar from 1886 at Wadham College, Oxford, he won a rowing blue (1889) and took second-class honours in classical moderations (1888) and *literae humaniores* (1890).

On completing his studies Cook remained in Oxford as a private tutor. Ralph Pulitzer, son of Joseph Pulitzer, proprietor of the New York *World*, was one of his pupils, which gave him the opportunity to travel widely in America and on the continent. This led to a career in journalism. In 1897 he was given a staff appointment on the *St*

*James' Gazette* and on 9 July the following year married Elizabeth Wilhelmina (*b.* 1866/7), fourth daughter of Pastor Link of Stuttgart. He was appointed editor in January 1900 in succession to Hugh Chisholm but resigned five months later after a dispute with the owner. He then joined the staff of the *Daily Telegraph*, writing columns on rowing and fencing under the pseudonym Old Blue. In 1910, on the retirement of William Senior, he was appointed editor-in-chief of *The Field*, predominantly a sporting paper for country gentlemen, and held the editorship until his death.

Cook was a well-known figure in the sporting world. At Oxford he had founded the university fencing club in 1891 and later became a leading figure in the administration of the sport. He joined the committee of the Amateur Fencing Association in 1904 and served as vice-president of the association from 1923 until his death. In 1903 he went to Paris as the non-playing captain of the first British fencing team to compete abroad, and in 1906 he filled a similar role at the intercalated Olympic games in Athens. While in Athens the Italians announced that they were withdrawing as hosts of the 1908 Olympic games, and Cook was one of the small group who met aboard Lord Howard de Walden's private yacht and decided to offer to hold the games in London. As a member of the council of the British Olympic Association, chaired by Lord Desborough, he played a major part in organizing the London games. He wrote a preface to the code of rules for the event, claimed to be the first such code for international competition, and was particularly involved in the attempt to codify the regulation regarding amateurism whereby each Olympic sport was governed by the same set of rules. As editor of the official report of the 1908 London games, he was given the task of refuting American claims of cheating by British officials. Elected a member of the International Olympic Committee in 1909, he resigned in 1915, when he failed to find sufficient support for his proposal that Germany, as an aggressor nation, should be excluded from the Olympic movement.

During the First World War Cook turned *The Field* in a propagandist direction, publicizing German war atrocities in Belgium and crusading against Prussian militarism. A collection of leading articles on such themes was published as *The Mark of the Beast* (1917). He also worked to support the British ambulance committee and was knighted in June 1916. A dominant theme of his wartime writings was his crusade for 'the preservation of true sportsmanship' (Cook, 284). After the war he urged Britain to withdraw from the Olympic games because of the lack of interest shown by the British sporting public (though he entered for the arts competition at the 1920 games in Antwerp, where he won a silver medal for literature). He was much concerned to maintain good relations between sportsmen in England and the USA. The necessity of preserving the amateur ethos in sport was one of his favourite themes. His views were elaborated in *Character and Sportsmanship* (1927), published in the wake of the general strike. He attributed the failure in Britain of extreme political movements of the left and right to the permeation of

the gentlemanly code of honour and responsibility, and celebrated the prime minister, Stanley Baldwin, as the embodiment of the virtues of the English squire.

Cook was himself something of a scholar-gentleman. He wrote learned accounts of *Old Provence* (1905) and *Old Touraine* (1906). His *The Curves of Life* (1914; repr. 1979) was a significant scientific study of spiral forms in nature and art, based on a wide knowledge of botany, conchology, anatomy, and art and architecture. He also wrote on such diverse subjects as tobogganing at St Moritz (1894), J. M. W. Turner's watercolours (1904), the history of English horse-racing (1905), and rowing at Henley (1919). His autobiography, *The Sunlit Hours*, appeared in 1925. He died suddenly of heart failure at his home, 54 Oakley Street, Chelsea, London, on 16 September 1928. His wife survived him.

IAN BUCHANAN

**Sources** T. A. Cook, *The sunlit hours: a record of sport and life* (1925) · *The Times* (18 Sept 1928) · *WWW* · Walford, *County families* (1919) · *The Field* (20 Sept 1928), 463–4 · m. cert.
**Archives** BL, corresp., as honorary secretary of the imperial peace memorial, with H. Campbell-Bannerman, Add. MS 41237
**Likenesses** Lafayette, photograph, 1925, repro. in Cook, *Sunlit hours*, frontispiece · K. Collings, drawing, 1926, repro. in T. A. Cook, *Character and sportsmanship* (1927), frontispiece
**Wealth at death** £1853 7s. 11d.: probate, 23 Nov 1928, *CGPLA Eng. & Wales*

**Cook, Sir Thomas** (*c.*1410–1478), draper and mayor of London, was the eldest son of Thomas Cook, draper, a warden of London Bridge (1440–57), and grandson of Robert Cook of Lavenham, Suffolk; the family were probably weavers and clothiers and the move to become drapers of London was a natural one. The post of alnager (inspector of woollen goods) in Lavenham and elsewhere in Essex was held by the two Thomases between 1432 and 1457, and the younger became a considerable power in the cloth industries of Essex and Suffolk, building on his father's successes. In the 1440s they were members of the mercantile party opposing the aspirations of the artisan tailors, clients of the drapers. Thomas the younger was on the common council of London by the 1440s and he had also married Elizabeth, one of the two daughters of the wealthy draper **Philip Malpas** (*d.* 1469). Philippa, the other daughter, married Ralph Josselyn, draper and mayor (1464–5). Malpas was a younger son of a Cheshire family who had been apprenticed to a London draper and made a prudent marriage to Juliana, daughter of the wealthy chandler, John Beaumond, and widow of the grocer, William Middleton (an executor of Beaumond). Spectacularly successful, Malpas was notorious for his business methods: he was convicted of usury in 1421. He was sheriff in 1439, and MP in 1432 and 1441, but was alderman only for the years 1448–50, and apparently disliked office. He and the Cooks were associated from the 1420s.

In the summer of 1450 London was threatened by the rebel forces of John Cade (*d.* 1450): at some time in June Cook received a safe conduct from Cade to negotiate with him on the city's behalf at Blackheath, but precisely what transpired is unknown. As a gesture of conciliation the city removed the unpopular Malpas from his aldermanry, and Malpas almost certainly saved his life by leaving the city before the rebels gained access on 3 July; his house, the Green Gate, was looted of a considerable fortune.

In the 1450s and 1460s Cook's business success continued, unaffected by the change of kings. He lent to the crown and secured the collectorship of customs at Southampton, possibly from Queen Margaret herself. He was himself a substantial importer of woad through Southampton. In 1453 he was sheriff; his ninth attempt secured an aldermanry (Vintry, 1456), moving quickly to Broad Street (1458). Both Cook and Malpas are likely to have been among the city's leading men who supported the Yorkist earls in July 1460, and, in Cook's case at least, the accession of Edward IV on 4 March 1461. Malpas, however, had panicked at the march of Queen Margaret's army on London after the second battle of St Albans on 17 February 1461, took ship, was captured by the French, and ransomed for 4000 marks, quarrelling with Cook in the process.

Cook's mayoralty from October 1462 to October 1463 saw him engaged in the major operation of placing a vault of brick and stone over the Walbrook River (onto which his Pope's Alley house backed) and raising gifts and loans for the king's campaigns in the north against the Lancastrians and the Scots. He was created a knight of the Bath at Queen Elizabeth's coronation (24–25 May 1465).

By the 1460s Cook's landed estate was considerable. In London he moved to a great house next to the Austin Friars, taking as his tenant for his previous house the Medici representative, Gherardo Canigiani. He and Malpas had been systematically building up an estate in the area of Havering, Essex, since the 1450s; with his neighbours there, Avery Cornburgh and Thomas Urswick (d. 1479), Cook secured for Havering a royal charter and the status of a liberty in 1465; he was also licensed to fortify his house at Gidea Hall and to enclose 200 acres.

In 1468 an invasion scare, prompted by the capture of Lancastrian agents, led to Cook's arrest, with many others, on a charge of treason. The accusation against Cook originated with John Hawkins, a servant of John, Lord Wenlock (d. 1471), who had confessed under torture. In the search for evidence many of his goods were confiscated and his property damaged. The trial opened on 4 July at Guildhall: on the instruction of the chief justice, Sir John Markham (d. 1479), Cook was acquitted of giving treasonable aid but not of concealing the plots revealed to him, the offence of misprision. The penalty was a fine of 8000 marks (£5333 6s. 8d.) set by the king, which shocked many, including the judges, even when compared with the value of some of the goods seized. Robert Fabyan (d. 1513), an apprentice of Cook whose father led the sureties for Cook's fine, recorded many details in his great chronicle of London years later; his overall judgement of Cook represents him as an arrogant man, and also endorses the trial's verdict as just. Cook successfully negotiated a release from the 800 marks surcharge of the 'queen's gold', a matter in which he was probably assisted by his son-in-law, John Forster, receiver-general of the queen. The stories of later chroniclers, which entirely exonerated Cook, blamed the proceedings against him on the enmity of Richard Woodville, Earl Rivers (d. 1469), the treasurer of England, and his wife, Jacquetta, duchess of Bedford, the looting of his property on their rapacity, and even the resignation of the trial judge on their revenge, cannot be substantiated. Despite his considerable losses at this time Cook remained a very rich man, and the death of Philip Malpas in 1469 after his other daughter, Philippa Josselyn, had died childless, further compensated Cook by bringing almost all Malpas's fortune to the Cooks. Malpas was buried in St Andrew Undershaft, London.

Edward IV's exile (1470–71) allowed Cook to have a brief revenge, but his attempt to claim compensation against Lord Rivers's heir in parliament, and his high-handed behaviour against those he thought had acted against him, seem to have cost him many friends, including his brother-in-law Ralph Josselyn—though their quarrels may have also been over property and loans. Cook regained his aldermanry and played such an important role in supporting the new Neville–Lancastrian regime in London that, on Edward's return, he fled abroad. He was captured by the Hanse, ransomed by Margaret of York, duchess of Burgundy (d. 1503), and returned, a sick man, to house arrest with his friend, Avery Cornburgh, in Essex. Pardoned in 1472, he was again on commissions in 1475.

Cook was adroit at keeping his Essex estate unencumbered despite considerable losses during his two 'troubles' which included his lands in other counties and his great house at the Austin Friars. The losses, debts, and lawsuits incurred as a result of his second 'trouble' probably far exceeded those of 1468. He was still a very wealthy man, however, when he drew up his will on 15 April 1478, shortly before his death at his house near the Austin Friars; he asked to be buried in the church of the Austin Friars and he remembered some Essex connections and relatives; he established an almshouse for ninety years and, like Malpas, wanted very public prayers for his soul in the city, although he did not feel obliged to spend Malpas's £1800 to help him through purgatory. Cook's will was designed to create a coherent estate in Essex for his eldest son, Philip (a young man whose lack of 'good rule' had been criticized in Malpas's will, and who remained unsteady); consequently it ignored both his wife's wishes over her Malpas lands and the interests of his surviving sons, John and William (he hoped they would be priests), and of his daughter, Joan, wife of John Forster, one of his major supporters from 1468 to 1472. Their lawsuits, and Elizabeth Cook's will of 1484, secured a more equitable distribution of the land, but nevertheless the heirs of Malpas and Cook, through Philip, remained the dominant landowners in Havering for 200 years.

A different sort of survival from the Cook household is a memoranda book belonging to John Vale of Bury St Edmunds, Sir Thomas's man of affairs (now BL, Add. MS 48031A), compiled partly at least from the varied contents of the Cook family archive, in 1478–84, and containing many, now unique, copies of political broadsides of the fifteenth century and literary texts, as well as letters received by Cook as mayor. The apprenticeship of the future chronicler and alderman, Robert Fabyan, over-lapped with the service of Vale, but Fabyan had no access to Vale's collection. ANNE F. SUTTON

**Sources** A. F. Sutton and L. Visser-Fuchs, 'The provenance of the manuscript: the lives and archive of Sir Thomas Cook and his man of affairs, John Vale', *The politics of fifteenth-century England: John Vale's book*, ed. M. L. Kekewich and others (1995), 73–123 [incl. references to main sources] · A. F. Sutton, 'Sir Thomas Cook and his "troubles": an investigation', *Guildhall Studies in London History*, 3 (1977–9), 85–108 · M. McIntosh, 'The Cooke family of Gidea Hall, 1460–1661', PhD diss., Harvard U., 1967 · M. McIntosh, *Autonomy and community: the royal manor of Havering, 1200–1500* (1986) [esp. chap. 6] · A. H. Thomas and I. D. Thornley, eds., *The great chronicle of London* (1938), xlii, lvii–viii, 204–8, 213–16, 222 · B. B. Orridge, 'Some particulars of Alderman Philip Malpas and Alderman Sir Thomas Cooke', *Transactions of the London and Middlesex Archaeological Society*, 3 (1865–9), 285–306 · M. Albertson, 'London merchants and their landed property during the reign of the Yorkists', PhD diss., Bryn Mawr, 1932, 91–4 · P. Nightingale, *A medieval mercantile community: the Grocers' Company and the politics and trade of London, 1000–1485* (1995), 507 · PRO, PROB 11/6, fols. 280–83 · private information (2004) · PRO, PROB 11/5, fols. 210–211v

**Archives** BL, Add. MS 48031A | PRO, ancient deed, his seal, E 326/2029

**Cook, Thomas** (1744/5?–1818). *See under* Boydell, John, engravers (*act.* 1760–1804).

**Cook, Thomas** (1808–1892), travel agent, was born on 22 November 1808 at 9 Quick Close, Melbourne, Derbyshire. He was the only child of John Cook (1785–1812), labourer, and his wife, Elizabeth (*d.* 1854), daughter of Thomas Perkins, a New Connexion Baptist pastor. The family was poor and their circumstances did not improve when Elizabeth married James Smithard soon after the death of her first husband in 1812. Thomas went to school until he was ten, when he began work as a gardener's boy on Lord Melbourne's estate. He received some further education at Sunday school, attending that of the Methodists until he was thirteen or fourteen, after which, as his mother wished, he joined that of the Baptists. At about the same time he started as an apprentice cabinet-maker with his uncle, John Pegg, who was also a strong Baptist. Described at this time as 'an earnest, active, devoted, young Christian' (*General Baptist Magazine*, 185), Thomas advanced quickly in the Sunday school to become a teacher and then the superintendent. On 26 February 1826 he was baptized by Joseph Foulks Winks, the New Connexion pastor at Melbourne, who influenced him considerably during this stage of his life.

**Itinerant village missionary** Just before his twentieth birthday Cook abandoned his apprenticeship to become an itinerant village missionary, on a salary of £36 a year (which was later reduced to £26 because he received so much hospitality from the faithful). His job was to spread the Word by preaching, distributing tracts, and setting up Sunday schools throughout the south midland counties. Thus began a career in travel. In 1829 Cook, a young man with a commanding presence and black penetrating eyes in which some discerned a gleam of fanaticism, met Marianne Mason (1807–1884). She was a 'very dapper' and sensible farmer's daughter who taught at the Baptist Sunday

Thomas Cook (1808–1892), by unknown photographer

school at Barrowden in Rutland (Thomas Cook Archive, 'Bishop reminiscences'). After a long courtship they married at Barrowden on 2 March 1833. The couple went to live at Market Harborough, near Leicester, where Cook had now set up in trade as a wood-turner, since the Baptist church could no longer afford to pay him as a preacher. All his life he remained a strict and ardent Baptist, although he was tolerant of other protestant sects. Religion gave him a strong desire to help the downtrodden and his political inclinations were liberal.

During the 1830s the burgeoning temperance movement gradually persuaded Cook that cheap strong liquor exacerbated the 'poverty, crime, strife and wretchedness' of the people (*Temperance Messenger*, 50). In 1836 both he and Marianne signed the pledge and decided that their workmen too should be denied alcohol on the premises. For the next few years Cook's own temperance crusade took precedence over both his business and his family, which now included a son, John Mason Cook [*see below*], born on 13 January 1834. (A second son, Henry, died as an infant in September 1835 and, after an interval of ten years, a daughter, Annie, was born.) Cook made speeches and published tracts inveighing against the demon drink. More significantly, he also arranged alternatives: wholesome forms of 'rational recreation' such as picnics at which revellers were sustained with 'biscuits, buns and ginger beer' (*Temperance Messenger*, 132). In 1840 he founded the *Children's Temperance Magazine*, the first English publication of its kind. On 5 July 1841 Cook organized and personally conducted a railway excursion from

Leicester to Loughborough for some 500 temperance supporters, who paid a shilling each. The journey was a great success and Cook afterwards looked back on it as 'the starting point of a career of labour and pleasure which has expanded into … a mission of goodwill and benevolence on a grand scale' (*Cook's Excursionist*, 13 Sept 1856).

**Early tours** Later in 1841 Cook moved to Leicester, which offered the advantages of good communications, a large Baptist community, and a radical corporation. It also provided a challenge in the shape of 700 beershops and public houses. Cook set up as a bookseller and printer, specializing in temperance literature but also producing such useful publications as his own *Leicester Almanack* (1842) and *Guide to Leicester* (1843). In addition he opened temperance hotels in Derby and Leicester (run by his mother and his wife respectively) and continued to organize excursions. In 1845, having won a reputation as an entrepreneur who could obtain cheap rates from the railway companies for large parties, he undertook his first profit-making excursion—to Liverpool, Caernarfon, and Mount Snowdon. Cook wrote a handbook which resembled in essential respects the modern tour operator's brochure. He also gave the 350 tourists his '*personal* superintendence' (*Handbook of the Trip to Liverpool*), while taking the opportunity to encourage them to climb Snowdon without 'the stimulus of alcohol' (*Cook's Excursionist*, 4 June 1856). The success of this tour made him determined to reach that bourn of contemporary romance, Scotland.

  Cook's first Scottish tour in the summer of 1846, although meticulously planned, was dogged by problems. Against expectations, the 500 tourists were unable to get off the train, which lacked a restaurant car and lavatories, at intervening stations; so they arrived at Fleetwood starving and bursting. There were not enough cabins on the steamer to Ardrossan and a storm soaked the deck passengers. Cook irritated them further by banging the temperance drum. A subsequent article in the *Leicester Chronicle* warned readers against future excursions arranged by the teetotal projector, who deserved a toss overboard into his '*favourite element*'. Cook was damaged by this attack but the collapse of his business in August 1846 was probably due more to competition from another temperance publisher. However, by 1848, for reasons which remain obscure, he had recovered sufficiently to be running three successful operations in Leicester: the temperance hotel, a bookselling business, and what can now be called a travel agency.

**Railway excursions** In the middle years of the century, as the country prospered and the railway system grew, Thomas Cook's tourist enterprise developed. In 1851 Cook arranged for 165,000 people to visit London for the Great Exhibition, which he described as 'a great School of Science, of Art, of Industry, of Peace and Universal Brotherhood' (*Cook's Excursionist*, 3 May 1851). This was followed by expeditions on which thousands of tourists viewed the cities, resorts, and beauty spots of England, Scotland, Wales, and Ireland. For these groups Cook provided cheap tickets, mapped out routes, supplied handbooks. He also chaperoned 'unprotected females', for whom tourism

became a step towards emancipation (*Cook's Excursionist*, 18 July 1860). Cook accompanied many parties himself, organizing them in such a peremptory fashion that he was nicknamed 'the General' (*Cook's Excursionist*, 3 Sept 1853). His clients were expected to find their own food and accommodation since Cook was reluctant to provide for the 'stomachs of Tourists' (*Cook's Excursionist*, 23 Aug 1858). As he often explained in his monthly journal the *Excursionist*, begun in 1851 and written in vigorous, self-revelatory prose, his main aim was to inculcate 'great moral and social lessons' (Thomas Cook Archive). Although his firm's profits were modest at this stage, Cook was able to abandon the printing trade, give considerable sums to poor relief, promote the erection of a Temperance Hall in Leicester, and finance the rebuilding of his Commercial and Family Temperance Hotel.

**Cook's foreign tours** The travel business could have been ruined in 1862, however, when the Scottish railway companies refused to issue any more group tickets for Cook's popular tours north of the border. With characteristic vision and 'wonderful strength of will' (*Barton Church Magazine*), Cook looked towards Europe, though his few previous forays across the channel had been financial failures. Now, with the help and encouragement of Joseph Paxton, he decided to exploit new rail links for the conveyance of large numbers of tourists to the continent. He set up an office in London and by September 1863 he had conducted 2000 visitors to France and 500 to Switzerland. Cook's continental tourists were provided not only with rail travel and a channel crossing via Newhaven and Dieppe (a route which he popularized), but also with accommodation in 'first-class establishments' and food acceptable to the 'thorough roast-beef-and-pudding-eating Englishman' (*Cook's Excursionist*, 28 Aug 1863).

  The 'Cook's tour' rapidly became a byword and its originator was hailed as the 'Napoleon of Excursions' (*Civil Service Gazette*)—though critics like Charles Lever accused Cook of swamping Europe with 'everything that is low-bred, vulgar and ridiculous' (*Blackwood's Magazine*, Feb 1865, 231). During the 1860s alpine journeys became increasingly popular and in 1864 parties began to venture into the newly united Italy. In 1866 the first Cook's tourists to America witnessed scenes of the recent civil war. At the end of the decade Cook took clients to even more exciting destinations: Egypt and the Holy Land, 'the greatest event of my tourist life' (*Cook's Excursionist*, 3 May 1869). He achieved a further ambition in 1872–3 when he conducted the first organized tourist party ever to go round the world. Cook hoped to 'pioneer the way for the golden age when nations shall learn war no more' (*Cook's Excursionist*, 29 July 1873). Certainly he blazed a trail which twenty further groups had followed by the time of his death.

**Final years** On the world tour, as on all others, Thomas Cook mixed 'Missions with business'. In a letter to his wife he explained that the practice 'has sweetened my journey and … improved my heart without prejudice to the mercenary object of my tour' (T. Cook to M. Cook, 24 March 1873, Thomas Cook Archive). In fact the firm's profits remained small. But the business began to change when John Mason Cook started full-time work with his father in 1865—to become a partner in what was subsequently known as Thomas Cook & Son in 1871. By then there were three English offices, manned by a growing staff and served by four 'travelling assistants'. While Thomas was away on his world tour the firm moved to grand new head-quarters in Ludgate Circus. In 1873 Thomas Cook & Son entered into a short-lived and ill-fated partnership with an American, E. M. Jenkins, to encourage the transatlantic side of the undertaking, in which Thomas became increasingly involved. By this time there had been frequent serious disagreements between father and son arising from their radically different approaches to the business. In 1878 a full-scale quarrel occurred, as a result of which Thomas retired to Thorncroft, the large house which he had built on the outskirts of Leicester, while John took charge of the firm.

Cook led a lonely life after the deaths of his unmarried daughter Annie (who drowned in her bath, apparently overcome by fumes from a new gas heater) in 1880 and his wife four years later. He continued to travel, however, making his final pilgrimage to the Holy Land in 1888. Much of his time and money were spent, as they had been throughout his career, in work for the Baptist church, the temperance movement, and other charities. He did not attend the firm's silver jubilee celebrations in 1891; whether this was because of blindness and physical incapacity or because John did not want him there is not clear. After suffering a stroke, Thomas Cook died at Thorncroft, Knighton, Leicester, on 18 July 1892, aged eighty-three. He was given a Baptist burial on 22 July in Leicester, where the flags (including that on the temperance hall) flew at half-mast.

**Thomas Cook & Son**  **John Mason Cook** (1834–1899), travel agent, was born on 13 January 1834 at Quaker's Yard, Market Harborough, the first of two surviving children of Thomas Cook and his wife, Marianne. He was brought up with Baptist, teetotal beliefs which he never changed. Since both his parents were wholly preoccupied by the temperance movement he may have had, as some allege, a 'pathetic' childhood. Certainly he was, as a mere boy, 'broken to the harness' of tourism by being required to officiate on his father's juvenile excursions (*Blackwood's Magazine*, Aug 1899, 211). But he received a basic education at a dame-school in Market Harborough and at a preparatory school in Leicester. In 1848 he left to work as a printer in Derby.

After a few months of hard labour and low pay Cook returned to Leicester to serve in his father's printing office. He also arranged and conducted more tours. Father and son did not work well together and in 1856 John Cook took up a post as superintendent of the Midland Railway's excursion traffic. Three years later he set up on his own as a printer in Leicester. He married a local girl, Emma Hodges, on 29 December 1861 and their first son, Frank, was born in 1862. Perhaps because of his growing financial responsibilities, John Cook agreed to rejoin his father's firm in 1865. He was put in charge of its new office at 98 Fleet Street, where he made an immediate impact.

**Farther afield**  John Cook pioneered Cook's tours to America, personally conducting his first party across the Atlantic in 1866. It was on his initiative that new offices were opened in Manchester, Brussels, and Cologne. He also introduced the popular system of hotel coupons, which tourists bought from Cook and exchanged for bed and board, thus preventing hoteliers from overcharging. It was to his incessant, painstaking toil that the firm largely owed its increased efficiency and profitability during the late 1860s. Yet only after much persuasion from his father did John consent to become a full partner in 1871. His reluctance was probably due to disputes between the two men, mainly over financial matters. Unlike Thomas, John believed that business should be kept separate from religion and philanthropy. He also upset his father by being more adventurous in investing money. He opened a hotel at Luxor and refurbished the Nile steamers of the khedive, from whom he obtained the passenger agency, thus helping to make Egypt a safer and more attractive destination. In 1872 he took advantage of Thomas Cook's prolonged absence to arrange the expensive move to large new premises, which soon proved to be indispensable. John Cook, a tall, thickset, heavily bearded man with an intimidating manner, imposed on his staff strict rules of dress, work, and conduct. But he was also a fair and benevolent employer.

During the 1870s Cook untiringly arranged new enterprises, nearly all of which proved to be profitable. The most lucrative was his creation, in 1878, of a foreign banking and money exchange department. Its business, especially through the improvement of credit notes, which he helped to develop into travellers' cheques, soon began to flourish. Railway coupons were another important facility, enabling passengers to book and pay for an entire international train journey in advance. Since railway companies accepted payments on a monthly basis, the firm as well as the customers benefited from this innovation. Meanwhile an angry correspondence raged between father and son which led to John's bringing about Thomas Cook's retirement. After taking charge in 1879 he paid his father a pension (probably £1000 a year) and rigorously excluded him from the business. Relations between them remained correct but distant.

**A passage from India** …  John Cook's first success as sole director was to build up the American side of Thomas Cook & Son after the dissolution of the partnership with E. M. Jenkins in 1878. During the 1880s he opened up new tourist destinations, among them India, which was not very popular, and Australia and New Zealand, which proved lucrative. He experimented with novel schemes such as improving the Mount Vesuvius funicular railway, which he purchased in 1887. Although the travel business became more competitive, Cook expanded the scope and increased the profits of his own firm. He concentrated on 'select' tours for a more exclusive clientele than that favoured by his father. He also sought out government patronage and was happy to accept official commissions like transporting the expedition to relieve General Gordon in 1884. The firm took the army from Cairo to Wadi Halfa, though he himself made a hazardous trip as far south as Dongola. With pardonable hyperbole some admirers said that if Cook had conducted the relief force all the way to Khartoum, Gordon would have been saved (*Daily Telegraph*; Royle, 554).

In 1887, at the behest of the India Office, which wanted to stop the exploitation of Muslim pilgrims, the firm took on the equally challenging task of transporting them between the subcontinent and Mecca. But the service was abandoned in 1893 when Cook's prices proved too high. There was no such problem about Cook's lavish arrangements for conducting Indian princes to London for Queen Victoria's silver and golden jubilees. Such public undertakings brought the firm prestige as well as profit—though the financial dispute with the war ministry which followed the death of Gordon may have cost Cook the knighthood he craved. Nevertheless at the firm's own golden jubilee in 1891 it was much praised for its services to the empire.

**A revolution in popular tourism** On this occasion John Cook enumerated the assets of his business: 84 offices, 85 agencies, 2692 staff (978 of them in Egypt), and 45 bank accounts. He rightly claimed to be personally responsible for its spectacular growth. But when he went on to speak of his belief 'that the world would be a pleasanter place of habitation if all the dwellers on its surface were brought closer together, and that international travel was one of the best preservatives against international wars' (*Cook's Excursionist*, 8 Aug 1891), Cook was echoing the ideals of his father. Although often at odds, the two men were complementary, Thomas providing the creative vision, John the executive drive. Between them, Thomas Cook & Son contributed signally to a revolution in popular tourism that changed the world.

John Cook also announced in 1891 that he wanted to hand over management of the business to his three sons, Frank, Ernest, and Thomas Albert (Bert), all of whom were already involved in it. Actually he could not bear to relinquish control. But because of deteriorating health he spent the winters in Egypt, where the firm enjoyed such a large share of the flourishing tourist trade that John Cook was often hailed as uncrowned king. There he supervised the construction of a fleet of splendid new Nile paddle-steamers, in which wealthy passengers enjoyed a sybaritic existence and were almost entirely insulated from Egyptian life. Cook showed the more charitable side of his nature, though, when in 1891 he built the first hospital for Egyptians at Luxor.

After going round the world to inspect the company's work in 1893, Cook gave much of his attention to special events and was particularly pleased to carry out royal commissions. His devotion to royalty—as well as to duty—may well have hastened his end. In 1898 he personally conducted Kaiser Wilhelm II to the Holy Land. The tour was arranged with the usual military precision but both men were affected by the 'excessive heat'. John Cook contracted dysentery and never really recovered. He died on 6 March 1899, aged sixty-five, at Mount Felix, his new residence in Walton-on-Thames. Like his father he was given a Baptist funeral in Leicester and buried in the family vault. He was survived by his wife.

The three grandsons of Thomas Cook carried on the business; and Ernest Edward *Cook was responsible for the banking and exchange department. Although the firm continued to prosper under their direction it was sold, quite unexpectedly, on 8 February 1928 to the Compagnie Internationale des Wagons-Lits of Belgium for £3.5 million. PIERS BRENDON

**Sources** *Cook's Excursionist* (1851–99) · P. Brendon, *Thomas Cook: 150 years of popular tourism* (1991) · J. Pudney, *The Thomas Cook story* (1953) · W. F. Rae, *The business of travel* (1891) · E. Swinglehurst, *Cook's tours: the story of popular travel* (1982) · A. Griffiths, 'John Cook', *Blackwood's Magazine*, 166 (Aug 1899) · J. A. R. Pimlott, *The Englishman's holiday* (1976) · E. Swinglehurst, *The romantic journey* (1974) · Thomas Cook Archive, Berkeley Street, London · *DNB* · 'The jubilee of Mr Thomas Cook', *General Baptist Magazine*, 78 (1876) [reprinted from *Derby Reporter*], 185 · *Temperance Messenger*, 2 (1841), 50, 132 · T. Cook, *Handbook of the trip to Liverpool* (1845) · *Leicester Chronicle* (4 July 1846) · *Barton Church Magazine* (Oct 1892) · *Civil Service Gazette* (14 May 1846) · 'Continental excursionists', *Blackwood*, 97 (1865), 230–33 · 'John Cook', *Blackwood*, 166 (1899), 211–23 · *Daily Telegraph* (4 March 1899) · C. Royle, *The Egyptian campaigns, 1882 to 1885*, rev. edn (1900), 554

**Archives** Thomas Cook Archive, Berkeley Street, London, letters to his wife | PRO, Colonel Ardagh MSS · PRO, Lord Cromer MSS · PRO, H. H. Kitchener MSS

**Likenesses** group portrait, photograph (at Pompeii), Thomas Cook Archive, Berkeley Street, London · photograph, Thomas Cook Archive, Berkeley Street, London · photograph (John Cook), Thomas Cook Archive, Berkeley Street, London · photograph (John Cook; with his wife and eldest son), Thomas Cook Archive, Berkeley Street, London · photograph (John Cook; in old age), Thomas Cook Archive, Berkeley Street, London · photograph, Hult. Arch. [*see illus.*] · wood-engravings, NPG; repro. in *ILN* (July 1891–July 1892)

**Wealth at death** £2731 7s. 2d.: probate, 8 Oct 1892, *CGPLA Eng. & Wales* · £622,534 3s. 4d.—John Cook: resworn probate, Feb 1900, *CGPLA Eng. & Wales* (1899)

**Cook, William**. *See* Cooke, William (d. 1824).

**Cook, Sir William Richard Joseph** (1905–1987), scientist and civil servant, was born on 10 April 1905 in Trowbridge, Wiltshire, the elder son and eldest of three children of John Cook, railway inspector, and his wife, Eva Boobyer. A successful scholar at Trowbridge high school, he went on to Bristol University and graduated BSc in 1925 with first-class honours in mathematics (specializing in applied maths). He took a diploma in education in 1926 and an MSc in 1927. Success as a part-time lecturer almost persuaded him to become a teacher, but he settled for the civil service, and joined the research department at Woolwich arsenal in 1928, as librarian.

After working for a time on the external ballistics of guns, Cook joined the new rocket programme in 1935, and by 1940 had become deputy controller of projectile development, where he was responsible for many successful military applications of rockets. At the end of the Second

World War he became first director of a new rocket establishment at Westcott, but uncertainty and disagreement about the future of the work unsettled him so much that in 1947 he moved to become director of physical research at the Admiralty, where, although the field was new to him, he was instrumental in pioneering major advances in underwater warfare technology. He became deputy chief scientific adviser, Ministry of Defence, in 1950, as well as chief of the Royal Naval Scientific Service. In 1954 the government decided to develop thermonuclear weapons and Cook, an ideal choice, was appointed to lead the programme, as deputy director at Aldermaston. The essence of his work was to test the bomb before a possible test ban treaty could be imposed. A crash programme, driven by Cook, culminated in a successful test series based on Christmas Island in 1957. He himself went to the island to play a vital role as directing scientist. Following this demonstration of British thermonuclear capability, he played a leading role in the successful negotiations to re-establish co-operation with the United States. Cook left Aldermaston early in 1958 to become member for engineering and development in the Atomic Energy Authority and took over the newly formed reactor group in 1961. Here he achieved a great deal, resolving problems in the advanced gas-cooled reactor, bringing the fast reactor to full power, and recommending the construction of a heavy-water steam-generating reactor.

Cook returned to the Ministry of Defence in 1964 where, as a deputy chief scientific adviser, he took responsibility for operational requirements and projects. His immediate problem was the disorganization that followed the cancellation of the fighter bomber TSR2. An Anglo-French project for a fighter aircraft quickly failed when the French withdrew, and was replaced by a joint British–German–Italian effort. After much difficult negotiation, in which Cook played a prominent part, the successful Tornado fighter was specified and produced. In 1968 he became chief adviser, projects and research, and set up a number of important international projects intended to reduce defence costs. He also initiated the studies which led eventually to the Chevaline system to improve the defence penetration of the Polaris missile. He retired in 1970 but soon became involved in commercial directorships, which kept him very busy for another fifteen years. Nationally the most important of these was Rolls-Royce, which had gone bankrupt in 1971. He was appointed to chair a committee to decide very quickly whether the RB211 engine should be continued, and it is largely to his credit that the engine eventually became the backbone of Rolls-Royce's civil programme. He was appointed a director when the new government-owned company was set up later in 1971. In addition to his directorships, he continued to chair, very effectively, the nuclear safety committees for another ten years. He was appointed CB in 1951, and KCB in 1970, having been knighted in 1968. He held honorary degrees from Strathclyde (1967) and Bath (1975). He was elected a fellow of the Royal Society in 1962.

Cook, known as Bill to his friends and colleagues, was slightly built and always neatly dressed. A man of great charm and ready wit, fond of his pipe and of a Scotch, he was known for his meticulous preparation for meetings, his ability to find and probe the weaknesses in a technical case, and his forceful but good-humoured pressure on all to give of their best. In 1929 he married Grace, daughter of Frederick Arthur Purnell, treasurer for Burton upon Trent council; they had one daughter. They were divorced in 1939, and in the same year he married Gladys, librarian at the Woolwich arsenal department, the daughter of Sydney Edward Allen, postman. They had one son and one daughter. When Gladys's health began to fail he looked after her devotedly. He died on 16 September 1987 in Westminster Hospital, London, following a massive stroke.

JOHN CHALLENS, *rev.*

**Sources** Lord Penney and V. H. B. Macklen, *Memoirs FRS*, 34 (1988), 443–61 · *The Times* (19 Sept 1987) · *Daily Telegraph* (22 Sept 1987) · personal knowledge (1996) · *CGPLA Eng. & Wales* (1988)
**Wealth at death** £189,951: administration with will, 19 Jan 1988, *CGPLA Eng. & Wales*

**Cooke**. *See also* Coke, Cook.

**Cooke family** ( *per. c.*1800–1865), engravers, artists, and publishers, came to prominence with **William Bernard Cooke** (1778–1855), who was born in Charles Street, Hatton Garden, London, the son of a German immigrant confectioner from Frankfurt am Main, Johann Bernhard Guck, who changed his name to John Bernard Cooke. His mother was Maria Anna White (*d.* 1821). An older brother of George Cooke [see below], with whom he frequently worked, W. B. Cooke was apprenticed to William Angus, engraver of *The Seats of the Nobility and Gentry in Great Britain and Wales* (1787–[1800]). He married, on 12 April 1804, Elizabeth Blundstone (*d.* 1830); there were no surviving children. His second wife was a sister of Anastasia Cromek, wife of the watercolourist Robert Hartley *Cromek, whose maiden name was Priestman; they married in 1831, and she died in 1840.

William Bernard Cooke was employed on John Norris Brewer's *The Beauties of England and Wales* (1805), and much of his work thereafter was in the same vein. Sir Henry Charles Englefield, bt, chose W. B. and George Cooke to engrave the illustrations to his *A description of the principal picturesque beauties, antiquities, and geological phenomena of the Isle of Wight and coast of Dorset* (1816) because of their truth to the original drawings and absence of engravers' invention.

W. B. Cooke opened a print gallery and shop at 9 Soho Square, London, with an exhibition entitled 'Engraving by Living British Artists under the Patronage of His Majesty' (1821), the catalogue claiming that:

> The Professors of the interesting and highly useful art have long felt the necessity [of] ... direct communication with its Patrons and Admirers ... and have invited their Brothers to co-operate by sending their work ... Under such auspices the British School of Engraving may confidently hope to arrive at a higher degree of Public estimation. (p. 1)

Subsequent exhibitions included drawings, some loaned by private collectors and some for sale, in 1822, 1823, and 1824.

*Picturesque Views of the Southern Coast of England* (1814–26) totalled forty-eight plates and thirty-two vignettes chiefly after drawings commissioned from J. M. W. Turner who closely supervised the proofs. Drawings by Alexander, F. L. T. Francia, Havell, Samuel Prout, and William Westall were included. The copperplates were engraved by, among others, W. B. and G. Cooke, E. Finden, E. Goodall, and W. Miller. It was acknowledged as a high point in the monochrome reproduction of watercolour drawings. The engravers worked in the line manner but were:

> a school truly indigenous, both in its style and its technical means … not … line-engraving at all, as practically all the work was done by etching … a wriggling wormlike line which is absolutely opposed to all the reasonable possibilities and conventions of graver work … in such contrast to the true ideals of the etcher's art that we would still be content to call its exponents line-engravers. (Hind, 221–2)

W. B. Cooke's dealings with Turner and John Constable show him to have had a keen business sense. His reputation rested on topographical, especially marine or coastal, subjects, and on antiquarian interests. Typical are Turner's five *Views in Sussex* (1819), Thomas Allason's *Picturesque Views of the Antiquities of Pola in Istria* (1819), James Hakewill's *A Picturesque Tour of Italy* (1820), T. L. Donaldson's *Pompeii … Including Recent Excavations* (1827), and *Vases, Altars &c from the … Louvre* (1828), drawn by W. B. Cooke and Thomas Boys, and engraved by Henry Moses. W. B. Cooke's apprentices were Frederick Smith, J. C. Allen, and W. Brandard. Samuel Redgrave wrote that he showed great ability and enterprise, published 'several of his own plates', but did not succeed (Redgrave, *Artists*, 96), a somewhat harsh verdict repeated by R. E. Graves. William Bernard Cook died at his home, 9 Camden Square, Camberwell, on 2 August 1855, of heart disease, and was buried on 8 August in Nunhead cemetery, London. His executors were Thomas Goff Lupton, engraver, and son.

**George Cooke** (1781–1834) was born on 22 January 1781 in Charles Street, Hatton Garden, London, a younger brother of W. B. Cooke, and apprenticed to James Basire (1769–1822) in 1795. He married, on 26 October 1808, Elizabeth Harriet Eglinton (1785–1882), with whom he had eleven children, the second being the marine painter Edward William *Cooke RA (1811–1880). George Cooke's wife kept a boarding-school, Albion House, Barnes, at which the daughters of Clarkson Stanfield RA and David Roberts RA were pupils and where he was drawing-master. His indentured apprentices were George Hollis, John Barnett, W. J. Cooke [see below], W. Miller, Thomas Shotter Boys, Percy Heath, Theo Lindsey Aspland, and F. R. Hay.

Basire, remembered as a neglectful master, produced for the *Oxford Almanack* engravings of drawings by J. M. W. Turner, and George Cooke's enthusiasm for these led him to plan a published series of that artist's watercolours. He engraved fifteen of the plates for Turner's *Picturesque Views of the Southern Coast of England* (1814–26) but a disagreement with Turner over the disposal of proofs led to an acrimonious severing of relations. He worked with W. B. Cooke on many of the series mentioned above, and there were also

160 plates from his hand in John Pinkerton's *General Collection of Voyages and Travels* (1808–14) in which he had to make acceptable pictures from 'mere tracings … & abortions of art' (*Arnold's Magazine of the Fine Arts*, 1834, 555). He undertook the engraving of the 2000 aquatint plates for the publisher Conrad Loddiges & Sons' work *The Botanical Cabinet* (20 vols., 1817–33). His studio and family being fully employed in its regular appearance, he moved to a house adjoining the Loddiges at their Hackney nursery gardens.

George Cooke published *Views of London and its Vicinity*, in parts, in 1826–34, planned to illustrate the developing metropolis; his painter friends gave him drawings for engraving for which his son Edward William had made preliminary outlines to save established artists, including A. W. Callcott, David Roberts, Clarkson Stanfield, and Samuel Prout, time and labour. Projected as eighty plates, on copper, it was overtaken by similar works quickly produced on steel plates which, whatever the quality, gave proofs of unvarying clarity. Conservative dislike of steel led him to avoid it but rivals using it outdistanced him and prospered. Cooke meanwhile doggedly maintained traditional high-quality proofs from copper, supervising printing to ensure the best results. However, he reduced *London* to forty-eight plates, the last number being published posthumously, by his widow.

A great many books of the 1820s contain plates of picturesque scenery and topographical interest from George Cooke's hand. *Sunderland Iron Bridge*, after Edward Blore, with 'effect' by F. L. Francia, was produced for R. Surtees' *The History and Antiquities of … Durham*. He engraved after A. W. Callcott a view of Rotterdam, and had begun two further large plates of Antwerp and Dover, but by the failure of his agent in the financial crash of 1825–6 he lost money, putting an end to the venture as well as straitening his circumstances. His *Views of the Old and the New London Bridges* (1833), from his son Edward's drawings, was engraved and etched conjointly; although the work was very well received, George Cooke's name does not appear on the title-page.

George Cooke was a member of the Associated Society of Engravers whose aims included securing recognition by the Royal Academy for engravers to be full academicians. They also embarked on engraving and publishing selected paintings in the National Gallery. Cooke was also a member of the Graphic Society, the Calcographic Society, and the Artists' Joint Stock Fund. He died on 27 February 1834 of brain fever at his home, Albion House, Terrace, Barnes, Surrey. He was buried in St Mary's Church, Barnes, on 6 March. He was remembered for his 'buoyancy of spirit, industry, perseverance, temperance and unsullied integrity' (*Arnold's Magazine of the Fine Arts*, 1834, 560).

**William John Cooke** (*bap.* 1796, *d.* 1865), engraver, was baptized in London on 5 April 1796, the son of John Conrad Cooke (*b.* 1770, *d.* before 1829), eldest brother of W. B. and G. Cooke, and his wife, Mary Ann, *née* Harrison. He was apprenticed to his uncle George Cooke about 1810. He married in 1823 Mary Boys, sister of his fellow apprentice Thomas Shotter Boys, the lithographer.

A pioneer worker on steel, which his former master despised, W. J. Cooke won in 1826 the Isis gold medal of the Society of Arts for improvements in fluids for etching on steel and the invention of an 'apparatus for gradating tints'. He engraved drawings by Richard Parkes Bonington whom he met in 1825 and with whom he remained friends. *Rouen from Bon Secours* and *Chillon*, both small in size, were published in *Friendship's Offering* in 1826. Cooke was a frequent visitor to the house of his former fellow apprentice John Barnett, where Bonington died in 1828.

William John Cooke engraved mainly for the annuals *The Gem*, *The Amulet*, *The Bouquet*, and *Friendship's Offering*. He also contributed plates to *Stanfield's Coast Scenery* by Clarkson Stanfield (1836) and the *Oriental Annual*, after works by W. Daniell (1834). He also engraved plates after J. M. W. Turner's drawings of Nottingham, Plymouth, Newark Castle (Scotland), and the Thames at Mortlake, and *Calais Pier*, after David Cox, which was engraved for the *Gallery of the Society of Painters in Water Colours* (1832). His work is sometimes signed W. Cooke Junr. A set of W. J. Cooke's pencil studies (priv. coll.) recording the ruins of the Palace of Westminster after the fire of 1834 was proposed for engraving jointly with his cousin Edward, but never carried out.

In 1840 the decline in the fashion for illustrated annuals and the possible adverse effect of photography upon engraving in England caused W. J. Cooke to move with his family to Darmstadt. He made topographical drawings in England and Germany, perhaps with publication in view but died in Darmstadt on 6 April 1865. His family later returned to England. His son William Montague Cooke (*b.* 1824) evidently inherited artistic talent for he gave drawing instruction to the children of Princess Alice, princess of Great Britain and Ireland, and grand duchess of Hesse and by Rhine.                 JOHN MUNDAY

**Sources** *Exhibition of engravings by living British artists* (1821) [exhibition catalogue, W. B. Cooke's Gallery, London] · E. Shanes, *Turner's Picturesque views in England and Wales* (1979) · W. Thornbury, *The life and correspondence of JMW Turner* (1877), 633–6 · A. M. Hind, *A history of engraving and etching*, 3rd edn (1923); repr. (1927) · J. Munday, *E. W. Cooke, 1811–1880: a man of his time* (1996) · Redgrave, *Artists* · diaries of E. W. Cooke, RA, priv. coll. · *Arnold's Magazine of the Fine Arts* (1834), 553–60 · J. Roundell, *Thomas Shotter Boys* (1974) · A. Dubuisson, *R. P. Bonington* (1924) · minutes of the committee of polite arts, 31 Jan 1826, RSA · 'Cooke, William John', *DNB*

**Archives** BM, account book [W. B. Cooke] · John Murray, London, letters | Free Library of Philadelphia, autographs of engravers collection, MS letters

**Likenesses** G. Clint, portrait (W. B. Cooke), priv. coll. · G. Clint, portrait (G. Cooke), priv. coll. · E. W. Cooke, pencil drawing (W. B. Cooke), repro. in Munday, *E. W. Cooke*, 27 · photograph (G. Cooke; after G. Clint), NPG · photograph (W. J. Cooke)

**Cooke, Alexander** (*bap.* 1564, *d.* 1632), Church of England clergyman and religious controversialist, was born at Beeston, near Leeds, Yorkshire, the second son of William Gayle or Cooke, and baptized there on 3 September 1564. After Leeds grammar school he followed his elder brother, Robert *Cooke (1549/50–1615), to Brasenose College, Oxford, in 1581, graduating BA in 1585. In 1587 he was elected to a Percy fellowship at University College, proceeding MA in 1588 and BD in 1596. Cooke returned to Yorkshire, where his strongly anti-Catholic views were employed in preaching to the recusant prisoners in York Castle in 1600, and on 5 February 1601 he was instituted to the important royal living of Louth in Lincolnshire. Cooke was appointed one of the select preachers at the accession of James I in 1603, but in the following year his puritan principles landed him in trouble with the diocesan authorities at Lincoln and he was deprived of his living on 30 October 1604 for refusing to wear the surplice.

Cooke then again returned to Yorkshire to assist, in the capacity of curate, his brother Robert, who as vicar of Leeds was instrumental in establishing a vigorous protestant tradition there. The brothers made a formidable partnership which attracted the support of many of the leading townsmen so that, when Robert died in 1615, a group of them persuaded the archbishop of York, Tobie Matthew, to bypass the surviving owners of the advowson—also local worthies, who had hoped to appoint to the vicarage Richard Middleton, a chaplain to Prince Charles—and to place Cooke in the living instead. A suit in chancery followed. This was settled in Cooke's favour in August 1617 when the right of presentation was confirmed in a self-perpetuating body of twenty-five trustees, mostly local lay sympathizers of Cooke and his brand of churchmanship, but also including John Favour, vicar of Halifax, and other puritan clergy of the area associated with the exercise at Halifax at which Cooke had been a preacher.

Though it met with vociferous opposition from some quarters, Cooke's subsequent ministry in the town was both purposeful and authoritative; he preached against popular festivals, including Christmas, and was firm in his opposition to the alehouse, denouncing from the pulpit by name those who had failed to live up to his godly standards. More positively, his ministry produced a flowering of puritan piety in Leeds and its chapelries, best expressed in the charitable giving to the poor and in support for clergy and educational institutions during the 1620s and 1630s. This was given institutional direction through the committee for pious uses established for the parish in 1619, and Cooke's supporters also formed the nucleus of the corporation set up by royal charter in 1626 giving the town self-government and releasing it from control of the manor.

Cooke's renowned anti-Catholic views were well known in senior ecclesiastical circles and brought him to the attention of Matthew, who encouraged him to publish controversial works, the first of which, *Pope Joane: a dialogue betweene a protestant and a papist, manifestly proving that a woman called Joane was pope of Rome*, was published in 1610, and in the course of the well-known argument pilloried the views of Bellarmine. A second edition followed in 1625 and a French translation was published in 1633, but Cooke's most popular controversial work in his lifetime was his more substantial *Work for a Mass-Priest*, first published in 1617, and going through four further amplified editions in the author's lifetime.

In addition to his public opposition to popery, Cooke

was thought to be a vigorous critic of the Arminians in private. His controversial style also affected his pastoral ministry, which was disturbed between 1619 and 1622 by a cause in Star Chamber between Cooke and John Metcalf, the bailiff of Leeds manor, over a variety of issues which had much to do with the administration of local charities and the traditional loyalties of the latter in matters of religion. Notwithstanding these problems, Cooke's legacy to the religious and cultural temper of seventeenth-century Leeds was substantial and in the years immediately after his death several endowments were made to the outlying chapelries of the parish and a new chapel, St John's, established in the town. Cooke died in 1632 and was buried in his parish church on 23 June next to his brother Robert. He was survived by his wife, Anne, and three children, to whom he left his books, which later formed the nucleus of a library for St John's Chapel.

WILLIAM JOSEPH SHEILS

**Sources** G. Forster, 'From Elizabeth to Ralph Thoresby', *Religion in Leeds*, ed. A. Mason (c.1994), 29–42 · C. Cross, *Urban magistrates and ministers: religion in Hull and Leeds from the Reformation to the civil war* (1985) · Foster, *Alum. Oxon.* · R. Thoresby, *Ducatus Leodiensis, or, The topography of … Leedes* (1715) · R. Marchant, *The puritans and the church courts in the diocese of York, 1560–1642* (1960) · parish register (baptism), 3 Sept 1564, Beeston · parish register (burial), 23 June 1632, Leeds · will, Borth. Inst., Archbishop's Register 32, fol. 32v · J. A. Newton, 'Puritanism in Yorkshire, 1603–1640', PhD thesis, U. Lond., 1964
**Archives** York Minster Library, sermon notes in back of printed text of *Work for a Mass-Priest*
**Wealth at death** under £80: will, Borth. Inst., York Archbishop's Register 32, fol. 32v

**Cooke, Alice Margaret** (1867–1940), historian, was born at 24 Boston Street, Hulme, Lancashire, on 18 September 1867, the daughter of John Cooke, a cotton yarn agent, and his wife, Eliza Anderson Jackson. She attended a private school in Manchester and then, from 1883 to 1887, Manchester High School for Girls (Girls' Public Day School Trust), where she was first inspired to become a historian. A classmate remembered her as 'a hard worker, very earnest and conscientious, and already rather academic, with eyes set on her goal' (Horner and Haworth, 1). Because her parents did not want her to leave home, in 1887 she entered Victoria University of Manchester (Owens College), which had been open to women only since 1883. There she was an excellent student, earning the Bradford history scholarship in 1888 and a first-class honours degree in history in 1890. In that year she became the first woman to be awarded the Jones fellowship, the highest distinction in history conferred by the college. The fellowship enabled her to pursue her love of medieval history, leading to the publication of 'The settlement of the Cistercians in England' in the *English Historical Review* (1893), which was for long the standard account of these early monastic foundations.

In 1893 Cooke received the MA degree, the first to be awarded to a woman at Owens College, and became the first woman to be appointed a lecturer there. She was one of the first women appointed to a university-level academic post in Britain. At that time, provision for women

**Alice Margaret Cooke** (1867–1940), by Helen T. Cohen, 1898

students at Owens College was limited. As well as teaching she served as assistant tutor to women students from 1897 to 1901; in this capacity she raised money for a new women's union and was one of the founders and joint honorary secretary of Ashburne Hall, the first hall of residence for women at Owens, and she served as chairman of the women's athletic union. In 1897 she was elected a member of the court of governors of Victoria University. She lectured for university extension, supported the Manchester University settlement, and worked for the cause of women's suffrage. Furthermore, during this period she was invited by her friend Mrs Rylands to compile a catalogue of Earl Spencer's Althorp Library, which became the nucleus of the John Rylands Library, University of Manchester. She was also fond of cycling and travel.

From 1901 to 1903 Cooke was lecturer in history and head of the Aberdare hall of residence for women students at the University of South Wales and Monmouthshire, Cardiff. In 1903 she became the first woman entrusted with librarian's work at the Cambridge University Library, where she was invited to catalogue Lord Acton's library, a historical collection of 60,000 to 70,000 volumes. In Cambridge she lived on Clare Road near Newnham College, where she taught modern history from 1905 to 1907.

In 1907 Alice Cooke was appointed lecturer in history at Leeds University, where she was chosen over the young F. M. Powicke, later regius professor of modern history at Oxford. At Leeds, where she was appointed reader in 1919, she established the department of medieval history and played an important role in strengthening the library's medieval collections. During the First World War she patrolled the streets of Leeds by night as a policewoman, which may have contributed to a breakdown in her health in 1920.

After two years recuperating at home in Manchester, Cooke returned to Cambridge as director of studies in history at Newnham College, where she remained until her retirement in 1927. After her retirement she lived in Cambridge with Lena Ward, the daughter of her old friend Sir Adolphus Ward. Cooke was fond of Cambridge, but her health remained poor, and in 1934 she became a complete invalid after an accident. She was able to retire to Manchester, where, although not a Roman Catholic herself, she was taken in by a community of Catholic nuns, who cared for her until her death, at St Joseph's Hospital, Carlton Road, Whalley Range, Manchester, on 26 January 1940.

Because of her teaching responsibilities and poor health, Alice Cooke was not able to devote as much time to historical research as she might have wished. Nevertheless, as well as her seminal article on the Cistercians, she wrote forty articles on medieval history, beginning with the letter N, for the *Dictionary of National Biography*, and made several indexes to the *Cambridge Modern History*. In 1901 the Chetham Society published her edition of the manuscript 'Visitationes B.M.V. de Whalley'. While at Leeds she was commissioned to write the chapter on monasticism for the *Cambridge Medieval History*, but was unable to complete it because of illness; it was eventually published as 'A study in twelfth century religious revival and reform' in the *John Rylands Library Bulletin* (January 1925). After a trip to Assisi in 1909 Alice Cooke had become fascinated by St Francis, and published 'St. Francis of Assisi' in the *Church Quarterly Review* in October 1929. Her greatest contribution, however, was probably as a pioneer in women's education in her native Manchester and as a teacher. A former student at Leeds University recalled that Alice Cooke had 'acquired something of the saintliness and humility and the sublime joy of the early Franciscans, and was able to communicate a measure of this to her pupils' (Horner, 43).                              Fernanda Helen Perrone

**Sources** I. B. Horner and E. A. Haworth, *Alice M. Cooke: a memoir* (1940) • I. B. Horner, 'Alice Margaret Cooke (1867–1940)', *Newnham College Roll Letter* (1941), 39–44 • [A. B. White and others], eds., *Newnham College register, 1871–1971*, 2nd edn, 1 (1979), vol. 1 • M. Tylecote, *The education of women at Manchester University, 1883–1933* (1941) • C. Dyhouse, *No distinction of sex? Women in British universities, 1870–1939* (1995) • b. cert. • d. cert. • *CGPLA Eng. & Wales* (1940)
**Likenesses** H. T. Cohen [Mrs E. G. Atkinson], drawing, 1898, repro. in Horner and Haworth, *Alice M. Cooke*, frontispiece [*see illus.*]
**Wealth at death** £3191 14s. 6d.: probate, 29 April 1940, *CGPLA Eng. & Wales*

**Cooke, Anne**. *See* Bacon, Anne, Lady Bacon (*c.*1528–1610).

**Cooke, Sir Anthony** (1505/6–1576), educator and humanist, was the only son of John Coke or Cooke (1485–1516) of Gidea Hall, Essex, within the liberty of Havering-atte-Bower near Romford, and Alice Saunders (*d.* 1510), daughter of William Saunders of Banbury, Oxfordshire. He was

the great-grandson of Sir Thomas Cook, a wealthy draper, who was lord mayor of London in 1462–3.

John Coke died in 1516, leaving the eleven-year-old Anthony to be raised by his uncle Richard Cooke, a diplomatic courier under Henry VIII, and his stepmother, Margaret Pennington, a lady-in-waiting first to Katherine of Aragon and later to the Princess Mary. Some time before 1523 Anthony Cooke married Anne (*d.* 1553), daughter of Sir William Fitzwilliam of Gaynes Park, Essex, a London merchant, and widow of Sir John Hawes of London. In 1523 Cooke was admitted to the Inner Temple and was granted the use for life of the Essex chamber.

Almost nothing is known of Cooke's actions over the next twelve years. There are no further references to him at the Inner Temple but he apparently remained in England for much of this time. He appears in the one surviving Havering manor court roll for these years acting as an agent for his family's lands, and his landed inheritance may have occupied much of his time. A fourth share in the estate of his maternal great-grandfather, Sir Henry Belknap, fell to Cooke in 1521, when he was only sixteen, giving him valuable lands in Warwickshire and adjoining counties.

Cooke next appears in the 1530s. From 1531 he was regularly appointed a justice in the liberty of Havering, and he was one of the Essex gentlemen alerted during the Pilgrimage of Grace in 1536; he may also have served in Ireland in 1536–7. Called upon to provide troops for the army in Flanders in 1543 and France in 1544, he served as sheriff of Essex and Hertfordshire in 1544–5, and was named to several local commissions. In 1539 he had received his first appointment at court, being named one of the fifty 'spears' of Henry VIII's reconstituted bodyguard. He was present at the reception of Anne of Cleves in 1540 and of the admiral of France in 1546, and in the latter year was given a regular position at court as a gentleman of the privy chamber. He was made a knight of the Bath on 20 February 1547, and also sat for Lewes in that year's parliament. He subsequently served as a commissioner to inquire into heresies in Essex in 1549, and on the commission of 1552 to revise the ecclesiastical laws.

Cooke's greatest importance lies in the field of education, particularly of women, yet nothing is known of his own basic training. He was almost certainly self-taught. At some point, perhaps in the 1530s, he embarked on a serious study of the church fathers, and was sufficiently advanced by 1541 to complete a translation from the Latin of a sermon on prayer by St Cyprian, which he dedicated to the king. The dedication of the manuscript (it remains unpublished) suggests some familiarity with the 'new thought' of the humanist movement in England, although there is no evidence of Cooke's having studied with any of the humanists of his day. It praises Henry VIII for delivering his subjects from the 'captivity and bondage' of Rome but is not otherwise overtly protestant, although this may represent a deliberate attempt to avoid controversy.

Some time in the 1530s Cooke turned his attention to the education of his children, and especially that of his daughters. Enlightened opinion favoured some form of training for girls, but Cooke's five daughters received as good an education as that given to his four sons and probably better. Latin and Greek certainly formed part of their studies and they may also have received some training in Hebrew and modern languages. They read both early Christian writers and the works of contemporary protestant thinkers, and became well known for their scholarly abilities. The eldest daughter, Mildred *Cecil, who married the future Lord Burghley, was especially praised for her knowledge of Greek, while Anne *Bacon, the second wife of Lord Keeper Bacon, published works by Ochino and Jewel in translations from Italian and Latin respectively. Katherine *Killigrew, the wife of the diplomat Sir Henry Killigrew, was a strong protestant noted for her linguistic scholarship. She published nothing, but the formidable Elizabeth *Russell, who married successively the translator Sir Thomas Hoby and John, Lord Russell, second son of the second earl of Bedford, published her translation of a Latin treatise on the sacrament in 1605. The remaining daughter, Margaret, who became a maid-in-waiting to Queen Mary, married Sir Ralph Rowlett in 1558 as his second wife but died only a few weeks later.

The high point of Cooke's career has traditionally been seen as his appointment as tutor to Edward VI, although whether he ever actually held a formal post is uncertain. In 1550 John Hooper referred to Cooke as one of Edward's tutors along with John Cheke, and in May of that year Cooke received a life annuity of £100 in return for giving 'training in good letters and manners' to the king (HoP, *Commons, 1509–58*, 1.690). Cooke is never mentioned in Edward's journal, however, nor was he ever officially described as royal tutor. Most probably, Cooke began working with Edward in 1550 after the retirement of Richard Cox, another of the royal tutors, but as a companion and guide rather than as a formal teacher.

Cooke may have been slow to move towards religious evangelicalism, but his commitment had grown sufficiently strong by 1553 to lead him to an apparently self-imposed exile shortly after Mary's accession. While on the continent he travelled widely, making visits to Italy before settling in Strasbourg in 1555. There he attended lectures by Pietro Martire Vermigli (known as Peter Martyr) and was in contact with leaders of the reformed faith. Following Mary's death he returned to England, where many expected that he would be named to high office. He played an active part in the parliament of 1559 (in which he sat as a knight of the shire for Essex), but in some way seems to have become disaffected from the progress of the religious settlement, and in spite of his close connections with the highest echelons of the new government he was never granted an important position. He served on several religious commissions early in Elizabeth's reign and sat as a member for Essex again in 1563, but his participation in national affairs, whether political or religious, had virtually ended by that year, and he appears to have been largely absorbed in family matters in the last years of his life. His occupations included the extension of Gidea Hall, which Queen Elizabeth visited in 1568. In his will, drawn

up on 22 May 1576 and with a codicil added on 9 June, Cooke provided for the descent of his lands (estimated to be worth some £1100 per annum) to his sons Richard and William. All his surviving sons and daughters received bequests of plate, while each daughter was given her choice of books, two Latin and one Greek, from her father's library. The executors were headed by Bacon and Burghley, each of whom was to have £200 for his pains. His bequests in cash, totalling nearly £1200, bear witness both to Cooke's wealth and to his concern for his wider family—he remembered a number of grandchildren, including Robert Cecil, Anthony and Francis Bacon, and Thomas Posthumous Hoby. Surprisingly, perhaps, his will makes only the briefest possible provision for the well-being of his soul, and contains no charitable bequest at all. Cooke died on 11 June 1576, aged seventy, and was buried in St Andrew's Church at Romford. His effigy survives at St Edward's Church, Romford.                  DONN L. CALKINS

**Sources** M. K. McIntosh, 'Sir Anthony Cooke: Tudor humanist, educator, and religious reformer', *Proceedings of the American Philosophical Society*, 119 (1975), 233–50 • HoP, *Commons, 1509–58*, 1.689–91 • HoP, *Commons, 1558–1603*, 1.644–5 • R. M. Warnicke, *Women of the English Renaissance and Reformation* (Westport, Conn., Greenwood Press, 1983) • M. K. McIntosh, 'Some new gentry in early Tudor Essex: the Cookes of Gidea Hall, 1480–1550', *Essex Archaeology and History*, 9 (1977), 129–38 • will, PRO, PROB 11/59, fol. 72r–72v
**Archives** Hunt. L., corresp. and papers
**Likenesses** marble and alabaster effigy on family monument, 1576, St Edward's Church, Romford, Essex
**Wealth at death** nearly £1400 in cash gifts to family, friends, and servants; value of Cooke lands in 1580 approx. £1100 p.a.: will, PRO, PROB 11/59, fols. 72r–72v; McIntosh, 'Sir Anthony Cooke', 233–50

**Cooke, Benjamin** (1734–1793), organist and composer, was born on 28 November 1734 in London, probably at his father's premises in Covent Garden. He was the son of Benjamin Cooke (d. 1742/3), a music seller and publisher in New Street, Covent Garden, and his second wife, Elizabeth Wayet, whose family came from Nottinghamshire and who was sister-in-law to Lancelot 'Capability' Brown. Among the works which Cooke's father published was the first ever edition in score of the classic op. 6 concertos and trio sonatas (opp. 1–4) of Arcangelo Corelli, 'Carefully Corrected by several Eminent Masters, and revis'd by Dr. Pepusch'. Shortly after Cooke's eighth birthday his father died, and it was to Pepusch that young Benjamin's musical education was entrusted. Under him the boy made such rapid progress that he is said to have deputized for John Robinson, organist of Westminster Abbey, by the age of twelve. Through Pepusch he also became intimately involved in the affairs of the Academy of Ancient Music, and developed those antiquarian interests which were to remain with him for life. In 1749 the young Cooke took over from Samuel Howard as the academy's librarian, and three years later, on the death of Pepusch (who left him a gold piece worth 5 guineas in his will), Cooke stepped naturally into his shoes as its musical director. He continued in that role until 1789, when, in the face of mounting press criticism of the academy's performance standards, he was unceremoniously ousted by the members, and Samuel Arnold appointed in his stead.

By this date Benjamin Cooke had long been firmly ensconced at Westminster Abbey, where he succeeded Bernard Gates as master of the choristers in September 1757 and John Robinson as organist in July 1762; he had also held an appointment as a lay vicar there since 27 January 1758. On 22 May 1758 he married one of his pupils, Mary Jackson (1731/2–1784); according to her son, 'she was a most amiable and affectionate woman, and possessed good property' (Cooke, 11). Of their ten children, five died in infancy. A sixth (another Benjamin) showed an early talent for music, but died aged ten and a half on 25 January 1772. On 2 November 1760 Cooke had been elected a member of the society 'for the Support of Decay'd Musicians or their Families' (later the Royal Society of Musicians), and in April 1767 he joined the Catch Club, in whose annual competition for the composition of catches, canons, and glees he was later to win several prizes; he was also a member of the Madrigal Society (from 1769). In July 1775 Cooke took a doctorate of music at Cambridge (which degree he subsequently incorporated at Oxford). Though he refused at first to join a little club of musical graduates set up in 1790, he had apparently been reconciled to the fact that Arnold was also a member by December 1791, when he dined quite happily with a group of fellow 'graduates' (including Haydn, a recent honorary DMus of Oxford).

Not content with his Westminster Abbey appointments, it seems that Cooke had hopes of becoming organist of St Michael Cornhill, London, as well; but in a parish election for the post held in 1781 he was resoundingly beaten by Richard John Samuel Stevens. The following year, however, he trounced Charles Burney in a similar contest for the organistship of St Martin-in-the-Fields. As one of the eight assistant directors responsible for organizing the first great Handel commemoration festival at Westminster Abbey and the Pantheon in 1784, Cooke worked closely with Burney, and he received one of the commemorative medals that George III had ordered to be struck on the occasion. Though Cooke is said to have been 'extremely thin' when young, he evidently became quite corpulent in old age; he also suffered much from gout, but it was probably a heart attack that carried him off on 14 September 1793. He died at his house in Dorset Court, Parliament Street, Westminster, and was buried in the west cloister of Westminster Abbey on 21 September. His grave, which he shares with his wife, who died on 19 March 1784, his mother-in-law, and all ten children, is marked by a wall plaque on which is inscribed a canon of his own composition and an epitaph written by James Mathias, a fellow member of the Madrigal Society.

As a composer Benjamin Cooke is of no great importance. His output, however, was considerable, and includes a good deal of convivial vocal music, some of which—his glees in particular—reveals a modest but none the less genuine creative talent. He was also, it seems, not only a respectable scholar but also a good-natured and very likeable man, and Laetitia Hawkins's character reference is positively glowing. Her father, Sir John, was one of Cooke's oldest friends, and in the preface to his *General History of the Science and Practice of Music* (1776) he acknowledges Cooke's 'learning and ingenuity' in transcribing into modern notation some of 'the compositions of greatest antiquity' which he had felt obliged to include; indeed, there are several examples of such pieces among the large collection of Cooke's musical manuscripts now in the library of the Royal College of Music, London. Evidence of his studies in musical theory and other such matters survives in the British Library (Add. MS 29298) and in a very miscellaneous volume of 'Musical conjectures' (started in 1769) now in the Bodleian Library at Oxford (Tenbury collection). Cooke liked to deprecate his abilities as a teacher, but this 'did high injustice to his ability and diligence; self, or mutual instruction could never have produced such pupils as left the choir of Westminster Abbey while it was under his tuition' ('Memoir of Benjamin Cooke', 208). Among the many musicians who benefited from Cooke's tuition were Sir William Parsons, John Crosdill, both the elder and the younger Charles Knyvett, Reginald Spofforth, James Bartleman, Thomas Greatorex, and John Hindle.

Cooke's four surviving children all died unmarried, the two girls, Mary and Amelia, in 1819 and 1845 respectively. Henry (1766–1840) was professionally active in the General Post Office (as was his uncle, Charles Jackson); in addition to *Some Remarks on the Greek Theory of Tuning Instruments*, he published a short memoir of his father (1837) and edited two volumes of his organ pieces. Cooke's second surviving son, Robert *Cooke (1768–1814), succeeded him as organist of St Martin-in-the-Fields.

H. DIACK JOHNSTONE

**Sources** L.-M. Hawkins, *Anecdotes, biographical sketches, and memoirs* (1822), 225–35 · review, *The Harmonicon*, 1 (1823), 23–4, 36 · [J. S. Sainsbury], ed., *A dictionary of musicians*, 2 vols. (1825); repr. (New York, 1966) · 'Memoir of Benjamin Cooke', *The Harmonicon*, 9 (1831), 207–8 · H. Cooke, *Some account of Doctor Cooke, organist of Westminster Abbey, &c.* (1837) · J. L. Chester, ed., *The marriage, baptismal, and burial registers of the collegiate church or abbey of St Peter, Westminster*, Harleian Society, 10 (1876) · Highfill, Burnim & Langhans, *BDA* · B. Matthews, ed., *The Royal Society of Musicians of Great Britain: list of members, 1738–1984* (1985) · H. W. Shaw, *The succession of organists of the Chapel Royal and the cathedrals of England and Wales from c.1538* (1991) · *Recollections of R. J. S. Stevens: an organist in Georgian London*, ed. M. Argent (1992) · *The John Marsh journals: the life and times of a gentleman composer*, ed. B. Robins (1998) · parish register, Westminster, St Martin-in-the-Fields, 5 Dec 1734 [baptism] · will, PRO, PROB 11/1237, fols. 218v–220v

**Archives** Westminster Abbey, papers | Bodl. Oxf., Tenbury collection

**Likenesses** W. Skelton, line engraving, after 1775 (after unknown artist), NPG, AM Oxf., Hope collection

**Wealth at death** total unknown; incl. investments valued at £1000: will, PRO, PROB 11/1237, fols. 218v–220v

**Cooke, Charles** (1759/60–1816). *See under* Cooke, John (1730/31–1810).

**Cooke, Deryck Victor** (1919–1976), writer on music and composer, was born on 14 September 1919 at 32 Duncan Road, Leicester, the only child of Henry Victor Cooke, an army pensioner, and his wife, Mabel Judd. He began his musical studies with piano lessons. After leaving Wyggeston grammar school in Leicester he studied music under Patrick Hadley and Robin Orr as an organ scholar at Selwyn College, Cambridge, from 1938 to 1940, and, after war service in the Royal Engineers, from 1946 to 1947. He then joined the BBC where he started as a music presentation assistant (1947–56) and moved on to be a music producer (1956–7) and a music presentation writer (1957–9); after six years as a freelance writer he returned as a music presentation editor from 1965. In 1966 Cooke married Jacqueline Etienne; there were no children.

Cooke's main interests and expertise were focused on writing about Wagner, Bruckner, Mahler, and Delius. During the early days of the BBC Third Programme it became something of an event to hear a symphony by Bruckner or Mahler, whose relative importance as composers was even then judged by the authors of Master Musicians to warrant only the sharing of a volume in their biographical series. Cooke's writings include 'The Bruckner problem simplified', a series of articles in the *Musical Times* (1969) tracing and clarifying the complicated publication history of the various versions of the composer's symphonies.

Cooke will undoubtedly be remembered as the man who, in 1960, completed Mahler's tenth symphony, though his natural modesty led him to describe his project as 'a performing version of the draft for the Tenth Symphony' (Simpson). He had an innate sympathy for and an imaginative insight into Mahler's music and won considerable praise for the result, but he was always keen to point out that, had the composer lived on, he might well have made a wholesale revision of his sketches. Cooke's final version received its first complete public performance by the London Symphony Orchestra under Berthold Goldschmidt at a Henry Wood Promenade Concert on 13 August 1964, since when it has not only found its place in the concert hall repertory but has also been recorded several times. It was published in 1976.

In *The Language of Music* (1954) Cooke argued that music was literally a language of emotions which composers unconsciously built up over the ages. This was fairly controversial and was criticized for confining itself to tonal European music (he was unashamedly hostile to modernism). Over forty years later, however, support can still be found for his case and for that of his opponents. Cooke's major writings were posthumously collected and published in 1982 under the title *Vindications: Essays on Romantic Music*. In a substantial preface to the collection, Bryan Magee's personal memoir recalls Cooke's extensive knowledge of Wagner and his works, in particular the *Ring* and its 'metamorphosis of the musical material, together with an awareness of its psychological and dramatic import at every point' (Magee, 20). Cooke's intention was to write a multi-volume book in two main parts, the first an analysis of the dramatic text of the cycle, the other an analysis of the score. *I Saw the World End*, the first half of the first main part, is all that he achieved before his untimely death from a stroke at his home, 207 Melfort Road, Thornton Heath, Surrey, on 27 October 1976. According to the composer Robert Simpson in an obituary notice, the work remains 'one of the most significant of all books on Wagner' (*The Listener*).                          CHRISTOPHER FIFIELD

**Sources** B. Magee, memoir, in |D. V. Cooke|, *Vindications: essays on Romantic music* (1982) • R. Simpson, *The Listener* (4 Nov 1976) • *New Grove* • b. cert. • J. Sloboda, *The musical mind* (1985) • C. Gabriel, 'An experimental study of Deryck Cooke's theory of music and meaning', *Psychology of Music*, 6 (1978), 13–20 • P. Reed, ed., *On Mahler and Britten* (1995) • *WWW* • H. Carpenter, *The envy of the world: fifty years of the BBC Third Programme and Radio 3, 1946–1996* (1996) • *CGPLA Eng. & Wales* (1977)

**Archives** SOUND BL NSA, documentary recording • BL NSA, '1911: a year in musical history', T6849RTR2 • BL NSA, oral history interviews • BL NSA, performance recordings

**Wealth at death** £3269: administration, 18 July 1977, *CGPLA Eng. & Wales*

**Cooke, Edward** (*fl.* 1676–1678), playwright and translator, wrote *The Divine Epicurus, or, The Empire of Pleasure over the Vertues* (1676), translated from the philosopher Antoine Le Grand. In 1678 he produced *A Just and Seasonable Reprehension of Naked Breasts and Shoulders*, translated from the work of Jacques Boileau. Cooke's major work was *Love's Triumph, or, The Royal Union* (1678), a drama dedicated to Mary, princess of Orange, which portrays Oroondates, prince of Scythia, in love with Statira, and Artaxerxes, prince of Persia, in love with Berenice, and ends with nuptials.

Another Edward Cooke wrote *Bartas junior, or, The world's epitome: man, set forth in his 1. Generation, 2. Degeneration, 3. Rejuvenation*, published in London in 1631 though probably drafted twelve years earlier. He may also have been responsible for *Duello foiled, or, The whole proceedings in the orderly disposing of a design for a single fight between two valiant gentleman* (n.d.).                          F. D. A. BURNS

**Sources** *DNB* • *BL cat.* • E. Cooke, *Love's triumph, or, The royal union* (1678)

**Cooke, Edward** (*fl.* 1680–1682), legal writer and lawyer, about whose early life nothing is known, studied law at the Middle Temple, London, and first surfaced in the late 1670s and early 1680s, when he joined the polemical battle to exclude the openly Catholic James, duke of York, from the throne. Cooke's career as a whig writer began in 1680 with the publication of an anti-papal harangue entitled *A true and perfect narrative of the inhumane practices … of the Jesuits and papists toward protestants at home and abroad*. This work was dedicated to the earl of Shaftesbury, whose patronage he sought and on whom, Cooke believed, depended the 'advancement of the Protestant religion [and] the welfare of the kingdom' (Zook, 83). It was followed in 1682 by two tracts that aimed at strengthening the whig case for exclusion. One was a translation of Magna Carta (*Magna Carta, made in the ninth year of King Henry the Third … faithfully translated for the benefit of those that do not understand the Latin*) and the other an account of the royal succession down to the seventeenth century (*The History of Successions of the Kings of England*).

In 1682 Cooke also published his most significant work, *Argumentum antiNormanicum, or, An argument proving from ancient histories and records that William, duke of Normandy made no absolute conquest of England by the sword.* Written in defence of William Petyt's *The Antient Right of the Commons of England Asserted* (1680) and against Dr Robert Brady's attack on Petyt in *A Full and Clear Answer* (1681), it was printed anonymously and in the late seventeenth century often attributed to Petyt or his fellow whig William Atwood. Although later scholars have sometimes treated the work somewhat dismissively (see, for example, Pocock, and D. Douglas, *English Scholars*, 1939), other historians (such as Zook and Greenberg) have suggested that it enjoyed a high reputation among prominent whigs. Thus James Tyrrell, a close associate of the earl of Shaftesbury and John Locke, and in 1704 the first contemporary to identify Cooke publicly as the tract's author, quoted from it frequently. Moreover Brady, who counted among his sponsors Charles II and James II, deemed it worthy of rebuttal in his *Introduction to Old English History* (1684). Equally telling, in 1689 *Argumentum antiNormanicum* was considered sufficiently persuasive to merit republication as the Convention Parliament deliberated the revolution settlement, this time under the title *A seasonable treatise: wherein it is proved that King William, commonly called the conqueror did not get the imperial crown of England by the sword.*

As for the political ideas which Cooke put forward to justify first exclusion and later the revolution the full titles of both versions of *AntiNormanicum* tell much of the story. Like Atwood, Petyt, and Tyrrell, he found radical ancient constitutionalism perfectly suited to making the case against the late Stuart kingship. Constructed by parliamentarians such as William Prynne in the civil wars of the 1640s, this ideology rested primarily upon three medieval sources, the so-called laws of St Edward the Confessor, the *Modus tenendi parliamentum*, and the *Mirror of Justices*. To late Stuart whigs such as Cooke these works, which claimed to predate the arrival of the Normans in 1066, supported the major tenets of their ideology, namely, that since at least as early as the Saxon period England had been governed by an elected king with whom the people had made an enforceable contract; that ancient parliaments, which included both the Lords and the Commons, possessed the power to make law and control over-mighty sovereigns; and that parliament, or the people, retained the right to resist, depose, and replace a ruler who broke the terms of his agreement with the kingdom. Finally whigs such as Cooke insisted that these Saxon institutions had survived Norman conquest intact and lived on in their own day.

Scholars later discovered that St Edward's laws, the *Modus*, and the *Mirror* dated not from the Saxon period but from the early twelfth and early fourteenth centuries. But throughout the Stuart period all three were widely accepted as authentic statements of how things used to be (though legal antiquaries such as John Selden raised doubts about the authenticity of the *Modus* and *Mirror*). Indeed, St Edward's laws enjoyed the imprimatur of the foremost lawyers and antiquaries of the seventeenth century, including Selden, Sir Henry Spelman, and Sir Roger Twysden. It was then perfectly understandable that Cooke

and his fellow whigs looked to these sources and the version of history, law, and government that they spawned for ammunition in their struggle against the late Stuart kings. Cooke, for example, argued that medieval records, especially St Edward's laws, proved that William I governed not as a conqueror but rather as the heir and successor of his cousin St Edward. One need look no further than William's confirmation of the Confessor's laws—'his Magna Carta and the groundwork of all that followed'—as well as to the various confirmations of his successors (Cooke, *Argumentum antiNormanicum*, liv). First came Henry I's famous charter of liberties, followed by the confirmations of King Stephen, Henry II, and King John in Magna Carta. Then there was the new coronation oath in which all rulers from 1308 down to Cooke's own day swore to abide by St Edward's laws. To Cooke this steady drumbeat of royal confirmations meant that the Norman kings, like their Saxon counterparts, had reigned by right and election and by consultation with a full parliament. And what was true of the Saxons and Normans was true of all monarchs, including Charles II and James II. From this reasoning a conclusion vital to the anti-Stuart cause ineluctably followed: the two houses of parliament, which held the lion's share of legislative sovereignty, possessed rights to change the king, alter the kingship, and settle the kingdom as they thought fit.

The end of Cooke's life is as much a mystery as his early days. If he was the Edward Cooke to whom, along with Atwood, Petyt bequeathed £50 in his last will and testament, he was still alive in July 1705.

JANELLE GREENBERG

**Sources** M. S. Zook, *Radical whigs and conspiratorial politics in late Stuart England* (1999) · J. Greenberg, *The radical face of the ancient constitution: St Edward's laws in early modern political thought* (2001) · J. Reid, 'The jurisprudence of liberty: the ancient constitution in the legal historiography of the seventeenth and eighteenth centuries', *The roots of liberty: Magna Carta, ancient constitution, and the Anglo-American tradition of rule of law*, ed. E. Sandoz (Columbia, MO, 1993) · L. Schwoerer, introduction, *The revolution of 1688–1689: changing perspectives*, ed. L. Schwoerer (1992) · B. O'Brien, *God's peace and king's peace: the laws of Edward the Confessor* (Philadelphia, 1999) · J. Pocock, *The ancient constitution and the feudal law: a study of English historical thought in the seventeenth century. A reissue with a retrospect* (1987)

**Cooke, Edward** (*bap.* 1755, *d.* 1820), government official and political pamphleteer, was baptized on 27 June 1755 at Denham, Buckinghamshire, the third and only surviving son of William *Cooke (1711–1797), provost of King's College, Cambridge, and his wife, Catherine, the daughter of Richard Sleech, a canon of Windsor. He was educated at Eton College (1760–72) and, from 16 May 1773, at King's College, Cambridge, whence he graduated BA in 1777 and MA in 1785, and was a fellow from 1776 to 1786.

Cooke entered government service in 1778, when he became private secretary to Sir Richard Heron, the chief secretary of Ireland during the vice-royalty of John Hobart, second earl of Buckinghamshire, and in the course of the next twenty-two years he became the most prominent English member of the Dublin Castle secretariat. He was therefore private secretary to Heron's successors, William Eden and Richard Fitzpatrick. He held a succession of posts in the Irish administration and parliament from 1778—as second chamberlain of the exchequer (1778–86), clerk of the stationery stores (1781–4), second clerk of the House of Commons (1786–9, 1798), and education commissioner (1788)—before occupying the more influential positions of under-secretary for the military department, from 7 April 1789 to 1796, and for the civil department, from 5 June 1796 to 21 October 1801. In addition the Irish administration had him returned an MP for the nomination boroughs of Lifford (1789–90) and Old Leighlin (1790–1800) and topped up his official perquisites of £1414 per annum and, by 1801, a house in the Phoenix Park, with several sinecures. It is a measure of his standing as a leading member of the secretariat of Dublin Castle that, despite being English, he was unanimously voted the freedom of Dublin in 1796 and that of the Guild of Merchants in 1798.

Cooke's career in Ireland prospered because he was clever and ready to support British policy there. His intellect was widely admired: in 1782 Lord Mornington recommended him to the incoming chief secretary, William Grenville, on the ground of the 'very high character' he had acquired 'for his knowledge and talents in his line' (*Fortescue MSS*, 1.164); and in 1800 Lord Cornwallis, then viceroy, referred to him as 'a very clever fellow' (*Correspondence of … Cornwallis*, 3.310). He did not wear his intelligence lightly, however. Cornwallis was not alone in criticizing his lack of an 'accommodating temper' (ibid.), and Edmund Burke took such criticism to extremes with his remark that Cooke was 'a shallow hot headed puppy, proud and presumptuous, and ill behav'd' (*Correspondence*, 9.339). Cornwallis also alleged that by the time of his viceroyalty Cooke guarded his position at the castle jealously, failed to delegate to others, and, being 'no man of details himself', left ordinary business 'behindhand, and in great confusion' (*Correspondence of … Cornwallis*, 3.315). However, it has to be said that there was little love lost between the two men, Cooke being coruscating in his criticism of his chief's administration.

With the exception of Earl Fitzwilliam's administration in 1795, when he was temporarily dismissed because of his influence and his identification with Pitt's regime, Cooke served successive Irish administrations in a variety of ways. There is circumstantial evidence of his involvement in managing the Irish parliament for the castle in the early 1780s and no doubt of that role later, especially during the Regency crisis and, most notably, during the passage of the Union (1799–1800). In the last case he was, in his own opinion, the official most 'deeply engaged in all the promises' made to individuals to reward them for their support of the measure or to win that support (Cooke to Auckland, 8 Oct 1801, Sneyd MSS), and therefore involved in the irregular funding of them through the English secret service fund. He was also routinely called upon to advise and to frame policy with the British government: for example, on the commercial propositions in

1785; on the ramifications in Ireland of the Portland whigs' taking office in 1794; and, most importantly, on the Union, when he played a prominent role in drawing up the relevant bills and, on the eve of Pitt's resignation, in working up drafts of measures to enable Catholics to sit in the imperial parliament and to reduce the burden of tithe. Throughout the Union episode his frequent correspondence with Castlereagh, Grenville, and Auckland is a major source of information on the disposition of the Irish politicians and the progress of the measure. Indeed, his influence in Dublin and his connections in London made him the vital bureaucratic link between the Irish administration and the British government.

Cooke was most widely known, however, as a pamphleteer. There is a strong possibility that he was the author of *A Letter to a Venerated Nobleman Lately Retired from this Kingdom* (1795), in which Fitzwilliam was accused of setting back the Catholic question by his alleged indiscretions. He certainly wrote the anonymous *Arguments for and Against a Union between Great Britain and Ireland Considered* (1798), which was regarded as a statement of the government's thinking and was 'very universally read' (*Fortescue MSS*, 4.404). In this Cooke argued that the union would benefit both countries and eventually bring about political benefits for Catholics—a cause on which he had come to believe that concession 'risks nothing, and denial risks everything' (*Memoirs … of Viscount Castlereagh*, 4.41–6). He even went so far in a 'Most secret' letter to Grenville on 15 January 1799 as to advise the government that it should make it clear to the Catholic hierarchy that concession would be made 'at an early period' after the Union in order to secure its passage in Ireland. However, on an issue that became a matter of repeated controversy in parliament until 1829, he later denied that he had had any communications with Catholics or protestants in Ireland on the subject *before* Pitt declared his intention to retire. On the other hand, his commitment to Catholic relief after Union was sufficiently strong to determine him to resign his post and return to England as soon as he heard of the king's veto and Pitt's replacement by the anti-Catholic Addington. As he put it as early as 9 February 1801 (in words that tend to confirm Cornwallis's opinion of his temper):

> How can I, with my natural eagerness and indiscretion, (which official habits for twenty years have not been able to tame) sit a quiet, torpid, useless clerk at a desk, going through mere common drudgery, and disapproving every measure that is taken by the Government …? (ibid., 4.28)

Cooke's departure, however, was protracted and acrimonious. In the immediate aftermath of the change of ministers he remained determined to leave Ireland, stressing now the needs of his many relatives in England, but was persuaded to remain for the time being by Lord Hardwicke, the new viceroy, on the ground that he was the best person to oversee the fulfilment of the Union promises. Indeed Hardwicke and the new chief secretary, Charles Abbot, asked him to go to London in spring 1801 to help with the 'secret business' of filling up the holes in the Secret Service Fund made by Cooke's promises, from which the new Irish administration wished to keep its distance (Cooke to Auckland, 8 Oct 1801, Sneyd MSS). At approximately the same time, however, Cooke took severe umbrage at Abbot's being appointed Irish lord privy seal and at the appointment of a new fellow under-secretary—on the ground of their ignorance of the country. With family pressures mounting, he renewed his decision to leave Ireland and, unbeknown to Hardwicke and Abbot, used part of the time he spent in London to make an arrangement with Lord Pelham, one of his former chiefs in Ireland and the incoming home secretary, by which he would become Pelham's under-secretary and Sir George Shee would replace him in Ireland. Cooke argued later that he believed that, in the new post-Union conditions, the authority of the home secretary over Irish matters had increased and that he would, in effect, have a decisive say in all major appointments. He also alleged that, although he had asked Pelham to broach the subject with Hardwicke himself, Pelham had dissembled and enjoined him to keep quiet.

When the arrangement did become known, a serious row broke out which had public and personal dimensions. Contrary to Cooke's interpretation of the respective powers of the viceroy and the home secretary, Hardwicke saw himself as a king's representative who should settle policy in collaboration with the prime minister and the cabinet rather than act under the Home Office. He and Abbot therefore regarded Cooke's action as 'a most monstrous and inadmissible presumption' by a public servant who had no right 'to govern and dispose of Lords Lieutenants and Secretaries of State' as he pleased (Abbot to Hardwicke, 1, 6 July 1801, BL, Add. MS 35711, fols. 67, 76). They therefore vetoed the intended exchange of posts.

Cooke reacted bitterly. 'I do not deserve this after 23 years service here and my labours in the Rebellion and Union', he pleaded to Auckland (6 Aug 1801, BL, Add. MS 34455, fol. 425), and later he told Pitt that he had been excluded from the discussion of policy following Abbot's arrival in order to force his retirement. Abbot, for his part, accused Cooke of publicly criticizing the government both during and after his time in London, and of describing his own intended reforms of the Irish administration in exaggerated and alarmist terms. It was even suspected that Cooke had colluded with Lord Clare and others in feeding such alarms to the government's opponents at Westminster. The otherwise temperate Hardwicke had seen enough and, although it removed the master of the complicated Union promises from the castle, consented to Cooke's retirement, which took place on 21 October 1801; he received a salary of £1000 for the sinecure post of keeper of the records of the Irish parliament, two other sinecures worth £500 each, and the imminent reversion of a post worth £800 a year.

Following his return to England Cooke was unemployed until the formation of Pitt's second administration in May 1804, when he was appointed under-secretary to Lord Camden, the new secretary for war and the colonies. Camden knew of Cooke, for he had been Cornwallis's predecessor as viceroy and, more particularly, was the father-in-law of Lord Castlereagh, Cooke's chief during the making of the Union. There was considerable respect and friendship between Cooke and Castlereagh, and both men had taken part in the horse-trading involved in passing the Union. Cooke served the remainder of his career first as Camden's and then as Castlereagh's under-secretary for war and the colonies, from 1804 to 1806, and then as Castlereagh's secretary at the Foreign Office, from 1807 to 1809, and again from 1812 to 1817. Although he and Castlereagh corresponded in private frequently, the evidence of his influence is slight. Under Camden (1804–5) he evidently conducted the military and colonial business of the department single-handed, and he claimed to be one of the prime movers in making the ill-fated assault on Buenos Aires (1806–7) an object of war policy for which the Grenville administration was criticized. Later he was reputed to be the author of pamphlets defending George III's conduct leading to the resignation of the Grenville government and that of Castlereagh in his dispute with Canning (1809). In winter 1814–15 he accompanied Castlereagh to Vienna and to Italy, partly to support his chief in the peace negotiations and partly to further ongoing talks with Cardinal Consalvi about securing an agreement with the Vatican on a settlement of the Catholic question. Two years later, in 1817, he retired, to Castlereagh's very considerable regret.

Cooke had married, on 10 August 1791, Isabella (d. 1821x4), the daughter of Hamilton Gorges of Kilbrew, co. Meath, an Irish MP, who endowed her with a portion of £10,000. They had no children, and the absence of any evidence of a social life seems to suggest that Cooke was the dedicated 'civil servant'. He even thought like one: '*thinking*', he once remarked to Lord Clare regarding the Catholic question, 'ought perhaps to make but a small part of my duty'; and on another occasion he told Castlereagh that 'vanity, ambition, interest' were the dominant passions in all governments and that a belief in 'utopian systems' which 'will not do' was one of the weaknesses of politicians (*Memoirs … of Viscount Castlereagh*, 4.41–6, 50–52). He died at his home in Park Lane, London, on 19 March 1820. Much to the regret of historians, he left no papers behind him.

P. J. JUPP

**Sources** DNB • E. M. Johnston-Liik, draft biography, *History of the Irish parliament, 1692–1800*, 6 vols. (2002) • *Report on the manuscripts of Earl Bathurst, preserved at Cirencester Park*, HMC, 76 (1923) • *The manuscripts of J. B. Fortescue*, 10 vols., HMC, 30 (1892–1927) • *The journal and correspondence of William, Lord Auckland*, ed. [G. Hogge], 4 vols. (1861–2) • *The correspondence of Edmund Burke*, ed. T. W. Copeland and others, 10 vols. (1958–78), vols. 8–9 • *Memoirs and correspondence of Viscount Castlereagh, second marquess of Londonderry*, ed. C. Vane, marquess of Londonderry, 12 vols. (1848–53) • *Correspondence of Charles, first Marquis Cornwallis*, ed. C. Ross, 3 vols. (1859) • *The diary and correspondence of Charles Abbot, Lord Colchester*, ed. Charles, Lord Colchester, 3 vols. (1861) • *The later correspondence of George III*, ed. A. Aspinall, 5 vols. (1962–70) • *Annual Biography and Obituary*, 5 (1821) • BL, Fortescue MSS • PRO NIre., Castlereagh MSS • Keele University, Sneyd MSS

**Archives** BL, letters to Lord Auckland, Add. MSS 34418–34460, *passim* • BL, letters to Lord Chichester, Add. MSS 33101–33111, *passim* • BL, Fortescue MSS • BL, corresp. with Lord Hardwicke, Add. MSS 35728–35732, *passim* • Bucks. RLSS, corresp. with Scrope Bernard • CKS, corresp. with Lord Camden; letters to Sir George

Hill · Durham RO, corresp. with Lord Castlereagh · Keele University, Sneyd MSS, letters to William Eden · NA Ire., Fane MSS, corresp. with Lord Westmorland, etc. · PRO NIre., corresp. with Lord Caledon; corresp. with Lord Castlereagh · U. Hull, Brynmor Jones L., corresp. with Thomas Perronet Thompson · U. Nott. L., letters to Lord William Bentinck

**Likenesses** W. Ward, mezzotint, pubd 1799 (after W. Cuming), BM · J. Burnet, line engraving, pubd 1821 (after G. Sanders), BM, NPG

**Wealth at death** £9000: will record, 1824

**Cooke, Edward** (1772–1799), naval officer, was born on 14 April 1772, the son of Colonel George John Cooke of Harefield, Middlesex, and Penelope, only daughter of Sir William Bowyer, third baronet, and Anne Stonhouse. His brothers were General Sir George *Cooke, army officer, who commanded the first division at Waterloo, and Major-General Sir Henry Frederick Cooke, private secretary to the duke of York. Following the death of Edward Cooke's father, his mother married General Edward Smith, uncle of Admiral Sir W. Sidney Smith.

Cooke entered the navy and was made lieutenant on 14 September 1790. In 1793 he was appointed to the *Victory*, going to the Mediterranean as Lord Hood's flagship. In August he was entrusted with the negotiations with the royalist inhabitants of Toulon, a service which he conducted with skill and boldness, and which resulted in Lord Hood's obtaining possession of the town and arsenal. Cooke was then appointed Toulon's lieutenant-governor and served with the governor, Captain George Elphinstone (later Viscount Keith). He continued in this post until the town's evacuation at the end of December. His services were rewarded by promotion, and on 12 April 1794 he was advanced to the rank of post captain. He took charge of the landing for the siege of Calvi in June 1794, and played an active part in subsequent operations, his zeal drawing the praise of Nelson, under whose immediate orders he was serving.

On 7 October 1794 Cooke was appointed to the *Sibylle*, a fine (40-gun) frigate, recently captured from the French, and in her he went out to the Cape of Good Hope, from where he was sent on to the East Indies to escort home the China trade. In early January 1798, in company with Captain Charles Malcolm of the *Fox*, he reconnoitred the Spanish force in the Philippines with the hope, if possible, of capturing two richly laden ships reported as ready to sail from Manila. As they neared the islands it occurred to Cooke that they might pass themselves off as French. The *Sibylle*, a French-built ship, was easily disguised, as was the *Fox* once it had been repainted. Between them, Cooke and an officer on the *Fox* spoke fluent French and some Spanish.

On 14 January the two frigates were off Manila where they aroused no suspicion. The guardboats came alongside, and the Spanish officers were taken down to the cabin and hospitably entertained, while in the foremost part of the ship the Spanish seamen were stripped, and British sailors dressed in their clothes were sent away in the guardboats to capture what they could. They thus took the Spanish entirely by surprise and brought off three

large gunboats. By the time the townsmen and the garrison realized that the two frigates were British, Cooke and Malcolm, in friendly talk with the Spanish officers, had gained much confidential information. They then sent them on shore along with the 200 prisoners, and, with the three gunboats in tow, stood out of the bay.

In February 1799 the *Sibylle* was lying at Madras when Cooke learned that the French frigate *Forte* was in the Bay of Bengal, and on 19 February he put to sea in search of her. On the evening of 28 February the *Sibylle* was off the Sand-heads; about nine o'clock she made out three ships, which she understood to be the *Forte* and two recently captured country ships. The *Forte* supposed that the *Sibylle* was another merchant ship and ordered her to strike. The *Sibylle* closed at once, and, with her main yard between the enemy's main and mizen masts, poured in a broadside and shower of musketry with deadly effect. The *Forte* was taken by surprise; the terrible broadside was the first intimation that she had to contend with the largest British frigate on the station. For nearly an hour the two ships lay broadside to broadside at a distance seldom greater than pistol shot. At about 1.30 a.m. Cooke was wounded by grape shot to the chest and shoulder. The action was then maintained by Lucius Hardyman, the first lieutenant. At 2.30 a.m. the *Forte*, being entirely dismasted, and having lost 150 men killed and wounded, struck her colours. She was at the time the largest and most heavily armed frigate afloat, being about one-third larger than the *Sibylle*, and carrying 24-pounders on her main deck, as against the *Sibylle's* 18-pounders. By comparison the *Sibylle's* loss was comparatively slight.

The darkness of the night, and the superior discipline and training of the *Sibylle's* crew are principal factors in explaining what proved to be one of the eighteenth century's most brilliant frigate actions. Lucius Hardyman was immediately promoted commander, and in January 1800 captain, of the *Forte*. However, Cooke's wounds proved fatal. After lingering for some months in extreme agony he died at Calcutta on 25 May 1799. He was buried there with the highest military honours; a monument was erected to his memory by the directors of the East India Company.               J. K. LAUGHTON, rev. NICHOLAS TRACY

**Sources** *Naval Chronicle*, 2 (1799), 161–2, 378–84, 447, 540, 643 · N. Tracy, ed., *The Naval Chronicle: the contemporary record of the Royal Navy at war*, 5 vols. (1998–9), vol. 1, pp. 18, 36, 40–41, 54, 233, 236–8; vol. 2, pp. 109, 328 · captain's letters 'C', 1794, PRO, ADM 1/1619 · Cooke to Nepean, 23 May 1796 and 20 Dec 1799, PRO, ADM 1/1625 (313–15) · W. James, *The naval history of Great Britain, from the declaration of war by France in 1793, to the accession of George IV*, [5th edn], 6 vols. (1859–60), vol. 2, p. 365

**Cooke, Edward William** (1811–1880), marine artist and gardener, was born on 27 March 1811 in Chapel Street, Pentonville, London, the second of the eleven children of George *Cooke (1781–1834) [see under Cooke family], engraver and print publisher, and his wife, Elizabeth Harriet Eglinton (1785–1882). He was educated at Grove House School, Woodford, Essex, before receiving artistic training in the studios of his father, uncle, and family friends, during which he became deeply versed in works of the early nineteenth-century landscapists.

Cooke was almost obsessively interested in recording his natural and man-made environment. He early became a proficient botanical illustrator, drawing from nature from the age of nine in the celebrated Hackney nurseries of Conrad Loddiges & Sons and later assisting his father with aquatints for the Loddiges's *Botanical Cabinet* (1817–33). The marine artist Clarkson Stanfield employed him to make drawings of nautical details, while a friendship with the captain of the West Indiaman *Thetis* gave Cooke opportunities for study on board. As an etcher of marine subjects he developed an almost archaeological approach, recording as if aware that change was afoot. He published *Fifty Plates of Shipping and Craft* (1829), *Twelve Plates of Coast Sketches: Brighton* (1830), and *The British Coast* (1831), all of which were republished together in 1831 as *Sixty-Five Plates of Shipping and Craft* but bearing the date of 1829. In 1833 he and his father produced *Views of the Old and the New London Bridges*, twelve plates from his drawings of the subjects. His father's *London and its Vicinity* (1826–34) was engraved from watercolours by Augustus Callcott, J. S. Cotman, Stanfield, and Samuel Prout, all based on outline drawings made by the younger Cooke to relieve them of the preliminary labour.

Cooke and several of his father's other pupils moved in the circle of Richard Parkes Bonington, whose watercolour style Cooke emulated. He showed a single-minded devotion to minutely observed portraits of smaller working craft, recording their appearance in every country he visited; his travels abroad included tours of France from 1833, the Netherlands from 1837, western Italy from 1845–6, Venice from 1850, Sweden and Denmark in 1853, Spain in 1861, and Egypt in 1874. His scenes of Netherlandish coasts and waterways earned him the nickname Dutch Cooke among picture dealers (he often inscribed Van Kook on his boats); he was also dubbed Venetian Cooke for his portrayals of the craft of the Adriatic Sea and the lagoons, which he sometimes inscribed Il Lagunetto.

Cooke first exhibited at the Royal Academy and the British Institution from 1835; he was elected ARA in 1851 and RA in 1863. Critics in general reviewed his work favourably and, early on in his artistic career, he attracted the patronage of John Sheepshanks, Robert Vernon, and William Wells, all wealthy collectors of modern art. Many major British galleries and museums own works by him, but his important *Morning after a Heavy Gale* (exh. RA, 1857), which was well reviewed by Ruskin, is in a private collection in the USA. On 13 June 1840 he married Jane Loddiges (1812–1843), the younger daughter of George Loddiges; they had a daughter who died in infancy and two sons.

Cooke combined his artistic interests with scientific ones, displaying an early enthusiasm for geology. He was introduced to the use of the microscope by George Loddiges and attended the inaugural meeting of the Microscopical Society. He was a fellow of the Linnean Society from 1857 and of the Royal Society from 1863. He was very interested in photography and was an early collector of calotypes. A member of the Athenaeum, he also belonged to the Alpine Club and the dining clubs of several scientific as well as artistic societies, including the Palaeontological Society. Among his publications is the eccentric *Entwicklungsgeschichte—grotesque animals* (1872), illustrated with ingenious drawings mixing fur, feather, bone, shells, and other fragments to demonstrate, with humorous descriptions, his familiarity with natural history. Ruskin—a fellow enthusiast for the natural sciences—described him a little cruelly as 'the smallest clever man I ever knew … full of accurate and valuable knowledge in natural history with which he is always overflowing at the wrong times' (J. Ruskin, *The Works of John Ruskin*, ed. E. T. Cook and A. Wedderburn, 1903–12, 14.69).

As a gardener Cooke displayed a talent for artistic grouping combined with great knowledge and love of plants. A determined collector of ferns, he named both his two Kensington houses The Ferns. For his friend James Bateman he designed many features of the remarkable gardens of Biddulph Grange, Staffordshire, which still exist. His own gardens at Glen Andred, Groombridge, Sussex, spreading round a house built for him by Norman Shaw in 1868, were renowned for the rocks which he revealed by removing the topsoil.

Cooke found inactivity unbearable, according to his letters; Richard Redgrave described him as 'of a lively and genial disposition, restlessly active, a greater talker, and full of anecdote' (R. Redgrave and S. Redgrave, *A Century of Painters* 1890, new edn, 1947, 424). W. E. Oswell recalled him at work, writing of 'the alert restless figure, the clear wide-set blue eyes … the marvellously sure hand darting from palette to canvas' (W. E. Oswell, ed., *William Cotton Oswell, Hunter and Explorer: the Story of his Life*, 1900, 2.96). Cooke died from cancer of the liver and lung on 4 January 1880 at Glen Andred and was buried at the church in Groombridge on 10 January. Sales of his remaining works took place at Christies, London, on 22 May 1880 and 11 March 1882.                    JOHN MUNDAY

**Sources** J. Munday, *E. W. Cooke* (1996) • J. Dafforne, 'Edward William Cooke', *Art Journal*, 28 (1866) • MSS and diaries, priv. coll. • d. cert. • *The Times* (8 Jan 1880)
**Archives** Inst. EE, sketches made on board HMS *Agamemnon* on the Atlantic cable-laying voyage • NRA, priv. coll., diaries • RA, ledger, MS 405
**Likenesses** E. W. Cooke, self-portrait, pencil drawing, 1831, repro. in Munday, *E. W. Cooke* • R. Hannah, oil sketch, 1848, repro. in Munday, *E. W. Cooke* • W. L. Price, photograph, 1857, NMM • John & Charles Watkins, photograph, 1864, repro. in Munday, *E. W. Cooke* • J. & C. Watkins, carte-de-visite, NPG • wood-engraving, NPG; repro. in *ILN* (13 Aug 1864)
**Wealth at death** under £35,000: probate, 24 Jan 1880, *CGPLA Eng. & Wales*

**Cooke, Elisha** (1678–1737), politician and physician in America, was born on 20 December 1678 in Boston, Massachusetts, the only son of Elisha Cooke (1637–1715), also a physician and a long-time leader of the puritan or anti-prerogative faction in Massachusetts, and Elizabeth (1651–1715), daughter of Governor John *Leverett. Having been educated at Harvard College, from where he graduated in 1697, Cooke was appointed in 1698 clerk of the

**Elisha Cooke** (1678–1737), by N. Byfield, 1713

superior court on which his father sat. On 7 January 1703 he married Jane Middlecott (1682–1741×5?).

Elisha Cooke first assumed the political mantle of his father in 1714, when the old man had finally patched up his differences with Governor Joseph Dudley. Elisha promoted a private land bank to supply the country with paper money—which the legislature rejected—and thereby squared off against the governor's son Paul Dudley to inaugurate political factionalism for a new generation. The next year, however, the Boston town meeting chose Elisha as one of its four representatives. The success was temporary: in 1717 and 1718, Cooke was not re-elected.

Cooke responded by launching a political initiative that led to his faction's triumph in the province which continued until his death. He was aided by the blundering of the new governor, Colonel Samuel Shute, who foolishly tried to protect mast timber for the Royal Navy from the depredations of landowners, including Cooke and other representatives. To respond Cooke created the Boston caucus, the first political machine in British North America. The caucus first flexed its muscles in the 1720 Boston elections for representatives, where three of its leaders won election over Paul Dudley's virulent opposition. Until the mid-1730s, caucus politicians were almost invariably, and almost unanimously, elected to the legislature, in contrast to the tightly contested elections of the two previous decades. How did the caucus function? Writing more than fifty years later, the Revd William Gordon maintained that they 'used to meet, make a caucus, and lay their plan for introducing certain persons into places of trust and

power. When they settled it, they separated, and each used their particular influence within his own circle' (W. Gordon, *A History of the Rise, Progress, and Establishment of the Independence of America*, 1780, 1.105). Cooke was a notable drinker, and, while intoxicated, he had several times publicly accosted the governor. Even if he were not the 'Cataline of his Era' who disbursed over £9000 in bribes (as the loyalist Peter Oliver charged in the 1780s), Cooke did treat his minions to liquid refreshment and refrain from suing them for unpaid debts, traits emulated by his revolutionary successors four decades later.

Cooke also took to the press, publishing his *Just and Seasonable Vindications* (1720) and thereby initiating one of the intermittent pamphlet wars which enlivened the provincial political scene. Over the next two years the house challenged the governor on several issues: whether he had the right to veto their choice of a speaker (Cooke himself); the size of the executive's salary; and the governor's right to command the armed forces on the Maine frontier—then engaged in a minor war with the Abenaki Indians, led by French-Canadian priest Sebastian Rasle—rather than their direction by a committee of the house.

Whether Cooke had anything to do with the shot fired at Governor Shute that caused him to flee the province suddenly on 31 December 1722 is open to speculation. Shute had intimated that he would levy charges against the province which might lead to the revocation of the Massachusetts charter. Even before Shute's arrival, the charter had been under attack, prompting province agent Jeremiah Dummer's notable *Defence of the New England Charters* (1721). But in 1723 the assembly, upset that Dummer's brother William, the acting governor in Shute's absence, continued his predecessor's policies, replaced Jeremiah with Cooke himself. Cooke travelled to London to make the assembly's case in defence of the charter. His appearances before the Board of Trade were disasters, and various friends of New England wrote back that the agent's tavern brawls did not help his cause. The outcome of the negotiations was an explanatory charter which affirmed the governor's power to overrule the assembly on certain issues, including the choice of speaker, but which was accepted by the legislature as the best compromise to protect other aspects of the Massachusetts charter.

Cooke's behaviour abroad weakened his support in Boston. In 1726 and 1727 two prerogative men shared the four Boston seats with members of the caucus. Having returned to oppose the very explanatory charter he had just negotiated, Cooke was overruled by the assembly forty-eight to thirty-two. Tensions ran so high that for the first time the house of representatives recorded in its published journal how individual representatives voted.

Massachusetts's new governor, William Burnet (1728–9), again played into Cooke's hands. Required to insist that the representatives approve a guaranteed permanent gubernatorial salary equal to at least £1000 sterling each year, the assembly was convinced by Cooke that this claim threatened its power of the purse. By 1735 the representatives had persuaded the Board of Trade as well. For the rest of his life Cooke continued to dominate both town and provincial politics by exploiting the salary question on which Burnet and his successor, Jonathan Belcher (1730–41)—a Massachusetts native who hoped to persuade his countrymen where others had failed—had been instructed to insist. Cooke died in Boston on 24 August 1737, after which the caucus declined and the prerogative party became a formidable competitor under the guidance of Thomas Hutchinson. However, by courting the 'lower orders' and organizing the caucus, Elisha Cooke had created the first political machine in British North America; later, a similar institution was critical in organizing the resistance that led to the American War of Independence.                                  WILLIAM PENCAK

**Sources** C. K. Shipton, 'Cooke, Elisha', *Sibley's Harvard graduates: biographical sketches of those who attended Harvard College*, 4 (1933), 349–56 · W. Pencak, *War, politics and revolution in provincial Massachusetts* (1981) · M. L. Lustig, 'Cooke, Elisha', *ANB* · E. A. J. Johnson, 'Cooke, Elisha', *DAB* · Thwing index, Mass. Hist. Soc.
**Archives** Mass. Hist. Soc.
**Likenesses** N. Byfield, portrait, 1713, Peabody Museum of Salem, Massachusetts [*see illus.*] · sketch, priv. coll.; repro. in *Sibley's Harvard graduates*; crayon copy, American Antiquarian Society, Massachusetts, USA
**Wealth at death** over £63,000: Shipton, 'Cooke, Elisha'

**Cooke, Elizabeth**. *See* Russell, Elizabeth, Lady Russell (1528–1609).

**Cooke, Sir George** (1768–1837), army officer, was the son and heir of George John Cooke of Harefield, Middlesex, and his wife, Penelope, only daughter of Sir William Bowyer, third baronet; he was a grandson of George Cooke (*c.*1705–1768), protonotary of the court of common pleas and MP for Middlesex from 1750 to 1768, and great-grandson of Sir George Cooke (*d.* 1740) of Harefield, protonotary of the court of common pleas. The naval officer Edward *Cooke (1772–1799) was one of his two brothers. His second sister, Penelope Anne, married Robert Brudenell, sixth earl of Cardigan, and was the mother of James Thomas *Brudenell, seventh earl. Cooke was educated at Harrow School, and at Caen in Normandy. He was appointed ensign in the 10th foot guards in 1784, and lieutenant and captain in 1792. In March 1794 he joined the flank battalion of the guards in Flanders, and in June was appointed aide-de-camp to Major-General Samuel Hulse. He was present when the combined armies took the field and attacked the French posts in April, in the actions of 17 and 18 May, and at the affair at Boxtel on 15 September. In 1795 he joined the brigade of guards at Darley camp and became aide-de-camp to Major-General Edmund Stevens. In 1798 he was promoted captain and lieutenant-colonel in his regiment, and in August 1799 he went with it to the Netherlands. He was present in the action at the Zuype on 10 September, and in the battle on 19 September, when he was severely wounded.

From 1803 until the spring of 1805 Cooke was assistant adjutant-general in the north-west district. In 1806 he went to Sicily, returning to England in December 1807. On 25 April 1808 he received the brevet rank of colonel, and in

July 1809 he was employed in the expedition to the Schelde, from where he returned sick in September.

In April 1811 Cooke went to Cadiz, and on 4 June attained the rank of major-general, and succeeded to the command of the troops stationed there, which he retained until his return to England in July 1813. In November he returned to the Netherlands with the brigade of guards. He commanded the 1st division of the guards at Waterloo, and lost his right arm in the battle. He was appointed KCB on 22 June 1815, and colonel of the 77th foot on the following day. He also received for his share in the engagement the order of St George of Russia (third class) and the order of Wilhelm of the Netherlands (third class).

On 20 October 1819 Cooke was appointed lieutenant-governor of Portsmouth, a post which he resigned a few years later. On 19 July 1821 he obtained the rank of lieutenant-general, and on 23 December 1834 he was transferred to the command of the 40th regiment. His health was shattered by his military career, and he died of influenza, unmarried, at his house, Harefield Park, Harefield, Middlesex, on 3 February 1837. According to the *Gentleman's Magazine*, 'the poor of the village have lost in him a most benevolent and kind-hearted friend' (*GM*, 657).                     E. I. CARLYLE, *rev.* ROGER T. STEARN

**Sources** *GM*, 2nd ser., 7 (1837), 656–7 · *Army List* · GEC, *Peerage* · H. T. Siborne, ed., *Waterloo letters* (1891) · J. C. Ropes, *Campaign of Waterloo* (1893) · W. F. Vernon, *Notes on the parish of Harefield* (1872) · D. Gates, *The Spanish ulcer: a history of the Peninsular War* (1986) · R. Muir, *Britain and the defeat of Napoleon, 1807–1815* (1996) · A. J. Guy, ed., *The road to Waterloo: the British army and the struggle against revolutionary and Napoleonic France, 1793–1815* (1990)
**Likenesses** J. W. Pieneman, oils, Wellington Museum, London

**Cooke, George** (1781–1834). *See under* Cooke family (*per.* c.1800–1865).

**Cooke, George Albert** (1865–1939), biblical scholar and Church of England clergyman, was born in London on 26 November 1865, the eldest son of George Isaac Foster Cooke, a barrister of Lincoln's Inn, and his wife, Agnes Marian, daughter of Stephen Mackenzie, a surgeon, and sister of Sir Morell Mackenzie (1837–1892) and Sir Stephen Mackenzie (1844–1909). He was educated at Merchant Taylors' School (where Hebrew was still taught) and in 1884 gained a Hebrew scholarship to Wadham College, Oxford. He was awarded a second class BA degree in theology in 1888 and won various prizes for Hebrew in 1886 and 1888 and the Houghton Syriac prize in 1889. Also in 1889 he was ordained and became curate of Headington; in the same year St John's College appointed him senior scholar and Hebrew lecturer. He became chaplain (1890) and fellow (1892–9) of Magdalen College, and also held the cure of the university church (1894–6) and the rectorship of Beaconsfield (1896–9). While there he married in 1897 Frances Helen (*d.* 1932), daughter of Patrick Anderson, a man of business in Dundee; they had four daughters. From 1899 to 1908 Cooke was private chaplain to the duke of Buccleuch at Dalkeith, Midlothian, from 1904 to 1908 he was warden of the Community of St Andrew of Scotland, and from 1907 to 1908 was canon of St Mary's Cathedral, Edinburgh. In 1903 he published his most important work, a

*Textbook of North-Semitic Inscriptions*, which for the first time presented Hebrew and Aramaic epigraphy to English speaking students. He received an honorary degree of DD from Edinburgh University in 1911.

In 1908 Cooke returned to Oxford, where he succeeded T. K. Cheyne as Oriel professor of the interpretation of holy scripture, canon of Rochester Cathedral, and fellow of Oriel College. While in Oxford he undertook short commentaries for the Cambridge Bible on the books of Judges and Ruth (1913), and Joshua (1918). In 1914 he was appointed regius professor of Hebrew and canon of Christ Church, Oxford, a position which he resigned in 1936 in order to become rector of a parish of only ninety-five persons at Bettiscombe-with-Pilsdon, near Bridport, Dorset. It was here that he wrote his most ambitious works, the large-scale *Critical and Exegetical Commentary on the Book of Ezekiel* (1937) and *The Prayer Book Psalter Revised* (1939), which attempted to preserve Coverdale's prose style within a more accurate biblical translation. Cooke died suddenly at the Imperial Nursing Home, Cheltenham, on 9 September 1939, following an operation.

HOPE DANBY, *rev.* GERALD LAW

**Sources** *Oxford Magazine* (26 Oct 1939), 22 · *The Times* (13 Sept 1939) · *The Times* (11 Sept 1939) · personal knowledge (1949) · private information (1949) · *CGPLA Eng. & Wales* (1940)
**Archives** University of Bristol Library, special collections, diaries | NL Scot., corresp. with T. and T. Clark
**Likenesses** H. Riviere, portrait, 1935, Christ Church Oxf.
**Wealth at death** £3448 19s. 2d.: probate, 17 Jan 1940, *CGPLA Eng. & Wales*

**Cooke, George Boughey** (1807–1863), actor, was born in Manchester on 7 March 1807. In early life he was placed with the mercantile firm of Hoyle & Co., but his interests lay in the theatre. After performing the role of Othello in amateur theatricals, he left the firm and in March 1828 began his professional career at Walsall theatre, under the management of Chamberlayne. He remained with Chamberlayne for eighteen months, playing in Coventry, Lichfield, and Leamington. He then joined other managements and appeared successfully at Margate, at Doncaster in 1832, and at Edinburgh in October 1835, as Old Crumbs in Douglas Jerrold's *The Rent Day*. In July 1837 he was at the Strand in London, then under the management of W. J. Hammond, playing Mr Wardle in W. T. Moncrieff's adaptation *Sam Weller, or, The Pickwickians*. He accompanied Hammond to Drury Lane in October 1839 but had rather a disastrous season at that theatre.

Cooke married in 1840 Elizabeth Stuart, the sister of a well-known actor. After playing at Liverpool, Manchester, and Birmingham, he appeared at the Marylebone in 1847, when that theatre was under the management of Mary Amelia Warner. Here he played the Old Shepherd in *The Winter's Tale*, Sir Oliver Surface in *The School for Scandal*, and Colonel Damas in *The Lady of Lyons*. He later enjoyed a long engagement at the Olympic Theatre, where he remained until his death, and became a favourite with the public in the original comic roles he played in Wilkie Collins's *The Lighthouse* (1857), John Oxenford's *The Porter's Knot* (1858), *Retained for the Defence* (1859), and *Uncle Zachary* (1860), and

many other plays. He died on 5 March 1863, committing suicide by cutting his throat at his residence, 51 Cambridge Street, Pimlico, London. He had been suffering for a long time from 'a dropsical disease'.

Cooke was a genial actor, skilled in the impersonation of old men, generous uncles, good-natured guardians, and similar such sketches of character.

JOSEPH KNIGHT, *rev.* NILANJANA BANERJI

**Sources** Adams, *Drama* · *Sunday Times* (8 March 1863) · *The Era* (8 March 1863) · *Theatrical Times* (16 Sept 1848) · Hall, *Dramatic ports.*
**Likenesses** plate, repro. in *Theatrical Times* · print, Harvard TC
**Wealth at death** under £300: probate, 30 March 1863, *CGPLA Eng. & Wales*

**Cooke, George Frederick** (1756?–1812), actor, claimed to have been born in Westminster, London, on 17 April 1756. The truth about his birth and parentage is unverifiable; perhaps the most probable scenario is that he was born out of wedlock in Dublin, possibly in a military barracks, the son of Eliza or Allison Renton and a British military man, possibly one James Moore. Little is known of his early life. He probably moved with his mother to Berwick upon Tweed, where her two sisters lived; he received some education there, and on his mother's death about 1764 was apprenticed to a printer, John Taylor. It was in Berwick too that Cooke saw his first dramatic performance, given by strolling players in the town hall about 1766. By 1769 he had been involved with amateur theatricals, and in 1771 obtained his release from Taylor and travelled to London, where he continued his amateur performances. In November 1771 he sailed to the Netherlands, probably as a cabin boy, but returned to Berwick early in 1772.

Over the next twenty-seven years, and despite two brief London engagements, it was as a provincial actor that Cooke made his mark: few major British actors have had to wait so long to earn recognition in the capital city. The date and place of his first professional appearance are uncertain, though it was most probably Lincolnshire between 1773 and 1775. For the next few years he was a strolling player, appearing in such towns as King's Lynn, Stamford, Brentford, and, during the summer of 1777, Hastings. In the spring of 1778 he took part in three benefit performances during the off-season at London's Haymarket Theatre, as Castalio in Thomas Otway's *The Orphan* (9 April), Modely in Charles Johnson's *The Country Lasses* (29 April), and Lovewell in Garrick and Colman's *The Clandestine Marriage* (30 April). Other than two additional benefits at the Haymarket in 1779, these were his last appearances in London for over twenty years. He returned to the provinces to continue his theatrical apprenticeship, where his early roles were predominantly in comedy.

Among Cooke's notable provincial engagements in the next few years were periods in Manchester, Lancaster, Preston, Liverpool, Chester, York, Hull, Leeds, Newcastle upon Tyne, Sheffield, and Buxton. In York on 29 July 1786 he first appeared with Sarah Siddons, with whom he would later frequently appear at Covent Garden in London. In 1787 he joined Joseph Austin and Charles Whitlock's company in Manchester as a leading player; he had previously appeared with them in supporting roles. By

**George Frederick Cooke** (1756?–1812), by Gilbert Stuart, 1811

1794 he was a provincial star, with prestigious engagements to follow, beginning in Dublin, where his first role was Othello on 19 November 1794. His initial success there was modest, but by the spring of 1800 he had been dubbed 'the Dublin Roscius' by the London press.

This formative period was critical for Cooke, for not only did he master over 300 roles, he also developed a major problem with alcohol, a reputation for unreliability, and domestic difficulties—conditions that would plague him throughout his career. For example, in the summer of 1795, following a period of dissipation (and no doubt drunk at the time), he enlisted in the army, but was soon discharged through the efforts of the Portsmouth theatre manager. He married his first wife, Alicia Daniels (*b.* 1777), an actress, on 20 December 1796, though at least two other actresses had previously called themselves Mrs Cooke (one appears by this name in playbills as early as February 1775, another in 1784). Daniels had her marriage to Cooke annulled on 4 July 1801, after Cooke had finally made the move to a major London theatre.

In February 1800 Cooke was invited to join the Covent Garden company for the 1800–01 season, and he made his début there on 31 October 1800 as Richard III, the role that would become his most famous. The critics were split in their opinions. Some preferred the more studied and refined style of Cooke's contemporary and competitor at Drury Lane, John Philip Kemble, while others considered Cooke a true original, one who did not imitate other actors but did in some respects resemble the great David Garrick. During his first season Cooke made his first London appearances in such notable roles as Shylock (10 November), Sir Archy MacSarcasm in Charles Macklin's

*Love-à-la-mode* (added as an afterpiece to *The Merchant of Venice* on 13 November), Iago (28 November), Macbeth (5 December), Kitely in Ben Jonson's *Every Man in his Humour* (17 December), the title role in Kotzebue's *The Stranger* (27 January 1801), and Sir Giles Overreach in Massinger's *A New Way to Pay Old Debts* (28 March). The following season he added two significant roles to these: Stukely in Edward Moore's *The Gamester* (27 November 1801) and Sir Pertinax McSycophant in Macklin's *Man of the World* (10 April 1802). These ten became his great parts, repeated frequently. For this auspicious first London season he managed to control his drinking. Thereafter, however, apologies for his 'indisposition' became more and more common.

For the next eight years Cooke invariably took summer provincial engagements between London seasons, including several in Scotland and Ireland and in theatres in the midlands familiar from his apprentice days. The summers became something of a respite from his troubled winter seasons in London. His appearance in London for his second season was delayed, probably by a genuine illness, and on this occasion his apology was accepted, even though many believed his absence was caused by drunkenness.

Although it was not one of his principal roles, Cooke performed King Lear for the first time in London during his second season (8 January 1801), but it was not repeated during that season. On 11 May for the first time it was recorded publicly that his drunkenness prevented his performance. A note written on a theatre playbill in the British Library declares that 'Cooke attempted to perform but was too inebriated to proceed beyond a few speeches' as Orsino in Matthew Lewis's *Alphonso, King of Castille*. Such occurrences now became commonplace. To complicate further Cooke's career and reputation, John Philip Kemble was engaged by Covent Garden in 1803, thus bringing their rivalry to the same stage.

Cooke's most discouraging season was that of 1805–6, when he appeared on only fifty nights in a season of 212 nights and presented no role more than six times. The press made frequent reference to his misdeeds, as they would in the next season, even though it was his least controversial in years. When he failed to appear in Manchester in June 1807 despite an advance payment, Cooke, unable to return the advance, was confined in Appleby prison, Westmorland, from 17 August until 30 December 1807. While he was frequently in financial straits and a poor manager of his funds, his alcoholism complicated his finances, and he was known to squander large sums of money. Numerous anecdotes record examples of his generous gifts to women in distress and to other unfortunates. The most positive result of his four and a half months in prison was the diary and journal of his career, which was the closest thing to an autobiography he ever undertook.

Perhaps chastened by the experience, Cooke performed his professional duties without incident between January and July 1808; he returned to Covent Garden in March 1808 and performed there for at least forty-eight nights in what remained of the season. Back in Edinburgh, on 21

September 1808 he married Sarah Harvey Lamb, the daughter of John Lamb of Newark, Nottinghamshire. Little is known of her or of the marriage, not even of its dissolution (it seems to have lasted less than a year). When Cooke returned to London for the 1808–9 season, Sarah accompanied him. It was a difficult period. Covent Garden had been destroyed by fire on 19 September 1808, and the company was forced to perform elsewhere. According to Arnold Hare, Cooke took Sarah back to Newark in February 1809, and she never returned. By then Cooke's London career was almost over: 1809–10 was to be his last season. He was frequently required to perform during the period of the Old Price riots which began in September 1809. His final London appearance was as Shylock on 22 June 1810. With his career at a low point and, according to his first biographer, William Dunlap, discontented with his position in London, where he was constantly undermined by a hostile press, Cooke was easily persuaded by the American actor–manager Thomas A. Cooper to appear in the United States under the aegis of the New York Park Theater. He sailed from Liverpool on the *Columbia* on 4 October 1810, having made his final English performance without fanfare or comment before a small country audience in Preston on 17 August.

Cooke made his début in New York on 11 November as Richard III. His reception was the most enthusiastic yet accorded an actor in the United States, and, although his reputation for drunkenness and debauchery preceded him, he was generally on his best behaviour, sobered after the long voyage, and shepherded by the playwright and manager William Dunlap during his 160 performances in New York, Boston, Baltimore, Philadelphia, and Providence. His appearance as Sir Giles Overreach in Providence on 31 July 1812 was to prove to be his final performance on the stage. The visit was a lucrative one for the managers of the theatres that hosted Cooke, with receipts totalling about $250,000. But Cooke himself received only $20,000, and this, coupled with anger over the devious terms on which he felt he had been taken to America, left him resentful and drove him back to the bottle. Although he fully intended to return to England, where he had accepted an invitation to rejoin the Covent Garden company, the Anglo-American War of 1812–14 and the subsequent American embargo on foreign-bound ships left him stranded in the United States. With his health steadily declining, Cooke returned to New York city, where he died on 26 September 1812, of cirrhosis of the liver, at the Mechanics' Hall, a well-known tavern at the corner of Broadway and Robinson Street (later Park Place). At his deathbed was his new American wife, Violet Mary Behn, the widow of a German merchant and the daughter of James Bryden, keeper of the Tontine Coffee House in New York. They had married on 20 June 1811. On 27 September 1812 Cooke's remains were placed in the strangers' vault of St Paul's Church. Edmund Kean, an admirer of Cooke's, had the actor's body reburied at the church and erected an elaborate monument during his first American tour, in 1821.

Cooke's accomplishment as an actor of the first order should overshadow his tainted personal reputation and quixotic career. Arguably he was the first true British romantic actor, ranking in the annals of the stage with the small group of great actors of the late eighteenth and early nineteenth centuries. He was the first major foreign star on the American stage, and his appearance there marked the inception of the star system in the United States. Even after age and debilitation had all but destroyed him, Cooke's figure continued to make an impression on those who saw him on or off stage. He was 5 feet 10 inches tall, broad-chested, and had a prominent nose in shape between Roman and aquiline, expressive eyes, and (when in possession of his faculties) a dignified, self-possessed, and courteous manner, and he fascinated observers. Yet underneath this exterior was a coarseness that coloured his acting, and his voice, which was not particularly pleasant, was even hoarse on occasion. Some critics believed his awkward, grotesque movements limited his scope of characters. But in the tradition of his great predecessors David Garrick and Charles Macklin, Cooke brought a new natural style to the stage: he spoke poetry like prose and delivered soliloquies as if thinking aloud. Although he created few important new roles, he did establish a reputation for playing a line of characters noted for their grim humour, sardonic sarcasm, specious menace, savage ferocity, and baleful guile.

DON B. WILMETH

**Sources** D. B. Wilmeth, *George Frederick Cooke: Machiavel of the stage* (1980) • A. Hare, *George Frederick Cooke: the actor and the man* (1980) • W. Dunlap, *The life of George Frederick Cooke* (1813) • *The diaries of William Dunlap, 1766–1839*, ed. D. Barck, 3 vols. (1931) • G. F. Cooke, diaries and journals, Harvard TC • playbills, BL • Highfill, Burnim & Langhans, *BDA*, vol. 3

**Archives** American Antiquarian Society, Worcester, Massachusetts, US newspapers • BL, playbills • Harvard TC, diaries and journals • NYPL for the Performing Arts, Billy Rose Theatre collection, MSS • Theatre Museum, London, Enthoven collection, playbills • Theatre Museum, London, notebooks

**Likenesses** J. Green, oils, exh. RA 1801 (as Iago), Garr. Club • S. De Wilde, oils, 1806, Garr. Club • G. Stuart, oils, 1811, Garr. Club [*see illus.*] • T. Sully, oils, 1811, Pennsylvania Academy of Fine Arts, Philadelphia, Pennsylvania • W. Dunlap, miniature, 1813, Harvard TC • S. De Wilde, watercolour (as Richard III), Garr. Club • O. Humphry, miniature, Royal Collection • C. R. Leslie, oils (as Richard III), Garr. Club • T. Phillips, oils (as Shylock), Garr. Club • H. Singleton, oils (as Kitely in *Every man in his humour*), Garr. Club • T. Sully, oils, Garr. Club • pencil drawing, Garr. Club • prints, BM • prints, NPG

**Wealth at death** $2000: letter from Joseph Fay, 24 Sept 1812, New York county surrogate court, book 50, p. 261

**Cooke, George Leigh** (*bap.* 1779, *d.* 1853), Church of England clergyman and natural philosopher, was baptized on 12 September 1779, the son of Samuel Cooke, rector of Great Bookham, Surrey, and his wife, Cassandra. He entered the University of Oxford in 1797 as a commoner of Balliol College, and was elected the same year a scholar of Corpus Christi College, of which he afterwards became a fellow and tutor. He graduated BA on 6 November 1800, MA on 9 March 1804, and BD on 12 June 1812. In 1810 he was elected Sedleian professor of natural philosophy; he resigned his fellowship to marry, on 26 October 1815, Anne, the eldest daughter of William Hay of Russell

Square, London. From 1818 to 1826 he was keeper of the archives of the university. He also held the office of public preacher, and was several times public examiner.

Cooke was presented to the rectory of Cubbington, Warwickshire, in 1820, and to Wick Rissington, Gloucestershire, and Hunningham, Warwickshire, in the same year. A sociable man, Cooke was the probable founder, and for many years the secretary, of the Literary Dining Club, frequented by the university's most distinguished scholars. An obituarist described him as 'a zealous clergyman, a kind and benevolent landlord and an honourable gentleman' (*GM*, 1853). He published in 1850 *The first three sections and part of the seventh section of Newton's 'Principia', with a preface recommending a geometrical course of mathematical reading, and an introduction on the atomic constitution of matter and the laws of motion.*

Cooke died at Cubbington on 29 March 1853, leaving a widow and several children, of whom Samuel Hay Cooke (1818–1877) and George Theophilus Cooke (*b.* 1820) both graduated at Oxford and took holy orders.

[ANON.], rev. ANITA MCCONNELL

**Sources** *GM*, 2nd ser., 40 (1853), 94 • Boase, *Mod. Eng. biog.* • *GM*, 1st ser., 85/2 (1815), 464 • *Clergy List* (1848) • *Hist. U. Oxf.* 5: *18th-cent. Oxf.* • Foster, *Alum. Oxon.*

**Cooke, George Wingrove** (1814–1865), legal and historical writer, eldest son of Thomas Homans Cooke, who came from a Devon family, was born at Bristol. He studied law under Andrew Amos at London University, and was called to the bar at the Middle Temple in January 1835. He was at the same time completing his classical education at Jesus College, Oxford, where he took his BA in 1834.

From the first, Cooke was a prolific writer, rarely needing to correct or retouch what he had written. While still an undergraduate he wrote *Memoirs of Lord Bolingbroke*, which was published in 1835. Clearly written from a whig standpoint, the book was unfavourably reviewed by John Croker in the tory *Quarterly Review*, but was strongly defended in the *Edinburgh Review*.

Encouraged by this success, Cooke went on to publish a *History of Party from the Rise of the Whig and Tory Factions to the Passing of the Reform Bill* (1836–7) and a *Life of the First Earl Shaftesbury* (1836), edited from the materials collected by Andrew Kippis, Benjamin Martyn, and others.

For many years after settling in London, Cooke was employed by the tithe commutation commission in defining the principles and supervising the mechanism for the composition of tithes. He also worked for the enclosure commission in a similar capacity. These years were marked by the preparation and publication of a number of legal treatises, dealing with subjects as diverse as agricultural tenancies and poll booths.

However, Cooke also turned his holidays to advantage by publishing the narratives of his long vacation travels. Most of these appeared anonymously, but in 1855, at the height of the Crimean War, he visited the Crimea, and on his return to his own country vividly described what he had seen in *Inside Sebastopol* (1856). Soon afterwards, the

managers of *The Times*, to which he was a frequent contributor, dispatched him to China as the special correspondent on the outbreak of the second Chinese war in 1857. His dispatches, narrating the progress of the British expedition and the details of life among the Chinese, were republished in book form in 1858, and sold well in several editions.

One of Cooke's holiday expeditions took him to Algiers, where he enquired into the intentions of the French, and speculated as to their prospects of colonization. The results of his investigations appeared as a series of letters in *The Times*, published in 1860 as *Conquest and Colonisation in North Africa*.

Cooke made two unsuccessful attempts to enter parliament as a Liberal: for Colchester in 1850 and for Marylebone in 1861. In 1862, he was appointed to a commissionership in the copyhold commission. Given to overwork, Cooke fell ill in June 1865. On the morning of 18 June he died of a heart attack at his house, 25 Cheyne Walk, Chelsea, London.                 W. P. COURTNEY, rev. JONATHAN HARRIS

**Sources** *The Times* (20 June 1865), 7 • *GM*, 3rd ser., 19 (1865), 256–7 • *Men of the time* (1862), 180–81 • Foster, *Alum. Oxon.*
**Archives** BL, corresp. with Richard Bentley and related business papers, Add MSS 46612 and 46649, *passim* • UCL, letters to Lord Brougham
**Likenesses** wood-engraving (after photograph by Maull & Polyblank), NPG; repro. in *ILN* (15 July 1865)
**Wealth at death** under £4000: probate, 26 July 1865, *CGPLA Eng. & Wales*

**Cooke, Henry** (*d.* 1672), singer, composer, and choirmaster, was 'bred up' in the Chapel Royal according to Anthony Wood, but Joseph Bridge's suggestion that his father was John Cooke of the chapel, formerly a vicar-choral at Lichfield, is speculative. Cooke joined the royalist army in the civil wars; it is uncertain whether he was the Lieutenant Henry Cooke of Colonel George Goring's regiment in 1640, but if he was it must be doubtful whether he could, as sometimes stated, have been the Henry Cooke who in 1642 scratched his name on a window in the Jerusalem chamber at Westminster. He reached the rank of captain, and retained the title; the will of the musician Thomas Ford, in which he was forgiven a debt, shows that he was using it by 1648.

Cooke was in London by 1651, when John Playford listed him in *A Musicall Banquet* among teachers 'For the Voyce or Viole'. A letter of 1656 from the musician George Jeffreys indicates that Cooke's pupils included the children of Christopher, first Baron Hatton, whose principal residence was Kirby Hall in Northamptonshire. Hatton's ownership of much Italian music may have helped to familiarize Cooke with the Italian style; John Evelyn's diary entry for 28 October 1654 describes him as 'the best singer, after the *Italian* manner, of any in *England*', an opinion endorsed in the 1664 edition of Playford's *Introduction to the Skill of Musick*. Another influence may have been Walter Porter, a member of the Chapel Royal before the wars, who visited Italy and claimed an association with Monteverdi. In 1656 Cooke provided some of the music for two stage works by William D'Avenant, *The First Days Entertainment at Rutland-*

*House* and *The Siege of Rhodes*, singing the part of Solyman in the second—a performance remembered well enough for Mrs Coleman to impersonate it for Samuel Pepys on 31 October 1665. Pepys's view, recorded on 13 February 1667, was that Cooke was 'a vain coxcomb', although 'as to voice and manner, the best I ever heard yet; and a strange mastery he hath in making of extraordinary surprizing closes, that are mighty pretty'. In spite of a distaste for Cooke's bragging, Pepys was often in his company, and in 1664 employed one of his choristers, Tom Edwards, as a musical servant.

At the Restoration in 1660 Cooke became a gentleman of the Chapel Royal and one of the musicians for the lutes and voices, receiving additional payments for training two singing boys in the private musick. On 29 June he was sworn in as master of the children of the Chapel Royal, with responsibility for enlisting and training choirboys and seeing that they were fed, clothed, cared for, and taught to read and write Latin and play instruments. Cooke travelled throughout England to recruit boys at intervals for the rest of his life, with authority from January 1661 to impress them. The necessity appears in Matthew Locke's statement, in *The Present Practice of Musick Vindicated* (1673), that for over a year after the chapel was reopened cornetts and men singing falsetto were substituted for boys' voices, 'there being not one Lad, for all that time, capable of Singing his part readily'. Cooke's duties were carried out with vigour and patent success, but in the face of financial difficulties that began as early as October 1661. By 1668 the boys' clothes were 'so worn out that they keep within doors', and Cooke was called before the privy council. It was not until 1670 that the king resolved to have the boys clothed 'as formerly', and Cooke agreed to arrange a loan for the purpose.

Cooke was among the composers who provided the chapel with a new repertory, writing some thirty anthems, nearly all of the verse type, and other devotional pieces. Most of these are lost. Pepys commented favourably on anthems by Cooke on 12 August 1660 (when Cooke himself sang) and the following 7 October. Ashmole noted Cooke's part in composing and performing music for the St George's feast at Windsor on 17 April 1661; and on 23 April Cooke and his choristers were at Charles II's coronation in Westminster Abbey, when three of his anthems were performed. On Sunday 14 September 1662 Pepys heard 'Cookes new Musique' and wrote:

> This the first day of having Vialls and other Instruments to play a Symphony between every verse of the Anthem; but the Musique more full than it was the last Sunday, and very fine it is. But yet I could discern Captain Cooke to overdo his part at singing, which I never did before.

Cooke's surviving anthems show no great gift for composition, but they are carefully tailored to the resources at his disposal, and contain innovations, afterwards developed by younger men, in the independence of instrumental passages, contrasting scorings, and the disposition of performers within the chapel. Cooke wrote four undistinguished court odes and also a handful of songs and catches, of which four were published in *Catch that Catch Can* (1667).

In 1663 Cooke successfully petitioned the king for an augmentation of the pay of the gentlemen and children of the chapel, and in the same year was chosen as a steward of the annual chapel feast. From early in 1663 he signed orders as deputy marshall of the Corporation of Musick, a society composed of royal musicians and claiming wide powers to regulate professional music-making; he was one of four members deputed on 31 May 1664 to attend a fruitless meeting with musicians of the City of London, who claimed similar powers. Cooke afterwards became marshall, probably in 1666 (when there is a gap in the records), following the death of Nicholas Lanier. Before that, in August 1664, he had obtained a further official appointment as a composer in the private musick.

Little is known of Cooke's family. His wife was named Mary and brought him land at Pluckley, in Kent; a daughter of the same name predeceased him. In 1672 his daughter Katherine married his pupil Pelham *Humfrey, who became master of the children on Cooke's death but died in 1674; Katherine's second husband was named Darcey. A third daughter, Amey, was married first to Bartholomew Tothill and then to Arthur Browne. Cooke's will suggests residence at both Westminster and Hampton. His Westminster house may have been in Little Sanctuary, where 'Widow Cooke' lived after his death. In 1669 he had lodgings at 'the further end' of the old bowling alley at Hampton Court, which in 1671 it was decided to demolish.

On 24 June 1672 Cooke asked to be replaced as marshall of the Corporation of Musick because of illness, and on 6 July he made his will; he added a codicil a few days afterwards. Most of his possessions were left to the members of his family. The will disposed of his house in Westminster, a house and land at Hampton, his land at Pluckley, and houses in Longditch, Westminster, a street in which people named Cooke lived, though it is not known whether they were related to him. He also left plate and jewellery, 120 pieces of gold, and well over £1000 owed to him in wages and allowances. Cooke died on 13 July 1672, presumably at Westminster, and was buried on 17 July close to his daughter Mary in the east cloister of Westminster Abbey, 'near the steps'. His widow, who he wished to be buried near him, made her will on 16 March 1696; it was proved on 16 June by her daughter Katherine.

JOHN HARLEY

**Sources** Lord Chamberlain's papers, PRO, LC3, LC5, LC9 [calendared in A. Ashbee, *Records of English court music* (1986–96), vols. 1, 5, 8] • Chancery copies of patents, PRO, C66 [calendared in A. Ashbee, *Records of English court music* (1986–96), vols. 5, 8] • Treasury minute books, PRO, T29 [calendared in A. Ashbee, *Records of English court music* (1986–96), vol. 8] • A. Wood, Bodl. Oxf., MS Wood D 19 (4) • J. D. Shute, 'Anthony A Wood and his manuscript Wood D 19 (4) at the Bodleian Library, Oxford: an annotated transcription', PhD diss., International Institute of Advanced Musical Studies, Clayton, Missouri, 1979 • J. C. Bridge, 'A great English choir-trainer: Captain Henry Cooke', *Musical Antiquary*, 2 (1910–11), 61–79 • E. Peacock, ed., *The army lists of the roundheads and cavaliers*, 2nd edn (1874) • G. Jeffreys, letter, 11 Dec 1656, BL, Add. MS 29550, fol. 275 • Evelyn, *Diary* • Pepys, *Diary* • the cheque books, St James's Palace, archive of Her Majesty's Chapel Royal • A. Ashbee and J. Harley, eds., *The cheque books of the Chapel Royal*, 2 vols. (2000) · J. L. Chester, ed., *The marriage, baptismal, and burial registers of the collegiate church or abbey of St Peter, Westminster*, Harleian Society, 10 (1876) · minute book of the Corporation of Musick, BL, Harley MS 1911 · A. Ashbee, ed., *Records of English court music*, 5 (1991), 5 · overseers' accounts, parish of St Margaret, 1672–3, City Westm. AC, E185–E186 · will, PRO, PROB 11/343, sig. 143 [6 July 1672 with codicil *c.*9 July, proved 19 Nov 1672; additional copy in Lord Chamberlain's papers. LC9/258, fol. 72] · will, 16 March 1696, PRO, PROB 11/432, sig. 91 [proved 16 June 1696; will of Mary Cooke, wife] · P. Dennison and B. Wood, 'Cooke, Henry', *New Grove*, 2nd edn, 6.385–7 [incl. work list] · will, PRO, PROB 10, box 698, 12 Nov 1648, proved 20 Nov 1648 [will of Thomas Ford] · *A brief introduction to the skill of musick … the fourth edition* (J. Playford, 1664) · E. Ashmole, *The institution, laws and ceremonies of the most noble order of the Garter* (1693) · M. Locke, *The present practice of musick vindicated* (1673) · *A musicall banquet* (J. Benson and J. Playford, publishers, 1651) · A. Ashbee and D. Lasocki, eds., *A biographical dictionary of English court musicians, 1485–1714*, 2 vols. (1998)

**Wealth at death** houses in Westminster; house and land at Hampton, Middlesex; land at Pluckley, Kent; plate and jewellery; 120 pieces of gold; plus over £1000 owed to him in wages and allowances: will, PRO, PROB 11/343, sig. 143

**Cooke** [ *formerly* Macook, Cook], **Henry** (1788–1868), minister of the Presbyterian Church in Ireland, was born on 11 May 1788, the fourth and youngest child of Jane Howe, the second wife of John Macook, a tenant farmer of the Grillagh, near Maghera, in co. Londonderry.

**Education and ordination**   Henry's early education was in a series of 'hedge' schools, and later he recalled how he and a Roman Catholic companion 'tended the peaceful flocks with Vergil or fought again the battles of Homer' (Kennedy, 70). This classical education was supplemented at home by his mother's vivid accounts of the battles of his protestant forefathers for 'faith and freedom'. His son-in-law and biographer, J. L. Porter, tells us that to her 'Henry was indebted for most of those anecdotes and incidents of Irish history which in after years he recited with such pathos and power' (Porter, 2). His boyhood experiences, in the disturbed confusion surrounding the 1798 rising, left impressions on his mind which inclined him towards the conservative principles which he adopted in later life.

In 1802 the fourteen-year-old Henry Macook matriculated in the University of Glasgow and began his studies for the ministry. In spite of his failure to graduate in arts he was accepted as a student for the ministry by the Root presbytery in 1807 and licensed the following year by the Ballymena presbytery. Although he was only twenty years of age he was soon called to the congregation of Denain in co. Antrim as assistant and successor to the Revd Robert Scott, being ordained and installed on 10 November 1808. If his university career had been undistinguished, his first pastorate was inauspicious, ending in resignation after only two years. Cook, who had now discarded Mac from his name but had not yet added the letter 'e', was young, poor, and lonely, living in lodgings on a pittance of £25 a year, and in November 1810 he resigned to become the tutor in the family of Alexander Brown, a farmer, of Kells, near Ballymena. This interruption of his ministerial career proved short-lived, however, and on 22 January 1811 he was installed in the nearby Donegore congregation by the

Henry Cooke (1788–1868), by Sir Daniel Macnee, *c.*1856

Templepatrick presbytery. Donegore had rejected an apparently more attractive candidate in the brilliant Henry Montgomery (1788–1865), destined to be Cooke's great opponent in the conflict which divided the synod of Ulster in the 1820s. The peace of the synod had been threatened for almost a century by the tensions between conservatives or Old Lights, who held tenaciously to traditional Calvinism, as enshrined in the Westminster formularies, and liberals or New Lights, who espoused a latitudinarian theology and opposed the obligation of ordinands to subscribe to the Westminster confession of faith. Cooke's Old Light theology had been one of the reasons for his discomfort in Denain, where his predecessor had been New Light, while Henry Montgomery's biographer, J. A. Crozier, claims that it was Montgomery's unequivocal New Light preaching which led to his rejection by Donegore. Donegore, unlike Denain, preferred Old Light. In Donegore Cooke made a fresh start, and his marriage in 1813 to Ellen Mann (*d.* 1868) of Toome gave his life a new stability. His gifts as a preacher began to blossom and in December 1814 he was invited to preach in Belfast on behalf of the rapidly growing town's recently founded house of industry. The occasion was a success, Cooke's sermon was printed, and his name begins to appear in newspaper accounts of special sermons for Bible societies and Sunday schools. Conscious now of the deficiencies in his earlier education, he returned to his studies, and between 1815 and 1818 an indulgent congregation allowed him to spend two winters in Glasgow and one in Dublin, largely in medical studies. This was not unusual at a time when, according to an observer of the Ulster scene, 'most Presbyterian ministers were physicians and surgeons likewise' (Gamble, 222).

**Emergence as a champion of orthodoxy** While in Dublin Cooke was involved in preaching on Sundays in Carlow and Stratford-on-Slaney, where Presbyterian congregations were being formed. This kind of outreach was characteristic of the evangelical movement, which was breathing new life into the dry bones of Irish protestantism and which was to lead to what was called the protestant crusade in Ireland. Dublin was the headquarters of the Irish evangelical movement, in which Dr Benjamin McDowell, the senior minister of the Presbyterian Mary's Abbey congregation, had been prominently involved, and Cooke's sojourn in Dublin and his associations with the Mary's Abbey congregation strengthened his evangelical and Old Light convictions.

To the disappointment of his Donegore congregation, Cooke moved to Killyleagh in co. Down soon after his return from Dublin, being installed there by the Dromore presbytery on 8 September 1818. He had been recommended to the Killyleagh congregation by his New Light predecessor there, the Revd W. D. H. McEwen, who described him as 'not bigoted in his opinions' and having 'too much good sense not to be charitable towards those who differ from him in sentiment' (McCreery, 228). Yet within three years of his arrival in Killyleagh he had emerged as an uncompromising champion of orthodoxy. One reason for this was the influence of a ruling elder in the Killyleagh congregation, Captain Sidney Hamilton Rowan. Rowan was the son of the local landlord, the United Irishman Archibald Hamilton Rowan. Captain Rowan shared his father's vigour and public spirit but differed from him in theology and politics. He was an ardent evangelical, and Alexander McCreery, a later minister in Killyleagh, claimed that 'to him [Rowan] primarily and mainly is attributable the influence which brought forward Dr. Cooke as the exponent and defender of evangelical doctrine' (ibid., 366). In 1821 an English Unitarian missionary, the Revd John Smethurst, visited Killyleagh in the course of a preaching tour in Ulster. Rowan and Cooke attended his lecture and Cooke, encouraged by Rowan, announced that he would reply to the Unitarian on the following Sunday evening. So enthusiastic was the response of a crowded congregation to Cooke's polemic that he pursued Smethurst through the province, attacking his teaching.

Few Irish Presbyterians were unitarians in 1821 but some were Arians, who rejected the full deity of Christ, and it was the appointment of an Arian, William Bruce, as professor of Greek and Hebrew in the Belfast Institution in 1821 which drew Cooke into the arena of public theological controversy once more. The Belfast Academical Institution, founded in 1810 to meet the urgent need in Belfast and Ulster for higher education of some kind, had already been a target for conservative political suspicion. Its founders included well-known Belfast radicals such as Dr William Drennan and Dr R. J. Tennent, which led the Ulster-born tory statesman Lord Castlereagh to suspect that the college would be the centre of radical influence. In particular Castlereagh feared that if, as its founders hoped, the institution became the training college for Ulster's Presbyterian ministers, this would defeat his policy of discouraging radicalism and encouraging loyalism among the ministers, some of whom had been implicated in the United Irish movement and the 1798 rising. Castlereagh, one of the architects of the Act of Union, had thrown the weight of his influence against arrangements to train Presbyterian students for the ministry in the institution, but he had failed because the college authorities and the Presbyterian synods had stood together for academic and ecclesiastical freedom. There were now three Presbyterian synods in Ulster for, during the eighteenth century, covenanters and seceders from Scotland had planted congregations and formed presbyteries in opposition to the increasingly liberal or New Light Synod of Ulster. All three had agreed to allow their students for the ministry to be educated in the institution and had appointed divinity professors to enable them to take their full course of training in Belfast. This had been a success, and when Cooke attacked Arian influences in the institution at the 1822 meeting of the synod of Ulster in Newry he found that few members of synod believed that a crusade against Arianism was necessary or desirable. Nevertheless Cooke persisted, rallying supporters, particularly among the Presbyterian laity.

**Cooke's campaign against Arianism** Cooke's election as moderator of the synod in 1824 gave him opportunities to ventilate his convictions, particularly when he was called upon to give evidence to parliamentary committees and government commissions of inquiry, including one into the affairs of the Belfast Institution. His allegations that the institution was becoming a 'seminary of Arianism' were publicized and provoked warm controversy. He survived attacks upon his evidence at the annual meeting of the synod in 1825 and succeeded in persuading the synod to demand increased influence in future appointment in the college. This the institution authorities refused to concede, insisting that the synod had already sufficient influence in appointment through the *ex officio* vote of its moderator. The institution was popular among Presbyterians who saw no evidence of Arian influences on their students for the ministry, and, at the meeting of the synod in 1826 in Ballymena, Cooke found the tide of majority opinion flowing against him as strongly as it had been with him the previous year. His campaign against Arianism in the institution had ended in defeat. The publication in 1827 of evidence given to the commission of inquiry into the affairs of the institution, however, gave him an opportunity to attack ministers of the synod who had avowed their Arian convictions. These included Henry Montgomery and William Porter, the clerk of the synod. When the synod met in Strabane in 1827 Cooke insisted that the reaffirmation of their church's Trinitarian faith was necessary, and in spite of Henry Montgomery's eloquent plea for liberty of conscience and the right of private judgement the overwhelming majority of the members of synod agreed, thus isolating the small minority of Arians and those opposed to doctrinal statements as tests of faith. The rejection, in 1826, of Cooke's allegations of Arian influences in the institution had not implied any approval of Arianism, and this was made clear by the 1827 synod's affirmation of its Trinitarian faith.

The following year the synod, meeting in Cookstown, was persuaded to set up a committee to examine the orthodoxy of students for the ministry, and it was clear that no Arian would be accepted in future. This led Montgomery and his party to publish a remonstrance against the proceedings of the synod, threatening to secede if their objections were not met, and in 1830 seventeen ministers and their congregations withdrew from the synod of Ulster to form the Remonstrant Synod. Before the separation took place, however, there was a final confrontation between the two parties, involving once more the Belfast Institution. The appointment of a Scot, John Ferrie of Glasgow University, to the chair of moral philosophy in the institution was attacked by Cooke on the grounds of Ferrie's doubtful orthodoxy. Montgomery, in reply, attacked Cooke's consistency and integrity because in his evidence to the institution commission of inquiry he had stated that he had never known of any Arianism in Glasgow, but now he was querying the orthodoxy of the former Glasgow University chaplain.

Cooke chose to interpret this as a charge of perjury, as his evidence had been given on oath, and, in the words of the radical Presbyterian journalist James McKnight, 'on this rhetorical hypothesis, he made, to the feeling of the audience, an appeal unequalled in the annals of oratory' (*Londonderry Standard*, 24 Dec 1875). This was hyperbole, of course, but, coming from a journalist who did not admire Cooke, it is a tribute to his remarkable oratorical powers. The withdrawal of the remonstrants left Cooke on a pinnacle of influence in the synod of Ulster, and the historian W. D. Killen, who was ordained in 1829, has judged that

> The popularity enjoyed in this period by the pastor of Killyleagh, was such as perhaps has never been attained by any other minister in this country and wherever he appeared either on the pulpit or on the platform he was sure to attract an overwhelming audience. (Reid, 3.462)

He refused a call to the Mary's Abbey congregation in Dublin in 1828, but in 1829 his admirers in Belfast, disappointed that he had not been invited to be the first minister of the new congregation in Fisherwick Place, built May Street Church to provide him with a pulpit in their growing town. His rejection by the Fisherwick Place congregation was clear evidence, however, that he was *persona non grata* in some quarters, and not all of them Arian or New Light. When Jefferson College, Pennsylvania, made him an honorary DD in 1829, the *Northern Whig* commented that 'in consequence of distance' the college had discerned 'literary and scientific attainments which, in consequence of our too near approximation to the luminary, we are unable to discern' (14 Dec 1829).

**Political influence** In his evidence before both houses of parliament in 1824, Cooke had queried the commitment of a majority of Irish Presbyterians to Catholic emancipation, in spite of the synod's declaration in its favour in 1813. This brought him into conflict with liberal Presbyterians but made him a hero with the opponents of emancipation. During the controversy in the synod he was prepared to play the Orange card, as when in Coleraine in 1825 he appealed improperly 'to those galleries, crowded with the freemen of my native county ... for a unanimous and cordial verdict of acquittal' (*Northern Whig*, 7 July 1825). It was alleged that the Orangemen in the galleries in Coleraine and in Strabane in 1827 may have influenced the outcome of the debates. Henry Montgomery claimed that it was by uniting evangelicalism and Orangeism that Cooke acquired his extraordinary popularity and influence.

The historian of the Belfast Institution, John Jamieson, has argued that Cooke's real objective in attacking the institution was the destruction of political liberalism in his church. Certainly, after his victory in the synod, Cooke became increasingly identified with the political interests of the protestant establishment in Ireland. He and his great ally, Robert Stewart of Broughshane, were among the few Presbyterians who opposed the concession of Catholic emancipation in 1829. He waged a relentless and ultimately successful campaign against the Irish national education system, introduced by a reforming whig government in 1831 to end Protestant proselytization of Roman Catholics through education by uniting all children for secular education and separating them for religious instruction. He advocated protestant political union in response to the challenge of post-emancipation Irish Roman Catholicism, antagonizing Presbyterian radicals by publishing the 'banns of marriage' of presbytery and prelacy at a great conservative demonstration at Hillsborough in co. Down in 1834.

Cooke was a determined supporter of the principle of religious establishments against voluntarism, which demanded the separation of the church and state. He liked to describe himself as a minister of the Church of Scotland in Ireland and was delighted when full communion between the Church of Scotland and the synod of Ulster was restored in 1836 following legislation in the synod to reintroduce subscription to the Westminster formularies for ordinands. In 1837 Trinity College, Dublin, made him an LLD for his services to the cause of religious establishments. The restoration of subscription in the synod of Ulster was a step on the road to union with the Secession synod, which took place in 1840. But union with the Seceders diminished Cooke's authority in what was now the general assembly of the Presbyterian Church in Ireland, and in the 1840s he was confronted by a renaissance of Presbyterian liberalism. In 1843, angered by the Disruption of the Church of Scotland and problems relating to the legality of marriages by Presbyterian ministers, the general assembly passed a resolution calling for better representation of Presbyterian interests in parliament, to which Cooke responded by withdrawing from the assembly until the resolution was rescinded in 1847. His absence from the assembly did not prevent his involvement in the negotiations between his church and the government over the foundation of the Queen's Colleges.

Cooke had finally succeeded in breaking his church's links with the Belfast Institution, and he played a significant part in an agreement between church and government by which the government endowed chairs in theological subjects for a Presbyterian college and the church recognized the Queen's Colleges for their ministerial students' pre-theological education. Cooke was considered as a possible first president of the Belfast Queen's College, but his increasingly strident anti-Catholicism ruled him out. A Presbyterian, the Revd P. S. Henry of Armagh, was appointed, and Cooke succeeded him as agent for the distribution of the *regium donum* at a salary of £320 a year. He was also appointed professor of sacred rhetoric and catechetics by the general assembly in the Presbyterian theological faculty in 1847 and president of the Presbyterian Theological College, which was opened in 1853. Compelled by the law of the church to resign his May Street pastorate, he continued a constant supplier of the pulpit until his retirement in 1867. He had been moderator of the general assembly in 1841 and was so honoured again in 1862.

Cooke continued to champion the causes of political Conservatism and unionism. His greatest political triumph was in 1841 when Daniel O'Connell, visiting Belfast to advocate the repeal of the union, declined to accept Cooke's challenge to debate the subject, and he was hailed as the 'cook who dish'd Dan'. It is often said that Cooke changed the political outlook of the Ulster Presbyterians from the radicalism and republicanism of the eighteenth century to Conservatism and unionism in the nineteenth, but this must be qualified. Irish Presbyterians may have become unionists, but they did not become Conservatives until Gladstone made home rule Liberal Party policy in 1886. Cooke's criticisms of the tenant-right movement in the 1850s, which was supported by many Presbyterian tenant farmers, lost him much popularity, and few Presbyterians shared his support for the Church of Ireland or responded to his deathbed appeal to Ulster's electorate to vote tory and save the Church of Ireland from disestablishment in 1868. He died at his home, 124 Ormeau Road, Belfast, on 13 December 1868, his wife and most of his thirteen children having predeceased him. He was accorded a civic funeral and burial on 18 December in Balmoral cemetery, Belfast; in 1876 his statue was placed in the centre of that city. Many of his sermons and addresses were published, but are regarded as failing to convey the dramatic impact of his oratory.

**Assessment** Few have articulated as effectively as Henry Cooke the distinctive and emotive emphases of nineteenth- and twentieth-century Ulster protestantism—evangelicalism, anti-Catholicism, and unionism in politics. Irish Presbyterians have traditionally honoured him as the Athanasius of their church, but many have deplored his identification of the interest of protestantism with unionism. J. L. Porter's biography is indispensable but uncritical, while John Jamieson, the historian of the Belfast Academical Institution, debunks him as a self-seeking demagogue. A study by R. F. G. Holmes (1981) is sympathetic but not uncritical.    FINLAY HOLMES

**Sources** J. L. Porter, *The life and times of Henry Cooke, D.D.*, [new edn] (1875) • F. Holmes, *Henry Cooke* (1981) • *Belfast News-Letter* (14 Dec 1868) • *Banner of Ulster* (17 Dec 1868) • R. F. G. Holmes, 'Henry Cooke, 1788–1868', MLitt diss., University of Dublin, 1970 [full bibliography, incl. Cooke's pubd addresses and sermons] • R. F. G. Holmes, 'Dr Henry Cooke: the Athanasius of Irish presbyterianism', *Religious motivation: biographical and sociological problems for the church historian*, ed. D. Baker, SCH, 15 (1978), 367–80 • *Belfast News-Letter* (1814–76) • *Northern Whig* (1825–50) • *Banner of Ulster* (1842–52) • records of Henry Cooke, Presbyterian Historical Society of Ireland, Church House, Belfast • J. A. Crozier, *The life of the Rev. Henry Montgomery* (1875) • J. Jamieson, 'The influence of the Rev. Henry Cooke on the political life of Ulster', MA diss., Queen's University, Belfast, 1951 • J. Jamieson, *The history of the Royal Belfast Academical Institution, 1810–1960* (1959, [1960]) • R. Allen, *The Presbyterian College, Belfast, 1853–1953* (1954) • A. McCreery, *The Presbyterian ministers of Killyleagh* (1875) • J. S. Reid and W. D. Killen, *History of the Presbyterian church in Ireland*, new edn, 3 (1867) • R. F. G. Holmes, *Magee, 1865–1965* (1965) • J. Gamble, *A view of society and manners in the north of Ireland in the summer and autumn of 1812* (1813) • D. Kennedy, 'Education and the people', *Social life in Ireland, 1800–45*, ed. R. B. McDowell (1957)

**Archives** Presbyterian Historical Society of Ireland, Belfast, archives | BL, corresp. with Lord Aberdeen, Add. MSS 43248–43249 • BL, corresp. with Sir Robert Peel, Add. MSS 40380–40559 • U. Edin., New College, letters to Thomas Chalmers

**Likenesses** D. Macnee, oils, *c*.1856, Ulster Museum, Belfast [*see illus.*] • group photograph, *c*.1863 (with the Presbyterian College Faculty), Union Theological College, Belfast, Faculty Room • McFarlane and Erskine, lithograph, pubd 1873 (after photograph), BM • statue, 1876, central Belfast • W. Holl, stipple and line engraving (after photograph), NPG • C. Turner, mezzotint (after J. Syme), BM • marble bust; presented to May Street Church, Belfast, in 1841 • oils, Ulster Museum, Belfast • photograph, repro. in Porter, *Life and times of Henry Cooke*

**Wealth at death** under £200: probate, 2 Nov 1869, *CGPLA Ire.*

**Cooke, John** (*d.* in or before **1614**), playwright, was the author of a comedy entitled *Greene's Tu quoque, or, The Cittie Gallant*, published in 1614 with a preface by Thomas Heywood. Another edition appeared in 1622 and there is also an undated quarto, possibly from as late as 1640. The play was performed at court by Queen Anne's men on 9 and 11 November 1611. The noted clown Thomas Greene took the part of Bubble, the Cittie Gallant, who constantly has on his lips the words 'Tu quoque', hence the origin of the first title. Entered in the Stationers' register under date 22 May 1604 is 'to William Cotton, Fyftie epigrams written by J. Cooke, Gent'; two editions of this survive, both undated.

Cooke may have been the John Cooke who stood surety to a loan of £20 to several of the shareholders in the Whitefriars syndicate (manager of the King's Revels company of actors). The loan was made on 16 October 1607 by William Cooke, a haberdasher. A link between Cooke and this company might explain the explicit borrowings in *Tu quoque* from *Ram Alley*, Lording Barry's Whitefriars play. It has been argued that Cooke may have been writing for the Whitefriars syndicate about the time of *Ram Alley* (1607–8) and may simply have reappropriated his own scenes from that play when he wrote *Tu quoque* (Bly, 361).

Heywood's *A Pleasant Conceited Comedie, wherein is Shewed, how a Man may Chuse a Good Wife from a Bad* is attributed, in a manuscript note on the title-page of a British Museum copy of the edition of 1602, to Joshua Cooke, whose name is otherwise unknown. John Cooke died before the publication of *Tu quoque* in 1614.

A. H. BULLEN, rev. MATTHEW STEGGLE

**Sources** J. Cooke, *Greene's Tu quoque, or, The cittie gallant*, ed. A. J. Berman (1984) • *The control and censorship of Caroline drama: the records of Sir Henry Herbert, master of the revels, 1623–73*, ed. N. W. Bawcutt (1996) • W. W. Greg, *Dramatic documents from the Elizabethan playhouses* (1931) • M. Bly, 'John Cooke: a playwright connected to the Whitefriars', *N&Q*, 243 (1998), 360–61

**Cooke, Sir John** (1666–1710), lawyer, was born on 29 August 1666, the third son of John Cooke of Whitechapel, London, surveyor of the customs, and his wife, Mary Bathurst. He was admitted to Merchant Taylors' School in 1673, and from there was elected to St John's College, Oxford, in 1684. While still a student, being a supporter of William III, he obtained a lieutenant's commission in an infantry regiment, and served in Ireland at the time of the battle of the Boyne. On returning to Oxford he resumed his studies, and graduated BCL in 1691 and DCL in 1694.

He was admitted as an advocate of the court of arches on 20 October 1694, and three days later became a member of Doctors' Commons. On 19 December 1695 he married Mary (*d.* 1709), the only daughter of Matthew and Mary Bateman, of London; the couple had one daughter. In 1699 Cooke served as counsel for Archbishop Tenison in the House of Lords to justify the archbishop's deprivation of Dr Thomas Watson from the bishopric of St David's. Cooke was almost certainly the author of the anonymous pamphlet *A Summary View of the Articles Exhibited Against the Late Bishop of St. David's* (1701), which defended the archbishop's proceedings against Watson and countered the claim that a bishop could only be deprived in a synod. Robert Ferguson, who wrote in support of Watson, described this pamphlet as 'scurrilous and virulent' and its author as a 'mercenary tool' of the archbishop (Ferguson, 64).

On 21 May 1701 Cooke received the honour of knighthood, and on 26 July of that year William III appointed him advocate-general. His competitor for that position was Dr Thomas Lane, who had been a captain of horse on King James's side at the battle of the Boyne, where he was wounded. When told that both men were good advocates but that 'the first fought against you, the other fought for you', the king said: 'Oh, I will have my own fellow soldier' (Lansdowne MS, 987/201). In 1702 Cooke served as a commissioner to negotiate a union between England and Scotland, and in the same year he was named to the renewed commission for building St Paul's. On 11 March 1703 Archbishop Tenison appointed Cooke to succeed Dr George Oxenden as official principal and dean of the arches. He also named him as his vicar-general, and as dean and commissary of the peculiars belonging to the archbishop.

In 1706 Cooke was appointed clerk of the pipe in the exchequer. He died at his house in Great Knight Rider Street, London, on 31 March 1710, and was buried at St Mary's, Whitechapel, on 2 April.

THOMPSON COOPER, rev. BRIAN P. LEVACK

**Sources** [J. Cooke], *A summary view of the articles exhibited against the late bishop of St. David's and of the proofs made thereon* (1701) • G. D. Squibb, *Doctors' Commons: a history of the College of Advocates and Doctors of Law* (1977), 89, 117, 185, 226 n.l. • *Le Neve's Pedigrees of the knights*, ed. G. W. Marshall, Harleian Society, 8 (1873), 475 • 'Remains of Sir John Cook', in Bishop Kennett's collections, vol. 53, BL, Lansdowne MS 987/201 • Mrs E. P. Hart, ed., *Merchant Taylors' School register, 1561–1934*, 1 (1936) • [R. Ferguson], *A large review of the summary view of the articles exhibited against the Bishop of St. David's and of the proofs made thereon* (1702), 64 • G. H., *The extraordinary case of the Bishop of St. David's* (1703), 9 • Foster, *Alum. Oxon.* • C. J. Robinson, ed., *A register of the scholars admitted into Merchant Taylors' School, from AD 1562 to 1874*, 1 (1882), 280 • M. J. Simmonds, *Merchant Taylor fellows of St John's College, Oxford* (1943), 43–4 • *APS*, 1702–7, appx, pp. 145–204 • *CSP dom.*, 1700–02, p. 352, 392; 1702–3, pp. 313, 484 • *State trials*, 14.455, 469 • *The history of the reign of Queen Anne, digested into annals* (1711), 9.412–13 • 'Sir John Coke's opinion about the Danish ship', BL, Add. MS 37354, fol. 465

**Archives** BL, Add. MS

**Likenesses** portrait, St John's College, Oxford

**Cooke, John** (1730/31–1810), publisher, first appears, according to the *Dictionary of National Biography*, as an assistant to Alexander Hogg, one of the first to publish cheap 'Paternoster Row numbers', or standard popular works issued in weekly parts. In this line of publishing Cooke made a fortune, successively setting up shop in London at the sign of the King's Arms in Great Turnstile, Holborn (1756), opposite St Clement's in the Strand (1758), and at Shakespear's Head, first behind the chapter house in St Paul's Churchyard (1759), then in Paternoster Row (1761 onwards). Religious works, practical manuals, and jest books dominated his work; nearly half of fifty-four titles in his *c.*1770 catalogue contain the words 'complete' or 'universal', as in *The Complete English Brewer* and *The Gardener's Universal Guide*. His folios and quartos were sold in parts, each 6*d.* number 'enriched' with a copperplate-engraving. Keen attention to advertising these illustrations was displayed in his catalogue of *c.*1784, a sign that his son Charles Cooke [*see below*] was now active in the concern. Depictions of torture and 'general Scenes of Pagan Barbarity and Popish Cruelty', for example, adorned Southwell's *New Book of Martyrs*. Likewise the *Universal Family Bible* (called Southwell's, though compiled by Robert Sanders) was 'embellished' with 100 plates 'taken from the finest Paintings of the most esteemed Masters'. The many editions of this title reportedly netted the publisher £30,000.

On 18 January 1773 Cooke was made a freeman and liveryman of the Musicians' Company, and was made steward in 1778. Between 1774 and 1782 he served on the city's common council for the ward of Farringdon Within. He died at his home in York Place, Kingsland Road, London, on 25 February 1810, aged seventy-nine.

**Charles Cooke** (1759/60–1816), publisher, was bound to the stationer Henry Cooke on 4 April 1775. He was freed on 9 April 1782, and was made a liveryman of the Stationers' Company the following month. He succeeded to his father's business about 1789, and further refined the art of serial publication. Illustrations had been made integral to a series of pocket editions by John Bell in his *Poets of Great Britain* (109 vols., 1776–82). Cooke's innovation was to apply this formula to several genres in a co-ordinated fashion. By marketing parallel series of novelists, poets, essayists, historians, and devotional authors—in uniform pocket editions, all 'Superbly Embellished'—and by adding plays to his list (he bought up Bell's British Theatre), Cooke became the first purveyor of a full range of English classics. One series alone, the *Select British Poets* (56 vols., 1794–1805), included more than 200 engravings. Commissions on this scale lend credibility to the claim that, in the annals of book illustration, Cooke helped to provide 'the first steady market for the work of English engravers and artists' (Amory, 140). The engraver Abraham Raimbach thought him a 'rather pompous gentleman publisher', inclined to 'dispense his patronage among the hungry artists, with an air of conscious superiority' (*Memoirs and Recollections*, 25). For 2s. Cooke offered deluxe imprints on vellum paper with hand-coloured stipple engravings, and for 1s. a 'superior edition', but the 'cheap edition' was his stock-in-trade. 'How I loved those little sixpenny numbers', testified Leigh Hunt about his boyhood enthusiasm;

> I doted on their size; I doted on their type, on their ornaments, on their wrappers, containing lists of other poets, and on the engravings from Kirk. I bought them over and over again, and used to get up select sets, which disappeared like buttered crumpets; for I could resist neither giving them away, nor possessing them. (Hunt, 77)

By 1803 Cooke had amassed a fortune sufficient to build at Walthamstow 'a sort of baronial mansion', as the bibliographer T. F. Dibdin called it (Dibdin, 749), overlooking the countryside—whence its name, Belle Vue. A description of the house, dubbed Cooke's Folly by locals, is given along with a picture in Bosworth's *Some Walthamstow Houses* (pp. 31–8). Between 1805 and 1816, like his father, Cooke was a member of the common council for the ward of Farringdon Within. He died on 16 April 1816, aged fifty-six, leaving a widow, Sarah. THOMAS BONNELL

**Sources** *GM*, 1st ser., 80/1 (1810), 386 · *GM*, 1st ser., 86/1 (1816), 382 · I. Maxted, *The London book trades, 1775–1800: a preliminary checklist of members* (1977) · L. Hunt, *The autobiography of Leigh Hunt*, ed. J. E. Morpurgo (1949) · H. Amory, '"Proprietary illustration": the case of Cooke's *Tom Jones*', *An index of civilization*, ed. R. Harvey, W. Kirsop, and B. J. McMullin (1993), 137–47 · *Memoirs and recollections of the late Abraham Raimbach*, ed. M. T. S. Raimbach (1843) · T. F. Dibdin, *The library companion* (1824) · G. F. Bosworth, *Some Walthamstow houses and their interesting associations* (1924) · *Enumeration of Cooke's pocket editions of the most esteemed works in the English language* (1804) · *A catalogue of useful and entertaining books, printed for, and sold by J. Cooke* [1770] · *A new catalogue of useful, important, instructive and entertaining books, printed for, and sold by J. Cooke* (1784?) · *DNB* · 'The cheap movement in literature', *Book Lore* (June 1886), 10–12 · Nichols, *Illustrations* · Nichols, *Lit. anecdotes* · Stationers' Company, court book, Stationers' Hall, London, R 407 · list of freemen of the Musicians' Company, 1743–1831, GL, MS 3098 · D. F. McKenzie, ed., *Stationers' Company apprentices*, [3]: *1701–1800* (1978), no. 1981

**Archives** Bodl. Oxf., John Johnson collection · Liverpool Central Library, Hornby collection

**Wealth at death** ample: Dibdin, *Library companion*; Maxted, *London book trades* · income from *Universal Family Bible* at least £30,000: *GM* (1810), 386; (1816), 382

**Cooke, John** (1738–1823), Church of England clergyman, was educated at Trinity College, Cambridge (BA 1761, MA 1764), and was presented to the rectory of Denton, Buckinghamshire, on 2 August 1773. He was also chaplain to Greenwich Hospital, and a commissioner from 1773 until his death on 4 May 1823 at Greenwich Hospital.

Cooke published a number of works, including *An Historical Account of the Royal Hospital for Seamen at Greenwich* (1789). The sermon he preached at the opening of the chapel of the hospital on 20 September 1789, on the suitable theme of the preservation of St Paul from shipwreck on the island of Melita, was also published. In 1799 he wrote an account of the voyage of John, earl of Sandwich, round the Mediterranean (together with a memoir of the earl's life). He was survived by his wife, whose name is not known. J. M. RIGG, *rev.* ROBERT BROWN

**Sources** *GM*, 1st ser., 93/1 (1823), 260, 572

**Cooke, John** (*c.*1756–1838), physician, was born in Lancashire but was descended from a family from Edith Weston, Rutlandshire. He was educated at the school established by Philip Doddridge at Northampton, and at first intended to become a dissenting minister. He preached at Rochdale and at Preston but later turned his attention to medicine. He studied at Guy's Hospital in London, at Edinburgh, and at Leiden, where he graduated MD in 1781. His thesis was on the use of cinchona bark in cases where there was no rise of temperature.

Cooke settled in London and became physician to the Royal General Dispensary in Bartholomew Close. In April 1784, after a drawn-out contest with John Whitehead, he was elected physician to the London Hospital, an office he held for twenty-three years. He delivered the first clinical lectures ever given in that institution. In June the same year he was admitted a licentiate of the Royal College of Physicians. In 1799 he was requested by the lord mayor of London to investigate the death of two men thought to have died of the plague. Cooke showed that the fears were groundless. In 1807 he was elected FRCP, and ten years later he became a fellow of the Royal Society. He was censor at the College of Physicians in 1811 and 1820, and he delivered the Croonian lectures in 1819, 1820, and 1821, and the Harveian oration in 1828. He was president of the Medico-Chirurgical Society in 1822 and 1823.

In 1820 Cooke began the publication of *A Treatise on Nervous Diseases*, which was continued in 1821 and completed in 1823. An American edition, in one volume, was published in Boston in 1824. This work, based on Cooke's Croonian lectures, gives an account of the existing knowledge of hemiplegia, paraplegia, paralysis of separate nerves, epilepsy, apoplexy, lethargy, and hydrocephalus internus. Although it contains no important addition to medical knowledge, it shows considerable clinical acquaintance with the subject.

During his latter years Cooke gave up practice and went little into society. A fellow of the Antiquarian Society he was well-read and a classical scholar, and throughout life he studied and enjoyed Homer. He died at his house in Gower Street, London, on 1 January 1838.

NORMAN MOORE, rev. CAROLINE OVERY

**Sources** Munk, *Roll* · T. J. Pettigrew, *Medical portrait gallery: biographical memoirs of the most celebrated physicians, surgeons … who have contributed to the advancement of medical science*, 4 vols. in 2 [1838–40], vol. 1, pp. 1–4 · R. W. Innes Smith, *English-speaking students of medicine at the University of Leyden* (1932) · A. E. Clark-Kennedy, *The London: a study in the voluntary hospital system*, 2 vols. (1962–3)
**Likenesses** W. Holl, stipple, Wellcome L.; repro. in Pettigrew, *Medical portrait gallery*

**Cooke, John** (1763–1805), naval officer, entered the navy at the age of thirteen, on the *Eagle*, Lord Howe's flagship on the North American station; having remained in her through her whole commission, he was promoted lieutenant on 21 January 1779. He was then appointed to the *Superb*, with Sir Edward Hughes, in the East Indies; he was obliged to invalid from there, and was then appointed to the *Duke* with Captain Gardner, who went out to the West Indies and took a distinguished part in the action off Dominica on 12 April 1782. After the peace (treaty of Versailles, 1783) Gardner was for some time commodore at Jamaica, Cooke remaining with him as first lieutenant of the *Europa*. In 1790 he served for some time as a lieutenant of the *London*, flagship of Vice-Admiral Sir Alexander Hood, and in February 1793 was appointed first lieutenant of the *Royal George*, bearing Sir Alexander's flag. At Lord Howe's battle of 1 June 1794 in the north Atlantic he served as commander, having been promoted on 21 February that year, and a few weeks later, on 23 June, was made a captain. He then served for a year in Newfoundland as flag captain to Sir James Wallace, in the *Monarch*; on his return home he was appointed, in the spring of 1796, to command the *Nymphe*. On 9 March 1797 his ship, in company with the *San Fiorenzo*, captured the two French frigates *Résistance* and *Constance*. These were returning to France after landing a band of convicts in Fishguard Bay, in memory of which the *Résistance*, a fine vessel of forty-eight guns, received the name of *Fisgard* when recommissioned for the British navy. When the mutiny broke out in April and May the *Nymphe* was at Spithead, and her crew joined the mutineers. On Cooke's attempting to give assistance to Rear-Admiral John Colpoys, he was ordered by the mutineers to go on shore; nor was it thought expedient for him to rejoin the ship. Clearly he was not a 'popular' officer. Two years later he was appointed to the *Amethyst*, which he commanded in the channel until the peace of Amiens. In October 1804 Cooke was invited by Sir William Young, the commander-in-chief at Plymouth, to come as his flag captain; but a few months later, having applied for active service, he was appointed to the *Bellerophon*, in which he joined the fleet off Cadiz in the beginning of October 1805. To be in a general engagement with Nelson would, he used to say, crown all his military ambition. In the battle of Trafalgar (21 October 1805) the *Bellerophon* was the fifth ship of the lee line, and was thus early in action; in the thick of the fight Cooke received two musket balls in the chest. He fell, and died within a few minutes, saying with his last breath, 'Tell Lieutenant Cumby never to strike'. He was buried at sea. A monumental tablet to his memory was placed by his widow, of whom nothing is known, in the parish church of Donhead in Wiltshire.

J. K. LAUGHTON, rev. ANDREW LAMBERT

**Sources** K. Breen and R. L. DiNardo, 'Commissioned sea-officers of the Royal Navy', *Mariner's Mirror*, 81 (1995), 485 · 'Biographical memoir of the late John Cooke', *Naval Chronicle*, 17 (1807), 354–66
**Archives** NMM, letters to his brother, written before the battle of Trafalgar when in command of HMS *Bellerophon*
**Likenesses** L. F. Abbott, oils, NMM · oils, NMM

**Cooke, Joseph** (1775–1811), religious reformer and founder of the Methodist Unitarian Movement, was born near Dudley, Worcestershire, on 8 May 1775. His parents were poor, and his education was 'not what is generally esteemed a learned one' (Ashworth, 11). In 1799 he married Martha (1772/3–1849); they had three sons and two daughters.

Converted to Methodism at an early age, Cooke took up local preaching so successfully that he was taken on trial as an itinerant preacher by the Methodist conference meeting in 1795 and was appointed to Redruth in Cornwall, to St Austell in 1796, and in 1798 to Burslem, Staffordshire. In 1799 he was admitted as a full preacher and served acceptably in Brecon and Chester circuits. In August 1803 he went to Rochdale circuit, which was centred on the Union Street Chapel. Constant itinerancy helped secure uniformity, as a preacher did not remain long enough to impress upon the members his particular views or methods. However, Cooke had his own views, and his rational and orderly method of examining the Bible and the tenets of Methodism soon attracted wide and popular attention.

Two sermons preached at Rochdale early in 1805 caused immediate trouble, and complaints led to Cooke's being called to account at the conference held at Sheffield in August. The sermons centred on justification by faith and the witness of the spirit. John Wesley had taught early in his career that unless a justified sinner felt his sins were forgiven by personal assurance, his way of life was of no avail to salvation; Cooke preached that when someone believed and was penitent, but was not conscious of God's pardon, he was still freely forgiven. Wesley seemed to follow this line later in his life, but Methodists were split on the matter and Cooke had touched a raw nerve. He strongly defended himself, and after much discussion stated that he would leave these matters alone for one year. On this basis he was appointed to the Sunderland circuit. However Cooke did preach on these subjects and published the two controversial sermons in Rochdale only months afterwards, with a contentious preface.

At the 1806 conference Cooke was expelled with accusations on both sides of bad faith. He returned to Rochdale with a wife and family to support and no income. However, many of his hearers at Union Street Chapel seceded, and in the same year opened Providence Chapel in the High Street in which he could minister. At the opening service he stated: 'This chapel was built and opened, not for the purpose of preaching any system of doctrines taught by man, but for the purpose of communicating those truths, which after a diligent and impartial enquiry, may appear to me to be contained in the Scriptures' (McLachlan, *Methodist Unitarian Movement*, 16–17). Cooke was feeling his way theologically, and 'if he did not arrive at Unitarianism by the time of his death, at least he moved steadily in that direction' (ibid., 16).

Cooke preached widely in remote parts of Lancashire north of Manchester, and particularly at Newchurch in Rossendale, where a room was opened at Mill End in 1807 by his supporter John Ashworth (1779–1852), another ejected Methodist local preacher. By late 1809 Cooke had developed tuberculosis, and died in Rochdale on 14 March 1811. He was buried in the aisle of Providence Chapel. All his children had died by 1834, and there were no descendants.

Cooke had started what became known as the Methodist Unitarian Movement (the Cookites), developed in the next decade by Ashworth, James Taylor (d. 1856), and James Wilkinson (1787–1858). The Cookites first came to the attention of Unitarians as a result of an article in the *Monthly Repository* in May 1815. In 1818 the minister of the old Presbyterian congregation in Rochdale stated 'May not Mr Cooke be considered as the father of Unitarianism in the town?' (*Monthly Repository*, April 1818, 262). The movement revivified the old Presbyterian chapels in the area, and while by the 1840s it was spent as a separate force, its dynamic had made a significant impact on old dissent in Lancashire. A high proportion of the Rochdale Pioneers who in 1844 laid the basis for the modern co-operative movement were strongly influenced by the distinctive Methodist Unitarian approach to religion.

ALAN RUSTON

**Sources** J. Ashworth, *An account of the rise and progress of Unitarian doctrine at Rochdale, Newchurch, in Rossendale and other places formerly in connection with Rev. Joseph Cooke* (1817) · H. McLachlan, *The Methodist Unitarian movement* (1919) · H. McLachlan, *Essay and addresses* (1930), 213–29 · E. Wilbur, *A history of Unitarianism in Transylvania, England, and America* (1952), 335–6 · *Monthly Repository*, 10 (1815), 313–22 · *Monthly Repository*, 13 (1818), 262 · *Christian Reformer, or, New Evangelical Miscellany*, 2 (1816), 233–8, 461–7 · *Christian Reformer, or, Unitarian Magazine and Review*, new ser., 5 (1849), 637–8 [obit. of Martha Cooke] · *Christian Reformer, or, New Evangelical Miscellany*, 4 (1818), 57–67 · J. Cooke, *Two sermons preached at the Methodist Chapel, Rochdale*, 2nd edn (1806) · A. Ruston, 'New light on Joseph Cooke', *Transactions of the Unitarian Historical Society*, 21/3 (1995–8), 205–12
**Likenesses** photograph (after painting), repro. in McLachlan, *Methodist Unitarian movement*, frontispiece

**Cooke, Katherine**. *See* Killigrew, Katherine (c.1542–1583).

**Cooke, Linen**. *See* Cooke, Robert (d. c.1726).

**Cooke, Mary Lamley** (1841–1916), peace campaigner, was born on 3 August 1841 at Gastard in Wiltshire, eldest of the three children of James Cooke (1809–1888), schoolmaster and private tutor, and his wife, Phoebe (1811–1890). By the age of twenty-one James Cooke was headmaster of the Friends' school at Wigton, but he preferred private tutoring. The family moved to Darlington, where he taught the family of Joseph Pease, and then, after a short period in Manchester, to Cork. In her early years Mary Cooke also taught, though she devoted most of her time to taking care of her parents. She did, however, develop an early interest in the peace cause and was secretary of the Cork Peace Association. After her father's death in 1888, she moved with her mother to Wandsworth, to live with her brother's family, and embarked upon a career of peace advocacy.

In 1890 Cooke became the assistant secretary of the Peace Union, the central association of a network of more than thirty local Christian absolute pacifist groups set up by Priscilla Hannah Peckover and run mostly by Quaker women. The secretary at the time was another Quaker activist, Ellen Robinson (1840–1912), with whom Cooke travelled around the country addressing meetings in favour of international arbitration, mutual disarmament, and the involvement of women in the peace cause (Cooke took over as secretary in 1903 after Robinson retired). In 1896 she began to edit a peace journal, *War or Brotherhood?* (begun in 1889 as *Messiah's Kingdom*, the organ of the short-lived interdenominational Christian Union for Promoting International Concord). *War or Brotherhood?* was often more outspoken on political events than the peace committee of the Society of Friends, of which Mary Cooke was also a core member. In 1899, for example, the journal called for an immediate and specific protest against the Second South African War when the Society of Friends was unwilling to make such a protest. Although she had no party political influence, Cooke, along with influential Friends such as Edward Grubb and J. W. Graham, played a part in reminding Quakers of the importance to their faith of pacifism, at a time when the peace testimony was not central to the identity of many Friends and when the largely Quaker-funded Peace Society was increasingly moribund. *War or Brotherhood?* ceased publication in 1909, but Cooke continued to write pamphlets, in particular for use in schools.

With John Frederick Green (1855–1932) Cooke was joint honorary secretary of the first four occasions of the National Peace Congress (1904–7) and of the National Peace Council, which was originally set up to organize the congresses. The initial impetus for these gatherings came from the Friends' peace committee, which proclaimed 'the desirability of more closely uniting those interested in the promotion of Peace in the United Kingdom, with the object of a national growth of the Peace Movement'. During the Edwardian period the National Peace Council and the National Peace Congress were successful in co-opting many representatives and bodies of progressive opinion into the specifically organized peace movement. As this demonstrates, Mary Cooke, though an absolute pacifist, was keen to collaborate with non-absolutist peace activists both in Britain and abroad: as a delegate from the Peace Union and the Friends' peace committee she attended the international peace congresses which were held most years from 1889 to 1913, and at which were aired a variety of peace ideologies.

A frail, slight figure with a pronounced stoop, Mary Cooke was quiet and lacked a natural buoyancy of temperament. She was, however, a highly respected minister at the Kingston monthly meeting and sat on Friends' committees dealing with a variety of social subjects. Her pacifism was unshaken by the war, and she was soon to travel to a women's international congress at The Hague when laid low by illness. She died in Letchworth on 4 January 1916.

PAUL LAITY

**Sources** 'Dictionary of Quaker biography', RS Friends, Lond. [card index] · *Friends' Quarterly Examiner*, 50 (1916), 188–97 · *The Friend*, new ser., 56 (1916), 24 · *War or Brotherhood?*, 7–22 (1889–94) · P. Laity, 'The British peace movement, 1896–1916: ideas and dilemmas', DPhil diss., U. Oxf., 1995

**Wealth at death** £419 2*s*. 6*d*.: probate, 21 Feb 1916, *CGPLA Eng. & Wales*

**Cooke, Mildred**. *See* Cecil, Mildred, Lady Burghley (1526–1589).

**Cooke, Mordecai Cubitt** (1825–1914), naturalist and mycologist, was born on 12 July 1825 at the post office in Horning, Norfolk, the eldest in the family of five sons and three daughters of Mordecai Cooke (1799–1869), village shopkeeper, and his wife, Mary (1803–1885), postmistress and village herbalist, daughter of William Cubitt, schoolmaster, of Neatishead, Norfolk. Cooke was educated at the village dame-school until he was ten, and then to the age of thirteen by his uncle, James Cubitt, a Baptist minister, first in Ilford and later in Stratford upon Avon. He then spent a year at a commercial school at Neatishead before being apprenticed for five years to a wholesale draper in Norwich.

In 1844 Cooke moved to London, where he obtained employment as a clerk. Then, influenced by his aunt Naomi Treen (*née* Cubitt), a teacher at a Pestalozzian elementary school, he obtained in 1851 the post of master at Holy Trinity national school, Lambeth, where he was allowed to pioneer revolutionary teaching methods in natural history and to set up a school museum. He published influential articles in the *School and the Teacher* and helped to found a museum for London teachers. In 1859 he passed first class in botany in the first examination for teachers organized by the Department of Science and Art, his sole academic qualification. The same year he resigned from teaching, undertook a variety of part-time jobs, and published his first books; in 1862 he joined the civil service on the staff of the India Museum, where he remained until 1880.

Cooke was slight in build with grey eyes, red hair, and luxuriant red moustache and beard. On 4 January 1846 he married Sophia Elizabeth (1823–1897), daughter of Abraham Biggs, tobacconist, who brought with her her two-year-old illegitimate daughter, Annie Elizabeth Thornton Biggs (1844–1920). Cooke had no children with his wife, but from the age of seventeen Annie bore him three sons and a daughter. In 1871 Annie left Cooke to marry his step-second cousin, John Quincey Cubitt, but by 1875 had left Cubitt and returned to Cooke, bringing with her her young daughter by Cubitt. She then had two more sons and a daughter by Cooke before finally leaving him about 1890, taking with her Cubitt's daughter and Cooke's two youngest sons. Cooke gave her an allowance and she remained in touch with the family. Sophia apparently never left Cooke and died in 1897.

Cooke's lifelong passion for natural history began in childhood, and he made it his prime duty to popularize the subject, writing fourteen books for the layman. In 1862 he founded the Society of Amateur Botanists; in 1865 he was co-founder, with his publisher Robert Hardwicke, and editor, of the immensely popular magazine *Science Gossip*, and soon afterwards founded the Quekett Microscopical Club. He regarded fieldwork as of fundamental importance in the study of natural history.

Cooke's interest in fungi began while he was teaching, and in 1862 he published the first popular book on toadstools, *A Plain and Easy Account of British Fungi*. This was followed by *Rust, Smut, Mildew and Mould* (1865), on plant pathogenic fungi, which was used in teaching in America. He was now in close touch with the Revd M. J. Berkeley, the 'father of British mycology', whom he eventually succeeded as Britain's leading mycologist. As Cooke's name became known through his huge output of taxonomic works, especially the two-volume *Handbook of British Fungi* (1871) and the journal *Grevillea*, which he founded in 1875 and edited himself, he entered into a vast correspondence with distinguished mycologists worldwide. In 1880 he was seconded to the Royal Botanic Gardens, Kew, as its first cryptogamic botanist, and redoubled his mycological studies, publishing, among much else, his monumental eight-volume *Illustrations of British Fungi* (1881–91). In all he published about 350 books and papers.

In 1892, with an international reputation, Cooke retired, having sold his herbarium to Kew, but he continued to write, his *Fungoid Pests of Cultivated Plants* (1906) being very well received. He became a scientific adviser to the Royal Horticultural Society and travelled the country attending the fungus forays of natural history societies and popularizing fungi among the public.

Cooke could never forget his humble origins. He lived in an unfashionable part of London (from 1870 until 1898 at 146 Junction Road, Kentish Town), and had no financial reserves. He was ill at ease with the gentleman scientists of his day and was treated as a mere technician by many, and consequently never achieved any position of responsibility. Scientifically, however, he was no respecter of persons, and entered vigorously into the polemics of the day. He was happiest at the field meetings of natural history societies and the subsequent festivities, where he could give free rein to his talents as a ballad singer and after-dinner speaker. He was a considerable artist, illustrating many of his own books. Though a strict Baptist, teetotaller, and political progressive in his youth, he later left organized religion, enjoyed alcoholic refreshment, and joined the Primrose League. The modest honours he received were mainly from natural history societies, but in 1873 he was awarded the honorary degree of MA by Yale University, in 1902 the Victoria medal of honour by the Royal Horticultural Society, and in 1903 the gold medal of the Linnean Society. He was an honorary member of American, French, and Italian scientific societies.

Having become progressively weaker and almost blind,

Cooke died on 12 November 1914 at his daughter's home at Dunluce, 38 Lindley Avenue, Southsea, Hampshire, and was buried in the same grave as his wife, Sophia, in Islington cemetery. A clump of toadstools is carved on his headstone.　　　　　　　　　　　　MARY P. ENGLISH

**Sources** M. P. English, *Mordecai Cubitt Cooke: Victorian naturalist, mycologist, teacher and eccentric* (1987) · J. Ramsbottom, 'Mordecai Cubitt Cooke, 1825–1914', *Transactions of the British Mycological Society*, 5 (1914–16), 169–85 · m. cert. · d. cert. · private information (1993, 2004) [family MSS]
**Archives** BL OIOC, papers, MSS Eur. B 38–40 · RBG Kew, autobiographical notes · RBG Kew, herbarium · RBG Kew, corresp. and papers | NHM, corresp. with C. E. Broome and M. J. Berkeley · Norwich Central Library, Cookes of Horning MSS, W. C. Cooke
**Likenesses** photograph (aged forty-eight), RBG Kew · photograph, NHM, Quekett Microscopical Club · photograph (aged seventy-eight), British Mycological Society, Kew
**Wealth at death** £813 15s. 6d.: probate, 2 Dec 1914, CGPLA Eng. & Wales

**Cooke, Robert** (d. 1593), herald, was purportedly the son of a tanner. As a youth he was said to have been a member of the household of Sir Edmund Brudenell, a great collector of pedigrees. He matriculated at St John's College, Cambridge, in 1553, graduated BA in 1558, and proceeded MA in 1561. In January 1562 he was appointed Rose Blanche pursuivant, and he then became Chester herald. In May 1567 he became Clarenceux king of arms, and in that office he was an assiduous maker of visitations to register coats of arms and pedigrees in southern England, visiting his whole province at least once. Between 1584 and 1586 he was acting Garter king of arms between Sir Gilbert Dethick and his son William, and in that capacity he served on the embassy to deliver the Order of the Garter to Henri III of France. A dispute with one of the earl marshal's servants over a gratuity provides evidence that Cooke expected to succeed Sir Gilbert Dethick permanently as Garter, but despite the apparent patronage of the earl of Leicester, who also seems to have been responsible for Cooke's appointment as Chester herald, this fell through and William Dethick succeeded his father instead.

Cooke's tenure as Clarenceux was troubled, beginning with the orders issued in 1568 by the duke of Norfolk as earl marshal, controlling grants of arms made by the provincial kings of arms (Clarenceux and Norroy) and securing their records for the College of Arms. It culminated in a bitter dispute with the younger Dethick over the latter's attempts as Garter both to encroach on the traditional rights of the provincial kings to grant arms and to make his own visitations throughout England.

As a result of Dethick's attacks biographers have often discounted the accusations against Cooke in the understandable but *ad hominem* belief that Dethick is an untrustworthy witness. However, 'Lant's observations' on the officers of arms seem to bear Dethick out, at least in part. Regarding Cooke's linguistic deficiencies, an entry in the French chancery records suggests that one of the two gold chains supposedly given to Cooke by the French king was actually intended for his interpreter, suggesting that Cooke's French was inadequate for his diplomatic duties.

A more telling charge, though a common one among heralds, is that Cooke gave arms and crests 'without number to base and unworthy persons for his private gain only without the knowledge of the E[arle]. Marshall' ('Lant's observations', fol. 68v). Cooke himself answered this indirectly in a treatise on granting arms by arguing that decaying nobility possibly envied men of mean birth whose virtue none the less outshone the older aristocracy's.

Cooke seems to have made excellent financial business out of granting arms, though he may have displeased Queen Elizabeth by making too many supposedly unworthy gentlemen: Ralph Brooke, York herald, writing to Sir Robert Cotton in 1614, says that Cooke gave more than 500 coats of arms and that both Dethicks gave more. This may be an understatement, possibly a very substantial one. Yet Dethick also claims that even with this lucrative source of income in fees, Cooke nevertheless dissipated a £1000 gift from the queen.

'Lant's observations' also accuse Cooke of burying knights as if they were barons 'and some no Gentlemen as Esq$^{re}$' ('Lant's observations', fol. 68v). He did bury Sir Philip Sidney magnificently as a baron, but this seems justified by Sir Philip's title from the French crown. Sir William Dugdale denounced Cooke's employment of a painter–stainer as the start of that profession's encroachments on the herald's prerogatives to marshal aristocratic funerals. Cooke also kept his official books as his own property, contrary to orders; it is likely, however, that like many of his colleagues, he still considered these his own papers. At his death his books, precedents, visitations, and pedigrees were bought for the College of Arms. Finally, if all this were not enough, Dethick also alleged that Cooke married another man's wife.

As well as heraldic compilations, visitations, precedencies, heraldry treatises, and ordinaries of arms, Cooke wrote 'The armorie of nobiliti' on the English baronage with Robert Glover of Somerset and Thomas Lant, then Portcullis. This survives in several copies, most notably BL, Royal MS 18 C. XVII, a fine painted folio with colour portraits of each sovereign of varying accuracy: the portraits of Mary I and Elizabeth I were 'cutte out by reason of y$^e$ inconsiderate vnseemlynes of y$^e$ picture' (Cooke and others, 'The armorie of nobiliti', fols. 155v, 158v).

Whereas Noble praised Cooke for his diligence, later writers have been more critical. Sir Anthony Wagner condemns Cooke's pedigrees for their 'amateurishness', though he also notes that Cooke adopted Glover's improved pedigree form and apparently initiated the practice of making a pedigree official by having it signed by the person registering it. Whatever his failings, Cooke should not be judged wholly by the critical standards of later ages, especially as many of the charges against him stemmed from acrimony among Elizabethan heralds. He died and was buried at Hanworth in Cheshire in August 1593, leaving a daughter, Catherine, who married John Woodnote of Shavington, Cheshire.　　　　　J. F. R. DAY

**Sources** R. Cooke and others, 'The armorie of nobiliti', BL, Royal MS 18 C. XVII · R. Cooke, 'A briefe treatis w$^{ch}$ sheweth that the

giveing of armes is no wayes hurtfull to ye com[m] wealth', BL, Lansdowne MS 255, fol. 190v • BL, Burghley papers, 1593 [Cooke's books bought for the College of Arms, 1593], Lansdowne MS 75, fols. 68 ff. • R. Brooke, York herald, letter to Sir Robert Cotton, BL, Cotton MS Faustina, E. i, fol. 141 • William Dethick to Lord Burghley, BL, Cotton MS Faustina, E. i., fol. 140v • 'The grevaunces of Thomas Lant als Portcullis pursuivant of arms', BL, Cotton MS Faustina, E. i., fol. 133 • 'Clarenceux [Cooke] and Norroy [Flower] their answer delivered to the erle marshall in defence of their authorite to graunt arms, 1585', BL, Cotton MS Faustina, E. i., fols. 166 ff. • W. Dethick, petition to Elizabeth I, BL, Burghley papers, Lansdowne MS 108, fol. 179 • Dethick to the 'LLL Deputes' for earl marshal, BL, Burghley papers, Lansdowne MS 108, fol. 181 • 'Lant's observations', BL, Harley MS 6591, 'Officers and offices of armes', fol. 68v [in table form] • Cooper, *Ath. Cantab.*, vol. 2 • W. H. Godfrey, A. Wagner, and H. Stanford London, *The College of Arms, Queen Victoria Street* (1963) [incl. list of officers of arms] • P. Gwynn-Jones, *The art of heraldry: origins, symbols and designs* (1998) • M. Noble, *A history of the College of Arms* (1804) • A. Wagner, *Heralds of England: a history of the office and College of Arms* (1967) • A. R. Wagner, *The records and collections of the College of Arms* (1952) • Venn, *Alum. Cant.*, 1/1.386
**Archives** BL, notes on medieval peers, charters, and seals, Egerton MS 3872 • BL, Baronage of England and Wales, Visitation of Kent and the Armour of Nobility, Add. MSS 5504, 5532; Royal MS 18 C XVII • Bodl. Oxf., Baronage compilation • Coll. Arms, heraldic collections, pedigrees, and historical miscellanies • PRO
**Likenesses** T. Dawes, Rouge Croix, group portrait, c.1578 (Procession of the Order of the Garter), repro. in Wagner, *Heralds of England* • T. de Brij, engraving (after T. Lant), repro. in J. F. R. Day, 'Death be very proud: Sidney, subversion, and Elizabethan heraldic funerals', *Tudor political thought* (1995) • M. Gheeraerts, group portrait, engraving (after T. Dawes) • T. Lant, Coll. Arms, Sidney's funeral roll • portrait?, repro. in J. Dallaway, *Inquiries into the origin and progress of the science of heraldry in England* (1793)

**Cooke, Robert** (1549/50–1615), Church of England clergyman, was the son of William Gayle, also known as Cooke, of Beeston, Leeds, where he was baptized on 23 July 1550. (The name Cooke seems to have originated from the employment of generations of the Gayle family.) After attending Leeds grammar school, he matriculated at Brasenose College, Oxford, on 5 April 1567, aged seventeen, graduated BA on 27 June 1573, and was unanimously elected as a probationer fellow on 2 December that year. Appointed proctor in 1582, he carried out his duties conscientiously. A speech given on 10 April 1583 on his resignation vividly described the state of the university and the difficulties and animosity Cooke had encountered as proctor. Apparently he was not too discouraged. He proceeded BTh in 1584 and was appointed college bursar shortly afterwards.

Highly respected for his learning and skill in debate, Cooke seemed set for a long university career. But in June 1590 he resigned his fellowship and on 18 December was instituted vicar of Leeds on the presentation of the parishioners. He succeeded the aged Alexander Fawcett, who may have had popish sympathies and seems not to have been a preaching minister. Cooke's arrival signalled more than a routine change in personnel. Since 1570 protestant sympathies had been gradually gaining ground. The energetic town merchants were seeking to further the town's economic, political, and religious development, and with the aid of Henry Hastings, third earl of Huntingdon, who negotiated a reduction in price, they were able to secure the advowson in 1588. Cooke's uncle, Ralph Cooke, was a

leading figure in Leeds, but his appointment shortly afterwards may also have reflected the earl's influence. In his new position, ironically, Cooke found himself in a dispute with Christ Church, Oxford, over property in the town, to which both the parish church and the college had claims. The matter was resolved in 1596 by Matthew Hutton, archbishop of York.

Cooke's brand of puritan piety seems to have agreed well with the hopes of many of his influential parishioners; there is evidence from wills of the affection and respect in which they held him. He also found it necessary to arrange for the construction of galleries in the church, but these proved inadequate to accommodate the growing numbers of townspeople who attended Sunday services. Cooke also became a trustee of Wakefield grammar school.

Cooke was a zealous opponent of Catholicism; his *Censura quorundam scriptorum* (1614), dedicated to William James, bishop of Durham, strove 'to detect the numerous forgeries and unauthorized insertions made by Roman Catholic editors or transcribers in the works of the Fathers' (Taylor, 77). A manuscript once in the Leeds museum of Ralph Thoresby contained 'A learned disputation between Robert Cooke, B.D., and Cuthbert Johnson, alias William Darrell, before his majesty's council, and other learned men at York, an 1610'. Latterly Cooke was assisted by a curate, his brother, Alexander *Cooke, a militant puritan who would succeed him as vicar. On 20 July 1614 he was collated by Bishop James to the sixth prebend of Durham Cathedral. Robert Cooke died in Leeds on 1 January 1615, and was buried at Leeds parish church the following day.                                   STEPHEN WRIGHT

**Sources** R. Thoresby, *Vicaria Leodiensis, or, The history of the church of Leedes in Yorkshire* (1724) • R. Thoresby, *Ducatus Leodiensis, or, The topography of … Leedes*, ed. T. D. Whitaker, 2nd edn (1816) • *The diary of Ralph Thoresby*, ed. J. Hunter, 2 vols. (1830) • J. Crossley, note, *N&Q*, 4th ser., 11 (1873), 514 • R. V. Taylor, ed., *The biographia Leodiensis, or, Biographical sketches of the worthies of Leeds* (1865) • J. T. Cliffe, *The Yorkshire gentry from the Reformation to the civil war* (1969) • *Thoresby Miscellany*, Thoresby Society, 1 (1891) • J. W. Kirby, 'The rulers of Leeds: gentry, clothiers and merchants, c. 1425–1626', *The Thoresby Miscellany*, 18, 22–49, Thoresby Society, 59 (1985), 22–49 • R. Cooke, *Censura quorundam scriptorum* (1614) • *Reg. Oxf.*, 2.70 • [F. Madan], ed., *Brasenose College quatercentenary monographs*, 1, OHS, 52 (1909) • W. Bristow, *Musaeum Thoresbyanum* (1816)

**Cooke** [Cook], **Robert** [*called* Linen Cooke] (d. c.1726), vegetarian and author, the elder son of Robert Cooke, came of a family that settled in co. Cork in the early seventeenth century and prospered in the linen and other trades, particularly in Cork city and the town of Youghal. Reliable information on Cooke's genealogy and life is virtually limited to two sources: a biographical entry in *The Antient and Present State of … Waterford* (Dublin, 1746), whose author, the Dungarvan pharmacist Charles Smith, presumably knew Cooke at least by reputation; and a brief article in the magazine *The Patrician* for 1847 based on information supplied by a descendant of Cooke's brother William.

Cooke's grandfather Peter Cooke—allegedly of Norfolk

origin—was the first of his family to settle in co. Cork. His eldest son, Thomas, was father of another Thomas, an active Quaker, who died in 1706 having made a fortune in the linen trade which enabled him to acquire much land, including Dungallane near Kilworth: renamed Castle Cooke, it was the seat of the Cooke-Collis family down to 1921. Peter's second son, Robert Cooke, who served as an officer in the cavalry regiment raised among the protestant settlers of Munster by Roger Boyle, Lord Broghill, settled at Cappoquin, co. Waterford. Robert Cooke, later known as Linen Cooke, was his elder son. The younger son, William Cooke (d. 1742) of Camphire, was mayor of Youghal in 1708 and married a niece of the faith healer Valentine Greatrakes, 'the Stroker'.

Cooke inherited Cappoquin from his father but fled to England with many other protestant settlers upon the Catholic take-over of Ireland in 1689 and was among those outlawed as absentees by the Irish parliament of James II. He lived for a time at Ipswich, Suffolk, but returned to Ireland after the Williamite victory of 1691. He was twice married: his first wife was a woman of Bristol (a port with which he had commercial links); his second wife, Cicely, with whom he had three sons—John (of Youghal), Robert, and Josiah—and two daughters, appears to have survived him.

Like his cousin Thomas, Robert Cooke was a member of the Society of Friends, but he left it to pursue his own solitary quest for a relationship with the Almighty. In 1691 he published a pamphlet or broadside (partially reproduced by Smith) in which he explained his vegetarian and theological opinions. 'I am a Christian and a Protestant', he declared:

> and my Religion is to fear God and to keep his Commandments, to keep my soul undefiled from the worldly evil nature. I abhor the evil and love the good and have fellowship therein with all in every sect or gathered or scattered people. (Smith, 372)

In 1695 he was in correspondence with the Dublin merchant and Quaker Anthony Sharp.

Smith states that Cooke would 'neither eat fish, flesh, butter, &c., nor drank any fermented liquor, nor wore woollen cloaths, or any other produce of an animal' (Smith, 371) and relates anecdotes of his eccentricity. Cooke chose white cows rather than black and always had his coach drawn by white horses. On one occasion his servants caught a fox which had killed some of his poultry: Cooke assembled his employees and tenants, and having delivered a lengthy harangue on the fox's crime, ordered it to run the gauntlet of rods before letting it go. In his pamphlet Cooke declared that killing an animal would have done violence to his conscience, 'that innocent life in me', while he preferred 'water for drink and pulse (viz.) corn (and other vegetives) for food, and linen and other vegitives for rayment' as 'cleanest and wholesomest, and warm, and strengthening, and nourishing, and healthful' (ibid., 374). Cooke died at Cappoquin Castle about 1726, aged 'upwards of four score' (Smith, 374). In his will he directed that he should be buried with the family of his son

John 'in the cathedral or church called *tempul* in Youghal' and stipulated, perhaps unnecessarily, that his shroud be made of linen ('Fragments of family history').

JULIAN C. WALTON

**Sources** C. Smith, *The antient and present state of the county and city of Waterford* (1746), 371–4 · 'Fragments of family history: Robert Cooke, esq., called "Linen Cooke"', *The Patrician*, 4 (1847), 64–5 · *DNB* · R. ffolliott, 'Some account of the family of Large and their connections', 1958, Irish Genealogical Research Society, London, 78–84 [chap. 3: 'Cooke-Collis of Castle Cooke'] · Burke, *Gen. GB* (1848) [see also successive edns] · R. L. Greaves, *Dublin's merchant-Quaker: Anthony Sharp and the community of Friends, 1643–1707* (1998), 118–19, 244–5, 315 · will of Thomas Cooke, proved 7 Sept 1706, prerogative grant book, 1704–6, NA Ire. [reproduced in ffolliott, 'Some account'] · W. King, *The state of the protestants of Ireland under the late King James's government* (1691)
**Archives** NL Ire., Joly pamphlets, no. 2143

**Cooke, Robert** (1768–1814), organist and composer, was born in Westminster, London, the second son of the organist and composer Dr Benjamin *Cooke (1734–1793) and his wife, Mary Jackson (d. 1784). He succeeded his father as organist of St Martin-in-the-Fields in 1793 and was appointed organist at Westminster Abbey on the death of Samuel Arnold in 1802; by 1805 he was master of the choristers there. Cooke was one of the first members of the Philharmonic Society. His religious compositions include an evening service in C (1806) and a collection of chants for daily use in Westminster Abbey. He published a collection of eight glees in 1805, and three of his thirty-three glees won Catch Club prizes. He drowned in the River Thames near Millbank on 22 or 23 August 1814, and it was assumed he had taken his own life. He was buried in Westminster Abbey.

EDWARD HERON-ALLEN, rev. ANNE PIMLOTT BAKER

**Sources** *New Grove* · H. W. Shaw, *The succession of organists of the Chapel Royal and the cathedrals of England and Wales from c.1538* (1991), 336 · D. Baptie, *Sketches of the English glee composers: historical, biographical and critical (from about 1735–1866)* [1896], 71–2 · J. S. Bumpus, *A history of English cathedral music, 1549–1889*, 2 vols. [1908], 318–20 · [J. S. Sainsbury], ed., *A dictionary of musicians*, 2 vols. (1824)

**Cooke, Robert** (c.1820–1882), Roman Catholic priest, was born in Waterford about 1820. He studied medicine for a time but, during a visit to France, joined the Roman Catholic congregation of the Oblates of Mary Immaculate. After being ordained a priest he was stationed at the residence of the Catholic convert A. P. De Lisle, Grace Dieu Manor, Leicestershire, where he spent much of his time preaching in the open air in the surrounding towns and villages. In 1847 he was sent to Everingham Park, Yorkshire, and established missions at the nearby towns of Howden and Pocklington. In 1851 he moved to Leeds, where he founded another new mission in the town. Cooke then visited Ireland and established a house of the Oblates at Inchicore; he later founded another at Kilburn in London.

In 1875 Cooke published: *Catholic Memories of the Tower of London*, and in 1879 and 1882 the two volumes of a biography of the founder of his order entitled *Sketches of the life of Mgr. de Mazenod, bishop of Marseilles, and founder of the Oblates of Mary Immaculate, and of the missionary labours of the*

*French Oblates of Mary Immaculate*. His last missionary endeavour was in the East End of London, where he founded the church of the English Martyrs, Tower Hill. He died in Tower Hill on 18 June 1882.

DAVID HUDDLESTON

**Sources** Gillow, *Lit. biog. hist.* · BL cat. · *The Tablet* (24 June 1882) · *The Athenaeum* (31 May 1879), 697

**Cooke, Roger** (*b.* 1552, *d.* after 1612?), alchemist, was born on 1 February 1552. In 1567, at the age of fourteen, he became an assistant to John Dee, with whom he lived for the next fourteen years. Most of the little that is known about Cooke is derived from the diary of John Dee. Cooke seems to have assisted Dee in his alchemical experiments, and may have scryed (crystal gazed) for him. On 28 December 1579 Dee revealed an alchemical secret to Cooke, but on 12 July 1581, when Cooke was not invited to witness an alchemical experiment, they argued. On 5 September Cooke asked Dee's permission to leave him; he departed two days later. Dee describes Cooke as of a melancholy nature, and sought to rectify the ill sentiment between them by promising Cooke £100 as soon as he could afford it, as well as 'some pretty alchemical experiments, wheruppon he might honestly live' (*Private Diary*, 13).

No records of Cooke's life for the two decades after he left Dee have been located, though he seems to have had some association with Francis Anthony, the London medical practitioner and alchemist. On 30 September 1600 Cooke returned to Dee, 'offred and promised his faithfull and diligent care and help, to the best of his skill and powre, in the processes chymicall, and that he will rather do so then to be with any in England' (*Private Diary*, 63). Dee agreed, and on 1 November Cooke began his distillations. The reconciliation was short-lived, however, and on 2 February 1601 Dee's son, Arthur, discovered that Cooke was plotting against Dee; despite a series of further reconciliations, Cooke departed for London on 2 March of that year.

This is probably the same Roger Cooke who was employed by Henry *Percy, 'the Wizard Earl', in building and running a still house in the Tower between 1606 and at least 1609. He might also be the Roger Cooke who assisted the experiments of Cornelis Drebbel at the court of Rudolf II and returned to England late in 1612. He seems not to have written anything, and nothing is known about his death.

LAUREN KASSELL

**Sources** *The private diary of Dr John Dee*, ed. J. O. Halliwell, CS, 19 (1842) · J. Roberts and A. G. Watson, eds., *John Dee's library catalogue* (1990) · J. W. Shirley, 'The scientific experiments of Sir Walter Ralegh, the Wizard Earl and the three magi in the tower, 1603–1617', *Ambix*, 4 (1949–51), 52–66 · Bodl. Oxf., MS Ashmole 423, fol. 294 · L. E. Harris, *The two Netherlanders: Humphrey Bradley and Cornelis Drebbel* (1961), 144

**Cooke, Sir Samuel Burgess Ridgway** (1912–1978), judge, was born on 16 March 1912 at 23 Kensington Road, Lancaster, the only child of Samuel Cooke (*d. c.*1948), railway clerk, and his wife, Jessie Lennox Ridgway (*d.* 1966), a teacher. Scholarships enabled Cooke to enter Lancaster Royal Grammar School and then in 1930 Gonville and Caius College, Cambridge. He took firsts in both classics

and the law tripos and in 1934, holding left-wing views, was president of the Cambridge Union Society. On 28 July 1934 he married Nancy Isabel Bulmer (1910–2000); they had two sons.

In November 1936 (having been placed first in the bar final examination and awarded a certificate of honour) Cooke was called to the bar by Lincoln's Inn, and in 1938 he entered the office of the parliamentary counsel. Cooke took particular pride in his contribution to the drafting of the 1944 Butler Education Act and the Crown Proceedings Act 1947 (which removed ancient obstructions to pursuing legal claims against the government).

The post-war years saw changes, both personal and professional, in Cooke's life. His first marriage had broken down, and on 10 January 1945 he married the poet and writer Diana Witherby (*b.* 1915) with whom he was also to have two sons. Professionally, his Whitehall colleagues were not alone in recognizing his abilities, and in 1946 he did not feel able to resist an invitation to re-enter private practice from the chambers of Patrick Devlin KC (subsequently Lord Devlin).

The expertise which Cooke had acquired in the parliamentary counsel office was soon put to use in his work during 1947 on legal aspects of the independence of India and Pakistan as constitutional adviser to the viceroy, Lord Mountbatten. After returning from India, Cooke rapidly built up an impressive and broadly based practice at the bar. He continued to advise the crown on matters of importance, but the bulk of his practice was in high-class commercial advisory work. He was also a powerful and lucid advocate, highly regarded for the research and scholarship which underpinned his arguments.

Cooke took silk in 1960 and was elected a bencher of Lincoln's Inn in 1966. In 1967 he was knighted, and in that year Lord Chancellor Gardiner invited him to accept appointment as a judge of the High Court, Queen's Bench Division. On the bench he was careful, meticulous, and unfailingly courteous to all those who appeared before him. But Cooke had already begun to show symptoms of a disease of the nervous system—not diagnosed at the time—which affected his balance and his speech. The ebullient and gregarious barrister with epicurean tastes and a liking for fast cars and National Hunt racing was transformed into a quiet and apparently retiring personality.

Cooke had never enjoyed certain aspects of the life of a judge on circuit, and in the circumstances it was no doubt something of a relief when, in January 1973, Lord Chancellor Hailsham offered him appointment as chairman of the Law Commission (the body, established by the Law Commissions Act 1965 to undertake systematic development and reform of the law). Cooke immediately faced difficult decisions, not least in dealing with the legacy of projects undertaken in the enthusiasm of the commission's early years but which had not been brought to successful completion. For example, the Law Commission had lavished much intellectual effort on attempts to codify the law of contract, but under Cooke's chairmanship it was decided to concentrate on examining those aspects of contract law (such as exemption clauses) which seemed in practice to give rise to injustice or particular difficulty. A second problem was how best to make progress with the commission's massive project on the law governing the ownership of matrimonial property. Cooke persuaded the commission that comprehensive legislation imposing co-ownership as found in European community of property systems would necessarily be so complex as to jeopardize its acceptability. But his role at the commission was not limited to retrenchment. Under his chairmanship the commission began work which eventually led to much important legislation (for example, the Enduring Powers of Attorney Act 1985), but the most important report completed under his leadership in terms of impact on the development of English law may well have been the *Report on Remedies in Administrative Law* (1976). The new procedure (introduced by rules of court) gave the judiciary the impetus to create what has now become a distinctive and greatly expanded system for the judicial review of administrative actions.

The ideological climate of the mid-1970s was profoundly different from that which had influenced the commission's founders, committed as they had been to ambitious schemes for major institutional change; and the fact that the Law Commission survived as a respected and effective mechanism for law reform can in large measure be attributed to Cooke's ability as an effective manager of change at a crucial period. It is true that the increasingly apparent effects of Cooke's illness made it impossible for him to emulate the presentational achievements of his predecessor Sir Leslie (later Lord) Scarman, but Cooke's legal skills won the respect of all with whom he had dealings, while the sense of humour and personal modesty which had endeared Sammy Cooke to both lay and professional clients at the bar made him greatly loved by colleagues and the commission's staff.

Cooke died after a long illness at his country home, Rectory Farm, Plumpton, near Towcester, Northamptonshire, on 12 April 1978. He was buried on 15 April at Weedon Lois church, Towcester.                                    S. M. CRETNEY

**Sources** *The Times* (14 April 1978) • *The Times* (21 April 1978) • *Daily Telegraph* (14 April 1978) • J. Venn and others, eds., *Biographical history of Gonville and Caius College*, 5: *Admissions from 1911 to 1932* (1948) • 1934, records of Cambridge Union Society • archives, Lincoln's Inn, London • *WW* • *British Imperial Calendar and Civil Service List* (1938) • Archives of Royal Grammar School, Lancaster • *India: the transfer of power, 1942–7*, 9–12 (1980–83) • *8th to 13th annual reports of the law commission, 1972–1978*, HMSO • R. T. Oerton, *A lament for the law commission* (1987) • S. M. Cretney, *Law, law reform and the family* (1998), chap. 1 • private information (2004) • d. cert. • b. cert.
**Likenesses** photograph, Lincoln's Inn, London • photograph, law commission, London
**Wealth at death** £133,102: probate, 3 July 1978, *CGPLA Eng. & Wales*

**Cooke, Sophia** (1814–1895), missionary and schoolmistress, was born in the Norfolk village of Hilborough, on 27 February 1814, attended school in Bury St Edmunds, and was a governess in Suffolk for twenty years before leaving England in March 1853 to become superintendent of the Chinese Girls' School in Singapore as agent for the Society for Promoting Female Education in the East. Tall, blonde, blue-eyed, with a lively sense of humour, she was immediately welcomed into the expatriate British community, but felt her main mission was among Asians. The only other protestant missionary in Singapore at that time was a self-supporting independent, Benjamin Keasberry, who worked among the Malays.

In 1856 Sophia Cooke (a lifelong Anglican) persuaded the Anglican chaplain to begin mission work among the Chinese and invited a presbyterian Chinese catechist from Amoy (Xiamen) to conduct Singapore's first Chinese-language services in her school compound. Providing a sound general education, along with Christian teaching and practical housewifery skills, the Chinese Girls' School was also a refuge for orphans and adolescents rescued from prostitution. Many school leavers went on to spread the Christian message and minister to the poor and sick in Singapore, China, and as far afield as Korea. Except for her own salary Sophia Cooke had to raise all the funds for the school and for outside charity work. Much came from bazaars of handwork provided by well wishers in Britain, with whom Sophia Cooke kept up an indefatigable correspondence, while expatriate Singapore businessmen gave willingly to her good causes.

The school was the most important of many charitable works. Sophia Cooke organized regular Bible classes for Chinese women, policemen, soldiers, and others, and each week she devoted one day to visiting Asian wards in the general and military hospitals. In 1865 she established the first of two 'ragged schools' for indigent mothers and children, and ten years later she started the YWCA in Singapore on an informal basis. In 1882 she opened the Sailors' Rest near the docks; this offered cheerful surroundings, cheap beds, and food, as well as Bible classes which she conducted herself, winning many converts.

Initially enjoying excellent health, it was nearly ten years before Sophia Cooke took her first home leave, but in 1869 she became seriously ill and subsequently had to spend extended periods of sick leave in England. Defying acute rheumatism and failing sight, she continued to work a six-day week, holding Bible readings and visiting the sick. Too frail to climb the stairs to Chinese tenements, she was carried upstairs by police constables.

After being confined to bed for just a fortnight, Sophia Cooke died of erysipelas in Singapore on 14 September 1895 and was buried the same day. With policemen as pall bearers, the funeral was attended by many soldiers, sailors, and Chinese families, in addition to leading officials and clergy of all denominations. The following Sunday a memorial service was held in St Andrew's Cathedral, Singapore.

Sophia Cooke was a capable, practical missionary, admired and respected alike by pupils, policemen, sailors, soldiers, officials, and business people, and encouraging all Christians to work together for the welfare of others.

C. M. TURNBULL

**Sources** E. A. Walker, *Sophia Cooke, or, Forty–two years' work in Singapore* (1899) • W. Makepeace, G. E. Brooke, and R. St J. Braddell, *One hundred years of Singapore*, 2 vols. (1921); repr. (1991) • J. A. B. Cook,

*Sunny Singapore* (1907) • C. B. Buckley, *An anecdotal history of old times in Singapore*, 2 vols. (1902); repr. in 1 vol. (1965); new edn (1984) **Likenesses** photograph, repro. in Makepeace, Brooke, and Braddell, *One hundred years of Singapore*, vol. 2, p. 460

**Cooke, Sir Thomas**. *See* Cook, Sir Thomas (*c*.1410–1478).

**Cooke, Sir Thomas** (*c*.1648–1709), merchant, was the son of Thomas Cooke, hat maker. He was apprenticed in the Goldsmiths' Company in 1664 and later flourished in that line of business, partly through lucrative connections in Cadiz, later also by branching out into banking, bullion dealing, and property ownership. He married, on 7 February 1672, Elizabeth Horne, and together they had two sons and four daughters. Between 1675 and 1684 he was established for trade at the Griffin in Exchange Alley. In 1683 he was elected as a committeeman of the East India Company, rising to become deputy governor by 1690, and governor for the first of several terms of office in 1692. At the same time he fostered his personal interests by lending bullion to the company and by trading on his own account in East India merchandise. In 1691 he became prime warden of the Goldsmiths' Company, in 1692 an alderman for Queenhithe ward, and in 1694 sheriff of the City of London.

Cooke became tainted with the suspicion of Jacobitism following his vote in 1702 at the common council along with other East India merchants against the City's address denouncing Louis XIV's recognition of the pretender James Stuart. In 1693 and 1703 he stood, unsuccessfully, as the tory candidate for mayor, but when he was elected mayor in 1704 he asked to be excused from this office on grounds of ill health. In fact at this time he was largely occupied with East India Company affairs. Because of his authoritarian personal style he became known in his heyday as the 'dictator' of the company. In 1691 he married one of his daughters to Sir Josiah Child, second baronet, a leading businessman whose influential father was the greatest shareholder in the East India Company. Cooke was also an associate of the London speculative builder Nicholas Barbon, with whom he projected to build over Little Lincoln's Inn Field in 1693. In 1693 he was in a position to make a bid to farm the land tax for £3 million. He was elected as MP for Colchester in 1694. Such was his reputation as an expert on bullion that he was appointed in 1695 to the parliamentary committee established to consider the export of silver.

Between 1688 and 1691 a power struggle between 'old' and 'new' interests in East India trade broke out among London merchants and spilled over into court and parliament. Both sides sought to control the monopoly of trade with the East Indies. The old company interest (Cooke's) was blamed for incautious policy and consequently disastrous military actions against the Mughal empire, infringing the original company mandate for peaceful trade. The new interest had become bitter at the extent of personal influence wielded by Child as chairman and a handful of all-powerful company men including Cooke who manipulated affairs to their own advantage. In 1691 Cooke held some £40,000 worth of company stock, while Child held £51,000. Between them this amounted to holdings of about 15 per cent of the total shares. The battle for the company was tinged by fights between the major political and constitutional factions. The old interest was identified to some extent with the crown, the house of Stuart, an aggressive turn in foreign policy, and authoritarian politics in general. Annual gifts to the crown (before and after 1689) were a central element of company policy.

The company's charter was due for renegotiation in 1690. Following the fall of James II and the accession of William and Mary in 1689 the future of the trade seemed most uncertain. A Commons committee was set up to investigate the company and make recommendations about its future status and regulation. The committee reported in 1690 and recommended against renewal of the company charter on its existing terms. A period of intense lobbying, cajoling, and bribery then followed. Private interests and political passions combined to produce a maelstrom of intrigue. Whig financiers, including those behind the Bank of England, pressed for a new company or an open trade with the East. These opponents of the old company established a new Scottish East India Company through the Edinburgh parliament (though financed with English money). Child and Cooke eventually saw off this challenge, but not without generating formidable enemies in the process. The old company interest survived, then, but at some cost to Cooke's later career and reputation.

A crop of financial scandals in and around parliament burst forth in early 1695 and focused public attention afresh on the question of corruption in the political world forged by the revolution of 1688, presenting an opportunity to settle old scores. Henry Guy, secretary to the Treasury, was accused of taking 200 guineas as a bribe and sent to the Tower. Sir John Trevor, speaker of the Commons, was found to have received 1000 guineas from the City of London for his help in passing a local bill. In this heated atmosphere attention turned to the East India Company, where larger quarry was thought to lie. Investigations into the company's affairs, in train since 1693, had turned up unaccounted disbursements totalling £90,000 or more. Most of the money had passed through Cooke's hands and he was thus called upon in parliament to explain these payments. His performance under interrogation was highly emotional; at times he broke down into tears. Cooke ultimately refused to be called to account in this manner and consequently was ordered to be taken to the Tower of London. A bill threatening heavy penalties should he persist with his intransigence was rushed through the Commons. The bill met with some resistance in the Lords, but Cooke was finally persuaded to strike a deal with his pursuers. He agreed to reveal all publicly in return for an indemnity against future prosecution, and made disclosures to a special joint committee of the Lords and Commons on 23 April 1695. The same day an act of indemnity was passed through the exchequer chamber. A written account of disbursements paid for special services submitted by Cooke was found unsatisfactory and he was faced with detailed questioning. Francis Tyson had received a lump sum of £10,000 and several tallies of £1000. Cooke claimed that this money had been delivered via Child to William III as a 'customary present'. The duke of Leeds (who had earlier spoken for Cooke in the Lords) was accused of having taken a gift of some 5500 guineas and threatened with an impeachment for corruption and the betrayal of his office as a privy councillor. It was also revealed that several of the king's closest advisers led by the duke of Portland had accepted about £50,000 in bribes in order to keep the king on the side of the old company.

The outcome of these protracted proceedings was that Cooke's name was blackened but his career not yet over. In the elections of 1695 he stood again for election but lost his Colchester seat by a narrow margin; he was able to regain it for the parliaments of 1698–1702 and 1702–5. He lost his seat on the committee of the East India Company until 1698 and faced financial retrenchment, selling in 1697 his Hackney manor house. His fortunes revived somewhat in his later years, and he continued to use his personal and political influence in the old East India Company interest still at threat from the new whig financiers. The year 1698 saw the ending of the old company's monopoly in East India trade and the triumph of the interests behind the earlier Scottish East India Company. This setback, however, was not to be the end of Cooke and the old interest, who were able to gain, through last-minute intrigues, incorporation within the new company and to continue to trade as before, even excluding its rivals in the new company from some markets. Conflict between the two interests eventually gave way to plans for a merger, which finally came into being in 1709. While plotting to take control of the new company in the autumn of 1708, Cooke was struck by a severe apoplectic fit that left him unable to attend meetings or to conduct his own affairs. This was to be the end of a remarkable business career. He died on 6 September 1709 following a second fit of apoplexy, leaving his wife and eldest son, John, to deal with the disposal of his estate.          R. D. SHELDON

**Sources** 'Cooke, Thomas', HoP, *Commons, 1690–1715* [draft] · *The examination and informations upon oath of Sir Thomas Cooke and several other persons* (1695) · papers rel. to Cooke's examination before the committee of both houses, 1695, BL, Add. MS 61358, fols. 180–2216 · W. R. Scott, *The constitution and finance of English, Scottish and Irish joint stock companies to 1720*, 3 vols. (1910–12) · A. Browning, *Thomas Osborne, earl of Danby and duke of Leeds, 1632–1712*, 1 (1951) · H. Horwitz, 'The East India trade, the politicians and the constitution', *Journal of British Studies*, 17/2 (1977–8), 1–18 · will, PRO, PROB 11/511, sig. 240

**Archives** BL, papers relating to examination before committee of both houses, Add. MS 61358, fols. 180–2216 · BL, letters to Governor Pitt, Add. MS 22851, fols. 135–40; Add. MS 22852, fols. 53, 55, 173

**Wealth at death** wealthy: will, PRO, PROB 11/511, sig. 240

**Cooke, Thomas** (1703–1756), translator and writer, was born on 16 December 1703, at Braintree, Essex, the son of John Cooke (*d.* in or after 1728), an innkeeper, and his wife, Rebeckah. His father, according to Pope, was a Muggletonian. Cooke was educated at Felsted School, where he excelled in classics. While quite young he was introduced to Thomas Herbert, eighth earl of Pembroke,

who employed him and encouraged him in his classical studies. In 1722 Cooke went to London to earn his living by his pen, contributing articles to the daily papers, and attaching himself to the whigs. He came to know Thomas Tickell, Ambrose Philips, Leonard Welsted, Richard Steele, and John Dennis. Dennis was the subject of a letter (24 January 1734) from Cooke to John Baker of St John's College, Cambridge, published some fifty years later in the *European Magazine* (February 1786, 91–2). In it Cooke gave an account of Dennis's acute poverty and the gifts of money from several prominent people, including the earl of Pembroke and Horace Walpole. Appended to the letter is a transcription of a Latin document detailing Dennis's birth, paternity, education, death, and burial. John Nichols, signing himself M. Green, one of his known pseudonyms, reprinted most of Cooke's letter which formed part of the Baker collection in the Harley MSS in the British Library (7031) in the *Gentleman's Magazine* (1st ser., 65, February 1795, 105–6).

Cooke's earliest publications were a poem on the death of the duke of Marlborough (1722), a translation of the poems of Moschus and Bion, and *Albion, or, The Court of Neptune, a Masque* (1724). In 1725 he issued anonymously a poem entitled *The Battle of the Poets*, attacking Pope, Swift, and their friends, and eulogizing the writers of his own school. He continued the campaign by publishing in the *Daily Journal* (6 April 1728) notes on Pope's version of the Thersites episode in the second book of the *Iliad*, proving to his own satisfaction that Pope was no Greek scholar. Pope resolved to pillory Cooke in the *Dunciad*, but news of his intention reached Cooke, and he, taking alarm, wrote two letters to Pope (11 August and 16 September 1728), repudiating his connection with the offensive publications. With the second letter he forwarded a copy of his newly issued translation of Hesiod. In letters to Lord Oxford, Pope showed some sign of accepting Cooke's denial, but when the *Dunciad* appeared at the close of the year, Cooke occupied a place in it (B ii. 138), and was held up to ridicule in the notes. By way of reply Cooke reissued his *Battle of the Poets* and his letters on the Thersites episode, with new and caustic prefaces, in 1729. The volume was entitled *Tales, Epistles, Odes, Fables, &c.*, and contained several other of Cooke's published poems, some translations from the classics, 'proposals for perfecting the English language', and an essay on grammar. Pope was here described as 'a person who with but a small share of learning and moderate natural endowments has by concurring and uncommon accidents acquired as great a reputation as the most learned and exalted genius could ever hope'. In 1731 Cooke collected a number of the letters on the political and literary controversies of the day he had contributed, under the pseudonym of Atticus, to the *London Journal* in 1729 and 1730, and dedicated the book to Horace Walpole. Letter 5 is on 'the controversy betwixt the poets and Mr. Pope'. Pope renewed his attack on Cooke in his *Epistle to Dr. Arbuthnot*, l.146 (1735).

Cooke tried his hand at every kind of literary work. In 1726 he published *The Bath, or, The Knights of the Bath*, a poem suggested by the revival of that order, to which was added the now very rare *Scandalous chronicle, or, A ballad of characters, written for the use of the poets, and proper to be sung at their next sessions*; *Philander and Cydippe*, a poem; and an edition of Marvell's works, with a memoir. Subsequently he issued separately a long series of odes, with dedications addressed to Lord Chesterfield and other persons of influence. William Oldys says that Cooke compiled *Seymour's Survey of London* in 1734. In this same year he wrote a short *Life of King Edward III of England*. And about this time he contributed to the *Weekly Oracle*, numbers 54 and 56 on the Phalaris controversy being by him. Four years later he wrote the preface to the poem by Samuel Wesley the younger entitled *The Battle of the Sexes*. Another edition of Cooke's collected poems appeared in 1742.

Cooke achieved a wider and deserved reputation by his translations from the classics. In 1728 he translated Hesiod, the first translation in English; his early patron, the earl of Pembroke, and Lewis Theobald contributed notes. Each of the two volumes bears the dedication to a notable personage, and the practice of seeking and acquiring a dedicatee continued for all his subsequent writings. He was thereafter known as Hesiod Cooke. The edition was reissued in a number of early anthologies. An edition of Terence, with an English translation (3 vols.), followed in 1734, and a translation of Cicero's *De natura deorum*, with elaborate critical apparatus, in 1737. In 1741 Cooke produced an edition of Virgil with English notes and a Latin paraphrase, and in 1754 appeared the first and only volume—a translation of the *Amphitruo*—of the long-promised edition of Plautus. Samuel Johnson said that Cooke was soliciting subscriptions for this book for twenty years, and that the proceeds of his canvass formed his main source of income. Cooke, according to Sir Joseph Mawbey, said that Johnson was 'half a madman, half a scholar, three parts a Roman Catholick, and a compleat Jacobite' (*GM*, 1st ser., 61, 1791, 1184).

Cooke was extremely successful in obtaining subscribers to his projected edition of Plautus's plays, according to Isaac Reed, editor of the *European Magazine* (December 1791, 406–7). When the first, and only, volume of the Plautus was published in 1746, there were 713 subscribers. Eighteen years earlier, in 1728, Cooke managed to get only 174 subscribers to his translation of Hesiod. In the intervening years he had sharpened his techniques. Reed, in the *European Magazine* piece cited above, reprinted two letters from Cooke to prospective subscribers in which his methods are clearly seen.

Cooke also wrote for the stage. In 1728 he helped his friend John Mottley with *Penelope, a Dramatic Opera*. The *Triumphs of Love and Honour*, with a prologue by Sir Robert Henly, then a student of the Inner Temple, was acted at Drury Lane on 18 August 1731, and was published in the same year with an essay 'on the stage, and on the advantages which arise to a nation from the encouragement of the arts'. The essay, with long criticisms of Shakespeare's *King Lear* and Addison's *Rosamond*, was also issued separately. *The Eunuch, or, The Darby Captain*, a musical farce

adapted from Terence, was performed at Drury Lane on 17 May 1737, with Charles Macklin in the part of Captain Brag. In 1739 Cooke published a tragedy called *The Mournful Nuptials*, together with 'some considerations on satire and on the present state of our public entertainments'. It was acted under the title of *Love the Cause and Cure of Grief, or, The Innocent Murderer* at Drury Lane on 19 December 1743. His most successful effort was *The Battle of the Poets, or, The Contention for the Laureat* (1730), a new act introduced into Fielding's *Tom Thumb*, acted six times and republished in 1744, with a prologue by Sir Robert Henly, according to Sir Joseph Mawbey. Mawbey also stated that he had offered Garrick a manuscript play by Cooke entitled 'Germanicus', but Garrick declined it. Cooke subsequently wrote songs for Vauxhall, and dialogue and songs for John Rich's production of Theobald's very popular *Harlequin, a Sorcerer*. About 1742 Cooke took part in Colley Cibber's theatrical quarrel, and issued, under the pseudonym Scriblerus Quartus, *The Bays Miscellany, or, Colley Triumphant*, which included two new satiric dialogues, 'Petty Sessions of the Poets' and 'The contention of the Laurel as it is now acting at the New Theatre at the Hay-Market', together with a reprint of the *Battle of the Poets*. In 1743 an extravagantly eulogistic epistle in verse addressed by Cooke to the countess of Shaftesbury appeared, together with a prologue and epilogue on Shakespeare, the former spoken by Garrick at Drury Lane on 21 January, before and after *The Merchant of Venice* for his benefit, and the latter by Mrs Woffington. Cooke formed a fine collection of printed plays, which he sold to Mrs Oldfield, the actress, and after her death it was purchased (1737) by Queen Caroline for £200.

About 1741 Cooke became editor and author of the well-known *Craftsman*, in succession to Nicholas Amhurst. In 1748 his free criticisms of the Pelham administration led the duke of Bedford, a secretary of state, to proceed against him for libel, and he was placed under the care of a parliamentary messenger for several weeks, but received no further punishment. Religious discussions interested Cooke, and he approached them from an advanced point of view. In 1748 he published anonymously a letter (addressed before 1732 to Archbishop Wake) 'concerning Persecution for Religion and Freedom of Debate, proving Liberty to be the support of Truth and natural property of Mankind', which was prefixed to *A Demonstration of the Will of God by the Light of Nature*. This work was dedicated to the third earl of Shaftesbury, and portions of it criticize the argument of Samuel Clarke (1675–1729), with whom Cooke was for the most part in agreement. In 1756 he supplied Dr Leonard Howard, rector of St Saviour's, Southwark, with some unpublished poems and old correspondence as material for the second volume of Howard's collection of *Ancient Letters*. Among Cooke's correspondents were men prominent in the church and in the universities, as well as a number of writers.

Cooke was always in debt, and his difficulties increased with his years. He died in great poverty on 29 December 1756 at a small house in Lambeth, which he was in the habit of describing to casual acquaintances as a magnificent mansion. He was buried on 1 January 1757. A few literary friends subscribed to his funeral expenses, and contributed to the support of his widow, Anne, a sister of Charles *Beckingham, and his only child, a daughter, Elizabeth. Anne died in March 1757, and Elizabeth in the autumn of 1758 in the Lambeth workhouse. Cooke, though of a convivial temper, had a cynical humour; he introduced Samuel Foote to a club as 'the nephew of the gentleman who was lately hung in chains for murdering his brother'. Sir Joseph Mawbey, to whom Cooke left his manuscripts, contributed a long anecdotal biography, with copious extracts from his commonplace books, to the *Gentleman's Magazine* for 1791, 1792, and 1797. There he described Cooke as of a 'bold and daring temper' and 'blunt, and sometimes coarse', as well as 'not infrequently dictatorial and assuming, which often disgusted strangers, and made him feared by many' (*GM*, 1st ser., 61/2, 1791, 1092; 62/1, 1792, 30).

SIDNEY LEE, rev. ARTHUR SHERBO

**Sources** *GM*, 1st ser., 61 (1791), 1090–94, 1178–85 • *GM*, 1st ser., 62 (1792), 26–30, 214–21, 313–16 • *GM*, 1st ser., 65 (1795), 105–6 • *GM*, 1st ser., 67 (1797), 566 • *European Magazine and London Review*, 9 (1786), 91–2 • *European Magazine and London Review*, 20 (1791), 406–7 • A. Sherbo, '"Hesiod" Cooke and the subscription game', *Studies in Bibliography*, 41 (1988), 267–70
**Archives** Yale U., Beinecke L., commonplace book | BL, letters to the duke of Newcastle, Add. MSS 32690–32866 • BL, letters to Sir Hans Sloane, Sloane MSS • Bodl. Oxf., letters to Mr Nourse
**Likenesses** W. Hogarth, bust, Museo Pembrokiana; repro. in T. Cooke, ed. and trans., *The works of Hesiod*, 1 (1728), frontispiece

**Cooke, Thomas** (1722–1783), Church of England clergyman and eccentric, born in Hexham, Northumberland, on 23 October 1722, was the son of John Cooke, a shoemaker at Hexham. He received his education as king's scholar at Durham School, and afterwards entered Queen's College, Oxford (22 February 1743), where he never took a degree. He obtained the curacy of Embleton, Northumberland, and soon was brought into notoriety by the singularity of his religious notions. He maintained that the Jewish ceremonies were not abrogated by the Christian dispensation, and insisted on the necessity of circumcision, supporting his doctrine by his own practice. At this period he assumed the names of Adam Moses Emanuel.

On being deprived of his curacy Cooke moved to London, where he was known as the Bearded Priest, on account of his unusual appearance. Calling himself 'a Minister of Christ's Universal Catholick Church' (Baker, 1.145–6) and urging the necessity of double Sabbath observance and regular mortification, he preached in the streets, and became an author; but as his unintelligible jargon did not sell he was reduced to great distress. Resorting to desperate shifts to relieve himself, he became notorious for soliciting subscriptions for works that were never published, and for helping himself to meals that had not been bought for him, contending that 'the goods of fortune should be held in common by all God's creatures' (ibid.), and producing a range of Latin, Greek, and Hebrew authorities in justification for his conduct. For

two or three years he was confined in Bethlem Hospital (Bedlam).

On his release Cooke travelled through Scotland and went to Ireland in 1760. Ultimately he returned to the north of England, and until a few years before his death subsisted on a pension allowed him by the Society of the Sons of the Clergy. Here he occupied himself with writing odes, letters, epigrams, and strictures of one kind or another. His last undertaking involved a plan for the alteration of St Nicholas's Church in Newcastle, and 'a project for making, what he called, a grand universal Church upon true evangelical principles' (Baker, 1.145–6). His death, which occurred at Newcastle upon Tyne on 15 November 1783, is said to have been occasioned by his copying the ascetic practices of Origen too closely.

Cooke published two dramatic works: *The King cannot Err* (1762), a comedy, and *The Hermit Converted, or, The Maid of Bath Married* (1771), also a comedy. Neither piece was ever performed on the London stage.

THOMPSON COOPER, rev. RICHARD SHARP

**Sources** D. E. Baker, *Biographia dramatica, or, A companion to the playhouse*, rev. I. Reed, new edn, rev. S. Jones, 1 (1812), 145–6 • M. A. Richardson, ed., *The local historian's table book … historical division*, 5 vols. (1841–6), vol. 2, p. 283 • Foster, *Alum. Oxon.* • IGI
**Likenesses** line engraving (after Walker), BM

**Cooke, Thomas** (1763–1818), writer on physiognomy, was born in Sheffield on 20 March 1763. He was employed in trade early in life, but when he was twenty-two years old he began the study of physiognomy and later became a popular and widely respected physiognomist with a large circle of curious enquirers. His papers were collected and published only posthumously, under the title of *A Practical and Familiar View of the Science of Physiognomy* (1819), and his work was illustrated with the first series of lithographic drawings produced by the London Lithographic Institution from copies of drawings in the writings of Johann Caspar Lavater (1741–1801) and Petrus Camper (1722–1789). A lithographic silhouette of Cooke forms the frontispiece to the book. A believer in the free agency and moral accountability of man, he claimed in this work that the practice of physiognomy produced an intellectual and social knowledge of human character: it effected a 'moral and religious sentiment' and a 'philosophical and rational thought'. According to his friend, I. G. Marshall (later editor of his writings), 'his remarks were always communicated in a serious and earnest manner, and were sometimes marked by a singular union of impressive wisdom and kindness' (*A Practical and Familiar View*, 3). Cooke died in Manchester on 26 July 1818.

C. W. SUTTON, rev. LUCY HARTLEY

**Sources** T. Cooke, *A practical and familiar view of the science of physiognomy* (1819)
**Likenesses** Lithographic Institution, silhouette, lithograph, 1819, repro. in Cooke, *Practical and familiar view … of physiognomy*

**Cooke** [Cook]**, Thomas** (1807–1868), optician, the eldest son of James Cook, a shoemaker, and his second wife, Jane, was born at Allerthorpe in the East Riding of Yorkshire on 8 March 1807. His education was limited to two years at the national school, after which he was put to his father's trade. But inspired by accounts of Captain Cook's voyages, he took up the study of mathematics and navigation, and was on the point of becoming a seaman when his mother's tears persuaded him to seek a less hazardous livelihood. Further study enabled him to open a village school, and it was here that he met Hannah Milner, a pupil, who in 1831 became his wife. He moved to York in 1829 and for the next seven years supported himself by teaching, while continuing to devote his spare moments to the study of mathematics and practical mechanics. Optics attracted him, and to make practical use of his knowledge he constructed a reflecting telescope. Since the requisite metals cost money he turned to refractors, finding cheap material in the thick bottom of a glass tumbler. He developed methods of shaping and polishing, and eventually succeeded in producing a reasonably good achromatic telescope; the instrument was later purchased by Professor John Phillips of Oxford, his lifelong friend and patron.

With a growing family to support, Cooke decided to embark on a full-time career as an optical instrument maker, and by March 1837 he had opened his first shop, at 50 Stonegate, York, selling refracting and reflecting telescopes, microscopes, opera glasses, spectacles, eyeglasses, optical lenses, single- and double-barrelled air-pumps, electrical machines, barometers, thermometers, spirit levels, hydrometers, globes, sundials, and mathematical instruments. His first important order was from William Gray FRS for an equatorial telescope with a lens of 4½ inch diameter; this was followed in 1851 by a commission from Hugh Pattinson of Gateshead for one of a 7 inch aperture, lent in 1856 to Professor Piazzi Smyth for his expedition to Tenerife. These successes added so much to Cooke's reputation and business that in 1855 he built a new factory, known as the Buckingham Works, in Bishophill, York. It was one of the earliest scientific instrument manufactories in the country. Here Cooke made most of his own machine tools, the lens-grinding equipment was powered by steam, and metals were cast in his own foundry. He also attended exhibitions at home and abroad, often being awarded medals for the excellence of his workmanship. In 1860 he constructed an equatorial telescope for Prince Albert, later erected at Osborne House on the Isle of Wight. But his largest enterprise was undertaken for Robert Stirling Newall, a manufacturer of submarine cables at Gateshead. Cooke committed himself to the onerous task of producing a huge telescope with an object-glass 25 inches across and of the highest quality in design and finish. The optical part of the commission was completed early in 1868, but Cooke, worn out by the anxieties induced by so vast an undertaking, died on 19 October 1868 at the Buckingham Works from 'disease of the nerves'. He was buried at York cemetery. The great telescope was mounted in the following year and was completed at Newall's estate at Ferndean near Newcastle in 1871. At that time it was the world's largest refractor. It was subsequently transferred to Cambridge University observatory and later to the Greek national observatory in Athens. A pair of 5 foot transit instruments constructed by Cooke for the Indian Trigonometrical Survey was described by Lieutenant-Colonel Strange before the Royal Society in 1867. They were among the largest portable instruments of their class. Cooke also invented an excellent automatic engine for the graduation of circles, and was the first to devise machinery for engraving figures upon them. He perfected the astronomical clock, and built nearly one hundred turret clocks for public institutions and churches.

Cooke restored Britain to the forefront in the field of practical optics. By his methods of grinding and polishing lenses their production was rendered easy and cheap, and his object-glasses were acknowledged to be extremely fine, both in definition and colour. His construction methods brought comparatively large instruments within the reach of an extensive class of amateur astronomers. His excellent system of equatorial mounting reduced the problems of flexure, torque, and vibration. Admirable workmanship was combined, in all his instruments, with elegance of design. Simplicity, truthfulness, and modesty distinguished his private character. He was admitted a member of the Royal Astronomical Society in 1859, served on its committee in 1865–6 and contributed to its proceedings a paper, 'On a new driving-clock for equatorials' (*Monthly Notices*, 28, 1867–8, 210–13). In his will he bequeathed 'everything' to his wife and the business was continued by two of his four sons, Thomas and Frederick.

A. M. Clerke, *rev.* Alison J. Brech

**Sources** A. McConnell, *Instrument makers to the world: a history of Cooke, Troughton & Simms* (1992) · S. Smiles, *Men of invention and industry* (1884) · *Monthly Notices*, 29 (1868–9), 130–35 · [J. Scott], 'York astronomers and instrument makers', *Yorkshire Gazette* (7–21 Feb 1925); (7 March 1925) · R. G. W. Anderson, J. A. Bennett, and W. F. Ryan, eds., *Making instruments count* (1993) · D. W. Dewhirst, 'The Newall telescope', *Journal of the British Astronomical Association*, 80 (1969–70), 493–5 · 'The Newall telescope', *Nature*, 1 (1869–70), 408–10 · I. Fletcher, 'On the photospheres of the sun', *Monthly Notices*, 25 (1864–5), 231–2 · C. Feinstein, ed., *The British Association York, 1831–1981* (1981) · parish register (baptism), Allerthorpe, Yorkshire, 9 March 1807

**Archives** Borth. Inst., Vickers Instruments archive | FILM Borth. Inst.

**Likenesses** photograph, *c.*1865, Borth. Inst., Vickers Instruments archive

**Wealth at death** under £5000: probate, 14 April 1869, *CGPLA Eng. & Wales*

**Cooke, Thomas Potter** (1786–1864), actor, was born on 23 April 1786 in Titchfield Street, Marylebone, Middlesex, the child of Joseph Cooke, a surgeon 'of great respectability' (*Actors by Daylight*, 24, 1838, 186), and his wife, Mary. After Joseph Cooke's death in 1793 his wife seems to have gone into service, and Cooke himself to have become an errand boy; however, seeing a nautical melodrama fired him with enthusiasm to join the navy. Having been provided with clothing by the Marine Society, he was entered as a 'servant' under the name Thomas Cook on the muster-roll of HMS *Raven* on 30 July 1796, giving his age as thirteen, the minimum age for entry into the service. The *Raven* took part in the siege of Toulon and was under Admiral Jervis's command at the battle of Cape St Vincent (14 February 1797), when Cooke probably worked as a powder monkey.

Thomas Potter Cooke (1786–1864), by Charles Baxter, 1835 [as William in *Black-Eyed Susan* by Douglas Jerrold]

He narrowly escaped death when the *Raven* was later wrecked off Cuxhaven and the crew struggled to survive by clinging to the wreckage for two days and nights in intensely cold weather. Cooke managed to reach the shore but suffered a near-fatal attack of rheumatic fever. He was eventually able to return to sea, however, serving aboard HMS *Prince of Wales*, which took part in the blockade of Brest.

In 1802 came the peace of Amiens and on 27 April the end of Cooke's naval career. He joined a travelling circus 'at a modest salary of fifteen shillings a week' (Stirling, 2.107), turned to the stage for a living, and made his first appearance in January 1804 at the Royalty Theatre in Wellclose Square, then used by Philip Astley as his winter quarters. Impressed no doubt by Cooke's fine physique and athletic prowess, Astley engaged him for several seasons at his Amphitheatre, and he also appeared at the Lyceum and in Dublin. Cooke had a talent for arranging pantomimes and theatrical spectacles, and in 1809 R. W. Elliston recruited him as stage manager for the Surrey Theatre. He first made his mark as actor there in the role of Roderick Dhu, a fierce highland chieftan, in T. J. Dibdin's *The Lady of the Lake* (24 September 1810). He stayed with Elliston until 1816 and thereafter obtained engagements at various London theatres, including Drury Lane, building up a reputation but without any very notable triumphs, apart from a German character Hans Ketzler, a 'wonderful admixture of cowardice and courage' (*ILN*, 1853, 319), in George Soane's *The Innkeeper's Daughter* (Drury Lane, 7 April 1817). In 1819 he married Louisa Maria Ann Cremer of Brompton, who was, according to *The Drama*, 'a lady of great accomplishments and large property' (*Drama*, 4, 58) and with whom he had one daughter.

In 1820 Cooke was engaged at the Lyceum Theatre (English Opera House), where he made a great hit as Ruthven, the demonic protagonist of Planché's *The Vampire* (9 August 1820) and again as Dirk Hatteraick in the same dramatist's adaptation of *Guy Mannering, the Witch of Derncleugh* (1821); in the latter role he finely displayed 'that determined ferocity that might be supposed to belong to

the captain of a daring band of robbers' (*Drama*, 1, 1821, 201). In July 1823, when he was still at the Lyceum, Cooke's skills as 'a pantomimist of the first rank' (Stirling, 2.106) brought him sensational success in the non-speaking role of the Monster in *Presumption, or, The Fate of Frankenstein* (28 July 1823), R. B. Peake's adaptation of Mary Shelley's novel. He was to perform this role 365 times in all during his career, including eighty at the Porte St Martin Theatre in Paris in 1825–6 (during which time he suffered one of those attacks of gout that plagued him throughout his life). Another triumph in a similarly silent role, the spectral Vanderdecken in Fitzball's *The Flying Dutchman* at the Adelphi (4 April 1826), confirmed Cooke's excellence in supernatural roles. According to the *Illustrated London News*

> others played ghosts and demons with unquestionable success; but how mechanically and solidly. … It was he who first infused them with a true poetic element—gave them a dreamy indistinctness—a vague suggestive shadow, which, while it chained the senses, set the imagination loose. (*ILN*, 1853, 319)

Cooke was already noted for his excellence in sailor roles (the heroic British seaman Jack Gallant, for example, in Moncrieff's *Shipwreck of the Medusa* at the Coburg on 19 June 1820, and Philip in J. B. Buckstone's hugely successful *Luke the Labourer* at the Adelphi on 17 October 1826) before his reputation in this respect made a quantum leap with his creation of the role of the patriotic English coxswain Long Tom Coffin in Fitzball's *The Pilot* (Adelphi, 31 October 1825), adapted from Fenimore Cooper's novel. Cooke's performance in this role (which he was to play 562 times in all) was 'highly picturesque' and gave to the stage figure of the sailor 'a new feature of thoughtfulness and mystery, and a tinge of the romantic' (*The Stage*, 8, 1829, 73). In his *Road to the Stage* (1827) Leman Rede mentions a 'characteristic touch' of Cooke's in his Coffin performance, 'invariably recognised, and applauded': 'previous to commencing his combat with the [American] Sergeant he pauses to take tobacco, and afterwards when he has driven his adversary from him, claps his sword into his mouth while he hitches up his trousers', thereby illustrating 'cool habitual bravery' (Rede, 104). Even his Tom Coffin was eclipsed, however, by his Sweet William in Douglas Jerrold's *Black-Eyed Susan*. First performed at the Surrey on Easter Monday 1829, it had a phenomenal run of over 300 nights there and, from 30 November for over two weeks, Cooke also acted William at Covent Garden every night after finishing his Surrey performance: 'a hackney cab brought the triumphant William in his blue jacket and white trousers from the Obelisk to Bow Street' (*GM*, 3rd ser., 16, 1864, 676). Cooke's William, featuring the superlative hornpipe which was one of his trademarks, became a veritable national institution, and in 1853, when he was giving a season at the Standard Theatre in the East End, the *Illustrated London News* recorded that he had played the part 785 times during his career. This tailor-made role brought out all his powers—his athleticism and heartiness and, in the final scenes, his ability to invest his sailor figures with both pathos and dignity. Above all, he embodied the nautical:

His hitch, his swing, his back-handed wipe, his roll—in short, his every look, gesture and motion are redolent of the blue water and the lower deck; and all this is qualified by … a degree of feeling which is far more like truth than acting. (*London Literary Gazette*, 3 Oct 1829, 654)

After William, he created only one more major role, another sailor, Harry Hallyard in J. T. Haines's *My Poll and my Partner Joe* (Surrey Theatre, 31 August 1835). His immense popularity continued unabated, however, and he generally took short engagements at different theatres to perform the repertory of his most celebrated roles.

In 1849 Cooke applied for, and was awarded, the naval general service medal with a St Vincent clasp in respect of his service aboard the *Raven*. In 1857 Henry Morley considered his Tom Coffin at the Adelphi 'a marvel': 'the singing voice has gone, and that is all … For about five minutes of hornpipe the veteran's breath is good and his feet are as nimble as they were when they twinkled for the pleasure of our forefathers' (Morley, 164). His last appearances were at Covent Garden on 29 October 1860, for the benefit of the Dramatic College, founded as a retirement home for actors (Cooke was deputy master), and at the Princess's Theatre on 2 May 1861 for the benefit of an actor's widow. His wife's death in 1863 shook him severely, and he moved from his home at 38 Woburn Square to live with his married daughter, Mrs Hugh Cumming, at 37 Thurloe Square, where he died (from what the death certificate describes as 'decay of nature') on 4 April 1864. He was buried in Brompton cemetery, London on 10 April. His obituary in *The Era* acclaimed him as someone who, 'by the high character of his private life, has reflected so much credit on the Profession he adorned' (*The Era*, 10 April 1864). Having always practised 'strict economy' he had 'amassed a large fortune' (Stirling, 2.107), and in his will left £2000 to the Dramatic College to be invested to provide a prize for 'the best Drama on a Nautical or National subject', the copyright to be retained by the college, with a further £1000 to fund an annual dinner for the college's inmates and officers on 23 April, the birthday he proudly shared with Shakespeare. A. R. Slous's *True to the Core: a Story of the Armada* (Surrey Theatre, 8 September 1866) was the first prize drama, and there was another award in 1868 (J. S. Dilley and James Albery's unperformed *The Mate of the Mountjoy*), but funds proved insufficient to sustain the competition, and the college itself came to a rather ignominious end in the late 1870s. MICHAEL SLATER

**Sources** *The Era* (10 April 1864) · *ILN* (15 Oct 1853), 319 · *Drama, or, Theatrical Pocket Magazine*, 4 (1823), 58–9 · K. Douglas-Harris, *Naval medals, 1793–1856* (1987) · W. J. Nichols, 'The acting of T. P. Cook', *Nineteenth Century Theatre Research*, 5/2 (1977) · E. Fitzball, *Thirty-five years of a dramatic author's life*, 2 vols. (1859), vol. 1, pp. 136ff., 154ff. · *The Stage*, 8 (1829), 73f. · *The biography of the British stage, being correct narratives of the lives of all the principal actors and actresses* (1824) · *GM*, 3rd ser., 16 (1864), 676 · J. Winton, *Hurrah for the life of a sailor!* (1977), 45–51 · *Actors by Daylight*, 1/24 (1838), 185–7 · E. Stirling, *Old Drury Lane*, 2 (1881), 105–11 · R. Foulkes, 'The Royal Dramatic College', *Nineteenth Century Theatre Research*, 13 (1985), 63–83 · H. Morley, *The journal of a London playgoer from 1851 to 1866* (1866) · L. Rede, *The road to the stage* (1827) · LMA, X023/015

**Archives** Bath Central Library, corresp. · Royal Naval Museum, Portsmouth
**Likenesses** C. Baxter, miniature, 1835; Sothebys, 11 Oct 1994, lot 121 [*see illus.*] · Mayall, photograph, 1853 (as Long Tom Coffin in *The pilot*), NMM; repro. in *Theatre Notebook*, 34 (1980) · H. Watkins, print, c.1856–1859, NPG · engraving, repro. in *Actors by Daylight*, 135 · engraving (as William; after photograph by Mayall), repro. in *ILN*, 320 · photograph (in old age), repro. in F. Whyte, *Actors of the century* (1898), facing p. 130 · prints, Harvard TC
**Wealth at death** under £25,000: probate, 13 July 1864, *CGPLA Eng. & Wales*

**Cooke, Thomas Simpson** [Tom] (1782–1848), singer and composer, was born in Dublin, and received his first musical instruction from his father, Bartlett Cooke, an oboist at the Smock Alley Theatre. He performed a violin concerto in public at the age of seven. He later studied composition with Tommaso Giordani, and in 1797 was engaged as leader of the orchestra at the Crow Street Theatre, Dublin, for which he composed several overtures and songs. He also kept a music shop from 1806 to 1812.

After several years Cooke's ambitions led him to appear in a new capacity, as a dramatic singer, and he chose for his début the role of the Seraskier in Storace's *The Siege of Belgrade*. His success was such that he sang the same part in London at the English Opera House at the Lyceum Theatre on 13 July 1813. On 14 September 1815 he began his long connection with the Drury Lane Theatre, when he appeared as Don Carlos in Linley's *The Duenna*. For almost twenty years he held the post of principal tenor, and from about 1821 he was director of music. During this period he composed music for more than fifty productions at the theatre, including a version of *Oberon* (1826). For some time, after about 1823, he appeared alternately as a singer and as orchestral leader. He was a member of the Philharmonic Society, and occasionally served as leader of the orchestra or conductor at its concerts. He also belonged to the Royal Academy of Music, though he was not one of the original members. From 1828 to 1830 he was one of the music managers of Vauxhall Gardens, and until 1838 he sang as principal tenor at the chapel of the Bavarian embassy in Warwick Street. He was engaged by Alfred Bunn to direct the music and conduct at both Covent Garden and Drury Lane.

Cooke adopted, with substitutions of his own, many successful foreign operas for the English stage, including *Abou Hassan* (Drury Lane, 4 April 1825), after Weber; *The White Lady* (Drury Lane, 9 October 1826), after Boieldieu; *The Jewess* (Drury Lane, 16 November 1835), based on Halévy; and *The Siege of Corinth* (Drury Lane, 8 November 1836), after Rossini. One of his last works for the stage was the vaudeville *The Follies of a Night*, with words by Planché, which was first performed at Drury Lane on 5 October 1842. Of all his compositions, the song 'Love's Ritornella', from *The Brigand Chief* (Drury Lane, 18 November 1829), was perhaps his most popular. From about 1830 onwards he spent much of his time composing glees, and several examples of his works won prizes at the catch and glee clubs. *Six Glees for Three and Four Voices* were published in

**Thomas Simpson Cooke (1782–1848),** by John William Gear, pubd 1830 [as Signor Cremona in *The Vaudeville of the Statue Lover, or, Opera Mad* ]

1844, and others were issued individually. As early as 1828 he published a treatise entitled *Singing Exemplified in a Series of Solfeggi and Exercises, Progressively Arranged* (which was reviewed in the *Quarterly Musical Magazine and Review* in that year), and he subsequently became a widely popular singing master. Among his many distinguished pupils were Maria Tree, Elizabeth Rainforth, and, perhaps the most eminent, John Sims Reeves (1818–1900), whose first London appearance at Drury Lane in 1842 was made under the auspices of Cooke.

In 1846 Cooke was appointed leader for the final two years of the Concerts of Ancient Music, succeeding John David Loder in that capacity. He was renowned as a musician for his versatility; he played the violin, flute, oboe, clarinet, bassoon, horn, cello, double bass, and piano, and was also a man of great wit. He died on 26 February 1848 at his home in Great Portland Street, London, and was buried at Kensal Green cemetery. His eldest son, Henry Angelo Michael (Gratton) Cooke (1809–1889), was a successful oboist and bandmaster.

J. A. F. MAITLAND, rev. DAVID J. GOLBY

**Sources** B. Carr, 'Cooke, Thomas Simpson', *New Grove* · book review, *Quarterly Musical Magazine and Review*, 10 (1828), 371–4 · J. Warrack and E. West, 'Cooke, Tom', *The Oxford dictionary of opera* (1992) · *GM*, 2nd ser., 29 (1848), 559
**Archives** Folger
**Likenesses** J. W. Gear, engraving, pubd 1830 (as Signor Cremona in *The vaudeville of the statue lover, or, Opera mad*), NPG [*see illus.*] · T. Lupton, mezzotint, pubd 1839 (after G. Clint), BM, NPG · prints, NPG · prints, Harvard TC

**Cooke** [Coke], **William** (*d.* 1553), judge, is said to have been born in Chesterton, near Cambridge, where he had a house, and to have attended Cambridge University, although the latter point is dubious. His parentage is obscure, but his father may have been the East Anglian attorney called William Coke who was likewise a member of Gray's Inn. He was admitted to Gray's Inn in 1528, probably from Barnard's Inn, and became an ancient in 1536. A collection of moots in the inns of court and chancery from about this time, bearing his name, is in the British Library (Harley MS 5103). He was elected to read in Gray's Inn in 1544, but managed to evade the duty until 1546, when he read as serjeant-elect; a copy of the reading, which was on the Statute of Tithes of 1540, is also in the British Library (Hargrave MS 92, with the disputed cases in Hargrave MS 253). He was steward of the manor of Chesterton in the 1540s, was elected recorder of Cambridge in 1546, having already been a justice of the peace for the county since 1542, and is said to have acted as steward of courts for several Cambridge colleges. His creation as a serjeant, delayed by the king's death, took place in February 1547. Three years later he was appointed one of the king's serjeants, and on 16 November 1552 one of the justices of the common pleas. He occupied his place in Westminster Hall for less than one year, dying on 24 August 1553. There is an elaborate monument in the church of Milton, Cambridgeshire, where he was lord of the manor from 1548 and where he was buried, with brasses depicting him in his judicial robes with his wife, Alice, and a long Latin inscription. The motto *Plebs sine lege ruit* ('People come to ruin without law'), which occurs on the brass, was used for the rings at the serjeants' call the previous year. He had two sons, Thomas and Henry, and three daughters, Agnes, Mary, and Dorothy.

J. H. BAKER

**Sources** Foss, *Judges*, 5.298–9 · Baker, *Serjeants*, 169, 506 · Sainty, *King's counsel*, 15 · Cooper, *Ath. Cantab.*, 1.114 · will, PRO, PROB 11/36, sig. 19 · PRO, CP 40/1152, m. 1 · W. Lack, H. M. Stuchfield, and P. Whittemore, *The monumental brasses of Cambridgeshire* (1995) · *VCH Cambridgeshire and the Isle of Ely*, 3.59; 9.15, 27, 180 · BL, Hargrave MS 92, fol. 104 · BL, Hargrave MS 253, fol. 45*v* · BL, Harley MS 5103 · PRO, REQ 1/4, fol. 145*v*
**Archives** BL, collection of moots, Harley MS 5103
**Likenesses** brass effigy on monument, *c.*1553, Milton church, Cambridgeshire

**Cooke, William** (1709–1780), antiquary and numismatist, was born at Barnard Castle in co. Durham on 16 August 1709, the eldest son of John Cooke (*d. c.*1714), apothecary and surgeon there, and citizen and member of the Barber–Surgeons' Company of London. In 1719 Cooke's mother, Lucy, obtained his admission to Christ's Hospital whence he proceeded as a Moses exhibitioner to Pembroke College, Cambridge, in June 1726. In 1730 he graduated BA and in 1733 MA, taking orders as a priest in 1731. He was instituted to the living of Enford, Wiltshire, in 1733, and held it until his death. He was also rector of Oldbury on the Hill and Didmarton, Gloucestershire, and by 1754 had been appointed chaplain to the earl of Suffolk.

Cooke's first publication, which came out in 1746, was a translation of the works of Sallust, with a life of the historian and a summary account of the relevant period of

Roman history. In 1752 he was incorporated a member of St Mary Hall, Oxford, and in 1754 his *Enquiry into the Patriarchal and Druidical Religion, Temples, &c.*, appeared, arguing for the close kinship of the Hebrews and ancient British, on the basis of archaeological, religious, and cultural similarities, as well as such feats of comparative philology as seeing 'Hartlepool' as 'a manifest corruption of *Heracleopolis*' and deriving the Welsh toponym element *aber-* from Apher, the companion of Hercules. The book, which drew upon the works of Stukeley for its data and those of John Hutchinson for its spirit, fitted into a well defined eighteenth-century category of erudite, druid-inspired fantasies. A second, revised edition appeared in 1755. A desire to reconcile classical mythology with Christian reason also led him, about 1760, to undertake a revised edition of Samuel Boyse's *New Pantheon*, which he described as a work intending to divest heathen theology of 'the Marvellous'. Further editions came out until the seventh and last in 1777.

Cooke died at Enford on 25 February 1780. For some time previously he had suffered from ill health, but managed to complete and send to press a laborious numismatic work, which was corrected and published by his son in two volumes in 1781 as *The Medallic History of Imperial Rome*. Prefaced by a lengthy list of subscribers, it applies coins to the illustration of Roman history and the lives of the emperors. The plan of the book is good but the engravings very poor, and most of the coins seem to have been previously published in other works. The name of Cooke's wife is not known; his son William matriculated from New College, Oxford, in 1765, aged nineteen, and graduated BA in 1768.

W. W. WROTH, rev. C. E. A. CHEESMAN

**Sources** Nichols, *Lit. anecdotes*, 2.264–7 · *GM*, 1st ser., 50 (1780), 154 · Christ's Hospital presentation papers, vol. 14, GL, microfilm 12818A/14, bundle 42 · Christ's Hospital children's registers, vol. 7, GL, microfilm 12818/7, 228 · admission book, Pembroke Cam., MS Eα, 154 · R. C. Hoare, *The history of modern Wiltshire*, 2/1: *Hundreds of Everley, Ambresbury, and Underditch* (1826), 23 · Foster, *Alum. Oxon.* · *Corrections and additions to the Dictionary of National Biography*, Institute of Historical Research (1966)

**Cooke, William** (1711–1797), college head and dean of Ely, was born in St James's, Westminster, on 15 October 1711, the son of William Cooke. He was sent to Harrow School in 1718, and placed upon the foundation at Eton College in 1721. In 1731 he matriculated as a scholar from King's College, Cambridge, and became a fellow in 1734. He graduated BA in 1735, and soon afterwards became an assistant master at Eton. In May 1743 he was unanimously elected headmaster, but he found his health too weak for the place, and in 1745 took the college living of Sturminster Marshall, Dorset. On 28 January 1746 he married Catherine, daughter of Richard Sleech, canon of Windsor.

In 1748 Cooke was elected a fellow of Eton College, and resigned Sturminster on being presented to the rectory of Denham, Buckinghamshire; he was also bursar of Eton. In 1765 he proceeded DD, and was appointed chaplain to the earl of Halifax. In 1768 he accepted the rectory of Stoke Newington. On 25 March 1772 he was unanimously elected provost of King's College, Cambridge. He was vice-

chancellor of the university in 1772–3. The antiquary William Cole had a low opinion of Cooke's abilities and claimed that Eton had been glad to lose him, but Cooke doubtless had provoked Cole's scorn by raising the rent of his cottage at Milton. In April 1780 he received a prebend in Ely, and on 9 August 1780 was appointed to the deanery.

Cooke published a few sermons, in one of which (1750) he provoked a slight controversy by defending Thomas Sherlock against Conyers Middleton in his interpretation of 'a more sure word of prophecy' in the second epistle of Peter. Cooke also published anonymously a small collection of poems entitled *Musae juveniles* (1732). He died at Bath on 20 October 1797.

Of Cooke's twelve children, Catherine married Bishop Samuel *Hallifax (1733–1790), and one of his sons, Edward *Cooke (bap. 1755, d. 1820), became secretary at war in Ireland. Another son, **William Cooke** (bap. 1749, d. 1824), Church of England clergyman and classical scholar, was baptized at Eton on 8 May 1749. He matriculated from King's College, Cambridge, in 1765 and graduated BA in 1770. A fellow of his college from 1768 to 1786, he was regius professor of Greek in the university from 1780 to 1792. He published an edition of Aristotle's *Poetics* in 1785, to which was appended the first translation of Gray's *Elegy* into Greek verse. Ordained deacon on 1 September 1779 and priest on 23 June 1785, he was appointed rector of Hampstead-with-Hessingham in Norfolk in 1785. He published a few sermons, two of which examined the nature of moral liberty and civil liberty. His principal work was *The Revelations Translated, and Explained throughout* (1789), in which he compared Revelation to Sophocles' *Oedipus tyrannus* and to Homer. He soon afterwards became mentally deranged and died on 3 May 1824.

LESLIE STEPHEN, rev. S. J. SKEDD

**Sources** Venn, *Alum. Cant.* · R. A. Austen-Leigh, ed., *The Eton College register, 1698–1752* (1927) · R. A. Austen-Leigh, ed., *The Eton College register, 1753–1790* (1921) · A. Austen-Leigh, *King's College* (1899), 204–7, 222 · Nichols, *Lit. anecdotes*, 9.154–5, 629, 630 · *GM*, 1st ser., 67 (1797), 901, 953 · *GM*, 1st ser., 68 (1798), 774 · *GM*, 1st ser., 94/2 (1824), 183

**Archives** NL Scot., letters to Lord Hailes

**Likenesses** S. Harding, stipple, pubd 1798, BM, NPG

**Wealth at death** bequests amounting to several thousands of pounds

**Cooke, William** (bap. 1749, d. 1824). *See under* Cooke, William (1711–1797).

**Cooke, William** (1757–1832), legal writer, second son of John Cooke, was born at Calcutta, where his father was an administrator. He was educated at Harrow School and was admitted a student of Lincoln's Inn on 19 November 1777. He was called to the bar there in November 1782, and in 1785 published *A Compendious System of the Bankrupt Laws*. He soon obtained a considerable practice in chancery and bankruptcy, and in 1816 was made KC and bencher of his inn.

In 1818 Cooke was commissioned by Sir John Leach to proceed to Milan for the purpose of collecting evidence concerning the conduct of Queen Caroline. He reached

Milan in September of that year, and reported the result of his investigations in July 1819. The report, which was forthwith laid before the cabinet, led to the introduction of the celebrated bill of pains and penalties against the queen in the House of Lords on 5 July 1820: this accused Caroline of 'licentious behaviour', and proposed to dissolve her marriage. About this time Cooke began to be much troubled by frequent attacks of gout, which caused him to abandon court practice. He continued, however, to practise as a chamber counsel until 1825, when he retired from the profession. He was one of the witnesses examined before the commission on chancery procedure in 1824.

During the last few years of his life Cooke resided at his house, Wrinsted Court, Frinsted, Kent, where he died on 14 September 1832. His work on the *Bankrupt Laws* passed through eight editions by 1823, and was, during his life, the standard authority on the subject. Cooke is often erroneously credited with the works of the writer William Cooke (*d.* 1824). J. M. RIGG, rev. ROBERT BROWN

**Sources** W. P. Baildon, ed., *The records of the Honorable Society of Lincoln's Inn: admissions*, 1 (1896) · J. Gorton, *A general biographical dictionary*, 3 vols. (1841) · *The public and private life of Lord Chancellor Eldon, with selections from his correspondence*, ed. H. Twiss, 3 vols. (1844) · *GM*, 1st ser., 102/2 (1832), 286 · E. Hasted, *The history and topographical survey of the county of Kent*, 4 vols. (1778–99) · 'Memoirs of William Cooke', *Legal Observer*, 4 (1832), 374–5 · 'The late Wm Cooke, esq. KC', *Legal Observer*, 6 (1833), 101 · Venn, *Alum. Cant.*

**Cooke, William** (*d.* 1824), writer, was descended from an old family originally from Cheshire, but for some time settled in Cork. He was educated at Cork grammar school, and afterwards by a private tutor. At the age of nineteen he married a lady of considerable fortune, but squandered a large portion of it, and lost nearly all the remainder in his business, that of a woollen manufacturer. His first wife died after about three years, and later in life he married his second wife, Maria, identified only as a sister of a late Major Galway.

In 1766 Cooke left Cork for London with strong recommendations to the duke of Richmond, the marquess of Lansdowne, Edmund Burke, and Oliver Goldsmith, whose friendship he retained through life. He was called to the bar at the Middle Temple in 1777, and for one or two years went on the home circuit, but already occupied himself chiefly with literature. His earliest publication was a poem entitled *The Art of Living in London*, which met with some success, and in 1807 he published another of greater pretension, entitled *Conversation*, in the fourth edition of which, published in 1815, he introduced the characters of several of the members of the well-known literary club in Gerrard Street, Soho, such as Burke, Samuel Johnson, Sir Joshua Reynolds, and Goldsmith.

Contemporary biographical accounts usually present Cooke's relationship with Goldsmith as amicable and mutually congratulatory. Some twentieth-century commentators, however, suggest that Cooke's 'anecdotes' or 'reminiscences' of Goldsmith were less than charitable, and show a tendency to paint the more famous author as

something of a simpleton. To one of Goldsmith's biographers, R. M. Wardle, Cooke was a 'goon' who was often among those who were 'more interested in telling an effective story (and perhaps incidentally suggesting an intimacy with the great) than in checking the accuracy of their information' (Wardle, 5, 190, 290). It seems, however, that Goldsmith maintained his friendship with Cooke, regardless of the latter's own inconsistencies.

Cooke also authored *Elements of Dramatic Criticism* (1775); *The Capricious Lady*, a comedy, altered from Beaumont and Fletcher's *Scornful Lady* (1783); *Memoirs of C. Macklin* (1806), the actor, including a history of the stage during Macklin's lifetime; and *Memoirs of Samuel Foote, with some of his Writings* (3 vols., 1805). He died at his house in Piccadilly on 3 April 1824, at a very advanced age.

T. F. HENDERSON, rev. GRANT P. CERNY

**Sources** R. M. Wardle, *Oliver Goldsmith* (1957), 5, 190, 290 · D. E. Baker, *Biographia dramatica, or, A companion to the playhouse*, rev. I. Reed, new edn, rev. S. Jones, 1/1 (1812), 147–8 · will, Middlesex April 207 (1824), PRO, PROB 11/1684 [Erskine], fols. 51–2 · *GM*, 1st ser., 94/1 (1824), 374–5 · [J. Watkins and F. Shoberl], *A biographical dictionary of the living authors of Great Britain and Ireland* (1816) · J. Ginger, *The notable man: the life and times of Oliver Goldsmith* (1977)
**Likenesses** print, 1807 (after A. Pope), BM; repro. in *Monthly Mirror*

**Cooke, William** (1807/8–1886), circus manager, was the second son of Thomas Taplin Cooke (1782–1866) and Mary Ann (*née* Thorpe). He was twice married. His first wife was Mary Ann Spicer (1808/9–1874); they had five children, the eldest of whom, William Henry (1833/4–1905), became an important partner in his business affairs from the 1850s. His second wife was Sarah Saunders, with whom he had two children.

Between 1853 and 1860 Cooke managed Astley's Amphitheatre in London, continuing its long-established equestrian tradition by producing circus entertainments. At Astley's he earned recognition for producing Shakespearian plays, such as *Macbeth* and *Richard III*, as equestrian dramas. In addition to managing the London house at this period, Cooke also ran a company that toured the provinces during the 'tenting season'. The 1858 season was a notable failure for him and his tenting company as they sought to rival a visiting American horse-tamer by demonstrating before provincial audiences the secrets of horse-taming; suspicion was aroused by these so-called secrets in communities such as Norwich and Cheshire where a sound knowledge of horse-taming prevailed, at least among grooms. Cooke's financial position at this stage is unclear, but there is some speculation that he steadily lost money during his years as manager of Astley's. In 1860 he retired from the management of Astley's and the report in *The Era* gives an indication of the negative market forces affecting Cooke and possibly other impresarios in the 1850s:

we are not in Mr Cooke's confidence and are therefore ignorant of the cause which induces him to retire from the position which he has held with such credit to himself … but with all the spirit and skill as a manager, it is not difficult in these free trade days to perceive what anxiety and responsibility must attend the conduct of a high priced and restricted theatre, whose lessee, unable to meet the economy of the times, is compelled to keep up exclusive and protectionist prices.   (*The Era*, 5 Feb 1860, 11)

After his retirement from Astley's, Cooke established the Victoria Riding Establishment in Church Road, Wimbledon.

Cooke's other major achievement was his role in creating the first equestrian friendly society, the Dramatic Equestrian and Musical Agency and Sick Fund Association, a society established in 1855 on the progressive principle, common among other such organizations in this period, of 'sooth[ing] the hours of sickness, accident, and old age while elevat[ing] the profession' (*The Era*, 29 July 1855, 10). The agency was important since it provided for performers who were traditionally excluded from those friendly societies set up by established theatres, such as Drury Lane and Covent Garden, and by the Actors' Benevolent Fund which catered to the élite of the acting profession. As such it was resorted to by employees of the circus, who could afford its relatively reduced subscription rates. In addition to being a founder member of the organization, Cooke sat on its board of trustees for many years, and was appointed a life governor along with his first wife, Mary Ann. Cooke died at the age of seventy-eight at his residence, 149 Acre Lane, Brixton, on 6 May 1886. He was survived by his second wife.

BRENDA ASSAEL

**Sources** *The Era* (5 Feb 1860), 11 · Lambeth Archives, London, William Cooke MSS, with 1858 Route Book · clippings file: Astley's, 1853–60, Theatre Museum, London · biography file, William Cooke, Theatre Museum, London · *The Era* (29 July 1855), 10 · *Chester Courant* (14 July 1858), 8 · *Chester Courant* (21 July 1858), 8 · *Norfolk News* (28 Aug 1858), 5 · d. cert. · *CGPLA Eng. & Wales* (1886)
**Archives** Lambeth Archives, London · Theatre Museum, London, biography file | Theatre Museum, London, Astley's production files
**Wealth at death** £137 13s. 4d.: probate, 1 June 1886, *CGPLA Eng. & Wales*

**Cooke, William Bernard** (1778–1855). *See under* Cooke family (*per. c.*1800–1865).

**Cooke, Sir William Fothergill** (1806–1879), developer of electric telegraphy, was born on 4 May 1806 at Ealing, Middlesex, one of two sons and two daughters of William Cooke (1776/7–1857), surgeon, and his wife, Elizabeth Ann, *née* Fothergill. In 1822 William Cooke was elected physician to Durham Infirmary, a post he held until 1842. His son attended Durham School in 1822–3, then Edinburgh University, before entering the Indian army, becoming an ensign. After five years in India he resigned his commission on grounds of ill health, and took up his father's profession, studying anatomy at Paris and then at Heidelberg, under Professor Münke. He prepared the wax models which his father used for his own anatomy lectures in 1842.

Electric telegraphy came to Cooke's notice while he was at Heidelberg, several people having demonstrated its feasibility. Professor Münke's lectures included a demonstration of telegraphic apparatus on the principle introduced by Baron Schilling in 1835. Hitherto, such experiments had been confined to the classroom and laboratory;

**Sir William Fothergill Cooke (1806–1879)**, by unknown photographer, 1870s

Cooke realized the commercial possibilities, and conceived the idea of using the invention in connection with the various railway systems then developing. He abandoned his studies and devoted himself entirely to telegraphy. In 1836 he returned to England and conducted experiments with his friend and solicitor, Burton Lane. Cooke found that, although his apparatus worked across a room, it would not work through 1 mile of wire. He sought help from Michael Faraday and Peter Roget; neither could assist, but Roget, who knew of the work of Charles *Wheatstone, referred Cooke to him.

Cooke and Wheatstone first met on 27 February 1837, by which time Cooke was negotiating with the Liverpool and Manchester Railway Company for the use of his (Cooke's) telegraphs. After one or two interviews, in which Wheatstone seems to have frankly revealed to Cooke all the work he had done towards perfecting the electric telegraph, a partnership was agreed upon between them, and duly entered into in May 1837. Wheatstone had neither taste nor leisure for business details, while Cooke possessed a good practical knowledge, much energy, and business ability of a high order. Wheatstone and Cooke's first patent, 'for improvements in giving signals and sounding alarms in distant places by means of electric currents transmitted through electric circuits', was signed by William IV on 10 June 1837. Cooke now proceeded to test the utility of the invention, the London and Blackwall, the London and Birmingham, and the Great Western Railway companies successively allowing the use of their lines for the experiment. It was found, however, that with five needles and five line wires the expense was too great, and in that form the electric telegraph was abandoned. In 1838 an improvement was effected whereby the number of needles was reduced to two, and a patent for this was taken out by Cooke and Wheatstone. Before a parliamentary committee on railways in 1840, Wheatstone stated that he had, conjointly with Cooke, obtained a new patent for a telegraphic arrangement. The new apparatus required only a single pair of wires instead of five, and was greatly simplified. The telegraph was still too costly for general purposes. In 1845, however, Cooke and Wheatstone succeeded in producing the single needle apparatus, which they patented, and from that time the electric telegraph became a practical instrument, and was speedily adopted on all the railway lines of the country. In the meantime, a bitter controversy arose between Cooke and Wheatstone, each claiming the chief credit of the invention. Cooke contended that he alone had succeeded in reducing the electric telegraph to practical usefulness at the time he sought Wheatstone's assistance, and on the other hand Wheatstone maintained that Cooke's instrument had never been, and could never be, practically applied. More of the actual work of invention was no doubt done by Wheatstone than by his partner, though Wheatstone agreed that he could not have succeeded commercially without Cooke's 'zeal and perseverance and practical skill'. An arrangement was arrived at in 1843, by which the telegraph patents were assigned to Cooke, with the reservation of a mileage royalty to Wheatstone. Subsequently, Wheatstone sold all his rights in Great Britain, Ireland, and Belgium to Cooke for £30,000. In 1846 the Electric Telegraph Company was formed in conjunction with Cooke, the company paying Cooke £120,000 for the earlier patents.

On 5 June 1838 Cooke married Anna Louisa (d. 1891), daughter of Joseph Wheatley, a solicitor, at Treeton near Rotherham, Yorkshire; they had one daughter. For some years Cooke employed himself very actively in the practical work of telegraphy, but after his separation from Wheatstone he did not achieve much in the way of invention. He tried to obtain an extension of the original patents, but the judicial committee of the privy council decided that Cooke and Wheatstone had been sufficiently remunerated, and that the electric telegraph had not been so poor an investment as they had been led to believe by the press, the shareholders having received a bonus of £15 per share, besides the usual dividend of four per cent on £300,000. The Albert gold medal of the Society of Arts was awarded on equal terms to Cooke and Wheatstone in 1867; and two years later Cooke was knighted, Wheatstone having had the same honour conferred upon him the year before. Cooke subsequently lost all the money he had made from the telegraph in unsuccessful mining ventures in north Wales. A civil-list pension of £100 p.a. was granted to him in 1871. He died at Castle Street, Farnham, Surrey, the home of his son-in-law, on 25 June 1879. He was survived by his wife.

JAMES BURNLEY, rev. BRIAN BOWERS

**Sources** G. Hubbard, *Cooke and Wheatstone and the invention of the electric telegraph* (1965) · B. Bowers, *Sir Charles Wheatstone* (1975) · Inst. EE, Cooke and Wheatstone papers · personal information (2004) · d. cert. · *CGPLA Eng. & Wales* (1886) · New Brentford registers, LMA
**Archives** Inst. EE, archives, corresp. and papers, SC MSS 7 · PRO, papers relating to construction of telegraphs
**Likenesses** photograph, 1870–79, Sci. Mus. [*see illus.*] · M. Thomas, oils, c.1876, Inst. EE · photograph, repro. in F. H. Webb, ed., *Extracts from the private letters of the late Sir W. F. Cooke* (1895)
**Wealth at death** £16: administration, 1 Sept 1886, *CGPLA Eng. & Wales*

**Cooke, William John** (*bap.* **1796**, *d.* **1865**). *See under* Cooke family (*per. c.*1800–1865).

**Cookes, Sir Thomas**, second baronet (*bap.* 1648, *d.* 1701), benefactor, was baptized on 6 December 1648 at Feckenham, Worcestershire. He was the elder son of Sir William Cookes (*c.*1616–1672) of Norgrove, Worcestershire, and his second wife, Mercy, *née* Dinely (1628/9–1694). William Cookes, a royalist descended from an old, wealthy Worcestershire family, was created a baronet on 24 December 1664: an honour which cost him £1095.

Thomas Cookes matriculated from Pembroke College, Oxford, as a gentleman commoner on 7 June 1667, and was admitted to Lincoln's Inn on 26 June 1669. He succeeded to the baronetcy on the death of his father in July 1672, and on 28 August 1672 he married Mary Windsor (1658/9–1695), daughter of Thomas *Windsor, Lord Windsor (later first earl of Plymouth), and niece of the celebrated George Savile, marquess of Halifax (1633–1695). Cookes's bride was aged thirteen or fourteen; he was twenty-three. His seat was Bentley Pauncefote at Tardebigge, Worcestershire, but he owned property in sixteen west midlands parishes and in London: an inheritance perhaps all the larger because his younger brother, William, died in 1673, aged twenty-two.

Lady Mary Cookes died on 3 January 1695. On 6 December 1695 the widower married another young bride, Lucy (*b.* 1681), daughter of Bernard Whalley of Billesley, Warwickshire, and his wife, Lucy, *née* Baldwin. Both of Sir Thomas's marriages were childless, but he preserved his name through educational charities. He endowed and virtually refounded Bromsgrove School in 1693 and did the same for Feckenham School in 1696. More significantly, by the terms of his will, made on 19 February 1697, he left £10,000 in trust to endow a new college in Oxford University or to add to an existing foundation there. At this new or augmented foundation, as yet unnamed and unlocated, preference would be given to Bromsgrove and Feckenham schools and to Cookes's kin in the election of scholars and fellows. The archbishop of Canterbury, three other bishops, and all twenty-five heads of Oxford colleges and halls were named as trustees of the benefaction.

When Sir Thomas's intentions for Oxford became known, the claims of Gloucester Hall were pressed by its principal, Benjamin Woodroffe (1638–1711), who by the end of 1698 obtained a charter of incorporation (which proved to be invalid in law) and drew up confused statutes for the new college in terms that temporarily antagonized Cookes. The case for Balliol College was then put by its future master John Baron (c.1669–1722). Both claimants approached Sir Thomas directly, both preached highly partisan sermons on charity in Feckenham church (Baron in 1699, Woodroffe in 1700), and both produced printed arguments in 1702.

Cookes died on 8 June 1701 and was buried on 10 June beside his first wife in Tardebigge church. His will was proved on 9 July 1701, but the trustees were politically divided and very slow to interpret and execute his intentions regarding the gift to Oxford. In 1707 they decided that it should go to Magdalen Hall, but Simon Harcourt (1661?–1727), the lord keeper, decreed in the court of chancery on 31 October 1712 that it had been Cookes's intention that his charity, now swollen by interest to £15,000, should go to Gloucester Hall. The trustees reluctantly accepted his decree on 16 November 1713, and Gloucester Hall was formally incorporated as Worcester College on 29 July 1714. One witness in the chancery case declared that Cookes 'was a very wavering and unsteady and humoursome man in the managing of his affairs' (Worcester College Archives, deposition of William Cookes, April 1712, 7), and others testified to the same effect. However, Harcourt had probably correctly divined Sir Thomas's settled wishes, even though his own primary concern was to increase his political influence in the university by ensuring that his chaplain, Richard Blechinden (1668–1736), became principal of Gloucester Hall on Woodroffe's death in 1711 and subsequently provost of Worcester College. Blechinden was a far less colourful character and a less able scholar than Woodroffe, but a more competent man of affairs.

Cookes left a fee-simple estate of about £3000 p.a. and a personal estate of £40,000, including the £10,000 for Oxford. His will stipulated arrangements for his burial beside his first wife, but made no mention of the woman he had married just over a year before making the will: presumably she already had an adequate settlement. After Cookes's death she married Charles Knotsford of Queenhill, Worcestershire. Cookes's residuary legatee and executor was his nephew and godson, Thomas Winford (1673–1744), who took his uncle's name and, on the death in 1702 of his own father, a baronet, became Sir Thomas Cookes Winford; he was MP for Worcestershire from 1707 to 1710 and supported Gloucester Hall's claim to his uncle's gift.

JAMES SAMBROOK

**Sources** L. M. Sutherland, 'The foundation of Worcester College, Oxford', *Oxoniensia*, 44 (1979), 62–80 • parish registers, Tardebigge; 28 Aug 1672 [marriage]; 6 Dec 1695 [marriage]; 10 June 1701 [burial], 5 July 1672 [burial: Sir William Cookes] • Lord keeper's decretal, 31 Oct 1712, Worcester College, Oxford, box 28 (1) • Depositions, April 1712, Worcester College, Oxford, box 28 (1) • W. C. Metcalfe, ed., *The visitation of the county of Worcester* (privately printed, Exeter, 1883) [in 1682 and 1683] • Foster, *Alum. Oxon.* • *VCH Worcestershire*, 3.117, 119, 198, 227–8, 233; 4.148, 510–11, 531 • W. P. Baildon, ed., *The records of the Honorable Society of Lincoln's Inn: admissions*, 1 (1896), 304 • GEC, *Baronetage*, 3.301 • J. Nichols, *The history and antiquities of*

the county of Leicester, 2/2 (1798), 737 • T. Nash, *The history and antiquities of Worcestershire* (1781), 1.440–43, 2.403, 408 • H. E. M. Icely, *Bromsgrove school through four centuries* (1953), 23–30 • *Hist. U. Oxf.* 5: *18th-cent. Oxf.*, 94, 298–9 • M. Dickins, *A thousand years in Tardebigge* (1931), 156–8 • A. H. Barrett, 'Worcester's first provost', *Worcester College Record* (1986), 20–26 • *London Magazine*, 16 (1747), 243 • parish register, Feckenham, 6 Dec 1648 [baptism]
**Archives** Worcester College, Oxford, documents relating to the Cookes benefaction, boxes 28 (1), (2)
**Likenesses** M. Dahl, oils, Bodl. Oxf. • attrib. J. Nost, double portrait, monumental effigy (with his wife), Tardebigge church, Worcestershire • oils, Worcester College, Oxford
**Wealth at death** left fee-simple estate of approx. £3000 p.a. and personal estate of £40,000, incl. £10,000 for new foundation at University of Oxford: Lord Keeper's decretal, 31 Oct 1712, Worcester College, Oxford, box 28 (1)

**Cookesley, William Gifford** (1802–1880), classical scholar, son of John Cookesley, was born at Brasted, Kent, on 1 December 1802. He was educated at Eton College and at King's College, Cambridge, which he entered as a scholar in 1821. He graduated BA in 1826, MA in 1829, and held a fellowship from 1824 until 1831. Cookesley was an early member of the University Cricket Club, which was founded in 1820. He played in the first match against Oxford in 1827, but failed to score in a game which was unfinished owing to rain. He was ordained deacon in 1827 and priest in 1835. On 20 March 1831 he married Augusta, daughter of John Davy Foulkes. From 1829 until 1854 he was an assistant master at Eton. In 1857, having served a curacy in Ipswich, he was appointed vicar of Hayton, Yorkshire. He became incumbent of St Peter's, Hammersmith, in 1860, and rector of Tempsford, Bedfordshire, in 1868. He died there on 16 August 1880, his wife having predeceased him. He was survived by a daughter.

Cookesley published a number of school editions of classical authors, including several of Pindar (1838, 1844, 1851). He also produced some volumes of sermons, and various theological books and pamphlets, including works against popery (1849), on Jews in parliament (1852), and on Mosaic miracles (1853), and a volume of criticisms of Bishop Colenso's views on the Pentateuch (1863).

W. W. WROTH, rev. RICHARD SMAIL

**Sources** Venn, *Alum. Cant.* • Boase, *Mod. Eng. biog.* • *The Athenaeum* (21 Aug 1880), 240 • W. J. Ford, *The Cambridge University Cricket Club, 1820–1901* (1902) • *GM*, 1st ser., 101/1 (1831), 365
**Archives** BL, Disraeli MSS • BL, letters to W. E. Gladstone, Add. MSS 44361–44454 • Bodl. Oxf., letters to Benjamin Disraeli • Bodl. Oxf., letters to S. L. Giffard
**Wealth at death** under £1000: administration, 15 Sept 1880, *CGPLA Eng. & Wales*

**Cookson family** (*per. c.1700–1863*), industrialists and bankers, came to prominence with **Isaac Cookson** (*bap.* 1679, *d.* 1743), glass and iron manufacturer, who was baptized in Penrith on 3 March 1679, the third of seven children of William Cookson (c.1635–1712), a brazier, and his wife, Alice. William was occasionally cautioned for religious dissent and non-attendance at church. By 1704 Isaac had moved to Newcastle upon Tyne, where he became a merchant adventurer; however, nothing is known of the details of his early business interests. He married Hannah Buston (1681/2–1760) on 6 April 1709, but no details of her family, or of when their five children were born, are extant. The Cookson family worshipped at the Hanover Square congregation of dissenters, founded by Richard Gilpin before 1700.

By 1721 Isaac Cookson was established in the iron trade. In that year he entered into partnerships, first with his eldest brother, **William Cookson** (*bap.* 1668, *d.* 1744), and second with Joseph Button, a Gateshead stationer in whose house Daniel Defoe stayed during his *Tour through the Whole Island*. The brothers' partnership was for the building of an iron furnace at Little Clifton, near Workington, on land leased from Lord Lonsdale. The furnace was supplied with water power from the River Marrow, ironstone from Branthwaite, and coal from Cookson's mines at Clifton and Greysouthen. The ironworks appears to have been a success. The lease was renegotiated in 1735 for £240 for a further twenty-one years and, in 1750, the lessors considered the works to be 'carrying on to very great proffit for the casting and making of Pots and other Uttensals of cast iron' (Hedley and Hudleston, 13–14).

Isaac Cookson's original partnership with Joseph Button concerned the leasing, in March 1721, of a founding house for casting iron and brass wares at the east end of old Trunk Staith, Gateshead, from William Cotesworth. The partnership was later extended for thirty-one years from 1 September 1729, the partners agreeing to share the 'art, trade and mystery of carrying on iron foundries at Clifton [Cumberland], Gateshead and Newcastle' (Hedley and Hudleston, 25). The capital employed was £4800, of which Cookson's share was £3900.

The first evidence of Isaac Cookson's interests in glass manufacturing is in 1728, when he entered into partnership with Joseph Airey, a Newcastle mercer and fellow member of the Hanover Square congregation. Airey, Cookson & Co. took over the Dagnia flint glasshouse in the Closegate, Newcastle, after the death of Onesiphorus Dagnia. This glasshouse was still operating as Airey, Cookson & Co. in 1801. In the late 1730s Isaac Cookson was part of a separate partnership to develop a crown glasshouse at Bill Quay, South Shields, on land he had originally leased in 1722, and appears to have acted as a sleeping partner in this enterprise by leasing the land for building. The main partners were his eldest son, John Cookson [*see below*], Thomas Jeffreys and James Dixon, merchants of Snow Hill, London, and Francis Hawkes the elder, a glassmaker of Vane Hall, Surrey. This partnership appears to have been reinforced by marriage: James Dixon married Isaac Cookson's daughter Hannah in 1738. By 1740 the partnership was advertising the best crown glass to be sold at its London warehouse, the Old Swan, London Bridge.

Isaac Cookson died in Newcastle upon Tyne in 1743 and his brother William a year later, in 1744. It is not known how the Little Clifton ironworks partnership was continued after their deaths. In his will, drawn up on 13 November 1740, Isaac Cookson left 'all and every my goods and chattels, rights and credits' to his son John Cookson, who was his sole executor, with the 'special condition, trust and confidence' (Hedley and Hudleston, 20) that annual payments of £80 be made to his widow during her lifetime. Hannah was also to have the family's silver plate, linen, beds, and other furniture, although she was required to release her dower money to her son within three months of her husband's death. Isaac Cookson's other sons, Isaac and Joseph, were to receive £2000 and a one-eighth part of the crown glasshouse at South Shields plus its stock, money, debts, glass bottles, pots, clay work, and tools. His daughters, Sarah Cookson and Hannah Dixon, were to receive £1200 and £300 respectively.

William Cookson, who was baptized in Penrith on 25 November 1668, had two sons and four daughters with his first wife, Esther Wren, whom he married on 30 December 1691 and who died soon after the birth of their youngest child in 1705. No children were born of his second marriage, on 5 August 1708, to Susanna (*d.* 1736), widow of John Stenhouse. William Cookson was buried in Penrith on 25 December 1744. Of the five elder children nothing is known. However, the youngest child, **Isaac Cookson** (*bap.* 1705, *d.* 1754), who was baptized in Penrith on 11 November 1705, became a notable Newcastle goldsmith, being apprenticed, in 1720, to Francis Batty, and taking over Batty's shop, the Gold Ring, in The Side, following his master's death in 1728. In the 1740s Cookson became a partner in an ultimately unsuccessful lead smelting and refining partnership. This involved mining and smelting lead at Acton Burn, Blanchland, and refining lead and silver at Elswick, Newcastle. Cookson negotiated the lease for the Elswick refining house for fourteen years from May 1743, but it was apparently not renewed after his death. On 23 May 1734 Isaac Cookson married Susanna Gilpin (*d.* 1746) of Whitehaven. They had one daughter, Esther (*b.* 1737). Isaac Cookson died intestate in 1754 and was buried at Newcastle upon Tyne on 22 August 1754.

**John Cookson** (1712/13?–1783), merchant, glass and iron manufacturer, mine owner, and banker, was the eldest son of Isaac Cookson (*d.* 1743) and Hannah Buston. His date and place of birth are unknown, although it seems likely that he was born in Newcastle in 1712 or 1713. On 9 February 1728 he was apprenticed to Joseph Airey, a mercer and his father's partner in the Closegate flint glasshouse. John Cookson was enrolled by the Merchant Adventurers on 13 March 1728 and given his freedom on 27 April 1738. Prior to this, on 20 January 1736, he was granted leave to travel to improve his skills.

John Cookson's first known business venture was in 1738 as a partner in the South Shields crown glasshouse. Prior to 1740 he sold, for £375 paid by their father, a sixteenth share in the business to his brother Joseph. Joseph Cookson was living in South Shields in 1740 and may have managed the family's business interests there, which included salt pans and a ballast quay as well as the glasshouse. In 1746 John and Joseph Cookson were listed among the six owners of the plate and crown glasshouse and salt pans at South Shields.

On 27 July 1743, immediately after he had inherited his father's estate and thus become a wealthy man, John Cookson married Elizabeth, daughter of Walter Lutwidge of Whitehaven. Reputedly, as part of the marriage settlement, Cookson bought an estate at Whitehill, near

Chester-le-Street. Here, in partnership with John Button, the son of his father's iron trade partner, he built a blast furnace with the intention of coking local coal and making steel. In the long term, as a steel works, Whitehill was unsuccessful, although, as a foundry, it successfully made high quality cannon in the 1780s. Despite this, in the 1750s Whitehill was part of Cookson's diverse industrial interests which made him one of the most important businessmen in the region. His letters of this period demonstrate a mature grasp of these businesses, which included salt and alum refining and coal and lead mining as well as iron and glass making. These interests extended from Newcastle and South Shields to Chester-le-Street, Hexham, Cumberland, and north Yorkshire, and included Newcastle's trade with London and Glasgow.

By the mid-1750s John Cookson's status as a wealthy businessman of varied interests led him to become one of four partners in Newcastle's first bank. This was established in Pilgrim Street in 1755, the prime mover being a fellow Newcastle merchant, Ralph Carr. Joseph Airey, Cookson's apprentice master and partner in the Closegate glasshouse, was also a partner. By a deed of co-partnership, drawn up for ten years from 1 January 1756, each partner was to provide paid-up capital of £500. This investment was substantially repaid in profits—Cookson is estimated to have made £880 in 1758, £823 in 1771, and £1250 in 1776.

It is not, therefore, surprising that, in drawing up his will in 1774, having left his banking interests to his eldest son, Isaac (1745–1831), and his estates and mines to his wife in her lifetime, then to Isaac, Cookson was able to make very generous financial provisions for five of his six younger children. John Cookson (1754–1802), who subsequently became a London barrister, Thomas Cookson (1757–1775), of the Indian Civil Service, who died before his father, and Joseph Cookson (1763–1800), who subsequently became a captain in the Life Guards, were to receive £10,000 each. The two unmarried daughters, Hannah, who subsequently married Richard Ellison, MP for Lincoln, and Sarah, were to receive £5000 each. There was no legacy to his eldest daughter, Elizabeth, whose portion probably went to her on marriage to a London banker, Samuel Castell, in 1769.

John Cookson died on 17 December 1783; his will was proved in London on 19 April 1784. His eldest son retired from what had become known as the 'Old Bank' in 1796. However, the family's interests in the coal, glass, and iron industries prospered in the early nineteenth century. Isaac Cookson's estate was valued at £300,000 in 1846. Three of his sons—John Cookson (1773–1857), of Whitehill, Isaac Cookson (1776–1851), of Meldon Park, Northumberland, and Thomas Cookson (1779–1863), of The Hermitage, Chester-le-Street—became landed industrialists, creating the basis for further diversification of the Cookson family's industrial interests in the latter part of the century. However, the key figure in the Cookson family's business affairs, and indeed one of the key figures in the business history of north-east England, was John Cookson. His achievements were to diversify his father's broadening

industrial interests, ensure a landed base, create new business opportunities with existing partners, develop financial stability via banking, and provide for his younger children's futures by marriage and/or careers in the established professions. No great eighteenth-century magnate could have done more.       J. D. BANHAM

**Sources** W. P. Hedley and C. R. Hudleston, *Cookson of Penrith, Cumberland, and Newcastle upon Tyne* (1966) · M. Phillips, *A history of banks, bankers and banking in Northumberland, Durham, and North Yorkshire* (1894), 177–9, 188–90 · M. A. V. Gill, *A handbook of Newcastle silver* (1978), 7, 9 · F. W. D. Manders, *A history of Gateshead* (1973), 64–5 · J. Rush, *A Beilby odyssey* (1987), 27, 54 · H. J. Powell, *Glass-making in England* (1923), 94 · A. Clow and N. Clow, *The chemical revolution* (1952), 278 · D. J. Rowe, *Lead manufacturing in Britain* (1983), 19–20, 133–47 · A. E. Smailes, *North England* (1960), 142 · C. Evans, 'Manufacturing iron in the north east during the eighteenth century: the case of Bedlington', *Northern History*, 28 (1992), 178–96, esp. 192–3 · P. Riden, 'Some unsuccessful blast furnaces of the early coke era', *Historical Metallurgy*, 26 (1992) · C. M. Ross, 'The development of the glass industry on the rivers Tyne and Wear, 1700–1900', 2 vols., PhD diss., U. Newcastle, 1982 · J. D. Banham, 'Business development and banking in north east England, 1755–1839', PhD diss., University of Sunderland, 1997
**Archives** Corning Museum of Glass, New York, Rakow Library, letter-book, record no. 45276 [John Cookson] · Northumbd RO, Newcastle upon Tyne, Cookson (Meldon) MSS, ref. ZCK · Tyne and Wear Archives Service, Newcastle upon Tyne, letter-book, accession no: 1512/5571 [John Cookson] · U. Durham L., Cookson MSS

**Cookson** [*née* Davies], **Dame Catherine Ann** (1906–1998), writer, was born on 20 June 1906 at 5 Leam Lane, South Shields, co. Durham, the illegitimate daughter of a domestic servant, Catherine Fawcett (1883–1956), known as Kate. Catherine was brought up by her grandmother and stepgrandfather (Rose Fawcett, *née* McConnell, and John McMullen), in a strong Irish Catholic family, and believed for the first eight years of her life that the McMullens were her parents and that Kate was her sister. She learned the truth from children in the street. Her childhood was marred by alcoholism, unemployment, and poverty: she made regular trips to the pawnshop for her mother and scavenged for wood and coal on the banks of the Tyne. The story she later told in *Our Kate* and earlier unpublished manuscripts portrays a family in which physical and sexual abuse were common: Catherine's mother admitted to Catherine before she died that she had been abused by both her stepfather and her half-brother. Catherine, in turn, claimed to have been sexually assaulted by a lodger and to have been emotionally and physically abused by her mother when under the influence of alcohol. At times she hated Kate so much that she fantasized about killing her. In unpublished autobiographical manuscripts Catherine writes of 'tragic secrets' and 'things so terrible' that they can never be told.

Always known at this stage as Kitty or Katie McMullen, Catherine did not discover until she was given a copy of her birth certificate in her late twenties that her real name was Catherine Ann Davies and her official date of birth 27 June 1906. Kate had registered her daughter's birth later than the legal time allowed, and falsified her date of birth to avoid the penalty. She also claimed to be married to Catherine's father, named on the certificate as Alexander

Dame Catherine Ann Cookson (1906–1998), by Chris Hay, 1987

Davies, commission agent, in a vain attempt to avoid the stigma of illegitimacy. He is believed to have been Alexander Davies Pate (1879–1948), a handsome labourer of Scots–Irish descent with a passion for gambling, who already had a wife in Newcastle and later bigamously married another. Catherine clung to the fantasy that her father had been a 'gentleman' and rarely admitted that she knew his true identity. She inherited her father's good looks and red gold hair as well as his charismatic personality and ability to tell stories. Less welcome was the rare blood disorder she also inherited from him—hereditary haemorrhagic telangiectasis—from which he eventually died and whose symptoms blighted Catherine's life.

Educated at St Peter and St Paul's Roman Catholic School at Tyne Dock, Jarrow, Catherine left school because of ill health before she was thirteen and followed her mother into domestic service. She was already writing stories and trying to get them published but, realizing that her lack of education was a restriction, she began to educate herself by a programme of reading and night classes. At various times she also took lessons in bookkeeping, elocution, fabric painting, juggling, French, and music in an effort to better herself and was eventually rewarded by the offer of a job in the workhouse laundry at Harton in South Shields. More senior posts followed at Tendring in Essex and at Hastings in Sussex, where Catherine finally settled. There she bought her first house, run initially as a lodging-house with help from her mother and a friend, Nan Smyth (Annie Smyth; 1895–1969), with whom Catherine had an intense and ambiguous relationship. Although they were together for nine years, 'We lived together; we slept together', Catherine always denied that it was anything other than a close female friendship. Nan kept letters which she later used to try to disrupt Catherine's marriage to Thomas Henry Cookson (1912–1998), an Oxford mathematics graduate teaching at Hastings grammar school who came initially as a lodger to the house Catherine and Nan were sharing. Tom was a

protestant and Catherine had to face considerable opposition from the priests, her mother, and Nan Smyth before they were able to marry on 1 June 1940 at St Mary's Star of the Sea Catholic Church in Hastings. Catherine claimed that Nan had threatened to shoot her on the morning of the wedding if she allowed it to take place.

During the war Catherine Cookson accompanied her husband on his postings around the country as an RAF instructor. She earned a living as a skilled illustrator for J. Arthur Dixon and continued a programme of self-education, helped by Tom who drew up a reading list and taught her English grammar. Religious doubts and a series of stillbirths and miscarriages affected Cookson's mental health, which was already shaky following the breakup of her friendship with Nan Smyth. She became ill with severe depression and was admitted to St Mary's Hospital in Herefordshire, where she had several sessions of electroconvulsive therapy. She was never able to have a child and allowed her Catholic faith to lapse.

After the war the Cooksons returned to Hastings and Catherine Cookson joined the Hastings writers' circle and began to try to get her work published. Her first, autobiographical, novel, *Kate Hannigan*, was taken up by agent John Smith at Christy and Moore and published by Macmillan in 1950. Though she was devastated when her second was rejected, she quickly began the series of Jarrow novels that made her famous as a novelist of the social history of the north-east of England. The 'Cookson novel' became a genre in its own right. Fame was slow to come, however, until *The Round Tower* won the Winifred Holtby award in 1969.

Cookson also wrote many nineteenth-century historical novels, such as *The Glass Virgin* and *The Black Velvet Gown*, children's books, and humorous novels such as the Mary Ann series based on her own childhood. The story of her own and her mother's life, *Our Kate*, which was published in 1969, is a much edited version of the memoir she had begun in 1956 after the death of her mother, with whom she had had a difficult and often turbulent relationship. It was a very powerful story, portraying an illegitimate girl growing up in one of the poorest communities in the Western world, struggling with family problems such as poverty, illiteracy, abuse, and alcoholism, to become one of the best-selling novelists of all time.

With the sale of *Katie Mulholland* to America and publication of the Mallen trilogy in 1973, Cookson's books began to dominate the best-seller lists. Characteristically, she gave much of her wealth to charity. She returned to live in the north-east, first at Corbridge in Northumberland, then in the village of Langley, and finally at 23 Glastonbury Grove in Jesmond, Newcastle upon Tyne. She continued to struggle with ill health, both mental and physical. In particular haemorrhagic telangiectasis caused spontaneous bleeding from nose, mouth, and stomach and necessitated frequent trips to hospital and frequent blood transfusions. Catherine gave many hundreds of thousands of pounds to fund genetic research into the condition. She was cared for by her devoted husband Tom who, she admitted, had 'given up his life' so that she could write. Although now a multi-millionaire (she once described herself as 'the best paid bastard in the business!'), Cookson was still haunted by religious doubts and the shame of her illegitimate birth. She remained loyal to her roots, insisting that she had always been 'a child of the Tyne', her novels recording the rise and decline of the industries on its banks across a period of nearly 200 years.

Catherine Cookson herself soon became one of the region's most profitable industries as interest in her novels attracted tourists into the area. South Shields declared itself 'Catherine Cookson country', and a replica of her old home (demolished under a slum clearance programme) was re-erected in the town museum. During the 1980s and 1990s her books were made into films for television and reached an even wider audience, being translated into sixty-eight languages. She wrote a total of 103 books—89 novels, 10 children's books, and 4 autobiographical works—continuing to dictate fiction until her ninetieth year.

Cookson was given an honorary MA by the University of Newcastle upon Tyne in 1982 and an honorary doctorate by the University of Sunderland in 1990. St Hilda's College, Oxford, made her an honorary fellow in 1997. In 1985 she was appointed OBE, and in 1993 she was made a dame of the British empire.

Cookson was reconciled to the Roman Catholic church in the last year of her life and died at her home in Jesmond on 11 June 1998, from heart failure. She was cremated later in June at the West Road crematorium, Newcastle. Her husband died just seventeen days later, and the bulk of their joint estate was left to a charitable trust.

Several of her novels were published posthumously, including *A House Divided*, *Rosie of the River*, *The Silent Lady*, *The Blind Years*, *Riley*, *The Thursday Friend*, and her rejected second novel, *Kate Hannigan's Girl*. Catherine Cookson's will failed to appoint a literary executor. This resulted in some confusion over manuscripts still unpublished and in major disagreements between her agents Anthony Sheil (who represented Cookson for almost thirty years) and Sonia Land of Sheil Land Associates Ltd, which were resolved when Anthony Sheil left the agency. Sheil Land Associates Ltd continued to represent the Cookson estate after her death.      KATHLEEN JONES

**Sources** K. Jones, *Catherine Cookson: the biography* (1999) · unpublished MSS, Boston University · autobiographical tapes, priv. coll. · personal knowledge (2004) · private information (2004) · b. cert. · m. cert. **Archives** Boston University, literary MSS and papers · U. Newcastle, Catherine Cookson collection | South Shields Museum and Art Gallery, Catherine Cookson collection | SOUND U. Newcastle **Likenesses** A. Reynolds, photograph, 1973, Hult. Arch. · C. Hay, photograph, 1987, NPG [*see illus.*] **Wealth at death** £8,994,174: probate, 4 Sept 1998, *CGPLA Eng. & Wales* · £8,476,174: publication of will in *Newcastle Journal*

**Cookson, George** (1760–1835), army officer, sixth son of Captain Thomas Cookson RN (*d.* 13 Nov 1775), and grandson of William Cookson of Wellington, Shropshire, was born at Farnborough, Hampshire, on 29 April 1760. He entered the Royal Navy in 1773, and served with his father, but after his father's death in 1775 Lord North gave him a cadetship to the Royal Military Academy, Woolwich, which he entered in 1777. He became second lieutenant, Royal Artillery, in 1778, and lieutenant in 1780. His early service was principally in the West Indies, and on one occasion, in 1785, he commanded all the artillery on the Black River (on the Spanish main in South America) until its evacuation. In November 1792 he was promoted captain-lieutenant, and in 1793 accompanied the duke of York's army to the Netherlands. He opened the first British battery against the city of Valenciennes, and commanded the British gunners in the trenches and at the successful storming of that city. On the conclusion of the campaign he was promoted captain and appointed to the command of no. 7 company, 5th battalion. He served two years at Gibraltar (1797–8), and in 1800 was made brevet major. In that year he commanded the Royal Artillery with General Maitland's expedition against Belle Île, which afterwards joined the force sent against Ferrol under Sir James Pulteney, and was eventually incorporated with the artillery under Sir Ralph Abercromby's command in the Mediterranean. Cookson was appointed to manage the landing of the field pieces in Abercromby's disembarkation on the coast of Egypt, and he was so rapid that the guns were in action almost as soon as the infantry, and did great service in covering the landing of the rest of the army. During the whole Egyptian campaign Cookson greatly distinguished himself, especially at the siege of Alexandria, when for a time he commanded all the fifty-two guns employed at the siege, and in the attack on the castle of Marabout on 22 August, when he was publicly thanked by Sir Eyre Coote. On 29 October 1801 he was made commandant of the ancient Pharos, and appointed to command all the artillery in Egypt, and he was afterwards presented with a gold medal by the grand vizier, an honour conferred on no other artillery officer.

After his return to England Cookson was promoted lieutenant-colonel, and in September 1804 was appointed to command the artillery in the Dublin district. He had made the acquaintance of Lord Cathcart in the Netherlands, and at that general's special request he was appointed to command the artillery accompanying the expedition to Hanover in 1805. The expedition, however, did nothing, and after its failure Cookson returned to Dublin. He was again, at Cathcart's request, ordered to accompany that general's more important expedition to Denmark in 1807, and commanded the batteries on the right during the bombardment of Copenhagen; but he received no recognition of his services on this occasion, though the officer commanding the artillery, Colonel Blomefield, was made a baronet. In October 1808 he embarked in command of the forty-eight guns and 1200 artillerymen ordered to form part of Sir David Baird's army intended for the Peninsula, and when Baird joined Sir John Moore, Cookson took command of all the horse artillery with the combined army. He commanded it with great ability throughout Moore's retreat, and especially distinguished himself at the action off Benevente on 29 December 1808, when General Lefevre-Desnouettes was taken prisoner. At the close of the retreat, 3 miles from Corunna, he successfully blew up two great magazines of powder, containing some 12,000 barrels, to save them from the enemy, but he missed the battle of Corunna, as he had embarked with the horse artillery the night before.

In April 1809 Cookson received the command of the artillery in the Sussex district, which he held until 1 August 1814, except in July 1809, when he commanded the artillery in South Beveland during the Walcheren expedition up to the fall of Flushing. Few artillery officers saw more varied service than Cookson, but as he did not serve in the post-Corunna Peninsula campaigns or at Waterloo he was never even made CB for his services. He was promoted in regular course colonel on 17 March 1812, major-general on 4 June 1814, and lieutenant-general on 22 July 1830.

Cookson was married three times. In 1786 he married Ann Helena (1766–1789), daughter of Dr Thomas Weir of Jamaica; they had no children. In 1791 he married Sarah (1769–1798), daughter of John Parker, banker, of Hornsey and London. They had three children: two died young and George (b. 1793), an officer in the 3rd guards, was killed at the battle of Fuentes d'Oñoro on 5 May 1811. Cookson married in 1807 Margaret, only daughter of William Remington; they had a large family and she survived him. He died at Esher, Surrey, on 12 August 1835.

H. M. STEPHENS, rev. ROGER T. STEARN

**Sources** J. Philippart, ed., *The royal military calendar*, 3 vols. (1815–16) · *GM*, 2nd ser., 4 (1835), 428 · Fortescue, *Brit. army*, vol. 4 · A. J. Guy, ed., *The road to Waterloo: the British army and the struggle against revolutionary and Napoleonic France, 1793–1815* (1990) · R. Muir, *Britain and the defeat of Napoleon, 1807–1815* (1996) · T. C. W. Blanning, *The French revolutionary wars, 1787–1802* (1996)

**Cookson, Henry Wilkinson** (1810–1876), college head, was born on 10 April 1810 at Kendal, Westmorland, the sixth son of Thomas and Elizabeth Cookson. Wordsworth was one of his godfathers. He was educated at Kendal grammar school and at Sedbergh School, then under the headmastership of Henry Wilkinson, an old friend of the family from whom he derived his second baptismal name. In October 1828 he entered Peterhouse, or St Peter's College (as he always preferred to style the most ancient college in the University of Cambridge). His private tutors were Henry Philpott, who as bishop of Worcester was to pronounce the last words over his grave, and the famous William Hopkins of Peterhouse. He graduated BA as seventh wrangler in 1832, MA in 1835, and BD and DD in 1848. Elected a fellow of his college in 1836, Cookson was appointed tutor in 1839; his pupils included William Thomson (later Lord Kelvin). He was proctor in 1842.

In 1847 Cookson succeeded Dr Hodgson as master of his college, and also as rector of Glaston in Rutland until 1867 when the two offices became separated under the new college statutes. In 1855 he married Emily Valence, elder

Henry Wilkinson Cookson (1810–1876), by Lowes Cato Dickinson

daughter of Gilbert Ainslie DD, master of Pembroke College. They had one daughter. Cookson died, after an illness of a few days, on 30 September 1876, in Peterhouse lodge, Cambridge; he was buried in the churchyard of the college benefice of Cherry Hinton, near Cambridge.

Cookson was one of the most influential members of his university. With his mathematical abilities he combined strong scientific sympathies and distinct literary tastes. He rendered substantial service to the Cambridge Philosophical Society, of which he was president in 1865–6. A staunch protestant, in 1870 he defended the maintenance of religious tests in the university; it was no secret that in 1867, through Lord Derby, he was offered the bishopric of Lichfield, which he declined. In politics a Conservative, he was an energetic chairman of the committee in support of Anthony Cleasby during the parliamentary election for one of the university seats in February 1868. He was elected vice-chancellor on five occasions (1848, 1863, 1864, 1872, and 1873) and was almost continuously a member of the council of the senate from its institution in 1856 onwards. His 'unerring eye for the bye-paths of university business … earned him the nickname "the artful dodger"' (Brooke, 53). Although he became proverbial at Cambridge for prudence and caution, he was hardly less distinguished by a genuine enthusiasm for progress, and especially for the extension of the studies of the university, and an increase in the number of its professorial chairs. Thus he drew particular satisfaction from the practical results of university administration, such as the augmentation of the Woodwardian Museum, the enlargement of the botanical garden, and the erection of new museums; and he was one of the first to advocate the application of a proportion of the funds of the colleges to the endowment of new professorships. Altogether, he had no slight share in the remarkable development of Cambridge after 1850.        A. W. WARD, *rev.* M. C. CURTHOYS

**Sources** *Cambridge Chronicle* (7 Oct 1876) · *Saturday Review*, 42 (1876), 475–6 · Venn, *Alum. Cant.* · C. N. L. Brooke, *A history of the University of Cambridge*, 4: *1870–1990*, ed. C. N. L. Brooke and others (1993), 53 · *CGPLA Eng. & Wales* (1876)
**Archives** CUL, letters to Lord Kelvin; letters to Sir George Stokes · NRA, priv. coll., corresp. with S. H. Walpole
**Likenesses** L. C. Dickinson, portrait, Peterhouse, Cambridge [*see illus.*] · C. G. Scott, mural brass, Cherry Hinton church, Cambridge
**Wealth at death** under £5000: probate, 21 Nov 1876, *CGPLA Eng. & Wales*

**Cookson, Isaac** (*bap.* **1679**, *d.* **1743**). *See under* Cookson family (*per. c.*1700–1863).

**Cookson, Isaac** (*bap.* **1705**, *d.* **1754**). *See under* Cookson family (*per. c.*1700–1863).

**Cookson, James** (*bap.* **1751**, *d.* **1835**), Church of England clergyman, was baptized on 14 April 1751 at Martindale, Westmorland, the son of John Cookson. He received his academic education at Queen's College, Oxford, where he matriculated in 1777. He graduated BA on 13 June 1781, and proceeded MA on 13 July 1786. Meanwhile he had been instituted, in September 1785, to the family-owned rectory of Colemore with Priors Dean, Hampshire, to which he was inducted the following October. Colemore and Priors Dean were both small livings with fewer than 200 inhabitants. He was also for many years curate of the neighbouring village of Steep, and about 1796 was presented to the vicarage of Harting, Sussex. Popular report says that he was put into the last-named living under a bond of resignation, and that when asked to resign he said 'his conscience did not allow him to do so'. As incumbent of Colemore he was also a trustee and frequently acting curate of East Tistead.

Despite the cares of three parishes some miles apart, Cookson found time for writing. His first work was entitled *Thoughts on Polygamy* (1782) and consisted of reflections on the institution of marriage and its obligations. He outlined the laws relating to it, and particularly discussed 26 Geo. II, ch. 33, commonly called the Marriage Act. Cookson also commented on the Revd Martin Madan's *Thelypohthora*, and suggested a scheme for the prevention of prostitution. His next work was *A New Family Prayer-Book* (1783). This was followed in 1784 by *The Universal Family Bible*. Between the appearance of the last two works Cookson had become master of Churcher's College, Petersfield, through the recommendation of Lord Clanricarde, a local Hampshire landowner. In 1784 Churcher's College was a small establishment, with only a dozen boys in residence.

Cookson was of eccentric habits, and is said once to have announced in church, 'I have forgotten my sermon, but I will read you a true account of the battle of Waterloo.' In 1814 he was elected a fellow of the Society of Antiquaries.

He died on 6 January 1835 at Petersfield, and was buried on 12 January in the chancel of Colemore church, Hampshire.

GORDON GOODWIN, *rev.* WILLIAM GIBSON

**Sources** J. Hervey, *History of Colemore and Priors Dean* (1857) · *GM*, 2nd ser., 3 (1835), 441 · *BL cat.* · Foster, *Alum. Oxon.* · W. R. Ward, ed., *Parson and parish in eighteenth-century Hampshire*, Hampshire RS, 13 (1995) · *IGI* · private information (1887)

**Cookson, John** (1712/13?–1783). *See under* Cookson family (*per. c.*1700–1863).

**Cookson, William** (*bap.* **1668**, *d.* **1744**). *See under* Cookson family (*per. c.*1700–1863).

**Cookworthy, William** (1705–1780), porcelain manufacturer and Quaker minister, was born on 12 April 1705, the eldest child of William Cookworthy (1670–1718), a Quaker serge maker of Kingsbridge, Devon, and his wife, Edith (*d.* 1759), daughter of John and Mary Debell of St Martin by Looe, Cornwall. After his father's death, Cookworthy's mother was left in severely straitened circumstances after the loss of money invested in South Sea stock. In 1720 the young Cookworthy began an apprenticeship with the Quaker apothecaries Timothy and Sylvanus Bevan of Plough Court, London, walking from Devon to save the coach fare. The Bevans recognized his outstanding skill and took him into partnership at the end of his apprenticeship—the firm of Bevans and Cookworthy, wholesale chemists and druggists, being established in Plymouth under Cookworthy's management in 1726. His principal customers were doctors and apothecaries in the three south-western counties and the naval fraternity in Plymouth.

On 12 February 1736 Cookworthy married Sarah, daughter of Peter and Elizabeth Berry of Fullerns, Somerset, at Taunton Friends' meeting-house. They had five daughters. Sarah Cookworthy died on 11 September 1745. His wife's death was a turning point in Cookworthy's life. In his grief he withdrew temporarily from business and spent several months in retirement at Looe. Thereafter, his brother Philip took over the day-to-day management of the business, leaving Cookworthy freer to devote his energies to his religious work and his china clay experiments.

Cookworthy was the first to recognize that the twin ingredients of Chinese porcelain, kaolin for the body and petuntse for the glaze, were to be found in the china clay and moorstone (or 'growan', as it was known locally) of the Cornish moors. His interest in the chemistry of porcelain can be traced to 1745, when he met the discoverer of china clay in Virginia. It was probably between then and 1748 that Cookworthy discovered the china clay and moorstone deposits on Tregonning Hill, Germoe parish, Cornwall. By 1758 his porcelain-making experiments had resulted in a successful firing of clay from Tregonning Hill, but it was the discovery of an abundant deposit of high-quality china clay and moorstone at Carloggas, St Stephen parish, near St Austell, that proved to be the turning point. Thomas Pitt (later Lord Camelford), the owner of the Carloggas estate, helped Cookworthy to obtain a patent to manufacture porcelain using the Cornish ingredients in 1768 and provided finance for his experimental work. In 1768 Cookworthy opened a porcelain factory at Coxside, near the quayside at Plymouth. It was a small concern with share capital of under £300, half provided by Cookworthy and other local men, and half by a group of Quakers from Bristol, where Cookworthy had been involved in a china works for several years. The market for the blue and white china produced at Plymouth included exports to America.

In 1770 the Plymouth factory closed, apparently because of difficulties with maintaining quality. The numerous pieces classed as seconds suggest that Cookworthy had been unable to acquire a sufficiently skilled workforce in Plymouth. The business was transferred to 15 Castle Green, Bristol, where porcelain was manufactured under Cookworthy's supervision until 1773, when he decided to sell his interest in the factory and his patent rights to Richard *Champion, his business partner. Champion continued to make porcelain in Bristol until 1778, when—his capital spent—he closed the factory. He later sold Cookworthy's patent to a syndicate of Staffordshire potters, who exploited Cornish china clay for the production of bone china. True porcelain manufacture, pioneered by Cookworthy, virtually ceased in Britain with the closure of the Bristol works.

Cookworthy was also well known as a Quaker minister and religious thinker. He emerged from his period of retirement during his bereavement with strengthened faith; thereafter he adopted the traditional 'plain' dress and speech of the Quakers, though he continued to move in scientific and literary circles. Between 1745 and 1747 he took an unpopular stance, urging his Quaker neighbours in Plymouth not to compromise their pacifist principles by dealing in 'prize goods' from captured vessels. From that time he became an active Quaker minister, travelling widely in the three south-western counties, representing Devon Friends at the yearly meeting in London for the first time in 1748, and becoming the mainstay of Plymouth meeting.

Cookworthy believed firmly in the importance of the central Quaker doctrine: the power of the divine inner light operating on the human heart. This led him to explore beyond the Quaker fold to the writings of others who stressed the mystical side of religion. His publication in 1751 of a translation of Muralt's *L'instinct divin* as *The Divine Instinct Recommended to Men* was the prelude to translations of the writings of Emanuel Swedenborg, the Swedish visionary. He was perhaps attracted by Swedenborg's belief that personal relationships, particularly those of man and wife, survived beyond the grave. Cookworthy published *The Doctrine of Life* in 1763, the first of Swedenborg's works to appear in English, and collaborated with Thomas Hartley (d. 1784) in the translation of Swedenborg's *Heaven and Hell* (published 1778), accompanying Hartley on a visit to Swedenborg in London. That Cookworthy's faith was highly individual and could not be bound by the confines of Quaker orthodoxy is highlighted by an episode on his deathbed: he took bread and

wine, inviting his daughters to join him, saying that he felt it his duty to follow the scriptural injunction despite the Quaker testimony against ritual sacraments.

Cookworthy was a polymath, more scholar than businessman, his reputation for absent-mindedness and his 'mild but intellectual countenance' (Selleck, 228) confirming the impression of a man absorbed in study. A linguist, he was fluent in Latin and French, and his circle of acquaintances was wide and extended well beyond fellow Quaker intellectuals such as John Fothergill to include such figures as John Smeaton, who lodged with him during the building of the Eddystone lighthouse, and Captain James Cook, who, with Joseph Banks and Daniel Solander, dined with him before sailing from Plymouth in 1768. Cookworthy's willingness to embrace unorthodox beliefs, seen in his attraction to Swedenborg, was also visible in the scientific field. He firmly believed that divining rods could locate metallic lodes, and contributed an essay advocating their use to William Pryce's *Mineralogia Cornubiensis* (1778).

Cookworthy's scholarship drew comment from those who knew him. The naval officer John Jervis was reported as saying that no one could be in Cookworthy's company 'without being the wiser and better for it' (Selleck, 170). A young American who spent a whole day discussing politics, religion, and history with Cookworthy in 1776 found in him

> the most sensible Learned kind Man I ever knew … an amazing Memory, excellent Delivery, and a Stile that we no where else meet with, catholic in the extreme, deep in Argument, meek, humble … in short the most refind and accomplished Man.   (Morgan, 109–10)

Cookworthy fell ill in May 1780 and died at his home in Notte Street, Plymouth, on 17 October 1780, aged seventy-five. He was buried in the Quaker burial-ground at Plymouth on 21 October.                ANGUS J. L. WINCHESTER

**Sources** *DNB* · A. D. Selleck, *Cookworthy, 1705–80, and his circle* (1978) · J. Penderill-Church, *William Cookworthy, 1705–1780* (1972) · 'Dictionary of Quaker biography', RS Friends, Lond. [card index] · K. Morgan, ed., *An American Quaker in the British Isles* (1992)
**Archives** Devon RO, chemical notebook | BL, letters to Lord Camelford, Add. MS 69323 · Swedenborg Society, Swedenborg House, London, letters
**Likenesses** J. Opie, cartoon, *c.*1779, repro. in Penderill-Church, *William Cookworthy* · J. Opie, oils, 1779, City Art Gallery, Plymouth · C. Fox, drawing (after a cartoon by Opie), repro. in Selleck, *Cookworthy … and his circle* · attrib. J. Opie, pencil drawing, City Art Gallery, Plymouth · engraving, repro. in Bristol and Frenchay Monthly Meeting of Society of Friends, album, vol. 1, p. 32 · silhouette, RS Friends, Lond.

**Cool, Jacob** [Jacobus Colius; called Ortelianus] (1563–1628), scholar and writer, was born on 31 December 1563 in Antwerp, the son of Jacob Cool or Cole (d. 1591), merchant, and Elisabeth Ortelius (d. 1594), sister to the Antwerp map maker and geographer Abraham *Ortelius (1527–1598). Both his parents belonged to the Dutch-Walloon refugee community in London and like them Cool settled in Lime Street, where he followed in his father's footsteps as a cloth merchant, specializing in silk production and the silk trade. However, it was Cool's learned interests in theology, history, poetry, art, numismatics, and botany which came to dominate his life and which formed the basis for his many friendships with scholars such as William Camden, Emanuel van Meteren, Carolus Clusius, and the royal botanist Mathias de Lobel, who later became his father-in-law. Surprisingly, although he seems to have been a competent Latinist from an early age, Cool does not appear to have received any formal schooling. He was largely self-taught, except for a period during the late 1580s when he was educated by his uncle Abraham Ortelius, who evidently inspired his lifelong interest in history and in his collection of Greek and Roman coins and medals, and who provided him with the nickname Ortelianus by which he became known within the republic of letters. Between 1584 and 1586 Cool wrote a short treatise on letter combinations to be found in different figures, 'Tractatus de scriptis in fictis characteribus legendis'; another two unpublished works, written in 1588, 'Fasti triumphorum et magistratuum Romanorum' and 'Graeca numismata externorum regum', were on numismatics, about which he continued to correspond regularly with the Augsburg collector and numismatist Adolph Occo.

In 1592 Cool travelled widely in Germany and the Netherlands. That year and the next, as a liberal but firm Calvinist, he seems to have been temporarily in conflict with his uncle Ortelius, who held Familist and spiritualist views. In 1594 he married his first wife, Maria, daughter of Lodewijk Theus, an elder of the Dutch church in London, but by 30 November that year she was dead. In 1597 he went on a grand tour, seeing the major cities in southern Germany, in Italy, where he travelled as far as Naples, and in the United Provinces, *en route* visiting many of the leading intellectuals of the day, with whom he later regularly corresponded. Among them were the Bohemian humanist and intelligencer Jacob Monau and the son of the famous Leiden printer Franciscus Raphelengius, Franciscus junior; Franciscus Raphelengius himself expressed his admiration for Cool's elegant Latin. That Cool was a Latin scholar and poet of some capacity can be seen from the *Lacrymae* he wrote on the occasion of his uncle Abraham Ortelius's death in 1598 and from the verses attached to one of the later editions of Ortelius's great work, *Theatrum orbis terrarum*.

Cool's first two published works appeared in 1606. His deep scholarly interest in botany is demonstrated by his *Syntagma herbarum encomiasticum*, published in Leiden in 1606 under the Latin form of his name, Jacobus Colius; it is noteworthy that the Leiden botanist Carolus Clusius thought highly of Cool's botanical learning. The same year Cool married Louisa, daughter of the royal botanist to James I, Mathias de Lobel. Cool's Calvinist faith is prominent in his long descriptive poem about his personal experience of the outbreak and horrors of the plague in London in 1604, *Den staet van London in hare groote peste* (published in Middelburg in 1606), as in his two later works, on the interpretation of Psalm 104, *Paraphrasis … vanden CIV Psalm*, and on how to die as a good Christian, *Of Death, a True Description*.

For many years Cool played a prominent role within the Dutch community in London. In 1604 he provided the poetry for the community's triumphal arch and tableaux in connection with James I's coronation entry, and he was one of the leading members of the community who contributed poetry to the elegy for its learned minister Simon Ruytinck, who had died in 1621, which was published in Leiden in 1622. From 1624 he served the Dutch church in London as an elder. At the coronation of Charles I in 1625 Cool was made supervisor of the design for the then planned triumphal arch by the community. Here his contacts with leading English artists such as the poet Ben Jonson and the painter Francis Cleyn proved extremely useful to the church, and both were recruited for the work.

Cool died a very wealthy man on 20 May 1628: apart from his house in Lime Street and his house in Highgate, together with their furniture, jewellery, and paintings, he left more than £5000 in money and a number of large silver gilt cups, not to mention his considerable library, and his collection of prints, statues, antique coins, and medals, much of which he had inherited from Abraham Ortelius. His wife, Louisa, survived him, but there were no children from either of his marriages.

OLE PETER GRELL

**Sources** GL, MS 7397/7 · J. H. Hessels, ed., *Ecclesiae Londino-Batavae archivum*, 1: *Abrahami Ortelii at virorum eruditorum ad eundem et ad Jacobum Colium Ortelianum epistulae* (1887) · J. A. van Dorsten and K. Schaap, 'Introduction', in J. Cool, *Den staet van London in hare groote peste* (1962) · J. A. van Dorsten, '"I.O.C.": the rediscovery of a modest Dutchman in London', *The Anglo–Dutch renaissance: seven essays* (1988), 8–20 · O. P. Grell, *Dutch Calvinists in early Stuart London: the Dutch church in Austin Friars, 1603–1642* (1989) · O. P. Grell, *Calvinist exiles in Tudor and Stuart England* (1996)

**Wealth at death** very wealthy: will, Hessels, ed., *Ecclesiae Londino-Batavae archivum*

**Cooley, Thomas** (1740/41–1784), architect, is said to have been born in England; his parentage is unknown. He was apprenticed to a London carpenter named Reynolds, and subsequently became clerk to William Grenell, master joiner in the office of works. By 1763 he had become a pupil of Robert Mylne and by 1765 he was working as Mylne's clerk. Cooley reputedly devoted all his spare time to the study of architecture: he competed for premiums awarded by the Society of Arts, winning third prize in 1763 and second prize in 1764 and 1765. He also exhibited designs at the Free Society of Artists between 1765 and 1768.

In March 1769 Cooley won the Dublin Royal Exchange competition, a success which, according to Dublin rumour, was due to Mylne's influence with the committee. He moved to Dublin to supervise the execution of the exchange and settled in the city for the rest of his life. In 1775 he succeeded Joseph Jarratt as clerk and inspector of civil buildings at the barrack board. He enjoyed the patronage of Richard Robinson, archbishop of Armagh, who employed him as his architect for building projects in the city and diocese of Armagh: these included the archbishop's palace (1770), the public library (1771), the royal school (1774), and the gaol (1780). It was to Cooley's office that Robinson sent the young Francis Johnston from Armagh to train in the profession; after Cooley's death Johnston succeeded him as the primate's architect. In

Dublin itself, in addition to the Royal Exchange, Cooley designed the chapel of the Hibernian Military School in Phoenix Park (1771), Newgate prison (1773–81), and the north and west ranges of the west court of the Four Courts, begun in 1776 and completed after his death by James Gandon. His two major country house commissions were Caledon House, co. Tyrone (1779), for James Alexander, later first earl of Caledon, and Rokeby Hall, co. Louth, designed shortly before his death for Archbishop Robinson and carried out by Francis Johnston. His participation also seems to have been crucial in the design of Ardbraccan, co. Meath (1773–5), for Henry Maxwell, bishop of Meath.

When Gandon arrived in Ireland in 1781, he pronounced that Cooley and Thomas Ivory were the only two architects 'properly so called' (Mulvany, 49–50) in Dublin. In Cooley's architecture the richness and elaboration of the Dublin Royal Exchange, a domed structure with a giant Corinthian order on two façades, is unique. A rational sobriety prevails in his other buildings: their quality depends on interval and balance, and their restrained style prepares the visitor for interiors which often exhibit a sophisticated manipulation of architectural elements and an innovative elegance of detail unmatched by other Irish architects of the time.

Cooley was said to have 'supported an unimpeached character for integrity' (*Freeman's Journal*) but was also thought to be supercilious. He died of a bilious fever in Anglesea Street, Dublin, in 1784 in his forty-fourth year, leaving a son, William, and a daughter; his wife had predeceased him in January 1779. His collection of books, drawings, prints, antique medals, a camera obscura, and other items was sold at auction in April 1784. William Cooley married Emily, daughter of his father's executor, the sculptor Richard Cranfield; their son Thomas Cooley (1795?–1872) was a portrait painter in Dublin.

A. M. ROWAN

**Sources** 'Anecdotes of the fine arts in Ireland: Mr Thomas Cooley', *Anthologia Hibernica* (July 1793), 35–6 · [W. Papworth], ed., *The dictionary of architecture*, 11 vols. (1853–92) · E. McParland, *James Gandon: Vitruvius Hibernicus* (1985) · R. Dossie, *Memoirs of agriculture, and other oeconomical arts*, 3 (1782), 420–21 · *Public Register, or, Freeman's Journal* (5–7 Jan 1773) · *Faulkner's Dublin Journal* (21–3 Jan 1779) · *Faulkner's Dublin Journal* (24–7 April 1784) · A. E. Richardson, *Robert Mylne* (1955), 63, 66–7 · J. Gandon and T. J. Mulvany, eds., *The life of James Gandon* (1846) · R. McKinstry, R. Oram, R. Weatherup, and P. Wilson, *The buildings of Armagh* (1992) · *North Leinster*, Pevsner (1993) · Graves, *Soc. Artists*

**Archives** Armagh Public Library | Irish Architectural Archive, Dublin, RIAI Murray collection

**Cooley, William Desborough** (1795?–1883), geographer and controversialist, was probably born on 16 March 1795 in Dublin, the son of William Cooley (*b.* 1772/3), a Dublin barrister, and grandson of the architect Thomas *Cooley. Educated privately and then from 1811 to 1816 at Trinity College, Dublin, he developed an interest in the history of discovery, physical geography and surveying, and the mathematics which went with it, the last interest leading to later publications on Euclid.

Cooley's life from 1816 to the early 1830s is obscure, but he then emerged on the London literary scene as an editorial associate on *The Athenaeum*, a writer for the *Foreign Quarterly Review* who had revealed the false claims of J. B. Douville to discoveries in Angola, and the author of a *History of Maritime and Inland Discovery* in 1830–31 which remained standard for about forty years. He offered his services to the *Edinburgh Review* as a controversial writer on Irish subjects but the editor restricted him to geographical and African subjects on which he contributed eleven major reviews in three years. One of these, in 1835, revealed the existence of the then unknown Lake Tanganyika and distinguished what later became known as the Bantu and their languages. At this time Cooley was in contact with W. F. W. Owen and J. B. Emery, who had surveyed east Africa's coasts, and with two visiting Arab traders and their African servants who knew the interior. Collating their information with what little was available from Portuguese sources and from ancient authorities and then 'rectifying' it all, Cooley built up a picture of east Africa's geography which was set out in a major article with a map for the *Journal of the Royal Geographical Society* in 1845 and elaborated in a book, *Inner Africa Laid Open*, in 1852. Practical exploration now began to show that some of the details were wrong but Cooley became notorious for refusing to accept travellers' findings. He denied, for example, that there was snow on the summits of Kilimanjaro and Mount Kenya (though he had revealed the existence of these mountains) and he insisted that lakes Tanganyika and Malawi were connected as one water. When Livingstone mentioned particular Ngoni peoples, he said they did not exist. Perhaps demolishing Douville's claims had given Cooley too much of a taste for contradicting explorers, while his Irish background and combative temperament set him at odds with the English geographical establishment. More serious was his failure to realize that history moves on: for example, locations of peoples correctly deduced from sixteenth-century sources were no longer necessarily correct. In the end, his stubbornly held views made his geography absurd.

The problem was compounded by Cooley's relationship with the Royal Geographical Society. A member from its origin in 1830, he was elected to the council in 1832 and became a vice-president in 1835. He used his position to try to organize some exploring expeditions but none came to full fruition. He blamed the society and also accused the secretary, Alexander Maconochie, of mishandling the subscriptions—a grievance which still rankled forty years later. Cooley had to resign from his offices. Although he continued freely, and not altogether unjustifiably, to criticize the society in its years of prosperity for using the popularity of the great explorers to increase its fashionable appeal, he was given free membership and, at its instance, a £100 civil-list pension in 1859. Meanwhile, a stream of articles in *The Athenaeum* and other periodicals commented learnedly, forcefully, and not always mistakenly on the work of explorers in Africa and elsewhere.

Foremost among Cooley's positive achievements was the formation in 1846 of what he originally proposed to call the Columbus Society—a body which would make available to its subscribers in printed form records of important voyages and travels of the past. The idea arose partly out of Cooley's displeasure at the Royal Geographical Society's failure to act in this area and his own failure to make much of a success of a publication series entitled The World Surveyed. Renamed the Hakluyt Society, with Cooley as its first secretary and the editor of one of its earliest publications, the new body soon established itself as one of the country's major text-publishing learned societies and has flourished ever since. Increasing deafness and the pressure of other work led Cooley to resign the secretaryship in 1849, but he continued on the council until 1859.

It is a pity that the promising concepts which bore fruit in Cooley's *Physical Geography* of 1876 were not developed further. His other achievements may be said to be his attempts to bring rigour into what passed for geography in Britain in the mid-century. He was not wrong to criticize Livingstone's misreading of Herodotus which led to delusions about the 'fountains of the Nile'. Nor was he wrong in his *Claudius Ptolemy* of 1854 to question the credulous acceptance of ideas like the 'mountains of the moon' on the alleged authority of Ptolemy. Cooley did useful work on Somaliland and its history and on Arabic source materials for west Africa. His ideas on Africa, however misplaced some of them were, raised awareness and promoted serious study of the continent and its peoples. The information he acquired for his 'discoveries' of the 1830s and 1840s has remained useful evidence for historians of Africa.

Having lived for many years in comparative poverty, Cooley died of bronchitis on 1 March 1883, at 55 Crowndale Road, Somers Town, London. He is thought to have been unmarried.                                    ROY BRIDGES

**Sources** R. C. Bridges, 'W. D. Cooley, the RGS and African geography in the nineteenth century', *GJ*, 142 (1976), 27–47, 274–86 [incl. bibliography] · R. C. Bridges, 'William Desborough Cooley and the foundation of the Hakluyt Society', *Compassing the vaste globe of the earth: studies in the history of the Hakluyt Society, 1846–1996*, ed. R. C. Bridges and P. E. H. Hair, Hakluyt Society, 183 (1996), 51–78 · *The Athenaeum* (10 March 1883), 315 · *Proceedings* [Royal Geographical Society], new ser., 5 (1883), 232–3 · *DNB* · W. D. Foster, 'The Hakluyt Society, 1846–1946: a retrospect', *Richard Hakluyt and his successors*, ed. E. Lynam, Hakluyt Society, 2nd ser., 93 (1946), 141–70 · d. cert.
**Archives** RGS, notes on African travel | BL, letters from Heinrich Barth, Add. MS 32117 · BL, letters to Macvey Napier, Add. MSS 34616–34619 · RGS, letters to Royal Geographical Society
**Likenesses** photograph, c.1850, RGS
**Wealth at death** £1078 8s. 9d. in England: Irish probate sealed in England, 16 April 1883, *CGPLA Eng. & Wales*

**Coolidge, William Augustus Brevoort** (1850–1926), mountaineer, was born in New York on 28 August 1850, the son of Frederick William Skinner Coolidge, a merchant, of Boston, Massachusetts, and his wife, Elisabeth Neville Brevoort, a New Yorker whose family had made a fortune in the fur trade. Coolidge and his sister were raised by their mother and their aunt, Marguerite Claudia (Meta) Breevort (1825–1876). He was educated at St Paul's School, Concord, New Hampshire, privately in Paris, and

at Elizabeth College, Guernsey, before entering Exeter College, Oxford, in 1869. There he won the university Taylorian French scholarship in 1871, and obtained a first class in modern history in 1873 and a second class in jurisprudence in 1874. In 1875 he was elected to a fellowship of Magdalen College, Oxford, which he held until his death. Coolidge taught history at Magdalen and lived in Oxford until 1896, except for a year (1880/81) as professor of English history at St David's College, Lampeter. He was ordained deacon in 1882 and priest in 1883, holding decidedly high-church theological opinions. When at Oxford he regularly acted as honorary curate at South Hinksey between 1883 and 1896. But 'he chose a manner of life which made it for long periods difficult to perform clerical functions' (*DNB*).

Coolidge's principal devotions were climbing in and writing about the Alps. He first climbed there in 1865 with his aunt Meta Brevoort, one of the first female mountaineers. The two were well known for their climbs in the Dauphiné and in the Alps in winter. Coolidge gained a reputation as the 'young American who climbs with his aunt and his dog' after Christian Almer, his Swiss guide, gave him Tschingel, a beagle, in 1868. At the age of seventy Coolidge published a list of some 1750 of his own climbing expeditions between 1865 and 1900, including some 900 high ascents. He was equally scrupulous in recording each of Tschingel's sixty-six major peaks and passes, nearly all of which were canine first ascents. He employed this same obsession with accuracy of detail as an editor and author of guidebooks and reference works. He edited the *Alpine Journal* from 1880 to 1889 and, with William Martin Conway, a series of climbing guidebooks to the Alps. He also edited or revised several other alpine guidebooks and contributed thousands of articles to encyclopaedias and journals throughout Europe.

But Coolidge was meticulous to a fault. His self-righteousness, pugnacity, and impatience in correcting the mistakes of others led to numerous public quarrels with other members of the Alpine Club, such as William Edward Davidson and Edward Whymper. These pedantic disputes often degenerated into bitter internecine rivalries. Coolidge's vanity was also remarkable: one of his Christmas cards consisted in its entirety of his *Who's Who* entry within a border of edelweiss.

Although he did not wear his learning lightly, Coolidge's historical writing is of a high quality. His works are erudite but bibliographical in focus. *Swiss Travel and Swiss Guidebooks* (1889) is a solid study of the subject, with a separate section on the history of Zermatt. Often considered his major work, *Josias Simler et les origines de l'alpinisme jusqu'en 1600* (1904) reprints Josias Simler's *De altibus commentarius* (1574), in the original Latin and in French translation, with additional sources and editorial commentary. The introduction to Simler contains Coolidge's historical sketch on mountaineering before 1600. *The Alps in Nature and History* (1908) discusses the topography and peoples of the Alps, and the political and mountaineering histories of the region. *Alpine Studies*

(1912) collects some of his essays, including one on Tschingel.

In 1896 Coolidge moved permanently to Grindelwald, where he lived first at Am Sandigenstutz with the family of Christian Almer and later at Chalet Montana with a servant and a library of over 26,000 volumes. He never married. He died of a heart attack at Grindelwald on 8 May 1926; a memorial service was held for him there three days later.  PETER H. HANSEN

**Sources** R. W. Clark, *An eccentric in the Alps: the story of W. A. B. Coolidge, the great Victorian mountaineer* (1959) · A. Lunn, 'Memories of Coolidge', *Alpine Journal*, 60 (1955), 437–9 · A. L. Mumm, *The Alpine Club register*, 2 (1925)
**Archives** Alpine Club, London, corresp. and papers · Magd. Oxf., corresp. and papers · Zentralbibliothek, Zürich | Alpine Club, London, G. W. Young MSS · CUL, W. M. Conway MSS
**Likenesses** photographs, repro. in Clark, *Eccentric in the Alps*
**Wealth at death** £7411 16s. 4d.: probate, 6 April 1927, CGPLA Eng. & Wales

**Cooling** [Colinge], **Richard** (d. 1697), government official, was from a family apparently of Shropshire origins, and with several members in government service. Wood was of the opinion that he 'was originally, as it seems, of All Souls' College' (Wood, *Ath. Oxon.: Fasti*, 2.285–6). He was to claim that he had undertaken 'hazardous services' towards the restoration of Charles II, and had assisted in preparations for the subsequent coronation (*CSP dom.*, 1677–8, 120). More certainly, by 5 July 1660 he was acting as secretary to the lord chamberlain, the second earl of Manchester, and was one of the persons incorporated MA at Oxford with Manchester, on 8 September 1665. He continued to act as secretary to successive lord chamberlains until April 1697, while building up a collection of other offices. Thus he was appointed a commissioner for licensing hackney coaches in 1670 and acted as clerk of the robes and wardrobes from 26 September 1680 and, having vacated this post by March 1685, again from 1689. Perhaps a clerk-in-extraordinary to the privy council from 1679, he was sworn a clerk-in-ordinary on 21 February 1689. Pepys was acquainted with him, and regaled by him with court gossip. His attitude to office seems appropriately expressed in his reported comments that 'his horse was a Bribe, and his boots a bribe, and … he was made up of bribes, as an Oxford scholar is set out with other men's goods when he goes out of town' (Pepys, 8.369); a colleague remarked, at his death (17 June 1697), that he 'had the reputation of a "griping" officer to little purpose' leaving little in property and hefty debts (*CSP dom.*, 1697, 203). He bequeathed to his wife ('now liveing'; PRO, PROB 11/440), Mary (*née* Cullum), son Charles, and daughters Mary and Anne (he appears to have had at least one other son, Richard) little more than the residue of leases on some small properties, mostly in Shropshire, and of his house in Suffolk Street, London.  R. M. ARMSTRONG

**Sources** Pepys, *Diary* · J. C. Sainty and R. Bucholz, eds., *Officials of the royal household, 1660–1837*, 1: *Department of the lord chamberlain and associated offices* (1997), 2–3, 88–9 · will, PRO, PROB 11/440, fols. 23–5 · Wood, *Ath. Oxon.: Fasti* (1820), 285–6 · *CSP dom.*, 1660–97
**Likenesses** engraving, Magd. Cam. · mezzotint, BM · pencil and watercolour drawing, NPG
**Wealth at death** sums invested in exchequer and leases of Shropshire property; comment at death suggests £500 debts: *CSP dom.*, 1697, 203; will, PRO, PROB 11/440, fols. 23–5

**Coomaraswamy, Ananda Kentish** (1877–1947), art historian, was born on 22 August 1877 in Colombo, Ceylon, the only child of Sir Mutu Coomaraswamy (1834–1879), barrister, politician, and scholar of Buddhism and Hinduism, and his wife, Elizabeth Clay Beeby, the elder daughter of William John Beeby, of Kent. His father was the son of Gate Mudaliyar A. Coomaraswamy, the first Tamil member of the legislative council which had been established in Ceylon as a result of the recommendations of the Colebrooke commission. Sir Mutu Coomaraswamy was the first Hindu to qualify as a barrister in England, and was the senior unofficial member of the legislative council. He was knighted at Osborne by Queen Victoria in 1874, the first Tamil to be knighted. When Ananda was two he was taken to England by his mother, who was a Catholic and a descendant of one of Queen Victoria's ladies-in-waiting. His father had intended to follow his family to England, but died in May 1879 on the day he was due to depart.

In 1889 Coomaraswamy entered Wycliffe College, Stonehouse, Gloucestershire, after which he studied at University College, London, graduating in 1900 with first-class honours in mineralogy and botany. On 19 June 1902 he married Ethel Mary Partridge (1872–1952) [*see* Mairet, Ethel Mary], daughter of James Partridge, dispensing chemist, of Barnstaple; she later played a central role in the revival of hand-weaving in Britain. Following his election to a fellowship at University College in 1903, Coomaraswamy was director from 1903 to 1906 of the mineralogical survey of Ceylon. In 1906, as a result of his detailed scientific investigations, in the course of which he discovered a new mineral, thorianite, he was awarded an honorary DSc by London University. He retired from the mineralogical survey in the same year in order to devote himself to private study. Taking a keen interest in the arts of Ceylon and India, he played a major part in initiating the movement for national education, the teaching of vernaculars in all schools, and the revival of Indian culture. He was also president of the Ceylon Social Reform Society and a member of the Ceylon University Association. In 1910 he helped to found the India Society. In 1910–11 he was in charge of the art section of the huge United Provinces Exhibition held in Allahabad, India. Soon after, his first marriage having ended in divorce, he married Alice Richardson, an English student of Indian music who went by the name Ratan Devi. They had a son, Narada, and a daughter, Rohini.

In 1917, following the donation of the Dennison W. Ross collection to the Museum of Fine Arts, Boston, Massachusetts, Coomaraswamy was invited to take up the post as the museum's research fellow in Indian, Persian, and Muhammadan art, a position he held until his death. During his many years in Boston he not only developed the museum's Indian holdings, the largest in the United States, but established his reputation as a leading specialist in the history of Indian art and as an interpreter of Indian culture to the West. His second marriage having

Ananda Kentish Coomaraswamy (1877–1947), by Maull & Fox

ended shortly after the move to America, he married, thirdly, in November 1922, Stella Bloch (1898–1999), an American artist, and (this marriage having also ended in divorce) fourthly, on 18 November 1930, an Argentinian woman, Luisa Runstein, with whom he had a son, Rama, who became an eminent surgeon.

In endeavouring to explain the meaning of a particular work, Coomaraswamy would place it in its cultural context, at the same time evaluating the aesthetic, religious, philosophical, and metaphysical factors contributing to its structure. During the course of his life, in which he was influenced by the metaphysical writings of the Frenchman René Guénon, he wrote extensively on the arts and crafts of India and Ceylon, Rajput painting, Vedic literature and philosophy, the thoughts of Buddha, Hindu and Buddhist myths, Buddhist iconography, and Indian dance and music. He wrote some 913 papers and articles between 1908 and 1947, and his *History of Indian and Indonesian Art* (1927) is regarded as a definitive study. His aesthetic credo was expressed in such writings as *The Transformation of Nature in Art* (1934) and *Figures of Speech or Figures of Thought* (1946), in which the similarities and disparities between Eastern and western European ideologies were underlined. His *Catalogue of the Indian Collections in the Museum of Fine Arts, Boston* was published in five volumes (1923–30).

AKC (the acronym by which he was generally known) was a scholar of unusual breadth, recognized internationally as a leading Indologist, art critic, historian, and linguist. Throughout his life he was a believer in the concept of unity and remained a strong supporter of Ceylonese

culture, which he considered to be undervalued by the Ceylonese people. An essentially private person, he discouraged prospective biographers, telling one: 'I consider the modern practice of publishing details about the lives and personalities of well-known men is nothing but a vulgar catering to illegitimate curiosity' (Sandrasagra). He had hoped to return to Ceylon after his retirement, but died in Needham, Massachusetts, on 9 September 1947. His collected works were later published by the Indira Gandhi National Centre for the Arts, New Delhi, and he was commemorated by an annual Ananda Coomaraswamy memorial oration at the Indian Cultural Centre, Colombo, and by an annual Ananda Coomaraswamy award by the American Association of Asian Studies.

G. R. SEAMAN

**Sources** *Encyclopaedia Britannica* · R. Fernando, 'The primordial tradition: a tribute to Ananda Coomaraswamy', kataragama.org, Dec 2001 · M. Sandrasagra, 'Going against the stream: the relevance of Ananda Coomaraswamy in the 21st century', kataragama.org · R. Lipsey, ed., *Coomaraswamy*, 3: *His life and work* (1977) · 'Dr Ananda K. Coomaraswamy', www.freeindia.org/biographies · *WWW* · Burke, *Peerage* · *Debrett's Peerage* · m. cert. [Ethel Partridge]
**Archives** CUL, letters and notebooks | Princeton University Library, New Jersey, corresp. and papers, incl. letters to his third wife, Stella Bloch
**Likenesses** S. Bloch, pencil drawings, Princeton University Library, Stella Bloch papers · Maull & Fox, photograph, GS Lond. [*see illus.*] · photographs, Princeton University Library, Stella Bloch papers

**Coombe, Thomas** (1747–1822), Church of England clergyman and American loyalist, was born on 21 October 1747 in Philadelphia, Pennsylvania, the son of Thomas Coombe (*c*.1720–1799) and his wife, Sarah, *née* Rutter. His father was health officer of the port of Philadelphia, a friend of Benjamin Franklin, and actively interested in natural philosophy. Coombe was baptized in Christ Church, Philadelphia, on 14 November 1747. He attended the College of Philadelphia (subsequently the University of Pennsylvania), where he received an AB in 1766 and an AM in 1768. Valedictorian of his college class, Coombe demonstrated literary ability as an undergraduate by translating some of the Latin poems of his master John Beveridge, which appeared in the latter's *Epistolae familiares*, published in Philadelphia in 1765. Coombe travelled to England in 1768, seeking ordination, as there was no bishop in the colonies to perform the rite, and stayed temporarily at the lodgings of his father's friend Benjamin Franklin, at 36 Craven Street, Strand. He was ordained deacon on 11 February 1769, and priest on 21 December 1771 at the Chapel Royal, St James's Palace, by Richard Terrick, bishop of London. In 1771 Coombe was appointed chaplain to Charles Watson-Wentworth, second marquess of Rockingham, whom he served until his return to America the following year to be an assistant minister at Christ Church and at St Peter's, Philadelphia. He was elected a member of the American Philosophical Society on 15 January 1773.

Coombe married, first, Sarah (Sally) Ann Leake (1752?–1778), daughter of Bernard Badger and Susannah Riché of Hempstead, Long Island, New York, on 13 May 1773. On 21

May 1774 Sally bore twins, a son, John Riché Coombe (*d.* 12 May 1855), and a daughter. A further son, Henry Coombe, died on 3 October 1776, aged one year; two years later Sally died, on 17 October 1778. Coombe married his second wife, Elizabeth Chassereau (1758–1829), on 8 September 1784 at St Martin-in-the-Fields, London; she was the daughter of François Chassereau and his wife, Honor, *née* Williams, of London. Three children of this second marriage are identified in Coombe's will: Thomas (1796–1876), Charlotte, and Elizabeth.

Early in his career Coombe distinguished himself as an eloquent preacher. In a sermon delivered on 20 July 1775, a general fast day appointed by the continental congress, he advocated the cause of the colonies. His sermon, which aroused much attention, was printed and received wide circulation in editions published in Philadelphia, Baltimore, and Newport. Like many of his Anglican colleagues Coombe conscientiously believed that his oath of allegiance to king and parliament required at ordination did not permit him to swear to uphold the Declaration of Independence. At the outbreak of the American War of Independence Coombe and forty other rich and prominent persons were arrested by the executive council of Philadelphia on the charge of having 'uniformly evinced a disposition inimical to the cause of America' (Bronson, 554–7). He was held in the masons' lodge in Philadelphia and sentenced to imprisonment at Staunton, Augusta county, Virginia, in 1777. Many prominent Philadelphians came to his defence and protested the harshness of the decree. Coombe pleaded ill health, which rendered his removal impracticable. After the arrival of the British army in Philadelphia in 1777 he was granted permission to go to New York. Three of the English commissioners who had arrived in New York in 1778 with the intention of settling the dispute between the colonists and England—Frederick Howard, fifth earl of Carlisle, William Eden, later first Baron Auckland, and George W. Johnstone, governor of West Florida—granted Coombe authorization to sail for England in 1779, where he passed the remainder of his life.

Both in Philadelphia and in London, Coombe was recognized as a scholarly, persuasive, and powerful preacher. Josiah Quincy jun. said that one of Coombe's extemporary prayers, 'in point of sentiment, propriety of expression, and true sublimity', excelled anything of that kind that he had ever heard (J. Quincy, *Memoir of the Life of Josiah Quincy, Junior*, 1825, 121). Several of his sermons and addresses were published. He enjoyed the company of many distinguished friends, including Benjamin Franklin, Sir Joshua Reynolds, Samuel Johnson, Oliver Goldsmith, John Jortin, and James Beattie.

After a period of service as chaplain (from 1780) to Lord Carlisle, Coombe accompanied Carlisle upon his appointment as lord lieutenant of Ireland (1780–82) and was soon made his private secretary. Under the eye of his patron Coombe obtained in 1781 the rectory of Donagh-Henry, co. Tyrone, which he later resigned. In the same year he was admitted to the degree of doctor of divinity from Trinity College, Dublin. At the dissolution of the government of

Lord North in 1782 he returned to England with Lord Carlisle.

In 1789 Lord Auckland asked Coombe to accompany him to The Hague as chaplain to his embassy, a post which he declined. For many years he served as preacher at the Mayfair Chapel in Curzon Street. In 1794 he was appointed a chaplain to George III. Under the continuing auspices of Carlisle he was preferred to a prebendal stall at Canterbury in 1800. A year later he was presented by the dean and chapter of the cathedral to the vicarage of St Mildred, Tenterden, Kent, a post which he was permitted to resign to his son John in 1806. In 1808 the dean and chapter of Canterbury appointed Coombe rector of the united parishes of St Michael Queenhithe and Trinity the Less, in London, which he served for fourteen years, until his death.

Coombe's claim to the title of poet rests on his publication *The Peasant of Auburn, or, The Emigrant: a Poem* (1783). Dedicated to Oliver Goldsmith the work is an imitation of Goldsmith's *Deserted Village*; it recounts the unhappy fortunes of the emigrant from 'sweet Auburn' when later, on the banks of the Ohio River, his bright hopes darkened to desolation, war, and death. The volume includes a number of shorter poems.

Coombe easily adapted his career and life to London. To his contemporaries he was more of an Englishman than an American, and a clergyman of character and talent rather than a poet. He was an active and outspoken member of the committee for the abolition of the slave trade. Coombe died a wealthy man on 15 August 1822 at his home in Hereford Street, London. His will, proved on 22 August 1822, indicates an estate valued at more than £30,000. He granted to his wife £14,500, the leasehold for the house and stable in Hereford Street, his plate, and his household furniture. To each of his four surviving children he bequeathed £4500; his library of about 300 volumes he divided between his sons John and Thomas. To his son from his first marriage, the Revd John Riché Coombe, he bequeathed a gold snuffbox.                    JAMES B. BELL

**Sources**  *GM*, 1st ser., 92/2 (1822), 188–9, 276–7 • W. W. Bronson, *The inscriptions of St Peter's church yard, Philadelphia*, ed. C. R. Hildeburn (Camden, NJ, 1879) • *The papers of Benjamin Franklin*, 15–21, ed. W. B. Willcox (1972–8); 29, ed. B. B. Oberg and others (1992); 35, ed. B. B. Oberg and others (1999) • will, PRO, PROB 11/1660, sig. 426 • J. B. Bell, 'Anglican clergy in colonial America ordained by bishops of London', *Proceedings of the American Antiquarian Society*, 83 (1973) • *The diary of Elizabeth Drinker*, ed. E. F. Crane, 3 vols. (1991), 2 • H. M. Jenkins, ed., *Pennsylvania, colonial and federal: a history, 1608–1903*, 3 vols. (1903), 2 • trustees' minutes, College of Philadelphia, 20 May 1766 • A. E. Coombe, *Genealogy of Coombe, showing their descent from Edward 1st Plantagenet, king of England* (1856) • *Philadelphia Evening Post* (19 Oct 1778) • T. P. James, *Memorial of Thomas Potts junior* (1874), 368 • *University of Pennsylvania: biographical catalogue of the matriculates of the college, together with lists of the members of the college faculty and the trustees, officers and recipients of honorary degrees, 1749–1893*, Society of the Alumni (Philadelphia, 1894) • 'Biographical file of members of the American Philosophical Society', MS, American Philosophical Society, Philadelphia

**Likenesses**  H. Benbridge, oils, *c.*1769–1770

**Wealth at death**  over £30,000: will, PRO, PROB 11/1660, sig. 426

**Coombes, Bert Lewis** [*formerly* Bertie Louis Coombs Griffiths] (1893–1974), coalminer and author, was born at 30 Dudley Road, Wolverhampton, Staffordshire, on 9 January 1893, the only child of James Coombs Griffiths, grocer, and his wife, Harriett Thompson, the family coming to use the surname Cumbes or Coombes. He spent a part of his youth (and received all his education) in Treharris, Glamorgan, where his father worked at the local colliery. By 1905–6 the family had taken the tenancy of Blenheim Farm, Madley, Herefordshire, Coombes working first as a farm labourer and later as a groom. In 1910 he left the countryside to travel to Resolfen, Glamorgan, to find work as a collier's helper. He spent the rest of his working life in the coal industry, later as a repairer and ambulance man. On 29 September 1913, at St David's parish church, Resolfen, he married Mary Rogers (1892/3–1970), the daughter of John Rogers, a check-weigher and a local trade unionist. They had a daughter and a son. Coombes settled into the local community, acquiring a working knowledge of Welsh, helping to found the Resolfen cricket club, and joining the St John Ambulance Association. He took up the violin, participated in the formation of the Resolfen orchestra, and became active in trade union matters.

In the early 1930s Coombes began to experiment with writing. Initially his ambition was to be a novelist, and, in addition to reading widely in the library of the local miners' institute, he took National Council of Labour Colleges courses in English and joined the British Scribbler writing circle. After a difficult period of apprenticeship, his early success (1937–8) was in short story writing, particularly for John Lehmann's *New Writing*, and his 'Twenty tons of coal' was to win lasting acclaim (*New Writing*, 3, 1939). Coombes's stories were bolstered by short pieces of non-fiction as well as by reviews. In 1939 two major works of non-fiction followed: *I am a Miner*, published as Fact pamphlet no. 23; and *These Poor Hands: the Autobiography of a Miner Working in South Wales*. *These Poor Hands* was published by Victor Gollancz and was selected to be the Left Book Club's book of the month for June 1939. It sold almost 80,000 copies within a year and was discussed by Left Book Club local groups across Britain, as well as attracting an international readership, impressed by its grittily realistic depictions of mining work allied to a forceful critique of private ownership.

Despite growing literary success, Coombes resisted the temptation to leave the mines for a full-time writing career. Partly this was because he felt writing was insufficiently secure as an occupation, but more significantly he believed that he could be useful in writing about mining only if he remained a miner with first-hand experience of conditions underground and in mining communities—a point developed in his exchange with Virginia Woolf in *Folios of New Writing* (1940–41). Much of his output in the 1940s was of a documentary nature: articles for *Fortnightly*, *New Writing*, *Geographical Magazine*, and the *New Statesman*. His *Those Clouded Hills* (1944) anatomized the coal industry for the benefit of a transatlantic readership, and he contributed radio scripts for the wartime service run by the Ministry of Information. His Penguin 'Special' *Miners Day*

(1945) was a more informal but still observational account of mining life. Coombes used the proceeds from such publications to take up farming on a small scale: first at Ynysgron Farm near Glynneath and later at Nantyfedwen Farm near Onllwyn.

Coombes's greatest political impact came with the publication of the 'Plan for Britain' issue of *Picture Post* (4 January 1941). Coombes's 'This is the problem' was a passionate indictment of the capitalist political and economic system, pleading for 'great changes in the men and women who run this country' and for 'new ideas and new methods'. The issue was an enormous success and contributed to Coombes's growing renown as an 'authentic' working-class voice in wartime Britain.

Labour's general election victory in 1945 and subsequent coal nationalization appeared to vindicate much of Coombes's writing. He continued to publish short stories and non-fiction pieces, often in the National Coal Board's magazine *Coal*, as well as making occasional forays into radio with documentaries and short plays. He collaborated with Jack Lindsay in writing the play *Face of Coal: a Provocative Documentary* (Scala Theatre, London, 1946), and continued to write regular articles for his local newspaper, the *Neath Guardian* (1940–71). By the 1950s, however, his ideas no longer appeared to have such contemporary relevance, and continued efforts to publish a novel failed. Apart from his local journalism, Coombes's last contribution to British publishing was his winning entry in a *Daily Mirror* essay competition in 1955, advocating international friendship.

A series of accidents underground and the demands of running a small farm, combined with a steady decline in the health of his wife, Mary, contributed to Coombes's retreat from the public eye. Nevertheless, in 1963 the National Union of Mineworkers (South Wales Area) paid tribute to his 'outstanding contributions to working-class literature' (*Neath Guardian*, 11 Oct 1963), and *These Poor Hands* was republished in 1974 with a foreword from the veteran Labour politician and miners' leader James Griffiths. Coombes died of cerebral thrombosis at the Adelina Patti Hospital, Craig-y-Nos, Brecknockshire, on 4 June 1974, and was buried a few days later in St David's churchyard, Resolfen, Glamorgan. He may not have been a writer of outstanding literary talent, nor always an easy man to like. He guarded his writing time jealously, and was both impressively organized and of almost inexhaustible energy. His gift was in his ability to capture a sense of the harshness, injustice, and humanity that could be found in Britain's mining communities.                    CHRIS WILLIAMS

**Sources** B. Jones and C. Williams, *B. L. Coombes* (1999) • B. Nield, 'Coombes, Bert Lewis', *DLB*, vol. 4 • D. Smith, 'Underground man: the work of B. L. Coombes, "miner writer"', *Anglo-Welsh Review*, 53 (1974), 10–25 • C. M. Baggs, 'A "war-time mirror to Welsh life"? B. L. Coombes and the *Neath Guardian*', *Morgannwg*, 34 (1990), 78–93 • *With dust still in his throat: B. L. Coombes anthology*, ed. B. Jones and C. Williams (1999) • P. Lester, 'By these poor hands: the writings of B. L. Coombes', *London Magazine, a Monthly Review of Literature*, new ser., 33/9–10 (1993–4), 60–70 • B. Lipman, 'Bert Coombes', *Planet*, 23 (1974), 17–20 • R. L. Ortega, *La crisis economica de 1929 y la novelistica de* *tema obrero en Gran Bretaña en los anos treinta* (1974) · J. Calder, *Chronicles of conscience: a study of George Orwell and Arthur Koestler* (1968) · b. cert. · m. cert. · d. cert. · *CGPLA Eng. & Wales* (1974)

**Archives** U. Wales, Swansea, literary MSS, newspaper cuttings, scrapbook of reviews | Princeton University, New Jersey, John Lehmann papers, corresp. · U. Hull, *Dictionary of labour biography* archive · U. Texas, John Lehmann papers, corresp.
**Likenesses** photograph, Princeton University, John Lehmann papers, Box 93 Folder II · photographs, U. Wales, Swansea, B. L. Coombes archive · photographs, Hult. Arch. · photographs, repro. in *Picture Post* (4 Jan 1941) · sketch, repro. in B. L. Coombes, *Miners Day* (1945)
**Wealth at death** £7348: probate, 1 July 1974, *CGPLA Eng. & Wales*

**Coombes, Robert** (1808–1860), oarsman, was born at Vauxhall, Surrey, and was apprenticed at an early age as a waterman on the Thames. His first sculling victory came in July 1836 and during the next fifteen years he established himself as one of the principal professional scullers of his time. Although he was only 5 feet 7 inches tall and his rowing weight was normally under 9 stone, his skill often allowed him to beat men of greater strength and weight. Coombes's greatest achievements as a sculler were in the professional championship of England, a race held at infrequent intervals whenever a suitable challenger emerged. He was beaten at his first attempt on 1 November 1838 by the holder, Charles Campbell, but he defeated Campbell easily on 19 August 1846, the first time the championship was rowed over the Putney to Mortlake course on the Thames in London. He won the title twice more, beating Robert Newell on 29 September 1847 and Tom Mackinnery on 7 May 1851. He lost the championship to Thomas Cole, a younger man, on 24 May 1852 by only half a length. He challenged Cole again on 14 October of that year but lost once more; it was his last important sculling race.

Coombes also excelled in fours. He stroked a Thames four that beat Henry Clasper's crew on the Tyne on 16 July 1842, a race that prompted Clasper to develop the first keelless, outrigged boat. Two years later, on 21 June 1844, Coombes's crew lost to Clasper's at the Royal Thames regatta in London, although it won the fours championship on the final day. Using a boat similar to that designed by Clasper, Coombes won the championship for a second time in 1846 and again in 1849. On the latter occasion Clasper was the stroke, and this was the only time Coombes sank his differences with his Tyne rival. It was claimed in the press at the time 'that circumstances, not inclination exactly, conduced to this union'.

Coombes's expertise attracted the attention of the university oarsmen. He trained the losing Oxford crew for the 1840 boat race and the victorious Cambridge boat in 1846. There were two races in 1849, and Coombes coached Cambridge on both occasions: Cambridge won the first but lost the second. When he was asked to coach the 1852 Cambridge crew, Coombes found himself at the centre of a fierce argument about the use of professional watermen in the training of university oarsmen. Oxford had expressed disquiet on the issue in 1846 and 1849 but on this occasion T. S. Egan, for many years the mentor of Cambridge rowing, was also concerned at Coombes's presence and defected to Oxford, where he trained a crew that won the boat race with ease. It was a decisive moment for certain amateur oarsmen, mainly those from the universities and the more important metropolitan clubs, who subsequently tried to distance themselves from the professionals and any oarsmen of working-class origin. Coombes was never again involved with a boat race crew but he explained his training methods at the end of a small volume published in 1852, *Aquatic notes or sketches of the rise and progress of racing at Cambridge by a member of C. U. B. C.*

Later in life Coombes fell into poverty and began to suffer various mental disorders, and in 1859 he was admitted to the Kent Lunatic Asylum at Barming Heath, Maidstone. He died there on 25 February 1860. He was buried at the expense of his friends in Brompton cemetery on 7 March; the funeral was attended by the leading London watermen. ERIC HALLADAY

**Sources** W. B. Woodgate, *Boating* (1888), chap. 16 and appx · G. C. Drinkwater and T. R. B. Sanders, *The university boat race*, ed. C. Gurdon (1929), 159–63 · R. D. Burnell, *The Oxford and Cambridge boat race* (1954), 42–4, 53 · E. Halladay, *Rowing in England: a social history* (1990), chap. 1 and appx 1 · *Newcastle Courant* (22 July 1842) · *Newcastle Journal* (23 July 1842) · *Newcastle Journal* (14 July 1849) · *The Times* (24 June 1844) · *The Times* (15 Oct 1852) · *Bell's Life in London* (23 Aug 1846) · *Bell's Life in London* (4 March 1860) · *ILN* (29 May 1852) · *The Field* (3 March 1860) · d. cert.
**Likenesses** portrait, NPG; repro. in *ILN*, 436
**Wealth at death** died in poverty

**Coombes, William Henry** (1767–1850), Roman Catholic priest, was born on 8 May 1767, at Meadgate in Camerton, Somerset, where his family was well established. His grandfather had been the local blacksmith, and it seems likely that George Coombes, the landlord of the Camerton Inn, was William Henry's father. It was probably his uncle, the Revd William Coombes, vicar-general of the western district, who sent him to the English College at Douai, where he was admitted on 22 July 1779. He was ordained priest in 1791 and taught at the college in 1792–3. During the tumult of the French Revolution, Coombes twice escaped from Douai, the second time successfully, reaching Austrian lines on 20 October 1793. On his arrival in England he was appointed professor of theology at Old Hall Green College. He was an accomplished Greek scholar, and in 1797 he published *Sacred Eloquence*, a selection of readings from the Greek fathers. This was followed in 1799 by the publication of an account of his escape from Douai. He also published some letters on Catholic matters in William Cobbett's *Register*, under the pseudonym of 'the British Observer', between 1804 and 1806. On 12 December 1801 Pope Pius VII conferred upon him a DD.

In 1810 Coombes accepted the mission at Shepton Mallet, which he held for the next thirty-nine years. From his arrival until the sisters moved to Westbury near Bristol in 1830, he acted as spiritual director to the adjacent Convent of the Visitation, which undoubtedly stimulated his interest in the history of the order. In 1812 he published a translation of Jacques Marsollier's *Life of St Francis of Sales*; this was followed by another translation, *The Spiritual Entertainments of St Francis of Sales* (1814), which he dedicated to the Visitation sisters. In 1830 he published his own *History of the Life of St Jane Frances de Chantal*. He also published a polemical work, *The Essence of Religious Controversy* (1827), and a protest about those clauses in the 1829 Catholic Relief Bill which related to monastic institutions. In June 1849 he retired to Downside Abbey, where he remained until his death on 15 November 1850. He was buried in the Downside cemetery. Little is known of his character, although the vicar of Camerton, the irascible John Skinner, recorded that Coombes caused 'much unnecessary trouble' over the collection of his uncle's tithes in 1807 (Coombs, 262). Lady Jerningham, who became acquainted with Coombes in Bath in 1808, described him as 'A good Grecian and clever, agreable [*sic*] also and pious. Not conceited, always wears spectacles' (E. Castle, ed., *The Jerningham Letters*, 1896, 1.326).                ROSEMARY MITCHELL

**Sources**  G. Oliver, *Collections illustrating the history of the Catholic religion in the counties of Cornwall, Devon, Dorset, Somerset, Wilts, and Gloucester* (1857) · P. R. Harris, ed., *Douai College documents, 1639–1794*, Catholic RS, 63 (1972) · Gillow, *Lit. biog. hist.* · [J. Skinner], *Journal of a Somerset rector, 1803–1834*, ed. H. Coombs and P. Coombs, rev. edn (1971) · *DNB*

**Cooper**. *See also* Couper, Cowper.

**Cooper family** ( *per.* **1854–1994**), accountants, came to prominence as the result of the achievements of four of the sons of Emanuel Cooper (1794/5–1851), who was one of the founders of the London and County Bank, its deputy chairman from 1841, and a well-known advocate of the abolition of slavery. He was also a staunch Quaker, but was dismissed by the bank in 1848 having advanced himself some £16,000 which he was unable to repay. The bank's records contain a pitiful letter from his widow requesting money to keep her from penury. The request was dismissed, but is consistent with complaints made by Francis and Ernest in later life that they did not have enough to eat in their childhood days.

Emanuel and his wife, Elizabeth (*née* Ranson), had thirteen children. The four sons who were to found and for many years dominate their accountancy practice were: his eldest son, **William Cooper** (*c*.1826–1871), public accountant; his second son, **Arthur Cooper** (1833–1892), chartered accountant; **Francis Cooper** (1845/6–1893), chartered accountant; and his seventh son and youngest child, **Ernest Cooper** (1847–1926), chartered accountant. It also appears that the other three brothers and two or three of the sisters occasionally helped out in the early days.

William and Arthur started off as clerks in London in the office of Quilter, Ball & Co., which is thought to have had the largest accountancy practice in England in the middle of the nineteenth century. William left to set up a practice in his own name at 13 George Street, London, in 1854. The firm's name was changed to W. and A. Cooper in 1858, soon after the admission of Arthur to the partnership in 1857, and Cooper Brothers & Co. in 1860. Francis was probably admitted to partnership in 1871 and Ernest a year later, having each initially trained with the family firm.

William died in 1871, seventeen years after founding the firm, and was succeeded as senior partner by Arthur. Arthur was privately regarded by the family as the ablest of the four brothers, followed by Francis, who suffered from diabetes and died in 1893 at the age of forty-seven. In 1910 two of the second-generation Coopers were admitted to the partnership: Arthur's son Harold Arthur Cooper (resigned in 1913 and killed in action in France in 1916), and Francis's son (Francis) D'Arcy Cooper, son of Francis and his wife Ada Frances, daughter of Henry Power, surgeon. Ernest's son Stuart Ranson Cooper became a partner in 1921 and retired in 1946.

The original Cooper brothers had well-earned reputations for uprightness and honesty in their business dealings; and this may have stemmed from a religious commitment instilled in them by their Quaker parents. They were initially active in the days prior to the formation of professional accounting bodies in England and Wales. Ernest, who was a colourful writer, made the following often quoted characterization (some might say caricature) in relation to the accountant's position in 1864:

> We could hardly, South of the Tweed, claim to be a profession. There was absolutely no organisation or co-operation, no Institute or Society, no examinations, very few articled clerks, no newspaper, no library, no benevolent fund, and not even a dining club or golf club. … Our social position was not enviable. We may disregard the then current gibes, that if an accountant were required, he would be found at the bar of the nearest tavern to the Bankruptcy Court in Basinghall Street, and that an accountant was a man who had failed in everything else … but an accountant was regarded as associated with and dependent upon insolvency, and I well remember that to be seen talking to or having your office entered by an accountant, was to be avoided, particularly in the stressful times of 1866.   (Cooper, 554)

This has been one of the cornerstones of the conventional view of late Victorian accountants: as being almost entirely reliant on fraud and liquidation work, until the more widespread growth of the limited liability company requiring audit towards the end of the nineteenth century. Recent research, however, suggests that, while some firms were heavily reliant on liquidation and fraud, others, including Cooper Brothers itself, had a much wider portfolio.

Liquidation work was clearly of importance to the company, however, with Arthur, for example, liquidating the Oriental Commercial Bank and acting as receiver of the Swedish and Norwegian Railway Company. Indeed, his obituary in *The Accountant* suggested that as trustee in bankruptcy he probably had more and larger estates than any other London accountant. In focusing on this area, Arthur was undoubtedly playing to his strength. Sir John Hollams (considered one of the finest lawyers of this period), who worked a great deal with Arthur, judged him to have a remarkable legal brain 'honed on and critical in insolvency work' (Jones, 'Cooper, Arthur', 777).

Arthur died in 1892 and Ernest, who is known to have been in part educated abroad at a Roman Catholic school, took over as senior partner. This change in due course released an important constraint on the firm's development: Arthur had insisted that partners must be able personally to supervise all the firm's work. Under the new regime branches were opened, beginning with Liverpool in 1920 and an overseas office in Brussels in 1921. With the growth of professional firms reflecting the success of their clients, the introduction of William Hesketh Lever to Ernest Cooper by the District Bank was a key event, and it is thought that Ernest prepared the 'Accountants' report' for the prospectus issued by Lever Brothers Ltd on becoming a public company in 1894.

Ernest's experience as an accountant had its lighter and its darker sides. When he was on a visit to Hamburg to carry out an investigation in 1874, an attempt was made to bribe him (he was invited to 'name his price'); and in 1892 he won £2000 in damages from a newspaper (resulting in its bankruptcy) for unjustified criticism of his role as special manager and trustee of Barker's Bank. In 1927 the firm was sacked as auditors of Marconi's Wireless Telegraph Company amid public controversy. Cooper Brothers had qualified the company's accounts commencing 1920 with respect to the value placed by the directors on the shares held in associated companies and patents. It may be that the wording of their audit report was insufficiently clearcut, a criticism which has been levelled against the accountancy profession on numerous occasions over the years. It is certainly known that, when Marconi's financial position deteriorated and reorganization proposals were under consideration in 1927, a group of shareholders demonstrated against the auditors and opposed their reappointment. The resignation of Cooper Brothers drew the following comment from the leader writer of *The Accountant* (2 April 1927) which also has a perennial ring about it:

> In the present case, we say roundly, the ultimate blame lies on shareholders who year after year have slumbered while their watch dog dutifully barked. They have now roused themselves to find that the house has been burgled, and it does them little credit that their only action is to buy two new watch dogs.

Of the four brothers, it was Arthur and Ernest who were active in the establishment of professional accounting organizations. A member of the élite Institute of Accountants in London, formed in 1870, Ernest wrote a letter to its officers in 1877 criticizing the lack of technical facilities and its poor performance in attracting new membership relative to the Society of Accountants in England (formed in 1872). Arthur had been a council member of the Institute of Accountants since 1876, and the firm's official history suggests that the concerted efforts of these two brothers probably played a significant part in the formation of the most important accountancy body outside Scotland. This was the Institute of Chartered Accountants in England and Wales (ICAEW), which was formed from the merger of five accountancy bodies already established south of the border, including the Institute of Accountants.

Arthur Cooper was a member of the ICAEW's first council, vice-president in 1882–3, and president in 1883–4. His proficiency in legal matters enabled him to devise by-laws designed to regulate members' conduct at a time when this fledgeling profession was struggling to raise its status, and he was a member of an institute committee appointed to make recommendations to the Board of Trade about the Bankruptcy Bill which finally resulted in the act of 1883. Ernest was elected to the council in 1891, was president from 1899 to 1901, and remained on the council for a total of thirty-three years. Indeed, ever since the ICAEW was formed, at least one of the firm's partners has been a council member.

In 1869 Arthur Cooper married Maria, daughter of Edward Joseph Cole, a merchant; they had three sons and three daughters. He died on 22 August 1892 at Cuorabelle, Westgate-on-Sea, during a short break from the office. Ernest married Edith Isabella Henderson and they had a son and a daughter. Ernest died on 4 January 1926 at East Court, East Grinstead.

There is some evidence that Cooper Brothers suffered more than most accountancy firms 'by the calls of the Services' during the First World War, and the key figure in their early post-war revival was the highly talented Sir (Francis) D'Arcy *Cooper (1882–1941), whose resignation as senior partner in 1923 to become vice-chairman of the soap manufacturers Lever Brothers was a major set-back and judged to be an important contributory factor to the firm's slow rate of growth in the inter-war period. The last partner to bear the Cooper name was Vivian Rupert Vaughan, son of Harold Arthur Cooper and grandson of Arthur, who was admitted to partnership in 1935, retired in 1973, and died in 1994.

The partnership founded by the Cooper brothers has been one of the leading firms of accountants since the early days of the profession. It was in the vanguard undertaking insolvency work and, in 1886, it was the seventh largest firm in terms of the number of quoted company audits. Its success probably owes much to Emanuel's injunction to his family to hold together like a bundle of sticks which cannot be broken. The most significant partner in the years after the Second World War was Henry Alexander *Benson, Baron Benson. The nephew of Sir (Francis) D'Arcy and grandson of Francis Cooper, Benson was admitted to partnership in 1934 and became joint senior partner in 1946 following the retirement of Stuart Cooper who, although able, was not in favour of rapid growth. The firm was subsequently the subject of a whirlwind expansion, sometimes attracting criticism and envy from competitors directed at what were considered to be overtly commercial practices. The firm was renamed Coopers and Lybrand following merger with the American firm of Lybrand, Ross Bros. and Montgomery in 1973 and became one of the largest such firms in the world. It merged with Price Waterhouse in 1998 to form PriceWaterhouseCoopers. JOHN RICHARD EDWARDS

**Sources** *A history of Cooper Brothers, 1854–1954* (1954) · H. Benson, *Accounting for life* (1989) · E. Cooper, 'Fifty-seven years in an accountant's office', *The Accountant* (22 Oct 1921), 553–63 · J. R. Edwards, 'Cooper, Sir Francis d'Arcy', *DBB* · E. Jones, 'Cooper, Ernest', *DBB* ·

E. Jones, 'Cooper, Arthur', *DBB* • E. Jones, 'Benson, Henry Alexander', *DBB* • *The Accountant* (27 Aug 1892), 657 [obit. of Arthur Cooper] • *The Accountant* (9 Jan 1926), 56–7 [obit. of Ernest Cooper] • private information (2004) • *Accountancy*, 116 (July 1995), 18–19 • d. certs. [Arthur, Emanuel, Ernest and Francis Cooper] • *CGPLA Eng. & Wales* (1893) [Francis Cooper]

**Wealth at death** £32,223 10s. 8d.—Arthur Cooper: resworn probate, March 1893, *CGPLA Eng. & Wales* • £26,386 5s. 8d.—Francis Cooper: resworn probate, June 1893, *CGPLA Eng. & Wales* • £194,403 9s. 3d.—Ernest Cooper: probate, 1926

**Cooper, Abraham** (1787–1868), battle and animal painter, was born on 8 September 1787 at Red Lion Street, Holborn, London. His father was a tobacconist and later became an innkeeper at Holloway and for a time at Edmonton, but with little financial success. Cooper attended a local school and showed an early aptitude for drawing, especially horses and dogs, attracting the attention of a Mr Phillips, for whom he painted watercolour portraits of his horses. At thirteen Cooper went to work for his uncle, William Davis, manager of Astley's circus, famous for its spectacular equestrian dramas, providing the boy with opportunities to study horses at first hand. However, he refused an equestrian role with John Kemble at Covent Garden about 1809, and from this year determined to become an artist. About this time, wishing to have a portrait of a horse he had often ridden, Cooper bought a small book on oil painting and set about the task himself. The horse's owner, Henry Meux, seeing the finished picture, *Frolic*, was so delighted with it that he insisted on buying it for his own collection. William Davis knew the celebrated horse painter Benjamin Marshall. The generous Marshall, appreciating Cooper's talent, addiction to hard work, and personal charm, freely gave him studio space, encouragement, and instruction, and introduced him to prospective patrons. Cooper also studied and copied illustrations in the *Sporting Magazine* and became a contributor in 1811 with a portrait of a pointer, *Basto*, described as a very staunch young dog. During his lifetime Cooper provided 189 subjects which were engraved in the magazine. He exhibited first in 1812 at both the Royal Academy and the British Institution. Initially his subjects were horses, dogs, and some wild animals, but from 1815 he started showing meticulously researched battle paintings, often of the civil war, usually including mounted soldiers. He was elected an associate of the Royal Academy in 1817, and it was said that his painting shown in 1820, *The Battle of Marston Moor*, led to his election as Royal Academician that year. Becoming an academician within seven or eight years of taking up oil painting was a remarkable achievement. Between 1812 and 1868–9 Cooper exhibited 332 pictures at the Royal Academy (and seventy-three at the British Institution). Although only a quarter of these paintings were battle scenes, he was acknowledged as the country's principal battle painter, with a similar standing to Peter Hess in Germany and Horace Vernet in France. A slightly plaintive correspondent of the *Art Journal* wrote that 'Between the years 1828 and 1831 the artist seems to have been so much occupied with painting portraits of famous racers, hunters, and roadsters, as to leave no time

for pictures of a more important character' (*Art Journal*, 1863, 90). With changes of taste, the twentieth-century public largely forgot his battle pictures, but his many racehorse portraits, perhaps lacking some of the vibrancy of those by his mentor Marshall, came into vogue as well as providing a valuable and accurate record for turf historians. Two of his most famous racehorse portraits, both exhibited at the Royal Academy, were the winners of the St Leger in 1836 and 1837. Lord George Bentinck's Elis with John Day up and the trainer John Doe with his hack was followed by Mango, the property of Bentinck's great rival Charles Greville, clerk to the privy council. Cooper's conversation piece *The Day Family*, exhibited in 1838, shows the artist as a master of portraiture, both human and equine, and composition in placing the six figures of the celebrated racehorse trainer and his family, two horses, and a mule carriage in a natural grouping. This painting was bequeathed by Sir Abe Bailey to the National Gallery of South Africa. A very similar version, also dated 1838, is in the Tate collection. Cooper was particularly adept at catching the character of Arab horses and *Adonis*, his portrait of George III's favourite charger which had been imported from Hanover to improve the royal stud, is a perceptive study of this attractive breed. He painted coursing and shooting scenes, but the hunting field only on rare occasions. He also gave lessons to J. F. Herring (1795–1865) and to William Barraud (1810–1850), and his son, Alexander Davis Cooper (*fl.* 1837–1888), must have benefited from his father's advice in his genre painting and illustrations of scenes from Shakespeare. Abraham Cooper lived throughout his life in or near London, dying at his home, Woodbine Cottage, Woodland Street, Greenwich, on 24 December 1868. He was buried in Highgate cemetery. His obituary in the *New Sporting Magazine* remembers him as 'a guileless pleasant gentleman with little jealousy in his nature' (*New Sporting Magazine*, 100), which probably accounted for his personal effects being valued for his widow, Frances, at less than £200.     CHARLES LANE

**Sources** J. Dafforne, 'Abraham Cooper', *Art Journal*, 25 (1863), 89–91 • S. A. Walker, 'An animal painter of 100 years ago', *Country Life*, 146 (1969), 1652–3 • Graves, *RA exhibitors* • Graves, *Brit. Inst.* • *Sporting Magazine*, 38 (June 1811) • *New Sporting Magazine*, 154 (Aug 1869), 100–02 • S. Walker, 'Abraham Cooper', *British Racehorse*, 22/3 (Sept 1970), 332–40 • *CGPLA Eng. & Wales* (1869) • *Art Journal*, 31 (1869), 45

**Likenesses** C. H. Lear, pencil drawing, *c.*1845, NPG • C. W. Cope, drawing, 1862, NPG • C. W. Cope, drawing, 1864, NPG • Elliott & Fry, carte-de-visite, NPG • F. H. R., line engraving (after W. Mulready), NPG • J. Jackson, pencil and watercolour drawing, Newport Museum and Art Gallery, South Wales • J. H. Robinson, etching (after W. Mulready), BM, NPG; repro. in J. Pye, *Patronage of British art* (1845) • J. Thomson, stipple (after J. Jackson), BM, NPG • C. E. Wagstaff, stipple (after A. D. Cooper), BM, NPG

**Wealth at death** under £200: probate, 11 Jan 1869, *CGPLA Eng. & Wales*

**Cooper, Alexander** (*bap.* **1609**, *d. c.*1660), miniature painter, was baptized at the church of St Nicholas Cole Abbey, in the City of London, on 11 December 1609, the second son of Richard Cooper (*b.* 1577) and Barbara, sister of John *Hoskins (*c.*1590–1665), the miniaturist; Richard and Barbara had married at the same church on 1 September 1607. Following Richard Graham's biographical note on Samuel *Cooper (1607/8–1672) historians have until recently believed that Alexander was the elder of the two brothers (Edmond, 'Limners and picturemakers', 99; Edmond, 'Samuel Cooper', 84). Graham also states that Samuel and Alexander were brought up by Hoskins, so it is assumed that Richard and Barbara died while the children were in infancy. Little is known of their upbringing or training but the Dutch chronicler Joachim Sandrart suggests that Alexander learned the art of miniature painting from Peter Oliver—'Oliverii hujus discipulus longe celeberrimus' ('[he was] by far the most celebrated pupil of this Oliver'; Sandrart, 312). Both boys must have benefited greatly from the expertise of their uncle.

Historians have also believed that Alexander Cooper went abroad in the early 1630s and passed the rest of his life in northern Europe, dying romantically in Stockholm in 1660, 'alone, while at work, and with his brush in his hand' (Williamson, 90–91). The notion that Cooper died thus in Sweden may have derived from documents in the Swedish royal archives recording applications for payment of salary from the king of Sweden, such as those of 1651–3 (transcribed in Foster, 1, appx, 91–3), in which Cooper apparently claims to be terminally ill. The language of such applications is, however, conventional and does not necessarily indicate that Alexander was on the point of death. In the second application Cooper signals his intention of returning to England or of going to Tuscany but he seems to have remained in Sweden or Denmark until about 1656. In June 1658 he was in York with members of his extended family, signing a deposition in a probate case and claiming to have been resident at his brother's house in Covent Garden 'for these two yeares last past' (Edmond, 'Samuel Cooper', 83–5). He is not mentioned in any of the later documents relating to the Hoskinses and the Coopers, so he may indeed have died about 1660, probably in England rather than in Sweden.

The earliest work in the Victoria and Albert Museum, London, that is plausibly attributed to Cooper dates from about 1628–30. From the 1630s there is a group of portraits of Elizabeth of Bohemia and her family and household in the Bode Museum, Berlin. A portrait of Charles Louis, count palatine, datable to about 1632 (V&A), is signed with the initials AC. These sitters were all patrons of Peter Oliver and could have been painted in the Netherlands or, since they are not necessarily from the life, in London, where the English sitters painted by Cooper in these years would have been. In the 1630s Alexander Cooper may have contributed to the output of the Hoskins studio. About 1642, when his brother was becoming established in London, Sandrart records that he was in Amsterdam and that he brought with him portraits of the 'aulae Anglicanae' (Sandrart, 312). This is usually taken to mean the luminaries of the English court in London but possibly refers to the English courtiers of Elizabeth and Frederick of Bohemia in The Hague. Thereafter documentary evidence of payments to him and the identities of sitters place him

consistently, until the mid-1650s, on the continent—in the Netherlands, Sweden, and Denmark—the recipient of quite lucrative royal patronage. He is documented as receiving erratic payments in the Swedish royal accounts from 1647 to 1657 (Williamson; see also Cavalli-Björkman, *Svenskt Miniatyrmaleri*, 18–25). Cooper is referred to as 'court painter' from 1647 in Sweden (Cavalli-Björkman, 'Cooper', 7).

The stylistic evidence tends to confirm Sandrart's statement that Cooper was Oliver's pupil. His work projects into the mid-century the brightness and hard focus of Hilliard and Oliver, as in the *Frederick III of Denmark* of 1656 (Rosenborg Castle, Copenhagen), which was by then slightly archaic in the context of the English miniature but was directly analogous in appearance to the continental enamel. His backgrounds are often in the flat colours of the sixteenth-century tradition; they include unconventional colours such as lavender or grey, sometimes lightened or shaded behind the figure, and on occasion even showing a curious non-naturalistic variant of a technique of floating wet washes into one another, originally developed by Hilliard to simulate the sheen of silk curtains in the background of the miniature. No landscape background by Cooper is known, which suggests that he was out of touch with the Hoskins studio during this phase of activity. Unlike Oliver or Hoskins he worked with a hatching stroke, shorter and much less graphic than that of his brother but firm and precise. The surviving œuvre is, however, small and much of it spread through the royal collections of the states in which he worked, including especially that of Sweden (Nationalmuseum, Stockholm). In the Victoria and Albert Museum and in other English collections there are few signed works to give a solid indication of stylistic criteria, and there are disturbing variations in technique among the works attributed to him that pass through the saleroom.                JOHN MURDOCH

**Sources** [R. Graham], 'A short account of the most eminent painters both ancient and modern, continued down to the present times, according to the order of their succession', in C. A. Du Fresnoy, *De arte graphica / The art of painting*, trans. J. Dryden (1695), 227–355; 2nd edn (1716) • M. Edmond, 'Limners and picturemakers', *Walpole Society*, 47 (1978–80), 60–242 • M. Edmond, 'Samuel Cooper, Yorkshireman—and recusant?', *Burlington Magazine*, 127 (1985), 83–5 • J. Sandrart, *Academia nobilissimae artis pictoriae* (1683) • G. C. Williamson, *The history of portrait miniatures*, 1 (1904) • J. J. Foster, *Samuel Cooper and the English miniature painters of the XVII century*, 2 vols. (1914–16) • G. Cavalli-Björkman, *Svenskt miniatyrmaleri: en konstbok fran Nationalmuseum* (Stockholm, 1981), 18–25 • G. Cavalli-Björkman, 'Alexander Cooper in the Nationalmuseum', *Nationalmuseum Bulletin*, 1/3 (1977), 7 [Stockholm] • J. Murdoch, *Seventeenth-century English miniatures in the collection of the Victoria and Albert Museum* (1997), esp. 235–50

**Cooper, Sir Alfred** (1838–1908), surgeon, born at Norwich on 28 December 1838, was the son of William Cooper, at one time recorder of Ipswich, and his wife, Anna Marsh. In April 1850 Cooper entered Merchant Taylors' School, then in Suffolk Lane, London. He was later apprenticed to W. Peter Nichols, surgeon to the Norfolk and Norwich Hospital, and sometime mayor of Norwich. In 1858

Cooper became a student at St Bartholomew's Hospital, London. He gained his MRCS on 29 June 1861, and in the same year he passed the licence of the Society of Apothecaries. These two qualifications formed the usual route to practice at this time. He then went to Paris with Thomas Smith (1833–1909), to improve his anatomical knowledge. He was appointed a prosector to the examiners at the Royal College of Surgeons.

Cooper started practice in Jermyn Street, London, eventually establishing a fashionable private practice. He remained an enthusiastic operator, serving several voluntary hospitals. He was surgeon to St Mark's Hospital for Fistula, City Road, from April 1864 until 1897, to the West London Hospital from 1867 to 1884, to the Royal Hospital for Diseases of the Chest, City Road, and to the Lock Hospital, Soho. At this hospital he gained a broad knowledge of syphilis. On 4 July 1882 he married Lady Agnes Cecil Emmeline Duff (d. 1925), third daughter of James, fifth earl of Fife, and sister of Alexander, the first duke of Fife; Lady Agnes had been married first to Viscount Dupplin (they divorced in 1876), and secondly to Herbert Flower (d. 1880); Cooper and Lady Agnes had three daughters and a son, the politician (Alfred) Duff *Cooper (1890–1954).

In 1884 Cooper published *Syphilis and Pseudosyphilis*, which was revised in a second edition in 1895. He also wrote *A Practical Treatise on Disease of the Rectum* (1887), which he revised with F. Swinford Edwards as *Diseases of the Rectum and Anus* (1892). Cooper was admitted FRCS Edinburgh in 1868, and FRCS England on 9 June 1870. He became a close friend of William Alexander, twelfth duke of Hamilton, and the duke presented him with Cooper Angus Lodge, Whiting Bay, in the Isle of Arran, which he made his home when he retired from London.

In 1874 Cooper travelled to St Petersburg with the prince of Wales, later Edward VII, on the marriage of Alfred Ernest Albert, duke of Edinburgh. In recognition of his services he was appointed by the tsar a chevalier of the order of St Stanislas. In 1893 he was appointed surgeon-in-ordinary to the duke of Edinburgh when he became duke of Saxe-Coburg and Gotha. Cooper was knighted at Edward VII's coronation in 1902.

Cooper gained a wide knowledge of the world, partly as surgeon to kings and princes, partly in the out-patient rooms of hospitals, and partly through his expertise in syphilis. He was highly regarded by the profession and was trusted as a broadminded confidant by his patients. He was elected twice to the council of the Royal College of Surgeons of England, serving from 1895 to 1905. On one occasion his name was at the top of the poll, and he was consequently co-opted as vice-president.

From early in his career Cooper served as surgeon to the Inns of Court rifle volunteers, 'The devil's own', and he retained a deep interest in the reserve forces throughout his life. He obtained the volunteer decoration for long service and eventually served as surgeon-colonel to the Duke of York's Loyal Suffolk hussars. Cooper was also an active freemason. He held high office in the United Grand Lodge of England and was instrumental in founding the Rahere Lodge, which was the first masonic body to be associated with a hospital.

Cooper died at Villa St Jacques, Menton, France, on 3 March 1908, and was buried in the English cemetery there. He was survived by his wife.

D'A. POWER, rev. STELLA BUTLER

**Sources** *St Bartholomew's Hospital Journal*, 15 (1907–8), 105–6 • *The Lancet* (21 March 1908), 901–2 • *BMJ* (14 March 1908), 660–61 • V. G. Plarr, *Plarr's Lives of the fellows of the Royal College of Surgeons of England*, rev. D'A. Power, 1 (1930), 267–8 • Burke, *Peerage* • *CGPLA Eng. & Wales* (1908)
**Likenesses** Spy [L. Ward], caricature, watercolour lithograph, NPG, Wellcome L.; repro. in *VF* (30 Dec 1897)
**Wealth at death** £14,130 18s. 5d.: resworn probate, 22 May 1908, *CGPLA Eng. & Wales*

**Cooper, Alice Jane** (1846–1917), headmistress, was born in Cartwright Street, Doncaster, Yorkshire, on 4 August 1846, the eldest of the four daughters of the Revd John Thomas Cooper (d. 1877), a Unitarian minister, and his wife, Anne, formerly Barrow (d. 1892). Like many Unitarians she was deeply involved in education. Having succeeded in the new Cambridge higher local examination, she was second mistress from 1875 to 1876 at Nottingham Hill High School for Girls, one of the first two schools established by the Girls' Public Day School Company in 1873. From 1876 until 1895 she was the first headmistress of Edgbaston High School for Girls, an early example of a proprietary high school for girls and the first to offer public secondary schooling to girls in Birmingham.

Alice Cooper entered fully into the objectives of the nonconformist 'industrial squirearchy' of Birmingham that had established this non-sectarian school for girls to provide the best education available. Concerned with every aspect of school life, she refused to copy any narrowing contemporary educational practices. Establishing a broad curriculum, she discouraged cram and rote learning and disapproved of external examinations before the age of sixteen or seventeen. She did much to promote the very successful teaching of science at Edgbaston, although, as she pointed out in the 1894 *Journal of Education*, elsewhere girls particularly often suffered badly from the lack of scientific equipment.

Miss Cooper was also a pioneering headmistress in her encouragement of cricket and other games, callisthenics, gymnastics, Ling exercises, sensible clothing, and drama—in 1889, for example, her correspondent Lewis Carroll saw a performance of *Alice in Wonderland* at the school. She stimulated a variety of other extra-curricular activities, including a school magazine, *Laurel Leaves*, and founded The Link for old girls. She thus laid the foundations of a very successful, rapidly growing high school for the wealthier middle class, from which many girls left to join the increasing band of women university students.

The innovative attitudes of both headmistress and council of the school were shown in 1882 when Miss Cooper was sent to the USA to report upon educational methods there. In her detailed report on the large and varied number of educational institutions she visited, while not converted to common state primary schools, she extolled the schools' better equipment, separate classrooms, and specialized facilities, approved of the encouragement of questioning attitudes in pupils, and displayed a cautious preference for co-education.

Miss Cooper, like other women reformers, did much to promote the professional training of teachers for secondary education as her fellowship of the College of Preceptors and membership of the 1874 Association of Headmistresses illustrated (the latter met at Edgbaston High in 1889). She attended Edward Thring's conference of headmistresses at Uppingham in 1887. On the board of managers of the Birmingham Day Training College, established in 1890, she supported this method of training elementary teachers and, approving of greater links between elementary and secondary schooling, made the novel suggestion that high school girls could use such colleges and thence teach in the higher grade elementary schools. She wished to extend such training to secondary teachers, wanting all women teachers, public or private, to gain a university qualification. This would be followed by teacher training based on university departments and schools together, with public financial support if necessary. She also supported travelling scholarships for teachers, secretarial and commercial classes for women, and co-education in higher education. She argued strongly and often for the better payment of schoolmistresses and was one of the headmistresses who gave evidence to the Bryce commission on secondary education in 1894–5. There she argued strongly for more equal funding for girls' schools, better science facilities, properly thought-out technical education for girls, and, above all, a good general, liberal education for girls of all classes, because girls gained less education than boys from their 'career in life'. She also argued for local councils of education in large towns.

In 1895, to widen her educational activities, Alice Cooper resigned as headmistress. From 1891 to 1915 she was a member of the council of Somerville College, one of the earliest colleges for women in Oxford, and non-denominational. In 1897 she became tutor to women students taking the training course for teachers in secondary schools run by the Oxford University delegacy of local examinations, and was the first woman to be employed by an Oxford delegacy in an academic role. She was on the committee of the Association for Promoting the Education of Women in Oxford and by 1910 was assistant lecturer in education. Teacher training in Oxford took time to gain support, but Miss Cooper's teaching was reported to be 'highly appreciated by her students, men as well as women' (Delegacy for the Training of Secondary Teachers, *Memorandum for the Information of Members of Convocation*, 1912, 7). At her death Edgbaston High School endowed a bursary at Somerville for a former Edgbaston student intending to teach.

Miss Cooper's writings include 'On the training of the memory', a paper for the 1881 *Kindergarten Papers* of the Froebel Society (of which she was a member), in which she characteristically stressed the importance of a scientific basis for teaching and of questioning in learning. With E. A. Sonnenschein she wrote *Part II Analysis and Syntax of an English Grammar for Schools*, highly praised in the USA and in Germany. In 1890 a course book, *English Examples and Exercises*, was added, to which Miss Cooper contributed 'Part II analysis'. She was one of only three women among the impressive array of authors in this Parallel Grammar Series.

In 'Technical education for girls', published in the Board of Education's *Special Reports on Educational Subjects*, 1896–7, Miss Cooper examined how to make girls' technical subjects in higher grade schools 'organic parts of a well-ordered whole', a favourite subject of hers. She wanted homecrafts, including nursing, to be taught scientifically and interrelated with general subjects in order to produce skilled, self-reliant, resourceful craftswomen who would be able to make their adult leisure and home duties more interesting. She also wanted to introduce the teaching of citizenship as she had at Edgbaston. Although in some respects keeping to a gendered curriculum, therefore, Miss Cooper wanted all females to be prepared for the fuller life, duties, and occupations formerly reserved for men.

In appearance 'dowdy and grey', with rather square features, Miss Cooper had an invigorating personality, a gift for speaking, and a lively zest for knowledge and travel. She died suddenly at her home, Cestria, Ledborough Lane, Beaconsfield, Buckinghamshire, on 17 June 1917.

RUTH WATTS

**Sources** J. Whitcut, *Edgbaston high school, 1876–1976* (1976) · *The Inquirer* (23 June 1917) · *The Inquirer* (Oct 1852) · *The Inquirer* (March 1877) · *The Inquirer* (17 March 1877) · *The Inquirer* (6 Feb 1892) · *The Inquirer* (31 Jan 1931) · *The Inquirer* (4 Feb 1933) · M. Bateson, ed., *Professional women upon their professions* (1895) · G. Walford, ed., *The private schooling of girls past and present* (1993), 33–78 · 'Royal commission on secondary education: minutes of evidence', *Parl. papers* (1895), vol. 44, C. 7862-I · G. E. Evans, *Vestiges of protestant dissent* (1897) · J. Sondheimer and P. R. Bodington, eds., *GPDST, 1872–1972: a centenary review* (1972) · J. S. Pederson, *The reform of girls' secondary and higher education in Victorian England* (1987) · d. cert.
**Likenesses** pastel, 1895, Edgbaston High School for Girls
**Wealth at death** £625 14s. 5d.: administration, 1 Aug 1917, *CGPLA Eng. & Wales*

**Cooper, Andrew** [Anthony] (*fl.* **1660**), poet, details of whose life are scarce, is best known as the author of *Stratologia, or, The History of the English Civil Warrs, in English Verse*, printed in London in 1660. Written from an observer's perspective, and signed 'A.C.', the verse examines the principal events of the civil war from its causes until the execution of Charles I, and concludes by predicting further upheaval:

> blood for blood
> Cryes out aloud, and will be understood,
> Revenge whereof although the Gods delay,
> It's with more Fury, that they may repay.
> (p. 171)

Cooper's 'Epistle to the reader' (sig. A3v) warns of taut, blunt, and violent language, due in part to the poem's themes, but also to Cooper's own background. Wounded three times before the age of eighteen, he had had his education interrupted by military demands:

> When first for Oxford, fully there intent,
> To study learned Sciences I went.
> Instead of Logicke, Physicke, School-converse,
> I did attend the armed Troops of Mars.
> (ll. 13–16)

The succeeding verses are a product of periods of imprisonment, but Cooper articulates hopes to supplement his first volume with a sequel:

> And if thou shalt accept these first Essayes,
> Shortly perchance we may in smoother Layes
> The second part of our sad Annals sing,
> Till the blest Restauration of our King.
> (ll. 29–32)

The verse itself is dedicated to the Honourable Conyers Darcy (1622–1692) of Hornby Castle, Yorkshire. Cooper, stimulated by Darcy's faith and valour, eulogizes the achievements of Darcy's regiment, and acts as a witness to the personal cost of his allegiance, in terms of physical wounds and financial risk:

> Your sufferings since the Warres who hath not known
> You paid both for your Souldiers, and your own
> Loyalty, nor would your brave mind submit
> To imposition, till much mov'd to it
> By your most vertuous Lady's prayers and tears
> Your name the last in that black Roll appears.
> (ll. 25–30)

An earlier text, *A Speedy Post; with More News from Hull, York and Beverley*, printed in London for John Thomas in 1642, has been attributed to Cooper on the basis of his close involvement in the battles of the civil war. The author, Andrew Cooper, provides a detailed news report of events surrounding the arrival in York of Charles I, and his courting of support prior to his departure from the city in August. Initially focusing on a recent skirmish in Anlaby, Cooper then relates the daily polarization of the two parties, the anxious gathering of conscripts, and the tangible prologue of conflict: 'the Country hereabout is put in a great feare, if civill Warrs begin amongst us, that ruin and distruction will befall this Kingdome, which God of his mercy prevent' (p. 6). He ends with prayers for unity and concord, and with the promise of future instalments and literary undertakings. Both Sir Egerton Brydges and Thomas Corser have speculated that the poet was related to Anthony Ashley Cooper, created earl of Shaftesbury in 1672.      ELIZABETH HARESNAPE

**Sources** Wing, *STC* · *BL cat.* · A. C. [A. Cooper], *Stratologia, or, The history of the English civil warrs* (1660) · A. C. [A. Cooper], *A speedy post; with more news from Hull* (1642) · E. Brydges, *Restituta, or, Titles, extracts, and characters of old books in English literature*, 4 vols. (1814–16), vol. 3, pp. 331–3 · T. Corser, *Collectanea Anglo-poetica, or, A … catalogue of a … collection of early English poetry*, 4, Chetham Society, 77 (1869), 441–3 · A. Browning, *Thomas Osborne, earl of Danby and duke of Leeds* (1913) · M. W. Helms, P. A. Bolton, and P. Watson, 'Darcy, Hon. Conyers', HoP, *Commons, 1660–90* · *CSP dom.*, 1678, earl of Danby to Williamson, 12 Oct 1678, 458 · *CSP dom.*, 29/407/22, Darcy to Williamson, 12 Oct 1678 · *CSP dom.*, 29/407/23 · *DNB*

**Cooper, Anthony Ashley**, first earl of Shaftesbury (1621–1683), politician, was born shortly after 3 a.m. on 22 July 1621 at the house of his grandfather, Sir Anthony *Ashley,

Anthony Ashley Cooper, first earl of Shaftesbury (1621–1683), by Samuel Cooper, *c.*1672

baronet, in Wimborne St Giles, Dorset, 'the eldest child then living' (Christie, vol. 1, appx 2, p. xxv) of Sir John Cooper, baronet (*d.* 1631), of Rockbourne, Hampshire, and his wife, Anne Ashley (*d.* 1628) of Wimborne St Giles. He was baptized on 3 August and given both names of his maternal grandfather in fulfilment of a promise his parents had made to Sir Anthony. Anthony had a younger sister, Philippa (1623–1701), and a younger brother, George (*b.* 1625), about whom little is known. His father, created a baronet in 1622, represented Poole in the parliaments of 1625 and 1628, supporting an attack on the Arminian tendencies of the bishop of Winchester, Richard Neile, in February 1629. Both his parents died while Anthony was still a child; his mother on 20 July 1628, his father on 23 March 1631.

Through birth and through his relatives' and his own marriages Cooper became connected to some of the most powerful families in England. The Coopers and the Ashleys were of minor gentry stock, but both families had steadily built up their landed possessions over the generations, and the marriage between John and Anne in 1616 united extensive neighbouring estates in Dorset, Hampshire, and Wiltshire, as well as outlying properties in Somerset, Staffordshire, Derbyshire, and Middlesex. In 1622, two years after the death of his first wife, Sir Anthony Ashley, now aged seventy, married nineteen-year-old Philippa Sheldon, who was related to George Villiers, marquess of Buckingham, then the most powerful figure at court. In 1629 Sir John Cooper took as his second wife Mary, the widow of Sir Charles Moryson and one of the daughters of Sir Baptist Hicks, to whose great commercial fortune she was coheir. Mary's grandson from her first marriage was Arthur Capel, first earl of Essex. Cooper himself married three times over the course of his life. On 25 February 1639 he married Margaret (d. 1649), third daughter of Thomas *Coventry, first Baron Coventry, Charles I's then lord keeper; she brought with her a dowry of £4000; the marriage also connected him with George Savile, later first marquess of Halifax, whose father married Margaret's sister. Margaret was Cooper's own choice as bride, and he appears to have been genuinely in love with her. The marriage, however, brought no children. Margaret had two miscarriages (in 1646 and 1647) and gave birth to a stillborn girl in December 1647; she was seven and a half months into her fourth pregnancy when, on 10 July 1649, she 'fell suddenly into an apoplectical convulsion fit' and died (Christie, vol. 1, appx 2, p. lii). Cooper's second wife was Lady Frances Cecil (1633–1652), eldest daughter of David Cecil, third earl of Exeter, whom he married on 15 April 1650 when she was still only seventeen. The couple had two sons: the first, Cecil, died in childhood; the second, Anthony Ashley, eventually became second earl of Shaftesbury. Frances died on 31 December 1652, aged only nineteen. On 30 August 1655 Cooper married Margaret (bap. 1627, d. 1693), sixth daughter of William Spencer, second Baron Spencer of Wormleighton, sister of the first earl of Sunderland (who had been killed at Newbury fighting for the king in 1643), and the niece of Thomas Wriothesley, fourth earl of Southampton; she also brought a dowry of £4000. Although the marriage remained childless, it appears to have been happy.

**Inheritance and early life** Cooper's inheritance was troubled. His father, as a result of heavy gambling and extravagant spending, had run up debts in excess of £35,000. In addition most of his lands were held by knight service, which meant that his heir and estates would pass into the hands of the court of wards. Sir John's two trustees, Edward Tooker (who had married one of Sir John's sisters) and Sir Daniel Norton (a colleague of Sir John's in the Commons and the husband of Cooper's godmother), bought the wardship of the boy from the king for £3000, but found themselves still under the authority of the court of wards when it came to selling land to meet Sir John's debts. Sir Francis Ashley, the younger brother of Sir Anthony, then the king's serjeant-at-law, persuaded the court to sell some of the richest parts of the estate, which enabled Sir Francis and two of the commissioners for the sales to pick up several properties at less than market value. Cooper later estimated his loss from what he called 'the injustice and oppression of that Court' at £20,000 (Christie, vol. 1, appx 1, p. viii). He was far from being reduced to poverty, however; a survey made in 1638 calculated that a yearly revenue of £2349 15s. 9d. from the lands remaining to him was improvable to over £7000.

As he was growing up Cooper was exposed to a number of puritan influences. His first tutor was Aaron Guerdon, a noted puritan selected for him by his grandfather, who felt the youth 'could not have too deep a dye of religion' (Haley, 12). Following his father's death the young Sir Anthony Cooper, bt, as he now became, went to live at Southwick, near Portsmouth, with his father's trustee, Sir Daniel Norton, a man of puritan leanings who had joined the attack on Arminianism in the parliament of 1629. Here he was tutored by a man called Fletcher, about whom we know only that he was an excellent teacher of grammar. When Sir Daniel died in early 1636 Cooper joined the household of the other trustee, Edward Tooker, at Maddington, near Salisbury, where he was put into the care of a third tutor, an MA from Oriel College, Oxford, who left so little impression that later in life Shaftesbury was unable to remember his name. In March 1637 Cooper entered Exeter College, Oxford, where he studied under its rector, Dr John Prideaux, regius professor of divinity, a strong upholder of the Calvinist doctrine of predestination and another vehement opponent of Arminianism, before entering Lincoln's Inn on 18 February 1638, where he was exposed to the puritan preaching of Dr Edward Reynolds and Joseph Caryll.

Following his marriage to Lord Coventry's daughter in February 1639 Cooper, being still a minor and therefore not yet having come into possession of his property, moved into his father-in-law's household, and apart from occasional visits to Wimborne St Giles lived in the lord keeper's houses at Durham House in the Strand and at Canonbury in Islington. He inherited the short stature of his grandfather and as an adult was markedly below average height. He was also plagued by ill health, suffering from an internal condition which left him with a permanent dull aching pain on his left side, but which invariably flared up during the middle of the day to cause a bout of such intense pain that he was forced to lie down wherever he was. Portraits reveal a man with marked features, though by no means unattractive, and a face that shows character, composure, and intelligence. Although his education had been unsystematic he attained the educated gentleman's usual knowledge of the classics, history, and law.

**Early political career and civil war politics, 1640–1650** In March 1640 Cooper was chosen to serve as member for Tewkesbury for the Short Parliament (13 April–5 May) when still a minor, thanks in part to the influence of the Coventrys, whose family seat was at nearby Croome D'Abitot in Worcestershire. However, he was not asked to stand for Tewkesbury again in October 1640 at the elections for what was to become the Long Parliament, the Coventry connection probably working to his disadvantage at a time when opinion in the country was hardening against those associated with the court. In December he contested the by-election for the borough of Downton in Wiltshire, but a double return was made, and although (according to Cooper's own account) the committee of privileges decided in his favour its report never came before the Commons. When civil war broke out in 1642 Cooper at first tried to avoid taking sides. Although he left London after the king's departure from Whitehall in January 1642 he did not join the court, instead making his way to Rufford, Nottinghamshire, to stay with his brother-in-law, Sir William Savile. He was present in the county when Charles I raised his standard at Nottingham on 22 August and rode from Rufford to Nottingham to see the king, though whether or not he actually witnessed the ceremony is unclear. He left with the king for Derby on 13 September, but 'only as a spectator', he later claimed in his autobiographical sketch, 'having not as yet adhered against the Parliament' (Christie, vol. 1, appx 2, p. xxvii); indeed, he did not accompany Charles beyond Derby, but instead retired northwards, away from the scene of military operations.

In spring 1643, however, with the expected speedy resolution to the conflict not having materialized, Cooper decided that he should return to Dorset, make his choice, and take part in the upcoming campaign. During that summer he threw in his lot with the royalists and at his own expense raised a regiment of foot and a troop of horse, of which he became a colonel and captain respectively. Nevertheless he hoped for a compromise settlement. According to a later memoir written by John Locke he went to see the king at Oxford and asked to be allowed to treat with the parliamentary garrisons, starting in his own country of Dorset, offering to restore things to 'the same posture they were before the war' and promising a free parliament to 'do what more remained to be done for the settlement of the nation' (*Works of John Locke*, 1812, 9.267). Cooper did begin some private negotiations for the surrender of Dorchester but had achieved nothing when the royalist victory at Roundway Down in mid-July, followed by the fall of Bristol, changed the military balance in the area. By 2 August royalist troops under the command of Lord Carnarvon were at the gates of Dorchester and Cooper was one of three royal commissioners appointed to treat with the town the next day. Dorchester surrendered without resistance in return for being spared plunder and punishment; Weymouth and Portland soon followed suit. However, the terms of the surrender were betrayed by Prince Maurice, whose troops arrived in the area shortly afterwards and immediately set about plundering both Dorchester and Weymouth. Carnarvon resigned his command in disgust, while Cooper and Maurice were said to have exchanged 'some pretty hot words' (ibid.). Maurice next tried to stop Cooper's appointment as governor of Weymouth and the Isle of Portland—a commission promised him by Maurice's predecessor as commander of the royalist forces in the west, the marquess of Hertford—on the grounds of inexperience. Cooper was able to persuade the chancellor of the exchequer, Edward Hyde (the future earl of Clarendon), to intercede with the king on his behalf, and in the end Charles agreed to confirm the commission; at the same time, however, the king wrote to Hertford to express concern over Cooper's youth and lack of military experience, urging the marquess to use his influence with Cooper to persuade him to resign as soon as he could without losing face. Cooper remained in the post for the rest of the year and was compensated with other honours, being made sheriff of Dorset and president of the council of war for that county. Locke's memoir claims that Cooper now made another attempt to bring the civil war to an end and framed a design to raise a third army of clubmen in several parts of the kingdom 'to suppress the armies on both sides' (*Works of John Locke*, 1823, 9.268). Locke's account is problematic, however, since the clubmen movements did not emerge until 1645; moreover, there is no firm evidence to suggest that Cooper was involved in the formation of the clubmen in the west country at this later date.

Early in 1644 Cooper resigned all his commissions under the king and on 24 February presented himself at parliament's quarters at Hurst Castle. Clarendon alleged that it was pique at being forced to give up the governorship of Weymouth that led Cooper to quit the king's party, but this seems unlikely, since going over to parliament meant giving up the shrievalty and turning down an offer of a peerage (both of which were more prestigious honours than the governorship of a small port) as well as leaving the greater part of his estates in Dorset, Somerset, and Wiltshire behind enemy lines. In his autobiographical sketch penned in January 1646 Cooper claimed that he took this step because he saw that the king's aim was 'destructive to religion and the state' (Christie, vol. 1, appx 2, p. xxix); indeed, others left the royalist cause at this time, out of concern about the increasing Catholic influence at court, Charles's truce with the Catholic rebels in Ireland, and the general view at royalist headquarters that a settlement must be imposed by conquest. When examined before the committee of both kingdoms in London on 6 March 1644 as to his reasons for coming over Cooper said that he believed the royalist side had no intention of 'promoting or preserving .. the Protestant religion and the liberties of the kingdom'; that he was 'fully satisfied … of the justness' of parliament's proceedings; and that he was willing to take the solemn league and covenant, now the general test of loyalty following parliament's recent treaty with the Scots (Christie, 1.50).

On 10 July 1644 the Commons gave Cooper permission to leave London and join the county committee for Dorset and on 3 August the Dorset committee granted him a commission to command a brigade of horse and foot in Dorset with the title of field marshal-general. His first action was in the taking of Wareham, which capitulated on 10 August. On the 14th both houses of parliament voted to add him to the committee for governing the army in Dorset, and on the 22nd the Commons agreed that he should be allowed to compound for his sequestrated estates by payment of a £500 fine (though the fine was never paid and was later discharged by Oliver Cromwell). Back in Dorset, Cooper played an active role on the county committee, many of whose letters carry his signature first. On 25 October he was appointed commander-in-chief of a parliamentary force of 1500 men to oppose the royalist forces in the area under the command of Sir Lewis Dyve. He led the attack on the home of Sir John Strangways at Abbotsbury, west Dorset, in early November, went on to take Sturminster and Shaftesbury, and in December assisted in the relief of Colonel Robert Blake at Taunton. Taunton, however, was to be Cooper's last military action. Although a parliamentary committee sent him instructions in May 1645 to besiege Corfe Castle nothing ever came of this because the troops he was to use were occupied elsewhere. His military retirement may have had something to do with the new modelling of the army and the passage of the self-denying ordinance on 3 April 1645; although not a sitting MP Cooper still regarded himself as rightful member for Downton and may have thought it unwise to jeopardize his claim to the seat by retaining his commissions. Indeed, in autumn 1645 he did try to gain admission to parliament as member for Downton through his original petition, though the Commons resolved that 'no Person that hath been in actual War against this Parliament' should 'be admitted to sit as a Member' (*JHC*, 4, 1644–6, 260). Yet he may have been forced to cease military service because of ill health; in June and July 1645 he spent six weeks in Tonbridge with his wife where 'he drank the waters', and in February 1646 he underwent two minor surgical procedures—having 'a nerve and vein cut' on both occasions (Christie, vol. 1, appx 2, pp. xxxi, xxxiii)—which left him confined to his chamber for several days.

Cooper nevertheless continued to serve in local office. In October 1645 he resumed his place on the Dorset county committee, often serving as chairman. In December the committee sent him to Ottery St Mary, Devon, to ask the general of the parliamentary army, Sir Thomas Fairfax, for troops to assist in the besieging of Corfe Castle; Cooper's role, however, was exclusively civil, and he was not present when Corfe Castle finally surrendered in April 1646. In December 1646, after the end of the first civil war, parliament appointed Cooper high sheriff for Wiltshire, a post he held until 11 February 1648, when he was replaced by his uncle, possibly for reasons of ill health. In July parliament made him one of the commissioners for the militia in Dorset and also a commissioner for the rate for Ireland for Dorset.

It was towards the end of the first civil war that Cooper began his investments in commerce and overseas plantations. On 23 March 1646 he records in his diary signing 'articles concerning my plantation in Barbadoes' (Christie, vol. 1, appx 2, p. xxxiv), while at the beginning of the next month he notes that two local boys bound themselves to him to serve there for seven years. Cooper had a joint share in a plantation of 205 acres, which employed twenty-one white servants and nine adult black slaves. Investments in the sugar plantations led him to acquire a quarter share in a small slave ship, the *Rose*, which was involved in the triangular trade between England, Guinea, and the West Indies. He sold his share of the Barbados plantation (105 acres) in 1655 for £1020.

Unfortunately Cooper's diary, which runs from 1646 to 1650, remains silent on the great political issues of these years. It is normally thought that his sympathies lay with the presbyterians, though this needs qualification. He was not a religious presbyterian; he never advocated a policy of rigid conformity, and retained throughout his life a distaste for ecclesiastical authority. In his youth he had been friends with the noted puritan preacher William Strong, who was presented to a living near Wimborne in 1640 and who after the first civil war was to gather an Independent congregation which met in Westminster Abbey. Later in life Cooper was to have as his chaplain the Scottish Independent divine Robert Ferguson. He appears to have supported the cause of the political presbyterians in parliament against the army officers in 1647–8, but he nevertheless showed himself willing to serve the Commonwealth at the local level after the regicide in January 1649. Thus in February 1649 the new regime made him a JP of the quorum for the counties of Wiltshire and Dorset and of oyer and terminer for the western circuit (though he was not actually sworn in until 16 August, perhaps hinting at some initial qualms about serving). In April he was appointed commissioner to regulate the contribution paid by the counties of Wiltshire and Dorset, and in January and February 1650 he not only subscribed the engagement of loyalty to the new regime but agreed to serve on a commission tendering the engagement to others.

**Interregnum career, 1652–1660** No more is heard of Cooper until 17 January 1652, when the Rump Parliament named him to an extra-parliamentary commission of twenty-one, headed by Sir Matthew Hale, for the reform of the law. The Hale commission, which was dominated by moderates, made a series of well reasoned proposals for law reform designed mainly to appeal to the middle ground, although none of them was to be implemented. On 17 March 1653 the Rump pardoned Cooper 'of all Delinquency' (*JHC*, 7, 1651–9, 268), thereby opening the door for him to sit in parliament. Cromwell dissolved the Rump on 20 April, but Cooper was nominated to serve in the Barebones Parliament which assembled on 4 July, where he sat for the county of Wiltshire. He was made a member of the council of state on 14 July and appointed to a number of important committees, including the committee 'for the business of the law', which was intended to pick up where the Hale commission had left off, and he was among those present at a conference with the envoys of the United Provinces on 21 July when Cromwell put forward proposals for a close union between the two commonwealths. He firmly aligned himself with the moderates in the assembly, voting against abolishing tithes before an alternative maintenance had been worked out (15 July) and opposing the passage of a further bill for the sale of delinquents' estates (30 August). On 27 August he reported from the council of state to parliament on the case of the former Leveller John Lilburne, who had been banished by the Rump under pain of death, but who had since returned to England where he had been found 'Not Guilty of any crime worthy of death' by an Old Bailey jury who had taken it upon themselves 'to be Judges of matter of law, as well as matter of fact' (*State trials*, 5.446–7). Cooper made no recommendation as to what to do with Lilburne, though parliament decided that Lilburne should continue in prison. Cooper was re-elected to the council of state when the time arrived to renew the body at the beginning of November, and supported a committee recommendation that tithes be continued when the issue again came before the assembly on 3 December. When the assembly voted on 10 December, by a majority of just two, to reject the committee's recommendation he joined with those who decided to turn up early on the morning of Monday 12 December 1653 to vote their own dissolution.

Within four days a new constitution, the 'Instrument of government', establishing Cromwell as lord protector, was installed, and under its terms Cooper was named as one of fifteen members of the new council of state (though he never received his allotted salary of £1000 per annum). He was thus a member of the council which, in March 1654, approved the removal of John Lilburne to Jersey, where the writ of habeas corpus would not run: a loophole in the law which ironically was to be stopped by the so-called Shaftesbury Act of 1679. In the elections to the first protectorate parliament in summer 1654 he was chosen by three constituencies—Wiltshire, Poole, and Tewkesbury—opting to sit for the more prestigious county seat, where he had emerged victorious after a fierce partisan contest. Under the new constitution Wiltshire had ten MPs, and the election that July came to be disputed between two rival slates of ten candidates: one a group of determined republicans, headed by Edmund Ludlow; the other a mixture of Cromwellian partisans, presbyterians, and erstwhile cavaliers, headed by Cooper. So many voters showed up on election day that the poll had to be switched from Wilton to Stonehenge. There Cooper urged the electorate to choose 'such as were of healing spirits', not those who 'were for putting of all things into confusion and disorder' (Firth, 1.388–9), and the under-sheriff eventually declared his slate elected, though Ludlow alleged electoral malpractice and claimed that his own party were in the majority.

The first protectorate parliament spent much of its existence debating the detailed terms of the 'Instrument of government', though unfortunately the records do not provide much insight into where Cooper stood on the issues involved. On 27 November 1654 he was one of the tellers against a motion for restoring the old 40-shilling freehold county franchise, which the instrument had replaced by a voting qualification of £200 worth of real or movable property. On 23 December he supported a proposal that Cromwell should be offered the title of king, as part of a last-ditch effort to prevent the protector from breaking with his parliament and ruling through a standing army; however, it failed to generate much interest and was not even pressed to a division. Shortly afterwards Cooper broke with Cromwell. He attended the council for the last time on 28 December and was not present when it next met, on 5 January 1655. That same day parliament voted an entirely inadequate sum for the army, and a few days later Cooper moved a resolution to make illegal the collection or payment of revenue not authorized by parliamentary grant. Cromwell dissolved the parliament on 22 January. Ludlow alleged that Cooper moved into opposition because Cromwell refused to let him marry his daughter, Mary, but there is no contemporary corroboration for this. Instead Cooper's change of sides was probably motivated by a genuine concern about political developments under the protectorate.

The exiled Charles II thought that Cooper had turned royalist, and on 26 February 1655 wrote offering forgiveness and reward if he would help secure a restoration. Cooper did not reply and remained aloof when Colonel Penruddock launched his royalist rising in the west country in March 1655. Elected to serve for Wiltshire in the second protectorate parliament (which met on 17 September 1656), he was among about one hundred members whom the council of state refused to allow to sit, and together with sixty-four similarly excluded members he signed a letter of protest to the speaker, which was delivered by the presbyterian Sir George Booth. His was also one of ninety-eight names appended to a printed remonstrance against Cromwell that appeared a few days later, accusing the protector of having 'assumed an absolute arbitrary sovereignty' and charging anyone who approved of the exclusion with being a 'Capital enemy to the Commonwealth' (*To All the Worthy Gentlemen*), though the work appears to have been written by a disgruntled Commonwealth man, who affixed the names of the excluded members without authority. Cooper finally took his seat on 20 January 1658, following Cromwell's acceptance of a revised version of the *Humble Petition and Advice* (which stipulated that the excluded members should be allowed to return), and took the oath of fidelity to the protector as chief magistrate of the Commonwealth. That same month Cromwell discharged the fine of £500 imposed on Cooper by the Long Parliament for delinquency. Cooper joined with the opposition to the 'other house' which had been created by the petition and advice, and a frustrated Cromwell dissolved this parliament on 4 February.

Nothing more is heard of Cooper until the calling of Richard Cromwell's parliament in early 1659, which was elected according to the old system of county and borough representation for English members, though still with the new Scottish and Irish members provided for by the 'Instrument of government'. Cooper was returned for both Wiltshire and Poole, but as before chose to sit for the former. The house spent most of its time debating the validity of the existing constitution, where Cooper sided with the republicans, challenging the *Humble Petition and Advice* and insisting that the bill to recognize Richard Cromwell should contain additional clauses limiting the powers of the protector, particularly with regard to the key issues of control over the militia and the negative voice. Although the house agreed that before the Bill of Recognition was committed it could declare additional clauses binding the protector's power to be part of the bill, the Cromwellians managed to deflect the issue by insisting that the position of the 'other house' be settled first. The house agreed that it should be part of the Bill of Recognition to declare that parliament was to consist of two houses, but fell into endless debates about the composition and powers of the 'other house'. Cooper wanted the question of whether the second chamber should consist of the old lords or the new ones nominated by Oliver Cromwell determined first (making clear his own hostility to the new lords), though some of the opposition thought it better to impose bounds on the 'other house' before settling the question of membership. As a way through the impasse supporters of the government proposed that the house should transact with the 'other house' as a house of parliament, with the proviso that this should not 'exclude the rights of the old peers that have been faithful'. In a speech on 7 March Cooper condemned this as a trick, for by pretending to safeguard the rights of the old peers it in reality destroyed their claim to constitute the upper house. The house then turned to debating the right of the Scottish and Irish members to sit. In discussing the Scots, Cooper insisted he was 'as much for the Union as any man' and would have the Scots 'have as fair a legislature as may be', but objected to the way in which they were brought in 'upon the interest of the Chief Magistrate' (*Diary of Thomas Burton*, 4.189). Those who wanted the Scottish and Irish members to continue to sit, however, carried the day. On 28 March the house returned to the question of whether it should transact with the 'other house'. Again Cooper condemned the idea, alleging that if they gave 'this other House' the right of veto over business transacted in the Commons it would effectively give the protector 'a whole negative' to block whatever proceedings he did not like (*Diary of Thomas Burton*, 4.284). In the end the 'other house' was recognized, though only for the duration of the existing parliament. Cooper also opposed a bill purporting to end the excise and customs duties after the protector's death, which was a thinly veiled attempt to confirm the protector's right to levy these for life, urging members not to settle the revenue before they knew what their money would go to support. The debate was adjourned, but never resumed, and the bill failed.

Richard Cromwell dissolved parliament on 22 April 1659, and the Rump Parliament, which had been forcibly dissolved by Oliver Cromwell in 1653, was restored on 7 May (Richard Cromwell resigned as protector on 24 May). Cooper again tried to revive his claim to sit for Downton, the matter being referred to a committee which never reported. He was, however, appointed to the council of state on 19 May as one of the ten non-members in an executive body of thirty-one. Some of the republicans on the council objected to his sitting, suspecting him of royalist sympathies; to allay any suspicion he asked to be tendered the oath of loyalty to the Commonwealth 'without a single person, kingship or house of peers' (Haley, 113). That same month he rejected a second personal advance from Charles II. He sat on the council until 11 July, when he returned to Wimborne to attend to his estates. In August he was arrested on suspicion of complicity in Sir George Booth's unsuccessful presbyterian royalist uprising in Cheshire—Booth was a known friend and was reported to have been in correspondence with Cooper—but on 14 September the council found him not guilty of any involvement.

Thus exonerated, Cooper resumed his seat on the council, but he opposed the army's suspension of the Rump on 13 October 1659 and stopped attending the council of state two days later. When the army replaced the council of state with its own committee of safety on the 25th he threw in his lot with the republicans Thomas Scott, Sir Arthur Hesilrige, Henry Neville, and five others who continued to meet secretly as the rightful council of state. On 9 November he and Scott unsuccessfully tried to induce London's common council to petition for the restoration of the Rump. The secret council now came to see General George Monck, commander of the forces in Scotland, as their main hope. On 16 November Cooper and Hesilrige met three of Monck's commissioners in London and urged that Monck should declare for the recall of the Rump, claiming that he would have the support of all the inferior officers and common soldiers stationed near London. That same day appeared a printed remonstrance, with Cooper's one of the 450 names appended, protesting against the interruption of the parliament by the army and calling for the restoration of the Rump 'and the settlement of this Nation upon the constant succession of Parliaments' (*The Remonstrance*, 3). While waiting for Monck the secret council secured the support of the garrison of Portsmouth (3 December), commanded by Cooper's long-term friend Colonel Whetham, and Cooper was given a commission to command all the forces in London expected to join the revolt against the committee of safety. He was arrested on suspicion of planning to raise the counties of Wiltshire and Dorset, but since his plot involved London and not the west country, he was truthfully able to deny all such allegations and was released after giving his word not to leave London without permission. He now slipped into hiding in the City, where he and his colleagues launched a conspiracy to seize the Tower of London, with the help of the lieutenant of the Tower, Colonel Fitch, on 12 December. Tipped off in advance, the committee of safety had Fitch arrested and the plot came to nothing, but Cooper, Scott, and others wrote an open letter to General Charles Fleetwood, commander-in-chief of the army, on 16 December defending the attempt and insisting that the Rump was the only authority which could 'be hoped to make the sword subservient to the civil interest, and settle the government in the hands of the people by successive and free parliaments unlawfully denied to them' (Christie, vol. 1, appx 5, p. lxxvii).

Developments were soon to play into Cooper's and his allies' hands. With the fleet under admiral Lawson having already declared for the Rump, on 23 December troops assembled at Lincoln's Inn Fields and resolved to stand by parliament and follow the orders of the council of state. The Rump reassembled on 26 December and appointed Cooper one of the seven commissioners to have temporary control over the armed forces (until Hesilrige returned on the 28th) and one of the three to have temporary control of the Tower (until his friend Colonel Morley was made lieutenant on 7 January 1660). On 2 January Cooper was one of the ten non-members voted to a new council of state; three days later a committee was set up to report on the disputed Downton election, and on 7 January he was finally allowed to take his seat in the Long Parliament, some nineteen years after his original election. On his admission to the house he took the engagement of 1649 to be faithful to the Commonwealth. When an additional clause was put to the council of state renouncing Charles

Stuart he declined to take it, but so did the majority of the council, including impeccable republicans like Colonel Hutchinson; he still made no attempt to engage in correspondence with the exiled court, and in mid-January Hyde wondered whether Cooper would 'ever serve the King' (Ogle, 4.517). Nevertheless Cooper had begun to break company with his former republican allies, and according to the royalist agent, John Mordaunt, the Rump became divided into two irreconcilable parties, one headed by Cooper, the other by Henry Neville. When the Rump set about remodelling the army regiments to remove officers who had supported the committee of safety they gave Cooper Fleetwood's regiment (18 January), which he proceeded to fill 'with officers for his turn' (Firth, 2.206). With Monck now on his march south from Scotland, Hesilrige and Scott offered Cooper command of the army to march against him, but he refused, saying he had given Monck his 'word to be his friend, and therefore could not break it' (Christie, 1.205). Upon Monck's arrival in London, Hesilrige and his supporters on the council of state, in an attempt to ruin Monck's credit, urged the general to punish the City for recent disturbances and for threatening to withhold taxes until there was a free parliament by dismantling the gates and arresting eleven prominent citizens. Cooper made a desperate effort to dissuade Monck from taking such action, though in vain. Having dutifully carried out his commands on 10 February, Monck then learned that the Rump, instead of confirming him as commander-in-chief as promised, had decided to appoint five commissioners to control the army. Cooper, together with Lady Monck and some other friends, now convinced the general of the need to 'take some vigorous course' if he was to prevent his ruin (Christie, 1.208). On 11 February Monck marched with his own troops into the City and sent the Rump a letter reminding them that his army had undertaken not only to restore the parliament but also to vindicate the people's liberties and demanding that writs be issued out within a week to fill all the vacant seats. When the Rump decided to place restrictions on who should be allowed to stand Cooper urged Monck to restore the secluded members. This was done on 21 February with Cooper, as colonel of Fleetwood's regiment, commanding the escort. Two days later parliament appointed Cooper to a new council of state which consisted entirely of presbyterians and others who had played no part in the regicide and were not committed to a republic. The Long Parliament finally voted its own dissolution on 16 March 1660.

It was only now that Cooper began to draw closer to the royalist cause; in late February Lady Willoughby reported to Hyde that Cooper was a 'firm friend to the King', and a letter from Charles II to Cooper in mid-March about procuring the 'peace and happiness of the nation' this time received a 'civil' response (Ogle, 4.573, 600, 660). Cooper may initially have favoured a conditional restoration, since in mid-April he attended a meeting of the 'presbyterian knot' at Sussex House, who were pressing for a settlement along the lines of the treaty of Newport negotiated with Charles I in 1648. However, as MP for Wiltshire in the Convention Parliament, which met on 25 April, he

decided to acknowledge an unconditional restoration, and was one of twelve voted by the Commons on 8 May to go to The Hague to invite Charles II to return.

**The Restoration and the Clarendon administration, 1660–1667**
Cooper accompanied Charles II on his triumphal return to England in late May and was among those who received a special recommendation from Monck for a place on the privy council. Further support for his appointment came from the incoming treasurer, the earl of Southampton, who was thought to be more than capable of keeping his nephew by marriage on the path of loyalty. Thus at Canterbury on 27 May Charles named Cooper to his new privy council; two days later he appeared at the head of his regiment of cavalry at Blackheath, where the army assembled to welcome Charles back into the capital. He availed himself of the free pardon offered by Charles's declaration of Breda of 4 April, and received a formal pardon on 27 June. He was granted further pardons under the great seal on 10 February and 8 June 1661.

Although not one of the inner ring of the privy council, known as the committee on foreign affairs, as a member of the Convention Cooper acted as an important spokesman for the government. On 4 July he helped defeat a motion that those who served under the protectorate should refund their salaries—'he might freely speak', he said, 'because he never received any'—claiming that the proviso was 'dangerous to the peace of the nation' (Cobbett, *Parl. hist.*, 4.78) and pointing out that it reached important members of the new royal administration, such as General Monck and Admiral Montagu. On 16 July he successfully argued for a postponement of the discussion of a bill to settle religion, the government wanting to address what in its view were more urgent matters first. In the debates over the Indemnity Bill (passed 29 August), which was to decide who should be exempted from the general pardon, Cooper urged lenity. He saved Hesilrige's life, arguing that only those who had been guilty of shedding Charles I's blood should be punished; he also signed a certificate in favour of Colonel Hutchinson, another former republican colleague, and spoke in favour of the regicide Colonel George Fleetwood. As a member of the special commission for the trial of the regicides excluded from the general amnesty, however, he took part in the sentencing to death of a number of former colleagues and associates: Hugh Peters, who had served with him on the law reform commission of 1652–3; Major-General Harrison, who had sat with him on the council of state in 1653; and Thomas Scott, an ally in the revived Rump of 1659 and one who towards the end of that year had joined with him in the conspiracy to seize the Tower. In November he spoke out against the revival of the court of wards (abolished by the Long Parliament in 1641), at whose expense he had suffered in his youth, and supported the continuance of the Long Parliament's excise duties to compensate the crown for loss of revenue from former rights of wardship. As a privy councillor he served on numerous committees, including the committee to deal with the plantations and the council for trade, being one of the government's hardest workers. His reward came on 20 April

1661, when in the coronation honours Charles II created him Baron Ashley of Wimborne St Giles. He took his seat in the Lords on 11 May and two days later he was appointed chancellor of the exchequer and under-treasurer (probably owing the latter appointment to the influence of his uncle Southampton).

Some biographers have claimed that Ashley vehemently opposed the Corporation Act (passed 19 December 1661), which restricted municipal offices to Anglicans, but there is no firm evidence to support this; he was not even present at the decisive conference between the Lords and Commons on the act on the 19th. Indeed, at this stage he appears to have supported the government's desire for greater control over the towns, remarking at one Lords committee meeting in early February 1662 that 'the greatness of corporations' was 'inconvenient to monarchy' (Seaward, 151). Nor did he intervene in the debates over the Act of Uniformity (passed May 1662), and when the Lords debated the Commons' amendments making the act more stringent he was not recorded as being present. He did, however, support efforts to alleviate the plight of dissenters. He was a member of a Lords committee in July 1662 that tried to insert a clause into a bill allowing for late subscription to the Act of Uniformity that would have made it possible for moderate dissenters to conform, though the amendment was rejected by the Commons. He joined Sir Henry Bennet, the earl of Bristol, and Lord Robartes in advising Charles to issue his first declaration of indulgence on 26 December 1662 in favour of peaceable nonconformists and loyal Catholics, and when parliament made Charles withdraw the indulgence in February 1663, denying the legality of the dispensing power on which it was based, he supported Robartes's efforts to introduce a bill to allow the king to dispense protestant nonconformists (though not Catholics) from the Act of Uniformity. In the face of opposition to the Dispensing Bill from lord chancellor Clarendon, Ashley proclaimed in the Lords on 12 March how unfortunate the king was that 'the great Officers of the Crown' should oppose 'such a Prerogative' (the dispensing power) as perhaps 'would be found to be inherent in him without any Declaration of Parliament', adding that he wondered why they would not trust the king (*Life of … Clarendon*, 2.471). Clarendon, stung by the attack, described the bill as 'Ship-Money in Religion, that Nobody could know the End of' (ibid., 2.473). The bill was dropped in committee, but Clarendon's outspoken remarks cost him favour with the king.

Ashley had not always seen eye to eye with the lord chancellor since the Restoration. In 1661–2 he had joined with Bristol in opposing Charles's proposed marriage to Catherine of Braganza and the consequent commercial treaty with Portugal, which had been backed by Clarendon, because the match brought England into the French orbit, implying, as it did, support for the Portuguese in their struggle for independence from France's rival Spain. Following the clash over the Dispensing Bill Ashley seemed to be the rising star at court: in April 1663 the French ambassador observed how Ashley was 'perfectly in the King's graces' and predicted that he, Bristol, Bennet,

and 'the rest of that clique' might 'well give trouble to the Chancellor' (Christie, 1.272). Ashley still retained some connections with the chancellor. For example, on 24 March 1663 the two men were among the nine named as joint proprietors of the projected colony of Carolina. Nor did Ashley support Bristol's rash attempt to impeach Clarendon in July. Nevertheless he continued to be associated with the chancellor's reputed enemies: it was during this time that he first struck up a political association with the earl of Lauderdale, and by early 1664 Ashley was firmly identified as part of Lauderdale's anti-Clarendonian cabal.

Ashley's sympathy for dissent led him to try to soften the impact of the Conventicle Bill which came before the Lords on 28 April 1664 and he was a member of a Lords subcommittee that managed to mitigate the harshness of the penalties originally suggested by the Commons. On 24 December, following the outbreak of renewed hostilities with the Dutch, he was appointed treasurer of the prize commission, accountable to the king alone; Clarendon, jealous of Ashley's growing influence, objected to the bypassing of the normal exchequer routine, but was forced to back down. Clarendon remained confident 'that few men … had a worse Opinion of [Ashley's] Integrity' than Charles himself (*Life of … Clarendon*, 2.466); on the surface, however, Ashley seemed genuinely in the royal favour. Indeed, on 10 August 1665 Charles did him the honour of a surprise visit to his house at Wimborne, and a couple of weeks later both the king and queen were entertained there. It was now that Ashley met the king's teenage illegitimate son, James, duke of Monmouth, for the first time.

In the brief parliamentary session of October 1665, held at Oxford because of the plague, Ashley unsuccessfully opposed Sir George Downing's appropriation proviso to the Subsidy Bill, restricting the use of the money thus raised to the sole purpose of carrying on the Dutch war, on the grounds that the precedent, once set, might deprive ministers of any flexibility over how to use the money received from parliamentary taxation. According to his own, later account, he also supported his uncle Southampton's attempt to block the passage of the Five Mile Act, which forbade ejected nonconformist ministers from coming within 5 miles of any town or their former parish, though the records of the Lords do not list him as among the bill's opponents. When Ashley returned to Oxford in June 1666, seeking relief from his internal abscess by drinking the local spa water, he chanced to make the acquaintance of John Locke, beginning what turned out to be a lifelong friendship. When Ashley took up residence in Exeter House, off the Strand in London, in spring 1667, he invited Locke to live in his household.

In the parliamentary session of 1666–7 Ashley joined the duke of Buckingham in supporting the passage of the Irish Cattle Bill, designed to prevent the importation into England of Irish fat cattle. As a landowner he was concerned about the effect the Irish imports were having on cattle breeders in his native south-west, but he also used the occasion to strike out at the lord lieutenant of Ireland,

James Butler, duke of Ormond—either from a personal antipathy to Ormond, a jealousy that Irish peers might rise above English ones, or as a subterfuge to attack the high-church party at court (of which Ormond was one). He followed this up by proposing in the committee of privileges that Irish peers should lose any right to precedence over English commoners, and was rumoured to be preparing a bill to alter the Irish book of rates so as to force Ireland to import foreign commodities only through England. The Irish Cattle Bill passed the Lords on 23 November 1663 by a vote of 63 votes to 47 (noticeably all the bishops voted against it), but the matter did not rest there, since the Lords had replaced the word 'nuisance' in the bill, which would have prevented the king from granting dispensations from it, with the legally more innocuous words 'detriment and mischief'. The Commons refused to accept this, and were supported by a minority of peers, including Ashley and Buckingham, who argued that it did not take away from the royal prerogative to make laws indispensable, since most laws made for the king's benefit were, such as the laws against treason. In the end the word 'nuisance' was reinserted and the bill became law on 14 January 1667.

The dispute over the Irish Cattle Bill represents the first time that Ashley stood on the same side as a discontented majority in the Commons against the court interest. As such it temporarily cost him royal favour. When the treasurer, Southampton, died in May 1667, Charles, instead of appointing Ashley, who was under-treasurer, as his successor, put the Treasury into commission; he did, under protest, name Ashley as one of the commissioners, though not as one of the quorum. Following the failures of the Dutch war Clarendon himself was now in trouble, and was stripped of the chancellorship on 31 August. Yet despite having been at odds with the former chief minister on many issues for several years Ashley did not seek to reingratiate himself with the king by supporting the attempted impeachment of Clarendon in November, which was backed by Charles himself and pressed in the Lords by Ashley's former political allies Buckingham, Bristol, and Bennet (now earl of Arlington). Indeed, he successfully opposed a motion to commit Clarendon to the Tower on a general charge of treason, arguing that he could not be committed unless detailed charges were brought.

**The administration of the cabal, 1668–1673** The administration that succeeded Clarendon's is normally referred to as the 'cabal', following the initial letters of the ministers who signed the phoney treaty of Dover of 1670—Clifford, Arlington, Buckingham, Ashley, and Lauderdale. In fact, the five never formed a coherent ministerial team. Initially Arlington and Buckingham ran the government, though there were rivalries between the two. Ashley was out of favour following Clarendon's fall, and it was some time before he obtained a leading place in the king's councils; although he continued as chancellor of the exchequer and a commissioner of the Treasury, he had still not been placed on the king's inner cabinet, the

so-called committee of foreign affairs. The fall of Clarendon suggested that the time might be right to modify the religious settlement erected at the Restoration, and Ashley joined with Buckingham, Arlington, and the latitudinarian Bishop Wilkins of Chester to persuade Charles to endorse schemes for the comprehension of more moderate dissenters within the established church; two government-backed comprehension bills were drafted in October 1667 and February 1668, though they came to nothing. However, in May 1668 Ashley fell desperately ill. From the detailed notes kept by John Locke it appears that Ashley was suffering from a hydatid cyst of the liver, which now ruptured. (The condition is caused by a parasite transmitted through dogs or sheep.) Locke advised an operation, which was performed by a surgeon named Knollys on 12 June and undoubtedly saved Ashley's life. More dubiously it was decided that the tube which had been inserted during the operation to drain fluid from the abscess should remain permanently there, to allow for possible further drainage: hence later tory pamphleteers christened Shaftesbury 'Tapski', an allusion to the copper tap affixed to the end of the tube (the Polish ending because tories accused Shaftesbury of wanting to make England an elective monarchy like Poland).

It was at this time that Ashley resumed his interest in colonial affairs. Back in July 1660 he had been placed on the privy council's standing committee on trade and plantations, and later that year had helped set up the council of trade and council for foreign plantations, though these latter two bodies rapidly became moribund. When the standing committees of the privy council were reorganized in January 1668 Ashley was again placed on the committee for trade and plantations and, once he had recovered from his operation, was influential in resuscitating the council of trade, which received its commission in October. He became an *ex officio* member of the revived council for foreign plantations, set up on 30 July 1670, and president of the council of trade and foreign plantations when the two councils were merged in September 1672 (he continued to serve until April 1676, when the council was superseded by a committee of the privy council). He invested in the Hudson's Bay Company (chartered 1670), being appointed its deputy governor on 24 November 1674, and was instrumental in setting up the Bahama Adventurers' Company in autumn 1672. His darling, however, remained Carolina, and in 1669 he helped draw up the fundamental constitutions of Carolina, a copy of which in Locke's hand is preserved among the Shaftesbury papers.

On the domestic front Ashley joined Arlington and Buckingham in supporting the proposal for a political union with Scotland in 1669 and was at last admitted to a meeting of the committee of foreign affairs that June to discuss the terms, which he had had a hand in drawing up. Some progress was made over the next year, but when the Scots refused to consider a reduction in their existing parliamentary representation in any combined parliament the scheme was dropped. Despite Ashley's sympathy for the plight of dissenters he did not join with those peers who signed a formal protest against the passage of the 1670 Conventicle Act, though he probably supported the amendments by which the Lords reduced the penalties the Commons wanted to impose for attendance at non-conformist conventicles.

By now the question of the succession had already begun to occupy people's minds. Catherine of Braganza remained childless and the heir to the throne was therefore still Charles's brother, the duke of York, whose Catholicism was already suspected. Following the fall of Clarendon, Ashley joined Buckingham and the earl of Carlisle in trying to persuade Charles to declare his eldest illegitimate child, James, duke of Monmouth, legitimate. When that failed, attention turned to trying to persuade Charles to divorce his wife and remarry. Hence the significance of the Roos Remarriage Bill, which came before the Lords in March 1670. Lord Roos had already obtained a divorce in the ecclesiastical court and his children had been declared illegitimate by parliament, but he was now seeking an act to allow him to remarry; if parliament could establish its competence to pass such an act the implications for a potential royal divorce were obvious. In the debate in the Lords on 28 March Ashley spoke strongly in favour of the bill, taking the line that marriage was a civil contract, not a sacrament, and therefore should be managed by the civil magistrate. The measure passed, though Charles was never to avail himself of the precedent.

Ashley was kept out of the negotiations for the secret treaty of Dover, signed on 22 May 1670, whereby in return for French subsidies Charles promised to announce his own conversion to Catholicism and join with France in an attack against the Dutch republic. Since preparations for war could hardly be kept secret, a mock treaty (*traité simulé*) was concluded for the benefit of Ashley, Buckingham, and Lauderdale, omitting the so-called Catholic clauses (of which only Arlington and Clifford among the cabal had any knowledge). Ashley had reservations about a French alliance (he had initially asked for time to think it over), but he was also concerned about Dutch commercial competition, and when in July, as one of the royal commissioners appointed to discuss a projected treaty on overseas trade with the Dutch ambassador, it became obvious to him that any concessions from the Dutch in the East Indies or elsewhere could only be won by force, he fell in with the plan. The *traité simulé* was signed by the five members of the cabal on 21 December; Ashley, Buckingham, and Lauderdale, however, insisted on adding a number of Dutch territories to the English share of the spoils, to ensure future English control of the mouths of the Scheldt and Rhine, much more than the French had initially bargained for.

In 1671 Ashley was one of the peers who pressed for a reduction of the duty on sugar imposed by the Commons' Supply Bill, fearing that the new rate would have an adverse effect on colonial sugar planters. The Commons objected to the Lords' attempt to interfere in a money bill, and the bill was lost when the king prorogued parliament on 22 April. That September Ashley and Clifford were together responsible for a momentous change in the administration of the customs when they proposed abandoning the traditional practice of employing customs farmers and suggested that the revenue should be collected by the king's own commissioners instead. The change was well received by London merchants and eventually redounded to the king's profit. In the short term, however, Charles was desperately short of money to fight the Dutch war. The government therefore decided upon the stop of the exchequer in January 1672, which involved stopping the repayment of loans to bankers out of the proceeds of taxes. Although many contemporaries blamed Ashley, the policy was in fact Clifford's; Ashley opposed it as being against 'common justice', 'the law', and the king's 'constant promises', and predicted that it would 'ruin thousands' and depress trade (Christie, 2.59).

The declaration of war against the Dutch was preceded by the issuance of a declaration of indulgence on 15 March 1672, suspending 'all manner of penal laws in matters ecclesiastical' against both protestant nonconformists and Catholics, and allowing the former to take out licences to hold their own religious meetings in public (Kenyon, 407). The government believed it necessary to conciliate the nonconformists lest they side with their Dutch co-religionists once war was declared, and Ashley strongly supported the measure. The declaration of war was followed by new honours for the members of the cabal, to induce them to remain united behind the controversial royal policy. Ashley became earl of Shaftesbury and Baron Cooper of Paulet, the patent being dated 23 April 1672, and on 17 November he was appointed lord chancellor. When parliament reconvened on 4 February 1673 Shaftesbury, in his new official capacity, gave a lengthy address justifying the royal policy in which he urged the need for large supplies in order to prosecute the war, accused the Dutch of being the common enemies of all monarchies and their only rivals in trade (declaring in one famous outburst, 'Delenda est Carthago, Carthage must be destroyed'), defended the stop of the exchequer (while urging the Commons to consider what might be done to help the bankers who had been affected by it), and vindicated the declaration of indulgence.

The Commons unanimously voted a supply of £1.26 million to be raised over a period of eighteen months, but demanded the redress of a number of grievances before it would enact the Supply Bill. Prior to the reconvening of parliament Shaftesbury, as lord chancellor, had issued writs to fill thirty-six seats that had fallen vacant during the prorogation. Although there were precedents, normally such writs were issued by the speaker, and since the great majority of the newly elected members were supporters of the court Shaftesbury's initiatives looked like an attempt by the government to pack parliament. Colonel Giles Strangways, an old Dorset rival, led the attack, and the elections were declared void. The Commons also demanded that Charles withdraw the indulgence. Shaftesbury advised the king to send an answer to the Commons maintaining the ecclesiastical supremacy but denying any claim to suspend laws in which the properties, rights, and liberties of the subject were affected and offering to concur with any bill presented to him for liberty of conscience; the Commons refused to accept this, however, and in the end Charles himself backed down and cancelled the indulgence. The Commons then presented an address against the growth of popery and proceeded to promote a Test Act (enacted 20 March 1673), requiring all holders of civil and military office to take the Anglican sacrament and make a declaration against transubstantiation. Despite his championship of the indulgence Shaftesbury supported the Test Act, though there was nothing necessarily inconsistent in this; even dissenters at this time realized that the most they could hope for was religious liberty, not full civil liberty. Shaftesbury took the Anglican sacrament together with the duke of Monmouth at St Clement Danes Church in the Strand, with Shaftesbury's secretary, John Locke, serving as witness to both. Shaftesbury supported a bill for the ease of dissenters when it came before the Lords towards the end of March, though he wanted to insert a clause giving the king power to issue proclamations on religious matters and he objected to the Commons' proposal to restrict the ease to those who were willing to subscribe to the Thirty-Nine Articles, which would have excluded many sectaries. The adjournment on 29 March put a stop to further debate on the bill, and parliament failed to pick up on the measure when it reconvened in October.

The failure of the indulgence and the passage of the Test Act meant the days of the cabal were numbered. For the time being, however, Shaftesbury remained in office, despite moving closer to the political opposition in parliament. Although some, including the king, suspected his loyalty, it is highly unlikely that he was involved in any intrigues with the Dutch against the English government, though now he was certainly keen to end the war and in favour of negotiating peace directly with the Dutch. The failure of the duke of York to take the Anglican sacrament at Easter 1673, moreover, reignited Shaftesbury's concern about the prospect of a Catholic successor. In June a letter of his to the duke urging him to change his religion was circulated. The succession issue became more pressing when York decided to take the Italian archduchess Mary of Modena (a French protégée) as his second wife in autumn 1673; James had two daughters by his first wife, Anne Hyde (d. 1671), both of whom had been brought up as protestants, but a son by his second would take precedence in the succession and raised the prospect of a never-ending succession of Catholic kings. The marriage had been celebrated by proxy, and Mary had still not arrived in England when parliament reconvened on 20 October. York was anxious that parliament should be prorogued immediately for a few days, to prevent the Commons protesting against the match; Shaftesbury, however, deliberately retarded the summons of the lower house before the Lords, which gave the Commons time to draw up an address to the king urging that the marriage not be consummated. It was too late to put a stop to the marriage, however, so Shaftesbury now revived the idea of trying to persuade Charles to divorce the queen and take a second

wife. He also joined with Arlington, Ormond, and secretary Henry Coventry in advising Charles to send his brother away from court. York was incensed and pressed the king to dismiss Shaftesbury from office. Charles, who had become increasingly suspicious of Shaftesbury's loyalty over the last few months and now had reason to believe he was intriguing with Scottish malcontents in order to stoke up opposition to Lauderdale in the upcoming session of the Scottish parliament, agreed that his lord chancellor would have to go. On Sunday 9 November he sent secretary Coventry (Shaftesbury's brother-in-law) privately to Exeter House with two warrants, one for the seals, and the other for a royal pardon for all crimes committed before 5 November; Shaftesbury is reported to have said 'It is only laying down my gown, and putting on my sword' (Christie, vol. 2, appx 3, p. xliii n.).

**Country politician, 1674–1678** It was not clear at first that Shaftesbury's fall from favour would be permanent. Towards the end of November 1673 Arlington tried to broker a reconciliation with the king, and even persuaded the French ambassador that Shaftesbury might be won back with an appropriate bribe. Shaftesbury refused such overtures, protesting that he would not 'be a friend to the French King' and support 'an interest that was so apparently destructive to [Englishmen's] religion and trade' (Christie, vol. 2, appx 3, p. xliv). According to the Venetian secretary he instead set himself up 'as the organ of the Spanish party' and offered the king friendship with Spain, peace with the Netherlands, reconciliation with parliament, and money to defray the expenses of the last war, if he would 'repudiate the queen and make a second marriage, so as to exclude by his own offspring the suspected progeny of the duke of York' (*CSP Venice, 1673–5*, 183).

In the parliamentary session which began on 7 January 1674 Shaftesbury's main preoccupation was the threat of popery and the prospect of a Catholic succession. On the 8th he gave an impassioned speech warning that there were more than 16,000 Catholics in the London area ready to rebel, prompting the Lords to address the king for a proclamation ordering all papists to depart 10 miles from the capital, and four days later he proposed that every peer should take the oath of allegiance before entering the house, including the duke of York. Shaftesbury was now co-ordinating tactics with a group of malcontent peers—including Carlisle, Fauconberg, Holles, Salisbury, Buckingham, and Halifax—who met at Holles's house to discuss what measures to introduce in parliament. The fruits of their efforts were revealed on 24 January when Salisbury moved for a bill to provide for the education of York's children as protestants, Carlisle proposed that in future neither the king nor any prince of the blood should marry a Catholic without the consent of parliament, and Halifax called for the disarming of all Catholics. The Lords responded by appointing a committee to prepare a bill for securing the protestant religion. When, on 10 February, the house came to debate the clause in the proposed bill forbidding a prince of the blood from marrying a Catholic without parliamentary consent Carlisle and Halifax proposed that the penalty for its breach should be exclusion from the succession. Shaftesbury spoke strongly in favour of the measure, insisting that there were precedents, though the proposal was dropped in the face of opposition from the bishops and the lord keeper, Sir Heneage Finch. Shaftesbury and Carlisle were next said to be considering proposing that York's regiments of guards be disbanded, while Shaftesbury also accepted responsibility for presenting a petition that Ireland was in danger from a French invasion; when Charles learned that the opposition peers were intending a direct attack on York, and might even seek to accuse him of treason, he speedily prorogued parliament (24 February). It would be wrong to create the impression that party lines were irreconcilably drawn in this session, however. Shaftesbury and his presbyterian associates, Holles, Carlisle, Fauconberg, Clare, and Salisbury, together with Charles's new leading minister, the earl of Danby, supported a Comprehension Bill sponsored by the bishop of Winchester and backed by six other bishops, which would have removed some of the presbyterian ministers' chief objections to the Act of Uniformity. The bill passed the Lords but was lost with the prorogation.

On 19 May 1674 Shaftesbury was expelled from the privy council; he was subsequently removed as lord lieutenant of Dorset and ordered to leave London. Successive prorogations meant that parliament did not meet again until 13 April 1675. Early in the new year there was talk that Shaftesbury was to be brought back into favour by the court, and might even be appointed vicar-general in ecclesiastical affairs, a position previously held only by Thomas Cromwell. On 3 February, however, Shaftesbury wrote a letter to the earl of Carlisle, which was widely circulated in manuscript, where he stated that the only advice he could offer the king would be to call 'a new Parliament', and that he would not return to court until he saw that 'the King thinks frequent parliaments as much his interest as they are the people's right' (Christie, 2.201). With Danby having determined upon an alliance with Anglican royalists and a strict enforcement of the penal laws against both Catholics and protestant nonconformists, even York began making overtures for a possible alliance with Shaftesbury's group of disaffected peers. By early April an astonished Venetian secretary could report that Shaftesbury (who was back in town for the upcoming parliamentary session) and York were reconciled, and that Holles 'and the rest of the confederates [had] all assured the duke of their desire to serve him' (CSP Venice, 1673–5, 391). When parliament assembled later that month Danby brought forward his notorious Test Bill, which would have required all office-holders and members of both houses to declare against the lawfulness of resistance and swear never to endeavour the alteration of the government in either church or state. Shaftesbury led the opposition to the test in a lengthy series of debates which lasted over several weeks, maintaining that resistance to those commissioned by the king could, in some circumstances, be legitimate and that endeavouring to alter the church so as to restore it, say, 'to what it was in Queen Elizabeths days

might consist with his being a very good Protestant' (Letter, 22). Yet despite all Shaftesbury's efforts opponents of the test were in the minority in all divisions. The bill got held up, however, as a result of a jurisdictional dispute between the Lords and Commons over the case of Shirley v. Fagg, the central issue of which involved whether the Lords had the right to hear appeals from lower courts when they involved members of the Commons. Shaftesbury did his best to ensure that the two houses remained at loggerheads over the case, thus causing a deadlock to business and leaving Charles with no alternative but to prorogue parliament (9 June). In a surprising development Shaftesbury was admitted to kiss the king's hand on 13 June. The reconciliation was probably York's doing; he apparently promised Shaftesbury that he could procure a new parliament and Danby's dismissal, while Charles, who never liked committing himself to one minister, welcomed the chance to keep other options open. In the end Danby succeeded in blocking the initiative and Shaftesbury was ordered away from court again on the 24th.

In July 1675 Giles Strangways, MP for Dorset, died, which meant there would be a by-election once parliament reconvened in October and the speaker authorized the sending out of a writ. At first Shaftesbury said he would back Lord Digby, the son of the earl of Bristol, but when he learned that Digby was corresponding with the court he threw his support behind Thomas Moore of Hawkchurch, the principal supporter of conventicles in the county. Digby felt betrayed and at a chance meeting in late August threatened Shaftesbury with his sword, saying: 'You are against the King, and for seditions and factions, and for a commonwealth, and I will prove it, and by God, we will have your head next Parliament' (Christie, 2.215). Shaftesbury brought an action for scandalum magnatum against Digby and obtained £1000 in damages; he gave the money to help rebuild the town of Northampton, which had been badly damaged in a fire. Digby nevertheless won the by-election by a large majority of over 1700 votes to 520, and in the subsequent session of parliament Digby's father, Lord Bristol, also launched a verbal attack on the earl, for which he was forced to apologize.

Shaftesbury must have spent some of summer 1675 preparing A Letter from a Person of Quality to his Friend in the Country, a 15,000-word pamphlet attacking Danby's test which began by accusing 'the High Episcopal Man, and the Old Cavalier' of conspiring since the Restoration to make 'the Government absolute and Arbitrary' and establish divine right monarchy and episcopacy, not 'bounded or limited by humane Laws' (Letter, 1). The pamphlet caused quite a stir when it hit the streets in November: at first it sold for just 1 shilling, but it was soon fetching 20 shillings. There has been debate as to whether the tract was really Shaftesbury's work or Locke's, or whether the earl dictated it and his secretary wrote it down, though it was probably a collaboration of some sort. When parliament reconvened on 13 October Shaftesbury did his best to revive the dispute over Shirley v. Fagg, in the hope that if another session ended in deadlock the king would be forced to dissolve parliament and call new elections. He was probably one of those who persuaded Shirley to bring in his petition again, and when Danby tried to divert it Shaftesbury gave a lengthy speech (20 October) in which he linked the interests 'of the Poorest man in *England*' to the preservation of the rights of the upper house, since no prince, Shaftesbury claimed, 'ever governed without *Nobility* or an *Army*', and that if you did not have the one you would inevitably have the other (A. A. Cooper, earl of Shaftesbury, *Two Speeches*, 1675, 7). He ended with a stinging attack on the bishops, accusing them of not believing the king was '*King by Law*' but that monarchy was '*of Divine Right*' (ibid., 10): if this be true, he said, 'our *Magna Charta* is of no force, our Laws are but Rules amongst our selves during the Kings pleasure' and 'All the Properties and Liberties of the People, are to give way, not onely to the interest, but the will and pleasure of the Crown' (ibid., 11). On 20 November, in a premeditated move, Shaftesbury seconded Lord Mohun's motion that in order to bring the dispute over *Shirley* v. *Fagg* to an end, the king should dissolve parliament. When the motion, which was also supported by York and the Catholic peers, was narrowly defeated by a vote of 50 to 48, Shaftesbury and twenty-one other peers entered a protest, on the grounds that 'according to the ancient Lawes and Statutes of this Realm … there should be frequent and new Parliaments' and that the actions of the Commons had made it impossible for the two houses to work together (*JHL*, 13, 1675–81, 33). Charles prorogued parliament two days later until 15 February 1677. Shaftesbury was probably involved in the publication of *Two Seasonable Discourses Concerning the Present Parliament* (1675), purporting to consist of arguments used in the debates of 20 November, which predicted that a new parliament would vote the king money, preserve the church, grant dissenters liberty of conscience, and deliver Catholics from the penal laws if they were deprived of access to court and prevented from holding office and bearing arms.

In mid-February 1676 Charles sent the secretary of state, Sir Joseph Williamson, to Shaftesbury with a message to leave town; Shaftesbury refused to go, protesting that he meddled with nothing but his own private business. When he was subsequently seen receiving visits at Exeter House from opposition MPs and discontented elements in the City, Danby urged Charles to send Shaftesbury to the Tower; Shaftesbury was saved because Williamson refused to sign the necessary warrant. Exeter House was proving too expensive to keep up, however, now Shaftesbury was no longer lord chancellor, and he moved out in the summer. After spending a few months in the west country he moved into Thanet House in Aldersgate Street in the autumn. Shaftesbury was still in London when, at the shrieval election at the Guildhall on 24 June, linen draper Francis Jenks made a sensational speech urging the common council to petition the king for a new parliament, arguing that as a result of the fifteen-month prorogation the present one was *ipso facto* dissolved because two statutes from Edward III's reign required parliaments be held every year. Although government pamphleteers accused Shaftesbury of being behind the initiative, it was

Buckingham who had put Jenks up to it; Shaftesbury opposed the step as premature. He did, however, decide to pursue the idea in the upcoming session of parliament. He and his allies printed and dispersed a number of pamphlets outlining their case; one, *Some considerations upon the question, whether the parliament is dissolved, by its prorogation for 15 months?*, answered the objection that the prorogation of parliament was a matter solely for the royal prerogative by insisting not only that parliament could restrict that but that it could even 'bind, limit, restrain and govern the Descent and Inheritance of the Crown it self' (Holles, 26). Shaftesbury tried to convince York that this had been put in at the last minute without his knowledge; Buckingham, on the other hand, told York that Shaftesbury 'had drawn it, and caus'd it to be inserted' (Clarke, 1.505). When parliament met on 15 February Buckingham, backed by Shaftesbury, Salisbury, and Wharton, proclaimed that in accordance with the statutes of Edward III no parliament was legally in existence; the motion was rejected, and when the four refused to ask pardon for their action they were sent to the Tower. Shaftesbury tried petitioning for his release, to no effect, and so in June he brought a writ of habeas corpus before king's bench; the judges, however, determined they had no jurisdiction in the matter, since the prisoner was being held by a superior court while parliament was in session. Although Charles freed Buckingham, Salisbury, and Wharton shortly thereafter, he was determined to humble Shaftesbury, while Shaftesbury remained determined not to apologize. What seems to have changed Shaftesbury's mind was the raising of an army in England, supposedly to be used in a war against France but which many thought was the first step in a design to establish a standing army. On 25 February 1678 he finally made a full submission, begging the king's and the house's pardon, and apologizing for bringing his action of habeas corpus. He was released the next day. During his stay in the Tower, Shaftesbury compiled a list of the political sympathies of the lay peers and members of the House of Commons, marking those whom he thought of as his allies with a 'w' for 'worthy' and his enemies with a 'v' for 'vile', using double or triple letters to signify extra degrees of worthiness or vileness.

Early in 1678, when it looked as if Charles might declare war on France, the French ambassador approached Russell, Holles, and Buckingham offering Louis XIV's help in securing a dissolution of parliament; Russell, in return, promised to work to prevent further votes of supply and promised to engage Shaftesbury in the affair. Shaftesbury must have known of these discussions, since Russell visited him in the Tower on several occasions, but it is doubtful whether the suggested meeting between Shaftesbury and the French ambassador ever took place upon Shaftesbury's release. Indeed, far from wanting to help the French king neutralize Charles II on the foreign policy front, in March Shaftesbury joined with Buckingham, Holles, Halifax, and others in urging the Lords to join with the Commons in addressing the king to declare war immediately on France. When war was not forthcoming Shaftesbury supported the Commons in pushing for a speedy disbandment of troops, and on 25 June he signed a protest against a Lords' amendment to the Disbanding Bill delaying the date at which the forces were to be disbanded. Charles prorogued parliament on 15 July; it was not to reconvene until 21 October, which was after Titus Oates had made his revelations of a supposed popish plot to murder the king and massacre English protestants. Shaftesbury played a prominent role in the Lords in prosecuting the plot, being a member of nearly all the important committees. On 2 November he proposed that the Lords should demand that York be removed from the king's presence, though he did not press the matter to a division. He supported the Test Act designed to exclude Catholics from both houses of parliament, and on 29 November was one of three peers who entered a protest against the Lords' refusal to concur with a Commons address for removing the queen and her retinue from court after Oates had accused her of being involved in the plot. With Danby now under threat of impeachment, the king prorogued parliament on 30 December; on 24 January 1679 he dissolved it. Outside parliament Londoners were already beginning to view Shaftesbury as the great hero of the opposition to the court. When on 9 November 1678 the king promised MPs he would pass any bills that would make them safe in the reign of his successor, so long as they did not impeach the right of the succession, his speech was mistakenly reported as a resolution in favour of a protestant successor or the duke of Monmouth, prompting celebratory bonfires throughout the capital where crowds 'drank healths to the King, the Duke of Monmouth, and Earl of Shaftesbury, as the only three pillars of all safety' (*Ormonde MSS*, new ser., 4.473). The citizens held Shaftesbury in such esteem that, fearing a Catholic plot against his life, they paid for a special guard to protect him.

**The exclusion crisis and the first whigs, 1679–1683** Shaftesbury emerged as one of the leading figures in the whig campaign to exclude the duke of York from the succession in the three successive parliaments which met between 1679 and 1681. It would be wrong, however, to see him as the leader of a coherent and well-organized whig party. The whig movement was never that cohesive, and Shaftesbury's control over it was far from complete; indeed, he often found himself at odds with other prominent figures in the political opposition to Charles II and the duke of York. Although he tried to use his patronage to influence elections where possible, he did not have a strong enough regional power base to secure the return of a large clientele of compliant MPs. Shaftesbury's precise role in co-ordinating the activities of the whig press is also unclear. Danby was informed that Shaftesbury 'could have what he pleased printed, and that in a night's time' (Haley, 499); Shaftesbury certainly had close contacts with a number of whig printers, though he did not have his own printing press in Thanet House, as Danby thought, and the older view that he was the guiding spirit behind much of the whig propaganda that poured forth from the

presses undoubtedly exaggerates his influence. Shaftesbury was not even a member of the famous Green Ribbon Club that met at the King's Head tavern in Chancery Lane, which is known to have played some role in co-ordinating the whig propaganda campaign (though it should be noted that a number of his relatives and dependants were, including his trusty steward, Thomas Stringer). Shaftesbury kept his own clubs at the Swan in Fish Street, the Angel tavern near the Old Exchange, the Queen's Arms, and the Nag's Head. It has even been claimed that the term 'exclusion crisis' is a misnomer, since the battle lines were not drawn solely over whether or not to pass an exclusion bill: some whigs were willing to entertain other expedients to resolve the problem of the Catholic succession; Shaftesbury himself continued to push for a royal divorce and even tried to persuade Charles to make Monmouth his heir, though both schemes, it should be recognized, were attempts to exclude York from the succession by other means.

Before the meeting of the new parliament on 6 March 1679 Shaftesbury drew up another list of lay peers and MPs predicting how they would align themselves politically. He estimated that in the Commons the court could count on 32 per cent of the members, the opposition 61 per cent, with the remaining 7 per cent being doubtful. He also produced a document, 'The present state of the kingdom', in which he voiced his concern over the power of France, the Popish Plot, and the evil influence exercised on the king's affairs by Danby, the duchess of Portsmouth (the royal mistress), and York, who Shaftesbury claimed designed 'to introduce a military and arbitrary government in his brother's time' (Christie, 2.314). The paper, probably intended as a pamphlet, was never published, though Shaftesbury did deliver a dramatic speech on the state of the nation in the Lords on 25 March, in which he warned of the double threat of popery and arbitrary government to the three kingdoms and castigated the record of the royal administration in Scotland under Lauderdale and in Ireland under Ormond. Shaftesbury supported the efforts of the Commons to bring Danby to account and voted for the Bill of Attainder when it passed the Lords on 14 April by the narrow margin of 39 to 36 votes. He subsequently tried to neutralize Danby's allies on the episcopal bench by moving that the bishops should not be allowed to sit in the Lords in capital trials.

Charles thought that Shaftesbury 'was only angry in revenge, because he was not employed' (*Burnet's History*, 302), and so, on 21 April 1679, decided to appoint him lord president of a reconstructed privy council, with a salary of £4000 a year. Shaftesbury soon made it clear, however, that he was not being bought off. A few days later, when he unsuccessfully opposed a motion in the Lords that protestant nonconformists, including Quakers, should be administered the same oaths of allegiance required of Roman Catholics, he protested that he would never have taken office 'if he had thought he could not succeed in a matter of such consequence' and 'that he desired his post in the Council only that he might .. take care of the safety and interests of the whole nation' (Christie, 2.328). He pressed the case in council for excluding York and 'making the succession to go on, as if he was dead'; Essex and Halifax urged limiting the powers of a popish successor instead, but Shaftesbury insisted that this was 'much more prejudicial to the crown than the exclusion of one heir', since it 'changed the whole government, and set up a democracy instead of a monarchy' (*Burnet's History*, 303). Shaftesbury's right-hand man in the Commons, William, Lord Russell, introduced an Exclusion Bill in the lower house on 11 May, which passed its second reading on 21 May, though to block the bill and to stop any further proceedings against Danby, Charles at first prorogued (27 May) and then dissolved parliament (3 July). On both occasions Shaftesbury is reputed to have said that he would have the heads of those who advised it. The only measure of any note to come out of this parliament was the Habeas Corpus Amendment Act, sometimes known as the Shaftesbury Act, which aimed to stop up certain loopholes in the traditional habeas corpus procedure; it passed on the last day of the session by 57 votes to 55, but only because Lord Grey of Warke (jokingly at first) decided to count one particularly fat peer as ten, and no one spotted the error.

Shaftesbury decided to stay on the privy council for the time being, telling his friends that he did so 'only to be a tribune for the people there' (Haley, 530); according to lord chancellor Finch, Shaftesbury 'joined with the Duke of Monmouth' on the council to 'obstruct all' until they were 'at the top of all affairs' (*Diary of … Sidney*, 2). The earl nevertheless found the duke a frustrating man to deal with. When Monmouth led the government forces against the rebellious Scottish covenanters in June 1679 Shaftesbury was said to be 'ill pleased' with Monmouth's decision to inflict a quick and decisive victory over the covenanter army at Bothwell Bridge, since if the rebellion had been more drawn out it might have forced Charles to recall parliament (Haley, 536). Nevertheless, in early August Shaftesbury and Monmouth were observed to be meeting 'very often' (*Hastings MSS*, 2.388), and on one occasion they apparently proposed to the earl of Bath, Danby's ally, that they would help secure Danby's release from the Tower if he would reveal how York had on a number of occasions urged the king to rule through armed force. Nothing came of the suggestion, and on 19 August Shaftesbury left for Dorset. Two days later, however, Charles fell ill; with the king's brother in exile in Brussels, Essex and Halifax feared a coup by Monmouth and advised York to make a speedy return. Charles soon recovered and sent both York and Monmouth out of the country, but in early October he allowed his brother to change his place of exile from Flanders to Scotland. Shaftesbury, now back in London, summoned an extraordinary meeting of the council to discuss the duke's move, acting on his own authority as president while the king was away at Newmarket. This proved the final straw for Charles and on 14 October he informed Shaftesbury that his attendance at the council was no longer required.

It was about this time that the Meal Tub Plot, an attempt by a group of Catholics to frame Shaftesbury and other opposition leaders for treason, came to light. When revealed as a sham its leading informer, Thomas Dangerfield, changed his story and claimed that the Catholics had offered him money to kill the king and the earl of Shaftesbury. The revelations led to renewed talk on the council about the need to bring forward the meeting of parliament; a new parliament had been due to convene in October 1679, but the elections that summer had gone badly for the court and the king had prorogued it until 26 January. When Charles refused to meet parliament any earlier Essex resigned his commissionership of the Treasury, fuelling speculation that Shaftesbury was his intended replacement. Indeed, in early November the earl of Sunderland did try to broker a reconciliation between Shaftesbury and the king, but Shaftesbury made it clear that he would only return to office if Charles would 'leave to Parliament all that concerned the Queen and the Duke of York' (*Ormonde MSS*, new ser., 4.558). Shaftesbury now decided to launch a petitioning campaign to pressure the king into meeting parliament and held a series of meetings with other whig peers at the Swan tavern in Fleet Street to plot tactics. As a preliminary he wrote to Monmouth urging him to return from exile; the duke arrived back in London late on the night of 27 November, to scenes of widespread celebrating throughout the capital. The first petition was delivered to the king on 7 December, signed by Shaftesbury and fifteen other whig peers, asking that parliament be allowed to meet on 26 January 1680. This was followed by a monster petition in the name of the inhabitants of Westminster and Southwark, signed by some 20,000 people (including Shaftesbury), delivered to the king on 13 January, and several provincial petitions. When the king prorogued parliament again and recalled his brother from Scotland instead, Shaftesbury wrote a letter to his friends on the council (30 January) urging them to resign; four did.

On 24 March 1680 Shaftesbury told the council of information he had received concerning a planned Catholic uprising in Ireland backed by French aid. The Irish plot was not new—there had been unsubstantiated rumours to this effect for years—but these latest revelations afforded Shaftesbury the opportunity to highlight the continuing Catholic threat at a time when popular anxieties over the Popish Plot was beginning to flag. The secretary of state, Henry Coventry, was convinced the Irish stories were a complete fabrication, designed for their effect on public opinion, but although Shaftesbury showed no qualms about exploiting them for this end there is no concrete evidence that he was guilty of subornation of witnesses. The government had no option but to launch an inquiry, and in the end the plot cost the life of Oliver Plunket, the Catholic archbishop of Armagh.

On 13 May 1680 the king again fell ill, prompting concerns about the security of the protestant religion should he suddenly die. According to a later confession by the Rye House plotter and Monmouth rebel Ford, Lord Grey of Warke, a series of meetings was held at Shaftesbury's house (involving Monmouth, Russell, Grey, and others) where plans were laid for an uprising in the city, although these were abandoned when the king recovered. Other whig accounts, however, insist that there was no talk of an uprising prior to the third Exclusion Parliament (in Oxford) of March 1681, and since Grey himself could not remember whether the king's illness was before or after the Oxford parliament, his testimony may not be trustworthy. With the king back to full health Shaftesbury and his allies decided to strike again at the duke of York. On 26 June he and fourteen others (peers and commoners) went to Westminster Hall to present an indictment to the Middlesex grand jury against the duke as a popish recusant; the grand jury also had ready a petition for the calling of parliament, but before they could do anything they were dismissed for interfering in matters of state. Shaftesbury tried again four days later, but was prevented once more by the dismissal of a second grand jury.

By mid-September 1680 Shaftesbury was holding meetings at Thanet House to prepare for the upcoming parliamentary session, which began on 21 October. He took his seat in the Lords on the 23rd and immediately called for a committee to be set up to investigate the Popish Plot. He spoke passionately in support of the Exclusion Bill on 15 November when it came before the Lords where he became locked in debate with his kinsman Halifax, who favoured limitations. The result was always a foregone conclusion, however, given the number of court peers and the dead weight of the bishops, and the Lords rejected the bill on its second reading by a vote of 63 to 30. The following day Essex proposed a Bill of Association, modelled on that of 1585 to protect Queen Elizabeth from assassination by protestants, and Shaftesbury was appointed to a subcommittee to consider it. Halifax suggested banishing York for five years; Shaftesbury replied that the best way of protecting the kingdom had been rejected, and that the only other remedy was for the king to divorce and remarry. The Lords set aside 23 November to discuss the proposal, but Shaftesbury was absent that day due to gout; when he returned on the 24th he surprisingly suggested that all expedients should be tabled for the time being, apparently convinced that financial stringency would eventually force the king to give in to exclusion. Shaftesbury gave a violent speech in the Lords on 23 December reiterating his support for exclusion; in this he attacked York, expressed distrust of the king, and urged that no taxes be voted until 'the King shall satisfie the People, that what we give is not to make us Slaves and Papists' (A. A. Cooper, earl of Shaftesbury, *A Speech Lately Made by a Noble Peer of the Realm*, 1681). With the Commons threatening to impeach some of his judges and actively pursuing the Irish plot Charles decided to prorogue parliament on 10 January; eight days later he dissolved it and announced his intention to call another at Oxford on 21 March. The only bill that was ready to receive the royal assent was that repealing an act of 1593 against sectaries; Charles secretly ordered the clerk not to present it to him, however, and thus even this measure was lost.

On 25 January 1681 Shaftesbury, Essex, Salisbury, and others presented a petition to the king signed by sixteen peers asking that parliament might sit at Westminster rather than Oxford, though to no avail. According to Grey's later account Shaftesbury, Russell, Monmouth, and others thought about staying in London, ready to raise the City in support of parliament if the king issued another dissolution. If Shaftesbury did ever contemplate this it was not for long, for by the end of January he was making arrangements for his accommodation in Oxford. In the forthcoming parliamentary elections, several constituencies drew up instructions to their newly elected MPs, advising them what measures to support at Oxford, many of them calling explicitly for a commitment to exclusion. The fact that a draft set of instructions survives in the Shaftesbury papers has led some historians to conclude that Shaftesbury was largely responsible for co-ordinating the campaign. This is questionable, however; a comparison between the draft and the actual addresses reveals significant differences, and the constituency instructions, rather than being dictated to the localities by a central whig party machine, appear to have been the result of local initiatives. As a prelude to the meeting at Oxford, Shaftesbury and his supporters brought another indictment against York for recusancy, this time at the Old Bailey, on 26 February. The grand jury found the bill true, but York's defence counsel asked for a delay until Easter week before their client was declared convicted, and in the end the prosecution lapsed.

In his opening speech to the Oxford parliament Charles insisted that he would not depart from the succession but would listen to any expedient that might 'remove all reasonable Fears that may arise from the Possibility of a Popish Successor coming to the Crown' (*JHL*, 13, 1675–81, 745). Shaftesbury's first move was to call for an inquiry into why the bill repealing the act of 1593 had not been passed. Then on 24 March he announced that he had received an anonymous letter containing an 'expedient' which would 'comply with the King's speech, and satisfy the people too'; when shown to the king it turned out to be a proposal for settling the crown on Monmouth. Charles was furious, protesting that this expedient would 'trample over all laws of God and Man'; Shaftesbury replied by asking for 'leave to make it as lawful as we can' (Haley, 634). Later that day Charles asked Shaftesbury 'whether no other expedient could be found out instead of the Exclusion'; Shaftesbury replied 'no, and that the whole nation seemed to be of that opinion' (*Ormonde MSS*, new ser., 6.6–7). The Commons brought in an Exclusion Bill on Saturday the 26th; two days later Charles dissolved the parliament. Much of the short life of the Oxford parliament was taken up discussing whether to impeach Edward Fitzharris, accused initially of a design of trying to fasten upon Shaftesbury a libel he had concocted himself against the king but who was now offering to make startling revelations about York's involvement in the Popish Plot. Charles wanted Fitzharris left to the common law and permanently silenced by being sentenced to death; by initiating impeachment proceedings the Commons hoped to give Fitzharris the opportunity to reveal all he knew before parliament. On the 26th the Lords voted not to agree to the impeachment. Shaftesbury was one of twenty peers who signed a protest.

Following the dissolution of the Oxford parliament the whigs' hopes fell back on the corporation of London bringing pressure on Charles to call another parliament. To increase his influence in the City, Shaftesbury procured admission as a freeman of the Skinners' Company on 3 May 1681. By now, however, the government was on the offensive; on 2 July Shaftesbury was arrested on suspicion of high treason, the main witnesses against him being the very informants whom Shaftesbury had used in the Irish plot, and was sent to the Tower. The government also ordered his papers to be seized, though nothing particularly incriminating was found, except for an anonymous draft of an association. Monmouth immediately went to visit Shaftesbury in the Tower; the king responded by ordering that Shaftesbury be kept close prisoner and allowed visits only from his wife and children.

Shaftesbury petitioned the Old Bailey that he be brought to trial or bailed under the terms of the Habeas Corpus Act, but the judges declared that they had no jurisdiction over prisoners in the Tower and that he would have to wait until the next term began in the king's bench in October. In late September he offered to retire either to his country estate, beyond seas, or to Carolina if he were released (and if the last, proposing that the king should give him £3000 to meet the cost of transporting himself and his family there). Charles said he would leave Shaftesbury to the law. On 24 October Shaftesbury moved for a writ of habeas corpus at king's bench, whereupon he was told that bail would be granted if there was no prosecution before the end of the term. Shaftesbury's case finally came before a grand jury on 24 November. His indictment accused him of having said, on 18 March 1681, that he and his supporters in parliament would compel the king to accept the Exclusion Bill and the bills for relief of dissenters, that armed men had been prepared, that the king 'deserved to be deposed', and that he (Shaftesbury) would 'never desist, until he had brought this kingdom of England into a commonwealth' (*State trials*, 8.777). The first piece of evidence produced was the draft association found among his papers which accused York of complicity in the Popish Plot and engaged subscribers to do all they could to prevent him from coming to the throne. A succession of witnesses then appeared, most of whom had been informants in the Popish and Irish plots, to testify to the treasonable remarks Shaftesbury was supposed to have made. The government's case was not a strong one. There was no convincing proof that Shaftesbury had ever intended to use force against the king; the association was not in the earl's handwriting, and was unsigned and undated; the law required that prosecutions for uttering treasonable words had to be made within six months, making Shaftesbury's alleged words out of date; and the witnesses against him were people whom even the government thought had previously perjured themselves. Yet because jury panels were selected by the London sheriffs, both of whom at this time were whig, there was never much likelihood that the grand jury would find the bill true and send the case to trial; Shaftesbury's grand jury comprised prominent exclusionists and whig merchants,

many of them with known dissenting sympathies, and predictably brought in a verdict of ignoramus. The news prompted bonfire celebrations in London, with crowds roaming the streets shouting 'No Popish Successor, No York, A Monmouth' and 'God bless the Earl of Shaftesbury' (*CSP dom.*, *1680–81*, 583), while there was similar rejoicing in other parts of the kingdom when news of Shaftesbury's deliverance reached the provinces. Shaftesbury was released on bail on 28 November, to commemorate which Shaftesbury's supporters had a medal coined showing the earl on one side and on the other the Tower, with the sun emerging from a cloud and the word 'Laetamur' ('let us rejoice'). When Shaftesbury reappeared in court on 13 February 1682 to answer his bail the prosecution against him was completely dropped.

Another royal illness that May prompted Shaftesbury to call an emergency meeting at Thanet House, attended by Monmouth, Russell, Grey, Sir Thomas Armstrong, and Major John Manley, to discuss what they should do were Charles to die; the group decided they would raise a rebellion with a view to summoning parliament to determine the succession, though the plan was dropped when Charles recovered. That summer Shaftesbury held talks with the earl of Argyll, the condemned Scottish traitor who had been hiding in London after his escape from Edinburgh Castle, about the possibility of funding a rebellion in Scotland, though nothing materialized since neither trusted the other. So far Shaftesbury and other radical whigs appear to have contemplated only how to act upon the king's unexpected death. They decided to take a more proactive stance following the confirmation of two tories as sheriffs elect that July, which ensured future tory control over the impanelling of London juries. No longer could dissident whigs expect to escape the clutches of the law at the hands of ignoramus juries and Shaftesbury himself faced the prospect of another treason charge on the basis of the draft association found among his papers which had not been mentioned in his previous indictment. Shaftesbury held a series of meetings at Thanet House, where plans were laid for co-ordinated rebellions in different parts of the country to try to force the king to come to terms. As preliminaries Monmouth would make a progress to Cheshire to gauge the level of support in the north-west; Russell would sound out the west country; Grey was to canvas Essex; and Shaftesbury would be responsible for London. Monmouth's progress that September was a great success, though on his return he was seized at Stafford and brought back to London under arrest, where he was released on bail. Shaftesbury wanted Monmouth to return to Cheshire immediately and launch a rebellion, but Russell advised against it and Monmouth declined to go.

Following the installation of the new tory sheriffs on 28 September 1682 Shaftesbury left Thanet House and went into hiding in the city, staying first in a house in Wood Street belonging to a merchant named Watson, where lodging was arranged for him under the pseudonym Mr Tucker; then at the house of Robert Ferguson, the fiery Scottish nonconformist clergyman, known best for his career as a plotter; and then with a sea captain named Tracy in Wapping. Shaftesbury had another meeting with Monmouth and Russell just before he left Thanet House in late September, and once more argued the case for an immediate insurrection, this time based on London alone, but Russell insisted they should wait for the west country, which would soon be ready. At the beginning of October Shaftesbury had a meeting with Lord Howard of Escrick at Watson's place in Wood Street, in which he said he had 10,000 men ready to fight for him in London (his 'ten thousand brisk boys'; State trials, 9.431; Grey, 30), complained of the recalcitrance of Monmouth and Russell, and urged Howard to lead an uprising in Essex, though Howard refused to commit himself until he had consulted the other peers. By now Shaftesbury was beginning to lose patience, and opened discussions with John Wildman and other conspirators about the possibility of assassinating the king and the duke of York on their return from the races at Newmarket later that month. When this project collapsed he turned once more to Monmouth, and finally the conspirators agreed to set a date of 19 November to launch co-ordinated uprisings in London, Cheshire, and the west county. Having had no communication from the south-west, however, it was decided at the last minute—at a meeting at which Shaftesbury was not present—to postpone the rebellion.

Shaftesbury now decided it was time to flee the country. Before he left he made provision for the repayment of his debts and the disposal of his estates to his wife and his eldest grandchild, Anthony Ashley *Cooper, the future third earl. The exact date of Shaftesbury's departure is unknown, but it was some time after 20 November and before the 26th when he landed at the Brill; by the 28th he was in Rotterdam and on 2 December he reached his final destination, Amsterdam. There his health quickly deteriorated; by the end of December he was finding it difficult to keep down any food, and on 17 January 1683, realizing he was dying, he made his will, which was witnessed by Thomas Dare. On the night of the 20th, in a last conversation with Robert Ferguson, who had travelled to the Netherlands with him, he apparently declared himself to be a professed Arian. The next day, Sunday 21 January, at about noon, he died in Amsterdam. Since in his will he had expressed a desire to be buried at Wimborne St Giles his body was embalmed before being shipped back to Dorset on 13 February, and was buried at Wimborne on the 26th. According to his steward, Stringer, Shaftesbury's debts in 1683 totalled £9724, including interest owed. The sum was considerable, but the capital value of his estates, which brought in annual rents of over £3000 per annum, must have been considerably more. Interestingly, he borrowed some £7600 from just six individuals between May 1680 and July 1682, which one biographer has interpreted as 'a collusive arrangement designed to guard against the possible confiscation of his estates by nominally mortgaging it all to friends' (Haley, 725), but which equally well might suggest efforts to raise ready cash in order to fund armed resistance.

**Reputation** Shaftesbury has enjoyed a somewhat tarnished historical reputation. Although Locke's epitaph for the earl praised him as 'a strenuous Defender [and] vigilant Preserver [of] Liberty in both Civil, and Ecclesiastical affairs', who 'most happily consulted [the] Publick Interest' and never allowed 'self-interest [to] influence his Actions' (Locke, 'Epitaph'; Works of John Locke, 1812, 9.281), few contemporaries were so generous. His political opponents regarded him as a shallow opportunist who was quick to change sides when it suited his personal ambitions. A satirical catalogue of books of 1666 included a title 'How to look backwards, and forwards, of this side, and that side and every, written by the Lord Ashley' (Seaward, 213). To John Dryden, in his famous character assassination of the whigs, Shaftesbury was 'the false Achitophel', 'A Name to all succeeding Ages Curst', who was

Restless, unfixt in Principle and Place,
In Power unpleas'd, impatient of Disgrace.
(Dryden, 6)

Modern biographies have been more sympathetic, keen to see consistency in Shaftesbury's many volte-faces and to envisage the earl as a man motivated by political principle. It would be wrong to be too naïve in an assessment of the earl: Shaftesbury was undoubtedly a wily operator who was not above saying or doing things for calculated political effect or abandoning former friends and allies as he mapped out a new direction for himself. Yet he clearly was a man of principles, who throughout much of his long political career was prepared to make personal sacrifices in pursuit of what he believed to be the public interest. Throughout his life he retained an abiding distrust of clerical authority (particularly the pretensions of the high-church bishops) and was a consistent supporter of toleration for dissent. Although far from being a modern liberal (his views on the role of the Lords as well as his constitution for Carolina betray an aristocratic conception of politics), he was nevertheless a firm believer in the rule of law and the sovereignty of parliament, and a passionate spokesman for the rights of the people against what he sincerely saw as the threat of arbitrary government. None of his changes of side brought him personal gain; indeed, invariably they cost him office (or the promise of an office) and not infrequently the loss of income too. Burnet, who knew Shaftesbury well, says that 'he was not ashamed to reckon up the many turns he had made; and he valued himself upon the doing it at the properest season, and in the best manner' (Burnet's History, 64). Shaftesbury may not have been the leader of the first whig party, but he undoubtedly was a great political leader—better 'at opposing, and running things down', than 'in building up' perhaps, but a man who 'had a wonderful faculty in speaking to a popular assembly' and 'a particular talent to make others trust to his judgment', which made him unrivalled among contemporaries, according to Burnet, 'in the art of governing parties, and of making himself the head of them' (ibid.).

TIM HARRIS

**Sources** K. H. D. Haley, The first earl of Shaftesbury (1968) • W. D. Christie, A life of Anthony Ashley Cooper, first earl of Shaftesbury, 1621–1683, 2 vols. (1871) • The works of John Locke: in ten volumes, 11th edn, 9

(1812); new edn, corrected, 9 (1823) · JHC, 4–8 (1644–67) · JHC, 8–9 (1660–87) · The memoirs of Edmund Ludlow, ed. C. H. Firth, 2 vols. (1894) · Diary of Thomas Burton, ed. J. T. Rutt, 4 vols. (1828); repr. (1974) · To all the worthy gentlemen who are duely chosen for the parliament (1656) · The remonstrance and protestation of the well-affected people (1659) · Calendar of the Clarendon state papers preserved in the Bodleian Library, ed. O. Ogle and others, 5 vols. (1869–1970) · Cobbett, Parl. hist., vol. 4 · State trials, 9.430–37 [Howard's confession] · Clarendon, Hist. rebellion · The life of Edward, earl of Clarendon … written by himself, 3 vols. (1759) · CSP dom., 1635–82 · CSP Venice, 1673–5 · J. P. Ferris, 'Cooper, Sir Anthony Ashley', HoP, Commons, 1660–90, 2.121–4 · [A. A. Cooper, earl of Shaftesbury and J. Locke?], A letter from a person of quality to his friend in the country (1675) · [D. Holles, Baron Holles of Ifield], Some considerations upon the question, whether the parliament is dissolved, by its prorogation for 15 months? (1676) · F. Grey, Baron Grey of Warke, The secret history of the Rye House plot and Monmouth's rebellion (1685) · B. Worden, The Rump Parliament, 1648–1653 (1974) · A. Woolrych, Commonwealth to protectorate (1982) · P. Seaward, The Cavalier Parliament and the restoration of the old regime, 1661–1667 (1989) · A. Swatland, The House of Lords in the reign of Charles II (1996) · J. P. Kenyon, The Stuart constitution, 1603–1688 (1966) · Calendar of the manuscripts of the marquess of Ormonde, new ser., 8 vols., HMC, 36 (1902–20), vols. 4, 6 · Report on the manuscripts of the late Reginald Rawdon Hastings, 4 vols., HMC, 78 (1928–47), vol. 2 · Lady Newton, ed., Lyme letters, 1660–1760 (1925) · R. North, Examen (1740) · J. Dryden, Absalom and Achitophel (1681) · J. Locke, 'Epitaph for Shaftesbury', PRO, 30/24/6A/385 · R. Morrice, 'Ent'ring book', DWL, Morrice MS P · M. Cotterell, 'Interregnum law reform: the Hale commission of 1652', EngHR, 83 (1968), 689–704 · T. Harris, London crowds in the reign of Charles II (1987) · M. Knights, Politics and opinion in crisis, 1678–81 (1994) · J. Scott, Algernon Sidney and the Restoration crisis, 1677–1683 (1991) · R. Hutton, Charles the Second: king of England, Scotland and Ireland (1989) · R. Hutton, The Restoration: a political and religious history of England and Wales, 1658–1667 (1985) · R. L. Greaves, Secrets of the kingdom: British radicals from the Popish Plot to the revolution of 1688–89 (1992) · Pepys, Diary · O. Airy, ed., Essex papers, CS, new ser., 47 (1890) · The life of James the Second, king of England, ed. J. S. Clarke, 2 vols. (1816) · Bishop Burnet's History of his own time, new edn (1857) · Diary of the times of Charles the Second by the Honourable Henry Sidney (afterwards earl of Romney), ed. R. W. Blencowe, 2 vols. (1843) · J. R. Jones, 'Shaftesbury's "worthy men": a whig view of the parliament of 1679', BIHR, 30 (1957), 232–41 · sacrament certificates, 1673, LMA, MR/RS/2/217–218 · GEC, Peerage

**Archives** BL, corresp. and papers · muniment room, Wimborne St Giles · NRA, priv. coll., papers · PRO, corresp. and papers, PRO 30/24 · Surrey HC, notes · V&A NAL, corresp. and papers | Bodl. Oxf., letters to John Locke

**Likenesses** English school, oils on copper, 1600–99, NG Ire. · S. Cooper, miniature, c.1672, priv. coll. [see illus.] · A. Blooteling, line engraving, 1673, BM · R. White, line engraving, 1680, BM, NPG · G. Bower, silver medal, BM · attrib. J. Greenhill, oils, Althorp, Northamptonshire · oils (after J. Greenhill), NPG; repro. in Haley, First earl of Shaftesbury, frontispiece

**Wealth at death** personal debts totalled £9724; estates brought in annual rents of over £3000 p.a.

---

**Cooper, Anthony Ashley**, third earl of Shaftesbury (1671–1713), philosopher and author, was born on 26 February 1671, at about eight o'clock in the evening, at Exeter House in the Strand, London, and baptized on 7 March at St Clement Danes. He was the first son of Anthony Ashley Cooper, later second earl of Shaftesbury (1651–1699), landowner, and Lady Dorothy Manners (d. 1698), third daughter of John *Manners, eighth earl of Rutland. Exeter House was the town residence of his grandfather Anthony Ashley *Cooper (1621–1683), who was already an important politician and, elevated as first earl of Shaftesbury in 1672, would dominate the next decade as leader of the

**Anthony Ashley Cooper, third earl of Shaftesbury (1671–1713),** by John Closterman, c.1700–01 [left, with an attendant]

whig opposition. By contrast Cooper's father was an ailing, reclusive, and somewhat mysterious figure, known, if at all, for the description of him as 'a shapeless Lump' in Dryden's poetic attack on the exclusionists, Absalom and Achitophel (1681). Torn between the active, political model of the first earl and the retiring figure of the second, the third earl found a resolution in writing Characteristicks of Men, Manners, Opinions, Times (1711), which endorsed both the aspiration to virtuous political action and the ideal of aloof self-knowledge and autonomy.

**Childhood and adolescence** The first earl of Shaftesbury, disappointed in his own son, looked to his grandson to assure the family's future. In 1674 the first earl prevailed on his son to relinquish guardianship of the future third earl. John Locke, physician and philosopher, who lived in the Shaftesbury household, had earlier watched over the infant's health and, from 1674, was responsible for his education. In the second half of the 1670s Locke entrusted the boy to Elizabeth Birch, a governess, who, fluent herself in Greek and Latin, laid the foundations for his competence in ancient languages. In the early 1680s he seems to have received instruction directly from Locke, who, in the third earl's later account, governed him according to the principles enunciated in *Some Thoughts on Education* (1693).

When the first earl died in exile early in 1683 authority over Cooper, to whom the title Lord Ashley now passed, returned to his parents. They promptly sent him to Winchester College, where he was enrolled from 1683 until no later than early 1686. The tory atmosphere of the school was inhospitable to such a scion of whiggism, and the experience contributed to his lifelong antipathy to formal institutions of education. In 1687 he began a continental tour, guided by a Scottish tutor, Daniel Denoune, and accompanied by Sir John Cropley, who remained an intimate throughout his life, and Thomas Sclater Bacon. After a stop in the Netherlands, where they visited the exiled Locke, and an extended stay in Paris, they spent almost a year in Italy, where Ashley devoted himself to acquiring knowledge and taste in the polite arts. Because of the hostilities between Britain and France that became inevitable once James II had been forced to leave England late in 1688 the party returned to England via central Europe, passing through Vienna, Prague, Dresden, Berlin, and Hamburg. Ashley's notes on his time abroad suggest his well-developed whig sensitivities, since they register suspicion of royal courts, Catholicism, clerics, and especially France. He was abroad in 1688 but commented in a letter to his father that he was thankful for:

> our late Purges from those promoters of y$^t$ Interest y$^t$ was to have Enslav$^d$ us to y$^e$ Horridest of all Religions, & to y$^e$ Service of the Usurpations & treacherys of that Neiboring Crown y$^t$ has Aim$^d$ so long att y$^e$ Subjection of all Europe. (Lord Ashley to the second earl of Shaftesbury, 3 May 1689, PRO 30/24/21/229)

**Early study and writings** Lord Ashley returned to England in the spring of 1689 and resisted the encouragement of at least one prominent whig to stand for the Commons in 1690. Rather he spent the early 1690s mixing serious study with the leisured pursuits typical of a young aristocratic gentleman. This is a poorly documented period compared to the last fifteen years of his life, for which hundreds of letters survive along with notebooks on personal, philosophical, and artistic topics. He inherited many acquaintances and friends from his grandfather and Locke. He knew such Locke associates as Edward Clarke, Walter Yonge, and Damaris Masham. He also established a lifelong friendship with John Somers, to whom he wrote or dedicated many of his mature writings. It was also through Locke that he knew Benjamin Furly, the Quaker merchant and intellectual broker in Rotterdam with whom he corresponded extensively. Furly in turn brought him into contact with continental scholars and men of letters, including Jean Le Clerc, Philip von Limborch, and Pierre Bayle, who introduced him to Pierre Des Maizeaux.

At the same time Ashley associated with Britons of his own generation who shared a principled whiggism that combined aristocratic, classical republican, commonwealth, and country elements into a critique of the whig leadership. His enduring friendship with Robert Molesworth dated from the 1690s. So did his patronage of John

Toland, with whom he had an uneasy relationship until in 1703 he concluded that Toland was too unpredictable and irresponsible an ally. His acquaintances also included Charles Davenant, Andrew Fletcher, Walter Moyle, William Stephens, and John Trenchard.

Lord Ashley pursued his reading of history, philosophy, and the classics during the 1690s. His correspondence with Locke from these years broached philosophical topics but also conveyed his quest for a philosophical identity independent of that of his famous mentor. His earliest publications appeared at the end of the decade, enunciating important themes of his later writing. His introduction to a 1698 edition of sermons by the latitudinarian Benjamin Whichcote gave Ashley the opportunity to criticize both the philosophical egoism of Thomas Hobbes and also the egoistic calculation underpinning Christian teachings about future rewards and punishments. In the next year the first version of *An Inquiry Concerning Virtue*, on which Ashley had been working since the early 1690s, appeared. It is probably true that, as the fourth earl maintained, John Toland published the *Inquiry* without permission, using the manuscript that Ashley had circulated among his friends. However, the fact that a few years later Ashley, by then third earl of Shaftesbury, encouraged Pierre Des Maizeaux to translate this version casts doubt on the fourth earl's story that Toland's piracy so angered Ashley that he tried to buy up extant copies. Besides, the main ideas of the *Inquiry* were ones to which the mature Shaftesbury remained committed: that moral norms had an ontological reality independent of religious prescription and that the foundations for human happiness were not in selfishness or pleasure but in virtue itself.

**Political activity in the reigns of William III and Anne** In 1695 Ashley was finally induced to enter politics. He was elected to the seat for Poole, Dorset, in May 1695, when the incumbent, Sir John Trenchard, died. That parliament was dissolved before Ashley could attend but he stood for the seat again, in the elections for the new parliament that autumn, and took his seat on 21 November. The 1695–8 parliament marked a period of taxing activity for Ashley in the Commons. Although he followed 'court' leadership on some matters he identified with 'country' members and frequently declared his independence of party. He worked to advance legislation associated with the country, most notably raising property qualifications for MPs, protecting the rights of those accused of treason, and disbanding the king's military forces after the signing of the treaty of Ryswick in September 1697. His speech in favour of the Treason Bill, which provided legal counsel for those accused of treason (a provision from which his own grandfather would have benefited in the 1680s), gave rise to a noteworthy anecdote. According to Abel Boyer, he:

> rose up in order to speak for it, and having begun his Speech, he industriously feign'd to be so surpriz'd that for a while he could not go on. But having recover'd himself, he took occasion from his very Surprize, to enforce the Necessity of allowing Council to Prisoners, who were to appear before their Judges; since he, who not only was unaccus'd and

innocent, but one of their Members, was so dashd when he was to speak before that august Assembly.   (Boyer, 3.117)

Whether spontaneous or premeditated his remark was regarded as a forceful rhetorical flourish which carried weight in the bill's passage in January 1696.

Ashley rather unexpectedly refused to stand again after this parliament was dissolved in 1698 and instead spent a year in the Netherlands. He returned to England in May 1699 and went to the family home, St Giles's House in Wimborne St Giles, Dorset, where his father died on 2 November, at the age of forty-eight. Two months later the third earl of Shaftesbury appeared for the first time in the House of Lords. For the remaining years of William III's reign he attended parliament assiduously. In the debates about the fate of Spain, the growth of French power, the partition treaties, and the impeachment of the whig lords who had negotiated them Shaftesbury found himself identifying more closely than he had with the whig leadership and relinquishing the oppositional posture that he had earlier adopted. His pamphlet *Paradoxes of State* (January 1702) argued that the threat of France made obsolete the distinction between court and country and left only one polarity in English politics, between those committed to quashing French ambitions and those not. Shaftesbury worked strenuously on behalf of whig candidates in the west country in the elections for the last two of William's parliaments, with notable success in the election of 1701–2. William recognized Shaftesbury's contributions and may have gone so far as to offer him a ministerial position. However, the political scene was disrupted in March 1702 by William's death. Anne's accession ended Shaftesbury's political prospects; indeed in 1702 she deprived him of the vice-admiralty of Dorset, which his father and grandfather had held before him. Thereafter the political climate, as well as his health, kept Shaftesbury from actively engaging in politics, although he remained a keen observer and at times, such as 1706 when a country amendment to restrict placemen in parliament was attached to the Regency Bill, a vigorous adviser.

**Psychic biography** Shaftesbury's fitful political career is primarily interesting as an illustration of the tensions within post-1688 whiggism as its fundamental commitment evolved from radicalism to the defence of a standing regime. None the less his political concerns are important in understanding the writings on which his influence rests. These writings were also significantly inflected by Shaftesbury's psychic history. His decision to abandon parliament and the country in 1698 for a year of study and reflection in Rotterdam was symptomatic not just of fatigue and poor physical health but of psychological stress, for which there is remarkable evidence in the notebooks that he began keeping at this time.

These notebooks were in part a commonplace book, assembling extracts from the Roman stoics Marcus Aurelius and especially Epictetus, and in part a diary of personal rumination and discovery. The notebooks show him struggling for personal autonomy and control in a social world that ineluctably pulled him in diverse directions and often compromised his integrity. His conflicts reflected the tension between, on one side, the social and political expectations imposed on him by his inherited social position and the model of his grandfather and, on the other, his individual temperament, which, borrowing from his father, was oriented toward privacy, contemplation, and study. Shaftesbury wrote extensively in these notebooks during 1698 and 1699, and again in 1703 and 1704, when he resumed residence in Rotterdam at a distance from his social and political obligations.

Though Shaftesbury endured periodic anxieties until the end of his life he appears to have reached a certain degree of psychological resolution during the first decade of the eighteenth century. He reaffirmed his commitment to a political vocation but recognized that he would fulfil it as a writer of whiggishly disposed works. He also affirmed his identity as a philosopher, but one whose ideas and methods were quite distinct from those of Locke.

**Assembling *Characteristicks*** From the early 1700s Shaftesbury was experimenting with genres and subjects situated on the borders of the topical, the political, and the philosophical. However, it was in the second half of the decade that he began publishing pieces, in different genres and of successively increasing length and complexity, that became the components of his chief work, the *Characteristicks*.

The first of these was prompted by the appearance in London in 1706 of the so-called 'French prophets', refugees from the remote Cévennes region of the Massif Central, where a millennially inspired protestant revolt against Catholic and royal authority had broken out in 1702. By 1707 the refugees had several English followers and apologists, whose prophetic activities Shaftesbury witnessed that summer. He drafted *A Letter Concerning Enthusiasm* in the autumn, although it was not published until spring 1708. While the *Letter* did ridicule the extravagancies of enthusiasts it also offered a positive interpretation of enthusiasm conceived as the morally orienting affective and imaginative capacity of individuals.

The *Letter* provoked a number of responses, including pamphlets by Mary Astell and Edward Fowler, bishop of Gloucester. These responses stimulated Shaftesbury to write *Sensus communis: an Essay on the Freedom of Wit and Humour*, published in 1709. *Sensus communis* defended and elaborated the earlier work by articulating an ideal of free and open public discourse as a programme for human progress and refinement. Shaftesbury grounded this programme on the human potential for solidarity and co-operation, itself founded in natural human sociability. In the same year he published *The Moralists: a Philosophical Rhapsody*. Organized as a tale of philosophical conversion this dialogue pitted a sceptic against a theist in a discussion vindicating a highly stoic vision of cosmic, social, and human order under the presidence of a supreme intelligence.

Finally, in 1710, Shaftesbury published *Soliloquy, or, Advice to an Author*, in which he treated the importance of arts and letters in society and the conditions in which they thrive. While apparently remote from his strictly ethical concerns the *Soliloquy* formulated publicly the sort of self-discursive technique for attaining self-knowledge that Shaftesbury had already explored in his notebooks. Thus the *Soliloquy* was indirectly related to many of Shaftesbury's chief philosophical concerns.

It is not clear exactly when Shaftesbury decided to bring together these four publications and the earlier *Inquiry*. By 1710 he was revising all of them, some significantly. In addition he wrote a set of five miscellanies to accompany and comment on the earlier writings. The result was the first edition of *Characteristicks of Men, Manners, Opinions, Times*, published by John Darby in three volumes in 1711. Over the next two years Shaftesbury polished *Characteristicks*, making many revisions, largely stylistic, in the text. He also commissioned a set of engravings to adorn the new edition and illustrate emblematically the philosophical and political meanings of the text. These were based on drawings which Shaftesbury had commissioned from Henry Trench, an Irish artist based in Rome, and had carried out in London by the distinguished Huguenot engraver Simon Gribelin. These fine graphics, in addition to greater care in the layout and typography, made the second edition of *Characteristicks* (1714) a splendid piece of book art.

**Interpreting *Characteristicks*** *Characteristicks* was a complex as well as composite book, a work of philosophy in a polite mode. It aimed centrally to convey a notion of philosophy as a form of ethical training. It mocked scholasticism, which survived, moribund but not quite dead, in the universities. More importantly it criticized those philosophical 'innovators', namely René Descartes, Thomas Hobbes, and John Locke, who themselves sought to demolish scholasticism. If they took their inspiration from mathematics and natural philosophy Shaftesbury took his from social and aesthetic experience. If they helped to make epistemology the central task of philosophy, Shaftesbury insisted on philosophy's ethical core. Assigning him paternity for the idea of moral sense, as philosophers have often done, has tended to assimilate him inaccurately to the epistemology-centred project of philosophy that he rejected. He opposed two traits of modern philosophy in particular: first, philosophical egoism, the postulate that the solitary individual was the starting point for social and ethical thinking; and, second, nominalism, the notion that ethical and other standards were largely conventional in character. In addition he found modern philosophy too dry, abstract, and demonstrative to address the moral formation of gentlemen.

Characterizing modern philosophy as revived epicureanism Shaftesbury aligned his own project with stoicism. He believed humans to be situated in a morally orderly cosmos and, by virtue of their natural sociability, capable of ethical virtue and political solidarity. These commitments were shaped by extensive readings in classical philosophy, where he found Socrates and Xenophon (rather than Plato), Marcus Aurelius and Epictetus, the most potent models. He also absorbed modern influences, especially those of moderate English churchmen such as Jeremy Taylor, Henry More, Richard Cumberland, and Benjamin Whichcote. Since his outlook depended on an orderly cosmos in which an intricate pattern of interdependence supported an ethics of reciprocity, he was highly theistic in his outlook. He did defend freethinking and scepticism as forms of intellectual practice, but he was wary of some kinds of deism. In particular he rejected any hint of materialism or nihilism, which he regarded as conducive to atheism.

As far as received religious opinion was concerned Shaftesbury was deeply sceptical of many claims made on behalf of the traditional Christian God and especially critical of ecclesiastical institutions. His moral thought aimed to secure the ontological reality of an ethical standard, not only against nominalism but against the position—closely related to nominalism, in his view—that ethics had to be founded in revealed religion. He was particularly anxious to show the inadequacy of the doctrine of future rewards and punishments as the ground for human ethical behaviour, since it founded supposedly moral behaviour on an essentially egoistic calculation of future benefit.

In addition, like anti-clerical writers from James Harrington onwards, Shaftesbury identified priestcraft as a malevolent force in the world, propagating superstition and spiritual subjection to the acquisitive worldliness of priests. He traced the deleterious impacts of priestcraft through world history and assigned high-church Anglicans a pedigree extending back through the Catholic church to classical Rome and even ancient Egypt. Bedevilled by priestcraft, human spiritual history was also marred by enthusiasm. Adapting the critique of enthusiasm, initially used against puritans and others who, it was said, relied too heavily on the spirit to make religious or philosophical claims, Shaftesbury carried it in new directions by suggesting that the high-church clergy were enthusiasts whose delusions authorized fanatic persecution. At the same time he wished to recuperate enthusiasm as that capacity, first limned by Plato, of being genuinely inspired by the divine and, for Shaftesbury, of being moved and drawn to the moral and aesthetic imperatives laced into the very structure of the universe by the supreme intelligence.

For Shaftesbury, avoiding the poles of superstition and enthusiasm was requisite for a correct philosophical temper. However, his criticism of spiritual perversion also had a political valence. Both superstition and persecuting enthusiasm helped to explain high-church bigotry, which he identified with toryism. He desired a moderate, inclusive, and tolerant religious establishment, controlled by the magistrate. Shaftesbury conspicuously cited such Anglican writers as Jeremy Taylor and John Tillotson, whom he deemed friendly to his own ecclesiology, and, according to the fourth earl, he actually attended Church of England services when his health permitted (fourth earl of Shaftesbury, sketch of the life of the third earl, Shaftesbury papers, PRO 30/24/21/226, p. 8).

This ecclesiastical position was one important element in Shaftesbury's vision of the whig polity that the 1688 revolution had made possible. The other was a patriotic whig libertarianism defined against a toryism that he linked with Stuart and French absolutism. Though deeply concerned with politics, his writings did not use the intellectual equipment that have made the writings of Hobbes and Locke canonical among students of the history of political discourse. In fact he was dismissive of the natural law tradition and its trappings (the state of nature, natural law, contract), and his references to republicanism and British constitutionalism tended to brevity.

Shaftesbury's main approach to politics was ethical and cultural; he promoted liberty by offering an account of liberty's culture. The heart of this culture was free and open discussion in a public arena. He found a model for such discussion in polite conversation, that is, edifying though pleasant interaction among free and equal gentlemen. Within the élitist terms of a gentlemanly society his version of polite conversation endorsed equality, reciprocity, and scepticism. When he asserted that all politeness was founded in liberty, he extended the reach of polite conversation to a generalization about culture as a whole. Thus he was critical of authoritarianism, whether ecclesiastical or governmental, and any dogmatic claims to certainty that had not been adequately tested. Throughout *Characteristicks* Shaftesbury used cultural history to explore the intertwined histories of politics and culture and to show how repeatedly in history priestly and royal regimes proved the enemy, and liberty the foundation, of the advancement of arts and letters.

Shaftesbury elaborated these ideas with persuasive force but without demonstrative rigour throughout the components of *Characteristicks*. The work's composite organization and discursive style explain why historians of both philosophy and political discourse have tended to neglect it. While *Characteristicks* was a collection its composite and digressive character was also a matter of design. The miscellanies, written specifically for the collection, were the most digressive of all the components and declared the cognitive value of the lack of system. This lack supported the philosophical, political, and cultural goals of the work by providing a textual embodiment of diversity, open-endedness, and freedom. Thus *Characteristicks* was meant not just to advertise a cultural model but also to actualize its parameters for the sake of its readership's moral and cultural edification.

**Final years** By the time *Characteristicks* appeared in the spring of 1711 Shaftesbury had already set in motion plans to exit the English scene. He had long deferred marriage, having enunciated repeatedly a strong desire to remain single; he preferred, it seems, to imitate Theocles, the philosophical hero of *The Moralists*, who lived a sober country life, devoted to study and enthusiastic contemplation, punctuated only by the visits and high-minded conversation of select gentlemen. Shaftesbury's sexual orientation has been a matter of some speculation; aside from his undoubted homosocial propensities, one of his letters, recounting an infatuation with a young man, suggests homosexual longings and attachments (Shaftesbury to Maurice Ashley, his brother, written 22 Jan 1705, posted 24

Dec 1705 [sic], PRO 30/24/20/110). However, he also recognized the obligation imposed by his social station to continue his line. With the assistance of Robert Molesworth in 1708 and 1709 he tried to negotiate an alliance with Lady Anne Vaughan, the daughter of John Vaughan, third earl of Carbery. When that effort failed, he settled quickly on a bride of less conspicuous wealth and status, Jane Ewer (1689?–1751), daughter of Thomas Ewer, squire of Bushy Hall in Hertfordshire. The marriage took place on 29 August 1709 and, on 9 February 1711, achieved its chief objective when the countess gave birth to a son, Anthony Ashley Cooper, who survived to become the fourth earl and assure the line.

By then, however, Shaftesbury's health was seriously deteriorating and he was about to make a final retreat. At several points during his life doctors diagnosed the particular weakness of his lungs and his tendency to asthma; his papers contain many prescriptions to relieve a variety of ills. These respiratory difficulties had long affected his living arrangements, particularly when he was not staying at St Giles's. In the 1690s, when he was in London, he occupied a residence near Red Lion Square. However, after he assumed his title and his health began to weaken he bought a house in Little Chelsea on what is now the Fulham Road; to the west of London, this site offered relief from London smoke. In 1709 he rid himself of the Chelsea house in favour of one in Reigate, Surrey, which offered greater distance from London air. However by the time that the first edition of *Characteristicks* was nearing publication he decided he would have to seek an entirely new and more salubrious climate if he was to survive. Giving up the house in Reigate he took one in Kensington, where he lodged his son and, for himself, made arrangements to go to Italy.

Shaftesbury sailed from Dover with the countess and a small retinue on 2 July 1711. Their route took them through Paris, Dijon, Lyons, Grenoble, Turin, Florence, and Rome to Naples, where they arrived on 15 November 1711 NS. They promptly set up a household in a *palazzo* in Chiaia, overlooking the Bay of Naples. After recovering from the damage to his health by the long journey Shaftesbury engaged in visiting sites in and around Naples and in socializing with local aristocrats and virtuosi. As noted above, he put considerable effort into preparing the second edition of *Characteristicks*.

In Italy, Shaftesbury also turned his attention more intently on the visual arts. He collected prints and paintings and he issued a major commission to Paolo de Mattheis (1662–1728), a prominent Neapolitan painter influenced by Luca Giordano and Carlo Maratta. The result was *The Judgment of Hercules*, a huge canvas which hung in St Giles's House until sold in 1980 to the Ashmolean Museum, Oxford. However, the image was well known in the eighteenth century as engraved by Simon Gribelin in 1714. Shaftesbury's commission included elaborate instructions about the nature and meaning of the scene to be represented. These were first published in French in the learned *Journal des Sçavans* in 1712 and then, in English, in 1713 as *A Notion of the Historical Draught or Tablature of the Judgment of Hercules*. (The *Notion* also appeared in volume 3 of the second edition of *Characteristicks*.) Shaftesbury also wrote *A Letter Concerning the Art, or Science of Design* (included in some copies of the second edition of *Characteristicks* and in all copies from the fifth edition in 1732), in which he described the promise of British culture under post-1688 conditions. He had a larger project in hand, namely, *Second Characters*, a companion to *Characteristicks*, which would have included both the *Notion* and the *Letter*, along with a commentary on *The Picture of Cebes*, a Socratic dialogue about painting (dating from the first century AD) and a long new treatment of the arts, notes for which he left in manuscript.

Shaftesbury's health declined toward the end of 1712 and he died in Chiaia on 15 February 1713 NS. His remains were returned to England and he was buried in the church at Wimborne St Giles; the granite monument there represents a sarcophagus, over which stands a female figure of 'Polite Literature mourning the death of her most distinguished votary'. At his death his landed estate had a rent roll of some £4000 a year; the inventories of his possessions, taken at his death, were £2003 for St Giles's House (excluding paintings, other art works, and the library) and £284 for the house at Kensington. He left little debt, largely because he fretted much about expenses after he inherited his title and sought to live within his means. Yet his papers also record regular benevolence to the needy in the St Giles's neighbourhood, and he extended considerable patronage to a number of young men, including Michael Ainsworth, Pierre Coste, Paul Crell, and Joseph and Thomas Micklethwayte.

**Shaftesbury's influence**  Shaftesbury's writings attracted a number of trenchant critiques in the eighteenth century, most notably those of Bernard Mandeville, George Berkeley, Joseph Butler, and William Warburton and his circle, including John Brown. Shaftesbury was charged with underestimating the power of human selfishness, failing to provide an adequate criterion of virtue, mistaking his aristocratic tastes for an ethical programme, overestimating ridicule as a test of truth, undermining order through his anticlericalism, and proffering a deistic hostility to revelation.

However, such critiques also suggested the extent to which a Shaftesburian moral and aesthetic tenor shaped the age's intellectual and cultural climate. Before 1800 *Characteristicks* went through twelve English-language editions, and selections of his letters were published six times. Shaftesburian ideas and themes appeared frequently in periodicals and poetry, most notably that of Alexander Pope, James Thomson, and Mark Akenside. In the gentlemanly class Shaftesbury found enthusiastic readers, such as the soldier and statesman James Stanhope, who was the first in a line of Shaftesburians inspired by the pursuit of virtue and taste. Seeking to integrate ethics and aesthetics into the education of the gentleman Shaftesbury belonged to a European lineage of courtesy writers stretching back to Baldassare Castiglione. The broad reach of Shaftesbury's writings influenced taste in painting, architecture, and gardens, deep into the century.

Shaftesbury's writing also contributed to the shape of contemporary philosophical and social thinking. His enquiries concerning virtue and religion, liberty and order, private autonomy and social cohesion, taste and beauty, were a starting point for writers throughout Britain. His most influential interpreter was Francis Hutcheson, who, settling in Dublin in the 1720s, was befriended by Robert Molesworth and exposed to Shaftesbury's writing. In his publications of the 1720s Hutcheson converted Shaftesbury's insights into a more formal approach to ethics and aesthetics, which he imported to Scotland when appointed professor of moral philosophy at Glasgow University in 1730. Either directly or as mediated by Hutcheson, Shaftesbury inspired William Wishart, George Turnbull, David Fordyce, and James Burnett, Lord Monboddo, among other Scots. While Hutcheson and others responded to Shaftesbury's specifically ethical positions Shaftesbury's more general concern with the nature and growth of politeness shaped the Scottish Enlightenment's attempt to define the norms and operations of a modern commercial and civil society. In England, meanwhile, although defended by Richard Fiddes, Henry Coventry, and Charles Bulkley and echoed by Viscount Bolingbroke, Shaftesbury found his greatest continuator in his nephew James Harris, in whose career scholarship, cultivation, and civic and political activism combined to promote a progressive whiggish culture. Shaftesbury was also eagerly absorbed by a range of North Americans, from Jonathan Edwards and the American Samuel Johnson to Thomas Jefferson and Ezra Stiles.

Shaftesbury's highly wrought prose style had always been susceptible to criticism and even ridicule, as commentaries by Berkeley, Adam Smith, George Campbell, and Hugh Blair make clear. However in the second half of the eighteenth century such criticisms betokened a decline of Shaftesbury's persuasiveness in general. The highly sympathetic article on Shaftesbury in the *General Dictionary, Historical and Critical* (1739), signed by Thomas Birch, although largely written by James Harris in co-operation with the fourth earl of Shaftesbury, proclaimed that the essays in *Characteristicks*:

> are not only perfectly finished in themselves, according to the nature and genius of that species of writing to which each belongs, but … all together they form a complete whole, whose parts have a certain order and relation to each other, and which cannot be inverted without the whole's being injured.  (Birch, 183)

However Andrew Kippis, in the second edition of the *Biographia Britannica* of 1789 (which expanded on the *General Dictionary*), provides evidence of Shaftesbury's declining stature:

> For a considerable time he stood in high reputation as a polite writer, and was regarded by many as a standard of elegant composition. His imitators, as well as admirers, were numerous, and he was esteemed the Head of the School of

sentimental Philosophy. Of late years, he has been as much depreciated as he was heretofore applauded.   (Kippis, 290)

On the continent Shaftesbury's influence arrived later and lasted longer than in Britain. He became known initially through learned journals, then through the mediation of such writers as Pope and Bolingbroke, and finally through translations of *Characteristicks* itself. Denis Diderot was deeply impressed by Shaftesbury, translating the *Inquiry Concerning Virtue* (1745) and then plundering the rest of *Characteristicks* for his *Pensées philosophiques* (1746). In the *Encyclopédie* Diderot juxtaposed Lockean penetration and truthfulness with Shaftesburian genius. Similarly Montesquieu ranked Shaftesbury, with Plato, Montaigne, and Malebranche, as one of the four great poets. It was no doubt this poetic quality that caught the imagination of Shaftesbury's German readers, who included Justus Möser, Johann Gottfried von Herder, and Moses Mendelssohn, who modelled his own philosophical dialogue on *The Moralists*. Similarly Gotthold Lessing's *Laokoon* (1766) took off from Shaftesburian aesthetic premises.

Shaftesbury provided a model for polite gentlemen in his own connoisseurship, which was sparing but highly deliberate. He was intimately involved in designing the two important portraits of him, which conveyed characteristic messages. Both were painted by John Closterman at St Giles's House, in 1700 and 1701. A full-length double portrait of Shaftesbury and his brother Maurice Ashley as philosophers in antique garb affirmed the unity of nature and culture, virtue and taste. Meanwhile a full-length portrait of Shaftesbury, with a servant beckoning from behind a curtain in the background, endorsed the equal claims of action and contemplation, politics and philosophy.   LAWRENCE E. KLEIN

**Sources** PRO, Shaftesbury MSS · Earl of Shaftesbury [A. A. Cooper], *Characteristics of men, manners, opinions, times*, ed. L. E. Klein (1999) · R. Voitle, *The third earl of Shaftesbury, 1671–1713* (1984) · L. E. Klein, *Shaftesbury and the culture of politeness: moral discourse and cultural politics in early eighteenth-century England* (1994) · S. Grean, *Shaftesbury's philosophy of religion and ethics* (1967) · T. Fowler, *Shaftesbury and Hutcheson* (1882) · *The correspondence of John Locke*, ed. E. S. De Beer, 8 vols. (1976–89) · S. O'Connell, 'Lord Shaftesbury in Naples, 1711–1713', *Walpole Society*, 54 (1988), 149–218 · M. Cranston, *John Locke* (1957) · K. H. D. Haley, *The first earl of Shaftesbury* (1968) · A. O. Aldridge, 'Shaftesbury and the deist manifesto', *Transactions of the American Philosophical Society*, new ser., 41 (1951), 297–385 · C. Robbins, *The eighteenth-century commonwealthman* (1959) · T. Birch, 'Third earl of Shaftesbury', *A general dictionary, historical and critical*, 9 (1739), 179–86 · A. Kippis, 'Anthony Ashley Cooper, third earl of Shaftesbury', *Biographia Britannica, or, The lives of the most eminent persons who have flourished in Great Britain and Ireland*, ed. A. Kippis and others, 2nd edn, 4 (1789), 266–98 · E. Ludlow, *A voyce from the watch tower*, ed. A. B. Worden, CS, 4th ser., 21 (1978), 17–55 · F. Paknadel, 'Shaftesbury's illustrations of *Characteristicks*', *Journal of the Warburg and Courtauld Institutes*, 37 (1974), 290–312 · D. H. Solkin, *Painting for money: the visual arts and the public sphere in eighteenth-century England* (1992), 1–77 · H. Schwartz, *The French prophets: the history of a millenarian group in eighteenth-century England* (1980) · J. Hutchins, *The history and antiquities of the county of Dorset*, 2 vols. (1774) · J. A. I. Champion, *The pillars of priestcraft shaken: the Church of England and its enemies, 1660–1730* (1992) · GEC, *Peerage*, new edn, vol. 11 · Burke, *Peerage* (1967) · A. Boyer, *The history of King William the Third*, 3 vols. (1702–3) · H. Caygill, *Art of judgment* (1989), 38–102 · K. Downes, 'The publication of Shaftesbury's "Letter concerning design"', *Architectural History*, 27 (1984), 519–23 · [M. Rogers], *John Closterman: master of the English baroque* (1981) [exhibition catalogue, NPG, 24 July – 4 Oct 1981] · *JHC* · *JHL* · C. T. Probyn, *The sociable humanist: the life and works of James Harris, 1709–1780* (1991) · *DNB*

**Archives** PRO, corresp. and papers, 30/24 | BL, Add. MSS · Bodl. Oxf., letters to John Locke · CUL, letters to Michael Aynsworth · Glos. RO, letters to Benjamin Furly, etc.

**Likenesses** J. Closterman, double portrait, oils, 1700–01 (with Maurice Ashley), NPG · J. Closterman, oils, *c*.1700–1701, St Giles's House, Wimborne St Giles, Dorset [*see illus.*] · J. Barry, group portrait, etching and line engraving, 1795 (after J. Barry), NG Ire. · S. Gribelin, line engraving (after J. Closterman), BM, NPG; repro. in A. A. Cooper, earl of Shaftesbury, *Characteristicks of men, manners, opinions, times*, 3rd edn (1723) · J. Hopwood, stipple, NPG

**Wealth at death** landed estate with rent roll of £4000 p.a.; £2003 St Giles's House, Wimborne St Giles, Dorset (excl. paintings, other art works, and library); £284 house in Kensington; negligible debt: PRO, Shaftesbury MSS, 30/24/22/6 [account books], inventories of his possessions, taken at his death

**Cooper, Anthony Ashley-, seventh earl of Shaftesbury** (1801–1885), philanthropist and politician, was born on 28 April 1801 at 24 Grosvenor Square, London, the fourth child and eldest son of Cropley Ashley-Cooper, sixth earl of Shaftesbury (1768–1851) from 1811 and chairman of committees in the House of Lords from 1814, and his wife, Lady Anne Spencer-Churchill (1773–1865), daughter of the fourth duke of Marlborough. He had an unhappy childhood, with parents who were distant and severe, and he also found his first school, Manor House, Chiswick, which he attended from 1809 to 1813, to be uncongenial. He flourished more at Harrow School, where he was educated from 1813 to 1816, and at Christ Church, Oxford, where he matriculated in 1819 after a period of two years boarding with a clergyman at Eckington in Derbyshire. He gained a first-class degree in classics in 1822, took his MA in 1832, and was made DCL in 1841.

**Election to parliament and marriage** Lord Ashley, as he was styled in his father's lifetime, was a handsome, seriousminded, and ambitious young man. In later life he was to trace his religious convictions back to the childhood influence of a family servant, Maria Millis, and his philanthropic zeal to his teenage encounter with a pauper funeral on Harrow Hill. Nevertheless in the 1820s his character and beliefs were by no means fully formed. At Oxford he became a close friend of George Howard, later Viscount Morpeth, an association which gave him, despite his own tory family loyalties, a strong link to the whig circles of Castle Howard and Devonshire House, to whose cultivated and worldly tone he appears to have conformed. He was abroad on an extended grand tour from 1823 to 1825.

Ashley was first elected to parliament in 1826 as MP for Woodstock, a pocket borough controlled by his uncle, the duke of Marlborough, and he initially identified himself strongly with the duke of Wellington, whom he greatly admired. He accordingly turned down the offer of office from Canning in April 1827, but early in 1828 he accepted from Wellington a commissionership at the India Board of

Anthony Ashley-Cooper, seventh earl of Shaftesbury (1801–1885), by George Frederic Watts, 1862

Control. He sought to promote humanitarian and administrative reform in India, and also in 1828 took a leading part in securing legislation to protect lunatics. He was subsequently appointed to the metropolitan commission in lunacy and became its chairman in 1833.

On 10 June 1830 at St George's, Hanover Square, Ashley married Lady Emily (Minny) Cowper (1810–1872), daughter of Emily, Countess Cowper, an alliance which strengthened his personal ties with the whigs, although it did not subvert his own tory convictions. It is very probable that Minny's natural father was not Earl Cowper but Lord Palmerston, and indeed, after Earl Cowper's death in 1837, her mother married Palmerston in 1839. Ashley's own marriage was a stable and devoted one, and he and Minny had six sons, including (Anthony) Evelyn Melbourne *Ashley, politician and biographer, and four daughters, born between 1831 and 1849.

In the general election of 1830 Ashley was returned for Dorchester. The subsequent fall of the Wellington administration left him out of office, and he turned down the offer from Palmerston of an under-secretaryship in the Foreign Office. He took a prominent part in the opposition to parliamentary reform, most notably through successfully contesting the Dorset by-election in the autumn of 1831. He was to represent the county until 1846.

In January 1833 Ashley was persuaded to take over from Michael Sadler, who had lost his seat in the general election of 1832, the parliamentary leadership of the campaign for factory reform and shorter hours of work. Ashley proposed to limit to ten hours a day the time worked in factories by children and young people. He met with strong opposition, but, following investigations by a royal commission, the Factory Act of 1833 was passed as a government measure. It provided for higher limits on hours, and a lesser measure of regulation, however, than Ashley and the Ten Hours Movement had advocated.

In the short-lived Peel administration of 1834–5 Ashley served as a civil lord of the Admiralty. His career, however, was already setting a course towards a stance independent of the expectation of office. This was to enable him to pursue his religious, moral, and social concerns without restriction. In the event, although he accepted a post in the royal household in 1839 when Peel unsuccessfully attempted to form a government, Ashley turned down the offer when it was renewed in 1841, and was never to hold government office again.

**Evangelical crusader in politics, 1835–1846**  Ashley's growing sense of himself as a lone crusader was undergirded in the course of the 1830s by a deepening of his religious commitment. He had always been a sincere and pious Christian, but his beliefs now assumed an unambiguously evangelical character, sustained in particular by his friendship from 1835 with the leading divine Edward Bickersteth. Ashley became convinced of the imminence of the premillennial second advent of Christ, an expectation which for him engendered a sense not of fatalism, but rather of the urgency of saving souls and of reforming national life so as to mitigate the impact of the coming divine judgment. This conviction remained fundamental to the intensity and passion with which he pursued his numerous concerns.

Accordingly from the later 1830s Ashley came to take a prominent role in relation to distinctively religious matters, both inside and outside parliament. He supported measures for Sunday observance, and in February 1836 took the chair at the inaugural meeting of the Church Pastoral Aid Society. He was to remain its president for the rest of his life. Meanwhile he became preoccupied with the spiritual condition of the Jews, central as they were to the unfolding of his apocalyptic vision, and he took a leading part in the movement that led to the creation of a protestant bishopric of Jerusalem in 1841. This development, which appalled John Henry Newman, confirmed Ashley's position as a conspicuous opponent of the Oxford Movement, and in 1841–2 he was chairman of the committee that successfully promoted the election to the professorship of poetry of James Garbett against the Tractarian Isaac Williams. He continued to campaign against high-church tendencies within the Church of England, and in 1845 deplored the passing of the Maynooth Act which he perceived as disastrously compromising the nation by committing it to the indefinite support of a Roman Catholic institution.

Ashley's spiritual fervour reinforced his endeavours for national social and moral improvement. He was concerned to sustain the probity of British policy overseas, being critical of military conduct in Afghanistan, and of the opium trade with China. He opposed the annexation of Sind in 1843 and in the same year regretted government inaction when the French forcibly annexed Tahiti. Meanwhile, in 1840 he strenuously supported legislation to protect children employed as chimney sweeps, and in 1842 he secured the passing of the Mines Act. A further government measure of factory reform was enacted in 1844, although it did not satisfy Ashley, who had unsuccessfully endeavoured to extend its provisions. He took more satisfaction from securing legislation in 1845 to control the employment of children in cotton printworks. Also in 1845 he was responsible for further significant legislation on lunacy, which greatly improved the regulation of treatment. Ashley was subsequently elected permanent chairman of the lunacy commission, which acquired powers covering the whole of England and Wales, and held the office until his death.

Ashley's sympathy with the oppressed increasingly set him at variance with his constituents, especially following a speech at Sturminster Newton in November 1843 in which he criticized landowners as well as manufacturers for their treatment of their labourers, tenants, and other dependants. His remarks on this occasion also led to a permanent estrangement from his father, with whom his relations had never been easy. In early 1846 his political position in Dorset became untenable when, in full agreement with Sir Robert Peel, he was convinced of the necessity for the repeal of the corn laws. He accordingly resigned his seat.

**Philanthropy** The enforced break in Ashley's parliamentary career lasted some eighteen months and reinforced him in a shift of emphasis from political to voluntary philanthropic activity. He became a leading figure in an extensive range of societies. Some, such as the Irish church missions to Roman Catholics and the British and Foreign Bible Society, stemmed from specifically evangelical spiritual imperatives; others, such as the Society for Improving the Condition of the Labouring Classes, reflected a broader social conscience, but for Ashley all were expressions of his Christian zeal to proclaim the gospel and to prepare the ground for it by advances in living and working conditions. He was increasingly concerned with education, primarily for moral and spiritual reasons, and one of his main motives for seeking to limit the hours worked by children was to provide them with more time to receive instruction. He had accordingly been disappointed at the failure in 1843 of an attempt to legislate for the provision of education in factories, but committed himself to voluntary efforts in this sphere, notably from 1844 through his presidency of the Ragged School Union. From the late 1840s he actively promoted schemes for supporting the emigration of young people whose prospects in Britain were poor.

Ashley by no means abandoned the parliamentary sphere, however. In the spring of 1847 he had the satisfaction of seeing the enactment of a Ten Hours measure, through the agency of John Fielden and others, and at the general election in July he was himself returned to the Commons, as MP for Bath. Factory reform continued to engage his energies, as the implementation of the 1847 act

proved problematic, and in 1850 he conceded a compromise which in effect allowed ten and a half hours. Meanwhile in 1848 he was appointed a commissioner of the newly formed Board of Health, in which role he laboured strenuously during the cholera epidemic of 1849. He campaigned for the closure of overcrowded city burial-grounds and for the improvement of water supplies to the metropolis.

**Evangelical peer** On the death of his father on 2 June 1851 Ashley succeeded to the title, as seventh earl of Shaftesbury, and to the family estates, amounting to over 20,000 acres in Dorset, Hampshire, and Wiltshire. Although he initially felt that the House of Lords was a complete political backwater, Shaftesbury took an active part in its proceedings and used his position there to further his religious and social objectives. He continued to hold himself aloof from government office, although in 1855, under intense personal as well as political pressure, he came close to accepting the chancellorship of the duchy of Lancaster from Palmerston. However, while in the event he did not join the cabinet, his father-in-law's accession to the premiership gave Shaftesbury a significant informal role as an adviser on ecclesiastical appointments, and he obtained a noticeable increase in the proportion of evangelicals on the bench of bishops. In 1861 Palmerston honoured his wider public services with the conferment of the Order of the Garter.

Despite such recognition and achievement, these were years of painful struggle for Shaftesbury. On a personal level the death of his beloved second son, Francis, in 1849 cast a long shadow over the succeeding decades, and three further children were to predecease their father. The family estates at Wimborne St Giles in Dorset were heavily encumbered with debt and much in need of improvement. Shaftesbury failed for a long time adequately to gain control of the problems he inherited. Eventually he achieved a substantial improvement in the social condition of his tenants and dependants, but his own financial position remained insecure.

Shaftesbury's evangelical convictions continued to permeate his public life. He was alarmed by the advance of Catholicism in England, and took a prominent role in condemnation of the episcopal hierarchy set up by the pope in 1850, and supported the subsequent activities of the Protestant Alliance. He was also hostile to modern biblical scholarship as promoted by the broad-church party and in 1866 was, notoriously, to condemn J. R. Seeley's *Ecce homo* as 'the most pestilential book ever vomited from the jaws of Hell' (Hodder, 3.164). More positively, he enjoyed some satisfaction in the later 1850s from the partial success of his efforts to facilitate and promote informal religious services to attract the working classes. His strong sense of national accountability to God led him to be a passionately engaged observer of the Crimean War and the Indian mutiny, on which some of his pronouncements appeared extreme and ill-considered. His protestant sympathies predisposed him to a strong and active identification with the cause of Italian unification. He was a staunch opponent of slavery and accordingly a supporter of the north in the American Civil War. Meanwhile he maintained his strenuous but not always successful efforts to improve social conditions in Britain, seeking to extend the regulation of child labour to other areas of employment, and to improve the conditions of lunatics.

Palmerston's death in 1865 removed not only Shaftesbury's personal link to real political influence, but also a weighty check to the forces of constitutional change which he feared so much. In 1866 he was again offered the chancellorship of the duchy of Lancaster, this time by Lord Derby, but again refused: although anxious to 'stem the tide of Democracy', he wished to do this in his own way without the constraints of office. The disestablishment of the Church of Ireland in 1869 particularly depressed him, and, while he recognized the necessity for the Education Act of 1870, he was disappointed to feel that the ragged schools he had done so much to build up were being superseded.

**Old age and death** Shaftesbury's wife's death in 1872 reinforced his self-image as a lonely old man left behind by the tide of history. Nevertheless, life and a measure of energy still remained to him, and he laboured on for the causes to which he had committed himself. Through his presidencies of numerous societies he was a central figure in the fabric of evangelical philanthropy and religious life. From the late 1860s he took up the cause of mission to the costermongers (street traders) of London, and also promoted the use of ships for housing and training homeless boys. The legislative initiative in matters of social reform had now passed to others, but he took a keen interest in developments in the regulation of employment, lunacy, and housing. His role was more central in continuing evangelical resistance to the advance of ritualism and rationalism and he was a leading promoter of the Public Worship Regulation Act of 1874. His firm stand against biblical criticism was sustained and he opposed the ecclesiastical and academic preferment of its exponents, but reacted more positively to the increase of scientific knowledge. Even in his seventies he was capable of taking new initiatives, notably in relation to the control of vivisection.

Shaftesbury suffered from various recurrent minor ailments, but his general health remained good, allowing him to continue a high level of public activity almost to the end of his life. His final illness began in the summer of 1885 and culminated with inflammation of the lungs leading to his death at 12 Clifton Gardens, Folkestone, Kent, on 1 October. His death was followed by widespread expressions of public grief. The funeral was held at Westminster Abbey on 8 October and the large crowds present in the streets and the numerous philanthropic and religious organizations represented were testimony to the esteem with which the 'poor man's earl' had come to be regarded by all social classes and a wide range of interest groups. He was interred on 9 October in the parish church on his estate at Wimborne St Giles in Dorset.

Shaftesbury was commemorated by J. E. Boehm's statue in Westminster Abbey (1886) and by the *Eros* monument (Alfred Gilbert, 1893) in Piccadilly Circus. His life and achievements attracted widespread interest, as indicated by the remarkable sales of Edwin Hodder's three-volume memoir (1887). The years following his death also saw the publication of numerous popular and pious biographies confirming his image as a heroic crusader for improving the conditions of the downtrodden and for the proclamation of the Christian gospel. Shaftesbury was held up to late Victorian and Edwardian manhood as a role model of noble Christian endeavour. Twentieth-century accounts of his life, notably that of the Hammonds (1923), by contrast adopted a more secular tone, recognizing his substantial contribution as a social reformer, but playing down his religious motivation.

Shaftesbury, whose portrait by Watts is in the National Portrait Gallery, had a tall, graceful figure, with blue eyes and dark curly hair, which he retained into old age. In the 1830s he was described as a 'complete *beau idéal* of aristocracy'. This comment on his appearance might also be applied to his whole outlook and career. He was deeply conscious of rank, and his social engagement was of a fundamentally paternalist kind. He was motivated on the one hand by Christian zeal for human dignity, the salvation of lost souls, and preparation for the millennium, and on the other by an awareness that only through mitigating the worst extremes of oppression and injustice could the class he represented sustain its social and political position. His deepest commitments were to Conservatism in politics and to evangelicalism in religion, but he was too rugged an individualist ever to be a true partisan or the successful leader of a coherent movement. His character was flawed by tendencies to impetuosity and anger and to self-pity and depression, but his outstanding qualities were tremendous integrity, courage, and persistence, and a passionate concern for the welfare of his fellow human beings. He had the ability on occasions to stir the conscience of the nation, and the dedication to back up high-profile public action with unremitting conscientious labour, notably in the spheres of lunacy, education, and public health. Even if his achievements fell short of his own exacting standards, they were very substantial and became a source of enduring inspiration to others.

JOHN WOLFFE

**Sources** E. Hodder, *The life and work of the seventh earl of Shaftesbury*, 3 vols. (1887) · U. Southampton L., Shaftesbury MSS · G. B. A. M. Finlayson, *The seventh earl of Shaftesbury* (1981) · G. Battiscombe, *Shaftesbury: a biography of the seventh earl, 1801–1885* (1974) · J. L. Hammond and B. Hammond, *Lord Shaftesbury* (1923) · *Random recollections of Exeter Hall in 1834–1837, by one of the protestant party* (1838) · *The Times* (2 Oct 1885) · *The Times* (9 Oct 1885) · *The Times* (10 Oct 1885) · GEC, *Peerage*

**Archives** Duke U., Perkins L., corresp. · NRA, priv. coll., corresp. and papers · St Giles House, Dorset · U. Southampton L., diaries, corresp., and papers | Bishopsgate Institute, London, letters to George Howell · BL, corresp. with Lord Aberdeen, Add. MSS 43242–43254, *passim* · BL, corresp. with Charles Babbage, Add. MSS 37184–37200, *passim* · BL, letters to Francis Bonham, Add. MS 40617 · BL, letters to Stanley Lees Giffard, Add. MS 56368 · BL, corresp. with W. E. Gladstone, Add. MS 44300 · BL, corresp. with Sir Robert Peel, Add. MS 40483 · Bodl. Oxf., corresp. with Lord Kimberley · Bodl. Oxf., letters to earl of Clarendon · Bodl. Oxf., letters to Benjamin Disraeli · Bodl. Oxf., letters to Sir William Napier · Bodl. Oxf., letters to Samuel Wilberforce · CKS, letters to Edward Stanhope · Devon RO, letters to Sir Thomas Dyke Acland · Herts. ALS, corresp.

with Lord Lytton · HMC, corresp. and MSS · Hunt. L., letters to Lord Aberdare · Hunt. L., letters to Frances Cobbe · LPL, corresp. with Lord Selborne · LPL, corresp. with A. C. Tait · priv. coll., letters to Lord Harrowby · PRO, letters to Lord Cairns, PRO30/51 · PRO, corresp. with Lord John Russell, PRO30/22 · Pusey Oxf., corresp. with E. B. Pusey · U. Durham L., archives and special collections, corresp. with the third Earl Grey · U. Southampton L., letters to Lord Palmerston · U. Southampton L., letters to duke of Wellington · UCL, corresp. with Sir Edwin Chadwick · University of Dundee, archives, corresp. with Lord Kinnaird · University of Sheffield Library, letters to A. J. Mundella · W. Yorks AS, Leeds, letters to Matthew Balme · Worcs. RO, corresp. with Lord Lyttelton

**Likenesses** attrib. F. Grant, oils, *c*.1840–1850, Palace of Westminster, London · M. Noble, marble bust, 1859, Wimborne St Giles parish church, Dorset · G. F. Watts, oils, 1862, NPG [*see illus.*] · J. E. Boehm, plaster bust, 1875, NPG · J. Collier, oils, 1877, NPG · J. E. Millais, oils, 1877, British and Foreign Bible Society, London · Annan & Swan, photogravure (after a photograph by Bassano), NPG · Ape [C. Pellegrini], caricature, chromolithograph, NPG; repro. in *VF* (13 Nov 1869) · Ashford Bros & Co., carte-de-visite, NPG · J. Doyle, caricatures, drawings, BM · W. J. Edwards, stipple (after F. Sandys; Grillion's Club series), 1855, BM, NPG · G. Hayter, group portrait, oils (*The House of Commons, 1833*), NPG · H. Hering, carte-de-visite, NPG · F. C. Lewis, stipple (after J. Slater; Grillion's Club series), BM, NPG · Lock & Whitfield, woodburytype photograph, NPG; repro. in T. Cooper, *Men of mark: a gallery of contemporary portraits* (1876) · Maull & Co., carte-de-visite, NPG · attrib. Maull & Polyblank, photograph, NPG · W. Merrett, plaster bust, Guildhall Art Gallery, London · H. Robinson, stipple (after G. Richmond), BM, NPG · T. Rodwell, oils, Broadlands, Hampshire · F. Sargent, pencil drawing, NPG · J. Thomson, stipple (after W. C. Ross), BM; repro. in H. T. Ryall, *Portraits of eminent conservatives and statesmen* [in pts, 1836–46] · carte-de-visite, NPG · prints (after photographs), BM, NPG

**Wealth at death** £32,352 1s 4d.; in 1883 had estates of 17,317 acres in Dorset; 3250 in Hampshire, 1218 in Wiltshire worth £16,083 p.a. or £16,440 inclusive of copyholds: probate, 11 Dec 1885, Burke, *Peerage*; CGPLA Eng. & Wales

**Cooper, Arthur** (1833–1892). *See under* Cooper family (*per.* 1854–1994).

**Cooper, Sir Astley Paston**, first baronet (1768–1841), surgeon, was born on 23 August 1768 at Brooke Hall, Norfolk, about 7 miles from Norwich, the fourth son and sixth child of the ten children born to the Revd **Samuel Cooper** (*bap.* 1739, *d.* 1800), and Maria Susanna Bransby (1737–1807) [*see* Cooper, Maria Susanna], daughter of James Bransby, a gentleman from Shotesham, about 3 miles from Brooke. Both families were solidly middle-class; Samuel Cooper studied at Magdalene College, Cambridge (BA, 1760; DD, 1770), and was ordained a priest in 1763. He was the author of several volumes of sermons, commentaries, and poems, and, from 1781, the incumbent of a large parish in Great Yarmouth. His wife wrote children's books and sentimental novels. Their surviving sons were successful (the eldest, Robert Bransby, was an author and member of parliament), but their five daughters and one son died young from consumption. Astley Cooper later requested that his own post-mortem examination should include particular attention to his lungs, where evidence of old tuberculosis was found.

**Education and early career** As a youth Cooper was a notorious prankster, with little inclination to book learning. He found his early education, mostly at home and locally, a desultory experience, but his thoughts turned towards

Sir Astley Paston Cooper, first baronet (1768–1841), by Sir Thomas Lawrence, 1828

surgery after a dramatic accident claimed the life, from bleeding, of a foster brother, and his subsequent witnessing of an impressive operation for the stone by a Mr Donnee, surgeon to the Norfolk and Norwich Hospital. Cooper's maternal grandfather had been a prosperous surgeon in Norwich, and his uncle William Cooper was senior surgeon at Guy's Hospital in London. Accordingly, in August 1784, Cooper was articled to his uncle, arrangements being made for him to reside in the house of Henry Cline, surgeon at nearby St Thomas's Hospital. A student of John Hunter, Cline quickly became Cooper's patron and the formal apprenticeship was switched to him. Cooper also attended Hunter's lectures and acquired from both his mentors an aptitude for dissection and experimentation that never left him.

Cooper's London studies were interrupted by a serious attack of fever, requiring convalescence in Great Yarmouth during the summer of 1787, and by a seven-month stay from the autumn in Edinburgh, where he attended the lectures of James Gregory, James Hamilton, William Cullen, and Joseph Black, and actively participated in two debating societies. Back in London for the 1788 academic session Cooper resumed his pupillage with Cline and his attendance at Hunter's lectures. He became Cline's anatomy demonstrator the following year, and in 1791 Cline invited him to share in the lectures of his combined course on anatomy and surgery. In the same year Cooper became engaged to Anne Cock, the only daughter of a wealthy retired merchant then living in Tottenham in north London—a friend of Cline and an early patient of Cooper. Mr Cock dying on the very day of their proposed marriage, the young couple delayed a month before marrying privately, in December 1791. Although the marriage was by all accounts happy, its subsequent tone was set by the fact that Cooper delivered his anatomy lecture as usual on the evening of his wedding. The Coopers resided for several years in a house in Jefferies Square which his father-in-law had purchased and equipped for them, in addition to providing his daughter with a dowry of £14,000.

Besides learning anatomy from Cline, Cooper also absorbed some of his republican, democratic principles. These were tried but not obliterated by four months that the Coopers spent in revolutionary Paris from June 1792. They witnessed the atrocities of the reign of terror, and Cooper attended the lectures and operations of the surgeons Desault and Chopart; much later he wrote that revolutions may be good for posterity, but not for the existing generation. They returned to London in September, just two months before the birth of their only child, Anna Maria, who died in March 1794. They subsequently adopted a daughter, Sarah, who was the same age as their dead child, and a son, Astley, who was a nephew of Cooper's.

**Establishing a reputation**  Cooper's financial security enabled him to devote the 1790s almost exclusively to his teaching at St Thomas's and to his dissections. He wisely separated the lectures in anatomy from those in surgery, the latter necessitating attendance in the surgical wards of the hospital. It took him some time to distance himself from the philosophical style of Hunter's own surgical lectures, but the latter's death in 1793 left Cooper and John Abernethy of St Bartholomew's Hospital as the main rivals for the Hunterian crown. As Cooper's surgical experience deepened, his lectures became more practical in their orientation, based primarily on his own cases. He was a systematic note-taker, and this, combined with a prodigious memory, enabled him to develop a comprehensive course in surgery. He was a doer rather than a reader, and during three decades his surgical lectures were central educational features for thousands of medical students attracted by the London hospitals and their medical teachers. As was common in an era when student fees constituted an important source of income for teachers, Cooper did not rush to publish a textbook. However, the successive compilations based on his mature lectures, beginning with *Outlines of Lectures on Surgery* (1820), between them had gone through ten editions by 1839, in addition to four American editions and several German translations. More than many textbooks, these volumes represented print versions of what Cooper actually taught. Despite the print edition of the first of these publications, Thomas Wakley shrewdly chose Cooper's lectures to reproduce in the first issue of his new journal, *The Lancet*, in 1823.

From 1793 until 1796 Cooper was also lecturer in anatomy at the Company of Surgeons (after 1800 the Royal College of Surgeons). In 1797 he took over the larger house at 12 St Mary Axe, vacated by Cline. This provided more room for both his experimental work and for his comparative

and human dissections. He accidentally left behind a live viper in his old house and once dissected an elephant in the front garden of his new one, throwing a carpet over the railings to conceal it from public view. He moved to Broad Street in 1806 and then to New Street in 1815. In 1800 his uncle resigned as surgeon to Guy's Hospital and Cooper applied for the post. Advised by the hospital's secretary that his chances would be much improved were he to renounce his earlier political views and continued association with friends of democratic principles, Cooper decided on reflection that a surgeon should be a man for all parties and discontinued any active involvement in politics. He was comfortably elected to the Guy's post, and the income from his surgical practice almost doubled within the year.

**Pre-eminent London surgeon**  Although Cooper always took his teaching seriously, he also practised his craft among all classes. Tall and handsome, and with an easy manner, he attracted a large number of wealthy and influential patients, including Lord Liverpool, the duke of York, the duke of Wellington, and the prince of Wales, who, as George IV, created him baronet in 1821 following the successful removal of a painful cyst from the king's scalp. By Cooper's request the baronetcy descended to his adopted nephew, also named Astley Cooper. Much of his practice would now be considered medical rather than surgical, and he was known as a good diagnostician who trusted only a few medicines. His income in his peak years exceeded £20,000, and he was once given 1000 guineas after a successful removal of a bladder stone. His practice was of such legendary profitability that an impostor successfully practised for a time under his name in south London.

Within the limits of surgery before anaesthesia and antiseptics, Cooper was an outstanding operator, precise and quick. He himself wrote that he was not so good when delicacy was required, as in cataract surgery, but he was prepared to take on most of what was then the surgical repertoire. He could even innovate. Like Hunter before him, Cooper was especially interested in the surgical treatment of arterial aneurysms, and used animals to investigate the development of collateral circulation following the surgical occlusion of an artery. He operated on patients suffering from carotid aneurysms, the second of his patients surviving for thirteen years, though an even more dramatic operation to tie the aorta in a patient with an aortic aneurysm resulted in his patient's death forty hours later. He also successfully ligated the external iliac artery for a patient with a femoral aneurysm. He advocated the use of catgut in arterial surgery, that suturing material having the advantage of being gradually absorbed.

Cooper's standing was recognized by his surgical colleagues. He was elected professor of comparative anatomy at the Royal College of Surgeons in 1813, a post he resigned two years later. He became a member of the court of examiners of the college in 1822, and he served as president twice, in 1827 and 1836. He was also a vice-president of the Royal Society, to whose fellowship he had been elected in 1802, and won the society's Copley medal. His publications reflected his twin passions of anatomy and surgery, his first monograph, on hernias (published in two parts between 1804 and 1807), being stimulated by his own inguinal hernia which he had noticed while still a student. The description of the anatomy of the inguinal area was especially important. Cooper also produced treatises on fractures and dislocations (1822; sixth edition, 1829), the diseases of the breast (1829) and testis (1830), and the anatomy of the thymus gland (1832) and the breast (1840). He paid particular attention to high-quality illustrations, drawn by a succession of artists that he himself employed. His monographs contain a number of his notable surgical and anatomical observations and are based almost entirely on his own work, done singly or with various of his pupils and associates.

Cooper was loyal to his articled pupils, and such was his influence that he expected them to land the top jobs. Wakley assaulted this nepotism in the early volumes of *The Lancet*. Later, when Cooper's nephew Bransby Cooper did not succeed his uncle as anatomy lecturer at St Thomas's Hospital when he retired in 1825, Cooper prevailed on the Guy's secretary to establish a separate school there, with Bransby teaching anatomy and another pupil, Aston Key, becoming the lecturer in surgery. The museum at St Thomas's, which he had built up, stayed behind; instead Cooper helped Guy's to establish its own anatomical and surgical museum. Many of its specimens came from his dissections, often supplied by body snatchers. Cooper was quite open about the inadequate number of bodies for anatomy teaching available through legal means, before the Anatomy Act of 1832. He famously remarked to the House of Commons select committee on anatomy in 1828 that no dead person, however exalted, was safe from the activities of the resurrectionists: 'The law only enhances the price, and does not prevent the exhumation.'

**Winding down** Cooper began to suffer from occasional dizzy spells in the 1820s, and his wife's death in 1827 prompted him to retire from all his London activities. He had already purchased an estate at Gadesbridge, near Hemel Hempstead, where his wife had lived for several years. He soon tired of farming, however, and after marrying Catherine Jones in 1828 entered into a kind of Indian summer. He became adept at treating farm animals, especially horses, which he acquired lame and nursed and fed back to saleable health. He reopened his London surgical practice, this time in Conduit Street, and went on several continental tours, where he met many leading medical figures. He also received honorary degrees from Oxford and Edinburgh.

Cooper was a man of enormous energy who generally dissected for two or three hours before breakfast. Temperate in his habits, he was nevertheless sociable and active in several societies, including the Physical Society at Guy's, the Medico-Chirurgical Society, of which he was a founder member, and the Pow-Wow, a medical dining club started by John Hunter. He was a good athlete who

valued the role of sport, and he hosted shooting parties at his estate.

Cooper's health gave way in 1840, and after developing signs of congestive heart failure he died in Conduit Street on 12 February 1841. He had left instructions for a postmortem examination to be conducted, and he directed his dissectors to pay particular attention to several points associated with his own medical history and to publish the autopsy report. He was buried on 20 February in the chapel of Guy's Hospital. His will endowed an essay competition at Guy's; a memorial statue was erected in St Paul's Cathedral, and his fine portrait by Sir Thomas Lawrence is in the possession of the Royal College of Surgeons.                    W. F. BYNUM

**Sources** B. B. Cooper, *The life of Sir Astley Cooper*, 2 vols. (1843) • R. C. Brock, *The life and work of Astley Cooper* (1952) • R. Richardson, *Death, dissection and the destitute* (1987) • J. F. South, *Memorials* (1884) • 'Brief memoir of Sir Astley Paston Cooper', *The Lancet* (20 Feb 1841), 764–7 • S. S. Sprigge, *The life and times of Thomas Wakley*, [new edn] (1899) • S. C. Lawrence, *Charitable knowledge: hospital pupils and practitioners in eighteenth-century London* (1996) • *DNB* • Venn, *Alum. Cant.* [Samuel Cooper] • *GM*, 1st ser., 70 (1800), 89, 177

**Archives** McGill University, Montreal, Osler Library of the History of Medicine, lecture notes • RCS Eng., corresp., lecture notes, and papers • Royal College of Physicians of Edinburgh, lecture notes • Wellcome L., letters • Wellcome L., lecture notes | BL, corresp. with Sir Robert Peel, Add. MSS 40359–40390 *passim* • Lincs. Arch., corresp. with Charles Lowe • U. Southampton L., letters to duke of Wellington • Yale U., Beinecke L., letters to T. J. Pettigrew

**Likenesses** H. Meyer, stipple, 1819 (after F. Simonau), NPG • J. S. Agar, stipple, pubd 1825 (after A. Wivell), BM, NPG • T. Lawrence, oils, 1828, RCS Eng. [*see illus.*] • Robinson, stipple, pubd 1829 (after Penny), NPG • J. Towne, bust, 1841, Guy's Hospital, London; copies, RCS Eng. • E. H. Baily, statue, *c.*1842, St Paul's Cathedral, London • H. Weekes, bust, *c.*1844, RCS Eng. • F. Chantrey, pencil drawing, NPG

**Wealth at death** exact sum unknown: will, PRO, PROB 11/1942, sig. 123

**Cooper, Bryan Ricco** (1884–1930), politician in Ireland and army officer, was born on 17 June 1884 at Jutogh, in the canton of Simla, India, the eldest son of Major Francis Edward Cooper (1859–1900), of the Royal Field Artillery, and his wife, Ella (d. 1924), the daughter of Major-General Maunsel Mark Prendergast, another officer of the Indian army. His family were members of the former Anglo-Irish ascendancy and were major landowners in co. Sligo, where their family seat was Markree Castle, near Collooney. Cooper's paternal grandfather, Edward Henry Cooper (1827–1902), was MP for Sligo county from 1865 to 1868.

Cooper's time at Eton College reputedly alerted him to his Irishness, while his future engagement in the Irish literary revival was presaged in his enthusiasm for the theatre and reputation for bookishness. When he was sixteen his father wrote from the Second South African War (in which he was later killed in action) urging him to join the Royal Artillery. This he duly did, and he was trained at the Royal Military Academy, Woolwich. Cooper was made a captain in 1905; his military career before the First World War was notable primarily for his decision to resign in May 1914 in protest at the possibility that the army might

**Bryan Ricco Cooper** (1884–1930), by Chancellor

be used to coerce Ulster into accepting home rule. This reflected his prominent role in the Unionist campaign against the third Home Rule Bill, in which he served as secretary to the Irish Unionist Alliance from 1912 to 1914. Cooper's writings reveal his preoccupation with the difficulties faced by members of his class in finding a role for themselves in an Irish society whose system of land tenure had been transformed by pressure from a highly politicized Catholic majority. Resistance to this made one a pariah, acquiescence made one irrelevant. His own recourse to Unionist activism indicated that a commitment to a separate Irish cultural identity, as evinced by his interest in the literary revival, did not necessarily translate into a commitment to Irish nationalism. Fêted by members of the Kildare Street Club, Dublin, the focus of southern Irish unionism, Cooper was the successful South County Dublin Unionist candidate in January 1910, but he lost the seat to his nationalist rival in December. On 19 March 1910 he had married Marion Dorothy (*b.* 1890), daughter of Edward Stanley Handcock of Fulmer, Buckinghamshire, and a relation of the earls of Castlemaine. They had three sons and one daughter.

With home rule and some form of partition increasingly likely, Cooper's constructive intelligence turned to its implementation. Distrusting nationalist intentions, he urged that some provision be made for both the representation of southern unionists in a Dublin parliament and for the continuation of the land purchase scheme. Cooper moderated his position further still with John Redmond's commitment of the Irish National Volunteers to the war effort in August 1914. Faced with the patriotism of his fellow countrymen, Cooper worked as an inspecting officer, beginning the process whereby he emerged as one of the foremost conciliators of the former ascendancy.

During the war Cooper served with the tenth (Irish) division in Gallipoli and Macedonia, and was made temporary major in 1915. He later wrote a history of the campaign, *The Tenth (Irish) Division in Gallipoli* (1917; reprinted 1993), that celebrated the unity in the ranks of protestant and Catholic, Unionist and nationalist. On his return he became press censor for Ireland and built up good working relationships with nationalist editors. The reorganization of the censorship regime under the provisions of the Defence of the Realm Act in August 1919 attracted Cooper's criticism for its failure to distinguish between extreme and moderate nationalist papers. Reconciled to some form of home rule and keen that constitutional nationalism might recover its popularity, Cooper was none the less increasingly impressed with Sinn Féin. This was compounded by his growing disillusionment with British tactics in Ireland, which he considered a major factor in the escalation of the Anglo-Irish War. Writing in 1920, he urged that Unionists reconcile themselves to Sinn Féin so that they could make their contribution to Irish government. 'If we, the descendants of the men who sat in Grattan's Parliament and filled the ranks of Charlemont's Volunteers, persist in turning away from our people we shall perish and our fate will be deserved' (Robinson, 128). His first marriage having ended in divorce (1920), on 23 February 1925 he married Lillian Stella, divorced wife of Frederick Newman Edward Fitzpatrick the elder, daughter of Captain George Rawden Maurice Hewson of Dromahair, co. Leitrim, and also a childhood friend. In 1927, having lived on the Vico Road in Dalkey since 1921, he reopened Markree Castle.

Cooper was a poet and playwright too, but overall, his contribution to Irish literature was undistinguished. If his poetry was influenced by Douglas Hyde's translations from Gaelic, his drama tended to the whimsical—with short pieces often on historical and political themes. His collection *The Collar of Gold* (1920) is of interest chiefly for the biographical insight given by the exchange, in 'The chief secretary—a statement of ideas', between Arthur Wellesley and the Robert Emmet-like Derek Ponsonby. Set in post-union Ireland (1808), they dispute the role of the Irish aristocracy. Ponsonby felt they should offer themselves as patriotic leaders; Wellesley asserted their centrality to the civilizing ethos of the British empire: 'But he [the Englishman] lacks understanding, and that we the Irish can give him' (p. 104). Cooper was on good terms with W. B. Yeats and other members of the literary élite (Oliver St John Gogarty visited him on his deathbed, Lennox Robinson wrote his biography), and periodically his plays were put on at the Abbey Theatre.

The final decade of Cooper's life was dominated by his constructive role in the politics of the Irish free state. He successfully contested the South County Dublin constituency as an independent candidate in August 1923 and is remembered as a popular and active member, making a notable contribution to the public accounts committee and travelling in 1926 to Canada and Australia as a free state representative. Kevin O'Higgins characterized Cooper's role as the 'moderator of my undue rigidity', while Governor-General Timothy Healy saw him as the 'invisible mender' of old antagonisms, social and political (Robinson, 152–3). Cooper's posthumous reputation rests on this role as a healer, and his genial and attractive personality no doubt smoothed his entry into an otherwise hostile environment. Moreover, the austere and conservative mien of the Cumann na nGaedheal governments and the non-co-operation of anti-treatyite republicans with the new regime made for an atmosphere suited to Cooper's considerable ability and lightness of touch. Finally he could play the benevolent patrician. Following De Valera's decision to return to constitutional politics Cooper abandoned his stance as an independent in an effort to shore up support for Cumann na nGaedheal at the general election of 1927. He came head of the poll for South County Dublin, a reflection of the large number of protestants living in the constituency. For the last year or so of his life Cooper battled illness before dying in his sleep at his home in Dalkey on 5 July 1930. He was survived by his second wife.                                MATTHEW KELLY

**Sources** L. Robinson, *Bryan Cooper* (1931) · D. Gwynn, *The Irish free state, 1922–1927* (1928) · P. Buckland, *Irish unionism*, 1: *the Anglo Irish and the new Ireland, 1885 to 1922* (Dublin, 1972) · *WWW, 1929–40* · Burke, *Gen. Ire.* (1958) · *CGPLA Eng. & Wales* (1931) · m. cert. (1925) · d. cert.
**Likenesses** Chancellor, photograph, repro. in Robinson, *Bryan Cooper* [see illus.]
**Wealth at death** £33,944 14s. 8d.: probate, 16 Sept 1931, *CGPLA Éire*

**Cooper, Charles Alfred** (1829–1916), journalist and newspaper editor, was born in Kingston upon Hull on 16 September 1829, the eldest son of Charles Cooper, architect. He was educated at Hull grammar school and, needing employment on the early death of his father, became a journalist on the *Hull Advertiser*; he was soon the paper's sub-editor and manager. In 1852 he married Susannah (d. 1887), the eldest daughter of Thomas Towers of Hull; they had one son. Despite his position he felt unable to enliven the *Advertiser* and in February 1861 went to London to join the parliamentary reporting staff of the *Morning Star*. The next year he became its sub-editor. It was at that time partly owned by John Bright, who powerfully influenced the development of Cooper's Liberalism. In 1866 he began to act as London correspondent of *The Scotsman* and in May 1868 moved to Edinburgh to become assistant to Alexander Russel, its editor. On Russel's death in 1876 he was *de facto* editor during the unhappy editorship of Robert Wallace, and succeeded him at the end of that year. Cooper built on his London experience by introducing the 'London letter', for long a feature of *The Scotsman*, and developed the paper's literary tradition with a weekly 'Review of books'. He strongly supported Gladstone's Midlothian

campaigns and became the confidant of Lord Rosebery, their organizer. He became Rosebery's source of Scottish political information during the latter's spells in London and in return received much political information on metropolitan affairs. Cooper was a strong devolutionist, supporting the campaign for a secretary of state for Scotland and for 'local-national bodies' for England, Scotland, and Ireland, but in 1886 (after printing a scoop of the supposed content of the Home Rule Bill on 29 March) Cooper, like John Bright, came out against Gladstone's proposals. The break was not immediate or unfriendly, but by the autumn of 1886 *The Scotsman* was a Unionist paper, and remained so under Cooper's editorship, becoming jingoistic during the Second South African War. In 1886 he declined a knighthood. After retiring as editor at the end of 1905, Cooper travelled to Egypt and South Africa—earlier such journeys had been recorded in *Seeking the Sun* (1892) and *By the Castle to the Cape* (nd). He lived in Bournemouth, where he died on 15 April 1916 at Pine Grange, Bath Road; he was buried in the Dean cemetery, Edinburgh, on 19 April. Cooper was first president of the Sir Walter Scott Club and a keen angler, on one day catching 139 trout weighing a total of 141 pounds. He was the only English editor of *The Scotsman*.          H. C. G. MATTHEW

**Sources** C. A. Cooper, *An editor's retrospect: fifty years of newspaper work* (1896) · [M. Magnusson and others], *The glorious privilege: the history of The Scotsman* (1967) · *WW* · R. R. James, *Rosebery: a biography of Archibald Philip, fifth earl of Rosebery* (1963) · Gladstone, *Diaries* · *The Scotsman* (20 April 1916)
**Archives** NL Scot., letters to James Logie Robertson · NL Scot., corresp. with Lord Rosebery

**Cooper, Charles Henry** (1808–1866), biographer and antiquary, was born at Great Marlow, Buckinghamshire, on 20 March 1808, the eldest of the ten children of Basil Henry Cooper (1783–1823), solicitor, and Harriet (1787–1860), daughter of Charles Shoppee of Uxbridge. He was educated at home until he reached his seventh year, when he was sent to a school kept by a Mr Cannon at Reading. There he remained to the end of 1822. From an early age he evinced a passion for reading, and as his father possessed an extensive library, he was able to lay the foundation of his ample stock of historical and antiquarian knowledge. In 1826 he settled at Cambridge, and applied himself diligently to the study of the law. He married at Ely on 17 September 1834 Jane (1805–1890), third and youngest daughter of John and Elizabeth Thompson of Prickwillow, Cambridgeshire, and they had eight children, of whom only the biographer Thompson *Cooper (1837–1904), his brother John William LLD (1845–1906), of Trinity Hall, Cambridge, and their sister Harriet Elizabeth survived.

On 1 January 1836, when the Municipal Corporations Act came into operation, Cooper was elected coroner of the borough, though he was not admitted a solicitor until four years later. In 1849 he was appointed town clerk of Cambridge, which office he held until his death. In 1851 he was elected a fellow of the Society of Antiquaries. A fine speaker, he acquired an extensive practice as a solicitor. In 1855 he was engaged in the Cambridge arbitration which

Charles Henry Cooper (1808–1866), by E. Monson, 1859

resulted in the Award Act of the following year to settle differences between the university and borough, and he was complimented for his learning and acumen by the arbitrator, Sir John Patteson. In a busy public life he supported liberal and progressive measures, such as the founding of the public library and improvements to Addenbrooke's Hospital.

Cooper is now better known, however, for his elaborate works relating to the history and topography of Cambridge and the biography of distinguished members of the university. His first book was *A New Guide to the University and Town of Cambridge*, published anonymously in 1831. It was superior to most works of its class, especially in its architectural descriptions. In 1842 the first volume appeared of the *Annals of Cambridge*, which was followed by three other volumes, dated respectively 1843, 1845, and 1852, and by a portion of a fifth (pp. 1–128) in 1853, completed by his son John, and finally published in 1908 with additions, corrections, and an index.

This work is arranged chronologically, and contains an account of the history of the university and town from the legendary times of Cantaber to 1856. It was brought out in parts by subscription amid great difficulties. Many of the academic authorities opposed its publication, as they mistakenly believed that it would in some way deprive the university of its ancient privileges. In 1858 the first volume appeared of a more ambitious work, *Athenae Cantabrigienses*, written jointly by Cooper and his eldest son, Thompson. The idea of the book was suggested by Anthony Wood's *Athenae Oxonienses*. It contains carefully

written memoirs of the worthies who received their education or were incorporated at Cambridge University, and, like the companion work of Wood, is arranged in chronological order according to the date of death. The first volume dealt with the period 1500–85, and the second, published in 1861, extends to 1609. Part of a third volume, extending to 1611, was printed but not published, though several of the memoirs in this unfinished volume were afterwards reproduced in abbreviated form in Thompson Cooper's *Biographical Dictionary*. Like the *Annals*, this work, which was at once recognized as a valuable addition to British biographical literature, was published by private subscription. After Cooper's death the university offered to pay for the printing of the remainder of the *Athenae*, but his two sons, after making some further progress with the manuscript, were forced by the pressure of their own work to abandon the undertaking. It was, however, completed and finally published by G. J. Gray in 1913.

Cooper's last work was *The Memorials of Cambridge* (3 vols., 1858–66). Cooper originally intended to base it on John Le Keux's work of the same title, but during its progress it was altered so extensively that it may be regarded as substantially a new work. Cooper was a constant contributor to the *Gentleman's Magazine*, the *East Anglian*, *Notes and Queries*, the local press, and the proceedings of the antiquarian societies of London and Cambridge. He always ungrudgingly assisted in any literary undertaking. Thomas Carlyle, in his *Life and Letters of Cromwell*, acknowledged the value of the information given to him by Cooper, as did many other writers. Cooper died at his residence, 29 Jesus Lane, Cambridge, on 21 March 1866 and was buried at Mill Road cemetery, Cambridge, on 26 March. Most of the books in his library were sold by Sotheby between 28 and 30 October 1891. He left in manuscript a 'Memoir of Margaret', about the mother of Henry VII. This work, written in 1839, was edited and published in 1874 by the Revd J. E. B. Mayor 'for the two colleges of her foundation'—Christ's and St John's. Mayor, who for thirteen years was Cooper's intimate literary friend, described him shortly after his death as 'the town's chief ornament', admired for 'his intelligence, his ready memory, his rare familiarity with English history, topography, and biography, his wide range of reading, his large and statesmanlike view of persons and events', who shared his knowledge generously and whose death left a void that could not be filled (Mayor, *Cambridge Chronicle*, 8). He also predicted that Cooper's historical works would be cited more often than any other Cambridge books of his day. So it has proved to be.

THOMPSON COOPER, *rev.* JOHN D. PICKLES

**Sources** CUL, Cooper MSS, Add. MS 7512 · J. E. B. Mayor, 'To Swann Hurrell, esq.', *The Reliquary*, 7 (1866), 37–40 · J. E. B. Mayor, *Cambridge Chronicle* (24 March 1866), 8 · *Men of the time* (1865) · *GM*, 4th ser., 1 (1866), 910–12 · d. cert. · *Cambridge Chronicle* (31 March 1866)

**Archives** Cambs. AS, Cambridge, Cambridgeshire MSS, notes relating to various aspects of Cambridge history · CUL, biographical notes on Cambridge alumni and notes for *Annals of Cambridge*; collections relating to Cambridge town and university

**Likenesses** Farren, photograph, *c.*1858, Cambridge Central Library · W. Mayland, photograph, 1858, Cambridge Central Library · E. Monson, photograph, 1859, Cambridge Central Library [*see illus.*] · T. Butler, marble bust, 1868, Guildhall, Cambridge · H. Wiles, marble bust, 1868, Cambridge Central Library

**Wealth at death** under £2000: probate, 5 April 1866, *CGPLA Eng. & Wales*

**Cooper, Charles Purton** (1793–1873), lawyer and antiquary, was the son of Charles Cooper, linen draper, of St Dunstan, Kent, and Fleet Street, London. He was educated at Wadham College, Oxford, where he matriculated in 1810 and was a contemporary of Richard Bethell, first Lord Westbury. He graduated BA in 1814 with a double first class in honours, gaining his MA on 5 July 1817. He was called to the bar at Lincoln's Inn on 18 November 1816, and, after practising with success as an equity draughtsman, was appointed a king's counsel in 1836. He was queen's serjeant for the duchy of Lancaster from 1834 to his death. In 1837 he became a bencher of Lincoln's Inn, and in 1843 presented to the society two thousand volumes of civil and foreign legal works, having previously presented a hundred and fifty volumes of American law reports. He was treasurer of his inn in 1855, and master of the library in 1856.

Cooper's enthusiasm for the cause of legal reform attracted the attention of Lord Brougham, who introduced him to the Holland House circle and the heads of the whig party and on 12 March 1831 appointed him secretary of the second record commission. During his period of office Cooper bought and printed so many books that the commission's debt, over and above the £400,000 voted by parliament, rose to £24,000. The commission lapsed on 20 June 1837 on the king's death. Lord Holland recommended Cooper for the post of solicitor-general but R. M. Rolfe, later Lord Cranworth, was appointed.

Cooper played an active part in public affairs in his own county, Kent, where he resided at Denton Court, near Canterbury. He appeared as a whig candidate for Lambeth in 1850, but withdrew from the contest. In 1854 and 1857 he unsuccessfully contested Canterbury. He was proposed as a candidate for West Kent in 1855, but declined to stand. His great knowledge of jurisprudence and legal antiquities procured him a fellowship of the Royal Society on 6 December 1832, and the degree of LLD from the Roman Catholic University of Louvain and from Kiel. He was elected a fellow of the Society of Antiquaries in June 1825 and was a corresponding member of the royal academies of Lisbon, Munich, Berlin, and Brussels.

Cooper enjoyed a leading practice in the court of Vice-Chancellor Knight-Bruce, but he openly quarrelled with that judge, quitted his court, and lost his practice. As business fell off he endeavoured, without success, to obtain government assistance for a project for digesting and sifting all the law reports down to that date. He eventually retired to Boulogne, where, after unsuccessfully attempting to carry on his projects of legal reform, he died of paralysis and bronchitis on 26 March 1873, aged eighty.

Cooper was a prolific writer. He published a large number of varied legal works, including *An Account of the Public*

*Records of the United Kingdom* (2 vols., 1832), three volumes of reports of cases, texts on the court of chancery, conveyancing, solicitors' costs, municipal corporations, and the custody of lunatics. In 1860 he published memoranda of his proposals to classify the law reports and digest the statute book. He also published a letter on the pope's apostolic letters of 1850, a pamphlet on the government and the Irish Roman Catholic members (1851), and a work on freemasonry.     J. A. HAMILTON, *rev.* BETH F. WOOD

**Sources** *Law Times* (5 April 1873), 427 · *Solicitors' Journal*, 17 (1872–3), 431 · *The Times* (2 April 1873), 5 · Ward, *Men of the reign* · Boase, *Mod. Eng. biog.* · Allibone, *Dict.* · Foster, *Alum. Oxon.* · W. P. Baildon, ed., *The records of the Honorable Society of Lincoln's Inn: the black books*, 4 (1902)

**Archives** PRO, corresp., letterbooks, and papers [30/10] · PRO, collection of French diplomatic papers, 30/41 | BL, corresp. with John Allen, Add. MS 52189 · BL, Egerton MSS, corresp. with Sir Frederick Madden, 2838–2843 · Bodl. Oxf., corresp. with Sir Thomas Phillipps · PRO, letters to John Allen, 30/26/110

**Cooper, Charlotte**. *See* Sterry, Charlotte (1870–1966).

**Cooper, Christine Elisabeth** [Tina] (1918–1986), paediatrician and expert on child abuse, was born on 21 July 1918 at Fontana, 45 Rickmansworth Road, Watford, Hertfordshire, the eldest daughter of William Francis Cooper (1878–1950), analytical chemist and physician, and his wife, Christine Maud, *née* Jones (1894–1919). Tina, as she was affectionately known, was only six months old when her mother died of influenza; her stepmother, whom her father married in 1920, was Eileen, *née* Hall (1902–1976), her late mother's first cousin. The Cooper family was comfortably off, and Tina's upbringing, and that of her two stepsisters and unofficially adopted stepbrother, to whom she was very close, were entrusted to a strict but devoted nanny. The family moved to Surrey in 1924, the year that Tina started her formal education. She attended Keeldar, Kingston Hill, Surrey, from 1924 to 1927, Surbiton high school (1927–30), and St John's, Bexhill, to 1935, and then went to a finishing school, Beau Soleil, Lausanne, Switzerland (1935–6). Her subsequent training as a nursery nurse, at Cromwell House, Mothercraft Training Society, in Highgate, Middlesex, from 1936 to 1938, hardened Tina's resolve to contribute more significantly to the welfare of children, only achievable, she considered, via a career in medicine.

But her schooling was a poor foundation for a medical career, and it was hard work, resolve, and academic success at Apps and Thomas's crammer in Notting Hill, London, that gained Tina her place at Girton College, Cambridge, in 1939. A prizewinning undergraduate, she undertook her clinical training at the Royal Free Hospital, London, qualifying MB, BChir (Cantab.) in 1945. She subsequently held the posts of house physician, senior house officer in obstetrics, and finally first assistant in the children's department there. She was awarded the DCH (London) in 1948.

Paediatrics was, at this time, an underdeveloped speciality, but one in which Tina was determined to pursue a career, and in 1949, to the dismay of her family, she moved to

Newcastle upon Tyne as senior registrar to the distinguished paediatrician James Spence, in the department of child health at Newcastle General Hospital. By 1952 she had been appointed consultant, a post which she occupied with distinction until her retirement in 1983.

Throughout her medical career, and in the face of some criticism, Tina adhered to a philosophy of family orientated paediatrics, believing that childhood problems could not be assessed in isolation, and that account had to be taken of environmental and parental influences. She also had an enduring concern for the emotional as well as the physical needs of children, particularly those who were neglected or deprived, and in the 1960s this led her to examine the extent and nature of child abuse. She was apparently influenced by the seminal work of the American paediatrician C. H. Kempe, who in 1961 identified the abused child as a medical phenomenon as well as the victim of a crime often perpetrated by a parent or guardian. While many of her medical colleagues in Britain not only resisted Kempe's ideas, and were also reluctant to accept that child abuse was as widespread and damaging as his research indicated, Tina became one of the first child specialists in Britain to recognize the prevalence, and the physical, psychological, and sexual nature, of child abuse. With her close friend Alfred White Franklin she was a member of the original Tunbridge Wells study group on child abuse founded in 1973 which guided national policy in the 1970s. Other friends who were involved in the subject included Anna Freud and Dermod MacCarthy.

Renowned, indeed admired, for her boundless energy and seemingly inexhaustible capacity for work, Tina involved herself, alongside her post as consultant, with innumerable bodies concerned with the welfare of deprived and disadvantaged children. From 1960 she worked with the Association of British Adoption and Fostering Agencies and in 1969 was invited by the Home Office to sit on the departmental committee on adoption (the Houghton–Stockdale committee), contributing significantly to the report which formed the foundation of the 1975 Children's Act.

Tina was a founder member of both the British Association for the Prevention of Child Abuse and Neglect (BASPCAN), established in 1979, and the International Society for the Prevention of Child Abuse and Neglect, becoming the second chairman, after A. W. Franklin, of BASPCAN. The medical advisory committee of the National Society for the Prevention of Cruelty to Children benefited from her wide experience, as did the National Children's Bureau, the advisory panel of the National Foster Care Association, and the social committee of the Council of Europe, for whom she was a consultant expert on child abuse.

As a teacher Tina was inspirational, and her contributions to medical journals and books were considerable. Her skill as an expert witness was widely recognized, and gave her the opportunity to become involved in many access and custodial cases. Although unmarried herself,

she was an advocate of maternity leave for women doctors, and was able to use her position on the council of the Medical Women's Federation between 1970 and 1976 to champion this and other causes. Her concern for children extended beyond both social paediatrics and the British Isles: a two year secondment to Sierra Leone in 1964 earned Tina the OBE in 1967 for her work in establishing basic child health services throughout the country. In the words of a colleague there, 'She saved many lives and endeared herself to many by her directness, sympathy and warmth' (*BMJ*, 1109). She was elected FRCP in the same year.

Amazingly, Tina still found time to pursue her wide interests. She had a passion for, and deep understanding of music, particularly opera. She loved combining travel with work, but found cultural travel equally stimulating, and had an encyclopaedic knowledge of Venice and Florence. An avid reader, she had an extensive library of books on history, philosophy, art, and travel, most of which she had read. Her unique collection of works on the subject of child abuse and adoption were bequeathed to the Walton Library at the University of Newcastle upon Tyne.

Tina was a tall, attractive, and imposing woman, and although many who met her formally were awed by her presence, she was essentially a warm, caring person with infinite patience and empathy, and an extraordinary gift with children. Above all, she was deeply attached to her family, godchildren, and friends, and enjoyed nothing better than sharing a seaside holiday with them.

After her retirement in 1983 Tina continued the work she loved—consulting, advising, and lecturing—until just before she died, of cancer, at her home, 3 Kenton Road, Gosforth, Newcastle, on 1 September 1986. Her cremation took place on 8 September 1986, and her ashes were scattered in the churchyard of Gosforth church, Newcastle.

SUSAN L. COHEN

**Sources** Munk, *Roll* · M. Howell, *Medical Woman*, 5/3 (winter 1986), 20–21 · *Child Abuse Review*, 1/4 (winter 1986), 2 · F. Bamford, 'Dr Christine Cooper, an obituary', *Adoption and Fostering*, 10/4 (1986), 10 · *Medical Directory* (1986) · *The Lancet* (20 Sept 1986), 699 · *The Times* (6 Sept 1986), 17 · *BMJ* (25 Oct 1986), 1109–10 · K. T. Butler and H. I. McMorran, eds., *Girton College register, 1869–1946* (1948), 1.552 · private information (2004) [Dr R. Cooper, F. Slade] · H. Hendrick, *Child welfare, 1872–1989* (1994) · b. cert. · d. cert. · M. Jay and S. Doganis, *Battered: the abuse of children* (1987) · A. W. Franklin, ed., *Child abuse: prediction, prevention and follow-up* (1977)
**Likenesses** photograph, repro. in Howell, *Medical Woman*, 20
**Wealth at death** £121,223: probate, 7 Nov 1986, *CGPLA Eng. & Wales*

**Cooper, Christopher** (1655?–1698), schoolmaster and Church of England clergyman, was according to Dobson, probably born in 1655 as he 'would be about 20 when he took his BA' (Dobson, 1.281). Cooper's birthplace is unknown, but it could well have been Buntingford in north Hertfordshire, where on the basis of the dedication of his *Grammatica* to Seth Ward, the bishop of Salisbury, it is thought that he was a charity boy of the local poorhouse. As a young man he evidently caught the attention of the Buntingford-born bishop, for it was Ward who enabled Cooper to go up to Cambridge: Cooper matriculated and was admitted to Corpus Christi College in 1672. He received his BA degree in 1676, proceeded MA in 1680, and was incorporated at Oxford in 1694. On 21 May 1676 he was ordained deacon in London. In view of his later career, it is likely that he was the Cooper who preached a sermon at St Michael's, Bishop's Stortford, on 11 March 1684. By the time his *Grammatica* was published in 1685, Cooper had already become headmaster of Bishop's Stortford grammar school in east Hertfordshire, and on 11 March 1686 he became vicar of St Michael's in the same town.

Cooper was responsible for two published grammars: the *Grammatica linguae Anglicanae* (1685) and *The English Teacher* (1687). The second, a translation of two parts of the first, has little grammar, but a great deal on pronunciation: it is for this work that Cooper is hailed by Dobson as the greatest of the seventeenth-century phoneticians, on the basis of the completeness and accuracy of his systematic analysis of a southern dialect of English, which Cooper sees as being the most acceptable as a standard. Dobson attributes Cooper's lack of scholarly fame to the fact that he neither was innovatory, nor tried to discover universal principles, the vogue of the time. Instead he devoted himself to 'the practical task of teaching English pronunciation, spelling and grammar' (Dobson, 1.280). Although Cooper's phonetic system reflects the typical seventeenth-century desire for symmetry and is therefore flawed to modern eyes, he was sufficiently precise in his aim to provide the 'vim et rationem' ('force and account') of letters, in emulation of the linguist John Wallis, to recognize that the short variants of the close tense vowels were closer to e and o than to i and u (Cooper, *Grammatica*, sig. A5r). Similarly he provides evidence for the survival of an (ou) diphthong, at least in his own speech, longer than has been previously thought. This is not just a reflection of spelling, for, according to Dobson, Cooper 'holds that we should not attempt to follow the etymon if it leads us to prefer a spelling which represents the pronunciation less well than an existing alternative would do' (Dobson, 1.284). Cooper's vowel system is clearly dependent on Wallis's previous work, but takes into account both the modifications of intervening phoneticians and well-observed differences in his own speech. Cooper remained living at Bishop's Stortford until his death there in 1698.

R. D. SMITH

**Sources** E. J. Dobson, *English pronunciation, 1500–1700*, 2 vols. (1968) · Venn, *Alum. Cant.* · Foster, *Alum. Oxon.* · C. Cooper, *Grammatica linguae Anglicanae: peregrinis eam addiscendi cupidis pernecessaria, nec non Anglis praecipuè scholis plurimùm profutura. Cum praefatione & indice, in quibus, quid in hoc libello perficitur, videatur* (1685) · *Cooper's Grammatica linguae Anglicanae, 1685*, ed. J. D. Jones (1911) · *Christopher Cooper's English teacher, 1687*, ed. B. Sundby (1953) · I. Michael, *English grammatical categories and the tradition to 1800* (1970)

**Cooper, Daniel** (1785–1853), merchant, was born at Bolton, Lancashire, one of at least two sons of Thomas Cooper and his first wife, Hannah. Little is known of his early life but in 1815 Cooper was convicted of theft and transported for life to the penal colony of New South Wales. He arrived in Sydney in 1816, and was granted a conditional pardon in 1818 which was made absolute in 1821. In 1819 he married Hannah Dodd (d. 1836), a fellow convict who had been sentenced to sixteen years' transportation in 1816. There were no children of the marriage.

Cooper opened a general store in Sydney, from which he diversified into shipping and brewing. In 1821 he became a partner in the firm of Hutchison, Terry & Co., which expanded from flour milling into general merchandising and banking. Cooper and another former convict, Solomon Levey, took over the firm in 1825, each investing £30,000. Levey had been sentenced to seven years' transportation in 1813, and had arrived in Sydney in 1815. He was granted an absolute pardon in 1819, when he married Ann, the daughter of William Roberts, a wealthy emancipist. Although she left Levey, her dowry allowed him to build up a flourishing business in real estate, retailing, shipbroking, sealing, rope making, and grazing. He was also a leading figure in the formation of the Bank of New South Wales, of which Cooper became a director in 1828. The firm of Cooper and Levey subsequently became a major merchant house in Sydney, combining a large retail trade with the import of goods and the export of wool, as well as having related interests as shipowners, shipping agents, and whalers. Both Cooper and Levey invested much of their profits in extensive holdings of land, which placed them among the largest squatters and holders of stock in New South Wales.

Expansion of the firm demanded a closer connection with London, in order to purchase goods for export to Sydney and to provide trade credit, a similar need to that faced by F. G. Dalgety. In 1826 Levey settled in London, with the purpose of opening a branch there, but he made the disastrous mistake in 1829 of joining Thomas Peel as a partner in his ill-fated scheme to develop the Swan River in Western Australia. Levey supplied £20,000 capital to the abortive venture. Fortunately for Cooper, much of his wealth was invested outside the firm in real estate, and he was able to escape from the crisis caused by Levey's ill-judged speculation. As a result Cooper took on new partners in Sydney, and returned to England in 1831 in order to purchase goods and to arrange shipping. Eventually the difficulties caused by Levey's involvement with Peel were resolved, in 1843, when Cooper reached a settlement with John Levey-Roberts, the son of Solomon Levey, who had opted for a life of leisure in Paris. Cooper died of disease of the heart at the Gloucester Hotel, Gloucester Place, Brighton, on 3 November 1853.

The bulk of Cooper's estate was left to his nephew, **Sir Daniel Cooper**, first baronet (1821–1902), merchant and philanthropist. The younger Daniel Cooper was also born at Bolton, Lancashire, on 1 July 1821, and he was the second son in the family of five sons and four daughters of his uncle's brother, Thomas Cooper, merchant, and his wife, Jane Ramsden. He emigrated to Sydney with his parents and then returned to London in 1835 to complete his education at University College School. Although he intended to become a lawyer, he abandoned his studies in 1841 as a result of ill health.

After a period with a Franco-American firm in Le Havre, Cooper joined his uncle's business in London in 1842. In the following year he became a partner in his brother-in-law's merchant house in Sydney, which he took over with his elder brother in 1848. He became sole proprietor of Cooper Brothers in 1852, which was by now one of the leading merchant houses in the city. Cooper prospered from the gold rush and owned considerable property in Sydney as well as extensive grazing lands. He was also a director of the Sydney Railway Company and of the Bank of New South Wales from 1847. He married Elizabeth Hill in 1846, and they had two sons and three daughters. His uncle's fortune and his own wealth made him a significant figure in New South Wales, where he became a leading Liberal member of the legislative council and assembly, serving as speaker between 1856 and 1860. In 1856 he started to construct Woolhara House, on the estate acquired by his uncle. He joined the senate of the University of Sydney in 1857, and was knighted in the same year.

Cooper returned permanently to England in 1861, and became much occupied with philanthropic activities. He gave generously to support the families of those killed in the Crimean War, and in the early 1860s he helped to organize relief funds for distressed textile-workers during the Lancashire cotton famine. Depicted as 'a little man—serene, smiling and graceful', Cooper had a broad and pale forehead. 'Looking at that head one could swear its owner was a heavy subscriber to Bethal Unions and a victim of begging letters' (Martin, 452). In 1863 he was raised to the baronetcy for his public services during the Lancashire distress and took Woolhara as his title.

Cooper also served as agent-general for New South Wales in England, and he was a leading participant in the controversies over the operation of the wool market in the early 1870s. The colonial sheep farmers were at this time attempting to wrest control of the wool market from their London consignees, which brought Cooper into conflict with Dalgety, the largest of the London-based wool importers. Dalgety denounced Cooper as a 'little Sydney blaguard' (Dalgety to Nichols, 10 Aug 1871), who was 'thoroughly unscrupulous, untruthful and pertinacious' (Dalgety to Blackwood, 5 Oct 1871). Dalgety was considerably annoyed by suggestions that the brokers and merchants in London were robbing and exploiting the colonial growers, and he fumed that

> Never in the annals of Commerce of London had there been a more disgraceful and dastardly attack … on a respectable body of men as that made by Sir Daniel Cooper, who merited the contempt and scorn of every right minded man for his conduct…. Yet in the Colonies he appears to have gained the admiration and gratitude of the Squatters … by his mendacity and trickery. (Dalgety to secretary of the Melbourne chamber of commerce, 10 Aug 1871, Australian National University, archives of business and labour, N39/42)

Dalgety and Cooper represented the change taking place in the operation of the wool market in the 1870s. Private partnerships such as Dalgety's firm faced increasing

difficulties in securing sufficient credit to provide funds to the squatters in the colonies, and to cover the sale of wool in London. By contrast Cooper represented the Bank of New South Wales, which had access to credit on more favourable terms; he marked the incursion into the City of London of colonial banks and pastoral finance houses. As well as acting as the agent-general for New South Wales in London, in 1881 Cooper was chairman of the London committee of the Sydney International Exhibition. He was appointed KCMG in 1880 and GCMG in 1888. Sir Daniel Cooper died at his London home, 6 De Vere Gardens, Kensington, on 5 June 1902. He was survived by his wife.

MARTIN DAUNTON

Sources J. W. Davidson, 'Cooper, Daniel', AusDB, vol. 1 · A. W. Martin, 'Cooper, Sir Daniel', AusDB, vol. 3 · G. F. J. Bergman, 'Levey, Solomon', AusDB, vol. 2 · R. F. Holder, Bank of New South Wales: a history, 1 (1970) · A. Barnard, The Australian wool market, 1840–1900 (1958) · M. J. Daunton, 'Firm and family in the City of London in the nineteenth century: the case of F. G. Dalgety', Historical Research, 62 (1989), 154–77 · d. cert. · d. cert. [Daniel Cooper] · F. C. Dalgety to C. Nichols, 10 Aug 1871, Australian National University, Canberra, Archives of Business and Labour, N39/42 · F. C. Dalgety to J. Blackwood, 5 Oct 1871, Australian National University, Canberra, Archives of Business and Labour, N39/42

Archives Bodl. Oxf., MSS Eng.a 2013–14, Eng.b.2047–9, Eng.c.3933–4514, Eng.d.2439–92, Eng.e.2790–7

Wealth at death £440,000—Daniel Cooper: AusDB · £150,531 2s. 2d.—Daniel Cooper: probate, 23 Aug 1902, CGPLA Eng. & Wales

**Cooper, Daniel** (1816/17–1842), naturalist, was born at 82 Blackfriars Road, Lambeth, the second son of John Thomas *Cooper (1790–1854), a teacher of chemistry at a private medical school and well known in London scientific circles, and his wife, Elizabeth ( fl. 1785–1840). He was intended for a medical career like two of his brothers, and was accepted for pupillage by a local physician, James Forbes Young, who shared and fostered his enthusiasm for natural history and for field botany especially. This enthusiasm led to Cooper's precocious authorship in 1836 of *Flora metropolitana*, a guide to the best places round London for botanical rarities (and for land and freshwater molluscs).

That same summer Cooper was chiefly instrumental in the founding of the Botanical Society of London. A frequent contributor of papers and exhibits to its early meetings, as initial honorary curator it fell to him to realize the society's central function as an agency for the postal exchange of dried specimens for herbaria. From the thousands of these sent in a selection had to be made, after sorting and relabelling, for a return parcel proportionate in size and interest to that sent. Cooper was through inexperience unequal to this very demanding task, and put into currency as a result numerous erroneous records which his successor, H. C. Watson, was to succeed in eliminating with only limited success.

Seeking to make a living as a naturalist, Cooper had meanwhile taken on numerous lecturing and writing commitments, including editing the short-lived *Microscopic Journal*, an abstracts service which he over-optimistically calculated would be rendered viable by the patronage of the recently founded Microscopical Society of London. A temporary post in the zoology department of the British Museum, assisting with its invertebrate collections, provided a further financial crutch. Having qualified as a surgeon, however, he decided to settle for the more secure and leisure existence offered by medical service in the army. Within just a few months, after joining a cavalry regiment at Leeds, phlebitis brought on by a slight injury led to his death at the barracks, at the age of only twenty-five, on 23 November 1842. He was buried at Quarry Hill church, Leeds, on 28 November. He is not known to have married.        D. E. ALLEN

**Sources** D. E. Allen, *The botanists: a history of the Botanical Society of the British Isles through a hundred and fifty years*, St Paul's Bibliographies (1986), 11–24 · *Microscopic Journal* (1842), 351–2 · *Annals and Magazine of Natural History*, 10 (1842), 419 · *Proceedings of the Linnean Society of London*, 1 (1838–48), 173 · J. F. Waller, ed., *The imperial dictionary of universal biography*, 3 vols. (1857–63)
**Archives** Museum of Holmesdale Natural History Club, Reigate, herbarium of J. A. Brewer, about 50 botanical specimens

**Cooper, Sir Daniel**, first baronet (1821–1902). *See under* Cooper, Daniel (1785–1853).

**Cooper, Sir (Francis) D'Arcy**, baronet (1882–1941), industrialist, was born in London on 17 November 1882, the only son of Francis *Cooper (1845/6–1893), chartered accountant [*see under* Cooper family (*per.* 1854–1994)], and his wife, Ada Frances, daughter of Henry Power, surgeon. Educated at Wellington College and on the continent, he was articled in the family firm, Cooper Brothers & Co., becoming a partner in 1910. On 3 June 1913 he married Evelyn Hilda Mary, daughter of Arthur Locke Radford, of Bovey House, Beer, Devon. Cooper enlisted in the army in 1915, received a commission in the Royal Field Artillery, and was badly wounded on the Somme. Later he served at the War Office before returning to his firm, where he rapidly established a reputation as one of the ablest members of his profession.

For many years Cooper Brothers & Co. had been auditors for Lever Brothers, which by 1920 was the largest company manufacturing oils and fats in the British empire, with extensive interests in many parts of the world. During the post-war boom, Lord Leverhulme had enormously expanded his business, not least by the purchase of other concerns, notably the Niger Company, and the slump of 1920 brought serious financial difficulties. Finding himself in 1921 under pressure from the banks, who were his principal creditors, Leverhulme called in Cooper who was able to retrieve a desperate situation. From then onwards Cooper's prestige in the Lever business steadily increased: in 1923 he became a director and joint vice-chairman, and within a week of Leverhulme's death in 1925 he was appointed chairman.

Cooper shirked no measures, however unpopular, which he deemed necessary to restore stability and confidence, and by 1929 he had achieved a large measure of success. In that year he completed complicated negotiations with the Margarine Union, the largest continental manufacturers of oils and fats. The business that emerged, under the name of Unilever, was one of the largest in the world. Much of the credit for its creation must go

to Cooper's patient and resolute diplomacy. No less remarkable was his success in reorganizing the new concern and guiding it through the economic troubles of the thirties. To weld into a unity a number of former competitors of several different nationalities was an arduous process, but he would allow no personal considerations or old affiliations to stand in the way of complete unification. Beginning with little technical knowledge he showed a swift mastery of detail and a genius for shaping and executing policy, which earned him the respect of his new colleagues.

Had it not been for Cooper, the Lever business might well have shared a fate that has often befallen the creations of dynamic personalities who have failed to provide against their own decline or economic changes. Cooper's qualities, notably of judgement and foresight, became increasingly indispensable to business enterprise during the twenties. By substituting an orderly system of management for personal autocracy, Cooper proved himself a leading member of the rising class of professional managers of large-scale business.

Tall and powerfully built, Cooper possessed a natural habit of command which compelled respect. But he had also an unaffected humanity and a simple hatred of anything savouring of dishonesty, which endeared him to those who worked with him. He was, said Leverhulme, one of those men who 'most resemble a warm fire and people naturally come up to him for warmth', and he had a gift for developing a sense of responsibility in subordinates. As Cooper overcame his natural shyness, his humour and a sense of style, derived from a love of good literature, made him an effective and engaging speaker. Believing that the conduct of modern business called for the best talent available, he gave valuable service as a member of the Cambridge University appointments board (1929–40) and did much to strengthen ties between the universities and industry. He received honours from Norway and Belgium, countries with which the Lever business had important connections, and also from Bulgaria. In the years immediately before the Second World War his services were increasingly in demand in connection with government economic policy and from 1940 he was principally occupied as chairman of the executive committee of the Export Council of the Board of Trade. He paid a useful visit to the United States in the autumn and was created a baronet in 1941. The Coopers had no children and the baronetcy became extinct when Cooper died at his home, Westridge, Coppice Lane, Reigate, on 18 December 1941.        CHARLES WILSON, *rev.*

**Sources** C. Wilson, *The history of Unilever: a study in economic growth and social change*, 2 vols. (1954) · *Port Sunlight News* (Oct 1936) · *Port Sunlight News* (May 1938) · private information (1959) · d. cert.
**Archives** Bodl. RH, corresp. with Lord Lugard
**Likenesses** G. Harcourt, oils, 1936, Unilever House, Blackfriars, London
**Wealth at death** £648,012 4s. 4d.: probate, 9 March 1942, *CGPLA Eng. & Wales*

**Cooper** [*née* Manners], **Diana Olivia Winifred Maud** [*known as* Lady Diana Cooper], **Viscountess Norwich**

**Diana Olivia Winifred Maud Cooper** [Lady Diana Cooper], **Viscountess Norwich** (1892–1986), by Emil Otto Hoppé, 1916

(1892–1986), actress, society hostess, and author, was born on 29 August 1892 in London into the Manners family where she was accepted as the third of three daughters and the fifth of five children. Her assumed father was Henry John Brinsley Manners, marquess of Granby, later eighth duke of Rutland MP (1852–1925), and her mother was (Marion Margaret) Violet (1856–1937) [see Manners, (Marion Margaret) Violet], artist, daughter of Colonel Charles Hugh Lindsay. It was generally believed, and certainly by Diana, that her true father was Henry John Cockayne (Harry) *Cust (1861–1917), politician, journalist, and brother of the fifth Baron Brownlow. She received no formal education, but was educated at home by governesses and the culture of her surroundings. She learned much, including great drifts of poetry, which she remembered to her dying day. In her voluminous correspondence and in the drafts for her books, her prose was vivid and imaginative, and her idiosyncratic spelling added to its charm.

At ten years old, Diana contracted Urb's disease, a form of paralysis, and for five years was a semi-invalid. She never complained, but, because of her illness, was certainly over-indulged by the family. In 1910 she formally came out and took her place at the centre of that so-called golden generation, soon so largely to perish in war. At this time her beauty was first acknowledged. She was hailed 'queen of beauty', but also acquired some notoriety. She and her immediate circle dubbed themselves the 'corrupt coterie', and lived their lives of privilege to the full and sometimes to excess. Diana was much criticized when, at a party on the Thames in 1914, Sir Dennis Anson swam for a dare and was drowned; this tragedy haunted her all her

life. When the First World War came in 1914, Diana Manners trained as a member of the voluntary aid detachment at Guy's Hospital. She was hard-working and conscientious, and acted as a nurse at Guy's and at the hospital established by her parents in their London house in Arlington Street.

Diana had many suitors and mourned the deaths of several of them in the fighting. (Alfred) Duff *Cooper (1890–1954), at first in the Foreign Office and then in the Grenadier Guards, was among her most ardent admirers. In 1916 she promised to marry him, but was prevented by lack of money and opposition from her ambitious mother. Even the DSO, to which Duff Cooper was appointed in 1918, failed to overcome this opposition. Eventually, however, agreement was given and they were married on 2 June 1919. It was a marriage which never staled. Diana had many who loved her and Duff was frequently unfaithful; but for each the relationship with the other remained the most important thing in their lives.

To earn money Diana acted in two unmemorable films before her marriage and gained the reputation of a hard-working actress as well as a transcendent beauty. Marriage and Duff Cooper's wish to enter politics increased the need for money and Diana was glad to accept Max Reinhardt's offer to play the Madonna in a mime play, *The Miracle*. This was first staged in the USA from November 1923 to the following May, and again for the following three autumns and winters. It toured Europe in 1927, and London and the provinces in 1932; the last performance was in January 1933. *The Miracle* was a phenomenal success, and Diana Cooper's triumphant part in it was remembered as long as she lived. The money earned allowed her husband to enter parliament, as MP for Oldham, in 1924.

On 15 September 1929 Diana had a son, John Julius. He was her only child and she took a close and intelligent interest in his education. Once *The Miracle* was ended, she was primarily concerned with her husband's career rather than her own, and she gave him powerful support, as chatelaine of Admiralty House (Duff Cooper became first lord of the Admiralty in May 1937). There she first had the opportunity to display her outstanding talent as a hostess in a splendid setting. In the 1930s the Coopers were friendly with Edward VIII and Mrs Simpson and accompanied them on the cruise of the *Nahlin* in 1936. They were spoken of as belonging to Mrs Simpson's camp, but this was never the case.

Diana supported Duff throughout the Second World War, even accompanying him to Singapore and the Far East against convention, and in the face of opposition. When in Britain, they lived in the Dorchester Hotel and at Bognor in a house given to Diana by her mother, where she found complete happiness running a smallholding farm. In January 1944 Duff Cooper became British representative to the French committee of liberation in Algiers and in November British ambassador in Paris. His wife was unfailingly at his side; her French was fluent but inaccurate, and she was by no means a conventional ambassadress, but she gave the embassy a glamour possessed by none other. With her remarkable ability to get on with people, she collected a group of artists and writers known as 'La Bande'; it was said with criticism that some of them had collaborated with the Germans. While at the embassy Diana Cooper discovered and rented the house 'she loved best in the world', the Château St Firman at Chantilly. On leaving the embassy at the end of 1947, contrary to convention and to the aggravation of their successors, the Coopers returned to live at Chantilly.

In 1952 Duff Cooper was created Viscount Norwich, but Diana would have none of it, announcing in *The Times* that she wished to retain her former name and title, so Lady Diana Cooper she remained. In 1953 Duff Cooper was taken violently ill; he recovered, but died on 1 January 1954 on a cruise to Jamaica. He was buried at Belvoir Castle, but Diana did not attend the funeral: she never attended the funerals of those she loved. Her life had been centred round Duff for thirty-five years, and she was distraught without him.

Diana lived for a further thirty-two years. She disliked getting old, but found solace in writing a three-volume autobiography, which was a resounding success. She gained much comfort from John Julius, her grandchildren, and her many friends. She retained her love of travel and her interest in people: she still enjoyed each new experience, even, it seemed, two burglaries, when she displayed her courage and her enduring star quality. She is remembered mostly for her outstanding beauty, but for most people this obscured the fact that she was a shy, very clever, and sometimes extremely funny woman. She died on 16 June 1986, at her London home, 10 Warwick Avenue.                    CHARTERIS OF AMISFIELD, *rev.*

**Sources** P. Ziegler, *Diana Cooper* (1981) · D. Cooper, *The rainbow comes and goes* (1958) · D. Cooper, *The light of common day* (1959) · D. Cooper, *Trumpets from the steep* (1960) · *The Times* (17 June 1986) · *CGPLA Eng. & Wales* (1987)

**Archives** BL, corresp., Add. MSS 70704–70720 | HLRO, corresp. with Lord Beaverbrook

**Likenesses** E. O. Hoppé, photograph, 1916, NPG [*see illus.*] · photographs, 1923?–1944, Hult. Arch.; *see illus. in* Reinhardt, Max (1873–1943) · B. MacKennal, bronze bust, National Gallery of Australia

**Wealth at death** £172,971: probate, 8 Oct 1987, *CGPLA Eng. & Wales*

**Cooper, (Arthur William) Douglas** (1911–1984), art historian and collector, was born at 49 Sloane Gardens, Chelsea, London, on 20 February 1911, the first of three sons (there were no daughters) of Arthur Hamilton Cooper, captain in the Essex regiment and of independent means, and his wife, Mabel Alice Smith-Marriott. His parents were British, but the family fortune had been made, generations back, in Australia. His estrangement from his national background was to constitute a lifelong theme. He chose to live in France for much of his adult life and was always severely critical of the British for what he saw as their ignorance about and failure to patronize the great art of the twentieth century.

Cooper was educated at Repton School, Derbyshire, and at Trinity College, Cambridge, where in 1930 he obtained a third class in the French section and a second (division 2)

in the German section of the modern and medieval languages tripos. He then went briefly to the Sorbonne and to the University of Freiburg, concentrating on the study of art history. In 1932 he decided to devote one third of his inheritance to the creation of an art collection which would represent the development of the four major cubist artists—Pablo Picasso, Georges Braque, Juan Gris, and Fernand Léger—from 1906 to 1914. He proceeded to build his collection with such alacrity and concentration that it was essentially formed by 1945.

Cooper's early experiences in the Second World War, serving with a French ambulance unit, are recorded in *The Road to Bordeaux* (1940), written with Denis Freeman. Subsequently he obtained a commission with the Royal Air Force, working in intelligence and (drawing upon his linguistic skills) interrogation. From 1944 to 1946 he was deputy director of the monuments and fine arts branch of the Allied Control Commission for Germany, helping to identify, protect, and repatriate works of art.

Cooper's residences in London included 8 Groom Place (decorated with furniture designed by the painter Francis Bacon), and 18 Egerton Terrace (shared with Basil Amulree, a noted gerontologist and a friend since Cambridge days). It was in 1949, while on holiday with Lord Amulree and an art historian, John Richardson, that Cooper discovered and subsequently purchased the dilapidated Château de Castille in Argilliers, Gard. That grand eighteenth-century house, filled with Cooper's impressive collection and animated by his own colourful and controversial personality, became a popular end to a pilgrimage for members of the art world. Léger was among the first house guests; Picasso was a neighbour in the south of France and a frequent visitor. In 1954 Cooper published a catalogue of the art collection of the industrialist Samuel Courtauld. His introduction reveals that he viewed this collector of post-impressionism as a role model, imitating his concentration on a single school in his own focus on the cubists. However, he also collected major groups of works by Paul Klee and Joan Miró and works by other modern artists (many of whom he knew personally), including César, Cocteau, Giacometti, Guttuso, Hockney, Hugo, Marini, Masson, Matisse, Modigliani, De Staël, Graham Sutherland, and Ubac. Later works of Braque (*Atelier VIII*, for example), Léger, and Picasso also formed part of the collection. In 1963 five drawings by Picasso, including three studies relating to Manet's *Déjeuner sur l'herbe*, were executed in enlarged format, in concrete and stone, on a loggia wall in the garden of Castille.

Cooper's was by no means an easy personality and even his friendships often had bitter endings. His lifelong friendship with Picasso concluded in alienation, capped rather tragically (even after the artist's death) with a vicious commentary on his late work exhibited in Avignon in 1973. Cooper's campaign in the 1950s against the Tate Gallery and its director, Sir John Rothenstein—whom he accused of favouring English above contemporary French art—was so sustained that it provoked the hard-pressed Rothenstein into a physical assault on his critic at a public function. Contentiousness characterizes many of his numerous reviews and letters which frequently appeared in the *Burlington Magazine* and the *Times Literary Supplement*. A prolific and formidable scholar and critic, in his early years he wrote under the pseudonym Douglas Lord. His contributions to the study of cubism remain landmarks in that field. His bibliography includes, notably, *Fernand Léger et le nouvel espace* (1949), *Pablo Picasso: les déjeuners* (1962), *Picasso, théâtre* (1967), and *Juan Gris: catalogue raisonné de l'œuvre peint* (1977). He also organized numerous important exhibitions culminating in two extraordinary presentations: 'The cubist epoch' at the Los Angeles County Museum and the Metropolitan Museum in 1970, and 'The Essential Cubism' at the Tate Gallery in 1983. He wrote extensively about other nineteenth-century and twentieth-century artists, including Klee, Degas, Turner, and Van Gogh.

Cooper was a lecturer at the Courtauld Institute, Slade professor of fine art at Oxford (1957–8), and Flexner lecturer at Bryn Mawr (1961). His honours included membership in the Real Patronato of the Prado Museum and he was made a chevalier of the Légion d'honneur. He died on 1 April 1984 in the Royal Free Hospital, Camden, London. He was unmarried but in 1972 he had adopted a son, William Augustine McCarty-Cooper, aged thirty-five.

DOROTHY KOSINSKI

**Sources** D. Kosinski, *Douglas Cooper und die Meister des Kubismus* (1987–8) [exhibition catalogue, Kunst Museum, Basel, and Tate Gallery, London] · J. Richardson, 'Remembering Douglas Cooper', *New York Review of Books* (25 April 1985), 24–6 · D. Kosinski, *Picasso, Braque, Gris, Léger, Douglas Cooper collecting cubism* (Houston, 1990) [exhibition catalogue, Museum of Fine Arts, Houston] · 'Douglas Cooper, British art historian', *Annual Obituary* (1984), 210–11 · R. Shone, 'Douglas Cooper: unpublished letters to the editor', *Burlington Magazine*, 128 (1986), 481–3 · d. cert.
**Archives** Getty Research Institute for the History of Art and the Humanities, Los Angeles, corresp. and papers | Tate collection, corresp. with John Banting [corresp. relating to Unit One] · TCD, corresp. with Thomas Bodkin

**Cooper, (Alfred) Duff**, first Viscount Norwich (1890–1954), diplomatist and politician, was born at 9 Henrietta Street, Cavendish Square, London, on 22 February 1890. His father, Sir Alfred *Cooper (1838–1908), was a fashionable London surgeon who specialized in the sexual problems of the upper classes and was celebrated for his skill, discretion, and conviviality. Dr Cooper in 1882 married Lady Agnes Cecil Emmeline Flower (1852–1925), sister of the first duke of Fife. Lady Agnes was an adventurous lady who had already eloped with two husbands; one of them she deserted, the other died. The marriage produced four children who survived to maturity, three girls and finally Duff (as he was always known: the name Alfred was never used).

**Education, Foreign Office, and marriage** After unhappy passages at two preparatory schools Duff Cooper went to Eton College, where he enjoyed himself greatly without achieving any particular distinction. His prodigious memory and precocious literary skills enabled him to gain respectable academic results without too much hard

(Alfred) Duff Cooper, first Viscount Norwich (1890–1954), by Man Ray, 1930s

work, and the same proved true at New College, Oxford, where he got a second-class degree in history (1911) and narrowly missed a first. More importantly, to his mind at least, at Eton and Oxford he made close friends among a group of young men who were intelligent, cultivated, notably self-indulgent, and for the most part high-born. With them he learned to drink too much, gamble for stakes higher than he could afford, and pursue beautiful women—tastes which he cherished throughout his life and which brought him vast pleasure. Almost all these friends were to die in the First World War.

After two abortive efforts, Cooper passed into the Foreign Office in October 1913. When war was declared he was working in the commercial department; neither this, nor the contraband department in which he also served, entertained or stimulated him. He did not actively seek to escape from the Foreign Office to do military service, but when in June 1917 he was released to join the army he welcomed the opportunity. 'I am not afraid of death', he wrote in his diary at the time, 'though I love life and should hate to lose it' (Duff Cooper, *Old Men Forget*, 61).

This nevertheless seemed the most probable outcome, for the life expectancy of a subaltern in the Grenadier Guards was short indeed. Cooper spent only six months at the front, but this was long enough for him to prove himself exceptionally courageous, resourceful, and a natural leader of men. In the allied advance on the Albert Canal in August 1918 he acquired both a minor wound and, most unusually for a second lieutenant, the DSO. He left the army with relief but also with great distinction.

Cooper returned to the Foreign Office, shone, and after a

period in the Egyptian department became private secretary to the parliamentary under-secretary. Far from satisfying him, this promotion merely fed the appetite he had been nurturing ever since he became a diplomatist: to leave the Foreign Office and enter politics. Only a lack of money held him back. Salvation came through his wife. On 2 June 1919, in spite of much initial opposition from her family, he had married Lady Diana Manners [see Cooper, Diana Olivia Winifred Maud (1892–1986)], formally daughter of the eighth duke of Rutland but in the view of most people, including herself, child of the notorious philanderer and literary eminence Harry Cust. Lady Diana was one of the great beauties of the age and a woman of striking intelligence and wit. Their marriage was sublimely happy if by conventional standards irregular. Duff Cooper was endlessly promiscuous, and his wife endlessly tolerant, secure in her certainty that, however often he might stray, she was unchallenged as the most important woman in his life.

**Politician and biographer** Lady Diana was eager to see her husband launched on a political career, but her financial resources were equally limited. Then, in 1923, she was engaged to play the part of the Madonna in Max Reinhardt's extravagant pantomime *The Miracle*. The rewards for her work were substantial, sufficient to embolden Cooper to leave the Foreign Office. In July 1924 he resigned; within three months he had been adopted as Conservative candidate for the two-member constituency of Oldham and returned triumphantly with a majority of several hundred over the Liberal candidate, Edward Grigg, and of 13,000 over the sitting Labour member.

It was quickly clear that Cooper was not for long to remain a humble back-bencher. His maiden speech—on the Egyptian question—was a spectacular success; 'Brilliant' said H. A. L. Fisher, who followed him in the debate, 'perfect in form and distinguished by a liberality and generosity of spirit' (Charmley, 46). He was soon accepted as one of the more formidable debaters and orators among the younger Conservatives and was mentioned with such figures as Anthony Eden and Harold Macmillan as a coming man on the liberal wing of the party. In January 1928 he was appointed financial secretary to the War Office—not the job he would have chosen, but fortunate for him in that his easy-going secretary of state, Sir Laming Worthington-Evans, was happy to allow him a considerable degree of independence. If the Conservatives had remained in power he would probably soon have won promotion, but he was to enjoy little more than a year in office; at the general election in the spring of 1929 Labour became the largest party and Cooper was one of the many Conservatives who lost their seats.

Defeat had its consolations. Duff Cooper had long been attracted by the personality and career of Talleyrand, and resolved to devote some of his newly gained leisure to writing a biography of the French statesman. Rarely can subject and author have been more satisfactorily matched: Cooper shared Talleyrand's scepticism, his broadness of vision, his intelligence, his dislike of cant, and, above all, the pleasure he got from the more civilized features of social life. Cooper wrote slowly, but with considerable panache and elegance, and rarely needed substantially to revise his earliest draft. It was 1932 before the book was published, but it was then received with great enthusiasm, has been constantly reprinted, and, though not the fruit of prolonged historical research, is still considered one of the most illuminating and enjoyable of twentieth-century biographies.

Success carried its own hazards. The executors of Earl Haig's estate were inspired by it to invite Cooper to take on the official biography of the field marshal. The assignment was financially rewarding but not suited to Cooper's talents; when it appeared in two volumes in 1935 and 1936 it was widely criticized for being inadequately considered and being biased in favour of its subject. The years in opposition, however, bore other fruits; in September 1929, after ten years of marriage, Diana Cooper produced a son, John Julius. He was the only child.

**War Office, Admiralty, and resignation over Munich** In March 1931 Cooper returned to the House of Commons after a by-election in the St George's division of Westminster. No one doubted that a Conservative would be returned for this seat, but the prime minister, Stanley Baldwin, had many enemies in the party, notably the empire free traders backed by the press barons, lords Beaverbrook and Rothermere, and these were running an 'independent Conservative' candidate, Ernest Petter. It was a bitter campaign, marked by Baldwin's denunciation of the press barons as wanting 'power without responsibility, the prerogative of the harlot throughout the ages'. At the end of it Cooper emerged triumphant with a majority of nearly 6000.

Within a few months Cooper was back in office, once again at the War Office, as under-secretary to the aged and fainéant Lord Crewe. He shone sufficiently to earn a transfer in June 1934 to the Treasury as financial secretary, traditionally accepted as a staging post on the way to the cabinet. This brought him into close contact with the then chancellor, Neville Chamberlain, who, according to Sidney Herbert, 'valued your judgment and wise reticence' and was 'full of optimism about your future' (Charmley, 77). But Chamberlain also saw reason to warn him to be less vehement in his denunciations of Nazi Germany. Cooper had recently visited Germany, had attended a Nuremberg rally, and had been appalled and alarmed by what he saw. He warned Churchill that Hitler was preparing for war and continually urged the need for rearmament at a time when this was unfashionable if not politically incorrect.

After the general election of November 1935 Cooper was appointed to the cabinet as secretary of state for war and was sworn of the privy council. He was one of the few cabinet ministers who Edward VIII felt was sympathetic to his cause in the abdication crisis of 1936. Cooper urged the king to avoid a confrontation with the government until after his coronation and was prepared to contemplate the possibility of a morganatic marriage, ideas which held no appeal for Baldwin and Chamberlain. Both temperamentally and politically Cooper felt himself increasingly at odds with the Conservative leadership, and he was pleasantly surprised when in May 1937 Chamberlain became prime minister and invited him to become first lord of the Admiralty. In this post he proved an unequivocal success: he relished the opportunities it afforded for high living aboard the official yacht *Enchantress* but also worked hard on the nuts and bolts of naval affairs and fought the navy's corner against the parsimonious chancellor of the exchequer, John Simon. Chamberlain increasingly viewed him as an indiscreet and belligerent firebrand, and Cooper was already largely isolated in the cabinet before the Munich crisis brought matters to a head.

In autumn 1938 Chamberlain returned from a meeting with Hitler bearing 'peace with honour' at the price of the dismemberment of Czechoslovakia. In Cooper's view the peace would be only transitory and the dishonour so gross that he could not bear to be associated with it. On 3 October he denounced the Munich agreement in the House of Commons and resigned from the government. Arguments over the merits and demerits of appeasement continue to rage, but no one has ever disputed that Cooper's action was high-principled and courageous and involved great personal sacrifices, both political and financial.

On the back benches once more, Cooper joined the Conservative dissidents who were grouped loosely around the former foreign secretary, Anthony Eden. His opposition to the government was muted, and his weekly articles for the *Evening Standard*—his main source of income during this period—were more concerned with the need for a strong Anglo-French alliance at the heart of a united western Europe than with such issues as appeasement. When war broke out and Churchill joined the government, Cooper was offered no job; instead he left for the United States on an extensive lecture tour in which he propagandized vigorously for the cause of the democratic powers.

**Office under Churchill** Among other things Cooper predicted that Hitler would attack through Belgium in 1940 and that Churchill would subsequently become prime minister. At the time the prophecy seemed far-fetched, but when it was fulfilled in May he found himself recalled to power as minister of information. It was not a task that he relished, and his discomfiture was made worse by the hostility of the press, who portrayed him as the enemy of free speech and an arch—if ineffective—spin-doctor. When he tried to establish the state of popular morale his investigators were called 'Cooper's snoopers' and the enterprise was generally derided; his term in office is best remembered for his outspoken arraignment of P. G. Wodehouse, who had made some singularly ill-advised but essentially harmless broadcasts on the German radio from Berlin. It was a great relief to Cooper when, in July 1941, he was appointed chancellor of the duchy of Lancaster, traditionally the odd-job man of the cabinet.

Cooper's odd job took him to Singapore on an ill-defined mission which led to his appointment, after the Japanese attack on Pearl Harbor in December 1941, as resident cabinet minister with responsibility for Far Eastern affairs. He was authorized to form a war cabinet but found neither the civil nor the military authorities disposed to accept his leadership and was pleased when Wavell's appointment as supreme commander made his continued presence in Singapore unnecessary. He had been given neither the powers nor the time to affect the situation but returned to Britain to find himself unfairly associated in the public mind with the defeats in south-east Asia and the abject surrender of Singapore. For the next eighteen months he was under-employed, serving as chairman of the cabinet committee on security but free to devote much time to his writing and to weekends at Bognor, where his wife busied herself with the running of a small-holding.

From this relative inactivity Cooper was rescued by an invitation to take on a task which was close to his heart and which was to occupy him for the rest of his professional career. In December 1943 he was appointed British representative to the French committee of national liberation in Algiers, on the understanding that he would be the first post-war ambassador in Paris as soon as events made this possible. His most urgent and enduring responsibility was to maintain a working partnership with the Free French leader, General de Gaulle, and in particular to patch up the often turbulent relations between de Gaulle and Churchill. Cooper found de Gaulle exceedingly difficult to deal with but considered Churchill almost equally impossible; it is greatly to his credit that at the operating level the relationship between the two governments remained more or less satisfactory.

**Ambassador to France** In September 1944 Cooper moved to Paris, and on 18 November he presented his letters of credence as British ambassador. For the next three years, thanks in large part to the maverick brilliance of his wife, the entrée to the British embassy was one of the most sought-after privileges in the social and political world in Paris. It was complained, with some justice, that Lady Diana's glittering gatherings contained too few worthy trade unionists and civil servants and too many people who, because of their wartime record, should not have been received in an official residence. The fact remained that parties at the embassy were tremendous fun and that Cooper's obvious love of Paris and the French made him as popular as any British ambassador has ever been.

Cooper's views on global affairs were resolutely Eurocentric, and he was passionately convinced that a Franco-British alliance should be the corner-stone of British foreign policy. He did not find it easy to convince Churchill's government of this priority. When Labour won the general election of July 1945 Cooper thought it probable that he would swiftly be replaced, but the new foreign secretary, Ernest Bevin, liked Cooper and thought that he was doing a good job. His work as ambassador was actually made easier by the change of administration. On 4 March 1947 his efforts were crowned by the signature of a treaty of alliance between Britain and France at Dunkirk. At the end of the same year he left the embassy, his passage being made less painful by the award of the GCMG (1948) and, in July 1952, his elevation to the peerage as Viscount Norwich, of Aldwick, Sussex, a choice of title which caused some adverse comment among the dignitaries of the East Anglian capital. He bequeathed to the embassy a large part of his extensive library, housed in a handsome room which he had persuaded the office of works to install.

**Retirement and assessment**  The Coopers' choice of a retirement home—to the dismay of the new ambassador, who would have preferred not to have had his predecessor so close to Paris—was the Château de St Firmin in the park at Chantilly. Cooper took on several business assignments, notably on the board of the International Wagons-Lits, but his main occupation was writing. During the war he had found the time to write the life of the Old Testament hero King David; now, in 1949, he added an imaginative and entertaining study of Shakespeare's early life, *Sergeant Shakespeare*. In the same year he published a selection of his own poems. His only novel, *Operation Heartbreak* (1950), was based on a real-life incident in the Second World War and was viewed unenthusiastically by the cabinet office, who tried to stop its publication on the ground that it breached security. Finally, in 1953, his autobiography, *Old Men Forget*, appeared, an eloquent, stylish, and in many ways revealing account of a life that was not totally successful in worldly terms but was never dull. By now his health was faltering. He had already suffered a dangerous haemorrhage in May 1953. At the very end of that year he embarked with his wife on the French liner *Colombie* on a cruise to Jamaica. On new year's eve he had another haemorrhage, and he died on board at 3.30 p.m. on 1 January 1954. He was buried five days later at Belvoir Castle, Leicestershire, the home of his wife's family. His son, John Julius, the writer and broadcaster, succeeded him.

'I love the sunlight but I cannot fear the coming of the dark' Cooper wrote in his autobiography (Duff Cooper, *Old Men Forget*, 384). Courage and joy in living were the most conspicuous features of his personality; if he had had less of either he might have achieved higher office but his life would have been far less fulfilled. He can fairly be accused of an extravagantly short temper, self-indulgence, and an inordinate appetite for wine, women, and gambling, but he was never mean or in the least ignoble; at times, indeed, he showed true nobility. He was a great-spirited patriot, too proud to court popularity, too reserved to command it readily, but a man whose honesty, generosity, and public spirit were never put in question.

PHILIP ZIEGLER

**Sources**  priv. coll., Duff Cooper MSS · J. Charmley, *Duff Cooper* (1986) · D. Cooper, *Old men forget: the autobiography of Duff Cooper* (1953) · D. Cooper, *The rainbow comes and goes* (1958) · D. Cooper, *The light of common day* (1959) · D. Cooper, *Trumpets from the steep* (1960) · P. Ziegler, *Diana Cooper* (1981) · CGPLA Eng. & Wales (1954) · GEC, *Peerage*, vol. 14, p. 802

**Archives**  BL, diaries, reserved MS 94 · CAC Cam., corresp. and papers · priv. coll., MSS · UCL, school of Slavonic and east European studies, album relating to Czechoslovakia | BL, corresp. with Lady Caroline Duff, reserved MS 94 · Bodl. Oxf., letters to Margot Asquith · CAC Cam., corresp. with Sir E. L. Spears · CUL, corresp. with Sir Samuel Hoare · Herts. ALS, letters to Lady Desborough · HLRO, corresp. with Lord Beaverbrook · King's Lond., Liddell Hart C., corresp. with Sir B. H. Liddell Hart · Lpool RO,

corresp. with earl of Derby | FILM BFI NFTVA, news footage · IWM FVA, actuality footage · IWM FVA, news footage

**Likenesses**  M. Ray, photograph, 1930–39, NPG [*see illus.*] · W. Stoneman, photograph, 1938, NPG · H. Coster, photographs, *c.*1939–1940, NPG · C. Beaton, photographs · J. Lavery, oils, priv. coll. · D. Low, double portrait, chalk caricature (with Lady Diana), NPG · Quiz [P. Evans], mechanically reproduced caricature, NPG; repro. in *Saturday Review*, 141 (1926) · group photograph, Hult. Arch.

**Wealth at death**  £ 14,303 7*s*. 0*d*. in England: probate, 21 April 1954, CGPLA Eng. & Wales

**Cooper, Edith Emma** (1862–1913). *See under* Bradley, Katharine Harris (1846–1914).

**Cooper, Edward** (*d.* 1725), print seller, became the most distinguished print publisher of his generation and a leading figure in the art world. Nothing is known of his early life, but he first appeared as publisher of a portrait of Thomas Thynne in an advertisement in the *True Protestant Mercury* on 21 February 1682. He first began to challenge Alexander Browne's command of the mezzotint publishing business in 1684, and in 1686 he obtained a royal privilege protecting his plates against copies for a term of fourteen years. By this time he was already employing the talented engraver John Smith and cultivating certain leading portrait painters, notably Willem Wissing, Frederic Kerseboom, Godfrey Kneller, and (soon after) Michael Dahl. He also published contemporary landscapes, still lifes, and 'fancies' by Robert Robinson, Bernard Lens the younger, and Jan vander Vaart, and old master paintings, undertaking such important initiatives as a set of mezzotints of the Raphael cartoons (1707).

Mezzotint was the characteristic staple of Cooper's publishing business, but he also issued some engravings. He was co-publisher with Richard Tompson of Peter Vandrebanc's etchings of the ceilings in the north range at Windsor Castle (1682–6?) and publisher of Dirck Maas's large etching of *The Battle of the Boyne* (1691). He also reissued some old plates, including a set of twenty-five *Birds and Beasts*, after Francis Barlow, later stolen during the view of the sale that followed his death. As a retailer, Cooper dealt in old master prints, imported Italian prints, and was named in advertisements as a principal distributor of such important English undertakings as Nicolas Dorigny's Raphael cartoons and James Thornhill's prints of his designs for the cupola of St Paul's.

However, Cooper's business in art was not confined to prints: he also sold paintings and artists' materials and was widely acknowledged as an art expert. In 1703 he valued Robert Hooke's print collection and by 1711 he was distributing catalogues of important auction sales of paintings; it is likely that he was the cataloguer and possibly the auctioneer of many of these sales. One at least, in 1719, was of pictures 'collected by Mr Edward Cooper' (*Daily Courant*, 21 Jan 1719). He mixed with the leading connoisseurs in the country. In 1714 he was steward at the feast of the exclusive club the Virtuosi of St Luke, 'the earliest organized group of art experts and art advisers in this country' (Bignamini, 21). Cooper was a member from at

**Edward Cooper** (*d.* 1725), by Peter Pelham, 1724 (after Jan van der Vaart)

least 1714 to 1720. He was also one of George Vertue's trusted informants about art history.

Cooper remained at the Three Pigeons in Bedford Street, between Covent Garden and the Strand, until his death. He married Priscilla and they had at least three children, Elizabeth, John, and Priscilla. Portraits of all the family were engraved in mezzotint. Cooper's decision to retire was signalled by the advertisement of a sale of 'the large and curious collection of prints and drawings of Mr Edward Cooper (who is leaving off the business)' in the *Daily Courant* of 2 February 1723. At this point he published his own portrait, engraved by Pelham after vander Vaart, showing a corpulent man holding a proof mezzotint. John vander Vaart was mentioned as a 'dear friend' in Cooper's will. This document indicated substantial affluence: he left a second house to his wife. He died early in 1725, and his death was followed by another sale, of household goods and shop goods, including a 'four-Wheel'd Chaise' as well 'as Copper-Plates, Paints, Pictures, fine Colours, &c. likewise several sorts of Materials belonging to Painting, Printing, &c.' (*Daily Post*, 1 May 1725). Prints published by Cooper may be found in the British Museum, London, and the Yale Center for British Art, New Haven, Connecticut.

His son **John Cooper** (*d.* 1729/30), art auctioneer, was the leading figure in this field during the 1720s, as well as co-publisher of Hogarth's *Hudibras* (1726) and publisher of *The Hampton Court Beauties* (1727). It would appear that father and son fell out, since John was left in Edward's will 'one shilling British money and no more by reason I have already given him a greater part or share out of what I had than by his behaviour to me he hath deserved'. John

Cooper was probably the auctioneer whose widow was Elizabeth Cooper, compiler of *The Muses Library* and author of *The Rival Widows* (1735).

During his long career Edward Cooper provided employment for most mezzotint engravers of the time. Of his regular employees, Isaac Beckett, John Smith (1652–1743), William Faithorne the younger, Bernard Lens (1659/60–1725), Jan vander Vaart, and Peter Pelham are separately noticed. **Robert Williams** (*fl.* 1680–1704), engraver, born in Wales, was a pupil of Theodore Freres, and had the misfortune to have his leg amputated. He worked chiefly for Cooper, occasionally publishing his own mezzotints. **Francis Kyte** (*fl.* 1710–1745), engraver, at first worked exclusively for Cooper and later also for John Bowles. He was pilloried for forging a bank note in 1725 and this may have been the reason why at this time he sometimes Latinized his name to Milvus. It is fairly certain that he was the same person as the 'rather good' (Waterhouse, 212) portrait painter with dated work in the 1740s, some of which was published.               TIMOTHY CLAYTON

**Sources** *True Protestant Mercury* (21 Feb 1682) · *Daily Courant* (21 Jan 1719) · *Daily Courant* (2 Feb 1723) · *Daily Post* [London] (1 May 1725) · *Daily Post* [London] (8 May 1725) · *Daily Post* [London] (24 May 1725) · *Country Journal, or, The Craftsman* (24 Jan 1730) · will; codicil 25 Jan 1725, proved March 1725, PRO, PROB 12/95 602 · will, PRO, PROB 11/631 [John Cooper] · A. Griffiths, 'Early mezzotint publishing in England: Peter Lely, Tompson and Browne', *Print Quarterly*, 7 (1990), 130–45 · T. Clayton, *The English print, 1688–1802* (1997) · A. Griffiths and R. A. Gerard, *The print in Stuart Britain, 1603–1689* (1998) [exhibition catalogue, BM, 8 May – 20 Sept 1998] · I. Bignamini, 'George Vertue, art historian, and art institutions in London, 1689–1768', *Walpole Society*, 54 (1988), 1–148 · J. C. Smith, *British mezzotinto portraits*, 4 vols. in 5 (1878–84) · J. Ganz, *Fancy pieces: genre mezzotints by Robert Robinson and his contemporaries* (1994) · Waterhouse, *18c painters*

**Likenesses** P. Pelham, mezzotint, 1724 (after J. vander Vaart), BM [*see illus.*]

**Wealth at death** considerable: will, PRO, PROB 12/95, 602

**Cooper, Edward Herbert** (1867–1910), novelist, born at Trentham, Staffordshire, on 6 October 1867, was the eldest son of Samuel Herbert Cooper of New Park, Trentham, later of Newcastle under Lyme, Staffordshire, and his wife, Katharine, daughter of the Revd Edward James Justinian George Edwards and granddaughter of the bibliographer James Edwards. While at a preparatory school at Hoddesdon, Hertfordshire, Cooper contracted a chill, which caused an illness that lasted seven years and left him partially disabled. Prepared for Oxford by a private tutor, he matriculated at University College on 18 October 1886, took third-class honours in history in 1889, and graduated BA in 1890.

After a false start in chartered accountancy in London, and in politics as secretary of the Suffolk Liberal Unionist Association at the general election of 1892, Cooper found his feet as a writer. His first novel, *Geoffrey Hamilton*, a rather plotless work but with some good Oxford autobiographical tales, was published in 1893. It was followed in the same year by *Richard Escott*, and then by the stronger work *The Enemies* (1896), about Ireland after the Parnell affair. Later that year Cooper joined in Paris the staff of *Galignani's Messenger*, and acted as Paris correspondent for the *New York World*. *Mr Blake of Newmarket*, an excellent sporting story, and *The Marchioness Against the County*, a social satire, were both published the following year, in 1897. *Mr Blake* drew a letter of praise from Lord Rosebery, and *The Sportsman* called it 'the best exposition of turf life that we know'.

But although Cooper dabbled in a variety of genres, producing twenty-three works, he found his greatest success as a children's writer. In 1899 he began a series of imaginative stories for the young, told by a pretty little rich girl, Wyemarke. They were: *Wyemarke and the Sea Fairies* (1899); *Wyemarke and the Mountain Fairies* (1900); *Wyemarke's Mother and Sent to the Rescue, or, Wyemarke's Adventures in South America* (1903); and *My Brother the King* (1910). The tales owed much to the suggestion of Lewis Carroll, but there was originality in their execution. Cooper also aided the philanthropist Benjamin Waugh in practical efforts to protect children from cruelty.

Meanwhile, Cooper travelled a great deal in search of better health. In 1898, supported by two sticks, he made the ascent of Mont Blanc as far as the Col du Goûter, and in 1901 he visited Finland. He afterwards wrote in the London press on Finland's constitutional struggle, and the following year assisted in the preparation of the English version of N. C. Fredericksen's *Finland: its Public and Private Economy*. In 1903 he returned to London, and was for three years special reporter on the *Daily Mail*.

Cooper, whose features were marked by a rare refinement, bore his physical disabilities with courage and cheerfulness. He had an inveterate addiction to gambling: while cheering on his favourite horse at the Newmarket racecourse on 26 April 1910 he suffered an apoplectic seizure and died. He was buried in Kensal Green cemetery, London. He was unmarried.

G. LE G. NORGATE, rev. KATHARINE CHUBBUCK

**Sources** J. Sutherland, *The Longman companion to Victorian fiction* (1988) · Foster, *Alum. Oxon.* · R. L. Wolff, *Nineteenth-century fiction: a bibliographical catalogue based on the collection formed by Robert Lee Wolff*, 5 vols. (1981–6) · *The Athenaeum* (30 April 1910), 527 · *The Times* (29 April 1910) · *Daily Telegraph* (29 April 1910) · *Staffordshire Sentinel* (7 May 1910)
**Likenesses** engraving, repro. in *Lady's Pictorial* (7 May 1910)

**Cooper, Edward Joshua** (1798–1863), landowner and astronomer, was born in May 1798 at St Stephen's Green, Dublin, the eldest of the three sons of Edward Synge Cooper (d. 1830), a landowner, and his wife, Anne, the daughter of Harry *Verelst, governor of Bengal. He attended school in Armagh, where he became acquainted with the astronomical observatory, and Eton College, and then spent two years from 1816 at Christ Church, Oxford, without taking a degree. His education was completed by ten years of travel.

By his constant practice of determining with portable instruments the latitudes and longitudes of the places he visited, Cooper accumulated a mass of unpublished geographical data. In the summer of 1820 he met Sir William Drummond at Naples, and, by the latter's interest in ancient zodiacs, was induced to visit Egypt to obtain accurate copies of them. He accordingly ascended the Nile

as far as the second cataract in the winter of 1820–21, and brought home with him the materials of a volume entitled *Views in Egypt and Nubia*, printed for private circulation at London in 1824. A set of lithographs from drawings by Bossi, a Roman artist engaged by Cooper for the journey, formed its chief interest.

Cooper's eastward excursions reached as far as Turkey and Persia, and in 1824–5 he traversed Denmark, Sweden, and Norway, as far as the North Cape. Following his travels he regarded Munich and Nice as the best adapted spots in Europe for astronomical observation. He subsequently undertook important astronomical work in the vicinity of both cities, and at Nice a large refractor was established in the 1890s.

On his father's death in 1830 Cooper succeeded to his position as manager of the family estates at Markree, Collooney, co. Sligo, Ireland, and decided to erect an observatory there. He visited Cauchoix in Paris in 1829 and by 1831 was able to purchase from him an object-glass 13⅓ inches across and 25 feet in focal length, the largest then in existence. Used at first on a wooden stand, it was mounted equatorially by Thomas Grubb of Dublin in 1834. Cast iron was employed for the first time as the material of the tube and stand. A dome of the requisite size was considered then not to be feasible, and the instrument was set up in the open air. A 5 foot transit by Troughton, a meridian circle 3 feet in diameter, fitted with a 7 inch telescope, ordered in 1839 on the occasion of a visit to the works of Ertel in Bavaria, and a comet seeker (a short-focus, wide-angle refracting telescope), likewise by Ertel, acquired in 1842, were successively added to the equipment of what was authoritatively described in 1851 as 'undoubtedly the most richly furnished of private observatories' (*Monthly Notices of the Royal Astronomical Society*, 11, 1850–51, 104).

Cooper worked diligently in the observatory himself when at Markree, and obtained in March 1842, in Andrew Graham, an assistant who gave a fresh impulse to its activity. In their joint work in 1842–3 the positions of fifty stars within two degrees of the pole were determined; later the systematic meridian observations of minor planets were set on foot, and on 10–12 August 1847 an experiment was successfully made of determining the difference of longitude between Markree and Killiney, 98 miles distant, by simultaneous observations of shooting stars. A ninth minor planet was discovered by Graham on 25 April 1848 and named Metis, its detection having ensued from the adoption of a plan of work laid down by Cooper. Meteorological registers were continuously kept at Markree for thirty years from 1833, and many of the results were communicated to the Meteorological Society. In 1844–5 Cooper and Graham made together a tour through France, Germany, and Italy. The great refractor formed part of their luggage, and, mounted on a wooden stand with altitude and azimuth movements, was used to sketch the Orion nebula and to detect independently, at Naples on 7 February 1845, a comet already observed in the southern hemisphere.

From the time that the possibility of further planetary

discoveries had been recalled to the attention of astronomers by the finding of Astraea on 8 December 1845, Cooper had it in view to extend the star maps then in progress at Berlin so as to include stars of the twelfth or thirteenth magnitude. A detailed acquaintance with ecliptical stars, however, was indispensable for the facilitation of planetary research—Cooper's primary object—and the Berlin maps covered only an equatorial zone of thirty degrees. He accordingly resolved on the construction of a set of ecliptic star charts to twelfth or thirteenth magnitude of four times the linear dimensions of the *Horae* prepared at Berlin. The intention was to show fainter stars so that fainter minor planets could be detected. Observations for the purpose were begun in August 1848, and continued until Graham's resignation in June 1860. The results were printed at government expense in four volumes with the title *Catalogue of Stars Near the Ecliptic Observed at Markree* (1851–6). The approximate places were contained in them of 60,066 stars (epoch 1850) within three degrees of the ecliptic, only 8965 of which were already known. A list of seventy-seven stars missing from recent catalogues, or lost in the course of the observations, formed an appendix. The maps corresponding to this extensive catalogue, presented by his daughters after Cooper's death to the University of Cambridge, have remained unpublished. For this notable service to astronomy, in which he took a large personal share, Cooper received in 1858 the Cunningham gold medal of the Royal Irish Academy. He had been a member of that body from 1832, and was elected a fellow of the Royal Society on 2 June 1853.

The elements and other data relative to 198 cometary bodies, gathered from scattered sources during several years, were arranged and published by Cooper in a volume entitled *Cometic Orbits, with Copious Notes and Addenda* (1852). Although partially anticipated by Galle's list of 178 sets of elements appended to the 1847 edition of Olbers's *Abhandlung*, the physical and historical information collected in the notes remain of permanent value. The preface contains statistics of the distribution in longitude of the perihelia and nodes of both planetary and cometary orbits, showing what seemed more than a chance aggregation in one semicircle. Communications on the same point were presented by Cooper to the Royal Astronomical Society in 1853, to the Royal Society in 1855, and to the British Association in 1858.

Cooper succeeded to the proprietorship of the Markree estates on the death in 1837 of his uncle Joshua Cooper. He was Conservative member of parliament for co. Sligo from 1830 to 1841, and again from 1857 to 1859. He was twice married, first to Sophia L'Estrange, of Moystown, King's county, who died having given birth to a son who also died, and second to Sarah Frances (d. 1863), the daughter of Owen Wynne of Haslewood, co. Sligo, with whom he had five daughters. Cooper died, shortly after his wife, at Markree Castle on 23 April 1863.

According to W. Doberck, Cooper was a kind as well as an improving landlord; his private life was blameless, and

he united attractiveness of manner to varied accomplishments. He kept up to the last his interest in scientific pursuits, and numerous records of his work in astronomy were printed in the *Monthly Notices*, the *Astronomische Nachrichten*, and other journals. He imparted his observations of the annular eclipse of 15 May 1836 to the Académie Royale des Sciences in Paris. For some years after his death the Markree observatory was completely neglected. It was restored in 1874, when W. Doberck was appointed director, and the refractor began to be employed, according to Cooper's original intention, for the study of double stars. However, little was done in this field, though meteorological observations were continued into the 1890s. In 1927 the 13 inch telescope, then nearly 100 years old, was sold for use in teaching science at a Jesuit seminary in Hong Kong. It was damaged during the Second World War, and the Cauchoix lens is now preserved in good condition at the Manila observatory. At Markree Castle only the observatory walls remain.

A. M. CLERKE, rev. P. A. WAYMAN

**Sources** Burke, *Gen. Ire.* · W. Doberck, 'The Markree observatory [pts 1–2]', *The Observatory*, 7 (1884), 283–8, 329–32 · *Proceedings of the Royal Irish Academy*, 8 (1861–4), 485–6 · *The Times* (27 April 1863) · *PRS*, 13 (1863–4), 1
**Archives** RS | CUL, maps of Markree catalogue
**Likenesses** attrib. M. Ward, watercolour, *c.*1857 (after photograph), Northern Ireland National Trust · photograph, *c.*1860, priv. coll. · portrait, repro. in T. O'Rorke, *History, antiquities and present state of the parishes of Ballysadare and Kilvarnet* (1878)
**Wealth at death** under £1000 in England: Irish probate sealed in London, 15 June 1863, *CGPLA Eng. & Wales*

**Cooper, Sir (Thomas) Edwin** (1874–1942), architect, was born at 44 Nelson Street, Scarborough, on 21 October 1874, the eldest child of Samuel Cooper, carriage proprietor, and his wife, Ann, daughter of Thomas Pickering, an agricultural labourer. Cooper's father died during his childhood, and his mother, recognizing his talent for drawing, encouraged him towards his future career. Cooper was articled to the architectural firm Hall and Tugwell in Scarborough from 1885 to 1889, and after further experience with W. Penty and Walter Brierley in York he went to London to Goldie, Child, and Goldie for a further two years. Cooper returned to Scarborough in 1893 with his friend and fellow pupil Herbert Davis to found a practice as Hall, Cooper, and Davis with John Hall, an older architect in the town. On 14 July 1898 Cooper married Mary Emily (b. 1873/4), the daughter of Henry Wellburn, merchant of Scarborough; they had a son and a daughter. Hall, Cooper, and Davis opened a London office in 1895, but local commissions in the north gave Cooper a good start, and included in Scarborough Westwood higher grade school (1897) and Scarborough College, Filey Road (1898). These were eclectic brick buildings, showing signs of Brierley's controlled Romanticism. Cooper travelled in France and Italy, and expressed admiration for the works of Baldassare Peruzzi and Michele Sanmicheli, both of whom were generally admired by Edwardian leaders of revived classicism.

In 1903 Cooper became a fellow of the RIBA, and became a partner of Samuel Bridgeman Russell until 1910, when he set up on his own. By then Cooper had consolidated his technique for competition designs for large public buildings. In 1905 John Belcher selected his design for the rebuilding of Hull Guildhall, on an awkward narrow site, and the building was constructed, faced in Portland stone, between 1906 and 1914. Its emphatic horizontals of cornice and basement enclose an engaged Corinthian colonnade, which became one of Cooper's hallmarks. The terminal piers of the building are crowned with baroque sculptural groups by Albert Hemstock Hodge. Russell and Cooper's design for the County Hall competition in London was similar in mood, and Cooper was among a small group of architects who formed the Classical Society, chiefly in protest against the assessors' selection of Ralph Knott. The centrepiece from this design reappeared in the winning scheme by Cooper for the Port of London Authority's new headquarters on Tower Hill in 1912. His elevational style had by then turned towards the currently fashionable American-influenced Beaux-Arts movement, with 'neo-Grec' detailing. Cooper became the favourite architect of Hudson Kearley, first Viscount Devonport, the chairman of the authority, who brought him many later commissions, including the port facilities at Tilbury, where Cooper designed the fine baggage hall (1921–2), whose simple interior achieved a genuine Roman grandeur.

On the completion of the Port of London Authority building, Cooper was knighted in 1923. Contemporaries praised the efficiency of his planning, the tight control of the construction, and the rich ornamental detail of the main rooms. Sir Aston Webb, who had assessed the competition, wrote that it 'contains many novel features of plan which will make it a model for buildings of this class in the future' (Webb to Lord Devonport, 17 Sept 1917, RIBA BAL, Cooper MSS, CoE 1/3). C. H. Reilly described it as 'a very bold attempt by a brave man to use Roman baroque architecture to express the majesty of our present day commerce' (*Country Life*, 14 Oct 1922, 465). That such an attempt had not fully succeeded was tacitly admitted even by one of Cooper's greatest admirers, A. E. Richardson, in the *Dictionary of National Biography*, where he wrote:

> Had the Edwardian period been truly receptive of the classic point of view, it is possible that a return to the qualities of eighteenth-century architecture would have followed. Scholarship, grace, and general culture, however, were lacking, and no individual architect, however earnest, could hope to make up for these deficiencies in his own work.

Cooper's Marylebone town hall, also won in competition in 1911, was joined in 1937 by the public library next door, in a slightly simplified style. In the City of London, Cooper designed offices for the Banque Belge, Bishopsgate (1919; now dem.) and for Spillers Ltd in St Mary Axe (1922–3). In 1925 Cooper was commissioned by Lloyds of London to build their new headquarters in Leadenhall Street (completed 1928). The design problem involved planning on an awkward site to an unusual brief. Lloyds itself occupied the back part of the site, with only a small frontage on Leadenhall Street, although the remainder of the street elevation was soon redeveloped by Cooper as Royal

Mail House. He composed an entrance front with a pediment and clever use of relief planes and sculpture, which led down a long corridor to the 'Room', the large open floor space where the business of Lloyds is traditionally transacted, around the central feature of the Lutine bell, which Cooper housed in a wooden Greek revival structure. This, together with the original Leadenhall Street façade, is the only piece of Cooper's work to have survived the redevelopment of the site 1981–5. Lloyds was decorated with ceiling paintings by William Walcot (who also drew many perspectives of Cooper's buildings) and Fred Taylor. Cooper's last major City building, on a prominent corner site facing the Mansion House, was the National and Provincial Bank, Princes Street, a Renaissance-style palazzo building with a grand Corinthian order.

After an initial design by Giles Gilbert Scott had been rejected as impractical, Cooper offered his services free for the Star and Garter Home (for war veterans) on Richmond Hill (1921–5), conceived in a Wren-like mixture of red brick and Portland stone. His obituarist in *The Times* complained that it 'comes perilously near to a vulgarisation of the tradition of Wren. There is a relationship between style and scale to which Cooper appeared to be insensible' (*The Times*, 25 June 1942). Cooper became a specialist in medical and hospital buildings, several of which were funded by his big business patrons, such as Lord Devonport. He worked at St Thomas's Hospital, St Mary's, and the Dreadnought Seamen's Hospital. He also designed buildings at Cranleigh School, Bryanston, and Bedales. Cooper's small domestic *œuvre* is understated and cold in character.

Cooper was elected ARA in 1930 and RA in 1937. He was treasurer of the Royal Academy and in this role succeeded in attracting financial support. He also participated in the formation of the Royal Academy plan for London during the war, and succeeded Sir Edwin Lutyens as president of the Incorporated Association of Architects and Surveyors, a rival body to the RIBA, in 1937. He refused to pay the standard fee to the Architects' Registration Council, on its establishment in 1933, and was therefore technically not legally entitled to the designation of architect.

A. E. Richardson wrote in appreciation that

> From the three-dimensional standpoint, Cooper's buildings are models of ingenuity. Everything seems to be combined within a small compass; both deep below ground and soaring skywards. The aim was to produce comprehensive perspective effects internally and rigid academic symmetry externally. (*DNB*)

Cooper's reputation did not last well in the post-war climate of modernism, and his work has none of the appeal which led to a revival of interest in Lutyens, even though most of his buildings survive and give good service. His chief assistant, Terence Heysham, continued the practice and built a new 'Room' for Lloyds in Lime Street (1950–57).

Details of Cooper's personal character and private life are hard to find. His *Times* obituary described him as 'a pink-faced, silver-haired man of episcopal appearance' (*The Times*, 25 June 1942). When receiving the royal gold medal for architecture in 1931, Cooper said, 'I oftimes think that the less an architect has to say on any matter where he is concerned personally the better' (*The Builder*, 6 March 1931, 440). His friends often urged him to work less hard for the sake of his health. He died of a heart attack while at work at 4 Verulam Buildings, Gray's Inn, London, on 24 June 1942. His wife survived him.

ALAN POWERS

**Sources** DNB · *RIBA Journal*, 49 (1941–2), 154 · *The Builder*, 163 (1942), 3 · *Architect and Building News*, 171 (1942), 2, 24 · papers, including press cuttings books, RIBA BAL, CoE 1–4 · A. Powers, 'Corinthian epics: the architecture of Sir Edwin Cooper', *Thirties Society Journal*, 2 (1982), 13–18 · *The Times* (25 June 1942) · 'Presentation of royal gold medal', *The Builder* (6 March 1931), 440 · b. cert. · m. cert. · *WW*
**Archives** RA, diploma work · RIBA BAL, corresp. and papers · RIBA BAL, designs for stonework
**Wealth at death** £126,402 5*s*. 7*d*.: 23 Dec 1942, *CGPLA Eng. & Wales*

**Cooper** [*née* Price], **Elizabeth** (*b*. in or before **1698**, *d*. **1761**?), playwright and anthologist, was the daughter of Aubrey Price (*d*. 1698) and his wife, Bridget Claypoole (*c*.1674–1738), daughter of John Claypoole, Oliver Cromwell's son-in-law and master of horse, and his second wife. Both her mother and grandmother were unfortunate in choosing the men in whom they placed their trust: though Blanche Claypoole had brought to her marriage perhaps £10,000, Bridget, already an orphan and her parents' only heir, was at or shortly after Elizabeth's birth a widow and a pauper. Where Elizabeth was born, brought up, and educated remains unknown, but both her parents during their brief marriage and she herself after her own marriage inhabited various parishes in Westminster. On 25 February 1722 she married John Cooper (1691–1729), a successful auctioneer in Covent Garden of major art and book collections such as those of the duke of Portland and Dr Woodward. They had six children, including one who died in its first year, before John Cooper's death in 1729 (when she may have been pregnant with a seventh). Their house (cum auction rooms) in the Great Piazza was visited by scholars such as Thomas Birch, and it was presumably through a shared interest in the contents of the books and manuscripts passing through that she came to know the writer and theatrical entrepreneur James Ralph and the antiquary William Oldys. John Cooper's own art collection was sold at auction in 1730, as well as the house, the latter perhaps to the auctioneer Christopher Cock (immortalized by Fielding), with whom Cooper had sometimes been associated.

In the 1730s Elizabeth Cooper seems to have been seeking a means of financial support. Early in 1734 she acted as a member of the company at Drury Lane in Ralph's *The Cornish Squire* and a pantomime, *Cupid and Psyche, or, Columbine Courtezan*. That April she organized a benefit for herself at Lincoln's Inn Fields, Colley Cibber's *The Careless Husband*, with herself playing Lady Easy. Her activities then expanded to playwriting: in 1735 appeared at Covent Garden *The Rival Widows*, in which she played the lead for her

two benefits, and the following year at the Haymarket *The Nobleman*, which reached the third night benefit but which was never printed. Fielding's *Pasquin* was that season the sensational hit at his and Ralph's theatre, the Haymarket, and though Ralph had foregone production of one of his own plays to extend its run, he is said to have urged that Mrs Cooper's play be produced. But then came Walpole's Licensing Act, which closed the Haymarket and ended Fielding's dramatic career and incidentally Mrs Cooper's as well.

Cooper then turned to compiling an anthology of English poetry from the eleventh century (Edward the Confessor) to the sixteenth (Samuel Daniel). For this she borrowed books from William Oldys and sought unpublished manuscripts from poets' families. Cooper added biographical information about the poets and gave brief critical assessments of the works. The volume, called *The Muses Library*, is competent in every respect and remains well worth reading. It has been credited by reputable modern scholars as the model for Samuel Johnson's format in his *Lives of the Poets* and as the chief inspiration for Thomas Chatterton's antique style. Elizabeth Cooper planned a further volume, of poetic theory, but unhappily the first failed to sell well, and the project collapsed.

The last record of Cooper, in a letter of disputable date (probably 1742), places her in St James's. J. Yeowell wrote that she died on 5 August 1761, but David Baker wrote in 1764 'Of this Lady, who is still living, and whom we must rank among the Female Geniuses of this Kingdom' (Baker, sig. H1*r*).

YVONNE NOBLE

**Sources** Blanche Claypoole and Bridget Price suits as plaintiffs in chancery, 1688–1708, PRO · E. Cooper, letter to Thomas Birch, 24/10/[1742?], BL, Add. MS 4303, fol. 79 · [D. E. Baker], *The companion to the play-house*, 2 (1764) · *A literary antiquary: memoir of William Oldys … together with his diary*, ed. J. Yeowell (1862) · A. H. Scouten, ed., *The London stage, 1660–1800*, pt 3: *1729–1747* (1961) · B. H. Bronson, 'Thomas Chatterton', *The age of Johnson: essays presented to Chauncey Brewster Tinker*, ed. F. W. Hilles (1949) · R. Wellek, *The rise of English literary history* (1941) · W. A. Littledale, ed., *The registers of St Bene't and St Peter, Paul's Wharf, London*, 2, Harleian Society, register section, 39 (1910)

**Cooper, Elizabeth** (*fl*. **1865–1874**), historian, made her début as a writer in 1865 with the publication of *A Popular History of America*. Her subsequent works were biographies. In 1866 she published *The Life and Letters of Lady Arbella Stuart* (2 vols.), a laudatory portrait of an altruistic protestant heroine destroyed by court intrigues. It was based on original documents, some of which belonged to Sir Thomas Phillipps, the famous bibliophile. A pause in publication ensued, probably because Cooper became ill around 1869 (in her dedication to her next work she described herself as 'the hapless victim of a neglected and torturing malady'). In 1874 she published *The Life of Thomas Wentworth, Earl of Stafford*, the first scholarly biography of the seventeenth-century statesman. According to the reviewer for *The Spectator*, the work showed that she had 'industry and care, but wants the grasp of imagination which is needed for her difficult subject'. He concluded, however, that the work had 'real merits', praising in particular her account of Wentworth's government of Ireland (*Spectator*, 471–2). Very little else is known of Cooper's life. She appears to have lived mainly in or near London, and was unmarried at the time of her publications.

ROSEMARY MITCHELL

**Sources** Allibone, *Dict.* · *The Spectator* (10 April 1874), 471–2 · letters to Sir Thomas Phillipps, 1865–70, Bodl. Oxf., Phillipps-Robinson MSS · *The letters of Lady Arbella Stuart*, ed. S. J. Steen (1994), 103–4
**Archives** Bodl. Oxf., notes and extracts from state papers relating to earl of Stafford | Bodl. Oxf., Phillipps-Robinson MSS

**Cooper, Ernest** (1847–1926). *See under* Cooper family (*per.* 1854–1994).

**Cooper, Fanny** (1814–1872). *See under* Lacy, Thomas Hailes (1809–1873).

**Cooper, Francis** (1845/6–1893). *See under* Cooper family (*per.* 1854–1994).

**Cooper, Frank** (1844–1927), marmalade manufacturer, was born on 12 November 1844 over his father's shop at 46 High Street, Oxford, the eldest surviving son of Francis Thomas Cooper (1811–1862), hatter and tea dealer, and his wife, Decima (1819–1857), daughter of Isaac Stone. Both parents came from the market town of Thame, 13 miles east of Oxford, where Francis's father had been an innkeeper and Decima's a builder. Encouraged by his brother Henry, who worked for the London tea-importing firm of Ridgways, Francis had for several years combined his hatter's business with an agency for Ridgways' teas; but in 1845 he abandoned the hatter's trade to become a grocer and dealer in tea and coffee. In 1856, after the decline and near closure of Oxford's former main coaching inn, the Angel, Francis Cooper moved his family and business across the road into two adjacent properties, formerly belonging to the Angel, at 83–4 High Street, with his shop in the spacious, pillared former coffee room of the hotel at no. 84.

Following his father's death in 1862, the seventeen-year-old Frank Cooper and a widowed aunt were left in charge of the grocery shop. His mother had died five years earlier, and the family was cared for by a resident cousin from Thame. In 1872 Frank married Sarah Jane Gill (1848–1932), daughter of John Gill, a Worcestershire farmer; she was connected on her father's side with the Gills and Wards, prominent Oxford coal-dealing and ironmongering families. Frank and Sarah had five children, one of whom died in 1903. Sarah Jane Cooper is traditionally credited with the manufacture of the first batch of Seville orange marmalade, which went on sale in the shop, in stoneware jars, in the spring of 1874. 'Her insistence on using Seville oranges … and her method of presenting the coarse-cut, chunky but well-macerated peel, produced a high-quality and excitingly bitter-tasting marmalade' (Allen, 33). Popular among undergraduates as a feature of the new, lighter breakfasts and as a source of energy for athletes in training, the distinctive 'Oxford' marmalade became something of a late-Victorian cult food. Other Oxford grocers, and some of the colleges, followed the Coopers' example

in manufacturing and selling their own marmalade; but the Coopers remained well ahead, adding jam to their output in the early 1880s, and mounting an extensive advertising campaign which stressed the purity of their marmalade and included sending samples to the smarter military messes, London clubs, and leading department stores. By 1884 Frank was displaying the royal arms, as a purveyor of marmalade to the prince of Wales, the future Edward VII; and in 1911–12 tins of Oxford marmalade accompanied Captain Scott on his Antarctic expedition. A miniature jar of Frank Cooper's Oxford marmalade later found a place in Queen Mary's dolls' house at Windsor Castle.

Despite the increasing success of his marmalade business, Frank Cooper continued as a grocer and wine merchant until 1919, living on the premises of his shop in the High Street, until 1907, when he moved with Sarah Jane to a newly built Edwardian house, 155 Woodstock Road, Oxford. The jam and marmalade continued to be made on the shop premises, under Sarah Jane's supervision, until early in 1903, when (probably as a result of strictures on manufacturing conditions in the 1901 Factory Act) their production moved to a purpose-built factory in Park End Street, Oxford.

In 1913 Frank Cooper sold his personal interest in the manufacturing business for £26,559 15s. 6d. to a newly constituted limited company, Frank Cooper Ltd, directed by himself, his sons, and his son-in-law. All the ordinary and preference shares were held by Cooper and members of his family. The eldest son, William Frank Cooper (1874–1952), manager of the factory, became managing director; the youngest, Maurice, became company secretary; and the second son, Arthur, an engineer, sat on the board. This eventually included a few non-family members, but the business remained for the most part family-owned. Frank Cooper, as governing chairman, attended every board meeting of the company during the remaining fourteen years of his life, and regularly appeared at the factory in his chauffeur-driven Daimler car. Always careful, he was renowned among the workforce during his last years for his thriftiness, and had few obvious interests outside the business. He died at home in Oxford on 26 July 1927, leaving an estate valued at £47,848 3s. 11d. He was survived by his wife. The company remained independent until the early 1960s, when it merged with Brown and Polson Ltd, part of the American-owned CPC group of companies. A purpose-built factory, which was opened at Wantage, Berkshire, at this time, finally severed the manufacturing link between Cooper's marmalade and Oxford.

BRIGID ALLEN

**Sources** B. Allen, *Cooper's Oxford: a history of Frank Cooper Ltd* (1989) · m. cert. · d. cert. · parish register (baptism), Oxford, St Peter-in-the-East, 8 Dec 1844
**Archives** Oxon. RO, Oxfordshire Archives | CPC, Esher, Surrey, Morrells Archives
**Likenesses** photograph, 1895–1900, repro. in Allen, *Cooper's Oxford*, 66
**Wealth at death** £47,848 3s. 11d.: probate, 26 Aug 1927, *CGPLA Eng. & Wales*

**Cooper, George** (1820–1876), organist, was born on 7 July 1820 at Lambeth, London. His father, also named George Cooper (*d.* 1843), was assistant organist at St Paul's Cathedral. Cooper's early proficiency, arising from assiduous practice on an old pedal harpsichord, came to the notice of Thomas Attwood, the chief organist of the cathedral, who on several occasions made him extemporize at the festivals of the Sons of the Clergy. On one such occasion he is said to have earned the praise of Mendelssohn. At the age of eleven the younger George Cooper often took the service instead of his father, and in 1834 he received the appointment of organist of St Benet Paul's Wharf. Two years later he became organist of St Anne and St Agnes, Aldersgate, and on Attwood's death, in March 1838, he succeeded his father as assistant organist of St Paul's Cathedral. His father, who had resigned at that time, died in 1843, on which occasion Cooper also obtained his post at St Sepulchre's. In the same year he was appointed singing master and organist to Christ's Hospital. In September 1856 he became organist of the Chapel Royal, in succession to J. B. Sale, who had just died. This appointment, together with those at St Paul's, St Sepulchre's, and Christ's Hospital, he retained until his death.

Cooper published a book of *Organ Arrangements*, an *Organist's Assistant*, an *Introduction to the Organ*, and an *Organist's Manual* (1851). In 1862 he revised the music for W. Windle's *Church and Home Metrical Psalter and Hymn Book*, contributing several tunes of his own. On the death of Henry John Gauntlett in February 1876 he undertook to complete the musical editing of *Wesley's Hymns*. He had finished the task by the time of his death, but the book appeared posthumously in 1877. Cooper died at his home at 14 Heathcote Street, Mecklenburg Square, London, on 2 October 1876. He was survived by his wife, Eleanor Cooper.               J. A. F. MAITLAND, *rev.* NILANJANA BANERJI

**Sources**  Grove, *Dict. mus.* · Brown & Stratton, *Brit. mus.* · H. W. Shaw, *The succession of organists of the Chapel Royal and the cathedrals of England and Wales from c.1538* (1991) · W. Cowan and J. Love, *The music of the church hymnary and the psalter in metre* (1901) · *CGPLA Eng. & Wales* (1876)

**Wealth at death**  under £1500: probate, 30 Nov 1876, *CGPLA Eng. & Wales*

**Cooper, Giles Stannus** (1918–1966), playwright, was born on 9 August 1918 in Carrickmines, Dublin, the elder child and only son of Guy Cooper (1889–1941), naval officer and colonial civil servant, and his wife, Winifred, *née* Warren (1888–1977), a talented painter who had studied at the Beaux-Arts in Paris. Both families belonged to the Anglo-Irish landed gentry, with a tradition of service in the armed forces at home and in the empire, as well as membership of the Westminster and later the Dublin parliament. The Coopers, originally farmers from East Anglia, acquired large tracts of land in Ireland in the seventeenth century, though by the twentieth their estates consisted only of Markree Castle and a 1000 acre farm in co. Sligo. Giles Cooper's father, a younger son, trained as a naval officer, saw action in the First World War, then entered the colonial service and became attorney-general of the Seychelles. This establishment background throws light on

Cooper's later devastating critique of post-colonial England and its disintegrating values.

Cooper's education, at Arnold House, Hampstead, London, Seafield School, Bexhill, Sussex, and Lancing College, conformed to a then-typical pattern for children of fathers serving overseas of boarding-schools and long separations from his parents. Apparently unperturbed by this regime, he enjoyed boxing, shooting, acting, and above all writing, especially for the stage, although a later play, *Unman, Wittering and Zigo*, presents a very dark picture of public-school life. His father, intending him for the diplomatic service, sent him abroad to learn modern languages, but after a post-school year studying French in Grenoble, Cooper decided to follow his own bent. Persuading his father to let him off Cambridge and the Foreign Office, he went instead to drama school, the Webber Douglas School of Singing and Drama, London. However, the Second World War broke out a few weeks after he qualified as an actor, and by 1942 he was an infantry officer on a troopship bound for Singapore. In Cape Town an ailment kept him ashore while his comrades sailed on unawares to years of Japanese captivity which few survived. Cooper himself was re-routed to Burma, where for two years his battalion fought under harrowing conditions in the jungle. He rarely mentioned his experiences there: he struck acquaintances as the typical 'officer and a gentleman'—courteous, cheerful, and excellent company while basically stoical and reserved. But just as outward convention veiled inner subversion, so beneath the laughter in his work and conversation lay a sombre view of human frailty owing much to what a relative has called his 'very nasty war'.

Demobilized in 1946 with the rank of captain and a recurrent kidney weakness, Cooper started a modest career as an actor which introduced him to Gwyneth Lewis (1916–1991), an assistant stage manager just out of the WAAF. She was the daughter of Canon Lewis of Llandaff Cathedral. They married on 15 February 1947 and had two sons: Guy (*b.* 1948) and Richard (*b.* 1955). Those were lean times for struggling freelances, but a characteristically jovial trait of Cooper's was to keep a supply of rockets handy for celebrating pleasant surprises.

One of these, after only moderate success with writing for the theatre, was the immediate enthusiasm Cooper met with as a script writer for radio. His first radio play, *Fools Rush In*, was broadcast in 1949, and thanks to the perspicacity of such BBC directors as Donald McWhinnie, Cooper soon emerged as a supreme exponent of pure radio, producing a seemingly inexhaustible stream of bizarrely original ideas carried out with virtuoso variation of form and technique. *The Disagreeable Oyster*; *Under the Loofah Tree*; *Unman, Wittering and Zigo*—the very titles amaze. *Mathry Beacon* (1958), a realistic fantasy about a group of people maintaining a remote anti-aircraft gun-site long after the war is over, won the Prix Italia. In little more than a decade a score of Cooper's plays were broadcast on television or radio. He was made an OBE for 'services to broadcasting'.

Cooper never gave up on the theatre—*Everything in the*

*Garden*, a corrosive debunking of suburban respectability, was staged by Peter Hall in London in 1962 and adapted for Broadway by Edward Albee after the author's death—but Cooper's 'natural' medium was radio. The apparently bourgeois points of departure that may have obscured his originality on the stage, in the 'kitchen-sink' era of attacking the status quo from without, could on radio be suggested and outsoared within seconds, making way for a display of Cooper's distinctive dramatic economy. He exploited the possibilities of the medium to the full, his particular background and temperament adding a sardonic poise and elegance all his own. But on 3 December 1966, at a time when professional success and a family legacy had made financial worry a thing of the past, and he and his family were settled comfortably in rural Sussex, Giles Cooper died, at Kingston Hospital, Kingston upon Thames, Surrey, following a fall from a train. He was buried in Heyshott, Sussex. His *Six Plays for Radio*, published in one volume by the BBC in 1964, is a revelation, not sufficiently remembered, of radio writing as literature. Cooper's work has also been already honoured by an annual award named after him.                    BARBARA BRAY

**Sources** R. Cooper, unpublished memoir · personal knowledge (2004) · private information (2004) · BBC WAC · D. McWhinnie, *The art of radio* (1959) · W. Ash, *The way to write radio drama* (1985) · d. cert.

**Archives** BBC WAC, playscripts and MSS · Col. U.

**Wealth at death** £16,252: probate, 20 March 1967, *CGPLA Eng. & Wales*

**Dame Gladys Constance Cooper** (1888–1971), by Dorothy Wilding, 1940

**Cooper, Dame Gladys Constance** (1888–1971), actress and theatre manager, was born at Lewisham in London on 18 December 1888, the eldest of the three daughters of Charles William Frederick Cooper, journalist and editor of *Epicure*, founded by himself, and of his second wife, Mabel, daughter of Captain Edward Barnett of the Scots Greys. She was educated first at home by a French governess, then briefly at school in Fulham, and from the age of seven she began regular photographic modelling for the studio of Downey's in Ebury Street. In the autumn of 1905 she was taken by a schoolfriend to an open audition at the Vaudeville Theatre and, somewhat to her own surprise, she was offered the title role in a tour of *Bluebell in Fairyland* by E. Seymour Hicks that opened at Colchester on her seventeenth birthday. Within another year she had joined George Edwardes's company at the Gaiety, signing a contract for £3 (rising to £5) a week to play as cast, primarily in small singing and dancing roles in such musicals as George Grossmith's *The Girls of Gottenberg* (1907) and *Havana* (1908), and J. T. Tanner's *Our Miss Gibbs* (1909).

Gladys Cooper was not, however, the kind of Gaiety girl who was taken to Romano's by wealthy young men about town; her ambition was to be a serious actress, though all thoughts of a career were interrupted when one night she was seen on stage by Herbert John Buckmaster, a 26-year-old who had served in the Second South African War, then working for Ladbroke's. Within days he had arranged an introduction to her, and they were married on 12 December 1908, much to the disapproval of her parents who felt

that at nineteen she was still too young to leave home. For a year or so after the marriage she continued to work at the Gaiety, but then came the birth in July 1910 of Joan, the first of her two children with Buckmaster. When she returned to the stage after that it was at last to the straight theatre; she began to get small roles in comedy at the Royalty Theatre and she then joined Sir George Alexander for a revival of Oscar Wilde's *The Importance of Being Earnest* (1911) at the St James's. Her first real break came in 1912 with a small but showy last-act role in *Milestones* by Arnold Bennett and Edward Knoblock that ran for eighteen months; during this time she would also take on many other roles at other theatres in other plays, provided that they finished early enough in the evening to allow her to get back to the Royalty for her entrance in *Milestones*. When that run ended she went into *Diplomacy* by B. C. Stephenson and Clement Scott (1913) at Wyndham's, which lasted another year, throughout which she played for the first time with the man who was to become the most constant and beloved of her stage partners, Gerald Du Maurier. By now she was earning £40 a week, and the strain was beginning to show on her marriage to a man who was still only earning about half that from Ladbroke's; then, however, came the First World War. Buck, her husband, joined the cavalry and went to France with the Royal Horse Guards, while she spent the Christmas of 1914 also at the front, though with a concert party organized by Seymour Hicks. By now she was carrying her second child, John, who was born in June 1915.

It was in the following year, 1916, that Gladys Cooper

first began to act at the theatre that she was later to manage, the Playhouse, on the corner of the Embankment and Northumberland Avenue by Charing Cross—a building that was for the next fifteen years to become her professional home. By 1917 she had joined Frank Curzon in its management, thereby becoming the only woman other than Lilian Baylis at the Old Vic to run a West End London theatre before the Second World War, and the plays that she presented, acted in, and sometimes unofficially directed there were to include four W. Somerset Maugham premières (*Home and Beauty*, *The Letter*, *The Sacred Flame*, and *The Painted Veil*) as well as revivals of Knoblock's *My Lady's Dress*, Pinero's *The Second Mrs Tanqueray*, and Louis N. Parker's adaptation of *Magda*.

Herbert Buckmaster returned from the war in 1918 to find that the chorus girl that he had married a decade earlier had now become a professional actress and theatre manager, neither of which were attributes he was looking for in a wife. Accordingly and amicably they were divorced in 1921; he was to marry twice more and to make an eventual home at Buck's Club, which he had founded in Clifford Street and where fifty years after their divorce Gladys Cooper would still frequently be found at parties given by him to celebrate yet another first night. They were always to be the best of friends.

Gladys Cooper spent the 1920s bringing up her two children and running the Playhouse; in 1928 came a second marriage, to Sir Neville Arthur Pearson, second baronet (*b.* 1898); with him she had her third and last child, Sally, but it was to be a short-lived marriage (dissolved in 1937) and by the early 1930s there was little to keep her in England. Changing theatrical tastes brought an end to her years of success at the Playhouse; Maugham had ceased to write plays, and despite her discovery of such interesting new works as *The Rats of Norway* by Keith Winter (which gave Laurence Olivier one of his early stage successes in 1933) and a West End success in *The Shining Hour* (1934), also by Winter, Gladys Cooper began to feel that she had lost touch with London theatregoers. The bright young things for whom she had worked so hard and successfully in the 1920s were no longer thronging the stalls, and she herself had by now fallen in love with the actor Philip Merivale (1886–1946), who was to become her third and last husband; his already successful career on Broadway encouraged Gladys to try her luck there too. Gladys Cooper's philosophy was always cut-and-run, and by the middle 1930s the London where she had once been a definitive *Peter Pan*, where she had run her own theatre and had brought up her elder children, was a place of the past. America was where she would now live and, despite a catastrophic Broadway start in which she played (unsuccessfully) both Desdemona and Lady Macbeth opposite Merivale (whom she married in Chicago in April 1937), it was indeed America that was to become her home for the second half of her long life.

Gladys Cooper returned to London in 1938 for another brief and unsuccessful Shakespeare season (this in the Open Air Theatre, Regent's Park) and a West End run in *Dodsworth*, by now always appearing in partnership with Merivale. They returned to New York for Dodie Smith's *Spring Meeting* (1938) on Broadway and then, in the autumn of 1939, came an offer from Alfred Hitchcock. He was making his first-ever Hollywood film, *Rebecca* (1940), and wanted Gladys Cooper for the small role of Max de Winter's sister, opposite Laurence Olivier; she went out to California for three weeks and stayed for thirty years. She fell immediately and totally in love with the sun, the sea, and the surroundings of California. Though she was never there to get the leading roles that an actress of her stage distinction might have expected, she went under contract to MGM and played in a total of thirty films between 1940 and 1967, of which the most distinguished were *Now Voyager* (for which she got an Oscar nomination in 1943), *Separate Tables* (1958), and *My Fair Lady* (1964). Though Philip Merivale died in California in 1946, Gladys Cooper was to live on there alone, making a home for herself and those of her many relatives and friends seeking (however temporarily) a place in the Californian sun. During the 1950s and 1960s she also began with increasing frequency to return to the London stage, first in *Relative Values* (1951) by Noël Coward and then in such later successes as *The Chalk Garden* (1955) and the revival of Maugham's *The Sacred Flame* (1967). She bought a house on the regatta stretch of the Thames at Henley and, as the old English colony in California began to disappear, spent more and more of her time back home again amid children, grandchildren, and great-grandchildren. In 1967 she was appointed DBE, a year later she celebrated her eightieth birthday, and, on 17 November 1971, having just played in another revival of *The Chalk Garden*, she died at home in Henley only a month away from the start of her eighty-fourth year. She left one son (John Buckmaster, himself for some time an actor); two daughters, both of whom married actors (Joan married Robert Morley in 1940, Sally married Robert Hardy in 1961); five grandchildren; two great-grandchildren; and the unforgettable memories of one of the most remarkable and resilient actresses of her generation.

SHERIDAN MORLEY, *rev.*

**Sources** S. Morley, *Gladys Cooper* (1980) · G. Cooper, *Gladys Cooper* (1931) · S. Stokes, *Without veils* (1953) · personal knowledge (1986) · *The Times* (18 Nov 1971) · J. Parker, ed., *Who's who in the theatre*, 6th edn (1930)
**Archives** University of Southern California Library, Los Angeles, special collections department, corresp. and papers
**Likenesses** photographs, 1909–71, Hult. Arch. · J. Collier, oils, 1915, Garr. Club · B. Park, chlorobromide print, 1922, NPG · C. Moffat, chlorobromide print, *c.*1924, NPG · R. S. Sherriffs, ink and wash caricature, 1938, NPG · D. Wilding, bromide print, 1940, NPG [*see illus.*] · G. Argent, photographs, 1970, NPG · A. Broom, group portrait, photograph, NPG · C. Buchel, oils, NPG · C. Buchel & Hassall, lithograph, NPG · D. Wilding, photographs and postcards, NPG · A. Wysard, pencil and watercolour drawing, NPG
**Wealth at death** £38,157 in England and Wales: probate, 7 April 1972, *CGPLA Eng. & Wales*

**Cooper, Grey** (*c.*1726–1801), politician, was the eldest son of William Cooper, physician, of Newcastle upon Tyne, and Mary Grey of Alnwick. He received a legal education at the Middle Temple, London, and was called to the bar in 1751. On 5 October 1753 he married Margaret Grey (*d.* 1755), daughter of Sir Henry Grey, first baronet, of

Howick. Following her death he married Elizabeth Kennedy (1733/4–1809) of Newcastle upon Tyne on 19 July 1762; they had two sons and two daughters. In 1775 he assumed the baronetcy of the Coopers of Gogar, supposedly created in 1638, on the grounds that he was the great-grandson of the Revd James Cooper, brother of the second baronet, but both the title and his claim to it are disputed (GEC, *Baronetage*, 2.446–7).

By 1765, when Cooper entered politics, his legal practice was earning him an estimated £1000 per annum. His advocacy of the duke and duchess of Atholl in their petition to sell their sovereignty of the Isle of Man made a strong impression in the House of Commons. The same year he defended the Rockingham administration in two pamphlets entitled *A Pair of Spectacles for Short-Sighted Politicians* and *The Merits of the New Administration Truly Stated* in response to the criticisms levelled in an anonymous pamphlet, *An Honest Man's Reasons for Declining to Take Any Part on the New Administration*, thought to have been written by Charles Lloyd, George Grenville's private secretary. These publications brought him to the attention of the administration and in October 1765 he was appointed secretary to the Treasury after protracted negotiations concerning his pension, for he wished to be fully compensated for the loss of his legal practice which he would have to give up on taking office. Rockingham granted him an annuity of £500 per annum and engineered his election as MP for Rochester. Cooper continued as joint secretary to the Treasury for the next sixteen years under the successive governments of Pitt, the duke of Grafton, and Lord North, but he went out of office on the downfall of the last ministry in 1782. Under North he managed the electoral interests in the Cornish boroughs and the duchy revenues, but on the whole his business was restricted to financial matters. He represented Grampound from 1768 to 1774 and Saltash from 1774 to 1784, both in Cornwall, and he returned to office briefly as a lord of the Treasury in the Fox–North coalition government. He failed to be nominated for the government seat of Saltash at the general election in 1784 and he was out of parliament until February 1786, when he was elected MP for Richmond on the Dundas interest. During the debates in 1787 on the commercial treaty with France he took an active part in the opposition and 'yielded to few in his accurate knowledge of the complicated interests which it included' (*Memoirs of … Wraxall*, 4.398). On this and Pitt's other financial measures he directed a keen and searching criticism. At the height of his career in the early 1780s his income from his office and accumulated sinecures earned him over £5500 per annum. In addition he had managed to secure for his sons under a reversionary patent the post of auditor of the land revenue in virtually every county in England, which was worth about £2000 per annum. Cooper did not stand for parliament in 1790 but he continued to be involved in politics and went over to Pitt in 1793. Hoping for return to office, he had to be content with his nomination in 1796 as a privy councillor. A volume of his verse dedicated to his friend the poet William Mason was published in 1780. Cooper died very suddenly at Worlington, Suffolk, on 30 July 1801, and was buried in the church there, where a monument was erected to his memory. His widow died at Worlington on 3 November 1809, aged seventy-five.

W. P. COURTNEY, *rev.* HALLIE RUBENHOLD

**Sources** R. Christie, 'Cooper, Sir Grey', HoP, *Commons* · R. Welford, *Men of mark 'twixt Tyne and Tweed*, 3 vols. (1895) · J. Hutchinson, ed., *A catalogue of notable Middle Templars: with brief biographical notices* (1902) · Watt, *Bibl. Brit.* · *GM*, 1st ser., 71 (1801), 769–70 · *GM*, 1st ser., 79 (1809), 1084 · *The historical and the posthumous memoirs of Sir Nathaniel William Wraxall, 1772–1784*, ed. H. B. Wheatley, 5 vols. (1884), vol. 1, p. 428; vol. 3, p. 56; vol. 4, pp. 398, 402; vol. 5, p. 99 · G. Thomas, earl of Albemarle [G. T. Keppel], *Memoirs of the marquis of Rockingham and his contemporaries*, 2 vols. (1852), vol. 1, pp. 309–10 · *The Grenville papers: being the correspondence of Richard Grenville … and … George Grenville*, ed. W. J. Smith, 4 (1853), 157 · Nichols, *Illustrations*, 6.700–01 · *Report on the manuscripts of Mrs Stopford-Sackville*, 1, HMC, 49 (1904), 102–3 · GEC, *Baronetage*

**Archives** BL, letters to Lord Auckland, Add. MSS 34412–34460 · BL, letters to Frederick Haldimand, Add. MSS 21706–21707 · BL, letters to Lord Hardwicke, Add. MSS 35614–35659 · BL, letters to Sir Robert Murray Keith, Add. MSS 35510–35534, *passim* · BL, corresp. with Lord Liverpool, Add. MSS 38206–38309, 38406–38471, *passim* · BL OIOC, corresp. with Philip Francis, MSS Eur. C 8, D 18, E 12–22, F 5–6 · NL Scot., letters to Henry Dundas · Sheff. Arch., corresp. with Edmund Burke · U. Mich., Clements L., corresp. with Thomas Gage · U. Nott. L., letters to the third duke of Portland

**Likenesses** J. Sayers, caricature, etching, and mezzotint, pubd 1769, NPG

## Cooper, James (1846–1922),

**Cooper, James** (1846–1922), Church of Scotland minister and ecclesiastical historian, was born at Elgin, Morayshire, on 13 February 1846, the eldest son of John Alexander Cooper, a merchant, afterwards a farmer at Spynie, Elgin. His mother, Ann, daughter of James Stephen of Old Keith, was descended from the Gordons and Stuarts of Birkenburn. Educated at Elgin Academy and at Aberdeen University (1863–70), where he graduated MA in 1867, Cooper was licensed to preach in 1871. In 1873 he was ordained at St Stephen's Church, Broughty Ferry, and in 1881 was translated to the East Church of St Nicholas, Aberdeen; in 1898 he became regius professor of church history at Glasgow University.

Cooper was an energetic pastor and a faithful preacher. He introduced Holy Week services at St Stephen's, revived the daily service at Aberdeen, and was the first to institute a women's guild. Shortly after his induction to the East Church in Aberdeen his 'high church' doctrine and practices were challenged by some of the elders. The final verdict of the presbytery in the 'East Church case', however, represented a vindication of Cooper's position as belonging within the reformed tradition of the kirk. Passionately interested in church architecture and antiquities, he founded the Aberdeen Ecclesiological Society and later served four times as president of the Scottish Ecclesiological Society. He was also an active member of the Church Service Society, for which he produced an edition of 'Laud's liturgy' in 1904. He had previously edited the chartulary of the East Church, Aberdeen, for the New Spalding Club (1888–92).

Cooper reflected his upbringing in the episcopalian north-east of Scotland by being a lifelong advocate of the union of the Church of Scotland and the Church of England, a 'United Church for the British Empire'. He was the first secretary of the Scottish Church Society, founded in 1892 to advance Catholic doctrine, and he became one of the leaders of the 'Scoto-Catholic' party in the kirk. He took a prominent part in the negotiations for presbyterian reunion in Scotland, and secured what he considered to be an adequate safeguard for the Catholic faith in the new constitution of the kirk set out in the 'articles declaratory' of 1921. He was elected moderator of the general assembly in 1917, a tribute to the high regard in which he was held in the Church of Scotland.

As professor Cooper exercised a strong personal influence over students by his sincerity and piety; his cultured mind, varied interests, and generous hospitality also brought him a large circle of friends. He published a large number of sermons, addresses, and pamphlets, and in 1907 brought out *Confessions of Faith and Formulas of Subscription*. On 4 January 1912 he married Margaret (*d.* 1947), eldest daughter of George Williamson, a farmer at Shempston in Morayshire; they had no children. He received the freedom of Elgin (1917) and honorary degrees from the universities of Aberdeen (1892), Dublin (1909), Durham (1910), Oxford (1920), and Glasgow (1922). He died at Braemoriston, Elgin, on 27 December 1922, and was buried in Urquhart churchyard on 30 December.

W. FULTON, *rev.* D. M. MURRAY

**Sources**  H. J. Wotherspoon, *James Cooper: a memoir* (1926) • W. Fulton, 'The late Dr James Cooper: an appreciation', *Aberdeen University Review*, 10 (1922–3), 132–6 • J. M. Kirkpatrick, 'James Cooper, 1846–1922', *Church Service Society Annual*, 17 (1947), 3–11 • F. Franklin, 'James Cooper, 1846–1922', *Fathers of the kirk*, ed. R. S. Wright (1960), 261–73 • J. F. Leishman, *Linton leaves* (1937) • D. M. Murray, 'James Cooper (1846–1922) at Glasgow: presbytery and episcopacy', *Traditions of theology in Glasgow, 1450–1990*, ed. W. I. P. Hazlett (1993), 66–74 • D. M. Murray, 'James Cooper and the East Church case at Aberdeen, 1882–3: the high church movement vindicated', *Records of the Scottish Church History Society*, 19 (1975–7), 217–33 • D. M. Murray, 'Cooper bibliography', *The Record of the Church Service Society*, 29 (1995), 34–40 • D. M. Murray, *Freedom to reform: the 'Articles Declaratory', 1921* (1993) • G. Quig, 'The divinity staff at Glasgow University in 1903', *Records of the Scottish Church History Society*, 3 (1927–9), 210–19 • *The Times* (28 Dec 1922) • *Glasgow Herald* (28 Dec 1922) • *Fasti Scot.* • 'A man greatly beloved', *Transactions of the Scottish Ecclesiological Society*, 7/2 (1923), 4–25

**Archives**  U. Aberdeen L., special libraries and archives, corresp. and papers | Church of England Record Centre, Bermondsey, London, letters to F. C. Eeles • NA Scot., Sands MSS • U. Edin., New Coll. L., Balfour MSS • U. Edin., New Coll. L., White MSS • U. Glas., Church Service Society MSS

**Likenesses**  H. Mackenzie, oils, Church of Scotland assembly hall, Edinburgh

**Wealth at death**  £8888 13s. 2d.: confirmation, 9 March 1923, *CCI*

**Cooper, James Davis** (1823–1904), wood-engraver, was born on 18 November 1823 at Pratt's Place, Lambeth, London, the second son of George Cooper (*d.* 1843). His father was a church organist in London at St Sepulchre's, Snow Hill, and an assistant organist at St Paul's Cathedral. James was a pupil at the City of London School in 1837 and then, at the age of fourteen, left to train as a wood-engraver in the studio of Josiah Whymper in Canterbury Road, Lambeth. As an apprentice he showed considerable talent and quickly became skilled as a wood-engraver, eventually becoming one of the leading engravers of the sixties, a

period when book and periodical illustration flourished. Cooper made engravings of the work of many of the prominent artists of the time, including Miles Birket Foster, Dante Gabriel Rossetti, and Arthur Hughes, and provided illustrations for books by such notable figures as Darwin, Huxley, Livingstone, and Stanley. He also had the distinction of engraving illustrations for books by Queen Victoria, among them *Our Life in the Highlands* (1868). On 20 July 1848 he married Jane Eleanor, the daughter of Benjamin Ovington, a clerk in the Bank of England. They had three sons and four daughters. From 1848 Cooper lived at 10 Ely Place, Holborn, and by the following year he had established his own wood-engraving business. He later moved to Camberwell, and by 1855 he was working at 26 Great James Street, Bedford Row. Finally, by 1860 he had established a workshop at 188 Strand, where he worked until retirement.

Among Cooper's early works were engravings for an edition of *Robinson Crusoe* (1847) after drawings by Charles Keene (who was also trained by Whymper) and thought to be Keene's first published illustrations. Cooper often pursued his own ideas for books, finding a publisher and commissioning artists; in this way he was able to encourage and forward the careers of a number of talented illustrators, such as Robert Barnes, E. M. Wimperis, and William Small. During the 1850s and 1860s he provided wood-engravings for books produced in association with the printer Richard Clay, including a number of fine engravings for *The Farmer's Boy* (1858), after drawings by Birket Foster. His reputation was such that H. G. Bohn included him in his supplement to W. A. Chatto and J. Jackson's *Treatise on Wood-Engraving* (2nd edn, 1861) and featured examples of his engraving from *Childe Harold's Pilgrimage* (1859), after drawings by Percival Skelton, and *Select Poems and Songs of Robert Burns* (1858), after drawings by Birket Foster and Harrison Weir. Cooper produced engravings for many other notable books, among them *Favourite English Poems* (1859), Mrs Barbauld's *Hymns in Prose* (1863), *Pictures of English Life* (1865), and *Gulliver's Travels* (1865), after drawings by T. Morten. In particular he is known for his collaboration with Randolph Caldecott, who had his first success in book illustration with an edition of Washington Irving's *Old Christmas* (1876) followed by *Bracebridge Hall* (1877), both projects initiated by Cooper and published by Macmillan. Much of the success of these books was due to the excellent craftsmanship Cooper showed in his faithful interpretation of Caldecott's drawing and his skill in achieving the integration of text and image in the design of the page. In 1883 the two men collaborated on an edition of *Aesop's Fables*.

In 1857 Cooper took out a patent (no. 710) for his invention of an engraving technique which, through a reversal of the usual process, produced a relief printing surface by cutting out the areas to print black and then making an electrotype, filling in the recessed areas. This produced raised lines which, when ground, formed an even printing surface. However this 'improvement' never came into general use.

Cooper was also in demand as an engraver for magazines and periodicals, and contributed to the *Illustrated London News* and magazines such as the *British Workman*, *The Quiver*, *London Society*, *Friendly Visitor*, and *The Builder*, in which he showed his ability for engraving architectural subjects. His work appeared in the *Art Journal* from about 1863 and the *English Illustrated Magazine* in the 1880s. A most prestigious commission was for engravings of cloud effects from drawings by Ruskin which appeared in the *Art Journal* in 1884. Cooper is especially named in the text for having executed them to Mr Ruskin's satisfaction.

Towards the end of his life Cooper complained of being 'half-blind', as he suffered from cataracts, which forced him into retirement some years before his death, at the age of eighty. By all accounts he was a kind and genial man, 'jovial and breezy in manner' (*DNB*), with a lively intelligence to his last days. He died at Rothesay, his final home, in North Road, Highgate, Middlesex, on 27 February 1904, and was buried in March in the Great Northern London cemetery.　　　　　　　M. J. Andrews

**Sources** *The Times* (4 March 1904) · *The Builder*, 86 (1904), 259 · R. K. Engen, *Dictionary of Victorian wood engravers* (1985), 54 · W. Chatto, J. Jackson, and H. G. Bohn, *A treatise on wood-engraving*, 2nd edn (1861), 550–51 · *DNB* · H. Blackburn, *Randolph Caldecott: a personal memoir of his early art career* (1886); new edn (1890), 68, 95, 109, 134, 145 · 'Mr Ruskin on "The storm-cloud"', *Art Journal*, new ser., 4 (1884), 105–8 · E. de Maré, *The Victorian woodblock illustrators* (1980), 93, 95 · P. Goldman, *Victorian illustration* (1996) · *The reminiscences of Edmund Evans*, ed. R. McLean (1967), 55 · G. S. Layard, *The life and letters of Charles Samuel Keene* (1892), 11 · P. Muir, *Victorian illustrated books* (1971), 113, 165 · *The Portfolio*, 18 (1887), 166 · *Art Journal*, new ser., 24 (1904), 170 · *CGPLA Eng. & Wales* (1904)
**Archives** Macmillan (Publishers), Basingstoke, Hampshire, archive, MSS and corresp. · U. Reading, MSS
**Likenesses** R. Caldecott, cartoon (with Caldecott), repro. in Blackburn, *Randolph Caldecott*, 134
**Wealth at death** £2839 13s. 7d.: probate, 15 March 1904, *CGPLA Eng. & Wales*

**Cooper, Joan Davies** (1914–1999), social worker and civil servant, was born on 12 August 1914 at 38 Fairfield Square, Droylsden, Manchester, the only daughter and elder child of Valentine Holland Cooper (1885–1942), area manager, and Louisa Wynnefred Gardner (1885–1977), teacher. Born into a Moravian community, she professed no religion in later life. The values of her early upbringing, however, her mother's example, and the effects of the economic depression awoke the social conscience that inspired her to become one of the great social workers of her century.

Educated at Fairfield high school and the University of Manchester, Joan Cooper initially undertook teaching appointments with which she combined an interest in probation and social work. After joining Derbyshire education department in 1941, she worked with children who had been evacuated from their homes. She became assistant director of education in 1944, and in 1948 made the significant transition to the post of children's officer for east Sussex. She was in the forefront of that talented band, largely women, which faced the challenges and seized the opportunities of creating children's departments in local authorities following the 1948 Children Act. They met difficulties, and sometimes hostility, in seeking to modernize systems of child care dominated by the values of the poor law and the vested interests of large institutions. Cooper concentrated unswervingly on meeting the needs of the vulnerable and deprived children the new department had been created to serve. She sought ideas from the continent and North America, introduced training for staff, and developed both foster care and small residential homes. Greatly respected by her peers she was elected president of the Association of Children's Officers in 1954, and served on the National Advisory Council on Child Care at the Home Office.

In 1965 Cooper was recruited as chief inspector of the children's department at the Home Office. The appointment of an outsider to such a post was rather unusual at the time. However, she settled naturally to the role of civil servant without compromising her professional dedication to the welfare of children and their families. She contributed to important and progressive policies: the community development and urban aid programmes, the white papers leading to the Children and Young Persons Act of 1969, and the Local Authority Social Services Act of 1970. She transformed the children's inspectorate into an agency for change, infusing its existing function of professional audit with an ethos of creativity, innovation, and leadership.

Integration of the social services in 1971 was accompanied by similar changes in central government. The children's department left the Home Office for the Department of Health and Social Security, and Cooper became director of the new social work service there. The dominant health culture of the department was antipathetic to the concept of inspection, even in the creative form practised by the children's inspectorate. She worked selflessly to unify the new service and to provide social services departments with professional guidance and support during an extraordinary period of turbulence and growth. She was appointed CB in 1972.

Retirement in 1976 signalled a change in focus, not a withdrawal. Characteristically Cooper threw herself into sustained support for voluntary organizations, both national and local. She began a long association with the University of Sussex as visiting research fellow, and wrote *The Creation of the British Personal Social Services* (1983). From 1984 to 1986 she again assisted government as chair of the Central Council for Education and Training in Social Work. At the end of her life she led the group that planned the fiftieth anniversary celebrations of the Children Act of 1948.

All Cooper's adult life was spent in public service. Social work for her was a moral activity that demanded rigorous intellectual application. Her personal and professional authority provided a beacon to social workers in an ethically confused society. Her influence was enhanced by articles, books, and public speaking, as well as through the positions she held. A private person, fiercely independent, she was warm and generous in her relationships, encouraging younger colleagues and maintaining contact to the end of her life with children who had been in her care as a children's officer. Unmarried, she lived most of her adult life in Lewes, which she loved. She died at Brighton General Hospital on 15 January 1999, of pneumonia following a stroke, and was cremated at Brighton crematorium on 26 January. WILLIAM UTTING

Sources B. Holman, *Child care revisited: the children's departments, 1948–71*, Institute of Childcare and Social Education UK (1998) · *The Independent* (2 Feb 1999) · *The Times* (5 Feb 1999) · personal knowledge (2004) · private information (2004) [brother]
Archives U. Sussex, papers
Likenesses photograph, repro. in *The Times*
Wealth at death £273,910—gross; £272,550—net: probate, 8 April 1999, *CGPLA Eng. & Wales*

**Cooper, John** (*d.* **1729/30**). *See under* Cooper, Edward (*d.* 1725).

**Cooper, John** (1793–1870), actor, was born in Bath, the son of a tradesman. After playing Alonzo in E. Young's *The Revenge* in a private theatre, he appeared on the Bath stage, on 14 March 1811, as Inkle in *Inkle and Yarico* and subsequently in two or three other parts. Following a short visit to Cheltenham, he appeared on 15 May 1811 at the Haymarket in London as Count Montalban in John Tobin's *The Honeymoon*, and, besides playing other characters, was the original William Wyndham in W. Dimond's *Royal Oak* and Hartley in Theodore Hook's *Darkness Visible*. He then joined Andrew Cherry, the manager of several Welsh theatres, after whose death in 1812 he played in the north of England and Scotland. In Edinburgh he acted Edgar to Edmund Kean's King Lear, and was in Glasgow the original Virginius in Sheridan Knowles's tragedy of that name. In November 1820 he made his first appearance at Drury Lane, as Romeo, and was well received. In the course of the opening season at Drury Lane he played Antony in *Julius Caesar*, Tullus Aufidius in *Coriolanus*, Joseph in *The School for Scandal*, Richmond in *Richard III*, Iago to Kean's Othello, and many other parts.

Around 1825 Cooper married the widowed actress Mrs Dalton, originally Miss Walton, of Dublin. During the twenty-five years which followed his services were generally in request at Covent Garden, the Haymarket, the English Opera House, and the Surrey. A steady, capable, and eminently conscientious actor, but heavy and mechanical, he played during this period a singularly large number of parts, some of them of leading importance. He was the original Duke of Sheridan Knowles's *Love* at Covent Garden in 1839. Among his best parts were Iago and the Ghost in *Hamlet*. Cooper was also a great favourite in the York and Lincoln circuits, which he quitted for Norwich. There he was appointed stage-manager in 1843, in which year his wife died in London. In September 1845 the Norwich circuit passed into the hands of W. J. A. Abingdon, and Cooper joined Charles Gill at Newmarket. Next he was engaged by Knowles, the proprietor of the Theatre Royal, Manchester, and made his début there as Menenius in *Coriolanus*. Cooper was also popular in Hull and Leeds, and finally played under Charles Kean at the Princess's Theatre in London, performing such characters as Henry IV in *Henry IV, Part I*, the Duke of York in *Richard II*, and Kent

in *King Lear*. On retirement from the Princess's in 1859 he withdrew from the stage and lived on his savings. At the end of his life he lived at 6 Sandringham Gardens, Ealing, and he died on 13 July 1870 at Tunbridge Wells, where he had gone for his health.

JOSEPH KNIGHT, *rev.* NILANJANA BANERJI

Sources *The Era* (14 July 1870) · *The life and reminiscences of E. L. Blanchard, with notes from the diary of Wm. Blanchard*, ed. C. W. Scott and C. Howard, 2 vols. (1891) · T. Marshall, *Lives of the most celebrated actors and actresses* [1846–7] · 'Memoir of John Cooper', *Oxberry's Dramatic Biography*, 5/69 (1826), 73–86 · Adams, *Drama* · *The biography of the British stage, being correct narratives of the lives of all the principal actors and actresses* (1824) · *Era Almanack and Annual* (1892) · Hall, *Dramatic ports.* · Genest, *Eng. stage* · *London Magazine and Theatrical Inquisitor*, 3 (1821) · *Macready's reminiscences, and selections from his diaries and letters*, ed. F. Pollock, 2 vols. (1875) · J. W. Cole, *The life and theatrical times of Charles Kean … including a summary of the English stage for the last fifty years*, 2 vols. (1859)
Likenesses J. W. Gear, pencil, pen-and-ink drawing (as John of Paris), NPG · portrait, repro. in *Era Almanack and Annual* · portrait, repro. in J. Cumberland, *Cumberland's British theatre with remarks, biographical and critical* (1832) · portrait, repro. in 'Memoir of John Cooper', *Oxberry's Dramatic Biography* · portrait, repro. in *The Drama* (1821) · portrait, repro. in W. Oxberry, *The new English drama* (1822–3) · prints, Harvard TC · prints, BM, NPG

**Cooper, John** (1833/4–1920), animal trainer, was born in Bread Street, Birmingham, the son of a well-known carrier. Orphaned at the age of ten, he ran away with Hilton's menagerie. After a spell with Manders's menagerie, he became apprenticed to the animal trainer Thomas Batty. In 1852, with Batty in Leeds, Cooper distinguished himself by coolly securing the collar of a lion which had broken free. Batty's men had stood by, paralysed with fear, and Mrs Batty fainted. He was billed the next day as 'the youngest lion Tamer in the world'. Eventually his fame as a lion tamer reached the continent, and he joined the German menagerist Renz. Altogether he spent seventeen years abroad, visiting every town of note in Europe. In 1871 he was presented with a carved pipe by Victor Emmanuel II of Italy. In addition to his group of lions, Cooper became the proprietor of trained elephants. After returning to Britain, in the mid-1870s he joined James W. Myers's American circus, and remained with them until Myers sold up in 1882. Cooper then decided to retire, and sold his animals in 1883, but his love of the profession was so strong that he joined Edmonds's (previously Wombwell's) menagerie, as a trainer and exhibitor. With Edmonds he travelled England, Wales, Germany, Belgium, the Netherlands, and Denmark. His performances with the lions and leopards, in each cage, lasted twenty minutes and people stood spellbound.

Cooper was a gentle, quiet, and unassuming man whose wonderful control over his animals was legendary. He was the surest tamer of his day, dispensing with all kinds of glitter, and performed in plain evening dress, often without even a switch in his hand. He had a large, dark beard, and beautiful blue eyes. Eventually he retired to Penzance, but then he returned to the midlands, first to Cotteridge, Birmingham, and finally to a commodiously furnished house in Wolverhampton, surrounded by an extensive library, oil paintings, and presentations from crowned heads. He was said to have owned property in Birmingham. He died, unmarried, on 15 April 1920, at his home, 2 Cleveland Road, Wolverhampton; according to his death certificate he was eighty-six. He was buried at Penn Fields.             JOHN M. TURNER

**Sources** *Chums* (28 Aug 1895), 13 · *World's Fair* (24 April 1920), 7 · *World's Fair* (28 March 1925), 10 · G. Speaight, *A history of the circus* (1980), 84 · J. L. Middlemiss, *A zoo on wheels* (1987), 27 · d. cert.
**Likenesses** engravings (after photographs by Burgoyne and Möbus), repro. in *Chums*
**Wealth at death** £2050 4s. 11d.: probate, 27 July 1920, *CGPLA Eng. & Wales*

**Cooper, John** [Jack], **Baron Cooper of Stockton Heath** (**1908–1988**), trade unionist, was born on 7 June 1908 at 26 Dundonald Avenue, Stockton Heath, Cheshire, the son of John Ainsworth Cooper, bricklayer, and his wife, Annie Lily, *née* Dukes, daughter of George Harry Dukes, spade plater, and sister of Charles Dukes, first and only Baron Dukeston, general secretary of the National Union of General and Municipal Workers (GMW). Jack Cooper, as he was always known, was educated at the local Stockton Heath primary, from which he won a place at Lymm grammar school, Cheshire—an unusually successful achievement for a working-class boy in those days, and an early indication of a sharpness of mind that was later to bring him considerable prominence.

Cooper's first job after leaving grammar school was as a general hand at Crosfields soapworks in Warrington, where he started in 1924 at the age of sixteen. He swiftly became a member of his uncle's union. Dukes was then Lancashire district organizer—a key post in one of the union's strongest regions. That was the first step on the trade union ladder which, eventually, would take both Dukes and Cooper to the most senior position in the union. After filling a number of lay posts in the union Cooper became a full-time official in 1928, albeit in a junior capacity, at the age of twenty. Even so he had already shown considerable ability in recruiting members to the union, and six years later he was appointed to the post once held by his uncle—Lancashire district organizer. From that point Cooper's future was marked out as a potential leader of the union—such was the strength of his family connection. On 11 August 1934 he married Nellie Spencer (*b.* 1903/4), a shop assistant, and daughter of Paul Spencer, a cold storage manager, of Warrington. There were three daughters of the marriage.

The big move for Cooper was when he became southern district secretary of the union in 1944. But in the intervening ten years as Lancashire district organizer he played an increasingly prominent role in local politics, and was a member of Manchester city council from 1936 to 1942. That was a powerful combination of Labour politics and trade union influence, which established Cooper's credentials for promotion to a national platform. That followed with his move to London in 1944. From then on it was clear that he was destined to play a powerful role in the direction of the union. Charles Dukes retired in 1946 to enter the House of Lords and be succeeded by Tom Williamson—who also had family connections.

Cooper was brought more closely into the political affairs of the union, and in 1949 he was elected to the London county council (LCC). A year later he won the parliamentary seat of Deptford, in south-east London, a Labour stronghold with powerful trade union links. Attlee was in his final spell as leader of the Labour Party and prime minister, and Cooper was given early preferment by Attlee—himself a member of the GMW. Cooper was appointed parliamentary private secretary to Patrick Gordon Walker, secretary of state for Commonwealth affairs. He lost his seat at Deptford in the 1951 general election but was given a token compensation by becoming an LCC alderman in 1952 as well as national chairman of his union, to be followed one year later by nomination as GMW representative on the Labour Party national executive committee. He remained on the party executive for four years and was a strong supporter of Hugh Gaitskell in his fight against the Bevanites and the Labour left. Throughout this period Cooper remained district secretary of the union's southern region, a post he retained until 1961. Yet even before becoming general secretary he was already a significant figure on the right wing of labour politics, and his role was still further enhanced when he joined the TUC general council in 1959. By then he was very much the heir apparent to Williamson, and when Williamson retired in 1961 Cooper was duly elected to succeed—a unique element being that he was the second member of the Dukes family connection to inherit the highest post in the union.

An extraordinary hiatus in Cooper's hitherto smooth career occurred in June 1959 at the GMW annual conference in Scarborough. With Cooper in the chair and Williamson as general secretary the conference delegates caused a sensation by voting with left-wing rebels for unilateral nuclear disarmament. By 150 votes to 126, with 75 abstentions, the GMW aligned itself with left-wing unions such as Frank Cousins's Transport and General Workers. The whole event was vastly out of character, politically and tactically. Cooper was blamed for the way he handled the vote—especially allowing seventy-five delegates to abstain because they were absent from the hall, probably in the tea room. The Labour leadership, including Gaitskell, were thrown into confusion, and the vote was corrected only by the device of an extraordinary recall conference which, under pressure, duly reversed the decision on nuclear disarmament. Nevertheless, it left a hugely embarrassing cloud over the union. However, in later years Cooper atoned for any error of judgement in 1959 by his unswerving support for right-wing policies, politically and industrially.

Yet there was a radical streak to Cooper. During his earlier years on the TUC general council he argued strongly for greater industrial discipline, sterner measures against unofficial strikes, a more rational wages policy—he was one of the first union leaders to propose a form of incomes policy which he considered would be an advantage to the lower-paid. At the same time he began to advocate, and put into practice, some of the earliest moves to modernize trade union structure. He promoted training facilities for his members, inaugurated a research department, and bought a new headquarters for the union (Ruxley Towers, near Esher, Surrey) in which he set about modernizing the entire organization. He even attempted to co-ordinate activities with two of his major rival unions—the Transport and General Workers and the Amalgamated Engineering Union. That move came to nothing, but he did succeed in moving his union into commercial investments, using union funds to buy industrial and commercial shares, as well as supporting the newly fledged Trade Union Unit Trust set up by Lord Hirshfield. He was chairman of the TUC in 1970–71, when the unions campaigned against the Heath government's Industrial Relations Bill—though privately he actually agreed with a number of the proposals in that legislation. Cooper previously had given firm backing to Barbara Castle's legislative proposals in *In Place of Strife* in 1969, despite the disapproval of most of his colleagues on the TUC leadership.

Cooper was not a good orator but rather a sound organization man and negotiator; had he possessed the platform style of the more impassioned Labour and trade union leaders he might well have left a more lasting impression. But his political moderation always seemed to apply the brake on his speaking style. He retired as general secretary of the National Union of General and Municipal Workers in 1973. In his later years he was appointed a part-time member of the National Bus Company, a director of Yorkshire Television, and a member of the Meat and Livestock Commission and of the Thames Conservancy Board. He was chairman of the British Productivity Council from 1965 to 1966 and of the National Water Council from 1973 to 1977. He was made a life peer by Harold Wilson in 1966 though, subsequently, this did not prevent him voting for the abolition of the upper house.

In many ways the most unorthodox aspect of Cooper's life came towards the end when, in 1969, he divorced his wife of thirty-five years to marry a childhood sweetheart, Mrs Joan Rogers, whom he had last met forty-five years earlier when she was thirteen. He fell under her spell again and in 1969 she became the second Lady Cooper. He died at Chessington, Surrey, on 2 September 1988 after a heart attack. He was survived by his second wife and by the three daughters of his first marriage.

GEOFFREY GOODMAN

**Sources** WWW, 1981–90 · *Daily Telegraph* (13 Sept 1988) · *The Times* (14 Sept 1988) · *The Guardian* (14 Sept 1988) · Trade Union Congress general council annual reports · G. Goodman, *The awkward warrior: Frank Cousins, his life and times* (1979) · H. A. Clegg, *General union: a study of the National Union of General and Municipal Workers* (1954) · E. A. Radice and G. H. Radice, *Will Thorne: constructive militant* (1974) · b. cert. · m. cert., 1934 · *CGPLA Eng. & Wales* (1988)
**Likenesses** photograph, repro. in *Daily Telegraph* · photograph, repro. in *The Times* · photograph, repro. in *The Guardian*
**Wealth at death** £95,297: probate, 18 Oct 1988, *CGPLA Eng. & Wales*

**Cooper, John Astley** (*bap.* 1858, *d.* 1930), propagandist for athleticism, baptized on 21 April 1858, was the oldest of the six children of the Revd Astley Cooper, the English-born vicar of St Mary's Church, Adelaide, Australia, and his wife, Fanny. The family returned to England in 1870 and Cooper matriculated as a non-collegiate student at the University of Oxford in 1878 but did not take a degree. Little is known about his professional or private life, although he claimed to be a company director and travelled to Africa on business at least once.

Cooper was an enthusiastic imperialist who first gave public expression to his views in July 1891, when he anonymously published an article entitled 'Many lands—one people' in *Greater Britain*. Later that year he put forward his proposals for an Anglo-Saxon Olympiad the aim of which was to provide a new bond for an empire threatened (as he saw it) by both internal divisions and foreign rivals. He advocated the strengthening of a 'great network of a common literature, fine arts, academic studies and athletic exercises', of which the latter was the most important. His views were crudely Darwinistic, and presented the English-speaking race as having a God-given responsibility for the extension of civilization; in this work the United States was envisaged as very much a junior partner to the British empire. When J. A. Froude supported him in *The Times* in 1892, Cooper's ideas received a much wider airing; and the British national and provincial press was matched in its enthusiasm by that of the empire.

Despite this, and despite the refining of his views in such journals as the *Nineteenth Century*, Cooper's proposals foundered because of apprehension about the likely costs and because of widespread apathy. He was also pushed out of the limelight by the growing acceptance of Pierre de Coubertin's proposals for an international Olympiad, which would serve as a peacemaker between imperial rivalries. Cooper returned to obscurity until 1908, when the Olympics were held in London and he was able to claim them as a triumph of his ideas. He also claimed to have invented Empire day, more usually ascribed to Reginald Brabazon, twelfth earl of Meath.

Cooper subsequently found another outlet for his views in the Royal Colonial Institute and its journal *United Empire*. He reiterated his views, if anything more crudely, in its pages in 1910, at a time of growing international uncertainty. His last known contribution came after the outbreak of the First World War, when his jingoism and assumptions about the automatic superiority of the British were presented again in *United Empire* (vol. 7, 1916), in his lecture 'The British imperial spirit of sport and the war'. This rambling panegyric to militant athleticism appeared just before the battle of the Somme revealed how tenuous such claims were.

Cooper hit a popular vein of assumed superiority which events called into question. Although he disappeared from the public press after 1916 many of his ideas survived the war and came to fruition with the establishment of the British empire games, first held at Hamilton, Ontario, Canada, in August 1930. Cooper died on 4 February 1930, aged seventy-three, at 2 Beach Houses, Beach Road, Westgate-on-Sea, Kent, survived by his wife, Agnes.

J. R. LOWERSON

**Sources** K. Moore, 'A neglected imperialist', *International Journal of the History of Sport*, 8 (1991) · J. A. Mangan, *The games ethic and imperialism* (1986) · J. Lowerson, *Sport and the English middle classes, 1870–1914* (1993) · *Wellesley index* · Foster, *Alum. Oxon.* · census returns, 1881 · d. cert.

**Cooper, John Gilbert** (1722–1769), writer, was born on 24 August 1722 at Lockington, Leicestershire, the eldest of five children of John Gilbert (*bap.* 1672?, *d.* 1773) and Dorothy (*bap.* 1695, *d.* 1727), daughter of William and Martha Bainbrigge. His father inherited the estate of a relation, John Cooper of Thurgarton Priory in Nottinghamshire, on condition that he took Cooper's name and arms. He therefore introduced a private bill into the House of Lords; this received royal assent on 5 May 1736, after which date father and son both took the name John Gilbert Cooper.

Gilbert Cooper received his early education in Sutton Coldfield, proceeding to Westminster School in 1733, and to Trinity College, Cambridge, as a fellow-commoner in 1740. He studied at Gröningen University for eight months from February 1743, after which he toured the United Provinces and Germany, returning to England in May 1744.

Gilbert Cooper's poetic career began in 1742, with the anonymous publication of a poem, *The Temples of Virtue and Pleasure*. *The Power of Harmony*, a philosophical poem heavily influenced by Lord Shaftesbury's *Characteristicks* and Mark Akenside's *The Pleasures of Imagination*, followed in 1745. Gilbert Cooper also contributed extensively to *The Museum* (1746–7), a periodical published by Robert Dodsley and edited by Akenside; his contributions were usually signed Philaretes.

On 22 October 1748 Gilbert Cooper married Susanna (1723×5–1751), the eldest daughter of William Wright, recorder of Leicester. His father now settled on him lands in Nottinghamshire and Lincolnshire, and Gilbert Cooper began extensive works on Thurgarton Priory, to which he and his family moved early in 1751. The marriage produced three children: Henry (1749), who died aged one day, and for whom Gilbert Cooper wrote a Latin epitaph, much criticized for its pomposity and apparent insincerity; Susanna (1750–1802); and John (1751–1822). His wife died on 10 November 1751, seven weeks after the birth of John.

Gilbert Cooper became embroiled in a literary controversy on the publication of his historical work, *The Life of Socrates* (1749). In it he showed little respect for established scholarship; and in particular he singled out the works of William Warburton for attack. Warburton retaliated in a note to *An Essay on Criticism* in his edition of Pope (1751), and Gilbert Cooper swiftly replied in a pamphlet, *Cursory Remarks on Mr Warburton's New Edition of Mr Pope's Works*, complaining that Warburton's comments had been personal. His complaint is undercut by his own, very personal, attack on the future bishop's work as 'nothing but [what] the inflamed Brain of a rank Monk could conceive, or the Oyster-selling Maids near *London-Bridge* could utter' (p. 5). Dr Johnson was perhaps recalling this controversy when he retorted, on hearing that Gilbert Cooper had

called him 'the Caliban of literature', 'I must dub him the Punchinello' (Boswell, *Life*, 2.129).

Gilbert Cooper's next work, *Letters Concerning Taste* (1754), was the first book-length contribution in English to the subject. The perspective adopted is both philosophically informed and critically analytic, an approach which was to prove influential. In the later 1750s he turned again to the publication of poetry, including *Epistles to the Great, from Aristippus in Retirement* (1757); *The Call of Aristippus* (1758); and a translation of Jean-Baptiste-Louis Gresset's mock-heroic tale of a nunnery parrot, *Ver-vert* (1759). These three works are in a French metre introduced into English by Gilbert Cooper, in which octosyllabic couplets are interspersed irregularly among octosyllabic lines rhyming on different patterns. He published nothing new after 1759, although a manuscript comedy, 'The Lover's Resolution', dated 1762, survives (Nottinghamshire County RO, M9660), and in 1764 the Dodsleys published a selection of his poetry.

From November 1755 Gilbert Cooper lived mainly in London, where he became actively involved in the Society for the Encouragement of Arts, Manufactures, and Commerce; he is said to have resigned when he failed to be elected as the society's vice-president. Gilbert Cooper died at his house in Mayfair on 14 April 1769, having suffered from kidney stones, and was buried on 21 April at Thurgarton.                                                                 ROBIN DIX

**Sources** [J. Gilbert Cooper], 'Anecdotes concerning the life and writings of John Gilbert Cooper esqr', Notts. Arch., M9659 · *DNB* · A. Chalmers, ed., *The general biographical dictionary*, new edn, 32 vols. (1812–17) · J. V. Price, 'Cooper, John Gilbert', *The dictionary of eighteenth-century British philosophers*, ed. J. W. Yolton, J. V. Price, and J. Stephens (1999) · A. Kippis and others, eds., *Biographia Britannica, or, The lives of the most eminent persons who have flourished in Great Britain and Ireland*, 2nd edn, 5 vols. (1778–93) · R. A. Davenport, 'The life of John Gilbert Cooper', *The poems of Cooper and Cotton*, The British poets, 72 (1822) · 'Life', *Poetical works of John Gilbert Cooper*, Bell's Edition: the Poets of Great Britain, 10 (1794) · A. Chalmers, 'The life of Gilbert Cooper', *The works of the English poets from Chaucer to Cowper*, ed. A. Chalmers, 15 (1810) · K. J. H. Berland, 'Bringing philosophy down from the heavens: Socrates and the new science', *Journal of the History of Ideas*, 47 (1986), 299–308 · R. Dix, 'John Gilbert Cooper: a poet in search of his metier and meter', *Age of Johnson*, 13 (2002), 255–81
**Archives** Notts. Arch., autobiography, letters received, MS play, family bibles, etc. | Bodl. Oxf., letters to Robert Dodsley, MS Eng. misc. d. 174
**Wealth at death** claimed father's estates in Nottinghamshire and Lincolnshire settled on him in 1748, but family finances complex: [Cooper], 'Anecdotes', Notts. Arch., M9659

**Cooper, John Newton** (1923–2000), racing car engineer, was born at 49 Fassett Road, Kingston upon Thames, Surrey, on 17 July 1923, the son of Charles Newton Cooper (1893–1964), motor engineer, and Violet Elsie (*née* Paul). Educated at Surbiton county school, he left at fifteen to become apprenticed to one of his father's toolmaking companies. He moved on to another company specializing in naval equipment, then spent the Second World War as an aircraft instrument maker, serving in the RAF in 1944–5.

John Cooper had grown up in the world of motor racing,

as his father, who ran a garage in Surbiton, had maintained Kaye Don's Wolseley Viper Brooklands racer. When Cooper was eight his father had made him a half-scale car and at twelve he was given a lightweight Austin Seven special. After the war John Cooper and a friend built a small racing car, a single-seater with rear-mounted engine, for the new 500 cc racing class. The Cooper 500 performed creditably in the motor-sport season of 1947 and in response to demand two initial batches each of twelve replicas were built and the Cooper Car Co. Ltd was established in 1948. The rear-engined Cooper 500 virtually dominated Formula 3 racing until the formula came to an end in 1958: some 360 cars had been built by 1956. John Cooper successfully raced the works car for several years before leaving the circuit to become Cooper racing manager, and he remained co-director of the Cooper F1 racing team until 1969. The company progressed successfully to Formula 2 and then to Formula 1, winning the world championship in 1959 and 1960. Charles Cooper ran the manufacturing business as a tight ship, with dingy works premises and poorly paid staff, yet without losing their loyalty. John Cooper's attitudes were more relaxed than his father's, and his longer-term vision resulted in frequent quarrels between them. Yet father and son together have been praised for setting the pattern of the modern grand prix car. The innovator can expect to be challenged and despite the early Formula 1 successes Cooper, partly as a result of its cautious attitude towards expansion, found itself overtaken by Colin Chapman's Lotus Cars. Two major setbacks to the Cooper Car Co. occurred in the early 1960s: in 1963 John Cooper was badly injured when his prototype twin-engined Mini-Cooper somersaulted to destruction on the Kingston bypass. This accident was followed on 2 October 1964 by the death of his father at the age of seventy. John took a long time to recover from his injuries and in 1965 he sold the business to the Chipstead Motor Group.

However, the Cooper–Mini link, although responsible for John's accident, kept the name of Cooper in the forefront of sporting motoring for the rest of his life. Alec Issigonis, the designer of the innovatory Mini, was an old acquaintance, and John Cooper became very interested in the motor-sport potential of the little transverse-engined car. Issigonis did not share this enthusiasm but a Cooper-tuned Mini impressed George Harriman, the chairman of the British Motor Corporation (BMC). An agreement for a trial production of 1000 Mini-Coopers, with royalties for Cooper, was quickly reached; project ADO 50, the 997 cc Mini-Cooper, was launched in July 1961. The model achieved outright wins in the Monte Carlo rallies of 1964 and 1965; took the first three places in the 1966 rally, but suffered a controversial disqualification; then achieved first overall in 1967. By the time British Leyland, which had taken over BMC, discontinued the Mini-Cooper in 1971 some 150,000 cars had been built. On the closure of the Cooper racing team at the end of 1969 John Cooper moved to the south coast, where he opened John Cooper Garages Ltd at Ferring, near Worthing, Sussex.

A new chapter in the Mini-Cooper's history began in 1985, when the showing of a Cooper-converted Mini in Japan resulted in 1000 orders and the production of a British conversion kit at the time of the Mini's thirtieth anniversary (1989). The launch of the 1275 cc Mini-Cooper, initially a limited run of 1000 as a Rover special product, resulted and was followed by mainstream production and an agreement that an S-conversion pack produced by Cooper would receive full Rover warranty. The take-over of Rover by BMW meant that development to meet tighter emission regulations could be undertaken. Mini-Cooper activity flourished, and the business was moved a few miles from the Ferring Garage to East Preston. Mini production ended shortly before John Cooper's death, but both he and his son had been involved from the outset in the design of the new-generation Mini, which was launched at the 2000 motor show.

Cooper married Pauline (Paula) Marie Brady (b. 1924/5) on 25 June 1947. They had three children: two daughters, one of whom predeceased him, and a son, Michael, who continued the business and the Cooper involvement with the Mini. To the purist 'the Cooper conception of a Grand Prix car … could hardly be called "design", for it was an obvious development of something that had started out as a convenient compromise' (Clutton and others, 231). However, this cautious judgement in no way detracts from John Cooper's and the Cooper family's achievements—the Cooper 500, the grand prix cars of the 1950s, and the Mini-Cooper line, which gave a much needed fillip to Britain's troubled motor industry. John Cooper, who was president of the British Racing and Sports Car Club, was appointed CBE in 1999 for his services to British motor racing. He had been suffering from cancer for some time before his death on 24 December 2000. His funeral service took place at Arundel Cathedral. Many tributes were paid, not only to his engineering skill, but also to the warmth, openness, and charm of his personality.

RICHARD A. STOREY

**Sources** *The Times* (26 Dec 2000) · *Daily Telegraph* (27 Dec 2000) · *The Independent* (27 Dec 2000) · *The Scotsman* (27 Dec 2000) · *The Guardian* (5 Jan 2001) · 'Tribute to John Cooper CBE 1923–2000', *MiniWorld* (April 2001), 19–29 · C. Clutton, C. Posthumus, and D. Jenkinson, *The racing car: development and design*, rev edn (1962) · G. N. Georgano, ed., *The Beaulieu encyclopaedia of the automobile* (2000) · b. cert. · m. cert.

**Likenesses** photograph, repro. in *Daily Telegraph* · photograph, repro. in *The Times* · photograph, repro. in *The Independent*

**Cooper, John Thomas** (1790–1854), chemist, was born on 29 June 1790 in Greenwich. He studied medicine and for a short while was a general practitioner, but, unable to cope with the anxiety and fatigue involved, turned to chemistry. He was married to Elizabeth ( *fl.* 1785–1840) though further details are unknown; their second son, the naturalist Daniel *Cooper, predeceased his father. Until 1842 he made his living from lecturing as well as from selling chemicals, acting as a consultant analytical chemist, and devising or improving scientific instruments.

As early as 1810 he delivered popular lectures on chemistry in Mount Street, Lambeth. He later lectured on chemistry at the Russell Institution, at the Aldersgate school of medicine, and at the school of medicine in Webb Street, Southwark (founded by Edward Grainger), a position he occupied until 1842 when the school closed. Following this he devoted himself solely to the other aspects of professional chemistry.

In his business of selling chemicals Cooper was at one time the sole supplier of iodine in Britain and a successful preparer of potassium and sodium when the price of these elements was 10 and 12 guineas per ounce. In 1825 he used matches with heads made of sulphur and phosphorous.

In the course of his career Cooper invented several scientific instruments and made improvements to many more. In 1823 he published details of an improved apparatus for analysing organic bodies and also an account of a new hydrometer. For these two inventions he was respectively awarded, in 1823, the large silver medal and the gold Vulcan medal of the Society of Arts, of which he was a member between 1815 and 1829. With the optical instrument making company founded by William Cary he invented the oxy-hydrogen microscope, which he had perfected by 1835 and which was manufactured and retailed by Edward Montague Clarke. In 1839 he invented a baroscope which formed the subject of his only paper in the *Philosophical Transactions of the Royal Society* and the topic of his first Friday evening discourse at the Royal Institution. His only other Royal Institution discourse, in 1841, was on electroplating. In 1840 he published a paper recommending the use of copper instead of platinum in the electric cell recently invented by William Robert Grove; this suggestion led Robert Wilhelm Bunsen to invent his own cell. In 1843 he published improvements to William Hyde Wollaston's refractometer. He was also the first to employ Canada balsam for mounting microscopic objects, an invention of important practical use.

As a consultant analytical chemist Cooper appeared in trials (including the Severn and King insurance case in 1820) to give expert testimony. In 1827 he carried out some chemical experiments for the subcommittee of the joint Royal Society and board of longitude committee to improve optical glass. This subcommittee (which comprised John Frederick William Herschel, George Dollond, and Michael Faraday) was responsible for making optical glass and determining its properties. In the late 1840s and early 1850s Cooper's analytical services were retained by various London water companies in their fight with Edwin Chadwick. He published some of the analyses that he performed, such as of calculi (1816), zinc ores (1820), and ancient ruby (1824). One of the results of these kinds of activities was that he made several chemical discoveries. For instance, in 1817 he described some new compounds of platinum and two years later a method to separate lime and magnesia. He independently discovered iodoform (though it was originally thought of as the sesqui-iodide of carbon) about 1823, but because Cooper failed to publish it the credit went to Georges-Simon Serullas. One interest that he had which seems not to have stemmed from his analytical work was in the Fraunhofer lines of the solar spectrum. In 1831 he published a method

of observing them and in 1839 announced, in a note published in the *Proceedings of the Royal Society*, that the infrared spectrum also contained Fraunhofer lines.

Cooper was described in the *Gentleman's Magazine* as having an unostentatious character, which doubtless accounts for the paucity of information about him, but he was, nevertheless, well-known in London's scientific community; he was one of the founders of the Chemical Society in 1841, and is said also to have had a connection with the Spitalfields Mathematical Society. He died after a long and painful illness on 24 September 1854 at his home, 82 Blackfriars Road, London, and was buried in Norwood cemetery. He was survived by a son and a daughter.

FRANK A. J. L. JAMES

**Sources** *Quarterly Journal of the Chemical Society*, 8 (1856), 109–10 · *GM*, 2nd ser., 42 (1854), 521 · J. R. Partington, *A history of chemistry*, 4 (1964) · *The jubilee of the Chemical Society of London: record of the proceedings, with an account of the society, 1841–1891*, Chemical Society of London (1896) · R. F. Bud and G. K. Roberts, *Science versus practice: chemistry in Victorian Britain* (1984) · RS, Cooper MSS · *The correspondence of Michael Faraday*, ed. F. A. J. L. James, 1–2 (1991–3) · *Catalogue of scientific papers*, Royal Society, 2 (1868), 42
**Archives** RS, Herschel MSS

**Cooper, Joshua Edward Synge** (1901–1981), cryptanalyst and intelligence officer, was born on 3 April 1901 in Fulham, the son of Richard Edward Synge Cooper, a chartered engineer, and his wife, Mary Eleanor, youngest daughter of William Burke. Joshua was the eldest of five children, four sons and a daughter, all brought up in England, but both parents came from Ireland, the Coopers being a well-known family associated with Castle Markree in co. Sligo. Joshua's great-grandfather was the astronomer Edward Joshua Cooper FRS.

Cooper was educated at Shrewsbury School and took a scholarship in classics to Brasenose College, Oxford. After taking a third class in classical honour moderations in 1921 he entered King's College, London, to read Russian and Serbian in which he took a first in 1924. In 1925 he was one of a small number of graduates recruited into the Foreign Office to work in the Government Code and Cypher School (GCCS) by its director, A. G. Denniston. It is said that these recruits were not told at their interviews the kind of work in which they would be engaged. In 1934 he married Winifred Blanche de Vere, daughter of Thomas Frederick Parkinson, a civil engineer in India. They had two sons, the elder of whom died in 1956.

Also in 1934 the Air Ministry decided that, like the Royal Navy and the army, the Royal Air Force needed to have its own stations to intercept the signals of potential opponents, and in 1936 Cooper, who was already a distinguished cryptanalyst in GCCS, was seconded to the Air Ministry as head of AI 1(e) to analyse the intercepted material. He remained head of what became known as the air section until 1943, when he was transferred back to the Foreign Office. At the beginning of this period the role of his section (like GCCS) was seen simply as that of cipher-breaking, and the section only received enciphered messages, the plain language being analysed elsewhere.

Cooper changed this curious arrangement and thus prepared for the wartime work against the Luftwaffe. With the outbreak of war, and the great increase in Luftwaffe traffic, a number of bright young men and women, service and civilian, were assigned to its analysis at Bletchley or at the interception stations. Cooper was their mentor and inspiration.

The air section and its associated stations provided immediate and longer-term information to the Air Ministry and RAF commands on every aspect of the operations of the Luftwaffe. For example, in 1939–40 there were serious questions about the size of the Luftwaffe resulting from differing views in the Air Ministry and the Ministry of Economic Warfare. Winston Churchill appointed Sir John Singleton to conduct an inquiry and this was followed by studies by F. A. Lindemann. It was finally agreed that there had been a substantial overestimate of German strength, because the basic unit of the Luftwaffe, the Staffel, had been wrongly assessed by the Air Ministry as consisting of twelve aircraft. It was the air section which demonstrated conclusively that the true size was nine, and Cooper himself presented the evidence in these inquiries.

In his subsequent career at Government Communications Headquarters (GCHQ) ending up as an assistant director in charge of GCHQ's research work, Cooper demonstrated the great range of his mind and his ability to comprehend in fields such as mathematics and physics which were outside those in which he had been educated. He realized very early the potential significance of the postwar development of computers and ensured that his colleagues understood it too.

Cooper was not an administrator but was always admired and beloved by those who worked for him and with him; his mannerisms were endearing, his eccentricities much embellished in the telling. The latter arose from his concentration on the subject occupying his mind. With his extraordinary memory and instant recall, he would resume a conversation without preamble or reference after a lapse of weeks. He retired in 1961 and published *Russian Companion* in 1967 and *Four Russian Plays* in 1972. He was always very close to his brother Arthur R. V. Cooper, the distinguished Chinese scholar, and shared ideas with him based on their complementary knowledge of languages.

Cooper took it as axiomatic that the safety of Britain and its citizens in peace and war depended on the effectiveness of its intelligence services; and that, to be effective, this work must remain secret—he deplored the spate of wartime reminiscences—and must be with malice toward none. Cooper, who was appointed CMG in 1943 and CB in 1958, died at Amersham, Buckinghamshire, on 14 June 1981.                    D. R. NICOLL, *rev.*

**Sources** R. Lewin, *ULTRA goes to war: the secret story* (1978) · *The Times* (18 June 1981) · N. West, *GCHQ* (1986) · F. H. Hinsley and others, *British intelligence in the Second World War*, 1 (1979) · private information (1990) · personal knowledge (1990) · *CGPLA Eng. & Wales* (1981)

**Wealth at death** £2542: probate, 10 Sept 1981, *CGPLA Eng. & Wales*

**Cooper, Lettice Ulpha** (1897–1994), writer, was born at 133 Monton Road, Eccles, Lancashire, on 3 September 1897, the eldest child of Yorkshire parents, Leonard Cooper, a constructional engineer and merchant, and Agnes Helena, *née* Fraser. From the age of seven she wrote and told stories, greatly encouraged by her father, who made her feel that books mattered. She was educated by a governess at the family home near Leeds, before attending St Cuthbert's, a boarding-school in Southbourne, and Lady Margaret Hall, Oxford, where she read classics in 1916–18.

Returning to Yorkshire, Lettice Cooper joined the family engineering firm. Her first novel, *The Lighted Room*, appeared in 1925 and was one of ten novels written while she was living at home. Of these, *The New House* (1936), a fine and technically accomplished work which takes place within one day, was described by Lettice Cooper as 'a novel of feelings and relationships, rather than a portrait of a place' (Virago publicity form), and won her the accolade 'Chekhov in Yorkshire' from the *Manchester Guardian* of the time.

*National Provincial* (1938) was written shortly after Lettice Cooper joined the Labour Party and is a vivid demonstration of her socialist principles. Though her family were 'staunchly Conservative', Lettice Cooper's own political views were shaped at Oxford and were confirmed during the depression when she worked in a centre for unemployed men. An extensive portrait of Leeds during the 1930s, *National Provincial* dramatizes the political differences and shades of feeling during that period of flux. The novel found many admirers, including Lady Rhondda, who invited Lettice Cooper to join the staff of *Time and Tide*, where she was associate editor for a year in 1939. She was joined in London by her sister Barbara, also a writer (she was John Lehmann's secretary for some twenty years, beginning in 1939), with whom she shared a flat in Swiss Cottage.

The Second World War interrupted Lettice Cooper's writing career. She joined the public relations division of the Ministry of Food and was also an air raid warden. In 1947 she became the fiction reviewer of the *Yorkshire Post*, a position she was to hold for the next ten years. During those years, and until the 1970s, Lettice Cooper made annual trips to Florence to visit Lionel Fielden, the creator of All India Radio. Her close friendship with Fielden, who was homosexual and referred to her as his 'cover girl', was highly important in Cooper's life. Florence, a city she much loved, provides the setting for *Fenny* (1953). A Book Society choice on publication, the novel explores the emotional and political development of a young English governess, alongside the growth of fascism and the Second World War.

Lettice Cooper's other work includes a biography of Robert Louis Stevenson (1947)—she was president of the Robert Louis Stevenson Society from 1958 to 1978 and its vice-chair for the last three of those years—a monograph on George Eliot (1951; rev. 1960, 1964), and numerous children's books. She wrote for three hours every morning and said that she had 'never wanted to do anything else' (*Ham and High*, 18 July 1986). Lettice Cooper was committed not only to writing, but to writers. For some years she sat on the executive committee of the English PEN Club and chaired it from 1976 to 1978. With Brigid Brophy, Maureen Duffy, Francis King, and Michael Levey, she was a founding member of the Writers' Action Group, which successfully campaigned for public lending right. In 1978 she was appointed OBE for her work with the group.

On the strength of an Arts Council bursary Cooper wrote a detective story, *Tea on Sunday* (1973), and *Snow and Roses* (1976), a compassionate account of the miners' strike in 1972. The last of Lettice Cooper's twenty adult novels, *Unusual Behaviour*, appeared in 1986. Her profile had not been high for many years but the reissue of *The New House*, *National Provincial*, and *Fenny* in 1987 introduced her earlier work to a new audience in her ninetieth year. In the same year she received the freedom of the city of Leeds.

Lettice Cooper was always engaging and willing to be engaged. Her frank, open smile suggested the qualities of warmth and integrity her nature amply demonstrated. Throughout her long career her convictions and enthusiasms remained undimmed. Her interest in psychoanalysis—she underwent analysis for many years, and was an ardent Freudian—is reflected in a body of fiction which focuses as much on the inner lives of her characters as on their outward circumstances, and was repeatedly praised for its perceptiveness. The ways in which individuals react to change—be it social, cultural, political, or emotional—is a recurrent theme of her work. Some years after the death of her sister, Lettice Cooper moved to Norfolk to live with her brother, the writer Leonard Cooper. She died, unmarried, on 24 July 1994 at Coltishall Hall, Wroxham Road, Coltishall, Norfolk.    LYNN KNIGHT

**Sources** M. Duffy, introduction, in L. Cooper, *The new house* (1987) · F. King, introduction, in L. Cooper, *Fenny* (1987) · L. Cooper, *National provincial* (1987), preface · *The Times* (26 July 1994) · *The Guardian* (27 July 1994) · *Ham and High* (18 July 1986) · publicity form, 6 June 1987, Virago archives, Lettice Cooper publicity file · J. Vinson and D. L. Kirkpatrick, eds., *Contemporary novelists*, 2nd edn (1976) · P. Parker and F. Kermode, eds., *The reader's companion to twentieth-century writers* (1995) · b. cert. · d. cert.
**Archives** Eccles Library, Lancashire, MSS
**Likenesses** photograph, *c*.1987, Virago archive file
**Wealth at death** under £125,000: probate, 19 Sept 1994, *CGPLA Eng. & Wales*

**Cooper** [*née* Bransby], **Maria Susanna** (1737–1807), writer and poet, was born on 20 August 1737 in Shotesham, Norfolk, the eldest daughter (and heir) of James Bransby and Anna Maria Paston. In 1761 Maria Susanna married the Revd Samuel *Cooper (*bap.* 1739, *d.* 1800) [*see under* Cooper, Sir Astley Paston], who was appointed rector at Yelverton, Norfolk, shortly after their marriage. The couple continued to live in the Shotesham area, with her father for the first six years of their marriage and then at Brooke Hall.

Most of Maria Susanna Cooper's publications were interspersed with the births of her ten children and the deaths of six of them, and her eldest son and editor,

Bransby Cooper, connects his mother's writing career with her domestic role: 'The entertainment and instruction of her children, [and] a sense of duty … were [her] principal motives' (B. Cooper, introduction, in M. S. Cooper, *Moral Tales*, 1811). Bransby mentions that her earliest publications were children's books published with John Newbery, but no further information about these is available. Her literary reputation was based on her epistolary novels, described by Bransby as 'exemplify[ing] the female character in the several stations of life' (Cooper, 1.20). The first, *Letters between Emilia and Harriet*, was published in March 1762, also the year of Bransby's birth (21 February 1762). Five more children were born before the publication of her best-known work, *The Exemplary Mother, or, Letters between Mrs Villars and her Family* (2 vols.), in 1769: Samuel Lovick (4 February 1763), William Houman (4 September 1764), Charlotte Maria (18 September 1765), Marianne, and Astley Paston *Cooper (23 August 1768). This publication was followed by the birth of three daughters, Anna Maria, Margaret Bransby, and Anna Maria Inyon, all of whom died in infancy of consumption, and one son, her final child, Beauchamp Newton.

Maria Susanna Cooper continued to publish despite her family tragedies. Two epistolary novels appeared in 1775, *The Daughter* (a revised version of *Letters between Emilia and Harriet*) and *The History of Fanny Meadows*, and in 1776 she published *Jane Shore to her Friend—a Poetic Epistle*. In 1781 the Revd Samuel Cooper was appointed curate of Great Yarmouth and the family moved there. A new edition of *The Exemplary Mother* appeared in 1784. Within a few years Maria Susanna lost her remaining two daughters to consumption: Charlotte Maria in January 1786 and Marianne in 1789. Her husband died on 7 January 1800 and her youngest son, Beauchamp Newton, died from consumption in 1802. In October 1806 Maria Susanna went to live with Bransby at his home, Furney Hill, in Dursley, Gloucestershire. She died there on 3 July 1807. At his mother's request Bransby arranged for the publication of newly revised editions of her novels as well as of *Moral Tales* (1811) and *The Wife, or, Caroline Herbert* (1813).

Maria Susanna Cooper's epistolary novels are resolutely didactic, an effect she tried to safeguard by presenting her earliest works as actual collections of letters. In the 'Advertisement to the reader' for *The Exemplary Mother*, she distinguished between 'the most unnatural Characters and the most improbable Adventures' of many novels and her own work, 'containing the Exhibition of a genuine Character in the common Occurrences of *real* Life' in order that it might 'correc[t] Vice by the Goodness of its Precepts, and … strengthe[n] Virtue by the Amiableness of its Examples'. Maria Susanna Cooper's name never appeared on the title-page of her works, although after her literary success they appeared as 'By the author of The Exemplary Mother' and she did begin to sign her prefatory letters. For all her caution about appearing in print, she allows her characters to defend 'the female right to the use of the *pen*': 'writing [is] … a more rational employ' than other pastimes and, furthermore, '[t]he men … will scarcely be afraid of women, because they are capable of being agreeable companions, and useful friends' (*The Exemplary Mother*, 1.59, 61). JEANNE WOOD

Sources B. B. Cooper, *The life of Sir Astley Cooper*, 2 vols. (1843) · parish register, Shotesham, All Saints · 'Alphabetical catalogue, or list of books published in May, 1813', *Critical Review*, 4th ser., 3 (1813), 560 · *GM*, 1st ser., 32 (1762), 147 · Blain, Clements & Grundy, *Feminist comp.* · 'Cooper, Sir Astley Paston', *DNB* · E. W. Pitcher, 'Maria Susanna Cooper (1738–1807): the "exemplary mother" from Norfolk', *American Notes and Queries*, 17 (Sept 1978), 35–6

**Cooper, Myles** (1736/7–1785), Church of England clergyman and American loyalist, was born near Broughton in Furness, Lancashire, the son of William and Elizabeth Cooper, and was baptized probably on 19 February 1737 at Holy Trinity Church, Millom, Cumberland. He matriculated at Queen's College, Oxford, on 27 February 1753, aged sixteen, and proceeded BA (1756) and MA (1760); in 1767 he was granted a DCL by diploma. During 1760–61 he was a schoolteacher in Kent. Having returned to Queen's College as chaplain in 1761 he published, with collaborators, a volume of secular verse, *Poems on Several Occasions* (1761).

In 1762 the governors of King's College (subsequently Columbia University) in New York city, anticipating the retirement of the founder and first president of the institution, Samuel Johnson, and advancing the Anglicization of the college, asked Thomas Secker, archbishop of Canterbury, to recommend a clergyman as a successor. The request was sent to the Revd Edward Bentham, a canon of Christ Church, Oxford, and later regius professor of divinity in the university, who selected Cooper. The 25-year-old joined a band of Queen's College graduates who had accepted clerical posts in America.

Having arrived in New York on 30 October 1762 Cooper was immediately appointed by the governors as an assistant to Johnson as well as professor of moral philosophy and fellow of the college. He immersed himself also in the affairs of the Anglican church in New York, New Jersey, and Connecticut; he was elected president of the 1765 annual convention of the New York and New Jersey clergy. At the college he strengthened the library and provided intellectual leadership.

Under Cooper's aegis the curriculum, rules of conduct, and discipline of the college were revised, following the practices of Queen's College. The restructured procedures of the college imitated practices at Oxford University rather than those at Harvard, Yale, and Princeton. Whereas in the previous curriculum science and mathematics had been stressed, emphasis was now placed on Aristotelian principles of ethics, poetry, and politics and on Latin and Greek grammar and logic. Cooper's guidance inspired the governors to enhance the college in other ways; James Jay, brother of the revolutionary leader John Jay, sought financial support in England, while Cooper appointed new members of faculty and started a medical school. The college also received an endowment of land in Gloucester county (later part of Vermont). These measures may have contributed to the rise in the number of undergraduates entering King's College during this

period. Cooper published in Latin his lectures on Aristotelian ethics, *Ethices compendium* (1774). In recognition of his services and leadership the governors of King's College granted him an LLD in 1768.

Probably half the college's students and alumni alive in 1776 were loyalists at the outbreak of the war of independence. Included in this assembly were Cooper, four of the five faculty members between 1770 and 1777, and more than two-thirds of the governors. On the eve of the war college authorities sought a 'Royal Charter for the College constituting it a University'. The college would be an instrument for Anglicization, for 'cementing the Union between Great Britain and the Colonies', and for providing for the education of native colonists for the ministry. Cooper travelled to England in 1771, seeking the charter, grants of land, legal privileges comparable to those of Oxford and Cambridge, and royal funding for professorships. His efforts garnered more land grants, meagre funding for professors' salaries, and reduced quitrents on college lands. He pressed London authorities for the appointment of an American bishop, believing that a resident prelate would provide supervision over college affairs, subdue external critics, and superintend the provincial clergy. He returned to New York in 1772 without British officials having taken action on either a charter for the college or the appointment of a bishop. He brought with him, however, a valuable collection of books for the college library, donated by the Clarendon Press at Oxford University.

Cooper was the target of rising popular objections to English policies. As head of the college and as an Anglican clergyman he was a prominent symbol of imperial power and influence in the political turmoil of revolutionary New York. In April 1775 he was one of five New Yorkers to be warned in a public letter that 'Repeated insults and unparalleled oppressions have reduced the Americans to a state of desperation'. Fearing for his life, Cooper fled for a few days to a British warship anchored in New York city harbour but soon returned to his duties. About midnight on 10 May 1775 a mob invaded the campus, and Cooper, aroused by a student, escaped half-dressed through a rear exit and sought safety in the home of a friend. The next day he boarded a British vessel; on 25 May 1775 he sailed for England.

A poem that appeared in the *Gentleman's Magazine* for July 1776 recounted Cooper's New York experience; he provided his interpretation of the causes of the American War of Independence in a sermon preached at Oxford on 13 December 1776. As a loyalist he was granted a royal pension of £200 per annum for life, later reduced by half. He resumed his fellowship at Queen's College, where he lived for several years. At the end of 1777 he was appointed senior minister of the episcopal chapel in Edinburgh. According to his will he also held two other benefices—as rector of Cowley, in Gloucestershire, and vicar of Neen Savage, in Shropshire. A bachelor, late in life he supported several orphaned children in his family.

A large man of cultivated tastes, Cooper enjoyed good food and wine. He died among friends at a luncheon in

Edinburgh on 20 May 1785. A man of his times, an active and persuasive leader of the state church in New York, Cooper unswervingly embraced his ordination oath of allegiance to the crown and parliament. His will, proved at London on 6 October 1785, bequeathed nearly all his estate, valued at more than £2000, to his nephews and nieces, children of his brother Major John Cooper of the Cumberland militia and his sister, Esther Warrington of Carlisle.　　　　　　　　　　　　　JAMES B. BELL

**Sources** Col. U., Clarence H. Vance MSS · LPL, Fulham Palace MSS · D. C. Humphrey, *From King's College to Columbia, 1746–1800* (New York, 1976) · R. McCluer Calhoon, *The loyalists in revolutionary America, 1760–1781* (New York, 1973) · J. R. Magrath, *The Queen's College*, 2 (1921) · *GM*, 1st ser., 46 (1776) · E. R. Fingerhut, 'Cooper, Myles', *ANB* · will, PRO, PROB 11/1134, sig. 497 · *IGI* · Foster, *Alum. Oxon.*
**Archives** Col. U., Clarence H. Vance MSS · LPL, Fulham Palace MSS
**Likenesses** J. S. Copley, oils, Col. U.; repro. in J. D. Prown, *John Singleton Copley* (1966), vol. 1
**Wealth at death** over £2000: will, PRO, PROB 11/1134, sig. 497

**Cooper, Richard, the elder** (*bap.* 1696?, *d.* 1764), engraver, was probably the son of Richard Cooper (*b.* 1667) and his wife, Sarah, *née* Turner, baptized at St Andrew's, Holborn, London, on 12 February 1696. He studied engraving under John Pine and had some contact with Louis Cheron, who taught drawing at the academies in Great Queen Street and St Martin's Lane. On the death of his father he inherited enough money to travel to Italy, where he began a collection of prints and drawings. About 1725 he moved to Edinburgh, originally at the invitation of a Mr Guthrie whom he had met in Rome, and who was probably either the painter Alexander Guthrie or the Alexander Guthrie who was secretary to the board of trustees.

Cooper's arrival in Edinburgh precipitated some remarkable developments in the city's cultural life. In 1725 he engraved the music for Allan Ramsay's *Collection of Scots Songs*, and over the next thirty years his studio engraved almost all the music published in Scotland. He was a founder in 1729, and the first treasurer, of the Edinburgh School of St Luke, the earliest academy of artists in Scotland. Other signatories to the founding indenture included the poet Allan Ramsay, the bookseller James Balfour, the art dealer Andrew Hay, the painters John Alexander and Richard Chalmers, the architect William Adam, and the decorator James Norie. The school probably originated through the interaction between Cooper and the academic staff of Edinburgh University, notably Alexander Monro, and from 1731 until at least 1733 the school met at the university. In 1735 Cooper bought a large plot of land in St John Street and established a private academy close to his house. In that year he became first junior and then senior warden of the Canongate lodge of freemasons. He was made a burgess of Edinburgh in 1736 'for good services done and performed to this City' (Watson, 44). Cooper had quickly established a flourishing business as a general engraver of tickets, music, portraits, views, maps, and book illustrations, having more or less a monopoly of engraving business in the city. He made botanical

Richard Cooper the elder (*bap.* 1696?, *d.* 1764), by Jeremiah Davison

studies for James Justice and anatomical studies for Alexander Monro. He also sold prints and related items such as wallpaper and acted as an interior decorator to various noblemen and institutions. In 1736 he took Robert Strange as a boarding apprentice. Strange was not entirely pleased when Cooper's marriage, on 24 December 1738 to Ann Lind (*d.* 1775), the daughter of an Edinburgh merchant, brought about changes in the big house in St John Street, and very shortly a son, also Richard Cooper [*see below*]. Samuel Taylor was apprenticed to Cooper in 1738 and Andrew Bell in 1741. A second son, George, was born in 1742. The School of St Luke probably ceased to function in 1745, when most of the members who had not already died came under suspicion of treason, and Cooper's pupil Strange fled to France.

Cooper, however, remained in Edinburgh. In 1747, after years of determined opposition from the town council and the clerical and university authorities, he completed the building of a theatre on his land in Canongate (which through ancient burgh status was legally outside the jurisdiction of the town council). He leased his theatre for twenty-five years to the managers of the Canongate Concert Hall but took an active part in its operations, employing William Delacour as a scene-painter. He continued to prosper. In 1749 he bought the house of the Incorporation of Tailors in Canongate and in 1751 he bought the dean's house in Restalrig village. By now he was acting as drawing-master to various noble ladies, while his studio continued to produce anatomical and medical illustrations and most of the maps and prints of any consequence that were produced in Scotland. He made a will in 1757 leaving all his stock in trade to his son Richard. Cooper died, aged sixty-seven, on 20 January 1764 and was buried in Restalrig parish churchyard.

The younger **Richard Cooper** (*b*. 1740?, *d*. after 1817) was born in Edinburgh and trained under his father before, in 1758, following Robert Strange to Paris to study under the famous French engraver J. P. Le Bas. He moved to London in 1761 and launched a proposal for a print of Van Dyck's *The Children of Charles I*, and he exhibited figure drawings and engravings at the Society of Artists and at the Free Society until 1764. *The Children of Charles I* was published in 1763 and favourably noticed in the *Critical Review*. Cooper then travelled in Spain and was the first British engraver to record old masters in Spanish collections. In 1768 he succeeded Alexander Cozens as drawing-master at Eton College, then in 1771 went to Italy, travelling with Thomas Merriman, and visiting Venice, Capua, and Naples, where he was patronized by Sir William Hamilton in 1772–3. The Edinburgh banker Robert Alexander assisted him in getting to Rome, where he became friendly with the Runciman brothers and developed a style of landscape painting close to that of Alexander Runciman. A series of tinted drawings of Rome and its vicinity earned him the nickname the English Poussin. He also became a friend and associate of the painter Jacob More, subsequently acting as More's executor. Cooper painted many Italian views, particularly of Rome, Tivoli, and Naples, some of which were exhibited at the Society of Artists in 1783.

On 11 August 1777 Cooper married Frances Ramsay in Edinburgh; it is not clear whether he took up residence in Edinburgh, but in 1778 he exhibited Italian views at the Royal Academy. About 1787 he settled in Charles Street, in Westminster's fashionable district of St James, and devoted himself to drawing and exhibiting numerous examples of his work at the Royal Academy up to 1809. He taught drawing to Princess Charlotte (1796–1817). He is thought to have died some time after 1817.

TIMOTHY CLAYTON and ANITA McCONNELL

**Sources** J. Rock, 'An important Scottish anatomical publication rediscovered', *Book collector*, 49 (2000), 27–60 · D. Macmillan, *Scottish art, 1460–1990* (1990) · D. Irwin and F. Irwin, *Scottish painters at home and abroad, 1700–1900* (1975) · J. C. Guy, 'Edinburgh engravers', *Book of the Old Edinburgh Club*, 9, 79–113 · J. Dennistoun, *Memoirs of Sir Robert Strange, knt*, 2 vols. (1855) · J. Ingamells, ed., *A dictionary of British and Irish travellers in Italy, 1701–1800* (1997), 239 · Graves, *Soc. Artists* · R. V. Tooley, *Tooley's dictionary of mapmakers*, ed. J. French, rev. edn, 1 (1999), 298 · C. B. B. Watson, ed., *Roll of Edinburgh burgesses and guild-brethren, 1701–1760*, Scottish RS, 62 (1930) · E. Harris, *British architectural books and writers, 1556–1785* (1991) · *DNB*
**Archives** NA Scot., letters to J. Gray
**Likenesses** J. Davison, portrait, Scot. NPG [*see illus.*]

**Cooper, Richard** (*b*. **1740?**, *d*. after **1817**). *See under* Cooper, Richard, the elder (*bap*. 1696?, *d*. 1764).

**Cooper, Robert** (**1649/50–1732**), mathematician and Church of England clergyman, was the second son of the seven children born to Robert Cooper of Kidderminster, Worcestershire, and his wife, Elizabeth. He entered Pembroke College, Oxford, as a servitor in 1666, aged sixteen,

graduated BA in 1670, and was elected fellow through the influence of Dr Hall, master of Pembroke. Cooper is credited by Wood (Wood, *Ath. Oxon.*, 4.749) as the author of the anonymous tract *Proportions Concerning Optic-Glasses, with their Natural Reasons Drawn from Experiments* (1679), which expounds in simple fashion the laws governing reflection and refraction through glass. Elsewhere this work has been attributed to Obadiah Walker, who had an interest in mathematics but who never put his name to his own works, and also to Abraham Woodhead, who had no scientific interests. The likeliest explanation is that it was found among Walker's papers at his death in 1678, and that Cooper, who was a competent mathematician, edited it and passed it to Woodhead, who was a delegate of the university press, for publication. Five hundred copies were printed.

The anonymous 'General introduction to geography' which prefaced the first volume, published in 1680, of Moses Pitt's multi-volume but incomplete *English Atlas* has also been attributed to Cooper. The author of this text includes an explanation of the calculations for latitude and longitude and other aspects of mathematical geography.

On 8 April 1681 Cooper, who was considered an able preacher, was presented to the rectory of Harlington, Middlesex, where he resided at least part of the time until his death. From 1698 he was also archdeacon of Dorset. Cooper never married. He died in March 1732 and was buried at Harlington, where his tomb bears the incorrect death date of 1722, which is corrected on a memorial inside the church. He left his books to his nephew Robert Pyre, vicar of Heath, and over £1500 in South Sea shares to his sister Rachel and various nieces. He also requested that £100 promised to Pembroke College towards the cost of the chapel then under construction should be paid.

ANITA McCONNELL

**Sources** J. R. Burton, *A history of Kidderminster* (1890), 92, 152 · F. Madan, *Oxford literature, 1651–1680* (1931), vol. 3 of *Oxford books: a bibliography of printed works* (1895–1931); repr. (1964), 370–71, 380–81 · PRO, PROB 11/657, sig. 80 · 'Monumental inscriptions at the church of St Peter and St Paul, Harlington, Middlesex', typescript, London Society of Genealogists, MX/M/vol.3 · *VCH Middlesex*, 3.271 · Wood, *Ath. Oxon.*, new edn, 4.749 · Foster, *Alum. Oxon.*
**Wealth at death** books to nephew; over £1500 in South Sea shares to sister and nieces; £100 to Pembroke College, Oxford

**Cooper, Robert** (*fl*. **1800–1836**), printmaker, flourished in the first part of the nineteenth century, but nothing is known of his parentage, early life, or training. Although he did design a few of his own prints, he was primarily a reproductive engraver of portraits who worked variously in stipple and line engraving as well as in etching. Given the early nineteenth-century fashion for collecting historical portraits, he found much employment contributing prints to illustrated antiquarian publications such as Edmund Lodge's *Portraits of Illustrious Personages of Great Britain* (1821–34) and Henry Tresham's and William Young Ottley's *British Gallery of Pictures* (1808–18). While most of these modest historical portraits are formulaic in pose and handling, Cooper was able to provide a level of novelty by employing various engraving techniques such as the delicate stipple effect that can be seen in his series of plates for Sir Robert Naunton's *Fragmenta regalia* (1824), an anecdotal account of the court of Queen Elizabeth. His plates also embellished the pages of luxury editions of more light-hearted reading material: they can be found in copies of Sir Walter Scott's *Old Mortality*, the fashionable periodical *La Belle Assemblée*, and the picturesque *Scenery of the Rivers of Norfolk* (1834), after paintings by James Stark. Apart from working to order for publishers, Cooper also executed a number of privately issued plates for the duke of Buckingham, all of which were portraits after artists such as Van Dyck and Velázquez apart from the portrait of the duke of Buckingham himself, which was taken from a modern work by George Lethbridge Saunders. His best-known work for this patron is surely his version of the Chandos portrait of Shakespeare, a subject which was in keeping with Cooper's preference for portraits of contemporary actors and actresses, which were eventually published as a series of hand-coloured etchings entitled *British Theatrical Gallery* (1822–5).

Although it is not clear when, it seems that Cooper also went into business as a picture dealer and publisher. However, judging from Southgate's auction of his stock of prints and the sale of his 'capital mahogany press' (*Catalogue*) between 31 October and 2 November 1826, it would appear that he was unsuccessful in this venture. Somewhat unscrupulously, this sale also included many impressions from the private plates Cooper had executed, as well as 'reworkings of subjects popularized by other artists' (ibid.), such as West's *Death of Wolfe* and an unfinished large engraving of *Christ Bearing the Cross*, after Mignard. He is known to have shown work at the Associated Engravers' exhibition in 1821, and is thought to have still been living in 1836.                    LUCY PELTZ

**Sources** Bryan, *Painters* (1903–5) · *Catalogue of the valuable collection of engravings of Mr. Robert Cooper … sold by Mr Southgate, 22 Fleet Street, Tues October 31, 1826* (1826) [sale catalogue, 31 Oct 1826] · Redgrave, *Artists*

**Cooper, Samuel** (1607/8–1672), miniature painter, was born probably in Blackfriars, London, the elder child of Richard Cooper (b. 1577) and Barbara Hoskins (b. c.1590), who were married on 1 September 1607 at the church of St Nicholas Cole Abbey, near Blackfriars. Barbara, the daughter of John Hoskins, at that time an inmate of the Fleet prison although the family was of substance, was the sister of John *Hoskins (c.1590–1665), the miniaturist. Richard Cooper was originally from York, where the family retained its geographical base. About 1610 Richard and Barbara seem to have died or otherwise relinquished the charge of their children, so Samuel and his brother, Alexander *Cooper (bap. 1609, d. c.1660), were brought up by their uncle John Hoskins, evidently in the neighbourhood of Blackfriars, a district much favoured by artists and craftsmen because of its traditional freedom from the trade restrictions imposed in the rest of the City by the livery companies. There Richard Graham, who knew Cooper

Samuel Cooper (1607/8–1672), self-portrait, 1645

and was his earliest biographer, records that Samuel 'derived the most considerable Advantages, from the *Observations* which he made on the Works of *Van Dyck*' (Graham, 375–6). His earliest signed miniature, c.1635, is a portrait of Van Dyck's mistress Margaret Lemon, now in the Institut Néerlandais, Paris.

**Early years and marriage** By 1634 the Hoskins household had moved to Bedford Street, in the fashionable new development of Covent Garden, where Cooper wrote out for the king's physician, Sir Theodore Turquet de Mayerne, who attended Hoskins as his doctor and commissioned his portrait from him, 'tout le secret de lenluminure' (Edmond, 'Limners and picturemakers', 100–01). About 1635 Cooper's hand is evident in miniatures presented as the work of his uncle (see portraits of the earl of Dorset and the earl of Holland in the Victoria and Albert Museum, London) but his own signed *œuvre* does not begin until 1642; early biographers state that he 'spent several years of his life abroad' (Graham, 375–6). He was widely accomplished. Samuel Pepys recorded (on 10 July 1668) that he spoke French, and Richard Graham that 'he was reckon'd one of the best *Lutenists* … in his Time' (ibid.). By 1642 he was certainly in England, living in King Street, Covent Garden.

In 1642 Cooper married Christiana (1623–1693), daughter of William Turner of Towthorpe, near York, and of his wife, Thomasina. Christiana had a sister, Edith (b. 1643), who became the mother of the poet Alexander Pope. In 1650 Cooper moved with his wife to one of the most substantial houses in Henrietta Street, also in Covent Garden, and lived there until his death. There were no children of the marriage.

**Major works** Through his uncle Samuel Cooper was introduced from the start to the royal and courtly clientele of miniature painting, but never worked under his own name for Charles I, since Charles and his court left London for Oxford about the time that Cooper arrived. By the mid-1640s he was adapting himself and his style successfully to suit the prevailing conditions of patronage in London during the civil wars and interregnum, building a reputation for good likenesses, brilliant execution, and great personal charm. His 'parliamentary' output—portraits of men in armour usually against a dark background, and women whose *tenue* remained relatively unaffected by the circumstances of war—culminated in the paintings of Oliver Cromwell in the early 1650s: 'Mr Cooper. the painter … desires you to excuse him one month longer, as he has some work to finish for Lord General Cromwell and his family', wrote Miles Woodshaw to Lord Conway on 7 November 1650 (Long, 85). Cooper seems to have taken various likenesses of Cromwell for various purposes, including formal portraiture, for which he made the *ad vivum* sketch now in the collection of the duke of Buccleuch and on which Lely may have relied for the surviving oil painting (Birmingham City Museum and Art Gallery). There are also images made apparently for use on medals or coins, a good example of which is an *ad vivum* profile in the National Portrait Gallery. Claimed likenesses of other members of the Cromwell family, including the sons Richard and Henry, are very doubtful but there is a miniature by Cooper, descended from the Claypoles, traditionally identified as Elizabeth Claypole, Cromwell's younger and favourite daughter, dated 1653, in the collection of the duke of Buccleuch, which has been considered by the National Portrait Gallery to provide authority for other possible images of Elizabeth. These might include the small, bright, and highly finished miniatures by Cooper—also of the mid-1650s—one of which was given by Lord Lee of Fareham to the Chequers Trust, and the other, finer version of which is now in the Victoria and Albert Museum (Murdoch, cat. no. 74). It is particularly interesting that these miniatures, if they are correctly identified, suggest the extent to which the protector's family (but not he) adopted after 1653 a personal style similar to that of the French royal family and court, where enamel portraits, set in expensive boxes or personal jewels, provided a fashionable means of courtly self-presentation. Arguably, however, for the historian of English visual culture in the revolutionary years it is portraits such as the *Sir William Palmer* of 1657 (V&A), apparently alluding to Rembrandt in their colouring, that show most vividly Cooper's probing and intelligent engagement with the individuality of his sitters as distinct from their class or official status. A similar ability to characterize as well as portray is occasionally evident in the work of other contemporary English artists such as William Dobson (*bap.* 1611, *d.* 1646). It shows a tendency in the development of English painting and in the understanding of human nature that is surely related to the interest in inductive study of appearances and symptoms characteristic of English seventeenth-century thinking about ways of truly knowing a subject.

Soon after the Restoration, however, Charles II sat to Cooper for a new likeness used for the production of numerous finished miniatures, most of which were not finished to Cooper's normal high standard, which suggests that Cooper was again so pressed with business that the replication of the new king's image required studio assistance. Of these official portraits the best and largest is probably that of the king in Garter robes at Goodwood House, Sussex. The king also sat to Cooper for a profile for the new coinage. John Evelyn, the diarist and art connoisseur, records for 10 January 1662:

> Being call'd to his Majesty's closet when Mr. Cooper, the rare limner, was crayoning of the King's face and head, to make the stamps by, for the new mill'd money now contriving, I had the honour to hold the candle whilst it was doing, he choosing the night and candle-light for the better finding out the shadows. During this his Majesty discours'd with me on several things relating to painting and graving.   (Evelyn, *Diary*, 3.309–10)

Drawings in red and black chalk, now in the Royal Collection, are probably results of this sitting. Such an emphatic chiaroscuro was necessary in designs intended for the low-relief die-maker but normally Cooper painted in the full light of his studio. His portrait of James, duke of York, of 1661 (V&A) is an excellent example of the development in his orthodox miniature portraiture at this period. It is bright and direct in its lighting, and subtly enriched in its representation of the sitter's complexion; it shows also the enlargement of the oval to nearly 3½ inches, which became increasingly the norm for miniatures until the mid-eighteenth century.

Cooper's professional pre-eminence was confirmed by his appointment as king's limner in 1663. Such was his charm and perceived eminence that his clients tended to become his friends and willing advocates. His circle of acquaintance seems to have included most of the intellectual and artistic élite of the period; Richard Graham recorded that he was known to 'the greatest Men of *France*, *Holland*, and his *own country*, and by his *Works* more universally known in all the parts of *Christendom*' (Graham, 376). When Grand Duke Cosimo III of Tuscany sat to him in 1669 Cooper was described in the official journal of the visit as 'un piccinetto tutto spirito e cortesia. E ancor egli assai ricco, e in casa non sta meno honorabilmente di Lelley, lavora sopra un tavolino coperto di velluto' ('a tiny man, all spirit and courtesy, very well-off and not less honourably set up in his house than Lely, and working on a table covered in velvet'; Crino, 148). The style in which Lely lived was famous. Pepys, as well as Evelyn, watched Cooper at work, the experience of seeing the genius in action being highly valued. Charles Beale, another diarist, recorded his death: 'Sunday, May 5 1672, Mr Samuel Cooper, the most famous limner in the world for a face, died' (Vertue, *Note Books*, 4.169).

**Reputation** Cooper died thus at the height of his powers, busy with commissions from the king and the duke of

York, in his fine house on Henrietta Street. Interestingly he may have converted to Roman Catholicism, for he chose not to be buried in his own parish but in the church of St Pancras, in which many converts were buried at this time. His tomb bears the initials of the pre-Reformation monumental inscription 'Cuius animae propricietur deus' (Edmond, 'Samuel Cooper', 83–5). It also states his age at death as sixty-four.

As a miniaturist Cooper was the pioneer of a method of painting the human face using a firm hatching stroke applied with the tip of the brush in red and brown, which he developed evidently while still working within the orbit of his uncle John Hoskins. The method requires considerable assurance of hand and is particularly well fitted for a draughtsman capable of seizing a sitter's likeness rapidly. In contrast to the delicate stipples of the earlier tradition of Nicholas Hilliard and Isaac Oliver the hatching style is demonstrative and painterly; its stylistic relationship to the 'new' portraiture of Mytens and Van Dyck has often been observed. Other elements of the composition, such as architectural or landscape backgrounds, are often painted with an almost aggressive or careless breadth. Examples of early exercises in this style are the portrait of the earl of Holland against a stormy sky (Ham House, Richmond, Surrey) and that of the fourth earl of Dorset, after Van Dyck (V&A), which bears the Hoskins monogram but is surely by the young Cooper. The somewhat harsh painterly style of the late 1630s becomes very disciplined in the 1640s, the hatching in the face firm and clear, and subordinated to the need to produce a good characteristic likeness. The backgrounds are neatly painted, often plain dark brown with perhaps a flush of light reflected from the studio window behind the sitter's left shoulder. Sometimes the background is divided, as though the sitter is posed against a window or door to the outside world. This phase, during which the standard Cooper signature is the separate initials SC divided by a colon, gives way progressively to an interest in fine finish, with the brush strokes disappearing into a smooth, illusionistic surface, and, in 1653, a new signature: a loose monogram of the conjoined initials, usually with a date, appears for the first time.

By the early 1650s Cooper was responding to the French developments in fine enamel portraiture, sometimes reducing the size of his ovals and increasingly aiming at a fine, 'invisible' *facture*, as in the portraits said to be of Elizabeth Claypole. Alongside these, however, there seem to be signs of a division in his *œuvre* between the miniatures, which are made according to the rigorous professional discipline of the sittings, and his sketches or graphic work, in which, in common with other draughtsmen of the time, he allowed an interest in brilliant execution to be predominant. They are probably opportunistic or alternative views of sitters, quickly executed as the artist tried his subject in different positions. Many such 'unfinished' works were extant in his studio at his death, variously interpreted as either awaiting the finishing touches or as pattern likenesses, preparatory to the multiplication of finished works. More probably, however, they

were always intended to be autonomous, a different kind of art recording the direct experience of the studio, and contrasting with the necessary formality of the finished miniatures.

In the finished miniatures of the 1660s, as the standard size of the oval was increased to some 3½ inches and large, rectangular, 'cabinet' miniatures were demanded by the most important sitters, other ways of maintaining the illusionistic surface had to be developed. The brush strokes accordingly begin to be blended together, with considerable amounts of gouache and with a final glaze of red in the cheeks, to create an effect of vividness that sometimes startled contemporaries: 'I must confess I do think the colouring of the flesh to be a little forced', wrote Samuel Pepys, whose eye would have been conditioned by twenty years of looking at the sober, 'sad-coloured' portraiture of the interregnum (Pepys, 136). Unfortunately, however, except in the private collection at Welbeck Abbey, Nottinghamshire, few unfaded Cooper miniatures of any period now survive.

For all aspects of his *œuvre* a full representation of Cooper's stylistic range, including an interesting group of the 'unfinished' works deriving ultimately from the estate of his widow, may be seen in the Victoria and Albert Museum. The most brilliant of the surviving 'sketches'—of sitters who had been of importance to the king—were, however, acquired from Christiana Cooper by Charles II in June 1673, when Christiana was granted a pension of £200 a year. They remain in the Royal Collection and include portraits of two royal mistresses—Barbara Villiers, duchess of Cleveland, and Frances Stuart, duchess of Richmond—of extraordinary delicacy in representing the different formal properties of the beauty exemplified by these famous women. Cooper's ability thus to analyse, even when the imperatives of flattery might seem to be at their sharpest, extends to the contrasting images of James Scott, duke of Monmouth (equally famous for his personal beauty), and George Monck, duke of Albemarle, the subtle soldier–politician, his gaze resting on something just to the artist's right. Unlike the sober portraiture of the 1640s and 1650s these are not character studies but are more neutral, more a matter of vision and record. Already in the seventeenth century they were understood as the raw material of history, compiled first-hand by an observer of rare sensitivity. Thomas Carlyle considered that *ad vivum* portraits were among the most valuable of historical documents, and in all these images the fortunes of those caught up in the great events of the seventeenth century become indeed more accessible to the imagination.

The whole group of unfinished miniatures, presumably including those acquired for the king, was seen soon after Cooper's death by the London agent of Grand Duke Cosimo III, who had been so impressed by the artist's genius and style in 1669 and who persisted in trying to acquire examples of his work until 1683. Cooper's widow, however, did not really need to sell, and the remaining miniatures 'which I shall have by me att the tyme of my decease' were bequeathed by her to John Hoskins, the son of the miniaturist and evidently a miniaturist himself

(Edmond, 'Limners and picturemakers', 111–12). Some of them, possibly left in the Henrietta Street house at Christiana's death (24 August 1693), passed to the house's next inhabitant, the goldsmith Michael Rosse, husband of the miniaturist Susannah-Penelope Rosse (daughter of the miniaturist Richard Gibson), where they continued to exercise influence over both the practice and the connoisseurship of art in England. (An incomplete list of those included in the sale of Michael Rosse's collection, 2 April 1723, is printed in D. Foskett, *Samuel Cooper*, 1974, 100–06.)

Like his predecessors Peter Oliver and John Hoskins and many contemporaries Cooper worked also in 'crayon', as Evelyn called it—'dry colour' in Edward Norgate's vocabulary, or 'pastel', as it is now normally known. A drawing in this fragile medium, once believed to be a self-portrait, is in the Victoria and Albert Museum. Its quality, perhaps due to retouching, is unimpressive and it is probably not by Cooper but may be a portrait of him in the late 1650s by his cousin 'Jack's son', the younger Hoskins. The black chalk drawing of Thomas Alcock in the Ashmolean Museum, Oxford, to which could perhaps be added that of Charles II in the Royal Collection and a famous study of a dead baby from a group of Hoskins family portraits that survive in the Harford Collection (exhibited at the Cooper exhibition, National Portrait Gallery, 1974, nos. 136–9), are on the other hand very beautiful and suggest that, had any genuine Cooper pastels survived in comparable condition, they also would be of beautiful quality.

Apart from the pastel in the Victoria and Albert Museum the only plausible image of Cooper is the miniature in the Royal Collection, recently rehabilitated as a self-portrait by Graham Reynolds on the grounds of its inscriptions, its long traditional identification, and its iconography (Reynolds, *Miniatures*, no. 106, pp. 129–30). If Reynolds is right it would show Cooper in February 1645, aged about thirty-seven, an exceptionally attractive man with curly dark brown hair and vivid brown eyes, wearing a crisply laundered lace collar over an embroidered silk coat of discreet but luxurious quality. It helps to substantiate his reputation for charm and suggests an astonishing degree of economic self-confidence in a young man who was just beginning to establish himself in a luxury trade against a background of civil war and the puritan critique of conspicuous urban consumption.  JOHN MURDOCH

**Sources** [R. Graham], 'A short account of the most eminent painters both ancient and modern, continued down to the present times, according to the order of their succession', in C. A. Du Fresnoy, *De arte graphica / The art of painting*, trans. J. Dryden (1695), 227–355; 2nd edn (1716), 375–6 • [B. Buckeridge], 'An essay towards an English school of painters', in R. de Piles, *The art of painting, and the lives of the painters* (1706), 398–480 • B. S. Long, *British miniaturists* (1929) • A. M. Crino, 'Il ritrovamento della miniatura di Cosimo III di Toscane, eseguita da Samuel Cooper a Londra', *Rivista d'Arte*, 29 (1954), 148 • M. Edmond, 'Limners and picturemakers', *Walpole Society*, 47 (1978–80), 60–242 [Edmond provides full references to her primary sources in parish and probate registers] • M. Edmond, 'Samuel Cooper, Yorkshireman—and recusant?', *Burlington Magazine*, 127 (Feb 1985), 83–5 • J. Murdoch, *Seventeenth-century miniatures in the Victoria and Albert Museum* (1997) • A. G. Reynolds, 'Was Samuel Cooper influenced by Rembrandt?', *Victoria and Albert Museum Bulletin*, 2/3 (July 1966), 97–103 • Pepys, *Diary*, vol. 9 • Evelyn, *Diary*,

3.309–10 • tombstone, St Pancras Old Church • A. G. Reynolds, *The sixteenth and seventeenth century miniatures in the collection of her majesty the queen* (1999), no. 106, pp. 129–30
**Likenesses** S. Cooper, self-portrait, 1645, Royal Collection [*see illus.*] • S. Cooper?, self-portrait?, pastel drawing, V&A • watercolour drawing (after S. Cooper), NPG

**Cooper, Samuel** (*bap.* **1739**, *d.* **1800**). *See under* Cooper, Sir Astley Paston, first baronet (1768–1841).

**Cooper, Samuel** (**1780–1848**), surgeon and writer, was born on 11 September 1780, the second son of a businessman who had made a fortune in the West Indies, but who died when his three sons were still young. He was trained by Dr Burney at Greenwich Hospital, and in 1800 entered St Bartholomew's Hospital, where he showed great promise. In 1803 he became MRCS, and settled in Golden Square, London. In 1806 he gained the Jacksonian prize at the Royal College of Surgeons for the best essay; his subject was diseases of the joints. In 1807 he published his *First Lines of Surgery*, which went through seven editions. In 1809 the first edition of his great *Surgical Dictionary* appeared, and it achieved instant popularity. During Cooper's lifetime seven large and carefully revised editions appeared.

In 1810 Cooper married a Miss Cranstoun (*d.* 1811), but she died in the following year, leaving a daughter, who afterwards married Thomas *Morton, surgeon to University College Hospital. After his wife's death Cooper in 1813 entered the army as surgeon, and served at the battle of Waterloo. Afterwards he devoted his attention to editing the successive editions of his two principal works. He also ran a successful surgical practice. In 1827 he became a member of the council of the Royal College of Surgeons, and from 1831 was surgeon at University College Hospital and professor of surgery in the college. In 1845 he was elected president of the Royal College of Surgeons, and in 1846 fellow of the Royal Society. In 1848 he resigned from both his posts in protest at the appointment of James Syme as professor of clinical surgery. Cooper died of gout on 2 December 1848.

Besides his principal works Cooper wrote a book on *Cataract* (1805), and edited the third and fourth editions of Mason Good's *Study of Medicine*. He delivered the Hunterian oration in 1834. The *Dictionary* was translated into French, German, and Italian, and several times was republished in America.

G. T. BETTANY, *rev.* CHRISTIAN KERSLAKE

**Sources** *The Lancet* (9 Dec 1848), 646 • *GM*, 2nd ser., 31 (1849), 320 • G. L. Cooper, 'Biographical preface', in *Cooper's dictionary of practical surgery and encyclopaedia of surgical science*, new edn, ed. A. Lane and others, 2 (1872) • J. F. Clarke, *Autobiographical recollections of the medical profession* (1874), 323–6 • V. G. Plarr, *Plarr's Lives of the fellows of the Royal College of Surgeons of England*, rev. D'A. Power, 2 vols. (1930) • *The Lancet* (15 April 1848), 425, 428 • *The Lancet* (22 April 1848), 459 • *The Lancet* (29 April 1848), 482–4 • *The Lancet* (6 May 1848), 503–4, 508–11 • *The Lancet* (13 May 1848), 527–8, 531–3 • *The Lancet* (10 June 1848), 648 • *The Lancet* (24 June 1848), 696
**Likenesses** A. Morton, oils, exh. RA 1838, RCS Eng. • T. Butler, marble bust, *c.*1851, RCS Eng. • Beynon & Co., lithograph (*Alumni of University College Hospital*), Wellcome L. • T. Bridgford, lithograph, Wellcome L.

**Cooper** [*née* Coombe], **Selina Jane** (1864–1946), suffragist and socialist, was born on 4 December 1864 in Callington, Cornwall, the sixth of seven surviving children of Charles Coombe, railway labourer and later railway subcontractor, and his wife, Jane Uren, dressmaker. In 1876, after her father's sudden death from typhoid fever, eleven-year-old Selina, her widowed mother, and youngest brother moved up to Barnoldswick in north-east Lancashire where cotton mills offered jobs to impoverished families like the Coombes.

Selina Coombe became a half-timer: she combined part-time school with working as a creeler in the cardroom, supplying bobbins onto which fleecy strands of cotton were wound prior to spinning. On her thirteenth birthday even her half-time schooling ended forever, and the 1881 census records sixteen-year-old Selina as 'Cotton Operative'. Shortly afterwards she left the cardroom to care for her mother, now bedridden; and in 1883 they moved to nearby Brierfield, squashed between Burnley and Nelson, both fast expanding weaving towns. Here Selina worked as part-time nurse, part-time washerwoman until her mother's death in 1889. Returning to the mill, she entered Tunstills' winding rooms and joined a trade union—the large Burnley Weavers' Association. Other aspects of Selina Coombe's life, however, like those of so many other working-class women of her generation, remain shadowy.

Nelson and Burnley became early centres of socialism, and Selina Coombe was among the many millworkers drawn into the heady movement. On 24 October 1896 the Revd Leonard of nearby Colne Independent Chapel, a socialist, conducted the marriage of Selina Coombe and Robert Cooper (1869–1934), cotton weaver and founder member of the Nelson Social Democratic Federation (SDF). Their son John Ruskin was born on 21 May 1897 but died of acute bronchitic convulsions on 24 September 1897: this private sorrow haunted Selina long afterwards. However in 1899 Leonard offered the Coopers escape into the countryside, managing a new Co-operative Holiday Association centre at Keld in Swaledale. On their return, their daughter Mary was born on 8 March 1900; and about new year 1901 the Coopers moved to nearby 59 St Mary's Street, Nelson—where all three lived for the rest of their lives.

In 1898 Selina Cooper was elected president of the new Brierfield branch of the Women's Co-operative Guild, so gaining invaluable experience as a public speaker and finding a springboard for the suffrage campaigning which now swept her up. About 1900 she began collecting signatures locally among women cotton factory workers for a petition protesting that their denial of the franchise was 'unjust and inexpedient' (Liddington, 102). On 18 March 1901 she accompanied the 29,359-signature petition down to Westminster, informing the Lancashire MPs meeting the deputation that women have 'to educate their children, but if they are not interested in national life, how could they impart to their children a knowledge of true citizenship?' (ibid., 105). At this gathering Selina Cooper,

Selina Jane Cooper (1864–1946), by E. Buck

fast emerging as a talented speaker, met influential members of the National Union of Women's Suffrage Societies (NUWSS) including the society's president, Millicent Fawcett, and the Leeds socialist Isabella Ford.

The Coopers' home became a focus for local campaigns. In February 1901 Selina Cooper was elected a poor-law guardian, her candidature supported by both the SDF and the Independent Labour Party (ILP). In 1903 she helped launch the Lancashire Women Textile Workers' Representation Committee, and in 1906 organized the Nelson Suffrage Society which met in the Coopers' small front room.

Selina Cooper's belief in both socialism and women's suffrage was tested in 1905 and again in 1907 at Labour Party conferences when, as an ILP delegate, she seconded a women's suffrage resolution—only to be defeated by an adult suffrage amendment. Disenchanted, suffragists like Selina Cooper distanced themselves from the Labour Party—and from the increasingly militant Women's Social and Political Union. Instead, from 1906–7 she worked as a NUWSS organizer, deploying her considerable speaking skills nationally—including supporting the young Bertrand Russell, suffrage candidate at the 1907 Wimbledon by-election.

However in 1912 a new Labour–suffrage alliance was

forged, triggered by the obduracy of Herbert Asquith's Liberal government and helped by ILP lobbying of the Labour Party. Along with other radical suffragists—Ada Nield Chew, Annot Robinson, Ellen Wilkinson—Selina Cooper now became in tremendous demand as a speaker; helped by the NUWSS's new election fighting fund, she stumped the country, supporting Labour by-election candidates and lobbying the giant Miners' Federation to put its might behind women's suffrage.

On the outbreak of war suffrage campaigning was suspended. Selina and Robert Cooper, like other ILP members, opposed the war and supported local conscientious objectors; in 1917 Selina bravely led a Women's Peace Crusade procession through Nelson, despite scuffling and jeering. But unlike other internationalist suffragists, Selina Cooper did not resign from Mrs Fawcett's NUWSS; and once women over thirty were enfranchised in 1918 the NUWSS encouraged her (rather unrealistically, given her feminism and her anti-war stance) to stand for parliamentary selection in a Lancashire constituency.

In 1923 and again in 1924 Selina Cooper did stand for election—as Labour candidate for Nelson town council; an outspoken socialist and known supporter of birth control, she was not elected. However, nominated by the Nelson Weavers, she was appointed a magistrate in 1924; and in 1930 she was co-opted onto the Burnley guardians (a district within Lancashire's new public assistance committee). As unemployment rose in 1931, Selina Cooper JP found herself outnumbered on a magistrates' bench 'swarming with manufacturers' (Liddington, 369) after a Nelson Weavers' demonstration against strike-breakers led to a mounted police charge and an arrest. Later that year, amid economic and political crisis, grassroots socialists like Selina Cooper found their convictions shaken to the core by Labour leadership betrayal. 'Philip Snowden and MacDonald took place of a God in those days. And when they tumbled, my mother', Mary Cooper recalled '… got very sad' (ibid., 377).

In 1933 Selina Cooper spoke in London's Central Hall on married women's right to work—'the married women of the north beg their sisters in the south to help them face the "new menace" which is threatening our position as women workers' (Liddington, 402)—sitting down to thunderous applause. Recently widowed, she was invited in 1934 by a new pro-communist Women's World Committee Against War and Fascism to join a small delegation to Nazi Germany to visit four women prisoners; on her return she told about the grim realities of Nazism. A supporter of the Popular Front in the late 1930s, in 1940 Selina Cooper joined the more marginal People's Convention initiated by the Communist Party; she was soon expelled from the Labour Party, so finding herself for the first time in half a century cast outside mainstream labour politics. It was a bitter blow.

Selina Cooper died at home on 11 November 1946 shortly before her eighty-second birthday, and was cremated three days later. The memorial meeting was attended not only by Coombe and Cooper relatives, but also by Nelson's mayor and councillors, fellow magistrates, and members of the public assistance committee, Nelson Labour Party, women's co-operative guilds—and even one or two from the far-off Edwardian days of the Nelson Women's Suffrage Society.

Memories of the campaigns of Selina Cooper and her associates faded rapidly after the First World War, overlain by the more dramatic suffragette narratives of the Pankhursts. However, her papers were preserved by her daughter, and rediscovered in 1976; and in 1996, to mark the fiftieth anniversary of her death, a memorial exhibition and lecture about Selina Jane Cooper were organized in Nelson.   JILL LIDDINGTON

**Sources**  J. Liddington, *The life and times of a respectable rebel: Selina Cooper, 1864–1946* (1984) • Lancs. RO, Cooper MSS • Oral history interviews with Mary Cooper, Tameside Local Studies Library, Stalybridge, Manchester Studies Oral History Tapes • J. Liddington and J. Norris, *One hand tied behind us: the rise of the women's suffrage movement* (1978) • b. cert. • d. cert. • *CGPLA Eng. & Wales* (1946) • parish register (baptism), Callington, Cornwall, 25 March 1870
**Archives**  Lancs. RO, corresp., papers, and photographs, PDX 1137 | SOUND Tameside Local Studies Library, Stalybridge, Manchester Studies Oral History Tapes, Mary Cooper tapes
**Likenesses**  E. Buck, photograph, Women's Library, London [*see illus.*] • photographs, Lancs. RO, Cooper MSS, PDX 1137 • portraits, Lancs. RO, Cooper MSS, PDX 1137
**Wealth at death**  £423 4s. 11d.: administration, 7 Dec 1946, *CGPLA Eng. & Wales*

**Cooper, Susan Vera** [Susie] (1902–1995), potter, was born at Stansfield, near Burslem, Staffordshire, on 29 October 1902, the youngest of the seven children of John Cooper (d. 1914), JP, and his wife, Mary-Ann, née Adams. The year of her birth was that in which Arnold Bennett's *Anna of the Five Towns* was published; Susie Cooper, too, was to become a Potteries heroine—the only woman to own, manage, and design for her own potworks. Comfortably off, her parents ran a farm and retail business. As a child, Susie Cooper could always be 'kept good' with a drawing book. She attended a local school, then Mollart School, Hanley, a private establishment, which she left in 1917, to help with the family business. She also enrolled for evening classes in drawing at Burslem School of Art, and in 1919 won a scholarship for full-time training at the school, when she came under the influence of Gordon Forsyth, formerly an art director of leading pottery firms and from 1920 superintendent of art education in the district.

Through Forsyth Susie Cooper was taken on by Gray's Pottery, a decorating firm. Originally she had had ambitions to go to the Royal College of Art in London, but decided instead to make her career in the Potteries. In 1923, as a piece-worker, she helped decorate Forsyth's range of 'Gloria Lustre' wares, which were exhibited on Gray's stand at the British Industries' Fair. Promoted to resident designer, she was given her own backstamp for use on wares—a miniature image of an ocean liner with the words 'Designed by Susie Cooper'. Her patterns were shown at an industrial art exhibition at the Victoria and Albert Museum, London, in 1923; at the British Empire Exhibition at Wembley in 1924; and on Gray's stand in the

Susan Vera [Susie] Cooper (1902–1995), self-portrait, c.1933

British pavilion at the Paris 'Exposition … des Arts Décoratifs' of 1925 which was to give its name to art deco.

By the late 1920s Cooper was designing brilliantly enamelled cubist patterns not unlike those of her near-contemporary, the ceramics designer Clarice Cliff. But, dissatisfied with the way large areas of paint tended to flake, Cooper designed the 'banded' wares which were to be among her specialities. As a sideline she designed screen curtains for the neo-baroque Odeon, Marble Arch, London—a falling leaf pattern in gold, commissioned by the London interior design company Skilhorn and Edwards.

On her twenty-seventh birthday, Cooper left Gray's Pottery to set up on her own, with £4000 raised from her family. It was an unpropitious time to be starting any new business. The first premises she rented in Tunstall closed down after three months when the landlord went bankrupt after the Wall Street crash. Cooper next rented a Burslem works from Doulton & Co. and gathered a workforce of ten paintresses. In April 1930 she took her first advertisement in the *Pottery Gazette*, offering 'Elegance with Utility'. Her first independent pattern was 'Bronze chrysanthemums'. Her stand at the 1931 British Industries' Fair was very successful. By then she was decorating blank wares from Harry Wood; she moved into his Crown Works in Burslem which were to be her headquarters for almost half a century.

In 1932 Cooper's most familiar backstamp of a leaping deer was introduced—a quintessential art deco motif which remained in use until the mid-1960s. The streamlined 'Kestrel' shape was shown at the British Industries' Fair, where Queen Mary bought a breakfast-in-bed set from her and the princess royal purchased a triangular lamp decorated with clowns. By March 1933 Cooper had become prominent enough to be interviewed by the *Manchester Evening News*. The article noted that she was already exporting to Norway and South Africa: exports were always an important aspect of the firm's output. What also emerged clearly from the interview was Cooper's concern to train and look after the girls on the shop floor. That

month she also patented a 'Kestrel' tureen with a lid that doubled as a serving plate. Just before the 1933 British Industries' Fair opened, the John Lewis store in London placed a substantial order for wares from her, the beginning of a happy relationship.

In 1934 Cooper began using the technique of tube lining: slip (liquid clay) was squeezed out of a bag on to the ware in the manner of icing. She also designed wall masks, including one of Greta Garbo and one of herself, though the latter was never put on sale.

Contemporary photographs record Cooper's striking, almost film-star looks. In 1934 she also introduced her popular polka-dot pattern and crayon designs. In 1935 she was invited to exhibit at the Royal Academy's 'Art in Industry' show. She introduced lithographic patterns, admired by the art historian Nikolaus Pevsner in an article of 1936. Cooper was never a purist, and always had a feeling for popular taste. In 1937 she designed her very popular, if somewhat schmaltzy, 'Dresden spray' pattern, which lasted until the late 1950s. Distinct from this canny commercialism was a terracotta figure she made called *Lummox*—a suffering woman with bowed head, inspired by a book by the American writer Fanny Hurst. Also in 1937 the Burslem Pottery, of which she had become a director in 1933, was renamed the Susie Cooper Pottery Ltd. She introduced her streamlined 'Falcon' shapes, with aerographing (spraying on colour) and *sgraffito* (scratching designs through the glaze). On 28 April 1938 she married the architect Cecil Barker (1908/9–1972), with whom she had a son, Timothy, in 1943. He became a boat-builder, incorporating a Susie Cooper ceramic plaque in one boat. 'We both make vessels', she remarked.

By the late 1930s Susie Cooper's firm was one of the success stories of British industry. Imperial Airways were using her wares on their London–Paris flights. She was commissioned to make services for the experimental Peckham health centre and for Peter Jones's restaurant in Chelsea, both in dramatically modern buildings. In 1939 she was made a royal designer for industry. In spite of wartime restrictions, new patterns were introduced, including 'Black leaves' and 'Tigerlily'. But in 1942 a serious fire caused a close-down at her pottery until the end of the war.

Cooper was on the selection committee for the 'Britain can make it' exhibition at the Victoria and Albert Museum, London, in 1946 and exhibited wares herself. In the 1950s she expanded into porcelain, buying the Jason China Company, Longton. A 'Quail' shape was designed for the royal pavilion at the 1951 Festival of Britain. By 1952 her workforce had risen to 250. In the *New Statesman* of 27 March 1954, an American buyer was quoted as saying that: 'Britain is losing the design battle. Except for Susie Cooper you haven't a designer who can keep up with modern American styles.' In that year she designed a plaque to mark the bicentenary of the founding of the Royal Society of Arts. From 1956, responding as usual to changes in taste, Cooper introduced neo-classical patterns and a fluted shape. In 1957 a second bad fire caused a hiatus in production. Her husband resigned from his architectural firm and worked for her business full-time. In 1958 she designed the ultra-simple 'can' shape, a harbinger of the less whimsical styles of the 1960s. She bought the Crown Works in 1959. Gradually earthenware was phased out and the switch to bone china was complete by 1964.

In 1956 Cooper's firm was taken over by Wedgwood but she continued as a designer in the division of Susie Cooper Ltd, responding to the 'swinging sixties' with such vibrant patterns as 'Carnaby Daisy' and 'Harlequinade'. But she found that Wedgwood 'wouldn't take risks'. In her view too much attention was paid to the salesmen's view of what would sell and what wouldn't. She felt keenly the loss of control and the cramping of her freedom to design whatever she chose. Her husband died in 1972 aged sixty-three, and she resigned as director of Susie Cooper Ltd.

However, Cooper was asked to design lustre ware to celebrate the queen's silver jubilee in 1977; and in 1978 Wedgwood held a Susie Cooper retrospective exhibition at Sanderson's Exhibition Gallery, London, entitled 'Elegance and utility'. In 1978 she was appointed OBE for services to British industry. In 1980 Wedgwood, to her distress, closed the Crown Works, whereupon she moved to William Adams of Tunstall, part of the Wedgwood group. In 1982 her eightieth birthday was marked by a celebratory show at the Stoke-on-Trent Museum and Art Gallery. With the growing interest in art deco, she had become a cult figure among collectors, and a Susie Cooper collectors' group with its own newsletter was formed. Because she had made so much, in so many styles, and all of it marked, her work was an ideal collector's quarry.

In 1985 Cooper was saluted, with Clarice Cliff and the slightly earlier potter Charlotte Rhead, in a Channel 4 television series, *Pottery Ladies*. The following year she and her son left the Potteries to live on the Isle of Man. Interest in her work was unabated. In 1987 the Victoria and Albert Museum organized a travelling exhibition of 'Susie Cooper productions' and, to accompany it, Wedgwood revived three of her 1930s patterns. She received an honorary doctorate from the Royal College of Art.

Cooper began a new and eccentric art form, 'seed paintings', a sort of recycling of nature into art. An exhibition of her work in this curious medium was held at the Stoke-on-Trent museum in 1990. To celebrate her ninetieth birthday in 1992, Wedgwood staged a show at their visitors' centre, Barlaston, and she produced a limited edition of ninety of a porcelain model of a leaping deer. She died at Douglas, Isle of Man, on 28 July 1995. Her work, covering seven decades, mirrored and to some extent influenced the changing styles of twentieth-century decorative art. A key figure in both art deco and the 1950s 'contemporary' style, she designed some 4500 patterns and 500 new shapes. Examples of her work can be seen at the Wedgwood Museum, Barlaston, Staffordshire, in the Victoria and Albert Museum, and at the Design Museum, London. BEVIS HILLIER

**Sources** A. Eatwell, *Susie Cooper productions* (1987) [exhibition catalogue, V&A, 3 June – 6 Sept 1987] • B. Youds, *Susie Cooper: an elegant affair* (1996) • A. Casey, *Susie Cooper ceramics: a collector's guide* (1992) • J. Hay, *Art deco ceramics* (1996) • D. Critchlow, 'Susie Cooper, an artist who brings beauty to many homes', *Manchester Evening News* (1 March 1933) • A. Woodhouse, *Elegance and utility: the work of Susie Cooper RDI, 1924–1978* (1978) [exhibition catalogue, Sanderson's Exhibition Gallery, London] • C. Buckley, *Potters and paintresses: women designers in the pottery industry, 1870–1955* (1990)

**Archives** FILM *Pottery Ladies*, Channel 4, 1985

**Likenesses** S. V. Cooper, self-portrait, ceramic mask, *c*.1933, NPG [*see illus.*] • photograph, RSA, Archive of Royal Designers for Industry • photograph, repro. in *The Times* (1 Aug 1995) • photograph, repro. in *The Independent* (1 Aug 1995)

**Cooper, Thomas** (*c*.1517–1594), theologian and bishop of Winchester, was born in Catte Street, Oxford, to poor parents; his father is said to have been a tailor.

**Schooling and early career** Cooper rose from being a menial servant at Magdalen College, Oxford, to admission to the college school as a chorister in 1530–31, when he was over twelve. Nothing is known of his childhood except that it was hard and he was diligent. Taught grammar by Thomas Robertson, he was bright enough to proceed to a training in rhetoric and in 1539 to a probationary fellowship at Magdalen, which, when he graduated BA, became permanent in 1540. By 1543 he had proceeded MA. But fellows were required to be ordained and Cooper was neither in sympathy with the theology of the time nor happy to commit himself to a life of celibacy. Like his friend and near contemporary the martyrologist John Foxe, he resigned his fellowship in 1545 and took on the task, with considerable misgivings, of revising Thomas Elyot's dictionary, which contrived to put into English the words, phrases, and technical terms encountered in classical Latin. Cooper doubted his skill, but Thomas Berthelet, the printer of the dictionary, reassured him that no one else was up to the task. By 1548 he had completed and published his first revision with the addition 'augmented and inriched with above xxxiii thousand words and phrases, very nedeful for the knowlage of the latin tonge' (Starnes, 69).

About 1546 Cooper married a woman named Amy (possibly Royse) and in 1549 set about completing Thomas Lanquet's unfinished *Chronicle*—a universal history from the beginning of the world. At just this moment in his career, when he might have become no more than a hack author, he was offered the mastership of the school at Magdalen which provided a salary and some status. However, Edward VI's privy council raised radical proposals about whether the colleges of the university should support schools. Cooper and thirty-one fellows vigorously resisted these and enlisted the help of Cranmer and the city of Oxford. It was the first of many occasions in Cooper's career on which he had to promote the case for good learning.

At this time Cooper also faced personal problems which became the gossip of Oxford. His wife seems to have had affairs with at least two men which provoked ribald verses directed at her and a remarkable tribute by Sir John Harington to him. Cooper refused to divorce his wife, and Harington, observing that Amy Cooper was 'too light for his gravitie', added that 'His lyfe in Oxford was very commendable and in some sort saint-lyke; for if it be saintlike to live unreproachable, to bear a cross patientlie, to forgive injuries freely this man's example is sampleless in this age' (Harington, 2.88–9).

Cooper certainly needed patience. His wife threw into the fire the early drafts of his own dictionary, the *Thesaurus*, eventually published in 1565, and his position as headmaster was also imperilled by the accession of Queen Mary. He recognized that he must either go abroad, as many of his contemporaries had done, or else support his family in other ways. In 1556 he supplicated for the degree of bachelor of medicine and was given leave by the university to practise as a doctor. He thus became part of a small but important group of Elizabethan bishops 'in waiting' who experienced the Tudor church only from within and were not disposed to judge it or reform it to the patterns of the continent.

Following the accession of Elizabeth, Cooper was reappointed to the headship of Magdalen College School in 1559. His skills as a teacher were praised by William Camden, who acknowledged the debt he owed to Cooper 'in whose school I both confesse and rejoice that I received education' (Camden, 540). His second edition of Lanquet's *Chronicle*, which took the history to the reign of Queen Elizabeth—now called Cooper's *Chronicle*—appeared in 1560. He was probably ordained by this time, but no record survives. Could he now catch the eye of the Elizabethan establishment and move from his native city?

**Elevation to Lincoln** Cooper wrote in defence of Bishop Jewel on the sacrament in 1562, and published his own *Thesaurus* in 1565. When the queen visited Oxford in 1566 she heard and enjoyed not only a Latin oration from Cooper but also disputations on theological subjects which he had arranged for her. He recognized her interest in theology, and shortly afterwards himself proceeded to the degrees of BTh and DTh, both on 18 March 1567. In that year he was also elected vice-chancellor (against the wishes of the earl of Leicester, who was chancellor) and introduced popular celebrations, mainly of feasting and bell-ringing, to celebrate the queen's accession day. Also in 1567 he became dean of Christ Church and was tutor to Sir Philip Sidney; surviving accounts show that Sidney lived in his house until midsummer 1570. In 1569 Parker and Grindal recommended Cooper for the deanery of Gloucester, which was 'not so far distant from Oxford, so he may very well have due regard to both charges' (*Pepys MSS*, 161). In the event Cooper had hardly been appointed—there is no record that he was ever installed—when the see of Lincoln became vacant. His elevation was swift. He was elected on 4 February 1571, and consecrated on the 24th. Installed by proxy in the cathedral in March, he was installed in person on 28 June.

The diocese of Lincoln was vast, stretching from Lincolnshire to Hertfordshire; Cooper chose to live for most of his tenure of the see at Buckden, near Huntingdon, which was conveniently situated on the Great North Road. The immense task before him was essentially that of converting both priests and people to the peculiarly English form of protestantism and liturgy enacted by statute. This tested his skill as a teacher to the uttermost. Characteristically, he set about his task by preaching both nationally and in his diocese, by publishing easily comprehensible books, and by attempting to organize the clergy into group exercises in scriptural exegesis which were intended to promote better and more obviously biblical preaching.

Cooper preached at St Paul's Cross in 1572, and was accused by an adversary of maintaining an ignorant ministry, of defending the 'unjust lordship of bishops', of 'magnifying' the prayer book, and of misusing the scriptures by 'wringing' them from 'their natural sense and meaning'. All this was attributed to Cooper's ignorance of the church in Europe because, his critic suggested, 'I have heard you were never yet out of this realm' (Strype, 2.287–302). Undaunted, Cooper forged ahead, publishing in 1573 *A Briefe Exposition of such Chapters of the Old Testament as Usually are Redde in Church* (STC 5684). As the title suggests, the book gives an exposition of the text for each Sunday of the Christian year 'whereby the unlearned reader may not only the sooner attaine to the true sense and meaning of the holy ghost, the author of the scriptures but also learne some godly instruction of the same' (Cooper, *A Briefe Exposition*, preface). Parker wrote to Burghley asking that it be commended by the council: 'It would doe well. The rather for that the simpler [*sic*] the doctrine is to the people the sooner they may be edified and in obedience reposed' (BL, Lansdowne MS 19, no. 9).

**Diocesan reformer** In the wake of his primary visitation of 1574 Cooper ordered the clergy who were not graduates to meet on alternate Thursday mornings for carefully regulated exposition of scripture, keeping closely to the text, with specially selected moderators judging the performance and correcting errors, noting absentees, and inquiring into the lives of participants. His orders were precise and survive for both Hertfordshire and Buckinghamshire. These exercises (often known as 'prophesyings') were later commended by Archbishop Grindal, but were condemned by the queen on the ground that they could move out of the control of the bishops and be used to promote presbyterianism. Instructed to have them repressed in Welwyn, Cooper wrote a very careful reply, pointing out that he had asked the shire gentlemen and those ministers he trusted to report to him about them. Neither they nor the JPs had heard 'of any disorder there but that it was in all parts both moderately and godly us'd' (BL, Add. MS 29546, fol. 41v). His remonstrations fell on deaf ears and he was forced to dissolve all exercises in the south of his diocese except at Aylesbury. He was nevertheless apprehensive that reports of disorderly exercises might come from the northern parts of the diocese, not least because those in favour at court 'not only by their well doings but by the discrediting of others well doings' were a hazard. He remained vigilant for those who 'made means to publish fantasticall opinions' (ibid., fol. 42v), especially in Leicester, and particularly criticized laity who attended exercises but who would not come to sermons.

It was Archdeacon John Aylmer who cast doubt on Cooper's sanguine report on prophesyings. The bishop himself was probably all too aware of the indifferent standard of education among his clergy. The battle not just for a passive assent but also for an active understanding of the Elizabethan settlement required all Cooper's energy and pedagogic skills. His injunctions following his visitation in 1577 required records to be kept of the number of sermons preached in every parish, and he insisted on the celebration of communion four times a year. Children over six were to be catechized for an hour before evensong. Ministers were to apply themselves to the study of scripture and to note 'wholesome sentences' for use in preaching (Kennedy, 2.46).

Cooper had a hard time with his cathedral chapter. It had been reformed under his predecessor, Bullingham, and looked as though it might become a centre of evangelism. John Whitgift was dean, John Aylmer was archdeacon of Lincoln, and Michael Reniger was subdean and chancellor. All three were learned and enthusiastic reformers and were for a time in residence. But Cooper was quick to spot that there was no divinity lecturer as there had been in Bishop Longland's time, and that the senior residentiaries were greedy for the perquisites of residence and the more lucrative prebends: Aylmer received Corringham, Whitgift Nassington, both worth considerably more than that given to Cooper's son-in-law, Dr John Belley, now his vicar-general. Aylmer was also in dispute with the bishop about the share of each in judicial fees which was eventually settled by a return to the practice of the fifteenth century. For Cooper this was just an irksome distraction from the real business: how could he prevent a slipping back to the old ways of the Church of Rome?

Cooper saw Catholics as those who 'winke with both eyes, and without offence suffer the Clergy of Rome, shameless Simony, incontinence, drunkeness, Dice playing, hunting, Necromancie, ambition, bribery', and much else that he utterly abhorred (Cooper, *Certaine Sermons*, 47; STC 5685). His visitation of his diocese in 1577 uncovered a number of recusants: the women of Bedfordshire were a difficult bunch, and the wife of William Mordaunt he described as 'a verie obstinate woman' (PRO, SP 12/117, no. 13). In Huntingdonshire a JP had his house in Cooper's diocese but his parish church in that of Peterborough so he could dodge both bishops. In Lincolnshire the bishop was not convinced of the sincerity of another JP who went to church 'starkly and seldom' and used the convenient excuse of sickness (ibid.). In 1580 the council congratulated him on 'how discretlie he hath travaled in discovering the offences of the principall Recusants' (*APC, 1580–81*, 106).

Cooper's vigour in promoting reform and suppressing dissent clearly marked him out for further promotion. Under his rule the diocese of Lincoln saw an increase in ordinations and a marked improvement in the learning of the clergy. In June 1579 he declined translation to Norwich on the ground that such a move would bring him neither an appreciable increase in stipend nor a less demanding cure. A more advantageous translation became a possibility with the death of John Watson of Winchester in 1584.

**Translation to Winchester** Cooper's passage to the diocese of Winchester was unusually speedy: he was translated from Lincoln on 12 March 1584 and confirmed in his new see by Archbishop Whitgift on the 23rd. His were trusted hands, and the state of the Winchester diocese was in need of them. Writing to Lord Burghley in January 1584 Robert Bennet, master of St Thomas's Hospital in Winchester, pleaded that the diocese required:

a man full of wisdome, faithefulness and spirit in his calling, that maie as in his place soo in giftes of diligence, zeale, wisdome, government, and hospitalitie strive before the rest and that the vacation be not longe, lest the insolence of recusantes growe to too great an height of pride. (BL, Lansdowne MS 40, no. 23)

In April 1584 Cooper became the prelate to the Order of the Garter, a perquisite of the holder of the see, and was invested with the appropriate robes. It was a long way for a poor tailor's son to have come.

The task facing Cooper was daunting. The diocese, which comprised Hampshire, Surrey, and the Channel Islands, presented problems different from those of Lincoln. The inadequacy of incumbents was common to both sees, but in Winchester the central problem was that of the recusants who could turn traitor with disastrous consequences in a diocese that bordered on the channel. In May 1584 Cooper told Burghley that his archdeacon reported at least 400 obstinate recusants in Hampshire alone, and a single parish had forty or fifty. The slackness of the churchwardens meant that this was an underestimate. Cooper asked for increased powers to deal with them, and suggested names for ecclesiastical commissioners.

In 1587 Cooper conducted a personal visitation of his diocese: he was at pains to see that preachers who were deemed satisfactory were well deployed and helped by clergy of 'the inferior sort' who were to catechize and read homilies. They were to attend to their 'exercises' with a view to public preaching, and those whose university degree exempted them from exercises were 'to beware of innovation in their ministry' and see that holy communion was celebrated at least three times a year. They were also required to wear the surplice 'not from any holiness therein but for obedience and reverence' (Hants. RO, MS 21 M65/B1/18). The same orders were repeated throughout Hampshire and the Isle of Wight. All ministers were forbidden to frequent fairs, markets, taverns, and ale houses, and were ordered to 'abstain from filthy drunkenness' (ibid.). In 1590 he isolated four sorts of minister for special blame: the ignorant, those whose lives were in contradiction to the gospel, those who were negligent in their duties, and those who executed their duties 'perversely or frowardly' (Hants. RO, MS 21 M65/B1/19).

What Cooper might find perverse or froward others might not. In 1586 John Udall, the puritan lecturer in Kingston, Surrey, was accused of holding conventicles and was tried and condemned to death, though pardoned in 1592 at Whitgift's request. The sheriff of Surrey, Sir William More of Loseley, brought a petition to parliament from the inhabitants of South Farnham lamenting the failings of the ministry there; yet it was Cooper who complained to More about the vicar of Farnham's insufficiency in 1589 and noted the failure of his parishioners to attend church in 1591. Nor was More above presenting to the parish of Compton a cleric whom the bishop judged to be of insufficient learning and thus no preacher.

The real anxiety for Cooper, however, was the problem posed by recusants who were by 1585 harbouring priests from Douai and Rome to minister to the Catholics of the land and who were smuggled in along the channel coastline. The Hampshire prisons were full of recusants whom Cooper treated with little mercy. He would not allow them burial in church ground and even suggested that the able should be sent to swell the earl of Leicester's army in the Low Countries. Jesuits were known to avoid Winchester, but neither the death penalty, severe fines, nor imprisonment deterred the Catholics. Cooper, an ecclesiastical commissioner, examined and handed over to the secular authorities for execution two priests from Rheims and a labourer who had assisted them, and others were sent to London for trial. In 1587 there were more than 100 in the common prison for Surrey; Cooper wrote desperately in 1589 'that the people do fall away in Religion by the evil example of such Recusants as have liberty' (*APC, 1589–90*, 124).

Part of Cooper's anxiety lay in the assumption that as the Armada approached, English Catholics would support the Spaniards. In this he was wrong, but that did not stop him pressing hard on his clergy to make sure they all contributed in money or in kind to the defence of the realm. For this he was held up as an example to other diocesans. Behind Cooper's energetic involvement in national defence lay his fervent loyalty to the queen: he was asked to write a prayer for use in the army, while in 1589 he was also engaged in writing *An Admonition to the People of England*. This, however, was not directed against papists but against the parallel threat, as he saw it, from extreme puritans.

**Target for Marprelate** Though seditious books were under severe penalty after 1586, there were a number of illegal attacks on the church, which senior churchmen attempted to answer. The deaths in 1588 of both John Field and the earl of Leicester goaded a weakened but committed puritan party into producing a series of tracts under the pseudonym of Martin *Marprelate, beginning with two of the most important: the *Epistle* in October 1588 and the *Epitome* in the following month. It is probable that from the first Cooper intended his *Admonition* to constitute a broad defence of the Elizabethan settlement, and that he subsequently added a preliminary section to it specifically dealing with the issues raised by the Marprelate tracts. The result was that he became embroiled in a dispute in which his opponent showed all the wit and personal insult of the street-pamphleteer, while Cooper laboured under the self-imposed handicap of neither descending to personal detail nor lowering his tone to match that of his adversary.

Cooper knew that his *Admonition*, presented as the work of 'T. C.'—the bishop's own initials but taken by others (who had clearly not read the book) for Thomas Cartwright—would have little effect against Marprelate's wit: 'The dartes, I confess, of deceitfull and slanderous tongues, are very sharpe, and the burning of woundes made by them, will as hardly in the hearts of many bee quenched, as the coales of juniper' (Cooper, *Admonition*, 4). His primary argument is that the government of the church is not laid down by scripture but is expedient to the government of the land. Contrasting the different arrangements for European protestant churches, he observes:

> I doubt not but … directed by the spirite of God to retain this liberty, that in external government and other outward orders they might choose such as they thought in wisedome and godlinesse to bee most convenient for the state of the Country and disposition of the people.   (ibid., 64–5)

In England to be without bishops would be 'not just Marprelate, but Mar-prince, Mar-state, Mar-law, Mar-magistrate' (ibid., 31). He defends his episcopal colleagues from the charges against them and repeats often that 'Men are fraile, and in danger to sinne though they have otherwise great graces' (ibid., 20). Bishops, however, have no monopoly of frailty, and to bring them into 'contempt' at a time when the enemies of the realm have lately been defeated shows an ingratitude for 'the mightie workes of God and his marvellous mercies' (ibid., 29). He argues that bishops have experience and learning that many of their critics do not, and he condemns 'our hasty divines that in three yeeres study think … to have more learning then all the Bishops in England' (ibid., 54).

Cooper's argument was moderate. He claimed no divine right through apostolic succession for the bishops, nor did he deny their fallibility. But he was convinced that the church had improved under Elizabeth, and that such improvement was put at risk by extremists who quibbled over details (such as the sign of the cross in baptism) and who refused in consequence to enrich the church with their teaching or other abilities. They also made legitimate reforms seem unwise since they were asking for so many changes at a time when the Spaniards threatened far more decisively the whole fabric of English protestantism, of which both presbyterianism and episcopalianism were a part. Moderation after this fashion was to be reasserted by Richard Hooker, possibly a pupil of Cooper at Magdalen.

Within three months of the appearance of the *Admonition* Marprelate replied to it with *Hay any Worke for Cooper* (published on 23 March 1589). Not only did the pamphleteer revel in the publicity that the bishop had given to his tracts, but he also took the opportunity to hurl personal abuse at the bishop. Cooper was said to be 'very choleric and peevish' (Marprelate, 20); the old matter (though significantly no new matters) of his wife's infidelity was brought to public attention; he was accused of ignorance, and of being addicted to card-playing and gambling. It all pained Cooper. He was an old man by 1590, and by 1592 was beginning to have to absent himself from committees and the House of Lords (which he had previously attended regularly) seemingly on health grounds. Marprelate's taunts were savage precisely because Cooper was a formidable adversary. He was a strong defender of that peculiarly English form of protestantism, eventually to be designated Anglicanism, even before it existed. Writing in 1583, he displayed his heart on his sleeve when he wrote:

> For this I dare saye that synce the very age of the Apostles unto this tyme we lyve in, there was never any Churche upon thearthe that had so perfecte trewthe of doctryne nor so synceare admynystratyon of Sacraments without supersticyon, as thanked be God, the Churche of Engeland now hathe. Thearfore the dangerusnes of these latter daies consydered, we should raythur yelde most hearty thankes to god for the greate blessings that we have, then to murmur at some smale blemyshes or imperfectyons that remayne. (BL, Stowe MS 159, fol. 153v)

In sum, much of Cooper's support for the English church lay in his conviction that scripture should not be interpreted literally, but rather with a view to restoring the usage of the early church. With this went a profound respect and love for the service of holy communion. As a diocesan he ordered its celebration three or four times a year, as a visitor to his old college he rebuked the fellows for the carelessness and the irreverence shown to it. In his sermons he could write more warmly: 'For in deede wee teach I believe that it is one of the sweetest and most excellent comfortes that Christ at his departure left unto his people' (Cooper, *Certaine Sermons*, 33). In his utter certainty that faith and the fruits of belief were a seamless robe, neither existing without the other, Cooper was at one with his adversaries.

Marprelate did not, however, confine his attack on Cooper to the *Admonition*. The bishop was a lexicographer, initially in his adapting Elyot's *Dictionary*, and then in compiling his own *Thesaurus*. Marprelate accused him of plagiarism, and also implied both that he had failed to acknowledge Elyot's original contribution and that he had lifted much of the *Thesaurus* from the French dictionary of Robert Stephanus (1552) and the German dictionary of John Frisius (1556). It is certainly true that Cooper borrowed widely and used, for instance, William Turner's herbal dictionary and those of others. It has been observed that Cooper's 'contemporaries and successors were inclined to judge him by a higher standard than they applied to the average' (Starnes, 98). The subtlety of Cooper's English usage and the fact that he gave a large number of English words that might translate the Latin not only served to enrich English, but made for a more accurate understanding of Latin. Thus 'Salve multum' (Plautus) is given by Cooper as 'God speed you heartily, God give you an hundred good tomorrows' (Redhead, 54).

**Financial matters** More telling still was Marprelate's gibe that Cooper was a 'petty pope' (Marprelate, 23). The people of Leicestershire had noticed a certain lordliness in his demeanour and wished that he would come to them without any entourage and pomp. Yet it is difficult to find

evidence that before his last years in Winchester Cooper conducted himself like a wealthy man. His wife may have had property and he may have made some money as a physician, but the diocese of Lincoln yielded an income of less than £900. The expenses of servants and travel were heavy, which no doubt explains why the bishop used his son-in-law as his deputy: it kept the money in the family.

Winchester was two or three times the value of Lincoln. On his translation to Winchester Cooper was granted the temporalities, calculated at £2793, retrospectively from Michaelmas 1583. This was a generous restitution but Cooper claimed that, not being 'riche in myself' and not having any other office *in commendam*, he would 'hardlie be hable to live' unless he was allowed to pay his first fruits over a period of five years at the rate of £500 per annum (BL, Egerton MS 1693, fol. 115r–v). His petition was granted, and Cooper also asked for, and received, £530 from the executors of his predecessor, John Watson. By 1587, however, he was at full stretch financially. He evaded the expense and responsibility of a projected queen's progress in 1586. He was complaining as late as 1590 to William More that litigation pending on his estate over fishing and other rights was making a heavy demand on him:

> I could not but make this complaint unto you, being at this time more troubled with quarrelous matters than I have [been] in all my life to stand the charges in all things I shall not be able to beare it, unless I give over housekeeping cleane. (Redhead, 193)

Yet the bishop did not die a pauper; indeed his successor excused his own payments for the defence of the realm on the grounds that he was not as rich as Cooper. Cooper's will shows that by the time of his death he was hardly short of housekeeping money. He had accumulated much silver gilt; his collection of armour (for his contribution to the defence of the realm) included 72 pikes, 6 cases of pistols, 29 daggers, and considerable ammunition. At Farnham he had 12 geldings and 5 'stone' horses, and at Waltham at least 7 other horses. All those may have been the necessary perquisites of an active bishop. More remarkable was Cooper's note 'of such ready money as I have in possession this 9 April 1594'. It included 'one bagge £150; in one other bagge £140, in one other bagge £160', and £480 in further bags (Foster, *Lincoln Episcopal Records*, 343). What he did not have—and he defended episcopal wealth for this reason—were estates or even a house for his widow. But there was a little. He mentions 'graunts, assignmentes and assurances' made to himself and his wife by his brother-in-law Robert Royse 'of and in twoe meadowes parcel of the Ferme of Mydly by Oxford' (ibid., 339).

As he lay dying in 1594 Cooper was careful to double-check his last arrangements, adding codicils to his will: his wife was to enjoy most of his wealth, but the remainder was to go to his grandchildren through his sons-in-law. His will also recognizes the claim of old and infirm servants and gives a glimpse of his love for the son-in-law who had served him so well; Cooper's devotion to learning was apparent in the gift of his books to Winchester Cathedral Library.

**Cooper and the Elizabethan church** Cooper was one of a number of Elizabethan bishops whose learning, hard work, and pastoral involvement shaped the church in England in the late sixteenth century—one of those whose 'wainscoted face' (Marprelate, 71) may have expressed the strain of a long life often lived against the grain. He had withstood the onslaughts of Mary's reign, come to terms with a termagant wife, and devoted much of his life to sheer hard work. He served the University of Oxford well, but the church established in England in Elizabeth's reign was his real love. He served it in his writing and by his sermons, but above all by his ability to teach his clergy as he had initially taught his Magdalen pupils. There is a suspicion that his so-called grandeur was the shyness of a man unused to the heights to which he had been raised. He served his country not only by sitting on commissions and in the Lords, but also in the meticulous way in which he answered enquiries, whether about his 'exercises' or about defence or recusants. Though Marprelate sought to smear him, his rigorous pastoral care and the quality of his writings and sermons suggest that the smear was unjustified.

Cooper died at Winchester on 29 April 1594. He was buried on the south side of the cathedral with an inscription, now removed, but whose words survive and suggest the profound respect in which he was held. His exercise of the office of a bishop commanded superlatives for learning, generosity, and vigilance. The conclusion to his pithy but elegant Latin obituary may be translated as proclaiming that 'the earth has covered his body but his spirit is above the stars, Heavenly souls enjoy a heavenly peace' (Foster, *Lincoln Episcopal Records*, xix). Cooper would have liked that.                              MARGARET BOWKER

**Sources** BL, Lansdowne MSS 19, 40; Egerton MS 1693; Add. MS 29546 • PRO, state papers domestic, Elizabeth I, SP 12/117 • Hants. RO, MSS 21 M65/B1/18–19 • C. W. Foster, ed., *Lincoln episcopal records, in the time of Thomas Cooper … bishop of Lincoln*, CYS, 11 (1913) • C. W. Foster, ed., *The state of the church in the reigns of Elizabeth and James I*, Lincoln RS, 23 (1926) • J. V. Redhead, 'Thomas Cooper and the Elizabethan church', MLitt diss., U. Newcastle, 1975 • *The Marprelate tracts, 1588–1589*, ed. W. Pierce (1911) • T. Cooper, *An admonition to the people of England*, ed. E. Arber (1895) • T. Cooper, *Certaine sermons wherin is contained the defense of the gospell* (1580) • T. Cooper, *A briefe exposition of such chapters of the Old Testament as usually are redde in church* (1573) • *APC, 1588–93* • W. D. Macray, *A register of the members of St Mary Magdalen College, Oxford*, 8 vols. (1894–1915) • W. H. Frere and W. P. M. Kennedy, eds., *Visitation articles and injunctions of the period of the Reformation*, 3, Alcuin Club, Collections, 16 (1910) • W. P. M. Kennedy, ed., *Elizabethan episcopal administration*, 2, Alcuin Club, Collections, 26 (1924) • De W. T. Starnes, *Renaissance dictionaries: English–Latin and Latin–English* (1954) • J. Strype, *Annals of the Reformation and establishment of religion … during Queen Elizabeth's happy reign*, new edn, 2 (1824) • *Report on the Pepys manuscripts*, HMC, 70 (1911) • J. Harington, *Nugae antiquae*, ed. T. Park and H. Harington, 2 vols. (1804) • Wood, *Ath. Oxon.*, new edn, vol. 1 • F. Heal, *Of prelates and princes: a study of the economic and social position of the Tudor episcopate* (1980) • P. Collinson, *The Elizabethan puritan movement* (1967) • P. Collinson, *Godly people: essays on English protestantism and puritanism* (1983) • B. D. Till, 'Episcopacy in the works of the Elizabethan and Caroline divines', *The historic episcopate*, ed. K. M. Carey (1954) • W. Camden, *Britannia*, trans. P. Holland (1610) • P. Lake, *Anglicans and puritans? Presbyterianism and English conformist thought from Whitgift to Hooker* (1988)

**Archives** Folger, Loseley MSS
**Wealth at death** see inventory, Foster, ed., *Lincoln episcopal records*, 342–3

**Cooper** [Cowper], **Thomas** (b. 1569/70, d. in or after 1626), Church of England clergyman and writer on witchcraft, was born in London and attended Westminster School, apparently with help from the Fishmongers' and Skinners' companies. On 17 December 1586, aged sixteen, he matriculated as a queen's scholar from Christ Church, Oxford, graduating BA on 14 December 1590, and proceeding MA on 19 June 1593 and BD on 14 April 1600. Soon afterwards he was appointed by the mayor and corporation of the city of Chester, probably as a lecturer, to replace William Harrison, recently selected as one of the queen's preachers for Lancashire. On 1 August 1601, on presentation of the dean and chapter of Christ Church Cathedral, Cooper was admitted as vicar of Great Budworth, Cheshire, remaining until 1604; on 8 May he became vicar of Holy Trinity, Coventry. On 28 November 1605 the mayor and Lord Harington wrote from the city to Robert Cecil concerning 'Mr Cowper a minister, who stated in a sermon that the papists had contrived nine plots against the King and state' (*CSP dom., 1603–10*, 263). Cooper repeatedly drew attention to God's deliverance of the nation from the Gunpowder Plot. In his first treatment of this theme, *A Brand Taken Out of the Fire, or, The Romish Spider …, with his Webbe of Treason* (1606), there appeared dedications to Lady Harington, to Princess Elizabeth (then in the care of Lord and Lady Harington), and to the Coventry authorities. Relations with the city fathers appear to have soured, for later Cecil was in receipt of another missive from Coventry, this time from Cooper, claiming that for three years his sermons there had remained unpaid. He signed *The Converts First Love Discerned* (1610) from 'my poor house at Coventry, this 10 April 1610', but had resigned by the year's end.

It seems probable that soon afterwards Cooper moved to London, for *The Estates of the Hypocrite and Sincere Christian* (1613) and later works were dedicated to city people or institutions. In the preface to *A Familiar Treatise, Laying Down Cases of Conscience* (1615) the dedicatees, Lady Rumney, Mr Springham, Mr Slaney, Mr Parkhurst, Mr Clarke, Mr Vincent, Mr Mosley, and Mr Thaire, were among Cooper's 'Christian auditors and loving neighbours' and 'the instrument of my settling in the Citie, and exercise of my calling'. In 1615 also appeared *The Blessing of Japheth*, dedicated to Sir Thomas Hayes, mayor of London, the aldermen and sheriffs, and the commissioners for plantations in Ireland and Virginia. There followed *The Mysterie of the Holy Government of our Affections* (1619), addressed to 'Sir Thomas Smith, most worthie governor of the East Indian Company' and his colleagues. Here as elsewhere Cooper makes plain that for him the material and spiritual ends of trade and colonization meshed perfectly. He acted for another company, the Grocers', in supplying two visitation sermons, published in 1619, at the free school at Oundle, Northamptonshire.

In 1617 Cooper issued *The Mystery of Witch-Craft*, the book for which he is chiefly known. Against those who saw in astrology a key to the orderliness of the world, he argued on their own scientific terrain: 'The rules of this art have no foundation in experience' (Thomas, 418). But God was the great architect of order; his providence, together with the efforts of Satan, lay behind the unexpected events which sometimes disrupted the world. Cooper rejected the purveyors of traditional magic, the 'good' witches and cunning men of rural England, who sought to achieve results directly by spells and divinations, and thus to assume among the common people the authority of God. He was convinced, however, of the real existence of witchcraft and, like other Calvinists of the new generation, he accepted the widespread European view that witches had made a pact with the devil. Earlier, while at Great Budworth, he had been involved in a case in which a Northwich child had been 'afflicted by the power of sathan, and (as it was conceived) through the confederacie of some witches thereabout' (Cooper, *Mystery of Witch-Craft*, A3r).

In *The cry and revenge of blood: expressing the nature and haynousnesse of wilfull murther … committed at Halsworth in high Suffolk* (1620) appears a remarkable woodcut depicting the exhumation of bodies and the murderer at work with a large cudgel, urged on by a black, satanic figure, horned and taloned, with wings like those of a bat. Cooper attended the trial at Bury assizes, and the book was based on his notes (a representation of the hanging appears at page 59). A preface to Lord Chief Justice Henry Montagu recalled his 'gratious clemency in releasing a poor distressed neighbour, at my request' who had 'provoked your honour's just displeasure'; the work was signed from 'my house in Whitecrosse street', London, on 24 August 1620.

After 1622, when he issued *The Wonderful Mysterie of Spiritual Growth*, dedicated to Lionel Cranfield, the flow of Cooper's publications abruptly ceased. Despite all the great names which had appeared in his works, there can be no doubt that the author was the Thomas Cooper, bachelor in divinity, who, having been appointed a preacher to the fleet by Captain Richard Gyffard, was, in September 1626, in the embarrassing position of having to petition the duke of Buckingham for an advance on his wages (£5 a month) for transport to Portsmouth. After this nothing is known of him.               STEPHEN WRIGHT

**Sources** Foster, *Alum. Oxon.* · *Old Westminsters* · E. Axon, 'The king's preachers in Lancashire, 1599-1845', *Transactions of the Lancashire and Cheshire Antiquarian Society*, 56 (1941-2), 67-104 · K. Thomas, *Religion and the decline of magic* (1991) · G. Ormerod, *The history of the county palatine and city of Chester*, 2nd edn, ed. T. Helsby, 1 (1882) · W. Dugdale, *The antiquities of Warwickshire illustrated*, rev. W. Thomas, 2nd edn, 1 (1730) · T. Cooper, *The mystery of witch-craft: discovering the truth, nature, occasions, growth and power therof, together with the detection and punishment of the same* (1617) · CSP dom., 1603-26 · T. Cooper, *The cry and revenge of blood: expressing the nature and haynousnesse of wilfull murther … exemplified in a most lamentable history thereof, committed at Halsworth in high Suffolk and lately convicted at Bury assizes* (1620)

**Cooper, Thomas** (1759-1839), political writer and college head, was born in Westminster on 22 October 1759, the son of Thomas Cooper, who was entitled to bear heraldic

**Thomas Cooper (1759-1839),** by Asher Brown Durand, 1829 (after Charles Cromwell Ingham)

arms. He matriculated from University College, Oxford, in February 1779, but did not take a degree; well known in later life as a freethinker, he is said to have refused to sign the Thirty-Nine Articles. He attended anatomical lectures in London during the summer of 1780 and subsequently took a clinical course at the Middlesex Hospital. In the same year he entered into a partnership of calico printers at Raikes, near Bolton, and about 10 miles from Manchester. The register of alumni of Oxford states that in 1787 he became a barrister from the Inner Temple, but his name does not occur on its list of graduates. He travelled the northern circuit, which included Lancashire, between 1787 and 1790. By 1785 he was living south of Manchester at Woodheys, Altrincham, Cheshire, but later removed to Lever Hall, Bolton, which placed him nearer the dye works. He was married to Alice Greenwood in St George's parish, Hanover Square, London, several years before settling in Lancashire. They had five children before her death in October 1800.

In early adulthood Cooper distinguished himself as a humanitarian thinker and a philosophical radical. In 1787 he published *Letters on the Slave Trade*, an essay denouncing slavery as 'the most diabolical exertion of political tyranny, which the annals of oppression can exhibit an instance of' (p. 4). That same year he published *Propositions Respecting the Foundation of Civil Government*, a paper asserting that government had originated in the consent of the people who retained in perpetuity a right to alter the government at their will. As vice-president of the Manchester Literary and Philosophical Society and a founder member of the Manchester Constitutional Society, he befriended Thomas Walker, Samuel Jackson, James Watt jun., and others who were to join him in the ill-fated parliamentary reform movement. He also carried on a vigorous correspondence with the notorious radical John Horne Tooke. In the spring of 1792, while in Paris on business together with James Watt jun., son of the inventor, he was requested to establish contact with the revolutionary societies of France on behalf of the Manchester Constitutional Society. He and Watt duly paid a visit on Robespierre and the Jacobins, which earned them a rebuke in parliament from Edmund Burke. Upon his return to England Cooper published his *Reply to Mr. Burke's Invective*, a scathing attack on hereditary government in the spirit of Thomas Paine's better-known *The Rights of Man*. 'Kings and Nobles', Cooper wrote, 'have flourished at the expense of the People, who have been universally regarded merely as the Footstools of their pride, and the means of their gratification'. He went on to prescribe a democratic remedy: 'If the good of the People … is to be the Object of Government, THEY MUST BE THEIR OWN GOVERNORS—they must adopt, *in fact*, the government of the MANY by the MANY' (Cooper, *Reply to Mr. Burke's Invective*, 13, 28).

In 1793, discouraged by official repression of reform in England, Cooper paid an initial visit to America with an eye towards possible resettlement. While he was away, his calico-printing firm was forced into bankruptcy by its creditors. In 1794, his fortunes at a low ebb, he and a friend, the renowned scientist Joseph Priestley, quit their native country for Pennsylvania and together settled their families in Northumberland county. Unlike Priestley, who had lost all taste for public controversy, Cooper soon re-entered political life in the service of the Jeffersonian party working in close association with newspaper editor William Duane and lawyer A. J. Dallas, later to be secretary of the treasury under James Madison. A polemical tract targeting President John Adams, head of the rival Federalist Party, resulted in his prosecution for libel under the sedition law in the spring of 1800 and earned him a short stay in the Philadelphia gaol. He was later rewarded by his party with public office, serving first as a land commissioner and after 1804 as president judge of one of the state's common pleas districts. When the state party split over legal reform, he sided against the radical faction that wanted to open the practice of law to persons without formal training and to make judges subject to popular election. In 1811 his opponents succeeded in having him removed from the bench. The experience led him to conclude that popular democracy was 'not quite so perfect in practice as it is beautiful in theory' (Cooper, *Narrative*, 6). He expanded his critique of democracy in a letter dated July 1815 which circulated privately among his friends. 'Experience has taught us all', he lamented, 'that there is a perpetual and almost irresistible inclination among the people to cheat themselves, and to be cajoled and cheated by others'. Contemptuous of the 'aristocracy of talent', popular opinion, he wrote, was 'harsh and violent, as well as unreflecting: prone to sacrifice its friends to its flatterers, and to commit injustice in the wantonness of power, as well as through mistake or resentment' (extract of a letter to a student at law, Madison MSS, 76.4).

Cooper became professor of chemistry at Carlisle College in 1812. Four years later he moved to the University of Pennsylvania. His friend Thomas Jefferson subsequently invited him to join the faculty at the University of Virginia, but Cooper's philosophical materialism and obvious contempt for religious establishments made him unacceptable to the state legislature. In 1819 he moved to Columbia, South Carolina, as professor of chemistry at South Carolina College. The following year he was named president of the college, and although his tenure was plagued by opposition from the community on account of his controversial religious opinions, he retained the support of the board of trustees until his retirement in 1834. Not long after his arrival in Columbia he was again enmeshed in political controversy. During the Anglo-American War of 1812–14 he had supported a protective tariff; however, in the 1820s he rallied to the defence of *laissez-faire*. High tariffs on imported goods designed to protect the infant industries of the north were a sore point with the southern states, whose economic well-being depended on agricultural exports to Britain. Adopting the southern point of view, he denounced the tariff as a grave political threat that 'forebode no good to Union'. The protectionists, he wrote, sought unfair advantage: 'Their object is monopoly; to make the farmer sell at the manufacturer's price, and buy at the manufacturer's price'. His condemnation of northern manufacturing interests anticipated the critique of capitalism levelled at a later date by George Fitzhugh, the famous apologist for slavery. Like Fitzhugh, he deplored the effects of factory labour on the working man and complained that it was immoral 'to increase the wealth of a few capitalists, at the expense of the health, life, morals, and happiness of the wretches who labour for them' (Cooper, *On the Proposed Alteration of the Tariff*, 5, 11). In a less polemical vein, he also wrote *Lectures on the Elements of Political Economy*, an influential textbook espousing the doctrine of *laissez-faire*. The tariff controversy came to a head in 1832 when a special convention in South Carolina declared the new federal import duties null and void within the state. The nullification crisis was ultimately defused by a timely act of congress that lowered the tariff and at the same time affirmed the supremacy of the federal government. Cooper remained dissatisfied, however, and recommended in 1834 that the southern states contemplate secession from the union in order to protect their interests, including black slavery, which he now defended as a just and necessary institution. He is best remembered today as the 'schoolmaster of state's rights' to the generation of South Carolinians that fought the American Civil War.

Over the course of his life Cooper published numerous books and essays on a wide variety of topics, including (in addition to politics) metaphysics, religion, science, economics, and law. His legal writings include a treatise on the bankruptcy law of America compared with that of England (1801), the first American edition of the *Institutes of Justinian, with Notes* (1812), *Tracts on Medical Jurisprudence* (1819), and a *Treatise on the Law of Libel and the Liberty of the Press* (1830). He devoted his last years to a revision of *The*

*Statutes at Large of South Carolina* (5 vols., 1836–9). He died in Columbia on 11 May 1839 and was buried in the Guignard plot, Trinity churchyard, Columbia.

STEPHEN L. NEWMAN

**Sources** S. L. Newman, 'Thomas Cooper, 1759–1839: the political odyssey of a bourgeois ideologue', *Journal of Southern Studies*, 24/3 (autumn 1985), 295–305 · D. Malone, *The public life of Thomas Cooper, 1783–1839* (1926); repr. (1961) · H. M. Ellis, 'Thomas Cooper — a survey of his life', *South Atlantic Quarterly*, 19 (1918) · M. Kelley, 'Additional chapters on Thomas Cooper', *University of Maine Studies*, 2nd ser., 15 (1930) · T. Cooper, *Reply to Mr. Burke's invective, against Mr. Cooper and Mr. Watt in the House of Commons, on the 30th of April 1792* (1792) · T. Cooper, *Narrative of the proceedings against Thomas Cooper, Esquire* (1811) · L. Cong., manuscript division, Madison MSS · T. Cooper, *On the proposed alteration of the tariff* (1823) · T. Cooper, *Letters on the slave trade* (1787)
**Likenesses** A. B. Durand, engraving, 1829 (after C. C. Ingham), NPG [*see illus.*] · steel engraving, repro. in T. Cooper, *Lectures on the elements of political economy* (1831)

**Cooper, Thomas** (1805–1892), Chartist and religious lecturer, was born on 20 March 1805 in Leicester, the illegitimate son of a dyer. His mother continued working as a dyer after the early death of Cooper's father, which indicates that the relationship was more than transitory. Living in Gainsborough with his mother and half-sister Ann, Cooper began, outside his hours at the free school, what became an astonishing programme of self-education. By the age of twenty he could recite thousands of lines of poetry (including the first three books of *Paradise Lost*), and was conversant with a huge number of historical and theological texts, as well as Latin, Greek, and French. These achievements profoundly shaped him as a man. He was capable, in later life, of being pedantic and autocratic. Whether as the secretary of the Lincoln Choral Society in 1836 or as the compiler of a proposed volume of Chartist hymns in 1845, Cooper was a man who did not like to be challenged. It should be noted, however, that he was also honest and generous; he had a reputation for giving away money.

Not content with being known as a shoemaker who could recite poetry, Cooper opened, in 1828, a school and continued with this occupation for the next eight years. This was not enough, however, for such an energetic and passionate man. When not in his school, he was preaching in the villages around Gainsborough. He soon quarrelled, however, with his Wesleyan Methodist superiors, who he believed were not working as hard as he was. These arguments led to his departure from Gainsborough for Lincoln and, in due course, to a break with the Methodists. In the cathedral city Cooper embarked on what seemed like a new life. He married and became involved in the mechanics' institute and the choral society. His marriage to Susanna Chaloner (1801–1880) lasted from February 1834 until her death on 1 February 1880, but remained childless. It was also in Lincoln that Cooper began work as a journalist: he gave up schoolmastering and became a bold critic of the cathedral clergy for the *Lincoln, Rutland and Stamford Mercury*.

When Cooper left Lincoln for London in 1839, it was to begin a long-desired literary career. He had already published by subscription a small volume of religious verse, but was unable to find a publisher in the capital for his historical novel; when *Captain Cobler* (1850) eventually appeared, it was from a radical press. Cooper could only return to newspaper work, and, in 1840, accepted employment on the *Leicestershire Mercury*. In Leicester Cooper embraced ultra-radicalism, became an enthusiastic admirer of Feargus O'Connor, and made the town a Chartist stronghold. The old leaders were no match for Cooper, who established himself as a preacher, the organizer of an adult school, and the editor of a series of Chartist journals, notably the *Midland Counties Illuminator* and *The Commonswealthsman*. He was arrested after the riots in the Potteries in 1842, and was sentenced the following year to two years in prison.

Cooper emerged from Stafford gaol in 1845, a changed man. In London, where he now lived, he remained a firm supporter of the 'six points', but, after quarrelling with O'Connor over money and political strategies, he took on the role of an independent Chartist. In this capacity he became a prominent advocate of religious radicalism, a lecturer for Giuseppe Mazzini's Peoples' International League, and, in the *Plain Speaker* (1849) and *Cooper's Journal* (1850), a tenacious campaigner for co-operation between middle- and working-class radicals. Cooper earned his living in the late 1840s and early 1850s by lecturing; he spoke mainly about historical and literary topics. These years did also see a determined attempt to establish himself as a successful writer. *The Purgatory of Suicides*, written in prison and over 900 stanzas long, was published in 1845. Though few read it from beginning to end, its poetic ambition impressed not only the readers of the Chartist press but also Carlyle, Disraeli, and Kingsley. The *Purgatory* was a vindication of Cooper's radical beliefs, but he was unable to find a publisher for a Chartist novel. He produced instead two innocuous novels, *Alderman Ralph* (1853) and *The Family Feud* (1855). A collection of short stories, *Wise Saws and Modern Instances* (1845), was his best attempt at prose fiction.

For more than two decades after 1856, when he announced his renunciation of free thought (he was baptized at Friar Lane Baptist Chapel, Leicester, on 12 June 1859), Cooper travelled throughout Britain as a religious lecturer. A well-known figure, he attracted large audiences. He estimated that by 1866, when he fell ill, he had given more than 3300 discourses; by this time his wife had gone to live with relatives and he no longer had a permanent home. The lectures Cooper gave in his later years were accompanied by a series of texts such as *The Bridge of History over the Gulf of Time* (1871), all of which had good sales. Cooper also brought out his long-contemplated autobiography in 1872. This is generally recognized as the best memoir of a Victorian artisan. With its delightful portrait of the early years of a highly intelligent working-class boy, its informative descriptions of the lower echelons of Victorian literary and intellectual life, and its often neglected sections on the work of a popular itinerant preacher, this brisk and honest book emphasizes that Cooper should be remembered as more than simply 'the Leicester Chartist'. Thomas Cooper died on 15 July 1892 at his home, 13 St Mary Street, Lincoln, having lived in the city since he retired from lecturing. His grave, in Washingborough Road cemetery, Lincoln, was restored in 1993.

STEPHEN ROBERTS

**Sources** T. Cooper, *The life of Thomas Cooper, written by himself*, [new edn] (1872); repr. with introduction by J. Saville (1971) · S. Roberts, 'Cooper, Thomas', *DLB*, vol. 9 · S. Roberts, 'Thomas Cooper in Leicester, 1840–1843', *Leicestershire Archaeological and Historical Society Transactions*, 61 (1987), 62–76 · S. Roberts, 'The later radical career of Thomas Cooper in Leicester, c. 1845–1855', *Leicestershire Archaeological and Historical Society Transactions*, 64 (1990), 61–72 · S. Roberts, 'Thomas Cooper: a Victorian working class writer', *Our History Journal*, 16 (Nov 1990), 12–26 · Boase, *Mod. Eng. biog.*
**Archives** BL, letters · Internationaal Instituut voor Sociale Geschiedenis, Amsterdam, corresp. · Lincoln Central Library, letters and papers, incl. MS of *Purgatory of suicides*; notebook · Lincs. Arch., corresp. and papers · Lincs. Arch., discourse on John Wickliffe · PRO, Treasury solicitor MSS, 11/600–602 · Staffs. RO, assize case papers; minutes and notebooks | Bishopsgate Institute, London, letters to Thomas Chambers and Thomas Tatlow · BL, letters to Freshney, fragments of *Purgatory of suicides*, Add. MS 56238 · Bodl. Oxf., letters to Benjamin Disraeli · Co-operative Union, Holyoake House, Manchester, letters to G. J. Holyoake · Leics. RO, letters to William Jones
**Likenesses** F. Bryant, cabinet photograph, NPG · H. Linton, woodcut (after H. Anelay), NPG · drawing, repro. in *North Staffordshire Mercury* (15 Oct 1842) · portrait, repro. in W. E. Winks, *Lives of illustrious shoemakers* (1883) · portrait, repro. in *ILN* (23 July 1892), 102

**Cooper, Thomas Frederick** [Tommy] **(1921–1984)**, comedian, was born on 19 March 1921 at Caerphilly, Glamorgan, the elder of the two sons of Thomas Cooper, coalminer, and his wife, Catherine Gertrude Wright. Although born in Wales, Cooper was brought up mainly in Exeter (where he attended Radcliffe College) and Southampton, where he began his working life as an apprentice shipwright. He received his first magic kit at the age of eight, and performed with it in small shows at his school and then in the canteen at his work. He described this experience later:

> I had awful stage-fright. It's terrible. You can't talk and every trick went wrong. They were all laughing like mad and I was nearly in tears. Afterwards, though, I thought it wasn't such a bad idea and I started to do it on purpose.   (Nathan, 168)

This became the centrepiece of his act which lasted throughout his comedy career—the series of conjuring tricks which went disastrously wrong.

Cooper spent seven years in the Horse Guards, including service in the Middle East where he first obtained the fez which became a trademark of his stage costume. He performed in NAAFIs during the Second World War, and then attempted to break into show business when back in civilian life. Like a number of other former service performers he found his first regular work at the Windmill Theatre in London in the late 1940s. He was soon successful. He appeared in the revue *Sauce Piquante* in 1950, had his first appearance at the London Palladium in 1952, and performed in the first of his many royal command performances in 1953. He was in great demand for theatre and cabaret in Britain and abroad but it was television

Thomas Frederick [Tommy] **Cooper** (1921–1984), by Michael Dyer, 1976

which gave him his greatest success. From 1952 he appeared on television, starting with *It's Magic*, followed by four other series in the 1950s and 1960s, and then *Tommy Cooper*, *Cooper*, *The Tommy Cooper Hour*, *Just Like That*, and *Cooper's Half Hour* through the 1970s and early 1980s. On 24 February 1947 he married Gwen, daughter of Thomas William Henty, farmer. They had a daughter and a son. From 1967 until his death he also had a relationship with his personal assistant, Mary Fieldhouse, who wrote of it in *For the Love of Tommy* (1986).

Alongside his magic 'tricks', the other main set piece in Tommy Cooper's performance was a maniacal monologue in which he would change hats constantly to keep in character. He would invariably lose his place, and the whole recitation would descend into chaos. The key to Cooper's act was described as a 'brilliantly deceptive air of under-rehearsed confusion' (Fisher, 69), and indeed the deception was complete, because although his obituary in *The Times* described him as an 'outstanding natural comedian', it was his 'serious, almost monk-like, dedication' to improving his craft that most impressed those close to him (Fieldhouse, 25). Magic remained also his 'hobby and his relaxation' throughout his life (Nathan, 167). Cooper's comic character was most often compared to that of a clown rather than comedian. His large figure (6 ft 3 in. and 15 stone), his constant use of facial expressions and gestures, and his somewhat ridiculous costume made an impressive visual impact which worked both in person and on television. Cooper had a heart attack in 1977, followed by further health problems. He died at Westminster

Hospital, London, on 15 April 1984 after collapsing during the broadcast of a live television show from Her Majesty's Theatre. His wife survived him. MARC BRODIE

**Sources** M. Fieldhouse, *For the love of Tommy: a personal portrait of Tommy Cooper* (1986) · J. Fisher, *Funny way to be a hero* (1973) · *The Times* (16–17 April 1984) · T. Cooper, *Just like that*, 3rd edn (1994) · D. Nathan, *The laughtermakers: a quest for comedy* (1971) · T. Vahimagi, ed., *British television: an illustrated guide*, 2nd edn (1996) · *DNB* · *CGPLA Eng. & Wales* (1984)
**Archives** FILM BFI NFTVA, 'Tommy Cooper', ITV, 16 Sept 1986 · BFI NFTVA, 'Just like that', Channel 4, 28 Dec 1987 · BFI NFTVA, *Parkinson: the interviews*, BBC1, 9 Aug 1995 · BFI NFTVA, *Heroes of comedy*, Channel 4, 13 Oct 1995 · BFI NFTVA, 'Unforgettable Tommy Cooper', ITV1, 2 Sept 2001 · BFI NFTVA, current affairs footage · BFI NFTVA, performance footage
**Likenesses** photographs, 1953–80, Hult. Arch. · M. Dyer, photograph, 1976, NPG [*see illus.*] · photographs, repro. in Fieldhouse, *For the love of Tommy*
**Wealth at death** £327,272: probate, 29 Aug 1984, *CGPLA Eng. & Wales*

**Cooper, Thomas Henry** (1813–1881), surgeon and botanist, was born in December 1813 at Lewes, Sussex, the second of four sons of Thomas Cooper, a solicitor in that town, and Lucy Elizabeth Durrant. He probably attended Lewes grammar school and at fifteen was apprenticed to a surgeon in Marylebone, Middlesex. He subsequently studied at the Middlesex Hospital and, from 1832, at University College, London, where he attended the botanical lectures of Lindley. Through the good offices of the latter he was elected a fellow of the Linnean Society in 1834, the year in which he gained his licence to practise. He was married and had two daughters; the surname of his wife, Annie Elizabeth, who outlived him, is unknown.

Cooper's claim to notice is as the once-supposed author of useful early catalogues of the higher plants of Sussex and Nottinghamshire. The first of these was published as a seventeen page appendix to the second volume of T. W. Horsfield's *History, Antiquities, and Topography of the County of Sussex* (1835), and was notable for the unusual device of presenting the data in three successive ways: by habitats, topographically, and finally with the plant names arranged in the newly fashionable natural system, which had been ardently embraced by Lindley. A long list of records for the rarer species followed, seemingly on Cooper's own authority. Years later, however, it emerged that these had been lifted almost in their entirety (without clear acknowledgement) from a catalogue provided by William Borrer, a veteran Sussex botanist with a high reputation nationally.

Cooper treated another local expert, Dr Godfrey Hewitt, in just the same way during a brief spell in Nottingham a few months later. He was at that time seeking to impress his botanical seniors and obtain one of the few academic posts in the subject. He boldly sought to compete against Lindley for the professorship of botany at the Society of Apothecaries in 1835 but the best he was able to achieve, and that after some years, was lecturing at an agricultural school in Hoddesdon, Hertfordshire.

By that time botany was a mere prop to what had returned to an essentially medical career. That was to prove not undistinguished, culminating in Cooper's appointment as physician to the Great Western and Metropolitan railways and then election as FRCS. Perhaps significantly, though, all mention of his botanical past was suppressed from his entry in the professional directories. He spent his final years in Slough, where he died on 25 December 1881. D. E. ALLEN

**Sources** D. E. Allen, 'The plagiarisms of Thomas Henry Cooper', *Journal of the Society of the Bibliography of Natural History*, 9 (1978–80), 275–9 · student records, UCL · *CGPLA Eng. & Wales* (1882)
**Archives** RBG Kew, specimens
**Wealth at death** £864 14s. 8d.: probate, 13 March 1882, *CGPLA Eng. & Wales*

**Cooper, Thomas Mackay**, Baron Cooper of Culross (1892–1955), judge, was born in Edinburgh on 24 September 1892, the elder son by a second marriage of John Aitken Cooper, burgh engineer of Edinburgh, and his wife, Margaret Mackay, from Dunnet. His father, who came from Culross, died when Tom Cooper was eight. At nine he entered George Watson's College and left at sixteen, *dux* of the school, medallist in English, Latin, and Greek, with second place in mathematics and winner of the North American prize for dynamics and chemistry. He passed to Edinburgh University, taking first place in its open bursary list, and graduated MA with first-class honours in classics (1912) and LLB with distinction (1914). For a time during the war he worked in the war trade department in London and for his services was appointed OBE in 1920.

Cooper had passed advocate in 1915 and on returning to the bar in 1919 made rapid progress. He had the advantage, through a maternal uncle, of valuable legal connections, but he had also gifts of advocacy and a knowledge of many technical subjects which pointed to an assured forensic career. He took silk in 1927. After eight years of large senior practice he was elected Conservative member for West Edinburgh in May 1935 and appointed solicitor-general for Scotland. In October of the same year he became lord advocate and was sworn of the privy council. He proved himself to be one of the most efficient and popular lord advocates that Scotland had ever had. In June 1941 he succeeded Lord Aitchison as lord justice-clerk with the judicial title of Lord Cooper, and in January 1947 he became lord justice-general and lord president of the Court of Session. Serious illness overtook him in the late summer of 1954 and he resigned office in December. He had received his barony in June 1954, but, because of illness, he was never able to take part in the business of the upper house: his sole appearance there was the occasion of his introduction, undertaken with great difficulty in March 1955.

Cooper had a well-equipped legal mind. His judgments were vigorous, penetrating, and lucid. As a lawyer he will stand favourable comparison with the most eminent of his predecessors. He was a steadfast supporter of the principles of Scots law, and frequently commented on the unfortunate intrusion into these principles of English legal conceptions and precedents. Perhaps the most publicized of his judgments was that given shortly before he retired, in an action challenging the adoption for Scotland of the numeral II in the title of Queen Elizabeth (*MacCormick* v. *HM Advocate*, 1953). Though the action failed on certain preliminary pleas, Lord Cooper took occasion to criticize the English principle of the sovereignty of parliament in relation to the treaty of union between Scotland and England. He was active in the formation in 1934 of the Stair Society to study and advance the history of Scots law, and made a number of contributions to its publications, the chief being *Regiam majestatem* (1947). Independently of the society he published in 1944 *Select Scottish Cases of the Thirteenth Century*. A member of the Scottish History Society from 1934, he gave, as its president (1946–9), four addresses which he published under the title of *Supra crepidam* (1951), and which he claimed to be merely addresses by an amateur to specialists on their own subject. It has been said that his keen perception as a historian is best seen in these addresses. Numerous other addresses and contributions to periodicals, collected in *Selected Papers, 1922–1954*, published by his brother in 1957, after his death, show his breadth of view and width of learning, as also the spirit of a reformer. He was an original member of the Scottish committee on the History of Parliament and latterly chairman of its executive committee until his death. When a judge, he was called on to be chairman of a number of government committees on Scottish problems; the most important, on hydroelectric development in Scotland (1941–2), resulted in the setting up of the North of Scotland Hydro-Electric Board. He was a trustee of the National Galleries of Scotland from 1947, for a short time (1946–9) chairman of the Ancient Monuments Board for Scotland, and, as lord president, a trustee *ex officio* of the National Library of Scotland.

Cooper was a man of restless energy, great industry, keen intellect, and a rapid worker. He had a scientific bent of mind, with the genius for the practical application of his knowledge. He was a fellow of the Royal Society of Edinburgh and its vice-president (1945–8), a fellow of the Society of Antiquaries (Scotland), a fellow of the Royal Astronomical Society, and a member of the Astronomical Society of Edinburgh, which lent him a telescope which he had erected in his garden. Essentially a friendly man, Cooper was nevertheless shy, not a man of the world or socially inclined, although drawn to men with whom he could talk on a basis of common understanding. He was happy with very young children, whom he would amuse with drawings and stories, but his interest in them evaporated when they left childhood. He loved animals and never failed to hold converse with a cat. He had some interest in music and art, taught himself to play the piano and organ, and engaged in sketching. He was devoted to his mother, with whom he made his home for substantially the whole of his life, and whom he survived by less than four years. He died in Edinburgh, unmarried, on 15 July 1955.

Cooper was an honorary LLD of Edinburgh, Glasgow, and St Andrews, and received an honorary doctorate of Paris University, a signal honour for a Scottish judge. He was an honorary master of the bench of the Middle Temple and honorary member of the Society of Public Teachers of Law, of the Institution of Municipal Engineers, and of the Edinburgh Merchant Company.

KEITH OF AVONHOLM, *rev.*

**Sources** *The Scotsman* (16 July 1955) · *Scots Law Times* (30 July 1955) · private information (1971) · personal knowledge (1971)
**Archives** NL Scot., letters to A. D. Gibb
**Likenesses** W. Stoneman, photograph, 1937, NPG · W. O. Hutchison, oils, 1956, Parliament Hall, Edinburgh
**Wealth at death** £127,645 1s. 8d.: confirmation, 22 Oct 1955, CCI

**Cooper, Thomas Sidney** (1803–1902), animal painter, was born on 26 September 1803 in St Peter's Street, Canterbury, Kent, the second of two sons and three daughters. Of his parents nothing is known except that his father abandoned the family when Cooper was about five. Cooper had an early and continuing devotion to drawing, and one of his first memories was sketching the cathedral bell-tower. He could not afford pencils and paper for sketching, so he used his school slate until George Cattermole happened to see him drawing and gave him a large quantity of paper and a dozen pencils. Having no knife, Cooper asked passers-by to help sharpen his pencils and thus met Manners Sutton, archbishop of Canterbury, who promised 5s. for a copy of one of his drawings of Canterbury Cathedral, but actually paid £5. By the age of twelve Cooper was apprenticed to paint coaches for the uncle of his schoolfriend William Burgess. When he was sixteen a Mr Doyle, a scene-painter for a travelling theatre, taught him scene painting and perspective. In 1823 Cooper's maternal uncle, a minister named Elvey, invited him to London, where he studied at the British Museum and in the Royal Academy Schools, which he entered in 1824. After nine months, Cooper was back in Canterbury, where he established himself as a drawing-master.

In the summer of 1827 Cooper and his friend Burgess sailed from Dover to Calais. They visited Gravelines, Dunkirk, Bruges, Ghent, and finally Brussels, painting signboards and portraits in exchange for their lodging. Cooper worked in pencil, watercolour, and lithography. The backgrounds of Cooper's portraits drew attention, and he began to concentrate on the study of landscape and animals. He became acquainted with the Flemish animal painter Eugène Verboeckhoven, who introduced him to the great seventeenth-century Dutch animal paintings of Paulus Potter and Aelbert Cuyp. Thereafter Cooper was sometimes referred to as an 'English Cuyp' or a 'British Paulus Potter'. Verboeckhoven was also responsible for encouraging Cooper to paint in oils.

While in Brussels, from 1827 to 1831, Cooper met Charlotte Pearson (1810–1842), the daughter of one of the most respectable of its English residents. They married on 1 October 1829 and had four children: Maria Charlotte (1830–1859), Lucy Elizabeth, later Mrs Coxon (1831–1904), Georgina Mary (1833–1868), and Thomas George (1836–1901). The revolution of 1830 made life in Belgium difficult and Cooper, his pregnant wife, and first daughter returned to England in spring 1831, landing at Dover with £13.

Drawing on his continental success, Cooper produced some topographical views of London, which were bought by Ackermann's in the Strand, as well as some of his lithographs. Having previously exhibited on the continent, in 1833 Cooper showed his first pictures in London, with the Society of Artists in Suffolk Street and at the Royal Academy, where his only entry was entitled *Landscape with Cattle*. Cooper faithfully portrayed various breeds of cattle, and the Victorian public loved his pictures of unspoiled countryside populated by placid cows and sheep. He became known as 'Cow' Cooper to distinguish him from Abraham 'Horse' Cooper. One of the great Victorian art patrons, Robert Vernon, commissioned *Farmyard with Cattle* from Cooper, which, together with another example of his work, is now in the Vernon collection at the Tate Britain, London.

Cooper was a prolific exhibitor and also showed at the New Watercolour Society and the British Institution. He exhibited many paintings at the Royal Academy, where he showed 266 pictures in an unprecedented and unbroken record from 1833 until 1902, when four landscapes with cattle appeared in the spring exhibition following his death. Cooper also showed paintings at international exhibitions, notably the Manchester Art Treasures of 1857, the Paris International of 1878, and the Manchester Jubilee of 1887. He enjoyed bountiful success and was elected an associate of the Royal Academy in 1845 and a Royal Academician in 1867. In 1861 a reviewer wrote that he was 'the painter of bucolics, and reigns supreme in the farm-yard, the sheep-fold, and the pasture' (*Art Journal*, 1861, 133).

In 1847 Frederick Richard Lee invited Cooper to visit him in Devon and the two decided to paint in collaboration, with Lee painting the landscape and Cooper adding the flocks and herds. From 1848 to 1856 their paintings appeared under both their names at the Royal Academy exhibitions. Cooper also worked in conjunction with other landscape painters, including Thomas Creswick and James Baker Pyne.

Cooper always maintained a home and a studio in London, and in 1848 purchased land at Harbledown, near Canterbury, where he built a house he named Vernon Holme, in honour of his early patron. After the death of his first wife in 1842 Cooper remained a widower until 1863, when he married Mary, daughter of William Cameron of Canterbury. They had one son, Nevill Louis (1864–1936). Soon after the death of Cooper's mother in 1865, he bought the house where he was born and some adjacent properties, which he developed into a picture gallery and school of art. In 1882 Cooper presented to the city of Canterbury the Sidney Cooper Gallery of Art, now known as the Royal Museum and Art Gallery. This museum holds the most important collection of his paintings, drawings, and lithographs, as well as his personal memorabilia.

In addition to the museum in Canterbury and Tate Britain in London, there are paintings by Cooper in many provincial English museums. The Royal Collection includes two paintings by Cooper: *The Entrance to Carisbrooke Castle* (1837), which he presented to Queen Victoria for her jubilee in 1887, and *The Victoria Cow*, a royal commission of 1848 when he was asked to paint the royal stock at Osborne. In 1901 Cooper was appointed CVO by Edward VII.

Although he was still painting in his ninety-ninth year, there was a gradual decline of Cooper's strength in his last few months and he died at his home, Vernon Holme, on 7 February 1902, survived by his second daughter, Lucy, his second wife, Mary, and his son Nevill. His funeral was held on 13 February at Canterbury Cathedral, and he was buried in the churchyard of St Martin's, Canterbury. The contents of Cooper's studio were sold by Christie, Manson, and Wood from 12 to 15 April 1902.

DELLA CLASON SPERLING

**Sources** T. S. Cooper, 'Memoir of T. S. Cooper, A.R.A.', *Art Journal*, 11 (1849), 336–7 • *The Times* (8 Feb 1902), 6 • T. S. Cooper, *My life*, 2 vols. (1890) • S. Sartin, *Thomas Sidney Cooper, C.V.O., R.A., 1803–1902* (1976) • *DNB* • *Art Journal*, new ser., 22 (1902), 125 • Graves, *RA exhibitors* • Graves, *Artists* • C. Forbes, *The Royal Academy (1837–1901) revisited: Victorian paintings from the Forbes collection* (New York, 1975), 32 • K. J. Westwood, *Thomas Sidney Cooper: his life and work* (1991) • 'Thomas Sidney Cooper', *The dictionary of art*, ed. J. Turner (1996) • *CGPLA Eng. & Wales* (1902) • S. C. Hutchison, 'The Royal Academy Schools, 1768–1830', *Walpole Society*, 38 (1960–62), 123–91, esp. 177
**Archives** priv. coll., letters • Royal Museum and Art Gallery, Canterbury, memorabilia
**Likenesses** T. S. Cooper, self-portrait, 1832 • W. Scott, oils, *c*.1841, NPG • J. P. Knight, oils, 1843, Royal Museum • W. W. Ouless and J. P. Knight, portrait, exh. RA 1869, Mappin Art Gallery, Sheffield • T. G. Cooper, etching, exh. RA 1884 • W. W. Ouless, oils, 1889, Royal Museum • G. J. Stodart, stipple, pubd 1890 (after J. Scott, *c*.1841), BM, NPG; repro. in Cooper, *My life*, 1 (1890), frontispiece • Elliott & Fry, carte-de-visite, NPG • G. Goursat, caricature, watercolour drawing, AM Oxf. • H. S. Mandelssohn, photograph, NPG • W. W. Ouless, oils, Aberdeen Art Gallery, MacDonald collection • R. W. Robinson, photograph, NPG; repro. in *Members and associates of the Royal Academy of Arts* (1891) • F. Walker, group portrait, pen-and-ink drawing (*Four men at cards*), NPG • J. & C. Watkins, carte-de-visite, NPG • wood-engraving, NPG; repro. in *ILN* (6 July 1867)
**Wealth at death** £47,413: probate, Oct 1902, *CGPLA Eng. & Wales*

**Cooper, Thomas Thornville** (1839–1878), traveller and promoter of trade, the eighth son of John Ibbetson Cooper, coal fitter and shipowner, and his wife, Elizabeth, *née* Douglas, was born on 13 September 1839, at Bishopwearmouth, co. Durham. He was educated at the Grange School, Bishopwearmouth, and then by a tutor in Sussex. There his health failed, and he was advised to take a voyage to Australia where he decided to remain, making several journeys into the interior of the country. In 1859 he went to India, and worked in Madras for Arbuthnot & Co. In 1861 he threw up the appointment and went to Sind to visit a brother who was resident there. In the following year he visited Bombay and then went by way of Beypore and Madras to Burma, where he studied Burmese. In 1863 he rejoined his brother, who was now in Shanghai; there Cooper joined the Shanghai volunteer corps and took his share in the protection of the city against the Taiping insurgents. After the suppression of the uprising the question of the commercial penetration of China, and particularly the route through to India, became an issue of concern to British merchants, especially as the construction of the Suez Canal drew to a close. Anglo-French rivalry in this area was keenly felt, and all of Cooper's travels must be seen against this background.

In 1868 Cooper left his position as a solicitor's clerk with Edward Lawrence, and undertook an attempt to penetrate through Tibet to India. He successfully canvassed for funds from the merchants of Shanghai to support his journey, although many believed he was merely seeking a free journey home, with some good shooting on the way. After being thwarted in his original travel arrangements by the French consul in Hangchow (Hangzhou) he left that city on 4 January with a Christian Chinese interpreter known as George Philips, travelling by way of Chungking (Chongqing), Chengtu (Chengdu), Kangding, and Litang to Paan. From this point he had hoped to reach Rima on the Luhit Brahmaputra in eight days, but the Chinese authorities forbade him to continue his journey westward. He therefore decided to take the route to Bhamo via Dali, then the capital of the Muslim rebel state, the Pingnanguo, known to the British as the Panthay kingdom (1855–73). He struck southwards, following the valley of the Lancang Jiang, and reached Zegu on the western bank of that river—the most westerly point that had then been reached by any traveller from China in the region of the great rivers north of Bhamo. At this point he was within 100 miles of Manchi, on the upper Irrawaddy, which had been visited by Lieutenant Wilcox from India in 1826. Still continuing his journey southward Cooper arrived at Weisi (Weixi), nearly due west of Likiang (Lijiang), where he obtained passports for Dali. At a distance of three days' journey from Weisi, however, he was stopped by a tribal chief who had just switched allegiance from the Muslim rebels and who refused to allow him to proceed. He was compelled, therefore, to return to Weisi, where he was imprisoned and threatened with death by the civil authorities on suspicion that he was in communication with the Panthays. For five weeks he was kept a close prisoner, but was afterwards (6 August) allowed to depart. Finding it impossible to continue his exploration further, he returned to Yaan (Ya'an). Proceeding down the Min River he struck the Yangtze (Yangzi) at Ipin (Yibin), and from there descended the river to Hangchow, where he arrived on 11 November 1868.

Although Cooper had failed to reach India from China, he was lauded in Shanghai, and after he had written an initial report on his trip, published under the title *Journal of an Overland Journey from China towards India* (1869), he attempted almost immediately to reverse the process, and to enter China from Assam. Again taking Philips with him, he left Sadiya in October 1869, and passing up the line of the Brahmaputra, through the Mishmi country, fighting malaria and fortified by visions of Allsopp's Best India Pale Ale, he reached Prun, a village about 20 miles from Rima. Here he again met with such determined opposition from the authorities that he was obliged to turn back. Almost immediately afterwards he returned to England and published several articles and the accounts of his journeys *Travels of a Pioneer of Commerce* (1871) and *The Mishmee Hills* (1873). In 1872 he agitated for the India Office

to allow him to accompany a Panthay mission led by Liu Daohang, which had visited London, back to the frontier of Yunnan, where Cooper would in his personal capacity investigate trading possibilities with the rebels. On arriving at Rangoon he learned that the uprising had been crushed, and his mission was therefore at an end; he had, however, made good use of his expenses on the way, a box at the opera in Vienna being deemed vital for the self-styled 'Equerry to His Highness Prince Hassan'. The viceroy, Lord Northbrook, appointed him political agent at Bhamo. Unfortunately ill health obliged Cooper to return almost immediately to England, where he was attached to the political and secret department of the India Office as a copyist, and supported his two unmarried sisters on his salary.

In 1876 Cooper was sent to India with dispatches to the viceroy and presents for distribution in connection with the imperial durbar at Delhi; he was appointed officiating political agent at Bhamo in April 1877. In November of the same year he received W. J. Gill and William Mesney after the successful termination of their journey from Yunnan. At Bhamo, on 24 April 1878, while reading, Cooper was shot through the heart and lungs by a soldier of his guard, whose enmity he had aroused through the infliction of a series of punishments. He was buried just outside the station compound. His debts were such that little remained of his estate for his sisters.

Cooper was certainly courageous, and inspired affection among his friends. No mere traveller, he styled himself, even in his will, the 'Pioneer of Commerce', and the vision of opening a market for Assam tea and Manchester goods in Yunnan was a constant in his public and private utterances. He was a successful self-publicist (if a self-important one who habitually acquired official-sounding titles), but at root he was a freelance imperial activist, ever ready to solicit funds for his ventures, whose connections with the India Office were tenuous, and of whom officials were wary. ROBERT BICKERS

**Sources** DNB · BL OIOC, L/P&S/7/18, fols. 1021–88 · BL OIOC, L/P&S/5/594, fols. 141a–273 · *North China Herald* (1868–78) [articles on, and letters by, T. T. Cooper] · B. L. Evans, 'The Panthay mission of 1872 and its legacies', *Journal of Southeast Asian Studies*, 16 (1985), 117–28 · T. J. [sic] Cooper, *Journal of an overland journey from China towards India* (1869) · T. T. Cooper, *Travels of a pioneer of commerce* (1871) · T. T. Cooper, *The Mishmee hills* (1873) · W. J. Gill, *The river of golden sand*, ed. E. C. Baber (1883) · *India List, Civil and Military* (March 1877) · CGPLA Eng. & Wales (1879)
**Archives** BL OIOC, L/P&S/7/18; L/P&S/5/594
**Likenesses** line drawing, repro. in Gill, *River of golden sand*, 108
**Wealth at death** under £200: administration with will, 5 Sept 1879, CGPLA Eng. & Wales

**Cooper, Thompson** (1837–1904), biographer and journalist, born at Cambridge on 8 January 1837, was the eldest son of Charles Henry *Cooper (1808–1866), the Cambridge antiquary, and his wife, Jane, the youngest daughter of John Thompson of Prickwillow, Cambridgeshire.

A younger brother, John William Cooper (1845–1906), who graduated from Trinity Hall, Cambridge (LLB 1866, LLD 1880), was called to the bar from Lincoln's Inn in 1868, but lived in Cambridge almost all his life, taking a prominent part in municipal affairs. He revised his father's *Annals of Cambridge*, to which he added a fifth volume. He died at Cambridge on 10 November 1906.

Thompson Cooper, educated at a private school kept at Cambridge by the Revd John Orman, was articled to his father, who had become a solicitor in 1840, but the law was only nominally Thompson's vocation. His real inheritance from his father was a love of biographical and antiquarian research, and he was elected FSA at the age of twenty-three. He married young, his wife (*d.* 1896) being a widow with two young daughters, though they had no further children. He was converted to Roman Catholicism.

While still a boy Cooper began to collect material for a work modelled on the *Athenae Oxonienses* of Anthony Wood. His father collaborated in the project, and in 1858 they published the first volume of *Athenae Cantabrigienses*, containing memoirs of those eminent alumni of Cambridge who died between 1500 and 1585. A second volume, published in 1861, carried the work forward to 1609.

In 1861 Cooper began his career in journalism as subeditor of the *Daily Telegraph*. In 1862 he was made its parliamentary reporter. He became an authority on the history of shorthand, publishing a manual on the Mason-Gurney system as early as 1858. A long connection with *The Times* lasted from 1866 until his death. He was one of its parliamentary reporters from 1866 to 1886, when he was appointed to write the daily summary of the debates in the House of Commons—a task requiring unusual accuracy, conciseness, and familiarity with parliamentary and public affairs. In 1898 he took on the less arduous duties of summary-writer in the House of Lords.

Cooper was associated with the *Dictionary of National Biography* from its inception. In 1883 Leslie Stephen appointed him to compile the lengthy lists of proposed entries which were published every six months in *The Athenaeum* to elicit information and comment. He himself wrote 1423 entries—much the largest contribution by any one author. He specialized in Roman Catholic subjects, but was also responsible for Cambridge graduates of early date, modern journalists, and shorthand writers. His literary and historical insight was not profound, but he had the gift of serendipity and never lost his zest for research.

In 1869 Cooper projected a new periodical, the *Register and Magazine of Biography*, but it ceased with the completion of one volume. His *Biographical Dictionary*, mainly of Englishmen, which first appeared in 1873, incorporated some of the material he had collected for the then unpublished third volume of *Athenae Cantabrigienses* (finally published, with additions and corrections, together with an index, by G. J. Gray in 1913). He also wrote the text for a series of contemporary profiles entitled *Men of Mark* (1876–83), and was responsible for four editions of *Men of the time* (1872, 1875, 1879, and 1884). He was a frequent contributor to *Notes and Queries* from the age of sixteen until the year before his death. Cooper died at his house, 38 Loughborough Road, Brixton, London, on 5 March 1904, and was buried, with Roman Catholic rites, in Norwood cemetery, London.                     A. A. BRODRIBB, *rev.* G. MARTIN MURPHY

**Sources** *The Times* (6 March 1904) · *The Tablet* (12 March 1904) · G. Fenwick, *The contributors' index to the Dictionary of National Biography, 1885–1901* (1989) · G. Fenwick, *Leslie Stephen's life in letters* (1993) · *N&Q*, 10th ser., 1 (1904), 246 · *The Journalist* (March 1903) · private information (1912) · *CGPLA Eng. & Wales* (1904)
**Wealth at death** £1594 1s. 7d.: resworn probate, 1904, *CGPLA Eng. & Wales*

**Cooper, William** (*fl.* 1640–1681), clergyman and ejected minister, may have been the man admitted as a sizar at Emmanuel College, Cambridge, in 1628, graduating BA in 1632 and MA in 1635, and there is reason to suppose he may have then spent time in the Netherlands. It is hard to be sure of anything about William Cooper's early life, but he is probably not to be identified with the Oxford BA (1634) from Gloucestershire (who was possibly the man nominated on 1 March 1648 to Long Marston in that county), nor with the lecturer of St Michael the Belfries, York, one of several nominated or recommended by parliament on 1 March 1642. It is scarcely credible that the parliamentarian and future ejected minister can have been the man who in April 1643 was sequestered from the parish of St Thomas the Apostle in London and ordered to be committed to the Fleet because (among other things) he called the troops of the earl of Essex 'rebels and traitors to the king' and 'refused to give the sacraments to his parishioners unless they would come up to the rails' (*JHL*, 1643–4, 21–2).

Ironically, however, the Cooper who is the subject of this article appears to have owed his first English benefice to the patronage of none other than William Laud. In February 1640 he was granted a licence to marry Susannah Le Maire, a native of Amsterdam and daughter of John Le Maire, a painter. Le Maire, if Edmund Calamy is to be believed, having 'given good content to Archbishop Laud, begged the favour of some presentation for his son in law', who was accordingly installed in the vicarage of Ringmere, Sussex. Whatever the reason, Laud certainly did present Cooper to Ringmere during an episcopal vacancy; installed before 20 October 1640, he apparently resigned early in the following year.

From 1644 to 1648 Cooper served as chaplain to Elizabeth, queen of Bohemia, during her residency at The Hague. It is clear that he was acting during those years in the interest of the parliamentarians. Shortly after his return to England he was requested by the council of state, on 15 May 1649, to preach at the funeral of Dr Isaac Dorislaus whose 'execrable murder' had just occurred (*CSP dom.*, *1649–50*, 141). On 21 June the council recommended to the revenue committee 'that what remains due to Mr Cooper, late minister to the Queen of Bohemia, may be paid to him, he having done special service in the time of his being there, besides his service in the way of the ministry' (ibid., 201). It seems that this 'special service' may have had to do with Cooper's father-in-law, for some years later, in a letter to Thurloe of August 1655, Cooper indicated that Le Maire was acting as an agent for the protectorate government. In the same letter he also urged Thurloe to press on Cromwell the interests of 'Alderman Searl, Mr Heycocks, and other honest men of the borough of Southwark, relating to their adventure for Ireland, wherein they are disappointed, and none but his highness can relieve them'; Cooper's statement that these men had 'been often here in person' suggests they were using him as a means of access to the corridors of power (Thurloe, *State papers*, 3.705).

Cooper's connection with the borough of Southwark had originated soon after his return from The Hague. His sermon before parliament on 29 August 1649 celebrated the relief of Dublin and the victory of Michael Jones over Ormond, and appeared as *Jerusalem Fatall to her Assailants* under the name of 'William Cooper, minister of the gospel at St Olave's Southwark'. For Ireland, Cooper was conventionally anxious that the Rump Parliament remember that firm magistracy be complemented by 'a good ministry', which may 'effectually pluck up every bitter root that beareth gall and wormwood, as Popery and prophaneness'. But for England he had some surprisingly radical aspirations, complaining that 'some cry for bread to feed their bodies, others cry for bread to feed their souls … some grow rich upon others poverty, and some proud by others riches', urging his hearers to 'unload heavy burdens, take off every yoke, and let the oppressed go free' (Cooper, *Jerusalem*, 29–30).

Cooper went on to play a prominent role in the ecclesiastical politics of the protectorate. He was a morning lecturer at Westminster Abbey in 1654 and appears in its accounts as having been in receipt of £25 for the year 1658. On 20 March 1654 he was named a national commissioner for the approbation of public preachers. Also in that year he served as assistant to the commission of triers for the London ministry, and was named to the Surrey commission on 29 September 1657. The following summer, according to Robert Baillie, he was engaged in high-level discussion of proposals to strengthen the ministry. After the death of Oliver, Richard Cromwell received a letter from General George Monck recommending Cooper as one of 'the gravest sort of moderate presbyterian divines' whom the new protector should hear at Whitehall 'as often as those of other judgements' (Thurloe, *State papers*, 7.387). In early 1659, together with Calamy and other presbyterians, Cooper wrote to Richard Baxter urging him to be active in the struggle against Independency. The last protectorate parliament selected three presbyterians, and only one Independent, to preach at the opening session, and picked 'Cooper, a Presbyterian, to pray every day' (Abernathy, 23). Cooper also acquired an assistant: on 5 May John Cooke of King's College, Cambridge, was ordained for his ministry at St Olave's, Southwark, on the authority of the fourth classis of London. On 14 March 1660, after the return of its secluded members, the Long Parliament named Cooper as one of its ministerial 'Approvers'.

The Restoration marked no abrupt change in Cooper's fortunes. His living at St Olave's, Southwark, was confirmed by royal grant on 30 July 1660. On 11 December 1661 the denization was granted of Susannah, his wife. Between April and August that year Cooper was one of the presbyterian representatives at the Savoy conference, but

the negotiations, aimed to secure their inclusion within the restored Church of England, came to nothing. On 2 June 1662 Secretary Edward Nicholas was informed that William Cooper had presented Lord Chancellor Clarendon with a petition for the king on behalf of the presbyterians 'for a connivance or grace of toleration which they say his Majesty may do by his prerogative', and that he had acted in this matter as spokesman for his co-religionists (Bosher, 258).

In 1662 Cooper was ejected from St Olave's, Southwark, and moved to Somerset, where he took the Oxford oath in 1666. On 22 July 1672 he was licensed as a presbyterian preacher at Crewkerne, and also at his own house at Long Load, Somerset. Here a close colleague was James Stephenson, ejected minister, of Martock, where Cooper had an estate. Both men were selected as overseers of the poor but successfully cited their episcopal ordination as a reason why they should be granted exemption. Cooper contributed a preface to *Cases of Conscience Practically Resolved* (1673), by another Somerset minister, John Norman, 'late minister of Bridgwater'. But he had fallen far since the days of his national prominence, and was bitter against the failure of his hopes for a godly commonwealth. In 1677 he wrote angrily against 'churches grown corrupt and degenerate in doctrine and manners' and recalled the old ideal, 'the desire of our souls to have them reduced to their ancient and primitive purity' (Cooper, *The Good Man Perished*, 7). But there was worse to come—Cooper was one of the dissenting ministers imprisoned during the tory reaction of 1681. The manner and date of his death are not known.

STEPHEN WRIGHT

**Sources** *Calamy rev.*, 134–5, 463 · Thurloe, *State papers* · Venn, *Alum. Cant.* · R. S. Bosher, *The making of the Restoration settlement: the influence of the Laudians, 1649–1662* (1951) · G. R. Abernathy, *The English presbyterians and the Stuart restoration, 1648–1663* (1965) · *CSP dom.*, 1649–50; 1661–2 · E. Calamy, ed., *An abridgement of Mr. Baxter's history of his life and times, with an account of the ministers, &c., who were ejected after the Restauration of King Charles II*, 2nd edn, 2 vols. (1713) · W. Cooper, *Jerusalem fatall to her assailants, discovered in a sermon before the honourable House of Commons, August 29 1649* (1649) · W. Cooper, *The good man perished upon the earth* (1677) · J. L. Chester and J. Foster, eds., *London marriage licences, 1521–1869* (1887) · Foster, *Alum. Oxon.* · C. E. Surman, ed., *The register-booke of the fourth classis in the province of London, 1646–59*, 2 vols. in 1, Harleian Society, 82–3 (1953) · C. H. Firth and R. S. Rait, eds., *Acts and ordinances of the interregnum, 1642–1660*, 2 (1911) · G. L. Hennessy, *Chichester diocese clergy lists* (1900) · *Report of the Deputy Keeper of the Public Records*, 46 (1885), appx · *The letters and journals of Robert Baillie*, ed. D. Laing, 3 vols. (1841–2) · G. L. Turner, ed., *Original records of early nonconformity under persecution and indulgence*, 3 vols. (1911–14) · *VCH Somerset*, vol. 4 · *JHL*, 6 (1643–4), 1–14

**Cooper, William** (*bap.* 1639, *d.* 1689), bookseller and writer on the occult sciences, was born in Leicester, the son of John Cooper and his wife, Elizabeth. He was baptized on 5 June 1639 at the parish church of St Martin in Leicester. Following his father's death, Cooper moved to London and, on 29 September 1655, began an eight-year apprenticeship to William Wells, stationer, under whom he developed the occupational interests and skills that would serve him throughout his life. On 14 November 1669 Cooper married Mary Cleere at the church of St

Bartholomew-the-Less, near Little Britain, the important centre of the London book trade where Cooper was to conduct his varied enterprises at a shop under the sign of the Pelican. His primary interests were occult, scientific, and medical books written in English, and his *Catalogue of Chymicall Books*, first issued in 1673, is an invaluable guide to book production in these specializations.

Records of books printed by and for Cooper, covering the period 1669–89, and published lists of books available for purchase in his shop suggest that he enjoyed a flourishing business. He was interested in alchemy and chemical medicine and had a special preference for works by the pseudonymous Eirenaeus Philalethes, George Starkey, whose *Secrets Reveal'd, or, An Open Entrance to the Shut-Palace of the King* (1669) was the first volume printed for sale by Cooper. It was followed by additional Philalethean works, editions of other alchemical authors, and collections of alchemical tracts, such as the *Aurifontina chymica* (1680), dedicated to Charles II, and the *Collectanea chymica* (1684). In addition to works ranging from ephemerides to editions of William Barton's *Select Hymns*, Cooper also published scientific and technical titles such as those of Thomas Houghton and Gabriel Plattes on mining and William Simpson's works on spas and mineral waters.

Cooper was, in all likelihood, the author of *A philosophicall epitaph in hierogliphicall figures … published by W. C. esq with a catalogue of chymicall bookes* (1673). This curiously complex work features an engraved title-page and symbolic illustrations for which Cooper provides interpretive commentary; these are followed by his own translations of Johann Friedrich Helvetius's *Briefe of the Golden Calfe*, Johann Rudolph Glauber's *The Golden Ass Well Managed*, and *Jehior, the Day Dawning*, usually attributed to Paul Felgenhauer. The book's addresses to the reader and dedications to Robert Boyle and Elias Ashmole, the latter alluding to past illness and unspecified 'Long troubles', reveal that Cooper seriously believed in alchemy, in both its physical and esoteric aspects. In his commentary, Christian, millenarian, cabbalistic, and neoplatonic ideas are intermingled, but his approach to physical alchemy and physic is primarily that of Paracelsus and Van Helmont.

As the final section of the *Philosophicall Epitaph* of 1673, Cooper added *A catalogue of chymicall books which have been written originally, or translated into English*. Not narrowly 'chymicall' in coverage, this list includes sixteenth- and seventeenth-century books on magic, astronomy, physic, and pharmacy—both Galenical and Paracelsian—Rosicrucianism, and 'chemical philosophy', as well as many works which, in their empirical and inductive emphasis, were more closely allied with the 'new science'. The *Catalogue* contains more than 180 main entries that provided the basis for two expanded and corrected versions. In 1675 he compiled a *Second Part* containing additional book entries, and a *Third Part* consisting of a ten-year index to items published in the *Philosophical Transactions of the Royal Society* which pertain to 'Chymistry, or the Study of Nature by Art in the Animal, Vegetal or Mineral Kingdoms'. In 1688, he added a *Continuation or Appendix to the Second Part*,

consisting of corrections, rectifications, or additions of books entries up to that year. Now exceedingly rare, this *Continuation* brought the total number of main entries to approximately 430. By extending his booklist thirteen years beyond the 1675 edition, Cooper provided a much fuller inventory of books that had been published and were available for purchase in late Restoration England. The earliest work listed in the *Catalogue* is Hieronymous von Braunschweig's *Vertuose Boke of Distyllacyon of the Waters of All Manner of Herbes* (1527), and one of the latest, and the only entry by a female writer, is Mrs Mary Trye's *Medicatrix, or, The Woman-Physician* (1675).

Primarily as the result of a large number of extant sale catalogues, knowledge of Cooper's activities as England's first book auctioneer is more complete than for any other aspect of his life. His auctioneering began on 31 October 1676 with the sale of the Lazarus Seaman library, included at least twenty-two sales, and ended in June 1688; his printed catalogues contain much additional information on the frequency and dates of his sales, his clients (who included Nathan Paget, Milton's doctor, and Richard Davis, Oxford bookseller), and estimates of the number of books included in certain of the sales. He was keenly aware of his historic role in this new method of bookselling in England, which was patterned after those used in Leiden and Amsterdam, and established a format and procedures to regulate this business. His auctioneering fame and that of his sometime partner Edward Millington are humorously celebrated in George Smalridge's Latin poem *Auctio Davisiana Oxonii habita, per Gul. Cooper & Edward Millington bibliopol* (1689). Cooper died in February 1689. His widow, Mary, succeeded to the business.

STANTON J. LINDEN

**Sources** [W. Cooper], *A philosophicall epitaph in hieroglphicall figures … published by W. C. esq with a catalogue of chymicall bookes* (1673) · S. J. Linden, *William Cooper's A catalogue of chymicall books, 1673–88* (1987) · P. Ash, 'Fathers of auctioneering', *Estates Gazette* (22–9 Dec 1962), 866–9, 916–19; (5–12 Jan 1963), 51–6, 121–7 · H. R. Plomer and others, *A dictionary of the printers and booksellers who were at work in England, Scotland, and Ireland from 1668 to 1725* (1922); repr. (1968) · J. Lawler, *Book auctions in England in the seventeenth century, 1676–1700* (1898); repr. (Detroit, 1968)

**Cooper, William** (1822–1868), promoter of the co-operative movement, was born in Rochdale, the son of James Cooper, a weaver, and his wife, Susan (*née* Taylor); he was probably the eldest of six children. Cooper had little formal education, but was drawn to discussion of political and economic issues. Influenced by the work of Robert Owen, he joined the Rochdale branch of the Rational Society in the early 1840s and retained Owenite ideals from then on. Cooper also supported the Chartist land plan promoted by Feargus O'Connor. He is, however, most associated with consumers' co-operation and the widespread dissemination of the inspiring example of the Rochdale Pioneers society.

Cooper worked first as a fustian cutter, but by the time of his marriage on 21 July 1844 to Betty Smith he was a hand-loom weaver, producing flannel for Ashworths of

Church Style. In August 1844 Cooper attended the meeting which established the Rochdale Society of Equitable Pioneers [see Rochdale Pioneers] and in December was appointed its cashier. Cooper served in the shop which opened for evening business on 21 December 1844, working alternate weeks with Samuel Ashworth, the society's first salesman. By 1851 Cooper was superintendent to two shopmen and the store kept more conventional trading hours. Cooper's responsibilities grew with his appointment in 1849 as secretary to the Rochdale Pioneers. In 1855 this carried a weekly salary of 21s. rising to 25s. as and when his efforts merited it. Cooper remained secretary and cashier until his death.

Cooper's position within one of the principal co-operatives of the day led to involvement with other projects. In 1850 he was a founder of the Rochdale District Co-operative Corn Mill Society, whose early history he published in 1860. He was also a promoter of the Rochdale Co-operative Manufacturing Society launched in 1854 and unsuccessfully defended the principle of bonus to labour against shareholders interested in returns on invested capital. As secretary to the Pioneers society Cooper also maintained an extensive, and international, correspondence both with politicians and intellectuals interested in such working-class initiatives, and with individuals and co-operatives seeking inspiration and advice to sustain their own operations. His propagandism extended to numerous newspaper contributions and speeches to local societies. Cooper was thus a forerunner to the Co-operative Union in advising on, and promoting, co-operative expansion during the mid-nineteenth century. He assisted infant societies in drafting their rules and also operated a small printing business supplying rule books, ledgers, and stationery.

Cooper was involved with efforts to extend co-operation to wholesaling, thus forging new bonds between local consumers' societies and extending co-operative influence throughout the distributive system. In 1850 the Rochdale Pioneers established a wholesale department, hoping to develop a broad-based wholesale operation from an initial association with their strong retail society. Cooper was appointed, with John Healey, to attend to the wholesale business. This operation had a troubled existence amid concerns from Rochdale that their society was taking commercial risks and external allegations of unfair dealing. Attempts to establish a larger operation were further checked by the collapse of a parallel organization, the Central Co-operative Agency (CCA), with premises in London and Manchester. The CCA failed in 1857 and the Rochdale wholesale department closed the following year. Cooper's proposal of March 1859 that it be reopened was rejected, but initiatives were afoot that led to the modern Co-operative Wholesale Society.

Development of wholesale trading as a joint venture between co-operatives was handicapped by the 1852 Industrial and Provident Societies Act. This restricted societies' ownership of land and property and the establishment of educational funds, and precluded limited liability status. It was, however, the prohibition on one society investing in another which, in the context of the development of wholesale trading, finally prompted action. Efforts to amend the 1852 act united northern working-class co-operators and middle-class Christian socialists. As secretary to the organizing committee Cooper played a central role, assuming chief responsibility for an estimated 1600 items of correspondence. Cooper also gave evidence to the parliamentary enquiry considering revision of industrial and provident society legislation and assisted E. V. Neale in drafting amendments to the 1852 act. After the passage of a new act in 1862, the North of England Co-operative Wholesale Society (later the Co-operative Wholesale Society) was established. Cooper remained involved and in 1863 was one of twelve individual members admitted to the wholesale society to circumvent continuing restrictions on the scale of investment by one co-operative in another.

Cooper's role in the development of national co-operative initiatives also included service as secretary to the Co-operative Congress Board and involvement in the establishment of the Co-operative Insurance Company in 1867. He was active in canvassing opinion regarding the foundation of the company and became its first secretary. Cooper's work was cut short, however, by his death on 31 October 1868. He contracted typhus, which had already killed his daughter Elizabeth, and died at his home, 115 Oldham Road, Rochdale. Cooper, a lifelong secularist, was interred at Rochdale cemetery on 3 November 1868; he was survived by his wife and three of his six children. His estate and effects were valued at under £600. At the quarterly meeting of the Co-operative Wholesale Society following his death £20 was voted to a Cooper memorial fund. Tributes emphasize Cooper's unselfish commitment to co-operation; indeed Holyoake referred to him as 'the drudge of co-operation' (*Rochdale Observer*). But Cooper was also 'a roystering sort of lad' (quoted in Bonner, 494) and exhibited considerable zeal and personal energy in his promotion not only of co-operation but also of other progressive causes including the abolition of slavery in the American south and extension of the British parliamentary franchise.                    MARTIN PURVIS

**Sources** G. J. Holyoake, *Self-help by the people: the history of the Rochdale Pioneers, 1844–1892*, 10th edn (1900) · P. Redfern, *The story of the C.W.S., 1863–1913* (1913) · *Rochdale Observer* (7 Nov 1868) · family and census details derived from the unpublished research of Mrs Dorothy Greaves, Toad Lane Co-operative Museum, Rochdale · G. D. H. Cole, *A century of co-operation* (1945) · H. F. Bing and J. Saville, 'Cooper, William', *DLB*, vol. 1 · letters and other papers (uncatalogued), National Co-operative Archive, Rochdale, William Cooper MSS · A. Bonner, *British co-operation: the history, principles, and organisation of the British co-operative movement*, rev. edn (1970)

**Archives** Co-operative College, Manchester, National Co-operative Archive · Man. CL, Manchester Archives and Local Studies, Rochdale Equitable Pioneers MSS, minute book, board meetings and general meetings, 8/1844 to 2/1851, MF 870 · Rochdale Public Library, Rochdale Equitable Pioneers Society MSS, minute book, 7/1856 to 12/1863, C/CO-OP/1 1/1/1

**Likenesses** group portrait, photograph, 1865 (with Rochdale Pioneers), Rochdale Pioneers Museum, Rochdale; *see illus. in* Rochdale Pioneers (*act.* 1844)

**Wealth at death** under £600: probate, 26 Nov 1868, *CGPLA Eng. & Wales*

**Cooper, William** (*c*.1826–1871). *See under* Cooper family (*per.* 1854–1994).

**Cooper, William Durrant** (1812–1875), antiquary, was born on 10 January 1812 in High Street, Lewes, Sussex, the son of Thomas Cooper (1789–1841), solicitor, and his wife, Lucy Elizabeth, *née* Durrant (*d.* 1867). He was educated at Lewes grammar school until at the age of fifteen he was articled to his father; he was admitted attorney and solicitor at the Michaelmas term of 1832.

Cooper's evidence in 1833 to a House of Commons committee on the negligent way in which he had found incumbents keeping parish registers reveals an early interest in archives, albeit to prove title to property. In the following year he published a substantial history of parliamentary elections in all the Sussex constituencies; this reappeared as an appendix to *The History … of … Sussex* (1835) by T. W. Horsfield (1792–1837). It was followed by a short *Glossary of the Provincialisms in Use in Sussex* (1836; 2nd edn, 1853).

The electoral history signalled also active engagement in politics, in the whig cause. After helping John Easthope (1784–1865) in his unsuccessful attempt to win the Lewes seat in 1837, Cooper moved permanently to London and joined the parliamentary staff of the *Morning Chronicle*, of which Easthope was a proprietor. He subsequently worked for *The Times*, but in time abandoned journalism to concentrate on his legal practice, chiefly conveyancing and parliamentary agency. Some of the offices he held may have been in recognition of political support: the duke of Norfolk made him auditor of Skelton Castle, Yorkshire (in 1843), and his steward for the borough of Lewes (in the mid-1860s). He had joined the Reform Club in 1837 and was appointed its solicitor about 1870. His most lucrative office was probably that of solicitor to the vestry of St Pancras, London (1858).

Cooper's greater love, however, was history and associated literary pursuits, particularly editing documents of the sixteenth and seventeenth centuries. Removal to London permitted active involvement in the national antiquarian societies. In 1841 Cooper was elected a fellow of the Society of Antiquaries and not only published four papers in *Archaeologia* but also gave sterling service on the finance committee. The council of the Camden Society he joined in 1846, and between 1853 and 1862 he edited two volumes and contributed to two of the society's *Miscellanies*. He edited a volume of plays, *Ralph Roister Doister … and the Tragedie of Gorbaduc*, for the Shakespeare Society (1847) and published privately (1844) seven letters by or associated with Laurence Sterne, which he found in the muniment room at Skelton Castle.

Cooper contributed six papers to the journals of the London and Middlesex, Kent, and Surrey archaeological societies. Having joined the Sussex Archaeological Society within its first year (1846–7), his contributions were more prolific: one, two, or three articles to all but one of the first twenty-five volumes (1848–73) of the society's *Collections*. As editor in 1859–65 he was known for the copious notes he added to other authors' contributions. His most sustained piece of work was the *History of Winchelsea* (1850): his father's family had come from the neighbouring parish of Icklesham.

In 1872 Cooper was stricken by an attack of paralysis, but he lingered for three years longer, before dying on 28 December 1875 at 81 Guilford Street, Russell Square, London, his home since at latest 1848. He was never married, and latterly lived with his spinster sister.

JOHN H. FARRANT

**Sources** H. Campkin, 'The late William Durrant Cooper … and the late Mark Antony Lower', *Sussex Archaeological Collections*, 27 (1877), 117–51 [incl. list of pubns] · 'Select committee on parochial registration', *Parl. papers* (1833), 14.528, no. 669 · Sussex Archaeological Society, Lewes, Lower MSS
**Archives** Sussex Archaeological Society, Lewes, draft lectures and articles | Sussex Archaeological Society, Lewes, letters to Mark Lower
**Wealth at death** under £3000: probate, 18 Jan 1876, *CGPLA Eng. & Wales*

**Cooper, William Ricketts** (1843–1878), orientalist, was born at 7 Devonshire Buildings, Great Dover Road, St Mary Newington, in south London, on 12 March 1843, the son of Daniel Cooper, farmer, and his wife, Anne Pernell Brooks. He began life as a designer of carpet patterns and became a missionary in London. Then, under the influence of Samuel Birch (1813–1885), and Joseph Bonomi the younger (1796–1878), whose assistant he became at the Sir John Soane's Museum, he directed his varied energies to the study of Egyptian antiquities and Assyriology. Without being strictly a scholar, he accomplished a great deal of valuable work. He was one of the principal originators in 1870 of the Society of Biblical Archaeology and was active and enthusiastic as the society's secretary from its foundation. He lived at 5 Richmond Grove, Barnsbury, London, until delicate health compelled him in 1876 to retire to 7 Trinity Terrace, Ventnor, on the Isle of Wight. He inspired the archaic classes conducted by A. H. Sayce (1845–1933) and Sir Peter le Page Renouf (1822–1897), and the publication of the valuable series of translated Assyrian and Egyptian documents, entitled Records of the Past. He was named a fellow of the Royal Asiatic Society in 1875 and was also a fellow of the Royal Society of Literature. He published, among other works, *Serpent Myths of Ancient Egypt* (1873); *The Resurrection of Assyria* (1875); *Egypt and the Pentateuch* (1875); *The Archaic Dictionary* (1876); *The Horus Myth and Christianity* (1877); and *A Short History of the Egyptian Obelisks* (1877; 2nd edn, 1878). According to E. A. Wallis Budge, Cooper was tall in stature, but his stoop made him appear of only medium height; he had finely cut features and a large aquiline nose and was nicknamed 'the Etruscan', as he resembled a figure on an Etruscan sarcophagus in the British Museum. Cooper died in Ventnor on 15 November 1878.

STANLEY LANE-POOLE, *rev.* M. L. BIERBRIER

**Sources** *The Athenaeum* (23 Nov 1878), 657 · E. A. W. Budge, *By Nile and Tigris*, 1 (1920), 7–8 · *Proceedings of the Society of Biblical Archaeology*, 1 (1878), 10 · *Journal of the Royal Asiatic Society of Great Britain and Ireland* (1879), ix–x · *CGPLA Eng. & Wales* (1879)

**Archives** RIBA BAL, MS index compiled by him of the drawings in the museum of Sir John Soane
**Wealth at death** under £3000: probate, 23 Jan 1879, *CGPLA Eng. & Wales*

**Cooper, William White** (1816–1886), oculist, was born on 17 November 1816 at Holt, Wiltshire, of unknown parentage. Following his arrival in London about 1834, he enrolled as a student at St Bartholomew's Hospital, and at the same time he became a private pupil of Edward Stanley, surgeon at St Bartholomew's. Cooper's notes of the lectures of Professor Richard Owen at the Royal College of Surgeons were so outstanding that Owen awarded him a prize; the notes were published as *Lectures in the Comparative Anatomy and Physiology of the Invertebrate Animals* (1843). Cooper became MRCS in 1838, and spent a year or two on foreign travel—his visit to Madeira resulting in his *Invalid's Guide to Madeira* (1840).

In 1845 Cooper became FRCS, and in the same year he married on 9 December Mary Elizabeth (*b.* 1823/4), daughter of Samuel Poyser of Derby. He associated with the ophthalmic surgeon John Dalrymple, and gained a large practice. He was one of the original staff of the North London Eye Institution, and was subsequently ophthalmic surgeon to St Mary's Hospital, Paddington. Cooper gained a reputation as a careful, steady, and neat operator, judicious and painstaking in treatment. His book *On Wounds and Injuries of the Eye* (1859) was the first to treat this subject and was comprehensive for its time. In 1859 Cooper was appointed surgeon-oculist to Queen Victoria, who regularly sought his advice on government matters connected with his specialism.

In the autumn of 1884 Cooper suffered blocked veins in his leg. Under the best treatment, he appeared to rally but then, on 29 May 1886—the day on which his knighthood was announced—he fell victim to acute pneumonia. He died at his home, 19 Berkeley Square, Westminster, London, on 1 June. He was survived by his wife and his eldest son, who had followed him into the medical profession.

G. T. BETTANY, rev. ANITA MCCONNELL

**Sources** *The Lancet* (19 June 1886), 1187–8 · d. cert. · m. cert. · *CGPLA Eng. & Wales* (1886)
**Wealth at death** £28,806 3s. 2d.: probate, 24 July 1886, *CGPLA Eng. & Wales*

**Coote, Sir Charles**, first baronet (*d.* 1642), soldier and political administrator, was the elder of the two sons of Sir Nicholas Coote and his second wife, Eleanor Stanhope. Sir Nicholas had been a retainer of the duke of Norfolk, in whose cause he struck the attorney-general, for which he was fined £20,000. He spent some time in prison and at last was obliged (with his son's permission) to sell off part of his estates to pay the fine.

Charles is said to have been at Cambridge in 1591, and then served as a captain under Charles Blount, Lord Mountjoy, in 1600–03, the concluding three years of the Nine Years' War; in 1605 he was appointed provost-marshal of Connaught for life. His marriage about 1610 to Dorothea, daughter of Hugh Cuffe of Cuffeswood, co. Cork, brought them four sons and a daughter.

Coote was sworn onto the privy council and promoted vice-president of Connacht in 1620, and created a baronet of Ireland the following year. In 1621, too, Coote was appointed sovereign of the newly created corporation of Jamestown, strategically situated on a crossing of the River Shannon in co. Leitrim. The landmark 1622 commission on the government of Ireland queried why the royal revenue in Connacht was 'strangely lost and reduced to nothing' (Treadwell, 201) and criticized the cost of fortifying the tiny settlement with a large bastioned *enceinte*. Some commissioners suggested that Coote financed his recent meteoric rise through embezzlement of the composition rent in Connacht; he was, they said, 'a stirring man fuller of wit than judgement, very pragmatical but his own ends so much in his eye as he is become an eye sore to the country who have grievously complained against him for extortion' (Canny, 255).

Coote, however, was protected by his patron George Villiers, from 1623 duke of Buckingham. Firmly ensconced as James I's favourite, Buckingham was able to ward off Coote's many enemies and he even extended his Jamestown contract to include Charlestown in adjacent co. Roscommon. Coote picked up many properties scattered throughout the midlands as these were planted from 1620 onward. These included Castlecoote on another river crossing on the Roscommon–Galway border and Dowbally in co. Cavan where he built a large ironworks. He set up another ironworks at Drumanlasse in co. Leitrim. Further south he acquired an estate of 500 acres at Castlecuffe and another of 400 acres at Mountrath, both in the north of Queen's county (Laois). In contrast to Jamestown, Mountrath developed into a model plantation nucleated settlement based on the Coote's works for the manufacture of linen, fustian and woollen cloth. Coote was returned for Queen's county in the 1639–41 parliament.

The usually dominant office-holding faction to which Coote belonged was closely connected through marriage alliances and business interests and was headed by Richard Boyle, earl of Cork; 'all birds of a feather and the earl of Cork's party' (Perceval-Maxwell, 87–8). In 1630 Coote went to London to lobby for a plantation of Ormond and the following year, in concert with Cork, he proposed a plantation of Sligo, Roscommon, and Mayo. Coote's advocacy of plantation was more sympathetically received following the appointment of Lord Deputy Wentworth in 1633. The following year Coote was appointed as one of the commissioners 'to secure defective titles', this being the legal mechanism whereby peacetime land confiscations could be set in train.

The origins of the October 1641 rising can be traced in part to the instability and resentment provoked by these plantations. Despite his advanced age—he was described in 1627 as being 'old and infirm' (*CSP Ire.*, 1625–32, 220)—Coote was appointed as governor of Dublin in November 1641 and commissioned to raise a regiment. He led successful attacks on insurgent positions surrounding the city, south towards Wicklow in November 1641 and north towards Swords and Kilsallaghan in January and February 1642. However, his killing of innocent civilians on the

Wicklow expedition came at a politically inopportune time when the Old English palesmen were debating whether to join the insurgents. If Bellings, a normally restrained Irish commentator, is to be believed, one such incident involved 'his calling a simple country fellow from the plow to have him blow his pistoll, which the simple man, in obedience to Sir Charles Coote's command, performs readily, he shoots him in the mouth and kills him' (*Irish Confederation*, ed. Gilbert, 1.35). Reports of such alleged atrocities gave credence, in Irish Catholic eyes, to rumours that the government planned to massacre them.

Otherwise, Coote proved to be an active and successful military commander, most notably in leading a cavalry detachment to relieve the midland garrisons of Birr, Borris, and Knocknamease in April 1642, 'after surmounting incredible difficulties and a march of forty eight hours without the intermission of more than three hours rest' (Carte, 3.314), in the teeth of stiff insurgent resistance. On rejoining the main army he participated in a follow-up victory at Kilrush when an insurgent army tried to block the return of Ormond's army to Dublin. Ormond left Coote to garrison Naas. Subsequently Coote helped to capture Philipstown (Daingean) and Trim. On 7 May 1642 he was shot dead while repelling an insurgent counter-attack on Trim, 'whether by the enemy or by one of his own troopers, was variously reported' (Archdall, 2.67). His eldest son, Charles *Coote (c.1610–1661), succeeded him as second baronet and in 1660 was created first earl of Mountrath.

PÁDRAIG LENIHAN

**Sources** M. Perceval-Maxwell, *The outbreak of the Irish rebellion of 1641* (1994), 67, 87–8 · T. Carte, *An history of the life of James, duke of Ormonde*, 3 vols. (1735–6), vol. 3, p. 314 · M. Archdall, *The peerage of Ireland* (1779), vol. 2, pp. 62–7 · *CSP Ire.*, 1603–6, 149; 1625–32, 149, 195, 217, 220, 340, 471–2, 477, 605, 646; 1633–47, 64, 79, 130 · *History of the Irish confederation and the war in Ireland ... by Richard Bellings*, ed. J. T. Gilbert, 1 (1882), 35 · J. T. Gilbert, ed., *A contemporary history of affairs in Ireland from 1641 to 1652*, 1 (1879), 18 · deposition of Philip Sergint, TCD, MS 815 (Queen's county), p. 90 · deposition of Chidley Coote, TCD, MS 814 (King's county), p. 90 · V. Treadwell, *Buckingham and Ireland, 1616–28* (Dublin, 1998), 200–03 · A. de Vlieger, *Historical and genealogical record of the Coote family* (1900) · A. Clarke, *Prelude to restoration* (1999) · B. McGrath, 'A biographical dictionary of the membership of the Irish House of Commons, 1640–1641', PhD diss., University of Dublin, 1997, 111–13 · N. Canny, *Making Ireland British 1580–1650* (2001), 254–5, 359, 371, 374

**Coote, Charles, first earl of Mountrath** (c.1610–1661), army officer and politician, was the eldest son of Sir Charles *Coote, first baronet (d. 1642), of Castle Coote, co. Roscommon, and Dorothea, daughter of Hugh Cuffe, of Cuffe's Wood or Cuffeswood, co. Cork. Little is known of his early years, but he was knighted in 1626 and in the 1630s he supported his father's work as provost-marshal of Connaught, and was returned as MP for Leitrim in the Irish parliament of 1640. Before 1630 he married Mary (d. in or before 1645), daughter of Sir Francis Ruish. He married second, before May 1645, Jane (d. 1684), daughter of Sir Robert Hannay, baronet.

At the outbreak of the Irish rising of 1641 Coote was left to defend the family estates in Connaught, while his father joined the main army at Dublin. When his father

was killed in May 1642 Coote was nominated to succeed him as provost-marshal, and in February 1643 he joined a delegation to Oxford which tried to persuade Charles I to send supplies to the west of Ireland. The subsequent cessation of arms agreed between the king and the confederate Irish, and the appointment of lords Wilmot and Dillon as joint presidents of Connaught, seem to have confirmed Coote's doubts about royalist intentions. In April 1644 he was one of the protestant agents who attended the king once again, demanding that he repudiate the cessation of arms, condemn popery, confiscate rebel estates, and impose further plantation in Ireland. Their proposals caused consternation at Oxford, and Coote and his colleagues were accused of intending 'only scandal upon the king and his ministers' (Lord Digby to Ormond, 6 May 1644, Bodl. Oxf., MS Carte 10, fol. 532). The agents received a warmer reception in London, and by August Coote had declared his support for the parliamentarian cause.

In October 1644 Coote was nominated by parliament as their lord president of Connaught, and the post was confirmed in February 1645. In the interim he joined Sir Robert King, Sir John Temple, and other Irish protestants in advising parliament on its Irish policy. In May 1645 he was finally given leave to return to Ireland, and joined forces with the 'Laggan' army in western Ulster, with whom he recaptured Sligo, and advanced into Connaught, capturing eighteen towns by the end of the year. In the spring of 1646 Coote and his allies persuaded Viscount Ranelagh to defect to parliament, and narrowly failed to arrange a mutiny at Athlone. In May he besieged the earl of Clanricarde in Portumna Castle in southern Galway. Coote's successes were soon shattered by the defeat of the Ulster Scots at Benburb in June 1646. He withdrew to Belfast, and begged parliament to send effective support to northern Ireland. The independents, who now controlled Irish affairs through the new lord lieutenant, Viscount Lisle, tried to conciliate Coote, but they were more concerned to send reinforcements to Dublin and the Munster garrisons. In March 1647 Coote sent agents to parliament to bring the 'very sad condition' of Connaught to their notice, and to 'prevent that torrent which carrieth all to Munster' (*Egmont Diary*, 1.366, 379). After Lisle's commission ended in April, Coote received more help from Westminster. In July £8000 was allocated to Connaught, and in October Coote was appointed vice-admiral of the province. The threat of Irish intervention in the second civil war prompted parliament to send further supplies, and Coote was made governor of Londonderry.

The trial and execution of Charles I seem to have made little impact on Coote. During the winter of 1648–9 he joined the Ulster commander George Monck in a purge of the British officer corps, and he imposed the engagement on Londonderry soon afterwards. These moves did not go unchallenged, however, and in May 1649 Coote was besieged in Londonderry by his former allies in the Laggan regiments. Relief was slow in arriving, and when he was eventually reinforced the immediate danger had passed. From early 1650 Coote played a crucial role in bringing northern Ireland under parliament's control. He defeated an Irish army at Scarrifhollis in July 1650, and, working with the New Model brigade under Robert Venables, ravaged Ulster, before invading Connaught in 1651, capturing Athlone and Portumna, and, after a long siege, taking the surrender of Galway in April 1652. Despite his victories, Coote was criticized by the parliamentary commissioners, who thought the Galway articles too lenient. They were also suspicious of his continuing association with the Ulster Scots and with former royalists. It was not a surprise when most of Coote's northern regiments (including those under the command of his three brothers) were disbanded in the reduction of the Irish army in 1653.

Coote retained the presidency of Connaught, however, and during the later 1650s he was able to extend his political influence over much of Connaught and western Ulster. In the elections for the protectorate parliaments of 1654, 1656, and 1659 he was able to return his own candidates to at least six seats in each parliament. He himself was elected for Galway and Mayo, although he only took his seat in 1659. During this period he also became allied to a number of men of national importance, including Lord Broghill (Roger Boyle), Sir Hardress Waller, and William Jephson. Of particular importance was his friendship with Henry Cromwell, who governed Ireland from the summer of 1655. In October 1656, for example, Henry Cromwell supported Coote's efforts to secure the renewal of his patent as lord president; a year later he recommended Coote for a peerage and a seat in the 'other house', although without success. Coote soon returned the favour: in 1658 he acted as Henry Cromwell's agent in the settlement of his newly acquired estates in Galway, and in the 1659 parliament he was a staunch supporter of the protectorate, and acted as teller in favour of recognizing the other house.

The fall of the protectorate in May 1659 left Coote vulnerable. He was reappointed as colonel of foot by the republican regime in July 1659, but he did not support the new government, and was involved in the coup of December 1659, capturing Galway for the Irish officers. In January 1660 he was appointed one of five commissioners to govern Ireland for parliament, and he was a central figure in the Dublin Convention. It was during the meeting of the convention that Coote began to support the restoration of the monarchy as the best option for stability in Ireland. As early as the summer of 1659 he had been accused of 'declaring for the Scot's king's interest' (Warner, *Nicholas Papers*, 4.156), and he worked closely with his former colleague George Monck during the winter of 1659–60, but his first direct contact with the court in exile came only in February 1660, when he sent Sir Arthur Forbes to wait on Charles II in the Netherlands. A reply, acknowledging his support, was penned by the king in March.

After the Restoration, Coote was well rewarded. In July 1660 he was reappointed president of Connaught; in August his estates were confirmed; and in September he was created Baron Coote of Castle Cuffe, Viscount Coote of Castle Coote, and earl of Mountrath. As lord justice of Ireland from October 1660, he governed Ireland with Lord

Broghill (now earl of Orrery) and Sir Maurice Eustace. During 1661 he proved an effective manager of the Irish parliament, influencing elections and steering proceedings to ensure that (in his own words) 'all things are now fully restored to their ancient order' (BL, Egerton MS 2537, fol. 345). His death in Dublin from smallpox on 18 December 1661 was (according to Orrery), 'a great blow to this kingdom' (*CSP Ire.*, 1660–62, 479). This was not an exaggeration. In the following months, the rule of the lords justices gave way to the lieutenancy of the duke of Ormond, and the Irish protestants found their ambitions increasingly frustrated. Mountrath was buried on 6 February 1662 at St Patrick's Cathedral; he was succeeded by his eldest son, Charles, from his first marriage. He was survived by his wife, who afterwards married Sir Robert Reading, bt.

PATRICK LITTLE

**Sources** P. Little, 'Coote, Sir Charles', HoP, *Commons, 1640–60* [draft] · *Report on the manuscripts of the earl of Egmont*, 2 vols. in 3, HMC, 63 (1905–9) · Bodl. Oxf., MSS Carte 10–14, 16, 23, 24, 63 · BL, Lansdowne MS 823 · J. Lodge, *The peerage of Ireland*, 4 vols. (1754) · *CSP dom.* · *CSP Ire.* · PRO, SP 28/93 · *JHC* · R. Dunlop, *Ireland under the Commonwealth* (1913) · *The memoirs of Edmund Ludlow*, ed. C. H. Firth, 2 vols. (1894) · *The Clarke papers*, ed. C. H. Firth, 4 vols., CS, new ser., 49, 54, 61–2 (1891–1901) · *The Nicholas papers*, ed. G. F. Warner, 4 vols., CS, new ser., 40, 50, 57, 3rd ser., 31 (1886–1920) · GEC, *Peerage*
**Archives** BL, Lansdowne MS 823 · BL, corresp. with Sir Philip Percival, Egmont MS I · Bodl. Oxf., Carte MSS

**Coote, Charles** (*bap.* 1760, *d.* 1835), historian and biographer, was the son of John *Coote (1733/4–1808), a bookseller of Paternoster Row, London, and the author of several dramatic pieces, who died in 1808; his mother was Jane, *née* Weaver (*d.* in or before 1808). He went to St Paul's School in 1773, matriculated from Pembroke College, Oxford, in 1778, took the degree of BA in 1782, and on 30 December 1784 was elected a scholar on the Benet or Ossulstone foundation in that society. He proceeded MA in 1785, BCL by commutation on 10 July 1789, DCL on 14 July following, and was admitted a member of the College of Advocates on 3 November in the same year. He devoted his attention to literature rather than to law, and was for some time editor of the *Critical Review*. To adopt his own words, 'even after his enrolment among the associated advocates he for some years did not dwell within the circuit of the college, and when he became a resident member he rather patiently awaited employment than eagerly sought it' (Coote, 133). Coote was

> of a retired disposition, with much of that eccentricity and indolence which often accompany literary merit, he passed through his profession with credit and respect, but without that emolument which was perhaps due to his abilities, had they been much exerted. (*GM*)

Not being an able speaker he was rarely employed as an advocate, but he frequently acted as a judge in the court of delegates.

Coote's first work was *Elements of the Grammar of the English Language* (1788; 2nd edn, 1806), a work of some interest; he then wrote *The History of England from the Earliest Dawn of Record to the Peace of 1783* (9 vols., 1791–8), to which he added in 1803 another volume, bringing down the history to the peace of Amiens in 1802. He then published two classical histories (1794 and 1796), followed by a *History of the union of the kingdoms of Great Britain and Ireland: with an introductory survey of Hibernian affairs traced from the times of Celtic colonisation* (1802), which sold poorly. His most distinctive work was *Sketches of the lives and characters of eminent English civilians, with an historical introduction relative to the College of Advocates* (1804), in which he included himself. He added six volumes to Mosheim's ecclesiastical history in 1811, and published a history of ancient Europe (3 vols., 1815), and various other updatings of other authors' historical works.

Coote had been married, but was for many years a widower. He died at Islington, London, on 19 November 1835, survived by two daughters and three sons, one of whom was the historian Henry Charles *Coote.

THOMPSON COOPER, *rev.* H. C. G. MATTHEW

**Sources** *GM*, 2nd ser., 5 (1836), 92 · Foster, *Alum. Oxon.* · [C. Coote], *Sketches of the lives and characters of eminent English civilians, with an historical introduction relative to the College of Advocates* (1804)

**Coote, Sir Colin Reith** (1893–1979), newspaper editor, was born on 19 October 1893 at Fenstanton in Huntingdonshire, the eldest of three sons, one of whom died in infancy (there were no daughters) of Howard Browning Coote (1865–1943), landlord, coal merchant, and later lord lieutenant of Huntingdonshire, and his wife, Jean Reith, daughter of Alexander Reith Gray, of Aberdeen. From childhood a French-Swiss governess gave Colin Coote a love for France and its language. He was educated at Rugby School and Balliol College, Oxford, where he obtained a second class in *literae humaniores* in 1914.

Sir Colin Reith Coote (1893–1979), by Walter Bird, 1962

Soon after Coote had taken his degree the First World War broke out, and he obtained an immediate commission in the 4th battalion of the Gloucestershire regiment. Transferred to the Italian front, he was promoted captain and won a DSO (1918)—rare for an officer below field rank. He was gassed and three times wounded. In 1917 Neil Primrose, Liberal MP for the Isle of Ely, was killed in action. Coote was given leave to contest the by-election as a Liberal candidate. Having won it, he returned to the front. A year later, demobilized, he was re-elected as a Coalition Liberal (and the youngest member in the Commons) in the 'coupon' election of 1918. His four years in parliament, during which he shared a house with his lifelong friend Walter Elliot, became a useful experience, but journalism was beckoning. His freelance writing was noticed. Already bilingual in French and English, Coote had added mastery of Italian during his war service. Though he was without formal experience as a journalist, he caught the eye of G. Geoffrey Dawson. When he lost his seat in 1922 he was appointed Rome correspondent of *The Times*.

Four years in Rome gave Coote an insight into the city that persuaded him to write two books—*Italian Town and Country Life* (1925) and *In and about Rome* (1926). It was also the time of the rise to power of the efficient young Mussolini. The distaste implanted in Coote's liberal mind for a regime of that kind decisively shaped his judgements a decade later at the time of Munich. By nature a commentator rather than a news-gatherer, he made his mark in Rome by his interpretation of events. In 1926 *The Times* called him back to the House of Commons, this time to write the newspaper's sketch of parliamentary proceedings. That helped to develop his intimacy with politics. It also enhanced his facility for writing clean English as fast as a pen could travel. Coote wrote his copy and his innumerable private letters in a minute but beautifully legible handwriting with few pauses or corrections, successive lines sloping from the left margin. In 1929 he became a *Times* leader writer, mainly on politics but sharing responsibility for a range of other subjects at home and abroad. The rise of the dictators presented difficulties for him over his newspaper's editorial policy. *The Times* endorsed the so-called appeasement policy of Neville Chamberlain and Viscount Halifax. Coote's detestation of fascism and national socialism was absolute. He did not resign, but withdrew from foreign leader-writing, increasingly confining himself to home topics. At odds with his friend Walter Elliot, he came to detest Chamberlain and to abhor Munich. When war came, his knowledge of military matters served his newspaper well enough for a time; but an invitation in 1942 to join the *Daily Telegraph* was a welcome signal.

Coote joined as a leader writer. Now forty-nine years of age with twenty years of varied experience, an immense range of public friendships, and a grasp of national and international politics, he was an acquisition. Three years later he was appointed deputy to Arthur E. Watson, editor since 1924. When Watson retired in 1950, Coote was invited by Viscount Camrose to succeed him. Though more of a writing editor than Watson had been, he had the qualities to lead a staff of journalists and to keep a national newspaper on course. Tall, good-looking, and urbane, he could when he chose bring great charm to bear. In a more Olympian mood, he could make someone he thought mistaken feel very small indeed. After retiring in 1964 he described one essential duty of an editor in these terms: 'to keep his paper independent of all outside influences, British or Foreign, commercial or political'. Another duty, he thought, was 'to maintain the English language'. In both these respects he lived up to his precepts. His term as editor, from 1950 to 1964, coincided with the conservative regimes of 1951–64. Yet his wide political sympathies led him to observe more than once that among all the political leaders he had known (and he claimed the friendships of ten prime ministers) he liked best Churchill and Hugh Gaitskell. His editorship also fell into the period of Great Britain's dalliance with Europe. Like many of his generation who had spent youthful years in the First World War, Coote was an ardent European as well as an active protagonist for Anglo-French accord. Under his influence the *Daily Telegraph* strongly advocated joining the European Common Market.

On main issues Coote's basic political principles and moral values were founded on rock. On particulars and intermediate values he always liked to seek the views of his staff experts, and if they were soundly presented he would always accept them. Lord Camrose occasionally teased Coote about his old Liberal blood, but in so far as this was ever reflected in the editorial columns of the *Daily Telegraph* it did the newspaper no harm whatever. Coote's relations with Lord Camrose and, after 1954, with W. M. Berry (later Lord Hartwell) were amicable. The greatest quality that an editor can possess, Coote wrote after retiring, is luck. During his time as editor a rapid rise in the standards of life of the average citizen was reflected in the fortunes of the newspaper with which he was associated. Between 1950 and 1964 the circulation of the *Daily Telegraph* rose from 971,000 to 1,319,000. He received a knighthood in 1962.

Coote believed in and practised the civilizing qualities of a balanced life. He was an enthusiastic golfer with a low handicap, and an authority on good wine and food. At dinner parties given by Coote and his wife in their Hampstead home, guests were feasted. One of the attributes that made him good company was his readiness with the right sort of remark for all occasions. One illustration of this occurred in a London street when Coote, after dodging a bus, landed on all fours on a traffic island. Picking himself up and shaking off the dust, he came face to face with Sir William Haley. 'Good morning', said Coote coolly. 'How appropriate to find the editor of *The Times* in the middle of the road.' His humour, never broad, was frequently astringent.

Apart from his two books on Italy, Coote put together a volume called *Maxims and Reflections of Winston S. Churchill*

(1947) and wrote *A Companion of Honour: the Story of W. Elliot* (1965).

Coote was three times married. In 1916 he married Marguerite Doris, daughter of Colonel William Henry Wellstead, of the Royal Engineers, of Tranby Lodge, Hessle, East Riding of Yorkshire; they had two daughters. This marriage was dissolved and in 1925 he married Denise, daughter of Emile Dethoor, of Doulieu, France; they had no children. She died in 1945 and in 1946 he married Amalie, daughter of Samuel Lewkowitz, businessman, of Amsterdam. They adopted Amalie's nephew, who became a correspondent for the *Daily Telegraph* and was killed in a flying accident a few months after Coote died at his London home, 16 Bigwood Road, on 8 June 1979.

DEEDES, *rev.*

**Sources** Lord Burnham [E. F. L. Burnham], *Peterborough Court: the story of the Daily Telegraph* (1955) · G. Astor, ed., *Fleet Street* (1966) · C. R. Coote, *Editorial: the memoirs of Colin R. Coote* [1965] · *Daily Telegraph* (9 June 1979) · private information (1986) · personal knowledge (1986)
**Archives** NL Scot., corresp. and working papers for biography of Walter Elliot | King's Lond., Liddell Hart C., corresp. with Sir B. H. Liddell Hart
**Likenesses** W. Bird, photograph, 1962, NPG [*see illus.*]
**Wealth at death** £75,159: probate, 21 Aug 1979, *CGPLA Eng. & Wales*

**Coote, Edmund** (*d.* 1609), schoolmaster and author, was the son of Thomas Coote of Steeple Bumstead, Essex, and his wife, Anne Cole. Admitted pensioner at Peterhouse, Cambridge, on 24 March 1576, he graduated BA in 1580 and proceeded MA in 1583. On 8 October 1592 he married Barbara Cooke in the church of St Mary-the-Less which adjoined his college. The couple had a daughter, Hester, baptized there in 1594.

On 5 June 1596 Coote was appointed master of the King Edward VI Free School in Bury St Edmunds, but on 18 May the following year he resigned, for reasons which the governors' register does not reveal. During his brief tenure he published his pedagogical manual *The Englishe Scholemaister* (1596), whose thoroughly practical approach to the teaching of English explains its ensuing popularity. Coote's elaborate title-page summarizes his purpose—to assist the teacher of the elementary literacy skills in 'the distinct reading and true writing of our English tongue'. The text opens with a fourteen-point statement of 'The Schoole-maister his profession', followed by a 'Preface for the direction of the reader', among whom he included 'men and women of trades (as tailors, weavers, shopkeepers, seamsters and such other) as have undertaken the charge of teaching others' (sig. A3r). Coote then proceeds via the letters of the alphabet, syllables, and two- and three-syllable words to offer a mode of spelling lesson, with an older pupil 'opposing' a younger. The importance of pronunciation is emphasized by objecting to such habits as pronouncing 'my naunt for mine aunt and thy nuncle for thine uncle', together with the injunction 'Take heed also you put not id for ed as unitid for united' and 'ignorantly writing a cup a wine for a cup of wine, and other like absurdities' (ibid., 31). A seven-page catechism with proof texts in the margin is followed by

'Sundry Necessarie Observations for a Christian' in the form of a series of moral maxims, a set of prayers for use at various times of the day, and a group of versified psalms. A half-page introduction to numbers is cut short in order to leave space for a 22-page list of 'hard words (especially from the Latin and French)' (ibid., 72–94). Coote's was not the first such book to be published. It was, however, by far the most popular, and continued to be printed throughout the seventeenth century, reaching a fifty-fourth edition in 1737.

After leaving Bury St Edmunds, Coote taught at Hunsdon, Hertfordshire, although the circumstances of his appointment are unknown. A son, Samuel, was baptized there in 1607. Coote died in 1609, and was buried on the same day as his wife, 13 February 1609, at St Mary's Church in the adjacent parish of Sawbridgeworth.

KENNETH CHARLTON

**Sources** B. Daniellson, 'A note on Edmund Coote: prolegomena for a critical edition of Coote's *Englishe Scholemaister*', *Studia Neophilologica*, 32 (1960), 228–40 · B. Daniellson, 'A second note on Edmund Coote', *Studia Neophilologica*, 33 (1961), 282–4 · T. A. Walker, *A biographical register of Peterhouse men*, 1 (1927) · Venn, *Alum. Cant.* · Cooper, *Ath. Cantab.*, 2.243 · J. W. Donaldson, *Retrospective address read at the tercentenary commemoration of King Edward's School, Bury St Edmunds, 2nd August 1850* (1850) · *Westminster Review*, new ser., 40 (1871), 565–6 · E. J. Dobson, *English pronunciation, 1500–1700*, 2 vols. (1957), vol. 1, pp. 33–7, 322 · I. Michael, *The teaching of English from the sixteenth century to 1870* (1987) · N. Carlisle, *A concise description of the endowed grammar schools in England and Wales*, 2 vols. (1818)

**Coote, Sir Eyre** (1726–1783), army officer, was the fourth son of the Revd Chidley Coote of Ash Hill, Kilmallock, in co. Limerick, and Jane, daughter of George Evans of Bulgaden Hall, co. Limerick, and sister of the first Lord Carberry.

**Early career, 1744–1757** It is assumed that he was brought up in Ireland, but nothing is known until the eighteen-year-old Coote was appointed ensign in Blakeney's or the 27th foot, the Inniskilling regiment, on 8 June 1744. Coote's military career began most inauspiciously when he took part as regimental colour bearer in the action near Falkirk on 17 January 1745 against the forces of Charles Edward Stuart. The ill-led, inexperienced regiment was routed in this battle; Coote was swept along in the panic retreat and reached Edinburgh ahead of his comrades still clutching the colour. In the ensuing court martial Coote was one of the four officers who underwent an exemplary trial for cowardice. Rather than being cashiered, he suffered the lesser penalty of suspension from the service, and his reappearance in the *Army List* of 1748 as a half pay cornet in the earl of Rothe's dragoons, with his commission still dated 1744, indicates that he was eventually forgiven for his conduct at Falkirk and subsequently. He may have seen service with the dragoons in Germany at the tail-end of the War of the Austrian Succession. On 18 April 1749 the half pay Coote transferred back on to the active list as a lieutenant by exchanging into the 37th foot under orders for Minorca. The regiment returned to England in 1755; Coote had received his captaincy in June that year and transferred again, this time to Adlercron's 39th foot,

Sir Eyre Coote (1726–1783), attrib. Henry Robert Morland, *c.*1763

currently serving in India. He sailed in November 1755 in command of a reinforcement for the 39th, and joined the regiment at Madras in the late summer of 1756.

Coote had arrived at an opportune moment to distinguish himself. The opening of the Seven Years' War entailed renewed Anglo-French conflict in India, primarily in the Carnatic around Madras and Pondicherry. In addition, Coote found himself immediately pitchforked into a crisis in Bengal, where the Calcutta council of the East India Company had provoked the local Mughal governor (nawab), Siraj ud-Daula, to attack the settlement and to throw the British out of the province. Madras decided to send a naval–military expedition under Admiral Charles Watson and Colonel Robert Clive to recover the situation. Captain Coote commanded one of the three companies detached from the 39th to join the company's troops and marines, which left Madras on 17 October, arriving at the mouth of the Ganges on 30 November. The force met little resistance in its progress up the river, retaking Fort William, Calcutta, without a fight on 2 January 1757. Belatedly, Siraj ud-Daula arrived outside Calcutta early in February with 40,000 men, apparently to cow the presumptuous British. But a daring, if ill-managed, march in the early morning mist right through the nawab's camp by a force of 2000 men led by Clive, with Coote in command of the Europeans, sufficiently alarmed Siraj to come to terms, restoring the company's position and paying damages.

The nawab, still hostile to the British, would have done well to protect their rivals the French, but he weakly allowed Watson and Clive to take the French base of Chandernagore early in March. Clive put Coote in command of the French fort. Then, when Clive joined a conspiracy brewing in Siraj's army against him led by Mir Jafar, his leading general, he promoted Coote temporary major and appointed him to command the advance guard in the march to the nawab's capital, Murshidabad, to supplant Siraj ud-Daula with Mir Jafar. Forty miles short of the capital, on the field of Plassey, Clive's 3000-strong force, which was supposed to have been joined by Mir Jafar's host, was confronted by the nawab with 50,000 men (including Mir Jafar) and fifty guns served by French artillery men. Coote was the most forceful and in a minority in Clive's council of war in arguing to accept battle; after reflection Clive was persuaded to agree. Siraj ud-Daula, destabilized by his justified fear of treachery in his own ranks, lost the battle of Plassey on 23 June 1757 in his own mind before ever a shot was fired, and not many had to be fired in an action later often celebrated as the beginning of the raj. Coote commanded one of the European divisions that pursued the retreating Mughal army. Clive later installed the grateful Mir Jafar as the new nawab and gave Coote his first independent command with orders to capture a fleeing French unit up the Ganges. Although the French eventually evaded him by escaping into the next province (Oudh), Coote had demonstrated his nerve, persistence, and leadership in keeping a small mixed force (750 men and 2 guns) of Europeans and Indians to a vigorous pursuit for 200 miles through alien and fairly hostile country at the height of the monsoon.

**Middle years, 1758–1772** Like other veterans of Plassey, Coote had made a small fortune due to the largesse of Mir Jafar, and the gloss of the victory gave his career a great boost. Back in England before Clive at the end of 1758, Coote was feted in polite society and consulted as an India expert by William Pitt the elder, the leading figure in the coalition government. A year later the East India Company made Coote the next commander-in-chief of their forces in India to succeed Clive, and the king made him a lieutenant-colonel and gave him a new regiment (the 84th foot). Coote arrived back at Madras on 27 October 1759 and, finding the Anglo-French War was still in progress, took the field at the head of the Madras army. He was lucky, in his first major independent command, that he came to the conflict at a point where, after years of material inferiority in men and money, the British had a superiority at sea as well as on land and were now backed up by the resources of Bengal, while having deprived the French of theirs from the Northern Circars, a small territory, nominally owned by the nizam of Hyderabad, abutting the northern Carnatic. None the less, the arduous campaign Coote conducted between November 1759 and January 1761, when the starving garrison in the French headquarters at Pondicherry finally surrendered to him after a prolonged blockade and siege, marked him out as a highly competent tactician who led from the front (the sepoys titled him Coote Bahadur, Coote the Hero). His crowning victory over the French at Wandiwash (22 January 1760) was the biggest battle fought between the Europeans in India. He was, however, criticized at the time by the Madras council and later by his French opponent, the

comte de Lally, for his lack of strategic vision when he failed to follow up his victory with an immediate march on Pondicherry while the French were demoralized and ill prepared to resist him. He preferred to spend another year reducing other forts in the Carnatic before finally closing in on the French capital.

On 9 March 1761, exercising his right as commander-in-chief of British forces in India, Coote sailed to Bengal with his regiment. He found that the council, Mir Jafar not having proved to their taste, had replaced him with his son-in-law Mir Kasim as nawab. Shortly after, Coote was sent up country to mediate in a dispute between Mir Kasim and his provincial chief at Patna. He failed in this, instead quarrelling with Mir Kasim over who should guard Patna's gates; diplomacy was never Coote's strong suit. Coote sailed for home in June 1762 and on the way married, on 8 July 1763, Susannah Hutchinson (d. 1812), universally admired daughter of the governor of St Helena. Back home in England, he bought an estate near Fordingbridge in Hampshire. In January 1764 a grateful East India Company presented him with a sword studded with diamonds and worth 700 guineas for his services in India, and in 1765 he was made a full colonel by the king. In 1768, in eighteenth-century fashion, he 'bought' himself one of the Leicester parliamentary seats, sitting for the constituency until 1774, when he transferred to Poole, nearer home, until 1780. He appears to have played little part in parliamentary affairs, presumably seeing his seat simply as a status symbol and patronage asset. He sided with the Laurence Sulivan clique against Clive's friends in the house in the great feud which raged among the East India Company's directors in these years.

In 1769 the directors reappointed Coote as their commander-in-chief in the east and to be associated with the three commissioners they hoped would reform their corrupt administrations in India. This visit was brief and unhappy for all concerned. With no wars to fight, Coote, his ego in high gear, created political mayhem at Madras and Calcutta. His three commissioner colleagues were lost on the voyage out, throwing Coote's surviving independent powers into question; his loosely worded commission as commander-in-chief led him to claim military independence from the civilian governors who traditionally held the same titles in their presidencies to assert ultimate civil control over the army. Outfaced by the civilians, Coote returned home overland via Aleppo in summer 1771. Warren Hastings wrote feelingly of Coote to the chairman of directors after this sorry episode: 'May success and Honor attend him in any other part of the world, but God forbid that he should ever return to any part of India' (Hastings to Laurence Sulivan, 10 Feb 1772, BL, Add. MS 29126, fol. 125). Coote, none the less, found favour in Britain when he was knighted on his return.

**Later career, 1773–1783** For five years (1773–8) Coote, with his new regiment the 27th foot, acted as commandant of Fort George in Scotland, where James Boswell and Samuel Johnson visited him on their famous tour and Boswell characterized him as a 'most gentleman-like man' (Sheppard, 103). Further promotions made him major-general in 1775 and lieutenant-general two years later. In 1778, with war in America and possibly with the French in India, Coote once again was given the command-in-chief of the king's and company's forces there. He arrived at Madras with his wife in the last week of 1778 and, after reviewing the military establishment, in March 1779 he sailed on to Bengal to join the company's new supreme government in the east. He was immediately plunged into an intense political conflict at Calcutta, where Hastings was now governor-general, but could not get his way on policy owing to a hostile majority of non-company British government appointees on the council led by Philip Francis. But Hastings still held considerable executive authority and ensured that Coote was given all the independence in the military department (with considerable patronage) he could desire. Hastings was probably pleasantly surprised that Coote, who had resolved to stay out of politics, restored Hastings's power by falling in with all his non-military proposals. The chagrined Francis bitterly railed: 'Coote is despised by all parties; his faculties—if he ever had any are gone' (ibid., 115).

A year later (October 1780) Coote was drawn down to the Carnatic once more to take command of the Madras army after the disaster it had suffered in August at the hands of Haidar Ali, the dynamic ruler of Mysore. He had invaded the province with a reputed 100,000 men the previous month and destroyed a large company detachment, while the main British force nearby disintegrated due to logistical collapse. Haidar was not able to take the major British-held forts in the province, but most of the smaller ones, garrisoned only by the nawab's troops, fell easily to him, and he asserted a stranglehold on the central Carnatic. Coote inherited a highly demoralized and greatly outnumbered army. His inadequate bullock supply for logistical support and lack of effective cavalry made it very difficult for him to venture far from the coast, where food was brought to him by sea. Even this supply route was unreliable owing to monsoon storms and with the arrival of a hostile French fleet which contested command of the coastal waters with a Royal Navy squadron.

In the circumstances it would have been remarkable if Coote, with a field force of 8500 men at first, had just managed to survive in the field, occasionally relieving the few British-held blockaded forts in the interior. These were, in fact, of no use to him as magazines for an extended campaign because they were too far apart to sustain his marches; they still had to be maintained, however, to ensure the political credibility of the nawab as effective ruler of the Carnatic and the military credibility of his British backer. And Coote did more. Haidar, despite having a much larger army but one much inferior in discipline and tactical control, had wisely adopted a policy of logistical attrition. His tens of thousands of light cavalry stripped the country of food around the British garrisons, threatened any supply columns which were not heavily protected, and made a desert around Coote's army when he tried to move it around. None the less, on four occasions Haidar allowed himself to be drawn into battle with Coote and was worsted each time. Arguably the action

Coote fought at Porto Novo on 1 July 1781 was his finest. His army was in a very tight position, hemmed in on the coast, almost bereft of supplies and outnumbered ten to one. After carefully reconnoitring the ground, under fire, Coote coolly marched across Haidar's front behind some low sandhills, pinned his centre with well-placed artillery on one of the hills, and launched an infantry assault on his left flank which drove the Mysorean host from the field. It was a manoeuvre reminiscent of, perhaps inspired by, Frederick the Great's outstanding battle at Leuthen in 1757. However, as on other occasions, Coote for want of cavalry and sufficient transport was unable to exploit Haidar's withdrawal by inflicting a destructive rout on him. Nevertheless, by simply remaining undefeated in the field, he denied Haidar any claim to be in control of the Carnatic.

Coote's inability to drive Haidar out of the Carnatic occasioned a prolonged and bitter dispute with the civilian governor of Madras, Lord Macartney, which, as in 1760, calls into question Coote's strategic judgement. Macartney was critical of his alleged indulgence to his officers and men in allowing them so many followers that they outnumbered the fighting men four to one, making his army difficult to sustain in the field. The governor went on to suggest a far bolder strategy than the soldier was willing to entertain, to wit to draw Haidar out of the Carnatic by attacking his supply bases as Haidar was theirs. Macartney wanted to split Coote's army into two, ignore Haidar's forces in the Carnatic, and attack Mysore from the east at two points, while an amphibious Bombay force landed on Haidar's Malabar Coast in the west. Dividing his force in the face of a vastly larger and fleeter enemy army was anathema to Coote. Besides, as a king's officer (Coote, unlike some of his other British army colleagues such as the great Stringer Lawrence, never switched to the company's service), he put a higher priority on destroying the small French force (but with possibly more to come) which had established itself with strong naval support on the Coromandel Coast, south of Pondicherry. Coote's imperious character, bolstered by powers given him by the supreme council at Calcutta to have a wide independence in conducting military operations, ensured that he had his way. His relations with the civilian Madras government were as bad as they had ever been with the company's authorities. He hardly ever freely consulted them, and railed at Madras constantly for its failure to keep him adequately supplied, even though, for a variety of political reasons and Haidar's effective strategy, it was impossible to do so.

**Death and reputation** The strategic dispute was never properly resolved because Coote, after a sojourn at Calcutta during the monsoon of 1782–3, trying to recover his health, shattered by dedicated toil in the field, died on 27 April 1783, shortly after his return to Madras. The war with France ended a few months later, Coote's dilatory successor, General James Stewart, having failed to take the French stronghold at Cuddalore before a truce intervened. And Macartney, now free of Coote, was able to bring Tipu Sultan, Haidar's successor, to terms later that year by carrying out his converging strategy of squeezing Mysore from two directions and because the Mysoreans were being threatened by their inveterate Indian enemy the Maratha confederation.

Coote's qualities as a general were considerable: brave and cool on the battlefield and a great tactician. His strategic ability may have been over-cautious and unimaginative, though critics probably underplayed the stress under which Coote and his armies, always ill supplied and outnumbered, laboured. Several observers believed his powers were in decline in the last two years of his life. Macartney characterized him at this period as 'soured by disappointment, grown old, impaired in health, jealous and fractious' (Wylly, 276). Beloved of his sepoys, Coote was exceptional in his time in his care for ordinary soldiers and his concern to mention them in dispatches when merited; his presence always significantly raised the army's morale. Coote's unflagging commitment to his duty to the end, as well as his choleric temperament, probably brought on the stroke which killed him. He hardly ever got on with his civilian colleagues, and he was certainly venal, though this was common at the time in British India. After his death he was buried in Madras, but later his wife took his body back to England for interment in the parish church of Rockbourne, near his estate, on 14 September 1784. The couple had no children, and on Lady Coote's death in 1812 the estate passed to his nephew, also Sir Eyre *Coote. Coote's portraits (one is in the National Portrait Gallery) depict in full life a tall, robust man with strong but ill-proportioned features. There is a monument to him symbolizing a winged victory figure in Westminster Abbey.

           G. J. BRYANT

**Sources** DNB · consultations of Madras select committee and Bengal select committee, 1755–83, BL OIOC · E. W. Sheppard, *Coote Bahadur: a life of Lieutenant-General Sir Eyre Coote* [1956] · H. C. Wylly, *A life of Sir Eyre Coote* (1922) · M. M. Drummond, 'Eyre, Coote', HoP, *Commons, 1754–90*

**Archives** BL OIOC, corresp. and papers, MSS Eur F 190 · BL OIOC, MSS Eur Orme, corresp. · BL OIOC, corresp. and papers relating to India, Home misc. series · BL OIOC, journal (microfilm), reel 606 · NAM, plans and journals · National Archives of India, New Delhi, official papers | BL, corresp. with Warren Hastings, Add. MSS 29117–29192, *passim* · BL, corresp. with Lord Macartney, Add. MSS 22439–22440, 22454 · BL, letters to Lord North, Add. MS 61865 · BL OIOC, corresp. with John Carnac, MSS Eur F 128 · Bodl. Oxf., corresp. with Lord Macartney, MSS Eng hist b 173–6, c 66–70, 110, *passim* · NL Scot., corresp. with James Stuart and papers · NRA, priv. coll., corresp. with Norman Macleod

**Likenesses** attrib. H. R. Morland, oils, c.1763, NPG [*see illus.*] · P. S. de Loutherbourg, group portrait, oils, 1802 (*The landing of British troops at Aboukir, 8 March 1801*), Scot. NPG · T. Hickey, oils, Government House, Madras · J. T. Seton, oils, BL OIOC · medallion (after J. Nollekens), BM · portrait, NPG; repro. in Sheppard, *Coote Bahadur* · portrait, Oriental Club, London; repro. in Sheppard, *Coote Bahadur* · statue; formerly at the India office, Whitehall

**Wealth at death** substantial estate: Sheppard, *Coote Bahadur*

**Coote, Eyre** (*bap.* 1759, *d.* 1823), army officer and colonial administrator, was baptized on 20 May 1759, the second son of Dr Charles Coote (*d.* 1796), of Shaen Castle, Queen's county, dean of Kilfenora, and his first wife, Grace (*d.* 1767), the daughter of Thomas Tilson and the widow of Thomas Cuffe. His elder brother, Charles Henry Coote

(1754–1823), was MP in the Irish parliament for Queen's county from 1776 to 1783 and from 1797 to 1801, and for Maryborough from 1783 to 1797, and sat for Queen's county at Westminster from 1801 to 1802, when he succeeded a distant cousin as second Baron Castle Coote; he was an ardent campaigner for the union of Great Britain and Ireland and a supporter of administration. His uncle was the army officer Sir Eyre *Coote (1726–1783). The family had substantial property in Queen's county.

Educated at Eton College between 1767 and 1771, Coote matriculated at Trinity College, Dublin, on 1 November 1774, but did not take a degree. He was commissioned ensign and lieutenant in the 37th regiment of foot in 1776, and immediately embarked for service in the American War of Independence, first participating in the battle of Brooklyn, in August 1776. He served through the subsequent middle colonies campaigns, and saw action at the battles of Brandywine (11 September 1777), Germantown (4 October 1777), and Monmouth Court House (28 June 1778) and expeditions to the Chesapeake and Rhode Island. He was promoted captain on 10 August 1778. Commanding a company of the 37th, he participated in the southern campaign (1780–81) under Charles Cornwallis, second Earl Cornwallis. Having been captured at Yorktown, Virginia (October 1781), he returned to Britain and advanced rapidly, becoming major of the 47th foot (1783) and lieutenant-colonel of the 70th (1788). On 9 November 1786, at St Marylebone, Coote married Sarah (*d.* 1795), the daughter of John Rodbard; they had three daughters, all of whom died before their father. In 1790 he became MP for Ballinakill and in 1797 he moved to Maryborough, but his military career was always his priority.

Coote's advance through the army was helped by his family's wealth, including the fortune amassed by his uncle Sir Eyre Coote, of whom he was the eventual heir, but it was his natural leadership ability, professional military skill, and tactical acumen that resulted in commands of increasing responsibility and complexity. As war with revolutionary France unfolded, Britain took advantage of French inability to defend her West Indian sugar islands. Under General Sir Charles Grey, Coote, promoted colonel on 24 January 1794, commanded the light infantry battalion. After arriving off Barbados on 6 January 1794, Grey commenced operations against French islands, among them Barbados and Martinique. Coote particularly distinguished himself in the assault on St Lucia on 2 April 1794. Assigned to storm a redoubt and two artillery batteries adjacent to the island's main fortification, Morne Fortuné, Coote's battalion took the French garrison by surprise using only bayonets, killing thirty enemy defenders with no British losses.

As a consequence of his service in the West Indies, Coote advanced rapidly. While participating in the disastrous allied Netherlands campaign of 1794–5, his brigade effectively covered the retreat from the Waal River, thus reducing potential allied losses in the face of a vigorous French counter-attack (10 January 1795). Coote was appointed aide-de-camp to King George III following a second West

Indies expedition under Sir Ralph Abercromby in 1795; the following year he was promoted brigadier-general and took command of the camp at Bandon, Ireland. On 1 January 1798 he was raised to major-general, and soon afterwards he was given command of Dover camp, the primary staging point for the British army's continental operations.

In 1798 Coote was placed in command of a 1400 man operational force with the task of destroying the locks at Saas in the Netherlands, thereby closing a new canal between Bruges and Ostend, through which troops and supplies intended for an invasion of Britain could easily move. Despite Admiralty concerns that led to minimal co-operation from the navy, the expedition accomplished the mission, but bad weather delayed re-embarkation as the troops gathered on the beach. Overwhelming French forces assaulted their defensive position. With Coote severely wounded, the second in command surrendered.

Following his exchange, Coote returned to Dover, but soon he commanded a brigade in the Helder expedition (August 1799). Despite his brigade's excellent performance at the battle of Bergen (19 September 1799), the enterprise ultimately failed. Commanding a brigade in Sir Ralph Abercromby's Egyptian expedition, Coote took part in the successful landing at Abu Qir (8 March 1801). Between April and August he besieged Alexandria with 6000 troops while the bulk of the army marched on Cairo. Though severely depleted by disease, Coote's force captured Fort Marabout (21 August), which led to the city's eventual capitulation.

Coote appears to have been a popular commander and highly successful in a subordinate role; however, Abercromby regarded him as ill-suited for overall field command. None the less, Coote received a knighthood of the Bath for his Egyptian service (19 May 1802) as well as the newly created order of the Crescent from the Turkish sultan, Selim III. The treaty of Amiens in 1802 halted his plans for a military expedition to South America. The same year he succeeded his brother as MP for Queen's county in the Westminster parliament. In the Commons he supported Henry Addington's administration, but advocated preparations for renewed conflict with France. He continued to support the ministry following Pitt the younger's return to power in 1804, but voted for the censure of Henry Dundas, Viscount Melville, in April 1805. On 25 October 1805 he married Katherine (d. 1821?), the daughter of John Bagwell, MP for co. Tipperary. They had one son.

That same year, promoted lieutenant-general, Coote commanded 7000 troops staged at Cork to reinforce either the West Indies or England, depending on French operations. Once the invasion threat subsided, in 1806 he was appointed lieutenant-governor and commander-in-chief in Jamaica, but he resigned in April 1808 because of deteriorating health. During this period he is said to have had a child with one of his slaves, Sally. The relationship was publicized in 1995 and again in 2001 when a descendant, United States army officer Colin Powell, became secretary of state. Assigned as second in command to John

Pitt, second earl of Chatham, for the Walcheren Island campaign commencing in July 1809, with tactical command of the army's left wing, Coote commanded the siege of Flushing while Chatham advanced on Antwerp. He was relieved in October, his troubling erratic, eccentric behaviour (credited to a tropical malady from his West Indian service) prevented any further military command, even though he was promoted general in 1814. That year he applied for a peerage in recognition of his and his uncle's military services, but he received only a GCB, on 2 January 1815.

Coote served as MP for Barnstaple from 1812—an opponent accused him of 'the most open bribery' (Fisher)—until the 1818 parliamentary dissolution. He spoke where he could apply his military experience, praising the contribution of Irish Catholic soldiers to Grey's expedition to the West Indies during the debates on Catholic relief in 1813, and opposing any attempt to reduce the authority of the East India Company in India. His political career was ended by controversy. On 25 November 1815 he was charged with indecent conduct before the lord mayor of London, having allegedly paid boys from Christ's Hospital to be flogged. The lord mayor dismissed the case, but the army commander-in-chief, Frederick, duke of York, convened a military inquiry on 18 April 1816. His friends argued that Coote was suffering from mental illness, the consequence of the Jamaican sun, the premature deaths of his daughters, and heredity, but the inquiry concluded that his eccentric behaviour had been unworthy of an officer and a gentleman, and not caused by mental illness. Coote was dismissed from the army despite the protestations of many prominent officers and degraded from the Order of the Bath in spite of his previous excellent service. No longer a knight or an officer, Coote continued to decline physically and mentally. He did not stand for parliament again, and lived abroad and at West Park, Hampshire, which he inherited in 1812, until his death, on 10 December 1823. Despite the sad disgrace of the general, the Coote family continued the tradition of parliamentary service; his only son, also Sir Eyre Coote (1806–1834), eventually served as MP for Clonmel. Coote's estate, according to the codicil to his will dated 17 September 1817, stood at more than £16,000, the bulk of which went to his son and heir.

STANLEY D. M. CARPENTER

**Sources** DNB · Burke, *Gen. GB* (1939) · Fortescue, *Brit. army*, vols. 4–7 · P. Mackesy, *British victory in Egypt, 1801: the end of Napoleon's conquest* (1995) · will, PRO, PROB 11/1682, sig. 138 · *The diary of Sir John Moore*, ed. J. F. Maurice, 2 vols. (1904) · E. Coote, transcripts of letters to Prince William of Gloucester, NAM, Acc. 8806–8828 · letter to Brownrigg, 16 March 1801, NAM, Abercromby MSS · *JHC*, 67–79 (1812–24) · P. A. Symonds, 'Coote, Sir Eyre', HoP, *Commons, 1790–1820* · R. A. Austen-Leigh, ed., *The Eton College register, 1753–1790* (1921) · Burtchaell & Sadleir, *Alum. Dubl.* · D. R. Fisher, 'Barnstaple', HoP, *Commons, 1790–1820*, 2.101–5 · *The Times* (16 Oct 1995) · *The Times* (23 Dec 2000)

**Archives** Hants. RO, corresp. · NAM, journal and MSS | BL, corresp. with Lord Chichester, etc., Add. MSS 33102–33105 · BL, corresp. with Lord Hardwicke, Add. MSS 35733–35763 · NAM, letters to duke of Gloucester · St Ant. Oxf., Middle East Centre, letters to duke of Gloucester

**Likenesses** A. Cardon, stipple, pubd 1805 (after W. Lodder), BM, NPG · H. R. Cook, engraving (after W. Lodder), repro. in *European Magazine*, 57 (1810), 243 · M. A. Shee, oils, NAM
**Wealth at death** over £1600: will, PRO, PROB 11/1682, sig. 138

**Coote, Henry Charles** (1815–1885), historian, was the son of Charles *Coote (*bap.* 1760, *d.* 1835), historian. He was admitted a proctor in Doctors' Commons in 1840, practised in the probate court for seventeen years, and, when that court was thrown open to the whole legal profession in 1857, became a solicitor. He wrote several books on professional legal subjects, including *Practices of the Ecclesiastical Courts* (1846) and *Practice of the High Court of Admiralty* (1860). He was best-known as a historian, however, and devoted much of his leisure to the study of early English history, folklore, and foreign literature. He frequently travelled to Italy, and was an accomplished linguist. He was a fellow of the Society of Antiquaries, a founder of the Folklore Society, and an industrious contributor to learned periodicals.

Coote's name was chiefly associated with his attempts to prove that the Roman settlers in Britain were not wiped out by the Germanic migrations of the fifth century, and that the laws and customs observed in Anglo-Saxon England were mainly of Roman origin. This theory was first advanced by Coote in articles published in the *Gentleman's Magazine*, and in 1864 the material was expanded into a small volume entitled *A Neglected Fact in English History*. Little attention was paid to Coote's researches until 1870, when E. A. Freeman fiercely attacked them in *Macmillan's Magazine*. Coote was stimulated to revise his work, and in 1878 he published a larger volume entitled *The Romans in Britain*. The importance of Coote's conclusions were acknowledged by Frederic Seebohm in his *English Village Community* (1883). Several papers on the same subject were contributed by Coote to the *Transactions of the London and Middlesex Archæological Society*. Coote's interpretation of the fall of Roman Britain and the creation of the Anglo-Saxon kingdoms was a small counterpoise to the then prevailing whig historiography, itself driven in part by contemporary liberal politics. The notion of continuity of institutions and ideas between the Roman and Germanic eras, though put in an extreme and over-simplified form by Coote, became one of the key concerns of research in the field in the later twentieth century.

Coote's last published work was a paper in the January 1885 issue of the *Folklore Quarterly Journal*, to which he was a very frequent contributor. Stricken with paralysis about 1882, he owed his partial recovery to the devoted nursing of his wife, Fanny Coote, but then died suddenly at his home, 13 Westgate Terrace, Redcliffe Square, West Brompton, London, on 4 January 1885. He was buried at Kensal Green on 10 January.

[ANON.], *rev.* NILANJANA BANERJI

**Sources** *The Athenaeum* (17 Jan 1885), 86 · *The Athenaeum* (24 Jan 1885), 122 · *CGPLA Eng. & Wales* (1885)
**Wealth at death** £5190 11s. 9d.: resworn probate, Nov 1885, *CGPLA Eng. & Wales*

**Coote, Holmes** (1817–1872), surgeon, was born in London on 10 November 1817, the second son of Richard Holmes Coote, a barrister of the court of chancery. He was educated at Westminster School, and at the age of sixteen was apprenticed to Sir William Lawrence, surgeon to St Bartholomew's Hospital. In 1845 Coote won a prize at the Royal College of Surgeons for his essay, 'On the anatomy of the fibres of the human brain, illustrated by the anatomy of the same parts in the lower vertebrata'. His first book, *The Homologies of the Human Skeleton* (1849), placed human anatomy in the context of the archetype skeleton of the naturalist Richard Owen. It was not a significant contribution.

As demonstrator of anatomy at St Bartholomew's medical school, Coote taught in the dissecting room until elected assistant surgeon in 1854. In 1863 he was elected full surgeon to the hospital. In 1855 the governors agreed to allow him to serve in the Crimean War as civil surgeon in charge of casualties at Smyrna. After returning from the war he published *A Report on some of the More Important Points in the Treatment of Syphilis* (1857). His experience in the Crimean War formed the basis for his interest in the problems of bones and the treatment of wounds, and he published several papers on bone and joint diseases and on the importance of careful management in the treatment of wounds in *St Bartholomew's Hospital Reports*. In 1867 he published a volume entitled *On Joint Diseases*. His published work did not break new ground and he was not an investigator of any calibre. His strengths were as a teacher and interpreter.

Tall and strongly built, Coote was reportedly kind to both colleagues and patients and enjoyed good food and company. He married twice. Coote never succeeded in establishing a very extensive practice and consequently was not well off. While only in his fifties he looked older than his years, and suffered from mental problems, including delusions of boundless wealth. He died from 'general paralysis of the insane' (syphilis) on 21 December 1872, while an in-patient of Blacklands House private lunatic asylum, Chelsea, London.

NORMAN MOORE, *rev.* STELLA BUTLER

**Sources** L. Holden, *St Bartholomew's Hospital Reports*, 9 (1873), xxxix–xliii · V. G. Plarr, *Plarr's Lives of the fellows of the Royal College of Surgeons of England*, rev. D'A. Power, 2 vols. (1930) · personal knowledge (1887) · d. cert.
**Likenesses** E. Edwards, photograph, 1868, Wellcome L.

**Coote, John** (1733/4–1808), bookseller and publisher, was born in Horsham, Sussex. Nothing is known of his parents, early life, or education. Probably in the latter half of 1757, Coote entered the London book trade as partner of John Cooke (1730/31–1810), bookseller. Cooke, who later specialized in publishing books in weekly numbers, was then publishing jest-books and chronicles of crime. According to newspaper advertisements, in 1756 Cooke's business was located at the King's Arms in Great Turnstile, Holborn, but by October 1757 Cooke and Coote had moved to the King's Arms without Temple Bar, opposite Devereux Court in the Strand (*Public Advertiser*, 6 Oct 1757); late in 1757 they moved near by to a shop opposite St Clement Danes in the Strand. The partnership lasted less than a year.

On 7 March 1758 John Coote married Jane Weaver in the church of St Clement Danes. About this time Coote established his own shop near St Paul's Cathedral, at the King's Arms (subsequently no. 16), Paternoster Row, on the north side of the street, near Queen's Head Passage. His former partner relocated next door, at Shakespeare's Head (no. 17). The Cootes had seven children, six of whom outlived their father. The first four were all baptized in the parish of St Faith under St Paul's. The eldest child was a son, Charles *Coote (*bap.* 1760, *d.* 1835), baptized on 4 September 1760, who became a historian and biographer. Three daughters followed: Mary, baptized on 8 July 1762; Elizabeth, baptized on 23 May 1764; and Catharine, baptized on 29 August 1766. Records of the other three children have not been located. Mary, who died in 1801, achieved some reputation as a miniature painter (*GM*).

Coote had ambitions as a playwright and songwriter. John Nichols described him as 'a facetious companion', and remembered that he wrote in rapid succession an opera and five farces but lacked 'that weight of interest which was requisite to bring them on the stage'; three, however, were printed (Nichols, *Lit. anecdotes*, 3.719). Soon after moving to Paternoster Row, Coote began publishing books and pamphlets. Among his earliest publications was Arthur Young's political pamphlet *The Theatre of the Present War in North America* (1758), for which Coote paid the author with books valued at £10 (Gazley, 7–8). Coote also continued his interest in the stage, publishing in 1758 *The Theatrical Review: for the Year 1757, and Beginning of 1758*. In May 1759 he was granted a royal licence to print the two-volume *New Geographical Dictionary* (1759–60), a work published in numbers. To produce it, he invested, in the conventional words of his licence petition, 'very great Labour and expence in purchasing Books in various languages, and employing learned and ingenious Men, to write and compile' (PRO, SP 36/142); newspaper advertisements claimed that the plates alone cost him £800. Coote also joined in publishing enterprises with other booksellers. For several years he worked closely with George Kearsly, with whom he published Tobias Smollett's novel *The Adventures of Sir Launcelot Greaves* in March 1762 (*London Chronicle*, 30 March–1 April 1762). Coote and Kearsly were both involved in publishing plays, including five editions of Samuel Foote's comedy *The Minor* in 1760 and 1761. Coote's success in the trade enabled him to acquire large shares of literary property. Thomas Mortimer's entry on Coote in *The Universal Directory* (1763) states that he purchases 'any valuable Manuscripts that are offered him; and is a Proprietor in several considerable Copies [copyrights]'. Coote later sold some of his copyright shares and stock: in 1767 he received £1000 for the copyright and approximately 180,000 printed numbers of Rider's Bible (1763–7), plus the 'Stretch' Bible, and in 1770 he received over £400 for seven-sixteenths of the copyright and seven-sixteenths of the remaining 12,766 volumes of Voltaire's *Works* (1761–70).

In April 1758 Coote began publishing the *Weekly Magazine, and Literary Review*, which survived for sixteen weeks. Then in May 1759 he petitioned for a royal licence to print the *Royal Magazine, or, Gentleman's Monthly Companion* (PRO, SP 36/142, fol. 54). This monthly magazine, which commenced publication in July 1759 and ran until December 1771, was Coote's first sustained effort in periodical proprietorship and publishing. Within a year, advertisements in newspapers were naming him as a publisher–proprietor of four of the twelve magazines then being published monthly in London, for example the *Daily Advertiser*. But ten years later he was deliberately hiding most of his proprietorships from public view. In 1770 Coote founded the *Lady's Magazine* and hired John Wheble to publish it. He then sold the periodical for £500 in 1771. Wheble's printed account of the subsequent July 1771 court trial concerning the right to publish the *Lady's Magazine* brought to light Coote's secret proprietorship of seven magazines. Wheble claimed that in 1771 Coote was controlling not only the *Royal Magazine*, but also the *Universal Museum*, *Court Miscellany*, *Oxford Magazine*, *Freeholder's Magazine*, *Court and City Magazine*, *Gentleman's Museum*, and *Every Man's Magazine*. As early as 1761 Coote had occasionally ordered articles to be duplicated concurrently in his magazines. This strategy eventually permitted him to oversee the simultaneous production of eight or more periodicals in varying stages of growth or decline. During cross-examination in the 1771 trial, Coote was asked why he had not used his own name in the imprint of the *Lady's Magazine*; he answered, 'I was then [1770] Publisher of several Magazines, and it is a conceived notion amongst people, that if they do publish three or four, they are made up one of the other' (*Lady's Magazine*, 1, July 1771, 47).

The exposure of Coote's proprietorships may have contributed to the collapse of his business. A commission of bankruptcy against him was sealed on 12 November 1772 (PRO, B 4/21). Coote left Paternoster Row, but he did recover from bankruptcy. His certificate was granted on 14 August 1773, and he paid dividends to creditors in June 1774 and July 1775. In 1775 or 1776 he returned to business on a smaller scale, opening a shop at 14 Red Lion Street, Clerkenwell. In 1777 he sold both the *Sentimental Magazine* and the *Monthly Miscellany* from those premises. That year he also published an edition of John Gay's *Fables* and a 'new edition' of Smollett's *Roderick Random*. In 1778 he brought out a 'new edition' of James Hervey's *Meditations and Contemplations*. The publication of the last three works suggests that Coote took advantage of the change in copyright law made in 1774 and began reprinting popular titles in an effort to increase his profit, but his new bookselling venture failed to flourish.

Little is known about Coote after 1778. Land tax records for Clerkenwell, Middlesex, dating only from 1780, reveal that he resided in Compton Street from 1780 to 1781 and in St John's Square from 1782 to 1787. Coote died in London on 20 October 1808 'in his 75th year', according to his obituary in the *Gentleman's Magazine*. He had outlived his wife and died intestate. Administration of his estate, valued at less than £100, was granted to his eldest son, Charles, on 28 April 1809. At the time of his death Coote was living in White Lion Street, Pentonville, in the parish of St James, Clerkenwell (LMA, DL/C/441). His name, however, does not appear in the register of burials for the parish.

In John Coote's obituary John Nichols wrote that 'His talents rose above mediocrity; and he evinced fertility in the invention of schemes, but did not possess sufficient steadiness or patience to carry them into effect, or beneficial execution' (*GM*). Nevertheless, for perhaps a dozen years, from 1759 to 1771, Coote was a familiar publisher on the London scene. His ambition to succeed in the book trade led him to hazard his money on promising new works that he probably commissioned, and on new periodicals. However, his decision to hide his proprietorships succeeded beyond his expectations: his name had become obscure even before his death.

BARBARA LANING FITZPATRICK

**Sources** G. E. Bentley, Jr., 'Copyright documents in the George Robinson archive: William Godwin and others, 1713–1820', *Studies in Bibliography*, 35 (1982), 67–110 · *DNB* · B. L. Fitzpatrick, 'Physical evidence for John Coote's eighteenth-century periodical proprietorships: the examples of Coote's *Royal Magazine* (1759–71) and Smollet's *British Magazine* (1760–67)', *Analytical and Enumerative Bibliography*, new ser., 11/3 (2000), 211–58 · J. G. Gazley, *The life of Arthur Young, 1741–1820* (Philadelphia, 1973) · *The poetical works of Charles Churchill*, ed. D. Grant (1956) · I. Maxted, *The London book trades, 1775–1800: a preliminary checklist of members* (1977) · Nichols, *Lit. anecdotes* · *GM*, 1st ser., 78 (1808), 1041 · H. R. Plomer and others, *A dictionary of the printers and booksellers who were at work in England, Scotland, and Ireland from 1726 to 1775* (1932) · G. Pollard, 'The early poems of George Crabbe and the *Lady's Magazine*', *Bodleian Library Record*, 5 (1954–6), 149–56 · *IGI* · PRO, SP 36/142; B 4/21 · LMA, DL/C/441

**Coote, Richard**, first earl of Bellamont (1636–1701), politician and colonial governor, was the only son of Richard Coote, Baron Coloony (1620–1683), landowner and Irish peer, and his wife, Mary (*d.* 1701), daughter of Sir George St George of Carrickdrumruske, co. Leitrim, and sister of the first Baron St George. Little is known of his early life. On 19 August 1680 Coote was licensed to marry Catherine (1665?–1738), daughter of Bridges Nanfan of Birtsmorton, Worcestershire. Upon the death of his father on 10 July 1683 Coote succeeded to the barony.

In 1687 Coote fled to the Netherlands and sought the patronage of William of Orange. For fleeing to William, King James had him attainted by the Irish parliament in May 1689. But he had cast his fortune well, and after the revolution of 1688 he was rewarded with the office of treasurer for Queen Mary II, the governorship of co. Leitrim, and 77,000 acres of forfeited land, and was made first earl of Bellamont on 2 November 1689. He had also become a friend of the whig junto, who were happy to see him installed in the House of Commons representing Droitwich in 1689. An ardent whig, he got into trouble in 1693 for attacking Lord Coningsby for corruption. Coningsby was a particular favourite of King William, so Bellamont lost his position in the royal household.

Coote was always in need of funds and preferment, and in 1695 the whig lords finally got William to assent to his being named governor of Massachusetts. When the salary was deemed insufficient, he was made governor of New York and New Hampshire as well. His financial condition also involved him in what proved to be a dangerous scheme. Robert Livingston, a New York merchant, and William Kidd, a celebrated pirate, put forward a scheme in 1695 that would be financed by Bellamont, Livingston, and the whig lords Shrewsbury, Somers, Orford, and Romney, and with the king a secret partner. The scheme was to have Kidd go out and capture the pirates who were bedevilling English trade and return with their booty to be processed outside the Admiralty courts to the benefit of the partners. Meanwhile, Bellamont immediately fell into the partisan politics of New York. The rebellion of Jacob Leisler at the time of the revolution of 1688 lingered, with vicious political infighting between the Leislerians and the anti-Leislerians. Bellamont tried to remain a friend to both sides but found himself allied with the Leislerians. Massachusetts offered no relief as he fought with the colony's leaders about trade regulation, his salary (which the legislature cut), and a new law against piracy.

The real danger to Bellamont's career, however, came from his relationship with Kidd. The latter had gone off to the Indian Ocean, where he committed piracy and consorted with pirates on the island of St Maries, just off Madagascar. His progress had enraged the East India Company, which conducted a campaign against him in England. What made this dangerous was that the whigs had lost power and the tories saw Kidd's actions as a way of embarrassing the whig junto that had supported him. The government sent out notices to the colonies in November 1698 ordering the arrest of Kidd, who was on his way back to North America. Bellamont was in Boston when Kidd gingerly sailed into New York, where his partner Robert Livingston brought him up to date. Kidd started to negotiate with Bellamont while sailing off Connecticut. Bellamont had to balance the fact that he was still in partnership with the whig lords and Kidd, versus his orders from the government to arrest him. Kidd arrived in Boston, where, after talking to him, Bellamont had him arrested. He then went on the hunt for the money and goods Kidd had been leaving with friends and relatives. Kidd and his recovered loot were sent to England, where he testified in the Commons about the partnership. He never gave the tories the evidence they wanted, and he was hanged for piracy after trial. Before Kidd was put to death Bellamont had died in Bowling Green, New York, on 5 March 1701. He was buried in New York; in 1790 his casket was placed in St Paul's churchyard, New York.

ROBERT C. RITCHIE

**Sources** L. H. Leder, *Robert Livingston, 1654–1728, and the politics of colonial New York* [1961] · J. D. Runcie, 'The problem of Anglo-American politics in Bellamont's New York', *William and Mary Quarterly*, 26 (1969), 191–217 · R. C. Ritchie, *Captain Kidd and the war against the pirates* (1986) · S. H. Friedelbaum, 'Bellamont: imperial administrator during the 17th century', PhD diss., University of Columbia, 1955 · P. U. Bonomi, *A factious people: politics and society in colonial New York* (1971) · R. C. Ritchie, *The duke's province: a study of New York politics and society, 1664–1691* (1977) · E. B. O'Callaghan and B. Fernow, eds. and trans., *Documents relative to the colonial history of the state of New York*, 15 vols. (1853–87) · E. B. O'Callaghan, ed., *The documentary history of the state of New York*, 4 vols. (1850–51) · J. R. Broadhead, *The history of the state of New York, 1609–91*, 2 vols. (New York, 1853) · B. Fernow, *Calendar of council minutes 1668–1783* (1902) · *CSP col.* · *DNB*

**Archives** BL, Add. MSS • Bodl. Oxf., letters to John Locke • Hunt. L., letters to Lord Bridgewater; Ellesmere & Blathwayt MSS • New York Historical Society, Bellamont MSS; de Peyster MSS • PRO, Colonial Office 5 (New York) • PRO, CO 324 • Surrey HC, letters to Lord Somers

**Wealth at death** probably in debt: will, proved 25 Feb 1705

**Cop** [Cope], **Michel** (*c*.1501–1566), religious author, mistakenly known as Michael Cope, was conjectured without conviction by Anthony Wood, who describes him as 'a zealous Calvinist of Geneva' (Wood, *Ath. Oxon.*, 1.192), to have been a member of the Oxfordshire family of Cope of Hanwell. The undoubted fact that two of his works, both of them religious and evangelical in character, were published in English in the mid-sixteenth century subsequently led to the understandable assumption that Cop must have been one of the colony of English protestants who sought refuge in Calvin's city during the reign of Mary Tudor. In fact Cop was the second of three sons of the distinguished physician Guillaume Cop, a native of Basel who migrated to France, where he obtained the prestigious position of king's physician. Two of Cop's sons, Michel and Nicolas, were soon drawn into the humanist–evangelical circle which flourished in the capital in the early 1530s. In 1534 Nicolas Cop, who had obtained the prestigious position of rector of the University of Paris, attained notoriety as the preacher of the famous sermon which, by injudicious support for views propounded by the reformers, caused a conservative backlash which engulfed many of the Paris evangelicals. Many were forced to flee, including Calvin and both the brothers Cop. Michel Cop repaired first to Basel, before moving, in 1545, to Geneva, where he was swiftly promoted to the ministry. He served as a minister, and a firm supporter of Calvin, until his death in 1566. An accomplished and urbane author, in 1556 he published his *Exposition sur les proverbes de Salomon*, and the following year his master work, *Le livre de l'Ecclésiaste, autrement dit le Prescheur*, swiftly also published in English translation as *A Faithful and Familiar Exposition of Ecclesiastes* (1557). The *Salomon* also enjoyed an English life, the printer Luke Harrison being licensed to print *An Exposition upon the Fyrste Chap. of the Proverbis of Salomon by Mygchell Coope* in 1564. In Geneva, Cop married one Ayma Waremberg; he was created a *bourgeois* of the city on 25 October 1554. He died on 18 September 1566.

ANDREW PETTEGREE

**Sources** C. H. Garrett, *The Marian exiles: a study in the origins of Elizabethan puritanism* (1938) • H. Heyer, *L'Eglise de Geneva, 1555–1909* (Nieuwkoop, 1974) • STC, 1475–1640, nos. 5723, 5723.5 • W. G. Naphy, *Calvin and the consolidation of the Genevan reformation* (1994) • St Andrews French sixteenth-century religious book project files [project in progress] • Wood, *Ath. Oxon.*, new edn, vol. 1

**Copcot, John** (*d.* 1590), college head, is said to have been born in Calais, a report given colour by the occasional appearance of his name in French forms, such as Copequot. He matriculated as a pensioner at Trinity College, Cambridge, on 16 November 1562, took up a scholarship there the following year, and was admitted to a fellowship in 1567. Copcot graduated BA in 1567 and MA in 1570. He was appointed a university preacher in 1576, and was awarded his BTh in 1577 and his doctorate in 1582. He acquired several ecclesiastical livings, including the rectory of St Dunstan-in-the-East in 1580 and that of Orwell, Cambridgeshire, in 1586; in that year also, on 4 August, he was installed as prebendary of Sidlesham, in the diocese of Chichester.

Copcot was a determined defender of the Church of England, preaching at Paul's Cross in 1584 against criticism of its liturgy and government which had appeared in Dudley Fenner's *Counter-Poyson*. In a published extract from this sermon, he is said to have cited the epistle to the Corinthians to prove that 'For lack of discipline, no man ought to depart from the church' (Fenner, no pagination). In 1586–7 he served as vice-chancellor of Cambridge University, despite his not holding a college mastership. Opposition to his forthright views undoubtedly reinforced the resentment occasioned by this breach of tradition. His appointment gave rise to an anomaly: within his own college Copcot was subject, as a fellow, to the discipline of its master, John Still, but outside its walls Still, like the other college heads, had to defer to the authority of the vice-chancellor.

Copcot proved eager to use his powers. Mutual jealousies and jurisdictional disputes had increasingly soured relations between town and university. When John Edmunds (alias Mere), the mayor of Cambridge, impounded some hogs belonging to the bailiff of Jesus College, the vice-chancellor and college heads acted to ban all dealings between him and members of the university. Copcot also sought to stem the tide of puritan radicalism, flowing strongly at this time, which had given rise to some alarming manifestations. In July 1587 he wrote to Lord Burghley, the chancellor of the university, about one Ralph Durdon of Pembroke College, whom he had imprisoned in the Tolbooth the previous November, and who remained there still, for he had circulated papers 'interpreting the Revelation of St John the Divine after his own fancy', and had 'named himself Elias, and being at liberty would be preaching very disorderly whither he could come' (*Masters' History*, 141). While vice-chancellor Copcot also became embroiled with the fellows of Christ's College in disputes arising from efforts to reform its lax finances, and to discipline the radical puritan Sampson Sheffield. Copcot sought to use the visitorial powers of the vice-chancellor to confront both problems, but the delaying powers of the fellows proved too strong. His attempt to continue his efforts beyond the tenure of his vice-chancellorship was in breach of the statutes, and led to a successful appeal to the chancellor, Lord Burghley.

It was nevertheless on the recommendation of Burghley that on 6 November 1587, Copcot was elected master of Corpus Christi College. His was a turbulent tenure, fully in keeping with his character and record, though other factors certainly contributed to the contentious atmosphere in Cambridge in the late 1580s. Perhaps the most notable dispute concerned Anthony Hickman, expelled in 1588 by the master and five of the eight fellows on the grounds that he was 'proud, idle, contentious, studied not, and condemned those that did'; but it was also reported that

Copcot and his party 'bore an ill will indeed to him, occasioned by his opposing the election of the said master this year' (Strype, *Annals*, 3/2.113). The legal case for expulsion seems to have been weak, for Hickman's appeal to Secretary Walsingham won the support of three college heads and several prominent civil lawyers. When enquiry was made as to the grounds of the expulsion, Copcot refused all explanation, asserting the right of the college to act independently in such matters. The case was then passed to Archbishop Whitgift, whose rejection of Hickman's case may have owed something to the fact that Copcot was then his chaplain. A further appeal, to Lord Burghley, was batted back to Whitgift, who remained obdurate. So did Copcot, for Hickman was not restored until 1591, under the new mastership of Jegon.

Despite his taste for political contention Copcot is said to have been 'not only a great proficient in and lover of literature himself, but an encourager of it in others' (*Masters' History*, 136), and 'a great critic in the Latin language' (Cooper, *Annals*, 2.94). To the library of Corpus Christi College he presented an edition of the works of Bellarmine. Copcot corresponded often with John Drusius, the scholar in classical languages, who recorded that he became emaciated through long hours of study. He died, probably in Cambridge, in early August 1590.                STEPHEN WRIGHT

**Sources** J. Strype, *Annals of the Reformation and establishment of religion … during Queen Elizabeth's happy reign*, new edn, 4 vols. (1824) • *Masters' History of the college of Corpus Christi and the Blessed Virgin Mary in the University of Cambridge*, ed. J. Lamb (1831) • Venn, *Alum. Cant.* • J. Strype, *The life and acts of John Whitgift*, new edn, 3 vols. (1822) • Cooper, *Ath. Cantab.* • *Fasti Angl., 1541–1857*, [Chichester] • C. H. Cooper and J. W. Cooper, *Annals of Cambridge*, 5 vols. (1842–1908) • D. Fenner, *A defence of the reasons of the Counter-poyson for maintenance of the eldership against an aunswere made to them by Doctor Copequot in a publike sermon* (1586)

**Cope, Alan** (d. 1578), Roman Catholic ecclesiastic, gave his origin as the diocese of London. He was educated at Magdalen College, Oxford; he matriculated in 1549, he received the degree of MA in 1552, and was unanimously chosen senior proctor of the university in 1558. He then studied civil law and graduated BCL in 1560, being 'esteemed for his great erudition' (Gillow, *Lit. biog. hist.*, 1.561). Some time after this, realizing that he would no longer be permitted to practise his Roman Catholic faith openly, he resigned his preferments and fled to Flanders. In 1561 his name appears, annotated as 'late scholar of Oxford', in a list of 'Recusants which are abroad and bounde to certayne places' signed by Bishop Grindal of London and others. He entered the university at Louvain, where he matriculated in 1563, and he was still known to be in Flanders in February 1570. In 1566 he allowed his name to appear as author of the Antwerp-published *Dialogi sex contra summi pontificatus*, an attack on Bishop Jewel and others that had, in fact, been written by Nicholas Harpsfield during his imprisonment in the Tower of London. This subterfuge was to avoid further aggravation of Harpsfield's situation in England.

By 1570 Cope was in Rome and was ordained to the diaconate in the Lateran basilica by Bishop Goldwell on 23

December. There remains no record of his priestly ordination. He continued his studies, gaining doctorates in divinity and canon law and in 1572 published at Louvain his *Syntax historiae evangelicae*—a life of Christ taken from the accounts of the evangelists. In 1576 he is listed for the first time as having rooms in the English Hospice, which was three years later to become the English College. In 1577 and 1578 he is also listed as one of the two *camerarii* ('councillors') of the hospice. Pope Gregory XIII appointed him a canon of St Peter's and his finances were further augmented by a pension of 40 florins a year provided by Jane, the English-born duchess of Feria. He died at Rome in 1578 and was buried in the chapel of the English Hospice. The exact date of his death is uncertain. The college celebrated his anniversary with an annual mass on 16 June, while the Douai diaries record receiving news of his death on 14 October. He left his books to the English Hospice in Rome, and a number of volumes inscribed with his name are still to be found on the shelves of the college's library. He is recorded as 'leaving behind him a most admirable exemplar of virtue, which many did endeavour to follow, but could not accomplish their desires' (Wood, *Ath. Oxon.*, 1.456).                PETER E. B. HARRIS

**Sources** G. Anstruther, *The seminary priests*, 1 (1969) • Gillow, *Lit. biog. hist.*, vol. 1 • P. Hughes, *The Reformation in England*, rev. edn, 3 vols. in 1 (1963) • *DNB* • A. Gasquet, *A history of the venerable English College, Rome* (1920) • D. A. Bellenger, ed., *English and Welsh priests, 1558–1800* (1984) • T. F. Knox and others, eds., *The first and second diaries of the English College, Douay* (1878) • Wood, *Ath. Oxon.*, new edn, 1.455–6

**Cope, Sir Alfred William** (1877–1954), civil servant, was born in Kennington, London, on 14 January 1877, the eldest of eleven children of Alfred Cope, bottle merchant, and his wife, Margaret Elizabeth Dallimore. He joined the civil service as a boy clerk in the customs and excise, the lowest possible rung of the Whitehall ladder in one of its least prestigious departments. In 1896 he became a customs detective, in 1908 he was made a preventive inspector, and soon afterwards he was placed in charge of investigations throughout the London area, pursuing smugglers and illicit distillers. Contemporaries said there was always something of the sleuth about him. Cope was, however, also a gifted administrator and organizer, and it was these attributes rather than his talent for clandestine work which saw his translation from the arcane world of customs and excise enforcement into the Whitehall mainstream. In 1919 he was appointed second secretary in the Ministry of Pensions, with the task of bringing order to a department on the verge of collapse. In itself this promotion was a remarkable achievement for a man of modest origins and limited education who had entered the civil service at the humblest rank. The magnitude of his Whitehall success was, however, destined largely to be forgotten because of the dramatic course of the last two years of his public service career, in which he became a key figure in the framing of the Anglo-Irish settlement of 1921–2.

Cope's ability and his unconventional background appealed to the powerful head of the civil service, Sir Warren Fisher. In May 1920 Fisher brought Cope as one of two assistants on an inspection of the Irish administration, which was showing signs of collapse under the pressures of the Anglo-Irish War. Fisher then advised Lloyd George to transfer a number of high-calibre Whitehall officials to Dublin, led by Sir John Anderson, in order to effect fundamental reform. Cope became an assistant under-secretary in Dublin Castle. His main task was to develop lines of communication to the Irish separatist leadership in order to explore possibilities for a settlement. He, Anderson, and other officials soon became convinced that the existing policy of thoroughgoing coercion of the separatist movement was futile, and that efforts should be made to reach an accommodation with Irish nationalism based on dominion home rule and protections for Unionist Ulster: they made their views plain to a meeting of cabinet ministers on 23 July 1920, although strains within the coalition government meant that their arguments were discounted.

Nevertheless, supported by Anderson, by Fisher, and by Lloyd George, Cope persisted in probing the possibilities for compromise even as the Anglo-Irish War intensified. He did this with zest, courage, and initiative, on occasion having to shake off British intelligence agents as he travelled to clandestine meetings. His Dublin Castle colleague Mark Sturgis kept a diary in which he paints a vivid picture of 'Andy' Cope's relentless hunt for a means of ending the Anglo-Irish conflict, sometimes infuriating the police and army in the process. Cope won the respect and confidence of the separatist leaders, and after playing a key role in the negotiation of the July 1921 truce he became the main point of liaison between the British government and the emerging twenty-six-county state. He also established, organized, and staffed the new Northern Ireland administration, and at one point in 1921 was believed to be London's choice for the crucial post of permanent secretary of the ministry of finance in Belfast. However, his views on policing sectarian conflict made him suspect in Ulster Unionist eyes, and the idea was dropped. An intense and excitable man, he worked tirelessly to bring the Anglo-Irish treaty of December 1921 to fruition, and in the tense days leading up to the outbreak of civil war in Dublin in June 1922 he ensured that the pro-treaty provisional government got the resources necessary to confront anti-treaty forces, and oversaw the arrangements for the final transfer of civil authority to the government of the Irish Free State.

Despite his high standing as a result of his achievements in Ireland, Cope chose not to return to the more sedate world of pensions administration in Whitehall. Instead he retired towards the end of 1922. He was appointed KCB, having been created CB in 1920. Cope then became general secretary of the National Liberal Party, but he found his hero Lloyd George a difficult employer and in 1924 he resigned. He played one further part in Anglo-Irish relations, giving private advice to the Irish government during the 1925 boundary commission crisis. He went into business as managing director of a group of collieries, where he experienced modest success before retiring in 1935. When war came in 1939 he briefly returned to Whitehall as a volunteer worker under his old chief Sir John Anderson, but soon stood aside. He died on 13 May 1954 at his home, 11 Westdown Road, Seaford, Sussex.                                    EUNAN O'HALPIN

**Sources** *DNB* · J. McColgan, *British policy and the Irish administration, 1920–22* (1983) · T. Jones, *Whitehall diary*, ed. K. Middlemas, 3 (1971) · E. O'Halpin, *Head of the civil service: a study of Sir Warren Fisher* (1989) · Sturgis diary, PRO, 30/59/1–4 · *CGPLA Eng. & Wales* (1954)
**Wealth at death** £25,295 10s. 5d.: probate, 3 Sept 1954, *CGPLA Eng. & Wales*

**Cope, Sir Anthony** (1486/7–1551), landowner and courtier, was the second recorded son of William Cope (*c.*1440–1513), cofferer to Henry VII, of Bedhampton, Hampshire, and Hanwell, Oxfordshire, and an unknown second wife. His father married three times, and Anthony had at least one elder half-brother, Stephen, one brother, and four younger stepsisters (one of whom became Stephen's wife) who were the daughters of William Cope's third wife, Johane Spencer. Anthony Cope was educated at Oxford, according to Wood, who speculates that he attended Oriel College; he does not appear to have graduated. He then travelled in Germany, France, and Italy, visiting various universities, acquiring considerable learning, and writing several books there. These may have included the translation of writings by Galen and Hippocrates that Erasmus refers to in 1516 as made by Cope.

Aged twenty-six on his father's death in 1513, Cope inherited the manor of Hanwell, near Banbury, and other property near by. He completed Hanwell Hall, the mansion that his father had begun there. Much of it was demolished in the late eighteenth century, but surviving portions and earlier drawings show that it was brick-built in the latest court style, two storeys high around a central courtyard, with towers at the corners. At an unknown date he married Jane, daughter of Matthew Crews, of Pynne, in Stoke English parish in Devon, and left one known son, Edward, and one daughter, Anne.

By 1530 Cope had prospered sufficiently, probably from extensive cattle farming, to secure from his elder half-brother Stephen renunciation of his remaining interest in the manor of Hardwick and other property in and around Banbury, and near by in Northamptonshire, and was able to establish himself as a significant gentleman in Oxfordshire. By 1531 he was on the commission of the peace there, and served on it regularly, as well as on the commission for gaol delivery. By about 1530 he was also escheator for Oxfordshire and Berkshire, and in that capacity was soon courting Thomas Cromwell in his correspondence, urging that the king had few friends in the shire, and offering to keep Cromwell's hawks for him. This led in June 1534 to the grant to himself and three others of the wardship of Sir William Spencer's heir, an undoubted source of profit. Later he vainly tried to gain the bishop of Lincoln's fee farm of Banbury by reporting the escape of convicts from the bishop's custody. However, he was one of the Oxfordshire commissioners for the *valor ecclesiasticus* in 1535, and in 1537 was summoned to bring twenty troops for suppressing the northern rising. His loyalty was undoubted, and had already been rewarded with the estates of Brooke Priory, Rutland, at the dissolution of the smaller monasteries: in 1538 he was recorded as having been receiving a fee from Kenilworth Abbey. Meanwhile he enclosed land. Bishop John Longland of Lincoln protested to Cromwell in 1539 that his tenants were wronged thus, and that Cope would not meet him privately to settle their dispute. He was able and willing to lend money and foreclose on the security, as the courtier Sir Ralph Langford lamented in 1543, apparently from the Fleet prison. He continued to rise in service and status in the shire, taking twelve foot soldiers in the vanguard to France in 1544.

By 1540 Cope was probably adopting protestant views. On 2 September he confronted the vicar of Banbury, John Pitt, before the privy council, and was commended for doing so. As the council told Cope to use his learning at the appropriate time and place, it would appear that the dispute had been theological, and his views somewhat reformed. He had become a courtier, and was one of the esquires in attendance at the magnificent gathering on Blackheath where Henry VIII met Anne of Cleves on 3 January 1541. When the king married Katherine Parr in July 1543, Cope became part of her household, as, successively, keeper of her hawks, vice-chamberlain, and ultimately chamberlain, in charge of thirty-eight people, a position he held until her death in September 1548. In 1544 he published *The Historie of Two of the Moste Noble Capitaines of the Worlde*, English lives of Hannibal and Scipio Africanus based on Livy and other Latin writers. Several times reprinted, it is dedicated to Henry VIII, and no doubt there is an element of flattery in the praise lavished on the king for his having subdued the Roman hydra. But *A Godly Meditacion upon XX Select … Psalms* of 1547, a new year's present written for the queen, shows a knowledge of the work of Calvin and Luther, referring to God's elect and just reprobation, and to Katherine's 'godly purpose in the reading and study of holy Scripture and the advancement of the true Word of God' (Cope, xxvii). Of sin he writes that 'remedy have we none, but to fly from Thy wrath into the bosom of Thy most dearly beloved SON JESUS CHRIST, making him a bulwark and a shield of defence between thine anger and our offences' (ibid., 12–13). Such language sounds truly evangelical, though since Edward VI was clearly about to succeed a degree of opportunism may also have been present.

Probably knighted at Edward's coronation Cope became a commissioner under the Chantries Act, and was sheriff of Oxfordshire and Berkshire for 1547–8. Thus in July 1547 he was deeply involved in the repression of the Oxfordshire revolt against enclosures and the more protestant policies of the new government, led by both craftsmen and conservative priests. He oversaw the hanging of some of the ringleaders, and the setting of their heads atop the highest buildings in their communities. He died, probably at Hanwell Hall, on 5 January 1551, and was buried in the chancel of Hanwell church. His wife, to whom he bequeathed £100 and an annuity of 100 marks, survived him.
ELIZABETH ALLEN

Sources LP Henry VIII, vols. 2/1, 5–8, 10, 11/2, 13/1, 14/2, 15–18/1, 19/1, 20/1, 21/1; addenda, 1 · DNB · A. Cope, Meditations on XX select psalms,
ed. W. H. Cope (1848) · *Visitations of Hampshire, 1575, 1623, and 1686, ex MSS Phillips* (1854), 16–17 · VCH Oxfordshire, 10.43, 45–6, 55, 97 · Hants. RO, 43M48, 102–6, 108, 126 · CSP dom., 1547–80, 126–7 · APC, 1547–50, 474 · J. R. H. Weaver, ed., *Some Oxfordshire wills*, Oxfordshire RS, 39 (1958), 47 · D. Loades, *The Tudor court* (1986), 67 · A. Beesley, *The history of Banbury* (1841), 194 · PRO, PROB 11/34, fols. 235r–235v · G. J. Armytage, ed., *The visitation of the county of Rutland in the year 1618–19*, Harleian Society, 3 (1870), 20 · *Oxfordshire*, Pevsner (1974), 632

Archives Hants. RO, papers
Wealth at death £100, and 100 marks annuity to widow: will, PRO, PROB 11/34, fols. 235r–235v; estate title deeds, Hants. RO; LP Henry VIII, 11/2, 209, 1536

**Cope, Sir Anthony, first baronet** (1548x50–1614), politician, was probably born at Hardwick Manor, near Banbury, Oxfordshire, the son of Edward Cope (d. 1557), gentleman farmer, and Elizabeth, his wife (d. 1587), daughter of Walter Mohun of Overstone and Wollaston, Northamptonshire. He was the second of four sons and three daughters who survived their father's early death. All were then under the joint guardianship of their mother and her father.

Beginning with Cope's grandfather and namesake, Sir Anthony *Cope, the family had been convinced protestants. On Elizabeth Cope's marriage in 1561 to her second husband, George *Carleton, a new and radical protestant influence affected Anthony. By 1571 he had inherited the family seat of Hanwell, Oxfordshire, from his elder brother, William, and, with business acumen, persuaded his two younger brothers to consider parting with their shares of property in Banbury in return for annuities, when of age. This was an early step in building up substantial property and lands in and around Banbury, and elsewhere in Oxfordshire, besides estates in Northamptonshire, Lincolnshire, and Surrey. At an unknown date he married Frances (d. 1599/1600), daughter of Rowland Lytton of Knebworth, Hertfordshire, with whom he had four sons and three daughters who survived until adulthood. The marriage of his daughter Elizabeth in 1603 to Richard Cecil, second son of the marquess of Exeter, shows his rise in status; and Cope played host to the earl of Leicester at Hanwell in August 1585.

In 1571 Cope began a parliamentary career which excluded only one parliament up to his death, at first as the MP for Banbury. In it he worked with a group of radical protestants including Peter Wentworth and George Carleton, combining defence of freedom of debate in the Commons (in 1581) with advocacy of further church reform. By 1586 he was deeply committed to presbyterianism, as is attested by his choice of John Dod as rector of Hanwell. Dod was invited to preach, and approved by the people and neighbouring ministers, in Presbyterian fashion, before settling as their minister. He often invited the presbyterian Thomas Cartwright to preach there. Cope was linked to the puritan synod held in early 1587 to further church reform. On 27 February, defying Elizabeth I's ban on parliament's discussing this, he proffered a bill to presbyterianize the Church of England, with a revised Geneva prayer book attached. The queen had both bill and book seized, and on 2 March Cope and other puritan MPs were imprisoned in the Tower of London. This marks the end of his conspicuous parliamentary activity in her reign.

However, Cope's friendships and political alliances were unaffected by his imprisonment. In August 1591 the privy council ordered Hanwell Hall to be searched for material which might have been intended to be moved in parliament, especially over the succession, because Peter Wentworth had been staying there. When the latter hoped for release from a consequent sojourn in the Tower, he named Cope as a friend he would like to dwell with. Cope continued to work locally for 'further reformation'. In 1589 he supported prominent Banbury puritans in suppressing May games in the hundred. He presented Robert Cleaver, a radical puritan, to the neighbouring parish of Drayton, and, as Cleaver stayed there after being deprived for non-subscription to the three articles of 1604, may have supported him. Cope resisted recognizing Dod's similar deprivation from Hanwell, so that he also remained in place. Robert Harris, unordained, came as preacher, and eventually succeeded Dod as rector, suggesting he was 'called' by the congregation like his predecessor. Cope probably found a niche for Dod with his cousin Sir Edward Cope at Canons Ashby, but ensured him a house in his will should he be driven out of his ministry.

Cope was increasingly involved in county affairs, serving as sheriff three times. He became a JP, and received special commissions from Elizabeth I. He was among those ordered to examine Lady Babington and others who had received the Jesuit Edmund Campion, and to search their homes for Roman Catholic material. In August 1592 he became the gaoler of those influential local recusants imprisoned in Banbury Castle. He guarded them vigilantly, but humanely. In 1596, when many were re-arrested, he economized by charging them board and lodging to pay their guards rather than paying it himself, leading to a prolonged rent strike. He was knighted late in 1592 or early 1593, and henceforth was periodically appointed a deputy lieutenant of Oxfordshire. By 1600 his standing was such that he was one of only seven Oxfordshire gentry selected by the queen to provide one armed horseman each to serve in Ireland, as 'of best abilitie [wealth] and of speciall note for their good mind and forwardnes to do her service' (APC, 1599–1600, 434–5, 438–9). On the death of his first wife he married, on 7 April 1600, Anne, née Paston (bap. 1553, d. 1637), widow first of Sir George Chaworth and then of Sir Nicholas Le Strange. His son and heir, William, subsequently married Elizabeth Chaworth, her daughter, thus consolidating both lands and relationships, as Anne had no children with Sir Anthony.

Cope was sufficiently wealthy and influential to entertain James I and Queen Anne for a night at Hanwell Hall in 1605, and the king arranged to return in August 1612. On 29 May 1611 Sir Anthony was created baronet. This meant he had a clear income of £1000 a year, and, according to John Chamberlain, cost £10,000. On Prince Henry's death in 1612 he was one of ten baronets chosen to carry black bannerols around the 'chariot' bearing the coffin. Since baronets were created to defend and better Ulster, Sir Anthony was granted 2000 acres at Dirribarde and Killarie, and acquired a further holding in co. Tyrone. A son built houses and a bawn for defence, but the buildings lacked settlers in Sir Anthony's lifetime. On a further 3000 acres at Derrycrevy and Dromullie, in co. Armagh, he had a fine castle built, apparently by English workmen who settled there; and a further 'plantation' was soon established. Thus he played an effective part in the protestantization of Ulster. Since he left all his Irish estates to his second son, Anthony, a Cope dynasty settled there.

As knight of the shire from 1604, in the 1606–7 session of James I's parliament Cope resumed campaigning on church matters—for the restoration of ministers deprived for non-subscription, for a preaching ministry, and for the reduction of the powers of the court of high commission. He argued that only legislation should control church practice. He helped draw up a petition to the king on ecclesiastical grievances, and was one of those who presented it. One of his last speeches, in May 1614, was on clerical non-residence, which he denounced with fire:

> Popery hath hatched up this Monster, which will eat out the very Bowels of the Church ... A Soul-murthering Non-resident is as dangerous to the Soul, as a Murtherer of the Body to it ... If we were upon our sick Bed, we would do otherwise than now.—Not to be satisfied with the Bill; but to petition the King that the Soules of his Subjects might be precious with him: and that the Parliament might not be dissolved till some Course [was] taken about this. (JHC, 482–3)

Cope was generally an active and respected MP, sitting on many committees for revising bills, and representing the Commons in learning the Lords' views on the union of England and Scotland in 1607. Then he also joined the senior committee of privileges. His radicalism led him to argue repeatedly that redress of grievances should precede voting of subsidies, as on 9 May 1606, when widespread support for this delayed the presentation of the subsidy bill to the Lords. He vigorously attacked Cowell's *Interpreter* on 24 February 1610, darkly suggesting that confederates, perhaps from overseas, were involved. Thus he advocated the rule of law against use of the royal prerogative.

Cope fell ill in June 1614 and died on 6 July, probably at Cope Castle, his brother Walter *Cope's mansion in Kensington, Middlesex. He was buried at Hanwell, Oxfordshire. The reputed portrait of him at Knole, Sevenoaks, Kent, postdates his death.

ELIZABETH ALLEN

**Sources** JHC, 1 (1547–1628) • J. E. Neale, *Elizabeth I and her parliaments*, 1: *1559–1581* (1953), 182, 413 • J. E. Neale, *Elizabeth I and her parliaments*, 2: *1584–1601* (1957), 148–9, 152, 157 • APC, *1581–2, 1586–7, 1591–3, 1596–1600* • CSP dom., *1581–90; 1595–7; 1611–18* • *Calendar of the manuscripts of the most hon. the marquis of Salisbury*, 4, HMC, 9 (1892), 295; 6 (1895), 58, 516; 7 (1899), 303–4; 10 (1904), 323; 11 (1906), 392 • CSP Ire., *1611–14* • CSP, *1603–24* [Carew] • Hants. RO, MSS 43M48/122 (1), 123, 126, 129, 132, 136, 148, 153, 156, 159, 168, 172, 206, 211, 214, 216, 219 • J. Nichols, *The progresses, processions, and magnificent festivities of King James I, his royal consort, family and court*, 1 (1828), 518; 2

(1828), 421–2, 451, 460, 498 · S. Clarke, *The lives of two and twenty eminent divines* (1660), 200–01 · S. Clarke, *A collection of the lives of ten eminent divines* (1662), 278–81 · A. Hughes, *List of sheriffs for England and Wales: from the earliest times to AD 1831*, PRO (1898), 109 · V. Sackville-West, *Knole* (1969), 18 · Hanwell parish register, 1586, Oxfordshire Archives · parish register, Bishopsgate, St Helen's, 7 April 1600, GL [marriage] · parish register, Paston, Norfolk RO · *Visitation of Hampshire ex MSS Phillips* (1854), 17 · memorial inscription of Sir Anthony Cope and his wives, Hanwell church · will, PRO, PROB 11/127, fols. 174v–175r · HoP, *Commons, 1558–1603* · record of Anthony Cope's livery, 28 May 1571, PRO, Ward 9/63, fols. 68–9 · S. Adams, ed., *Household accounts and disbursement books of Robert Dudley, earl of Leicester, 1558–1561, 1584–1586*, CS, 6 (1995), 293, 295

**Archives** Hants. RO, papers of the Copes of Bramshill, 43M48, 13M50, 2M55

**Likenesses** effigy, alabaster, Hanwell church · portrait? (posthumous), Knole, Kent

**Wealth at death** considerable: will, PRO, PROB 11/127, fols. 174v–175r

**Cope, Charles West** (1811–1890), history painter, was born on 28 July 1811 in Park Square, Leeds. His father, Charles Cope (d. 1827), painted landscapes in watercolour; his mother was said to be a gifted amateur in the same medium. They named their children after eminent artists whom the father knew personally: Ellen Turner after J. M. W. Turner; Charles West, about a year younger, after Benjamin West. Charles's mother died soon after his birth, and the boy was sent for two or three years to foster parents at Woodhouse Moor and then to London. He attended a boarding-school in Camberwell Grove and lived with an aunt during the holidays.

From 1818 to 1827, Cope passed through a painful period. Bullies at Mr Terry's school in Great Marlow subjected him to a prank that broke his elbow and left him with a permanently crooked left arm; in the grammar school at Leeds a severe master treated all the boys as hopeless dunces. The widowed father encouraged his son as best he could: he took him on an excursion to Teesdale, where the boy picked up a lifelong passion for fly-fishing; and he urged him to develop his artistic talent. At sixteen, with his father's support, Cope entered Henry Sass's academy of art in Bloomsbury. In 1827 his father died after a stagecoach accident, and Sass consented to administer the estate and act as guardian to Charles and Ellen.

**Early artistic experience** Cope worked hard at drawing and in 1828 gained admittance to the Royal Academy Schools. He won a silver medal (1829) at the Society of Arts and a second medal (1831) at the academy's life school. With awakening inquisitiveness, he read widely and in 1832 travelled to Paris, where he studied the paintings in the Louvre. In 1833 he exhibited for the first time at the Royal Academy *The Golden Age*, which was not sold. On the advice of William Hilton, then keeper of the schools, he set out in September 1833 for Italy; he stayed for nearly two years, examining the pictures in galleries and churches. He spent six months at Rome and as many at Florence; he travelled widely, as far south as Naples looking with special attention at frescoes and observing at close hand an eruption of Vesuvius. Of his many new acquaintances—Italian, German, English—one, the painter William Boxall, became a good friend.

Charles West Cope (1811–1890), self-portrait, 1879

On returning to London, Cope lodged in Russell Place, Fitzroy Square, and painted *Paolo and Francesca* (exh. RA, 1837), which was sold to the Art Union, and *Osteria di campagna between Rome and Ancona* (exh. RA, 1838), sold for 150 guineas and given in 1878 to the Walker Art Gallery, Liverpool. The *Osteria*, with about twenty figures—*vettura* travellers at their repast and German students in the background—attracted attention to a 'new man'. Cope joined the Etching Club as an original member; the etchers, most of them future Royal Academicians, experimented with the medium, discussed their plates, sold a few, and enjoyed simple suppers together. Cope and Richard Redgrave formed a close friendship; other particular friends—non-members of the club—included John Sheepshanks, known to Cope since boyhood as a benevolent patron of living artists, and the portrait painter George Richmond. Cope moved from Russell Place to a spacious room built for B. R. Haydon off Lisson Grove and painted there a large altarpiece (exh. RA, 1840) for presentation to the new St George's Church at Little Woodhouse, Leeds. This work won a prize of 50 guineas at Liverpool.

On a fishing expedition to Greta Bridge and the valley of the Tees, Cope met at a friend's house a young lady named Charlotte Benning (d. 1868): the two fell in love. Her father, a busy country surgeon, showed sympathetic understanding; her stepmother insisted, however, on evidence that the young artist was respectable. In spite of her misgivings, the Bennings made plans for the wedding; on 1 September 1840 Charles and Charlotte were married, with Richard Redgrave as best man. There was a last-minute contretemps: the bridegroom forgot to bring the ring to church, and Redgrave had to run and fetch it from the inn. The happy couple drove away 'amid acclamations'; but Mrs Benning, tearfully hugging the bride, exclaimed, 'Oh, you poor victim!' (Cope, 143).

The couple proceeded first to London and then to the house of friends near Staines. Cope attended a meeting of the local Board of Guardians, of which their host was chairman, and began a painting entitled *Poor Law Guardians, Board-Day Application for Bread* (exh. RA, 1841). The contemporary subject drew attention, notably in *The Times*; but the picture was not sold: 'Abundant praise', Cope recalled, 'but no solid pudding' (Cope, 143). Two years later it went for 100 guineas to the holder of an Art Union prize. In 1841 Cope repeated for Lord Lansdowne a *Mother and Child* first painted at Florence in 1834 and sold to William Beckford; and the Copes, with their own first child, a son named Charles, moved into a new house in Hyde Park Gate, next door to Richard Redgrave.

**Work for the houses of parliament** The year 1841 was marked also by an event that affected Cope's career for the ensuing twenty-five years: the establishment of the Royal Fine Arts Commission, with Prince Albert as president and Charles Lock Eastlake, later Sir Charles, as secretary. Sir Robert Peel, the initiating force, stated the purpose: 'Investigation whether the Construction of the new Houses of Parliament can be taken advantage of for the encouragement of British Art' (Peel to Queen Victoria, 12 Oct 1841, BL, Add. MS 40432). In April 1842 the commission announced its first competition for artists, inviting cartoons in chalk or the like, uncoloured, for frescoes based upon subjects chosen from English history or from the works of Spenser, Shakespeare, or Milton. Cope submitted *The First Trial by Jury*, one of 141 cartoons in the Westminster Hall exhibition of 1843; and the judges awarded to him one of the three highest premiums of £300. In this year he was elected an associate of the Royal Academy.

To the competition in 1844, for painters in fresco, with free choice of subject matter, Cope sent *The Meeting of Jacob and Rachel*, and he was one of the six artists selected to prepare designs for six arched compartments in the House of Lords. His subject, announced in July, was *Edward the Black Prince Receiving the Order of the Garter from Edward III*. Cope began his sketches, but on 30 September informed Eastlake of a worrying predicament: Sir Harris Nicolas, historian of the orders of knighthood, declared 'positively that no such thing ever did occur, and that it is an historical absurdity' (BL, Add. MS 40452). Eastlake circulated copies of Cope's letter. Peel hardly knew what to say, at first; he would see the prince, and meanwhile recommended consultation with the three historian-commissioners—Henry Hallam, T. B. Macaulay, and Lord Mahon—who failed to respond promptly. Eastlake nudged Peel, and Peel came to a decision: the investiture *might* have occurred. Prince Albert agreed that it was not 'an historical absurdity'. Cope resumed his sketching, and the finished work was eventually ready for the opening of parliament in 1847. The artist was elected a Royal Academician in 1848 and a member of the Athenaeum in 1849. When Redgrave's sketches for another compartment

were judged unacceptable, the subject was reassigned to Cope, who completed *Prince Henry, Later Henry V, Acknowledging the Authority of Chief Justice Gascoigne* in 1849.

Cope now took up an assignment in the Upper Waiting Hall. The commission had announced the plan in 1845: at £400 each, eight frescoes based on works by English poets. The first list included Chaucer, Spenser, Shakespeare, Milton, Dryden, and Pope. Chaucer was assigned to Cope; Milton, to John Callcott Horsley. Both artists saw the need for further knowledge of fresco-painting; and in 1849 they spent about three months on the continent, studying works by Giotto and other *frescanti*, ancient and modern. At Florence, Cope met William Dyce, travelling with the same purpose. At Munich he admired the frescoes of Heinrich Hess in the new basilica of St Boniface and conferred twice about the technique of fresco with Hess himself, professor of painting and director of all the art collections in the city.

For the 'Poets' Hall', Cope chose to execute in fresco *Griselda's First Trial of Patience*, based on the Clerk's Tale and completed in 1852. The commission added Scott and Byron to the list of poets and offered the Byronic subject to Cope; he finished *The Death of Lara* in 1854. By that time the poetical frescoes had begun to suffer ruinously from blisters caused by damp and dirt; the colours were dropping away as dust. 'I feel how much of life', Cope said in his *Reminiscences*, 'has been wasted in, as it were, writing in the sand' (Cope, 257).

Cope faced yet another assignment: by 1847 the commission had planned for the peers' corridor eight illustrations of 'the virtues and heroism of some of the actors in the great Civil War, four of them on the Royalist side, and four on that of the Parliament' (Cope, 255). By 1853, however, none of the several aspirants had produced acceptable sketches. Eastlake enquired whether Cope would submit a sketch, with the understanding that, if it proved satisfactory, he might be employed to paint the whole series. Cope sketched *The Embarkation of a Puritan Family for New England*. The commissioners approved, and Cope agreed to terms paralleling those for E. M. Ward's complementary series in the commons' corridor: £600 for each of eight frescoes in portable slate-backed frames. The Copes saw *The Embarkation* safely installed in October 1856 before going on a celebratory shopping spree. His work for the peers' corridor continued for a decade: in 1857 he finished *The Burial of Charles I*; in 1859 *The Parting of Lord and Lady William Russell*; in 1861 *Charles I Erecting his Standard at Nottingham*; in 1862 *Basing House Defended by the Cavaliers*; in 1864 *The Expulsion of the Fellows of a College at Oxford for Refusing to Sign the Covenant*; in 1865 *The Setting out of the Train Bands to Raise the Siege of Gloucester*; and finally, in 1866, *Speaker Lenthall Asserting the Privileges of the Commons Against Charles I*. They have been described as 'supreme achievements of the Victorian vision of the British past, brilliant recreations of lost moments of time within the Artist-Antiquarian tradition' (Strong, 141).

**Other activities** 'I had little time left for oil-painting', Cope wrote in his *Reminiscences*, 'and what I did execute consisted mostly of small pictures of a domestic character, done from my own children, so that Mr Tom Taylor in his criticisms dubbed me "Poet Laureate of the Nursery"' (Cope, 157). The numerous examples of such works include *The Young Mother* (exh. RA, 1846) and *Mother and Child* (exh. RA, 1853), both bought by Sheepshanks and now in the Victoria and Albert Museum, London. But Cope still painted historical scenes, including the reception of Cardinal Wolsey in 1530 at Leicester Abbey (exh. RA, 1848), commissioned by the prince consort and placed in Osborne House; the martyrdom of Laurence Saunders in 1555 (exh. RA, 1851); and Princess Elizabeth lying dead in 1650 at Carisbrooke Castle (exh. RA, 1855).

Cope also showed two oil versions of his fresco subjects: *The Embarkation* (exh. RA, 1856), sold in 1864 to the National Gallery of Victoria, Melbourne, and *Lord and Lady William Russell* (exh. RA, 1861). From Shakespeare he drew several subjects: *King Lear and Cordelia* (exh. RA, 1850), for I. K. Brunel's Shakespeare room; *Othello Relating his Adventures* (exh. RA, 1851) and *Cordelia Receiving the News of her Father's Ill-Treatment* (exh. RA, 1859). Five Copes, including three from the Sheepshanks collection, went to Paris for the Universal Exhibition in 1855, and five reappeared among the art treasures at Manchester in 1857.

Cope found time to go fishing with Mark Pattison, but he was increasingly busy at the academy. He had served on the council and the committee of arrangement. In 1863 he appeared as a witness before the Royal Academy commission; in 1866 he was elected to the professorship of painting, a post which he held until 1875. On 28 July 1868 he suffered a grievous blow, the death of his beloved Charlotte, mother of his ten children. With his son, Charles, and his wife, he made a brief trip to Belgium for a change of scene, but 'Work alone', he recalled, 'could divert my thoughts' (Cope, 269). He sent three pictures to the academy in 1869, and he accepted appointment in 1870 as examiner in painting at the schools of art in South Kensington.

During the 1870s Cope completed two paintings destined for institutions: *Mr Guy and Dr Mead Considering the Architect's Plans for the Proposed New Hospital* (exh. RA, 1871), presented to Guy's Hospital; and *The Council of the Royal Academy—Selection of Pictures* (exh. RA, 1876), placed in the academy. In 1876 he travelled to the United States to represent the academy at the centennial exposition in Philadelphia, and chaired the international committee that judged paintings and awarded medals. In 1879 he left his house in Hyde Park Gate and stayed first with his daughter, Margaret, in Herefordshire. Then he went to Charles and his wife at Maplestead, Essex, and there met Eleanor Smart, an old family friend and sister of a former pupil. 'She took pity', Cope said, 'on my solitude' (Cope, 335). They were married on 19 November 1879 at Barnet, with Charles and the bride's brother officiating, and soon settled in a house at Maidenhead.

**Death and assessment** Cope sent his last pictures to the Royal Academy in 1882 and became in 1883 an honorary retired member; but he continued to go up to London for varnishing days and liked to arrange large family gatherings, with lunch, for the private views. At Maidenhead he amused himself by painting, bicycling about the countryside with a sketchbook, and going on the river. After a brief illness he died on 21 August 1890 at Bournemouth, with his wife and four of his children at his side. Several of the ten children had predeceased him. The eldest survivor, the Revd Charles Henry Cope, edited and completed *Reminiscences of Charles West Cope* (1891), adding a chronological list of paintings, some letters (1843–4) about work on *Edward the Black Prince*, the evidence given before the Royal Academy commission (1863), and a version of his father's report to the Royal Academy (1876) on his experiences at Philadelphia. The third son, Arthur Stockdale Cope, followed his father into the Royal Academy and the Athenaeum.

Charles West Cope was a highly proficient artist and a worthy academician: he had a good eye, drew well, and learned all that he then could about various techniques, especially fresco. The critics generally, although at times impressed by his accomplishments or touched by his tender domestic scenes, discerned no remarkable flair and no compelling reason to extol him. John Ruskin, for example, had little more to say about Cope's picture of Princess Elizabeth lying dead than that it was a 'very beautiful and well-chosen subject, not ill painted' (Ruskin, 20). On the other hand, Prince Albert and Sir Charles Eastlake recognized Cope's strengths—his talent for dramatic narrative in a lucid and monumental style which was virtually an English reinvention of Italian Renaissance fresco—and many artists had warm professional and personal regard for him. Daniel Maclise, fellow painter of frescoes in the new houses of parliament, wrote in 1849 that Cope's cartoon of Prince Henry and Chief Justice Gascoigne was 'learnedly drawn and practically designed, and suited admirably for the monumental character of fresco art' (O'Driscoll, 98). The words come close to predicting why, in the national memory, Cope's most important works would be his frescoes in the House of Lords and the peers' corridor.　　DAVID ROBERTSON

**Sources** C. H. Cope, *Reminiscences of Charles West Cope* (1891) • *DNB* • D. Robertson, *Sir Charles Eastlake and the Victorian art world* (1978) • T. S. R. Boase, 'The decoration of the new Palace of Westminster, 1841–1863', *Journal of the Warburg and Courtauld Institutes*, 17 (1954), 319–58 • R. J. B. Walker, *A catalogue of paintings, drawings, sculpture and engravings in the palace of Westminster*, 4 vols. (1959–62) • S. C. Hutchison, *The history of the Royal Academy, 1768–1986*, 2nd edn (1986) • F. M. Redgrave, *Richard Redgrave, C.B., R.A.* (1891) • J. C. Horsley, *Recollections of a Royal Academician* (1903) • W. J. O'Driscoll, *A memoir of Daniel Maclise* (1871) • J. Ruskin, *Notes on some of the principal pictures exhibited in the rooms of the Royal Academy*, 3rd edn (1855) • G. Scharf, *Art treasures of the United Kingdom* (1857) • F. T. Roberts and F. Hicklin, eds., *Summary catalogue of British paintings: Victoria & Albert Museum* (1973) [catalogue, V&A] • *The taste of yesterday: an exhibition of paintings and sculpture from the gallery's reserve collection, Walker Art Gallery* (1970) [exhibition catalogue, Walker Art Gallery, Liverpool, 1970] • R. Strong, *Recreating the past: British history and the Victorian painter* (1978) • *CGPLA Eng. & Wales* (1890)

**Archives** RA, minutes of the council and of the general assembly • V&A, MSS, English 86.0.8

**Likenesses** W. L. Price, photograph, albumen print, c.1857, priv. coll.; repro. in J. Maas, *The Victorian art world in photographs* (1984) • C. W. Cope, self-portrait, oils, 1879, NPG [see illus.] • A. S. Cope, oils, 1884, Aberdeen Art Gallery • Done and Ball, photograph (in later life), repro. in Cope, *Reminiscences*, frontispiece · R. Redgrave, watercolour drawing, V&A · Sem [G. Goursat], caricature, watercolour drawing, AM Oxf. · J. & C. Watkins, carte-de-visite, NPG · cartes-de-visite, NPG

**Wealth at death** £28,230 8s. 6d.: probate, 7 Oct 1890, *CGPLA Eng. & Wales*

**Cope, Edward Meredith** (1818–1873), classical scholar, was born on 28 July 1818 in Birmingham. He first went to school in Ludlow, but then moved to Shrewsbury, where his headmasters were Samuel Butler and B. H. Kennedy. Cope entered Trinity College, Cambridge, in 1837. He was elected a scholar in 1839 and won the Porson prize in the same year. He graduated BA (first classic) in 1841 and MA in 1844. In 1842 he was elected a fellow of Trinity, becoming a tutor and lecturer in Greek in 1845. He was a proctor in 1859. He was ordained deacon in 1848 and priest in 1850, but although he regularly assisted various Cambridge contemporaries with their parish duties, he found the work of the educational clergy more congenial than that of the parochial.

At Trinity, Cope was a conscientious and respected lecturer. His main subjects were the Greek tragedians, historians, and orators, although in later years he lectured regularly on Plato and Aristotle. His learning and industry were notable, but, as he confessed to friends, he found it impossible to rewrite material once he had made up his mind on a topic, and this led to a certain diffuseness and lack of clarity in his work.

In the vacations Cope was an indefatigable traveller with an excellent knowledge of European languages. He regularly spent the summer walking in the Alps, and kept extensive and detailed vacation journals which remain unpublished.

In 1854 and 1855 Cope contributed articles to the first two volumes of the *Journal of Philology* criticizing Grote's views on the sophists in his *History of Greece*. Notes and corrections by Cope were included by Grote in a later volume. In 1864 he published a literal translation of Plato's *Gorgias*, and a similar version of the *Phaedo* was edited after his death by H. Jackson.

Cope's most important works were on Aristotle's *Rhetoric*. He published an introduction in 1867, and an edition with an extensive commentary was completed by J. E. Sandys and published in 1877. This edition is unusual for its time in the detail of its explanatory notes, which include frequent translations. Cope carefully relates the ideas of the *Rhetoric* to other passages in Aristotle and to later writers on the subject, from whom he quotes extensively. His work remains one of the chief sources of information on ancient rhetoric after more than a century.

In 1867 Cope was a candidate for the professorship of Greek at Cambridge; the votes of the electors were divided and as the vice-chancellor and the master of Trinity, on whom the election then devolved, differed, the appointment lapsed to the chancellor, who gave the chair to B. H. Kennedy. There is no doubt that his disappointment on this occasion preyed on Cope's mind, and was one of the causes of the acute mental illness which led to

his retirement in 1869. His mind gave way and he died, unmarried, at Ticehurst, Sussex, on 4 August 1873, and was buried on 14 August in Birmingham.

H. R. LUARD, *rev.* RICHARD SMAIL

**Sources** H. A. J. Munro, 'Edward Meredith Cope', *The Rhetoric of Aristotle*, ed. E. M. Cope and J. E. Sandys, 1 (1877), xiii–xx · Venn, *Alum. Cant.* · *CGPLA Eng. & Wales* (1873)

**Wealth at death** under £30,000: probate, 7 Oct 1873, *CGPLA Eng. & Wales*

**Cope, Sir John** [Jonathan] (1690–1760), army officer, was the only son of Lieutenant-Colonel Henry Cope (*b.* 1645), of Icomb, Gloucestershire, a retired army officer, and Dorothy Waller, the widow of an excise man. John (or Jonathan) Cope was disinherited owing to the disapproval of his grandfather William Cope of Henry Cope's choice of wife; after attending Westminster School he was therefore obliged to make his own way in the world. Cope responded to this challenge with spectacular success. In 1706, during the War of the Spanish Succession, he was appointed page to Thomas Wentworth, third Baron Raby, Queen Anne's ambassador at Berlin. Raby was colonel of the Royal regiment of dragoons, in which he obtained Cope a cornet's commission on 14 March 1707. Upon joining his regiment in Spain, Cope made a favourable impression and in June 1708 was invited to serve as aide-de-camp to Major-General James Stanhope, the commander-in-chief. Stanhope's patronage ensured that Cope thereafter enjoyed accelerated promotion. In October 1710 Cope secured a captaincy in the 3rd foot guards—an appointment that carried the army rank of lieutenant-colonel. By the war's close in 1713 Cope was brevet colonel of Wynne's foot, outranking many officers with longer service.

On 16 December 1712, at St Anne and St Agnes, Aldersgate, London, Cope cemented his social position by marrying Jane Duncombe, sister of Anthony Duncombe, later first Baron Feversham, and niece of the former lord mayor of London Sir Charles Duncombe. In 1722 Cope entered parliament as MP for Queenborough. He later represented Liskeard (1727–34) and Orford (1738–41), voting consistently in support of Walpole's administration. He may have been the John Cope who married Elizabeth Waple at St Anne and St Agnes on 31 August 1736; if so, his first wife was dead by this date.

During these years of peace Cope's army career continued to prosper. In June 1737 he secured the colonelcy of the regiment that subsequently became the 9th dragoons; he was colonel of the 7th dragoons from 1741 until his death. He was promoted to brigadier-general in 1735; appointment to major-general followed four years later. By 1743, after Britain intervened in the War of the Austrian Succession, Cope ranked as lieutenant-general. Despite his enduring reputation as a cowardly incompetent, described by one critic as 'a little, dressy, finical man' (*Memoirs*, 179), Cope played a creditable role in the ensuing German campaign. That June he prevented the capture of the British contingent's commander, John Dalrymple, second earl of Stair, after his escort was surprised by enemy hussars. Cope's gallant conduct was noted by James Wolfe, the future conqueror of Quebec, in a letter to his father of 21 June 1743. Cope participated in the defeat of the French at Dettingen, and in the subsequent mood of euphoria was created a knight of the Bath.

Upon the outbreak of the 1745 rising, Cope commanded in Scotland. Although his regular troops were scarce and of poor quality, he was persuaded to advance into the highlands and confront Charles Edward Stuart without delay. Having concentrated his forces at Stirling, he marched for Fort Augustus. On hearing that the Jacobites intended to defend the perilous Corrieyairack Pass, on 26 August Cope called a council of war and accepted its recommendation to head for Inverness instead. Though understandable, Cope's decision was heavily criticized as it allowed the Jacobites to capture Edinburgh. It was reported that this 'false step' led the delighted Young Pretender to drink Cope's health and exclaim: 'if all the Usurper's Generals follow his Example, I shall soon be at St. James's' (Henderson, 34–5). Naval transports rendezvoused with Cope's troops at Aberdeen and ferried them down the coast to Dunbar. His force disembarked on 18 September, and on the following day marched towards Edinburgh. The Jacobite army advanced to meet him.

On 20 September the two armies made contact near Prestonpans, where Cope arrayed his troops in a strong defensive position. That night a local Jacobite sympathizer indicated a route by which Cope's flank could be turned. The Jacobite approach was detected by Cope's outposts, so allowing time to organize a line of battle. However, when the highlanders launched their broadsword charge at daybreak on 21 September, Cope's redcoats bolted with scarcely a show of resistance. Cope struggled to rally them, exclaiming 'For Shame, Gentlemen; don't let us be beat by such a set of Banditti' (*Report of the Proceedings*, 61). Collecting 450 dragoons, Cope retreated to Berwick. News of Prestonpans caused consternation in London and Cope became the scapegoat for the government's dismal showing during the opening phase of the 'Forty-Five. The public clamour against him was so great that, when a court of inquiry was held in September 1746, it was predicted that he would 'meet with the justice he deserved' (ibid., iv). However, after examining more than forty witnesses, the generals composing the court were unanimous in their opinion that Cope was blameless. As Horace Walpole observed in a letter to Sir Horace Mann of 14 October 1746, 'Cope is come off most gloriously, his courage ascertained, and even his conduct, which everybody had given up, justified' (Walpole, *Corr.*, 19.320). Yet it was Cope's supposed incompetence that passed into legend: the *Dictionary of National Biography* described his part in the campaign against the Jacobites as 'ludicrous', and cited the rousing Jacobite song 'Hey, Johnnie Cope! are ye waukin yet?' Thus Cope's nearly four decades of distinguished service were eclipsed by one incident that condemned him to lasting (and undeserved) ridicule.

Plagued by gout, Cope never again held a field command; in 1751 he was appointed to the staff in Ireland. After Prestonpans, according to gossip, Cope wagered that his successor would share his fate, and collected £10,000 when Lieutenant-General Henry Hawley was duly beaten at Falkirk in January 1746. Cope died in London on 28 July 1760 and was survived by his second wife, Elizabeth, executor of his will. His only son, James Cope, MP for the Duncombe family borough of Downton from 1754, and a career diplomat, had died in 1756.                    STEPHEN BRUMWELL

**Sources** I. Burton and A. N. Newman, 'Sir John Cope: promotion in the eighteenth-century army', *EngHR*, 78 (1963), 655–68 · *The report of the proceedings … of the board of general officers, on the examination into the conduct, behaviour and proceedings of Lieutenant General Sir John Cope* (1749) · A. N. Newman, 'Cope, John', HoP, *Commons, 1715–54* · *Scots Magazine*, 22 (1760) · *LondG* (9–12 July 1743) · A. Henderson, *The history of the rebellion MDCCXLV and MDCCXLVI*, 5th edn (1753) · *Memoirs of the life of Sir John Clerk of Penicuik*, ed. J. M. Gray (1892) · Walpole, *Corr.* · K. Tomasson and F. Buist, *Battles of the '45*, 2nd edn (1967) · S. Reid, *1745: a military history of the last Jacobite rising* (1996) · R. Wright, *The life of Major-General James Wolfe* (1864) · *DNB* · *GM*, 1st ser., 30 (1760), 394 · J. A. Cannon, 'Cope, James', HoP, *Commons, 1754–90* · IGI

**Archives** NL Scot., papers related to board of enquiry into his conduct of Scottish campaign · NL Scot., report on military operations and related Jacobite material | BL, John, second Lord Carteret, corresp. and papers · BL, letters to Lord Strafford, Add. MSS 22231, 31134–31135, 31141, *passim* · BL, Titley papers · BL, corresp. with Charles Whitefoord and Whitefoord's defence of him, Add. MS 36592 · Derbys. RO, corresp. with Sir Robert Wilmot · Hunt. L., letters to Lord Loudoun · NL Scot., corresp. with Lord Tweeddale · U. Nott. L., letters to Henry Pelham

**Likenesses** satirical print, 1745 · G. Townshend, pen-and-ink caricature, c.1751–1758, NPG · G. Townshend, pencil caricature, c.1751–1758, NPG

**Cope, Michael**. *See* Cop, Michel (c.1501–1566).

**Cope, Richard** (1776–1856), Independent minister, was born near Craven Chapel, Regent Street, London, on 23 August 1776. Before he was twelve he began work as a clerk in the excise, and subsequently served in various establishments until he became a student at the theological college, Hoxton Academy, in March 1798. After remaining there for more than two years, he received an invitation from the Independent congregation at Launceston in Cornwall. He preached his first sermon there on 28 June 1800 and was ordained in the church on 21 October 1801. He married a Miss Davies at St James's Church, Piccadilly, on 30 June 1801; they had five sons and two daughters. Cope remained in the post at Launceston until 1820, having concurrently kept a boarding-school with great success. In June 1819 he helped to form the Home Missionary Society with his colleague Ingram Cobbin.

From 1820 to 1822 Cope filled the post of tutor in the Irish Evangelical College, Manor Street, Dublin, and also preached in many towns in the north of Ireland on behalf of the Irish Evangelical and London Missionary societies. After this brief change of occupation, he returned to England as minister of Salem Chapel, Wakefield, where he served from 1822 to 1829; he was subsequently minister of Quebec Chapel, Abergavenny, from 1829 to 1836, and of New Street Independent Chapel at Penryn, in Cornwall, from April 1836 until his death. He died at Penryn on 26 October 1856, and was buried on 31 October.

The degree of MA was conferred upon Cope at Marischal College, Aberdeen, on 12 March 1819, and the degree of LLD in 1826. He was elected FSA on 13 February 1824. His

*Autobiography and Select Remains* (1857) was edited by his son. Cope also published several sermons and other works including *Adventures of a Religious Tract* (1820) and *Entertaining Anecdotes* (1828).

W. P. COURTNEY, rev. DAVID HUDDLESTON

**Sources** R. J. Cope, ed., *The autobiography and select remains of the Rev. Richard Cope* (1857) · *Congregational Year Book* (1857) · R. Tudur Jones, *Congregationalism in England, 1662–1962* (1962)
**Likenesses** R. Woodman, stipple, pubd 1826, NPG · engraving, repro. in Cope, ed., *Autobiography and select remains* · stipple, BM, NPG; repro. in *Evangelical Magazine* (1815)

**Cope, Sir Walter** (1553?–1614), administrator, was probably born at Hardwick Manor, near Banbury, Oxfordshire. His father was Edward Cope (*d.* 1557), a gentleman farmer, and his mother, Elizabeth (*d.* 1587), daughter of Walter Mohun of Overstone and Wollaston, Northamptonshire. On their father's early death he was the third son of a family consisting of four sons and three daughters. He was entered at Gray's Inn in 1570. With no resources except a £12 annuity, he became gentleman usher to William Cecil, and an official of the court of wards in 1574, doubtless through Burghley's influence as master. He was concerned with its financial aspects. Additionally, in 1580 he became the court's feodary for Oxfordshire, though he left to his deputy much of the work of ensuring that the crown received its dues from tenants-in-chief who were minors. He held this post at least until Elizabeth's death, and in 1601 became also the feodary for the city of London and Middlesex, a post he continued to hold under James I. The latter was especially lucrative as feodaries were paid a percentage of the revenue they brought to court. At an unknown date Cope married Dorothy (*d.* 1638), daughter of Richard Grenville of Wotton Underwood, Buckinghamshire, and Mary, *née* Gifford.

Having the gift of making himself indispensable, Cope continued to serve Lord Burghley, for by 1593 he was described as his secretary and was thus known as a great person in England by Magistrate Valladares of Lisbon. Both positions made him a person well worth cultivating, and led to gifts in addition to his wards fees. He was also able to buy wardships and thus gain from managing wards' lands, as in the case of Thomas Hoardson of Folkestone. He acquired an estate in Dunsden, Oxfordshire, which he sold to his brother Anthony *Cope in 1591, buying West Town Manor in Kensington, Middlesex, in 1592, and subsequently all the other manors there, helped by a share in Overstone from his mother. He had also become the trusted friend of Sir Robert Cecil, and continued to be involved in national administration as Burghley sickened and died in 1598. He accompanied Cecil on a diplomatic mission to France, examined suspects in Essex's rebellion, and gave advice on emergency finance when customs collection was behindhand in 1601. He was also involved in personal errands for Cecil, including oversight of the improvements to the Theobalds water supply.

On James I's accession in 1603 Cope journeyed north to welcome him, and was thus knighted at Worksop. He continued to combine national affairs with his work as Cecil's factotum: he arranged for Burbage's company to revive *Love's Labours Lost* to entertain Queen Anne at Cecil's house; advised James I on the most acceptable way of establishing a lottery, by raising money for charity; and went on a diplomatic mission to Brussels and Holland. He was so influential that Dudley Carleton pleaded with him for help when suspected of involvement in the Gunpowder Plot, and later in gaining an embassy. He began building Cope Castle (later Holland House), an imbroglio of Dutch gables and Italianate ornament, in Kensington in 1605, with an extensive park containing exotic trees imported by John Tradescant. He repeatedly entertained the king and queen there. John Chamberlain complained in 1608 that he was not allowed to touch even a cherry because the queen was expected. He was on sufficiently close terms that, after Prince Henry died in 1612, James I spent the night there, and Prince Charles, Princess Elizabeth, and the elector palatine came next day to join him.

Cope continued to advance in favour under James I. In June 1609 he was made chamberlain of the exchequer, a virtual sinecure, for life; in October he was granted a sixth of all fines given the king in the next twenty-one years; and in 1611 or 1612 he was made public registrar-general of commerce, and keeper of Hyde Park with Cecil, from 1605 earl of Salisbury, further profitable offices. Thus he was able to marry his only known child and heiress, Isabel, to Sir Henry Rich, later earl of Holland. But the death of his patron, Salisbury, in 1612, left Cope isolated; perhaps the more so as he and his fellow executor disputed the validity of his will. As his dead friend and master was vilified, Sir Walter's career faced eclipse. Courageously, he wrote a vindication to present to the king, *An Apology for the Late Lord Treasurer*, in resonant prose: 'I held it base to flatter him in his life: I will not now begin to flatter him in his grave. To offer such incense to the dead, I account the basest kind of sacrifice' (Gutch, 119–20). Perhaps Chamberlain was right to suggest that Cope was also putting forward his own qualifications to become master of the court of wards. In November 1612 the king granted him the office. This gave him precedence over all officials except privy counsellors, and probably an income of about £5000 a year. He increased the annual revenue from the sale of wards and marriages, which stood at £12,491 in his second year. He purposed to act honestly, and was concerned to raise revenue. This was his zenith.

Cope was an MP in at least two Elizabethan parliaments, and those of 1604 and 1614, sometimes clearly through the Cecil interest. He was an active member, especially in matters of religion and also of finance. In 1604 he suggested that composition for the feudal right of purveyance should be set at £30,000 p.a., strongly backing the rule of law: 'Cords bind Beasts, Words bind Men, Treaties bind Kings abroad, and Laws at home' (*JHC*, 1.984). He opposed impositions by prerogative on merchants, and resisted pressure in 1611 to consider subsidies before discussing redress of grievances. He was involved in considering what to do with the 1604 *Form of Apology*, and thus must have favoured it. He acted with independence of mind despite his closeness to Salisbury and desire for advancement from James I. Yet, as an influential figure, he was consulted before the speaker agreed to answer a question about Bate's case. The Addled Parliament ended his membership of the house ingloriously. Sir Thomas Parry, chancellor of the duchy of Lancaster, had offered one of the Stockbridge seats to him, and fraudulently altered the return when the electors refused to accept his nominees. Thus his election was annulled.

Cope invested in a number of overseas trading companies, including the Virginia and East India companies. Of the former he was a director, and persuaded others to invest in it. Another excursion into business was to prove disastrous. In May 1607, with his brother Sir Anthony, Arthur Ingram, Sir Thomas Lake, and others, he joined a syndicate to buy former church property in crown hands for £37,333 6s. 8d. A further contract was undertaken in November; another in May 1608 for rectories worth £75,000; and yet others in 1611, 1612, and 1613. Clearly, from Ingram's shady financial reputation, this was not a noble attempt to re-endow plundered livings: it was speculation, in a market which, by 1613, was glutted. Cope's involvement in Ingram's alum monopoly and the crown commission investigating it was dubious, and unprofitable. The probable portrait of him in 1612 shows an elegant, dignified, but anxious man.

Less than a month after Sir Anthony's death Sir Walter Cope was suddenly taken ill. According to Chamberlain, his brother's loss, rumours of losing the mastership of the wards, and his financial commitments after Sir Anthony's death had combined to break his heart. His will reflects anxiety about paying all his debts; and on 30 July 1614 he died at Cope Castle, reputedly with over £26,000 to settle. He was buried at Kensington parish church on 1 August. His probable portrait, perhaps by John de Critz the elder, hangs at Hatfield House.                    ELIZABETH ALLEN

**Sources** PRO, WARD 5/33; 8/47/4; 9/14, fols. 9, 16; 9/107, fol. 279; 9/112, fols. 118v–119r; 9/221, fol. 263; 9/275; 9/448, Oxfordshire section · *Calendar of the manuscripts of the most hon. the marquis of Salisbury*, 4, HMC, 9 (1892), 405; 6 (1895), 23; 8 (1899), 16; 9 (1902), 75, 79; 11 (1906), 70, 396; 12 (1910), 407; 16 (1933), 415; 17 (1938), 374; 19 (1965), 218 [see also other references] · *JHC*, 1 (1547–1628) · *CSP Spain, 1587–1603* · *CSP dom., addenda, 1580–1625; 1603–18* · *The letters of John Chamberlain*, ed. N. E. McClure, 1 (1939) · *Calendar of chancery patent rolls (6 James 1)*, List and Index Society (1975) · *Calendar of chancery patent rolls (8 James 1)*, List and Index Society (1976), 45, 51 · A. F. Upton, *Sir Arthur Ingram, c.1565–1642: a study in the origins of an English landed family* (1961) · Hants. RO, 43M48/120, 122 (1), 126, 136, 137, 218, 219 · H. E. Bell, *An introduction to the court of wards and liveries* (1953) · HoP, *Commons, 1558–1603* · J. Gutch, ed., *Collectanea curiosa*, 2 vols. (1781), 119–31 · T. K. Rabb, *Enterprise and empire: merchant and gentry investment in the expansion of England, 1575–1630* (1967), 270 · H. S. Passmore, 'Life and times of Sir Walter Cope', lecture to the Kensington Society, 1958, 1 · [T. Birch and R. F. Williams], eds., *The court and times of James the First*, 1 (1848), 165, 263, 333 · *London: northwest*, Pevsner (1991) · J. Nichols, *The progresses, processions, and magnificent festivities of King James I, his royal consort, family and court*, 1 (1828), 88 · *Visitation of Hampshire … Ex MSS Phillipps* (1854), 17 · J. Foster, *The register of admissions to Gray's Inn, 1521–1889, together with the register of marriages in Gray's Inn chapel, 1695–1754* (privately printed, London, 1889), 40 · T. K. Rabb, *Jacobean gentleman: Sir Edwin Sandys, 1561–1629* (1998), 159, 184–5 · E. R. Foster, ed., *Proceedings in parliament, 1610*, 2 (1966), 82–4 · E. Auerbach and C. Kingsley Adams, *Paintings and sculpture at Hatfield House* (1971), 78–80, 143 · Northants. RO, MS Y2 5312 · G. Lipscomb, *The history and antiquities of the county of Buckingham*, 4 vols. (1831–47), vol. 1, p. 600 · will, 1614, PRO, PROB 11/25, fols. 529r–530v · M. Prestwich, *Cranfield: politics and profits under the early Stuarts* (1966), 32 · A. Haynes, *Robert Cecil, first earl of Salisbury* (1989), 75 · transcript of bills, Hatfield House, 58/3, 285
**Archives** Hatfield House, Hertfordshire, MSS
**Likenesses** J. de Critz the elder?, oils, 1612, Hatfield House
**Wealth at death** Kensington estate, based on Cope Castle (Holland House) to daughter; reputedly owed £26,000 (perhaps exaggerated), which he hoped to clear with assets; was owed money; widow received £3500: *Letters*, ed. McClure vol. 1, pp. 554, 560, 580; will, 1614, PRO, PROB 11/25, fols. 529r–530v

**Cope, Sir (Vincent) Zachary** (1881–1974), surgeon and medical historian, was born in Kingston upon Hull on 14 February 1881, the youngest of ten children (of whom three died in early childhood) of Thomas John Gilbert Cope, a minister of the United Methodist church in Brougham Street, and his wife, Celia Ann Truscott, daughter of a dairy farmer and general dealer in St Austell. His education was entirely in London and he passed from Westminster City School, where he was head boy, to London University, graduating BA in 1899. From there he won a scholarship to St Mary's Hospital medical school, where his teachers included Augustus Waller and Almroth Wright. He graduated MB BS in 1905 with distinctions in surgery and forensic medicine, and proceeded to train in surgery at St Mary's Hospital. He was appointed consultant surgeon at St Mary's in 1911 and became a popular clinical teacher. In 1912 he also became surgeon to the Bolingbroke Hospital, where he remained until his retirement in 1946.

During the First World War, Cope served from 1916 to 1918 as a surgeon with the rank of captain in Mesopotamia, in a campaign notable for the problems caused by ill health in the forces, including the death from cholera of the commander Sir Stanley Maude. Cope was mentioned in dispatches in 1918. During his time away he made many useful observations, which became the basis of his first book, *Surgical Aspects of Dysentery* (1920). In the following year he published *The Early Diagnosis of the Acute Abdomen*, a sound text which addressed the urgency of dealing with the condition and met the needs of the advances in abdominal surgery at the time. Cope supervised all fourteen editions of this work in the next fifty years; the last, published in 1972 when the author was ninety years old, was distinguished by being shorter than the first. The text had an international reputation and was translated into five languages, among them Greek in an unauthorized edition.

In 1941 Cope was appointed sector officer of no. 6 sector of the emergency health service and in the post-war years he was a successful chairman of a number of influential inquiries and committees, playing an important part in the hospital survey and in the national registration of the professions auxiliary to medicine. The reports were published between 1949 and 1952, during which time he also edited two substantial volumes of the official medical history of the Second World War, those on medicine and pathology (1952) and on surgery (1953). For these public services he was knighted in 1953.

Cope's retirement years were much occupied by the writing of medical history, which often added to the current knowledge of familiar persons and events. He combined a readable style with an awareness of the importance of social history. He published two histories of his own medical school at St Mary's Hospital (1954 and 1955), an account of the Royal College of Surgeons of England (1959), two historical reviews of abdominal surgery, and two collections of essays. In addition he compiled biographies of Sir Henry Thompson, bt (1951), William Cheselden (1953), Florence Nightingale (1958), Sir John Tomes (1961), and Almroth Wright (1966). In his earlier years he gave numerous lectures, notably the Arris and Gale lecture (1922) of the Royal College of Surgeons of England, and he was also the college's Hunterian professor on four occasions (1916, 1920, 1925, and 1927). Although he may have preferred executive roles to high office, he was nevertheless vice-president of both the British Medical Association and the Royal College of Surgeons of England; he was also honorary librarian of the Royal Society of Medicine and president of the Medical Society of London. His contributions to medical history were marked by an honorary fellowship of the Worshipful Society of Apothecaries, and he was a director of Pitmans, the medical publishers.

Cope was short in stature, and stood on a small platform while operating. In his professional life he avoided controversy and intrigue. He was fond of composing light verse, both as a *memoria technica* in surgical teaching, and to mark personal events and public occasions. He was an early motoring enthusiast and owned a car from 1916 onwards.

Cope was twice married: first in 1909 to Agnes Dora (d. 1922), daughter of James Newth, a glazier's diamond manufacturer, of Ruislip; they had no children. In 1923 he married Alice May (d. 1944), daughter of Charles John Watts, engineer, of King's Lynn; they had one daughter. Cope died in Oxford on 28 December 1974.

DAVID HAMILTON, rev.

**Sources** *BMJ* (11 Jan 1975) · *The Lancet* (11 Jan 1975) · W. Lefann, *Medical History*, 19 (1975), 307–8 · unpublished autobiography, priv. coll. · private information (1986)
**Archives** St Mary's Hospital, London, MSS · Wellcome L., notebooks and papers | Wellcome L., corresp. with Charles Singer
**Likenesses** W. Stoneman, photograph, 1956, NPG
**Wealth at death** £42,730: probate, 20 Feb 1975, *CGPLA Eng. & Wales*

**Copeland** [*née* Fenzi]**, Ida** (1875/6?–1964), politician, was born in Italy about 1875 or 1876, according to the age recorded at her death, though her marriage certificate indicates 1880 or 1881. She was the daughter of Camillo Fenzi (d. August 1883) of Florence, and his wife, Evelyne Isabella, daughter of Sir Douglas Strutt *Galton. She was brought up in Italy but came to live in England while still young. After her father's death her mother married, in 1898, Leonard D. Cunliffe of Juniper Hill, Mickleham, near Dorking, in Surrey. Ida lived there until, on 28 July 1915, she married Richard Ronald John Copeland (1884–1958) of Kibblestone Hall, Staffordshire, the second son of Richard

Pirie Copeland. They had two sons (born in 1918 and 1920). From 1913 her husband was president and chairman of the Spode-Copeland firm of bone china manufacturers, and travelled widely abroad to obtain orders for its products.

Throughout her life Copeland was interested in all forms of social welfare, and especially in youth training. She was active in the girl guide movement in Staffordshire, serving as division commissioner for the north-west of the county from 1918, while her husband was a county commissioner for the Boy Scouts Association. She was also on the International Council of Girl Guides, 1920–28. In 1920 she became chairman of the Stoke division of the Women's Unionist Association. She was adopted as Conservative candidate for Stoke at the 1931 general election, when one of her opponents was Sir Oswald Mosley, leader of the New Party. Mosley came from an old Staffordshire family and his wife, Lady Cynthia Mosley, had won Stoke for Labour in 1929. Although he spent less than a week campaigning in the constituency, directing his efforts instead at a national campaign, Mosley met with enthusiastic support there, especially among younger voters. In spite of this, and to the amazement of her supporters, the electoral tide ran in Copeland's favour. She benefited from her husband's position as a leading china manufacturer in the Potteries, while her 'moderate and straightforward appeal' won her an audience even outside factory gates (*The Times*, 23 Oct 1931). She won by an impressive majority of 6654 votes.

Copeland made her maiden speech in May 1932 on import duties, which she approached 'entirely from the point of view of the pottery industry' (*Hansard 5C*, vol. 265, col. 1204). It was an industry under threat from foreign competition and she welcomed the protection that tariffs afforded. She believed that overseas manufacturers paid starvation wages to their workers, and it was with a critical eye on the opposition benches that she asked:

> Can we allow goods manufactured under those conditions to come into this country and lower the standard of living of our own people? I say 'no', and I firmly believe that, if we raise these tariffs, the time will come when our industry will be on its feet again. (*ibid.*, col. 1206)

She made another plea for protection of the china industry in December 1933 after reports that Australian and New Zealand markets were being flooded by cheap Japanese goods, including skilful imitations of British wares: 'the competition is so severe that it threatens to sweep the English Potteries right out of those countries' (*Hansard 5C*, vol. 283, col. 1790). She wanted the British government to compel the dominion governments, in their own interests as much as in Britain's, to take action to prevent this 'dumping'. This was, though, a sensitive matter and the official response was sympathetic without being specific.

In her short time in the Commons, Copeland made several lucid and well-informed speeches, and was responsible for numerous written questions on a range of topics from price levels in the telephone network to speed limits on roads. But her principal focus was the defence of home and dominion industries, in particular the pottery and china trade, from foreign competition. She could not prevent a Labour resurgence at Stoke at the November 1935 general election. Though her vote was only marginally down on the 1931 figure the Labour vote was significantly up, and she lost by 2125 votes to the Labour candidate she had beaten in 1931.

Copeland did not stand for parliament again, but remained active in public life. She chaired the Staffordshire Anglo-Polish Society from 1943 and was awarded the Polish gold cross of merit in 1952. She also resumed her work on the International Council of Girl Guides in 1940. In 1949 she was made a sister of the order of St John of Jerusalem. She was also a fellow of the Royal Society of Arts and a silver medallist of that society in 1934.

In 1937 Copeland inherited the Trelissick estate at Feock, 4 miles south of Truro, in Cornwall, and she and her husband created a notable garden there. In March 1956 she gave 376 acres of Trelissick to the National Trust. She was remembered by friends as a generous and kindly woman, and as a strong character who did not suffer fools gladly. She had a keen sense of humour and of the ridiculous, enjoyed languages, travel, small boat sailing, and pottery, and led an active life until three years before her death. She died on 29 June 1964, at the Highlands, Ticehurst, Sussex.                                        MARK POTTLE

**Sources** WWW · WWBMP · Burke, *Gen. GB* (1935) · m. cert. · d. cert. · R. Copeland, 'Copeland, Richard Ronald John', *DBB* · *CGPLA Eng. & Wales* (1964) · *The Times* (16 Oct 1931) · *The Times* (23 Oct 1931) · *The Times* (29 Oct 1931) · *The Times* (22 March 1956) · *The Times* (11 July 1964) · *Hansard 5C*, vols. 265, 283 · F. W. S. Craig, *British parliamentary election results, 1918–1949*, rev. edn (1977) · P. Brookes, *Women at Westminster: an account of women in the British parliament, 1918–1966* (1967) · R. Skidelsky, *Oswald Mosley* (1990) · C. Rallings and M. Thrasher, *British electoral facts, 1832–1999* (2000) · R. Fedden and R. Joekes, *The National Trust guide* (1973)

**Likenesses** photograph, repro. in *The Times* (29 Oct 1931)

**Wealth at death** £97,496: probate, 16 Oct 1964, *CGPLA Eng. & Wales*

**Copeland, Ralph** (1837–1905), astronomer, was born on 3 September 1837 at Moorside Farm, Woodplumpton, Lancashire, the youngest of several sons of Robert Copeland (d. c.1840), a yeoman farmer and part owner of a cotton mill, and his wife, Elizabeth Milner. He attended a small weaver's school, and then Kirkham grammar school. He was briefly apprenticed into the cotton mill of an older brother in Blackburn, but in 1853 emigrated to Australia, first as a shepherd in Victoria, then at gold diggings in the Omeo district. Here he developed an interest in astronomy. In 1858 he returned to England via Cape Horn, in the meantime studying John Herschel's *Outlines of Astronomy* and observing Donati's comet. He became an apprentice in the locomotive firm of Beyer, Peacock & Co. of Manchester, and with some workmates set up a small observatory with a 5 inch Cooke refractor at West Gorton. His first published observation was of an occultation of $\kappa$ Cancri on 26 April 1863.

Copeland resolved to abandon engineering because of depression in the cotton trade and retrain as an astronomer, although in 1859 he had married his cousin Susannah Milner. He spent some months improving his German in a village in Hesse, then in 1865 matriculated at the University of Göttingen to study under Klinkerfues, Weber, and Stern. In 1866 he had the misfortune to lose his wife and was left with a small daughter and an infant son. The following year he became a volunteer observer at the Göttingen observatory and, in anticipation of the long-term project for a great star catalogue, organized by the German Astronomische Gesellschaft and involving some seventeen observatories (part of which appeared as the *First Göttingen Catalogue* in 1869), he began with Carl Börgen (later director of the Wilhelmshaven observatory) up to January 1869 a series of observations of star places down to ninth magnitude in the declination zone 0° to -1° with the Reichenbach transit circle. However, these were made before the plans by the Gesellschaft had been finalized and were not accepted by its council, although they remain a valuable list.

Copeland, eager for adventure, was then invited to accompany Börgen on a German Arctic expedition under Captain Koldeway to explore the east coast of Greenland as far north as possible. During the preparations they took their degrees of doctor of philosophy, Copeland's dissertation being 'Über die Bahnbewegung von α Centauri' (1869). They carried out geodetic, meteorological, auroral, terrestrial magnetism, and natural history studies beyond 75° N, published in two volumes (1874), and on their return Copeland with others received the order of the Red Eagle from Kaiser Wilhelm I.

In January 1871 Copeland was appointed assistant at Lord Rosse's observatory at Birr Castle, Ireland. In December he got married again, to Theodora (1847–1937), the daughter of the distinguished orientalist Professor Theodor Benfey of Göttingen; they had three daughters and a son. For the first two years he was occupied mainly with observations of the moon's radiant heat with the 3 foot reflector. In 1874 he was elected fellow of the Royal Astronomical Society and became assistant to Dr Robert Ball at the Dunsink observatory, Dublin, but was immediately granted leave of absence to accompany James Ludovic, Lord Lindsay, to Mauritius to observe the transit of Venus, the results of which were only partly successful in cloudy conditions. The yacht *Venus* called in briefly at the small uninhabited island of Trinidad (or Trindada) in the south Atlantic, where Copeland discovered the giant tree fern *Cyathea Copelandi* high in the interior.

In 1876 Copeland was appointed director of the great observatory at Dun Echt in Aberdeenshire belonging to Lord Lindsay (later the twenty-sixth earl of Crawford), succeeding David Gill. He was singularly well suited to this, having expertise in its variety of instruments and a love of scientific and rare literature. There he assisted Lindsay in building up his great astronomical library, now the Crawford collection of the Royal Observatory, Edinburgh. The first five or six years were spent in reducing the backlog of the Mauritius observations, issued in 1885 as volume 3 of Dun Echt Observatory Publications.

Copeland became devoted to the main instrument at Dun Echt, the 15 inch Grubb refractor, and the spectroscope. Schmidt's nova in Cygnus was found on 2 September 1877 to have its spectrum reduced to a single emission line—a notable discovery. Every comet visible from the observatory was then studied, some of their elements and ephemerides computed, and astronomical news sent worldwide through the Dun Echt *Circulars*. The comets of 1881 and 1882 proved especially interesting: 1882I (Wells) exhibited strong sodium D lines and was visible in monochromatic sodium light with the slit open.

Copeland was appointed to take charge of the Jamaica station for the successful transit of Venus collaborative programme of 6 December 1882; then at Crawford's expense he undertook an exploratory mission to test the potential of the seeing conditions in the Andes of Bolivia and Peru. Here he discovered five new Wolf–Rayet stars and studied the peculiar variable $\eta$ Argus. Back at Dun Echt he employed a new spectroscope to study emission lines in the supernova in the Andromeda spiral, the emission spectrum of the variable $\gamma$ Cassiopeiae, and in the Orion nebula found the D3 line later identified as Helium. During this eventful period many observations by Crawford, Copeland, and their German-trained assistants Ludwig Becker and Jacob Gerhard Lohse were published in *Astronomische Nachrichten*, in *Monthly Notices*, and in *Copernicus* (3 vols., 1881–4), edited by Copeland and J. L. E. Dreyer, which, although printed in Dublin, was recognized as the 'organ' of Dun Echt.

The happiest years were soon over. Lord Crawford, learning of government plans to suppress the Royal Observatory on Calton Hill, Edinburgh, on the retirement of Charles Piazzi Smyth, offered to present his entire instrument collection and library to the nation on condition that a new royal observatory be built to house them. Copeland accepted the joint posts of astronomer royal for Scotland, director of the observatory, and professor of astronomy at Edinburgh University. He was faced with the task of choosing the most suitable site—Blackford Hill—and unlike his predecessors he was, after a struggle, successful in instituting rigorous courses in astronomy for the new BSc degree. The new observatory was not completed until April 1896, so Copeland had to move between what was left of Dun Echt and the limited resources at Calton Hill. However, he was able to observe Thomas Anderson's discovery, Nova Aurigae (1892), and at the British Association's Cardiff meeting in 1891 suggested that the bright streaks on the moon were caused by lines of minute glassy spherules—an extraordinary anticipation.

In 1896 Copeland went to Vadsø in Finnmark, Norway, for the total solar eclipse, with a 4 inch, 40 foot focal length Dallmeyer lens built into a huge camera. It was cloudy, but he had the compensation of meeting Nansen. Much more successful were the 1898 eclipse expedition to India and the 1900 expedition to Spain. The observation and issue of the *Circular* for Anderson's Nova Persei (1900) proved to be Copeland's last notable work. The following year a bout of influenza was followed by increasingly severe attacks of angina. Copeland refused to retire. He died at the observatory residence in Edinburgh on 27 October 1905 and was buried on 30 October in Morningside cemetery. He was a robust, adventurous man, sporting a long white beard, and was held in great affection by his colleagues. He was elected fellow of the Royal Society of Edinburgh in 1890, and was a member of the Scottish Meteorological Society and a director of the Ben Nevis (meteorological) observatory.

DAVID GAVINE

**Sources** J. L. E. Dreyer, *Monthly Notices of the Royal Astronomical Society*, 66 (1905–6), 164–74 · H. Macpherson, *Astronomers of to-day and their work* (1905) · *The Scotsman* (28 Oct 1905) · H. A. Brück, 'Lord Crawford's observatory at Dun Echt, 1872–1892', *Vistas in Astronomy*, 35 (1992), 81–138 · *DNB*
**Archives** Royal Observatory Library, Edinburgh, corresp. and papers | Birr Castle, Birr, corresp. with earl of Rosse · RAS Library, letters to Royal Astronomical Society · RGS, letters to Sir David Gill
**Likenesses** A. J. Ramsay, photograph, repro. in Brück, 'Lord Crawford's observatory at Dun Echt', 107 · bas-relief bust, Royal Observatory, Edinburgh · photograph, repro. in Brück, 'Lord Crawford's observatory at Dun Echt', 101 · photograph, repro. in MacPherson, *Astronomers of today*, 70 · photograph, repro. in J. Ogilvie, *An address on the occasion of inaugurating the memorial in the village of Rothiemay to the astronomer James Ferguson FRS* (1907) · photographs, Royal Observatory, Edinburgh · wood-engraving (after a photograph by J. E. Munro), NPG; repro. in *ILN* (16 Feb 1889)
**Wealth at death** £1040 17s. 5d.: confirmation, 25 Jan 1906, *CCI*

**Copeland, Thomas** (1781–1855), surgeon, son of William Copeland (1747–1787), curate of Byfield, Northamptonshire, was born in May 1781. He studied under Mr Denham at Chigwell in Essex, and in London under Edward *Ford, his maternal uncle, before attending medical classes in Great Windmill Street and at St Bartholomew's Hospital. On 6 July 1804 he was admitted a member of the Royal College of Surgeons, and on the 14th of the same month was appointed an assistant surgeon in the 1st foot guards. He embarked with his regiment for Spain under Sir John Moore, and was present at the battle of Corunna in 1809.

On his return to England and retirement from the army, Copeland succeeded to his uncle's practice following the latter's death in September that year. Copeland also inherited his residence, 4 Golden Square, London, and having been appointed surgeon to the Westminster General Dispensary he soon made some influential connections, chiefly among the aristocracy. In 1810 he brought out *Observations on the disease of the hip-joint, by E. Ford; edited and revised with additions, by T. Copeland*. In the same year he published *Observations on some of the Principal Diseases of the Rectum*, a work which ran to three editions. His new and scientific treatment of these diseases established his reputation and justly earned him the distinction of being the founder of rectum surgery; as a consulting surgeon his opinion was in great demand in the West End of London. Copeland was the first to suggest the removal of the septum narium by means of an ingeniously contrived pair of forceps, in cases where its oblique position obstructed the passage of air through the nostrils.

Copeland was elected FRS on 6 February 1834, and in

1843 he became honorary FRCS. For a time he was a member of the council of the Royal College of Surgeons, and he became surgeon-extraordinary to Queen Victoria in 1837. He moved to 17 Cavendish Square, London, in 1842, but his failing health caused him to reduce his practice. Copeland was also the author of *Observations on the symptoms and treatment of the diseased spine, more particularly relating to the incipient stages*, published in 1815; a second edition appeared in 1818 and the work was translated into several European languages. Among his contributions to professional journals was a paper entitled 'History of a case in which a calculus was voided from a tumour in the groin' (*Transactions of the Medico-Chirurgical Society*, 3.191). Copeland's career was marked by a keen observance of professional etiquette, and by courtesy and friendship towards his fellow practitioners. Copeland died from an attack of jaundice at Brighton on 19 November 1855. His wife died on 5 December 1855. He left £180,000, bequeathing £5000 both to the Asylum for Poor Orphans of the Clergy and to the Society for the Relief of Widows and Orphans of Medical Men.          G. C. BOASE, rev. IAN LYLE

**Sources**  GM, 2nd ser., 45 (1856), 91 · *Medical Circular* (13 July 1853), 31 · T. J. Pettigrew, *Medical portrait gallery: biographical memoirs of the most celebrated physicians, surgeons … who have contributed to the advancement of medical science*, 4 vols. in 2 [1838–40] · *London and Provincial Medical Directory* (1856)
**Likenesses**  W. Drummond, lithograph (after T. Stewardson), BM; repro. in *Portraits of members of the Athenaeum*, 2 vols. (1836) · W. and F. Holl, stipple (after H. Room), Wellcome L., BM, NPG; repro. in T. J. Pettigrew, *Medical portrait gallery: biographical memoirs of the most celebrated physicians, surgeons … who have contributed to the advancement of medical science*, 4 (1840) · oils, Wellcome L.
**Wealth at death**  £180,000: DNB

**Copeland, William John** (1804–1885), historian and Church of England clergyman, was born at Chigwell, Essex, on 1 September 1804, the elder son of William Copeland, a surgeon. He entered St Paul's School, London, in 1815 and Trinity College, Oxford, in 1824, where he held a scholarship but was prevented by ill health from entering for honours and, like J. H. Newman, did not obtain the expected first-class degree. He took his BA in 1829, MA in 1831, and BD in 1840. In 1829 he was ordained to the title of St Olave Jewry but soon moved to Hackney, where he came into contact with the Hackney Phalanx of traditional high-churchmen, which included John James Watson, Watson's brother Joshua, Henry Handley Norris, and Thomas Sikes.

Elected a fellow of Trinity in 1832, Copeland threw himself into the circle that produced the Tracts for the Times, which included another fellow of the college, his close friend Isaac Williams. Copeland filled many college posts—tutor, rhetorical lecturer, and vice-president—being, in addition, curate of St Mary Magdalen, Oxford (1835–7), and Begbroke (1838–9), and helping Newman in an unofficial capacity at St Mary's. He became an authority on the Anglican divines of the seventeenth and eighteenth centuries, publishing an article on the non-jurors (*British Critic*, 21, Jan 1837, 39–75), the edition of Bishop Cosin in the Library of Anglo-Catholic Theology (of which

he was an increasingly disillusioned superintending editor from 1840 to 1843), and the historical appendix to the published edition of Pusey's condemned sermon (1843). A respected classicist, he translated the *Homilies of S. John Chrysostom on the Epistle to the Ephesians* for the Library of the Fathers (1840).

In March 1840 Copeland became curate at Littlemore, without giving up his rooms in Trinity, spending much of his time there following Newman's resignation of St Mary's and remaining alone after the secessions of 1845. Despite many doubts at the time, he devoted himself to parish work at Garsington and the college living of Farnham, Essex, of which he was rector between 1849, when he resigned his fellowship, and his death there on 26 August 1885. He was buried on 29 August. He left his estate to his nephew, William Copeland Borlase MP.

A celibate priest of great humour and sympathy, of wide-ranging and deep friendships, Copeland was quite content in parish life. A small man in the side-whiskers and clerical dress of an earlier age, he judged the later ritualists kindly, looking beyond controversial dress and ceremonial to their missionary activity. A chance meeting with Newman on 3 June 1862 led to the resumption of their friendship and correspondence, Copeland editing Newman's Anglican sermons as *Parochial and Plain Sermons* (8 vols., 1868) and *Selection Adapted to the Seasons* (1878).

Copeland's reserve, perfectionism, and lack of ambition meant that he published little, to the exasperation of his friends. From 1860 until his death, Pusey, Newman, and Edward Churton urged him to write a history of the Oxford Movement. Pusey felt that Copeland alone could do justice to its context, origins, and early history (Pusey to Copeland, 28 March 1866, Liddon Bound Volumes, 79/89). He possessed a formidable memory and gathered a large number of sources, from which he provided much of the historical material for Pusey's reprinted edition of Tract 90 (1865). However, only fragments of the proposed 'Narrative of the Oxford Movement' were dictated before his prolonged final illness left him paralysed and confused. The historiography of the movement might have been very different had it been completed. The young men involved in the disputes in Oxford in the 1830s and 1840s would have been placed in the context of an older generation working largely outside the university by one who was among the last surviving witnesses. Newman's dating the start of the movement to 1833 might not have gained such unqualified acceptance, and a more nuanced picture of the Church of England in the first third of the nineteenth century would have emerged. Copeland's library was sold, but his invaluable collection of Tractarian papers was put at the disposal of H. P. Liddon and R. W. Church and was later given to Pusey House.

K. E. MACNAB

**Sources**  Pusey Oxf., Copeland papers · D. A. Bell, working papers for unfinished biography of Copeland, Pusey Oxf., Bell papers · W. J. Copeland, *A narrative of the Oxford movement*, ed. D. A. Bell and K. E. Macnab [forthcoming] · R. W. Church, *The Guardian* (2 Sept 1885) · *The letters and diaries of John Henry Newman*, ed. C. S. Dessain and others, [31 vols.] (1961–) · *The autobiography of Isaac Williams*, ed. G. Prevost, 3rd edn (1893) · DNB · R. B. Gardiner, ed., *The admission* registers of St Paul's School, from 1748 to 1876 (1884) · J. Menet, *Rest in the tabernacle of God: a sermon preached … the day after the funeral of the Rev. William John Copeland* (1885)

**Archives** Pusey Oxf., corresp. and papers | Birmingham Oratory, Newman MSS · Keble College, Oxford, Keble MSS · LPL, Williams dep · priv. coll., Churton MSS · Pusey Oxf., Churton MSS · Pusey Oxf., Liddon bound volumes · Pusey Oxf., Pusey MSS
**Likenesses** Dolamore & Bullock, photograph, c.1870, repro. in S. L. Ollard, *A short history of the Oxford Movement*, 2nd edn (1932)
**Wealth at death** £4093 10s. 4d.: probate, 15 Dec 1885, CGPLA Eng. & Wales

**Copeland, William Taylor** (1797–1868), pottery manufacturer, was born on 24 March 1797 at Lincoln's Inn Fields, London, the son of William Copeland (1765–1826), partner of the potter Josiah Spode II, and his wife, Mary (d. 1837), *née* Fowler. He was brought up in the family home in Leyton, Essex, where he continued to reside for many years. On 29 April 1826 he married Sarah (1799–1860), daughter of John Yates, a potter. They had ten children, of whom a daughter and four sons, William Fowler Mountford (1828–1908), Edward Capper (1835–1875), Alfred James (1837–1921), and Richard Pirie (1841–1913), survived Copeland.

Copeland entered the Spode-Copeland business on 19 July 1824 and was taken into partnership when his father died. Following the death of Josiah Spode in 1827 he became sole owner of the London business, and in 1833, owner also of the pottery at Stoke-on-Trent. In that year he went into partnership with Thomas Garrett, manager of the Stoke pottery, the firm being known as Copeland and Garrett. This partnership was dissolved in 1847 and the firm then traded as W. T. Copeland, late Spode. In 1867 his sons joined him in partnership as W. T. Copeland & Sons.

Although he did not achieve the aesthetic eminence of Wedgwood, Copeland produced wares whose artistic quality raised the standard of ceramic manufacture. With the aid of his art director Thomas Battam (1810–1864), one of a family of ceramic artists, he gained worldwide renown. Copeland's artistic triumph came with the production of the refined statuary porcelain, or parian, introduced about 1842, and his reputation was further enhanced when this product was shown at international exhibitions. He employed eminent sculptors including John Gibson, whose *Narcissus* was commissioned by the *Art Union Magazine* in 1846. 1859 saw the appointment of the remarkable flower painter Charles Hurten. In 1866 Copeland was appointed china and glass manufacturer to the prince of Wales.

Copeland was active in the promotion of machinery. His attempt in 1847 to introduce a mechanized 'Jolley' (a device to shape the interior of cups and deep bowls) was thwarted, but he was the first to install the newly patented Needham and Kite filter press in 1856. Copeland was the only manufacturer willing to undertake the exacting commission to tile the cupola of the Imperial Library, Paris, which opened in 1868. He also supported the formation of the schools of design in London and Stoke, the latter opening in 1847.

Copeland was also active in local and national politics.

He was elected alderman for Bishopsgate ward in 1828 and immediately served as sheriff of London and Middlesex in 1828–9. In 1835 he was elected lord mayor, the third youngest man to hold that office. He was a member of the Goldsmiths' Company and its master in 1837–8. He was for seven years president of the royal hospitals of Bridewell and Bethlem; he was a member of the Irish Society, which managed the City's Irish estates, president of the Honourable Artillery Company, a director of the London and Birmingham Railway Company, and a major investor in Fenton Park colliery. He was widely recognized as a generous man, supportive of charitable institutions, and upright in his dealings.

Copeland contested the borough of Coleraine in 1831 and 1833 as a Liberal and was seated on petition in both years. He retained the seat until the general election of 1837 when he joined the Conservatives and was returned for Stoke-on-Trent. He was defeated in 1852 but held the seat once more from 1857 to 1865. He was never an active debater in the house.

A keen sportsman, Copeland kept a stud of racehorses at his country residence, Russell Farm, Watford, Hertfordshire. He had another house at Cliffe Bank, Stoke, but spent much of his time in London. His health failed in the early months of 1868, and although he recovered enough for his doctors to consider him out of danger, he suffered a relapse. He died at Russell Farm on 12 April 1868, and was buried in the new cemetery in Watford six days later.

R. E. GRAVES, rev. HELEN L. PHILLIPS

**Sources** Keele University, Spode-Copeland Archive · P. A. Halfpenny, ed., *Spode-Copeland, 1733–1983: potters to the royal family since 1806* (1983) [exhibition catalogue, City Museum and Art Gallery, Stoke-on-Trent, 1983] · R. Copeland, *Spode and Copeland marks* (1993) · R. S. C. Copeland and V. Wilkinson, *The Copeland china collection* (1989) · *Art Journal*, 30 (1868), 158 · *City Press* (18 April 1868), 5c · *Staffordshire Advertiser* (6 May 1826) · priv. coll., Alan Townsend archive and research · *Evening Sentinel* (30 Dec 1871), 4 · D. Stuart, ed., *People of the potteries: a dictionary of local biography* (1985) · L. Whiter, *Spode* (1970) · A. B. Beaven, ed., *The aldermen of the City of London, temp. Henry III–[1912]*, 2 vols. (1908–13)
**Archives** Keele University, Spode-Copeland Archive
**Likenesses** Mrs C. Pearson, oils, 1835, probably Spode · J. F. Herring, portrait, 1842 (*Scene on Cannock Chase*) · W. M. Tweedie, oils, exh. RA 1866, Bridewell Royal Hospital, Surrey
**Wealth at death** under £20,000: probate, 1868, CGPLA Eng. & Wales

**Copeman, Sydney Arthur Monckton** (1862–1947), medical scientist, was born at home on 21 February 1862 in the cathedral close at Norwich, the son of Arthur Charles Copeman (1824–1896), canon and rural dean of Norwich, and his wife, Mary Metcalfe (1834–1927), daughter of deputy lieutenant Charles Metcalfe JP, of Inglethorpe Hall, Emneth, Norfolk. He was the eldest of seven sons and five daughters, in that birth order, who all achieved a prominence in their chosen careers as physicians, priests, colonial governors, matrons of hospitals, and headmistresses. His father had qualified in medicine (MB, London) in 1848, having in 1844 been gold medallist of his year in anatomy and physiology; he practised only briefly before taking

Sydney Arthur Monckton Copeman (1862–1947), by Walter Stoneman, 1921

holy orders, and in addition to his ecclesiastical duties took on being chairman of the Norfolk and Norwich Hospital and chairman of the building committee of the new hospital; he was active in the foundation and management of very many clerical, educational, and humane works centred in Norfolk. Copeman's maternal grandfather held lordships of five manors, and was also from a clerical and landowning family.

Copeman was educated at King Edward VI School, Norwich, and at Corpus Christi College, Cambridge, where he obtained a second class in the natural sciences tripos in 1882. He then went to St Thomas's Hospital, London. He graduated MB (1886) and MD (1890) at Cambridge, and was elected FRCP in 1899, proud of having become MRCP by examination though not primarily a clinician. On 12 July 1899 he married Ethel Margaret (1869–1944), youngest daughter of Sir Thomas William Boord, bt, of Wakehurst Place, Sussex (later managed by the National Trust and Royal Botanic Gardens, Kew). Their first house was 57 Redcliffe Gardens, London, where two of their three children were born. Their eldest child was William Sydney Charles *Copeman (1900–1970).

Copeman was initially encouraged to pursue medical research while an undergraduate by Sir Michael Foster, the first professor of physiology at Cambridge. He took the post of demonstrator in physiology and morbid anatomy at St Thomas's Hospital, and later became assistant lecturer in physiology and research scholar of the British Medical Association, with clinical access to patients and laboratory space. He published, within four years of qualification, seventeen papers on haematological subjects, including one in collaboration with Sir Charles Sherrington and two with W. S. Bristowe.

These lines of research, Sherrington reported, were 'cut short … to my loss' (MacNalty and Craigie, 38), after Copeman was recruited by Dr Richard Thorne Thorne, principal medical officer of the Local Government Board. From 1891 Copeman's career was in public health, with the medical department of the Local Government Board. With no Medical Research Council or other scientific grants, he welcomed a paid post to allow him further opportunities to pursue his researches, which by now were embracing work on the relationship of variola to vaccinia (cowpox). These researches were aided in the early stages by a gift of £400 from Sir Joseph Lister, which Copeman later repaid. The rosebowl that Lister gave Copeman as a wedding present was donated to the Royal College of Physicians by his son, W. S. C. Copeman, in gratitude for Lister's friendship; Lister was his 'unofficial' godfather.

Copeman's experimental work and publications for the next eight years were concentrated chiefly on vaccinia and smallpox viruses; he enquired into their nosological importance in man and in animals. Was vaccinia or cowpox in nature a variety of attenuated smallpox, i.e. variola minor or alastrim? How was this relevant to the development of an efficient vaccine against smallpox? Copeman was also pursuing, concurrently, another aspect that was of supreme importance to world health—a method for rendering bacteriologically pure the virus vaccine raised in the calf. In 1889 the royal commission on vaccination had broadly recommended single-dose vials of vaccine rendered bacteriologically pure, provided the process of creating it free of contamination allowed no loss of efficiency of the active agent. For four decades scientists in many countries had been experimenting with heat treatments and with the addition of chemicals. Copeman suggested the use of glycerine before the royal commission on vaccination in 1893. He freely acknowledged that during the previous forty years variations along these lines had been advocated and tried and that a great variety of methods had been employed but without satisfaction. The worry about the vaccine transmitting erysipelas (caused by common staphylococci and streptococci), and the remoter syphilis and leprosy, was specifically questioned in the report by the royal commission on vaccination in 1896. The methods of vaccination then in use—by transmitting material from arm to arm, or, since the days of Edward Jenner, from the calf's belly to the patient (as was still practised on the continent), or as lymph and exudate dried onto ivory points creating a scab crammed with unwanted micro-organisms—were methods to be deplored on the obvious grounds of microbiological hygiene.

However, in the Milroy lectures at the Royal College of Physicians in 1898, Copeman could now detail the methods he had devised to raise the pure vaccine: 'I at length found [success] in the addition to the lymph, or rather the vesicular pulp, obtained from a vaccinated calf, of a steril-ized 50 per cent solution of glycerine in distilled water' (S. M. Copeman, 155). The long-term effectiveness and reli-ability of the virus in the vaccine was preserved, and the dangers of passing on bacterial infection were abolished. Copeman's improved methods allowed the vaccine to be stored for a long period in glass vials and transported round the world. The manufacture of the vaccine, the glycerinated lymph, was now simple and cheap. The Vac-cination Act of 1898 gave statutory authority, and the vac-cination order (1898) of the Local Government Board effected Copeman's methods for the raising, production, and purification of glycerinated calf lymph. A new labor-atory was provided in Chelsea, London, for its production, but to accommodate the vastly increased work the gov-ernment lymph establishment was founded at Hendon in 1907. Copeman thus transformed vaccination against smallpox into a sure and safe operation. His methods of vaccine production continued to be employed until small-pox was eliminated from the globe in 1977.

The important point about Copeman's career was that he was employed to do contract research—taking on pub-lic health problems given to him by his employers. In many ways he carried on the tradition of investigative work established for the medical department by John Simon in the 1860s and 1870s. According to his obituarists he was also a pioneer in immunization against diphtheria, and his presidential address for the epidemiological sec-tion of the Royal Society of Medicine in 1926 concerned serum prophylaxis of measles.

> The remarkable thing about Copeman was that he made time to do so much in so many varied fields of activity and did it with little effort or appearance of haste. This characteristic was apparent in his literary work. He wrote easily and his writing displayed clarity of thought and diction. His scientific work was pursued under many difficulties for as a medical officer he was always liable to interruption in the middle of important experiments, in order to conduct some medical inspection, to hold a public enquiry or to go abroad at a moment's notice on the Crown's Service. Yet he always returned to research work with unabated energy.   (MacNalty and Craigie, 45)

Copeman wrote nearly a hundred meticulous scientific papers and official reports concerning public health, infant and child mortality, household sanitation, food storage, waste disposal, and pollution by sewage and chemical effluents. He investigated outbreaks of scarlat-ina, typhus, and enteric fevers, incriminating milk, water, and ice-cream sources, particularly with regard to pollu-tion of underground water supplies by contamination from soil and subsoil. Many of his reports resulted in dras-tic reforms. He investigated an outbreak of a mysterious, lethal, epidemic skin disease, the nature of which is still unknown; encephalitis lethargica; the epidemiology and natural history of ascaris gut infestations; and the cause of lead poisoning from drinking-water supplies. He travelled extensively in England and on the continent investigating and advising on the safety of manufacturing processes, explosive and poisonous gases from ferro-silicone manu-facture, and 'offensive nuisances' from India-rubber and linoleum manufacturers.

Copeman conducted ingenious experiments on blue-bottles and houseflies, their breeding in horse manure and how to control this, and the range of their transmis-sion of infection, tracking individual flies over large dis-tances 1000 yards or more to rubbish tips. Cancer was a later interest. As a member of the council of the Zoo-logical Society of London he developed its work on scien-tific lines and promptly dealt with an outbreak of anthrax, and he discovered a colony on London's Primrose Hill of a rare, burrowing parasitic fly. He was a founder of the Medical Research Club (Council), a councillor of the Royal College of Physicians, a knight of grace of the order of St John and a member of the chapter-general of the order, a liveryman of the Society of Apothecaries, and, after retirement, a member of the London county council. Other honours and distinctions were the fellowship of the Royal Society (1903), the Cameron prize of the University of Edinburgh (1899), the Fothergillian gold medal of the Medical Society of London (1899), the Buchanan gold medal of the Royal Society (1902), the Jenner medal of the Royal Society of Medicine (1925), and the gold medal of the International Faculty of Sciences (1938).

'Copeman was tall and of distinguished appearance', and apparently elegant and so notably well-dressed (wear-ing a black, tall silk hat even on field work) as to attract special mention in the Westminster medical school stu-dent magazine. 'He was of generous and kindly dispos-ition, ever ready to help his younger colleagues … well read, a man of wide culture and a delightful companion' (MacNalty and Craigie, 45). A high Anglican, he was a regu-lar communicant. His wife, Ethel, helped him to prepare his work for publication, and assisted with his foreign cor-respondence in French, German, and Italian. She died on 24 April 1944. Copeman died at his home in King's Gar-dens, Hove, Sussex, on 11 April 1947, and was buried at Brighton parish church. A memorial service was held on 7 May 1947 at the church of the order of St John of Jerusa-lem. In 1996 an English Heritage blue plaque was erected outside Copeman's house in Redcliffe Gardens, on the 200th anniversary of Edward Jenner's discovery of vaccin-ation against smallpox.

PETER W. MONCKTON COPEMAN

**Sources** A. S. MacNalty and J. Craigie, *Obits. FRS*, 6 (1948–9), 37–50 · *Journal of Pathology and Bacteriology*, 59 (1947), 706–16 · P. W. M. Copeman, 'Extinction of the speckled monster celebrated in 1996', *Journal of Medical Biography*, 6 (1998), 39–42 · P. W. M. Cope-man, 'S. Monckton Copeman's centenary', *BMJ* (8 Sept 1962), 668–9 · J. A. Dudgeon, *Journal of the Royal Society of Medicine*, 73 (1980), 581–6 · S. M. Copeman, *Vaccination: its natural history and pathology* (1899) · bap. cert. · m. cert. · d. cert. · *BMJ* (19 April 1947), 546 · *BMJ* (17 May 1947), 700 · private information (2004)
**Archives** Nuffield Oxf., corresp. with Lord Cherwell
**Likenesses** W. Stoneman, photograph, 1921, NPG [*see illus.*] · F. Eastman, portrait, repro. in Copeman, 'Extinction of the speckled monster' · photograph, repro. in *Journal of Pathology and Bacteriology* · photograph, repro. in *Fellows of the Royal Society*, 6 (Nov 1948), 37–50

**Wealth at death** £71,502 19s. 10d.: probate, 11 Sept 1947, *CGPLA Eng. & Wales*

**Copeman, William Sydney Charles** (1900–1970), rheumatologist and historian, was born on 29 July 1900 at the house of his grandfather, Wakehurst Place, Ardingly, Sussex, and was baptized in its private chapel. He was the only son of Dr Sydney Arthur Monckton *Copeman (1862–1947) and Ethel Margaret (1869–1944), daughter of Sir Thomas William Boord MP. He was educated at Lancing College, Sussex, before becoming an ensign in the Coldstream Guards (1917–18). After medical training at St Thomas's Hospital, London, Copeman qualified with the conjoint diploma in 1924, graduated MB BChir from Gonville and Caius College, Cambridge, in 1925, and MD with honours in 1936. He became MRCP (1926) and FRCP (1937). Copeman became assistant étranger to the professor of paediatrics at the Sorbonne in Paris, worked as house physician in the Hospital for Sick Children, Great Ormond Street, London, and was medical registrar to out-patients in St Mary's Hospital, London. Speaking perfect French he learned his medicine in France and England at a time when the rheumatic disorders were receiving some attention, in France in particular; this was the start of his serious interest in these disorders. Nearly forty years later he wrote in the preface to the third edition of his *Textbook of Rheumatic Diseases* (1964, first published 1948) that:

> when The Royal College of Physicians of London appointed their first special committee to survey the rheumatic diseases in 1933 this field of medicine was derelict. Since that time academic interest in all branches of rheumatology has gradually become world wide and is rapidly increasing.

That this transformation had come about arose to a remarkable degree from his own activities. Rheumatology was a neglected subject in Britain and most other countries before the Second World War. The particular study of diseases of the musculo-skeletal locomotor system, rheumatology, was not recognized as a medical speciality in its own right, as was the study of diseases of other systems. It is to the outstanding credit of Copeman that he realized what needed to be done to remedy this situation.

In March 1936 in Peto Place, London, six doctors met under the chairmanship of Dr Matthew Ray to form the committee for the study and investigation of rheumatism, which became the Heberden Society in 1937. Copeman became its president in 1949–50 and was its honorary librarian from 1950 until his death. He was awarded the Heberden medal in 1939. Copeman was also involved with the Empire Rheumatism Council, founded in 1936 as a voluntary organization to finance research and education on the rheumatic disorders. This organization changed its name to the Arthritis and Rheumatism Council and later to the Arthritis Research Campaign (ARC).

In 1937 Copeman was appointed to the rheumatism department at the West London Hospital. He was also physician to the British Red Cross Rheumatism Clinic at Peto Place. He later became consultant physician to the West London Hospital, and to the Middlesex Hospital when it took over Peto Place, as well as to the Hospital of St John and St Elizabeth, the Home for Incurables, Putney, and the Star and Garter Home, Richmond. He also had a large private practice. Copeman published a series of papers on the use of cortisone and ACTH (adrenocorticotrophic hormone) in rheumatoid arthritis and in 1950 became chairman of the Medical Research Council committee on steroids. He was also the first to describe rheumatoid arthritis of the arytenoid joints, and fat micro-herniation as a cause of non-articular rheumatism. In addition Copeman was editor of the *Annals of Rheumatic Diseases*.

In the Second World War he was a lieutenant-colonel in the Royal Army Medical Corps; he was mentioned in dispatches twice and was appointed OBE. He became adviser in medicine to Malta command in 1943. At the Royal College of Physicians, Copeman served as secretary to the college committee on chronic rheumatic diseases (1935–7) and was its chairman thereafter. He was councillor (1955–8), FitzPatrick lecturer (1958 and 1959), and member of the library committee (1958–60) and of the committee to revise the by-laws of customs of the college. He was elected a vice-president in 1969. Copeman became a Hunterian professor of the Royal College of Surgeons in 1949, and delivered the Thomas Vickery lecture in 1963. He was sometime master of the Society of Apothecaries and served on the court for many years. He also took a keen interest in the history of medicine and played a part in the foundation of the faculty of the history of medicine and pharmacy and in 1964 of the British Society for the History of Medicine, of which he was president 1967–9. His publications in this area include *Doctors and Disease in Tudor Times* (1960) and *Apothecaries: a History of the Worshipful Society of Apothecaries of London, 1617–1967* (1968).

Copeman was president of the British branch and past president of the European Ligue Contre le Rheumatisme and was an honorary member of the American, French, Spanish, Argentinian, Brazilian, Norwegian, Danish, and Dutch rheumatism societies and associations. His desire for a national rheumatological research institute came about in 1966 due to the generosity of Mathilda and Terence Kennedy, which led to the foundation of the Kennedy Institute. Copeman served as its chairman from 1967 until his death.

In spite of his busy medical life Copeman was essentially a home-loving man. He and his wife, Helen (1903–1980), daughter of William Bourne of Garston Manor, Watford, Hertfordshire, whom he married on 15 November 1931, had two daughters and a son, Peter, a consultant dermatologist in London. Both their son and son-in-law, Oliver Dawson, became active members of the ARC.

Will Copeman was a tall, slim, handsome man who never lost his military guardsman's appearance. Warm-hearted and generous, he was excellent company at any medical or social gathering; he had a keen sense of humour. He was particularly dependent on his friends and colleagues and was sensitive to their feelings; he was seldom sure that he was in the right and would ask others for their honest opinion and, moreover, usually acted on it. After an evening in his company one left with intellectual and psychological batteries charged, with new ideas to consider and new plans to think over. Copeman was internationally recognized as a pioneer in the field of rheumatic diseases. He died at his home, 12 Hyde Park Place, London, on 24 November 1970 and was buried at St Margaret's Church, Ockley, Surrey, on 1 December.

F. DUDLEY HART

**Sources** A. E. Porritt and F. D. Hart, 'W. S. C. Copeman: his importance in contemporary medicine', *Annals of the Rheumatic Diseases*, 51 (1991), 283–8 · Munk, *Roll* · *BMJ* (5 Dec 1970), 625 · *The Lancet* (5 Dec 1970) · b. cert. · *WWW*
**Likenesses** photograph, 1968, RCP Lond. · photograph, repro. in *BMJ* · photograph, repro. in *The Lancet*
**Wealth at death** £87,025: probate, 9 Feb 1971, *CGPLA Eng. & Wales*

**Coper, Hans Joachim** (1920–1981), potter, was born on 8 April 1920 in Chemnitz, Saxony, the second son of Julius Coper, a prosperous Jewish businessman, and his wife, Erna (*d.* 1969). Coper's childhood was deeply affected by the increasing harassment of Jewish citizens throughout the 1930s, something that led to the family's moving from Chemnitz to Dresden, and subsequent difficulties in his early education. His father committed suicide in 1936, and his brother emigrated to Canada in 1937. Coper spent a short period studying textile engineering in Dresden before emigrating to England in 1939. In 1940 he was interned as an enemy alien and sent to Canada, volunteering to return to England to join the Pioneer Corps in 1941. Soon after the war Coper met the émigré Viennese potter Lucie *Rie and with no prior knowledge of pottery joined her studio as an assistant to make ceramic buttons for the fashion industry. Her studio was a meeting-place for European artists and architects and Coper was greatly encouraged in this urbane atmosphere to extend both his ceramic and his drawing skills. Rie's reputation as a potter was based on her austere tableware designs of black and white glazed teapots and coffee cups, decorated with minimal cross-hatching or parallel lines, and Coper helped to throw and decorate them. The tableware stood out at this period against the more orientalist functional pots, heavily glazed in rich earth colours, that were espoused by Bernard Leach and his followers. Coper's developing abilities were recognized by Rie and many of these tableware pieces carry both their personal sealmarks on them.

Coper also began to make less functional ceramics alongside this tableware. These pieces were distinctive and already displayed his sensibility; in particular his fascination with the archaic pots of Greece coupled with an interest in the abstract mark making of such contemporary painters as Marino Marini and Ben Nicholson. The exterior surfaces of these pots were rarely glazed; rather they have dry abraded surfaces into which lines have been scored to make abstracted designs of birds or fish, or patterns reminiscent of webs or nets. Their forms were simple, often bowls or beakers or compounds of two more shapes brought boldly together: all the component parts of his pots were thrown on the potter's wheel, something he believed strongly gave intensity and vigour to the forms. Above all these potters shared the interest in archaic ritual so current among contemporary sculptors. Coper's palette of colours was muted: ochres, browns, and black predominated in these first pots as they were to do throughout his career, their tonality highlighting their connections with more overtly sculptural materials like stone rather than with ceramics. These pots of Coper's made a considerable impact when exhibited at the Festival of Britain in 1951, and subsequently at exhibitions in London with Rie at the Berkeley Galleries in 1954 and 1956. His work began to be collected by notable patrons and it is a marker of his burgeoning reputation that in the first monograph on studio pottery by Muriel Rose published in 1955 ten of Coper's pots were illustrated.

Coper had married Annie Penelope Karaiskos in October 1943 and had a daughter, Ingrid, in 1944. Their marriage was short-lived, a relationship with Dorothy Frances (Francesca) Zobel, formerly Nicholas, starting also in 1943, with two children, Anya and Laurens, being born in 1944 and 1948. In 1954 Coper met the photographer Jane Gate, with whom he was to live for the rest of his life. Jane Gate's photographs of Coper provide a remarkable archive of images of his work in progress in his studios. They married in 1974.

In 1959 Hans Coper moved to a newly inaugurated arts centre at Digswell in Hertfordshire where he was given a studio and flat. Digswell was founded to strengthen connection between the arts and architecture, and in the five years that Coper lived there a substantial proportion of his work was focused on making architectural ceramics. These included cladding tiles for both the exterior and interior of buildings as well as designs for washbasins and lavatories. This kind of work revealed Coper's interest in exactitude and problem solving, as well as a rare sense of engagement with the hardware of buildings. It was during this period that Coper also received the two most significant architectural commissions of his life. The first was to make the candlesticks for the new Coventry Cathedral, designed by Basil Spence, a brief that specified that they should be 'in scale with the huge concrete altar … an ordinary design would look puny. That is the pitfall' (Whiting, 19). It was a pitfall that he avoided. Coper made them 7 feet tall, slotting multiple thrown sections together on metal rods, a technique that reflected his grasp of engineering as much as of ceramics. His handling of scale is impressive, the candlesticks retaining great presence in their positioning in front of a vast Graham Sutherland tapestry. Spence was to be behind Coper's other great commission, that of two massive candlesticks for the meeting-house at Sussex University (now installed on a Henry Moore altar in St Stephen Walbrook, London). They were conceived as a bowl form raised above a tapered drum-like foot. Glazed with a matt manganese surface, they are magisterial in their austerity.

In 1961 Coper started teaching part-time at Camberwell School of Arts and Crafts at the suggestion of Lucie Rie, and at the Royal College of Art in London in 1966. His teaching made a considerable impression on his pupils, who included some of the most significant ceramicists of the 1970s, such as Elizabeth Fritsch, Glenys Barton, and

Alison Britton, though their new school of hand-built work often vibrantly painted shared little with Coper's aesthetic. A man of considerable good looks, tall and slightly hunched through a stiffened spine, and with an almost hieratic intensity of manner, Coper inspired great loyalty among those he taught. He was not given to inanity or unnecessary pleasantry when discussing work, and many record that it was his gravitas about the making of ceramics that was so inspirational. The devotion he inspired was described by Barton: 'I suddenly felt an urgent need to have something better to show him the next time he came' (Barton, 54).

Coper returned to London in 1963 and the subsequent four years were to prove some of the most fertile of his life. Coper's characteristic way of working was to make numerous pots in a very small series of forms, intensely revising the shapes and their decoration, and discarding much of his work. When exhibiting his work he preferred to show pots of widely differing scale and tone together to create a complex of formal resonances. His composite forms grew more complex, involving many different thrown sections and sometimes also joining a disc at the rim or at the intersection of two forms. Many of his pots were concerned with contrasting ellipses and flattened volumes, sometimes dramatically indenting or squeezing the forms. Their surfaces were subtler with a pale cream slip used in contrast with the black interiors. Function was no longer of significance (though he continued to suggest that they could be used for flowers or candles), as he developed his increasingly distinctive vocabulary of shapes and surface.

In 1967 Coper had his most important joint European exhibition at the Boymans Museum in Rotterdam with Lucie Rie, for which he made some of the largest pieces of his career. In 1969 he showed with the weaver Peter Collingwood at the Victoria and Albert Museum, London. In this exhibition he showed elongated forms mounted on very small drum-like bases for the first time. With their submerged anthropomorphism these pots became known as his 'Cycladic' pots owing to their resemblance to the archaic figures that partly inspired them. For this exhibition he wrote sparingly about his work, the only time which he did so and about which subsequently he had serious misgivings:

> My concern is with extracting essence rather than with experiment and exploration. The wheel imposes its economy, dictates limits, provides momentum and continuity. Concentrating on continuous variations of simple themes I became part of the process; I am learning to operate a sensitive instrument which may be resonant to my experience of existence now—in this fantastic century. Practising a craft with ambiguous reference to purpose and function one has occasion to face absurdity. More than anything, somewhat like a phantom piano-tuner, one is trying to approximate a phantom pitch. (Houston, 99)

Coper moved to Somerset in 1967. His reputation, always high among a small group of collectors, had now become considerable in Europe and America. Though his work now fetched more money, the intense scrutiny under which he put his work meant that the few pieces he sold brought him no great affluence. He continued to live in an electively spartan manner. It was only after his death that his work became the most expensive of studio ceramics and the subject of fervent speculation. From 1974 there were increasing signs of physical deterioration in his co-ordination, with motor neurone disease diagnosed in 1975. Coper made fewer and fewer pots until in 1979 he ceased completely; he died in Frome, Somerset, on 16 June 1981.

Since his death Coper's reputation among critics and ceramicists has remained steadfast: his work has continued to be perceived as having the greatest sculptural presence among studio potters. Principal collections of Coper's works include those in the Victoria and Albert Museum, and the Crafts Council, London; the Metropolitan Museum, New York; and the Boymans Museum, Rotterdam. EDMUND DE WAAL

**Sources** T. Birks, *Hans Coper* (1983) · M. Coatts, *Lucie Rie and Hans Coper: potters in parallel* (1997) [exhibition catalogue, Barbican Art Gallery, London, February–May, 1997] · T. Harrod, *The crafts in Britain in the 20th century* (1999) · J. Houston, ed., *Craft classics since the 1940s* (1988) [exhibition catalogue, Crafts Council Gallery, London, 19 Oct 1988 – 8 Jan 1989] · D. Whiting, 'Coper at Coventry: Hans Coper and the Coventry Cathedral candlesticks', *Studio Pottery*, 20 (April–May 1996), 19 · L. Campbell, *To build a cathedral: Coventry Cathedral, 1945–1962* (1987) · O. Watson, *British studio pottery: the Victoria and Albert Museum collection* (1990) · G. Barton, *Crafts*, 54 (1982), 54 · *CGPLA Eng. & Wales* (1982) · b. cert. [Laurens Coper]
**Likenesses** J. Coper, photographs, repro. in Birks, *Hans Coper*
**Wealth at death** £421,530: probate, 5 April 1982, *CGPLA Eng. & Wales*

**Coperario, Giovanni**. *See* Coprario, John (*d.* 1626).

**Copinger, Walter Arthur** (1847–1910), jurist and author, was born on 14 April 1847 in Clapham, the second son of Charles Louis George Emanuel Copinger (1821–1866), colonel in the American army, and his wife, Mary, widow of George James, and daughter of Thomas Pearson of Shepperton, Middlesex. Educated at the private school of John Andrews at Wellesley House, Brighton, he entered University College, Durham, but left without completing his course to join the office of a relative who was a solicitor in London. He did not remain there long. In 1866 he was admitted a student of the Middle Temple, and after spending a short time in the chambers of T. Bourdillon, a well-known conveyancing counsel, he was called to the bar on 26 January 1869.

After his call to the bar Copinger turned his attention to the law of copyright, and in 1870 he published his *Law of Copyright in Works of Literature and Art*. The work went through several editions and was revised in the 1920s; a tenth edition appeared in 1965. Also in 1870 Copinger settled in Manchester, and began practice as an equity draftsman and conveyancer, and in the chancery court of the county palatine of Lancaster. His work as a conveyancer increased so rapidly that he soon ceased to take court work and became the leading conveyancer out of London. At the same time he was widely consulted on questions of copyright. He had a strong grasp of the intricacies of the law, especially that relating to real property. He was sharp, and had a good memory, powerful concentration, and an easy style of draftsmanship. Pupils found his chambers an admirable school of training: he was said to have the power of making law live. On 3 September 1873 he married Caroline Agnes, eldest daughter of Thomas Inglis Stewart, vicar of Landscove, Devon; they had two sons and three daughters.

Amid his heavy professional work Copinger continued to write on legal subjects, more particularly on conveyancing. Between 1872 and 1886 he published several large works on this and related topics. In 1876 he published *An Essay on the Abolition of Capital Punishment* which, to his amusement, was so enthusiastically received by the abolitionists that his intention to publish another pamphlet demolishing all the arguments in the first was abandoned.

In 1888 Copinger was appointed lecturer in law in the Owens College, Manchester, and in 1892, upon the resignation of Professor Munro, he became professor of law, and finally dean of the faculty of law in the Victoria University, Manchester. He received the Lambeth degree of doctor of laws from Archbishop Benson in 1889, and that of MA from the Victoria University in 1905. He was president of the Manchester Law Society's library.

Copinger pursued versatile interests with untiring industry. Besides being an expert in old property law, he was also a keen bibliographer and antiquary, and took a deep interest in theology. Unfortunately all his bibliographical and historical work lacks the essential quality of minute accuracy. Largely owing to his efforts, supported by Richard Copley Christie, the Bibliographical Society was founded in London in 1892; he was the society's first president, and held the office for four years, doing much to establish the society on a firm basis. Between 1895 and 1898 he published his most important bibliographical work, the *Supplement to Hain's Repertorium bibliographicum*, comprising 7000 corrections of and additions to the collations of fifteenth-century works described or mentioned by Hain, and a list of nearly 6000 works not referred to by Hain. This work extends to upwards of 1630 closely printed double-column pages. Copinger contributed several papers to the *Transactions of the Bibliographical Society*, including an exhaustive monograph on the fifteenth-century printed editions of Virgil. In 1892 he published a bibliographical account of 124 editions of the Latin Bible printed between 1450 and 1500. At The Priory, Greenheys, Manchester, his home at the time, he set up a small press, at which he printed four bibliographical works for private circulation.

Copinger was equally keenly interested in genealogy, heraldry, and manorial history. In 1882 he published his *History of the Copingers or Coppingers*, in which he traced the descent of his family from the Danes in the tenth century, when they appear to have settled in Suffolk and in the south of Ireland. His last years were devoted almost exclusively to the history of Suffolk. Between 1902 and his death he produced a stream of work on this subject, including a five-volume general history of Suffolk and a work on the manors of Suffolk which ran to seven volumes. He also published work on heraldry.

In religion Copinger was an Irvingite, and for a number of years was the angel, or minister, of the Catholic Apostolic church in Manchester. His interest in theology was wide and deep. The work which he valued most among his writings was his huge treatise on *Predestination, Election, and Grace* (1889). He also wrote six other works on theological subjects.

Copinger mainly found all the relaxation which he allowed himself in a change of work; but music always attracted him. He played several instruments, including the piano and violin, and found time to compose a number of musical pieces, including a collection of seventy-five original hymn tunes.

Copinger was an ardent book collector, and accumulated a considerable library. It was rich in early printed books, Bibles, manuscripts, and printed editions of Thomas à Kempis's *Imitatio Christi*, hymnbooks, Elzevier editions, and general works of reference. Genial and affable, he was always ready to place his knowledge and his library at the disposal of any student.

Copinger died, a widower, at his home, Ormonville, Lower Broughton, Salford, on 13 March 1910 from pneumonia following an attack of influenza, and was buried at Birch, Rusholme, Manchester.

HENRY GUPPY, *rev.* CATHERINE PEASE-WATKIN

Sources 'Professor W. A. Copinger', *Manchester Faces and Places*, 8 (1896–7), 8–12 • *Manchester University Magazine*, 7, 182–4 • W. A. Copinger, ed., *History of the Copingers or Coppingers* (1882) • *Manchester Guardian* (14 March 1910) • *The Athenaeum* (26 March 1910), 369 • private information (1912) • personal knowledge (1912)

Likenesses A. Brothers & Co., photograph, repro. in *Manchester Faces and Places* • group portrait, photograph, repro. in H. B. Charlton, *Portrait of a university* (1951), 62

Wealth at death £25,355 19s. 11d.: probate, 30 May 1910, *CGPLA Eng. & Wales*

**Copinger, William** (*d.* 1416), clerk and supposed theologian, was a member of a family settled at Buxhall, Suffolk, where he was himself buried. His will is dated 20 January 1412, and was proved on 2 March 1416. Bale attributes to Copinger, whom he describes as *doctor*, a treatise *De vitiis et virtutibus*, with incipit 'Vani sunt omnes homines in quibus non est scientia dei', and a *sacramentale*, both of which he found in a manuscript at Balliol College, Oxford. In this he was followed by Pits, who dubs Copinger a *magister insignis*, and by Tanner. The volume Bale saw was Balliol College, Oxford, MS 83, which contains an abbreviation of *De vitiis et virtutibus* by the mid-thirteenth-century French Dominican Guillaume Peyraut, and also the *sacramentale* of Guillaume de Mont Lauzun. The colophon of the former is signed Toppynger (or perhaps Toppyng), who, however, was clearly the transcriber, not the author, of the work in question, and whose name Bale misread, replacing its capital letter 'T' with a 'C'. Bale also endowed his inadvertent creation with a first name, William, perhaps through a confusion with the William Copinger who was successively a scholar of Winchester College and New College, Oxford, and who proceeded BCL in 1542.

R. L. POOLE, *rev.* HENRY SUMMERSON

Sources R. Sharpe, *A handlist of the Latin writers of Great Britain and Ireland before 1540* (1997), 721 • Bale, *Index*, 122 • J. Pits, *Relationum historicarum de rebus Anglicis*, ed. [W. Bishop] (Paris, 1619), 852 • Tanner, *Bibl. Brit.-Hib.*, 199 • Emden, *Oxf.*, 4.136 • Wood, *Ath. Oxon.: Fasti* (1815), 116 • BL, Add. MS 19165, fol. 53

**Copisarow, Maurice** (1889–1959), chemist, was born at Biruch in Russia on 16 August 1889, the son of Elkana (Conan) Copisarow, who following military service was a rabbinical scholar, and his wife, Sarah. After emigrating to England in 1908 Copisarow was taken under the wing of Chaim Weizmann, then a lecturer in chemistry at the University of Manchester, later first president of Israel. Copisarow obtained his MSc in 1914; a joint paper with Weizmann published in 1915 dealt with new phthalides of the benzene, naphthalene, and carbazole series. He was naturalized in that year.

Copisarow's research was original and independent; even from 1914 he published papers mostly without collaborators, very occasionally with a junior colleague. At first his work was in the field of synthetic organic chemistry, for example on new applications of the Friedel Craft reaction, but even in the early years he developed wider interests which gradually absorbed his whole attention. His work on the structure and mode of oxidation of carbon led to a series of papers on the subject of allotropy.

At Manchester, Copisarow was Dalton research scholar (1914–16), honorary research fellow (1916–19), and in 1925 obtained his DSc. His research was interrupted, however, when for financial reasons he was obliged to accept a variety of external tasks. He worked as temporary demonstrator in the chemistry department, on behalf of the research committee of the Royal Society, and for the government Department of Scientific and Industrial Research. During the First World War he worked for the Ministry of Munitions.

In the summer of 1915 Copisarow was sent by Professor H. B. Dixon, with the support of Weizmann, to organize the analytical section of the newly installed trinitrotoluene (TNT) plant at the government factory at Gorton. He set out to discover the cause of a series of disastrous explosions in the TNT plants of northern England and Scotland, in which several hundred workers had been killed since the beginning of the war. He soon found the Woolwich arsenal testing specifications to be inadequate, limited as they were to the conditions of nitration and a few tests of the product. New problems were the purification of TNT; the action of alkalis thereon; the related question of inherent acidity; and the utilization of rapidly accumulating residues. These led to extensive research, partly published in *Chemical News*, but the most significant paper was held back until after the armistice, at the express wish of Lord Moulton. This work was instrumental in substituting steam treatment of crude TNT for the hazardous alkali wash. Copisarow also discovered methods for converting the dangerously unstable waste products generated by the production of explosives into gelatinous dynamite, chloropicrin, and khaki dyes.

During three years with the Ministry of Munitions, Copisarow was on the so-called coal tar chemical testing staff, stationed at Manchester University. In 1919–22 he was on the research staff of British Dyestuffs Corporation. Among his research was a paper entitled 'Carbazole-blue and carbazole-violet' (*Journal of the Chemical Society*, 117, 1920, 1542–50), and he took out a patent on the industrial production of carbazole as a base for hydron blue. This was acquired by Levinstein Ltd. He also developed a continuous process for the conversion of toluene and the xylenes to benzene. On 10 December 1919 Copisarow married Eda Cohen, of Manchester. They had a daughter and a son, Sir Alcon Charles Copisarow, who in 1964–6 was chief scientific officer of the Ministry of Technology, and from 1995 chairman of the Eden Trust.

As early as 1917 Copisarow's eyesight had begun to fail and the deterioration was doubtless accelerated by continued contact with such toxic materials as phosgene, chloropicrin, and TNT. He had eight unsuccessful eye operations, and lost the sight of both eyes shortly after 1925. Owing to this and general bad health he had no employment after 1922. Between 1925 and 1927 he had several major operations for gastric and duodenal troubles and was artificially fed for a period of six months. His indomitable character was clearly displayed in these extremely adverse circumstances. Finding himself in need of an income, Copisarow first of all set to work with his wife to establish a successful business connected with furs. He set up a laboratory in his attic and continued experimental work, which led to the publication of a series of papers on the most varied topics, all of which were characterized by the highest originality. After 1932 the effect of the slump in trade compelled the Copisarows to realize and utilize all their small means, to resort to mortgages and borrowing on life policies. Nevertheless they managed to bring up and educate their two children.

In later years Copisarow's practical approach to problems was replaced by theoretical writings. He considered a number of topics, among them the mode of synthesis of marble and alabaster. He provided evidence which justified the replacement of the igneous theory of Sir James Hall by a new hydrothermal conception of the formation of marble. He also developed his ideas on rock formation in other directions, focusing particularly on the effects of silica in a number of its forms. He also wrote on the fundamentals of periodicity and the co-ordination of physical and chemical periodic structures, and on mineral arborial growth, its range and bearing on the form of organic structures. In the unrelated field of physiological chemistry his studies of the biochemical causes of malignant growth and possible control of carcinoma were discussed in a comprehensive review article, 'History of human cancer', published in the *Edinburgh Medical Journal* (1952). Copisarow was very interested in enzymes and wrote about their action in relation to malignant growth and radiation, and to influenza and other viruses. The high quality of his writings, after he had lost most of his sight, was quite remarkable.

Among many agricultural topics which Copisarow studied were the preservation of fruit and vegetables, natural and artificial fertilizers, destruction of bracken, and a method for making new materials from woody and other cellulosic starting-points. During the Second World War he was able to use this knowledge to help the war effort, and was as a consequence placed on the civil list in recognition of special services to his country. Finally, an essay on the ancient Egyptian, Greek, and Hebrew concepts of the Red Sea, published soon after his death in *Vetus Testamentum*, showed that Copisarow's erudition was not entirely confined to scientific matters.

In the difficult circumstances of his later life it was impossible to complete much of his work, but his papers teem with original ideas. Physical infirmity deprived him of the opportunity fully to develop his undoubted scientific ability. Copisarow died of a coronary thrombosis at his home, 1 Gildridge Road, Manchester, on 15 April 1959.

ROBERT ROBINSON, *rev.* K. D. WATSON

**Sources** *Nature*, 184 (1959), 315 · *The Times* (24 April 1959), 17 · personal knowledge (1971) · private information (1971, 2004) [Sir Alcon Copisarow, son] · d. cert. · m. cert.

**Wealth at death** £157 7s. 0d.: administration, 8 Oct 1959, *CGPLA Eng. & Wales*

**Copland, Alexander** (1774–1834), building contractor, was born on 14 May 1774, in the parish of St Martin-in-the-Fields, London, the only surviving son of Alexander Copland (1736–1793), builder, and his wife, Barbara (1734–1790?), daughter of Richard Smirke of Wigton, Cumberland—probably the grandfather of the architect and artist Robert Smirke (1781–1867)—and widow of Richard McCartney.

Copland was educated at a school at Sowerby, near Thirsk, Yorkshire, and in November 1784 bound as an apprentice to Richard Holland, surveyor, at the Stationers' Company. He entered the Royal Academy Schools in November 1788. Apart from small legacies, his father bequeathed him all his leasehold and personal estate, said by Smirke to be worth £10,000. Copland was admitted to the freedom of the Stationers' Company on 5 April 1796, and on 30 April married Lucy (*d.* 1849), only daughter of William Giffard of Turnham Green, Middlesex. They had three sons and one daughter.

Copland's significance lies in his being the earliest of the great building contractors. He was called on to build barracks, often in country areas, with great rapidity, and based his operations in London, where he largely recruited a workforce of hundreds of men of all trades—though never more men on a site than could work to advantage—whom he supplied with tools, in contrast to the tradition by which the artisan supplied his own. He enforced a new degree of labour discipline, ascribing his success in completing work on schedule to his having 'always employed a great many more Superintending Clerks and Foremen than is usual for the number of men, in order to compel the workmen to do their duty' ('Commissioners of military inquiry', 2.47).

Copland's career progressed through personal contacts. His brother-in-law, Henry Hemsley, a surveyor in the barrack office, gave the crucial impetus when in 1796 he asked him to supply prefabricated barrack buildings for the West Indies. The government then decided, in view of the war with revolutionary France, to build temporary wooden barracks throughout the country, and in August 1796 Copland was employed to build one at Chelmsford, Essex, for 2400 men, in only five weeks. He built another in three weeks at Weymouth for 300 cavalry and officers, prior to the king's visit in 1798. Thereafter he was extensively employed by the barrack-master-general in the Isle of Wight, 1798–1802, where he employed 700 men; in the Channel Islands (1799, for Russian troops evacuated from Holland); and in Weeley (Essex), Winchester, and elsewhere. In all, by 1805 a total of twenty-six barracks at a charge of £1,464,629, were executed by Copland's own firm, save for about £4000 of stonework on the prestigious Windsor barracks.

These barracks were contracted for on the basis of 'measure and valuation'. So generous were the valuations of the barrack office surveyors that Copland was able to make very large profits; an independent valuation of his Silverhill bill in 1805, allowing a 15 per cent profit margin, reduced it by 48 per cent. Copland's work at Radipole, Dorset, in 1804, was attacked as 'a most glaring instance of imposition' ('Commissioners of military inquiry', 2.52). The rubble foundation of the stables employed mortar made of muddy sand without a proper proportion of lime; repairs estimated at £2600 were required within the year, 'which could not have been the case, had the Builder performed his Contract with common honesty' ('Commissioners of military inquiry', 2.52).

Barrack building, however, was by no means his only activity. John Sanders of the barrack office was architect of two major contracts, for the Duke of York's Asylum, Chelsea (1801–03), and for the Royal Military College, Sandhurst (1807–12), and probably also of a third, the guard house in Hyde Park (1798). The first of these contracts no doubt brought Copland into personal touch with the duke of York, whose town house in Piccadilly, mortgaged to the banker Coutts, he proposed in 1801 to develop as a residential hotel. Eventually Copland paid £37,000 in instalments in 1802–5 to become absolute purchaser of York House. In association with the architect Henry Holland (cousin of Richard), and Holland's nephew, the builder Henry Rowles, Copland converted it into residential chambers known as Albany, erecting also two parallel rows of chambers in the gardens, the first purpose-built residential apartments of their kind.

In addition, like his father, Copland built houses for the upper end of the London market. From at least 1799 he was also a timber merchant, and about 1806 entered into partnership in that trade with Rowles. In 1807 and 1808 Copland built houses which were let at from £102 to £150 per annum on Rowles's Upper Cadogan Place estate, subsequently selling them on. He also worked on Covent Garden theatre (1809), designed by his cousin, Sir Robert Smirke (but not, as often claimed, on the great hall of Christ's Hospital, where he merely, as a governor, served on the responsible committee).

Copland leased building sites from Rowles, and from about 1811 joined him in exploiting Westminster Abbey's Tothill Fields estate; in 1827 and again very shortly before his death he invested over £2000 in leases in the neighbourhood of Vincent Square, but probably as a land speculation rather than for building, for both men had retired from contracting by 1821. Their firm (sometimes including the name of Holland), nevertheless continued at Narrow-wall (later Belvedere Road), Lambeth, until Copland's death. By 1808 Copland had acquired, in addition to his residence and premises at 67 St Martin's Lane, a yard in Horseferry Road, Westminster, to which he soon added others in Millbank, on the river. The latter he gave up when in 1812—the year in which he also moved from St Martin's Lane to Great George Street—he established workshops and a house on a 10,000 square yard site in Horseferry Road, which contained also sawpits and brickworks.

Copland also appears in an 1817 list of architects practising in London, but his only known work is the ornate thatched cottage of 1818 'in the Elizabethan style, built after the manner of one at Virginia Water belonging to … George IV' (*Life and Letters of Captain Marryat*, 2.130), on his Langham estate, Norfolk, in the planning of which he was assisted by his son Frank, then a pupil in the office of Sir John Soane (1753–1837). His library was sold at Sothebys in 1837.

Copland, handsome and self-confident, early used his profits in adopting an aristocratic manner of life, with country seat and town house; he entertained extensively, rode to hounds, and sent his three sons to Eton. In 1801 he purchased for £10,000 the bulk (some 76 acres) of the estate at Gunnersbury, Middlesex, formerly the property of Princess Amelia. He immediately erected a house, enlarged in 1816, where pastimes included cricket and archery. In 1810 he bought a 1000 acre estate at Langham, Norfolk, which in June 1830 he exchanged for Sussex House, Hammersmith, the property of his old friend Captain Marryat, the novelist. He moved in 1812 from St Martin's Lane to a large house, 29 Great George Street, Westminster (subsequently the National Portrait Gallery), where, despite frequent attacks of gout, he entertained liberally, culminating in 1832 in a grand ball.

Almost as soon as the continent was open to English travellers, in September–October 1814 Copland toured northern France and Belgium. In 1819 he took his family and two servants on a four-month tour of Wales, the Lakes, Scotland, and north-east England, bearing introductions to several noblemen. In 1820–22 he sent his eldest son on an unusually comprehensive European tour, and a family tour in three carriages, accompanied by three servants, through France and Switzerland to Italy, followed between August 1823 and May 1824. Copland was a magistrate for Middlesex but in 1820 paid a fine rather than serve as sheriff of London. On his eldest son's marriage in 1826 he settled £300 a year on him and gave a reception for 350 guests. To a younger son he advanced £6000 to purchase a commission in the Queen's Bays. Copland was also a generous benefactor to hospitals, being elected treasurer of the Charing Cross Hospital.

His children's travel diaries show Copland to have been keenly interested in the works of both man and nature, alike enthusiastic about visiting Crawshay's Welsh ironworks, Smirke's new Lowther Castle, and Staffa's caves. He was, too, a committed family man, keen that wife and children share such experiences, and visiting his mother's birthplace to enquire into her family. Copland died in his Westminster house, 29 Great George Street, on 12 July 1834, and was buried in the chancel vault of St Martin-in-the-Fields.      M. H. PORT

**Sources** 'Commissioners of military inquiry: fourth report', *Parl. papers* (1806–7), 2.47, 52, 82b, 169–92, 325, no. 99 · priv. coll., Copland family MSS · will and affidavit of Alexander Copland, PRO, PROB 11/1839, fol. 671 · will and affidavit of Alexander Copland senior (*d.* 1793), PRO, 11/1238, fol. 542 · ratebooks, 1810–20, St Margaret and St John, Westminster · *London Directory* (1799–1835) · Christ's Hospital, court minute book, 1813–33, GL, Guildhall MS 12806/14 · St Katharine's Dock Co. minute book 1, Museum of London, Port of London Authority archives · *Life and letters of Captain Marryat*, ed. F. Marryat, 2 (1872), 130 · Burke, *Gen. GB* · *Court and private life in the time of Queen Charlotte, being the journals of Mrs Papendiek*, ed. V. D. Broughton, 2 vols. (1887) · S. Birkenhead, *Peace in Piccadilly: the story of Albany* (1958) · D. Lysons, *The environs of London*, 2nd edn, 2/1 (1811), 145 · LMA, Westminster Abbey muniments, Middlesex Deeds Registry
**Archives** priv. coll., diaries | priv. coll., Copland family MSS
**Likenesses** portrait, *c.*1805, priv. coll. · W. J. Newton, miniature, 1828, priv. coll. · photograph (after a portrait), Albany, Piccadilly, London · portrait (as a boy), priv. coll.
**Wealth at death** see will, PRO, PROB 11/1839, fol. 671

**Copland, James** (1791–1870), physician, was born in November 1791 in the Orkney Isles. The eldest of nine children, he went to school at Lerwick, and in November 1807 entered the University of Edinburgh. His studies were at first directed towards theology, but after a time he changed to medicine, and graduated MD in 1815. He went to London in August of that year, and spent eighteen months going round the London hospitals, to study the surgical practices. Being offered an appointment as medical officer to the settlements of the Royal African Company, he sailed early in 1817 for the French trading fort of Goree, and then continued to Senegal, the Gambia, and Sierra Leone, learning all he could of the diseases of the country. Soon after leaving Sierra Leone he was able to make use of his newly acquired knowledge, for three-quarters of the crew fell ill with fever, and in the midst of the epidemic a gale carried away the masts of the ship. Following the storm Copland landed and by various means made his way along the coast to the British fort of Cape Coast, where he lived for some months; he returned to England in 1818. He then travelled through France and Germany, again looking at medical practice, and was back in England by 1820. In the same year he took a house at Walworth and became a licentiate of the Royal College of Physicians. He wrote on the medical topography of west Africa for the *Quarterly Journal of Foreign Medicine* (1820), on human rumination, on yellow fever, on hydrophobia, and on cholera for the *London Medical Repository* (1821); he then engaged in a discussion on chronic peritonitis in the *London Medical and Physical Journal*, about whether the disease was caused by tubercle or merely by chronic inflammation.

In 1822 Copland took a house in Jermyn Street and

became editor of the *London Medical Repository*, to which he also continued to contribute. In 1825 he issued a prospectus for an encyclopaedia of medicine. At the same time he lectured on medicine at a medical school then existing in Little Dean Street; somewhat later he took up a similar post at the Middlesex Hospital. His further proposals for an encyclopaedia were ultimately successful; the first part was issued in 1832, and Copland's *Dictionary of Practical Medicine*, in three volumes, and covering every part of medicine, was completed in 1858. It earned him £4000. The advances in medical techniques had been so great that the publishers then urged him to prepare a supplement, for which he was paid £1000. His achievement earned Copland the epithet of 'the Johnson of medicine' (Clarke, 410), whom, it was said, he to some degree resembled (ibid., 420).

In 1832, following an outbreak of cholera in Britain, Copland's earlier article on cholera was published as a separate book, *Pestilential Cholera, its Nature, Prevention, and Curative Treatment*; cholera was a disease which Copland believed to be spread by contagion. Copland was elected FRS in 1833, and fellow of the Royal College of Physicians in 1837. He built up a considerable practice and wrote more on medicine than any fellow of the college, in his own day or previously. He was respected in the college and was Croonian lecturer in 1844, 1845, and 1846; Lumleian lecturer in 1854 and 1855, and Harveian orator in 1857. He was president of the Pathological Society, but did not obtain the respect of the practical morbid anatomists who attended its meetings, and who were often led to smile when the president claimed as his own numerous modern discoveries in pathology. Copland gave up practice about a year before his death. He died at Hertford House, Brondesbury Road, Kilburn, London, on 12 July 1870. Nothing is known of his wife, but a son and a daughter were named as executors to his will.

NORMAN MOORE, rev. ANITA McCONNELL

**Sources** T. J. Pettigrew, *Medical portrait gallery: biographical memoirs of the most celebrated physicians, surgeons … who have contributed to the advancement of medical science*, 4 vols. in 2 [1838–40], vol. 1, p. 109 · J. F. Clarke, *Autobiographical recollections of the medical profession* (1874), 324–6, 410–20 · *Medical Circular*, 4 (1854), 299, 317, 333
**Likenesses** H. Room, oils, RCP Lond.
**Wealth at death** under £1500: resworn probate, Nov 1870, CGPLA Eng. & Wales

**Copland, Patrick** (*c*.1572–*c*.1651), philanthropist, was born in the burgh of Aberdeen, the son of John Copland, a merchant. He attended Aberdeen grammar school and Marischal College, Aberdeen. He appears to have gone then to England, and in 1612 joined the East India Company as chaplain on its tenth voyage. It was during this time that Copland's profound belief in the role of education in the process of civilization began to manifest itself. On his return from his first voyage with the company he was entrusted with the care and education of a young Bengali boy brought back to England. He taught the boy to read and write, and instructed him in the principles of Christianity, with a view to using him in the attempted conversion of his people.

In 1621, returning on the *Royal James* from his second voyage, Copland encountered some ships bound for Virginia and learned of the lack of churches and schools in the colony. This encounter had a profound effect on his future interests. He conducted a vigorous campaign to raise funds for a proposed college at Henrico, where the children of American Indians would be educated as part of the process of colonization and to which the planters of Virginia might also send their children. For his efforts, Copland was made a free brother of the Virginia Company, and in July 1622 was chosen rector-elect of the proposed college. However, news of massacres in the colony, followed by the king's dissolution of the company in 1624, ended the plans for the college and Copland's involvement with it. Instead, along with his wife, daughter, and others, he left in 1626 for the Somers Islands (Bermuda) where they planned to use a £300 bequest transferred from the Virginia Company to the Somers Islands Company to found a school.

For much of his life Copland was a presbyterian, and was opposed to the restoration of episcopacy in Scotland under James VI. Throughout his life he was indefatigable both as a letter writer and as a preacher, and his most famous sermon, 'Virginia's God be thanked' (1622), was a model of Calvinist exhortation to active citizenship and colonizing zeal. Preached to the assembled members of the Virginia Company at the church of St Mary-le-Bow, Cheapside, in April 1622, in thanksgiving for the safe arrival of eight of their ships in the colony, it was at one time (1929) the most valuable printed sermon in existence.

Copland's involvement in the colonization of the New World did not prevent him from taking an intense interest in education in his own native town, and—over three instalments, made in 1616, 1622, and 1627—he contributed 6000 marks Scots for the founding of a chair of divinity at Marischal College. His regular correspondence with the burgh council on the matter of his divinity professorship and on the personnel of the college in general evidences close connections with the Scottish protestant intellectual diaspora both in London and on the continent. Walter Donaldson, one-time principal of the academy at Sedan, was a kinsman, and Copland was also acquainted with Robert Boyd, Robert Howie, and Thomas Reid, Latin secretary to James VI and I and a fellow benefactor of Marischal College.

In the Somers Islands, Copland eventually led a movement towards congregationalism, for which he was imprisoned for a time in 1647. In 1648 the colony moved to Eleuthera, in the Bahamas. After three years, the difficulties of sustaining life on Eleuthera persuaded them to return to Bermuda, where Copland is thought to have died, impoverished, shortly afterwards.

SHONA MacLEAN VANCE

**Sources** *Council register*, Aberdeen City Archive, vols. 47–52/1 · L. B. Taylor, ed., *Aberdeen council letters*, 6 vols. (1942–61), vols. 1–3 · *Fasti academiae Mariscallanae Aberdonensis: selections from the records of the Marischal College and University, MDXCIII–MDCCCLX*, 1, ed. P. J. Anderson, New Spalding Club, 4 (1889) · P. J. Anderson, 'Mr Patrick

Copland', *Scottish Notes and Queries*, 5 (1891–2), 1–3 • J. Gammack, 'Rev. Patrick Copland', *Scottish Notes and Queries*, 7 (1893–4), 107–8 • E. D. Neill, *Memoir of Rev. Patrick Copland, rector elect of the first projected college in the United States: a chapter of the English colonization of America* (1871) • *CSP col.*, vols. 2–4, 9 • J. F. Kellas Johnstone and A. W. Robertson, *Bibliographia Aberdonensis*, ed. W. D. Simpson, Third Spalding Club, 1 (1929)

**Wealth at death** very poor: Gammack, 'Rev. Patrick Copland'

**Copland, Patrick** (1748–1822), natural philosopher and university teacher, was born early in 1748 in the parish of Fintray, Aberdeenshire, and baptized there on 22 March 1748. He was the first of three children and the only son of Samuel Copland (*c*.1716–1795), minister of the parish of Fintray, originally from nearby Tough, and his wife, Jean (*née* Copland), a distant relative from Aberdeen.

Copland entered Marischal College, Aberdeen, with a minor bursary in 1762. There he was taught natural philosophy by George Skene and moral philosophy by James Beattie; both were members of the philosophical society of Aberdeen that was responsible for the common-sense school of philosophy. After graduating AM in 1766, Copland went back home to pursue natural philosophy, in particular mechanical science. In 1774 he was asked by Skene to return as his assistant. Skene resigned six months later, and on 25 February 1775 Copland was appointed regent and professor of philosophy at Marischal College. He remained a professor there until a month before his death in 1822; though from 1779 until 1817 he held the title of professor of mathematics.

Professor Copland was a tall, handsome man, and when young was regarded as the principal beau in Aberdeen. Nevertheless, he remained a bachelor until he was thirty-nine. On 27 September 1787 he married Elizabeth Ogilvie (1767–1852), almost twenty years his junior, the eldest daughter of Dr David Ogilvie, a surgeon in the Royal Navy. The Coplands had three sons: Alexander (*b*. 1788), John (*b*. 1789), and Charles (*b*. 1791), followed eight years later by Mary (*b*. 1799), who married Dr Alexander Murchison in 1821. In 1803 Copland purchased Fountainhall House, Aberdeen, from the estate of George Skene. Copland was a mild and unassuming man. He had a taste for pictures, a love of the theatre, and an ear for music that led him to build his own large pipe organ in 1789. Above all, he was devoted to natural philosophy. For services to Marischal College he was awarded an honorary LLD in 1817.

Copland introduced into university education the large-scale use of demonstration apparatus in teaching natural philosophy, a trend that lasted for almost 200 years. He gave extensive education to tradesmen, especially in mechanics, and he acted as an academic consultant to the municipality, to industrial contacts, and to members of the aristocracy. In 1782 he was elected a corresponding member of the Society of Antiquaries of Scotland. In 1785 he was one of the non-resident founding members of the Royal Society of Edinburgh, and in 1807 was elected a member of the Linnean Society. These interests remained peripheral: Copland was exceptional for specializing in mechanical science. He built up in the college his own workshop, which he equipped with lathes and many hand tools, including taps and dies by Ramsden, whom he knew

personally. There Copland himself made to a high professional standard a great many pieces of demonstration equipment in wood and metals. Just before his death his collection and his tools were sold to Marischal College, and a number of items survive there. In 1783 Copland obtained a grant to employ a mechanic, John King, to make models of machinery; he may be the earliest university technician in the country. King stayed at Marischal for about eight years before returning to clock making.

Copland was acknowledged to be the best teacher in the university in his day. About 2000 students benefited from his lectures, which were planned around his exceptional collection of demonstration equipment covering almost all of the disciplines within natural philosophy. Among his students was James Stephen, grandfather of Leslie Stephen, the founder of the *Dictionary of National Biography*. Copland's demonstration equipment was also the basis for his extramural adult education classes. These preceded by many years and were deeper in content than those of better-known 'pioneers' such as George Birkbeck and others who promoted the rise of mechanics institutions in the 1820s. Copland's classes began in 1785 and continued for twenty-eight years, being given approximately biennially. Each course consisted of about eighty lectures of one and a half to two hours. The success of these efforts to educate tradesmen has been considered a significant influence in the founding of London's Royal Institution in 1800. Partly for this initiative and partly for his consultative work he received a royal pension in 1803.

Copland raised a public subscription in 1780 to construct the first publicly funded astronomical observatory in Scotland equipped with modern instruments. The observatory was situated on the Castlehill, near Marischal College, and was furnished with instruments by Dollond, Ramsden, and Troughton. Copland excited popular imagination when at the observatory site he released hydrogen balloons as early as March 1784. With John King he constructed to an unusual design by James Ferguson an elaborate astronomical clock, which survives at the university. He appointed as assistant keeper Andrew Mackay, who became a notable teacher and writer on navigation.

Copland's interests in applied natural philosophy led him to become an early example of what would now be called a consultant physicist. He advised the town on obtaining improved fresh water supplies, and in 1804 put forward proposals for what would have been one of the very first municipal sand and gravel slow filtration beds, had it been implemented. He also gave advice on standards of length, weight, and volume measure, and made accurate comparative determinations for them. He advised town and county on matters of surveying, and made the earliest measurements of the height of the Deeside hills by barometric means. He probably introduced the process of liquid chlorine bleaching into Britain. After seeing the process demonstrated by Saussure in his laboratory in Geneva in May 1787, Copland explained it to Aberdeen industrial chemists. They developed the process into a commercially viable technique, which prevented the grant of a restrictive patent to a Liverpool company in

1788 and thereby aided the spread of modern bleaching methods.

Copland achieved a national reputation. Although he left no scientific papers or patents as tangible records of his work, in his own way he influenced many contemporaries through his actions and his teaching. He died on 10 November 1822 at his home, Fountainhall House, from a large growth, probably throat cancer. He was buried in St Nicholas's churchyard, Aberdeen, on 20 November.

JOHN S. REID

**Sources** J. S. Reid, 'Patrick Copland, 1748–1822: connections outside the college courtyard', *Aberdeen University Review*, 51 (1985–6), 226–50 · J. S. Reid, 'Patrick Copland, 1748–1822: aspects of his life and times at Marischal College', *Aberdeen University Review*, 50 (1983–4), 359–79 · J. S. Reid, 'The Castlehill observatory, Aberdeen', *Journal for the History of Astronomy*, 13 (1982), 84–96 · J. S. Reid, 'The remarkable Professor Copland', *Bulletin of the Scientific Instrument Society*, 24 (1990), 2–5 · *The memoirs of James Stephen, written by himself for the use of his children*, ed. M. M. Bevington (1954), 176–94 · U. Aberdeen, MSS 2886, 2999 · [A. Cruikshank], *Vanishing Aberdeen* (1984), 7–10 · U. Aberdeen, MSS M203–M205; MSS 438–439, 2944, M174 [notes from Copland's lectures] · U. Aberdeen, MS 3123/2 [lecture notes attributed to Copland] · parish register (baptism), Fintray, Aberdeenshire, 22 March 1748 · *Aberdeen Journal* (20 Nov 1822), 3 · Copland family records

**Archives** U. Aberdeen, 'The description and use of mathematical instruments'; lecture notes | W. Sussex RO, letters to duke of Gordon

**Likenesses** J. Moir, oils, 1817, priv. coll.

**Copland** [Coplande], **Robert** [Roberte] (*fl.* **1505–1547**), translator and printer, began his career in Wynkyn de Worde's shop. Because in his poem *Hye Way* one of the beggars tells 'Copland' that he is:

> And lyke your maystershyp
> of the north

Francis suggested a northern origin for the printer (Francis, 9), but Hazlitt's reading 'If it please your mastership, of the north' is more likely (*Remains of the Early Popular Poetry*, 4 vols., 1864–6, 1.336). It has been suggested that Copland was Caxton's apprentice, because of Copland's statement in his preface to *Kynge Appolyn of Thyre* (before 1510) that he was 'gladly folowynge the trace of my mayster Caxton begynnyng wyth small storyes and pamfletes and so to other'. In addition, about 1505 Copland had called his translation *A Complaynt of them that be to Soone Maryed* his 'fyrst werke'. If he were between twenty and twenty-four in this year, however, Copland's birth date would lie between 1485 and 1481—too late for him to have been Caxton's apprentice before the latter's death in 1491. Hence Copland's reference to 'my mayster' probably indicates only his respect for the patron and employer of his own undoubted master, Wynkyn de Worde. Anthony Wood's belief that 'R. Copland and E. More had as it seems spent some time in Oxon, in the condition of poor scholars' (Wood, *Ath. Oxon.*, 1.249–50) is refuted by Copland's own statement that 'in scole nor countre / I never take effect' (*The Castell of Pleasure*, C6v). The will of Cecilye Clowgh, 'wedow of the parisshe of Seynt Bride the Virgin', tentatively dated 28 January 1543, provides a bequest to 'my ostis Coplonde' (Darlington, 84), who was perhaps the printer's wife, in view of the date and the parish, since

Copland's sign of the Rose Garland faced on Fleet Street, near Fleet Bridge, in that large extramural parish (*The Tryumphant Vyctory*, 1532, colophon).

For about a decade before he began work as a printer Copland translated French light reading which de Worde published. First, about 1505, he produced a pair of *malmarié* laments, *A Complaynt of them that be to Soone Maryed* and *The Complaynte of them that ben to Late Maryed*, the latter certainly, the former possibly, by Pierre Gringore. To each of these he attached an acrostic verse envoi displaying his own name, ROBERTE (-US) COPLAND(E), imitating a French authorial fashion. In 1508 he revised, partly retranslated, and wrote verse for the popular compendium of physical and spiritual advice, *The Kalender of Shepeherdes*. Some time before 1510 he produced his translation *Kynge Appolyn of Thyre*, and on 6 February 1512 his translation *The Knyght of the Swanne*, or *Helyas*, appeared; for both of these romances he supplied prose prefaces. After he began work as a printer, in 1514, he continued to produce translations: his version of a French dance manual, *The Maner of Dauncynge of Bace Daunces after the Use of Fraunce*, was published on 22 March 1521. Later, in 1524, he brought out *The Begynnynge and Foundacyon of the … Knyghtes Hospytallers*, a translation of the account by Guillaume de Caorsin (*c.*1430–1501), together with the *Syege of Rodes*, from the eyewitness account of 1522 by Jacques de Bourbon, both commissioned by the grand prior of the knights of Malta in England. On 7 August 1528 *The Secrete of Secretes* appeared, his translation of the medieval encyclopaedic compilation, and in the same year Copland produced the first English printed navigational route book, *The Rutter of the See* (1528). The next year saw the appearance of a short guide to daily living: *The Maner to Lyve Well* was printed in thirty-six editions of books of hours between 1529 and 1556, and thus played a considerable part in the emergence of English in this popular devotional manual. His later translations included a 1532 news dispatch on the current fighting in Styria, *The Tryumphant Vyctory of the Imperyall Mageste agaynst the Turkes*; a compendium of four surgical tracts (among them the first printing of Galen in English, *The Questyonary of Cyrurgyens*, 1542); and, about 1545, a version of the popular memory treatise by Pietro Tommai (Peter of Ravenna), *Fenix* (1491). Copland's translation, *The Art of Memory* (*c.*1545), was the first complete text devoted to classical mnemonic theory to appear in English. This list of his translations demonstrates Copland's centrality as a conduit for French popular literature; at the same time it suggests the utility of his translated works of information.

Copland's first printing was also for de Worde, with whom he shared the printing of two previously published and successful texts, one religious (*The Deyenge Creature*, 1514), the other legal (*The Justices of Peas*, 1515). It may be that the older printer here planned a large edition and commissioned part of it from his employee, as the younger man's introduction to the craft. Copland printed in all thirty-five editions (disregarding ephemera like indulgences and images of pity), and of this number several items which bear his colophon were probably printed for de Worde. After the latter's death in 1534 or 1535, ten books, almost a third of Copland's output, were printed for other men, a record which indicates a continuing lack of capital.

Copland many times showed himself acutely aware of early printing's technical concerns as it attempted to accommodate its inheritance from a manuscript tradition. He served as de Worde's corrector for *Ipomydon* in 1518 ('Syth that no wryter / wolde take it to amende'), and, as William Herbert noted, he was the first printer to use the comma in addition to the virgule (early January 1534, in Erasmus's *Funus* and John Colet's *A Ryght Fruteful Monycion*). He warns printers against overzealous changes:

> Correccyon
> I agre
> but there a pause, Folowe your copy
> and lette thamendynge alone.
> (*Guystarde and Sygysmonde*, 1532, D2v)

The criticisms he put into Quidam's mouth in the preface to *The Seven Sorowes* (*c.*1526) demonstrate his sensitivity to the accurate transmission of text. 'By my soule the prynters make such englyshe, so yll spelled, so yll poynted, and so pevyshe, that scantly one cane rede lynes tow, But to fynde sentence, he hath ynough to do' (A3). Most tellingly, he printed Chaucer's *Parliament of Fowls* from manuscript (Bodl. Oxf., MS 638) rather than depending primarily on an earlier edition, claiming that in so doing he had 'losed' the text from 'ruynous domage', amended the poetry to 'thylke same langage that Chaucer to the gave', and thus made it possible for lovers of Chaucer to 'his mynde avewe'.

In his writing Copland's personal voice registers strongly, even in the ephemeral verses which preface many of his publications and in the 'go little book' envois which conclude them. In 1518, for instance, he apologized to *The Castell of Pleasure*'s author for adding his own 'verses incorrect':

> Without your lycence
> yf I dyde them impresse, Pardon I praye you
> of this my homelynesse.

In this editorial verse he several times commented on the decay of reading: 'Bokes be not set by theyr tymes is past I gesse' (*Castell*, *Assemble of Foules*, *Guystarde and Sygysmonde*). But it is in his three longer poems that his skill in the creation of dramatic situation and character through dialogue is best displayed. *The Seven Sorowes that Women have when Theyr Husbandes be Deade* (written about 1526) provides a parody of religious meditation on the seven sorrows of the Virgin, but the conventionally lascivious widow's emotions and thoughts are presented sympathetically, with an interior focus rare for the period. The tone shifts somewhat uneasily between psychological realism and conventional misogynist fun. The short, amusing *jeu d'esprit Jyl of Braintfords Testament* (*c.*1535) might be labelled a very late English fabliau owing to its scatological jokes and bequest of farts theme. *The Hye Way to the Spyttell Hous*, written between 1529 and 1534, is a depiction of the life of

the (often criminal) poor who went to London's St Bartholomew's Hospital, and makes a central contribution to the early modern English discussion of poverty as a social problem. It contains the first printed version of thieves' cant in England and thus anticipates the later sixteenth-century work of Thomas Harman, John Awdely, and Thomas Dekker. The poem is indebted in its second section to Robert de Balsac's *Le chemin de l'ospital* (1502), a catalogue of fools.

Copland worked in a period for which almost no Stationers' Company records survive, but he is glimpsed as one of a group of colleagues when, on 25 October 1526, the bishop of London, Cuthbert Tunstall, warned thirty-one members of the book trade against printing Lutheran books. Copland's lifelong connection with de Worde is further shown by his appointment as one of two overseers for the latter's will and by a bequest of 10 marks in books, perhaps equivalent to a year's income. The lay subsidy assessment taken in the printer's ward of Farringdon Without on 4 April 1544 records his worth as 20s., a low figure, though these assessments were sometimes suspect. Near the end of his life Andrew Boorde's *Breviary of Helthe*, dated 15 July 1547, refers to another book of Boorde's, his *Introduction of Knowledge*, 'whiche hath been longe a pryntynge for lacke of money and paper and it is in pryntynge with pyctures at Roberte Coplande prynter' (Duff, 30). In his *Pryncyples of Astronamye*, which Copland printed (1547?), Boorde refers again to this work: 'Introduction of knowledg a boke of my makyng the whiche ys aprintyng at old Robert Coplands the eldist printer of Ingland the which doeth print thes yere mi pronosticacions'. This evidence, combined with the *Short-Title Catalogue*'s assignment of a Copland-printed herbal to the same probable date, suggests that Copland was still active in this year. He perhaps died before its end, however, since in 1547 his successor, William *Copland (*d.* 1569), printed *A Fruteful … Instruction* for Richard Kele (the *STC* lists an additional group of four books which may be assigned to 1548 and to either Robert or William Copland).

MARY C. ERLER

**Sources** *Poems: Robert Copland*, ed. M. C. Erler (1993) [incl. complete lists of poetry, prose, trans., and printing] • M. C. Erler, 'Printers' copy: MS Bodley 638 and the *Parliament of fowls*', *Chaucer Review*, 33 (1999), 221–9 • M. C. Erler, 'Suleyman's 1532 Vienna campaign: an English news dispatch', *Slavonic and East European Review*, 65 (1987), 101–12 • M. C. Erler, 'The first English printing of Galen: the formation of the Company of Barber-Surgeons', *Huntington Library Quarterly*, 48 (1985), 159–71 • M. C. Erler, 'The maner to lyve well and the coming of English in François Regnault's primers of the 1520s and 1530s', *The Library*, 6th ser., 6 (1984), 229–43 • *STC, 1475–1640*, nos. 5728–34, 3.45 • I. Darlington, ed., *London consistory court wills, 1492–1547* (1967), 84 • J. Ames, T. F. Dibdin, and W. Herbert, eds., *Typographical antiquities, or, The history of printing in England, Scotland and Ireland*, 4 vols. (1810–19), vol. 3, pp. 111–26 • W. G. Moore, 'Robert Copland and his *Hye way*', *Review of English Studies*, 7 (1931), 406–18 • W. G. Moore, 'The evolution of a sixteenth-century satire', *A miscellany of studies in romance languages and literatures presented to Leon E. Kastner*, ed. M. Williams and J. A. de Rothschild (1932), 357–60 • Wood, *Ath. Oxon.*, new edn, 1.249–50 • E. G. Duff, 'The printer of Borde's *Introduction of knowledge*', *The Library*, new

ser., 8 (1907), 30–33 · F. C. Francis, *Robert Copland* (1961), 9 · lay subsidy assessment, PRO, E 179/144/123
**Likenesses** printer's mark, repro. in Erler, ed., *Robert Copland: poems*
**Wealth at death** lay subsidy valuation of 20s. in 1544: PRO, E 179/144/123

**Copland, William** (d. 1569), printer, was believed by Dibdin (Ames, Dibdin, and Herbert, 3.127) to have been the younger brother of Robert *Copland (fl. 1505–1547); he is more likely to have been Robert's son. After Robert's death, probably in 1547, William continued as printer in the same house. On 24 November 1546 he had received a licence to marry Joanne Tyddeswell of St Bride's. Though he may have begun printing as early as 1545 his earliest dated book, *A Fruteful and a Very Christen Instruction for Children*, printed for Richard Kele, appeared in 1547. An original member of the Stationers' Company, Copland was named in the charter of 1557. On 12 March of the same year he was brought before the privy council and ordered to deliver to the printer J. Cawood for burning all the copies which he had printed of Cranmer's *Recantation*. The Stationers' register, which covers only the second decade of his career, records that he was fined four times—Herbert calls his behaviour 'as regular as most of his associates' (Ames, Dibdin, and Herbert, 1.128)—and that he took an apprentice, Robert Jonnes, in May or June 1562. Copland's career falls into three periods: he first printed at Robert Copland's old shop, the Rose Garland in Fleet Street, from 1547 to early 1558; he then printed at the Three Crane Wharf in the Vintry, in the parish of St Martin, from some time before October 1558 to possibly 1562; and he was in Lothbury, opposite St Margaret's Church, from about 1563 to 1567.

During his twenty-year career Copland produced over 150 books, many of them for other printers. His work includes a remarkable number of popular items, romances in particular, which had been first published by Wynkyn de Worde and even by Caxton. Among them are *The Four Sons of Aymon*, which Caxton had translated and published in 1490, de Worde about 1505, Notary about 1510, and William Copland (three editions for other printers) in 1554; *Sir Bevis of Hampton*, first printed by de Worde in 1500 and then five more times before William Copland printed two editions in the 1560s; *Valentine and Orson* (de Worde c.1510; William Copland c.1555 and c.1565); and *The Seven Wise Masters of Rome* (Pynson 1493; de Worde 1506?; William Copland c.1555). The list of popular books owned by the sixteenth-century Coventry collector Captain Cox includes many of Copland's titles and it is likely that Cox possessed Copland's actual editions. What may have been Copland's last project, *A Dyaloge betweene ij Beggers*, was registered to him between 22 July 1567 and 22 July 1568, but no copy survives.

Because of his connection with Robert Copland, and Robert's with Caxton's heir, Wynkyn de Worde, William Copland represents the fourth in a direct line of succession from England's first printer. He provided a connection between popular reading taste of the late fifteenth century and that of the seventeenth, continuing to make

available works such as Caxton's translation of Le Fevre's *Recuyell of the Historyes of Troye* (1475?) which first appeared at Bruges and which saw seven more editions, including Copland's, before 1636. The date of his death is not known, but he was buried on 30 May 1569 in the parish of St Margaret, Lothbury, London. Shortly afterwards the wardens of the Stationers' Company 'Payd for the buryall of coplande vjˢ' (Arber, *Regs. Stationers*, 1.392). Whether this payment indicates impoverishment or merely recognition of an original member has been disputed; the former may be more likely since only one other contemporary burial payment is printed by the register's editor.

H. R. TEDDER, *rev.* MARY C. ERLER

**Sources** STC, 1475–1640 · E. G. Duff, *A century of the English book trade* (1905) · Arber, *Regs. Stationers*, vol. 1 · J. Ames, T. F. Dibdin, and W. Herbert, eds., *Typographical antiquities, or, The history of printing in England, Scotland and Ireland*, 4 vols. (1810–19), vol. 3, pp. 127–72 · J. L. Chester and G. J. Armytage, eds., *Allegations for marriage licences issued by the bishop of London*, 2 vols., Harleian Society, 25–6 (1887) · APC, 1554–6, 247–8 · *Captain Cox, his ballads and books, or, Robert Laneham's letter*, ed. F. J. Furnivall (1871) · *Poems: Robert Copland*, ed. M. C. Erler (1993) · G. S. Fry, ed., *Abstracts of inquisitiones post mortem relating to the City of London*, 1: 1485–1561, British RS, 15 (1896) · marriage licence, Principal Registry of the Family Division, London, consistory court of 1446–1560, Liber vicarii generalis, vol. 2, fol. 7r · parish register, St Margaret Lothbury, GL, MS 4346/1, 30 May 1569 [burial] · private information (2004) [A. Hill-Zenk]

**Copleston, Edward** (1776–1849), bishop of Llandaff and moral philosopher, was born on 2 February 1776 at Offwell in Devon, where his father, John Bradford Copleston, was rector. He was educated at home until the age of fifteen when, in 1791, he won a scholarship to Corpus Christi College, Oxford. Further meritocratic progress ensued: the chancellor's prize for Latin in 1793, a fellowship (by invitation) at Oriel College in 1795, the English essay prize in 1796, a college tutorship in 1799. He was destined for a traditional career as an Oxford don, albeit an educationally reforming one: he was one of six Oriel fellows who gratuitously conducted the first examinations under the examination statute of 1800. Ordination followed in 1800 and the vicarage of St Mary the Virgin, Oxford, usually held by an Oriel fellow, together with further college and university preferment. He became professor of poetry in 1802, and as senior treasurer of Oriel for six years from 1806 substantially improved the college's finances. His genealogical hobbies led to his election as a fellow of the Society of Antiquaries of London in 1804. He never married.

In his thirties Copleston entered a wider public stage. This was principally due to his successful support in 1809 for the candidacy for the office of university chancellor of the pro-Catholic politician Lord Grenville. As a result, not only did he gain prominence in the university (he was elected unopposed provost of Oriel in 1814, succeeding Provost Eveleigh, one of the sponsors of the examination statute) but also entry to the liberal tory political world. He became a frequent visitor to Dropmore, Grenville's country house, and to Althorp, the home of the second Earl Spencer. In the 1820s he was consulted by Robert Peel

**Edward Copleston** (1776–1849), by Thomas Phillips, 1820

and William Huskisson on financial questions. It was also in this period that he wrote his most important publications: on education (the *Three Replies to the Calumnies of the Edinburgh Review*, 1810–11), economics (the letters to Sir Robert Peel on the currency and pauperism, 1819), and theology (the *Inquiry into the Doctrines of Necessity and Predestination*, 1821).

**An Anglican polemicist** Copleston's promotion of educational reform, political economy, and Christian apologetics all served an essentially conservative enterprise: to ensure the continued existence of an Anglican ruling élite and the dominance of Anglican institutions. Thus his *Three Replies* were a defence of Oxford University and a classical education against the charges of the Edinburgh Reviewers (contained in a series of articles by John Playfair, Richard Payne Knight, and Sydney Smith) that the university neglected, to the detriment of the country, the new social sciences as well as the physical sciences. In political economy he was a champion of the gold standard, and attacked the inflationary speculation of the wartime years. He sought to return the economy to the order of nature. In his theological writings he attacked the external threats to Anglican orthodoxy, in particular the Calvinist doctrine of predestination. However, his methods were liberal: he utilized new means for conservative ends.

Copleston recognized that a university education served a national purpose and that the English universities were answerable to public opinion. He was not, therefore, averse to reform in order, as he wrote in the *Three*

*Replies*, that 'the lifeblood of England' might be 'invigorated by healthy food'. Not only did he support the introduction of the new examination statute, as noted above, he also supported the abolition of closed scholarships and fellowships, and developed the tutorial system which made Oriel famous. Through his teaching he sought to develop an Anglican meritocracy. This involved changes to the curriculum; he almost singlehandedly promoted the teaching of logic at Oxford, albeit deductive Aristotelian logic rather than the Baconian inductive reasoning favoured by the Edinburgh Reviewers, as well as reviving the analogical reasoning of Joseph Butler (1692–1752). Although he believed that the Oxford trinity of logic, divinity, and mathematics should exclusively form the basis of a degree, he supported the teaching of the new natural and social sciences outside the colleges by means of university professors. Paradoxically, in view of the attacks of the Edinburgh Reviewers, through his admiration for the work of Dugald Stewart and in particular his *Elements of the Philosophy of the Human Mind*, Copleston introduced the work of the late Scottish Enlightenment to Oxford, and so too, it is generally considered, to the first Oxford political economists: Nassau Senior (1790–1864) and Richard Whately (1787–1863).

In his *Letters to Robert Peel* on the gold standard and the poor laws, Copleston characteristically began with the assertion that it was only by reference to the first principles of the science of political economy that it was possible to sustain an argument about practical measures. By clearing away the undergrowth of false reasoning and by applying the deductive method to a few axiomatic truths it was possible to reach certain conclusions. In this way, despite the existence of the evils of unemployment and poverty, it was possible to see the divinely created order even in the current economic chaos. Thus, he argued, political economy was emphatically not a secular science. In his *First Letter* he attributed the economic dislocation of post-Napoleonic war England to the depreciation of the currency, and urged the government to remove such obstacles as it was able to the self-correcting mechanism of nature. In his *Second Letter*, although he agreed with the evangelical John Bird Sumner (1780–1862) that economic life was one of the trials of man, and thus that governments should not effect by human laws what God had provided by the laws of nature, he did not concede that misery was the necessary consequence. He argued that it was possible to provide by law for the preservation, but not the propagation, of life. He thus tempered the apparent 'evil' of Malthus's natural check to population growth. The object of the poor laws was not radically inconsistent with the principle of population where it embodied the Christian duty of charity but did not usurp the natural order by encouraging population growth. Moreover, as the state of society improved, so would the standard of poor relief. However, Copleston's liberality in the face of demands for the abolition of poor-law relief should not be exaggerated: he opposed public works programmes and the purchase of land for cultivation by the poor, and approved of checks being imposed on the administration of relief by justices of the peace. The purpose of his support for relief was better to punish vagrancy and mendicity.

**Theological and philosophical writings** In theological matters Copleston applied the principles of natural theology to the interpretation of revealed religion in order to demonstrate the reasonableness of revelation. He argued, invoking the aid of the eighteenth-century Bishop Butler, that if the difficulties of revealed religion were no greater than those of nature, and the divine creation of the latter were acknowledged, those difficulties should not be regarded as objections to the credibility of revelation but as evidence of its truth. Thus in his *Enquiry into the Doctrines of Necessity and Predestination* (1821) he argued that just as in the natural world free will is compatible with divine order, by analogy in the revealed world the existence of divine foreknowledge is compatible with man's exercise of choice and the punishments and rewards which God administers as a result. The Calvinist error in construing the biblical passages on divine foreknowledge as evidence of predestination was, according to Copleston, to place too human a construction on them. The Calvinist forgot that God's attributes are described imperfectly, in human terms only, since it is impossible for man to know the true nature of the divine. Indeed this was not the purpose of the Bible—which was to teach man how to feel and act towards God, not to explain his nature. However, by restoring 'the pure substance of the Gospel' in this way, Copleston arguably diminished its strength in the long run by opening it to the critical scrutiny of the natural sciences.

Copleston's writings were chiefly ephemeral in nature and do not reflect his breadth of interests nor do justice to his importance in the intellectual life of the country. His principal intellectual legacy, in the best Oxford tradition, was his students, who wrote the substantial works which his occasional pieces anticipated. Copleston was the leader of the early Noetic school at Oxford, centred around Oriel College, and so called from the Greek *noesis*, meaning reason. This school was responsible to a large degree both for the intellectual revival of the university and a distinctive Anglican apologetic which, in the 1820s, combined a 'high' view of the church, as an externally visible, divinely appointed society, with a rational defence of the Christian creed. His main disciple was Richard Whately (1787–1863), fellow of Oriel and archbishop of Dublin. His books on logic and rhetoric in particular owed much to Copleston, who at one stage had contemplated writing a treatise on logic and who, in his pamphlet published in 1809, *The Examiner Examined, or, Logic Vindicated*, a review of Henry Kett's *Logic Made Easy* (1809), had declared that logic was 'the guide for Reason'. Whately also wrote an introductory treatise on political economy which Copleston was equipped, but failed, to provide. Another student was Baden Powell (1796–1860), also a fellow of Oriel, whom he recommended for the Savilian chair of geometry. His controversial views on the non-divinely ordained nature of the sabbath (also shared with Whately) Copleston foreshadowed in a book review of William

Buckland's *Reliquiae diluvianae* (1823). Renn Dickson Hampden (1793–1868), fellow of Oriel, regius professor of divinity, and bishop of Hereford, was a third pupil, whose Bampton lectures for 1833 continued Copleston's revival at Oxford of the works of Bishop Joseph Butler.

At the height of his Oxford dominance Copleston is said to have been of august and commanding presence: he was physically fit, a noted equestrian, and tireless walker (he once walked all the way from Oxford to Offwell). He had the air and polish of a man of fashion, rather than of a university don, as befitted a member of the Alfred, a London club much patronized by senior clergy and superior lawyers, and a guest of society drawing-rooms. His sonorous voice was much imitated by undergraduates. He was also capable of rudeness and irritation when his quickness of mind was not followed by others. Above all, he was noted for his precision of thought, a characteristic trait of the Oriel common room at that time, which attributed much intellectual error to incorrect definitions and loose reasoning.

**Bishop of Llandaff** With such talents and connections, it is perhaps surprising that Copleston did not achieve greater ecclesiastical preferment. He became dean of Chester in 1826, and in 1827 dean of St Paul's and bishop of Llandaff, one of the poorest sees, with no episcopal residence and a net income in 1828 of only £924; he resigned the provostship of Oriel in January 1828. Part of the explanation may be that in the 1820s he was caught in the cross-fire between the Canningites (with whom he was associated and whom he praised in his publications) and the ultratories, with the result that he was passed over for the see of Oxford in 1826 which instead went to Peel's candidate and former tutor, Charles Lloyd. It may also have been the result of his anti-sabbatarian views, with which William Howley, then bishop of London and subsequently archbishop of Canterbury, who was consulted by the king on the Oxford bishopric, was not in sympathy. From the 1820s onwards he also began to suffer from the depression which in his later years is said to have clouded his intellect.

As bishop of Llandaff, Copleston participated in the conference at Lambeth which determined the form of declaration which was to replace the sacramental test abolished by the repeal of the Test and Corporation Acts in 1828. He also amended the declaration in the House of Lords by inserting the words 'upon the faith of a Christian', turning it into a religious test designed to exclude non-Christians from office and provoking the protests of the whigs Lord Holland and Henry Brougham. He supported Catholic emancipation in 1829, but this, however, was the limit of his liberalism. Although much consulted by the whig governments of the 1830s on ecclesiastical appointments, he was never truly in sympathy with their politics. He voted against the Reform Bill on its second reading in the Lords in October 1831, although he subsequently changed his mind; he opposed the abolition of church rates in the 1830s, and was not in favour of substituting a payment out of the consolidated fund; he disapproved of non-denominational Christian education; he opposed repeal of the corn laws and the Jew Declaration Bill, and voted against the increase in the grant to Maynooth College in 1845. His friend and former pupil, Richard Whately, was right to term him in the context of post-Reform politics 'a most decided tory'.

Copleston's diocese, which had been predominantly rural, had a rapidly expanding population due to the development of the south Wales coalfields and the coal ports of Newport and, subsequently, Cardiff. In response he encouraged the construction of both parsonage houses, to encourage a resident clergy, and churches. Between 1827 and 1853 the number of cures without a resident minister fell by approximately 60 per cent. He also promoted parochial schools and reformed the administrative structure of the diocese: a deanery was created in 1840 and a second archdeacon appointed in 1844. On average he personally expended in occasional donations and subscriptions connected with his diocese, both public and private, sums greater than his annual episcopal income. Such activities, however, were unequal to the task of stemming the growth of Welsh dissent. Nor did they exempt him from the charge that, by failing to present Welsh speakers to Wesh benefices, he had weakened the church. However, as much of the population growth was due to English immigration, and as he only had twelve livings in his personal gift, such a failure (denied by his biographer), if true, can scarcely have had the consequence alleged.

Copleston's theological and economic views in the 1840s were unaltered from those he expressed in the 1820s. He opposed the 'mysticism' of the Tractarians and their opposition to science and literature. He saw the Irish famine of 1846 as a providential message of the truth of Malthusianism. In his later years he became increasingly irritable and oversensitive as his health deteriorated: he gave up horse-riding in 1844. Copleston died on Sunday 14 October 1849 at Hardwick House, near Chepstow, and was buried on 23 October in the lady chapel of Llandaff Cathedral, the first bishop to be buried there since 1674.

Copleston's life exemplified the transitional position which he occupied in early nineteenth-century England. By comparison with many of his contemporaries he was a liberal reformer, promoting both the revival of learning and liberal politics at Oxford. But he chose not to pursue the consequences of the liberal speculations which he encouraged in his pupils. He had no desire to see either the natural or social sciences displace classical learning at Oxford, nor reason undermine Anglican doctrinal truth. He wished only for a revivified English establishment, which, instead of retreating into reaction, was capable of fighting new heresies on their own territory. This, however, was a task principally undertaken by his students.

Richard Brent

**Sources** W. J. Copleston, *Memoir of Edward Copleston, DD* (1851) · R. Whately, 'Introduction', in E. Copleston, *Remains* (1854) · W. Tuckwell, *Pre-Tractarian Oxford* (1909) · T. Mozley, *Reminiscences, chiefly of Oriel College and the Oxford Movement*, 2 vols. (1882) · *Letters of the earl of Dudley to the bishop of Llandaff* (1840) · A. M. C. Waterman, *Revolution, economics and religion: Christian political economy, 1798–1833* (1991) · B. Hilton, *The age of atonement: the influence of evangelicalism on social and economic thought, 1795–1865* (1988) · P. Corsi, *Science and religion: Baden Powell and the Anglican debate, 1800–1860* (1988) · *Hist. U. Oxf.* 6: *19th-cent. Oxf.* · U. R. Q. Henriques, *Religious toleration in England, 1787–1833* (1961) · M. Brock, *The Great Reform Act* (1973) · N. Gash, *Mr Secretary Peel: the life of Sir Robert Peel to 1830*, new edn (1985)

**Archives** Devon RO, corresp. · NL Wales, corresp. | BL, letters to Philip Bliss, Add. MSS 34568–34581 · BL, corresp. with Lord Grenville, Add. MSS 59416, 69109, 69112, 69145 · BL, corresp. with Robert Peel, Add. MSS 40344–40584 · Bodl. Oxf., letters to Richard Heber · Glos. RO, letters to John Neale · NL Wales, letters to Revd Dr T. Hughes; letters to his family · Oriel College, Oxford, corresp. with Edward Hawkins; letters to Renn Dickson Hampden

**Likenesses** J. Downman, pencil and watercolour drawing, 1810, AM Oxf. · T. Phillips, oils, 1820, Oriel College, Oxford [*see illus.*] · W. Behnes, marble bust, 1843, Oriel College, Oxford · attrib. M. A. Shee, oils, CCC Oxf.

**Copleston, Frederick Charles** (1907–1994), philosopher and Jesuit, was born on 10 April 1907 at Claremont, Trull, near Taunton, Somerset, the elder son of Frederick Selwyn Copleston (1850–1935), civil servant in India and high court judge in Rangoon, and his second wife, Norah Margaret, daughter of Colonel Charles Little, whom he had married in 1902 after the death of his first wife in 1895. The family, which claimed to have lived in the west country since the time of William the Conqueror, had strong roots in the Church of England. John Copleston was provost of King's College, Cambridge (1681–9), Edward *Copleston was bishop of Llandaff (1827–49). His uncle, Reginald Stephen *Copleston, was bishop of Calcutta (1902–13).

Freddie Copleston, as he was widely known, was educated at Marlborough College from 1920 until 1925, where he was a contemporary of John Betjeman, Louis MacNeice, and Anthony Blunt, though he regarded them as much more intellectually inclined than he was himself. Towards the end of his time at Marlborough he decided to become a Roman Catholic, a decision which was not welcome either to the school authorities or to his family, who had the greatest difficulty in understanding what seemed like a renunciation of a centuries-old family tradition in favour of an unattractive and alien form of Christianity. He went up to St John's College, Oxford, in 1925, but preoccupation with his new religious beliefs and perhaps too much time rowing for the second eight led to him taking a disappointing third in classical moderations. Much to his father's relief, he did obtain a reasonable second in Greats in 1929. His philosophy tutor was the well-known J. D. Mabbott, but Copleston's philosophical views were more in sympathy with what even then was a somewhat old-fashioned neo-Hegelian idealism. Some of his friends remarked that it seemed incongruous that the recent convert to Catholicism should at the same time be seeking an all-encompassing philosophical type of world view.

Upon leaving Oxford, Copleston was accepted as a candidate for the priesthood by his home diocese of Clifton, and went to Oscott College on the outskirts of Birmingham to begin his studies. After a year there, however, he decided instead to join a religious order, and became a Jesuit novice in the autumn of 1930. In 1932 he went to Heythrop College, near Chipping Norton, Oxfordshire, which

Frederick Charles Copleston (1907–1994), by unknown photographer

was then the Jesuit house of studies, where he was ordained priest in 1937. In 1938 he went to Germany to complete his Jesuit training, and only just managed to escape back to Britain before the outbreak of war in 1939. The war put paid to the plans for him to study for a doctorate in philosophy at the Gregorian University in Rome, and he found himself instead lecturing at Heythrop to the few young Jesuits who were not serving in the armed forces.

The rural quiet of Oxfordshire did at least give him time to write. He produced his first philosophical books, monographs on Nietzsche and Schopenhauer. More importantly, it was then that he began what was to be his life's major task, the nine volumes of *A History of Philosophy*. Originally conceived as a three-volume survey for his Jesuit students (for whom philosophy at that time was studied merely as a background to the study of theology), it soon developed into a much more ambitious project, aimed at philosophy undergraduates who were studying the subject for its own sake, and needed something much more detailed. The final volume of the set appeared in 1975, some thirty years after the first. Copleston was firmly of the view that one had no right to disagree with a philosopher until one had accurately understood, and indeed truly appreciated the value of, what that philosopher had written. Accordingly, his history consciously aimed at an accurate, and as far as possible impartial, account of the writers he included. Despite its occasional unevennesses

(he later described the first volume as 'deplorable'), it is a monumental achievement. Its lucidity and directness of style make it an easily accessible and reliable introduction to its subjects which has few, if any, comparable rivals.

In addition to lecturing at Heythrop, Copleston taught in the Gregorian University in Rome for one semester each year for many years, starting in 1952. He also found time to broadcast: in 1948 there was a famous radio debate with Bertrand Russell on the existence of God, and in the following year another with A. J. (Freddie) Ayer on the merits of logical positivism. Radically different though their philosophical views were, the two Freddies got on extremely well together, and their friendship lasted for many years, ending only with Ayer's death. Copleston was, perhaps not unreasonably, fairly unimpressed with the analytic philosophy current in Britain in the 1950s and 1960s. Though one looks in vain in the pages of the *History* for clues to Copleston's own views, his preference for some continental writers, especially perhaps Jaspers and Blondel, rather than their British contemporaries can be seen in his *Contemporary Philosophy: Studies of Logical Positivism and Existentialism* (1956).

In 1970 Heythrop College was re-founded as one of the colleges of the University of London, with Copleston as its first principal, a post which he held until his retirement in 1974. Academic administration was neither his forte nor at all to his taste, but he successfully presided over the considerable change in ethos required when a Jesuit house of studies became a university college at the service of the wider community. His students and his younger colleagues welcomed his unassuming manner, his constant encouragement, and his often mischievous sense of humour.

In retirement, spent partly at Campion Hall, Oxford, and partly at the Jesuit residence in central London, Copleston continued to write, and was internationally much in demand as a lecturer, notably at Santa Clara University in California. *Philosophies and Cultures* (1980) was a scaled down version of what he had hoped might be a history of the history of philosophy; and his Aberdeen Gifford lectures, published as *Religion and the One: Philosophies East and West* (1982), is a work of high—unfashionably high—metaphysics, evidence of the fact that his youthful interests had never really been abandoned. In 1986 he published *Philosophy in Russia: from Herzen to Lenin and Berdyaev*, followed in 1988 by *Russian Religious Philosophy: Selected Aspects*. He regarded these as incomplete, but better than nothing given the lack of any comparable treatment in English. He lamented that the really interesting philosophers were not really Russian, and the interesting Russians not really philosophers.

Copleston was honoured with membership of the British Academy (1970), a personal professorship in the University of London (1972), an honorary fellowship at St John's College, Oxford (1975), and several honorary doctorates, including awards from Santa Clara, Uppsala, and St Andrews. He was appointed CBE in 1993. He had long suffered from cancer, though for several years it did not seem to inconvenience him unduly. He died peacefully at

St Thomas's Hospital, London, on 3 February 1994, and was buried on 12 February in Kensal Green Roman Catholic cemetery, London.                    GERARD J. HUGHES

**Sources** F. C. Copleston, *Memoirs* (1988) · Jesuit Archives, 114 Mount Street, London · personal knowledge (2004) · G. J. Hughes, 'Frederick Charles Copleston, 1907–1994', *PBA*, 87 (1995), 277–86 · G. J. Hughes, ed., *The philosophical assessment of theology* (1988) [incl. bibliography of Copleston's works] · b. cert.
**Archives** Boston College, Massachusetts | SOUND BL NSA, performance recording
**Likenesses** W. E. Narraway, oils, 1974, Heythrop College, Kensington Square, London · photograph, repro. in Hughes, 'Frederick Charles Copleston' · photograph, British Academy [*see illus.*]
**Wealth at death** £125,000: probate, 3 May 1994, *CGPLA Eng. & Wales*

**Copleston, Reginald Stephen** (1845–1925), bishop of Calcutta, was born at Barnes, Surrey, on 26 December 1845, to Reginald Edward Copleston and his wife, Anne Elizabeth, *née* Sharpe. His father was rector of Barnes and a relative of Edward Copleston, the bishop of Llandaff. He was educated at Merchant Taylors' School, London. In 1864 he won a postmastership at Merton College, Oxford, where he became a leading contributor to the *Oxford Spectator* and was twice president of the union. He was elected to a fellowship at St John's College in 1869 and appointed tutor in 1870, in which year his textbook *Aeschylus* was published.

Copleston was ordained priest in 1875 and was appointed the fourth bishop of Colombo by Lord Carnarvon, the colonial secretary; he was then consecrated in Westminster Abbey on 28 December, at the earliest possible age. In Ceylon the inexperienced 'Boy Bishop' immediately plunged into a conflict with the missionaries of the evangelical Church Missionary Society (CMS), who had been operating virtually independently; Copleston, however, believed that he had the responsibility for co-ordinating all of the church's work in his diocese. The CMS was also hostile to the 'high-church' ritualist views held by Copleston. The dispute became a major controversy, reverberating in England as well as Ceylon. In 1879 Copleston refused to license new CMS missionaries or ordain their candidates. The dispute was only settled as a result of mediation by a committee of English bishops under Archbishop Tait in 1880.

The next major challenge which Copleston had to face arose from the British government's decision in 1881 to disestablish the church in Ceylon. This meant that it would cease to provide ecclesiastical subsidies (including clerical salaries) but set the diocese free to manage its own affairs. Copleston readily accepted that the church of a small minority should not be maintained out of public funds, and made successful efforts to raise alternative funding. He also instituted a synod, including lay members and with a Ceylonese majority, for the administration of the diocese; after his move to India in 1902 he also took steps to develop synodical government there, which paved the way for the eventual independence of the Anglican church in south Asia. In 1882 he married Edith Chenevix Trench (*c*.1845–1943), daughter of Richard Chenevix *Trench, archbishop of Dublin. They had one son and two daughters.

Copleston was the ablest bishop of Colombo in the colonial period, and his translation to Calcutta, as the metropolitan of the Anglican church in India and Ceylon, was widely welcomed. He consistently emphasized the importance of the corporate life and unity of the church despite the ethnic and linguistic differences among its members. He was critical of British racism, calling for Indians to be treated with greater understanding and respect. He encouraged the development of local leadership for the church, strongly supporting the controversial appointment of the first Indian bishop, V. S. Azariah, to an independent diocese (Dornakal), rather than acting as an assistant bishop in the diocese of Madras who would minister only to Indians. Unimpressed by much of the 'higher criticism' of the Bible, and insisting that the Book of Common Prayer should be exactly translated into the languages of south Asia, Copleston was conservative in many respects, but he was equally concerned that Christianity should not seem foreign to Asians. Thus he criticized undue attachment to uniformity and sanctioned new forms of service to meet local needs.

Copleston was president of the Ceylon branch of the Royal Asiatic Society for sixteen years. He produced a substantial study of Buddhism, *Buddhism Primitive and Present in Magadha and in Ceylon* (1892; revised edn, 1908), which was highly regarded at the time. In it he considered the Buddhism both of the original texts and as practised in contemporary Ceylon. Generally in his appraisals of both Buddhism and Hinduism he stressed their differences from Christianity—in opposition to the argument that they might be seen as foundations for it. He agreed that the missionary should start with 'the truth which his hearers already hold' ('Buddhists and Christian morality', 1), but argued that it is found in what is common to human nature rather than in the doctrines specific to Buddhism or Hinduism.

*Buddhism* was Copleston's only major work, but other publications included the pamphlet *Ceylon: Historical Sketch* (1906), two papers for the Pan-Anglican congress of 1908, and several episcopal charges and sermons.

Copleston was a brilliant linguist who quickly learnt to preach in the diverse languages of Ceylon and eastern India. Tall and athletic, he had a powerful presence and was concerned to uphold the authority of the bishop while respecting the convictions of others. He resigned from Calcutta in 1913 and lived at Putney, London, until his death there, at his home, 25 St John's Road, on 19 April 1925. He was buried at Putney Vale cemetery on 22 April. His wife survived him, dying in 1943.

MICHAEL LAIRD

**Sources** *The Times* (21 April 1925) · *The Guardian* (24 April 1925) · M. E. Gibbs, *The Anglican church in India, 1600–1970* (1972) · F. L. Beven, *A history of the diocese of Colombo* (1946) · C. P. Williams, *The ideal of the self-governing church* (1990) · R. S. Copleston, *The obligations of Christianity and civilisation to the heathen* (July 1878) [sermon] · R. S. Copleston, *A charge delivered at his ... visitation of the diocese of Calcutta* (1905); (1909) · R. S. Copleston, Sermon preached in St Paul's Cathedral, Calcutta, January 5th 1913 · R. S. Copleston, 'Buddhists and Christian morality', in *Pan-Anglican papers*, Pan-Anglican Congress

(1908) · R. S. Copleston, 'The missionary's equipment in India', in *Pan-Anglican papers*, Pan-Anglican Congress (1908) · R. S. Copleston, 'The relation of Hindu philosophy to the gospel', *Church Missionary Review*, 64 (1913) · R. S. Copleston, *A charge delivered at his … visitation of the diocese of Colombo* (1886); (1897); (1900) · C. S. Grimes, *Towards an Indian church* (1946) · *Journal of the Ceylon Branch of the Royal Asiatic Society*, 17 (1901–2), 84–8 · C. H. C. David, *A short history of the Church of England in Ceylon* (1906) · K. M. De Silva, *A history of Sri Lanka* (1981), 343 · MSS on the Ceylon question, Church Missionary Society · Bodl. RH, United Society for the Propagation of the Gospel archives · BL OIOC, Curzon MSS · private information (2004) [archivist, St John's College, Oxford; librarian, Colombo Diocesan Library, Sri Lanka] · *CGPLA Eng. & Wales* (1925) · b. cert.
**Archives** Bodl. RH, United Society for the Propagation of the Gospel MSS · Colombo Diocesan Library, 368/3 Bauddhaloka Mawatha, Sri Lanka · LPL, corresp. and papers, MSS 2966–2967 · PRO, Ceylon MSS | BL, corresp. with W. E. Gladstone and Lord Gladstone · BL OIOC, Curzon MSS · CUL, corresp. with Lord Hardinge · LPL, corresp. with Edward Benson · LPL, corresp. with A. C. Tait · NL Scot., Blackwood MSS; Minto MSS · U. Birm. L., letters to Church Missionary Society, ref. CMS/W
**Likenesses** photograph, LPL; repro. in S. A. Walker, *Dignitaries of the Church*, 2 vols. [1889–90] · portrait, Diocesan Conference Hall, Colombo, Sri Lanka · portrait, Bishop's Committee Room, Colombo, Sri Lanka · portrait, St Thomas College, Mount Lavinia, Sri Lanka
**Wealth at death** £7377 7s. 10d.: probate, 6 June 1925, *CGPLA Eng. & Wales*

**Copley, Anthony** (b. 1567, d. in or after 1609), writer and conspirator, was the third son of Thomas *Copley (1532–1584) and his wife, Catherine Luttrell (d. in or after 1590). John *Copley (c.1577–1662) was his younger brother. When his father went abroad, he remained in England. In 1582, however, 'being a yonge student of Furneval's Inne under the charge of a kinsman … Mr T[homas] Southwell, who is now himselfe beyond sea, him unwitting, I stole away' (BL, Lansdowne MSS, vol. 66, no. 47). He joined his parents in Rouen, where he stayed for two years. A kinsman, the Jesuit Robert Southwell, procured him a pension of £10 from Pope Gregory XIII, and he was sent to Rome. There he spent two years until, in 1585, Gregory died and the pension was not renewed. Copley returned to Flanders, where Hugh Owen obtained him a pension of 20 crowns from the duke of Parma. As he admitted on his return to England in 1590, 'since that time till now … I have served the king of Spaine in his warres in Flanders' (ibid.). Copley was arrested shortly after his arrival in England, and it was from prison, on 6 January 1591, that he wrote this to William Waad, clerk of the privy council. In the same letter he sought the queen's pardon and employment, swearing loyalty 'to my prince and country' (ibid.). He proved his loyalty in a series of letters detailing the whereabouts and activities of English Catholic fugitives and the unscrupulous, harsh conduct of his former patron, Parma. In a dramatic role reversal the former Spanish pensioner besought God to favour queen and kingdom against Philip II, who 'sware … he would utterly ruine her Majestie and Ingland' (ibid., nos. 25, 47).

During the 1590s Copley, who was entitled to a £30 annuity by his father's will, married and lived with his wife at Roughay, Horsham parish, in Surrey; by 1604 they had children. Here, according to Richard Topcliffe's report to the queen, on 26 June 1592, he early manifested his volatility and unreliability:

> Anto[ny] Coplaye, the most desperayte yowthe that lyvethe … Bee most familiare with [Robert] Southewell. Coplay did shoote at a gentilman the Last summer, and killed an Oxe with a muskett and in Horsham Churche threwe his dagger at the parishe Clarke … There lyvethe not the lyke I think in England for sudden attemptes. (BL, Lansdowne MSS, vol. 72, no. 39)

He also remained under suspicion 'because he doth avouch himself to be a papist' (*APC*, 22.168). In December 1591 he was committed a close prisoner to the Fleet prison and questioned about certain speeches to which he had confessed.

Despite such suspicions, during Elizabeth's reign Copley was a moderate Catholic loyalist, hostile to the Jesuits and in search of toleration. In 1595 and again (this time without his name but with many 'late, true, and wittie accidents') in 1614 appeared *Wits, Fittes and Fancies Fronted and Entermedled with Presidentes of Honour and Wisdom*. This piece of prose consisted of jests, tales, and sayings mostly translated from a Spanish work, *La floretta spagnola*. The 1595 edition included *Love's Owl*, a poetic dialogue between 'Love and an Olde Man', and in the following year he published a poem entitled *A Fig for Fortune*. Both works were of little artistic merit but politically revealing about Copley's position. He dedicated the latter to another loyalist Catholic, Anthony Browne, Viscount Montague, and, at the same time, this 'Elizian out-cast of Fortune' sang the praises of his protestant 'soveraigne Ladie Eliza' (*A Fig for Fortune*, sigs. A4–A4v). This 'versified allegory … is a barely concealed plea for Catholic toleration, couched in terms of hyperbolic praise, with an argument at once elaborate and transparent' (Shell, 134). Then, in 1601, he took the side of secular priests in their controversy with the Jesuits. In particular Copley supported one of them, his friend William Watson, who had already appeared in print, with his pamphlet *An answere to a letter of a Jesuited gentleman, by his cosin, Maister A.C., concerning the appeale [against the arch-priest George Blackwell], state, Jesuits*. In it Copley identified 'Jesuitisme and Spaine' and defended the 'Seminarie-Bees' of 'our English hive'. Next year appeared *Another Letter of Mr. A. C. to his Disjesuited Kinseman Concerning the Appeale, State, Jesuits*. This was followed by a *Letter of his apologeticall for himself against the calumnies contained against him in a certain Jesuiticall libel intituled 'A manifestation of folly and bad spirit'*. There is, however, no record of the publication of his promised 'forthcoming Manifestation of the Jesuit's Commonwealth'.

In 1603 Copley became involved with Watson and others in the Bye plot. Its purpose was to seize the new king, James I, and compel him to grant toleration to the Catholics. Implementation of the plan on 24 June was frustrated by lack of Catholic armed support due, Copley claimed, to the Jesuits, who also informed the government. On 2 July a proclamation denounced the 'wicked purpose' of 'so ungracious and traiterous a minde' and ordered Copley's arrest. When his sister refused to harbour him he surrendered and made, in the bishop of London's words, 'so ample and full' confession (*Salisbury MSS*, 15.187). At the conspirators' trial at Winchester, on 15 November 1603, it was variously reported that 'Copley did deal more ingenuously' than the rest (Kempe, 375) and that he was 'a man of a whining speech, but a shrewd invention and resolution' (*State trials*, 2.64). His confession, also used against Sir Walter Ralegh at his trial, helped to secure the conviction of most of the Bye conspirators who were duly sentenced to death. Copley was pardoned, possibly because he provided further information. He was, however, banished from the realm. On 6 July 1604 he bade farewell to Robert Cecil, to whom he felt bound 'for his life and goods'. He added that 'The little he has of his own is necessarily left to his wife and children' (*Salisbury MSS*, 16.165). When Copley went into exile, he journeyed to Jerusalem with Ambrose Vaux. He was later in Brussels (1605), the English College at Rome (January–April 1606 or 1607), and The Hague (1608). He was still alive in 1609. It is not known if his wife or any of his children survived him.                    MICHAEL A. R. GRAVES

**Sources** *Calendar of the manuscripts of the most hon. the marquis of Salisbury*, 24 vols., HMC, 9 (1883–1976), vols. 15–17, 20 • J. Strype, *Annals of the Reformation and establishment of religion … during Queen Elizabeth's happy reign*, new edn, 4 (1824), vol. 4 • *State trials*, vol. 2 • Lansdowne MSS, BL, vols. 63, 64, 66, 72 • A. C. [A. Copley], *An answere to a letter of a Jesuited gentleman, by his cosin* (1601) • A. Copley, *A fig for fortune* (1596) • A. Copley, *Wits, fittes and fancies: also 'Love's owle', an ideal conceited dialogue* (1595); rev. edn, *Newly corrected and augmented, with many wittie accidents* (1614) • *Proclamation ordering the arrest of Anthony Copley for conspiring against the king* (2 July 1603) • 'Waad, William', *DNB* • 'Watson, William', *DNB* • *Dodd's Church history of England*, ed. M. A. Tierney, 5 vols. (1839–43), vol. 4 • *DNB* • K. C. Dorsey, *The life of Father Thomas Copley: a founder of Maryland* (1885) • *Letters of Sir Thomas Copley … to Queen Elizabeth and her ministers*, ed. R. C. Christie, Roxburghe Club, [130] (1897) • A. J. Kempe, ed., *The Loseley manuscripts* (1836) • A. Shell, *Catholicism, controversy, and the English literary imagination, 1558–1660* (1999)
**Archives** BL, Lansdowne MS

**Copley** [*née* Beuzeville; *other married name* Hewlett], **Esther** (1786–1851), writer, was born on 10 May 1786, probably in London, the youngest daughter of a prosperous Spitalfields silk manufacturer, Peter (Pierre) Beuzeville (1741–1812), and his wife, Mary (Marie) Griffith Meredith (1744–1811), both of French Huguenot descent. Her father retired from business and settled at Henley-on-Thames where, on 15 April 1809, she married James Philip Hewlett (1779/80–1820), curate of the evangelical parish of St Aldates, Oxford, and also chaplain at Magdalen and New College. They had three sons and two daughters. After Hewlett's early death she married in 1827 William Copley (*d.* 1857), who was ten years her junior. Copley was a Baptist minister, and succeeded James Hinton (1761–1823) at the Baptist chapel in New Road, Oxford; Esther had become a member of New Road Chapel, before she remarried, and may well have participated in the growth of missionary activities, including Sunday and day schools and preaching in outlying Oxford villages, which the energetic Hinton pioneered.

Esther Copley (1786–1851), by unknown photographer

Esther Hewlett was from 1815 a prolific author, publishing tales for children, tracts, works of domestic economy, and sacred history and biography. *Cottage Comforts* (1825), one of her earliest works, reached its eighth edition by 1831 and its twenty-fourth by 1864; a household management manual addressed to the labouring classes, it included chapters on renting and furnishing a cottage, brewing and baking, keeping animals, care and education of children, and the treatment of illnesses. Although it opened with a sententious section on the virtues essential to domestic comfort, *Cottage Comforts* was full of practical advice (the author had tried out her own recipes) and was forthright on such subjects as childbirth and constipation. *Catechism of Domestic Economy* (1850), *The Comprehensive Knitting Book* (1849), and *The Young Servant's Friendly Instructor* (1827) were works in the same genre. Mrs Copley's genuine concern for the working classes was further evidenced in *Hints on the Cholera morbus* (1832), a pamphlet published during the cholera epidemic of the early 1830s; offering practical advice on how to avoid cholera and how to nurse those infected, it was reissued in 1849 under the title of *Cholera Preventible*.

Like such women writers as Harriet Martineau and Eliza Meteyard, Mrs Copley attempted to inculcate principles of morality and domestic economy through fiction. She was the author of collections of tales for young people (both working class and middle class), such as *The Old Man's Head, or, Youthful Recollections* (1823), *My Mother's Stories, or, Traditions and Recollections* (1838), and *Family Experiences and Home Secrets* (1851); the contents of the latter had originally appeared in the *Family Economist*. *The Poplar Grove, or, Little Harry and his Uncle Benjamin* (1841), in which the Dawson family achieve comfort and prosperity through hard work, foresight, and benevolence, is one of her more developed stories of the same ilk.

Among many works written for children, Mrs Copley produced *Scripture Natural History for Youth* (1828), *Scripture History for Youth* (1829), and *Scripture Biography* (1835). Her most significant work, *A History of Slavery and its Abolition*

(1836), was also intended for children. More than 500 pages in length, the *History* austerely informed its readers that the origin of slavery was to be found in 'human depravity' (*History*, 12). But this theological explanation did not prevent Mrs Copley from tracing the course of slavery from scriptural times to her own day. Her youthful audience was spared neither graphic descriptions of the sufferings of black slaves in the West Indies nor lengthy accounts of the proceedings of the anti-slavery movement. Ironically, only three pages were devoted to the role of ladies' anti-slavery societies in a work which was, in itself, a witness to the significant commitment of nonconformist women to the anti-slavery cause.

The Copleys lived for a time at St Helier on the island of Jersey, until William was asked to become minister at Eythorne in Kent, a post he took up between 1837 and 1839. During his ministry, the chapel was active and well organized; however, Copley seems to have become an alcoholic. Esther Copley attempted to support him, apparently writing his sermons for him and ensuring that he performed his Sunday duties. Eventually he resigned his charge, possibly after a call to a chapel in the midlands, and left both Eythorne and his wife in 1843. She remained in the village until her death there on 17 July 1851. She had left the Baptist chapel in 1844, probably as a result of her marital problems; two of her sons took holy orders in the Anglican church, but Esther Copley seems to have returned to her denomination and died a Baptist. She was buried at Eythorne. A plaque commemorating Esther Copley, her parents, and her siblings was dedicated on 19 October 1997 at the United Reformed church in Henley-on-Thames.                        ROSEMARY MITCHELL

**Sources** D. M. Lewis, ed., *The Blackwell dictionary of evangelical biography, 1730–1860*, 2 vols. (1995) • [E. Copley], 'Biographical sketch of Mrs Copley', in E. Copley, *The complete cottage cookery*, 11th edn (1859), v–x • Allibone, *Dict.* • Foster, *Alum. Oxon.* • W. Stevens and W. W. Bottoms, *The Baptists of New Road, Oxford* (1948), 12–16 • W. J. Oldfield, 'Index to the clergy whose ordination, institution, resignation, licence or death is recorded in the diocesan registers of the diocese of Oxford … 1542–1908', 1915, Bodl. Oxf., MS Top. Oxon. c. 250 • IGI • D. C. A. Agnew, *Protestant exiles from France in the reign of Louis XIV, or, The Huguenot refugees and their descendants in Great Britain and Ireland*, 2nd edn, 2 (1871), 351ff • W. P. Clark, *Eythorne: our Baptist heritage* (1981), 44–6 • d. cert.
**Likenesses** engraving (after photograph), repro. in Copley, 'Biographical sketch of Mrs Copley', frontispiece • photograph, priv. coll. [*see illus.*]

**Copley, Sir Godfrey**, second baronet (*c.*1653–1709), politician, was the eldest son of Sir Godfrey Copley, first baronet (1623–1678), of Sprotborough, Yorkshire, and his first wife, Eleanor (*d.* 1659), daughter of Sir Thomas Walmesley of Dunkenhalgh, Lancashire. Although nothing is known of Copley's early education, he was admitted to Lincoln's Inn in 1674 and to the Inner Temple in 1681. In 1678 he succeeded his father as the second baronet. Thereafter his place of residence alternated between Sprotborough and his London residence at Red Lion Square. He was married twice, first, on 14 October 1681, to Catherine Purcell (*b. c.*1657), daughter and coheir of John Purcell of Nantriba, Montgomeryshire—they had three sons and daughters,

Sir Godfrey Copley, second baronet (*c.*1653–1709), by John Smith, 1692 (after Sir Godfrey Kneller, *c.*1690–92)

though only a daughter survived him—and second, in 1700, to Gertrude Carew (*bap.* 1682, *d.* 1736), daughter of Sir John Carew of Antony, Cornwall. The second marriage remained childless.

Copley was an active member of the Royal Society, of which he became a fellow in 1691, and served on the society's council on several occasions. His interest in science and antiquities was accommodated by healthy financial circumstances. He also regularly attended the London taverns that served as meeting-places for politicians. These two interests provided him with a wide circle of acquaintances that included many leading politicians as well as men of letters such as Dr Hans Sloane and Ralph Thoresby.

Politically, Copley was a country tory back-bencher, who on occasion expressed his independence in relation to party politics. His early parliamentary career was uneventful, though after his election for Aldborough, Yorkshire, in 1679 a rumour was spread that he was a Roman Catholic, owing to his connection through his maternal grandfather with Catholic interests in Lancashire. Having represented Aldborough until 1681, Copley did not return to parliament until 1695, when he was elected for Thirsk, another Yorkshire constituency, which he represented for the remainder of his life. From 1695 onwards he was a very active MP, taking a particular interest in financial affairs. His legal training was also evident in his parliamentary activity, especially in the debates surrounding the attainder of the Jacobite conspirator Sir John Fenwick in 1696. Copley spoke on several occasions, warning of the consequences of dispensing with the legal requirement of evidence from two witnesses, emphasizing the danger of setting precedents in the method of the attainder, and pointing out that parliament could not ignore 'the eternal rules' of equity, justice, reason, and conscience (Cobbett, *Parl. hist.*, 1116). In keeping with these sentiments, Copley attended Fenwick to the scaffold. Copley also spoke in several debates relating to the Anglican church, of which he was a member, and which he believed was in less danger than was believed by many of his contemporaries.

In 1701 Copley was elected as one of the commissioners to be named in the bill of accounts. This new parliamentary commission was included in the bill on the instigation of tory back-benchers, including Copley, who hoped to prove the charges that millions of pounds, granted for the war with France, remained unaccounted for. In the following year he was again elected to the commission, which he proceeded to serve on until 1704. During Copley's time as a commissioner Ralph Thoresby visited him at Sprotborough and noted that although Copley received him kindly he had to return to London in a few days, owing to the commission's heavy workload. However, Copley did find time to show Thoresby his new canal, his house, his many paintings by great masters, and certain mathematical instruments of which Copley had a good understanding. In 1704 Copley precluded himself from any further service on the commission by accepting the office of comptroller of army accounts, which he held until his death. After 1704 he was less active in parliament, probably due to his closer association with the government, although he continued to adhere to his country principles on occasion.

Copley died at Red Lion Square, London, on 9 April 1709 of a 'quinsy', or inflammation of the throat, which was considered to be a rare ailment, and was buried at Sprotborough on 23 April. In his will of 14 October 1704 he made substantial financial provision for his second wife and his daughter, Catherine, as well as leaving £100 to the Royal Society for the benefit of scientific knowledge. Although the first financial award was not made until 1731, in 1736 the society decided to use the bequest to fund an annual gold medal award, named after Copley. In time the Copley medal became regarded as the highest scientific distinction bestowed by the society, and is still awarded to this day. Copley's estates were put in trust for his cousin, Lionel Copley, though they were eventually inherited by Copley's grandson Joseph Moyle, the son of Catherine, who took his grandfather's surname by act of parliament.

C. I. McGRATH

**Sources** HoP, *Commons, 1690–1715* [draft] • GEC, *Baronetage*, vol. 3 • W. Yorks. AS, Leeds, Yorkshire Archaeological Society, Copley MSS • Sheff. Arch., Copley papers • Cobbett, *Parl. hist.*, vol. 5 • *The diary of Ralph Thoresby*, ed. J. Hunter, 2 vols. (1830) • *Dugdale's visitation of Yorkshire, with additions*, ed. J. W. Clay, 2 (1907) • Nichols, *Illustrations*, vols. 1, 4 • M. Y. Bektas and M. Crosland, 'The Copley medal: the establishment of a reward system in the Royal Society, 1731–1839', *Notes and Records of the Royal Society*, 46 (1992), 43–76 • M. Hunter, *The Royal Society and its fellows, 1660–1700: the morphology of an early scientific institution* (1982) • *The parliamentary diary of Sir Richard Cocks, 1698–1702*, ed. D. W. Hayton (1996) • H. Horwitz, *Parliament, policy and politics in the reign of William III* (1977)
**Archives** Sheff. Arch., incl. family MSS and corresp. • W. Yorks. AS, Leeds, Yorkshire Archaeological Society, incl. family MSS and corresp. | BL, letters to Hans Sloane, Sloane MSS 4036–4041, 4058 • Hunt. L., Stowe MSS, James Brydges diary • Notts. Arch., Newcastle account book, DD3P10/2/2
**Likenesses** J. Smith, mezzotint, 1692 (after G. Kneller, *c.*1690–1692), BM [*see illus.*] • G. Kneller, portrait
**Wealth at death** see HoP, *Commons, 1690–1715* [draft]

**Copley** [*alias* Luttrell], **John** (*c.*1577–1662), protestant convert and Church of England clergyman, was born at Louvain in the Spanish Netherlands, the fourth and youngest surviving son of Thomas \*Copley (1532–1584) of Gatton, Surrey, and Roughay, Sussex, a coheir of Lord Hoo and Hastings, whose title he used, and of his wife, Catherine, *née* Luttrell (*d.* in or after 1590), whose family had lands in East Anglia; Anthony \*Copley was his elder brother. His family had fled England as recusants but John was taken back there at nine days old to be nursed and educated. He stayed with a conformist uncle named Southwell, worshipping as an Anglican, but from his seventh year was also taught the Roman Catholic faith. When he was nine he and his mother went to Liège. The following year he started at King's College, Douai; then he continued his education successively at Valenciennes, the English College, Douai, and the Jesuit English College at St Omer, where he was one of the first to enter in 1593 and remained until about 1595. His mother returned to England, where in May 1596 she conformed.

About this time, while on a voyage, Copley and five fellow students were captured by an English ship near Calais and taken to London, where his relation Lord Howard of Effingham, as lord admiral, and Archbishop Whitgift entertained them. Copley was handed over to Bishop Aylmer and instructed in Anglican doctrine, but was soon freed on his friends' surety, and described himself as indulging in worldly pleasures while continuing to receive the Roman Catholic sacraments. However, in October 1599 he was admitted to the English College in Rome, and ordained sub-deacon, deacon, and priest in 1602. In September he left for England via Douai. He worked diligently as a seminary priest, sometimes under the name Luttrell, in the Roman Catholic London district, befriending many and initially with a strong conviction that he was serving God.

The Gunpowder Plot was a watershed for Copley. Convinced that the priests connected with it, whose guilt he assumed, would not have acted without papal authority, he was deeply disillusioned, considering that the pope would rather be the vicar of hell than the vicegerent of Christ. In July 1606 he was banished, with twenty-three other priests, and arrived at Douai. He was shocked by the acquiescence of the Jesuits abroad in the plot, regarding Roman Catholic teaching on the pope's power to depose rulers as totally unacceptable. He soon returned to England, but in May 1607 was arrested at Flushing; in October was indicted for hearing mass in Newgate gaol.

By this time Copley had read extensively in protestant polemic, the better to refute it. This stirred up doubts, fuelled by his reading of Bellarmine's *Controversies*. Some protestants challenged him to satisfy them on disputed points from scripture, the early fathers, or natural reason, which he was unable to do: his studies convinced him that the Anglican position was right. This led to a spiritual crisis in which 'my poore soule [was] environed with perplexed assaults of flesh and bloud' (Copley, 10). His struggle 'to overcome these conflicts between truth and falsehood' was aggravated by ties with numerous friends and recusant relatives, and by the thought of the distress apostasy would cause his converts. Once released from prison he became a chaplain to his kin the Cottons, but had to leave in 1610 owing to friction within the household. In 1611 his inner turmoil led to a spiritual Damascus experience, and Anglicanism. He was then chaplain to the Sussex-based Anthony Maria Browne, Viscount Montague. While in his service Copley fell in love with his future wife, Rebecca Moone, and they were married in St Margaret's, Westminster, on 10 December 1611. Commentators as different as John Chamberlain and archpresbyter George Birkhead concluded that it was a woman's love which had enticed Copley from Catholicism.

In *Doctrinall and Morall Observations Concerning Religion* (1612) Copley argued his new theological position moderately, with much reference to Roman Catholic works and those of the early fathers supporting his view, as well as personal testimony. In July, James I pardoned him for activities regarded as treasonable under the 1586 Act against Seminary Priests. Birkhead had already concluded four months previously that Copley had betrayed to the government all he knew of the activities of Catholic missionaries. Although he averred he would not inform against priests, it seems that Copley did subsequently inform against lay Catholics. In October, Archbishop Abbot, on whom he had attended following his conformity, presented him to Bethersden vicarage in Kent, which he resigned when Abbot collated him to the rectory of neighbouring Pluckley in 1616. Rebecca Copley died, and was buried there on 10 March 1623. Copley married again, on 9 February 1624 at St Mary Abbots, Kensington, Alyce Boucher, a widow, who died in 1638: on his death he left a third wife, Martha. All marriages were apparently childless.

In the 1630s Copley repeatedly conflicted with Sir Edward Dering at Pluckley over alleged wrongful appropriation of tithes and other rectorial matters. Dering's petition to Archbishop Laud in 1637 that Copley be removed to another living was fruitless, apparently owing to Copley's own obstruction. On 29 March 1642, together with Dr Richard Sheldon and Mr Higgins, Copley was summoned to the House of Commons accused of supporting a Kentish petition initiated by Dering which favoured the prayer book, royal control over the militia, and a synod of divines, but he denied any connection, and the Commons took no further action in the case. However, in September 1643 his benefice was sequestrated. Copley was restored to Pluckley in 1660, but may never have returned there as he died in Ashford, Kent, where he was buried on 3 June 1662. By his will, dated 19 September 1658, he left what he termed his 'small estate' (valued at £91 8s., including debts) to his wife, Martha (Canterbury Cathedral Archives and Library, DC6/PRC 17/71/246).   ELIZABETH ALLEN

**Sources** G. Anstruther, *The seminary priests*, 1 (1969), 87 · J. Copley, *Doctrinall and morall observations concerning religion* (1612) · A. Kenny, ed., *The responsa scholarum of the English College, Rome*, 1, Catholic RS, 54 (1962), 19–21 · M. C. Questier, *Conversion, politics and religion in England, 1580–1625* (1996), 48, 83, 112, 118 · M. C. Questier, *Newsletters from the archpresbyterate of George Birkhead*, CS, 5th ser., 12 (1998), 38, 137, 150, 157, 228 · *Walker rev.*, 214 · register of Archbishop Abbot, LPL, vol. 1, fols. 394r, 419r · S. P. Salt, 'The origin of Sir Edward Dering's attack on the ecclesiastical hierarchy, c.1625–40', *HJ*, 30 (1987), 21–52, esp. 24–9 · *CSP dom.*, 1633, 568; 1636–7, 446–7 · *JHC*, 2 (1640–42), 503–5, 510, 515 · W. Kelly, ed., *Liber ruber venerabilis collegii Anglorum de urbe*, 1, Catholic RS, 37 (1940), 116 · E. H. Burton and T. L. Williams, eds., *The Douay College diaries, third, fourth and fifth, 1598–1654*, 1, Catholic RS, 10 (1911), 74 · A. Kenny, ed., *The responsa scholarum of the English College, Rome*, 2, Catholic RS, 55 (1963) · D. A. Bellenger, ed., *English and Welsh priests, 1558–1800* (1984), 51 · parish register, Pluckley, CKS · parish register, Bethersden, CKS [transcript] · inventory of Copley's goods, CKS, PRC 11/19/52 · archdeacon's transcripts of Ashford parish register, Canterbury Cathedral and City Archives · *DNB* · will, Canterbury Cathedral and City Archives, DC6/PRC 17/71/246
**Wealth at death** £91 8s. moveables, incl. debts to him: inventory, CKS, PRC 11/19/52

**Copley, John** (1875–1950), printmaker and painter, was born on 25 June 1875 at his parents' home, Fallowfield, in Manchester, the only child of William Crawford *Williamson (1816–1895), professor of botany at Manchester University and founder of palaeobotany, and his second wife, Annie Copley Heaton (1840?–1929?). Copley was always his working name but was formalized by deed poll only in 1927. He was educated at Manchester grammar school, Manchester School of Art (he saw Ford Madox Brown paint the town hall frescoes), and the Royal Academy Schools in London (1892–7). He then spent three years in Italy. His first lithographs were published in 1906. In 1910 he helped Joseph Pennell set up the Senefelder Club for the revival of lithography as a creative medium, and was its secretary from 1911 to 1915. Here he met his wife, Ethel Léontine Gabain (1883–1950), also a lithographer. They married on 28 June 1913 and had two sons: Peter (*b*. 1915) and Christopher (1918–1940). Copley produced 252 lithographs between 1909 and 1938 drawn on stone; almost all were in black and white and all were printed by him in editions of twenty to thirty.

In perception, technical skill, and imaginative power Copley became perhaps the outstanding lithographer of the first half of the twentieth century in England. After his early complex colour works failed to sell, he found that black and white lithography was the ideal medium to record the activity of humankind, which he saw sometimes with sardonic humour, for example in *A Lavatory* (1909), sometimes with social concern, as in *Recruits* (1915). He loved the backstage life of the theatre, which he recorded in *Footlights* (1911), and delighted in the odd moment glimpsed: *Seen from an Omnibus* (1931). 'He had the photographer's ability to freeze an action and hold it in perpetual potentiality' (Taylor, 4). In 1930 he received the chief award and medal at the first International Exhibition of Lithography at the Art Institute of Chicago.

Copley throughout his life was semi-invalid with a heart condition: for two years, 1925–7, he and his family lived in Italy for his health, at Alassio. Lithographic stones not being available, he turned there to copper plates, and from 1930, when working a lithographic press became too strenuous, he concentrated on etching and resumed painting. Between 1927 and 1950 he made 131 etchings, and the process affected his art profoundly. Instead of following the precise technique that had become characteristic of British etching he used bold expressive outlines and decorative hatching. As the painterliness of lithography was replaced by the precision of etching so his mental attitudes became both more introspective and also more daring; there was a blackish humour and an existential unease in his enquiries into the human condition. In 1939 war broke out and his wife became seriously ill, and in 1940 his younger son died tragically: subsequently his images seemed to grow in power and foreboding, as in *Figures in the Wind* (1940) and *London Snow* (1940). A series made in the Scottish highlands explored the fierce darkness and sudden light of mountain storms, of which *Cairngorms* (1943) and *Loch Morlich: after Rain* (1943) are memorable examples. One of his last etchings, *In my Studio* (1949), is a self-portrait in which he looks at his aged self with penetrating curiosity. All his prints were signed in pencil 'John Copley', sometimes with the addition of 'imp.', meaning printed by him: he had his own press and did all his own printing. Between 1910 and 1918 he often placed by the signature a printed drawing of a yew tree, thus identifying that it was made at Yews, the house he lived in during those years and which had fine yew trees in the garden. In 1998 the lithographic prints mentioned above sold at between £2500 and £3500, while the etchings fetched between £1000 and £2000. Other prints sold at between £250 and £700. Copley earned his living solely as an artist, making paintings as well as prints. In 1938 his paintings were exhibited jointly with those of his wife at the Colnaghi Galleries.

Though a Mancunian, Copley never seemed a very English artist. It has been said that a stranger shown his prints would have no clue to their origin. He is an unclassifiable, original European, part of no fashion, school, or aesthetic movement. With passion and integrity he sought his own path, and had his own technique for transferring the shape of things and of living people onto plain paper. His obituarist noted that:

> there was a feeling behind [his work] of a consistent judgement of life that might be called stoical if it were not so intense in feeling, with a sense of tragedy that never became sentimental. There was something of the mystic in his temperament and sometimes his work reminded one of Blake. (*The Times*, 18 July 1950)

He held no rigid political or religious views. In 1935 he participated in the Artists' International Exhibition against War and Fascism. In the 1945 general election, in an uncharacteristic moment of dogmatic certainty, he voted Communist.

In his last years Copley found a rare new energy: besides working and caring lovingly for his increasingly ill wife,

he was, in 1948, elected president of the Royal Society of British Artists, a conservative body shaken into life by his wide-ranging exhibitions which he invited film stars—notably Vivien Leigh—to open. He organized exhibitions for foreign artists (a de Chirico show electrified London), concerts, and picture-hire schemes. More especially, he arranged open assemblies for young contemporaries and students, and many then young artists benefited from, and also acknowledged, Copley's influence on their work, particularly Carel Weight, Paul Hogarth, Michael Ayrton, and Patrick Heron.

Copley and his wife, Ethel Gabain, worked closely but not imitatively together, sharing studio space all their lives. He often said, almost jokingly, to his son, 'If anything happens to your mother I shan't want to stay around'. She died early in 1950. He organized a memorial exhibition of her paintings, said one day, 'There is no more for me to do', and five months after her, on 17 July 1950, he died peacefully at his home, 10 Hampstead Square, London, where they had lived for thirty years. Examples of his work may be found in the print rooms of the British Museum and the Victoria and Albert Museum; the municipal galleries of Manchester, Bradford, and Liverpool; the National Gallery of Canada; the Galleria Moderna, Rome; the Uffizi, Florence; and the library of the City of Boston.

PETER COPLEY

**Sources** H. Wright, *The lithographs of John Copley and Ethel Gabain* (1924) · *Lithographs, Copley and Gabain* (1920) [exhibition catalogue] · *Recent lithographs, Gabain and Copley* (1929) [exhibition catalogue, 1929] · R. A. Walker, 'The lithographs of John Copley', *Print Collectors' Quarterly*, 13 (1926), 273–96 · *John Copley and Ethel Gabain* (1985) [exhibition catalogue, Garton and Cooke Gallery, London, 13 Nov – 6 Dec 1985; incl. articles by P. Copley and G. Cooke] · C. Weight, *The Artist* (Oct 1950) [reprinted in *John Copley: an exhibition of etchings and lithographs* (1990)] · G. Cooke and J. R. Taylor, *John Copley, 1875–1950* (1990) [exhibition catalogue, Yale U. CBA, 6 Feb – 1 April 1990] · *The Times* (18 July 1950) · private information (2004) · personal knowledge (2004) · CGPLA Eng. & Wales (1950) · WWW · d. cert.

**Archives** Art Institute of Chicago · Yale U. CBA | LUL, corresp. with T. S. More and family

**Likenesses** E. Gabain, lithographs, 1914 (*The printer*), priv. coll. · E. Gabain, lithograph, 1918 (*The chequered scarf*), priv. coll. · J. Copley, self-portrait, lithograph, 1933, priv. coll. · J. Copley, self-portrait, etching, 1949 (*In my studio*), priv. coll. · J. Copley, self-portrait, etching, 1949 (*The pink vase*), priv. coll. · photographs, priv. coll.

**Wealth at death** £13,441 6s. 7d.: administration with will, 1 Nov 1950, CGPLA Eng. & Wales

**Copley, John Singleton** (1738–1815), portrait and history painter, was born in Boston, Massachusetts, on 3 July 1738 at Long Wharf, the first and only child of Mary Singleton (c.1710–1789) and Richard Copley, shopkeepers who emigrated from Ireland some time in the mid-1730s. Richard Copley died some time in the mid-1740s, but his widow and son continued the family business of cutting and selling tobacco until 1748.

**America, 1738–1774** Copley's formal education during his childhood remains a mystery. But his home on Long Wharf, the centre of Boston's thriving merchant economy, which accounted for 40 per cent of the total volume of colonial American shipping, was a *de facto* classroom

**John Singleton Copley (1738–1815),** self-portrait, 1780–84

that taught Copley market lessons that he would later apply to his artistic career.

In 1748 Copley's widowed mother married Peter Pelham (1695–1751), an émigré English artist and schoolteacher who had arrived in America in 1727. Pelham had been married twice before and had four sons and a daughter of his own. Ten-year-old Copley and his mother moved into Pelham's house on Lindel's Row, which was in a district of artisans near the centre of Boston. A half-brother, Henry Pelham (1749–1806), born the next year, would become a miniaturist, printmaker, and map maker of some reputation.

Copley's artistic education must have begun at about this time. He learned to mezzotint, a print technique that generates form in tonal areas rather than in lines, from his stepfather, who had achieved prominence in London and Boston for his work in that medium. Copley's first artistic effort, a mezzotint of the Revd William Welsteed, was printed in 1753 from the rescraped plate his stepfather had used to produce his own portrait of the Revd William Cooper ten years earlier. Peter Pelham also opened his library of English prints to his stepson and probably arranged to have Copley visit the studio of John Smibert (1688–1751), the leading artist of Boston during Copley's childhood. The ambitious late baroque pictures (241 painted in Boston) of this Scottish émigré, who arrived in Boston in 1729 after pursuing a moderately distinguished career in London, had established a new standard of excellence for many American colonial artists. Smibert's studio also offered Copley a look at English and European prints, theoretical treatises on art, and plaster casts from the antique. As a result, Copley's first paintings, of 1754, were mythological works: *The Forge of Vulcan* (priv. coll.), *Galatea* (Museum of Fine Arts, Boston), and *The Return of Neptune* (Metropolitan Museum of Art, New York), all based on European prints and more consistent with

baroque English taste than the traditional American taste for portraits.

Pelham also passed entrepreneurial skills on to his stepson. Like most household producers in Boston, Pelham, and later Copley, had to be marketing tacticians capable of identifying, satisfying, and at times creating the desire to own works of fine art. Copley in particular was at the forefront of the process of Anglicization, in which the newly wealthy merchant élite of Boston began to covet and consume luxury English goods, or facsimiles of them, including portraits in the formal English style. Even in his early twenties, the marketwise Copley competed with the English rococo artist Joseph Blackburn, then resident in Boston, for commissions. He imitated Blackburn's technique so successfully that the English artist was forced to return home in 1763, leaving the 25-year-old Copley in control of the burgeoning market for paintings in Boston.

Without the benefit of an art academy or further instruction from Pelham, who died in 1751, Copley taught himself, often by imitating the English prints that could be bought or viewed in Boston. He studied prints after paintings by Sir Godfrey Kneller, Thomas Hudson, and Sir Joshua Reynolds. For example, his *Mrs Daniel Hubbard* (1764; Art Institute of Chicago), is explicitly based on John Faber's print after a Hudson portrait of Mary Finch, Viscountess Andover (*c*.1746). The prints were of twofold importance in Copley's self-improvement: first for teaching him contemporary compositional patterns, and second for providing knowledge of current English imagery that allowed his upmarket Anglophile clients to be persuasively portrayed as sophisticated English ladies and gentlemen.

In the late 1750s and early 1760s, Copley developed his signature style, which was descriptive and marked by meticulous detail, crisp lines and edges, strong colour, and dramatic tonal contrasts. His portraits of *Mary and Elizabeth Royall* (*c*.1758; Museum of Fine Arts, Boston), *Moses Gill* (1764; Rhode Island School of Design, Providence, Rhode Island), and *Nathaniel Sparhawk* (1764; Museum of Fine Arts, Boston) are exemplary. He was so fastidious in his technique that Gilbert Stuart once commented on a realistic passage in Copley's *Epes Sargent* (1760; National Gallery of Art, Washington): 'Prick that hand and blood will spurt out' (S. Benjamin, *Art in America*, 1880, 20). Copley's sitters often mentioned the numerous sittings he required, one recalling the twenty visits needed for *Mr and Mrs Thomas Mifflin* (1773; Philadelphia Museum of Art). Though he often based his compositions on English prints, he could not learn English brush technique from them, and as a result his paintings veered away from the fluid effects of the artists of London, such as Reynolds and Thomas Gainsborough, who preferred painterly brushwork and atmospheric veiling. In that way he was like other artists, such as Joseph Wright of Derby and Tilly Kettle, who were working in provincial areas of Britain.

In an effort to improve his art and to acquire an English metropolitan manner in his early career, he shipped his portrait of his half-brother Henry Pelham, *Boy with a Squirrel* (1765; Museum of Fine Arts, Boston), to London for exhibition at the Society of Artists the following year. Reynolds said it was 'a very wonderfull Performance', but noted 'a little Hardness in the Drawing, Coldness in the Shades, An over minuteness' (Jones, 41–2). Benjamin West also praised Copley's painting, but thought it 'too liney, which was judged to have arose from there being so much neetness in the lines' (ibid., 44). Reynolds and West agreed that Copley must leave America to study in Europe and London before, as the former phrased it, 'your Manner and Taste were corrupted or fixed by working in your little way at Boston' (ibid.).

The exhibition, however, did result in Copley's election as a member of the Society of Artists in London. In 1767 Copley sent to London a second picture, *Young Lady with a Bird and Dog* (Toledo Museum of Art, Ohio), but to English academic eyes he again missed the mark. Citing first the overall detailing and the opacity and brightness of colour, West added that 'Each Part being … Equell in Strength of Coulering and finishing, Each Making too much a Picture of its silf, without that Due Subordanation to the Principle parts, viz they head and hands' (Jones, 56–7). He repeated the admonition to come 'home' to London 'before it may be too late for much Improvement' (ibid., 60).

Though Copley wrote back to lament a situation in America in which he had to paint pictures in a place where 'the people regard it no more than any other usefull trade … like that of a Carpenter, tailor or shew maker, not as one of the most noble Arts in the World' (Jones, 65–6), he was, none the less, extremely popular in the late 1760s, producing some of colonial America's most memorable images. Among them are the merchants *John Hancock* (1765; Museum of Fine Arts, Boston), *Nicholas Boylston* (1767; Harvard University, Cambridge, Massachusetts), and *Jeremiah Lee* (1769; Wadsworth Athenaeum, Hartford, Connecticut); the ladies *Mrs Samuel Quincy* (c.1761; Museum of Fine Arts, Boston), *Mrs Thomas Boylston* (1766; Harvard University), and *Rebecca Boylston* (1767; Museum of Fine Arts, Boston); the ministers *Myles Cooper* (1768; Columbia University, New York) and *Nathaniel Appleton* (1761; Harvard University); and the artisans *Paul Revere* (1768; Museum of Fine Arts, Boston) and *Nathaniel Hurd* (c.1765; Cleveland Museum of Art, Ohio).

In the 1760s Copley also pioneered miniature and pastel painting in America, in both of which he was self-trained. His experimental oil on copper miniatures of the late 1750s were superseded about 1762 by a more delicate watercolour on ivory technique (for example, *Jeremiah Lee*, c.1769; Metropolitan Museum of Art, New York). Copley drew about fifty-five pastels in America, beginning in 1758 (for example, his *Self-Portrait*, 1769; Winterthur Museum, Winterthur, Delaware).

By 1771 Copley had become so renowned in New England and along the Atlantic seaboard that he was invited to New York city, where he spent six months and reached the pinnacle of his American fame with portraits so powerful and austere that they bear more resemblance to the French neo-classical art of Jacques-Louis David than to

contemporary English painting. His portraits of *Mrs Thomas Gage* (1771; Putnam Foundation, Timken Museum, San Diego) and *Samuel Adams* (c.1770–72; Museum of Fine Arts, Boston), painted in Boston, are among the most arresting pictures painted in colonial America.

In 1769 Copley married Susannah Farnham Clarke (1745–1836), the daughter of Richard Clarke, the official agent of the British East India Company in Boston, and purchased a 20 acre farm on Beacon Hill, next to the estate of John Hancock. Political events, especially the Stamp Act of 1765, the Townshend Acts of 1767, the non-importation movements that they provoked, and the Boston massacre of 1770, led to the destabilization and polarization of Boston society. Copley had friends and clients in both tory and whig factions. On the one hand he counted radical whigs such as Samuel Adams, John Hancock, and Paul Revere as his friends, actually painting Adams as a political firebrand. On the other hand, he had married into a prominent tory family and painted many tories, including Thomas Gage, the British commander in North America and the colonial governor of Massachusetts from 1774 to 1775. Copley, however, never labelled himself politically and rarely expressed a clear political position. But he did have a political opinion, namely that he felt threatened, both personally and professionally, by the growing crisis, and wished the clock could be turned back a decade or two to when America was under the invisible benefaction of English rule. He claimed to dissociate himself from partisan politics in the higher name of art, and began, as early as 1766, to imagine himself emigrating, breaking the 'shackels' of relentless portrait painting, and abandoning the comforts of his annual income of 300 guineas.

The defining event in Copley's decision to emigrate was the Boston Tea Party of 1773. Because his father-in-law had been importing tea under an exclusive contract with the East India Company, a situation that was emblematic of British control of American markets, he was under ferocious whig attacks led by Samuel Adams. Copley attempted to forestall political action against the Clarkes, but after Adams exhorted 8000 Bostonians at South Church in November of that year, a group of activists disguised as Mohawks boarded Richard Clarke's tea ship and dumped all 342 casks in the harbour. That and other pre-Revolutionary events traumatized the Copley and Clarke families. Copley himself was threatened by marauding whigs; the retaliatory Coercive Acts and Boston Port Bill ruined the economy; British warships began filling the harbour; and Copley knew he had to leave the city, which he did on 10 June 1774, lamenting the inevitable 'Civil War', as he called it. In May of 1775, war having broken out, his wife, three children, and the Clarkes left for England. His mother, Mary, half-brother, Henry Pelham, and sickly infant son, Clarke, remained in Boston.

**Britain, 1774–1815** After a 21-year career in America, Copley moved on to a fourteen-month tour of the continent, largely in Italy, and then to a highly successful second career of some forty years as a portrait and history painter in

London. Though John Adams had lauded him as 'the greatest Master that ever was in America' (L. H. Butterfield, ed., *Adams Family Correspondence*, 1963, 2.103), he was known in London only as the author of two exhibition pictures and as a correspondent with Benjamin West; on the continent he was unknown entirely. In order to adapt to and succeed in his new cultural environment he embarked on a study of antiquity and the old masters, long beyond the age at which English artists had done so. Travelling with the English artist George Carter, he set off late in 1774 for Rome via Rouen, Paris, Lyons, Marseilles, Toulon, Antibes, Genoa, Pisa, and Florence. He studied the work of Raphael in particular, unapologetically basing his first European painting, *The Ascension* (1775; Museum of Fine Arts, Boston) on the Italian's late *Transfiguration*. Late in 1775 he travelled via Parma, Venice, the Tyrol, Mannheim, and Cologne to London, where he joined his wife and three eldest children: Elizabeth (*b.* 1770); John Singleton *Copley, later Baron Lyndhurst (*b.* 1772); and Mary (*b.* 1773). His son Clarke died in Boston, and a third daughter, Susanna, was born.

In 1776, at the age of thirty-eight, Copley settled into a house on Leicester Fields, was elected associate of the Royal Academy, and submitted his portrait *Mr and Mrs Ralph Izard* (1775; Museum of Fine Arts, Boston) to the Royal Academy's annual exhibition. Ever ambitious, he submitted four more pictures to the Royal Academy in 1777, including the large *Copley Family* (1776–7; National Gallery of Art, Washington) which was attacked in the London press. His English portrait style was a modification of his American style, keeping many of the poses, the sharp light and dark contrasts, and bright colouring he was accustomed to, but now loosening the brushwork somewhat, reducing the details, attempting more group portraits, and concerning himself more with the representation of social rank. Exemplary works are *Sir William Pepperell and his Family* (1778; North Carolina Museum of Art, Raleigh), *Clark Gayton, Admiral of the White* (1779; NMM), *Henry Laurens* (1782; National Portrait Gallery, Washington), *William Murray, First Earl of Mansfield* (1783; NPG), *The Three Youngest Daughters of George III* (1785; Royal Collection), *Richard, Earl Howe, Admiral of the Fleet* (*c.*1791–1794; NMM), *Baron Graham* (*c.*1804; National Gallery of Art, Washington). During this period Copley was elected Royal Academician (1779); saw the birth (1782) and death (1785) of his third son, Jonathan; and the death of his daughter Susanna (1785). He moved to George Street near Hanover Square, London (1783), visited Ghent, Flanders, Brussels, and Antwerp (1787), and lost the election for the presidency of the Royal Academy to Benjamin West (1792). It was remarkable that Copley, whose artistic education had taken place thousands of miles from London, would vie for the president's chair of the Royal Academy. But it was equally understandable that he would lose, for he thought of himself, more so than his peers at the Royal Academy, as an autonomous professional with a style of his own. Decades of self-reliant work in Boston, without the company of professional colleagues, had set him on that path, as had his innately independent thinking.

Copley's primary artistic goal in London was to paint historical subjects, which Reynolds and others considered the highest branch of painting. He painted seven religious subjects. Prominent among them were *The Tribute Money* (1782; RA), which was his belated diploma picture for the Royal Academy; *Samuel Relating to Eli the Judgements of God on Eli's House* (1780; Wadsworth Atheneum, Hartford, Connecticut); and *Saul Reproved by Samuel for not Obeying the Commandments of God* (1798; Museum of Fine Arts, Boston). He once painted a subject from literature, *The Red Cross Knight* (1793; National Gallery of Art, Washington), from Edmund Spenser's *The Faerie Queen*.

Copley's primary focus, however, was on contemporary history painting, on which he intended to build his artistic reputation. His first, and most spectacular and novel, was *Watson and the Shark* (1778; National Gallery of Art, Washington), which the London press favourably reviewed. Unlike most contemporary history paintings that depicted heroic subjects of national magnitude, for example, Benjamin West's *The Death of General James Wolfe* (National Gallery of Canada, Ottawa; replica, Royal Collection), Copley's picture was commissioned by Brooke Watson, a merchant and, later, lord mayor of London, and is concerned with a macabre and wholly personal episode in Watson's young adulthood. In 1749 the fourteen-year-old Watson, who was then a crewman on a British ship, went for a swim in Havana harbour, where he was attacked by a shark that mutilated his right leg below the knee. Copley's picture depicts the climactic moment of the shark wildly pursuing its already injured prey moments before a group of fellow crewmen drive it away and pull Watson from the waters. Despite the idiosyncratic and biographical nature of the subject, Copley based passages of the picture on old master paintings, according to the theoretical dictates for history painting advocated by Reynolds and practised by West. For example, the man in the prow who is about to jab the shark with a boat hook suggests traditional pictures of St Michael casting out Satan; the crewmen reaching out of the boat towards Watson are based on figures in Raphael's *Miraculous Draught of Fish*; and the wild-eyed figure of Watson flailing in the water is adapted from another in Raphael's *Transfiguration*.

As a tale of physical trial and emotional trauma, followed by salvation, the subject of *Watson and the Shark* was more in the literary tradition of Daniel Defoe's *The Life and Strange Surprizing Adventures of Robinson Crusoe* (1719) than it was in the pictorial tradition of English history painting. The theme of triumph over adversity must have been on Watson's mind when he commissioned the picture, however, for he bequeathed it to Christ's Hospital, London, with the hope that it would 'hold out a most usefull Lesson to Youth' (will of Brooke Watson, 1807, PRO).

Copley's next historical subject, the *Death of the Earl of Chatham* (1779–81; Tate collection), incorporated portraits of fifty-five of England's noblemen. It shows William Pitt, first earl of Chatham, collapsing in the House of Lords on 7 April 1778 during his reply to the duke of Richmond's speech in favour of American independence. Not only did

Copley break with tradition by combining history painting with portraiture, he also marketed his picture in a novel way, by renting a private venue for its exhibition, which was in direct competition with the Royal Academy's annual exhibition of 1781. He charged for admission and earned more money from prints made after the painting and marketed for him by the print publisher John Boydell.

Boydell commissioned and eventually paid Copley £800 for *The Death of Major Peirson* (1782–4; Tate collection), which was again exhibited privately and for profit at 28 Haymarket. Boydell also arranged for the accompanying print sale. A highly dramatic picture, painted at the peak of Copley's powers, it depicts the events of 6 January 1781 when Peirson valiantly died leading his troops during the French invasion of the island of Jersey. Copley carefully researched the details of the town's appearance and correctly recorded the uniforms, but in accord with Reynolds's theory of history painting he also idealized Peirson's death, turning him into a modern Patroclus. The picture's composition was based on the tripartite structure of Benjamin West's *The Death of General James Wolfe* (1771) but now made more densely populated and physically animated.

The *Peirson* attracted the interest of George III, who reportedly devoted three hours to study of its 'various excellencies, in point of design, character, composition, and colouring' (*Morning Herald and Daily Advertiser*, 22 May 1784). The picture, with its brilliant reds and whites, theatrical lighting, and sophisticated composition, all put to the service of glorifying English heroics, captured the patriotic imagination of viewers who eagerly looked to military events, such as the defence of Jersey in 1781 and the defence of Gibraltar in 1782, that would ease their sense of the impending loss of America. The corporation of London rewarded Copley for the *Peirson* with a commission for a huge picture, *The Siege of Gibraltar* (1783–91; Guildhall Art Gallery, London), for a final sum of £1100. The picture glorifies British magnanimity in the midst of battle as officers risk their lives in the aftermath of victory to rescue the enemy from their exploding ships. General George Augustus Eliott (later Lord Heathfield) is depicted large on a white horse, directing the rescue.

To display the picture, which took eight years to paint, Copley had to erect a tent in Green Park, London. He said that 60,000 came to see it, paying the 1s. admission price ('Anecdotes of artists of the last fifty years', *Library of the Fine Arts*, 4, July 1832, 25). Four years later Copley exhibited at Spring Gardens *Charles I Demanding in the House of Commons the Five Impeached Members* (Boston Public Library). Earlier in subject than his previous history paintings, the exhibition of the picture was not well attended. In 1799 Copley attempted a last private showing of a historical picture, *The Victory of Lord Duncan* (1798–9; Dundee Art Galleries and Museums), which depicts the surrender at the battle of Camperdown of the Dutch Admiral DeWinter to Admiral Duncan on 11 October 1797.

After 1800 the quality of Copley's work was in decline. One version of *The Offer of the Crown to Lady Jane Grey* (1807–

8; Somerset Club, Boston) was well received at the Royal Academy. But his *George IV* (1804–10; Museum of Fine Arts, Boston), an equestrian portrait, was poorly composed and highly criticized. In the early nineteenth century he became preoccupied with petty squabbles with clients and fellow artists. He went into debt. Commissions became scarce. His half-brother Henry Pelham drowned in Boston in 1806. Finally, his health deteriorated and he became feeble in both mind and body. His *Battle of the Pyrenees* (1812–15; Museum of Fine Arts, Boston) and *The Siege of Dunkirk* (1814–15; College of William and Mary, Williamsburg, Virginia) were inept. When the young American artist Samuel F. B. Morse visited Copley in 1811, he wrote:

> He is very old and infirm … His powers of mind have almost entirely left him; his late paintings are miserable; it is really a lamentable thing that a man should outlive his faculties. He has been a first-rate painter, as you well know. I saw at his room some exquisite pieces which he painted twenty or thirty years ago, but his paintings of the last four or five years are very bad. He was pleasant, however, and agreeable in his manners. (E. L. Morse, ed., *Samuel F. B. Morse: his Letters and Journals*, 1914, 1.47)

Copley suffered a stroke at dinner on 11 August 1815. He was left paralysed and incapable of speaking. He died at his home in George Street, London on 9 September 1815, and was buried in Croydon, Surrey. After his death, the family was supported by John Singleton Copley junior, a lawyer, who was elected to parliament in 1818, made Baron Lyndhurst in 1827, and was the first lord chancellor to have been born outside Britain.

Copley was the greatest and most influential painter in colonial America, producing about 350 works of art. With his startling likenesses of persons and things, he came to define a realist art tradition in America. His visual legacy extended throughout the nineteenth century in the American taste for the work of artists as diverse as Fitz Hugh Lane and William Michael Harnett. In Britain, while he continued to paint portraits for the élite, his great achievement was the development of contemporary history painting, which was a combination of reportage, idealism, and theatre. He was also one of the pioneers of the private exhibition, orchestrating shows and marketing prints of his own work to mass audiences that might otherwise attend exhibitions only at the Royal Academy, or who previously had not gone to exhibitions at all.

PAUL STAITI

**Sources** C. Rebora and P. Staiti, *John Singleton Copley in America* (1995) • E. Neff, *John Singleton Copley in England* (1995) • J. Prown, *John Singleton Copley*, 2 vols. (1965) • G. Jones, ed., *Letters and papers of John Singleton Copley and Henry Pelham, 1739–1776* (1914) • S. Rather, 'Carpenter, tailor, shoemaker, artist: Copley and portrait painting around 1770', *Art Bulletin*, 79 (1997), 269–90 • *Catalogue of the very valuable collection of pictures of the Rt. Hon. Lord Lyndhurst, deceased* [Lyndhurst sale; sale catalogue, Christies] • A. T. Perkins, *A sketch of the life and list of the works of John Singleton Copley* (1873) • M. B. Amory, *The domestic and artistic life of John Singleton Copley* (1882) • B. N. Parker and A. B. Wheeler, *John Singleton Copley: American portraits in oil, pastel and miniature, with biographical sketches* (1938) • J. T. Flexner, *John Singleton Copley*, rev. edn (1948) • A. Frankenstein, *The world of Copley, 1738–1815* (1970) • W. Craven, *Colonial American portraiture* (1986) • R. B. Stein, 'Copley's *Watson and the shark* and aesthetics in the

1770s', *Discoveries and considerations: essays on early American literature and aesthetics, presented to Harold Jantz*, ed. C. Israel (Albany, NY, 1976), 85–130 · T. J. Fairbrother, 'John Singleton Copley's use of British mezzotints: a reappraisal prompted by new discoveries', *Arts Magazine*, 55 (1981), 122–30 · E. Miles, *John Singleton Copley's 'Watson and the shark'* (1993) · G. B. Warden, 'John Singleton Copley's Boston', *Apollo*, 91 (1970), 48–55 · C. Troyon, 'John Singleton Copley and the grand manner', *Journal of the Museum of Fine Arts, Boston*, 1 (1989), 96–103 · J. W. Shank, 'John Singleton Copley's portraits: a technical study of three representative examples', *Journal of the American Institute of Conservation*, 23 (1984), 130–52 · R. H. Saunders, 'Genius and glory: John Singleton Copley's *The death of Peirson*', *American Art Journal*, 22/1 (1990), 4–39 · M. Lovell, '"To be conspecuous in the croud"; John Singleton Copley's *Sir William Pepperell and his family*', *North Carolina Museum of Art Bulletin*, 15 (1991), 30–43 · M. Lovell, 'Mrs. Sargent, Mr. Copley, and the empirical eye', *Winterthur Portfolio*, 33/1 (1998), 1–39 · A. Abrams, 'Politics, prints, and John Singleton Copley's *Watson and the shark*', *Art Bulletin*, 61 (1979), 265–76 · B. Novak, *American painting of the nineteenth century* (1969) · E. G. Miles and others, *American paintings of the eighteenth century* (1995) [catalogue, National Gallery of Art, Washington, DC] · E. Wind, 'The revolution of history painting', *Journal of the Warburg Institute*, 2 (1938–9), 116–27 · E. Wind, *Hume and the heroic portrait*, ed. J. Anderson (1986)

**Archives** Glamorgan RO, Cardiff · L. Cong., corresp. · Metropolitan Museum of Art, New York, MSS · Museum of Fine Arts, Boston, Massachusetts, MSS · PRO, MSS, CO 5/38, CO 5/39 · RA, letters

**Likenesses** J. S. Copley, self-portrait, pastel drawing, 1769, Winterthur Museum, Delaware · J. S. Copley, group portrait, exh. RA 1777 (with his family), National Gallery of Art, Washington, DC · J. S. Copley, oils, 1780–84, Smithsonian Institution, Washington, DC · J. S. Copley, self-portrait, oils, 1780–84, Smithsonian Institution, Washington, DC, National Portrait Gallery [see illus.] · G. Stuart, oils, c.1784, NPG · W. Daniell, soft-ground etching, BM, NPG · H. F. du Pont, drawing, Winterthur Museum, Delaware · H. Singleton, group portrait, oils (*Royal Academicians*, 1793), RA

**Copley, John Singleton**, Baron Lyndhurst (1772–1863), politician and lord chancellor, was born at Beacon Hill, Boston, Massachusetts, before the American War of Independence and died in London after the outbreak of the American Civil War.

**Early years and education** Copley was born on 21 May 1772, the elder son of the distinguished portrait painter John Singleton *Copley (1738–1815) and Susannah Farnham (1745–1836), the daughter of Richard Clarke, a loyalist and principal agent of the East India Company in Boston. As a result of the increasing political turmoil of the early 1770s his father's income dwindled. In June 1774 Copley sen. left for England and Italy, to 'enjoy a long-denied visit and return after the tempest [of colonial unrest] had blown itself out' (Prown, 1.87). His wife and three of his four children went to England in May of the following year. Neither Copley sen. nor his wife ever returned to America. In 1783 the family moved to 25 George Street, Hanover Square, London. No. 25, later enlarged with the purchase of no. 24, was to be the younger Copley's London home for the remainder of his life.

Educated at a private school, Manor House, in Chiswick, Copley entered Trinity College, Cambridge, in 1790. His academic career was distinguished: a first-class classicist and second wrangler in the mathematical tripos (1794), 'having adopted the subject within these nine months, whereas several of my opponents have been labouring for

John Singleton Copley, Baron Lyndhurst (1772–1863), by Thomas Phillips, 1836

years', he was elected, by examination, to a fellowship of his college, which he held from 1795 to 1804. His affection for Trinity and the university remained undiminished and he regarded his election as high steward (1840) as one of the chief honours of his life.

As an undergraduate it was said that he became a 'mighty Jacobin' and a fervent supporter of the French Revolution. But in his account, to the vice-chancellor, of his travels in the United States he professed himself a 'fierce aristocrat' and extolled that country as the 'country to cure your Jacobins. Send them over and they will return quite converted' (Amory, 145). His contemporaries at the bar, such as Sir Thomas Denman, then a friend, would have been surprised to read this protestation. Viscount Althorp was present during the debate on the second Reform Bill and heard Lyndhurst's vehement protest that he 'never was a Whig':

[the Attorney-General (Denman)], who stood next to me, pressed my arm tightly, saying, Villain! No he was a Democrat. When I was a young man, he took me to a dinner of the friends of the people. The violence of the speeches startled me, and I could not help observing that I thought his friends went too far, for there must be some honest Tories. 'No', he (Lord Lyndhurst) answered, 'it is impossible; an honest Tory is a contradiction in terms'. (Le Marchant, 350–51)

Copley was welcomed in Boston by relatives and friends. But the visit was tinged with disappointment for he vainly sought to recover the family lands on Beacon Hill; he was advised to compromise his father's claims and did so, accepting a sum of about £4200. On his return from the United States he decided to become a barrister, but his limited means compelled him to spend the next seven years learning the mysteries of special pleading in the chambers of the immortal William Tidd. It was only a loan of £1000 from Gardiner Greene, a Boston merchant, married to his eldest sister, Elizabeth, which enabled him to be called to the bar by Lincoln's Inn in 1804. He then joined the midland circuit.

**Early career to 1826** Copley appeared to have all the talents for immediate success: he was distinguished in appearance, clever, articulate, and 'among his many natural gifts, the rich melodious tone of his voice was not the least' (Le Marchant, 351). But his progress was relatively slow. By 1807 his mother, to whom he was devoted, could write that: 'his prospects are satisfactory, and remove our anxious concern on that score … He has made a great advance and says, he must style himself, as others do, "a lucky dog"' (Amory, 284–5). His income was, however, only 'satisfactory' for some years thereafter.

Copley came into prominence in 1812 with his defence of one of the leading Luddites, John Ingham, who was indicted at the Nottingham assizes and charged with the capital offences of rioting and the destruction of machinery. The acquittal, which was hugely popular, was on a technicality since the indictment misdescribed the trade of Ingham's employers. In the following year Copley became a serjeant-at-law, a recognition of his growing professional reputation. *Bovill* v. *Moore*, in 1816, was a particularly important landmark. In that case, he mastered the specifications of the patent which his client's machine had allegedly infringed. His command of the facts and law persuaded the jury to reject the plaintiff's claim. Thereafter he was the acknowledged leader of his circuit. The increased income was particularly welcome after the death of his father in 1815. The burden of supporting the London family fell upon him, as did the moral obligation, which he gradually discharged, of paying off his father's many creditors.

It was the trial in 1817 for high treason of Watson and Thistlewood, two of the Spa Fields rioters, which brought Copley to the attention of tory ministers. His address to the jury, ridiculing the indictment that they had levied war against the king, helped to secure their acquittal. Lord Campbell, who vilified Lyndhurst in his *Lives of the Lord Chancellors*, described his address as 'one of the ablest and most effective ever delivered in a court of justice' (Campbell, 8.17). Henry Crabbe Robinson was equally impressed: 'He said nothing that was not to the purpose. There was no idle or superfluous passages in his speech' (H. C. Robinson, *Diary, Reminiscences and Correspondence*, 1869–70, 2.361).

Such successes led to the crown retaining Copley in a number of state trials for treason. The tories had few able lawyers in the House of Commons, and Lord Castlereagh, who had sat through Watson's trial, realized that Copley was an obvious candidate. In March 1818 he accepted Lord Liverpool's invitation to enter the house, and became a member for the rotten borough of Yarmouth in the Isle of Wight, before being returned for Ashburton at the general election later the same year. In October 1819 he was knighted, and switched seats again in 1826 to the University of Cambridge. Denman and other whigs never forgave his 'dereliction of principle' (Arnould, 63); 'he had no more formed opinion that Toryism was true than he had that Mahometanism was true' (Bagehot, 3.232, 236).

Copley may have given no pledge to Liverpool; but he consistently supported the government. His political advancement was swift. In February 1819 he became chief justice of Chester and king's serjeant and, in June of that year, solicitor-general, succeeding Sir Robert Gifford. In the house he defended Castlereagh's six bills but did not otherwise take an active part in debates. He was one of the counsel who led the prosecution of the Cato Street conspirators for high treason (1819) and in the same year supported the bill of pains and penalties against Queen Caroline, earning the praise of her counsel, Denman, for his able cross-examination. In January 1824 he succeeded Gifford as attorney-general.

**Master of the rolls, lord chancellor, and chief baron of the exchequer, 1826–1834** In September 1826 Copley succeeded Gifford as master of the rolls, a judicial office which he could hold while retaining his seat in the house. On Lord Eldon's resignation in the following year he was appointed lord chancellor and was raised to the peerage as Baron Lyndhurst of Lyndhurst. He served successively under Canning, Goderich, and Wellington. The tory government fell in 1830 and Earl Grey took office. With Lord Brougham's support, Grey surprisingly offered Lyndhurst the office of chief baron of the exchequer. After consulting the duke of Wellington, Sir Robert Peel, and Lord Aberdeen, he decided to accept the offer, knowing that he 'should be subjected to so much obloquy and abuse' (Lyndhurst MSS, Trinity College, Cambridge); 'a judicial office, wholly unconnected with politics' (Martin, 295) was his apologia. He took his seat in January 1831. £7000 p.a. was more attractive than a pension of £4000 to a man who spent too freely. Wellington well knew that 'he cannot live without place, as he has no property and he has already expended *three years* beforehand his salary' (A. Aspinall, ed., *Three Early Nineteenth Century Diaries*, 1952, 4 n. 2). Lady Lyndhurst's influence over Grey, who even toyed with the possibility of keeping Lyndhurst as lord chancellor, may have been instrumental in securing Lyndhurst's appointment; indeed Arbuthnot suspected that Lyndhurst was already intriguing with the whigs. Possibly Lyndhurst had led Grey to believe that he would not actively oppose government bills and, in return, may have been offered the reversion to the office of lord chief justice. But if any bargain was made, it was soon to be broken.

Greville predicted that 'the public will gain by the transaction, because they will get a good judge' (*Greville Memoirs*, 2.89). That prediction proved to be true, for

Lyndhurst's brief tenure as chief baron (1830–34) earned even Campbell's praise. He revived a moribund court which became popular with suitors. Whitwell Elwin records he had the 'power of summing up evidence with such terseness, completeness and exactness from memory alone' (Martin, 283).

Nowhere were these skills better demonstrated than in *Small* v. *Attwood* in 1832, a dispute which centred on the sale, allegedly induced by the seller's fraudulent misrepresentations, of coal and iron mines in Staffordshire. At the trial, which lasted twenty-one days, Lyndhurst was confronted with a web of tangled facts, complex calculations, and voluminous documents and depositions. But his judgment 'was entirely oral, and without even referring to any notes … Never once did he falter or hesitate, and never once was he mistaken in a name, a figure, or a date' (Campbell, 8.73). It was 'one of the ablest judgments ever delivered' (*Greville Memoirs*, 2.330).

Lyndhurst was not a judge who revelled in the niceties of fine legal argument. His judgments do not contain an 'ample exposition of the principles applicable to other disputes'. He was one of those judges:

> who always decide on the particular case before them rightly, who have a nice insight into all that concerns it, are acute discerners of fact, accurate weighers of testimony, just discriminators of argument. Lord Lyndhurst is perhaps as great a judge in this kind as it is easy to fancy. If a wise man had a good cause, he would prefer its being tried before Lyndhurst to its being tried before anyone else. (Bagehot, 3.159, 180–81)

Lyndhurst never pretended to be a 'chancery man'. Unlike Eldon he was not concerned to establish himself as a master of equitable doctrines. As chief baron, he assigned most of the equity business to Baron Alderson, and from the woolsack he delivered few memorable legal speeches.

Lyndhurst became very influential in the House of Lords. Disraeli said he was a 'pleader rather than an orator, and never a debater' (Monypenny, 1.330). Sir Denis Le Marchant commented that he was:

> always a complete master of his argument, his premises being so skilfully laid that his conclusions were almost irresistible: nothing could be more clear, distinct and logical than his handling of a subject—at least according to his view of it; but he grappled with no difficulties he was not sure to overcome. (Le Marchant, 351)

His mind was a lawyer's mind. Hence, Wellington's comment: '[you are] not only the first speaker in the House of Lords, but … the first in your own profession' (Amory, 371–2). Lyndhurst rarely appealed to the emotions. Irony and sarcasm were his telling weapons. So, he looked upon 'what proceeded from [Wetherell on the Catholic Relief Bill, 1829] rather as the ravings of a disordered imagination, than as emanations from an enlightened and sagacious understanding' (*Hansard 2*, 21, 1829, col. 192).

As solicitor-general and lord chancellor Lyndhurst spoke against Catholic emancipation in 1827 and in its favour in 1829. In 1827 he argued that concessions should be granted only if the Catholic community offered 'security' that civil liberties would not be usurped, the authority of the church would not be endangered, and there would be no 'foreign interference' (*Hansard 2*, 16, 1827, col. 905ff.)—an argument which Denman dismissed as 'bad—politically, morally, and intellectually' (Arnould, 1.201). In 1829 Lyndhurst's defence of the government's volte-face was equally vigorous. Change, consistent with 'security', was necessary if Ireland was to be governed without coercion; and that security had now been offered and accepted. These were higher considerations than personal consistency. The ultras were not mollified. They combined with the whigs to bring down Wellington's government.

The 1831 and 1832 debates on the first and second reform bills were passionate. Lyndhurst was condemned for viewing '[questions] only through the medium of party' (Le Marchant, 351); the interventions of this 'unblushing lawyer' (Kriegel, 178) were sneering, factious, mischievous, and imprudent. In his speeches on the Reform Bill, in language reminiscent of Burke, he cautioned against change. 'Our constitution is not the work of a day.' The Reform Bill would destroy the 'nice balance' of the constitution. There would be an 'entire change in the persons who are to elect and, consequently, an entire change in the persons elected'; and the rights and privileges of the monarchy and the church would be endangered (*Hansard 3*, 8, 1831, col. 283 ff.). It was his wrecking amendment to the 1832 bill, to postpone discussion of the disfranchising clauses until the enfranchising clauses had been disposed of, which made a collision between the two houses inevitable (Le Marchant, 418–19). His confident assertion, that 'we are no less representative of the nation than the House of Commons' (*Hansard 3*, 34, 1832, col. 888ff.), was particularly galling. The amendment was passed, and Grey resigned. On the tories failing to form a government, he resumed office. A constitutional crisis was only averted when, confronted with the threat to create enough peers to secure its enactment, the tory peers withdrew their opposition.

**Lord chancellor twice more, and opposition in the Lords** After his brief sojourn as lord chancellor in Peel's 100 days' administration in 1834, Lyndhurst was once more in opposition. The sessions of 1835 and 1836 were almost as tumultuous as those of 1831 and 1832. In 1835 Lyndhurst confided to Disraeli that the movement, which sought the radical reform of the country's institutions, could be stopped. He opposed any reform of municipal government, possibly in the hope of bringing down the government; so the tory-dominated House of Lords, encouraged by his speeches, drastically amended the Municipal Corporations Bill of 1835, which had won the broad support of Peel in the lower house. When the bill was once more debated in that chamber, Lord John Russell accepted some of its amendments, as did Peel who was anxious to reach a compromise. The House of Lords passed the bill in its amended form.

The debate on the Irish Municipal Corporations Bill of 1836, which Peel had unsuccessfully sought to amend, was even more heated. Lyndhurst infuriated O'Connell by saying that the Irish protestants 'had to contend with a population alien to Englishmen, speaking, many of them, a different language, professing a different religion, regarding the English as invaders, and ready to upset them on the first opportunity' (*Hansard 3*, 30, 1837, col. 734; 33, col. 297; 34, col. 297). Once again he invoked the independence of the House of Lords as the justification for its intervention. The government abandoned the bill after a conference failed to reach agreement.

On Disraeli's suggestion, in the same year Lyndhurst gave his first 'summary of the session'; it was a telling catalogue of ill-considered bills, subsequently withdrawn. It was more restrained than his earlier speeches, and even praised by Holland as one of the 'best speeches he had ever heard in Parliament' (*Greville Memoirs*, 3.362). But his acerbic attack on the government, in 'language reflecting on the Commons' (ibid.), was bound to be resented by his opponents.

Lyndhurst's combative speeches, praised by Disraeli in his *Vindication of the English Constitution* and in the *Morning Post*, won him parliamentary admirers. In 1835 and 1836 there was talk that the king wanted him as prime minister. But the king knew that he was 'inextricably bound' to Peel (Monypenny, 1.329); and a number of tory peers had second thoughts about the proposal to desert Peel for Lyndhurst. It is doubtful whether Lyndhurst sought, except momentarily, the burdens of the highest office. Disraeli may have exaggerated Lyndhurst's political support; three years earlier Holland had described the notion of his leadership of the tories as 'absurd' (Kriegel, 235), but Disraeli perceived that Lyndhurst's 'own disinclination [to become prime minister] alone stands in the way' (Monypenny, 1.304). The source of that 'disinclination' was, not only his lack of high political ambition, but also the legacy of the fiery exchanges in the house during these years. In January 1837 he told Greville, on his return from a delightful four months in Paris:

> I suppose the Government will get on; I'm sure that I shall not go on in the House of Lords this year as I did the last. I was induced by circumstances and some little excitement to take a more prominent part than usual last session; but I don't see what I got by it except abuse. (*Greville Memoirs*, 3.378)

Lord Holland and Viscount Melbourne vociferously complained about the bitterness of Lyndhurst's invective. But he chose to ignore their taunts of want of principle, which culminated in the prolonged hoots which greeted his appearance under the gallery of the House of Commons during its debate on the Irish Bill in 1837. Holland was told that he felt these insults 'most acutely' (Kriegel, 356); but, commented Greville, he 'neither attempted to stir, nor changed a muscle of his countenance' (*Greville Memoirs*, 3.389).

Lyndhurst was true to his words. After the furore of the Irish Bill, the years 1838–40 were quieter years. He was more active in the judicial business of the house, although his 'summary of the session' of 1839 was enlivened by his

description of a discredited government, clinging to office.

In 1841 Lyndhurst became lord chancellor for the third time, in Peel's administration. Lyndhurst and Peel were never intimates. Disraeli wrote that Lyndhurst was jealous of Peel (Monypenny, 1.301–2). There is little evidence to support that view and their formal exchange of letters was invariably cordial. But Lyndhurst was not alone in thinking that Peel was an austere colleague. It may be that he was less influential in the cabinet, which Peel dominated, than he was in the House of Lords. But even in the house he played, politically, a more muted role. His interventions were generally confined to matters of legal reform, such as the Copyright Bill of 1843 and the ill-fated Charitable Trusts Bill of 1845. Not surprisingly, the attacks of his political opponents now became less vituperative.

Peel resigned in July 1846, leaving a party bitterly divided over the repeal of the corn laws. Lyndhurst's attempt to reunite it failed dismally. By the end of that decade Lyndhurst was totally blind; in 1850 a cataract operation partially restored his sight and a second was to follow. Nevertheless a year later he was on his feet in the House of Lords. He refused to take office in the first Derby administration of 1852. Lyndhurst enjoyed being an elder statesman, denouncing Russian aggrandizement (1853) and speaking passionately in 1859 and 1860 on the state of the national defences. These speeches of an octogenarian were admired for their undiminished force and clarity.

Lyndhurst did not welcome political change. But he earned praise as a law reformer. In the debate on the Juvenile Offenders Bill of 1838 Lyndhurst had drawn a dramatic picture of the horrific treatment of young children in reformatories; and in the following year he proposed the modification of the common law which gave a wife, separated from her husband, access to the children only with his permission. In 1853 and 1858 he supported the admission of Jews into parliament, demonstrating that the words of the oath, 'without mental reservation and on the true faith of a Christian', were inserted to exclude, not Jews, but Roman Catholics. In 1857, in the debate on the amendment of the divorce laws, his study of the church fathers enabled him to refute the bishop of Oxford, who had invoked St Augustine as authority for the dogma of the indissolubility of marriage. The previous year he had mocked Campbell's bill prohibiting the sale of obscene books, paintings, and prints. Correggio's *Jupiter and Antigone* would be confiscated, as well as Ovid's *Art of Love*; and Dryden's poem 'Sigismonda and Guiscerdo' 'must be placed in [Lord Campbell's] *Index Expurgatorius*' (*Hansard 3*, 146, 1856, col. 330ff.). The last time he spoke in the house was in 1861 in the debate on Lord Kingsdown's act for the establishment of the validity of wills of personal estate.

**Personal life** On 13 March 1819 Lyndhurst married Sarah Garay Thomas, daughter of Charles Brunsden and niece of his friend Sir Samuel Shepherd, whose marriage of six weeks to Lieutenant-Colonel Charles Thomas of the Coldstream Guards ended with his death at Waterloo. She was then aged twenty-four or twenty-five, Lyndhurst forty-seven. Three of their five children died in infancy. Two daughters survived. Sarah Elizabeth (1821–1865) married Henry Selwin-Ibbetson, later Lord Rookwood. Sophia Clarence (1828–1911) married Hamilton Beckett; they had one son and two daughters.

Lady Lyndhurst was a handsome, striking woman, with intelligent black eyes, 'so like one of Leonardo da Vinci's pictures' (A. F. Stewart, *The Diary of a Lady in Waiting: Lady Charlotte Bury*, 1835, 200), whose 'passion leads her to the universe of clever men only' (Lady Dorchester, *Recollections of a Long Life: Lord Broughton* (*John Cam Hobhouse*), 1910, 3.107). Indeed her various 'affairs' with the powerful and the wealthy, including the duke of Devonshire (J. Lees-Milne, *The Bachelor Duke, 1790–1858*, 1991, 88, 91–2, 102, 110) and Lord Dudley (J. Gore, *Creevey's Life and Times, 1768–1838*, 1934, 253–4, 363), and her attempted 'rape' by the king's brother, the duke of Cumberland, intrigued the London salons (ibid., 307–9). Mrs Arbuthnot, a high tory, found her 'a singularly vulgar woman' (*The Journal of Harriet, Mrs Charles Arbuthnot, 1822–1832*, 1950, 2.258–9). Lady Holland, a whig, was somewhat kinder; she was 'good hearted' and 'good natured' but 'with odd sallies … from coming into the *beau monde* when her ways were formed for another class' (earl of Ilchester, ed., *Elizabeth, Lady Holland to her Son, 1821–1845*, 1946, 91). Even Lyndhurst's adoring sister, Mary, admitted that 'perhaps she had too high an opinion of the attractions of the world' (Amory, 351). She was quite manipulative. 'Having known what poverty is' (earl of Ilchester, ed., *The Journal of the Honourable Henry Edward Fox, 1818–1830*, 1923, 359), she set out to charm whig grandees to secure her husband's advancement and her security. In turn they vainly hoped that her pro-reform views would persuade her husband not to oppose political change.

Lady Lyndhurst died, suddenly, in Paris on 15 January 1834. Mary wrote to her sister Mrs Greene that 'her brother was heartbroken'. 'What a melancholy change have a few short months made in the family! Then all was bustle, gayety, and happiness, but now, alas! quite the reverse' (Amory, 351). But the less charitable doubted Lyndhurst's faithful devotion to 'Dolly', as she was affectionately called.

In many quarters Lyndhurst's personal reputation was no higher than that of his deceased wife. In 1840 William Whewell, soon to be master of Trinity, opposed Lyndhurst's election as high steward of the university, not only on the ground that he was a 'political adventurer', but also because of the many scandalous rumours about his private life which made him 'quite unfitted to hold academic office' (D. A. Winstanley, *Early Victorian Cambridge*, 1940, 100). Lyndhurst was quickly comforted after his wife's death. Within months he met Lady Henrietta Sykes, Disraeli's lover, who introduced him to Disraeli; so began a long friendship between the two men. For a short time Henrietta may well have been Lyndhurst's kept mistress. Disraeli and others agreed with her judgement that 'where women are concerned never was there a greater fool' (Blake, 118).

George Street was one of the centres of London fashion. The licence and ribaldry of Lyndhurst's conversation attracted adverse comment, as did his appearance which was more that of a cavalry colonel than a lord chancellor, dressing as he did in 'white Russia duck trousers, strapped under his boots of polished leather and in a becoming frock coat' (Lee, 124). At a great fancy ball in June 1835 he appeared as a marshall of France, and his guests were eighty of the 'supremist ton and beauty'. Disraeli wrote to his sister: 'you can conceive nothing more splendid and brilliant than his house illuminated, with a banquet to a company so fancifully dressed' (Disraeli, *Letters*, 2, no. 408).

Paris was Lyndhurst's second home. He loved the company of its politicians and men of letters. On his return from Paris in January 1837 he told Greville that:

> he had never passed such an agreeable time as the last four months; not a moment of *ennui*; had become acquainted with a host of remarkable people of all sorts, political characters of all parties, and the *littérateurs*, such as Victor Hugo, Balzac, &c., the latter of whom … is a very agreeable man. (*Greville Memoirs*, 3.378)

Lyndhurst visited Paris almost every year, and was just as much at ease in the Parisian as in the London *haut monde*. On one such visit, in 1835, he dined with Louis Philippe, and twenty years later he met Louis Napoleon and the empress, remaining in 'active conversation, no other person present, for more than an hour' (Lee, 244). One of the Parisian 'political characters' was Lewis Goldsmith, whose daughter Georgiana (1807?–1901) Lyndhurst was to marry on 5 August 1837, much to the surprise of family and friends. Disraeli found her very different from Sarah:

> Without being absolutely pretty, her appearance is highly interesting … She is very little, but her appearance is elegant and delicate. She is not all national in the vulgar sense, her features being very small … Her manner calm and assured, yet tinged with a certain degree of reserve not unbecoming. (Disraeli, *Letters*, 3, no. 733)

It proved a very happy marriage. The couple spent their leisure time in Turville Park, near Henley-on-Thames, which Lyndhurst leased, and its small farm gave him much pleasure. Their one daughter, Georgiana Susan (1838–1926), married Sir Charles Du Cane MP; they had two sons and three daughters.

**Later years and reputation** Historians have described Lyndhurst as a 'somewhat enigmatic figure' (Blake, 115). He died in the determination that this should be so, for he burnt nearly all his private papers. Condemned for his 'conversion' to tory principles, a Proteus whose 'path to power was through the wreck of all political consistency' (Arnould, 1.408), once he entered the house as a tory he became an unswervingly loyal party man. He would not have gone to the stake for a principle his party had abjured. So it was that he was first against and then for the defendant's right to counsel in felony trials; against and within two years for Catholic emancipation; against any reform of the franchise, and within a year for some reform; for the corn laws, and shortly afterwards against the corn laws: 'He took up the opinions of the existing Government and advocated them, and to the end of his life would have thought it "nonsense and rubbish" to act otherwise' (Bagehot, 3.232, 236).

For many Lyndhurst appeared a paid advocate, who

could not be trusted to be true to a principle. Campbell contemptuously accused him of repudiating 'all the opinions and sentiments which he had before entertained and expressed' and castigated him, as solicitor-general, for piloting the detested Six Acts through the House of Commons. In a bitter and splenetic passage, he remarked that Lyndhurst's conduct had been compared to that of 'the mercenary soldier ready to obey every command of his superior officer' (Campbell, 8.30–31). Campbell then went on to quote three lines from Lucan's *The Civil War (Pharsalia)*:

> Pectore si fratris gladium iuguloque parentis
> Condore me iubeas …
> … invita peragam tamen omnia dextra.
> (Tell me to plunge my sword into my brother's breast
> Or in my father's throat …
> And I shall do it all with this right hand,
> Though it go against the grain.)
> (ibid., 1.376–8)

Lyndhurst did have some political convictions. He firmly believed that the House of Lords was a vital part of the constitution; he opposed the creation of life peers because he feared that governments would create them for political purposes, thereby further eroding its authority and independence. But he came to perceive, as he did not in the 1830s, that there were limits to its powers. In 1858 he described its role in these words:

> it is also a most important part of our duty to check against the rash, inconsiderate, hasty, and undigested legislation of the other House, to give time for consideration and for consulting and perhaps modifying the opinions of the constituencies, but I never understand, nor could such a principle be acted upon, that we were to make a firm, determined and persevering stand against the opinion of the other House of Parliament, when that opinion is backed by the opinion of the people, and least of all, on questions affecting, in a certain degree, the constitution of that House and popular rights. (*Hansard 3*, 149, 1858, cols. 1754–6)

Lyndhurst's intellectual pre-eminence was widely recognized. Disraeli said his mind was not original. But Disraeli judged him as a politician and, as a politician, he did not seek to originate; but he 'corrected, perfected, or improved much' (*QR*, 126, 1869, 29). He never ceased to be intellectually curious. After he had entered his ninetieth year, he went through the problems of Euclid to ascertain whether he was still capable of effort in mathematics. The posthumous sale of his library included classical, English, and French authors, although it was said that he read little before his retirement. At a later sale there were Old Master engravings and drawings, and paintings by his father, Titian, Van Dyck, Tintoretto, Canaletto, and Paulus Potter.

Lyndhurst 'both looked, and was, a great man' (Bagehot, 3.232). Disraeli described his brow as 'majestic'; his deep-set eyes, gleaming 'with penetrating fire'; he was a 'high-bred falcon'. 'Indeed nothing could be finer than the upper part of his countenance … Nothing could be more beautiful. It was that of the Olympian Jove.' But 'the lower part of his countenance betrayed the deficiencies of his character; a want of high purpose, and some sensual attributes' (Monypenny, 1.333). It was commonly said that

'the soubriquet of "Mephistopheles" admirably suited him; the mocking sneer was quickly followed by the genial smile'.

Lyndhurst was condemned for his lack of *gravitas*, yet it was this very lack of *gravitas* which even political opponents could find endearing. Only the most salacious claimed that he was corrupt; in 1829 he successfully initiated criminal libel indictments against newspapers which alleged that he had sold church appointments and trafficked in political offices. A formidable political opponent, he was, in Brougham's view, 'free from all jealousy or petty spite' (Martin, 507). He took pains to placate Eldon; he enjoyed the company of radicals like Robert Wilson and Roebuck; he and Edward Ellice, a passionate Liberal, were 'great friends here [in Paris]' (C. C. F. Greville, *Journals of the Reigns of George IV and William IV*, 3.379); Brougham attacked him in the *Edinburgh Review* and became his closest friend; Sydney Smith and Macaulay, loyal whigs, gratefully acknowledged his patronage. Nor did Lyndhurst, a devout Anglican, at least in later life, bear any religious grudges; he supported, it is true because it was expedient to do so, the Catholic Relief Bill, and, from conviction, the admission of Jews to parliament. Such a man would never sacrifice a colleague or friend for political or legal advancement.

Lyndhurst was content with the honours he enjoyed and the influence he exercised in the House of Lords; he was, lamented Henrietta Sykes, 'too unambitious' (Blake, 118). His love of society never left him; and society welcomed him for his gaiety and kindness. Granville, no tory, affirmed that he was totally without intellectual or social vanity. At Turville Park and George Street, surrounded by family, he entertained artists, authors, scientists, and beautiful and gifted women as well as politicians. Never bored, cosseted by a devoted wife, sister, and three daughters, supported by his friends, he was in 1863, as he was in 1791, 'naturally a friend to gaiety', continuing despite infirmity to 'love to see what is to be seen' (Amory, 116–18). Lyndhurst died peacefully on 12 October 1863 at his house, 25 George Street, Hanover Square, London. He was buried on 17 October in Highgate cemetery and later, in 1865, reinterred in Kensal Green cemetery.

GARETH H. JONES

**Sources** M. B. Amory, *The domestic and artistic life of John Singleton Copley* (1882) · D. Lee, *Lord Lyndhurst: the flexible tory* (1994) · J. D. Prown, *John Singleton Copley*, 2 vols. (1966) · J. Campbell, *Lives of the lord chancellors*, 8 vols. (1845–69), vol. 8 · T. Martin, *A life of Lord Lyndhurst* (1883) · *The Times* (13 Oct 1863) · Lord Holland [H. R. V. Fox] and J. Allen, *The Holland House diaries, 1831–1840*, ed. A. D. Kriegel (1977) · J. Ridley, *The young Disraeli* (1995) · R. Blake, *Disraeli* (1966) · W. F. Monypenny, *The life of Benjamin Disraeli*, 1 (1910) · *Benjamin Disraeli letters*, ed. J. A. W. Gunn and others (1982–), vols. 1–3 · *Hansard 2* · *Hansard 3* · W. Bagehot, 'What Lord Lyndhurst really was', in *The collected works of Walter Bagehot*, ed. N. St John-Stevas, 3 (1986), 232–7 · J. Arnould, *Memoir of Thomas, first Lord Denman*, 1 (1873) · *The Greville memoirs, 1814–1860*, ed. L. Strachey and R. Fulford, 8 vols. (1938) · D. Le Marchant, *Memoir of John Charles, Viscount Althorp, third Earl Spencer*, ed. H. D. Le Marchant (1876) · HoP, *Commons, 1790–1820*, vol. 3

**Archives** Glamorgan RO, Cardiff, corresp. and papers · Hunt. L., letters · New York Historical Society, legal notebook · Trinity

Cam., corresp. and papers | BL, corresp. with Lord Aberdeen, Add. MSS 43238–43252; corresp. with William Huskisson, Add. MSS 38750–38754; letters to Sir Robert Peel, Add. MSS 40316, 40442 • Bodl. Oxf., letters to Benjamin Disraeli • Exeter Cathedral, letters to Henry Phillpotts • PRO, corresp. with Lord Ellenborough, PRO 30/12 • U. Nott. L., letters to fifth duke of Newcastle • U. Southampton L., letters to duke of Wellington • UCL, corresp. with Lord Brougham • W. Sussex RO, corresp. with Lady Caroline Maxse

**Likenesses** J. S. Copley senior, group portrait, 1776 (*The Copley family*), National Gallery of Art, Washington, DC • J. S. Copley senior, oils, 1793, National Gallery of Art, Washington, DC • T. Phillips, oils, 1836, NPG [*see illus.*] • F. Roffe, watercolour drawing, *c.*1836, NPG • D. Wilkie, group portrait, oils, 1837 (*The first council of Queen Victoria*), Royal Collection • HB [J. Doyle], group portrait, lithograph, pubd 1839 (*HB discovered in his studio*; after his portrait), NG Ire. • H. W. Pickersgill, oils, *c.*1839, Lincoln's Inn, London • W. Behnes, bust, 1844, Trinity Cam. • G. Richmond, chalk drawing, 1851, NPG • J. E. Mayall, photographs, 1861, NPG • G. F. Watts, oils, 1862, NPG • Count D'Orsay, Hughenden Manor, Buckinghamshire • G. Hayter, group portrait, oils (*The trial of Queen Caroline, 1820*), NPG • G. Hayter, group portrait, oils (*The House of Commons, 1833*), NPG • J. Partridge, group portrait (*The fine arts commissioners, 1846*), NPG • T. A. Prior, group portrait, line engraving (after T. Lawrence and A. Wivell), NG Ire.

**Wealth at death** under £18,000: probate, 19 Nov 1863, *CGPLA Eng. & Wales*

**Copley, Lionel** (*d.* 1675), ironmaster, was the younger son of William Copley of Wadworth (*d.* 1658), and Ann (*d.* 1645), daughter of Gervase Cressy of Birkin. His paternal great-grandfather, Sir William Copley, had acquired the Sprotborough estate in the West Riding of Yorkshire through marriage. His grandfather, Christopher Copley, a younger son of Sir William, purchased an estate a few miles away at Wadworth. This passed to Copley's father and then to his elder brother, Christopher, a colonel in the parliamentary army during the civil war. Copley lived at Rotherham before he inherited the Wadworth estate upon the death of his brother (by 1664). He was normally referred to as 'Lionel Copley of Rotherham and Wadworth, esquire'. Copley married Frizalina (1610/11–1696), the daughter of George Ward of Capesthorne, Cheshire, and the widow of John Wheeler of London. They had two sons, Lionel and William, and two daughters, Castiliana and Ann.

In the 1570s and 1580s George Talbot, sixth earl of Shrewsbury, had erected charcoal blast furnaces and forges on his estates in and around Sheffield and Rotherham, thus starting an era in the local iron industry that was to last until the mid-eighteenth century. His son, Gilbert, the seventh earl, leased these ironworks to the Copleys during the early seventeenth century. It is uncertain how involved were Copley's father and brother before he himself became the leading ironmaster in south Yorkshire, ranking with George Sitwell (1601–1667) of Renishaw Hall, the dominant figure in the north-east Derbyshire and north Nottinghamshire iron industry.

During the civil war Copley 'suffered great losses by the forces of the Earl of Newcastle' (PRO, C5/22/27), the royalist commander in Yorkshire and the east midlands. After the parliamentary victory his fortunes recovered. In 1652 he spent nearly £4000 on acquiring the leases of Chapel and Rockley furnaces and Kimberworth forge. In 1656 he took a lease of the Kimberworth Park coal pits at £100 per annum, and in 1661 he renewed his lease to three forges and two furnaces at Wardsend. A rental of Sheffield manor in 1664 notes his leases of Ecclesfield furnace, the ironworks at Attercliffe and Wadsley, and rights to cordwood in the coppices. In 1666 he renewed his leases to Chapel furnace and the forges at Attercliffe, Rotherham, and Wardsend. At that time he was paying £100 per annum rent for Attercliffe forge and the furnace and forge at Wadsley. He was also involved in the early steel industry in south Yorkshire, but the only information that has come to light about his activities is the mention of a steel furnace at Kimberworth in the hearth tax returns for Lady day, 1672, owned by 'Willm Hellefeild or Mr Copley' and taxed on four hearths (Goodchild Collection, Wakefield).

Copley made his will on 20 November 1675 and died in London on 7 December. His body was taken back to Wadworth for burial in the parish church, where his grave was commemorated by a simple stone, set among other monumental inscriptions to various members of his family. A few months after his death, his son Lionel married Anne Boteler of Hertfordshire. Their son, another Lionel, inherited the Wadworth estate and was the heir to Sir Godfrey Copley of Sprotborough. Copleys lived at Sprotborough until the 1920s but with the deaths of Lionel Copley and George Sitwell, control of the ironstone mines, charcoal woods, furnaces, forges, and an outlet for sales via the river port of Bawtry passed to a different group of gentry ironmasters, and Copley's son and namesake left the district to become governor of Hull and afterwards of Maryland.                    DAVID HEY

**Sources** D. Hey, *The fiery blades of Hallamshire: Sheffield and its neighbourhood, 1660–1740* (1991), 169–174, 185 • J. Hunter, *South Yorkshire: the history and topography of the deanery of Doncaster*, 1 (1828), 251–2 • PRO, C5/22/27 • Hearth tax returns for Lady day, 1672, Wakefield Metropolitan District Council Library, Balne Lane, Wakefield, J. F. Goodchild Collection

**Archives** Sheff. Arch., deeds and papers, Copley family

**Copley, Thomas** (1532–1584), landowner and Roman Catholic exile, was born between February and May 1532, eldest son of Sir Roger Copley (*d.* 1549), landowner and member of the Mercers' Company, and his second wife, Elizabeth (*d.* 1559/60), daughter of Sir William *Shelley of Michelgrove, Sussex, judge of common pleas. He was related to Elizabeth I by common descent from Thomas, last Lord Hoo and Hastings, and he was a kinsman of both William Cecil Lord Burghley and Francis Walsingham. In 1547 he was admitted to the Inner Temple where, in 1561, he served as marshal for its 'grand and solemn Christmas' (Inderwick, 219). His father had settled the manor and parliamentary borough of Gatton, Surrey, on his mother. She controlled elections and returned Thomas to the Marian parliaments of April and November 1554, and the parliament of 1558. After her death he returned himself to the Elizabethan parliaments of 1559 and 1563–7.

To his inheritance, which included Gatton, the Maze (Southwark), and estates in Sussex and Lincolnshire, Copley added the Surrey manors of Chipstead, Colley, and Merstham. He was extravagant as he acknowledged, spending on 'costly building, chargeable music, horses, and such like vanities' (*CSP dom.*, *1580–1625*, vol. 27, no. 55). He was also impulsive. During the Inner Temple reader's dinner in 1556, when London's lord mayor was present, Copley and others made off with the mayoral sword of honour. They were imprisoned and expelled from the society. He was readmitted only after his 'humble suit and submission' (Inderwick, 187). When, on 5 March 1558, during the childless Catholic Mary's last parliament, he spoke out as an ardent protestant in defence of Princess Elizabeth's right to succeed her, he was imprisoned, although he pleaded his youth as a mitigating circumstance. Instead of contracting the expected marriage alliance with his powerful neighbours, the Howards of Effingham, later that year, about July, he married Catherine (*d.* in or after 1590), the Catholic daughter and coheir of Sir John Luttrell of Dunster, Somerset.

When Princess Elizabeth became queen Copley enjoyed royal favour. He was appointed commissioner of the peace for Surrey (1559–68) and in 1561 Elizabeth was godmother to his heir, Henry. However, about 1563, according to the Spanish ambassador, he converted to Roman Catholicism. Robert Persons (*Relation of a Trial between the Bishop of Evreux and the Lord Plessis Mornay*, 1604) attributed his conversion to the errors which he detected in Bishop Jewel's *Apology* (1562 in Latin, 1564 in English). Copley was fined and imprisoned for recusancy. In 1569 he advised his fellow justices that he could not subscribe to the supremacy and uniformity acts and in 1570 he went abroad without royal licence. By then his translations from the church fathers entitled *Certaine Treaties … Touching the Doctrine of Good Workes* (1569) and *A Treatise of Justification* (1569) had been published in Louvain. Copley's stated intention was to achieve religious unity; his *Certain Treaties* was a defence of justification by faith and good works rather than a vituperative attack on protestants.

Copley remained abroad, moving between the Low Countries, France, and Spain, until his death. During that time he frequently corresponded with the queen, Burghley, Walsingham, and others about his dilemma: although a devout Catholic he was a loyal subject whose unauthorized absence made him liable to statutory forfeiture of property for life. Necessity, he protested, obliged him to serve foreign princes. His integrity and loyalty, however, were widely doubted. 'A prime man among the English Fugitives' (Camden, 372), he was paid a Spanish pension, ennobled by Philip II as grand master of the Maes (Maze in Southwark) and lord of Gatton, made a baron and knight by the French king, and granted Spanish letters of marque against the Dutch rebels. Meanwhile the Howards benefited from his property and he received no income from it. He died on 25 September 1584 at the Spanish military camp near Antwerp. As his eldest son had died young he named his son William as his heir in his will (1576), and bequests were made to his daughters, Margaret, Helen, and Mary. In a codicil of 1577 provision was also made for his youngest sons, Anthony *Copley and John *Copley.

**Thomas Copley** (*b.* 1594, *d.* in or after 1652), Jesuit and colonist in America, was born in Madrid, eldest son of William Copley (1565–1643) and Magdalen Pickering (*d.* 1610), and grandson of Thomas Copley, the Roman Catholic exile. His family returned to Gatton in 1603, but eight years later he left for Louvain, where John Gerard had become rector of the Jesuits there. Copley made his noviceship at Liège and was admitted to the society; perhaps at that point, he surrendered his rights as heir to his younger brother William. By 1623 or 1624 'Father Copley [who] hath newly taken orders and come from beyond seas' was recorded as living in London (Dorsey, 41). Thereafter nothing is known of him until the 1630s. He was still in London in December 1634, when he petitioned Charles I that he was 'an alien born' and therefore should not be molested or arrested for his religion 'whilst following occasions which concern his father and his own estate' (*CSP dom.*, *1634–5*, vol. 278, no. 1). The king granted a warrant which afforded him personal protection until, in 1637, he sailed for the Maryland settlement, which had been established four years earlier.

Copley's life in Maryland was one of contrasts. He transported forty-eight men which enabled him to claim and receive 10,000 acres of land. As a Jesuit father he was prominent in establishing stations such as St Inigoes, St Thomas Manor, and Mattapony, in the new colony, ministering to settlers and providing spiritual counsel. At the same time, contrary to proprietary instructions to keep religion a private matter, he was active in worldly affairs on behalf of the Society of Jesus, importing goods to exchange with Indians for pelts, bringing out 'servants' and taking up more land, owning houses, suing and being sued in the lawcourts, and claiming cash and chattels at the death of men whose transportation he had funded. The proprietor, Lord Baltimore, approved of proposed laws, presented to the Maryland assembly in 1637–8 and 1638–9, to limit the Jesuits' political and economic activities. Copley appears to have been actively involved in marshalling resistance to them. Late in his life (August 1650) he demanded 20,000 acres of land for transporting sixty men to Maryland and in 1651 he was defendant in a lawsuit. He was unsuccessful in both. In November 1652 he bound himself to pay the debts of one Paul Simpson. He died in Maryland, though his date of death is uncertain and his burial place is unknown.

The alias Philip Fisher has been ascribed to Thomas Copley by Foley, McCoog, Land, and others, but it was not accepted by Copley's biographer, Katherine Dorsey.

MICHAEL A. R. GRAVES

**Sources** *CSP dom.*, *1566–1625*; *1631–7* · K. C. Dorsey, *The life of Father Thomas Copley: a founder of Maryland* (1885) · N. Davie, 'Prêtre et pasteur en Angleterre aux XVIe et XVIIe siècles: la carrière de John Copley (1577–1662)', *Revue d'Histoire Moderne et Contemporaine*, 43/3 (1996), 403–21 · *HoP, Commons, 1558–1603*, 3.650–51 · *VCH Surrey*, vols. 1, 3 · *DNB* · J. Strype, *Annals of the Reformation and establishment of religion … during Queen Elizabeth's happy reign*, new edn, 1/2–2 (1824) · F. A. Inderwick and R. A. Roberts, eds., *A calendar of the Inner Temple records*, 1 (1896) · will, PRO, PROB 11/68, sig. 13 · *JHC*, 1 (1547–1628), 33–81 · A. J. Kempe, ed., *The Loseley manuscripts* (1836) · G. Camdeno [W. Camden], *Annales rerum Anglicarum et Hibernicarum regnante Elizabetha* (1615) · L. B. Larking, ed., *Proceedings principally in* *the county of Kent in connection with the parliaments called in 1640, and especially with the committee of religion appointed in that year*, CS, old ser., 80 (1862) · *CSP for.*, 1577–8 · A. C. Land, *Colonial Maryland: a history* (1981) · D. W. Jordan, *Foundations of representative government in Maryland, 1632–1715* (1987) · *Seventh report*, HMC, 6 (1879), 608a, 628a · HoP, *Commons, 1509–58*, 1.694 · R. C. Christie, introduction, in *Letters of Sir Thomas Copley … to Queen Elizabeth and her ministers*, ed. R. C. Christie, Roxburghe Club, [130] (1897); repr. (New York, 1970), xl

**Copley, Thomas** (b. 1594, d. in or after 1652). *See under* Copley, Thomas (1532–1584).

**Coppack, Thomas** [Tom] (1895–1981), shipowner, was born on 14 August 1895, at East View, High Street, Connah's Quay, Flintshire, the fourth child and second son of Thomas Coppack (c.1867–1940), shipowner, of Connah's Quay, and Elizabeth Ann Butler (d. 1956) of Burton Stather, Lincolnshire, daughter of a shipbuilder. He was always known as Tom. The family had its origins in Norway, and Coppack is a corruption of the Norwegian name Kopeck. It was a maritime family in a maritime community, long settled on the Dee. Connah's Quay was one of the many busy ports which were concerned with the important coastal trade. Coppack's paternal grandfather, Captain John Coppack, had retired from the sea to become a shipowner about 1860. His firm, using the extensive development of the local brick, tile, and coal industries, found good business for its schooners, and also undertook the agency work for other vessels which they loaded. To this they added ship chandlery and ship repairing in association with members of the Butler family from Burton Stather. In the 1880s Captain Coppack ventured successfully into small steam coasters, whose higher cost made it much more important to keep them busy. Captain Coppack retired in the 1890s, and was succeeded by his second son, Thomas, and, for a time, the captain's brothers. Many other relatives were also seafarers. In 1910 the firm owned six steamers, seven sailing vessels, and a tug.

Coppack had his only formal education at St Mark's church school, Connah's Quay, although the family attended the Methodist chapel; later they moved to the Anglican church. However, his father's recurrent asthma meant that he started in the firm's office when he was eight years old. He had expected to go to sea, and he did make a number of voyages in the firm's ships, but his father's illness, and probably his own aptitude, brought him increasingly into management together with his eldest brother, John William (who died in the 1960s and with whom he shared membership of freemasonry). Between 1916 and 1919, Coppack served in the Royal Navy as a signalman, mostly with convoy commodores. On his return, he married Elsie, daughter of John Jones, a builder, of Shotton, near Connah's Quay. They had two daughters.

His early practical experience gave Coppack a thorough knowledge of the coasting trade, where owners needed to know the characteristics of the many ports, the different types of cargo, the vessels employed, as well as the capacities of the men in their employ. His father was a hard driver of both his ships and his men, but in 1926 ill health finally compelled him to retire and Coppack and his elder brother became the principals of the firm, buying out three other brothers. They maintained the strict regime which had given Coppacks such a good name for reliable service in such ventures as the potato trade from western France to England, where quick delivery of perishable cargoes was necessary. Coppack, with great aptitude for the complex calculations and judgements involved in arranging satisfactory charters, dealt with that department.

The First World War ended the era of commercial sail on the coast, and the Coppacks sold their last schooner in 1922. Henceforth they owned nothing but the smaller type of steam coaster with a single hatch, usually having four or five at any given time. The firm still traded in many familiar Irish sea passages, such as Connah's Quay bricks and tiles or Point of Ayr coal to all parts of Ireland, and stone from the north Wales quarries to Liverpool and elsewhere; but coasters, like deep sea tramps, were always open to the charter taking them further afield and so they still participated in the spring fruit and potato business from the Channel Islands and Brittany. Attention to the cleanliness of holds also gained them regular china clay cargoes from Cornwall to Grimsby.

Between the wars was a difficult period with boom and slump, and a collapse of rates but not of expenses, a pattern repeated after 1945. The coasting business in general gradually contracted: although the agency business remained active, the local industries no longer had such extensive connections and cargoes became very local, while the disadvantages of Connah's Quay became too evident. However, the firm had many regular shippers and the business remained viable. The Coppacks kept trading until 1965 when Tom Coppack retired in favour of his nephew and niece.

Coppack was slim, about 5 feet 8 inches tall, with dark, wavy hair. He had a quick mind, and there was usually a twinkle in his eye. His equable personality and unremitting attention to detail could get the best out of men. Although the firm never sought a national place, Coppack was a coasting shipowner of much repute. In retirement he wrote a fascinating autobiography, *A Lifetime with Ships* (1973), which charts a vanished era of maritime history. He lived at or near Connah's Quay all his working life, but after the death of his wife he moved about 1980 to Sheffield to live with his surviving daughter. He died in Nether Edge Hospital, Sheffield, from bronchopneumonia and cerebrovascular problems on 23 November 1981.

A. W. H. PEARSALL

**Sources** T. Coppack, *A lifetime with ships* (1973) · private information (2004) · R. S. Fenton, *Cambrian coasters: steam and motor coaster owners of north and west Wales* (1989) · d. cert. · m. cert. · CGPLA Eng. & Wales (1982)
**Archives** Clwyd RO
**Likenesses** photograph, repro. in Coppack, *A lifetime with ships*, pl. 1
**Wealth at death** £25,000: probate, 7 Jan 1982, CGPLA Eng. & Wales

**Coppard, Alfred Edgar** (1878–1957), short-story writer and poet, was born on 4 January 1878 at 35 St John's Street,

Folkestone, Kent, the eldest child and only son of the four children of George Coppard (*d.* 1887?), a journeyman tailor, and Emily Alma Southwell, who had been a housemaid. They were 'shockingly poor', although as Coppard was to recall in his unfinished autobiography, published posthumously, the two rooms comprising his first home were 'snug enough' (Coppard). But it was not until they moved to Brighton, when Coppard was five, that their fortunes improved sufficiently for them to live for a time as sole tenants of a house. Supposed ill health terminated Coppard's schooling at nine, but it was his father's death which made it necessary for him to go out to work as an assistant to a street vendor of paraffin and firewood. Perhaps because of this poverty, Frank O'Connor described Coppard's early life as 'cruel' (O'Connor, 171), although in his autobiography Coppard characteristically expressed its freedom and pleasures. By the time he was twenty, Coppard had worked for an auctioneer, a cheesemonger, a soap agent, and a carrier. He next spent several years in the office of an engineering firm, and then in 1907 moved to Oxford as confidential clerk in the Eagle ironworks (attached to Lucy's factory). On 5 August 1905 Coppard married Lily Annie (*b.* 1881/2), daughter of Albert Richardson, a plumber, of Brighton. After her death he married Winifred May, daughter of Dirk de Kok, solicitor, of South Africa; they had a son and a daughter.

It was on 1 April 1919 that Coppard gave up his business occupation and became a full-time professional writer. '"All Fools" Day was truly the congenial date of it', he recalled (Coppard), for he had saved only £50. Indeed, his office colleagues thought he was 'daft'. Nevertheless, many years later he was honoured by his old firm, which showed great pride in his literary achievement.

Coppard's early enthusiasm for reading and study had not lessened while he was a clerk, and he gained sufficient success as a spare-time athlete to use the prize-money to buy books and shape himself for his literary vocation. He appreciated the atmosphere of Oxford, where he 'was fired, though not by any more worthy muse than the spirit of rivalry' (Coppard). The deep impression made on his creative mind by Chekhov, Maupassant, Thomas Hardy, Katherine Mansfield, and the short stories of Henry James had already determined him to concentrate on the genre of the short story. But in his first three months as a freelance he sold only 'one little tale, one little poem, and received twenty rejections' (Coppard). It was therefore a timely relief and encouragement when an American periodical paid him £50 for 'The Tiger', a piece of a few thousand words.

In 1921 Coppard's first collection, *Adam and Eve and Pinch Me*, was published by Harold Taylor, the young owner of the Golden Cockerel Press, who had been impressed by Coppard's early efforts. This volume was the forerunner of a lengthy series of collected short stories. Coppard received early praise from Ford Madox Ford, who wrote: 'He is almost the first English prose-writer to get into English prose the peculiar quality of English lyric poetry—the fancy, the turn of the imagination, the wisdom … and the

beauty of the great lyricists' (Ford, 173). Coppard was an innovator in the English short story: he frequently presented a woman's point of view, and his writing strongly conveys the mystery and unpredictability of life. Like many short-story writers, he showed a preference for the misfit and the underdog. The hatred and dismay that he was made to feel by injustice and cruelty caused him to become prominent in the peace movement.

Coppard ranks with contemporaries such as Seán O'Faoláin and T. F. Powys in the history of the short story, although his best work is closer in spirit to that of Thomas Hardy. Poetry as well as prose occupied him from the outset, and *Hips and Haws*, the first of five volumes of lyrics, came out in the same year as his second book of stories, *Clorinda Walks in Heaven* (1922). However, Coppard's verse is undistinguished, and his finest poetry is to be found in his short stories. Between 1921 and 1951 hardly a year passed without a publication bearing the imprint A. E. Coppard: *Fishmonger's Fiddle* (1925), *The Field of Mustard* (1926), *Silver Circus* (1928), *Nixey's Harlequin* (1931), *Crotty Shinkwin* (1932), and *Dunky Fitlow* (1933) are the titles he invented for what proved to be his best successes. *It's me, O Lord!* was the title given to the first part of his autobiography, published a few months after his death of a heart attack in the Royal Northern Hospital, Islington, London, on 13 January 1957.

Coppard's closing years were heartened by the Book of the Month Club of America, which issued his *Selected Tales* (1946) to its vast membership, the first occasion on which it had made a work of this kind its leading choice. The undergraduates of Oxford paid him tribute with a celebration of his seventy-fifth birthday, attended by many distinguished personages, including Sir Maurice Bowra, the vice-chancellor. Coppard's many friends appreciated his twinkling eyes and a face suggesting the kindest of laughter. His last home, at Hillside, Duton Hill, Dunmow, Essex, delighted him, with its encircling trees, and birds so tame that he would pretend to be cross with them whenever they became too obtrusive. He spent a term on a rural council, and shared his second wife's enthusiasm when she was appointed assistant county medical officer in mid-Essex. She died in 1969, having become popular on television in frank discussions of family problems.

THOMAS MOULT, *rev.* CLARE HANSON

**Sources** A. E. Coppard, *It's me, O Lord!* (1957) • F. O'Connor, 'The price of freedom', in F. O'Connor, *The lonely voice* (1963), 170–86 • H. E. Bates, 'Katherine Mansfield and A. E. Coppard', in H. E. Bates, *The modern short story: a critical survey* (1941), 122–47 • private information (1971) • personal knowledge (1971) • F. M. Ford, *It was the nightingale* (1934), 140–41, 173–5
**Archives** BL, journal, Add. MS 70637 • Ransom HRC, papers • Syracuse University, New York, corresp. and literary MSS • U. Reading L., corresp. • Yale U., Beinecke L., papers | Col. U., letters to Cyril Clemens • Col. U., letters to George Coppard • U. Aberdeen L., letters to J. B. Chapman • U. Leeds, Brotherton L., letters to Cecil Lay and Joan Lay
**Likenesses** R. Gibbings, woodcut, 1928, V&A; repro. in A. E. Coppard, *Count Stefan* (1928) • H. Coster, photographs, 1931, NPG • T. Van Oss, oils, priv. coll.
**Wealth at death** £1056 1*s.* 10*d.*: probate, 12 March 1957, *CGPLA Eng. & Wales*

**Coppe, Abiezer** (1619–1672?), Baptist preacher and Ranter, was born on Sunday 30 May 1619, and baptized on 1 June at St Mary's, Warwick, the eldest known child of Walter Coppe (*b.* 1593, *d.* in or after 1667), who was probably a literate artisan, perhaps working with animal hides. After the Restoration Walter Coppe secured a seat in the middle aisle of his parish church and was rated at three hearths in Jury Street ward, Warwick.

**Early life and education** If his later confession is to be believed Abiezer Coppe's youth was marked by a godly litany of zealous devotion: fervent prayer 'by heart', memorizing 'much of the Scripture'; frequent and 'most secret' fasting; and abasement before God. At thirteen he began to 'take and keep' a daily register of his sins, setting them down in a book. To prevent his tongue from speaking sinful words he bridled his mouth, writing upon 'Scrouls of Parchment' the inscription '*Yea yea, nay, nay*' (Matthew 5: 37), which he 'sewed about' his wrists (Smith, 134–5). As a native of Warwick, Coppe was able to attend the town's free school. At fifteen it appears that Coppe began taking lessons given by the recently appointed master of Warwick School, Thomas Dugard. In his diary entry for 18 October 1634 Dugard noted that Coppe and two other boys had received instruction from a Greek New Testament and Homer; further entries in this diary indicate Coppe's progress. Some of Dugard's pupils went on to attend university and it may have been through Dugard's connections that Coppe secured a place at Oxford.

At an unknown date Abiezer Coppe was admitted at All Souls College, Oxford. He matriculated on 20 May 1636, but according to the antiquary Anthony Wood, Coppe continued at All Souls 'but for a short time' (Wood, *Ath. Oxon.*, 3.959) before becoming one of the postmasters (a class of poor scholars) of Merton College; Wood thought Coppe's tutor at Merton was Ralph Button (1611/12–1680). Button was, in Wood's estimation, a 'rigid presbyterian' but also a 'good scholar' and a 'noted Tutor' (ibid., 3.381; Wood, *Ath. Oxon.: Fasti*, 2.158). Coppe's studies at Oxford, however, were curtailed and he left the university without a degree. He returned to Warwick with his ties to Dugard intact and his eyes no doubt set on the ministry. In 1641 Dugard recorded that his former protégé, though probably unlicensed, was permitted to preach on Palm Sunday and at five Tuesday lectures.

**The civil war and imprisonment in Coventry** On 9 June 1644, after heavy fighting the two previous days, the royalist stronghold of Compton House in Warwickshire fell to local parliamentary forces under the command of Colonel William Purefoy. It seems that by this date Coppe, perhaps through Dugard's influence, had been appointed a chaplain under the command of Major George Purefoy. Coppe was to be stationed with the garrison at Compton House, receiving an initial payment of £35 for thirty-five weeks' service in February 1645. He was present at the muster of the garrison on 23 April 1646, but may have left the army in June 1646 when parliament's troops were removed from Compton House. Richard Baxter, who was at that period preacher to the garrison at Coventry, recalled 'I

heard of no opinion that he vented or held, but, the Necessity of Re-baptizing, and Independency, and was a sharp Reproacher of the Ministry' (Baxter, 148).

This deprecating image of Coppe as a fiery, sectarian preacher is seemingly confirmed by apparent autobiographical allusions in Coppe's later prophetic writings. Recounting the spiritual tribulations of a young man 'void of understanding', Coppe describes his bewitchment by the whore of Babylon (Revelation 17: 5), a flattering, deceitful figure that hunts after him, following him 'from street to street, from corner to corner, from grosse Protestantisme to Puritanisme, & c. at length from crosse in baptisme, and Common-Prayer-Book to Presbyterianisme'. Accounting the 'eating of a bit of bread, and drinking a sip of wine perhaps once a moneth' a vain form of religion, the young man quickly passes to 'Independency, and from thence perhaps to Anabaptisme' (Coppe, *A Second Fiery Flying Roule*, 19–21).

Baxter reckoned that Coppe 'continued a most zealous Re-baptizer many years, and re-baptized more then any one man that ever I heard of in the Countrey, witnesse *Warwickshire*, *Oxfordshire*, part of *Worcestershire*, & c.' (Baxter, 148). Although this may be an exaggeration—perhaps stemming from Coppe's alleged boast that he had 'baptized seven thousand people'—it is clear that Coppe was a 'leading man' and his standing within the Baptist churches was confirmed by his association with Hanserd Knollys and William Kiffin (Wood, *Ath. Oxon.*, 3.960; Smith, 147). When Knollys and Kiffin travelled from London to Coventry in the autumn of 1646 to engage in a public disputation with two local ministers, it was Coppe who acted as their scribe. Coppe, moreover, was to revel in the impending day of judgement that he believed awaited those who had maltreated 'the Lords Servants; (who come from a farr and strange countrey,)' (Smith, 54). He recalled that they had subjected one servant to stoning, the Old Testament penalty prescribed for blasphemy (Leviticus 24: 16) and Coppe's reworking here of a parable in the gospels (Mark 12: 1–9) resonates with the punishment meted out to Knollys who, by his own testimony, had been driven by this means from the pulpit. Coppe, too, suffered at the hands of persecutors and was imprisoned in Coventry gaol for his 're-baptizing'. Such was the significance of his case that on 28 November 1646 the governor and committee at Coventry wrote to the House of Commons concerning him. Afterwards Coppe claimed that he 'sustained a 14 weeks close imprisonment' without 'bail or mainprize'—suggesting that he was detained without charge (Smith, 129; Coppe, *A Second Fiery Flying Roule*, 20).

**Conversion experience and moral attitudes** In his twenty-eighth year Coppe underwent a profound transformation, an experience that he came to represent as a spiritual passage from death to life. Reflecting upon his former sanctity, his 'prayers tears, sighs, groans, watchings, fastings, humiliations', Coppe recalled his 'self-seeking' in first observing and then scorning 'carnall' gospel ordinances (Smith, 135; Coppe, *A Second Fiery Flying Roule*, 21–2). Hinting at the necessity of having a contrite, 'soft heart', Coppe recounted how 'God in his infinite wisdome' had laid low his vanity and levelled his pride—which is the 'true and pure levelling' (Smith, 74, 141; Coppe, *A Second Fiery Flying Roule*, 22). Reading Obadiah's prophecy of the burning of the house of Jacob (Obadiah 1: 18) as an allegory of the incendiary appearance of the Lord of hosts upon his 'fierce, rugged flesh', Coppe narrated how his 'hatred, strife, envy, malice, evil surmizing' was utterly consumed by the '*Cœlestiall* Fire' of God's love:

> First, all my strength, my forces were utterly routed, my house I dwelt in fired; my father and mother forsook me, the wife of my bosome loathed me, mine old name was rotted, perished; and I was utterly plagued, consumed, damned, rammed, and sunke into nothing, into the bowels of the still Eternity (my mothers wombe) out of which I came naked, and whereto I returned again naked.   (Smith, 78, 45; Coppe, *A Fiery Flying Roll*, preface)

Coppe lay a while 'rapt up in silence'. At length he heard with his 'outward care' a most 'terrible thunder-clap, and after that a second'. Upon the second thunderclap 'I saw a great body of light, like the light of the Sun, and red as fire', which infused him with great awe and joy. And so he lay 'trembling, sweating, and smoaking (for the space of half an houre)' before the immanent presence of the Lord. He was finally reassured that God would take him to heaven, but not before he had drunk a 'bitter cup; where-upon (being filled with exceeding amazement) I was throwne into the belly of hell' (Coppe, *A Fiery Flying Roll*, preface). Later he recovered, and in a further vision a 'most strong, glorious voyce uttered these words, *The Spirits of just men made perfect*'. Coppe professed that the 'visions and revelations of God' were 'stretched' out before him and within him 'for the space of foure dayes and nights, without intermission' (ibid.). Baxter, however, considered that he 'was in a long trance & hath seene strange Satanicall delusions' (DWL, Baxter MS, *Treatises*, 3.67, fol. 302r).

Coppe emerged from these experiences a resurrected man, with a new name. The 'day *star*' was risen in his heart (2 Peter 1: 19), and as his erotic coupling of '*love*' and '*dove*' suggests (Song of Solomon 5: 2) Coppe imagined that the 'day of the Lord' was at hand (Isaiah 13: 6) (Smith, 52, 47). In the manner of John in the book of Revelation, Coppe presented a powerful vision of the impending apocalypse; similarly he reworked the story of the 'filthy blinde Sodomites' who failed to recognize two angels in their midst (Genesis 19: 11) into a prophecy that '*Sodome* must be burnt, *Lot* must be saved, *flesh* must die & be crucified, and the *Spirit* live and dwell in the Saints' (Coppe, *A Fiery Flying Roll*; Smith, 63). Already

> There are Angels … come downe from Heaven, in the shapes and formes of men, who are full of the vengeance of the Lord; and are to poure out the plagues of God upon the Earth, and to torment the Inhabitants thereof.   (Coppe, *A Fiery Flying Roll*, 8)

Coppe claimed that he himself had been 'plagued and tormented beyond expression' and he affirmed that he had 'rather behold one of these Angels pouring out the plagues of God, cursing; and teaching others to curse bitterly'. Adopting the mantle of an angel (in the form of a man), he inveighed against the hypocrisy of carnal religious observance, announcing that 'To the pure all things are pure' (Coppe, *A Fiery Flying Roll*, 8).

Supposing that he had undergone instantaneous transformation Coppe reportedly set about enacting his new principles. It was to be said of him that thinking he was 'above Ordinances' and that he was 'a childe of God' he began to live 'very loosley', cursing and swearing, 'spreading blasphemies, and committing base lewd sins' (*Severall Proceedings in Parliament*, 16, 11–18 Jan 1650, 213). Baxter likewise charged Coppe with unnamed 'filthy lascivious practices', amazed that 'such a man should have any followers' and that professedly God fearing men and women should join him in 'roaring, drinking, whoring, open full-mouthed swearing ordinarily by the Wounds and Bloud of God, and the fearfullest Cursing that hath been heard, as if they were all possessed with Divels' (Baxter, 148). Many of these allegations echo, and in some instances perhaps derive from, pronouncements in Coppe's writings. Coppe maintained 'It's meat and drink to an Angel [who knows none evil, no sin] to sweare a full mouth'd oath' (Coppe, *A Second Fiery Flying Roule*, 13). In a similar tone he noted that there was a time 'to be merry' (Ecclesiastes 8: 15), a time to partake of the spiritual feast: 'To the fatted calfe, ring, shoes, mirth, and Musicke, & c. which is the *Lords Supper indeed*' (Smith, 62, 66).

Coppe pointed to the fact that Michal had clearly adopted an inappropriate stance in disapproving of her husband King David's dancing uncovered before the ark of the covenant in celebration of its return to Jerusalem (2 Samuel 6: 16), a reference which is significant in this context, for it partly anticipates the allegation that it was usual for Coppe to preach 'stark naked' by day and to lie drunk with a wench 'stark naked' at night (Wood, *Ath. Oxon.*, 3.960). This association of nudity with sexual licence, though itself familiar from hostile accounts of adult baptism rituals, is suggestive in its depiction of Coppe as an adulterer, for Coppe delighted in citing the scriptural precedent of Hosea, 'who went in to a whore' (Hosea 1: 2).

**Publications, preaching, and associates, 1649**  On 12 November 1648 Coppe received a fraternal letter from Mistress T. P., probably Thomasine Pendarves (*bap.* 1618, *d.* in or after 1671), daughter of Thomas Newcomen of Dartmouth and wife of John Pendarves, minister of St Helen's, Abingdon. Coppe responded in a work published as *Some Sweet Sips, of Some Spirituall Wine* (1649) with an epistle to his 'Deare Sister, in the best fellowship' and with a '*Preparatory*' epistle intended 'only, and primely for that precious *Princesse* … another late converted *Jew*, and for the Saints at *Abingdon*' (Coppe, *Some Sweet Sips*, 45, 10). These modes of address, together with Coppe's rendering of the initials T. P. into Hebrew, indicate Coppe's identification of the heirs of Abraham born to him by 'a *freewoman, Jerusalem which is above*' (Galatians 4: 26) with 'the Israel of God, the seed of the Lord' (Smith, 55). This adoption of '*Spiritual Israel*' as an emblem for '*the Land of the living*' is a recurring feature of Coppe's *Some Sweet Sips*. As its title implied,

Abiezer Coppe (his name spelled in Hebrew) *A late converted JEW*, sought to offer the '*bewildered Israelites*' who read this book a taste of liberty and happiness 'from spirituall Canaan'. For like the two Israelite spies of his title (Numbers 13: 23), Coppe believed that he had returned from the Holy Land bearing spiritual grapes of 'great worth, and weight' (ibid., 42, 60, 68–9).

Perhaps shortly after Christmas day 1648 Coppe believed that the '*word of the Lord*' came expressly to him, commanding him to 'Go up to *London*, to *London*, that great City, write, write, write'. This he revealed in *A Fiery Flying Roll* (1649). As he began to write Coppe beheld a hand with 'a roll of a book' therein (Ezekiel 2: 9), 'which this fleshly hand would have put wings to, before the time'. Immediately the roll was snatched out of his hand and thrust into his mouth. Like the prophet Ezekiel Coppe was forced to eat the roll—though whereas for Ezekiel the roll was 'in my mouth as honey for sweetness' (Ezekiel 3: 2), for Coppe the roll tasted 'as bitter as worm-wood'. There it lay 'broiling' and 'burning' in his stomach. When Coppe arrived in London about the beginning of January 1649, the 'most excellent Majesty' within him unexpectedly set his 'forme' in many 'strange' postures: this, on his account, received a mixed reception. Imagining that he had been set as 'no small signe and wonder in fleshly *Israel*' (Isaiah 8: 18), Coppe recalled how he fell down before the feet of cripples, beggars, and lepers, kissing their feet and 'resigning up' his money to them (Coppe, *A Fiery Flying Roll*, preface, 1, 13). In *A Second Fiery Flying Roule* (1649) Coppe remembered how at the prison in Southwark he sat, ate, and drank with gypsies, hugging and kissing them, putting his hand 'in their bosomes, loving the she Gipsies dearly' (Coppe, *A Second Fiery Flying Roule*, 11). Contrasting with this demeanour was Coppe's '*strange and lofty carriage towards great ones*'. In the open streets of London and Southwark, with his hand 'fiercely' stretched out, his hat 'cockt up', his eyes set 'as if they would sparkle out', sometimes 'gnashing' his teeth and with a 'mighty loud' voice he charged the coaches of 'men and women of the greater ranke', proclaiming the 'notable day of the Lord' to them. Thus he acted, day and night, 'for the space of 12. or 13. dayes', without a finger lifted against him, a hair of his head touched, or a hand laid on his clothes (Coppe, *A Fiery Flying Roll*, Contents, 14–15).

While in London, Coppe was said to have 'appeared in a most dreadful manner' before a group calling itself 'My one flesh' (Clarkson, 25). Suggestively, this conventicle was known to Giles Calvert, a publisher and bookseller, who issued Coppe's *Some Sweet Sips*. About this time Coppe read and transcribed *John the Divine's Divinity*, probably by John File. It was printed for Calvert with a preface by Coppe dated 13 January 1649. Two or three days later Coppe preached an inflammatory sermon in the church at St Helen, Bishopsgate. Before a large assembled congregation he caused an uproar by blaspheming and cursing for an hour, allegedly saying 'a pox of God take al your prayers hearing, reading, fasting'. Although 'guarded by a party of his own', it seems that Coppe was jostled in the pulpit by some angry Baptists (*The Ranters Ranting*, 1650, 6). Rather

than face charges of blasphemy before a magistrate (a felonous and capital offence under the provisions of an ordinance of May 1648) he probably fled into hiding the next day.

In spring or summer 1649 Coppe may have visited John Pordage, rector of Bradfield, Berkshire. Another of Pordage's guests was Richard Coppin, to whose allegedly blasphemous book *Divine Teachings* (1649) Coppe contributed a preface. Some time after 7 June, when a lavish thanksgiving dinner was consumed at Grocers' Hall while 'hundreds of poor wretches dyed of hunger' (Coppe, *A Fiery Flying Roll*, 12), Coppe completed the writing of *A Fiery Flying Roll*. The roll had been broiling and burning in Coppe's stomach, but now it was spewed forth as a blazing text, proclaimed on the title page as 'A Word from the Lord to all the Great Ones of the Earth.' (ibid., title page) and 'the last WARNING PIECE at the dreadfull day of JUDGEMENT' (ibid.). Revelling in the reversal of the old order, in the passing of episcopacy, monarchy, and the House of Lords, the 'excellent Majesty' dwelling in Coppe proclaimed that, as in Ezekiel 21: 27, '*I overturn, overturn, overturn*'. Disavowing both 'sword levelling' and 'digging-levelling', he inveighed against all blood shed in the name of honour, rank, and propriety. The blood of the righteous, the blood of the 'hellishly murdered' Levellers 'shot to death' in Burford churchyard on 17 May 1649, would be avenged. For the Levellers who had died 'Martyrs for God and their Countrey' were but 'shadows of most terrible, yet glorious good things' to come. God himself was the 'mighty Leveller', whose coming was imminent (Coppe, *A Fiery Flying Roll*, 1, 2, 4, 11).

On Sunday 30 September 1649, while riding through an open field, Coppe recounted that he met a poor, deformed man. Moved by the beggar's plight, Coppe was tempted to give him 6*d*. Having only a shilling coin, he asked the beggar for change, but when the beggar replied that he had none, Coppe rode away without giving him anything. But then, by God's judgement he 'was struck down dead' and 'my money perish with me'. The tale, which Coppe claimed was a 'true story', illustrates that he believed he was living in the 'last daies' (James 5: 3) when cankered gold and silver would rise up like fire in judgement against those that forbore from casting all into 'the Treasury' (Mark 12: 43). For only those who accounted nothing their own, who had 'ALL THINGS common' (Acts 2: 44), would have '*treasure in heaven*' (Matthew 19: 21) (Coppe, *A Second Fiery Flying Roule*, 4, 6, 16, 22, 4). Towards the end of the year Coppe completed the writing of *A Second Fiery Flying Roule: to All the Inhabitants of the Earth; Specially to the Rich Ones*. As with *A Fiery Flying Roll* he believed that the word of the Lord came expressly to him. The two rolls were printed in London, probably by the same printer though at different times, and issued together by an anonymous publisher 'in the beginning of that notable day, wherein the secrets of all hearts are laid open; and wherein the worst and foulest of villanies, are discovered, under the best and fairest outsides' (Coppe, *A Fiery Flying Roll*, title-page).

**Coppe—'the great Anabaptist' or 'the great Ranter'?** On 18 December 1649 the council of state issued warrants for the apprehension of Coppe and the seizure of his 'Mad, and Blasphemous Bookes, called the fyery flyinge Role' (PRO, SP 25/63, 408). By 8 January 1650 he had been taken into custody and imprisoned in Warwick. On 10 January a party of soldiers hurried '*the great Anabaptist*' from Warwick to Coventry gaol (*A Perfect Diurnall of some Passages and Proceedings*, no. 6, 14–21 Jan 1650, 42). On 1 February the House of Commons ordered that all printed copies of *A Fiery Flying Roll* 'be burnt by the Hand of the Hangman, at the *New Palace Yard*, at *Westminster*; the *Exchange*, in *Cheapside*; and at the *Market Place*, in *Southwark*' (*JHC*, 6.354). The next day the council of state ordered that Coppe be brought to London, but he seems to have languished in the noxious conditions of his confinement and 'being not well, desired he might not take the journey as yet, least it should cost him his life' (*A Perfect Diurnall of some Passages and Proceedings*, no. 9, 4–11 Feb 1650, 76). By late March several denunciations of Coppe's professed doctrines had appeared. Gerrard Winstanley condemned 'the Ranting Practise' as a 'Kingdome that lies in objects; As in the outward enjoyment of meat, drinke, pleasures, and women' (*The Works of Gerrard Winstanley*, ed. G. Sabine, 1941, 399), while the London Baptist churches were likewise quick to issue a collective epistle censuring the abominations espoused by their former co-religionist and his associates.

On 6 March Andrew Wyke, a Baptist preacher and possibly pastor to a Baptist congregation at Colchester, arrived in Coventry with his kinswoman. He may have brought money with him, collected by provincial Baptist churches, to help pay for Coppe's prison debts. He was soon joined by Joseph Salmon, formerly chaplain to Commissary-General Henry Ireton's regiment of horse and a comrade of Coppe's. Both were swiftly committed to Coventry gaol for the misdemeanour of swearing and for defying an order prohibiting the visiting of Coppe. On 19 March Coppe was transferred to Newgate on the instructions of the council of state. Under suspicion of blasphemy and treason against the state, Coppe wrote to Salmon and Wyke assuring them that:

> Newgate … is noe prison to mee while I am inthroned in my Triple heart wch is but one & triangular, which is as firme as a stone, when I my selfe (‡ heere & there ˣ and everywhere) raise uppe my selfe … (Smith, 117)

An act of 10 May for suppressing incest, adultery, and fornication was followed on 28 June by an act against profane swearing and cursing and on 9 August by an act against blasphemy that prescribed six months' imprisonment without bail or mainprize for a first offence—a more lenient sentence than the death penalty decreed by Mosaic Law and an ordinance of 2 May 1648. Although this legislation can be seen as part of a wider programme designed to further the cause of godly reformation in doctrine and manners, it is also evident that the impetus for these measures came from a parliamentary majority's desire to extinguish 'the several abominable Practices of a

Sect called Ranters' (*JHC*, 6.427). Coppe was still more specific, claiming he had been informed that the acts against adultery and blasphemy 'were put out because of me; thereby secretly intimating that I was guilty of the breach of them' (Coppe, *Remonstrance of the Severe and Zealous Protestation of Abiezer Coppe*, 1).

On 27 September Lawrence Clarkson, author of an 'impious and blasphemous' book called *A Single Eye All Light, No Darkness*, was brought before a parliamentary committee 'for suppressing licentious and impious Practices, under pretence of Religion, Liberty, & c.' (*JHC*, 6.474). In his published spiritual autobiography Clarkson was to write disingenuously how, during his examination, he confessed to knowing Coppe, 'and that is all, for I have not seen him above two or three times' (Clarkson, 31). On 1 October, seventy-four days after parliament had ordered the MP for Warwick to convey to the council of state their concern that Coppe be 'speedily' brought to trial, Coppe, again described as 'the great Ranter', was brought before the same committee that had examined Clarkson (*JHC*, 6.444; *The Weekly Intelligencer of the Common-Wealth*, 2, 1–8 Oct 1650, 16). It was said that when Coppe appeared he refused to remove his hat in deference. In the manner of David before Achish, the king of Gath (1 Samuel 21: 10–15), Coppe 'disguised himself into a madnesse'. When questioned he seemed to talk to himself, 'which some thought to be Gods just judgement upon him' (ibid.; *The Routing of the Ranters*, 1650, 2). At other times he flung apples, pears, and nutshells about the room. The committee sent him back to Newgate: there was to be no public trial.

**Recantations?** By 3 January 1651 Coppe had completed, not so much for his 'own sake (for my pure innocence supports me)', but for the 'sakes of others' *A Remonstrance of the Sincere and Zealous Protestation of Abiezer Coppe* (1651). Written as 'a Preamble to a farther future Declaration', this brief yet defiant pamphlet was Coppe's unrepentant response to the Blasphemy Act (Coppe, *Remonstrance*, 1651, title-page, 1). On 30 May he penned a 'humble Petition' to the parliament and council of state. Lamenting his '*sore, tedious, and long continued imprisonment*', an apologetic Coppe emotively recounted the misfortunes his '*poor disconsolate wife*' and '*small innocent children*' had suffered on his account. Appended to this supplicatory epistle was a tract entitled 'Truth asserted against, and triumphing over error'. Here Coppe presented a refutation of the 'several blasphemous opinions' hinted at in 'the *Fiery flying role*'. Yet rather than acknowledge authorship of this work, Coppe contented himself with a catalogue of 'severall Errors' (some of which he denied having been 'tackt or tainted' with 'in the least degree') and a casuistical assertion of the several 'contrary Truths' (Smith, 125, 127, 128, 137, 151, 155, 157).

On 22 June, John Dury and some unnamed persons conferred with Coppe. They found him to be 'ingenuously open' in what he said and 'truly penitent' for what he had done. The next day Dury wrote to Coppe inviting him to explain his views on matters such as sin, God's law, resurrection, and judgement. Mindful that Coppe might profess repentance outwardly only to gain his liberty, Dury warned him not to dissemble. In response Coppe sought to convince Dury of the sincerity of his repentance, remarking that he had been persuaded that never had any man 'lien more under the wrath and heavy displeasure of God for sin, then I have done'. That same day Coppe also replied to the proposals of the Commonwealth propagandist Marchamont Nedham. Coppe assured Nedham that he had made the necessary changes to his recantation 'by deleating what might prove offensive', 'altering, correcting, and amending other things', and by 'explicating some other things that might appear dubious, or difficult' (Smith, 146–7, 152, 156–7). Some time after 28 June, perhaps through the intervention of Dury and Nedham, Coppe was finally released from Newgate.

On Sunday 21 September 1651 Coppe preached near Witney, Oxfordshire. His text, apparently, was 'There is a time to sing, and a time to dance' (Ecclesiastes 3: 4). Some who heard him thought he said 'that the whole Scripture from the beginning of genesis to the end of the Revelations was to be understood allegorically' (Tickell, 80). On 23 September he preached a recantation sermon on Isaiah 42: 24 at Burford church from the very pulpit where in 1649 Cornet Henry Denne had preached obedience to the Commonwealth after witnessing the execution of three of his fellow mutineers in the churchyard. Before Coppe was able to ascend the pulpit, however, he found his place usurped by John Tickell, minister of St Helen's, Abingdon. Preaching what appears to have been a prepared sermon on Galatians 1: 8–9, Tickell took the opportunity to insinuate that Coppe was accused for having preached a false gospel, and when his own address appeared as *The Bottomless Pit Smoaking in Familisme* (1651) he observed that in his sermon Coppe 'againe and againe' made 'assertions of divine truth under execrations'. While he suspected Coppe's conversion, Tickell contented himself with the thought that 'God is his judge and knowes his heart' (Tickell, 32, 34, and 'To the reader').

**Last work and final years** Towards the end of February 1655, while lodging at The Mermaid by the Mews at Charing Cross, George Fox recalled that Colonel Packer and his officers came in with Coppe and 'a great company of ranters', who having ordered drink and tobacco 'bowed & scraped on to another' (*Journal of George Fox*, 1.165). This portrayal of Coppe as an obsequious man who indulged his carnal appetite is typical of Fox and his censorious accounts of Ranter behaviour. The reference to William Packer, however, a Baptist army officer and preacher, may suggest that by this date Coppe had been re-embraced by some within the Baptist fold.

In January 1657 there appeared a broadside, *Divine Fireworks, or, Some Sparkles from the Spirit of Burning in this Dead Letter*. This warning was delivered 'In *ABHIAM*', perhaps a contraction for 'In Ab(iezer ?) I am' *cf.* Exodus 3: 14, ('I AM THAT I AM'). The author prophesied the coming that year of the 'roaring ramping Lyon, with the sharp two-edged Sword' (Revelation 5: 5, 19: 15) and the 'consuming fire' (Hebrews 12: 29). The proclamation of this message, given by one who with fear and trembling claimed to have seen

'the Lord the King', may have coincided with Coppe's assumption of the prophetic name Hiam.

After this Coppe is lost to view, until, on 13 February 1667, Abiezer Hiam, alias Coppe of the city of London, having subscribed to the Thirty-Nine Articles of Religion, was granted licence to practise medicine and surgery. Of the four physicians who provided Coppe with letters testimonial, two were prominent Baptists. It may be that for the remainder of his life Coppe practised medicine under the name Hiam. On 23 August 1672 one Hiam was buried at St Mary's, Barnes, Surrey. Although no one named Hiam is recorded either as a tenant of the manor of Barnes, or in the surviving hearth tax returns for the parish, there seems little reason to doubt that the dead man was Coppe.

In 1680 there appeared a broadside, *A Character of a True Christian*, the purported author of which was 'Abiezar Copp'. Its style, however, conforms to no known work by Coppe. Some years later Anthony Wood compiled a brief biography of Coppe as part of his monumental *Athenae Oxonienses*, 2 vols. (1691–2). Drawing on manuscripts, printed texts, and oral testimony of sometimes questionable veracity, Wood's depiction of Coppe as a lascivious blasphemer has exercised a lasting influence. Some anecdotes, notably the tales of Coppe's misdeeds as an undergraduate and later as a Ranter, appear little more than prurient gossip. Other statements, such as the remark that, after the Restoration, Coppe preached in conventicles, though as yet unsubstantiated, seem more credible. Wood brought Coppe's life to an end by surmizing that he was 'brought low by certain infirmities which he had contracted in his rambles by drinking and whoring'. He mentioned Coppe's burial as 'Dr Higham on the south side of the body of the church' at Barnes, 'under the seats' (Wood, *Ath. Oxon.*, 3.961–2). This church was largely destroyed by fire in 1978, however, and Coppe's bones may now lie under the Langton chapel in the rebuilt church.

ARIEL HESSAYON

**Sources** A. Hessayon, 'After-clap: Abiezer Coppe (1619–1672)', [forthcoming] · N. Smith, ed., *A collection of Ranter writings from the seventeenth century* (1983) · Foster, *Alum. Oxon.* · R. Baxter, *Plain scripture proof of infants church-membership and baptism* (1651) · Wood, *Ath. Oxon.*, new edn · H. Knollys, *The life and death of that old disciple of Jesus Christ and eminent minister of the gospel, Mr Hanserd Knollys*, ed. W. Kiffin (1692) · A. Coppe, *A fiery flying roll* (1649) · A. Coppe, *A second fiery flying roule* (1649) · [C. Fowler], *Daemonium meridianum: Satan at noon* (1655) · R. Coppin, *Truths testimony* (1655) · *A perfect diurnall of some passages and proceedings* (1650) · JHC · L. Clarkson, *The lost sheep found* (1660) · *The routing of the Ranters* (1650) · J. Tickell, *The bottomless pit smoaking in familisme* (1651) · D. Lysons, *The environs of London*, 4 vols. (1792–6), vol. 1 · *The journal of George Fox*, ed. N. Penney, 2 vols. (1911)

**Copper family** (*per.* 1845–2000), folk singers, of Rottingdean on the Sussex coast, 4 miles to the east of Brighton, came to prominence with the brothers James Copper and Thomas Copper, the sons of John Copper and his wife, Charlotte. They are among the most important performers of English traditional song ever to have been recorded. A selection of their songs appeared in the first number of the *Journal of the Folk Song Society* in 1899, and members of the family were still performing their unique repertory in their characteristic style of two-part harmony early in the twenty-first century. The family's songs and the context in which their tradition survives have been richly documented, most notably in sound recordings and in the writings of Bob Copper.

**James Copper** (1845–1924) was always known as Brasser Copper. He was married to Frances, and worked on the large downland farm of William Brown, eventually rising to the important and prestigious managerial position of head bailiff. His brother **Thomas Copper** (1847–*c*.1936) started his working life on a farm and worked up to the post of head carter. Later he became a pub landlord, taking over tenancies first in Rottingdean and later at Chailey on the Sussex Weald. This shift from farm work to pub tenancy was a recurring theme in the lives of the Copper family during the twentieth century.

Rottingdean, in the late nineteenth and early twentieth centuries, was an unusual place containing simultaneously three interacting but distinct economies with their related social groups. The village was at once a farming and, in a minor way, fishing community, a popular resort catering for the developing trade in holiday-making and tourism, and a residential refuge for well-heeled and eminent Victorians and Edwardians. Copper family members earned their livings in agriculture until its diminishing importance and the rise of alternative economic opportunities encouraged them into other livelihoods. The Coppers sustained traditional attitudes and a positive view of customs inherited from the past, including singing and mumming.

The influx of a significant group of well-to-do people into Rottingdean was greatly aided by the development of fast and efficient rail links between London and Brighton. Many nineteenth-century villages attracted a residential social élite of incomers, but in Rottingdean this was a particularly significant artistic and political group. Residents of the late Victorian and Edwardian periods included the artist Sir Edward Burne Jones, the writer Rudyard Kipling, the future prime minister Stanley Baldwin, and the Unionist politician Sir Edward Carson. It was while staying at the home of the latter that Kate Lee, secretary of the newly formed Folk Song Society, collected songs from James and Thomas Copper in 1898.

Lee's publication of the Coppers' songs and her account of the experience might have been the last records of the Coppers. Lee died in 1905, and no other of the early folk-song collectors seem to have visited the Coppers after her. In spite of fast-changing social, economic, and cultural conditions, however, the Coppers maintained their singing tradition sufficiently for it to re-emerge from obscurity in the 1950s.

James 'Brasser' Copper had two sons: **(Francis) John William Copper** (1880–1952) and **James Dale Copper** (1882–1954), known as Jim. This next generation of Copper brothers kept up the family involvement with agricultural work. Jim Copper 'inherited' his father's position of

farm bailiff, and John Copper was a head shepherd. They continued the tradition of singing at social gatherings and for amusement. John Copper died on 12 May 1952 in the Royal Sussex County Hospital, Brighton. Jim Copper died on 19 May 1954. They each had a son significant to this account. John Copper's son was **Ronald Copper** (*c*.1913–1979), known as Ron. He was a carpenter and later a publican, having the licence of the Queen Victoria in Rottingdean. Robert James Copper (*b*. 1915), known as Bob, was the son of Jim Copper and his wife, Daisy Louise Clark. He was variously a barber, a fisherman, a guardsman, a policeman, and finally a publican and author.

Bob and Ron Copper were cousins and friends who spent a lot of time together. They learned the old way of singing from their fathers and, in spite of some hostility in the inter-war years from people who thought their songs old-fashioned and drear, regularly sang together. At times Bob lived away from the Rottingdean area, as a guardsman in London in the 1930s and subsequently as a policeman in Worthing. The singing tradition could then have petered out, but Bob maintained a strong contact with his father and his cousin Ron, and singing was part of their shared time together. During the late 1930s and the years of the Second World War, partly under the influence of a friend, the writer Barclay Wills, Bob Copper formed the resolve that the family singing tradition and songs were worth preserving.

In 1949 Jim Copper heard one of the songs he knew in the programme *Country Magazine* on BBC radio (although he did not much like the way in which it was performed). He wrote to the BBC saying that he had heard one of the songs regularly performed by members of the Copper family. The letter attracted the attention of the producer Francis Collinson, who had a long-standing interest in folk music and later wrote significant books on Scottish music. Collinson 'collected' songs from the Coppers and arranged for Jim and Bob Copper to appear on a live broadcast of *Country Magazine*. This was the start of the Copper family's emergence into public view, mainly through the connection with the BBC and such people as Brian George, Peter Kennedy, and David Thomson, who produced a programme called 'The life of James Copper' in 1951. Four of the family appeared at the Albert Hall in 1952, a far cry from the parlours, taprooms, and open country that had usually been their places of performance. This was the start of public performances by members of the family on an international stage that have continued into the twenty-first century.

Bob Copper made contact with the BBC at a very opportune moment. Stirrings of interest in recording what remained of the traditional music of Britain and Ireland led to an extensive recording project, and in 1954 Bob Copper joined the staff of the BBC as a field collector on a series of short-term contracts. Using an ironically named 'Midget' tape recorder he recorded traditional singers in Hampshire and Sussex and gathered some fascinating material. He later documented his experience in his book *Songs and Southern Breezes* (1973), and in the LP sound recording of the same title (1976). His affability and his personal understanding of the lives and backgrounds of the people he recorded made him an ideal folk-song collector, comparable to Alfred Williams in an earlier generation.

Bob and Ron Copper were extensively recorded in the 1950s and 1960s. These recordings show their great musical empathy, built on years of singing together. Ron died in 1979, but long before this Bob had started singing with younger members of his family. In 1971 Bob Copper produced his first book, *A Song for every Season*, the first of several works dealing with the family, its singing tradition, and its social and historical context. The book was a great success and won the Robert Pitman literary prize for best new author, an interesting achievement for someone in his late fifties. Publication of the book and the subsequent set of recordings of the same name drew considerable attention to the Copper family. More books followed, along with radio and television broadcasts, films, and documentaries. Yet in spite of their success in the later twentieth century the Coppers never lost a feeling for an appropriate context for their songs, and regularly chose to share their music with audiences in back rooms of pubs as well as taking it on to more public stages.

Bob Copper's writing, romantic and nostalgic as it sometimes is, has a sharpness of observation that makes it indispensable reading for people interested in English traditional music and social history. The sound recordings, both of the Copper family themselves and of singers whom Bob Copper recorded in the 1950s, provide rich insights into aspects of traditional music-making in southern England. The family repertory contains songs that originated at different periods and includes some unusual and archaic material. Without the activities of members of the Copper family in sustaining and promoting their musical tradition, understanding in this field would be much poorer; theirs was a unique contribution.

VIC GAMMON

**Sources** B. Copper, *A song for every season* (1971) • B. Copper, *Songs and southern breezes* (1973) • B. Copper, *Early to rise* (1976) • B. Copper, *Across Sussex with Belloc* (1994) • B. Copper, *Bob Copper's Sussex* (1997) • *The Copper family song book—a living tradition* (1995) • C. J. Bearman, 'Kate Lee and the foundations of the Folk-Song Society', *Folk Music Journal*, 7 (1995–9) • K. Lee, 'Some experiences of a folk song collector', *Journal of the Folk Song Society*, 1 (1899) • V. Gammon, 'Folk song collecting in Sussex and Surrey, 1843–1914', *History Workshop Journal* (1981) • b. cert. [Robert James Copper] • *CGPLA Eng. & Wales* (1952) [Francis John William Copper] • personal knowledge (2004) • private information (2004) [Reg Hall] • 'Come write me down: early recordings of the Copper family of Rottingdean', Topic Records, 2001, TSCD534 [CD and two booklets]
**Wealth at death** £648 6s. 4d.—(Francis) John William Copper: probate, 1952, *CGPLA Eng. & Wales*

**Copper, James** (1845–1924). *See under* Copper family (*per.* 1845–2000).

**Copper, James Dale** (1882–1954). *See under* Copper family (*per.* 1845–2000).

**Copper, (Francis) John William** (1880–1952). *See under* Copper family (*per.* 1845–2000).

**Copper, Ronald** (*c.*1913–1979). *See under* Copper family (*per.* 1845–2000).

**Copper, Thomas** (1847–*c.*1936). *See under* Copper family (*per.* 1845–2000).

**Coppin, George Selth** (1819–1906), actor and politician, born at Steyning, Sussex, on 8 April 1819, was the only child of George Selth Coppin (1794–1854) and his wife, Elizabeth Jane Jackson (1789–1869). His father, of a Norwich family, gave up medical practice for the stage and became a theatrical manager.

As a child the son showed proficiency on the violin and played juvenile characters on the stage. At the age of seventeen Coppin took to his profession seriously, and in November 1837 he was a minor member of the Sheffield stock company, playing Osric to the Hamlet of the young starring tragedian Gustavus Vaughan Brooke. Having developed into a capable low comedian, he was engaged at the Queen's Theatre, Manchester, early in 1841, and in August of that year began an engagement at the Abbey Street Theatre, Dublin. For a time he sang comic songs nightly between the pieces, accompanying himself on the violin. Here he met a fascinating American actress, Maria Watkins Burroughs, the wife of a provincial actor–manager, with whom he eloped to Australia. They landed at Sydney in March 1843 and lived together until Maria's death on 10 August 1848. Coppin acted at the Royal Victoria Theatre, and made a lot of money which, however, was lost in commercial enterprises, and he left Sydney in debt.

In January 1845 Coppin began an engagement at Hobart Town, and in March commenced theatrical management at Launceston, where he had a prosperous season. Three months later he took his company to Melbourne, where he rented the Queen's Theatre Royal, and made his first appearance there in June, when he played Glavis in Bulwer-Lytton's *The Lady of Lyons* and Crack in *The Turnpike Gate*. Thereafter he moved to Adelaide, where he converted a billiard room in less than two months into a 700-seat theatre, which he opened in November 1846. Here within three or four years he made a fortune from various enterprises, including a tavern and racehorse breeding, only to lose it by speculations in copper mining. After passing through the insolvency court in 1851, he returned to Melbourne and spent a fortnight at the gold diggings: he determined that entertaining the miners would be more profitable than mining himself. Following a short engagement in Melbourne, in 1852 he commenced management at the Great Malop Street theatre, Geelong, where he rapidly made another fortune. He returned to Adelaide, paid his creditors in full, and sailed for England in January 1854. His first appearance was made at the Haymarket, London, in June. Later he fulfilled engagements at Birmingham, Manchester, Edinburgh, and Dublin. While

**George Selth Coppin (1819–1906)**, by Falk Studios, *c.*1905

at Birmingham in August he induced G. V. Brooke to sign articles to star under his management for 200 nights in Australia and New Zealand.

After returning to Melbourne, Coppin reappeared at the Queen's Theatre in December 1854, and the following month began a successful engagement at the Victoria Theatre, Sydney. In June 1855 he opened the new Olympic Theatre, Melbourne, popularly known as 'the Iron Pot', under his own management, and played Colonel Damas in *The Lady of Lyons* and Mr Trotter Southdown in Tom Taylor's *To Oblige Benson*. In August 1855 Coppin married Harriet Hilsden, *née* Bray (*b.* 1820), a widowed sister-in-law of Brooke. Meanwhile Brooke's tour proved highly prosperous, and Coppin joined him in purchasing the Theatre Royal, Melbourne, which they opened in June 1856. About the same period they acquired the freehold of the Cremorne Gardens Amusement Park; they also owned four hotels. At the Theatre Royal they organized the first grand opera season in Australia. The partnership was dissolved in February 1859, Brooke continuing the management. Coppin then built the Pantheon Theatre; but owing to Brooke's difficulties he resumed control of the Theatre Royal in December 1860.

Harriet Coppin had died on 2 September 1859 following the birth of the couple's third child. On 4 June 1861 Coppin married Harriet's daughter by her first marriage, Lucy Hilsden; they were to have two sons and five daughters. In 1862 he lost control of the Theatre Royal, but in September of that year he completed a new theatre, the Haymarket. A second bankruptcy followed, but he brought out Mr and Mrs Charles Kean to Melbourne in October 1863, and then took them to Sydney, with the result that he paid his creditors in full. After touring with the Keans in America (1864–5) he reappeared at the Haymarket, Melbourne (January 1866), in a variety of characters, including Daniel White in H. T. Craven's *Milky White*.

In 1871 Coppin went into partnership with Messrs Harwood, Stewart, and Hennings in the management of the Melbourne Theatre Royal, but suffered a considerable loss through the burning of the uninsured building in March 1872. He immediately took a ninety-nine years' lease of the site and rebuilt the theatre, subsequently transferring the property to the Theatre Royal Proprietary Association, Ltd, of which he remained managing director until his death. At this house in November and December 1881 he gave farewell performances for twelve nights. His last appearance was on 9 December 1881 as Bob Acres in Sheridan's *The Rivals* and Crack in *The Turnpike Gate*.

During the same period Coppin was also engaged in politics. In 1858 he was elected first to the Richmond municipal council and then to the legislative council of Victoria for the south-western province, but he resigned his seat on leaving the colony in 1864 for his American tour. During this time he helped to pass the Transfer of Real Property Act and to introduce Post Office Savings Banks. He advocated the federation of the colonies and intercolonial free trade and opposed the payment of members. He unsuccessfully sought election in 1866, but from 1874 to 1877 and from 1883 to 1888 he was member of the legislative assembly for East Melbourne. He was then returned to the legislative council, unopposed, for Melbourne (1889–95). He was twice elected chairman of the Richmond municipality, and for two years was chairman of magistrates in that district. His political commitments entailed periodical retirement from the stage, as low comedy and political office were deemed incompatible.

A man of immense energies and extraordinarily diverse interests, Coppin left the mark of his talents upon the colony of Victoria. As early as 1870 he advocated acclimatization, and was the first to import camels and English thrushes into Australia. About 1861, in association with Charles Gavan Duffy, he founded the beautiful watering place Sorrento-on-the-Sea, 40 miles south-east of Melbourne, where Mount Coppin was called after him, and where he maintained a home until his death. In 1868 he built a magnificent residence, Pine Grove, Richmond Hill, Melbourne, where he died on 4 March 1906.

[ANON.], *rev.* NILANJANA BANERJI

**Sources** *AusDB* · B. Burke, *A genealogical and heraldic history of the colonial gentry*, 2 (1895) · J. H. Heaton, *Australian dictionary of dates and men of the time* (1879) · B. Hunt, ed., *The green room book, or, Who's who on the stage* (1906) · T. A. Brown, *History of the American stage* (1870) · *Illustrated Australian News* (10 Sept 1872) · *Melbourne Punch* (16 May 1861) · *The Age* [Melbourne] (2 Nov 1889) · R. M. Sillard, *Barry Sullivan and his contemporaries: a histrionic record*, 2 vols. (1901) · J. B. Howe, *A* *cosmopolitan actor* • W. J. Lawrence, *Life of G. V. Brooke* (1890) • *Theatrical Journal*, 16/801 (1855) • private information (1912)

**Likenesses** Falk Studios, photograph, *c.*1905, State Library of Victoria, Melbourne, La Trobe picture collection [*see illus.*]

**Wealth at death** £9709: *AusDB*

**Coppin, John**. *See* Copping, John (*d.* 1583).

**Coppin, Louisa** (1845–1849), supposed ghost, was born on 7 September 1845 at Ivy House, 34 Strand Road, Londonderry, the third child of Dora (*d.* 1866) and **William Coppin** (1805–1895). William Coppin was born on 9 October 1805 and was a surveyor for ships and engines of the Board of Trade and of the Londonderry emigration board. An important figure in the River Foyle shipbuilding industry, in the mid-nineteenth century he employed 500–700 men. His most significant construction was the steamer *Great Northern* (1842), ahead of its time in being screw-propeller driven; but despite conversion to naval specifications, it failed to win a government contract. Although he subsequently built several smaller vessels, after a disastrous dockyard fire in 1846 Coppin turned his attention to salvage. In the same year he failed to refloat SS *Great Britain*, which had run aground off Dundrum Bay, co. Down. Nevertheless, he successfully raised more than 140 ships. Between 1857 and 1886 he also lodged several patents for effective maritime and rail inventions.

Coppin had had several paranormal experiences and his daughter Louisa, or Little Weesy as she was known, began her extraordinary posthumous career in October 1849, five months after her death at Ivy House on 27 May 1849 from gastric fever. She allegedly appeared to her family as 'a ball of bluish light', revealing the position of Sir John Franklin's lost polar expedition by means of 'writing on the wall', stating: '*Erebus* and *Terror*, Sir John Franklin, Lancaster Sound, Prince Regent Inlet, Point Victory, Victoria Channel' and 'a complete Arctic scene' (Skewes, 1889, 74–5). The Admiralty ignored this advice, but a desperate Lady Franklin proved receptive to this unorthodox guide when approached by Captain Coppin in May 1850 and went on to direct searches to the south, as Weesy had suggested, previous searches having been too far north.

The story of Little Weesy was not made public until 1889, thirteen years after Lady Franklin's death, when J. Henry Skewes, vicar of Holy Trinity, Liverpool, published a verbose, inaccurate, and sensationalist book entitled *Sir John Franklin, the true secret of the discovery of his fate: a 'Revelation', 'A little child shall lead them'*. Its first edition was reviewed in the *Pall Mall Gazette* of 9 May 1889, which provoked Admiral Sir Leopold McClintock to write denying any influence of Weesy's apparition upon his largely successful *Fox* expedition three decades earlier. Both McClintock and Sophia Cracroft, Lady Franklin's niece, were anxious to state that paranormal advice had never been heeded in the Franklin search. Skewes's second edition of 1890 included a supplement which proved that it had; but by quoting a letter from W. Parker Snow of the *Prince Albert*, published in the *Morning Star* of 19 October 1860 to support his claim, he unwittingly also showed that he had enormously embellished Weesy's message to fit the facts retrospectively. This embellishment included the use of place names such as Victoria Channel, which were not in use until after Weesy's apparent message. Miss Cracroft was even quoted by Skewes as suggesting to William Coppin in the 1850s that the story should be published by Charles Dickens in *Household Words*—an idea which he wisely vetoed on grounds of family privacy.

No relevant correspondence with Captain Coppin, nor the vital chart drawn by his daughter Ann, supposedly on Weesy's instructions, exists among Lady Franklin's papers at the Scott Polar Research Institute, though other documents there confirm the use of other mediums. Moreover, Ann Coppin had been presented with a book inscribed: 'in memory of her deep sympathy in the Arctic expedition. From her sincere friend, Jane Franklin, Nov., 1863' (Skewes, 1890, 313). As Lady Franklin's biographer, Frances Woodward, summarizes her faith in psychics: 'there is reason only to grieve that a fine mind should be thus prostrated' (Woodward, 267). It therefore appears certain that the more conventionally Christian Sophia Cracroft deliberately destroyed all primary evidence of Weesy's role, probably at the time of her aunt's death in 1875.

William Coppin died aged almost ninety, on 17 April 1895, and was interred with the rest of his family, including Louisa, in the graveyard of St Augustine's Church, Londonderry. Ivy House, which he had built in 1840, and where the Weesy apparitions took place, was demolished in 1994, despite the efforts of the Foyle Civic Trust to save that historic site. RALPH LLOYD-JONES

**Sources** A. Malley and M. McLaughlin, *Captain William Coppin* (1992) • J. H. Skewes, *Sir John Franklin: the true secret of the discovery of his fate*, 1st edn (1889) • J. H. Skewes, *Sir John Franklin*, 2nd edn with supplement (1890) • *Morning Star* (19 Oct 1860) • *Pall Mall Gazette* (9 May 1889) • *Pall Mall Gazette* (11 May 1889) • *Liverpool Courier* (4 June 1889) • *Liverpool Mercury* (4 June 1889) • *Liverpool Mercury* (16 June 1889) • *Liverpool Mercury* (22 June 1889) • *Liverpool Daily Post* (6 June 1889) • *St Stephen's Review* (13 July 1889) • *St Stephen's Review* (9 Nov 1889) • F. J. Woodward, *Portrait of Jane, a life of Lady Franklin* (1951) • R. Lloyd-Jones, 'The paranormal Arctic: Lady Franklin, Sophia Cracroft and Captain and "Little Weesy" Coppin', *Polar Record*, 37 (2001), 27–34

**Coppin, Richard** (*fl. c.*1645–1659), nonconformist preacher and writer, about whom little is known except what he recounts in *Truths Testimony* (1655), was probably from Kent, and grew up to be an unexceptional pious believer within the established church. He was probably a student at Oxford but left without taking a degree; no record survives of his matriculation.

Probably in the mid- to later 1640s and while he was living in London, Coppin was attracted successively to Presbyterianism, Independency, and the Baptists, rejecting each in turn as manifestations of spiritual tyranny or forms of worship that were merely human inventions. He turned instead—probably about 1648—to a purely personal religion which was marked by a principle of saying or writing nothing 'that should perish or come to an end'. This represented the beginning of Coppin's ministry of preaching the redemption of all things, a message that was both anti-clerical and anti-university. He operated as a preacher, claiming that any money he received was turned over to the poor, in or near the Thames valley in

Berkshire and Oxfordshire, where he encountered the hostility of local puritan ministers, most of whom were predestinarians and Baptists if not also Fifth Monarchists. By this time Coppin was part of a group of radical puritans all of whom had 'risen above ordinances' to await the coming of a higher spiritual order. Among these was the Ranter Abiezer Coppe, who influenced Coppin's beliefs and provided a preface for Coppin's extensive discussion and defence of his beliefs, *Divine Teachings*, published in London in 1649. This group would have been identified at the time as 'Seekers' and, in Coppe's account, had established a well-developed network across several towns and villages in the area. The response of the ministers in Berkshire was to contain Coppin's impact with the lure of a preferment in return for his recantation and a perhaps ill-conceived attempt to buy up every copy of his book.

*Divine Teachings* is a remarkable work of religious enthusiasm, with its firm belief that the Holy Spirit or Christ had come to live within the meek and uneducated. Coppin argued that clergy would be punished while thieves and murderers would go free. Also evident in this text is the marked habit of controlled allegorical interpretation of the Bible, a central feature that infuriated the presbyterian divines with whom he disputed and who labelled him variously as a Familist and a Jesuit. Coppin's ideas are distinctive but are also related to many of those in the radical puritan diaspora. He believed that God and Christ are in all men, and that election pertains to God's choosing of Christ as the saviour of mankind, from which universal salvation follows. For him, the subject of reprobation is not the person but all the evil qualities in mankind that will finally be removed with the resurrection of God in man; death is the state of not recognizing these inner presences, the devil is the not-God that dwells within people, and the wrath of God is a purging of sin from all people. All of this Coppin describes in terms of images: the image of God in man and the possibility of seeing the 'Vision of God'.

Coppin continued as an itinerant preacher but his activities led to a series of encounters with the law. Preaching at Burford and Evenlode in the summer of 1651, he found himself in conflict with another group of ministers led by Ralph Nevill and was brought to trial under the terms of the Blasphemy Act at Worcester the following March. The judge was sympathetic but the jury was not: Coppin was found guilty and bound over until the next assizes. A similar dispute at Enstone in Oxfordshire resulted in a summons to the Oxford assizes in March 1653; once again, despite a sympathetic judge, Coppin was declared guilty and was only discharged at the following assize. The following year Coppin found himself set against both minister and magistrates in Stow on the Wold, Gloucestershire, which led predictably to another appearance at assizes, this time at Gloucester in summer 1654. However, on this occasion, the judge considered the charges to be insubstantial and Coppin was acquitted. During this period Coppin published, among other works, *Saul Smitten for not Smiting Amalek*, an allegorical interpretation of scripture written to demonstrate how the Bible had prophesied the fall of the Rump Parliament in April 1653. Coppin approved of many of the reforms that the succeeding Barebone's Parliament called for, although his own desire for complete religious tolerance would have been far too much for most of that assembly's representatives.

Coppin published his spiritual autobiography and defence of his beliefs, *Truths Testimony*, in 1655. In the summer of that year he returned to Kent, where he succeeded the former Ranter Joseph Salmon, who had preached on Sundays in Rochester Cathedral for most of the early half of the decade. Where Salmon had been carefully guarded in his sermons in order to avoid interference, he correctly predicted that Coppin would draw attention to himself. By October a group of local ministers had organized regular preaching against Coppin's alleged assertions about the sinful nature of Christ, that all mankind was the body of Christ, that all would be redeemed, and that there would be no resurrection of the body. Coppin was duly examined on 24 December by Major-General Kelsey and several justices, and was found to have breached the terms of the Blasphemy Act; he and his supporters were described by Kelsey as 'church and state Levellers'. Coppin was imprisoned in Maidstone for six months: 'I will delight myself with the worst of men as well as with the best' was his response (Hill, 222). Two publications, *A Blow at the Serpent* (1656) and *Michael Opposing the Dragon* (1659), both in much the same vein as his previous writings, represent the last evidence of his activities.

Coppin was one of the first in England to preach universal salvation; the Digger Gerrard Winstanley may have preceded him in this but only just. Although he denied being a Ranter, Coppin's writings, especially *Divine Teachings*, were influential among Ranters, and his beliefs may have gathered a small group of followers by the early eighteenth century. Some of his writings were republished in the 1760s when they were the focus of both admiration and opprobrium.                    NIGEL SMITH

**Sources** A. L. Morton, 'Coppin, Richard', Greaves & Zaller, *BDBR*, 174–5 · C. Hill, *The world turned upside down* (1975) · N. Smith, ed., *A collection of Ranter writings from the seventeenth century* (1983) · J. C. Davis, *Fear, myth and history: the Ranters and the historians* (1986) · N. Smith, *Perfection proclaimed: language and literature in English radical religion, 1640–1660* (1989) · R. Coppin, *Truths testimony* (1655) · Wing, *STC* · A. L. Morton, *The world of the Ranters: religious radicalism in the English revolution* (1970)

**Coppin, William** (1805–1895). *See under* Coppin, Louisa (1845–1849).

**Copping** [Coppin], **John** (*d.* 1583), shoemaker and religious radical, is of unknown origins. By 1576 he was living in Bury St Edmunds where, with his companions Elias Thacker, a tailor, and one Tyler, he proved a thorn in the side of the ecclesiastical authorities in the diocese of Norwich. Well before the radical separatist Robert Browne came to Bury, and as early as 1576, Thacker had been imprisoned by the bishop's commissary, John Dey, for 'his disobedyence to the ecclesiasticall lawes of this royalme' (BL, Lansdowne MS 27, fols. 52*r*–53*v*). He refused to allow his child born in August 1578 to be baptized by any minister 'except he be a preacher and then also without godfathers and godmothers' (ibid.) and was reported to the privy council for asserting that the queen was perjured. Copping appears to have been in and out of Bury gaol from 1576 until his execution in 1583. Sir Robert Jermyn and Sir John Heigham confessed that they had sought to have Copping and his associates released from prison so long as there was some hope of persuading them out of their radical opinions, but once they realized that this policy had failed they 'gave them up to their froward wylls' and became 'ernest suters' to Edmund Freake, bishop of Norwich, and the assize judges to have them removed from the gaol in Bury 'for feare of infectyng others' (BL, Lansdowne MS 37, fol. 59r).

Given the increasingly antagonistic relationship between Bishop Freake and the godly Suffolk gentry, the presence and radical critique by such laymen of the established church proved an acute embarrassment for the close alliance of godly magistracy and ministry within Bury St Edmunds, already sensitive to the charge levelled at them by their conformist opponents that they had truncated the required services to little more than Genevan psalms and sermons. The presence and preaching of Robert Browne in Bury by the summer of 1581 undoubtedly made this critique more pointed and powerful. Between 1581 and 1583 there appears to have been considerable support for the Brownist cause in Bury St Edmunds. In 1581 Freake reported that some inhabitants gathered 'to the number of an hundred at a tyme in privat howses and conventicles' to hear Browne preach, 'not without danger of some ill event' (BL, Lansdowne MS 33, fol. 26r). Freake's fears were realized in the following year when, thanks to some careful detective work by Richard Bancroft, the future archbishop, it was discovered that some of the more radical inhabitants had organized the effort to paint the first part of the scriptural warning of the angel to the church at Thyatira (Revelation 2: 19) around the queen's arms in the parish church of St Mary, with its covert implication that, for all Elizabeth's works and love and service and faith, she was a Jezebel who caused her servants to commit fornication and eat meat sacrificed to idols.

This scandalous caption seems to have proved the last straw for the authorities and matters came to a head at the summer assizes held in Bury in 1583. On 30 June Elizabeth issued a proclamation declaring 'sundry seditious, schismatical and erroneous printed books … set forth by Robert Browne and Richard [Robert] Harrison' to be called in and 'burned or utterly defaced' and that those that were 'so hardy as to put in print or writing, sell, set forth, receive, give out, or distribute any more of the same or such like seditious books it libels' would 'answer for the contrary at their uttermost perils' (Hughes and Larkin, 2.501–2). The exemplary punishments meted out at the assizes held in Bury over the next few days followed swiftly. Both Copping and Thacker were indicted and convicted for 'dispersinge of Browne's bookes and Harrisons bookes' (BL, Lansdowne MS 38, fols. 162r–163v), and while the assizes were still in session both men were executed,

Thacker on Thursday 4 July and Copping on Friday 5 July. Small bonfires to the number of forty books were made at both executions. The severity of the penalties was entirely in keeping with the fierce temper of Sir Edward Anderson, chief justice of the common pleas, who saved a copy of one of Robert Harrison's *Three Formes of Catechismes* (1583) from the flames and presented the same to Bancroft, who attended the assizes and had been instrumental in revealing the extent of radical sentiment in the town. The other assize judge, Lord Chief Justice Sir Christopher Wray, wrote a full account to Lord Burghley of the proceedings in Bury in which he apologized for troubling 'your Lordship with a tedious matter' and expressed the hope that the 'example of this assizes' would bring an end to the separatist movement in and around Bury (BL, Lansdowne MS 38, fols. 162r–163v). However, probate evidence, and in particular a number of bequests to the widows Copping, Thacker, and Tyler made by some Bury testators as late as 1589, seems to indicate that the movement managed to survive in some form.            JOHN CRAIG

**Sources** BL, Lansdowne MSS 27, no. 28; 33, nos. 13, 20; 36, no. 65; 37, no. 38; 38, no. 64 • CUL, Baker MS Mm.1.47, p. 332 • J. S. Cockburn, *A history of English assizes, 1558–1714* (1972) • P. Collinson, 'The puritan classical movement in the reign of Elizabeth I', 2 vols., PhD diss., U. Lond., 1957, chap. 9 • J. Craig, *Reformation, politics and polemics: the growth of protestantism in East Anglian market towns, 1500–1610* (2001), chap. 3 • P. L. Hughes and J. F. Larkin, eds., *Tudor royal proclamations*, 2 (1969) • D. MacCulloch, 'Catholic and puritan in Elizabethan Suffolk', *Archiv für Reformationsgeschichte*, 72 (1981), 269–78 • D. MacCulloch, *Suffolk and the Tudors: politics and religion in an English county, 1500–1600* (1986), 199–211 • A. Peel, 'Congregational martyrs at Bury St Edmunds: how many?', *Transactions of the Congregational Historical Society*, 15 (1945–8), 64–7

**Coppinger, Edmund** (*c*.1555–1591), prophet, was the impoverished younger son of a fervently protestant Suffolk gentry family. He does not appear to have taken a university degree, though two of his brothers were at St John's College, Cambridge. Henry was rector of Lavenham between 1578 and 1622, and Ambrose was MP for Ludgarshall in 1586 as well as 'chiefe officer' to the earl of Warwick, the well-known champion of the puritan cause. It was through Ambrose that, around 1588, Edmund made the acquaintance of the presbyterian leader Thomas Cartwright. Some time before 1591 he had acquired a minor post in the royal household and was living chiefly in London. There he developed a firm friendship with a Yorkshire gentleman named Henry Arthington, with whom he shared a belief that the Church of England was in need of far-reaching reform. Both were noted for their religious zeal, and their 'itching eares' carried them to the sermons of godly preachers all over the city (Cosin, 2). It was in the context of the imprisonment and trial of Cartwright and other puritan ministers that Coppinger and Arthington were introduced to the Northamptonshire maltster William Hacket, with whom they began to formulate an ambitious and risky scheme for 'the deliverye of ther restrained bretheren' (*Kenyon MSS*, 608), the overthrow of the bishops, and 'th'expelling of dumme ministers all at one clappe' (Throkmorton, sig. A2v). Coppinger initially sought sanction for this 'secret project' from key figures in the puritan movement, but when his importunate overtures were sharply rebuffed he and his accomplices turned fiercely against them. He also pestered the queen and her close advisers with letters, and used his connections to arrange an interview for Hacket and himself with Lord Burghley, who dismissed them 'without further adoe' and accused Coppinger of building 'castels in th'ayre' (Cosin, 30; Throkmorton, sig. A4r). Coppinger had a series of close encounters with God in his dreams, during which he was 'inwardlie ravished in spirit'. The strange groans he made in his sleep led his bedfellows to suspect him 'not to bee well in his wittes', an opinion shared by Thomas Cartwright, who believed Coppinger suffered from 'some crazing of the braine' and on one occasion threatened to confine him in Bridewell or Bedlam (Throkmorton, sigs. A4v, A3v).

As a result of these experiences Coppinger became convinced that he and Arthington were prophets of mercy and judgment, divinely appointed lieutenants of Hacket, the new messiah and supreme king of the earth. As a consequence, their plot to depose the queen, replace several privy councillors, and establish presbyterian discipline in England gathered momentum.

Always the more energetic and proactive of the two disciples, Coppinger organized the publication and dissemination of hundreds of pamphlets and broadsides on the eve of the planned insurrection. On 19 July 1591 he and Arthington moved through the streets of London proclaiming 'newes from heaven', before mounting a cart in Cheapside and announcing the second coming of Christ in the guise of William Hacket. A tumult ensued, and shortly afterwards all three were arrested. By this time Coppinger seems to have been completely mentally deranged, though in his *Conspiracie, for Pretended Reformation* (1591) Richard Cosin alleged that he had feigned madness in the hope of escaping the full rigour of the law. He died in Bridewell on Thursday 29 July, twenty-four hours after Hacket's execution for treason, following a hunger strike which he had begun seven or eight days before. According to Arthington, who recanted and wrote a narrative of his 'seduction' in 1592, prior to his death Coppinger had 'detested Hacket and asked pardon of the almightie' (Arthington, 7). The episode was used by spokesmen for the ecclesiastical establishment as propaganda against the puritan movement, and was held up as an example of the dangers of religious enthusiasm.

ALEXANDRA WALSHAM

Sources R. Cosin, *Conspiracie, for pretended reformation* (1591) • *The manuscripts of Lord Kenyon*, HMC, 35 (1894), 607–9 • T. Phelippes, to Henry Saintmains (?), 19 July 1591, PRO, State Papers Domestic, Elizabeth, SP 12/239/93 • APC, 1590–91, 293, 297, 299–300, 319, 325 • Venn, *Alum. Cant.*, 1/2.395–6 • H. Arthington, *The seduction of Arthington by Hacket especiallie* (1592) • [R. Bancroft], *Daungerous positions and proceedings* (1593) • J. Throkmorton, *The defence of Job Throkmorton, against the slaunders of Maister Sutcliffe* (1594) • T. Cartwright, *A brief apologie of Thomas Cartwright* (1596) • R. Hooker, *Of the lawes of ecclesiasticall politie* (1597), bk 5, dedication to Archbishop John Whitgift • J. Stow, *The annales of England … untill this present yeere 1592* (1592), 1288–90 • LPL, Fairhurst MSS, MS 2008, fol. 29r • A. Walsham, '"Frantick Hacket": prophecy, sorcery, insanity, and the Elizabethan puritan movement', *HJ*, 41 (1998), 27–66

**Coppinger, Richard William** (1847–1910), naval surgeon and naturalist, born on 11 October 1847 in Dublin, was the youngest of the six sons of Joseph William Coppinger, a solicitor of Farmley, Dundrum, co. Dublin, and his wife, Agnes Mary, only daughter of William Lalor Cooke, a landed proprietor of Fortwilliam, co. Tipperary. The father's family was long settled at Ballyvolane and Barryscourt, co. Cork, and was said to descend from the first Danish settlers in Cork city. Coppinger received his medical education in Dublin, graduating MD at the Queen's University in 1870. Entering the medical department of the navy, he was appointed surgeon to HMS *Alert*, which, with HMS *Discovery*, left Portsmouth on 29 May 1875 under the command of Captain George S. Nares on a voyage of exploration towards the north pole. The *Alert* reached a higher latitude than had ever been touched before, and Coppinger distinguished himself as the naturalist in charge of one of the sledging parties. On the return of the *Alert* to England in October 1876 he was specially promoted staff-surgeon and awarded the Arctic medal. Coppinger again served as naturalist in the *Alert* on her four years' exploring cruise in Patagonian, Polynesian, and Mascarene waters from 1878 to 1882. He married, on 8 January 1884, Matilda Mary, daughter of Thomas Harvey Browne, a landed proprietor of Sydney, New South Wales. They had three sons and one daughter; she survived her husband.

In 1889 Coppinger was appointed instructor in hygiene at the Haslar Royal Naval Hospital at Gosport, where he was a most successful teacher, his knowledge of bacteriology being in advance of the time. On 13 March 1901 he was appointed inspector-general of hospitals and fleets, and was for three years in charge at Haslar. On 15 May 1904 he was placed on half pay, and, disappointed at not being made director-general of the medical department of the navy, he retired in 1906.

Coppinger wrote *The Cruise of the Alert, 1878–82* (1883); 'Some experiments on the conductive properties of ice made in Discovery Bay, 1875–6' (*PRS* 27, 1878, 183–9); and 'Account of the zoological collections made in the years 1878–1881, during the survey of HMS *Alert* in the Straits of Magellan and the coast of Patagonia' (*Proceedings of the Zoological Society*, 1881). He also contributed to the parliamentary paper containing the report of the Admiralty committee (1877) on 'The outbreak of scurvy in the Arctic expedition, 1875–6' (*Parl. papers*, 1877, 56, 557), and to the *Report on the zoological collections made in the Indo-Pacific Ocean during the voyage of HMS Alert 1881–2* (British Museum, Nat. Hist., 1884). He died at his residence, Wallington House, Fareham, on 2 April 1910, and was buried at Fareham cemetery.          H. D. ROLLESTON, *rev.* ANDREW LAMBERT

Sources *BMJ* (30 April 1910), 1090 • private information (1912) • CGPLA Eng. & Wales (1910)
**Wealth at death** £3439 13s. 5d.: probate, 4 May 1910, CGPLA Eng. & Wales

**Coppock, James** (1798–1857), election agent, was born at Stockport on 2 September 1798, the eldest son of William Coppock, a mercer of that town. He was educated at the school of the Revd Mr Higginson, Unitarian minister of

Stockport. After serving an apprenticeship in his father's business, he was placed as a clerk with a wholesale haberdasher in London. He afterwards ventured a small amount of capital as a partner in a silk firm, but, owing to commercial disasters following on the French Revolution of 1830, he lost it all. He married in 1829.

After careful consideration, Coppock resolved to enter the legal profession, and in 1832 articled himself to a solicitor in Furnival's Inn. He was admitted on the roll of attorneys in 1836. He had always been an active politician, and took a prominent part in the contest during the first election for Finsbury after the Reform Act of 1832. After the second general election under the act, on the formation of the County Registration Society by the Liberal Party, with branches throughout England, Coppock was appointed secretary, with a residence in the society's rooms at 3 Cleveland Row, St James's. These rooms were the rendezvous of agents and solicitors from all parts of the country, and, by his rapid decisions and sound judgement, Coppock quickly became a power in politics. With F. R. Bonham on the Conservative side and Joseph Parkes with him on the radical, Coppock was a founder of centralized political organization.

When, a few years later, the society's operations ceased, Coppock took the lease of the premises in Cleveland Row, and established himself as a solicitor and parliamentary agent. From this time forward there was scarcely a contested return before the House of Commons in which he had not an active interest. The coolness and daring with which he fought his opponents with their own weapons became proverbial. He helped to establish the London Reform Club and, after briefly serving as its secretary in 1836, he was elected an honorary life member, and appointed its solicitor.

Although in his day no man was a fiercer partisan, Coppock was respected by friend and foe. In the August before his death he received the appointment of county court treasurer, but business, both private and public, of a harassing nature accumulated, and the strain of overwork was too great. He died at his house in Cleveland Row, London, on 19 December 1857.

ALBERT NICHOLSON, rev. H. C. G. MATTHEW

Sources  Stockport Advertiser (23 Dec 1857) · The Times (21 Dec 1857) · Ward, Men of the reign · N. Gash, Politics in the age of Peel (1953)

**Coppock, John Terrence** [Terry] (1921–2000), geographer, was born on 2 June 1921 at 121 Colum Road, Cardiff, the second of three sons of Arthur Leslie Coppock (1890–1962) a secondary schoolmaster, and his wife, Margaret Valerie, née Phillips (1896–1981). He was educated at the Victoria primary school, Penarth (1926–32) and the Penarth county grammar school (1932–7), where he started his love affair with geography. His parents could not support him at university, so in 1938 he became a clerical officer in the county court branch of the Lord Chancellor's Department office in the Rhondda valley. In 1939 he joined a territorial battalion of the Welch regiment and in 1941 he was commissioned lieutenant in the Royal Artillery with which he served in the Middle East until 1946. The experience gave him an acute awareness of new geographies and an appetite for travel.

In 1946 after demobilization Terry Coppock (as he was known) returned to the civil service but realized very quickly that despite rapid promotion he was not really a civil servant. He was particularly frustrated at being unable to enter the administrative class because he did not have a degree. Having sought advice about his future career, in 1947 he was admitted as an exhibitioner to Queens' College, Cambridge, later graduating as a scholar with first-class honours in geography after only two years. In 1949 Professor Clifford Darby appointed him university demonstrator at University College, London. Finding himself required to teach a course in the regional geography of western and central Europe, Coppock prepared himself by bicycling round France, Belgium, and the Netherlands in the long vacation. At University College he became an assistant lecturer in 1950, a lecturer in 1952, and a reader in 1964. During these years he met Sheila Mary Burnett (d. 1990) and they were married in 1953. They had two children, John and Helena.

Coppock's research, under the influence of Clifford Darby, focused on agricultural activity and rural land use change. He undertook a land use survey of the Chilterns which proved a turning point in his career. The work involved analysing very large sets of data drawn from the agricultural census, and for this Coppock was quick to grasp the potential of computer technology to process vast quantities of spatially referenced data. This stimulated his interest in the application of computers in mapping and in geographical information systems (GIS). He delivered a conference paper on the subject as early as 1953, and published his first paper on 'Electronic data processing in geographical research' in the Professional Geographer in 1962. In the 1960s Coppock's team developed a computer mapping system (CAMAP) for the preparation of his Agricultural Atlas of Scotland (1976) and Coppock himself went on to develop the world's first MSc course in GIS in the department of geography at Edinburgh. He is widely recognized as a founding father of GIS and was the first editor of the International Journal of GIS (1986–93). His research was empirical rather than theoretical. He believed in accumulating large amounts of data, ensuring that they were accurate, and, where they were not, making explicit their deficiencies. He was then prepared to make informed judgements and firm recommendations. These qualities later enabled Coppock to provide intellectual leadership to several public commissions concerned with public policy and planning.

Between 1963 and 1964 Coppock and his family were in Nigeria, where he was a visiting lecturer at the University of Ibadan. He travelled widely in eastern and southern Africa and considered this travel to have given him a valuable perspective for comparative and systematic analysis. Shortly after returning from Nigeria, and after publishing his Agricultural Atlas of England and Wales, Coppock became the first holder of the Ogilvie chair at the department of geography in the University of Edinburgh in 1965. By then he had become one of the first scholars to recognize the growing importance of tourism and recreation to both economy and landscape, and the possible conflict between farming and tourism, especially in remote areas. In 1966 he established the tourism and recreation research unit (TRRU) within the University of Edinburgh to address these problems. The TRRU undertook important data-gathering surveys and produced reports about an activity that had become one of Scotland's main economic sectors.

Recognition of Coppock's enthusiasm and ability to produce sound policy and relevant work led to his being invited to serve on numerous bodies, including the natural resources advisory committee (1965–6), the nature conservation committee (1965–71), the Natural Environment Research Council (1967–73), the Scottish joint committee on information systems (1968–72), and the select committee on Scottish affairs. He was also chairman of the International Geographical Union (IGU) commission on agriculture and food production (1976–8) and chairman of the IGU working group on international environmental maps.

Coppock was president of the Institute of British Geographers (1973–4), was elected a fellow of the British Academy in 1975, served as one of its vice-presidents (1985–7), and was awarded the CBE for services to geography (1987). He retired in 1986 having published twelve books (five with co-authors) and 120 papers, and edited six books alone or with others. His career was dominated by research: he was not known for his teaching skills and he shunned administration. He was at his best with his many graduate students whom he unselfishly encouraged and helped. Their work greatly benefited from his critical scrutiny, his impeccable editorial skills, and his demand that they write in clear, precise English.

Immediately after retiring Coppock was appointed secretary and treasurer of the Carnegie trust for universities in Scotland, founded by Andrew Carnegie in 1901 to give financial help to Scottish university staff and students. Coppock was ideally suited to the work, being fair, balanced, and apolitical. In 1999 he was awarded honorary doctoral degrees by the universities of Edinburgh and Glasgow for his contributions to British geography and Scottish higher education. He saw his main contribution as having been in academic and policy-related work that contributed to maintaining or even improving the natural environment. His love of nature was revealed in his diary, in which he claimed that the most exhilarating experience of his life was snorkelling along the Great Barrier Reef, where he was privileged to witness nature in its most splendid glory.

Coppock was a prudent man, whose dynamism and love of work were universally recognized. With his lanky frame he was an accomplished badminton player well into his seventies. He also enjoyed listening to classical music and watching cartoons and football on television. After having suffered from lupus disease for three years Coppock died in Edinburgh on 28 June 2000.

LYNDHURST COLLINS

**Sources** b. cert. · *The Scotsman* (14 July 2000) · *The Independent* (7 July 2000) · *The Independent* (31 July 2000) · *The Guardian* (10 July 2000) · personal knowledge (2004)
**Likenesses** photograph, repro. in *The Scotsman* · photograph, repro. in *The Independent* (7 July 2000)
**Wealth at death** £143,753.90: confirmation, Scotland, 2000, *CCI*

**Coppock, Thomas** (*bap.* 1719, *d.* 1746), Jacobite chaplain, was born in Old Millgate, Manchester, and baptized on 13 December 1719. He was the third of four children of John Coppock, a tailor, and his wife, Esther, *née* Ogden, both from Manchester. In the 1730s he attended the local grammar school and in 1739 went on to Brasenose College, Oxford. After graduating BA in October 1742 he started an adventurous career which eventually led him to the scaffold in October 1746. Two propaganda pamphlets, published after his death, offer colourful stories of Coppock's progress as a Jacobite villain from a career as a quack doctor in Oxford to the execution site at Harraby Hill, Carlisle. Although most of the stories are of questionable reliability, it is almost certain that in November 1744 Coppock forged a testimony in order to obtain a curacy in Kent. The forgery was discovered nine months later and he had to return to his paternal home.

In November 1745 Coppock joined the Jacobite army, quickly becoming both the chaplain and the quartermaster of the Manchester regiment. On the way back north he stayed behind with his regiment at Carlisle, where he was captured and imprisoned. He gained some prominence as the 'rebel bishop of Carlisle' in the Hanoverian press, which exploited the fictitious story of his nomination by the Stuart pretender. After ten months in prison at Lancaster and Carlisle he was condemned for high treason in September 1746.

> It is observed, that he behaved very insolently on his trial; that when he was going from the bar, after having been found guilty, he said openly to the other rebel prisoners, 'Never mind it, my boys, for if our Saviour was here, these fellows would condemn him'. (*Scots Magazine*)

He wrote numerous petitions and also tried to escape twice, but in the end was hanged and quartered with eight other Jacobites in Carlisle on 18 October 1746. Afterwards his head was displayed at the English gate.

CHRISTOPH V. EHRENSTEIN

**Sources** *DNB* · B. Stott, 'Parson Coppock', *Transactions of the Lancashire and Cheshire Antiquarian Society*, 40 (1923), 45–75 · Foster, *Alum. Oxon.* · *Scots Magazine*, 8 (1746), 498 · *An authentick history of the life and character of Thomas Cappoch, (the rebel-bishop of Carlisle), who was executed for high treason at Carlisle, in the county of Cumberland, on Saturday the 18th of October, 1746* (1746) · *True copy of the dying declarations of Arthur Lord Balmerino, Thomas Syddall, David Morgan, George Fletcher, John Berwick, Thomas Theodorus Deacon, Thomas Chadwick, James Dawson, Andrew Blyde, Donald MacDonald, esq.; the Rev. Mr. Thomas Coppock, John Hamilton, Esq., James Bradshaw, Alexander Leith, and Andrew Wood* (1750) · [T. Coppock], *The genuine dying speech of the Reverend Parson Coppock, pretended bishop of Carlisle* (1746) · D. J. Beattie, *Prince Charlie and the borderland* (1995) · P. K. Monod, *Jacobitism and the English people, 1688–1788* (1989) · F. J. McLynn, *The Jacobite army in England, 1745: the final campaign* (1983) · [C. B. Heberden], ed., *Brasenose College register, 1509–1909*, 2 vols., OHS, 55 (1909)

**Coprario, John** (*d.* 1626), composer and musician, was, despite his name, evidently of English descent. Nothing is known for certain of his early life. Possibly he was the John Cowper who was installed as a chorister at Chichester Cathedral in 1575 (Dart). Anthony Wood's 'Notes on the lives of musicians' (Bodl. Oxf., Wood, D.19[4]) describes Coprario as 'an English man borne, who having spent much of his time in Italy was there called Coprario, which name he kept when he returned into England' (no specific evidence in confirmation of Wood's assertion is known, however). He was described by the late seventeenth-century writer Roger North as 'Coperario, who by the way was plain Cooper but affected an Italian termination'.

In 1602 William Petre paid Coprario 10s. for 'lessons hee brought mee'. Sir Robert Cecil paid Coprario £3 in connection with travel to the Low Countries in April 1603, and following his elevation to an earldom in 1605 (and subsequently to the position of lord treasurer) he became Coprario's regular patron. Cecil's musicians performed before Queen Anne on 31 October 1605, for which Coprario was paid £5. During the next few years frequent payments were made by the earl of Salisbury to Coprario for a range of musical tasks, including the teaching of a boy, George Mason, repair and maintenance of stringed instruments, and 'setting of musick'; there were several one-off payments (of £20 in 1610, and £10 in 1613) and fees were paid for hired musicians at entertainments (Charteris, 'Jacobean Musicians'). In 1613 Coprario attended Elector Frederick and Princess Caroline on their journey to Heidelberg, following their marriage (he had composed some music for Thomas Campion's *The Lord's Masque*, performed on 14 February that year, for which he was paid £20). Later patrons of Coprario were Edward Seymour, earl of Hertford, and Francis Clifford, earl of Cumberland. Thomas Fuller's *The History of the Worthies of England* (1662) claims that the composer William Lawes received his musical instruction under Coprario while the latter was in the employ of the earl of Hertford. The earl of Cumberland paid Coprario £11 in January 1617 following his return from Dubrovnik, for which records show that he was granted a permission 'to goe unto forraigne partes for one yeare about dispatch of his private occasions'; later that same year, Coprario was granted another pass enabling him to undertake a year-long journey to Germany (Hulse).

Chief among Coprario's patrons, however, was Charles, prince of Wales (later Charles I). According to Sir John Hawkins's *A General History of the Science and Practice of Music* (1776) he was the music teacher of the children of James I; Charles Burney's *A General History of Music* (1776) specifies that he taught the future Charles I to play the viol. This much is speculative, though in 1618 Coprario received of Charles the sum of £50, evidently in recognition of musical services rendered, and on 25 March 1622 there began a series of annual stipendiary payments to Coprario as one of the 'musicians-in-ordinary' to the prince of Wales. In the same year, a small group known as 'Coprario's music' was established within Charles's household, probably for the express purpose of performing Coprario's consort fantasias. When he became king in

1625, Charles made Coprario his composer-in-ordinary, but this appointment, the climax of his career, was short-lived. He was replaced by Alfonso Ferrabosco the younger in July 1626 'in the place of John Copreario deceased' (Charteris, *John Coprario*): his death, in London, must have occurred about June of that year.

Coprario's output for string consort consists in the main of fantasias, a genre of composition akin to the fugue or canon (in which the separate strands of the polyphony imitate each other) which Thomas Morley, writing in his *Plain and Easy Introduction to Practical Music* (1597), had termed 'the chiefest kind of musicke which is made without a dittie'. Coprario left examples in two, three, four, five, and six parts. If these works are traditional in idiom, his 'fantasia-suites' break new ground. Here, the fantasia is followed by several dance pieces (to which it is connected in mode). Moreover, these works include prominent parts for the violin (rather than the older viol) and organ, tending at times towards a texture not dissimilar to that associated with the continuo bass, which had recently emerged in Italy, but elsewhere granting the keyboard part an essential, rather than merely subsidiary, accompanimental function. There are also works for the lyra viol (a special kind of consort bass viol, capable of playing melody and chordal accompaniment textures simultaneously). Anthony Wood (Bodl. Oxf., Wood, D.19[4] no. 106) later described Coprario as 'one of the first authors that set lessons to the viol lyra-way, and composed lessons not only to play alone, but for two or three lyraviols in consort, which hath been approved by many excellent masters'.

While Coprario will always be best-known as a composer of instrumental consort music, he also produced many secular vocal pieces. He was clearly familiar with a good deal of published Italian madrigal repertory from the end of the sixteenth century (including works by Marenzio, Anerio, Vecchi, and others), for he appropriated a large number of titles from such works in his forty-nine five-part instrumental settings for viol consort known today as 'instrumental madrigals'; some of these pieces are actually based on the madrigals from which the titles are borrowed. Eight other similar works survive (for six viols), in three of which text is underlaid throughout, suggesting that they may have originated as vocal rather than instrumental pieces. There survive twenty-one genuinely vocal three-part villanellas, settings of Italian texts extracted in the main from Gorzani's *Primo libro di napolitane* (1570); three madrigals of rather more elevated pretensions (including one to a text by Petrarch); a lute song, 'Send home my long strayd eyes to mee' (words by Donne); and three songs contributed to Thomas Campion's *Masque of Squires* ('The Earle of Somerset's Masque'), presented in December 1613. Coprario's *Funeral Teares* (1606) was written in memory of Charles Blount, earl of Devonshire, and contains seven settings of melancholic verse, possibly of Coprario's own composition, for solo voice or duet with the accompaniment of lute and bass viol. He could also capture the elegiac mood, as shown by the items written for Campion's *Songs of Mourning: Bewailing the Untimely Death of Prince Henry* (1613). More devotional in intent are the settings 'Ile lie me downe' and 'O Lord how doe my woes encrease' included in Sir William Leighton's *Teares or Lamentations of a Sorrowful Soule* (1614).

Coprario wrote a short musical treatise, 'Rules how to compose', possibly about 1617. It was compiled to instruct the young William Lawes, whom the earl of Hertford had taken 'from his Father, and bred him of his own cost … under his Master Giovanni Coperario' (Ashbee and Lasocki). This was never published (the holograph survives in the Huntington Library, San Marino, California), but was evidently quite widely circulated in copies; it was clearly still influential in the 1650s and 1660s, when Christopher Simpson based some examples in his *The Principles of Practical Musick* (1665) on Coprario's. There is a strong similarity between Coprario's 'Rules' and Campion's *A New Way of Making Fowre Parts in Counter-Point* (1613–14), though which had the priority is unclear.      JOHN IRVING

**Sources** J. Pulver, 'Giovanni Coprario alias John Cooper', *Monthly Musical Record*, 57 (1927), 101–2 · W. L. Woodfill, *Musicians in English society from Elizabeth to Charles I* (1953) · *Roger North on music*, ed. J. Wilson (1959) · T. Dart, 'Music and musicians at Chichester Cathedral, 1545–1642', *Music and Letters*, 42 (1961), 221–6 · C. D. S. Field, 'The English consort suite of the seventeenth century', DPhil diss., U. Oxf., 1971 · R. Charteris, 'Jacobean musicians at Hatfield House, 1605–1613', *Royal Musical Association Research Chronicle*, 12 (1974), 115–36 · R. Charteris, *John Coprario: a thematic catalogue of his music with a biographical introduction* (New York, 1977) · P. Holman, *Four and twenty fiddlers: the violin at the English court, 1540–1690* (1993) · L. Hulse, 'The musical patronage of the English aristocracy, c.1590–1640', PhD diss., U. Lond., 1993 · J. Hawkins, *A general history of the science and practice of music*, 5 vols. (1776) · Burney, *Hist. mus.* · A. Ashbee and D. Lasocki, eds., *A biographical dictionary of English court musicians, 1485–1714*, 2 vols. (1998)

**Copsi** [Coxo], **earl of Northumbria** (*d.* 1067), magnate, first appears as the deputy of Tostig, earl of Northumbria (1055–65), and, according to a text on the earls of Northumbria incorporated into the *Historia regum Anglorum* attributed to Symeon of Durham, was responsible for the government of the earldom. Copsi's origins are obscure but his name (probably the Old Norse Kofsi or Cofsi in Yorkshire Domesday Book) and the location of lands granted by him to the church of St Cuthbert suggest that he was a Yorkshire thegn. Symeon of Durham records a gift of several manors in north Yorkshire together with the church of St Germanus at Marske which had been dedicated by Æthelric, bishop of Durham (1042–56). Tostig's relations with members of the comital house of Bamburgh were strained and it is likely that Copsi's gift to St Cuthbert, like those of Tostig and his wife, was designed to bolster support for the regime north of the Tees. Copsi's gift was accompanied by the presentation of a silver cup which, Symeon noted, the church of St Cuthbert retained as a remembrance of the donation.

Copsi was expelled with Tostig by the Northumbrians in 1065. The twelfth-century source, Gaimar, suggests that in the spring of 1066 Copsi met Tostig at Thanet bringing seventeen ships with him from Orkney. Subsequently they seem to have joined with Harold Hardrada's invasion force and Copsi may have fought with his lord and the Norwegians at the battle of Stamford Bridge on 25 September 1066, although, unlike Tostig and Harald Hardrada, he survived. Copsi made his submission to King William at Barking early in 1067 along with earls Eadwine and Morcar. Morcar had been appointed to the earldom of Northumbria after Tostig's downfall and 'because he was burdened with other matters' (Symeon of Durham, *Opera*, 2.198). Morcar handed control over the north of the earldom (that is the land north of the Tyne), to Osulf, the representative of the native comital house of Bamburgh. On Morcar's arrest by William, Copsi was granted Osulf's earldom and in February 1067 he ventured north and forced Osulf to take refuge in the woods and mountains. There Osulf managed to gather together a band of supporters and they attacked Copsi while he was feasting at the ancient comital manor of Newburn-on-Tyne. Copsi escaped but was trapped in the nearby church (possibly now St Michael's, Newburn). The Northumbrians set fire to the church and when Copsi emerged he was decapitated by Osulf. Copsi's death occurred on 12 March, only five weeks after his appointment to the earldom. The Norman sources, which call him Coxo, suggest that some of Copsi's men had tried to persuade him to abandon his oath of fealty to the Conqueror and that his refusal to do so had driven them into opposing and finally murdering him. For both William of Poitiers and Orderic Vitalis, Copsi was the very model of a faithful vassal, a 'statesman-like and honest man' (Ordericus Vitalis, *Eccl. hist.*, 2.207), and his death was eloquent testimony of his steadfast loyalty. His career highlights the very real difficulties which the later Anglo-Saxon and early Norman kings experienced in their attempts to govern Northumbria.

     WILLIAM M. AIRD

**Sources** Symeon of Durham, *Opera*, vol. 2 · Symeon of Durham, *Libellus de exordio atque procursu istius, hoc est Dunhelmensis, ecclesie / Tract on the origins and progress of this the church of Durham*, ed. and trans. D. W. Rollason, OMT (2000) · Guillaume de Poitiers [Gulielmus Pictaviensis], *Histoire de Guillaume le Conquérant / Gesta Guilelmi ducis Normannorum et regis Anglorum*, ed. R. Foreville (Paris, 1952), 237, 269–71 · Ordericus Vitalis, *Eccl. hist.*, vol. 2 · *Lestorie des Engles solum la translacion Maistre Geffrei Gaimar*, ed. T. D. Hardy and C. T. Martin, 2 (1889), 5165–8 · J. Morris, ed., *Domesday Book: a survey of the counties of England*, 38 vols. (1983–92), vol. 30 [Yorkshire; in 2 pts] · C. R. Hart, *The early charters of northern England and the north midlands* (1975) · M. H. Dodds, ed., *A history of Northumberland*, 13 (1930) · W. M. Aird, 'St Cuthbert, the Scots and the Normans', *Anglo-Norman Studies*, 16 (1993), 1–20 · A. Williams, *The English and the Norman conquest* (1995) · F. S. Scott, 'Earl Waltheof of Northumbria', *Archaeologia Aeliana*, 4th ser., 30 (1952), 149–215

**Copson, Edward Thomas** (1901–1980), mathematician, was born on 21 August 1901 at 46 Northumberland Road, Coventry, the elder son of Thomas Charles Copson, motor engineer, and Emily Read. He was educated at King Henry VIII School, Coventry, and St John's College, Oxford, where he gained a double first in mathematics and graduated BA in 1922. He was a lecturer at the University of Edinburgh in 1922–30 (taking a DSc degree there in 1928), and at the University of St Andrews in 1930–34. For one year (1934–5) he was assistant professor at the Royal Naval College, Greenwich, but he returned to Scotland a year later on his appointment as professor of mathematics at University College, Dundee. In 1950 he was appointed to the regius chair of mathematics in the University of St Andrews, and apart from serving as a research fellow at Harvard in 1957–8, remained there until his retirement in 1969. In the period 1954–7 he was master of St Salvator's College, St Andrews.

In his many years in Scotland, Copson played an active role in the Edinburgh Mathematical Society and the Royal Society of Edinburgh. In the former he served twice as president (1930–31 and 1954–5) and was elected an honorary member in 1979. He was elected a fellow of the Royal Society of Edinburgh at an early age and was a member of council for several years and its vice-president in 1950–53. He was awarded the Keith prize by the society in 1941.

On 11 July 1931 Copson married Beatrice Mary, the elder daughter of Sir Edmund *Whittaker. They had two daughters. Copson made substantial contributions to both classical mathematical analysis and applied mathematics. His analysis papers are devoted mainly to the theory of partial differential equations, but there are also papers on the theory of sequences, series, inequalities, special functions, Fourier theory (including dual integral equations), Marcel Riesz's multiple integrals of fractional order, and harmonic Riemann spaces. The range of his papers in applied mathematics is equally impressive, embracing gas dynamics, sound waves of finite amplitude, electrostatics, and diffraction problems. Although his research papers were well received, his international reputation rests mainly on his *An Introduction to the Theory of Functions of a Complex Variable* (1935), which remained a standard work for over half a century, and on *The Mathematical Theory of Huygens' Principle* (1939), written with Bevin B. Baker, the second edition of which, in 1950, was the first account in English of the modern theory of hyperbolic partial differential equations. He contributed two volumes to the Cambridge Tracts in Mathematics and Mathematical Physics: *Asymptotic Expansions* (1965) and *Metric Spaces* (1972). His final major publication was *Partial Differential Equations* (1975). His library of mathematical books is now housed in the Mathematical Institute of the University of St Andrews.

Copson died on 16 February 1980 in King's Cross Hospital, Dundee, after a short illness, and was cremated at Dundee crematorium on 21 February. He was survived by his wife.                                    IAN N. SNEDDON

**Sources** private information (2004) · personal knowledge (2004) · *Bulletin of the London Mathematical Society*, 13 (1981), 566–7 · d. cert. · m. cert.

**Archives** U. St Andr., Mathematical Institute

**Coral** [*formerly* Kagarlitsky], **Joseph** [Joe] (1904–1996), bookmaker, was born on 11 December 1904 into a Jewish family in Warsaw, Poland. His father, Abraham Kagarlitsky, died when he was very young; his mother, Jessica, took Joe and his two brothers to London, before the First World War, and they settled in the East End. The family soon changed its name to Coral, a name drawn from R. M. Ballantyne's novel *Coral Island*. During his school years Joe was afflicted by polio which badly affected both his arms,

Joseph Coral (1904–1996), by unknown photographer, 1969

but his remarkable flair for mathematics had been strongly apparent. On leaving school at fourteen he took a job with a lamp-maker, just as the First World War came to an end. It was there that he made his first entry into the world of betting; he became a bookie's runner: that is, someone who runs bets for his colleagues and workmates on behalf of the local bookmaker. Off-course ready money (cash) betting on horse-racing had been illegal since 1853, and the bookie's runner was a pivotal figure in the culture of working-class betting and gambling.

Coral soon understood that the bets were money in the bookmaker's pocket. The punters rarely made claims for winnings due. 'I would notice', he recalled, 'that it was only once in a blue moon that there would be a claim the next day. I thought "you must be mad to give it to the bookmaker"' (McGrath). He began to stand bets himself, and to make his own profits. He was sacked from the lamp-maker's workshop for, in Coral's words, 'concentrating on the wrong ledger'. He went to work at a small London advertising agency. The Saturdays off enabled Coral to build up a local network of punters based at a billiard hall in Stoke Newington, and he was soon established as a local bookmaker. Billiards and snooker also remained his lifelong hobbies. In 1927 he left advertising to set up his own pitch at the White City greyhound racing track in Haringey, north-east London. The introduction of the electric hare from the United States of America in 1926 thus assisted Coral's career: it created a legal context for track-side betting.

In common with so many bookies Coral maintained both a legal and an illegal trade. The legitimate side of the business was greyhound racing and credit betting with cheques, where no ready money changed hands, but the most lucrative wing of his business was street betting. Coral stated that he would go out every morning with the aim of increasing his trade. He drank in local pubs, took shaves with the local barbers, and informally plied his trade with those publicans, barbers, shopkeepers, and others willing to take bets on his behalf. Other locals took bets for Coral from pitches in streets and in back alleys. By 1930 he was a cash-in-hand employer of between seventy and eighty agents who collected ready-money bets for him. By that year he had also taken over the pitches of Bill Chandler, a popular Hoxton bookie, who was unable to compete with Coral.

The illegality of street betting bred criminal interference, and the dog tracks were unofficially controlled by gangs. Coral's success attracted the attention of the notorious London mafia, the Derby Sabini gang. During the late 1920s Coral was violently intimidated by Derby Sabini himself. According to Coral, 'I shoved an old rusty pistol that wasn't even loaded into his guts and told him "F * * * off or you'll get this through the belly"' (*The Times*). This gesture earned Coral both the freedom to conduct his business without overt menaces and the respect of the local punters.

Coral was one of the largest regional bookmakers in England by 1939. War interrupted the betting business, owing to the huge reductions in the racing calendar, but Coral was still busy. He opened a credit betting office in Stoke Newington in 1941, and moved the office to London's West End four years later. After the war, moreover, Coral was one of a number of bookmakers who advertised betting by post in the major sporting newspapers such as the *Sporting Life* and the *Sporting Chronicle*. 'Sporting' newspapers were really betting newspapers. Betting by post was legal because no cash changed hands, only cheques or postal orders. The illegal business continued to thrive, however, but the 1950s witnessed a thawing of official attitudes to betting and gambling. During an era of full employment and affluence the paternalistic concern of church and government lest the working classes gamble themselves into poverty was misplaced. The police, moreover, took the opportunity to argue to the royal commission on betting, lotteries and gaming of 1949–51 that the law was unworkable, and that illegal betting was a thriving open secret which rendered futile any attempts to restrict it through intervention. This change of thinking led to the Betting and Gaming Act of 1960, which finally legalized off-course cash betting, and introduced the licensed betting office to the high streets and back streets of England and Wales.

Initially Coral, along with other large bookmakers such as William Hill, for example, had been unenthusiastic about legalization. A major requirement of the 1960 act was that any new betting office needed to show 'unstimulated demand' before being granted a licence. One way was to convert existing business premises to a licensed betting office. Coral paid to have the sweetshop of one of his agents turned into a betting shop. The most efficient way, however, to negotiate the new law was to buy up other offices, and by 1962 Coral had twenty-three shops. Subsequently during the 1960s the corporate structure of bookmaking became more fully fledged, and bookmaking firms became public companies, operating on a legal and commercial basis. Corals became a public limited company in 1963, and diversified into casinos, bingo halls, and hotels. The firm was bought, in 1970, by the brewing, hotels, and entertainments group Bass. The motives for the take-over were clear: Corals' annual profits were £1.5 million in that year. He remained president of the bookmaking firm and a major company director, and took some important subsequent initiatives.

By the mid-1970s expansion had produced 650 Corals bookmakers' shops, and by the end of the decade Corals was one of the 'big four' bookmaking firms. It retained that status into the 1990s. In 1992 Corals entered into an arrangement with the tote, the pool betting system based at the racecourses, whereby pool bets could be placed at Corals outlets. The company had also been one of the British bookmaking operations that ventured into Europe at that time; the aim was to take advantage of the continental punter's dissatisfaction with the lack of choice engendered by the municipal and state monopoly over betting. There were thirty-six Corals shops in Belgium by the end of 1992, taking bets on British and other countries' horse- and dog-racing.

Coral had married his wife, Dorothy Helen, in 1927. They brought up three sons, two of whom, Bernard and Nicholas, pursued careers in the family business from the early 1950s. Joe Coral died in University College Hospital, Camden, London, on 16 December 1996 from lung cancer, having suffered from dementia for some years. His address at death was a comfortable flat in Gloucester Place, Marylebone, London. A spokesman of the modern firm of Coral told the *Sporting Life* that 'we shall not see his like again'—a cliché appropriate for many earlier bookmakers and certainly for him: Coral's was a powerful rise from poverty to prosperity. In circumstances of considerable adversity, he had taken his chances and opportunities, and had reaped the results of wealth.

MARK CLAPSON

**Sources** *The Times* (19 Dec 1996) · C. McGrath, *Sporting Life* (17 Dec 1996) · *The Guardian* (19 Dec 1996) · R. Munting, *An economic and social history of gambling in Britain and in the USA* (1996) · C. Chinn, *Better betting with a decent feller: bookmakers, betting, and the British working class* (1991) · naturalization certificate, PRO, HO334/370/BNA 27966 · d. cert. · Companies House (search) Coral (Turf Accountants) Ltd, 01316563
**Likenesses** photograph, 1969, repro. in *The Times* [see illus.] · photograph, repro. in *The Guardian*
**Wealth at death** £305,022: probate, 1996, CGPLA Eng. & Wales

**Coram, Thomas** (*c.*1668–1751), philanthropist, was born in or near Lyme Regis, Dorset, but no baptismal record is

Thomas Coram (*c.*1668–1751), by William Hogarth, 1740

extant. His parents were probably John Coram (*bap.* 1629) and his wife, Spes (*d.* 1677), of that town, John Coram being in merchant shipping. Thomas Coram's earliest years can only be conjectured from autobiographical comments in letters written late in life. He wrote that his mother died when he was young and he went to sea in his eleventh year, that his father remarried and moved to Hackney, and that he, Thomas, was later apprenticed by his father to a Thames-side shipwright.

In 1691–2 Coram was engaged by the government to audit the tonnage of troop and supply transports to Ireland. His abilities attracted the attention of London merchants, who in spring 1694 put him in charge of an enterprise to establish a new shipyard in Boston, Massachusetts. New England was a promising area at that time for a young man of obscure antecedents, but Coram was a staunch Anglican in a puritan colony. For the next ten years he built ships in Boston and Taunton, but attracted enemies, resulting in prolonged litigation and an attempt on his life. On 27 June 1700 he married Eunice Wait (Wayte; 1677–1740) of Boston. Coram claimed it was a happy marriage, though apparently childless, and his letters suggest loving relationships with the Wait family.

Coram's ten-year sojourn in New England made him an ardent mercantilist. His first project on his return to England in 1704 was to lobby for an act to encourage the importation of naval stores from North America in order to reduce dependence on Scandinavia (3 & 4 Anne c. 10). Thereafter he appears to have commanded merchant ships during the War of the Spanish Succession, acquiring the title of captain in consequence. His interest in the North American colonies led him to identify corrupt practices in contracting naval stores from there, and Boston harbour's need for a lighthouse. In 1712 he was elected to a role in a private corporation, Trinity House, Deptford, which combined public responsibilities with charitable purposes. His election signified Coram's growing reputation as a public servant knowledgeable in naval affairs.

After the treaty of Utrecht (1713) Coram unsuccessfully promoted the colonization of lands in what later became upper Maine. Using discharged soldiers, Coram believed the colony could strengthen a vulnerable frontier and provide hemp and timber for the Royal Navy. In 1719 he visited Hanover to scout for timber. His ship, the *Seaflower*, fell victim to German wreckers out of Cuxhaven; none the less he was able to effect changes in regulations that allowed for the importation of timber from Germany for use by the navy.

While living at Rotherhithe and pursuing his business interests in London, Coram regularly travelled a route on which he saw abandoned children, some dead, others dying. In 1722, motivated by an enduring blend of Christian benevolence, practical morality, and civic spirit, he decided to take action. Inspired by examples of foundling hospitals on the continent, he advocated one for London. However, failure attended these first efforts. In February 1727 he sought employment by the privy council, and his appeal was forwarded to the Admiralty. It is uncertain whether he was given a sinecure, but he used the Navy Office for his letters. While Coram is now best-known for the Foundling Hospital project, during the 1720s he continued to be interested in colonization ventures north of Massachusetts, at various times in the region of Maine, and later in Nova Scotia; these attracted both considerable support and opposition, the latter from those with prior economic interests there. With the support of Thomas Bray, with whom the Corams for a time lived, Coram also turned his attention to additional philanthropic ventures, including missionary work in North America, the development of parochial libraries there, aid for imprisoned debtors, and a colonial programme in the region of the Savannah River, in what became the royal colony of Georgia.

In 1732 Coram assisted the hatters of London to obtain protection for their industry (5 Geo. II, c. 22) and declined recompense beyond a hat. In the same year he became a trustee for the new colony of Georgia, incorporated by royal charter, and thereupon took an active role in raising funds and seeing off colonists at Gravesend and Dover. In 1734 he fell foul of the colony's founder, James Oglethorpe, and his supporters, primarily over his opposition to restrictions enacted to deny the right of female inheritance in the colony. He publicized his opposition, was cut by his opponents, and ceased an active role in the colony's future. Yet by this time Coram had acquired a reputation for knowledge of colonial affairs. In 1735 Horace Walpole wrote to his brother Robert, the prime minister, that Coram was the 'honestest, the most disinterested, & the most knowing person about the plantations I ever talked with' (W. Coxe, *Memoirs of the Life and Administration of Sir Robert Walpole*, 1798, 3.243).

Coram had by now a wide set of acquaintances, experience in petitions, and persistence, but his efforts to promote a foundling hospital initially attracted only modest interest, and opposition from those who believed a hospital would increase illegitimate births. Moreover Coram, the promoter, was poorly educated, relatively rough-mannered, advanced in years, and lacked a patron, as well as wealth and pedigree. The turning point in his campaign was the 'ladies petition' of 1729, signed by peeresses, and the patronage of Queen Caroline. Coram's comment on the men who had been initially apathetic was that he might as well have asked them to 'putt down their Breeches and present their Backsides to the King and Queen' (Coram to Colman, 22 Sept 1738, 'Letters of Thomas Coram', 43). The saltiness and candour of Coram's language, offensive to some, was a thread throughout his long career, contributing to litigation in New England and his eventual ostracism by the other governors of the Foundling Hospital.

Coram's petitions came before the king in council on 21 July 1737. A committee of the privy council was charged to consider, and Coram was given the responsibility for finding the first governors. He recommended 375 individuals, approximately half of whom he personally approached, his two criteria for selection being wealth and influence. Of the governors 89 were peers, 35 country gentlemen, 66 merchants, and 72 MPs. In addition Coram was required to raise funds to cover costs. The Foundling Hospital charter was signed by the king on 14 August 1739, and the first meeting of the governors was held at Somerset House that November. Coram scouted sites for the hospital, designed a corporate seal, researched foundling hospitals on the continent, and inspected temporary quarters in Hatton Garden. At that site the hospital opened its doors on 25 March 1741. Later that year irregularities at the hospital were aired publicly and Coram was implicated in having been indiscreet in his criticisms. Details are murky, but Coram's active participation in the hospital's governance ended in the spring of 1742. The new purpose-built hospital, at Lamb's Conduit Fields, began to receive children on 1 October 1745.

In his last years Coram witnessed a number of other successes: the lighthouse for Boston harbour was built, the Georgia trustees decided to permit female inheritance, and a civilian settlement was established in Nova Scotia. In addition the London hospital prospered, not only as a home for foundlings but as a centre for the capital's fashionable society, who combined benevolent gestures with an enjoyment of art works donated by leading British artists including William Hogarth, Francis Hayman, and Joseph Highmore, and the attendance (from 1750) of

annual concerts organized by George Frideric Handel (like Hogarth, a hospital governor). In mid-July 1740 Coram's wife died, but Coram remained active to the end. Although heavy-set, he ate and slept well and could walk 10 to 12 miles in a day. He retained his interest in philanthropies even though his earlier causes were now the work of others. William Hogarth's oil on canvas portrait of Coram (1740), replete with symbols of his mercantilist and philanthropic interests, shows a man with natural, flowing white hair, ruddy cheeks, rugged features, and purposeful eyes. He had made his living building ships and transporting naval stores, but he had laid nothing aside for his later years. In 1749 his supporters raised a subscription for his maintenance.

Alongside his successes Coram also faced the failure of several projects, among them a refuge for impoverished New Englanders stranded in London, a hostel for vagrants, a foundling hospital for Westminster, and an Anglican college in Massachusetts. One of his last efforts was a scheme—in tune with his latitudinarian and patriotic ethos of philanthropy—to promote the education of Native American girls as a means of spreading Christianity and strengthening the bonds of empire. He died, aged about eighty-three, at his lodgings on Spur Street, off Leicester Square, London, on 29 March 1751, and in accordance with his wishes he was buried, on 3 April, in the vault under the Foundling Hospital chapel.

If the oft-told story is true that Coram sat in the Foundling Hospital arcade in his last years distributing gingerbread to the children, it was a momentary rest from more active projects. His greatest achievement was to provide the template for eighteenth-century philanthropy of a secular foundation modelled on the joint-stock company, of which the Foundling Hospital was the first and finest expression.

JAMES STEPHEN TAYLOR

**Sources** R. K. McClure, *Coram's children: the London Foundling Hospital in the eighteenth century* (1981) · R. K. McClure, 'The captain and the children', PhD diss., Columbia University, 1975 · 'The letters of Thomas Coram', *Proceedings of the Massachusetts Historical Society*, 56 (1922–3), 15–56 · H. B. Fant, 'Picturesque Thomas Coram', *Georgia Historical Quarterly*, 32 (1948), 77–104 · R. Brocklesby, *Private virtue and publick spirit display'd in a succinct essay on the character of Thomas Coram* (1751) · R. H. Nichols and F. A. Wray, *The history of the Foundling Hospital* (1935) · H. Compston, *Thomas Coram, churchman, empire builder and philanthropist* (1918) · J. Brownlow, *Memoranda or chronicles of the Foundling Hospital* (1847) · H. A. Hill, *Thomas Coram in Boston and Taunton* (1892) · G. F. Jones, ed., *Henry Newman's Salzburger letterbooks* (1966) · *GM*, 1st ser., 21 (1751), 141, 183 · J. Hutchins, *The history and antiquities of the county of Dorset*, 2 vols. (1774) · D. T. Andrew, *Philanthropy and police: London charity in the eighteenth century* (1989)

**Archives** Mass. Hist. Soc., letters | Foundling Museum, London, family MSS, records · Harvard U., Houghton L., Harvard Univ. MSS, 'Memorial on Foundling Hospital'

**Likenesses** W. Hogarth, oils, 1740, Foundling Museum, London [*see illus.*] · wash drawing, 1740 (after W. Hogarth, 1740), NPG · B. Nebot, engraving, 1741, Foundling Museum, London · J. Macardell, mezzotint, 1749 (after W. Hogarth), BM, NPG

**Wealth at death** next to none: Brocklesby, *Private virtue*

## Corbaux, Marie Françoise Catherine Doetter [Fanny]

(1812–1883), painter and biblical critic, was the daughter of the statistician and mathematician Francis Corbaux

FRS (*c.*1769–1843), an Englishman who lived much abroad. Her sister, Louisa Corbaux (*b.* 1808), was also an artist. In 1827 her father's health was affected by financial losses and she immediately turned her early artistic talent to lucrative purpose. As women were not admitted to the Royal Academy Schools at this time (an exclusion which she campaigned to remove), and probably lacking funds for a private master, she taught herself by copying works in the National Gallery and the British Institution. She exhibited forty-eight works at the Society of British Artists (1828–40), eighty-six at the Royal Academy (1829–54), fifteen at the British Institution (1830–41), seven at the Royal Manchester Institution (1830–45), twenty-one at the Liverpool Academy (1832–54) and thirty-eight at the New Society of Painters in Water-Colour (1832–54); she was also represented by two works at the Paris Universal Exhibition in 1855. Most of her paintings were miniature portraits—on which she relied initially for her living—and larger figure compositions in watercolour. In the latter she favoured female subjects and, specifically, during the 1830s and early 1840s, literary heroines in emotional scenes from the works of Shakespeare, Scott, Byron, Letitia Elizabeth Landon, Felicia Hemans, and Caroline Norton.

In the late 1840s and early 1850s Corbaux turned increasingly to the Bible as a source, depicting Naomi, Ruth, Leah, Rachel, Hagar, Hannah, and Miriam. The Bible was also the subject of her contributions to periodicals during this period. One series, called 'Letters on the physical geography of the Exodus', appeared in *The Athenaeum* and another, 'The Rephaim', giving the history of this nation, in the *Journal of Sacred Literature*. In addition she wrote an introduction to *The Exodus Papyri* (1855) by D. I. Heath.

Recognition came early: between 1827 and 1830 Corbaux was awarded five medals by the Society of Arts, including the large silver medal (1827) and the gold Isis medal (1830) for original miniature portraits, and the large silver Isis medal for an original historical composition in watercolour (1829). She was elected an honorary member of the Society of British Artists in 1830 and a member of the New Society of Painters in Water-Colour in 1839. A number of her pictures were engraved: for *The Keepsake* (1834, 1839, 1844), *Heath's New Gallery of British Engravings* by C. Heath (1846) and *Heath's Book of Beauty* (1843), and for the almanac *Emlény* (1839), published in Budapest. In addition she designed the illustrations in *Finden's Byron Beauties* (1836), Thomas Moore's *Pearls of the East, or, Beauties from Lalla Rookh* (1837), and J. C. von Schmid's *Cousin Natalia's Tales* (1841). She herself lithographed her portrait of the opera singer Emma Albertazzi (exh. Society of British Artists, 1838; impression British Museum, London). Her exhibits were regularly mentioned in periodicals such as *The Athenaeum*, *The Spectator*, the *Art Union* and the *Art Journal*. In 1837 *The Spectator* commented that:

> Miss Corbaux is one of the first paintresses of the day: she excels both in oil and watercolours, and her power in watercolour painting especially is very great: she designs with taste and skill, paints with great depth and brilliancy of colouring, and has a truly intellectual feeling for her art. (18 Feb 1837, 164)

In 1871 she received a civil-list pension of £50.

Corbaux and her sister, Louisa, often exhibited from the same London addresses: from 5 Hercules Buildings, Lambeth, between 1828 and 1837, and from 59 Upper Norton Street, Portland Place, between 1839 and 1851. After a long illness she died, unmarried, at her home, 2 Lansdowne Terrace, East Hove, Sussex, on 1 February 1883.

CHARLOTTE YELDHAM

**Sources** E. C. Clayton, *English female artists*, 2 (1876), 68–70 · *Men of the time* (1862) · G. Vapereau, *Dictionnaire universel des contemporains*, 5th edn, 2 vols. (Paris, 1880) · *Engraved Brit. ports.* · Graves, *Artists* · Graves, *RA exhibitors* · Graves, *Brit. Inst.* · J. Johnson, ed., *Works exhibited at the Royal Society of British Artists, 1824–1893, and the New English Art Club, 1888–1917*, 2 vols. (1975) · E. Morris and E. Roberts, *The Liverpool Academy and other exhibitions of contemporary art in Liverpool, 1774–1867* (1998) · exhibition catalogues (1830–45) [Royal Manchester Institution] · C. Yeldham, *Women artists in nineteenth-century France and England*, 1 (1984), 281–3 · *The Year's Art* (1884), 217 · *The Spectator* (18 Feb 1837), 164 [review] · CGPLA Eng. & Wales (1883) · DNB

**Archives** BM, department of prints and drawings, works · Courtauld Inst., Witt Library, works | Bodl. Oxf., corresp. with Sir J. G. Wilkinson

**Likenesses** J. Goodman, portrait, exh. *c.*1836 · J. Goodman, portrait, exh. *c.*1844

**Wealth at death** £4965 15*s.*: probate, 6 March 1883, CGPLA Eng. & Wales

**Corbeil, William de** (*d.* 1136), archbishop of Canterbury, was probably born in Corbeil, a small town on the Seine a little way upstream from Paris, now absorbed in Évry Corbeil-Essonnes. He could have been born about 1070, in the reign of Philippe I of France. Nothing is known about his parents or upbringing, but two brothers, Ranulf and Helgot, appear much later in his company.

**Early career in Normandy and England** William de Corbeil first emerges in 1104 as a clerk of Ranulf Flambard, bishop of Durham and previously William Rufus's factotum, at the inspection of the 'incorrupt' body of St Cuthbert on 24 August before its translation to a new tomb in the almost completed new cathedral. He could have attached himself to Flambard in 1101, when the bishop returned from exile in Normandy. And after Henry I had restored to the bishop the royal free chapel of St Martin, Dover—a secular college—Flambard granted William a canonry in it, worth, possibly, £70 a year.

At some point William transferred his allegiance to Canterbury. Symeon of Durham, who admired the clerk, remarks that he had been in frequent and familiar contact with Archbishop Anselm, a relationship that unless formed abroad can be dated to 1107–9. William's desertion of Durham, however, may have been connected with a visit he made to the famous school of Laon between 1107 and 1112, when Waldric, formerly King Henry's chancellor, was bishop. According to the Laon account of a begging tour made by a party of its canons probably in 1123, these were warmly welcomed at Canterbury and lodged in St Augustine's Abbey by Archbishop William, a very old friend, who a good time before, while he was tutoring the sons of Ralph, King Henry's chancellor, had stayed for many days in the bishop's palace at Laon so as to attend Master Anselm's lectures. Ralph was indeed royal chancellor in succession to Waldric; but it would simplify the story if the boys' father was Ranulf Flambard. While still engaged in his studies the clerk had had an influential religious experience. When lying desperately ill in a house in Dover, he had a vision of being attacked by two successive mobs of devils and being rescued by the Virgin Mary, with the help of the archangels Michael, Gabriel, and Raphael. This, he explained some time between 1116 and 1120 to Alexander, the Canterbury monk who replaced Eadmer as Anselm's intimate and recorder of his master's words, made him, when already thinking of abandoning the secular life, even more devout. Every day, while a student, he recited the little office of Our Lady, and later he celebrated masses *de angelis* (votive masses for a special, private intention) frequently, and with great devotion.

**Election to Canterbury**  By 1116 William had entered the service of Anselm's successor as archbishop, the nobly born Ralph d'Escures, whom he had probably first met at the Durham ceremonies in 1104, when Ralph was the exiled abbot of Sées. Ralph took William with him on his calamitous and fruitless journey to Rome of 1116–17 concerning the consecration of Thurstan, archbishop-elect of York. A week's stay at Sutri as the guests of Henry I's son-in-law, the emperor Heinrich V, may have been the only consolation for the many disasters which could have finally decided the clerk to enter a religious order. Some time in 1118 he became a regular canon at Holy Trinity Priory, Aldgate, in London, founded in 1107–8, where later he was followed by one of his brothers. In 1121 Richard de Belmeis, bishop of London (d. 1127), founded an Augustinian priory at St Osyth in Essex, and appointed William as its first prior; and when Ralph d'Escures died on 20 October 1122, William was eventually, and surprisingly, elected in his place.

Episcopal elections were traditionally held in the royal court, according to a procedure regulated since 1107 by the 'compromise of Bec', and since 1122 influenced by the imperial concordat of Worms. Henry summoned a traditional 'national' council to Gloucester for the beginning of February 1123. As well as the barons and royal servants, the bishops and abbots were there in force—even Thurstan of York was present. Since the Christ Church monks claimed that they had the sole right to elect their archiepiscopal abbot and were determined to get a monk, while a powerful party among the bishops, led by Roger, bishop of Salisbury, and including Richard of London, was implacably opposed to both propositions, and insisted that the diocesan bishops should have a say in the choice of their metropolitan, the two days' debate was lively, with the king supporting the bishops and the barons the monks.

In the end Henry secured a compromise: the monks could choose from four clerks put forward by the bishops. On 4 February, most reluctantly, the monks opted for the one they considered the least unsuitable. William, although not a monk, was at least a regular canon. And Symeon of Durham claims that the Canterbury monks,

because of William's familiarity with Anselm, knew him to be a good and well educated man. The king, too, was assured by Thurstan of York and Athelwold, prior of Nostell, Yorkshire, that William was indeed a most suitable candidate, a man distinguished by his scholarship, good character, and religion.

**The dispute over primacy**  William inherited a dispute between the metropolitans of Canterbury and York over primacy and some related matters with which he was already familiar. The basic papal policy on this subject was to keep the two metropolitans in equilibrium. By subjecting the Scottish bishops to York the two provinces had been made geographically equal, and by confirming similar privileges to both archbishops the primacy was being reduced to a title of honour. English kings seem to have had no fixed views on the matter. In 1123 Thurstan's long-standing refusal to make a profession of obedience to Canterbury was punished by the substitution of William Giffard of Winchester as William's consecrator at Canterbury on 18 February. The feud thus rekindled was to last until William's death. In 1123 both archbishops took their cases to Rome. William sought a pallium, Thurstan the quashing of William's election on the grounds of various irregularities, including the rejection of his services. In the end, on 21 May, Calixtus II—bowing to the pressure of Henry I and the emperor Heinrich V, with both of whom, because of recent concordats, he wished to remain on good terms—confirmed William's election and granted him the pallium. But, after a dossier of forged papal privileges produced by Canterbury had been laughed out of court, the matter of the primacy was, as usual, deferred.

In 1125 Calixtus's successor, Honorius II, sent to England a legate, the formidable cardinal-priest Giovanni da Crema, who in April 1121 had commanded the papal forces at the siege of Sutri, to deal with all the English problems. And in the autumn in Normandy king and legate produced a radical compromise which both archbishops were ordered to accept. Canterbury should surrender to York the bishoprics of Chester, Bangor, and the unnamed diocese of St Asaph; Thurstan should accept Canterbury's primacy verbally, and his successor should make a written submission. But when the legate and the parties appeared before Honorius at Rome, William objected to the terms, and the pope, who cared only for his own primacy, substituted his own solution, which probably also suited the king. At the end of the year he made William his vicar and legate in England (within which was comprised Wales) and Scotland, thus giving him a personal superiority dependent solely on papal grant. The office could be revoked at will, and lapsed automatically on the grantor's death. William's legation would subsequently be in abeyance for two years after Honorius died in 1130. But since William had not abandoned his claim to the primacy and its associated privileges, he had not suffered final defeat. And Thurstan remained defiant. At the king's Christmas court at Windsor in 1126, York not only claimed the right to crown Henry, but also had his cross carried before him in the royal chapel. His claim, however, was unanimously rejected, and his cross-bearer and cross were ejected from the chapel. Subsequently both parties coexisted uneasily.

**A reforming archbishop** On his return from his fairly successful visit to Rome in 1123, William was enthroned, wearing his pallium, at Canterbury on 22 July. And on the same day he performed as metropolitan his first consecration of a bishop—Alexander to Lincoln. He and Thurstan had arrived too late at Rome to attend Calixtus's Lateran Council (18–27 March), which signalled the renewal of the papal drive for reform. But in 1125 Giovanni da Crema was commissioned by Honorius not only to settle the Canterbury–York dispute but also to publicize the relevant conciliar decrees. On Easter day, to demonstrate his authority, he celebrated high mass in Canterbury Cathedral. The monks regarded William's demotion as a punishment for their having a clerk rather than a monk as archbishop, but observed scornfully that the legate arrayed himself in full pontificals although he was merely a cardinal-priest. Then, after making a widespread visitation of the kingdom, on 8 September Giovanni held a council at Westminster, and in the presence of both archbishops, twenty bishops, and some forty abbots promulgated seventeen canons, mostly based on the First Lateran Council. Those that caused most alarm in the audience were the condemnation of any hereditary claim to a father's church, prebend, or benefice (canon no. 5), and the prohibition of the presence of any woman, except a permitted relation, in a clerical household (canon no. 13).

In 1127 William, fresh from his visit to Honorius II and himself a papal legate, took up the cause. He was clearly an enthusiastic reformer. On 13–16 May he held at Westminster a legatine council to which Thurstan refused to go, and to which Ranulf Flambard, taken ill, sent proctors. In a crowded and disorderly assembly eleven canons were issued. The decree not only that priests, deacons, subdeacons, and all canons who refused to dismiss their wives or concubines were to be degraded and deprived of their benefices (canon no. 5), but also that their women should be expelled from the parish (unless they had contracted a lawful marriage), judged by the bishop, and, in the last resort, condemned to slavery (canon no. 6), was received with hostility. And two years later, in October 1129, King Henry presided over a national council at Westminster, attended by both archbishops, at which he added his authority to the prohibition of clerical wives. They were all to be dismissed by 30 November. William's gullibility in conceding justice in this matter to the king, who simply allowed unchaste priests to keep their women at the cost of a fine to the royal exchequer, was blamed by the chronicler Henry, archdeacon of Huntingdon.

**Provincial and diocesan** William was a disciplinarian, and it would seem that he stood up for his rights within his own province. He treated the Welsh bishops just like the English. In 1124 he and Bishop Alexander of Lincoln quarrelled, apparently over Canterbury's claim to a peculiar in the latter's diocese known later as the deanery of Risborough, Oxfordshire; and they crossed to Normandy to litigate before the king. This discord probably contributed

to the disparaging verdict pronounced on the archbishop by Henry of Huntingdon, in Alexander's diocese, in his *Epistola de contemptu mundi*: 'No one can sing his praises because there's nothing to sing about' (Huntingdon, *Historia Anglorum*, 608–9). But in his own diocese William was clearly an active pastor; and he sometimes used Bernard of St David's as a suffragan. An Augustinian canon himself, he was particularly interested in the reformation of collegiate churches, and he looked askance at Benedictine communities. His relations with his own chapter, although he was a doughty champion of Canterbury's rights, were probably cool. But he received the dedication of a spiritual letter from Elmer, who became prior of Christ Church in 1128, with whom he was obviously on excellent terms. He succeeded, if only with difficulty, in getting a profession of obedience from Hugh of Trottiscliffe, in 1126 elected abbot of St Augustine's, Canterbury, and he seems to have restored the decayed nunnery at Minster in Sheppey. Moreover he put regular canons into St Gregory's outside Northgate, Canterbury.

In his last years William attempted to reform St Martin's, Dover, in which he himself had held a canonry, a church that the king had granted to the archbishop and church of Canterbury on the occasion of the cathedral's dedication in 1130. William built a fine new church outside Dover and, when dying, sent bishops John of Rochester and Bernard of St David's, Helewise, archdeacon of Canterbury, and Elmer, prior of Christ Church, to conduct an advance party of regular canons drawn from Merton Priory into the church. But they were intercepted by the insubordinate Christ Church sub-prior, Jeremiah, who forbade the canons' entry, on the grounds that St Martin's belonged to the monks, not the archbishop, and appealed to Rome. William's agents gave way; and as soon as the archbishop died, the monks, taking sweet revenge, sent twelve of their own number to colonize Dover.

Dover was only one of William's building works. After King Henry had granted him Rochester Castle he improved it by constructing what Gervase of Canterbury described as a remarkable keep. And, taking over from Bishop Ernulf of Rochester, who died in 1124, he brought both Canterbury and Rochester cathedrals to completion. On Sunday 4 May 1130, with the king and queen and David, king of Scots, among the large and distinguished congregation, he dedicated his own cathedral. The splendour of the ceremony, claimed the monk Gervase, was without equal since the dedication of King Solomon's temple. And on the following day William consecrated Rochester Cathedral.

**The accession of Stephen and death of Archbishop William** King Henry died in Normandy on 1 December 1135, and was buried by William on 4 January following in the late king's foundation at Reading. Meanwhile the part he played in the succession of Henry's nephew, Stephen, inflicted serious damage on William's reputation. On 1 January 1127 he had sworn with the other bishops and abbots and the barons to acknowledge Henry's daughter, the Empress Matilda, as the heir to the throne. But in 1135, after some prevarication and debate, perhaps because he was overborne by that powerful pair of bishops, Henry of Winchester and Roger of Salisbury, William accepted Stephen's *coup d'état* and, together with them, crowned him at Westminster, probably on 22 December. He secured, however, from the new king two important concessions in writing: the coronation charter, which confirmed the rights of the king's barons and vassals, and the Oxford charter of April 1136, which elaborated Henry I's coronation charter of 1100, especially as regards the freedom of the church. That Stephen soon showed little respect for ecclesiastical liberties does not diminish the value of these royal undertakings. One more step had been taken on the road to Magna Carta.

William did not long survive Henry I. While attempting to complete his reform of St Martin's, Dover, he fell seriously ill at his manor of Mortlake, Surrey, and, deeply chagrined by the opposition of his monks, had himself carried to Canterbury. It was probably there that he died, on 21 November 1136; he was buried in the north transept of his cathedral. His conduct throughout his career had been mostly admirable, and his achievements were by no means negligible. He was a devout man, in the circle that fostered the cult of the Virgin Mary; and it was at the Council of Westminster in 1129 that the feast of the Immaculate Conception was generally authorized. He was a zealous reformer and his three visits to Rome were exceptional. William of Malmesbury considered him a courteous man, temperate in behaviour, and contrasted his sobriety with the flamboyance of the 'modern' bishop. But most of the contemporary chroniclers were prejudiced against him, and grudging in their tributes. His enacted reforms were unpopular. The author of *Gesta Stephani*, although allowing him the countenance of a dove and the dress of a monk, accused him of hoarding money. Monastic writers could not accept that a clerk or canon could be a proper archbishop of Canterbury; and those who supported the excluded Matilda, and later her son, Henry II, branded him a perjurer and a traitor. That he should, nevertheless, have been regarded favourably by Hugh the Chanter of York, and generally held to be basically a decent and religious man, must be considered a remarkable tribute.            FRANK BARLOW

**Sources** *The historical works of Gervase of Canterbury*, ed. W. Stubbs, 2 vols., Rolls Series, 73 (1879–80) · Symeon of Durham, *Opera* · *Hugh the Chanter: the history of the church of York, 1066–1127*, ed. and trans. C. Johnson, rev. edn, rev. M. Brett, C. N. L. Brooke, and M. Winterbottom, OMT (1990) · J.-P. Migne, ed., *Patrologia Latina*, 217 vols. (1844–55), 977 · Alexander, 'Alexandri monachi Cantuariensis liber ex dictis Beati Anselmi: miracula', ed. R. W. Southern and F. S. Schmitt, *Memorials of St Anselm* (1969), 266–8 · K. R. Potter and R. H. C. Davis, eds., *Gesta Stephani*, OMT (1976) · *Willelmi Malmesbiriensis monachi de gestis pontificum Anglorum libri quinque*, ed. N. E. S. A. Hamilton, Rolls Series, 52 (1870) · John of Worcester, *Chron.* · Henry, archdeacon of Huntingdon, *Historia Anglorum*, ed. D. E. Greenway, OMT (1996) · D. Whitelock, M. Brett, and C. N. L. Brooke, eds., *Councils and synods with other documents relating to the English church, 871–1204*, 2 (1981) · R. Foreville, *L'église et la royauté en Angleterre sous Henri II Plantagenet, 1154–1189* (Paris, 1943) · D. Bethell, 'William of Corbeil and the Canterbury–York dispute', *Journal of Ecclesiastical History*, 19 (1968), 145–59 · D. L. Bethell, 'English Black monks and episcopal elections in the 1120s', *EngHR*, 84 (1969), 673–98 · R. Anstruther, ed., *Epistolae Herberti de Losinga, Osberti de Clara, et Edmeri* (1846)
**Likenesses** seal, BL; Birch, *Seals*, 1171

**Corbet, Clement** (*c*.1576–1652), civil lawyer, was the sixth of eight sons of Sir Miles Corbet (*d*. 1607) of Sprowston and his first wife, Katherine, daughter of Sir Christopher Heydon. His father was high sheriff of Norfolk in 1591 and was knighted at the sacking of Cadiz in 1596. Corbet was admitted a scholar of Trinity Hall, Cambridge, on 7 December 1592, took the degree of LLB in 1598, held a fellowship at his college from 1598 to 1611, and was created LLD in 1605. In May 1607 Corbet was appointed professor of law at Gresham College, London, and occupied that chair until November 1613. He was already chancellor of the diocese of Chichester when he became master of Trinity Hall in October 1611 at the early age of about thirty-five, immediately after the death of John Cowell. On 9 May 1612 Corbet was admitted a member of the College of Advocates at Doctors' Commons. He was vice-chancellor of Cambridge University in 1613–14.

In 1613 Corbet married Elizabeth Kemp (*d*. 1644), through whom he held Saham-Toney manor, Norfolk; they raised a family, of whom a son, Samuel, and at least four daughters survived him. The focus of Corbet's life moved to Norfolk in 1624 when he became registrar of audience and consistory courts at Norwich, continuing to adjudicate on civil litigation in the consistory court even after the abolition of the episcopacy in 1646. In 1625 he resigned the mastership of Trinity Hall and leased a house in the precincts of Norwich Cathedral, where he was appointed vicar-general and principal official to Matthew Wren, bishop of Norwich. Corbet sought a uniform and orthodox church, to which end he encouraged Wren to be more severe with the puritans. He died on 28 May 1652 and was buried in the chancel of Belaugh church, Norfolk. Samuel erected a monument to his parents, describing his father as 'a hammer of schism', but he was otherwise not a conspicuous figure.

THOMPSON COOPER, *rev.* ANITA MCCONNELL

**Sources** B. P. Levack, *The civil lawyers in England, 1603–1641* (1973) · W. Harvey, *The visitation of Norfolk in the year 1563*, ed. G. H. Dashwood and others, 1 (1878), 35 · J. Ward, *The lives of the professors of Gresham College* (1740); repr. (1967) · C. Crawley, *Trinity Hall: the history of a Cambridge college, 1350–1975* (1976) · A. E. Corbet, *The family of Corbet*, 2 vols. (1914–20), vol. 2 · G. D. Squibb, *Doctors' Commons: a history of the College of Advocates and Doctors of Law* (1977), 169 · will, PRO, PROB 11/224, sig. 217
**Likenesses** portrait, Trinity Hall, Cambridge

**Corbet, Denys** (1826–1909), Guernsey patois poet, was born on 22 May 1826 in the Vale parish, Guernsey, the first of the two children of Peter Corbet, a seafarer, and his wife, Susan, *née* de Beaucamp. According to a family tradition Peter Corbet drowned while Denys was still young, and the family struggled. In one poem Corbet records that he was looked after

> Par un respectâblle vier couplle
> D'mes près parents
> ('by a respectable old couple of my relations'; Corbet, 179)

He became a schoolmaster in the Forest parish and complained in verse of the sorry condition of the humble teacher. He married, according to one source, in 1852, Elizabeth Wellington, the daughter of a gardener; there were four sons and two daughters of the marriage.

Corbet played many parts in the life of his parish. He gave assistance in field surveys, painted pedigree Guernsey cows, and served as *connétable*. He translated a French text on the cultivation of grapes in greenhouses, and two of his essays—'Witchcraft' and 'Local superstitions, omens, signs and warnings'—were published in the *Transactions of the Société Guernesiaise* (1880 and 1882). A French critic inferred from his writings that he was a deist, a socialist, a good Anglo-Saxon democrat, and probably a freemason (Lebarbenchon, 65, 81). As a patois poet Corbet consciously followed in the tradition of Georges Métivier, to whom he dedicated his first volume. This appeared in 1871 with the punning title *Les feuilles de la forêt* ('Leaves from the forest'); fourteen of the poems were in patois, the rest in French and English. That volume was followed by a collection entitled *Le jour de l'an de 1874*, evidently successful as there were subsequent collections of *Le jour de l'an* for 1875, 1876, and 1877. The final volume to appear was *Les chànts du drain rimeux* (1884): Corbet was conscious that he was the last ('drain' means 'dernier') of the patois poets. Most of this work was given over to a lengthy description (over 8000 lines) about a journey through the ten parishes of Guernsey. In this highly original poem Corbet reminisced about the past and meditated about changes in the economic and social life of the island. He welcomed many of the changes of modern life—such as better roads, improved housing, steamships, photography, and telegraphy.

In both the nineteenth and twentieth centuries islanders have tended to admire Métivier rather than Corbet, and have enjoyed Corbet primarily as a 'poète-chroniqueur' of the good old days. In 1988 a fine appreciation of Corbet was published by the French scholar R. J. Lebarbenchon. The latter considered Corbet's work 'parmi les plus originales et personnelles' ('among the most original and personal') in the genre of patois poems (both insular and Norman) (Lebarbenchon, 81). Corbet not only evoked the past—part of which he admired—but also displayed an awareness of what had been wrong in the past. He had a lively appreciation of changes that were necessary: 'philanthrope, pacifiste, partisan du progrès, apôtre de l'instruction publique, il se classe aussi parmi les modernes et a foi en *l'avenir*' ('philanthropist, pacifist, supporter of progress, apostle of public education, he ranks also among the moderns and has faith in the future'; ibid., 81).

When Corbet died at Le Mont Marché, Forest, Guernsey, on 21 April 1909 he was remembered both as an artist and as a poet. At the end of the twentieth century his work was known to very few in his native island, and he was, almost certainly, better appreciated by Norman critics.

GREGORY COX

**Sources** R. Lebarbenchon, *La grève de Lecq: Guernesey et Jersey* (Cherbourg, 1988) · M. de Garis, 'Denys Corbet, le drain rimeux', *Report and Transactions* [Société Guernesiaise], 16 (1955–9), 361–8 · D. Corbet, *Les chànts du drain rimeux* (1884) · *Gazette de Guernesey* (24 April 1909) · Greffe records, Royal Court, Guernsey
**Likenesses** photograph, repro. in D. Corbet, *Les feuilles de la forêt* (1871), frontispiece

**Corbet, Edward** (1601×3–1658), Church of England clergyman, was born at Pontesbury in Shropshire; his parents' names are unknown. He matriculated at Merton College, Oxford, on 16 November 1621, when he was said to be aged nineteen, graduated BA on 4 December 1622, was made a fellow in 1624, and proceeded MA on 25 June 1628. He became proctor on 4 April 1638. In the late 1630s he distinguished himself at Merton, where he became sub-warden under Sir Nathanael *Brent, by his resistance to the innovations of Archbishop Laud. In particular, Corbet consistently refused to bow before the communion table.

Corbet, who like Brent was absent from Merton by the time the king arrived in Oxford in 1642, was chosen as a member of the Westminster assembly of divines and as a parliamentary preacher. On 28 December 1642 he preached before the Commons a sermon entitled *God's Providence* (1643), which demonstrates his speculative approach to theology. When Isaac Bargrave died in January 1643 the rectory at Chartham, Kent, was left vacant, but Laud, who at that time was in the Tower, refused to grant Corbet the living. In the resulting dispute parliament bypassed Laud's authority and instituted Corbet in the rectory by ordinance in May. The next month, citing Corbet's case, parliament sequestered Laud's 'estate' pending the resolution of the charges against him. Like Brent, Corbet subsequently gave evidence at Laud's trial, detailing newly erected crucifixes as well as the command to bow upon entering the chapel at Merton.

Corbet continued at Chartham until 1646 when he returned to Oxford as one of the seven ministers appointed by parliament to preach royalist scholars into obedience, an assignment he found little to his liking. He was also elected one of the visitors of the university, 'yet seldom or never sat among them' (Wood, *Ath. Oxon.: Fasti*, 2.117). In January 1648 Corbet was installed as public orator and canon of the second stall in Christ Church, in place of Henry Hammond, who had been ejected by the visitors, but being 'a person of conscience and honesty' (ibid.), he resigned both places the following August. On 12 April 1648 he proceeded DD. On the death of Thomas Soame, Corbet was presented to the valuable rectory of Great Hasely, near Oxford.

By early 1649 Corbet had married Nathaniel Brent's daughter, Margaret. Together they had three children, Edward (who matriculated at Oxford on 16 November 1666 at the age of seventeen), Martha, and Margaret. His wife, Margaret, died in 1657, 'little above 28 years of age' and was described by Henry Wilkinson in his funeral sermon for her as both loving and wise. Corbet himself died in London on 5 January 1658 aged about fifty-five. He was buried on 14 January in the chancel of Great Hasely, near his wife, having requested that John Conant, rector of Exeter College, preach his funeral sermon. By his will he bequeathed books to the Bodleian Library and libraries of

Merton College and Shrewsbury School, and left the education of his son to Henry Wilkinson and of his daughters to his cousin Elizabeth, wife of Sir Francis Butler of Hertford.　　　Mark Robert Bell

**Sources** J. Rushworth, *Historical collections*, 2nd edn, 3/2 (1692), 330, 338 • Foster, *Alum. Oxon.* • *CSP dom.*, *1638–9*, 46, 68; *1639–40*, 508–9; *1640–41*, 325 • E. Hasted, *The history and topographical survey of the county of Kent*, 3 (1790), 156 • Wood, *Ath. Oxon.: Fasti* (1815), 405, 500; (1820), 80, 100, 117–18, 159 • Wood, *Ath. Oxon.*, new edn, 1.xxx; 2.226; 3.325, 795; 4.343 • W. Prynne, *Canterburies doome, or, The first part of a compleat history of the commitment, charge, tryall, condemnation, execution of William Laud, late arch-bishop of Canterbury* (1646) • H. Wilkinson, *The hope of glory … at the funeral of … Margaret Corbet* (1657) • B. Brook, *The lives of the puritans*, 3 (1813), 266–7 • D. Neal, *The history of the puritans or protestant nonconformists*, 2 (1754), 503 • PRO, PROB 11/273, fols. 44r–46r • *Fasti Angl., 1541–1857*, [Bristol], 90 • *Walker rev.* • R. S. Paul, *The assembly of the Lord: politics and religion in the Westminster assembly and the 'Grand debate'* (1985) • J. F. Wilson, *Pulpit in parliament: puritanism during the English civil wars, 1640–1648* (1969) • Tai Liu, *Discord in Zion: the puritan divines and the puritan revolution, 1640–1660* (1973) • *Hist. U. Oxf. 4: 17th-cent. Oxf.*, 711, 721, 726

**Corbet, Gabriel** (*fl.* 1427–1454), merchant, was a Venetian mariner, perhaps originally called Gabriele Corbizzi, who was already established as a trader in Southampton by 1427. In 1431, after petitioning parliament, he was granted letters of denization by the crown, ostensibly because of the service he had done for Henry V and Henry VI upon the seas, but he also paid 40s. into the hanaper for the privilege. He spent the rest of his life in Southampton, and evidently became a modestly successful merchant and respected citizen of the town. Some time before 1440 he married Mabilla, but there is no record of whether she, too, was of Italian birth. They do not appear to have had any children; a Thomas Corbet who was living and trading in Southampton at the same time as Gabriel, but who was probably not a burgess of the town, may possibly have been a brother or a cousin.

Corbet's business as a merchant shows little evidence of specialization in either commodities or markets. In the earliest surviving Southampton port book, that for 1427/8, he appears as mainly concerned with the coastwise trade in wheat, although he also imported some five tuns of wine in a Genoese carrack. His interest in the wine trade continued into the 1430s but he can also be found trading in oil, pepper, kerseys, salt herring, and other fish. On occasion he also acted as pledge for the customs and other dues of some of the Genoese visiting Southampton. His inland customers were spread out over the south of England, from Wells to London, but were most commonly located in Salisbury or Alton.

In 1440 Corbet and his wife were jointly granted by John Fyssmark and his wife, Isabella, a large property called The Cheynes in Coleye Lane in Southampton; this was, in fact, a stone warehouse with cellars beneath, adjacent to the Town Quay on the Southampton waterfront, a good location for a merchant. It was also very near the shop over the Watergate belonging to William Soper (*d.* 1459), a leading citizen and keeper of the king's ships (1420–42). Corbet himself lived in a house rented from Soper in English Street, not far from the Franciscan church, even though he owned in his own right two small houses further up English Street near St Lawrence's Church. It was perhaps Corbet's association with Soper and his friends and associates, Robert Aylward and Walter Fetplace, that ensured his election to office in the corporation of Southampton. He was first a collector of the subsidy in the parish of the Holy Rood in 1434–5, and later town steward in 1441 and 1442 and water bailiff (collector of the local customs and port dues) in 1443.

Corbet's rise to prosperity in the years around 1440 should probably be associated with the determination of the Southampton merchants at that time to capture the Italian trade at London's expense. And his most important office, that of sheriff, to which he was elected in 1453, when Aylward was mayor, needs to be seen in a similar context. A. A. Ruddock has connected Aylward's mayoralty with a struggle which seems to have gone on in the 1450s within the ruling oligarchy of Southampton merchants, between those who shared the anti-alien feelings then sweeping through merchant circles in London, and those who wished to remain on good terms with the Italian community. Aylward and Fetplace (who was mayor when Corbet was water bailiff) had unusually close connections with the foreign merchants, and would have seen Corbet as a natural supporter of their party in the town.

Corbet was unusual among the Italians living and working in Southampton at this period in taking out letters of denization and becoming involved in the public life of the town. This may have been because in his early life as a mariner he had become involved with Soper in the affairs of the king's ships, and, encouraged by a group of powerful friends in the town, had subsequently taken the decision to settle permanently in England. In the Southampton terrier of 1454 Corbet was recorded as living on English Street, Southampton. It is not known when or where he died.　　　Susan Rose

**Sources** A. B. Wallis Chapman, ed., *The Black Book of Southampton*, 3 vols., Southampton RS, 13–14, 17 (1912–15), vol. 1, p. 21; vol. 2, pp. 72, 76 • A. A. Ruddock, *Italian merchants and shipping in Southampton, 1270–1600*, Southampton RS (1951), 160, 169 • L. A. Burgess, ed., *The Southampton terrier of 1454*, Southampton RS, 15 (1976), 49, 51, 56, 83 • H. W. Gidden, ed., *The book of remembrance of Southampton, 1303–1620*, 1, Southampton RS, 27 (1927), 3, 66 • H. W. Gidden, ed., *The stewards' books of Southampton*, 2 vols., Southampton RS, 35, 39 (1935–9), vol. 1, p. 7; vol. 2, p. 50 • P. Studer, ed., *The port books of Southampton … 1427–1430*, Southampton RS, 15 (1913), 18, 20, 31, 39, 47, 70 • B. Foster, ed., *The local port book of Southampton, 1435–36*, Southampton RS, 7 (1963), 8, 28, 44 • H. S. Cobb, ed., *The local port book of Southampton, 1439–1440*, Southampton RS, 5 (1961), 4–5, 66, 95, 103 • O. Coleman, ed., *The brokage book of Southampton, 1443–1444*, 2 vols., Southampton RS, 4, 6 (1960–61), vol. 1, pp. 46, 61, 65, 76, 78, 84, 119; vol. 2, pp. 156, 172, 200, 210, 227, 230, 232, 281, 291, 293, 308 • E. A. Lewis, ed., *The Southampton port and brokage books, 1448–9*, Southampton RS, 36 (1993), 30, 55, 142 • J. M. Kaye, ed., *The cartulary of God's House, Southampton*, 2, Southampton RS, 20 (1976), 380 • E. O. Blake, ed., *Cartulary of the priory of St Denys near Southampton*, 2 vols., Southampton RS, 24–5 (1981), vol. 1, p. xci • *CPR, 1429–36*, 117, 459; *1452–61*, 164 • P. Nightingale, *A medieval mercantile community: the Grocers' Company and the politics and trade of London, 1000–1485* (1995)

**Corbet, Henry** (1820–1878), agricultural editor, was born on 31 December 1820 and educated at Bedford School. He hoped to go to university but was unable to do so because of family difficulties. During the early 1840s he lived in London and first came to public attention in November 1846 when he was appointed secretary of the London (or Central, as it was then styled) Farmers' Club in succession to Thomas Thorp. The issue of tenant right was one of the great concerns of the club during its early years. In 1848 Corbet collaborated with William Shaw, the editor of the *Mark Lane Express and Agricultural Journal* and founder of the Farmers' Club, to produce a digest of the agricultural customs of England and Wales that had been reported to Phillip Pusey's select committee on tenant right, the proceedings of which were never formally published. Corbet was also awarded a prize by the Wenlock Farmers' Club for an essay on tenant right which came to be regarded as a definitive statement on the subject.

Shaw left abruptly for Australia in 1852 and Corbet was invited to write for the *Mark Lane Express*; he soon took over as editor. He established a reputation for a combative, forthright style of writing, and while tenant right remained one of his most abiding concerns he also campaigned on a range of issues such as the abolition of the malt tax, the reform of the game laws, county expenditure and county rates, the need for effective government action to counter the spread of animal disease, and the sale of sub-standard and adulterated animal feedstuffs. Apart from leading articles in the *Mark Lane Express*, the six papers that he gave to the London Farmers' Club between 1860 and 1870 offer insights into Corbet's style and opinions.

Although Corbet took a close interest in all aspects of agricultural progress he was more sceptical about the potential of agricultural science than many of his contemporaries. His particular expertise was in the appraisal of farm livestock, and he was much in demand as a stock judge at agricultural shows. The depth of his knowledge of stock was evident in his report on the livestock exhibited at the Royal Agricultural Society of England's 1872 Cardiff show and in his essay, 'Heads', for the Bath and West Society. Corbet was also an enthusiastic sportsman and edited the *Steeplechase Calendar* between 1845 and 1848. Later he wrote extensively for *The Field*, *Bell's Life*, and *All the Year Round*; a selection of these writings was published as *Tales and Traits of Sporting Life* (1864).

Despite Corbet's criticisms of the lack of a unified system of tenant right and the operation of the game laws, he was essentially conservative in many of his views about the countryside. He spoke out against trends in country sport of which he disapproved, such as the fashion for large-scale pheasant shooting or the overexploitation of two-year-old horses on the turf, and he saw fox-hunting as a cohesive social force. As he concluded in his address, 'Foxes *versus* rabbits', to the London Farmers' Club (May 1869):

> let us try our best to keep one old English pastime amongst us pure and undefiled. We have scared the wolf from our woods and forests, we have banished the bustard from our plains, and the very grouse fly before the shepherd and his flock; but it will be a bad day for this country when a fox can no longer be routed from his lair to 'Die in the open as a good'un should do!' (*Farmer's Magazine*, 3rd ser., 35, June 1869, 515–16)

Corbet was active in a number of agricultural institutions. He was secretary of the Total Repeal Malt-Tax Association, helped to reform the constitution of the Smithfield Club in the early 1860s, and was for many years auditor to the Royal Agricultural Society of England. In 1871 he, with his brother Edward, established the Alexandra Park Horse Show. He was made a member of the council of the Royal Agricultural Benevolent Institution and of the committee of Lord Vernon's French Farmers' Relief Fund, and in 1876 was elected a member of the Agricultural Society of France in recognition of services to agriculture. In December 1875 he suffered a severe stroke, which left him paralysed and unable to continue his work.

Corbet was best-known for his editorship of the *Mark Lane Express*, which achieved under him 'an individuality and a reputation for thoroughness and independence' ('Noteworthy agriculturists: Mr. Henry Corbet'). But the paper—like the London Farmers' Club—carried little political influence. His antipathy towards the central chamber of agriculture (founded in 1866 in the wake of the disastrous outbreak of 'cattle plague') further fragmented the agricultural interest at a time when it was becoming marginalized in an increasingly urban and industrial economy. Although his anecdotes and strong sense of the ludicrous made him good company, his acerbic style and tendency towards personalized attacks—as, for example, in his denunciation of Samuel Sidney, the secretary of the Islington Agricultural Hall Company—made him a number of enemies.

On his retirement from the London Farmers' Club Corbet was presented with 100 guineas; his poverty led to another collection, and he was presented with a further £350 in May 1878. After the long illness which followed his stroke, he died at his home, 22 Walpole Street, Chelsea, on 29 December 1878 and was buried close to his father at Chepstow on 4 January 1879.            NICHOLAS GODDARD

**Sources** 'Noteworthy agriculturists: Mr. Henry Corbet', *Agricultural Gazette* (15 May 1876) · 'Death of Mr. Henry Corbet', *Farmer's Magazine*, 3rd ser., 55 (1879), 105 · N. Goddard, 'A contrast in style: an appreciation of two Victorian agricultural journalists', *Agricultural History Review*, 44 (1996), 180–90 · K. Fitzgerald, *Ahead of their time: a short history of the London Farmers' Club* (1967) · H. Corbet, *Tales and traits of sporting life* (1864) · H. Corbet, 'Heads', *Journal of the Bath & West Society*, 3rd ser., 2 (1871), 98–116 · H. Corbet, 'Report on the exhibition of livestock at Cardiff', *JRASE*, 2nd ser., 8 (1872), 373–404 · d. cert.

**Likenesses** engraving (after a photograph), repro. in *Agricultural Gazette*, 627 · engraving (after a photograph), repro. in *Farmer's Magazine*, 3rd ser., 53 (April 1878), frontispiece

**Wealth at death** under £4000: probate, 17 Jan 1879, *CGPLA Eng. & Wales*

**Corbet, Sir John**, first baronet (*bap.* 1594, *d.* 1662), politician, was baptized on 20 May 1594 at Stoke upon Tern, Shropshire, the second son of Richard Corbet (*d. c.*1602) of Stoke upon Tern and his wife, Anne, daughter of Sir Thomas *Bromley, lord chancellor from 1579 to 1587. He may have been the John Corbet recorded as graduating BA at Cambridge in 1612 and he was a student at Lincoln's Inn in 1615. The date of his knighthood is not recorded, but he was made a baronet on 19 September 1627. He was a justice of the peace in Shropshire during the 1620s and 1630s. Corbet's family had been a significant presence in the shire since the mid-sixteenth century when his grandfather Reynold *Corbet acquired the estates at Stoke and Adderley by marriage to Alice Gratewood, coheir to Sir Rowland Hill. John Corbet succeeded his elder brother, Richard, about 1618 and established his principal residence at Adderley. In 1620 he married Ann (d. 1682), daughter of Sir George Mainwaring of Ightfield, Shropshire: they would have ten sons and ten daughters.

Corbet's main claim to fame was his involvement in two celebrated local disputes during the 1630s. The first of these was a quarrel over honour and precedence with his near neighbour, Robert Needham, second Viscount Kilmorey, of Shavington. Disputes had arisen with Kilmorey's father over rentals, rights of way, and whether the Needhams were entitled to set up seats in the chancel of the parish church at Adderley where Corbet owned the rectory. Corbet was able to obstruct the elder Kilmorey's efforts to have a chapel consecrated for his use at Shavington, and when both received titles in 1627 he contested his claim to local precedence by insisting that 'an English Baronet was as good as an Irish Viscount'. However, the second viscount used his contacts at court to turn the tables when he succeeded his father in November 1631. Suits in king's bench and the court of arches secured his right of way across Corbet's estate and enabled him to go ahead with consecrating his chapel. Corbet attempted to retaliate in 1633 by having one of his servants, an Irish footboy, buried in the chancel at Adderley, immediately adjacent to the tomb of the first viscount. Kilmorey regarded this as a deliberate attempt to bring 'great scandall and disrepute' on 'his name and familie' (Harrod) and immediately appealed to the earl marshal's court where he secured an order to remove the footboy's body. He then pressed home his advantage by obtaining a licence from Archbishop Laud to build his own family chapel adjacent to the chancel at Adderley. Corbet was apparently beaten on all fronts, but the dispute rumbled on and in March 1642 led to an armed affray as Lady Corbet used her servants to deny Kilmorey and his family access to the chapel. The quarrel was finally subsumed in the events of the civil war in which Corbet and Kilmorey took opposite sides.

The second dispute was over the more public issue of the crown's right to raise fees to pay the muster master, responsible for training the county militia. At a quarter sessions held at Shrewsbury on 7 April 1635 the grand jury presented these as 'a great grievance and oppression'. Timothy Tourneur, esquire, one of the justices and steward to the county's lord lieutenant, the earl of Bridgewater, immediately rebuked the jury for meddling in matters which did not concern them, whereupon Corbet called for the statute book, asked the clerk of the court to read out the section referring to the petition of right, and

attacked Tourneur for trying to prevent the grand jury from carrying out its duty. Corbet's intervention apparently had the support of most of the justices present but the matter was reported to Bridgewater, a privy councillor. Corbet was summoned to London and required to answer for 'making speeches to his Majesties disservice and the animating of others to refuse the payment of the muster master's fee' (Cope). He apparently refused to back down and on 10 June was imprisoned and bound over to appear for trial in Star Chamber. The trial never took place, but he remained in the Fleet prison for six months and was removed from the commission of the peace. He took his revenge in February 1641 when he petitioned against Bridgewater's proceedings in the Long Parliament. In June the Commons declared that imposing the fee for the muster master was contrary to the petition of right, that Corbet's arrest had been illegal, and that he should receive reparation. In September the Lords took order to proceed with the impeachment, although they did not go through with it.

Corbet's return as knight of the shire for Shropshire in the Long Parliament was probably a result of the reputation he earned for standing up for the liberties of the subject; but although he sat right through until 1648, when he was one of the members secluded at Pride's Purge, he made little impact on proceedings. In February 1642 he was one of the MPs chosen to conduct negotiations with the king over the militia ordinance and in March he presented a petition from Shropshire before the Commons. At the local level he was nominated as one of the leaders of the parliamentary committee for Shropshire in June 1642 and later on as colonel-general of the forces to be raised there. During July and August he was active in the county attempting to execute the militia ordinance but after this he returned to London, where he appears to have remained for much of the war. He has been identified as working during 1643–5 with 'the middle group' in the Commons and in religious terms he was a presbyterian, being listed as one of the elders for Shropshire. After his seclusion from parliament in December 1648 he took little further role in public affairs. He died in June 1662 and was buried in the chancel of the parish church at Market Drayton, Shropshire. His widow died on 29 October 1682.

RICHARD CUST

**Sources** Keeler, *Long Parliament*, 142 · J. Burke and J. B. Burke, *A genealogical and heraldic history of the extinct and dormant baronetcies of England, Ireland, and Scotland* (1838), 132 · H. T. Weyman, 'Shropshire members of parliament', *Transactions of the Shropshire Archaeological Society*, 4th ser., 11 (1927–8), 153–84, esp. 172–3 · private information (2004) [M. D. G. Wanklyn] · H. D. Harrod, *The history of Shavington* (1891), 24–73 · E. S. Cope, 'Politics without parliament: the dispute over muster masters' fees in Shropshire in the 1630s', *Huntington Library Quarterly*, 45 (1982), 271–84 · *Fourth report*, HMC, 3 (1874), 99b · W. H. Coates, A. Steele Young, and V. F. Snow, eds., *The private journals of the Long Parliament*, 3 vols. (1982–92), vol. 1, p. 436; vol. 2, p. 2; vol. 3, p. 284 · M. Jansson, ed., *Two diaries of the Long Parliament* (1984), 8 · D. Underdown, *Pride's Purge: politics in the puritan revolution* (1971), 371 · J. H. Hexter, *Reappraisals in history* (1961), 167–70 · Venn, *Alum. Cant.* · *JHL*, 5 (1642–3), 269–70 · IGI
**Archives** Shrops. RRC, Kilmorey/Shavington muniments

**Corbet, John** (1603–1641), religious polemicist and Church of Scotland and Church of Ireland minister, was probably born in the Gorbals, Glasgow, the son of William Corbet, a portioner of the city. He graduated MA from Glasgow University in 1623, and as 'a Person of Good learning' was subsequently employed as a schoolmaster at Renfrew (*Fasti Scot.*, 3.331). He was ordained as minister of Bonhill, Dunbartonshire, in 1637 but his tenure was destined to be both brief and racked with controversy. As a supporter of episcopacy he refused to acknowledge the authority of the general assembly of 1638 and aroused the suspicion and animosity of the solidly presbyterian synod of Dumbarton. After vacillating, in an attempt to retain his position, he finally refused to subscribe to the assembly's declaration against the bishops and fled to Ireland, leaving behind him his heavily pregnant wife and four young children to follow later. In his absence he was deposed from the ministry on 16 April 1639.

Once settled in Dublin, Corbet found powerful patrons in the form of John Bramhall, bishop of Derry, and Thomas Wentworth, earl of Strafford. Indeed, it was to this latter figure that he dedicated his pamphlet *The Ungirding of the Scottish Armour* (1639). This work was intended as a direct, and highly critical, response to the Revd Alexander Henderson's *Instructions for Defensive Arms* (1639). Rejecting both the legality of rebellion against 'great King Charles' and the validity of the national covenant, it attacked 'the Flood of our Scottish Disorders and Uproares', while thoroughly vindicating the role of the episcopate (Corbet, iv, vii).

Having thus endeared himself to the authorities in Ireland, Corbet appeared to be the ideal candidate to fill the recently vacated, and highly lucrative, post of dean of Raphoe, Donegal. However, this sinecure fell within the gift of Archibald Adair, bishop of Killala, who objected strongly to the scathing language that had been employed in Corbet's anti-Scottish diatribe. As Gilbert Burnet recounted it this resulted in a stormy interview between the two men in which Adair bitterly mocked and reviled his junior, pointing out that in Scottish dialect a Corbet, or Corby, signified a raven and that 'it was an ill bird that defiled its own nest' (Burnet, 109), although John Vesey told it slightly differently. Storming back to Dublin 'full of wrath' Corbet lodged a complaint with Bishop John Bramhall against Adair's language and conduct, which was instrumental in having the latter removed by the high commission from his see (Burnet, 109–12; Reid, 1.262; Vesey, xxiv).

The following year saw the publication of Corbet's *The Epistle Congratulatorie of Lysimachus Nicanor of the Society of Jesu, to the Covenanters in Scotland* (1640). In this bitter and 'very smart Book' (Burnet, 109) Corbet upbraided the covenanters and used the character of a fictional Jesuit to express satisfaction at the troubles in Scotland, and on sixteen separate counts, to draw close parallels between the pretended doctrines of the presbyterians and the Society of Jesus. Having been rewarded in 1640 with the ministry of the parishes of Killabin and Ballintubride, in Queen's county, Corbet appears to have been caught unawares by the suddenness and ferocity of the outbreak of the Irish rebellion of October 1641. His house was sacked by the insurgents and, though he sought refuge in the arms of his wife, he was cut to pieces by the blows of two Gaelic swineherds; his wife seems to have survived.

JOHN CALLOW

**Sources** J. S. Reid and W. D. Killen, *History of the Presbyterian church in Ireland*, 1 (1834) · J. Corbet, *The ungirding of the Scottish armour, or, An answer to the informations for defensive armes against the kings majestie* (1639) · A. Stevenson, *The history of the church and state of Scotland*, 2 (1754) [incl. A. Henderson's 'Instructions for defensive arms', pp. 686–95] · *Fasti Scot.*, new edn, vol. 3 · [R. Baillie], *Letters and journals*, ed. R. Aiken, 2 vols. (1775), vol. 1 · J. Ware, *De Hibernia et antiquitatibus ejus, disquisitiones in quibus praeter ea quae de Hibernia antiqua explicantur* (1654) · *A collection of tracts and treatises illustrative … of Ireland*, 2 vols. (1860) · G. Burnet, *The life of William Bedell D.D., bishop of Kilmore in Ireland*, 2nd edn (1736) · J. T. Gilbert, ed., *A contemporary history of affairs in Ireland from 1641 to 1652*, 3 vols. (1879–80) · H. Kearney, *Strafford in Ireland, 1633–41: a study in absolutism* (1959); repr. (1989) · J. Vesey, 'Life of Bramhall', in *The works of the most reverend father in God, John Bramhall, D.D.*, ed. J. Vesey (1676)

**Corbet** [Corbett], **John** (1609–1670), politician and judge, was the eldest son of Richard Corbet, gentleman of Halston, Shropshire. He was educated at Shrewsbury School and entered Gray's Inn on 6 June 1627. On 11 February 1639 he was called to the bar and about November 1641 he married Abigail (*d.* 1696), daughter of the alderman and later lord mayor Isaac *Penington. He is known to have inherited his father's lands at Pontesbury, Shropshire, and was possibly a presbyterian in religion.

Corbet entered the Long Parliament as a recruiter member for Bishop's Castle about February 1646, having been recommended by Samuel More, the son of his deceased predecessor and his own cousin. He joined his namesake, Sir John Corbet, bt (*d.* 1665), who had sat for the county of Shropshire from the beginning of the Long Parliament in November 1640. In parliament Corbet initially assumed a decidedly pro-army stance and in the summer of 1647 he chaired a committee set up to hear charges of delinquency against Lord Inichquin's agent, Sir Philip Perceval, and upwards of thirty other members who had had suspicious contacts with the king. He was subsequently one of fifty-eight members who fled to the army in late July 1647 in the face of popular pro-royalist violence in London. Corbet survived Pride's Purge in December 1648 and the Rump subsequently named him to the high court of justice set up to try the king on 6 January 1649. However, like the majority of the common-law bar and bench, he distanced himself from the proceedings and neither served on the court nor signed Charles's death warrant. In February 1649 he registered his dissent to the Long Parliament's vote of 5 December 1648 in favour of continued negotiations with the king and accordingly took his place in the Rump Parliament.

During the years of the Commonwealth Corbet was active both in government and the law. In the Rump he was part of a group of lawyers including Bulstrode Whitlocke and Thomas Widdrington who united in common opposition to proposals for legal reform. He became an ancient of his inn on 24 May 1650 and was elected to the council of state on 19 November 1651. Later, in May 1652, he became chair of the parliamentary committee for Ireland. As a lawyer he was not permitted to sit in the Barebone's Parliament, but his legal career appears to have flourished during the interregnum. On 29 June 1653 he was appointed chief justice of the great sessions in Wales for Brecknockshire, Glamorgan, and Radnor. On 21 May 1658 he became a bencher of Gray's Inn and the following year was made a serjeant-at-law, possibly as a prelude to further promotion to the bench at Westminster. However, this promotion never materialized.

Following the Restoration, in August 1660 Corbet resigned his office. It is likely that his rank of serjeant was not confirmed. He died in 1670 and was buried on 7 February that year at Pontesbury. Corbet's wife, Abigail, lived until 1696, at which time his familial lands at Pontesbury fell to Nicholas Lechmere, husband to Corbet's daughter Judith.                                    D. A. ORR

**Sources** H. A. Nenner, 'Corbet (or Corbett), John', Greaves & Zaller, *BDBR*, 1.175 · G. Yule, *The independents in the English civil war* (1958), 93 · B. Worden, *The Rump Parliament, 1648–1653* (1974), 30 · D. Underdown, *Pride's Purge: politics in the puritan revolution* (1971), 82–3, 371 · *VCH Shropshire*, 3.250–52; 8.274 · Baker, *Serjeants* · Foster, *Alum. Oxon.*

**Corbet, John** (*bap.* **1619**, *d.* **1680**), clergyman and ejected minister, was baptized on 14 February 1619 at Holy Trinity, Gloucester, the son of Roger Corbet, a shoemaker of Gloucester. He matriculated from Magdalen Hall, Oxford, in 1636 and graduated BA on 5 July 1639 (in 1658 he supplicated for the degree of BD). In 1640 he was appointed rector of St Mary de Crypt, Gloucester, and he was for two years (1641–3) usher at the attached grammar school, of which his undergraduate contemporary at Magdalen Hall, John Biddle, afterwards imprisoned for his anti-trinitarianism, was then master. When Gloucester was garrisoned by the parliamentarian army Corbet was appointed chaplain to the governor, Colonel Edward Massey. 'Out of abundant respect to my deare native place' and because 'the Action of these times transcends the Barons Warres, and those tedious discords between the House of *Yorke* and *Lancaster*', in 1645 he published *A historicall relation of the military government of Gloucester: from the beginning of the civill warre betweene king and parliament, to the removall of Colonell Massie* (sig. A2v).

On 15 December 1646 Corbet became curate of St James's, Duke's Place, London, but he had given up this post by November 1647. After staying briefly in Bridgwater, Somerset, he was appointed preacher at Chichester Cathedral, Sussex, on 19 September 1648. On 7 May 1656 he became rector of Bramshott, Hampshire. In 1654 he was appointed an assistant to the Sussex commission for approbation of public preachers (or triers), and in 1658 to the Hampshire commission.

Following the Restoration, in *The Interest of England in the Matter of Religion* (1660) Corbet argued that 'the Upholding of both Parties by a just and equal Accommodation' is 'more desireable, and more agreeable to the State of *England*, then the absolute Exalting' of either the presbyterians or the episcopalians (title-page). In his reply, *Interest Mistaken, or, The Holy Cheat* (1661), Roger L'Estrange denounced presbyterianism as a seditious movement acting under 'the Masque of Religion' (title-page). It was this opinion which prevailed, and following the Act of Uniformity in 1662 Corbet gave up a stipend of £200 per annum and left the established church 'to keep the Peace of his Conscience' (*Reliquiae Baxterianae*, 3.96, para. 206/1).

Following his ejection Corbet moved to London and 'lived privately, taking no employment till his first wife died' (Wood, *Ath. Oxon.*, 3.1265); of this first marriage, nothing is known. He then lived in the house of John Micklethwaite, a future president of the College of Physicians knighted in 1681, serving him as chaplain. In 1664 Corbet was reported to be preaching in Ironmongers Lane and at the Seven Stars, Ludgate Hill. In 1668 he was nominated by Thomas Manton 'in the roome of Mr. [William] Jenkyns' as a delegate in discussions concerning comprehension of nonconformists within the established church (Keeble and Nuttall, letter 760). In the episcopal returns of 1669 he was reported to be preaching at Fernhurst, Sussex, and at Chipping Barnet, Hertfordshire. About this time he married his second wife, Frances (*d.* in or after 1685), a daughter of William Twisse, prolocutor of the Westminster assembly, and he joined the household of Alderman Webb, of Totteridge, Hertfordshire, as his chaplain.

It may have been Corbet's presence in Totteridge which led Richard Baxter to choose it as his place of residence in the autumn of 1669 following his release from prison that summer. He had first met Corbet in 1642 when he took refuge in Gloucester for three months, and the two became lifelong friends who never had 'one displeasing word' (Baxter, *Sermon*, 27). When, in June 1670, Baxter and his wife, Margaret, took their second, larger, house in Totteridge, Corbet and his wife, Frances, moved in with them, and the two wives became as closely attached as their husbands.

Corbet left Totteridge early in 1672 when the declaration of indulgence offered the chance for renewed public ministry. 'His old flock at *Chichester*' invited him to return (Baxter, *Sermon*, 28) and he was licensed there as a presbyterian on 1 May 1672. At some point thereafter he engaged in oral disputation with Peter Gunning, then bishop of Chichester, at which Gunning inveighed against nonconformists as seditious schismatics, without allowing Corbet the right of reply, to the subsequent disapproval of John Tillotson, afterwards archbishop of Canterbury. In a letter to Gunning of 11 December 1679, Baxter recommended to the bishop *The Kingdom of God among Men* (1671) by 'your old troubled Neighbour Mr. *Jo. Corbet*', if Gunning would 'better understand us' (Keeble and Nuttall, letter 1037).

Corbet, like Baxter, was committed to moderation in

ecclesiastical affairs and to the incorporation of non-conformity within the established church. He consistently argued that the unity of the catholic Christian church lies in its confession of faith, not in any 'one ritual or set Form of Sacred Office, one policy or model of Rules and Orders', on which the New Testament is silent (*Point of Church-Unity*, 20). In his published works he wrote as one 'not eager for any Party, … with charity towards real Christians of all Parties', taking up Baxter's phrase 'meer Christianity' to define this interdenominational faith (*Kingdom of God*, sigs. A3–A3v, A4). In his prefatory epistle to Corbet's posthumous *An account given of the principles & practices of several nonconformists. Wherein it appears that their religion is no other than what is profest in the Church of England* (1682) Baxter, noting 'the agreement of all here written … with what I have Published', added 'But as we were of one Mind and Heart, our agreement is no wonder' (sig. A2). The *Account* is a classic defence of the nonconformists' faith as conscientious and practical protestantism, of 'healing principles' and the same 'Catholick Spirit' as the established church (Corbet, *Account*, 23), against caricatures of it as 'a mixture of folly and villany … turbulent and seditious' (ibid., 1). Like Corbet's anonymous *Discourse of the Religion of England* (1667) and *The Point of Church-Unity and Schism Discuss'd* (1679), and the tracts in his *Remains* (1684), the *Account* is marked by succinctness, lucidity, and accessibility. Baxter, both more prolix and more contentious than Corbet, so valued him as 'one of the most Calm, as well as Judicious Nonconformists' that he submitted the manuscript of his *Cure of Church Divisions* (1670) to him before publication 'and altered every Word that he wished to be altered' (*Reliquiae Baxterianae*, 3.72, para. 155). Corbet encouraged Baxter in the composition of his eirenical *Catholick Theologie* (1675), and Baxter consulted him in the course of negotiations with Tillotson and Edward Stillingfleet in 1675. He described Corbet as 'a Man of extraordinary Judgment, stayedness, moderation, peaceable Principles, and blameless Life, a solid Preacher, well known by his Writings' (ibid., 3.96, para. 206 (1)). These writings included the first volume of John Rushworth's *Historical Collections* (1659), which was 'much of his Composure' (ibid.), and later his *Self-Imployment in Secret* (1681), prefaced by John Howe, a collection of Corbet's private meditative and introspective papers, frequently reprinted. Calamy is a partial witness, but his testimony to Corbet is quite exceptional among his accounts of the ejected nonconformist ministers: 'A great Man every way' (Calamy, *Abridgement*, 2.333).

Corbet made his will in Chichester on 30 January 1679. It mentions property in Chichester and elsewhere in Sussex, and refers to his wife, Frances, his sons John and Samuel, his daughter Susannah, his brother Arthur, and his sister Jane Thomas. Corbet was 'many Years afflicted … with the Stone, which at last was his death' on 26 December 1680, probably in London (Calamy, *Abridgement*, 2.335). He was buried in St Andrew's, Holborn, London, on 31 December, Baxter preaching the funeral sermon. Following his death his 'Exemplary Wife' lived with Richard and Margaret Baxter as Margaret's companion until the latter's death in June 1681 (*Reliquiae Baxterianae*, 3.189, para. 66). In a letter to Richard Baxter of 1 November 1685 Frances Corbet writes that she often thinks to herself 'if it were now with me, as it was in times past, how glad I should be', and she looks forward to 'a safe, and a comfortable death' (Keeble and Nuttall, letter 1154). N. H. KEEBLE

**Sources** J. Corbet, *A historicall relation of the military government of Gloucester: from the beginning of the civill warre betweene king and parliament, to the removall of Colonell Massie* (1645) · J. Corbet, *An account given of the principles & practices of several nonconformists. Wherein it appears that their religion is no other than what is profest in the Church of England* (1682) · J. Corbet, *Remains* (1684) · R. Baxter, *A sermon preached at the funeral of … Mr. John Corbet* (1681) · *Reliquiae Baxterianae, or, Mr Richard Baxter's narrative of the most memorable passages of his life and times*, ed. M. Sylvester, 1 vol. in 3 pts (1696) · *Calendar of the correspondence of Richard Baxter*, ed. N. H. Keeble and G. F. Nuttall, 2 vols. (1991) · E. Calamy, ed., *An abridgement of Mr. Baxter's history of his life and times, with an account of the ministers, &c., who were ejected after the Restauration of King Charles II*, 2nd edn, 2 vols. (1713) · *Calamy rev.* · Wood, *Ath. Oxon.*, new edn · G. L. Turner, ed., *Original records of early nonconformity under persecution and indulgence*, 3 vols. (1911–14) · R. L'Estrange, *Interest mistaken, or, The holy cheat* (1661) · W. Kennett, *A register and chronicle ecclesiastical and civil* (1728) · Foster, *Alum. Oxon.*

**Archives** DWL, Baxter letters

**Corbet, Matthew Ridley** (1850–1902), landscape painter, was born on 20 May 1850 at South Willingham, Lincolnshire, the son of the Revd Andrew Corbet and his wife, Marianne Ridley, through whom he was descended from the Ridleys of Blagdon, Northumberland. Educated at Cheltenham College, Corbet was originally intended for a military career. Instead, he was apprenticed to Alexander Davis Cooper, a painter of landscape and literary subjects. Corbet studied art at Heatherley's School of Art and at the Slade School of Fine Art in London, where he was among the first intake of students. He then went on to the Royal Academy Schools. Corbet worked at first as a portraitist, influenced by the example of George Frederic Watts; portraits by him appeared at the Royal Academy summer exhibitions during the second half of the 1870s. Later in his career he seems to have restricted himself to painting friends, his last exhibited portrait being a likeness of the painter Walter Maclaren, shown at the Royal Academy in 1889; in the 1890s he made portraits of members of the family of the amateur artist George Howard, ninth earl of Carlisle.

Corbet spent a period of years away from England during the first half of the 1880s, devoting himself to landscape painting. In 1880 he travelled to Egypt, where he made oil sketches of the desert. By the winter of 1880–81 he was established in Rome, living at via di San Basilio 20 and joining a group of young artists in the city which included the sculptor Alfred Gilbert and the American painter Elihu Vedder. In Rome Corbet soon encountered the Italian painter Giovanni Costa, from whom he learned how to refine his landscape compositions by the use of subdued and harmonious colour. In the winter of 1883–4 Corbet was one of the group of painters of different nationalities—all of whom revered Costa—who formed the so-called Etruscan school. Later, Corbet's paintings

**Matthew Ridley Corbet** (1850–1902), by John McLure Hamilton, 1893

were shown with those of Costa at the exhibitions 'In arte libertas'.

Although the city of Rome and the Roman Campagna were Corbet's favourite painting grounds in the first half of the 1880s, he also made painting expeditions into the south, joining the community of artists that formed around Charles Caryl Coleman at Capri about 1882, and to the countryside near Perugia, where he shared a rented farm house with Gilbert and his family. In 1885 Costa settled at Bocca d'Arno in Tuscany. Corbet made frequent visits to Costa, staying with him or lodging at the Albergo Ascani at Marina di Pisa. Over the following years Corbet made a thorough exploration of the countryside of the coastal plain between Leghorn and Viareggio, as well as of the hills inland around Volterra and to the north of Lucca. That Corbet knew how to capture the characteristic effects of the Italian countryside in a delightful way was commented on by an obituarist:

> His knowledge of Italy is not that of a tourist; it is that of a poet-painter, whose imagination is stirred by the cadence of the hills, the magic of dark cypresses silhouetted against the evening sky, the elusive beauty of olive-clad slopes, the 'temper' of that country whose every valley, as mists steal silently across, is charged with memories. (*Art Journal*, 93)

From about the mid-1880s Corbet seems to have established a pattern of life between Italy and London. In the winter months he occupied a studio in The Avenue, off the Fulham Road. He had probably first met Sir Coutts Lindsay—the proprietor of the Grosvenor Gallery—in Rome, and from 1880 he was invited to send works to the Grosvenor summer exhibitions. In 1888 he transferred to the New Gallery, along with other progressive painters at the time when the Grosvenor was seen to be losing its position as the most interesting of the London summer exhibitions. In 1889 he won a bronze medal for his painting *Sunrise* at the Paris Universal Exhibition. Corbet was also a regular exhibitor at the Royal Academy, from where two of his landscapes, *Morning Glory* (one of a small number of English landscapes by Corbet) and *Val d'Arno*, were bought by the trustees of the Chantrey bequest, in 1894 and 1901

respectively (both Tate collection). In January 1902 Corbet was elected an associate member of the Royal Academy.

On 17 March 1891 Corbet married Edith Jane Murch, *née* Edenborough (*b.* 1846/7), the widow of the painter Arthur Murch and herself a landscape painter and an Italophile. They lived together in London at 54 Circus Road, St John's Wood, and it was there that Corbet died on 25 June 1902, following an attack of pleuro-pneumonia. His wife survived him, and his ashes were later taken to South Willingham. CHRISTOPHER NEWALL

**Sources** 'M. Ridley Corbet: the new associate of the Royal Academy', *Magazine of Art*, 26 (1901–2), 236–7 · *Art Journal*, new ser., 22 (1902), 92–3, 264 · *DNB* · I. McAllister, *Alfred Gilbert* (1929), 58–68 · C. Newall, introduction, *The Etruscans: painters of the Italian landscape, 1850–1900* (1989) [exhibition catalogue, Stoke-on-Trent Museum and Art Gallery, 1989] · b. cert. · m. cert. · d. cert.

**Likenesses** A. Gilbert, portrait medal, 1881, Musée d'Orsay, Paris · J. M. Hamilton, oils, 1893, NPG [*see illus.*] · E. Onslow Ford, bust

**Wealth at death** £2360 2*s.*: probate, 13 Aug 1902, *CGPLA Eng. & Wales*

**Corbet, Miles**. *See* Corbett, Miles (1594/5–1662).

**Corbet, Reynold** (*c.*1510–1566), judge, was the third son of Sir Robert Corbet (*d.* 1513) of Moreton Corbet, Shropshire, and Elizabeth, daughter of Sir Henry Vernon of Haddon, Derbyshire. The Middle Temple records no longer exist for most of the period of his membership, but he must have been admitted in the early 1530s and he became a bencher in 1552. Like Brooke, Dyer, and a number of other judicial contemporaries, he was trained as a pupil in the Middle Temple office of John Jenour. His reading in Lent 1552, on offices before escheators, was attended by Chief Justice Mountagu and three future chief justices (Serjeant Saunders, Brooke, and Dyer). Already as a junior barrister he had served as member of parliament (first for Wenlock, in 1542, and then for Shrewsbury), and had become recorder of Shrewsbury in 1547. He was also a justice of the peace for Shropshire.

At an unknown date Corbet married Alice, the daughter of John Gratewood of Wollerton, Shropshire. In 1553 he became a member of the council in the marches, and in 1558 a judge on the Anglesey circuit; soon after that he received a serjeant's writ, and was created at the general call in April 1559. On 16 October 1559 he was appointed a puisne justice of the queen's bench, and sat there for seven years. Dyer came close to accusing him of partiality in 1560 when, in the case of Lord Powis, he was the only judge supporting the plaintiff, Vernon, a member of his mother's family. He died on 19 November 1566, and was buried according to his testamentary directions at Stoke upon Tern, Shropshire, where there is an alabaster effigy in judicial robes, with his wife and children; around his shield of arms is a ribbon with the motto 'Corona lege fulcitur' ('The crown is secured by the law'). His opinion in *Stowell* v. *Lord Zouche* had the strange distinction of being reported posthumously by Plowden; although he died before he was able to deliver it in court, an autograph draft was found in his study.

By his will, made at Stoke on 26 August 1566, Corbet

made Alice his sole executor, and appointed as one of his overseers his elder brother Sir Andrew Corbet (*d.* 1578), barrister of the Middle Temple and vice-president of the council in the marches. Though seated at Stoke, he also had property in Cheshire and Staffordshire. He left six sons and five daughters. His grandson Sir John *Corbet, the politician, was created a baronet in 1627; the title became extinct in 1750.      J. H. BAKER

**Sources** HoP, *Commons, 1509–58,* 1.700 · Baker, *Serjeants,* 171, 506 · Sainty, *Judges,* 30 · will, PRO, PROB 11/49, sig. 1 · Foss, *Judges,* 5.475–6 · W. R. Williams, *The history of the great sessions in Wales, 1542–1830* (privately printed, Brecon, 1899) · *Reports from the lost notebooks of Sir James Dyer,* ed. J. H. Baker, 1, SeldS, 109 (1994), 35–36 · *Les commentaries, ou, Les reportes de Edmunde Plowden* (1571), fol. 375v · R. Tresswell and A. Vincent, *The visitation of Shropshire, taken in the year 1623,* ed. G. Grazebrook and J. P. Rylands, 1, Harleian Society, 28 (1889), 138 · inquisition post mortem, PRO, C142/145/26, 28 · A. E. Corbet, *The family of Corbet,* 2 vols. (1915–18)

**Likenesses** alabaster effigy on monument, *c.*1566, Stoke upon Tern church, Shropshire · oils (Reynold Corbet?), repro. in Corbet, *Family of Corbet,* 2, facing p. 269; Sothebys, 1946

**Corbet, Richard**. *See* Corbett, Richard (1582–1635).

**Corbet, Robert** (*d.* 1810), naval officer, is probably best remembered for the controversy associated with his later career and the circumstances surrounding his death. Born of an old Shropshire family, Corbet was commissioned a lieutenant on 22 December 1796, and served with distinction in command of the cutter *Fulminante* during the operations on the coast of Egypt in 1801; he was subsequently promoted commander on 29 April 1802. Upon the outbreak of the war against Napoleon in 1803 Corbet was given the brig *Bittern* and sent to the Mediterranean where he came under the command of Vice-Admiral Nelson. His activities on that station, and particularly his 'officer-like and regular' conduct (*Dispatches and Letters,* 6.363) attracted Nelson's support, and in April 1805 Nelson promoted him acting captain of the frigate *Amphitrite.* Four months later Corbet was transferred to the frigate *Seahorse* (38 guns) and, following the battle of Trafalgar, he was sent to the Jamaica station where his promotion to post captain was finally confirmed on 25 May 1806.

In November 1806 Corbet commissioned the frigate *Nereide* at Portsmouth and in March 1807 he was sent to escort transports carrying troops for the ill-fated campaign in the River Plate. After the withdrawal of British troops the *Nereide* returned to the Cape of Good Hope station. In August 1808 she was sent for refit to Bombay, where Corbet assumed the duties of a senior officer, thereby attracting the displeasure of his commander-in-chief, Sir Edward Pellew. The crew of the *Nereide* also raised a complaint against Corbet for cruelty, and Corbet responded by demanding a court martial. A shortage of post captains on the East India station meant that the frigate had to return to the Cape for the trial to take place. This was not explained to the crew and, believing that their complaint had been ignored, they mutinied. The mutiny was suppressed and when the ship arrived at the Cape, ten of the ringleaders were tried, found guilty, and sentenced to death. Nine were subsequently pardoned and one hanged. The trial of Corbet then took place. By

1809 Corbet had acquired a reputation for such brutality that it was noted that his seamen deserted even in hostile territory.

Corbet was certainly a very severe commander. Between August 1806 and March 1807, for example, he ordered 134 floggings in just 211 days, with an average of seventeen lashes on each occasion. This was a brutal record by contemporary standards. At his court martial Corbet defended himself by stating that he was following the usual custom at sea even though 'the consequences in two instances have been unpleasant' (Lavery, 403). Corbet justified his actions by arguing that he had inherited a poorly disciplined crew and that 'Severity must depend upon circumstances, and whenever I have been severe, circumstances have rendered it necessary' (ibid., 404). Corbet was subsequently acquitted on all counts except that of having caused men to be 'started' (casually beaten) with sticks of an improper size, and for this alone he was reprimanded. As a wider consequence of the court martial, however, the Admiralty implemented steps to prohibit 'starting'.

Corbet and the *Nereide* were immediately returned to the Cape of Good Hope station, where they were attached to a squadron under the command of Commodore Josias Rowley. In September 1809 Rowley ordered a detachment of his ships, together with troops from the island of Rodriguez, to attack the French-held harbour of St Paul's on the Isle Bourbon which had become a rendezvous for French cruisers. Corbet, having a strong previous acquaintance with the islands, was given responsibility for landing the troops. After several days French forces abandoned St Paul's and the harbour was captured, together with the French frigate *Caroline.* The *Caroline* was renamed *Bourbonnaise* and taken into the Royal Navy. Corbet, in recognition of his services at St Paul's, was given command of her and ordered to return to Plymouth; he arrived in the spring of 1810 and was immediately appointed to the more powerfully armed frigate *Africaine.* Corbet's reputation as a harsh captain was now so well known that the crew of that frigate promptly mutinied, refusing to hear him read out his commission. The mutiny was quelled after the frigate *Menelaus* was brought alongside and her guns run out in threat.

By the early part of September the *Africaine* was on station in the Indian Ocean. On 12 September the frigates *Africaine* and *Boadicea,* together with the sloop *Otter* (16 guns) and the gun brig *Staunch,* gave chase to two French frigates, the *Iphigénie* and *Astrée,* off the Isle Bourbon. During the night the *Africaine* out-sailed the other British vessels which were unable to close with her. At 2.20 a.m. on 13 September Corbet, apparently concerned that the French frigates might escape to Port Louis, engaged the *Astrée,* firing a double-shotted broadside into her starboard quarter. The *Astrée* immediately returned the fire, and on her second broadside Corbet was mortally wounded when a round shot struck off his right foot above the ankle and a splinter caused a compound fracture of the thigh on the same leg. After ten minutes the *Astrée,* having suffered some damage, surged ahead to escape from the *Africaine's* guns. The *Iphigénie* by this time had ranged up on the lee-ward side of the *Astrée*, and the *Africaine*, now commanded by Lieutenant Joseph Tullidge, ranged forward to engage her. As she did so the wind began to fall, leaving the *Africaine* with the *Iphigénie* on her starboard side and the *Astrée* on the larboard bow.

Both French frigates now took full advantage of their positions. By 4 p.m. the *Africaine* was in serious trouble, having lost her jib-boom, foremast and mizen-topmast. Her remaining officers were also either wounded or dead. By 4.45 p.m. the becalmed *Africaine* could only man six of her guns, and with the *Boadicea* still 4–5 miles away Tullidge decided to strike the ship's colours. At the end of the action the *Africaine* had lost 49 dead and 114 wounded out of a crew of 295. Corbet himself had his leg amputated below the knee during the action, but died six hours later as a result of the wound.

Rumours about Corbet's death may have begun to circulate almost immediately. In his *Naval History of Great Britain* (1822) William James noted that there were many who insisted that Corbet was wounded by his own men, and had torn the bandages from his wounds rather than survive to face the loss of his ship (James, 5.183). In 1823 Edward Brenton wrote that because Corbet was hated by his men they

> would not defend their ship or *his* honour, because they had been ill treated,—a bad reason, but a true one. I have been told that they cut the breechings of their guns, and put *no shot* in them after the first or second broadside.     (Brenton, 2.370)

A decade later Basil Hall claimed that the crew of the *Africaine* had refused to reload their guns, preferring to be mown down by the French broadsides. Hall's comments invoked a spirited defence of Corbet by Captain Jenkin Jones, who had been on board the *Africaine* at the time of Corbet's death. Jones's account made Hall publicly retract his earlier comments, and even today the account constitutes a warning against reaching a hasty conclusion about Corbet, whose professional advancement clearly owed much to his skill and reputation for courage. Nevertheless, Corbet's system of discipline was at times exceptionally severe, and it is this as much as the circumstances of his death which has ensured his notoriety.

J. K. LAUGHTON, *rev.* TOM WAREHAM

**Sources** J. Jones, 'Character and conduct of the late Capt. Corbet vindicated, in a letter to the editor', *United Service Journal*, 3 (1832), 162–71 [incl. response from Captain Basil Hall and a letter from Captain Thomas Bennett RN] • captain's log, HMS *Nereide*, 16 Aug 1806–30 Sept 1808, PRO, ADM 51/1941 • B. Lavery, ed., 'Court martial on Captain Corbet of HMS *Nereide*, 1809', *Shipboard life and organisation, 1731–1815*, Navy RS, 138 (1998), 401–8 • W. James, *The naval history of Great Britain, from the declaration of war by France in 1793 to the accession of George IV*, [8th edn], 6 vols. (1902) • *Naval Chronicle*, 25 (1811), 157, 160–61, 176, 245 • B. Hall, *Fragments of voyages and travels*, 2nd ser., 3 (1832), 322 • *The dispatches and letters of Vice-Admiral Lord Viscount Nelson*, ed. N. H. Nicolas, 7 vols. (1844–6) • E. P. Brenton, *The naval history of Great Britain, from the year 1783 to 1836*, 2 vols. (1837) • J. D. Grainger, ed., *The Royal Navy in the River Plate, 1806–1807*, Navy RS, 135 (1996) • D. Syrett and R. L. DiNardo, *The commissioned sea officers of the Royal Navy, 1660–1815*, rev. edn, Occasional Publications of the Navy RS, 1 (1994)

**Archives** BL, letters to Lord Nelson and others, and log of HMS *Bittern*, Add. MSS 34919–34929 • PRO, letters to Admiralty

**Corbet, William** (1779–1842), revolutionary and soldier, was born at Ballythomas, co. Cork, on 17 August 1779, one of eight children in a protestant family. He was well educated by his father, who was a classical scholar and schoolmaster. He and his brother Thomas entered Trinity College, Dublin, in 1794. At college he took more interest in politics than in his work, and became a member of the Society of United Irishmen and a friend of T. A. Emmet and Hamilton Rowan. He was also a leading debater in the Trinity College Historical Society, of which he was for some time secretary, and was one of the students who signed the address to Grattan in 1795 in support of Catholic emancipation. In 1798 there was an inquiry by Lord Clare, the chancellor of the university, and Patrick Duigenan into the conduct of the undergraduates; it was alleged that a treasonable song had been sung at a social meeting in Corbet's rooms. Lord Clare asserted the existence of an assassination committee, and Corbet was solemnly expelled with eighteen others, including T. A. Emmet. He subsequently became more deeply involved in revolutionary politics and fled to France, where he received a commission as captain, and was appointed to accompany the staff in Humbert's expedition to Ireland in 1798. He was on the same ship as Napper Tandy, which did not land in Ireland, and he therefore got safely back to France. He was then made an adjutant-general, and while he was at Hamburg, planning another descent upon Ireland, he was arrested there, contrary to international law, by Sir James Craufurd, the English resident, together with Napper Tandy, Blackwell, and Morres, in November 1798. After being confined for some months at Hamburg, he was sent off to England in an English frigate in September 1799. Lord Grenville did not quite know what to do with these prisoners; Bonaparte loudly denounced their arrest, and declared his intention of executing certain English prisoners at Lille if any harm came to them; and they were held in Kilmainham prison at Dublin without being brought to trial. From Kilmainham, Corbet and Blackwell made their escape in 1803, and after many risks and adventures arrived safely in Paris. Corbet gave an account of his escape in his autobiography, published in Paris in 1807, and Maria Edgeworth used the episode in her novel *Ormond* (1817).

Corbet's commission of 1798 was recognized, and he entered the Irish Legion, from which he was soon transferred as a captain to the 70th French regiment of the line. With the French army he served in Masséna's expedition to Portugal, and greatly distinguished himself in the retreat from Torres Vedras and especially at the battle of Sabugal. When Marmont succeeded Masséna he took Corbet onto his staff, and after the battle of Salamanca, Clausel made him *chef de bataillon* of the 47th regiment. He served in this capacity until 1813, when Marmont summoned him to Germany to join his staff, where he served throughout the campaigns of 1813 and 1814; he was made

a commander of the Légion d'honneur. After the first abdication of Napoleon he was promoted colonel in January
1815, and acted as chief of the staff to General d'Aumont at
Caen. After the second restoration he was placed on half
pay, and was looked upon with disfavour by the Bourbons
because of his friendship with General Foy, the leader of
the opposition, whose acquaintance he had made in
Spain. In 1828 he accompanied Marshal Maison in his
expedition to the Morea, in the face of the opposition of
Lord Stuart de Rothesay, the British ambassador at Paris.
His services in Greece were extensive. After serving as governor of Navarino, Messina, and Nauplia, he relieved
Argos from Colocotroni's attack. This victory was of the
greatest importance; it finally overthrew the Russian
party, upset the schemes of Count Capo d'Istria, and practically placed King Otho upon the throne. Corbet was
rewarded by being made a knight of the order of St Louis
and of the Redeemer of Greece, and was promoted
general of brigade. He succeeded General Schneider as
commander-in-chief of the French forces in Greece in
1831, and returned to France in 1832 with them. He was
soon after promoted general of division, and commanded
at Caen and Tulle. Corbet died, unmarried, at St Denis on
12 August 1842.          H. M. STEPHENS, *rev.* GERARD MCCOY

**Sources** R. R. Madden, *The United Irishmen: their lives and times*, 3rd
ser., vol. 1 (1846), 15–62 • R. Hayes, *Biographical dictionary of Irishmen
in France* (1949) • *The Times* (Sept 1842)
**Archives** TCD, corresp. and family papers
**Likenesses** T. W. Huffain, aquatint etching, NG Ire.; repro. in
Madden, *United Irishmen*, facing p. 15 • group portrait, coloured
lithograph, NPG • mezzotint, NPG

**Corbett, Edward James** [Jim] **(1875–1955)**, hunter and
conservationist, was born at Naini Tal, India, on 25 July
1875, the eighth child of Christopher William Corbett
(1822–1881), a postmaster, and his wife, Mary Jane (1837?–
1924), *née* Prussia, widow of Charles Doyle. From childhood, Jim (as he was commonly known) was closely
acquainted with the life of the jungle, spending many
nights alone in it and growing accustomed to the cries and
calls of bird and beast, and studying their natural history.
He also hunted, shooting birds and, later, big game, killing
his first leopard at the age of eleven. Initially educated by
his mother and half-sister Mary, he progressed to the Diocesan Boys' School (now Sherwood College), Naini Tal. He
had ambitions to be an engineer but a lack of family
money prevented this and, in 1895, he joined the Bengal
and North-Western Railway as a fuel inspector at Bihar;
later he was promoted to trans-shipment inspector at
Mokameh Ghat, Bengal. In the First World War, with the
rank of captain, he helped to recruit a labour corps of
Kumaoni hillfolk, and commanded his own unit of 500 in
France in 1917: he brought 499 safely home. Promoted to
major, he served in the Waziristan campaign of the Third
Anglo-Afghan War (1919–21).

A legacy enabled Corbett to quit the railways and buy
into the partnership of a Naini Tal hardware and estate
agency business, and devote his time to the welfare of the
people of the Kumaon region. He and his sister Maggie,
with half-sister Mary, ran a surgery at Kaladhungi, the

Edward James Corbett (1875–1955), by J. G. Laithwaite, 1940

family winter home in the *terai*. Near by was the dilapidated village of Choti Haldwani. Corbett bought the village and surrounding farmland, turning them into a successful and much admired model community which still
exists. He built (with his own hands, working alongside
the local people) a wild-pig-proof stone wall 6 feet high
and 6 miles long, designed and installed a field irrigation
system, and experimented with agriculture, bringing in
seeds and cuttings from trips he made to British East
Africa, where he hunted in Kenya and Tanganyika with his
lifelong friend Sir Percy Wyndham. Not all his experiments were fruitful. Introduced African bananas, grape-
fruit, vines, and coffee all failed miserably but a large-
kernelled maize was a considerable success.

In Naini Tal, Corbett's estate agency business flourished
by the letting of houses during the hot summer to Europeans escaping the heat of the plains. This business success in turn afforded him the opportunity to return to the
jungle to hunt. He was an expert shot and keen angler,
especially for mahseer. Over the 1920s he gradually realized the damage being done to the environment of
Kumaon by deforestation and increasing human population, and he began to preach conservationist theories and
to criticize British policies. His theories were dismissed
but he continued to pursue them, publish them, and
cause controversy, often to his detriment. He took against
shooting for sport and turned to big game photography,
using both still and movie cameras. With the infinite
patience and courage of a hunter, using bait animals and
his ability to call up leopards and tigers by imitating their
calls, he took the first moving pictures of a rare white tiger
at a distance of 30 feet, without a telephoto lens.

Although eschewing shooting, Corbett accepted
responsibility for hunting down man-eating tigers and
leopards, much to the anxious chagrin of his sister Maggie, with whom he lived all of his life and whose obsessive
possessiveness of her brother prevented him from marrying. Between 1907 and 1945 he dispatched at least twelve
man-eaters. Wiry and incredibly fit, he endured terrible
hardships and sometimes illness in the execution of his
errands of mercy. He frequently went without adequate

sleep or food for days on end, and spent many long nights hunched on a makeshift platform in a tree overlooking a kill, sometimes the gruesome remains of the most recent human victim. He was in continual danger and more than once was nearly killed. His resolve and bravery became legendary and brought him the deepest affection and even worship of the Kumaoni people, who still regard him as a *sadhu* or holy man. He maintained that no tiger or leopard was by nature a man-eater but became one through injury or by the effect of human environmental factors such as careless hunting or habitat destruction.

During the Second World War, Corbett was too old for active service but he was, from 1940 to 1942, actively involved in the recruitment of over 1400 soldiers for a Pioneer Corps. Later, with the rank of lieutenant-colonel, he trained British troops in jungle survival techniques in readiness for the invasion of Burma. His survival lessons included warning against bathing in jungle pools because they often housed sleeping pythons and the issuing of silk stockings to combat troops as the fine mesh of the silk prevented leeches from gaining purchase on the skin: the latter recommendation was not officially sanctioned.

Under the instigation of Lady Violet Haig, wife of the provincial governor, Corbett wrote a thin, privately published booklet on his man-eater hunting escapades. Entitled *Jungle Stories*, it was modest yet thrilling and filled with jungle lore as well as ripping-yarn excitement. This developed into three commercially published books: *Man-Eaters of Kumaon* (1946), *The Man-Eating Leopard of Rudraprayag* (1948), and *The Temple Tiger* (1954).

In 1947 Corbett and his sister Maggie decided to leave India and settle at Nyeri, Kenya, living near relatives and renting a cottage in the grounds of the Outspan Hotel, which had originally been built for Lord Baden-Powell. Corbett was made an honorary game warden, and devoted much of his time to photographing and filming wildlife, and to writing. In addition to the works already mentioned, he published the autobiographical *My India* (1952), *Jungle Lore* (1953), and *Tree Tops* (1955), an account of the visit of Princess Elizabeth and the duke of Edinburgh to the famous game-viewing lodge near Nyeri. He was with the royal party on the night the princess ascended to the throne. Of his books in English well over 2 million have been sold, with translations in eighteen languages.

Tall, slim, and blue-eyed, Corbett was a handsome, scrupulously honest, and modest man, kind and generous, and beloved and admired by all who knew him, no matter what their rank. He was awarded the volunteer decoration (1920), the kaisar-i-Hind gold medal (1928), the OBE (1942), and the CIE (1946), and was granted the freedom of the forests in India, a privilege given only once previously to a European. In 1957 the Indian government renamed the Hailey National Park, the famous tiger sanctuary in Garhwal, the Corbett National Park 'in memory of one who had dedicated his life to the service of the simple hill folks of Kumaon'. Corbett died at the Mount Kenya Hospital, Nyeri, on 19 April 1955, and lies in the same cemetery as Baden-Powell, at St Peter's Church, Nyeri. He is today considered one of the earliest conservationists and the father of the movement to save the tiger from extinction.                                    MARTIN BOOTH

**Sources** M. Booth, *Carpet sahib: a life of Jim Corbett* (1986) · *DNB* · private information (2004) · personal knowledge (2004) · *CGPLA Eng. & Wales* (1956)

**Archives** Oxford University Press, MSS

**Likenesses** J. G. Laithwaite, photograph, 1940, BL [*see illus.*] · photographs, priv. coll. · photographs, repro. in Booth, *Carpet sahib*

**Wealth at death** £13,553 12s. 6d. in England: probate, 4 Feb 1956, *CGPLA Eng. & Wales*

**Corbett, Harry** (1918–1989), children's entertainer, was born on 28 January 1918 at 27 Edmund Street, Horton, Bradford, Yorkshire, the elder son of James William Corbett (1884–1960), coalminer, and his wife, Florence (1884–1948), daughter of Harry Ramsden of Bradford, founder of the fish and chip dynasty. Harry Corbett was educated at elementary school and at the Carlton high school, Bradford. He also received piano lessons from a private tutor from the age of seven and became a promising pianist, encouraged by his parents, who bought him a Steinway grand for £300. He was also greatly influenced by his uncle, Harry *Ramsden, the entrepreneur and showman who transformed his father's business into 'the biggest fish and chip shop in the world' (Mosey and Ramsden, 5), and his first public performance in his early teens was playing the piano at the opening of Ramsden's new fish and chip restaurant at Guiseley in 1931, where he subsequently often entertained diners as an amateur pianist.

For a time Corbett considered a musical career, but suffered in his teenage years from hereditary deafness and decided to leave school at sixteen to begin an electrical engineering apprenticeship with Crompton Parkinson at Guiseley, where his own father had acquired a fish and chip shop after retiring from mining. Corbett worked for Crompton Parkinson for thirteen years and then joined the Vulcan Boiler Insurance Company as an engineer surveyor, where he remained for a further five years. He retained his interest in music, however, and in 1939 formed a trio, the Rhythmists, with his younger brother, Leslie, as saxophonist and a friend as drummer. He also took up amateur conjuring and magic in 1940. In 1942 he met Marjorie Kathleen Maud Hodgson (1922–1995), a lively nineteen-year-old waitress at his uncle's restaurant. They were married in a joint wedding ceremony with his brother and his bride at Guiseley parish church on 8 July 1944, at the insistence of their mother. Their father, it later emerged, had been a lapsed Catholic, but neither son professed any particular religious affiliations.

Corbett's career changed direction in 1948, when he purchased a glove puppet teddy bear on Blackpool's north pier for 7s. 6d. to entertain his two young sons. He incorporated the puppet into his conjuring act and the bear made its stage début at Pudsey Conservative Club in 1948. After attracting the attention of a television producer at the Manchester Radio Exhibition in 1952 he subsequently appeared on BBC television's *Talent Night* on 3 May 1952. The *Sunday Express* of 4 May enthused: 'five minutes on the

Harry Corbett (1918–1989), by Count Zichy for Baron Studios, 1954 [with Sooty]

television screen last night established Harry Corbett's teddy bear as a rival to Muffin the Mule' (Tibballs, 24). On 18 October 1952, with the support of his wife, he turned professional, giving up his job as a £15 per week electrical engineer. The bear, originally known as Teddy, was rechristened Sooty after the application of chimney soot to its ears and nose to give the bear more character. The untimely death of Annette Mills in 1955 resulted in the demise of his nearest rival, Muffin the Mule, and a whole generation of children with a very limited choice in television viewing became enraptured by the antics of the mischievous bear, which was given its own television show in 1956. Corbett's mobile pianist's fingers enabled him to manipulate the puppet with dexterity in what was essentially a music-hall routine with Corbett acting as straight man to the impish bear. Sooty, who spoke only in inaudible whispers to his long-suffering presenter, made Corbett's life a misery by ruining his conjuring tricks, spraying him with water, pelting him with flour, and hitting him on the head with a balsa wood hammer in the tradition of Punch and Judy, much to the delight of his audience of children.

Five years later another puppet, Sweep, joined the act, operated by Corbett's brother, Leslie, who provided the doleful and rather dim dog's distinctive squeaky voice by blowing through a reed. Subsequently other characters were also added, including Butch the dog, Ramsbottom the snake, and Soo, a cute panda, the first female character, operated by Corbett's wife. Her introduction to the show, however, created a furore. Corbett's initial suggestion that Sooty should be provided with a girlfriend had been dismissed on the grounds that it would be introducing an undesirable sexual element into the children's programme. Predictably the tabloid press had a field day, and the BBC establishment was eventually obliged to relent to Soo's inclusion on condition that the two characters never touched. However, the new character subsequently attracted further controversy when feminist critics complained that she was too often portrayed doing all the housework; as a corrective she was allowed to mend Sooty's motorbike, while Sooty made fairy cakes with

Sweep. Moreover, Sooty had also been required to desist from dealing hammer blows to his presenter's head after a father had been injured by his impressionable young son imitating the bear's antics.

The sensitivity to public opinion which was required of Corbett, who wrote all his own scripts, illustrated the influence achieved by the character at the peak of its popularity. The puppets became known internationally and a growing business built up around them through the sale of themed merchandise. By 1973 Corbett, who had earned a mere 12 guineas for each of his first six programmes with the BBC, was reputedly earning an annual £40,000. Sooty was later adopted as a mascot by Corbett's native city of Bradford, and a Sooty museum was opened in the nearby town of Shipley. Sooty's success was due in no small measure to the personality of its presenter. Corbett was a natural stage and television performer with a genuine affection for children, who loved the sound of children's laughter. With his receding hair, neatly combed back, revealing a rounded, genial countenance, he always appeared on stage and screen wearing a smartly pressed suit in full knowledge that it would require laundering after each performance. His self-effacing, softly spoken, gentle manner appealed to children. His most memorable catch-phrase, 'Izzy wizzy, let's get busy', and his weary, resigned farewell at the end of each show, 'Bye, bye, everybody, bye bye', became incorporated into the vocabulary of child rearing in the 1950s. Shrewdly, Corbett always ensured that his audience was on the side of youthful mischief against a grown-up desire for peace and quiet.

In 1968 Corbett reluctantly severed his links with the BBC after a new controller had insisted upon the need for a presenter with a more youthful image, offending Corbett by suggesting that he disguise his baldness by wearing a wig and modify his northern accent to help generate increased overseas sales of the programme. Corbett had cosmetic surgery to remove some of the puffiness from around his eyes, and negotiated a new £30,000 contract with Thames Television. After Corbett suffered a severe heart attack in London at Christmas 1975 his younger son, Matthew (b. 28 March 1948), a professional actor, stepped into his shoes, eventually buying out his father for £35,000, and ultimately selling his interests in the character to Guinness Mahon, a subsidiary of the Bank of Yokohama, for nearly £1.5 million in 1998. After relinquishing his television performances Harry continued his one-man stage shows, mainly in south-west England where he had purchased a 300-year-old thatched farmhouse at Child Okeford, Dorset, in 1966. He was appointed OBE for his charitable work in 1976 and died in his sleep on 17 August 1989 at his home, Pilgrims Farm, Child Okeford, Blandford Forum, after playing to a capacity audience at Weymouth Pavilion on the previous evening. He was cremated on 25 August at Poole, Dorset, following a funeral service conducted by the rector of Child Okeford. He was remembered as a man of simple pleasures who, when he was not entertaining children, enjoyed a quiet game of golf and a weekly fish and chip supper with his wife at a local public house. His death attracted relatively scant television and press coverage for someone who had created a British institution. Indeed, at the time of his death Sooty was already in the record books as the longest running television show in the world. However, in 1996 Corbett and his mischievous bear appeared on a series of Royal Mail postage stamps to celebrate fifty years of children's television.　　JOHN A. HARGREAVES

**Sources** G. Tibballs, *The secret life of Sooty* (1990) · *The Times* (21 Aug 1989) · *Daily Telegraph* (19 Aug 1989) · *The Guardian* (19 Aug 1989) · *Bradford Telegraph and Argus* (19 Aug 1989) · *Wharfedale and Airedale Observer* (22 Aug 1989) · *Yorkshire Life* (Sept 1992) · *Pennine Magazine* (Dec 1983–Jan 1984) · Yorkshire TV, *A big hand for Sooty* (1998) · J. Evans, *Guinness TV encyclopaedia* (1995) · private information (2004) [M. and L. Corbett, sister-in-law and brother; M. Corbett, son] · D. Mosey and H. Ramsden jun., *Harry Ramsden*, 2nd edn (1994) · b. cert. · m. cert. · d. cert. · b. cert. [mother] · m. cert. [parents] · d. certs. [parents]
**Archives** FILM BBC WAC · BFI NFTVA, *This is your life*, Thames, 21 Feb 1988 · BFI NFTVA, current affairs footage · BFI NFTVA, documentary footage · BFI NFTVA, performance footage · Yorkshire TV, *A big hand for Sooty* | SOUND BL NSA, performance footage
**Likenesses** Count Zichy for Baron Studios, photograph, 1954, NPG [*see illus.*] · photographs, 1955–82, Hult. Arch. · portrait on postage stamp, 1996 (with Sooty) · photograph (with Sooty), repro. in *Guardian* · photographs, repro. in Tibballs, *The secret life of Sooty* · photographs, repro. in Mosey and Ramsden, *Harry Ramsden*
**Wealth at death** £80,918: probate, 6 Dec 1989, CGPLA Eng. & Wales

**Corbett, John** (1817–1901), chemical manufacturer and philanthropist, born at The Delph, Brierley Hill, Staffordshire, on 12 June 1817, was the eldest son in a family of five sons and one daughter of Joseph Corbett and his wife, Hannah. The father, originally a Shropshire farmer, moved to Staffordshire to become a carrier of merchandise by canal boats. John, after attending as a child Mr Geary's school at Brierley Hill, helped on his father's boats from the age of ten to twenty-three. He devoted his leisure to an unaided study of mechanical problems, and in 1840, at the mature age of twenty-three, was apprenticed for five years to W. Lester, chief engineer of Messrs Hunt and Brown of the Leys ironworks, Stourbridge. In 1846 he reluctantly abandoned the career of an engineer to become his father's partner, and under the name of Corbett & Son a prosperous business was carried on, a large fleet of boats being maintained between the Staffordshire district and London, Liverpool, Manchester, and other commercial centres. In 1852 the business was sold, the advent of railways threatening to decrease canal traffic, and Corbett then bought the Stoke Prior salt works near Droitwich. In April 1856 he married Anna Eliza, daughter of John O'Meara of co. Tipperary. They had two sons and four daughters.

Salt had been discovered at Stoke Prior in 1828 but efforts to extract it had been frustrated by the local geology. Corbett was aware that he was taking a risk in purchasing the premises of two defunct companies, which faced each other across the Worcester and Birmingham Canal. With a firm grasp of the mechanical, commercial, and economic problems, however, Corbett completely transformed the enterprise. He installed new brine pits lined with cast-iron cylinders to prevent the inflow of fresh water, and introduced a novel process whereby a system of pipes doubled the intensity of both the fire-heat and steam, yielding a whiter, more finely grained salt than was obtainable elsewhere, the size of the grain or crystal depending on the temperature at which the brine was evaporated. Fifty canal boats were acquired, and tributaries were excavated from the canal to the warehouses in which the salt was stored in lofts. A railway was laid down within the works, to carry coal to and salt from such places as could not be reached by water, and a wagon factory, a foundry, fitting shops, sawmills, and a brickyard were established. As many as seven depots were established in London. Corbett himself supervised all details. Within twenty-five years he raised the annual output of salt from 26,000 tons to 200,000 tons, and built up the most perfect system of salt manufacture in the world. Corbett enjoyed excellent relations with his workpeople. He built model houses, gardens, schools, a club house, lecture room, and dispensary. In 1859 he abolished female labour at the works, and in order that the family incomes should not suffer, increased the men's rates of pay, an act of generosity commemorated by a window placed by public subscription in Stoke Prior church. He sold the works in 1889 to the Salt Union.

Corbett was interested in politics on the Liberal side. In 1868 he contested Droitwich unsuccessfully against the Conservative candidate, Sir John Pakington, but the voters reversed their decision in 1874, when Corbett defeated Pakington and was elected. He kept the seat in 1880; in 1885, when the old borough was merged in the mid-Worcestershire division, he was returned unopposed for that constituency. In the Commons, though never prominent in debate, he showed interest in questions of local taxation, advocated alterations in the laws of land tenure, and was an early advocate of women's suffrage. Opposed to Irish home rule, he joined the ranks of the Liberal Unionists in 1886 and was returned by a large majority in that interest in July 1886. He retired at the dissolution of 1892.

Corbett acquired from Lord Somers a large estate at Impney near Droitwich and from Athelston Corbet (not a relative) a second estate at Ynysmaengwyn near Tywyn in Merioneth. On the Impney property he erected a residence in the style of a French château of the time of François I. Having an interest in transport systems, he was a director of various canal companies and of the River Severn Navigation. He was elected an associate of the Institution of Civil Engineers in 1876. A generous supporter of philanthropic institutions in the midlands, Corbett presented land and buildings for Corbett Hospital to Stourbridge in 1892 and Salters' Hall, a building capable of holding 1500 people, to Droitwich. He also contributed generously to the funds of Birmingham University, of which he was a governor, to the University College of Wales, and to the Bromsgrove Cottage Hospital; he helped in the development of Droitwich as a health resort by the erection of St Andrew's Brine Baths (1889), and by the restoration of the old Raven Hotel and the building of the Worcester Hotel; he presented a church clock to Brierley Hill and placed memorial windows in the church there to his father and mother. To the development of Tywyn he contributed by the erection of a fine esplanade, a massive sea wall, and the provision of water and sewage systems. Corbett died at Impney on 22 April 1901.

S. E. FRYER, *rev.* ANITA MCCONNELL

**Sources** *The Times* (24 April 1901) · *Mining World* (27 April 1901) · J. Murray, *Worcestershire: handbook for travellers* (1894) · *Oil Trade Review* (4 Jan 1868) · *VCH Worcestershire*, 2.231, 263 · *PICE*, 145 (1900–01), 355–6 · *John Corbett* (privately printed, Stourbridge, [1893]) · B. Middlemass and J. Hunt, *John Corbett: pillar of salt* (1985) · d. cert.
**Archives** NL Wales, personal papers · Worcs. RO, deeds; estate, legal, and financial papers
**Likenesses** H. T. Wells, portrait, exh. RA 1895 · E. O. Ford, bust · photograph, repro. in *John Corbett Esq of Impney*
**Wealth at death** £412,972 5s. 4d.: administration, 28 Aug 1901, CGPLA Eng. & Wales

**Corbett, Sir Julian Stafford** (1854–1922), naval historian, the second son of Charles Joseph Corbett, architect and property developer, and his wife, Elizabeth, *née* Byrne, was born on 12 November 1854 at Walcot House, Kennington Road, Lambeth, London. He was educated at Marlborough College (1869–73) and at Trinity College, Cambridge (1873–6), where he gained a first class in the law tripos in 1876. In 1877 he was called to the bar and practised for five years, although he found the work irksome. In 1882 he abandoned it and, having private means, travelled extensively, visiting among other places India and the United States. In 1886 Corbett found in fiction an outlet for his literary ability: his first novel, *The Fall of Asgard* (1886), was quickly followed by *For God and Gold* (1887) and *Kophetua the Thirteenth* (1889). He was also drawn towards biography, contributing to the English Men of Action series the life of Monk in 1889, and in the following year that of Drake. In 1894 he reverted to fiction, his next novel being *A Business in Great Waters* (1895).

During this period Corbett continued to travel, visiting Norway frequently, and almost invariably spending the winter in Rome. His taste for sport and travel induced him in 1896 to accompany the Dongola expedition to the Sudan as special correspondent of the *Pall Mall Gazette*. His experiences were much less exciting than he had anticipated, but the campaign undoubtedly set him thinking about the conduct of war as a subject for his pen. In 1898 he produced his first serious contribution to historical literature, *Drake and the Tudor Navy*. As he had already written two novels on this theme as well as a biography, the choice of subject was natural enough, but his experiences as a war correspondent had sharpened his perceptions. A critical and popular success, the book was notable not only for its comprehensive use of archival material, but for Corbett's understanding of the relationship between national policy and the use of naval power. Although he was to develop a deep knowledge of sailing battle tactics, his insistence on the primacy of national strategy was to be an abiding theme in his work.

*Drake and the Tudor Navy* opened a new chapter in Corbett's life, but he was still uncertain about his future direction. His researches had brought him into touch with the Navy Records Society, recently founded by Sir John Knox Laughton, who persuaded him to edit a volume connected with Drake, *Papers Relating to the Navy during the Spanish War, 1585–1587* (1898). At forty-five Corbett was hesitating whether to resume the role of the novelist or to follow his friends' advice and stand for parliament, when his marriage on 7 February 1899 to Edith Rosa (*b.* 1870/71), only daughter of George Alexander, cotton manufacturer, of Manchester, made up his mind. At his wife's request, he decided to devote himself to serious historical writing.

The first fruit of this decision was *The Successors of Drake* (1900). Two years later (1902) Corbett edited for the Navy Records Society Sir William Slyngsbie's contemporary *Relation of the Voyage to Cadiz, 1596*. From 1900 onwards, at first with articles in the *Monthly Review*, he began to comment on contemporary defence matters, focusing initially on the need to integrate the efforts of both army and navy. He soon became involved in the movement for naval educational reform, which brought him into contact with Lieutenant Herbert Richmond and Admiral Sir John Fisher. In 1902 Corbett became lecturer in history to the Royal Naval War College, just established at Greenwich, and in 1903 was selected to deliver the Ford lectures at Oxford. In 1904 he presented the results of recent research in *England in the Mediterranean, 1603–1714*, a comprehensive study of naval strategy. Naval tactics next engaged his attention, and for the centenary of Trafalgar (1905) he prepared for the Navy Records Society *Fighting Instructions, 1530–1816*, a collection of documents illustrating the art of handling battle fleets in the days of sail. But at the War College it was strategy rather than tactics that his audiences required, and in 1907 he completed another notable contribution to the subject, *England in the Seven Years' War*. Benefiting from Corbett's study of the work of Clausewitz, this was a book which, more than any of its precursors, analysed the complex relationship between naval power and national policy.

During Fisher's term as first sea lord (1904–10), he called on Corbett to support many of his innovations, notably the *Dreadnought* and the battle cruiser, with historical argument in the public press and in material for government committees. Corbett did much to assist the admiral but he was always careful to limit himself to judgements which could fairly be deduced from historical analysis. In 1908, he edited for the Navy Records Society volumes dealing with *Views of the Battles of the Third Dutch War* and *Signals and Instructions, 1776–1794*, the latter a supplement to his *Fighting Instructions*. He also found time to write numerous articles and pamphlets, including *The Capture of Private Property at Sea*, reprinted by A. T. Mahan in *Some Neglected Aspects of War* (1907). But Corbett was chiefly engaged upon a new study, *The Campaign of Trafalgar*, published in 1910. His most important work so far, it disappointed some reviewers, who were expecting more emphasis on Corbett's controversial treatment of Nelson's tactics. They received instead what may be called the first staff history of a naval campaign. Nevertheless, Corbett's tactical assessments were sufficiently controversial to cause the formation of an Admiralty committee on the subject in 1912. Its findings largely vindicated him.

Corbett's continuing work at the War College and his revision of his associated pamphlet *Strategic Terms and Definitions used in Lectures on Naval History* (1906; the 'green pamphlet') caused him to present the essence of his doctrine in *Some Principles of Maritime Strategy* (1911). At the same time he was editing for the Navy Records Society the *Private Papers of George, Second Earl Spencer* (1913–14), which threw new light on naval administration in Nelson's day. On the appearance of the second volume of this work, he was awarded the Chesney gold medal by the Royal United Service Institution (1914).

When the First World War broke out Corbett offered his services to the Admiralty. In addition to organizing the collection of material for the history of the struggle at sea, he wrote pamphlets to press the allied cause with neutrals and supplied statements of historical parallels for the assistance of the naval staff. He also helped in drafting a number of key staff documents. His work in 1914–15 included advising on both the Dardanelles campaign and what Lord Fisher later termed his 'Baltic project'. In 1917 he was knighted.

Shortly before the war Corbett had undertaken to write a two-volume classified history of the naval campaigns of 1904–5; this was completed in 1915 under the title *Maritime Operations in the Russo-Japanese War, 1904–06*. This confidential work suffered from its timing and its very limited distribution. It received little or no official attention, despite the significance of much of Corbett's analysis to the First World War at sea. However, the experience that he gained was to prove invaluable in compiling the official history of the current naval war and strengthened the historian's hand when seeking access to materials and dealing with cabinet and Admiralty over the issue of censorship. The friendship of Maurice Hankey, secretary of the cabinet and the committee of imperial defence, proved of critical importance, but Corbett's path was not an easy one. All three volumes of *Naval Operations* (1920, 1921, and 1923) which Corbett wrote were marked by delay, debate, and attempts at suppression, particularly the last, which dealt with the battle of Jutland. He was forced to tread carefully, making his assessments implicit and leaving criticism often unstated. Even then the Admiralty disclaimed agreement with Corbett's narrative of Jutland, complaining that the 'tendency to minimise the importance of seeking battle' was in conflict with the navy's views. This misinterpretation of Corbett's insistence on a utilitarian approach to command of the sea had been a recurring theme in the previous decade. It had brought him into conflict with Lord Sydenham of Combe immediately after Jutland when the latter blamed Corbett's teachings for the indecisive result.

In 1921 Corbett delivered the Creighton lecture at King's College, London, sketching in outline the subject which he had put aside to chronicle the Russo-Japanese War, and to which he always hoped to return—'Napoleon and the British navy after Trafalgar' published in the *Quarterly Review*, in April 1922. But his plans were frustrated. The strain and bitterness of the controversies over *Naval Operations* had taken their toll and Corbett died quite suddenly,

of heart disease, at Manor Farm, Stopham, Pulborough, Sussex, on 21 September 1922, only two weeks after delivering the manuscript of the third volume of *Naval Operations*. He was survived by his wife and by one son and one daughter.

Corbett had a natural bent for history, collected rare books and manuscripts, and wrote in a cultured and arresting style. There was as much of the philosopher in him as the historian. It was fortunate that his career was undetermined when the Royal Naval War College was instituted. Finding in him the instrument it needed, it inspired the series of monographs and histories which won for Corbett a wide measure of esteem and, for the Royal Navy, a more profound understanding of its purpose. G. A. R. CALLENDER, *rev.* JAMES GOLDRICK

**Sources** B. Ranft, 'Sir Julian Corbett', *Maritime strategy and the nuclear age*, ed. G. Till (1984) • D. M. Schurman, *Julian S. Corbett, 1854–1922: historian of British maritime policy from Drake to Jellicoe*, Royal Historical Society Studies in History, 26 (1981) • D. M. Schurman, *The education of a navy: the development of British naval strategic thought, 1867–1914* (1965) • D. M. Schurman, 'An historian and the sublime aspects of the naval profession', *Dreadnought to Polaris: maritime strategy since Mahan*, ed. A. M. J. Hyatt (1973) • D. M. Schurman, 'Julian Corbett's influence on the Royal Navy's perception of its maritime function', *Mahan is not enough: the proceedings of a conference on the works of Sir Julian Corbett and Admiral Sir Herbert Richmond* [Newport, RI, 1993], ed. J. Goldrick and J. B. Hattendorf (1993), 51–63 • P. M. Stanford, 'The work of Sir Julian Corbett in the Dreadnought era', *United States Naval Institute Proceedings*, 77 (Jan 1951) • J. T. Sumida, 'The historian as contemporary analyst: Sir Julian Corbett and Admiral Sir John Fisher', *Mahan is not enough*, ed. J. Goldrick and J. Hattendorf (1993) • b. cert. • m. cert. • d. cert. • *CGPLA Eng. & Wales* (1922)

**Archives** King's Lond., Liddell Hart C., corresp. and papers • NMM, corresp. and papers • priv. coll. | BL, corresp. with Lord Keyes • CAC Cam., corresp. with Lord Fisher • NMM, Richmond, Slade MSS

**Wealth at death** £63,636 5s. 6d.: probate, 20 Dec 1922, *CGPLA Eng. & Wales*

**Corbett, Miles** (1594/5–1662), politician and regicide, was probably born in Sprowston, Norfolk, where several generations of the Corbett family are buried, the second son of Sir John Corbett, baronet (*d.* 1628), who married a daughter of Sir Arthur Capel. A pedigree compiled between 1655 and 1659 lists Thomas Corbett, usually referred to as Miles's father, as his great-uncle; Sir Thomas Corbett, Miles's elder brother, was still living in the 1650s. Miles Corbett matriculated as a pensioner at Christ's College, Cambridge, in 1612, and subsequently was admitted to Lincoln's Inn. His father was imprisoned for nearly a year in Westminster gatehouse for refusing to pay or support the collection of the forced loan of 1628: Miles was recorder of, and in 1628 MP for, Great Yarmouth, where he prepared a petition calling for the town to be excused payment of the loan.

Corbett was elected for Great Yarmouth in the Short and Long parliaments of 1640. Edmund Ludlow praised him for 'joyning constantly with those who most eminently appeared for the cause of God and their country' over thirty-seven years. As a close colleague, Ludlow appears to have had access to Corbett's posthumous 'confession' (Ludlow, *Voyce*, 300). Corbett's opinion of his own diligent and faithful service stemmed from the many committees on which he efficiently served, as did his opponents' accusations of Corbett's arbitrariness, and a posthumous reputation as a cynical self-server. He chaired the committee which prepared a bill against scandalous ministers (22 March 1641), the committee for examinations, and that which drew up charges against Archbishop Laud. In 1644 he was created one of two clerks of the court of wards and, with Robert Goodwin, was granted the registrar's office in chancery in place of Walter Long in 1648.

Corbett was a target of presbyterian stalwarts who responded to radical Independents who deprecated their commitment to liberties by accusing men like Corbett of arbitrary, self-seeking tactics. Denzil Holles called Corbett's committee for examinations a 'continual horse-fair … even like dooms-day itself, to judge persons of all sorts and sexes' (Holles, 1.265). Corbett was also satirized in 1645 in *A most learned speech spoken in the House of Commons by Miles Corbet, taken in short hand by his clarkes*. The presbyterians accused Independents of captious proceedings which furnished huge estates, while the latter protested that their constancy had wasted them.

Corbett was named to the high court of justice to try Charles I, attended one session, and signed Charles's death warrant [see also Regicides]. In October 1650 he was appointed one of four civil commissioners in Ireland, landing in Waterford in late 1650. A carefully worded letter to the commanders in Ireland presented Cromwell's assumption of power in 1653 as a sign of God's displeasure at the progress of his reformation, but Corbett kept his place under the protectorate. Appointed to the council in Ireland in August 1654, he opposed Irish elections that year, claiming unsettled military and climatic conditions. As a member of the council he was appointed one of its commissioners to hear and determine cases of proposed transplantation to Connaught. In July 1655 he was created chief baron of the exchequer of Ireland.

Corbett's religious stance was shaped as one of a group of gentlemen at the inns of court influenced by the preaching of Preston and Ussher, and he was a particular friend of the Independent divine William Bridge. His extant professions, albeit composed shortly before his death, testified to his submission to providence, citing it as the key to his political actions. As an Irish commissioner he tried to use calls for days of humiliation to rally the godly, warning that the Lord should not find any 'beateing his fellow servants' (J. Mayer, 'Inedited letters of Cromwell, Colonel Jones, Bradshaw and other regicides', *Transactions of the Lancashire and Cheshire Historic Society*, new ser., 1861, 239–41, 241–3, 258–60).

Under the restored Rump, Corbett regained the post of Irish commissioner, managing the affairs of the army, and conducting a campaign described by Clarendon as the systematic replacement of presbyterians. Yet men such as Corbett were 'odious to the army as well to the people' (Clarendon, *Hist. rebellion*, 213), enabling presbyterians and royalists to move against them. In December 1659 (along with Ludlow and his fellow commissioners Jones and Tomlinson) Corbett was impeached by Sir Charles Coote,

president of Connaught, for maintaining in Ireland the interest of the republican party in England.

Corbett was returned for Great Yarmouth for the Convention Parliament in 1660, but lost his place in a double return. He then fled to the Netherlands, where he was betrayed by Sir George Downing, later expressing his bitterness towards a state supposedly sympathetic to the English republic. He was imprisoned in the Tower, dragged on a sledge to Tyburn, one of nine regicides to be partially hanged, disembowelled, and quartered and died, aged sixty-seven, on 19 April 1662, 'very cheerfully' and unrepentant (Pepys, 3.66). He described himself as grey-haired and, while escaping most scabrous, anti-Rump satire, was deemed 'bull-headed, splay-footed, bacon-faced Corbet' (*Lucifer's Lifeguard*, 1662). He was close to his wife, Mary, who survived him, and had several children including a son, John, to whom he wrote the day before his death that he bequeathed him his cause and his faith, but no estate.

SARAH BARBER

**Sources** Norfolk RO, MS 15577. 43. B · M. Corbett, 'Confession', Norfolk RO, MC 46/4/1, 488x1 · M. Corbett, letter to J. Corbett, 18 April 1662, Norfolk RO, MC 1304/1, 809x4 · 'Some occasional speeches of Mr Miles Corbett one the Sabbath before his death', Norfolk RO, MC 1304/2, 809x4 · W. Bridge, letter to M. Corbett, 30 Jan 1659, Norfolk RO, 46/3, 488x1 · *CSP dom., 1651–2* · *JHC*, 5 (1646–8) · Clarendon, *Hist. rebellion*, vol. 6 · E. Ludlow, *A voyce from the watch tower*, ed. A. B. Worden, CS, 4th ser., 21 (1978) · R. P. Cust, *The forced loan and English politics, 1626–1628* (1987) · R. Spalding, *Contemporaries of Bulstrode Whitelocke, 1605–1675*, British Academy, Records of Social and Economic History, new ser., 14 (1990) · C. V. Wedgwood, *The trial of Charles I* (1964) · *The memoirs of Edmund Ludlow*, ed. C. H. Firth, 2 vols. (1894) · D. Holles, 'Memoirs of Denzil, Lord Holles', *Select tracts relating to the civil wars in England*, ed. F. Maseres, 1 (1815) · Pepys, *Diary*

**Archives** Norfolk RO, MC 46/4/1, 488x1; MC 1304/1, 809x4

**Likenesses** R. Cooper, line engraving, BM, NPG · engraving (after scarce print in Col. Dowdeswell's collection published in 1810)

**Wealth at death** apparently none: Norfolk RO, Norwich, MC 1304/1, 809x4

**Corbett, Richard** (1582–1635), bishop of Oxford and of Norwich, and poet, was born at Ewell, Surrey, the son of Vincent Corbett (d. 1619), a nurseryman at Whitton, near Twickenham, and his wife, Benet (d. 1634). He was educated at Westminster School before going up to Broadgates Hall, Oxford, in 1598. Later that year he was elected a student at Christ Church, where he graduated BA on 20 June 1602 and proceeded MA on 9 June 1605. In 1612 he was senior student at Christ Church and served as junior proctor, pronouncing funeral orations in the university for both Prince Henry and Thomas Bodley. On 26 March 1613, in defiance of the canons of 1604, he was ordained deacon and made priest on the same day by John Bridges and at much the same time he identified himself with the emerging anti-Calvinists in his Passion Sunday sermon for 1613 when he 'insisted upon the Article of Christ's descending into Hell, and therein grated upon Calvin's manifest perverting of the true sense and meaning of it' (P. Heylin, *Cyprianus Anglicus*, 1668, 68). In 1616 he was recommended for election to the projected Chelsea College. For his Oxford BD on 8 May 1617 he defended the tenet that sacraments do not confer grace *ex*

Richard Corbett (1582–1635), attrib. Simon Luttichuys

*opere operato*, a discussion of the possible misinterpretation arising from article 30 of the Thirty-Nine Articles; he proceeded DD on the same day. In 1618 Corbett left Oxford for a tour of France, described in a letter to his friend and student contemporary at Christ Church, Sir Thomas Aylesbury, and the following year he inherited some landed property in the City of London after his father's death.

It was in 1620, however, that Corbett's ecclesiastical career began to gather momentum. In Aylesbury he was fortunate to have a ready supplicant at court: having been secretary to the earl of Northampton when he was lord high admiral, Sir Thomas was retained when the Howards fell from power by Northampton's successor as admiral, George Villiers, then marquess of Buckingham. In 1620 Corbett became not only rector of Puttenham, Hertfordshire, and a canon of Salisbury, but also in June dean of Christ Church; his 1622 poem 'A New Yeare's Gift to my Lorde Duke of Buckingham' (BL, Harley MS 1221, fol. 75*v*) makes it clear that he regarded Buckingham as the agent for his securing the deanery. Much of Corbett's poetry was aimed at post-hunting, and it was as a poet rather than a priest that his Oxford friends celebrated his elevation at Christ Church ('In admissionem decani Corbet oratio'; Christ Church, Oxford, MS 325, fol. 8). About 1620 Corbett married Alice (1602–1628), daughter of his subdean, Dr Leonard *Hutten (1556/7–1632), the antiquary, and his

wife, Anne Hamden. A journey north undertaken by Corbett and his father-in-law one August inspired *Iter boreale*, Corbett's most widely circulated poem.

By 1621 Corbett was also a royal chaplain and from that time was routinely listed among the twenty-one annual Lent preachers at court. He was not always at ease in the royal pulpit. During the 1621 summer progress he was called to preach before James I at Woodstock and there mangled his words and managed to tie the strings of his preaching bands with the royal ring he had just received, an event which still provoked comment years later. Corbett's friendship with Buckingham allowed him sufficient intimacy to help dissuade the duke from inclining to Catholicism during 1622 and 1623. Soon after the abortive negotiations for the Spanish match Corbett wrote to his patron on 23 February 1624, again seeking his help toward further promotion in the church; but when, on 30 July 1628, shortly before Buckingham's assassination, Corbett was nominated to the vacant see of Oxford it was primarily to make room in the deanery for Dr Brian Duppa, at the behest of the queen's chamberlain, the fourth earl of Dorset.

In the absence of any official residence for the bishop of Oxford, Corbett continued to live at Cassington, where he had become rector in 1622, despite repeated attempts to have his first fruits remitted and to regain the use of Gloucester Hall, Oxford. For a time Corbett seems to have been more concerned about his accommodation than his episcopal ministry: the only occasion on which he is recorded as consecrating other bishops was at the Croydon consecration of William Piers, for Peterborough, in October 1630, and from a letter from Archbishop Abbot to Secretary Dorchester it emerges that he had to be sent for by authority. It was presumably at Laud's request that Corbett assisted at the baptism of the duke of York at St James's in November 1633; Corbett had clearly sought to endear himself to Laud—when the latter became chancellor of the university he was among the first in Oxford to write to congratulate him, sending him congratulatory verses by way of cultivating his patronage (Christ Church, Oxford, MS 325, fol. 35).

Contemporaries knew Corbett as a wit, 'as his poems, jests, romantic fancies, and exploits which he made and performed extempore showed' (Wood, *Ath. Oxon.*, 2.594), but as a prankster he was not always so much liked and even as a bishop he could be inclined to inappropriate behaviour in the wine cellar if John Aubrey is to be believed (*Brief Lives*, 1.186). He was later remembered, in the high table gossip of one college, more for his *bons mots* than for action. In November 1634 the subject of the positioning of the holy table came up for discussion in the Queen's College and it was recalled that the conformist Corbett had said that 'he could not away with any ticktack conformity' (diary of Thomas Crosfield, Queen's College, MS 390, fol. 174*v*). He also apparently complained that George Birkhead at Bletchingdon let his church 'lay more undecent' than Corbett's own stable but that it had been made good with marble (ibid.). In the diocese he insisted upon decorous church order in his primary visitation of 1629, asking expressly whether 'any man or boy in time of divine service cover his head, or sit with his hat upon his head … or doth not use all other gestures and behaviours in time of divine service required in that 18 cannon'.

As his chaplains Corbett appointed men as gregarious as himself—William Strode, the university orator, and Thomas Lushington, in whose favour he resigned his prebendal stall at Salisbury. Both men followed Corbett from Oxford when on 7 May 1632 he was translated to the see of Norwich to make room for John Bancroft (who would do so much financially for the diocese and to assist Laud's buildings at St John's College). Corbett was bishop of Norwich for little more than three years, during which he made little impression on the vast diocese and may have inclined towards lax toleration. Whereas at his Oxford visitation Corbett had relied predominantly on those of John Howson (in 1619), his 1633 articles for the diocese of Norwich conformed closely to the 1619 set issued by John Overall. However, he followed Laud's policy of closing stranger churches, turning out the Walloon congregation that had used the bishop's chapel since 1619. He insisted upon the conformity of George Burdett, the truculent lecturer of Great Yarmouth, who had failed to make his Easter communion in 1633 and had roundly prayed that God was to be worshipped spiritually and not with any physical gestures. Corbett also encouraged his clergy to support the rebuilding of St Paul's Cathedral, admonishing one synod to bear in mind the benefits that all of them had had from sheltering in it.

Corbett died in Norwich on 28 July 1635, 'like a Roman, bravely' (PRO, SP 16/298/10) as George Garrard reported to Viscount Conway, at the comparatively young age of fifty-three. By his will, drawn up three weeks earlier, he left £1000 to his daughter Alice (1625–1682) and the residue of his estate to his son Vincent (*b.* 1627). Probate was granted on 5 September to the executrix, Corbett's mother-in-law, Anne Hutten, to whose care the children had been entrusted, their mother having died of smallpox in April 1628. Corbett was buried in Norwich Cathedral.

Nicholas W. S. Cranfield

Sources Foster, *Alum. Oxon.* · *The poems of Richard Corbett*, ed. J. A. W. Bennett and H. R. Trevor-Roper (1955) · PRO, SP 16 · BL, Harley MS 7000 [Stave 402] · BL, diocesan letters, Norwich, Harley MS 464 · diary of Thomas Crosfield, Queen's College, Oxford, MS 390 · Westminster Abbey Muniments, Book 15 · PRO, Lord Chamberlains' Books, LC 5/132 · Wood, *Ath. Oxon.*, new edn, 2.594 · *Brief lives, chiefly of contemporaries, set down by John Aubrey, between the years 1669 and 1696*, ed. A. Clark, 1 (1898), 186 · PRO, PROB 11/169 [fols. 33–33v] · *Reg. Oxf.*, 2/1.213 · Oxfordshire Archives, Oxf. Dioc MSS, e. 9, fol. 77v · Bodl. Oxf., MS Rawl. D. 853, fol. 172 · *The works of the most reverend father in God, William Laud*, 4, ed. J. Bliss (1854), 292 · Morgan L., St Paul's Cathedral MSS, i, fol. 59 · Christ Church Oxf., MS 325 · *Fasti Angl., 1541–1857*, [Ely]

Archives BL, corresp., Harley MSS 464, 7000 · Norfolk RO, synodal address

Likenesses attrib. S. Luttichuys, portrait, Christ Church Oxf. [*see illus.*] · portrait, Christ Church Oxf.

**Corbett, Thomas** (*d.* 1751), secretary of the Admiralty board, was the eldest son of William Corbett (*d.* 1699), a barrister at the Middle Temple, London, and Eleanor Jones, third daughter of Colonel John Jones of Nanteos, near Aberystwyth. After attending Westminster School he is recorded on 24 March 1704 as serving unofficially as an ordinary seaman on board the *Ranelagh*, the flagship of Rear-Admiral George Byng. This was the start of a close association with Byng that was to take Corbett to the secretaryship of the Admiralty board. The *Ranelagh* was part of the allied fleet in the Mediterranean during 1704 and was present at the successful attack on Gibraltar and the battle of Malaga (13 August). On 14 December Corbett was rated as Byng's clerk and four days later moved with Byng to the *Barfleur*. Corbett continued to move with Byng as his clerk and on 29 December 1705 he was appointed his secretary. On 8 November 1709 Byng was appointed to the Admiralty and on 6 December Corbett became Admiral Matthew Aylmer's secretary on board the *Royal Sovereign*, where he remained until 19 October 1710. Corbett resumed his career with Sir George Byng, now admiral of the white, when the latter took over command in the channel in July 1711, and joined him as his secretary on board the *Cumberland* on 22 July.

Byng returned to shore in September 1711 and Corbett was discharged on 28 December. Early in 1712 Corbett went to Utrecht to try to obtain a post among the diplomats who were gathering for the preliminary peace negotiations. A particular opportunity arose in March, with rumours of a vacancy of secretary to Thomas Wentworth, third earl of Strafford, the chief English plenipotentiary for the peace negotiations, but by August, Corbett was disappointed. All the while he reported his progress back to Byng. The disappointment was made worse on 30 September 1712 when Strafford became first lord of the Admiralty and, as the political crisis around the succession mounted, Byng was dismissed from the Admiralty commission on 19 January 1714.

After the Hanoverian succession Byng returned to the Admiralty on 14 October 1714 and Corbett was appointed a clerk to the board on 17 January 1715. Corbett maintained a close attachment to Byng. In a fulsome dedication to his translation of Michelet's *Mediterranean Pilot*, published in 1715, Corbett called Byng 'the best of friends' and he accompanied the admiral on the summer operations during the Jacobite rising. In 1716 Corbett was appointed secretary of Greenwich Hospital. Byng, who after 1718 was styled Viscount Torrington, left the Admiralty on 30 September 1721, but Corbett kept his post. Torrington was treasurer to the navy and probably played an important role in advancing Corbett to the post of chief clerk on 15 March 1723, despite the general convention of seniority. After the accession of George II, Torrington returned to the Admiralty in the commission appointed on 2 August 1727. The post of deputy secretary was revived for Corbett on 27 July 1728, probably reflecting the fact that the secretary, Josiah Burchett, at the age of sixty-two, was beginning to feel the strain of service.

It may be assumed that Corbett's role became more significant after his appointment as deputy secretary. The administrative records are not clear on this, but there are circumstantial indicators to suggest that Corbett possessed both the social status and professional expertise to make him a valued member of the Admiralty office. The twenty-one volumes of precedents that currently bear his name, some of which have annotations that appear in the hand of Torrington's successor, Sir Charles Wager, are testimony to his grasp of Admiralty affairs. He was confident enough to address both Torrington and George Anson as friends. When the duke of Bedford was brought into government as first lord of the Admiralty on 27 December 1744, his parliamentary supporters quickly came to appreciate Corbett's professionalism. Henry Legge, writing to Bedford on 17 August 1745, wrote of Corbett,

> We go on very lovingly and comfortably with our monocular secretary: when one comes to be better acquainted with him, he is not as bad as he looks for. It is true he has but one eye, but then he takes more exact aim at the matters in question with the remaining one.   (*Correspondence*, 1.37)

In the 1734 election, Corbett became member for Saltash in Cornwall, a borough controlled by the Admiralty, which he represented until April 1750. In the House of Commons, Corbett spoke for the ministry on a number of occasions. Six years after Torrington's death he published *An Account of the Expedition of the British Fleet to Sicily* (1739), including the victory at Cape Passaro which had earned Byng his title. The work, which was partly based on personal papers provided by the second Viscount Torrington, reflects Corbett's closeness to his patron. In the year following publication of his book Corbett married Mary Lloyd of Duke Street, London; they had one daughter.

With Burchett ailing and under pressure from the demands of the war that broke out with Spain in 1739 Corbett was appointed joint secretary with him on 29 April 1741, thereby reviving the practice that had periodically existed in wartime until it had been abolished in 1705. Burchett could not continue long and retired on 14 October 1742, leaving Corbett as sole secretary. Corbett retained the office until his death, but his declining health led to the establishment of a new post of second secretary, given to John Clevland, on 1 August 1746 to assist with the expanding workload. Corbett held the office of secretary to the Admiralty board for a shorter period of time than his distinguished eighteenth-century colleagues, Burchett, Clevland, and Philip Stephens, but his service to the board stretched over thirty-six years and his knowledge was clearly valued by the commissioners. He died on 30 April 1751.                                   RICHARD HARDING

**Sources** Royal Navy Museum, London, Corbett MSS, Admiralty collection, MS 121 · will, PRO, PROB 11/787, sig. 135 · *The Byng papers: selected from the letters and papers of Admiral Sir George Byng, first Viscount Torrington, and of his son, Admiral the Hon. John Byng*, ed. B. Tunstall, 3, Navy RS, 70 (1932), 11–20 · PRO, ADM 6/13, fol. 212v; 27 July 1728 · E. Cruickshanks, 'Corbett, Thomas', HoP, *Commons* · *Correspondence of John, fourth duke of Bedford*, ed. J. Russell, 3 vols. (1842–6)

**Archives** PRO, Adm. MSS · Royal Naval Museum, London | TCD, letters to John Baker

**Likenesses** T. Hudson, portrait; formerly at Admiralty, 1932 · G. Kneller?, portrait; formerly at Admiralty, 1932

**Wealth at death** books, plates, pictures, freehold and copyhold estates: will, PRO, PROB 11/787, sig. 135

**Corbett, Thomas Godfrey Polson**, second Baron Rowallan (1895–1977), chief scout of the British Commonwealth and empire, was born at Hans Place, Hans Crescent, Chelsea, London, on 19 December 1895, the second of three children and the elder son of Archibald Cameron Corbett, first Baron Rowallan (d. 1933), and his wife, Alice Mary (d. 1902), daughter of John Polson of Castle Levan, Gourock, director of the firm Brown and Polson. Corbett's father, a Scottish businessman and landowner, for many years a Liberal MP and a notable benefactor of the city of Glasgow, was created Baron Rowallan in 1911. Corbett was educated at Eton College and joined the Ayrshire yeomanry at the age of eighteen. He served in Gallipoli, Egypt, and Palestine in the First World War. After the second battle of Gaza he transferred to the Grenadier Guards, and suffered a severe leg wound on the western front. He was awarded the MC, but was invalided out of the army. His brother was killed in action.

In 1918 Corbett married Gwyn Mervyn (1899–1971), eldest daughter of Joseph Bowman Grimond, of St Andrews, Fife, a Conservative MP from a Dundee jute family. They had five sons (one of whom was killed in action in 1944) and a daughter. On leaving the army Corbett devoted himself to the family estate in Ayrshire and became a successful breeder of pedigree dairy cattle. He campaigned for the eradication of tuberculosis in cattle and was instrumental in the promotion of a government scheme for improvement in this area. Between 1929 and 1931 he was president of the Ayrshire Cattle Herd Book Society of Great Britain and Ireland and he was later president of the Royal Highland Agricultural Society. In 1936 he led a committee involved in the improvement of livestock in the Scottish islands and crofting areas. His interest in cattle was lifelong and in 1963 he played an active part in the campaign to eliminate brucellosis.

The family firm of Brown and Polson also engaged Corbett's attention and in due course he became its chairman. He inherited the title of Baron Rowallan on his father's death in 1933. He devoted much time to public service and to the Boy Scouts, and he interested himself in hospitals and in the problem of juvenile employment. He also maintained close links with the Territorial Army and in 1939 he was called upon to raise and train a new battalion of the Royal Scots Fusiliers. Led by Rowallan, the battalion went to France in April 1940 and saw fierce action before being evacuated in June. In spite of the inevitable problems arising from a shortage of experienced officers and NCOs, the battalion left the French coast better equipped than it had arrived, having collected arms and ammunition abandoned by others.

Thereafter Rowallan's leg wound confined him to home service. He commanded a young soldiers' battalion, where his training methods gained notable success with many of the toughest and least disciplined youngsters. Later, at a pre-OCTU training centre, he showed that many borderline or failed candidates could be brought up to the standard required in officers, and there is no doubt that the methods which he, with others, devised in wartime had immense influence on the training of young people in the post-war era, especially in the Outward Bound schools, the Duke of Edinburgh's award scheme, the Boy Scouts, and the cadet forces of the armed services.

Rowallan retired from the army in 1944 with the rank of lieutenant-colonel and was appointed chief scout of the British Commonwealth in 1945 after the early death of Lord Somers. He had become district commissioner for north-west Ayrshire in 1922 and from 1944 was commissioner at Scottish headquarters for leader training. As chief scout he devoted himself to reforging the international links broken by the war and to recovery and consolidation at home following the loss of many young leaders. He built on Lord Somers's 'post-war commission', introducing air scouts and replacing rovers by senior scouts. He travelled widely throughout the Commonwealth, being of an apparently iron constitution, though his leg wound necessitated a walking-stick.

Tall, well-built, and always wearing a kilt, Corbett had a fine presence. He was a resourceful and effective speaker to large audiences of boys, never consulting a note and making good use of anecdote to illustrate the value of scout training. He was, however, more at home in the company of adult leaders than of boys and he sometimes gave vent to his intolerance, to youngsters who did not achieve the standard he expected. He had great personal charm and a hearty laugh, though not perhaps a great sense of humour. He took endless trouble to write long letters of thanks and appreciation to all and sundry in his mostly illegible handwriting.

Rowallan remained chief scout until 1959, having seen the movement grow throughout the world and, in the United Kingdom, achieve a membership of nearly 600,000. He was governor of Tasmania from 1959 to 1963. He was appointed KBE in 1951 and KT in 1957, and he received honorary degrees from three universities: McGill (1948), Glasgow (1952), and Birmingham (1957).

Rowallan died in the Nuffield Nursing Home, Glasgow, on 30 November 1977, and was buried at Fenwick cemetery. He was succeeded in the barony by his eldest son, Arthur Cameron Corbett (*b.* 1919).

WILLIAM GLADSTONE, rev.

**Sources** Lord Rowallan, *The autobiography of Lord Rowallan, KT* (1976) · *The Times* (1 Dec 1977) · *The Times* (20 Dec 1977) · Scout Association Archives, London · personal knowledge (1986)
**Archives** NL Scot., corresp. and papers | Scout Association, London, archives
**Likenesses** J. A. Hampton, photograph, 23 Aug 1951, Hult. Arch. · Karsh, photograph, repro. in Rowallan, *Autobiography of Lord Rowallan*, 1 · photographs, repro. in Rowallan, *Autobiography of Lord Rowallan*, 100–01

**Corbett, Thomas William** (1888–1981), army officer, was born on 2 June 1888 at Naini Tal in India, the son of Thomas Bartholomew Corbett, a postmaster, and his wife, Emily Harriet. He was educated at St Paul's School, Darjeeling (1897–1904), and the Royal Military College, Sandhurst (1905–7), passing out near the top of his class. On 10 January 1907 Corbett was commissioned second lieutenant and after a year with a British unit he joined Hodson's Horse, an Indian cavalry regiment. Between November

1914 and March 1918 he served on the western front, was twice promoted (captain 1915, brevet major 1917), and was awarded an MC and bar. On 28 October 1915 he married Flora Margaret (1878/9–1951), daughter of David Gold, who had previously divorced Alistair Maxwell Macdonell. In 1918–19 Corbett served as a brigade major with the Egyptian expeditionary force in Palestine before entering the Staff College, Quetta, in October 1920. In 1922 he was promoted major and held various staff appointments in southern command and at army headquarters (AHQ) India. Early in 1930 he transferred to the 2nd lancers (Gardner's Horse) and on 24 January he was appointed an instructor at the Staff College, Quetta, where he established a close friendship with Claude Auchinleck. He attended the senior officers' school, Belgaum, in 1932, before returning to his regiment, and was promoted brevet lieutenant-colonel in 1933. In September 1934 he returned to instruct at the Staff College, where he was awarded a viceroy's certificate for rescue work during the May 1935 earthquake, and was promoted colonel on 1 July 1935. On 2 August 1938 he took command of the Sialkot brigade area with the rank of temporary brigadier, and in January 1940 he was appointed brigadier, cavalry, at AHQ in New Delhi where he oversaw the conversion of Indian cavalry regiments into armoured units. Corbett was promoted acting major-general on 22 April 1940 and was instrumental in organizing and training the 1st Indian armoured division and in developing a tactical doctrine for the Indian armoured corps. He was made a CB in 1941.

In January 1942 Corbett took command of 4th Indian corps in Iraq, with the rank of acting lieutenant-general. Shortly afterwards, on 15 March 1942, he was appointed by Auchinleck (now General Sir Claude) to the key post of chief of general staff (CGS), Middle East, to the surprise of many senior British service officers in London and Cairo who knew nothing about this Indian cavalryman. As the situation in the western desert deteriorated Corbett acted as an intermediary between the commander-in-chief and his hard-pressed field commanders. When Major-General Neil Ritchie was relieved, Auchinleck briefly considered Corbett as general officer commanding Eighth Army, but then decided to take command in the field himself.

While the commander-in-chief was absent Corbett remained at general headquarters Cairo as his representative, carrying out its routine business and preparing the city and the Nile delta for defence. His inexperience of higher command, however, meant that Corbett, now clearly out of his depth, failed to impress Churchill and many senior officers who met him. In particular, his lacklustre efforts to instil a warlike spirit among the large number of troops in the rear areas exposed him to considerable criticism. Along with Auchinleck, Corbett was dismissed in the 'Cairo purge' in August 1942 and returned to India where he briefly commanded 7th Indian division. Corbett retired from the Indian army in 1943 and became involved in farming in Kenya. Following his first wife's death in 1951, he married in 1952 Sara (Sally) N. E. Withers (*née* Raymond), widow of Lieutenant-Colonel H. H. C. Withers. They had a daughter. On 28 December 1981 he died of bronchopneumonia at Panthill, Spithurst, near Barcombe, near Lewes.

Corbett was an intelligent and hardworking Indian army soldier, staff officer, and instructor, who played a key role in organizing the Indian armoured corps. However, he was clearly out of his depth when appointed CGS, Middle East, a post for which he lacked sufficient experience.                                    T. R. MOREMAN

**Sources** *Indian Army List* · CAC Cam., Corbett MSS · BL OIOC, Cadet MSS, L/MIL/9/305, fol. 167 · d. cert. · m. cert. · *WWW* · R. Parkinson, *The Auk. Auchinleck victor of Alamein* (1977) · P. Warner, *Auchinleck the lonely soldier* (1981) · I. S. O. Playfair, *The Mediterranean and Middle East*, 3: *British fortunes reach their lowest ebb* (1960) · J. Connell, *Auchinleck* (1959) · *CGPLA Eng. & Wales* (1982)

**Archives** CAC Cam., papers

**Wealth at death** under £25,000: probate, 4 May 1982, *CGPLA Eng. & Wales*

**Corbett** [Corbet], **William** (*bap.* 1680?, *d.* 1748), violinist and composer, was possibly the William Corbett, son of Henry and Sarah, baptized at St Margaret, Westminster, on 18 July 1680. St Margaret's is cited in Corbett's will as his family's parish. The coat of arms depicted in one of his portraits suggests Shropshire ancestry. His early musical training remains a mystery, although it is likely that he enjoyed a period of study in Italy. He quickly established himself in England as a composer and instrumentalist, assisted by his natural flair for self-promotion and the presentation of the novel in performance and composition that he demonstrated throughout his career.

Corbett was given a benefit at York Buildings, London, on 17 March 1699, and his op. 1, a set of twelve trio sonatas in the Italian style, was published in Amsterdam (possibly *en route* for or from Italy) about 1700. Already associated with Thomas Betterton's company at Lincoln's Inn Fields as a composer and performer, he wrote music and songs (published three years later) for Shakespeare's *Henry IV* performed there on 9 January 1700 and also given in Oxford that same year. Incidental music and songs for other productions followed in 1703. He was also actively involved in the long-running and pioneering London concert series organized by Thomas Britton, and his pupils included the Scottish violinist and composer William McGibbon.

Benefits and concerts featuring Corbett's own music followed in 1704–5, at York Buildings and Lincoln's Inn Fields. He was leader of the band at the opening of the Queen's Theatre in the Haymarket on 9 April 1705 and held that position for a number of years (although not during the period 1707–10). He wrote the overture and act tunes for the semi-opera *The British Enchanters* by George Granville, Baron Lansdowne, given there on 21 February 1706 with eleven further performances, and his contributions were published during the same year. His annual salary of £40 at the theatre was equalled only by the violinist John Banister. He held a benefit on 18 March 1706 and performed a new Italian solo, billed as 'the first he ever play'd in public' (Edwards, 'Espionage', 327), on 19 March 1707 at York Buildings. In addition to giving frequent performances there, he appeared at Nottingham races (August

William Corbett (*bap.* 1680?, *d.* 1748), by John Simon (after J. Austen, *c.*1728)

1707 and 1709), York (August 1709), the duchess of Shrewsbury's, Kensington, Home's Dancing School, and Hickford's music room. As the lord chamberlain's records testify, Corbett also remained a member of the royal band from the end of 1709 until his death in 1748, gaining prestige, money, and freedom during this period.

With the appointment of a new band following the production of Handel's *Rinaldo* at the Queen's Theatre in 1711, Corbett lost the post of leader. However, contrary to Sir John Hawkins's version of events, Corbett did not then leave for Italy. He remained in England, performing (notably at court on Queen Anne's birthday in 1712) and composing. His op. 4, consisting of twelve trio sonatas in two books, appeared in 1713, and 'Hail happy day', a song to commemorate the coronation of George I, in 1714. The ode *Lost is my Love* also dates from about this time.

On 25 March 1713 Corbett shared a benefit with the Italian opera singer Anna Lodi, *née* Signoni, of Milan, the widow of Francesco Lodi. It was the first concert to be given in Hickford's New Room in James Street, and also featured a new mandolin concerto. He made other concert appearances there the following month and held further joint benefit concerts with Lodi in 1714 (28 April) and 1715 (26 April). It was not generally known that Corbett had in fact married Signora Lodi in 1703. Corbett and Lodi had a daughter in 1713 and lived together, presumably in London, until the end of 1715, when Anna parted from him. Corbett followed her to Milan, via Amsterdam, and there they settled in September 1716. The daughter remained with relatives in London.

The pay that Corbett continued to receive in absence

from the royal band (said to be an annual stipend of £300) gave rise to the story, kept alive by Hawkins, that Corbett was serving as a spy on James Francis Edward, the Pretender. However, this money may have been intended to fund his valuable collection of music and instruments accrued during his extensive travels around the great cities of Italy, and there is no conclusive evidence either way.

Back in England on 18 March 1724, Corbett played at the New Haymarket Theatre on the *viol de venere* (a variant of the viola d'amore with twenty-two strings), which, it was claimed, had never previously been heard in England. On 16 May the first of Corbett's sales of instruments, music, and other items was advertised, and during the same month the *Session of Musicians* ridiculed his new instrument.

At some time after September 1724 Corbett returned to Milan with his daughter. He continued to tour Italy, and the family settled in Bologna in 1726. The cantata *Lost is my Love* dates from this period. However, the death of George I in 1727 required Corbett to return to London and renew his oath of allegiance to the crown. A benefit, billed as the only opportunity to hear him during his stay, took place on 20 March 1728 at Hickford's room and featured his 'new Bizzaria's', op. 8, as well as pieces on the viola d'amore and the supposedly all-new 'chamber horns'. Corbett published the first instalment of his op. 8, *Le bizzarie universali, a quatro*, his most significant and curious works, while in London in June 1728. These twelve string concertos were written 'on all the new Gusto's in his Travels thro' Italy' (title-page) and so reflected the general penchant for Italian music. A second edition, dedicated to Corbett's patron Richard, first Baron Edgcumbe, appeared in 1742 entitled *Concerto's, or, Universal Bizzaries … in VII Parts* and consisting of thirty-five concertos in three volumes. Competent and assured, these works combine effective instrumental writing, contemporary Italianate features, and parody. Each is prefixed with the name of an Italian city or European country. By this time Corbett had been granted a royal privilege, giving his music copyright protection for fourteen years. An advertisement for the sale of his instruments appeared in 1728, and he joined his family in Milan in September of that year.

Corbett's eventful private life then took a turn for the worse. By pretending to arrange a concert tour on which he was to be accompanied only by his daughter, he compounded an earlier controversy caused by his sister-in-law's staying with him in Rome in 1730, before the arrival of his wife and daughter. Such indiscretions led to his family going into hiding in May 1731 and living off valuables they had taken from the home. Corbett petitioned in passionate terms for their return; but while his efforts provide details of their relationship, they were ultimately in vain. He departed from Italy probably during the summer of 1731. Royal Archives place him back in England and present at court from 1732.

Several of Corbett's new '*Bizzaria Universall*' concertos, with the composer playing first violin, were given on 8 March 1734 at York Buildings, where a benefit was held the following month. Billed as lately arrived from Italy, he presented 'An essay of different kinds of harmony, intermix'd with some pieces on the new Viol D'Venere'. His last solo recitals took place in 1739. Concerts on 4 and 11 August of that year featured the *viol de venere*, viola d'amore, and 'viol volubile'. On 28 August 1739 he became one of the original members of the Royal Society of Musicians. In 1741 he tried, once again, to sell part of his collection of music and instruments, but without success.

Although often accompanied by controversy and subject to bouts of impetuosity, Corbett was evidently an extremely talented musician. He died, probably in London, on 7 March 1748. His will (dated 3 March 1747) was proved on 19 April by Richard Dawson, Daniel Cogdell, and Bridget Bohannon, widow. He requested a private burial in his family grave in the churchyard of St Margaret, Westminster, 'at some short time' (Highfill, Burnim & Langhans, *BDA*) before midnight, with only two coaches in his cortège. The will includes a sum for his brother-in-law, Isaac Wattlington, late of St Leonard, Shoreditch, although for some reason his sister Ann, referred to as Wattlington's wife, was to receive 1s. only 'if demanded' (ibid.), and Corbett's wife and daughter are not mentioned. The largest bequest, his collection of music, instruments, and other valuables, was left to Gresham College 'to be deposited and put in a Room belonging thereto' (ibid.), although Corbett's connection with the college remains a mystery. He provided £10 annually for Bridget Bohannon to be curator of the collection during her lifetime. Items included Cremonese and Stainer violins, a violin played by Corelli (destined for Giardini), a viola, a cello, double basses, bows, a harpsichord, and pictures, candlesticks, Italian silks, and music books. Included in the music were three sets of concertos, seven books of operas, and fifty-three individual concertos, some of which were to be given to deserving foreign performers but not sold on any account. Nevertheless, internal squabbles resulted in Gresham's turning down the bequest, and the collection was sold at auction in 1751: the instruments at Mercer's Hall, and the books and manuscripts at a house in Silver Street, Golden Square, which Corbett appears to have been renting at the time of his death.

DAVID J. GOLBY

**Sources** O. Edwards, 'Espionage, a collection of violins … a fresh look at William Corbett', *Musical Quarterly*, 73 (1989), 320–43 • Highfill, Burnim & Langhans, *BDA* • J. Hawkins, *A general history of the science and practice of music*, new edn, 2 (1853), 807, 822–3 • Burney, *Hist. mus.*, new edn, 2.693–4, 985, 990, 995, 997–8 • O. Edwards, 'Corbett, William', *New Grove*, 2nd edn, 6.446 [incl. list of works] • O. Edwards, 'English string concertos before 1800', *Proceedings of the Royal Musical Association*, 95 (1968–9), 5–6 • H. D. Johnstone and R. Fiske, eds., *Music in Britain: the eighteenth century* (1990), vol. 4 of *The Blackwell history of music in Britain*, ed. I. Spink (1988–95)

**Archives** BL, Robinson papers, Add. MS 23782, fols. 23 and 24 • PRO, state papers, series 85/13 Italy, document no. 74, fols. 153–4

**Likenesses** J. Simon, mezzotint (after J. Austen), BM • J. Simon, mezzotint (after J. Austen, c.1728), BM [see illus.]

**Wealth at death** see will, Highfill, Burnim & Langhans, *BDA*, 489; Edwards, 'Espionage'

**Corbie, Ambrose**. *See* Corby, Ambrose (1604–1649).

**Corbie, Gerard**. *See* Corby, Gerard (1558–1637).

**Corbie, Ralph**. *See* Corby, Ralph (1598–1644).

**Corbishley, Thomas** (1903–1976), Jesuit and writer, was born at Preston on 30 May 1903, the second of four sons and second of five children of William Corbishley, master painter and decorator, of Preston, Lancashire, and his wife, Catherine Bamford. He was educated at Preston Catholic College. From this Jesuit secondary school he entered the noviciate of the Society of Jesus at Roehampton on 7 September 1919. After studying scholastic philosophy at St Mary's Hall, Stonyhurst, Lancashire, he went up to Campion Hall, Oxford, in 1926 to read classics. He took a first both in honour moderations (1928) and in *literae humaniores* (1930), an uncommon achievement for one who had not studied Greek at school. On leaving Oxford he joined the teaching staff of Stonyhurst College for three years before beginning his course of theology in 1933 at Heythrop College, then at Chipping Norton.

By the time of his ordination in September 1936 Corbishley had amassed an extensive knowledge of the New Testament which later informed his spiritual conferences, sermons, and counselling. In the area of doctrine he made a special study of the genuineness of Christ's human knowledge.

It was at this time that Corbishley made his only important contributions to classical scholarship: an essay on the date of the Syrian governorship of M. Titus in the *Journal of Roman Studies* (1934) and another on the census of Quirinius in the *Journal of Theological Studies* (1935). These two essays contained crucial implications for the chronology of the life of Jesus.

Corbishley's early years as a priest were occupied mainly with the academic preparation of Jesuit students for their strictly professional studies. At the outbreak of war in 1939 he became actively engaged in the Sword of the Spirit movement, an inter-church activity, jointly sponsored by Archbishop William Temple and Cardinal Arthur Hinsley, which anticipated the ecumenical movement launched by the Second Vatican Council. It was not unexpected that ecumenism should become the principal preoccupation of his last twenty years.

In 1945 Corbishley was appointed master of Campion Hall in succession to Martin D'Arcy, who had transferred the private hall from a building in St Giles' leased from St John's College to a hall in Brewer Street, which was the only contribution by Sir Edwin Lutyens to the architecture of Oxford. In 1958 Corbishley left the university to become superior of the Jesuit church in Farm Street, Mayfair. On the expiration of his term of office in 1966 he remained on the staff at Farm Street until his death.

Corbishley acknowledged that the greatest single influence in his life had been the personality and writings of his fellow Jesuit, C. C. Martindale, who in the inter-war period had revolutionized hagiography by showing that true sanctity could exist along with hereditary and human weaknesses. Like Martindale, Corbishley deserted purely academic studies and spread his interest widely, as the

titles of his better known books witness: *Roman Catholicism* (1950), *Religion is Reasonable*, a collection of mainly Oxford conferences (1960), *The Spirituality of Teilhard de Chardin* (1971), and *One Body, One Spirit* (1973), which was chosen as the archbishop of Canterbury's Lenten book. A versatile popular theologian, he believed that he had something to contribute to the moral and theological discussions of his day.

Both at Oxford and in London Corbishley devoted himself to many Christian causes such as the needs of Polish and Hungarian exiles, the Oxford University joint action committee against racial intolerance, the Council for Christians and Jews, and Oxfam, to which he gave valuable guidance when it was establishing its policy of granting money for family planning programmes. But he is best-known for his work in the ecumenical movement. While seeking closer understanding between the churches he came in for much criticism from ultra-conservative Roman Catholics. An enthusiastic pioneer, he sometimes stretched traditional discipline to breaking point in his eagerness to hold out a hand of friendship to fellow Christians of all denominations. Unassuming and tolerant, he was well fitted to represent his church in ecumenical discussions.

Corbishley died in London on 11 March 1976. On the following 17 May his life and work were commemorated at evensong in Westminster Abbey. In his address on this occasion Alan Booth spoke of Corbishley as 'one of the truly distinguished minds of our day who chose deliberately to occupy himself in the chores of faithful, very practical little efforts to heal the great wounds of mankind' (personal knowledge).                    PHILIP CARAMAN, *rev.*

**Sources** *The Times* (12 March 1976) • personal knowledge (1986) • *CGPLA Eng. & Wales* (1977) • *WWW*
**Likenesses** photograph, repro. in *The Times*
**Wealth at death** £1079: administration with will, 4 May 1977, *CGPLA Eng. & Wales*

**Corbould, Edward Henry** (1815–1905), watercolour painter, born at 70 St John Street, Fitzroy Square, London, on 5 December 1815, was the eldest son of Henry *Corbould (1787–1844), painter and draughtsman, and his wife, a Miss Pickles of Chelsea, and a grandson of Richard *Corbould (1757–1831), painter and illustrator. His brothers were Francis John Corbould (1819–1884), a sculptor, and the twins Henry Heath and Alfred Hichens Corbould, born in 1821: one became a surgeon, and the other an artist. All four were educated at King's College School, London, where the younger brothers were taught drawing by John Sell Cotman.

Edward Corbould was taught by his father, and studied at Henry Sass's drawing school in Bloomsbury before entering the Royal Academy Schools in 1834. In that year his watercolour the *Fall of Phaeton* won a gold medal at the Society of Arts, but his prize entries in the following two years were models, a *St George and the Dragon* and a *Chariot Race from Homer*. His first exhibits in the Royal Academy, in 1835, also included a model, but thereafter he abandoned sculpture. However, in 1889, when the London corporation invited designs for sculpture for Blackfriars Bridge (a project never carried out), he produced drawings of colossal groups. With rare exceptions, such as the oil painting *The Canterbury Pilgrims* (exh. RA, 1874), he worked in watercolour, or claimed to. In fact, at least from 1851—when he contributed one of the few paintings shown at the Great Exhibition—he often used the 'new silica colour and a glass medium' invented ten years previously by Thomas Miller of Long Acre.

Corbould also exhibited at the New Watercolour Society, later the Royal Institute of Painters in Water Colours, from 1837, being elected a member in that year. In 1861 he resigned over financial mismanagement, but returned after failing to win election to the Old Watercolour Society. He finally retired from active membership in 1898, having exhibited about 250 works. Corbould's highly wrought exhibition pieces—sometimes harsh in colour and rigid in composition—were very obviously intended to face down oil paintings on their own terms; numerous prints of his works were published. His sketches owe something to the works of the German Nazarene school, employing strong pen outlines and light colour washes. Corbould was also a prolific book and magazine illustrator, working on many standard nineteenth-century editions of authors such as Chaucer, Edmund Spenser, and Walter Scott. Many of his illustrations were mere hackwork, and the historian of 1860s illustration Gleeson White dismissed the work of Corbould and other contributors to the 1870 volume of *Cassell's Magazine* with the remark that it would be kindest to ignore it.

In 1840 Corbould drew the portrait of the queen for the new penny black stamp, from Wyon's medal, and he also designed stamps for Trinidad, Mauritius, Ceylon, and Van Diemen's Land. In 1842 his *The Woman Taken in Adultery* was bought by the prince consort, who subsequently presented a number of his works to the queen, and in 1851 he was appointed 'instructor of historical painting to the royal family'. For the next twenty-one years he taught various members of the family, and many of his best works were acquired by them. His duties could be time-consuming: in 1862 he wrote to J. J. Jenkins from Osborne:

> Here I am a prisoner but I hope to get up to town on Saturday night. The Princess Alice has made me promise to 'stay over Saturday'. Surely HRH never understands that I am to be visible here on the Monday? I shall only understand *till* Saturday evening. (Royal Watercolour Society archives)

Corbould was married three times: his first marriage on 28 September 1839 to Fanny Jemima (d. 1850), daughter of the engraver Charles *Heath (1785–1848) [see under Heath family], produced three daughters. The eldest, Jemima, married the painter Francis John Wyburd (1827–1909), and the second, Isabel Fanny, Mrs G. H. Heywood, had two artist daughters. His second marriage, to Annie Middleton Wilson (d. 1866), took place on 7 August 1851; the couple had two sons, Ridley Edward Arthur Lamothe (1854–1887) and Victor Albert Louis Edward (b. 1866), who became a doctor. He married thirdly, on 15 January 1868, Anne Melis

Sanders, daughter of Ellis Lee Sanders, with whom he had a further son and daughter.

Between 1851 and 1853 Corbould's brother Alfred built Eldon Lodge, at 8 Victoria Road, in the new suburb of South Kensington, but Edward was then by far the more prosperous of the two and in the 1860s he took over the property. He extended it, creating a worthy neighbour for Leighton House and its artistic fellows on Campden Hill: Corbould's studio measured 26 feet by nearly 25 feet, was proportionately high, and panelled with English and continental oak carving dating from the middle ages to the Gothic revival. Below was an equally sizeable picture store. While the hall was tiled in the manner of Pugin, the dining-room was in the Adam style, and the study was fashionably japanesque.

After the death of Prince Albert, the queen employed Corbould to colour photographs of him; he was responsible for the image of Albert the Good in knightly armour receiving his crown of glory, which hung as a memorial in the Albert Room at Windsor Castle. However, by the mid-1870s Corbould's historical paintings were out of fashion. On 6 May 1875 the queen noted in her journal that she 'thought him much aged and altered' (Royal Archives, Windsor), and thereafter she not only paid £50 p.a. towards his son's school fees, but from 1891 a personal allowance, continued by Edward VII. He died at Eldon Lodge on 16 January 1905. As well as the watercolours and albums in the Royal Collection, there are examples of his work in the British Museum and the Sydney Art Gallery.

HUON MALLALIEU

**Sources** G. C. B. Poulter, *The Corbould genealogy* (1935) • *Art Journal*, 26 (1864), 98 • *Art Journal*, new ser., 25 (1905), 286, 379 • *Daily Graphic* (19 Jan 1905) • *Daily Chronicle* [London] (21 Jan 1905) • DNB • Wood, *Vic. painters*, 2nd edn • D. Millar, *The Victorian watercolours and drawings in the collection of her majesty the queen*, 2 vols. (1995) • Tate collection • Bankside Gallery, London, Royal Watercolour Society archives • Graves, *RA exhibitors* • King's College School, London, archives • G. White, *Illustration in the sixties* (1908) • m. certs. • d. certs.
**Wealth at death** £5249 2s. 8d.: probate, 29 June 1905, CGPLA Eng. & Wales

**Corbould, Henry** (1787–1844), draughtsman and book illustrator, was born in London (or possibly Robertsbridge, Sussex) on 11 August 1787, the third son of Richard *Corbould (1757–1831); he was baptized on 11 September 1787 at St Andrew's, Holborn. His father was a prolific book illustrator and a landscape artist, and his mother, Charlotte, according to Joseph Farington's diaries, was a daughter of the Heath family of engravers: it is therefore unsurprising that both Henry and his elder brother George (1786–1846) displayed youthful artistic talent. They both trained in painting with their father, and from 1801 both 'Master' Corboulds had begun exhibiting at the Royal Academy. While George was eventually apprenticed to the line engraver James Heath, Henry was admitted to the Royal Academy Schools on 29 March 1805 at the age of seventeen. Having already shown a preference for subjects such as *Paris and Menelaus Fighting for Helen* (exh. RA, 1803), his neo-classical taste was no doubt consolidated by his training under Johann Heinrich Fuseli and his friendship with fellow students such as Francis Chantrey and Richard Westmacott. During his time at the Royal Academy Schools Corbould gained some recognition. In 1807 he was awarded a silver medal for a life study, and he received support from more established academicians such as John Flaxman and Benjamin West, who employed him as a model for several religious paintings.

It is not clear exactly when Corbould left the Royal Academy Schools, but in April 1812 he married a Miss Pickles of Chelsea, and three years later she gave birth to Edward Henry *Corbould, the first of their four sons. It is perhaps as a result of these family commitments that Corbould chose not to pursue a career as a history painter—concentrating his efforts instead on perfecting a delicate, rather feminine, neo-classical style which suited the purposes of refined Regency book illustration. During the remainder of his career he was 'extensively employed by publishers to make drawings for engravings, and the number of his designs, which adorn many books amount to several hundreds' (Britton, 2.172). This is also reflected in those works he continued to send to the Royal Academy exhibition, which were predominantly compositions of a sentimental and literary genre, commissioned to illustrate the novels of Walter Scott or the poetry of Byron and Crabbe. As was the case with J. F. Dove's edition of Fanny Burney's *Cecilia, or, Memoirs of an Heiress* (1825), many of Corbould's illustrations were turned into steel-engravings by his cousin Charles Heath; in other instances they were reproduced in fashionable media such as lithography and stipple engraving.

Aside from gaining a reputation for designing some of the most 'graceful and effective productions of the age' (*Art Union*, 7, 1845, 37), Corbould was renowned as an antiquarian draughtsman, and his commitment to this study is confirmed by his membership of both the Society of Dilettanti and the Society of Antiquaries. According to his obituary in the *Art Union*, he was 'distinguished by courteous and gentlemanly manners', and these qualities must have assisted his easy movement in such varied social circles. He also worked for the aristocracy; from early in his career he had been employed to draw the antiquities in the duke of Bedford's and Lord Egremont's marble collections for private publication in lavish presentation volumes such as *Outline Engravings and Descriptions of the Woburn Abbey Marbles* (1822). These noblemen undoubtedly appreciated Corbould's manners and had confidence in his abilities after his employment, by the trustees of the British Museum, in a long-term project to produce similar transcriptions of the Elgin marbles for *Description of the Marbles of the British Museum* (1845).

Corbould died on 9 December 1844 at Robertsbridge and was buried at Etchingham church in Sussex. The cause of his death remains a matter of some confusion. Most biographers blame a fall from his horse, while John Britton records that Corbould was a victim of an accident on the Eastern Counties Railway, when a train fell from an embankment, killing a number of passengers. Corbould was survived by his four sons; however, judging from an obituary in the *Literary Gazette* which mentions his engagement to Lady Chantrey, the widow of his old friend the sculptor Sir Francis Chantrey, it would appear that his wife had died some time earlier. Certainly, in his will, written in 1832, he directed that his property was to be divided equally among his children, with no mention of their mother; he also bequeathed a diamond shirt pin—'a very trifling token of my love and esteem'—to Charles Heath's wife, and the choice of one of his pictures 'with its frame' to his brother Richard.                    LUCY PELTZ

**Sources** *Art Union*, 7 (1845), 37 • Bryan, *Painters* (1866) • Redgrave, *Artists* • J. Britton, *The autobiography of John Britton*, 3 vols. in 2 (privately printed, London, 1849–50), vol. 2, p. 172 • Graves, *Artists* • Graves, *RA exhibitors* • Farington, *Diary* • H. Hammelmann, *Book illustrators in eighteenth-century England*, ed. T. S. R. Boase (1975) • S. Houfe, *The dictionary of 19th century British book illustrators and caricaturists*, rev. edn (1996) • S. C. Hutchison, 'The Royal Academy Schools, 1768–1830', *Walpole Society*, 38 (1960–62), 123–91 • *Literary Gazette* (21 Dec 1844), 831 • Mallalieu, *Watercolour artists* • *Monthly Magazine*, 33 (1812) • *Richard Corbould, 1757–1831, illustrator: a glimpse of the common life of Georgian England* (1984) [exhibition catalogue, Spink and Son, London, 7 Feb – 2 March 1984] • Thieme & Becker, *Allgemeines Lexikon* • J. Turner, ed., *The dictionary of art*, 34 vols. (1996) • IGI • will, PRO, PROB 11/2010, sig. 23
**Likenesses** C. Skelsey, medallion on monument, *c.*1844, Assumption and St Nicholas Church, Etchingham, Sussex

**Corbould, Richard** (1757–1831), artist, was born in London on 18 April 1757, and baptized at St Edmund the King and Martyr, Lombard Street, on 24 April, the son of George Corbould and his wife, Anne. He painted, both in oils and watercolours, portraits, landscapes, still life, and history; miniatures on enamel and ivory, also on porcelain; and occasionally he etched. He was thought very clever at imitating the style of the old masters, and yet could show an originality of his own. He first appears as an exhibitor in 1776 at the Free Society of Artists, to which he sent *The Morning*, after Claude Lorrain, a stained drawing, *A Bunch of Grapes*, and another landscape. In 1777 he sent a miniature to the exhibition of the Royal Academy, and continued to exhibit there numerous pictures in varied styles up to 1811. These included *Cottagers Gathering Sticks* (1793); *The Millennial Age: Isaiah Xi. 6, 8* (1801), a picture very much admired at the time; and *Hero and Leander* (1803). With his wife, Charlotte, he had two sons, Henry *Corbould (1787–1844) and George Corbould, also notable painters. He last appeared as an exhibitor in 1817 at the British Institution.

It is, however, as a designer of illustrations for books that Corbould is most widely known. He was largely employed by publishers, and his illustrations, engraved by the best artists, showed both skill and judgement. He contributed to Cooke's pocket editions of English classics (1795–1800), including illustrations for Richardson's *Pamela*. He also illustrated children's books and non-fiction. Corbould lived for some years in John Street, Tottenham Court Road, but later in life moved to the north of London. He died at Highgate on 26 July 1831, and was buried in the churchyard of St Andrew's, Holborn, London.

L. H. CUST, *rev.* RUTH STEWART

**Sources** *Richard Corbould, 1757–1831, illustrator: a glimpse of the common life of Georgian England* (1984) [exhibition catalogue, Spink and

Son, London, 7 Feb – 2 March 1984] • Redgrave, *Artists* • Graves, *Artists* • *GM*, 1st ser., 101/2 (1831) • *IGI* • H. Hammelmann, *Book illustrators in eighteenth-century England*, ed. T. S. R. Boase (1975)
**Archives** V&A NAL • W. Yorks. AS, Leeds, sketchbooks
**Likenesses** H. Edridge, pencil and ink drawing, BM

**Corbridge, Thomas of** (*d.* 1304), archbishop of York, presumably came from Corbridge in Northumberland, a small town adjacent to the archbishop of York's liberty of Hexhamshire. No details survive of his parentage and early years but he became a master, and then a doctor, of theology, and Oxford has been claimed (though without definite proof) as the place of his university education. Indeed his erudition and scholarship, not just in theology but in all the liberal arts, were remarked on by chroniclers. There were several clerks in the York diocese with the territorial surname of Corbridge in the late thirteenth and early fourteenth centuries, but no precise relationship can be established.

Throughout his career before his elevation to the archbishopric Corbridge had very strong connections with York, and indeed, rather surprisingly, is not known to have held any ecclesiastical preferment outside the city; no evidence of any parochial preferment has been found. He was a canon of York Minster in the time of Archbishop Giffard (*r.* 1266–79)—in 1277 he occurs as the prebendary of Osbaldwick—and is found as a clerk of Archbishop Wickwane in 1279 when he was commissioned to proceed in the matter of the election of Robert of Scarborough as dean of York. He acted for the archbishop as his proctor in Rome in 1281, in the course of the latter's bitter dispute with the bishop of Durham, and he was also active in the perennial source of conflict between the two English archbishops over the carrying of their respective primatial crosses erect in the other province. He succeeded Wickwane as chancellor of York Minster, and in 1280 vacated his prebend of Osbaldwick for the richer minster prebend of Stillington, which he held until his own appointment to the archbishopric. He continued to act as an archiepiscopal clerk after the succession of Archbishop Romeyn in 1286, but he later came into conflict with the archbishop in 1290 over his own promotion to the sacristy of the chapel of St Mary and the Holy Angels, a twelfth-century foundation adjacent to the minster in York. Romeyn appointed him as sacrist and Corbridge resigned (conditionally, it is claimed) the chancellorship of the minster. The archbishop then promoted Thomas of Wakefield, at that time subdean of York, to chancellor. Unfortunately Corbridge had difficulty in entering upon the sacristy and tried to resume the already filled chancellorship. Romeyn excommunicated him and Corbridge appealed to the pope, but in 1291 the excommunication was revoked and he was able to obtain peaceful possession of the sacristy.

Following the death of Archbishop Henry Newark on 15 August 1299, Corbridge was elected his successor on 12 November by a majority of the canons of York Minster. Having obtained royal assent from Edward I, who was present in York at the time, the archbishop-elect set off for the Roman curia to obtain papal confirmation and consecration. Pope Boniface VIII set aside the election but provided Corbridge as archbishop, consecrating him on 28 February 1300. The royal mandate for the restoration of the temporalities of the see was issued on 30 April.

As a diocesan Corbridge seems to have been exemplary, if the evidence of his register and related archival material is taken into account. The itinerary constructed from his recorded acts shows that for his years as archbishop he was in his diocese for almost all of the time, except for brief attendances at parliament. Almost immediately he undertook a systematic visitation of parishes and religious houses in his diocese, and when this had been completed during 1300–01, began a second series of visitations in late 1302. The 106 folios of his register bear testimony to an efficient and methodical administrator.

Like so many other medieval archbishops, Corbridge's defence of archiepiscopal claims led inevitably to conflict with others—with the archbishop of Canterbury over the primatial cross business and the attempt by Canterbury to visit the York archiepiscopal jurisdiction of Churchdown in Gloucestershire; with the provost of Beverley over visitations; and with Edward I over the patronage of the sacristy of the chapel of St Mary and the Holy Angels. In this last-mentioned conflict he found himself between competing papal and royal claims. Upon Corbridge's consecration as archbishop the pope had provided his own nephew, Francisco Gaetani, to the new archbishop's vacant prebend of Stillington and the sacristy of St Mary and the Holy Angels, and in due course an archiepiscopal mandate was issued for Gaetani's admission. In the meantime, during the vacancy of the see, King Edward had presented one of his own clerks, John Bussh, to the same positions, since in a vacancy the archiepiscopal patronage belonged to the crown. Gaetani gave up the sacristy in 1303, and the archbishop appointed Gilbert Seagrave in his place, notwithstanding Bussh's claims. Corbridge thereupon found himself arraigned by Bussh in the royal courts, and the king was led to seize the archiepiscopal temporalities. Bussh eventually proved his case against the archbishop (the papal provisions being rejected by the courts) and gained possession in 1304, shortly after Corbridge's death. According to Walter of Guisborough, Corbridge's death was brought on by the hard treatment to which he was subjected by the king and courts in this case.

In his relations with Antony (I) Bek, bishop of Durham (*r.* 1284–1311), Corbridge had more success than his predecessors. The bishop's conflict with the prior and convent about rights of visitation over his cathedral priory involved the archbishop in the matter of appeals, but Corbridge and Bek were able to come to an agreement about such appeals to the papal curia, which specifically states its purpose as that of avoiding the bitter quarrels of the time of archbishops Wickwane (1279–85) and Romeyn (1286–96).

In 1304 Corbridge fell ill at his residence at Laneham in Nottinghamshire, where he had been staying since early

July, and died there on 22 September following. From his register it is clear that he continued to transact business until five days before his death. He was buried in Southwell Minster.

DAVID M. SMITH

**Sources** Chancery records · Emden, Oxf. · C. T. Clay, ed., York Minster fasti, 2 vols., Yorkshire Archaeological Society, 123–4 (1958–9) · J. Raine, ed., The historians of the church of York and its archbishops, 3 vols., Rolls Series, 71 (1879–94) · W. H. Dixon, Fasti Eboracenses: lives of the archbishops of York, ed. J. Raine (1863) · The register of Thomas of Corbridge, lord archbishop of York, 1300–1304, ed. W. Brown and A. H. Thompson, 2 vols., SurtS, 138, 141 (1925–8) · The register of William Wickwane, lord archbishop of York, 1279–1285, ed. W. Brown, SurtS, 114 (1907) · The register of John le Romeyn … 1286–1296, ed. W. Brown, 2 vols., SurtS, 123, 128 (1913–17) · The chronicle of Walter of Guisborough, ed. H. Rothwell, CS, 3rd ser., 89 (1957) · R. Brentano, York metropolitan jurisdiction and papal judges delegate, 1279–1296 (1959) · A. H. Thompson, 'The chapel of St Mary and the Holy Angels, otherwise known as St Sepulchre's Chapel, at York', Yorkshire Archaeological Journal, 36 (1944–7), 63–77, 214–48 · R. M. Haines, 'Canterbury versus York: fluctuating fortunes in a perennial conflict', Ecclesia Anglicana: studies in the English church of the later middle ages (1989), 69–105 · CEPR letters, vol. 1
**Archives** Borth. Inst., register, Reg. 6

**Corby** [Corbie], **Ambrose** (1604–1649), Jesuit, was by his own account born in Yorkshire on 25 December 1604, the youngest of the four sons of Gerard *Corby or Corbie (1558–1637) and his wife, Isabella Richardson (d. 1652). Both his parents were Catholic converts and future religious, while his two surviving brothers, Robert Corby and Ralph *Corby, became Jesuits and his two surviving sisters Benedictine nuns. Educated first in Yorkshire, at the age of twelve he entered the English College at St Omer, where he studied humanities and was reported 'among the first rather than the last in class' (Kenny, 2.348). On 11 October 1622 he entered the English College, Rome, and received minor orders on 16 September 1625 before ill health caused him to return to join his father in the Low Countries. He was admitted into the Society of Jesus at Watten on 7 September 1627, and successively taught syntax, rhetoric, and grammar at St Omer from 1628. Ordained priest on 22 September 1633 he undertook his Jesuit theological studies at Liège and his tertianship at Ghent. He again taught humanities at St Omer before his profession of the four vows on 15 August 1641. Appointed minister at Ghent in 1644 he was sent to Rome the following year, where he served as confessor in the English College. He was the author of Narratio gloriosa mortis … P. Henricus Mors (1645), an account of the recently executed English Jesuit Henry Morse, and of Certamen triplex (1645), comprising accounts of Morse and his fellow Jesuits and fellow sufferers Thomas Holland and Corby's own brother Ralph. An English translation of the latter work was published in 1858. He also wrote a brief account of his father, subsequently published by Foley in 1877. He died in Rome on 11 April 1649.

THOMPSON COOPER, rev. R. M. ARMSTRONG

**Sources** H. Foley, ed., Records of the English province of the Society of Jesus, 7 vols. in 8 (1875–83) · T. M. McCoog, English and Welsh Jesuits, 1555–1650, 2 vols., Catholic RS, 74–5 (1994–5) · T. H. Clancy, A literary history of the English Jesuits: a century of books, 1615–1714 (1996) ·

A. Kenny, ed., The responsa scholarum of the English College, Rome, 2 vols., Catholic RS, 54–5 (1962–3)

**Corby** [Corbie], **Gerard** (1558–1637), Roman Catholic exile, was the son of Ralph Corby (fl. 1591), a wealthy dealer in surface coalmining at Hett in co. Durham. Although his mother was a Catholic recusant, Gerard was brought up a protestant, but was converted to Roman Catholicism through meeting missionary priests. About 1585 he married Isabella Richardson (1552–1652), also a convert, and they went to live in exile in Kildare, Ireland, in the service of Lady Kildare. They had seven children, four sons and three daughters. The eldest daughter died in infancy; three of their sons, Ambrose *Corby, Ralph *Corby, and Robert, joined the Society of Jesus. Their son Richard died when a student at the Jesuit college at St Omer, and their two daughters, May and Catharine, became Benedictine nuns at Brussels. Gerard and his wife at length went into permanent exile in the Spanish Netherlands, where they agreed to separate and to consecrate themselves to religion. He accordingly entered the novitiate of Society of Jesus at Watten as a lay brother in 1628. In 1633 Isabella, when turned eighty, became a professed Benedictine nun at Ghent, the house having been founded from Brussels in 1624. She died there a centenarian on 25 November 1652. Gerard became blind five years before his death, which occurred at Watten on 18 September 1637, on the ninth anniversary of his entry into the society.

THOMPSON COOPER, rev. G. BRADLEY

**Sources** T. M. McCoog, English and Welsh Jesuits, 1555–1650, 1, Catholic RS, 74 (1994), 146 · J. A. Myerscough, The martyrs of Durham and the north-east (1956), 135–41 · P. Prime, 'Blessed Ralph Corby', Stonyhurst Magazine, 27 (1944) · H. Foley, ed., Records of the English province of the Society of Jesus, 3 (1878), 62–8 · Gillow, Lit. biog. hist., 1.563 · H. Chadwick, St Omer to Stonyhurst (1962), 162 · A. Corbie, The threefold conflict by three priests of the English province of the Society of Jesus, trans. W. B. Turnbull (1858)
**Archives** Archives of the British Province of the Society of Jesus, London, Angliae vol. v. 11. 18

**Corby** [Corbie], **Ralph** (1598–1644), Jesuit, was the son of Gerard *Corby (1558–1637) and his wife, Isabella Richardson (d. 1652), and was born on 25 March 1598, at Maynooth, co. Kildare, his parents having been compelled to retire to Ireland from co. Durham to escape persecution for recusancy. He was taken at five to England by his parents and he spent his childhood in the bishopric of Durham or in Lancashire. Afterwards he studied at the English College in St Omer (1613–19), at St Gregory's College, Seville (1619–21), and at St Alban's College, Valladolid (1621–5), where he was ordained priest about 1624. He entered the Society of Jesus at Watten in 1625. Two of his brothers, Ambrose *Corby (1604–1649) and Robert Corby, also joined the society. About 1631 he was sent to the English mission, and worked in Yorkshire and in co. Durham. He was arrested by parliamentary soldiers at Hamsterley Hall, near Ebchester, co. Durham on 8 July 1644, when vesting for mass; he was conveyed by sea to London and committed to Newgate on 22 July, together with John Duckett, a secular priest. At their trial at the Old Bailey on 4 September they both admitted that they were priests; they were condemned to death and were executed at Tyburn on 7 September 1644. Corby was beatified by Pius XI on 15 February 1929. Corby's remains were burned by order of the sheriff. THOMPSON COOPER, *rev.* G. BRADLEY

**Sources** A. Corby, *Certamen triplex a tribus societatis Jesu ex provincia Anglicana sacerdotibus, T. Hollando, R. Corbaeo, H. Morsaeo* (Antwerp, 1645) • H. Foley, ed., *Records of the English province of the Society of Jesus*, 3 (1878), 59–98 • J. Brodrick, *Blessed Ralph Corby* (1933) • P. Prime, 'Blessed Ralph Corby', *Stonyhurst Magazine*, 27 (1944) • R. Challoner, *Memoirs of missionary priests*, ed. J. H. Pollen, rev. edn (1924), 461–6 • T. M. McCoog, *English and Welsh Jesuits, 1555–1650*, 1, Catholic RS, 74 (1994) • G. Anstruther, *The seminary priests*, 2 (1975), 72 • M. Murphy, *St Gregory's College, Seville, 1592–1767*, Catholic RS, 73 (1992), 61 • G. Holt, *St Omers and Bruges colleges, 1593–1773: a biographical dictionary*, Catholic RS, 69 (1979), 73
**Archives** Stonyhurst College, Lancashire, Stonyhurst MSS, Anglia A. vol. 5, 18
**Likenesses** miniature, St Mawgan's Carmelite Convent, Lanherne, Newquay, Cornwall

**Corbyn, Thomas** (1711–1791), pharmaceutical chemist, was born on 13 February 1711 in Worcester, the son of John Corbyn and his wife, Candia, daughter of John and Cecilia Handley of Pontypool. His parents were members of the Society of Friends. He was apprenticed for eight years from September 1728 to Joseph Clutton, citizen and apothecary of London. His time finished, he continued to work with Clutton and did not apply for his freedom of the Society of Apothecaries until April 1743, the year in which his employer died. Mrs Clutton decided to continue the business herself, and as the sole surviving son, Morris Clutton, was only four years into his apprenticeship with his father, Corbyn was brought into the business. A co-partnership was finally formed when Mrs Clutton remarried and Morris Clutton gained his freedom of the Society of Apothecaries in July 1747. Each partner put in about £2000.

Joseph Clutton had spread his pharmaceutical interests beyond the confines of London; for example, he had been the 'chymical' supplier to the county hospital in Winchester since 1739. Some years before Clutton's death, Corbyn had been sending letters to overseas correspondents. From extant letter-books it is known that by 1741 Corbyn had developed a good trade with the American colonies, in February sending 'Jesuit's Bark', rhubarb, and cinnamon to Virginia, and soon after importing drugs such as senega. Corbyn was a staunch upholder of the purity of drugs, though well aware of the increased profits he could make if he descended to adulteration. In 1750 he wrote to John and Esther White in Pennsylvania, 'The simple drugs are the best of their kind, and the composition not only true, but curiously prepared, and charg'd reasonable according to the market price' (Western MSS 5435–5460). In 1752 Corbyn married Sarah Garret of Colchester; they had two daughters and a son. In 1754 he wrote to his cousin, John Corbyn, a doctor in New England, 'I don't know any thing particularly new & valuable in Physick. My wife has br[ough]t me a new girl now ab[ou]t 6 weeks old and thrives well' (ibid.).

Corbyn's probity both at home and abroad was an important factor in the success of the firm. When Morris Clutton died in 1754, a balance sheet shows that the concern had increased in value from about £4000 to some £14,000 in the seven years of the partnership. Corbyn also seems to have had no difficulty in raising the necessary capital to buy out Clutton's heirs. For a while he ran the firm alone but by 1762 he had entered into agreements with John Brown and Nicholas Marshall. When Marshall died in 1776 he was replaced by John Beaumont, and ten years later Beaumont's brother-in-law, Josiah Messer, joined the group. They in turn were followed by Beaumont's son, Abraham, and two more Josiah Messers—strong evidence of the close Quaker network both in business and family life. The most important partner, however, proved to be George Stacey, John Beaumont's son-in-law and the first of a dynasty of Staceys.

Corbyn had an excellent relationship with his suppliers, customers, and agents, but he expected prompt payment and did not hesitate to say so. He saw the necessity for taking out insurance, and in 1788 he published in the *Morning Chronicle* an article entitled 'Advantage of insurers or underwriters to merchants and traders exporting goods'. He also produced a catalogue, *Chemical and galenical medicine truly prepared and sold with all sorts of drugs, by Thomas Corbyn. Chemist and druggists, at the Bell and Dragon in Holborn, London. 1 month [January] 1789.*

Corbyn remained an active Quaker. In the severe winter of 1767 he joined with a number of other Friends in John Fothergill's scheme for the relief of the poor. Fish and potatoes were purchased at wholesale prices and sold at a small loss from established warehouses. He was, however, severe, authoritarian, and uncompromising in his attitudes, so much so that he was nicknamed 'the Quaker pope'. He clashed with William Cookworthy in Plymouth over disownment and the implementation of rigid discipline. However, James Jenkins wrote that he frequently lent money to young men starting in business—and not infrequently lost it.

Towards the end of his life, Corbyn moved from High Holborn to Bartholomew Close, where he died a widower on 14 February 1791. In his will he bequeathed sums of 5 to 50 guineas to his partners and employees, and to his Quaker friends and executors, and nearly £2000 in government securities to relatives and the Society of Friends. His son, John, already a partner, was to receive the property in Holborn and Coldbath Fields provided he paid £4200 to the executors. The residue of the estate was divided equally between all three children. The life and career of Thomas Corbyn shows that the expanding drug trade of the eighteenth century was based on greater trust and probity than is often thought. JUANITA BURNBY

**Sources** 'The monthly and two-week meetings of Society of Friends—a digest', typescript, RS Friends, Lond. • R. Porter and D. Porter, 'The rise of the English drugs industry: the role of Thomas Corbyn', *Medical History*, 33 (1989), 277–95 • T. D. Whittet and J. Burnby, 'The firm of Corbyn and Stacey', *Pharmaceutical Journal*, 228 (1982), 42–8 • 'A chapter of drug history', *Chemist and Druggist* (25 Jan 1896), 164–6 • A. L. Short, 'Corbyn, Stacey & Co', *Pharmaceutical Journal*, 199 (1967), 211–12 • W. H. Boorman, 'Corbyns and the county hospital Winchester, Hampshire', *The Indian Journal of*

*Hospital Pharmacy*, 1 (1962), 54 · minutes of the Apothecaries' Society of London, MS 8200/6 · James Jenkins's diary, RS Friends, Lond., ff 274 et seq MS · A. D. Selleck, *Cookworthy, a man of no common clay* (1978) · Wellcome L., Wellcome Corbyn MSS, Western MSS 5435–5460

**Archives** Camden Public Library, London, rates books of St Andrew's, Holborn, above bars · GL, records of the Society of Apothecaries of London · Wellcome L., Wellcome Corbyn MSS, Western MSS 5435–5460

**Wealth at death** over £25,000: will, PRO, PROB 11/1201/62

**Corcoran, Michael** (1827–1863), army officer, was born at Carrowskill, co. Sligo, Ireland, on 21 September 1827, the son of a British army captain. Commissioned into the Irish constabulary in 1845, he resigned in 1849 and emigrated to America, working as a clerk in the New York city post office. He joined the 69th New York militia, becoming colonel in 1859. At the outbreak of the civil war he was under court martial for refusing to parade the 69th in honour of Prince Albert. However, he was allowed to rejoin his regiment and led them at the first battle of Bull's Run, where he was wounded and made prisoner. Exchanged on 15 August 1862, he was made a brigadier-general, and raised an Irish legion. He took part in the battles of Nausomond and Suffolk in North Carolina in 1863, and checked the advance of the Confederates on Norfolk. He died, from the effects of a fall from his horse near Fairfax, Virginia, on 22 December 1863.

H. M. CHICHESTER, rev. M. G. M. JONES

**Sources** M. M. Boatner, *Cassell's biographical dictionary of the American Civil War, 1861–1865* (1973) · F. S. Drake, *Dictionary of American biography, including men of the time* (1872)

**Likenesses** photograph, 1861, repro. in W. C. Davis, *First blood: Fort Sumter to Bull Run*, The Civil War (1983) · painting, repro. in F. N. Boothe, *Great generals of the American Civil War and their battles* (1986)

**Corcoran, Timothy Joseph** (1872–1943), Roman Catholic priest and educationist, was born at Honeymount, near Roscrea, co. Tipperary, Ireland, on 17 January 1872, the first of seven children, five boys and two girls, born to Thomas Corcoran (1848–1922) and his wife, Alice Gleeson (1846–1911). Timothy, known as Tim, greatly admired his father, who managed an extensive farm and was the first chairman of north Tipperary county council. From 1878 he attended the local national school at Lisduff, and after fifth grade he was sent to the national school at Roscrea. In 1885 he moved to the Jesuit boarding-school at Tullabeg, near Tullamore, King's county, and in the following year transferred to another Jesuit boarding-school, Clongowes Wood College, co. Kildare, where he laid a strong foundation for his future studies in classics, history, and English literature. He entered the noviciate of the Irish province of the Society of Jesus, St Stanislaus College, at Tullabeg, in 1890, and after two years took his vows, followed by two years of instruction and study with a view to teaching in Jesuit schools.

In 1894 Corcoran was appointed to Clongowes as a teacher. The college was in the forefront of intermediate prize lists, and his teaching ability contributed to the school's successes. He combined firm discipline with an aptitude for methodical teaching, and had a special gift for map making. In 1901 he was sent to Louvain, Belgium, to study philosophy at St John's College. He continued there until 1904, but his main interest was in studying for his BA degree from the Royal University of Ireland, which he obtained in 1903, taking a first in history and economics, and also obtaining a double gold medal award for Latin verse and English verse. His time at Louvain meanwhile deepened his sense of being European and widened his knowledge of the educational systems of different countries.

Corcoran taught for two more years at Clongowes, during which time he also took the higher diploma in education, winning the gold medal award, from the Royal University. He next went to study theology at the Jesuit theologate, Miltown Park, Dublin. But his sights were set on obtaining a position in the new National University, constituted by the Irish Universities Act of 1908. He was appointed professor of the theory and practice of education, then a relatively new subject, in University College, Dublin, a constituent college of the university, in 1909. The initial problem was to get any students to apply for his courses, though eventually a small group was formed. It included Eamon De Valera, the future revolutionary and president of Ireland, who was said to be the new professor's first pupil. Corcoran repaid De Valera with a lifelong loyalty to him as a political leader, and appears to have played an important part in securing his appointment as chancellor of the National University in 1921. Loyalty to friends and causes to the point of fierceness was a feature of his character.

In 1911 Corcoran obtained the degree of DLitt for his 'Studies in the history of classical teaching, Irish and continental, 1500–1700', and the following year he founded *Studies*, the Jesuit quarterly review. There, and in another Jesuit publication, the *Irish Monthly*, he published a wide range of articles on educational topics. His writing on the subject of history manifested a desire to inculcate in youth a pride in their locality, country, and language—even though he himself had little Irish—and reflected an almost devout sense of nationhood. This, to an extent, was a reaction to the more colonial type of history which had hitherto prevailed. Indeed, he deliberately sought to wean students away from things English, including English educational methods, and to direct their attention to the European mainland, aiming to renew former links between Ireland and the continent. His attitude towards John Henry Newman reflected something of this outlook. He appreciated Newman as a great churchman and writer, but he held that the *Idea of a University* imaged the Oxford of Newman's day, a preserve of the ruling caste, and was far removed from the needs of the mass of the Irish people and from the tradition of the ancient Irish centres of learning and of the medieval universities.

In 1916 Corcoran published his *State Policy in Irish Education*, which established his reputation for pioneering work in a new field of historical writing, and was the basis for his lectures in Irish educational theory and history. With a view to giving Irish education a place in its own right, he also published over many years a series of booklets and pamphlets by himself and his students, some of which dealt with educational experiments in Ireland, while others presented the views of the great educationists in their own words. The 1920s were a time of great productivity, not just in his work as professor and as adviser on education to the new state, but also as a writer. He published four books, and numerous articles in periodicals such as *Thought*, *Studies*, and the *Irish Monthly*—to which he contributed some hundred articles on education from 1923 to 1932. His publications are listed in *Sources for the History of Irish Civilization* (ed. R. J. Hayes, 1970, 1.694–9). In addition he wrote under a variety of pseudonyms in the *Catholic Bulletin* from 1923 to its demise in 1939. These articles and reviews were frequently marked by a polemical, abrasive vehemence.

Corcoran's impact on education structures in the new Irish state was of particular significance. His influence through the commissions of education set up in 1921 was many-sided, but he is notably associated with new history and geography programmes, and with the requirement that Irish language teaching should be obligatory from the first days of primary education. He insisted that all school subjects be imbued with 'Catholic truth'. This last involved teacher training in 'Catholic philosophy'. His insistence that Irish should be taught to the youngest classes by native speakers proved quite impractical as there were few teachers available. The very largeness of conception in his programme for secondary schools created problems for many teachers and pupils, but such considerations, or practical criticism of his views on the teaching of Irish, received little sympathy from him. He stretched himself to the full and expected the same from others.

A fellow Jesuit, Cyril Power, who had experienced the educational system before and after Corcoran's reforms, remarked that they

> led to a widening of courses in Mathematics, to more texts in Classics, to a broader approach in History and to the development of Irish History and Geography, and to a special emphasis on the Irish language. Generally, the new courses were no longer as narrow, petty, and grammatical as they had been. (Power and Morrissey)

Corcoran was also a gifted teacher, in Power's view, but he could be aloof, rough, and rude, and 'always wanted his own way' (ibid.). No doubt part of his aloofness and abruptness of manner was a shield for shyness. Tributes from past students after his death, however, suggested that many had experienced the human being behind the carapace. He was very close to his own family and took their financial troubles to heart; he assisted them out of his own salary without reference to his religious superiors. Something of that sense of family he extended to his students and to the teaching staff in his department.

Just before Christmas 1941 Corcoran suffered a paralytic stroke. He never taught again, though he did not resign as professor until September 1942. He died at St Vincent's Nursing Home, St Stephen's Green, Dublin, on 23 March 1943, and was buried at Glasnevin cemetery. He had helped to change the educational system of his country,

and had opened up the study of education in Ireland; through his own writings and those of his students he remained a source of influence. He was a successful director of research, although much of his historical work was apologetic. As a personality, his indefatigable energy and machine-like observance of punctuality combined with his innate forcefulness to produce an outsize, almost epical figure seemingly invulnerable to the dislike and criticism he generated.            THOMAS J. MORRISSEY

**Sources** Irish Jesuit Archives, Dublin · *Irish Province News* (July 1943), 754 · J. G. Deegan, 'An assessment of the contribution of Reverend Professor Timothy Corcoran, S.J. to the development of education in Ireland', MEd diss., University College, Cork, 1981 · J. O'Neill, D. F. Gleeson, and M. Beaumont, 'Father T. Corcoran, S.J.', *Studies*, 32 (1943) · C. Power and T. Morrissey, interview, 4 Sept 1974 · H. Delany, 'The hidden persuaders: T. J. Corcoran, S.J., D.Litt., and the national programmes 1922 and 1926', MEd diss., TCD, 1981 · P. Durkin, 'The contribution of T. J. Corcoran to Irish educational policy and provision', DipEd diss., TCD, 1983
**Archives** Archives of the Irish Province of the Society of Jesus, Dublin
**Likenesses** photograph, 1912, Archives of the Irish Province of the Society of Jesus, Dublin · S. Keating, oils, 1942, University College, Dublin

**Corda, Oswald** (*d.* 1434), author and prior of the Charterhouse, Perth, was almost certainly born in Bavaria, though some sources state that he was English or Scottish. He may have studied at Paris before being admitted to the Charterhouse of Hortus Christi near Nordlingen in Bavaria *c.*1405, and transferred to the Grande Chartreuse in May or June 1414. While at the mother house, possibly in 1410 but more probably in 1417, he completed his major work, the *Opus pacis* (extracts from which are edited by Lehmann), on the correction of texts. His work circulated extensively, but not exclusively, within his own order: of ten extant manuscripts, two are Benedictine and eight are Carthusian. Between April 1424 and April or May 1429 he conducted a close correspondence (edited by Glorieux) with Jean Gerson (*d.* 1429), chancellor of the University of Paris, in which Corda addressed to him many questions on practical and spiritual subjects and developed an already fruitful relationship between the *doctor christianissimus* and Corda's own order. Corda may have translated some of Gerson's treatises from French into Latin, though other works have been attributed to him by mistake. He became vicar of the Grande Chartreuse, apparently between 1424 and 1427, and first prior of the Charterhouse of Vallis Virtutis at Perth in 1429. The circumstances of his appointment to the latter office are unknown, but it is likely that he was chosen by the authorities at the Grande Chartreuse, following their grant of permission for the foundation of the Perth Charterhouse in a letter of 19 August 1426. As prior, Corda advanced James I's new foundation, acquired a contemporary reputation for learning and sanctity, and, according to the acts of the Carthusian general chapter, died in office on 15 September 1434, though less official and less reliable sources give the year as 1437.            W. N. M. BECKETT

**Sources** J. Hogg, 'Oswald de Corda: a forgotten Carthusian of Nordlingen', *Analecta Cartusiana*, 55/3 (1982), 181–5 · P. Lehmann, 'Bücherliebe und Bücherpflege bei den Kartäusern', *Miscellanea

*Francesco Ehrle*, 5 (1924), 364–89 · J. Gerson, *Oeuvres complètes*, ed. P. Glorieux, 2 (Paris, 1960) · P. Glorieux, 'Gerson et les Chartreux', *Recherches de Théologie Ancienne et Médiévale*, 28 (1961), 115–53 · M. G. Sargent, 'The transmission by the English Carthusians of some late medieval spiritual writings', *Journal of Ecclesiastical History*, 27 (1976), 225–40 · J. Hogg and others, eds., *The chartae of the Carthusian general chapter*, Analecta Cartusiana, 100/1–24 (1982–94) · W. Bower, *Scotichronicon*, ed. D. E. R. Watt and others, new edn, 9 vols. (1987–98), vol. 8 · Bale, *Cat.* · T. Petreius, *Bibliotheca Cartusiana, sive, Illustrium sacri Cartusiensis ordinis scriptorum catalogus* (1609) · Tanner, *Bibl. Brit.-Hib.* · C. Le Couteulx, *Annales ordinis cartusiensis*, 7 (1890) · L. Le Vasseur, *Ephemerides ordinis cartusiensis*, 3 (1891)
**Archives** University of Basel, corresp. with Jean Gerson, MS A.viii.32

**Cordell, Charles** (1720–1791), Roman Catholic priest, was born on 5 October 1720, the son of Charles Cordell of Holborn, London, and his wife, Hannah, *née* Darell, of Scotney Castle, Sussex, and Calehill, Kent. Educated at Dame Alice's school at Fernyhalgh, Lancashire, he entered the English College at Douai in March 1734, and was ordained priest at Arras in December 1744. He was chaplain at Arundel Castle 1748–55 and then at Red Hall, an estate also owned by the Howards, at Roundhay, Leeds, Yorkshire. On 10 June 1765 he took charge of the secular chapel in Newgate Street, Newcastle upon Tyne, where he continued until his death.

Cordell was a Jacobite in politics but an ecclesiastical progressive. He was admired for his preaching skills and he was an advocate of an English liturgy. His first literary effort was the controversial publication, at his own expense, of a four-volume edition of *The Divine Office for the Use of the Laity* (1763). To the further disapproval of the bishops, he introduced Sunday vespers in English at the chapel in Newcastle and in 1780 he issued a second edition of his *Divine Office* in a more convenient two-volume format; it was reissued in Manchester in 1806. Pope Clement XIV (the Franciscan Giovanni Ganganelli) suppressed the Society of Jesus in 1773 and Cordell reprimanded William Warrilow, his colleague and former Jesuit missioner in Newcastle, for criticizing the pope in the local press; relations between them never recovered. Cordell pursued his interest in Clement: in 1776 he published translations from the French as *The Life of Pope Clement XIV* and in the following year two volumes of *Interesting Letters of Pope Clement XIV*. In a *Letter* of 1785 he attacked the former Jesuits John Thorpe and John Jones, who had published *A Candid and Impartial Sketch of the Life and Government of Pope Clement XIV* (1785) which vilified the pontiff.

Cordell's later publication of translations from the French of some obscure works prompted Henry Rutter, a fellow missioner in the area, to remark that he had *cacoethes scribendi*; Rutter also questioned Cordell's wisdom because many unsold copies of the books were left on Cordell's hands (Gooch, *Revival*). Cordell was influential in the development of the book trade in Newcastle. His scholarly reputation led to an offer of the presidency of the English College at St Omer in 1778 but he declined it. Cordell became odd, though whether this was a symptom of eccentricity or illness is unclear; Rutter said that Cordell was never invited to participate in Holy Week services

because he would create confusion, and he reported that in his later years Cordell was unable to carry out any ecclesiastical duty and had asked to be buried in his garden (ibid.). Cordell died on 26 January 1791 and was buried in St John's Church, Newcastle.      LEO GOOCH

**Sources** G. Anstruther, *The seminary priests*, 4 (1977), 72 · Gillow, *Lit. biog. hist.* · L. Gooch, *The revival of English Catholicism* (1995) · L. Gooch, *Paid at sundry times: Yorkshire clergy finances in the eighteenth century* (1997), no. 15 · F. Blom and others, *English Catholic books, 1701–1800: a bibliography* (1996)
**Wealth at death** bequeathed only small artefacts of little value: will, 28 April 1791, summarised in Anstruther, *Seminary priests*

**Cordell, Sir William** (1522–1581), lawyer and speaker of the House of Commons, was the eldest son of John Cordell, originally from Edmonton, who had become the principal servant to Sir William Clopton (d. 1531) of Kentwell in Long Melford, Suffolk, and Lincoln's Inn. His mother was Emma, daughter of Henry Webb of Kimbolton, Huntingdonshire. He was probably brought up in Clopton's household, and sent to Lincoln's Inn through his influence. A William Cordall was admitted to Gray's Inn in 1534, but can hardly have been the same person. The future master of the rolls was only sixteen when he joined Lincoln's Inn in 1538, and was called to the bar while still very young in 1544. He became a bencher in 1553 and gave a reading in 1554. Besides his extensive private practice, he was a founder member of the Russia Company, and his standing in society became sufficient to require a grant of arms for his father in 1548 and another for himself (quartering Webb) in 1549.

Cordell's election to the bench of his inn coincided with his appointment as solicitor-general to Mary I in 1553, a position that he held until 1557 when he became master of the rolls and a member of the privy council. He served in five parliaments between 1545 and 1571, and was speaker in 1558, when the queen knighted him. He was executor to Queen Mary, to Cardinal Pole, and to Archbishop Parker. Elizabeth I did not include him in her reduced privy council, but he continued as master of the rolls until his death in 1581.

Cordell married Mary (d. 1584), granddaughter of his father's master, being the daughter of Richard Clopton of Groton, and was able to buy the manor of Long Melford for himself from the crown in 1554. There he built Melford Hall, which was completed in 1559 and where he received Elizabeth I in 1578. However, he left no surviving children of his own. He founded a hospital of the Holy Trinity at Long Melford, and supported the foundation of St John's College, Oxford, of which he was the first visitor.

Cordell was responsible for a set of chancery ordinances in 1574, and for reorganizing the six clerks in 1578, but a historian has described his tenure as 'a praiseworthy record of competence' in contrast with the more enthusiastic tenure of Sir Thomas Egerton at the end of the century. Egerton was later to complain that Cordell had surrendered the House of Converts to the crown, and given up some rights of the office in connection with the public records. Cordell died at The Rolls in Chancery Lane on 17 May 1581, and was buried in Long Melford church, where there is an alabaster effigy in armour. There is also a three-quarter length portrait in Melford Hall, which shows that he had a short face with reddish hair and beard. He left numerous small charitable bequests including £20 to be distributed among the poor scholars of Cambridge and Oxford 'unto suche as be moste towardes in vertewe and learninge'. His legacies included a jewel with a unicorn's horn, which he settled to go in succession, and a book on parchment 'conteyninge a matter betweene King Henrie the seaventhe and Edmonde Dudley esquier', which he left to Sir William Cecil. His executors were his sister Jane (d. 1604), George Carew, and his brother Edward (d. 1594), a six clerk in Chancery. On the failure of his issue, his lands were inherited by Jane, who married Richard Allington.

J. H. Baker

Sources HoP, Commons, 1509–58, 1.702–3 · Foss, Judges, 5.476–8 · Cooper, Ath. Cantab., 1.431–3 · W. Hervey, The visitation of Suffolke, ed. J. J. Howard, 1 (1866), 47 et seq., 245 et seq. · will, PRO, PROB 11/63, sig. 42 · W. J. Jones, The Elizabethan court of chancery (1967), 58–60 · W. Hervey, The visitation of Suffolk, 1561, ed. J. Corder, 1, Harleian Society, new ser., 2 (1981), 28–9 · Sainty, Judges, 150 · W. P. Baildon, ed., The records of the Honorable Society of Lincoln's Inn: the black books, 1 (1897) · CPR, 1553–4, 217–19; 1554–5, 203 · D. MacCulloch, ed., The chorography of Suffolk, Suffolk RS, 19 (1976), 54–5, 116

Likenesses oils, c.1560–1570, Melford Hall, Suffolk · C. Cure, alabaster tomb effigy, c.1581, Holy Trinity Church, Long Melford, Suffolk

**Corden, William, the elder** (1797–1867), painter, was born at Ashbourne, Derbyshire, on 28 November 1797. He was apprenticed at the china works at Derby under Robert Bloor, where he was employed to paint portraits, landscapes, and flowers on china. He painted much of a dessert service with illustrations after John Thurston for William Tegg's edition of the plays of Shakespeare (1812). On 25 September 1816 he married at St Alkmund's, Derby, Hester Simpson. About 1820, on completing his apprenticeship, Corden began to concentrate on portrait painting, painting first his employer, Bloor, and his wife. In 1820–21 Corden painted figure subjects on a dessert service for the third Lord Henley-Ongley. The sixth duke of Devonshire acquired Berlin porcelain plates which Corden was allowed to copy; one, with a view of Chatsworth, may be from Corden's design. He seems to have been among the painters who decorated with landscapes and figures the enormously elaborate Rockingham dessert service (144 plates and 56 large pieces), made at Swinton between 1830 and 1837 for William IV, at the cost of £5000. It was first used at Queen Victoria's coronation celebrations (Royal Collection).

Careless in firing, Corden was not technically a very good enamel painter, but was an excellent colourist. At Coalport, where he worked from 1820, Corden painted portraits onto blanks made in the factory for outside decoration. These china plaques became a popular new genre, especially in Derby and Nottingham. From 1824 Corden had a London address and exhibited three times at the Royal Academy; 'Hebe', on porcelain, was shown in 1826, and, in 1836, his last exhibit was a copy on china of

Sir Thomas Lawrence's portrait of Sir Walter Scott (Royal Collection).

In July 1829 Corden was commissioned to paint one of the king's pages, a Mr Batchelor, at Windsor. He also painted Admiral Sir Edmund Nagle for George IV in 1829. Illness prevented the king from sitting to him, but the Marchioness Conyngham employed him at Windsor. Corden had settled at Windsor by 1836 where, in June 1838, he drew Queen Victoria on the East Terrace, and copies were made in miniature of his drawing (Royal Collection). A similar portrait (Art Journal, 1901, 99) was there described as the first sketch made of her after her accession and was extensively copied by him on ivory and porcelain. For Queen Victoria, Corden painted very many life-size oil copies after portraits in the Royal Collection. In 1844 Prince Albert arranged that Corden should visit Coburg to copy Saxe-Coburg family portraits.

From 1854 Corden was again employed in the Staffordshire potteries. There he worked with the miniature painter and photographer, Mr Scaife of Baker Street, on a project (which proved unsuccessful) to combine enamelling with photography. Corden died at Nottingham on 18 June 1867.

His son, **William Corden the younger** (1819–1900), painter, was born in Derby, where he was baptized at St Alkmund's Church on 19 August 1819; he moved with his family to Windsor in 1829. He studied and worked with his father and they travelled together to Coburg in 1844 where he painted six watercolour views of the town for Prince Albert. The younger Corden was sent to Lisbon in 1850 by Queen Victoria and the prince to copy the portrait of Ferdinand, king consort of Portugal, by Ferdinand Krumholz. Instead it was arranged that he should himself paint full-lengths of Queen Maria II and her husband (Royal Collection). Corden was constantly employed by Queen Victoria to copy portraits in her collection, usually as presents. These included about fifty by F. X. Winterhalter and others by such artists as H. von Angeli, A. Graefle, H. R. Graves, G. Koberwein, R. Lauchert, J. Lucas, and J. Sant. Corden also painted photographs of watercolours for the queen. He exhibited eight works, including subject pictures, at the Royal Academy, between 1843 and 1855, and one at the British Institution. William Corden the younger died on 7 September 1900 at Salisbury Terrace, Newbury, Berkshire. His son, Victor Milton Corden (c.1860–1939), painter of landscape and military subjects, who was baptized on 28 July 1860 at Datchet, Buckinghamshire, when his mother's name was recorded as Elizabeth, also worked for Queen Victoria.

Delia Millar

Sources A. Cox and A. Cox, Rockingham pottery and porcelain 1745–1842 (1983) · A. Wallis and W. Bemrose, The pottery and porcelain of Derbyshire (1870) · B. S. Long, British miniaturists (1929); repr. (1966) · D. Foskett, A dictionary of British miniature painters, 2 vols. (1972) · O. Millar, The later Georgian pictures in the collection of her majesty the queen, 2 vols. (1969) · J. Haslern, The old Derby china factory (1876), 113–16 · Jewitt's ceramic art of Great Britain, 1800–1900, rev. edn, rev. G. A. Godden (1972) · D. G. Rice, The illustrated guide to Rockingham pottery and porcelain (1971) · B. Hughes and T. Hughes, English porcelain and bone china, 1743–1851 (1955) · O. Millar, The Victorian pictures in *the collection of her majesty the queen*, 1 (1992), 57–8 · *IGI* · d. cert. [William Corden the younger]

**Corden, William, the younger** (1819–1900). *See under* Corden, William, the elder (1797–1867).

**Corder, Stephen Pit** (1918–1990), university professor, was born on 6 October 1918, at 4 Bootham Terrace, York, the second of the two sons of Philip Corder (*b.* 1885), schoolmaster, and his wife, Johanna Adriana van der Mersch (*b.* 1887). His father was English and his mother Dutch. Pit, as he was known to colleagues, attended the Quaker school, Bootham, in York. At Merton College, Oxford (1936–9), he read modern languages. Corder's father belonged to an old Quaker family and was himself a master at Bootham School. After Oxford, Corder taught at Ayton (Quaker) school until he was called up for military service in the Second World War. Having registered as a conscientious objector, he was awarded exemption conditional on his working with the Friends' Ambulance Unit (FAU). He served with the FAU throughout the war period in Finland and Egypt. In 1946 Corder married Nancy Proctor (*b.* 1916). Second cousins, they maintained his mother's house in the Lake District during their years abroad. They had two sons and a daughter.

After the war Corder joined the British Council, and served in Austria, Turkey, Colombia, and Jamaica. At the time the council was rapidly expanding its English teaching operations worldwide. For this purpose it needed a cadre of specialists. Corder's background in language studies and his own interest in the work led in 1957 to his joining the newly established school of applied linguistics in the University of Edinburgh to study for the postgraduate diploma in applied linguistics. After that year he was seconded for a period to the Nigerian ministry of education in order to develop language teaching materials for television. Then in 1961 he was outposted by the British Council to the University of Leeds, where Peter Strevens, with whom he had served in the FAU, was developing postgraduate training in English language teaching. In 1964 he resigned from the British Council on appointment as director of the school of applied linguistics at the University of Edinburgh. There he remained for the rest of his career, serving successively as senior lecturer, professor of applied linguistics, head of the department of applied linguistics, and head of the very large department of linguistics, which had more than thirty academic staff. He was a founder member of the British Association of Applied Linguistics, following Peter Strevens as its second chair, president of the International Association of Applied Linguistics for two successive periods of three years each, a member of the British Council's English teaching advisory committee, and the first holder of a university chair in applied linguistics in the UK (and possibly in the world). He was promoted to a personal chair in 1971 and was created emeritus professor on retirement in 1983.

The Edinburgh school (later department) of applied linguistics had been set up in the late 1950s with government funding under the Colombo plan to provide at an advanced level research-based training for English teachers from the former colonies. Corder quickly brought together a young and enthusiastic team of academic researchers, and with them developed the influential teaching materials that became internationally known through the four volumes of the *Edinburgh Course in Applied Linguistics*, published by Oxford University Press (1973–7). As academic applied linguistics swiftly expanded to other universities, many of Corder's students were appointed to lead the new departments.

Corder's publications chart his own intellectual development, moving from the very traditional (and successful) textbook *An International English Practice Book* (1960), through the early attempt to integrate language teaching with situation in *The Visual Element in Language Teaching* (1966), on to the magisterial defining of a coherent linguistic discipline in *Introduction to Applied Linguistics* (1973), and finally to the innovative cognitive approach in his later papers, brought together in *Error Analysis and Interlanguage* (1981). It was these papers in which he offered a view of language learning that captured the imagination of researchers internationally, providing them with a rationale for investigation that remains hugely productive. What Corder pointed to was both daring and obvious, but he was the first to provide the necessary explanation: namely, that the learning of a second or foreign language is developmental, that it follows a sequence that can be checked, and that it can be studied by analysing the errors that learners make. These errors, he insisted, are signs of positive thinking rather than of negative inadequacy. Corder's claim that the learner's language, which, following a seminal paper by Larry Selinker (1972), he termed 'interlanguage', is a language in its own right is now generally accepted.

In spite of the esteem of his colleagues in British applied linguistics, in the late 1970s and 1980s Corder seems to have found himself increasingly isolated intellectually. In part this reflected his growing dissatisfaction with the British tradition of English language teaching, to which applied linguistics was initially attached and which Corder himself had done so much to promote in his early career and in the *Edinburgh Course in Applied Linguistics*. That approach he came to see as finally wanting, considering that its attempt to marry bits of theory to practical issues was ultimately incoherent. What was needed, he seems to have thought, was a proper marriage between practice and theory. His dissatisfaction also reflected both his own excitement in ideas, his moving on always to new ventures, and his lack of interest in anything empirical, whether in practice or in research. Language teaching as such did not engage him, thereby absolving his students and younger scholars from any responsibility for the ever-increasing gap between language teaching practice and language acquisition research. Neither was he personally excited by research. That he left to his students. What really mattered to Corder was the sudden poetic or artistic insight, 'the incision of inspiration which cut through the clutter of established thought' (Widdowson, vi).

Corder's ideas were influential but he did not establish a

'school'. He inspired by example and by his own intellectual curiosity. He belonged to a very British tradition of speculative curiosity. His hobbies showed that, just as much as did his intellectual interests. His craftsmanship in wood, his music, and his home-making and family were as important to him as his career. He was a man of conviction, clear about his place in the world. That is why he could move from one phase of his career to another with finality. After a series of mild heart attacks he retired in 1983, and when he and his wife moved back to the Lake District he donated all his academic books to his department. They and the rest of his academic life had provided a temporary vehicle for his speculation. He did not look back. Corder died of a heart attack on 27 January 1990 at his home, Burnside Cottage, Braithwaite, near Keswick. He was survived by his wife and children.

ALAN DAVIES

**Sources** A. Davies, *Newsletter* [British Association of Applied Linguistics], 36 (1990), 33–5 · H. G. Widdowson, *Applied Linguistics*, 11/4 (1990), v, vi · A. P. R. Howatt, 'The academic works of S. Pit Corder (1918–1990): a bibliography', *Applied Linguistics*, 12/1 (1991), 96–101 · R. Mitchell, *Notes on the history of the British Association of Applied Linguistics* (1997) [occasional paper of the BAAL] · S. P. Corder, 'Teaching linguistics: Edinburgh', 1974, U. Edin., department of theoretical and applied linguistics · A. Davies, 'British applied linguistics: the contribution of S. Pit Corder', *Foreign/second language pedagogy research*, ed. R. Phillipson and others (1991), 52–60 · A. Davies, C. Criper, and A. P. R. Howatt, eds., *Interlanguage* (1984) · *CGPLA Eng. & Wales* (1990) · L. Selinker, 'Interlanguage', *International Review of Applied Linguistics*, 19 (1972), 200–31 · private information (2004) [Nancy Corder, widow] · b. cert. · d. cert.

**Wealth at death** £93,316: probate, 28 March 1990, *CGPLA Eng. & Wales*

**Corder, Susanna** (1787–1864), biographer, was born in Stoke Newington, Middlesex, the daughter of John Corder and Ruth Marriage, both Quakers. A delicate child, she was educated from 1797 to 1799 at Ackworth School in Yorkshire. About the age of twenty, after a period of spiritual depression, she experienced a deepening of her religious commitment. She nursed her mother devotedly until her death, after which she decided to pursue a career in teaching, to which she had long felt called. From 1817 to 1824 she taught at a school at Suir Island, Clonmel, Ireland, which she enjoyed. In 1824 she returned to England and, with the help of William Allen and other leading Quakers, started a school for girls at Fleetwood House in Stoke Newington, which was modelled on the Irish establishment.

Corder's school was a progressive one: the curriculum included astronomy, experimental philosophy, physics, and natural history, as well as more traditional subjects such as writing, arithmetic, history, French, and needlework. Greek, Latin, German, and Italian were offered as extras, and William Allen gave lectures on chemistry and lent his telescope for the use of the pupils. In 1827 the wide range of subjects offered was celebrated in some doggerel verses by one Joseph Pease, who referred to the 'astounding variety of stores intellectual imbibed by pupils at the "N[ewington] Nunnery"' (Shirren, 163). By that date the number of pupils had risen from twelve to twenty-five.

If the curriculum was liberal, the general regime of the school was not. In her youth Susanna Corder had experienced 'much conflict of mind on the subject of dress' (*Annual Monitor*, 43) and had adopted the full austerity of traditional Quaker dress. Accordingly, her pupils were required to wear stiff Quaker bonnets, which exposed them to the ridicule of their contemporaries at a neighbouring school. The religious needs of pupils were catered for extravagantly: copious spiritual readings and talks were given by such visitors as Allen and Sarah Grubb. The high days and holidays of the school year consisted of visits to the British Museum and attendance at the yearly meeting in London.

The ethos of the school reflected the essential conservatism of Susanna Corder's religion. She herself was described as 'an embodiment of perfection as regards propriety of manner, costume, and doctrine of the medieval section of the Friends' Society' (Shirren, 162). She became an elder of the local meeting soon after her return to Stoke Newington, and it was in this capacity that she signed a warning letter to John Wilkinson, whose heterodox views produced a schism among the Stoke Quakers in 1836. She was also on the revising committee of the Morning Meeting for fifteen years. In 1841 she published *A Brief Outline of the Origin, Principles, and Church Government of the Society of Friends*, in which her strong adherence to the traditional Quaker dress, manners, and doctrine was clearly manifested.

Susanna Corder retired between 1840 to 1845, and moved to Chelmsford, where she spent the rest of her life. She now turned entirely to her writing. Corder had already published her most successful work, *Memorials of Deceased Members of the Society of Friends* (2nd edn, 1839), which went through at least six revised editions. These sketches of the lives of eighteenth- and nineteenth-century English and American Quakers concentrated on their spiritual experiences, opinions, and work, and often recounted their edifying deaths in great detail. Her subjects were largely obscure; one was her own pupil Ann Backhouse, who had died at the age of nineteen. Corder's emphasis on the inner spiritual lives of her characters—rather than their (often unspectacular) public careers—no doubt helped to ensure a roughly equal balance of male and female subjects: the second edition (1839) included twenty-seven men and twenty women. Corder's most significant work, however, was her 1853 biography of the prison reformer Elizabeth Fry, which she wrote at the request of Fry's family. Based largely on Fry's diaries, from which it quotes continually and extensively, the *Life* succeeded in tracing the inner spiritual journey of a well-known public figure; it still remains an important source for Fry's life. Three years later Corder wrote a memoir of Priscilla Gurney, Fry's sister.

Susanna Corder also published *Christian Instruction in the History, Types, and Prophecies of the Old Testament* (1854), an 'epitome of Scriptural history and doctrine' (p. iii). The text of this work—which, as Corder herself said, does not rival the 'impressive sublimity of the beautifully simple style of the Sacred Volume' (ibid., 1)—shows the author's usual tendency towards an earnest and ponderous verbosity. She also wrote several pamphlets, including one advocating the exercise of spiritual gifts by women (1839), which reached a third edition. Susanna Corder died on 28 February 1864 at her home in Chelmsford, and she was buried in Chelmsford on 3 March.

Rosemary Mitchell

**Sources** 'Dictionary of Quaker biography', RS Friends, Lond. [card index] · A. J. Shirren, *The chronicles of Fleetwood House* (1951), 159–66 · *Annual Monitor* (1864), 42–51 · *The Friend*, new ser., 4 (1864), 98 · B. Marshall, *Emma Marshall: a biographical sketch* (1900), 12–13 · J. Sherman, *Memoir of William Allen FRS* (1851) · *CGPLA Eng. & Wales* (1864)

**Wealth at death** under £5000: probate, 4 May 1864, *CGPLA Eng. & Wales*

**Corder, William** (1804–1828), murderer, was born in Polstead, Suffolk, on 22 June 1804, the son of John Corder, farmer, and his wife, Mary. He attended the local village school and then an academy at Hadleigh. At that time he was described as slender with a stoop. He took off for London and met up with some undesirable companions, among whom was Hannah Fandango, a young prostitute whose pimp was Samuel 'Beauty' Smith. In 1824 his father summoned him home to work on the farm and there he met **Maria Marten** (1801–1827), the daughter of a local mole-catcher. Maria had already borne an illegitimate, short-lived child fathered by William's brother, Thomas. William and Maria soon produced another child, which lived only two weeks. On his frequent visits to the house where Maria still lived with her parents, Corder was pressed to marriage by Maria's father and stepmother, Anne, and to this he agreed. His disreputable friends from London then embarrassingly turned up in Polstead. Corder convinced Maria that the police were searching for her in connection with the illegitimate children and that they must run away secretly to escape them. She dressed in male attire and took with her female garments. Both were seen leaving the Martens' house on 18 May 1827 separately in the direction of the barn where they had conducted their courting and which was to become notorious as the 'Red Barn'. There Corder murdered Maria, by shooting her with a pistol, stabbing her many times with a knife, and finally suffocating her with her own handkerchief. He continued to visit the Martens and put forward various and conflicting excuses for Maria's absence, saying she was the companion to a lady in Yarmouth or Ipswich and too busy to write, then that they were going to London to be married, and later that they were married and living in the Isle of Wight. Mrs Marten then began to have dreams that Maria's body was buried in the barn and a search in April 1828 revealed that this was indeed so.

Corder had by now married at St Andrew's, Holborn, in November 1827, a respectable schoolmistress, Mary Moore; he had placed an advertisement in the *Morning Herald* of 13 November 1827, which generated an enormous response. Mrs Corder had set up a school for ladies in Brentford, and there Corder was arrested and brought for trial at Bury St Edmunds. The trial was a public sensation, and extensively reported in *The Times*. Corder pleaded not

William Corder (1804–1828), by unknown engraver, pubd 1828 [in Bury gaol a few days before his trial]

guilty, and said that Maria had shot herself and died while he was seeking help; he claimed to have hidden her body through fear of a murder accusation. However, a great deal of evidence was brought forward to prove his guilt. Chief Baron Alexander summed up against Corder and the jury brought in a guilty verdict. In court Corder, who was said to be aged about forty (but who was in fact twenty-four), and who was 5 feet 5 inches tall, with fair hair, a large mouth and eyes, and a turned-up nose, appeared in a frock coat with a velvet collar, black waistcoat, and blue trousers. He was hanged and, apparently unusually, drawn and quartered on 11 August 1828, having admitted his guilt and asking his wife's forgiveness. She had been regularly in court and visited him assiduously in gaol.

The execution was witnessed by a huge crowd, estimated at ten thousand; even more came to listen to sermons preached near the Red Barn. Corder's body was flayed, the skin tanned, and the skeleton preserved in the local hospital where the surgeon, George Creed, carried out the autopsy. The skeleton, from which it is possible that the skull was removed and replaced by that of an unknown person, ended up in the Hunterian Museum in London. The real skull is reputed to have changed hands many times, bringing with it bad luck to any owner. The tanned skin was used to cover a book by J. Curtis about the crime; the Moyse's Hall Museum, Bury St Edmunds, had the object, along with other relics such as Corder's scalp and a replica of the death mask (the original of which was in Norwich Castle), at the end of the twentieth century.

The murder was the subject of various contemporary peepshow productions, including one by Lord George Sanger, and many broadsheets (for example those published by J. Catnach) and 'penny dreadfuls'. Ceramics of the Red Barn were also made shortly after the trial. A 'serial' book by W. Maginn entitled *The Red Barn* appeared in 1828. Theatrical performances on the subject were widely given, such as *The Red Farm, or, The Well of St Marie*, adapted from the French of D'Ennery and Lemoine by W. T. Moncrieff and first produced at Sadler's Wells on 29 August 1842. Another play on the subject of the murder was put on at the Elephant and Castle in the 1920s. A film was made by MGM in 1935, *Maria Marten, or, The Murder at the Red Barn*. A melodrama by Brian J. Burton, *The Murder of Maria Marten, or, The Red Barn*, was published in 1964. These works, along with a stream of novels and non-fiction, testify to the lasting impact of this sordid crime.

ALSAGER VIAN, *rev.* J. GILLILAND

**Sources** P. Haining, *Buried passions* (1992) · *The Times* (8 Aug 1828) · *The Times* (9 Aug 1828) · *The Times* (10 Aug 1828) · *The Times* (12 Aug 1828) · J. H. H. Gaute, *The new murderers' Who's Who* (1989) · R. H. Lewis, *Victorian murders* (1988) · D. McCormick, *The Red Barn mystery* (1967) · J. Curtis, *An authentic and faithful history of the mysterious murder of Maria Marten* (1828) · D. Gibbs and H. J. M. Maltby, *The true story of Maria Marten* (1949) · R. Arnold and others, *Maria Marten: murder in the red barn* (1966) · D. McCormick, *The Red Barn mystery* (1967) · R. Church, *More murder in East Anglia* (1990) · H. M. Walbrook, *Murders and murder trials, 1812–1912* (1932) · W. Maginn, 'The red barn', a tale, founded on fact (1828) · H. Swales, 'Maria Marten', *Suffolk Fair*, 1/6 (Aug/Sept 1971) · J. Hines, 'The doctor who scalped a killer', *East Anglia Monthly*, 1/16 (Feb 1978)
**Archives** Moyse's Hall Museum, Bury St Edmunds · Norwich Castle · Suffolk RO
**Likenesses** engraving, pubd 1828, NPG [*see illus.*] · death mask, Norwich Castle Museum · effigy, Madame Tussaud's, London · portrait, repro. in J. Timbs, *English eccentrics and eccentricities* (1877), 316 · prints, BM, NPG

**Corderoy, Jeremy** (*b.* 1562/3), religious writer, was the son of a Wiltshire gentleman. He matriculated in February 1581, aged eighteen, at St Alban Hall, Oxford. After taking his degree in arts he proceeded to his MA (Hart Hall, 1584) and continued to reside there to study theology. He took holy orders and in July 1590 was appointed junior chaplain of Merton College, a post in which he is recorded alongside Robert Brierley until 1595 and which he may have held for at least thirteen years and possibly longer. Although not fellows, both were granted borrowing rights in the newly shelved college library.

Both Corderoy's published works are framed as theological disputations between a scholar of orthodox convictions and religious controversialists. The earlier, *A Short Dialogue* (1604), is an attack on church papistry and sets out to establish that no one may be saved without good works.

It was issued in a second corrected edition in 1604 and reprinted a decade later. The second discourse, *A Warning for Worldlings* (1608), was dedicated to Lord Chancellor Ellesmere and was an appeal for support against the 'outragious dealing of Atheists'. In the latter disputation the 'scholler' would appear to be Corderoy himself, and he writes of his not having been preferred to any living, since, although two had been offered to him, they were not such as he could enter into with a good conscience. Wood slightly observed that 'his life and conversation was without exception' (Wood, *Ath. Oxon.*, 2.47). The date and place of Corderoy's death are unknown.

ALSAGER VIAN, *rev.* NICHOLAS W. S. CRANFIELD

**Sources** J. M. Fletcher, ed., *Registrum annalium collegii Mertonensis, 1567–1603*, OHS, new ser., 24 (1976) · G. H. Martin and J. R. L. Highfield, *A history of Merton College, Oxford* (1997) · J. Corderoy, *A short dialogue wherein is proved that no man can bee saved without good workes*, 2nd edn (1604); repr. (1615) · J. Corderoy, *A warning for worldlings* (1608) · Foster, *Alum. Oxon.* · Wood, *Ath. Oxon.*, new edn, 2.47

**Cordiner, Charles** (1746?–1794), Scottish Episcopal clergyman and antiquary, lived most of his life in Banff, and became minister of St Andrew's Chapel there in 1769. Few other biographical details concerning him survive. He died at Banff on 18 November 1794, leaving a widow and eight children. James *Cordiner (1775–1836), the educator and author of *A Description of Ceylon* (1807), was his third son.

Cordiner's significance centres on two publications: *Antiquities and Scenery of the North of Scotland, in a Series of Letters to Thomas Pennant* (1780) and *Remarkable ruins and romantic prospects of north Britain, with ancient monuments and singular subjects of natural history* (2 vols., 1788–95). Both works, relying on visual and verbal description, were early contributions to the construction of a romantic image of the Scottish highlands; and both were conceived as supplements to Thomas Pennant's very successful Scottish tours of 1769 and 1772. Pennant claimed to be responsible for Cordiner's work, noting:

> When I had published the last volume of my tours in Scotland, I reflected that there were certain parts which I had not been able to visit. I prevailed on Mr. Cordiner to undertake the tour which appeared in 1780 … He afterwards published, and continues to publish, in numbers, the most remarkable ruins, and subjects of natural history he met with in his journies [*sic*] through the northern parts of his country. (*General Collection*, ed. Pinkerton, 3.66–7)

Cordiner's earlier work follows the narrative pattern of the tour used by Pennant, but the later work—published in parts, one every three months, each containing two plates of landscape, one of antiquities, and one of marine animals—is a miscellany of illustrations with commentary. His choice of subjects appears to derive from a circular Pennant distributed to Scottish clergymen prior to his 1772 tour indicating topics on which he sought information. The drawings in both books were Cordiner's own work, and the engraver working with him was Peter Mazell, who also did the engravings for Pennant's tours.

JEFFREY R. SMITTEN

**Sources** T. Pennant, 'A tour in Scotland, 1769', *A general collection of the best and most interesting voyages and travels in all parts of the world*, ed. J. Pinkerton, 3 (1809) • T. Pennant, 'A tour in Scotland and voyage to the Hebrides, 1772', *A general collection of the best and most interesting voyages and travels in all parts of the world*, ed. J. Pinkerton, 3 (1809) • *Scots Magazine*, 56 (1794), 735 • L. F. Powell, 'The tours of Thomas Pennant', *The Library*, 4th ser., 19 (1938–9), 131–54 • P. Womack, *Improvement and romance: constructing the myth of the highlands* (1989) • B. Knight, introduction, in T. Pennant, *A tour in Scotland, 1769*, ed. B. Knight (1979) • *DNB*

**Cordiner, James** (1775–1836), Scottish Episcopal clergyman in Ceylon and India, was born probably in Banff, one of eight children of the Episcopalian minister and antiquary Charles *Cordiner and his wife, Jean Shand. He was educated locally, and then at King's College, Aberdeen, where he graduated MA in 1793. In 1797, while still a divinity student, he was appointed to superintend the Military Male Orphan Asylum at Madras, for Eurasian sons of British soldiers. In October, *en route* for India, he was ordained deacon by the bishop of Carlisle.

Cordiner reached Madras by way of Bombay in June 1798 and remained at the asylum until the following April. At that time he was introduced to the Hon. Frederick North, later fifth earl of Guilford, and the first civil governor of Ceylon. As the chaplain to the garrison of Colombo had recently died, Cordiner was invited by North to take his place. He also became chaplain to the 51st regiment, having previously acted as chaplain to the 80th. He was chaplain from 1799 to 1804 and during this time he was also principal of all the schools on the island. As the only episcopalian clergyman on the island he conducted services at Government House each Sunday. He was also responsible for the formation of three schools in Colombo for Sinhalese, Tamil, and European pupils. In 1800 he made a six-month tour of the island with the governor, after which he made an official report on the schools. When Cordiner left Ceylon in 1804 he was presented with a piece of plate worth 200 guineas.

Cordiner set sail for England and reached Dover in February 1805; he then returned to his native north-east Scotland. While living at Peterhead he prepared his two-volume *Description of Ceylon* (1807) for the press. The work, which was handsomely illustrated with engravings taken from Cordiner's own drawings, described his experiences of the country including his observation of an elephant hunt, pearl fishing, and cinnamon cultivation, as well as a tour of the island. The second part of the work described, on the basis of second-hand information, details of military operations in 1803. A further work, *A Voyage to India* (1820), completed his descriptions of his life in the East.

In May 1807 Cordiner became second minister of St Paul's Episcopal Chapel, Aberdeen, a collegiate charge. He was promoted from second minister to first minister in the following year. In November 1834 ill health prompted him to retire from his ministerial duties. He died in Aberdeen of congestion of the lungs on 13 January 1836, and was buried locally in St Nicholas churchyard. Not much is known of the personal life of this man, whose claim to distinction lay in the fact that he visited Ceylon just as it was being brought under British administration, and published elegant descriptions of his experiences. He had married and had a son, Charles, who later became a Church of Scotland minister in the *quoad sacra* parish of Kininmonth, Aberdeenshire. His obituary emphasized his cheerful disposition, his humility, and his eagerness to avoid giving offence (*Aberdeen Journal*, 20 Jan 1836).

H. M. CHICHESTER, *rev.* LIONEL ALEXANDER RITCHIE

**Sources** *Aberdeen Journal* (20 Jan 1836) • J. Cordiner, *A voyage to India* (1820) • J. Cordiner, *A description of Ceylon … with narratives of a tour round the island in 1800, the campaign in Candy in 1803, and a journey to Ramisseram in 1804*, 2 vols. (1807) • A. E. Smith, ed., 'Register of St Paul's Episcopal Chapel, Aberdeen, 1720–1793', *The miscellany of the New Spalding Club*, 2, New Spalding Club, 34 (1908), 101–3 • W. Cramond, ed., *The annals of Banff*, 2, New Spalding Club, 10 (1893), 110, 359 • *DNB* • *Fasti Scot.*, new edn, 6.225
**Likenesses** W. Bond, stipple, pubd 1819 (after A. Birnie, 1819), NPG; repro. in Cordiner, *Voyage to India*, facing frontispiece

**Cording, John Charles** (*bap.* 1810), clothing manufacturer, was baptized on 11 May 1810 at St Clement Danes, Westminster, London, the son of John Cording and his wife, Mary *née* Wilson, who married on 11 September 1806 at St Martin-in-the-Fields, Westminster. His father may have been the John Cording, jeweller, of the Strand whose bankruptcy was recorded in *The Times* (15 February 1826). Cording founded the business, Cordings, from his home with his mother and sister, Ellen, and in 1839 the first Cordings shop opened at 231 Strand, London. From here Cordings developed waterproof garments such as the Dreadnought coat which came with a warrant that it was able to withstand the effects of any climate. Company records show that among the shop's customers at this time were the duke of Connaught and other peers of the realm. In 1871 Cordings kitted out Sir Henry Morton Stanley in preparation for his expedition to Africa in search of the scientist Dr Livingstone. In 1890 the business transferred to 19 Piccadilly, London, where workshops were set up on the premises for the manufacture of footwear and tailored goods. In 1902 the prince of Wales, later George V, appointed Cordings as one of his outfitters, as did his son, Edward, prince of Wales, in 1922. In 1902 the firm also became a limited company trading under the name J. C. Cording & Co. It continued to enjoy royal patronage from Edward VIII when he became duke of Windsor and from Queen Elizabeth the queen mother, as well as from Mrs Simpson, later duchess of Windsor. They were all supplied with Cordings' patented brand of waterproof boots called the Newmarket. The range of Idstone boots was also patented in the 1920s. Under different ownership, the company continues to trade at 19 Piccadilly.

CATHERINE HORWOOD

**Sources** company records, Cordings, London • *IGI* • *The Times* (15 Feb 1826) • *The standard royal book* [1912]

**Core, Philip McCammon** (1951–1989), artist and writer, was born in Dallas, Texas, on 7 June 1951. He spent his early childhood in Delhi, where his father, an alcoholic journalist, was temporarily vice-consul, before returning to New Orleans, where at the age of six he went to school

Philip McCammon Core (1951–1989), self-portrait, 1984

at the military academy. When he was seven he won first prize in the Vieux Carré artists' open competition.

Although New Orleans was to remain a profound influence on Core's life with its atmosphere of southern Gothic and dandyism, he escaped his family at the first opportunity, in 1963, by winning a scholarship to Middlesex School in Concord, Massachusetts, one of the pre-eminent east coast preparatory schools. From there he went to Harvard University in 1969. He led a colourful undergraduate life making experimental films and designing for a New York boutique, and spent a year in Paris. Here, under the auspices of Philippe Jullian, whom he helped research for his book *The Symbolists* (1973), he met surviving members of the Cocteau set. In 1973 Core graduated *cum laude*, with an honours thesis on the Belgian symbolist Fernand Khnopff, and later that year left for Europe to study for a postgraduate course at the Ruskin School of Drawing, at Oxford, where he designed a ceiling painting for the Oxford Union. Hating Oxford, he transferred to the Academia degli Belli Arti in Florence in 1974; he settled in London later that same year. In Oxford, Florence, and London he cultivated friends who were members of the *demi-monde*. He had a great capacity both for making friends and for falling out with them.

From the beginning Philip Core's literary and artistic work explored his homosexuality, and appeared in the gay press. His art often featured a 'specific type of male, sometimes as threatening, sometimes as innocent as an animal' (Melly, *Philip Core*, 6). Core's first British exhibition was 'Heroes and Monuments' at the Hammond Lloyd Gallery, London, in 1976; it was followed in 1979 by 'Pieces of

Conversation' at the Francis Kyle Gallery, which consisted of fictive conversations between some of his (mainly literary) heroes, including a conversation between Evelyn Waugh and Nancy Mitford, and Warhol playing chess with Marcel Duchamp.

Core's career as a painter looked as if it might take off, but unfortunately his patience and artistic technique never quite matched the grandeur of his visual ambition. In his third exhibition, 'Novels without Words' (1980), he successfully combined his interests in pop art and baroque fiction, but thereafter his work tended to be large-scale and too slapdash. In order to support himself financially, he sought commissions including *The Ideal Party* (1980) a commemorative mural, rapidly lost, over the entrance to the Ritz Hotel, London, of seventy-five famous guests spanning the hotel's history; an immense cyclorama commissioned by BBC television's *Omnibus* (1984); and a group portrait of the cast of the film version of *Brideshead Revisited*.

Core, however, had an alternative métier in the 1980s as a broadcaster on radio programmes such as *Kaleidoscope* for BBC Radio 4, since he was able to talk with encyclopaedic authority about almost any subject. The breadth of his intellectual interests also made him an excellent journalist. When, for example, *The Independent* was founded in 1986, he was commissioned by James Fergusson to write for the newspaper obituaries of controversial subjects such as the photographer Robert Mapplethorpe and the graffiti artist Jean-Michel Basquiat, thereby contributing to the death of the po-faced official obituary. He also flourished as the paper's photographic critic. In 1984 he published two books, one a dictionary entitled *Camp: the Lie that Tells the Truth* and the other *The Original Eye: Arbiters of Twentieth-Century Taste*. Both demonstrated his exceptionally wide knowledge of the byways of twentieth-century culture.

But it is as much as a person as for his work that Philip Core deserves to be remembered. He lived in a flat which he painted entirely black near the Elephant and Castle, London, from which he would make excursions which were sometimes grand and more often *louche*. He dyed his hair blonde in the manner of Andy Warhol. Indeed, he might have become, like Warhol, a cult figure in later life, but was one of the first people to be diagnosed as having AIDS, at a time when the disease was scarcely known in Britain. Towards the end of his life he was involved in a case with the board of customs and excise concerning the import of visual material which it regarded as pornographic. Shortly before his death he wrote a characteristically perceptive description of himself in the catalogue of an exhibition held at the Watermans Art Centre in Brentford, Middlesex:

> I am not a great artist, only someone who loves painting, drawing and making things with his hands above all else; someone who has, by some curious gift of heredity, become possessed of articulacy and intransigence in equal degree; someone who knows what they love and feels no shame about it.

Philip Core died on 12 November 1989 at the Westminster

Hospital, London, of bronchopneumonia brought on by AIDS, and was cremated at Mortlake cemetery, London. In the 1990s, as a tribute, the composer Patrick Nunn wrote *Hextych*, a work based on Core's paintings.

CHARLES SAUMAREZ SMITH

**Sources**  G. Melly, introduction, in *Philip Core: paintings, 1975–1985* (1985) [exhibition catalogue] · *The Independent* (14 Nov 1989) · *Daily Telegraph* (15 Nov 1989) · G. Melly, 'Shocking to the Core', *The Observer* (30 Oct 1988) · d. cert.
**Likenesses**  P. M. Core, self-portrait, acrylic on canvas, 1984, repro. in *Philip Core: paintings* [*see illus.*]
**Wealth at death**  £57,438: administration, 13 July 1990, *CGPLA Eng. & Wales*

**Corehouse**. For this title name *see* Cranstoun, George, Lord Corehouse (*d.* 1850).

**Corelli, Marie**. *See* Mackay, Mary (1855–1924).

**Corey, Giles** (*d.* **1692**). *See under* Salem witches and their accusers (*act.* 1692).

**Corey, John** (*fl.* **1699–1735**), actor and playwright, was, according to the *Biographia dramatica*, 'descended from an ancient family in Cornwall, but was himself born at Barnstaple, in Devonshire' (Baker, 148). It has been suggested that he may alternatively be the son of the actress Katherine *Corey, *née* Mitchell, and her husband, John Corey, baptized at St Clement Danes on 26 April 1668 (Highfill, Burnim & Langhans, *BDA*). *Biographia dramatica* records that he abandoned the study of law at the New Inn for a career on the stage. It is possible that this change of direction coincided with, or was precipitated by, the production of his first play, *A Cure for Jealousy*, at Lincoln's Inn Fields during the 1699–1700 season. This slight comedy, set in and around Covent Garden, was eclipsed by the success of George Farquhar's *The Constant Couple*, but it was published in 1701, the year in which Corey made his first recorded appearance as an actor, in the undemanding role of Faithless in Charles Johnson's *The Gentleman Cully*. His name continued to appear on playbills until the close of the 1734–5 season at Drury Lane, invariably in secondary roles. He was, however, sufficiently esteemed by Thomas Betterton to be granted a solo benefit on 4 July 1704. It was also in 1704 at Lincoln's Inn Fields that his second and last play, *The Metamorphosis*, was performed. This unremarkable farce was derived from the sub-plot of *Albumazar*, a comedy presented to James I at Trinity College, Cambridge, in 1614. Its provenance suggests that Corey was, for an actor, uncommonly well read, and may have been of service to his successive theatrical managers by proposing additions to the repertory. Without some such supplementary source of income, his modest status as an actor would barely have sustained him.

Corey's traceable career is representative of that of a jobbing player in the early years of the eighteenth century. Beginning with the joint company under Betterton, he moved with the patent holders to the Queen's Theatre from 1705 to 1708, then to Drury Lane from 1708 to 1714, but advanced only to the Player King in *Hamlet* and Malcolm in *Macbeth*. Most summers until 1727 found him working on the booth stages of London's fairs. Perhaps in the hope of better roles, he shifted allegiance from Drury Lane to John Rich's Lincoln's Inn Fields from 1714 to 1719, and was rewarded with Laertes, in which he made little impact. He returned to Drury Lane, and, with the exception of a season at Goodman's Fields in 1732–3, remained there until his last recorded appearance, as the Lord Chamberlain in *Henry VIII*, on 8 May 1735. He was, says the *Biographia dramatica*, 'a just and sensible speaker, yet being but low in stature, and his voice none of the best, he was ever obliged to work against the stream, and labour with difficulties'. No details of his private life seem to have survived, and it is eloquent of Corey's unobtrusiveness that Colley Cibber, who acted with him often and became his manager, makes no reference to him in his *Apology*. It may also say something of his quality that, when Theophilus Cibber engineered a walkout of actors from Drury Lane in May 1733, Corey did not join the exodus.

PETER THOMSON

**Sources**  Highfill, Burnim & Langhans, *BDA* · D. E. Baker, *Biographia dramatica, or, A companion to the playhouse*, rev. I. Reed, new edn, rev. S. Jones, 3 vols. in 4 (1812)

**Corey** [*née* Mitchell], **Katherine** (*b. c.*1635), actress, was born Katherine Mitchell to parents whose names are as yet unknown, and was already a widow when in 1662 she married John Cory or Corey (*b. c.*1637); he was perhaps the dramatist John Corye whose *The Generous Enemies* was performed by the King's Company about June 1671. It has been suggested that the John Corey baptized at St Clement Danes in 1668, probably their son, was John *Corey, later an actor and playwright. She was one of the first actresses on the English stage, appearing for the first time in theatrical records in the roster of the King's Company in 1661–2. In a lawsuit of March 1689 she claimed that she was 'the first, and is the last of all the Actresses that were constituted by King Charles the Second at His Restauration', though cases have been made for awarding the title of 'first English actress' to others (Highfill, Burnim & Langhans, *BDA*, 3.495). Her first recorded role (as Mrs Coary) was Julia in John Ford's *Love's Sacrifice* (before August 1664), though she may have been the Mrs Covey listed for the production of John Wilson's *The Cheats* performed in 1663.

Mrs Corey played mostly comic roles, specializing in older women and widows. One of her most famous was Widow Blackacre in William Wycherley's *The Plain Dealer*, a role she originated in 1676. She also played Margery Pinchwife's maid, Lucy, in *The Country Wife* (1675), and in 1677 Sysigambis in Nathaniel Lee's *The Rival Queens* and Octavia, the scorned wife of Antony, in Dryden's *All for Love*. With other actors from the King's Company she may have performed in Edinburgh in 1679, staying perhaps until 1682. After the union of the two London companies in that year she played Mopsophil in Behn's *The Emperour of the Moon* (1687), Teresia in Thomas D'Urfey's adaptation of George Chapman's *Bussy D'Ambois* (1691), and Mrs Teazall in Thomas Southerne's *The Wives' Excuse* (1691). Her salary peaked at the good sum of 30s. per week, as admitted by the 1694 'reply of the patentees' over the playhouse rebellion of that time. The reply notes that the actress Elinor Leigh receives that amount, 'being as much as ever Mrs Cory had who was Extraordinarily well received by the Audience' (Milhous, *Thomas Betterton*, 245).

One interesting story about Corey may indicate her court connections as well as her brand of comedy. While performing Sempronia in Ben Jonson's *Catiline's Conspiracy* in late 1668 or early 1669, she apparently impersonated the court intriguer Lady Harvey, which caused offence. Lady Harvey had her imprisoned, though one of the king's mistresses, Lady Castlemaine, as Samuel Pepys notes, 'made the King to release her, and to order her to act it again worse than ever the other day' while the king was in attendance. Results show the hazards of being an early performer: 'my Lady Harvy provided people to hiss her and fling oranges at her. But it seems the heat is come to a great heighth, and real troubles at Court about it' (Pepys, 9.415).

The only other trouble relating to Corey and her career occurred in 1689: apparently Henry Killigrew had tried to set up a new company under the new monarchs William and Mary and had invited Corey to be a member, along with other popular comedians such as Anthony Leigh and James Nokes. Because of their insurrection, all the players involved were discharged from the company. All were subsequently readmitted, except for Corey, who petitioned to the lord chamberlain in March. He readmitted her, 'like the rest of the rebels', to the company on 11 March (Milhous, *Thomas Betterton*, 53). Her last performance seems to have been as Morossa in Anthony Rivers's *The Traytor* (1692), and her disappearance from cast lists after that date indicates that she probably retired after the 1691/2 theatrical season. No death date is known, and very little information exists about Corey beyond these professional details. In sum her career seems to have been one of success. Never the tragedy heroine or the flirtatious ingénue, Corey built a solid, long, popular career in strong comic supporting roles.                CHERYL WANKO

**Sources** Highfill, Burnim & Langhans, *BDA* · Pepys, *Diary* · J. Milhous and R. D. Hume, eds., *A register of English theatrical documents, 1660–1737*, 1 (1991) · C. Visser, 'Theatrical scandal in the letters of Colbert de Croissy, 1669', *Restoration*, 7 (1983), 54–7 · E. Howe, *The first English actresses* (1992) · J. Milhous, *Thomas Betterton and the management of Lincoln's Inn Fields, 1695–1708* (1979)

**Corey, Martha** (*d.* 1692). *See under* Salem witches and their accusers (*act.* 1692).

**Corfe, Arthur Thomas** (1773–1863), organist, third son of Joseph *Corfe (1740–1820), was born on 9 April 1773, at Salisbury, where his father was later organist. In early life he was a pupil of a Mr Antram of Salisbury, and in 1783 he became a chorister of Westminster Abbey under Benjamin Cooke. He was for some time a pupil of Clementi for the piano. In 1796 he married Frances, the daughter of J. Davies, vicar of Padworth, Berkshire; they had fourteen children. In 1804, on the resignation of his father, Corfe succeeded him as organist of Salisbury Cathedral, and by 1813, if contemporary accounts are to be believed, he had moulded the choir into a state of remarkable perfection.

In 1828 he organized and undertook at his own risk a festival at Salisbury, which took place with very great success on 19–22 August of that year. He himself conducted the whole of the performances, and the organ was played for him by his eldest son, **John Davies Corfe** (1804–1876), who was organist of Bristol Cathedral from 1825 for more than fifty years, as well as the long-time conductor of the Bristol Madrigal Society Choir, at that period one of the most famous choirs in England. Among the solo singers at the festival were Mary Ann Paton, Rosalbina Caradori-Allan, and John Braham.

Corfe's work as a composer was not remarkable. He wrote a service, a few anthems, songs, and glees, as well as some piano pieces. He also published arrangements of different kinds, and a book on *The Principles of Harmony and Thorough-Bass*. Towards the end of his life his health showed signs of failing, but he attended the daily service regularly until the end. On 28 January 1863 he was found dead at his house, in the close at Salisbury, early in the morning, kneeling by his bedside as if in prayer. He was buried in the cloister of the cathedral, where a tablet was erected to his memory by his thirteen surviving children.

Several of Corfe's sons were choristers at Magdalen College, Oxford. His fourth son, George Corfe, became resident medical officer at the Middlesex Hospital, and wrote several medical treatises. Another son, **Charles William Corfe** (1814–1883), took the degree of DMus at Oxford in 1852, and was organist of Christ Church, Oxford, from 1846 to his retirement shortly before his death on 16 December 1883. He was appointed choragus to the university in 1860, and published several glees, partsongs, and anthems.                J. A. F. MAITLAND, *rev.* NILANJANA BANERJI

**Sources** Grove, *Dict. mus.* · Foster, *Alum. Oxon.* · Brown & Stratton, *Brit. mus.* · D. Baptie, *A handbook of musical biography* (1883) · 'Grand musical festivals', *Quarterly Musical Magazine and Review*, 10 (1828), 135–82, esp. 140 · *GM*, 3rd ser., 14 (1863), 394 · *CGPLA Eng. & Wales* (1863) · *CGPLA Eng. & Wales* (1876) [John Davies Corfe] · *CGPLA Eng. & Wales* (1884) [Charles William Corfe]
**Wealth at death** under £8000: probate, 28 Feb 1863, *CGPLA Eng. & Wales* · £4000—John Davies Corfe: probate, 4 Feb 1876, *CGPLA Eng. & Wales* · £4177 3s. 1d.—Charles William Corfe: probate, 4 Feb 1884, *CGPLA Eng. & Wales*

**Corfe, Charles William** (1814–1883). *See under* Corfe, Arthur Thomas (1773–1863).

**Corfe, John Davies** (1804–1876). *See under* Corfe, Arthur Thomas (1773–1863).

**Corfe, Joseph** (1740–1820), singer and organist, was born in Salisbury on 25 December 1740 and baptized on 9 February 1741, the son of Joseph Corfe (*b.* 1705). The family had evidently lived there since 1692, when his paternal grandfather (John, (*d.* 1743)) was appointed a lay vicar of the cathedral. Of the five sons in the next generation, all but Corfe's own father were musicians. It is hardly surprising therefore that the boy was brought up as a chorister under Dr John Stephens, then organist of Salisbury Cathedral, and subsequently apprenticed to him. In 1759 Corfe was made a tenor lay vicar, and, with the encouragement of James (Hermes) Harris, he became increasingly involved in the musical life of the city; he also sang regularly at the

Three Choirs festival between 1764 and 1768 (and elsewhere later). On 14 April 1766 he married Mary Bernard, and the first of their six children, four sons and two daughters, was born the following year; only three, however, were still alive when Corfe made his will in 1814.

When Stephens died in December 1780 Corfe made an unsuccessful bid for the organistship of the cathedral, which post eventually came his way on the death of the victorious candidate, Robert Parry, in July 1792. In the meantime, however, his vocal ability (supported no doubt by the interest of Robert Lowth, bishop of London, to whom he had been introduced by Harris) had gained him, in February 1783, a place as gentleman of the Chapel Royal. Six months later he was elected a member of the Royal Society of Musicians, in whose admissions records he is described as 'Director of the Concert' at Salisbury. This latter appointment—regarded by some simply as a consolation prize for his earlier having failed to gain the cathedral organistship—evidently gave rise to much acrimonious dispute among local music lovers, a vivid account of which is to be found in the diary of John Marsh. From numerous other references in the same source, it is clear that Corfe was not only an accomplished vocal soloist, but also a competent organist and violinist who could, as need arose, play the double bass as well.

Though a service in B♭ and one or two anthems were still in use some fifty years after his death, Corfe is of no consequence as a composer, and most of his published work consists of arrangements, either of Scottish folksongs or of music by well-known composers of the period (such as Sacchini, Paisiello, Haydn, and Pleyel); for example, three sets of *Twelve Glees* (1791–8) and two volumes of *Sacred Music* (1800?). He was also the author of *A Treatise on Singing* (1799) and a book entitled *Thorough Bass Simplified* (1805). In November 1804 Corfe resigned his post of organist of Salisbury Cathedral in favour of his eldest surviving son, Arthur Thomas *Corfe (1773–1863), a pupil of Benjamin Cooke and Clementi. Another son, John (b. 1769), had been active on the London musical scene as singer, cellist, and double bass player in the Drury Lane orchestra, but was apparently dead by 1799. Joseph Corfe himself died at his home in Salisbury on 29 July 1820 and was buried in the north-west transept of the cathedral.

H. DIACK JOHNSTONE

**Sources** Highfill, Burnim & Langhans, *BDA*, vol. 3 · [J. S. Sainsbury], ed., *A dictionary of musicians*, 2 vols. (1825); repr. (New York, 1966) · H. W. Shaw, *The succession of organists of the Chapel Royal and the cathedrals of England and Wales from c.1538* (1991) · *The John Marsh journals: the life and times of a gentleman composer*, ed. B. Robins (1998) · B. Matthews, ed., *The Royal Society of Musicians of Great Britain: list of members, 1738–1984* (1985) · *New Grove* · [Clarke], *The Georgian era: memoirs of the most eminent persons*, 4 vols. (1832–4) · *Grove, Dict. mus.* (1878–90) · J. D. Brown, *Biographical dictionary of musicians: with a bibliography of English writings on music* (1886) · Brown & Stratton, *Brit. mus.*

**Wealth at death** left £4700 in 3 per cent annuities to his youngest surviving son: will, 1814, Highfill, Burnim & Langhans, *BDA*

**Corfield, William Henry** (1843–1903), sanitarian, born on 14 December 1843 at Shrewsbury, was the eldest son of

Thomas Corfield, chemist, and his wife, Jane Brown. Educated at Cheltenham grammar school, he gained a demyship in natural science at Magdalen College, Oxford, and matriculated on 12 October 1861; he gained a first class in mathematical moderations in 1863. While studying at Oxford Corfield was selected by C. G. B. Daubeny to accompany him to Auvergne, France, where he investigated the volcanic landforms in the Montbrison district. He graduated BA at Oxford in 1864, and from 1865 to 1875 he held the Sheppard medical fellowship at Pembroke College, Oxford. Corfield entered University College, London, as a medical student in 1865; in 1866 he won the Burdett-Coutts scholarship at Oxford for geology, and in 1867 he was elected Radcliffe travelling fellow.

Influenced by Sir Henry Acland and by George Rolleston, Corfield had by this time directed his attention to hygiene and sanitary science. He spent some time in Paris, where he attended Apollinaire Bouchardat's lectures and studied hygiene under Professor Berthelot at the Collège de France. He proceeded afterwards to Lyons, worked in clinical medicine and surgery, and made a special study of the remains of the aqueducts of ancient Lugdunum. He also visited some of the medical schools in Italy and Sicily. He graduated MB at Oxford in 1868 and MD in 1872. In 1869 he was admitted MRCP, and in 1875 he was elected FRCP. He became a fellow of the Institute of Chemistry in 1877. Corfield married in 1876 Emily Madelina, youngest daughter of John Pike FSA; they had six children.

Meanwhile in 1869 Corfield had been appointed professor of hygiene and public health at University College, London, and in 1875 he opened the first laboratory in London for the practical teaching of hygiene. In memory of E. A. Parkes, in 1876 Corfield actively helped to found a museum of practical hygiene, which was situated first at University College, then at Margaret Street, Cavendish Square, and after 1909 at Buckingham Palace Road, Westminster. Corfield was medical officer of health for Islington (1871–2), and for St George's, Hanover Square (1872–1900), and he was at one time president of the Society of Medical Officers of Health.

A member of the committee appointed in 1869 by the British Association for the Advancement of Science to inquire into the treatment and utilization of sewage, Corfield worked as reporter to the committee until 1875, and he became an ardent advocate of land filtration and sewage farms. At the Royal Society of Arts in 1879 he delivered the Cantor lectures, entitled 'Dwelling houses, their sanitary construction and arrangements'; in 1893 he gave the Harveian lecture before the Harveian Society of London, entitled 'Disease and defective house sanitation'; and in 1902 he gave the Milroy lectures at the Royal College of Physicians of London, 'On the aetiology of typhoid fever and its prevention'.

Corfield shares with Rogers Field the honour of being a pioneer in house sanitation and of being the first to enunciate the hygienic principles of a healthy home. Public interest was aroused in 1871 when the prince of Wales (the future Edward VII) contracted typhoid fever at Londesborough Lodge, Scarborough. For the next thirty years

Corfield enjoyed a large consulting practice throughout England, in connection with the sanitation of public and private buildings. In 1899 he was the first holder of the newly established office of consulting sanitary adviser to the office of works.

With John Netten Radcliffe, Corfield was joint secretary of the Epidemiological Society from 1870 to 1872, and he was president in 1902–3. He was also president of the public health section of the British Medical Association meeting held at Bristol in 1894 and of a section of the sanitary congress of the Sanitary Institute held at Newcastle upon Tyne in 1896, and he originated the successful International Congress of Hygiene held in London in 1891. He represented the office of works at the International Congress of Hygiene and Demography, of which he was honorary president, at Paris in 1900; and he presided at the conference held by the Sanitary Institute at Paris in August 1900 under the auspices of the Société Française d'Hygiène.

Corfield belongs to the second generation of sanitary reformers in England. Entering professional life after a general education, he took up the subject of public health where it had been left by Edwin Chadwick, John Simon, Sir George Buchanan, Netten Radcliffe, Richard Thorne-Thorne, and others, and carried it forward into the twentieth century.

Corfield was a collector of rare books and a connoisseur of bindings. His library was especially rich in works on fishing. He was also a lover of prints, and made a fine collection of Bewick woodcuts. For more than twenty years he was chairman of the committee of the Sunday Society, which promoted the opening of museums, picture galleries, and public libraries on Sunday. Corfield died on 26 August 1903 at Marstrand in Sweden, during a visit for his health.

In addition to his numerous appointments and large practice Corfield published many works, mostly on sanitary dwelling arrangements and the problems presented by sewerage. *Laws of Health* (1880) reached nine editions, and *Dwelling Houses: their Sanitary Construction and Arrangements* (1880) and *Disease and Defective House Sanitation* (1896) were both translated into other European languages.

D'A. POWER, rev. RICHARD HANKINS

**Sources** *The Lancet* (12 Sept 1903) · *Journal of the Sanitary Institute*, 24/3 (1903), 503 · *Medico-Chirurgical Transactions*, 87 (1904), cxxxi–cxxxiv · *Transactions of the Epidemiological Society of London*, new ser., 22, 160 · private information (1912) · Munk, *Roll* · *BMJ* (12 Sept 1903), 627–8 · *CGPLA Eng. & Wales* (1903)
**Likenesses** lithograph; replica, Wellcome L.
**Wealth at death** £12,868 8s. 11d.: probate, 15 Oct 1903, *CGPLA Eng. & Wales*

**Corio** (*fl.* AD 15–20). *See under* Roman Britain, British leaders in (*act.* 55 BC–AD 84).

**Cork**. For this title name *see* Boyle, Richard, first earl of Cork (1566–1643); Boyle, Richard, first earl of Burlington and second earl of Cork (1612–1698); Boyle, Richard, third earl of Burlington and fourth earl of Cork (1694–1753); Boyle, John, fifth earl of Cork and fifth earl of Orrery (1707–1762); Boyle, Mary, countess of Cork and Orrery (1746–1840); Boyle, William Henry Dudley, twelfth earl of Cork and twelfth earl of Orrery (1873–1967).

**Cork,** Sir **Kenneth Russell** (1913–1991), accountant, was born on 21 August 1913 in Finchley, Middlesex, the youngest of the three sons of William Henry Cork (1885–1940), chartered accountant, and his wife, Maud Alice, *née* Nunn. After leaving Berkhamsted School in 1930, he joined his father's City accountancy firm, W. H. Cork & Co., which specialized in bankruptcy, and qualified as a chartered accountant in 1937, in which year, on 12 June, he married Nina (*b.* 1915/16), daughter of Ernest Alfred Oswald Theodore Lippold, furniture manufacturer. They had one son (Sir Roger Cork, lord mayor of London in 1996–7), and one daughter. In 1937 W. H. Cork, Gully & Co. was formed, to do audit work for W. H. Cork & Co., and Kenneth Cork became a partner, with H. J. Gully, in this new firm. He enlisted in the Honourable Artillery Company in 1938, and spent the war in north Africa and Italy, reaching the rank of lieutenant-colonel, in charge of all the catering services at allied forces headquarters and the Army Catering Corps in Italy in 1944.

His father and H. J. Gully had died during the war, and Cork became senior partner in W. J. Cork Gully in 1947. He began to take on insolvency work, and soon moved from audit and accountancy work to specialize in receivership. By the 1970s, W. J. Cork Gully was the largest insolvency practice in Britain, and 'the mere mention of Cork's name struck terror into the hearts of businesses everywhere' (Levin, 233). Cork felt this was unfair, as his philosophy was that receivership did not necessarily lead to failure, and he preferred to try to save an insolvent business and sell it as a going concern, rather than to put it into liquidation, which would mean closing it down and disposing of its assets, as was the usual practice. For example, when Brentford Nylons went bankrupt in 1976, Cork managed to keep the factory going, and sold it to Lonrho, saving 3000 jobs. W. J. Cork Gully was called in to investigate and deal with most of the major bankruptcies of the 1960s and 1970s, including that of Rolls Razor, which made cheap washing machines for John Bloom, and crashed with a £4 million deficit in 1965, and that of Emil Savundra's Fire, Auto, and Marine Insurance Company, which left 400,000 British motorists without cover, in 1966. This investigation took eleven years, before the firm was able to rescue £1 million for the creditors. Another major case was that of the Stern Group, dealing in residential property, which collapsed in 1974 with debts of over £170 million. In 1980 a new firm, Cork Gully, was formed in a merger with the insolvency department of Coopers and Lybrand, with Cork as senior partner, and it became a division of Coopers and Lybrand. One of the first cases taken on by the new firm was that of the De Lorean Motor Company, which had built a factory in Belfast to manufacture sports cars for sale in America, financed by the British government. When the government called in Coopers and Lybrand to review the desirability of continued support, Cork headed the investigation, and as a result of his report the government put the Belfast factory into receivership.

Cork played an important part in the government of the City of London. He was elected to the common council in 1951 for Billingsgate ward, and as chairman of the music committee in 1957 he was responsible for planning the Barbican Arts Centre. In 1970 he was elected alderman by Tower ward, and he served as lord mayor of London from 1978 to 1979. He was also a member of the Wilson committee set up by the government in 1977 to review the country's financial institutions, and in the same year he became chairman of the insolvency law reform committee, to investigate insolvency law in the United Kingdom. The committee decided to write a new law, rather than to try to amend the existing law, with the object of making it easier for an insolvent business to be sold as a going concern, which would preserve jobs, and would also be in the best interests of the creditors. The principle behind the Cork report, published in 1982, was that a business is a national asset, and all insolvency schemes must be aimed at saving a business. In drafting the 1985 Insolvency Act, the government did not accept the report in its entirety, but picked bits out of it, including the idea of appointing an administrator to try to save businesses threatened with bankruptcy. In his foreword to the 1991 edition of *A Practitioner's Guide to Corporate Insolvency and Corporate Rescues*, Cork wrote: 'a good insolvency practitioner is coming to be regarded not simply as the undertaker to a business which has failed, but as a source of advice to struggling businesses which hope to avoid collapse'. That this was the case was to a large extent a result of his example.

Cork retired from Cork Gully in 1983, and although he continued to take an interest in insolvency—he published the *European Insolvency Practitioners' Handbook* in 1984—he became interested in venture capital and the creation of new businesses (rather than his previous work of rescuing old ones), and was chairman of Advent Eurofund (1983–91), Advent Capital (1985–91), and Advent Management (1988–91). He also helped to set up the youth enterprise scheme, to lend venture capital to young people.

Always interested in the arts—he was chairman of the Royal Shakespeare Company from 1975 to 1985, and it was he who persuaded the Royal Shakespeare Company to make the Barbican its London home—Cork was vice-chairman of the Arts Council from 1986 to 1987, and chaired the Arts Council inquiry into theatre in England, which produced its report, *Theatre is for All* (known as the Cork report) in 1986. An expert in finance for the arts, in this report he argued the case for public investment in the arts.

Cork was a devout member of the Church of England, who liked to listen to the Bible on his journey into the City, and he preached at St Paul's Cathedral during his year as lord mayor. He loved sailing, and always said he would have preferred to skipper a rum-runner in the south seas to joining the family firm. Appointed GBE in 1978, he was the first accountant to have his portrait hung in the National Portrait Gallery, a few days before his death on 13 October 1991, in the London Clinic. He was cremated at Chilterns crematorium, Amersham, on 21 October, following a funeral at the church of Sts Peter and Paul, Great Missenden, Buckinghamshire.

ANNE PIMLOTT BAKER

**Sources** K. Cork, *Cork on Cork* (1988) · H. Levin, *John de Lorean* (1983) · J. Connell and D. Sutherland, *Fraud: the amazing career of Dr Savundra* (1978) · *The Times* (16 Oct 1991) · *The Independent* (16 Oct 1991) · *CGPLA Eng. & Wales* (1992) · WWW
**Likenesses** photograph, 1978, Hult. Arch. · D. Poole, oils?, 1979, repro. in Cork, *Cork on Cork*, following p. 116 · J. Whittall, oils, 1991, NPG · photograph, repro. in *The Times*
**Wealth at death** £1,915,124: probate, 4 March 1992, *CGPLA Eng. & Wales*

**Corker, James** [*name in religion* Maurus] (1636–1715), abbot of Lambspring, was the son of Francis Corker (*d.* 1667), vicar of Bradford, a royalist who changed sides and became a spy against the royalists during the interregnum. He was brought up as an Anglican, but was converted to Catholicism, abhorring his father's disloyalty to the monarchy, and, joining the English Benedictines, was professed in the monastery of St Adrian and St Denis at Lambspring in Lower Saxony on 23 April 1656. He was sent on the English mission in the Benedictine south province in 1665, and for twelve years he was chaplain to Mrs Frances Cotton, a relative of Sir Robert Cotton, and later to Queen Catherine of Braganza at the Savoy. In 1677 he was appointed Benedictine censor of books, setting about the task of building up a library for the use of young Benedictine missioners while he continued to be a generous benefactor to the English Benedictine houses on the continent.

Being alarmed at the narrative of Titus Oates and his party, who had included him among those concerned in the pretended Popish Plot and had intimated that a papal bull appointed him bishop of London, Corker concealed himself for several months, but on the eve of the opening of parliament in October 1678 he was arrested in his lodgings by Titus Oates as part of a plan to discredit the queen through her chaplains and was committed prisoner to Newgate. On 18 July 1679 he was tried at the Old Bailey with Sir George Wakeman and the two monks William Marshall and William Rumley, but their innocence was so evident that the jury returned a verdict of not guilty. Corker was detained, however, on account of his being a Catholic priest, and on 17 January 1680 was tried for high treason in having taken holy orders from the see of Rome. Despite a well-rounded speech given in his defence he was found guilty and was sentenced to death, but was reprieved by the king and remained in Newgate until 1685. In prison he was confessor and spiritual guide to many of the Popish Plot prisoners, and published accounts of the trials, dying speeches, and devotions of those who died on the scaffold, including *Stafford's Memoires* (1682) and *A Remonstrance of Piety and Innocence* (1683). It is stated that during his confinement there he reconciled more than a thousand persons to the Catholic church, and was a great comfort to many in distress. He said that he was comforted when under sentence of death by the hope that his sufferings would expiate the guilt of an ancestor in accepting Nostell Priory. In prison he acted as spiritual director to the unfortunate St Oliver Plunket, Catholic archbishop of Armagh, who allowed him to view his last speech. He was elected president-general of the English Benedictines in 1680, being installed as such on 15 September 1681 in Newgate prison by Dom John Huddleston, and in the following year he was made cathedral prior of Canterbury. This same year was published anonymously his *Roman Catholick Principles in Reference to God and the King*, which had been written in prison and which soon became recognized as the clearest formulation of Anglo-Gallican principles by clarifying the duties which Catholics owed to their monarch. In 1683 he was responsible for the exhumation of the quartered remains of St Oliver Plunket and supervised their transfer to Lambspring.

On the accession of James II Corker was restored to liberty, but the king was reluctant to have him become Benedictine president again in 1685 because of his involvement in the Popish Plot, and Corker became briefly Benedictine procurator in Rome. In 1685 too he became the administrator of a bursary at the school in Lambspring provided by his patron Frances Cotton so that a student might be educated in the mystical teachings of Dom Augustine Baker. He returned to London and was appointed resident ambassador of the elector of Cologne to the court of St James on 31 January 1688. This office had been held in the past by abbots of Lambspring. On the occasion of his reception at court he was publicly accompanied by six other monks in the Benedictine habit, on the instructions of the king, which gave offence to some. During the reign of James II he was responsible for receiving the poet John Dryden into the Catholic church, and established a chapel in the Savoy.

Owing to a dispute with the Jesuits Corker was persuaded by the king to remove to St John's, Clerkenwell, and having first obliged the Jesuits to pay him what his chapel had cost him, there built

> a mighty pretty convent, which the revolution of 1688 pulled down to the ground, to his very great loss, for as he was Dean of the Rosary [confraternity] he melted down the great gold chalice and patten to help towards this building, supplying the want of them with one of silver just of that make. He counted this convent, for the conversion of souls, amongst those things which the Holy Fathers of the Church allow the church treasures to be spent on. (Weldon, 5.312)

The chapel had only a brief existence, being the first object of attack by the populace when the news reached London of the safe landing of William, prince of Orange. On Sunday 11 November 1688 a crowd assembled round the building and was about to demolish it when a military force arrived. The monks succeeded in removing most of their furniture before any report of their intentions got abroad, but the last two carts were stopped in Holborn, and all that they contained was publicly burned in the middle of the street.

Forced to seek refuge on the continent, Corker became chaplain to the English Benedictine nuns in Paris between 1688 and 1690, to whom he donated an arm of St Oliver Plunket as a relic. There he was the spiritual director of the nun Dame Justina Gascoigne, a disciple of Dom Augustine Baker. On 21 September 1690 he was installed as fourth abbot of Lambspring, having been appointed titular abbot of Cismar in 1689, and helped to consecrate the new abbey church on 26 May 1691. In this he had a monument erected in 1693 to St Oliver Plunket in the crypt and donated to the church a set of vestments made from James II's royal robes. As abbot he was often at loggerheads with his community, attempting to force a German model of stricter Benedictine observance, such as obtained in the Bursfeld congregation, on the monks, and was absent for long periods in the Netherlands, France, Italy, and England. He found himself briefly under arrest in England in 1694 on account of some money he had earlier borrowed when an ordinary missioner. The impostor William Fuller met him on one of his journeys

> accoutred more like a Dragoon than a ghostly Father, having on him a Red Coat, with a swinging Belt about a foot broad about his Wast, a terrible large long sword, a Campaigne Wig, and a laced Hat, and he looked most Furiously. (W. Fuller, *The Whole Life of Mr William Fuller*, 1703)

Finally, on 27 July 1696 he resigned the abbacy and returned for good to England to continue his favourite task of making converts. There, about 1698, he wrote his *Rational Account … by M. B.* which explained his conversion to Catholicism and which elicited William Wake's reply, *The Church of Rome No Guide* (1700). It was followed about 1710 by another apologetical tract, *Queries to Dr. Sacheverell from North-Britain*. Retaining his title of abbot of Cismar, he lived 'in a recluse solitary manner' at 'Stafford House, near the park'; his room was lined with books and 'ghastly pictures drawn dead with ropes about their necks', representing the victims of the Popish Plot (*DNB*). He died at Paddington, Middlesex, on 22 December 1715 and was buried at St Pancras. GEOFFREY SCOTT

**Sources** *The tryals of Sir George Wakeman, William Marshall, William Rumley, James Corker* (1679) • T. Tickle-foot [F. Smith], *Some observations upon the late tryals of Sir George Wakeman, Corker and Marshal* (1679) • T. A. Birrell, 'James Maurus Corker and Dryden's *Conversion*', *English Studies*, 54 (1973), 461–9 • T. A. Birrell, *Catholic allegiance and the Popish plot* (1950) • J. Kenyon, *The Popish Plot* (1972) • Gillow, *Lit. biog. hist.* • D. Lunn, *The English Benedictines, 1540–1688* (1980) • G. Scott, *Gothic rage undone: English monks in the age of Enlightenment* (1992) • C. C. Vigurs, 'Francis Corker', *Bradford Antiquary*, new ser., 6 (1933–9) • *Walker rev.* • Ampleforth Abbey, York, Allanson MSS • B. Weldon, 'Memorials', Douai Abbey, Woolhampton, Berkshire, English Benedictine Congregation Archives • *DNB* • A. Allanson, *Biography of the English Benedictines* (1999)
**Archives** Douai Abbey, Woolhampton, Berkshire, B. Weldon, 'Memorials', vols. 2 and 4

**Corkery, Daniel** [ *pseud.* Lee] (1878–1964), Irish nationalist and writer, was born at 1 Gardiner's Hill, Cork city on 14 February 1878, the son of William Corkery (d. 1883), a carpenter whose family had lived in Cork city for several generations, and Mary Barron (d. 1923), the daughter of a Waterford sea captain, who kept a small shop after her husband's death. Corkery suffered from a bone deformity which left one leg shorter than the other. Corkery was educated by the Presentation Brothers at their South Monastery School, won a King's scholarship, and trained as a pupil teacher; he became a full-time teacher in 1905 and underwent a year's training at St Patrick's College, Drum-condra, in 1906–7.

Corkery developed an interest in the Gaelic League in 1901 under the influence of D. P. Moran's weekly paper *The Leader*. (He had previously been only vaguely aware of the existence of an Irish language.) Between 1901 and 1910 Corkery wrote regularly for *The Leader* under the pen-name Lee, with the aim of improving Irish artistic standards and giving Cork a civic culture drawing on the everyday life of the city and the Gaelic traditions of the surrounding countryside. He also taught primary classes in St Francis' national school in the city centre (1905–13) and St Patrick's national school on the North Side (1913–18), both in slum areas. He complained about teaching overcrowded classes of poor children in an examination-oriented system which gave little time for encouraging individual creativity, and tried to encourage team sports, gave drawing lessons, and formed a school choir. His pupils included the future sculptor Seamus Murphy and Michael O'Donovan (Frank O'Connor).

In 1908 Corkery became the leading figure of the Cork Dramatic Society, an amateur group intended as a Cork counterpart to the Abbey. Between 1909 and 1913 it produced eighteen original plays (including five by Corkery). Despite its eventual demise it marked the beginning of Cork's Little Theatre tradition. At this time Corkery was primarily a cultural nationalist who saw separatism as impracticable; he argued the subject with Terence Mac-Swiney, whom he had met through the Gaelic League. Although they admired each other's dedication and intellectual ambitions, they also disagreed about the possibility of Irish culture expressing itself through English as well as Irish (MacSwiney thought this impossible) and the plays of J. M. Synge, which Corkery publicly defended.

Corkery had begun to publish short stories in magazines; in 1916 some were collected as *A Munster Twilight*. This and the publication of his novel *The Threshold of Quiet* the following year established his literary reputation. At the same time he was moving towards Sinn Féin; this led to his being refused the headmastership of his school in 1918, and he resigned to become a travelling instructor with the co. Cork technical instruction committee. In 1918 he was offered a Sinn Féin parliamentary candidacy.

Corkery was deeply affected by the sense of cultural and national revival of the War of Independence period (1919–21), in particular by the death on hunger strike of Mac-Swiney as lord mayor of Cork which attracted worldwide attention. His response to this period is expressed in his second short-story collection, *The Hounds of Banba* (1920), and *The Labour Leader* (1920), a play loosely based on the activities of James Larkin, whom he greatly admired. He also wrote at this time *Three Plays* (1920; a play about the Easter Rising, which was excluded by military censors and published in 1942) and a book of verses, *Ui bhreasail* (1921). He hoped to found a school of local writers incorporating some of his younger associates, notably O'Connor and Sean O Faolain.

Corkery opposed the Anglo-Irish treaty of 1922 as a betrayal of the ideals of the rising and supported the defeated republicans in the ensuing civil war. In 1924 he published his best-known book, *The Hidden Ireland*. This study of the Gaelic poetry of eighteenth-century Munster has been criticized for romanticizing its subject and ignoring the extent to which the poets it described spoke for a class of strong farmers with aristocratic pretensions rather than the Irish-speaking people as a whole, but its evocation of cultural loss, and its insistence on the impossibility of understanding Ireland without knowledge of Gaelic culture, made it an inspiration to many later Irish artists and intellectuals.

The appearance of *The Hidden Ireland* strengthened Corkery's literary reputation (further increased by his third and strongest short-story collection, *The Stormy Hills* (1929)) and opened a breach with his disciples O'Connor and O Faolain, who disliked his calls for the subordination of individuality to an idealized national tradition. This was exacerbated by Corkery's attacks on Sean O'Casey and Liam O'Flaherty for what he saw as vulgarity and cynical hostility to the idealism of the War of Independence period, and by his publication of *Synge and Anglo-Irish Literature* (1931), a partial retraction of his earlier praise of Synge, which although often narrow and incoherent, raises important questions about Irish literature in English. Its insistence on the link between Catholicism and Irishness was particularly controversial. (Corkery idealized the culture of medieval Catholic Europe, but his own religious beliefs are the subject of some controversy. Some friends believed he was a secret agnostic; he certainly had a strong anti-clerical streak, usually confined to private conversation.) By 1931 Corkery had decided it was impossible to have a distinctive Irish culture in English, since it would be distorted by the dominance of the English literary market. This led him to devalue most Irish literature in English, including his own (though he published one further short-story collection, *Earth out of Earth* (1939)). He later published some small works outlining his views on the revival of the Irish language, and a play in Irish, *An doras dunta*.

Corkery was appointed professor of English in University College, Cork, in 1931 after a bitter contest with O Faolain, and held the position until 1947. He was awarded a DLitt in 1948, served in the Irish Senate, 1951–4, and sat on the Irish Arts Council, 1952–6. He continued to produce journalism, and was recognized as a significant influence by many Irish artists and a major presence in the intellectual life of Cork (where he continued to encourage local talent). The Irish-language poet Sean O Riordain, who had an ambivalent relationship with him, said that he towered over the intellectual life of Cork like a mountain. He painted extensively in watercolours all his life, and attained a minor reputation for the handling of colour in his late work, most of which is in private ownership.

Corkery never married; his unmarried sister Mary kept house for him. Towards the end of their lives, as they grew increasingly frail (Corkery became almost blind some time before his death) they spent the winter months with their niece in Passage West, co. Cork, where Corkery died suddenly of a heart attack on 31 December 1964. He was buried in January 1965 at St Joseph's cemetery, Cork city.

Daniel Corkery's critical views remain controversial. Some critics see him as a cultural commissar embodying the narrowness of de Valera's Ireland, others praise him as a pioneering post-colonial critic. Through his role as developer of others' talents and popularizer of Gaelic culture, as well as his own limited but distinctive literary output, he secured a lasting place in Irish cultural history.

PATRICK MAUME

**Sources** University College, Cork, Corkery MSS · University College, Dublin, Terence MacSwiney MSS · *The Leader* [Dublin] (1901–10) [Corkery articles] · *The Leader* [Dublin] (1915–20) [Corkery articles] · P. Maume, *'Life that is exile': Daniel Corkery and the search for Irish Ireland* (1993) · G. B. Saul, *Daniel Corkery* (1973) · S. O Tuama, 'Daniel Corkery', in S. O Tuama, *Repossessions* (1995) · F. O'Connor, *An only child* (1961) · F. O'Connor, *My father's son* (1968) · University College, Dublin, C. P. Curran MSS · Sean O Riordain's diary, University College, Dublin · *Feasta* (1940/49–1950/59) · L. M. Cullen, *The hidden Ireland: reassessment of a concept* (1988) · P. Walsh, *Strangers: a correspondence between John Hewitt and Daniel Corkery* (1996) **Archives** Cork Municipal Museum, MSS, L313 · University College, Cork, corresp. and literary papers | NL Ire., Thomas MacDonagh MSS · PRO NIre., John Hewitt MSS · University College, Dublin, C. P. Curran MSS · University College, Dublin, Terence MacSwiney MSS | SOUND Radio Telifis Éireann, Dublin, archives · RTE, Cork, archives **Likenesses** J. Higgins, bronze bust, 1908, University College, Cork · W. Sheehan, oils, 1918, priv. coll. · S. Murphy, bust, 1934, Crawford Art Gallery, Cork · S. O'Sullivan, pencil drawing, repro. in *Feasta* (c.1950) · photographs (with friends and family members), University College, Cork, Corkery MSS

**Corkine, William** (*fl.* 1610–1617), composer, brought out two volumes of accompanied solo songs, both with other music for instruments. His first, *Ayres, to sing and play to the lute and basse violl, with pavins, galliards, almains and corantoes for the lyra violl*, appeared in 1610. The newly fashionable lyra viol was played from tablature like a lute, but chords were restricted to adjacent strings because of the use of a bow. Corkine's *The second booke of ayres, some to sing and play to the base-violl alone, others to be sung to the lute and base violl, with new corantoes, pavins, almaines: as also divers new descants upon old grounds, set to the lyra-viol* (1612) begins with songs for voice and bass viol alone, in which both parts have an equal importance, rather than being a melody and its harmonic bass. The setting of John Donne's 'Break of Day' is particularly successful. Corkine combined the new chordal lyra viol techniques with traditional 'divisions', in which a relatively slow-moving melodic line was divided into running passage work, and here he used the entire compass of the instrument. This is evident in the 'new descants upon old grounds' in his setting of the melody for 'Come live with me and be my love'.

Describing himself as 'a poor man indebted to many', Corkine dedicated parts of his books to different people, seven in all, rather than inscribing each volume to a single patron. One of his dedicatees was Edward Herbert, later Lord Herbert of Cherbury, whose own manuscript lute book indicates that he was himself no mean player. A song, 'What booteth Love', for voice and three instruments (probably viols), was included in a 1956 recording, but the original was lost sight of until it was rediscovered in 1983 by David Greer, who also found a second song, 'Sad is the time', in the same source. This is a combined volume of John Dowland's first three printed books of ayres, into which the manuscript songs were introduced (Greer). In 1617 a passport was issued by the privy council to a certain George Vincent 'to goe over to the Prince of Poland, and to carry over with him to the sayd Prince his master these musicians', including one 'Wm Corkin', perhaps indicating the pronunciation of his name (Limon, 101).

IAN HARWOOD

**Sources** W. Corkine, *Ayres, to sing and play to the lute and basse violl* (1610); facs. edn (1970) · W. Corkine, *The second booke of ayres* (1612); facs. edn (1970) · *New Grove* · G. Nelson, 'The lyra-viol variation sets of William Corkine', *Chelys*, 17 (1988), 17–23 · P. Walls, 'Lyra viol song', *Chelys*, 5 (1973–4), 71 · D. Greer, 'Two songs by William Corkine', *Early Music*, 11 (1983), 346–9 · J. Limon, *Gentlemen of a company* (1985)

**Corlett, John** (1841–1915), sporting journalist, was born at Winthorpe, Nottinghamshire, on 8 April 1841, the son of Sergeant-Major John Corlett of the 6th dragoon guards and his wife, Eleanor. According to his entry in *Who Was Who* he was educated by his father. At the age of sixteen he entered the wholesale grocery firm of Joseph Travers & Son in the City of London and by the time he was twenty-one he had reached the headship of a department. He was already a horse-racing enthusiast and he began sending articles to the growing number of papers specializing in sport. These included the well established *Bell's Life*, which by the middle of the 1860s had been joined by *The Field*, *The Sportsman*, the *Sporting Life*, and the *Sporting Times*; it was with the last of these that Corlett became inextricably linked.

Corlett's big chance came in 1867, when he was given a job on *The Sportsman*. From then until 1874 he wrote under the *noms de plume* of Vigilant and The Wizard. His style was direct and vigorous but he was a master of the subject of horse-racing and this was what attracted readers. He was one of the earliest and most successful of the relatively new profession of sporting journalists who contributed to the growth of modern sport as an integral part of the popular culture of the British.

The *Sporting Times* first appeared on 11 February 1865 as a weekly chronicle of racing, literature, and the theatre. Horse-racing was the hobby of its owner, Dr Joseph Henry Shorthouse (*d.* 1883), and Corlett bought it in 1874 for £50. Its circulation at that time was probably in three figures but Corlett's energy and leadership gradually pushed it up to 20,000. He achieved this by promoting accuracy and good fellowship but also by affecting a flippant and bacchanalian outlook. The staff were presented as terrible dogs whose weekly copy was wrung out of them at the last minute over huge Fleet Street lunches. Racing authority, plain patriotism of the 'if you see a foreigner heave half a brick at him' type, and a humour which has not travelled well down the racecourse of history attracted a readership of young and not so young men from club, mess, and smoking room. The paper became known as the *Pink 'un* probably as the result of an economy measure which led to its appearance on pink paper from April 1876. It was the *Sporting Times* which published the mock obituary notice for English cricket after the England team's defeat by the Australians at the Oval in August 1882, thus setting off the train of events which led to the legend of the Ashes. Corlett eventually sold the paper in 1912.

Corlett was a Conservative who lived mostly in rural Surrey and Kent, looking and living the part of a local squire and JP. He called Gladstone the 'grand old humbug'. He was not greatly attracted to new ideas, did not like the gramophone, and refused to use the telephone in his Fleet Street office. He was happily married on 12 December 1868 to Mary, daughter of Charles Stebbing of Newmarket, and was devastated by her death in 1909. One son was killed in the Second South African War and a second was wounded in France in 1915. Corlett died of heart failure at his home, Park House, Walmer, Kent, on 23 June 1915. He was buried next to his wife at East Sutton, near Sutton Valence.

TONY MASON

**Sources** J. B. Booth, *Old Pink 'un days* (1924) · J. B. Booth, *The Pink 'un world* (1938) · T. Mason, 'Sporting news, 1860–1914', *The press in English society from the seventeenth to nineteenth centuries*, ed. M. Harris and A. Lee (1986) · *The Field* (26 June 1915) · *Sporting Times* (26 June 1915) · *Sporting Times* (10 July 1915) · *The Sportsman* (25 June 1915) · *The Sportsman* (28 June 1915) · *The Times* (24 June 1915) · H. Cox, *Who's Who in Kent, Surrey and Sussex* (1911)
**Wealth at death** £28,228 19s. 1d.: probate, 30 Sept 1915, CGPLA Eng. & Wales

**Cormac mac Airt** [Cormac ua Cuinn, *called* Cormac Ulfhota] (*supp.* **196/7–267**), legendary king and sage, features prominently in early Irish tradition. According to the annals of the four masters, he became king of Tara in the year 227 and reigned until 266. However, Irish annalistic records at such an early period are not to be taken as historically authentic, and it is likely that Cormac was a purely legendary figure.

Cormac was reputed to be the grandson of another prominent mythological king, *Conn Cétchathach (Conn the Hundred-Battler). His father was Art, often called Art Oenfher (Art of the One Man), evidently because he had only one son. Cormac was conceived as a result of a single encounter between Art and Achtán, the beautiful daughter of the druid Olc Aiche; Art was then killed at the battle of Mag Mucrime. When Cormac was born, in 196 or 197, his grandfather Olc Aiche put magical protection on him against wounding, drowning, fire, witchcraft, and wolves.

Soon afterwards, Cormac was abducted by a female wolf and suckled by her. He was rescued by a hunter named Luigne Fer Trí, who kept him for a year. His mother Achtán then discovered where he was and brought him to Fíachnae Cassán, the foster father of Art. While he and his mother were on their journey northwards at night, the wolves of Ireland attempted to recapture the boy. However, he was saved by the intervention of a herd of wild horses. Cormac was fostered by Fíachnae Cassán for thirty years. The purpose of the association of Cormac with Luigne Fer Trí was to assert an alliance between the Uí Néill (who claimed Cormac as their ancestor) and the Luigni and Corco Fírthri of northern Connacht and also of the neighbourhood of Kells.

On a suitably auspicious day, Cormac set out for Tara with his father's sword and ring and assembly garment. As he approached Tara he saw a woman who was weeping. On enquiring the cause, it was explained to him that the woman was the owner of some sheep which had broken into the queen's woad garden and eaten the leaves off the plants. The king, Mac Con, had ordered that the sheep be forfeit for their offence. Cormac immediately pointed out that the judgment should have been 'one shearing for another', that is, that the woman should merely have had to forfeit the shearing of her sheep in recompense for the shearing of the woad plants. When Mac Con was informed of Cormac's judgment, he realized that he had been guilty of an injustice and that Cormac was the rightful king. According to another version of this episode, the side of the house in which Mac Con made his false judgment collapsed. Cormac subsequently assumed the kingship.

Because of his justice, Cormac's reign was characterized by peace and plenty. The rivers teemed with fish, the woods with mast, and the plains with honey. Tara was restored by Cormac so that it was grander than ever before and he added the most magnificent palace ever built there. The tale *Esnada Tige Buchet* ('The melodies of the house of Buchet') describes his meeting with Eithne of the Long Side, who became his wife. She was a daughter of Catháer Mór, king of Ireland, and was fostered by Buchet, a rich hospitaller in Leinster. However, the frequent visits of her twelve brothers reduced Buchet to penury and he and his wife were forced to flee to Kells (Cenannas), where they lived in a hut in the woods. Eithne loyally stayed with her foster father and looked after his bull and seven cows—all that remained of his wealth. She continued to honour him by reserving for him the best milk, rushes, and water. Cormac sent a message to Buchet asking for Eithne as his bride, but he replied that only her father, Catháer, could give her in marriage. Cormac ordered that Eithne be brought to him by force and had intercourse with her that night. She escaped the following morning, but was pregnant with a son, Cairpre Lifechair. Subsequently she became Cormac's queen, but only after a large bride-price had been paid to her foster father, Buchet. Cormac gave him all that he could see from the ramparts of Kells, including cows, oxen, horses, and tenantry.

The sources constantly stress the wisdom of Cormac: it is said that only Solomon son of David was wiser. He is also reputed to have embraced Christianity and to have refused to worship stones or trees. According to one Middle Irish text, only three Irishmen became Christians before the coming of St Patrick. The first was Conchobar mac Nessa, the second was Morann mac Cairpri Cinn Chaitt, and the third was Cormac mac Airt. A ninth-century collection of wise observations is attributed to Cormac. It is entitled *Tecosca Cormaic*, 'The teachings of Cormac', and consists of a series of replies to questions posed by his son Cairpre. Cormac advises in some detail on the proper qualities and behaviour of a king and stresses the importance of fostering poetry, learning, and art. He extols the virtues of receiving instruction from one's elders, but also describes how he acquired wisdom by solitary meditation: 'I was a listener in woods, I was a gazer at stars'. He replies to his son's queries on such topics as proper behaviour at a feast, types of weather, care of the body, and how to plead a law case. Much of the text is devoted to a discussion of different psychological types and gives some general observations on human behaviour. In reply to his son's query 'How do you distinguish women?', Cormac launches into a bitter diatribe, accusing them of jealousy, silliness, haughtiness, greed, sulkiness, and many other vices. This is one of the most savagely anti-female passages in medieval literature.

Cormac is associated with technical innovation as well as learning. According to one tradition, he impregnated a slave named Cíarnait. As her pregnancy advanced, she became unable to carry out her duty of grinding the corn for the king's household in a hand-quern. Cormac therefore sent for a millwright from overseas, who constructed the first mill built in Ireland. There are some references in the sources to Cormac's prowess as a warrior, but in general he does not feature as a military hero and there are accounts of his being forced into exile on at least two occasions. In one text he is also said to have been blinded in one eye, a blemish which made him ineligible for the office of king. A further reference to his physical characteristics is found in the epithet Ulfhota, which may be translated as 'of the Long Beard'.

Because of the five magical protections placed on him by his maternal grandfather, Cormac was not vulnerable to most forms of death. However, his death occurred none the less, due to an accident while feasting in the house of Spelán the hospitaller at Clettech, on the Boyne in Meath. A salmon bone had fallen into a bowl and had been inadvertently kneaded into bread which was given to Cormac. As he ate, the crowd outside watched a fight between two warriors. A sudden roar was raised, which startled Cormac. He swallowed a piece of bread with the bone in it and it stuck in his throat and killed him. Because of his Christian beliefs, Cormac had ordered that he was not to be buried in the pagan site of Brug na Bóínne, but at Ros na Ríg, near Slane, in Meath, with his face towards the east. His people disregarded his instructions. However, the River Boyne (Bóinn) rose up and carried his body three times to Ros na Ríg. On the third occasion his people followed his wishes and raised a gravemound for him at Ros na Ríg.

FERGUS KELLY

**Sources** T. Ó Cathasaigh, *The heroic biography of Cormac mac Airt* (1977) · M. Dillon, *The cycles of the kings* (1946); repr. (1994) · K. Meyer, *Tecosca Cormaic: the instructions of King Cormac mac Airt* (1909) · W. Stokes, ed. and trans., 'The songs of Buchet's house', *Revue Celtique*, 25 (1904), 18–39 · W. Stokes, 'A note on Esnada tige Buchet', *Revue Celtique*, 25 (1904), 225–7 · D. Greene, 'Esnada Tige Buchet', *Fingal Rónáin and other stories*, ed. D. Greene (1955), 27–44 · K. Meyer, 'The expulsion of the Déssi', *Ériu*, 3 (1907), 135–42 · E. Gwynn, ed. and trans., 'Temair III', *The metrical dindshenchas*, 1, Royal Irish Academy: Todd Lecture Series, 8 (1903); repr. (1991), 14–27 · W. Stokes, 'The battle of Mag Mucrime', *Revue Celtique*, 13 (1892), 426–74 · 'Senchas na relec', *Lebor na hUidre / Book of the dun cow*, ed. R. I. Best and O. Bergin (1929), 127–32 · M. L. Sjoestedt, 'Forbuis Droma Damhghaire', *Revue Celtique*, 43 (1926), 1–123 · M. L. Sjoestedt, 'Siège de Druim Damhghaire', *Revue Celtique*, 44 (1927), 157–86

**Cormac mac Cuilennáin** (*d.* 908), king of Munster and bishop, belonged to one of the lesser branches of the Éoganacht and his assumption of the kingship of Munster seems likely to have been a compromise arrangement (Byrne, 214, 292). It is likely that his marriage to *Gormlaith (*d.* 948) is a later fiction. The fullest version of his biography is to be found in the seventeenth-century compilation, the annals of the four masters. According to this, he was brought up by the sage, Snedgus of Dísert Díarmada, who died in 890. In 902 he assumed the kingship of Munster in place of Cenngégán. Five years later he and Flaithbertach led a Munster force against Flann Sinna, high-king of Ireland, at Mag Léna. After defeating him, they marched on into southern Meath and also defeated the men of Connacht and brought home hostages from the Uí Néill. The victories brought no lasting peace. In 908 Flann with Cerball, king of Leinster, and Cathal, king of Connacht, brought a great army against Cormac at Belach Mugna (Ballymoon, Kildare). The annals record the doom-laden prophecies accompanying Cormac and his death is described in detail (Radner, 153–9). The Munstermen were subject to great slaughter. As Cormac was escaping on horseback, his horse slipped on the blood-covered road; it fell backwards crushing the king, breaking his back and neck. As he fell, Cormac said, 'In manus tuas, Domine, commendo spiritum meum' ('into your hands, Lord, I commend my spirit'). In the coda of the annal entry, he is described as:

> a scholar in Irish and in Latin, the wholly pious and pure chief bishop, miraculous in chastity and prayer, a sage in government, in all wisdom, knowledge and science, a sage of poetry and learning, chief of charity and every virtue; a wise man in teaching, high king of two provinces of all Munster in his time. (Radner, 159)

This description is supported by the wide range of works attributed to Cormac. They include the *Lebor na cert* (the 'Book of rights'), *Sanas Cormaic* ('Cormac's glossary'), the manuscript compilation known as the psalter of Cashel, and numerous poems and tales (for a selection, see the indexes of the catalogues by Flower and by Abbott and Gwynn). However, recent scholarship has tended towards the view that many of these attributions should be treated with scepticism. *Lebor na cert* consists of sections on each of the kingdoms of Ireland in which two poems detail the stipend received by the provincial king from the king of Ireland and the stipend paid to the provincial king by the tribes of the province. At various times the work has been attributed en bloc to Cormac or he has been seen as one of the contributors. However, Dillon has demonstrated that the work is a compilation of poems on the rights of provincial kings, probably put together in the reign of Brían Bóruma in the eleventh century. At some stage it had been thought that *Lebor na cert* had been part of the psalter of Cashel and this was used as part of the argument for connecting it with Cormac. The psalter of Cashel is no longer extant though a number of works claim, in their scribal colophons, to be derived from it. The contents list of the psalter has been reconstructed by Ó Riain and he has argued that a link between Cormac and the psalter cannot be demonstrated before the last quarter of the fourteenth century.

One particular link which has been broken by Ó Riain's work is that between the psalter and an early fragment of 'Cormac's glossary' in the Bodleian Library (MS Laud 610). 'Cormac's glossary' (entitled *Sanas Cormaic* in the Yellow Book of Lecan version) is an encyclopaedic form of alphabetical glossary on Irish words; it contains not only explanations of difficult words, and in some cases lengthy tales explaining the origin of a word, but also etymological explanations of simple words in a style probably derived from Isidore of Seville. There are several versions of this glossary extant; they divide into two groups, a short version and a longer one with extra entries at the end of many of the letters. Sometimes the work is attributed to a Cormac, but the evidence for its connection with Cormac mac Cuilennáin would be entirely circumstantial were it not for a marginal gloss in the prose Dindsenchas (explanations of place names) on Tara at page 159a of the Book of Leinster, where an entry on Tara which is identical with an entry in 'Cormac's glossary' is glossed 'Corm[ac] m[ac] Cul[ennáin]' (Russell, 10–11). Supporting evidence, though circumstantial, is offered by the use of *sanas* in the title of the glossary: it basically means 'secret' and is not used of any other glossary; but it does occur in references to the secret council of the king of Munster. However, even if Cormac mac Cuilennáin can be linked to this glossary, it is not clear what role he played in its creation. It has emerged from recent work that material in 'Cormac's glossary' can also be found in other early glossaries and that the glossarial tradition can be traced back to a very early period of Irish scholarship. Indeed the etymological techniques employed can be found in Isidore and Jerome. The growth of glossaries was ongoing and it would seem that 'Cormac's glossary' represents a fairly late stage in the process. If Cormac had anything to do with the glossary attributed to him, it was at best as a compiler of pre-existing glossarial material, not as a collector of hard words directly from texts. Moreover, it seems that after Cormac's input the process of growth continued throughout the manuscript tradition right up to the period of the extant manuscripts.

Many of the poems and tales attributed to Cormac await re-evaluation, although it seems that there was a tendency to attribute works to him in order to enhance their status and that of the manuscript containing them. In contrast to the prevailing trend, Breatnach has recently attributed the *Amra Senáin*, a poem in praise of St Senán, to Cormac on the basis of the historical associations in the poem and language and vocabulary also attested in 'Cormac's glossary'.

PAUL RUSSELL

**Sources** AFM · J. N. Radner, ed., *Fragmentary annals of Ireland* (1978) · F. J. Byrne, *Irish kings and high-kings* (1973) · M. Dillon, 'On the date and authorship of the *Book of Rights*', *Celtica*, 4 (1958), 239–49 · P. Ó Riain, 'The psalter of Cashel: a provisional list of contents', *Éigse*, 23 (1989), 107–30 · Cormac mac Cuilennáin, *Sanas Cormaic: an old-Irish glossary*, ed. K. Meyer (1912), vol. 4 of *Anecdota from Irish manuscripts*, ed. O. J. Bergin and others (1907–13) · P. Russell, 'The sounds of a silence: the growth of Cormac's Glossary', *Cambridge Medieval Celtic Studies*, 15 (1988), 1–30 · L. Breatnach, ed., 'Amra Senáin', *Sages, saints and storytellers: Celtic studies in honour of Professor James Carney*, ed. D. Ó Corráin, L. Breatnach, and K. McCone (1989), 7–31 · S. H. O'Grady, R. Flower, and M. Dillon, *Catalogue of Irish manuscripts in the British Museum*, 3 vols. (1926–53) · T. K. Abbott and E. J. Gwynn, eds., *Catalogue of the Irish manuscripts in the library of Trinity College, Dublin* (1921) · M. Ní Dhonnchada, 'On Gormfhlaith daughter of Flann Sinna and the lure of the sovereignty goddess', *Seanchas: studies in early medieval Irish archaeology, history and literature in honour of Francis J. Byrne*, ed. A. P. Smyth (2000), 225–37 · M. Ní Mhaonaigh, 'Tales of three Gormlaiths in medieval Irish literature', *Ériu*, 52 (2002), 1–24 **Archives** Bodl. Oxf., MS Laud 610

**Cormac mac Eogain** (*fl.* 6th cent.). *See under* Connacht, saints of (*act. c.*400–*c.*800).

**Cormac Ó Luinín.** *See* Lynegar, Charles (*fl.* 1708–1731).

**Cormac ua Liatháin** (*fl.* late 6th cent.). *See under* Meath, saints of (*act. c.*400–*c.*900).

**Cormack, John** (1894–1978), protestant agitator and local politician, was born on 7 July 1894 in Edinburgh, the eldest child of the four sons and three daughters of Donald Cormack (1865–1937), a clerk and former soldier, and his wife, Mary McPhail (*c.*1870–1951). The family moved to Liverpool for a time but returned to Edinburgh, where Cormack had an elementary school education. He enlisted in 1909 as a boy soldier, serving in his father's regiment, the Argyll and Sutherland Highlanders.

Cormack remained for thirteen years in the army, survived First World War service in France, and was in the Rhineland army of occupation, and then in Ireland during the Anglo-Irish war (the 'troubles'). In October 1918 he married Mary Ross—they had three daughters and a son, but the marriage broke up in the early 1930s—and took his discharge as corporal in 1922. He probably held higher acting rank earlier and was also a drum major. He returned to Edinburgh, where he worked as a Post Office sorter and driver for ten years until suspended after allegations (which he said were malicious) of stealing postal orders. No charges followed and wrangling ensued, but he lost his job.

Cormack's leisure activities made him a controversial figure. His father was a Baptist whose lay preaching included meetings on the Mound, then Edinburgh's speakers' corner. Although the emphasis was evangelical there were occasional confrontations with Roman Catholics, whose controversialists also pitched their pulpits there. John Cormack developed his own militancy, joining the fringe of a widespread Scottish protestant movement in which new anxieties were grafted on to the traditional doctrinally based hostility to the Roman church. One of these was demographic alarm at Irish immigration, another dislike of the 1918 Education Act by which the state assumed responsibility for Catholic education but allowed the hierarchy considerable influence. But closest to Cormack's experience was resentment at the perceived alliance of the Roman church and Sinn Féin which he had witnessed in the Irish troubles. The Argylls, whose turbulent beat included the Knock pilgrimage, resented the hostility they faced from priests and seminary students.

Cormack developed a taste for historical and theological polemic, enlivened with denunciations of priestly delinquencies. He joined the Scottish Protestant League, a vehicle for protest driven by the unstable Alexander Ratcliffe, but seceded in 1930. In 1933 he was co-founder of the Protestant Action Society, and joined an Orange lodge, though he was intermittently at odds with that movement. Cormack combined leadership and 'loner' qualities. He deployed effective techniques of oratory and demagoguery, adaptable to indoor or outdoor use and displayed on the Mound for thirty years. During the 1930s his meetings provoked confrontation, especially among those who came to be provoked. In 1935 he led protests in Edinburgh against a Roman Catholic young men's conference and a eucharistic congress. These brought tens of thousands to the streets, as protesters and spectators, and involved turbulence, intimidation, and violent clashes. He also used his position on the city council, after his election for North Leith in 1934, to oppose the granting of the freedom of Edinburgh to the Australian prime minister, Joseph Lyons, and the American ambassador Joseph Kennedy, carrying protests from the council chamber to the ceremonies themselves. He campaigned on education and the replacement of Catholic municipal workers by unemployed protestants, though his causes also included slum clearance, nurses' pay, and a civic airport.

It was remarkable that such protests should flourish not only on Clydeside, with its sectarian traditions, but in Edinburgh, where the Roman Catholic minority represented only 9 per cent of the population and the dominant middle-class protestantism was hostile to all demonstrative militancy. Cormack's success, most evident when Protestant Action took 31 per cent of votes in the Edinburgh local elections in 1936, perhaps reflected an Edinburgh working-class search for a cause of its own, at a time when it was less affected by socialism than most of urban Scotland. It also reflected the economic frustrations and political styles of the 1930s.

But the tide of protestant militancy, also evident in Glasgow, soon ebbed. Ratcliffe's personal cult, which also moved towards antisemitism, decayed rapidly. Cormack lost his council seat in 1937, though he was returned for South Leith in 1938. He remained a councillor (and a phenomenon) until his retirement in 1962. The ill will he provoked in his prime surrounded him into the war years. The Roman Catholic archbishop unsuccessfully urged the Scottish Office to act against him for the alleged incitement by him of attacks on Italian businesses in 1940, a charge of which he was innocent, though he denounced Italian as well as Irish Catholicism and was hostile to Poles, even when they were allies. However, Cormack was insulated from Nazism and fascism, as well as communism and Scottish nationalism. He was not antisemitic, but he sympathized with Jews as victims of the Inquisition. His suspicion that 'once a Catholic, always a Catholic' (irritating protestant campaigners working with former monks and disillusioned priests) extended to Hitler and Mussolini.

Cormack failed to become Leith's MP when he stood as an independent candidate at the general election of 1945, coming last with under 2500 votes out of a total poll of over 32,000. Thereafter he mellowed and concentrated on developing the substance and image of robust independence. On Edinburgh corporation he was a one-man party, co-operating with the ruling progressives (Conservatives, Liberals, and right-wing independents, Roman Catholics among them). He became health convener and a bailie, and was also a magistrate, achieving a kind of aldermanic status, though later than his seniority suggested. Militancy, isolation, and perhaps his plebeian origins excluded him in 1950s Edinburgh from the possibility of becoming lord provost. His personal credit was raised by his advocacy of Leith interests and his exemplary fairness on the magistrates' bench, together with a reputation (which his simple lifestyle, in a modest flat, bore out) for eschewing personal advantage. Now a dormant volcano, he became a local worthy. The Catholic historian of protestant protest described his transition 'from ogre to institution' (Gallagher, 159). Heart trouble in 1964 silenced his oratory. He died in Edinburgh on 17 June 1978 and was cremated at Warriston, Edinburgh, on 20 June.

R. D. KERNOHAN

**Sources** T. Gallagher, *Edinburgh divided: John Cormack and no popery in the 1930s* (1987) · S. Bruce, *No pope of Rome: anti-Catholicism in modern Scotland* (1985) · J. Cormack, 'If I were dictator of Edinburgh', *Glasgow Daily Record* (6 Oct 1937) · private information (2004) [family] · records of Charlotte Baptist Chapel, Edinburgh

**Archives** Edinburgh Central Reference Library, Protestant Action election literature · priv. coll.

**Likenesses** cloth banner (after photograph, *c*.1980), Loyal Orange Lodge No. 188, Edinburgh; repro. in Gallagher, *Edinburgh divided* · photograph, repro. in *The Scotsman* · photograph, repro. in *Edinburgh Evening News* · photographs, repro. in Gallagher, *Edinburgh divided*

**Cormack, Sir John Rose** (1815–1882), medical editor and physician, was born on 1 March 1815 at Stow, Midlothian, the only son of the Revd John Cormack (1776–1840), minister in the Church of Scotland, and his wife, Helen Rose, youngest daughter of John Rose, of Holm, Nairnshire. He attended the grammar school at Jedburgh before entering Edinburgh University in 1829 to study classics, mathematics, and philosophy. Cormack did not take his MA but stayed on to study medicine. In 1836 he won the university's Harveian prize for his 'Treatise on the properties of creosote'. He graduated MD in 1837, receiving a gold medal for a thesis on the presence of air in the organs of circulation. In the same year he was senior president of the Edinburgh Royal Medical Society, in which capacity he presided over its centenary celebrations. After graduating Cormack visited Paris, where he attended some medical lectures, before travelling in Spain and Italy.

Cormack then returned to Edinburgh to practise medicine. He was appointed physician to the Royal Public Dispensary, to the Fever Hospital, and to the Royal Infirmary. He became FRCPE in 1841. On 4 November 1841 he was married in London, at St George's, Bloomsbury, to Eliza

Anne, second daughter of William Hine, of Hampshire, Trelawney, Jamaica. They were to have four sons and seven daughters. Refused permission to give clinical lectures at the infirmary, Cormack resigned his post in 1845 and moved to Putney in south-west London, where he set up in practice as a general practitioner. In the 1850s he moved to central London. Although 'an amiable man of enterprising and industrious disposition', Cormack had limited success as a practitioner. A colleague, Charles Williams, attributed this to a lack of 'firmness and strength of character' (Williams, 411).

Cormack became a medical editor and author at a comparatively young age. In January 1841 he founded the *Edinburgh Monthly Journal of Medical Science*, which he edited until June 1846. In 1843 he wrote *The natural history, pathology, and treatment of the epidemic fever prevailing in Edinburgh and other towns*, and in 1848 he published a pamphlet on the Universities of Scotland Bill. In January of the following year he resumed his editorial activity, founding the *London Journal of Medicine*, which he edited until September 1852, at which point it was amalgamated with the *Provincial Medical and Surgical Journal* (*PMSJ*) to form the *Association Medical Journal* (*AMJ*—the *British Medical Journal* or *BMJ* from 1857). Cormack had been appointed to the part-time editorship of *PMSJ*, the weekly publication of the Provincial Medical and Surgical Association (PMSA—the British Medical Association or BMA from 1855), in the previous August. He took up his editorial duties with the association at an annual salary of £250, a sum he considered inadequate, in January 1853; he carried them out for a period of thirty-three months, tendering his resignation in August 1855.

Cormack was the first editor to produce the PMSA's journal in London, though he actually conducted most of his editorial work at his home, undertaking to be present at the journal office for no more than 75 minutes per week 'when not unavoidably prevented by other duties' (*AMJ*, 24 Nov 1852). In September 1854 he became *de facto* PMSA secretary. He was editor of the *AMJ* at a time when, through no fault of his, the association was riven with dissension about the journal's format, frequency and place of publication, high cost, and even its continued existence. Although Cormack's editorial regime was in many ways successful, he received much criticism, particularly from those PMSA members who resented the journal's transfer to London and its expansion to the point at which it threatened to become more important than the association which had established it. Matters came to a head at the PMSA's anniversary meeting at York in August 1855, when it was agreed that the editorship of the journal could not be held by the secretary of the association, and that the *AMJ* should revert to being the *PMSJ*. Despite having the support of many members, Cormack resigned both positions, though he remained a PMSA member. In 1856 he unsuccessfully applied to become medical officer of health for Holborn. Two years later he was also unsuccessful in an attempt to secure appointment as general medical registrar and secretary to the newly created General Medical Council.

In 1866 ill health prompted Cormack to move with his family to Orléans in France. In 1869, on the death of Sir Joseph Olliffe, physician to the British embassy, he then moved to Paris. He continued to write on medical subjects, though less prolifically than in the past. He translated volumes 2–5 of Armand Trousseau's *Clinical Lectures* (1868), and published a two-volume collection of his main papers under the title *Clinical Studies* (1876). In August 1870 he was awarded the degree of MD in Paris with a thesis entitled: 'De l'entrée de l'air dans les orifices béants des veines uterines considerée comme cause de danger et de mort subite peu de temps après la délivrance'. In reporting the award the *BMJ* stated that Cormack was the only physician in Paris to hold both British and French MD degrees.

Cormack was also in Paris when it was besieged during the Franco-Prussian War of 1870–71 and throughout the commune. He served as surgeon to the Ambulance Anglaise, tending to the war wounded and to British residents of the city. In December 1870 he described in the *BMJ*, for which he was war correspondent, how the previous week was 'in many respects the most eventful, exciting, and laborious week of my whole life' (*BMJ*, 17 Dec 1870, 664). In recognition of his work during the crises he received several awards. The French government made him chevalier of the Légion d'honneur in 1871, and in Britain, on 14 March 1872, he received a knighthood at Buckingham Palace. Cormack remained in Paris after the commune, becoming physician to the Hertford British Hospital, a post he retained for the rest of his life.

For some time before his death Cormack suffered from chronic disease of the prostate and bladder. In early 1882, in an attempt to recover his health, he spent several weeks in Monte Carlo, but on returning to Paris his condition deteriorated. He died at his home, 364 rue St Honoré, Paris, on 13 May 1882. His widow survived him by a few months.

P. W. J. BARTRIP

**Sources** *BMJ* (20 May 1882), 761 · *Medical Times and Gazette* (10 June 1882), 624 · *The Lancet* (20 May 1882), 847 · *The Times* (17 May 1882) · *DNB* · *Testimonials submitted to the General Council of medical education and registration, by J. R. Cormack* (1858) · *London Medical Directory* (1847) · P. Bartrip, *Mirror of medicine: a history of the British Medical Journal* (1990) · Edinburgh University, *Doctors of medicine, 1705–1845* (1846) · Boase, *Mod. Eng. biog.* · Allibone, *Dict.* · m. cert. · C. J. B. Williams, *Memoirs of life and work* (1884) · *GM*, 2nd ser., 17 (1842), 92

**Cormeau, (Beatrice) Yvonne** (1909–1997). *See under* Women agents on active service in France (*act.* 1942–1945).

**Cornbury**. For this title name *see* Hyde, Henry, Viscount Cornbury and fifth Baron Hyde of Hindon (1710–1753).

**Corneliszoon, Lucas** [*known as* Lucas Corneliszoon de Cock] (*b.* 1495, *d.* in or before 1552), painter, was born in Leiden, the third son of the painter Cornelis Engelbrechtszoon and his wife, Elysabeth Pietersdochter. Corneliszoon was presumably trained by his father and was noted by the painter and biographer Karel van Mander as a painter in oil and watercolours. His family were of prosperous burgher class and so there is reason to question the assertion that 'he could barely maintain himself in his native town by means of the art of painting' (van Mander, 129) and was thus compelled to take up cooking. He probably went to England during the reign of Henry VIII, as did several other artists from the Low Countries, although the only work which may be autograph and date from this time is an oval portrait of Sir Thomas Wyat (priv. coll.), which is inscribed 'Lucas Cornelii'. Van Mander, who mentions a number of his works still surviving in 1604, states that his paintings were much sought after by Englishmen who arrived in the Netherlands during the earl of Leicester's governorship (1585–7) and this statement may be based on van Mander's personal observation. Corneliszoon was back in Leiden on 16 June 1542, but the length of this visit cannot be determined and it cannot therefore be assumed that he did not spend a considerable amount of time in England. Attempts have been made to ascribe a number of works in various media to him, but these attributions remain inconclusive, especially because his identity has been confused with Jan (Wellens?) de Cock. Corneliszoon died before 27 June 1552. It is not known whom he married, but according to van Mander he had seven or eight children, who were living abroad, conceivably in England, at the time of his death, which may also have taken place in England.

SUSAN BRACKEN

**Sources** K. van Mander, *The lives of the illustrious Netherlandish and German painters*, ed. H. Miedema, 1 (1994) · J. D. Bangs, *Cornelis Engelbrechtsz.'s Leiden* (1979)

**Cornelius a Sancto Patricio**. *See* O'Mahony, Connor (1594–1656).

**Cornelius Tacitus**. *See* Tacitus (*b.* AD 56/7, *d.* in or after 113) *under* Julius Agricola, Gnaeus (AD 40–93).

**Cornelius, John** (*c.*1557–1594), Roman Catholic priest, possibly a son of Gervase Cornelius and Maud (or Mary) Buckingham, was born in Bodmin, Cornwall. His parents were Irish and, though living in the humblest station, are said to have sprung from the illustrious family of the O'Mahons. His patron, Sir John Arundell of Lanherne, sent him to Oxford. Elected a fellow of Exeter College on 30 June 1575 he was expelled for popery by royal commission on 3 August 1578. He arrived at the English College in Rheims on 26 September 1579. He was sent on to the English College in Rome on 9 February 1580, arriving on 1 April. Ordained deacon on 10 October 1581 he preached in the presence of Pope Gregory XIII on the feast of St Stephen, 26 December 1581. He departed for England in September 1583 shortly after his ordination to the priesthood. Sir John Arundell received him; in March 1588 he was living with Arundell at his house in Muswell Hill. After Arundell's death on 17 January 1591 Cornelius accompanied his widow, Anne, daughter of Edward, third earl of Derby, and formerly widow of Charles, seventh Lord Stourton, to Chideock Castle, Dorset.

Like his friend the Jesuit William Weston, Cornelius was a noted exorcist. According to the Jesuit John Gerard, Cornelius was

> so famous in preaching that all Catholics followed him as children do their nurse when they long for milk, and the man so full of the Apostle's charity, that with one fervent speech in imitation of the offer which St. Paul made to be '*anathema pro fratribus*', he expelled a devil out of a person whom he was exorcising. I know the time and place where it was performed; and where another wicked spirit confessed in a possessed person that his fellow was cast out by Cornelius his charity.   (Morris, 17–18)

On 14 April 1594, however, Sir George Trenchard raided Chideock Castle. After a search of five or six hours someone led the pursuivants to the priest hole where Cornelius was hiding. Thomas Bosgrave, a Cornish gentleman and kinsman of Sir John Arundell, was taken into custody at the same time, as were two servants of the Arundell family.

Imprisoned in Trenchard's house Cornelius met a number of protestant divines and engaged them in debate. One of these divines, named Charke (possibly William Charke), was 'easily their leader and principal in the whole of the county' (*Elizabethan Jesuits*, 224). According to More, Sir Walter Ralegh also discussed unspecified issues with Cornelius for one night in order 'to remove his doubts'. Despite Ralegh's displeasure at something Cornelius said about atheism the courtier promised to intercede with Elizabeth I on the priest's behalf. At the end of April, Cornelius was ordered to London, to Marshalsea prison, where, despite being tortured, he revealed nothing that would prejudice his benefactors. In late June he was remanded to Dorchester for trial, where he and his three companions were found guilty: Cornelius of high treason for being a priest and coming into the kingdom and remaining there, Bosgrave and the servants of felony for aiding Cornelius, knowing him to be a priest. They were executed at Dorchester on 3 or 4 July 1594.

Whether Cornelius died a Jesuit is somewhat controversial. In late 1588 Henry Garnet reported to Claudio Acquaviva, Jesuit superior-general, that John Cornelius wished to enter the Society of Jesus. Garnet, however, was reluctant to send him to the Spanish Netherlands. He feared that Jesuit authorities there would reject Cornelius's application on account of his health, and he was unwilling to take Cornelius away from his flock. Garnet admitted that Cornelius always lived with a Jesuit and would not suffer if his noviceship was postponed or, indeed, if he were allowed to make it in England. In a letter to Garnet some time after his capture Cornelius still hoped to be admitted into the society. After Cornelius's martyrdom, Garnet explained how much he had tried to console the priest, but it was not within his power to accept him into the society. However, on his own initiative Cornelius pronounced Jesuit vows before his execution and instructed three unnamed principal Catholics who witnessed the event to inform Garnet of what he had done.

THOMAS M. MCCOOG

**Sources** T. M. McCoog, *English and Welsh Jesuits, 1555–1650*, 2 vols., Catholic RS, 74–5 (1994–5) · T. M. McCoog, ed., *Monumenta Angliae*, 1–2 (1992) · H. Foley, ed., *Records of the English province of the Society of*

*Jesus*, 7 vols. in 8 (1875–83) • T. F. Knox and others, eds., *The first and second diaries of the English College, Douay* (1878) • G. Anstruther, *The seminary priests*, 1 (1969) • W. Kelly, ed., *Liber ruber venerabilis collegii Anglorum de urbe*, 1, Catholic RS, 37 (1940) • Foster, *Alum. Oxon.* • *The Elizabethan Jesuits: Historia missionis Anglicanae Societatis Jesu (1660) of Henry More*, ed. and trans. F. Edwards (1981) • *The condition of Catholics under James I: Father Gerard's narrative of the Gunpowder Plot*, ed. J. Morris (1871) • P. Caraman, ed., *William Weston: the autobiography of an Elizabethan* (1955) • P. Caraman, *Henry Garnet, 1555–1606, and the Gunpowder Plot* (1964) • J. H. Pollen, ed., *Unpublished documents relating to the English martyrs*, 1, Catholic RS, 5 (1908)

**Archives** Archives of the British Province of the Society of Jesus, London • Archivum Romanum Societatis Iesu, Rome
**Likenesses** C. Weld, pencil drawing (after seventeenth-century portrait formerly in the Gesù in Rome), Stonyhurst College, Lancashire; repro. in Foley, ed., *Records*, vol. 3, following p. 434; vol. 71, following p. 170 • line engraving, NPG

**Cornell** [*née* Gunn], **Muriel Amy** (1906–1996), athlete, was born on 27 September 1906 at 2 Western Road, Mitcham, Surrey, the daughter of Frederick William Gunn, master grocer, and his wife, Beatrice Minnie, *née* Loosemore. She attended Wimbledon county school, where athletics was not part of the curriculum, and came to the sport via her brother and her fiancé, Stanley Herbert (Stan) Cornell (*b.* 1903/4), a brush manufacturer (the son of Herbert Cornell, an accountant). Both men were founder members of Mitcham athletic club. In 1926 they encouraged her to join the newly formed women's section and, although she regarded herself primarily as a sprinter, she entered and won the long jump at an internal club competition in June of that year. Intrigued by her success—obtained despite being tired after running the 220 yards—she put in some practice, during which she leapt further than the existing world record. Mitcham's secretary then persuaded the organizer of that summer's British games at Stamford Bridge to include a woman's long jump, at which she broke the world mark officially.

Within two months of taking up long jumping, Muriel Gunn was representing Britain at the second women's world games at Göteborg in Sweden. However, her inexperience let her down. A potential winning leap was reduced by her leaving a mark in the sand behind her actual landing point when she turned to speak to an official before leaving the pit. She and the winner, the Japanese Kinui Hitomi, exchanged the world record several times during the 1920s. Domestically her British all-comers record of 19 feet 2½ inches, which she set at Birmingham in 1930 in a match against Germany, remained intact for twenty-three years. Before this she had increased the mark five times since she first broke the record. She married Stan Cornell on 15 August 1928.

Muriel Cornell was not just a long jumper. At the Women's Amateur Athletic Association (AAA) championships she won the 100 metres hurdles in 1927, the 100 yards in 1928, and the 80 metres hurdles in 1930. In 1928 she broke the world record for the 80 metres hurdles in the semi-final but was beaten in the final itself. Of course her forte was the long jump, for which she held the title from the inaugural Women's AAA meeting in 1927 through to 1931.

Cornell performed poorly at the trials for the Los Angeles Olympics of 1932, a matter later explained as being due to pregnancy. In January 1933 she gave birth to a daughter, Lorna, and then returned to competitive athletics, one of the first mothers to resume high standard track and field. Nevertheless a snapped Achilles tendon in a hurdle race ended her career as an athlete. She remained in the sport as a coach and administrator, serving for eleven years as secretary to the Women's AAA and managing the women's team at the 1936 Olympics in Berlin.

Cornell's seventieth birthday party was attended by Olympian Harold Abrahams, who presented her with a gold medal inscribed 'from a fellow long jumper'. She herself was never able to jump at the Olympics, as the long jump did not become a recognized event for women until the London games in 1948. She died on 8 March 1996 of pneumonia, in the East Surrey Hospital, Redhill, Surrey. Her husband predeceased her. WRAY VAMPLEW

**Sources** *Daily Telegraph* (14 March 1996) • b. cert. • m. cert. • d. cert. • *CGPLA Eng. & Wales* (1997)
**Likenesses** E. F. Corcoran, photograph, 1930, Hult. Arch. • J. Gouger, double portrait, photograph, 1931 (with Ruby Davis), Hult. Arch. • J. Gouger, photograph, 1931, Hult. Arch. • photograph, 1931, repro. in *Daily Telegraph*
**Wealth at death** under £145,000: probate, 1997, *CGPLA Eng. & Wales*

**Cornelys** [*née* Imer; *married name* Pompeati], (**Anna Maria**) **Teresa** [*known as* Madame Trenti, Mrs Smith] (**1723?–1797**), singer and impresario, was born in Venice, probably in 1723, to the Genoan actor and impresario Giuseppe Imer (*d.* 1758) and his wife. Many particulars of her life, especially before 1759, derive from Giacomo Casanova's *History of my Life*, a not wholly reliable source. Teresa and her older sister Marianna were trained as professional singers. Casanova (1725–1798) met Teresa for the first of several times about 1740 and says that being caught making love to her cost him a job. The outlines of her moderately successful career between 1741 and 1754, mostly as a *seconda donna*, can be traced through casts printed in opera librettos, though she almost certainly sang in other productions for which no book was printed. She is listed as Cleopatra in the libretto for the 1741 production of *Cesare in Egitto* in Verona, her earliest known performance. She sang Vitellia in *Tito Manlio* during the carnival season at Florence in 1742 in a company that included her sister. In Venice on 2 May 1742 she appeared as Barsene in the première of Gluck's *Demetrio*. In 1743 she sang Creusa in *Demofoonte* in Padua as well as Albina in *Alessandro Severo* and Araspe in *Farasmane re di Tracia* at Genoa, both with her sister. The Sartori index lists her as Dircea in *Demofoonte* in Turin in 1744, but the entry for the libretto is lacking.

At an unknown date about 1744–5 Teresa married the dancer Angelo Francesco Pompeati (*c.*1701–1768), with whom she had a son, Giuseppe (1746–*c.*1797). The sisters sang at the King's Theatre, Haymarket, in London during the 1745–6 season, when Gluck was the house composer. Teresa created the role of Iride in *La caduta de giganti*, sang Erifile in *Il trionfo della continenza*, an unknown role in *Artamene*, and Erissena in *Alessandro nell'Indie*. After this season the sisters' careers diverged, and there is a small gap in documentation of Teresa's engagements. In 1748 she went to Hamburg to sing Rosmiri in *Arsace* and Irene in *Bajazet*. According to Howard, she probably participated in the première of Gluck's *La contesa de'numi* in Copenhagen in 1749, and the next year she sang Aristea in *L'Olympiade* at Brunswick.

Then there is a blank in Teresa's career. Aspects of her life can be sketched in from Casanova, who, while acknowledging her intelligence, asserts that 'her good fortune had not depended entirely on her talent; her charms had contributed to it more than anything else' (Casanova, 3.243–4). The first instance he offers is that she became the mistress of Friedrich, margrave of Brandenburg-Bayreuth (1711–1763). In February 1753 she bore a daughter, baptized Wilhelmine Frederike. The child's paternity is uncertain, as is the total number of Teresa's children. About this time she and her husband separated permanently, and Casanova reports that she had begun an affair with a gentleman of the bedchamber, Théodore Camille, marquis de Montperny. Casanova admits to a very brief liaison he himself had with Teresa during a visit she made to Venice in 1753, and he eventually acknowledged paternity of a daughter known in London as Sophie Wilhelmina, who was Teresa's second or perhaps third child.

After resuming her career, Teresa appeared in 1754 as Animia in *L'huomo* at Bayreuth and as Asteria in *Bajazet* in Turin, where she placed her maiden name after that of her estranged husband and described herself as 'virtuosa di camera delle Loro Altezze Eccellenze e Reali di Barayt' (Sartori, 3.643). Casanova says that at an unknown date, presumably after this, the discovery of her affair with Montperny ended her tenure as the margrave's mistress. Casanova records what he says is the history she gave him of her next several years: she had 'gone to Brussels with a lover, where for a few days she had taken the fancy of Prince Charles of Lorraine, who gave her a special patent granting her the direction of all theatrical performances throughout the Austrian Netherlands' (Casanova, 5.138). Prince Karl Alexander of Lorraine was governor of the Austrian Netherlands between 1748 and 1756, and a 'Mlle Pompeati' was listed as 'directrice des spectacles en Flandre' among the subscribers to Robert Daubat's *Cent contredanses* (1757), but otherwise this part of her life is obscure. According to Casanova,

> with this patent she had embarked on the most extensive enterprises which had led her to spend enormous sums, so that in less than three years, after selling all her diamonds, her laces, her wardrobe, and everything she owned, she had been obliged to go to Holland to avoid being sent to prison. (Casanova, 5.138)

Casanova says he heard this story when he came across Teresa unexpectedly in 1758–9 in Amsterdam, where she was singing at public concerts around a circuit of Dutch cities in very reduced circumstances under the name Madame Trenti. He was no longer interested in her sexual favours but professed concern for the child Sophie, who was introduced to him as his own. He therefore agreed to

give Teresa money with which to move to Britain, where she thought she could make a better living, and he temporarily took charge of her son Giuseppe.

Teresa arrived in London in October 1759. She travelled with further financial help from another lover, the Dutch merchant Jan Cornelis Rigerboos (or Jan Rigerboos Cornelis), whose name she used during most of the rest of her life. No particulars about their relationship are known, though late in his memoirs Casanova alleges that she 'ruined' Rigerboos (Casanova, 9.162). Teresa chose London for a new beginning because she thought she had an entrée to musical circles through a cellist and double-bass player performing in the Dutch concerts. He called himself John Freeman and claimed to be a beneficed clergyman in the Church of England with many contacts who would be useful in her attempt to support herself via concerts in London (Survey of London, 33.74). There he used the name John Fermor (he appears as 'Sir Frederick Fermer' in Casanova, 9.163–4), and although he proved not to have the contacts needed, he did have money to lend.

In a lawsuit Teresa noted that together they gave a series of concerts at the Little Theatre in the Haymarket shortly after their arrival in October 1759. She worked hard at meeting potential aristocratic patrons for an ambitious scheme of subscription assemblies that she and Fermor had worked up together. As she did not yet speak English and was not in a position to be too choosy about her supporters, at the beginning she used the notorious Elizabeth Chudleigh as a spokesperson for the project, but other (at least slightly) more respectable ladies soon endorsed her plans. Horace Walpole names Elizabeth Percy, countess of Northumberland, Caroline Stanhope, countess of Harrington, and 'some other great ladies' (whom he disliked) as her eventual sponsors (Walpole, *Corr.*, 23.271).

Teresa leased Carlisle House, Soho Square, in May 1760 and began her 'entertainments' that autumn. The key to her success was limiting the subscription to the nobility and people vouched for by them. Aristocrats bought 5 guinea tickets to a series of gatherings to which only members of 'the Society' were admitted. Dancing and refreshments were available, but probably a more potent lure was gambling. Few records of the early meetings remain. A highly irregular pattern of advertising suggests that Teresa communicated with her subscribers principally by private means. Tickets were never available for sale to the general public, nor were her assemblies usually reviewed, as more public gatherings sometimes were. Encouraged by her success, she commissioned a major remodelling of the premises, between June and December 1761. To settle construction debts she gave large numbers of tickets, or the promise of the income from them, to certain creditors.

During the 1760s Teresa undertook several kinds of expansion. She engaged the best musicians available in London, and the Johann Christian Bach–Karl Friedrich Abel concert series began at Carlisle House in 1763–4; when it transferred in 1767–8 to her competitor, Almack's Rooms, she turned to Felice Giardini and Mattia Vento for music. She branched out to include concerts, balls, and masquerades among her 'entertainments', and boldly sang in oratorios in 1764 and 1765. A plan to open a parallel set of rooms in the City was bruited in 1766, but not well received. Further development of the Carlisle House property in 1768 included costly rooms with a Chinese motif and a Chinese bridge between buildings, probably designed by the cabinetmaker Thomas Chippendale. Teresa's balls and masquerades were increasingly both splendid and (perhaps undeservedly) notorious for loose conduct.

Writing to Horace Mann on 22 February 1771, Horace Walpole summarized her progress in retrospect:

> She took Carlisle House in Soho Square, enlarged it and established assemblies and balls by subscription. At first they scandalized, but soon drew in both righteous and ungodly. She went on building, and made her house a fairy palace, for balls, concerts and masquerades.

While he regarded 'her taste and invention in pleasures and decorations' as 'singular', he also acknowledged that 'of late years she has been the Heidegger of the age, and presided over our diversions' (Walpole, *Corr.*, 23.271).

Teresa's success was, financially at least, superficial. She was never able to accumulate capital or pay off her debts, so from as early as February 1762 she was constantly harassed by creditors' lawsuits. Casanova, visiting London in 1763–4, found her confined to the house except on Sundays, lest bailiffs arrest her. On 1 February 1768 she signed an agreement with four creditors that left her with only nominal control of the entertainments and an £800 expense budget, for a business that was valued at £20,000 (PRO, C12/1518/6). Still borrowing and finagling, in 1771 she took advantage of disagreements between the administration of the King's Theatre, Haymarket, and its imported stars, particularly Gaetano Guadagni, to expand into opera. Under the disguise of 'harmonic meetings' she, Guadagni, and the dancer Simon Slingsby presented fully costumed and at least semi-staged *opera seria* at Carlisle House. Performances of Vento's *Artaserse* on 24 and 31 January 1771 brought complaints from the opera managers at the Bow Street magistrates' court that they were violating the Licensing Act of 1737. The theatre managers supported these complaints, since their monopoly too would have been vulnerable, had this scheme succeeded. She was twice fined £50, but the rumour of a prosecution for running a bawdy house is not true. Several satirical pictures of Teresa were published about this time.

According to lawsuit testimony, Teresa cleared more than £3000 in 1771, though only £1300 by 28 October 1772 (PRO, C12/1518/6). The failure of her opera brought out creditors, and by October she had gone into retirement at 'The Hotel' in Southwark, in which she briefly had a part interest. The list of bankrupts in the *Gentleman's Magazine* of November 1772 described her as a 'dealer' (*GM*, 1st ser., 42, 1772, 544). On 22 December Carlisle House and its furnishings were sold to a consortium of her creditors (among them Chippendale) for £10,200 in what she claimed was a rigged auction. Her daughter deserted her

at this time and lived on the charity of various noble families for the rest of her life. Teresa was granted a £200 annuity after the auction, though how long it was paid is not clear. However, Carlisle House did not flourish after her demotion: she was unable to regain her public in the few masquerades to which her name was attached in the next five years.

Teresa 'remained in obscurity many years' under the alias Mrs Smith, according to her obituary (*GM*, 1st ser., 67/2, 1797, 890). She had recently reappeared, to the amusement of that writer, keeping a herd of asses in Knightsbridge, whose milk she occasionally offered as a 'public *déjeuné* for people of fashion' (ibid.). Again she managed to overspend: an allowance made her by her son, who was tutor to George Fermor, third earl of Pomfret, and the annuity provided by a member of the Cowper family were not enough to keep her out of the Fleet prison, where she died on 19 August 1797, still full of 'visionary projects' (*GM*, 1st ser., 67/2, 1797, 891). The generous assessment in the obituary seems remarkably apt: she was 'a distinguished priestess of fashion' (ibid., 890), who 'being of an enterprizing spirit, possessing a good understanding, great knowledge of mankind, and specious manners' (ibid.), was able to make Carlisle House 'the favourite region of amusement among the nobility and gentry' (ibid.) for more than ten years; she provided such 'diversified amusement' (ibid.) that for many years 'no other public entertainments could pretend to rival' (ibid.) Carlisle House. Despite her fall, her '*projecting turn*' (ibid., 891) kept her dreaming that she might recapture her position at the height of society. A female entrepreneur who could not control her expansionist tendencies, for more than a decade she directed fashionable entertainments for the British nobility, despite being a foreign adventuress and stage performer.　　JUDITH MILHOUS

**Sources** C. Sartori, *I libretti italiani a stampa dalle origini al 1800*, 7 vols. (Cuneo, 1990–94) · G. Casanova, *History of my life*, trans. W. R. Trask, 12 vols. in 6 (1966); repr. (1997) · S. McVeigh, *Concert life in London from Mozart to Haydn* (1993) · *The parish of St Anne, Soho*, 2 vols., Survey of London, 33–4 (1966) · P. Howard, 'Guadagni in the dock: a crisis in the career of a castrato', *Early Music*, 27 (1999), 87–95 · *GM*, 1st ser., 67 (1797), 890–91 · *GM*, 1st ser., 42 (1772), 544 · *Mrs Cornely's [sic] entertainments at Carlisle House, Soho Square* (1840?) · Highfill, Burnim & Langhans, *BDA* · M. R. Charters, 'Cornelys, Theresa', *New Grove*, 2nd edn · Walpole, *Corr.* · Cornelys v. Chamberlain, 1772, PRO, C12/1518/6 · Cornelys v. Fermor, 1763–4, PRO, C12/1471/1
**Archives** PRO, papers, C107/149
**Likenesses** portrait, 1 April 1771, BM · portrait, 24 Dec 1772, BM · portrait, 1 May 1773, BM · C. Bowles, portrait, BM
**Wealth at death** in debtors' prison: *GM* (1799), 890–91

**Corner, George Richard** (1801–1863), antiquary, born in the parish of Christ Church, Southwark, London, was the eldest of the six children of Richard Corner (d. 1820), a solicitor in Southwark, and Maria, daughter of James Brierley. He was educated at Gordon House, Kentish Town, and after having been admitted an attorney in 1824, followed his father's profession with success.

In 1828 Corner married Sarah, the youngest daughter of Timothy Leach of Clapham, with whom he had two sons and two daughters who survived him. About 1835 he was appointed vestry clerk of the parish of St Olave, Southwark, a parish in which he was greatly active, particularly during the 1832 cholera epidemic. On 28 November 1833 Corner was elected a fellow of the Society of Antiquaries, and from this date published many antiquarian papers, often connected with the history of Southwark. Of these the best-known were *A Concise Account of the Local Government of the Borough of Southwark* (1836) and *The Rental of St. Olave and St. John Southwark* (1838, 1851). His first communication to the Society of Antiquaries was made on 9 January 1834, when he pointed out in *Archaeologia* the distinction, not previously recognized, between the three manors of Southwark. He contributed other papers to *Archaeologia* from 1835 to 1860, including 'An account of excavations on the site of Roman buildings at Keston, near Bromley, in Kent' (vol. 36) and a paper on the abbot of Waltham's House, St Mary-at-Hill, London (vol. 36).

Corner was one of the original members of the Numismatic Society of London, founded in 1836, but apparently did not make a special study of coins. He left the society ten years later, in January 1846. He was also a member of the British Archaeological Association from the time of its establishment in 1843: he exhibited many antiquities before this society, and contributed accounts of them to its journal. Corner also showed great interest in the Archaeological Society of Surrey, and contributed to its *Proceedings*, as also to the *Sussex Archaeological Collections* (vol. 6), the *South London Journal* (1857), and the *Collectanea Topographica et Genealogica* (vols. 5, 7). He was also an occasional contributor to the *Gentleman's Magazine*.

In the last years of his life, Corner seems to have experienced 'difficulties occasioned … by family misfortunes'. He died suddenly on 31 October 1863, at Queen's Row, Camberwell, where he resided, and was buried in Nunhead cemetery. His brother Arthur Bloxham Corner (d. 1861) was her majesty's coroner and attorney in the court of queen's bench. Another brother, Richard James Corner, was appointed chief justice of the Gold Coast colony, and was joint author, with Arthur Bloxham Corner, of *Crown Practice* (1844). W. W. WROTH, rev. JOANNE POTIER

**Sources** *GM*, 3rd ser., 16 (1864), 528–30 · *GM*, 3rd ser., 15 (1863), 808 · *Proceedings of the Society of Antiquaries of London*, 2nd ser., 2 (1861–4), 392 · *Journal of the British Archaeological Association*, 20 (1864), 181–6 · Boase, *Mod. Eng. biog.* · R. A. G. Carson and H. Pagan, *A history of the Royal Numismatic Society* (1986), 57
**Archives** Bodl. Oxf., notes relating to the custom of borough English in Sussex · LMA, corresp. | BL, letters to Joseph Hunter, Add. MS 24867 · U. Edin. L., letters to James Halliwell-Phillipps

**Corner, John** (*fl.* **1788–1825**), printmaker, worked in London from the late eighteenth century to the end of the Regency. Nothing is known of this engraver apart from his *œuvre*. Working primarily in etching and stipple engraving, he specialized in portraiture, but most of his output is unremarkable and served to illustrate the cheaper end of the market for literature and periodical publications. He is best-known for his theatrical portraits for the *European Magazine* and *Bell's British Theatre*, and for his series of twenty-five portraits of artists published under the title

*Portraits of Celebrated Painters*. Although Redgrave criticized the heads in this last work as 'ill drawn, weak and ineffective', this series was stylish in its grouped medallion format and decorative devices (Redgrave, *Artists*, 99). Apart from these series Corner also etched a few history subjects and proudly 'engrav'd from the original by permission' a version of Edward Penny's moralizing, yet titillating, subject *Apparent Dissolution*. His daughter, Julia *Corner, was a children's writer. LUCY PELTZ

**Sources** Thieme & Becker, *Allgemeines Lexikon* · Bénézit, *Dict.* · Redgrave, *Artists* · *Engraved Brit. ports.*

**Corner, (Edred) John Henry** (**1906–1996**), botanist, was born on 12 January 1906 at 37 Harley Street, London, the son of Edred Moss Corner (d. 1950), surgeon, and his wife, Henrietta, *née* Henderson (d. 1966). He was educated at Arnold House, St John's Wood; Highfield School, Liphook, Hampshire; and Rugby School. Although a brilliant athlete, he eschewed sport in favour of botanical excursions. He won a scholarship to Sidney Sussex College, Cambridge, took a double first in the tripos in 1926, and won the Frank Smart prize in 1927 and the Frank Smart studentship in botany in 1928. For eighteen months, he was a research student of F. T. Brooks but did his own research on Discomycetes and started visiting Arthur Harry *Church in Oxford.

Corner believed that his stammer precluded him from any lecturing post, so in 1929 he accepted an appointment as assistant director of the Singapore Botanic Gardens, with an annual salary of £400. His research was largely on microfungi, notably practical matters such as the identity of rubber pathogens. By 1931, though, he had begun to study and record the Malayan forest as it was being felled, resulting in his *Wayside Trees of Malaya* (1940; 3rd edn, 1988). He also introduced coconut-collecting macaque monkeys to the gardens as plant-collectors. In 1934 he married Sheila Kavanagh Bailey, daughter of Dana Clark Bailey, a history teacher, of New York. They had a son and two daughters.

In February 1942 Singapore was surrendered to invading Japanese forces. Looting preceded the takeover, so the governor acceded to Corner's request that he be allowed to carry a note to the Japanese entreating them to preserve the scientific collections. A ship of Japanese technicians and officials had been sunk and they were replaced with British people: among them, Corner became a 'civil internee' in the botanic gardens. His internment gave him the opportunity for the elaboration of his 'Durian theory', a highly original hypothesis on the origin of modern plants, building substantially on the work of Church. He also began his study of the microscopic structure of seeds. His studies led on the one hand to his textbook, *The Life of Plants* (1964), and, on the other, to his influential *Seeds of Dicotyledons* (1976).

Corner returned to England in November 1945. In 1947–8 he was principal field scientific officer (Latin America) for UNESCO, stationed first in Rio de Janeiro and then, as executive secretary of the Hylean Amazon project, at Manaus. His attempt to establish a field institute failed, the leading Brazilian proponents being accused of compromising national security in setting up such an international venture.

In 1949 Corner was appointed lecturer in taxonomy at Cambridge. He became reader in plant taxonomy in 1959 and professor of tropical botany in 1966. He built on his account of figs in *Wayside Trees*, elaborating a classification of the genus *Ficus*. In concentrating on so large a genus he saw clearly, as he did in his seed work, the 'grades' of classification and the importance of clades that underpin modern phylogenetic work. His very readable *The Natural History of Palms* appeared in 1966. His lectures, despite the occasional stammer, were spell-binding: like his writing, they were original, iconoclastic, and hugely entertaining. His individualistic style was a hallmark of his teaching as of his research, and he instilled the same independence of thought into his research students. Like Church before him, he never ran a research group in the modern sense. Up until 1973 he had thirteen research students, almost all working on tropical angiosperm topics. So esoteric was Corner's style that, on his retirement in 1973, tropical botany withered in Cambridge.

Corner's first marriage ended in divorce in June 1952. On 9 April 1953 he married his daughters' nanny, Helga Dinesen Sondergaard (1912/13–1999), daughter of Dinus Larsen Sondergaard, a farmer, of Mors, Denmark. He was elected FRS in 1955 and was awarded the Darwin medal in 1960. In 1961 he led the Royal Society expedition to North Borneo and in 1965 that to the Solomon Islands. Among the many honours he received were the benefactor's medal of the British Mycological Society, the patron's medal of the Royal Geographical Society (1966), the gold medal of the Linnean Society of London (1970), the Victoria medal of honour of the Royal Horticultural Society (1974), and the Allerton award of the Pacific (later National) Tropical Botanical Garden, Hawaii (1981). He was made CBE in 1972. Emperor Hirohito of Japan and his son, Emperor Akihito, invited him to Japan twice: he was given the Golden Key of the city of Yokohama in 1985, the year in which he received the first Japanese international prize for biology (worth 10 million yen). In 1990 he published a biographical memoir of Emperor Hirohito, who was a keen biologist. In 1996 he was joint winner of the first de Bary medal of the International Mycological Association.

Corner was a man of imposing bearing and could be stubborn or irascible. He had little time for narrow specialists and especially decried what he saw as retrograde trends in biological teaching and research. Bureaucracy was anathema to him: in his view it hindered scientific progress. He kept up a vast correspondence and was a loyal supporter of those he thought worthy or worth encouraging. As a tropical botanist he was unique in carrying out research on both seed plants and fungi: his knowledge of botany and its literature was prodigious. Above all he was a developmental biologist: the study of development—process rather than 'characters'—was inculcated in him by Church. Corner's early move from mycology to angiosperms led him to be a conservationist:

the cause of rain-forest conservation pervaded his writing. In the 1940s he was one of the first to publicize the fate of tropical vegetation and he continued to do this for the rest of his life, though he considered his efforts on the executive board of the International Union for the Conservation of Nature 'fruitless'.

In retirement Corner returned to fungi, studying them in a laboratory set up at his home. He also wrote a harrowing account of the occupation of Singapore in *The Marquis: a Tale of Syanon-to* (1981) and other autobiographical pieces, including *Botanical Monkeys* (1992) and a major unpublished autobiography, *Moments botaniques*. In 1975 he was diagnosed with glaucoma and then cataract in both eyes: after 1983 he was unable to undertake further microscopic work. He declined physically and his eyesight deteriorated until he was almost blind. With his mental faculties still intact, he died of heart failure at his home, 91 Hinton Way, Great Shelford, Cambridgeshire, on 14 September 1996. He was survived by his wife, Helga, and the three children of his first marriage.

D. J. MABBERLEY

**Sources**  D. J. Mabberley, *Memoirs FRS*, 45 (1999), 77–93 • *The Independent* (21 Sept 1996) • *The Times* (2 Oct 1996) • D. J. Mabberley, 'A tropical botanist vindicated', *Gardens' Bulletin, Singapore*, 52 (2000), 1–4 • *WWW* • *CGPLA Eng. & Wales* (1996) • will • m. cert. [Helga Dinesen Sondergaard]
**Archives**  Botanic Gardens, Singapore • National Herbarium of the Netherlands, Leiden, papers and specimens, etc., on *Ficus* • priv. coll., papers and drawings on phanerogams • RGS, expedition diaries, papers, and drawings • Royal Botanic Garden, Edinburgh, mycological papers, drawings, specimens, books • U. Cam., department of plant sciences, herbarium specimens | CUL, letters to Robert Hill
**Likenesses**  photograph (in middle age), RS; repro. in Mabberley, *Memoirs FRS* • photograph (in old age), repro. in *Gardens' Bulletin, Singapore*, 29 (1977) • photograph (as a schoolboy), repro. in D. J. Mabberley, *Arthur Harry Church: the anatomy of flowers* (2000) • photograph, repro. in *The Independent*
**Wealth at death**  £610,760: probate, 14 Nov 1996, *CGPLA Eng. & Wales*

**Corner, Julia** (1798–1875), children's writer, was born in London, the daughter of John *Corner (*fl.* 1788–1825), a printmaker. Her first publication was a silver fork novel, *The Baronet* (1834), a rather uneven production in which a sprightly narrative is oddly interrupted by a dream-like murder scene. She continued to produce occasional novels throughout her literary career, including *The Brothers Basset* (1855) and *Culverley Rise: a Tale* (1861), both workmanlike productions of mid-nineteenth-century domestic realism.

Corner was, however, far more significant as the writer of history textbooks. In 1837, she produced a sequel to Richmal Mangnall's popular *Historical and Miscellaneous Questions* (1800), entitled *Questions on the History of Europe*. Then, in 1840, she published *The History of England* and *The History of France*, with Thomas Dean & Son, well-known publishers of juvenile works. These were the first volumes in a series known as Miss Corner's Historical Library (1840–48), which covered the history of European countries as far apart as Ireland and Turkey; some were illustrated from designs by Sir John Gilbert (1817–1897), a painter and illustrator as prolific in his production of historical images as Corner was of historical texts. Some volumes of the Historical Library were later reprinted as *Every Child's History*. The English volume in the series is a brisk, largely conventional narrative, although Corner was less credulous of traditional historical anecdotes and gave more space to social history than many contemporary textbook writers; the foreign volumes were more conservative in these respects. In 1850, a singularly productive year, Corner published (with Dean & Son) accounts for young children of the ancient Britons, Saxons, and Normans, followed by descriptions of England in the middle ages, the sixteenth and seventeenth, and eighteenth and nineteenth centuries. With Henry Bohn, she published *China* (1853) and *India* (1854).

Corner's other educational works for children included *The Picture Nursery Sunday-Book* (1852), *Merry Multiplication* (1867), and *The Play Grammar* (1848), the last of which was an admirably lucid (if rather challenging) guide to parsing. She also produced revised versions of historical textbooks by other authors, including Anne Rodwell's *A Child's First Step to the History of England* in 1853. But Corner also published lighter works, contributing in 1854 five or six tales to Dean's series of Simple Tales and Little Stories, including *Rose and her Bird* and *The Good Children*. In addition, she wrote many short plays for children, based on fairy stories and published in Dean's series of Little Plays for Little People. In the Preface to *The Little Play of Mother Goose* (1854), she claimed to have been inspired by seeing some children amusing themselves and their elders at Christmas by this 'innocent and lively recreation'. Conscious that some parents would object to home theatricals, she argued that amusement was an essential part of education and could be used to teach useful and moral lessons.

Julia Corner died unmarried, at her home, 92 Clarendon Road, Notting Hill, London, on 16 August 1875. Although well received by contemporaries, her publications brought her no lasting reputation; Allibone's *Critical Dictionary*, however, described her as 'one of the most useful writers of the age' (1.430). ROSEMARY MITCHELL

**Sources** Allibone, *Dict.* · Boase, *Mod. Eng. biog.* · *Men of the time* (1875) · *CGPLA Eng. & Wales* (1875)

**Wealth at death** under £200: probate, 9 Oct 1875, *CGPLA Eng. & Wales*

**Cornewall, Charles**. See Cornwall, Charles (*bap.* 1669, *d.* 1718).

**Cornewall, Folliot Herbert Walker** (*bap.* 1754, *d.* 1831), bishop of Worcester, was baptized Folliot Herbert Cornewall on 9 May 1754 at Ludlow, Shropshire, the second son of Frederick Cornewall (1706–1788), of Delbury, Shropshire, a naval officer and MP for Montgomery from 1771 to 1774, and his wife, Mary, daughter of Francis Herbert, a first cousin of Henry Arthur Herbert, first earl of Powis. His elder brother, Frederick Cornewall (1752–1783), was MP for Leominster from 1776 to 1780, and for Ludlow from 1780 until his death. Cornewall entered Eton College on 27

Folliot Herbert Walker Cornewall (*bap.* 1754, *d.* 1831), by William Owen, 1813

April 1765 and was admitted pensioner at St John's College, Cambridge, on 24 June 1772. He graduated BA in 1777. On 14 December that year he was ordained deacon by John Hinchcliffe, bishop of Peterborough, and on 20 December 1778 he was ordained priest. He proceeded MA in 1780, the same year that he was appointed chaplain to the House of Commons, nominated by the speaker, his second cousin Charles Wolfran Cornwall. His sermon before the House of Commons for 30 January, the anniversary of the execution of Charles I, was given and printed in 1782. Cornewall continued to accumulate preferment. He was rector of Frilsham, Berkshire, from 1781 to 1784, canon of Windsor from 1784 to 1793, master of Wigston's Hospital, Leicester, from 1790, and dean of Canterbury from 1793 to 1797. In Ludlow he was a common councilman from 1781 to 1797.

On the death of his brother in 1783 Cornewall inherited the estates of a relative, Francis Walker, and took the additional name of Walker. On 19 June 1787, at Taplow, Buckinghamshire, he married Anne (*d.* 1795), daughter of George Hamilton, canon of Windsor; they had two sons and two daughters. On 9 April 1797 Cornewall was consecrated bishop of Bristol. His fast sermon preached before the House of Lords was published in 1798. He was translated to the diocese of Hereford, a wealthier see than Bristol, on 28 January 1803. In 1805 he deputized for Richard Hurd, the elderly bishop of Worcester, on a confirmation tour, as the octogenarian Hurd was too infirm to travel. Following Hurd's death, he was nominated to succeed him. The prime minister, William Henry Cavendish Cavendish-Bentinck, third duke of Portland, wrote to

George III that Cornewall's character and learning were highly distinguished, that his appointment was 'much wished for by the principal gentry as well as clergy' (*Later Correspondence of George III*, 5.3668), and that his political opinions would help secure the diocese's loyalty to the administration. He was consecrated in 1808.

Cornewall died at home at Hartlebury Castle, Stourport, Worcestershire, on 5 September 1831, and was buried in the family vault at Delbury, Shropshire. The *Gentleman's Magazine* remembered him as 'possessed of fair scholarship, strong good sense, polished manners, and an amiable temper: … [he] passed a virtuous and exemplary life' (*GM*, 370).                    J. M. RIGG, *rev.* ANDREW ROBINSON

**Sources** J. B. Burke and J. Burke, *The royal families of England, Scotland, and Wales*, pt 2 (1847), 199 · Burke, *Gen. GB* (1858) · *GM*, 1st ser., 101/2 (1831), 290, 370 · R. Hole, *Pulpits, politics and public order in England, 1760–1832* (1989), 135, 137 · N. Sykes, *Church and state in England in the XVIII century* (1934) · *The later correspondence of George III*, ed. A. Aspinall, 5 vols. (1962–70), vol. 5, no. 3668 · L. B. Namier, 'Cornewall, Frederick (1706–88)', 'Cornewall, Frederick (1752–83)', HoP, *Commons, 1754–90* · Venn, *Alum. Cant.*
**Archives** BL, corresp. with earls of Liverpool, Add. MSS 38219–38320, 38470–38473, 38570, *passim*
**Likenesses** W. Owen, oils, 1813, NPG [*see illus.*] · oils, c.1830, Powys Castle, Montgomeryshire · G. Hayter, drawing, NPG · G. Hayter, group portrait, oils (*The trial of Queen Caroline, 1820*), NPG · oils, deanery, Canterbury

James Cornewall (*bap.* 1698, *d.* 1744), by unknown artist, 1730s

**Cornewall, James** (*bap.* 1698, *d.* 1744), naval officer and politician, was baptized on 17 November 1698 at Moccas, Herefordshire, the fourth son of Colonel Henry Cornewall (*d.* 1717) of Bradwardine, near Hereford, and the second son with his second wife, Susanna, daughter and coheir of Sir John Williams, second baronet, of Elham, Kent. James's half-brother and brother, Henry and Velters Cornewall, were MPs for Hereford and Herefordshire respectively, while his uncle Vice-Admiral Charles *Cornwall (formerly Cornewall) came to prominence for his role in the victory off Cape Passaro in July 1718.

Cornewall appears to have begun his career as a volunteer per order in the *Chatham* in March 1721, moving in the same rate to the *Torbay* in December of that year (PRO, ADM 6/477, pp. 326, 415). On 3 April 1724 he was promoted captain of the frigate *Sheerness*, in which for the next four years he was employed on the North American coast, principally at Boston, in protecting legitimate trade from piracy. He returned to England in August 1728 and two years later stood unsuccessfully as the parliamentary candidate for Weobley, Herefordshire. He was subsequently returned for that seat in April 1732 and held it until 1734. In December 1732 he was appointed to the frigate *Greyhound*. During the following summer he was employed in her on the Moroccan coast where, during 1733, he established friendly relations with the Salé corsairs and the bashaw of Tetuan. In the following March he returned to England and three months later he took command of the *Deptford* (50 guns) which served in the channel and along the Portuguese coast with Sir John Norris.

Early in 1737 Cornewall commissioned the *Greenwich*, in which he oversaw the regulation of trade on the west African coast. Rumours surfaced that he had carried slaves to Barbados, though this charge was not substantiated and led to nothing more than a caution addressed to his successor, George Anson. In March of that year he had been returned as MP for Weobley on petition; seldom in the house, he voted (for the administration) in only two divisions and did not contest his seat at the 1741 election. In 1739 he had been appointed to the *St Albans* (50 guns), in which between September and October, with the company of the *Weymouth*, he cruised off the Azores in quest of homeward-bound Spanish ships. Plans to send Cornewall on to the China seas and western Pacific to co-operate with Anson's squadron in the eastern Pacific came to nothing on account of the strain of the West Indian expedition. In 1741 he was appointed to the *Bedford* in which, a year later, he accompanied Vice-Admiral Thomas Mathews to the Mediterranean.

Cornewall was transferred to the *Marlborough* (90 guns) in 1743 and supported the *Namur* (Mathews's flagship) during its engagement with the Spanish flagship, *San Felipe*, and her seconds at the battle of Toulon (11 February 1744). The *Marlborough* and *Namur* bore the brunt of the encounter, the *Namur* being dismasted while the *Marlborough* was reduced to a wreck. The ship suffered heavy casualties (43 killed and 120 wounded) including Cornewall who died, unmarried, after his legs had been shot away, an injury which left him with life only 'to express the agony he was in, by shaking his head at the surgeon' (*Narrative of the Proceedings of his Majesty's Fleet in the Mediterranean*, 1744, 89). Writing in June 1747, Horace Walpole commented how 'in the present dearth of glory' Cornewall 'is canonized, though poor man! he had been tried twice the year before for cowardice' (*Letters of Horace Walpole*, 37.271). In the same year parliament voted to commemorate his actions with a 36 foot monument for Westminster Abbey, designed by Sir Robert Taylor and completed in 1755. Cornewall's cousin, Frederick Cornewall, then first lieutenant of the *Marlborough*, assumed command after Cornewall's death until he too was severely wounded. He later commanded the *Revenge* in the action off Minorca in 1756 and died in 1786.　　　　J. K. LAUGHTON, *rev.* PHILIP CARTER

**Sources** A. N. Newman, 'Cornewall, James', HoP, *Commons, 1715–54* · H. W. Richmond, *The navy in the war of 1739–48*, 3 vols. (1920) · Walpole, *Corr.* · J. Charnock, ed., *Biographia navalis*, 3 (1795), 263; 4 (1796), 130; 5 (1797), 3.263; 4.130; 5.288 · PRO, ADM 6/477, pp. 326, 415
**Likenesses** oils, 1730–39, NPG [*see illus.*] · line engraving (after medallion on monument), NPG · medallion on monument, Westminster Abbey

**Cornewall, John**, Baron Fanhope (*d.* 1443), soldier, was the son and heir of Sir John Cornewall (*d.* 1392?), third son of Sir Geoffrey Cornewall of Burford in Shropshire, reportedly with a niece of John de *Montfort, duke of Brittany (*d.* 1399), to whose service the elder Sir John was long attached. According to tradition, the younger John was born on a ship in St Michael's Mount Bay, Cornwall, as his mother made her way from Brittany to England, and he is occasionally described in the records, supposedly by reason of his birth at sea, as Green Cornewall. His date of birth is unknown but is likely to have been no later than the mid-1370s, for he was already a knight when he accompanied Richard II to his meeting with Charles VI at Ardres in 1396. As son of a younger son he had to make his own way in the world, and he followed his father's example in pursuing a military career. Richard II retained him at the generous annual fee of 190 marks, and he participated in the ill-fated Irish campaign of 1399. His first wife, Philippa (*d.* 13 Sept 1399), widow of Sir Richard Cergeaux (*d.* 1393) of Colquite in Cornwall, and daughter of Sir Edmund Arundel, eldest but bastardized son of Richard (II) *Fitzalan, earl of Arundel, brought him the enjoyment of her dower lands in Cornwall and he had the wardship of the other Cergeaux lands through royal grant.

Cornewall's substantial gains from Richard II's patronage proved no impediment to him when Henry IV took the throne. Indeed, Sir John had already established an association with the house of Lancaster for, in the 1390s, he was in receipt of an annuity of 40 marks from John of Gaunt, duke of Lancaster. This association was soon to become much closer. Soon after the deposition he contracted a spectacular marriage to *Henry IV's sister, *Elizabeth of Lancaster (1364?–1425), widow of John Holland, earl of Huntingdon (*d.* 1400). According to one chronicler, Cornewall came to her notice as a result of his prowess at a tournament at York in July 1400. The marriage made him a wealthy man for Elizabeth enjoyed a life annuity of 1000 marks by grant of her brother. Her voluntary disparagement did not exclude the couple from the fruits of royal

patronage. In December 1400 Sir John was given a life interest in her annuity and, through a petition presented in the first parliament of 1404, they won dower on the forfeited estates of her first husband. On 15 February 1405 the king stood godfather to their son.

In 1409, in a striking mark of royal favour, Cornewall was promised 400 marks per annum from Holland lands in Cornwall in the event of his wealthy wife's predeceasing him. In the following year he became a knight of the Garter, an elevation he must have owed to his renowned prowess on the tournament field and service on campaigns in Scotland and Wales. In 1412 he was one of the leaders of the French expedition under Thomas, duke of Clarence, and he went on to serve as one of the leading commanders in Henry V's conquest of Normandy. For Cornewall war was massively profitable, through both the capture of valuable prisoners, most notably Louis de Bourbon, count of Vendôme, at Agincourt, and ransom brokerage, a remunerative practice of which he was one of the leading exponents. But, although war brought him money and renown, it also ended his hopes of founding a dynasty. His only legitimate son was killed at the siege of Meaux late in 1421, and this personal tragedy marked the end of his active military involvement until his participation in the Calais campaign of 1436.

Earlier grants of royal patronage ensured that Cornewall's landed income was not significantly reduced by his wife's death in November 1425. The profits of marriage, royal patronage, and war provided him with the surplus wealth to purchase a large estate in Bedfordshire, centred on the lordship of Ampthill, acquired from Eleanor, widow of Almaric, Lord St Amand, at an unknown date before 1424. The great castle he built there survived to be described by the Tudor antiquary, John Leland, but is now entirely gone. Building must have been swift for by the end of 1429 the castle was fit to receive so great a prisoner as Charles, duke of Orléans, who remained there until August 1432. A month before Orléans left his charge his lengthy service to the house of Lancaster was recognized in his elevation to the peerage as Lord Fanhope, a title taken from a manor in Herefordshire he had purchased from the Chandos family and probably chosen in allusion to the privilege of parliamentary summons once enjoyed by that family. The later years of his career were uneventful, apart from his dispute with the other leading Bedfordshire magnate, Reynold, Lord Grey of Ruthin, over control of judicial administration in that county, which resulted in eighteen deaths in a disturbance at peace sessions at Bedford on 12 January 1439. He died without surviving legitimate children on 11 December 1443. Although his royal wife had been buried at Burford, he was buried in the chapel he had founded in the cemetery of the Friars Preacher near Ludgate in London. In his will he bequeathed 800 marks to be divided between his two bastard sons. His great Ampthill estate was sold to his friend, Ralph, Lord Cromwell, for as much as 5000 marks, reportedly a discount of £1000 against the market price.

　　　　　　　　　　　　　　　　　　S. J. PAYLING

**Sources** A. C. Reeves, *Lancastrian Englishmen* (1981), 139–202 · *Chancery records* · C. G. S. Foljambe and C. Reade, *The house of Cornewall* (1908) · GEC, *Peerage*, new edn, 5.253–4

**Corney, Bolton** (1784–1870), literary critic and antiquary, was born at St Lawrence, Thanet, on 28 April 1784 and baptized in the parish church of St Lawrence, the son of Henry Corney (*d.* 1801) and his wife, Mary Stock. It has been stated that he served for some time in the revenue service, but this is doubtful and little is known of his early life and education. In 1803 he obtained a commission as ensign in the 28th regiment of foot, and in 1804 a medal for good marksmanship inscribed 'Royal Greenwich Volunteers'. The middle portion of his life was spent at Maze Hill, Greenwich, where he held the post of first clerk in the steward's department at the Royal Hospital (*Navy List*, 1840, 138). From this he did not retire until about 1846 or 1847, when he married Henrietta Mary Pridham, elder surviving daughter of Captain (afterwards Admiral) Richard Pridham of Plymouth; he then moved to 29 The Terrace, Barnes, in Surrey.

In early life Corney formed an attachment to literature, and after his move to Barnes he plunged more deeply than ever into his bibliophilic researches, and lived and died literally in the midst of his books. In *Researches and Conjectures on the Bayeux Tapestry* (1836), he contended that the tapestry was not executed until 1205, and his view was adopted by Dr Lingard (J. C. Bruce, *Bayeux Tapestry Elucidated*, 11, 163). Edouard Lambert published a reply to Corney in *Réfutation des objections faites contre l'antiquité de la tapisserie de Bayeux* (1841). Corney's caustic criticism of Isaac D'Israeli in *Curiosities of Literature by I. D'Israeli Illustrated* (1837) prompted D'Israeli to reply in *The Illustrator Illustrated* (1838), whereupon Corney brought out a second edition of his work, 'revised and acuminated, to which are added, Ideas on Controversy, deduced from the practice of a Veteran; and adapted to the meanest capacity' (1838). The *London Metropolitan Magazine* thought the illustrations 'by far the best specimens of historical and bibliographical criticism that we have seen anywhere this many a day' (Allibone, *Dict.*). One hundred copies of the 'Ideas on controversy' were separately printed. *On the new general biographical dictionary: a specimen of amateur criticism, in letters to Mr Sylvanus Urban* (1839) was a collection of letters which originally appeared in the *Gentleman's Magazine*, in which he severely criticized the earlier portions of the well known biographical compilation published under the name of the Revd Hugh James Rose. In the 1860s he published *Comments on the evidence of Antonio Panizzi, esq., before the select committee of the House of Commons on the British Museum, AD 1860* (in 1856 Corney, who had often clashed with Panizzi, protested to Palmerston against Panizzi's appointment as principal librarian); *The Sonnets of William Shakspere: a Critical Disquisition Suggested by a Recent Discovery* (by V. E. Philarète Chasles, relating to the inscription which precedes the sonnets in the edition of 1609) (1862); and *An Argument on the Assumed Birthday of Shakspere: Reduced to Shape, 1864.*

Corney also edited, from a manuscript in his own possession, *An Essay on Landscape Gardening* by Sir John Dalrymple, one of the barons of the exchequer in Scotland (1823); *The Seasons* by James Thomson, with illustrations designed by the Etching Club (1842); Goldsmith's *Poetical Works, Illustrated, with a Memoir* (1846); *The Voyage of Sir Henry Middleton to Bantam and the Maluco Islands in 1604* (1855), for the Hakluyt Society, of which his son attested that he was one of the original founders in 1846; and *Of the Conduct of the Understanding, by John Locke* (1859). He was a frequent contributor to *Notes and Queries* and *The Athenaeum*, and he made special collections concerning Caxton, which he placed at the disposal of William Blades (Blades, *Life and Typography of William Caxton*, 7. xi, 282–5; 2.259). He was a member of the council of the Shakespeare Society and the Camden Society, one of the auditors of the Royal Literary Fund, and a long-time member of the Royal Society of Literature.

Corney died at his home, 29 The Terrace, Barnes, on 31 August 1870 from 'natural decay' and was buried in the parish cemetery on Barnes Common. He left an only son, Bolton Glanvill Corney, born in 1851, who became a member of the Royal College of Surgeons and was appointed government medical officer in Fiji.

THOMPSON COOPER, *rev.* CLARE L. TAYLOR

**Sources** Allibone, *Dict.* · private information (2004) · *CGPLA Eng. & Wales* (1870) · d. cert.
**Archives** U. Edin. L., letters to J. Halliwell-Phillips
**Wealth at death** under £2000: probate, 31 Oct 1870, *CGPLA Eng. & Wales*

**Cornford, Christopher Francis** (1917–1993), artist and writer, was born on 9 February 1917 at Conduit Head, Madingley Road, Cambridge, the second son of Francis Macdonald *Cornford (1874–1943), professor of ancient philosophy and author of best-selling studies of Plato, and Frances Crofts Darwin (1886–1960) [*see* Cornford, Frances Crofts], well-known poet and granddaughter of Charles Darwin. His elder brother, by just over a year, was the radical poet (Rupert) John *Cornford. There were five children, who grew up as members of the Darwin clan in 1920s Cambridge: Christopher's governess was Dorothy Bristow, who later became an influential art teacher. The Greek philosophy, the Darwin connection, the radicalism, the wit, and the visual art all resurfaced in later life. Educated at Stowe School (with John) and the Leys School, Cambridge, Cornford went to Chelsea College of Art in 1934 and was awarded an art teacher's diploma in 1937. He was a visiting instructor there and at Morley College from 1937 to 1939 and met his future wife, (Mary) Lucy Jameson (1912/13–1991), daughter of Julian Veitch Jameson, an indigo planter. They were married on 1 February 1941, and had two sons.

Together with his brother John (who went to Cambridge), Christopher joined the British Communist Party in the mid-1930s and marched against Oswald Mosley's blackshirts. John then joined the International Brigades to fight against Franco in Spain, and was shot and killed by the fascists on or just after his twenty-first birthday. Christopher never quite got over this tragedy: it confirmed him in a lifelong commitment to creating a better-organized society. He once said that he and his brother 'were always seeking the reality behind surface appearance' (personal knowledge). During the Second World War Christopher served in the Royal Artillery. From 1946 to 1953 he was master of painting in the department of fine art at King's College, University of Durham, then from 1955 to 1962 visiting instructor in drawing and architecture in the school of architecture at Cambridge.

But it was at the Royal College of Art in London's South Kensington, which he joined full-time in autumn 1962, that Christopher Cornford at last found a spiritual and intellectual home and a new set of causes with which to identify. He was appointed by his cousin Robin Darwin, who was then principal and a great believer in a dynastic approach to senior appointments, to take over (from Basil Taylor) the direction of the department of general studies. The department had been founded to offer courses on the history, philosophy, and criticism of art and design to all the practitioner students in the studios—some of whom had been over-specializing in art from an early age. Darwin was convinced that young artists and designers, if they were to succeed, ought to be equipped with 'amused and well-tempered minds'; the reformers of British art education (the Coldstream and Summerson committees) were simultaneously proposing an expansion of theoretical studies within art schools. Cornford's unusual mix of an excellent eye, drawing skills, scholarship, and personal modesty was very well suited to this role as intellectual troubadour.

Cornford assembled a supergroup of visiting authors (including Iris Murdoch and George Steiner) to supplement a committed team of staff tutors. The courses he conceived and directed and the long 'critical essays' which all students had to write about them as an integral part of their postgraduate studies became models in the post-1960s, national system; they also helped the Royal College of Art's progress towards university status, which it achieved on royal charter day in 1967. By the early 1970s he had introduced MA-by-thesis students into his department, and in the mid-1970s doctoral students.

Cornford's own research interests centred on theories of proportion in art and design (on which he lectured and supervised theses), and in particular the geometry of the 'golden section'. Although the Darwin years at the Royal College of Art (1947–72) were partly about establishing the college as the artistic equivalent of 'walking past the great court of Trinity on crisp autumn evenings' (as the principal, who became rector in 1967, put it), Christopher Cornford remained magnificently anti-establishment: he had a lot of sympathy after 1968 with the student radicals, most of whom, in Britain unlike continental Europe and America, came from art schools; in the 1970s he became an early green activist, hosting a seminal 'Design for need' conference in April 1976, and even staffed a fair-trade stall in the college for the sale of varieties of rice until his impressionistic approach to weights and measures led to its closure. After retirement in summer 1979 he became a characteristically active chairman of the Cambridge Campaign for Nuclear Disarmament and a mainstay of the University of the Third Age, as well as continuing to paint, write, and draw gentle political cartoons.

Cornford's most important legacy is in the minds and memories of successive generations of artists and designers graduating from the Royal College of Art. They remember his humanity, his support (he once missed a key faculty board meeting to attend a student picnic in Kensington Gardens), his inspirational seminars, and his extraordinary impish performances as public orator every convocation day in early July—performances which enlivened the proceedings and gave them a distinctive art school twist, through a combination of outrageous puns, a parody florid style, and misused quotations. His valedictory lecture of June 1979 was called 'The repeal of disillusion', and when he died at Addenbrooke's Hospital in Cambridge on 8 April 1993—after being admitted for heart surgery, only to discover that he had cancer of the spine—he had just finished drafting his *magnum opus* (begun twenty years earlier) on proportion in art and design. Lucy Cornford had died, after a debilitating illness, in 1991.                                    CHRISTOPHER FRAYLING

**Sources** C. Frayling, *The Royal College of Art* (1987) · C. Cornford, *In defence of a preoccupation*, RCA Papers, 1 (1975) · C. Cornford, *The repeal of disillusion* (1979) · C. Cornford, *The Cornford orations* (1979) · b. cert. · m. cert. · d. cert. · *The Independent* (5 May 1993) · *The Times* (5 May 1993) · personal knowledge (2004) · private information (2004)

**Archives** BL, corresp. with his mother, Add. MS 58412

**Cornford** [*née* Darwin], **Frances Crofts** (1886–1960), poet, was born in Cambridge on 30 March 1886, the only child of Sir Francis *Darwin (1848–1925) and his second wife, Ellen Wordsworth Crofts (1856–1903), daughter of John Crofts, of Leeds, and a great-niece of William Wordsworth. Ellen was a lecturer in English at Newnham College, Cambridge. Francis Darwin, then lecturer in botany at Cambridge, was the third son of Charles *Darwin, whom he had helped with his biological researches. Frances was half-sister to the writer and golfing expert Bernard Darwin, the only child of her father's first marriage. Her education was private, and during her childhood her chief associates were her cousins, the children of George Darwin and Horace Darwin. Her mother died when she was seventeen; her father then moved their home for a short time to London, but soon returned to Cambridge where Frances spent most of the rest of her life.

In the summer of 1908 members of the Cambridge Marlowe Dramatic Society arranged a performance of *Comus* as part of a Milton tercentenary celebration at Christ's College, where Frances Darwin met Francis Macdonald *Cornford (1874–1943), a fellow of Trinity College and afterwards Laurence professor of ancient philosophy at Cambridge, who had been cast for the part of Comus. They were married in 1909. Their home at Conduit Head off the Madingley Road soon became a meeting-place for artists and men of letters such as Will Rothenstein, Eric Gill, Lowes Dickinson, Bertrand Russell, and occasional visitors such as Rabindranath Tagore. The Cornfords had five children. Their eldest son, (Rupert) John *Cornford,

Frances Crofts Cornford (1886–1960), by Sir William Rothenstein, 1925

was killed in Spain, in December 1936. The second son, Christopher Francis *Cornford, became an artist and in 1963 was appointed the first dean of the Royal College of Art in London.

Frances Darwin, with intellect and artistic sensibility strongly represented in her forebears, started writing poetry at sixteen and subsequently published enough to entitle her to a distinguished place among the minor poets of the Georgian period and later years. Her first volume, *Poems* (1910), brought somewhat embarrassing fame for 'To a Fat Lady Seen from a Train', which became a standard anthology piece and was parodied by G. K. Chesterton. Rupert Brooke was one of her closest friends and she was always eager to profit by his criticism and that of others such as Christopher Hassall and Sir Edward Marsh. She was herself always ready to give help of the same kind to younger writers. One of her early books was a 'morality' play, *Death and the Princess* (1912). With the publication of later volumes of poetry, *Different Days* (1928), *Mountains and Molehills* (1934), and *Travelling Home* (1948), the quiet but distinctive quality of her work began to be recognized. She was not influenced by the poetic trends set by T. S. Eliot and Ezra Pound and her short, often epigrammatic, poems are characterized by visual acuity and quiet humour. In 1954 her volume *Collected Poems* was the official 'choice' of the Poetry Book Society and in 1959 she was awarded the queen's medal for poetry. She also tried her

hand with some success at verse translations, publishing *Poems from the Russian* (1943, assisted by Esther Salaman) and a selection (1950) from the French of Louis Aragon. Three of her books were decorated with woodcuts by her cousin Gwen Raverat, and one had cuts by Eric Gill.

Frances Cornford was of medium height and of brown complexion, with dark hair and eyes. Her appearance was striking and attractive rather than beautiful, her attractions being increased by her gentle friendliness, her amusing conversation, and her wish to enter with warmth and imagination into the feelings and emotions of her many friends. In the ordinary affairs of life she was endearingly vague and unpractical, with an extraordinary capacity for mislaying her possessions. She had not been baptized and was brought up without religion. Initially, she wrote as a troubled agnostic. Later, however, she accepted with deep conviction the faith of the Church of England. Her sensitive nature led to her suffering from several periods of deep depression, the first one following the shock of her mother's death. Each time, however, she made a good, though slow, recovery and she lived to the age of seventy-four; she died of heart failure at her home, 10 Millington Road, Cambridge, on 19 August 1960. She was buried at St Giles's cemetery, Cambridge.

GEOFFREY KEYNES, *rev.* SAYONI BASU

**Sources** *The Times* (22 Aug 1960) · A. Anderson, *A bibliography of the writings of Frances Cornford* (1975) · G. Raverat, *Period piece: a Cambridge childhood* (1952) · personal knowledge (1971) · private information (1971) · *CGPLA Eng. & Wales* (1960)

**Archives** BL, corresp. and papers, incl. journals and literary MSS, Add. MSS 56331–56347, 58381–58426, 59608 | BL, corresp. with Sir Sydney Cockerell, Add. MS 52710 · BL, letters to Albert Mansbridge, Add. MS 65620 · BL, letters to Sydney Schiff and Violet Schiff, Add. MS 52916 · Bodl. Oxf., corresp. with Gilbert Murray · CUL, letters to Sir Edward Marsh · Dartington Hall Trust Archive, Totnes, letters to Dorothy Elmhirst · King's AC Cam., letters to J. D. Hayward and John Maynard Keynes · King's Lond., Liddell Hart C., corresp. with Sir B. H. Liddell Hart · NYPL, letters to Edward Marsh · Tate collection, letters to Albert Rutherston [copies] · Trinity Cam., corresp. with F. M. Cornford

**Likenesses** W. Rothenstein, drawing, 1925, NPG [*see illus.*]

**Wealth at death** £21,116 17s. 2d.: probate, 13 Dec 1960, *CGPLA Eng. & Wales*

**Cornford, Francis Macdonald** (1874–1943), classical scholar, was born at Eastbourne, Sussex, on 27 February 1874, the second son of the Revd James Cornford (1840–1900), and his wife, Mary Emma Macdonald. He was educated at St Paul's School under F. W. Walker and at Trinity College, Cambridge, where his father had studied. He won a scholarship (1894), obtained a first class in both parts of the classical tripos (1895, 1897), and was bracketed equal for the chancellor's classical medal (1897). Among the important influences upon him were Henry Jackson, Arthur Woollgar Verrall, and Walter George Headlam.

**Pre-1914 Cambridge: friendship with Jane Harrison** Cornford considered becoming a schoolmaster but decided rather to follow an academic career, and in 1897 applied for the chair of Greek at the University College of South Wales in Cardiff. Although this application failed, he was subsequently elected a fellow of Trinity College, Cambridge, in 1899; the earlier possibility of a fellowship had been

Francis Macdonald Cornford (1874–1943), by Eric Gill, 1929

delayed because of Cornford's criticism of Jackson in a thesis. After his father's death in February 1900 Cornford took responsibility for his mother. In 1902 he was appointed assistant lecturer in classics at Trinity College and lecturer in 1904. Except for the period of the First World War, almost the whole of his adult life was to be spent in Cambridge.

Cornford was from the first dissatisfied with the somewhat narrow nineteenth-century Cambridge ideal of 'pure scholarship'. In an address to the newly established Cambridge Classical Society in November 1903—and published as a pamphlet, *The Cambridge Classical Course: an Essay in Anticipation of Further Reform* (1903)—Cornford (the first secretary of the society) advocated a more humane, less philological type of instruction, as well as a better co-ordinated intercollegiate lecture system in place of the semi-chaotic conditions then prevailing. He felt that:

> a course of lectures ought to be the outcome of recent first-hand work. When a man's mind is full of fresh ideas and quickened by the excitement of discovery, then is the time to lecture: there is the chance of interesting his class, while the discipline of exposition will test and clarify his thoughts.

Recognizing that lectures ought not to repeat what can better be obtained from books, Cornford always aimed at stimulating his classes by an original treatment of his subject; the better men appreciated this, but his methods were perhaps less well suited to the ordinary minds which

formed the majority of his audiences. Concurrently with lecturing he had a considerable amount of college teaching; but although he never compromised this work, his heart was from early days elsewhere, namely in writing books. Apart from the professorial lectures of his last years, it is as a writer rather than as a teacher that he is chiefly remembered.

One of the people who influenced Cornford's view of lecturing was the unconventional Jane *Harrison (1850–1928) of Newnham College. Cornford had attended her lectures in 1898 (soon after her return to Cambridge), and they became close friends. Cornford associated with Jane Harrison and Gilbert Murray, and together they formed a loose group; Murray recalled of them:

> we somehow had the same general aim and outlook, or something, and the work of each contributed to the work of the others. We were out to see what things really meant, looking for a new light our elders had not seen.
> (Stewart, 83)

Members of this group looked to the Near East for influences. In an attempt to get to grips with oriental languages, Cornford, Harrison, Arthur Bernard Cook, and James George Frazer were being given Hebrew lessons by Robert Hatch Kennett, the regius professor in Cambridge. Cornford and Harrison were also learning cuneiform, even taking texts on holiday to Marazion in Cornwall. Jessie Stewart recorded how she was presented with a Plasticine tablet on which Cornford had cut a cuneiform text, translated by Harrison, that celebrated the exploits of Stewart's black Russian poodle, Kapi (Stewart, 69).

What primarily interested Cornford in this period was the study of those primitive modes of thought and feeling which provided the background, largely unrealized, of the writers—poets, historians, and philosophers—of the classical age of Greece, and the investigation of the ritual forms in which those thoughts and feelings found outward expression. Out of this group's thinking emerged Cornford's first book, *Thucydides mythistoricus* (1907), a work dedicated to Harrison as 'a dream which but for help and understanding would have gone up the chimney with the smoke'. *Thucydides*, although highly original and stimulating, is probably the least convincing of Cornford's three books of this period; Gilbert Murray was to quote an Oxford philosopher, 'Much of the book is wrong, but I have learnt more from it than from any book I have read for years' (Murray, 422). Historians were not slow to challenge some of the book's arguments. An anonymous review in the *Journal of Hellenic Studies* (1907) noted that 'Mr Cornford has written a most brilliant essay, but cannot be said to have penetrated below the surface of his subject' (p. 307). John Percival Postgate, in an extensive review article, concluded that Cornford had 'combined scientific analysis with literary form and that he has invested the conclusions of a rationalist with all the charm of a mythistorian' (*Classical Quarterly*, 1907, 318).

Relations between Harrison and Cornford at this point were close. They frequently went on holiday together: Marazion in Cornwall and Southwold in Suffolk were two favoured spots, though they also travelled on the continent. Together they attended the first International Congress of Classical Archaeology in Athens in April 1905; around Cambridge they were also a regular sight on their bicycles, 'Francis very upright, with his usual rather Spanish dignity' (Stewart, 104). Both suffered from illness during 1907, which proved a turning point in their relationship. In May Cornford was struck down by appendicitis, a condition which had caused the death, in 1901, of Harrison's friend, R. A. Neil, tutor at Pembroke College. This fear may have induced Harrison's spell of blindness during Cornford's convalescence in Southwold that June.

Cornford had long played an active part in Cambridge life. In May 1897 he had supported degrees for women and helped to organize an undergraduate petition in its favour. He had been a member of the editorial committee of the *Cambridge Review* since 1897 and became editor in 1899; a number of his poems were published there between 1903 and 1908, including 'The academic dilemma' and 'A ballad of cadavers, or, The MATERIAL needs of the medical school'. He had a reputation for composing Latin valentines, represented by his *Quaestiones Valentinianae* (1902). Cornford prepared an anonymous flysheet, *Compulsory Chapel* (1904), which provoked a flysheet response from Russell Kerr Gaye—and eventually ended compulsory chapel at Trinity College in 1913. Pamphlets distributed in 1910 by William Chawner, master of Emmanuel College, promoted a rationalist position in the university, and in the wake of the controversy Cornford and Charles Kay Ogden were responsible for founding the Cambridge Society of Heretics. One of Cornford's lectures to the society was published as *Religion in the University* (1911).

Cornford was also active in wider circles, speaking on university education to the Oxford and London Fabian societies (1910). One of his long-lasting commitments was to the Working Men's College, then meeting in Great Ormond Street in London, for which he had helped to establish an annual summer course in Cambridge in 1901; George Macaulay Trevelyan, who introduced Cornford to the Working Men's College, recalled that 'Cornford was devoted to the men he met there, more I think than to the average of his pupils at Cambridge' (Trevelyan, 24).

**Microcosmographia academica and Frances Darwin** The wit and light satire of Cornford's vision for classics in Cambridge found fuller scope in *Microcosmographia academica* (1908), originally anonymous. It was a skit on university politics, 'one of the few university satires', it has been said, 'which have outlived their occasion'. It contained pictures of the 'Young Man in a hurry' who 'is afflicted with a conscience, which is apt to break out, like measles, in patches'. It also responded to the growth of science as a subject at Cambridge, noting the 'Adullamites' who 'inhabit a series of caves near Downing Street'.

The success of the *Microcosmographia academica* brought Cornford into contact with a young woman, an episode which was to alter his relationship with Harrison. Frances Darwin [*see* Cornford, Frances Crofts (1886–1960)], the

only daughter of Ellen Crofts (1856–1903), one of Harrison's closest friends at Newnham College, and the botanist Francis *Darwin (1848–1925), son of Charles Darwin, had recently returned to Cambridge after recuperation following her mother's death. Frances had been intrigued by *Microcosmographia academica*, and Harrison, a close family friend of the Darwins, arranged a tea party in Lent term 1908, so that Frances could meet Cornford. Their friendship developed during a production of Milton's *Comus* in July 1908 as part of the celebrations for Milton's tercentenary, supported by Cornford as treasurer of the Marlowe Society. During rehearsals the cousins Frances and Gwen Darwin persuaded the producers, Justin and Rupert Brooke, that Cornford, 'in spite of his great age' should be Comus (Stewart, 109). (The 'great age'—of thirty-four—is no doubt a hint at Cornford's view, expressed in *Microcosmographia academica*, that middle age started at thirty-five.) Cornford, who acted in the production anonymously, subsequently acquired the nickname Comus.

While accompanying Harrison, who was convalescing after surgery, to Braunton, Devon, Cornford successfully proposed to Frances Darwin. He was not insensitive to Harrison's feelings for him, and wrote to Frances, 'About Aunt Jane we shall have to be thoughtful. You see she and I were both rather lonely people, we foregathered and made friends and we have been a good deal together' (Stewart, 109). Their formal engagement was announced in early October 1908. That Christmas Frances painted a card showing herself, her father, Cornford, and Harrison, all bearing or leading pigs, in a direct reference to the Greek cult practice at the sanctuary of Demeter and Kore at Eleusis in Attica. In July 1909 they married in a register office. Their first child, Helena, was born in 1913.

Harrison found her relationship with Cornford strained. She seems to have hoped that one day they would marry, or that they could have continued in their semi-married status: 'I had come back from Death … just to find the man I always called my "Rock of Ages" slipping away from me' (Beard, 157). Cornford was now nicknamed Zeus and Frances Old One, the name given to one of Harrison's favourite toy bears. She and Cornford were, however, able to work together again. Cornford contributed a chapter on the origin of the Olympic games to Harrison's *Themis* (1912) as a refutation of Professor William Ridgeway's theories. He now concentrated on ancient philosophy and his next book, *From Religion to Philosophy: a Study in the Origins of Western Speculation* (1912), was dedicated to his father-in-law, Francis Darwin. The work is notable for its penetrating interpretation of the pre-Socratic thinkers. Gilbert Murray had contributed an essay, 'Excursus on ritual forms preserved in Greek tragedy', to Harrison's *Themis*. This was in part the inspiration for Cornford's *The Origin of Attic Comedy* (1914), which analysed the structure of Aristophanes' plays in order to detect the ritual sequence lying behind them.

During the First World War Cornford, who had been a member of the Cambridge University rifle volunteers, was soon enlisted and to the surprise of his friends Rupert

Brooke and Gilbert Murray became a musketry instructor at Grantham. In December 1915 Cornford's first son was born, named Rupert John in honour of Brooke, who had died that April. Now a commissioned officer holding the rank of captain, Cornford transferred to the Ministry of Munitions, of whose founding he wrote an anonymous satirical account, *The First Book of Munitions called Genesis*, 'in the style of the first chapter of Genesis, with the contrary views of Jahvist and Elohist strongly marked in accordance with a burning controversy of the time' (Murray, 431; copy in Trinity College Library). He was involved in the attempt to have Bertrand Russell restored to his fellowship at Trinity.

Cornford's return to life in Cambridge was dominated by Frances's serious bout of depression; this seems to have followed the birth of a third child, Christopher Francis *Cornford, later an artist and writer, in February 1917. Virginia Woolf observed to Vanessa Bell:

> The poor woman has a delusion that she must never be tired, and has now spent 2 years in going from rest cure to rest cure. She refuses to see either her husband or children. The doctors have at last sent her home, but think she may be incurable.  (*Letters of Virginia Woolf*, 2.377, no. 1068, 17 July 1919)

Gilbert Murray commented that this illness 'brought out [Cornford's] infinite practical helpfulness and patience' (Murray, 432). The Cornfords had two more children: a son born in 1921, and a daughter in 1924.

**Ancient philosophy**  On the death of Henry Jackson in 1921 Cornford was an unsuccessful candidate for the regius professorship of Greek. He presented a lecture, 'The beginnings of natural science: Euripides, *Melanippe the wise*, frag. 484 (N2)', described by Harrison as 'a beautiful sermon quite over their heads—the row of old cabmen who were electors looked bothered' (Harrison to Murray, 17 Nov 1921, Bodl. Oxf., MSS G. Murray). *Microcosmographia academica* was reissued under Cornford's name in 1922, and dedicated to Edward Granville Browne, Sir Thomas Adams's professor of Arabic. Cornford added a short preface, including the comment that the first edition had lacked a chapter on 'propaganda' which he 'defined as that branch of the art of lying which consists in very nearly deceiving your friends without quite deceiving your enemies'. Further editions appeared in 1933, 1949, 1953, 1964, and 1970.

Cornford's work now became more strictly concerned with ancient philosophy. He published important papers: 'Mysticism and science in the Pythagorean tradition' (*Classical Quarterly*, 16, 1922), and 'Anaxagoras' theory of matter' (*ibid.*, 24, 1930). He also prepared *Greek Religious Thought from Homer to Alexander* (1923), consisting of translated extracts with a valuable introduction. In 1927 he was appointed Brereton-Laurence reader in classics (with special direction to instruct in ancient philosophy). At the same time he assisted Philip Henry Wicksteed, who had been working on a translation of Aristotle's *Physics* but had been 'overtaken by paralysis and symptoms of approaching death' (Murray, 426), and took dictation of the manuscript. Cornford subsequently prepared the notes as two volumes in the Loeb Classical Library (1929–34), supplementing Wicksteed's free translation with an alternative rendering and masterly annotation.

Cornford was gaining an international reputation, and in 1928 was invited to lecture at Harvard, though he was again an unsuccessful candidate for regius professor of Greek at Cambridge. His academic contribution was finally acknowledged in 1931 when he was appointed first holder of the Laurence chair of ancient philosophy at Cambridge. His inaugural lecture was published as *The Laws of Motion in Ancient Thought* (1931). A series of four lectures presented for the board of extra-mural studies at Cambridge in August 1932 was published as *Before and after Socrates* (1932). In that same autumn he gave a series of BBC lectures under the title *Our Debt to the Past*, concluding with 'How Greece reconciled ethics and science'.

In 1935 came the first of the three great commentaries on Plato's later dialogues, all published in the International Library of Psychology, Philosophy and Scientific Method series, which crown Cornford's achievement and placed him in the forefront of modern Platonic scholars: *Plato's Theory of Knowledge: the Theaetetus and Sophist of Plato* (1935); *Plato's Cosmology: the Timaeus of Plato Translated and with a Running Commentary* (1937); and *Plato and Parmenides: Parmenides' way of truth and Plato's Parmenides; translated with an introduction and a running commentary* (1939). In his last years he produced an excellent translation of the *Republic* (1941), with interpretative summary, section by section, and a judicious pruning of the encumbrances of dialogue-form. Murray observed that this work reflected 'Cornford's own strong interest in the same problems as they recur in modern society' (Murray, 429). Cornford supported young scholars through the creation of the Cambridge Classical Studies series for which he served as one of the editors. Volumes included R. P. Winnington-Ingram's *Mode in Ancient Greek Music* (1936) and J. Enoch Powell's *The History of Herodotus* (1939).

Life at home had been varied. Frances had become well known as a poet, but their children had given them some concern. Gilbert Murray remembered:

> His relations with a series of brilliant children, whose opinions were at times vehemently opposed to his own, and whom he encouraged 'to sail away like ships' in pursuit of their own ideals, were a model to those parents who believe in the supreme power of affection and the value of freedom. (Murray, 432)

Cornford's eldest son, the poet (Rupert) John *Cornford, an active member of the Young Communist League, left for Spain and was killed near Córdoba in December 1936, on or just after his twenty-first birthday, while fighting against the forces of General Franco in the Spanish Civil War. Cornford contributed an essay on his son's childhood to Pat Sloan's *John Cornford: a Memoir* (1938).

Cornford received the honorary degree of DLitt from Birmingham University in 1937 and was elected FBA in the same year. He retired from his chair in 1939. His health then started to fail. His last two papers challenged what he saw as misguided contemporary theories. 'The Marxist view of ancient philosophy' was presented to the Classical

Association (summary in *Proceedings of the Classical Association*, 39, May 1942). He was due to give a paper, 'Was the Ionian philosophy scientific?', to the joint congress of the Hellenic and Roman societies in September 1942, but in the end it was read by Gilbert Murray; it was subsequently published in the *Journal of Hellenic Studies* (1942). Cornford died at his home, Conduit Head, Madingley Road, Cambridge, on 3 January 1943.

Professor W. K. C. Guthrie, a former student, added a foreword to the 1949 edition of *Microcosmographia academica* and published some of Cornford's works posthumously. A series of essays written between 1921 and 1943 appeared in *The Unwritten Philosophy and other Essays* (1950), along with a memoir. A more substantial work, *Principium sapientiae* (1952), contained Cornford's latest speculations on the origins of Greek philosophical thought. Fifty years after Cornford's death a tenth edition of the *Microcosmographia* was published with the further title *Cambridge's Classic Guide to Success in the World* (1993), and a foreword by Henry Chadwick. The satire's enduring qualities were reflected in the endorsement by Ray Bell, head of strategy development of British Telecom: 'For every young MBA in a hurry, it will save you years of struggling to find this out for yourself'. Cambridge University Press also issued an edition with an essay by Gordon Johnson on Cornford's Cambridge under the title *University Politics* (1994).

Frances Cornford described her husband at their first encounter at a concert about 1901: 'a tall dark man with hair parted in a stylised way like a wig' (Stewart, 105). Virginia Woolf's impression on meeting Cornford in Cambridge in early 1923 was of 'a military man, of upright bearing and manly spirit' although on a previous occasion 'he was wearing a French peasant's blouse and a red tie' (Woolf to Jacques Raverat, *Letters of Virginia Woolf*, 3.24, 30 March 1923). Gilbert Murray recalled that Cornford 'combined great personal charm and courtesy with a certain aloofness and apparent indifference to worldly values and received opinions' (Murray, 421).

Reginald Hackforth, rev. David Gill

**Sources** *The Times* (5 Jan 1943), 6 · [C. M. Brodribb], *TLS* (9 Jan 1943), 17 · K. G. [W. K. C. Guthrie], 'Dr F. M. Cornford: an appreciation', *The Times* (15 Jan 1947), 7 · D. S. Robertson, 'Francis Macdonald Cornford', *Cambridge Review* (30 Jan 1943), 164–5 · G. Murray, 'Francis Macdonald Cornford, 1874–1943', *PBA*, 29 (1943), 421–32 · D. K. Wood, 'F. M. Cornford', *Classical scholarship: a biographical encyclopedia*, ed. W. W. Briggs and W. M. Calder (1990), 23–36 · G. Johnson, *University politics: F. M. Cornford's Cambridge and his advice to the young academic politician* (1994) · S. Arlen, *The Cambridge ritualists: an annotated bibliography of the works by and about Jane Ellen Harrison, Gilbert Murray, Francis M. Cornford, and Arthur Bernard Cook* (1990) · J. Stewart, *Jane Ellen Harrison: a portrait from letters* (1959) · S. J. Peacock, *Jane Ellen Harrison: the mask and the self* (New Haven: Yale University Press, 1988) · M. Beard, *The invention of Jane Harrison* (2000) · F. M. Cornford, *Newnham College Roll Letter* (1929), 72–8 · *Selected papers of F. M. Cornford*, ed. A. C. Bowen (New York and London: Garland, 1987) · R. Ackerman, *The myth and ritual school: J. G. Frazer and the Cambridge ritualists* (1991) · R. Ackerman, *J. G. Frazer: his life and work* (1987) · G. Raverat, *Period piece: a Cambridge childhood* (1954) · *The letters of Virginia Woolf*, ed. N. Nicolson, 2–3 (1976–7) · G. M. Trevelyan, *An autobiography and other essays* (1949) · A. Robinson, *The life and work of Jane Ellen Harrison* (2002)

**Archives** BL, corresp. and papers, Add. MSS 58401–58411, 58427–58430 · Trinity Cam., corresp., notebooks, poems, and papers | Bodl. Oxf., corresp. with Gilbert Murray
**Likenesses** F. Darwin (later Cornford), painted card, 1908, repro. in Stewart, *Jane Ellen Harrison* · E. Gill, pencil drawing, 1929, Trinity Cam. [*see illus.*] · photograph, repro. in Murray, 'Francis Macdonald Cornford' · photograph, repro. in Robinson, *Jane Ellen Harrison*
**Wealth at death** £3340 9s. 1d.: probate, 28 April 1943, *CGPLA Eng. & Wales*

**Cornford, (Rupert) John** (1915–1936), poet and political activist, was born in Cambridge on 27 December 1915, the eldest son and second of the five children (three sons and two daughters) of Francis Macdonald *Cornford (1874–1943), professor of ancient philosophy at Cambridge University, and his wife, Frances Crofts *Cornford (1886–1960), the poet, daughter of Sir Francis Darwin. Through his mother he was a great-grandson of Charles Darwin. One of his brothers was the artist Christopher *Cornford. It was ironic that John Cornford should be named Rupert in memory of the poet Rupert Brooke, who had died in April 1915, for Cornford came to despise the school of Georgian poets, of whom Brooke was the supreme exemplar and his mother a loyal adherent. His father described him as 'a large, placid baby with very dark eyes and skin and thick black hair … good-tempered and easy to amuse, even when unwell', and he showed few indications, as a small boy, of the vigorous intellect and independence of mind that were to flourish so strikingly in adolescence. Initially Cornford was taught as a day boy in Cambridge, but at nine he was sent as a boarder to Copthorne Preparatory School in Sussex. Already he had developed an interest in military history, particularly in the campaigns of Napoleon. At fourteen he obtained a scholarship to Stowe School, which had existed for only six years. The first headmaster, J. F. Roxburgh, had been a pupil of Professor Cornford's at Trinity College, Cambridge.

Cornford's individualism caused him to refuse to join the Officers' Training Corps. At fifteen he was writing poetry under the avant-garde influence of Robert Graves, T. S. Eliot, and particularly W. H. Auden, from whom he solicited a letter of encouragement. His political theories were being shaped by reading *Das Kapital* and the *Communist Manifesto*, and at sixteen he won an exhibition to Trinity College, Cambridge. But, having outgrown Stowe and with time to kill before going up to Cambridge, he gravitated almost inevitably to the London School of Economics, where his active interest in politics began to overshadow his desire to be a poet. He joined the Young Communist League, and although he did attend lectures, he used his time in London to deepen his commitment to abolishing poverty by establishing communism in England. At this period Cornford had so separated politics from poetry that he even published a poem in *The Listener* under a pseudonym.

Cornford was still only seventeen when he entered Trinity in October 1933. During his three years at Cambridge he wrote only nine poems, for he was spending fourteen hours a day on political activities, and in March 1935 he became a full member of the Communist Party of Great Britain. Despite his insistence on Marxian analysis and his

(**Rupert**) **John Cornford** (1915–1936), by Ramsey & Muspratt, 1934 [with Ray Peters]

exhausting programme of extra-curricular activities, he achieved first classes in both parts of the history tripos (1935 and 1936). He found time too to father an illegitimate child, shortly afterwards abandoning both the child and its mother, Ray Peters, for the woman he might well eventually have married, Margot *Heinemann (d. 1992). In 1936 Trinity gave him a scholarship, and he planned to study the Elizabethans, but when the Spanish Civil War broke out on 18 July 1936, on a sudden impulse and without even saying goodbye to his family, he left for Dieppe. By 8 August he was in Barcelona, unable to speak a word of Spanish but armed with a press card.

Cornford is said to have been the first Englishman to enlist in the International Brigades to fight against Franco. During his first period in Spain he fell seriously and mysteriously ill, and spent some time in hospital. During three weeks' leave in England he resigned his Trinity scholarship and made a conscious decision to return to Spain for the duration of the war. He took part in the battle for Madrid, which began on 7 November 1936, and received a severe head wound. At this time his poetic inspiration returned, and some of his finest work was written in the last weeks of his life, including his most famous poem, 'Heart of the Heartless World'. The battle near Lopera in which John Cornford was killed was a shambles, and the precise circumstances and date of his death are not known. He may have died on 27 December 1936, his twenty-first birthday, or the day after. His body was never recovered.

John Cornford's poems appeared in *New Writing*, the *Cambridge Review*, and the *Student Vanguard*, and they were collected in 1938 in *John Cornford: a Memoir*, edited by Pat Sloan. His best work has a direct simplicity, benefits from its autobiographical inspiration, and stands as a worthy memorial to all who died in the Spanish Civil War. Cornford himself came to be regarded as much as a typically doomed and respected idealist of his generation as a poet.                                  MICHAEL DE-LA-NOY, rev.

**Sources** P. Stansky and R. Abrahams, *Journey to the frontier: Julian Bell and John Cornford, their lives and the 1930s* (1966) · P. Sloan, ed., *John Cornford: a memoir* (1938) · *John Cornford: collected writings*, ed. J. Galassi (1988)
**Archives** Trinity Cam., corresp., diaries, essays, and poems | BL, letters of and relating to Cornford, Add. MS 58412
**Likenesses** Ramsey & Muspratt, photograph, 1934, NPG [*see illus.*]

**Cornforth** [*other married names* Hughes, Schott], **Fanny** [*née* Sarah Cox] (**1835–c.1906**), artists' model and intimate companion of Dante Gabriel Rossetti, was born at Steyning, Sussex, on 3 January 1835, and baptized there on 1 February 1835, the daughter of William Cox (*bap.* 1814, *d.* 1859), a journeyman blacksmith, and his wife, Jane, *née* Woolgar (*bap.* 1814, *d.* 1847). Her youngest sister Fanny died in February 1847, and their mother two months later. The family moved to Brighton, where Sarah was in service at a respectable lodging-house in 1851; her father lived half a mile away with his second wife.

As she later told an American collector, Sarah Cox and a 'cousin' (probably her great-aunt) attended a fête, held in London at the Surrey Gardens in Walworth on 25 August 1856, to celebrate the return of the regiments of guards from the Crimea. Also in the crowd were Edward Burne-Jones, Ford Madox Brown, Cormell Price, and Dante Gabriel *Rossetti (1828–1882) who dislodged her hair 'as if it were an accident' (MS letter from Samuel Bancroft jun. to Caroline Kipling, 2 April 1899, Bancroft collection, Delaware Art Museum). On the following day Sarah, accompanied by her aunt, went at his invitation to Rossetti's studio 'and he put my head against the wall, and drew it for the head of the girl in the calf picture [*Found*]' (ibid.). The encounter was to change both their lives. By winter 1858 Sarah—living in Dean Street, Soho, London—was modelling for Rossetti, Burne-Jones, and J. R. Spencer Stanhope. Rossetti introduced her to the watercolourist and diarist George Price Boyce, and in the following spring they both helped her move to rooms in Tenison Street, Lambeth. Here she probably developed her acquaintance with Timothy Hughes (*c.*1831–1872), a part-time model and, like his stepfather George Cornforth, a turner or mechanical engineer. Courted by Boyce, Sarah remained attached to Rossetti, and in July 1859 Boyce sought consolation by commissioning him to paint her portrait. When it was seen by his friends three months later, Arthur Hughes expected that Boyce would 'kiss the dear thing's lips away' (Allingham and Williams, 67). *Bocca baciata*, described by Swinburne as 'more stunning than can be decently expressed' (*Swinburne Letters*, 1.27), marks a turning point in Rossetti's art, heralding the abandonment of his Pre-Raphaelite past.

Sarah almost certainly hoped for a future with Rossetti, and broke down when the news reached her of his marriage to Elizabeth Siddal in May 1860. Uncertain of her long-term security, she impulsively turned to Hughes, whom she married in that year at St John's, Waterloo, on 11 August. She maintained her career as a model, continuing to sit for Burne-Jones and Rossetti, amalgamating the names of her dead sister and husband's stepfather into a new professional identity: Fanny Cornforth. But she

**Fanny Cornforth** [Sarah Cox] (**1835**–*c*.**1906**), by Dante Gabriel
Rossetti, *c*.1860

remained committed to Rossetti, and was sharing lodgings with him at Lincoln's Inn within weeks of Siddal's
death in February 1862; a sketch which Rossetti made at
the time puts the nature of their relationship beyond
doubt. Fanny remained intimate with Rossetti for much of
the ensuing decade; her husband Timothy Hughes, a shadowy figure described by Gabriel as her 'incubus', died in
1872.

Rossetti took Fanny with him when he moved to Tudor
House, Cheyne Walk, Chelsea, in autumn 1862, and they
visited Paris together in 1863. Her existence was concealed
from his mother but was accepted by his brother and close
friends, who enjoyed Fanny's high spirits, good nature,
and untutored Sussex vernacular. J. A. M. Whistler and
William Bell Scott, the ambiguities of whose affairs
resembled Rossetti's own, were ready to receive her as a
guest; outside bohemia her role as his housekeeper satisfied the requirements of respectability. While at Tudor
House, Fanny sat for many of the works which now sustain Rossetti's reputation: *Fazio's Mistress* (1863; Tate collection), *Woman Combing her Hair* (1864; priv. coll.), *The Blue
Bower* (1865; Barber Institute of Fine Arts, University of Birmingham), and *Lady Lilith* (1866; Delaware Art Museum).
She may also have modelled for Frederick Sandys (1829–
1904), an occasional resident of Cheyne Walk.

Increasingly preoccupied with the image of Jane Morris,
Rossetti came to find Fanny's presence an embarrass-
ment, and in summer 1868 he established her at 36 Royal
Avenue, Chelsea. Yet she retained the keys of Tudor
House, and still saw herself as its chatelaine.

Throughout his frequent absences in the 1870s Rossetti
never ceased to regard Fanny as his responsibility—in September 1872, as yet unrecovered from a major breakdown,
he wrote from Scotland: 'you are the only person whom it

is my duty to provide for, and you may be sure I should do
my utmost as long as there was a breath in my body or a
penny in my purse' (*Letters to Fanny*, 37–9). Aware that it
would be impossible to support Fanny by conventional
means, Rossetti endowed her with pictures and money,
and on more than one occasion, correctly foreseeing disputes after his death, certified that she was the rightful
owner of the works in her possession.

In September 1877 the increasingly erratic Rossetti
informed Fanny that he could no longer provide for her,
and she impetuously threw in her lot with John Bernard
Schott (1837–1891). With Schott, a former publican and
the son of an army bandmaster, from the firm of Mainz
music publishers, Fanny left Royal Avenue to run the Rose
tavern in Jermyn Street. On 13 November 1879 they were
married, nine days after Schott had obtained a divorce
from his first wife. But as Rossetti's health declined, Fanny
once more willingly responded to his emotional
demands, by then bordering on dependence. In something of a return to the old days of their intimacy, in September 1881 Fanny accompanied Rossetti to the Lake District where, during his vain attempt to recover his health,
she probably tried to induce him to write a will in her
favour. She no doubt felt that she had the claims of a wife
in all but name, and later declared that she had given up
all for Rossetti. But when in a few months the end finally
came, no such provision had been made; the family kept
her at arm's length and were spared any personal embarrassment when her request to see Rossetti's body arrived
too late.

After Rossetti's death and in financial difficulties, Fanny
and Schott established the short-lived Rossetti Gallery in
Bond Street, London, hoping to sell the pick of her collection of Rossetti's manuscripts and drawings. In April 1884
they left the Rose tavern and moved to Kensington, where
Fanny devoted herself to raising her two stepsons, Cecil
and Frederick Schott. Cecil's talent as an artist had been
advanced by Rossetti, but his career cannot be traced after
his departure from George Frederick Watts's studio in
1896 for a new life in South Africa. John Schott died on 12
June 1891 and for the rest of her life, as she and Frederick
(1870–1898) moved through a series of rented rooms in
west London, Fanny came to be regarded as a Pre-
Raphaelite relic, the custodian of more than 120 portraits,
sketches, and studies. Artists and collectors such as Samuel Bancroft jun. (1840–1915), a Delaware industrialist,
and Charles Fairfax Murray (1849–1919) visited her, anxious to salvage her memories and the residue of her treasures.

After Frederick's death Fanny's faculties began to fail
and she gradually became dependent on John Schott's sister Rosa Villiers, who in 1905 removed her from her lodgings without disclosing her destination. There is neither
record of her death nor trace of her grave.

According to Rossetti's brother, Fanny Cornforth was 'a
pre-eminently fine woman, with regular and sweet features, and a mass of the most lovely blonde hair—light-
golden or "harvest yellow"'. But, he added, 'she had no
charm of breeding, education, or intellect' (*Family Letters*,

vol. 1, p. 203). These deficiencies never troubled, and may even have attracted, Rossetti himself, but came to exasperate his friends, who saw her as an unfortunate echo of his bohemian past, and 'a living denial of the legend they wished to create' (Drewery, Moore, and Whittick, 13). Finding concealment impossible, Rossetti's biographers dismissed Fanny as the personification of 'the sordid frailties of a great man' (Edmund Gosse to T. J. Wise, 2 Oct 1923, BL, Ashley MS 3854, fol. 30). By the 1950s her path to notoriety had culminated in assertions, based on a misapprehension of her age and what little was known of her circumstances, that she had once earned her living as a prostitute.

The facts of Sarah Cox's life show that, like Lizzie Siddal and Jane Morris, she was the daughter of a family of manual workers, fascinated by an older man of exceptional talent from a world beyond her experience. As Fanny Cornforth, she was the second artistic muse of Rossetti's career—the inspiration for his landfall on the shores of aestheticism and symbolism. Her persistent loyalty, and his inability ever to abandon her, combined to form the enduring bond between them.

Christopher Whittick

**Sources** A. Drewery, J. Moore, and C. Whittick, 'Re-presenting Fanny Cornforth', *British Art Journal*, 2/3 (spring/summer 2001), 3–15 · *Letters of Dante Gabriel Rossetti*, ed. O. Doughty and J. R. Wahl, 4 vols. (1965–7) · MS letter from Samuel Bancroft to Caroline Kipling, 2 April 1899, Delaware Art Museum, Wilmington, Samuel Bancroft collection, box 5 · *Dante Gabriel Rossetti's letters to Fanny Cornforth*, ed. P. F. Baum (Baltimore, 1940) · H. Allingham and E. Baumer Williams, eds., *Letters to William Allingham* (1911) · *The correspondence between Samuel Bancroft, Jr. and Charles Fairfax Murray, 1892–1916*, ed. R. Elzea (Wilmington, 1980) · J. Marsh, *Dante Gabriel Rossetti* (2000) · MS letter from Edmund Gosse to T. J. Wise, 2 Oct 1923, BL, Ashley MS 3854, fol. 30 · D. B. Elliott, *Charles Fairfax Murray* (2000) · *Dante Gabriel Rossetti: his family letters*, ed. W. M. Rossetti, 2 vols. (1895) · *The Swinburne letters*, ed. C. Y. Lang, 6 vols. (1959–62), Algernon Swinburne to William Bell Scott, 16 Dec 1859 · W. Sussex RO, MP 4486

**Archives** Delaware Art Museum, Wilmington, Samuel Bancroft collection, corresp. with D. G. Rossetti and S. Bancroft jun.

**Likenesses** D. G. Rossetti, portrait, 1859, Museum of Fine Arts, Boston · D. G. Rossetti, drawing, *c*.1860, AM Oxf. [*see illus.*] · D. G. Rossetti, portrait, 1865, Barber Institute of Fine Arts, Birmingham · D. G. Rossetti, portrait, 1870, Birmingham Museum and Art Gallery · E. Burne-Jones, portrait · J. R. S. Stanhope, portrait · photograph, JRL, Charles Fairfax Murray collection, MS 1282 photographs 3 · photograph, Delaware Art Museum, Wilmington · photographs, NPG

**Cornhill, Gervase of** (*c*.1110–1183/4), royal official, was probably the son and heir of the Roger, nephew of Hubert, who was sheriff of London in 1125, perhaps also in 1114–15, and who died in 1130 or shortly before, probably on pilgrimage to Jerusalem; Roger's widow was Ingenolda. A thirteenth-century pedigree makes Gervase the son of one Hubert of Caen, but this seems less likely, in view of successive royal grants of the manor of Chalk, Kent, to Roger and to Gervase; however, it may well have been Hubert of Caen who was Roger's uncle. Gervase derived his surname, with, presumably, substantial property in London, from the family of his wife, Agnes, daughter of Edward of Cornhill, who had been a member of London's

*cnihtengild*, an early association of eminent citizens. Though there is no direct evidence, there seems little doubt that Gervase himself, as well as his father and father-in-law, was a successful and rich London merchant, and the activities of his son Henry [*see below*] suggest that he traded in cloth. William of Canterbury describes Gervase as 'thinking of his usurious two-thirds and hundredths rather than of what was good and right' (Robertson and Sheppard, 1.100); this is a hostile source, but his acquisition of lands in Gamlingay, Cambridgeshire, through a mortgage is also evidence that he did business as a moneylender.

Gervase was named as justice of London on a charter of between 1136 and 1147 and on the seal he was still using in the 1170s. In 1155–7 and 1160–61, and perhaps also 1159–60, he was one of London's two sheriffs, and he was probably the Gervase who in 1174 presented a loyal address from the citizens to Henry II. He was sheriff of Surrey from 1163 until his death, and also of Kent from 1167 to 1174. In the latter role he was involved in the attempt to prevent Thomas Becket from landing at Sandwich in December 1170, allegedly at the instance of the archbishop of York and the bishops of London and Salisbury. From 1169 or 1170 to his death Gervase regularly served as an itinerant justice, in Devon as well as in Kent and Surrey.

Besides the properties in London, Chalk, and Gamlingay, Gervase acquired lands in Langham, Essex, and in Berkesden, Hertfordshire, both probably in the 1140s, and later held lands in East Horndon, Essex, and in Ashtead and elsewhere in Surrey. He quitclaimed property at Greenwich and Lewisham to St Peter's Abbey, Ghent, between 1161 and 1168, and granted his lands at Berkesden to Holy Trinity Priory, Aldgate, before 1154. He died between Michaelmas 1183 and Michaelmas 1184, leaving at least three sons: Henry; Ralph, sheriff of Kent (1191–2) and Surrey (1191–4), who married Alice, daughter and heir of Robert of Hastings, in or before 1191 and died in 1199 or 1200; and Reginald [*see below*].

**Henry of Cornhill** (*c*.1135–1192/3), royal official, was the eldest son of Gervase, and inherited his lands and, presumably, his business interests. By his marriage to Alice, daughter of William de Courcy, he acquired the barony of Stogursey and twenty-five and a quarter knights' fees mostly in Somerset, Dorset, Oxfordshire, and Northamptonshire. From 1175 at the latest he was employed by the king's household as an agent for buying cloth and other goods. He had custody of the escheated honours of Rayleigh (1181) and Boulogne (1183) and succeeded his father as sheriff of Surrey; he was also a sheriff of London in 1187–9. Present at Henry II's death at Chinon, he was confirmed in his offices by Richard I and, in close attendance on the king in 1189–90, had charge of preparing his fleet for the crusade, for which a special account was rendered in the exchequer. In 1190 he became sheriff of Kent, on paying 100 marks, and keeper of the exchange for all England except Winchester. Closely associated with the chancellor, William de Longchamp, he shared his downfall in October 1191 and was deprived of his offices. He died between Michaelmas 1192 and Michaelmas 1193, when his brothers answered for his debts in the exchequer. His daughter Joan, who married Hugh de Neville (d. 1234) in 1195 or soon after, was his sole heir; his widow married Warin Fitzgerald in or soon after 1193.

**Reginald of Cornhill** (c.1140–1209/10), royal official, was a younger son of Gervase, and on Henry's downfall he and his brother Ralph paid 100 marks to hold Henry's offices until the king's return to England; in 1192 he succeeded Ralph as sheriff of Kent and held the office for the rest of his life. Until his death he continued as a purchaser of goods—luxury items rather than basic commodities—for the king's household. He was responsible for assessing or collecting scutage (1199) and tallage (1200) in several counties, and, jointly, for the duty of one-fifteenth on imports and exports in 1203–4, the recoinage of 1205, and the organization of the king's ships from 1205 to 1208, in which he worked with William of Wrotham (d. 1217). From 1201 onwards he served as a justice in many counties. He built up a substantial estate, especially in Kent, mostly by purchase. His wife is named in 1200 as Matilda; after his death, between Michaelmas 1209 and Michaelmas 1210, his son Reginald paid 10,000 marks to succeed as sheriff of Kent, and for his own and his father's debts.

P. D. A. Harvey

**Sources** W. R. Powell, 'English administrative families in the 12th and 13th centuries with special reference to the Cornhill family', BLitt diss., U. Oxf., 1952 • J. H. Round, 'Gervase de Cornhill', *Geoffrey de Mandeville: a study of the anarchy* (1892), 304–12 • H. C. M. Lyte and others, eds., *Liber feodorum: the book of fees*, 3 vols. (1920–31) • *Reg. RAN*, vol. 3 • J. C. Robertson and J. B. Sheppard, eds., *Materials for the history of Thomas Becket, archbishop of Canterbury*, 7 vols., Rolls Series, 67 (1875–85) • C. N. L. Brooke and G. Keir, 'The sheriffs and justices of London and Middlesex, c. 1030–1216', *London, 800–1216: the shaping of a city* (1975), 371–4 • R. Ransford, ed., *The early charters of the Augustinian canons of Waltham Abbey, Essex, 1062–1230* (1989) • W. Farrer, *Honors and knights' fees … from the eleventh to the fourteenth century*, 3 vols. (1923–5) • I. J. Sanders, *English baronies: a study of their origin and descent, 1086–1327* (1960) • *Pipe rolls*, 29–30 Henry II; 5 Richard I; 11–12 John • *Curia regis rolls preserved in the Public Record Office* (1922–), vol. 1, p. 370

**Cornhill, Henry of** (c.1135–1192/3). *See under* Cornhill, Gervase of (c.1110–1183/4).

**Cornhill, Reginald of** (c.1140–1209/10). *See under* Cornhill, Gervase of (c.1110–1183/4).

**Cornhill, William of** (d. 1223), bishop of Coventry, belonged to a London family who rose in the service of Henry II and his sons. He was probably the nephew, or possibly the son, of Reginald of Cornhill (d. 1209/10), a close adherent of John, and doubtless owed his elevation to this fact.

About 1204 William of Cornhill's name begins to appear frequently in the records as a royal clerk and an officer of the exchequer. His first ecclesiastical preferment was the rectory of Maidstone to which he was presented in 1205 by the king. The following year he was made *custos* of the vacant bishopric of Winchester and abbey of Malmesbury, and in 1206 he acquired a similar role in relation to the see of Lincoln. On 30 June 1207 the king made him archdeacon of Huntingdon and a prebendary of Chichester: he presumably paid the price of 500 marks for these

promotions (*Rotuli de oblatis et finibus*, 412). In 1208 Cornhill served as a royal justice, and for the next two years was in constant attendance on the king, being appointed royal chamberlain in succession to Hubert de Burgh (d. 1243) and Peter des Roches (d. 1238). On occasions he transmitted orders for the preparation of royal letters, which consequently bore the mark 'per W. de Cornhill'. One of the most trusted of John's advisers (though sometimes out of favour), in 1207 he was appointed assessor for the thirteenth in Lincolnshire, while in 1208, as part of the king's response to the interdict, he was given custody of the clergy's lands in the diocese of Lincoln. In 1213 there is evidence for his participating in the marriage market, when he was granted the right to dispose of the heirs and widows associated with two rich estates—this was the usual type of secular reward for John's servants. Finally, some time before 9 July 1214, through the king's influence, he was elected bishop by both the monks of Coventry and the canons of Lichfield, though he continued to be called archdeacon of Huntingdon until at least 16 August, and probably did not resign this office until he received the temporalities of his see on 20 October of that year (his successor as archdeacon is first recorded on 15 November). He was consecrated by Archbishop Stephen Langton (d. 1228) at Reading on 25 January 1215 (*Ann. mon.*, 2.282), the king making him a large grant of venison from Windsor Forest towards his consecration feast.

Cornhill remained active on the side of John until the very end of the reign; he went on unsuccessful missions to persuade both the Londoners and the Welsh princes to support the king (Rymer, *Foedera*, 1.121, 127) and accompanied him to Runnymede, being named in Magna Carta as one of the magnates by whose advice it was issued. He was present when the legate Guala crowned Henry III at Gloucester on 28 October 1216. Of his acts as bishop little is recorded, almost certainly because the practice of keeping episcopal records on rolls did not become prevalent in his diocese, unlike that of Lincoln. Cornhill attended the Fourth Lateran Council in 1215 and has been said by some modern scholars to have been so influenced by it, and the principles of church government enunciated there, that he was responsible for the *Constitutiones cuiusdam episcopi*, one of the earliest sets of diocesan constitutions (BL, Cotton MS Vespasian E.iii; *Councils & Synods*, vol. 2, ed. F. M. Powicke and C. R. Cheney, 2 vols., 1964, 2.781–97). C. R. Cheney, however, considered that Hereford diocese was the more likely origin of this document. Cornhill granted the canons of Lichfield the privilege of electing their own dean.

In September 1221 Cornhill was deprived of speech by a sudden stroke of paralysis during an ordination service. He died on 19 August 1223, and was buried in Lichfield Cathedral, where his coffin was discovered in 1662. The prior of Coventry's contemporary epitaph was 'Vir simplex et liberalis, fidelis regi et utilis regno' ('a generous low-born man, faithful to the king and of service to the realm'; Dugdale, *Monasticon*, 6.1242).     M. J. Franklin

**Sources** H. E. Savage, ed., *The great register of Lichfield Cathedral known as Magnum registrum album*, William Salt Archaeological

Society, 3rd ser. (1924, [1926]) · Dugdale, *Monasticon*, new edn · *Ann. mon.* · F. M. Powicke and C. R. Cheney, eds., *Councils and synods with other documents relating to the English church, 1205–1313*, 2 vols. (1964) · C. R. Cheney, 'The earliest English diocesan statutes', *EngHR*, 75 (1960), 1–29 · *Chancery records* (RC) · T. D. Hardy, ed., *Rotuli de oblatis et finibus*, RC (1835) · *Fasti Angl., 1066–1300*, [Lincoln] · Rymer, *Foedera*, new edn, 1.121, 127

**Archives** BL, Cotton MS Vespasian E.iii

**Cornish, Charles John** (1858–1906), naturalist and journalist, was born on 28 September 1858 at Salcombe House, near Sidmouth, the residence of his grandfather, Charles John Cornish JP DL. He was the eldest son of Charles John Cornish (1834–1913), then curate of Sidbury, Devonshire, and his first wife, Anne Charlotte Western (1831–1887); the geographer Vaughan *Cornish was his brother. He was brought up at Debenham, Suffolk, where his father became vicar in 1859. In 1872 he entered Charterhouse School as a gownboy, and left in 1876. After receiving private tuition, he entered Hertford College, Oxford, as a commoner in 1881, and was elected Brunsell exhibitioner in 1882, and Lusby scholar in 1883. He obtained his blue in association football, a second class in classical moderations in 1883, and a second class in *literae humaniores* in 1885. After leaving Oxford he was appointed assistant classics master at St Paul's School, London, a post which he held until his death. In 1893 he married Edith, eldest daughter of Sir John I. Thornycroft FRS, and they had one daughter. In 1896 he founded the school field club.

Soon after going to London Cornish started to write occasional articles on natural history and country life. In 1890 he became a regular contributor to *The Spectator*, and, later, to *Country Life*; many of his articles reappeared in book form. The work for which he was best known was *Life at the Zoo* (1895); his final work, *Animal Artisans and other Studies of Birds and Beasts*, was published posthumously in 1907 with a prefatory memoir by his widow.

Cornish's country tastes and love of shooting and fishing were fostered by his father, in whose family they were traditional. His artistic and literary gifts he inherited from his mother. His powers of observation were unusually keen and rapid, his memory remarkably good, and he had vivid powers of expression. His literary energy, which continued through twenty years, stimulated public interest in natural history and country life, and helped to give these subjects an assured place in English journalism. He died at 114 Marine Parade, Worthing, Sussex, on 30 January 1906, from an illness originating in an accident he suffered when shooting, many years before. After cremation his ashes were interred at Salcombe Regis, near Sidmouth, and a mural tablet to his memory was placed in the parish church.

VAUGHAN CORNISH, rev. V. M. QUIRKE

**Sources** personal knowledge (1912) · *The Times* (31 Jan 1906) · *The Times* (5 Feb 1906) · E. Cornish, 'Memoir', in C. J. Cornish, *Animal artisans and other studies of birds and beasts* (1907)

**Wealth at death** £2809 10s. 8d.: resworn probate, 14 March 1906, CGPLA Eng. & Wales

**Cornish, Francis Warre Warre-** (1839–1916), schoolmaster and author, the second son of the Revd Hubert Kestell

Cornish (1803–1873), vicar of Bakewell and formerly fellow of Exeter College, Oxford, and his wife, Louisa, daughter of the Revd Francis Warre (1775–1854), DCL, was born at Cheddon Fitzpaine, Somerset, on 8 May 1839. He adopted the surname Warre-Cornish in 1892. He went to Eton College as a colleger, was Newcastle scholar in 1857, and passed in the same year to King's College, Cambridge, where he was a fellow, 1860–67. After graduating third classic in 1861, he returned to Eton as an assistant master in the same year. He was appointed vice-provost and librarian in 1893, resigned in April 1916, and died at Englefield Green, Surrey, on 28 August 1916.

Warre-Cornish was a singularly attractive man. Small and frail, with a gentle voice and quiet manners, he was not the typical schoolmaster. He was no martinet and was not methodical. But boys who wished to learn were inspired by his fine scholarship and his literary and historical knowledge, and in this he followed the tradition of William Johnson Cory, whose letters and journals he edited in 1897. As a housemaster, he was inclined to leave his boys to govern themselves; but their attachment to him was shown by a strong *esprit de corps*.

Warre-Cornish had a wide knowledge of books and bindings and made a special study of Aldines. He was a good musician. As an author he was versatile. Industrious in research, he wrote clearly and with distinction, and had a power of vivid portraiture. His chief work was a useful *History of the English Church in the Nineteenth Century* (1910). He also wrote a *History of Chivalry* (1901), a *Life of Oliver Cromwell* (1882), *Jane Austen* in the English Men of Letters series (1913), and a translation of Catullus (1904), besides minor books and many reviews in the *Quarterly Review* and elsewhere. *Sunningwell* (1899) and *Dr Ashford and his Neighbours* (1914) were in a different vein, graceful fictions, with little plot, embodying a slightly ironical view of life, expressed with a peculiar charm and sympathy.

Warre-Cornish married in 1866 Blanche, daughter of the Hon. William Ritchie, legal member of the council of the viceroy of India, and his wife, Augusta, daughter of Thomas Trimmer. A niece of W. M. Thackeray, she wrote two moderately successful novels, *Alcestis* (1871) and *Northam Cloisters* (1882), and contributed to periodical literature. She was a brilliant conversationalist and hostess; her drawing-room, distinctively decorated with William Morris wallpaper, played an influential part in Eton life. She was a convert to Roman Catholicism and contributed with Shane Leslie (who depicted her as Mrs Thackeray in his novel *The Oppidan*) to *Memorials of Robert Hugh Benson* (1915). Her daughter Charlotte, one of eight children, was a Catholic convert and married a fellow of King's College, Cambridge, Reginald Balfour (1875–1907), also a convert. Charlotte Balfour was the author or translator of a number of religious works published between 1910 and 1946. Another daughter, Mary (d. 1953), who married Sir Desmond *MacCarthy, was also an author.

HENRY BROADBENT, rev. M. C. CURTHOYS

**Sources** *WWW* · Venn, *Alum. Cant.* · *Wellesley index* · F. C. Burnand, ed., *The Catholic who's who and yearbook* (1909) · private information

(1927) • personal knowledge (1927) • T. Card, *Eton renewed: a history from 1860 to the present day* (1994)

**Archives** BL, corresp. with Macmillans, Add. MS 55116 • King's AC Cam., letters from him and his wife to Henry Bradshaw; letters to Oscar Browning • St Deiniol's Library, Hawarden, letters to W. E. Gladstone • Trinity Cam., letters to Henry Sidgwick

**Likenesses** Spy [L. Ward], caricature, chromolithograph, NPG; repro. in *VF* (26 Sept 1901)

**Wealth at death** £2326 12s. 2d.: probate, 2 Jan 1917, *CGPLA Eng. & Wales*

**Cornish, Henry** (d. **1685**), local politician, was apparently a native of Wiltshire and was originally of 'a mean servile condition', according to a detractor (*CSP dom., Jan–June 1683*, 315). A cloth factor resident in London, perhaps from as early as 1659, he became a freeman of the Haberdashers' Company in 1668 and served as its master in 1680–82. After 1671 he lived in Cateaton Street, Cheapside, in the parish of St Lawrence Jewry. He carried on his business there, eventually with partners Thomas Cornish and John DeVink, one of his sons-in-law. He also maintained a country house at Bromley, owned other London properties, and possessed lands in Somerset. An occasional conformist, he probably had presbyterian preferences: a daughter married a son of Henry Ashurst, the city's most prominent presbyterian layman, and Cornish had business connections to the dissenting Foley family of Worcestershire. His relationship to a contemporary west country dissenting divine of the same name (an ejected canon of Christ Church, Oxford) is unknown.

In May 1679 Cornish was one of the first to sign a city petition intended to encourage parliamentary adoption of a bill to exclude James, duke of York, from the succession. For the remainder of Charles II's reign he took a leading part in civic politics. The election of Cornish and Slingsby Bethel as sheriffs of London and Middlesex in June 1680 signalled a seizing of the political initiative in the city by those who would soon be called whigs. It was also intended to promote accommodation between the state church and reformed protestants outside the church. However, neither Cornish nor Bethel had qualified by taking the oaths intended to prevent dissenters from holding office, so their elections were disallowed. Despite the king's appearances in the city to assist the secretary of state, Leoline Jenkins, in promoting loyalist candidates, Cornish and Bethel headed the poll in a second election. By that time they had also satisfied the religious tests. Jenkins 'fear[ed] more from Cornish' than from Bethel, although Bethel was generally regarded as a republican (*CSP dom.*, *1679–80*, 620). Charles declined to knight either of the new sheriffs, as would have been customary. Cornish was also returned as alderman for Vintry ward in 1680, and he was eventually accepted by the court of aldermen despite loyalist objections.

Bethel and Cornish were not friends: they clashed almost immediately over the choice of an under-sheriff. Bethel insisted upon the attorney Richard Goodenough, whom Cornish openly distrusted as hostile to the government. He was also offended by Bethel's much ridiculed

frugality in office, insisting that he would, during his shrievalty, provide the accustomed hospitality. Politically, however, the two sheriffs were partners and tribunes of the civic whig movement and regarded themselves as accountable to the electors who chose them. They were quite useful to Shaftesbury and the parliamentary whigs because they impanelled the urban juries with an eye towards the prosecution of those accused of complicity in the Popish Plot. They also co-operated in an unsuccessful scheme to grant the civic freedom to Shaftesbury and the duke of Buckingham so that they might, in time, assume magisterial office in London.

In 1681 Cornish was instrumental in securing the deposition of the Irish informant, Edward Fitzharris, with whose fanciful revelations Shaftesbury hoped to revive fears about Catholic plotting. He was faulted by fellow whigs for immediately informing the king about Fitzharris's information. When the crown sought to silence Fitzharris through a treason prosecution Cornish and Bethel delayed summoning a jury. According to Cornish's testimony at the trial, Charles had told him that Fitzharris was actually employed by the court. After being condemned Fitzharris charged Cornish and other whigs with suborning his evidence about plotting, but when Cornish and Bethel officiated at Fitzharris's execution they sought to encourage further revelations. Cornish facilitated whig efforts to petition for another parliament after the brief sitting at Oxford in March 1681. He helped select the London jury that threw out the crown's treason case against Stephen College, 'the protestant joiner'. After the crown's unsuccessful treason prosecution of Shaftesbury, Cornish was said to be collecting depositions for ministerial impeachments.

Cornish was similarly visible in the controverted events of 1682–3 in which the crown recovered control of the corporation of London. In January 1682 he was named to the committee to defend the civic charter against the crown's *quo warranto*, and he was one of the whig aldermen who refused to co-operate in legal actions against conventiclers. An organizer for whig candidates Thomas Papillon and John Dubois during the protracted shrieval election of 1682, he was indicted, with other leading civic whigs, for a riot. When tory sheriffs supported by the crown were declared elected by the loyalist lord mayor, despite a poll that favoured their rivals, Cornish protested. He told the lord mayor that the citizens would not be 'baffled' by such 'encroachments on their privileges' or 'suffer an Arbitrary unjust one to Rule' in London (Library of Congress, London newsletters, 8.121, 28 Sept 1682). But Cornish himself was baffled in the ensuing election for a new lord mayor: he and a whig colleague headed a poll for the office only to see the court of aldermen adjust the results in favour of loyalist Sir William Prichard.

Cornish was present at strategy sessions throughout 1682 in which civic and parliamentary whigs discussed responses to what they perceived as Charles's infringements upon electoral rights. He was, for instance, a late arrival at a gathering in November 1682 at the home of merchant Thomas Shepherd where the duke of Monmouth, Lord Russell, Lord Grey, Robert Ferguson, and Colonel John Rumsey apparently discussed an urban insurrection that was subsequently aborted. In April 1683 Cornish met Thomas Papillon and John Dubois just before his former assistant, Richard Goodenough, arrested Lord Mayor Prichard for failing to respond to a whig suit on behalf of Papillon and Dubois as the legitimate sheriffs. Goodenough had earlier been privy to a scheme to assassinate Charles II, restore parliamentary government, and get Cornish made mayor of London. In May 1683 Cornish was fined 1000 marks after he and his whig colleagues were found guilty of riot in the 1682 shrieval election. Undaunted, he toured the clothing towns of Wiltshire and eastern Somerset, where he was met by enthusiastic crowds and looked into purchasing an interest in the parliamentary borough of Hindon.

Cornish was implicated in some of the revelations about whig plotting that were heard before the privy council during the summer of 1683. He was apprehended four times in the next two years, once on suspicion of distributing pamphlets that suggested the earl of Essex had been murdered by the government, and again during Monmouth's rebellion against James II. The capture of Richard Goodenough after Monmouth's rebellion sealed his fate: the crown now had another witness willing to support Colonel John Rumsey's claim that Cornish had been involved in the conspiracies against Charles II's life in 1682–3. Arrested and found guilty in a hasty trial, he was executed on 23 October 1685, before his Cheapside house. He was comforted by Dr Benjamin Calamy, the vicar of his parish, who had sought to save him, and Cornish claimed from the scaffold that 'the crimes laid to my charge were falsely and maliciously sworn against me by the witnesses' (*State trials*, 11.451). James eventually granted Cornish's estate and his remains, which were displayed over Guildhall and the city gates, to his widow, Elizabeth, and to his children. He was buried at St Lawrence Jewry in November 1687. An inventory drawn up after his death included more than a hundred accounts with credits and debts amounting to £87,000, a figure that indicates the considerable scale of his business.

Although lords Grey and Howard regarded Cornish as a plot participant, most of his whig contemporaries regarded him as the victim of judicial murder. Robert Ferguson and Thomas Shepherd insisted that he was not yet present when rebellion was discussed at Shepherd's house in November 1682. What he knew about subsequent whig conspiracy is unclear. Some plotters regarded him as too cautious, and some exiles doubted his commitment to their cause. Gilbert Burnet regarded Cornish as 'a plain, warm, honest man' who was manifestly innocent (*Bishop Burnet's History*, 2.248). The circumstances of his death secured his place in the pantheon of whig martyrs that included Algernon Sidney and Lord Russell. His attainder for treason was reversed after the revolution of 1688, and the foreman of his trial jury was burnt in effigy by a London crowd in December 1689. His London son of

the same name followed him in business, held a government place under William III, and was briefly MP for Shaftesbury in Dorset. GARY S. DE KREY

**Sources** H. A. Nenner, 'Cornish, Henry', Greaves & Zaller, *BDBR*, 1.177–8 · J. R. Woodhead, *The rulers of London, 1660–1689* (1965), 52 · R. L. Greaves, *Secrets of the kingdom: British radicals from the Popish Plot to the revolution of 1688–89* (1992) · *CSP dom.*, 1679–85; 1687–9 · *State trials*, vols. 9–11 · L. Cong., manuscript division, London newsletters collection, 7, fols. 65–69 (22, 24, 26, 29 June, 1 July 1680), fols. 72–77 (10, 12, 15, 17, 20, 22 July 1680), fol. 80 (29 July 1680), fols. 83–84 (5, 7 Aug 1680); 8, fols. 38 (6 April 1682), 81 (8 July 1682), 121, 123 (28, 30 Sept 1682) · Newdigate newsletters, 26 June–5 July 1680, Folger, L.c.952–7; 15–22 July 1680, L.c.961–4; 27–9 July 1680, L.c.966–7; 5 Aug 1680, L.c.969; 8 June 1681, L.c.1085 · W. A. Shaw, ed., *Calendar of treasury books*, 8, PRO (1923), 382, 437, 472, 494, 572, 652–3 · *Bishop Burnet's History*, 2.247–9, 278–9, 289; 3.65–6 · *The tryals of Henry Cornish … and Elizabeth Gaunt* (1685) · *DNB*

**Likenesses** J. Savage, group portrait, line engraving (*Anti-papists*), BM · engraving, repro. in T. B. Macaulay, *The history of England from the accession of James I*, ed. C. H. Firth (1985), 655 · line print, NPG

**Wealth at death** household goods in London and Bromley houses, value approx. £200; £47,038 owed to him; £36,867 owed by him; six houses in St Stephen's Coleman Street, London; lands in Chew Magna and Mells, Somerset: Shaw, ed., *Calendar of treasury books, 1685–89*, 472, 652–3

**Cornish, Joseph** (1750–1823), Presbyterian minister and religious writer, was born at Taunton, Somerset, on 16 December 1750, the youngest of seven children of Joseph Cornish (*d.* 1776), woollen-dresser, and his second wife, Honour Ham (*d.* 1769). His parents' attachment to the dissenting ministry of Thomas Amory at Pauls Meeting and Tancred Street, Taunton, may indicate a long-standing family connection, especially given the publication in 1731 of *A sermon preach'd at the ordination of the Rev. Mr. Thomas Amory, and Mr. William Cornish, at Taunton, Somerset, Oct. 7, 1730*. Certainly, two of his father's eight brothers were Presbyterian ministers: John at Leather Lane, London, and James at Dulverton, Somerset.

Cornish received a classical grounding locally from a clergyman named Patch and from a Mr Glass of Westminster School. In 1765 he became one of the first pupils of Joshua Toulmin, the learned Baptist minister who had recently accepted a call to the Mary Street meeting-house in Taunton and who, in September 1767, gained him admission as a foundation student in Coward's academy, Hoxton. The divinity tutor was Samuel Morton Savage, a moderate Calvinist, who was assisted by Andrew Kippis and Abraham Rees, both Arians. While at Hoxton, Cornish began his lifelong adherence to what he called the 'very high Arian scheme', associated with Samuel Clarke (*Monthly Repository*, 18, 1823, 617). Shortly before leaving the academy in 1772, Cornish published *A Serious and Earnest Address to Protestant Dissenters*, which went through three large editions, and his pointed and telling *Brief and Impartial History of the Puritans*, later revised by Samuel Palmer, the editor of Calamy's *Nonconformist's Memorial*, in 1797. In 1772, at the suggestion of Philip Furneaux, Cornish also applied unsuccessfully for the afternoon lectureship at Salters' Hall in succession to Hugh Farmer.

Amory, impressed by Cornish's learning, recommended

him to George's Meeting, a small Presbyterian congregation at Colyton, east Devon, which had been vacant for four years since the departure of Matthew Anstis for Bridport, Dorset, in 1768. Toulmin had also served there from 1761 until 1765. As Colyton was relatively near his father's home, Cornish began his ministry there in July 1772 despite a unanimous call to Epsom, which he had occasionally supplied from Hoxton. He subsequently received Presbyterian ordination at Taunton on 11 May 1773.

Cornish never married and was to stay at Colyton for the remaining fifty-one years of his life. During his long ministry the meeting-house was enhanced by a new entrance with iron gates, built about 1800, a burial-ground, in use from 1832, and an organ, installed in 1820. His stipend at Colyton, including endowment, averaged no more than £40 per annum, but until 1783 he boarded with Mr Slade, one of his leading hearers, whose house was 'the chief resort of various ministers visiting the town'. The charge was under £20 a year and Cornish therefore always found it possible 'to spare something for charitable purposes' (*Monthly Repository*, 18, 1823, 619). At the same time he saved hard to clear the debts arising from the failure of his late father's business that had been ruined by the American war, and as soon as he was able to do so he honoured his father's memory by paying every creditor in full. Calls from Tewkesbury late in 1781 and from Banbury in 1792 offered the prospect of a larger income, but Cornish resisted such temptations out of regard for his existing friends.

Cornish's finances were improving as a result of running a classical school, which he opened at Colyton in 1782. He initially taught in the gallery of his meeting-house, but the undertaking proved so successful that at Christmas 1796 he was able to buy a house and take boarders. The school was not confined to dissenters and continued in one shape or another until Christmas 1819. Some of his students proceeded to careers as surgeons or in the Royal Navy; others became clergymen.

As minister and schoolmaster Cornish earned much local affection and he was on intimate terms with three successive vicars of Colyton, George Nutcombe, Richard Buller, and Frederick Barnes. He was long remembered for 'his peculiar bachelor habits, his quaint old world courtesy, his chivalry to women, and his never-failing kindness to children' (Murch, 22). In old age some of those children recalled 'a man in knee breeches, black silk stockings and shoes, with a fund of true humour and joke', someone who was 'always the scholar and the gentleman' (Evans, *Colytonia*, 22). He showed a particular fondness for his apple trees, whist parties, children's tea parties, and long walks up Colyton Hill and in Shute Park.

Cornish remained a particularly active writer until the 1790s, several of his works being published locally in Taunton, where Mrs Jane Toulmin was long engaged as a bookseller. As a writer he is a good specimen of the class of men to whom dissent meant religious liberty rather than sectarian organization or theological system. His works sold rapidly and addressed not only theological questions but also practical religion, religious biography, and classical learning. He was paid a much needed 5 guineas for the copyright of *A Blow at the Root of All Priestly Claims* (1775) by John Johnson of St Paul's Churchyard. In *A Letter to the Venerable Bishop of Carlisle [Edmund Law]* (1777) he argued for extensive alterations to the liturgy and Thirty-Nine Articles. He wrote an improved account of the life of Thomas Firmin, the seventeenth-century philanthropist, with the help of Andrew Kippis and Joseph Bretland; his defence of Firmin's decision to remain within the established church was criticized by the Unitarians. Cornish also projected a 'Life of John Lilburne', but the work, though announced, was never published. His last works were an article 'On the decline of Presbyterian congregations', published in the *Monthly Repository* (1819), and some short pieces, foremost among which was a supportive letter of September 1798 which he sent, together with 5 guineas, to Thomas Williams, who had been imprisoned for selling Paine's *Age of Reason*.

Cornish's comments on dwindling congregations appear to have been based upon first-hand experience. By 1793 he had successfully built up a following at Colyton of 'about eighty', but on 28 April 1814 four neighbouring ministers wrote to him suggesting that he should retire in favour of a Calvinistic successor (Polwhele, 2.314). He flatly refused, quoting in his defence John Lavington, himself a high Calvinist, 'Should the number of your hearers lessen, do not be discouraged so as to grow remiss in your endeavours: remember Jesus Christ preached an excellent sermon to one woman' (Murch, 336). Consequently, a new meeting-house was built in 1819 for the Calvinistic dissenters. Cornish continued to discharge his ministerial duties until August 1823, when he was attacked by illness. He assisted at the Lord's Supper on 5 October, but died four days later. He was buried beneath the entrance to his meeting-house on 17 October, and a memorial tablet to his memory was placed above the spot. James Manning, minister of Exeter, officiated and subsequently published an abridged version of Cornish's autobiography in the *Monthly Repository* (1823). His death was 'universally lamented' 'by men of all parties' who had come to respect his charity, classical scholarship, instruction of youth, and writing (Murch, 336, 342). Among Cornish's benefactions was a sum of £400 given to the London Presbyterian Fund.                    PATRICK WOODLAND

**Sources** 'Memoir of the late Rev. Joseph Cornish of Colyton, drawn up by himself', ed. J. Manning, *Monthly Repository*, 18 (1823), 617–23 · *Monthly Repository*, 11 (1816), 649–54 · J. Cornish, 'On the decline of presbyterian congregations', *Monthly Repository*, 14 (1819), 77–80 · 'Letters between Rev. Jos. Cornish of Colyton and Mr T. Williams', *Monthly Repository*, 17 (1822), 586–8 · L. Holden, *Monthly Repository*, 18 (1823), 635 · J. Murch, *A history of the Presbyterian and General Baptist churches in the west of England* (1835) · G. E. Evans, *Colytonia, a chapter in the history of Devon: being some account of the Old and George's Meetings, Colyton from 1662 to 1898* (1898) · G. E. Evans, 'Colyton: the old parsonage', *Devon Notes and Queries*, 5/8 (1909) · parish registers, Wilton and Taunton St Mary, Som. ARS · IGI · R. Polwhele, *The history of Devonshire*, 3 vols. (1793–1806), vol. 2, p. 314 · *Trewman's Exeter Flying Post* (23 Oct 1823) · DNB

**Wealth at death** over £400; £400 bequeathed to London Presbyterian Fund: Murch, *A history*; *Monthly Repository* (1823); *DNB*

**Cornish, Sir Samuel**, baronet (*c*.1715–1770), naval officer, was believed by John Charnock to have risen from modest origins, and to have served his apprenticeship on a collier before being appointed to an East Indiaman (Charnock, 5.139). However, it remains possible that these details relate to his father. Cornish is known to have entered the navy as a volunteer 'per order' in 1728. He was commissioned lieutenant in the *Litchfield* on 12 November 1739, and on 11 November 1740 he moved, with Captain Charles Knowles, to the *Weymouth*, in which he served in the ill-conducted combined operation at Cartagena during March and April 1741. On his return to England he was appointed to command the bomb-ketch *Mortar*; and on 12 March 1742 he was posted flag captain of the *Namur* under Vice-Admiral Thomas Mathews, with whom he served in the Mediterranean.

On 21 September 1742 Cornish was appointed to command the *Guernsey* (50 guns); he continued in her until the end of the war, doing occasional good service in the destruction of the enemy's privateers, and taking part in the action off Toulon on 11 February 1744. His part in that discreditable engagement occasioned no comment, which must be considered an achievement in the light of the number of careers destroyed on that day and in the subsequent courts martial. On 9 March 1749, as a 'gentleman well skilled in mathematicks and natural knowledge', Cornish was elected to the Royal Society (record of election of members). In 1755 he commissioned the *Stirling Castle* for service in the channel, and in 1758 he was transferred to the *Union* (90 guns), and was ordered by Lord Anson to wear a distinguishing pennant.

On 14 February 1759 Cornish was promoted rear-admiral of the white, and in May he was sent out to the East Indies with a small squadron to reinforce Vice-Admiral George Pocock. Having been delayed on passage by the need to escort East India Company ships to Trincomalee, he was not present at Pocock's engagement with D'Aché on 10 September 1759, but after consultations with the governor, George Pigot, and the council at Fort St George, Madras, Cornish undertook operations to clear the coast of Coromandel; this established his reputation as a commander able to co-operate effectively with the army. Pocock had resigned his command of the station to Rear-Admiral Charles Steevens, and when Steevens died on 17 May 1761, Cornish succeeded him. He immediately found himself embroiled in a dispute with the East India Company over the plunder taken at the surrender of the French fortress of Pondicherry, in which Cornish betrayed an ominously unconstructive attitude which certainly suggests that his or his father's earlier dealings with the company had left bitter feelings. This bitterness affected his relations with Madras when he was asked to assist in the creation and execution of a plan to seize the French post on Mauritius, the Île de France, but his professional competence in combined operations and respect for the military officers of the company enabled him to overcome his feelings.

**Sir Samuel Cornish, baronet** (*c*.1715–1770), by Tilly Kettle, exh. Society of Artists 1768 [*An Admiral in his Cabin, Issuing his Orders*; right, with Captain Richard Kempenfelt and Thomas Parry]

The plan Cornish prepared was a model of its kind, but when Spain was drawn into the war it was laid aside in favour of a proposal to capture the Spanish port of Manila. Cornish commanded the seven ships of the line and three frigates carrying Colonel William Draper's troops. By posting a frigate in the Strait of Malacca Cornish ensured that no news of the impending strike reached Manila prior to the fleet's arrival on 23 September 1762. The city walls were breached on 5 October and on the following day the place was taken by storm. Draper did his utmost to put a stop to the spoliation of the town, and with Cornish agreed to accept a ransom of $4 million. The hinterland, however, was soon raised against the British, and Cornish, who had taken the position of governor of Cavite, quarrelled over the means of defence, the collection of the ransom, the administration of justice, and measures to be taken to secure the Spanish Acapulco galleons. With the conclusion of the treaty of Paris, Manila was returned to Spain.

Cornish, who had been advanced to vice-admiral of the blue on 21 October 1762, returned to Europe in February 1763 before news of the peace treaty was known in Asia, and he participated in an unsuccessful campaign to persuade the government to use forceful means to obtain payment of the Manila ransom. A pamphlet written to support this claim, *A Plain Narrative of the Reduction of Manila*, although published anonymously, appears to have been his work. Despite this disappointment he had acquired a comfortable income from prize money. In 1765 he purchased the manors of Sharnbrook, Tafte, and Temple Hills in Bedford. The duke of Norfolk supported his election as MP for Shoreham, a seat he held from December 1765 until his death, and on 9 January 1766 he was created a baronet, taking his style as Sir Samuel Cornish of Sharnbrook. About this time he married Susan, daughter of James Gambier of Holborn and sister of Admiral James Gambier; they had no children. Cornish died on 30 October 1770, whereupon his title became extinct and his estate passed to his nephew, Samuel Pitchford, captain in the navy, who took the name Cornish.

J. K. LAUGHTON, *rev.* NICHOLAS TRACY

**Sources** N. Tracy, *Manila ransomed: the British assault on Manila in the Seven Years' War* (1995) · N. Tracy, 'Vice-Admiral Sir Samuel Cornish and the conquest of Manila, 1762', MPhil diss., U. Southampton, 1967 · K. C. Leebrick, 'Troubles of an English governor', *The Pacific ocean in History*, ed. H. M. Stephens and H. E. Bolton (1917) · [S. Cornish], *A plain narrative of the reduction of Manila and the Philippine islands* (1764) · 'Narrative of the proceedings of His Majesty's fleet in the Mediterranean … from the year 1741 to March 1744', NMM, TUN 179 · J. Charnock, ed., *Biographia navalis*, 5 (1797), 139–49; 6 (1798), 445–6 · D. Syrett and R. L. DiNardo, *The commissioned sea officers of the Royal Navy, 1660–1815*, rev. edn, Occasional Publications of the Navy RS, 1 (1994) · J. Brooke, 'Cornish, Samuel', HoP, *Commons* · muster books, *Weymouth*, PRO, ADM 36/4603 · *Norfolk*, PRO, ADM 51/643 [captain's log] · *Stirling Castle*, PRO, ADM 51/934 [captain's log] · *Weymouth*, PRO, ADM 51/1058 and 51/4392 [captain's log] · high court of admiralty, PRO, HCA 32 · wills, Principal Registry of the Family Division, London, 1770/391 [S.V. Cornish] · election certificate, RS

**Likenesses** T. Kettle, group portrait, oils, exh. Society of Artists 1768, priv. coll. [*see illus.*] · photogravure (after T. Kettle), BM

**Cornish, Vaughan** (1862–1948), geographer, was born on 22 December 1862 at Debenham, Suffolk, the third and youngest son of Charles John Cornish (1834–1913), vicar of Debenham, and his wife, Anne Charlotte Western (1831–1887). His father's cousin was F. W. Warre-Cornish and his elder brother was the naturalist Charles John *Cornish. He was educated first at home and then, when he was seventeen, at St Paul's School, London. After working as a private tutor he studied chemistry at Victoria University of Manchester. While a student he presented a paper to the British Association with Percy Kendall in 1887; he graduated BSc with first-class honours in 1888, and proceeded MSc in 1892 and DSc in 1901.

In 1891 Cornish married Ellen Agnes (1853–1911), the daughter of Alfred Provis, an artist, of Kingston Lisle, Berkshire. In the same year he became director of technical education for Hampshire county council. Living in a cliff-top house near Branksome Chine, between Bournemouth and Poole, he began his studies of waves, and in 1895 he resigned from his job to devote himself to research. In this he was encouraged and financially supported by his wife, who had private means. Ellen was trained as an engineer, and the couple exercised their scientific interests through worldwide travel, giving up a permanent home. Ellen died in 1911, and is recalled in Cornish's *The Travels of Ellen Cornish: being the Memoir of a Pilgrim of Science* (1913) and *Kestell, Clapp and Cornish* (1947). Cornish's global experience would later inform his survey of *The Beauties of Scenery* (1943). In 1913 he married Mary Louisa, the daughter of William Richards Watson, rector of Saltfleetby, and the widow of his second cousin, the

Vaughan Cornish (1862–1948), by unknown photographer

explorer Ernest Ayscoghe Floyer, whose notice he contributed to the *Dictionary of National Biography*. They settled in Camberley, Surrey, though Cornish continued to travel extensively. There were no children of either marriage.

Cornish's research on surface waves, to which he gave the label 'kumatology', was primarily observational, and often carried out in extreme conditions. He was awarded the Royal Geographical Society Gill memorial prize in 1901. Books such as *Waves of the Sea and other Water Waves* (1910) and *The Waves of Sand and Snow* (1914) document sand waves in the Libyan desert, wind-blown snow in Canada, and water waves below Niagara and in the mid-Atlantic. Cornish also studied British tidal bores, shooting the first film of the Severn bore in September 1901 from a boat anchored in mid-stream and tracking the Trent 'eagre' by car in 1922. His results were summarized in *Ocean Waves and Kindred Geophysical Phenomena* (1934), with theoretical elaborations by Harold Jeffreys. He illustrated his work with his own photography, for which he won awards at the St Louis Exposition in 1904 and the Franco-British Exhibition in London in 1908. He later collected his work in *The Photography of Scenery* (1946), with a companion volume of *Sketches of Scenery in England and Abroad* (1949). The aesthetic concerns which dominated his later career were already strong in his physical geographic research.

In 1907 and 1910 Cornish visited the construction site of the Panama Canal, which he described in *The Panama Canal and its Makers* (1909) as a spectacular landscape of engineering and which proved a key inspiration for his political and strategic geography. He promoted Britain's imperial mission and position in *Naval and Military Geography* (1916), *Imperial Military Geography* (1920), and *A Geography of Imperial Defence* (1922), and lectured to officers in wartime on the western front and at Scapa Flow, an experience recalled in *Geographical Essays* (1946). Cornish's imperial geography was also a racial geography, proposing the migration of 'British stock' through the empire to safeguard the future of the 'white races'. He argued for a geographical eugenics in the *Eugenics Review* (1925), asking 'which Nations are now the most useful part of the Human Community'. Strategic concerns also informed his well-received historical geography of *The Great Capitals* (1923), which argued for the 'forward position' of capital cities as a focal point of internal and foreign communications. His *Borderlands of Language in Europe* (1933) further argued that polyglot areas reflected periods when the 'Historic Frontier of Christendom' had remained stationary. Cornish was president of the geographical section E of the British Association in 1923.

From around 1918 Cornish began to formulate an 'aesthetic geography', later citing Sir Francis Younghusband's 1920 address to the Royal Geographical Society on natural beauty and geographical science as a key inspiration. In his 1928 presidential address to the Geographical Association on harmonies of scenery (*Geography*, 1928) he proposed a 'science of scenery' which would enable the geographer to assess and advise on the beauty of landscape. *Nature* devoted an editorial to his work in March 1928. Cornish explored the workings of the eye in *Scenery and the Sense of Sight* (1935) and in reviews of landscape art exhibitions for *Nature* between 1929 and 1942. He termed himself a 'Pilgrim of Scenery', and his nature-mysticism received fullest expression in *The Poetic Impression of Natural Scenery* (1931) and *The Churchyard Yew and Immortality* (1946). His mystical and aesthetic geography extended the patriotic concerns of his imperial geography by presenting landscape as a key element of national identity, the 'proper' experience of which would improve the citizen. Cornish was active in the Council for the Preservation of Rural England (CPRE), for whom he gave evidence to the national parks committee in 1929 and produced *The Scenery of England* (1932). He proposed national parks in *National Parks and the Heritage of Scenery* (1930) and *The Preservation of our Scenery* (1937), and put preservationist principles into practice after inheriting land in Salcombe Regis, Devon, in 1938, described in his CPRE pamphlet *The Farm upon the Cliff* (1939) and *The Scenery of Sidmouth* (1940). Cornish entered into agreements to preserve the cliff-top South Combe farm in perpetuity, and as owner of Thorn Farm erected a stone to explain the communal folk meaning of the Salcombe Regis thorn, discussed in his *Historic Thorn Trees in the British Isles* (1941).

Cornish was intensely proud of his family, minor gentry of the Sidmouth district of Devon since the fifteenth century. He regarded land as a source of family as well as national identity and was devoted to family history. He wrote the entry in the *Dictionary of National Biography* for his elder brother, Charles, edited *Reminiscences of Country Life* (1939) by his brother the Revd James George Cornish, and published two works on family history, *A Family of Devon* (1942) and *Kestell, Clapp and Cornish* (1947). Cornish was somewhat austere yet courteous, and his reserve thawed when he discussed his lifelong interests. He died at the Willersley Nursing Home, Park Road, Camberley on 1 May 1948, and was buried alongside his first wife in Salcombe Regis churchyard.

Under the terms of his will of 4 August 1945 the Vaughan Cornish bequest was established at the University of Oxford to enable graduate students of the university to pursue studies 'relating to the beauty of scenery as determined by nature or the arts in town or country at home or abroad'. G. R. CRONE, *rev.* DAVID MATLESS

**Sources** A. Goudie, 'Vaughan Cornish: geographer', *Transactions of the Institute of British Geographers*, 55 (1972), 1–16 • B. Waites, 'Vaughan Cornish, 1862–1948', *Geographers: biobibliographical studies*, 9, ed. T. W. Freeman (1985), 29–35 • D. Matless, 'Nature, the modern and the mystic: tales from early twentieth century geography', *Transactions of the Institute of British Geographers*, new ser., 16 (1991), 272–86 • D. Matless, 'A modern stream', *Society and Space*, 10 (1992), 569–88 • K. Dodds, 'Eugenics, fantasies of empire and inverted whiggism: the political geography of Vaughan Cornish', *Political Geography*, 13 (1994), 85–99 • D. Matless, *Landscape and Englishness* (1998) • D. Matless, 'Visual culture and geographical citizenship', *Journal of Historical Geography*, 22 (1996), 424–39 • V. Cornish, *The travels of Ellen Cornish: being the memoir of a pilgrim of science* (1913) • V. Cornish, *A family of Devon* (1942) • *CGPLA Eng. & Wales* (1949)

**Archives** Geographical Association, Sheffield, photographs • RGS, corresp. • U. Oxf., VCB/1, BEQ/66 | Bodl. Oxf., corresp. with J. L. Myres, MS Myres 9, fols. 66–91

**Likenesses** photograph, RGS [*see illus.*]

**Wealth at death** £14,916 9s. 9d.: probate, save and except settled land, 22 Jan 1949, *CGPLA Eng. & Wales*

**Cornish Giant, the**. *See* Payne, Antony (*d.* 1691?).

**Cornthwaite, Robert** (1818–1890), Roman Catholic bishop of Leeds, was born in Preston on 9 May 1818, son of William and Elizabeth Cornthwaite, and was sent to St Cuthbert's College, Ushaw, in 1830. In 1842 he went to the English College, Rome, to complete his theological education and was ordained priest on 9 November 1845. In the following year he began work as a mission priest in Carlisle before returning to Rome as rector of the English College in 1851, where he remained for six years. Conflict between Cornthwaite and Louis English, formerly president of the Collegio Pio (which was united with the English College in 1855), seems to have led to Cornthwaite's resignation. Nevertheless, Pius IX recognized the value of his work there and shortly after his resignation Cornthwaite received a papal honour which gave him the title of monsignor. From 1857 to 1861 he worked in the Darlington mission, becoming both canon theologian and secretary to the bishop of Hexham, before being appointed bishop of Beverley. He was consecrated on 10 November 1861.

Cornthwaite was a convinced ultramontane and, on taking charge of Beverley, made clear his determination to ensure that all in the diocese understood the importance of loyalty and obedience to the pope. He showed his own devotion to the papacy at the Vatican Council in 1869–70, when he was one of only three English bishops consistently to support the definition of papal infallibility. Cornthwaite also had a high view of the priestly life and cared for the well-being and sanctification of his clergy, organizing annual retreats for them, and stressing the importance of days of meditation and self-examination. He soon gained the reputation of being an efficient administrator and organizer, bringing order to diocesan affairs. Cornthwaite also believed strongly in the importance of education, placing the provision of schools before churches, and was the only English bishop to establish a successful diocesan seminary for the education of priests. The foundation stone of St Joseph's seminary was laid in 1876; it was opened in 1878, the year in which the bishop had to reconcile priests and people to the division of Beverley, a diocese encompassing the whole of Yorkshire, into the two new dioceses of Leeds and Middlesbrough. Despite much initial opposition this was finally accepted and Cornthwaite became bishop of Leeds.

Although he seems to have recovered from a stroke in 1864, Cornthwaite's health gave cause for concern from the late 1880s and a coadjutor was appointed in February 1890. The bishop died on 16 June 1890. After a funeral service at St Anne's Cathedral, Leeds, he was buried in the cemetery attached to the church of Mary Immaculate, Sicklinghall. Cornthwaite was regarded not only as an able administrator but as a man of sanctity and prayer who hid a tender heart beneath a cool and reserved exterior. Perhaps his greatest achievement lay in welding together the different elements of the Catholic community in Yorkshire, so that secular priests, members of religious orders, old Catholic gentry, converts, and Irish immigrants were able to work together to create a revived and flourishing Catholic church.

JENNIFER F. SUPPLE-GREEN

**Sources** Leeds Diocesan Archives, Cornthwaite MSS · F. J. Cwiekowski, *The English bishops and the First Vatican Council* (1971), 102–4, 136–9 · R. Carson, *The first hundred years—diocese of Middlesbrough, 1878–1978* (1978), 19–26 · *The Tablet* (26 Oct 1889) · *The Tablet* (1 March 1890) · *The Tablet* (21 June 1890) · *Leeds Mercury* (17 June 1890) · *Leeds Mercury* (21 June 1890) · *Leeds Mercury* (25 Feb 1890) · J. F. Supple-Green, *The Catholic revival in Yorkshire, 1850–1900* (1990), 25–60
**Archives** English College, Rome, papers as rector · Leeds Diocesan Archives, corresp. and papers · Westm. DA | Ushaw College, Durham, letters to C. Newsham
**Likenesses** oils, bishop's house, Leeds
**Wealth at death** £207 11s. 11d.: probate, 11 Dec 1890, *CGPLA Eng. & Wales*

**Cornwall**. For this title name *see* Reginald, earl of Cornwall (d. 1175); Richard, first earl of Cornwall and king of Germany (1209–1272); Edmund of Almain, second earl of Cornwall (1249–1300); Gaveston, Piers, earl of Cornwall (d. 1312); John, earl of Cornwall (1316–1336).

**Cornwall** [*formerly* Cornewall], **Charles** (*bap.* 1669, *d.* 1718), naval officer, was baptized on 5 August 1669 at Eyre, Herefordshire, the son of Robert Cornewall (1646–1701) of Berrington, and his wife, Edith Cornwallis (*d.* 1696). He entered the navy in 1683, commanded two prizes in 1691–2, and on 19 September 1692 was made post

captain of the sloop *Portsmouth*. In 1693 he commanded the *Adventure* (44 guns), and accompanied Admiral Edward Russell to the Mediterranean; he remained there until 1696, at about which time he married Dorothy Hanmer; they had eight sons and seven daughters. This was Cornwall's second marriage; details of his first wife are unknown. On 18 January 1695 he shared in the capture of the French ships *Trident* and *Content*. Captain James Killigrew of the *Plymouth*, the senior officer present, was killed in the action, and Cornwall was promoted to command the *Plymouth*.

Cornwall left the navy at the peace of Ryswick (1697), having latterly commanded the *Kent*, and in 1701 he attempted unsuccessfully to enter parliament for Herefordshire, at which time it was said that he possessed an estate of £10,000–£12,000 and an annual income of £500–£600. He returned to naval service in command of the *Shrewsbury* in 1701, but resigned after a few months in order to settle the complicated family affairs caused by the sudden death of his father. Although appointed to the *Exeter* in 1702, he was unwilling to serve in her if he was to be effectively a 'second captain' under John Leake, who was appointed to command the Newfoundland station; Cornwall protested that 'their sending a private captain to command … me in my own ship [was] a modest way of terming me a blockhead' (*Portland MSS*, 8.102), and he rejected a proposed transfer to a smaller ship. Because of the chequered nature of his recent career, and his uneasy political relationship with Robert Harley, he was finding it difficult to obtain suitable employment, despite regular requests to leading ministers. However, in 1705 he was appointed to command the *Orford*.

In the *Orford* Cornwall again went out to the Mediterranean, where he remained for the next two years, under the command, first, of Sir Cloudesley Shovell, and afterwards of Sir Thomas Dilkes. In the autumn of 1707 he commanded a detached squadron on the coast of Naples. In March 1708 he returned to England, and in 1709 he changed his name to Cornwall in an attempt to distinguish between different branches of his family. He sat as a whig MP, first for Bewdley—1709–10—and later for Weobley, from 1715 until his death. In December 1709 he was appointed to command in the Downs and off Dunkirk; and in October 1710 he left England in command of the *Dreadnought*, in charge of the trade for the Levant. This he escorted safely to Smyrna, and by December 1711 he was again in England where his strong political leanings excluded him from further employment under the tory administration.

At the accession of George I Cornwall was appointed comptroller of storekeeper's accounts at the Navy Board; he retained this post until promoted rear-admiral on 16 June 1716. In the following October he became commander-in-chief in the Mediterranean, with instructions to take appropriate measures to prevent the depredations of the Salé corsairs, and to enter into a treaty with the emperor of Morocco. In this work he was occupied for the next year, residing at Gibraltar, where a quarrel—one which was to become increasingly bitter—sprang up between Cornwall and the governor; it arose out of the soldiers' unwillingness to admit the admiral's authority even in matters relating to the ships in the port. The blame for this may have lain chiefly with the governor, who maintained that either he or Cornwall was 'the vilest fellow upon earth', and permitted, if he did not encourage, his officers to 'drink damnation to the admiral and the negotiation he was conducting'. Cornwall too may have used strong language, for he seems to have been a man of hot temper; but the correspondence between the two ended in the admiral's expressing determination to refer the matter to the king or to the speaker of the Commons. He seems to have been prevented from doing so by his being called away from Gibraltar on active service. He had been promoted vice-admiral in March 1718, and in June he hoisted his flag in the *Shrewsbury*, as second in command of the fleet under Sir George Byng, before playing a prominent part in the victory off Cape Passaro on 31 July. Afterwards he shifted his flag to his former ship, the *Argyle*, convoyed the prizes to Port Mahon, and sailed for England. His health had been poor for some time, and after putting into Lisbon on the homeward passage he died there on 7 October 1718. He was buried in Westminster Abbey.

Among Cornwall's sons, Jacobs was the father of Charles Wolfran *Cornwall, who was named after Charles's uncle, another naval captain, Wolfran Cornwall, who had been a prominent Williamite agent during the revolution of 1688. Cornwall's younger brother, Frederick (*d.* 1748), vicar of Bromfield for forty-six years, was the grandfather of Folliott H. W. Cornwall, bishop of Worcester. J. K. LAUGHTON, *rev.* J. D. DAVIES

**Sources** HoP, *Commons* [draft] · J. Charnock, ed., *Biographia navalis*, 2 (1795), 410–12 · *The manuscripts of his grace the duke of Portland*, 10 vols., HMC, 29 (1891–1931), vol. 8, pp. 91–2, 102, 116–17 · NMM, Sergison MSS, SER/136 · PRO, ADM 6/424 · PRO, ADM 7/549 · D. Syrett and R. L. DiNardo, *The commissioned sea officers of the Royal Navy, 1660–1815*, rev. edn, Occasional Publications of the Navy RS, 1 (1994) · *Pattee Byng's journal, 1718–1720*, ed. J. L. Cranmer-Byng, Navy RS, 88 (1950)

**Cornwall, Charles Wolfran** (1735–1789), speaker of the House of Commons, was born on 15 June 1735 and baptized ten days later at St Thomas's Church, Winchester, the only son of Jacobs Cornwall (1709/10–1736), of Berrington, Herefordshire, and his wife, Rose (1706/7–1783), the daughter of Robert Fowler, of Barton Priors, Hampshire. His paternal grandfather was Vice-Admiral Charles *Cornwall (*bap.* 1669, *d.* 1718). Educated at Winchester School from 1748 and trained for the law at Lincoln's Inn from 1755 and Gray's Inn in 1757, he was called to the bar in 1757. He then became involved politically with his cousin Charles Jenkinson, later first earl of Liverpool, whose influence secured him the post of commissioner for examining the German accounts in 1763. The following year, on 17 August, he married Jenkinson's sister Elizabeth (*bap.* 1730, *d.* 1809), who was the daughter of Colonel Charles Jenkinson and Amarantha Cornwall. They had no children.

After quitting office in 1765 Cornwall came under the influence of both Lord Rockingham and Lord Shelburne, and at the latter's recommendation he entered parliament in May 1768 as one of the MPs for Grampound, Cornwall. In the Commons he quickly established himself as a frequent and effective spokesman for the opposition, specializing in East India affairs. When Lord North offered him the opportunity to supervise and regulate the East India Company's activities in Bengal in 1773, Cornwall declined, but within a few months he succumbed to North's more attractive offer of a pension of £500 from West Indies revenues. Cornwall formally crossed the floor of the house when he accepted a place at the Treasury board in 1774, and thereafter he defended the government's American policy, despite his misgivings about the conduct of the war. In October 1774 he was returned as MP for the Treasury seat of Winchelsea, which he exchanged for another Cinque Ports seat, Rye, in April 1784.

On 31 October 1780 Cornwall was elected speaker of the Commons and it was hoped, according to Nathaniel Wraxall, that 'a sonorous Voice, a manly as well as imposing Figure, and a commanding Deportment' would ensure success (*Historical and Posthumous Memoirs*, 1.374–5). Wraxall went on to denounce Cornwall's record as speaker and accused him of being both drunken and bored, a caricature perpetuated by the writers of the satirical *Rolliad*. This was a distorted view of Cornwall's record for, though he never achieved distinction as speaker, his frequent and well-informed interventions from the chair demonstrated initiative and judgement. He called MPs to account for unparliamentary behaviour and ruled on procedural matters, such as allowing the innovation of parliamentary questions in May 1783. Re-elected in 1784, he even had the temerity to vote against a government measure on 27 February 1786 when, after an all-night debate on a motion in favour of fortifying the dockyards, the division was tied. He also held the office of chief justice in eyre north of the Trent from 1780 until his death and was sworn of the privy council on 8 November 1780.

Cornwall died in office on 2 January 1789 at his house in Privy Garden, Whitehall, and was buried on 12 January at the church of St Cross Hospital, Winchester, where a monument was erected to him. One obituarist praised him for having conducted himself with 'an affability, dignity, and rectitude of conduct highly becoming his elevated situation' (*GM*). An aphorism conveyed to a later speaker asserted that 'Mr Speaker Cornwall said of his office: "It is laborious, but not so painful as being forced to defend measures for which I was not properly responsible, and which I did not approve"' (Sidmouth MSS).

WILLIAM HUNT, *rev.* CLARE WILKINSON

**Sources** P. D. G. Thomas, *The House of Commons in the eighteenth century* (1971) · C. Wilkinson, 'The practice and procedure of the House of Commons, *c.*1784–1832', PhD diss., U. Wales, Aberystwyth, 1998 · J. Debrett, ed., *The parliamentary register, or, History of the proceedings and debates of the House of Commons*, 45 vols. (1781–96) · Devon RO, Sidmouth papers · *The historical and the posthumous memoirs of Sir Nathaniel William Wraxall, 1772–1784*, ed. H. B. Wheatley, 5 vols. (1884) · J. Brooke, 'Cornwall, Charles Wolfran', HoP, *Commons, 1754–90* · *GM*, 1st ser., 59 (1789), 87

**Archives** BL, corresp. with Charles Jenkinson, Add. MSS 38201–38580, *passim*
**Likenesses** J. Sayers, etching, pubd 1784, BM, NPG · T. Gainsborough, oils, *c*.1785–1786, National Gallery of Victoria, Melbourne · J. Sayers, etching, pubd 1786, NPG · portrait, Palace of Westminster, London, Speaker's House · portrait, NPG

**Cornwall, Gerard of**. *See* Gerard of Cornwall (*supp. fl. c*.1350).

**Cornwall, Sir James Handyside Marshall-** (1887–1985), army officer and linguist, was born in India on 27 May 1887, the only son and elder child of James Cornwall, postmaster-general of the United Provinces, India, and his wife, Agnes Hunter. He was educated at Rugby School, where he was not happy. In 1905 he went to the Royal Military Academy at Woolwich, which at the time was known as 'The Shop'; its atmosphere was better suited to his temperament. In 1907 he was commissioned into the Royal Field Artillery and posted to Edinburgh, whence, during his first spell of annual leave, he travelled to Germany to study German. He later passed the civil service commission examination as a first-class German interpreter. This was the first of the eleven interpreterships he was to gain. Before the First World War he passed as first-class interpreter in French, Norwegian, Swedish, Hollander Dutch, and Italian.

On the outbreak of war Cornwall was ordered to join the intelligence corps, 'a formation of which I had never heard', and was sent to Le Havre. After the débâcle at Le Cateau he was, rather surprisingly, given command of a squadron of the 15th hussars. In February 1915 he was appointed GSO3 (intelligence) at 2nd corps headquarters in the Second Army, with the rank of captain. In January 1916 he was promoted to the rank of temporary major and was sent to the general headquarters of the British expeditionary force (BEF) as GSO2 (intelligence). This was his first encounter with Sir Douglas Haig, who had recently taken over command of the BEF from Sir John French. Cornwall soon realized that the information given to Haig by his chief intelligence staff officer, Colonel John Charteris, was based more on what he thought his chief would be pleased to hear than on a realistic assessment of the situation. He spent two frustrating years at general headquarters, from which Charteris was eventually transferred. In January 1918 Cornwall was posted to the War Office as head of the MI3 section of the military intelligence directorate, where he remained until the armistice. He won the MC in 1916 and was appointed to the DSO in 1917.

In January 1919 Cornwall was sent to Paris as ex officio member of the general staff delegation at the peace conference. There he struggled, along with Reginald Leeper and Harold Nicolson, with the knotty problems of the new boundaries of Europe. Then followed a spell as student at the Staff College. From 1920 to 1925 he was employed in several jobs in the Middle East, which gave him the opportunity to polish up his Turkish and modern Greek. While encamped in the Izmit peninsula he met Marjorie Coralie Scott Owen (*d*. 1976), who was driving an

**Sir James Handyside Marshall-Cornwall** (1887–1985), by Walter Stoneman, 1936

ambulance for a Red Cross mission to White Russian refugees. They were married in Wales in April 1921. She was the daughter of William Scott Owen.

In 1927 the Baldwin government sent a force to China to protect British life and property in the Shanghai international settlement. Cornwall's position as brigade major in the Royal Artillery (Shanghai defence force) enabled him to learn Chinese and to travel extensively in the Far East with his wife. In the same year he inherited a small estate in Scotland from his maternal uncle, William Marshall, on condition that he should assume the surname of Marshall. As Marshall was one of his forenames, this was achieved by the simple insertion of a hyphen. From 1928 to 1932 he held the post of military attaché in Berlin, where Sir Horace Rumbold was ambassador.

In 1934, after two years as commander of the 51st Highland division, Royal Artillery, based at Perth, Scotland, Marshall-Cornwall was promoted major-general, which, under the peculiar system of those days, left him without a job. The next four years were mainly spent travelling in Europe, India, and the United States. There followed two years in Cairo as head of the British military mission to Egypt, where, not surprisingly, he qualified as an interpreter in colloquial Arabic. In 1938 he was promoted lieutenant-general and was put in charge of the air defence of Great Britain. The year 1940 found him in France helping to evacuate British troops from Cherbourg. He himself boarded the last ship to leave that port when Rommel was only 5 kilometres from the harbour. In

1941, as the only senior serving officer who spoke Turkish, he was sent by Winston Churchill to Turkey in an attempt to persuade the Turks to join the war. He was not unhappy at the failure of this mission, convinced, as he then was, that the Turks would have been more of a liability than an asset to the allied cause.

Marshall-Cornwall took over western command in November 1941, but was dismissed in the autumn of 1942 for going outside the proper channels to secure the safety of the Liverpool docks. He spent the rest of the war with the Special Operations Executive and then MI6.

Retired from the army in 1945 at the age of fifty-eight with the rank of full general, Marshall-Cornwall was still very much in the prime of life, and his later years were as active as his military career had been. Between 1948 and 1951 he was editor-in-chief of captured German archives at the Foreign Office. Arms dealing, writing military history, and presidency of the Royal Geographical Society (1954–8) were among the various activities which crowded the many years left to him.

Short of stature and slight of build, Marshall-Cornwall's outstanding intellect and phenomenal memory more than compensated for his modesty and lack of self-advertisement. He said that towards the end of his life his memory began to fail him, and he was annoyed to find on revisiting Turkey in 1982 that 'all my Turkish was completely outdated'. But anyone reading his autobiography, *Wars and Rumours of Wars* (1984), written in his ninety-seventh year, will deduce that he retained near perfect recall until the end.

The Marshall-Cornwalls had three children. Their only son was killed in France in 1944. He is buried on the spot where he fell in a Normandy orchard, subsequently purchased by Marshall-Cornwall to protect his son's grave, which he visited each year on the anniversary of the death. Their elder daughter died aged fourteen in 1938 after an operation for appendicitis in Switzerland.

Marshall-Cornwall was appointed CBE in 1919, CB in 1936, and KCB in 1940. He died on 25 December 1985 at Birdsall Manor, Malton, Yorkshire, the home of his younger daughter.

LEO COOPER and T.R. HARTMAN, *rev.*

**Sources** J. Marshall-Cornwall, *Wars and rumours of wars* (1984) · personal knowledge (1990) · private information (1990) · *The Times* (27 March 1985) · *WWW* · B. Karslake, *1940 the last act: the story of the British forces in France after Dunkirk* (1979)
**Archives** SOUND IWM SA, oral history interview
**Likenesses** W. Stoneman, photograph, 1936, NPG [*see illus.*]
**Wealth at death** £75,060: probate, 19 Feb 1986, *CGPLA Eng. & Wales*

**Cornwall, John of** (*d.* in or after **1198**), theologian, says of himself that he studied under Master Theoderic, who is presumably the Thierry of Chartres who taught at Paris and died after 1156, and also that he studied at Paris under Peter Lombard, who became bishop of Paris in 1159, and Robert de Melun (*d.* 1167), who left to become bishop of Hereford by 1163. He was apparently present at the Council of Tours in 1163, which was presided over by Pope Alexander III. John in turn left France and became master of a

school. Gerald of Wales (*d.* 1220x23) recounts that John once lampooned the ignorance of parish clergy in the public auditorium of his school: he told the story of a clerk who asked what *busillis* meant, without understanding that at the turn of a page the opening words of one of the gospel readings (*in diebus illis*: 'in those days') had been separated.

This school was probably in Oxford, although definite evidence is lacking, and there is the difficulty that more than one person named Master John of Cornwall may have left his mark on some of the ecclesiastical business transacted there. It may be he who witnessed a charter granted in London by Richard of Ilchester (*d.* 1188), bishop-elect of Winchester, in 1173. He was certainly recommended to Henry II by Master Gerard Pucelle (*d.* 1184) as a proper person to be made bishop of St David's in 1176 on account of his knowledge of the Welsh language, but Geoffrey Ridel, bishop of Ely (*d.* 1189), argued before the king that this knowledge should count against him. He witnessed a decision by papal judges-delegate in a case concerning Guisborough Priory, Yorkshire, heard at Oxford between 1174 and 1180. In 1183–4 he appears sufficiently frequently in witness lists in the *acta* of Walter de Coutances, bishop of Lincoln (*d.* 1207), to suggest that he was a member of Walter's *familia*; Walter was a fellow Cornishman and had been archdeacon of Oxford as well as treasurer of Rouen, of which he became archbishop in 1184. Preferment seems to have followed for John in the form of the archdeaconry of Worcester, where he appears in 1197. He acted as a judge-delegate in settlement of a suit between Osney Abbey, Oxford, and Jordan of Hambledon, probably at Oxford, in October 1192. He was for a second time recommended for the see of St David's in 1198, by Gerald of Wales, again unsuccessfully. It is not known when he died, but if he was identical with the John of Cornwall recorded as a canon of Rouen, he was still alive in 1202.

John of Cornwall undertook an exposition of the prophecies of Merlin. Geoffrey of Monmouth (*d.* 1155), in his *History of the Kings of Britain*, book 7, had earlier stimulated a fresh range of writing about Merlin, and John's is one of the most interesting examples. His work is in the form of a poem of 139 hexameters and of a prose commentary on the first 105 lines; both are written in Latin, but in the commentary Celtic words and phrases appear. Less than a third of the verse prophecies come directly from Geoffrey of Monmouth; the remainder are presumably taken directly from independent Celtic sources. The work suggests a lively interest in the fate and endurance of the Celtic peoples and church. The prophecies have a political character and relate to events in recent English history, such as King Stephen's capture at Lincoln in 1141, as well as to places in Cornwall. According to John in his preface, his work was requested by Robert, bishop of Exeter; this could be either Robert Warelwast (1138–55) or Robert of Chichester (1155–60). Either way, this suggests a date of composition in the 1150s.

John of Cornwall's *Eulogium ad Alexandrum Papam III* is an informative contribution to a lively debate about Christ which attracted the attention of the more speculative theologians in the 1150s. John wrote his work in opposition to the doctrine held by Gilbert de la Porrée, bishop of Poitiers, Peter Abelard, and for a time Peter Lombard, that the humanity of Christ was only a garment (*habitus*) with which the Word clothed itself. The doctrine that Christ was not a man, and that as man Christ was not anything, was debated in the presence of Pope Alexander III at Tours in 1163. *Eulogium* is used in the sense of a wise discourse or proposition. John declares his own belief that Christ was a man: as God, Christ was an incorporeal substance, but as man, he was a bodily creature.

The *Eulogium* was written rather hastily, when the Third Lateran Council, held in 1179, was imminent, and with the intention of pressing Alexander to issue, in place of his earlier admonitions, a solemn condemnation of two of the three opinions concerning the union of the two natures in Christ which had been set forth earlier by Peter Lombard in his *Sentences*, book 3, 6.2–4. John of Cornwall presents these before attacking the masters who advocate the second and the third opinions which amount, in John's view, to a denial that Christ had a human soul and flesh. He then introduces authors who favour the first opinion, which is that Christ was both God and a man with a rational soul and human flesh. These are Anselm of Canterbury (*d.* 1109), Bernard of Clairvaux, Hugh of St Victor, Achard of St Victor (*d.* 1171), Robert de Melun, and Maurice, now bishop of Paris.

John of Cornwall writes that he himself has been slowly converted to the first theory after listening to the attacks on Peter Lombard delivered in lectures and disputations by Robert de Melun and Maurice. He presents texts from scripture and the church fathers and gives reasons in support of his appeal to the pope to restore agreement 'by a general, everlasting decree' (*Eulogium*, 299). John later added a *Retractatio* in order to clarify some of his statements and quotations and to add, in a preface, a transcript of Alexander's first decretal on the subject, censuring Peter Lombard; this had been issued at Veroli on 28 May 1170, and sent to William, archbishop then of Sens but now (from 1176) of Rheims. The *Eulogium* must have been composed between 1176 and 1179, and revised before 1181, the year of Alexander III's death.

Fragments of John's theological teaching survive in two glosses on the *Decretum* preserved in Cambridge, Gonville and Caius College, MS 676, which appears to come from the Oxford schools. Other works that have been ascribed to John are: a treatise on the mass in Cambridge, Corpus Christi College, MS 459 (*incipit* 'In virtute sancte crucis et sacramenti altaris', ascribed to John but in fact by Richard de Prémontré); an *Apologia de Christi incarnatione*, also called *De verbo incarnato* or *De homine assumpto*, which treats of the same subject as the *Eulogium* but is possibly the work of a canon of St Victor, Paris; and a commentary on the *Posterior Analytics* which is ascribed to John of St Germans, a later master, not identical with John of Cornwall (though the two have been confused). John is also credited by Bale with *Disceptationes quaedam*, *Epistolae*, and *Commentarii scripturarum*, of which nothing is known; and also (but

conjecturally) with an unprinted work, *De diversa consuetudine legendi sacram scripturam*, which is found in BL, Royal MS 8 G. ix and which was written by one who attended lectures given by Peter Lombard and perhaps Robert de Melun.

DAVID LUSCOMBE

**Sources** E. Rathbone, 'John of Cornwall: a brief biography', *Recherches de Théologie Ancienne et Médiévale*, 17 (1950), 46–60 • 'A new edition of John of Cornwall's *Prophetia Merlini*', ed. M. J. Curley, *Speculum*, 57 (1982), 217–49 • 'The *Eulogium ad Alexandrum Papam tertium* of John of Cornwall', *Mediaeval Studies*, 13 (1951), 253–300 • Emden, *Oxf.*, 1.489–90 • *Gir. Camb. opera*, 1. 133; 2. 343 • D. M. Smith, ed., *Lincoln, 1067–1185*, English Episcopal Acta, 1 (1980), xlvi–xlvii [witnesses to nos. 301, 313, 317, 319, 323] • M. J. Franklin, ed., *Winchester, 1070–1204*, English Episcopal Acta, 8 (1993), 104 • *Fasti Angl., 1066–1300*, [Monastic cathedrals], 106 • A. G. Rigg, *A history of Anglo-Latin literature, 1066–1422* (1992), 47 • G. F. Warner and J. P. Gilson, *Catalogue of Western manuscripts in the old Royal and King's collections*, 1 (1921), 227 • Bale, *Cat.*, 1.215

**Cornwall** [Bryan], **John** (*d.* 1349), schoolmaster and grammarian, described himself in his will as 'John Bryan of Cornwall [Cornubia]', making it likely that he originated in that county. He occurs as an inhabitant of Oxford in 1341 and as master of a grammar school there between 1344 and 1349, his school lying between Catte Street and Schools Street, opposite the city wall and near the present-day north range of the Bodleian Library. His pupils included the young scholars of Merton College, Oxford, and he also paid dues for selling ale. He made his will on 8 June 1349, instructing his executors to dispose of his school, pay his debts, and employ the rest of his estate in pious works for his soul and that of his wife, Agnes. She evidently predeceased him and they seem to have had no surviving children. He was dead by 8 July, when the will was registered.

Oxford was a major centre of resort for school, as well as university, education in England during the later middle ages, and Cornwall appears to have been one of the most influential Oxford (and therefore English) schoolmasters of this period. According to the historian Ranulf Higden, writing in the 1320s, it was the custom in English grammar schools for children to be taught Latin through the medium of French and to construe Latin into French rather than English. John Trevisa, who translated Higden into English in 1387, observed that this custom had changed since the black death of 1348–9, 'For Johan Cornwal, a mayster of gramere, chaynegde the lore in gramerscole and construccion of Freynsch into Englysch', in other words employing the English language for teaching purposes (Sisam, 148–9). Trevisa, who studied at Oxford in the 1360s and was also a Cornishman, may have overestimated Cornwall's influence in this respect, since there are signs that English was used in schools in the twelfth and thirteenth centuries, but he may well be correct that Cornwall promoted and typified the adoption of English for all vernacular purposes, which took hold in schools during the second half of the fourteenth century.

Cornwall was the author of a treatise on Latin grammar entitled *Speculum gramaticale*. It is dated 1346 and also describes its author as J. Bryan of Cornwall. The work is a lengthy and detailed survey of Latin grammar and syntax, illustrating its points with *latinitates* (model Latin sentences) which show the parts of speech in use. It appears to have had at least a modest circulation. The sole surviving manuscript (Bodl. Oxf., MS Auct. F.3.9, pp. 1–180) was written in the first half of the fifteenth century and belonged to Coventry Cathedral priory, but another recorded copy was owned by John Bracebridge, schoolmaster of Lincoln in 1406, who gave it to Syon Abbey, Middlesex. Some of Cornwall's *latinitates* refer to everyday life and current affairs, following a strategy common among late medieval grammarians, and the use of English in schools is reflected by the inclusion of English glosses and translations of a few of the Latin sentences.

NICHOLAS ORME

**Sources** 'Speculum gramaticale', Bodl. Oxf., MS Auct. F.3.9 · extracts from Cornwall's will, Bodl. Oxf., MS Twyne 23, 335–6 · H. E. Salter, *Survey of Oxford*, 1, ed. W. A. Pantin, OHS, 14 (1960), 86 · R. W. Hunt, 'Oxford grammar masters in the middle ages', *Oxford studies presented to Daniel Callus*, OHS, new ser., 16 (1964), 163–93 · Emden, *Oxf.*, 1.490 · K. Sisam, ed., *Fourteenth century verse and prose* (1955), 148–9
**Archives** Bodl. Oxf., MS Auct. F.3.9, pp. 1–180
**Wealth at death** extracts from will: Bodl. Oxf., MS Twyne 23, 335–6

**Cornwall, Michael of** [Michael le Poter, Michael Blaunpayn] (*fl.* 1243–1255), poet, has left no mark on the historical record apart from his verses. He appears to have studied philosophy and taken a master's degree, perhaps at Cambridge. In 1243 he wrote a short humorous poem to the doctors caring for the broken leg of the royal counsellor John Mansell, threatening them with the king's displeasure should the cure go badly. He studied rhetoric under Master Henry d'Avranches, with whom in 1254–5 he contested the series of flytings for which both poets have been best known. Michael and Henry competed in exchanging exaggerated insults and accusations of plagiarism conveyed in elaborately rhymed Latin verse; unfortunately, only Michael's side survives. Michael won the first contest, which was judged by the bishop of Ely. In a parody of the procedure of the ecclesiastical courts, Henry appealed the decision before the official of the archbishop of Canterbury in St Mary-le-Bow on 5 February 1255: this is only the second appeal case known to have been heard by the incipient court of arches. By this time Michael resided in London, where, he alleges, Henry and an accomplice broke his strongbox and stole not only his savings but a book of his verses, which Henry plagiarized. Michael triumphed in the second round as well; the outcome of the third and longest competition, before the king's half-brother Aymer de Valence and other judges, is not known. Other fanciful details of Michael's life, such as his title of dean of Utrecht, are due to the attribution to him of some of Henry's verses by Robert Cotton's librarian, Richard James. A short religious poem by him also survives, headed 'Magister Michael le Poter de Cornubia'; the name Blaunpayn ('White Bread') was given to him by the antiquarians.

In the flytings Michael defended his Cornish heritage against Henry's slurs, claiming the special favour of King Arthur and even punning on Henry's name in Cornish.

Some of his complex rhyme schemes, rare in Latin, may possibly have been based on Celtic models; they also occur in his other surviving work, a brief poem on the fall. Michael championed England against Henry's Norman stock, with a topical passage in which a feeble, disconsolate Normandy alternately hurls empty defiance and laments her domination by the usurping French king. The patrons of the flytings span the deep political division between the Poitevin and Savoyard parties, showing that Michael's nationalism did not express itself in adherence to a political faction at court. Of his career after the flytings nothing is known; J. C. Russell's claim that he wrote a chronicle of the barons' wars is very doubtful.

PETER BINKLEY

**Sources** A. Hilka, ed., 'Eine mittellateinishe Dichterfehde: *Versus Michaelis Cornubiensis contra Henricum Abrincensem*', *Mittelalterliche Handschriften: Festgabe zum 60. Geburtstag von Hermann Degering*, ed. A. Bömer and J. Kirchner (Leipzig, 1926), 123–54; repr. (Hildesheim, 1973) · P. Binkley, 'The date and setting of Michael of Cornwall's *Versus contra Henricum Abrincensem*', *Medium Aevum*, 60 (1991), 76–84 · A. G. Rigg, *A history of Anglo-Latin literature, 1066–1422* (1992), 193–208 · *The shorter Latin poems of Master Henry of Avranches relating to England*, ed. J. C. Russell and J. P. Heironimus (1935); repr. (1970), 149–57

**Cornwall, Peter of** (1139/40–1221), scholar and prior of Holy Trinity, Aldgate, was born on his father's estates in or near Launceston, Cornwall, the son of Jordan of Trecarrel (*d. c.*1180), sometime *praepositus* (or provost) of Launceston. In his *Liber revelationum*, book 1, chapter 6, he gives some account of his father's character, and he relates stories concerning his grandfather Ailsi and his uncles, Jordan's brothers, of whom the two eldest, Bernard and Nicholas, were *scriptores* in the royal chapel in the time of Henry I. Peter also mentions his kinship by marriage to Reginald de Dunstanville, earl of Cornwall; whence it has been conjectured that Peter's mother was a sister of the earl's wife, Beatrice, daughter of William fitz Richard of Cardinan, the most important of the local nobility.

Little is known of Peter's early career. He studied in London where his teacher was Master Henry of Northampton, a canon of St Paul's, who was often in residence during the 1170s and 1180s. Godfrey de Lucy, later bishop of Winchester, is once referred to as his fellow student. After 1170 he was received as an Augustinian canon by Prior Stephen at Holy Trinity, Aldgate—the mother house from which the priory in his home town of Launceston had been founded. In Stephen's company he attended a synod in London, where a sermon preached by Gilbert Foliot, bishop of London, provided the inspiration for Peter's first work of scholarship, the massive *Pantheologus*, completed in 1189. In this book he presented a great quantity of biblical material organized by subject as an aid for preachers, using the method of treating a scriptural theme *per distinctiones*—that is, presenting interpretations of words schematically, according to the various senses in which they could be interpreted. Of the extant copies, there is one complete set in a contemporary hand, BL, Royal MSS 7 E.viii, 7 C.xiii, 7 C.xiv; this belonged to the library of

Rochester Cathedral priory and may have been a presentation copy from Peter to his friend Gilbert de Glanville, bishop of Rochester.

In 1197 Peter succeeded Stephen as prior of Holy Trinity, Aldgate, one of the three major religious houses in London. He continued in office until his death on 7 July 1221, and was buried at the priory. He was a conscientious administrator and was remembered as a great teacher. In 1210 Peter and his friend Benedict, abbot of Stratford Langthorn, acted as intermediaries between King John and Stephen Langton, archbishop of Canterbury, unsuccessfully seeking a reconciliation and an end to the interdict.

Peter of Cornwall is now remembered principally for his scholarship, which was of a compilatory rather than an original nature. His *De reparatione lapsus generis humani* (Som. ARS, MS DD/AH 66/17) is dedicated to Gilbert de Glanville. This work is referred to in the *Liber disputationum contra Symonem Iudeum* (Eton College, MS 130, fols. 92–226v), which Peter dedicated to Stephen Langton in exile during the interdict (1208–11). The biblical compilation intended to introduce the latter work does not survive. Peter's personal manuscript of his *Liber revelationum* (LPL, MS 51) is an immense collection of visions relating to the next life, compiled between 1200 (in which year he was aged sixty) and 1206. It is largely derivative, but it contains some stories written from his own experience and that of his personal acquaintances, including an account of his family and its devotion to St Stephen's Church, Launceston. These personal stories, together with the prefaces to his theological compilations, provide the principal evidence for his career.      RICHARD SHARPE, *rev.*

**Sources** R. W. Hunt, 'The disputation of Peter of Cornwall against Simon the Jew', *Studies in medieval history presented to F. M. Powicke*, ed. R. W. Hunt, W. A. Pantin, and R. W. Southern (1948), 143–56 · P. L. Hull and R. Sharpe, 'Peter of Cornwall and Launceston', *Cornish Studies*, 13 (1985), 3–53 · R. W. Hunt, 'English learning in the late twelfth century', *TRHS*, 4th ser., 19 (1936), 19–42

**Cornwall, Richard of** ( *fl.* 1237). *See under* Cornwall, Richard of ( *fl. c.*1238–*c.*1259).

**Cornwall, Richard of** [Richard Rufus of Cornwall] ( *fl. c.*1238–*c.*1259), Franciscan friar and theologian, presumably came from south-west England. He studied arts at Paris before he entered the Franciscan order in 1238 (not in 1230 as is sometimes assumed). After returning to England to make his profession of vows he went on to study theology at Oxford. In 1248 Giovanni da Parma, the minister-general, gave him permission to continue his studies at Paris, but, probably because of ill health, Richard stayed at Oxford, where he lectured on the *Sentences* about the year 1250. In 1253 he decided to avail himself of the general's permission after all, and to transfer to Paris. The reason probably was that in March of that year the Franciscan community gave Thomas of York permission to incept in theology and become their official lector at Oxford, although Thomas was much younger and less well prepared for the job.

In Paris Richard lectured on the *Sentences* once more, although accounts vary as to whether he did so 'cursorily', essentially giving a running commentary on the text, or 'solemnly', in greater depth. However, in 1256, when Thomas of York was transferred to Cambridge, Richard of Cornwall returned to England, succeeding Thomas to become fifth lecturer to the Oxford convent. He is last mentioned in November 1259, when he was bequeathed a habit and a copy of the canonical epistles by Martin de Sancta Cruce, master of the hospital of Sherburn near Durham. Although he was respected by his fellow Franciscan Adam Marsh, who in 1253 tried to find a secretary for him, he owes his fame to the fact that in 1292 Roger Bacon called him a bad and stupid man, and an inventor of some serious philosophical errors.

It is now generally accepted that the lecture course on the first three books of the *Sentences*, preserved in Oxford, Balliol College, MS 62, and partly also in BL, Royal MS 8 C.iv, represents Richard of Cornwall's Oxford lectures. His other major work is an abbreviation and critical assessment of Bonaventure's commentary on the *Sentences*, preserved complete in Vatican City, Biblioteca Apostolica Vaticana, MS Lat. 12993 (books 1–2), and Assisi, Sacro Convento, MS 176 (books 3–4), and in part in other manuscripts. It is a matter of debate, whether he composed the abbreviation in Paris in the years 1253–6, or in Oxford during his years as lector. But since it is likely that Bonaventure did not prepare the final version of his commentary before 1256, the latter solution seems more probable. If so, Richard was a pioneer in introducing the teaching of the Paris schools to Oxford.

A number of Richard of Cornwall's disputed questions, one of which is explicitly ascribed to *magistrum ruffum cornubiensem*, can be found in two collections that reflect the teaching of the Franciscan school at Paris in the second quarter of the thirteenth century. One of these, preserved in Assisi, Sacro Convento, MS 138, was certainly used, and perhaps even compiled, by Bonaventure himself, whose pencilled notes are scribbled all over the margins.

Far less certain is the attribution to Richard of four other works. The first is a collection of *Abstractiones*, written by a Ricardus Sophista in England before 1250 (Bodl. Oxf., MS Digby 24, fol. 90r, and other manuscripts). Although it has not yet been possible to identify the author, it must be said that there are no parallels between this work and the two *Sentences* commentaries. The second is a commentary on Aristotle's *Metaphysics* written in Oxford about 1235. Although this work, which survives in four manuscripts, is in one of them ascribed in a contemporary hand to a Master Richard (probably even Rufi de Cornubia), the opinions defended in it are flatly contradicted in the Oxford *Sentences* commentary, so that the two works can hardly have been written by the same author. The conclusion must be either that this commentary is spurious or, more radically, that all the other works attributed to Richard are probably not his, with the exception of the one disputed question explicitly attributed to him, a solution that so far has not met with general approval. It seems most unlikely that a Franciscan friar, studying theology, should have written a philosophical work at the same time.

In 1992 the claim was made that two early commentaries on Aristotle, on the *Physics*, and the *Posterior Analytics*, preserved in Erfurt, Bibliotheca Amploniana, MS qu.312, represented the result of Richard's training in the arts at Paris. Much of the argument depends on accepting the authenticity of the *Metaphysics* commentary. But even if these two works are not Richard's, it is still possible to characterize him as a theologian whose main concern was the introduction of Aristotelian natural philosophy into the tradition of Christian theology, especially on such questions as the status of theology as a science, God's knowledge of things outside himself, and the eternity of the world. As such he was a pioneer at Oxford, where, in Grosseteste's shadow, a more traditional approach to theology had prevailed until then.

Another **Richard of Cornwall** (*fl.* 1237) is mentioned in two letters by Robert Grosseteste. He was recommended to the bishop by Cardinal Aegidius Hispanus, and given a prebend in the diocese of Lincoln probably in 1237. Grosseteste encouraged him to take the care of souls very seriously. It is not certain whether this prebendary is identical with the subdeacon Richard of Cornwall, whose lack of fluency in the English language is mentioned in a letter of Adam Marsh to Grosseteste in 1248.

PETER RAEDTS

**Sources** *Fratris Thomae vulgo dicti de Eccleston tractatus de adventu Fratrum Minorum in Angliam*, ed. A. G. Little (1951) · R. Bacon, *Compendium of the study of theology*, ed. T. S. Maloney (1988) · P. Raedts, *Richard Rufus of Cornwall and the tradition of Oxford theology*, Oxford Historical Monographs (1987) · T. Noone, 'Richard Rufus of Cornwall and the authorship of the *Scriptum super metaphysicam*', *Franciscan Studies*, new ser., 49 (1989), 55–91 · R. Wood, 'Richard Rufus of Cornwall on creation: the reception of Aristotelian physics in the west', *Medieval philosophy and theology*, 2 (1992), 1–30 · S. T. Brown, 'The eternity of the world discussion at early Oxford', *Mensch und Natur im Mittelalter*, ed. A. Zimmermann and A. Speer, 2 vols., Miscellanea Mediaevalia, 21 (1991), 1.259–80 · *Roberti Grosseteste episcopi quondam Lincolniensis epistolae*, ed. H. R. Luard, Rolls Series, 25 (1861) · J. S. Brewer and R. Howlett, eds., *Monumenta Franciscana*, 2 vols., Rolls Series, 4 (1858–82) · R. Wood and R. Andrews, 'Causality and demonstration: an early scholastic *Posterior Analytics* commentary', *The Monist*, 79 (1996), 325–56
**Archives** Balliol Oxf., MS 62 · Biblioteca Apostolica Vaticana, Vatican City, MS Lat. 12993 · Bibliotheca Amploniana, Erfurt, MS qu.312 · BL, MS Royal 8 C.iv · Bodl. Oxf., MS Digby 24, fol. 90r · Sacro Convento, Assisi, MSS 138, 176

**Cornwallis**. For this title name *see* individual entries under Cornwallis; *see also* Bacon, Jane, Lady Bacon [Jane Cornwallis, Lady Cornwallis] (1580/81–1659).

**Cornwallis, Caroline Frances** (1786–1858), author and feminist, was born on 12 July 1786 at Wittersham, Kent, the second of two daughters of Revd William Cornwallis (1751–1827), rector of Elham and Wittersham in Kent. Her mother, Mary (*née* Harris), wrote a number of religious works, including *A Preparation for the Lord's Supper … Intended for the Use of Ladies* (1826; 3rd edn, 1838), which revealed views similar to those of the evangelical Hannah More. Caroline Cornwallis demonstrated remarkable

intellectual capacity as a child and wrote prodigiously from the age of seven. In 1803 her sister, to whom she had been extremely close, died following the birth of her first child. In her grief, Cornwallis pledged herself to a frugal way of life, devoting herself to scholarship and to her parents, and living 'as if there had been no gaieties in the world' (Cornwallis to Miss Liscomb, 25 Dec 1844; Cornwallis, 268). During this period, despite poor health, she learned many languages, including Latin, Greek, Hebrew, German, Anglo-Saxon, and Ancient Egyptian, as well as studying philosophy, science, history, law, theology, and politics. In 1826 she moved to Pescia, Italy, where she was lent a house by a close friend, the historian Jean Charles L. Simonde de Sismondi. The change in environment and beauty of the Italian landscape appear to have given her a new zest for life. However, she continued to study as hard as ever, focusing on mineralogy and Tuscan law. In 1827 she travelled to England to be with her mother, following the death of her father, and returned to Italy in 1829 before settling permanently in Kent, where she owned farm property.

In 1842 Cornwallis's first published work appeared, *Philosophical Theories and Philosophical Experience, by a Pariah*. This formed the first volume of an ambitious project, Small Books on Great Subjects. The aim was to popularize difficult subjects for a general readership and was the result of a collaboration between Cornwallis and a small group of unnamed friends, whom she called the ABC Society. The majority of the twenty-two volumes, covering a remarkable variety of subjects, including philosophy, chemistry, theology, grammar, geology, and criminal law, were written by Cornwallis herself, and enjoyed a wide readership in both Britain and America.

A committed Christian, Cornwallis also wrote on the decline of Christianity and the need for it to be understood as a philosophical system based upon rational principles (see, for example, her contribution to the Small Books series, *On the State of Man Subsequent to the Promulgation of Christianity*, 1851–4). She had earlier been involved in the production of her mother's theological works, though she came to describe herself as an episcopalian, distancing herself from her mother's evangelicalism. In 1846 Cornwallis wrote a historical novel, *Pericles*, which received some favourable reviews, but she did not carry out her intention of writing a sequel.

In the latter part of her life Cornwallis became particularly interested in schemes to prevent crime, arguing firmly that prevention was better than punishment. The solution she most favoured was the establishment of 'ragged schools', offering a basic education to the most destitute of children. She suggested that school meals might be provided and that children should also be instructed in a trade. In 1853 her essay on juvenile delinquency was bracketed with that of Micaiah Hill for a prize of £200 offered by Lady Byron. Cornwallis believed that the suffrage might be extended to all classes of society once education was enjoyed by all.

Throughout her life Cornwallis felt frustrated and inhibited by the position of women within contemporary society. She longed to have enjoyed the academic opportunities open to men of her class and chafed against the domestic duties which had distracted her from her studies. By the 1840s her private letters reveal that such feelings were developing into a deeply held feminist consciousness—comparing women's position to that of black slaves and calling for women's emancipation and the vindication of their rights. These sentiments were given their fullest expression in two seminal articles on the inequities of married women's legal position which appeared in the advanced Liberal journal the *Westminster Review* in 1856 and 1857. Written at the height of the bitter debates then raging in parliament over proposed changes to married women's legal rights, the anonymous essays became widely cited and proved to be very influential. It is by these essays that Cornwallis is best remembered. She used her extensive grasp of the workings of the law to trace the development and social purposes of the system of common law. With the use of telling examples she argued that by denying property rights to married women the law revealed itself to be a relic from a 'semi-barbarous' age. Cornwallis maintained that such a system degraded not only marital relations but the whole tenor of society. She advocated legal reform based upon the principle of the 'inalienable rights' of every human being. Only then, she insisted, might women make their full contribution to society. At the time of writing the articles Cornwallis was extremely ill, but she persevered in their composition, believing that it was a cause 'of the deepest import to the highest interests of humanity' (*Selections*, vii).

In addition to her scholarly interests Cornwallis was also artistically gifted—a favourite pastime was to create models from wax. However, this interest was overshadowed by her great passion for science. She was extremely knowledgeable on contemporary developments and discoveries. She was friendly with Michael Faraday, who, she was pleased to report with characteristic self-confidence, 'allows me to question his notions' (Cornwallis to Miss Mansfield, 1844; *Selections*, 260). A single woman (she turned down a marriage proposal from Sismondi), Cornwallis enjoyed the companionship of a circle of many such accomplished friends. She was particularly close to David Power QC, the author of several works on electoral law, and to Samuel Birch, the orientalist, who shared her views on women's position. She was cousin to the mother of Dorothea Beale, the celebrated pioneer of girls' schools, and while Miss Beale did not know Cornwallis personally, she claimed that her relative's literary achievements had been a great inspiration to her. Cornwallis was described as 'large-featured, tall and thin' (*DNB*), though in her self-portrait she presented herself as tall and rather glamorous, with striking eyes. She suffered from debilitating illness for much of her life and was often bedridden. However, this physical weakness was greatly belied by her vigorous and dominant personality. Cornwallis died at her home, Sidwells, Goudhurst, Kent, on 8 January 1858, and was buried in the churchyard of Linton, near Maidstone.

KATHRYN GLEADLE

**Sources** *Selections from the letters of Caroline Frances Cornwallis*, ed. M. C. Power (1864) · *DNB* · E. Raikes, *Dorothea Beale of Cheltenham* (1908) · *Wellesley index* · will, 1 Dec 1837 [with later codicils] · *GM*, 1st ser., 96/1 (1826), 504 · d. cert.
**Archives** Yale U., Beinecke L., commonplace book
**Likenesses** C. Cornwallis, self-portrait
**Wealth at death** under £7000: probate, 11 Feb 1858, *CGPLA Eng. & Wales*

**Cornwallis, Sir Charles** (*c.*1555–1629), courtier and diplomat, was the second son of Sir Thomas *Cornwallis (1518/19–1604), and his wife, Anne (*d.* 1581), daughter of Sir John Jerningham or Jernegan of Somerleyton, Suffolk. Cornwallis's father was a noted Catholic who had taken part in the coup which gave Mary I the throne, and under her was appointed a privy councillor and comptroller of the household. Despite his religion he raised both his sons as protestants, perhaps realizing that they would need to conform in order to advance. Cornwallis matriculated from Trinity College, Cambridge, in 1566, and in 1578 he married Anne (*bap.* 1551, *d.* 1584), daughter and coheir of Thomas Fincham of Fincham, Norfolk, and widow of Richard Nicholls of Islington, Norfolk. Their union produced two sons, including Sir William *Cornwallis the younger, essayist, before Anne died. In 1585 Cornwallis married Anne (*d.* 1617), daughter of Thomas Barrow of Barningham, Suffolk, and widow of Sir Ralph Shelton, of Shelton, Norfolk.

Cornwallis pursued a life at court and he had a meteoric rise under the patronage of Robert Cecil, earl of Salisbury, to whom he was connected by marriage. On 11 July 1603 he was knighted. The following year he was elected MP for Norfolk, and he was allowed to retain his seat in the Commons even when, the next year, he was appointed resident ambassador to Spain. He had an uncomfortable trip to Madrid, being ill and confined to a litter for most of the journey, as well as quarrelling over precedence with the earl of Nottingham, who had been sent to Spain to ratify the 1604 peace treaty. Cornwallis's main task in Madrid was to oversee the provisions of the treaty which allowed the English to practise their religion in private and protected merchants from the harassment of the Inquisition. He was required to deal with many complaints from English merchants that their goods had been seized by the Spanish under the pretence of searching for forbidden protestant literature. While in Madrid he provided valuable intelligence on Spain for Salisbury and busied himself writing treatises on the state of the country, the history of Aragon, the structure of the Spanish court, and the wealth of the nobility (BL, Add. MSS 4149, 39853). From 1607 he petitioned to be relieved from his post, claiming poverty and harassment from English Catholic exiles. He was finally granted leave to return to England in 1609.

Cornwallis resumed his place in the Commons when he returned and in 1610 was appointed treasurer of the household to Henry, prince of Wales. He was often in attendance upon Henry and found him an impressive figure, later writing 'A discourse of the most illustrious Prince Henry, late prince of Wales' (1641). It was rumoured in 1612 that he would be made master of the court of wards but after the deaths of Henry and Salisbury the same year he received no further court or government office. In 1613 he was appointed a commissioner to investigate the elections to the Irish parliament and while there he set down his views on the people and the nation, describing them as 'naked barbarians' (BL, Add. MS 39853, fol. 2v).

Upon his return to England, Cornwallis sought election to the 1614 parliament for Eye in Suffolk but before he arrived there he learned that the election had already taken place. During the parliament John Hoskins bitterly denounced the Scots and their influence over James I and, when questioned, claimed that he was echoing the views of Cornwallis, whom he had met on the road to Eye. Called before the privy council, Cornwallis denied that he had suggested Hoskins attack the Scots but his guilt was seemingly confirmed when a letter was published in London in which he asked the king for forgiveness. He was committed to the Tower and on his release in June 1615 retired to the country to live at his ancestral home, Brome Hall, Suffolk, and at Harborne, Staffordshire. His second wife died in 1617 and three years later on 29 April 1620 he married Dorothy, daughter of Richard *Vaughan of Nyffryn in Llŷn, Caernarvonshire, bishop of London, and widow of Bishop John Jegon of Norwich. Cornwallis died at Harborne on 21 December 1629, survived by his wife.

CHRIS R. KYLE

**Sources** HoP, *Commons* [draft] · P. Croft, 'Englishmen and the Spanish Inquisition, 1558–1625', *EngHR*, 87 (1972), 249–68 · A. Clarke, 'Pacification, plantation, and the Catholic question, 1603–23', *A new history of Ireland*, ed. T. W. Moody and others, 3: *Early modern Ireland, 1534–1691* (1976), 187–232, esp. 211–17 · BL, Add. MS 4149, fols. 132–58 · BL, Add. MS 39853, fols. 1–5, 21, 23–24v, 29v–69 · *APC, 1613–14*, 174–5, 188 · *JHC*, 1 (1547–1628) · W. Harvey, *The visitation of Norfolk in the year 1563*, ed. G. H. Dashwood and others, 1 (1878), 43, 114; 2 (1895), 370, 394, 405 · *The letters of John Chamberlain*, ed. N. E. McClure, 1 (1939), 540–43 · P. McGrath and J. Rowe, 'The recusancy of Sir Thomas Cornwallis', *Proceedings of the Suffolk Institute of Archaeology*, 28 (1958–60), 226–71 · BL, Stowe MS 574, fols. 59–61v · PRO, SP 14/77/42, 43; 14/80/115 · J. W. Stoye, *English travellers abroad, 1604–1667* (1952), 331–57 · J. P. Malcolm, *Londinium redivivum, or, An antient history and modern description of London*, 4 vols. (1802–7), vol. 1, p. 305 · Suffolk RO, Iveagh MSS, Cornwallis MS 1/2 · M. K. Dale, 'Cornwallis, Sir Thomas', HoP, *Commons, 1509–58*, 1.708–9
**Archives** BL, corresp. and papers, Add. MS 39853 · BL, Cotton MSS, corresp. · BL, Harley MSS, papers relating to negotiations in Spain, etc. · Bodl. Oxf., 'Embassy to Spain' [copy] · Harvard U., life of Prince Henry · Hunt. L., corresp. and papers · LUL, 'Discourse of the estate of Spaine' · NL Scot., life of prince of Wales [copy] | BL, letters to Sir Thomas Edmonds, Stowe MSS 168–171
**Likenesses** print (Sir Charles Cornwallis?), repro. in W. Cornwallis, *Essayes* (1632) · print, NPG

**Cornwallis, Charles**, first Marquess Cornwallis (1738–1805), governor-general of India and lord lieutenant of Ireland, the sixth child and eldest son of Charles Cornwallis, fifth Baron and first Earl Cornwallis (1700–1762), and his wife, Elizabeth (d. 1785), daughter of Charles 'Turnip' *Townshend, second Viscount Townshend (1674–1738), was born in Grosvenor Square, London, on 31 December 1738. Lord Townshend, his maternal grandfather, was brother-in-law to Sir Robert Walpole. The family's origins are obscure, possibly Irish, though both the name and the Cornish choughs that adorn the family arms suggest a

Charles Cornwallis, first Marquess Cornwallis (1738–1805), by John Smart, 1792

Cornwall connection. In the fourteenth century Thomas Cornwallis (d. 1384), a sheriff of London, and his son John settled the family at Brome, near Eye, in Suffolk. By the mid-sixteenth century, the Cornwallises had consolidated their position by exceptional loyalty to the crown, a trait which Charles Cornwallis inherited. Sir Thomas *Cornwallis (1518/19–1604) built the family manor, Brome Hall. His grandson Sir Frederick (d. 1662), who had fought for Charles I, followed Charles II into exile. After the Restoration he was rewarded by being made treasurer, privy councillor, and, in 1661, first Baron Cornwallis of Eye. His status as a peer was supportable in part because he had inherited in 1660 the estate of Culford, also in Suffolk, near Bury St Edmunds, but it was not until the first marquess's time that the family achieved a fortune to match its acres. Charles Cornwallis's father has been described by his son's biographers as 'a loyal but plodding servant of the crown' (Wickwire and Wickwire, *War of Independence*, 15), who held no office of the first rank. Nevertheless, he was well connected at court and, through his wife, to Walpole, and in 1753 he was created Earl Cornwallis and Viscount Brome. In 1768 the same connections helped secure the election of a younger brother, Frederick *Cornwallis (1713–1783), as archbishop of Canterbury.

**Early life and education** Charles Cornwallis, styled Viscount Brome during his father's lifetime, attended Eton College for at least a year; in December 1753 he was listed in the sixth form. He always viewed Eton with affection, and in 1790 he joined the new Eton Club in Calcutta. A passionate hunter and sportsman, he yearned for military glory from childhood, but his chances of an army career were almost scuppered at Eton when Shute Barrington, later bishop of Durham, struck him in the eye during a hockey game. The injury eventually healed, leaving him with slightly skewed vision and a permanently quizzical look. On 8 December 1756 he obtained a commission as an ensign in the 1st foot guards. He had matriculated at Clare College, Cambridge, in Easter 1756, but he sought a military education and in 1757, with the king's permission, he toured the continent with a Prussian officer, Captain H. G. de Roguin, and studied at the Turin military academy. At Geneva in the summer of 1758, he learned that the guards had been ordered to join Prince Ferdinand of Brunswick for the defence of Hanover against the French and Austrians. Having missed joining his regiment, he attached himself as a volunteer to Frederick's army, and for his forwardness was rewarded with appointment as aide-de-camp to the marquess of Granby. He served Granby for over a year, and was at the battle of Minden. In August 1759 he was made captain in the 85th regiment and in June 1761 he was promoted lieutenant-colonel of the 12th regiment. He and his regiment served with distinction at the battle of Kirch Denkern on 15 July 1761 and, in the following summer, at the battles of Wilhelmstadt and Lutterberg.

Meanwhile, Cornwallis had also embarked upon a political career both conventional and yet curiously principled. With a number of siblings and his own military career he urgently needed lucrative office, but he disliked politicking and always put his own sense of honour and personal loyalties above party. Elected MP for the family scot and lot pocket borough of Eye, Suffolk, in January 1760, he inherited the earldom following his father's death on 23 June 1762, and sat in the Lords from the following November. In many ways a natural conservative, especially in his views on the hierarchical ordering of society, he nevertheless allied himself with the Rockingham whigs. He was loyal to the crown and establishment but, in the manner of the old country whigs, whose mantle the Rockinghamites claimed, he was wary of overweening monarchical power and 'big', financially irresponsible government. In 1763 these views, and his friendship with the duke of Newcastle, sent him north to Scotland to rally support for the whig opposition. They also led him to support Wilkes in his battle against charges of sedition. Government spies reported that the two men had met privately in autumn 1763 and in November Cornwallis was one of seventeen peers who signed Lord Temple's protest against the Commons' resolution that 'the privilege of parliament does not extend to cases of seditious libel'. In 1765 he voted with the Rockinghamites against the imposition of the Stamp Act on the American colonies, and when Rockingham won government later that year he was rewarded for his support by being made an aide-de-camp to the king and a lord of the bedchamber. He relinquished the latter in return for the promise of a regiment, and in March 1766 became colonel of the 33rd foot. In 1766 he also voted with the Rockinghamites to repeal the Stamp Act and to outlaw general warrants (by which the previous government had arrested Wilkes and confiscated his property). But he was not a blind follower of party, and when Rockingham attempted to ameliorate

the implications of the Stamp Act's repeal by passing the Declaratory Act, which asserted Britain's right to legislate for the colonies under all circumstances, Cornwallis joined the five peers who voted against it. Moreover, when the ministry fell in August 1766, Cornwallis did not go into opposition. One of his closest friends was Lord Shelburne, alongside whom he had fought in Germany, and who had also opposed the Declaratory Act. Shelburne was willing to serve in Chatham's new administration and in December 1766, following his friend's lead, Cornwallis accepted from the government the chief justiceship in eyre south of the Trent. In 1768, when Shelburne resigned from the government, Cornwallis also withdrew his support and thereafter did not align himself with any political grouping. Nevertheless, he continued to receive the government's favours, and in 1769 he resigned his chief justiceship to obtain the office of vice-treasurer of Ireland. On 21 November 1770 he was made a privy councillor, and on 10 January 1771 constable of the Tower of London. In 1770 'Junius' publicly attacked him for an unprincipled love of sinecures, but other observers were surprised that Cornwallis remained in royal favour when he had never hidden his opposition to the king's well-known opinions on America and a free press. The probable explanation is that, of all the whigs, George III respected this sober young earl, who stated his beliefs openly but also undertook to put his duty to his monarch and country above all else.

Cornwallis's withdrawal from active politicking in the late 1760s was prompted by more than just an awareness that he was not very good at it. On 14 July 1768 he married Jemima Tulikens (1747–1779), daughter of Colonel James Jones of the 3rd regiment of foot guards. It was a love match. The daughter of a professional soldier, Jemima brought no dowry, but she was an elegant beauty who returned her husband's adoration. They had few years together before her premature death, but these years, and their children, Mary (1769–1857) and Charles (1774–1823) [*see below*], gave Cornwallis his greatest happiness. After his youthful passion for action and glory, he came soon to prefer the comforts and consolations of domesticity to every other existence. At the peak of his career only his devotion to duty prevented him from refusing the high commands and offices that dragged him from his beloved family.

**Cornwallis in America** This duty was tested to the full when hostilities broke out in America in 1775. Cornwallis, promoted major-general on 29 September 1775, promptly offered his services against the rebellion, even in a subordinate position. He had consistently opposed the policies that had sparked the rebellion, and his wife begged him not to go, but to him his duty was clear. He sailed from Cork on 12 February 1776 in command of seven regiments, including the 33rd, which, after ten years in his care, had earned a reputation as one of the finest and most disciplined regiments of foot. Throughout the long years of war ahead, the loyalty of the rank and file to Cornwallis was undoubted. He displayed a rare humanity in his attention to their interests and sufferings, which they repaid in obedient service and genuine grief at his final defeat at Yorktown.

Cornwallis arrived at the Cape Fear River in North Carolina on 3 May, too late to help restore royal government there. After a hapless assault on Charles Town, commanded by Sir Henry Clinton, Cornwallis and Clinton shipped their troops up to New York to reinforce the commander-in-chief, General Sir William Howe. Under Howe, Cornwallis commanded the reserve wing of the army that defeated Washington in the battle of Long Island on 27–8 August. Hotly engaged in the fighting himself, he afterwards refused to condemn Howe for not having pressed home his advantage and for allowing Washington's army to escape across the East River to Manhattan. This reluctance to criticize Howe damned him in the eyes of other British officers, notably Clinton, but he stood by it. In later years his defence of Howe possibly owed something to a consciousness of his own missed opportunities in the war. The first of these occurred after the battle of Fort Lee, on 18 November. Chasing Washington's army south across New Jersey, Cornwallis almost caught up with his quarry on the banks of the Raritan at New Brunswick on 1 December, but there he stopped, acting on orders from Howe to go no further. His critics argued that with just one more push he could have caught Washington and defeated his weary troops, but Cornwallis always insisted that the week-long chase had stretched his own men to the limit and that immediately fording a river and fighting a battle was beyond them. A month later, however, he was given another chance against Washington when Howe ordered him to Trenton, near Princeton, to avenge a defeat Washington had inflicted on the Hessians in British service. Bogged down in winter mud and harried by sniper fire, Cornwallis's 8000 men took a whole day, 2 January 1777, to march the 10 miles from Princeton to Trenton. Arriving at twilight, with a swollen waterway, the Assanpink Creek, between him and Washington's men, Cornwallis decided to rest his men rather than attempt an assault in the dark. Fatally, however, he failed to put the proper outposts in place, and while his men rested in the village of Trenton, Washington again escaped, under cover of darkness. Another furious pursuit by Cornwallis came too late to catch him, and in shock the British pulled back to the Raritan River. The winter campaign was over. It was of this affair that Clinton was to observe famously that Cornwallis was guilty 'of the most consummate ignorance I ever heard of [in] any officer above a corporal' (Wickwire and Wickwire, *War of Independence*, 98).

After Trenton, Washington declined to be drawn into an open fight, and for much of the spring of 1777 Cornwallis was bogged down in minor skirmishes in and around New Brunswick, where he commanded the garrison. Perhaps frustrated by this limited warfare, he supported Howe's decision in the summer to attack Philadelphia, even though it meant diverting the war effort from New Jersey and New England, and split the British forces into three smaller, weaker camps at Philadelphia, Albany, and Manhattan. Washington obliged the British by fighting for

Philadelphia, and Cornwallis shone militarily at the battle of Brandywine on 11 September 1777, a classic British battle of cannonading followed by an orderly bayonet charge. Subsequent attempts to draw Washington into open battle failed, however, and in December, with winter closing in and campaigning slowing, Cornwallis was granted permission to go home on leave.

Cornwallis returned to Philadelphia in the spring of 1778 as lieutenant-general and second in command to Sir Henry Clinton, now commander-in-chief in America. The entry of the French into the war after General Sir John Burgoyne's surrender at Saratoga (17 October 1777) convinced Cornwallis that a bold plan of occupation of ports where the French might disembark and vigorous aid to the southern loyalists was essential for the British to regain the initiative. But Clinton frittered away the remainder of the campaigning season in small predatory expeditions. Cornwallis then returned to England again on learning of the dangerous illness of his wife, who died on 16 February 1779. Despite his personal distress, he returned to America. Only then was he able to put into operation his bolder plans. Clinton and Cornwallis moved their operations to South Carolina in May 1780 and quickly captured Charles Town. Following Clinton's return to New York, Cornwallis held the south against the American armies for the rest of the year, defeating General Gates at Camden on 16 August 1780. In 1781 Cornwallis decided to strike a decisive blow by marching north to Virginia, the most important insurgent colony, in an attempt to link up with Clinton. He contrasted a successful battle in Virginia which 'may give us America' with a 'defensive [plan], mixed with desultory expeditions' (*Correspondence*, 1.87). On his way north, Cornwallis was ordered by Clinton to establish himself at Yorktown, though he realized his force was not strong enough to hold such an exposed post. Washington recognized Cornwallis's mistake and joined with the French to attack the British on 14 October 1781. When Clinton finally sailed from New York on 24 October, it was already too late. Cornwallis had been forced to surrender on 19 October and the American War of Independence was effectively at an end.

From his very first campaign most of the problems which were to dog Cornwallis until the final defeat at Yorktown in 1781 were in evidence. The British were hampered by long lines of communication and their desire to fight throughout the thirteen colonies. These problems were exacerbated by the entry of France and Spain into the war from 1778. British military and political co-ordination were threatened by personal and political rivalries. Cornwallis's own relations with Clinton had quickly deteriorated. He was also in conflict with the colonial secretary, Lord George Germain. In addition, parliament and the ministry were hampered by the king's intervention. There were intractable difficulties in America. The British defeated the continental army in almost every major engagement, but could not destroy the American will to fight. The Americans, supported by an increasing proportion of the civil population as British armies visited hardship and brutality on them, simply regrouped, avoiding battle wherever possible. The loyalist militias were regarded with more or less undisguised contempt by Cornwallis and his brother commanders. On the other hand, Cornwallis never seems properly to have understood the spirit of independence which animated his enemies. While at a local level the British maintained their military superiority, their intelligence was poor, and despite his efforts Cornwallis found it difficult to guarantee the troops ample supplies. All the same, the conduct of the war and military administration revealed some constants in Cornwallis's attitudes and approach. In principle, he had sympathized with American liberties, but his essential allegiance to royal authority shone through. He disliked and distrusted settlers, having no time for either loyalist or republican 'banditti'. He was to have little more time for the non-official British in India or the ascendancy élites in Ireland. During his brief period of administration in the Carolinas he was to insist on the sanctity of private property and the unfettered rights of the landlord, another theme which was to resurface in India and Ireland. The best that can be said of Cornwallis's American career was that he emerged as a good commissary general, if a flawed strategist. From the outset he had devoted himself to logistics and to supplying and feeding his men. He seems to have remained genuinely popular among his troops. This concern was to serve him well in the conditions of warfare during the Indian campaigns, with its vast distances and huge armies of camp followers.

The political world in Britain was dimly aware of these deficiencies, so Cornwallis was never really blamed for the collapse in America. As early as May 1782, when still on 'parole', he was asked to go to India as governor-general, but, distrusting the ministry, he refused. He resigned as constable of the Tower in January 1784 when his political friend Lord Shelburne lost office to William Pitt. Having again refused the offer of India when pressed by Pitt and Dundas, he went off on a short military mission to Frederick the Great in August and September 1785.

**Cornwallis in India, 1786–1793** Cornwallis was the first governor-general appointed under the terms of William Pitt's East India Act (1784). According to its author, the act's intention was 'to give the crown the power of guiding the politics of India with as little means of corrupt influence as possible' (Moon, 229). Cornwallis was appointed over the only other serious candidate, Lord Macartney, previously governor of Madras, who had made far too many enemies among the East India Company directors for ministerial comfort. Cornwallis's reputation as a good soldier who had been put in an impossible position at Yorktown and his probity attracted Pitt and Henry Dundas, the dominant minister in the new Board of Control for India. Cornwallis had seen the effects of divided control in America and he insisted on enhanced powers in India. Having been assured that he would, if necessary, be able to override his council and that he would also be appointed commander-in-chief in India, Cornwallis accepted the office in February 1786.

Both military efficiency and probity were indeed very valuable commodities in India in these years. The sultans of Mysore had battered the enfeebled Madras administration with constant sallies into their territory over the past quarter of a century. In 1782 the presidency had nearly collapsed under the assault of Tipu Sultan. The lax two-year rule of Sir John Macpherson as governor-general had fully exposed the extent of the corruption and peculation which was thought not only to be undermining the East India Company's reputation, but even to be weakening the British constitution itself. Cornwallis later remarked that Macpherson's government 'was a system of the dirtiest jobbery' (*Correspondence*, 1.371). What he found in India when he arrived in October 1786 strengthened his already strong aversion to the untrammelled activities of British subjects overseas, who he believed were undermining the crown. Cornwallis's relations with Dundas in his first few years, however, were to be rendered difficult by Macpherson's attempts to return to India and by ministers' apparent willingness to countenance this. Back in England, Macpherson, presumably irritated by Cornwallis's stoic reputation, circulated a story to the effect that the new governor-general was on the point of marrying a sixteen-year-old girl. Pained that Dundas had given credence to this, Cornwallis complained that if he had so far forgotten his duty 'at the age of forty-nine … forgetting likewise his grey hairs and rheumatism' (ibid.), then Macpherson's return would be of little note as his own administration would already be sliding into a similar decadence.

Fighting corruption consumed much of Cornwallis's time in India. It was to have long-term consequences not only for the nature of British rule but for the place of Indians within colonial government and society. On an early visit up-country to Benares he remarked that almost all the company's servants were involved in commerce under the names of friends and relatives and that they used their parallel position as judges and collectors to undermine the company's interests, becoming 'the greatest oppressors of the manufacturers' (*Correspondence*, 1.271). Cornwallis moved urgently to ensure that company servants were not involved in private trade and he separated the judicial from the revenue-collecting branch of government in the districts. Yet the root of this corruption, Cornwallis thought, lay in close British dealings with Indians. In Benares, he asserted, 'The Rajah is a fool, his servants rogues, every native of Hindostan (I really believe) is corrupt and Benares six hundred miles from Calcutta' (ibid.). Later, in Bengal, he castigated a British official who had 'a strong propensity for jobbery and intrigue … [and] has formed connections with the worst black people in Bengal' (ibid., 2.134). Before 1791 Cornwallis therefore instituted a new system of law courts in which Indian agency was greatly decreased. He introduced 'European principles' into legal judgments, dispensing with measures of Muslim law (shariʿa) such as the right of relatives of a murdered man to play a role in sentencing. He also brought the local Indian police in Calcutta, and later across the whole of Bengal, more closely under British supervision. The governor-general's strong aversion to the administration of 'natives of influence' effectively created a racially divided government, whereas under Warren Hastings a mere ten years before, Indians could still reach major administrative positions.

Scarcely had Cornwallis begun to see the fruits of his reform measures than he was forced to spend the best part of 1791 and 1792 in the field in southern India fending off the threat from Tipu Sultan of Mysore. Tipu feared British encirclement and had repeatedly spurned British offers of treaty relationships on the grounds that other princes had lost independence by entanglement with the Europeans. Seeing a build-up of British influence on the south-west coast of India, Tipu had moved, in December 1789, against a British ally, the raja of Travancore. Cornwallis did not trust the abilities of the Madras government and its army; he was suspicious of his Indian allies, the Marathas and the nizam of Hyderabad, and he felt that, in view of the outbreak of the French Revolution, this was a good time to try to restrain what he saw as the enmity and implacable ambition of Tipu Sultan. Hesitating to intervene prematurely, Cornwallis only took command in Mysore in late 1790, worried by early military set-backs to the company's forces. By April 1791 he had taken Mysore's key city, Bangalore, and captured 'vast numbers of cannon' and a huge quantity of grain. But not until more than a year later (25 February 1792) did Cornwallis finally force Tipu to accept peace terms, and even then the sultan was only obliged to cede half his territory, outlying districts which included much of the kingdom's poorer and less productive land.

A logistical commander *par excellence*, Cornwallis found himself in a potentially vulnerable condition throughout the campaign. His advance was several times delayed by his massive baggage train and army of camp followers. But the baggage train was necessary because the Mysoreans adopted a scorched earth policy and destroyed all villages and crops. The Maratha light horse which was sent to deal with the still powerful Mysorean light cavalry failed dismally. Cornwallis had few maps and charts and 'a lack of all satisfactory information' (*Correspondence*, 2.20). Terrain and weather were also against him. The monsoon made the countryside treacherous and in the 1791 campaign he had found it impossible to get his heavy cannon across the wide and boulder-strewn flood plain of the Kavery River which protected Tipu's final redoubt, the fortress city of Seringapatam. When, during the spring campaign of 1792, Cornwallis effectively defeated Tipu in front of Seringapatam, the governor-general did not risk an all-out attack on the city, sensing the underlying weakness of his own position. His troops were exhausted, his allies were unreliable, and disease had broken out among his European troops. Politics counselled otherwise also. He did not want to build up his dangerous allies, the Marathas and Hyderabad, too much. A balance of power in south India was better, with Tipu's wings neatly clipped. Cornwallis was also enough of a politician to see that the significant body of British opinion which rightly believed that Tipu had been antagonized by long-term British

ambitions in the south would protest if the sultan was destroyed. The imminence of war with France was also a strong argument for strategic caution. The view of some that Cornwallis had simply shrunk from the final battle was less easy to maintain, given the huge loss of territory and massive indemnity which Tipu had been forced to accept.

The India Act of 1784, spurred by claims that Warren Hastings's government had been despotic, noted the complaints that 'diverse rajahs, zemindars and other native landholders had been deprived of their lands, jurisdictions and privileges'. On arriving in India, Cornwallis was plunged into a long-standing official debate about the best way to administer the system of land taxation which the British had inherited from the Mughals. This was to culminate in the governor-general's permanent settlement of the land revenues of Bengal in 1793, his most important act in the view of economic and social historians. Philip Francis had broached the idea of a permanent settlement in the 1770s, but opinion remained divided. John Shore, Cornwallis's ablest aide on the financial side of government, collected a huge amount of data on the nature of tenures and the past history of landholding during 1788 and 1789. Ultimately, Shore came down on the side of a ten-year settlement with the landholders rather than permanency. It was Cornwallis's personal intervention, therefore, which in 1793 set the Bengal revenues at £3 million and ensured that 'they [the zemindars] and their heirs and lawful successors will be allowed to hold their estates at such an assessment for ever' (*Selections from the State Papers*, 1.206). In this Cornwallis was inspired by pragmatism. War with France seemed inevitable, and it was important for the British government to placate the Bengal countryside and put itself into a position in which it could count on stable revenues for some years ahead. But Cornwallis was not entirely immune to the teachings of theory. He appears to have believed that, while Indian politics were decadent and corrupt, Indian landlords were nevertheless motivated by an underlying spirit of economic rationality. Some have perceived the indirect influence of Adam Smith here. Given stability, the landlords would invest in the land, succour the peasantry, and boost the sluggish internal trade of Bengal. Later administrators, Indian nationalists, and modern historians have often blamed Cornwallis for abandoning the Bengal cultivators to a rapacious landlord class. But this is unjust, as he believed that the zemindars' rights could coexist with an equally inviolable peasant right of occupancy. Only under the later dispensation of regulation 7 of 1799, when Cornwallis had long left India, was the balance tipped decisively in favour of the landlords. As the 'permanency' was pushed through the cabinet and court of directors against considerable opposition, Cornwallis's first tenure of the governor-generalship was ending. Within six months of France's declaration of war on Britain in February 1793, he was homeward-bound from Madras on the *Swallow*, after accepting the capitulation of the French enclave of Pondicherry.

On his return to Britain Cornwallis was rapidly enlisted

in an attempt to boost the allies' ailing fortunes against the French republican armies. Fending off attempts to make him a local field marshal in central Europe to replace the duke of York, who was regarded as incompetent, Cornwallis was persuaded in February 1795 to become master-general of the ordnance, with a seat in cabinet. His task was to prepare the defences of England against an expected French invasion, but there were more imminent dangers threatening other British dominions. In February 1797 he was again sworn in as governor-general of India with a brief to suppress the mutiny which was brewing among white officers of the company's armies. Their unrest resulted from plans which Cornwallis, as part of his programme of Indian reform, had devised to transfer the company's troops to the crown. In the event, timely pecuniary concessions from the court of directors quelled the discontent and Cornwallis did not embark.

**Lord lieutenant of Ireland (1797–1801)** The threat of an uprising in Ireland, aided by the French, had clouded Britain's war counsels for months. By early 1798, with the United Irishmen in open rebellion, Pitt's need for a cool-headed administrator in Ireland had become urgent. With his extensive military and administrative experience, Cornwallis was the obvious choice, but he was unenthusiastic when Lord Spencer floated the idea that he should become both commander-in-chief and lord lieutenant: 'I said, You are too good to me, to wish to place me in so easy a situation' (*Correspondence*, 2.334). Nevertheless, by early June he had accepted Pitt's entreaty to take up the double burden, while retaining his cabinet post as master-general of the ordnance. The immediate military responsibilities were not as onerous as expected. On 21 June, the day after he arrived in Dublin, generals Lake and Moore defeated the rebels in battles at Vinegar Hill (Enniscorthy) and Wexford. Cornwallis had only to take the field once, in a short campaign against General Joseph Humbert's French invasion force which landed in late August. It surrendered to Cornwallis near St Johnstown on 8 September.

Rebellion aside, Cornwallis was appalled at the task before him in Ireland. His primary duty, he believed, was to strengthen the empire by coaxing Ireland into a lasting and peaceful co-existence with Britain. To his shame and anger, however, he found that the most ardent champions of the British connection were the least likely advocates of peace and conciliation. It was the loyalists, he decided, who, by their hatred of Catholics, had succeeded in transforming a small Jacobinical rebellion against church and state into a religious civil war. He marvelled at the bloodlust of the loyalist troops, complaining variously that they 'delight in murder', or that 'murder appears to be their favourite pastime' (*Correspondence*, 2.355, 357). Worse, however, was the attitude of the leading protestants. There was little to be looked for in the Irish parliament, he informed the duke of Portland, as both houses were 'adverse to all acts of clemency'. Left to their own devices

Irish MPs would 'pursue measures that could only terminate in the extirpation of the greater number of the inhabitants, and in the utter destruction of the country' (ibid., 2.358). Even his own dinner guests partook of this barbaric 'system of blood', enlivening the viceregal table with the happy news of the murder of yet another Catholic priest. Within ten days Cornwallis had concluded that 'the life of a Lord-Lieutenant of Ireland comes up to my idea of perfect misery' (ibid., 2.356). By the following April, even India looked attractive. 'Sincerely do I repent that I did not return to Bengal', he lamented to his brother (ibid., 3.93).

Cornwallis's one source of consolation in Ireland was the young Viscount Castlereagh, an Ulsterman and MP for County Down who shared his faith in the efficacy of clemency and conciliation. Castlereagh had been acting chief secretary in Ireland since March 1798 and in November Cornwallis pressed to have him confirmed in the post. By unwritten law the Irish chief secretary was almost never Irish, but Cornwallis asked for an exception to be made in this case because, as he put it, Castlereagh was 'so very unlike an Irishman' (*Correspondence*, 2.439). It was a clumsy compliment: Cornwallis meant that of all the leading protestants he had met, only Castlereagh seemed willing to put the future of his nation above personal ambition and religious prejudice. Perhaps Cornwallis relied upon Castlereagh's judgement and local knowledge too much. Certainly it was during these years that the chief secretaryship began to rival the lord lieutenancy in executive importance at Westminster. From the outset Castlereagh shared Cornwallis's view that it was essential 'to soften the hatred of the Catholics to our Government'. This meant conceding religious and political rights to Catholics—a change that could safely be accommodated only within the confines of an Irish union with Britain, as this would have the effect of reducing Catholics to a manageable minority of the population. A union might even save Ireland's protestants from the consequences of their own actions, though Cornwallis did not look for gratitude from them: 'they arrogate to themselves the exclusive knowledge of a country, of which, from their mode of governing it, they have, in my opinion, proved themselves totally ignorant' (ibid., 2.404–5). Pitt and his ministers agreed that union was the only way forward for Ireland, and Cornwallis and Castlereagh were authorized to sound out Irish attitudes towards it. Cornwallis was soon disappointed to learn, however, that there was no intention of granting concessions to Catholics at the same time. He pleaded his case in an impassioned letter to Pitt of 17 October. Where was the sense, he asked, in making an alliance with a small party in Ireland which already enjoyed Britain's protection and, moreover, had exploited it 'to wage eternal war against the Papists and the Presbyterians … about nine-tenths of the community' (ibid., 2.418)? Pitt sympathized, but denied that it was either practicable or proper to link Catholic emancipation to the union. The lord lieutenant would have to be satisfied with the undertaking that no clause in the act of union would explicitly bar Catholics from future participation in parliament.

Cornwallis was never fully reconciled to this position, and henceforth his faith in the union as a panacea for Ireland's ills wavered. After the initial vote against the union in the Irish parliament in January 1799, he left it up to Castlereagh to negotiate most of the payment—in money, patronage, and honours—required to persuade a majority of Irish MPs to end their institution and associated perquisites. To Cornwallis this was jobbery, not compensation, and he recoiled from it, even while allowing that it had to be done. He concentrated instead on wooing Ireland's Catholic voters to back the union. His relations with the Catholic bishops were cordial, even sympathetic, and with their blessing he toured the southern market towns drumming up support for the union among Catholic professionals and merchants. In London, however, complaints grew louder that he did not communicate freely with the cabinet. He had previously excused himself on the grounds that, as a newcomer to Ireland, he found it hard to come to definite conclusions. In fact he had formed his opinions within days of arriving; he simply did not see his way clear to implementing them with the unpromising material of the Irish parliamentarians. He allowed that none of the MPs or their backers had legitimate or rational grounds for opposing the union. In his eyes, all were in pursuit of their 'own private objects of ambition or avarice' (ibid., 3.8). To the chagrin of his fellow unionists, and in spite of his studied attempts at courtesy, Cornwallis's disdain for the government's friends was visible to all. Edward Cooke, the civil under-secretary, complained that half the battle for the union was occasioned by Cornwallis's 'total incapacity, self-conceit and muleishness' (McDowell, *Ireland*, 699). Protestants resented his disapproval of their severity towards Catholics, Cooke explained, feeling that Cornwallis did not understand their difficulties. This failure to find common ground with the loyalists was another indication that, for all his time in America and India, Cornwallis remained essentially metropolitan in outlook, unable to empathize with the concerns and culture of a colonial class.

Cornwallis may have hated the horse-trading that preceded the Irish parliament's vote for union in June 1800, but he was determined to salvage some honour from the proceedings. When, a few days after the victory, Portland wrote brusquely saying that he and Castlereagh had been too liberal in their offers of peerages to secure support for the union and that he would have to find a way of extricating the government from their promises, he was furious and threatened to resign. The cabinet and George III backed down. Pitt had hoped that, once union was a fact, a united cabinet might be able to persuade the king of the wisdom of Catholic emancipation. Like Cornwallis and Castlereagh, he had hinted to Catholics that emancipation was imminent, though he had also quietly promised anti-papist peers that they could safely vote for the union. With the union safe, however, the cabinet's flimsy undertaking to Cornwallis and Castlereagh to grant Catholics relief fell apart and, lacking vital support, Pitt dared not broach the issue with the king. His ministerial malcontents were not so reticent. They spent the months before the union parliament was due to meet stiffening George's resolve against emancipation until, on 29 January 1801, he declared his implacable opposition to any measure of relief. This, added to the dissension in the cabinet, guaranteed that Pitt could never force a relief bill through the Lords. Already ill with worry about the war and the national debt, he seized the opportunity to resign. A few days later, in mid-February, Cornwallis and Castlereagh followed him out of office, Cornwallis also resigning as master of the ordnance. Naively underestimating the anti-Catholic feeling in the cabinet, Cornwallis had let himself become almost cheerful about the imminence of emancipation, and his disappointment was correspondingly bitter. To General Ross at the ordnance he explained that he could no longer serve an administration 'so blind to the interest, and indeed to the immediate security of their country, as to persevere in the old system of proscription and exclusion in Ireland' (*Correspondence*, 3.337). He had to remain in Dublin until May, when his successors arrived to take office, but once freed he looked forward to exchanging the detested factionalism of public life for a quiet retirement at Culford.

**Peace with France** However, in early July 1801, with rumours of a French invasion, Cornwallis was prevailed upon to accept the command of the eastern district, with headquarters at Colchester. He grumbled, but was settled there within the week. Towards the end of September, and with much more enthusiasm, he agreed to serve as the British plenipotentiary to negotiate peace with France. With his son, Viscount Brome, he sailed from Dover on 3 November. He was favourably received in Paris by Napoleon Bonaparte on the 10th but, finding that further talks with the first consul eluded him, he moved at the end of the month to Amiens to open negotiations with the French plenipotentiary, Napoleon's elder brother Joseph, and his formidable adviser Charles de Talleyrand. As ever, Cornwallis's sense of duty informed his undertaking, but perhaps pride played a part too. Pitt is said to have observed that Cornwallis had always wanted to head a diplomatic mission, which, if true, was a measure of Cornwallis's delusion, for he was not a natural diplomat. To bluff or hedge or lie was anathema to him, and his scrupulous adherence to a notion of gentlemanly conduct rendered him helpless before the wily charm and intrigues of the elder Bonaparte and Talleyrand. Soon his lugubrious pen was complaining of the French negotiators' want of candour and 'unsteadiness and tergiversation', and of the little dependence that could be placed on private conversations with them (*Correspondence*, 3.439). Too late, it dawned on the British plenipotentiary that he was 'too much a *John* to delight in foreign society' (ibid., 3.406).

Cornwallis was further handicapped in the negotiations by the unhelpful terms of the preliminary articles signed in London and the extent of his own military knowledge. Even before the Austrians' defeat at Marengo (14 June 1800), which deprived Britain of her last ally, he had shuddered at the sight of British raw recruits being sent off to battle, fatally lacking in training, discipline, and hope. Whereas politicians suspected that Britain's war effort was unsustainable, Cornwallis knew it for a painful, bloody fact. By January 1801, when Austria agreed terms with France, he was desperate for peace. It is unfair, however, to say that he underestimated France's own need for peace. His biggest fear was that Bonaparte would be swept from power before the definitive treaty could be signed. He was not helped by the conciliatory terms of the treaty preliminaries that Britain had agreed before his departure; nor was Lord Addington's flailing government able to infuse him with either confidence or authority. In the end he settled for a 'peace that will not dishonour the country and will afford as reasonable a prospect of future safety as the present very extraordinary circumstances of Europe will admit' (*Correspondence*, 3.437). The peace of Amiens was signed in March 1802, though in the meantime many of the considerations which had led the British to agree the preliminaries had evaporated.

**Return to India, death, and character** For three years after Amiens Cornwallis led the peaceful country life which he had desired for so long. Then, abruptly, he was again sent to India as governor-general, arriving with great misgivings in July 1805. After the hectic career of expansion embarked on by Richard Wellesley which had tripled the company's debts, the directors yearned for peace in India. After a rapid assessment Cornwallis decided to make immediate overtures to the Maratha leaders, Holkar and Shinde, although the outgoing commander-in-chief, Gerard Lake, regarded this as a virtual capitulation. Historians of the imperial era criticized Cornwallis for a move which would have allowed central India to slip back into its pre-colonial 'anarchy', but this has since been disputed. Besides, Cornwallis knew that the company's troops were on the point of mutiny because their pay was seriously in arrears following the collapse of the company's credit on the Indian money market. But peace on these terms was never concluded because, after only two months in India, Cornwallis fell ill on his way up-country and died on 5 October 1805 at Ghazipur, near Benares. He was buried just outside this small town and a monument to him in the style of a classical temple was erected on a high bluff overlooking the River Ganges.

A corpulent man of rather severe appearance, Cornwallis has often been treated by historians as a leader of outstanding competence rather than brilliance, promoted again and again because Britain possessed so few outstanding proconsuls at this time of international emergency. Cornwallis's formal minutes do indeed seem staid and orotund, his devotion to duty almost too classical for his contemporaries or for the post-colonial age to bear. The charge of dullness is, however, belied by the vigour of his less official letters to his friend General Ross and to Dundas, and that of mere competence by the clarity and persuasiveness of his vision. Cornwallis should be seen as a transitional figure. His devotion to the crown had at its heart something archaic. It rose in part from his peculiar position in aristocratic society as a man who was independent yet without patronage: 'Here was no fortune to be mended ... Here was no beggarly mushroom kindred to be provided for. No crew of hungry followers, gaping to be

gorged!' (Moon, 231), as Dundas colourfully proclaimed of him in parliament. At the same time, Cornwallis's career also pointed forward to the new Victorian type of crown servant. He saw the world in stark colours of race and moral independency. Indians were corrupt; Americans little more than banditti; the Irish tiresome and petulant. Yet this was not the racism of high imperialism with its urge to 'improve'. Still less was Cornwallis a harbinger of colonial capitalism. Caste and the Muslim religion were, he wrote to the bishop of Salisbury, 'insuperable bars' to the progress of Christianity in India. His reverence for the principle of property came not from a desire to encourage a vigorous market in land, but from his sense that a society's moral worth was underpinned by agrarian stability.

**Cornwallis's son** Cornwallis's only son, **Charles Cornwallis**, second Marquess Cornwallis (1774–1823), landowner, styled Viscount Brome until he inherited on his father's death in October 1805, was born on 19 October 1774 at Culford, Suffolk, and educated at Eton College (*c*.1783–4, 1786–9) and St John's College, Cambridge (admitted October 1792, MA 1794). His health was delicate and his father did not want him to have a military career. He was a tory MP for the family pocket borough of Eye, Suffolk (1795–6), and for Suffolk (1796–1805). He married, on 17 April 1797, Lady Louisa Gordon (1776–1850), daughter of Alexander *Gordon, fourth duke of Gordon, and his wife, Jane, *née* Maxwell: 'having expressed to the Duchess some hesitation about marrying her daughter on account of supposed insanity in the Gordon family, he received from her the gratifying assurance that there was not a drop of Gordon blood in Louisa!' (GEC, *Peerage*, 3.457). They had five daughters. He was a captain in the Suffolk yeomanry from 1795 to 1802 and colonel of the Suffolk militia from 1802 until his death. He was master of the buckhounds from 1807 until his death. Following disease, for which he was about to visit the continent, he died on 9 August 1823 at his residence in Old Burlington Street, London, and was buried at Culford, Suffolk. At his death the marquessate became extinct. James *Cornwallis (1743–1824), bishop of Lichfield and dean of Durham, became fourth earl.

C. A. Bayly and Katherine Prior

**Sources** BL OIOC, Home misc. · *Correspondence of Charles, first Marquis Cornwallis*, ed. C. Ross, 3 vols. (1859) · *Selections from the state papers of the governor-generals of India: Lord Cornwallis*, ed. G. Forrest, 2 vols. (1926) · F. Wickwire and M. Wickwire, *Cornwallis and the War of Independence* (1971) · F. Wickwire and M. Wickwire, *Cornwallis: the imperial years* (1980) · R. B. McDowell, *Ireland in the age of imperialism and revolution, 1760–1801* (1979) · N. K. Sinha, *The economic history of Bengal from Plassey to the permanent settlement*, 2 vols. (privately printed, Calcutta, 1956–62) · S. Islam, *The permanent settlement in Bengal: a study of its operations, 1790–1819* (Dacca, 1979) · R. Guha, *A rule of property for Bengal: an essay on the idea of permanent settlement* (Paris, 1963) · R. Datta, *Society, economy and the market: commercialisation in rural Bengal, c. 1760–1800* (Delhi, 2000) · W. K. Firminger, *Historical introduction to the Bengal portion of the 'fifth report'* (Calcutta, 1917) · I. Lee, *Castlereagh* (1951) · J. W. Derry, *Castlereagh* (1976) · R. B. McDowell, 'The Irish executive in the nineteenth century', *Irish Historical Studies*, 9 (1954–5), 264–80 · P. J. Marshall, *Bengal—the British bridgehead: eastern India, 1740–1828* (1987), 2/2 of The new Cambridge history of India, ed. G. Johnson and others · P. J. Marshall, '"Cornwallis triumphant": war in India and the British public in the late eighteenth century', *Trade and conquest: studies on the* *rise of British dominance in India* (1993) • M. Hasan, *History of Tipu Sultan*, 2nd edn (1971) • J. Ehrman, *The younger Pitt*, 1–2 (1969–83) • P. Moon, *The British conquest and dominion of India* (1989) • R. Callahan, *The East India Company and army reform, 1783–1798* (1972) • *The private record of an Indian governor-generalship: the correspondence of John Shore*, ed. H. Furber (Cambridge, Massachusetts, 1933) • A. Aspinall, *Cornwallis in Bengal* (1931) • HoP, *Commons, 1754–90* • GEC, *Peerage* • Venn, *Alum. Cant.* • *DNB*

**Archives** BL OIOC, Home misc. series, corresp. and papers relating to India • CKS, corresp. and papers • NMM, letter-books • PRO, corresp. and papers, PRO 30/11 • Suffolk RO, Ipswich, entrybook | BL, letters to Lord Hardwicke, Add. MSS 35642–35752, *passim* • BL, letters to Warren Hastings, Add. MSS 29170–29171 • BL, corresp. with J. Murray, Add. MS 40073A • BL, corresp. with duke of Newcastle, Add. MSS 32911–33110 • CKS, corresp. with Lord Camden; letters to James Cornwallis; letters to William Pitt • Devon RO, corresp. with Lord Sidmouth • NA Scot., corresp. with Sir Archibald Campbell • NAM, letters to Alexander Ross • NL Scot., letters to Henry Dundas • NRA, priv. coll., letters to Lord Lansdowne • NRA, priv. coll., letters to Norman MacLeod • NRA, priv. coll., letters to Lady Waldegrave • Port Eliot, St Germans, Saltash, corresp. with wife [Charles Cornwallis] • PRO, letters to William Pitt, PRO 30/8 • U. Nott. L., letters to duke of Newcastle

**Likenesses** oils, 1742, priv. coll. • T. Gainsborough, oils, 1783, NPG • J. Gillray, etching, 1792 (*The Bengal levée*), BL OIOC • R. Home, oils, 1792, Government House, Madras • J. Smart, pencil and wash drawing, 1792, NPG [*see illus.*] • J. Bacon, statue, 1793, BL OIOC • W. Beechey, oils, exh. RA 1799, priv. coll. • A. W. Devis, oils, exh. RA 1799, priv. coll. • M. Brown, group portrait, oils, Oriental Club, London • J. S. Copley, oils, Guildhall, London • J. C. Ross, statue on monument, St Paul's Cathedral, London • H. Walton, oils on copper, Moyses Hall Museum, Bury St Edmunds • bust, Westminster Abbey • busts; formerly in Calcutta, Madras

**Cornwallis, Charles**, **second Marquess Cornwallis** (**1774–1823**). *See under* Cornwallis, Charles, first Marquess Cornwallis (1738–1805).

**Cornwallis, Edward** (1713–1776), army officer and colonial governor, was born in London on 22 February 1713, the sixth of seven sons of Charles, fourth Baron Cornwallis (1675–1722), and his wife, Lady Charlotte Butler (*d.* 1725), daughter and heir of Richard *Butler, first earl of Arran. His twin brother was Frederick *Cornwallis (1713–1783), archbishop of Canterbury. He was educated at Eton College from 1725 to 1728. Two years later—on 20 October 1730—he entered the army as an ensign. In July 1731 Cornwallis became a lieutenant in the 8th regiment of foot, a captain in April 1734, and rose to major in the 20th foot on 31 March 1742. On 9 December 1743 he was elected MP for the family seat of Eye in Suffolk.

From 1742 until 1745 Cornwallis's regiment was in Flanders, where he joined it in 1744 after five years as a diplomatic courier. After Fontenoy he became lieutenant-colonel of Bligh's regiment, which was recalled to Britain to stem the Jacobite advance. After the fall of Carlisle Cornwallis was sent with a detachment to reinforce Chester, and the regiment was in the thick of the hand-to-hand fighting at Culloden. In 1747 Cornwallis's loyal service and connections made him groom of the bedchamber to George II, a sinecure he was to hold until ousted by political intrigue in 1763. More plums were on the way, for on 23 March 1749 he became colonel of the 24th regiment and resigned his seat in the Commons to become governor of Nova Scotia. This was to be a step to greater things, for he stipulated that he would serve for three years at the most.

Indeed, Nova Scotia was no sinecure. The few white inhabitants, mainly French and Catholic, resented British rule and had intermarried with local Native Americans. Moreover, the long dispute over the borders with New France was nearing a crisis, just as the fortress of Louisbourg was being returned to France. Cornwallis was instructed to consolidate British claims by establishing a new base on the peninsula and plant posts within the contested region across the Bay of Fundy.

Cornwallis threw himself into the task with all the vigour and directness of a soldier. He established Halifax on Chebucto Bay, planted posts at the St John's River and on the isthmus, and went to war with the Mi'kmaqs. The result was a little local war in which the British were effectively confined to the peninsula. Cornwallis campaigned successfully for military reinforcements, less successfully for naval ones, aimed to destroy the Mi'kmaqs and favoured expelling the Acadian settlers altogether—a policy actually carried out in 1755. At the time the Board of Trade rebuked him for aggression and still more for overspending; but although Cornwallis was no diplomat and disliked financial administration, he was a conscientious and hard-working governor. In 1751 his health gave way under the strain and he resigned.

At home Cornwallis returned to politics and to extending his family connections. In 1752, apparently at the king's request, he stood for and won one of the Westminster seats in the House of Commons. On 17 March 1753 he married Mary, daughter of Charles *Townshend, second Viscount Townshend. Throughout the 1750s he was connected with Thomas Pelham-Holles, duke of Newcastle, with whose support he successfully defended his seat in 1761.

Cornwallis's connections may have protected his military career during the Seven Years' War. His regiment had been posted to Minorca, but when war broke out Cornwallis was home on leave. He sailed with Byng, and was one of the fateful council of war which advised the admiral to abandon the relief of the island. Exonerated by a court of inquiry, he joined Hawke and Mordaunt's abortive raid on Rochefort—which did little good to his reputation. Nevertheless, he became a major-general in 1757, a lieutenant-general in 1760, and governor of Gibraltar in 1762. Compared with Nova Scotia, Gibraltar was an enormous plum, but the work involved probably killed him. Tortuous diplomacy to guarantee food imports from north Africa, maintaining and improving the fortifications, collecting intelligence of Spanish military and naval forces, and counter-espionage all took their toll. He bombarded ministers with requests for more troops, and for warships to protect the rock from the sea. By 1765 he was suffering from 'a disorder in my head which has plagued me several years at times has grown so much worse as to often stupefie me …' (Cornwallis to the earl of Halifax, Gibraltar, 17 May 1765, CO 91/14)—perhaps a brain tumour. He was allowed leave from June 1765 until October 1767, and again from June 1769 until January 1771. He left Gibraltar for the last time in June 1773 and died in England on 14 January 1776; he was buried at Culford, near Bury St Edmunds, Suffolk. He left his estates, including his house at Essington in Hertfordshire, to his nephew Charles *Cornwallis, first Marquess Cornwallis (1738–1805), and all his personal property to his wife.     JOHN OLIPHANT

**Sources** PRO, CO 217, 218, 221 · PRO, CO 91, 20 · R. R. Sedgwick, 'Cornwallis, Hon. Edward', HoP, *Commons, 1715–54* · L. B. Namier, 'Cornwallis, Hon. Edward', HoP, *Commons, 1754–90* · PRO, SP 42/100 · PRO, WO 64, 65 · BL, Add. MSS 32821, 32852, 32883, 32914 · PRO, WO 71/129 · S. Reid, *A military history of the last Jacobite rising* (1996) · B. Tunstall, *Admiral Byng and the loss of Minorca* (1928) · J. M. Beck, 'Cornwallis, Edward', *DCB*, vol. 4 · will dated at Essington, Hertfordshire, PRO, PROB 11/1016/57 · BL, Add. MS 37883, fol. 88
**Archives** BL, corresp. | NAM, letters to Lord Townshend
**Likenesses** G. Chalmers, portrait, 1755, priv. coll. · Reynolds, portraits, before 1760 · Ekhardt, portrait · engraving (after Reynolds), priv. coll.
**Wealth at death** estates; house in Hertfordshire: will, PRO, PROB 11/1016/57

**Cornwallis, Frederick** (1713–1783), archbishop of Canterbury, was born in London on 22 February 1713, the seventh son of Charles, fourth Baron Cornwallis of Eye (1675–1722), politician and army officer, and his wife, Lady Charlotte Butler (*d*. 1725), daughter of Richard Butler, first earl of Arran. He was the twin of the military commander Edward *Cornwallis (1713–1776). After an education at Eton College (1725–8) he matriculated at Christ's College, Cambridge, in 1732 and graduated BA in 1737. In 1739 he was ordained deacon and became a fellow of his college; he was ordained priest in 1742. At Cambridge, according to a contemporary source, he was not only a 'studious man', but 'always consistent, decent and beloved' (*Kentish Parson*, 40). He clearly adapted well to the effects of a palsy that deprived him of the use of his right hand and he graduated DD at Cambridge in 1748; according to one source, he came close to election as master of Christ's College (ibid., 73–4).

Meanwhile, Cornwallis's aristocratic connections had assisted him to a series of ecclesiastical preferments. He became rector of Chelmondiston, Suffolk, in 1740, and of Tivetshall in Norfolk two years later. Proof that he was a rising clergyman came in 1746 when he was made chaplain to George II and a canon of Windsor. He became a prebendary of Lincoln in 1747, canon of St Paul's Cathedral in 1750, and dean of the cathedral in 1766. His geniality of manner and avoidance of theological controversy helped to make him a suitable candidate for the bench, and in 1750 he became bishop of Lichfield and Coventry through the patronage of the duke of Newcastle. On 8 February 1759 Cornwallis married Caroline, daughter of William Townshend and granddaughter of Charles, second Viscount Townshend. She shared his intellectual interests. There were no children and she died on 5 January 1809.

Cornwallis's attempts to obtain translation to Worcester or Salisbury were unsuccessful, but friendship with the duke of Grafton helped to secure his nomination as archbishop of Canterbury in 1768 on the death of Thomas

*Frederick Cornwallis* (1713–1783), by Nathaniel Dance, 1768

Secker. He immediately won popularity among his diocesan clergy by his conviviality. A letter to the *Gentleman's Magazine* immediately after his death, from a Kentish vicar (Samuel Denne), praised his 'liberality of soul' in abolishing 'that odious distinction of a separate table for the chaplains' (*GM*, 1st ser., 53, 1783, 280) for clergy dinners at Lambeth Palace. He displayed a similar gregariousness in his diocesan visitations. There were some, indeed, who believed that he carried merriment too far and George III, apparently prompted by the evangelical countess of Huntingdon, chided him for proposing to hold a 'rout' at Lambeth (Rowden, 331). As archbishop, Cornwallis played little part in debates in the House of Lords, though he lent consistent support to Lord North's administration. He expressed sympathy with some of the campaigners for amendment to the Thirty-Nine Articles test for clerical and university subscription, but consultation with his fellow bishops convinced him that he should not endorse the Feathers tavern petition of 1772. He led the episcopal contributions to the fund for the dispossessed American episcopalian clergy in 1776 and gave general succour to the Society for the Propagation of the Gospel. One of his very few publications was a sermon to that society preached on 20 February 1756, in which he expressed the standard fears about the subversion of the American colonies by Spanish Catholicism. However, he did not share the contemporary paranoia over 'popery' and on 6 June 1780 Lambeth Palace was in some danger from the Gordon rioters.

Cornwallis died after a short illness on 19 March 1783 at Lambeth Palace and was buried in Lambeth church eight days later. He was a conscientious administrator and an entirely conventional Georgian churchman. A recent historian has observed: 'As a consequence of the complaisant Establishmentarianism of the likes of Cornwallis, the Church would lay itself open to the incursions of Evangelical thought and the reaction of "Orthodoxy" which culminated in the Oxford Movement' (Young, 79). That he published little, however, did not reflect a lack of intellectual interests, and both he and his widow bequeathed valuable items to the archiepiscopal palaces at Lambeth and Croydon. Perhaps his most appropriate epitaph was provided by the Revd John Denne of Maidstone who, on Cornwallis's translation to Canterbury, commented: 'We have now got what we wanted—a gentleman' (*Kentish Parson*, 124).

G. M. DITCHFIELD

**Sources** A. W. Rowden, *The primates of the four Georges* (1916) · *GM*, 1st ser., 48 (1778), 438 · *GM*, 1st ser., 53 (1783), 273–4, 280 · *GM*, 1st ser., 79 (1809), 92 · R. A. Austen-Leigh, ed., *The Eton College register, 1698–1752* (1927), 84 · J. Peile, *Biographical register of Christ's College, 1505–1905, and of the earlier foundation, God's House, 1448–1505*, ed. [J. A. Venn], 2 (1913), 225–6 · *A Kentish parson: selections from the private papers of the Revd Joseph Price, vicar of Brabourne, 1767–1786*, ed. G. M. Ditchfield and B. Keith-Lucas (1991) · Nichols, *Lit. anecdotes*, 8.14–15 · Nichols, *Illustrations*, 3.500–05 · E. Hasted, *The history and topographical survey of the county of Kent*, 2nd edn, 12 vols. (1797–1801) · Venn, *Alum. Cant.*, 1/1.399 · B. W. Young, *Religion and Enlightenment in eighteenth-century England: theological debate from Locke to Burke* (1998), 79 · *Fasti Angl., 1541–1857*, [Canterbury] · N. Sykes, *Church and state in England in the XVIII century* (1934)

**Archives** LPL, accounts and visitation papers | BL, letters to the second earl of Hardwicke, Add. MSS 35608–35619 · BL, Liverpool MSS · BL, corresp. with the duke of Newcastle, Add. MSS 32720–33090, *passim* · Hunt. L., Hastings MSS, HA 1628 · LPL, Society for the Propagation of the Gospel MSS

**Likenesses** portrait, 1750, Audley End House, Essex · N. Dance, oils, 1768, LPL [*see illus.*] · oils, *c.*1785–1799, Audley End House, Essex · engraving, repro. in *The New Christian's Magazine*, 16 (2 June 1783) · line print, BM, NPG

**Wealth at death** all to widow: will, PRO, PROB 11/1102, fols. 120r–120v; printed with appraisal 'no real estate', *GM* (1783), 280 · rich; left substantial library and collection of prints, which widow bequeathed to Lambeth Palace: Rowden, *Primates of the four Georges*, 345, 347

**Cornwallis, James**, fourth Earl Cornwallis (1743–1824), bishop of Lichfield and Coventry, was the third son of Charles Cornwallis, first Earl Cornwallis (1700–1762), and his wife, Elizabeth Townshend (*d.* 1785), daughter of Charles *Townshend, second Viscount Townshend of Raynham, and was the younger brother of Charles *Cornwallis, first Marquess Cornwallis (1738–1805). He was born in Dover Street, Piccadilly, London, on 25 February 1743, and was educated at Eton College and Christ Church, Oxford, where he graduated BA in June 1763, before being given a fellowship at Merton, from which college he took the MA degree in 1766. On leaving Oxford he entered as a member of the Temple, and intended practising at the bar, but on the advice of his uncle Frederick *Cornwallis (1713–1783), archbishop of Canterbury, he changed his mind and was ordained.

Cornwallis commenced his career in the church by acting as chaplain to his cousin Lord Townshend, lord lieutenant of Ireland, until in 1769 he was presented by his uncle to the living of Ickham, Kent, to which that of the neighbouring parish of Adisham was added the following year. In this same year (1770) he was made a prebendary of Westminster, rector of Newington, Oxford, and then of Wrotham, Kent. On receiving this last appointment he resigned the livings of Ickham and Adisham, but six months later he was for the second time inducted as rector of Ickham, a dispensation having been granted which allowed him to hold the rectory of Wrotham conjointly with that of Ickham and the chapel of Staple. In 1771 he married Catharine, daughter of Galfridus Mann of Newton and Boughton Malherbe, and sister of Sir Horace Mann. They had a daughter, Elizabeth, two children—Charles and Susan—who died in infancy, and a son, James.

In 1773, having in the meantime again resigned the living at Ickham, Cornwallis became, still by his uncle's patronage, rector of Boughton Malherbe in the same county. From being a prebendary of Westminster he was preferred in 1775 to the deanery of Canterbury, while he continued to hold his parochial cures, and at about the same time he received the honorary degree of DCL from his university. In 1781 he was consecrated bishop of Lichfield and Coventry, and then at length retired from his Kentish livings. On the translation of Bishop Douglas of Carlisle to the see of Salisbury in 1791, Cornwallis succeeded him as dean of Windsor, a position which three years later he exchanged for that of dean of Durham.

The bishops of Lichfield lived at Eccleshall Castle rather than the more modest palace in the close. Although the house at Eccleshall adjoined the churchyard, Cornwallis insisted on driving through the town in his four-horse carriage to the church gates, and no one left the church before him after services. A turnpike was set up near his gate, whereupon he moved to Richmond, Surrey: from thence he made a visitation every three years. This resulted in more than 1200 confirmations at one time in Stafford and 700 in Tamworth. It is said that Cornwallis's example encouraged widespread pluralism in the diocese. He wrote a subservient letter to Pitt in 1791 asking for the deanery of St Paul's but received a crushing reply. Between 1777 and 1811 he published five of his sermons.

In August 1823 the second Marquess (and third Earl) Cornwallis died; the marquessate became extinct, but the earldom reverted to James Cornwallis. The bishop was by now in his eighty-second year, and on 20 January 1824 he died at Richmond. He had been bishop of Lichfield for nearly forty-three years, and was buried in his cathedral. According to the *Gentleman's Magazine*, his funeral cortège was splendid, going from Richmond to St Albans where it stayed one night and proceeding to Lichfield on the following day. Cornwallis's memorial tablet in Lichfield Cathedral states merely that he was 'Highly respected throughout his diocese'.

ALSAGER VIAN, *rev.* PAT BANCROFT

**Sources** W. Beresford, *Lichfield* [1880] · *GM*, 1st ser., 94/1 (1824), 279 · Foster, *Alum. Oxon.* · *VCH Staffordshire*, 3.69 · chapter act books, 1781–1824, Lichfield Cathedral Archives, Lichfield · BL, Add. MS 19167, fol. 142 · *Fasti Angl.* (Hardy) · GEC, *Peerage* · E. Hasted, *The history and topographical survey of the county of Kent*, 4 vols. (1778–99)

**Archives** PRO, letters to William Pitt, PRO 30/8
**Likenesses** J. Goldar, line drawing, BM, NPG; repro. in *The New Christian's Magazine* (1783) · H. W. Pickersgill, mezzotint, BM, NPG · attrib. G. Romney, oils, Canterbury Cathedral, deanery · W. Ward, engraving (after H. W. Pickersgill), Lichfield Cathedral Library · W. Ward, mezzotint (after H. W. Pickersgill), BM, NPG

**Cornwallis, Jane**. *See* Bacon, Jane, Lady Bacon (1580/81–1659).

**Cornwallis, Sir Kinahan** (1883–1959), diplomatist, was born on 19 February 1883 in New York, the son of Kinahan Cornwallis, journalist and writer, and his wife, Elizabeth Dickinson Chapman, of Hartford, Connecticut. He was educated at Haileybury College and at University College, Oxford; he graduated with a second-class degree in jurisprudence in 1905, before going on to study Arabic. Cornwallis was a renowned athlete, representing Oxford against Cambridge at athletics for four consecutive years, and was president of the Oxford University Athletic Club from 1904 to 1906. On leaving Oxford in 1906 he joined the Sudan civil service. After postings in Khartoum and Kassala, his knowledge of Arabic and Arab affairs was recognized by the Egyptian government, which first borrowed him in 1912 for service in the ministry of finance, and then, in 1914, made him a permanent member of their civil service. He remained there for the rest of his career, being seconded at different times to the army, the foreign office, and the Iraq government. On 14 October 1911 he married Gertrude Dorothy Bowen (d. 1958), second daughter of Sir Albert Edward Bowen, first baronet, businessman and public servant. There were two sons and one daughter of the marriage, which was dissolved in 1925.

On the outbreak of war in 1914, Gilbert Clayton at general headquarters intelligence had Cornwallis commissioned in the Egyptian army and took him into his own office; in 1915 he became a member of the Arab bureau where D. G. Hogarth was then director. A year later he accompanied Hogarth and Ronald Storrs to Jiddah in order to confirm with Sherif Hussein of Mecca the outbreak of the Arab uprising against Ottoman rule; during the event one of Hussein's sons, Feisal, accompanied by T. E. Lawrence, led an Arab force alongside allied forces in the occupation of Palestine and Syria and, specifically, in the capture of Damascus in October 1918. Cornwallis succeeded Hogarth as director of the Arab bureau in 1916, and he took over as regular editor of the *Arab Bulletin*, a series of wide-ranging summaries of confidential information on the Arab world, to which he contributed *Asir before World War I: a Handbook* (1916). Lawrence immortalized Cornwallis in his *Seven Pillars of Wisdom* (1935) as being at this stage of his career:

> a man rude to look upon, but apparently forged from one of those incredible metals with a melting point of thousands of degrees. So he could remain for months hotter than other men's white-heat, and yet look cold and hard.
> (Lawrence, 58)

Cornwallis inspired trust and confidence at all levels, while his kindness, courteousness, and innate leadership evoked the loyalty of all those who served him. Having become a lieutenant-colonel in 1916, he was awarded the DSO in 1917, and appointed CBE in 1919.

Cornwallis's appointment in 1919 as a political officer with the Egyptian expeditionary force occupying Syria marked the beginning of a long collaboration and close friendship with Feisal. While the allies gathered at the Paris peace conference, Feisal attempted to create an independent Arab state. However, as determined by an Anglo-French agreement in 1916, and by negotiations of the allies in Paris, British forces evacuated Syria in November 1919 and left France with a free hand to expel Feisal and establish mandatory rule. Feisal protested, and Cornwallis was assigned the task of persuading him to accept a compromise. When, the following year, an uprising in Mesopotamia persuaded British officials that its inhabitants were as determined to establish self-government as Britain was to reduce its military responsibilities, Cornwallis was deputed by Lord Curzon to offer Feisal a newly created throne at Baghdad. Feisal especially asked that Cornwallis accompany him on his journey from Jiddah to his new kingdom in June 1921. This attachment lasted for fourteen years, during which Cornwallis remained permanently in Baghdad at the ministry of the interior (where he exerted influence over the political administration and the military) and acted as a personal adviser to King Feisal. While the British mandate operated, Cornwallis helped construct the new state of Iraq: his great influence with the tribes and ruling members of the Iraq government enabled him to carry on the Iraq civil service originated by Sir Arnold Wilson with the aim of training Iraqis for independence.

Cornwallis also worked untiringly to bring about the Anglo-Iraqi treaty of 1930, which led to the independence of Iraq while safeguarding essential British strategic interests in communications and oil. British advisers clearly continued to exert much influence in independent Iraq, and the extent to which a precarious balance was maintained at that period between King Feisal, the Iraqi government, and the British authorities is surely a testament to Cornwallis's abilities. 'Among us', wrote Freya Stark, 'he held quiet authority which no one dreamt of gainsaying, made up of wisdom and kindness and courage' (Stark, 2). During these years Cornwallis's appointment as CMG in 1926, his knighthood in 1929, and his advancement to KCMG in 1933 underlined the recognition he received in London. After the signing of the treaty Cornwallis continued at Baghdad to advise on the workings of the new state, but King Feisal died in 1933 and was succeeded by his popular, though inexperienced, son, Ghazi I. Upon the admission of Iraq to the League of Nations in 1932, there followed continuous efforts on the part of the government to reduce both the number of foreign advisers and their influence; many contracts were simply not renewed. Cornwallis retired in 1935 and, as a special mark of the royal family's appreciation for his long and distinguished service, he was invested with the first class of the order of Rafidain (order of the Two Rivers) by King Ghazi. On 19 July 1937 he married, as his second wife, Margaret (Madge)

Clark, only daughter of Harry Ralph Clark, of Lymington, Hampshire.

The outbreak of war in 1939 found Cornwallis in the Middle East division of the Ministry of Information. In April 1941 he returned to Baghdad as ambassador, in succession to Sir Basil Newton. He arrived at a critical period: an army coup had forced the regent and the pro-British politicians to flee the capital and had brought to power an apparently pro-axis government under Rashid Ali al-Gaylani. The status of the 1930 Anglo-Iraqi treaty was of immediate concern, and Cornwallis's first task was to demand that British troops be allowed transport through the country. Realizing that the new regime was widely supported, Cornwallis proceeded with caution; but when negotiations with Rashid Ali's government deteriorated, British military intervention duly restored power to the old ruling coalition. On 31 May an armistice was signed. When the mayor of Baghdad and two officers came to surrender, and asked that the independence of the country still be respected, Cornwallis is said to have replied:

> Many years ago I fought, together with King Feisal the lamented who was my friend, for the freeing of the Arabs, and together we built up the Kingdom of Iraq. And do you think that I would willingly see destroyed what I have helped to build? (Stark, 163)

But the crisis through which Iraq had passed would have profound repercussions: the humiliation of being placed under British military occupation for the duration of the war played a formative role in the Iraqi revolution of 1958 and the overthrow of the monarchical regime which Cornwallis had done so much to foster.

Cornwallis, who was advanced to GCMG in 1943, remained as ambassador until March 1945. After returning to England he continued at the Foreign Office as chairman of the Middle East committee, and in 1946 he went with Lord Stansgate to Cairo on the commission to discuss a new Egyptian treaty; but ill health beset him and he retired altogether in that year. He died at his home, Castle Mill House, North Warnborough, near Basingstoke, Hampshire, on 3 June 1959. He was survived by his second wife and by the daughter and one son of his first marriage, his younger son having been killed in action in 1945.

MARTIN BUNTON

**Sources** DNB · *The Times* (4 June 1959) · F. Stark, *East is west* (1946) · T. E. Lawrence, *Seven pillars of wisdom: a triumph* (1935) · R. Storrs, *Orientations*, 2nd edn (1945) · *The letters of Gertrude Bell*, 2 (1927) · P. P. Graves, *The life of Sir Percy Cox* (1941) · P. W. Ireland, *Iraq* (1937) · *WWW*, 1951–60 · Burke, *Peerage*
**Archives** St Ant. Oxf., Middle East Centre, corresp. with A. E. Kinch · U. Durham L., Sudan archive, letters to Sir Harold MacMichael; corresp. with Sir Reginald Wingate | FILM BFI NFTVA, news footage
**Likenesses** W. Stoneman, photographs, 1933–47, NPG · F. Stark, photographs, 1941, St Ant. Oxf., Middle East Centre; repro. in Stark, *East is west*
**Wealth at death** £94,724 3s. 3d.: probate, 21 July 1959, CGPLA Eng. & Wales

**Cornwallis, Sir Thomas** (1518/19–1604), administrator, was the eldest son of Sir John Cornwallis (c.1491–1544), steward of the household of Prince Edward from 1538 to 1544, and his wife, Mary, daughter of Edward Sulyard of

Sir Thomas Cornwallis (1518/19–1604), attrib. George Gower, c.1577

Otes, Essex. He was admitted to Lincoln's Inn in 1539. Thomas had married Anne (d. 1581), daughter of Sir John Jerningham of Somerleyton, Suffolk, by 1540 and was knighted at Westminster on 1 December 1548. In the summer of 1549 he joined other East Anglian gentry under the command of William Parr, first marquess of Northampton, to quell the rebellion led by Robert Ket. Cornwallis was taken prisoner when the rebels captured Norwich, but regained his freedom after the earl of Warwick defeated Ket's forces. Perhaps because of that assistance to the government, in 1553 Cecil listed Cornwallis as a supporter of Queen Jane. As sheriff in that year of Norfolk and Suffolk, Cornwallis was swept up in the succession crisis of July 1553. In response to Northumberland's letter, he had dutifully proclaimed Lady Jane at Ipswich, but Thomas Poley's declaration of Mary the same day left him wondering which side to support. According to Wingfield's account he stood at 'the crossroad' as he weighed Mary's legitimate claim and local popularity against the armaments and 'the wealth of the entire kingdom together with the nobility' (MacCulloch, *Vita*, 255–6). Reliable news indicating the possibility of violence and London's dissatisfaction with Northumberland induced Cornwallis to change his mind. He proclaimed Mary and rushed to swear allegiance as she made her way to Framlingham Castle on 12 July. Mary rewarded him with a seat on her council and appointed his wife to her household as a lady of the privy chamber.

Cornwallis represented Gatton, Surrey, in Mary's first

parliament, but his increasingly onerous assignments often took him away from the court and council. In October 1553 he was appointed with Sir Robert Bowes to treat with the Scottish commissioners on border matters, and a code of march law was agreed by them at Berwick on 4 December. Cornwallis played a leading part in attempts to defuse Wyatt's rebellion. On 22 January 1554 Mary sent him with Sir Edward Hastings to Dartford to confer with Wyatt, whom they were instructed to tell that she 'marvelled' at his 'unnatural stire and commotion' for 'thimpeachment of the marriage' (PRO, SP 11/2/9). Nothing came of these approaches, and in March Cornwallis served on the commission for Wyatt's trial. In the previous month he was dispatched with Lord William Howard and Sir Edward Hastings to bring the Princess Elizabeth from Ashridge in Hertfordshire to London. They found her 'willing and conformable' although she tried to delay the journey on the grounds of her recent illness. When his political allies, the conservative and Catholic members of the council, suggested sending Elizabeth to the Tower, Cornwallis joined the princess's supporters in opposing that plan. As a councillor and MP for Grampound, Cornwall, in Mary's second parliament he joined those who tried to block Gardiner's plan for a speedy Catholic restoration. On 7 May 1554 he was appointed treasurer of Calais under his cousin, Sir Thomas Wentworth, second Lord Wentworth; he remained there until about two months before the town fell into the hands of the French in January 1558. The suspicions of Sir Thomas's complicity with the French which are recorded in the lines:

> Who built Brome Hall? Sir Thomas Cornwallis
> How did he build it? By selling of Calais.

appear to have been unfounded. Wentworth, Cornwallis, and others at Calais had warned the queen of the weakness of the garrison, and urgently requested a larger force.

On 25 December 1557 Cornwallis was made comptroller of the household in the place of Sir Robert Rochester, and in the following month he was elected MP for Suffolk. In her will Mary named him one of her six assistant executors. But at the end of 1558 Elizabeth removed him from his post in the household as well as from the privy council, and he retired to Suffolk. As a Catholic, a trusted servant of Mary, and a client of the duke of Norfolk, he was an object of suspicion after the northern rising in 1569. Cornwallis was arrested with his son-in-law Sir Thomas Kitson, and both men were interrogated about their involvement with Norfolk and their religious practice. After remaining in custody for a year Cornwallis made his submission on 20 June 1570, protesting loyalty to the queen. He agreed to conform to the extent that 'Almyghte God wyll gyve me grace to be further persuadyd' (PRO, SP 12/43/10). Cornwallis exemplified that generation of Catholics who were torn between their loyalty to the crown and their faith. The question of religious preference, loyalty, and preferment split his family as well. His sons William, whose unsuccessful attempts to forge a career at court caused his father considerable concern, and Charles *Cornwallis, later ambassador to Spain, conformed, while his wife and

daughters remained Catholic. Cornwallis attended church for a time, but while others prayed on their knees, he was reported to have sat reading Catholic devotional works. By 1578 he had returned to recusancy, and he had become involved in what became the long-running dispute over the legitimacy of the secret marriage of his youngest daughter, Mary, a devout Catholic, to the young earl of Bath. His long-standing friendship with Lord Burghley could not solve Mary's problem, but it did protect Cornwallis and his family from the most severe consequences of recusancy.

Cornwallis remained recusant while also continuing to protest his loyalty to the crown. In a letter to Lord Burghley, dated 9 July 1584, transmitting a copy of his letter to the bishop of Norwich justifying his non-attendance at church, he asserted that 'no action of his life discovered a disobedient or unquiet thought towards her majesty', but 'much unquietness bredd in myselfe to satisfy Hir Majesty' (PRO, SP 12/172/17). His name, along with the female members of his family, continued to appear on Suffolk recusant rolls until his death on 24 December 1604 in the eighty-sixth year of his life. Wingfield had described him in 1553 as 'a young man of ready eloquence and conspicuous worth', and a portrait of 1590 depicts a handsome and sensitive man. He was buried on 28 December in the church in Brome, Suffolk, where the inscription on the monument erected to his memory notes his loyalty to the crown.

ANN WEIKEL

**Sources** D. MacCulloch, 'The *Vita Mariae Angliae Reginae* of Robert Wingfield of Brantham', *Camden miscellany, XXVIII*, CS, 4th ser., 29 (1984), 181–301 • P. McGrath and J. Rowe, 'The recusancy of Sir Thomas Cornwallis', *Proceedings of the Suffolk Institute of Archaeology*, 28 (1958–60), 226–71 • A. Simpson, 'The courtier', *The wealth of the gentry, 1540–1660: East Anglian studies*, new edn (1963), 142–78 • D. E. Hoak, 'Two revolutions in Tudor government: the formation and organization of Mary I's privy council', *Revolution reassessed: revisions in the history of Tudor government and administration*, ed. C. Coleman and D. Starkey (1986) • A. Weikel, 'Sins of the fathers?: the marriage of Mary Cornwallis', *Recusant History*, 23 (1996–7), 16–26 • *The private correspondence of Jane, Lady Cornwallis, 1613–1644*, ed. Lord Braybrooke (1842), xxxii–xxxiv • HoP, *Commons, 1509–58*, 1.708–9 • *DNB* • *CSP Spain, 1554–67* • *APC, 1552–8* • *CPR, 1553–8* • will, PRO, PROB 11/105, sig. 11 • PRO, state papers, domestic, Mary I, SP 11/2/9; SP 11/3/21 • PRO, state papers, domestic, Elizabeth I, SP 12/43/10; SP 12/172/17 • BL, Cotton MS Caligula B.IX, fol. 2; Harleian MS 6994, fol. 78; Lansdowne MS 103, fol. 2 • W. A. Shaw, *The knights of England*, 2 vols. (1906) • D. MacCulloch, *Suffolk and the Tudors: politics and religion in an English county, 1500–1600* (1986) • W. P. Baildon, ed., *The records of the Honorable Society of Lincoln's Inn: admissions*, 1 (1896)

**Archives** Suffolk RO, Ipswich, corresp. and papers, HA411, boxes 1, 3–4, 5, 7–8, 72–3 | BL, Lansdowne MSS • CUL, Hengrave MSS • PRO, state papers, Mary I, Elizabeth I

**Likenesses** attrib. G. Gower, oils on panel, *c.*1577, Audley End, Essex [*see illus.*] • monument, Brome church, Suffolk

**Wealth at death** see will, PRO, PROB 11/105, sig. 11; PRO, C 142/290/99

**Cornwallis, Thomas** (1663–1731), commissioner of lotteries, was born in Brome, Suffolk, on 31 July 1663, the fourth son of Charles, second Baron Cornwallis (1632–1673), and his wife, Margaret, *née* Playsted (*d.* 1669). The Cornwallis family had a long tradition of service to the royal household. In April 1676 Thomas and his elder brother William were admitted fellow-commoners of Corpus Christi College, Cambridge. Thomas left Cambridge without taking a degree and in January 1680 obtained a commission as ensign in the 1st foot guards. He was promoted captain in 1683, serving in Portsmouth in succession to his brother Frederick. Between 1685 and 1687 he captained a company of grenadiers in the regiment known as 'our Holland'.

In 1710, when the system of parliamentary lotteries was reintroduced after a break of ten years, Cornwallis was appointed one of the managers and directors at a salary of £200 p.a., and retained this position for the remainder of his life. The lottery was intended to raise £150,000 by sales of £10 tickets, the majority of which earned 5s. annually, the few winning tickets being worth up to £1000 annually, for thirty-two years. Such was its popularity that two lotteries were run each year to 1714, when Jacobite troubles brought proceedings to a temporary halt. When they recommenced in 1719 Cornwallis's own annuity was raised to £400, with an additional pension of £100. The lottery was run erratically until 1726 when many of the tickets remained unsold and it then ceased until 1731.

Cornwallis was childless, though twice married, first to Jane, widow of Colonel Vernam, and second, on 18 April 1723, to Anne, daughter of Sir Hugh Owen and widow of John Barlow of Lawrenny, Pembrokeshire. He died at his home in St James Street, Westminster, on 29 December 1731. His widow died at Bath on 7 April 1732.

ANITA McCONNELL

**Sources** J. Redington, ed., *Calendar of Treasury papers*, 6 vols., PRO (1868–89), *1710, 1718* · *Masters' History of the college of Corpus Christi and the Blessed Virgin Mary in the University of Cambridge*, ed. J. Lamb (1831), 271 · J. Ashton, *A history of English lotteries* (1893), 51–60 · C. Dalton, ed., *English army lists and commission registers, 1661–1714*, 1–2 (1892–4); repr. (1960) · wills of Anne and Thomas Cornwallis, PRO, PROB 11/651 sig 101

**Cornwallis, Sir William, the younger** (*c*.1579–1614), essayist, was probably born in Fincham, Norfolk, eldest child of Sir Charles *Cornwallis (*c*.1555–1629), diplomat and court official, and his first wife, Anne Nicholls (*bap.* 1551, *d.* 1584), daughter of Thomas Fincham of Norfolk. An unconfirmed report suggests that he studied at Queen's College, Oxford. He married Katherine Parker (1582?–1634) on 26 August 1595; they had eleven children. Serving in the earl of Essex's Irish campaign, he was knighted on 5 August 1599. Whether or not he was involved in Essex's rebellion, he lived quietly for the rest of Queen Elizabeth's reign and was for a time in Edinburgh, where he introduced Sir Thomas Overbury to Robert Carr. Confusion of Cornwallis with his uncle, Sir William the elder (*b.* before 1566, *d.* 1611), has made nonsense even of recent discussions of his work, attributing to him his uncle's greater age, retired life, and friendship with Ben Jonson. In 1600 and 1601 he published two volumes of familiar *Essayes*. About 1600 he began writing paradoxical essays, some published posthumously as *Essayes, or Rather, Encomions* (1616) and *Essayes of Certaine Paradoxes* (1617). Among the latter is his encomium of Richard III, dedicated in an extant manuscript to John Donne. Other works include a verse epistle to Donne, an elegy on the

death of Prince Henry, and *Discourses upon Seneca the Tragedian*.

Cornwallis writes as a gentleman amateur on such subjects as ambition, resolution, youth, essays and books, and humility. His tone is meditative, his style fluent but discursive, his periods short and balanced. Illustrative examples are drawn from his own experience, though with evident modesty. He is concerned with self-improvement, particularly for statesmen, stressing stoic virtues such as resolution, fortitude, and endurance. His method is influenced by Montaigne, his ethics by Seneca. The paradoxes range from satirical praise of misfortunes (the French pox, debt) to what seem at least partly serious defences of historical figures (Julian the Apostate, Richard III). The essay on Richard III is the first extant attempt at a defence of that king. There have been suggestions (Zeeveld; Kincaid and Ramsden), based on the changes in the manuscript versions, that Cornwallis was adapter rather than author of this work. Though limited to excusing Richard for reason of state rather than disproving the accusations against him, it influenced later defenders, beginning with Sir George Buck.

On James I's accession in 1603, Cornwallis became a member of the king's privy chamber. He won favourable notice from the earls of Northampton and Salisbury and from Sir Henry Wotton, and they tried to persuade his father—who complained of Cornwallis's extravagance—to support him more liberally. In 1605 he carried dispatches to England from Spain, where his father was resident ambassador. Sir William was MP for Orford, Suffolk, in 1604 and 1614. During the earlier tenure he spoke in parliament supporting the union of England and Scotland. He received a gift of £2000 from the king in 1612, but when he died in the summer of 1614 his widow complained that she and their eight surviving children had been left destitute. He was buried on 1 July in St Martin-in-the-Fields, London.

Cornwallis vies, with Sir Francis Bacon, for the distinction of being the first familiar essayist in English and, with his friend John Donne, for that of being the first English paradoxical essayist. In each case it is impossible to tell who wrote first. He was a pioneer in using Montaigne. Popular in his own time, he is rarely noticed now, obscured by his more famous and older contemporaries. However, the essay tradition, as it re-emerged in the eighteenth and nineteenth centuries, is nearer to Cornwallis's method than it is to Bacon's.

ARTHUR KINCAID

**Sources** R. E. Bennett, 'The life and work of Sir William Cornwallis the younger', PhD diss., Harvard U., 1931 · P. B. Whitt, 'New light on Sir William Cornwallis, the essayist', *Review of English Studies*, 8 (1932), 155–69 · *Essayes by Sir William Cornwallis the younger*, ed. D. C. Allen (1946) · *The private correspondence of Jane, Lady Cornwallis, 1613–1644*, ed. Lord Braybrooke (1842) · R. E. Bennett, 'Sir William Cornwallis', *TLS* (20 Nov 1930), 991 · A. N. Kincaid and J. A. Ramsden, introduction, in W. Cornwallis, *The encomium of Richard III*, ed. A. N. Kincaid (1977) · W. G. Zeeveld, 'A Tudor defense of Richard III', *Proceedings of the Modern Language Association of America*, 55 (1940), 946–57 · W. L. MacDonald, 'The earliest English essayists', *Englische Studien*, 64 (1929), 20–52 · R. E. Bennett, 'Four paradoxes by Sir William Cornwallis, the younger', *Harvard Studies and Notes in Philology and Literature*, 13 (1931), 219–40 · R. E. Bennett, 'Sir William

Cornwallis's use of Montaigne', *Proceedings of the Modern Language Association of America*, 48 (1933), 1080–89 · R. L. Colie, *Paradoxia epidemica* (1966)

**Archives** Hunt. L., discourse on Richard III | Bodl. Oxf., Tanner MSS

**Likenesses** engraving, *c*.1632 (William and Charles Cornwallis?), repro. in W. Cornwallis, *Essayes* (1632), frontispiece

**Wealth at death** widow complained she was destitute: *APC*, 1 July 1614

**Cornwallis, Sir William** (1744–1819), naval officer, was born at Eye, Suffolk, on 20 February 1744, the fourth son of Charles, fifth Baron and first Earl Cornwallis (1700–1762), a royal household official, and his wife, the Hon. Elizabeth Townshend (*d.* 1785), daughter of Charles *Townshend, second Viscount Townshend. He entered Eton College in 1753 and joined the navy in 1755, under the patronage of the duke of Newcastle.

**Early career** Cornwallis's first ship, the *Newark*, went to North America under Admiral Edward Boscawen to intercept a French reinforcement for Canada; she was present at the capture of Louisbourg in 1758, and at the battle of Quiberon Bay. Shortly afterwards Cornwallis went to the Mediterranean. In December 1760 Cornwallis moved into the flagship of Admiral Charles Saunders, and on 5 April 1761 he was appointed lieutenant. After the death of his father in June 1762 and the retirement of his father's patron Newcastle, Cornwallis's mother and eldest brother, Charles *Cornwallis (now second Earl Cornwallis), expressed some anxiety about his career, but he was able to secure peacetime employment through his ability, presence of mind under fire, and family interest. In July 1764 he was promoted commander, and on 20 April 1765 he was made captain by the new Rockingham ministry, which his brother supported. Cornwallis was an early convert to the divisional system whereby each lieutenant took charge of a division of the ship's company, which he introduced aboard his first captain's command. Cornwallis knew the value of his political friends and family, all of whom were whigs. In 1768 he was returned as MP for the local family constituency of Eye in Suffolk, a seat he retained until 1774. In 1784 Lord Howe (at that time first lord of the Admiralty) persuaded him to stand as the government candidate at Portsmouth. In 1790, after Howe left the Admiralty, Cornwallis returned to Eye, and he remained in parliament until January 1807.

Cornwallis was appointed to the *Pallas* in 1774, and, operating on the west African coast, he arrested several rebel American vessels, which were loading gunpowder in the African rivers. In 1776 he moved to the West Indies and North American stations, before going home. Moving to the *Lion* (64 guns) in August 1778 Cornwallis returned to the West Indies in time to take part in the battle of Grenada on 6 July 1779. The *Lion*, in the van, suffered severely, being effectively dismasted, but Cornwallis managed to spread some sails on the stumps of his masts and limp to Jamaica. While the *Lion* was refitting Cornwallis met Horatio Nelson. A shared commitment to the highest professional standards, and a dynamic approach to tactical problems cemented a warm personal relationship that would

**Sir William Cornwallis (1744–1819)**, by Daniel Gardner, 1781

last until Nelson's death. The following March Cornwallis commanded a small squadron cruising in the Windward passage. Off Monte Christi he encountered a French convoy escorted by a more powerful squadron, which attacked him on 21 March. Although heavily outnumbered Cornwallis kept up a running fight throughout the day, until reinforcements arrived the following morning and the French broke off. At the end of the year Cornwallis returned to England, with Nelson, more dead than alive after the Nicaragua expedition, as a passenger. In the spring the *Lion* joined Admiral George Darby's fleet for the second relief of Gibraltar.

**Later career and 'Cornwallis's retreat'** In August 1781 Cornwallis took the *Canada* (74 guns) to North America. The attempt to relieve his brother at Yorktown proving futile, the *Canada* was detached to Admiral Samuel Hood in the West Indies. Cornwallis took a prominent part in the three major battles of 1782: St Kitts on 26 January, and the battles off Dominica on 9 and 12 April. On 12 April, in the Saints passage, Admiral George Rodney caught de Grasse with his fleet badly formed, exploited a shift in the wind to break through his line, and imposed close action. Although he took the enemy flagship, Rodney's hesitant conduct of the latter stages of the battle, when he restrained Cornwallis from pursuing a broken, fleeing enemy, excited the derision of a young whig captain, already predisposed to find fault with a tory officer. The *Canada* returned home that autumn, and with Cornwallis's high reputation, and his political friends in office, he was appointed to the yacht *Royal Charlotte* in March 1783, an honorary command he held until October 1787. In September 1787 he was appointed colonel of marines. When his brother Earl Cornwallis was appointed governor-general of Bengal, Cornwallis was sent out as commodore and commander-in-chief in the East Indies in October 1788; and when the French Revolutionary War broke out Cornwallis seized all the French ships within reach, and helped capture the French trading posts at Chandernagore and Pondicherry. He reached England in April 1794.

After his promotion to rear-admiral on 1 February 1793 Cornwallis hoisted his flag in the Channel Fleet in May 1794. He missed the battle of 1 June 1794 because he was escorting a convoy. On 4 July he became a vice-admiral, and in December he moved to the new three-decker *Royal Sovereign* (100 guns). On 16 June 1795 Cornwallis was cruising off Ushant with his flagship, four battleships, and two frigates when a powerful French force of nine battleships and nine frigates under Vice-Admiral Villaret-Joyeuse came into contact early. Cornwallis hauled off and formed a line ahead. The French closed, two of the British ships sailing badly. At daylight on 17 June the French were closing in three divisions, one directly astern and one on each quarter. At 9 a.m. two French ships opened fire, damaging the rigging of the *Mars*. Seeing she was falling to leeward and might be cut off, Cornwallis wore round to support her in his flagship, and ran down to engage the enemy. This bold move caused four French ships steering to attack the *Mars* to pause, enabling her to regain the line of battle. Desultory firing continued until 6 p.m. Shortly after 6.30 the French ships shortened sail and made off to the east, victims of a classic *ruse de guerre*. Cornwallis had detached the frigate *Phaeton* (Captain Robert Stopford), who pretended he was in communication with the main British fleet. 'Cornwallis's retreat' was a monument to his resolve and his skill. In October Cornwallis joined an admiral's revolt, protesting against new regulations which removed soldiers serving on warships from naval discipline. This strained relations with the first lord, Earl Spencer. Cornwallis was ordered to take command of the West Indies fleet and proceed with the army transports in February 1796. When the *Royal Sovereign* was damaged in a collision, Cornwallis, having seen his fleet safely into the Atlantic, returned to Spithead. The Admiralty ordered him to proceed in a frigate. Although willing to proceed as soon as the *Royal Sovereign* was repaired, he declined to go in a frigate, his health being precarious. He was court-martialled for disobedience, and although censured for not proceeding in a ship of the original squadron, he was acquitted. Cornwallis struck his flag and had no more service while Spencer remained at the Admiralty. On 14 February 1799 he became a full admiral, and bought a country seat, Newlands, near Milford in Hampshire.

**Blockade of Brest**  In February 1801 Earl St Vincent became first lord, and selected Cornwallis to replace him in command of the Channel Fleet. The *Ville de Paris* (110 guns), the largest ship in the service, would carry his flag, with little interruption, for the next five years. St Vincent had already drilled the Channel Fleet to the highest standards of seamanship and initiative, but Cornwallis's blockade of Brest was a masterpiece of naval operational art in the age of sail. Denying the French access to stores and supplies exhausted the large Franco-Spanish fleet, while effective British victualling arrangements ensured that the only limits on his fleet were seamanship and human endurance, qualities that Cornwallis possessed in abundance. This was vital, for the collapse of the second coalition left Britain once again single-handedly fighting France. The blockade of Brest was the hub around which British strategy revolved, covering operations in the Baltic and Mediterranean, protecting shipping, and preventing an invasion. At the peace of Amiens Cornwallis came ashore briefly, but St Vincent reappointed him to the channel command before war resumed, and he was on station off Ushant on 17 May 1803, the day before war was declared. The command wore out even the best officers, and Cornwallis went ashore twice for his health, being relieved by Sir Charles Cotton in July and August 1804, and Lord Gardner between April and July 1805. Cornwallis was now sixty, of medium height, and rather stout with a florid complexion.

In the early stages of the blockade St Vincent and Cornwallis were eager to take the initiative, and considered a combined attack on Brest; but there were never enough troops. Cornwallis hoped to attack the fleet in Brest Roads with fireships, but this plan was blocked by Admiral Gambier, the petty and spiteful first sea lord who made the last eighteen months of Cornwallis's sea career a severe trial of his less than perfect patience.

When William Pitt returned to office in May 1804, Henry Dundas, Lord Melville, replaced St Vincent. Melville was soon afterwards succeeded by Admiral Lord Barham, who provided the central direction of the 1805 campaign, but left his commanders to use their initiative on the basis of the available intelligence. Throughout 1805 Napoleon's plans were constantly shifting to meet each new set of circumstances, and may have had more to do with disguising his intention of attacking Austria, and pinning down the British, than invading the British Isles. In early 1805 he planned a grand raid on the British West Indies. This and all subsequent schemes collapsed in the face of coherent British strategic and tactical doctrine, superior British leadership, and his own ignorance of the peculiar problems of war at sea. The major French movement of 1805, Villeneuve's cruise to the West Indies, planned as an attack on trade and colonies, only belatedly became part of an invasion scheme. When Barham divined that Villeneuve was not returning to the Mediterranean he directed Cornwallis to detach Vice-Admiral Sir Robert Calder to pick up the ships blockading Rochfort and Lorient and intercept Villeneuve off Cape Finisterre (Spain). In mid-July Cornwallis stretched to the south to search for Villeneuve, leaving Brest with only a frigate screen for eight days; he had correctly calculated that Admiral Ganteaume would not come out. He did not make contact with Villeneuve, and returned to his post depressed, having once again missed the chance of a battle. On 13 August Calder rejoined the flag, after his inconclusive battle with Villeneuve on 22 July. Nelson, returning from the West Indies, fell in with him on 15 August, and left his squadron with Cornwallis. Cornwallis now commanded thirty-six battleships. The centre was safe, but there were no British battleships in the Mediterranean, and precious few south of Brest. Although Cornwallis's main task was to hold the mouth of the channel, to prevent an invasion of Britain or Ireland, he recognized that French fleets could now control the Mediterranean, which had been abandoned by Nelson, or cruise against British trade.

Cornwallis had to balance these conflicting priorities, and in this crisis he demonstrated his true worth as a strategist of genius. Cornwallis was convinced that Villeneuve, with at least twenty-five sail, was either at Ferrol or already moving south. While Allemand's small Rochefort squadron was supposed to have joined Villeneuve, if it had not it would pose a serious threat to trade. Something had to be done. The initial concentration at the centre had been correct, but with Ganteaume held inside Brest, and morally already beaten, it was time to take the initiative. This led to the most controversial decision of Cornwallis's career. On 16 August, the day after Nelson had reinforced him, Cornwallis divided his fleet. He sent half his ships, under Calder, to Ferrol, to blockade Villeneuve, or to pursue him if he left. Calder had twenty battleships. Barham, who had anticipated the movement, was quick to approve. In fact Cornwallis had not divided his fleet quite as much as mere numbers would suggest. The seventeen ships remaining with his flag included ten three-deckers, including the three most powerful ships in the navy. Against this Villeneuve had twenty-nine ships, but only one three-decker. The relative effectiveness of the two fleets ensured that Cornwallis, as St Vincent had recognized, would not be beaten by any number of French and Spanish ships. Even Ganteaume in Brest only had three three-deckers. Consequently the risk in dividing the Channel Fleet was small, and the prize to be secured was vast. The fleet that Cornwallis detached under Calder was the one that Nelson led at Trafalgar. Had it not been sent Villeneuve would have been able to operate against trade, as Barham feared, return to Toulon, or go to Sicily as Napoleon desired. Between 1803 and 1805 British strategy had been complicated by the sheer number of French and Spanish battleships. Now they were at sea they could be destroyed.

Throughout the campaign Cornwallis knew that every other squadron would, in an emergency, fall back on him. He was also in possession of superior intelligence of French movements. Consequently he knew that if Villeneuve came north to Brest, Calder would be hot on his heels. This understanding proved critical when Ganteaume finally tried to leave Brest on 21 August, following peremptory orders from Napoleon. He had twenty-one battleships, Cornwallis had seventeen. At 4.30 the following morning Cornwallis led the fleet towards the French in a single line. The French made sail, but when the British closed, they went about and ran for the harbour under the cover of heavy shore batteries. Cornwallis tried to cut off a flagship at the rear of the French line, but Ganteaume scrambled back. Cornwallis was slightly wounded by a shell fragment. Once again he had demonstrated exemplary skill. His aggression, based on well-founded confidence, was tempered by a cool head, and informed by strategic wisdom. Although Cornwallis would have preferred to let Ganteaume out to sea, where he could be destroyed, the strategic situation required that he be driven back into harbour. Cornwallis's greatness lay in his ability to see the big picture, and adapt his tactics accordingly. He had to be content with a partial action, the moral significance of which was as great as any fleet battle. Recognizing there was now no danger of an invasion, Cornwallis quickly instructed Calder to pursue Villeneuve if he left Ferrol, and warned Collingwood to expect him off Cadiz.

The position off Brest was complicated by the extended cruise of Allemand's squadron, which was sufficiently powerful to overwhelm any of the extremely valuable commercial and military convoys then on passage. Cornwallis detached five battleships in early September, and at the end of the month took the entire fleet in pursuit, but Allemand's luck held. The Channel Fleet was back off Ushant on 8 October. Within days Barham reported Napoleon's invasion of Germany; the crisis of the naval war had passed. After Trafalgar Cornwallis regretted that he had not been able to speak with Nelson that summer. Cornwallis's inshore division, under Sir Richard Strachan, searching for Allemand, captured the last fugitives from Trafalgar, but Allemand got home, unscathed, on Christmas eve 1805. After Trafalgar the Channel Fleet was divided to meet Barham's overriding concern for the defence of trade. When the blockade was relaxed for the winter, to reduce the damage to the fleet, two French battle squadrons escaped from Brest. They achieved nothing; one was destroyed off San Domingo in January, the other suffered severely from the weather.

**Final years and reputation** Deeply affected by the death of Nelson, exhausted in mind and body, and convinced there would be no more fleet actions, Cornwallis became paranoid. The 'ministry of all the talents' replaced him with St Vincent and he hauled down his flag on 22 February 1806. The death of his brother Charles in 1805, followed by that of his flag captain, John Whitby, on 6 April 1806, ended Cornwallis's earthly ambitions. He saw no further service, and effectively retired from public life, giving up his seat in parliament in early 1807. He spent his remaining years at home, with his horses and parrots, latterly in the company of Whitby's widow. He had never married, had few close friends, and little interest in society. At the peace he was made GCB. He died on 5 July 1819, at Newlands, near Milford, Hampshire, leaving his estate to Mrs Whitby. He was buried in Milford churchyard, alongside Captain Whitby, in an unmarked grave.

Cornwallis lacked the polish and refined manners of his elder brother, preferred the company of other naval men, and considered outward show to be vulgar. He was devoted to the Church of England, and loathed blood sports. Universally admired and respected by his officers, and loved by the sailors, his nicknames were complimentary. The sailors called him Billy Blue, from his constant use of the Blue Peter to keep the fleet at short notice when anchored in Torbay, and Billy-go-tight in mocking tribute to his relative abstemiousness and florid complexion. His fellow admirals used Billy. Given to depression and ill humour, he was always cheered by the prospect of action. Professional to the core of his being, Cornwallis demonstrated the highest qualities of an admiral; his leadership, vision, and determination were unsurpassed, and only the accident of history, the one that denied him a great battle, has kept him out of the pantheon of naval immortals. Although he never had the opportunity to win a great victory, his pivotal role in the years of maximum danger, between 1800 and 1805, reflected leadership, judgement, and professional qualities of the highest order. Like his friend Nelson he had the insight to function at the highest level, and the steadiness to do so at the one place where the war could be lost. Rather than defeating a French fleet he secured a greater victory, defeating Napoleon's strategy. His blockade of the coast of Brittany, through all seasons and all weathers, remains the ultimate achievement of seapower in the age of sail. He held the centre, around which the greatest contest between land and sea power yet waged was played out.                    ANDREW LAMBERT

**Sources** G. Cornwallis-West, *Life of Admiral Cornwallis* (1927) · *Report on manuscripts in various collections*, 8 vols., HMC, 55 (1901–14), vol. 6 · J. Leyland, ed., *Dispatches and letters relating to the blockade of Brest, 1803–1805*, 2 vols., Navy RS, 14, 21 (1899–1902) · A. T. Mahan, *The influence of sea power upon the French Revolution and empire*, 2nd edn., 2 vols. (1893) · E. Desbrieve, *The naval campaign of 1805* (1933) · J. S. Corbett, *The campaign of Trafalgar* (1910) · *Letters and papers of Charles, Lord Barham*, ed. J. K. Laughton, 3, Navy RS, 39 (1911) · *Letters of … the earl of St Vincent, whilst the first lord of the admiralty, 1801–1804*, ed. D. B. Smith, 2 vols., Navy RS, 55, 61 (1922–7) · GEC, *Peerage*

**Archives** New York Historical Society, corresp. and papers · NMM, corresp., journals, and papers · University of Minnesota, Minneapolis, Ames Library of South Asia, letter-books and naval papers, incl. report of Mahe incident [microfilm copies in BL OIOC] | BL, corresp. with T. Graves, Add. MS 40667 · Keele University Library, corresp. with John Whitby and Mrs Whitby · NL Scot., letters to Viscount Melville · NMM, corresp. with Lord Barham · NMM, corresp. with Lord Sandwich · PRO NIre., corresp. with Lord Castlereagh

**Likenesses** D. Gardner, portrait, 1781, priv. coll. [*see illus.*] · F. Haward, stipple, pubd 1784? (after D. Gardner), BM · C. Warren, line engraving, pubd 1805? (after T. Unwin), BM · Roberts, stipple (after J. Barry), BM, NPG · W. N. Skinner (after D. Gardner), NMM

**Wealth at death** over £50,000 in stock, plus property: will, PRO, PROB 11/1618

**Cornwell** [*other married names* Whiteman, Robinson], **Alice Ann** (1852–1932), goldmining industrialist and newspaper proprietor, was born on 1 January 1852 at 18 Bakers Row, West Ham, Essex, one of at least three daughters of George Cornwell, railway guard, and his wife, Jemima Ridpath. At the age of nine she emigrated with her parents to Dunedin, New Zealand. She remained there until the age of seventeen when she left with her parents for Victoria, Australia. Her father became a builder and railway contractor and, later, a gold prospector. While in Victoria, on 4 December 1875 Alice married John Whiteman (*d.* 1892), a politician and poet, and on 17 February 1877 she gave birth

to a son, George Frederick Francis Carl. There was, however, a great disparity in age between Alice and her husband, and a formal separation took place subsequently.

Alice Cornwell, as she was known, returned to England, and after studying at the Royal Academy of Music, where she won several gold medals and composed a number of popular songs and pianoforte pieces, taught music at Queen's College. Following the death of her mother, however, she went back to Australia where her father was then occupied in mining speculations and losing money. Alice Cornwell made herself acquainted with the geology of the goldfield, and convinced herself, and persuaded others, that payable 'reefs' underlay her father's property. Sufficient capital was raised and a shaft sunk: and a vein of gold was struck apparently within a foot of the point at which she had indicated its existence. This discovery was made in the teeth of strong local scepticism and proved to be one of the richest strikes in Victoria: the establishment of the Midas mine in Sulky Gully, Ballarat, led to her becoming known as 'Princess Midas'. The Midas Mine Company was later floated on the London stock market.

With the riches from her goldmine, Alice Cornwell became a well-known and flamboyant figure in Melbourne and London. In late October 1887 *The Times* reported a private view of the Midas gold nugget that Alice Cornwell had arranged at 32 Queen Victoria Street, London. Called the 'Lady Loch', after the wife of the governor of Victoria, it weighed 617 oz, measured 1 foot by 8 inches, and was valued at £2537. *The Times* reported that it was the seventh largest nugget found at Ballarat since 'the Midas gold field has been opened up through the perseverance of Miss Cornwall [as her name was popularly misspelt]' (*The Times*, 29 Oct 1887).

In 1887 Alice Cornwell bought the *Sunday Times* from the FitzGeorge family. Her aim was partly to publicize her next mining venture, the British and Australasian Mining Investment Company, but the editorship was also intended as a present for Frederick Stannard ('Phil') Robinson, a war correspondent whom she was to marry in 1894.

Returning to Australia in the following year, Alice Cornwell's next speculative venture was the purchase of the Wyong estate at a cost of £280,000. This covered 17,000 acres between Sydney and Newcastle and offered excellent prospects for coalmining. Alice Cornwell was also involved in the development of a harbour at Port Adelaide.

In an interview published in Victoria in 1888, Alice Cornwell commented on the prospects for the newspaper she had bought. 'I bought *The Sunday Times*, a Conservative paper. It would be called Liberal out here, for mostly what is Conservative at home is Liberal in Victoria, and so *vice versa*.' She added that when she had bought the paper it was only a scissors and paste affair, with hardly any original news, but after being placed under the management of Phil Robinson it began to be a splendid paper, 'and when I left its circulation was rapidly increasing' (Hobson, Knightley, and Russell, 50). However in reality although the price of the *Sunday Times* was reduced to 1*d.* in a bid to undercut *The Observer* and to fight it out with a new rival, *The People*, also priced at 1*d.*, the circulation remained unresponsive. Although a charming writer, Phil Robinson was a reluctant editor, and left to join Alice Cornwell in Victoria, where he also gave a series of lectures. While he was in Australia, the temporary editorship of the *Sunday Times* was in the hands of Joseph Hatton.

The late 1880s saw the height of Alice Cornwell's fame. She was the subject of a novel entitled *Madame Midas* (1888) by Fergus Hume. This was later turned into a play, which led to a lawsuit in Australia by John Whiteman, then still her husband. Then in July 1889 Alice Cornwell was featured in *Men and Women of the Day*, where she was described as 'singularly earnest and sincere … a woman who has adopted a role unprecedented among her sex'. The article deemed her to be 'one of the most remarkable women of her time' (p. 80).

After over five years as a newspaper proprietor, and having lost money through her mining failures, Alice Cornwell sold the *Sunday Times* in 1893 to Frederick and Rachel Beer. She settled in England and, known formally as Mrs Stannard Robinson, became a successful breeder and exhibitor of pugs, and in 1894 founded the Ladies' Kennel Association. To give publicity to the organization she launched the *Ladies' Kennel Journal*. A keen supporter of the organization was the princess of Wales, later Queen Alexandra.

Alice Cornwell's son became a professional actor at the age of nineteen, changing his name to Sydney Carroll, and for many years was a well-known writer on the theatre, and film critic of the *Sunday Times*. Alice Cornwell died of cancer of the kidney on 7 January 1932 at 19 Palmeria Square, Hove. Her second husband predeceased her.

D. M. GRIFFITHS

**Sources** private information (2004) · H. Hobson, P. Knightley, and L. Russell, *The pearl of days: an intimate memoir of the Sunday Times, 1822–1972* (1972) · D. Griffiths, ed., *The encyclopedia of the British press, 1422–1992* (1992) · *Kennel Gazette* (June 1994) · *Men and Women of the Day*, 2 (1889), 77–80 · *The Times* (29 Oct 1887) · H. J. Gibbney and A. G. Smith, eds., *A biographical register, 1788–1939: notes from the name index of the 'Australian dictionary of biography'*, 1 (1987) · b. cert. · d. cert. · F. Hume, *Madame Midas: realistic and sensational story of Australian mining life* (1888) · P. Mansfield, 'Alice Cornwell—mining speculator', *Ballerat Historian*, 3/2 (Sept 1986), 17–22
**Archives** priv. coll.
**Likenesses** photograph, Hult. Arch.

**Cornwell, James** (1812–1902), educational writer, born in east London on 4 August 1812, was one of nine children of James Cornwell, silk manufacturer, and his wife, Mary Blake. Up to the age of fifteen he was mainly self-taught. He then studied at the model school of the Borough Road Training College of the British and Foreign School Society, and by August 1829 was a fully-fledged student. In the early part of 1830 he was sent as a teacher on supply to the society's schools at Brighton and Chelmsford, and in October to Lindfield in Sussex. He returned to the college in January 1833 for a short period of training.

In April 1835 the society appointed Cornwell organizer of country schools, his duty being to 'organize new schools' and assist newly appointed masters in obtaining

'good discipline by moral means'. In October 1839 he was appointed normal schoolteacher and inspector, and from 1835 worked both in the training college and as an inspector outside. In 1846, when the training department of the institution in Borough Road was recognized by the privy council as a grant-earning normal college, Cornwell was appointed by the British and Foreign School Society its head teacher or principal. Under his care the institution greatly developed and took a high position among the training colleges of the country. His lectures were clear, pertinent, and accurate, and he showed much ability in practical teaching. His principles and methods of school management anticipated later developments.

Cornwell married on 19 November 1840 Mary Ann Wilson of Besthorpe, Nottinghamshire; they had one daughter. He continued his own studies, obtaining an external degree from London University and in 1847 he received a PhD from a German university. In 1860 he became a fellow of the Royal Geographical Society.

In 1841 Cornwell began to publish school books, which enjoyed a universal vogue. With J. T. Crossley, J. G. Fitch, and Henry Dunn, he established the standard type of secular school book which came into general use in the second half of the nineteenth century. His first, *A New English Grammar* (1841), produced in collaboration with Dr Alexander Allen, had reached a twenty-third edition by 1855, and their *Grammar for Beginners* (1855) went through ninety editions. He collaborated with Fitch in publishing *The Science of Arithmetic* (1855). His *School Geography* (1847; 90th edn, 1904) had an enormous sale, though its relentless presentation of facts about the countries of the world, which were to be committed to memory, made it a rather unattractive volume.

Cornwell resigned from the principalship of Borough Road College at a comparatively young age in 1856, and lived in semi-retirement for nearly half a century, writing new works or revising his former ones for the series of school books entitled Dr Cornwell's Educational Series. He was fond of music and the study of nature. For sixteen years he lived at a house he built for himself, Loughborough Park Villa, Brixton, before moving to Purbrook, Crescent Wood Road, Sydenham, where he died on 12 December 1902. He was buried in Norwood cemetery.

ELIZABETH LEE, *rev.* M. C. CURTHOYS

**Sources** *The Times* (15 Dec 1902) · G. F. Bartle, *A history of Borough Road College* (1976) · M. Sturt, *The education of the people* (1967), 230–32
**Likenesses** J. R. Dicksee, portrait, 1903, Borough Road Training College, London
**Wealth at death** £25,425 17*s.* 5*d.*: probate, 24 Jan 1903, *CGPLA Eng. & Wales*

**Cornwell, John Travers** (1900–1916), naval hero, was born on 8 January 1900, at Clyde Cottage, Clyde Place, Leyton, Essex, the son of Eli Cornwell (1852–1916), tram driver and soldier, originally from Newmarket, and his wife, Lily King (*d.* 1918). His siblings included at least two brothers (one of whom was killed in action in August 1918) and a sister. He was educated at Walton Road School, Manor Park, Essex. As a boy he was a keen member of the St

**John Travers Cornwell (1900–1916),** by unknown photographer

Mary's Mission Boy Scout troop at Manor Park until it was disbanded in 1914; posthumously he became a hero of the scout movement, which instituted a Cornwell badge for high character and devotion to duty, and a Cornwell memorial fund to provide scholarships for badge-winners.

Cornwell wished to join the Royal Navy after school but his parents preferred a civilian life for him, and he became a delivery van boy for Brooke Bond & Co., tea merchants. After the outbreak of the First World War his parents relented, and he joined the navy at Devonport on 27 July 1915. During nine months at a training school at Dartmouth he took to seamanship, although gunnery training on HMS *Vivid* proved more challenging. A photograph taken at this time shows keen features, and an attentive, resolute expression. He joined a new light cruiser, HMS *Chester*, on its commissioning day at Cammell Laird's Birkenhead yard, 1 May 1916, and was at sea for only a month before his death.

At the battle of Jutland, on 2 June 1916, Boy First Class Cornwell was stationed at an exposed gun on *Chester*, where he was mortally wounded early in the fight when a shell burst overhead. He remained standing alone at his post, quietly awaiting orders, with the gun's crew lying dead and wounded about him, until the end of the action. Dying shortly afterwards, he was buried in a common grave at Grimsby, Lincolnshire. In his dispatch reporting the battle Sir David Beatty mentioned the courage and patient sense of duty of the boy, who was immediately extolled by publicists, journalists, and public figures as a

model of obedience, selflessness, and fidelity for the young. 'The imperishable boy Cornwell', in Leo Maxse's words, became 'a national hero' (*National Review*, 68, Oct 1916, 193). It was suggested that his photograph should be hung in every elementary school 'so that the lustre of his deed may shine where boys and girls are quick to catch the reflection of lofty and honourable conduct' (*The Spectator*, 15 July 1916, 68). Lord Beresford urged in parliament on 26 July 1916 that Cornwell should receive the Victoria Cross posthumously: 'An honour paid to Cornwell's memory would be an example to the boys of the Empire at their most susceptible age' (*Hansard 5L*, col. 921). Partly as an exercise in patriotic propaganda the boy's remains were re-interred with much pomp in Manor Park cemetery, East Ham, on 29 July 1916. He was gazetted VC on 15 September 1916. His father died five weeks later, and his widowed mother received the cross from George V at Buckingham Palace on 16 November 1916. Cornwell was the youngest ever naval VC, although Arthur FitzGibbon in 1860 had been three months younger at the time of his heroism during a military campaign in China.

30 September 1916 was declared Jack Cornwell day in British elementary schools; penny stamps were printed bearing his portrait; rousing verses were circulated about him; £18,000 was raised in his memory for the Jack Cornwell ward of the Star and Garter Home for Disabled Servicemen at Richmond. Posthumous portraits were made by Sir Robert Baden-Powell, Frank Salisbury, and Fortunino Matania; Matania's picture of the boy standing at his gun, published in *The Sphere* (18 November 1916), became iconic, and the gun itself was installed at the Imperial War Museum. A new-born boy was given the forenames Travers Cornwell as late as 1955.

RICHARD DAVENPORT-HINES

**Sources** *The Times* (7 July 1916), 5b · *The Times* (8 July 1916), 11d · *The Times* (11 July 1916), 9b · *The Times* (26 July 1916), 3a · *The Times* (31 July 1916), 3e · *The Times* (16 Sept 1916) · *The register of the Victoria cross* (1981) · J. Winton [Pratt], *The Victoria cross at sea* (1978) · *The Spectator* (15 July 1916) · *Hansard 5L*, cols. 920–21 · *The Family Record*
**Archives** Newham Archive and Local Studies Library, papers and photographs · Stratford Library, London
**Likenesses** photograph, 1915?, repro. in *Register of the Victoria cross*, 61 · R. Baden-Powell, portrait, 1916, probably Scout Association, London · F. Matania, 1916, repro. in Winton, *Victoria cross at sea*, facing p. 129 · Rembrandt, photogravure, 1916, repro. in *Teachers' World* (July 1916) · F. Salisbury, portrait, 1916 (commissioned by Admiralty) · photograph, 1916, Hult. Arch. · photograph, IWM [*see illus.*]

**Cornysh, William** (*d.* 1502). *See under* Cornysh, William (*d.* 1523).

**Cornysh** [Cornysshe], **William** (*d.* 1523), composer and court impresario, is of unknown parentage. It is likely that he was close kin, perhaps even a son, of **William Cornysh** [Cornysshe] (*d.* 1502), composer, also of unknown parentage. Nothing is known of the elder William's upbringing and musical education. On 25 March 1480 he either already was or was newly appointed as a member of the ensemble of four adult professional singers which since before 1400 had been employed at Westminster Abbey to enhance with polyphonic music the observance of the daily Lady mass and evening Marian antiphon performed in the lady chapel there. Composers of music in these genres had lately expanded its sonority and scope by adding boys' voices to the long-established performing ensemble of men's voices alone. Cornysh was now appointed to raise a team of six boys from the abbey's flourishing almonry school, whom he was to train as singing-boys and with whom he was to expand and modernize the resources of the existing lady chapel choir.

By 1485 Cornysh was renting from the abbey a substantial residence located in Sanctuary Yard, regranted to him in 1489 at a greatly reduced rent. Between 1489 and 1491 he married Joan and on 29 March 1491, four days after leaving the abbey's service, he renewed the lease on this residence in their joint names. As inducement for continuation of his goodwill towards the abbey he was permitted to continue paying only the much reduced rent. He retained possession for the rest of his life, and his widow after him until 1519.

Cornysh's new employment after 1491 is not known. However, his compositions include works which, for their ample scoring and great technical intricacy, seem unlikely to have lain readily within the competence of a small lady chapel choir. This consideration, taken with his need to make independent arrangements for possession of a settled domestic residence, suggests that in 1491 he moved not to a residential job at another church but to membership of one of the dozen or so peripatetic household chapel choirs, of the highest quality, maintained at this period by members of the nobility. It may have been at the instigation of such an employer that from Christmas 1499 Cornysh found himself in receipt of an annual pension of £5 6s. 8d., payable to him by Westminster Abbey in recognition of his past services there.

The attribution of certain works to one William Cornish junior in a manuscript of (apparently) 1501 discloses the existence at that time of an older composer of renown from whom the younger man needed to be distinguished. Eight major compositions attributed simply to William Cornysh were included in the Eton choirbook, a collection of Marian votive antiphons and Magnificats compiled between about 1502 and 1505; four survive complete, the remainder being incomplete or lost. The style of the surviving music is characteristic of a mature composer of the 1480s and 1490s, expansive in concept, ornate in detail, and requiring of its performers much virtuosity of vocal technique; it thus appears to be the work of a man born in the 1440s rather than thirty years later and (as first proposed by David Skinner in 1997) may be attributed to the elder William Cornysh. These works were well known and widely copied. (Further lost works attributed simply to Cornysh may be the work of either the older or the younger man of that name.)

Even if Cornysh the elder did not achieve the profundity of his greater contemporary John Browne or the extended control of sheer display manifested by Richard Davy, his work impresses for its boldness of execution and confidence of design. Further, *Stabat mater* exhibits refined deployment of vocal scoring for apparently calculated,

even affective, ends, while the 'Gloria patri' in the Magnificat includes one of the most memorably extrovert and virtuosic passages in all early Tudor music. *Ave Maria, mater Dei* and *Gaude virgo, mater Christi*, both for four men's voices, are in a style at once more concentrated and compact.

Cornysh died between 5 May and 29 September 1502; the fraternity of St Nicholas, the guild of parish clerks and professional church musicians of London and its hinterland, to membership of which he had been admitted during 1480–81, was informed. He was buried with death-knell and torches in St Margaret's churchyard, Westminster, of which his residence in Sanctuary Yard rendered him a parishioner. During the following year the churchwardens received from his widow a bequest of 6s. 8d., and in 1509 the abbey's almonry possessed a silver bowl donated by William Cornysh, 'syngar'.

William Cornysh the younger may have been the elder William's son, but not from his marriage to Joan. Both men have been confused with one another. Of Cornysh the younger's education and musical training nothing is known. By 1493 he had become a lay gentleman of the Chapel Royal, and so remained until his death.

The Chapel Royal was England's foremost ecclesiastical choir, and Cornysh's membership coincided with the beginning of its greatest flowering as a cynosure of liturgical and musical practice. Its personnel of forty professional singers (thirty men, ten boys) conducted the greater part of the daily ecclesiastical liturgy of Salisbury use. Extending to some five or six hours of work each day, this comprehended not only the intricately detailed complexities of the ever changing text, ritual, movement, and plainsong of the liturgy but also the ornate and extended polyphony of this period, composed for unaccompanied virtuoso voices in up to six independent parts.

On 29 September 1509 Cornysh was appointed to succeed William Newark as master of the choristers. The duties of this very exacting job extended to teaching fundamental music theory and notation, highly developed techniques of singing, all the intricacies of the liturgy, the basic Latin needed for their comprehension, and the vocal parts to be sung by the boys in the polyphonic repertory, including, for instance, masses by Robert Fayrfax, John Taverner, Hugh Aston, Thomas Ashwell, and John Marbeck. The boys were rewarded particularly for their execution of two great set pieces from the liturgical year, *Audivi vocem* at matins of All Saints, and *Gloria in excelsis Deo* at Christmas day matins. Cornysh supervised all arrangements for the choristers' boarding and feeding, and was responsible also for their recruitment, using a royal commission empowering him to take from other choirs their very best boys already fully trained. Gratuities paid to him by Thetford Priory, Norfolk, in 1511/12 and by Westminster Abbey in 1522 may well have been bribes to induce him not to take singing-boys from their respective lady chapel choirs.

Cornysh and the boys attended Henry VIII in France on the Thérouanne expedition of 1513 and at the Field of Cloth of Gold, held at Guînes between 7 and 24 June 1520.

Perhaps this latter occasion was the most demanding single event in Cornysh's entire career; at its climax the English and French chapels royal jointly sang high mass in (doubtless competitive) alternation, concluding the service with several motets, 'which was a heavenlie heareing' (Russell, 214). No sacred music set to Latin words can confidently be ascribed to Cornysh as composer. Nevertheless, certain settings of Lady mass sequences copied for the choir of King's College, Cambridge, in 1508/9 may well, from their late date, have been his work rather than that of his earlier namesake, as also may have been the four-part masses and single six-part mass recorded among that choir's repertory in 1529.

Cornysh married Joan (*d*. in or after 1523) before January 1513. As well as many cash rewards, some very large, he received from Henry VII and Henry VIII a grant of the administration of a territorial windfall to the crown (1494), monastic corrodies in the royal gift (Malmesbury Abbey in Wiltshire in 1495, Thorney Abbey in Cambridgeshire in 1496, Thetford Priory in 1523), and a lease of the manor of Hilden (near Tonbridge, Kent), with survivorship to his wife, Joan, and son, Henry, on 20 August 1523. His service at court was not uninterrupted; he wrote his poem 'A treatise between truth and information', dated July 1504, while incarcerated in the Fleet prison. This text constituted his claim that the charge laid against him by some informant was untrue and his resulting imprisonment unjust. Its use of imagery drawn from musical experience is of great interest, and although the style of Cornysh's writing lacks any conspicuous elegance, the concepts he conveys were generated with a noteworthy degree of intelligent imagination and perceptiveness.

This incident did not at all jeopardize Cornysh's future career in the royal household. Indeed, with Henry VIII he seems to have enjoyed terms of jovial familiarity sufficient to allow him, perhaps, some of the licence of a court jester. In March 1518 he was able, by exploiting his easy relationship with the king, to draw to Henry's attention a prevailing shortage of victuals for the court, making joking supplication for provision of 'a botell off haye and an horselofe' (PRO, SP 1/16, fol. 176*r*).

The skills and attributes which qualified men and boys for Chapel Royal employment were exclusively musical, and their duties as practitioners of liturgical observance can have left but limited time for extra-curricular activities. However, Cornysh exhibited a certain leaning towards theatrical enterprise, and he was fortunate to have been in service as an employee of the court at a period which, albeit briefly, proved particularly propitious for the exploitation of such inclinations. On 6 January 1494 the court discovered Cornysh's capacity for making a theatrical entrance when he executed a cameo performance costumed as St George, suddenly interrupting on horseback a play being performed by Henry VII's professional troupe of players. After declaiming his speech he led the gentlemen of the Chapel Royal in a lusty rendering of some setting of 'O Georgi Deo care', a text of somewhat martial character first set to music during the wars of Henry V. He made a substantial contribution to the disguisings mounted in November 1501 to celebrate the marriage of Arthur, prince of Wales, and Katherine of Aragon, devising a production consisting of three sequential dramatic pageants showing a degree of elaboration unprecedented at the English court. Further, it is possible that from 1505 until 1512 he and three or four Chapel Royal colleagues collaborated once a year to mount a play or other entertainment before the king. Cornysh, John Kite, and William Crane, particularly mentioned together (for their musical, not their theatrical, expertise) in Alexander Barclay's 'Second eclogue' of about 1513–14, appear to have belonged to this informal group.

Cornysh participated in pageants performed on 13 February 1511 and at new year 1512 and 1515; presumably he also coached those boys of the Chapel Royal who contributed songs and in 1515 joined him in recitation of the prologue. He next made both a foray upon dramatic writing and, despite the weight of his responsibilities as master of the choristers, a significant return to undertaking production. For the pageant on 6 January 1516 he shared responsibility for the creation of its central scenic structure, wrote some of the speeches, and acted the Herald. Further, he was credited with the production of a play presented in May 1516, and in 'Le gardyn de esperans' (twelfth night 1517) he, as usual, declaimed the prologue, assisted again by two of his boys.

With varying degrees of plausibility modern scholarship has sought to identify Cornysh as deviser and manager of several other examples of court spectacle at this time. Certainly he created two pageants for presentation before Charles V on 12 July 1520 at Calais, and he was responsible for not merely the production but also the writing of a major dramatic presentation mounted on 15 June 1522 as part of the celebrations marking the creation of an Anglo-imperial alliance against the French. In this unsubtle allegory characters including Amity, Prudence, and Might combined to bridle an unruly horse representing François I.

Cornysh also developed an intriguing production enterprise peculiarly his own. On 6 January 1516 he presented an interlude called 'The story of Troilus and Pandor' performed just by himself and, for the first time as actors, his Chapel Royal singing-boys. Thereafter he devoted much of that theatrical work with which he chose to supplement his primary Chapel Royal duties to the presentation at court on two or even three occasions per year of plays acted by himself and his boy choristers. These productions were relatively modest, all his expenses and expectations of reward being covered by a charge to the king of but £6 13*s*. 4*d*. There is record of nine such productions between new year 1517 and new year 1521. The entertainments of September 1519 specifically included 'a pastym that master kornyche mad', consisting of an interlude of evidently traditional character acted by seven of his choristers.

The Chapel Royal boys, of course, were never more than makeshift actors. In no sense were they ever subjected to transformation into a formally organized playing company; such pastimes could not be suffered to encroach upon their principal daily work as members of the sovereign's personal, and England's most prominent, professional liturgical and musical ensemble. Indeed, when in March 1518 something—most probably some distraction of his attention towards theatrical enterprise—was leading Cornysh to neglect his duties towards the musical training of the Chapel Royal boys and the general direction of the choir, Henry himself demonstrated to his choirmaster how the musical standards of his own chapel had begun to slip below those of Cardinal Thomas Wolsey's. After this incident it was only in their own plays mounted by Cornysh, and in no other type of production conducted at court, that the Chapel Royal boys participated. (The singing-boys not of the king's but of Wolsey's chapel played in 'Château vert' on 4 March 1522.)

Cornysh was involved in the secular as well as the ecclesiastical music-making of the court; in particular, he composed to texts in English, for use at court in non-ecclesiastical contexts. The most substantial extant piece is a four-part setting of 'Woefully arrayed', a meditation on the passion of Christ exhibiting a precociously skilful response to the mood of the text. Probably the 'carrall' for the composition of which Cornysh received a fee of 13s. 4d. from Elizabeth of York at Christmas 1502 was a further vernacular piece of comparable character.

The vagaries of survival mean that Cornysh is best known as a court composer for his lightweight vernacular partsong, to texts hinting strongly at the nature of their courtly milieu. After early endeavours engaging lengthy and complex repetition forms with integrated refrain or burden, the songs for the court of Henry VIII are far simpler, some being very slight indeed. At its best Cornysh's compositional style exhibits a degree of balance and poise belying its simplicity of structure, the inventive jollity of the songs of rustic merry-making complementing the reflectiveness of the songs of *fine amour*. Two surviving instrumental pieces are far more intellectual and rarefied. One fantasia is lengthy and contrapuntally intricate, while a briefer piece includes in its tenor four successive palindromes, respectively of fifteen, five, nine, and three pitches; the mathematical patterning is obvious, its significance utterly obscure.

Within his very limited circle of courtly pursuits Cornysh in his own time was probably a man of some consequence. In the longer run, however, most of his accomplishments appear but transitory. Renaissance ideals had as yet reached neither English music nor English letters; Cornysh was a late medieval figure who was merely quite good at quite a number of things which on the whole proved to have little long-term future. Unfortunately not a single word of any pageant or play written by him has survived. Yet he made one lasting contribution to English drama, namely the free-standing interlude of the type which from 1516 onwards was performed by his amateur choirboy actors. Hereby Cornysh invented a genre yielding particular and lasting satisfaction as entertainment, which both helped to keep alive the thread of occasional drama at court through the remaining years of Henry's reign and beyond, and also spawned a tradition which eventually contributed modestly to the flowering of English drama later in the century.

Cornysh retired as master of the choristers at Easter 1523, retaining his position as gentleman of the Chapel Royal until death. He died very soon after receiving his last mark of royal favour on 20 August 1523, for by 16 September his corrody from Thetford Priory had become available for award to a successor. Probate of his will was granted on 14 October. He requested burial in the nave of the chapel of the rood in East Greenwich, the location of his home, and he bequeathed his numerous properties and leases in Greenwich to Joan, his wife, and after her to their son, Henry (PRO, PROB 11/21, sig. 13).

ROGER BOWERS

**Sources** Westminster Abbey muniments, accounts of the warden of Lady Chapel (1479/80–1490/91) and of the almoner (1484/5–1519/20) · F. L. Harrison, ed., *The Eton choirbook*, 2nd edn, 3 vols., Musica Britannica, 10–12 (1967–73) · *Early Tudor magnificats*, 1, ed. P. Doe, Early English Church Music, 4 (1964) · D. Skinner, 'William Cornysh: clerk or courtier', *MT*, 138 (1997), 5–15 · J. Caldwell, *The Oxford history of English music*, 2 vols. (1991), vol. 1, pp. 201–14 · H. Benham, *Latin church music in England, c.1460–1575* (1977), 93–5 · F. Harrison, 'English polyphony, c.1470–1540', Ars Nova and the renaissance, 1300–1540 (1960), vol. 3 of *The new Oxford history of music*, 309–10, 318–28, 345–8 · J. Stevens, *Music and poetry in the early Tudor court* (1961); rev. edn (1979) · H. N. Hillebrand, 'The child actors: a chapter in Elizabethan stage history', *University of Illinois Studies in Language and Literature*, 11 (1926), 1–355 · *LP Henry VIII*, vols. 1–3 · A. Ashbee, ed., *Records of English court music*, 7 (1993) · *Music at the court of Henry VIII*, ed. J. Stevens, 2nd edn, Musica Britannica, 18 (1973) · J. Stevens, ed., *Early Tudor songs and carols*, Musica Britannica, 36 (1975) · W. Edwards, 'The instrumental music of Henry VIII's manuscript', *The Consort*, 34 (1978), 274–82 · S. Anglo, 'William Cornish in a play, pageants, prison and politics', *The Review of English Studies*, new ser., 10 (1959), 347–60 · E. Flügel, 'Kleinere mitteilungen aus Handschriften', *Anglia*, 14 (1892), 466–71 · W. R. Streitberger, *Court revels, 1485–1559* (1994) · F. Kisby, 'A courtier in the community: new light on the biography of William Cornysh, master of the choristers in the English Chapel Royal, 1509–1523', *Bulletin of the Society for Renaissance Studies*, 16 (1999), 8–17 · J. G. Russell, *The Field of Cloth of Gold* (1969) · will, PRO, PROB 11/21, sig. 13
**Wealth at death** see will, PRO, PROB 11/21, sig. 13

**Coronio** [*née* Ionides]**, Aglaia** (1834–1906), embroiderer, bookbinder, and art patron, was the first child and elder daughter of Alexander Ionides (1810–1890) and his wife, Euterpe, *née* Sguta (*b.* 1816). Alexander emigrated to England from Greece in 1827 to work in the Manchester business started by his father, Constantine Ionidis Iplikzis (1775–1852), which exported cottons to Turkey and Greece and imported a variety of goods into Britain. Alexander became a British subject and took an Anglicized surname from Ionidis. In later life he became managing director of the Banque of Constantinople and director of the Crystal Palace Company. From 1840 the Ionides family lived in Tulse Hill, London, moving in 1864 to a large house at 1 Holland Park. Both homes became the headquarters for a group of wealthy, influential Anglo-Greek families and through their interest and patronage of the arts, centres for artistic London society. The Ionides women were admired for their independent personalities and striking looks, especially Aglaia, who was tall and slender with a pale face and haunting black eyes, and her equally beautiful cousins Maria Zambaco and Marie Spartali, who were known as 'The three graces'. They were painted by D. G. Rossetti, G. F. Watts, and notably by Edward Burne-Jones in *The Mill*, completed between 1870 and 1882 (V&A).

From 1854 to 1866 Alexander Ionides served as the Greek consul-general in London, Aglaia acting as his official hostess. She became known as one of the most gracious, intelligent, and witty women of the period. In his 1894 novel *Trilby*, George Du Maurier describes his first impressions of her as 'so beautiful and stately and magnificently attired that they felt inclined to sink … on their bended knees as in the presence of some overwhelming Eastern royalty and were only prevented from doing so, perhaps, by the simple, sweet, and cordial graciousness of her welcome' (Ormond, 100).

After her marriage in 1855 to Theodore John Coronio (*c.*1828–1903) Aglaia lived at 1 Lindsey Row, moving in 1869 next to her parents at 1A Holland Park. Her daughter, Calliope, was born in 1856 and her son, John, a year later. She became a keen patron of the arts owning works by Rossetti, Whistler, and Fantin-Latour and she practised the arts of bookbinding and embroidery. The only known existing example of her work is a pair of embroidered curtains designed by William Morris in the 1870s. These and their design, which is marked with her name, are owned by the Victoria and Albert Museum.

Aglaia Coronio and William Morris became close friends and their long-lasting correspondence illustrates how deeply Morris confided in her. He visited her frequently and encouraged her artistic pursuits. In a letter to his wife, Jane, in 1870 he refers to her making 'quite a fine thing' of bookbinding (Kelvin, 1.128). He supplied her with embroidery threads and she, in return, secured for him samples of the rare, red dye kermes, and packets of unspun Levantine wool. Her refined tastes were also invaluable in the selection and arranging of textiles and drapery in the paintings of Edward Burne-Jones, another of her prodigies.

References to Aglaia's melancholic character portend her dramatic and tragic end. On 20 August 1906, the day following the death of her daughter, she committed suicide at her home in London by repeatedly stabbing herself in the neck and chest with her embroidery scissors.

LINDA PARRY

**Sources** D. S. Macleod, *Art and the Victorian middle class: money and the making of cultural identity* (1996) · C. Dakers, *The Holland Park circle* (1999) · L. Ormond, *George Du Maurier* (1969) · *The collected letters of William Morris*, ed. N. Kelvin, 4 vols. (1984–96) · F. McCarthy, *William Morris: a life for our time* (1994) · M. Tidcombe, *Women bookbinders, 1880–1920* (1996) · d. cert.
**Likenesses** E. Burne-Jones, oils (*The mill*), V&A · D. G. Rossetti, drawing, V&A · carte-de-visite, Hastings Museum and Art Gallery
**Wealth at death** £13,905 19s. 8d.: resworn probate, 13 Sept 1906, CGPLA Eng. & Wales

**Corri family** (*per. c.*1770–1860), musicians, were of Italian descent but settled in Britain, Ireland, and the USA and were particularly influential as music teachers and writers of teaching material.

The senior member was **Domenico Corri** (1746–1825), composer, music publisher, and teacher, born in Rome on 4 October 1746. His father, a confectioner, was employed in the palace of Cardinal Portocarero and sent Domenico, who showed early musical promise, for violin and singing lessons. By the age of ten the boy was performing in Roman theatre bands, although the cardinal took him under his wing and set about turning him away from music in favour of the church. His (rather covert) musical studies did continue, however, up to the cardinal's death. He then began harpsichord and composition lessons, put on private concerts (attended by Muzio Clementi), and, at his parents' expense, eventually boarded with and received tuition from the famous composer and singing teacher Nicola Porpora in Naples between 1763 and 1767. Following his teacher's demise Domenico returned to Rome, where he conducted concerts for the Roman and visiting British nobility. He lived for two years with the exiled pretender to the British throne, Charles Edward Stuart, who was also an amateur cellist. His opera *La raminga fedele* (now lost) appeared in 1770, and in September of that year Dr Charles Burney heard performances in Rome given by Corri and the miniaturist and soprano Alice Bacchelli (*d. c.*1800), a former pupil of Corri. The result of this encounter and the highly favourable impression made on Burney (relayed in his writings) was an invitation to them both from the music society of Edinburgh to perform at the St Cecilia's Hall concerts there as conductor and singer respectively. By the time this invitation had arrived they were married, and so they travelled to Edinburgh together, arriving in August 1771. They were warmly welcomed and an initial three-year contract became the beginning of an eighteen-year stay in the city. There was a sojourn to London when Domenico's opera *Alessandro nell' Indie* was given at the King's Theatre in 1774 (with his friend and former fellow pupil Venanzio Rauzzini making his début in the title role). It enjoyed some success, but according to Burney the 'young composer of genius' and his work did not receive the attention they deserved (Burney, *Hist. mus.*, 2.880). His wife performed in high-profile concerts at the new Hanover Square Rooms and elsewhere at this time. Back in Edinburgh, Domenico, now a successful performer and singing-master, took on risky managerial posts, including appointments at the Vauxhall Pleasure Gardens and the Theatre Royal, which resulted in financial disaster. Not to be deterred in an expanding market for music, he moved into publishing about 1779, setting up business in Bridge Street with his brother Natale Corri (1765–1822) and using the name of his eldest son, John (or Giovanni). Natale had been a singing teacher, guitarist, and composer in Rome, and may have travelled from Italy with his brother in 1771. He established himself in Edinburgh as a concert promoter as well as a practical musician and married one of the artists he promoted, the soprano Camilla Giolivetti, on 19 February 1794. Despite financial troubles about the turn of the century, Natale remained in business in Edinburgh until he travelled to the continent with his daughters in 1821. His own works included three keyboard sonatas with, as was common at the time, violin accompaniment

(1790?), *Scales for Practice and Fingering the Piano forte* (c.1815), and various arrangements of popular works.

About 1780 Domenico and his brother were joined by James Sutherland, and the firm Corri and Sutherland survived until Sutherland's death a decade later. Domenico published his harpsichord tutor (advocating scale practice) in 1784 and *A Complete Musical Grammar* three years later; both later appeared in modified versions. Natale took over the Scottish business, Corri & Co., when the Corris returned to and settled in London about 1790; there they entertained and enjoyed the company of the city's most eminent musical figures and visitors, including Dr Burney, Joseph Haydn, and, later, John Braham. Domenico continued to publish music in Soho, concentrating, as in Edinburgh, on songs and operatic numbers published both separately and in various collections (many bear the prince of Wales's feathers as a mark and appeared in association with the Edinburgh firm). As well as canzonettas by Haydn, four volumes of *A Select Collection of the most Admired Songs, Duetts*, arranged and edited by Corri and dedicated to Queen Charlotte, were published in Edinburgh and London between c.1779 and 1795. These were pioneering for British publications in providing written-out accompaniments rather than just a shorthand 'figured' bass. The collections (along with his writings) also provide useful information on contemporary vocal and keyboard performance practices, including ornamentation. Signora Corri appeared in Johann Peter Salomon's concerts in 1792 but may have retired soon afterwards. In 1794 the Corris were living together at 67 Dean Street, Soho, where Domenico established a publishing firm in partnership with his son-in-law, the acclaimed pianist and composer Jan Ladislav *Dussek (1760–1812). The firm Corri, Dussek & Co. also acted as agent for Broadwood's piano firm in Scotland (Dussek was intimately involved with Broadwood's extension of the piano keyboard) and appears to have thrived for a time, including Lorenzo da Ponte (Mozart's librettist) among its associates and investors. The German-born composer Ignace Pleyel too appears to have been connected in some way, judging by *Pleyel, Corri & Dussek's Musical Journal*, published by Corri, Dussek & Co. in London and Edinburgh (1797). Many of Dussek's works were printed by the firm. However, financial difficulties intervened once more, and towards the end of 1799 Dussek's debts prompted him to flee to Hamburg or Paris. Domenico was gaoled for a short time at Newgate prison as a result of the first of several bankruptcies, but managed to carry on the business alone; it was based at 28 Haymarket from about 1801 to 1804, when his son Montague [*see below*] took over. Corri's wife had died some time previously (the family's move from Scotland was partly due to her poor health), and he remarried on 3 April 1803 at St Martin-in-the-Fields. His second wife, Alice Henley, was an English music teacher. Domenico had earlier written a *Musical Dictionary* (1798), had composed and published a piano concerto (1800) and keyboard sonatas, including some with 'tambourine accompaniment' (Ward Jones and others), and had contributed a 'Bird Song' to Charles Dibdin's *The Cabinet* (1802). His five-act opera *The Travellers* was finally produced at Drury Lane in January 1806, following a long delay as a result of apparent reservations on the part of theatre impresarios (the work was conceived shortly after he had arrived in London). This has been attributed in part to the 'pseudo-Oriental' (ibid.) music used to accompany scenes set in China and Turkey that broke with his generally conservative, *galant* style. Domenico composed and taught (his pupils included the composer Isaac Nathan) for another decade or so before a decline in his health. His later compositions for the stage include music for the operatic farce *In and out of Tune* (1808), including the quartet 'Past Ten O'Clock', and for David Garrick's play *Lilliput* (1808). He continued to write for the keyboard (completing twenty-one sonatas in all) and to edit collections including a volume of hymns and psalms (c.1820). *The Singer's Preceptor* (1810), an important guide to the art of performance, also features Corri's autobiography to that date. He was 'subject to fits of insanity during the last six months of his life' (ibid.) and died in Hampstead, London, on 22 May 1825. Lorenzo da Ponte, rueful of his disastrous involvement with Corri's business (which caused a loss of 1000 guineas), questioned both his business acumen and honesty. His most enduring contribution remains his legacy as a pedagogue and writer.

The singer and composer Sophia Justina *Dussek (1775–1847) was Corri's daughter.

**(Philip) Antony Corri** [*later* Arthur Clifton] (1784?–1832), music teacher, singer, and composer, was a son of Domenico Corri and was born in Edinburgh. He made his name in London during the early part of the nineteenth century as a composer of songs and piano pieces and a teacher of lady amateurs. It was entirely natural therefore that he should produce duets for piano or piano and harp and a piano tutor, *L'anima di musica* (1810), one of the most comprehensive of the time. The latter was reissued in 1822, and a popular abridged version, *Original System of Preluding*, appeared about 1812 and was itself reprinted on several occasions. His other piano works include a sonata, with violin accompaniment, entitled *La morte di Dussek* (1812). Corri is also well known as a principal figure (along with Johann Baptist Cramer, William Dance, William Ayrton, and Charles Neate) in the founding of London's Philharmonic Society in 1813, at which time he was resident at 9 Portman Place, Paddington. His high standing within the society, as a singer as well as a composer, came to an abrupt end in December 1816 when, having 'made off with someone's wife' (Ehrlich), he was expelled in disgrace. He was also director of the Professional Concert at this time. He then emigrated to the USA, appearing in New York and Philadelphia and arriving in Baltimore towards the end of 1817. He was baptized there as Arthur Clifton on 31 December 1817 and married Alphonsa Elizabeth Ringgold the next day. Positions as organist and choirmaster at diverse churches (the First Presbyterian Church, 1818–23, and the First Independent Church, 1823–31) were complemented by teaching, performance, and theatre productions. He published compositions in Baltimore, including songs, pieces for piano, and a ballad opera (with Italianate elements), *The Enterprise, or, Love and*

*Pleasure* (1822). He appears to have charmed his way back onto the Philharmonic platform under his own name at some point, but died in Baltimore on 19 February 1832.

**Montague Philip Corri** (*c.*1784–1849), music publisher and composer, was born in Edinburgh, another son of Domenico Corri and possibly the twin brother of Philip Antony Corri. He initially chose painting and fencing (at which he became expert by the age of ten under the guidance of Domenico Angelo) over music and, perhaps as a reaction against family pressure, spent a period at sea. Music appealed to him a great deal more when he was about eighteen, and he mainly taught himself despite a few lessons from his father, Peter Winter, and Daniel Steibelt. In 1804 he took over his father's business which operated in association with various other traders until a new firm called Corri & Co. broke away. This published *The Library Newspaper & Musical Journal* in 1806, while based at 13 Oxendon Street, and about 1807 was located for a short time in Little Newport Street. The music dealership became bankrupt in 1811. Montague's instrumental career was also curtailed as the result of an accident which left one of his fingers dislocated. This may, however, have been to his long-term advantage, as he became a successful composer and arranger for the theatre and military bands, famous for the speed at which he could work under pressure. His work included music for plays and pantomimes at the Surrey, Astley's, and Cobourg theatres and the English Opera House (1812–14), written in collaboration with John Braham, Charles Edward Horn, and others. After a season as chorus master at the English Opera House (1816–17) he was employed for a short time by his uncle Natale Corri as manager of the Pantheon in Edinburgh. From then on he appears to have led a fairly itinerant lifestyle, living and working (in the theatre and as a fencing instructor) in Manchester, Liverpool, and Newcastle. He continued to compose songs and keyboard pieces, including numerous arrangements for piano solo and duet, and published a singing treatise (*c.*1830), a piano tutor (1835?), and, perhaps most interestingly, *A Complete Course of Instructions on … Arranging Music* (1835?). The story that Montague was shipwrecked during a voyage from Shields to London, losing everything, attributed to Brown and Stratton by *New Grove*, was first recorded by Sainsbury. He died in London on 19 September 1849. He was the father of William Charles Cunningham Corri (1834/5–1893), a song composer who was the father of Charles Montague Corri (1861–1941), an opera conductor at the Old Vic Theatre, London; Clarence Collingwood Corri (1863–1918), a composer principally of songs and operettas; and William Corri (*b. c.*1865, *d.* after 1905), also a song composer.

**Haydn Corri** (1785–1860), pianist, organist, and composer, was born in Edinburgh, a son of Domenico Corri. He presumably received keyboard lessons from his father from an early age. He established himself as an instrumentalist and travelled from London to Ireland in 1811 and in 1819–20 as an accompanist to Italian opera singers performing at the Crow Street Theatre in Dublin. He married the soprano Ann Adams (Adami) (1800–1867) in London on 15 July 1814, and they both settled in Dublin in 1821. She was employed as a singer at the new Theatre Royal, Hawkins Street, and he became an important figure in the musical life of Dublin. A popular keyboard and singing teacher (his *The Delivery of Vocal Music Simplified* appeared in 1826), he became organist and choirmaster of St Mary's, the pro-cathedral in Marlborough Street, in 1827, and retained the post until 1848. His compositions include sacred works for performance there, along with the staple fare of songs and arrangements. An adaptation of Cherubini's mass in A (originally composed in 1825 for the coronation of Charles X of France), for organ or piano with an added fourth voice part, was published about 1855. Haydn Corri died in Dublin on 12 February 1860. He was the father of two musicians: Patrick Anthony Corri (1820–1876), a singer, conductor, and composer and the father of the baritone Haydn Woulds Corri (1845–1876); and Henry Corri (1822–1888), a bass and conductor and the father of Ghita Auber Corri (1869/70–1937), a song composer and singer in the Carl Rosa Opera Company who married the playwright Richard Neville Lynn in 1899.

**Frances** [Fanny] **Corri** [*married name* Corri-Paltoni] (*b.* 1795/1801, *d.* in or after 1835), singer, was born in Edinburgh, one of the daughters of Natale and Camilla Corri. After singing lessons from her father she went to London for instruction from John Braham and Angelica Catalani. Frances embarked on a continental tour (1815–16) with Catalani, and her powerful singing style, along with impeccable intonation, was said to resemble closely that of the Italian soprano. Back in London, her King's Theatre début (17 January 1818), as the Countess in Mozart's *Le nozze di Figaro*, was a great success. Further engagements there and with the Philharmonic Society followed until she, along with her father and sisters, left for the continent in 1821. From Munich she travelled to Italy, where she settled and married the singer Giuseppe Paltoni. She gave performances in Milan at La Scala (1828–9) and toured widely and successfully, visiting Spain, Germany, and Russia. A performance of Bellini's *Norma* at Alessandria (1835) featured her last known appearance.

Among Natale's and Camilla's other daughters, little is known of the soprano Angelina Corri. Rosalie Corri (1803–*c.*1860), also a soprano, was taught by Rovedino; she sang alongside Frances in London at the King's Theatre and performed in Irish premières of Mozart operas in Dublin under the direction of Haydn Corri in 1819. She continued to perform in London, where she married William Geeson in 1825, and also appeared in Milan at the Teatro Re (1823). A charity concert was staged for the sisters in London in 1823, a year after their father's death (*DNB*).

DAVID J. GOLBY

**Sources** P. Ward Jones and others, 'Corri', *New Grove*, 2nd edn, 6.500–03 [incl. lists of works and bibliography] · C. R. F. Maunder, ed., *Domenico Corri's treatises on singing: a four-volume anthology*, 4 vols. (1993–5), vols. 3, 4 [incl. *The singer's preceptor* (1810); preface incl. autobiography] · H. A. Craw and B. Shaljean, 'Dussek, Sophia (Guistina)', *New Grove*, 2nd edn, 7.765–6 [incl. list of works and bibliography] · P. Ward Jones, 'Corri, Domenico', *The new Grove dictionary of opera*, ed. S. Sadie, 1 (1992), 960 · P. Ward Jones, 'Corri, Frances', *The new Grove dictionary of opera*, ed. S. Sadie, 1 (1992), 960 ·

J. Bunker Clark, 'Clifton, Arthur', *The new Grove dictionary of opera*, ed. S. Sadie, 1 (1992), 887 • W. H. Cummings, 'A neglected musical benefactor', *Proceedings of the Musical Association*, 7 (1880–81), 19–28 • Burney, *Hist. mus.*, new edn, 2.880, 901, 916 • Highfill, Burnim & Langhans, *BDA* • J. C. Kassler, *The science of music in Britain, 1714–1830*, 2 vols. (1979), 1. 216–21 • C. Ehrlich, *First philharmonic: a history of the Royal Philharmonic Society* (1995), 3, 8 • [J. S. Sainsbury], ed., *A dictionary of musicians*, 1 (1824), 177–9 • C. Humphries and W. C. Smith, *Music publishing in the British Isles from the earliest times to the beginning of the nineteenth century* (1970), 117–18 • *Musical World*, 38 (1860), 144 [Haydn Corri]

**Corri, (Philip) Antony** (1784?–1832). *See under* Corri family (*per. c.*1770–1860).

**Corri, Domenico** (1746–1825). *See under* Corri family (*per. c.*1770–1860).

**Corri, Frances** (*b.* 1795/1801, *d.* in or after 1835). *See under* Corri family (*per. c.*1770–1860).

**Corri, Haydn** (1785–1860). *See under* Corri family (*per. c.*1770–1860).

**Corri, Montague Philip** (*c.*1784–1849). *See under* Corri family (*per. c.*1770–1860).

**Corrie, Archibald**. *See* Gorrie, Archibald (1778–1857).

**Corrie, Daniel** (1777–1837), bishop of Madras, was born at Ardchattan, Argyll, on 10 April 1777, the second son of John Corrie and his wife, Anne McNab. George Elwes *Corrie (1793–1885), eventually his biographer, was a younger brother. His father was for many years curate of Colsterworth and vicar of Osbournby in Lincolnshire, and afterwards rector of Morcott in Rutland. Daniel appears to have received his early education partly at home and partly at the house of a friend of his father in London. He then went into residence at Cambridge, first at Clare College in October 1799 and afterwards from 1800 as an exhibitioner at Trinity Hall. He was ordained deacon in 1802 and priest in 1804, and graduated LLB in 1805. While at Cambridge he came under the influence of Charles Simeon, which affected him for the remainder of his life and led to his appointment to a chaplaincy in Bengal in 1806.

Corrie reached Calcutta in September 1806. He became the guest of the Bengal chaplain, David Brown, at whose house he renewed his friendship with Henry Martyn. During the following eight or nine years he held various chaplaincies in the North-Western Provinces, including those of Chunar, Cawnpore, and Agra, in all of them carrying out missionary work in addition to his duties as chaplain to the British troops. He founded churches and schools and did much to nurture the growth of the Anglican church in north India. He was a great supporter of the Church Missionary Society (CMS), of which he was a governor, and this led to tension with Bishop Middleton. He was a superior scholar in Hindi, which he wrote with elegance and spoke with ease. He translated a number of works into Hindi. On 16 November 1812 at Barrackpore he married Elizabeth Myers (1789–1836), only child of William Myers and Hannah Ayres. They had four children; a son and daughter died in infancy.

In 1815 Corrie was compelled by the state of his health, which had suffered much from the Indian climate, to visit England. The CMS asked him to preach and speak on its behalf and in 1816 he gave the anniversary sermon. He returned to India in 1817 and was soon promoted to the senior chaplaincy at Calcutta, where, first as secretary to the local CMS committee and afterwards as president of the Church Missionary Association, he continued his active services to the missionary cause. In 1823 he was appointed by Bishop Heber as archdeacon of Calcutta, in which capacity the administration of the diocese devolved upon him at three different times, following the deaths of Bishop Heber (1826), Bishop James (1828), and Bishop Turner (1831). In 1835, Madras and Bombay having been constituted separate sees under the Charter Act of 1833, Corrie was appointed the first bishop of Madras; he began his duties on 28 October 1835. He survived his installation little more than fifteen months, and died a few weeks after his wife, at Madras, after a few days' illness, on 5 February 1837; but short as the period was, it was long enough to impress the community of the Madras presidency with a very high estimate of the piety, devotion, and untiring zeal with which he had discharged his duties. After his death subscriptions were collected to erect a monument in the cathedral at Madras and to endow scholarships in the grammar school he had recently founded. Corrie's devotion to missionary work is enshrined in Weekes's impressive statue in the cathedral. Similarly in Bengal his thirty years of service were commemorated by marble slabs in two of the churches in which he had long been accustomed to minister, and scholarships were named after him in the Calcutta high school. As a missionary chaplain Corrie ranks with David Brown, Claudius Buchanan, Henry Martyn, and James Thomason. A gentle and humble man of great generosity, Corrie left his family poor by his gifts to others. Bishop Wilson, in his funeral oration, paid tribute to the much loved and respected Corrie as 'the parent of the CMS in India, the centre of union and the soul of all its operations'. A. J. ARBUTHNOT, *rev.* PENELOPE CARSON

**Sources** Venn, *Alum. Cant.* • G. E. V. H. Corrie, *Memoirs of the Right Rev Daniel Corrie* (1847) • H. Carey, ed., *Oriental Christian biography*, 1 (1850) • *Annual Register* (1837) • *GM*, 2nd ser., 7 (1837), 427 • A. Macnaghten, *Daniel Corrie, his family and friends* (1969) • H. Cnattingius, *Bishops and societies: a study of Anglican colonial and missionary expansion, 1698–1850* (1952) • M. E. Gibbs, *The Anglican church in India, 1600–1970* (1972) • D. Hughes, *Bishop Sahib: a life of Reginald Heber* (1986) • F. Penny, *The church in Madras*, 3 (1922) • M. A. Sherring, *History of protestant missions in India, 1706–1882* (1884)

**Archives** priv. coll., diary • U. Birm. L., special collections department, Church Missionary Society archives, corresp. and papers | Canterbury Cathedral, Canterbury Cathedral archives, corresp. with Henry Martyn • U. Birm. L., special collections department, letters to Major Phipps

**Likenesses** line engraving, pubd 1816, NPG • H. Weekes, group portrait, statue, 1842, Madras Cathedral • engraving, repro. in S. C. Woodman, *Memoirs*, frontispiece • lithograph, NPG • marble tablet, St Peter's Church, Colombo • portraits, repro. in MacNaghten, *Daniel Corrie* • stipple, NPG • tablet, St John's Church, Calcutta

**Wealth at death** very little; all left to daughters (brother if daughters died): will, 1834, BL OIOC L/AG/34/29/237

**Corrie, George Elwes** (1793–1885), Church of England clergyman and college head, was born at Colsterworth, Lincolnshire, on 28 April 1793, youngest of eight children of John Corrie (1746–1829), the curate there, and his first wife, Anne McNab (1751–1798). One of his three brothers, Daniel *Corrie, became bishop of Madras. The family was Scottish but a tradition claiming descent from Cluny Macpherson is decidedly improbable. Corrie was educated at home, followed country pursuits, and entered St Catharine's College, Cambridge in 1813. Upon graduating in 1817 he was elected to a fellowship and soon after, at what was for the time a young age, was made tutor of his college. He held that post until 1849, with growing distinction because his old-fashioned churchmanship in unsettled times, studied courtesy, and concern for the spiritual development of the young, gave an attractive tone to the society and greatly increased its numbers. He took a BD degree in 1831 (DD 1853), and filled most college offices, often holding several at the same time.

Corrie had a huge appetite for business and for ecclesiastical and theological scholarship, and in the years between 1845 and 1858 edited Latimer's *Sermons and Remains* and *The Homilies*, Nowell's *Catechism*, Twysden's *Historical Vindication*, Burnet's *History of the Reformation*, and Wheatly's *Common Prayer*. Other works included a timely *Historical notices of the interference of the crown with the affairs of the English universities* (1839), and a biography (with his surviving brother, Henry) of Bishop Corrie. The anonymous *On Endowments of the Parish Churches in England* (n.d. [*c*.1835]) is attributed to him. He also wrote for the Cambridge Antiquarian Society of which he was a founder and four times president, and was for many years president of the Cambridge Architectural Society. As Norrisian professor of divinity (1838–54) Corrie, a little under middle height, silver-haired, and with a patrician mien, was a strong influence on the Cambridge educated clergy. He was expected to succeed to the mastership of St Catharine's in 1845, but his pupil, Henry Philpott was elected. It was a grievous and unmerited disappointment to him. In 1849, however, his friend Bishop Turton of Ely (to whom he was chaplain) presented him to the mastership of Jesus College, Cambridge, and later added the rectory of Newton near Wisbech. He remained as active as before in college and comfortable in his parish, for at heart he was a country priest. Corrie theological prizes were established at St Catharine's and Jesus.

Corrie prided himself on consistent conservatism and spent much time and energy going against the tide of affairs in church and university. He opposed Catholic emancipation and the admission of dissenters to degrees, and cordially disliked both ritualists and radicals. As master of Jesus (and in 1850 as vice-chancellor), he refused to co-operate with parliamentary commissioners, and snubbed the chancellor, Prince Albert. He lived to see fellows married when he believed their duty lay in celibacy: he remained a bachelor. The last ditch was his spiritual home, and Adam Sedgwick, Prince Albert's local secretary, described him as 'obstinate as a mule … he, perhaps, never believes himself to be in the wrong' (Winstanley,

234). Yet he had a dry, sometimes self-conscious humour as in his letter to a railway company to say that proposals to bring 'foreigners and others' to Cambridge on Sundays were 'as distasteful to the authorities of the University, as they must be offensive to Almighty God and to all right-minded Christians' (Holroyd, 271–2). And when the 1877 commissioners asked about the main wants of the university he replied that the first was 'exemption from the disturbing power of Royal or Parliamentary Commissions'. Too frail to take much part in public affairs, he nevertheless retained his mental faculties until he died 'of natural decay' at Jesus lodge on 20 September 1885; he was buried at Newton. His large library was sold by Sothebys.

JOHN D. PICKLES

**Sources** M. Holroyd, *Memorials of the life of George Elwes Corrie* (1890) · A. Gray and F. Brittain, *A history of Jesus College, Cambridge*, rev. edn (1979) · A. Macnaghten, *Daniel Corrie, his family and friends* (1969) · D. A. Winstanley, *Early Victorian Cambridge* (1940)
**Archives** CUL · Jesus College, Cambridge, journal of a tour through France to Switzerland · LPL, lecture notes · St Catharine's College, Cambridge | U. Durham L., corresp. with Temple Chevallier
**Likenesses** F. Sandys, portrait, *c*.1860, Jesus College, Cambridge · portrait, St Catharine's College, Cambridge; damaged
**Wealth at death** £7738 15s. 6d.: probate, 16 Jan 1886, *CGPLA Eng. & Wales*

**Corrie, Joseph** [Joe] (1894–1968), miner and playwright, was born on 13 May 1894 at Limerigg, Slamannan, Stirlingshire, the eldest of three sons and four children of Joseph Corrie, grocer, and his wife, Mary McCleary, a farm servant from Sorbie, Wigtownshire. His father became a surfaceman in the Fife coalfield at Cardenden in 1896. Joe attended Auchterderran and Lochgelly schools. As a boy he was entranced by the 'penny geggies' (travelling theatres) which visited such mining communities. At fourteen he went down the pit, and his further education was provided in the Miners' Institute and the Workers' Educational Association. During the First World War he worked in Ayrshire, but after it he returned to Cardenden, began to write verse, and contributed articles to *The Miner* and *Forward*. His first book of poems was *The Road the Fiddler Went* (*c*.1925). He became a considerable popular poet, known particularly for *The Image o' God*.

During the miners' lockout in 1926 Corrie discovered a facility for writing one-act plays, such as *The Poacher* (published in 1927) and *The Shillin'-a-Week Man* (1927), which were used to raise money. His best-known three-act play, *In Time o' Strife* (1927), depicting a family's struggles during the strike, was first staged by the amateur Bowhill Players, who became the professional Fife Miner Players, and took this highly successful drama all over Scotland. An 'English' version was produced in Hackney, and it went to Germany and to Russia. The Scottish National Players had happily performed two of Corrie's plays but declined *In Time o' Strife*, perhaps because of its political content and a hectoring tone. Corrie publicly disputed this, and came to rely on performances by clubs in the Scottish Community Drama Association. He moved to Mauchline, Ayrshire, and threw himself into writing. He was incredibly prolific, producing close to 100 plays. These were generally in lowland Scots, and about everyday life; they were sometimes lightweight, but genuinely in touch with popular feeling. Corrie was one of the first working-class dramatists, and his work was revived later by agitprop theatre companies.

Corrie was a tall, handsome figure with a burly frame, and was gentle and reserved. He had married Mary McGlynn, from London, the secretary of the Workers' Drama Movement, on 12 July 1930, and their daughter, Morag, was born on 25 January 1932. Corrie remained a powerful working-class voice in Britain. Several later plays had radical themes, including *Hewers of Coal* (1936/7), and *Dawn*, banned by the lord chancellor as an anti-war play. His most effective mature work, *A Master of Men*, about the conflict between a mine manager, the mine owners, and the miners, was performed by the Glasgow Citizens' Theatre in 1944.

In 1938 the Corries moved to Surrey, then to London, and back to Surrey. They lived in Glenrothes after 1958. Corrie died at 31 Greenbank Drive, Edinburgh, of a heart condition on 13 November 1968, and was cremated. In 1985 his daughter opened a social centre in Cardenden, named the Corrie Centre, where a plaque proudly states how Corrie described the struggles and triumphs of life in 1920s Cardenden.                                    LOUIS STOTT

**Sources** L. MacKenney, *Joe Corrie: plays, poems and theatre writings* (1985) · A. Hutchison, *Corrie and Cardenden* [n.d.] · C. Ravenhall, 'Joe Corrie', in A. Reid and B. D. Osborne, *Discovering Scottish writers* (1997) · *The Scotsman* (14 Nov 1968) · *Fife Free Press* (16 Nov 1968)
**Archives** BBC WAC, corresp. with staff of BBC · NL Scot., additional papers · NL Scot., literary papers, diaries | U. Reading L., letters to Macmillan & Co.
**Likenesses** group portrait (with family), repro. in Hutchison, *Corrie and Cardenden* · photograph, Scot. NPG
**Wealth at death** £1637 8s.: confirmation, 19 Feb 1969, NA Scot., SC 70/1/1810/38–42

**Corrigan, Sir Dominic John**, first baronet (1802–1880), physician, was born in Thomas Street, Dublin, on 1 December 1802, the second son of John Corrigan, a well-known dealer in agricultural tools, and Celia O'Connor. At the age of ten Corrigan entered the lay college of St Patrick, Maynooth, where a local doctor, Talbot O'Kelly, kindled in the boy a passion for medicine. In 1820 he enrolled briefly in the school of physic in the University of Dublin (Trinity College), where he studied under professors Arthur Jacob, James Macartney, and John Crampton. During his time at Kirby's anatomy school in Peter Street (*c*.1820–*c*.1821) he became an amateur grave robber whenever fresh cadavers were in short supply. In old age he recalled the excitement of nocturnal forays into the paupers' cemetery next to the Royal Hospital, Kilmainham, where he and a few fellow students would dig up the coffins of the recently interred, extract the bodies, remove the shroud, wrap the bodies in sheets, and haul them back to the school for dissection. (This preceded the Anatomy Act of 1832, which regulated the supply of bodies to dissecting academies.)

One of Corrigan's ablest contemporaries, William Stokes, encouraged him to pursue his medical studies at Edinburgh University, from which he took his medical degree along with Stokes in 1825, after writing a thesis on scrofula or tuberculosis. Once back in Dublin he began to climb the tall ladder of medical and social success. Keen to excel in a profession dominated by members of the protestant ascendancy, who guarded the higher rungs with sectarian zeal, Corrigan faced formidable obstacles. His humble social origins and Roman Catholic faith stamped him firmly as an outsider with neither money nor connection. Promotion, in other words, would depend entirely on hard work and marked ability. He opened a modest practice at 11 Upper Ormond Quay, where most of his patients were indigents or paupers who could not afford to pay his fees. Appointed physician to the Sick-Poor Institute of Meath Street in the Liberties, one of Dublin's worst slum areas, he decided to specialize in diseases of the heart and lungs. Among the more important papers he published in the 1830s, 'On permanent patency of the mouth of the aorta' (*Edinburgh Medical and Surgical Journal*, 37, April 1832, 225–45) impressed doctors in London and on the continent. His work on heart murmurs, known then as *bruit de soufflet* and *frémissement cataire*, palpitations, aneurysms, and aortic valvular impairment did not prevent him from studying the epidemic diseases arising out of severe malnutrition.

Slowly but surely Corrigan's career prospered. He accepted posts at the Meath Dispensary, the Cork Street Fever Hospital, and the Charitable Infirmary in Jervis Street. He also became a lecturer at the Peter Street medical school as well as the Dublin school of anatomy, surgery, and medicine in Digges Street, and Apothecaries' Hall. As his income and patient list grew he moved his consulting rooms from Ormond Quay to 13 Bachelor's Walk, and then in 1834 to elegant quarters at 4 Merrion Square West, where his neighbours included some of Dublin's leading families. On 2 June 1829 he married Joanna Woodlock, the daughter of a wealthy Dublin merchant. They had three sons and three daughters, only one of whom survived beyond 1882.

In 1839 Corrigan was appointed physician-in-ordinary to the lord lieutenant of Ireland and a year later physician to the House of Industry Hospital, a post he held until 1866. But he failed in 1841 to secure the coveted regius professorship of physic at Trinity College. Corrigan's combination of medical expertise, drive, and personal charm soon attracted patients from the top tiers of landed and professional society. Among the élite who competed for his services were Lady Castlerosse, Lady Granard, and the marquess of Headfort. By the late 1850s he was earning well over £4000 a year and this wealth enabled him to treat the poor and carry out research on heart and lung diseases as well as cholera.

If Corrigan's researches led to no major medical breakthroughs, his eagle eye and practical turn of mind, combined with years of treating patients of all kinds and conditions, enabled him to explain with unusual clarity such diseases as pulmonary fibrosis, cirrhosis of the lung, aortitis, and heart murmurs. At a time when anaesthesia and antiseptic procedures were unknown in Dublin's hospitals he explored the symptoms and causes of aortic valvular insufficiency or impairment, which came to be called Corrigan's pulse. This water-hammer pulsation of the brachial and radial arteries was described by a later authority as 'a jerky pulse with a full expansion, followed by a sudden collapse, occurring in aortic regurgitation' (*Dorland's Dictionary*, 1387). Following in the footsteps of Stokes, Corrigan promoted the use of the stethoscope. However, like other physicians of his day, he prescribed opium to relieve inflamed joints and leeches for victims of fever.

In the early 1840s Corrigan lectured and published papers on the close connection between famine and fever. As he observed in an 1846 pamphlet, 'if there be no famine, there will be no fever' (O'Brien, *Conscience*, 188). This argument proved more than prescient in view of the devastating effects of the blight or fungus that struck the Irish potato crop between 1845 and 1849. In 1846 he joined the newly created central board of health, which was trying to cope with the huge public health crisis that overwhelmed Ireland's medical as well as economic resources. His aversion to financial waste moved him to recommend that dispensary doctors hired to treat fever victims be paid only 5*s.* a day. But because these men risked serious illness or even death from contagion this board-approved fee struck both the medical establishment and the public as stingy. Corrigan soon became the object of much abuse from the public for this paltry pay and a senior colleague, Robert James Graves of the Meath Hospital, not only accused him of parsimony but also blocked his bid to become an honorary fellow of the King and Queen's College of Physicians in Ireland in 1847, despite his admission to the Royal College of Surgeons of England in 1843. It took Corrigan years to recover from this blow. Not until 1855 did he become a licentiate of the college; a year later he was elected a fellow.

In 1847 the whig government officially recognized Corrigan's services to public health by making him physician-in-ordinary to Queen Victoria in Ireland—the first Catholic to be so honoured. Two years later Trinity College awarded him an honorary doctorate of medicine. He also served as a commissioner of lunatic asylums in Ireland from 1856 to 1868. In 1859, he reached the pinnacle of his career by becoming president of the College of Physicians—a position to which he was re-elected for an unprecedented five years. Once again he was the first Catholic to hold this office. To his lasting credit Corrigan negotiated the purchase from the Kildare Street Club of the site on which the college built its imposing headquarters. The first official meeting of the college in its new premises was held on 5 July 1864. During his presidency it awarded fellowships to graduates of any medical school in the British Isles or Europe.

Corrigan's colleagues honoured him with a portrait by Catterson Smith and an imposing statue by the sculptor John Henry Foley. The latter was installed in the entrance hall of the college on 3 June 1869 before a crowd of devoted medical colleagues and friends that included William Stokes. Appointed a commissioner of national education in 1859, Corrigan served as president of the Royal Zoological Gardens and the Irish Pharmaceutical Society. In January 1866 the government conferred on him a baronetcy of the United Kingdom and in the same year he became consulting physician and joined the board of the House of Industry (Richmond Surgical) Hospital. For more than twenty years he served with distinction on the General Medical Council in London. In 1871 he accepted the vice-chancellorship of the Queen's University of Ireland, having served as a senator since the 1840s.

Elected to parliament in 1870 as member for Dublin City, Corrigan spent more time in London, espousing traditional Liberal ideas and devouring sumptuous dinners at the Reform Club. His advocacy of the early release of Fenian prisoners and promotion of secular education in universities alienated the Catholic hierarchy—especially Cardinal Cullen. A true Christian, he attacked every form of sectarianism and dreamed of a national University of Ireland free from religious dogma and prejudice. But his ecumenical idealism had scant appeal, and once Gladstone's ambitious Irish University Bill of 1873 ran foul of religious zealots Corrigan decided to retire from parliament.

On the issue of female doctors Corrigan displayed some distinctly patriarchal prejudices. While he defended their right to attend medical school, he did not want women to practise medicine because he was convinced that such work would defeminize or 'unsex' them. This outlook did not, however, prevent the College of Physicians from registering five women as licentiates in 1877. A champion of stricter regulation of both the medical and pharmaceutical professions, he also worked hard to purify Dublin's water supply, being fully cognizant of the link between dirty water and sickness.

As he grew older and gout made travel painful, Corrigan spent more time in his suburban house, Inniscorrig, Dalkey, south of Dublin. Despite a mild stroke in 1878 that left him partially paralysed, he continued to see patients. But a second stroke at the end of December 1879 left him permanently disabled. Nursed by his wife and children during his final illness he died in his Merrion Square house on 1 February 1880. His funeral proved one of the biggest seen hitherto in the city. Following a service attended by hundreds of admiring patients, friends, and colleagues, he was buried in the family vault in St Andrew's Church, Westland Row, Dublin, on 5 February.

Noted for his ambition, compassion, and cheerful bedside manner, Corrigan also earned professional respect for his work on aortic inadequacy, heart murmurs, pulmonary fibrosis, and bronchial dilatation. A liberal in church–state relations and education, he opened wider the doors of his profession to fellow Catholics who were born without the privileges of the Colles, Cramptons, Graves, Smylys, Stokes, and other members of the Dublin medical establishment. With the death of his eldest grandson, John Joseph Corrigan (1859–1883), the baronetcy became extinct, but his name survives, emblazoned on the Beaumont Hospital in north Dublin; while visitors to the Royal College of Physicians on Kildare Street can still see his handsome features carved in marble and painted in oil in the elegant rooms that arose under his presidency. L. PERRY CURTIS JUN.

Sources E. O'Brien, *Conscience and conflict: a biography of Sir Dominic Corrigan, 1802–1880* (1983) · E. O'Brien, 'Sir Dominic Corrigan (1802–1880)', *Journal of the Irish Colleges of Physicians and Surgeons*, 10/1 (July 1980), 11–19 · D. Coakley, *Irish masters of medicine* (1992), 106–15 · J. B. Lyons, *Brief lives of Irish doctors* (1978), 79–83 · J. S. Doyle, 'Corrigan on fever', *Journal of the Irish Colleges of Physicians and Surgeons*, 10/1 (July 1980), 44–5 · F. R. Cruise, 'Sir Dominic Corrigan (1802–1880)', *Twelve Catholic men of science*, ed. B. Windle (1912) · J. D. Widdess, 'Corrigan's button', *Irish Journal of Medical Science*, 495 (1967), 137–40 · R. Mills and E. O'Brien, 'Corrigan bibliography', *Irish Journal of Medical Science*, 495 (1967), 50–52 · *Dorland's illustrated medical dictionary*, 28th edn (1994) · *BMJ* (7–21 Feb 1880) · *Freeman's Journal* [Dublin] (2 Feb 1880) · *Dublin Journal of Medical Science*, 69 (1880), 268–72, 330–31 · *The Lancet* (14 Feb 1880), 268–9 · *The Times* (2 Feb 1880), 6

Archives Royal College of Physicians of Ireland, Dublin, private papers

Likenesses prints and photographs, c.1855–1879, Royal College of Physicians, Ireland · J. H. Foley, plaster statuette, 1863, NG Ire. · S. C. Smith, oils, 1863, Royal College of Physicians, Ireland; repro. in O'Brien, *Conscience and conflict* · J. H. Foley, marble statue, 1869, Royal College of Physicians, Ireland; repro. in O'Brien, *Conscience and conflict* · Spex [J. F. O'Hea], caricature (*The Physic—all Baronet*), repro. in *Ireland's Eye* (11 July 1874), 174 · photo-engraving, on porcelain, Royal College of Physicians, Ireland; repro. in O'Brien, *Conscience and conflict* · wood-engraving, Wellcome L. · wood-engraving (after T. Cranfield), NPG; repro. in *ILN* (17 March 1866)

**Corro, Antonio del** (1527–1591), theologian, was born at Seville, the son of Antonio del Corro, doctor of law, and a prostitute. He entered the Observantine Hieronymite monastery of San Isidoro del Campo, near Seville, about 1547, and soon afterwards renounced the Roman Catholic faith. He ascribed this step to the influence of certain disclosures made to him by a member of the Spanish Inquisition, who also introduced him to the writings of Luther and Bullinger. He fled Spain about 1558 and spent the next nine years in Lausanne, where he studied at the university, and Flanders. Though not formally identifying himself with any protestant communion, he exercised ministerial functions for five years in Reformed communities in Béarn, Bergerac, and Montargis. Invited to Antwerp, he was chosen in 1566 pastor of the Walloon church, but the civil authorities, under Spanish influence, refused to confirm his settlement. In his defence he published *Lettre envoyée à la majesté du roy des Espaignes* (1567; English edn, 1577), addressed to Philip II of Spain, in which he explained his evangelical views and pleaded for liberty of conscience. He also set out to combat Lutheran triumphalism at Antwerp with a 'godly admonition', *Epistre et amiable remonstrance* (1567; English edn, 1569), recommending a greater moderation in the matter of eucharistic doctrine, with a view to protestant unanimity, in accordance with the ideas of John à Lasco.

On the arrival of a Spanish garrison at Antwerp in April 1567 Corro went to London with his wife, Marie Lenaerts (whom he had married about 1560), their sons John and James, and two servants, took up residence in a house belonging to the duchess of Suffolk in Cripplegate ward, and attached himself to the Italian congregation of the Strangers' Church. Soon after, by favour of Sir William Cecil and Robert Dudley, earl of Leicester, he became pastor of the Spanish congregation. As early as 1563 he had written from France, concerning the printing of a Spanish version of the Bible, to Casiodoro de Reina (also a native of Seville), the first pastor of the Spanish congregation in London. But when the letter arrived Reina was no longer in London, having fled under a charge of sodomy, and the Spanish congregation had been divided between the French and Italian churches, until the arrival of Corro with other exiles gave occasion for reviving it. On 16 January 1568 he addressed a letter to Archbishop Parker, accompanied by his two publications in French, which he thought would be good reading for two children of the archbishop, who were then learning that language. Doubts about the orthodoxy of Corro's trinitarian views were raised by the French pastors in London, led by Jean Cousin. In seven letters Corro laid the case before Beza at Geneva, who did not like 'the hot, accusing spirit of this Spaniard', and left the matter in the hands of Grindal, in whom, as bishop of London, was vested the superintendence of the Strangers' Church (*Bèze*, 10.47–51). Grindal recognized Corro's learning but disapproved of the spirit in which he acted.

On 17 March 1569 Corro was suspended by Grindal for slander and obstinacy, but not for any doctrinal aberration. Doctrinal differences then arose between Corro and Gerolamo Ferliti, pastor of the Italian congregation, the main charge being that in his teaching, and in his *Tableau de l'œuvre de Dieu* (1569), Corro showed Pelagian and universalist tendencies. Cecil continued to support his friend, and in May 1571 persuaded Edwin Sandys, Grindal's successor, to appoint Corro Latin reader in divinity at the Temple. He held this post for three years, but did not get on well with Richard Alvey, the master of the Temple, and was disliked for 'speaking not wisely on predestination and suspiciously uttering his judgement on Arianism' (*Correspondence of Matthew Parker*, 476). William Barlow, afterwards archdeacon of Salisbury, praised his eloquence and learning, but thought him wanting in respect for recognized authorities, and too great an admirer of Sebastian Castellio. On 5 March 1576 the earl of Leicester, chancellor of Oxford University, sent letters to the vice-chancellor and convocation asking that Corro might proceed DTh without fee. On 2 April convocation granted the request on condition 'that he purge himself of heretical opinions before the next act' (McFadden, 455, n. 1). Corro had already subscribed the Anglican articles before the privy council, but John Reynolds on 7 June wrote to Lawrence Humphrey, the vice-chancellor, reviving the charges against Corro and hinting that he was the source of the heresies of Francesco Pucci, an erratic Florentine who had given trouble to the university in the previous year. Corro's application was rejected on 13 June.

As Corro styles himself 'professor of sacred theology' in a publication as early as 1574, he may have had a foreign or a Lambeth degree. In 1578 he published a commentary on Ecclesiastes, *Sapientissimi regis Salomonis concio* (English edn, 1586), which was widely admired and used. In the summer of that year the earl of Leicester supported him in an application for a post at Oxford. After severe examination he was admitted as a divinity reader in 1579. At Oxford, Corro lived as a student in Christ Church, and became reader of divinity to the students in Gloucester, St Mary, and Hart halls. He was *censor theologicus* at Christ Church (1578–86), and matriculated as a member of Christ Church in 1586. In 1582 he obtained the prebend of Harlesden in St Paul's, London, and in 1585 was installed in Lichfield Cathedral as prebendary of Eccleshall. In 1586 he published a Spanish grammar, *Reglas gramaticales* (English edn, 1590), his only work in his native language, based on notes made about 1560 when he was tutor to the future Henri IV of France; most of its examples are drawn from scripture.

The charge of heresy was reiterated against Corro at Oxford in 1582, and has clung to his memory. Bonet-Maury places him among those who have rejected the doctrine of the Trinity, and McFadden asserts that one of his works, *Monas theologica* (unpublished in Corro's lifetime), 'is frankly unitarian', though he notes that Corro is essentially concerned with practical religion, not theological speculation (McFadden, 692–5). His published articles of faith (1574) are quite orthodox on that doctrine. Some of his London congregation may have been anti-trinitarian, but he does not seem to have been personally heterodox, except in the article of predestination and cognate doctrines, as held by Calvinists. He was a man of open mind, and a vigorous defender of toleration, not only among Christians but also toward Jews and Muslims; had his temper been less hot and his disposition more conciliatory, his career might have been brighter. Corro died in London on 30 March 1591, and was buried at St Andrew by the Wardrobe on 3 April. His wife and a daughter, Susan, survived him. In the eyes of posterity Corro has come to be perceived as 'a proto-Arminian … a pioneer of the intellectual reaction against John Calvin' (Collinson, 151), but this was also a perception current in his own lifetime. In the late 1570s Sir Henry Killigrew, Burghley's brother-in-law, was including regular reports on Corro's activities in his dispatches to William Davison, ambassador in the Netherlands, who shared his deep suspicions of Corro's theology, and when in 1585 Richard Hooker began preaching at the Temple, where Corro had briefly held sway, 'comparisons were at once drawn with the Spaniard' (ibid.).

ALEXANDER GORDON, *rev.* JONATHAN L. NELSON

**Sources** W. McFadden, 'The life and works of Antonio del Corro', PhD diss., Queen's University, Belfast, 1953 · A. G. Kinder, 'Antonio del Corro', in A. G. Kinder, *Bibliotheca Dissidentium*, 7 (Baden-Baden, 1986), 121–76 [incl. bibliography] · A. del Corro, *Lettre envoyée à la majesté du roy des Espaignes* (Antwerp, 1567) · *Bibliotheca Wiffeniana: Spanish reformers of two centuries from 1520*, ed. E. Boehmer, 3 vols. (1874–1904), vol. 3, pp. 1–146 · B. A. Vermaseren, 'The life of Antonio de Corro (1527–1591) before his stay in England', *Archives et Bibliothèques de Belgique*, 57 (1986), 530–68; 61 (1990), 175–275 · E. Boehmer, 'Antonio del Corro', *Bulletin Historique et Littéraire* [Société d'Histoire du Protestantisme Français], 50 (1901), 201–16 · H. Robinson, ed. and trans., *The Zurich letters, comprising the correspondence of several English bishops and others with some of the Helvetian reformers, during the early part of the reign of Queen Elizabeth*, 2, Parker Society, 8 (1845) · Wood, *Ath. Oxon.*, 1st edn, vol. 1 · *Correspondance de Théodore de Bèze*, ed. H. Aubert, 6 (Geneva, 1970–); 10 (1978) · *Correspondence of Matthew Parker*, ed. J. Bruce and T. T. Perowne, Parker Society, 42 (1853) · P. Collinson, *Archbishop Grindal, 1519–1583: the struggle for a reformed church* (1979) · A. G. C. A. Bonet-Maury, *Early sources of English unitarian Christianity*, trans. E. P. Hall (1884) · A. D. C. [A. del Corro], *Reglas gramaticales para aprender la lengua Espanola y Francesa* (1586) · A. del Corro, *The Spanish grammer: with certeine rule teaching both the Spanish and French tongues*, trans. J. Torrie (1590) · parish register, St Andrew by the Wardrobe, GL, MS 4501/1 [burial] · Certificaetbouck 43, Antwerp City Archives

## Corry, Henry Thomas Lowry

**Corry, Henry Thomas Lowry** (1803–1873), politician, was born in Dublin on 9 March 1803, the second son of Somerset Corry, the second earl of Belmore (1774–1841), and his wife, Lady Juliana (*d.* 1861), second daughter of Henry Thomas Butler, second earl of Carrick. He was educated at Eton College and Christ Church, Oxford, where he gained second-class honours in classics and graduated BA in 1823. He married, on 18 March 1830, Lady Harriet Anne (*d.* 1868), daughter of Cropley Ashley-Cooper, the sixth earl of Shaftesbury, and sister of the famous seventh earl, a Christ Church contemporary. They had two sons and two daughters.

Corry was elected as a Conservative for Tyrone county in June 1826, a family seat, and represented it until his death. He was comptroller of the household in Peel's 1834–5 administration and was sworn a privy councillor. He became a junior lord of the Admiralty in Peel's second ministry in 1841, and was appointed secretary to the Admiralty on the reconstruction of the government in December 1845. In the 1847 parliament he sat as a Peelite. When Derby was trying to form an administration in February 1851 Disraeli recommended Corry as someone with the reputation of a good administrator, who had addressed the house with fluency, clearness, and knowledge of his subject. He was offered a cabinet post, the Colonial Office, even though Derby felt this to be above his claims and his abilities. He refused and was left out when Derby formed a ministry a year later. He returned as secretary to the Admiralty in Derby's 1858–9 administration. In July 1866 he was appointed vice-president of the council on education. He proposed a modification of the revised code of 1862 to help smaller schools.

On the resignation of Cranborne, Carnarvon, and Peel in March 1867 Corry joined the cabinet as first lord of the Admiralty. In his first major speech on 1 April 1867 he emphasized the sole responsibility of the cabinet for naval dispositions, the reasons for which were sometimes not known even by the lords of the Admiralty. He initiated a programme of building iron-clads. His final months in office were overshadowed by ill health. He was the author of *Naval Promotion and Retirement, a Letter to the Right Hon. S. P. Walpole* (1863) and of *Three Speeches on the Navy, with Preface by Sir J. C. D. Hay, Bt, MP* (1872). Corry died at Hursley, Bournemouth, Hampshire, on 6 March 1873. His second son, Montagu *Corry, was Disraeli's private secretary and was raised to the peerage as Lord Rowton.

E. J. FEUCHTWANGER

**Sources** Burke, *Peerage* · Boase, *Mod. Eng. biog.* · Walford, *County families* · *Disraeli's reminiscences*, ed. H. M. Swartz and M. Swartz (1975) · *Disraeli, Derby and the conservative party: journals and memoirs*

of Edward Henry, Lord Stanley, 1849–1869, ed. J. R. Vincent (1978) • Hansard 3 (1858), 148–51; (1867) • McCalmont's parliamentary poll book: British election results 1832–1918, ed. J. Vincent and M. Stenton, 8th edn (1971) • J. B. Conacher, The Peelites and the party system (1972)
**Archives** PRO NIre. | Bodl. Oxf., letters to Benjamin Disraeli • Bodl. Oxf., Hughenden MSS • Bodl. Oxf., corresp. with Sir Robert Peel • Lpool RO, letters to fourteenth earl of Derby • NMM, corresp. with Sir Alexander Milne • PRO NIre., corresp. with Daniel Auchinleck • Som. ARS, letters to Sir William Jolliffe
**Likenesses** H. Gales, watercolour (The Derby cabinet of 1867), NPG • G. Hayter, group portrait, oils (The House of Commons, 1833), NPG • R. & E. Taylor, wood-engraving (after photograph by J. Watkins), NPG; repro. in ILN (22 March 1873)
**Wealth at death** under £30,000: probate, 9 April 1873, CGPLA Eng. & Wales

**Corry, Isaac** (1753–1813), politician, was born probably in Newry on 15 May 1753, the eldest son of Edward Corry (d. 1792), merchant and MP, and Catherine Bristow (1731–1818), daughter of Captain Charles Bristow of Crebilly, co. Antrim. He was educated at the Royal School, Armagh, under its celebrated headmaster, Dr Grueder, and he entered Trinity College, Dublin, on 8 July 1768, graduating BA in 1773. He was admitted to the Middle Temple on 18 October 1771 and called to the Irish bar in 1779. He was unmarried but had a long-term relationship with Jane Symms; they had six children.

Corry succeeded his father as MP for Newry in 1776 and represented the constituency almost continuously for thirty years, first in the Irish parliament and from 1802 to 1806 in the imperial parliament. Commercial interests were a prime concern for Newry, because of its flourishing linen trade and its hopes of becoming a major port for the coal trade, both for its citizens and, given the potwalloping nature of the constituency, for its representatives. As might be expected Corry was appointed to the linen board in 1783. The principal political interests in the town were those of the Needham family, who backed Corry, and Lord Hillsborough, who described the town in 1784 as 'very little short of the factious violence of Belfast' (Malcomson, 5). During the 1776–83 parliament Newry was divided by the issues of the movement for 'free trade' and the volunteers. In August 1780, when the Newry Volunteers were reviewed, Corry was a captain and adjutant-general.

In the early 1780s Corry supported the fifth earl of Carlisle's administration but otherwise was generally in opposition. He also supported parliamentary reform and was then a friend of Grattan. In 1783 he opposed the government for not safeguarding the country's interest over Ireland's exclusion from the Methuen treaty on Portuguese trade, the East India Company, and parts of the 1660 Navigation Act. On the issue of trade the government feared the capacity of Corry and Henry Flood to stir up national agitation. In March 1785 the Dublin Morning Post described Corry as a 'zealous watchman' of Irish interests and in 1787, at the time of the French commercial treaty, Corry emphasized the point that the Irish parliament should exercise their undoubted right and discuss it 'lest in the eyes of the British Minister they should appear altogether ignorant or neglectful' (Parliamentary Register, 7, 1787, 286). At the same time he admitted that the ultimate

decision had to be made in the British parliament. He also pointed out that although France could provide Ireland with a market for her goods—especially, it was hoped, linen—nevertheless there was 'an opposition of natural interests, an opposition of political constitutions, an opposition of national views and therefore of national councils and conduct' (ibid., 287). Like almost all of the Irish opposition he was anxious to retain the British connection, writing that 'next to the preservation of our constitution and keeping the country out of debt' the great object of his heart was 'to support the honour and interests of the British empire' (291–2).

In 1783 it was thought that after the election Corry would 'apply for office, as he lives expensively and does not pursue his profession, which is the law'. Although Henry Flood and Corry were not always in agreement, Flood's absence at Westminster gave Corry the leadership of the opposition. But although his oratorical skills were more than adequate he lacked Flood's pre-eminence. At this time it was thought that he placed his stakes too high, but in 1788 it was remarked that he 'speaks frequently, has Parliamentary talents, and [is] perhaps among the first in opposition' (Dublin Morning Post, 26 Jan 1788). These were gifts which no administration could afford to ignore, and he became surveyor-general of the ordnance in 1788, which carried with it a salary of £1000 p.a. for doing 'virtually nothing'; Corry, however, appears to have been fairly active in putting its affairs in order, much to the chagrin of the inmates. He probably got his instructions from the marquess of Buckingham, who, in both his viceroyalties, was determined to root out any waste or misdemeanours associated with inefficiency. The following year Corry was appointed a commissioner of the revenue. According to Richard Annesley, in April 1795 he 'attacked the FitzWilliam administration as vigorously as he had strongly supported it before' (Downshire MSS, D607/C/84).

Corry was made an Irish privy councillor on 18 August 1795. In 1798 he was elected chairman of the committee on ways and means, and finally in 1799 he was appointed chancellor of the exchequer and a lord of the Treasury in place of Sir John Parnell, who quarrelled violently with Pitt over the projected union, which he categorically refused to support. Although this decision was taken in London, Corry was blamed for Sir John's dismissal and for succeeding him. This was certainly irrational and probably very unjust as he was in fact the logical person to succeed Parnell both from abilities and experience. Furthermore, such a succession had precedents in the cases of Anthony Malone and John Foster. Under the 1793 Place Act Corry had to seek re-election on his appointment as chancellor and on 7 February 1799 the Catholic priest at Newry, Father Lennon, wrote to Archbishop Troy that 'Mr Corry was this day re-elected for the town of Newry' (Bolton, 136).

The national finances were in chaos and to help balance the budget Corry introduced a window tax, similar to that in England. This added to his unpopularity. Then, during a debate on the union on 18 February 1800, he accused Henry Grattan of 'living in familiarity with rebels and being a conniver at this plan to overthrow the country'—an opinion which was not unique to Corry (*Correspondence of … Cornwallis*, 3.196). At the end of the debate Grattan challenged him. Although Corry was slightly wounded in the duel, the opposition accused him of trying to assassinate Grattan. Further unfortunate coincidences followed: the marquess of Downshire, a fervent anti-unionist, committed suicide on 7 September 1801, and the marchioness appears to have blamed Corry together with Castlereagh, and vowed vengeance on them. Next, Sir John Parnell died of apoplexy on 5 December. Meanwhile, the representation for Newry had been reduced to one seat by the Act of Union and Corry was unlucky in the ballot that decided the continuing MP. At the time of the union he had agreed with Pitt and Castlereagh over the question of Catholic emancipation and this made it difficult to find him a seat, especially in view of the expressed hostility of the king, which brought him unwelcome notoriety. But as chancellor of the Irish exchequer he had to present the budget in parliament and he was returned, at Addington's instigation, for Lord Roden's borough of Dundalk.

In 1802 Corry was returned unopposed for Newry but he still aroused enmity, fuelled by a mixture of envy at his abilities and hostility to his origins. He presented the Irish budget to the Commons on 1 April 1801 and spoke only on Irish questions—principally on financial matters. He overcame the opposition of John Foster to the plan for Irish finance legislation by arguing that Ireland should adopt the English system. He carried the Irish Revenue Acts in the 1802–3 session but Foster refused to enlist with government while Corry remained. If he was to hold on to Newry he needed ever increasing patronage and his continual demands made him unpopular with the Irish administration. Finally, in May 1804, Corry was dismissed by Pitt in favour of Foster, but he was awarded £2000 p.a. in compensation. He was not a steady Pitt supporter, and, perhaps not surprisingly, he was critical of Foster's budget. He voted for Catholic relief on 14 May 1805. Unlike many Irish members he appreciated and enjoyed the Westminster scene.

Meanwhile the political scene in Newry altered. The Needham estate passed to the senior branch of the Needham family, the viscounts Kilmorey, and Lord Kilmorey, assisted by Lady Downshire, decided to return his brother General Francis Needham at the general election of 1806. Corry was powerless against such 'real' interest and he did not have the funds needed, in excess of £5000, to purchase a seat elsewhere. However, Lady Downshire was inclined to support the Grenville ministry and came to a formal agreement with Corry to give him £1000 towards his expenses should he be successful in Newry, and, if not, to bring him in for another borough. Corry failed against the Needham interest in Newry, but a seat at Newport, Isle of Wight, was purchased for him, with £4000 from Lady Downshire, and Corry was appointed to the Board of Trade. Six months later Grenville's ministry had fallen and there was another general election. Corry stood, again unsuccessfully, for Newry.

Corry did not come into parliament again. His health was declining and, although he had been given a generous, if erratically paid, pension, he felt bitter at his loss of office and a seat in parliament, for which he blamed Foster. He died at his house in Merrion Square, Dublin, on 15 May 1813 and was buried in St Patrick's Cathedral, Dublin. He was not without personal attractions. It was said in 1789 that:

> possessing from nature, a very pleasing exterior, Mr Corry loses not that advantage, by a slovenly neglect of it … His voice is remarkably good, clear, distinct, and melodious and equally adapted to thunder in the storm of impetuous eloquence, or to insinuate in the soothing accents of captivating persuasion.   (Malcomson, 6)

The story of the Corrys in the last quarter of the eighteenth century illustrates the exclusivity of the ascendancy, for whom wealth and birth counted more than talent.

E. M. JOHNSTON-LIIK

**Sources** E. M. Johnston-Liik, *History of the Irish parliament, 1692–1800*, 6 vols. (2002) • A. P. W. Malcomson, *Isaac Corry* (1974) • A. Aspinall, 'Corry, Isaac', HoP, *Commons, 1790–1820* • Burtchaell & Sadleir, *Alum. Dubl.* • J. L. J. Hughes, ed., *Patentee officers in Ireland, 1173–1826, including high sheriffs, 1661–1684 and 1761–1816*, IMC (1960) • *Index to privy counsellors, 1711–1910 (and partially from 1660)* [n.d.] • E. Keane, P. Beryl Phair, and T. U. Sadleir, eds., *King's Inns admission papers, 1607–1867*, IMC (1982) • H. A. C. Sturgess, ed., *Register of admissions to the Honourable Society of the Middle Temple, from the fifteenth century to the year 1944*, 1 (1949), 373 • J. Kelly, *Henry Flood: patriots and politics in eighteenth-century Ireland* (1998), 348, 368, 391, 438 • J. Kelly, *Prelude to Union: Anglo-Irish politics in the 1780s* (1992), 67, 152 • *Correspondence of Charles, first Marquis Cornwallis*, ed. C. Ross, 2nd edn, 3 vols. (1859), vol. 3, pp. 39, 195–6 • J. Kelly, *That damn'd thing called honour: duelling in Ireland, 1570–1860* (1995), 137, 140, 211–12 • R. B. McDowell, *Irish public opinion, 1750–1800* (1944), 79, 118, 141 • P. D. H. Smyth, 'The volunteers and parliament, 1779–84', *Penal era and golden age: essays in Irish history, 1690–1800*, ed. T. Bartlett and D. W. Hayton (1979), 113, n. 1 • G. C. Bolton, *The passing of the Irish Act of Union* (1966), 136–7 • W. A. Maguire, *The Downshire estates in Ireland, 1801–1845: the management of Irish landed estates in the early nineteenth century* (1972), 187 • *Memoirs and correspondence of Viscount Castlereagh, second marquess of Londonderry*, ed. C. Vane, marquess of Londonderry, 12 vols. (1848–53), vol. 2, p. 168 • *Drogheda Newsletter, or, Ulster Journal* (8–10 March 1800) • *Public Register, or, Freeman's Journal* (8 Sept 1796) • *Public Register, or, Freeman's Journal* (29 Aug 1799) • *Belfast News-Letter* (18–22 April 1794) • *Belfast News-Letter* (15 Jan 1798) • *Belfast News-Letter* (8 Oct 1799) • *Belfast News-Letter* (25 Feb 1800) • *Belfast News-Letter* (21 May 1813) • *Dublin Journal* (14–18 Oct 1783) • Dublin University Library, private members' bills, 386.s.39 • J. Porter, P. Byrne, and W. Porter, eds., *The parliamentary register, or, History of the proceedings and debates of the House of Commons of Ireland, 1781–1797*, 17 vols. (1784–1801) • R. G. Thorne, 'Newport, I. o. W.', HoP, *Commons, 1790–1820*, 2.185–6 • P. J. Jupp, 'Newry', HoP, *Commons, 1790–1820*, 2.646–9 • PRO NIre., Downshire MSS, D607/C/84

**Archives** BL, letters to Lord Hardwicke, Add. MSS 35728–35750, *passim* • Hants. RO, corresp. with W. Wickham • Hunt. L., letters to Grenville family • PRO NIre., Blackwood pedigree, T 618/333 • PRO NIre., Downshire MS D 607/C/84 • PRO NIre., Irish Volunteers MS MIC 474

**Likenesses** F. Wheatley, group portrait, oils (*The Irish House of Commons, 1780*), Leeds City Art Gallery • portrait, Castleward, co. Down

**Corry, John** ( *fl.* 1792–1836), writer, was a native of north Ireland. Nothing is known of his parentage or his education: he seems to have been self-taught. He worked as a journalist in Dublin, before establishing himself in 1792

in London, where he showed himself an author of astonishing versatility. Besides editing a periodical, he provided the letterpress for *The History of Liverpool*, published by Thomas Troughton in 1810, and in 1817 published *The History of Macclesfield*. A more ambitious undertaking was his *History of Lancashire* (1825), which was dedicated to George IV. This county history was a poor imitation of Matthew Gregson's *Portfolio* of 1817, and was immediately eclipsed by Edward Baines's *Gazetteer* (1824–5). Corry also wrote biographies of George Washington (1800), William Cowper (1803), and Joseph Priestley (1804), as well as children's books and satirical works. He was for some time an honorary member of the Philological Society in Manchester. Little is known about his life after 1825, although a letter from him dated 1836 has survived. His works have now fallen into complete obscurity.

GORDON GOODWIN, *rev.* JOANNE POTIER

**Sources** Allibone, *Dict.* · H. Fishwick, *The Lancashire library* (1875), 53–4 · C. R. J. Currie and C. P. Lewis, eds., *English county histories: a guide* (1994), 163–4, 221 · Bodl. Oxf., MSS Phillipps-Robinson b.121, fols. 176–9 · [J. Watkins and F. Shoberl], *A biographical dictionary of the living authors of Great Britain and Ireland* (1816)
**Archives** BL, corresp. with Sir Robert Peel, Add. MSS 40254, 40263, 40274, 40363, 40365, 40606, 40611 · Bodl. Oxf., letters to Sir Thomas Phillipps

**Corry, Montagu William Lowry**, Baron Rowton (1838–1903), politician and philanthropist, was born in London on 8 October 1838, the third of four children (second of two sons) of Henry Thomas Lowry *Corry (1803–1873) and his wife, Lady Harriet Anne Ashley-Cooper (*d.* 1868), second daughter of the sixth earl of Shaftesbury and granddaughter of the fourth duke of Marlborough; Corry's paternal grandfather was the second earl of Belmore, whose wife (his cousin) was a daughter of the second earl of Carrick. Monty Corry was educated at Harrow School and at Trinity College, Cambridge (BA 1861); he was called to the bar at Lincoln's Inn in 1863 and then joined the Oxford circuit. Successful in his profession and popular in society, he was also an occasional contributor to *The Owl*.

On 31 August 1865 at the duke of Cleveland's Raby Castle, Benjamin *Disraeli observed the handsome young man amusing some bored young women by dancing while singing a comic song, and told him, 'I think you must be my impresario'. On 29 June 1866, when Lord Derby was forming his third administration, Corry reminded Disraeli of their meeting, although he could 'scarcely presume to ask for the honour of being Private Secretary to yourself'. Disraeli, however, offered him the post, and on 11 July Corry wrote: 'it will be owing to no neglect on my part, if I fail to prove myself worthy of it'. True to his word, he served Disraeli faithfully both in and out of office until (and even after) Disraeli's death in 1881.

Disraeli quickly developed great confidence in Corry, and by the autumn of 1866 was praising his work and frankly discussing with him his views on men and affairs. Meanwhile, Corry began keeping Disraeli informed of the opinions current in society. In October Disraeli asked him to be the nominal editor of a collection of his speeches on parliamentary reform; it appeared in January 1867. One of

Montagu William Lowry Corry, Baron Rowton (1838–1903), by Heinrich von Angeli

Corry's first assignments was to protect Mrs Disraeli at Grosvenor Gate from the crowds agitating for reform in Hyde Park, when he concluded, 'she sympathizes with them'. He and Mrs Disraeli became close friends; from his watch by her deathbed in 1872 Disraeli wrote, 'She says she must see you'. With the termination of her life interest in her first husband's estate, Disraeli left the search for a new town residence entirely to Corry, who increasingly looked after Disraeli's personal affairs, such as (in 1874) the redecoration of Downing Street, and the purchase of a wedding gift for the countess of Pembroke. Corry nevertheless maintained his freedom to look after his own family, especially his frail unmarried sister, Alice, who after 1873 usually lived with him at 71 South Audley Street. Disraeli invariably bemoaned his absences.

Although he never sought any higher office, Corry became so much an extension of Disraeli (especially in domestic affairs) that, as Lord Carnarvon remarked in 1874, 'M. Corry is in fact Prime Minister.' He vetted political hopefuls, controlled access to the prime minister, suggested positions on major issues, and was Disraeli's link with the social world. After an invitation to Osborne in January 1868, he became friends with the queen, and established good relations with the court circle, as well as with the prince of Wales and his friends. Corry was privy to Disraeli's most confidential dealings, and attended him at cabinet meetings from an adjoining room, most famously in 1876, when Disraeli by a signal sent him to Baron Rothschild for a loan of £4 million to purchase the khedive of Egypt's shares in the Suez Canal. In May 1877, when Disraeli (now Lord Beaconsfield) was too ill to attend cabinet meetings, the queen summoned Corry to report to her.

The heavy workload undermined Corry's health with bouts of depression, most seriously in early 1878, when he went abroad with his sister. Beaconsfield had other secretaries, but 'no substitute for him'. Corry recovered in time to attend Beaconsfield at the Congress of Berlin in June and was present at the seven-minute meeting with Bismarck that broke the impasse with Russia in England's favour. Also in 1878, Corry negotiated with Longman the unprecedented sum of £10,000 for *Endymion*, Beaconsfield entrusting him with completing the novel if necessary.

Corry never married, but he had many affairs and several children, whom he provided for as their godfather; one of his daughters was Violet Manners, daughter of Violet *Manners, wife of the eighth duke of Rutland (Lambert, 79). The queen originally saw him as 'a man of pleasure', and Beaconsfield remarked, 'What a Lothario Monty is'. His most enduring liaison was with Lady Mary Dawson (from 1872 countess of Ilchester). Beaconsfield bemusedly tolerated this aspect of Corry's life; during one absence in 1879 he remarked to Lady Bradford: 'I want him, & could have commanded his presence, but I can't work with a man, perpetually sighing, & whose thoughts are in another place. In a week's time, I hope, he will think only of me' (Zetland, 2.243).

On leaving office in 1880, Beaconsfield told Lord Barrington that 'he chiefly deplored his fall from power on account of M. Corry, who in his opinion was fitted to fill any *Cabinet* office'. When Corry loyally declined the many posts offered him, Beaconsfield recommended him for a peerage, making sure that Corry's aunt, Lady Charlotte Lyster, would bequeath him her estate (listed in 1883 at 6300 acres yielding £5600 a year) to support the dignity. On 6 May 1880 he was controversially created Baron Rowton, of Rowton Castle, Shropshire, an unprecedented honour for a secretary. He continued (unpaid) as Beaconsfield's secretary, and was with his 'dearest Chief'—who typically addressed him as 'my dearest Monty'—when he died on 19 April 1881. Beaconsfield left all his private papers unconditionally to Rowton, who did much of the original work of putting them in order and preserved material (such as the Henrietta Sykes papers) which Sir Philip Rose wanted to destroy. Rowton was frequently the queen's guest, adviser, and link with her former prime minister and, after Beaconsfield's death, with parliament and the Conservatives.

During 1889 Rowton developed philanthropic interests; in November he accepted an active trusteeship of the Guinness Trust Fund for the provision of artisans' dwellings in London and Dublin and, after inheriting his aunt's estate in December, conceived the idea of a poor man's hotel. Against advice he invested £30,000 in the first Rowton House, opened on the last day of 1892 in Bond Street, Vauxhall. Rowton Houses Limited was incorporated in March 1894, and five more houses were opened by 1905, providing cheap but respectable accommodation for over 5000 men while realizing a modest profit.

Rowton was made a CB in 1878, a KCVO in 1897, and sworn of the privy council in 1900; he was also a deputy lieutenant for Shropshire. He died of pneumonia at his residence, 17 Berkeley Square, on 9 November 1903, and was buried at Kensal Green cemetery; he left his property to a nephew, but his title became extinct.

Lord Salisbury, who considered appointing Rowton to the Berlin embassy, said of him in 1895:

> He is charming, and sympathetically intelligent, without being what people call 'clever'. His disposition is most sociable, and he delights in knowing all about his friends' griefs and joys, and helping them. Art and nature are words that mean nothing to him, so his whole mind is turned to friends.

Disraeli's experience with Rowton is reflected in chapter 49 of *Endymion*:

> The relations between a minister and his secretary are … among the finest that can subsist between two individuals. Except the married state, there is none in which so great a degree of confidence is involved, in which more forbearance ought to be exercised, or more sympathy ought to exist.

Queen Victoria said that Rowton devoted himself to Disraeli 'as few sons ever do', and it is as Disraeli's model secretary that he will always be known.          M. G. WIEBE

**Sources** W. J. Jordan, 'Monty Corry: "the pattern private secretary"', *Disraeli Newsletter*, 6/1–2 (1981), 17–33 • R. Blake, *Disraeli* (1966) • W. F. Monypenny and G. E. Buckle, *The life of Benjamin Disraeli*, 6 vols. (1910–20) • Bodl. Oxf., Dep. Hughenden • *Letters of Disraeli to Lady Chesterfield and Lady Bradford*, ed. marquis of Zetland, 2 vols. (1929) • *The Times* (10 Nov 1903) • GEC, *Peerage* • 'Monty Corry, Lord Rowton', C. C. Petrie, *The powers behind the prime ministers* (1958), 11–30 • A. Lambert, *Unquiet Souls: the Indian summer of the British aristocracy, 1880–1918* (1984)

**Archives** priv. coll. | BL, Northcote MSS • Bodl. Oxf., Disraeli MSS • PRO NIre., Abercorn MSS

**Likenesses** H. von Angeli, oils, Hughenden Manor, Buckinghamshire [*see illus.*] • V. Granby, portrait, repro. in V. Granby, *Portraits of men and women* (1900) • Spy [L. Ward], cartoon, NPG; repro. in *VF* (3 March 1877), 134 • Spy [L. Ward], cartoon, NPG; repro. in *VF* (1880)

**Wealth at death** £183,612 11s.: probate, 19 Jan 1904, CGPLA Eng. & Wales

**Corsellis, Timothy John Manley** (1921–1941), poet, was born on 27 January 1921 at Hazelwood, North Park, Eltham, London, the son of Douglas Henry Corsellis, analytical chemist and barrister, and Helen Mary Corsellis, *née* Bendall. His father had served as a captain in the machine-gun corps during the First World War. Corsellis entered Winchester College in 1934 and some of his early poems appeared in *The Wykhamist Literary Supplement*. It was at Winchester that he formed the most influential friendship of his brief life, that with the poet Nigel Weir. A few months his senior, Weir was a linguist and naturalist whose open-faced idealism drew a questioning response from the younger boy. They fenced in the school gym, discussed their work, and gradually took up contrasting positions over the looming disaster of war which would destroy them both. Weir joined the celebrated Oxford University air squadron which his father had founded, and was awarded a half-blue for fencing; Corsellis became a member of ARP (air-raid precautions) and toiled in the East End of London. His 'Dawn after a Raid' vividly describes the confusion of homeliness and horror that was the blitz. A series of fine nature poems at this time included 'The Thrush', in which he confesses to Weir, 'I stopped his song'. On 8 August 1940 Weir shot down three German planes during the battle of Britain and won the DFC. He was killed flying in November, and his death left Corsellis isolated. 'In memoriam N.W.' thrusts aside the conventions of their uneasy relationship: it is an anti-war hero poem which sees Weir

> Moving among the Spitfires … And I pitied the German sons
> And I pitied his troubled soul.
> (Corsellis, 'In memoriam N.W.', *Poems*)

Corsellis's poetry reflects the nadir of the Second World War when the thoughts of so many people, especially the young, ran contrary to the official rhetoric. Reels of grinning soldiers in the news-cinema made him ask, 'Where are you going to, laughing men? For a holiday on the sea?' And when he himself joined the RAF he was crushed by the sordidness and inertia of the barracks; his poem 'Drill' perfectly encapsulating this common experience. He had little or no contact with other writers but a meeting with Stephen Spender resulted in an astute and moving appraisal of an established figure.

> I had expected an overwhelming greatness.
> Now I see you much as I am.
> You sit with a disturbance in your mind.
> (Corsellis, 'Stephen Spender', *Poems*)

Corsellis was a war poet who closely examined the ennui, boredom, and casual cruelty of his day. There are none of the literary references in his work which one might expect from such a young writer. In September 1939 Nigel Weir could write:

> There is a death, Elizabeth,
> for which we all must wait;
> and men and war can do no more
> than try to change the date.

Corsellis's fatalism was of a different kind. In no more than a handful of remarkable poems he was able to express certain attitudes towards the conflict which were common, though incoherent, during its darkest months. He is an uncomfortable realist who until he is able to make 'cartwheels in the sky' is plunged into all kinds of meanness. 'The sacrifice is greater than I ever expected.'

After training as a leading aircraftsman, Corsellis became a second officer in the Air Transport Auxiliary. This was a civilian organization connected to the Ministry of Aircraft Production. The twenty-year-old Corsellis was piloting a Magister aircraft L8268 on a ferrying flight from Luton to Carlisle on 10 October 1941 when it stalled in a turn and hit a tree near Annan, Dumfriesshire, and he was killed.

As with so many servicemen poets of the period, Timothy Corsellis first had his work published by the admirable Keidrich Rhys, himself serving as a gunner in the Royal Artillery. It belongs to the group of air force poets who include Henry Treece, John Pudney, and Vernon Watkins, while remaining distinctive and troubling. An edition of his collected poems has never been published. Corsellis's originality lies in his ability to reveal youthful disappointment with what was offered him. Barely grown

up, and lacking his friend Weir's strong sense of cause, he wrote poetry that is a severe indictment of the grim world into which the war cast him.

> Sometimes we pray to be hardened and callous,
> But God turns a deaf ear,
> And we know hate and sorrow—intimately,
> And we do not mind dying tomorrow.
> (Corsellis, 'Dawn after the Raid', *Poems*)

RONALD BLYTHE

**Sources** P. Ledward and C. Strang, eds., *Poems of this war by younger poets* (1942) [with an introduction by Edmund Blunden] · B. Gardner, ed., *The terrible rain: the war poets, 1939–1945* (1978) · R. Blythe, ed., *Writing in a war: stories, poems and essays of 1939–1945* (1982) · b. cert. · d. cert. · *CGPLA Eng. & Wales* (1942) · personal knowledge (2004) · private information (2004)
**Wealth at death** £2035 6*s.* 1*d.*: administration, 11 March 1942, *CGPLA Eng. & Wales*

**Corser, Thomas** (1793–1876), literary scholar and Church of England clergyman, the third son of George Corser, a banker, of Whitchurch, Shropshire, and his wife, Martha, daughter of Randall Phythian of the Higher Hall, Edge, Cheshire, was born at Whitchurch. From Whitchurch School he went in 1808 to the Manchester grammar school, and in May 1812 was admitted to Balliol College, Oxford, after being awarded one of the school exhibitions. He graduated BA in 1815, and MA in 1818. It was during his residence at Oxford, and through his intimacy with Dr Henry Cotton, sub-librarian of the Bodleian, that his love of early English poetry and Elizabethan literature was formed and his bibliographical tastes encouraged. In 1816 he was ordained to the curacy of Condover, near Shrewsbury, and in the following year received priest's orders, holding also the chaplaincy of Atcham Union at Berrington. From 1819 to 1826 he served as curate of the various parishes of Stone, Staffordshire, of Monmouth, and of Prestwich, near Manchester. In 1826, while curate of Prestwich, he obtained the incumbency of All Saints' Church, Stand, Manchester, where he continued for nearly fifty years. By his care and exertions the parish was early supplied with large and flourishing schools. He married on 24 November 1828 Ellen Lyon, the eldest daughter of the Revd James Lyon, rector of Prestwich.

Corser was one of the founders of the Chetham Society in 1843. Of the four works edited by Corser for the society—Chester's *Triumph* (1844), *Iter Lancastrense* (1845), Robinson's *Golden Mirrour*, and *Collectanea Anglo-poetica*—the most important are the *Iter* and the *Collectanea*. The first is an interesting account by Richard James, in verse, of his visit to Lancashire in 1636, amplified by the editor's research and diligence. The second is an alphabetical account, with extracts from each author, and elaborate biographical and bibliographical notices, of the editor's magnificent collection of early English poetry, which he had begun to form at an early age. The first part was issued in 1860. Corser's advanced age and infirmities interfered with the progress of the undertaking on the original scale beyond the letter C, and it was concluded at the fourth part (1869). But six further parts (1873–1880) were subsequently issued on a briefer plan. Corser died after the fifth part was published in 1873, and James Crossley edited the remainder. The work was a very valuable contribution to English bibliography, and the collection of books which formed its basis was sold in London in portions at different dates, from July 1868 to 1874, realizing upwards of £20,000. Corser was also a member of the Spenser, Camden, Surtees, Percy, and Shakespeare societies, and was elected FSA in 1850. In 1867 he suffered from an attack of paralysis; his eyesight failed, and he could write only with his left hand. He died at the Stand rectory on 24 August 1876. His wife had died on 25 April 1859, but at least one son and one daughter survived them.

G. C. BOASE, rev. NILANJANA BANERJI

**Sources** *Manchester Courier* (25 Aug 1876) · J. F. Smith, ed., *The admission register of the Manchester School, with some notes of the more distinguished scholars*, 3/1, Chetham Society, 93 (1874), 32–6 · *CGPLA Eng. & Wales* (1876)
**Archives** BL, letters to W. C. Hazlitt, Add. MSS 38898–38901 · Chetham's Library, Manchester, corresp. chiefly to and from Corser · U. Edin. L., special collections, corresp. with James Halliwell-Phillipps
**Wealth at death** under £25,000: probate, 13 Oct 1876, *CGPLA Eng. & Wales*

**Corss, James** (*fl.* 1658–1678), mathematician, was probably born and educated in Glasgow. The first formal record of Corss's activities is April 1658 when Edinburgh town council granted him permission to 'keip a publict school within this brugh for instructing of gentlemen and uthers in Arithmetique Geometrie Astronomie and all uther airts and Sciences belonging theirto' (Wood, 93). Advertisements indicate that Corss taught a wide range of applied mathematical topics:

> *Arithmetick* both Natural and Artificial, *Geometry*, in taking of heights, depths and distances, *Surveighing* of Ground, and all manner of Superficies and Solids; *Gunnery, Guadging, Dyalling, Drawing*, with the noble Arts of *Navigation* and *Trigonometry*: Together with *Astronomy*, in all the exquisite, practical, and demonstrative parts thereof, *viz*. In the most curious Calculations of the Diurnal Motions and Eclipses of the Luminaries. (J. Corss, *A New Prognostication for … 1675*, 1675, A3r)

In England such topics were widely available, but for early Restoration Scotland these were novel courses for a private teacher to offer. Corss's success can be measured by the fact that later in the century a growing number followed his pioneering attempts to teach practical mathematics to professionals and artisans.

From 1662 Corss annually compiled an almanac with astronomical data calculated for central Scotland. Almanacs had been published in Scotland since 1603, but Corss's was the first produced by an identifiable and native mathematical compiler. The Edinburgh publishers who printed his almanacs over the next sixteen years judged Corss's reputation for astronomical computation sufficient to acknowledge his authorship on the title-page. His successors, as compilers of Edinburgh published almanacs, James Paterson (*d.* 1694) and John Man (*d.* 1709), were heirs to that tradition. In contrast, Glasgow and Aberdeen almanacs were usually anonymous, at best stating the compiler's initials. Corss's first almanac was dedicated to the lord provost and baillies of Glasgow and earned its author a gratuity from the burgh. Next year

Edinburgh town council were dedicatees, with free copies given to members. There was no immediate reward, but in October 1664 James Corss 'mothimatician' was admitted burgess and guildbrother of Edinburgh, despite not having served an apprenticeship, and granted full remission of fees.

Corss's first book, *Ouranoskopia …, or, General Prognostication* (Edinburgh, 1662), included worked examples of the computations that underpinned the astronomical predictions of his almanacs. Referring, *en passant*, to the 'probability of the Heroick Hypothesis of Copernicus', he was explicitly aware that many still maintained that the earth was immovably fixed, but was nevertheless confident that earth 'hath a Motion, though insensible, by reason of the disproportion which our visual senses have to its vast magnitude' (Corss, sig. A 4r). In this context Corss discussed and illustrated the compromise Tychonic world system, which until the observations of James Bradley (1727–9), gave as good an account of observed phenomena as did the Copernican. Dedicated to the chancellor of Scotland, William Cunningham, earl of Glencairn, *Ouranoskopia* failed to elicit state patronage. In the introduction Corss lamented the poor level of mathematical attainment in Scotland and complained at the lack of encouragement given to those with numerate skills. Using phraseology long commonplace in England, he trumpeted the utility of mathematics to national and local government, landowner, merchant, and craftsman.

A second book, *Practical Geometry* (Edinburgh, 1666), was a similarly lucid text written for adult readers with basic numeracy skills. As the title-page announced, it was 'fitted for the ingenious of all Ranks and Professions, whether Military, or Civil: but principally for Artificers, Massons, Wrights, Surveyors of Lands or Buildings, Engineers, Military Architects, Gunners, Myners, and all other Students in the Mathematicks'. A wide range of practical applications was covered, and sustained the claim for the utility of geometry declaimed in the preface. In 1673, following a series of observations of the meridian altitude of the sun, Corss recalculated the latitude of Edinburgh to exactly 56°, against the 56°04′ previously accepted. The improved accuracy (55°56′ is the modern figure for central Edinburgh) is of less interest than his use of a quadrant of 6 feet radius, the limb divided to single seconds of arc.

George Liddell, subsequently professor of mathematics at Marischal College, Aberdeen, recorded that Corss's

> integrity of life, and accommodation to Mathematicall Students and Scholars was very well known: He was a Man not given to Ostentation, but lived content with the Talent that God had bestowed upon him, in the Mathematical Sciences, neither did he envy any person, altho their Gifts were above his. (Liddell, 3)

In 1678 Corss married Janet Boog in Edinburgh. In October or November that year his final work, an almanac for 1679, was published in the city. The date of his death is unknown.

D. J. BRYDEN

**Sources** J. Corss, *Ouranoskopia …, or, General prognostication* (1662) · W. M. McDonald, 'Scottish 17th century almanacks', *The Bibliotheck*, 4 (1963–6), 257–322, esp. 264–5 · D. J. Bryden, *Scottish scientific instrument-makers, 1600–1900* (1972), 1–4 · G. Liddell, *Certamen* *mathematicum* (1684) • E. G. R. Taylor, *The mathematical practitioners of Tudor and Stuart England* (1954), 239, 370, 375 • B. S. Capp, *Astrology and the popular press: English almanacs, 1500–1800* (1979) • M. Wood, ed., *Extracts from the records of the burgh of Edinburgh, 1655–1665*, [10] (1940), 93 • C. B. B. Watson, ed., *Roll of Edinburgh burgesses and guild-brethren, 1406–1700*, Scottish RS, 59 (1929), 119 • H. Paton, ed., *The register of marriages for the parish of Edinburgh, 1595–1700*, Scottish RS, old ser., 27 (1905), 70, 147

**Cort, Henry** (1741?–1800), ironmaster, was born in Lancaster and is usually assumed to have been the son of Henry Cort (d. 1747), a mercer and former mayor of Kendal. His exact date of birth is not known. According to the ambiguous inscription on his tombstone, he died in 1800 in 'the 60th year of his age', and 1740 has traditionally been accepted as the year of his birth. However, on the occasion of his first marriage, to Elizabeth Brown of St Giles-in-the-Fields, Holborn, whom he married at Crowhurst in Surrey on 21 April 1764, Cort gave his age as twenty-two. Whatever the circumstances of his birth, by 1765 Henry Cort was established in London as a naval agent, responsible for the disbursement of pay, allowances, and prize money to crews in the Royal Navy. His second marriage, in 1768, to Elizabeth Heysham (d. 1816), the daughter of Thomas Heysham, a steward to the duke of Portland, involved him more closely with the provision of naval supplies, and naval ironware in particular. His new wife's uncle, William Attwick of Gosport, owned a forge at Fontley, Hampshire, from where ironwares were supplied to the royal dockyard at Portsmouth. In time, Henry Cort invested in the Fontley works and in 1775 he took over its management, hoping to aggrandize the lucrative market for naval ironware.

At Fontley, Cort began to experiment with the techniques of rolling and refining iron for which he was to be renowned. His use of grooved rolls to produce hoops and bars of iron was the subject of his first patent (no. 1351) in 1783. Rolling allowed the production of malleable bar iron with a speed and uniformity of finish that was unattainable with the forge hammers that had previously been employed for the purpose. The process described in his second patent (no. 1420) in 1784 involved the use of coal as fuel in the decarburization of pig iron and its conversion thereby from a brittle material into a malleable iron. This process centred upon the stirring about and turning over of molten metal in the hearth of an air furnace so as to expose the iron evenly to an oxidizing current of air—hence the term 'puddling'. The effect of Cort's endeavours was to bring to an end the long search for an effective and expeditious coal-based refining technique, thus freeing the iron trade from its dependence upon charcoal as a source of energy. Together, the puddling and rolling methods made for an enormous increase in forge capacity and established the global supremacy of the British iron industry in the early nineteenth century.

Cort publicized his patent methods extensively in the mid-1780s, staging demonstrations and tests at ironworks in the midlands and Scotland and in the royal dockyards. In the late 1780s the first large-scale application of puddling and rolling was under way at the Cyfarthfa works of Richard Crawshay in Glamorgan. And when in April 1789 the Navy Board advertised its new bar-iron contracts, it stipulated that only iron manufactured according to Cort's patents would be considered. At this point, however, nemesis struck. His developmental work had been funded by an old associate, Adam Jellicoe, deputy paymaster of the navy, whose son Samuel was Cort's business partner. Jellicoe senior had advanced money from the official balances in his hands to Messrs Cort and Jellicoe. In 1789 these questionable transfers were discovered and the treasurer of the navy moved to recover £27,500 from Cort, who, quite unable to meet these demands, was gazetted bankrupt. The intervention of his friends secured a pension of £200 per annum from the government in 1794, but he remained an undischarged bankrupt until his death at lodgings in Devonshire Street, London, on 23 May 1800. He was buried in Hampstead churchyard. His second wife, the mother of his sixteen children, survived him.

Cort's patents were forfeit to the state at the time of his bankruptcy, though the government made little or no effort to collect the royalties due. As a result the British iron industry was able to exploit Cort's processes unhindered; in recognition of this, the leading British ironmasters were persuaded to enter into a subscription for his widow's benefit in 1811. The following year Cort's sons Henry and Coningsby petitioned the House of Commons for some recompense for their father's efforts in developing puddling, which, they asserted, had proved such a vital element of national prosperity. A committee of the house investigated the matter. Several witnesses were examined, the most damaging of whom, Samuel Homfray of Merthyr, had been one of the earliest users of the puddling technique. Homfray denied the novelty and worth of Cort's contribution to metallurgy, and the petition of his sons was rejected accordingly. However, Homfray's testimony was disingenuous. Although it was true that Cort's methods had to a degree relied upon an ingenious adaptation and concatenation of techniques already in experimental use in the iron trade, most of his peers had no doubt of the genuine originality of his contribution. It was puddling and rolling, not one of the rival techniques current in the 1780s, which remained the basis of iron refining for decades afterwards, until wrought iron was superseded by mass-produced steel in the second half of the nineteenth century. CHRIS EVANS

**Sources** R. A. Mott, *Henry Cort: the great finer* (1983) • E. W. Hulme, 'Henry Cort, founder of the iron puddling process, and his family', *N&Q*, 197 (1952), 77–82 • C. Evans, 'Iron puddling: the quest for a new technology in eighteenth-century industry', *Llafur*, 6/3 (1994), 44–57 • C. K. Hyde, *Technological change and the British iron industry, 1700–1870* (1977)
**Archives** Sci. Mus., Weale MSS
**Likenesses** bas-relief on monument, St John's Church, Hampstead, London • lithograph, BM • medallion, Sci. Mus.
**Wealth at death** undischarged bankrupt

**Cort, Henry Francis de** (1742–1810), landscape painter, was born at Antwerp, and first studied painting under W. Herreyns. On 16 May 1769 he entered the studio of the landscape painter Hendrik Joseph Antonissen, and on 16 May 1770 he was admitted a master in the guild of St Luke at Antwerp. His chief works were topographical paintings of towns and landscapes; in some of these he was assisted by his fellow pupil Ommeganek, who painted the figures for him. Leaving Antwerp he proceeded to Paris, entered the academy there, and was elected a fellow in 1781. There he painted some views of Chantilly, and was appointed painter to the prince de Condé. In 1788 he returned to Antwerp, and took an active part in reorganizing the school of painting there, acting as secretary to the newly constituted academy. He contributed six pictures to the first exhibition of the new academy held in 1789. Shortly after this he arrived in England, with some of his pictures, and in 1790 exhibited seven pictures at the Royal Academy. During the following twelve years he contributed numerous landscapes to the Royal Academy, particularly of the west of England. A total of sixty-three paintings were exhibited. In 1806 he contributed three landscapes to the first exhibition of the British Institution. Although his status does not seem to have been very high, his landscapes were much valued by private collectors, being agreeably coloured and treated in the Italian manner, very much in vogue at the time. His sepia drawings were also much admired. G. H. Harlow was one of his pupils. He died in London on 28 June 1810, and was buried in St Pancras old cemetery.                L. H. CUST, rev. MICHAEL MARKER

**Sources** Waterhouse, *18c painters* · Bénézit, *Dict.*, 4th edn · Redgrave, *Artists* · Graves, *RA exhibitors* · private information (1888)

**Corvan, Edward** [Ned] (1830–1865), entertainer and songwriter, was born in Liverpool of Irish parents, but was brought up from the age of four in Newcastle upon Tyne. Three years after the move his father, Matthew Corvan, a mason, died, and the young Corvan tramped the streets in search of odd jobs to help the family budget. He was eventually apprenticed to a sail maker but as a stage-struck teenager he forsook his indentures to join the company of Billy Purvis's music-hall, the Victoria Theatre, in the capacities of small-part actor, scenery painter, orchestra violinist and *entr'acte* singer. He soon began to write his own songs on local topics, setting them in time-honoured fashion to existing traditional or popular tunes. He achieved considerable success with items as disparate as 'Jimmy McKenny', a lament for a fairground and racecourse drummer and conjuror, and 'He wad be a Noodle', a good-humoured but sharp reproach to those who volunteered for the militia.

In 1849 Corvan moved to the newly opened Olympic Music Hall as resident singer and songwriter. In addition he played the violin—his standard was up to Paganini's *Carnaval de Venise*—and did impromptu cartoons in chalk on a blackboard. He adopted costume, either male or female, appropriate to his songs, delivered prose monologues between verses, and engaged in impromptu repartee with members of his audiences. In what was probably his best-loved song, 'The Toon Improvement Bill, or, Ne Pleyce noo ti Play' (a complaint at the loss of recreational space when Newcastle Central Station was built in 1849) he came on 'as a schoolboy in a white pinafore, with leathern belt, and trundling his hoop'. The comment is from

an eye-witness, who adds that Corvan had 'a bony, muscular frame, surmounted by a head which suggested a certain kind of rough power, and a countenance whose expression betokened infinite good nature and a rare fund of comicality', and that 'his appearance on the stage created quite a *furore*, altogether eclipsing the other performers' (Embleton Smith, 522).

Corvan married Isabella Arrowsmith on 17 March 1851. His health was not good, and he died from tuberculosis at Haddoch's Court, Newgate Street, Newcastle, on 31 August 1865. He was buried in an unmarked grave in St Andrew's cemetery. In his lifetime Corvan had performed all over the Tyneside area. He was celebrated both for the skill of his performances and for the fervour of his advocacy of the cause of working men and women, who were the protagonists of his songs. His subjects included sports such as rowing (a local passion), prize-fighting and horse-racing; the seamen's strikes of 1851 and the Hartley pit disaster of 1862; enforced emigration and adverse economic conditions. The tenor of his songs varied widely, from comic to satirical, from elegiac to indignant. Their language was the Tyneside vernacular, with sometimes irritating adaptations of standard spelling. They appeared as street ballads, singly or in groups of ten or twelve, were often reprinted, but gradually fell out of favour, although one turned up in oral tradition in Aberdeenshire in 1907. The first man on Tyneside to make a full-time profession of writing and singing local songs, Corvan retains a place in scholarly writing on the subject.         ROY PALMER

**Sources** J. Embleton Smith, 'Ned Corvan', *Monthly Chronicle* (Nov 1891), 522–3 · K. Gregson, *Corvan: a Victorian entertainer and his songs* (1983) · D. Harker, 'The making of the Tyneside concert hall', *Popular Music*, 1 (1981), 27–56 · D. Harker, 'Thomas Allen and "Tyneside Song"', *A choice collection of Tyneside songs*, ed. T. Allen (1972) [prefatory essay in 1972 repr. of 1891 book] · M. Vicinus, *The industrial muse: a study of nineteenth-century British working-class literature* (1974) · R. Middleton, *Studying popular music* (1990) · m. cert. · d. cert.
**Archives** South Shields Public Library, broadsides · U. Newcastle, broadsides
**Likenesses** portrait, repro. in Embleton Smith, 'Ned Corvan' · portrait, repro. in Harker, 'Making of the Tyneside concert hall'

**Corvo.** For this title name *see* Rolfe, Frederick William, styled Baron Corvo (1860–1913).

**Corvus, Joannes** (d. 1546), painter, is known from inscriptions formerly on the frames of two portraits, the first of Bishop Fox (Corpus Christi College, Oxford), the second of Mary Rose Tudor (1531) at Sudeley Castle, Gloucester, which read 'Joannes Corvus Flandrus faciebat'. Of his parents, nothing is known. It is generally accepted that the artist is identical with Jan Raf, who entered the Bruges Painters' Guild in 1512 and who rented a stall in the Pandt market there in 1514. He emigrated to England after this date and his name was subsequently recorded in a variety of spellings; he may be identical with the John Raff (Raufe, Rauff, Rauffe) who worked on decorations for the Greenwich revels in 1527 and for Westminster Palace in 1531. Sir Roy Strong suggested that two Elizabethan paintings of the festivities at the Field of the Cloth of Gold (the Royal Collection) may reflect these designs, although this remains conjectural. Equally uncertain is Max J. Friedländer's suggestion that the artist may be responsible for a drawing (Musée du Louvre, Paris) and a panel portrait of Charles Brandon, duke of Suffolk, husband of Mary Rose Tudor, in middle age (priv. coll.). Lionel Cust suggested Corvus was the 'Master John' referred to in the privy purse expenses of Henry VIII's daughter, the future Mary I, for the year 1544. However, the only surviving portrait of Mary bearing this date (NPG) bears little stylistic relationship to Corvus's other portraits. The artist is probably identical with 'Jehan Raf, peintre de Flandres', who produced a map of England in 1532 and a 'pourtraict de la ville de Londres' in 1534 for Francis I of France as well as the 'John Raven, born in Flanders' of London who was granted denizenship on 13 May 1544. The artist's will was made on 24 May 1546 (and proved on 20 July 1546), leaving his equipment to his son, Laurens. Inadequate and uncertain documentation make it difficult to create a satisfying outline of Corvus's life while the extensive nineteenth-century retouching of his two surviving autograph paintings makes it impossible to discern the qualities of his work which attracted the attention of the royal families of England and France. Nevertheless, his career demonstrates the close artistic links between the Netherlands and England during the period while his surviving works underline the reasons why Holbein should have achieved such pre-eminence.

P. G. Matthews and Elizabeth Drey-Brown

**Sources** R. A. Parmentier, 'Bronnen voor de geschiedenis van het Brugsche schildersmilieu in de XVIe eeuw, XXXIV: Jan en Laurens Rave', *Revue Belge d'Archéologie et d'Histoire de l'Art*, 18 (1949), 191–7 · E. Auerbach, *Tudor artists* (1954), 53, 160, 182 · J. C. Wilson, 'The participation of painters in the Bruges "Pandt" market', *Burlington Magazine*, 125 (1983), 476–9 · M. J. Friedländer, 'Ein vlämischer Porträtmaler in England', *Gentsche Bijdragen tot Kunstgeschiednis*, 4 (1937), 5–18 · R. Strong, *Holbein and Henry VIII* (1967), 24–6 · F. Lugt, *Inventaire général des dessins des écoles du nord: publié sous les auspices du cabinet des dessins: maîtres des anciens Pay-Bas nés avant 1550* (1968) · N. Toussaint, *Les primitifs flamands et leur temps*, ed. B. De Patoul and R. Van Schoute (1994), 574–5 · will, LMA, MS DL/C/355 [probate in the consistory court of London], fol. 92r (M/F x 19/13)

**Cory, Annie Sophie** [*pseud.* Victoria Cross] (**1868–1952**), novelist, was born on 1 October 1868 in Rawalpindi, Punjab, the youngest of the three daughters of Colonel Arthur Cory (*bap.* 1831, *d.* 1903), an army officer and later newspaper proprietor, and his wife, Elizabeth Fanny Griffin (1834–1916), daughter of Alfred Griffin (1811–1867), a barrister and landowner; Annie sometimes used her mother's maiden name, calling herself Vivian Cory Griffin. The poet Adela Florence *Nicolson (1865–1904), was her middle sister. Her sisters went to school in Richmond, Surrey but there is no evidence that she did. Her father resigned from the army in 1876, becoming editor and co-proprietor of the *Civil and Military Gazette* in Lahore until 1882; in 1884 he moved to Karachi to become editor and proprietor of the *Sind Gazette*. Annie Sophie matriculated at London University aged nineteen in 1888, but although she passed the intermediate examination in arts as an external student in 1890, partly qualifying herself for a BA pass degree, she did not graduate, either because

she failed the final examination or because she abandoned her course of study.

Cory's first traceable publication as Victoria Cross was 'Theodora: a Fragment', which was published by John Lane in the *Yellow Book*, 4 (January 1895), an extract from a very daring manuscript novel she had offered him, which was not to appear until 1903, when Walter Scott published it as *Six Chapters from a Man's Life*. In August 1895 Lane published *The Woman who Didn't* by 'Victoria Crosse' in the Keynotes series. Many critics have been misled, as no doubt were some contemporaries, into believing that the book was written as a riposte to Grant Allen's *The Woman who Did*, published in the same series in February 1895. In fact it is very different, an account of a brief unconsummated encounter on board ship between an officer in the Indian army and an unhappily married woman, and the title seems to have been a bit of clever marketing. The titillating evocation of sexual desire was to be the main selling point in the fiction of Victoria Cross (as she called herself on the title-page of *Paula: a Sketch from Life* (1896), and from then on). The reticence which characterizes *The Woman who Didn't* was shaken off in such works as *Anna Lombard* (1901), one of her best-sellers (she claimed it had sold 6 million copies by 1928), about an Englishwoman torn between her lust for an Indian and love for an Englishman. She marries them both, and eventually murders her child by the former to save her marriage to the latter. *Five Nights* (1908), about a woman's affair with her painter cousin, made Elinor Glyn's *Six Weeks* (1907) seem pretty tame. Her books are ostentatiously nonconformist in their attitude to marriage, often have spiritualist or mystical elements, but are dubious about religious conformity. Like many feminists of her generation Cory was a keen anti-vivisectionist (being a patron of the British Union for the Abolition of Vivisection), and she opposed conventional medicine, denouncing the pernicious effects not only of vaccination but also of appendicectomy. Another conspicuous theme is a horror of childbearing, in its effects both on women's bodies and on relationships between men and women. Surviving correspondence with T. Werner Laurie, Cory's main publisher, indicates that her books had very large sales, especially in cheap form, into the early 1920s. Several were dramatized or filmed. Thereafter, although she went on publishing until 1937, her popularity declined. Her work is extraordinarily uneven; it often focuses on the disabling effects of gender roles in a way that is startling for its date. It can be witty, but it can also be pretentious and absurd. Even in the 1930s, by which time her power to shock the conventional had declined, she was capable of producing intermittently fascinating work, such as *A Husband's Holiday* (1932), about a prim woman who disguises herself as a coarse one to win her husband back, only to realize that he is not worth it; and the futurist *Martha Brown, MP* (1935), set in a world in which women rule and men are dim, shallow, and whining. Her letters indicate that she was convinced of her own greatness; perhaps if she had been less isolated from her contemporaries it might have been better for her work.

Her adult life seems to have been luxurious and peripatetic but almost devoid of friendships outside her family. Her father's death in 1903 was followed in 1904 by the death of her brother-in-law General Nicolson and the suicide of his widow. Cory and her mother set up home with the latter's brother Heneage Mackenzie Griffin (1848–1939), who had made a fortune mining in the USA. They travelled widely, especially after her mother's death in 1916. They were in England during the First World War, but thereafter spent their time in the grand hotels of the Italian lakes and the south of France, mostly at the Riviera Palace Hotel, Menton. Heneage Griffin died in September 1939 and his niece spent the war in Geneva. She died in a nursing home, the Clinica Capitanio, in Milan on 2 August 1952, her novels out of print and forgotten, leaving a large estate to be the subject of litigation between rival claimants. CHARLOTTE MITCHELL

**Sources** S. M. Knapp, 'Victoria Cross', *Late-Victorian and Edwardian British novelists: second series*, ed. G. M. Johnson, DLitB, 197 (1999) • *IGI* • *CGPLA Eng. & Wales* (1955) [Arthur Cory, Annie Sophie Cory, Elizabeth Fanny Cory, Heneage Griffin] • U. Reading, John Lane and T. Werner Laurie archives • Burke, *Gen. GB* • private information (2004) [Anthony Griffin] • U. Hull, Brynmor Jones L., British Union for the Abolition of Vivisection archive • K. Beckson and M. S. Lasner, 'The *Yellow Book* and beyond', *English Literature in Transition, 1880–1920*, 42 (1999), 401–32
**Archives** Ransom HRC | BL, Lord Chamberlain's plays • BL, Society of Authors archive • NYPL, Berg collection • U. Reading, John Lane and T. Werner Laurie archives, corresp.
**Likenesses** two photographs, repro. in Knapp, 'Victoria Cross', x
**Wealth at death** £87,304 10s. 8d.: administration, 1955

**Cory, Sir George Edward** (1862–1935), chemist and historian, was born on 3 June 1862 at 9 Palatine Place, Stoke Newington, London, the son of George Nicholas Cory and his wife, Susannah Emma Flowers. His father followed a variety of occupations and never settled long in one place. Cory's early schooling was consequently fragmentary, and at the age of thirteen he was put to work. During the next few years he employed all his spare time in studying, using popular manuals and self-educators, and in 1879 he entered St John's College, Hurstpierpoint, where he remained for three years. He then went to work for Sir William Siemens at Woolwich, where he was engaged first in testing transatlantic cables, and then in electric lighting; he helped to install the first arc lamps in London, at the Savoy opera-house.

With the aim of resuming his academic studies, in 1884 Cory began teaching at St John's College, and moved subsequently to Northwich grammar school, and then to a private school in Cambridge. In 1886 he became a non-collegiate student and attended university lectures for the science tripos (in chemistry, physics, and anatomy), taking his BA two years later and an MA in 1892. He was admitted to King's College in 1888, and was university demonstrator in chemistry (1888–91). He was elected a fellow of the Chemical Society and began to study for a medical degree, but never completed it.

In 1891 Cory went to South Africa to take up the post of vice-principal of Grahamstown public school. He became public analyst for the Eastern Province, and in 1894 was appointed lecturer (later professor) in chemistry at St Andrew's College, Grahamstown, where he designed a new laboratory. In 1904 he became the first professor of chemistry at the newly founded Rhodes University College, Grahamstown. In 1895 he married, in South Africa, Gertrude Blades, the second daughter of C. M. Blades, the public analyst for Northwich, Cheshire. They had three sons and three daughters.

Cory's strong interest in the history of the Eastern Province—where the first British settlers had arrived in 1820—soon grew into a systematic research programme, displacing any chemical studies and becoming his life's work. He interviewed elderly settlers and native African chiefs, photographed historical sites, and sought out collections of historical documents housed throughout the region. The work, aided by financial support from the estate of Cecil Rhodes and from the Union government, was eventually published in six volumes entitled *The Rise of South Africa* (5 vols., London, 1910–30; vol. 6, Cape Town, 1940). Cory also edited the diary of the Revd Francis Owen, an early missionary (1926).

Cory earned wide recognition as a historian. He was awarded an honorary DLitt from Cambridge in 1921, and in the following year he was knighted for services to science and literature. He visited England in 1922, when he was elected a fellow of the Royal Historical Society. He was awarded the gold medal of the Royal Empire Society in 1933. A cheerful and kindly man, he presented a somewhat dishevelled appearance, and enjoyed singing, walking, and bowls. He was known as a vivid speaker and a good teacher.

In 1925 Cory retired from Rhodes University College where—despite his historical interests—he was still professor of chemistry. He was then appointed professor emeritus. He was subsequently also appointed as honorary archivist to the Union government of South Africa, and moved to Cape Town, where he worked daily at the Cape Archives until shortly before his death in Cape Town on 28 April 1935. K. D. WATSON

**Sources** *DSAB*, vol. 2 • *The Times* (29 April 1935), 16e • *WWW* • *Nature*, 135 (1935), 984 • private information (2004) • J. J. Withers, *A register of admissions to King's College, Cambridge, 1797–1925* (1929) • Venn, *Alum. Cant.* • 'Foreword', G. E. Cory, *The rise of South Africa*, 6 (1940) • b. cert.
**Archives** Rhodes University, Grahamstown, South Africa, Cory Library for Historical Research, papers
**Likenesses** J. H. Amshewitz, portrait, 1923, Rhodes University, Grahamstown, South Africa, Founders Hall • N. Lewis, caricature, 1926, Owl Club, Cape Town; repro. in *Owl Club Annual* (1926) • C. Ayliff, pastels, Rhodes University, Grahamstown, South Africa, Cory Library • M. Kottler, bronze bust, Rhodes University Library, Grahamstown, South Africa • M. Walgate, sculptured head, Cape Archives, Cape Town, South Africa • J. Wheatley, portrait, University of Cape Town, Smuts Hall • photographs, Rhodes University, Grahamstown, South Africa, Cory Library

**Cory, Isaac Preston** (1801/2–1842), writer, was the son and heir of Robert Cory FSA, an attorney at Great Yarmouth and mayor of the town in 1815. His father's library of topographical, architectural, and miscellaneous works was sold on the latter's death in 1840. Cory was educated at the grammar schools at Saffron Walden and Norwich before matriculating at Clare College, Cambridge, in 1820. Five of his brothers were subsequently educated at Cambridge. In 1821 he migrated to Gonville and Caius College, where he was elected to a scholarship in 1822. Graduating BA in 1824 (as thirteenth wrangler) and MA in 1827, he was elected in 1824 to a fellowship of Caius, which he held until his death. He was Hebrew lecturer at Caius from 1839 to 1841. His chief academic work was a compilation of *Ancient fragments of the Phoenician, Chaldean, Egyptian, Tyrian, Carthaginian, Indian, Persian, and other writers* (2nd edn, 1832; rev. edn, 1876). In 1832 he was called to the bar at Lincoln's Inn, and subsequently published a *Practical Treatise on Accounts* (1839), which described methods of bookkeeping and discrepancies between the law and reality of commercial practice. It was reprinted in 1980. He died, unmarried, at Blundeston, Suffolk, on 1 April 1842 aged forty.

M. C. CURTHOYS

**Sources** Venn, *Alum. Cant.* · *GM*, 2nd ser., 17 (1842), 565 · will, PRO, PROB 11/1962/318

**Cory, John** (1828–1910), coal broker and philanthropist, was born on 28 March 1828 at Bideford, the eldest of five sons of Richard Cory (1799–1882), merchant, and Sarah, both of Bideford. The father was the owner and master of a small vessel in the coastal trade, and his decision in the 1830s to open a store as ship's chandler and provision merchant in Cardiff proved to be decisive in the family fortunes. In the early 1840s the business was moved to the new Bute Dock, and shipbroking and coal agency were added to its activities. The two elder sons, John and Richard, joined their father as shipowners, brokers, coal exporters, and colliery agents, trading first as Richard Cory & Sons from 1856 and, when their father retired in 1859, as Cory Brothers & Co. It was as coal exporters and shipowners that John and his brother were most directly involved in the business of the region, which was then growing fast enough to absorb their attention: they especially used their knowledge of freight rates and insurance to take over some of the financial risks from the colliery sales agencies. The firm's shipping and coal business steadily increased, and the universal demand for south Wales steam coal for navigation led John Cory to conceive the idea of establishing coal depots, offices, and agencies in all major overseas ports. One of the earliest was established at Port Said on the opening of the Suez Canal in 1869. At the time of Cory's death the firm had acquired about a hundred of these depots, located on the maritime routes to India, China, South Africa, and South America, and was the leading supplier of steam coal for shipping. The firm also moved into coalmining. It acquired the Resolfen colliery and in 1869 the Pentre colliery in the Rhondda, and floated them in 1873 as the Cardiff and Swansea Smokeless Steam Coal Co. This led Cory into some financial difficulties: with the collapse of the coal boom in the early 1870s, there was a slump in share values and in 1875 there were even half-hearted accusations of fraud from disappointed shareholders. However, the company's fortunes revived and it was able to acquire the Gelli

and Tynybedw collieries in the Rhondda (1884); Aber colliery (1893); Dunraven (1896); and Wyndham and Penllwyngwent (1906); and it took back direct control of Pentre and Resolfen (1894). In separate enterprises the two brothers also partnered their brother-in-law, Thomas Beynon, in promoting a profitable sale of shares in the Newport Abercarn Black Vein Steam Coal Co. in 1873 and, with other partners, sank the Penrikyber colliery in the Cynon valley between 1872 and 1878. John Cory was thus, from the 1870s on, a substantial coal owner; but although a member, he played no active part in the Coalowners' Association. He also played no direct role in the management of the collieries; instead he installed salaried managers and left himself free to exercise overall control over the company's activities from its Cardiff office at Oscar House, where a staff of more than 100 was employed by the time of his death, and where the day began with the partners and heads of departments meeting for prayer. In 1883 Cory became associated with other Rhondda coal owners to promote the Barry dock and railway. He afterwards held a large interest in that concern and became vice-chairman of its company. Although Cory Brothers was a limited company from 1893 entire control remained in the hands of the family; and John Cory served as chairman. The range of the productive and commercial interests of Cory Brothers in the coal trade gives credence to the claim that they were, before 1914, the largest private railway-wagon owners in Britain.

On 19 September 1854 Cory married Anna Maria (*d.* 1909), daughter of the Monmouthshire coal owner John Beynon, of Newport; they had one daughter and three sons. An alderman on Glamorgan county council and a long-serving member of the Cardiff school board, he was also an active philanthropist. Cory was one of the first to sign the pledge, and was one of Cardiff's leading advocates of teetotalism. However, although temperance and evangelical causes benefited particularly, his largesse was not confined to these. In part the nature of the causes Cory supported reflected the family's religious shift (the father moved from the established church to the United Methodists, John became a Wesleyan, and his brother became a Baptist). During his lifetime, he funded a project for a garden village (Glyn-Cory) on his estate, provided Maendy Hall at Tonpentre for the Salvation Army, and financed the Cory Hall in Cardiff, which was opened on 9 September 1886 and was designated a temperance hall during the 1890s. This building, which was demolished in the 1980s, was characteristic of Cory's search to give his wealth useful public expression. At his death, Cory left more than £798,777, and just as he had given consistently and lavishly during his life so he listed thirty-five separate legacies, totalling £89,000, in his will. The largest was a £20,000 bequest to the Salvation Army, in three separate donations for its foreign, general, and rescue work. Equally significant were gifts of £1000–£5000 to home and foreign missionary societies, Bible societies, the YMCA, Cardiff Infirmary, orphanages, and sailors' rest houses in various ports. In his will Cory also requested that his children, as a matter of honour and affection to their father, give to charities at least 10 per cent of their income from his legacies—an indication of the scale of his own practice.

Cory died at his estate at Dyffryn, St Nicholas, near Cowbridge, on 27 January 1910 only five months after his wife, Anna, had died; he was buried at the parish church at St Nicholas.                                         JOHN WILLIAMS

**Sources** *South Wales Daily News* (10 Sept 1886) • *Western Mail* [Cardiff] (31 July 1875) • *DWB* • M. J. Daunton, *Coal metropolis: Cardiff, 1870–1914* (1977) • J. H. Morris and L. J. Williams, *The south Wales coal industry, 1841–1875* (1958) • R. H. Walters, *The economic and business history of the south Wales steam coal industry, 1840–1914* (1977) • W. G. Dalziel, *Monmouthshire and South Wales Coal Owners Association* (1896) • D. Moore, ed., *Barry: the centenary book* (1984)
**Likenesses** W. G. John, bronze statue, 1905, Gorsedd Gardens, Cardiff • W. G. John, marble bust, NMG Wales
**Wealth at death** £798,777 6s. 10d.: probate, 31 March 1910, *CGPLA Eng. & Wales*

**Cory, Thomas** (*d.* 1656), lawyer and legal official, is said to have been born at Great Franson in Norfolk, where he lived for a time; details of his family and early life are unknown. He practised as an attorney in Lyon's Inn until 1638, by which time he had amassed a sufficient fortune to be able to purchase the principal clerical office in the legal system, that of chief protonotary of the court of common pleas. His fortune may have been derived in part from his marriage (at an unknown date) to Judith, daughter of Sir Christopher *Clitherow, lord mayor of London. He seems also to have been a shrewd speculator, with investments in the East India Company. Sir Richard Hutton said he was 'un bon clerk' (*Diary of Sir Richard Hutton*, 111). As chief protonotary he was the immediate successor to Richard Brownlow, who had gained sufficiently from the position to establish his descendants in the nobility. According to Hutton, Cory had to pay to the agents of the marquess of Hambleton £9500 for the office, as Hambleton possessed the right of nomination under an arrangement between Chief Justice Finch, to whose office the appointment properly belonged, and the king. The appointment took effect on 9 October 1638 and was confirmed by letters patent the following year. Cory's unpublished reports, written in a crabbed court hand, cover the period 1636 to 1654; they contain a description of his own admission ceremony on the first day of Michaelmas term 1638, when he was sworn in by the second protonotary, given the round cap of office, installed in his place, and presented with his first fee as a token of seisin. Upon this promotion he was admitted to the Inner Temple where, by the king's express command, he continued to occupy Brownlow's office and was elected an associate of the bench of the inn. He purchased the manor of Hutton Hall, near Brentwood in Essex, from George White and settled there; he also owned property in Shenfield. Cory died on 16 December 1656, leaving an only daughter, Elizabeth, and he was buried in Hutton church. In common with other protonotaries Cory had collected precedents of pleading; some of these were printed in *Placita Latine rediviva* (1661). He is also the reputed author of *The Course and Practice of the Court of Common Pleas* (1672), a treatise on procedure.

J. H. BAKER

**Sources** J. H. Baker, *The legal profession and the common law: historical essays* (1986), 250–52, 255 • *The diary of Sir Richard Hutton, 1614–1639*, ed. W. R. Prest, SeldS, suppl. ser., 9 (1991), 111–12 • P. Morant, *The history and antiquities of the county of Essex*, 1 (1768), 195 • PRO, PROB 11/261, fols. 90–91 [Cory's will] • F. A. Inderwick and R. A. Roberts, eds., *A calendar of the Inner Temple records*, 2 (1898) • PRO, C66/2844, m.6 • Lincoln's Inn, London, MS Misc. 586 • BL, MS Hargrave 23, 123 • Inner Temple, London, MS Misc. 30 (79)
**Archives** BL, book of entries, MS Hargrave 123 • BL, reports, MS Hargrave 123 • Lincoln's Inn, London, reports, MS Misc. 586
**Likenesses** bust on monument, *c.*1656, Hutton church, Essex

**Cory, William Johnson** (1823–1892), poet and schoolmaster, was born William Johnson at Torrington, Devon, on 9 January 1823, the second son of Charles William Johnson, formerly an indigo planter in India, and his wife, Theresa, daughter of the Revd Peter Wellington Furse of Halsdon, Devon, and a great-niece of Sir Joshua Reynolds. His elder brother, Charles Wellington Johnson (1821–1900), assumed his mother's surname of Furse; he was well known from 1894 until his death as canon and archdeacon of Westminster. William Johnson received his education at Eton College, where he was elected king's scholar in 1832 and Newcastle scholar in 1841, and at King's College, Cambridge, where he was elected to a scholarship on 23 February 1842. In 1843 he gained the chancellor's medal, 'won by a casting vote', for an English poem on Plato. In 1844 he won the Craven scholarship, succeeded to a fellowship at King's in February 1845, graduated BA, and in September of that year was appointed an assistant master at Eton, where he remained for upwards of twenty-six years.

Eton in 1845 still had very large forms ('divisions') taught in unsuitable rooms, and Johnson, who was extremely short-sighted and weak-voiced, did not easily keep order. The main activities in class were the testing of lessons previously prepared and the hearing of recitations ('saying lessons'). The master had the duty of talking about the set texts or the background history and geography; Johnson could fascinate responsive boys, drawing parallels from modern history and literature out of his amazingly well-stocked mind.

The most constructive work was done in smaller groups of boys under their tutor, who might be in charge of them throughout their school career. Here Latin prose and verses were composed, and Johnson produced suitable textbooks for this purpose. The most famous, *Lucretilis*, was used at Eton for 100 years; the sapphics and alcaics were said by H. A. J. Munro to be the best since Horace and were reprinted in the 1940s. (The boys produced their own versions, working from English texts.) Also a tutor would give 'private business' to his pupils, and 'Sunday private', in which he could range off the syllabus. Johnson excelled at this, taking immense pains to encourage his pupils to think over a wide area. He also wrote perceptively about them—his most often quoted judgement being on the future prime minister, A. P. Primrose, the fifth earl of Rosebery: 'he is one of those who likes the palm without the dust'. His tutorial letters to parents set a lasting standard for his successors.

Johnson also contributed to educational theory. Two

William Johnson Cory (1823–1892), by unknown photographer

pamphlets, *Eton Reform* and *Eton Reform II*, written in reply to criticisms, define his view of the purpose of school life: 'You go to a great school not so much for knowledge as for arts and habits'—which include taste and discrimination, the art of expression, the art of entering quickly into another person's thought, and the habits of attention and accuracy, of submitting to censure and reputation, and of mental courage and mental soberness. In 1867 he contributed an essay, 'Education of the reasoning faculties', to Dean F. W. Farrar's *Essays on a Liberal Education*, in which he mentions some of the ways he tries to develop his pupils' ability to think rationally, including the analysis of argumentation found in sermons and newspapers. A pamphlet, *Hints for Eton Masters*, published only in 1898, circulated among his friends; along with much else that was wise, it encouraged the boys' freedom, a distinguishing feature of Eton. His influence was to some extent surprisingly close to the muscular Christians, then becoming important in education. For he loved action from boys, which he could not himself match. He was an imperialist, even if a liberal in the whig tradition at home. Yet he differed from the caricatural muscular Christian by his love of music and learning, and the scepticism of his Christianity.

Johnson was considered as a possible professor of history at Cambridge, though he himself would have preferred political economy, a subject which he began to teach at Eton when the curriculum for older boys was expanded. He taught many of the ablest boys in the school and had, as the senior assistant master, progressed to teaching the second classical division.

In April 1872 Johnson suddenly resigned at Eton, and no one can be quite sure of the exact circumstances of his resignation. There is no question, however, that he was dangerously fond of a number of boys. Although he probably did not allow his affections to take any physical form, he permitted intimacies between the boys. This conduct was brought to the notice of the headmaster, James Hornby, who demanded Johnson's resignation, and Johnson retired quietly to the family home, Halsdon, which he had leased from his brother. He also resigned the fellowship of King's; his influence there had been on the side of opening up the college from its traditional Etonian exclusiveness. Wanting a fresh start, he changed his surname to Cory. In 1878 he went to Madeira for his health, and there married, in August, a twenty-year-old Devon neighbour, Rosa Caroline Guille (*b.* 1858), whose father was rector of Little Torrington. The couple had a son, Andrew. While in Madeira he wrote an idiosyncratic *Guide to Modern English History*, covering the period from 1815 to 1835, without the aid of reference books. It was published, but never brought to a conclusion, on his return from Madeira in 1882. The family settled in Hampstead, London, where he taught some girls gratis, who found him still a magical teacher. He died at his home, 4 Rosslyn Villas, Pilgrim's Lane, Hampstead, on 11 June 1892, after a period of gradually declining health, and was buried at Hampstead on 16 June; his wife survived him.

Johnson's poetry was mostly written at Eton, published privately and anonymously in two slim editions in 1858 and 1877 and then somewhat enlarged in 1891. His most famous lines, 'Heraclitus', were a translation of a Greek construe thrown off for his pupils, illustrating the excellence of his ear. Many other of the better pieces were inspired by particular boys; the words of 'The Eton Boating Song' were written in 1865 for an ephemeral published by his pupil Everard Primrose and later set to music by another old pupil, Algernon Drummond. Curiously his literary judgement was unorthodox, for example placing Tennyson above Shakespeare.

Some of Johnson's best writing is found in his letters and journals, of which a selection was published by Francis Warre Cornish in 1897. A certain censorship was exercised by a young Old Etonian, Reginald Brett (later second Lord Esher), who was with him at Halsdon at the crisis of his life, but even so there is still much of interest which Cornish did not like to make public. Johnson remains therefore someone probably known to few general readers. His main influence has been exerted through a large number of distinguished pupils, and through a chain of gifted teachers who knew him or were inspired by his writing.
TIM CARD

**Sources** A. C. Benson, biographical note, in W. Cory, *Ionica*, 2nd edn (1891) · W. Cory, *Eton reform*, 2 pts (1861) · F. Compton MacKenzie, *William Cory: a biography* (1950) · J. Carter, 'The Eton boating song', *Etoniana*, 118 (1966), 282–5 · J. Carter, 'Indian summer of an Eton master', *Etoniana*, 122 (1969), 343–7 · Eton, Cory MSS · correspondence with Reginald Brett, second Lord Esher, 1868–92, Churchill College, Cambridge · d. cert.

**Archives** Eton, corresp. and papers | CAC Cam., corresp. with Reginald Brett · Hunt. L., letters to Frederick James Furnivall · King's Cam., letters to Henry Bradshaw · King's Cam., letters to Oscar Browning · NL Scot., corresp. with Lord Rosebery
**Likenesses** C. Furse, oils, 1891, Eton · photograph, repro. in F. W. Cornish, ed., *Extracts from the letters and journals of William Cory* (1897), frontispiece [*see illus.*]
**Wealth at death** £10,410 6s. 10d.: probate, 9 Aug 1892, *CGPLA Eng. & Wales*

**Coryate, George** (*d.* 1607), Latin poet, was born in St Thomas's parish, Salisbury, where his family appears to have been long settled; educated at Salisbury Free School and Winchester College, he proceeded to New College, Oxford, where he became a probationary fellow on 15 December 1560 (some months after Michael Maschiart, a fellow Latinist of his native parish), perpetual fellow in 1562, BA in March 1564, MA in July 1569, and BD on 12 July 1582. He was appointed vicar of Hilmarton, Wiltshire, in 1567, rector of Donington in 1570, and in June of the same year rector of Odcombe, Somerset, the place that his peripatetic son was to immortalize. While remaining at Odcombe, he obtained some further preferments, culminating in a prebend at York, 1595. According to H. Hatcher (writing in Hoare's *Modern Wiltshire*), he married one Henrietta Cooper; he later married Gertrude Williams(?) (*d.* 1645), and they had one child, Thomas *Coryate (1577?–1617).

Coryate was 'much commended in his time for his fine fancy in Latin poetry, and for certain matters which he had written' (Wood, *Ath. Oxon.*, 1.774), as quoted by several contemporary writers of unimpeachable seriousness; 'at a time when a talent for Latin poetry was an enviable accomplishment, he was celebrated for his Latin verses' (Hoare, 6.619). His son Thomas published the *Posthuma fragmenta poematum Georgii Coryati Sarisburiensis* at the end of his celebrated *Crudities* (1611), with a dedicatory letter to Henry, prince of Wales, explaining his motives for rescuing his father's work 'ex Cimmeriis illis tenebris' ('from outer darkness'). George himself, shortly before his death, had expressed the hope that his early writings might be printed; his friends had sought publication as a memorial. He had been honoured by the notice of James Middendorp, and the philosopher John Case had quoted his lines on Oxford and Cambridge (Case, 153), written about forty years previously, along with many others 'de descriptione Angliae, Scotiae, et Hyberniae'. At least 2000 lines, composed in his prime, 'elegantibus sane ac a viris eruditis non parum laudatis' ('elegant, applauded by the learned') had vanished, through the author's carelessness or the action of time and bookworms ('tineis edacibus corrosis'). Thus 'Thomas Coryatus Odcombiensis, peregrinans pedesterrimus' begs Henry's favour against snapping critics, 'virulentos Momorum morsus'.

The first group of surviving verses were written at Winchester, for Queen Elizabeth's visit in August 1560; Coryate urges her to marry, in elegiacs clever and lively enough to earn a reward. At Oxford he paraphrased the Psalms (a common way of combining devotion with neo-Latin virtuosity); sixteen virtuoso acrostic lines survive, dedicating that exercise to the queen. In 'Viridis draconis

triumphus' Coryate laments William Herbert, earl of Pembroke, then turns to his son Henry (who made him his chaplain); he shows skill in handling about 100 hexameters, which do at least demonstrate the superior elegance of Latin, when compared with the accompanying vernacular fourteeners, 'The Pembroke dragon, greene of hue, good reader, here behold'.

Astronomical verses by Coryate to the chancellors of the universities (Leicester and Burghley) were recited in New College hall, neatly comparing them to the two polestars (Coryate, 1905 edn, 2.397). Burghley received several other sets of verses, with medical advice on the power of song, and gave Coryate 40s.; his poem of thanks refers to 'illustrissima tua uxor' (the learned Mildred, Lady Burghley), and her poem to Buchanan. Coryate complained to Burghley, in forty-two elegiacs, of 'Pseudocausidicos se injuste opprimentes' ('false advocates unjustly accusing him'; ibid., 2.399). He wrote also to Lord Keeper Puckering. Bishops Jewel and Piers of Salisbury are each mourned as his 'Maecenas optimus'. He puns wittily on Piers (later archbishop of York) and Perseus. Epitaphs include a clever multiple acrostic on Anne Clifton; another commemorates eight members of the Worsley family, two blown up by gunpowder. Archbishop Whitgift received an elaborate acrostic. Coryate's various patrons were not fools; he showed mastery of a valued accomplishment. He died at the parsonage at Odcombe on 4 March 1607; his son preserved his body until 14 April, when he was buried in the chancel at Odcombe. Thomas could no doubt thank his father for the fluency in spoken and written Latin, as well as the confident eccentricity, with which he toured Europe.

D. K. MONEY

**Sources** Wood, *Ath. Oxon.*, new edn, 1.774 · Foster, *Alum. Oxon.* · T. Coryate, *Coryats crudities* (1611); repr. 2 vols. (1905) · R. Benson and H. Hatcher, *The history of modern Wiltshire*, ed. R. C. Hoare, 6 (1843) · J. Case, *Speculum moralium quaestionum* (1585) · *DNB*

**Coryate, Thomas** (1577?–1617), traveller and writer, was the only son of George *Coryate (*d.* 1607), rector of Odcombe, Somerset, and his wife, Gertrude (*d.* 1645), whose maiden name may have been Williams. Doubt about his year of birth arises from Winchester College's *Register of Oaths, 1576–1639* (fol. 73v), which indicates 1579; Coryate himself believed 1577 to be correct. A scholar at Winchester from July 1591, he went up to Gloucester Hall, Oxford, in 1596, matriculating on 11 June, aged nineteen. He studied there for about three years and left without taking a degree, but with a retentive memory, much learning, excellent knowledge of Greek and Latin texts, fondness for rhetoric, aptitude for histrionics, curiosity to see the world, and a thirst for personal fame.

Coryate was acquainted with several influential families in the neighbourhood of Odcombe and refers to Sir Edward Phelips of Montacute and his son Sir Robert as his patrons. It was probably through them that he joined the household of Henry, prince of Wales. There he met many eminent people of the day, and played the role of unofficial, and probably unpaid, court jester.

In May 1608 Coryate sailed from Dover to Calais and made his way to Paris, which he found even filthier and smellier than London. At Fontainebleau he was befriended by members of Henri IV's garde écossaise and saw more of the royal household than would normally have been permitted to chance visitors. He journeyed on to Lyons, through Savoy to Turin, Milan, Mantua, and Padua. His description of how Italians shielded themselves from the sun resulted in apparently the first mention of 'umbrella' in English literature. Table forks, almost unknown in England, were in general use in Italy; Coryate acquired one, imitated the Italian fashion of eating and continued to do so frequently when he came home.

It is wrongly stated that Coryate's European travels were mainly on foot. He did walk extensively, often unaccompanied, carrying no weapons but a staff and a knife; one day in May 1608 between 5 a.m. and 6 p.m. he walked 36 miles. His other modes of travel were boat, horseback, coach, and cart; over the Mont Cenis Pass he was carried in a 'chaise à porteurs'.

Arriving in Venice on 24 June 1608 Coryate presented two letters of introduction to the English ambassador, Sir Henry Wotton, who, perhaps impressed by the letter which mentioned that Coryate was remotely related to the earl of Essex, did him many kindnesses. These included rescuing him in the ambassadorial gondola from a threatening crowd of Jews who objected to Coryate preaching Christianity to their rabbi. Later he was to risk reprisals for antipathy to Roman Catholic rites and, during his Eastern travels, for proclaiming against Islam. After six weeks of intensive quest and recording of information, he left Venice on 7 August by boat to Padua, then walked to Vicenza, Verona, and Bergamo.

Coryate arrived in Zürich by boat and reached Basel on foot at the end of August. While in Switzerland he heard the story of William Tell. Coryate's admirable rendering appears to be the earliest in English. Arriving in Strasbourg by boat he then got lost, alone and on foot, in the Black Forest, but the sole threat of armed violence experienced in Europe was from a German peasant, who resented Coryate picking grapes from a vineyard. He was hospitably received in Heidelberg and walked to Mainz. After a detour to visit Frankfurt's fair he sailed down the Rhine, with a brief stop at Cologne, and continued by water down what was the temporary truce line between the armies of Spain and the United Provinces. After calling on the English merchants established at Middelburg he was entertained by the English garrison at Flushing. Thence he embarked on 1 October and landed in London on 3 October 1608. With the rector's permission Coryate hung his shoes in Odcombe church.

Coryate drew on his experiences in writing *Coryats Crudities* (1611), which was intended to encourage courtiers and gallants to enrich their minds by continental travel. It contains illustrations, historical data, architectural descriptions, local customs, prices, exchange rates, and food and drink, but is too diffuse and bulky—there are 864 pages in the 1905 edition—to become a vade-mecum. To solicit 'panegyric verses' Coryate circulated copies of the title-page depicting his adventures and his portrait, which

had been engraved by William Hole and which he considered a good likeness. About sixty contributors include many illustrious authors, not all in verse, some insulting, some pseudonymous. Prince Henry accepted the dedication but insisted that all were published. There then appeared *The Odcombian Banquet*, a pirated version of the 'verses' with a scurrilous preface. John Taylor may have been responsible; certainly thereafter he heaped versified ridicule on Coryate. *Coryats Crambe* (1611), presented as 'the second course to his Crudities', is a slim miscellany, including orations made to the royal family when Coryate presented copies of *Crudities*. According to *Thomas Coriate Traveller for the English Wits* (1616), Coryate belonged in the early 1610s to the Mermaid Club, a group of 'sireniacall gentlemen, that meet on the first Friday of everie moneth, at the Mermaide in Breadstreet' (*STC*, 5812). He was its beadle, and the members provided him with a mock passport before he departed on his Eastern travels.

On 20 October 1612 Coryate sailed for Constantinople. During a protracted voyage he visited, among other places, Alexandria Troas, then thought to be the site of Troy, where a companion dubbed him 'the first English Knight of Troy'; he responded with an oration. Arriving in Constantinople towards the end of March 1613, he presented a letter of introduction to the English ambassador, Paul Pindar, who treated him kindly and during Coryate's ten-month stay frequently included him in his suite on state occasions. He now learned Turkish and Italian, the lingua franca of the Levant, having previously relied mainly on Latin; few but his countrymen knew English. In January 1614 he sailed from Constantinople, disembarking at Iskenderun, the port of Aleppo. On 15 March he left Aleppo to walk with a caravan mainly of Christian pilgrims, guarded against Arab attack by Turkish troops. After spending four blissful days in Damascus he arrived in Jerusalem on 12 April in time for Easter. There he toured the sights and, like many pilgrims, had crosses tattooed on his wrists. After visiting Nazareth, Bethlehem, Jericho, and the River Jordan he walked back to Aleppo.

Intending to write a great travel book, Coryate remained in Aleppo from May to September writing up his notes. He sent these home, where, drastically abbreviated, they were eventually published by Samuel Purchas in his *Purchas his Pilgrimes* (1625). Coryate's decision then to walk to India was primarily to confirm that the Odcombian Legstretcher, as he had been termed, was the greatest walker in the world. Joining an enormous caravan, he was robbed of much of his money at Diyarbakır, spent six days inspecting the ruins of Tabriz and continued via Qazvin to Esfahan. There he spent two months and left notes accumulated since leaving Aleppo, notes which disappeared. He joined another caravan in February 1615, walked via Kandahar, Multan, Lahore, and Delhi to the official Mughal capital, Agra, only to find that the emperor Jahangir was then resident at Ajmer, a further ten days' march. Arriving there in mid-July 1615 he measured his walk from Jerusalem: 2700 miles in ten months by his reckoning. He must actually have walked at least 3300 miles, during which he spent only 50s., seldom drinking anything but water, often living reasonably well for 1*d.* sterling per day.

Excepting Father Thomas Stephens, Coryate was the first Englishman to visit India with no thought of trade. At Ajmer he was warmly welcomed by the East India Company's servants and lived at their expense and that of Sir Thomas Roe, England's first ambassador to the Mughal court, with whom Coryate had become acquainted in England. In December 1615 Coryate accompanied the welcoming party which met Roe outside Ajmer, and made another oration. He earned his keep by entertaining Roe and the merchants with his tales. He explained his fourteen-month stay in Ajmer by the necessity to learn Persian and continue studying Turkish and Arabic. With these, and fluent Hindustani, he would travel, and solicit donations by flattering and amusing the rich and powerful. One of the two versions of *Thomas Coriate Traveller for the English Wits* published in 1616 was subtitled 'greeting. From the court of the great Mogul'. About August 1616 he made an oration in Persian before Jahangir, who rewarded him with 100 silver rupees.

In September 1616, when Roe and his immediate attendants accompanied the emperor on his progress towards Mandu, Coryate resumed his wanderings, having sent a final missive to England from Agra on 30 October, published in 1618. He reached as far north as Kangra, and besides other places visited Hardwar, where the Ganges issues from the Himalayan foothills. He was back in Agra in July 1617 and continued to the ruined city of Mandu, some 400 miles to the south. There he found Roe installed in a deserted mosque and was introduced to his chaplain, Edward Terry, with whom he shared a room, and a tent when the emperor continued his progress towards Ahmadabad. Publishing nearly forty years later (*Voyage to East India*, 1655 edn, 57), Terry gives a convincing character sketch, but is unreliable about Coryate's itinerary, confusing what had been achieved with Coryate's relation of his future plans. In November Coryate decided to leave the camp and make for the East India Company's factory at Surat in Gujarat. There, in December 1617, he died of dysentery, exacerbated, according to Terry, by the merchants plying him with sack. There is conflicting evidence about where he was buried. Coryate, yearning for lasting fame, dreaded lying in an unmarked grave, but the site of his interment has been durably, if inaccurately, commemorated because a large, domed tomb in the Islamic style, a landmark for sailors near the anchorage off Surat, is shown on British admiralty charts as 'Tom Coryat's tomb'.

MICHAEL STRACHAN

**Sources** M. Strachan, *The life and adventures of Thomas Coryate* (1962) • T. Coryate, *Coryat's crudities*, new edn, 3 vols. (1776) • T. Coryate, *Coryats crudities* (1611); repr. 2 vols. (1905) • W. Foster, *Early travels in India, 1583–1619* (1921) [incl. annotated texts of Coryate's letters from India] • T. Coryate, *Coryats crudities* (1611); repr. (1978) • A. Kippis and others, eds., *Biographia Britannica, or, The lives of the most eminent persons who have flourished in Great Britain and Ireland*, 2nd edn, 4 (1789) • Wood, *Ath. Oxon.*, 2nd edn • F. Schott, *Itinerarium Italiae* (1655) • L. Guicciardini, *Descrittione di tutti i paesi bassi* (1567) • T. Fuller, *The worthies of England*, ed. J. Freeman, abridged edn (1952), 502 • M. Strachan, *Sir Thomas Roe, 1581–1644: a life* (1989) • *DNB* • *STC, 1475–1640* • E. Terry, *A voyage to east India* (1655)

**Archives** BL, copy of *Crudities* [incl. only known holograph letter, to Sir Michael Hicks]

**Likenesses** probably W. Hole, engraving, BL; repro. in T. Coryate, *Coryates crudities* • W. Hole, line engraving, BM, NPG; repro. in T. Coryate, *Coryates crudities* (1611) • W. Hole, line engraving, BL; repro. in T. Coryate, *Coryates crudities* • woodcut, NPG; repro. in T. Coryate, *Thomas Coriate traveller for the English wits* (1616) • woodcut, repro. in T. Coryate, *Thomas Coriat to his friends in England* (1618), letter to his mother from Agra

**Coryndon, Sir Robert Thorne** (1870–1925), colonial governor, was born in Queenstown, Cape Colony, on 2 April 1870, one of six children born to Selby Coryndon (1835–1885), a lawyer, and Emily Caldecott (*d.* 1889), daughter of a Cape politician. He was educated at a number of South African schools, finishing off his secondary school career at Cheltenham College (1884–7), then returning to the Cape to work in the law firm of his uncle Alfred Caldecott. Office routine was too confining for an outdoorsman like Coryndon, and when his mother died in July 1889, he joined the Bechuanaland border police. This élite force, recruited from the ranks of well-to-do Cape families—euphemistically known as the 'Top Hat Brigade'—signified Coryndon's entry into the imperial world of Cecil Rhodes. He was to become one of Rhodes's 'twelve apostles' or 'young lambs'.

The British government's reliance on the British South Africa Company to execute its imperial schemes proved critical for Coryndon's future in the colonial service. In 1890, after being transferred to the company's police, Coryndon was a member of the pioneer column to Mashonaland, part of the territory later known as Southern Rhodesia. While the Rhodesian incursion effectively ended his police career, it did not, as with most of the invading force, mean life as a European settler. The twenty-year-old joined the administration instead, soon working as a surveyor and cartographer with the surveyor-general's department in Salisbury. Late in 1892 Coryndon accepted a commission from Lionel Walter Rothschild to collect specimens of flora and fauna, taking leave of absence from his post in the administration. He captured two white rhinoceroses, which were dispatched to the British Museum (Natural History) in Kensington and to Rothschild's museum at Tring. His precise recording of all his kills, and the technically proficient sketches he executed—he is credited with the first ever drawings of the ancient ruins of Zimbabwe—stand in marked contrast to his later lack of attention to bureaucratic procedures as a top-level colonial administrator.

The Rothschild contract was cut short by the Matabele (Ndebele) campaign of 1893; Coryndon joined a volunteer burgher force under Major Forbes. After Lobengula's defeat Coryndon took up big game hunting professionally, and on occasion drove the postal cart from Salisbury to Kimberley. Less than three years had elapsed when the Rhodesian adventurer became involved in the second, more formidable, conflict with the Matabele, who were this time joined by some Shona groups in the 1896–7 uprising. Coryndon was in charge of a party of Beal's scouts but saw action only once before succumbing to pneumonia. While in hospital he learned of the death in the rising of his younger brother John Selby (1877–1896), a trooper with the Salisbury Rifles. Discharged in November 1896, Coryndon took up a position as one of Rhodes's private secretaries, and accompanied his employer to face the hearings on the Jameson raid (1896–7). Rhodes then offered his amanuensis the choice of either managing one of his estates or becoming resident adviser to King Lewanika of Bulozi (Barotseland). Coryndon, portentously, chose the latter.

Coryndon's move to Barotseland (North-Western Rhodesia, later part of Northern Rhodesia) marked the beginning of a career spanning almost three decades as an imperial pro-consul. He was the first administrator of Barotseland, which meant negotiating with Lewanika on political authority, instituting a tax regime, and abolishing slavery. He received little guidance from his British South Africa Company overseers; in turn, he was regarded by an official at the South African high commission as 'a remote and at times disturbing figure … no office man' (Coryndon MSS, Bodl. RH, MSS Afr. s.633 10/1/31–33). It was Coryndon's ability to survive in the bush that had attracted Rhodes. Muscular and 5 feet 9 inches tall, the professional hunter was renowned for his feats of physical strength, including tearing in half a deck of cards with his powerful hands, and for his skills in carpentry and building. The two men were reputed to have met on the postal run to Kimberley, although Rhodes already knew Coryndon as his father's son in élite Cape society. Yet they were never really close, and Coryndon's Barotseland experience created a greater distance between them.

In April 1907 Coryndon took up his appointment as resident commissioner of the new protectorate of Swaziland as the direct representative of the British government. He was to remain there until 1916. After many itinerant years in the Rhodesias where, he claimed, 'I did not spend three consecutive months in one place' and 'with no real foothold' in England, the new resident commissioner regarded Swaziland as 'the first real home I have ever had' (University of Zambia, Coryndon MS 4). It was in 1909, during his Swazi appointment, that he married Phyllis Mary, daughter of James Worthington of Lowestoft, Suffolk, and sister of his Barotseland colleague Frank. They had three sons and one daughter.

Coryndon's main duty in the high commission territory was to oversee the land partition between the Swazi and European concessionaires, a partition considered unfavourable by the Swazi royals when it was announced in October 1907. The new resident commissioner, while not responsible for the recommendations of the land commission (1904–7), was responsible for their implementation. For his role, he earned the Swazi nickname Msindazwe (translated as 'he who sits heavily upon the land' or 'he who exerts tremendous influence over the land'). As in Barotseland, Coryndon was charged with setting up an administrative infrastructure, initiating tax

collection and ensuring a smooth relationship with the indigenous authority.

In 1914 Coryndon's Rhodesian experience, along with his immersion in the Swazi land settlement, earned him the chairmanship of the Southern Rhodesian native reserves commission, known as the Coryndon commission. The Colonial Office was anxious for a final settlement of the land question before the anticipated incorporation of the settler territory into the Union of South Africa. The highly controversial Coryndon commission smacked of being a company affair, and the chairman's connections with the British South Africa Company, coupled with the recommendation that African reserves be diminished by over 1 million acres, sparked a torrent of criticism. Yet it was Coryndon's aversion to segregation, stemming from his belief that tribalism was retrogressive, that inspired the commission report, ratified by order in council in 1920.

The Rhodesian inquiry virtually filled the last two years of Coryndon's Swazi appointment. A brief stint as resident commissioner of Basutoland (1916–17) was followed by his first governorship, Uganda (1917–22). In Uganda he complained again about a lack of direction in policy, especially economic policy. The post-war slump virtually wiped out European plantation agriculture, but Coryndon acceded to European demands for political representation and established the first executive and legislative councils (1921). The governor placed his economic faith in Lancashire cotton, encouraging peasant production while simultaneously endeavouring to control the chiefs whom he denigrated as a plutocratic, corrupt class hindering economic progress. Coryndon's reputation as a governor of 'Native territories' preceded his appointment to the governorship of Kenya (1922–5), and so he was initially distrusted by the vociferous white settler community—who referred to him as 'policeman Bobby Coryndon'—then embroiled in a controversy over Asian political rights. Yet Coryndon's antagonism towards Indians, deriving from his belief that the Asian community blocked African economic progress, and his objections to 'tribalism', coincided with settler aspirations. Indigenous production and settler agriculture both fared well under the governor, although his so-called dual policy (the complementary interests of white and black) has been characterized as a disguise for his support of settler hegemony. The 1923 Devonshire declaration pronouncing African paramountcy ended the Indian crisis but put paid to settler hopes for self-government. Although Coryndon set up local native councils for African regional government (1924), he was commonly regarded as a spokesman for settler interests at the time of his death in Nairobi from acute pancreatitis on 10 February 1925. He was buried the next day at the new cemetery in Nairobi. Lady Coryndon survived him.

Coryndon left little in the way of published works, and certainly no philosophical rationale of colonialism. He was the type who wanted to 'get on with the job', something which has been associated with an imperious, dictatorial manner. He often criticized both the British South

Africa Company and the Colonial Office for poor pay and benefits, and for lack of imperial vision. He was made a CMG in 1911 and promoted KCMG in 1919.

CHRISTOPHER P. YOUÉ

**Sources** C. P. Youé, *Robert Thorne Coryndon: proconsular imperialism in southern and eastern Africa, 1897–1925* (1986) · Bodl. RH, Coryndon MSS, MS Afr.s.633 · V. Harlow, E. M. Chilver, and A. Smith, eds., *History of East Africa*, 2 (1965) · P. Duignan, 'Sir Robert Coryndon: a model governor (1870–1925)', *African proconsuls*, ed. L. H. Gann and P. Duignan (1978), 313–52 · E. A. Brett, *Colonialism and underdevelopment in east Africa* (1973) · G. Caplan, *The elites of Barotseland, 1878–1969* (1970) · R. Palmer, *Land and racial domination in Rhodesia* (1977) · private information (2004) · University of Zambia, Lusaka, Zambia, Coryndon MSS · *DNB*
**Archives** Bodl. RH · University of Zambia, Lusaka, Zambia | BL, corresp. with Lord Gladstone, Add. MSS 46071–46081 · Bodl. RH, Sir Sidney Henn MSS, Afr. s.715
**Likenesses** photographs, Bodl. RH, Robert Thorne Coryndon Papers; repro. in Youé, *Robert Thorne Coryndon*

**Coryton, William** (1580–1651), politician, was the eldest son of Peter Coryton of Coryton and Newton Ferrars, Devon, and his wife, Joan, daughter of John Wreye of Milton, Cornwall. Nothing is known of his early years and he did not attend university. He married Elizabeth (*d.* 1656), daughter of Sir John Chichester de Raleigh and Anne, daughter of Sir Robert Dennis; they had four sons and seven daughters.

Coryton was a critical figure in the west-country political network of the Herbert earls of Pembroke, and was vice-warden of the stannaries, deputy lieutenant, and *custos rotulorum* of Cornwall. He sat in all parliamentary sessions between 1624 and 1629, usually being returned for Cornwall. There he was a leading member of the Pembroke interest and linked to Sir John Eliot and the earl of Warwick. A bitter opponent of Buckingham, he opposed Arminianism in the church and favoured war with Spain. Believing in the conciliar and legislative authority of parliament, he espoused traditional concepts of purging evil counsellors but under Charles I came to put pressure upon the constitutional notion that the king could do no wrong. In parliament in 1624 he sought, while supporting war, to link supply to redress of grievances. In 1625 he addressed both financial and religious issues. In 1626 he helped assemble the Pembroke faction, attacked Buckingham, and wanted redress before supply. He was a leading opponent of the forced loan, arguing its illegality in a treatise, 'A relation of so much as passed between the lords of the council and Mr Coryton at the council table'. He respected the royal prerogative but appealed tellingly to statute and Magna Carta. Having challenged the council to try him, he was the ringleader in the *five knights' case* and was committed to the Fleet prison in July 1627. His stand over the loan caused the loss of his county offices and vice-wardenship, thanks to Buckingham's influence. The stannary appointment went to John, later Lord Mohun, friend of the duke's local agent and Coryton's enemy Sir James Bagg.

In the elections of 1628 Coryton traded on local factionalism and his fame as a loan refuser. Released from prison, in the Commons he again attacked Buckingham and supported due process legislation (eventually the petition of right), becoming distrustful and confrontational towards the king. A prominent speaker in 1629, he attacked Arminianism and accused the king of protecting evil advisers. Part of the demonstration in the house on 2 March, he was arrested and interrogated with Eliot and others. In consummate fashion he pleaded a lapse of memory about events in the Commons, but offered information about the Eliot group's plans. Like the others he entered a plea of parliamentary privilege when charged in Star Chamber, but in May submitted to the king and was released, the earl of Pembroke probably interceding. Coryton was therefore not one of those, including Eliot and Selden, who fought a constitutional battle in the courts in 1629–30. Pembroke effected his reinstatement to the stannaries, where his administration was controversial.

Arrested in 1637 on a charge of false imprisonment in a case apparently deriving from Pembroke business interests, Coryton was later released. He was elected to the Short and Long parliaments, but expelled from the latter after being found guilty of falsifying returns. He again lost the vice-wardenship and the deputy lieutenancy of Cornwall as well as the stewardship of the duchy. A gentleman of the privy chamber, Coryton was a royalist colonel in the first civil war, raising a regiment in Cornwall. By 1645–6 he was negotiating with Hugh Peter for local royalist composition, surely in the process securing his own estates. He changed sides and assisted the parliamentarian reduction of the county, eventually compounding in 1647. He died on 1 May 1651 and was buried in the church of St Mellion near Plymouth. His wife survived him by five years. His son John was a royalist colonel, created baronet after the Restoration.

Coryton was politically sophisticated, capable of pragmatism and sharp practice as well as principled dissent—not the stuff of which martyrs are made. His life was a microcosm of the early seventeenth-century English political world in its troubled complexity, with tensions between establishment and dissent, politics and ideology, centre and locality, loyalty to monarchy and suspicion of Charles I, and royalism and parliamentary power.

L. J. REEVE

**Sources** *DNB* · L. J. Reeve, *Charles I and the road to personal rule* (1989) · L. J. Reeve, 'The legal status of the petition of right', *HJ*, 29 (1986), 257–77 · R. P. Cust, *The forced loan and English politics, 1626–1628* (1987) · T. Cogswell, *The blessed revolution: English politics and the coming of war, 1621–1624* (1989) · M. Jansson and W. B. Bidwell, eds., *Proceedings in parliament, 1625* (1987) · W. Notestein and F. H. Relf, eds., *Commons debates for 1629* (1921) · *CSP dom.*, 1627–31 · *Devon and Cornwall Notes and Queries*, 18 (1934–5), 355–8 · S. R. Gardiner, *History of England from the accession of James I to the outbreak of the civil war*, 10 vols. (1883–4) · C. Russell, *Parliaments and English politics, 1621–1629* (1979) · C. Russell, *The causes of the English civil war* (1990) · C. Russell, *The fall of the British monarchies, 1637–1642* (1991) · *State trials* · D. Brunton and D. H. Pennington, *Members of the Long Parliament* (1954) · R. E. Ruigh, *The parliament of 1624: politics and foreign policy* (1971) · J. L. Vivian, ed., *The visitations of Cornwall, comprising the herald's visitations of 1530, 1573, and 1620* (1887), 102 · J. L. Vivian, ed., *The visitations of the county of Devon, comprising the herald's visitations of*

*1531, 1564, and 1620* (privately printed, Exeter, [1895]) • P. R. Newman, *Royalist officers in England and Wales, 1642–1660: a biographical dictionary* (1981) • M. Coate, *Cornwall in the great civil war and interregnum, 1642–1660* (1933), 226 • N. Tyacke, *Anti-Calvinists: the rise of English Arminianism, c.1590–1640* (1987) • P. R. Newman, *The old service: royalist regimental colonels and the civil war, 1642–1646* (1993) • K. M. Sharpe, ed., *Faction and parliament: essays on early Stuart history* (1978) • R. Lockyer, *Buckingham: the life and political career of George Villiers, first duke of Buckingham, 1592–1628* (1981)

**Archives** Cornwall RO, corresp. and MSS • NRA, priv. coll., corresp. | PRO, state papers domestic, Charles I (SP 16)

**Wealth at death** fined £1244 for delinquency 5 April 1647: Coate, *Cornwall*, 226

**Cosby, Alexander** (1547–1596). *See under* Cosby, Francis (d. 1580).

**Cosby, Arnold** (d. 1592). *See under* Cosby, Francis (d. 1580).

**Cosby, Francis** (d. 1580), soldier and planter in Ireland, was the second son of John Cosby of Hermaston, Lincolnshire, and Mabel Agard. Arrived in Ireland by 1548, he distinguished himself as a soldier in the midlands, writing detailed accounts of his exploits against the Gaelic clans of O'More and O'Connor to Lord Deputy Bellingham. His career as landholder began in Kildare with a grant of Vicarstown, and he served as constable of Monasterevin and sheriff of the county. In 1558 Cosby was appointed general of the kerne, a troop of Gaelic footsoldiers in the crown's pay. Combining effectively the roles of soldier and settler, Cosby became one of the most significant newcomers in Leix (Laois), or Queen's county. His landed base was the suppressed abbey of Stradbally in Queen's county, and his military presence was confirmed by his appointment as governor of Maryborough, and seneschal of Queen's county. His growing strength in the region was aided by a strategic alliance with Rory Oge O'More, who was conducting a war of attrition against the settlement.

Cosby's social position was boosted through propitious marriage alliances. His first wife was Lady Mary Seymour, daughter of the first duke of Somerset. His son Alexander [*see below*] married Dorcas Sidney, niece of Sir Henry Sidney, under whose governorship Francis prospered. Catherine, a daughter of Francis and his second wife, Elizabeth Palmer, married into the newly settled Moore family, and there were also close ties with their fellow planters the Hartpoles.

In the mid-1570s Cosby's rejection of Rory Oge's clientship sparked a vicious war, marked by the kidnapping of Alexander and a notorious act of retribution. In March 1578, along with Robert Hartpole, Cosby invited dozens of leading O'Mores to a parley at the great rath of Mullaghmast in Queen's county. Encircled by troops, the Gaelic men and women were massacred by bullet and sword. His participation in the slaughter caused Cosby to be demonized in the folk history of the region. After the subsequent assassination of Rory Oge, Cosby tightened his grip in the midlands. When the Baltinglass revolt began in 1580, he led the kerne against the viscount and his Gaelic ally, Feagh MacHugh O'Byrne. Against the advice of Cosby, Lord Deputy Grey marched the English army into the valley of Glenmalure in co. Wicklow on 25 August 1580. In a bloody encounter with the rebels Francis Cosby and many other English troops were killed.

**Alexander Cosby** (1547–1596) succeeded to the estates. In 1587 he was sheriff of Queen's county, and he was an active campaigner for the security of the plantation. He and Dorcas had two sons and two daughters. Alexander was, with his son Francis, killed by the O'Mores at the battle of Stradbally Bridge on 19 May 1596. He was buried at Stradbally. **Arnold Cosby** (d. 1592), Francis Cosby's second son, served under the earl of Leicester in the Low Countries, and was executed in 1592 for causing the death of John, second Baron Bourke of Castleconnell, at Hounslow.          COLM LENNON

**Sources** W. Fitzgerald, 'Genealogy of the Cosbys of Stradbally', *Journal of the Kildare Archaeological Society*, 5 (1906–9), 316–17 • V. P. Carey, 'John Derricke's *Image of Irelande*, Sir Henry Sidney and the massacre at Mullaghmast, 1578', *Irish Historical Studies*, 31 (1998–9), 305–27 • V. P. Carey, 'Gaelic reaction to plantation: the case of the O'More and O'Connor lordships of Laois and Offaly, 1570–1603', MA diss., National University of Ireland, Maynooth, 1982 • C. Brady, *The chief governors: the rise and fall of reform government in Tudor Ireland, 1536–1588* (1994) • T. Dowling, 'Annales Hiberniae', in *The annals of Ireland by Friar John Clyn and Thady Dowling: together with the annals of Ross*, ed. R. Butler, Irish Archaeological Society (1849) • *CSP Ire., 1574–85* • J. O'Hanlon and E. O'Leary, *History of the Queen's county*, 1–2 (1907–14) • J. G. Crawford, *Anglicizing the government of Ireland: the Irish privy council and the expansion of Tudor rule, 1556–1578* (1993) • 1548, PRO, SP 61/1, nos. 41, 46–51 • W. M. Hennessy, ed. and trans., *The annals of Loch Cé: a chronicle of Irish affairs from AD 1014 to AD 1590*, 2 vols., Rolls Series, 54 (1871), 2.396–7 • D. O'Byrne, *The history of the Queen's county* (1856) • *DNB*

**Cosby, Sir Henry Augustus Montagu** (1743–1822), army officer in the East India Company, only son of Captain Alexander Cosby (d. c.1760), a direct descendant of Francis *Cosby (d. 1580) of Stradbally, Queen's county, was born at Minorca, where his father was stationed. Alexander Cosby was a distinguished officer who, after serving in the duke of Montagu's regiment, and on the staff in Germany and Minorca, went on half-pay, and was sent to India by the directors of the East India Company in 1753 to reorganize their troops. He served as second in command to Major Stringer Lawrence (1697–1775) in the Madras presidency, and was transferred to Bombay, where he acted as second in command at the capture in 1759 of Surat, of which he was appointed commandant, and where he died soon after.

Henry Cosby first saw service when only thirteen, as a volunteer at the capture of Gheria, the stronghold of the Maratha pirate Angria, by Colonel Clive and Rear-Admiral Charles Watson in 1756. In 1760 he joined the East India Company's Madras regiment of Europeans, which his father had disciplined, as an ensign. He was at once employed in Colonel Eyre Coote's advance on Pondicherry, and at its capture he distinguished himself by saving the life of the major commanding the 79th regiment, who offered him an ensigncy in it, which he refused. Cosby was at the siege of Vellore, and on being promoted lieutenant was sent with a detachment of Europeans and sepoys to Masulipatam, where he remained in command until 1764. In the same year he resigned his command in order to serve at the siege of Madura under Colonel

Charles Campbell, and in 1767 he was promoted captain and appointed to the 6th battalion of Madras sepoys, which he commanded at the battles of the Chengama and of Errore, and at the siege of Arlier, where he was wounded in 1768. In 1771, under Brigadier-General Joseph Smith, he commanded the troops which stormed Vellore on 27 September, and was appointed governor there; a year later he went on the staff as brigade-major, and in 1773 he was promoted lieutenant-colonel and appointed the first adjutant-general of the company's troops in Madras. As such he served under General Smith at the second siege of Tanjore in 1775, and negotiated the raja's surrender. He was sent home with the dispatches announcing its capture by Smith, the commander-in-chief at Madras. In 1777 he returned to Madras, and, after successfully commanding a force against the celebrated palegar Bom Rauze, resigned his staff appointment in December 1778 for the lucrative appointment of commander of the nawab of Arcot's cavalry and attached troops. This force he thoroughly disciplined, and he played an important part at its head in the Second Anglo-Mysore War with Haidar Ali. His forced march in 1780 from Trichinopoly was a great military feat, though he was just too late to join Colonel William Baillie (d. 1782), who was defeated and forced to surrender at Polillur. His march managed to circumvent Haidar Ali, and he cleverly joined Sir Hector Monro, under whom he did important service. In October 1782 he was ordered to England on sick leave, but was taken prisoner at the Cape. He managed to save the most important dispatches on the Anglo-Mysore War with which he was entrusted, and for this was knighted by George III when he reached England on parole. In late 1784 he returned to India, and after commanding in Trichinopoly and Tinnevelly as brigadier-general, in 1786 he was appointed colonel of the 4th Madras Europeans, and finally left India in December 1786, after thirty years' continuous service. He had made a large fortune in India, and like other nabobs purchased a country house and estate: the beautiful seat of Barnsville Park, Gloucestershire, near Chepstow, which he greatly improved and embellished.

Cosby married first early in life Elizabeth Marsh (d. 1773) of the Marshes of Kent, and they had three sons and two daughters. The eldest son, Major Henry Smith, was killed at the siege of Seringapatam (1799); and the youngest son, Montague, lieutenant-colonel of Madras cavalry, died of cholera near Poona in 1820. In 1793 he married second Ann (who died at Clifton on 24 May 1817), daughter of Samuel Eliot of Antigua and eldest sister of Elizabeth, Lady Le Despencer. They had two sons and one daughter.

Following his return to England Cosby continued to take a keen interest in Indian affairs, then troubled and controversial. The company's army had grown in size and importance and its British officers formed a distinct interest group, determined to preserve its own system including promotion by seniority and opportunities for vast ill-gotten profits. They were aggrieved and resentful at the status of royal army officers in India. During the 1780s and 1790s George III, Pitt's government, and especially Henry Dundas and Lord Cornwallis, sought to bring the company's military force under royal control and to undertake reforms. However, their attempt was delayed and mismanaged. The company officers, bitter and insubordinate, organized against the proposals in India and England. In 1786 Cornwallis became governor-general of India. In December of the following year a meeting of company officers at the Crown and Anchor tavern, the Strand, London, elected a committee which chose Cosby, its most senior member, as chairman (1787–8). They met representatives of the company and the government, and accepted a compromise agreement. In 1794 Cornwallis returned from India with a new plan to reform the company army, transferring it to the king's service and ending lucrative perquisites including double batta, bazaar duties, and moneylending. The Bengal officers again organized against this and sent agents to London, who in August 1794 gained Cosby's support. He became chairman (1794–6) of a representative committee which met company officials and the government. In 1795 the committee issued a critique of Cornwallis's plan, with an introduction by Cosby alleging that the plan would 'render the Army desperate' (Callahan, 144). The directors opposed the plan and Dundas withdrew it, and finally a compromise was agreed which largely conceded the officers' demands. The company army was not incorporated into the royal army, and promotion by seniority continued. An establishment of general officers was created for each presidency and Cosby, at the request of the other officers on the committee, in 1796 (antedated to 1793) was made one of the first major-generals on the Indian establishment, although he had been absent from India more than the five years allowed by the new regulations. The coast army officers presented him with 'a handsome service of plate' (GM 92/1, 232). However, in the long term Cosby's and the other company officers' defeat of reform harmed the Indian army and contributed to the mutiny which finally, and so bloodily, ended the company's army.

Cosby was also appointed to command the depot which the East India Company intended to establish on the Isle of Wight in 1796 for the recruiting service of their European regiments, a scheme which was abandoned following disagreement between the company and Board of Control. In 1816 he was promoted lieutenant-general (antedated to June 1799). He died at Bath on 17 January 1822, and was buried in Bath Abbey; a monument to him was placed in the south transept of the abbey church.

H. M. Stephens, rev. Roger T. Stearn

**Sources** GM, 1st ser., 92/1 (1822), 94, 177–82, 229–32, 648 · GM, 1st ser., 87/1 (1817), 571 · Dodwell [E. Dodwell] and Miles [J. S. Miles], eds., *Alphabetical list of the officers of the Indian army: with the dates of their respective promotion, retirement, resignation, or death … from the year 1760 to the year … 1837* (1838) · J. Philippart, *East India military calendar*, 1 (1823) · R. Callahan, *The East India Company and army reform, 1783–1798* (1972) · Burke, *Peerage* (1889) · T. A. Heathcote, *The military in British India: the development of British land forces in south Asia, 1600–1947* (1995) · C. A. Bayly, *Indian society and the making of the British empire* (1988), vol. 2/1 of *The new Cambridge history of India*, ed. G. Johnson · H. H. Dodwell, ed., *British India, 1497–1858* (1929), vol. 4 of *The Cambridge history of the British empire* (1929–59)

**Archives** BL, journal of campaign in the Carnatic and corresp., Add. MSS 29898–29899 | NA Scot., letters to Henry Dundas, GD 51

**Cosby, Phillips** (1729/30–1808), naval officer, was born in Nova Scotia, the son of the lieutenant-governor, Colonel Alexander Cosby of Stradbally Hall, Queen's county, Ireland, and nephew of the governor, General Phillips. He went to sea in 1747 and served for several years as able seaman, midshipman and master's mate in, successively, the *Mermaid* (20 guns), the *Severne* (50 guns), the *Blandford* (20 guns), the *Torrington* (44 guns), and the *Centaur* (24 guns) under captains Pratten, Gayton, Noel, and Huchenson, among others, before gaining his lieutenant's certificate on 7 August 1754. His first commission was as fourth lieutenant of the *Monarch* (74 guns) on 28 January 1755, but he moved to the *Orford* (68 guns) on 22 March that year, and became the ship's third lieutenant on 14 May 1756. Cosby commanded a schooner at the siege of Louisbourg in 1758, and at the siege of Quebec the following year he was marine aide-de-camp to General James Wolfe, and was reputedly with Wolfe at the storming of the Heights of Abraham on 13 September 1759.

Cosby returned to England and became second lieutenant of the *Sterling Castle* (64 guns) on 5 February 1760. From 2 June 1760 he commanded the sloop *Laurel*, and then, from 11 February 1761, the sloop *Beaver*. He became a post captain on 19 May 1761, with his appointment to the *Hind* (24 guns), and moved to the *Isis* (50 guns) on 11 August 1762, serving in her until the peace in 1763. Next in the frigate *Montreal* (32 guns), to which he was appointed on 6 March 1766, Cosby served in the Mediterranean under Commodore Richard Spry, and was given the job of carrying the duke of York's body home from Monaco between September and November 1767. At Leghorn on 15 April 1769 his ship played host to Emperor Joseph II of Austria.

In 1771 Cosby was appointed receiver-general of St Kitts, at an annual salary of £1600. He resigned this lucrative post on the outbreak of war with France, obtained command of the *Centaur* (74 guns) on 14 February 1778, and fought in the battle of Ushant on 27 July. On 31 March 1779 he moved to the *Robust*, and between December 1779 and March 1780 he was involved in the siege of Charles Town. On 16 March 1781 Arbuthnot's squadron met Des Touches's off the Chesapeake: the *Robust*, which led the British line into action, was very severely damaged by the concentrated fire of the French squadron, and needed extensive repairs in New York and Antigua before her return to England in July 1782.

Between 22 July 1785 and 21 January 1789 Cosby in the *Trusty* (50 guns) was commodore and commander-in-chief in the Mediterranean, and in 1788 he led a mission to the emperor of Morocco, with whom he negotiated a treaty granting British vessels protection from the Barbary corsairs. Having been granted the sinecure of colonel of Marines on 24 September 1787, Cosby was promoted rear-admiral of the white on 21 September 1790 and given command of Cork in the *Fame* (74 guns). During the Russian armament (1791) Cosby commanded the *Impregnable* (98 guns), and in the following year he was port admiral at Plymouth, in the *St George* (98 guns). In October of that year he married Eliza Hurst, *née* Gunthorpe, the widow of an army agent.

On 15 April 1793, now a vice-admiral, Cosby sailed from Spithead in the *Windsor Castle* (98 guns) in command of a squadron sent to the Mediterranean to watch the French fleet in Toulon. From August to December he was third-in-command of Hood's Mediterranean Fleet. While at Leghorn in November 1793 his whole squadron narrowly escaped the fire and explosion on the *Scipio*. He moved to the *Alcide* (74 guns) on 11 April 1794, and returned to England on 12 November.

Cosby was head of the impress service in Ireland until the peace of 1801 and became admiral of the red on 9 November 1805. Prior to this he retired to Bath where he died in Alfred Street on 10 January 1808. He was buried six days later at the abbey church.     Randolph Cock

**Sources** *DNB* · *Naval Chronicle*, 14 (1805), 353–64 · *Naval Chronicle*, 19 (1808), 88 · lieutenant's passing certificate, PRO, ADM 107/4, 280 · commission and warrant books, PRO, ADM 6/18, 19, 20, 21 · corresp. from Commodore Phillips Cosby, 1785–1789, PRO, ADM 1/388 · W. L. Clowes, *The Royal Navy: a history from the earliest times to the present*, 7 vols. (1897–1903), vols. 3–4 · *GM*, 1st ser., 78 (1808), 92 · D. Syrett and R. L. DiNardo, *The commissioned sea officers of the Royal Navy, 1660–1815*, rev. edn, Occasional Publications of the Navy RS, 1 (1994)

**Archives** priv. coll., corresp. and papers · PRO, corresp. as commander-in-chief Mediterranean, ADM 1/388 · PRO NIre., letter-book, logbook, and order | NMM, letters to Sir Charles Middleton, MID/1/33

**Likenesses** Ridley, stipple, pubd 1805 (after miniature by Robinson), NPG

**Cosby, William** (*c*.1690–1736), army officer and colonial governor, was born at Stradbally Hall, Queen's county, Ireland, the sixth son of Alexander Cosby and Elizabeth, *née* L'Estrige. He married Grace Montagu, sister of the earl of Halifax and cousin to Thomas Pelham-Holles, duke of Newcastle; they had three children.

Cosby began his military career in 1705 as a cornet in Earl Cadogan's regiment of horse. In 1711 he served as a captain in Lieutenant-General Harvey's regiment of horse, and in 1717 was named colonel of the Royal Irish regiment of foot. He was named brigadier-general in 1735. He was appointed governor of Minorca in 1718, and served there for ten years. As governor, Cosby had appropriated a shipment of snuff from a Portuguese merchant, Bonaventure Capedevilla. Having been tried in London on the complaint of the merchant, Cosby was ordered to pay £10,000 in damages. Now impoverished he sought assistance from his wife's cousin the duke of Newcastle, southern secretary in charge of the American colonies. Cosby had already accepted the governor-generalship of the Leeward Islands when news reached Britain in 1731 of the death of New York and New Jersey governor John Montgomerie: in fact, Cosby was already on ship, ready to sail. Instead he returned to London and asked Newcastle for the vacant post, which promised a greater opportunity to make money.

Colonists were well aware that Cosby and all other governors came to New York to enrich themselves. They also realized that Cosby had received the post not because of merit but because of his family connection to Newcastle. Word of his dealings with the Portuguese merchant preceded him, and colonists in New York and New Jersey looked on Cosby with particular suspicion.

Cosby kept in office the agreeable merchant assembly elected in 1728 during the governorship of John Montgomerie. He allied himself with the merchant faction, as had Montgomerie, thereby alienating the landowning interest who again constituted the opposition. The assembly proved willing to co-operate with Cosby and voted five years' support, though some members baulked at giving Cosby a present of £1000. Instead they voted the governor only £750. Cosby invited those assemblymen who opposed the full gift to dinner and took that opportunity to berate them; the next day the assemblymen voted to increase his present to £1000.

Cosby then tried to collect money from Rip Van Dam, who as senior councillor had been acting governor from Montgomerie's death on 1 July 1731 until Cosby's arrival on 1 August 1732. Cosby's instructions authorized him to take half the salary and half the money from perquisites and fees that Van Dam had received during that period. Van Dam, with the backing of the opposition faction, refused to pay. Cosby tried to bring the matter before the colony's supreme court as an equity cause. On 9 April 1733 Chief Justice Lewis Morris, head of the landowner opposition, argued that the supreme court did not have the jurisdiction to try equity causes, but the other two judges, James DeLancey, son of the merchant Stephen DeLancey, and Frederick Philipse, son of the merchant Adolph Philipse, disagreed. Morris's objections meant that the cause was never heard and the issue remained unresolved. Morris had won a victory but paid a price: in August 1733 Cosby dismissed him as chief justice of New York and appointed James DeLancey in his place.

The opposition was further alienated by Cosby's decision to take a one-third share of all land grants. Landowners complained to the home government about Cosby's excessive greed and what they considered his mismanagement of the colony, but got little response. They realized that they would have to stir up support for their anti-Cosby campaign from New York's voting population. Voter support was needed so the landowning party's candidates could secure office during the next assembly election. Informing the public was difficult because Cosby controlled the colony's only newspaper, *The New York Gazette*. To carry their message across to voters the opposition established their own paper, *The New York Weekly Journal*, printed by John Peter Zenger. The paper carried articles and essays written by the opposition and published anonymously. It also published reprints from the opposition press in Britain, particularly those that stressed the importance of freedom of the press and of speech.

Cosby countered the opposition propaganda that appeared in the *Weekly Journal* as best he could, but eventually decided to prosecute the printer. Zenger was charged with seditious libel and imprisoned, with bail set at £400. Unable to raise the money, he remained in prison for eight months until his trial in August 1735. Defended by Philadelphia attorney Andrew Hamilton, Zenger was found not guilty by a jury of his peers, who accepted Hamilton's argument that truth was an adequate defence against charges of libel. James Alexander, who contributed many essays to the *Weekly Journal*, wrote an account of the trial that made it well known throughout Britain and its colonies. The trial eventually helped to set the precedent that truth was indeed an adequate defence against libel.

Perhaps because of his preoccupation with New York's tangled politics, Cosby spent little time in and paid less attention to New Jersey. He called the New Jersey assembly into session on only one occasion, in April 1733, and received a promise of financial support until 1738. Little business was conducted during Cosby's infrequent meetings with the New Jersey legislature.

Lewis Morris went to England to lodge personal complaints against Cosby, but was unsuccessful in convincing the Walpole ministry to recall the governor. Despite the notoriety created by the Zenger trial and other events, Cosby remained in post with the support of the Westminster administration. Despite the fact that he continued to govern, the campaign mounted against him had led New Yorkers to define and verbalize their opposition to arbitrary rule, and to define such basic rights as those of trial by jury and freedom of speech and the press. Constant appeals by the élite to the lower and middling sort, voters or not, led to the politicization of those groups, and did much to increase provincial disrespect for British authority. Cosby's governorship only came to an end with his death on 10 March 1736, from tuberculosis, in New York city, where he was buried. William Cosby, only one in a series of inept governors, damaged imperial relations and, in the long run, weakened the royal prerogative.                    MARY LOU LUSTIG

**Sources** board of trade MSS, PRO, colonial office MSS, Class 5, vols. 1050–1058 · secretary of state MSS, PRO, colonial office MSS, Class 5, vols. 1090–1093 · New York State Library, Albany, New York, colonial MSS, vols. 61–62 · E. B. O'Callaghan and B. Fernow, eds. and trans., *Documents relative to the colonial history of the state of New York*, 15 vols. (1853–87) · E. B. O'Callaghan, ed., *The documentary history of the state of New York*, 4 vols. (1849–51) · C. Z. Lincoln, ed., *Messages from the governors, 1683–1776* (1909) · *The colonial laws of New York from the year 1664 to the revolution*, 5 vols. (1894) · *CSP col.*, vols. 22–3 · W. A. Whitehead and others, eds., *Documents relating to the colonial, revolutionary and post-revolutionary history of the state of New Jersey*, 1–10 (1880–86) · *Minutes of the common council of the city of New York, 1675–1776* (1905) · C. Colden, 'History of Governor William Colby's administration and of Lieutenant-Governor George Clarke's administration through 1737', *The letters and papers of Cadwallader Colden*, 9 (1937), 283–355 · J. Alexander, *A brief narrative of the case and trial of John Peter Zenger*, ed. S. N. Katz (1963) · W. Smith, *The history of the province of New-York* (1757); repr. M. Kammen, ed., 2 (New York, 1972) · P. A. Stellhorn and M. J. Birkner, eds., *The governors of New Jersey, 1664–1974* (1982) · R. E. Cray, 'Cosby, William', *ANB* · E. P. Tanner, 'Cosby, William', *DAB*

**Wealth at death** wealth, if any, in New York land

**Cosgrave** [*née* Daly], **Mary Josephine** (*c*.1877–1941), local administrator and social worker, was born in Naas, co.

Kildare, the daughter of James William Daly and his wife, Jane. She was educated at the Convent of Mercy in Naas and later studied at St Andrews University, where she was awarded an LLA. From 1896 she taught in the training college of Our Lady of Mercy in Baggot Street, Dublin. She also worked as an examiner in English under the intermediate board of education, Ireland. On 9 July 1901 she married the barrister and journalist Maurice Joseph Cosgrave.

In 1922 Mary Cosgrave was elected to Rathmines urban district council, and she was a member of Dublin corporation from 1933 until her death. She sat on numerous committees, including the housing committee, the City of Dublin welfare committee, and the City of Dublin vocational education committee. She was also a committee member of the Cheeverstown Convalescent Home for Little Children and the National Children's Hospital. She was chairman of the Meath Hospital committee and the county libraries committee, and vice-chairman of Dublin county council until 1930. She also played a leading role in the Civics Institute. Cosgrave was a key figure in the Irish Women Citizens' Association, of which she was also chairman. She represented the National Council of Ireland at international congresses.

Cosgrave was interested in social work, particularly maternity and child welfare work. She was active in the Women's National Health Association of Ireland and served as president of that association from 1939. The association's campaign against TB led to her association with Peamount Sanatorium and she became president of the sanatorium committee in 1939. Cosgrave died at her home, Woodside, 17 Park Drive, Cowper Gardens, Rathmines, Dublin, on 17 November 1941.    MARIA LUDDY

Sources WWW · *Irish Times* (18 Nov 1941) · *Irish Press* (18 Nov 1941) · *Irish Independent* (18 Nov 1941) · census returns, 1901, NA Ire. · *CGPLA Ire.* (1942) · m. cert. · d. cert.

Wealth at death £2647 0s. 10d.: probate, 8 Jan 1942, *CGPLA Eng. & Wales*

**Cosgrave, William Thomas** (1880–1965), president of the executive council of the Irish Free State, was born at 174 James Street, Dublin, on 5 June 1880, the second son and second child of Thomas Cosgrave, licensed vintner, of 174 James Street, and his wife, Bridget Nixon. After schooling with the Christian Brothers he entered his father's business, soon turning also to share his father's interest in local politics.

In 1905 Cosgrave participated with Arthur Griffith in the founding of Sinn Féin and in 1909 was elected a Sinn Féin representative to Dublin corporation. He served this body for thirteen years, being elected chairman of its estates and finance committee in 1915, and being returned as an alderman in 1920. In 1916, as a lieutenant in the Irish Volunteers, he fought under Eamon Ceannt in the South Dublin Union, was captured and condemned to death, a sentence later commuted to life imprisonment. After one year in Portland prison he was released in the general amnesty of 1917.

Cosgrave entered national politics as a Sinn Féin

**William Thomas Cosgrave** (1880–1965), by Sir John Lavery, 1923

abstentionist, winning a two-to-one victory over the parliamentary party candidate, John Magennis, in the Kilkenny City by-election of August 1917. In October 1917 he became one of the honorary treasurers of Sinn Féin, and in December 1918 was returned unopposed in the general election, for Kilkenny North. At the meeting of the first Dáil Éireann on 2 April 1919 he was appointed minister for local government. In that year he married Louise (d. 1959), daughter of Alderman Flanagan, a farmer of Dublin; they had two sons.

In the elections of 1921, 1922, 1923, and June 1927 Cosgrave represented the Carlow–Kilkenny constituency. In the election for the sixth Dáil, in September 1927, he was returned for both Carlow–Kilkenny and Cork borough, topping the poll in each. He chose to sit for the Cork seat and in the elections of February 1932, January 1933, July 1937, June 1938, and June 1943 he topped the poll there on all occasions except 1938. He retired from Dáil Éireann in 1944.

Local government, the seat of much disruption of British administration, was perhaps the true revolutionary arena in the years 1919–21. The department's inspectors and numerous councillors waged a continuous, consciousness-raising battle with the official local government board, withholding allegiance yet striving to retain as many housing and employment moneys as possible. Inefficiency and mismanagement were other characteristics, however, and Cosgrave's experience undoubtedly affected the attitude of the independent Irish government towards local authorities in the years to come, when he himself was to be thrust into greater prominence. A determined advocate of the Anglo-Irish treaty of December 1921, which he felt represented the best settlement available, he accepted membership of the provisional government, established to receive power from Britain, in January 1922, becoming its chairman in August after the death of Griffith and Michael Collins. He added the office of president of Dáil Éireann in September 1922, finally becoming the first elected president of the executive council of the Irish Free State on 6 December 1922. He held also the ministry of finance, in 1922–3, and for short periods the Ministry of Defence, in 1924, and the ministry of external affairs, in 1927. Having steered the country through civil war during 1922–3, it was his responsibility to establish the domestic administration and the international reputation of his country, which had assumed a somewhat ambiguous 'dominion status' by the 1921 treaty.

Under Cosgrave's wise chairmanship an able cabinet team established full parliamentary, legal, and administrative processes on a foundation of probity and wide acceptance. Orthodox financial management and cautious economic development secured an equally sound reputation for integrity in these spheres. The government's main economic initiative, the harnessing of the River Shannon to generate electricity, also proved a resounding success, while the body established to control it, the Electricity Supply Board (established in 1927), set a pattern of semi-state authorities widely emulated in the future. The failure of the boundary commission to advance Irish unity provided both crisis and disappointment for the government in 1925, but the ensuing agreement with Britain in December of that year was, Cosgrave felt, 'a damned good bargain'. His subsequent policy of co-operation with Belfast and of promoting Irish unity through the attraction of good government set a realistic course all too soon interrupted.

Surviving other crises such as the army mutiny in 1924 and the assassination of his vice-president, Kevin O'Higgins, in 1927, Cosgrave enjoyed a personal triumph when he visited the United States and Canada in 1928. Already he had led his country into the League of Nations, in 1923, and at successive imperial conferences, notably 1926 and 1930, his ministers helped expand 'dominion status' into full sovereignty, a position given legal force in the 1931 Statute of Westminster.

With the state firmly founded at home and abroad, and successfully weathering the world depression, Cosgrave suffered defeat in February 1932, but watched with satisfaction the ensuing peaceful change from his administration to that of Eamon De Valera. An unflagging democrat, he recoiled in horror at aspects of the amalgamation of his foundering party with the neo-fascist Blueshirt movement in 1933. When the brief leadership of General O'Duffy ended in September 1934, however, Cosgrave soon returned (spring 1935) as head of the renamed Fine Gael, and led the parliamentary opposition until his retirement in January 1944. His interest in horse-racing

was then reflected in his chairmanship of the Irish racing board, from 1946 to 1956, and again from 1957.

Cosgrave received a number of honours during his lifetime, becoming a knight grand cross, first class, of the Pian order, in 1925, and gaining honorary doctorates from the Catholic University of America; Columbia, Cambridge, and Dublin universities; and the National University of Ireland. He died at his home Beechpark, Templeogue, co. Dublin, on 16 November 1965, and was buried in the Golden Bridge cemetery, Inchicore, co. Dublin, two days later. His elder son, Liam, became leader of Fine Gael in 1965, and subsequently taoiseach (prime minister) of a coalition government in 1973.

Regarded by Sir Winston Churchill as 'a chief of higher quality than any who had yet appeared', Cosgrave was throughout his life an unpretentious and modest man. Short in stature, with a shock of hair he retained into old age, he had a lively eye and a ready wit, with gifts of common sense, courage, coolness, good humour, and humanity, which won the respect and affection of opponents as well as supporters. A deeply religious man, courteous and considerate, and a reconciler, he proved more successful in office than as an opposition leader, his greatest work being done in the decade 1922–32. The parliamentary democracy then established against daunting odds remains his most fitting monument.

DAVID HARKNESS

**Sources** *Irish Times* (17 Nov 1965) · *The Times* (17 Nov 1965) · personal knowledge (2004) · M. Daly, *The buffer state: the historical roots of the department of the environment* (1997) · M. Cronin, *The Blueshirts and Irish politics* (1997) · F. S. L. Lyons, *Ireland since the famine* (1971) · *CGPLA Ire.*
**Archives** HLRO, corresp. with Lord Beaverbrook · PRO, corresp. with Lord Midleton · TCD, corresp. with Thomas Bodkin | FILM BFI NFTVA, news footage
**Likenesses** photographs, 1919–32, Hult. Arch. · J. Lavery, oils, 1923, Hugh Lane Municipal Gallery of Modern Art, Dublin [*see illus.*] · S. O'Sullivan, charcoal drawing, 1940, NG Ire., Dublin · L. Whelan, oils
**Wealth at death** £1137: administration, 24 Feb 1966, *CGPLA Éire.*

**Cosin, Edmund** (1510/11–1574?), college head, was born in Bedfordshire and entered King's Hall, Cambridge, as a Bible clerk. He held a scholarship or fellowship there at the time of his presentation by the college on 21 September 1538 to the vicarage of Grendon, Northamptonshire, a living he held until November 1541. Cosin graduated BA in 1534/5 and MA in 1540/41. About 1540 he took up a fellowship at St Catharine's College. Appointed a university proctor in 1545, he became a fellow of Trinity College, Cambridge, at its foundation the following year, and took his BTh in 1547.

Cosin was a zealous Roman Catholic and prospered especially during the reign of Queen Mary. In 1553, on the queen's presentation, he became rector of St Edmund's, North Lynn, in Norfolk, and the vicar of Trumpington, Cambridgeshire; in the following two years he was installed to three more livings in the county—to the vicarage of Holy Trinity Caistor and Oxburgh (1554), to the vicarage of Fakenham (1555), and, on presentation of Trinity College, to the rectory of Thrapland (1555). From 1553 to

1557 he acted as official of the archdeacon of Norfolk, and from 1555 as commissary of the archdeaconry. On 13 January 1554 the chancellor of Cambridge University, Stephen Gardiner, wrote successfully commanding the president and fellows of St Catharine's College to choose as their master 'Mr Cosyn, a man for his wisdom and honest behaviour very meet for that room' in place of Dr Sandys, whose marriage, 'contrary to the ecclesiastical laws and your statutes' had made the office void (Jones, 80). According to Strype, he 'was a busy man in that reign, and one in commission for prosecuting protestants' (Strype, *Parker*, 1.177). That Cosin was busy is beyond dispute, for in addition to filling his many positions he also acted as chaplain to Bonner, then bishop of London, and as assistant to Michael Dunning, chancellor of the diocese of Norwich. Cooper, however, reports that he was 'not active in the efforts to repress protestantism' (Cooper, *Ath. Cantab.*, 1.204).

In 1558 Cosin was appointed vice-chancellor of the university; illness made it necessary that the ceremony be conducted in his house, an omen perhaps. This was a bad year for an outspoken Roman Catholic to achieve his greatest public visibility: elected on 8 November, he resigned on the twenty-fifth, to be replaced by John Pory. Cosin also lost the mastership of St Catharine's—either through resignation or by order of the commission which visited the university in 1559—and was succeeded by John May. He relinquished his ecclesiastical benefices and lived quietly in Cambridge. On 20 November 1561, then aged fifty, he was admitted to rooms in Gonville and Caius College by its recent founder, John Caius. He appears as a pensioner there in 1564.

The rest of his life is obscure. A man named Edward Cosyn was named in 1567 as party to a conspiracy to depose Elizabeth and to enthrone Mary, queen of Scots. It is not at all certain that this was the former master; the conspirator may have been Edward or Edmund Cussen, a Catholic reported to be living abroad in 1576. Cosin of St Catharine's had very likely died by then, probably in 1574 since the will of Edmond Cosyn, proved on 8 July 1574, disposed of property at Chesterton, near Cambridge, where land had been granted in November 1556 to the master and fellows of St Catharine's. Other goods bequeathed were meagre, even for an ordinary parish clergyman, and the testator reveals neither his benefice nor place of residence; if this was the will of the former vice-chancellor, he died in straitened circumstances, possibly under the protection of sympathetic Catholic friends.

STEPHEN WRIGHT

**Sources** H. C. Porter, *Reformation and reaction in Tudor Cambridge* (1958) · W. H. S. Jones [W. H. Samuel], *A history of St Catharine's College, once Catharine Hall, Cambridge* (1936) · G. F. Browne, *St Catharine's College* (1902) · Venn, *Alum. Cant.* · Cooper, *Ath. Cantab.* · J. Strype, *The life and acts of Matthew Parker*, new edn, 3 vols. (1821), vol. 1 · J. Strype, *Ecclesiastical memorials*, 3 vols. (1822) · *Masters' History of the college of Corpus Christi and the Blessed Virgin Mary in the University of Cambridge*, ed. J. Lamb (1831) · will, PRO, PROB 11/56, sig. 30 · J. P. Collier, ed., *The Egerton papers*, CS, 12 (1840)
**Wealth at death** see PRO, PROB 11/56, sig. 30

**Cosin, John** (1595–1672), bishop of Durham, was born on 30 November 1595, the son of Giles Cosin, a wealthy Norwich citizen who was probably involved in the cloth trade, and his wife, Elizabeth Remington (*d.* 1644?). He studied first at Norwich grammar school and was then elected to a Norwich fellowship at Gonville and Caius College, Cambridge, in 1610, his father having died two years previously. He contributed verses in English to the *Epicedium Cantabrigiense* (1612), graduated BA in 1614, proceeded MA in 1617, was elected a junior fellow in 1620, and served as rhetoric praelector in 1620–21 and university preacher in 1622; he proceeded BD in 1623. However, despite the best efforts of Cosin and his supporters, he failed to succeed to a senior fellowship in 1624.

**Early career and contacts** In fact Cosin had already been developing important contacts and an alternative career outside Cambridge. About 1616 he was invited by both his diocesan, Lancelot Andrewes, and by John Overall (to whom he had been recommended by the bishop's nephew, John Hayward) to go to London to take care of their libraries. Advised by his tutor, John Browne, Cosin chose Overall, and from 1617 to 1619 served him not only as librarian but also as secretary. Overall exercised an important influence over the ideas of the young Cosin, who subsequently never missed an opportunity to salute his patron's memory. Near the end of his life, in 1669, he erected a tablet to Overall's memory in Norwich Cathedral, in which he described himself as 'devotissimus Discipulus'. Overall's devotion to the church's ceremonies and determined opposition to Calvinist doctrine can be glimpsed in Cosin's earliest extant sermons (the first delivered in Hayward's parish of Coton).

After Overall's death in 1619 Cosin came under the influence of another important anti-Calvinist ceremonialist, Richard Neile, then bishop of Durham, whose chaplain he became, and by whom he was appointed to the mastership of Greatham Hospital (1624)—which he swiftly exchanged for the rectory of Elwick (which was subsequently served by a curate)—and a prebendal stall in Durham Cathedral, where he regularly attended chapter meetings thereafter. In 1625 Cosin was appointed archdeacon of the East Riding of Yorkshire, and in 1626 rector of the rich living of Brancepeth in Durham. Brancepeth was his principal residence in the city (several of his sermons preached there survive), and he oversaw the lavish refurbishment of the church, complete with elaborate Gothic woodwork (destroyed by fire in the twentieth century). On 15 August 1626 he married, at St Margaret's, Durham, Frances, daughter of Marmaduke Blakiston (another Durham prebendary and the previous archdeacon of the East Riding).

While Cosin was active in Durham he became most famous initially for his activities in Bishop Richard Neile's circle in London. This was the so-called *Durham House group of anti-Calvinist divines who gathered around the bishop's London house in the Strand, and included such figures as John Buckeridge and William Laud. Cosin's

John Cosin (1595–1672), by unknown artist, *c.*1635–40

energies were swiftly employed in controversial directions as he became closely involved in the conflicts surrounding the works of Richard Mountague. It seems clear that Cosin's friendship with Mountague predated the latter's acquaintance with the rest of the Durham House group (perhaps arising through their mutual friend Augustine Lindsell). Mountague's first surviving letter to Cosin of January 1621 already assumes a close friendship, and his many subsequent letters to Cosin demonstrate a much greater confidence and familiarity than Mountague ever showed towards the rest of Neile's circle. Cosin played a decisive role in Mountague's two notorious publications, the *New Gagg* (1624) and the *Appello Caesarem* (1625), securing licences for both and introducing a number of changes into the latter work with the author's enthusiastic encouragement ('Add alter, do what you will … I refer the whole unto you as you please'; *Correspondence*, 1.34). He also acted on Mountague's behalf at the first session of the York House conference, where he was not only secretary but also intervened on several occasions to defend the absent author on points of detail. He also tackled Mountague's opponents in other ways, securing the calling in of Daniel Featley's anonymous book against him.

This was only one example of Cosin's more general employment at this time as an unofficial censor of puritan books: he also prompted official condemnations of the works of the puritan writers William Crompton and Edward Elton (the latter of whom had two of his books burnt), and helped to secure the calling in of another puritan work falsely attributed to Isaac Casaubon. He was accused of hovering around London systematically seeking to calumniate Calvinist writings 'and to procure them

either to be altogether suppressed, or to be so gelded and mangled, that the sale of them thereby was very much hindred' (Featley, 40, 'The printer to the reader' by Robert Mylbourne). About this time he also acted as a commissioner at the trial before high commission of the heterodox boxmaker John Etherington, allegedly maintaining that at the eucharist 'the very flesh of Christ was eaten with our teeth' (Etherington, 50).

It was also in 1626 that Cosin delivered a famous sermon at the consecration in Durham House chapel of Francis White as bishop of Carlisle. At this splendid occasion, presided over by bishops Neile and John Buckeridge among others, and with a congregation of some 500 people (including many distinguished courtiers), Cosin threw down a gauntlet on behalf of the Durham House group. He condemned the current obsession with preaching over the other priestly duties, and attacked 'they which preach as voluntary as the organ plays' and those 'who love not to hear of a law, of a working and a doing religion', the powers of vestries, the 'ceremony-haters of our day'. He declared that the Church of England suffered criticism from Roman Catholics:

> that we have a service, but no servants at it; that we have churches, but keep them not like the houses of God; that we have the Sacraments, but few to frequent them … that we have all religious duties … but seldom observed; all good laws and canons of the Church, but few or none kept; the people are made to do nothing; the old discipline is neglected, and men do what they list.

This was unacceptable: 'it should be otherwise and our Church intends it otherwise' (*Works*, 1.97). If Cosin was here setting out the programme of the Durham House movement he was also setting out his own personal programme which he can be seen implementing over the next fourteen years in Durham and Cambridge.

**Early writings and controversies** Not surprisingly Cosin soon had his enemies. But he first found himself in the glare of puritan opposition for his activities at court. Cosin's liturgical expertise had already been called upon at the coronation of Charles I, where he acted as master of ceremonies and directed the choir, and where his translation of the *Veni Creator* was employed. Opposition was aroused, however, by the publication of his celebrated *Collection of Private Devotions* in 1627. According to Cosin's account, this work was prompted by the concern that the French ladies-in-waiting who had accompanied Henrietta Maria to England chided the English ladies of the court because they did not follow any religious exercises in the way that the Catholics did. On the advice of Francis White (another member of the Durham House group) the king instructed Cosin to prepare a book of religious offices for the court ladies. Within three months Cosin had completed the *Collection*, essentially a primer, combining canonical observance of the hours of prayer with further prayers, expositions of the Lord's prayer, creed, and ten commandments, and other devotional material. While the Elizabethan primer of 1560 was Cosin's basic model he also used a wide range of other sources, even including an unacknowledged prayer of St Ignatius Loyola, and often drew upon the same medieval sources used by Cranmer for the Book of Common Prayer, thereby providing what was intended to be 'an integral and homogeneous *private* complement to the *common* prayer of the Church' (Cosin, *Collection*, xxxiii). The book sold rapidly, going through three editions in 1627 alone, and five more impressions before Cosin's death; some passages from it were adopted in the Scottish prayer book of 1637. But in the polarized religious politics of the period, and given Cosin's open support for Richard Mountague the year before, the book was soon attacked in pamphlets by the puritans Henry Burton and William Prynne, who claimed that the book was riddled with popery, and condemned in particular its endorsement of prayers for the dead (which was removed in a further edition), the proliferation of martyrs and saints' days, and the emphasis placed on the power of priestly absolution.

Cosin wrote an anxious defence against these charges to the licenser of the work, George Montaigne, but worse was to come—this time from Durham. It was here that one of Cosin's fellow prebendaries, Peter Smart, sought to demonstrate publicly how Cosin 'hath turned these his Popish theories and speculations [in the *Collection of Private Devotions*] into practice' (Smart, preface, sig. *2r). On 27 July 1628 Smart (who had held his stall since 1609) delivered a sermon in which he made a vitriolic attack on the recent beautifying of the cathedral and of its services by Cosin and his associates. Cosin in particular was singled out as 'our young Apollo, [who] repaireth the Quire and sets it out gayly with strange Babylonish ornaments'. He was also accused of having set up '50 glittering Angels round about the quire of Durham Church', of burning 220 candles in the cathedral on Candlemas day, of having the creed sung to the accompaniment of 'Organs, Shackbuts, and Cornets', and insisting on the wearing of copes during services, 'one of them having the picture of the Trinitie embroydered upon it' (ibid., sigs. 2v–3r, 24). It was also charged that Cosin had hectored worshippers who did not follow the correct actions in worship, urging gentlewomen 'can ye not stand ye lazy sowes?' (*Correspondence*, 1.194).

Smart's language was undoubtedly outspoken and he may at times have exaggerated the details, and have misrepresented as pure novelty what was often merely an intensification of existing practice. Nevertheless, more recent scholarship has confirmed many of his charges, particularly in the area of music (Cosin's speciality): it seems clear that choral polyphony was indeed displacing the more traditional congregational involvement in music, that texts such as the Sanctus, Gloria, and creed were being transferred wholly to the choir, and that the liturgy was being changed to accommodate more choral music. It is also indicative of the radical nature of these innovations that following the arrival in Durham later in 1628 of the new bishop, John Howson, who had himself supported Mountague and had had his own clashes with puritans, he sought a compromise, undid some of Cosin's

liturgical changes, and noted that Smart had been provoked by superstitious innovations, (although it is possible that Smart was an old college acquaintance of his).

In the meantime Smart had been suspended and his stall sequestered by a commission of the chapter. Smart failed in his attempt to indict the commission before the assizes, although his charges were raised in parliament as part of more general enquiries into the activities of the Arminian faction, supplemented by the damaging allegation that Cosin had remarked in a conversation in April 1628 that the king 'is not supreme heade of the Church of England next under Christ, nor haith he anie more poore [power] of excommunication than my man that rubs my horse['s] heeles' (*Correspondence*, 1.147). In a letter to Laud Cosin denied having said such words (which while technically correct were disastrous in tone) and the king ordered the prosecution dropped. The Commons, however, accused him of high treason, charged him with tampering with the prayer book, and condemned the *Collection* to be burnt and Cosin to be punished as an 'author and abettor of Popish and Arminian innovations'.

The dissolution of parliament and beginning of the personal rule came just in time for Cosin, and brought happier times. In 1630 he proceeded DD. The troubles at Durham continued for a while, partly in the face of renewed charges from Smart, partly as Cosin also fell out with both the dean, Richard Hunt, and the bishop, John Howson. Cosin, as usual, appealed to Laud and the king for support, and obtained it, with Howson receiving a stern royal rebuke. Cosin's closeness to the king was manifested still more clearly when Charles visited Durham in 1633, and it was Cosin who arranged the divine services and the king's reception. He was appointed a royal chaplain-extraordinary in June of the same year, although he was not made a chaplain-in-ordinary until April 1636. Having been an active commissary for Richard Neile in the latter's episcopal visitation of Chester in 1633, Cosin continued to serve as chaplain to Neile when he became archbishop of York, and preached the morning sermon at the consecration of St John's Church, Leeds, in 1634. In the meantime he became increasingly involved in the business of the Durham chapter, showing a particular zeal as treasurer in 1633–4 in vigorously reforming cathedral finances.

**Master of Peterhouse** Soon afterwards Cosin returned to Cambridge when he was appointed master of Peterhouse in 1635 by his old Durham House colleague Francis White, bishop of Ely (presumably at the king's behest, and against the fellows' own preference for Christopher Wren, brother of the previous master). Although in the following year Cosin took the university's side in opposing Laud's attempts to conduct a visitation of the university he may have written a memorandum sent to the archbishop in the same year which detailed the various irregularities in the religious life of the colleges that might usefully be reformed were such a visitation to take place. Certainly, Cosin did not hesitate to push his college in an even more vigorously Laudian direction, making his own sizeable financial contribution towards a marked embellishment of the chapel and its services. It was later complained that since he became master the college chapel 'hath bene soe dressed up and ordered soe Ceremoniously, that it hath become the gaze of the University & a greate invitation to Strangers' (BL, Harley MS 7019, fol. 71r). The altar, covered with bright silk, was placed on raised marble, and decorated with expensive new altar plate, including two gilt embossed candlesticks and a censor; elaborate hangings with cherubim, and a striking east window based on Rubens's 'Le coup de lance' were installed. There was, as might be expected, a notable increase in the use of music in the chapel services (apparently drawing heavily on Durham's musical repertory), and a new post of organist was established.

As one of the Laudian heads of college Cosin also played a partisan role in the vice-chancellor's court, condemning puritan attacks on the enhanced ritualism, and defending the more exuberant ceremonialist notions of junior fellows such as John Normanton (who soon afterwards converted to Roman Catholicism) and Sylvester Adams. Cosin defended Adams's teaching that confession to a minister was necessary for salvation with the reflection that such a position was not explicitly condemned in the Thirty-Nine Articles or Book of Common Prayer, and therefore could not be condemned by the court. This was to leave a very large latitude indeed to what opinions were to be regarded as orthodox. Cosin was himself made vice-chancellor in 1639, and rapidly made an impact. He oversaw the development of more elaborate services and decoration in the university church of Great St Mary's, including a large new chancel screen, and he introduced more rigorous regulations into its services, barring all those below the degree of doctor from the chancel, and lavishly decorating the altar. He also chose the church as the venue for an extraordinary sermon on Christmas eve 1639 at which he condemned Socinian and puritan Antichrists as 'Locusts ascending out of the bottomlesse pit, the very form of the beast, hellhounds' (BL, Harley MS 7019, fol. 63r). He was later attacked for his high-handed administration: it was alleged that he had prohibited the use of extemporary prayers in the university, while the corporation of Cambridge protested at his overbearing attitude towards the municipal administration of justice. Not all Cosin's activities were controversial: his lively interest in building and libraries led him to launch abortive plans for the building of a new commencement house and university library, the latter of which had raised some £8000 in subscriptions until the upheavals of the early 1640s frustrated the enterprise.

**Troubles of 1640–1644** The deteriorating situation in Scotland soon affected Cosin. While his loss of income from his Durham livings as a result of the bishops' wars was compensated with his appointment by the king as dean of Peterborough in November 1640, it was less easy for him to gain protection from his enemies in England. Attacks on his allegedly popish opinions had been heard in the northern high commission in 1634 and 1635, and the calling of the Short Parliament made it inevitable that Peter

Smart's charges would be renewed in a petition to the Commons—it was probably only the rapid dissolution of parliament that prevented further moves against him.

With the calling of the Long Parliament Cosin was soon in trouble. Smart's petition was presented once more within a week of the parliament's opening. Cosin strongly rejected the charges that he purposely turned to the east in celebrating communion, that he covered cushions and benches with crosses, that he had spoken scandalously of the reformers, and that he had denied the royal supremacy, but he was found guilty by a Commons committee and was judged unfit to hold his current positions. Cosin responded with spirit. When, on his bowing before the committee, one of them commented sarcastically 'Heere is no Altar, Dr Cosin', he replied 'Why then, I hope there shall be no Sacrifice' (CUL, MS Mm. 1.45, p. 36). The twenty-one articles of impeachment were taken up to the House of Lords in March 1641, and again received vigorous denials from the accused, although in some specific cases at least Cosin's defence was demonstrably untrue. Cosin's additional urging of the king's pardon granted to him in 1629 may have partly helped to ensure that the Lords did not take his case any further, although sheer weight of business may partly explain why he escaped further prosecution. The hostility of the crowds lining the stairs to the Commons chamber and the fact that Cosin's bail was fixed at the enormous sum of £10,000 demonstrate the importance attached to the charges against him.

There is little indication that Cosin was cowed by his treatment. In 1641 he was still showing his customary zeal at his new home of Peterborough, drawing up a complete inventory of chapter lands and leases, and drafting proposals for more rigorous rent collection even as parliament debated whether deans and chapters should be abolished altogether. On 25 March 1642 his wife died. Early in August his attempt to send money and college plate from Peterhouse to the king was foiled by a volunteer company of Cambridgeshire men under Oliver Cromwell. Soon afterwards he returned to Durham, and with the outbreak of war he was reportedly appointed to review for political content all sermons prepared for delivery in the area controlled by the duke of Newcastle. He seems to have left Durham after August 1643, and on 13 March 1644 he was ejected from his mastership of Peterhouse, but it is likely that he had already found his way abroad by this time, reportedly disguised as a miller.

**Exile** Cosin was appointed by the king to serve as chaplain to the protestant members of Queen Henrietta Maria's court in France, and for the next decade and a half he did what he could to keep the beleaguered protestant royalist exiles together, operating initially from quarters in the Louvre, and later in the residence of the English ambassador, Sir Richard Browne, whose chapel provided an important and visible base for the exiled Church of England. Thomas Fuller later praised Cosin for acting at this time as 'the Atlas of the Protestant Religion, supporting the same with his Piety and Learning, confirming the wavering therein, yea dayly adding Proselytes (not of the meanest rank) thereto' (Fuller, *Worthies*, 1.295). There were many conversions to Catholicism among royalist exiles, not least among members of Cosin's own college of Peterhouse (including his son-in-law Francis Blakiston), and in 1651 these were joined by Cosin's only son, John (who had been admitted to Peterhouse two years earlier, aged fifteen), much to his father's grief. In these circumstances Cosin embarked upon a series of written defences of the Church of England and her ceremonies, and attacks upon the church of Rome. He was involved in a formal disputation with Father Paul Robinson, prior of the English Benedictines in France, concerning the validity of Anglican orders, which was continued in written papers. Further private debates with Catholics led him to draw up a number of papers on the areas in dispute, including memorials against the authority of the Lateran Council of 1215, transubstantiation, Roman auricular confession, and communion in one kind. He also composed for foreigners a summary of the Church of England's doctrine and discipline, the *Regni Angliae religio catholica*, and other short papers summarizing the points on which Catholics and protestants agreed and disagreed. In 1656 he wrote a larger history of papal transubstantiation (first published after his death) and in the following year his most substantial single work, a *Scholastical History of the Canon of Holy Scripture*, which was immediately published and had gone through five editions by 1684. These scholarly endeavours were performed by Cosin in ever more straitened circumstances. After the execution of Charles I Cosin had all his pensions cut off, and was left impoverished. His health also deteriorated, and in 1654 his death was expected. His efforts to frustrate Henrietta Maria's attempts to secure the conversion, first of the duke of York, and then of the duke of Gloucester, made his position in Paris still more precarious. Assistance came from, among others, Sir Ralph Verney (to whom he had sent a copy of his *Collection* following the death of Lady Verney in May 1650) but John Evelyn's predatory attempts to buy the library of the struggling cleric were rebuffed.

While Cosin continued as a redoubtable opponent of Roman Catholicism he also developed an interesting acquaintance with the archbishop of Trebizond, with whom after discussion of what they considered to be the same foundations of their religions, he agreed that they should retain communion and unity. The liturgist in Cosin must have been fascinated to hear the archbishop say St John Chrysostom's liturgy in a private chapel at the Louvre, and he approved the duke of York's private observation of the same. On the other hand he enjoyed increasingly amicable relations with the reformed church at Charenton, near Paris. In a letter of 1646 he still reflected that Genevans 'shall never have my approbation of their doings' (*Works*, 4.385), yet was already comparing their defects favourably with those of Rome—his love of the missal could not compensate for the dogmas of Tridentine Catholicism and the predatory behaviour of Roman priests towards the exiled Anglican community. As early as 1645 Cosin had reportedly buried a deceased royalist in the church at Charenton, employing the full prayer book service with the allowance of the Huguenots. In a famous

letter to Thomas Cordel, a royalist exile and tutor to Verney's children, Cosin approved intercommunion (although instructing him to request that he might receive kneeling), having studied the validity of Calvinist orders. In a later letter to Peter Gunning in 1657 he carefully limited his acceptance of Calvinist orders, emphasizing that he did not accept the validity of English presbyterian ordinations because England had rejected protestant episcopacy. But he clearly enjoyed amicable relations with the pastors at Charenton. Against Thomas Fuller's charges that he had not joined them he emphasized that the French ministers 'were very deserving and learned men, great lovers and honourers of our Church' (*Works*, 4.397–8), and he was happy to report that he prayed and sang psalms with them and heard their sermons, while in turn he baptized many of their children at the ministers' own request, conducted marriages for them, admitted two young Huguenots to English orders, and gave many of the Huguenots communion according to the Anglican rites (although there is no evidence that Cosin himself took communion at Charenton). His closeness to the Huguenots drew criticism from other exiled Laudians, and in particular from another former Cambridge head of college, Edward Martin, who complained bitterly of Cosin's influence and how his arguments undermined the integrity of the Church of England.

**Restoration** Edward Hyde wrote to Cosin in April 1660 advising his return to England. By June Cosin was back in Cambridge, while in Peterborough Cathedral he performed prayer book services well before the book was revived officially elsewhere, much to Hyde's displeasure. Further promotion was swiftly forthcoming, and on 2 December 1660 Cosin was consecrated bishop of Durham, his chaplain William Sancroft preaching the consecration sermon. As holder of this office Cosin stood at the king's right hand at the coronation service.

Cosin's skills as a liturgist were soon in demand. A revision of the prayer book was at the top of the religious agenda, and gave Cosin the opportunity to fulfil a lifelong interest, perhaps derived from Overall, whose reflections on the subject he copied into his notes. He had first been employed to enter corrections into a new printing of the prayer book as early as the 1620s at the command of Charles and Laud, and over the following thirty years had entered a series of observations into a number of prayer books in which he identified imperfections and inconsistencies in the existing liturgy and noted the alternatives provided by the Sarum missal and the first Edwardian prayer book. Cosin seems to have drawn up a further set entitled 'Particulars to be considered, explained and corrected in the Book of Common Prayer' in 1660, possibly having already seen Matthew Wren's 'Advices' for changes to be made to the prayer book. Cosin's own 'Particulars' draw especially on the 1549 prayer book, as well as his earlier notes, in emphasizing the need for greater clarity, order, and uniformity in the service. He proposed more systematic changes in the so-called Durham Book, drawn up in 1660 and 1661. Many of the proposed alterations detailed there were routine improvements, and overtly controversial issues were generally avoided. Nevertheless, many of Cosin's persistent concerns were addressed: for example, the communion table was to be placed permanently at the east end, singing in the creed and Sanctus permitted, the water in baptism to be blessed. However, Cosin's departure in August 1661 for his enthronement as bishop of Durham seems to have provided the opportunity for the introduction of further compromises into the draft revisions in the light of the Savoy conference, and the new prayer book that was ultimately approved by convocation contained barely two-fifths of the changes proposed by Cosin in the Durham Book. While Cosin was asked to provide a form of service for consecrating churches and chapels, it seems to have been rejected at the behest of Gilbert Sheldon, bishop of London, although Cosin used it himself in 1668.

At Durham Cosin maintained his links with Huguenots. Moïse Amyraut's *In orationem dominicam* (1662) is dedicated to him, and he received presentation copies of books from Jean Daillé in 1660 and 1664. Daillé wrote to an English friend of 'your Cosin, or rather ours' (*Works*, 4.399), and many French immigrants regarded him as an actual or potential patron for their writings and careers. In his diocese Cosin was recognizably the same vigorous, decisive, and somewhat overbearing administrator that he had proved himself in Cambridge. He was characteristically punctilious in pursuing and reviving all the rights and finances of the bishopric. He was personally very active at his first visitation, where he proceeded severely against Roman Catholic and protestant dissenters. His concern at the persistence of conventicles increased over the years: in 1670 he wrote approvingly of how in London conventicles had been 'ferretted out of every hole' by trained bands and troops (*Correspondence*, 2.243). Nevertheless, he did in a number of reported cases try to persuade nonconformists by argument and promises of preferment, even reportedly offering conditional ordination in private in the case of Richard Franklin, the ejected minister of Bishop Auckland. Cosin's struggles were not just with nonconformists. He quarrelled with the dean and chapter over the lease of church lands and the organization of the cathedral. He also clashed with local notables in his violent opposition to the election of parliamentary representatives for Durham, and he was swift to resume episcopal authority over the city, although he did rebuild the guildhall and grant a charter to a company.

Cosin was always at pains to point out that he had made good use of the financial resources that he had so vigorously reclaimed for the church. Even if he sometimes exaggerated the scope of his rebuilding works, they are still highly impressive. He presided over significant restoration at Durham Castle; at Auckland Castle he remodelled the great hall as a chapel, with Gothic-style screens and woodwork and a new set of altar plate for the chapel, while at Durham Cathedral he provided a new litany desk and reading desk, and some other woodwork there, including the extraordinary font cover, has been attributed to Cosin. He refounded the almshouses outside the cathedral on Palace Green as well as a smaller almshouse at Bishop Auckland, and rebuilt the assize courts in 1664, as well as repairing the bishop's house at Darlington. Perhaps most notable of all is the Cosin Library on Palace Green—completed in 1668 at a cost of £2500, opened the following year as a public library for clergy, gentry, and scholars, and still an invaluable resource for scholars in the twenty-first century. While most of Cosin's bounty was inevitably expended in Durham he also remembered his earlier homes by providing scholarships for the colleges of Caius and Peterhouse (along with an ornamental eastern facade of Peterhouse chapel in 1665). Isaac Basire later claimed that Cosin had spent £2000 every year of his episcopate on works of charity, which (allowing for a capacious definition of charity which would include ecclesiastical buildings and stipends) is likely to be accurate.

Following recurrent 'violent fits of the strangury' (Osmond, 299–301), Cosin died on 15 January 1672 in Pall Mall, London, whence his body was taken for burial, on 29 April 1672, at his own request in his chapel at Auckland Castle. The funeral sermon, preached by Isaac Basire, constitutes the first brief biography of the bishop. His will provides a full and itemized listing of all his building and charitable work, in order to demonstrate his claim that none of the £20,000 which he had received in fines and leases had been spent on himself or his children. He had three sons and four daughters. Two of his sons died in infancy, and the remaining son, who had for the second time deserted the Church of England for Catholicism, was left a bequest of £100, a sum which Cosin increased in a codicil written the following day. Three of his daughters survived him, and all made prominent marriages.

**Reputation and assessment** Not surprisingly Cosin was the darling of the later high-churchmen, especially on the strength of his first series of prayer book notes, first published by Nicholls in the early eighteenth century, and thereafter an important source for those defending the ritualistic interpretation of the ornaments rubric, which argued for the continued use of the eucharistic vestments of the first Edwardian prayer book. Cosin's various written works, sermons, and a selection of his correspondence were published in the Library of Anglo-Catholic Theology. His *Collection of Private Devotions* went through five printings between 1838 and 1867, and his version of the canonical hours was used by the nineteenth-century Church of England Sisterhood of Mercy of Devonport and Plymouth. This Anglo-Catholic adulation meant that he also received his fair share of criticisms too, most notably from J. T. Tomlinson, who, in *The Prayer Book Homilies and Articles* (1897), attacked Cosin's scholarship and what he dubbed 'the great Cosin Myth' which had led people to consider the first series of prayer book notes to express the 'mind of the Church' towards the meaning of the 1662 prayer book. Instead Tomlinson noted a string of errors in the first series of prayer book notes and pointed out that it was Matthew Wren rather than Cosin who was the more influential figure in the drafting of the 1662 prayer book.

Was Cosin the hero that the Anglo-Catholic movement made him? Cosin's deep attachment to Catholic tradition, and to the first Edwardian prayer book as offering a closer link to the Sarum missal, are undeniable. He was more than ready to contemplate changes to the Elizabethan liturgy in order to undo some of the damage (as he saw it) of the second Edwardian prayer book, and was always seeking ways of making prayer book services more patristic. In Durham and Cambridge he promoted an elaborate ceremonialism which was unquestionably novel in a number of its features (and in his liturgical innovations, and especially in his promotion of music, Cosin seems to have gone further than any of his Laudian colleagues). If the first and third series of prayer book annotations are accepted as genuine, then they would seem to reveal a lively sacramentalism, firmly anti-puritan, but also a deep interest in the writings of the moderate Jesuit Maldonatus, especially on the eucharist, where Cosin declared Maldonatus's exposition of the eucharistic sacrifice entirely acceptable. There is little obvious attempt here to condemn Roman Catholic excesses: indeed, Cosin maintained that the Church of England and Rome agreed in their liturgies (Smart claimed that Cosin had said that the Anglican service was a mass), which made it unnecessary and perverse for protestants to focus continually on areas of doctrinal controversy between the two churches. His close friendship with Mountague shows that he shared the latter's deeply polarized view of contemporary religious politics, and Cosin's deep antipathy towards puritan forms of piety is fully evident in his earliest sermons and the *Collection of Private Devotions*. Like Laud, Cosin also showed himself throughout his career to be an energetic, even zealous, administrator, determined to rebuild the financial resources of the church, and rigorous in his enforcement of ecclesiastical discipline.

However 'Anglo-Catholic' the early Cosin might appear, however, any analysis of his career must address the central question of whether his views changed as a result of his exile in Paris, becoming less Catholic and more reformed. In 1626 he stressed that presbyters could not ordain, and in the privacy of an earlier prayer book he had queried whether deficiencies in the formula of consecration meant that Calvinists had no real sacrament of the eucharist. Later his understanding of the Calvinist liturgy and powers of ordination manifestly altered. His writings and prayer book annotations after 1640 seem to display a livelier sense of the errors of Roman Catholics, and a more informed interest in and sympathy with Reformed authors, who are now regularly cited in support of Cosin's arguments. His second series of prayer book notes (composed after 1640) speak more favourably of Calvin in particular, but Cosin's real interest here and elsewhere was in the writings of the Lutheran syncretist Georg Calixtus, whose writings he acquired and enthusiastically annotated, and whose funeral sermon he carefully transcribed. These changes may generally be evidence more of a shift of polemical focus, and the development of a more informed understanding of foreign protestantism, rather than of a major alteration in doctrinal presuppositions, although some writers have detected a mellowing in his eucharistic doctrine.

It would be unwise to draw too great a distinction between the pre-exile Cosin and the later figure, however. The high level of continuity in his outlook on liturgical issues from the 1620s through to the 1660s may be evidenced by the considerable number of echoes of the *Collection of Private Devotions* in the Durham Book. But his assumptions of where his liturgical preferences placed him between the forces of Rome and protestantism undoubtedly shifted during his exile. This flexibility of approach makes him distinctive among Laudians, even if it did not make him a more tolerant diocesan. In his administration as bishop of Durham, Cosin showed himself as ready as any in his persecution of protestant dissenters. But he retained reserves of personal affability that transcended differences in churchmanship. In the 1660s he made extensive use of the Quaker builder and stonemason John Langstaffe. Back in the 1630s he had forged a friendship of sorts with his diocesan the Calvinist bishop Thomas Morton (who had been his opponent at the York House conference), whose portrait he later commissioned for his library. Both Joseph Mede and Thomas Fuller revised their earlier hostile assumptions regarding the sincerity of Cosin's protestantism. Richard Baxter's portrait of the new bishop of Durham at the Savoy House conference perhaps captures best some of the later Cosin's emollience. 'As he was of a Rustick Wit and Carriage', Baxter reported, 'so he would endure more freedom of our Discourse with him, and was more affable and familiar than the rest' (*Reliquiae Baxterianae*, 2.363).

ANTHONY MILTON

**Sources** The works of … John Cosin, ed. J. Sansom and J. Barrow, 5 vols. (1843–55) · *The correspondence of John Cosin D.D., lord bishop of Durham*, ed. [G. Ornsby], 2 vols., SurtS, 52, 55 (1869–72) · J. Cosin, *A collection of private devotions*, ed. P. G. Stanwood and D. O'Connor (1967) · J. G. Hoffman, 'John Cosin (1595–1672): bishop of Durham and champion of the Caroline church', PhD diss., University of Wisconsin, 1977 · W. H. D. Longstaffe, ed., *The acts of the high commission court within the diocese of Durham*, SurtS, 34 (1858) · P. H. Osmond, *A life of John Cosin* (1913) · M. Johnson, ed., *John Cosin: papers presented to a conference to celebrate the 400th anniversary of his birth* (1997) · G. J. Cumming, *The Anglicanism of John Cosin* (1975) · A. I. Doyle, 'John Cosin (1595–1672) as a library maker', *Book Collector*, 40 (1991) · CUL, MS Mm. 1.45 · BL, Harley MS 7019 · G. J. Cumming, ed., *The Durham Book: being the first draft of the revision of the Book of Common Prayer, 1661* (1961) · P. Smart, *The vanitie and downe-fall of superstitious popish ceremonies* (1628) · J. T. Tomlinson, *The prayer book homilies and articles* (1897) · [J. C. Hodgson], ed., *Northumbrian documents of the seventeenth and eighteenth centuries, comprising the register of the estates of Roman Catholics in Northumberland*, SurtS, 131 (1918) · J. G. Hoffman, '"The Arminian and the iconoclast": the dispute between John Cosin and Peter Smart', *Historical Magazine of the Protestant Episcopalian Church*, 48 (1979), 274–301 · J. G. Hoffman, 'John Cosin, prebendary of Durham Cathedral and dean of Peterborough, 1624–43', *Durham University Journal*, 78 (1985), 1–10 · J. G. Hoffman, 'John Cosin's cure of souls: parish priest at Brancepeth and Elwick, county Durham', *Durham University Journal*, 71 (1978), 73–83 · J. G. Hoffman, 'Another side of "Thorough": John Cosin and administration, discipline and finance in the Church of England, 1624–44', *Albion*, 13 (1981), 347–63 · J. G. Hoffman, 'The puritan revolution and the "Beauty of holiness" at Cambridge: the case of John Cosin master of Peterhouse and vice-chancellor of the university', *Proceedings of the Cambridge Antiquarian Society*, 72 (1984), 93–105 · A. Milton, *Catholic and Reformed: the Roman and protestant churches in English protestant thought, 1600–1640* (1995) · D. Featley, *Cygnea cantio*

(1629) • J. Etherington, *The defence of John Etherington* (1641) • Fuller, *Worthies* (1662) • P. Lake, *The boxmaker's revenge* (2001) • *Reliquiae Baxterianae, or, Mr Richard Baxter's narrative of the most memorable passages of his life and times*, ed. M. Sylvester, 1 vol. in 3 pts (1696) • F. P. Verney, *Memoirs of the Verney family*, 4 vols. (1892–9) • J. Venn and others, eds., *Biographical history of Gonville and Caius College*, 8 vols. (1897–1998) • IGI

**Archives** Durham Cath. CL, corresp. and papers • U. Durham L., corresp. and papers | U. Durham L., letters to Myles Stapleton **Likenesses** portrait, *c*.1635–1640, throne room, Auckland Castle [*see illus.*] • portrait, *c*.1665, Peterhouse, Cambridge • portrait, *c*.1670, loan library, Palace Green, Durham; copy, Durham Cathedral treasury • W. Dolle, line engraving, BM, NPG; repro. in I. Basire, *Funeral sermon* (1673) • copy of portrait at Auckland Castle, Peterhouse, Cambridge • oils, Durham Cathedral • portrait, Gon. & Caius Cam.

**Wealth at death** see will, repro. in *Correspondence*, ed. Ornsby, vol. 2, pp. 294-308

**Cosin, Richard** (1548?–1597), ecclesiastical lawyer, was born in Hartlepool, the son of John Cosin (*d*. 1547) of Newhall, co. Durham, a gentleman and soldier who was killed by the Scottish enemy or by mischance shortly after the battle of Pinkie (September 1547). His mother, Margery, daughter of Henry Pudsey of Bolton, soon afterwards married Roger Medhope of Skipton, where Cosin went to school. He matriculated as a pensioner of Trinity College, Cambridge, on 12 November 1561. Elected to a scholarship in 1563, he graduated BA in 1566 and became a fellow in the same year. He proceeded MA in 1569 and DCL in 1580.

Late in 1579 John Whitgift, formerly his tutor at Trinity and now bishop of Worcester, made Cosin his chancellor, an office that he continued to hold throughout his life, exercising it by deputy from 1584. Thus began a long professional partnership that would eventually place Cosin at the apex of the ecclesiastical court system. On Whitgift's translation to Canterbury he was appointed dean of the peculiar of St Mary-le-Bow and commissioned to exercise *sede vacante* jurisdiction throughout the province (10 December 1583). About this time Cosin was also appointed to the high commission. In 1584 he was elected MP for Downton, and served on a parliamentary committee considering appeals out of the ecclesiastical courts. In October 1585, at the request of Whitgift, he was made a member of Doctors' Commons, having already been admitted as an advocate in the court of arches in February 1581. In 1586 he was elected MP for Hindon, and in March 1587 was appointed, presumably to represent the church's position, to a committee dealing with a motion for promoting a learned ministry and for mitigation of Whitgift's proceedings against puritan ministers. He was MP for Downton again in 1589. Serving also as a chancery lawyer, he was sworn a master in ordinary in October 1588, having previously been a master extraordinary. In the same month Whitgift appointed him auditor (judge of the court of audience), vicar-general, and official principal; while in March 1590 he became official (customarily known as dean) of the court of arches and *ex officio* president of Doctors' Commons. In July 1595 he was confirmed as vicar-general, official principal, and dean of the arches, while the offices of auditor and dean of the peculiar of St Mary-

le-Bow were (with his agreement) assigned to Thomas Byng.

Owing to the loss of records of the southern high commission and of the court of arches there is only limited evidence of Cosin's practice as an ecclesiastical judge, but he is known to have taken a major part in proceedings against leading puritans. His career as a polemical defender of the church against puritan critics can be traced more clearly. *An Answer to the Two First and Principall Treatises of a Certeine Factious Libell* (1584) refuted William Stoughton's arguments that non-preaching ministers could not exercise a lawful ministry and that dispensations for holding benefices in plurality were unlawful; while *Ecclesiae Anglicanae politeia in tabulas digesta*, drawn up in the late 1580s but not published until 1604, reflected the conservative cast of Cosin's thinking on the church's constitution. *Conspiracie, for Pretended Reformation: viz. Presbyteriall Discipline* (1592) purported to expose a puritan plot behind the doings of the pretended messiah William (Frantic) Hacket in the previous year. Far more important was *An Apologie: of, and for Sundrie Proceedings by Jurisdiction Ecclesiasticall* (1591); only about forty copies were initially printed, but in 1593 Cosin published a greatly enlarged version to refute attacks on the use of *ex officio* oath made by Sir Robert Beale and the common lawyer James Morice. The *Apologie* became the standard defence of the jurisdiction of the church courts and high commission.

Shortly before his death Cosin purchased lands at Cote and Aston in Oxfordshire. These featured in his will, which included substantial bequests to Trinity College where Cosin had been, he recalled, 'an unprofitable student'. Whitgift was referred to as 'mine especiall good lord' (PRO, PROB 11/90, fol. 423*v*). Cosin died unmarried at his chambers in Doctors' Commons on 30 November 1597, and was buried at Lambeth on 9 December. Lancelot Andrewes preached the funeral sermon, while another future bishop, William Barlow (whose education Cosin had paid for), published in 1598 a Latin eulogy that praised Cosin for his extensive learning, marvellous powers of memory, and ready wit. Physically he was said to have been handsome, with a long beard and ruddy complexion, robust and well proportioned if a trifle stout, his presence lacking neither authority, dignity, nor grace. From his very appearance, claimed Barlow, one would readily believe him not only good, but great. The puritan victims of his sharp strictures no doubt harboured different views.                                    MARTIN INGRAM

**Sources** W. Barlow, *Vita et obitus … Richardi Cosin* (1598) • Cooper, *Ath. Cantab.*, 2.230–32, 549 • HoP, *Commons, 1558–1603*, 1.660–61 • G. D. Squibb, *Doctors' Commons: a history of the College of Advocates and Doctors of Law* (1977), 39, 86, 116, 163 • D. M. Owen, *A catalogue of Lambeth manuscripts 889 to 901 (carte antique et miscellanée): charters in Lambeth Palace Library* (1968), 24, 33, 36, 38 • Archbishop Whitgift's register, LPL, vol. 1, fol. 92; vol. 2, fols. 159–6 • PRO, PROB 11/90, sig. 111; 30/26/8, fols. 423–8; 30/26/8, fols. 35*v*–64 • PRO, PRO 30/26/8, fols. 35*v*–64*v* • Inner Temple Library, London, Petyt MS 538/54, fol. 19*r–v*; Barrington MS 29 (18), fol. 19; fols. 691*r*–6*r* • bishops' register, diocese of Worcester, 1571–1625, Worcs. RO, fols. 19–74 *passim* • consistory court acts books, 1581–6, 1587–94, *passim*; consistory court deposition book, 1574–82, Worcs. RO, Worcester diocesan archives, 794.011 [BA 2513/3–4]; 794.052, fols. 339*v*, 340*r*, 364*r*[2102/2]

**Cosslett, (Vernon) Ellis** (1908–1990), physicist and electron microscopist, was born on 16 June 1908 in Cirencester, Gloucestershire, the eighth child in the family of six boys and five girls of Edgar William Cosslett, carpenter, and his wife, Anne Williams. His father worked on the earl of Eldon's Stowell Park estate, and they lived in an isolated house on the site of the Roman villa at Chedworth. Because of illness, Ellis was already seven when he entered elementary school in Cirencester, 8 miles from home. At twelve he won a junior county scholarship to Cirencester grammar school, and in 1926 a county scholarship took him to Bristol University, where he obtained first-class honours in chemistry (1929).

In 1929 Cosslett was awarded an ICI research studentship to work for a Bristol PhD in chemistry. He spent the second year at the Kaiser Wilhelm Institute for Physical Chemistry in Berlin, and took full advantage of the opportunity, having acquired some German while an undergraduate. However, he did not know that at that very time the electron microscope was being invented by M. Knoll and E. Ruska only a few miles away. Witnessing the rise of the Nazi party had a traumatic effect, and he became a lifelong worker for left-wing causes, though he concealed these views from most of his colleagues. He obtained his PhD in 1932, and a London MSc in 1939.

Cosslett moved to London in 1935 to teach at Faraday House and research part-time on electron optics at Birkbeck College under P. M. S. Blackett, and later J. D. Bernal. In 1939 he was awarded a Keddey–Fletcher–Warr research fellowship but, in the autumn, Birkbeck was evacuated to Oxford, and he spent the Second World War years teaching physics to short-course officer cadets in the electrical laboratory of Oxford University. He maintained his interest in electron optics and became increasingly convinced of the possibilities of the electron microscope: although he had barely set eyes on one, he was a founder of the electron microscope group of the Institute of Physics in 1946.

In the same year Cosslett was awarded an ICI fellowship at the Cavendish Laboratory, Cambridge, where there was an electron microscope (EM), which had been received during the war under lend-lease arrangements with the USA. Cosslett's life's work was now beginning. Even before he was appointed lecturer in 1949 he started to attract bright young research students to his EM section, nearly all of whom made important contributions to electron microscopy then, and in their later careers. At its peak the section had forty members. Noteworthy projects which were brought to successful conclusions were: the X-ray projection microscope (1955), the X-ray scanning microprobe analyser (1959), a high voltage (750 kilovolts) electron microscope (1966), and, jointly with the Cambridge engineering department, a high resolution (to less than 0.2 nm) electron microscope (1979). Commercial developments followed from all these projects. Writing occupied much of Cosslett's time and he published four

books, including *Practical Electron Microscopy* (1951) and *Modern Microscopy* (1966), and many papers.

Cosslett was little involved with undergraduate teaching, and was not elected to a college fellowship until 1963; his college then was Corpus Christi. In 1965 he became reader in electron physics and was also awarded the ScD. Cosslett's achievements, which were considerable, lay not in proposing new principles, or the design and engineering of new instruments, but in drawing together the many diverse strands of the rapidly developing subject that embraced the whole of biology and material sciences. He was adept in attracting good students, guiding them towards rewarding projects, obtaining grants to finance them, and keeping them informed about work in progress in other laboratories all over the world. Early on, he very quickly built up an international reputation, and was a founder member and first secretary (1955) of the International Federation of Societies for Electron Microscopy.

In 1972 Cosslett was elected a fellow of the Royal Society; he was awarded its royal medal in 1979. He shared the Duddell medal of the Institute of Physics (1971), and received honorary degrees from Tübingen (DSc, 1963) and Göteborg (MD, 1974). He was an honorary fellow (1965) of the Royal Microscopical Society and served as president in 1961–3.

Cosslett was a mild-mannered and courteous man but there were fires within, which, on rare occasions and to the dismay of those present, would burst out spectacularly. Outside microscopy, interests that he shared with his second wife included mountain walking, listening to music, and gardening. In 1936 he married Rosemary, a teacher at Clifton Girls' College and daughter of James Stanley Wilson, graduate electrical engineer, of Barking, Essex. In 1940 the marriage was dissolved, and in the same year he married Anna Joanna, daughter of Josef Wischin, a railway official in Vienna. She was a microscopist who had recently arrived in London as a refugee; they had a son and a daughter. She continued with her research and played an important part in the EM section until her death in 1969. After some years of increasing disability, Cosslett died at his home, 31 Comberton Road, in the village of Barton near Cambridge on 21 November 1990.

DENNIS MCMULLAN, *rev.*

**Sources** T. Mulvey, *Memoirs FRS*, 40 (1994), 61–84 • V. E. Cosslett, 'The development of electron microscopy and related techniques at the Cavendish Laboratory, Cambridge, 1946–1979', *Contemporary Physics*, 22 (1981), 3–36 and 147–82 • personal knowledge (1996) • private information (1996)
**Archives** CAC Cam., corresp. and papers
**Wealth at death** £100,576: probate, 1 March 1991, *CGPLA Eng. & Wales*

**Cossor, Alfred Charles** (1861–1922), manufacturer of electronic and medical equipment, was born in Islington, London, on 8 July 1861, the elder son of Alfred Charles Cossor and his wife, Elizabeth, *née* Freeman. He joined his father's business making thermometers and barometers, in 1875, but left in 1890 to set up his own business as a scientific glass-blower in Clerkenwell. Cossor was then able to take advantage of the expansion in electrical studies during the final decade of the nineteenth century; colleges and research laboratories were a ready market for his sealed vacuum tubes. His customers included Sir William Crookes, who was investigating the properties of electrical discharges in a vacuum.

Crookes's researches were followed up by physicists in several countries. Röntgen, in Vienna, discovered the short-wavelength X-rays in 1895. The subsequent demand for X-ray tubes, both for research and for medical diagnosis, created a profitable market for Cossor's products; he later claimed, in his company's advertisements, that he was the first to make these tubes in Britain. Another important development from Crookes's work was Braun's invention of the cathode ray tube in Germany; here, again, Cossor claimed that his own cathode ray tubes were, in 1902, the first to be produced in Britain.

In 1892 Cossor married Alice, the daughter of George Parker, an estate bailiff. After her death he married Elsie Mary, *née* Vincent, in 1919.

All the devices produced by Cossor in the nineteenth century had been intended for medical or scientific research laboratories. But during the first decade of the twentieth century he started making apparatus for the rapidly growing commercial market. He supplemented his output of X-ray tubes with miniature electric light bulbs for surgical probes; he later marketed similar, but somewhat larger bulbs for miners' lamps and motor-car headlamps. He also made his first thermionic radio valve in 1907, but mainly as an experiment, for such valves had limited practical application while their use was the subject of patent litigation between the leading radio companies.

In 1908 Cossor formed a new limited company, A. C. Cossor. He was joined by a young Australian engineer, W. R. Bullimore, who took over the day-to-day running of the business. Cossor himself performed the less onerous duties of company chairman. By the outbreak of the First World War he had retired to Fawley in Hampshire, leaving Bullimore virtually in charge. The change in management came at about the same time as a large increase in orders for radio valves from the armed services, obliging the company to move to larger premises at Highbury in north London, where extra production capacity could be installed. Bullimore expanded radio component production after the war, and in 1922 launched a new range of high quality valves to coincide with the formation of the BBC. Expansion continued after Cossor's death with the manufacture of radio receivers and, in the late 1930s and 1940s, of television sets and radar equipment based on the company's valves and cathode ray tubes.

When he founded his business, Cossor was regarded by the few scientists who knew him as one of the country's best glass-blowers. At and after his death his name was recognized nationwide as a manufacturer of radio equipment for a large domestic market. Ironically, this increasing fame had been brought about mainly by Bullimore's enterprise rather than by Cossor himself!

Relieved of his business responsibilities, Cossor took an active part in local affairs at Fawley, serving as churchwarden and as harbour master. He was interested in the conservation of Fawley, and particularly in the restoration of the parish church. He was a member of the London lodge of freemasons. He died at his home, Fawley Cottage, Fawley, on 27 May 1922, survived by his second wife.

ROWLAND F. POCOCK

**Sources** F. Brittain, 'Cossor, Alfred Charles', *DBB* · K. Geddes and G. Bussey, *The setmakers: a history of the radio and television industry* (1991), 48, 114 · S. G. Sturmey, *The economic development of radio* (1958), 35 · d. cert. · *CGPLA Eng. & Wales* (1922)
**Wealth at death** £17,007 8s. 9d.: probate, 6 July 1922, *CGPLA Eng. & Wales*

**Costa, Alvaro Jacob** [Alvaro Rodrigues] **da** (1646–1716), merchant, was born in Lisbon, the only child of Fernão Mendes da Costa (1608–1670), an important New Christian merchant and government official from Trancoso, Beira Alta, Portugal. He was the son of his father's first marriage to Brites da Costa, daughter of Alvaro Rodrigues of Elvas. His father, widowed twice, was suspected, together with his third wife, Branca Rodrigues, of judaizing; Branca was finally condemned at the Lisbon *auto-da-fé* of 14 April 1666 and probably burnt at the stake. Fernão fled to London in 1662 or earlier with his son Alvaro, then a youth and reputedly a page-boy to Catherine of Braganza. In a list of good Catholics, Fernão is referred to as 'forced to leave Portugal for fear of the Inquisition and living in London' (Samuel, 1961, 42, n. 26); as such, he may well, as Samuel suggests, have been associated with Duarte da Silva in handling the dowry of Catherine of Braganza in 1662. He certainly arrived with substantial funds. The ledgers of Alderman Edward Backwell, goldsmith and banker, show for 1663 accounts in Fernão's name with a turnover of £30,490, and he was able to buy a huge quantity of pepper at an East India Company sale.

Da Costa himself is frequently referred to as the founding father of the Anglo-Sephardi community in London, though neither he nor his father was ever a professing Jew in the usual sense of the term. He remained uncircumcised, never figured in the synagogal records, and in his will of 1710 did not leave money for alms-giving to the synagogue, or ask to be buried in the Jewish burial-ground at Mile End. Indeed, he continued to profess Christianity, perhaps because initially he hoped to return to Portugal, perhaps from religious indifference or cynicism, and certainly through self-interest. As a Christian he could and did become a naturalized Englishman—the first Jew to do so—on 30 October 1667, as soon as he attained his majority, taking the sacrament as required, and swearing the prescribed Christological oaths of allegiance and supremacy.

Da Costa was admitted, on 5 August 1668, as a freeman of the East India Company, again taking the Christological oaths, and now in a position to promote his own, his family's, and his friends' mercantile interests. Chief among these was the import of diamonds from India. As well as cotton stuffs from there, he imported brazilwood from the Azores, and exported a variety of goods, such as coral from Italy to India, essential as a trade for diamonds, and hats, woollen cloth, and stockings for the South American trade via Lisbon, Seville, and the Canaries. He and his associates (principally his first cousins, Dr Fernando Moses *Mendes (1647–1724) and John Joseph Mendes da Costa (1655–1726), two other founding fathers of the Anglo-Sephardi community) acted as brokers for customers in Antwerp, Amsterdam, Paris, and other European centres, and were involved in shipments of bullion, thus moving from trade to finance. Da Costa dominated Jewish mercantile activities in the City of London for the next thirty years; he was, for instance, one of the two largest individual London importers of diamonds from 1669 to the end of the century. Despite the fact that he had certainly been baptized in Lisbon, as a young man of twenty-six he received adult baptism on 9 October 1672 at St Katharine by the Tower, thus confirming his allegiance to the established church, and parrying any charge of popery. He appears in the court books of the East India Company, buying and selling stock and having his knuckles rapped on occasion for allowing his name to be used by non-freemen ('interlopers') to avoid paying dues. He was one of the first Jews to subscribe to Bank of England stock (7 December 1696).

As a naturalized Englishman, da Costa could hold absolute title to land, and was the first Jew to do so. In 1675 he bought a house on Highgate Hill (later known as Cromwell House), which he shared with his cousins, and in 1677 bought a house in Budge Row in the City. In 1667 he married his cousin, Leonor Mendes Gutiérres (1651–1727). Their three sons, Anthony Moses da *Costa, John Benjamin da Costa (1674–1752), and Fernando Joseph da Costa (1683–1753) were in their turn noted merchants; all were professing Jews, although Anthony was baptized on 12 January 1679. Da Costa died in early February 1716 and was, despite all, buried in the Jewish burial-ground at Mile End. His religious beliefs remain a mystery. Although Hyamson and others see him as a pillar of Anglo-Jewry, the evidence is against this. His ties with the Portuguese Jewish community seem to be based on ethnic identity and family solidarity rather than on any religious beliefs or practices.                    NORMA PERRY

Sources private information (2004) • E. B. Sainsbury, ed., *A calendar of the court minutes … of the East India Company*, 11 vols. (1907–38) • E. R. Samuel, 'The diamond trade in the late seventeenth century, with special reference to London', MPhil diss., U. Lond., 1978 • M. Woolf, 'Foreign trade of London Jews in the seventeenth century', *Transactions of the Jewish Historical Society of England*, 24 (1970–73), 38–58 • G. Yogev, *Diamonds and coral: Anglo-Dutch Jews and eighteenth-century trade* (1978) • N. Perry, 'Anglo-Jewry, the law, religious conviction and self-interest (1655–1753)', *Journal of European Studies*, 14 (1984), 1–23 • will, 23 March 1710, PRO, PROB 11/553, sig. 134 and PROB 11/555, sig. 242 • E. R. Samuel, 'The first fifty years', *Three centuries of Anglo-Jewish history*, ed. V. D. Lipman (1961), 27–44 • T. M. Endelman, *Radical assimilation in English Jewish history, 1656–1945* (1990) • N. Perry, 'Voltaire and the Sephardi bankrupt', *Jewish Historical Studies*, 29 (1982–6), 39–52 • A. M. Hyamson, *The Sephardim of England: a history of the Spanish and Portuguese Jewish community, 1492–1951* (1951) • 'Livro dos homens', Inquisição de Lisboa, Portuguese National Archives, fols. 420, 423 • 'Livro das mulheres', Inquisição de Lisboa, Portuguese National Archives, fol. 190v • 'Autos-da-fé, 1609–1704', Portuguese National Archives, 159/6/862 • IGI

Wealth at death very rich; left two houses; over £21,000 bequests; residue to sons: will, 23 March 1710, PRO, PROB 11/553, sig. 134

**Costa, Anthony Moses da** (1667×9–1747), merchant, the eldest son of Alvaro Jacob da *Costa (1646–1716), also a merchant, and Leonor Mendes Gutiérres (1651–1727), was born in Budge Row, in the City of London. He was baptized on 12 January 1679 at St Antholin, Budge Row, presumably because his father wished him to have the advantages of being a member of the established church. But he became a professing Jew. He was a member of the *mahamad* (governing body) of the Sephardi synagogue in Bevis Marks, 1720–21. He had been its *gabay* (treasurer) in 1710, and was a *parnas* (warden) in 1716, 1720, and 1730. He was presiding warden in 1735 and was on the board of deputies in 1739. On 13 August 1698 he married his second cousin Catherine Mendes (1679–1756) [*see* Costa, Catherine da], the daughter of Dr Fernando Moses *Mendes (1647–1724), and they had six children. Catherine is reputed to have been born and baptized in Somerset House, where her father was body physician to Queen Catherine; although there is no documentary evidence that, as is asserted, the queen was her godmother, the infant is at the least likely to have been named after her, as this is the first time that anyone in the family was called Catherine.

Like his father, da Costa was in his day prominent in the East India trade and was also a leading figure in banking and commerce. He owned Bank of England stock, but was never, as used to be said, a director. He aligned himself firmly with Jewish interests on occasion. From 1713 to 1717 he was involved in gradually persuading the East India Company to relax its attitude to non-company diamond merchants (many of whom were Jews), and in 1735 he successfully protested, with five other firms (four of them Jewish), against the reimposition of higher import duties on coral going into Madras. In 1739 he was one of the deputies who, albeit fruitlessly, prepared and presented a petition to the lord mayor and aldermen of the City asking for an increase in the number of sworn Sephardi brokers.

Besides engaging in the India trade, da Costa dealt in East India Company stock and was well known in the exchange and discount business. To his considerable cost he invested heavily in the South Sea Company. He could be litigious. In 1727 he applied for admission to the Russia Company (either because he was diversifying or because he wanted to bring a test case). Although there was no legal impediment to admitting a Jew, the company refused him entry—as a Jew. Justifiably indignant, he published a brief account of the affair. The following year he took legal steps to force the company to admit him but was defeated, as the company successfully petitioned parliament to emend its charter to provide for exclusion on the grounds of religion. In 1736, when he, again probably with justice, considered himself unfairly treated in a financial matter, he again resorted to print to publicize the injustice. About 1730 he was, together with two other noted Jewish merchants, appointed commissioner for the new colony of Georgia; the three raised a fair sum of money, but instead of handing the money over to Lord

Egmont and the other trustees, they spent it on sending out in 1733 forty emigrants, including two poor Ashkenazi families, of their own choice. By the time, a year later, that the trustees procured the surrender of their commissions, their protégés had already landed in Savannah.

Da Costa lived in style in his house in Winchester Street, off London Wall, and in the house on Highgate Hill that he had inherited from his father in 1716. He died on 3 March 1747, his fortune much diminished, probably as a result of his speculations in the South Sea Company. He was buried the following day, in the Jewish burial-ground at Mile End, as his will requested.

Catherine da Costa is notable as the first Anglo-Jewish miniaturist. From 1712 to 1730 she was a pupil of Bernard Lens, royal miniaturist and drawing master to the royal children. There is a signed miniature by her of Mary Stuart (probably copied from one by Bernard Lens) in Ham House, Surrey. Miniatures by her on ivory of her little son Abraham and of a cousin are in the Jewish Museum, Albert Street, London, and a full-length portrait of her father in his doctoral robes is now in the synagogue of the Spanish and Portuguese Jewish congregation in Ashworth Road, London. While Voltaire was in London (1726–8) to publish the *Henriade*, he became acquainted with Anthony and Catherine da Costa, and they both, together with six other members of the family, subscribed to the publication.

NORMA PERRY

**Sources** private information (2004) · E. Mendes da Costa, 'Genealogical notes', *GM*, 1st ser., 82/1 (1812), 21–4 [BL, Add. MS 29867] · G. Yogev, *Diamonds and coral: Anglo-Dutch Jews and eighteenth-century trade* (1978) · N. Perry, 'Voltaire and the Sephardi bankrupt', *Jewish Historical Studies*, 29 (1982–6), 39–52 · [A. da Costa], *The case of Mr Anthony da Costa with the Russia-Company* [1727] · [A. da Costa], *The case of Mr. da Costa with Mr. Monmartel, relating to a bill of exchange* (1736) · will, 9 March 1747, PRO, PROB 11/753, sig. 68 · N. Perry, 'City life in the 1720s: the example of four of Voltaire's acquaintances', *The secular city: studies in the Enlightenment, presented to Haydn Mason*, ed. T. D. Hemming, E. Freeman, and D. Meakin (1994), 42–56 · G. Rudé, *Hanoverian London* (1971) · A. M. Hyamson, *The Sephardim of England: a history of the Spanish and Portuguese Jewish community, 1492–1951* (1951) · L. R. Schidlof, *The miniature in Europe in the 16th, 17th, 18th, and 19th centuries*, 1 (1964) · parish register, London, St Antholin, 12 Jan 1679 [baptism] · will, PRO, PROB 11/753
**Wealth at death** much reduced (probably) by South Sea Disaster, 1720: will, PRO, PROB 11/753, sig. 68

**Costa** [née Mendes]**, Catherine** [Rachel] **da** (1679–1756), miniature painter, was born in London in 1679, the eldest daughter of Dr Fernando (Moses) *Mendes (1647–1724) and his wife, Isabel (Rachel) Henriques (d. 1691), daughter of Diego Rodrigues Marques. Mendes's parents were born in Portugal and married in London. Fernando Mendes was physician to Charles II and Catherine of Braganza and conformed to the Roman Catholic church as long as he held that office. Catherine was baptized at Somerset House and named after her godmother, the queen; like her mother she was given the Jewish name of Rachel. Fernando Mendes shared a household with his brother-in-law and cousin, Alvaro da Costa, at Budge Row in the City of London and at Highgate House (later called Cromwell House), where the children of both families were brought up as

Jews. Catherine married Alvaro's eldest son, Anthony Moses da *Costa (1667×9–1747), in synagogue on 13 August 1698. Like his father he was a prosperous merchant. Catherine learned miniature painting from Bernard Lens the younger (1682–1740) and was also one of the earliest artists to paint in watercolours on ivory. George Vertue wrote of her:

> One of the Da Costa Jews daughters learn't to limn of Bernard Lens for many years she having begun in 1712 continued to 1730—in this time she coppyd many pictors and limnings mostly all the remarkable pictors of Fame in England painted by Rubens, Vandyke and other masters which Mr Lens her instructor had copyd, all furnished a Room and are said to be done by herself which makes a very good collection for a Lady's Cabinet.   (BL, Add. MS 23079, fol. 26)

Catherine da Costa's full-length watercolour portrait of her father is at the Spanish and Portuguese Synagogue, Maida Vale. Most of her known paintings are miniatures of her family and friends. The most charming is her 1714 portrait of her only son, Abraham (1704–1760), at the age of ten, now in the Jewish Museum, London. This was painted on ivory with the background in oils, the hair and costume in gouache, and the hands and face in watercolour. Her gouache miniature on ivory of two young children holding an orange almost certainly depicts her grandchildren of the Suasso family, which supported the house of Orange (ex Sothebys, 16 March 1999). During Voltaire's visit to England, from 1723 to 1726, Anthony da Costa subscribed to his *Henriade* and Voltaire dined with the da Costas. He wrote, 'Madame Acosta dit en ma presence a un abbé qui vouloit la faire chrêtienne. Votre Dieu, est il né juif? Ouy. Est il mort juif? Ouy. Eh bien soyez donc juif' (Voltaire, *Notebooks*, 1968, 26).

Da Costa died on 11 December 1756 in London and was buried in the Portuguese Jews' new cemetery, Mile End, Middlesex. She bequeathed her miniatures to her son, Abraham, for life, to be divided after his death between the families of her four daughters. Some of these are in the Amsterdam Jewish Historical Museum. Catherine da Costa was a well-trained and accomplished amateur miniaturist and the earliest known English-born Jewish artist.

EDGAR SAMUEL

**Sources** A. Rubens, 'Early Anglo-Jewish artists', *Transactions of the Jewish Historical Society of England*, 14 (1935–9), 91–129 · A. Rubens, 'Francis Town of Bond Street (1738–1826) and his family with further notes on early Anglo-Jewish artists', *Transactions of the Jewish Historical Society of England*, 18 (1953–5), 89–111 · R. D. Barnett, *Catalogue of the permanent and loan collections of the Jewish Museum London* (1974), nos. 858, 902 · E. Mendes da Costa, genealogy of the Mendes da Costa family, BL, Add. MS 29867 · D. Foskett, *Miniatures: dictionary and guide* (1987) · N. Perry, 'Voltaire's first months in England: another look at the facts', *Studies on Voltaire and the Eighteenth Century*, 284 (1991), 115–38, esp. 134 · Voltaire, *La Henriade* (The Hague, 1728) · L. D. Barnett, ed., *Bevis Marks records, 2: Abstracts of the Ketubot or marriage contracts of the congregation from earliest times until 1837* (1949) · M. Rodrigues-Pereira and C. Loewe, eds., *Bevis Marks records, 6: The burial register (1733–1918) of the Novo (New) Cemetery of the Spanish and Portuguese Jews' Congregation, London* (1997) · BL, Add. MS 23079, fol. 26

**Costa, Catherine Rachel da**. *See* Mellish, Catherine Rachel (1710–1747).

**Costa, Emanuel Mendes da**. *See* Mendes da Costa, Emanuel (1717–1791).

**Costa** [*née* Murphy], **Margaret Mary** (1917–1999), restaurateur and writer on cookery, was born on 30 August 1917 in Umtali, Southern Rhodesia, where her father, Michael John Murphy, was a senior official in the customs and excise department of the Southern Rhodesian government. His job entailed frequent moves while she was growing up, including a time in Mozambique, before they moved to England in 1932. She spent two years at St Mary's Convent, Ascot, before winning an exhibition to Lady Margaret Hall, Oxford, in 1935 to read English. She changed to French in her second year and graduated with a second-class degree in 1938, which her tutors thought could easily have been a first, had she paid as much attention to her subject as to her social life.

Margaret Murphy worked during the early stages of the Second World War for the Royal Institute of International Affairs, then located in Oxford, before moving to a top-floor flat in Monmouth Street, Covent Garden, where she stayed for thirty years. During the latter stages of the war she acted as air raid warden for the surrounding Seven Dials area, and was an assistant principal in the civil service. Later she worked for the blind theatre manager Jack Pemberton, and also took parties of businessmen to France, acting as interpreter. In 1943 she began her career in journalism, submitting recipes to the *Sunday Pictorial*, where she also helped with the agony column. In the post-war years she became one of the first middle-class girls to hire herself out to prepare dinner parties in other people's houses and, despite food rationing, prospered. In 1950 she was working in advertising on food accounts. A friend of Raymond Postgate, she became part of the team that helped him with the early editions of the *Good Food Guide*.

On 30 January 1948 Murphy married, at the Église de Nôtre Dame de France in London, John (Bill) Costa (*b.* 1913/14), a Tin Pan Alley music publisher four years her senior. He was the son of Manolo Costa, a bank clerk. She kept his name throughout her writing career, though they divorced before 11 July 1958, when she married her second husband, a divorced actor, Richard St Helier Curnock (*b.* 1921/2), who was four years her junior. He was the son of George Corderoy Curnock, a journalist. Following their divorce she married, thirdly, on 1 November 1979, William James (Bill) Lacy, a chef from London's East End, and son of William James Lacy, a gardener. She sometimes said that her first husband insisted she cook only English food, and her second nothing but French. The third cooked for her. There were no children of any of the marriages.

Articles that Costa had written for *Farmer's Home* magazine were collected as *A Country Cook* in 1960, but her career really took off when, in 1965, she became the successor to the flamboyant, very successful Robert Carrier as the *Sunday Times* magazine's cookery writer. She wrote the column for twelve years, paying careful attention to the quality of ingredients and once writing a column, revolutionary for the times, solely about salt, pepper, and mustard. She had also come to the attention of Jane Montant, editor of the influential American food magazine *Gourmet*, and wrote an occasional column for her called 'London at Table', which resulted in Costa having an American following. In 1970 she published the book for which she was most celebrated, *The Four Seasons Cookery Book* (republished 1996), with its period, fancy dinner-party recipes, such as chilled avocado soup and duck with orange sauce.

Also in 1970, Costa and Bill Lacy opened their controversial restaurant, Lacy's, in Whitfield Street, just off Charing Cross Road, London. There she was front-of-house, welcoming her American fans, and serving them with her husband's signature dishes of smoked salmon with smoked trout pâté, lamb's liver with orange and Dubonnet, lamb with apricot sauce, and warm fruit salad. This was also the fashionable food of the time, and it so enraged some contributors to the *Good Food Guide* that the editor, Christopher Driver, decided to split the restaurant's entry into 'Love Lacy's' and 'Loathe Lacy's' columns. More importantly both for the history of restaurants and for the finances of Lacy's, they embarked upon a costly experiment in which they would open any bottle of wine on the list, no matter how expensive, and charge only for what was consumed. Trouble set in at once, as the system was, according to Nigel Slater, 'famously abused by her notoriously out-of-control waiting staff,' who drank what they considered their own rightful share before charging the cost to the customer (*The Guardian*). Eventually the Lacys lost the restaurant and virtually all their money, and were said at one point to be living in their car.

In 1984 Costa was diagnosed as having the early symptoms of Alzheimer's disease, and though Lacy struggled to support her in the years that followed, by the time of his death, five years before her own, she no longer recognized him. She ended her days in Bryher Court Nursing Home, 85 Filsham Road, St Leonards, Sussex, where she died on 1 August 1999.　　　PAUL LEVY

**Sources** *The Independent* (9 Aug 1999) · *The Times* (13 Aug 1999) · *The Guardian* (13 Aug 1999) · personal knowledge (2004) · private information (2004) · m. cert. [John Costa] · m. cert. [Richard St Helier Curnock] · m. cert. [William James Lacy] · d. cert.
**Likenesses** portrait, repro. in *The Independent*

**Costa, Sir Michael Andrew Angus** [*formerly* Michele Andrea Agniello] (1808–1884), conductor and composer, was born in Naples on 4 February 1808, the son of Pasquale Costa. He studied with his father, his maternal grandfather Giacomo Tritto, and Giovanni Furno, then at the Real Collegio di Musica with Niccolò Zingarelli; he also took singing lessons with Girolamo Crescentino. For the college he composed a cantata, *L'immagine* (1825), and two operas, *Il delitto punito* (1826) and *Il sospetto funesto* (1827). Other youthful works included an oratorio, *La passione*, a mass, *Dixit dominus*, and three symphonies. His opera *Il carcere d' Ildegonda* was written for the Teatro Nuovo in 1827, when he was also appointed accompanist at the Teatro San Carlo. His opera *Malvina* was composed for the latter in 1829. In the autumn of that year he was sent to England

Sir Michael Andrew Angus Costa (1808–1884), by unknown photographer

by Zingarelli, who had composed his *Cantico d'Isaiah Profeta, xii* for the Birmingham festival; but the directors, distrusting Costa's ability on account of his youth, refused not only to allow him to conduct the work but to pay him a fee unless he sang (as a tenor) at the festival. This he did, but with very moderate success. He was first heard on 6 October in the duet 'O mattutini albori' from Rossini's *La donna del lago*, with Fanny Ayton. On the subsequent days of the festival he sang two solos, besides taking part in ensemble numbers. The criticisms on his performance were unfavourable, and his master's work did not have much greater success. Zingarelli, according to *The Harmonicon*, 'would have acted with more discretion had he kept both his *sacred song* and his profane singer for the benefit of his Neapolitan friends. As a singer [Costa] is far below mediocrity, and he does not compensate for his vocal deficiencies by his personal address, which is abundantly awkward'. Clementi found Costa 'scoring' (probably arranging) a song from Bellini's *Il pirata*, and declared him to be a composer rather than a singer. Costa accompanied himself in this song, 'Nel furor delle tempeste', and the audience showed their displeasure in no uncertain manner.

Costa's real talent was soon recognized, however, and he was appointed *maestro al piano* at the King's Theatre in

London under Laporte's management. His ballet *Kenilworth* was produced here with considerable success in 1831, and in the following year he succeeded Nicholas Bochsa as director of music under the management of Monck Mason. Many of his most effective reforms of the abuses which had crept in among the orchestral players at the opera were now set in train, no doubt much to the disgust of the old members of the band, who on the morning after his début as conductor had presented him with a case containing seven miniature razors in mockery of his extremely youthful appearance. It was probably at this time that he introduced conducting with a baton. The ballet *Une heure à Naples* was his principal work of 1832, and in 1833 he wrote a similar work, *Sir Huon*, for Maria Taglioni, and the vocal quartet 'Ecco quel fiero istante'. In the same year he also became director of the Italian opera at the King's Theatre, winning glowing opinions for the improved standard of the orchestral playing. On 14 January 1837 a new version of *Malvina* was produced as *Malek Adel* at the Théâtre Italian in Paris, with Giulia Grisi, Emma Albertazzi, G. B. Rubini, Antonio Tamburini, and Luigi Lablache, though the London production at Her Majesty's in 1844 was more successful. He wrote another ballet, *Alma*, in 1842, and another opera, *Don Carlos*, in 1844, but was no more fortunate with these. His last major stage work was the ballet *Faust*.

In 1846 Costa, with some of the principal singers and 53 of the 80 members of the orchestra, moved to Covent Garden to found the Royal Italian Opera, and in the same year he was appointed conductor of the Philharmonic Society, where he remained until Wagner took over the 1854 season. In these roles he won the highest praise. On 22 September 1848 he was elected conductor of the Sacred Harmonic Society, a post he held until the society's dissolution in 1882. He directed the Birmingham festival in 1849 with very different results from those which followed his early efforts as a singer. The successive triennial festivals were conducted by him until 1879, as were the Bradford festival of 1853, the triennial Handel festivals at the Crystal Palace from 1857 to 1880, and the Leeds festivals from 1874 to 1880. He remained at Covent Garden until he quarrelled with the manager, Frederick Gye, in 1868, then returned to Her Majesty's; from 1871 until the amalgamation with Covent Garden ten years later he was conductor there under Henry Mapleson's management. He was knighted in 1869, and received many foreign decorations.

The most important of Costa's compositions are the two oratorios *Eli* and *Naaman*, first performed in Birmingham on 29 August 1855 and 7 September 1864 respectively. Though they owe their form, if not their very existence, to the success of Mendelssohn's *Elijah*, they contain many effective passages, attractive melodies, and, in the latter case especially, some fine choral writing. They long remained in the programmes of the Sacred Harmonic Society. The more successful was *Eli*, whose march became very popular; the more ambitious *Naaman* did not find such favour with either public or musicians. Rossini's comment in 1856 was, 'Ce bon Costa m'a envoyé une partition d'oratorio et un fromage de Stilton. Le fromage était très bon' ('That good Costa sent me an oratorio score and a Stilton cheese. The cheese was very good').

Since he lived at a time before faithfulness to a composer's intentions was considered the first qualification for a conductor, it is not surprising that Costa should have made additions to Handel's scores with a view to what he regarded as greater effect. He lacked the perception to see that the simple grandeur of the choruses in *Israel in Egypt* requires no help from modern brass instruments, and therefore inserted trombones and timpani at will here and also in the works of Mozart. Berlioz regarded this as 'slapping a trowelful of mortar on a Raphael', and Shaw also deplored his taste while respecting him for keeping 'his foot down so long on sloppy and vulgar orchestral work'. It must be remembered, however, that Costa reflected the taste of his time, and that but for him the national love of Handel would have been less. It is as a conductor that he is to be remembered, for he was the first master of the art who had worked regularly in England. Not long before his arrival the direction of the orchestra had been from a piano or by the first violin, or by a shared arrangement; the change to the present system had been pioneered by Spohr, but it was some time before conducting became a separate art. His chief characteristics were his indomitable will, his firmness and decisiveness of beat, and his indefatigable energy; he also possessed no small amount of diplomacy, which was of the greatest use in managing recalcitrant prima donnas and other mutinous persons. He vigorously opposed the deputy system among orchestral players. Though many musical subtleties lay beyond his reach, he never failed to realize the music's general effect. Meyerbeer, whose works he conducted at the 1862 Exhibition, called him 'the greatest *chef d'orchestre* in the world', and Verdi, originally hostile, came to find him 'one of the greatest conductors in Europe' and 'un uomo musicale, forte, possente' ('a musical man, strong and powerful'). Many others admired the precision and control of his conducting while noting his lack of emotion and tendency to fast tempos. Shortly before the 1883 Handel festival he suffered a stroke, and he died at 13 Seafield Villas, Hove on 29 April 1884.

J. A. F. MAITLAND, *rev.* JOHN WARRACK

**Sources** J. E. Cox, *Musical recollections of the last half-century*, 2 vols. (1872) • B. Lumley, *Reminiscences of the opera* (1864) • J. Ella, *Musical sketches* (1878) • N. T. Portacci, *Michele Costa* (1934) • G. B. Shaw, *London music as heard in 1888–89 by Corno di Bassetto* (1937) • A. W. Ganz, *Berlioz in London* (1950) • H. Berlioz, *Mémoires* (1870) • F. Walker, 'Rossiniana in the Piancastelli collection', *Monthly Musical Record*, 90 (1960), 203–13 • A. D. Corte, *L'interpretazione musicale e gli interpreti* (1951) • 'Musical festivals', *Quarterly Musical Magazine and Review*, 10 (1828), 453–71, esp. 470 • *The Harmonicon*, 7 (1829), 273
**Archives** BL | Yale U., Beinecke L., letters to T. J. Pettigrew
**Likenesses** J. P. Dantan, bust, 1834, Musée Carnavalet, Paris, France • lithograph, pubd 1835 (after drawing), BM, NPG • C. A. Tomkins, mezzotint, pubd 1862 (after C. Perugini), BM, NPG • Bassano, photograph, NPG • J. E. Mayall, woodburytype photograph, NPG; repro. in T. Cooper, *Men of mark: a gallery of contemporary portraits* (1883) • D. J. Pound, stipple and line engraving (after photograph by Mayall), BM, NPG; repro. in *Illustrated News of the World* •

Spy [L. Ward], cartoon, NPG; repro. in *VF* (6 July 1872) • O. Tassaert, lithograph (after drawing by F. Bouchot), BM • G. Zobel, mezzotint (after photograph), BM • photograph, NPG [*see illus.*] • prints, NPG • two cartes-de-visite, NPG
**Wealth at death** £6789 11*s.* 10*d.*: probate, 18 June 1884, *CGPLA Eng. & Wales*

**Costain, Sir Richard Rylandes** (1902–1966), building contractor and industrialist, was born in Crosby, Liverpool, on 20 November 1902, the elder son of William Percy Costain (*d.* 1929), builder, and his wife, Maud May Smith. W. P. Costain was one of the five sons of Richard Costain (1839–1902), a Manxman who had founded and developed a small but well-equipped and successful building and contracting business in Crosby, into which he took three of his sons.

Costain was sent first to Rydal School at Colwyn Bay, then in 1911 to Merchant Taylors' School at Crosby. By the time he left there in 1920 the family firm, Richard Costain & Sons, had grown to considerable stature on Merseyside. It had built many thousands of houses for sale, artisans' flats for Liverpool corporation, houses and cottages for steelworks and other industries, army camps, munitions factories, churches, theatres, and college extensions. Costain automatically entered the family firm, first learning the trades of the joiner and the bricklayer. He took also a short architectural course in Rome. In 1922 W. P. Costain decided on a move to London, leaving his brothers to continue with the activities in Liverpool, so it was in London that Richard Costain cut his teeth as a builder, notably by working on the firm's large venture on the Kingswood housing estate in Surrey.

By 1927 Costain was joint managing director, and on the death of his father in 1929 R. R. as he was then widely known, became sole managing director. Speculative house building was at that period the firm's main activity, some ten thousand houses being built on eight estates. The London end of the business was floated as a public company in 1933. This marked a policy change; the company set out to be less dependent on house building and many building contracts were won for important public and industrial buildings and for blocks of flats. In 1934 important civil engineering contracts were won for the first time for sewage disposal works, and in 1935 for a variety of works in Persia.

A unique opportunity occurred in 1935 when proposals were made to build a huge block of flats, known as Dolphin Square, on the Embankment, on the site of the former army clothing depot. Costain took a personal decision in a matter of hours to seize the opportunity of purchasing this site and constructing what was not only the biggest block of flats in Europe, but the first to be conceived as a self-contained city community with its own shops and social amenities. He remarked to a colleague: 'in two or three years we'll either drive up to this spot in a Rolls-Royce, or we'll be standing here selling matches'.

This decision demonstrated Costain's spontaneity and courage and also the reputation and liking he had earned, for he was able in a few hours to gather the financial backing which this undertaking involved. His ability to size up a project was matched by his quick assessment of men. He was an inspired picker of staff, and a natural leader. He was short but sturdy in stature, with a forthright manner and a ready smile. He was good company, especially on the golf course, where he was an exceptional club golfer who twice reached the second round of the amateur championship; and at the bridge table, where he was brilliant.

On the outbreak of war in 1939 Costain offered his services to the government and was appointed deputy director of emergency works, later deputy director of works, in the Ministry of Works. After the war, when he was appointed CBE (1946), he returned as chairman to his company, which had become thoroughly experienced and well-equipped for contracting. He saw clearly the national need to earn foreign exchange and set himself the objective of obtaining a half of the company turnover abroad. It was, however, no longer possible to speak of 'the company', for with the launching or absorption of specialist activities, association with other companies in joint ventures, and the formation of subsidiaries and branches in many countries, it became the Costain Group.

Among many domestic contracts in the early post-war years, Costains was responsible for the Festival of Britain buildings and was involved in very large building and civil engineering works in many different countries. Chairman Dick, as he became affectionately known throughout the company, in 1950 replaced the centralized control which had been characteristic of a family business by a system of operating divisions, which led progressively to the structure of something like eighty autonomous companies within the group.

Costain did not keep himself exclusively to company affairs. In 1950 he was elected president of the London Master Builders' Association, and in the same year the government appointed him chairman of Harlow Development Corporation. This was the piece of public work which gave him the greatest satisfaction, and he devoted great efforts to seeing that the town was a well-balanced community. His work there was rewarded in 1954 by a knighthood.

From 1955 to 1957 Costain was president of the export group for the construction industries. Both for this group, and for his own company, he travelled extensively, for he believed in personal knowledge of his customer as well as his staff; he was also concerned with international consortia formed for specialist construction work in many countries. He took a particular interest and pleasure in Southern Rhodesia, where his contract for the construction of the Kariba Dam township frequently took him.

In 1927 Costain married Gertrude, daughter of William John Minto, with whom he had one son and two daughters. He died from coronary thrombosis at his home, Rylandes, The Sands, Farnham, Surrey, on 26 March 1966.

NORMAN KIPPING, rev.

Sources The Times (28 March 1966), 12e · private information (1981) · Bulletin [Costain Group] (June 1965) · personal knowledge (1981) · school register (Merchant Taylors' School, Crosby), 1875–1927, Society of Genealogists · d. cert. · The Engineer (1 April 1966), 519

Likenesses M. Codner, oils, Costain Group Headquarters, 111 Westminster Bridge Road, London · portrait, repro. in Engineer, 519
Wealth at death £58,521: probate, 13 Sept 1966, CGPLA Eng. & Wales

**Costard, George** (bap. 1710, d. 1782), writer on ancient astronomy, was baptized on 20 January 1710 at St Mary's Church, Shrewsbury, the son of the Revd Edward Coster, vicar of St Mary's, and his wife, Anne. Educated at Shrewsbury grammar school, in 1726 he matriculated at Wadham College, Oxford, from where he graduated BD in 1729, BA in 1731, and MA in 1733. He was chosen proctor of the university in 1742, but in 1777 he declined the wardenship of his college on the grounds of age. He was appointed curate of Islip, Oxfordshire, then promoted to be vicar of Whitchurch, Dorset. He became known for the erudition of his writing and in 1764 the lord chancellor procured for him the royal presentation to the vicarage of Twickenham, Middlesex, where he remained for the rest of his life.

While at Oxford, Costard began the studies in Hebrew, Arabic, and other oriental languages that with Greek and Latin gave him unparalleled access to the astronomical literature of classical and early modern eras. He maintained a wide correspondence with other scholars, and amassed a substantial library of ancient texts and mathematical works. From his investigation of the rise and progress of astronomy he concluded that the ancient Egyptians and Babylonians were merely observers, and that it was the application of Greek geometry that had raised it to a science. He derided the Chinese, however, believing that they exaggerated the antiquity of their texts. He also expounded on the identification of places and events mentioned in the Bible. From 1746 he sent numerous letters for publication in the Philosophical Transactions of the Royal Society. His mature views were published as The history of astronomy, with its application to geography, history and chronology, occasionally exemplified by the globes (1767), designed to show students how the subject could be investigated, as well as giving conclusions. From this work the 'Account of Arabian astronomy' was extracted for publication in the first volume of the Asiatic Miscellany printed at Calcutta in 1785.

Costard's admiration of classical Greece and democracy in general led him to regret any form of oppression that retarded the study of science. He lauded the developing state of oriental learning, which he believed would lead to a greater knowledge of the ancient world. He was popular in his parish, and the view of his obituarist in Monthly Review that he 'was left to live in obscurity, unpatronized and unpitied' hardly fits a man who was well known to orientalists and other men of culture. Costard died, unmarried, at Twickenham on 10 January 1782, supposedly in such poverty as to be 'indebted even for the discharge of the last sad duties that man owes to man … to the private charity of a few humble individuals; who while they wept over the ashes of their pastor, knew not the variety of his talents, or the extent of his acquirements' (Monthly Review, 419). He was buried in the south side of Twickenham churchyard, with no monument by his own request. No will or administration has been traced, but the sale of his library is known to have extended over three evenings: 434 books were offered, plus 20 manuscripts, mostly oriental, and 11 lots of scientific instruments, all by the best makers; a 3 foot reflecting telescope by Short and an electrical machine by Adams were the most valuable of these.                ANITA McCONNELL

**Sources** 'Memoir of the Rev. G. Costard', *GM*, 1st ser., 75 (1805), 305–7 · E. Ironside, *The history and antiquities of Twickenham* (1797) · R. S. Corbett, *Memorials of Twickenham* (1872), 121–2 · *Monthly Review*, 76 (1787), 419 · *GM*, 1st ser., 52 (1782), 46 · *N&Q*, 8th ser., 3 (1893), 186 · *A catalogue of the library and philosophical instruments of the late … George Costard* (1782) [sale catalogue, S. Paterson, 19–22 March 1782] · parish register, Shrewsbury, St Mary, 20 Jan 1710 [baptism]
**Likenesses** J. Basire, line engraving (after J. C. Barnes), BM, NPG; repro. in *GM* · engraving, repro. in 'Memoir of the Rev. G. Costard'

**Coste, Pierre** (1668–1747), translator and writer, was born on 27 October 1668 in Uzès (Cévennes), France, the second of sixteen children of Barthélemy Coste (1625–1707), a trader in woollen cloth, and his wife, Marguerite Verdier. At an early age Pierre lived with his maternal grandparents in nearby Anduze, where he attended school. In 1684 he went to the college and the academy in Geneva, where he studied with, among others, the philosopher Jean-Robert Chouet, a moderate Cartesian. In May Coste met Charles Pacius de la Motte (c.1667–1751), who became his lifelong friend and his biographer. Coste studied philosophy and theology at Lausanne from spring 1686 until April 1687, and then theology in Zürich until April 1688. He then studied theology at Leiden with Frederik Spanheim and Étienne Le Moine before going to live in Amsterdam. He was admitted as a proponent of the synod of Amsterdam on 23 August 1690. He was still mentioned as such in September 1697, but by this time he preached little and worked mainly as a corrector and author.

Coste made his writing début with an anonymous 'Discours sur la philosophie', a brief history of philosophy in *Cours entier de philosophie* (1691) by the Cartesian Pierre-Sylvain Régis. Then came Coste's first translation, rendering the second part of *Nouvelle bibliothèque des auteurs ecclésiastiques* (1692) into Latin. He presented himself as a historian with his *Histoire de la vie de Louis de Bourbon II, du nom, prince de Condé* (Cologne, 1693), which also contained a survey of European history from 1640 to 1688; it is a meticulous but not very inspiring work. Coste was also the translator of the first part of the biography of Oliver Cromwell by Gregorio Leti, Jean Le Clerc's father-in-law, which he translated anonymously from the Italian. It was published in Amsterdam in 1694. Le Clerc persuaded, and helped, Coste to translate John Locke's *Some Thoughts Concerning Education* (Amsterdam, 1695) into French. Locke later discovered who was responsible for the anonymous translation, of which he had a good opinion. Next Coste translated the first part of Locke's anonymous *The Reasonableness of Christianity* (Amsterdam, 1696).

After being delayed by illness, Coste left for England in August 1697 to accept a position at Oates, Essex, as the tutor of Francis Masham, the only son of Francis Masham and Damaris Cudworth, daughter of the philosopher Ralph Cudworth. His appointment had been recommended by Locke who had been staying with the Mashams since 1691; Coste also acted as Locke's secretary. In the summer of 1697 Coste had started the French translation of Locke's *An Essay Concerning Human Understanding* at the request of Schelte, a publisher in Amsterdam, and he now continued it under constant discussion with the author. Published in Amsterdam in 1700, it appeared to have won the praise of many, including Jean Le Clerc. At the same time Coste made a translation of *A Lady's Religion*, attributed to the theologian William Stephens, which was published in Amsterdam in 1698. A reprint of this work, to which Coste's translation of a second part was added, appeared in 1703. Coste then published extracts which gained wide attention from Locke's defence against Bishop Stillingfleet's criticism of passages in *The Reasonableness of Christianity* and in the *Essay* in the periodical *Nouvelles de la République des Lettres* (October–November 1699). He made a translation of the second part of Locke's *The Reasonableness* (Amsterdam, 1703), a work which had been delayed because, unknown to his employers, Coste was also occupied with other work, such as drawing up a defence of La Bruyère against Vigneul Marville (Bonaventure d'Argonne) and a review of Peter King's *The History of the Apostle's Creed* (in *Nouvelles de la République des Lettres*, November–December 1702). Coste commemorated Locke's death in 1704 by the famous 'Eloge' (ibid., February 1705) which contained a list of Locke's anonymous works. Locke had for some time shown a certain reserve towards Coste, especially because of the latter's sympathy for the Cartesian philosophical tradition. He had conspicuously passed over Coste in his will, and when it became clear that the remuneration for the translation of *Two Treatises* would be very meagre, Coste promptly stopped work on it. Neither did he translate Locke's *Posthumous Works*.

After Locke's death Coste left Oates. A translation of Damaris Masham's *A Discourse Concerning the Love of God* (1705), a work against the English theologian John Norris, and a review of Matthew Tindal's *The Rights of the Christian Church* in *Histoire des ouvrages des savants* (December 1705) date from this period. In 1706–9 Coste was at Chipley, Somerset, employed as the tutor of the two sons of Edward Clarke, who had been Locke's close friend. During this lonely stay Coste translated a work on insects by Francesco Redi from Italian into Latin (*De animalculis*, Amsterdam, 1708) and Xenophon's *Hieron* (Amsterdam, 1711) from Greek into French. He also annotated the Horatius translation by Jacques Tarteron SJ (Amsterdam, 1710). During 1709–10 Coste stayed for a while with Locke's pupil, the philosopher Anthony Ashley Cooper, third earl of Shaftesbury, on whose request he translated the latter's *Essay on the Freedom of Wit and Humour* (The Hague, 1710). As a refugee Coste was denied a French passport, so he was unable to accompany Shaftesbury on his continental journey; however, he revised a treatise in poor French that Shaftesbury had sent him, which appeared in the *Journal des Scavans* in November 1712. In 1711–12 Coste was in Cambridge as the tutor of John Hobard, later duke of Buckingham, with whom he visited The Hague, Utrecht, and Amsterdam in 1712–14, as well as Hanover, where he met Leibnitz. The latter added a letter to Coste to his 'Remarques' on Shaftesbury's philosophy (30 May 1712). On a collective passport Coste travelled with Hobard to Paris, Montpellier, and Bordeaux. Back in England Coste was tutor to Shaftesbury's son in Kensington. During the period 1714–22 Coste published a translation of Plautus's *Captivi* (Amsterdam, 1716), wrote a treatise on the reunion of all Christians for a reprint of his translation of Locke's *Reasonableness* (Amsterdam, 1715), supplied Dutch publishers with dedications to noble ladies for editions of Boileau's *Oeuvres* and Cornelius de Bruin's travel books (both published in Amsterdam in 1718), and on Newton's request he translated his *Optics* (Amsterdam, 1720), the translation being checked by the physicist Jean-Théophile Desaguliers.

In 1722 Coste became the tutor of Edmund Sheffield, second duke of Buckingham, with whom he left for France and Italy in 1726. He was engaged in writing the dedication and preface for an annotated edition of Racine (London, 1723), put considerable effort into corrections and annotations of Montaigne's *Essais* (Paris, 1724), and published an annotated edition of Theophrastus's *Characters* (1731).

There was much amusement when Coste, who was by now sixty-six, married Marie de Laussac, daughter of an army chaplain, in 1735. Apart from the first half of 1736, when they were staying at the duchess of Buckingham's house, the couple lived in Paris, where Marie died on 1 December that year. From then on Coste lived in England and France. In 1743 he became a member of the Royal Society and in the same year he edited a publication of La Fontaine's *Fables choisies* (Paris, 1743). On 24 January 1747 Coste died in Paris, where he was probably buried. His will mentions bequests totalling £2470.  J. J. V. M. DE VET

**Sources** M. E. Rumbold, *Traducteur huguenot Pierre Coste* (1991) · J. Locke, *Que la religion chrétienne est très raisonnable, telle qu'elle nous est représentée dans l'Écriture Sainte: discours sur les miracles … la vie de Coste et anecdotes sur ses ouvrages*, ed. and trans. H. Bouchilloux and M.-C. Pitassi (1999) · S. Mason, 'The afterlife of Pierre Coste' [forthcoming] · *The correspondence of John Locke*, ed. E. S. De Beer, 5–7 (1979–82), nos. 1917, 1940, 2107, 2285, 2480, 2601, 2609, 2746 · *The correspondence of Isaac Newton*, ed. H. W. Turnbull and others, 6 (1976), 228; 7 (1977), 497; letter 1365 · *Jean Le Clerc: epistolario*, ed. M. G. Sina and M. Sina, 4 (Florence, 1997), index, p. 581 · Jan de Vet, 'John Locke in de "Histoire des ouvrages des savants"', *Henri Basnage de Beauval en de 'Histoire des ouvrages des savants', 1687–1709*, ed. H. Bots, 2 (Amsterdam, 1976), 183–269 · H. Bots and L. van Lieshout, *Contribution à la connaissance des réseaux d'information au début du 18e siècle* (Amsterdam-Maarssen, 1984), 112, 138 · J. Almagor, *Pierre Des Maizeaux (1673–1754): journalist and English correspondent for Franco-Dutch periodicals, 1700–1720* (1989), 67, 87–8, 112, 116, 149 · B. Lagarrigue, *Un temple de la culture européenne (1728–1753): l'histoire externe de la 'Bibliothèque raisonée des ouvrages des savants de l'Europe'* (Nijmegen, 1993), 35–40, 69, 104 · J. Sgard and J. D. Candaux, eds., *Dictionnaire des journaux, 1600–1789*, 2 vols. (Paris, 1991), 605, 710, 1016 ['Histoire des ouvrages des savants', 'Journal des savants', 'Nouvelles de la république des lettres']

**Likenesses** portrait, repro. in P. Coste, *Histoire de la vie de Louis de Bourbon … prince de Condé*, 3rd edn, 2 vols. (The Hague, 1748)
**Wealth at death** £2470: Rumbold, *Traducteur*, 28, 162 n. 87, PRO, PROB 11/752, no. 35

**Costeley, Guillaume** (1530–1606), composer, was born at Fontanges in the Auvergne, France; nothing is known of his parentage or education. Having arrived in Paris probably by 1554, he rapidly established himself as the city's leading composer of chansons. By 1560 he had been appointed chamber musician and music tutor to Charles IX, and he mixed with the intellectual circle of Catherine de' Medici. His output, which is almost entirely secular, ceased after his retirement to Évreux, Normandy, in 1570. Theories that he was of Scottish or Irish parentage were once occasionally entertained, but were conclusively discredited by Maurice Cauchie in 1926. Costeley was twice married, first to Jehanne Blacquetot and second to Françoise Deshaies. He died at Évreux on 1 February 1606.  ROGER BOWERS

**Sources** I. Godt, 'Costeley, Guillaume', *New Grove* · M. Cauchie, 'Documents pour servir à une biographie de Guillaume Costeley', *Revue de Musicologie*, 7 (1926), 49–68
**Likenesses** engraving, repro. in Godt, 'Costeley, Guillaume'

**Costello, Dudley** [Dualtache] (*d.* 1667), soldier and outlaw, was of unknown parentage and background, the surname being very common in east Mayo, where the Costellos, reputedly Gaelicized descendants of early English settlers, had given their name to a barony. Nothing is known of his early life but a deposition taken in 1652 names Dudley and Thomas Costello, brothers, as having plundered English settlers late in 1641. This is difficult to reconcile with two letters written by Sir Charles Coote, parliamentary president of Connaught, in June 1647, which describe Thomas Costello and his brother Dudley as Catholics, 'but such as never did any prejudice to the Protestants' (*Egmont MSS*, 1.413). They had given his forces important assistance, controlled three fortresses which they were willing to surrender to parliament, and wanted only to be received into the state's pay. This alliance may prefigure the later pragmatic co-operation between Coote and Owen Roe O'Neill. Alternatively, it may have reflected a hostility towards Viscount Dillon, royalist commander in the region, whose family occupied the former lands of the Costellos. Coote reported that Dudley and Thomas had surrendered Dillon's brother, Captain Theobald Dillon, to him, and Dillon himself was later to claim that his estate had been ruined in Cromwell's time by the rebellion of Dudley Costello. By 14 February 1653, on the other hand, Dudley Costello, now a lieutenant-colonel, was part of the Catholic garrison at Inishbofin, where he was a signatory to articles of surrender guaranteeing transportation to Spain for himself and up to a thousand men, though the Commonwealth seems to have decided to transport them to Flanders.

By 6 May 1653 Costello was in Brussels, where he entered the Spanish service as colonel of a regiment to be composed of 732 men he had already brought from Ireland and a further 600 he was to recruit there. A subsequent grant of a Spanish pension (13 November 1658)

described him as having commanded a regiment in Lorraine, while a licence to return to England and Ireland on business (10 July 1660) identified him as a pensioner in the company of Colonel James Dempsey. Ormond later described him to Clarendon as 'a tall fellow, that was in Flanders when you and I were there' (Prendergast, 85). The Act of Settlement (1662) named Captain Dudley Costello as one of those who had served faithfully under the king's ensign overseas and were to be restored to their estates.

On 7 June 1666 Sir Arthur Forces, writing from co. Longford, reported that the outlaw Edmund Nangle was to be joined by Dualtache Costello, 'a man more considerable than himself for matters of action' (*Ormonde MSS*, 3.225). A proclamation on 25 June named Costello along with Nangle and others as having appeared in arms and committed robberies and murders in Connaught and Ulster. This resort to outlawry is normally attributed to an assumed failure to recover his estate. However Costello himself, writing to Viscount Dillon on 18 August, seems to indicate a personal feud, blaming relatives of Dillon for having had him proclaimed without a hearing and promising revenge.

When Nangle was killed in July 1666, leading an attack on Longford town reportedly with 200 men, Costello became leader of his band. In November he destroyed Cornet Ormsby's castle in co. Mayo, despite the resistance of a file of musketeers stationed there, and in December he burnt farms and villages in the baronies of Galen and Costello. On 3 March 1667 he was shot dead in an encounter with soldiers led by Captain Theobald Dillon at Castlemore, on the Mayo–Roscommon border. His head was mounted on St James's gate, Dublin, facing towards Connaught.                                      S. J. CONNOLLY

**Sources** J. P. Prendergast, *Ireland from the Restoration to the revolution, 1660 to 1690* (1887) • B. Jennings, ed., *Wild geese in Spanish Flanders, 1582–1700*, IMC (1964) • R. Dunlop, *Ireland under the Commonwealth* (1913) • M. Hickson, *Ireland in the seventeenth century, or, The Irish massacres of 1641–2, their causes and results* (1884) • *CSP Ire., 1660–62; 1666–9* • *Calendar of the manuscripts of the marquess of Ormonde*, new ser., 8 vols., HMC, 36 (1902–20), vol. 3 • *The manuscripts of his grace the duke of Portland*, 10 vols., HMC, 29 (1891–1931), vol. 1 • *Report on the manuscripts of the earl of Egmont*, 2 vols. in 3, HMC, 63 (1905–9), vol. 1, pt 2

**Costello, Dudley** (1803–1865), journalist and illustrator, was born in Sussex. His father, James Francis Costello, who became a captain in the 14th regiment on 25 May 1803, was born in the barony of Costello, co. Mayo; he died in 1814 or 1815, leaving his wife, Elizabeth, *née* Tothridge (*d.* 1846), and two children in impoverished circumstances. Dudley Costello was educated for the army at Sandhurst, from where he received a commission as ensign in the 34th regiment on 4 October 1821, but his regiment being in India and continuing there, he was placed on half pay on 27 September 1823. He joined the 96th regiment on 29 January 1824, served on the staff in North America and the West Indies, and as an ensign went on half pay on 10 September 1828. While residing in Bermuda he showed much literary talent by editing and writing a weekly journal entitled *The Grouper*, which he continued with limited means for a considerable period.

After his return to England, Costello joined his mother and his sister, Louisa Stuart *Costello (1799–1870), in Paris. He hoped that through the interest of George Canning, to whom he was related through Canning's mother, he might obtain some appointment which would prevent the necessity of a return to his regiment, but the death of Canning ended his chance of preferment. For some months he worked as an artist in the ichthyological section of the *Règne Animal* publication under Baron Cuvier. After this he devoted himself to copying illuminated manuscripts in the Bibliothèque Royale. His copies of the work of King René of Sicily, in English entitled 'Tournaments and their laws', are most accurate and beautiful, and were much admired in Paris. He continued in this line of work for some years, and he and his sister were in fact the first to call public attention to manuscript copying both in Paris and in the British Museum. He helped his sister with the illustrations to her *Specimens of the Early Poetry of France* (1835) and *The Rose Garden of Persia* (1845).

Costello returned to London in 1833. In 1838 he accepted the place of foreign correspondent to the *Morning Herald*, being a very good linguist, and for some time lived at Hanover. He afterwards divided his time between Paris and London, and in 1846 he was the foreign correspondent of the *Daily News*. For thirty years he was a contributor to many of the periodicals of the day, including *Bentley's Miscellany*, the *New Monthly Magazine*, *Household Words*, and *All the Year Round*. Selections from his journalism were later collected and published as *Holidays with Hobgoblins* (1861). In the course of his journalistic work he became acquainted with Charles Dickens, and performed in several of Dickens's amateur theatricals (1845, 1847, and 1850). He was also one of the first council members of Dickens's Guild of Literature and Arts. Costello became sub-editor of *The Examiner* under John Forster, and of his work in this capacity, Henry Morley remarked that he wrote 'all *but* the leaders and reviews, [compiled] the news, etc' (Solly, 200).

On 23 September 1843, Costello married Mary Frances, widow of J. D. Tweedy of Warley House, near Halifax. Soon after this, he produced one of his most popular books, *A Tour through the Valley of the Meuse* (1845), which, like his later *Piedmont and Italy, from the Alps to the Tiber* (2 vols., 1859–61), he also illustrated. In addition to his travel writing Costello wrote several novels, including *Stories from a Screen* (1855), *The Millionaire of Mincing Lane* (1858), and *Faint heart never won fair lady* (1859), but his fiction was inferior to that of his sister. His writing was never sufficiently remunerative; Louisa Costello gave him financial support, and he received a civil-list pension on 19 April 1861.

The death of Costello's wife on 1 May 1865 affected him deeply, and led to a breakdown in health from which he never fully recovered. A projected travel book on a journey to Spain did not serve to lift his depression, and he died of kidney disease at his home, 54 Acacia Road, St John's Wood, London, on 30 September 1865, and was buried in Highgate cemetery.

G. C. BOASE, *rev*. M. CLARE LOUGHLIN-CHOW

**Sources** *GM*, 3rd ser., 19 (1865), 659 · *Bentley's Miscellany*, 58 (Nov 1865), 543–50 · *The Examiner* (7 Oct 1865), 637 · *The letters of Charles Dickens*, ed. M. House, G. Storey, and others, 1–10 (1965–98) · Boase, *Mod. Eng. biog.* · W. G. Strickland, *A dictionary of Irish artists*, 2 vols. (1913) · H. Solly, *The life of Henry Morley* (1898) · A. Lohrli, ed., *Household Words: a weekly journal conducted by Charles Dickens* (1973) · *IGI*
**Archives** BL, letters to Sir Frederick Madden, Egerton MSS 2839–2846, *passim* · NL Scot., letters to William Blackwood & Sons
**Wealth at death** under £3000: probate, 26 Oct 1865, *CGPLA Eng. & Wales*

**Costello, John Aloysius** (1891–1976), taoiseach, was born in Rathdown Road, North Circular Road, Dublin, on 20 June 1891, the second of the three children (he had an elder brother and a younger sister) of John Costello, Land Registry clerk, of Rathdown Road, and his wife, Rose Callaghan. Educated at the O'Connell Schools, Dublin, and University College, Dublin, where he graduated in modern languages and law in 1911, he was called to the bar (King's Inns) in 1914, after winning the King's Inns Victoria prize in 1913. Making his career in the law he was called to the inner bar in 1925 and became a bencher of the Honourable Society of King's Inns in 1926. On 31 July 1919 he married Ida Mary (*d.* 1956), daughter of David O'Malley MD, of Glenamaddy, co. Galway; they had three sons and two daughters.

Closely associated with Hugh Kennedy, principal architect of the constitution of the Irish Free State and first attorney-general, Costello served as assistant law officer, provisional government, 1922, and assistant to the attorney-general in 1922–6, replacing Kennedy as attorney-general in the latter year, and serving in that capacity until the fall of the government of W. T. Cosgrave in February 1932. The two men shared a willingness to harmonize the laws of the Irish state with the prevailing moral values of the Catholic church, and censorship of films and books, a reduction in the number of licensed premises, the prohibition of literature advocating birth control, and the practical denial of divorce characterized these years. The anomaly of marriages recognized by the state but not the church lingered on, and Costello was to admit later that, although requested to, he had not prosecuted for bigamy a woman who married in a Catholic church in Ireland although previously married in a register office outside the state.

During these years, when rapid change was occurring in the British Commonwealth, the young Irish Free State did much to make dominion status synonymous with full sovereignty. At the League of Nations, and more especially in the Commonwealth conferences of 1926 and 1930, and at the 1929 conference on the operation of dominion legislation, which hammered out the terms of the Statute of Westminster of 1931, Costello played a significant role. Part of a team, he prepared the briefs for his political colleagues to present, and to Costello, as to Desmond FitzGerald, Kevin O'Higgins, and Patrick McGilligan, successive ministers for external affairs, much credit belongs. It was in these years too that much of Costello's reputation was secured: enduring friendships were forged, and the respect of political opponents won.

After the advent of Eamon de Valera as head of government in 1932 Costello sought to enter Dáil Éireann and did so successfully in the snap general election of January 1933, as a member for Dublin County. Representing Dublin Townships in 1937, he was returned there also in 1938, was unsuccessful in 1943, but swiftly returned in 1944, remaining in the Dáil until his retirement in 1969, his constituency changing in 1948 to Dublin South-east.

Costello was not leader of Fine Gael, the largest opposition party, when the February 1948 elections brought the possibility of an end to sixteen years of rule by de Valera's dominant Fianna Fáil. The man who filled that post, General Richard Mulcahy, was unacceptable to some of the potential members of a new coalition, however, and after deliberation Costello was approached to lead an alternative government. Much against his own inclination he agreed to serve, and for the next three years the qualities which commended him—his patience, integrity, no-nonsense directness, his loyalty, courage, and humanity—kept together an uneasy association of parties and individuals. That he succeeded surprised many, but there is no doubt that in surviving for so long he not only brought a renewed conviction to the Irish people that alternative government was possible, but he demonstrated the practicality of what had become a growing personal conviction. Tired of opposition for opposition's sake, tired too of what he felt was one-man rule dressed up as party government, he had increasingly felt the need for greater consensus in the making of constructive national policy. Inter-party government from 1948 to 1951 provided a working model, and one which he was to lead again from 1954 to 1957.

During his first period as taoiseach commendable progress was made, after the war and post-war years of stagnation, in the fields of housing and health, agriculture, and social welfare, but two major landmarks stand out. The first was the Republic of Ireland Act, which changed the title of the state to meet nationalist aspiration and so, it was hoped, to take the gun out of politics. The act, announced amid controversy in September 1948 and operative from Easter Monday 1949, removed independent Ireland from the Commonwealth and probably reinforced Northern Irish Unionist determination to remain within the United Kingdom. The second, even more controversial and also strengthening Ulster Unionism, was the attempt of the minister of health to make maternity welfare provision through a generous Mother-and-Child Bill in 1950. The bill brought an open conflict with the Roman Catholic hierarchy which led to the resignation of the minister of health in April 1951 (Costello himself took the portfolio) and soon to the breakup of this first attempt of coalition government, in May.

After acting as leader of the opposition from 1951 to 1954 Costello once more became taoiseach after the May 1954 elections. With experience of office behind him and with a more compact inter-party grouping, he nevertheless chose to continue his quiet form of leadership. He saw to the development of greater economic expertise in the service of the state, and to the provision of welfare services more in keeping with the expansionist Western world of the 1950s. Inflation and a resurgence of militant nationalist activity placed too great a strain on the coalition by 1957, however, and Fianna Fáil returned to power after the elections of March of that year.

On leaving office Costello once more built up a successful legal practice, retiring to the back benches in 1959 when Richard Mulcahy resigned the leadership of Fine Gael to James Dillon. During his last decade in the Dáil he helped to modernize further his party along social democratic lines.

Made a member of the Royal Irish Academy in 1948, and a freeman of the City of Dublin in 1975, and awarded the grand cross of the Pian order, 1962, Costello received honorary LLDs from Montreal, Ottawa, and Fordham, 1948; and the Catholic University of Washington, St John's University (New York), and Iona College, New Rochelle (New York), 1956.

To the end of his life Costello remained untouched by either public office or acclaim. Modest, accessible, helpful, he retained the tolerance and thoughtfulness that had always characterized him. His contributions to the consolidation of the infant state, to its continued enjoyment of parliamentary democracy, and to a more humane and progressive society will not be underrated by future historians. That he made his mark at all in these fields will have been his own reward. He died at his home, 20 Herbert Park, Ballsbridge, Dublin, on 5 January 1976, and was buried in Dean's Grange cemetery two days later. His son Declan also became attorney-general (holding the post from 1973 to 1977) and was subsequently a judge of the High Court (from 1977).      DAVID HARKNESS

**Sources** *Irish Times* (6 Jan 1976) · *Ireland To-day* (30 Jan 1976) · personal knowledge (2004) · J. Whyte, *Church and state in modern Ireland, 1923–70* (1971) · *Dáil Debates*, 67 · D. Fitzpatrick, *The two Irelands, 1912–1939* (1998) · *CGPLA Ire.* (1976)
**Archives** NL Ire., letters to W. G. Fallon · TCD, corresp. with Thomas Bodkin | FILM BFI NFTVA, current affairs footage
**Likenesses** D. Miller, photograph, 1948, Hult. Arch. · L. Whelan, oils, 1948, King's Inns, Dublin · three photographs, 1948–54, Hult. Arch. · S. O'Sullivan, charcoal, 1949, NG Ire. · S. O'Sullivan, pencil drawing, 1949, Dáil Éireann
**Wealth at death** £90,564: probate, 18 Feb 1976, *CGPLA Éire*

**Costello, Louisa Stuart** (1799–1870), miniature painter and author, was born in Sussex, the daughter of Captain James Francis Costello (*d.* 1814/15) of the 14th foot, a native of co. Mayo, and his wife, Elizabeth, *née* Tothridge (*d.* 1846). She was the only surviving sibling of the journalist and illustrator Dudley *Costello (1803–1865); another brother appears to have died at sea in 1813. After the death of her father Louisa went to Paris with her mother. There she helped to support the family by painting miniatures, reportedly funding her brother's education at the Royal Military College at Sandhurst and assisting him financially until his death. About 1820 Costello moved to London, where she continued to paint miniatures, some of which she exhibited at the Royal Academy between 1822

and 1839. Two extant watercolour portraits, of Mlle Sontag (1830; Victoria and Albert Museum) and Queen Victoria (1837; Royal Collection), are executed in a delicate, fashionable style reminiscent of the work of A. E. Chalon. In the 1820s Costello lived at addresses in Brompton, London, and Hammersmith, Middlesex, and by 1833 had moved to Brighton; she also seems to have frequently visited the continent, particularly France, during the 1820s and 1830s. Many of these trips may have been connected with her work as a copyist of illuminated manuscripts in both London and Paris; some examples are held in the British Museum.

From an early age Costello had pursued a parallel career as an author. Two books of poetry, published in 1815 and 1819, were followed in 1825 by a third, *Songs of a Stranger*, some of which were set to music and became popular. In 1835 she published *Specimens of the Early Poetry of France*, lyrical if rather fussy translations of a wide range of medieval French poets. This work made her literary reputation and attracted the attention of Thomas Moore, to whom it was dedicated, and Walter Scott. *The rose garden of Persia* (1845), highly ornamented with decorative borders deriving from original manuscripts held by the Asiatic Society, offered similar renditions of famous Persian poets. Although Costello worked from prose translations rather than the original works her interpretations were satisfactory; her paraphrases of sections of the *Quatrains* of ʿUmar Khayyam, for instance, compare creditably with the celebrated translation by Edward Fitzgerald.

Costello also published several novels, including *The Queen's Poisoner, or, France in the Sixteenth Century* (1841), a ponderous historical novel, and *Clara Fane, or The Contrasts of a Life* (1848), a curious mélange of romantic melodrama, domestic realism, farce, fantasy, and travel journal. Both novels suggest that she had no great talent for fiction, and both her historical biographies and her travel books are far more readable. Her biographies of royal and noble women—which clearly traded on the popularity of similar works by Lucy Aikin, the Strickland sisters, and Mary Anne Everett Green—were creditable examples of this literary genre and generally involved some original research. The four-volume *Memoirs of Eminent Englishwomen* (1844)—which included biographies of Bess of Hardwick, Arabella Stuart, Anne Clifford, Elizabeth of Bohemia, Lady Rachel Russell, Mary Beale, Lady Mary Wortley Montagu, and Susannah Centlivre—seems to have been researched mainly among the books and papers in the duke of Devonshire's library at Chatsworth. Some archival work was undertaken in public and private libraries in Brittany for her *Memoirs of Anne, Duchess of Brittany* (1855), the first full-length biography in English of that Renaissance French queen.

By far the most appealing of Costello's publications are her accounts of tours in Britain and on the continent, such as *A Summer amongst the Bocages and the Vines* (2 vols., 1840) and *Falls, Lakes and Mountains of North Wales* (1845). Well illustrated and lively they 'combine graphic description with that kind of anecdotical archaeology which varies the narrative of travel and adventure' (*The Athenaeum*).

*Summer*, for instance, mingles chatty accounts of local legends and antiquities with passionate outbursts on the deficiencies of French inns and the beauty of the Breton people. Costello also contributed essays and stories to periodicals, principally *Bentley's Miscellany* and *Household Words*, for both of which her brother Dudley also wrote. In 1843 Elizabeth Barrett Browning suggested to R. H. Horne that his *New Spirit of the Age* should include Costello, whom she described as highly accomplished.

Costello's publications won her a modest place in London society as a literary figure, and several friends of rank, including the family of the radical politician Sir Francis Burdett, who later supplemented her scanty literary earnings with a pension. She was also assisted by the grant of a civil-list annuity of £75 on 9 August 1852. Despite her 'pale pretty face and engaging conversation' (*The Athenaeum*) she never married, possibly because of her close-knit family relationships; one biographer comments acidly that 'Miss Costello's life was a long history of devotion to her mother and brother, neither of whom seems to have been particularly grateful' (Kunitz and Haycraft, 151). After the deaths of her mother (in 1846) and her brother (in 1865), she retired to Boulogne, a favourite haunt for impoverished but genteel English society. She died there, of cancer of the mouth, on 24 April 1870 at 20 rue Charles Butor; she was buried in the cemetery of St Martin. The last entry in her diary read 'Oblivion all'. ROSEMARY MITCHELL

**Sources** *The Athenaeum* (7 May 1870), 612 • W. G. Strickland, *A dictionary of Irish artists*, 2 vols. (1913); repr. with introduction by T. J. Snoddy (1989) • A. Lohrli, ed., *Household Words: a weekly journal conducted by Charles Dickens* (1973), 241–2 • Graves, *RA exhibitors* • D. Foskett, *Miniatures: dictionary and guide* (1987) • S. J. Kunitz and H. Haycraft, eds., *British authors of the nineteenth century* (1936) • G. Meissner, ed., *Allgemeines Künstlerlexikon: die bildenden Künstler aller Zeiten und Völker*, [new edn, 34 vols.] (Leipzig and Munich, 1983– ) • Blain, Clements & Grundy, *Feminist comp.* • L. Lambourne and J. Hamilton, eds., *British watercolours in the Victoria and Albert Museum* (1980), 83 • D. Millar, *The Victorian watercolours and drawings in the collection of her majesty the queen*, 1 (1995), 238 • *Wellesley index* • R. Welch, ed., *The Oxford companion to Irish literature* (1996) • *CGPLA Eng. & Wales* (1870)
**Archives** BL, business papers and corresp. with Richard Bentley's firm, Add. MSS 46613–46615, 46650, 46652, *passim*
**Wealth at death** under £600: probate, 13 June 1870, *CGPLA Eng. & Wales*

## Costello, William Birmingham

**Costello, William Birmingham** (1800–1867), surgeon and asylum keeper, was born near Dublin and commenced his medical education there. He completed his studies in Paris, where he lived from 1820 to 1829, working under the eminent surgeons C. L. S. Heurteloup, G. Dupuytren, and J. Civiale, and also acting as a private teacher of anatomy. He settled in London about 1829, specializing in treating the stone, and he was an early advocate in England of the operation of lithotrity (lithotripsy).

Costello published extensively in medical journals and invented various instruments. In 1830–31 he was associated with Michael Ryan, John Epps, and others in a short-lived private medical school in Brewer Street. He later became proprietor of Wyke House Asylum, near Isleworth, Middlesex, and published *An Address to the Visiting Justices of the Hanwell Lunatic Asylum* (1839) and *A Letter to Lord*

*Ashley on the Reform of Private Lunatic Asylums* (1845). His major work was the editorship of *The Cyclopaedia of Practical Surgery*, which commenced publication in parts in 1837 but faltered after the completion of the first volume in 1841. About 1847 Costello moved to Paris and concentrated on his *Cyclopaedia*, commissioning articles from leading French surgeons, which he translated into English. The work was finally completed in four volumes in 1861 but the bulk of the stock was destroyed in a fire.

Costello was married to (Henrietta) Leocadie Magnia Walker; by 1841 they had at least two children, the first of whom, a daughter, was born in 1837. Costello died in the Maison de Santé, in St Mandé, Paris, on 15 August 1867, impoverished by a succession of unfortunate speculations. JOHN SYMONS

**Sources** L. Hahn, *Dictionnaire encyclopédique des sciences médicales*, ed. A. Dechambre, 21 (1878), 34–5 • *The Lancet* (31 Aug 1867) • *Medical Times and Gazette* (31 Aug 1867), 245 • letter, *Medical Times and Gazette* (7 Sept 1867), 275 • *London and Provincial Medical Directory* (1852) • *London and Provincial Medical Directory* (1854) • *Diary of the late John Epps*, ed. Mrs Epps [1875], 181 • *The Lancet* (25 Sept 1830), 16 • *The Lancet* (19 March 1831), 800 • *The Lancet* (9 April 1831), 64 • *CGPLA Eng. & Wales* (1867) • b. cert. [of daughter]
**Archives** Wellcome L.
**Wealth at death** under £450: probate, 21 Nov 1867, *CGPLA Eng. & Wales*

**Costelloe, Rachel Pearsall Conn**. *See* Strachey, Rachel Pearsall Conn (1887–1940).

**Coster family** (*per. c.*1685–1764), copper smelters, came to prominence with **John** [ii] **Coster** (1647–1718). Born probably in the Forest of Dean, Gloucestershire, he was the second of three sons of John [i] Coster (1615–1678), iron-forge manager or smelter in the forest. John [ii]'s elder brother, Arthur (*d.* 1679), was involved in leasing property in Leigh Woods near Bristol in 1678 on behalf of Sir Clement Clerke (*d.* 1693) of Launde Abbey, Leicestershire, who was interested in experimental work in lead smelting. Under the management of Clerke's son Talbot, these experiments resulted in the successful introduction of coal to replace more expensive charcoal, thus lowering the production costs of lead. John [ii] was described in papers relating to a chancery action as 'chief agent' of the process by 1685, when he was thirty-eight. The work was abandoned in that year because patent rights were claimed by George Villiers, fourth Viscount Grandison (*d.* 1699), the entrepreneur with whom the Clerkes worked originally at Leigh Woods and whose attempts elsewhere to use coal for lead smelting had proved less successful.

The Clerkes' Bristol experiments then turned to the coal-fired smelting of copper under the management of John [ii] Coster, who was later acknowledged to have been mainly responsible for the success of these new smelting techniques. An adapted reverberatory furnace was used, which reflected, or 'reverberated', heat from a vaulted roof, and separated the coal and its gases from the melting ores below. Later the process proved applicable also to tin, but it was particularly significant in revitalizing English copper smelting, which previously had proved uneconomic and had been entirely abandoned. Its revival during the early years of the eighteenth century provided a basis for a thriving British industry in the production of copper and its alloy, brass.

John [ii] Coster went on to manage a copper-smelting works for the London partnership headed by William Dockwra (c.1635–1716), at Upper Redbrook on the River Wye. By the 1690s he was supplying, via the Thames, Dockwra's copper and brass works at Esher in Surrey. In the next decade he was developing his smelting methods, extending his activities to copper mining in Cornwall, where he bought ores extensively, and, still later, supplying the four major copper and brass companies, which, by then, had become established. In developing his own separate family business, he manufactured copper goods at watermills near Bristol, introducing water-powered rolling to the area. His headquarters were later established in the city.

John [ii] Coster was increasingly assisted by his three sons before his death at Upper Redbrook, Gloucestershire, on 13 October 1718. He left his wife, Mary (1664/5–1734), twenty shares in the Redbrook company, a mansion at Whitecliff, Monmouthshire, and two houses on College Green, Bristol. Both John and Mary Coster were included on an engraved family memorial erected by their son Thomas in All Saints' Church, Newland, the parish church of Upper Redbrook, where they were buried.

**Thomas Coster** (1684–1739), their eldest son, was born on 20 December 1684. He was married twice, first, in 1720, to Jane Rous, and second, to Astrea (d. 1738), daughter of Sir John Smith of Long Ashton, Bristol. While residing at College Green, Bristol, in 1734, Thomas Coster was elected tory member of parliament for the city. A petition to parliament from the mayor and corporation after the election asserted that invalid votes had been responsible for his defeat of the former whig member but was withdrawn when difficulty arose substantiating the claim, which appears to have arisen solely from political bias. In the Commons Coster actively represented local commercial interests, including presenting a petition on behalf of the Society of Merchant Adventurers of Bristol on 3 March 1738. He retained his seat until his death, some five years later, when the great bell of every parish church in the city is said to have tolled throughout the day.

At Bristol Thomas Coster's responsibility for extending the manufacturing operations of the family business in the city included the establishment in 1728 of an additional new mill site. He became a partner in the Bristol Brass Company when it assimilated the Upper Redbrook Copper Company in 1722. Thomas, like his father before him, had previously worked in close association with the Bristol company and now, also like his father, he continued to confine his business activities to the production of copper. By 1730 the brass company had closed the Redbrook smelting site in favour of its Bristol works.

An abandoned works at Melincryddan, near Neath, south Wales, provided a replacement smelting site for the Costers' own separate family business during the planning of a large new site at White Rock, Swansea. The site had many advantages and, with its accessibility for seaborne transport of copper ores and the existence of massive stocks of coal, Swansea would later become the centre of copper smelting in Britain. However, at that time Bristol still remained the country's main focus of copper production, and satisfied local demands for copper to alloy with zinc in order to maintain production of its large output of brass. White Rock was not completed until after Thomas's death, which occurred in Bristol on 30 September 1739, by which time he was the sole survivor of the Coster brothers.

Thomas Coster left £40,000 and his property to his only child, Jane (1720–1808), who in 1741 married John Hoblyn (d. 1751), after he had become an active partner in the family business. Although the male line of the Coster copper smelters ceased with Thomas, Jane, through her husband, extended the business involvement of the family. She erected a plaque to her father's memory in Bristol Cathedral.

Thomas Coster's two younger brothers were active mainly in Cornwall. **John** [iii] **Coster** (1688–1731) probably remained unmarried; and **Robert Coster** (1696–1736) married Grace, sister of Sir William Pendarves (1696–1765) of Cornwall. The brothers were concerned with mining management, new mining equipment, and the organization of buying and selling ore, with John [iii] taking much the senior role. In collaboration with his father, John [iii] registered a new type of engine for drawing water out of deep mines, under patent no. 397 in 1714. He and Thomas received an equal number of shares, together with much property in the family business, at the death of their father in 1718. John [iii] Coster died on 27 June 1731.

Robert Coster was still a minor when his father's will was made, and although he received a smaller share of his estate, he grew in influence with time. His wife, Grace Pendarves, inherited Cornish land and mining property from her brother, Sir William Pendarves, after his widow's death. Following Robert Coster's death, aged forty, on 31 March 1736, Grace married Samuel Percival (d. 1764), who then became a partner of the Coster business. Although the women of the family played no active role in the business, they in fact sustained it by bringing in new partners through their marriages. After Thomas Coster's death, the partnership was further expanded and eventually renamed the Samuel Percival and Copper Company. Following Percival's death in 1764, the then senior partner gave his name to the business as the John Freeman and Copper Company, which survived at Swansea in reduced form until about 1870.

Throughout these changes in name the business remained a direct descendant of that built up by the Costers, initiated by John [ii] Coster and made possible by his significant innovations in coal-fired smelting and his development of the reverberatory furnace. Apart from its other important eighteenth-century uses in tin and lead production, this furnace was ultimately adapted late in the eighteenth century by Henry Cort for his process of making 'puddled' iron, thus bringing British production of wrought iron to the fore in the early nineteenth century. By then the economic and technical development of copper smelting in the reverberatory furnaces of south Wales was leading the world in copper production.

JOAN DAY

**Sources** R. Jenkins, 'Copper works of Redbrook and Bristol', *Transactions of the Bristol and Gloucestershire Archaeological Society*, 62 (1940), 145–67 · J. Day, 'The Costers, copper-smelters and manufacturers', *Transactions* [Newcomen Society], 47 (1974–6), 47–58 · J. Day, *Bristol brass: a history of the industry* (1973), 48–57 · J. Morton, 'The rise of the modern copper and brass industry, 1690–1750', PhD diss., U. Birm., 1985 · R. O. Roberts, *The copper industry of Neath and Swansea*, South Wales and Monmouth RS, 4 (1957), 125–36 · R. O. Roberts, 'The smelting of non-ferrous metals', *Glamorgan County History*, 5 (1980), 47–96 · W. Pryce, *Mineralogia Cornubiensis* (1778) · D. B. Barton, *Copper mining in Devon and Cornwall* (1961) · S. R. Matthews, 'Coster, Thomas', HoP, *Commons*, 1715–54 · memorial, All Saints Church, Newland, Gloucestershire · memorial, Bristol Cathedral [Thomas Coster] · Bedford estate mine records, Devon RO [John (iii) Coster] · will (abstract), 16 Oct 1716, Sci. Mus., Rhys Jenkins papers [John (ii) Coster, proved 9 Dec 1718] · T. Latimer, *Annals of Bristol in the 18th century* (1893) [Thomas Coster]

**Archives** Sci. Mus., Rhys Jenkins papers · U. Lpool, Rhys Jenkins papers

**Wealth at death** land and premises at Redbrook, Gloucestershire; three houses at College Green, Bristol, and mills near Bristol; shares of Cornish mines; water engines, ores, and metal therein, and stock of Upper Redbrook copper works — John (ii) Coster: will, Sci. Mus., Rhys Jenkins papers · £40,000; plus property — Thomas Coster: Latimer, *Annals of Bristol*

**Coster, John** (1647–1718). *See under* Coster family (*per.* c.1685–1764).

**Coster, John** (1688–1731). *See under* Coster family (*per.* c.1685–1764).

**Coster, Robert** (1696–1736). *See under* Coster family (*per.* c.1685–1764).

**Coster, Thomas** (1684–1739). *See under* Coster family (*per.* c.1685–1764).

**Cosway, Baroness Maria Louisa Catherine Cecilia** [née Maria Louisa Catherine Cecilia Hadfield] (**1760–1838**), history painter and educationist, was born at her father's hotel, Hadfield's (or Carlo's), Lungarno Capponi, Florence, on 17 July 1760, the eldest of five surviving children of Charles Hadfield (1717?–1776) and his wife, Isabella Pocock (1730?–1809). She was baptized in Florence on 22 November 1760 by Everard Hutcheson, chaplain to the British factory at Leghorn, with Sir Brook Bridges and Lady Lucy Boyle as godparents, and was given the name Lucy after her godmother. In a shocking case of serial infanticide all her elder siblings had been murdered by a deranged maid-servant. This bizarre event profoundly affected her and can be seen as a major influence on her reaction to the early loss of her only child, Louisa (1790–1796), her intense Catholicism, and her later career as a pioneer of girls' education in Italy. Her younger brothers were the minor artist William Hadfield (*b.* 1761, *d.* before 1810) and George *Hadfield (1763–1826), a significant neo-classical architect who worked in Washington, DC. One of her sisters, Charlotte

**Baroness Maria Louisa Catherine Cecilia Cosway** (1760–1838), by Valentine Green, pubd 1787 (after self-portrait)

(*b.* 1766, *d.* after 1838), was a minor portrait miniaturist in London who in 1795 married the writer William Combe.

**Education** Schooled at a Florentine convent, Hadfield showed early signs of precocious talent; she began to study music at the age of six and drawing at ten. As the pupil of Violante Cerroti and Johann Zoffany from 1773, she copied paintings by old masters and contemporary artists in the Uffizi. Among the works that she studied were those by Correggio, Van Meiris, Trevisani, and Sir Joshua Reynolds (his self-portrait, 1775, had reached the Uffizi in the same year). Copies that she painted at this period of Raphael's *Large Cowper Madonna*, Correggio's *Virgin and Child with St Jerome*, and Rubens's *Four Philosophers* have been preserved (Fondazione Cosway, Lodi). Her work reached a level of quality such that on 27 September 1778 she was elected to the Florentine Accademia del Disegno. Her copying was encouraged by the painter Joseph Wright of Derby, and she met a number of artistic visitors passing through Florence, including the painters Edward Edwards and Henry Tresham, as well as the collector Charles Townley. She visited Rome on various occasions from 1777 to 1779, to study and copy artworks there. Staying with the family of the sculptor Thomas Banks she had:

> the opportunity of knowing all the first living Artists intimately; Battoni [sic], Mengs, Maron, and many English Artists. Fusely [sic] with his extraordinary visions struck my fancy. I made no regular study, but for one year and a half only went to see all that was high in painting and sculpture. (Cosway, autobiographical letter, fol. 1r)

She also visited Naples during April 1779 in the company of the artists Thomas Banks, Alexander Day, Henry Tresham, Prince Hoare, and James Northcote. The latter noted that 'she plays very finely on the harpsichord, and sings and composes music'. With her blond hair, blue eyes, and strong Anglo-Italian accent she was 'not unhandsome, endowed with considerable talents, and with a form extremely delicate and a pleasing manner of the utmost simplicity'; she was 'withal active, ambitious, proud and restless', having been 'the object of adoration of an indulgent father'. She had 'some knowledge of painting, the same of music, and about the same of five or six languages, but was imperfect in all of these' (Gwynn, 149–50).

After her father's death in 1776 Hadfield's mother decided to relinquish the family business in Florence and return to London with most of her offspring, and left in the summer of 1779. It seems that Hadfield's departure was reluctant. She later wrote to her husband's cousin Sir William Cosway:

> my mother recalled me [from Rome] to Florence to go with her to England. My inclination from a child had been to be a Nun. I wished therefore to return to my convent, but my mother was miserable about it and I was persuaded to accompany her.   (Cosway, autobiographical letter, fol. 1v)

**Move to England; and marriage** Maria Hadfield certainly had many letters of introduction to influential figures in the London art world—as she put it, 'for all the first people of fas[h]ion Sir J Reynolds, Cipriani, Bartolozzi [and] Angelica Kauffman' (Cosway, autobiographical letter, fol. 1v). According to Northcote it seems that her mother was determined to turn her into another Angelica Kauffman—in other words into a celebrated woman painter. However, money soon ran short and Hadfield, 'having refused better offers in her better days … from necessity married Cosway the miniature painter' (Gwynn, 149–50).

Richard *Cosway RA (bap. 1742, d. 1821) was an established artist in London. Noted for his diminutive stature, simian looks, and somewhat rakish reputation he was about to become the most fashionable miniaturist to Regency society. He had also established himself as an ambitious portraitist in oils, with his allegorical paintings exhibited annually at the Royal Academy during the 1770s. A virtuoso and collector, he maintained a busy studio in Berkeley Street at the heart of the fashionable West End and was able to provide Hadfield with a marriage settlement of £2800. The couple were married on 18 January 1781 at St George's, Hanover Square; Hadfield was given away—in the absence of her late father—by Charles Townley, while the register was signed by her mother and Thomas Banks. The 1780s was a period of exceptional artistic and social success for both Cosways within the circle of the young prince of Wales (later prince regent and then George IV). Maria Cosway organized extremely fashionable concerts, which attracted the bon ton of society, at which she sang and played the harp; a volume of music entitled Songs and Duets Composed by Mrs. Cosway was published in London in 1785. Key moments for the couple during this decade were their move to Schomberg House, in Pall Mall, during 1784; Richard Cosway receiving an honorific title from the prince of Wales in 1785; and their socially triumphant visit to Paris in 1786, when Maria met Thomas Jefferson, then American minister to France. This visit, and the one to Paris made by her alone the following year, were to a large extent engineered by the antiquarian Pierre-François-Hugues, Baron d'Hancarville, with whom she corresponded extensively. Cosway and Jefferson were introduced in Paris by the American history painter John Trumbull. In a letter of 21 May 1789 Jefferson wrote to Maria: 'Adieu my very dear friend. Be our affections unchangeable, and if our little history is to last beyond the grave, be the longest chapter in it which shall record their purity, warmth and duration' (Jefferson MSS, special collections, Alderman Library, University of Virginia, Charlottesville).

**Artistic ambitions** Maria Cosway exhibited her ambitious history paintings and 'in character' portraits at the Royal Academy exhibitions from 1781 to 1789 (as well as in 1796, 1800, and 1801). They were greatly influenced by the work of Angelica Kauffman, Sir Joshua Reynolds, and Henry Fuseli in terms of style, handling, and range of subject matter. Her interest in spiritual iconography was part of an increasing trend during the 1780s that was dominated by Fuseli and that received a mixed critical response. Cosway's subject pictures, based on mythological, literary, and biblical themes, were drawn from a variety of sources, including Homer, Virgil, Diodorus Siculus, Petrarch, Spenser, Shakespeare, Pope, Gray, Rogers, Macpherson (Works of Ossian), and Hannah Cowley, as well as from the Old Testament. Her most successful work was the portrait Georgiana, Duchess of Devonshire as Cynthia (exh. RA, 1782; priv. coll.), based on Spenser's Faerie Queene. This dramatic full-length composition shows the duchess flying through the night sky directly towards the viewer. One critic praised the 'elegant compliment' paid to the sitter, noting the painting's originality and delicacy, and also asserted that Cosway was 'the first of the female painters' and, regarding the male sex, only inferior to her husband and to Reynolds (Morning Chronicle, 9 May 1782). Other untraced paintings, such as Eolus Raising a Storm (exh. RA, 1782), Samson (exh. RA, 1784), The Deluge (exh. RA, 1785), and A Vision (exh. RA, 1786), were stylistically influenced by Fuseli and were generally considered failures by reviewers; all four were incorporated in the anonymous caricature of Cosway, entitled Maria Costive at her Studies (1786). More successful was the untraced painting The Hours (exh. RA, 1783), which was engraved in stipple by F. Bartolozzi (1788). An impression of this print was sent to the great neo-classical artist Jacques-Louis David, who in an untraced letter to Cosway praised both the composition and the artist very warmly (see Williamson, 45–6). David's influence can be seen clearly in the arrangement of figures and the prominent use of gesture in Cosway's unusual and successful representational painting The Death of Miss Gardiner (exh. RA, 1789; Musée de la Révolution Française, Vizille), although it shows lighting and handling that are characteristic of Reynolds's paintings. Engravings after her paintings, especially in mezzotint by

V. Green and S. W. Reynolds, and also in stipple by Bartolozzi, played a critical role in establishing her artistic reputation.

In her paintings Cosway wholeheartedly followed the impulse of her imagination, but her career as an artist was affected by her husband's attitude towards her. He portrayed his wife on numerous occasions, but in only one portrait drawing of her (c.1789; Fondazione Cosway, Lodi)—shown with a bust of Leonardo da Vinci—did he represent her with palette and brushes. Moreover he refused to allow her to sell her work. This, as she later admitted in her autobiographical letter of 1830 to Sir William Cosway, had a damaging impact on the quality of her output: 'Had Mr C. permitted me to paint professionally, I should have made a better painter, but left to myself by degrees instead of improving, I lost what I had brought from Italy of my early studies' (Cosway, autobiographical letter, fol. 1v).

**Motherhood and bereavement** On 4 May 1790, after a very difficult labour, Cosway gave birth to her only child, Louisa Paolina Angelica. The baby was named after her godparents, Princess Louisa of Stolberg, widow of Prince Charles Edward Stuart, and the exiled Corsican patriot General Pasquale de Paoli, who was an intimate friend and correspondent of her mother. Cosway, who may have been suffering from severe post-natal depression, was advised to travel to Italy for her health, and she reached Venice in September 1790. Extraordinarily she left behind not only her husband but also her new-born daughter, and was not to return to London for another four years. Among her surviving artistic compositions from this period a number show grieving or prostrate women, which suggests that these works reveal her state of mind. The first and most important of these is *Lodona*, an image of the dissolving water nymph, taken from Pope's poem *Windsor-Forest*, an untraced oil painted for Thomas Macklin's Poets' Gallery that was engraved in stipple by Bartolozzi (1792). Horace Walpole commented: 'surely it is odd to drop a child and her husband all in a breath' (Walpole, *Corr.*, 11.285). After copying artworks in Venice she visited Florence and Rome, before seeking admission to a convent in Genoa during 1793.

Cosway had returned to London by November 1794. Just over a year and a half later, on 29 July 1796, her daughter died of a fever. Both Cosways were devastated. Richard immersed himself in mysticism and magic. Maria became increasingly religious and involved with girls' education, concerns that were eventually to dominate the second half of her life. At the end of the decade Cosway painted for the Catholic Salvin family a huge altarpiece, *Exultation of the Virgin Mary, or, The salvation of mankind, purchased by the death of Jesus Christ* (1799; priv. coll.), a reduced replica of which also survives (exh. RA, 1801; Fondazione Cosway, Lodi); this composition had previously been engraved in mezzotint by V. Green (1800). In the same year she painted one of her most ambitious and original compositions, *The Birth of the Thames* (exh. RA, 1800; priv. coll.), which was later engraved in line by P. W. Tomkins (1802).

**Prints** Many of Cosway's prints were published by Rudolph Ackermann through his highly influential printselling business, *The Repository of Arts*. He also published *Imitations in Chalk* (1800; Yale Center for British Art, New Haven), a drawing book of her etchings after a selection of Richard Cosway's drawn sketches; two series of moral illustrations, known as *A Progress of Female Virtue* and *A Progress of Female Dissipation* (1800; BM), engraved by A. Cardon; and the series of twelve pen-and-wash illustrations to Mary ('Perdita') Robinson's pathetic autobiographical poem *The Winter Day* (c.1803), which were etched with aquatint by C. Watson (1803). The poem and accompanying designs were described by Ackermann as contrasting 'the evils of poverty and the ostentatious enjoyment of opulence'. He continued his introduction by describing Cosway's style, and his criticism may be applied to much of her work: 'Mrs Cosway's designs, it must be admitted, are sometimes eccentric, but it is the eccentricity of genius, and we have seen instances where she has snatched a grace beyond the reach of art'.

Of all the artistic projects that Cosway was involved at about the turn of the century the most demanding was that undertaken during her stay in Paris from 1801 to 1803. This was to copy and etch Dominique-Vivant Denon's reorganized display of the newly arrived old master paintings in the grand gallery of the Louvre (then known as the Musée Central), for which descriptive texts were provided by the entrepreneur Julius Griffiths. Eight folio-sized plates entitled *Galerie du Louvre* (1802) were published in Paris and made available to subscribers either in monochrome or hand-coloured. Cosway received assistance from the engraver Francesco Rosaspina, with whom she had an extensive correspondence; the original presentation volume of hand-coloured etchings with the names of the French and British subscribers survives (1801–3; Fondazione Cosway, Lodi). Despite signing the volume as the head of the Bonaparte family Napoleon himself was disparaging about the quality of Cosway's copies, a judgement with which she reluctantly concurred. (In 1807 she corresponded with the sculptor Antonio Canova about a cast (untraced) of his bust of Cardinal Fesch.)

**Pioneer of girls' education** As Cosway records in her diary, while staying in Paris she was intimate with members of the Bonaparte family, in particular Napoleon's mother, Letizia Ramolino, and her half-brother Cardinal Joseph Fesch (MS diary, Fondazione Cosway, Lodi). Under Fesch's patronage, as archbishop of Lyons, Cosway from 1803 fulfilled her desire to establish a girls' school at Lyons. The school continued until 1809, when Cosway moved to Lombardy to be close to her sister Elisabeth Hadfield (1769–c.1820). With patronage from Francesco Melzi, vice-president of the Cisalpine republic and later duke of Lodi, in 1812 she was able successfully to re-establish her girls' school as the Collegio delle Grazie at Lodi. It offered its pupils a religious and liberal education, provided tuition in music and art, and aimed, in pursuing the wishes of its founder, to produce 'good mothers'. In 1815 and from 1817 to 1822 she spent time in London nursing her ailing husband, who was increasingly suffering from religious delusions and eventually the strokes that caused his death. Despite their long separations the Cosways never divorced. In the year surrounding Richard's death, on 4 July 1821, Maria organized—through the auctioneer George Stanley and with the help of her friends and correspondents Sir Thomas Lawrence, Sir John Soane, and the antiquarian Francis Douce—a series of five sales of her husband's wide-ranging and curious collections: old master pictures, prints and drawings, objects of taste and virtu, as well as his extensive library. The auctions raised about £12,000, at least a third of which Cosway used to endow her school in Lodi. She also commissioned from Sir Richard Westmacott an elegant marble monument to her husband for the new St Marylebone Church. After touring Scotland in 1822 with her chief teaching assistant and faithful correspondent Annette Prodon she returned to her school. She brought with her most of her husband's drawings, which she had unsuccessfully exhibited at Stanley's in London during 1822 and which she later promoted vigorously in Italy. A few years later she commissioned Giovanni Paolo Lasinio, based in Florence, to engrave a group of Richard Cosway's finest drawings, which were published in *Raccolta di disegni originali scelti del portafogli del celebre Riccardo Cosway R.A.* (1826).

Cosway's work at her school in Lodi, where the Milanese and Lombard élite sent their daughters, was pioneering in the cause of girls' education in Italy. Notably the novelist Alessandro Manzoni sent one of his younger daughters, Vittoria, to the school from 1831 to 1835. This event was celebrated in a large oil painting by Gabriele Rottini, *Baroness Maria Hadfield Cosway Listening to Vittoria Manzoni* (c.1835; Fondazione Cosway, Lodi). In 1830 the school had been re-established as the Collegio delle Dame Inglesi, under the authority of the teaching order based in Austria. After visits to it by the Austrian emperor and empress Cosway was created a baroness by Francis I in 1834. She died on its premises on 5 January 1838 and was buried in the south transept of the adjoining church, Santa Maria delle Grazie. Later that year a tomb was erected there, and a marble bust of Cosway, by Gaetano Manfredini, was commissioned for the school (1839; Fondazione Cosway, Lodi).

Even by the standards of her time Cosway was a remarkable, 'all-accomplished' woman with an international reputation and an astonishing circle of friends and correspondents. She rose from being an innkeeper's daughter to be a baroness of the Austrian empire; and she transformed herself from an imaginative artist and musician into a pioneering educationist. Since 1945 Maria Cosway has been best-known for her romance with Thomas Jefferson while in Paris in 1786, which led to a life-long correspondence and was portrayed in the film *Jefferson in Paris* (1995), by Merchant Ivory Productions. She can now be seen both as a significant history painter and portraitist stylistically influenced by contemporaries such as Fuseli, and, as a woman artist, as an important successor to Angelica Kauffman. The exhibition at the Scottish

National Portrait Gallery, Edinburgh, and the National Portrait Gallery, London, in 1995-6 has helped to re-evaluate her varied artistic output. She can be considered as one of the most fascinating and versatile women of revolutionary and Romantic Europe.

STEPHEN LLOYD

**Sources** *Gazzetta Privilegiata di Milano* (11 Feb 1838) · G. C. Williamson, *Richard Cosway RA and his wife and pupils*, rev. 2nd edn (1905) · Graves, *RA exhibitors* · E. L. G. Charvet, 'Enseignement public des arts du dessin à Lyon 1804', *Bulletin du Comité des Sociétés des Beaux-Arts des Départements*, 35 (1912), 79–112 · H. P. Bullock, *My head and my heart: a little history of Thomas Jefferson and Maria Cosway* (1945) · M. Lozzi and A. Stroppa, *Il Collegio Cosway ieri e oggi* (1985) · J. Walker, 'Maria Cosway, an undervalued artist', *Apollo*, 123 (1986), 318–24 · E. Cazzulani and A. Stroppa, *Maria Hadfield Cosway*, rev. 2nd edn (1998) · S. Lloyd, 'The accomplished Maria Cosway', *Journal of Anglo-Italian Studies*, 2 (1992), 108–39 · S. Lloyd, ed., *Richard and Maria Cosway* (1995) [exhibition catalogue, Scot. NPG] · G. Barnett, *Richard and Maria Cosway: a biography* (1995) · J. Ingamells, ed., *A dictionary of British and Irish travellers in Italy, 1701–1800* (1997) [for entries on members of the Hadfield family] · T. Gipponi, ed., *Maria e Richard Cosway* (1998) · P.-M. Villa, *L'autre vie de Pascal Paoli* (Ajaccio, 1999) · S. Gwynn, ed., *Memorials of an eighteenth-century painter: James Northcote* [1898] · S. Hutchinson, 'The Royal Academy Schools, 1768–1830', *Walpole Society*, 38 (1960–62), 146 · M. Cosway, autobiographical letter to Sir William Cosway, 1830, V&A NAL, MS Eng. L. 961–1953

**Archives** Biblioteca Communale Laudense, Lodi, MSS · Fondazione Cosway, Lodi, MSS · Metropolitan Museum of Art, New York · V&A, MS Eng. L. 961–1953 | Biblioteca Communale Saffi, Forlì, Rosaspina MSS · Bodl. Oxf., Douce MSS · RA, letters to Ozias Humphry · Sir John Soane's Museum, London, Soane MSS

**Likenesses** R. Cosway, drawing, c.1781–1783, priv. coll. · R. Cosway, double portrait, etching, 1784 (with her husband), BM, NPG · F. Bartolozzi, stipple, pubd 1785 (after R. Cosway), BM · R. Cosway, double portrait, self-portrait, drawing, c.1785 (with M. Cosway), Fondazione Cosway, Lodi, Italy · F. Jeuffroy, glass paste profile, c.1786, Scot. NPG · V. Green, mezzotint, pubd 1787 (after self-portrait by M. Cosway), NPG [*see illus.*] · W. Birch, stipple, pubd 1789 (after R. Cosway and W. Hodges), BM, NPG · R. Cosway, drawing, 1789, Fondazione Cosway, Lodi, Italy · R. Thew, double portrait, stipple, pubd 1789 (with Mr Cosway; after R. Cosway), BM · L. Schiavonetti, stipple, pubd 1791 (after R. Cosway), BM, NPG · medallion, 1797, Museo Nazionale del Bargello, Florence, Italy · etching, c.1800, LMA · physionotrace (profile drawing), c.1801–1803, priv. coll. · G. Rottini, group portrait, oils, c.1835, Fondazione Cosway, Lodi, Italy · G. Manfredini, marble bust, 1839, Fondazione Cosway, Lodi, Italy

**Wealth at death** all residual money, art collections, and library left to the Collegio delle Dame Inglesi, Lodi: Cosway MSS, Fondazione Cosway, Lodi

**Cosway, Richard** (bap. 1742, d. 1821), artist and collector, was baptized in the parish church of Oakford, near Tiverton, Devon, on 5 November 1742, shortly after his birth, the exact date of which is not known. His parents were named as Richard and Mary Cosway, and his father was a schoolmaster in Tiverton (*Scots Magazine*). It does not appear that Cosway had any brothers or sisters.

**Early career, 1742–1759** As a child Cosway must have shown signs of talent as a draughtsman, since when he was a young teenager it was decided that he should further his artistic studies in London. In this venture he may well have been supported by his uncle Oliver Peard, who had been a mayor of Tiverton and was a leading merchant in this significant woollen manufacturing town. Cosway was

Richard Cosway (*bap.* 1742, *d.* 1821), self-portrait, *c.*1790

sent up to London at the end of 1754 to study under William Shipley, a drawing-master and portraitist who had recently established himself in the capital. He had just launched his Society for the Encouragement of Arts, Manufactures, and Commerce and was attracting talented young students. In the inaugural competition held by the society in 1755 Cosway won the first prize of £5 in the category of under-fourteen-year-olds for a drawing copy of the subject 'Compassion, taken from an original of Le Brun's'; (*Scots Magazine*), and in the following few years won other awards for drawing. He had also begun to train as a portraitist—in oils and miniatures—under the auspices of Shipley, to whom he was apprenticed and with whom he lived off the Strand. One of his finest early miniatures, *Thomas Cosway*—painted in the neat style of the so-called modest school—was of his cousin (ex Sothebys, London, 20 July 1981, lot 137), which the artist signed and dated in 1760. In that same year Cosway exhibited *William Shipley*, a confident head-and-shoulders oil portrait of his mentor (RSA; exh. Edinburgh, 1995) at the inaugural public exhibition of the Society of Arts. This significant pictorial statement, influenced by the oil portraiture of Thomas Hudson and Sir Joshua Reynolds, marked Cosway's emergence as a young artist.

**Career in the 1760s** Throughout the 1760s Cosway exhibited his work—oils, miniatures, and drawings—publicly in London, both at the Free Society of Artists from 1761 to 1764 and again two years later, while from 1767 to 1769 he returned to showing at the Society of Artists. Very few of his works have survived from this decade. An exception is the ambitious and large portrait miniature of an actress, *Miss Elliot in the Character of Pallas* (Fondazione Cosway, Lodi; exh. Edinburgh, 1995), that was shown at the Society of Artists in 1769. Two years earlier Cosway's miniature *Mrs Draper* had been praised by her literary admirer Laurence Sterne, in his famous work *The Journal to Eliza*. In 1775 the artist portrayed the same sitter in an oil painting (priv. coll.; exh. Edinburgh, 1995), where she is shown seated in his spectacular sitters' chair, designed by Matthias Lock (*c.*1755–60; V&A; exh. Edinburgh, 1995). This bold piece of studio furniture indicated Cosway's increasing confidence and flamboyant artistic persona. Well-known as a high-profile 'macaroni' at this period, he painted himself as such both in a miniature (Metropolitan Museum of Art, New York; exh. Edinburgh, 1995) and in an oil painting wearing fashionable 'Vandyke' dress (Attingham Park, Shrewsbury; exh. Edinburgh, 1995). Cosway's status as a society artist was consolidated by his move to the heart of the fashionable West End of London, when in 1768 he rented the studio and house of the recently deceased oil portraitist John Shackleton, at 4 Berkeley Street, just off Piccadilly, where he lived until 1784.

**Royal Academician: the 1770s** In 1769 Cosway was admitted as a student to the schools of the newly founded Royal Academy of Arts. The following year he exhibited three oil paintings there, and he was elected an associate academician. In 1771 he displayed a further three oils and a miniature, and he was elected Royal Academician. Cosway continued to show his ambitious oil portraiture at the academy's annual exhibitions (1770–87, 1798–1800, 1803, and 1806), rather than his more fashionable and prolific output of portrait miniatures and drawings.

A number of Cosway's little-studied oil paintings from the 1770s survive. These include *The Witts Family* (Tate collection; exh. Edinburgh, 1995), an unusual conversation piece that serves both as an allegory and as a memorial. This was exhibited at the Royal Academy in 1770 as *The portraits of a gentleman, his wife, and sister, in the character of Fortitude introducing Hope as the companion to Distress*. Equally influenced by the work of Sir Joshua Reynolds was Cosway's celebratory oil *The Carrick Family* (Castle Coole, Enniskillen). This was displayed at the academy the following year as *A lady and her daughters in the character of Virtue and Beauty directed by Wisdom to sacrifice at the altar of Diana* (engraved in mezzotint by J. R. Smith in 1773).

Perhaps Cosway's most successful painting from this decade not to have been exhibited publicly was a conversation piece painted in 1771–5, *Charles Townley with a Group of Connoisseurs* (Towneley Hall Art Gallery and Museums, Burnley; exh. Edinburgh, 1995). Letters (in the Townley papers, BM) from the artist to Charles Townley (1737–1805), the important collector of classical sculptures, reveal their close friendship and the lascivious interests of this circle of connoisseurs, who are shown in the picture admiring two statues of the nude Venus. Cosway resisted Townley's invitations to join him in Italy—probably owing to pressure of work—but the artist's Italophile tendencies were revealed in a letter to Townley—then in Italy—dated 24 February 1772:

Italy for ever say I—if the Italian women fuck as well in Italy as they do here, you must be happy indeed—I am such a zealot for them, that I'll be damned if I ever fuck an English woman again (if I can help it).   (Townley papers, BM)

Curiously, unlike so many of his artistic contemporaries, Cosway never visited Italy during his lifetime. This letter, with its emphatic statement of his sexuality, explicitly contradicts later historians' suggestions that Cosway was homosexual. As to Cosway's character, the critic William Hazlitt—in his brilliant descriptive cameo of the artist—recorded that his future wife Maria, when questioned in Paris during 1802 about her husband, stated that he was 'toujours riant, toujours gai' (Hazlitt, 'Old age of artists').

**Marriage and royal patronage: the 1780s**  In 1780 two events occurred that were to transform Cosway's already successful career as a fashionable society artist in London, principally active as a portraitist producing oils and miniatures. He met his future wife, Maria, *née* Hadfield [*see* Cosway, Maria Louisa Catherine Cecilia (1760–1838)], a talented artist and musician, who had recently arrived in the metropolis from her native Florence. In addition this was the year that Cosway first portrayed in miniature George, prince of Wales (1762–1830), later George IV, who had just turned eighteen and who was to become Cosway's most important patron over the next three decades.

Cosway's marriage appears to have been brokered by Charles Townley, who knew the Hadfield family in Florence, and who protected them in London, and also by Maria's mother Isabella, who was looking for a financially secure future for her daughter. It is very likely that Cosway settled the considerable sum of £2800 on his new wife. The couple were married at the fashionable church of St George's, Hanover Square, London, on 18 January 1781. Her father having died in 1776, Maria was given away in marriage by Charles Townley. Throughout the 1780s the Cosways established an intensely fashionable salon, first in Berkeley Street, and then after 1784 at their new home in the central apartment of Schomberg House in Pall Mall, where the Gainsboroughs were their immediate neighbours in the west wing.

Twenty years older than the prince of Wales when first he sat to the artist, Cosway not only helped create a fashionable and intimate pictorial image for the increasingly dissolute heir to the throne, but he also assisted in forming his young patron's aesthetic taste. The extensive manuscript list of unpaid portraits drawn up towards the end of Cosway's life in 1820 (which were in fact paid later that year) showed that the prince had commissioned work regularly from the artist over the period 1780 to 1808 (MS inventory, Fondazione Cosway, Lodi). These were chiefly portraits of the prince, mainly miniatures—sometimes of eyes only—but also drawings and paintings. There were also commissioned portraits of the prince's lovers—in particular of Mary, Mrs Perdita Robinson, and of Maria, Mrs Fitzherbert—as well as of most members of his family and close friends. In 1785 the prince allowed Cosway to sign his work with the extravagant Latin title *Primarius pictor serenissimi Walliae principis* ('principal painter to his

royal highness the prince of Wales'). Thereafter the miniatures were mostly signed this way on the back, with the finished portrait drawings being inscribed on the front and underneath the image.

**Portrait miniaturist**  The Royal Collection holds the finest and most extensive collection of Cosway's miniatures of the prince of Wales and his family. Other particularly important groups of the artist's small-scale work can be found in the Victoria and Albert Museum, London, the Fitzwilliam Museum, Cambridge, and the Huntington Library and Art Collections in San Marino, California. Cosway's mature style of miniature painting, which had evolved by 1785, can be described as the epitome of early Regency taste. Following on from the technical developments made by Jeremiah Meyer in the 1770s, Cosway expanded the size of the miniature portrait to about 3 inches in height. Like Meyer, he mastered the inherent luminosity of the ivory support allied to the natural translucency of the watercolour. He also developed highly characteristic compositional and technical traits within the miniature, which made his portraits notably alluring and flattering, often for a young and wealthy adult clientele. He enlarged the eyes in proportion to the head, and increased the size of the head in comparison with the body. He incorporated brilliant sky-blue and white cloudy backgrounds, thus subtly enhancing the isolated focus on the head and eyes of the sitter. He also developed a bravura technique that contrasted delicate stipple work in the face with more linear and expressive brushwork for the body and the sky. Two of the finest examples of his work from this period are *An Unknown Lady, called Mrs Fitzherbert* (Wallace Collection, London), datable to *c*.1785–90, and *Madame Du Barry* (National Gallery of Victoria, Melbourne), dated 1791.

Cosway enjoyed great facility as a painter and draughtsman, and he was a notably prolific artist, allegedly being able to undertake up to twelve separate portrait sittings a day for miniatures. During the 1790s and early 1800s as he matured as an artist, his miniatures lost some of their fashionable brilliance of the 1780s, but his work became more subtle, both in characterization and in execution. He became particularly adept at the combined use of monochrome shading and an increasingly limited application of pigment, especially in the sky backgrounds, which lends these portraits considerable psychological complexity. Outstanding examples of Cosway's late miniatures are *Arthur Wellesley, Later 1st Duke of Wellington* (V&A; exh. Edinburgh, 1995), signed and dated 1808; the actor *John Philip Kemble* (V&A; exh. Edinburgh, 1995), and the artist's last *Self-Portrait* (FM Cam., exh. Edinburgh, 1995), both of which can be dated from *c*.1805 to 1810.

Cosway's mature style of painting miniatures during the 1780s and 1790s was influential on a number of his contemporaries. He trained the two brothers Nathaniel Plimer (1757–1822) and Andrew Plimer (1763–1837), who both seemed to have worked for Cosway in the early 1780s. Among the more successful artists who adopted aspects of Cosway's style were Charlotte Jones (1768–1847); William

Wood (1769–1810); and Mrs Joseph Mee, *née* Anne Foldsone (*c*.1770x75–1851).

**Draughtsman** Alongside his lucrative business as a portrait miniaturist, Cosway developed in parallel his production of small-scale full-length portrait drawings, which were known as 'stained' or 'tinged' drawings, and were to be highly influential on other artists such as Henry Edridge and George Chinnery. These drawings were priced by Cosway at the same level as his miniatures, namely 30 guineas from the 1780s. These portraits on paper were made with detailed watercolour for the head, while more fluid draughtsmanship in graphite was applied for the body and the background landscape. Cosway produced these portrait drawings in considerable numbers between about 1790 and 1810. Particularly fine examples from the 1790s are *Princess Galetzin with her Two Daughters* (exh. Edinburgh, 1995), dated 1795, and *Caroline, Princess of Wales, with Princess Charlotte* (exh. Edinburgh, 1995), dated 1797 (both Royal Collection), which were commissioned by the prince of Wales.

Cosway's drawn self-portraits are remarkable statements of his technical virtuosity as a draughtsman. His *Self-Portrait with Busts of Michelangelo and Rubens* (Fondazione Cosway, Lodi; exh. Edinburgh, 1995), datable to *c*.1789, a richly detailed full-length composition in pen and ink, is a complex artistic manifesto, where Cosway presents himself as a sophisticated Rubensian courtier–artist and virtuoso. Pendent to it is equally rich study *Maria Cosway with a Bust of Leonardo* (Fondazione Cosway, Lodi; exh. Edinburgh, 1995). About 1800 Cosway drew himself in a searching and Fuselian *Self-Portrait Leaning on his Hand* (priv. coll.; exh. Edinburgh, 1995).

Cosway was a prolific draughtsman throughout his career, and works on paper by him can be found in many British, European, and American museums. One complete sketchbook with 119 drawings survives (BM; exh. Edinburgh, 1995). About 700 sheets survive in the Fondazione Cosway at Lodi, near Milan, where they had been taken by Maria Cosway in 1822, the year after Cosway's death. These drawings can be grouped into various categories, whether finished or compositional sketches: studies for portraits; figure studies; classical, allegorical, and historical scenes; religious imagery; angels, motherhood, and children. Cosway worked in various media, usually pen and ink or graphite, though occasionally in black chalk or sometimes adding wash or watercolour.

Two key early subject drawings by Cosway are the rococo fantasy in watercolour *Rinaldo and Armida* (*c*.1772) and the dramatic Fuselian *Perseus and Medusa* (both Graphische Sammlung Albertina, Vienna; exh. Edinburgh, 1995), which is monochromatic and can be dated to the second half of the 1780s. The former work is directly related to a small oil panel by Cosway exhibited at the Royal Academy that year (priv. coll.; exh. Edinburgh, 1995). Both drawings were acquired by Albert von Sachsen-Teschen—after 1785 but during Cosway's lifetime. His major achievement as a draughtsman during the 1790s was the series of at least ten pen-and-ink drawings illustrating Musaeus's classical poem *Hero and Leander*, using Sir Robert Stapylton's translation of 1647, Cosway's copy of which survives (Fondazione Cosway, Lodi). Especially notable for their intense fusion of classical, Renaissance, and neo-classical motifs are *Hero and Leander in the Temple* (AM Oxf.; exh. Edinburgh, 1995), *Hero and Leander by the Hellespont* (BM; exh. Edinburgh, 1995), and *Hero's Dream* (priv. coll.; exh. Edinburgh, 1995). After 1800 Cosway increasingly turned to graphite interpretations of religious subjects from the New Testament, where he strove to infuse a profound spirituality with a close study of the work of Correggio and of Michelangelo's late drawings. The merging of these concerns is clearly seen in the late, masterly drawing *The Death of Leonardo da Vinci in the Arms of Francis I*, datable to *c*.1815 (priv. coll.; exh. Edinburgh, 1995).

It appears that Cosway drew for practice and for his own pleasure. The portfolios of his own drawings were intended to be seen—by himself and his close artist and collector friends—alongside his famous collection of old master drawings. Certainly this was how the two collections of drawings were appreciated by Sir Thomas Lawrence. After seeing these works in 1811, Lawrence wrote revealingly to his friend the artist Joseph Farington, reappraising Cosway:

> What are Mr. Phillips, and Mr Owen, and Sir William Beechey, and Mr Shee's in mere colouring, when compar'd to the knowledge—the familiar acquaintance with study; and often happy appropriation and even liberal imitation of the Old Masters, the fix'd Landmark of Art, of this little Being which we have been accustom'd never to think or speak of but with contempt? (Lawrence MSS, LAW/1/289, RA)

**Reproductive prints** Like most of his contemporary artists, Cosway collaborated with reproductive engravers to promote his subject compositions and portraits, whether miniatures, drawings, or oil paintings. Throughout his more than fifty-year-long career 163 separate prints were produced from Cosway's compositions. He tended to have some of his oil paintings reproduced in the heavy tonal contrast of mezzotint, as with the baroque pastiche *Europa*, engraved by J. R. Smith in 1776, or the dramatic *Lady Hume*, engraved by V. Green in 1783. His more delicate miniatures and drawings were engraved in the fashionable stipple manner by among others F. Bartolozzi, L. Schiavonetti, the Condé brothers, A. Cardon, and J. Agar. Occasionally Cosway worked with the line-engravers, notably William Sharp, who reproduced four of Cosway's compositions, including three miniatures: *George, Prince of Wales* (1790; exh. Edinburgh, 1995), and the pair *William, Duke of Clarence* and *The Hon. Thomas Erskine* (1791), depicting the prince's younger brother and the Scottish lawyer—later lord chancellor. Sharp also engraved Cosway's unlocated religious composition *Christ's Passion*, which was also commissioned in 1791 for Thomas Macklin's great project of an engraved Bible.

Some of Cosway's more sentimental subjects were reproduced during the 1780s by commercial stipple-engravers, such as F. Bartolozzi, as well as Jean Condé (*d.* 1794)—a pupil of Jacques-Louis David—and his younger brother Pierre Condé (1767/8–1840). The key instance of this type of composition and reproduction was Cosway's mannered and erotic *Docet Amor* or *The Origin of Painting*, which was engraved by J. Condé and published by Cosway himself in 1791 (exh. Edinburgh, 1995). The latter was an image of iconographical significance for Cosway as he used it as the frontispiece for the private contract sale catalogue of his old master paintings also published that year.

Three series of Cosway's drawings were engraved and published, two during his lifetime and one posthumously. In 1785 six of his compositions relating to education were engraved in the chalk manner. In 1800 about forty of his subject drawings were reproduced in soft-ground etchings by his wife, Maria, and were published by R. Ackermann as a drawing book, entitled *Imitations in Chalk*. In order to promote her late husband's artistic reputation in Italy, Maria engaged the line engraver Giovanni Paolo Lasinio to reproduce fifteen of Cosway's drawings, published as *Disegni scelti dai portafogli del celebre Riccardo Cosway* (Florence, 1826).

**Collector, connoisseur, and virtuoso** Cosway was an outstanding and highly respected collector, connoisseur, and virtuoso of the late eighteenth and early nineteenth centuries, though his two collections of old master paintings may not have been as important as that of Reynolds, nor his extensive assemblage of old master prints and over 2500 drawings as remarkable as that of Lawrence. Cosway was a wealthy artist–collector, who sought out paintings and works on paper of the highest quality and interest by the leading artists of the Italian Renaissance and the Flemish and Dutch schools.

Among Cosway's most important paintings, prints, and drawings were a number by his greatest artist hero, Rubens. These included the oil sketches *King James VI & I Uniting the Kingdoms of Scotland and England* (Birmingham Museums and City Art Gallery; exh. Edinburgh, 1995), and *The Rape of Ganymede* (priv. coll.; exh. Edinburgh, 1995). He also owned the large canvas *A View of the Escorial* (priv. coll.), which was then thought to be by Rubens, but which is now considered to have been painted by Pieter Verhulst from a sketch by Rubens. This was bought in 1791 from Cosway by his patron Lord Radnor. Similarly, Cosway sold Lord Radnor a major high Renaissance portrait on panel, then thought to be of 'La Fornarina' by Raphael, though now identified as *An Unknown Lady* by Sebastiano del Piombo (priv. coll.).

Cosway also collected the work of Rembrandt. He owned *A Franciscan Friar* (National Gallery, London) and the very important panel *Mountainous Landscape* by Hercules Seghers (Uffizi gallery, Florence), which Rembrandt had once owned and retouched. Among the Rembrandt drawings owned by Cosway the most important are the *Study after Leonardo's 'Last Supper'* (BM) and the portrait sketch *Jan Six* (priv. coll.). Probably the most unusual panel painting in Cosway's collection was *The Mass of St Giles* by the so-called Franco-Flemish master, working about 1500 (National Gallery, London). Cosway considered this work, which was highly unusual for the taste of the period, to be

by Mabuse and to represent St Thomas Aquinas performing mass in the abbey of St Denis.

Cosway also had an extraordinary eye for furniture, the decorative arts, sculpture, and armour, in particular items that were highly decorated and were said to have historical associations. Sir John Soane, who was a close friend of both the Cosways, bought a number of *objets d'art* and sculptures from Cosway's posthumous sale held at George Stanley's on 22–4 May 1821 and recorded in *A catalogue of the very curious and valuable assemblage of miscellaneous articles of taste and virtù*. He purchased the terracotta statuettes *Charles II* by Arnold Quellin, *Van Dyck* by Michael Rysbrack, and *James Craggs the Younger* by Giovanni Battista Guelfi, in addition to small classical bronzes. Some of these purchases can be identified among the objects still to be found in the Sir John Soane's Museum, London. Cosway also owned a very precious piece of Elizabethan silver-gilt, now known as *The Cosway Salt* (BM; exh. Edinburgh, 1995). The art critic J. T. Smith described the effects of the interiors at Stratford Place, where Cosway had moved in 1791:

> His new house he fitted up in so picturesque and, indeed, so princely a style, that I regret drawings were not made of the general appearance of each apartment; for many of the rooms were more like scenes of enchantment, pencilled by a poet's fancy than anything, perhaps, before displayed in a domestic habitation.   (Smith, 2.401–2)

In 1822 William Hazlitt equally appreciated the taste and artistic imagination of 'Fancy's Child'—as he referred to Cosway—in his well-known praise (at the expense of William Beckford's 'desert of magnificence' at Fonthill Abbey) of the collections and interiors at Stratford Place:

> What a fairy palace was his of specimens of art, antiquarianism and *virtù* jumbled all together in the richest disorder, dusty, shadowy, obscure with much left to the imagination (how different from the finical, polished, petty, perfect, modernized air of *Fonthill*!   (Hazlitt, *Works*, 12.95–6)

Arguably Cosway's greatest achievement as a collector and connoisseur occurred during his socially triumphant visit to Paris with Maria in summer 1786. (They returned to London in October that year after an art-buying tour of Flemish towns and cities.) This visit is now remembered for Maria's affair with Thomas Jefferson, who was then based in Paris as the American minister to France. Cosway was ostensibly working on a portrait commission from the prince of Wales's great friend, Louis-Philippe, duc d'Orléans (later known as Philippe-Égalité) to portray his children in a drawing (Musée Condé, Chantilly). Through his friendship with the antiquarian and adventurer, baron d'Hancarville, however, Cosway conceived the idea of presenting Louis XVI—for display in the Grande Galerie of the Palais du Louvre—with his four huge tapestry cartoons (Louvre, Paris). These were then thought to be by Raphael and Giulio Romano and to be for the *History of Camillus* tapestry cycle. (They are now thought to have been made by Giulio Romano's studio and followers and are known to be from the *Fructus belli* and the *History of Scipio* tapestry cycles.) Cosway's offer was gratefully accepted on behalf of the king by baron d'Angivillier, the master of the king's works. These Renaissance cartoons were widely admired by the leading French artists—especially by David—when they were unveiled in the Louvre in 1788.

In return for his magnificent gesture (the cartoons were thought to be worth about £10,000), on 18 July 1788 Cosway was presented by Louis XVI with four superb Gobelins tapestries from the *Don Quixote* series after Coypel's designs, as well as a Savonnerie carpet. This was an exceptional gift, of a kind normally reserved by the French for visiting foreign royalty and ambassadors, and is indicative of Cosway's extraordinarily high status at this time. In turn Cosway made the equally magnificent gift in 1789 of these tapestries to his foremost patron, the prince of Wales. They were intended to decorate one of the principal bedrooms at the prince's splendid London residence, Carlton House, and remain in the Royal Collection.

**Later career: 1790–1821** On 4 May 1790 Maria Cosway gave birth to the couple's only child, Louisa Paolina Angelica Cosway. She was named after her godfather, the Corsican patriot General Pasquale Paoli (1725–1807), who was an intimate friend of Maria, and who was portrayed by Cosway in a masterly Titianesque oil of 1798 (Palazzo Pitti, Florence). Louisa was also named after her godmother Princess Louisa of Stolberg, duchess of Albany (1753–1824), the widow of Prince Charles Edward Stuart (1720–1788). A few weeks after the birth, Maria travelled to Italy, apparently for health reasons, leaving her husband and daughter behind.

In 1791 Cosway decided to move from Schomberg House. That May he offered his old master paintings for sale by private contract. He published *A Catalogue of the Entire Collection of Pictures of Richard Cosway Esq., R. A.*, in which the descriptions of the works were probably written by himself. He then leased an elegant Adam-style mansion designed in 1773–5 by Richard Edwin (*d.* 1778) at 22 Stratford Place, on Oxford Street. This he filled with the residue of his art collections, to which he continued to add. Three years later, possibly owing to the lack of privacy on Oxford Street, he decided to move two doors along to 20 Stratford Place, a much quieter residence. He lived there until the last year of his life, when he rented a cottage at 31 Edgware Road, London.

Maria Cosway returned from Italy to her family in London in November 1794. After developing a sore throat, Louisa died of fever on 29 July 1796. Both parents were devastated by this loss and profoundly affected.

Cosway's eccentric spiritual explorations increased after Louisa's death. He had shown considerable enthusiasm for Swedenborgianism and Mesmerism in the 1780s and 1790s, while later he became a committed faith healer and astrologer. His extensive library, which was sold at auction just before his death, not only contained books on history, poetry, and the fine arts, but also 'a numerous Collection of early Works on Divinity' and an 'unusual assemblage of Treatises on Magic, Necromancy, Apparitions, Vampires' (Stanley's, London, 8–12 June 1821). The seriousness with which he held these interests can be seen in his two late self-portraits: the *Mystical Self-Portrait* (Worcester

Art Museum, Massachusetts; exh. Edinburgh, 1995), datable *c.*1805, and the full-length *Self-Portrait as Esau*, dated 1806 (Uffizi gallery, Florence; exh. Edinburgh, 1995). Both works contain overt references to Cosway's profound interest in freemasonry and religious mysticism during the later part of his life.

**Aristocratic patrons** During the period *c.*1780–1815 Cosway worked for three major aristocratic patrons, apart from the prince of Wales. The first was Jacob, second earl of Radnor (1750–1826), all of whose commissions from the artist between 1781 and 1812 are recorded in his estate account book (priv. coll.). Cosway portrayed his patron in miniature and in a full-length oil painting. He also portrayed Radnor's wife in a drawing and his children in oils, the most successful of which is the charming, pastoral composition *William, Third Earl of Radnor, with his Sister the Hon. Mary Anne Pleydell-Bouverie* (priv. coll.; exh. Edinburgh, 1995). Cosway also sold Lord Radnor a select group of important old master paintings from his private contract sale of 1791; these entered one of the most important aristocratic paintings collections to be formed in Britain during the eighteenth and early nineteenth centuries.

The second key aristocratic patron of Cosway's was William, third Viscount Courtenay (1768–1835), the young lover (Kitty) of William Beckford. Portraits were commissioned from the artist by Lord Courtenay between 1790 and 1812—as noted in the artist's bill, which was not paid until 1820 (Cosway MSS, priv. coll.). This list refers to many miniatures as well as an important group of full-length oils. Most notable are the extravagant, Van Dyckian fancy-dress portrait of Lord Courtenay, dated 1791 (engraved in mezzotint by C. Turner in 1809), and the romantic, seated group of three of his sisters, *The Hons. Sophia, Louisa and Mathilda Courtenay*, dated 1806 (both priv. coll.; exh. Edinburgh, 1995). Cosway was also commissioned to paint a large altarpiece, *The Supper at Emmaus*, in which he included his self-portrait in the guise of the innkeeper (priv. coll.).

Cosway's third major patron was George, marquess of Blandford, later fifth duke of Marlborough (1766–1840), a profligate bibliophile, who assembled a celebrated library at his house, White Knights, near Reading. Apart from commissioning miniatures, drawings, and prints of himself and his family from 1797 to *c.*1815, Lord Blandford also sat to Cosway in 1797 for an elegant, Lelyesque oil portrait (priv. coll.; exh. Edinburgh, 1995). He also commissioned a spectacular double portrait of two of his children playing with armour, *George, Earl of Sunderland, and his Brother Lord Charles Spencer* (priv. coll.; exh. London, 1995).

**Death and reputation** In 1801 Maria Cosway left her husband again to travel to Paris, Lyons, and Lodi in northern Italy. On hearing that he had been taken ill in 1815, she visited London to be with him. Though they never divorced, this long separation may have been caused by the effective breakdown of their marriage. Maria returned to London again in 1817 as Cosway's health weakened through a series of strokes. After he died of a seizure—in his carriage on 4 July 1821—Maria organized his grand funeral on 12 July at St Marylebone Church, where he was buried, and commissioned a marble memorial including a portrait roundel from Richard Westmacott (*in situ*). She stayed another year in London, arranging the series of sales of Cosway's art collections and possessions through the auctioneer George Stanley. Maria also attempted—unsuccessfully—to sell her husband's own drawings to George IV, and then mounted an exhibition of them at Stanley's auction room in London during spring 1822. After touring Scotland she returned to Italy to resume directing the girls' school she had founded in Lodi. She had taken to Lodi most of her husband's surviving drawings, as well as prints, miniatures, and paintings, both by him and a few of the old masters, and also some of his books and documents. Together with her own collection, these materials form the basis of the Fondazione Cosway collection at Lodi, which today cares for them after her school finally closed in 1978.

Richard Cosway can now be seen as one of the most significant and multi-faceted artistic personalities active in Regency Britain. Arguably he was the pre-eminent pupil of William Shipley, being a frequent prize winner at the latter's newly founded Society of Arts. Cosway was also an original oil portraitist and a sophisticated draughtsman of subject compositions. He was undoubtedly the most important, influential, and fashionable portrait miniaturist and draughtsman during the last two decades of the eighteenth century: his delicate style and flattering portrayals have come to epitomize Regency society. Cosway's flamboyant personality, eccentric mysticism, and brilliant marriage to Maria Hadfield during the 1780s brought him celebrity and notoriety. He can be justly called the principal recorder of the prince of Wales's image from 1780 to 1808, as well as having exerted a great influence on his patron's artistic taste and collecting during that period. Perhaps Cosway's greatest achievement, however, was as a connoisseur, virtuoso, and collector—particularly of old master paintings, prints, and drawings—who was admired and respected by his contemporaries, notably Lawrence, Soane, Douce, Beckford, and Hazlitt.

STEPHEN LLOYD

**Sources** [R. Cosway?], *A catalogue of the entire collection of pictures of Richard Cosway* (1791) • *A catalogue … of the capital collection of pictures the property of Richard Cosway* (1792) [sale catalogue, Christies, 2–3 March 1792] • *A catalogue of the pictures of Richard Cosway* (1821) [sale catalogue, Stanley's, London, 17–19 May 1821] • *A catalogue of the … library of Richard Cosway* (1821) [sale catalogue, Stanley's, London, 8–12 June 1821] • *A catalogue … of the drawings and prints of the late Richard Cosway* (1822) [sale catalogue, Stanley's, London, 14–22 Feb 1822] • *A catalogue of the … assemblage of miscellaneous articles of taste and virtù, the property of … Richard Cosway* (1821) [sale catalogue, Stanley's, London, 22–4 May 1821] • *A catalogue of the last portion of the … collection of pictures … of the late Richard Cosway* (1822) [sale catalogue, Stanley's, London, 8–9 March 1822] • W. Hazlitt, 'Fonthill Abbey', *London Magazine* (Nov 1822); repr. in P. P. Howe, ed., *The complete works of William Hazlitt*, 22 vols. (1930–34), 12.95–6 • W. Hazlitt, 'On the old age of artists', *The plain speaker*, 2 vols. (1826), 207–27; repr. in *The complete works of William Hazlitt*, ed. P. P. Howe, 21 vols. (1930–34), 18.173–179 • P. Lasinio, *Disegni scelti dai portafogli del celebre Riccardo Cosway* (Florence, 1826) • J. T. Smith, *Nollekens and his times*, 2 vols. (1828) • A. Cunningham, *The lives of the most eminent British painters*, 6 vols. (1829–33) • 'Recollections of Richard Cosway', *Library of the Fine Arts*, 4 (1832), 184–91 • F. B. Daniell, *A catalogue raisonné of the engraved works of Richard Cosway* (1890) • *Catalogue of miniatures, oil paintings, drawings and engravings by Richard Cosway, R.A.* (1895) [exhibition catalogue, Moncorvo House, London] • C. Williamson, *Richard Cosway R.A. and his wife and pupils* (1897); 2nd edn (1905) • G. C. Williamson, *Catalogue of the collection of miniatures, the property of J. Pierpont Morgan*, 4 vols. (1906–8) • Helen Matilda, countess of Radnor and W. B. Squire, *Catalogue of the pictures in the collection of the earl of Radnor*, 2 vols. (1909) • G. Reynolds, *English portrait miniatures* (1952) • J. Murdoch and others, *The English miniature* (1981) • R. Bayne-Powell, ed., *Catalogue of portrait miniatures in the Fitzwilliam Museum, Cambridge* (1985) • S. Lloyd, 'Richard Cosway, R.A.: the artist as collector, connoisseur and *virtuoso*', *Apollo*, 138 (1991), 398–405 • R. Walker, *The eighteenth and early nineteenth century miniatures in the collection of her majesty the queen* (1992) • S. Lloyd, 'Forming the taste of a prince: Richard Cosway and George IV's early collection', *Apollo*, 138 (1993), 192–4 • S. Lloyd and others, *Richard and Maria Cosway: Regency artists of taste and fashion* (1995) [exhibition catalogue, Scot. NPG, 11 Aug – 22 Oct 1995, and NPG, 17 Nov 1995 – 18 Feb 1996] • S. Lloyd, 'Fashioning the image of the prince: Richard Cosway and George IV', *'Squanderous and lavish profusion': George IV, his image and patronage of the arts*, ed. D. Arnold (1995) • G. Barnett, *Richard and Maria Cosway: a biography* (1995) • S. Lloyd, 'Richard Cosway: primarius pictor, virtuoso e collezionista', *Maria e Richard Cosway*, ed. T. Gipponi (Turin, 1998), 45–60 • *IGI* • *Scots Magazine* (Jan 1755), 47

**Archives** Fondazione Cosway, Lodi, MS inventory, indentures of assignment and legal documents • PRO, expired commissions, HO 73 • Royal Arch., MSS | BM, Townley MSS • priv. coll., Courtenay MSS • priv. coll., Combe MSS • priv. coll., Radnor MSS • RA, Humphry MSS • RA, Lawrence MSS • Royal Arch., Carlton House MSS • Sir John Soane's Museum, London, Soane MSS

**Likenesses** R. Cosway, self-portrait, miniature, *c.*1770, Metropolitan Museum of Art, New York • R. Cosway, self-portrait, oils, *c.*1770, Attingham Park, Shropshire • R. Cosway, double portrait, etching, 1784 (with his wife), BM, NPG • M. Bova, stipple, pubd 1786 (after R. Cosway), BM, NPG • gilt-bronze medallion, *c.*1786, Museo Nazionale del Bargello, Florence, Italy • J. Clarke, stipple, pubd 1788 (after R. Cosway), BM, NPG • R. Cosway, self-portrait, drawing, *c.*1789 (with busts of Michelangelo and Rubens), Fondazione Cosway, Lodi, Italy • R. Thew, stipple, pubd 1789 (after R. Cosway), BM, NPG • R. Cosway, self-portrait, oil on panel, *c.*1790, NPG • R. Cosway, self-portrait, pencil and wash, *c.*1790, NPG [*see illus.*] • R. Cosway, self-portrait, drawing, *c.*1800, priv. coll. • R. Cosway, self-portrait, drawing, *c.*1805, Worcester Art Museum, Massachusetts • R. Cosway, self-portrait, drawing, 1806, Uffizi Gallery, Florence • R. Cosway, self-portrait, watercolour on ivory, NG Ire. • G. Dance, pencil and chalk drawing, RA • H. Singleton, group portrait, oils (*Royal Academicians, 1793*), Royal Collection • R. Thew, engraving (after double portrait, self-portrait, with Maria Cosway by R. Cosway, 1789) • R. Westmacott, medallion on monument, St Mary's Church, Marylebone • J. Zoffany, group portrait, oils (*Royal Academicians, 1772*), Royal Collection • bronze medallion, V&A

**Wealth at death** approx. £12,000: Fondazione Cosway, Lodi, legal and estate MSS documents

**Cosworth** [Cosowarth], **Michael** (*fl.* **1576–1610**), translator, was born in London, according to the *Dictionary of National Biography*, one of the five children of John Cosworth, a London mercer and receiver-general of the duchy of Cornwall, and his wife, Dorothy, daughter of William Locke, a London alderman. The *Dictionary of National Biography's* suggested birth date of 1568, however, appears untenable given the beginning of Cosworth's university career in 1576. Cosworth was related to Richard Carew, whose wife, Juliana, was the granddaughter of a John Cosworth. The psalmist Henry Lok (or Locke) was also a relation of his.

Cosworth matriculated as a pensioner of St John's College, Cambridge, in December 1576 and graduated BA in 1580. In 1587 he was successively rector of Redruth and Duloe in Cornwall; he was rector of Sampford Courtenay, Devon, in 1589. Cosworth and his family eventually relocated to Cornwall. There he probably was employed as clerk for Sir John Bramston the elder. Sir John Bramston the younger reported that his father had a clerk named 'Cusworth … whom we called cousin' whose older brother was a justice of the peace (*Autobiography*, 13).

Michael Cosworth also tried his hand at translating some of the Psalms; in Holland's view his efforts are 'not without merit' (Holland, 229). Richard Carew wrote of Cosworth that:

> he addicteth himself to an ecclesiastical life, and therein joining Poetry with Divinity, endeavoureth to imitate the holy prophet David, whose Psalmes of his translation into English metre receiveth general applause beyond a great many other well-deserving undertakings of the same type. (*DNB*)

One of the more readily available samples of Cosworth's work can be found in the form of a poem, dedicated to Henry Lok and signed 'M.C.', preceding Lok's *Ecclesiastes* (1597). A few more poems by and to Cosworth, originally in Harley MS 6906, have been anthologized in E. Brydges' *Excerpta Tudoriana* (1814), most notably a poem dedicated to 'his best cousin, Mrs Barbara Loke, by Michael Cosowarth' (this seems to be his own spelling of his name) on the theme of 'kind and kindness', with gentle puns on the various meanings of 'kind' (Brydges, 48). In the same selection there is a poem by Henry Lok to 'his best cousin, Mr Michael Cosowarth' (ibid., 51). Richard Carew also dedicates two poems to his 'cousin, Michael Cosowarth'. The first of his dedications commends the author's rendering of the Psalms:

> These Psalms which from their native sense exil'd,
> … COSWARTH calls home with high-tun'd voice of his.
> (ibid., 49)

The second one, however, seems to aim at sweetening Carew's criticism of his cousin's poetic skills:

> And now I have, as 'twas thy kind desire,
> Unkindly gentle censure of thy skill …
> (ibid., 50)

There is some indication that Michael Cosworth reached old age: in his autobiography Sir John Bramston the younger mentions that, on a visit to Cornwall in 1640, he saw both the clerk named 'Cusworth' and 'his eldest brother … a Justice of Peace [who] had a good estate' (*Autobiography*, 13). If this brother is the same person as Edward Coswarth who was an active 'Justice of Peace for Cornwall' in 1605 (*CSP dom.*, *1603–10*, 231), by the time Sir John Bramston the younger visited Cornwall thirty-five years later the Cosworth brothers are unlikely to have been in their prime.

It is not known whether Michael Cosworth founded a family of his own, though Venn suggests he may have done. His date of death has not been recorded, but Venn notes that Cosworth made a will in 1610; however, this does not survive.

ARTEMIS GAUSE-STAMBOULOPOULOU

**Sources** Cooper, *Ath. Cantab.*, 2.430 · *The autobiography of Sir John Bramston*, ed. [Lord Braybrooke], CS, 32 (1845) · J. Holland, *The psalmists of Britain*, 1 (1843) · H. Lok, *Ecclesiastes* (1597) · E. Brydges, *Excerpta Tudoriana*, 1 (1814) · *CSP dom.*, *1603–10* · Boase & Courtney, *Bibl. Corn.* · Venn, *Alum. Cant.* · J. L. Vivian and H. H. Drake, eds., *The visitation of the county of Cornwall in the year 1620*, Harleian Society, 9 (1874), 50 · *DNB*
**Archives** BL, Harley MS 6906

**Cosyn, Benjamin** (*c*.1580–1653), organist and composer, about whose family, birth, and education nothing is known, married Margett Rowley on 16 December 1603 at St Julian's, Shrewsbury, suggesting origins in Shropshire. He is described in these records as 'musitian' (Shropshire County RO, register of marriages, 1603) and could by that date already have had contact with John Bull in Hereford. He was organist at St Laurence's, Ludlow, from 1621 to 1622, and had moved to London by 1622, when he was appointed fellow and organist at Dulwich College with a salary of about £10 per year. He left this post in 1624. Two years later he was appointed first organist of the Charterhouse. The House of Commons eliminated his post in 1643, anticipating the order a year later banning organs in churches. Cosyn petitioned successfully to receive a pension in consideration of 'poverty, ould age and misperfeccons of body' (LMA, MS G3/2A, fol. 48v). He lived in the nearby ward of Aldersgate at least from 1641 and was buried in St Botolph's on 14 September 1653.

Cosyn copied keyboard music into two manuscripts, in 1620 and 1652, preserving not only the majority of his own works but also music by Tallis, Byrd, Bull, and Gibbons as well as pre-Restoration composers (BL, royal music MS 23.1.4; Bibliothéque Nationale, Paris, réserve 1185). His output of over fifty keyboard works chronicles the shift in taste during the first half of the century from plainsong settings and pavane–galliard pairs to suites of allemandes, courantes, and sarabands. Musicologists have criticized Cosyn for his heavy-handed approach to ornamentation. At its best, his music for virginals demonstrates skill in elaborating popular tunes with brilliant passage work. He was dependent on inspiration found in the music of fellow composers, upon which he drew to create lively settings in the fashionable genres of his day.

ORHAN MEMED

**Sources** O. Memed, *Seventeenth-century keyboard music: Benjamin Cosyn*, 2 vols. (1993) · Dotted crotchet, 'The Charterhouse', *MT*, 44 (1903), 777 · D. Dawe, *Organists of the City of London, 1660–1850* (1983) · P. Willets, 'Benjamin Cosyn: sources and circumstance', *Sundry sorts of music books*, ed. C. Banks, A. Searle, and M. Turner (1993), 129–45 · R. Francis and P. Klein, *The organs and organists of Ludlow parish church* (1982)
**Archives** Bibliothèque Nationale, Paris, Réserve 1185 · BL, 'Cosyn Virginal Book', Royal Music MS 23.1.4 | Dulwich College, MSS relating to Dulwich College, MSS IX, X · GL, MSS relating to St Botolph Aldersgate, MSS 1461/1, 2050/1, 3710, 3854/1 · LMA, MSS relating to the Charterhouse, MSS AR5/40c, AR5/41, G1/5, G1/6, G3/2a, film 56/6, part II, film 56/6 section A · PRO, MSS relating to

Aldersgate ward, MSS E/179/252/1, E/179/252/14 · Shrops. RRC, MSS relating to Shrewsbury

**Cotchett, Thomas** (*bap.* **1677**, *d.* in or after **1713**), silk-throwing mill owner, was baptized at Mickleover on 16 April 1677, one of six children of Thomas Cotchett (*bap.* 1640, *d.* 1713/14), a barrister at Gray's Inn, and his first wife, Hannah Biddle (*d.* 1678). About 1704 Cotchett, described erroneously as a barrister and a London silk-reeler, built the first water-powered mill in England for preparing skeins of silk ready for weaving. It was the forerunner of the many later cotton- and wool-spinning mills which formed such a vital role in launching the industrial revolution.

Production of fine silk cloth increased in England during the seventeenth century, particularly after the revocation of the edict of Nantes in 1685 and the arrival of Huguenot refugees skilled in weaving. To obtain suitable silk threads, the silk had to be unwound from the cocoon, with eight or ten being reeled off together into a skein. This was still too fine, so that the requisite number of skeins had to be reeled together with a light twist to form 'tram', suitable for soft weft. For warp threads tram had to be further twisted and then numbers of these 'thrown' or twisted together in the opposite direction to form a strong, thick thread called organzine. The Chinese had developed machines for all these different stages based on the plain spindle. By the thirteenth century the Italians had evolved hand-operated machines in which the spindles were set around the circumference of a circle with reels above. These were improved in two ways: first, through being driven by water-wheels and, second, by adding a flyer to the spindle. With the flyer, winding the threads onto bobbins ready for throwing would have been much easier, but the Italians kept these machines a secret.

All the silk used by English weavers was imported in the thrown state, so the weaver did not have the flexibility for preparing his own warp or weft to suit the cloth he wanted. Cotchett saw an opportunity here and decided to build a water-powered silk-throwing mill. A date of 1702 has been given in early accounts but more likely is a date of 1704, when Cotchett leased water rights on an island in the River Derwent at Derby. On 20 October 1705 he borrowed £2400 from his father, and this was followed by a further £2000 on 26 June 1707. These sums must be connected with establishing his silk mill, which was constructed by the famous local millwright George Sorocold. The building contained 'double Dutch mills' driven by a water-wheel 13 feet 6 inches in diameter, but the precise nature of these machines is not known. By comparison with the Italian machines they were probably primitive forms of throwing machine, using plain spindles without flyers. It is also said that Cotchett used only a single machine, whereas three were necessary.

Cotchett was bankrupt in 1713 but his mill was taken over by Sir Thomas Lombe, who built another with Italian machines alongside the first. William Wilson, who became joint owner of these mills, wrote a description of them about 1739 in which he described Cotchett's section

as still containing its double Dutch mills in complete working order, so perhaps Cotchett's failure was commercial rather than technical. What is clear from this description and early pictures of Cotchett's mill is that here was the prototype for later multi-storey textile-spinning mills.

RICHARD L. HILLS

**Sources** F. Williamson, 'George Sorocold of Derby: a pioneer of water supply', *Journal of the Derbyshire Archaeological and Natural History Society*, 57 (1936), 43–93 · F. Williamson, 'Cotchett family of Derby', *Journal of the Derbyshire Archaeological and Natural History Society*, 60 (1939) · A. L. Reade, *Johnsonian gleanings*, 4 (privately printed, London, 1923) · A. Calladine, 'Lombe's mill: an exercise in reconstruction', *Industrial Archaeology Review*, 16 (1993–4), 82–99 · W. H. Chaloner, 'Sir Thomas Lombe (1685–1739) and the British silk industry', *History Today*, 3 (1953), 778–85 · S. D. Chapman, *The cotton industry in the industrial revolution* (1972) · A. Rees and others, *The cyclopaedia, or, Universal dictionary of arts, sciences, and literature*, 45 vols. (1819–20) [article on silk] · W. Hutton, *The history of Derby* (1791) · S. Smiles, *Men of invention and industry*, rev. edn (1890) · A. E. Musson and E. Robinson, *Science and technology in the industrial revolution* (1969) · D. Kuhn, *Science and civilisation in China*, ed. J. Needham, 5 (1988) · R. L. Hills, 'From cocoon to cloth: the technology of silk production', *La seta in Europa, sec. XIII–XX: atti della 'Ventiquattresima settimana di studio* [Prato, Italy, 1992], ed. S. Cavaciocchi (Florence, 1993), 51–90

**Coterel, James** (*fl.* **1328–1351**), gang leader, is assumed to have been a younger son of Ralph Coterel, a landowner in Cromford, Matlock, Tadington, and three other places in Derbyshire, who was dead by 1315. In his youth James was the leader of a gang that included his brothers John and Nicholas and also had links with other groups of criminals including that led by Eustace Folville. Nicholas Coterel's pardon as one of Thomas of Lancaster's adherents in April 1322, and the group's close link to members of the Bradbourn family who had also been among the earl's followers, indicates an affiliation to the opposition of Edward II's rule. John Kinnersley, a canon of Lichfield later accused of supporting the Coterels, had been a member of Thomas of Lancaster's council, and Richard Rolleston of Crich, one of their receivers, had probably been one of the earl's bailiffs. But although the Coterels' career of violence and crime began with the breakdown of Edward II's government, there are no indications of a political motive. By 1330 they had been accused of having pillaged estates of Henry, earl of Lancaster (*d.* 1345), in Derbyshire and Staffordshire, and of having committed two murders, and they had already formed associations with other criminals.

Between 1330 and 1332 James Coterel led a ring of gangs involved in murder, kidnapping, and extortion in the Peak District and northern Nottinghamshire. Despite his own attachment for murder at the Derbyshire eyre of 1330, and the outlawry of his associates in March 1331, Coterel was never arrested. This was due to the support he received in the area, especially from two religious communities, the dean and chapter of Lichfield and the priory of Lenton, Nottinghamshire. When a powerful commission of trailbaston justices, led by the chief justices of king's bench and common pleas, visited the midlands in 1332, he escaped arrest because he was warned by the prior of Lenton. The canons of Lichfield were repeatedly mentioned as receivers of Coterel's gang. This close connection with the dean and chapter of Lichfield, as well as with the Cluniac priory of Lenton, illustrates Coterel's standing in the High Peak District, where both these religious communities had previously clashed over conflicting claims to advowsons and tithes. James Coterel also benefited from Queen Philippa's patronage more than once. Through her influence he was able to purchase the wardship of a mill in Wormhill and lands in Tideswell in 1332—he still had property interests in the latter manor in 1339. When he received a pardon in 1351 it was again at the queen's request. It is likely that he obtained this support because Nicholas Coterel was bailiff of the queen's liberty in Derbyshire and Leicestershire, though Nicholas did not acquit himself well in that office, since he was summoned before the king's council to answer a charge of embezzlement in 1359. Although James Coterel repeatedly acted as tax collector for Lenton Priory in his later career, and was even entrusted with one arrest warrant in 1336 and another in 1350, when he and six others were instructed to find and capture three monks of Lenton who had left the priory, he still felt it necessary to obtain a pardon for extortions, oppressions, receivings of felons, usurpations, and ransoms in 1351. Nicholas Coterel was still alive in 1363, when the recognizance of a debt of £132 which he owed to John Folville and Robert Harrington was entered upon the close rolls, but the date of James's death is unknown. JENS RÖHRKASTEN

**Sources** J. Bellamy, 'The Coterel gang: an anatomy of a band of fourteenth-century criminals', *EngHR*, 79 (1964), 698–717 · J. C. Cox, 'Receipt roll of the Peak jurisdiction of the dean and chapter of Lichfield', *Journal of the Derbyshire Archaeological and Natural History Society*, 11 (1889), 142–56 · *Chancery records*

**Cotes, Francis** (1726–1770), portrait painter, was born on 20 May 1726 in the Strand, London, the eldest of four children of Robert Cotes (d. 1774), apothecary and former mayor of Galway, and his second wife, Elizabeth (b. c.1700, d. after 1775), daughter of Francis Lynn, chief secretary to the Royal African Company. Cotes's great-grandfather John Cotes held estates in Leicestershire, which he was forced to forfeit during the civil war, owing to his royalist allegiance. He moved to co. Roscommon, Ireland, where Cotes's grandfather, John, was born. The family retained strong English connections that resulted in Francis Cotes's father being appointed mayor of Galway by the crown. In 1717 he was tried for treason by the Irish parliament, and subsequently by Queen Anne's council, for failure to uphold the English government's repressive policy against the Roman Catholic community. Upon his acquittal, his political career over, he set up business in London, as an apothecary. His first marriage was to Anne Fowler, who died on 11 December 1722, their infant son Robert dying the following March. At the time of Francis Cotes's birth his father was living in the Strand, Francis's baptism being recorded on 29 May 1726 at the newly built church of St Mary-le-Strand. Following Cotes's birth, the family moved to Cork Street, Burlington Gardens, in Mayfair. Three further children were born: Robert, who died in infancy, Samuel *Cotes (1734–1818), and a daughter, Frances-Maria, who also died in infancy.

**Early years, 1741–1757** It is conjectured that Cotes entered into an apprenticeship with the painter George Knapton, about the time of his fifteenth birthday (Johnson, 2). In addition to learning his trade Cotes was probably introduced to the work of the old masters, Knapton having a reputation as a connoisseur as well as an artist with fashionable aristocratic connections. Indeed, it may have been at this time that Cotes painted a copy of 'the Virgin and Child in crayons from Guido', which he bequeathed to Knapton in his will. During the 1740s Knapton worked in oils and in crayons, then a fashionable medium for portraiture, influenced particularly by the Venetian pastellist Rosalba Carriera. Cotes had probably completed his apprenticeship with Knapton by 1747, the year of his first known signed and dated works, pastels of an unknown gentleman (Leicestershire Museums and Art Galleries) and Miss Catherine Wilson (priv. coll.). Cotes appears to have concentrated exclusively on pastels throughout the remainder of the 1740s and well into the 1750s. From the outset Cotes's clientele included distinguished members of the whig aristocracy, including Lady Georgiana Lennox, mother of Charles James Fox (1748; priv. coll.), Lord Carysfort (1751; priv. coll.), and the Hon. George Keppel, later third earl of Albemarle (1752; priv. coll.). At that time Cotes also painted pastel portraits of the Irish Gunning family, notably the sisters Maria and Elizabeth, then celebrated for their great beauty, and subsequently countess of Coventry and duchess of Hamilton and Argyll (NPG). Both portraits were engraved in mezzotint by James Mac-Ardell in 1752, and offered for sale to the public from Cotes's father's house in Cork Street, which he then presumably used as a gallery to promote his work.

**The middle period, 1757–1765** By the mid-1750s Cotes's pastel portraits assumed a greater sense of naturalism and individual character. In this he was particularly influenced by the Swiss painter Jean-Étienne Liotard (then working in England), and also by the German Anton-Raphael Mengs and the Frenchman Maurice-Quentin de la Tour. From this period date Cotes's portraits of Louis François Roubiliac (c.1757; priv. coll.), of Dr William Bromfield, and of his father (both 1757; RA). Cotes's opinions on technical aspects of pastels and their preservation are contained in an undated short paper he wrote on the subject, which was published posthumously by the *European Magazine* in 1797.

Cotes's first recorded oil painting, a signed and dated portrait of an unknown lady (priv. coll.), dates from 1753. However, its quality is poor compared to his pastels of the same period, and he resisted further forays into the medium at that time. Several years later Cotes was particularly impressed by the Scots artist Allan Ramsay, who returned to London from Italy in 1757, promoting a style of oil painting which sought to imitate the soft, velvety texture of pastels. Indeed, it was probably the influence of Ramsay, and his success in court circles, that persuaded Cotes to work increasingly in oils. When he took up oils again in the later 1750s Cotes quickly became accomplished in this medium, as demonstrated by his portrait of his fellow artist Paul Sandby, seated drawing by an open window (1759; Tate Collection). In 1760 Cotes exhibited at the inaugural exhibition of the Society of Artists, where he showed two portraits in oils and two in pastels. These included a pastel of the eminent royal physician Sir Edward Hulse (priv. coll.) and an oil painting of Anne Sandby, wife of Paul Sandby, in a landscape setting. This was engraved by Edward Fisher in 1763 as *The Nut-Brown Maid*, from the poem by Matthew Prior. During the 1760s Cotes continued to exhibit at the Society of Artists, his portraiture by now increasingly influenced by Joshua Reynolds. Cotes's portraits retained their own distinct decorative, rococo air, although his colours became bolder and less subtle, while his female portraits, as with Reynolds, often appeared in 'timeless' classical garments. This can be seen, for example, in his double full-length portrait, *Lady Stanhope and Lady Effingham as Diana and her Companion* (1765; York City Art Gallery), and his full-length portrait *The Duchess of Hamilton as Venus, Queen of Beauty* (1767; priv. coll.).

In 1763 Cotes took a lease on a house at 32 Cavendish Square. Situated on the south side of the square, it was described in the sale catalogue after his death as a 'Large and commodious House, With an elegant Suite of Five Rooms on the First Floor, and Coach Houses and Stabling' (Johnson, 156). The house, situated in a fashionable part of London, was remodelled by Cotes to include, in addition to his own studio, a room for pupils to paint in, and a gallery or 'Shew Room'. Two other prominent artists, George Romney and Sir Martin Archer Shee, subsequently leased it to use as their studio. Cotes had at least two pupils, John Russell and John Milbourne. Although Cotes and Russell became friends, Russell's excessive religious zeal apparently disrupted his master's household. Owing to the volume of work Cotes also now began to employ an assistant, Peter Toms, to paint the clothing in his oil portraits, although not his pastels. Toms was a professional 'drapery' painter, who had already been employed extensively by Reynolds in the 1750s. By this time Cotes apparently charged between 20 and 80 guineas for his portraits; less than Reynolds but more than Thomas Gainsborough. He increased his prices once more in 1768. In May 1764 Cotes was being favourably compared with Reynolds, 'and greatly to his Honour be it said, that he generally preserves a beautiful Correctness in his Pictures, which the latter Master too often neglects' (*Public Advertiser*, 2 May 1764). Just before his death in October 1764, Hogarth apparently told the painter Edward Edwards that Cotes 'excelled Reynolds as a portrait painter' (E. Edwards, *Anecdotes of Painters who have Resided or been Born in England*, 1808, facs. edn, 1970, 34). Even so, as it has since been pointed out, Cotes's interest in emulating Reynolds's grand-manner portraiture remained superficial, undertaken principally to appeal to current fashion rather than from any inner conviction (Johnson, 19).

During the 1760s Cotes continued to paint in pastels as well as oils, although unlike Reynolds he preferred to portray his female sitters in contemporary costume, such as *Maria, Dowager Countess of Waldegrave* (1764; priv. coll.), and *Laura Keppel* (*c*.1764; priv. coll.). By the mid-1760s Cotes was also gaining popularity as a painter of children, in both oils and pastels. Often he depicted them with a toy or plaything, for example, Selina Chambers cradling a doll (1764; V&A), Lewis Cage with a cricket bat (1768; priv. coll.), or Frances Lee with a knotted handkerchief in the shape of a rabbit (1769; Milwaukee Art Center Collection, Wisconsin). Cotes's male adult portraits of this period are often less successful than his women or children, relying on formulaic compositions, the subject invariably standing or leaning upon a cane in a parkland setting. Among such works are four portraits of Sir Francis Burdett in the same pose but in different-coloured clothing, presumably commissioned to hang in different rooms of his manor house (Johnson, 23). All but one (Ferens Art Gallery, Hull) appear to be largely the work of Cotes's drapery painter.

**Later works, 1765–1770** In 1765 Cotes married. Nothing is known about his wife other than her name, Sarah, and her physical appearance. He painted her portrait on at least two occasions, exhibiting a pastel of her with a small dog at the Royal Academy in 1770. Little is known of Cotes's private life, although he was evidently known by his fellow artists as Frank rather than Francis (Farington, *Diary*, 2.506). Aside from Knapton, Cotes was close to the watercolourist Paul Sandby and the sculptor Joseph Wilton, whom he remembered in his will as his 'worthy friend'. He was also friendly with the society hostess Mrs Hester Thrale, who later recalled being on 'very intimate' terms with him. On one occasion she mischievously asked the identity of a woman in one of his portraits, 'who is as eminent for her Ugliness methinks, as any one here for her Beauty'; to which Cotes replied with alarm: ''tis my own Wife, it is indeed; & I have been married to her but a fortnight' (K. C. Balderston, *Thraliana: the Diary of Mrs. Hester Lynch Thrale*, 1942, 2, 268). Cotes's surviving portraits of his wife portray her as not unattractive. The couple had no children, Mrs Cotes being her husband's executrix at his death and the chief beneficiary of his estate. Cotes's self-portrait in pastels, which he bequeathed to his father, is untraced, as is the large miniature painted by his brother, Samuel, from memory after his death. Two other portraits are known; an engraved profile head of 1768 by D. P. Pariset after a drawing by the French artist Pierre Falconet, and a drawing of him seated, reading a book, ascribed to Paul Sandby. In the former Cotes's face is plump, the nose long and pointed, with a slightly receding chin, although in the latter work, which dates from 1755 (Nottingham Castle Museum and Art Gallery), he presents an altogether leaner, more handsome, figure.

In 1765 Cotes was one of nine signatories to a petition to George III requesting a royal charter for the Society of Artists, an indication of his senior position within the organization. From this time Cotes concentrated increasingly on oil portraits at the expense of pastels, although he continued to produce some of his finest works in this medium, including a head-and-shoulders portrait of

Admiral Augustus Keppel, exhibited at the Society of Artists in 1765 (priv. coll.) and Lady Frances Hoare at a spinning wheel (c.1766–70; Stourhead House, Wiltshire). Although he continued to emulate Reynolds's grand manner, Cotes's preference was for more informal images. These are exemplified by his full-length portrait of Sir Griffith Boynton, casually standing by a casement, book in hand (1769; priv. coll., USA), and Mr and Mrs William Earle Welby playing chess, exhibited at the inaugural exhibition at the Royal Academy in 1769 (priv. coll.).

In 1767 Cotes began to attract royal patronage, resulting in a series of female portraits in oils and pastels. These included portraits of Princess Caroline Matilda (1766; priv. coll.), Princess Louisa, and two large double portraits, *Queen Charlotte with Charlotte Princess Royal* and *Princess Louisa and Princess Caroline* (the latter subsequently married Christian IV of Denmark (Royal Collection). Although the subjects were depicted in elaborate court dresses, they retain an air of intimacy, conveyed through a series of informal gestures, Queen Charlotte gesturing the viewer not to wake her sleeping child on her lap, Princess Caroline Matilda touching her sister on the shoulder in a show of affection. With the express permission of the queen Cotes exhibited a pastel version of her portrait with Princess Charlotte at the Society of Artists in 1767, insisting that it be hung in a prime position. The king and queen came to the exhibition especially to see Cotes's portrait, causing one critic to proclaim:

> How happy Cotes? Thy skill shall shine,
> Unrivall'd in thy class, almost divine;
> For royal Charlotte's finish'd form is thine!
> (*London Chronicle*, 5–7 May 1767)

This picture also prompted Horace Walpole to comment in his Royal Academy catalogue, 'Cotes succeeded much better in crayons than in oils' (Johnson, 46). It was perhaps not a coincidence that Reynolds refrained from exhibiting that year, presumably piqued at the favouritism shown by the royal family towards Cotes.

On 11 June 1768 John Russell recorded in his diary that Cotes was ill, suffering from 'the stone', either kidney or gallstones, an illness from which he had apparently suffered for some years. Russell noted that Cotes intended that week 'to go under the severe operation of being cut' (Johnson, 42). The operation was partially successful, allowing Cotes to continue painting for another two years. In August 1768 Cotes, along with other directors, resigned his membership of the Society of Artists. Over the next few months, together with Sir William Chambers, Benjamin West and George Moser, Cotes drew up plans for a Royal Academy of Arts. Their paper was presented by Cotes to the king, who gave his approval in December 1768. Cotes, who was elected onto the council of the Royal Academy, showed eighteen portraits there in the first two exhibitions of 1769 and 1770. These included portraits of the dukes of Gloucester (1769) and Cumberland (1770).

On 16 June 1769 Cotes drew up his will, witnessed by Peter Toms and his pupil John Milbourne. In the summer of 1770 Cotes, by now clearly in great pain, ingested a soap-based potion in order to dissolve his kidney or gallstones. The concoction poisoned him. He died on Thursday 19 July 1770 at Richmond, Surrey. He was buried there, on 25 July, at the parish church of St Mary Magdalene. John Russell noted in his diary that, although Cotes's death was not unexpected, 'yet the news affected me much that a man full of worldly honour and pride with schemes of Business should be cut off without leaving any Marks of knowing the salvation of Jesus' (Johnson, 44). Cotes's fellow academician, Mary Moser, reported the news of Cotes's death to the artist Henry Fuseli in Rome: 'Many a tear will drop on his grave, as he is not more lamented as an artist than a friend to the distressed' (Fuseli, *The Collected English Letters of Henry Fuseli* ed. D. H. Weinglass, 1982, 12). Cotes's will was proved on 30 July 1770, his trustees being Joseph Wilton and the wealthy amateur painter Theodosius Forrest. Cotes's principal beneficiaries were his wife, his parents, and his brother, Samuel. On 21–3 and 25 February 1771 Cotes's wife sold the house in Cavendish Square and its contents at auction through Langford & Son of Covent Garden.

MARTIN POSTLE

**Sources** E. M. Johnson, *Francis Cotes* (1976) · A. Smart, *Introducing Francis Coates, R.A. (1726–1770)* (1971) [exhibition catalogue, Nottingham University Art Gallery] · Francis Cotes sale catalogue (1771) [Langford & Sons, 21–3, 25 Feb 1771] · *GM*, 1st ser., 40 (1770), 345 · will, PRO, PROB 11/959, sig. 259, fols. 33r–34v
**Likenesses** attrib. P. Sandby, pencil and chalk drawing, 1755, Nottingham Castle Museum and Art Gallery · D. P. Pariset, stipple, 1768 (after P. Falconet), BM, NPG
**Wealth at death** wife held extensive house and contents sale: Johnson, *Francis Cotes*, appendix

**Cotes, Roger** (1682–1716), mathematician and astronomer, was born on 10 July 1682 at Burbage, Leicestershire, the second son of Robert Cotes, rector of Burbage, and his wife, Grace, daughter of Major Farmer of Barwell, Leicestershire. Besides his elder brother, Anthony (b. 1681), Roger had a younger sister, Susanna (b. 1683). He was first educated at Leicester School, where his talent in mathematics was noticed before he was twelve. The Revd John Smith, Cotes's uncle, therefore took him to his house so that he might personally forward him in his studies. Smith, married to Cotes's aunt Hannah Cotes, had a son, Robert *Smith (bap. 1689, d. 1768), whose life was to be closely linked to that of his cousin. Cotes later studied at St Paul's School, London, from where he corresponded with his uncle on mathematical matters. He was admitted as a pensioner to Trinity College, Cambridge, on 6 April 1699, and graduated BA in 1702. He was elected minor fellow in 1705, major fellow in 1706, and proceeded MA in the same year. In January 1706 he was nominated first Plumian professor of astronomy and experimental philosophy, though his election did not take place until 16 October 1707. His appointment was favoured by his influential mentor Richard Bentley, master of Trinity; by Newton's successor as Lucasian professor, William Whiston, who claimed to be in mathematics 'a child to Mr Cotes' (Whiston, 133); and by Newton himself. It was, however, opposed by the astronomer royal John Flamsteed, who favoured his former assistant John Witty. Cotes was elected fellow of the Royal Society on 30 November 1711, and was ordained deacon on 30 March and priest on 31 May 1713.

Cotes was the first occupant of the Cambridge chair established by Thomas Plume (1630–1704), archdeacon of Rochester, who bequeathed nearly £2000 to maintain a professor and erect an astronomical observatory. Plans for an observatory at Trinity had already been drafted by Bentley before Plume's bequest. The observatory was eventually housed over the king's or great gate at Trinity College, together with living quarters for the Plumian professor. Cotes lived there with his cousin Robert Smith, who worked as his assistant and later succeeded him to the Plumian chair. On his appointment Cotes raised a subscription to supplement the costs for the erection of the observatory and supervised its construction. Although it was operational in his time it was not completed until 1739, and was demolished in 1797. Between August and September 1703 a number of instruments had been destined for the observatory, and these were supplemented following Plume's endowment with a brass sextant by John Rowley worth £150 and a clock donated by Newton worth about £50, now in the master's lodge at Trinity College. Further, Cotes's design for a transit telescope is carefully described in a manuscript at Clare College, Cambridge. Bentley said the observatory was 'well stor'd with the best instruments in Europe' (Willis, 500); however, Stephen Gray, who worked there for a few months as Cotes's assistant, stated in a letter to Flamsteed: 'I saw nothing there that might deserve your notice' (Cohen, 'Neglected sources', 47).

The most notable observation by Cotes was that of the total eclipse of 22 April 1715 OS, reported by Edmond Halley in the Royal Society's *Philosophical Transactions*. Cotes 'had the misfortune to be opprest by too much company, so that though the heavens were very favourable, yet he missed both the times of the beginning of the eclipse and that of total darkness' (*PTRS*, 29, 1714, 253). In a letter to Newton, Cotes reported that his assistant Richard Waller, who had a method for determining the middle of the obscuration, 'called out to Me, *Now's the Middle*, though I knew not at that time what he meant' (Edleston, 182). However, Cotes was able to observe the occultation of three spots, the end of total darkness, and the end of the eclipse, as well as to produce for Newton drawings by himself and an 'ingenious Gentleman' showing a brilliant ring about a sixth of the diameter of the moon at the centre of a luminous cross. Another observation by Cotes of March 1716, this time of a 'Great Meteor', was published in 1720 (*PTRS*, 31, 60).

In 1709 Cotes became heavily involved in the work for which he is best remembered, namely the revisions for the second edition of Newton's *Philosophia naturalis principia mathematica*, the first being out of print. Although Newton originally thought this would be a relatively speedy matter, it was not until 1713 that the 750 copies of the revised edition appeared with the imprint of Cambridge University Press, recently revived by Bentley. Cotes

stated: 'I never think the time lost when we stay for his further corrections and improvements' (Edleston, 209). Indeed, virtually all aspects of Newton's work were thoroughly and painstakingly examined, including definitions and stylistic matters. Among the topics in which Cotes became most involved were the theory of tides, the theory of the moon's motion, and the determination of cometary paths. The last topic was of great importance, because the regularity of cometary motion in all directions and inclinations to the plane of the ecliptic was a powerful argument against the existence of vortices and fluids carrying the planets. Newton was lucky to have an editor such as Cotes, though their relations became strained during their collaboration: in his final version of the preface he failed to thank the Plumian professor. A preliminary draft, however, did contain a small tribute to him (*Correspondence of Isaac Newton*, 5.114).

After Cotes had proposed to sign his name to a preface composed by Newton, he was authorized by Newton and Bentley to sign his own preface, a lengthy and important essay outlining his own version of Newton's method. In a preliminary draft Cotes had stated that gravity was essential to bodies. However, Newton's ally Samuel Clarke, whose advice Cotes had sought before publication, suggested a number of corrections and warned him against such a statement. Cotes agreed that 'it would have furnish'd matter for Cavilling' (Edleston, 158), and claimed instead that gravity was one of the primary qualities of bodies, together with extension, mobility, and impenetrability. His preface was retained in the third edition of Newton's *Principia* (1726), was translated into English by Andrew Motte, and is now easily available in the revised edition by F. Cajori. In it Cotes outlined three methods for studying natural philosophy. The first, used by Aristotle and the Peripatetics, relied on 'occult', or hidden, qualities, and was entirely based on giving names to things. The second method was based on sounder assumptions, namely that all matter is homogeneous. Its adherents, however, though they rejected the proliferation of empty words, arbitrarily imagined occult fluids agitating with occult motions and pervading the pores of bodies, thus relying on fallacious hypotheses and chimeras: therefore their works were an ingenious romance. Although Cotes does not mention Descartes and the Cartesians, it is not difficult to identify them as his targets. Indeed, portions of the preface were specifically aimed at Leibniz and his 'Tentamen de motuum coelestium causis', though it was agreed by Cotes and Newton that Leibniz's name would not be mentioned. The third method relied on experimental philosophy. Its adherents assumed no arbitrary first principles and did not rely on hypotheses. From select phenomena they found the forces and their modes of operation, and then from the forces they were able to show the constitution of the remaining phenomena. In this fashion they were able to establish universal gravity. Needless to say, this was the method adopted by Newton and the Newtonians.

Cotes also published 'Logometria' (*PTRS*, 29, 1714, 5–47), a mathematical essay dedicated to Halley and announced by Cotes in a letter to Newton as containing 'a new sort of Constructions in Geometry which appear to me very easy, simple & general' (Edleston, 117). Although the problems there treated were not new, Cotes was able to provide interesting solutions. His essay was reprinted as the first part of the *Harmonia mensurarum* (1722), a posthumous work edited by his literary executor, Robert Smith, which established Cotes as probably the most talented British mathematician of the generation after Newton. Though the *Harmonia* provides not simply solutions but also methods, it is not for the faint-hearted, containing dozens of beautifully printed pages of mathematics, often without a single word of text. The review in the *Philosophical Transactions*, possibly by William Jones (*PTRS*, 32, 1722, 139–50), provides an extensive and helpful contemporary assessment. Cotes's work deals with the 'harmony' between measures of angles (trigonometric quantities) and measures of ratios (logarithms), which he tries to treat conjointly with a single notation. In his work he shows great interest and skill in the problem of quadratures, developing new methods often inspired by and related to his revision of Newton's *Principia*. His skill in this area can be traced back to his first surviving letter to Newton, when he was bold enough to correct the latter on two points (August 1709). His tables of quadratures in the *Harmonia* were more than an ingenious set of techniques, because the 'harmony of measures' he had found was of deep mathematical import. Smith was able to include the statement of one of Cotes's last achievements, the factorization theorem, which, thanks to a reference found in a letter of 5 May 1716 from Cotes to William Jones, he managed to rescue from among the papers left by Cotes at his death.

The *Harmonia* also contains three *opuscula mathematica* of considerable interest. In the first, *Aestimatio errorum in mixta mathesi*, Cotes studied the proportions among the least contemporary variations of the sides and angles of plane and spherical triangles. His work had important applications to astronomy and aroused considerable interest, especially among French astronomers such as J. J. de Lalande, N. L. de Lacaille, who translated Cotes's tract, and J. B. J. Delambre. The *Aestimatio errorum* ends with a brief discussion of how to find the most probable place of an object by weighing the errors of a number of slightly different observations. That discussion gained Cotes a place in the history of eighteenth-century error theory. The second *opusculum*, *De methodo differentiali Newtoniana*, develops the method of interpolation of curves described by Newton in the *Principia* (book 3, lemma 5), which was of considerable significance for cometography. Lastly, *Canonotechnia* is a further development of Newton's methods of interpolation and approximate integration which can be found in his *Methodus differentialis* (1711). Cotes's book ends with three brief applications and an explicatory note by Robert Smith.

Smith was also responsible for another posthumous edition of Cotes's works, *Hydrostatical and Pneumatical Lectures*, which went through three English editions between 1738 and 1775 and was translated into French by Lemonnier

(Paris, 1742). The course of lectures for which they had been written was begun by Cotes and Whiston in 1707, though Smith did not include the lectures prepared by Whiston. Smith's publication, which was prompted by the prospect of an unauthorized edition, provides an interesting picture of natural philosophy teaching at Cambridge in the eighteenth century.

Cotes died unexpectedly on 5 June 1716 of a 'Fever attended with a violent Diarrhoea and constant Delirium' (Edleston, lxxvi). He was buried on 9 June in Trinity College chapel, and Richard Bentley composed an epitaph inscribed on his memorial. In 1758 Robert Smith, by then master of Trinity College, arranged for the erection of a bust in his cousin's memory by Peter Scheemakers, which is now in the Wren Library. On the page reproducing Bentley's epitaph in his own copy of the *Harmonia mensurarum*, Smith wrote: 'Sir Isaac Newton, speaking of Mr. Cotes, said "If he had lived we might have known something"' (Gowing, 141). DOMENICO BERTOLONI MELI

**Sources** *Correspondence of Sir Isaac Newton and Professor Cotes*, ed. J. Edleston (1850) · R. Gowing, *Roger Cotes: natural philosopher* (1983) · 'An account of the book, intituled *Harmonia mensurarum*', *PTRS*, 32 (1722–3), 139–50 · *The correspondence of Isaac Newton*, ed. H. W. Turnbull and others, 5–6 (1975–6) · D. J. Price, 'The early observatory instruments of Trinity College, Cambridge', *Annals of Science*, 8 (1952), 1–12 · A. Koyré, *Newtonian studies* (1965), 273–82 · I. B. Cohen, *Introduction to Newton's 'Principia'* (1971) · I. B. Cohen, 'Neglected sources for the life of Stephen Gray', *Isis*, 45 (1954), 41–50 · R. A. Chipman, 'The manuscript letters of Stephen Gray, FRS, 1666/7–1736', *Isis*, 49 (1958), 414–33 · S. P. Rigaud and S. J. Rigaud, eds., *Correspondence of scientific men of the seventeenth century*, 1 (1841), 257–70 · W. Whiston, *Memoirs of the life and writings of Mr William Whiston: containing memoirs of several of his friends also* (1749) · R. Willis, *The architectural history of the University of Cambridge, and of the colleges of Cambridge and Eton*, ed. J. W. Clark, 4 vols. (1886) · *Isaac Newton's Philosophiae naturalis principia mathematica*, ed. A. Koyré, I. B. Cohen, and A. Whitman, 2 (1972), 817–26 · parish register (baptism), 25 July 1682, Burbage, Leicestershire

**Archives** CUL, Cambridge lectures on hydrostatics and pneumatics [fair copy] · Trinity Cam. · Whipple Museum, Cambridge, astronomical instruments | Clare College, Cambridge, Morgan MSS

**Likenesses** P. Scheemakers, marble bust, Trinity Cam., Wren Library; repro. in D. McKitterick, *The making of the Wren Library* (1995), 124

**Cotes, Samuel** (1734–1818), miniature painter, was the third son of Robert Cotes (*d.* 1774) of Westminster, London, a former mayor of Galway, Ireland, turned apothecary, and his wife, Elizabeth (*b. c.*1700, *d.* after 1775), daughter of Francis Lynn, chief secretary of the Royal African Company. Samuel's only surviving brother, Francis *Cotes (1726–1770), became one of the most fashionable portrait painters of his generation, apart from Gainsborough and Reynolds, working in both oil and pastel. Encouraged by his brother's considerable success Samuel abandoned his intended career as an apothecary and, instructed by Francis, trained instead as an artist. He painted portrait miniatures, usually on ivory and occasionally in enamel, and also drew full-scale pastel portraits. His earliest works date from *c.*1757, and by 1760 he was exhibiting at the Society of Artists in Suffolk Street, London. He continued to show his work there until 1768 and, from 1769 to 1789, at the Royal Academy. Cotes married, first, on 11 June 1768, Mary Creswick of Westminster, with whom he had a daughter who died in infancy. Following his wife's death he married, second, on 15 April 1780, Sarah Sheppard (d. 1814), an amateur artist.

In scale and format Cotes's early work falls within the bounds of what Reynolds called 'the Modest School' of miniature painting. However, his miniatures tend to be more than usually expressive for a proponent of this style, as demonstrated by that thought to be of Frances Dickson (1769; Kenwood House, London). His masterpiece, *Mrs Yates as Electra* (1769; V&A) dates from this early phase of his career; it was subsequently engraved in mezzotint by Philip Dawe. Painted on a much larger scale (15.2 cm x 12.7 cm) than that to which Cotes was accustomed, it foreshadows the increase in size of his miniatures from about 4 cm throughout the 1760s to 6–7 cm throughout the 1770s and 1780s. A more intimate and equally interesting miniature is Cotes's portrait of his mother, *Elizabeth Cotes* (1775; Sothebys, Derwydd Mansion, Llandeilo, Carmarthenshire, 5 September 1998, lot 134). His robust but rather unpretentious treatment of his subjects reflects his brother's influence. He also copied directly from Francis Cotes's full-scale portraits, as in his *Lady Ann Fitzpatrick* (1760; Kenwood House, London). It is believed that Cotes signed his works 'S. C.', using several strokes for the S, but it is almost certain that a true assessment of his oeuvre has been impaired by the mistaking of his work for that of other miniaturists sharing the same initials, such as Samuel Collins (1735?–1768) and Sarah Coote (exh. 1777–84). Confusion with Collins may also be responsible for the premise that Cotes worked for a time in Bath; he is known for certain to have been living in Cork Street, London, in 1763 and at 25 Percy Street, Rathbone Place, London, in 1769. He retired about 1789, many years before his death, which occurred 'in his 85th year' (*GM*) at Paradise Row, Chelsea, on 7 March 1818. His reputation seems undiminished by the difficulties of attribution that beset his work and Schidlof has declared him 'the best English miniaturist of the generation which preceded Cosway and Smart' (Schidlof, 1.168). The Victoria and Albert Museum, London, houses the largest collection of his miniatures on display.                                                    V. REMINGTON

**Sources** B. S. Long, *British miniaturists* (1929), 103–4 • L. R. Schidlof, *The miniature in Europe in the 16th, 17th, 18th, and 19th centuries*, 1 (1964), 168 • G. Reynolds, *English portrait miniatures* (1952); rev. edn (1988), 109–10 • *GM*, 1st ser., 88/1 (1818), 276–7 • parish registers, St Clement Danes, City Westm. AC, 11 June 1768 [marriage] • E. M. Johnson, *Francis Cotes* (1976), appx I [reproduces Cotes family pedigree from J. Nichols, *The history and antiquities of the county of Leicester*, 4 vols. (1795–1815), 4/1 (1807), 35] • Graves, *RA exhibitors* • S. Edwards, *Miniatures at Kenwood: the Draper gift* (1997) • *IGI*

**Likenesses** P. Sandby, watercolour drawing, Royal Collection

**Cotesworth, William** (c.1668–1726), merchant and industrialist, was born the second surviving son of Charles Cotesworth (1637–1687) of Eggleston, co. Durham, a yeoman farmer, and his wife, Anne (d. 1712). His eldest brother, Charles, remained on the land while Cotesworth himself was apprenticed in March 1683 to a prosperous Gateshead merchant and tallow chandler who died three years later, leaving his trade in the hands of his widow and inexperienced son. The bright young apprentice seemed to provide a welcome addition to the weakened firm and he was soon brought into partnership, paying only a token £20 towards the joint capital. On 9 May 1699 he married his partner's sister-in-law, Hannah Ramsay (1673–1710), and gained in prosperity with the passing years, allegedly by milking the partnership's capital to finance his private business ventures. Whatever the truth of this allegation, it is beyond question that the breakup of the firm in 1706 left him able to establish a successful independent business and to enter the capital-intensive salt and coal industries, while the fortunes of his former partner steadily declined.

Over the next few years Cotesworth's standing in the area grew rapidly, particularly through his friendship with the Liddell family of Ravensworth Castle in co. Durham, and through his activities as principal agent of the Regulation, a cartel formed in 1708 by several of the principal mine owners of the Tyne valley. His spectacular business success and increasing influence aroused resentment since they were felt to be out of keeping with his relatively humble background; and this resentment intensified when in 1712 he persuaded his wealthy brother-in-law, William Ramsay, to buy the strategically placed manors of Gateshead and Whickham, south of the Tyne. Cotesworth exploited this purchase to regulate the amount of coal coming onto the market from the new collieries south and west of Ramsay's estate, a policy that dragged his reluctant relative into open and often violent confrontation with the owners of these collieries. Meanwhile, his active loyalty to the Hanoverian government made him more enemies in an area where political divisions were deep and bitter. In 1715 the transformation from impoverished apprentice to landed gentleman was completed when Ramsay died, childless, leaving Cotesworth the bulk of his estate. He became a JP and, four years later, was appointed high sheriff of Northumberland. By this time he had retired from trade to concentrate on his extensive investments in land and industry, which by the early 1720s were estimated to yield a total annual income of more than £8000—a remarkably successful return on his original stake of £20. The satisfaction which he presumably felt in surveying his expanding business empire from his country house on the outskirts of Gateshead was nevertheless marred, by the deaths of his wife (1710) and of four of their seven children.

The years which marked the peak of Cotesworth's success, however, were also those in which he began to encounter difficulties in his 'great concerns'; thereafter he was forced to fight hard to keep his head above water, let alone advance any further. The last five or six years of his life were spent in a constant battle against illness as well as against enemies anxious to deprive him of the fruits of his success. In 1725 he survived an assassination attempt allegedly instigated by one of his bitterest rivals. His aggressive self-righteousness undoubtedly played a part in sowing the whirlwind that he was to reap in the 1720s, but other factors working against him were outside his control and might well have had similar effects on the careers of less belligerent men. In attempting to break into a high-risk, capital-intensive, and aristocratically dominated industry like coal, Cotesworth characteristically overreached himself, and the difficulties he encountered so overwhelmed him that he left his only surviving son, Robert (1702–1729), a muddled and encumbered inheritance. His achievements, however, should not be underestimated: in his final years he was the driving force behind the so-called 'grand alliance' which dominated the Newcastle coal industry for another hundred years and, despite the financial burdens imposed by protracted lawsuits, he was able to leave his heirs a respected position in society and a landed estate valued at £60,000.

William Cotesworth died after a long and painful illness and was buried on 15 December 1726 at St Mary's parish church at Gateshead. His will contained a final surprise: a codicil revealed to Robert Cotesworth and his sisters, Elizabeth (*b*. 1701) and Hannah (1706–1787), that in 1722 or 1723 their father had married his housekeeper, Hannah Watson (*d*. 1766). Their daughter, Henrietta (*c*.1723–1781), who was reputedly very like her father, in 1760 became sub-governess of the royal nursery.                                J. M. ELLIS

**Sources** J. M. Ellis, *A study of the business fortunes of William Cotesworth, c.1668–1726* (1981) · J. Ellis, '"A bold adventurer": the business fortunes of William Cotesworth, c.1668–1726', *Northern History*, 17 (1981), 117–32 · *The letters of Henry Liddell to William Cotesworth*, ed. J. M. Ellis, SurtS, 197 (1987) · E. Hughes, *North country life in the eighteenth century*, 1 (1952) · J. Ellis, 'The poisoning of William Cotesworth, 1725', *History Today*, 28 (1978), 752–7 · parish register (burial), Gateshead, St Mary, 15 Dec 1726
**Archives** Gateshead Public Library | Gateshead Public Library, Ellison MSS · North of England Institute of Mining and Mechanical Engineers, Newcastle upon Tyne, Buddle-Atkinson Collection, vol. 14 (Baker-Cotesworth letters) · Northumbd RO, Carr-Ellison (Hedgeley) MSS · U. Newcastle, Jacobite letters
**Likenesses** T. Gibson, portrait, *c*.1722, Hedgeley Hall, Powburn, Northumberland
**Wealth at death** £60,000 rental from property excl. charges on estate; also income from coal investments

**Cotgrave, John** (*bap.* 1611?, *d.* in or after 1655), anthologist, may have been the 'John sonne of Randolph Cotgrave' who was baptized on 2 April 1611 at St Gregory by St Paul's, London (GL, MS 10231, fol. 50). If so, his father was probably Randle *Cotgrave (*fl.* 1587–1630?), author of *A dictionarie of the French and English tongues* (1611) and husband of Margaret (*d*. 1639). Randle was employed as secretary to William Cecil, second earl of Exeter (*d*. 1640), but so far nothing has come to light about John's education or subsequent circumstances. Though the surname was not uncommon in London, he may possibly be the John Cotgrave who with his wife Anne baptized a son of his own name at St Clement Danes on 10 August 1645.

Cotgrave has been credited with editing *Le Mercure Anglois*, a French-language news-sheet friendly to the parliament that was issued in London by Nicholas Bourne and reached seventy-three numbers between June 1644 and December 1648 (Nelson and Seccombe, 197). During the interregnum he made his appearance as an anthologist. *The English Treasury of Wit and Language* was entered by

Humphrey Moseley in the Stationers' register on 16 January 1655 as the work of 'J. Cotgrave gent.', and George Thomason's copy bears the purchase date of 1 May (BL, E.1464(1)). This 300-page commonplace book brings together close on 1700 anonymous dramatic extracts mostly from Jacobean and Caroline plays. Local references are removed for aphoristic effect and prose passages rendered as verse, while among the topics treated are kingship, rebellion, and tyranny. In a copy, now slightly imperfect at the end, that formerly belonged to William Oldys (BL, 1451.c.49) the source of almost every quotation has been identified in ink by an unknown contemporary annotator.

In the same year 'J. C.' was responsible for *Wit's Interpreter, the English Parnassus*, a handbook of courtly expression and pastimes mainly for lovers. The publisher Nathaniel Brooke signed his address to the reader 19 May, though Thomason's copy (BL, E.1448) is dated to 7 May. The contents were allegedly 'ransackt from the private Papers of the *choicest Wits* of the three *Nations*', and the compiler claims that 'whilst … in town to attend the Press' he had removed any material that was brought to his attention as being already in print. The work consists of three separately paginated sections totalling some 650 pages, and opens with 'The art of reasoning, or, A new logick', followed by a series of dialogues and some patterns for letter writing. The main section comprises a large collection of mostly pre-civil war love songs and epigrams. Another edition came out in 1662, with a figured frontispiece and Brooke's earlier preface redated to 22 October 1661, and in 1671 appeared 'The 3d Edition with many new Additions', notably a section of games and recipes, but lacking 'The art of reasoning'.                                W. H. KELLIHER

**Sources** G. E. Bentley, 'John Cotgrave's *English treasury of wit and language* and the Elizabethan drama', *Studies in Philology*, 40 (1943), 186–203 · C. Nelson and M. Seccombe, eds., *British newspapers and periodicals, 1641–1700: a short-title catalogue of serials printed in England, Scotland, Ireland, and British America* (1987) · J. Hunter, 'Chorus vatum Anglicanorum', BL, Add. MS 24492, fol. 14 · P. Cotgreave, 'A note on Randle Cotgrave', *N&Q*, 240 (1995), 346–7

**Cotgrave, Randle** (*fl.* 1587–1630?), lexicographer, was the son of Randle Cotgrave (*c*.1535–1592), of Christleton, notary public, minor canon in Chester Cathedral, and registrar to the bishop of Chester, and Ellen Taylor (*d*. 1591) of Chester. Randle was the second son of five children—six, if George Cotgrave (*d*. 1608), not recorded in the pedigree made at the visitation of Cheshire of 1613, was indeed the third son. He was admitted foundress scholar of St John's College, Cambridge, on 10 November 1587, and subsequently became secretary to William Cecil, Lord Burghley, the eldest son of Thomas, first earl of Exeter. He may have been the Randle Cotgrave, husband of Margaret (*d*. 1639), who was the father of John *Cotgrave.

Cotgrave's only known work, *A Dictionarie of the French and English Tongues*, was first published in 1611, and went through another four editions (1632, 1650, 1660, 1673). The second edition included an English–French dictionary compiled by Robert Sherwood; subsequent editions were revised and enlarged by James Howell.

Two entries in the Stationers' register have fostered the notion that Cotgrave's *Dictionarie* was largely based on *A Dictionarie French and English* (1593) by Claudius Holyband (Claude Desainliens). The entries, dated 7 June 1608 and 27 April 1610, both deal with the transfer of rights of a 'Dictionarie in Frenche and Englishe Collected first by C. Holyband and sythenc[e] Augmented or Altered by Randall Cotgrave' (Arber, *Regs. Stationers*, 3.381 and 3.432). Cotgrave's *Dictionarie* may have originated in a project to revise and enlarge Holyband's work, and he may even have embarked on it. However, it has been convincingly argued that Cotgrave's word-list was derived from Jean Nicot's *Thresor de la langue françoyse* (1606), and that Holyband's *Dictionarie* was the most important of a number of other lexicographical sources on which he drew (Smalley, 71–98).

Such scant information as has survived about the preparation and publication of Cotgrave's work is contained in the *Dictionarie* itself, and in two extant letters, both addressed to Beaulieu, secretary to the British ambassador at Paris. The first, dated 27 November 1610, indicates that Cotgrave sent portions of his manuscript for 'light' and 'help' to Beaulieu, assisted by his friends in Paris, and on their return he forwarded them to a Mr Limery, 'to whom I am in this business exceedingly beholden'. Evidently Cotgrave found himself under time pressure, since he urged Beaulieu to return the papers speedily, as 'about a week before Christmas I shall have need of my P. … Those of R I shall be able to spare a fortnight or three weeks longer' (Hazlitt, 84–5). This suggests that he was working to a printer's schedule, and may possibly have supervised the printing himself.

In the second letter, dated 8 July 1612 (in which we learn that he was still in the service of Lord Burghley), Cotgrave requests payment of 22*s.* for two copies of his *Dictionarie* that he had recently sent to Beaulieu, as he had 'not been provident enough to reserve any of them, and am therefore now forced to be beholden … to a Mechanicall generation, that suffers no respect to waigh down a private gaine' (BL, Harley MS 7002, fol. 126). However, Cotgrave was rewarded with a gift of £10 when he presented a copy of his book to Henry, prince of Wales.

Cotgrave dedicated his book to Lord Burghley, and thanked him for dispensing with 'th'ordinarie attendance of an ordinarie servant', and so allowing him time to finish the work, but added that his 'desires have aimed at more substantiall markes; but mine eyes failed them, and forced me to spend much more of their vigour on this Bundle of words'. This could be an allusion to an abandoned project on Rabelais—perhaps a translation or glossary—judging from the 750 plus citations from his works in the *Dictionarie*. In his address to the French reader, Jean L'Oiseau de Tourval, a translator, portrays Cotgrave as a perfectionist who had to be persuaded by his friends to surrender his work to the printers. He also informs us that Cotgrave had to omit a sizeable proportion of his material, including reference data: 'Il pouvoit bien citer le nom, le livre, la page, le passage; mais ce n'eut plus icy été un Dictionaire, ains un Labirinte' ('He could have cited

author, title, page and passage; but this would no longer have been a dictionary—it would have become a labyrinth').

Consisting of 960 unnumbered pages in double column, containing more than 48,000 headwords, and in the region of 1 million words, Cotgrave's *Dictionarie* was, by a considerable margin, the most extensive French word-list of its time. It is well known to students of both English and French philology as well as to textual editors, and is the seventh most quoted source for earliest citations in the second edition of the *Oxford English Dictionary* (1989). Although Cotgrave must have employed assistants to perform routine tasks, his is the distinctive voice throughout the dictionary. His definition style is characterized by wordplay, rhythmical cadence, robust humour, and encyclopaedic intervention, and is frequently tinged with scepticism and world-weariness. His attitudes are informed by his wide-ranging enthusiasms, especially for the vernacular and the new learning, and also by his intolerance of corruption. As such, the *Dictionarie* provides an invaluable resource for cultural historians, giving access to fresh and often unanticipated insights into the beliefs, mores, and day-to-day life of the Jacobean world.

Almost nothing is known of Cotgrave's life after 1612. Cooper asserts that he 'flourished' in 1634, but this date cannot be confirmed. It is possible that he returned to Christleton, as on 26 August 1630 a 'Randle Cotgreve, gent.', with five others of Christleton, gave evidence on oath at the inquisition taken before Bishop John Bridgeman at Chester Castle.                                    JOHN LEIGH

**Sources** BL, Harley MS 1535, fol. 92 · BL, Harley MS 7002, fol. 126 · *Cheshire Sheaf*, 3rd ser., 4 (1902), 25–6, 34, 88–9 · *Cheshire Sheaf*, 3rd ser., 5 (1903), 24 · *Cheshire Sheaf*, 3rd ser., 15 (1918), 43, 47 · [W. C. Hazlitt], 'Inedited letter of Randle Cotgrave', *N&Q*, 3rd ser., 8 (1865), 84–5 · V. E. Smalley, *The sources of 'A dictionarie of the French and English tongues' by Randle Cotgrave* (1948), 14–54, 71–98 · Ches. & Chester ALSS, Alyn Arthur Guest Williams papers, DGW 2087, box 5, item 1v · Arber, *Regs. Stationers*, 3.381, 3.432 · BL, Harley MS 1424, fol. 37 · BL, Harley MS 1500, fol. 82 · BL, Harley MS 1505, fol. 36 · P. Cunningham, *Extracts from the 'Accounts of the revels at court'* (1842), xvi · K. Lambley, *The teaching and cultivation of the French language in England during Tudor and Stuart times* (1920), 187–94 · *The visitation of Cheshire in the year 1580, made by Robert Glover, Somerset herald*, ed. J. P. Rylands, Harleian Society, 18 (1882) · G. J. Armytage and J. P. Rylands, eds., *Pedigrees made at the visitation of Cheshire, 1623*, Lancashire and Cheshire RS, 58 (1909) · L. E. Farrer, *Un devancier de Cotgrave: la vie et les œuvres de Claude de Sainliens alias Claudius Holyband* (1908), 67–96 · J. Willinsky, *Empire of words* (1994), 221 · L. Sainéan, *La langue de Rabelais* (1923), 2.531 · C. H. Cooper, *Memorials of Cambridge* (1861), 2.113 · *Cheshire Sheaf*, 3rd ser., 4 (1902), 6–7, 30–31, 39–41, 47–9, 65–6, 117–18, 122–3 · *Cheshire Sheaf*, 3rd ser., 5 (1903), 94–5 · *Cheshire Sheaf*, 3rd ser., 15 (1918), 1–2 · *Cheshire Sheaf*, 4th ser., 1 (1966), 27 · M. Schmidt-Küntzel, 'Cotgrave et sa source Rabelaisienne', diss., 1984, 258

**Archives** BL, Harley MS 1535, fol. 92 · BL, Harley MS 7002, fol. 126

**Cotman, John Joseph** (1814–1878), artist, was born on 29 May 1814 at Southtown, Great Yarmouth, the third of the five children of John Sell *Cotman (1782–1842), artist of the Norwich school, and his wife, Ann (1783–1854), daughter of Edmund Miles of Felbrigg, Norfolk, and his wife, Mary. In 1823 John Sell Cotman returned to Norwich to set up a school of drawing in St Martin-at-Palace Plain, where the young John Joseph was his pupil. He was later sent to work in his uncle's haberdashery shop, but detested it and soon gave it up to pursue art. In 1834 John Sell Cotman was appointed drawing-master at King's College School, London, and John Joseph went with him to assist with teaching. He did not settle, and at the end of the year returned to Norwich to take over the family teaching practice from his brother Miles Edmund *Cotman; he remained in Norwich for the rest of his life. J. J. Cotman worked primarily in watercolour in a freely painted style, with rich, vibrant colours. He inherited his love of colour from his father, who on 20 February 1838 wrote to him 'you have a good eye for colour, one of *the very best* points in the game—*good taste*' (BL, Add. MS 37029). His subjects were mainly landscapes of local scenery or imaginary views, often painted on a large scale. He invariably dated and signed his work J. J. Cotman, particularly in the 1860s and 1870s when he was producing his most original work. He also occasionally painted in oils. There is a major collection of his work in Norwich Castle Museum and Art Gallery. He exhibited with various exhibitions in Norwich from 1831 to 1870, including the Norwich Society of Artists (1831–3), and in London with the British Institution (1852–6) and the Royal Academy (1853).

Portraits show Cotman as a handsome man, but his life was marred by an unstable temperament, which in later years was aggravated by bouts of deep depression and drinking. On 21 July 1847 he married Helen Anderson Cooper, the daughter of John Cooper, a Norwich silversmith; they had six children. By 1858 she was no longer able to tolerate his erratic behaviour and left him. Cotman became increasingly eccentric and to pay his debts was forced to pawn his possessions and sell family drawings. He died destitute on 15 March 1878 at the Norfolk and Norwich Hospital, following an operation for cancer of the tongue; he was buried at Norwich cemetery on 18 March 1878.                              NORMA WATT

**Sources** N. Watt, 'The struggle of John Joseph Cotman', *Norfolk Fair* (Dec 1978), 24–5 · W. F. Dickes, *The Norwich school of painting: being a full account of the Norwich exhibitions, the lives of the painters, the lists of their respective exhibits, and descriptions of the pictures* [1906] · A. W. Moore, *The Norwich school of artists* (1985) · S. D. Kitson, *The life of John Sell Cotman* (1937) · m. cert. · CGPLA Eng. & Wales (1881)
**Archives** Norwich Castle Museum · priv. coll., journal and family letters | BM, Reeve collection, Cotman family letters
**Likenesses** J. J. Cotman, self-portrait, chalk, c.1830–1839, priv. coll. · photograph, c.1850–1855, Norwich Castle Museum and Art Gallery · J. J. Cotman, self-portrait, chalk, 1870–78, Norwich Castle Museum and Art Gallery · J. J. Cotman, self-portrait, chalk, c.1870–1878, priv. coll.
**Wealth at death** under £50: administration, 24 Feb 1881, *CGPLA Eng. & Wales*

**Cotman, John Sell** (1782–1842), painter and etcher, was born on 16 May 1782 in the parish of St Mary Coslany, Norwich, the son of Edmund Cotman (1759–1843/4), hairdresser (later haberdasher) and his wife, Ann Sell (1763–1835). On 3 August 1793 he entered Norwich grammar school with a free place.

John Sell Cotman (1782–1842), by John Philip Davis, 1818

**Early career in London** In 1798 Cotman moved to London where he worked as an assistant to Rudolph Ackermann, publisher of engravings and dealer in the Strand. In 1799 he joined the circle of Dr Thomas Monro, presumably attending evening meetings at Monro's house in Adelphi Terrace. Here he followed J. M. W. Turner and Thomas Girtin, studying and copying drawings in Monro's collection, as they had done a few years earlier. Cotman exhibited for the first time at the Royal Academy in 1800, when his address is recorded as 28 Gerrard Street, Soho. The same year he was awarded the large silver palette by the Society of Arts.

In summer 1800 Cotman visited Bristol and from there made the first of two tours of Wales. The landscape of Wales made a lasting impression on the young artist, providing a rich source of inspiration throughout his career. On 27 January 1801 he was elected an honorary member of the Society of United Friars of Norwich and 'produced for the inspection of the Brethren some very masterly sketches of scenes in Wales' (Rajnai, 30). At this time he also became a leading member of the Sketching Society in London, a group of artists who aimed to establish a 'School of Historic Landscape'. His second tour, in 1802, was in the company of Paul Sandby Munn, a fellow artist who was also his landlord at 107 New Bond Street from 1802 to 1804. Cotman's biographer, S. D. Kitson, first suggested the itinerary of this tour, based entirely upon a comparison of Munn's dated drawings with works by Cotman. Kitson was proved correct in his hypothesis when their two signatures were discovered in the visitors' register of the inn at Capel Curig, dated 31 July 1802.

Munn accompanied Cotman at the start of his first tour of Yorkshire in 1803. Yorkshire's influence upon Cotman was to be as important to him as to Girtin and Turner. He met and was befriended by the Cholmeley family, staying with them at Brandsby Hall, north of York. He made a second tour in 1803 and his third and last tour of the area was in 1805, when he stayed with the Morritts of Rokeby Park on the River Greta and in the village of Greta Bridge. It was this last visit which most profoundly affected him: he produced a series of watercolours which are among the finest in the history of the British use of the medium. At this time his London address was 20 Woodstock Street, Bond Street.

**Norwich and Great Yarmouth, 1806–1834** In 1806 Cotman failed to be elected to membership of the recently founded Society of Painters in Water Colours (later known as the Old Watercolour Society) and this may have had some bearing on his decision to return to his native Norwich that year. He exhibited for the last time at the Royal Academy (from 71 Charlotte Street) and set up a school of drawing in Wymer (now St Andrew's) Street, Norwich. To announce his arrival he held a 'daring' (Cotman to Dawson Turner, 8 Dec 1806, Kitson, 99) retrospective exhibition of several hundreds of his works in his new premises. He also began to experiment with painting in oils and exhibited for the first time with the Norwich Society of Artists in 1807. In the following two years he is described as a portrait painter in the Norwich Society catalogues. On 6 January 1809 he married Ann (1783–1854), the daughter of Edmund Miles, a tenant farmer of Swift's Grove Farm, Felbrigg in Norfolk. Their eldest of five children, Miles Edmund *Cotman (1810–1858), was born on 5 February in the following year. In 1810 Cotman established his circulating collection of drawings for pupils to copy: initially some six hundred drawings, this was to grow to several thousands over his teaching career.

In 1810 Cotman became vice-president of the Norwich Society of Artists and exhibited once again in London, at the Associated Artists in Water Colours and at the British Institution. In 1811 Messrs Boydell & Co. published his first volume of twenty-six views in England and Wales, *Miscellaneous Etchings*. In the same year he moved to Great Yarmouth under the patronage of the polymath Dawson Turner, settling into a house at Southtown, facing the river. His only daughter, Ann, was born on 13 July 1811. Cotman's Yarmouth years are characterized by a prodigious workload as a teacher and as an etcher. Suffering from a 'dangerous illness' (Cotman to Francis Cholmeley, 1 June 1813, Holcomb and Ashcroft, 55) in 1813, he also underwent an eye operation in the spring of 1814. Sydney Kitson, in his account of Cotman's Yarmouth period, tends to emphasize the drudgery of Cotman's existence, apparently inflicted upon him by Dawson Turner. However, Kitson did not have the benefit of the Cholmeley correspondence covering this period, which is rich in enthusiastic references to his current projects and family circumstances. He employed apprentices to help him complete his publication projects, while he himself 'only finished the works and sketched abroad' (Cotman to Francis Cholmeley, 1 June 1817, ibid.) for some two or three

years. Publications produced during this period were *A Narrative of the Grand Festival at Great Yarmouth* (three etchings, 1814), *The Nelson Column at Yarmouth* (one etching, 1817), *Specimens of Norman and Gothic Architecture, in the County of Norfolk* (fifty etchings, 1817), *Specimens of the Castellated and Ecclesiastical Remains in the County of Norfolk* (fifty etchings, 1817?), *A Series of Etchings Illustrative of the Architectural Antiquities of Norfolk* (sixty etchings, 1818), *Engravings of the most Remarkable of the Sepulchral Brasses in Norfolk* (111 plates, 1819), and *Antiquities of Saint Mary's Chapel, at Stourbridge, Near Cambridge* (ten etchings, 1819). Cotman also contributed drawings for engraved illustrations published in two volumes of *Excursions in the County of Norfolk* (1818–19). Cotman's etched œuvre is an undoubted tribute to his mastery of that medium, inspired in his treatment of architecture (on his own admission) by Giovanni Battista Piranesi. He skilfully renders his subject matter with dramatic contrasts of light and shade, bringing his compositions to life with picturesque effects of detail and incident.

In 1817, probably at the instigation of Dawson Turner, Cotman went on his first tour of Normandy. This was followed by a second in 1818, when Dawson Turner's family joined him for a period. His third and last tour of Normandy took place in summer 1820. These tours are extremely well documented as, by prior agreement, Cotman wrote full accounts of his travels both to his wife and to Dawson Turner. Under Dawson Turner's guidance, the essential aim of the first two tours had been to gather material for the publication of his *Architectural Antiquities of Normandy*, with letterpress by Turner (two volumes, ninety-seven etchings, 1822). Cotman's purpose in undertaking the final tour had been partly for his health but also to produce a 'picturesque tour' of Normandy (Cotman to Francis Cholmeley, 25 Sept 1820, Holcomb and Ashcroft, 62), the southernmost region of which enchanted him and which he described as 'the Wales of France' (Cotman to his wife, 26 Aug 1820, Kay, 116). His last three years at Yarmouth were devoted to the 'Herculean labor' (Cotman to Francis Cholmeley, 23 July 1822, Holcomb and Ashcroft, 69) of publishing the *Architectural Antiquities of Normandy*, but his elegiac monochrome watercolour drawings inspired by the landscape remained unpublished.

In 1823 Cotman returned once again to Norwich, opening early the next year a school of drawing in his new residence, a three-storey red-brick Georgian house on St Martin-at-Palace Plain. He also exhibited again in London, at the British Institution. On 1 May 1824 he held a large sale of his drawings, mainly Normandy subjects, at Christies, London. In 1825 Cotman became an associate of the Society of Painters in Water Colours, exhibiting with them for the first time. During this period he became well established as a drawing master but also suffered from depressive illness, notably in 1826. The 1820s were not especially lucrative years for artists in Norwich. Having been vice-president of the Norwich Society of Artists (since 1828 called the Norfolk and Suffolk Institution for the Promotion of the Fine Arts) for two years (1831–2), Cotman was president in 1833, the year in which the society was disbanded at a meeting in his house.

**London, 1834–1842** In 1834 Cotman moved to London to take up the appointment of drawing master at King's College School. His new house at 42 Hunter Street, Brunswick Square, Bloomsbury, remained his home for the rest of his life. Moving to a new home once again occasioned a major collection sale: this time of paintings, drawings, prints, books, and miscellaneous items at his Norwich house at St Martin-at-Palace Plain, through Spelman, 10–12 September 1834. Cotman's new post came as the fulfilment of a lifelong ambition: 'Much as I have ever loved London I have never trod its gold paved streets feeling so much a man of business, and so much to belong to it, as now' (Kitson, 307). He remained successful as a teacher: two pupils who joined his class in 1837 were Dante Gabriel Rossetti and his younger brother William. The latter, writing with the benefit of hindsight in 1895, described Cotman as 'the most interesting pedagogue of all … an alert, forceful-looking man, of modest stature, with a fine well-moulded face, which testified to an impulsive nature, somewhat worn and worried' (Dickes, 391). 1838 saw the publication by Henry Bohn of Cotman's *Liber Studiorum* (forty-eight plates including forty softground etchings) and *Specimens of Architectural Remains in Various Counties in England, but Especially in Norfolk*, an omnibus edition of his etchings (excluding those of Normandy). The softground etchings of the *Liber Studiorum* are an especially original use of the medium, which recall the similar work of Claude and also J. M. W. Turner. In 1838 he exhibited for the only time with the Society of British Artists.

**Technique** The development of Cotman's technique as a draughtsman and as a watercolourist falls into periods that mirror those of his life. The phases of his career outlined above match the most significant elements of his development in this aspect of his creativity to an extraordinary degree, just as the patronage and initiatives of Dawson Turner affected his productivity as a teacher and etcher. His earliest drawings of c.1800 follow a traditional pattern which reflects his first exploration of technique in the company of fellow artists in the circles of Ackermann and Monro. His use of pencil c.1800–02 consists of quite heavy parallel strokes of hatching within the outline of the subject, to indicate light and shade. By 1804 his pencil work had become lighter and daintier, with idiosyncratic dashes, particularly to indicate foliage in the foreground. The drawings of 1805–7 develop tone with a softer pencil. From 1808–10 his lines take on a more chunky rhythm in parallel with the development of his watercolour technique, while his use of the pencil during the Yarmouth years often possesses a flow rather different from his more finished etchings. The Normandy monochrome drawings, often made with the help of a camera lucida, are more precise for this reason. His later drawing technique adopts a more flamboyant approach, especially noticeable by 1829, in which he uses the soft side of his pencil to create shadowed areas with rapid hatching. The subtle combination of vigour and apparent langour in these drawings reaches a climax in his late chalk drawings, again characterized by loose and speedy hatching.

Cotman's technique as a watercolourist was particularly rapid in its early development. His surviving watercolours of c.1800–03 show a traditional use of indigo, unless faded and thus reddish in tone. His early work compares with that of Thomas Girtin, particularly in the use of dot and dash accents applied with the brush. He also let his colour gather in pools to achieve effects of depth. By 1805–6 the Greta period watercolours demonstrate an absolute control of the medium. It has been debated to what extent Cotman's Greta watercolours were painted *en plein air*. He wrote to Dawson Turner on 30 November 1805 that he had been 'colouring from nature' (Kitson, 80) and this indicates an important stage in the development of his technique. However, it is unlikely that some of his most exquisite watercolours on large sheets of handmade paper were executed on the spot: they are surely the products of direct observation recollected in the tranquillity of the remembered experience, aided by on-the-spot drawings and colour notes. From c.1807–8 his use of wash achieved a purity that enabled him, by c.1810, to execute compositions of colour and form of almost abstract intensity. During his Yarmouth years his output in watercolour was often in monochrome, usually related to his printing projects. In the mid-1830s his use of colour intensified, often made semi-opaque with the addition to his pigment of a flour or rice paste. In the late 1830s he returned to painting in monochrome, achieving subtle effects of deep, soft-velvetlike black in his shadows.

**Death and posthumous reputation** Cotman made one last extended visit to Norfolk in autumn 1841, a trip which resulted in a final series of dated drawings from nature which act as a creative coda to his life's work. An entry in the diary of Robert Geldart (brother of the Norwich artist Joseph Geldart) for 20 June 1842 records his visit to the Cotmans in Bloomsbury: 'Old Cotman, who was seriously ill, showed us Normandy drawings in sepia' (Kitson, 363). On 22 July Ann wrote to her brother John Joseph *Cotman (1814–1878) a touching account of their father's last days. Neither family nor doctors could encourage him to eat or sleep: 'I am quite sure he does not wish to get well, or he would have made some effort to do so' (ibid., 364). Cotman died on 24 July 1842 at his Bloomsbury home of 'natural decay' with his son, Miles Edmund, at his side, and was buried in the churchyard of St John's Wood Chapel, Marylebone, on 30 July. His collection was dispersed through four subsequent sales: oils and drawings, Christies, 17–18 May 1843; library, Christies, 6 June 1843; Cotman collection sale, Spelman, Norwich, 16 May 1861; Cotman collection sale, Murrell, Norwich, 26–27 November 1862. Today his work can best be appreciated in the private collections of connoisseurs, the James Reeve collection at the British Museum, the Colman Bequest at Norwich Castle Museum and Art Gallery, and the Sydney Kitson Bequest at Leeds City Art Gallery. The Colman collection at Norwich includes a comprehensive group of his paintings in oil, a medium with which he experimented throughout his career.

Viewed in its entirety, Cotman's *œuvre* is a remarkable achievement in the history of British art. The quality of Cotman's work, like that of his Norwich contemporary John Crome, has sometimes been obscured by the copies and imitations undertaken by followers, pupils, and copyists. These notably include his sons Miles Edmund and John Joseph, both of whom supported him in his teaching. Nevertheless, the originality of his *œuvre*—in etching, in oils, and above all in watercolour—remains as an inspiration to artists today and represents a high point of quality in the history of nineteenth-century art in Britain, at its finest the equal of his celebrated contemporary J. M. W. Turner.                              ANDREW W. MOORE

**Sources** S. D. Kitson, *The life of John Sell Cotman* (1937) · M. Rajnai, ed., *John Sell Cotman, 1782–1842* (1982) · A. W. Moore, *John Sell Cotman, 1782–1842* (1982) · A. M. Holcomb and M. Y. Ashcroft, *John Sell Cotman in the Cholmeley Archive* (1980) · M. Rajnai and M. Allthorpe-Guyton, *John Sell Cotman, 1782–1842: early drawings (1798–1812) in Norwich Castle Museum* (1979) · M. Rajnai and M. Allthorpe-Guyton, *John Sell Cotman: drawings of Normandy in Norwich Castle Museum* (1975) · A. E. Popham, 'The etchings of J. S. Cotman', *Print Collectors' Quarterly* (9 Oct 1922), 236–73 · H. I. Kay, 'John Sell Cotman's letters from Normandy, 1817–1820', *Walpole Society*, 14 (1925–6), 81–122; 15 (1926–7), 106–30 · D. B. Brown, A. Hemingway, and A. Lyles, *Romantic landscape: the Norwich school of landscape painters* (2000) [exhibition catalogue, London, Tate Britain, 24 March – 17 Sept 2000] · A. Hemingway, 'The constituents of romantic genius: John Sell Cotman's Greta drawings', *Recent essays in British landscape, 1750–1880*, ed. M. Rosenthal, C. Payne, and S. Wilcox (1997), 183–203 · A. W. Moore, *The Norwich school of artists* (1985); 2nd impression (1995) · C. Miller and D. Boswell, *Cotmania & Mr. Kitson* (1992) · W. F. Dickes, *The Norwich school of painting: being a full account of the Norwich exhibitions, the lives of the painters, the lists of their respective exhibits, and descriptions of the pictures* [1906] · will, PRO, PROB 11/1966, sig. 531 · d. cert. · Rajnai Norwich School archives · private information (2004) [P. Wessels, Norwich Castle Museum]

**Archives** BL, family corresp., Add. MS 37029 | BL, letters to J. H. Maw, Add. MS 45883 · BM, Reeve collection, corresp. with P. Turner, Cholmeley family, and others · N. Yorks. CRO, Cholmeley family corresp., letters to the Cholmeley family · Norwich Castle Museum, corresp. with S. Bignold, H. Gurney, and A. M. Hall · NRA, priv. coll., letters to D. Turner

**Likenesses** C. Varley, drawing, *c*.1810, Graves Art Gallery, Sheffield · J. P. Davis, pencil drawing, 1818, V&A [*see illus.*] · H. B. Love, pencil and watercolour drawing, 1830, BM · H. B. Love, pencil drawing, 1830, NPG · A. Clint, oils, *c*.1833, Thetford town hall · J. J. Cotman, chalk drawing, 1841, NPG · M. Turner, etching (after J. P. Davis), repro. in Rajnai, ed., *John Sell Cotman*

**Cotman, Miles Edmund** (1810–1858), watercolour painter, was born on 5 February 1810 in Wymer Street, Norwich, the eldest of the five children of John Sell *Cotman (1782–1842), artist of the Norwich school, and his wife, Ann (1783–1854), daughter of Edmund Miles of Felbrigg, Norfolk, and his wife, Mary. He received instruction in painting and drawing from his father and—from 1823 until his father's death—worked as his assistant, first at his school of drawing in St Martin-at-Palace Plain, Norwich, and then at King's College School, London, where John Sell Cotman was appointed drawing-master in 1834. In 1836 he was officially recognized as assistant drawing-master.

At the precocious age of thirteen Cotman exhibited his work with the Norwich Society of Artists in 1823, continuing to show there until 1833. In London he exhibited with the Society of British Artists, the Royal Academy, and the British Institution between 1835 and 1856. He painted primarily in watercolour and his subjects were Norfolk landscapes and river and sea views, including several views of shipping on the River Medway; some he signed M. E. Cotman. He was a close follower of his father and sometimes confusion exists between their work, complicated by the fact that they also produced a few collaborative works. The son's neat, carefully executed watercolours often lack the lyrical quality of those of the father, who on 13 November 1835 wrote to his younger son, John Joseph *Cotman (1814–1878), that he was encouraging Miles Edmund to work in a more 'dashing and Sketch like' manner (BL, Add. MS 37029). Ultimately he did develop his own, more fluid style. He also painted in oil and was a printmaker, publishing a set of lithographs, *Fac-Similes of Twelve Sketches Made in Norfolk by the Late J. S. Cotman in the Year 1841*. Over twenty etchings by him are known, including a set of ten published by Charles Muskett of Norwich in 1846.

In 1842, following the death of his father, Cotman succeeded to his post at King's College School. Soon after, on 16 May 1842, he married a widow, Mrs Elizabeth Juby, *née* Worts; they had a son and two daughters. In 1843 he moved from the family home at 42 Hunter Street, Brunswick Square, London, and by 1851 he was living at 9 Hollis Place, Haverstock Hill, Middlesex. He frequently suffered from ill health brought on by overwork and by 1854 was forced to return to Norfolk where he lived with his brother John Joseph, before finally moving to North Walsham. He spent his remaining years, often in financial straits, teaching and painting. Eventually he 'succumbed to a diseased ankle' (Dickes, 419) and was admitted to the Norfolk and Norwich Hospital, where he died on 23 January 1858. There is a major collection of his work in Norwich Castle Museum and Art Gallery.          NORMA WATT

**Sources** C. F. Bell, 'Miles Edmund Cotman (1810–1858) with a catalogue of fifty drawings by him selected from the Bulwer collection', *Walker's Quarterly* [whole issue], 21 [1927] · W. F. Dickes, *The Norwich school of painting: being a full account of the Norwich exhibitions, the lives of the painters, the lists of their respective exhibits, and descriptions of the pictures* [1906] · A. W. Moore, *The Norwich school of artists* (1985) · S. D. Kitson, *The life of John Sell Cotman* (1937) · ... the valuable and genuine Cotman collection, including 120 water colour drawings, paintings, rare old engravings and etchings late the property of John Sell Cotman, deceased (1861) [incl. works by M. E. Cotman; sale catalogue, Messrs Spelman, Norwich, 16 May 1861] · BL, Cotman MSS, Add. MS 37029 · *The exhibition of the Royal Academy* (1845) [exhibition catalogue] · *The exhibition of the Royal Academy* (1851–4) [exhibition catalogues] · *The exhibition of the Royal Academy* (1856) [exhibition catalogue] · parish register (baptisms), St John Maddermarket, Norwich · *Norwich Mercury* (30 Jan 1858) · m. cert.

**Archives** BL, letters to J. J. Cotman and others, Add. MS 37029 · BM, Reeve collection, family letters

**Likenesses** L. Sothern, chalk drawing, 1835, Norwich Castle Museum and Art Gallery

**Wealth at death** indigent

**Cotta, Alix von** (1842–1931), promoter of women's higher education, was born in Brunswick, the eldest of three daughters of Carl Berhard von Cotta (1808–1879) and

Ilsabe Ida von Orges (1812–1902). She grew up in Freiberg, Saxony, where her father was professor of geology at the internationally renowned mining academy there. Her mother was 'gifted and charming' with a 'wide range of sympathies and interests' (Newnham College Roll, 50). Alix von Cotta was fluent in several languages, including English which she spoke with her sisters. In 1870 she began a lifelong correspondence with Penelope Lawrence, the founder of Roedean School. It is not known how von Cotta came to know Lawrence, but the latter is said to have been educated partly 'overseas'. They both attended Newnham Hall, Cambridge, 1876–8, von Cotta passing two groups in the higher local examinations, gaining distinctions in English literature and composition, French, German, and Italian, and a first class in Old English.

Bedford College, London, had been founded in 1849 as a non-denominational college for women. By 1878, when the college had an enrolment of 130, serious efforts were made to attract better-prepared students. To this end, a preparatory department was opened, and von Cotta invited to become its mistress of studies. Students studied Latin, French, English, and mathematics. She left after two years, returning to Germany, where she wrote journal articles mainly about the education and training of women.

Following mid-century debates about teacher training and the reform of the higher girls' schools in Germany, a number of institutions were opened to offer further education to young women. The most famous of these was the Victoria Lyceum in Berlin founded by an Englishwoman, Georgina Archer, with the active support and patronage of the Crown Princess Victoria. The Berlin scheme followed closely the model drawn up by the north of England Council for the Promotion of the Higher Education of Women by Anne Jemima Clough and Josephine Butler whereby lectures were given by university men to women above school age who wanted to continue their studies. Beginning in 1869, the scheme offered lectures on a variety of subjects but did not lead to any examination or qualification. As in England, demand was soon felt for more rigorous and structured instruction, followed by examinations suitable for women wanting to improve their teaching qualifications. Part-time courses began at the Victoria Lyceum in 1874 and attracted a small amount of support from the Prussian state. Crown Princess Victoria was particularly interested in the new women's colleges in England and, following the death of Georgina Archer, chose Alix von Cotta to head the lyceum in 1884 ahead of other candidates for the post, largely because she had studied at Newnham Hall.

Reformers wanting to gain admission for women to German universities made little headway at this time. Many women felt it was more important to compete with the overwhelming number of men who taught students in the upper grades of girls' public high schools. For this, women needed better access to better courses and university-level examinations. Such advanced courses were introduced by von Cotta at the Victoria Lyceum in 1888, first in history and German and later in English and French. Students sat a special examination supervised by the ministry of education. However, no courses in science subjects were offered since it was felt these should be left to male teachers. As late as 1905–06, 1160 men held posts as teachers for the upper grades in Prussia's 207 public high schools for girls, while the corresponding number of women teachers was 221.

The Victoria Lyceum was the largest college training women for senior posts in girls' high schools in Prussia. Alix von Cotta remained its director for over twenty years and through her personal influence aroused 'intellectual interest among women, inspiring them with higher ideals and stimulating them to take an active part in public service' (Newnham College Roll, 51). She retired in 1911 and died in December 1931 in Hanover.

RITA McWILLIAMS TULLBERG

**Sources** [A. B. White and others], eds., *Newnham College register, 1871–1971*, 2nd edn, 1 (1979), 61 · *Newnham College Roll Letter* (1933), 50 · J. C. Albisetti, *Schooling German girls and women* (1988) · W. Killy and others, eds., *Deutsche biographische Enzyklopädie*, 11 vols. in 12 (Munich, 1995–9) · M. J. Tuke, *A history of Bedford College for Women, 1849–1937* (1939)
**Archives** State Archives of the Geheimes, Staatsarchive Preussischer Kulturbesitz (GStA Pk), material relating to the Victoria Lyceum · State Archives of the Geheimes, Staatsarchive Preussischer Kulturbesitz (GStA Pk), HA Rep 76, Ministry of Culture IV, Section 14, Berlin, no. 17, vols. 1–6 · State Archives of the Geheimes, Staatsarchive Preussischer Kulturbesitz (GStA Pk), HA Rep 89, Civil Cabinett no. 22 400 · Women's Library, London, letters to Penelope Lawrence and other corresp.

**Cotta, John** (1575?–1627/8), physician, was the son of Peter Cotta (*d*. 1620), who is described in his will of 1619 as 'professor of Phisicke' in the city of Coventry, Warwickshire. His mother was most probably Susan, or Susanna, Winthrop (1552–1604), whose brother, Adam (father of the future first governor of the Massachusetts Bay Colony, John Winthrop the elder), refers to the Cottas of Coventry in his Latin pedigree and diary. In 1588 John Cotta was admitted a pensioner of Trinity College, Cambridge, proceeding BA in 1593. He subsequently removed to Corpus Christi where in 1596 he was granted his MA. He obtained his MD in 1604 and shortly afterwards took up permanent residence in Northampton where he had been in practice since about 1600. Here he soon established a successful practice among the local gentry which can be attributed in large part to the patronage and influence of the puritan Sir William Tate, who, like Cotta, was a native of Coventry. By his first wife Cotta had two sons, Peter (*bap*. 16 April 1607) and John (buried on 4 September 1609 before his first birthday). The family lived in the parish of All Saints, Northampton, which, like Coventry, was a hotbed of Jacobean puritanism, and there is little doubt that Cotta was fully sympathetic to the staunch puritanism of its rector and leading parishioners. In 1607, for example, it was alleged in Star Chamber that Cotta, along with other noted puritans in the town of Northampton, was busy spreading malicious libels against the ecclesiastical and secular authorities in the town who were then active in suppressing nonconformity in the borough. His puritanism is also evident in the Cotta family connections to the Hales of Coventry and the Tates of Delapré (originally of Coventry), through whose combined influence Cotta probably entered the circle of midlands godly gentry which formed his clientele.

Cotta was the author of numerous published works which provide interesting insights into the mind of a provincial puritan physician of the early seventeenth century. In 1612 he published *A Short Discoverie*, in which he condemned the activities of a whole host of unlicensed and amateur medical practitioners. William Lilly, the celebrated astrologer, later claimed that it was prompted by the activities of the Buckinghamshire parson–physician, Richard Napier. Foremost in Cotta's thinking was his utter abhorrence of any form of illicit intrusion into the field of professional medicine, with particular hostility reserved for those priest—physicians like Napier, whose activities Cotta saw as inimical not only to good medical practice but also to the orderly nature of early modern society. Moreover, by stressing the religious nature of the physician's vocation Cotta may well have been expressing a peculiarly puritanical concern with order in the medical market place since much the same set of beliefs informed the work of his successor and fellow puritan, James Hart, who lived and worked in Northampton during the 1620s and 1630s. In 1616 Cotta published *The triall of witchcraft, showing the true methode of the discovery with a confutation of erroneous ways* in which he attempted to confute some of the more unsound methods currently used by those intent on proving the existence of witches, though it was not, as some historians of witchcraft have suggested, a work of rational scepticism. Failure to grasp this point almost certainly reflects a fundamental misunderstanding of the central purpose of Cotta's book, which was not to debunk popular belief in witchcraft but rather to use the contemporary debate on the attributes of witches and demons as a viable tool with which to probe the boundaries of contemporary scientific and philosophical thinking. In particular, Cotta had read deeply in the literature of occult causation, and was especially indebted to the work of the French physician and reformed Galenist Jean Fernel, whose *Abditis de rerum causis* he frequently cited in defence of the existence of witchcraft. In the process Cotta also affirmed the view that the detection of demonic activity in the sublunary world was the sole province of learned professionals like himself who alone were capable of differentiating between fraudulent and genuine claims of bewitchment and possession. Finally, in 1623, Cotta entered the fray against the empiric Francis Anthony, publishing *Cotta contra Antonium* which attacked Anthony's grandiloquent claims for one of his nostrums, *aurum potabile*. In line with his earlier published work in opposition to medical charlatans, Cotta was clearly determined to defend the orthodox, university trained, Galenic physician from the aspersions of interlopers like Anthony, one of whose agents, John Markes, the parson of Gayton, Northamptonshire, had been busy in the region selling his wares to Cotta's wealthy patients.

Further evidence of Cotta's rich and well-connected clientele, particularly among the puritan gentry of Northamptonshire, is provided by the evidence which he gave at the inquest into the death by poisoning of Sir Euseby Andrew, of Charwelton, in 1620. Cotta clearly profited, both financially and socially, through this important network of prominent patrons, so much so that in 1625 he was able to marry into the gentry when he wed his second wife Anne Tresham, daughter of Sir Thomas Tresham of Newton, Northamptonshire. His mother-in-law, also Anne Tresham, was the sister of Sir William Tate, one of Cotta's oldest patrons and benefactors, whose home at Delapré Abbey was an important centre for the godly puritan gentry of the county. At the time of his second marriage, however, Cotta was once again living in his native Coventry, in the parish of St Michael's where he may have inherited his father's lucrative medical practice. Cotta died there some time between November 1627 and February 1628. His nuncupative will mentions briefly only three beneficiaries, his wife, Anne, his servant John Pierson, and one Robert Cotta. An extensive inventory of his household goods survives, though unfortunately his library, valued at under £40, is not itemized.

PETER ELMER

**Sources** Venn, *Alum. Cant.* · wills of P. Cotta (proved 1620) and J. Cotta (proved 1628), Lichfield RO, B/C/11 · *The Winthrop papers*, ed. W. C. Ford and others, 1 (1929) · J. J. Muskett, *Evidences of the Winthrops of Groton, co. Suffolk, England* (privately printed, Boston, MA, 1894–6) · index of marriage licences, 1598–1684, Northants. RO · parish registers, Northampton, All Saints, Northants. RO, 223 P/1/6C and 36C · PRO, STAC 8/205/20 · J. Cotta, 'The poysoning of Sir Euseby Andrews', *Tracts relating to Northamptonshire* (1881) · W. Lilly, *Mr William Lilly's history of his life and times* (1715)
**Wealth at death** £271 16s. 8d.: will and inventory, Lichfield RO B/C/11, 1628

**Cottam, Thomas** (1549–1582), Jesuit, was the son of Lawrence Cottam, gentleman, of Dilworth and Tarnaker, Lancashire, and Anne, daughter of Mr Brewer, or Brewerth, of Brindle, who after her husband's death married William Ambrose, gentleman, of Ambrose Hall in Woodplumpton. Cottam entered Brasenose College, Oxford, graduated BA on 23 March 1569, and proceeded MA on 11 July 1572; he then undertook the direction of a noted free grammar school in London. He was converted to the Roman Catholic faith by Thomas Pounde of Belmont (afterwards a Jesuit priest), and proceeded to Douai, arriving on 22 May 1577; there he taught philosophy and studied theology for two years. He was ordained deacon on 19 December 1577, and travelled to England for four months, returning to the college on 14 May 1578.

Ardently desiring to take part in the mission to the East Indies, Cottam left Douai on 16 February 1579 for Rome, where he was admitted to the Society of Jesus, and entered the noviciate of Sant' Andrea on 8 April 1579. In the sixth month of his noviceship he was attacked by violent fever, and was sent back to his own country by his superiors on medical advice. At Lyons, the sickness increasing, he seemed too weak for the society, and did not continue with his noviciate. Cottam left Lyons for Douai College (then temporarily at Rheims) on 25 March

1580 in the company of a spy named Sledd. Sledd gave the following description of Cottam to the authorities: 'about 30 yeres of adge—of a meane stature—leane and slender of body. His face full of freckells. His bearde rede and thine & hathe a worte or mole about an inche from his mouthe one his cheke one the right side' (Talbot and Aveling, 208). He was ordained priest on 28 May 1580 and was sent to England on the mission. Also in the group were John Hart and William Rishton, priests, and Humphrey Ely, who was carrying a reprinted copy of *Regnans in excelsis*. On his arrival at Dover between 16 and 18 June 1580 he was immediately arrested, having been recognized from Sledd's marks. Ely was not known, and was commissioned to bring Cottam as prisoner before Lord Cobham, the governor of the Cinque Ports; Cottam gave himself up to save Ely from suspicion. Cottam was committed to the Marshalsea prison on 27 June 1580, where he was tortured, and thence he was removed on 4 December to the Tower of London, where he underwent the tortures of the rack and the 'Scavenger's Daughter'.

Cottam was indicted on 28 June 1581 under the new statute, but not tried until 20–21 November at Westminster Hall with Edmund Campion and others. Foley gives a detailed account of the trial. Cottam's execution was deferred until 30 May 1582, when he was drawn on a hurdle from Newgate to Tyburn with his companions William Filbie, Luke Kirby, and Laurence Richardson, priests. After refusing a last minute pardon if he would acknowledge the queen as supreme head of the church, he was hanged, drawn, and quartered. There is some doubt about whether he was readmitted to the Society of Jesus shortly before his execution. He was beatified by Pope Leo XIII on 29 December 1886. His portrait was engraved in company with those of twenty-four other Jesuits; it was published in Rome as a sheet: 'Effigies et nomina quorundam e Societate Jesu, qui pro fide vel pietate sunt intersecti, ab anno 1549 ad annum 1607'. Cottam is to be distinguished from Thomas Cottam of Chester, who arrived at the English College at Valladolid on 10 July 1593, was ordained on an unknown date, and died there in 1597.

THOMPSON COOPER, *rev.* CERI SULLIVAN

**Sources** J. H. Pollen, ed., 'Official lists of prisoners for religion during the reign of Queen Elizabeth', *Miscellanea, I*, Catholic RS, 1 (1905), 47–72, 7 · J. H. Pollen, ed., 'Four papers relative to the visit of Thomas Sackville, afterwards earl of Dorset, to Rome in 1563–4', *Miscellanea, II*, Catholic RS, 2 (1906), 1–11, esp. 10 · E. Henson, ed., *The registers of the English College at Valladolid, 1589–1862*, Catholic RS, 30 (1930), 25 · L. Hicks, ed., *Letters and memorials of Father Robert Persons*, Catholic RS, 39 (1942), 25, 87–8 · C. Talbot, ed., *Miscellanea: recusant records*, Catholic RS, 53 (1961), 208, 240 · *Letters of William Allen and Richard Barret, 1572–1598*, ed. P. Renold, Catholic RS, 58 (1967), 22 · T. M. McCoog, *English and Welsh Jesuits, 1555–1650*, 1, Catholic RS, 74 (1994), 148 · T. F. Knox and others, eds., *The first and second diaries of the English College, Douay* (1878), 121, 131–2, 141, 150, 166, 261 · *The Elizabethan Jesuits: Historia missionis Anglicanae Societatis Jesu (1660) of Henry More*, ed. and trans. F. Edwards (1981), 34, 161–6 · W. Allen, *A briefe historie of the glorious martyrdom of XII reverend priests, executed within these twelve monethes for confession and defence of the Catholicke faith* (1582), sigs. B6r–C3r, bvi r–v · D. de Yepes, *Historia particular de la persecucion de Inglaterra* (1599), 387–403 · Foster, *Alum. Oxon.* · H. Foley, ed., *Records of the English province of the Society of Jesus*, 2 (1875), 149, 164–9 · G. Anstruther, *The seminary priests*, 1 (1969), 392, 576 · Gillow, *Lit. biog. hist.*, 1.574–5

**Likenesses** engraving, 1607? · line engraving, NPG

**Cottawamago**. *See* Blackfish (1729?–1779).

**Cottenham**. For this title name *see* Pepys, Charles Christopher, first earl of Cottenham (1781–1851).

**Cotter, George Sackville** (1755–1831), poet and translator, was the fourth son of Sir James Cotter, baronet (1714–1770), and Arabella, widow of Colonel Cassaubon, MP for Carrig, co. Cork, and daughter and coheir of the Right Honourable John Rogerson, lord chief justice, king's bench. He was educated at Westminster School, of which he was captain in 1770, and in 1771 he was elected to Trinity College, Cambridge. He was a scholar in 1772 and graduated BA in 1775 and MA in 1779. Having taken holy orders in 1778, he became vicar of Kilmacdonough, and rector of Kilcreddan-Garrivoe and Ightermorragh, diocese of Cloyne from 1797 to 1831. He was also the curate of Cloyne in 1781 and the vicar of Kilmichael, co. Cork from 1784 to 1797. He married Margaret, daughter of Bayley Rogers, physician and banker of Cork; they had at least four sons.

In 1788 Cotter published two volumes of *Poems*, dedicated to Lady Shannon, and consisting of a poem in two books, entitled *Prospects*, and a collection of odes and other fugitive pieces. In 1826 he published a translation of Terence for the use of schools, in the preface to which he states that when at Westminster School he had been an actor in three of Terence's comedies. In the following year he printed seven of the plays of Plautus, 'translated literally and grammatically, and cleared of objectionable passages'. The later years of his life were spent at Youghal, co. Cork, and he died on 4 April 1831.

T. F. HENDERSON, *rev.* REBECCA MILLS

**Sources** Venn, *Alum. Cant.*, 2/2.146 · *Old Westminsters*, 1.216 · H. R. Luard, ed., *Graduati Cantabrigienses*, 6th edn (1873), 117 · Burke, *Peerage* (1848) · Allibone, *Dict.* · J. Foster, *The peerage, baronetage, and knightage of the British empire for 1880*, [pt 2] [1880] · D. J. O'Donoghue, *The poets of Ireland: a biographical dictionary with bibliographical particulars*, 1 vol. in 3 pts (1892–3) · Watt, *Bibl. Brit.*

**Cotter, Sir James** (d. 1705), army officer and colonial governor, was the second son of Edmond Cotter (d. 1660), landowner, and Elizabeth Connell, the daughter of John Connell of Barryscourt. Little is known of Cotter's early life, though he may have served with the royalists during the English civil war. His first confirmed action seems to have been involvement in an abortive attempt to assassinate a number of those involved in the execution of Charles I, who were then living as exiles in Vevey, Switzerland. However, on 11 August 1664 Cotter and two fellow Irishmen succeeded in shooting dead the regicide John Lisle on his way to church in Lausanne. Although Cotter himself neither led the mission nor actually carried out the killing, his involvement in the murder seems to have provided the foundation upon which his future advancement was based. Popular tradition says he received a knighthood and a commission in the army for this service, though the former claim is unsubstantiated.

In July 1666 Cotter did indeed receive a commission, but in 1667 he was captured by the French during an attempted invasion of the island of St Kitts in the West Indies. Despite accusations concerning his poor conduct in battle and of fraternization with his captors, Cotter returned to England in May 1668 and successfully petitioned for relief and back payment. Having resigned his commission in November 1673, Cotter was granted a number of administrative posts in the West Indies. Though these were held in trust by his elder brother, and exercised by deputies, they proved very profitable. Following a further mission to Switzerland in 1676, during which he provided a report on the activities of Edmund Ludlow and his remaining fellow regicides, Cotter returned to the West Indies. In 1679 he married Margaret Stapleton, the daughter of Sir William Stapleton, a fellow Catholic Irishman, with whom Cotter had fought at St Kitts and who was now the governor of the Leeward Islands. By April 1681 Cotter had assumed the rank of colonel, and was governor of the island of Montserrat, whose administration was dominated by Irishmen.

In September 1682 Cotter travelled to England on leave, apparently never returning to the West Indies. Earlier that year, following his petitioning, he had been awarded a pension of £200 annually from the Irish revenue. Cotter then seems to have returned to Ireland, purchasing land in co. Cork to enlarge the small estate he had already established. In September 1683 he was admitted a freeman of the city of Cork, and in 1684 was acting as a magistrate in the county. Further acquisitions of land followed, and in 1686 he acted as sheriff of co. Cork. Cotter's possible participation at the battle of Sedgemoor in 1685 may have resulted in his being knighted, but again there is no proof to this effect. In 1688 he married for a second time; his wife was Ellen Plunkett (d. 1698), the daughter of Lord Louth, with whom he subsequently had seven children.

From March that year Cotter's proven loyalty to the crown and his position in the Irish Catholic élite led to his taking on new responsibilities. These included his appointment as a lieutenant-colonel in a Jacobite regiment. He was also elected as a member for Cork city in the 'patriot parliament' of 1689, and appointed the governor of Cork by James II on 11 February 1690. Following the flight of James II, Cotter's wife and eldest son, also James *Cotter, were removed to France as Cotter himself assumed command of the Jacobite forces in the southwest. His military exploits throughout the war met with mixed results, but under the subsequent treaty of Limerick he retained his lands.

Opposition to this was countered by declarations of support from the protestant inhabitants of Cork city and Sir Richard Cox. Cotter then turned to the life of a country gentleman, allegedly becoming a patron of Gaelic bards and musicians. He was also accused of sheltering a Catholic bishop despite the enactment of legislation excluding the hierarchy from Ireland. He died in comfortable circumstances in 1705 at Rockforest, co. Cork, where he was buried. The details of Cotter's life suggest he was a man of energy and opportunism, with a durable loyalty to both the crown and his religion. Ultimately, it may be that his career and reputation contributed to the fate of his son James, hanged for rape in 1720.     NEAL GARNHAM

**Sources** NL Ire., Cotter MSS [transcripts], MS 711 · G. de P. Cotter, 'The Cotter family of Rockforest, co. Cork', *Journal of the Cork Historical and Archaeological Society*, 2nd ser., 43 (1938), 21–31 · B. Ó Cuív, 'James Cotter, a seventeenth-century agent of the crown', *Journal of the Royal Society of Antiquaries of Ireland*, 89 (1959), 135–59 · D. H. Akenson, *If the Irish ran the world: Montserrat, 1630–1730* (1997) · A. Marshall, *Intelligence and espionage in the reign of Charles II, 1660–1685* (1994), 279–300

**Archives** NL Ire., MS 711 [transcripts]

**Wealth at death** considerable: NL Ire., MS 711

**Cotter, James** (*c*.1689–1720), Jacobite agitator and rapist, was born in co. Cork, Ireland, the eldest of seven children of Sir James *Cotter (d. 1705), army officer and colonial administrator, and his second wife, Ellen Plunkett (d. 1698), daughter of Lord Louth. The elder Cotter's career had received something of a fillip during Charles II's reign owing to his involvement in the murder of the regicide Lord Lisle in Lausanne in August 1664. The profits accrued from the offices and pension that were subsequently bestowed on him resulted in Cotter's acquiring some property in north Cork to add to the small estate he had been bequeathed by his father, Edmond. Despite his involvement on the Jacobite side during the revolution of 1688, his estates remained intact and were inherited by his son.

On the death of his father the younger Cotter eventually became the ward of Lord Netterville, a local protestant proprietor. However, despite the censure of the Irish House of Commons, his actual care was delegated to a Catholic tutor. By 1710 Cotter had married Margaret Mathew, the daughter of Major George Mathew, a local Catholic landlord, and was already acquiring a reputation as a Jacobite troublemaker. In 1707 he had been involved in an election riot in Tralee, co. Kerry, and in 1713 he was noted as one of the ringleaders in the severe disturbances that accompanied elections in Dublin. Following the accession of George I to the throne, rumours circulated regarding both a potential rebellion in Ireland and an invasion, some of which implicated Cotter as a potential conspirator. In August 1718 he became involved in an incident near Fermoy, co. Cork, which led to his being accused of raping one Elizabeth Squibb. A prosecution was instigated by Edward Fenn, a Quaker and a relation of Squibb's. Although Cotter finally surrendered for trial in July 1719, legal proceedings were delayed. Then at his trial on 17 March 1720 he was convicted and sentenced to death. Despite calls for a pardon by both the grand and petty juries, letters of support from leading protestant gentlemen of the county, an appeal for clemency from the family of the victim, an attempted escape, and the nocturnal demolition of the gallows on the eve of the date set for his execution, Cotter was finally hanged at Cork on 7 May 1720; he was buried the following day in Carrigtwohill. His death caused considerable popular hostility, much of it focused on the Irish Quaker community, who were seen as responsible for his downfall.

Cotter entered local folklore immediately, and in later

years was celebrated in Gaelic poetry and popular song as a constant opponent of the protestant ascendancy and a religious and political martyr. Even into the late nineteenth century his execution was cited in popular literature as a symbol of the ruthless suppression of Irish nationalism and Catholicism by the Anglicized protestant state. In recent years most historians have continued to see Cotter's case as at least an example of local religious and political intolerance which resulted in a judicial assassination. However, such conclusions ignore the fact that Cotter was in fact almost certainly guilty of rape, a crime frequently punished by death. In addition, Cotter's father was widely known to have been responsible for the murder of Lord Lisle, the grandfather of Henrietta, duchess of Bolton, wife of the then lord lieutenant of Ireland. This latter fact was seen by at least one contemporary as crucial in circumventing local calls for mercy and guaranteeing Cotter's execution. The lack of precise and unquestionable evidence concerning Cotter's alleged crimes, and the myths and speculation that have grown up around the man, probably mean the exact details of the situation must remain uncertain; but the assertion that he was the victim of a local protestant cabal does seem untenable.

NEAL GARNHAM

**Sources** transcripts, NL Ire., Cotter MSS, MS 711 · B. Ó Buachalla, 'The making of a Cork Jacobite', *Cork: history and society—interdisciplinary essays on the history of an Irish county*, ed. P. O'Flanagan and C. G. Buttimer (1993), 469–98 · N. Garnham, 'The trials of James Cotter and Henry Baron Barry of Santry: two case studies in the administration of criminal justice in early eighteenth-century Ireland', *Irish Historical Studies*, 31 (1998–9), 328–42 · B. Ó Cuiv, 'James Cotter, a seventeenth-century agent of the crown', *Journal of the Royal Society of Antiquaries of Ireland*, 89 (1959), 135–59
**Archives** NL Ire., MSS, MS 711 [transcripts]
**Wealth at death** lands: NL Ire., Cotter MSS, MS 711, p. 156

**Cotter, Patrick** [ *performing name* Patrick O'Brien] (**1760/61– 1806**), giant, was born at Kinsale, co. Cork. He grew to be more than 8 feet tall (accounts vary from 8 feet 3½ inches to 8 feet 7 inches), and from his late teens was exhibited in England as the Irish Giant. He was originally tied to a showman who gave him £50 a year for three years for the right to show him, but after a disagreement Cotter was thrown into debtors' prison for a fictitious debt. He was bought out by a benevolent stranger, and thereafter exhibited himself for his own profit. The first certain notice of his exhibition is at a Mr Shenstone's tavern, the Full Moon, at Stokes Croft, Bristol, on 19 July 1783. Like other Irish giants of the period, he took the professional name O'Brien, claiming descent from Brian Bóruma, king of Ireland, and has sometimes been confused with another giant, Charles Byrne, who also took the name O'Brien. Cotter displayed himself around the country for some twenty years: in 1785 he was in London in a variety programme at Sadler's Wells, alongside performing animals, and in 1798 he was in a booth at Bartholomew fair. Extraordinary size had its conveniences: it is recorded that 'once in Bath, on a cold night, he terrified a watchman by quietly reaching up to a street lamp, and taking off the cover to light his pipe' (*N&Q*, 2nd ser., 11, 1861, 396); he made a tidy sum from his career, and in 1804 retired into

Patrick Cotter (1760/61–1806), by John Kay, 1803

private life. But Cotter's size had more disadvantages in an era which regarded physically exceptional individuals as freaks: the same source observes that he seldom went out during daylight, to avoid comments and taunts. He died in his lodgings in Hotwells Road, Clifton, on 8 September 1806 at the age of forty-five, and was buried in the Roman Catholic chapel in Trenchard Street, Bristol. In his will Cotter left legacies of more than £3000, mainly to his mother, Margaret Cotter, and strict instructions as to the details of his burial. Like Byrne, he was afraid that anatomists would seek to acquire his corpse, which, according to the memorial tablet in the chapel of his burial, was 'buried in the solid rock at the depth of twelve feet, and his body was secured with iron bars, so as to render removal impossible'.

K. D. REYNOLDS

**Sources** Highfill, Burnim & Langhans, *BDA* · *GM*, 1st ser., 76 (1806), 983 · *N&Q*, 2nd ser., 11 (1861), 369, 396 · *DNB* · H. Wilson, *Wonderful characters*, 3 vols. (1821) · *Kirby's wonderful … museum*, 6 vols. (1803–20), vol. 2, pp. 332–7
**Likenesses** T. Rowlandson, etching, pubd 1785, BM · J. Kay, caricature etching, 1803, NPG [*see illus.*] · A. Van Assen, etching (after J. Perry), BM, NPG; repro. in *Kirby's wonderful museum*, 2, 332 · group portrait, etching (*Five remarkable characters*), BM · group portrait, line engraving (*30 extraordinary characters, etc*), BM
**Wealth at death** left legacies and instructions for goods valued at approx. £3400, plus gold watch, diamond buckle, etc.: will, Highfill, Burnim & Langhans, *BDA*

**Cotterell** [Cottrell], **Sir Charles** (**1615–1701**), courtier and translator, was born in Wilsford, Lincolnshire, on Good Friday, 7 April 1615, and baptized there two days later, the only son (there were four daughters) of Sir Clement Cotterell (1585–1631) and his wife, Anne Alleyne (d. 1660). His father was appointed muster-master of Buckinghamshire in 1616 and groom-porter to James I in 1619, and was knighted in 1620, all through the Villiers interest: he was 'A creature of the Lord of Buckinghams' (*Letters of John Chamberlain*, 2.275).

Cotterell matriculated from Queens' College, Cambridge, in 1629. After his father's death in 1631 he completed another year at university but did not proceed to any degree. In June 1632 he began touring the continent with Richard Boyle, Viscount Dungarvan (heir of the earl of Cork), and William Russell (later third earl of Bedford). Shortly after returning to England he was engaged to take the earl of Pembroke's sons Charles and Philip Herbert on their travels. Though the tour was marred by the death of Charles, Cotterell entered Pembroke's service on his return in 1636.

Although Cotterell served in the privy chamber troop against the Scots his first real opportunity for advancement came with the death in July 1641 of the master of the ceremonies, Sir John Finet. Sir Balthasar Gerbier had the reversion to Finet's place and Cotterell replaced him as assistant master on 30 July. At about this time in Oxford, William Dobson painted himself in jovial company with Gerbier and Cotterell. Soon, however, these friends parted acrimoniously as Gerbier fled abroad while Cotterell continued courtly and military service.

In the summer of 1642 Cotterell married Frances (1614–c.1657), daughter of Edward West of Marsworth, Buckinghamshire, and half-sister of the architect Roger Pratt. Soon afterwards Cotterell was at Nottingham to witness the raising of the king's standard, whence he journeyed into Wales to raise men, taking a company to Shrewsbury. In December 1643 he was promoted to the rank of major and, having fought at Edgehill, at both battles of Newbury, and at Alresford, was knighted in Oxford on 21 March 1645. There he collaborated with William Aylesbury ('his constant friend'; Wood, *Ath. Oxon.*, 3.441) to translate, at the king's request, Davila's *Storia delle guerre civile*, published in 1647. In March 1649, following the king's execution, Cotterell accompanied Aylesbury and the duke of Buckingham into exile. His wife and elder daughter Frances (Frank) travelled with him, but an infant daughter, Anne [see Dormer, Anne], remained in England. Aylesbury's desertion in 1650 left Cotterell managing the duke's affairs. Based in Antwerp he housed prominent royalists while fighting a losing battle against Buckingham's most rapacious creditor, Henry Jermyn. About this time his first son, Clement, was born.

By 1652 Cotterell had moved to The Hague to become steward to Elizabeth of Bohemia as he was completing his translation of La Calprenède's novel *Cassandre*. Its first appearance in 1652 eclipsed a rival undertaking by George Digby and the version remained popular in England until well into the eighteenth century. In the winter of 1652 he went to Heidelberg to negotiate on Elizabeth's behalf with her son, the elector Karl Ludwig (Charles Lewis). He established an excellent relationship with the elector and

in 1654 named his second son, Charles Lodowick Cotterell [*see below*]. Meanwhile the Cotterells' youngest daughter, Elizabeth, was born about 1652, and their daughter Frank died on the last day of 1653.

Cotterell resigned his stewardship in September 1655. While Elizabeth attributed this to 'a pett he tooke' (Wendland, 69), money seems to have been the major reason. On 1 November, Charles II appointed Cotterell adviser to the duke of Gloucester (the term 'governor' did not please the youth). A month earlier Lady Cotterell had sailed for England, carrying the infant Charles Lodowick with her, but not until the second half of 1656 was Cotterell permitted to follow her there, where she died, probably early the next year. After returning to the continent Cotterell participated in three campaigns in Flanders alongside Prince Henry, effectively administering his regiment, and served Gloucester and York at Dunkirk in 1658.

On 29 May 1660 Cotterell returned with the royal party to London where he was sworn master of the ceremonies on 5 June. As a favour to Karl Ludwig he placed the elector's illegitimate son Ludwig von Selz in Gloucester's household, but tragedy struck that September when both youths died of smallpox. He had immediately sought a position as Elizabeth of Bohemia's agent in England and, though this was never formalized, he provided assistance to her in London until her death. In 1661 he procured both the wardenship of Merton College, Oxford, and a knighthood for his brother-in-law Thomas Clayton.

Cotterell was now suitor to an attractive young widow, Anne Owen. Her friend Katherine Philips agreed to support his cause if he would help her husband, James Philips, MP for Cardigan, who had been suspended from the Commons, accused of having been one of those who sentenced Colonel John Gerard to death in 1654. Though they may have known each other previously, this seems to be the origin of the friendship between Cotterell and Philips, a young poet, who was known in her salon as Orinda. Although his suit for Owen (Lucasia) failed, and James Philips, albeit exonerated, resigned his seat (to be replaced in 1663 by a deeply reluctant Cotterell), Cotterell became a major figure in Orinda's literary circle. She dubbed him Poliarchus, after a character in Barclay's *Argenis*. Poems she wrote were published without permission in November 1663, and he suppressed the edition as best he could. However, following her death editions of her poems were published and several times reprinted, though Cotterell's precise involvement is uncertain. Orinda's letters to him, probably sold by his son Charles Lodowick, were published as *Letters of Orinda to Poliarchus* in 1705.

Cotterell spent a month as envoy-extraordinary to Brussels in 1665 and on 26 June 1667 he was appointed master of requests. That same year, building on earlier work by Napier and Pascal, he devised a calculating machine similar to ones by Hooke and Morland. In 1668 Anne Cotterell married Robert Dormer, and in 1670 her sister Elizabeth married William Trumbull, the future secretary of state. Against his father's wishes Cotterell's elder son, Clement, attended the earl of Sandwich on his flagship at the battle of Sole Bay in 1672 with his friend Sir Charles Harbord. These 'two valiant and most accomplish[ed] youths, full of virtue and Courage' (Evelyn, 3.616), were killed with the admiral and buried in Westminster Abbey. This left Cotterell with the task of training his dissolute and troubled second son, Charles Lodowick, to succeed him.

In 1678 Cotterell was one of the committee appointed to translate Edward Coleman's letters during the Popish Plot scare. Generally, however, he had been an inactive MP during his parliamentary career and did not contest his seat in 1679. There may also have been a less scrupulous side to Cotterell. In 1671, according to testimony in the case of *Elam Mossam ex parte Thomas Neale* v. *Lady Theodosia Ivie* (1684), he had turned a blind eye to a forged mortgage in order to recover £1250 owed to him by Lady Ivie.

With the king's permission Cotterell resigned his office on 27 December 1686 in favour of his son Charles Lodowick. Though his reasons were his great age and ill health, his last years were many, albeit quiet. On 18 December 1688, in the company of John Evelyn and his old friend Sir Stephen Fox, he watched James II leave London. In 1693 he published a translation of a Spanish work of piety. Mainly he seems to have devoted himself to caring for his extensive family. After a sickness of some ten days, Cotterell died at 6 p.m. on 7 June 1701 at his home in St Martin's Lane, Westminster. His daughter Lady Trumbull, his son Charles Lodowick, and his faithful servant Robert Cary were at his bedside. He was buried two days later under his pew in the church of St Martin-in-the-Fields, Westminster. Though somewhat self-serious, Cotterell seems to have been well regarded by those who knew him. After meeting him at the home of the painter Dankerts, Pepys described Cotterell as 'ingenious' (Pepys, 9.504). Gregorio Leti lavished praise on him, believing he represented everything that any court in the world could seek in a master of ceremonies, describing him as 'd'humor benigno, dolce, e quieto: assiduo nelle visite, di buon Consiglio, di vita esemplare, d'ottimo discorso' ('of kind disposition, soft and gentle, assiduous in his visits, of wise counsel, exemplary lifestyle, and the best conversation'; Leti, 378).

**Sir Charles Lodowick Cotterell** [Cottrell] (1654–1710), courtier, second (but only surviving) son of Sir Charles Cotterell, was born at The Hague on 10 August 1654 and baptized there three days later. When several months old he was sent to be raised in England. He matriculated in 1671 at Merton College, Oxford, where his uncle was warden, and then went travelling on the continent, where he attended Lord Berkely's embassy at Paris in 1675 and began a translation in 1676 of Wicquefort's newly published *Mémoires touchants les ambassadeurs*. On 31 January 1677 he married Elizabeth Burwell (1656–1689). His distant relative Sir Thomas Browne described the young man as 'That honest heartie Gentleman' (*The Works of Sir Thomas Browne*, ed. E. L. Keynes, 1931, 6.152), but Cotterell was clearly a disappointment to his father, who upbraided him frequently for his indolence and self-indulgence. Although he assumed the duties of master of the ceremonies upon his father's resignation in December 1686,

and was then knighted in February 1687, he was not an assiduous official.

After Cotterell's first wife, who had borne seven children, died in 1689, he married Elizabeth (d. 1741), the daughter of Challoner Chute, on 16 June 1691. His eldest son, Charles, was appointed assistant master of the ceremonies on 17 August 1702, and was called upon more and more to stand in for him in his ceremonial duties. Laziness was clearly a factor, since Charles Lodowick was to be found in the dissolute company of Elihu Yale, but it is clear that he was showing signs of mental instability. His son Charles wrote in 1703 that, 'his melancholy continues and sometimes encreases he turns every thing that's said as a reflection upon him' (BL, Add. MS 72519, fols. 3v–4r). Charles died in 1707, leaving the reversion of the office of master of the ceremonies to the second son, Clement *Cottrell (1686–1758). Following the death of Prince George of Denmark on 28 October 1708 Charles Lodowick published a chapbook eulogy, *The Whole Life and Glorious Actions of Prince George of Denmark*. It was a final flourish. Debt ridden, he died of dropsy at his soon to be repossessed home in St Martin's Lane, Westminster, on 9 July 1710 and was buried at St Martin-in-the-Fields two days later. Shortly before, his heir wrote of his father, 'I pray God Almighty touch his heart with a true sense of the vileness of his past life … & give us his children grace, in the future conduct of our lives, to avoid those errors he has run into' (BL, Add. MS 72519, fol. 22v).

RODERICK CLAYTON

**Sources** Rousham, Oxfordshire, Rousham MSS, F 1–3, 5, 11; MC 5–6, 8 · *The collected works of Katherine Philips*, 2, ed. P. Thomas (1990) · P. Souers, *The matchless Orinda* (1931) · L. Naylor and G. Jagger, 'Cotterell, Charles', HoP, *Commons, 1660–90*, 2.138–9 · Wood, *Ath. Oxon.*, new edn · *CSP dom., 1641–89* · *Report on the manuscripts of the marquis of Downshire*, 6 vols. in 7, HMC, 75 (1924–95), vol. 1 · will, PRO, PROB 11/460, no. 77 · PRO, SP 77/83 · Wilts. & Swindon RO, MSS 865/391, 865/392 · A. Wendland, ed., *Briefe der Elisabeth Stuart, Königin von Böhmen an ihren Sohn, den Kurfürsten Carl Ludwig von der Pfalz, 1650–1662* (Tübingen, 1902) · J. C. Fox, *The Lady Ivie's trial* (1929) · G. Leti, *Il teatro brittanico*, 2nd edn, 5 vols. (Amsterdam, 1684), vol. 2 · *The letters of John Chamberlain*, ed. N. E. McClure, 2 (1939) · W. A. Shaw, *The knights of England*, 2 vols. (1906) · Venn, *Alum. Cant.* · Foster, *Alum. Oxon.* · Pepys, *Diary* · Evelyn, *Diary* · City Westm. AC, MF 10 · F. W. Cass, *Monken Hadley* (1880) · *Remarks and collections of Thomas Hearne*, ed. C. E. Doble and others, 3, OHS, 13 (1889) · BL, Add. MS 72519

**Archives** NRA, priv. coll., corresp. and papers · priv. coll. | BL, letters to Sir William Trumbull and Lady Trumbull, D/ED/C12

**Likenesses** W. Dobson, group portrait, oils, c.1640–1649, Albury Park, Guildford · W. Dobson, oils, c.1640–1649, Rousham, Oxfordshire · G. Kneller, oils, 1685, Rousham, Oxfordshire · J. Riley, oils, 1687, Rousham, Oxfordshire · W. Dobson, group portrait, Alnwick Castle, Northumberland · W. Dobson, miniature, Rousham, Oxfordshire · P. Lely, portrait · J. Riley, oils · R. Williams, mezzotint (after J. Riley), BM, NPG

**Cotterell, Sir Charles Lodowick** (1654–1710). *See under* Cotterell, Sir Charles (1615–1701).

**Cotterell, William** (1697/8–1744), Church of Ireland bishop of Ferns and Leighlin, was the third son of Sir Charles Lodowick *Cotterell (1654–1710) [*see under* Cotterell, Sir Charles] and his second wife, Elizabeth (d. 1741), only daughter of Chaloner Chute, of The Vyne, near

Basingstoke. William's half-brother was Sir Clement *Cottrell, master of ceremonies; his grandfather was Sir Charles *Cotterell. He was educated at Pembroke College, Cambridge, where he was admitted, aged eighteen, on 22 December 1716, graduating BA in 1720 and MA four years later. In 1725, on the death of Dean John Trench, he was presented to the deanery of Raphoe, co. Donegal, and the degree of DD was conferred upon him by diploma from the University of Oxford on 1 March 1733. The mention of Cotterell's name in Jonathan Swift's correspondence (30 July 1733) suggests that he was on intimate terms with the author. In March 1743 he became bishop of Ferns and Leighlin but held the see for little more than twelve months before he died, unmarried, in London on 21 June 1744. He was buried at St Anne's Church, Soho, London.

B. H. BLACKER, rev. PHILIP CARTER

**Sources** Venn, *Alum. Cant.* · H. Cotton, *Fasti ecclesiae Hibernicae*, 1–2 (1845–8) · *The correspondence of Jonathan Swift*, ed. H. Williams, 5 vols. (1963–5)

**Cottesford, Thomas**. *See* Cottisford, Thomas (d. 1555).

**Cottesloe**. For this title name *see* Fremantle, Thomas Francis, first Baron Cottesloe, and Baron Fremantle in the nobility of the Austrian empire (1798–1890); Fremantle, John Walgrave Halford, fourth Baron Cottesloe (1900–1994).

**Cottingham, Lewis Nockalls** (1787–1847), architect, was born at Laxfield, Suffolk, on 24 October 1787 and baptized on 24 November in Laxfield parish church, the son of John Cottingham (b. c.1762), farmer, and his wife, Elizabeth, *née* Johnson (b. 1762), the daughter of a surgeon. His ancestors included a master carpenter at York Minster in 1457 and the abbot of St Mary's, York, in 1483. Cottingham excelled in arts and science and then, in his own words, 'trained with a country architect and builder' in Ipswich before continuing his studies in London from 1810 'in the various branches of the art' (Cottingham to Fishmongers' Court, 15 Feb 1832). He started his own business as architect–surveyor in 1814, while living at 66 Great Queen Street, Lincoln's Inn Fields. From 1822 to 1840 he was surveyor to the Cooks' Company, and in 1828 moved to 43 Waterloo Bridge Road, Lambeth, part of an extensive estate he designed for John Field in 1825, where he lived and housed his museum. In 1822 he married Sophia Cotton (d. 1871), second daughter of Robert Turner Cotton, architect, of Finsbury; they had two sons, Nockalls Johnson [see below] and Edwin Cotton, and a daughter, Sophia.

Cottingham's great interest from 1810 onwards was the study of medieval architecture, its recording, preservation, and revival, and to this end he worked as an antiquary, archaeologist, restorer, collector, and Gothic revival architect and designer. Influenced by John Carter, fierce critic of the work of ignorant restorers, Cottingham published volumes of working drawings: *Plans of Westminster Hall* (1822) and *Plans, Elevations, etc. of the Magnificent Chapel of King Henry VII at Westminster Abbey etc.* (2 vols., 1822–9). These were dedicated to 'the young architects … for whose use and improvement the work is principally

dedicated' ('Preface' to *Plans, Elevations, etc.*). He also published *Working Drawings of Gothic Ornament* (1823) and *The Ornamental Metal Worker's Director* (1823), reissued in 1824 and 1840 as *The Smith and Founder's Director*.

As a preservationist, Cottingham's campaign saved the lady chapel of St Saviour's Church, Southwark, in 1832 and he supported efforts to save the fifteenth-century Crosby Hall in Bishopsgate, London. He published lithographs he made of Bishop Sheppie's tomb discovered in Rochester Cathedral in 1825, and accounts of his discoveries of encaustic tiles in the chapter house, Westminster, and lead coffins of the knights templar at Temple Church were published in *Archaeologia* (*Archaeologia*, 29, 1841, 390–91, 399). Cottingham's engravings of the tiles were published in J. G. Nichols, *Examples of Inlaid and Encaustic Tiles* (1843), and a large part of his archaeological survey of Temple Church appeared in William Burge, *The Temple Church* (1843).

Cottingham's museum of medieval art contained a library and 31,000 items, including models, casts of monuments, architectural features from demolished buildings, furniture, stained glass, and decorative arts. It was described by Henry Shaw in *A Descriptive Memoir* (1850) and in Shaw's preface to the *Catalogue of Sale* (Messrs Foster & Sons, 3 November 1851). Efforts to save it as a national collection failed and it was dispersed. The museum was influential as the first major collection of its kind in England, arranged chronologically with educative intent, and was visited by architects, aristocracy, and literary figures such as Sir Walter Scott.

Cottingham, as a leading medievalist, worked extensively in church restoration at Rochester Cathedral (1825–40), St Albans Abbey (1832–3), Armagh Cathedral (1834–42), Hereford Cathedral (1841–7), the Norman tower and St Mary's Church, Bury St Edmunds (1842–6), and many parish churches, including those of Ashbourne, Derbyshire (1839), Roos, Yorkshire, Great Chesterford, Essex, Milton Bryan, Bedfordshire (1841–2), Louth, Lincolnshire, Kilpeck, Herefordshire, and Market Weston, Horringer, and Theberton in Suffolk (1844–6). He won the competition to restore Magdalen College chapel, Oxford, in 1829, and built St Helen's Church, Thorney, Nottinghamshire (1845–9), in a robust Norman revival style. He brought innovative engineering skill, a careful archaeological approach, and a respect for existing fabric to his works of restoration.

In domestic architecture Cottingham moved from the neo-classicism of his Lambeth estate to full Gothic revival with Snelston Hall, Derbyshire (1827), for his patron John Harrison, and designed the Snelston estate village, taking the vernacular as a source of style. He had eminent patrons, and undertook medieval revival extensions and designs at Brougham Hall, Westmorland, for Lord Brougham (1830–47), Coombe Abbey, Warwickshire, for the earl of Craven (1833), Elvaston Castle, Derbyshire, for Lord Harrington (1834), Matfen Hall, Northumberland, for Sir Edward Blackett (1835–7), and Adare Manor, co. Limerick, for Lord Dunraven (1840). He built Gothic revival schools at Tuddenham, Suffolk, and Great Chesterford,

Essex (1846), and extended Clifton Hall, Nottinghamshire, and the General Hospital, Bury St Edmunds. He built the savings bank and Bank Cottage, Bury St Edmunds (1844) in the Tudor revival style. He also entered competitions for the Salters' Hall (1821), the Fishmongers' Hall (1832)—where he won third prize—and the Houses of Parliament (1836). He exhibited regularly at the Royal Academy and his skill as a watercolourist is evident in the (unpublished) book of designs for Snelston village (1821), and the elevations of Coombe Abbey (exhibited 1834).

Highly eminent in his own time, Cottingham fell into obscurity by the early twentieth century, his work included in the general condemnation of all nineteenth-century restorations. His significance lies in his influence as an early nineteenth-century promoter of an archaeological Gothic revival. He died at his home, 43 Waterloo Bridge Road, on 13 October 1847, and was buried in the family vault at Croydon parish church, Surrey, on 22 October.

Cottingham's will stipulated that his elder son, **Nockalls Johnson Cottingham** (1823–1854), should continue his practice. This he did, completing works at Hereford Cathedral, the churches of Barrow, Suffolk, and Ledbury, Herefordshire, the Norman tower at Bury St Edmunds, and the building of St Helen's Church, Thorney. He had attended King's College School in the Strand (1832–5), where he was taught drawing by J. S. Cotman. He trained in his father's office with another pupil from the school, Calvert Vaux. Nockalls Cottingham was successful as a stained-glass designer, and at Hereford Cathedral he designed windows for the lady chapel, including the east triplet (made by Hardmans of Birmingham, 1847–51). He died on his way to America, possibly to work with Calvert Vaux on designs for Central Park, New York, when the steamship *Arctic* foundered off Cape Cod on 27 September 1854.

L. H. CUST, rev. JANET MYLES

**Sources** Art Union, 9 (1847), 377–8 • The Athenaeum (16 Oct 1847) • J. Myles, L. N. Cottingham, 1787–1847, architect of the Gothic revival (1996) • H. Shaw, A descriptive memoir: museum of mediaeval architecture and sculpture, founded by the late L. N. Cottingham, Esq., FSA (1850) • L. N. Cottingham and N. J. Cottingham, nineteen letters to William Brougham, 1844–6, UCL, Brougham MSS • L. N. Cottingham, eight letters to the Fishmongers' Court, 30 Sept 1831–17 March 1832, GL, MS F843, File 14 • Cooks' Company, minutes of proceedings, July 1822–Sept 1834, GL, MSS 31114–31115 • W. Burge, The Temple Church: an account of its restoration and repairs (1843) • L. N. Cottingham, GM, 2nd ser., 15 (1841), 18 • The Builder, 5 (1847), 502–3 • The Builder, 8 (1850), 257 • The Builder, 9 (1851), 710, 742 • GM, 1st ser., 95/1 (1825), 76–7 • GM, 1st ser., 95/2 (1825), 226 • GM, 2nd ser., 18 (1842), 521 • GM, 2nd ser., 17 (1842), 193 • GM, 2nd ser., 19 (1843), 406 • The Ecclesiologist, 5 (1846), 162 • The Ecclesiologist, 9 (1848–9), 202–3, 415 • The Ecclesiologist, 16 (1855), 8–15 • The Ecclesiologist, 14 (1853), 7 • The Ecclesiologist, 22 (1856), 144 • parish register (baptism), Laxfield, Suffolk, 1787 • d. cert. • Suffolk RO, FC 80 • Colvin, Archs. • prints, V&A [note on drawing of a font]

**Archives** Armagh Cathedral Library, drawings • BM, plans for Lambeth estate and sketchbooks • Castle Howard, Yorkshire, archive • Col. U., Avery Architectural and Fine Arts Library, sketchbooks relating to Stratford and surrounding towns • Derbys. RO, drawings for Snelston Hall • Essex RO • GL, Fishmongers' Hall competition designs • Hereford Cathedral Library • Lloyds TSB, London, archive • Magd. Oxf., archives • Medway Archives and Local Studies Centre, Rochester, Kent, notes on repairs to Rochester Cathedral • NL Wales, Belmont Abbey collection, bundle 29 • RIBA, Houses of Parliament competition, etc. • Rochester Cathedral Archive • Salters' Hall, London • Suffolk RO, vestry book of St James • V&A, furniture, drawings, notebook | LPL, Incorporated Church Building Society archive • Northumbd RO, Blackett MSS • priv. coll., Stanton family collection • PRO NIre., Beresford MSS • PRO NIre., Dunraven MSS • UCL, Brougham MSS

**Wealth at death** estate (house / museum, incl. enormous collection and library) to widow and business to son: will, PRO, PROB 11/2072

**Cottingham, Nockalls Johnson** (1823–1854). *See under* Cottingham, Lewis Nockalls (1787–1847).

**Cottington, Francis**, first Baron Cottington (1579?–1652), diplomat and politician, was baptized at Pitcombe, Somerset, the third son of Philip Cottington (*d.* in or after 1611) of Godminster, near Pitcombe, and his wife, Jane, daughter of Thomas Biflete, also of Somerset. The Cottingtons were long-established minor landowners and sheep farmers in eastern Somerset, engaged in the production and marketing of broadcloth. Francis Cottington did not go to university. He was educated privately, at home and in the household of the former French ambassador Sir Edward Stafford, probably a kinsman of his mother, whose household he joined in the later 1590s. Through Stafford's recommendation, in the spring of 1605 Cottington entered the service of Sir Charles Cornwallis, the English ambassador at Madrid, where he became proficient in Spanish under the tutelage of Nicholas Ousely, and knowledgeable in the Spanish aspects of English diplomacy which, in subsequent years, made him indispensable to the king's service.

**Early career, 1605–1628** Cottington remained in Spain until July 1611, gaining promotion to the rank of junior secretary in 1607 and serving as agent from September 1609, following Cornwallis's departure. Indeed, Cornwallis's frequent illnesses required Cottington to deputize for him from an early stage of his employment, and his hard work was recognized by Cornwallis's successor, Sir John Digby. The frustrations he encountered in attempting to secure redress of English merchants' grievances—not all of which he regarded as worthy cases—combined with his own illnesses, the deaths of several embassy staff, and a short period of imprisonment in 1609, led him to wish for an end to his employment in Spain. He spent only four months in England, however, before returning in December 1611 as consul in Seville, although aware of what he described as 'some disgrace of the quality of the employment' (*Downshire MSS*, 3.164). His second spell in Spain proved to be brief, however, as Philip III refused to accept protestants as consuls.

In September 1613 Cottington obtained a clerkship-in-ordinary of the privy council for £400, after serving for three months as a clerk-extraordinary. His knowledge of Spanish affairs was undoubtedly a factor in his selection, as James's favourite, the earl of Somerset, and other privy councillors supportive of a Spanish marriage for Prince Charles were keen to use him as an intermediary with the Spanish ambassador, count Gondomar. His third term in

Francis Cottington, first Baron Cottington (1579?–1652), by unknown artist, 1634?

Madrid, from January 1616, supposedly for a short spell during Sir John Digby's absence, became another six-year stay, during which, as chargé d'affaires, he worked to further negotiations for the planned Spanish match, made more complicated by the crisis in Bohemia. His dispatches were reported to the new favourite, the marquess of Buckingham, by the secretary of state, Sir Thomas Lake, as 'worth his Majesties reading' (Gardiner, *Fortescue*, 80–81), suggesting that Cottington already enjoyed a degree of access to the king and his closest advisers, including Buckingham, to whom he sent a number of reports in 1618–19. His prolonged stay in Madrid, although keeping him physically distant from court, resulted from James's desire that the new ambassador, Sir Walter Aston, receive the benefit of his advice, and rumours in October 1621 that he would replace Sir Thomas Murray as secretary to Prince Charles, and the appointment itself, which followed his return to England in the autumn of the following year, reflected the king's confidence in him and the importance of the Spanish marriage intended for the prince. The appointment was accompanied in February 1623 with the grant of a baronetcy. Cottington's duties seem to have been somewhat loosely defined, involving him in administrative work arising from privy council business as well as secretarial work for the prince. His expertise in Spanish affairs—as the court prepared for the return of Gondomar—made him useful to the secretaries of state, one of whom, Sir George Calvert, was his kinsman. John Chamberlain noted the king's habit of consulting Cottington on Spanish affairs and, when he was required to offer an opinion on the prince's proposed journey to Spain, James clearly trusted him to give sound advice.

Also in February 1623 Cottington made an advantageous marriage to Anne (*d.* 1634), widow of Sir Robert Brett and daughter of Sir William Meredith, and a distant relative, through her mother, Jane, of the secretary of state Sir Francis Windebank. With her he had a son and four daughters, all of whom died before him. He first sat in parliament in 1624, owing his seat at Camelford to duchy of Cornwall influence after disappointments at Chester, Warwick, and Bury St Edmunds. His election for Bossiney (1625) and Saltash (1628) owed much to the influence of Buckingham and his client Sir James Bagg, but Cottington made little contribution to debates. His support for Digby, now earl of Bristol, during the 1625 parliament displeased Buckingham, but Charles in August 1626 apparently intended him for the post of secretary to Queen Henrietta Maria before admitting the prior claim of his mother's old secretary, Sir Robert Ayton. Charles also gave Cottington land and an annuity in 1625, and in June 1628 made him keeper of the king's game at Hampton Court.

**Chancellor of the exchequer, 1629–1641** On better terms with Buckingham by 1628, Cottington nevertheless found a more secure foothold at court following the duke's death, as Lord Treasurer Richard Weston, later earl of Portland and arguably the greatest beneficiary of Buckingham's demise, saw in him a valuable associate. He was sworn of the privy council on 12 November 1628 and became chancellor of the exchequer on 20 March 1629 on Newburgh's appointment as chancellor of the duchy of Lancaster. Cottington was the obvious choice as ambassador to Spain in 1629–31, holding a more cautious view of the negotiations than the over-optimistic Weston. In addition to the treaty of November 1630 which ended the Anglo-Spanish conflict, Cottington negotiated the secret treaty of January 1631 for the partitioning of the United Provinces, never implemented, and probably not taken seriously by Cottington himself. He became Baron Cottington of Hanworth on 10 July 1631.

During the 1630s the range of Cottington's duties was impressive. His membership of committees and commissions was matched only by that of Windebank, and involved him in a wide range of business, revealed in the state papers domestic. He took a particularly keen interest in the business of the board of the admiralty, to which he was appointed in November 1632, and he headed the rump of the government left in London in the summer of 1633, during the king's coronation visit to Scotland. Throughout the 1630s he regularly received reports from English diplomats abroad who evidently regarded him as a key figure in Charles I's dealings with the Habsburg powers, and an effective means of communication with the king. His removal from the foreign affairs committee in 1635 should not be taken to mean exclusion from deliberations on foreign affairs as Charles's appointments to that body did not necessarily reflect familiarity with policy. His appointment as master of the court of wards and liveries in March 1635 brought him another major office, which he ran efficiently, resulting in a substantial increase in revenue. Cottington may well have nursed ambitions for this post for several years: rumour had linked his name with the mastership in December 1631, and it is possible that Charles granted him this office during Portland's final illness as advance compensation for denying him the lord treasurership.

Cottington's appointment as master enabled him to do a couple of good turns for his friend, Lord Deputy Thomas Wentworth, most important of which was the grant of the wardship of William Wentworth; the second was the appointment of Wentworth's cousin Rowland Wandesford to the attorneyship of the court. Cottington's knowledge of financial affairs was particularly valued by Wentworth, who by 1634 was in the habit of forwarding relevant Irish business to Cottington in the first place, prompting the chancellor to warn his friend not to ignore the lord treasurer. Wentworth also appreciated, and benefited from, Cottington's understanding of political developments at court and broadly shared his pro-Spanish sympathies. Their relationship was not without its tensions, but it remained an important political association. In contrast, by the mid-1630s Cottington did not enjoy a good working relationship with Wentworth's key ally and correspondent, Archbishop William Laud, who clashed with the chancellor over the soap monopoly, the Star Chamber case of *Pell* v. *Bagg*, and the prosecution of Bishop John Williams of Lincoln. Charles's decision to place the treasury in commission following Portland's death, with Laud and Cottington as its head commissioners, gave Laud the opportunity to launch an investigation into the state of royal revenues in an attempt to discredit Cottington and damage his chances of succeeding Portland; the resulting unpleasantness convinced the king of the need to find some other candidate. The queen's informal visit to Hanworth, Cottington's Middlesex home, in the summer of 1635 probably confirmed his place as chancellor of the exchequer; earlier hints to Wentworth and remarks made by his friend the newsletter writer George Garrard suggest that Cottington was aware—as Laud was not—of the king's leanings towards Bishop William Juxon. True to his declared intention to indulge himself in leisure pursuits more often under Portland's successor than had been possible while serving under his old friend, Cottington spent the summer of 1636 hawking on his Hanworth estate, where he entertained Wentworth during the lord deputy's visit to England, visiting the earl of Salisbury, gaily dressed, at Hatfield, and participating in the king's visit to Oxford, where he was observed in close conversation with Laud. The king's failure to send Cottington any expressions of condolence on the death of his wife in February 1634 was bitterly noted in a letter to Wentworth; however, the chancellor continued to stand high in royal favour and successfully defended before the king in council Captain Walter Stewart's action in sailing for Dunkirk in July 1636 without stopping long enough at Dover to unload two-thirds of his valuable cargo of silver, presenting this as a necessary gesture to reassure Spain, suspicious of recent English dealings with France. Summer 1636 was marred for Cottington not by political developments but by a personal tragedy—the death of his only son.

Despite Cottington's characteristically disarming comments in February 1637 that he had become 'no more a leader, butt doe meddle with myn own particular duties only' (Strafford papers, 16/139), a more realistic appraisal of his position was offered by the earl of Clare, who, anticipating Juxon's appointment as lord treasurer, believed that the chancellor would nevertheless be required to 'do the business' (*Letters of John Holles*, 3.479). Cottington's financial expertise was indeed much needed during the king's preparations for war against his rebellious subjects in Scotland and his place at the centre of government was confirmed by his appointment in July 1638 to the committee for Scottish affairs, which grew into the council of war in December 1639. He supported Wentworth, now earl of Strafford, in negotiations with the Spanish ambassadors in an attempt to secure subsidies from Philip IV. In April 1640 he sat in the House of Lords and reported on his examination of the earl of Loudoun, having secured Commons seats at Hindon, Wiltshire, for Garrard and for Sir Miles Fleetwood, receiver-general of the court of wards. Having failed to persuade the City to lend the crown £100,000, Cottington turned instead to the purchase on credit of pepper from the East India Company to provide much-needed immediate money. His energetic approach to the king's financial difficulties matched that of Strafford, with whom he worked closely, and who may have stood with him as surety in the pepper deal. In May and June he gained additional responsibilities as constable of the Tower and lord lieutenant of Dorset, once again heading the government left behind in London when the king marched north in August. He sat in the House of Lords occasionally during the first session of the Long Parliament, defending Strafford in the spring of 1641, but recognizing that he might be in some danger himself he then resigned his offices. The mastership of the wards went to Lord Saye and Sele. The chancellorship of the exchequer was placed in commission, and Cottington retired to his Wiltshire property, Fonthill Gifford, in the summer of 1641 and remained there during the first months of the war.

**War and exile, 1642–1652** Cottington might have hoped to escape the attentions of the king's enemies by retiring to Wiltshire but the harassment he experienced in December 1642 turned into a more serious threat the following spring as parliament tightened its grip on most of southwest England. He joined Charles at Oxford in 1643, the most experienced of his advisers, and served him as a privy councillor, councillor of war, and lord treasurer; in January 1644 he was also reinstated as master of the wards. Following the king's defeat Cottington oversaw the surrender of Oxford in June 1646, probably leaving the city with the rest of the court. By now most of his property, amassed since the late 1620s and located mainly in southern England, had been appropriated by parliament and either sold or leased, although parliamentarian sequestrators were not able to discover the full extent of his wealth. His whereabouts for much of the rest of 1646 are not certain but, not allowed to compound for his delinquency, he left England in the latter part of the year without licence, and took up residence at Rouen. As lord treasurer he continued to try to raise money for the royalist cause and was sworn councillor to Charles II in May 1649. The new king sent Cottington, at his request, together with Edward Hyde, as ambassador-extraordinary to Philip IV, and Cottington arrived in Spain for the last time in September 1649. He found, however, that his reputation as a friend of Spain counted for little; he failed to secure financial assistance for the royalist cause from Philip IV, whose unwillingness to offend the Rump, evidently growing in strength following its victory at Dunbar, caused him to demand that they leave Madrid.

Cottington parted from Hyde in March 1651 and went to Valladolid, where he spent the months before his death on 19 June 1652, having finally converted to the Catholic faith, not, in Clarendon's opinion, because of any great zeal for that faith, but rather because he intended to live out the rest of his days in Spain, and he 'conformed to that which the province he held obliged him to' (Clarendon, *Hist. rebellion*, 5.152). In 1607, during his first stay in Spain, Cottington had been targeted unsuccessfully for conversion by Father Joseph Creswell, who was aware of his younger brother Edward's Jesuit training. Evidence to support the claim that Cottington underwent conversion during periods of illness, once in Spain in 1623, and later in the 1630s, is scant, and the Catholic bishop Richard Smith does not seem to have regarded him as trustworthy. Cottington's willingness to raise revenue in the shape of recusancy fines suggests that, while in government at least, his sympathies for Catholics had its limits. Likewise his affection for Spain—which meant he was likely to remain in favour with both James I and Charles I—was not at the expense of English interests, despite his portrayal by contemporaries, both hostile and friendly, as 'Don Francisco', the practitioner of 'Spanish tricks' (Strafford papers, 10b/70; 6/92). He was a hardworking, efficient, and devoted servant of the crown, whose expertise in diplomacy brought him into government, and whose abilities in financial administration helped him stay there. A witty, clever man who delighted in making jokes at the expense of his colleagues, Cottington avoided treating others with malice and remained respected by most of those who knew him.

Several years after the death of his wife, Cottington appears to have considered remarriage, but his plans met with no success. His will, made three days before his death, left whatever might be recovered of his English estate to his nephews and bequeathed money and jewels to religious houses in Valladolid. He was buried, according to his wishes, in the chapel of the English College in that city until it might be possible for his removal to England. In June 1678 his great-nephew Charles Cottington arranged for the re-burial of Lord Cottington's remains beside those of his wife in St Paul's Chapel, Westminster Abbey.                                        FIONA POGSON

**Sources** *CSP dom.*, *1611–40* · PRO, SP 14/123/15; 14/133/59; 14/134/80 · PRO, SP 16 · PRO, SP 94/18/124 · PRO, SP 94/19/170–71 · PRO, SP 94/14/65–6 · *CSP Venice*, *1636–9* · Strafford papers, Sheff. Arch., Wentworth Woodhouse muniments, 3/52–3; 3/203; 6/92; 8/427; 10b/70; 12/71; 13/219; 15/253; 16/19 and 139; 18/33 and 152; 21/138 · S. Antiquaries, Lond., Cottington and Meredith MS 203 · NA Scot., Hamilton MSS, GD 406/1/1234 · NL Wales, Wynn papers, no. 1433 · *Sixth report*, HMC, 5 (1877–8) · *The manuscripts of the earl of Westmorland*, HMC, 13 (1885); repr. (1906) · *The manuscripts of the Earl Cowper*, 3 vols., HMC, 23 (1888–9), vol. 2 · *Report on the manuscripts of the marquis of Downshire*, 6 vols. in 7, HMC, 75 (1924–95), vols. 2–3 · M. J. Havran, *Caroline courtier: the life of Lord Cottington* (1973) · Clarendon, *Hist. rebellion*, vols. 1, 5 · R. Scrope and T. Monkhouse, eds., *State papers collected by Edward, earl of Clarendon*, 3 vols. (1767–86), vols. 1–2 · S. R. Gardiner, ed., *Letters and other documents illustrating the relations between England and Germany at the commencement of the Thirty Years' War*, 2 vols., CS, 90, 98 (1865–8) · *The Nicholas papers*, ed. G. F. Warner, 1, CS, new ser., 40 (1886) · M. A. E. Green, ed., *Calendar of the proceedings of the committee for advance of money, 1642–1656*, 2, PRO (1888), 578–81 · *The Fortescue papers*, ed. S. R. Gardiner, CS, new ser., 1 (1871) · *Letters of John Holles, 1587–1637*, ed. P. R. Seddon, 3, Thoroton Society Record Series, 36 (1986) · A. J. Cooper, 'The political career of Francis Cottington, 1605–52', BLitt diss., U. Oxf., 1966 · A. MacFadyen, 'Anglo-Spanish relations, 1603–25', MA diss., U. Lpool, 1960 · J. K. Gruenfelder, *Influence in early Stuart elections, 1604–1640* (1981) · B. Quintrell, 'The Church triumphant? The emergence of a spiritual lord treasurer, 1635–1636', *The political world of Thomas Wentworth earl of Strafford, 1621–1641*, ed. J. F. Merritt (1996), 81–108 · J. W. Stoye, *English travellers abroad, 1604–1667*, rev. edn (1989) · E. S. Cope and W. H. Coates, eds., *Proceedings of the Short Parliament of 1640*, CS, 4th ser., 19 (1977) · H. Sydney and others, *Letters and memorials of state*, ed. A. Collins, 2 (1746) · *Memorials of affairs of state in the reigns of Q. Elizabeth and K. James I, collected (chiefly) from the original papers of … Sir Ralph Winwood*, ed. E. Sawyer, 3 vols. (1725), vol. 3 · R. C. Hoare, *The history of modern Wiltshire*, 4 (1822) · GEC, *Peerage* · M. C. Fissel, *The bishops' wars: Charles I's campaigns against Scotland, 1638–1640* (1994) · J. H. Elliott, 'The year of the three ambassadors', *History and imagination: essays in honour of H. R. Trevor-Roper*, ed. H. Lloyd-Jones, V. Pearl, and B. Worden (1981), 165–81 · W. R. Prest, *The rise of the barristers: a social history of the English bar, 1590–1640* (1986) · F. Pogson, 'Making and maintaining political alliances during the personal rule of Charles I: Wentworth's associations with Laud and Cottington', *History*, new ser., 84 (1999), 52–73 · G. Bankes, *The story of Corfe Castle* (1853) · J. L. Chester, ed., *The marriage, baptismal, and burial registers of the collegiate church or abbey of St Peter, Westminster*, Harleian Society, 10 (1876) · will, PRO, DEL 9/1, mm. 223–225

**Archives** NL Scot., accounts of expenses in Spain · S. Antiquaries, Lond., corresp. and papers, MS 203 | BL, letters to Edward Proger, RP 278(3) · BL, letters to William Trumbull, Add. MS 72281; Stowe MS 169 · PRO, SP 94/16–18, 22–24, 27, 30–31, 34–37 · Sheff. Arch., letters to Lord Strafford

**Likenesses** attrib. P. van Somer, portrait, *c*.1616, repro. in E. Lodge, *Portraits of illustrious personages of Great Britain*, 4 vols. (1821–34), vol. 3 · oils, 1634?, NPG; version, Clarendon collection [on loan to Council House, Plymouth] [*see illus.*] · R. Dunkarton, mezzotint (after P. van Somer), BM, NPG · effigy, Westminster Abbey, chapel of St Paul · pen and wash drawing, NPG

**Wealth at death** income in late 1630s probably more than £3000 p.a.: Havran, *Caroline courtier*, 109 · bequeathed 1200 ducats each to three servants; plus £20 annuity; five religious establishments in Valladolid received 100 reals each; some jewellery and plate: will, PRO, DEL 9/1, mm. 223–5

**Cottisford, John** (*d.* 1540), college head, was born in the late fifteenth century, and was either from the Oxfordshire village of Cottisford, or from nearby Launton. He seems to have gone to Lincoln College and was a BA by 1505 and MA by 1510, and then proceeded to become a bachelor and subsequently doctor in theology by 1525. His slow progress was probably due to his involvement in the administrative affairs of the college, of which he was a fellow in 1509–19, its bursar in 1513, sub-rector in 1516 and 1518, and subsequently rector from 1519 to 1539. He was also a senior proctor of the university, and in 1527 became the chancellor's commissary until 1532; in this connection he was heavily involved in the questions to the University of Oxford about the royal divorce. He was on a select committee with the bishop of Lincoln, John Longland, and some carefully chosen theologians. Not surprisingly, the committee favoured the dissolution of the marriage and Cottisford was made canon and first prebendary of Henry VIII's college.

Like many others Cottisford had difficulties keeping on the right side of the ecclesiastical establishment. The chancellor of the university, William Warham, and the visitor of Lincoln College, Bishop Longland, were both anxious to rid the university of Lutherans. It was Cottisford's responsibility in 1528 to imprison Thomas Garrett who was a prominent disseminator of Lutheran tracts: Cottisford was courteous enough to lock Garrett, during evensong, in his own lodgings, but he escaped. Cottisford was reported to have gone 'as pale as ashes' (*Acts and Monuments*, 5.423) but Garrett was later apprehended and Longland comforted Cottisford that the escape had had the beneficial effect of implicating other heretics. This time Cottisford imprisoned Garrett, with others, in a cellar under the college normally used for preserving salt fish, where some of them died. Cottisford was not to escape censure so easily again. He was rebuked by Longland for allowing a protestant curate to preach in a college rectory in Oxford, but was also suspected by Thomas Cromwell of having had something to do with an attack on one of his more protestant servants.

Cottisford was a very private man, and only one book of his survives. There is very little evidence to suggest a great interest in either scholarship or, surprisingly, the college, though it may be that he was unwilling to trust others in such contested times. When the college was visited in 1530 Cottisford, like the other fellows, dined alone, and was said to neglect divine office and to keep the college treasures, charters, and archives in his own rooms. There is also little to suggest that he influenced the other fellows. It may have been that his wish to move into a less exposed position led him to accept the prebendary of All Saints in Hungate, and to take up residence in Lincoln Cathedral in September 1538, although he did not resign as rector until January 1539. This was an unexpected move as he had tended to gather livings in a small radius from Cottisford, but it is possible that the promise and advanced grant of the chancellorship of Lincoln Cathedral lured him. His new position was short-lived: he was present at chapter for the whole of 1539 but on 11 June 1540 he was reported as 'being sick' (Cole, 2.36), and on 20 September 1540, he was reported as being 'out of town' (Cole, 2.39). He was dead by 14 December 1540, when his brother accepted the administration of his estate.

MARGARET BOWKER

**Sources** V. Green, *The commonwealth of Lincoln College, 1427–1977* (1979) · Emden, *Oxf.* · R. E. G. Cole, ed., *Chapter acts of the cathedral church of St Mary of Lincoln*, 2, Lincoln RS, 13 (1917) · *The acts and monuments of John Foxe*, new edn, ed. G. Townsend, 5 (1843–9) · DNB · Vetus Registrum; accounts, 1510–38, Lincoln College, Oxford

**Cottisford** [Cottesforde], **Thomas** (*d.* 1555), clergyman and evangelical reformer, was born at Winchester and studied at both Oxford and Cambridge. In his 'Epistle to an Englyshe Marchaunt' of Winchester, written from Marian exile, he thanked the addressee for his gifts 'whan I was a student at Oxforde' (*Accompt*, 66). No university record of his degrees survives, though he was described as MA in 1553. He became a chaplain to Bishop Goodrich of Ely in 1538, and shared his reforming views. In January 1541 he was in trouble with the privy council for distributing a letter of Melanchthon's attacking the Act of Six Articles, and was imprisoned in the Fleet. Goodrich was a patron to him: at some date in the early 1540s he presented him to the rectory of Walpole, Norfolk, which Cottisford resigned in May 1544. The next month he was presented to the benefice of Littlebury in Essex. In 1547 he was offered a more public role as one of the preachers accompanying the royal commissioners visiting the dioceses of Salisbury, Exeter, Bath and Wells, Bristol, and Chichester.

During Edward's reign Cottisford is most visible as a translator for the new protestant regime. He had already in 1543 published a translation of Zwingli's confession of faith, which was reprinted in 1548. In the early 1550s he may have had a hand in the translation of John a Lasco's liturgy, though this was never published. In 1553 he compiled the important protestant primer intended to replace the 1545 version. The preparative for prayer asks the reader to 'in thy faithful prayers remember Thomas Cottesforde' (Ketley, 377). Two attractive promotions may represent his reward for this work. On 20 May 1553 he was collated to the rectory of St Martin Ludgate, London, and on 10 July 1553 he was made prebendary of Apesthorpe in York Minster.

On Mary's accession Cottisford fled abroad, first to Copenhagen and then to Emden, probably accompanying a Lasco and the Dutch congregation from London. In Copenhagen he wrote his 'Epistle to an Englyshe Marchaunt', which was later published with a reprint of his translation of Zwingli. This letter addresses the issue of confession, and shows an interesting concern for private as well as general confession as a means of giving men knowledge of their sins. A second epistle appended to the Zwingli text is addressed to a godly lady and concerns adult baptism, perhaps reflecting the deep concern of the Dutch congregation about this issue. At Emden, Cottisford may have had a hand in the preparation of a new edition of Cranmer's defence of the eucharist. He was certainly responsible for translations of two works of Marten Micronius, former minister of the London Dutch congregations, and he wrote a metrical version of confession based on Daniel 9 that was sung by the congregation following a Lasco's models. He thus made a significant contribution to the appropriation of congregational singing by the English church. His writings suggest determination to maintain the faith in exile, but pessimism about the state of England: 'what an infinite nombre', he wrote in the preface to

Zwingli's *Confession*, 'are now suddenly turned backe to worship the beast' (*Accompt*, preface, fol. 5). At some point in 1555 Cottisford moved on to Frankfurt, where he died, on 6 December, and was buried. FELICITY HEAL

Sources *The accompt rekenynge and confession of the faith of Huldrik Zwinglius*, trans. T. Cotsforde [T. Cottisford] (1555) · A. Pettegree, *Marian protestantism: six studies* (1996) · D. MacCulloch, *Thomas Cranmer: a life* (1996) · J. Ketley, ed., *The two liturgies set forth ... in the reign of King Edward VI*, Parker Society, 19 (1844) · R. A. Leaver, 'Goostly Psalmes and Spirituall Songes': English and Dutch metrical psalms from Coverdale to Utenhove, 1535–1566 (1991) · C. H. Garrett, *The Marian exiles: a study in the origins of Elizabethan puritanism* (1938) · Emden, *Oxf.*, 4.141–2

**Cottle, Amos Simon** (1768?–1800), poet and translator, was born in Gloucestershire, the elder brother of Joseph *Cottle (1770–1853) and son of Robert Cottle (*d.* 1800) and his wife, Sarah (1739–1813), from Trowbridge. He received a classical education at John Henderson's school at Hanham, near Bristol, entered Magdalene College, Cambridge in 1795, and graduated BA in 1799.

Cottle's principal work was *Icelandic Poetry, or, The Edda of Saemund, Translated into English Verse* (1797), probably made from a Latin version. It is a free translation in often trite octosyllabic couplets. It is preceded by a critical introduction of slight value, and a poetical address from Southey to the author, which contains a panegyric of Mary Wollstonecraft, 'who among women left no equal mind'.

Several of Cottle's minor poems, mainly sonnets, but including a Latin ode on the French conquest of Italy, are contained in his brother's *Malvern Hills, with Minor Poems and Essays* (1829).

Amos Simon Cottle died at his chambers in Clifford's Inn on 28 September 1800.

RICHARD GARNETT, rev. JOHN D. HAIGH

Sources J. Cottle, *Malvern Hills with minor poems and essays*, 4th edn, 2 vols. (1829), 2.259 · Venn, *Alum. Cant.*, 2/2 · *GM*, 1st ser., 70 (1800), 1007 · Allibone, *Dict.* · [J. Watkins and F. Shoberl], *A biographical dictionary of the living authors of Great Britain and Ireland* (1816)
Likenesses W. Palmer, oils, 1787, NPG

**Cottle, Joseph** (1770–1853), bookseller and author, was born on 9 March 1770 in Barton Alley, Bristol, second of the seven children of Robert (*d.* 1800) and Sarah Cottle (1739–1813) from Trowbridge; Amos Simon *Cottle was his elder brother. Robert, descended from a Cornish gentry family, was a tailor and draper in Bristol who in 1771 moved to the corner of St James's, Barton. In March 1798 he became master corn-measurer to Bristol. From 1778 to 1780 Joseph was educated at Richard Henderson's school at Hanham, near Bristol, where his love of reading was stimulated. Before 1791 he had read more than a thousand volumes of English literature. His classics master John Henderson encouraged him to become a bookseller. Cottle opened his shop as printseller, stationer, binder, and bookseller on 9 April 1791, at High and Corn streets, Bristol.

In late 1794 Robert Lovell introduced Coleridge and Southey to Cottle. The poets were in Bristol courting the Fricker sisters and preparing for Pantisocracy (as they called their scheme to marry and set up a community on

the Susquehanna River). Cottle generously offered Coleridge and Southey 30 guineas for the copyright of their poems. He offered Southey an additional 50 guineas and fifty copies for *Joan of Arc* (1796). Cottle helped arrange the Pantisocracy lectures, selling tickets at his shop, and began an album of poems and letters of Southey, Coleridge, and Wordsworth (25 May 1795–1844). He introduced them to Hannah More, and commissioned portraits of Coleridge and Southey by Peter Vandyke (1795), and pencil sketches by Robert Hancock (1796), publishing Hancock's *Southey* and *Coleridge* in 1796, and Hancock's *Lamb* and *Wordsworth* in 1798.

Cottle facilitated Coleridge's marriage with the promise of a guinea and a half for every additional hundred lines of poetry. He published Coleridge's periodical *The Watchman* (1796), enlisted subscribers, and lent Coleridge money. In 1798 Cottle formed a partnership with the master printer Nathaniel Biggs (*fl.* 1795–1810) at St Augustine's Back, Bristol (until 1800). Biggs probably printed Coleridge's *Poems* in 1796, certainly printed them in 1797, and as Biggs and Cottle printed the *Lyrical Ballads* (1798). Biggs and Cottle also printed Southey's *Poems* (1799) and *Thalaba the Destroyer* (1801).

In 1807 Cottle introduced Thomas De Quincey to Coleridge and channelled De Quincey's anonymous £300 loan to Coleridge. Hurt by Coleridge's failure to express public gratitude and by Coleridge's rough treatment of *Alfred*, Cottle wrote the *Early Recollections ... Coleridge* (1837). Southey, the Coleridges, and others tried to stop publication. Hannah More's coachman Charles Tidy won a settlement of £1000 from Cottle for remarks in them. Cottle revised them as *Reminiscences of ... Coleridge and ... Southey* (1847). Cottle's distortions and suppressions, however, rendered both unreliable.

Cottle helped purchase Edith Fricker's wedding ring and paid Southey's marriage fees. His sisters lodged Edith while Southey went to Lisbon (1795). After Southey's return (1796), Cottle helped support him and Edith. He published Southey's *Poems* (1797) and *Letters Written ... in Spain and Portugal* (1797). Southey edited *The Annual Anthology* (1799–1800) with contributions by Cottle, Coleridge, Lamb, himself, and others, printed by Biggs. Cottle interested Southey in the plight of Chatterton's sister. The two collaborated on an edition of Chatterton's works, printed and published by Biggs and Cottle in 1803, which brought Mrs Newton £500.

Coleridge introduced Cottle to Wordsworth in Bristol in August 1795. *Lyrical Ballads*, for which copyright Cottle paid Wordsworth 30 guineas, was printed and published by Cottle on 18 September 1798, his greatest achievement. However, it was a commercial catastrophe, and instrumental in Cottle's failure as a publisher, the whole edition being sold to John and Arthur Arch in London within five days of its publication. Later Cottle gave Wordsworth the copyright.

In 1798 Cottle retired as a bookseller, but continued publishing. In 1800 he began selling his copyrights to T. N. Longman. Between 1791 and 1800 he had sold, printed, or published 114 works, mainly religious writings, medical tracts, topical pamphlets, and some literature—his own *Poems* (1795) and *Malvern Hills* (1798), for example—priced between 3s. and 8s., in congeries with Joseph Johnson, Benjamin Flower, and H. D. Symonds, among others. Now he composed eighteen works, principally poems, religious verse, and essays. *Alfred* (1800) and *The Fall of Cambria* (1808) drew sarcasm from Byron in *English Bards and Scotch Reviewers* (1809), but were regularly republished and widely reviewed.

Cottle, a bachelor, was a keen Calvinist dissenter, later joining the Broadmead Baptist Church and Zion Congregational Church. He supported anti-slavery, the Spitalfields weavers, and orphan girls. From 1794, ill health forced him to walk with two sticks until he died. John Dix, visiting Cottle in 1845, described his head as rather flattened, with spectacles and benevolent features. His grand-niece Miss S. E. Green remembered him as deeply religious, with long hair, a skull-cap, aquiline nose, bushy eyebrows, and weak blue eyes (B. Cottle, 23). Nathan Branwhite's lost miniature (c.1810) appears in Basil Cottle's life. Robert Hancock's half-length portrait (1800) is in the National Portrait Gallery, London.

Cottle died of natural causes at his home, Firfield House, Wells Road, Knowle Hill, near Bristol, on 7 June 1853 and was buried at Arnos Vale cemetery. *The Times* (10 June 1853) characterized him as extensively known by his own literary labours and greatly honoured and loved for his distinguished personal worth. He had the good fortune, and foresight, to publish the early works of some great poets.

RALPH A. MANOGUE

**Sources** B. Cottle, *Joseph Cottle of Bristol* (1987) · *The letters of William and Dorothy Wordsworth*, ed. E. De Selincourt, 2nd edn, rev. C. L. Shaver, M. Moorman, and A. G. Hill, 8 vols. (1967–93), vols. 2–3 · J. Dix, *Pen and ink sketches of poets, preachers, and politicians* (1846) · R. Holmes, 'The Romantic Circle', *New York Review of Books* (10 April 1997) · A. D. Boehm, 'Was Joseph Cottle a liberal bookseller?', *English Language Notes*, 32/3 (1995), 32–9 · J. Feather, *The provincial book trade in eighteenth-century England* (1985) · DNB · *The Times* (10 June 1853), 5, col. 5 · J. Cottle, *Early recollections; chiefly relating to the late Samuel Taylor Coleridge, during his long residence in Bristol*, 2 vols. (1837) · J. Cottle, *Reminiscences of Samuel Taylor Coleridge and Robert Southey* (1847) · W. E. Gibbs, 'Unpublished letters concerning Cottle's *Coleridge*', *Publications of the Modern Language Association of America*, 49 (1934), 208–28 · Boase, *Mod. Eng. biog.* · *New letters of Robert Southey*, ed. K. Curry, 2 vols. (1965) · *Henry Crabb Robinson on books and their writers*, ed. E. J. Morley, 3 vols. (1938) · *The life and correspondence of Robert Southey*, ed. C. C. Southey, 6 vols. (1849–50) · *Selections from the letters of Robert Southey*, ed. J. W. Warter, 4 vols. (1856) · W. Haller, *The early life of Robert Southey, 1774–1803* (1966) · d. cert. · G. Lamoine, 'Letters from Joseph Cottle to William Wordsworth, 1828–1850', *Ariel: a Review of International English Literature*, 3/2 (1972), 84–102
**Archives** Bodl. Oxf., corresp. · Bodl. Oxf., corresp. and poems, MS 25432, fol. 462 · Bristol Reference Library, corresp. · FM Cam., corresp. · Harvard U., autograph file · NYPL · University of Bristol, corresp. | BL, letters to Thomas Cadell, Add. MS 34486, fols. 24, 26 · BL, corrected proofs of Samuel Taylor Coleridge's 'Ode on the departing year' addressed to Cottle on proofs of his *Poems on various subjects* (1797), Ashley MS 408, fol. 65 · BL, letters to G. Cumberland, Add. MS 36500, fols. 64, 141; 36509, fol. 310; 36507, fol. 260; 36509, fol. 130; 36512, fol. 160; 36513, fols. 180, 280 · BL, corresp. with Joseph Haslewood on the Rowley MSS, Add. MS 22308 · BL, corresp. with Thomas Poole, Add. MS 35344, fols. 204–18 · Bodl.

Oxf., letters to Bulgin, bookseller · Bristol Reference Library, letters, mainly to Robert Southey
**Likenesses** R. Hancock, pencil and wash drawing, 1800, NPG · N. Branwhite, miniature, c.1810, repro. in Cottle, *Joseph Cottle of Bristol*, cover; now lost

**Cottle, Thomas John** (1761–1828), plantation owner and philanthropist, was the eldest of the four children of Thomas Cottle (1726–1765), solicitor-general of St Kitts, Leeward Islands, West Indies. Cottle inherited the Round Hill plantation on the neighbouring island of Nevis from his father. He became a member of the Nevis island council in 1794, and was its president at various periods between 1803 and 1816. In February or March 1803 he married Frances Huggins, daughter of Edward *Huggins. They had three children, one of whom died in infancy.

Nevis gained notoriety in 1810 when Cottle's father-in-law, an irascible planter, subjected thirty-two of his slaves, men and women, to a brutal flogging in Charlestown market place. This was witnessed by a number of visitors to the island and led to a public outcry in England. Cottle wrote a defence of Huggins's general character, published in 1811, but this may have said more for his family loyalty than for his stance on the treatment of slaves, as he did not condone the punishment nor support slavery in principle, although he opposed immediate abolition in the interest of the colonial economy and the interests of the landed proprietors. Though a slave owner himself, Cottle, a devout Anglican, stood out from the vast majority of his fellow planters by his efforts to improve the working conditions of his slaves and by paying Methodist missionaries to educate them and convert them to Christianity.

Such missionaries had been preaching and teaching in the fields since the mid-eighteenth century but the established church had been slow to show any enthusiasm for a ministry to slaves: it was not until 1792 that the Church of England established the Society for the Conversion and Religious Instruction and Education of the Negro Slaves on the West Indian islands under the auspices of Beilby Porteus, bishop of London. As a result, colonial governors were directed to persuade their legislative councils to pass laws ameliorating the conditions of their slaves. Missionary chaplains and schoolmasters were sent out to convert and instruct them, and a local Slave Amelioration Act was passed in Nevis in 1798. However, by 1812 Nevis still possessed no schools for slaves.

In that year the desultory ministry was shaken up by the arrival of Daniel Davis as rector of St Paul's, Charlestown, himself a planter's son from St Kitts who, while preparing for ordination at Oxford, had become convinced of the evil nature of slavery. Davis's evangelism not only led to the establishment of nineteen schools for slaves on Nevis, but inspired Cottle to build a chapel on his estate. The five parish churches of Nevis were too small even for the planters and their families, many of the plantations, like Round Hill, being far from any church. Cottle's chapel at Round Hill would not simply be a place where slaves could meet, segregated from the parish church, but a place where his own family and his slaves could worship together. The first service was held in the church on 5 May

1824. Davis duly reported to the Conversion Society: 'Mr Cottle made it a holiday for all his slaves, they consequently attended, as did many of the ladies and gentlemen of the island' (LPL, Christian Faith Society F/1, p. 96). The Cottle Church, as the picturesque ruins of its walls and gables are now known, was the first Anglican church in the Caribbean to be built specifically for members of both the white and black communities. Cottle's example was followed from an unexpected quarter by Peter John Huggins, son of the notorious Edward and brother of Frances Cottle, who built a chapel for his slaves on the neighbouring estate of Montravers. Soon the building of such chapels became general practice in other British islands, many of them subsequently becoming parish churches.

Cottle died on Nevis on 1 February 1828 and a memorial tablet was erected at his church, commemorating

> a fond father and an affectionate husband, a kind relative and sincere friend, and to his negroes a mild and humane master ever anxious to promote their temporal benefit, and proving his regard to their external happiness by the erection of this chapel for their improvement.

The tablet was later removed to the nearby parish church of St Thomas, where it remained at the end of the twentieth century pending its return to the Cottle church following the stabilization of the ruin.

CLIVE MITCHELL

Sources G. P. J. Walker, *Cottle Church, an incident in the life of pre-emancipation Nevis* · G. P. J. Walker, *The life of Daniel Gateward Davis, first bishop of Antigua* (1992) · extract from *Pedigree of Cottle of Round Hill, Nevis, West Indies* [stamped 'Local History Collection Woodstock Public Library' (presumed Woodstock, Ontario, Canada). MS annotation: '*Pedigree … by W. H. Cottell* (1891)'] · PRO, Colonial Office MSS, CO 152/100 · minutes of the Nevis island council, 1794–1828, Nevis Historical and Conservation Society, Charlestown, Nevis
Archives LPL, letters from D. Davis to the Conversion Society · Nevis Historical and Conservation Society, Charlestown, Nevis, minutes of the Nevis island council, 1794–1828

**Cottnam** [*née* How], **Deborah** (*c*.1727–1806), schoolmistress, was born probably at Canso, Nova Scotia, the only daughter of the four known children born to Edward How (*c*.1702–1750), merchant and JP, and his first wife, who died *c*.1743. Deborah's father subsequently married Mary Magdalen Winniett on 9 July 1744 in Annapolis. Deborah spent her childhood in Canso, an isolated fishing community and garrison outpost located on the far north-eastern tip of peninsular Nova Scotia. Her father was a prominent citizen in the community, as its principal merchant, JP, and militia officer, and was also an influential interlocutor with French and Mi'kmaq interests throughout the region; his frequent travels and the family's strong Massachusetts ties—the children may have been partly educated in the Boston area—brought a certain rough ambience to the household. About 1742 Deborah married Ensign Samuel Cottnam (*d.* 1780) of the 40th foot; their first child, Martha Grace, was eleven days old when Canso fell to the French in May 1744. The settlement was burnt and the garrison families were taken prisoner to the fortress at Louisbourg, Île Royale (Cape Breton Island), from where they were soon discharged to Boston.

Little is known about Mrs Cottnam's activities in the next three decades. Her husband, who was promoted captain, was present at the second fall of Louisbourg in 1758 and remained there until 1760, when he resigned his commission on grounds of ill health. From 1764 he worked as a merchant in Salem, Massachusetts, but in 1773 he and his family moved to Nova Scotia, where they lived probably in Windsor, with Martha Grace, who by that time had married Winckworth Tonge. Mrs Cottnam and her unmarried daughter Grissey Eliza returned to Salem where, by July 1774, they had opened a school for young ladies. The onset of war prompted them to move to Halifax, where their 'Female Academy' was once more in business by 1777. Their boarding- and day school educated the daughters of colonial officers and loyalist gentry; among its pupils were the daughters of Joseph Frederick Wallet DesBarres and of the Revd Dr Mather Byles. The curriculum centred on reading, writing, arithmetic, and French, but dancing and sewing were also taught. Under Grissey's supervision the girls were instructed in both practical and decorative needlework; their intellectual studies included topics such as 'Locke upon inate ideas' (Byles MSS, Rebecca Byles, 20 Feb 1784). It is clear that Mrs Cottnam provided her pupils with a stimulating intellectual education; Rebecca Byles, for one, was 'imploy'd in translating a very long Sermon … from French into English; & in reading Pamela and Terences Plays in French; [also] in hearing Popes Homer' (ibid., 6 Jan 1779). Mrs Cottnam certainly seems to have earned both respect and admiration from her pupils. Her few surviving letters reveal a loquacious correspondent who was alive to the world around her, and her poems display a dignified verse style in the classical tradition of the time. Rebecca Byles contrasted her own experience with what she regarded as the poor education received by boys in the colonies, and concluded:

> Girls … have the best Education the place affords, and the accomplishment of their Minds is attended to as well as the adorning of their persons; in a few years I expect to see Women fill the most important Offices in Church and State. (ibid., 24 March 1784)

The Cottnam family finances were always precarious. Early property investments in Nova Scotia and Massachusetts were either sold for debt or lost to the vicissitudes of war. Following Samuel's death in 1780 Mrs Cottnam petitioned the Nova Scotia government for additional land, citing her late husband's 'avow'd [loyalist] principles & fix'd attachment to Government' (land MSS, 1785). She received 1000 acres, but in a remote location which she could neither settle on nor sell profitably. The unsupportive attitude of the Halifax establishment no doubt persuaded her to accept the invitation from some loyalist families in Saint John, New Brunswick, to open a school there in 1786. She and Grissey were happier in Saint John but their financial problems continued; Grissey regretted that her mother was 'reduced at her year to the dreadful necessity of earning a scanty subsistence … in keeping a school … with difficulty gaining a sufficiency to live with decency' (How MSS, vol. 474, 241). Their fortunes improved a little in 1793, following the death of Edward

How's widow, whose annual £100 government pension was transferred to Mrs Cottnam. Mrs Cottnam had returned to Halifax by 1794 and her final years were spent quietly within the family circle at Windsor, where she died on 31 December 1806 and was buried in the Old Parish Burying-Ground. Her obituary in the *New Brunswick Royal Gazette* (21 January 1807) noted that she had 'taught girls for forty years'; although the exact date of when she started teaching remains uncertain, it is clear that her career exemplified the best of the dame-school tradition in colonial America.                    LOIS K. YORKE

**Sources** Nova Scotia Archives and Records Management, Halifax, How MSS, MG 1, vols. 472–4A · Nova Scotia Archives and Records Management, Halifax, Byles MSS, MG 1, vol. 163 · records of the 40th regiment, Tredegar Park muniments, Gould MSS · registry of deeds, Hants county, Nova Scotia · Nova Scotia Archives and Records Management, Halifax, land MSS, RG 20, ser. A · L. S. Loomer, 'The Cottnam brothers', Nova Scotia Archives and Records Management, Halifax, John V. Duncanson MSS, MG 1, vol. 2653 · Mass. Hist. Soc., Robbins MSS, 1774–7 · G. Davies, 'Consolation to distress: loyalist literary activity in the maritimes', *Acadiensis*, 16/2 (spring 1987), 51–68 · *Weekly Chronicle* [Halifax] (9 Jan 1807) · *Essex Institute Historical Collections*, 48–9 · *New Brunswick Royal Gazette* (21 Jan 1807) · L. K. Kernaghan, 'How, Deborah (Cottnam)', *DCB*, vol. 5

**Archives** Nova Scotia Archives and Records Management, Halifax, How MSS, MG 1, vols. 472–4A

**Cotton family** (*per. c.*1650–1802), ironmasters, together with the kindred families of *Hall and *Kendall, played a leading role in the development of the iron industry in Britain between the mid-seventeenth century and the second half of the eighteenth century. Members of the family were at the centre of extended partnerships which dominated iron production in Yorkshire, Staffordshire, Cheshire, and the north-west of England. These partnerships were consolidated by marriage between members of the families involved, occasionally accompanied by formal marriage agreements safeguarding the interests of forthcoming children.

Like the Spencer–Fownes partners in the south Yorkshire ironworks, the Cotton family originated in Shropshire, possibly from near Hodnet. Three children of Thomas [i] Cotton (*d.* 1671) and his wife, Ann, became involved in the iron industry in various ways. **William** [i] **Cotton** (*d.* 1675) married Eleanor, daughter of William Fownes (*d. c.*1647) of Kenley, and they had eleven children. Cotton became general manager for the partnership. An elder brother, Edward Cotton (1624–1669), also moved to Yorkshire and was involved at the partnership's Wortley forges. A sister, Elizabeth *Hall, *née* Cotton (*d.* 1679), married Michael *Hall (1623/4–*c.*1670) [*see under* Hall family], and after her husband's death became personally involved in the iron industry in Denbighshire.

When his mother-in-law, Elizabeth Fownes (*née* Spencer) [*see* Spencer family] of Wortley forges, died in 1658, William [i] Cotton inherited her mines in Denbighshire, and a property at Haigh, in the parish of Darton in Yorkshire, bought in 1656 out of the profits of the Shropshire ironworks. William [i] and Eleanor Cotton also inherited a fifth share in Elizabeth Fownes's personal estate and her stock in the ironworks in Shropshire and Yorkshire.

However, having entered the iron industry on his own account, Cotton ceased to act for the Spencer family partnership in 1667. He had already leased Colne Bridge forge near Huddersfield and he built a slitting mill there; in this he was partnered by a cousin, Thomas Dickin. In Wales he became partner of the Myddeltons of Chirk Castle from about 1662. They had a forge at Mathrafal in Montgomeryshire and the Denbighshire works (Ruabon furnace and Pont-y-blew forge), where Cotton's brother-in-law Michael Hall acted as clerk at Ruabon. Following her husband's death, Cotton's sister Elizabeth Hall had the oversight of Ruabon furnace during the 1670s, for which she was paid £30 a year, together with a 'riding allowance' for her involvement in sales of iron and in charcoal procurement.

William [i] Cotton was a staunch nonconformist and was a friend of the Revd Oliver Heywood. Cotton died on 13 March 1675, probably at Nether Denby, and was buried at Penistone, eight dissenting ministers in attendance, amid 'great lamentation'. His will made provision for an annuity to the ministers of the West Riding and for a bequest to his brother-in-law, the dissenting minister George Fownes. He wished his three younger sons, including Daniel, to be educated for the ministry. An older son, Thomas [ii] Cotton (1653–1730), who was already a pupil at Richard Frankland's academy, married the daughter of Leonard Hoare and was ordained by Oliver Heywood in 1696. Cotton's widow, Eleanor, survived until 1699. She died in Cheshire, where two of her children were established—Daniel Cotton [*see below*], now an ironmaster, and Joanna, who married her ironmaster cousin Thomas *Hall (1657–1715) [*see under* Hall family] in 1697. However, Eleanor Cotton was buried alongside her husband at Penistone.

Cotton's eldest son, **William** [ii] **Cotton** (1648/9–1703), was paid for drawing up the accounts of the Myddelton works in January 1674 and he continued the Denbighshire partnership until 1690. He disregarded the instructions in his father's will to sell the stock in Colne Bridge forge and the Haigh estate. On the contrary, he and Dickin took over Kirkstall forge and Barnby furnace in 1675, when the first Spencer partnership at length collapsed, and built a slitting mill there. Though the forges supplied bar iron for general purposes, the building of slitting mills shows that the production of rod iron, for which cold-short iron made from coal measure ironstone was suitable, was one of Cotton's main products. In the 1660s, while his father was manager of the Spencer–Fownes partnership, a slitting mill was set up near Wigan to supply the south Lancashire nail trade. Judging from its function during the period of the Spencer accounts it is clear that Colne Bridge mill was set up to supply this Lancashire market, while most of the Kirkstall output went to the nail trade of south Yorkshire. After 1684, with a new partner, Denis Hayford of Wortley, Cotton was also able to supply bar and rod iron in the Birmingham area from Lord Paget's works (Abbots Bromley and Cannock forges and Rugeley slitting mill), the lease of which they took over in that year. Rugeley was one of the largest slitting mills in the country.

After the death of Richard Foley of Longton, Cotton and Heyford acquired the Cheshire works (Lawton furnace, Warmingham and Cranage forges, and Cranage slitting mill). In addition to smelting local north Staffordshire ores, Lawton furnace used haematite ores from Furness, which had to be carried right across the Cheshire plain for smelting. The production of the valuable tough iron which these ores yielded was greatly eased by the building of a more accessible furnace at Vale Royal in 1696. Cotton's personal links with the north-west went back considerably beyond this, because on 2 October 1677 he married Barbara, daughter of Thomas Curwen of Sellapark, Cumberland. Their only child died in infancy. With tough and 'mixed' as well as cold-short pig iron available, much of the Cheshire product was sold as bar iron. However, a plating mill at Street (just north of Lawton furnace) enabled some of the Warmingham product to be sold locally as salt pan plates. Much of the Cranage product, especially the rod iron, went to Lancashire, but in addition to local markets the Cheshire works also supplied customers in Wrexham and in north Staffordshire.

Together with Hayford and William Simpson, Cotton also ran Knottingley forge and Bank furnace, so by the end of the century he had control of most of the Yorkshire works, and it seems to have been he who finally settled the elder branch of the family in Yorkshire at Haigh Hall. William [ii] Cotton was also involved with Hayford and other partners in the 'Company in the North', a shear-steel producing project in Durham, based on Blackhall mill on the Derwent. In 1748, together with Joshua Copley, Cotton's younger son, Joshua (1694–1753), a Newcastle ironmaster, was involved in selling the lease of the steel furnace at Derwentcote, so Cotton involvement in this steelmaking enterprise perhaps continued up to then.

Cotton's first marriage was celebrated at the Anglican church of St Crux in York, but his second wife, **Anna Cotton** [née Westby] (d. 1721), of Ravenfield, whom he married on 27 March 1683, was a woman as strongly nonconformist as had been his father. Both offered hospitality to Oliver Heywood and his sons and were ready recipients of the nonconformist tracts which he procured. Not until Oliver Heywood lay on his deathbed in 1702 was any child of the Cotton family baptized at the parish church of Darton.

Cotton and his second wife had four surviving children, and on his death, which occurred on 6 May 1703 when he was fifty-four, Anna and her brother-in-law **Daniel Cotton** (c.1660–1723) of Church Hulme in Cheshire, acted as guardians for these children, all of them minors. Daniel Cotton had an £8848 share in the Cheshire ironworks in 1701 and was manager of the new Vale Royal furnace. In 1707 the Cheshire ironworks were amalgamated with the Staffordshire works, a Foley family concern, and Daniel Cotton obtained a sixth share in the former and a seventh share in the latter. About this time he took over the management of Cranage forge and Lawton furnace, near the Staffordshire border. In 1709 he and his cousin Edward *Hall of Cranage [see under Hall family] commenced mining at Crossgates in Furness, a prelude to the establishment in 1711 of Cunsey furnace near Lake Windermere, in

which Daniel was one of the shareholders. The partnership of William Rea of Monmouth at Cunsey suggests that the later pattern of trade, in which only a small part of the tough pig iron produced there was used locally, the bulk of it being shipped to the Severn estuary to supply the south Wales and Stour forges, was envisaged from the start. Meanwhile, near the Shropshire border, Doddington furnace had been brought into the partnership about 1710 and in 1716, together with William Vernon, manager of Warmingham forge, Daniel Cotton repaired Madeley furnace, which was in blast again the following year.

Daniel Cotton married five times, but little is known about his wives. His first wife's name is not known, and on 31 December 1696 he married Sarah Nicols of Boleshall. A third wife was called Lydia, and on 28 August 1707 he married Sarah Booth of Twemlow. His fifth wife, Anne, survived him. He had at least one son and one daughter. Far from entering the nonconformist ministry, as did his elder brother Thomas, Daniel had his children baptized in the established church, gave a new peal of bells to the church at Holmes Chapel in 1709, and presented William Dugard to the rectory of Warmingham in 1714. Daniel Cotton died on 1 January 1723.

While the widowed Anna Cotton tried to safeguard her family's interests in Yorkshire against the encroachments of John Spencer (c.1655–1729) of Cannon Hall, the position of her family in the industry was consolidated by several judicious marriages. First, in 1708, her eldest daughter, Frances, married William Vernon, manager of Warmingham forge. In 1712 her second daughter, Anna, married Edward *Kendall (1684–1746) [see under Kendall family] of Stourbridge, joint manager with William Rea of Monmouth of the Staffordshire works. Meanwhile Elizabeth Hall of the Hermitage had married Ralph Kent of Kinderton, later to be a partner in the Cunsey works in Furness, and her cousin Elizabeth Hall of Cranage married Thomas Bridge, a Chester feltmaker; both of their sons, William and Edward Bridge, were eventually involved, along with the Vernons, in the expansion of the Cheshire partnership into Wales. Finally, in 1715, Anna Cotton's son **William Westby Cotton** (bap. 1689, d. 1749) married, on 1 September 1715, Mary Cotton of Church Hulme, Daniel Cotton's daughter. Anna Cotton died at Stourbridge on 8 July 1721, presumably at the home of her daughter and Edward Kendall. She was buried on 13 July at Darton. The death of his 'dear and worthy friend' was formally recorded by Oliver Heywood's successor, the Revd Thomas Dickinson, in their Northowram register.

William Westby Cotton's first entry into the iron trade was not in Yorkshire. In 1714, together with Edward Kendall, he took a lease of Kemberton furnace in Shropshire. Probably with her retirement in view, his mother had informed John Spencer in 1716 of her assignment of her share in Colne Bridge forge to her son, in partnership with her sons-in-law Edward Kendall and William Vernon. Spencer remained unco-operative, but in 1720 William Westby Cotton re-established himself in Yorkshire with a new furnace at Bretton, adjacent to Haigh Hall, run in conjunction with Kilnhurst forge on the Don, in a twenty-one-year partnership with his brother-in-law **Thomas** [ii] **Cotton** (*bap.* 1701, *d.* 1749) of Doddlespool (who was Daniel Cotton's son), Edward Hall of Cranage, and Samuel Shore of Sheffield. Rockley furnace was added to this partnership through a sixteen-year lease obtained in 1726.

William Westby Cotton obtained a corresponding share in the Staffordshire works, where, in addition to Doddington and Madeley furnaces, Cannock furnace was put in blast again during the 1720s. However, the depression of the 1730s hit the Staffordshire works severely and the 1732 lease of Cannock forge mentioned the furnace site as 'late used', which suggests it was again derelict. About this time Thomas [ii] Cotton moved from Doddlespool to Eardley End, nearer to Lawton furnace. In 1737 four of the forges were out of action; though Lea forge in Cheshire was in production in 1737, Thomas Coape, its clerk, left for the Spencer forges at Wortley in 1738, Thomas [ii] Cotton having no work for him. Small quantities of tin plate shipped down the Weaver Navigation by Thomas Cotton in the 1740s suggest that the tin-plate works had by now replaced the forge at Oakamoor. By 1750 Bromley forge was also out of action, but Cannock forge had by then resumed and Consall and Warmingham forges had even increased their production, each to 300 tons a year.

Thomas [ii] Cotton married Elizabeth Langley in 1724, and they had at least one son. Cotton's will of 1746 (Lichfield Joint RO, B/C/11) shows that he had disregarded the provision of his marriage agreement to lay out £2000 in the purchase of land for the settlement of sums on his sons, but that it still remained in his partnership with Edward Hall and others. If possible his executors were to increase his stock and maintain his leases for ten years, at least in the Staffordshire works, if not in those more remote, in the hope that his family would continue in the trade. In a desperate codicil he revoked most of the executorships (even that of his own son, Robert), confirming only that of his fellow ironmaster, Samuel Hopkins of Cradley. His worst fears were realized, however, and after 1750 the names Kendall and Hopkins replaced that of Cotton in transactions relating to the ironworks of Cheshire and north Staffordshire. Thomas [ii] Cotton was buried at Audley, Staffordshire, on 9 March 1749.

When a committee of the House of Commons reported to parliament in March 1738 on the damage likely to the English iron industry from the proposed lifting of the embargo on the import of bar iron from the North American colonies, William Westby Cotton was among the ironmasters whose evidence succeeded in prolonging the embargo. He died in August 1749.

**Thomas** [iii] **Cotton** (1723–1802) of Haigh, who was born on 4 April 1723, the son of Mary and William Westby Cotton, continued in the trade for some years after his father's death. However, the business was in decline, and of the furnaces in the Barnsley area, Bretton alone was still in blast in 1774. By 1794 Bretton was being run by Messrs Cook and Cockshutt, and it too was closed down in 1806. The Yorkshire Thomas [iii] Cotton married Rebecca Ackton in 1765 and died, childless, on 3 October 1802.

The Cotton family, in consolidating its partnerships by judicious marriages, was perhaps the most impressive example of the way in which ironmasters sought with considerable success to reduce the proneness to ruin through litigation, which had bedevilled the industry's progress during much of the sixteenth century and the seventeenth. Though parties to several chancery and Chester exchequer court cases, members of the family seem to have avoided initiating such suits themselves, even after 1703, when rivalry with the Spencer family was at its most intense. Not only was their influence felt in the iron trade throughout most of the north of England, their participation in the initiation of the steel industry on Tyneside and of tin-plate manufacture in the north midlands were interventions at crucial growing points in the British economy. The family also exhibited classic features of first, second, and even third generation enthusiasm for the trade, to the extent of female participation in management. This was followed by a rather surprising disinclination to meet the challenges faced by the iron industry in the later eighteenth century. The religious enthusiasm of the family followed a somewhat similar trajectory. BRIAN G. AWTY

**Sources** B. G. Awty, 'Charcoal ironmasters of Cheshire and Lancashire, 1600–1785', *Transactions of the Historic Society of Lancashire and Cheshire*, 109 (1957), 71–124 • J. Hunter, *South Yorkshire: the history and topography of the deanery of Doncaster*, 2 vols. (1828–31) • G. G. Hopkinson, 'The charcoal iron industry in the Sheffield region, 1500–1775', *Transactions of the Hunter Archaeological Society*, 8 (1960–63), 122–51 • B. L. C. Johnson, 'The Foley partnerships: the iron industry at the end of the charcoal era', *Economic History Review*, 2nd ser., 4 (1951–2), 322–40 • *The Rev. Oliver Heywood … his autobiography, diaries, anecdote and event books*, ed. J. H. Turner, 4 vols. (1881–5) • W. M. Myddelton, ed., *Chirk Castle accounts*, 2 vols. (1908–31) • I. Edwards, 'The charcoal iron industry of Denbighshire, c.1690–1770', *Transactions of the Denbighshire Historical Society*, 10 (1961), 1–49 • parish register, Holmes Chapel, 27 July 1701 [baptism, Thomas (ii) Cotton] • parish register, Audley, 9 March 1749 [burial, Thomas (ii) Cotton] • Sheff. Arch., Spencer–Stanhope papers • J. H. Turner, T. Dickenson, and O. Heywood, eds., *The nonconformist register of baptisms, marriages, and deaths* (1881)
**Archives** Sheff. Arch., Spencer–Stanhope papers
**Wealth at death** see Awty, 'Charcoal ironmasters'

**Cotton, Agnes** (1828–1899), social reformer and philanthropist, was born on 27 February 1828 at Walwood House, Leytonstone, Essex, the sixth of the seven children of William \*Cotton (1786–1866), merchant and director of the Bank of England, and Sarah (1790–1872), only daughter of Thomas Lane of Leyton Grange, Leyton, Essex, and his wife, Barbara. Her siblings included William Charles \*Cotton (1813–1879) [*see under* Cotton, Sir Henry], a clergyman and writer on bees; Sarah Acland (1815–1878), wife of Sir Henry Wentworth Acland; Phoebe (1817–1857), an illustrator; and Sir Henry \*Cotton (1821–1892), a lord justice of appeal. Both parents were evangelical Anglicans, heavily involved in philanthropic activities. Sarah and Phoebe Cotton received a rigorous academic education from their mother, although in 1842 Agnes was at boarding-school.

According to one account, after miraculously recovering from an illness at the age of fourteen, Agnes Cotton 'dedicated herself and her subsequent possessions to the service of God' (*Pastures Youth Centre*, 3). Surviving letters from the 1840s show that she was very devout and was influenced by the Oxford Movement. By the age of eighteen she was actively involved in philanthropy, both assisting the projects of family members and taking her own initiatives in connection with the care of local children.

Agnes Cotton was short and wore spectacles from about the age of seventeen. Surviving portraits in middle age show her in nun's dress, though not that of the Community of St John Baptist, Clewer, of which she may have become an associate. Gulielma Lister (*b.* 1860) recalled that, when she was a child living in Leytonstone, Cotton 'wore a black habit and veil' and 'we regarded her with horror as a "nun"'. However, Gulielma's father, Arthur Lister, very much admired Cotton and 'enjoyed her racy humour' (Lister and Lister, 2–3). By 1889 she was known in the locality as Sister Agnes (*Forest School Magazine*, 11–12).

In Lent 1865 Cotton began a 'small industrial home for destitute children' in Forest Place, Leytonstone, later described as 'the first Church of England home for fallen children'. In 1876 she purchased a property in Davies Lane, Leytonstone, which she renamed The Pastures and inhabited from 1877 to 1899. Between 1879 and 1881 Cotton had built beside it the Home of the Good Shepherd, with a chapel, schoolhouse, infirmary, and laundry, at a total cost of £9500. The initial aim of the home was to provide a special kind of care for girls who had been 'led into habits of impurity' (Cotton, 1), but not to be a reformatory for juvenile delinquents. Industrial training was provided in laundry work. Numbers rose from six to twenty in 1865, and to thirty by 1871. In 1882 the home was registered under the Criminal Law Amendment Act to receive forty girls, and certified to receive fifty in 1892.

In 1865 there were two male trustees, while by 1885 the home had acquired a more formal structure, with a male warden and an all-male council (which included five of Cotton's relatives). However, between 1865 and 1885, Cotton, known variously as 'mother', 'foundress', and 'superintendent', remained the chief organizer. To start with the home was financed through Cotton's own fortune and through the fund-raising and publicizing efforts of family and friends, both male and female. These included four people connected with houses of mercy in Soho, Hammersmith, Horbury, and Birmingham. A pamphlet written by Cotton and distributed in 1865 resulted in many gifts in kind from local tradespeople. However, by 1885 about half the school's income came from the Treasury and school boards.

Despite the rhetoric of 'love' and 'care' in the reports, and the approval expressed in guidebooks to Leyton, in 1894 widely publicized allegations of ill treatment were made. The Revd A. Drew, chairman of the industrial schools committee of the London school board, demanded a Home Office inquiry. Cotton was exonerated by Inspector William Inglis, who concluded that 'a better and kinder old lady does not live' (PRO, HO 45/9887/B17047/9). Nevertheless, her agreement with the London school board was terminated in 1895, and she formally resigned her industrial school certificate in 1897.

This conflict may have been caused by insufficient supervision, by Cotton's differing approach to discipline from that of Revd Drew, or because Cotton had become too old and infirm to manage the home effectively.

Agnes Cotton died, unmarried, on 20 May 1899 at The Pastures, Leytonstone. She was buried in the Cotton family vault in St John's churchyard, Leytonstone, on 24 May. The bulk of her personal effects and property were bequeathed in trust to her ward, Mary Agnes Hope; Elizabeth Amelia Bragg, spinster of Clapton, who had for many years helped Cotton with her work, received an annuity of £50. By previous arrangement, the home was taken over by the sisters of the Community of St John Baptist, Clewer, one of the new Anglican orders involved in 'rescue work'. The home survived until 1940, when it was evacuated to Northamptonshire and then dissolved.

Agnes Cotton's life's work shows a transition from informal charity undertaken with family members to the creation of a new kind of philanthropic institution which survived for eighty-five years. Initially supported by networks of family, friends, and clergy, by the 1880s her home was receiving much-needed state funding. However, in the long term a religious order proved to be a more secure form of support than the state.

Mary Clare Martin

**Sources** M. C. Martin, 'Women and philanthropy in Walthamstow and Leyton, 1740–1870', *London Journal*, 19 (1994), 119–50, esp. 127–39 [nn. 92–4, 100, 101, 109, 123, 135–8, 141, 159–62] · papers of William Charles Cotton, Bodl. Oxf., MSS Acland d.179, 17; d.189, 95, 108, 110–11, 113–14; d.194, 2–4, 18, 21, 48 · Leytonstone CIS, PRO, HO 45/9887/B17047 · M. L. Savell, *Some notes on the Cotton family of Leyton* (Leyton Public Libraries, 1963), 20–49 · M. S. Cale, '"Saved from a life of vice and crime": reformatory and industrial schools for girls, *c.*1854–*c.*1901', DPhil diss., U. Oxf., 1993, 145–50 · will, 1899, HM Probate Office, 95.10.0550 · d. cert. · E. M. Lister and G. Lister, 'Old Leytonstone: some memories', pamphlet coll., 1934, Local Studies Library (LBWF), L60 · 'A history of the school: part XI', *Forest School Magazine* (Easter 1889), 7–13 · A. Cotton, *A small industrial home is now at work at 15, Forest Place, Leytonstone, NE* (1865) · *Pastures Youth Centre*, London Borough of Waltham Forest (*c.*1960) · miscellaneous deeds, Essex RO, D/DU 322/7 · J. B. Atlay, *Sir Henry Wentworth Acland* (1903), 116, 193 · *St John Baptist, Clewer, Magazine* (autumn 1899), 17 · H. E. P. Grieve, 'Leyton', *VCH Essex*, 6.174–239, esp. 238 · private information · parish register (baptism), Leyton, St Mary, 8 April 1828 · parish register (burial), Leytonstone, St John's, 24 May 1899

**Archives** Convent of St John Baptist, Clewer | PRO, HO 45/9887/B17047

**Likenesses** photograph, 1893, Vestry House Museum, London Borough of Waltham Forest · photograph, repro. in Savell, *Some notes on the Cotton family*, 34

**Wealth at death** £7174 1s. 2d.: probate, 19 June 1899, *CGPLA Eng. & Wales*

**Cotton, Anna** (*d.* 1721). *See under* Cotton family (*per. c.*1650–1802).

**Cotton, Sir Arthur Thomas** (1803–1899), army officer and irrigation engineer, was born on 15 May 1803 at Woodcote, Oxfordshire, the ninth son of Henry Calveley Cotton (*d.* 1837) of Woodcote House, who served in the royal guards (postal service), and his wife, Matilda, daughter of John Lockwood of Dews Hall, Essex. Their other distinguished sons were Richard Lynch *Cotton DD, and Sir Sydney John

Sir Arthur Thomas Cotton (1803–1899), by Sir William Hamo Thornycroft, 1880

*Cotton. After boarding-school, aged fifteen, Arthur Cotton entered Addiscombe College, and at the end of 1819 he was commissioned in the Madras engineers.

**Early career** After serving with the Ordnance Survey at Bangor and the engineer depot at Chatham, Cotton went to Madras as an assistant engineer in 1821. Within a year he was posted to survey the Pamban Channel, as a potential shipping lane through Rama's (or Adam's) Bridge, the archipelago joining southern India with Ceylon. At Cotton's recommendation the passage was deepened and widened. However, it ultimately proved insufficient for increasingly larger vessels.

Cotton served in the First Anglo-Burmese War in 1824. He led the storming parties against seven forts and stockades, was present at most of the actions in the war, and was mentioned in dispatches. He later described the war as 'a very melancholy business inconceivably mismanaged' (H. M. Vibart, 344).

Returning from the war to Madras by sea, Cotton experienced a religious conversion. Always Anglican, he was thenceforth a committed evangelical Christian: his daughter wrote that 'his ever-abiding sense of God's presence was the secret and the mainstay of his life' (Hope, 548). In India he was the friend and supporter of missionaries, and sometimes himself conducted services. Later, on leave in England about 1830, he helped one of his brothers, an Oxfordshire clergyman, in his parish work.

**Indian irrigation, 1828–1862** In 1828 Cotton began work on his great achievement, the improvement and extension of irrigation in southern India. The chief projects on which he worked, or which owe their existence to his initiative, were works on the Cauvery and Coleroon rivers, located in the modern state of Tamil Nadu, and later works on the Godavari and Kistna rivers, located in the modern state of Andhra Pradesh.

The Cauvery had been used for irrigation, by banks and

canals, since ancient times all along its course, from its source in the Coorg mountains to its delta in Tanjore district. This system was fully operative when Tanjore came under British rule, but by 1828 it had become seriously impaired by the increasing tendency of the Cauvery waters to flow down the Coleroon, depleting the southern branch and its dependent branches and canals. Cotton, then a captain, was placed in charge of the works in Tanjore and the adjoining districts, with orders to improve the region's hydraulic system. Following several years of careful investigations, Cotton proposed the construction of two dams or anicuts (English corruption of *anai-kattu*, 'dam-building' in Tamil): the first at the head of the Coleroon and the second, a still larger work, 70 miles further down the river. Cotton ingeniously mastered the difficulty of building dams on unstable sandy river beds, partly by incorporating ancient Indian dam-building techniques. Such technical expertise he gained from examining the ancient Grand Anicut on the Cauvery near Trichinopoly.

The two dams proposed by Cotton, both major works, were built in the winter of 1835–6. Their great utility was at once recognized, and they provided lasting benefits. These major public works were also financially successful. A report forty-five years after their construction stated that the annual profit on capital expanded was 69 per cent for the upper anicut and nearly 100 per cent for the lower anicut. The increased value of private property, due to the works, was equally large. Moreover, the works permanently prevented further occurrence of famine, not only in the irrigated districts but also in the surrounding region.

Following a breakdown in health, Cotton went on leave to Van Diemen's Land. There he married on 29 October 1841 Elizabeth (1814–1907), daughter of John Learmonth, a large landed proprietor in Australia. They had one son, Alfred Fox (b. 1850), a major in the Indian Staff Corps, who died before his father, and one daughter, Elizabeth Reid, who married admiral of the fleet Sir James Hope and wrote the biography of her father. In 1845 Cotton proposed to the Madras government a project for building an anicut across the Godavari River a few miles below the town of Rajahmundry. The Godavari delta region was then in a most depressed condition. It had recently endured a terrible famine, the people were impoverished, and the region's revenue was always in arrears, as it had rested heavily on a precarious rainfall. The work Cotton designed for the Godavari, which had much more water than the Cauvery, was one of greater magnitude and presented more serious difficulties than the works on the Cauvery and Coleroon. It was a stupendous work, the longest dam of the anicut being longer alone than the two Coleroon anicuts put together. Moreover, unlike Tanjore and Trichinopoly, the Godavari district was comparatively destitute of irrigation canals, while in high floods the river overflowed its banks and flooded the surrounding country. The anicut was begun in 1847 and took five years to construct. An impressive subsidiary work was the Gannavaram aqueduct, built to conduct water over the tidal part of the river to a fertile island near its mouth. This was designed and built by one of Cotton's assistants, Lieutenant F. Haig.

Many of the Godavari irrigation canals were constructed for the dual purpose of navigation. The financial returns of the Godavari works, as represented by interest on capital, were considerably less than those received from the Cauvery and Coleroon works. The lower cost of the latter works was due in part to the pre-existence of a substantial network of distributive canals. The Godavari delta had lacked such a system. Up to 1880 the financial return on the Godavari works was variously computed from 12.69 to 14.92 per cent, according to the method of calculation. This was a satisfactory return on a public work. More importantly, the works acted to enhance the prosperity of the people. By 1890 the works irrigated more than 612,000 acres. They raised the exports and imports of the district from £170,000 in 1847 to £1,500,000 in 1887. They converted a district formerly continually plagued by extreme poverty and distress into one of the most prosperous districts in India. During the half-century following construction of the anicut, the population of the Godavari district more than doubled.

The anicut on the Kistna River at Bezwada was projected by Cotton, but was actually planned by Colonel Sir Henry Atwell Lake RE, afterwards distinguished in the defence of Kars during the Crimean War. Its construction, however, was supervised by Major-General Charles Orr RE, who trained under Cotton on the Godavari project: Orr had supervised construction of the Godavari anicut for several years, midway through its construction, while Cotton was on sick leave. The districts affected by the Kistna works (Guntur and Kistna) had long been in a depressed condition. The Kistna anicut constructed was 1300 yards long. A report of 1890 stated that the waters of the Kistna were distributed through 348 miles of navigable and 800 miles of unnavigable canals, the total cost of the anicut and the distributing canals was about £834,000, the number of acres irrigated was about 400,000, and the interest which the works yielded upon the capital expended was 14 per cent.

The three irrigation works described were only part of Cotton's contributions to India. He not only created great hydraulic works but established a model of Indian hydraulic engineering which continued to be followed in developing the resources of other Indian rivers. On several minor rivers in south-eastern India, including the Penner, Cotteliar, Paler, Cheyyar, and Vellar, anicuts and subsidiary works were subsequently constructed. Although less productive than those on the three larger rivers, these minor works still contributed to increasing the agricultural productivity of the country.

The success of Cotton's hydraulic schemes inspired more ambitious and challenging projects, such as the construction of a high dam along the Periyar River in the mountains of the modern state of Kerala. Completed in 1895, the Periyar Reservoir continues to supply water to a dry region in neighbouring Tamil Nadu.

Cotton's works proved to be effective in preventing or in mitigating famines. It is estimated that 4 million people died in the less protected districts of the Madras presidency during the great famine of 1877. In the districts protected by the great irrigation works on the Kauvery, Coleroon, Godavari, and Kistna rivers there were no deaths from famine. Furthermore, it is estimated that the surplus food exported from these districts was sufficient to save the lives of 3 million people.

Cotton's services were praised by the Madras government, which on 15 May 1858 stated of his work on the Godavari:

> Other able and devoted officers have caught Colonel Cotton's spirit and have rendered invaluable aid under his advice and direction, but for this creation of genius we are indebted to him alone. Colonel Cotton's name will be venerated by millions yet unknown when many who now occupy a much larger place in the public view will be forgotten. (Rundall, 187)

Cotton indeed is still revered by the people of south India. He is especially a folk hero in Andhra Pradesh, a state that has derived much benefit from his works. Monumental effigies of him are at various locations in the state and a barrage recently completed on the Godavari, that parallels and improves upon his original anicut, bears his name. Lieutenant-Colonel E. W. C. Sandes in his standard work, *The Military Engineer in India*, wrote:

> Arthur Cotton was sometimes too ambitious, over-confident, and careless in estimates, but he was a grand engineer—the best military engineer who ever served in the Irrigation Department south of the Jumna, and perhaps anywhere in India … the creator of works which saved many thousands of lives. (Sandes, 2.28)

In 1861, at the recommendation of Sir Charles Wood, the secretary of state for India, Cotton was knighted. In 1866 a KCSI (second class) was conferred upon him, and no further official award. His family and friends believed his services were never adequately recognized.

**Retirement and controversy, 1862–1899** Although Cotton retired from government service in 1862, broken in health, he continued to be frequently engaged in investigating and reporting on various irrigation projects, including some suggested by himself. Among those projects he suggested and strongly advocated were works on the Tungabhadra River, a major tributary of the Kistna, and on the Mahanadi River in Orissa. Involved in the former project was the construction of the Kurnool-Cuddapah Canal, which linked the Tungabhadra with the Penner River to the south. Both projects were undertaken by newly formed private irrigation companies, but they were great financial failures and the Indian government ultimately bought out the companies. Cotton believed these projects fell short largely because district officers failed to educate local people about the great benefit of irrigation for enabling them to cultivate more valuable crops than were possible without it. While Cotton's view holds some validity, the initial shortcomings of these projects were rooted more in their projectors' over-optimism and ignorance about the local climate, soils, geology, agricultural patterns, and society. Such features differed considerably from those in the delta tracts where Cotton's schemes were much more financially successful. However, while unsuccessful for a long time, the works on the Tungabhadra and Mahanadi that Cotton envisioned more than a century ago have ultimately acted to greatly enhance agricultural productivity in the Rayalaseema region of Andhra Pradesh and in Orissa.

In 1863 Cotton became engaged in a controversy with Sir Proby Cautley over the plan of the Ganges Canal, which had been constructed by the latter. After full investigation Cotton's criticisms, which had specific reference to the position of the canal head, were considered well grounded. The canal was partially remodelled at a cost, but much of the cost, totalling 55 lakhs of rupees, went towards requisite extension work.

Cotton strongly advocated improving water communications in India and believed that the rivers of India should be more extensively used. He objected to the focus on developing railways to the neglect of developing a system of inland waterways, which he deemed much more economically feasible. His views obtained little support, and his opponents declared that he had water on the brain. But there was much force in his arguments, and both the revenues of India and the national wealth would have benefited considerably had his advice been more acted upon at an earlier period. In 1878 he gave evidence before a Commons select committee on the expediency of constructing public works in India with money raised on loan, both as regards financial results and the prevention of famine. This committee was formed in the wake of a disastrous famine that had depopulated large areas in the Madras and Bombay presidencies. Some members of the committee were very hostile to Cotton's views, and he considered their report underrated the great importance of irrigation and of cheap water communication. This antagonistic attitude was maintained by some officials, but the 1899 famine in western India, unprecedented in extent and virulence, fostered a change in public opinion. In 1900 the viceroy, Curzon, practically admitted in a speech in the legislative council the correctness of Cotton's views.

Cotton retired from the army with the rank of general in 1877 and settled at Woodcot, Dorking. Thereafter he applied his ever-active mind to devising new methods for improving English agriculture. He had great faith in deep cultivation, and in a small plot of land next to his house at Dorking he carried out some remarkably successful experiments for 'improving the quality of food, relieving the country from absolute dependence upon foreign countries, and giving employment to those who at present get no work' (H. M. Vibart, 351). For the rest of his life he maintained a keen interest in Indian affairs. In a letter of November 1896 he wrote:

> What delights me is that, in spite of all mistakes, God has blessed India under our rule far beyond any man's imagination. If any man had written, when I went out, expressing a hope of anything approaching the present state of things, he would have been thought the greatest fool in India. (*DNB*)

His religious commitment continued. He was a member of the committees of the Church Missionary Society, the Bible Society, and the Irish Church Mission, and supported the Anti-Opium Society, anti-ritualism, and anti-popery; he was greatly interested in prophecy, and in his later years held strongly the 'Anglo-Israelite theory'. Cotton's publications included *Public Works in India* (1854).

In old age Cotton was afflicted by deafness, but otherwise maintained remarkable vigour, mentally and physically. He died at Woodcot on 24 July 1899, and was buried in Dorking. Shortly after Cotton's death the secretary of state for India in council granted Lady Cotton a special pension of £250 a year in recognition of her husband's services.

A. J. ARBUTHNOT, *rev.* PETER L. SCHMITTHENNER

**Sources** Lady Hope [E. R. C. Hope], *General Sir Arthur Cotton: his life and work* (1900) · H. Morris, *Sir Arthur T. Cotton: philanthropist and engineer* (1901) · A. J. Smithers, *Honourable conquests* (1991) · J. H. Bell, 'Memorandum on the engineering works … of General Sir A. T. Cotton', *Royal Engineers Journal*, 20 (1890), 205–9, 230–31, 247–9 · F. H. Rundall, *Royal Engineers Journal*, 29 (1899), 187 · E. W. C. Sandes, *The military engineer in India*, 2 (1935) · *Manual of the administration of the Madras presidency*, 3 vols. (Madras, 1885–93); repr., ed. C. D. Maclean (New Delhi, 1987–90) · D. R. Headrick, *The tentacles of progress: technology transfer in the age of imperialism, 1850–1940* (1988) · D. Hyland, *Indian balm* (1994) · 'Lord Curzon's famine policy', *Indian Engineering* (10 Nov 1900) · personal knowledge (1901) · private information (2004) · Burke, *Peerage* [Combermere] · biographical index, BL OIOC · d. cert. · H. M. Vibart, *Addiscombe: its heroes and men of note* (1894)
**Archives** BL, A. H. Layard MSS · BL, Florence Nightingale MSS
**Likenesses** W. H. Thornycroft, marble bust, 1880, NPG [*see illus.*] · engraving, repro. in Morris, *Sir Arthur T. Cotton* · monumental effigies, Hussein Sagar Tank Bund, Hyderabad, India · monumental effigies, near Rajahmundry, Andhra Pradesh, India · photograph, repro. in Sandes, *Military engineer in India*, facing p. 22 · photographs, repro. in Hope, *General Sir Arthur Cotton* · portrait, repro. in Hope, *General Sir Arthur Cotton*
**Wealth at death** £147 9s. 8d.: probate, 2 Sept 1899, *CGPLA Eng. & Wales*

**Cotton, Bartholomew** (*d.* 1321/2), chronicler and Benedictine monk, was probably a native of Cotton, near Stowmarket, Suffolk. He became a monk of Norwich some time before 1282–3, when he first occurs in the priory records. He is recorded as master of the cellar in 1282–4, and in connection with some priory business in 1288/9. The latest entry, in 1321/2, establishes the date of his death; it records payment by the chamberlain to the bearer of the brief giving notice of that event.

Cotton's earliest known literary work is a compilation made from the *Summa Britonis* or *Vocabularium Bibliae* (a lexicon of difficult terms and proper names in the Bible by Willelmus Brito). The colophon in the only known copy states that Bartholomeus de Cottune compiled it in 1291 (Cambridge, Corpus Christi College, MS 460, fol. 86). However, Cotton's fame rests on his *Historia Anglicana*, written in the course of the 1290s. It comprises three books: book 1, a history of Britain, extracted from Geoffrey of Monmouth; book 2, a history of England in two parts, 455–1066 and 1066–1298 respectively, the second part being preceded by a page of annals, from the creation to 1066; and book 3, a history of the archbishops and bishops of England. Book 3 is largely derivative, but has some value for the history of the bishops of Norwich, and a little for the archbishops of Canterbury. But the chronicle for the years 1291–8, which concludes book 2, is a source of primary importance, both for its narrative and for the many documents, a few otherwise unknown, that are cited in full. H. R. Luard edited books 2 and 3 for the Rolls Series in 1859. Book 3 of the *Historia* concludes with a colophon apparently written after Cotton's death, setting out his authorship and giving 1292 as the year of its completion. However, although the date supplied by the colophon indicates that Cotton concluded the whole *Historia* in that year, the fact that book 2 continues to 1298, and that the latest event recorded in book 3 is the consecration of John Salmon as bishop of Ely in 1299, without a stylistic change to suggest a change of authorship, make it probable that he continued the work later. The most complete manuscript of the *Historia Anglicana* now known is a fair copy from the early fourteenth century, BL, Cotton MS Nero C.v. Book 1, however, has become detached and is BL, Royal MS 14 C.i, folios 80–137.

The *Historia Anglicana* is commonly attributed to Cotton in its entirety. Nevertheless this comprehensive attribution is misleading. Luard demonstrated that Cotton copied verbatim the first section of the second part of book 2, that is the annals (creation–1066) and the chronicle as far as 1291, from a chronicle still preserved in Norwich Cathedral. Although local references prove that this chronicle was a Norwich production, it is not in Cotton's style. To 1262 the Norwich chronicle is nearly all extracted from well-known chronicles. John Taxster, a monk of Bury St Edmunds, was the source of the annals from 1258 to 1263, while for the period 1279–85 Cotton used the chronicle of St Benet's of Hulme attributed to John of Oxnead. The Norwich chronicle's annals for 1264–79 and 1285–91 are independent of all known chronicle sources and contain much unique information and some graphic details. For example, there is the description of the flight in 1289 of Thomas Weyland, chief justice of common pleas, after his indictment for harbouring two killers, to the Franciscan convent of Babwell, just outside Bury St Edmunds, of his assumption of a friar's habit, and of his and the friars' plight when beleaguered by the king's men. There follows a valuable account of the trial and punishment of others of the king's justices in 1290.

Cotton was an assiduous and judicious historian. For example, he was the first chronicler to recognize the growing importance of the Commons in parliament: he records that in 1294 four knights of each shire were summoned to come with power to bind their shires (*Historia Anglicana*, 254); Cotton's source was apparently a copy of the writ of summons which for the first time included the crucial formula, that knights were to come *cum plena potestate*.                                      ANTONIA GRANSDEN

**Sources** J. Greatrex, *Biographical register of the English cathedral priories of the province of Canterbury* (1997) · *Bartholomaei de Cotton … Historia Anglicana*, ed. H. R. Luard, Rolls Series, 16 (1859) · Tanner, *Bibl. Brit.-Hib.*, 202 · [H. Wharton], ed., *Anglia sacra*, 1 (1691), 397–417 · R. Pauli and F. Liebermann, eds., [*Ex rerum Anglicarum scriptoribus*], MGH Scriptores [folio], 28 (Stuttgart, 1888), 604–21 · A. Gransden, *Historical writing in England*, 1 (1974), 444–8 · M. Prestwich, *Edward I* (1988) · A. Gransden, ed. and trans., *The chronicle of Bury St Edmunds, 1212–1301* [1964], xxvii · N. R. Ker, 'Medieval manuscripts from Norwich Cathedral priory', *Transactions of the Cambridge Bibliographical Society*, 1 (1949–53), 1–28 · M. R. James, *A descriptive catalogue of the manuscripts in the library of Corpus Christi College, Cambridge*, 2 (1912), 388–90 · G. F. Warner and J. P. Gilson, *Catalogue of Western manuscripts in the old Royal and King's collections*, 2 (1921), 132–3

**Archives** BL, Cotton MS Nero C.v; Royal MS 14 C.i, fols. 80–137 · CCC Cam., MS 460, fol. 86

**Cotton, Charles** (1630–1687), poet and translator, was born at the family seat, Beresford Hall in Staffordshire, on 28 April 1630, the only child of Charles (*d.* 1658) and Olive, *née* Stanhope (1614?–1652?). His parents' marriage had caused a scandal when his father eloped with the young heiress and the marriage continued stormy, if one may judge by Olive's petition complaining of her husband's neglect, delivered to the House of Lords in 1647 (*Poems*, ed. Beresford, 14–15). The elder Charles, although a distinguished man with a circle of acquaintance which encompassed John Fletcher, Ben Jonson, Sir Henry Wotton, Izaak Walton, John Donne, Robert Herrick, Richard Lovelace, Sir John Davenant, and Lord Clarendon, none the less bequeathed his son an estate heavily encumbered by debt, and a reputation brilliantly summarized in Clarendon's memoir of him, which 'rendered his age less reverenced than his youth had been, and gave his best friends cause to have wished that he had not lived so long' (*Life of … Clarendon*, 1.36–7).

Of the younger Cotton's education, little is certainly known and there is no record of his having attended Oxford or Cambridge. It is likely that he was privately tutored and his affection for 'my dear Tutor' Ralph Rawson, who had been ejected from Brasenose in 1648, is asserted in a dedication ('An Ode of Johannes Secundus Translated', *Poems*, 1689, 547–8). In 1655 he and a companion were granted a pass for travel 'for improvement of their studies' to France, and he may well have extended his tour to include the sights of Europe.

Cotton's early compositions are typical of a cultured young gentleman of royalist tradition and sympathy. His first published poem was an elegy on Lord Hastings in the 1649 *Lacrymae musarum* which also ushered Dryden and Marvell into print; he may have been the 'C. C.' who in 1650 translated Hobbes's *De cive* into English. In 1651 he contributed a dedicatory poem 'To my Worthy Friend, Mr. Edmund Prestwich, on his Translation of Hippolitus', while by 1653 two of his love lyrics had been set by Edward Coleman and published in John Playford's *Select Musicall Ayres and Dialogues*. Although not published until 1664, Cotton's *Morall Philosophy of the Stoicks*, translated from the French of Guillaume Du Vair, was, he tells us in a 'Epistle Dedicatory', written in 1656 'by my Fathers command' (A4r); its celebration of friendship and moral endurance was apt for the royalist experience under Cromwell. In 1660 Cotton greeted the Restoration in prose, with what a contemporary unkindly described as 'the worst Panegyrick that ever was writ' (*Scriblerus Quartus*

Charles Cotton (1630–1687), by unknown artist

[T. Cooke], *The Bays Miscellany, or, Colley* [*Cibber*] *Triumphant*, [1730]).

Throughout his life Cotton moved in literary and social circles which had also sheltered his father; he answered Davenant's praise of the elder Charles in the former's *Gondibert* and he maintained his father's friendship with Richard Lovelace, who dedicated 'The Triumphs of Philamore and Amoret' to him, and was rewarded with both financial assistance and an elegy. Gilbert Sheldon, archbishop of Canterbury, was a distant relation and near neighbour, to whom Cotton dedicated his translated *History of the Life of the Duke of Espernon*, begun in 1666 and published in 1670. Thomas Ken, another neighbour, later bishop of Bath and Wells and famous as a nonjuror, was related by marriage to Izaak Walton, whose friendship with Cotton was celebrated by them both in print, as can be seen in the 1676 edition of *The Compleat Angler*, to which Cotton's 'Second part' is added. Their affection took more tangible form in the famous fishing house built by Cotton on his estate, whose lintel bore their intertwined initials; in his will Walton left a memorial ring to Cotton, a symbol of his almost paternal affection. Together, this group constituted a band of self-consciously Anglican anglers, finding solace and repose in a temporary retreat from public life. Other nearby friendly literati included his cousin Sir Aston Cokaine, who praised Cotton's writing and gratefully borrowed from his library, and the bibliophile William Boothby, whose recently discovered correspondence records several meetings in the last few years of Cotton's life.

Cotton's family circle seems to have been a similar source of content. He married his cousin Isabella Hutchinson (*d.* 1669) on 30 June 1656 (his poem 'The Separation' suggests that their blood ties caused some initial family opposition to the match) and they had nine children, of whom one son, Beresford, and four daughters survived infancy. Cotton's second daughter, Catherine, seems to have inherited her father's literary interests, to judge from her ownership inscriptions in several books surviving from his library. After Isabella's death in 1669, Cotton remarried. His marriage in 1674 to Mary, dowager countess of Ardglass, was childless.

Of Cotton's literary works, unquestionably the most successful in commercial terms was his *Scarronnides*, a scatological burlesque of Virgil, of which book 1 appeared in 1664 and book 4 the following year, thus completing the narrative of Dido and Aeneas. Samuel Pepys, collecting a copy of book 1 on the very day it was licensed, found it 'extraordinary good' (Pepys, 5.72) and the demand for reprints confirms his view: there were thirteen further editions of the two books combined between 1667 and 1807, and *Scarronnides* was also the star attraction of Cotton's *Genuine Works* (1715). Although Cotton's title recognizes his debt to Paul Scarron, whose *Virgile Travestie* had begun to appear in instalments in 1648, his is a wholly independent burlesque, whose wit depends on its close proximity to Virgil's Latin; parallels are noted on each page. It spawned a litter of imitators and earned the doubtful honour of a 'copycat' publication, the so-called 'Second book' of *Scarronnides* printed in 1692. A year earlier, the anonymous *The Valiant Knight*, a mildly pornographic fantasy, had been Cotton's first published venture into comic territory. A later attempt to capitalize on the success of *Scarronnides* with another classical burlesque, this time of Lucian in *Burlesque upon Burlesque, or, The Scoffer Scoft*, seems to have met with failure; the first edition of 1675 was only once reprinted (in 1686; some copies are dated 1687), although it does form part of the *Genuine Works*.

Burlesque, often featuring himself as a picaresque anti-hero, was a congenial mode for Cotton, who can be found stumbling down caverns in *The Wonders of the Peake* (1681), fobbed off with a nag to rival Quixote's Rozinante in 'A Voyage to Ireland in Burlesque', or offering a knowing self-characterization in his 'Epistle to Sir Clifford Clifton':

> For his stature, he's but a contemptible male,
> And grown something swab with drinking good ale;
> His looks, than your brown, a little thought brighter,
> Which grey hairs make every year whiter and whiter,
> His visage, which all the rest mainly disgraces,
> Is warp't, or by age, or by cutting of faces.
> So that, whether 'twere made so, or whether 'twere marr'd,
> In good sooth, he's a very unpromising bard:

The familiar verse epistle is among his favoured forms, with vivid examples to Sir Peter Lely (who painted his portrait), Walton, and John Bradshaw, whom he brackets with himself as 'wee Countrey-Bumkins' (*Poems*, ed. Beresford, 260):

> And now I'm here set down again in peace,
> After my troubles, business, voyages,
> The same dull Northern clod I was before, …
> Just the same sot I was e'er I remov'd,
> Nor by my travel, nor the Court improv'd;

The same old-fashion'd Squire, no whit refin'd, …
And now begin to live at the old rate,
To bub old ale, which nonsense does create,
Write lewd epistles, and sometimes translate
Old Tales of Tubs, of Guyen[n]e, and Provence,
And keep a clutter with th'old Blades of France, …
Which any will receive, but none will buy
And that has set H. B. and me awry.

Cotton here touches lightly both on his affection for his local district, which he also wryly eulogizes in *The Wonders of the Peake*, and on his fondness for translating French military memoirs; his 'old Blades' were the *History of the Life of the Duke of Espernon* (1670), the *Commentaries of Blaise de Montluc* (1674), and the posthumously printed *Memoirs of the Sieur de Pontis* (1694). 'H. B.' was his publisher and friend the bookseller Henry Brome. Other translations from the French include Corneille's *Horace* (1671).

Cotton's knowledge and love of his native countryside can be seen in ironic form in his epistles and burlesques, where the pose of a Restoration gentleman lends a certain detachment, or in more practical form in his translation of Triquet's gardening treatise *The Planters Manual* (1675), and his additional part to *The Compleat Angler*, 'Being instructions how to angle for a TROUT or GRAYLING in a clear stream' (his beloved River Dove), the work whose later canonization was the basis of Cotton's nineteenth-century fame. A more unaffectedly lyrical vein is seen in his several poems addressed to 'my most Worthy FATHER and FRIEND' ('Epistle Dedicatory' to *The Compleat Angler*) Walton, most notably in 'The Retirement' (*Poems*, ed. Beresford, 45):

Good God! how sweet are all things here!
How beautiful the fields appear!
How cleanly do we feed and lie!
Lord! what good hours do we keep!
How quietly we sleep!
What peace, what unanimity!
How innocent from the lewd fashion,
Is all our bus'ness, all our conversation!

These 'Stanzes Irreguliers' show the metrical mastery typical of Cotton's several experiments in the fashionable Pindaric ode. The posthumously published *Poems on Several Occasions* (1689) exhibits the full range of Cotton's work, encompassing love poetry, epigram (many in imitation of Martial), burlesque, political polemic (there is an unexpected savagery in his attacks on Cromwell in 'A Litany' and on the turncoat Waller in 'To Poet E. W.'), romance ('Philoxipes and Policrite'), and even epic ('The Battail of Yvry'). While several poems seem fully to engage with the literary fashions of the Restoration (those addressed to Aphra Behn and Katherine Phillips, for instance, or the lovely 'Elegy' on the prostitute 'M. H.'), Cotton's principal echoes are often of an earlier time: Shakespeare, Spenser, John Taylor the water poet. His copies of the two last survive, the Spenser heavily annotated. Recent years have seen the reappearance of several volumes from Cotton's library, at least three bearing the final inscription 'Tanquam explorator' which was also Ben Jonson's motto. A similar nostalgia can be seen in his praise of Chatsworth in *The Wonders of the Peake*, which rather seems a lament for the destruction of Bess of Hardwick's Elizabethan hall than a eulogy for the earl of Devonshire's neoclassical pile, despite being dedicated to the latter's countess.

The final work Cotton saw through the press was one of his most admired, his translation of Montaigne's *Essays* (three volumes, 1685–6), which immediately supplanted that by John Florio (1603) and was still being reprinted well into the twentieth century. In Montaigne, Cotton found a congenial mind and character, which he rendered in relaxed and conversational prose:

all I aim at is, to pass my time pleasantly, and without any great Reproach, and the Recreations that most contribute to it, I take hold of, as to the rest, as little glorious and exemplary as you would desire.

Another much reprinted work, whose attribution is less secure (Cotton did not own it in his lifetime) is *The Compleat Gamester*, first printed in 1674 and popular throughout the next century.

In the public life of his time, Cotton played a small but worthy part. Although his poems record his various, often uncomfortable travels, he resided mostly in the country, where he served as magistrate (from 1665) and revenue commissioner (1660) for both his native Staffordshire and the adjoining Derbyshire. He was widely regarded as an authority on the region and his help was acknowledged by the antiquary Robert Plot in his *Natural History of Staffordshire* (1686; see pp. 164–5). He held a brief commission as an army captain in 1667, but the vicissitudes of political life blocked this possible route to financial stability. All his life, even after his second marriage, to a woman of independent wealth, Cotton was short of money, being forced to seek parliamentary approval for the sale of his lands on several occasions (1659, 1665, 1675) and in 1681 eventually compelled to sell the family seat, although he seems to have continued to occupy it until his death. Cotton died, however, not at Beresford but in London, 'of a feaver' on 13 February 1687. Three days later he was buried in St James's, Westminster. He was survived by his second wife.

Cotton's later reputation has had its vicissitudes. In the eighteenth century he was renowned for burlesque and his lyrical poetry was barely known; the nineteenth century found the burlesques too gross, but Coleridge, Wordsworth, and Lamb rediscovered him as poet of nature, praising and imitating his 'Quatrains' of times and seasons, a characterization which, enhanced by his co-authorship of *The Compleat Angler*, brought him a continuing reputation into the twentieth century. Benjamin Britten set Cotton's 'Evening Quatrains' in his *Serenade for Tenor, Horn, and Strings* (1943). Only in 1992, however, did *The Valiant Knight* and *Scarronnides* appear in a modern edition and *The Scoffer Scoft* has still to do so. The 'Compleat' Cotton has yet to be reintegrated.                    PAUL HARTLE

**Sources** E. M. Turner, 'The life and work of Charles Cotton', DPhil diss., U. Oxf., 1954 • *Poems of Charles Cotton*, ed. J. Beresford (1923) • *Poems of Charles Cotton*, ed. J. Buxton (1958) • A. J. Chapple, 'A critical bibliography of the works of Charles Cotton', MA diss., U. Lond., 1955 • *Charles Cotton's works, 1663–1665*, ed. A. I. Dust (1992) • P. Beal, '"My books are the great joy of my life": Sir William Boothby, seventeenth-century bibliophile', *Book Collector*, 46 (1997), 350–78 · T. Zouch, *The life of Isaac Walton* (1823) · I. Walton and C. Cotton, *The complete angler … with original notes and memoirs by Sir H. Nicolas* (1836) · S. B. Beresford and W. Beresford, *A history of the manor of Beresford* (1908) · A. I. Dust, 'Charles Cotton: his books and autographs', *N&Q*, 217 (1972), 20–23 · *The life of Edward, earl of Clarendon … written by himself*, new edn, 3 vols. (1827) · Pepys, *Diary* · N. Malcolm, 'Charles Cotton, translator of Hobbes's *De cive*', *Huntington Library Quarterly*, 61 (1999–2000), 259–87 · E. Wilson, 'Charles Cotton's *The planters manual* (1675): a discovery rediscovered', *N&Q*, 248 (2003), 189–90

**Archives** NRA, letters and literary MSS | Derby County Library, Derbyshire collection · Yale U., Osborn collection

**Likenesses** P. Lely, oils, 1657, probably NPG · P. Lely, oils, 1667?, probably NPG · E. Ashfield, oils, 1674, priv. coll. · P. Audinet, line engraving, pubd 1815 (after Linnell), BM, NPG · G. Maite, mezzotint (after P. Lely), BM, NPG · W. W. Reyland, line engraving (after P. Lely), BM, NPG; repro. in I. Walton, *The complete angler, or, The contemplative man's recreation*, ed. J. Hawkins (1760) · portrait, priv. coll. [*see illus.*]

**Cotton, Sir Charles**, fifth baronet (1753–1812), naval officer, was born in June 1753, the third of the ten children of Sir John Hynde Cotton, fourth baronet (1717–1795), and his wife, Anne (*d.* 1769), daughter of Humphrey *Parsons, twice lord mayor of London, and his wife, Sarah. His grandfather, Sir John Hynde *Cotton, third baronet (*bap.* 1686, *d.* 1752), of Madingley, Cambridgeshire, was regarded as one of the chief supporters of the tory party and was a zealous opponent in parliament of Sir Robert Walpole's administration. Sir Charles's father was chosen as MP successively for St Germans, Marlborough, and the county of Cambridge between 1741 and 1774. After an education at Westminster School and (from 1770) Lincoln's Inn, Cotton entered the navy as midshipman aboard the *Deal Castle* (20 guns) on 24 October 1772; he went to North America in September 1775 in the *Niger* (32 guns), which supported the British army's evacuation from Boston in March 1776 and participated in the Long Island campaign of August 1776. In August 1777 he supported the landing of British troops in the Chesapeake as a lieutenant on the floating battery *Vigilant* (16 guns). On 10 August 1779 he received his commission as post captain for the *Boyne* (70 guns), which was second astern of Sir George Rodney's flagship at the battle of Martinique on 17 April 1780. After paying off the *Boyne* in England he assumed command on 21 April 1781 of the *Alarm* (32 guns), which embarked to the West Indies in February 1782; she was a repeating frigate at the battle of the Saints on 12 April 1782 and remained under Cotton's command in the West Indies until returning to England in 1783. Cotton resided at Madingley during the peace, and on 27 February 1788 he married Philadelphia (1763–1855), daughter of Admiral Sir Joshua Rowley. On 1 March 1793 he was appointed to the *Majestic* (74 guns) in the Channel Fleet. At the battle of 1 June 1794 the *Majestic* followed the flagship of Sir Alexander Hood through the rear of the French line and later took possession of the dismasted *Sans Pareil* (80 guns). Despite Hood's approbation, Cotton's name was omitted from Earl Howe's dispatches; consequently, the gold medal was not awarded to him, an indignity which he shared with

Sir Charles Cotton, fifth baronet (1753–1812), by Henry Hoppner Meyer, pubd 1812 (after James Ramsay)

others, including Sir Benjamin Caldwell and Cuthbert Collingwood.

Cotton succeeded to the baronetcy by the death of his father on 23 January 1795, and the earlier deaths of his two elder brothers. Sir Charles was commanding the *Mars* (74 guns) on 16 June 1795 when thirty French sail pursued a squadron under the Hon. William Cornwallis off the Penmarcks. Cornwallis placed the *Mars* astern of his flagship, where it engaged a succession of enemy ships of the line. Cornwallis, who earned reputation and fame from this masterly retreat, praised Cotton's intrepid conduct. On 20 February 1797 Cotton was advanced to flag-rank, and in March 1799 he hoisted his flag in the *Prince* (98 guns) as third in command in the Channel Fleet. In June, after Eustache Bruix's fleet escaped from Brest, Cotton followed it to the Mediterranean with twelve ships of the line and joined the squadron commanded by Lord Keith. Bruix's fleet returned to Brest on 11 August with Cotton and Keith in pursuit. Cotton was advanced to vice-admiral on 29 April 1802, and was again appointed to a command in the Channel Fleet on renewal of the war. His exertions off Brest in 1804 and 1805 helped frustrate the French effort to conduct a cross-channel invasion.

Before entering a period which was to be the highlight of his naval career, Cotton accepted an appointment as commander-in-chief of a squadron off the Tagus, where he supported the Portuguese struggle against the French army of occupation and assisted Sir Arthur Wellesley's littoral campaign, which culminated at Vimeiro on 21 August 1808. Cotton, now a full admiral, strongly objected to article 7 of the preliminary convention of Cintra, which recognized the port of Lisbon as neutral, and allowed the Russian squadron anchored there to remain unmolested or depart for Russia without being pursued for a specified period of time. Cotton and the Russian admiral subsequently agreed to a special convention, by which the ships would be delivered to an English port and restored within six months after the conclusion of peace. Before returning to England in December 1808 Cotton managed the transition of Lisbon into the British army's Iberian port of entry and prepared for an amphibious withdrawal of Sir John Moore's 30,000 troops. In March 1810 the Admiralty appointed Cotton to succeed Lord Collingwood in the Mediterranean. Under Cotton's command the Toulon fleet was effectively blockaded and the Royal Navy's support of the Spanish cause intensified as French military operations encroached upon the littorals of eastern Spain. In April 1811 Cotton was appointed to command the Channel Fleet in succession to Lord Gambier, but through a series of delays he did not hoist his flag at Plymouth until 8 October. Satisfied with the fleet's condition after an inspection cruise off the French ports, Cotton decided to exercise command that winter from Plymouth, and he died suddenly of apoplexy at Stoke House, Plymouth, on 23 February 1812. He was survived by his wife and four children: Maria, Philadelphia, Charles, and St Vincent *Cotton, sixth baronet. Cotton's body came to rest in the family vault at Landwade church, Cambridgeshire, on 13 April, and there is a monument to him in Madingley church.          PAUL C. KRAJESKI

**Sources** P. Krajeski, *In the shadow of Nelson: the naval leadership of Admiral Sir Charles Cotton, 1753–1812* (2000) · 'Biographical memoir of the late Sir Charles Cotton, bart., admiral of the white squadron', *Naval Chronicle*, 27 (1812), 352–97 · D. Horward, 'Portugal and the Anglo-Russian naval crisis, 1808', *Naval War College Review*, 34 (1981), 54–71 · J. Ralfe, *The naval biography of Great Britain*, 2 (1828); repr. (1972)
**Archives** Cambs. AS · NMM, corresp. and papers relating to memoirs · PRO | NMM, corresp. with Sir Samuel Hood · NMM, letters to Sir Richard Keats · NMM, letters to Charles Yorke
**Likenesses** G. Engleheart, portrait, 1794, Madingley Hall, Cambridgeshire · Landseer, Ryder, Stow, and L. Bartolozzi, line engraving, pubd 1803 (*Commemoration of the victory of June 1st, 1794*; after R. Smirke), BM, NPG · H. H. Meyer, mezzotint, pubd 1812 (after J. Ramsay), BM, NPG [*see illus.*] · Page, stipple, pubd 1812 (after miniature), NPG; repro. in 'Biographical memoir'

**Cotton, Daniel** (*c*.1660–1723). *See under* Cotton family (*per.* *c*.1650–1802).

**Cotton, George Edward Lynch** (1813–1866), bishop of Calcutta, was born at Chester on 29 October 1813. He was the son of Captain Thomas Davenant Cotton of the 7th fusiliers, who was killed at the battle of the Nivelle a fortnight after the birth of his son. His grandfather was George Cotton (*d.* 1805), dean of Chester.

Cotton was educated at Westminster School and at Trinity College, Cambridge, where in 1836 he took a first-class degree in the classical tripos. In the following year Dr Thomas Arnold appointed him an assistant master with charge of a boarding-house at Rugby School. Both at

George Edward Lynch Cotton (1813–1866), by Francis Holl? (after Eden Upton Eddis?, exh. RA 1854)

school and at university he was noted for his force of character, his quaint and grotesque humour, and his earnest religion. At Cambridge his religious views were evangelical, but at Rugby he soon came under the broadening influence of Arnold, and in the words of his biographer, 'thoroughly absorbed and reproduced in his own life and work the most distinctive features of Arnold's character and principles'. He was the original of the Young Master in *Tom Brown's School Days*. He remained at Rugby for fifteen years, gradually becoming an efficient master, devoted to the moral and intellectual training of his pupils. In 1845 he married his cousin, Sophia Anne, eldest daughter of the Revd Henry Tomkinson of Reaseheath in Cheshire; they had two surviving children, a son and a daughter. Mrs Cotton was to write her husband's biography after his death.

In 1852, having previously failed to be appointed headmaster of Rugby on the retirement of A. C. Tait, Cotton was appointed master of Marlborough College, which, though established only nine years before, already stood in urgent need of reform. Cotton, along with his friend C. J. Vaughan, headmaster of Harrow, is credited with introducing organized games into the centre of life in the English public schools. At the end of six years Cotton left Marlborough with a high reputation among public schools. His retirement was caused by his appointment as bishop of Calcutta, made on the recommendation of A. C. Tait, whose colleague he had been at Rugby, and to whom he had been examining chaplain while the latter was bishop of London.

Cotton was consecrated as the sixth bishop of Calcutta on 13 May 1858. He had no special knowledge of India, but his reputation as a moderate and broad-minded ecclesiastic and a man of calm judgement and sympathetic understanding recommended him for work in this diocese: calm statesmanship was called for by the condition of India in 1858. Although the rebellion which had swept the northern part of the country in the previous year had been practically suppressed, many questions remained to be answered, among them that of the attitude to be maintained by the new government of India towards Christian missions and the education of the Indian population. In some quarters the extension of education and the activities of missionaries were held partially responsible for the discontent which had turned mutiny into rebellion. In others it was held that too little had been done to promote Christianity, and that the introduction of Bible instruction in government colleges and schools ought no longer to be delayed. While helping the missionary cause and promoting other measures of importance in their bearing on religion and education in India, Cotton agreed with most officials that introducing Bible instruction into government schools would unnecessarily offend Hindu and Muslim sensibilities. On the subject of the education of Indians he came to the conclusion that the object to be aimed at was the gradual abolition of the government colleges and a great enlargement of the grants-in-aid to schools under private management, most of which at that date were mission schools. This he felt would be a better way of gaining Christian influence than the impracticable scheme of introducing the Bible into all existing government schools.

As metropolitan Cotton supervised the dioceses of Madras and Bombay as well as his own diocese. He exercised direct supervision over the Anglican chaplains who served the British troops and European congregations in India. To maintain contact with this scattered flock Cotton wrote regular pastoral letters and made extensive visitation tours. The bishop's licensing powers involved him in frequent negotiations with the two Church of England missionary societies, and he was sometimes called upon to settle disputes. Following the rebellion, the Society for the Propagation of the Gospel (SPG) raised funds to erect a church at Cawnpore as a memorial to the English men and women who had perished there. The Church Missionary Society (CMS) thought this was not appropriate work for a missionary body whose ministry was to the indigenous population. Cotton settled the matter by giving the money raised to the government, which built the memorial and in exchange gave over to the SPG a church building in the native district. On the issue of expanding the episcopate in India by creating missionary bishops, as advocated by the SPG, Cotton sided with the CMS secretary, Henry Venn, who argued that evangelism should be left to voluntary societies with visits by bishops to confirm, ordain, and superintend.

Another public incident which tested the bishop's ability to calm troubled waters erupted over the exposure of the ill treatment of poor peasants (ryots) by European indigo planters. James Long, a respected agent of the Church Missionary Society, translated and circulated a Bengali vernacular play, *Nil Darpan*, which depicted the planters as tyrants. This enraged the planters and their friends in government, and Long was tried and jailed for libel. Bishop Cotton was away from Calcutta at the time but wrote Long a letter in gaol, attempting a balanced assessment of responsibility. He also wrote a full account of the episode in the *Calcutta Christian Intelligencer* in September 1861.

The work which will always be most closely associated with his name is the establishment of schools for the Eurasian population of India and for Europeans who could not afford to send their children back to England for their education. It was not thought appropriate for Europeans to attend school with Indians, and people of mixed race were not welcomed by either Indians or Europeans. At a very early period in his episcopate Cotton was struck by the inadequacy of educational facilities for these children, and by the danger of leaving them uneducated while education was rapidly advancing among the Indian population. Cotton recommended a comprehensive scheme to the government in August 1860, and Governor-General Canning set forth a programme later in the year that provided grants-in-aid and government land for the establishment of a number of schools. The plan was to establish boarding-schools in the hills for 'the better placed members of the community' and day schools in the plains for the poorer sections. The boarding-schools were to approximate the model of an English public school, with religious teaching in conformity with the Church of England, modified by a conscience clause for dissenters. The day schools were to impart the practical education thought suitable for the sons of English and Eurasian artisans and railwaymen. Boarding-schools were started in Simla, Darjeeling, and Mussooree during Cotton's episcopate. Day schools in the plains were undertaken only later. Many of these schools were called by Bishop Cotton's name and are monuments to this part of his work.

The vast size of the Calcutta diocese and the consequent need for additional bishops for the Punjab and Burma was much felt by Cotton, although the creation of additional bishops took place after his episcopate. Another ecclesiastical reform, originating from Madras, which received his support was an increase in the pensions of government chaplains and the limitation of their service to twenty-five years, which both enabled and compelled them to retire before they were incapacitated for duty. Although liberal in his views on ecclesiastical questions Cotton could hardly be called a broad-churchman in the usual sense of the term. He never forgot that he was a bishop of the Church of England, and that it was his duty not 'to lose sight of the chief peculiarities and distinctive merits of the English church in pursuit of an unpractical pretence at unity'. Thus, while he was ready to meet nonconformists and dissenters on common ground and to surrender all exclusive and offensive church privileges, such as the sole validity of marriages by episcopal clergy, and to meet them as far as possible in concessions such as the loan of

English churches to Scottish regiments in cases of absolute necessity, he was not prepared to make churches or burial-grounds common; on one occasion he observed that in all such matters every concession came from the church side, and none from the nonconformists.

Cotton's death resulted from an accident. On 6 October 1866, when boarding in the dusk a steamer from which he had landed to consecrate a cemetery at Kushtia, on the River Gorai, a branch of the Ganges, his foot slipped on a platform of rough planks which he was crossing; he fell into the river and, carried away by the strong undercurrent, was never seen again.

A. J. ARBUTHNOT, rev. DAVID W. SAVAGE

**Sources** S. A. Cotton, *Memoir of George Edward Lynch Cotton* (1871) · G. G. Bradley, *The parting of Miletus* (1866) · J. A. Mangan, *Athleticism in the Victorian and Edwardian public school* (1981) · M. E. Gibbs, *The Anglican church in India, 1600–1970* (1972) · A. A. D'Souza, *Anglo-Indian education* (1976) · T. E. Yates, *Venn and Victorian bishops abroad: the missionary policies of Henry Venn and their repercussions upon the Anglican episcopate of the colonial period, 1841–1872* (1978) · C. P. Williams, *The ideal of the self-governing church* (1990) · G. Oddie, *Social protest in India: British protestant missionaries and social reform* (1979)

**Likenesses** portrait, 1858, Marlborough College, Wiltshire · F. Holl?, line and stipple engraving (after E. U. Eddis?, exh. RA 1854), NPG [*see illus.*] · wood-engraving, NPG; repro. in *ILN* (10 Nov 1866)

**Wealth at death** under £12,000 (in England): probate, 16 Jan 1867, *CGPLA Eng. & Wales*

**Cotton, Henry** (c.1545–1615), bishop of Salisbury, was the fourth of six sons of Sir Richard *Cotton (b. in or before 1497, d. 1556) of Cotton Hall, Warblington, near Havant, Hampshire, and Jane Onley (d. 1585) of Northamptonshire; there were also three daughters. Sir Richard was a follower of John Dudley, duke of Northumberland, in 1556 willing his soul to God without the intercession of saints; however Henry's eldest brother, Sir George Cotton (1538–1610), became a noted recusant. The future Queen Elizabeth I, then twelve, became Henry Cotton's godmother, and his family has been described as 'the most eminent' of any Elizabethan bishop, most being 'far better equipped intellectually than socially to lead the church' (Berlatsky, 37, 57). Cotton's assets were concentrated in the latter sphere rather than the former. He was first educated at Guildford grammar school and was relatively old when he attended Magdalen College, Oxford, as a commoner from 1566. He graduated BA in 1569, proceeding MA in 1572. His additional degrees of BTh (1586) and DTh (1599) coincided with his elevation to a royal chaplaincy and a bishopric: in the latter case an Oxford delegation to Salisbury argued that since 'to be a bishop is a greater thing in the church than to be a doctor' he might as well enjoy the latter dignity too (Holland, sig. A4r).

Ordained by Robert Horne, bishop of Winchester, in 1574, Cotton was made canon of the sixth prebend at Winchester in 1577. He was also provided to the rectory of Havant, where his mother rented the manor and eventually bequeathed him the lease in 1585, when the 'trustie' Henry rather than one of his more 'chargeable' brothers was appointed her executor (PRO, PROB 11/68/39). About 1580 Cotton became an unusually junior royal chaplain,

and from 1585 featured regularly on Lent court preaching lists. Retaining Havant (£24 6s. 10½d. p.a.), he acquired the vicarage of Wanborough in the diocese of Salisbury (£21 p.a.), and then in 1584 the rectory of Calbourne, Isle of Wight, in Winchester diocese (£19 12s. 6d. p.a.). In 1589 he relinquished Calbourne for the rectory of Meonstoke, Hampshire (£46 2s. 10d. p.a.).

Cotton is said to have had nineteen children, of whom four sons and three daughters survived to be mentioned in his will: John (bap. 1581); Francis (bap. 1583); Henry (1587–1622), who, although blind, graduated from Brasenose College, Oxford, and became precentor at Salisbury under his father; William (bap. 1588); Jane Hungerford; Mary Holdruppe (married Andrew Holdruppe in 1608); and Elizabeth Shelley. Their mother, who according to Sir John Harington was named Patience, must have died after Cotton's consecration, since she was buried in Salisbury Cathedral. Cotton's second wife, Elizabeth, seems to have been a widow, to have outlived him, and then to have married Edward Reade, esquire. She brought him a substantial dowry of £700, but, her husband complained in his will, it needed recovery 'by lawe … at my great charge'.

By his own account Cotton was baulked of the deanery of Winchester by a 'promise made to another', presumably Martin Heton, the successful candidate in 1589 (*Salisbury MSS*, 6.207). He was recommended in 1596 by the crown to replace Thomas Bilson as warden of Winchester College. Both Winchester and New colleges complained that he had never belonged to a Wykehamist foundation, and an effort to solve the situation by 'meanes w.ch wer never hearde of before', 'a simple old man' being 'terrified' into resigning his fellowship specifically in Cotton's favour (PRO, SP 12/259/9.IV, 243/106), gave new grounds for offence. Both Bilson and Thomas Sackville, Baron Buckhurst, chancellor of Oxford University, who called Cotton 'a man worthy of a far better place' (PRO, SP 12/259/9), expressed support in principle but dissuaded Elizabeth from persisting in advancing his claims.

Thus Cotton had received no previous appointment more elevated than his Winchester canonry when on 12 November 1598 he was consecrated bishop of Salisbury. The see had proved difficult to dispose of after the death of John Coldwell in 1596, since the latter had granted Sir Walter Ralegh a 99-year lease of the see's principal manor of Sherborne and Ralegh was now pressing for its full conveyance to himself in perpetuity. On such terms several candidates (including Lancelot Andrewes and Robert Bennet, dean of Windsor) refused it outright, but Cotton proved compliant. When Bennet openly criticized Cotton for accepting such humiliating terms he was rapped over the knuckles by Sir Robert Cecil. Ralegh pledged himself to guarantee that Cotton should retain Meonstoke *in commendam*, but even this meagre concession was finally denied him. He had to fight hard to obtain favourable terms for the payment of his first fruits, eventually securing ten six-monthly instalments over a period of five years.

Cotton enforced concessions to the see from Salisbury corporation, and sought to recover the chancellorship of the Order of the Garter. As part of a dispute with his diocesan chancellor, Cotton succeeded in regaining what he claimed his predecessors had neglected, 'the sole allowance of my clergy, wherein my chiefest charge consists', so as to deal with 'very bad and insufficient curates' (*Salisbury MSS*, 10.161). He was especially concerned with the conversion of Roman Catholics, and took an active but sceptical interest in the pin-vomiting of the alleged Berkshire witchcraft victim Anne Gunter.

In 1608 Edward Seymour, earl of Hertford, thanked Cotton for preaching 'a good sermone' (Murphy, 114), and after his elevation he was still enlisted as a court Lent preacher in 1599, thrice in 1600, in 1603, in 1607, and lastly in 1610. A regular Wiltshire JP in 1600–04, he never reappeared after 1609. Active in the parliaments of 1601, 1604, and 1605–6, with attendance rates over 80 per cent and participation in a variety of committees (appropriately including bills concerning the west country and recusancy), he attended only 15 per cent of sessions in 1606–7 and 30 per cent in 1610, before pleading sickness on 28 February 1611 and never returning. He seems to have conducted his last ordination in March that year; in April, with 'sundrie infirmities … weakeninge this my earthlie tabernacle' Cotton made his will (PRO, PROB 11/125/49). In this he continued his episcopal predecessors' 'serious neglect' of the Salisbury poor (Heal, 261), though he was more generous to his mother's almshouses at Havant, while Winchester, where he 'spent the greatest parte of my tyme', was to have his plate. £25 of the £575 he left in cash went to charity and £550 to his family.

Cotton lingered on for another four years. He managed to conduct institutions at Salisbury until 29 March 1615, dying in the bishop's palace there on 7 May. He was buried in the cathedral. He had perhaps been more notable as an ecclesiastical careerist, benefiting to an unusual degree from the personal interest of Elizabeth I, than for any obvious spiritual qualities. Yet Harington's story that Cotton seized the property of a debtor while offering to return it to him if he proceeded to his long neglected confirmation suggests that Cotton took his pastoral role at least as seriously as his material advancement. Except for the notorious Sherborne transaction, an exacerbation of extant arrangements prejudicial to his see, he seems to have been a reasonably conscientious bishop.

JULIAN LOCK

**Sources** F. O. White, *Lives of the Elizabethan bishops of the Anglican church* (1898) · S. H. Cassan, *Lives and memoirs of the bishops of Sherborne and Salisbury, from the year 705 to 1824*, 3 pts (1824) · J. Harington, *A briefe view of the state of the Church of England* (1653), 95r–97 · *Calendar of the manuscripts of the most hon. the marquis of Salisbury*, 24 vols., HMC, 9 (1883–1976) · state papers domestic, Elizabeth, PRO, SP 12 · F. Heal, *Of prelates and princes: a study of the economic and social position of the Tudor episcopate* (1980) · K. Fincham, *Prelate as pastor: the episcopate of James I* (1990) · K. Fincham, ed., *Visitation articles and injunctions of the early Stuart church*, 1 (1994) · Salisbury espiocal register, Wilts. & Swindon RO, D1/2/19 · episcopal registers, Winchester, Hants. RO, 21M65/A1/26, fols. 103v, 107r; 21M65/A1/27, fols.11r, 13r · parish register, Winchester, St Swithin over Kingsgate, Hants. RO, 74M81/1 · W. P. W. Phillimore and J. Sadler, eds., *Wiltshire parish registers: marriages*, 7 (1908) · exchequer, first fruits office, composition books, PRO, E334/8, 10–12 · faculty office register, LPL, F1/B, fol. 103v · will, PRO, PROB 11/125, sig. 49 · will of Jane Cotton, PRO, PROB 11/68, sig. 39 · will of Sir Richard Cotton, PRO, PROB 11/38, sig. 23 · J. A. Berlatsky, 'The social background of the Elizabethan episcopate, 1558–1603', PhD diss., Northwestern University, 1970 · D. J. Dawson, 'The political activity and influence of the House of Lords, 1603–29', BLitt diss., U. Oxf., 1950, 210 · *N&Q*, 10th ser., 4 (1905), 56, 114–15 · T. Holland, *Oratio … cum … Henricus … episcopus Sarisburiensis gradum doctoratus in theologia susciperit* (1599) · HoP, *Commons, 1509–58*, 1.711–13 · *JHL*, 2 (1578–1614) · E. R. Foster, ed., *Proceedings in parliament, 1610*, 1 (1966), 189 · Foster, *Alum. Oxon., 1500–1714*, 1.334 · P. E. McCullough, *Sermons at court: politics and religion in Elizabethan and Jacobean preaching* (1998), appx [incl. CD-ROM] · J. Sharpe, *The bewitching of Anne Gunter* (1999) · M. Ingram, *Church courts, sex, and marriage in England, 1570–1640* (1987), 64 · W. B. Wildman, *A short history of Sherborne* (1930), 170–72 · E. Edwards, *The life of Sir Walter Ralegh … together with his letters*, 1 (1868), 464–5 · O. Manning and W. Bray, *The history and antiquities of the county of Surrey*, 1 (1804), 80 · J. Britton, *History and antiquities of the cathedral church of Salisbury* (1814), 47–8 · C. R. Everett, 'An episcopal visitation of the cathedral church of Sarum in 1607', *Wiltshire Archaeological and Natural History Magazine*, 50 (1942–4), 170–87 · W. P. D. Murphy, ed., *The earl of Hertford's lieutenancy papers, 1603–1612*, Wilts RS, 23 (1969), 114

**Archives** Wilts. & Swindon RO, episcopal register, D1/2/19 | BL, corresp. with E. Seymour, Add. MS 5496 · BL, letters relating to Winchester College, Lansdowne MS 87

**Wealth at death** £575 in cash bequests; plus mother's lease of Havant manor; also at least 140 oz of plate: will, PRO, PROB 11/125/49

**Cotton, Henry** (1790–1879), ecclesiastical historian, was born in Buckinghamshire on 31 March 1790, a son of the Revd William Cotton, of Chicheley, Berkshire. In 1802 he went to Westminster School and in 1807 he entered Christ Church, Oxford, where he was awarded a first class in classics in 1810, and became Greek reader. He graduated BA in 1811 and proceeded MA in 1813. While at Christ Church he attracted the notice of the dean, Cyril Jackson, and it was probably through Jackson's influence that Cotton was appointed in 1814 sub-librarian of the Bodleian Library. He was also a student of Christ Church. He took holy orders, was created DCL in 1820, and was instituted as vicar of Cassington, Oxfordshire, where he served from 1818 to 1823. He resigned from the Bodleian in 1822.

In 1823 Cotton moved to Ireland as domestic chaplain to Richard Laurence shortly before Laurence became archbishop of Cashel. Cotton married Mary Vaughan Laurence, the archbishop's daughter. In June 1824 he was instituted as archdeacon of Cashel.

In 1832 he was appointed treasurer of Christ Church, Dublin; and in 1834 he was elected dean of Lismore.

Most of Cotton's many publications related to his research into editions of the Bible; they include *A List of Editions of the Bible in English from 1505 to 1820* (1818; 2nd edn, 1852), *Memoir of a French New Testament, with Bishop Kidder's Reflections on the same* (1827; 2nd edn, 1863), *A Short Explanation of Obsolete Words in our Version of the Bible* (1832), and *Rhemes and Doway: an attempt to show what has been done by Roman Catholics for the diffusion of the holy scriptures in England* (1855). His major work, however, was his *Fasti ecclesiae Hibernicae*, published in six volumes between 1851 and 1868; it was later superseded by the work of Canon J. B. Leslie and other scholars.

Failing eyesight induced Cotton to retire from the active ministerial duties, and he resigned the deanery of Lismore and the archdeaconry of Cashel in 1850. His wife died in 1866. In 1872 he became almost totally blind, and he died at his home, The Hall, Lismore, on 3 December 1879. He was buried in the graveyard of Lismore Cathedral. 	B. H. BLACKER, rev. MARIE-LOUISE LEGG

Sources J. B. Leslie, 'Fasti of Christ Church Cathedral, Dublin', Representative Church Body Library, Dublin · W. P. Courtney, *The Academy* (13 Dec 1879), 429 · *Irish Ecclesiastical Gazette* (3 Jan 1880) · *Old Westminsters*, vols. 1–2 · Foster, *Alum. Oxon.* · *Men of the time* (1865)
Archives Bodl. Oxf., notebooks · Representative Church Body Library, Dublin, corresp. and papers | BL, letters to Philip Bliss, Add. MSS 34570–34581
Wealth at death under £80,000: probate, 2 Feb 1880, *CGPLA Ire.*

**Cotton, Sir Henry** (1821–1892), judge, was born at Walwood House, Leytonstone, on 20 May 1821, the second son of William *Cotton (1786–1866) and his wife, Sarah Lane. Sarah Acland was his eldest sister and Agnes *Cotton his youngest. He was educated at Eton College, where he won the Newcastle scholarship in 1838. He matriculated at Christ Church, Oxford, where he was a student from 1837 until 1852. Having obtained second-class honours in classics and a first in mathematics in 1842, he graduated BA in 1843, and he entered as a student at Lincoln's Inn the same year. He was called to the bar in 1846. In August 1852 he married Clemence Elizabeth, daughter of the Revd Thomas Streatfield of Chart's Edge, Kent; they had five sons and three daughters.

Cotton quickly acquired a large practice in the equity courts, and through the influence of his father was appointed standing counsel to the Bank of England. In December 1866 he took silk and attached himself to the court of Vice-Chancellor Richard Malins, where he shared the leadership with W. B. Glasse. Among the important cases in which he was engaged were the liquidation of Overend, Gurney & Co.; *the King of Hanover* v. *Bank of England*; *Rubery* v. *Grant*; *Dr Hayman* v. *Governors of Rugby School*; and *the Republic of Costa Rica* v. *Erlanger*. In 1872 he was appointed standing counsel to the University of Oxford, and shortly afterwards only went into court on a special retainer. In June 1877, on the death of Lord Justice Sir George Mellish, he was appointed a lord justice of appeal, and subsequently sworn of the privy council, and knighted (July 1877). In the same year the University of Oxford conferred upon him the honorary degree of DCL. As a judge he was learned, painstaking, and courteous, and he enjoyed the reputation of being one of the strongest members of the appeal court. He retired from the bench in November 1890, when his health already showed signs of breaking down.

As a boy Cotton was keen on sports, though his stature was small. At Eton he was a 'wet bob' (an oarsman), and in later life specially distinguished as a figure-skater. For many years he took a grouse moor at Kinloch-Rannoch in Perthshire. While shooting there he damaged his right hand, which resulted in the amputation of the tips of most of the fingers. He was an active member of the Inns

of Court Volunteers from 1866 until his elevation to the bench. He died on 22 February 1892 at the estate which he had bought at Forest Mere, near Liphook in Hampshire, and was buried in the neighbouring churchyard of Milland.

Cotton's eldest brother, **William Charles Cotton** (1813–1879), writer on bees, was likewise educated at Eton before going to Christ Church, Oxford, where he held a studentship from 1834 to 1857 and graduated in 1836 with a first in classics and a second in mathematics. From boyhood he was devoted to the study of bees. At Oxford he was one of the founders of the Apiarian Society, of which he was the first secretary. In 1838 he printed two *Short and Simple Letters to Cottagers from a Bee Preserver*, which were afterwards expanded into an illustrated volume, *My Bee Book* (1842). Ordained in 1837, he became assistant curate to G. A. Selwyn at Windsor, and in 1842 went out to New Zealand as Selwyn's chaplain. During his time at Selwyn's mission at Waimate, Cotton established bee-keeping in the North Island of New Zealand, publishing *A Manual for New Zealand Beekeepers* (1848) and a Maori version, *Nga pi* (1849). Returning to England in 1848, he was increasingly afflicted by periods of insanity. In 1857 Christ Church appointed him to the living of Frodsham, Cheshire, where he had occasional periods of effectiveness. Breakdowns necessitated recuperative travels to the continent, where he came upon William Busch's *Schnurrdiburr*, which he rendered into verse and published as *Buzz-a-Buzz, or, The Bees* (1872, repr. 1982). Latterly his mind completely gave way, and he died, unmarried, on 22 June 1879 at the asylum in Chiswick, Middlesex, run by Thomas H. Tuke.
	J. S. COTTON, rev. M. C. CURTHOYS

Sources Boase, *Mod. Eng. biog.* · Burke, *Peerage* (1889) · *The Times* (23 Feb 1892) · J. Foster, *Men-at-the-bar: a biographical hand-list of the members of the various inns of court*, 2nd edn (1885) · private information (1901) · Foster, *Alum. Oxon.* · R. Etherington, 'William Charles Cotton: priest–missionary–beekeeper', *Journal of the Auckland–Waikato Historical Studies*, 36 (April 1980) · *CGPLA Eng. & Wales* (1879)
Archives Bodl. Oxf., letters to his brother, W. C. Cotton
Likenesses G. Richmond, chalk drawing, 1875, NPG · Barraud, photograph, NPG; repro. in *Men and Women of the Day*, 1 (1888) · Lock & Whitfield, woodburytype photograph, NPG; repro. in T. Cooper, *Men of mark: a gallery of contemporary portraits*, 5 (1881), pl. 32 · Spy [L. Ward], watercolour study, NPG; repro. in *VF*, 20 (1888), pl. 22 · portrait, repro. in *Green Bag*, 7 (1895), 380 · portrait, repro. in *ILN*, 100 (1892), 262 · woodburytype photograph, NPG
Wealth at death £59,144 0s. 4d.: probate, 21 April 1892, *CGPLA Eng. & Wales* · under £7000—William Charles Cotton: probate, 13 Sept 1879, *CGPLA Eng. & Wales*

**Cotton, (Thomas) Henry** (1907–1987), golfer, was born on 28 January 1907 at The Croft, Church Hulme, Congleton, Cheshire, the second son in the family of two sons and one daughter of George Cotton, an industrialist, inventor, and Wesleyan lay preacher, and his second wife, Alice le Poidevin, a native of Guernsey. His early childhood was spent in Peckham. He and his brother, Leslie, went to Ivydale Road school, Peckham, and, after their evacuation from London in the First World War, to Reigate grammar school. From there Cotton won a scholarship to Alleyn's School, Dulwich. The war over, George Cotton obtained junior membership for both boys at the Aquarius Golf

(Thomas) Henry Cotton (1907–1987), by unknown photographer, 1930s

Club, and both won the club championship before reaching their teens. From the time he left Alleyn's (after irritating the headmaster) to become a golf professional at sixteen, Cotton trod a path of his own. His aloofness lost him popularity with contemporaries, and his strong will brought him into conflict with golf's rulers, but he rarely deviated from his chosen course. His achievements were founded on intense application and self-reliance.

When Cotton entered his profession, the status of golf professional was barely above that of a senior caddy. By personal example Cotton did more than anyone of his time to alter that. He sought the best: silk shirts from Jermyn Street, limousines rather than taxis, and the best restaurants. Though he won three British open championships and many famous victories, his impact on his own profession was his greatest attainment. He was not long content to be the junior of six assistants at Fulwell Golf Club on 12s. 6d. a week. Within a year he had moved to an assistant's post at Rye. There he made friends with Cyril Tolley, a fine amateur golfer, who assisted his next move. At nineteen, Cotton went to Langley Park, the youngest head professional in the history of British golf.

At this point Cotton perceived that to reach the top in golf he must challenge American supremacy. With the blessing of his club, £300, and a first-class ticket on the *Aquitania*, he joined the 1928–9 winter season in America. A year later he was invited to Argentina to teach and play exhibition matches with a fellow professional. There

(Maria) Isabel Estanguet Moss (1902–1982) booked him for fifty lessons. The daughter of Pedro Estanguet, a wealthy landowner, and his wife, Epifania, and married to Enrique Moss, of Argentina's diplomatic service, Toots, as she became universally called, was five years older than Cotton. They formed a close partnership, which transformed both their lives. Eventually, on the annulment in Latvia in June 1939 of her first marriage, they married at a Westminster register office on 11 December 1939. They had no children, though there were two daughters from Isabel's first marriage. Passionately loyal to Cotton's interests, she became, when occasion demanded, his most trenchant critic, as well as a competent golfer herself.

Cotton won three open victories (1934 at Royal St George's, 1937 at Carnoustie, and 1948 at Muirfield). After seven years at Langley Park, he had taken a post at Waterloo, a fashionable club near Brussels. But after his first open win, he was persuaded by the sixth earl of Rosebery to build up the reputation of Ashridge Golf Club. The outbreak of the Second World War interrupted a career at the peak of success. Cotton joined the Royal Air Force, and suffered a regime which aggravated his stomach ulcer. After being medically discharged with the rank of flight lieutenant, he raised £70,000 for the Red Cross and other war charities from 130 matches which he organized. He took appointments first at Coombe Hill and then at Royal Mid-Surrey. From there he won his last open in 1948. That was the apogee of a career in which he had dominated tournament golf for some twenty years. He was also captain of the British Ryder cup team in 1947 and 1953. Though he had minor wins in 1953 and 1954, writing, teaching, and golf architecture became the main outlets for his energies. He wrote several books on golf, as well as designing thirteen golf courses in Britain and ten more abroad.

In 1963 Cotton went to Portugal, and on the Algarve coast created from a swamp the Penina golf course. This became his memorial, and he became virtually squire of the place until the Portuguese revolution of April 1974, during which he was expelled. Profoundly depressed by enforced exile, Cotton was rallied by his wife and they moved for a spell to Sotogrande in Spain. After a two-year interlude they returned to Portugal. There, at Christmas 1982, Toots died, ending half a century's close partnership. In 1987 Cotton entered King Edward VII Hospital, and was there told of his knighthood. He had been appointed MBE in 1946. During his convalescence he died suddenly from a heart attack at Beaumont House, Beaumont Street, Westminster, on 22 December 1987; he was buried at Mexilhoeira Grande in Portugal. He was knighted posthumously in the new year's honours of 1988.

Always an individualist, Cotton taught that golfing excellence demanded infinite pains. He believed in strong hands and could hit a succession of one-handed shots without regripping the club. A severe opponent, he was also an excellent host. Tireless in pursuit of his own goals, he freely shared with a generation of young golfers more insight into the game than any other figure of his time.

DEEDES, *rev.*

**Sources** H. Cotton, *This game of golf* (1948) • P. Dobereiner, *Maestro: the life of Henry Cotton* (1992) • personal knowledge (2004) • b. cert. • m. cert. • d. cert. • *The Times* (24 Dec 1987) • *The Independent* (24 Dec 1987)
**Likenesses** photographs, 1921–53, Hult. Arch. • photograph, 1930–39, NPG [*see illus.*] • J. A. A. Berrie, oils, 1938, Royal & Ancient Golf Club of St Andrews • photograph, repro. in *The Independent*

**Cotton, Sir Henry John Stedman** (1845–1915), administrator in India and positivist, was born in Kumbakonam, Madras presidency, south India, on 13 September 1845, the first of two sons of Joseph John Cotton (1813–1867), East India Company servant, and his wife, Jessie Minchin, daughter of a Madras barrister. In 1848 Henry and his younger brother, James, were taken to England and grew up in the care of a private school in Woodford, London, and with loving grandparents and family. In 1856 Henry entered Magdalen College School, Oxford, but transferred to Brighton College in 1859 because of parental concern over high-church influence at Oxford. He joined King's College, London, in 1861 and studied liberal arts, but as he was a less distinguished student than his brother, his father declined to send him on to Oxford. Instead, in 1865, he competed successfully in the Indian Civil Service public examinations and spent the next two years studying for India, participating in London literary and artistic groups, and mountaineering in the Alps. He became interested in positivism, attended lectures by Richard Congreve, leader of the British positivists, and in 1870 became a formal adherent. In 1867 he completed his India studies examinations, ranking twentieth overall among the forty-five entry students of 1865. On 1 August 1867, in a ceremony witnessed by the jurist C. H. Cameron and his wife, the photographer Julia Margaret Cameron, he married the attractive eighteen-year-old Mary, the daughter of James Ryan of Limerick. She accompanied him to India in September. The Cottons had three sons, born between 1868 and 1874. Mary Cotton returned to London with the children in 1874 and did not rejoin her husband until 1897. In India, Cotton was assigned to Bengal and served in district administration, the judiciary, and the Bengal government secretariat, rising to the position of chief secretary in 1891 and finally to the Assam chief commissionership in 1896.

As a positivist and advanced Liberal, Cotton did not fit the standard bureaucratic mould. Positivism was dedicated to the service of humanity and disapproved of imperialism. In 1872 Congreve stipulated that in future no positivist should serve the British raj and that those already there should assist India's 'transition from subjection to independence'. Cotton endorsed this view but was cautious because of the experience of his fellow positivist Indian Civil Service officer James C. Geddes, whose denunciations of British Indian policy earned him strong official displeasure and led, indirectly, to his early death in 1880. Not until 1883, in the context of the reformist policies of the Liberal viceroy Lord Ripon, did Cotton speak out forthrightly on Indian affairs. The occasion was an address to the London Positivist Society which he expanded in 1885 into a book, *New India, or, India in Transition*. The book was broadly critical of British rule, supported Indian nationalism, and viewed it as a key to ultimate independence. Welcomed by Western-educated Indians, the book alienated British officialdom. Cotton denied accusations of disloyalty made by India Office officials in London, but promised to avoid future public references to politics. His leadership of the Calcutta Positivist Society, held since Geddes's death, he transferred to Bengali hands. Officialdom was mollified, and Cotton's career advanced.

New difficulties arose during Cotton's appointment in Assam, where serious tensions existed between prosperous English tea planters and their Indian indentured labourers. Directed by the energetic, Conservative viceroy, Lord Curzon, to examine the labour situation, Cotton found conditions deplorable and meagre wages at levels set three decades earlier. Instead of his recommended 20 per cent wage increase, Curzon's government approved a further three-year wage freeze, followed by only small graduated increases. Meanwhile, Cotton officially criticized the established bias of the courts towards the English planters and promised more equitable justice. Planters demanded his dismissal and in February 1902 Curzon publicly repudiated Cotton's policies. Finding himself 'thrown to the wolves', Cotton, due to retire late that year, immediately resigned. Mainly to offset Indian criticism over the circumstances of his departure, Curzon arranged for a KCSI to be conferred on him in June 1902.

In Britain, Cotton joined the British committee of the Indian National Congress, the main organ of Indian nationalist opinion; in 1904 Congress elected him president of its twentieth anniversary session, and Indians gave him a hero's welcome. Elected to the Commons in the Liberal triumph of 1906, Cotton became a leader of a radical pro-India parliamentary group. He criticized his own government for refusing to revoke Curzon's Bengal partition of 1905, for sanctioning the deportation of Indian political activists in 1907–8, and for endorsing separate electorates for Muslims in the 1909 constitutional reforms. Handicapped by illness, Cotton was narrowly defeated in the general election of 1910. Despite health and financial problems, he continued to publish critical articles on policy in India. In 1911 he created a storm among the British-Indian establishment by publicly encouraging France to grant political asylum to the Indian revolutionary V. D. Savarkar, who had escaped British custody in Marseilles, while *en route* by ship for India, to stand trial. A positivist and pro-India enthusiast to the end, Cotton died on 22 October 1915 at his home, 45 St John's Wood Park, London, and was cremated three days later at Golders Green.  EDWARD C. MOULTON

**Sources** E. C. Moulton, 'Early Indian nationalism: Henry Cotton and the British positivist and radical connection, 1870–1915', *Journal of Indian History*, 60 (1982), 125–59 • H. Cotton, *Indian and home memories* (1911) • H. Cotton, *Indian speeches and addresses* (1903) • G. H. Forbes, *Positivism in Bengal* (1975) • m. cert. • *Guardian* (25 Oct 1915)
**Archives** BL OIOC, corresp. and papers, MS Eur. D 1202 | BL, letters to Richard Congreve, Add. MS 45228 • BL, corresp. with Lord Ripon, Add. MS 43618 • BL OIOC, Dufferin, Curzon MSS • National Archives of India, New Delhi, Gokhale MSS

**Likenesses**  H. G. Riviere, oils?, 1903, repro. in Cotton, *Indian and home memories* · photographs, repro. in Cotton, *Indian and home memories*
**Wealth at death**  £1769 4s. od.: probate, 1 Dec 1915, *CGPLA Eng. & Wales*

**Cotton, Jack** (1903–1964), property developer, was born at Edgbaston, Birmingham, on 1 January 1903, the third son of Benjamin Marcus Cotton and his wife, Caroline Josephine Rudelsheim. His father was an import–export merchant with a flourishing trade in silver plate cutlery to South Africa, and treasurer of Birmingham's chief synagogue. Cotton was educated at King Edward VI's Grammar School, Birmingham, and afterwards in the Jewish house at Cheltenham College. At the age of eighteen he was articled to a firm of Birmingham estate agents, and subsequently passed the examinations of the Auctioneers' Institute. Against his father's wishes his mother lent him £50, and on his twenty-first birthday he opened his own estate agency in Birmingham. He worked single-handedly as agent, auctioneer, rent collector, and typist until 1926, when he hired his first staff. Cotton married in 1928 Marjorie Rachel, daughter of Moss Mindelsohn. They had three sons and one daughter before separating in the 1940s.

In the early 1930s Cotton laid the basis of his fortune by acting as a middleman between farmers and speculative builders interested in suburban ribbon development around Birmingham. He also often acted for the builders in selling these houses. His first great development (undertaken with a Birmingham solicitor, Joseph Cohen) was the demolition of the grammar school in New Street where he had been a pupil, and its replacement with the office block called King Edward House. His redevelopment of the site of the Midland Conservative Club was another such scheme. Cotton and Cohen also led a syndicate which developed Birmingham's first block of luxury flats, Kenilworth Court, in 1935, but the market proved sluggish, and thereafter Cotton avoided residential developments. He became a rich man with a strong local reputation: when the Air Ministry needed a shadow armaments factory in the Birmingham area in 1938, it approached Cotton for help.

During the Second World War Cotton served in the Home Guard and was employed by the government in factory building. He was a British delegate of the World Jewish Congress in 1945, and visited the USA in the cause of Zionist emigration to Palestine. He was a benefactor of many Jewish charities, endowing chairs of architecture and fine arts at the Hebrew University in Jerusalem, and the chair of biochemistry at Israel's Weizmann Institute. He also gave £250,000 to the zoological gardens in Regent's Park, and £100,000 to the Royal College of Surgeons. He was nevertheless disappointed in his hopes of a knighthood.

Cotton moved to London after the war, living in a suite at the Dorchester Hotel on Park Lane, and operating in the London property market. After forming the City of Birmingham Real Property Company to redevelop blitzed sites in the midlands and elsewhere, he bought control in 1947 of a shell company with a quotation on the London stock exchange, Mansion House Chambers Ltd, and appointed his accountant as chairman. During the early 1950s he bought, sold, and reconstructed several property companies before consolidating his interests in 1955 in a company called City Centre Properties. Although he conceived and implemented all the deals, and was City Centre's major shareholder, he preferred to act through nominees and for many years kept off the boards of his companies. In 1958, at the insistence of institutional shareholders, he became chairman of City Centre.

Building restrictions imposed during the war were enforced until 1954, and Cotton made a fortune out of the shortage of office space. After he had built several office blocks for the civil service his schemes became so big that he could not finance them by himself. In 1955 he took Legal and General Assurance as a partner for a proposed £7 million development of the Monico site in Piccadilly, and in the following year initiated a development partnership with Pearl Insurance. This type of arrangement was widely copied. Cotton was also the first developer to realize that pension funds were ideal partners for property companies because their investment managers could take a longer view than those in insurance companies, especially as their investments were tax-free. In the early 1960s Cotton undertook major developments in association with the pension funds of companies such as ICI, Imperial Tobacco, and Unilever.

In 1958–9 Cotton launched a programme of developments in South Africa and the West Indies in which Barclays Bank (Dominion, Colonial, and Overseas) had a holding of 20 per cent. In 1959 City Centre took a half-interest in the $100 million scheme for the 59-storey Pan Am tower over Grand Central Station in New York. During 1960–61 City Centre merged with Walter Flack's Murrayfield Properties and Charles Clore's City and Central Investments to create the biggest property company in the world, called City Centre, with a stock market valuation (somewhat inflated) of £65 million. Cotton remained chairman.

Cotton's business methods proved inadequate for these new conditions. His staff had hitherto comprised only a few accountants, clerks, and typists who were seldom privy to his confidence. He kept the details of his deals in his head, or in a few files which were heaped on the spare bed in his suite at the Dorchester. After clashes with both Clore and institutional shareholders, Cotton relinquished City Centre's chairmanship in July 1963. His shares in the company (held by family trusts) were sold in November for about £8.5 million to a consortium headed by Kenneth Keith and Sir Isaac Wolfson. A month after leaving City Centre's board in February 1964, Cotton died of heart disease at Frilsham House, New Providence, Nassau, in the Bahamas, on 21 March 1964.

In business Cotton was quick, sharp, calculating, and opportunistic. His private character was ebullient and noisy. He disliked solitude and drank heavily in his later years. Having always shunned publicity, he was the object of intense journalistic interest after 1955, and often treated as a new King Midas. His suite at the Dorchester was a gathering place from which his truer friends were gradually driven away by sly sycophants, who would ply him with drink and tempt him to indiscretions. His consuming interest in life was property development; although he collected Impressionist paintings, his inspiration was chiefly pecuniary. Apart from the potential profit, the governing criterion of his developments was size, and even when he employed an architect such as Walter Gropius the results were seldom pleasing. Having disfigured many prime sites in London, Cotton conceived a need to redevelop Piccadilly, and from 1960 brought forward a series of grandiose proposals which fortunately were rejected. His most enduring monuments are therefore eyesores like the Big Top complex in Birmingham or the shopping centre at Notting Hill Gate in London.

RICHARD DAVENPORT-HINES

**Sources** R. P. T. Davenport-Hines, 'Cotton, Jack', *DBB* · S. Aris, *The Jews in business* (1970) · C. J. P. Booker, *The neophiliacs* (1969) · D. Channon, *The service industries* (1978) · *Daily Mirror* (23 March 1964) · E. L. Erdman, *People and property* (1982) · S. Jenkins, *Landlords to London* (1975) · O. Marriott, *The property boom* (1967) · A. Sampson, *Anatomy of Britain* (1962) · B. P. Whitehouse, *Partners in property* (1964) · *The Times* (23 March 1964) · b. cert. · *DNB*
**Likenesses** D. Low, drawings, 1960?, NPG
**Wealth at death** £1,176,074: probate, 19 June 1964, *CGPLA Eng. & Wales*

**Cotton, John** [John of Afflighem] (*fl. c.*1100), music theorist, was the author of a frequently cited and widely transmitted treatise, *De musica*, written about 1100. John and his treatise were long thought to be English on the strength of the opening words of a dedicatory letter with which the treatise begins, addressing 'Domini et patri suo venerabili Anglorum antisti [or episcopo] Fulgentio' ('To his venerable lord and father, Fulgentius, bishop of the English'; *Johannes Affligemensis*, 44). But evidence that John bore the surname Cotto or Cotton (itself not necessarily an English name) is slender; this name appears in only two of the nineteen principal manuscripts (in one of these it is an addition in a later hand), and it is not original to any of the surviving twelfth-century copies. Regarding Fulgentius, no English ecclesiastic of this name is documented, and scholars now generally accept that the dedication is to Abbot Fulgentius (1089–1121) of Afflighem, near Brussels. John may therefore have been a Lorrainer or a Fleming, and the name John Cotton has been rejected by many in favour of the coinage John of Afflighem, following the lead of Smits van Waesberghe. Nothing, however, rules out the possibility that Fulgentius (and John) were Englishmen residing abroad. Taking *fulgens* ('illustrious') as a descriptor rather than a name, Flindell has argued more speculatively that John was an English monk associated with the Norman abbey at Bec who dedicated his work to Anselm of Canterbury (d. 1109).

Whatever the nationalities of author and dedicatee, a solid case can now be made that geographically the treatise is Swiss-German in origin, having been written in the region between St Gallen and Bamberg. Decisive evidence for this conclusion has been drawn by Huglo from its tonary, and by Palisca from the provenances of the earliest surviving manuscript copies, the citations of uncommon chants or unfamiliar versions of chants, the mention of tonal letters to designate the modes, the earlier writers named by John, and the later medieval writers who quote John. The *De musica*, modelled on the *Micrologus* (*c.*1026–8) of Guido d'Arezzo, is directed to the boys of a choir school. It covers practical topics they would need to know for the performance and invention of plainchants and polyphony, including notation, pitch letter-names, intervals and their proportions, solmization syllables, transposition, the system of tetrachords, and the division of the monochord. The final four of its twenty-seven chapters comprise a tonary.

PETER M. LEFFERTS

**Sources** *Hucbald, Guido, and John on music: three medieval treatises*, ed. C. V. Palisca, trans. W. Babb (1978) · *Johannes Affligemensis: De musica cum tonario*, ed. J. Smits van Waesberghe (1950) · M. Huglo, 'L'auteur de traité de musique dédié à Fulgence d'Afflighem', *Revue Belge de Musicologie*, 31 (1977), 5–19 · M. Huglo, *Les tonaires: inventaire, analyse, comparaison* (1971) · J. Smits van Waesberghe, ed., *Codex Oxoniensis Bibliothecae Bodleianae Rawlinson C 270, pars A 'De vocum consonantiis' ac 'De re musica'* (1979) · E. Flindell, 'Joh[ann]is Cottonis', *Musica Disciplina*, 20 (1966), 11–30 · E. Flindell, 'Joh[ann]is Cottonis, corrigenda et addenda', *Musica Disciplina*, 23 (1969), 7 · J. Smits van Waesberghe, 'John of Afflighem or John Cotton?', *Musica Disciplina*, 6 (1952), 146–53

**Cotton, John** (1585–1652), minister in America, was born on 4 December 1585 in Derby, the son of Roland Cotton, a lawyer, and his wife, Mary (*née* Hurlbert). He studied at Derby grammar school from the ages of nine to thirteen and then matriculated sizar at Trinity College, Cambridge. He graduated BA in 1603 and a year later he migrated to Emmanuel College, proceeding MA in 1606 and accepting a fellowship. Over the next six years he served as head lecturer, dean, and catechist of the college. During most of that period Thomas Hooker, another future New Englander, was also a member of the fellowship. It was during his stay at Cambridge that Cotton began to assume the character of a puritan. The preaching of William Perkins pricked his conscience while he was still an undergraduate. Ordained in 1610, his preaching was at first noted for an ornate and learned style, but he was gradually affected by the example of Richard Sibbes and adopted the more plain and direct style of that clergyman. Those who had appreciated Cotton's more florid preaching were disappointed in this change, but John Preston's contemporary biographer reported that Cotton's plain preaching had a strong influence on Preston, at the time a fellow of Queens' College and later master of Emmanuel. The statutes of Emmanuel were devised so as to encourage fellows into pastoral cures after a relatively brief time at the university and so in 1612, having obtained his BD two years earlier, Cotton departed Cambridge to become vicar of St Botolph's, Boston, Lincolnshire. Soon afterwards he married Elizabeth Horrocks.

**English ministry** At St Botolph's Cotton combined an effective pastoral ministry with service to aspiring clergymen and young ministers. He refused to conform to liturgical practices that he felt were not justified in scripture, including making the sign of the cross in baptism, wearing the surplice, and kneeling to receive communion. Twice, in 1615 and 1621, his nonconformity led to brief suspensions from his ministry, but his positive relations with his diocesan bishops and the strong support of the Boston community led to the suspensions being lifted on both those occasions. He was on particularly good terms with Bishop John Williams of Lincoln, but became more vulnerable towards the end of the 1620s as Williams himself became alienated from Charles I.

In addition to his Sunday sermons Cotton preached in the early morning on Thursdays and Fridays and on Saturday afternoons. His preaching was such as to attract believers from the surrounding countryside, including Anne Hutchinson, who travelled 24 miles on many occasions to feast on Cotton's sermons. Many of his English sermons were published, though not until after he had migrated to Massachusetts. On occasion, as in his *A Commentary on First John* (1656), he spoke of the imperfections of the Church of England, but he was far more critical of separatism. He tended to direct his words to those members of his congregation who had received a saving experience of God's grace, using affective language and analogies to evoke a sense of God's love to his saints. This was especially noticeable in his *Brief Exposition of the Whole Book of Canticles* (1642). Yet, in his English sermons in particular, Cotton did preach God's law in his attempts to reach out to those members of the congregation who had not yet experienced God's grace. In *The Way of Life* (1641), for example, he discusses the preparatory graces whereby a sinner recognizes his sinfulness and loathes himself, yet is enabled by grace to follow the preacher's guidance in praying and humiliating himself before God. In 1618, troubled both by the popularity of Arminian doctrines of man's positive role in the process of salvation and by the rigour of William Perkins's formulation of strict predestination, Cotton composed a manuscript treatise on God's decrees which he shared with a neighbouring minister. Cotton stressed the demonstration of God's justice and grace in the decree of predestination and portrayed reprobation as non-election. He argued that God offered salvation to all and that those who are condemned are damned for refusing to do what they can do. This scribal publication came into the hands of William Twisse, who argued that Cotton's views came dangerously close to the Arminian heresy. While he later claimed that he had cleared Twisse's concerns before he left England, it is noticeable that Cotton steered clear of these matters in his later sermons and publications.

Reforming clergy like Cotton sustained themselves in part through the support of friends and fellow puritans, and correspondence was an important means of holding this network together. Cotton earned a reputation as a powerful adviser to embattled or confused clergy. John Norton, Cotton's successor in the Boston, New England, pulpit and his first biographer, wrote that 'he answered many letters that were sent far and near, wherein were handled many difficult cases of conscience, and many doubts by him cleared to the greatest satisfaction'

(Norton). His advice ranged from issues of ecclesiastical conformity to guidance on mixed dancing by clergymen, card-playing, and drawing names for valentines. This advice was a major factor in his growing eminence in the puritan community in the 1610s and 1620s.

Cotton also shaped young aspirants for the ministry by conducting an informal seminary in his household. Preston, now master of Emmanuel, recommended likely candidates, who included Thomas Hill, Samuel Winter, John Angier, and Anthony Tuckney. Students from the continent, such as Maximillian Teelinck, also journeyed to Boston to live with and study with Cotton. In his life of John Angier, Oliver Heywood related how when Angier was living with the Boston clergyman, Cotton took advantage of everyday occasions such as meals and rides through the countryside to converse and instruct his pupil.

**Migration** By the end of the 1620s Cotton was finding it increasingly difficult to ward off demands for his conformity and began to consider his choices. He was a friend of some of those who were promoting the Massachusetts Bay colony and in April 1630 he journeyed to Southampton to deliver the farewell sermon to the 400 emigrating settlers of the Winthrop fleet. Published as *God's Promise to his Plantation* (1630), the sermon contained a justification of the colonizing enterprise, an exhortation that the colonists live godly lives, and an encouragement to the conversion of the natives. But at that time Cotton was not prepared to leave England himself.

In April 1631 Cotton's wife, Elizabeth, died after eighteen years of marriage and between January and September the following year he married Sarah (*née* Hawkridge), widow of John Story. Shortly afterwards the couple were separated when he was forced into hiding to avoid prosecution for nonconformity. Early in 1631 he had been cited to appear before the court of high commission. At about this time he and his old Emmanuel colleague Thomas Hooker, who was likewise under attack, were invited to the home of the Revd Henry Whitefield, at Ockley in Surrey, to discuss their nonconformist stance with Thomas Goodwin, Philip Nye, John Davenport, Twisse, and other friends who sought to persuade them to compromise their objections to church practice so that their ministry would not be lost to the English church. The tables were turned during the debates, with Cotton and Hooker persuading their friends, or some of them, of the idolatrous nature of some of the disputed church ceremonies and that under the changed circumstances of the day conformity was no longer an option. Goodwin, Nye, and Davenport quickly joined Cotton and Hooker in demonstrating their nonconformity, and all would soon depart England as a result.

Cotton resigned his Boston living in May 1633 and on 13 July sailed for New England with Hooker and the Revd Samuel Stone. He and others 'came to the judgement', he later wrote:

> that by the free preaching of the word and the actual practice of our church discipline we could offer a much clearer and fuller witness in another land than in the wretched and loathsome prisons of London, where there

would be no opportunity for books or pens or friends or conferences.　(Cotton, preface to *Answer … by John Norton*, 11)

He always remained sensitive, however, to the charge that he had abandoned his parishioners and the community of saints in England.

**Massachusetts ministry** Although while in England he had expressed his criticisms of what he feared were the separatist tendencies of New England congregational practice, following his arrival Cotton quickly accepted and helped to advance that system of church polity. He and his wife, Sarah, were admitted to the Boston, Massachusetts, church on 8 September 1633 and presented their son Seaborn, delivered on the Atlantic crossing, for baptism, having delayed until they were members of a congregational church. A fast was kept in the Boston church on 10 October and Cotton was invited to join John Wilson in the ministry in the office of teacher. According to John Winthrop, as a result of his preaching, in the months that followed 'more were converted and added to that church [t]hen to all the other churches in the Bay' (*Journal of John Winthrop*, 106). This is borne out by the records of the church which show that in the four months following Cotton's arrival the membership of the church grew from 80 to 124, with 93 additional men and women joining in 1634. This success, his reputation in England, and his location in the colony's foremost church elevated him quickly to the front ranks of the colonial clergy. He also continued to work for the reform of the Church of England through correspondence with friends in England and exiles in the Netherlands.

Cotton soon became a valued adviser to the magistrates of the Bay colony, who called upon his advice on various matters. He wrote a response to Lord Saye and Sele, Lord Brooke, and 'other persons of quality' who had written in 1636 to the newly arrived and elected governor, Henry Vane, seeking assurances that if they migrated they would be a hereditary aristocracy with seats in what they proposed to be a colonial House of Lords, holding veto power over all government actions. While Cotton assured them that they would be honoured and chosen magistrates, he spoke on behalf of the colonial leadership in rejecting the idea of a hereditary aristocracy. 'Where God blesseth any branch of any noble or generous family with a spirit and gifts for government', he wrote,

> it would be a taking of God's name in vain to put such a talent under a bushel, and a sin against the honor of magistracy to neglect such in our public elections. But if God should not to delight to furnish some of their posterity with gifts fit for magistracy, we should expose them rather to reproach and prejudice, and all the commonwealth with them, than exalt them to honor if we should call them forth, when God doth not, to public authority.　(Bush, *Cotton Correspondence*)

The colonial magistrates and freemen were divided over the desirability of the amount of judicial discretion to allow magistrates, with some favouring restricting such freedom with a code of law. While John Winthrop was the foremost exponent of discretion, Cotton sided with those favouring a code. Chosen by the legislature as a member of a committee charged with codification, Cotton in October 1636 presented 'a model of Moses his judicials' which sought to base colonial practice on scriptural patterns. Rejected in Massachusetts as departing too far from normal English practice, the code did become the basis for the laws of New Haven, the colony established by Cotton's friend John Davenport. Of opposite opinions regarding legal practice, Cotton did side with John Winthrop in believing that, although the cross in the English ensign was idolatrous, Salem's John Endecott had been precipitate in cutting it out without consultation with his fellow magistrates.

Cotton's strong opposition to separatism made him a leading opponent of Roger Williams and contributed to the latter's exile from Massachusetts Bay in 1635. Shortly afterwards, however, Cotton himself became involved in a crisis that threatened his own future in the colony. The trigger to the controversy was Anne Hutchinson, who had followed Cotton to the New World and to Boston. Having arrived when John Wilson had returned for a time to England, she was shocked upon Wilson's return by what she interpreted as the pastor's advocacy of a covenant of works. Listening to other clergy on lecture days, she and her supporters became convinced that all the colonial clergy except Cotton and her newly arrived brother-in-law John Wheelwright implied in their teaching that works could save. Seeking not the toleration of her own more spiritist opinions, but rather the establishment of her views (which she claimed were derived from Cotton) as a new orthodoxy, she soon gathered a substantial following in the Boston church. Most prominent among her supporters was Governor Vane. Cotton sympathized with Hutchinson's criticisms of clerical overemphasis on preparation and on sanctification as evidence of election. This and his efforts to heal the developing split led many of the clerical majority, particularly Thomas Shepard, to doubt Cotton's own orthodoxy.

Following Vane's defeat by John Winthrop in the 1636 gubernatorial election, the tide began to turn. Before a synod held in August 1637 at Cambridge, Massachusetts, his fellow clergymen presented Cotton with a set of questions intended to clarify his views and force him into the open if he indeed was the source of Hutchinson's teachings. The synod then proceeded to define a set of errors believed to be held by the Hutchinsonians, after which Cotton gradually began to distance himself from the faction. John Wheelwright was tried and banished for incendiary comments made in a fast-day sermon. Supporters of Wheelwright and Hutchinson were disarmed and in some cases banished. Anne Hutchinson herself was tried and convicted both by the colony's general court and by the Boston church and departed for Rhode Island. Cotton eventually fully dissociated himself from her extreme opinions, but temporarily lost much of his stature.

**Spokesman for congregationalism** The outbreak of the civil wars in England brought Cotton back to prominence. With Hooker and Davenport, he was invited to sit in the Westminster assembly of divines that had been called to reform the English church. They declined, choosing instead to advance the cause by sending to England written advice based on the New England experience. In tune with his fellow colonists Cotton supported the parliamentary cause and in particular the cause of congregational Independency being promoted by his friends Thomas Goodwin and Philip Nye, who helped to see colonial works into print in England. Cotton's major contributions were *The Way of the Churches of Christ in New England* (1641) and *The Keyes of the Kingdom of Heaven* (1644). Attacked by Robert Baillie, a Scottish proponent of a presbyterian settlement for England, he responded with *The Way of the Congregational Churches Cleared* (1648). Cotton advocated congregationalism but sought accommodation with the presbyterians and expressed that hope in one of his last works, *Certain Queries Tending to Accommodation* (1655).

While presbyterian critics of the New England way like Baillie branded the colonies as a spawning ground for heresies, sectarian critics deplored the intolerance of Massachusetts. Responding to a letter in which Cotton had tried to turn him back towards orthodoxy, Roger Williams attacked the Bay clergy in *Mr Cotton's Letter Lately Printed, Examined and Answered* (1644). Cotton responded in *A Reply to Mr Williams* (1647), but in the meantime Williams had published his famous *The Bloudy Tenent of Persecution* (1644) which was designed in part to warn English sects from trusting their congregational allies in the Independent movement. Cotton responded with *The Bloudy Tenent, Washed and Made White in the Bloud of the Lambe* (1647). Williams had the last word in *The Bloudy Tenent yet More Bloody* (1652). Throughout this exchange Cotton maintained a position in keeping with that of Thomas Goodwin, Nye, and other English congregationalists, that 'Dissenters in fundamentals, and that out of obstinacy against conscience and seducers, to the perdition of souls, and to the disturbance of civil and church peace' were not to be tolerated, whereas toleration should be extended to 'such Dissenters as vary either in matters of less weight, or of fundamental, yet not out of wilful obstinacy, but out of tendency of conscience' (Cotton, 'Answer to Williams', 89). This indeed was the practice in New England. Unity was expected but not uniformity. Various shades of interpretation of fundamentals were tolerated so long as they did not contradict the orthodox consensus and provided those differences were not forced by zealous proponents. Those who kept their dissent quiet were undisturbed, and those who proselytized fundamental errors were subject to efforts to persuade them before action was taken to rid the colony of their presence. In practice, of course, individuals like Williams and Hutchinson were not likely to agree to keep quiet views which they were convinced represented the true explanation of God's way.

While engaging directly in the English polemical debates, Cotton also shared in the crafting of New England's official statement of faith and practice, the Cambridge Platform of 1648, a document intended to more firmly establish the New England way in America and to advance its adoption in England. Crafted by a synod that first met in September 1646, the Platform adopted the Westminster confession of faith which had been drafted by England's Westminster assembly, and set out in detail the nature of congregational polity as practised in New England. The Revd Richard Mather was primarily responsible for drafting the statement, but he drew heavily on Cotton's work, and the Boston clergyman prepared an important preface to the document.

In the years leading up to the conflict in England Cotton had begun to preach on the coming of the millennium. He expounded on this theme in a series of prophetic weekday lectures in Boston between 1639 and 1640, published as *An Exposition upon the Thirteenth Chapter of the Revelation* (1655), followed in the next year by *The Powring out of the Seven Vials* (1642) and *The Churches Resurrection* (1642). These contained harsh attacks on the Roman Catholic church as the seven-headed beast described in the book of Revelation, and in the later sermons a conviction that as the last days approached it was especially necessary for New England to remain true to its covenant with God. These works were especially popular in England as puritans tried to make sense of the conflict in which they became immersed in the 1640s. As that struggle continued Cotton preached forcefully on behalf of the parliamentary cause and came to see Oliver Cromwell as an agent of God. Early in 1651 Cotton preached a fast-day sermon in Boston that justified Pride's Purge and the execution of Charles I, hailed Cromwell's victory over the Scots at Dunbar as 'A greate & wonderfull Deliverance', and praised acts of the Commonwealth government as 'great workes of god' (Cotton, quoted in Bremer, 'In defense of regicide', 122–3). Writing to Cromwell in July 1651 he expressed himself 'fully satisfied, that you have all the while fought the Lord's battles, and the Lord hath owned you, and honored himself in you' (Hutchinson, 233–4). In his response Cromwell acknowledged Cotton as one 'whom I love and honor in the Lord', asked for his prayers, and enquired 'How shall we behave ourselves after such mercies? What is the Lord a-doing? What prophecies are now Fulfilling?' (ibid., 236–7). Although other correspondence does not survive, Roger Williams later contended that Cotton's views had influenced Cromwell's western design.

While engaged with events across the Atlantic, Cotton continued to address himself to fostering the New England way. He was an overseer of Harvard College, and contributed to the maintenance of a schoolmaster in Boston. He continued to advise the magistrates. *The Grounds and Ends of the Baptism of Children* (1647) addressed an issue that was increasingly debated in the mid-century. He prepared a catechism, *Milk for Babes* (1646), for the instruction of youth. He wrote occasional poetry and perhaps contributed some of the translations in the *Bay Psalm Book* (1640). His *Singing of Psalms a Gospel Ordinance* (1646) was the most detailed explanation of the puritan view of the use of the psalms in worship.

In December 1652 a comet was seen by the people of Boston. It was interpreted as a portent when, on 23 December, before its disappearance, Cotton died; he was buried in the Boston town burying-ground. He had been taken seriously ill early in the month after catching cold while crossing on the ferry to Cambridge to preach for a few days, and was reported to have great swelling of his legs and body. He was survived by his wife, Sarah, who on 26 August 1656 married Richard *Mather (1596–1669); she died on 27 May 1676.

Cotton's passing was greatly mourned by his contemporaries, and his reputation was advanced by his successor John Norton's biography, *Abel being Dead yet Speaketh* (1658) and by the writings of his grandson Cotton *Mather (1663–1728). He was, along with Hooker and Davenport, the most widely known and respected of the first generation of colonial clergy, but not as representative of colonial theological orthodoxy as the other two. Unlike most of his colleagues, he tended in his sermons and writings to shy away from discussions of the processes of conversion and to dwell more on the mystical joy that filled those who were born again. Nevertheless, he was the most forceful and influential of all the New Englanders in his advocacy of congregational church practice.

FRANCIS J. BREMER

**Sources** E. Emerson, *John Cotton*, rev. edn (1990) • *The correspondence of John Cotton*, ed. S. Bush (2001) • J. Norton, *Abel being dead yet speaketh* (1658) • J. Cotton, 'Master John Cottons answer to Roger Williams', *The complete writings of Roger Williams*, repr. (1963), vol. 3 [1647] • S. Bendall, C. Brooke, and P. Collinson, *A history of Emmanuel College, Cambridge* (1999) • *The journal of John Winthrop, 1630–1649*, ed. R. S. Dunn, J. Savage, and L. Yeandle (1996) • T. Hutchinson, *A collection of original papers relative to the history of the colony of Massachusetts* (1769) • F. J. Bremer, 'In defense of regicide: John Cotton on the execution of Charles I', *William and Mary Quarterly*, 37 (1980), 103–24 • J. Cotton, preface, in *The answer to the whole set of questions of the celebrated Mr William Appolonius by John Norton*, ed. and trans. D. Horton (Cambridge, MA, 1958) • S. Bush, 'Epistolary counseling in the puritan movement: the example of John Cotton', *Puritanism: transatlantic perspectives on a seventeenth-century Anglo-American faith*, ed. F. J. Bremer (1993) • F. J. Bremer, *Congregational communion: clerical friendship in the Anglo-American puritan community, 1610–1692* (1994) • R. C. Anderson, ed., *The great migration begins: immigrants to New England, 1620–1633*, 1 (Boston, MA, 1995) • S. Bush, 'Cotton, John', *ANB* • L. Ziff, *The career of John Cotton: puritanism and the American experience* (1962) • W. K. B. Stoever, *'A faire and easie way to heaven': covenant theology and antinomianism in early Massachusetts* (Middletown, Connecticut, 1978) • T. D. Bozeman, *To live ancient lives: the primitivist dimension in puritanism* (1988) • T. Toulouse, *The art of prophesying: New England sermons and the shaping of belief* (1987)

**Archives** Boston PL, corresp. • Mass. Hist. Soc., corresp. • Massachusetts State Archives, Boston, corresp. • New England Historic Genealogical Society, Boston, corresp.

**Wealth at death** inventory of estate valued at £1088 4*s*. 0*d*., incl. £470 in real estate and books worth £150

**Cotton, Sir John**, third baronet (1621–1702). *See under* Cotton, Sir Robert Bruce, first baronet (1571–1631).

**Cotton, Sir John**, fourth baronet (*c*.1680–1731). *See under* Cotton, Sir Robert Bruce, first baronet (1571–1631).

**Cotton, Sir John**, sixth baronet (*d*. 1752). *See under* Cotton, Sir Robert Bruce, first baronet (1571–1631).

**Cotton, John** (1802–1849), pastoralist and ornithologist in Australia, was born at Balham Hill, Surrey, the third son of William Cotton (1759–1816), a prosperous clerk in the London custom house, and his wife, Catherine Savery (*d*. 1803). An older brother was the art collector William Cotton (1794–1863). Cotton had a good education as a boy,

attending Crediton grammar school, then travelling round Britain and later Europe with a tutor, and apparently attended Oxford for a short time, where he studied law without taking a degree.

Cotton became attached to a firm of solicitors in Lincoln's Inn Fields but spent most of his time in art galleries, drawing and studying birds. In 1835 he published privately *The Resident Song Birds of Great Britain*, illustrated and hand-coloured by himself, reissued in expanded form with a new title (*The Song Birds of Great Britain*) either in late 1835 or early 1836, as the title-page is usually dated. The book reveals considerable artistic and observational talent. In 1841 he became a fellow of the Zoological Society, having before then attended a lecture series by Nicholas Vigors on the quinarian system of classification (based on groups of five) and taken copious notes. Cotton continued to use this distinctive system of animal classification long after it was abandoned in Britain. In the same year his younger brother Edward emigrated to New South Wales and Cotton decided to follow his example, emigrating on 19 January 1843, with his wife, Susannah, *née* Edwards (*d*. 1852), and nine children; their journey is commemorated in his *Journal of a Voyage in the Barque 'Parkfield'* (1845) which includes several of his poems. He took properties on the Goulburn River, near Port Phillip, eventually amounting to 30,000 acres; the family camped on the site while building a house.

Cotton lived for only six more years, during which time he wrote detailed, illustrated letters to his brother William in Devon, giving some of the most complete descriptions of bush life that have survived. These letters describe not only the hardship of a settler's life but also the natural history and indigenous population of the area. Cotton also remarks on contemporary events and literature, including scientific texts like *Vestiges of the Natural History of Creation* in 1846. All his spare time was otherwise dedicated to preparing an account of the birds of Port Phillip. This was never published in his lifetime although the illustrations survive and were issued as *John Cotton's Birds of the Port Phillip District* in 1974. Cotton seems to have felt the field was too well trodden by the famous ornithologist John Gould. The specimens he sent to his brother and to the naturalist Robert Hudson (possibly a cousin) were ungraciously received and did not sell. In 1848, however, he contributed a list of local birds to the *Tasmanian Journal of Natural Science*. Some of his earliest paintings of birds were collected and published in three volumes after his death by Robert Tyas.

Cotton was well known in Australian natural history circles and maintained a genteel interest in science and art. He experimented with daguerreotypes with Frank Gilbert, his children's tutor. Cotton died on 15 December 1849 on his farm after being ill for a few weeks. His doctor recorded acute rheumatism followed by brain fever as the cause.

JANET BROWNE

**Sources** M. Casey, 'John Cotton, 1802–1849', *Journal of the Society of the Bibliography of Natural History*, 4 (1962–8), 85–91 • M. Casey, *An Australian story* (1962) • C. Finney, *Paradise revealed: natural history in*

*nineteenth-century Australia* (1993) · *Correspondence of John Cotton, Victorian pioneer*, ed. G. Mackaness (1953) · *AusDB*
**Archives** Victoria Museum | Mitchell L., NSW, Gunn MSS · State Library of Victoria, Melbourne, La Trobe manuscript collection, Cotton family MSS
**Likenesses** portrait, priv. coll.; repro. in Casey, 'John Cotton, 1802–1849'

**Cotton, Sir John Hynde**, third baronet (*bap.* **1686**, *d.* **1752**), politician and Jacobite sympathizer, was baptized on 7 April 1686, the first and only surviving son of Sir John Cotton, second baronet (*c.*1647–1713), of Madingley Hall, Cambridgeshire, and his wife, Elizabeth Sheldon (*d.* 1714). The family's losses as staunch royalists in the civil war had been repaired by the second baronet through a fortunate marriage to the daughter and coheir of the merchant Sir Joseph Sheldon, lord mayor of London in 1675–6. Education at Westminster School and Emmanuel College, Cambridge, prepared the young Cotton for a parliamentary career, and he duly entered the House of Commons in 1708 as one of the members for Cambridge, a borough he represented continuously until 1722. Tall and handsome, with an imposing figure, which epic over-indulgence eventually turned to fat, he was inhibited from making long speeches by a stammer, but developed a technique which enabled him to intervene effectively, if necessarily crisply, in debate. By 1712 he had established enough of a reputation among tory back-benchers to secure election to the abortive commission of inquiry into crown grants, and had also attracted the attention of Lord Treasurer Oxford, who appointed him to the Board of Trade, at £1000 per annum.

Office did not make Cotton a moderate; he remained an active member of the October Club and the Loyal Brotherhood, the political dining society established by the duke of Beaufort. But although he undoubtedly consorted with Jacobites, there is no positive evidence of personal commitment to the Pretender. Indeed, he was reported to have said that 'he had been privy to no design bringing in the son of King James upon the Queen's death, but said that when he returned to London after that event, he found his old friends turned Jacobites' (Burnet, 3.356). Thus he was all the more disgusted to find himself dismissed from office in December 1714. In parliament under George I he did not immediately take up a position of prominence within the tory party, and in the various Jacobite conspiracies, real and imagined, of the period 1715 to 1722 his name is notable by its absence. He did not lose his place as a JP until 1726. In the parliament of 1722 he served as knight of the shire, but lost this seat in 1727 and was forced back on the borough of Cambridge, though at great cost (reputedly some £8000). With tory morale low and the party lacking firm leadership Cotton came to the fore, and by 1733 he was being described as one of 'the leaders of the Tories', even as 'the very head … of the violent (some will say the Jacobite) party' (*Egmont MSS*, 1.361). When Beaufort revived the Loyal Brotherhood, Cotton was one of its most active members. But even at this point there is little to link him directly with the Pretender. It was only in the early 1740s that he took part in Jacobite

intrigues and corresponded with the court at St Germain. He may have had material as well as political motives, for, despite two lucrative marriages, he was notoriously parsimonious; it was a frequent complaint of the Cambridge corporation that he did not do business there, but 'sent to London or anywhere else where he could purchase the cheapest' (BL, Add. MS 5841, fol. 337). As a result his standing in the town collapsed, and in the 1741 election he was obliged to fall back on a pocket borough; he was returned on the Bruce interest at Marlborough. His participation in the negotiations for a Jacobite invasion in 1740–45 was marked by extreme caution, especially when it came to making any personal commitment. On the fall of Sir Robert Walpole in 1742 his name was put forward for a seat on the Admiralty board, but the appointment was vetoed by the king, and Cotton promptly redoubled his efforts in opposition. Eventually George II was obliged to accept him as treasurer of the chamber in the so-called broad-bottom administration of 1744. The legendary size of Cotton's backside offered an irresistible target for satire, and in one caricature ministers were depicted preparing to thrust him down the throat of a reluctant monarch, to the accompaniment of such observations as 'his bottom's damn'd broad' (BM, 2613). Cotton did not heed the Jacobites' call during the rising of 1745; in fact, he kept his place in government and ostentatiously proclaimed his loyalty to the Hanoverian dynasty when the rebellion was over. But he was still dismissed from office a year later and returned to opposition.

Cotton's first wife, Lettice (*d.* 1718), whom he married on 24 May 1714, was a daughter of the great ironmaster Sir Ambrose Crowley, and brought a portion of £10,000. Following her death (leaving one son, the future fourth baronet) on 3 June 1724 he married Margaret (*d.* 1734), the daughter and coheir of James Craggs the elder and the widow of Samuel Trefusis. Cotton died at his house in Park Place, St James's, London, in the night of 4 February 1752, and was buried with his ancestors at Landwade in Cambridgeshire, where his funerary monument praised his 'integrity and manly conduct', and successful avoidance of 'faction' and 'invective' (*East Anglian*, 1, 1814, 344)—an improbable combination of virtues given his role in the politics of the 1740s. His obituary in the *Gentleman's Magazine* stressed his incorruptibility rather than his moderation and emphasized his constancy to 'country' principles: 'he lived, he died a patriot' (*GM*, 1st ser., 22, 1752, 92).

D. W. Hayton

**Sources** E. Cruickshanks, 'Cotton, John Hynde', HoP, *Commons, 1715–54* · HoP, *Commons, 1690–1715* [draft] · W. Cole, 'Gens Cottoniana Cantabrigiensis', copies, BL, Add. MS 5841 · W. Cole, 'Gens Cottoniana Cantabrigiensis', Cambs. AS, Cotton of Madingley MS 588/F43 · Cambs. AS, Cotton of Madingley papers · Royal Arch., Stuart papers · *DNB* · E. R. Edwards and G. Jagger, 'Cotton, John', HoP, *Commons, 1660–90* · *Manuscripts of the earl of Egmont: diary of Viscount Percival, afterwards first earl of Egmont*, 3 vols., HMC, 63 (1920–23) · H. Walpole, *Memoirs of King George II*, ed. J. Brooke, 3 vols. (1985) · L. Colley, *In defiance of oligarchy: the tory party, 1714–60* (1982) · E. Cruickshanks, *Political untouchables: the tories and the '45* (1979) · C. H. Cooper and J. W. Cooper, *Annals of Cambridge*, 5 vols. (1842–1908) · *East Anglian*, 1 (1814), 344 · *GM*, 1st ser., 22 (1752), 92 ·

*Bishop Burnet's History* · parish register, Madingley, Cambs. AS, P114/2 [baptism], 7 April 1686

**Archives** Cambs. AS, Cotton of Madingley MSS, estate and family papers, and copy of Cole, 'Gens Cottoniana Cantabrigiensis' | Royal Arch., Stuart MSS

**Likenesses** G. Kneller, oils; formerly at Madingley Hall, Cambs.

**Wealth at death** rent roll of estate in father's lifetime £1870 p.a.: Cambs. AS, Cotton of Madingley MSS, 588/E4

---

**Cotton, Joseph** (1745–1825), merchant, the second surviving son of Dr Nathaniel *Cotton (1705–1788), was born at St Albans on 7 March 1745 and entered the Royal Navy in 1760. After passing the examination for lieutenant he left the navy and was appointed fourth mate in the marine service of the East India Company. After two voyages, one as mate on the *Deptford* in the late 1760s, he assumed command of the *Queen Charlotte*, East Indiaman, and made two further journeys to the East. He retired in 1782 on the large private fortune he had acquired in the company's service, and lived for the rest of his life at Leyton in Essex. In 1779 Cotton married Sarah Harrison (1751–1818), daughter of John Harrison (1721–1794), a director of the East India Company. This family connection ensured that he retained an active interest in company politics after his retirement, but he also devoted considerable attention to maritime affairs.

In 1788 Cotton was elected an elder brother of Trinity House, and in 1803 deputy master, which office he held for about twenty years. In 1803 Trinity House raised a corps of volunteer artillery 1200 strong, of which William Pitt (as master) was colonel and Cotton lieutenant-colonel, to safeguard the mouth of the Thames against a foreign fleet. Cotton compiled a *Memoir on the Origin and Incorporation of the Trinity House of Deptford Strond* (1818), published without his name on the title-page, though it was appended to the dedication to Lord Liverpool. Shortly before this time the administration of Trinity House had been the subject of a parliamentary inquiry, and the special object of this work was to explain the public duties of the corporation and to defend the management of its large revenues. Incidentally the book gave much detailed information about the development of the lighting of the English coast.

Cotton was a director of the East India Company from 1795 to 1823; he was also a director of the East India Docks Company (chairman in 1803), and a governor of the London Assurance Corporation. In 1814 the Society for the Encouragement of Arts and Manufactures awarded to him a silver medal for the introduction into the country of rhea, or China grass, an eastern fibre of great strength and fineness.

Cotton died at Leyton on 26 January 1825, and was buried, with his wife and many others of his family, in a vault in the churchyard of the parish church. He was survived by three sons, Joseph (1780–1828), John (1783–1860), and William *Cotton (1786–1866).

J. S. COTTON, *rev.* H. V. BOWEN

**Sources** *Lloyd's List and Shipping Gazette* (16 Nov 1928) · *Genealogist's Magazine*, 6 (1932–3) · *GM*, 1st ser., 95/1 (1825), 189 · personal knowledge (1887) · J. Cotton, *Memoir on the origin and incorporation of the Trinity Home of Deptford Strond* (1818) · J. Cotton, *A review of the shipping system of the East India Company* (1798) · will, PRO, PROB 11/1695,

sig. 62 · parish register, St Albans, St Peter, 29 March 1745 [baptism]

**Archives** BL, letters to second earl of Liverpool · BL, letters to second Lord Spencer, Add. MSS 38243–38327 · BL OIOC, journal, MS Eur. C 0556

**Likenesses** W. Ward, mezzotint, pubd 1808 (after T. Stewardson), BM · C. Turner, mezzotint, pubd 1818 (after portrait by T. Lawrence), BL OIOC, NPG · Chantrey, marble bust, Trinity House

---

**Cotton** [*née* Robson; *other married names* Mowbray, Ward, Robinson], **Mary Ann** (1832–1873), poisoner, was born at Low Moorsley, co. Durham, on 12 October 1832, the elder daughter of teenage parents, Michael Robson (d. 1846), miner, and his wife, Mary, *née* Lonsdale (d. 1867). She is reputed to have killed by the administration of arsenic at least eighteen people, although some estimates place the total considerably higher. There is no evidence that she was deranged; her motives were apparently the desire for improvement to her circumstances and for frequent changes of sexual partner.

Mary Ann Robson was a pretty child with dark hair and eyes; she was a chapel-goer and, in her teens, a teacher at a Wesleyan Methodist Sunday school. Rumour later circulated that as a child she had pushed a boy to his death down a pit shaft. Her father died in a pit accident in 1846; her mother subsequently married George Stott, and opened a school in Murton. Mary Ann had worked as a nursemaid for three years before returning to help her mother with the school and to learn dressmaking. On 18 July 1852, and already pregnant, she married William Mowbray, a 26-year-old labourer, at Newcastle register office. They travelled around the country for several years in search of work, producing several children, all but one of whom died, possibly from natural causes. About 1856 they returned to Hendon, near Sunderland, where three more children were born; the eldest of these four survivors died within the year. Mowbray took out a life insurance policy on the three remaining children and his own life, and died in September 1864; two of the children rapidly followed him, the cause of death being given as diarrhoea, a common killer in those times. No suspicions were aroused, and Mary Ann collected about £30 from the insurance.

The remaining child was sent to live with Mary Ann's mother, and the widow took up with one Joseph Nattrass, who soon left her to marry another woman. She became a nurse on the fever ward of Sunderland Hospital, where she earned praise for her work from the doctor in charge, and married, on 28 August 1865, a good-looking patient, George Ward, an engineer. She had hoped that this marriage would improve her social position, but Ward's ill health prevented him from working; he died from 'fever' in October 1866. A month later she became housekeeper to James Robinson, shipwright, a widower with five children, and soon became his mistress, bearing him a child. The youngest of the Robinson children died in 1867. At about this time Mary Stott asked Mary Ann to resume the care of her surviving daughter by her first marriage, and, after Mary Ann had removed a quantity of household goods from the Stott house, Mary Stott died unexpectedly on 15 March 1867. Mary Ann returned to Robinson and her prospects of marriage. Her daughter and two of the Robinson children died in the last days of April and early May 1867; despite the disapproval of his three suspicious sisters, Robinson married her on 11 August 1867 at Bishopwearmouth church. Another child soon arrived and departed, but a second was to survive its mother. In 1869 Robinson began to suspect, correctly, that his wife was cheating him over the housekeeping money and his building society savings; she departed with the baby (whom she soon abandoned with friends, and who was returned to its father), and never returned.

For a while Mary Ann lived with a sailor, whose possessions she stole while he was at sea, and early in 1870 she became housekeeper, and in due course mistress, to Frederick Cotton of North Walbottle, a widower with three children. (Mary Ann had known his sister, Margaret, when she was in service.) By April 1870 Margaret and the youngest Cotton child were dead, and Mary Ann was pregnant. Cotton married her, bigamously, on 17 September 1870 at St Andrew's Church, Newcastle. The family moved from Walbottle to Johnson Terrace, West Auckland, after neighbours accused Mary Ann of poisoning their pigs, to which she had taken a dislike. Cotton would not insure the family as Mary Ann had hoped, and by September 1871 she was grieving ostentatiously for Cotton and two of the children, and was in receipt of funds provided by sympathetic neighbours and free coal from local mine owners.

Again 'widowed', Mary Ann found that her former lover Joseph Nattrass, now a widower himself, was living nearby, and he became her lodger. He made a will in her favour, and, her fancy having been taken by an exciseman called Quick-Manning, by whom she was yet again pregnant, Nattrass died on 1 April 1872, leaving her £10 and a watch. Mary Ann's only encumbrance now was her seven-year-old stepson, Charles Edward Cotton. On poor relief herself, Mary Ann tried to have him placed with an uncle or in the workhouse. The master of the workhouse, a shopkeeper named Riley, became suspicious when she predicted that Charles, a scrofulous, macrocephalic child, whom the neighbours said she maltreated, would soon follow the rest of his family into the grave. When the boy died on 12 July 1872 Riley informed the local police, who held an inquiry. A slipshod autopsy did not reveal any sign of poisoning, and Mary Ann indignantly accused Riley of attempting to besmirch her reputation. But the doctor, who had visited Charles Edward the day before his death, carried out a second examination of the contents of the child's stomach. This revealed the presence of arsenic. The bodies of Nattrass and two of the Cotton children were exhumed and found to contain arsenic (Frederick Cotton's body could not be found). Mary Ann, who was deserted by Quick-Manning, was arrested and charged with the murder of Charles Edward Cotton.

The trial was postponed until after the birth of Mary Ann's baby in January 1873, eventually taking place before a smartly dressed audience between 5 and 7 March at the Durham assizes. The defence argued that the child had inhaled arsenic fumes from green paint on the wallpaper;

this defence was plausible, especially as there was no evidence that she had administered the poison, but evidence was offered that Mary Ann had purchased arsenic, ostensibly for treating bedbugs, and the results of the exhumations of the other victims were admitted as evidence. She was found guilty, and an appeal to the home secretary was refused. She was executed in Durham gaol, making no confession, on 24 March 1873 by the notoriously clumsy hangman William Calcraft, and hung choking for three minutes before she died. She was buried in the gaol on the same day. Her responsibility for the other deaths which had surrounded her was retrospectively surmised. Mary Ann Cotton, the 'Lucretia Borgia of the North', was, as far as can be ascertained, Britain's most prolific female killer; a street rhyme, beginning

Mary Ann Cotton
She's dead and she's rotten

kept the memory of her crimes alive in the north-east.

J. GILLILAND

**Sources** A. Appleton, *Mary Ann Cotton: her story and trial* (1973) · *The Times* (5 Oct 1872), 9f · *The Times* (7 Oct 1872), 10f · *The Times* (13 Dec 1872), 10d · *The Times* (26 Feb 1873), 11e · *The Times* (6 March 1873), 10f · *The Times* (7 March 1873), 11e · *The Times* (8 March 1873), 11e · J. Robins, *Lady killers* (1993) · J. Robins and P. Arnold, *Serial killers* (1993) · M. Farrell, *Poisons and poisoners* (1994) · J. H. H. Gaute, *Murderers' who's who* (1979), 73–5 · *Cox's reports of cases in criminal law*, 12 (1875), 400–03 · B. O'Donnell, 'Mary Ann Cotton, Britain's mass murderess', *The mammoth book of killer women*, ed. R. G. Jones (1993), 182–8 · T. Manners, *Deadlier than the male* (1995) · A. Vincent, *A gallery of poisoners* (1993) · D. Dunbar, *Blood in the parlour* (1964), 20–24 · R. S. Lambert, *When justice faltered* (1935), 108–37 · J. R. Nash, *Look for the woman* (1981), 106–8

**Likenesses** portrait, repro. in north of England newspapers, 1873 · print, repro. in *Illustrated Police News* (16 Nov 1872) · woodcut, repro. in Appleton, *Mary Ann Cotton*

**Cotton, Nathaniel** (1705–1788), poet and physician, was born in London to Samuel Cotton, a Levant merchant. No record of his birth survives, although a Nathaniel Cotton, son of Samuel and Mary Cotton, was baptized on 12 March 1706 in Bull Lane Independent Chapel, Stepney. Most histories of Cotton begin as Robert Anderson's 1795 sketch does—with laments on the deficit of biographical details. Cotton would no doubt smile at such objections. As he writes in 'An Epistle to the Reader', in his most famous (and originally, anonymous) work, *Visions in Verse*:

All my Ambition is, I own,
To profit and to please unknown.

Cotton trained as a physician in Leiden, under Hermann Boerhaave. He matriculated as a medical student on 23 September 1729, and graduated MD on 7 August 1730. His twenty-eight-page Latin thesis *Dissertatio medica inauguralis, de variolis* also bears this date. According to a *Gentleman's Magazine* memoir, on his return to England Cotton succeeded one Dr Crawley, of Dunstable, Bedfordshire, 'who received insane persons under his care'. About 1738 Cotton married Anne Pembroke (*d.* 1749). They had seven children, five of whom survived infancy, including Joseph *Cotton (1745–1825). About 1740 Cotton's practice moved to St Albans, where he kept a private madhouse called the Collegium insanorum on Dagnall Street near the abbey, and lived with his family on St Peter's Street. After his wife's death in 1749, on 22 August 1751 Cotton married Hannah Everett (d. 1772), and with her had a son, John, and two daughters, Elizabeth and an infant. Boerhaave's eclectic, holistic medical system, which combined aspects of botany, anatomy, and theology, remained influential on his student. Cotton's epistolary *Observations on a particular kind of scarlet fever, that lately prevailed in and about St. Alban's* (1749) displays conscientious observation and a reluctance to prescribe panaceas. Instead, Cotton discusses the efficacy of individualized treatments ranging from opiates to bleeding to 'draughts of *sperma ceti* and nitre' diluted in white wine whey, and recommends 'air and a restorative diet' for febrile patients suffering melancholy. Cotton's professional reputation was secured not by this tract, however, but by his association with the poets William Cowper and Edward Young. Cowper resided in Cotton's madhouse during his second period of mental illness, from December 1763 to 17 June 1765. In *Adelphi* Cowper hints at the doctor's methods for vanquishing the religious doubts which caused his madness. Cowper writes that he was 'closely confined' and 'narrowly watched' by servants, and that Cotton 'visited me every morning while I stayed with him … the Gospel was always the delightful theme of our conversation'. Bibles carefully placed on a garden bench and a window seat (opening to the story of Lazarus and Romans 3:25's promise of salvation) restored Cowper's faith in divine grace at critical moments (*Letters and Prose*, 1.33–9). Such care was not without an earthly price. In a letter to Joseph Hill dated 14 August 1765 Cowper mentions that he owes Cotton at least £140. Cotton, who 'was very fond of Dr Young's company and greatly venerated his mental abilities', also attended Young in his final illness, though as a friend rather than as the presiding physician; he describes Young's character and his deathbed 'martyrdom' in a touching letter to an unknown correspondent dated 5 April 1765.

As a moralistic poet Cotton achieved considerable contemporary acclaim. His *Visions in Verse for the Entertainment and Instruction of Younger Minds*, first published anonymously in 1751, was reprinted twelve times over the next forty years, and appeared in new editions and poetical miscellanies well into the next century. The nine Visions are allegories depicting Slander, Pleasure, Health, Content, Happiness, Friendship, Marriage, Life, and Death. Each stresses the importance of religious reflection, retirement, and contentment in one's assigned work and social station. 'Death, Vision the Last' contains a typical exhortation to self-examination:

> Explore thy Body and thy Mind,
> Thy station too, why here assign'd.

Cotton employs contemplative, beneficent graveyard imagery. As the narrator approaches Death, he is astonished to see its monstrous aspect become 'divinely fair'. Perhaps not coincidentally, it was this collection which recommended Cotton to Young's notice. Following his second wife's death in 1772 Cotton remained a widower.

He died at St Albans on 2 August 1788, and was buried with his wives in St Peter's churchyard, St Albans.

In 1791 Cotton's son the Revd Nathaniel Cotton published *Various pieces in verse and prose by the late Nathaniel Cotton, M.D., many of which were never before published*. Its two volumes collect the *Visions*, fables, occasional verses such as the frequently anthologized poem 'The Fireside', Horatian odes, and five sermons. The third sermon, concerning Psalm 19, verse 12, 'Who can understand his errors? Cleanse thou me from secret faults', offers an interesting parallel to Cowper's 'Self-acquaintance'. Cotton's fables refer to family members and seem intended for private use. In 'A Fable' gentle autobiographical satire unfolds as a poetic Owl, puffed with praise, hoots that he will replace Colley Cibber as poet laureate. His owl-wife begs him to abandon poetry for physic:

> Say you the healing art essay'd,
> And piddled in the doctor's trade;
> At least you'd earn us good provisions,
> And better this than scribbling visions.

Yet ultimately, as Cowper's testimony of Cotton's value as a 'religious friend' and physician confirms, the two professions were neither incompatible, nor—to judge by Cowper's bill and Cotton's will—unprofitable.

LESLIE RITCHIE

**Sources** N. Cotton, *Observations on a particular kind of scarlet fever, that lately prevailed in and about St. Alban's, in a letter to Dr. Mead* (1749) · N. Cotton, *Visions in verse, for the entertainment and instruction of younger minds*, 8th edn (1781) · N. Cotton, *Various pieces in verse and prose by the late Nathaniel Cotton, M.D., many of which were never before published*, 2 vols. (1791) · N. Cotton, *Dissertatio medica inauguralis, de variolis … pro gradu doctoratus, summisque in medicina honoribus et privilegiis … Nathanael Cotton, Anglo Brittannus. Ad diem 7 August* (1730) · 'Memoirs of Dr Nathaniel Cotton', *GM*, 1st ser., 77 (1807), 500–01 · R. Anderson, 'Life of Cotton', *The works of the British poets*, 11 (1795), 1105–8 · R. A. Davenport, 'The life of Nathaniel Cotton, M.D.', *The British poets. Including translatio … in one hundred volumes*, 72.139–41 · *The letters and prose writings of William Cowper*, ed. J. King and C. Ryskamp, 5 vols. (1979–86) · E. A. Underwood, *Boerhaave's men at Leyden and after* (1977) · *The correspondence of Edward Young, 1683–1765*, ed. H. Pettit (1971) · IGI

**Likenesses** W. H. Worthington, line engraving (after J. Thurston), BM; repro. in B. W. Procter, *Effigias poeticae, or, Portraits of the British poets* (1824)

**Wealth at death** over £1300 in moneyed legacies, plus small quantity of plate and jewels, plus house and sanitorium: will, PRO, PROB 11/1168, fols. 361*v*–362

**Cotton, Sir Richard** (*b.* in or before **1497**, *d.* **1556**), courtier and administrator, was the third son of John Cotton, a Shropshire gentleman, and Cecily, daughter of Thomas Mainwaring of Lightfield, Shropshire. He began his career as an attorney in the sheriff's court in London, but then entered the king's service, no doubt helped by his elder brother George.

George Cotton was the governor of Henry VIII's illegitimate son Henry Fitzroy, duke of Richmond, in the latter's household in Yorkshire, and by 1526 Richard Cotton had become the household's comptroller. In a series of outraged and vivid letters, Richard Croke, an outstanding Greek scholar who had been appointed the young duke's tutor, complained to Cardinal Wolsey that discipline in both the schoolroom and the household in general was in a deplorable state. The Cottons, he alleged, were conspiring with Sir William Parr, the duke's chamberlain, to undermine his authority with Richmond, luring him away from his studies with hunting and shooting, and falsifying the household accounts. No action followed either then or after Richmond's death, when Cotton was not available for the completion of his accounts. After the duke died, on 22 July 1536, the Cottons were supposed to have his body wrapped in lead and taken to Thetford for interment; on 5 August the duke of Norfolk reported to Cromwell how displeased the king was to hear that they had failed in their task. Perhaps Henry's liking for the brothers helped to allay his anger somewhat—in 1531 he had paid them more than £20 in lost wagers, probably for archery.

By 1536 Richard Cotton had been rewarded with the stewardships of Bedhampton and Bovey Tracey parks, in Hampshire and Devon respectively, and he was also receiver of the barony of Sherburn, Yorkshire. He continued to be employed in the north, but now in a more military capacity—by 21 October 1536 he had been sent by Cromwell to supply the troops deployed by the duke of Norfolk and Sir Anthony Browne against rebels in Lincolnshire. He described to Cromwell how he 'pacified with fair words' the men who were not satisfied with 8*d*. a day in wages, and his problems ensuring that the horsemen, many of whom were impoverished younger brothers, had sufficient fodder (*LP Henry VIII*, 11.831). Soon afterwards he was back at court, first as cofferer to the household of Princess Mary and Princess Elizabeth, and then in 1538 as Prince Edward's cofferer and comptroller; his brother George was vice-chamberlain. Cotton was granted leases of the manor of Bedhampton in 1537 and of the manor of Bourne, Lincolnshire, the following year. From 1538 he was a JP in Hampshire. By that year he had married Jane, daughter of John Onley of London and Catesby, Northamptonshire. They had six sons and three daughters.

Shortage of money appears to have been a problem in Prince Edward's household too—in summer 1538 Lady Bryan wrote to Cromwell about the difficulty of dressing the little prince in an appropriate fashion. Matters came to a head in 1540, when Cotton was called before the privy council on 6 October and 26 December to render account. By the time the audit was completed a year later, he had been replaced by John Ryther in both his offices. But he remained on the prince's council between 1541 and 1547, and did not lose any land. Princess Elizabeth became godmother to Cotton's son Henry in 1545.

The military and administrative strands of Cotton's career came together under Edward VI, at whose coronation he was knighted, but his advancement seems at first to have been held back by Protector Somerset. When Henry died Cotton had been cofferer of the royal household, but in 1547 he lost this position, again to Ryther, and was also removed from the Hampshire peace commission. Instead he served in France, as treasurer of Boulogne until 1550, apart from a spell surveying the northern garrisons in 1549. His fortunes revived when Somerset was superseded at the head of government by the duke of Northumberland, who clearly found Cotton congenial. In 1551 he was granted the rectory and park of Warblington in Hampshire, complete with a 'fair great old house' which became his main residence (HoP, *Commons, 1509–58*, 1.712). He was sheriff of Hampshire in 1551–2. The year 1552 was something of an *annus mirabilis* for Cotton: he surveyed Calais and Guînes in January, became a privy councillor in May, and soon after the king's visit to Warblington in August was made comptroller to the household following the death of Sir Anthony Wingfield. A second royal visit, by the Scottish queen-dowager Mary of Guise, followed in October. He was also made warden of Holt Castle. Early in 1553 he was recommended to the Hampshire electors by the crown as a man whose knowledge and experience fitted him for a seat in parliament. The fact that he was very busy, mainly on financial commissions, did not make Cotton neglectful of his own interests. He exchanged the manor of Bourne for those of West Molesey (formerly belonging to Sir Richard Page) and Newhall in Cheshire, and further expanded his Cheshire estates by acquiring lands from the dean and chapter of Chester in May 1553, apparently under duress. Soon afterwards, perhaps because Northumberland needed to build up support in the north-west, Cotton was licensed to retain fifty men. In the same year he became a member of the council for the marches in Wales.

Although Cotton witnessed King Edward's will and was a member of Queen Jane's council, he defected to Mary as soon as it was clear the tide was turning in the latter's favour. Despite losing his household office he became once more a JP for Hampshire, and served at Calais again between 1553 and 1555. His acquiring a power base in Cheshire was reflected in his election in 1554 as the county's MP. Cotton died at Warblington on 2 October 1556 and was buried at Warblington church. Of his fair house only an octagonal tower remains.

CATHARINE DAVIES

**Sources** HoP, *Commons, 1509–58*, 1.711–13 • *LP Henry VIII*, vols. 4–21 • *CPR, 1547–58* • *Literary remains of King Edward the Sixth*, ed. J. G. Nichols, 2 vols., Roxburghe Club, 75 (1857) • *APC, 1547–54* • F. Gastrell, *Notitia Cestrenses, or, Historical notices of the diocese of Chester*, ed. F. R. Raines, 1, Chetham Society, 8 (1845) • *The diary of Henry Machyn, citizen and merchant-taylor of London, from AD 1550 to AD 1563*, ed. J. G. Nichols, CS, 42 (1848) • C. Wriothesley, *A chronicle of England during the reigns of the Tudors from AD 1485 to 1559*, ed. W. D. Hamilton, 2, CS, new ser., 20 (1877) • *VCH Hampshire and the Isle of Wight* • D. E. Hoak, *The king's council in the reign of Edward VI* (1976) • A. Bryson, '"The speciall men in every shere": the Edwardian regime, 1547–1553', PhD diss., U. St Andr., 2001

**Archives** PRO, SP domestic and foreign, Henry VIII, Edward VI, SP 1, SP 10

**Wealth at death** see will, PRO, PROB 11/38/23

**Cotton, Richard Lynch** (1794–1880), college head, was born on 14 August 1794 at Whitchurch, Oxfordshire, the third of eleven sons (the other ten gained distinction in the army, navy, and the church; there were also three daughters) of Henry Calveley Cotton (1755–1837), youngest son of Sir Lynch Salusbury Cotton, fourth baronet, and Matilda (*d.* 1848), daughter and heir of John Lockwood of

**Richard Lynch Cotton** (1794–1880), by Samuel Bellin, pubd 1858 (after Sir William Boxall)

Dews Hall, Essex. His brothers included Sir Sydney John *Cotton (1792–1874) and General Sir Arthur *Cotton (1803–1899). He was educated at Charterhouse from February 1805 until April 1812. On 5 November 1811, he matriculated at Worcester College, Oxford, as Lady Holford exhibitioner, and was elected scholar on Clarke's foundation on 8 May 1815. He took a second class in *literae humaniores*, graduating BA in 1815, and taking his MA in 1818.

At Easter 1815 Cotton was elected fellow of Oriel College, Oxford, but gave up this fellowship when he was elected fellow of Worcester College on 7 May 1816. He filled the college offices of tutor (1822), dean, and bursar (1828). In 1824 he was appointed to the office of domestic chaplain to the earl of St Germans. On 9 December 1823 he secured the small college living of Denchworth, Berkshire, and remained vicar until January 1839, when he was appointed provost of Worcester College by the duke of Wellington, chancellor of the University of Oxford. Cotton, who replaced Dr Whittington Landon (provost, 1796–1839), was not the only candidate for the provostship. The vice-chancellor, A. T. Gilbert, strongly recommended the candidature of Richard Greswell, tutor of Worcester College, as a reward for his reform of the financial and electoral system of the college. On 27 June 1839, at St George's, Hanover Square, London, Cotton married Charlotte Bouverie (1807–1883), daughter of the Hon. Philip Bouverie (who assumed the name of Pusey) and his wife, Lady Lucy, and sister of Philip *Pusey and of Dr Edward Bouverie *Pusey of Christ Church, Oxford, the celebrated Tractarian leader. They had one daughter, Amelia Lucy.

Cotton resided at Worcester College from 1815 until 1880. During the 1820s he had the reputation among residents of the university of being one of the best preachers at the university church of St Mary the Virgin. In 1840 he was appointed select preacher to the University of Oxford, and from 1852 until 1856 he was vice-chancellor of the university. During his term of office a university commission was created, with the aim of reforming antiquated academic statutes and usages at Oxford. The commission helped frame the University Reform Act of 1854 which, much to Cotton's dismay, brought Oxford's Laudian constitution to an end. The 1854 act was a parliamentary affair outside his direct control, and he merely acknowledged, but did not answer, the commission's inquiries. During his vice-chancellorship, Cotton supported the building of the University Museum (the foundation stone was laid in 1855), though it required the expenditure of capital which he would have preferred to have donated to the erection of a hall for accommodating poor scholars.

Originally of considerable private means, Cotton was prodigious in his liberality and could never refuse beggars. He was a generous promoter and benefactor of church building in the area to the south and east of Oxford: he endowed churches at Skippen and Dry Sandford near Abingdon, and was instrumental in procuring the erection of Headington Quarry church, near Oxford, in 1847.

Cotton published only a few single sermons. His *Scriptural View of the Lord's Supper* and *The Way of Salvation Plainly and Practically Traced* were both published in 1837. His most substantial published work was *Lectures on the Holy Sacrament of the Lord's Supper* (1849). He also published funeral sermons for deceased undergraduate members of the college: John Pierce (1857); William Welch Burrows and John Haywood Southby (1861).

In theological terms, Cotton has usually been classed with the evangelical school within the Church of England. Yet, though he was claimed by the evangelical party, he was never a narrowly party man and is best regarded as a conservative protestant churchman. He viewed the Tractarian movement with alarm and was a close associate of that most implacable enemy of the Tractarians, C. P. Golightly. He was a zealous supporter of the scheme to erect a Martyrs' Memorial at Oxford in 1838, which many regarded as a means of embarrassing and exposing the Tractarians as subverters of protestantism. Cotton, however, did not emulate the example of some other heads of houses in persecuting known Tractarians in his college, and did not alter the dinner hour on Sunday in order to prevent undergraduates from hearing Newman preach in St Mary's, as was the practice with some other heads. He remained on close terms with high-churchmen attached to Worcester College, such as John Miller and Richard Greswell, and, at a later date, John William Burgon, author of an affectionate biographical memoir of Cotton in his *Lives of Twelve Good Men* (1888). Cotton was a great admirer of Miller's influential Bampton lectures, *The Divine Authority of Holy Scripture* (1817), which were also a source of inspiration for the Tractarians. Cotton's anti-

Tractarianism may have been softened by his early friendly relations with Newman and his relationship by marriage with Pusey. He was horrified in his last years by the defection to Roman Catholicism of his beloved daughter, Amelia Lucy, but he bore the trial with fortitude. A man of deep personal piety and habits of prayer, Cotton was catholic in his devotional and architectural tastes. His favourite devotional work was that of an eighteenth-century high-churchman, Bishop Thomas Wilson's *On the Lord's Supper*, while his own published writings focused on eucharistic devotion. He was also instrumental in the transformation of Worcester College chapel in the 1860s into the most gorgeous and ornate specimen of its type in Oxford.

Cotton was of small physical stature, but always enjoyed excellent health. He had a reputation in his early days as a fearless rider of horses; a habit which earned him the label of 'hard-riding Dick'—an allusion to the Border rider mentioned in Sir Walter Scott's *Marmion*. His character was amiable and without guile. He was earnest and solemn, but not without a certain, albeit ponderous, sense of humour, well exemplified in his protests to one parishioner at Denchworth for being a dissenter when his surname was Church.

Cotton died suddenly, at the provost's lodgings, Worcester College, on 8 December 1880. He was revered by those of all shades of opinion in the Oxford of his day and his funeral was attended by every chief resident of the university. He was buried in Holywell cemetery on 14 December. His wife survived him, dying on 2 July 1883, aged seventy-six.                    PETER B. NOCKLES

**Sources** [R. L. Arrowsmith], ed., *Charterhouse register, June 1769–May 1872* (1964), 78 · W. D. Parish, ed., *List of Carthusians, 1800 to 1879* (1879), 57 · Foster, *Alum. Oxon.* · MS 238—2 vols. of material compiled for J. W. Burgon and used in his *Lives*, Worcester College, Oxford, MSS 238, 251, 291, 295 · J. W. Burgon, *Lives of twelve good men*, 4th edn, 2 (1889), 6, 71–92 · J. W. Burgon, *Guardian* (29 Dec 1880) · W. R. Ward, *Victorian Oxford* (1965), 142 · [W. F. G. Gorman], *'Rome's recruits': a list of protestants who have become Catholics since the Tractarian movement* (1878), 14 · E. P. Wilson, 'An engraving of Provost Cotton, 1852, by Thomas Woollen Smith', *Worcester College Record* (1994), 34–9 · E. P. Wilson, 'Derby day at Worcester, 1853', *Worcester College Record* (1995), 42–56 · *CGPLA Eng. & Wales* (1881) · baptismal record · Worcester College, Oxford, records · parish register (marriage), London, St George's, Hanover Square, 27 June 1839 · burial record

**Archives** Worcester College, Oxford, MSS 238, 251, 291, 295 | BL, corresp. with W. E. Gladstone, Add. MSS 44362–44528 · Lpool RO, letters to fourteenth earl of Derby · Pusey Oxf., Liddon MSS

**Likenesses** T. W. Smith, drawing, *c.*1852, repro. in W. Tuckwell, *Reminiscences of Oxford* (1907), frontispiece · S. Bellin, mezzotint, pubd 1858 (after W. Boxall), BM, NPG [*see illus.*] · W. Boxall, oils, *c.*1858, Worcester College, Oxford

**Wealth at death** under £12,000: probate, 18 Feb 1881, *CGPLA Eng. & Wales*

**Cotton, Sir Robert**, fifth baronet (1669–1749). *See under* Cotton, Sir Robert Bruce, first baronet (1571–1631).

**Cotton, Sir Robert Bruce**, first baronet (1571–1631), antiquary and politician, was born at Denton, Huntingdonshire, on 22 January 1571, and baptized there five days later. He was the eldest son of Thomas Cotton (*b.* in or

Sir Robert Bruce Cotton, first baronet (1571–1631), by unknown artist, 1629

before 1544, *d.* 1592), of Conington, Huntingdonshire, and his first wife, Elizabeth (*d.* in or before 1579), daughter of Francis Shirley of Staunton Harrold, Leicestershire. His father had set up residence in Denton, 3 miles from Conington, so as not to inconvenience his own father. Cotton had a brother, Thomas, born in 1572, and three sisters. His father married, in 1579, Dorothy, daughter of John Tamworth of Hawsted, Leicestershire, and had three sons and three daughters with his second wife. Cotton attended Westminster School, where William Camden was a master and an early influence on his scholarly interests. On 22 November 1581 he matriculated at Jesus College, Cambridge, graduating BA in 1585/6. He was admitted to the Middle Temple on 3 February 1588, and attended there in 1589.

**The Society of Antiquaries** In the late 1580s Cotton joined with his former teacher William Camden and several others as an early member of the Society of Antiquaries. By this date he had already collected materials for a history of Huntingdonshire. He continued to live in London, although there is little evidence of his participation in the affairs of the society before the death of his father in 1592; this necessitated his return to Huntingdonshire to help manage the family estates. Cotton was certainly living at Conington in 1593 when his father's inquisition post mortem was taken. He must have married soon after this date because his wife, Elizabeth (*d.* 1658)—daughter and coheir of William Brocas of Theddingworth, Leicestershire—gave birth to a son, Thomas [*see below*], in 1594. During this stay in the country Cotton may have begun the extensive building work involved in reconstructing the hall at Conington. Cotton's return to London in 1598 coincided with a revival of the Society of Antiquaries, which had been in abeyance between 1594 and 1598 because of the presence of plague in the capital. Perhaps coincidentally the society's records were better organized on Cotton's return and they reveal nine of Cotton's contributions to discussions, most of which contain a significant etymological element. In the late 1590s there is evidence of Cotton lending his fellow antiquarians volumes of manuscripts from his developing library, and presumably he also contributed documents to facilitate discussion at the society's meetings. Cotton was involved in an initiative towards the end of Elizabeth's reign (possibly in 1602) aimed at placing antiquarian research on a more official footing. He joined in a petition to the crown for a permanent academy 'for the study of antiquity and history founded by Queen Elizabeth' (Sharpe, *Sir Robert Cotton*, 27), which suggested, among other things, that Cotton's library be merged with the queen's to form a national library. Despite murmurings of official favour, extending into the next reign, the plans did not win royal approval. It seems probable that ministers realized the growing potential of antiquarian research to cause them political difficulties, especially in a parliament where debate was dominated by the use of precedent to decide the questions of the day. Similar fears among those in power may have hastened the demise of the Society of Antiquaries, the last recorded meeting of which took place in 1607. It may have been the failure of the projected academy which encouraged Cotton to treat his own library as an open resource for scholars in order to stimulate their own research and publication, and for those interested in public affairs.

Cotton's antiquarian studies did not neglect fieldwork. In 1599–1600 Cotton accompanied Camden on a tour of northern England, surveying and collecting Roman remains from the area around Hadrian's Wall, material later added to an edition of Camden's *Britannia*. London was now his permanent residence, although he was appointed a JP for Huntingdonshire in 1601. Indeed in that year he was forced to write an appeal to secretary of state Robert Cecil to avoid the office of sheriff of Huntingdonshire and Cambridgeshire: in it he referred to his 'inability to such a charge, in regard a great part of my estate is in dowry, part apportioned by lease to ten children, and so a third part hardly remaining constraineth me to leave the country' (Mirrlees, 43–4).

Cotton sought advancement at court through his kinswoman Lady Hunsdon and her husband, George Carey, Lord Hunsdon. Cotton also seems to have begun to learn Italian from John Florio in the hope of forwarding his career in government circles. In summer 1601 he was talked of as a candidate for a diplomatic posting to Bremen to negotiate with the Danes. Lord St John of Bletsoe chose Cotton as one of a group of local gentlemen to be present at court when Maréchal de Biron, Henri IV's representative, waited on the queen in autumn 1601. On 4 October 1601 Cotton was elected to parliament for Newton, Isle of Wight, the governor of the isle being Lord Hunsdon. The Hunsdons were connected by marriage to Henry Howard, younger brother of the duke of Norfolk (*d.* 1572), and newly returned to court. In 1601 Howard commissioned Cotton to write a tract demonstrating from precedent that the English ambassador to France, Sir Henry Neville, should take precedence over the envoy from Spain in Calais to discuss an Anglo-Spanish treaty. In November 1602 Cotton was asked by Howard to produce a list of precedents relating to the office of earl marshal.

**Parliamentary activities** Cotton and Howard shared the objective of supporting James VI of Scotland's claim to succeed Elizabeth I. Cotton was aware of his own Scottish antecedents, tracing his roots back to Robert the Bruce, and following James's accession to the throne of England he added the Bruce to his signature, becoming Robert Bruce Cotton. Following the queen's death Howard commissioned Cotton to write a defence of James I's claim, and this service no doubt contributed to Cotton's knighthood on 11 May 1603. In June 1603 Cotton produced the first piece of advice to Howard on the desirability of peace with Spain, advice which continued the following year when Howard (earl of Northampton from March 1604) was appointed to negotiate a treaty with the Spanish.

By 1603 Cotton was living in the house in London of the newly widowed Lady Hunsdon, possibly as her lover, thus continuing a long association with Blackfriars. He was not reconciled with his wife until after the fall of the earl of Somerset in 1615. Cotton was elected to parliament for the county of Huntingdonshire in 1604, for which his grandfather had previously sat. He was appointed to numerous committees, including the committee on grievances. In the 1605–6 session Cotton was named to the committee of privileges and to the bill attainting the gunpowder plotters. The Gunpowder Plot and attendant trials saw Cotton edit and prepare for publication Northampton's tract, *A True and Perfect Relation of the Whole Proceedings Against the Late most Barbarous Traitors* (1606).

In the parliamentary session which began in November 1606 Cotton was again named to the committee of privileges. He was also an advocate of a full union of Scotland with England which came before parliament in the 1606–7 session, being named on 24 November 1606 to the joint conference with the Lords on the subject. His knowledge of precedents saw him named to many important committees in the Commons; indeed he was referred to in the journals as 'Sir Robert Cotton, a known antiquary' (Kyle). Further, through his relationship to Northampton he was able to advise and thus influence the privy council. About 1608 Cotton wrote a tract for Northampton, one of the commissioners for the earl marshalship, on the legality of duels: he found precedents for a ban on duels in cases touching personal honour.

From May 1608 to June 1609 Cotton served on a commission investigating abuses in the navy. His main role in this reform initiated by Northampton was to assemble witnesses and evidence. In 1609 Cotton corrected the proofs for John Speed's *History of England* (1611). Cotton was also involved in advising the French historian Jacques Auguste

De Thou on the history of Scotland in the second half of the sixteenth century, and particularly James VI's concern that the role of his mother (Mary, queen of Scots) be rehabilitated from the unfavourable interpretation of George Buchanan's *Rerum Scoticarum historia* (1582). Cotton's accounts suggest that his income was about £1000 p.a. after 1610. This was needed because about 1609 there began a five-year period in which fortuitous circumstances, namely death, saw Cotton able to add immeasurably to his library with works formerly in the possession of Lord Lumley (d. 1609), the earl of Salisbury (d. 1612), Prince Henry (d. 1612), William Dethick (d. 1612), and Northampton (d. 1614). This period also seems to see a quantitative leap in recorded borrowings from the library, which demonstrates its growing importance to contemporaries.

In parliament's session of 1610 Cotton's importance was demonstrated by his nomination in first place to the committee of privileges. In February he used a precedent from the reign of Henry IV to support the view that a subsidy should be granted to the king before grievances were redressed. Cotton's 'Means for raising the king's estate' was probably drawn up in 1610 or 1611 in the wake of the failure of the great contract to suggest ways in which the royal revenue could be increased. He considered how precedent could be used to revive certain prerogative rights. Another of Cotton's suggestions was a proposal for a new order higher than that of knight, but below that of a baron. These baronetcies were to be sold, and Cotton acted as an agent for their sale, acquiring one of the first batch himself on 29 June 1611. However, all did not go smoothly, particularly the place of baronets in the order of precedence. In 1612, with Cotton lying low in the country, they lost their suit to be considered ahead of the sons of barons. Such financial proposals were useful to Northampton following his appointment to the treasury commission following the death of the earl of Salisbury in 1612.

In 1613 Cotton produced a tract for the king on the influx of Jesuits into England. He recommended imprisonment for these priests, rather than execution, partly in order to avoid making them martyrs and partly out of mercy. Further he identified the fundamental loyalty of most English Catholics, and the need for the Church of England to meet the threat through invigorating its own teachings and institutions. About 1613 Cotton drew up a list of political maxims: included on this was the saying that 'religion bindeth a good subject to desire a sovereign and to bear with a bad one' (Parry, 'Cotton's counsels', 88). If these maxims were designed as a primer for governing action in parliament they remained redundant for the moment, as in the election of 1614 Cotton failed to gain a seat, being defeated for Huntingdonshire. The Commons did however make use of his library, by now situated in the New Exchange in the Strand, in their search for material on impositions.

Northampton died in June 1614 but by then Cotton had been able to transfer his talents to Theophilus Howard, second earl of Suffolk, and to Northampton's heir,

Thomas Howard, earl of Arundel. The intermarriage of the Howards with the new royal favourite, Robert Carr, earl of Somerset, also provided Cotton with a means of continuing his influence as an adviser to privy councillors. Cotton was a key agent in the negotiations begun in January 1615 with the Spanish envoy, Diego Sarmiento de Acuña, later conde de Gondomar, for a Spanish match for Prince Charles. It seems likely that Cotton was acting under instructions from the king (which he may have misinterpreted). Negotiations were broken off at the end of 1615, and Cotton was later examined about his role. By this date the policy and influence of Somerset was in ruins, his influence eroded by the rise of Sir George Villiers, the future duke of Buckingham. Investigations in September and October 1615 into the death of Sir Thomas Overbury implicated Somerset and his wife. They also revealed that Cotton had advised Somerset to sue out a general pardon in the summer of 1615, so that he could avoid being prosecuted over the affair. Further Cotton had tampered with Somerset's correspondence to give the impression that Somerset was innocent of involvement, but it eventually fell into the hands of the prosecution. Cotton was taken into custody on 29 December 1615, and he was not in London to attend Somerset's trial for murder. Cotton was released on 13 June 1616 without facing a trial and pardoned in July. His experiences apparently persuaded him to go back to living with his estranged wife (although he had a reputation for infidelity and was threatened with blackmail as late as August 1630). As such he was to become part of the court faction uneasy with, and then opposed to Villiers, now Viscount Buckingham. His pardon also covered the charge of embezzling public records, no doubt a sensible precaution in the days of haphazard record keeping, and the potential for trouble given Cotton's rapacious appetite for manuscripts. The fall of Somerset did not see Cotton bereft of political influence for he soon emerged as an adviser of Suffolk's, although he moved even closer to Arundel.

Cotton was not elected to parliament in 1621, but he did advise James I on the impeachment of the lord chancellor, Sir Francis Bacon, more especially on what the king's role was and what parliament could do of its own volition. On a related matter he drew up his 'Brief discourse concerning the power of Peers and Commons of parliament in point of judicature', which dealt with the right of the Commons to judge non-members. Cotton also produced precedents to support parliament's desire to discuss the proposed Spanish match for Prince Charles, and the associated matter of war. In August 1622 Cotton advised Arundel over his attempt to add the constable's powers to those of the earl marshal's, which he already exercised. In 1622 Cotton moved his residence to Cotton House, a four-storey building, containing twenty-one rooms, and which adjoined both the House of Commons and the Painted Chamber. Further, another side had a courtyard which led to a passage under the court of requests and into Old Palace Yard. Finally, the other side led into a garden which backed onto the River Thames. The library was to remain in Cotton House until after his death. Its new location facilitated easy access for parliamentarians wishing to search for material of use in debates in the adjacent House of Commons. It was also used by government servants because it contained many items of an official nature. Cotton's skills were still regarded as useful to the government. In March 1623 Cotton was named to the commission to inquire into the fees charged in the law courts, dominated by his friend Sir Henry Spelman. He also sat on the commission to inquire into buildings in London.

In 1624 Cotton was able to enter parliament for Old Sarum when the financier Sir Arthur Ingram opted to sit for York. Old Sarum's patron at this time was either the second earl of Salisbury, a dependent of Buckingham, or the earl of Pembroke, a leading privy councillor. In 1624 Cotton felt able to support Buckingham because they were united in opposing the Spanish match for Prince Charles. Thus on 3 March 1624 Cotton was willing to inform a conference with the Lords of the perfidy of the Spanish in 1615–16. It was most obvious in the tracts which Cotton wrote for the duke. 'Relation against ambassadors who have miscarried themselves' was designed to counteract the Spanish ambassadors, Coloma and Hinojosa, who had denounced Buckingham to the king as a traitor for plotting a coup and a design to marry his daughter to the son of James's daughter Elizabeth, and 'A remonstrance of the treaties of amitie and marriage' documented Spanish duplicity during the current negotiations.

**Loyalty in question** In the first parliament of Charles I's reign, called in 1625, Cotton sat for Thetford, a borough under Arundel's control, and duly attended the Oxford session. It is from this session that there survives a speech which may have been partly written by Cotton, and which suggests that Buckingham be impeached. The use of precedents in the speech is a hallmark of Cotton's, but it was probably meant for either Sir John Eliot or Sir Robert Phelips to deliver, although in the event no opportunity arose before the dissolution. Cotton's association with Buckingham's rivals probably accounts for the snub delivered to Cotton on the day of Charles I's coronation in February 1626, when the royal barge avoided landing at Cotton House, where Cotton was waiting to present the king with 'a book of Athelstan's' upon which the kings of England had anciently taken their coronation oath.

Between March 1626 and October 1628 Arundel was in the Tower, and thus Cotton was not able to find a seat at the 1626 election. However, Cotton was still consulted by the council over such matters as a scheme to debase the coinage; most notably on 3 September he spoke at the council against any scheme to alter the coinage. In December 1626 he sat on the commission to reform the navy. He provided the attorney-general with precedents for a forced loan in 1627. Also in 1627 a tract which Cotton claimed to have written in 1614 was published without his consent. *A Short View of the Long Life and Reign of King Henry III* offered a view of a king dominated by a corrupt favourite who eventually came to rule through his council in a wise manner, thereby offering an obvious parallel with Charles

I and Buckingham. Cotton was questioned over its appearance, but stated that it had been offered as advice to James I, specifically to urge on him the need to take the advice of all his council rather than rely on the favourite, Somerset. Although Cotton escaped punishment, not surprisingly Buckingham advised the king to close Cotton's library because it had become a source of precedents for use against him.

Cotton's tract *The Danger Wherein the Kingdom Now Standeth and the Remedy* was published in 1628 under Cotton's own name. Cotton argued that England was in grave danger when both Spain and France were hostile. His solution was not to call for the fall of Buckingham, but to call for a return to traditional governance, with the council at its centre—Buckingham taking his place along with the other great peers. This work may have helped council to decide to call parliament in 1628. Cotton stood for Westminster, where he had recently been made a JP, but lost to a Buckingham nominee. Instead he came in for Castle Rising on Arundel's interest. Cotton seems to have been interested in the procedure of the petition of right, rather than in its contents. When parliament sat in January 1629 Cotton probably did not take his seat.

In November 1629 Charles I ordered the closure of Cotton's library, and for a brief period he was imprisoned. Cotton thus paid the price for allowing his collections to be used for the production of arguments and precedents deemed detrimental to royal interests, although the official reason was the discovery in his library of a tract, 'A proposition for his majesty's service to bridle the impertinency of parliaments', which was perceived as advocating rule by an absolutist monarch. On 15 November 1629 Cotton was allowed access to his library in the company of the clerk of the council. Both men were to have their own keys, with both needed to gain entrance. Cotton was appointed on 17 April 1630 to a new commission on fees, even before receiving the general pardon of 29 May 1630. However, in July and again in October the library was searched for documents belonging to the crown, and the privy council ordered a catalogue to be compiled of the library's contents. In September Cotton and his son petitioned for renewed access, and indeed Cotton was petitioning for its return when he died, reputedly of grief at the loss of his library. On 4 May 1631 Cotton made his will 'at this present indisposition in my health'. In it he referred to 'the manuscript books and antiquities and other collections in my studies, being my labours for forty years' (will, PRO, PROB 11/159), which he left to his son, Thomas, stipulating that they remain to his grandson John [see below] and his heirs. He died on 6 May 1631 at Westminster, being attended on his deathbed by a broad range of clergymen: William Piers (an Arminian bishop), Richard Holdsworth (a puritan divine), and two moderates, Theophilus Field and John Williams. According to his wishes he was buried in Conington church on 13 May, his monument pithily remarking 'his pyre survives to light the world' (Smith, 46). His widow's will was proved on 18 May 1658.

**Reputation** Cotton published little under his own name during his life, which perhaps reflects his involvement in the political affairs of the time. He advised a succession of leading politicians of his day, including James I and Charles I. This accounts for the nature of many tracts published by James Howells in *Cottoni posthuma* in 1651. Cotton did however have time to talk to other antiquarians and scholars, engage in an extensive correspondence with his counterparts in foreign lands, and above all to act as a source for many scholars engaged in their own work. The published acknowledgements of seventeenth-century writers testify to his pre-eminent role as a facilitator of scholarship. At his death Cotton's library consisted mainly of Anglo-Saxon manuscripts, monastic registers, biblical works, including lives of the saints and martyrs, genealogies and heraldic materials, and state papers relating to England's domestic and foreign affairs (not to mention the artefacts which were kept at Conington). In the late 1620s Cotton began reorganizing his library, possibly prompted by the purchase by Charles I of twelve portraits of Roman emperors, in which the presses containing the volumes would be identified by busts of the twelve Roman emperors from Julius Caesar to Domitian, plus the imperial ladies Cleopatra and Faustina, which may have been later additions. By the time of his death it had about 800 volumes of manuscripts. John Selden, a frequent borrower from the library, and probably its protector during the civil wars, summed up Cotton's importance in 1623:

> [he] has deservedly won immortal fame both abroad and at home not only from his collection of books and manuscripts of the choicest sort acquired at vast expence but also through his kindness and willingness to make them available to students of good literature and affairs of state. (Smith, 59)

Or, in modern parlance, Cotton 'was a magnificent specimen of the full-blown Jacobean antiquary' (Parry, *Trophies*, 92).

**Sir Thomas Cotton**, second baronet (1594–1662), was the eldest son of Sir Robert Bruce Cotton and his wife, Elizabeth Brocas. He was born at Long Coombe, Oxfordshire, in 1594. He matriculated at Oxford on 16 April 1613, and was awarded a BA from Broadgates Hall on 24 October 1616. With his father absent from Huntingdonshire for most of the time Cotton gradually took over the tasks of estate administration. By 1619 he had begun to make entries in the Conington rentals, and in 1620 he married Margaret (1593–1622), daughter of Lord William *Howard. Howard was a nephew of Sir Robert Cotton's patron the earl of Northampton and an uncle of Sir Robert's patron the earl of Arundel. Like his kinsmen, Lord William shared the Cotton interest in antiquities. Cotton sat for Great Marlow in the 1624 and 1625 parliaments, for St Germans in 1628, and Huntingdonshire in the Short Parliament of 1640. On 17 April 1640 he was licensed to marry Alice (*b.* 1614/15), daughter and heir of Sir John Constable of Dormanby, Yorkshire, widow of Edmund Anderson of Eyworth and Stratton, Bedfordshire. Under his ownership access to the Cotton library was more limited than under his father, but he was able to protect it during the civil

wars and interregnum, despite his being widely perceived to be sympathetic with the royalist cause. Cotton was an improving landlord keen to maximize the income from his estate which reached £6000 p.a. at one point. Cotton died on 13 May 1662, and was buried at Conington.

**Sir John Cotton**, third baronet (1621–1702), was the only son of Sir Thomas Cotton, second baronet, and his first wife, Margaret Howard. Sir Robert Cotton MP (1644–1717) was his half-brother, being the first surviving son of his father's second wife. Cotton entered Magdalene College, Cambridge, in 1637, and spent the years 1639–42 travelling abroad. On 8 June 1644 he married Dorothy, daughter and heir of Edmund Anderson of Eyworth and Stratton, Bedfordshire, and the daughter of his stepmother, Alice Anderson. They had seven sons, who all predeceased him, and two daughters. Cotton took no part in the civil war, but was sympathetic to the royalists. On 20 October 1658 he married Elizabeth (1637–1702), daughter of Sir Thomas Honeywood of Markshall, Essex. They had one surviving son, Robert, who became the fifth baronet, and two daughters. He was elected to parliament in 1661 for Huntingdon, where he generally supported the court, peppering his speeches with classical allusions, and showing hostility to both dissent and popery. He sat in parliament for Huntingdonshire in 1685. He accepted the revolution of 1688, but he did not sit in parliament again. He died at Stratton, Bedfordshire, on 12 September 1702, and was buried at Conington, having seen to it that the Cotton library was bought for the nation by act of parliament, 12 & 13 William III, c. 7 (1701). This decision to sell the library may well have been based upon the fact that otherwise it would fall into the hands of his 'two illiterate grandsons' (Tite, 35) and been sold and broken up.

**Sir John Cotton**, fourth baronet (*c.*1680–1731), was the first son of John Cotton (*d.* 1681) and his wife, Frances, daughter of Sir George Downing, first baronet, of East Hatley, Cambridgeshire. Sir John Cotton (1621–1702), third baronet, was his grandfather. Cotton was returned to parliament for Huntingdon in 1705, only to be unseated on petition on 22 January 1706. In 1707 Cotton House, which was in some structural disrepair, was passed to the nation (6 Anne, c. 30). On 4 July 1708 Cotton married Elizabeth (1680–1722), daughter of the Hon. James Herbert, and a granddaughter of Thomas Osborne, first duke of Leeds. They had two daughters who predeceased their father. Cotton was again elected to parliament, in a by-election in December 1710 for Huntingdonshire. He did not stand in 1713. Cotton died, aged forty-two, on 5 February 1731, in North Street, Red Lion Square, London, home of a Mr Hanbury, presumably William Hanbury, the husband of his sister, Frances. He was buried in St George the Martyr, Lamb's Conduit Fields, London. The Conington estates were settled on his cousin **Sir John Cotton**, sixth baronet (*d.* 1752).

Sir John Cotton was the son of **Sir Robert Cotton**, fifth baronet (1669–1749), and his first wife, Elizabeth Wigston (1681/2–1745). His father had been an active Jacobite engaged in the rebellion in 1715, and then resident in France for some years before returning to England. Sir

Robert may have joined in Charles Edward Stuart's abortive expedition from Dunkirk in 1744. Sir John Cotton had inherited the settled estate of the fourth baronet, and was thus a substantial landowner before his father's death. He married Jane (d. 1769), daughter of Sir Robert Burdet, third baronet of Bramcote, Warwickshire. With his death on 27 March 1752, leaving four daughters (two unmarried at his death), the baronetcy became extinct. His widow died on 17 March 1769.                    STUART HANDLEY

**Sources** K. Sharpe, *Sir Robert Cotton, 1586–1631: history and politics in early modern England* (1979) · C. Kyle, 'Cotton, Sir Robert Bruce', HoP, *Commons, 1604–29* [draft] · C. G. C. Tite, *The manuscript library of Sir Robert Cotton* (1994) [Panizzi lecture, 1993] · T. Smith, *Catalogue of the manuscripts in the Cottonian Library, 1696 / Catalogus librorum manuscriptorum bibliothecae Cottonianae*, ed. C. G. C. Tite (1696); repr. (1984) · G. Parry, *The trophies of time: English antiquaries of the seventeenth century* (1995), 70–94 · H. Mirrlees, *A fly in amber: being an extravagant biography of the romantic antiquary Sir Robert Bruce Cotton* (1962) · GEC, *Baronetage* · N&Q, 3rd ser., 6 (1864), 449–51 · L. L. Peck, *Northampton: patronage and policy at the court of James I* (1982) · B. White, *Cast of ravens: the strange case of Sir Thomas Overbury* (1965) · P. Hyde, 'Cotton, Sir Robert Bruce', HoP, *Commons, 1558–1603* · Venn, *Alum. Cant.* · E. R. Edwards, 'Cotton, Sir John', HoP, *Commons, 1660–90* · C. Wright, ed., *Sir Robert Cotton as collector: essays on an early Stuart courtier and his legacy* (1997) · K. Sharpe, 'Re-writing Sir Robert Cotton: politics and history in early Stuart England', *Sir Robert Cotton as collector: essays on an early Stuart courtier and his legacy*, ed. C. Wright (1997) · N. Ramsay, 'Sir Robert Cotton's services to the crown: a paper written in self-defence', *Sir Robert Cotton as collector: essays on an early Stuart courtier and his legacy*, ed. C. Wright (1997), 68–80 · G. Parry, 'Cotton's counsels: the contents of Cotton's posthuma', *Sir Robert Cotton as collector: essays on an early Stuart courtier and his legacy*, ed. C. Wright (1997), 81–95 · will, PRO, PROB 11/159, fol. 520r [Sir Robert Bruce Cotton] · will, PRO, PROB 11/466, fols. 110–12 [Sir John Cotton, third baronet] · will, PRO, PROB 11/642, fol. 221 [Sir John Cotton, fourth baronet] · will, PRO, PROB 11/794, fol. 265 [Sir John Cotton, sixth baronet] · R. B. Manning, 'Antiquarianism and seigneurial reaction: Sir Robert and Sir Thomas Cotton and their tenants', *BIHR*, 63 (1990), 277–88 · D. W. Hayton, 'Cotton, Sir John', HoP, *Commons, 1690–1715* [draft] · will, PRO, PROB 11/947, fol. 177 [Lady Jane Cotton] · IGI
**Archives** BL, collections relating to courts of chancery and requests, Add. MS 46410 · BL, collections relating to Huntingdonshire, Lansdowne MS 921 · BL, Cotton MSS, corresp. and papers · BL, Harley MSS, papers · Hunt. L., papers on impositions and defence · Inner Temple, London, papers and transcripts · Northants. RO, speech to House of Commons · Yale U., Beinecke L., MSS and papers | Cambs. AS, Cambridge, Cambridge Antrobus papers
**Likenesses** oils, 1629, BM [*see illus.*] · G. Vertue, line engraving (after P. von Somer), BM; repro. in *Vetusta monumenta* · oils, second version, NPG

**Cotton, Roger** (c.1557–1602), draper and poet, was born in Whitchurch, Shropshire, the fifth of six sons of Ralph Cotton, esquire, of Alkington in the parish of Whitchurch, and his wife, Jane, daughter and heir of John Smith (or Tarbock) of Newcastle under Lyme, Staffordshire. It is probable that he was educated at the free school in Whitchurch, which his father had helped to set up. Of his five brothers at least two were drapers, including the youngest, Sir Allen Cotton (c.1558–1628), lord mayor of London in 1625–6. Roger Cotton too moved to London, being admitted a member of the Drapers' Company and setting

up in Canning Street: he was made free of the company on 16 November 1584. The Cotton family were close friends and financial supporters of the Shropshire-born Hebrew scholar Hugh Broughton, and Roger Cotton in particular was strongly influenced by Broughton's religious views. Under Broughton's guidance, Cotton 'read over the *Bible* twelve times in one year' (Lightfoot, sig. A4v), and some of the effects of that can be seen in his work.

Cotton's first publication was a prose tract entitled *A Direction to the Waters of Lyfe* (1590), signed 'Roger Cotton, Draper'. It contained a dedication to the 'most heavenly Orator' Broughton, and it was reprinted in 1592 and (as *A Direct Way to the Waters of Life*) in 1610. Two years later Cotton published *An armor of proofe, brought from the tower of David, to fight against Spannyardes, and all enimies of the trueth* (1592), a poem in six-line stanzas dedicated to Gilbert Talbot, earl of Shrewsbury. Cotton announces in the preface that the purpose of his poem is 'to incourage the weake and feeble in faith towards God', and covers much the same subjects as he did in his earlier prose work. In the same year Cotton also published *A spirituall song: conteining an historicall discourse from the infancie of the world, untill this present time setting downe the treacherous practises of the wicked, against the children of God describing also the markes and overthrow of antichrist*. This ambitious poem, in unusual five-line stanzas, is dedicated to Sir Francis Drake. Accompanying it are various shorter poems of an apocalyptically militant protestant nature.

At an unknown date Cotton married Katherine Jenkes of Drayton, Shropshire, and they had at least two sons, Samuel (presumably the Samuel Cotton, son of Roger, baptized at St Clement's Eastcheap on 9 September 1590) and Alexander (d. in or before 1602), and a daughter, Marie. Roger Cotton's will was proved on 29 May 1602, and it identifies him as 'citizen and draper of London, St Clement's, Eastcheap'. By his will, he left 50s. a year to be administered by the Drapers' Company in helping the poor of Whitchurch.

Two of Cotton's publications were among the texts which the eighteenth-century forger William Henry Ireland embellished with 'Shakespeare's' annotations such as: 'I lyke notte thatte worde Masterre Cotton' (Corser, 4.492–3). Nor have other literary critics been much kinder, Corser for instance remarking that Cotton's works are 'not remarkable for any display of poetical genius or talent, indeed far otherwise' (ibid., 4.488). Relentlessly anti-Catholic in tone, verbose, and studded with marginalia giving scriptural cross-references, they are among the least appealing of Renaissance devotional poetry.

MATTHEW STEGGLE

**Sources** T. Corser, *Collectanea Anglo-poetica, or, A … catalogue of a … collection of early English poetry*, 4, Chetham Society, 77 (1869), 484–96 · J. Lightfoot, preface, in H. Broughton, *The works of the great Albionean divine … Mr Hugh Broughton*, 4 vols. (1662) · P. Boyd, 'Boyd's register of apprentices and freemen of the Drapers' Company of the city of London', Drapers' Company Archives · will, PRO, PROB 11/99, sig. 31
**Wealth at death** £2 10s. p.a. bequeathed to poor of Whitchurch: will, PRO, PROB 11/99, sig. 31

**Cotton, Sir St Vincent**, sixth baronet (1801–1863), sportsman and gambler, was born at Madingley Hall, Madingley, Cambridgeshire, on 6 October 1801, the fourth child and second (but eldest surviving) son of Admiral Sir Charles *Cotton (1753–1812) and his wife, Philadelphia (1762/3–1855), eldest daughter of Sir Joseph Rowley. He saw little of his father, whom he succeeded as sixth baronet in 1812, and Lady Cotton was soon apprehensive about his 'impatience of controul'. He was educated at Westminster School (1815–17), and entered Christ Church, Oxford, in 1820 but took no degree. He joined the 10th hussars as a cornet in 1827, was gazetted lieutenant, served in Portugal, and retired on half pay in November 1830.

Cotton belonged to a rich, rowdy, aristocratic set who frequented the taverns of Tom Spring and Jem Burn in London. He was often involved in brawls, where his advice was 'to pitch into the big rosy men, but if you see a little lemon-faced nine-stone man, have nothing to do with him' (*Sporting Magazine*, 1863, 87). He became known for all-round sportsmanship: he hunted in Leicestershire, where few men rode harder or were better mounted; he played cricket for the MCC from 1830 to 1835 and later followed the game; and he was at home in the boxing and racing worlds, where he was known familiarly as Vinny Cotton, Sir Vincent Twist, or the Baronet. Active and fearless, powerfully built and 6 feet tall, he was 'no despicable candidate for Olympic fame' (*Sporting Magazine*, Jan 1839, 226). What most distinguished him was his love of and skill in coach driving, which had become a fashionable pursuit among young bloods. In 1836 he bought the Brighton *Age* from J. J. Willan and for three years he horsed and drove it professionally with great popular success and *élan*. Cotton entered fully into his role, regaled his audience with jokes, and took their tips politely. He kept cool in emergencies and had exceptionally strong arms which, his friends said, were his safety brake, and 'although not quite so showy or graceful a whip as some of his compeers, he was a steady and safe one' (Lennox, 229). The *New Sporting Magazine* of 1837 contained two articles in admiration of him, yet his life was hard, he had several bad accidents, and before he was forty he was wrinkled and toothless.

It was said with romantic exaggeration that Cotton drove the *Age* for a living after ruining himself. From his youth he had spent far beyond his means and was helplessly addicted to gambling, especially hazard. William Crockford reportedly said that he knew no equal to Cotton in his fondness for betting or in the recklessness of his approach, and that Cotton would sooner have a wager with a beggar on a doorstep than not bet at all, while Captain Gronow remembered the 'enormous stakes' for which he and others gambled. There were false reports in 1845 that Cotton had killed himself after losses at the Derby, and in 1846 he fled to Jersey to avoid arrest for debt. On his return, under a shower of writs, he was compelled by degrees to sell or mortgage his properties and put his financial affairs in other hands. At great cost and in distress increased by his backslidings and guilt, Lady Cotton and his sisters saved him from penury. He left Madingley

after his mother's death and spent his last years in retirement enforced by meagre funds and a ruined constitution. He became paralysed and had to be lifted into his carriage and strapped to his seat. On 24 January 1863, when he was dying, Cotton married his mistress, Hephzibah (d. 1873, aged fifty-three), daughter of Nathaniel Dimmick, in the hope that as his widow she would be socially respected. He died the next day of apoplexy at his home, 5 Hyde Park Terrace, Kensington, and the baronetcy became extinct. On 31 January he was buried at Brompton cemetery, as was his wife ten years later. JOHN D. PICKLES

**Sources** *Morning Post* (28 Jan 1863) · *Morning Post* (4 Feb 1863) · *New Sporting Magazine*, 12 (1837), 81–4, 421–2 · *Sporting Magazine*, 3rd ser., 41 (1863), 87–8 · Cambs. AS, Cotton papers · [A. Haygarth], *Frederick Lillywhite's cricket scores and biographies*, 2 (1862), 140 · W. P. Lennox, *Coaching* (1876), 229 · *The reminiscences and recollections of Captain Gronow, 1810–1860*, 2 (1889), 85, 112 · d. cert. · Brompton cemetery records

**Archives** Cambs. AS

**Likenesses** J. Ferneley, oils?, c.1831, repro. in *Cambridge Evening News* (10 Sept 1987), 19 · T. C. W., lithograph, BM · engraving, repro. in *New Sporting Magazine*, facing p. 421 · print, Bodl. Oxf., Johnson Coll.

**Wealth at death** under £800: administration, 25 Feb 1863, *CGPLA Eng. & Wales*

**Cotton, Stapleton**, first Viscount Combermere (1773–1865), army officer, was born on 14 November 1773, second son and fifth child of Sir Robert Salusbury Cotton, fifth baronet (c.1739–1809), of Combermere Abbey, Whitchurch, Shropshire, and his wife, Frances (d. 1825), daughter and coheir of Colonel James Russell Stapleton of Bodrhyddan, Denbighshire. He was born at the old seat of the Stapletons, Lleweni Hall, Denbighshire, where his father lived until he succeeded to the baronetcy in 1773. His father, MP for Cheshire for forty years, was devoted to country pursuits and very hospitable, which eventually caused him to sell the Stapleton estates for £200,000. At the age of eight Stapleton Cotton was sent to a grammar school at Audlem, a few miles away, where Vernon Harcourt, afterwards archbishop of York, was once a schoolfellow, and where his education was neglected. A quick, lively boy, he was known by his family as Young Rapid, and was continually in scrapes. Afterwards, he spent four years at Westminster School (entered 28 January 1785), his father then having a town house in Berkeley Square. Next he went to a private military academy at Norwood House, Bayswater, kept by Major Reynolds of the Shropshire militia, where he learned little more than cleaning his musket and equipment.

**Early army years** On 26 February 1790 Cotton obtained a second lieutenancy without purchase in the 23rd Royal Welch Fusiliers, and joined the corps in Dublin in 1791. He became first lieutenant on 16 March 1791, and served the regiment until 28 February 1793, when he was promoted to a troop in the 6th carabiniers, formerly the 3rd Irish horse. The drinking and duelling of its officers gave Cotton's friends concern, but his temperate habits and good temper kept him out of trouble. He embarked with his regiment in August 1793 and joined the duke of York's army just after the siege of Dunkirk; he took part in the

Stapleton Cotton, first Viscount Combermere (1773–1865), by Thomas Heaphy, 1817

campaigns of that year and the following spring, when he was present at Prémont and the cavalry battle at Le Cateau in 1794. A few days after the latter Cotton was promoted to a majority in the 59th foot, and on 9 March 1794 became lieutenant-colonel of the newly raised 25th light dragoons, then known as Gwyn's hussars. He commanded the regiment in the south of England, including at Weymouth, where he was noticed by George III and his family. In 1796 he went with his regiment to the Cape, arriving about July. The regiment then went on to Madras, and served through the campaign against Tipu Sultan of Mysore in 1799, including the siege of Seringapatam, during which Cotton appears to have become acquainted with Colonel Arthur Wellesley. Cotton's elder brother having died, his father procured for Cotton an exchange home. Accordingly, he joined the 16th light dragoons on the Kentish coast.

**Marriage and the cavalry** On 1 March 1801 Cotton married the beautiful Lady Anna Maria Pelham-Clinton (1783–1807), eldest daughter of the third duke of Newcastle and his wife, Anna Maria. Cotton and his first wife had no surviving children. He was later stationed with his regiment in Ireland. Cotton, who attained the rank of colonel on 1 January 1800, became a major-general on 30 October 1805, and for a time commanded a cavalry brigade at Weymouth under the duke of Cumberland. From 1806 to 1814 he was tory MP for Newark. His wife died in 1807 of consumption. In 1808 he was sent to Portugal with a brigade comprising the 14th and 16th light dragoons, and one squadron of the 20th light dragoons. The brigade served on the Portuguese frontier during Moore's campaign in Spain, and afterwards in the north of Portugal in 1809, including the operations against Oporto. Until the arrival

of Lieutenant-General Payne, Cotton commanded the allied cavalry. At Talavera he commanded a brigade and did notable service.

News reached Cotton of his father's death at the end of 1809, and in January 1810 he went home. A baronet with a substantial estate (which, through his father's unbusiness-like habits, was in much need of supervision), a man of fashion, and welcomed in society, Cotton had many inducements to remain at home. But he preferred his military career, his qualifications for which, owing, perhaps, to his youthful appearance and his modesty, were not always fully recognized. He was of moderate stature, sparely built, very active, and an excellent horseman. Splendidly dressed—his uniform and horse trappings were reportedly worth 500 guineas ransom—and ever foremost in danger, he was known as the Lion d'Or, but did not expose his men or fatigue his horses unnecessarily. Wellington, who recognized the necessity of husbanding his inadequate force of cavalry, said that in entrusting an order to Cotton he knew it would be carried out with discretion as well as zeal.

On rejoining the army in the summer of 1810 Cotton was appointed to the command of the 1st division, and afterwards to that of the whole of the allied cavalry, with the local rank of lieutenant-general. He attained the same rank in the British army on 1 January 1812. According to Sir Charles Oman, Cotton 'was hardly up to his position, though he earned his chief's tolerance by strict obedience to orders, a greater merit in the Duke's eyes than military genius or initiative' (Oman, 36). Among his more important services at the head of the cavalry—which constituted a separate division after May 1811—were the covering of the retreat from Almeida to Torres Vedras, from July to September 1810, in which not one baggage wagon was abandoned; the successful action at Llerena, on 11 April 1812, when he attacked and defeated a superior force of Soult's rear-guard; his action at Castrejon, near Salamanca, on 18 July 1812, when with Anson's brigade of cavalry and the 4th and light divisions he held Marmont's entire army at bay and defeated plans that would have jeopardized the whole British army; and his services at the battle of Salamanca, where he was second in command under Lord Wellington, and led the charge of Le Marchant's and Anson's heavy brigades. Wellington wrote of Cotton that he commanded the cavalry very well, and better than some who might be supposed cleverer than he. Wellington apparently objected to Lord Bathurst's idea of conferring a peerage on Cotton, for fear of offending Marshal Beresford, Cotton's senior in the army. A slow voyage made him three days late for the battle of Vitoria, but he commanded the allied cavalry throughout the ensuing campaigns in Spain and southern France until the peace, including the actions in the Pyrenees, at Orthez, and at Toulouse.

**Peerage, military service, marriages, and death** On his return home Cotton, who was already KCB (1812), on 17 May 1814 was raised to the peerage as Baron Combermere of Combermere, Chester, with a pension of £2000 a year for his own and two succeeding lives. He was also awarded

Hanoverian, Portuguese, and Spanish orders. On 18 June 1814, at Lambeth Palace, he married Caroline (c.1793–1837), second daughter of Captain W. Fulke Greville RN, and twenty years his junior. They had a son, Wellington Henry, second viscount (1818–1891), and two daughters. Among their common interests was music, Combermere having some vocal pretensions and his wife being an accomplished musician. On Napoleon's return from Elba, to Wellington's annoyance, command of the cavalry in Belgium was given, at the insistence of the prince regent, to Lord Uxbridge. However, after Waterloo Wellington invited Combermere to Paris, where he arrived on 18 July 1815, and commanded the allied cavalry in France until the following year, when the army of occupation was reduced. In 1815 he was made GCB.

In 1817 Cotton was appointed governor of Barbados and commander-in-chief in the Leeward Islands, which he held until June 1820. He tactfully restored friendly relations with the French West Indian islands, disturbed by a supposed discourtesy to the French flag by a British warship. From 1822 to 1825 he was commander-in-chief in Ireland. A new commander-in-chief in India being then needed, and an expedition against Bharatpur being likely, Combermere was selected by the directors of the East India Company, reportedly on the advice of Wellington. An expedition against the Burmese was under consideration, and the cabinet asked Wellington's advice. He replied, 'Send Lord Combermere.' 'But we have always understood that Your Grace thought Lord Combermere a fool.' 'So he is and a d—d fool; but he can take Rangoon' (R. Lewin, The Chief, 1980, 201). Combermere, who attained the rank of general on 27 May 1825, had by then started for India, leaving his wife at home. The attack on Bharatpur was successful; the great Jat fortress, a menace to British rule ever since Lord Lake failed against it twenty years before, was destroyed. Combermere was made a viscount in 1827, and on 16 September 1829 colonel of the 1st Life Guards, having already been colonel of the 20th light dragoons 1813–18 and of the 3rd light dragoons 1821–9. He remained in India for the customary five years, during nine months of which he acted as governor-general while Lord Amherst was away in the hills, and returned home in 1830.

On his return Combermere separated from his second wife, who died in January 1837. In 1838 Combermere married his third wife, Mary Woolley Gibbings (d. 1889), only child of Robert Gibbings of Gibbings Grove, co. Cork. They had no children. His last thirty years were passed in the performance of his parliamentary and social duties. An old-fashioned tory, he opposed Catholic emancipation, the Reform Bill, repeal of the corn laws, army short service, and other innovations. From 1840 he was provincial grand master of the freemasons of Cheshire. He was governor of Sheerness from 1821 until 1852. On Wellington's death he was made constable of the Tower of London, and in 1855 a field marshal. Suffering from a severe cold, Cotton died at Colchester House, Clifton, on 21 February 1865, and was buried in the family vault in the church at Wrenbury, Cheshire.    H. M. CHICHESTER, rev. JAMES LUNT

**Sources** Memoirs and correspondence of Field Marshal Viscount Combermere, from his family papers, ed. M. W. S. Cotton [Viscountess Combermere] and W. Knollys, 2 vols. (1866) • The dispatches of … the duke of Wellington … from 1799 to 1818, ed. J. Gurwood, 13 vols. in 12 (1834–9) • H. Graham, History of the sixteenth, the queen's, light dragoons (lancers), 1759–1912 (privately printed, Devizes, 1912) • M. Glover, History of the royal Welch fusiliers (1989) • Fortescue, Brit. army, 2nd edn, vols. 3–4 • W. F. P. Napier, History of the war in the Peninsula and in the south of France, 6 vols. (1886) • Marquess of Anglesey [G. C. H. V. Paget], A history of the British cavalry, 1816 to 1919, 1 (1973) • C. W. C. Oman, Wellington's army, 1809–1814 (1912); repr. (1968) • E. Longford [E. H. Pakenham, countess of Longford], Wellington, 1: The years of the sword (1969) • J. Paget, Wellington's Peninsular War (1990) • J. Lunt, Scarlet lancer (1964) • GEC, Peerage • Burke, Peerage
**Archives** Ches. & Chester ALSS, letters and papers relating to India • NAM, corresp. and papers • NL Ire., letters • Notts. Arch., corresp. and papers of his election agent relating to parliamentary election | BL OIOC, letters to Lord Amherst, MS Eur F 140 • Bodl. Oxf., corresp. with Colonel Doyle • Durham RO, letters to Lord Londonderry • Lpool RO, letters to fourteenth earl of Derby • NAM, letters to Jasper Nicolls • U. Nott. L., corresp. with duke of Newcastle • U. Southampton L., letters to first duke of Wellington
**Likenesses** T. Heaphy, chalk drawing, 1799, Stratfield Saye, Hampshire • T. Heaphy, watercolour drawing, 1817, NPG [see illus.] • M. M. Pearson, oils, 1823, NPG • C. Turner, mezzotint, pubd 1823 (after T. Heaphy), BM • J. Hayter, oils, 1839, NAM • J. P. Knight, oils, c.1845, Plas Newydd, Anglesey • W. Ross, oils, c.1850; formerly at United Service Club, London • Maull and Polyblank, photograph, c.1860, NPG • C. Marochetti, statue, 1864, Chester Castle: Agricola Tower and Castle Walls, Cheshire • portrait, NPG • portrait (as a youthful lieutenant-colonel of the 25th light dragoons), repro. in Memoirs and correspondence, ed. Cotton and Knollys; priv. coll. • portrait (aged ninety), repro. in Memoirs and correspondence, ed. Cotton and Knollys; priv. coll.
**Wealth at death** under £16,000: probate, 25 April 1865, CGPLA Eng. & Wales

**Cotton, Sir Sydney John** (1792–1874), army officer, was born on 2 December 1792, the second son of the fourteen children of Henry Calveley Cotton (1755–1837), of Woodcote, Oxfordshire, uncle of the first Viscount Combermere, and his wife, Matilda (d. 3 Feb 1848), the daughter and heir of John Lockwood of Dews Hall, Essex. Among his brothers were General Sir Arthur *Cotton (1803–1899), also of the Indian army, Admiral Francis Vere Cotton, Royal Navy, General Frederic Cotton, Royal Engineers, and Richard Lynch *Cotton (1794–1880), provost of Worcester College, Oxford.

On 19 April 1810 Sydney Cotton was appointed cornet without purchase in the 22nd light dragoons in India, in which regiment he became lieutenant on 13 February 1812. When the 22nd dragoons were disbanded, Cotton was placed on half pay, but continued in India, serving as aide-de-camp to Major-General Hare at Bangalore. He married in 1820 Marianne (d. 1854), daughter of Captain Halkett, late 22nd light dragoons, and they had two sons and two daughters. In 1822 he purchased a company—his only purchased step—in the 3rd regiment (the Buffs), then in New South Wales, and after its move to India served as aide-de-camp, and for a time as military secretary, to his kinsman Lord Combermere, commander-in-chief in India. In 1828 he was appointed major in the 41st in Burma, and subsequently exchanged to the 28th in New South Wales. He became a brevet lieutenant-colonel on 23 November 1841, and at about the same time was sent from

Parramatta, in charge of 500 male and female convicts, to re-form an old station at Moreton Bay, on the east coast. The district was opened to settlement soon afterwards, and later became the state of Queensland.

Cotton accompanied the 28th to Bombay when it was sent there on the news of the disasters in the Khyber Pass, but cholera prevented the regiment taking the field, although it was employed for a while under Sir Charles Napier in Sind when the amir threatened a renewal of hostilities a year later. Cotton became regimental lieutenant-colonel on 8 June 1843, and when the 28th was ordered home in 1848 effected an exchange with Colonel John Pennefather to the 22nd foot, with which he remained in India. He commanded a force sent as a reinforcement to the north-west frontier in 1853, during the agitation resulting from the murder of the British commissioner Colonel Mackesay at Peshawar, and proceeded with it to the Kohat Pass, where he brought the refractory tribes into submission. The same year he commanded the 22nd with a force under Brigadier Boileau, employed against the Bori Afridis, and in 1854 was dispatched with a force of 4500 men to punish the Mohmands. He became brevet colonel on 20 June 1854, and when the 22nd foot went home he exchanged to the 10th foot in Bengal. At the outbreak of the Indian mutiny Cotton was commanding in the Peshawar valley as first-class brigadier. Of moderate stature and spare active form, he was considered one of the best regimental officers in the army. His previous Indian experience may be summed up from his own words, in the preface to his memoir of service on the north-west frontier: he served in the Madras presidency for many years, in Burma for a time, in the Bombay presidency for many years, in Sind for a time, in the Bengal presidency, at two periods of his life, for a great many years, and at almost every station in the three presidencies where European troops were located. He served in a light cavalry regiment in the Carnatic and Mysore for over ten years, in command of a squadron in the Ceded and Conquered Provinces during the Pindari war of 1816–17, on the staff of a general officer at Bangalore for two years, in command of a station near Madras, as deputy adjutant-general and deputy quartermaster-general of the royal forces in Madras, as aide-de-camp to the commander-in-chief in India, and as military secretary. He served under Sir Charles Napier in Sind, and commanded a field brigade at Deesa in the Bombay presidency, and brigades at Ambala, Rawalpindi, and Peshawar in the Bengal command. The outbreak of the mutiny gave him his chance, and he took it. He was, as Lord Lawrence pronounced him to be, the right man for the place (Smith, 1.463). Cotton was dispatched to Sirana, in command of an expeditionary force, with Herbert Edwardes as political agent, to deal with a remaining clutch of mutineers established over the Yusufzai border; he successfully executed this task, the offenders being punished without rousing the hostility of the adjacent tribes. For his frontier services Cotton was made KCB. He became major-general on 26 October 1858, and was appointed colonel of his old regiment, the 10th foot, on 5 February 1863. For some years he commanded the north-western district with headquarters at Manchester. He became lieutenant-general on 20 April 1866, and was appointed honorary colonel of the 1st Cheshire rifle volunteers in 1869. On 10 May 1872 he was made governor of the Royal Hospital, Chelsea, in succession to Sir John Pennefather, and GCB on 24 May 1873. He died in London, at the Royal Hospital, Chelsea, on 20 February 1874.

Cotton was the author of several works, among them *Nine Years on the North-West Frontier* (1868). In it he expressed his views on various Indian questions. These were of particular value, coming as they did from an officer of the British service with an exceptionally long experience of Indian conditions, and who, moreover, possessed to a remarkable degree the confidence of his soldiers, gained for the most part as a result of his unceasing endeavours to improve the lot of the British soldier serving in India.

H. M. CHICHESTER, *rev.* JAMES LUNT

**Sources** S. Cotton, *Nine years on the north-west frontier of India, from 1854–1863* (1868) • *Annual Register* (1874) • F. Brodigan, *Historical record 28th foot* (1884) • Lady Edwardes, *Memorials of the life and letters of Sir Herbert Edwardes* (1886) • J. W. Kaye and G. B. Malleson, *Kaye's and Malleson's History of the Indian mutiny of 1857–8*, 6 vols. (1888–9) • Burke, *Peerage* (1959) [under Combermere] • R. B. Smith, *Life of Lord Lawrence*, 2 vols. (1883) • J. W. Kaye, *A history of the Sepoy War in India, 1857–1858*, 3 vols. (1864–76) • P. Moon, *The British conquest and dominion of India* (1989) • C. Hibbert, *The great mutiny, India, 1857* (1978) • T. A. Heathcote, *The military in British India: the development of British land forces in south Asia, 1600–1947* (1995) • CGPLA Eng. & Wales (1874)
**Archives** ING Barings, London, corresp. with the earl of Northbrook
**Likenesses** wood-engraving, NPG; repro. in *ILN* (1858)
**Wealth at death** under £450: administration, 31 March 1874, CGPLA Eng. & Wales

**Cotton, Sir Thomas**, second baronet (1594–1662). *See under* Cotton, Sir Robert Bruce, first baronet (1571–1631).

**Cotton, Thomas** (*bap.* 1701, *d.* 1749). *See under* Cotton family (*per.* c.1650–1802).

**Cotton, Thomas** (1723–1802). *See under* Cotton family (*per.* c.1650–1802).

**Cotton, William** (*d.* 1621), bishop of Exeter, was the elder son of John Cotton, a citizen of London, and Pery Cheyne. Between 1568 and 1574 he was a scholar of Queens' College, Cambridge, graduating BA in 1572 and proceeding MA in 1575. In 1578 he married, by licence dated 10 December, Mary, daughter of Thomas Hulme of the county of Chester and widow of William Cutler, citizen of London; they had two sons and four daughters. He had been ordained by Bishop Aylmer of London on 15 May 1577 and became the bishop's chaplain but lost some favour with Aylmer for not being efficient enough in finding preachers for Paul's Cross. He was a prebendary at St Paul's from 1577 and archdeacon of Lewes from 1578. He kept both appointments until 1598, adding to them the positions of vicar of St Margaret's, New Fish Street Hill (1578), rector of West Tilbury (1581), and rector of Finchley (1581), his principal home.

Nominated bishop of Exeter in 1598, Cotton was consecrated on 12 November that year, and reached Exeter on 16 May 1599. In Devon he continued the practice of accumulating livings and added the precentorship of Exeter Cathedral and the livings of Bratton Clovelly and Silverton to his episcopal office. He had been reluctant to take the bishopric, which he considered remote and poor, but was promised an early translation to a wealthier see. He later complained to his distant cousin, the antiquary Sir Robert Cotton, that 'I was set on and hastned from Lambeth to adventure upon this Westerne and turbulent people amongst many clamourous and malicious Rattleheadds, with promise that I should not warme my stoole before I should be removed', yet twenty-two bishops had been consecrated or translated 'and I sit still as one nailed to this stoole' (Boggis, 388).

Cotton found his palace in a poor state of repair and sued his predecessor, Gervase Babington, now bishop of Worcester, for dilapidations. He was anxious to appear an effective new broom and wrote to Sir Robert Cecil in January 1601 implying that the diocese was in a chaotic state and requesting an ecclesiastical commission. This was granted in 1602, renewed in 1604, and lasted until 1609. He was the main person behind this court and usually present at its proceedings held in the chapter house or in the palace or at Silverton. There is little evidence that it achieved more than could have been dealt with in the ordinary ecclesiastical courts of the diocese. However, Cotton boasted of its success. He claimed in 1606 that he had:

> reformed by the help of that Commission many factious preachers and reclaimed many Papists. Within these 10 days I have brought 8 or 9 recusants to the Church and within one year I hope to clear my diocese of that Popish faction as I have done the peevish. (*Salisbury MSS*, 18.297–8)

Roman Catholicism was not a problem in the Exeter diocese at this time, there being fewer than 100 Catholics in Devon and not more than twice that number in Cornwall; there is no evidence that these numbers changed during Cotton's episcopate. Puritanism was potentially a much greater problem but even here Cotton was not as active as his reputation suggests. The judgement of Thomas Fuller, who gathered information from Cotton's son, that 'the vigilancy of this stout and prudent prelate plucked up' puritanism 'by the roots before it grew to perfection' (Fuller, *Worthies*, 66), is not confirmed by the evidence. The formal requirement of subscription to the canons of 1604 over the following year led to only four ministers being deprived and to three being suspended. One of these ministers, Samuel Hieron, maintained that Cotton only urged subscription on men he did not favour. Cotton had some sympathy with the puritan outlook and his wife, Mary, who was of a godly disposition, was an intermediary for puritans with her husband. He claimed that he spent much time persuading those who privately dissented to accept canon 36, and he occasionally allowed a minister to omit part of the second article which stated that only public liturgy could be used in divine worship.

Cotton's episcopate is open to various criticisms.

Although he dropped his practice of ordaining a man deacon and priest at the same time when it was prohibited in the canons of 1603, he had started doing so again by 1607. He used all possible means to increase his income, granting dispensations for eating meat on fast days and for marriage licences in the uncanonical seasons. He quarrelled with the city and county of Exeter, presenting extreme grievances to them over their supposed restriction of his boundaries and liberties, but they refuted his claim. His use of patronage to benefit his sons called forth a rebuke from Archbishop George Abbot. As well as bestowing benefices on them, he made William canon and precentor of the cathedral and Edward canon and chancellor. This inevitably brought the factious relationship of Cotton and the dean, Matthew Sutcliffe, into the affairs of the cathedral chapter.

The only evidence of Cotton's absence from his see is his presence in London during the early days of the parliaments of 1601 and 1604. He usually spent at least eight months of the year at Silverton, conducting ordinations and institutions there and continuing to live there after he resigned the living to his elder son, William. He was at his palace only during the winter months and even then normally conducted ordinations in the palace not in the cathedral. Sets of visitation articles survive for 1599, 1610, and 1619. Those for 1610 and 1619 were very similar and did not follow the pattern of Archbishop Richard Bancroft's articles of 1605, which were addressed to Exeter and nine other dioceses. It is of particular interest that Cotton did not think it necessary to enforce inquiries, similar to Bancroft's, to uncover any shade of nonconformist.

Cotton died at Silverton rectory on 26 August 1621, having suffered from the stone and from a loss of speech which left him able to say only 'Amen, Amen' during his last few days, according to Fuller's account obtained from his son. He was buried on 31 August in the south choir aisle of Exeter Cathedral, where a monument was erected to his memory. He was survived by his wife, who died on 29 December 1629. MARY WOLFFE

**Sources** K. Fincham, *Prelate as pastor: the episcopate of James I* (1990) · J. A. Vage, 'The diocese of Exeter, 1519–1641: a study of church government in the age of the Reformation', PhD diss., U. Cam., 1991 · *Calendar of the manuscripts of the most hon. the marquis of Salisbury*, 10, HMC, 9 (1904), 450–51; 11 (1906), 26; 18 (1940), 297–8 · Devon RO, Chanter 42, 50, 761, 1129; ancient letter 103; Bere Ferrers C/W Acc 1815 PZ1–5; Clawton 3577A PW1 · Fuller, *Worthies* (1811), vol. 2 · R. J. E. Boggis, *A history of the diocese of Exeter* (1922) · *Report on records of the city of Exeter*, HMC, 73 (1916) · G. Oliver, *Lives of the bishops of Exeter, and a history of the cathedral* (1861) · Venn, *Alum. Cant.* · Foster, *Alum. Oxon.* · J. L. Vivian, ed., *The visitations of the county of Devon, comprising the herald's visitations of 1531, 1564, and 1620* (privately printed, Exeter, [1895]) · A. Duffin, *Faction and faith: politics and religion of the Cornish gentry before the civil war* (1996) · M. Stoyle, *Loyalty and locality: popular allegiance in Devon during the English civil war* (1994) · DNB · *Articles to be enquired of within the diocese of Exeter in the general and triennial visitation of the reverend father in God, William lord bishop of Exeter* (1610) · K. Fincham, ed., *Visitation articles and injunctions of the early Stuart church*, 2 vols. (1994–8)

**Likenesses** effigy on monument, Exeter Cathedral

**Wealth at death** no value given: will, PRO, PROB 11/138, sig. 78

**Cotton, William** (*d.* **1675**). *See under* Cotton family (*per.* c.1650–1802).

**Cotton, William** (**1648/9–1703**). *See under* Cotton family (*per.* c.1650–1802).

**Cotton, William** (**1786–1866**), merchant and philanthropist, was born on 12 September 1786 at Leytonstone, Essex, the third son of Joseph *Cotton (1745–1825), a mariner and merchant, and his wife, Sarah (1751–1818), the daughter of John Harrison, a merchant and director of the Bank of England. He was educated until the age of fifteen at Chigwell grammar school. Having been brought up in a milieu of high Anglicanism and shipping enterprise (his father was a long-serving director of the East India Company), he was drawn to the church, but entered instead the office of a friend of his father, Charles Hampden Turner. In 1807–8 he became Turner's partner and also joined him in the Limehouse firm of Huddart & Co., set up to exploit the steam-driven rope-making machinery invented by Captain Joseph Huddart. Cotton himself was of an inventive bent; he had several patents to his name, and he became a fellow of the Royal Society in 1821.

Cotton soon took over sole control of Huddart & Co., while also taking part in regular investments in shipping ventures which afforded him a substantial income but not, in his view, a vast fortune. The Huddart factory itself depended on the prosperity of shipping; it thrived in the post-war expansion of trade, and supplied both ropes (from Russian hemp) and sails (from Scottish flax yarn). By London standards this was an impressive integrated firm, with its huge rope-walks, using travelling engines, and a power-loom sailcloth factory which brought to east London 'a foretaste of the giant establishments at Manchester' (Bodl. Oxf., Acland papers d. 179). Yet by the 1830s it faced the competition of both steamships and chain cables. Characteristically, Cotton welcomed the former, as a likely aid to the diffusion of Christianity, but the latter threatened the firm's machinery with obsolescence. Nevertheless, deeply impressed by the perfection of Huddart's machinery, Cotton persuaded the Admiralty to buy it in 1838 (the Russian navy was also purportedly interested). The rope-making apparatus was moved to Deptford but, faced by artisanal dislike and technological change, it soon fell into disuse and was broken up. Cotton, appalled by the fate of 'one of the most beautiful pieces of machinery in the world' (Cotton, *Brief Memoir*, 31), attempted to buy the parts. In the same year (1838) Cotton wrote a memoir of Huddart, with an account of his inventions. He was awarded a Telford medal from the Institution of Civil Engineers for this work, which was privately printed in 1855.

The Limehouse factory continued to operate on a considerable scale in the early 1840s, but thereafter was gradually run down before closing in the mid-1850s. Its continued existence owed much to Cotton's strong sense of responsibility as an employer, a sense rooted in his religious beliefs but reinforced by temporary residence in industrializing Stockport during the early years of the century. This had led him to end the payment of wages in public houses, to play an active part in the London Hospital (he was elected chairman in 1827 and treasurer in 1837), and, above all, to show a keen interest in churches and schools for the working classes.

By the late 1830s Cotton's interests had shifted largely from his own business concerns to the work of public bodies, above all the Bank of England. Following in the steps of his maternal grandfather, he had become a director in 1822, and took a leading part in its management. As governor between 1842 and 1845 (his term unusually extended from two to three years), he worked closely with Sir Robert Peel and Henry Goulburn in the formulation and implementation of the Bank Charter Act of 1844. He shared in a Peelite dislike of speculation fed by overextended credit and paper currency, and his support proved invaluable when many within the bank, the City, and the country at large distrusted the act's overly rigid management of money. He remained, particularly in the wake of the commercial crisis of 1847, one of the act's strongest defenders, both publicly and within the bank. Cotton's mechanical ingenuity also served the bank well, for, when it faced the task of reweighing the nation's coinage (an essential part of the campaign for sound money), he devised in 1842 an automatic weighing machine for sovereigns. Suitably nicknamed 'the governor', it won a medal at the Great Exhibition of 1851, was long used at the bank, and was later placed in its museum.

Cotton married on 4 February 1812 Sarah, the only daughter of Thomas Lane, and devoted great attention and anxiety to the welfare of their seven children. Of his four sons, three attended Eton College and Christ Church, Oxford, and both William Charles *Cotton [see under Cotton, Sir Henry] and Henry *Cotton were elected students of Christ Church. The former, having alarmed his father by his closeness to E. B. Pusey in the 1840s, took ship to New Zealand as Bishop Selwyn's chaplain, before returning to devote himself to bee-keeping and the parish of Frodsham; Henry became lord justice in the Court of Appeal. Cotton's eldest daughter, Sarah, married in 1846 Henry Acland, regius professor of medicine at Oxford, and the son of his old friend and church ally Sir Thomas Acland. An unmarried daughter, Agnes *Cotton, social reformer and philanthropist, founded in 1865 the Good Shepherd Children's Home at Forest Place, London.

In all spheres of activity, Cotton was impelled by his sense of religious duty combined with a fear of the nation's spiritual decline. He held deeply that, 'until the rich do all they can for the poor, we are not competent to say that poverty is any bar to the spread of Christianity' (Cotton to Revd Henry Soames, 9 April 1845, Cotton MS 207), and not only set aside one-tenth of his income for charity, but devoted much time to the work of moral reform in early nineteenth-century London. This he valued above political action for, while favourable to gradual reform in church and state, he believed 'he is the best patriot who does most towards moral reform as rendering the country more worth[y] of that divine favour on which we must rely' (Cotton to W. C. Cotton, 7 March 1830, Cotton MSS). Dismayed above all by the rapid relative decline in churchgoing, Cotton had been one of the founders of the Church Building Society in 1818, and in the 1830s became Bishop Blomfield's leading adjutant in the Metropolis Churches Fund. His energetic canvassing was credited with the building of seventy-eight rather than the projected fifty churches. Bishop Blomfield afterwards referred to Cotton as his 'lay archdeacon'. Cotton himself paid particular attention to Bethnal Green, where the existing parish was subdivided into ten churches—the last, St Thomas's, built at Cotton's sole expense in memory of his son Joseph Edward.

To a later generation of social reformer this work appeared indiscriminate and overhasty, with Bethnal Green a byword for ill-judged ecclesiastical reform, but to others this was an exemplary contribution to the work of national renewal. Cotton later became a leading supporter of the London Diocesan Church Building Society and in the 1850s, on land belonging to the former Huddart works, he erected, as a conscientious ground landlord, the church of St Paul's, Bow Common, of which his son Arthur Benjamin became the first incumbent.

Cotton promoted a wide variety of charitable efforts, often in association with the group of prominent high-churchmen drawn from the 'Hackney Phalanx' and the club of 'Nobody's Friends'. He was thus one of the founders of the National Society in 1811, formed for establishing schools in which the principles of the Church of England should be taught, and also of King's College, London, in 1829. He actively supported the Society for Promoting Christian Knowledge (SPCK) and was a member for fifty years and a long-serving treasurer. He was similarly a patron of the Society for the Propagation of the Gospel, the Colonial Bishoprics Fund, and the Additional Curates Society. Other interests included Christ's Hospital, and in the 1840s he became a promoter of public baths, wash-houses, and model lodging houses. In Essex, where he lived and farmed, he chaired the quarter sessions and acted as high sheriff in 1838. In 1848 he received an honorary DCL from the University of Oxford, an unusual accolade for a City merchant.

Cotton died on 1 December 1866 at Walwood House, Leytonstone, where he had lived since 1813. He was buried in the churchyard of St John the Baptist, Leytonstone, a church he had helped to build. A memorial window placed in St Paul's Cathedral by public subscription was destroyed during the Second World War.

A. C. HOWE

**Sources** *GM*, 4th ser., 3 (1867), 111–13 · W. C. Cotton, 'William Cotton, Esq.', *Church Builder* (Jan 1867), 25–46 · 'A day at a rope and sail-cloth factory', *Penny Magazine* (26 Nov 1842), 465–72 · F. Temple, 'An account of Wallwood, Leytonstone, from 1200–1960', *Transactions of the Essex Archaeological Society*, 3rd ser., 1 (1961–5), 114–26 · I. Brunel, *The life of Sarah Acland* (1894) · 'Select committee of the House of Lords to inquire into … places of divine worship', *Parl. papers* (1857–8), 9.3–17, no. 387 · 'Secret committee on commercial distress', *Parl. papers* (1847–8), vol. 8/1, nos. 395, 584; vol. 8/2, no. 395; vol. 8/3, nos. 565, 565-II · GEC, *Peerage* · W. Cotton, *A brief memoir of the late Captn. Joseph Huddart, FRS, and an account of his inventions in the manufacture of cordage* (1855), 31 · Bank of England archives, London, Cotton MSS, MS 207 · d. cert.

**Archives** Bank of England, archives, London | BL, corresp. with Sir Robert Peel, Add. MSS 40469–40600 · Bodl. Oxf., Acland MSS, corresp. with his son William · NA Scot., letters to G. W. Hope

**Likenesses** M. Noble?, bust, exh. RA 1856, Bank of England, London · photographs, Bank of England, London · wood-engraving, Bank of England, London; repro. in *ILN* (13 July 1844)

**Wealth at death** under £70,000: probate, 7 Jan 1867, *CGPLA Eng. & Wales*

**Cotton, William Charles** (1813–1879). *See under* Cotton, Sir Henry (1821–1892).

**Cotton, William Edward** [Billy] (1899–1969), bandleader and radio and television broadcaster, was born on 27 May 1899 at 31 New Tothill Street, Westminster, London, the youngest of the ten children of Joseph Cotton, a water turncock, and his wife, Susan Harmer. He was educated at St Margaret's School, Westminster, where he excelled at boxing, swimming, cricket, and football. As a boy treble he sang in the choirs of St Margaret's and St Andrew's, Ashley Place, receiving 2s. for a funeral and a half-crown for a wedding. Although under age at the outbreak of the First World War Cotton managed to enlist in the Territorial Army and was posted to Malta and thence to the Dardanelles. In 1916 he joined the Royal Flying Corps but was hospitalized after crashing a Bristol aircraft while training. (His daredevil streak manifested itself years later when he delighted in 'buzzing' his son Bill's boarding-school while piloting his own aircraft.) After the war Cotton had various jobs including bus conducting, drumming with the Fifth Avenue Orchestra (named after an address in Neasden rather than New York!), and playing professional football for Wimbledon and Brentford. On 26 December 1921 he married Mabel Hope (1895–1989), daughter of Edward Gregory, a butcher. They had two sons, Ted (1923–1966) and Bill Cotton junior (*b.* 1928), who became a senior BBC television executive.

In 1925 Cotton formed his own dance-band—the London Savannah Band—for a summer season at Southport Palais. Cine-variety and gramophone sessions (including an early recording of George Gershwin's *Rhapsody in Blue*) followed. Despite an exhausting schedule of band engagements Cotton continued playing cricket and football, piloting his own aircraft, sailing a 40 foot motor cruiser, and motor racing at Brooklands and Donnington. He dismissed the band at the outbreak of the Second World War but, finding he was considered too old to fly Spitfires, he reformed it and took the musicians to France to entertain the troops. This morale-boosting exercise stood the players in good stead when they were invited in February 1949 to do a series of Sunday morning radio broadcasts on the Light Programme. The *Billy Cotton Band Show*, heralded by a fanfare and a cheery cry of 'wakey-WAKEY!'), quickly became a Sunday lunchtime institution. Broadcast live from the Aeolian Hall studios, it combined popular tunes with broad comedy. The vocalists were Alan Breeze, Kathie Kay, and Rita Williams and the Bandits. There was

William Edward [Billy] **Cotton** (1899–1969), by Yousuf Karsh

no studio audience: the musicians themselves (and the radio audience at home) supplied the laughs.

1950 saw the first of several royal command performance appearances. Cotton was quick to exploit the opportunities afforded by the introduction of commercial television, though he did not remain with ITV for long. In 1957 Cotton clinched a long-term deal with BBC light entertainment supremo Ronnie Waldman. The agreement—signed on a paper napkin in a Shepherd's Bush trattoria—secured the band's services on BBC television and radio for a number of years. While the wireless format remained broadly the same, the television shows expanded (under the direction of Brian Tesler) to include production numbers with chorus girls and star guests of the calibre of Peter Sellers and Bob Hope. Bill Cotton junior had directed the band on tour when his father suffered a nervous breakdown in 1954. He now took over production of the television series and even presented the radio programmes when his father suffered a stroke in 1962, the year in which he won the Variety Club of Great Britain's award as show business personality of the year. Cotton made a full recovery and continued to entertain right up to 1969 when, on 25 March, he collapsed at a Wembley boxing match, and was declared dead on arrival at Wembley Hospital. He was cremated and his ashes scattered.

Larger than life in both physique and disposition, Billy Cotton lived life to the full. Notwithstanding his limited education and inability to read music, he gave the impression of being able to succeed in whatever he turned his hand to. His approach to dance music was pragmatic: it brought him fame and fortune, while allowing him enough spare time to indulge his love of sport and adventure. His band, never as musically adventurous as those of Jack Hylton, Roy Fox, or Ambrose, nevertheless outlasted them and brought pleasure to millions. He was a tough but fair boss and many of his players stayed with him for three decades. In the studio he could be cantankerous and obstinate but his television persona was an accurate reflection of the cheerful cockney that he was at heart. His remarkable 44-year career as a bandleader spanned the development of electronic entertainment from crystal set to colour television. Relatively few complete recordings of his radio and television output survive but commercial gramophone recordings have been released on CD and merit consideration.                    ANTHONY WILLS

**Sources** private information (2004) [Bill Cotton junior] • B. Cotton, *I did it my way: the life story of Billy Cotton* (1970) • J. Maxwell, *The greatest Billy Cotton Band Show* (1976) • *Radio Times* (1949–69) • *CGPLA Eng. & Wales* (1969) • *The Times* (26 March 1969) • d. cert. • m. cert. • b. cert.
**Archives** BBC WAC | FILM BBC WAC • BFI NFTVA, documentary footage | SOUND BBC WAC
**Likenesses** Y. Karsh, photograph, priv. coll. [*see illus.*]
**Wealth at death** £23,630: probate, 21 Aug 1969, *CGPLA Eng. & Wales*

**Cotton, Sir William James Richmond** (1822–1902), businessman and politician, was born at Stratford-le-Bow, London, on 13 November 1822, the eldest son of William Cotton. He received a private school education before joining a solicitor's office and then becoming a leading partner in Culverwell, Brook & Co., leather, hide, and tallow brokers. In 1846 he married Caroline, the daughter of Charles Pottinger of Sunderland; they had twelve children. Cotton published in 1850 a poem called *Imagination* dedicated to Charles Dickens. He also wrote *Smash: a Sketch of the Times, Past, Present and to Come* (1860) referring to railway speculations at a time of commercial panic. Among his other interests he owned extensive iron ore mines in Norway, was director of the Liverpool and London and Globe Fire and Life offices, and served as chairman of the Staines and West Drayton Railway Company.

Armed with a fine business reputation, Cotton began his civic career in 1866 when he was elected alderman for Lime Street ward in the City of London. He served as alderman until 1892, the last four years in the ward of Bridge Without. He had also gained recognition as the deputy chairman and joint treasurer of the Lancashire and Cheshire Operative Relief Fund in 1861. Building on these foundations, he was elected sheriff of London and Middlesex in 1868–9, and was appointed magistrate for London and Hertfordshire, commissioner of lieutenancy for London, chairman of the City police committee, and commissioner of Inland Revenue for Hertfordshire. He was elected to the London school board in 1870, and served in the City area until 1879. He was also made chairman of the board of governors of the Mary Datchelor schools, member of the Thames Conservancy Board, governor of Christ's, St Bartholomew's, St Thomas's, Bridewell, and Bethlem hospitals, and a governor of Queen Anne's Bounty. In 1892 he was appointed chamberlain.

Cotton was lord mayor of London in 1875–6, and hosted a banquet to celebrate the homecoming of the prince of Wales from India at a reported cost of £50,000. This was one of the few remarkable events in an unremarkable year, although Cotton oversaw a fund for eastern war victims and a mass meeting held on the subject of the 'Bulgarian atrocities'. Closer to home, funds were raised for the sufferers of the floods of the Thames and the fens.

Above all, Cotton was an advocate for the City guilds. He was a member of the courts of the Furriers', Fanmakers', and Loriners' companies, master of the Haberdashers' and Saddlers' companies in his mayoral year, and master of the Turners' Company (1891–3). When the livery companies were under attack from Liberal opponents, Cotton became chairman of the City Guilds Defence Association and championed their cause in parliament. As a result he was a member of the 1884 royal commission appointed to inquire into the livery companies of the City of London, and both co-author of the dissenting minority report and sole author of an additional protest ('Commissioners … livery companies', 39.57–76). One of his main objections concerned the passages relating to technical education, a subject in which he took a more voluntarist stance.

It is not surprising, then, that as an unsuccessful Conservative candidate for Southwark in December 1868, Cotton campaigned on 'constitutional principles', opposing sitting members on the Irish question. Issuing 'a very liberal address', he won 2495 votes, despite putting his name forward only forty-eight hours before the poll. He was member of parliament for the City of London from 1874 (the first Conservative alderman to be elected for forty-four years) until standing down after the election of 1885. However, he increased his vote in the interim, and remained the most popular candidate. As a critic of Disraeli over his Russian policy, he was denied the customary baronetcy at the close of his year as lord mayor, the honour being conferred only on 5 July 1892. Cotton had a reputation for 'manly independence', a term that, placed alongside his business and civic achievements, may also serve as his epitaph. In spite of suffering from gout for twenty-five years, he served the public continuously until his death, following a relatively short illness, at his home, 9 Bramham Gardens, Kensington, London, on 4 June 1902.

PETER M. CLAUS

**Sources** A. B. Beaven, ed., *The aldermen of the City of London, temp. Henry III–*[1912], 2 vols. (1908–13) · *The Times* (6 June 1902) · *City Press* (7 June 1902) · *Dod's Parliamentary Companion* (1884) · J. E. Richie, *Famous City men* (1884) · I. W. Archer, *The history of the Haberdashers' Company* (1991) · *WWBMP* · W. J. R. Cotton, 'The City of London: its population and position', *Contemporary Review*, 41 (1882), 72–87 · E. Kilmurray, *Dictionary of British portraiture*, 3 (1981) · 'Commissioners appointed to inquire into the livery companies of the City of London', *Parl. papers* (1884), 39/1.57–76, C. 4073 · d. cert.
**Archives** GL, Noble collection
**Likenesses** wood-engraving, *c.*1875 (after photograph by Maull & Co.), NPG; repro. in *ILN* (6 Nov 1875) · Spy [L. Ward], watercolour study, NPG; repro. in *VF* (5 Sept 1885) · bust, repro. in *The Graphic* (6 Nov 1875)
**Wealth at death** £11,522 14s. 1d.: administration with will, 1 July 1902, *CGPLA Eng. & Wales*

**Cotton, William Westby** (*bap.* **1689**, *d.* **1749**). *See under* Cotton family (*per.* c.1650–1802).

**Cotton, Sir Willoughby** (1783–1860), army officer, was the only son of Admiral Rowland Cotton, a cousin of the first Viscount Combermere, and his wife, daughter of Sir Willoughby Aston bt. He was educated at Rugby School, where he led a rebellion in November 1797, when the boys burnt the headmaster's desk and books. On 31 October 1798 he was appointed an ensign in the 3rd foot guards, in which he became lieutenant and captain on 25 November 1799. He served with his regiment in Hanover in 1805. On 16 May 1806, soon after his return from Hanover, Cotton married Lady Augusta Maria Coventry (*d.* 1865), eldest daughter of George William Coventry, seventh earl of Coventry.

Cotton was deputy assistant adjutant-general of the reserve, commanded by Sir Arthur Wellesley, in the Copenhagen expedition of 1807, when he was present in the action at Kjöge, and was attached in the same capacity to the light division of the Peninsular army under General Crauford in the retreat to Torres Vedras and in the operations on the Coa. Upon his promotion to the rank of captain and lieutenant-colonel on 12 June 1811 he returned home, but rejoined the 1st battalion of his regiment in 1813. He was present at the battle of Vitoria, and commanded the light companies at the passage of the Adour, and the pickets of the 2nd brigade of guards in the repulse of the French sortie from Bayonne. He received the Peninsular medal, with clasps for Busaco, Vitoria, and the Nive.

On 17 May 1821 Cotton, then senior captain and lieutenant-colonel 3rd foot guards, and one of the dandies of the guards, obtained a lieutenant-colonelcy in the 47th foot in India, and on 25 July the same year became brevet colonel. The 47th followed Sir Archibald Campbell's expedition to Rangoon at the end of 1824, and Cotton, with the local rank of brigadier-general, played a prominent part in the Burma campaign of 1825–6, including the unsuccessful attack, made according to orders, on Danobyu. In Burma Cotton made the acquaintance of Henry Havelock, who became his aide-de-camp, and who later dedicated to Cotton his history of the Anglo-Afghan War of 1838–9. In 1828 Cotton exchanged to the 14th foot in Bengal, and was promoted to the rank of major-general on 22 July 1830. The same year he was made a knight of the Hanoverian order. From 1829 to 1834 he commanded the troops in Jamaica, which was under martial law from December 1831 to February 1832.

In 1838 Cotton was appointed to command the Bengal division of the army of the Indus commanded by Sir Henry Fane, and afterwards by Sir John Keane, which entered Afghanistan and captured Ghazni on 23 July 1839, when he commanded the reserve. In October 1839 he relinquished the command of the Bengal troops, then in camp near Kabul, for a command in the Bengal presidency. The same year he was appointed colonel of the 98th foot. In 1838 he was made KCB, and in 1840 GCB. On 23 November 1841 he became lieutenant-general. From 1847 to 1850 he was commander-in-chief and second member of council in the Bombay presidency. At the outbreak of the Crimean War, Cotton, despite his age (seventy-one) and corpulence, sought active employment (unsuccessfully). On 20 June 1854 he became a general. He was appointed to the colonelcy of the 32nd foot in April 1854. Cotton died at his residence, 15 Lowndes Square, London, on 4 May 1860. His wife survived him with two children, General Corbet Cotton and Augusta, widow of Colonel Henry Vaughan Brooke.

H. M. CHICHESTER, *rev.* JAMES LUNT

**Sources** Burke, *Peerage* [Combermere] · *Rugby School register* · *Hart's Army List* · J. W. Kaye, *History of the war in Afghanistan*, 3rd edn, 3 vols. (1874) · P. Macrory, *Signal catastrophe: the story of a disastrous retreat from Kabul, 1842* (1966) · J. A. Norris, *The First Afghan War, 1838–1842* (1967) · Fortescue, *Brit. army*, vols. 11–13 · H. Havelock, *Memoir of the three campaigns of Major-General Sir Archibald Campbell's army in Ava* (1828) · H. Havelock, *Narrative of the war in Affghanistan in 1838–39*, 2 vols. (1840) · B. Robson, *The road to Kabul: the Second Afghan War, 1878–1881* (1986) · G. R. Gleig, *Sale's brigade in Afghanistan: with an account of the seisure and defence of Jellalabad* (1846) · J. C. Pollock, *Way to glory: the life of Havelock of Lucknow* (1957) · *GM*, 3rd ser., 8 (1860), 628

**Archives** BL OIOC, corresp. in Burma; letter-book in Kabul; letters to Sir Thomas Munro · Durham RO, letters to Lord Londonderry · NAM, Combermere corresp. · NAM, corresp. with Jasper Nicolls · PRO NIre., corresp. with Earl Belmore

**Likenesses** J. Atkinson, watercolour drawing, *c.*1838, NPG · Count D'Orsay, pencil and chalk drawing, 1842, NPG

**Wealth at death** under £50,000: probate, 19 June 1860, *CGPLA Eng. & Wales*

**Cottrell** [Cotterell; *later* Cottrell-Dormer], **Sir Clement** (1686–1758), courtier and antiquary, was born on 2 April 1686 in St Martin's Lane, Westminster, and baptized at the church of St Martin-in-the-Fields two days later, on Easter day. He was the sixth of the seven children of Sir Charles Lodowick *Cotterell (1654–1710) [*see under* Cotterell, Sir Charles], courtier, and his first wife, Elizabeth Burwell (1656–1689), daughter of Nicholas Burwell of Gray's Inn (*c.*1620–1670) and Susan, his wife. William *Cotterell (1697/8–1744) was his half-brother.

Following the death of his mother when he was three, Cottrell lived largely at Rousham, Oxfordshire, with his aunt Anne, wife of Robert Dormer, and also at Easthamstead with his aunt Elizabeth and her husband, Sir William Trumbull. Early schooling at St Martin's Library preceded Eton College (1697–1704, King's scholar 1698) and Trinity Hall, Cambridge, where he matriculated in 1706 (scholar 6 January 1707). On 6 May 1707 he was sworn assistant master of the ceremonies in place of his deceased brother Charles, but he remained at Trinity Hall, where he was elected Lincoln fellow on 11 June 1709, before graduating LLB in 1710. That same year his father died, in consequence of which he was sworn master of the ceremonies and knighted on 14 and 28 July 1710 respectively.

Sir Charles Lodowick Cotterell's debts were considerable. The family's leased house in St Martin's Lane was forfeit to creditors, and its contents sold to the new tenant. Some portraits were smuggled out and other items subsequently reacquired, but the vast majority of books, paintings, and furniture were lost. Cottrell now determined to

'begin by being a very diligent attendant at Court' (Cottrell to Trumbull, 14 July 1710, BL, Add. MS 72519, fol. 23). He considered practising as a lawyer simultaneously, and attended the courts at Doctors' Commons as often as possible, but official duties precluded a double career.

On 14 April 1716 Cottrell married Bridget Sherborne (1696–1731), only daughter and heir of Davenant and Mary Sherborne of Pembridge, Herefordshire. The couple were presented with a personalized version of Elkanah Settle's *Thalia triumphans*, and the poet subsequently dedicated other royal birthday poems to each of them individually.

By his late thirties Cottrell's health was often poor. Gout was a frequent and excruciating affliction. In 1726 Fenton reported that 'Sir Clement is laid up by the surgeons, who have cut off from his back a large wen, which he used to complain of' (*Correspondence of Alexander Pope*, 2.415). Whenever possible, he would escape to his house in Twickenham, where he was, as Swift wrote, Pope's 'friend and Neighbour' (ibid., 3.378). They had known each other ever since Trumbull became one of Pope's earliest patrons. Besides those already mentioned, Cottrell mixed with many other leading literary, artistic, and scholarly figures of the day, such as Gay, Orrery, Hearne, and Sloane. Unable to inherit much of his father's library, he built up an impressive one of his own. It included a spectacular collection of prints and a body of manuscripts concerning precedence and protocol at the English court that he preserved and augmented with his own experiences. Such diligence earned a mock treatise on good breeding for 'Clement Quoteherald' from Horace Walpole (*Works*, 1.141–5). He was also a vice-president of the Society of Antiquaries.

'Tho' in the Court Interest, [Cottrell] is nevertheless a man of honour', wrote Hearne (*Remarks*, 11.355). Appropriately, perhaps, Cottrell's second daughter, Bridget (1719–1801), became a maid of honour to Princess Anne, and on the latter's marriage to the prince of Orange in 1734, Cottrell himself reconducted the prince, staying several months overseas. In 1738 he placed his two sons at the University of Gröningen.

Cottrell's closest friend was his cousin General James Dormer. When the latter died in 1741, unmarried and without children, he bequeathed the bulk of his estate to Cottrell, who now assumed the additional surname Dormer (though contemporaries often ignored this), and made Rousham his principal residence. About this time, he signed Pope's witty mock petition addressed to Lord Burlington, to save a tree from the improvements of William Kent, who, of course, had beautified Rousham considerably.

Cottrell still kept up an active social life in London, as evinced by his Dover Street house being so full of guests that Pope feared there was no room for him. Yet some sadness attended Cottrell's later years. His wife had died in 1731, his stepmother died in 1741, his second son, Robert, a marine, perished at sea in 1744, and an adult daughter, Mary, died in 1753. Between 1753 and 1755 he was named as party in a lawsuit brought by the daughter of his half-brother Stephen.

On 13 October 1758 Clement Cottrell died at Rousham: Walpole wickedly reported that he was 'supposed to have been suffocated by my Lady M[acclesfield]'s kissing hands' (Walpole, 31.10). Buried at Rousham, he was succeeded by his oldest son, Charles (1720–1779), the only son (along with four daughters) to survive him. Besides Robert and Mary, who predeceased him as adults, there were a further five infant deaths and five miscarriages.

Cottrell and his family were known for being relaxed and friendly. 'It seems to be the family of love', wrote Mrs Delany, 'they are such good-humoured people, that ceremony is thrown aside' (*Autobiography … Mrs Delany*, 2.220, 225). The antiquary Thomas Hearne noted Cottrell as 'a very bookish man … He is for retirement & for being free from noise and hurry, as much as his affairs will permit' (*Remarks*, 11.93). Cottrell was a large man—he weighed 13½ stone at the age of thirty-nine—and his portraits at Rousham by Michael Dahl and Thomas Hudson support the sense of a warm, even jovial, figure.

RODERICK CLAYTON

**Sources**  Rousham, Oxfordshire, Rousham MSS, F10–12; MC 7, 11–15; Mun. D. 14 · BL, Trumbull MSS, Add. MS 72519, fols. 3–89 · 'History of the Cottrell-Dormer family', Rousham, Oxfordshire, Rousham MSS · *The correspondence of Alexander Pope*, ed. G. Sherburn, 2–4 (1956) · *Remarks and collections of Thomas Hearne*, ed. C. E. Doble and others, 11 vols., OHS, 2, 7, 13, 34, 42–3, 48, 50, 65, 67, 72 (1885–1921), vols. 10–11 · Venn, *Alum. Cant.* · R. A. Austen-Leigh, ed., *The Eton College register, 1698–1752* (1927) · Walpole, *Corr.*, vols. 1, 15, 31 · *The autobiography and correspondence of Mary Granville, Mrs Delany*, ed. Lady Llanover, 1st ser., 2 (1861) · G. Lipscomb, *The history and antiquities of the county of Buckingham*, 4 vols. (1831–47), vol. 1 · PRO, LC 9/391; LC 5/3 · *The works of Horatio Walpole, earl of Orford*, ed. R. Walpole and M. Berry, 1 (1798)

**Archives**  priv. coll. | BL, Trumbull MSS

**Likenesses**  M. Dahl, oils, Rousham, Oxfordshire · T. Hudson, oils, Rousham, Oxfordshire

**Couch, Sir Arthur Thomas Quiller-** [*pseud.* Q] (1863–1944), writer and anthologist, was born on 21 November 1863 at Poul Street, Bodmin, Cornwall, the eldest of the five children of Thomas Quiller Couch (1826–1884), physician, and his wife, Mary (*d.* 1901), daughter of Elias Ford, yeoman, and his wife, Theophilas, of Abbots Kerswell, near Newton Abbot, Devon. The Quillers and Couchs had lived for generations in Polperro, Cornwall, earning their living largely from the sea. Q's grandfather Jonathan *Couch (1789–1870) was a doctor and noted naturalist.

Educated at Newton Abbot College, Devon, and Clifton College, Bristol, Quiller-Couch won a classics scholarship to Trinity College, Oxford, in 1882. While there he wrote for the *Oxford Magazine* and began using the pseudonym Q. After he obtained a second class in *literae humaniores* (1886), Trinity awarded him a one-year lectureship in classics. In 1887 Q published his first novel, *Dead Man's Rock*—an adventure story in the manner of Robert Louis Stevenson—and moved to London. At this time he was supporting his family, his father having died in 1884; audaciously, Q asked Louisa Amelia (*d.* 1948), second daughter of John Hicks of Fowey, Cornwall, to be his wife. They were married on 22 August 1889 and had a son, Bevil, and a daughter, Foy Felicia.

Sir Arthur Thomas Quiller-Couch (1863–1944), by Sir William Nicholson, 1934

In London Q combined work for Cassell, which published many of his novels, with freelance writing. When Cassell started a Liberal weekly, *The Speaker*, Q was appointed assistant editor, and provided a short story each week. Overwork led to ill health and in 1892 Q was happy to take his doctor's advice and move to the seaside. At Fowey, from a house called The Haven, he indulged his love of rowing and yachting for fifty years.

During the twenty years between leaving London and returning to university life in 1912 Q published nearly forty novels, short-story collections, and anthologies. His second book on Cornish themes, *The Delectable Duchy: Stories, Studies, and Sketches* (1893), was so popular that the title became a synonym for Cornwall. His facility with the style of R. L. Stevenson caused Stevenson's estate to ask Q to finish the draft of *St. Ives*, which he did with great skill (1898). He initiated the Oxford Books series with *The Oxford Book of English Verse, 1250–1900* (1900, revised and extended to 1918 in 1939). This volume soon became the standard anthology of English verse and sold nearly a million volumes during Q's lifetime. In 1903 he antagonized mainstream Methodists with *Hetty Wesley*, a sympathetic portrayal of Hetty's unhappy relationship with her famous family.

Q combined public service with his prodigious writing, working tirelessly for improvement in Cornish education, and holding numerous local offices. He spent over thirty years on Cornwall's education committee, which was established to create a countywide system of grammar schools provided for in the Education Act of 1902. His reward for his public service was a knighthood in 1910 and his appointment as the second King Edward VII professor of English literature at Cambridge University in 1912. In that year he was also elected a fellow of Jesus College, where he spent each term. There was scepticism about his selection inside and outside the university, but Q confounded the critics with his inaugural lecture, finely crafted, rich in learning, and grounded in the classics. For over a decade his lectures were filled to capacity and his published collections of lectures were immensely popular. In *On the Art of Writing* (1916), his 'On jargon' was a timeless and telling warning of the stultifying influence that jargon has on clear and concise writing. The preface to *On the Art of Reading* (1920) is equally apposite, with its 'The real battle for English lies in our Elementary Schools, and in the training of our Elementary Teachers'. Throughout his lectures Q championed his belief that literature was an art that must be practised. During the First World War he and his allies H. M. Chadwick, professor of Anglo-Saxon, and Dr Hugh Fraser Steward, fellow of St John's and later Trinity, campaigned for an independent English faculty. In 1917 they were successful, when an English tripos, separate from the medieval and modern languages tripos, was authorized by the university senate. The study of Anglo-Saxon, philology, and medieval literature became optional and literary criticism and comparative literature could be offered instead. In 1928, at Q's urging, the English tripos was divided into two parts and a paper on the English moralists was added.

After his son's death in occupied Germany in 1919 Q submerged his grief in work, and the next decade was filled with academic studies and collections of lectures, including most notably the introductions to Shakespeare's fourteen comedies for the New Shakespeare series (Cambridge, 1921–31). In 1931 Q withdrew from the project and left the series to his co-editor, John Dover Wilson.

Q's output declined precipitously in the 1930s, but recognition for his life's work included honorary degrees from the universities of Bristol (1912), Aberdeen (1927), and Edinburgh (1930), and an honorary fellowship at Trinity College, Oxford (1926). He was made freeman of Bodmin, Fowey, and Truro, and became mayor of Fowey in 1937–8. His friend and first biographer, Frederick Brittain, wrote of Q that he was celebrated for 'his hospitality, his conversation, his humour, his kindness of heart, and the care he took in choosing and wearing picturesque clothing' (*DNB*).

Q's successor in the professorship and an early English school graduate, Basil Willey, described his predecessor as:

> intensely and even sentimentally patriotic; unobtrusively but sincerely Christian; a passionate believer in liberal education, liberal politics, and the idea of the gentleman. All that he thought and said presupposed the unbroken continuity of the old Christian-Humanist tradition, the old class structure of society, the old sense of decorum, propriety and ceremony in human relations in literature. (Willey, *Cambridge and other Memories*, 20)

These traits, and an inability to treat adequately the darker human emotions, have dated Q's serious works for a world grown cynical and less secure in its verities. In other areas, however, Q's legacy remains: the creation of the grammar school system in Cornwall; the English faculty at Cambridge; the unsurpassed window on Cornwall

and the Cornish in his fiction; and the enduring power of the lectures. Books by Helene Hanff have twice renewed interest in Q's works: *84 Charing Cross Road* (1970; later made into a play and a film) and *Q's Legacy* (1986).

In late March 1944 Q fell while avoiding a vehicle in Fowey, and on 12 May, at his house in Fowey, he succumbed to cancer of the mouth, brought on by a lifetime of smoking. He was buried in Fowey on 15 May.

MICHAEL DOUGLAS SMITH

**Sources** F. Brittain, *Arthur Quiller-Couch: a biographical study of Q* (1948) • A. L. Rowse, *Quiller-Couch: a portrait of 'Q'* (1988) • *Memories and opinions by Q*, ed. S. C. Roberts (1945) • A. T. Quiller-Couch, *On the art of writing* (1916) • A. T. Quiller-Couch, *On the art of reading* (1920) • B. Willey, *Cambridge and other memories, 1920–1953* (1970), 12–20 • B. Willey, *The 'Q' tradition* (1946) • H. Carey, *Mansfield Forbes and his Cambridge* (1984) • E. M. W. Tillyard, *The muse unchained* (1958) • F. R. Leavis, *English literature in our time and the university* (1969) • D. J. Palmer, *The rise of English studies* (1965) • T. MacKillip, *F. R. Leavis: a life in criticism* (1995) • *DNB* • b. cert.
**Archives** Cornwall RO, corresp. and papers • Jesus College, Cambridge, letters and MSS; corresp. and papers, some relating to *The pilgrim's way* • Oxford University Press, archives • Royal Institution of Cornwall, Truro, family papers, books, memorabilia • Trinity College, Oxford, corresp. and papers, incl. literary MSS | BL, letters to William Archer, Add. MS 45295 • Bodl. Oxf., letters to Bertram Dobell • Duke U., Perkins L., letters to J. A. Manson • Jesus College, Cambridge, letters to F. Stanley Service • NL Scot., letters to Sydney Cockerell • NL Scot., letters to John Dover Wilson • U. Leeds, Brotherton L., letters to Clement Shorter
**Likenesses** L. Paul, watercolour drawing, 1920, NPG • W. Nicholson, oils, 1934, Jesus College, Cambridge [*see illus.*] • H. Lamb, oils, 1938, Truro City Art Gallery, Cornwall • H. Coster, photographs, NPG • H. Lamb, chalk sketch, NPG • Stereoscopic Co., photographs, NPG
**Wealth at death** £5431 0s. 9d.: probate, 12 Aug 1944, *CGPLA Eng. & Wales*

**Couch, Jonathan** (1789–1870), physician and naturalist, was born at Polperro, Cornwall, on 15 March 1789, the only child of Richard Couch (1739–1823) and Philippa, *née* Minards (1744–1833). After receiving a sound basic education at Mr Cole's school at Lansallos and Bodmin grammar school, and some years' pupillage with two local medical men, he entered the united hospitals of Guy's and St Thomas's in 1808. In 1809 or early in 1810 he returned to Polperro, which he rarely left afterwards. For sixty years he was the doctor and trusted adviser of the village and neighbourhood. In 1810 he married Jane Prynn Rundle who died the same year, leaving a daughter, Jane Rundle Couch. In 1815 he married Jane Quiller (1791–1857); they had five children, of whom Richard Quiller *Couch (1816–1863), Thomas Quiller (1826–1884), and John Quiller (*b.* 1830) became medical men. In 1858 Couch married his third wife, Sarah Lander Roose; they had three daughters.

Couch used the opportunities afforded to a naturalist at Polperro. He was given rare and unfamiliar marine specimens by the fishermen, and inspired others with similar interests, notably C. W. Peach, Matthias Dunn, and William Loughrin, to serious marine biology. He corresponded with Thomas Bewick about the latter's projected book on British fishes, which was never published, and helped William Yarrell to complete his *History of British*

*Fishes* (1836) by lending him coloured illustrations and notes.

Couch's principal work was done in ichthyology. In 1835 he obtained a prize for the best essay on the natural history of the pilchard, printed in the third report of the Royal Cornwall Polytechnic Society. He made a major contribution to ichthyology with *A History of the Fishes of the British Islands* (4 vols., 1862–5). The work was illustrated by hand-coloured engravings based on his own watercolours drawn from freshly caught specimens; it was the earliest book on British fishes to be illustrated in colour. The accuracy of the artwork enabled later workers correctly to identify some of the species which Couch, in common with his contemporaries, had misidentified. The text on the natural history of many of the sea fishes contained many original observations. Although he was knowledgeable about the faunistically rich western English Channel, his knowledge of the fishes of the northern fauna and particularly freshwaters was less certain. However, despite being resident in this distant Cornish village he was in correspondence with many of the leading scientists of the day both in Britain and in Europe and thus received help with the less familiar species.

Couch was a prolific contributor to scientific journals of the period and also to local and more popular publications. His interests were wide, embracing many of the current interests of the day, such as observations on the disease of the potato in 1845, and the metamorphosis of crustaceans. Several of his studies were into the biology of fishes of economic importance such as the pilchard and the mackerel, the mainstay of the Cornish fishing industry at that time, and were motivated by his concern for the welfare of the fishing community. He had a strong interest in the early history of Cornwall and wrote the *History of Polperro* which was published after his death by his son Thomas Quiller Couch.

Throughout his life Couch kept a series of notebooks in which he recorded observations of all kinds. This 'Journal of natural history' amounted to twelve volumes at his death, and forms an important record of social and economic matters from 1805 to 1870. The journal was acquired by the Royal Institution of Cornwall, Truro, towards the end of the twentieth century. His more personal account of his family and events in his life was published in the *Journal of the Royal Institution of Cornwall* in 1983.

Couch was a Wesleyan Methodist and his religious views influenced his social conduct and were reflected in much of his writing. His pastoral as well as his medical care of the community governed his life. As a local naturalist his conscientious and loving observation of nature made a lasting impression on science. He died at Polperro on 13 April 1870 and was survived by his third wife.

ALWYNE WHEELER

**Sources** [B. Couch], *Life of Jonathan Couch, FLS, etc of Polperro, the Cornish ichthyologist* (1891) · 'The private memoirs of Jonathan Couch, 1789–1870, of Polperro', ed. A. Wheeler, *Journal of the Royal Institution of Cornwall*, new ser., 9 (1982–5), 92–145

**Archives** Cheltenham Public Library, journal · Cornish Studies Library, Cornish Centre, Redruth, natural history of Cornish fishes · Linn. Soc., journals and papers · McGill University, Montreal, Blacker-Wood Library of Biology, natural history of Cornish fishes · NHM, drawings and notes on fishes · Oxf. U. Mus. NH, memoranda relating to stalk-eyed crustaceans · Royal Institution of Cornwall, Truro, journal, notes on natural history, and watercolour album | NHM, corresp. with Albert Gunther and R. W. T. Gunther · Royal Institution of Cornwall, Truro, corresp. with his son Richard Quiller Couch
**Likenesses** photograph, priv. coll.
**Wealth at death** under £450: probate, 8 June 1870, CGPLA Eng. & Wales

**Couch, Sir Richard** (1817–1905), judge, was born on 17 May 1817, the only son of Richard Couch of Bermondsey, London. Educated privately, he entered as a student of the Middle Temple on 10 January 1838, and was called to the bar on 15 January 1841. In 1844 he assisted in editing Blackstone's *Commentaries* (21st edn). In 1845 he married Anne (d. 1898), eldest daughter of Richard Thomas Beck of Combs, Suffolk; they had one son, Richard, who later became a barrister of the Middle Temple. For some years Couch practised on what was then the Norfolk circuit, and he was recorder of Bedford from 1858 to 1862. In the last year he became a judge of the high court of Bombay and on the retirement of Sir Matthew Sausse in 1866 he succeeded to the chief justiceship of the court and was knighted. In 1870 he succeeded Sir Barnes Peacock as chief justice of the high court of Calcutta. In 1875 Couch was appointed president of the commission of inquiry into the charge brought against Malharrao Gaikwad, the ruler of the major Indian state of Baroda, of poisoning the representative of the Bombay government at Baroda, Colonel Robert Phayre. The matter was an extremely sensitive one, as many Indians believed that Malharrao was being victimized by the colonial rulers. Also, the government of India, based in Calcutta, was seeking to utilize the crisis to extend its direct control over the princely states of the Bombay Presidency. The commission consisted of three British commissioners and three Indians, and in their verdict they were divided along those lines, the former, led by Couch, finding Malharrao guilty of the crime, the latter insisting on his innocence. The government of India promptly ignored the commission, deposed Malharrao, and, in 1876, took responsibility for dealing with Baroda State. By then, Couch had already resigned the chief justiceship. On his return to England he was sworn of the privy council, and in January 1881 he was appointed to the judicial committee as one of the two members who had experience of judicial work in the colonies. He acted in this capacity for twenty years, providing clear and sound, but hardly brilliant, judgments. He was elected a bencher of his inn in March 1881. He died at his residence, 25 Linden Gardens, Bayswater, London, on 29 November 1905, and was buried at Paddington cemetery.

C. E. A. BEDWELL, *rev.* DAVID HARDIMAN

**Sources** *The Times* (30 Nov 1905) · *Men and women of the time* (1899) · *WW* (1904) · I. Copland, *The British raj and the Indian princes* (1998), 142–53 · J. Foster, *Men-at-the-bar: a biographical hand-list of the members of the various inns of court*, 2nd edn (1885) · *Law Journal* (2 Dec 1905)

Sir Richard Couch (1817–1905), by Bassano

**Likenesses** Bassano, photograph, NPG [*see illus.*] · wood-engraving (*Trail of the Guicowar*), NPG; repro. in *ILN* (3 April 1875)
**Wealth at death** £43,439 4*s.* 8*d.*: probate, 20 Dec 1905, *CGPLA Eng. & Wales*

**Couch, Richard Quiller** (1816–1863), naturalist and medical practitioner, eldest son of Jonathan *Couch (1789–1870), naturalist, and his second wife, Jane *née* Quiller (1791–1857), was born at Polperro, Cornwall, on 14 March 1816. His brother Thomas Quiller Couch (1826–1884) was the father of Sir Arthur Thomas Quiller-Couch (1863–1944), professor of English literature. After receiving a medical education under his father and at Guy's Hospital, London, where he gained several honours and prizes, Couch returned to Polperro. Here he assisted his father, and employed his leisure in careful zoological study.

In 1845 Couch settled in Penzance as a medical practitioner, and a few years later became recognized as an able zoological observer. Within a few weeks of his arrival at Penzance he was elected one of the secretaries and curators of the Penzance Natural History and Antiquarian Society, and he was for many years its president. His annual addresses and many other papers on zoology by him were published in the society's *Transactions*. He contributed the third part (on the zoophytes) to *The Cornish Fauna*, written by his father, and an account of the natural history of west Cornwall to J. S. Courtney's *Guide to Penzance* (1845). He produced papers on zoophytes, Crustacea, and fish, including specifically his observations on the

zoophytes of Cornwall, the development of the frog, the metamorphosis of decapod crustaceans, and the natural history of the mackerel.

Couch was also interested in Cornish geology, and did useful work in developing the difficult subject of Cornish fossil remains. From 1848 onwards he was curator of the Royal Geological Society of Cornwall, and contributed several papers and annual reports to its *Transactions*. The diseases of Cornish miners were a subject of his careful investigation, and his papers on the mortality of miners in the *Polytechnic Reports* (1857–60) were considered at the time to be valuable, and were translated into French. He died suddenly on 9 May 1863, at Penzance, leaving a widow, Lydia Penneck Couch, and four children.

G. T. BETTANY, *rev.* YOLANDA FOOTE

**Sources** *Cornish Telegraph* (13 May 1863) · G. Bettany, *Western Morning News* (12 May 1863) · *GM*, 3rd ser., 15 (1863), 106–8 · J. Couch, *A history of Polperro* (1871), 25–7 · Boase & Courtney, *Bibl. Corn.*, 1.92–4, 3.1138 · *CGPLA Eng. & Wales* (1863)
**Archives** Royal Institution of Cornwall, Truro, corresp. with his father, Jonathan Couch, and William Rendle
**Wealth at death** under £3000: probate, 29 May 1863, *CGPLA Eng. & Wales*

**Couche, William** (1732–1753), Jesuit, was born on 5 February 1732 at Tolfrey, near Fowey, Cornwall, the eldest son of William Couche and his wife, Anne, daughter of Peter Hoskins of Ibberton, Dorset. He studied at the English College at St Omer and entered the Society of Jesus in 1749, but died prematurely of smallpox at Liège on 23 February 1753. Couche was a promising member of the Jesuit order. His life was written by his cousin, Ralph Hoskins, under the title 'De vita, virtutibus et morte Gulielmi Couche', and was preserved in manuscript at Stonyhurst College.

THOMPSON COOPER, *rev.* ROBERT BROWN

**Sources** Boase & Courtney, *Bibl. Corn.* · G. Oliver, *Collections illustrating the history of the Catholic religion in the counties of Cornwall, Devon, Dorset, Somerset, Wilts, and Gloucester* (1857) · G. Oliver, *Collections towards illustrating the biography of the Scotch, English and Irish members of the Society of Jesus* (1835) · Gillow, *Lit. biog. hist.* · H. Foley, ed., *Records of the English province of the Society of Jesus*, 7 vols. in 8 (1875–83) · G. Holt, *The English Jesuits, 1650–1829: a biographical dictionary*, Catholic RS, 70 (1984)

**Couchman, Sir Harold John** (1882–1956), army officer and surveyor, was born on 29 July 1882 in Haileybury, Hertfordshire, the youngest child of the two sons and two daughters of the Revd Henry Couchman (1839–1922), assistant master of Haileybury College, and his wife, Mary Jane Pooley (1843–1933). He was educated at Haileybury College and the Royal Military Academy, Woolwich.

Couchman was commissioned in the Royal Engineers in August 1900. He was transferred to India in 1902 and appointed to the geodetic branch of the survey of India in 1906. His initial duties were to assist with fieldwork for the magnetic survey of India and by the 1908–9 field season he was in charge of operations in south-west India. He subsequently took part in the regional gravity surveys of Burma (1910–11) and southern and central India (1912–14). By 1914 he had been appointed deputy superintendent at Dehra Dun. He took the principal part in the synthesis and interpretation of all the gravity observations made in India over the period 1908–13, making an excellent attempt to interpret these data in the light of evidence recently reported by the American geodesist J. F. Hayford, drawing upon similar surveys in the United States. In both cases, regional gravity anomalies were found to occur, associated with the depression of dense rocks forming the earth's mantle by the less dense roots of major mountain chains.

In spring 1914 Couchman was transferred to the headquarters office of the survey in Calcutta. He was recalled to active military duty in October 1914. Couchman was promoted lieutenant in 1903, captain in 1910, and major in 1916, and was acting lieutenant-colonel (1917–19). Between September 1915 and November 1918 he served in the 21st, 39th, and 47th divisions of the Royal Engineers in France and Belgium, and fought in the battle of Pilckem Ridge in 1917. Wounded in action, he was twice mentioned in dispatches, was awarded the MC (June 1916), and was appointed to the DSO (June 1918). In 1925 he married Evelyn Beatrice (1883–1977), the divorced wife of Brigadier Robert Henry Thomas and youngest daughter of Colonel William Lewis Clinton Baddeley, a retired military officer. They had no children other than his stepson, the diplomat Antony Clinton-Thomas (1913–1981).

Couchman had returned to the survey of India in 1919 and, with the exception of a period as deputy master, security printing (1926–9), he spent the rest of his career with the survey. He was director in Shillong, Simla, and Calcutta; then in 1933 he was appointed surveyor-general, a position he held until his retirement in 1937. He was promoted lieutenant-colonel in 1930 and brigadier in 1933, and he was knighted in 1937. He was a keen tennis player and won the doubles in the 1923 army lawn tennis championships. Couchman died on 30 November 1956 in St George's Hospital, Westminster, London, and was survived by his wife.                RICHARD J. HOWARTH, *rev.*

**Sources** R. H. Phillimore, ed., *Historical records of the survey of India*, 2 (1950) · H. L. Pritchard, ed., *History of the corps of royal engineers*, 5–7 (1951) · *The Times* (3 Dec 1956) · *CGPLA Eng. & Wales* (1957) · *The Haileyburian* (19 Dec 1922) · Haileybury College register · d. cert.
**Wealth at death** £4821 18s. 8d.: probate, 17 Jan 1957, *CGPLA Eng. & Wales*

**Coucy, Enguerrand (VII)** [Ingelram] **de, earl of Bedford** (*c.*1340–1397), magnate, was the only son of Enguerrand (VI) de Coucy, lord of the barony of Coucy in Picardy, and Catherine of Habsburg. His father died when he was in his fifth year, and his lands were placed in trust by Philippe VI until he came of age. He was first armed in the Picard campaign against the English in 1355. When Charles, king of Navarre, entered Paris in November 1357, he was in his company, and in 1358 he was prominent in the suppression of the *jacquerie*. In the treaty of Brétigny in 1360 he was named among the forty hostages for the ransom of Jean II, king of France, and at the end of October, after the ratification of the treaty and the liberation of the king, he sailed for England with the other hostages.

From an English point of view the years following form the most interesting part of Coucy's career. The French hostages, who included the four princes of the *fleur de lys*—the dukes of Anjou, Berri, Orléans, and Bourbon—were well treated and richly entertained. Coucy, according to Froissart, 'was in great favour with both French and English' (*Œuvres*, 6.392), and Edward III in 1363 restored to him the lands in Lancashire, Yorkshire, Cumberland, and Westmorland to which he had claim in the right of his great-grandmother Catherine de Balliol. In July 1365, with Edward's blessing, he married the king's eldest daughter, *Isabella (1332–1379). Following this he was elected knight of the Garter, and on 11 May 1366 he was created earl of Bedford, with a pension of 300 marks p.a. Isabella was some eight years his senior, and on her side it may have been a love match. From Edward III's point of view, however, a marriage alliance with one of the most powerful lords of Picardy had obvious advantages, especially in the event of hostilities reopening with the French; and the significance of Coucy's territorial position was further enhanced when, in 1367, he acquired from his fellow hostage Guy de Blois, as the price of the latter's release, the county of Soissons. A first daughter, Marie (Mary), was born to Coucy and Isabella in 1366, and a second daughter, Philippa, in the following year.

Coucy was in France when, in 1369, war broke out again between France and England. With his wide lands, held in England of Edward III and in France of Charles V, he found himself in an ambiguous position. Remarkably, this seems to have been recognized by both kings. Isabella, with Philippa, was allowed to return to England; and the English, in Knolles's Picard campaign of 1370, were careful to leave Coucy's territories unmolested. Coucy himself seems to have sought to avoid military commitment to either side. In 1369 he led an expedition to Alsace on his own account, in pursuit of his claim in his mother's right as coheir of Duke Leopold of Austria to a share in the Habsburg family lands; and from 1372 to 1374 he was in the service of the pope, Gregory XI, against the Visconti, sharing with John Hawkwood the laurels of the victory of Montechiari (1373). Coucy returned to France in 1374. When in 1375 the truce of Bruges opened an interlude in the Anglo-French fighting, Charles V, anxious to rid his kingdom of the free companies, encouraged him to try his fortune once more in Alsace, and promised 60,000 livres to subvent him. He succeeded in recruiting a substantial force, not only among the companies but also among the knighthood of Picardy, the Low Countries, and even England. His *routier* recruits however proved disorderly and mutinous, and in a winter campaign he was unable to take any places of significance. Finally, by the terms of an agreement of January 1376 with the Habsburgs, he was ceded the county of Nidau in return for the renunciation of all his other claims, and he returned to France.

In spring 1376 Coucy came once more to England. He was at the deathbed of the Black Prince in June, and attended his funeral. But he was already by now a councillor of Charles V, and in the late summer he returned to France. When in June 1377, simultaneously, the truces with the English ran out and Edward III died, he took the decisive steps that severed his English connection permanently. On 26 August he wrote to Richard II, renouncing all that he held of him in faith and homage, and returned to him his Garter. Isabella, his wife, who had come back with her daughter Philippa to England on the news that her father was dying, remained there. She died in 1379. Coucy's English lands were taken into the king's hands, ultimately passing with Philippa to her husband, Robert de Vere, earl of Oxford. In 1380 Coucy married Isabella, daughter of Jean, duke of Lorraine.

From 1377 until his death in 1397 Coucy was continuously prominent in French military and political affairs. He served against the English in Gascony under Louis of Anjou in 1377, and in 1380 as captain-general in Picardy co-ordinated resistance to Buckingham's *chevauchée*. In 1382 he fought with distinction at Roosebeke, where van Artevelde's Flemings were defeated; and in 1383 he served under Burgundy against Bishop Despenser's crusade to Flanders. In 1384 he led a force to support Louis, duke of Anjou, in his attempt to make good his claim to the throne of Naples; he took Arezzo, but on learning of Louis's death ceded the town to Florence for 40,000 florins and returned to France. In 1386 he mustered for the projected invasion of England, and in 1388 served in the French campaign against the duke of Gueldres. In 1390 he took part in the duke of Bourbon's Barbary crusade. In 1394–5, when Louis, duke of Orléans, in alliance with the Visconti, sought to intervene in Italian affairs, he captained his troops in Liguria. He joined the crusading army led by Jean de Nevers against the Turks in 1396, but in its great defeat at Nicopolis on 25 September he was taken prisoner by the Turks, and died in captivity at Brusa on 18 February 1397. His heart was brought back to France, and buried in the church of the Celestines that he had founded in 1390 at Villeneuve-les-Soissons.

Coucy's high knightly reputation, his great territorial possessions, and a marked political dexterity made him acceptable to all parties in the confused politics of France between 1380 and 1396. Remarkably, he was trusted alike by the dukes of Burgundy, Anjou, and Orléans, as well as by Charles VI's Marmouset councillors. In 1381, in 1388, and again in 1392 he played a vital part in the reconciliations of Jean (IV), duke of Brittany, with the crown of France. He was twice offered the constable's sword (in 1380 and 1392) but on each occasion refused; in 1389 he was created grand butler of France. He was revered, above all, as a great chivalric figure. He was the friend and occasional patron of the chronicler Froissart, and was praised by Deschamps; he founded his own order of chivalry, the order of the Crown (1379). His lands at his death passed to his daughter Marie, widow of Henri de Bar: the inheritance was sold by her to Louis d'Orléans. From his second marriage Coucy had a daughter, Isabella, who married Philippe, count of Nevers, son of the duke of Burgundy; his recognized bastard, Perceval, enjoyed the title of sieur de Coucy.      M. H. KEEN

**Sources** *Dictionnaire de biographie française*, 9 (1961) · B. Tuchman, *A distant mirror* (1978) · GEC, *Peerage* · *Œuvres de Froissart*, ed. K. de Lettenhove, 6–17 (1868–72) · *Oeuvres complètes de Eustache Deschamps*, ed. G. Raynaud, 7 (Paris, 1891), no. 1366 · *Polychronicon Ranulphi Higden monachi Cestrensis*, ed. C. Babington and J. R. Lumby, 9 vols., Rolls Series, 41 (1865–86); vol. 8, p. 365 · H. L. Savage, 'Enguerrand de Coucy VII and the campaign of Nicopolis', *Speculum*, 14 (1939), 423–42 · M. Duplessis, *Histoire de la ville et des seigneurs de Coucy* (1728) · H. Lacaille, 'La vente de la baronnie de Coucy', *Bibliothèque de l'École des Chartes*, 55 (1894)

**Coucy, Marie de**. *See* Marie (d. 1284).

**Coughlan, Laurence** (d. 1784), founder of Methodism in Newfoundland, was born in Ireland. His parentage is unknown. By birth a Roman Catholic, he converted to Methodism at Drummersnave, Leitrim, in 1753, and was soon afterwards recruited as an itinerant preacher, serving initially in Ireland and, on being transferred to England, at Whitehaven in Cumberland and Colchester in Essex. In 1760 he went back to Ireland and preached at Waterford, the port through which most Irish servants left for work in the Newfoundland fishery. He returned to London, and on 23 February 1762 married Anne Andrews in the parish of St Giles Cripplegate. Coughlan was by then a widower. He had already, to John Wesley's dismay, 'married and ruined' one woman, details of whom are unknown (J. Wesley to P. Hall, 6 Oct 1768, *Letters*, 5.109). Coughlan's lack of learning and his zealous evangelism were also distasteful to Wesley, who did not regard him as a fit person for ordination. In 1764 Coughlan none the less got himself ordained by Erasmus, the Greek Orthodox bishop of Acadia, who had turned up in London, whereupon his formal connection with Wesley's movement ceased.

Coughlan now had to find a new outlet for his talents. He was aware that large numbers of Irish emigrants lived in Newfoundland, where Roman Catholicism was the only proscribed religion. Undercover Catholic priests were known to work on the island and there were fears, both among residents in Newfoundland and officials in London, that popery might gain a footing. Late in 1765 a number of inhabitants of Conception Bay, on Newfoundland's Avalon peninsula, authorized the merchant George Davis, who was about to leave for England, to find a protestant minister to come and live among them. A church had been built in Harbour Grace, the main centre of population in the bay, and the parishioners were prepared to pay an annual salary of £100 to a new minister. Davis found Coughlan; and the following spring Coughlan, after being reordained priest by the bishop of Chester in April, sailed to Newfoundland. He returned to London in autumn 1766 with a petition from the inhabitants to the Society for the Propagation of the Gospel in Foreign Parts (SPG) asking that he be appointed missionary and given a stipend. The fishery was then experiencing difficulties and the inhabitants could not afford the promised £100. Coughlan was appointed SPG missionary in December. In September 1767, accompanied by his wife and daughter Betsey, he went back to Harbour Grace. This was his third transatlantic voyage, an arduous experience for one with 'dreadful apprehensions of the sea'. Regular boat travel was also a feature of his work of house-to-house preaching in a community linked often only by rough paths.

Coughlan was the first Anglican clergyman to serve in Conception Bay. There were now about 4500 residents in the bay, of whom about a quarter were Irish Roman Catholics. Harbour Grace and, a few miles to the north, Carbonear, were Coughlan's main locations for his preaching. To judge from his reports to the SPG, his record as a missionary was marked by success. He administered the sacraments to growing numbers, many of them Catholic emigrants attracted by Coughlan's proficiency in the Irish language. He held regular services, had a second church built, in Carbonear, and a third at Blackhead, 10 miles to the north. In addition he opened a school which he maintained during his ministry. But all this cloaked his true ambition, which was to be an instrument of evangelical conversion among the people. To this end he held private meetings, walked, preached, and toiled for (he claimed) nearly three years. Then an 'awakening' commenced and spread *like fire*. According to Coughlan, the revival occurred 'in a very wonderful manner', manifesting itself in public testimonies, extraordinary deathbed protestations of faith, and a widespread reformation of morals. Word soon spread that the people at Harbour Grace and Carbonear 'were going mad' (Coughlan, 9–14). Though an SPG-sponsored Anglican clergyman, Coughlan thought of himself as a Methodist. The movement he began established Methodism on the north side of Conception Bay, where, under another name (the United Church of Canada), it endures in the early twenty-first century.

Coughlan's orthodox parishioners certainly saw him as something other than Anglican. As the revival spread, his Methodist theology appeared more openly in sermons, offending many. His appeal was to common people; his efforts were resisted by the 'Gentry' (Coughlan, 14), whom he derided and later demonized. Resistance turned to hostility in 1770 when Governor John Byron appointed him justice of the peace, with extensive power over sabbath breakers, drunkards, adulterers, blasphemers, and papists. Coughlan was not slow to use this power. In 1771 he denounced a Roman Catholic merchant for living in adultery and tried to prevent his servants from working on Sunday. His commission as justice was revoked. Another quarrel, in 1772, over a merchant's right to sponsor a child in baptism, resulted in more complaints. Governor Molineux Shuldham asked the SPG to remove him. Late in 1773 he appeared before the SPG in London and resigned his mission. He had, however, left behind not a few 'soldier[s] of *Jesus Christ*', or lay preachers (Coughlan, 82) to continue his work.

Coughlan's subsequent career was as a preacher in the Countess of Huntingdon's Connexion, a sect of Calvinistic Methodists. He served in at least two of her London chapels, those at Cumberland Street and Holywell Street, near Shoreditch. He published two books, *An Account of the Work of God in Newfoundland* (1776), describing his missionary activity, and *A Select Collection of Psalms and Hymns* (5th edn., 1779). He died in 1784, according to Wesley 'utterly

broken in pieces, full of tears and contrition for his past unfaithfulness' (J. Wesley to J. Stretton, 25 Feb 1785, *Letters*, 7.260).                                                    PATRICK O'FLAHERTY

**Sources** L. Coughlan, *An account of the work of God in Newfoundland* (1776) · P. O'Flaherty, 'Coughlan, Laurence', *DCB*, vol. 4 · H. Rollmann, 'Laurence Coughlan and the origins of Methodism in Newfoundland', *The contribution of Methodism to Atlantic Canada*, ed. C. H. H. Scobie and J. W. Grant (1992), 53–76 · *A sermon preached before the incorporated Society for the Propagation of the Gospel in Foreign Parts* (1767–76) [annual proceedings] · *The letters of the Rev. John Wesley*, ed. J. Telford, 8 vols. (1931) · *Arminian Magazine*, 8 (1785), 490–92 [Coughlan's letter to Wesley, 4 Nov 1772] · C. H. Crookshank, *History of Methodism in Ireland*, 3 vols. (1885–8) · A. Young, *A tour in Ireland*, ed. C. Maxwell (1925) · C. Atmore, *The Methodist memorial* (1801) · W. Wilson, *Newfoundland and its missionaries* (1860) · J. Parsons, 'The origin and growth of Newfoundland Methodism', MA diss., Memorial University of Newfoundland, 1964 · P. O'Flaherty, *The rock observed: studies in the literature of Newfoundland* (1979)

**Archives** A. C. Hunter Library, St John's, Newfoundland · PRO, CO 194/16–30 · Provincial Archives of Newfoundland and Labrador, St John's, Newfoundland, SPG MSS A/B&C series; governor's corresp., GN 2/1A, vols. 4–7 | A. C. Hunter Library, St John's, Newfoundland, W. Smith, 'Rev. Laurence Coughlan: an address delivered to the Newfoundland Historical Society on March 20, 1942'

**Coulcher, Mary Caroline** (1852–1925), philanthropist, was born at Rickinghall Superior, Bolesdale, Suffolk, on 19 November 1852, the daughter of the Revd George Coulcher, rector of Wattisfield, Suffolk, and his wife, Jane Sarah, *née* Hawtayne. Little is known about Coulcher's early life, except that she was educated at Lymington House School, Clapham, London, and moved to Ipswich in 1870. A petite, bespectacled lady, renowned for her gentle nature and generous spirit, she never married, but instead devoted her life to the service of others through voluntary work with the order of St John of Jerusalem. The mission of St John's was to instruct citizens in administering first aid to the sick and injured, as well as providing for the adequate transport of sufferers to hospitals and to their homes, and it was due largely to Coulcher's pioneering efforts that one of the earliest branches of the organization was founded in Ipswich, in January 1880. Fundraising, so that appliances including stretchers, hampers, surgical haversacks, litters, and carriages could be purchased, was the major priority in the early years. This was a task that Coulcher, as secretary and treasurer, undertook with great zeal, even describing herself as 'the only authorised beggar' in her search for funds (Cole-Mackintosh, 26–7). Between 1893 and 1894 Coulcher established the Ipswich corps of the St John Ambulance Brigade and the Ipswich nursing corps, and it was these early achievements that earned her selection first as an honorary associate of the order of St John in 1894, and then admission as a lady of grace in 1899.

While the Ipswich centre flourished under Coulcher's supervision, she continued to pursue her two greatest ambitions. The first was to ensure that the Ipswich Association had a secure home, and to this end in 1903 she made a bequest of land that enabled the local St John's to move into permanent headquarters. This gift was fully secured ten years later, when Coulcher gave, entirely free of charge, the freehold of the property jointly to the St John Ambulance Association, the grand prior of the order of St John of Jerusalem, and the local trustees, to be used for ambulance purposes in perpetuity.

Coulcher's second ambition concerned the transportation of the sick and wounded. Tumbrils and horse ambulances were still generally used in Ipswich to transfer patients to hospital, but their jolting invariably caused further injury. Coulcher's response was to present the local association with its first motor ambulance in July 1914. Her philanthropic gesture was a great asset to the centre, enabling many more patients to be transferred to hospitals and nursing homes in comfort and safety. As devoted as she was to St John's, Coulcher still found time to travel extensively in Europe and Palestine, and to pursue her love of music. She also became involved in municipal work, and served as a Conservative councillor for the St Margaret's ward of Ipswich between 1910 and 1912.

The outbreak of the First World War in 1914 exerted considerable pressure on the first-aid and nursing movement. Under the umbrella of the joint war committee, which co-ordinated the work of St John's and the British Red Cross Society, the Ipswich branch was supervised by Coulcher. In her capacity as vice-president and lady district superintendent of St John Ambulance Brigade no. 10, eastern district, commandant of Broadwater Auxiliary Hospital, Suffolk, and for a short period in 1915 commandant of the Isolation Hospital, Ipswich, she made sure that her local organization responded effectively to the needs of this national emergency. She was appointed OBE in 1918, in recognition of services rendered in connection with the war, and her dedication and determination were further rewarded in 1920 when she was promoted CBE. The immense task of war work had a lasting effect on Coulcher, and by late 1919 her health was so undermined that she was forced to retire from active involvement with St John's. However, her commitment remained undiminished, and in 1924 she made a further gift to the Ipswich corps of a second motor ambulance.

Mary Coulcher, regarded as the mother of the St John's cause in Ipswich, died of arteriosclerosis and nephritis at her home, Beecholme, Lacey Street, Ipswich, Suffolk, on 15 June 1925, aged seventy-two. Her funeral took place on 18 June 1925 at the church of St Mary-le-Tower, Ipswich, where she had prayed for many years, and where her late brother, George Bohun Coulcher, had been minister; she was buried in the family grave in Ipswich cemetery. As a memorial, the county named a new ambulance after her.

SUSAN L. COHEN

**Sources** *First Aid*, 32 (1925–6), 6–7 · *East Anglian Daily Times* (16 June 1925), 7 · *WWW* · personnel index, joint war committee, British Red Cross Society Archives, London · b. cert. · d. cert. · R. Cole-Mackintosh, *A century of service to mankind*, 2nd edn (1994), 26–7 · *Report of the chapter general of the grand priory of the order of the hospital of St John of Jerusalem in England* (1909), 294–5
**Likenesses** photograph, Archives of the Order of St John; repro. in *First Aid and the St John Ambulance Gazette*, 7
**Wealth at death** £28,366 4s. 10d.: probate, 1 Oct 1925, *CGPLA Eng. & Wales*

**Coulshed,** Dame (**Mary**) **Frances** (1904–1998), army officer, was born at 49 Lynmouth Road, Ecclesall, Sheffield, on 10 November 1904, the daughter of Wilfred Coulshed, a chemist who died when she was six years old, and his wife, Maude Mullin, a teacher. She was educated at Parkfields Cedars School, Derby; the Convent of the Sacred Heart, Kensington; and St Charles College, Kensington. At the Sorbonne in Paris she studied French for several months, and in London in 1925 she obtained her teacher's certificate, studying early English literature, Elizabethan poetry, and geography. She also trained as a singer and was an associate of the London College of Music. The Carl Rosa Opera Company offered her a career in music but she declined and became a teacher of French, English literature, geography, and music at St Mary's Secondary School, Derby. Coulshed was softly spoken, blue-eyed, of medium height and small build, with gently waved auburn hair. She had a friendly manner, a sense of humour, a merry laugh, and a great deal of natural charm. She was an ardent Roman Catholic.

While strolling through Whitehall with her cousin in 1938 she was attracted by the first recruiting poster for the Auxiliary Territorial Service (ATS). '"That's it", I said, and when I returned to Derby I went to the Drill Hall and signed up', she recalled in 1985 during a recorded interview with Brigadier Eileen Nolan, a former director of the Women's Royal Army Corps (WRAC) (NAM, videotape 9401–154–1, 2). She was among the first to join the ATS, which came into existence by royal warrant on 9 September 1938. She attended a course for officers at the duke of York's headquarters, Chelsea, in September and October that year and was commissioned a one-pipper, a company assistant (equivalent to second lieutenant). She joined the 1st Derbyshire company of the ATS, attached to the 68th heavy anti-aircraft regiment.

The first autumn of the war found the ATS women in Derby living in billets and working under canvas on a bleak hillside to the north of the city where the Royal Artillery defended institutions such as Rolls-Royce and the Midland Railway. A great deal of prejudice had to be overcome in the early days of the ATS, but by 1941, she recalled, nobody spoke any more of women 'playing at soldiers' (NAM, videotape 9401–154–1, 2). After the 68th regiment was posted overseas the 1st Derbyshire company was moved to Nottingham and Coulshed went on to serve in Norfolk, Lincolnshire, and Yorkshire. As a junior commander (captain) in a searchlight company, she helped to organize the first 24-hour plotting teams in the war.

In 1941, when the War Office decided that women could be permitted to operate anti-aircraft guns, Coulshed applied successfully to be posted to one of the first mixed batteries. In 1942 she was appointed commanding officer of 32 anti-aircraft brigade group with the rank of senior commander (major) and in August 1943 she took command of 31 anti-aircraft brigade group. The greatest triumph of the ATS occurred during the flying bomb (V1) attacks, which began on 16 June 1944. Anti-aircraft emplacements were moved to Essex and Suffolk, where

Dame (Mary) Frances Coulshed (1904–1998), by Walter
Stoneman, 1957

the 'gun girls' lived under canvas on the desolate mud flats
throughout a cold and rainy autumn, and then to East
Anglia during the winter. The ATS women had to be on
duty twenty-four hours a day, but they had the consolation of knowing that the proportion of V1 rockets brought
down was steadily increasing until nine out of ten were
secured.

When the Luftwaffe ceased to be a serious strategic
threat members of the ATS were shifted to Belgium where
the V1 and V2 flying bombs posed a threat. Coulshed was
responsible for the selection of the first 4000 ATS women
to serve on the continent.

> I wanted desperately to go overseas but by 1944 I was a chief
> commander (lieutenant-colonel) and I was told that I was too
> senior to go abroad. I therefore asked to be demoted—ten
> times in all—and eventually I was ordered to report to
> London where I saw Leslie Whateley, who was then director
> of the ATS. She told me that I had been posted abroad but she
> had no idea where the posting was. (NAM, videotape 9401–
> 154-1, 2)

Coulshed discovered her destination was Brussels when
she peeked through a window on the aircraft as it was
landing.

She was demoted to senior commander (major) and was
appointed deputy assistant director, ATS, serving with
Twenty-First Army group as senior staff officer ATS to
general headquarters anti-aircraft troops. As such Coulshed was the first woman officer to join a mobile operational headquarters in wartime, and was responsible for

the women of the five mixed regiments in north-west Europe. Between 12 October 1944 and 15 March 1945, 5960 flying bombs struck Antwerp, killing 731 soldiers and 3515
civilians.

The winter of 1944 was very cold and the women manning the guns lived an arduous life in Nissen huts. For six
weeks one unit worked in solid frozen snow, eating iron
rations and dehydrated vegetables out of mess tins. When
a US sailor heard from his girlfriend about the rigours of
service in the ATS on a gun site he was so horrified that he
wrote to the queen with a copy to the prime minister. This
upset anti-aircraft command, but Coulshed was able to
reassure headquarters that the women were accustomed
to these conditions (Bidwell, 133). When hostilities ended
Coulshed arranged conversion courses to train her troops
as ordnance storewomen or clerks. Their standards
proved to be so high that there were demands for their services from the headquarters of the army of occupation in
Germany. 'In spite of the medals', she said, 'I was frightened by the flying bombs' (*Evening Standard*, 25 Aug 1950).

When the war in Europe was over Coulshed was promoted once more to chief commander (lieutenant-
colonel), and appointed assistant director ATS Twenty-
First Army group (headquarters lines of communication,
north-west Europe). In 1946 she returned to Britain and
was appointed deputy director of anti-aircraft command,
a position she retained until 1950 when she became deputy director of the WRAC. In 1951 she was appointed director with the rank of brigadier. (The WRAC replaced the
ATS on 1 February 1949.) A highly respected director of the
WRAC, Coulshed saw the strength of the corps expand
from 5800 to about 6500 before her retirement in 1954.

'I believe that women in the services should not become
hard and masculine and I've encouraged those under me
to retain their femininity', Frances Coulshed maintained.
'They all know that an Eton crop is one of the most
unpopular things I can see' (*Daily Dispatch*, 31 Aug 1954).
During her time as director she travelled to the Middle
East, Malaya, Singapore, Kenya, and Hong Kong. Appointed CBE in 1949, she was advanced to DBE in 1953. She
served as aide-de-camp to George VI (1951) and Elizabeth II
(1952–4).

After leaving the army she worked for some years in
telecommunications. Apart from singing and playing the
piano one of her hobbies was embroidery, and she drew
her own designs based on Greek patterns. She was also a
keen walker, especially over the Cumberland fells. She
had a large collection of books, prints, and old maps and
also collected porcelain and china (*Homes and Gardens*, February 1951). In retirement she lived modestly on her own
in her flat at 42B Westminster Palace Gardens, Artillery
Row, London. She loved cats, and on the day she died the
nursing home cat, which spent much of its time with her,
'sat disconsolately under her window throughout the day'
(*The Times*, 8 Oct 1998). She died at Holton, 49 West Heath
Road, Child's Hill, London, on 28 September 1998. She was
unmarried and left no close relatives.               ROY TERRY

**Sources** R. Terry, *Women in khaki* (1988) · S. Bidwell, *The women's
royal army corps* (1977) · J. M. Cowper, *The auxilliary territorial service*

(1949) · Coulshed papers, NAM · interview of subject by E. Nolan, videotape, NAM, tape 9401–154–1, 2 · *Daily Telegraph* (22 Oct 1998) · *The Independent* (21 Oct 1998) · *The Times* (8 Oct 1998) · *Evening Standard* (25 Aug 1950) · *Homes and Gardens* (Feb 1951) · *Daily Dispatch* (31 Aug 1954) · b. cert. · d. cert.

**Archives** NAM, corresp. and papers | FILM NAM, interview with Brig. Eileen Nolan, videotape 9401–154–1, 2

**Likenesses** W. Stoneman, photograph, 1957, NPG [*see illus.*] · photograph, repro. in *The Times* · photograph, repro. in *The Independent* · photograph, repro. in *Daily Telegraph* · portrait, NAM, Coulshed papers

**Coulson, Charles Alfred** (1910–1974), theoretical chemist, was born at Dudley on 13 December 1910, one of twin sons (there were no other children) of Alfred Coulson, who became principal of Dudley Technical College and later HM inspector of technical colleges in south-west England, and his wife, Annie Sincere, headmistress and daughter of the inventor Charles Lamb Hancock. Alfred Coulson acted as superintendent of the local Methodist Sunday school, and both Charles and his brother were brought up as staunch Methodists. Indeed, Charles Coulson's whole outlook was coloured by his immensely strong Christian faith; he became an accredited lay preacher in 1929 and subsequently vice-president of the Methodist conference (1959–60). His brother, John Metcalfe Coulson, became professor of chemical engineering at the University of Newcastle upon Tyne.

Coulson was educated at two local schools in Dudley and, following the family's move to Bristol in 1920, at the XIV Preparatory School in that city. In 1923 he was awarded a scholarship to Clifton College, and in 1928 gained an entrance scholarship in mathematics to Trinity College, Cambridge. During these years he was a good cricketer and an excellent chess player. He was elected to a college senior scholarship. In the mathematical tripos he obtained a first class in part one (1929) and was a wrangler in part two (1931). He then took part two of the natural sciences tripos, in which he also obtained a first (1932). He was later elected to a research scholarship, initially under R. H. Fowler and subsequently under J. E. Lennard-Jones, who directed him into the field which played such a dominant role in his subsequent researches—molecular orbital theory.

At Cambridge, Coulson became a leader of a group of Methodists within the university. They included Eileen Florence Burrett, a trainee teacher, and she and Coulson were married in 1938, just before he left Cambridge. She was the daughter of William Alfred Burrett, house furnisher in Leeds. They later had two sons and two daughters.

In 1934 Coulson was elected to a prize fellowship at Trinity for four years, and he obtained his PhD two years later. In 1938 he became senior lecturer in mathematics at University College, Dundee. During the Second World War he was a conscientious objector, and was the sole remaining lecturer in applied mathematics at Dundee. In 1945 he moved to the Physical Chemistry Laboratory in Oxford on an ICI fellowship, and was appointed a lecturer in mathematics at University College. He was then awarded the newly established chair of theoretical physics at King's

Charles Alfred Coulson (1910–1974), by Walter Bird

College, London, which he took up in October 1947. In 1952 he returned to Oxford to take up the Rouse Ball chair of mathematics and a professorial fellowship at Wadham College. He spent much energy organizing the new Mathematical Institute at Oxford, which was completed in 1963. In 1972 he became Oxford's first professor of theoretical chemistry, although he was already beginning to suffer the effects of his final illness. He founded a summer school of theoretical chemistry which was outstandingly successful.

Coulson was very productive in his research. The Royal Society, of which he was elected a fellow in 1950, recorded in his obituary more than four hundred publications in scientific journals. His early book, *Waves* (1941), went into several editions. The work which he did with W. E. Duncanson, on electronic structure of molecules in momentum space, was pioneering, and their papers continued to have great influence for many years. Coulson himself thought his most important work was that on the relationship between bond-order and bond-length. He also carried out significant research on hydrogen bonding, and was influential in promoting the description of solids as the limiting case of large molecules—a theory which later gave rise to the field of low-dimensional solids. In his foreword to the book *Orbital Theories of Molecules and Solids* (ed. N. H. March, 1974), dedicated to Coulson by his friends and colleagues, H. C. Longuet-Higgins describes the personal consequences of their association:

'Above all I was impressed by the simplicity of Coulson's thinking and by his determination to make things so clear that even a novice could grasp the essential ideas'. The professional consequences were a series of brilliantly influential papers by Coulson and Longuet-Higgins in the *Proceedings of the Royal Society*. The clarity and simplicity of Coulson's thinking is nowhere better exemplified than in his best-selling book, *Valence* (1952).

Coulson was an outstanding scientist and expositor and also a man of unusually wide interests. In 1962–8 he was a member of the central committee of the World Council of Churches and in 1965–71 he was chairman of Oxfam. His religious publications and television appearances made him well known to the public. He enjoyed a happy family life, and he and his wife opened their home to his students on many occasions. He was tall and imposing, and occasionally unconventional in his attire.

He had twelve honorary degrees, including a Cambridge ScD (1971), and was an honorary fellow or member of several British and foreign learned societies. His many medals included the Royal Society Davy medal (1970) and the Faraday (1968) and Tilden (1969) medals of the Chemical Society. Coulson enjoyed robust health until 1970, when he was operated on for cancer of the prostate. He recovered, but in July 1973 a routine hernia operation revealed regrowth of the tumour. He continued to work until five days before his death, which took place at home in Oxford on 7 January 1974. His wife survived him.

N. H. MARCH, rev.

**Sources** S. L. Altmann and E. J. Bowen, *Memoirs FRS*, 20 (1974), 75–134 · private information (1986)
**Archives** Bodl. Oxf., personal, religious, and scientific corresp. and papers · U. Leeds, Brotherton L., lecture notes, notebooks, etc. | Bodl. Oxf., corresp. with Dorothy Hodgkin · Bodl. Oxf., corresp. with W. Hume-Rothery
**Likenesses** W. Stoneman, photograph, *c*.1952, RS · photograph, *c*.1974, RS · W. Bird, photograph, RS [*see illus.*]

**Coulson** [*née* Kerr; *other married name* Colville], **Elizabeth** [*pseud.* Roxburghe Lothian] (**1818/19–1876**), novelist, was the daughter of Robert Kerr (*b.* 1788) and Elizabeth Ker. She claimed as a paternal ancestor Andrew Kerr, brother to Robert Kerr, the first earl of Ancrum (1578–1654). The Kerr family was Scottish—traditionally borderers and royalists.

After a very early period, when her parents—her mother, evidently, as well as her father—were absent on a two-year trip to India, leaving her and her infant sister with paid caretakers, Elizabeth Kerr spent parts of her youth in France, Devon, and (especially) the Isle of Jersey. She seems to have grown close to both her parents, though in different ways. Her posthumously published autobiographical novel, *Lizzie Lothian*, represents her mother as a rather Dickensian character, much taken up with needlework and befuddled by a linguistically learned family. Her father, contrastingly, seemed a darker figure. He had seen extensive military action during the Napoleonic wars; at Bergen op Zoom he was shot in a lung and in his left arm, which was afterwards useless.

I have heard him speak of sitting up at night to make foot-bandages for his men and himself, when they had been months without proper shoes, and the ice set in so that the whole land was deeply frozen … Nothing ever could, or ever did, make him regret his decision to serve the country well, 'jade though she be!'    (Coulson, xiii–xiv)

He felt patriotic sentiments not only for England but for Italy, becoming an ardent supporter, as did his daughter, of Italian nationalism. Partly because of these leanings, he hired as her tutor Dr Giglio, 'one of a party which had striven and had suffered for the cause' (ibid., v). Giglio taught her Italian, French, and Spanish, plus a smattering of Latin and Greek, while giving her a lifelong interest in Italian culture and history. When Giglio left, the travel writer H. D. Inglis, who was a regular guest at the Kerr house, took over much of Elizabeth's education. He published at least one of her essays in a collection of pieces on the Channel Islands, although it is not clear which part or parts were written by her. Some time in adolescence or young womanhood Elizabeth Kerr produced the sentimental and occasionally amusing *Lizzie Lothian* which ended with the lugubrious premature death of the heroine, partly from romantic loss, mainly from sheer sadness. As well as a writer, Elizabeth Kerr also became an ardent pianist.

Elizabeth Kerr's first marriage (3 October 1837) was to Thomas Colville (*d.* 1851) of Annfield, Stirling; they had two sons and three daughters and a son who died in infancy. After Colville's death on 19 February 1851, on 15 December 1853 she married her first cousin Edward Foster Coulson (*b.* 1804), son of George Coulson of Cottingham Castle, Yorkshire, and Jane Ker.

Towards the end of 1876 Elizabeth Coulson published an ambitious two-volume historical novel titled *Dante and Beatrice from 1282 to 1290*. Coulson's Beatrice is Beatrice Portinari, ancestor of the family depicted in the Portinari altarpiece (to which the author devotes one of numerous appendices). In love with Dante, but reserved for marriage with a rich, heartless merchant, and terrorized by the Inquisition, she dies young; the novel ends with her demise, from which Dante will draw a lifetime of inspiration. The book features a range of mostly corrupt but very entertaining ecclesiastical characters, including a gourmet hermit gamekeeper and a Victor Hugo-like inquisitor-seducer, who longs for Beatrice as Frollo for Esmeralda. Coulson incorporates many songs and poems, including a Tuscan hymn to Bacchus and, in a mad scene for a persecuted heretic, snatches of Ophelia-like ditties. There are many learned digressions, mostly based on personal investigations in libraries or at famous sites associated with Dante in Florence and its vicinity. *Dante and Beatrice* is at times a savagely anti-Catholic novel—indeed, Dante himself appears as a kind of proto-protestant—and the book was much criticized for its depiction of Catholicism. Contrastingly, though on a more modest scale, Coulson is philosemitic, mentioning in a footnote, with implicit approval, Cromwell's welcome to the Jews after their long absence from the British Isles. Noticed in *The Hour* and the *Daily News*, *Dante and Beatrice* was applauded by the

*Edinburgh Review* (in an essay on Capponi's *History of Florence*, April 1876, 490).

Three weeks after the appearance of *Dante and Beatrice*, on 23 January 1876, Coulson died at Bellaport Hall, Norton, Market Drayton, Shropshire. A year and a half later her widower published *Lizzie Lothian*, prefaced by an extensive memoir of the author. This preface is the main contemporary source of information about Coulson's life.

The only known surviving image of Coulson is a bust that her second husband said was made in Florence in 1873 'by Fuller'. It is the subject of the frontispiece to *Lizzie Lothian*. RICHARD MAXWELL

**Sources** *EdinR*, 143 (1876), 490 · E. Coulson [Roxburghe Lothian], *Lizzie Lothian* (1877) [with an autobiographical preface by E. Coulson] · d. cert. · *CGPLA Eng. & Wales* (1896)
**Likenesses** Fuller, bust, repro. in Coulson, *Lizzie Lothian*
**Wealth at death** under £100: probate, 25 May 1896, *CGPLA Eng. & Wales*

**Coulson, Walter** (1795–1860), newspaper editor and barrister, son of Thomas Coulson (1767–1845), master painter in the Royal Dockyard, Devonport, Devon, and his wife, Catherine, second daughter of Walter Borlase, surgeon, of Penzance, Cornwall, was born at Torpoint in Cornwall, on 9 April 1795. His birth was registered at Morice Square Baptist Church, Devonport, where his name was spelt Coulsen (*IGI*). It is not known where he went to school, but for five or six years from the age of fifteen or sixteen he was tutored by the philosopher Jeremy Bentham at Bentham's home in Queen Square Place, Westminster, London, and he acted as Bentham's amanuensis. Walter's elder brother Thomas (*d.* 1813, aged twenty-two) had also worked for Bentham, and Walter was succeeded by his cousin Henry Coulson. This relationship had come about through Jeremy Bentham's brother Sir Samuel, one-time inspector-general of naval works, who had met Thomas Coulson senior through his work in the dockyards.

Jeremy Bentham launched Coulson on his journalistic career in 1813, before he was twenty, by getting him a job as parliamentary reporter on the *Morning Chronicle* at a salary of '4 guineas a week all the year around' (*Correspondence of Jeremy Bentham*, 8.432). In the summer of 1820 Coulson was appointed editor of the evening newspaper *The Traveller*, founded in 1800, of which John Stuart Mill said 'under the editorship of an able man, Mr Walter Coulson, it had become one of the most important newspaper organs of liberal politics' (Mill, 61); it was also 'a bold advocate of political reforms' (*Press Club Catalogue*, 74). *The Traveller* was originally the trade paper of commercial travellers and it was distributed on their circuits, but it had become a 'literary and political organ of some celebrity' under the control of Colonel Robert Torrens, described as 'once famous as the Radical member for Bolton and a political economist of learning and ingenuity' (Atlay, 11). *The Traveller* merged with *The Globe* and, from 30 December 1822, it appeared as the *Globe and Traveller*. Atlay says there is no record of how the merger came about, but that Torrens took the main interest and brought Coulson with him. Atlay describes Coulson as 'a

man of taste and learning, with great social and convivial gifts' (ibid., 12). With Coulson as editor, the paper became more radical: 'Under his management the paper entered a new lease of life. Its political complexion assumed a character of "Liberalism" which was in advance of the Whigs of the pre-reform days' (ibid.). Coulson was promised £800 a year plus a share of the profits. Bentham said the sales tripled in the first three months under Coulson. He wrote to a friend: 'The paper is favoured by the Whigs: but his [Coulson's] principles are mine and he introduces into his paper, as much of them as such patrons will endure … what he does in this way is no small matter' (*Correspondence of Jeremy Bentham*, 10.80). Bentham went on to give several examples of Coulson's helping foreign radicals by publishing articles for them and allowing them to reprint *Globe* articles. Atlay says Coulson resigned in 1834 after the *Globe and Traveller* made a harsh attack on his friend Lord Chancellor Brougham (Atlay, 13). Barham said there had been 'a change of opinions leading the proprietors to take a more radical turn than suited [Coulson's] principles and to abuse his friend, Lord Brougham' (*Life and Letters*, 258–9). For Grant the *Globe and Traveller* had 'All at once … abjured its Liberalism of fully sixty years, and became a thorough-going Tory journal' (Grant, 2.72), but this assessment went too far, for Roberts says the prominent tone of the *Globe* was 'whiggish', though it had its 'radical moments': 'the two outlooks mixed almost promiscuously in its columns and, along with the paper's powerful addiction to political economy (a doctrine both Radicals and Whigs could agree on), led in the 1850s to Liberalism' (Roberts, 9). Though Coulson enrolled as a student at Gray's Inn, London, as early as 1813, he was not called to the bar until 26 November 1828. Wisely, he specialized in conveyancing, for he was no orator, and he quickly became one of the leaders of the chancery bar. He was recorder of Penzance, where his family still lived, from July 1836 to January 1838, and he was for many years parliamentary counsel to the Home department. He became queen's counsel in July 1851 and a bencher of Gray's Inn in November 1851. He was treasurer of Gray's Inn in 1853. Coulson represented his inn on the Council of Legal Education after it was set up in 1857 to oversee the training of barristers. Coulson had a lifelong interest in economics and, in June 1821, he was elected an original member of the Political Economy Club, whose membership was restricted to thirty people. He took an active part in its proceedings, proposing topics for papers and chairing debates. Coulson served on the Royal Commission for the Exhibition of 1851.

One of the many friends Coulson met through Bentham was Francis Place, 'the radical tailor of Charing cross' (Bain, 77). Another was the philosopher James Mill: Coulson was one of the select few who accompanied him on his famous Sunday walks. He was also a frequent guest at the evening parties given by the essayist Charles Lamb. Coulson was godfather to the first child of the critic and essayist William Hazlitt, though this did not deter him from acting for Hazlitt's wife in their divorce. The poet and editor James Leigh Hunt called him the 'admirable

Coulson' (*B. W. Procter*, 195); Crabb Robinson described him as 'a prodigy of knowledge' (*Diary*, 1.264–5); and others called him a 'walking encyclopedia' (Clarke, 26). In 1817 Bentham had peevishly criticized the coldness of Coulson's personality, but he admitted that Coulson had 'a good sound judgment but no affections public or private' (*Correspondence of Jeremy Bentham*, 9.94). However, Coulson proved himself a good friend to John Black, the eccentric editor of the *Morning Chronicle* who was dismissed in 1843: he was among the subscribers to an annuity for Black and he provided him with a cottage and a garden on his estate near Birling, Kent, at a nominal rent, 'where Mr Black lived in comparative comfort until his death about 15 years later [1855]' (Grant, 288–9). Coulson died, unmarried, aged sixty-five at his home, North Bank, St John's Wood, London, on 21 November 1860 and he was buried at Kensal Green cemetery. He left most of his estate to his younger brother William *Coulson, a distinguished surgeon, for life and then to William's two sons.

HUGH MOONEY

**Sources** G. C. Boase, *Collectanea Cornubiensia: a collection of biographical and topographical notes relating to the county of Cornwall* (1890), 169–71 · Boase & Courtney, *Bibl. Corn.*, 1.95, 3.1139 · *The correspondence of Jeremy Bentham*, ed. T. Sprigge and others, [11 vols.] (1968–), in *The collected works of Jeremy Bentham*, vol. 8, pp. 66, 287, 431–2; vol. 9, p. 94; vol. 10, p. 80 · J. B. Atlay, '*The Globe*': a sketch of its history (1903), 5–13 · S. Rosenberg, 'Some further notes on the history of *The Globe*: its editors, managers and proprietors', *Victorian Periodicals Newsletter*, 5/1 (1972), 40–47 · F. D. Roberts, 'Who ran the London *Globe* in the 1830s, 1840s, and 1850s?', *Victorian Periodicals Newsletter*, 4/2 (1971), 6–11 · J. Foster, *The register of admissions to Gray's Inn, 1521–1889, together with the register of marriages in Gray's Inn chapel, 1695–1754* (privately printed, London, 1889), 41 · *The Press Club newspaper catalogue* (1935), 74, 75 · J. S. Mill, *Autobiography* (1873), 61 · J. Grant, *The newspaper press: its origin, progress, and present position*, 2 (1871), 72, 289 · C. Mackay, *Forty years' recollections of life, literature and public affairs, from 1830–1870*, 2 vols. (1877) · *The life and letters of … Richard Harris Barham*, ed. R. H. D. Barham, new edn, 2 (1880), 258–9 · A. Bain, *James Mill: a biography* (1882), 77 · *Political Economy Club, 1821–1882* (1881), vol. 4, *passim* · *Annual Register* (1860), 404 · *The Times* (21 Nov 1860), 1 · *The Times* (23 Nov 1860), letter · *B. W. Procter (Barry Cornwall): an autobiographical fragment*, ed. C. P. [C. Patmore] (1877), 135, 196 · F. K. Hunt, *The fourth estate: contributions towards a history of newspapers, and of the liberty of the press*, 2 vols. (1850) · C. C. Clarke and M. C. Clarke, *Recollections of writers* (1878), 26 · *The correspondence of Leigh Hunt*, ed. T. L. Hunt, 2 vols. (1862) · *Memoirs of William Hazlitt*, 2 vols. (1867) · *IGI* · *Diary, reminiscences, and correspondence of Henry Crabb Robinson*, ed. T. Sadler, 3rd edn, 1 (1872), 264–5

**Archives** Cornwall RO, corresp. with cabinet ministers and family

**Likenesses** R. J. Lane, lithograph, 1841 (after F. Corbaux), NPG · R. J. Lane, lithograph, 1848, Gray's Inn, London

**Wealth at death** under £12,000: probate, 14 Dec 1860, *CGPLA Eng. & Wales*

**Coulson, William** (1739–1801), linen manufacturer, was born at Lisburn, co. Antrim. His father may have been Richard Coulson, and there is some evidence to suggest that his ancestors were English settlers in co. Tyrone during the early seventeenth century. Coulson was one of the few eighteenth-century linen manufacturers in Ireland to adopt and develop the technology of draw-loom weaving. Draw-looms, which had been in use for several centuries

in continental Europe, especially in the Low Countries and Saxony, enabled the weaving of elaborately figured cloth known as damask. Such cloth was purchased for use as table linen in the households of royalty and the nobility.

Coulson is believed to have established a factory, in the sense of a number of looms and workmen collected under one roof, about 1760. This type of operation and scale of business differed from other eighteenth-century Irish linen manufacture in several ways. First, the complex draw-looms were much more expensive to erect and to operate than the plain hand-loom; second, it took several months, or even years, for a draw-loom to be set up or 'mounted' according to a design and then for a cloth to be woven. For both these reasons draw-loom damask linen manufacturers centralized their production in premises where the workers were under their management rather than relying on domestic cottage production. In addition Coulson's damask weavers were employees working for wages rather than independent domestic weavers who sold their woven cloth at market.

Coulson is first recorded as being in business in 1764 in premises near the bridge over the River Lagan in Lisburn, possibly in the buildings which had been occupied by the Huguenot Louis Crommelin, who had settled in the town in 1698 and developed fine plain-linen weaving. In 1766 Coulson was granted a lease on ground nearer the market house in the town centre by Lisburn's landlord, Francis Seymour-Conway, earl of Hertford. Here he erected buildings and installed looms. Lord Hertford's patronage was significant for the advancement of Coulson's enterprise. Hertford moved within royal circles. In 1757 he was appointed a lord of the bedchamber, and in 1766 was appointed lord lieutenant of Ireland. One of his predecessors as lord lieutenant, the duke of Dorset, had established a precedent, when lord steward of the royal household in 1736, for the royal purchase of Irish linens for household use as a substitute for those from the Low Countries. Hertford was in a position to direct such custom to Coulson, while his ambassadorial role as lord lieutenant helped develop a clientele for Coulson which was drawn from the courts of Europe as well as the English royal household. The subsequent patronage of Queen Charlotte, wife of George III, in ordering a full set of Coulson's damask table linen, set the seal on his royal connections. Where royalty led, the nobility followed. Coulson married Ann Hannigan (1741–1790), probably about 1770. One of their sons, Hill (1777–1815), became a Church of Ireland clergyman; the others, John (b. c.1770), William (1774–1851), James (1778–1854), and Walter (1783–1836), continued the family firm. During the 1830s the business divided in two, with James setting up as James Coulson & Co. while the other brothers remained in partnership as William Coulson & Sons.

Coulson's initial scale of operation was modest and self-financed. However, in a petition presented to the trustees of the Linen and Hempen Manufactures of Ireland (the Irish linen board) during the 1780s, he asked that they grant him the means to establish eight damask looms with their mountings to supplement his existing sixteen damask looms. In order to weave wide cloths, each of these looms could have required up to three weavers and a draw-loom boy assistant. Coulson also employed weavers in fine plain linens and sheetings. Expansion continued, for in 1812 a contemporary described the business as employing up to 200 weavers and assistants working on fifty damask looms in the manufactory, and a further 300 workers weaving diaper and fine linen on plain looms both in the manufactory and as domestic cottage weavers. By this time the firm was a vertically integrated operation, probably without parallel in Irish damask production. Under a putting-out system Coulson supplied women hand spinners with flax to spin into yarn, and weavers in and outside the manufactory with the yarn to weave into cloth. His premises also included a yarn-boiling house, where the yarn was scoured before weaving, and a bleach green near the manufactory, where the cloth was finished for sale. He had a commercial address in Dublin and rooms in the White Linen Hall there, where he met foreign linen buyers.

Coulson had a distinctive sense of commercial awareness. This is apparent in the designs of his earliest extant cloths dating from the end of the century, which follow neo-classical forms of decoration. Like other forms of the decorative arts of the period, they were intended to provide harmony with the Adam style of architecture. William Coulson became the best-known eighteenth-century Irish damask linen manufacturer to specialize in producing neo-classical designs, which he customized with armorial bearings, pictorial scenes, mottoes, and emblems to suit his clients. In both these aspects of business he displayed entrepreneurial zeal on a par with some of the best-known of eighteenth-century English industrial producers.

Coulson died on 6 January 1801 and was buried the same month in the family plot in the graveyard of Lisburn Cathedral. Little is known of his personal life, other than that he was a member of the select vestry of Lisburn Cathedral in 1768. He was a well-read man, who subscribed to various books on accounting procedures published in Dublin. He obtained high standards of craftsmanship from his workers and he rewarded their skills by high wages and the provision of a pension for the weavers. The family business was carried on by his sons, eventually adopting the Jacquard mechanism which superseded the draw-loom and, much later, adding power-loom manufacture alongside hand-loom weaving. The firm obtained a royal warrant in 1811 from the prince regent and its pre-eminence in damask production for royalty, nobility, and statesmen continued into the twentieth century.

BRENDA COLLINS

**Sources** A. W. [A. Woods], 'Coulsons of Lisburn', *Belfast Municipal Museum and Art Gallery Quarterly Notes*, 56 (June 1938), 1–7 · Coulson family gravestone, Lisburn Cathedral graveyard · D. M. Mitchell, 'Looke to the keeping of the naperie: table linen in the courts of Europe in the 17th and 18th centuries', *Rencontres de l'École du Louvre* (autumn 1996) · E. R. R. Green, *The Lagan valley, 1800–50: a local history of the industrial revolution* (1949) · H. McCall, *Ireland and her staple manufactures* (1870) · J. Dubordieu, *Statistical survey of the county of* *Antrim* (1812) · B. J. Mackey, 'Centres of drawloom damask linen weaving in Ireland in the 18th and 19th centuries', *Leinendamaste* (Abegg-Stiftung, Riggisberg, 1999)
**Archives** PRO NIre., Foster MS D 562/5590

**Coulson, William** (*bap.* **1801**, *d.* **1877**), surgeon, younger son of Thomas Coulson (1767–1845), master painter in Devonport Dockyard, and his wife, Catherine Borlase, was baptized in Devonport in 1801. Walter *Coulson was an elder brother. After receiving some classical education at Penzance grammar school, Coulson spent two years in Brittany at St Pol de Léon (1816–18), where he became proficient in French language and literature. After serving as an apprentice to Mr Berryman, a Penzance surgeon, Coulson entered Edward Grainger's anatomy school in Southwark, London, in 1822, and attended St Thomas's Hospital, where he became dresser to Frederick Tyrrell. It was at about this time that he began working as a reporter for the newly founded *Lancet*; he continued to write for it throughout his career. From 1824 to 1826 he studied in Berlin, supplying the *Edinburgh Medical and Surgical Journal* with foreign correspondence; during this time he became friends with the poet Thomas Campbell. After some months' stay in Paris, Coulson returned to London and became a member of the Royal College of Surgeons on 26 September 1826.

Coulson was one of the founders of the Aldersgate Street school of medicine along with Frederick Tyrrell, William Lawrence, and others, and he worked for three years as demonstrator of anatomy. At the same time he worked as foreign editor for *The Lancet* and made many English translations from foreign works. In 1828 he was elected surgeon to the General Dispensary, Aldersgate Street, and in 1830 he became consulting surgeon to the City of London Lying-in Hospital. His investigations on puerperal affections of the joints at the lying-in hospital did much to improve the knowledge of their nature and pathology. They were published in the second edition of his work, *Diseases of the Hip Joint* (1841). In 1832 he, with his colleagues, resigned his connection with the Aldersgate dispensary over a disagreement with the committee, over its 'virtually putting up for sale all the most efficient offices of the charity' (Clutterbuck, *Memoir of G. Birkbeck, M.D.*, 1849, 9). In the same year he joined the medical board of the Royal Sea-bathing Infirmary at Margate, of which he long continued an active member.

Coulson's practice rapidly increased with his various publications, which, commencing in 1827 with a translation and notes to Milne-Edwards's *Surgical Anatomy* and a second edition of Lawrence's translation of Blumenbach's *Comparative Anatomy*, became more and more original in their character and culminated in those on the bladder and lithotrity. He was also a valued contributor and adviser in connection with the cyclopaedia and other publications of the Society for the Diffusion of Useful Knowledge. Coulson moved from his early residence in Charterhouse Square to a house in Frederick's Place, Old Jewry, where he commanded for many years perhaps the largest city practice. In 1840 he married Maria Bartram (*d.* 1876).

Coulson was elected among the first batch of fellows of

the Royal College of Surgeons in 1843; he became a member of the council in 1851, and in 1861 he delivered the Hunterian oration. When St Mary's Hospital, Paddington, was established, Coulson was elected senior surgeon. In July 1851 he performed the first operation at St Mary's with John Snow administering chloroform. Besides being a specialist and successful operator in diseases of the bladder, Coulson undertook a large proportion of more strictly medical cases. He retired from the staff of St Mary's in 1862. Combining successful practice with good finance and the inheritance of his brother Walter's fortune, he accumulated one of the largest fortunes ever made in practice—said to be a quarter of a million pounds.

Coulson was noteworthy for more than his surgical skill. He was a liberal, a disciple of Thomas Carlyle, F. D. Maurice, and John Stuart Mill; he was a friend of R. H. Barham, Francis Newman, and other leading literary men; and he was of sufficient individuality among such men to leave a distinct impress. Contemporary descriptions report his determination and generosity, and he was said to be marked by a strong belief in individuality, in duty, and in the fulfilment of promises. He was tall and vigorous-looking, with a heavy face, white hair, and gold spectacles. He died at 1 Chester Terrace, Regent's Park, London, on 5 May 1877, and was buried four days later at Kensal Green cemetery.

Coulson published several works on surgery which were popular in his day, perhaps the most significant being *On Diseases of the Bladder and Prostate Gland* (1838), which ran to a 6th edition in 1865.

G. T. BETTANY, *rev.* KAYE BAGSHAW

**Sources** D. Innes Williams, 'William Coulson: Victorian values handsomely rewarded', *Journal of Medical Biography*, 2 (1994), 132–6 · J. Kirkup, 'William Coulson: St Mary's first surgeon', *St Mary's Gazette* (April 1985), 22–3 · *The Lancet* (19 May 1877), 740–42 · Z. Cope, *The history of St Mary's Hospital medical school* (1954) · *Life and letters of Thomas Campbell*, ed. W. Beattie, 2 (1849), 448 · *CGPLA Eng. & Wales* (1877)
**Archives** Cornwall RO, family corresp. | UCL, letters to Society for the Diffusion of Useful Knowledge
**Likenesses** Maguire, lithograph, probably RCS Eng.
**Wealth at death** under £120,000: probate, 17 March 1877, *CGPLA Eng. & Wales*

**Coulton, David Trevena** (1810–1857), journalist, the son of James Coulton and grandson of the Revd J. Coulton, dean of Bristol, was born at Devizes, Wiltshire, on 3 October 1810. His father died when he was about twelve years old. Owing to delicate health he was educated under a private tutor. At an early age he began to contribute both poetry and prose to the periodicals, and in 1839 he founded *The Britannia* newspaper, the aim of which was to extend and popularize the principles of Conservatism and to uphold national protestantism as embodied in the institutions of the realm. As a journalist Coulton possessed considerable skill in the popular exposition of complex questions, and could expound on any argument with the unfaltering force of logic. Particularly noteworthy are his

writings in the first years of Sir Robert Peel's administration; they gave the government much needed independent support in its early stages.

Coulton withdrew from active journalism in 1847 and, having in 1850 sold *The Britannia*, married Sarah Boniface at St Bride's, Fleet Street, on 23 April. They settled at Goudhurst, Kent, where he took to farming, occasionally contributing to the *Quarterly Review*. He published an *Inquiry into the Authorship of the Letters of Junius*, and in 1853 a novel entitled *Fortune: a Story of London Life*. Yielding to the solicitation of friends, he undertook in 1854 to edit *The Press*, Benjamin Disraeli's newspaper dedicated to the propagation of tory political principles as well as to the aggrandizement of Disraeli himself, to both of which aims Coulton had largely to subscribe. Coulton's recreation was mechanics; he had great knowledge of physics and planned an atmospheric railway that captured the interest of many scientists of the day. Coulton died of bronchitis at Brighton on 8 May 1857, survived by his wife and two children.

T. F. HENDERSON, *rev.* NILANJANA BANERJI

**Sources** *The Press* (9 May 1857) · *The Press* (16 May 1857) · *GM*, 3rd ser., 2 (1857), 742 · *John Bull and Britannia* (16 May 1857) · *Art Journal*, 19 (1857), 228 · Allibone, *Dict.* · S. E. Koss, *The rise and fall of the political press in Britain*, 1 (1981) · J. Shattock, *Politics and reviewers: The Edinburgh and The Quarterly in the early Victorian age* (1989) · D. Griffiths, ed., *The encyclopedia of the British press, 1422–1992* (1992)

**Coulton, George Gordon** (1858–1947), historian and controversialist, was born at Tower Place, King's Lynn, Norfolk, on 15 October 1858, the third son and sixth child of John James Coulton, a solicitor of Yorkshire origins, and his wife, Sarah Radley. After early schooling at a dame-school at Lynn, the *lycée* at St Omer, and Lynn grammar school, he was sent to Felsted School from where, in 1877, he won a classical scholarship to St Catharine's College, Cambridge. He remembered his Cambridge years without affection, perhaps owing to the failure of health which in 1881 confined him to an *aegrotat* degree. Briefly a master at a preparatory school in Malvern, he then trained for holy orders under Charles John Vaughan, though already subject to doubts concerning the Thirty-Nine Articles. Ordained deacon in 1883, he held curacies at Offley and Rickmansworth, but his misgivings grew, and in 1885 he finally decided that he could not proceed to the priesthood. Coulton then held a series of teaching posts in public schools, an experience he seems to have found increasingly depressing, since about 1896 he attempted suicide. But his life was saved, and in that year he took up a tutoring job at a coaching establishment in Eastbourne which he ran with his college friend Henry von Essen Scott for thirteen years. He had been studying the middle ages since the mid-1870s, and his new position gave him time both for extension lecturing and for the methodical study of primary sources which made him one of the most learned medievalists of his age. It also financed foreign travel—it was in Switzerland that in 1903 he met Rose Dorothy (*b.* 1876/7), daughter of Owen Ilbert, of Thurlestone, Devon, and niece of the parliamentary draftsman

George Gordon Coulton (1858–1947), by Walter Stoneman, 1930

Sir Courtenay Ilbert. They married on 19 July 1904 and had two daughters.

During the first decade of the twentieth century Coulton began to publish and to establish his scholarly reputation, starting with a translation of Salimbene (1906; enlarged edn, 1907) and a book about Chaucer (1908). He followed these with two anthologies of medieval sources, *A Medieval Garner* (1910) and *Social Britain from the Conquest to the Reformation* (1918), in which he began the process of putting original historical material before the general public which constituted one of his most notable services to scholarship. In 1911 he had moved to Cambridge, following his election as Birkbeck lecturer in ecclesiastical history at Trinity College, and supported himself by private tutoring. The fall in student numbers during the war made his position financially precarious, but in 1919 he was elected to a lecturership in the English faculty, which he held until his retirement in 1934, and a fellowship of St John's College. A secure income provided the basis for further research and writing, and in the last twenty-five years of his life Coulton published several substantial books as well as a number of shorter ones: *The Medieval Village* (1925); *Art and the Reformation* (1928); *Inquisition and Liberty* and *Medieval Panorama* (both 1938); *Five Centuries of Religion*, published in four volumes between 1923 and 1950, the last appearing posthumously. From 1940 to 1944 he was guest lecturer at the University of Toronto. He was elected fellow of the British Academy in 1929 and received honorary

doctorates from the universities of Durham (1920), Edinburgh (1931), and Kingston, Ontario (1942). He died at his home, 201 Chesterton Road, Cambridge, on 4 March 1947; he was survived by his wife.

A bare account of Coulton's career and its achievements conveys no idea of its frequently embattled course. He was constantly embroiled in controversy, by no means all of it academic. Thus he was a strong supporter of the National Service League, advocating compulsory national service for home defence, and campaigned energetically for it; his book *The Case for Compulsory Military Service* (1917) runs to nearly 400 pages. But he was far more often in the public eye for his recurrent conflicts with a group of Roman Catholic historians and apologists prominent in the early twentieth century, all of whom, and particularly Cardinal Francis Gasquet, he repeatedly denounced for what he described as 'habits of literary dishonesty' (*The Monastic Legend*, 1905, 12 n. 2). The sense of outrage which runs through practically all Coulton's writings had several roots. One was an absolute commitment to truth, which in a historiographical context meant a scrupulous dependence on contemporary sources, accurately cited, and furious broadsides of reproof for those who transgressed against this basic standard. Then there was a measure of religious antagonism. After deciding not to become a priest Coulton moved to a rather elusive spiritual position, somewhere between deism and Christian agnosticism, which in its acceptance of doubt left him radically opposed to the certainties of ultramontane Catholicism. Unlike his opponents, moreover, he fully accepted the claims of modernism; indeed he actively promoted them. This third strand in his historical thinking he himself described as his determination 'to justify the main trend of modern culture' (*Ten Medieval Studies*, 3rd edn, 1930, vii), and he attacked Catholic writers like Gasquet and G. K. Chesterton because he felt that they had constructed a false image of the medieval past, as centuries in which religious devotion had bred social contentment, in order to use it as a rebuke to the present. Far from regretting his involvement in controversy, he regarded it as part of his duty as a historian.

The carelessness and tendentiousness of Gasquet and his followers fully merited correction, but there was a degree of naïvety about Coulton's obsession with truthfulness, unsurprising, perhaps, in a man who could denounce his six-year-old daughter as a liar for a fib about a rabbit's nest. He acknowledged that preachers and moralists might have overstated the evils of their age, but in practice usually ignored his own caveat, with the result that his claims for the realities of medieval life sometimes appear as overbalanced in one direction as those of his adversaries in another. This feeling of imbalance is accentuated by Coulton's pugnacious literary style, as great accumulations of evidence (he was said to have read the entire Rolls Series) are deployed to overwhelm his opponents. Many of his books have dozens of appendices in which the errors of his opponents are exposed at length; *The Medieval Village* concludes with fifty-eight pages devoted entirely to 'A rough list of misstatements and blunders in Cardinal Gasquet's writings'. Coulton's only novel, *Friar's Lantern* (1906), is a *jeu d'esprit* in which a young curate devoted to the idea of the middle ages as an age of faith is transported back to the fourteenth century, where he undergoes a series of harrowing experiences; it ends with a characteristic assurance from the author that 'there is scarcely an incident which I have not taken from the most unimpeachable sources' (p. 247), together with two documentary illustrations to underline the point.

In appearance Coulton was tall and thin, his height accentuated, in the eyes of a French journalist, by his wearing clothes that were too short and tight. In academic circles he was combative but not malicious, and often made friends with those who stood up to him in debate—for instance the young Maurice Powicke. His abundant energies were not confined to scholarship, however, and sometimes made him a trial to his family. In his daughter Mary's *Father: a Portrait of G. G. Coulton at Home*, a minor masterpiece of exasperated affection, he appears as 'a powerful intellect and personality which steadily sustained a small middle-class household and sporadically wrecked its peace' (Campion, 140), a man addicted to cocoa brewed according to an elaborate recipe entirely his own, which he drank in a study filled with home-made gadgets, and also given to eccentricities like the embarrassing habit of removing meat-bones from plates at other people's dinner parties in order to take them home for his cats.

Coulton deserves to be remembered for more than his personal idiosyncrasies, however, for he made important contributions to medieval history. Not the least of them was his own extensive scholarship. He supported his arguments with a vast array of citations, more often from printed texts than from unpublished sources, but still extending far beyond the government-sponsored publications which proliferated in western Europe about the end of the nineteenth century. He appreciated the value of the medieval sermons and theological treatises which were still being printed in the sixteenth and seventeenth centuries, and also made good use of literary sources. This substructure of knowledge gives lasting value to even his most contentious writings. He also contributed to a widening of the range of medieval studies by his attention to social and economic issues. He expressed admiration for a few great men, like St Francis, St Bernard, and Archbishop Eudes Rigaud, but was principally concerned to study the effects of institutions like monasticism on the lower orders of society.

Coulton believed in bringing the fruits of his learning to a wider public than one made up of his fellow academics. A fine public speaker (several of his books originated in lecture courses), and always lucid and vigorous in his writings, he deliberately conceived anthologies of sources and books like *Medieval Panorama* to this end. He also encouraged other scholars to publish, and through the series Cambridge Studies in Medieval Life and Thought, which he inaugurated in 1920, provided the means for younger historians like Eileen Power to make their first appearances in print. Here and elsewhere, Coulton's obsession with factual accuracy helped to raise standards of scholarship. It is at least partly owing to him that twenty-first-century historians who present a view of medieval society more favourable than any he would have countenanced himself do so from a basis of scholarship unknown to his adversaries. Coulton's passionate concern for truth had some curious side-effects, but overall it served him and his profession well.                    HENRY SUMMERSON

**Sources** G. G. Coulton, *Fourscore years: an autobiography* (1943) · S. Campion [M. Coulton], *Father: a portrait of G. G. Coulton at home* (1948) · F. M. Powicke, 'Three Cambridge scholars: C. W. Previté-Orton, Z. N. Brooke and G. G. Coulton', *Cambridge Historical Journal*, 9 (1947–9), 106–16 · H. S. Bennett, 'George Gordon Coulton, 1858–1947', *PBA*, 33 (1947), 267–81 · G. Christianson, 'G. G. Coulton: the medieval historian as controversialist', *Catholic Historical Review*, 57 (1972), 421–41 · D. Knowles, 'Cardinal Gasquet as a historian', in D. Knowles, *The historian and character*, ed. C. N. L. Brooke and G. Constable (1963), 240–63 · Venn, *Alum. Cant.* · private information (2004) · b. cert. · m. cert. · d. cert. · *CGPLA Eng. & Wales* (1947)
**Archives** St John Cam., corresp., sketchbooks, and papers · University of Chicago Library, corresp. and papers | BL, corresp. with G. K. Chesterton, Add. MS 73194, *passim* · BL, letters to M. D. M. Petre, Add. MS 45744 · BL, corresp. with Society of Authors, Add. MS 56684 · NA Scot., corresp. with Lord Lothian · U. Glas. L., letters to George Neilson
**Likenesses** W. Stoneman, photograph, 1930, NPG [*see illus.*] · photographs, repro. in Coulton, *Fourscore years* · photographs, repro. in Campion, *Father*
**Wealth at death** £1047 11*s*. 1*d*.: administration with will, 16 Aug 1947, *CGPLA Eng. & Wales*

**Counsell, John William** (1905–1987), actor, theatre manager, and director, was born at Beckenham, Kent, on 24 April 1905, the son of Claude Christopher Counsell, preparatory school headmaster, and his wife, Evelyn Fleming (*d*. 1941). He was educated at Sedbergh, and Exeter College, Oxford. A love of the theatre led to his becoming a member of the Oxford University Dramatic Society from 1923 to 1926. When he came down, he worked briefly in Whiteley's department store and as a tutor, before joining the Oxford Playhouse Company as assistant stage manager. He made his stage début at the Playhouse in 1928. He undertook two tours of Canada as stage director for Maurice Colbourne's Shavian Company in 1928 and 1929, was leading juvenile in Northampton and Folkestone repertory companies from 1929 to 1930, stage manager for Baliol Holloway's *Richard III* at the New Theatre in 1930, and was stage director, scenic artist, and finally producer at the Oxford Playhouse between 1930 and 1933.

In autumn 1933 he became producer and joint managing director of the Windsor Repertory Company, at the Theatre Royal, a jewel of a theatre that nestled opposite the walls of Windsor Castle, but they were under-funded and the venture floundered. He did not give up, however, re-launching the Windsor Repertory Company in 1938, converting the theatre back from its recent use as a cinema, and staging middlebrow plays, which were performed to a consistently high standard. Success was assured when, three weeks after the opening in 1938, George VI brought a party to see Clifford Bax's romantic play *The Rose without a Thorn*, prompting the headline:

'King sits in 3*s*. 6*d*. stalls'. Over the years the royal family frequently brought their guests to the theatre.

Counsell had met his future wife, Mary Antoinette Kerridge (1914–1999), an actress, in 1936, when he was stage manager of *No Exit* and she was the leading lady's understudy. She was the daughter of Ernest Kerridge, a timber merchant. Their romance was full of high drama. Used to treating the understudy as a 'perk' of the job, Counsell nevertheless fell in love, and on hearing that Mary was on the point of touring South Africa for six months in Ian Hay's *The Frog*, charmed his way into the production. To his dismay, she did not go, whereas he was committed. He remained determined to win her, and decided that only by achieving the re-opening of the Theatre Royal would he prove himself sufficiently. This done, he called her and they were married on 29 July 1939. During the war twin daughters were born, both of whom became actresses.

In wartime the Windsor Repertory Company played on despite the black-out and a bomb in the car park. Counsell left to serve in the Royal Artillery, while his wife effectively kept the theatre going. He began as a territorial reservist, and ended as a lieutenant-colonel, having served in north Africa, France, and Germany, and as a member of the planning staff of Supreme Headquarters Allied Expeditionary Force, where he was assistant to Neville Grazebrook and composed the instrument of German surrender, signed at Rheims by General Jodl, which officially ended the war. Other wartime experiences included facing problems of discipline from Signaller Spike Milligan, and drafting dispatches for General Eisenhower for the Tunisian and Italian campaigns.

In 1945 he resumed direction of the Theatre Royal. A good repertory audience had been established during the war, and they remained loyal throughout the 1950s and 1960s. There was hardly a distinguished actor who did not, at one time or another, play at Windsor, enjoying its reputation for popular productions, many of which were launched there and later went to London. Dame Sybil Thorndike, Ivor Novello, Robert Morley, Patrick Cargill, and the acting husband and wife team Michael Denison and Dulcie Gray all performed there. Counsell effectively launched Geraldine McEwan in *For Better, for Worse*, a comedy by Arthur Watkyn, in 1952. The Theatre Royal was very much a family concern, and there were occasions when all four Counsells appeared on stage together, John, Mary, and the twins Jenny and Elizabeth in productions such as Bernard Shaw's *You Never can Tell* (1962) and Oscar Wilde's *The Importance of being Earnest*. In 1958 the theatre transferred from a weekly to a fortnightly repertory system and later ceased to maintain a resident company. Counsell was proud that the theatre never sought a grant or subsidy.

Counsell also produced plays at the Playhouse, the Lyric, Hammersmith, the Duchess, the Vaudeville, Aldwych, and Savoy theatres. Notable productions were Marcelle Maurette's *Anastasia* at the St James's Theatre in 1953, the television production of which won Counsell the *Daily Mail* award for best television play of the year, and *Grab me a Gondola* in 1956, a musical comedy by Julian More and

James Gilbert, which he had commissioned for Windsor. In 1968 he took his family and fifteen actors on a bus and truck acting tour of North America with four plays. He was the author of some memoirs, *Counsell's Opinion* in 1963, and *Play Direction: a Practical Viewpoint* in 1973. In 1975 he celebrated his seventieth birthday by appearing as Canon Chasuble in *The Importance of being Earnest* with Dame Flora Robson in the cast. That year he was appointed OBE.

Counsell was among the last of the gentlemen actor–managers. Under his direction the Theatre Royal became an integral part of Windsor life, its annual pantomimes holding as strong a place in local hearts as Christmas itself. He was never particularly attracted by the avant-garde, knew what he wanted, and ran the theatre as a successful venture, often showing a healthy annual profit. He was a keen supporter of local ventures and was a director of Yehudi Menuhin's Windsor festival from 1969.

Counsell suffered a series of strokes and had to give up running the Theatre Royal in December 1984, his wife, Mary Kerridge, remaining on the board for some years. He died at Princess Margaret Hospital, Windsor, on 23 February 1987.      HUGO VICKERS

**Sources** J. Counsell, *Counsell's opinion* (1963) · *The Times* (25 Feb 1987) · *Daily Telegraph* (25 Feb 1987) · private information (2004) [family] · personal knowledge (2004) · F. Gaye, ed., *Who's who in the theatre*, 14th edn (1967) · *CGPLA Eng. & Wales* (1987) · m. cert.
**Wealth at death** £18,491: probate, 1987, *CGPLA Eng. & Wales*

**Coupar**. For this title name *see* Elphinstone, John, third Lord Balmerino and second Lord Coupar (1623–1704) [*see under* Elphinstone, John, second Lord Balmerino (*d.* 1649)]; Elphinstone, John, fourth Lord Balmerino and third Lord Coupar (1652–1736) [*see under* Elphinstone, John, second Lord Balmerino (*d.* 1649)]; Elphinstone, Arthur, sixth Lord Balmerino and fifth Lord Coupar (1688–1746).

**Couper, Archibald Scott** (1831–1892), chemist, was born on 31 March 1831 in the Townhead of Kirkintilloch, Dunbartonshire, the only surviving child of Archibald Couper, cotton manufacturer, and his wife, Helen Dollar. Because of poor health he was educated at home before enrolling at Glasgow University to study humanities and classical languages. He spent the summer of 1851 in Halle to acquire fluency in German and the following summer again went to Germany and spent some time at the University of Berlin in desultory study. After returning to Edinburgh he studied logic and metaphysics under Sir William Hamilton, who was well versed in German philosophy, then largely ignored in British universities. After yet another continental tour Couper returned to Berlin in 1855, now determined to study chemistry for reasons which are not clear. He studied with K. F. Rammelsberg, professor of inorganic chemistry, and attended F. L. Sonnenschein's lectures on chemical analysis. In August 1856 he moved to Paris where he engaged in independent research in the laboratory of Charles-Adolphe Wurtz, then one of the few first-rate chemical laboratories outside Germany.

There, in less than eight months, Couper wrote the

Archibald Scott Couper (1831–1892), by unknown photographer

three papers which are his main claim to fame. The first, 'Some derivatives of benzene', was a straightforward account of the preparation of two new bromine derivatives of benzene. The second was more theoretical, dealing with the constitution of salicylic acid. This was of interest to the eminent German chemist F. A. Kekulé, but he failed to repeat Couper's experiment: many years later Couper was proved perfectly correct. In the third paper, 'On a new chemical theory', Couper clearly enunciated a new theory of the linking of carbon atoms which marked a transition from the prevailing type theory to the modern structure theory. He deduced that carbon had a combining power (valency) of four or two and a unique capacity for joining itself to other atoms of its own kind—the secret of the existence of millions of organic (carbon) compounds. All three papers were published in *Comptes rendus de l'Académie des Sciences*.

Early in 1858 Couper asked C.-A. Wurtz to have this third paper presented to the Académie des Sciences but there was delay because Wurtz was not then an academician: J. B. A. Dumas eventually presented it on 14 June 1858. Meanwhile Kekulé published a virtually identical theory in the 19 May issue of *Liebig's Annalen*. Kekulé stated that his work was more significant and claimed priority. Bitterly disappointed, Couper complained to Wurtz and was told to leave the laboratory immediately. He returned to Edinburgh and became laboratory assistant to Lyon Playfair, professor of chemistry at Edinburgh University. He expounded his theory in two further papers but suffered a severe mental breakdown in May 1859. He was twice confined to an asylum and finally discharged in 1862. He never recovered, and for the rest of his life was incapable of intellectual work. He was cared for by his mother, who survived him, and for the remaining thirty years of his life roamed the neighbourhood aimlessly, he and his theory totally forgotten. He died, unmarried, on 11 March 1892 in Kirkintilloch.

Kekulé died in 1896, loaded with honours, and Richard

Anschütz, his successor as professor of chemistry at the University of Bonn, undertook a comprehensive biography. He came across Couper's papers and immediately recognized his genius; he devoted much effort over many years to restoring Couper to his rightful place in the chemical hierarchy. A memorial plaque was unveiled on Couper's old home in Kirkintilloch on the centenary of his birth. TREVOR I. WILLIAMS, *rev.*

**Sources** R. Anschütz, 'Life and chemical work of Archibald Scott Couper', *Proceedings of the Royal Society of Edinburgh*, 29 (1908–9), 193–273 · J. Kendall, *Great discoveries by young chemists* (1953), 81–94 · O. T. Benfey, *Great chemists*, ed. E. Farber (1961), 705–11 · *Journal of Chemical Education*, 56 (1979), 500–01 · DSB
**Likenesses** photograph, Royal Society of Chemistry, London [*see illus.*]
**Wealth at death** £804 5*s.* 5*d.*: confirmation, 22 Sept 1892, *CCI* · £448 2*s.* 9*d.*: confirmation ad omissa, 13 April 1897, *CCI*

**Couper, Sir George Ebenezer Wilson**, second baronet (1824–1908), administrator in India, born at Halifax, Nova Scotia, on 29 April 1824, was eldest of the six children of Sir George Couper, first baronet (1788–1861)—then military secretary to Nova Scotia's governor, Sir James Kempt—and his wife, Elizabeth (*d.* 1880), daughter of Sir John Wilson, judge of common pleas. The father was subsequently comptroller of the household and equerry to the duchess of Kent. The second son, Major-General James Kempt Couper (1827–1901), served in the Indian Staff Corps, and the fifth son, Henry Edward (1835–1876), captain of the 70th foot, saw service in the Indian mutiny of 1857.

In 1839, after education at Sherborne School and at Coombe, Surrey, Couper entered the Royal Military College, Sandhurst. Passing out with distinction in 1842, he was gazetted to the 15th regiment as an ensign, but on receiving a nomination to a writership in India he went instead to East India College, Haileybury, and, at the close of 1846, joined the Bengal civil service.

Couper was first posted to Dinajpur in eastern Bengal as an assistant magistrate, but was transferred to the Punjab on its annexation in 1849 and, at the relatively young age of twenty-five, was made assistant commissioner at Jhelum. Thereafter his rise through the ranks was rapid, something which the satirical *Charivari's Album* of 1875 attributed in part to the charmed childhood he had spent in the duchess of Kent's household. Certainly Couper had influential friends. Lord Dalhousie, governor-general and 'oldest and dearest friend' of his father, took a keen interest in him, and, as shown in his *Private Letters* (1910), reported frequently to his father on his progress. On 29 April 1852, while on furlough, Couper married Caroline Penelope (*d.* 1910), daughter of Henry Every of the Life Guards and his second wife, the Hon. Caroline Flower; she was granddaughter of Sir Henry Every, ninth baronet, of Eggington Hall, Burton upon Trent.

In 1853 Couper was transferred to Calcutta as undersecretary to the government of India, first in the home and finance department and then in the foreign department. On the annexation of Oudh in February 1856 he was appointed secretary at Lucknow to the chief commissioner, Sir James Outram, staying on to serve his successor, Sir Henry Lawrence. Through the uprising of 1857, of which Oudh was at the epicentre, Couper was with Lawrence, serving as his aide-de-camp as well as his chief secretary until the latter's death at the residency on 4 July. He continued these positions with Sir John Inglis, and finally, after the relief, with Outram again. During the siege of Lucknow, Couper put his early military training to good use and won high praise from his chiefs. He was the author, save for the mentions of himself, of Inglis's celebrated dispatch of 26 September 1857 reporting the death of Lawrence, which he later reprinted for private circulation with selections from his own speeches on the uprising, but omitting Inglis's references to himself (1896). He also wrote the text to Captain C. H. Mecham's *Sketches of the Siege of Lucknow* (1858).

The viceroy, Lord Canning, rejected Outram's recommendation of Couper as his successor to the chief commissionership of Oudh, on the ground that Couper had been only twelve years in the service. Instead, in April 1859, after furlough, Couper was posted to Allahabad as chief secretary to the government of the North-Western Provinces. On 18 May 1860 he was made a CB. In the following year he succeeded to his father's baronetcy and in December 1862 returned to Oudh as judicial commissioner. From April 1871 he acted as chief commissioner of the province, and was confirmed in the appointment in December 1873. In that office he presided over the revision of the land revenue assessments, pursuing the post-1857 'Oudh policy' and securing the position of the *talukdars* (local landed magnates), of whom he was an ardent supporter.

On the retirement of Sir John Strachey in July 1876, Couper was made acting lieutenant-governor of the North-Western Provinces, while retaining his control of Oudh, thereby accomplishing the amalgamation of Oudh with the larger province. On 17 January 1877 Couper became the first 'lieutenant-governor of the North-Western Provinces and chief commissioner of Oudh'. After two decades of cosseting by the British the *talukdars* were deeply suspicious of the change, and it was only Couper's assiduously cultivated image as the *talukdars*' friend that enabled its smooth implementation. Couper's administration became known for its conservation of resources or, as his detractors labelled it, its parsimony. His handling of a serious famine in 1877–8 invoked widespread public criticism, including a blistering assault conducted by the Anglo-Indian newspaper the *Statesman and Friend of India* on the administration's delay and meanness in establishing relief works for the starving. Couper was stung by the attacks, but stuck to his argument that economy in relief was both morally and financially sound; the tax rises necessary to fund widespread gratuitous relief for the indigent would, he believed, impoverish the independent classes in society and retard India's progress.

Economy notwithstanding, Couper initiated a policy of canal and light railway construction for the North-Western Provinces and Oudh, although some of the local

benefits of this were lost to a subsequent ruling by the government of India that railways should not be provincial undertakings. Couper also developed the provincial agricultural department so that it became a model for other provinces; and he encouraged Indian industrial enterprises, such as the 'Couper' paper mills at Lucknow.

Couper was created KCSI in January 1877, and CIE a year later. Due to retire in January 1882, he had hoped to extend his term by another year but, regardless of the appeals of the Oudh *talukdars*, Lord Ripon, the viceroy, was only prepared to offer him another three months. He therefore retired in April 1882. He declined the proposal of the Husainabad endowment trustees, Lucknow, to erect a statue in his memory, and as an alternative they built a clock tower, as a symbol of progress and order.

After residing at Cheltenham for a few years Couper settled at Camberley. He died on 5 March 1908, at 11 Duchess Street, Portland Place, London, and was buried in St Michael's churchyard, Camberley. Couper's wife died on 28 November 1910 and was buried beside her husband. They had five sons and four daughters; one of the latter, who lived for barely a month, was born in the Lucknow residency during the siege. The eldest son, Sir Ramsay George Henry, succeeded as third baronet.

F. H. BROWN, *rev.* KATHERINE PRIOR

**Sources** *Indian Civil Service List* (1880) · F. C. Danvers and others, *Memorials of old Haileybury College* (1894) · *Sir George Couper and the famine in the North-West Provinces* (1878) [repr. of articles and letters from the *Statesman and Friend of India*] · J. A. B. Ramsay, marquess of Dalhousie, *Private letters*, ed. J. G. A. Baird (1910) · BL, Ripon MSS · *Charivari's album* (1875) · C. H. Mecham, *Sketches of the siege of Lucknow* (1858) · Burke, *Peerage* (1939)
**Archives** NRA Scotland, priv. coll., corresp. and papers | Balliol Oxf., letters to Sir Louis Mallet · BL, letters to Lord Ripon, Add. MS 43615
**Likenesses** A. A. Khan, photograph, *c.*1855, BL · A. Ali, photograph, repro. in A. Ali, *Rajas and Taluqdars of Oudh* (1880) · Isca, lithograph, repro. in *Charivari's album*
**Wealth at death** £52,363 2*s.* 11*d.*: double probate, July 1908, CGPLA Eng. & Wales

**Couper, Robert** (1750–1818), poet and physician, was the son of a farmer at Balsier, in the parish of Sorbie, Wigtownshire. He was born on 22 September 1750, and entered the University of Glasgow in 1769 to study for the ministry of the Church of Scotland. Before he had completed his studies, however, his parents both died, leaving him in some financial hardship, and he accepted the office of tutor in a family in Virginia. He considered becoming ordained in the Episcopal church, but on the outbreak of the War of Independence in 1776 returned to Scotland. After studying medicine at the University of Glasgow he began practising in Newton Stewart, Wigtownshire. In 1788, after obtaining an MD, he settled in Fochabers, Morayshire, as physician to the duke of Gordon, patron of Burns and himself a poet. Soon after this Couper married a Miss Stott. In 1804 he published *Poetry Chiefly in the Scottish Language*, dedicated to the duchess of Gordon, consisting of poems on the seasons, odes, and songs, of which the best-known are 'Kinrara', also known as 'Red gleams the sun', and 'The Ewebughts, Marion'. Couper's other publications include a medical and a historical text, and a prose work, *The Tourifications of Malachi Meldrum* (1803). He left Fochabers in 1806, and died at Wigtown on 18 January 1818. T. F. HENDERSON, *rev.* SARAH COUPER

**Sources** D. Laing, 'Preface and notes', in W. Stenhouse, *Illustrations of the lyric poetry and music of Scotland* (1853) • IGI • C. Rogers, *The modern Scottish minstrel, or, The songs of Scotland of the past half-century*, 1 (1855) • L. Baillie and P. Sieveking, eds., *British biographical archive* (1984) [microfiche]

**Coupland, Sir Reginald** (1884–1952), historian, was born in London on 2 August 1884, the only surviving child of Sidney Coupland (1849–1930), consulting physician and lecturer at the Middlesex Hospital, London, and his wife, Bessie, daughter of Thomas Potter of Great Bedwin, Wiltshire. An elder brother died in early childhood, and Coupland himself suffered frequent ill health. A contemporary later recalled that he was 'always much taken up with his own health, and indeed with all his own concerns' (*The Times*, 13 Nov 1952). He was educated privately in Brighton and at Winchester College, where he edited a youthful collection of essays and poems, *Horae iuventutis* (1903). He then studied classics at New College, Oxford, where Alfred Zimmern was one of his tutors. As an undergraduate he was noted as an ardent Liberal—as was his father, who was a close friend and supporter of Stopford Brooke—but he also discovered, and was much influenced by, the idea of fellowship put forward by John Ruskin and the early William Morris. He obtained a second class in classical honour moderations in 1905 and a first class in *literae humaniores* in 1907. On the strength of his examination papers he was elected to a fellowship and lectureship in ancient history at Trinity College, Oxford, later the same year, and started work on an unpublished history of ancient Greece, in which he argued that the impermanence of the Greek city states was largely the result of their failure to combine.

Coupland's career was transformed by his coming into contact with Lionel Curtis, who was Beit lecturer in colonial history at Oxford from 1912 to 1913. Curtis persuaded Coupland to succeed him as Beit lecturer, and to join the Round Table, which had been formed as an imperial 'ginger group' in 1910. Coupland subsequently maintained a lifelong connection with the group, editing its eponymous journal from 1917 to 1919 and 1939 to 1941, and contributing many anonymous articles. On the eve of the First World War he was employed by Curtis to write the volume of Round Table Studies relating to Canada. A proof version (dated 1920) survives, but again the work was unpublished. During the war Coupland remained in Oxford, having been declared ineligible for national service on medical grounds. In 1915 he published an edition of *The War Speeches of William Pitt the Younger*. This was reissued, with a preface by Winston Churchill, in 1940.

Some surprise was expressed when in 1920 Coupland was elected to succeed H. E. Egerton as Beit professor and professorial fellow of All Souls College. In his inaugural lecture Coupland admitted his lack of the usual professorial stock-in-trade, but asked to 'be judged not by what he

has done but by what he means to do' (R. Coupland, *The Empire in these Days*, 1935, 6). His tenure of the Beit chair, which lasted until 1948, was indeed marked by a steady output of books, many of them published to public and critical acclaim. His first was *Wilberforce* (1923), a life which reflected his long-held belief that 'personality is the really interesting thing in history' (Symonds, 53). *Wilberforce* was followed by *Raffles* (1926), *Kirk on the Zambesi* (1928), and *Livingstone's Last Journey* (1945), in each of which Coupland developed his theme of the moral basis of British rule, based on imperial trusteeship and the evolution of the empire into a Commonwealth of self-governing nations. An interest in the problem of nationality was reflected in *The Quebec Act* (1925), a study which emphasized the far-sightedness of British policy in Canada. His *The American Revolution and the British Empire* (1930) argued that the British empire had been transformed in the half-century after the American War of Independence, through the rise of trusteeship, anti-slavery, and free trade. He wrote the book in order to help Americans in particular to 'begin to look at [the empire] from a new angle' (May, 236). The theme of trusteeship was further explored in what Coupland considered to be his most important historical work, *East Africa and its Invaders* (1938), a detailed study of east African history from antiquity to the death of Seyyid Said, and *The Exploitation of East Africa* (1939), which continued the story from 1856 until the establishment of the British protectorate in 1890.

Coupland was instrumental in securing the training of colonial service probationers at Oxford. Sir Ralph Furse later recalled that 'one of the most capable officers in the service' had told him that Coupland's lectures had been 'the greatest help': they had 'sustained his faith … and … been a touchstone by which to judge the stream of criticism … directed in recent years at British colonial policy and the men who execute it' (*The Times*, 24 Nov 1952). Coupland also played a key role in setting up the school of philosophy, politics, and economics, for which he devised the special subject on the political structure of the British empire. He was involved in the negotiations leading to the founding of Nuffield College, Oxford, of which he was a professorial fellow from 1939 to 1950. Less successfully, he was also associated with the schemes for a school of government or of African studies put forward by his Round Table colleagues. An abiding interest at Oxford was the Ralegh Club, founded by Curtis to provide a forum for the discussion of imperial problems. Under Coupland's professorship, the club attracted as speakers many of the empire's most distinguished proconsuls, statesmen, and critics.

Coupland played a role on a wider stage as a member of the royal commission on the superior services in India, appointed under the chairmanship of Lord Lee of Fareham in June 1923. This reported in March 1924 in favour of increasing Indianization of the civil service in India. For his services on this commission, Coupland was appointed CIE in 1928. He worked under Lord Peel as an adviser to the Burma round-table conference in 1931, and again as a member of the royal commission on Palestine, appointed in July 1936. Coupland was widely believed to have played a key role in the commission, and to have drafted its report, published in July 1937, which concluded that the Arab–Jewish conflict was intractable, and that the only lasting solution would be partition, the forcible transfer of population, and the retention of a buffer zone by Britain. The British government's rejection of such a policy following the report of the Palestine partition commission, under Sir John Woodhead, was a source of great disappointment to him.

In February 1941 Coupland was persuaded by his old Round Table colleague Leo Amery, now secretary of state for India, to conduct a study of the Indian constitutional question, under the auspices of Nuffield College. When Sir Stafford Cripps arrived in India on his mission of March to April 1942, Coupland served on his staff. He subsequently published a sketch, *The Cripps Mission* (1942), and a more substantial study in three volumes, *The Indian Problem, 1833–1935* (1942), *Indian Politics, 1936–1942* (1943), and *The Future of India* (1943). Coupland was one of the first British writers to discuss seriously the idea of partition, but he came down in favour of a loose confederation of regions, formed by groups of provinces and princely states. He again put forward this solution in *India: a Re-Statement* (1945).

Coupland was appointed KCMG in recognition of his many services in 1944. He retired from the Beit chair in 1948, and was succeeded by Vincent Harlow. He was elected a fellow of the British Academy in 1948 and a fellow of All Souls in 1952. Meanwhile he had started work on a multi-volume study of nationalism in the British empire. He handed the manuscript of the first volume to his publisher on 5 November 1952. The following day he died suddenly, as he embarked at Southampton on a fact-finding voyage to South Africa. He was buried in the chapel of All Souls College, Oxford, on 12 November 1952. He was unmarried. His *Welsh and Scottish Nationalism* was published posthumously, to wide acclaim, in 1954.

Coupland was small, slight, and in later years stooped, with a quiet voice and an earnest demeanour. Nevertheless, his contemporaries remembered his lively lectures and his entertaining company. His views often irritated those who did not share his own belief in the moral rectitude of British rule. When Mahatma Gandhi addressed the Ralegh Club in 1931, Coupland lectured him on the need for patience and co-operation. Gandhi replied that he was only a peasant, not a professor, but that this was not how he understood America and Ireland to have won their independence (Symonds, 54). Eric Williams, later prime minister of Trinidad, wrote that Coupland was 'the most tedious of British historians' (Williams, 154). This was unfair. Coupland's books were expertly crafted, and appreciated by a wide audience. He was a fluent writer, with a flair for narrative and an exceptional geographical and historical scope. Even in his own lifetime many of his views came to be seen as outdated, but his interpretations of east African and Indian history in particular have remained influential, as the most coherent exposition of a particular point of view. ALEX MAY

**Sources** *The Times* (7 Nov 1952) · *The Times* (13 Nov 1952) · *The Times* (24 Nov 1952) · J. Simmons, 'Sir Reginald Coupland, 1884–1952', *PBA*, 45 (1959), 287–95 · T. G. Fraser, 'Sir Reginald Coupland: the Round Table and the problem of divided societies', *The Round Table, the empire/commonwealth and British foreign policy*, ed. A. Bosco and A. May (1997), 407–19 · D. Lavin, *From empire to international commonwealth: a biography of Lionel Curtis* (1995) · A. C. May, 'The Round Table, 1910–1966', DPhil diss., U. Oxf., 1995 · J. E. Kendle, *The Round Table movement and imperial union* (1975) · P. B. Rich, *Race and empire in British politics* (1986) · R. Symonds, *Oxford and empire: the last lost cause?* (1986) · R. J. Moore, *Churchill, Cripps, and India, 1939–1945* (1979) · A. L. Rowse, *All Souls in my time* (1993) · E. Williams, *British historians and the West Indies* (1964) · *DNB* · *WWW*

**Archives** Bodl. RH, corresp. and papers, MSS Brit. Emp. s. 403 · Bodl. RH, African and West Indian travel journals, MSS s. 7–14 | Balliol Oxf., corresp. with A. L. Smith, Letters C 82 · BL, corresp. with Society of Authors, Add. MS 63227 · Bodl. Oxf., corresp. with L. G. Curtis, MSS Eng. hist. b. 224, c. 776–877 · Bodl. Oxf., Fisher MSS · Bodl. Oxf., Milner MSS · Bodl. Oxf., corresp. with Gilbert Murray · Bodl. Oxf., Round Table corresp., MSS Eng. hist. b. 224. c. 776–877 · Bodl. Oxf., letters to Sir Alfred Zimmern · Bodl. RH, corresp. with Lugard, MSS Brit. Emp. s. 30–90 · Bodl. RH, corresp. with J. H. Oldham, MS Afr. s. 1829 · Bodl. RH, corresp. with Margery Perham · NA Scot., Lothian MS, corresp. with Philip Kerr, GD 40/17 · Queen's University, Kingston, Ontario, Douglas Library, Grigg MSS

**Likenesses** Bassano, photograph, 1948, repro. in Simmons, 'Sir Reginald Coupland, 1884–1952' · W. Stoneman, photograph, 1949, NPG · F. A. de Biden Footner, drawing, 1971, community centre, Wootton, Berkshire · photograph, repro. in *The Times* (7 Nov 1952)

**Wealth at death** £18,625 9s. 2d.: probate, 17 Dec 1952, *CGPLA Eng. & Wales*

**Cour, Ethel Maud De la** (1869–1957), college head and soroptimist, was born in Edinburgh on 6 December 1869, the daughter of Lauritz Ulrich De la Cour, a foreign merchant, and his wife, Alice-Maria. Educated at Madame Froebel's school, Edinburgh, and at a finishing school at Lausanne, she was appointed assistant secretary of the Edinburgh School of Cookery and Domestic Economy in 1896. In her early years she worked under its honorary secretary, Jessie Melvin, and was closely involved with the school's main founders, Christian Guthrie Wright and Louisa Stevenson.

On Guthrie Wright's sudden death in 1907, Miss De la Cour was promoted superintendent of the Edinburgh school. At that time the school was engaged in important negotiations with the Scotch education department (SED) leading up to the major changes introduced by the 1908 Education (Scotland) Act. Under its terms Scottish school-board schools were given a duty to promote the physical well-being of children and were required to provide domestic education for female pupils. Miss De la Cour and Jessie Melvin, together with Grace Paterson of the Glasgow School of Cookery, secured departmental agreement on the formal qualifications to be required of a domestic science teacher. The Edinburgh school became a designated central institution and was thereby brought under the direct control of the SED. Shortly thereafter Miss De la Cour was appointed as the school's first principal, and under her leadership the school quickly trebled its output of trained and qualified domestic science teachers.

During the First World War Ethel De la Cour was very

active in various food conservation programmes necessitated by war-time shortages. Initially the attempt was made to confront the crisis through voluntary means, and she served as a member of the Edinburgh Patriotic Food League which campaigned on the subject. School staff gave demonstrations and public courses of instruction to encourage households (and particularly those with young children) to obtain the maximum benefit from restricted food supplies. In 1917 partial food rationing was introduced and Miss De la Cour was appointed to the Scottish food campaign committee which was responsible for overseeing the policy in Scotland. School staff devised many novel recipes, gave demonstrations all over the country, and provided special training courses for school teachers to enable them to pass on instruction to their local communities.

During the war years Miss De la Cour was also a member of the Scottish committee for women's training and employment. At this time the arrival of women in some of the industrial factories produced a great deal of tension and labour unrest, particularly in the greater Glasgow area. To tackle these problems courses were organized within the school to train the welfare supervisors appointed by firms employing female workers. These classes were an extension of a social science course developed in the school before the war and Miss De la Cour was less than pleased when, after the war, it was taken over by the University of Edinburgh and developed into a major field of study.

Miss De la Cour's war-time services were recognized in 1920 when she was appointed MBE. In the same year she became one of the first women to be made a justice of the peace of the city of Edinburgh. She was appointed OBE in 1929, when the citation recognized her contribution to domestic science education and as principal of the school. She was a founder member of the Edinburgh Soroptimist Club and its first president, 1927–30, and was a member of the National Council of Women (Edinburgh branch).

Ethel De la Cour retired as principal in 1930, but for the next twenty-seven years she retained a strong connection with the school (which became Queen Margaret College). In 1955 past and present students and friends of the school commissioned a portrait of her by Sir Stanley Cursiter. She died at her home, 43 Corstorphine Road, Edinburgh, on 25 April 1957.

TOM BEGG

**Sources** T. Begg, *The excellent women: the origins and history of Queen Margaret College* (1994) • *Edinburgh School of Cookery Magazine*, 2/32 (July 1929), 5–6 • *Edinburgh School of Cookery Magazine*, 2/34 (July 1930), 6–7 • *Edinburgh Evening News* (8 June 1955) • Queen Margaret College scrapbooks, Queen Margaret College, Edinburgh • *Scottish biographies* (1938) • b. cert., NA Scot. • *The Scotsman* (27 April 1957)
**Archives** U. Glas., Queen Margaret College archives
**Likenesses** S. Cursiter, oils, 1955, Queen Margaret College, Edinburgh
**Wealth at death** £16,907 10s. 6d.: confirmation, 12 July 1957, CCI

**Courci, John de**. *See* Courcy, John de (d. 1219?).

**Courcy, Affreca de** (d. in or after **1219**). *See under* Courcy, John de (d. 1219?).

**Courcy** [Courci], **John de** (d. **1219**?), conqueror of Ulster, styled by contemporaries prince of Ulster, is of uncertain parentage. He was without doubt a member of the well-known family who took their name from Courcy-sur-Dives in Calvados and who were lords of Stoke Courcy (Stogursey) in Somerset, since they were patrons of St Andrew's Benedictine priory there, and John himself founded the priory of St Andrew in Ards, Down (Black Abbey), as a dependent house of Stoke Courcy. William de Courcy (d. 1171), lord of Stoke Courcy in the mid-twelfth century, had a brother Jordan, and one of his charters was witnessed by both Jordan and John de Courcy, the latter possibly the conqueror of Ulster, since he too had a brother Jordan. This would make John a son of William de Courcy (fl. c.1125), who married Avice de Rumilly, daughter of William Meschin, lord of Copeland in Cumberland, and hence explain John's succession to part of William's estate at Middleton Cheney in Northamptonshire, though its small extent suggests his illegitimacy.

A contemporary description of Courcy is provided by Gerald of Wales, who says: 'John was fair-haired and tall, with bony and sinewy limbs. His frame was lanky and he had a very strong physique, immense bodily strength, and an extraordinarily bold temperament'. Although brave, he was impetuous, 'and had about him the air of an ordinary soldier rather than that of a leader, yet away from the battlefield he was modest and restrained, and gave the church of Christ that honour which is its due' (*Expugnatio*, 179–81). Nothing is known of Courcy's early life but the fact that most of those whom he established in Ulster appear to have come from Cumbria and its hinterland suggests that it was spent in this region. According to the *Song of Dermot and the Earl*, a *chanson de geste* on the English invasion of Ireland, Henry II while in Ireland in 1171–2 granted Ulster to Courcy 'if by force he could conquer it' (*Song of Dermot and the Earl*, ed. G. H. Orpen, 1892, 199), though there is no evidence for his presence there until the latter half of 1176 when he arrived with William fitz Aldelin, the king's representative. Courcy brought a retinue of ten knights who formed part of the Dublin garrison but, according to Gerald, he grew impatient with William's lack of initiative, and gathered together 22 knights and about 300 others and, in late January 1177, marched out of Dublin to invade Ulaid (which approximates to the modern counties of Down and Antrim); Roger Howden adds that this was done contrary to William fitz Aldelin's prohibition.

On the morning of the fourth day, about 1 February, Courcy arrived at Down (now Downpatrick), and most accounts agree that he was initially successful, forcing Ruaidrí Mac Duinn Sléibe, the king of Ulaid, to flee, taking booty from the surrounding countryside, and digging himself in in Downpatrick by building a castle and 'a dyke from sea to sea' (Mac Carthaigh's Book, 65), though the usually reliable annals of Tigernach report an early victory by the Ulaid, with many of Courcy's followers being slain and he himself captured. However, he soon recovered his position and Gerald notes a second battle at Downpatrick on 24 June, probably that described in Mac

Carthaigh's Book in which Courcy's men slaughtered the Ulaid and their allies and captured the archbishop of Armagh and precious relics.

At Downpatrick, Courcy encountered the papal legate for Ireland, Scotland, and the isles, Cardinal Vivian of St Stephen in Monte Celio, who, according to Gerald, sought to intervene between Courcy and Mac Duinn Sléibe by having the latter agree to the payment of an annual tribute, if Courcy and his men consented to leave. He failed in his mediation, however, and, according to William of Newburgh, the legate then encouraged the Irish to fight to preserve their freedom. Vivian had come to Downpatrick from the Isle of Man, where he had solemnized the marriage of King *Godred [see under Godred Crovan] to a daughter of Mac Lochlainn, king of Cenél nEógain, and Courcy himself married Godred's daughter, Affreca [**Affreca de Courcy** (d. in or after 1219)] (in 1180 according to the unreliable Dublin annals of Inisfallen). A dower charter survives granting Affreca her portion of Courcy's estates in Ulster and Northamptonshire, but two of his charters offer prayers for Beatrice de Vilers (a lady of the same name was heir to Warrington in Lancashire), who may have been a mistress.

In his second year in Ulster, Courcy experienced a number of rebuffs, one at the hands of the men of Fir Lí (a Gaelic lordship bordering the lower Bann), a defeat attributed by the Irish annals to the intervention of saints Patrick, Columba, and Brendan. Also, having raided in north Louth, he was pursued by its king, Murchad Ó Cerbhaill, and by Cú Uladh Mac Duinn Sléibe, and the annals record that 450 English and 100 Irish were killed. This is possibly the battle of Newry Bridge ('apud pontem Ivori') which Gerald of Wales describes as following Courcy's return from England (179), a visit not elsewhere recorded, though he was certainly in England again in 1185–6.

In 1179 Courcy granted the monastic site at Nendrum, Down, to the monks of St Bees in Copeland so that they might establish a cell there, while the Cistercian abbey at Inch, Down, on the early church site of Inis Cumhscraidh, was made a daughter house of Furness in Lancashire. In 1183 he granted ten carucates to St Werburgh's Abbey, Chester, who sent some of their community to establish a priory in the cathedral church of Downpatrick, while a priory of Augustinian canons was set up at Toberglory near Downpatrick, as a cell of St Mary's, Carlisle, and a house of Premonstratensian canons at Carrickfergus was made subject to the abbot of Dryburgh in Berwickshire, possibly pointing towards a connection with its founders, the Morville family. The most famous religious foundation dating from this era is his wife's foundation of the Cistercian Grey Abbey (Jugum Dei), Down, in 1193, a daughter house of Holme Cultram in Cumberland (the William de Courcy who was abbot of Holme in 1216 was presumably a relative). John de Courcy also founded a priory of Crutched friars at Downpatrick, the parent house of which is unknown, and he granted lands in Down to the archbishop of Dublin, St Thomas's Abbey, and the priory of Holy Trinity, Dublin.

Although there is no evidence that Courcy himself was responsible for changing the town's name to Downpatrick, he did alter the dedication of Down Cathedral from the Holy Trinity to St Patrick, an act for which (according to the romanticized account of his exploits in the Book of Howth) God later took vengeance by denying him his Ulster lordship. The life of St Patrick by Jocelin of Furness was written at his behest and was intended in part to prove the primacy of Armagh over Dublin. When John minted his own halfpence they bore, not the king's name, but 'Patricius', while it is possible, as peerage writers claim, that Patrick de Courcy, lord of Kinsale in the early thirteenth century, was his illegitimate son.

In 1185 Courcy discovered at Downpatrick, and formally translated, what he claimed were the bodies of saints Patrick, Brigit, and Columba, an event reported by Gerald of Wales and the Scottish chronicle of Melrose. Gerald believed that Courcy's conquest of Ulster was the realization of a prophecy of Columba and claimed that 'John himself keeps this book of prophecies, which is written in Irish, by him as a kind of mirror of his own deeds'. Gerald also, in concluding his account, stated that he was leaving 'the theme of his mighty exploits to be unfolded more fully by his own historians' (Expugnatio, 177, 181), while the Book of Howth mentions that a Latin biography of Courcy was in circulation in Ulster in the sixteenth century.

Though the archaeological evidence for the progress of John de Courcy's conquest is considerable, the documentary record is remarkably thin. The archbishop of Armagh, the bishops of Down and Connor, and the heads of the churches of Bangor and Saul, occur in Courcy charters, suggesting that he quickly gained clerical support, but it is clear too that he won the allegiance of some local secular lords. Roger Howden thought that there were Irish in his army when he launched his first assault on Downpatrick, and Mac Carthaigh's Book reports for 1179 that Ulaid was laid waste 'by John de Courcy and the Irish who were along with him' (69), and that in 1196 he plundered Louth in the company of Niall Mac Mathgamna of Airgialla. In the following year Courcy's brother Jordan was killed by an Irish adherent, and when he then set about expanding his lordship to the north-west his army contained some Irish and a contingent of Gallowaymen whose lord, Duncan of Carrick, was rewarded with a grant of Ulster lands.

Gerald states that when Henry II's son John visited the country as lord of Ireland in 1185 he 'decided to prove the worth of men who were veterans and had long experience in the conquest of that island, and entrusted the overall administration to John de Courcy', whereupon 'the kingdom immediately began to enjoy a greater measure of tranquility', adding that he then led expeditions to Cork and Connacht (Expugnatio, 243). No evidence exists for the former, but his less than successful intervention in Connacht in 1188 in the succession war among the Uí Chonchobair is noted in the annals. Charter evidence suggests that Courcy held on to the justiciarship for some time, perhaps until 1192, when Peter Pipard had the position. When the Lord John rebelled against King Richard in 1193–4, Courcy remained loyal, and he and Walter de

Lacy, lord of Meath, are found acting as Richard's representatives in Ireland in 1194–5 in opposition to Pipard, who was taken prisoner by them. In the same year the annals record that Courcy and Lacy sought 'to assume power over the English of Leinster and Munster' and intervened again in Connacht, in opposition to William de Burgh, where they made peace with Cathal Crobderg Ó Conchobhair (*Annals of Loch Cé*, 1.191). When Cathal was ejected from Connacht in 1200 he sought refuge with Courcy in Ulster, and in the following year Courcy and Lacy's brother Hugh invaded Connacht in support of Cathal but were defeated, and sixty or more of Courcy's men slain. He himself, according to the annals of Loch Cé, was 'struck with a stone, so that he fell from his horse … and he was taken to Dublin until he gave pledges for himself that he would obey the king of the Saxons' (ibid., 1.201–3).

At this point Courcy and the Lacys seem to have parted company and thereafter appear as firm enemies. Roger Howden claims that Hugh de Lacy treacherously captured him in 1201 but that Courcy's men secured his release. In 1203 and again in 1204 Lacy and the English of Meath defeated Courcy in battle at Downpatrick; on the first occasion he fled, on the second he was captured and, say the annals of Loch Cé, released only when he undertook to take the cross and go to Jerusalem. Government records indicate that Courcy agreed to submit to the crown and gave hostages as a pledge, but in spite of several earlier safe conducts it was only in the spring of 1205 that he went to England and had his English lands restored. However, Hugh de Lacy also went to court and was awarded the whole of Ulster on 2 May and the title of earl, which Courcy never held, on 29 May. Courcy rebelled, again forfeited his English lands, and went to the Isle of Man. There his wife's brother, King *Ragnvald, supplied him with a fleet of 100 ships and they launched an invasion of Ulster but failed to capture the castle of 'Rath' (probably Dundrum) from Walter de Lacy, whereupon Courcy took refuge in Tír Eoghain with Áed Ó Néill. Finally, on 14 November 1207, he received a licence to go to England and, although the Dublin chronicler has a lengthy and unlikely account of his movements at this point (including, though, a more likely stay with the monks of Chester), nothing further is heard of him until the summer of 1210 when he took part in King John's overthrow of Hugh de Lacy, the latter, like his ally William (III) de Briouze, having fallen foul of the king.

John de Courcy was never restored to his Ulster estate and seems to have lived out his days as a royal pensioner. On 30 August 1213 the Irish justiciar was ordered to provide some land by which to sustain his wife, Affreca, and on 22 September 1219 a similar order was made to provide her with her dower, from which it may be concluded that Courcy had only recently died. According to the Manx chronicle, Affreca was buried in Grey Abbey, Down, while Courcy, who had probably died in England, had expressed a wish to be buried in the Augustinian house of Canons Ashby in Northamptonshire. No legitimate children are recorded. SEÁN DUFFY

**Sources** Giraldus Cambrensis, *Expugnatio Hibernica / The conquest of Ireland*, ed. and trans. A. B. Scott and F. X. Martin (1978) · *Chronica magistri Rogeri de Hovedene*, ed. W. Stubbs, 4 vols., Rolls Series, 51 (1868–71), vol. 2, pp. 119–20; vol. 4, p. 25 · W. Stokes, ed., 'The annals of Tigernach [8 pts]', *Revue Celtique*, 16 (1895), 374–419; 17 (1896), 6–33, 119–263, 337–420; 18 (1897), 9–59, 150–97, 267–303, 374–91; pubd sep. (1993) · S. Ó hInnse, ed. and trans., 'Mac Carthaigh's Book', *Miscellaneous Irish annals, AD 1114–1437* (1947) · W. M. Hennessy, ed. and trans., *The annals of Loch Cé: a chronicle of Irish affairs from AD 1014 to AD 1590*, 2 vols., Rolls Series, 54 (1871) · R. Howlett, ed., *Chronicles of the reigns of Stephen, Henry II, and Richard I*, 1, Rolls Series, 82 (1884), 238 · G. Mac Niocaill, 'Cartae Dunenses, XII–XIII céad', *Seanchas Ardmhacha*, 5 (1969–70), 418–28 · J. Otway-Ruthven, 'Dower charter of John de Courcy's wife', *Ulster Journal of Archaeology*, 3rd ser., 12 (1947), 77–81 · H. S. Sweetman and G. F. Handcock, eds., *Calendar of documents relating to Ireland*, 5 vols., PRO (1875–86), vol. 1 · J. S. Brewer and W. Bullen, eds., *Calendar of the Carew manuscripts*, 5: *1603–1623*, PRO (1871) · J. T. Gilbert, ed., *Chartularies of St Mary's Abbey, Dublin: with the register of its house at Dunbrody and annals of Ireland*, 2 vols., Rolls Series, 80 (1884) · S. Duffy, 'The first Ulster plantation: John de Courcy and the men of Cumbria', *Colony and frontier in medieval Ireland: essays presented to J. F. Lydon*, ed. T. B. Barry and others (1995), 1–27 · G. H. Orpen, *Ireland under the Normans*, 4 vols. (1911–20), vol. 2, pp. 5–23, 134–44 · G. H. Orpen, ed. and trans., *The song of Dermot and the earl* (1892) · G. Broderick, ed. and trans., *Cronica regum Mannie et Insularum / Chronicles of the kings of Man and the Isles* (1979)

**Courson, Robert de** (d. 1219), cardinal, may have been a member of the Anglo-Norman family which came from Notre-Dame-de-Courson and which in 1086 held land of Ferrers in Berkshire. The evidence for connecting him with the Derbyshire Curzons (and for his birth at Kedleston) is late and fanciful, but there is no doubt that he was English. He studied at Paris in the 1190s (probably between 1190 and 1195), where his teacher in theology was Peter the Chanter (d. 1197), and where from 1200 he was called *magister*. He was a canon of Noyon from 1204, though resident in Paris, and of Paris from 1209 to 1211. Internal evidence suggests that he wrote the *Summa*, or *Penitential*, his sole surviving work, during the period when he was teaching at Paris, but none of his lectures survives. The *Summa*, of which there are fourteen extant manuscripts, exhibits three versions: a primitive, an alternate, and a final. It commences 'Tota celestis philosophia'. There are forty-six main divisions to the work, which is not complete and probably grew in scope as Courson went along. The author's prologue states that he will begin with penance, then deal with moral questions, and finally with those questions that concern faith. The penitential part occupies thirty-six sections out of forty-six (almost four-fifths of the total).

Courson's *Summa* shows that, like his mentor Peter the Chanter, he believed theology to be concerned essentially with moral and sacramental matters, and this position is reinforced by his later attitudes and activities as legate in France. During this period he also acted frequently as a papal judge-delegate. His experience, his background, and his training, plus his acquaintance with Pope Innocent III, made him highly suitable for active employment within the church. In 1211 he was mentioned as a candidate for the patriarchate of Constantinople, but the pope had other plans. In 1212 Courson was promoted cardinal-priest of San Stefano in Monte Celio, and in 1213 he was acting as a papal auditor, but in the same year he was sent to France as legate with a commission to prepare for the proposed general council and to preach the forthcoming crusade. Between 1213 and 1215 he convoked local councils at Paris, Rouen, Clermont, Montpellier, Bordeaux, and Bourges, in which he tested and publicized reforms already discussed by Peter the Chanter's circle, before their presentation at the fourth Lateran Council in 1215.

Courson proved himself a harsh and determined reformer of morals. As legate he kept up an endless tour of the countryside, judging and investigating. At Limoges he deposed the abbot of St Martial as incapable, and appointed an Englishman, Alelmus, in his place. It was said that this was done in return for payment: half the treasure of the church and a yearly payment to his canons at San Stefano. Innocent III's letters show that he played some part, too, in the quarrel between the lay brothers of Grandmont and their prior; the pope reproved him for, as he saw it, favouring the lay brothers. Courson incurred the hostility of many important churches for attacking their customs, and also that of some of the bishops who refused to attend the council at Bourges in May 1215. He therefore excommunicated them. He was active against usurers, public courtesans, and deriders of religion. He condemned simony and endeavoured to enforce celibacy among clerks. Not surprisingly he was involved in important marriage cases, notably those of Philip Augustus and Ingeborg of Denmark, and Erard of Brienne and Philippine of Champagne, and in 1214 negotiated a five-year truce between the kings of England and France.

Shortly before the opening of the Lateran Council, Courson produced statutes for the University of Paris. The statutes of August 1215, which formalized the decisions reached in 1212–13, incorporated the masters as a separate body. Masters in arts were to be at least twenty-one years old and to have completed at least six years' study; those in theology were to have attained the age of thirty-five and to have concluded a minimum of eight years' study. There followed a compulsory period of two years' lecturing in arts on prescribed texts. Licence was to be granted free of all conditions and payments. The statutes also regularized the chancellor's jurisdiction over licensing and imprisonment. Henceforth he was to grant licences in theology, canon law, and medicine to any candidate considered worthy by the majority of the masters. He could bestow licence on his own initiative, but he was not to exact an oath of obedience or payment for this, nor was he to imprison any clerk unjustly. In the preamble to the statutes, Courson spoke of having 'a special mandate from the pope to take effective measures to reform the state of the scholars at Paris for the better, wishing with the counsel of good men to provide for the tranquillity of the scholars in future' (Leff, 197). The statutes were a résumé of the events and settlements of the past rather than a programme for future development. Papal control had been substituted for episcopal control but otherwise there was no spectacular change. The statutes show that by 1215 dialectic and philosophy had virtually displaced all the other liberal arts. The ban on using Aristotle's works on metaphysics and natural philosophy, which had been introduced in 1210, was repeated; however, the teaching of ethics was permitted.

Jacques de Vitry mentions that Courson was a considerable preacher—'a star in the firmament of heaven' (*Historia occidentalis*, 102)—and he and Stephen Langton may have conducted a preaching campaign in Flanders against usury, especially around Arras and St Omer between April and July 1213. He preached the crusade against the Albigensians with vehemence and took the cross himself. He gained a reputation for zeal and is said to have burned heretics after the surrender of Marcillac. He urged the truce between England and France in 1213 in the interests of the proposed crusade. After the accession of Pope Honorius III, he went to preach the fifth crusade under the leadership of Cardinal Pelagius of Albano, and died on 6 February 1219 during the siege of Damietta. Besides the *Summa*, his statutes for the University of Paris, and a manuscript belonging to him (Paris, Bibliothèque Nationale, MS nouv. acq. lat. 2066), there survive several of his charters as cardinal and legate (Douët d'Arcq, *Collection de sceaux* ii (1867), no. 6125, and Troyes, Archives départementales de l'Aube, G 2592, pièces 2,3).

JANE E. SAYERS

**Sources** Innocentius III [Pope Innocent III], *Patrologia Latina*, 214–17 (1855) · P. Pressutti, ed., *Regesta Honorii Papae III*, 1 (Vatican City, 1888) · P. Pressutti, ed., *Regesta Honorii Papae III*, 2 (Vatican City, 1895) · V. L. Kennedy, 'The contents of Courson's *Summa*', *Mediaeval Studies*, 9 (1947), 81–107 · V. L. Kennedy, 'Robert Courson on penance', *Mediaeval Studies*, 7 (1945), 291–336 · G. Lefèvre, *Le traité 'De usura' de Robert de Courçon* (1902) · H. Denifle and A. Chatelain, eds., *Chartularium universitatis Parisiensis*, 1 (Paris, 1889) · J. W. Baldwin, *Masters, princes and merchants: the social views of Peter the Chanter and his circle*, 2 vols. (1970) · W. Maleczek, *Papst und Kardinalskolleg von 1191 bis 1216* (1984) · Rymer, *Foedera*, new edn, 1.121 · P. Guébin and E. Lyon, eds., *Petri Vallium Sarnaii monachi hystoria Albigensis*, 2 (Paris, 1930), 129, 185, 208, 217, 262 · *The Historia occidentalis of Jacques de Vitry*, ed. J. F. Hinnebusch (1972) · A. O. Anderson and M. O. Anderson, eds., *The chronicle of Melrose* (1936), 55–7, 72 · G. Leff, *Paris and Oxford universities in the thirteenth and fourteenth centuries* (1968) · A. Longnon, ed., *Obituaires de la province de Sens*, Recueil des historiens de la France, 6 (1923), 238

**Archives** Archives Départementales de l'Aube, Troyes, G 2592, pièces 2, 3 | Bibliothèque Nationale, Paris, MS nouv. acq. lat. 2066

**Courtauld family** (*per.* **1708–1780**), goldsmiths, came to prominence with **Augustin Courtauld** (1685–1751), the second son of Augustin Courtauld (1655–1706), a merchant from St Pierre in the Île d'Oléron near La Rochelle, and his first wife, Julia Giron (1661–1686), both Huguenots, who had four children. He was reputedly brought to England in 1687 as an infant, concealed in a basket of vegetables, to escape the persecution of the protestants. Romantic though this would have been, he was in fact left behind with his grandfather Pierre Courtauld and only joined his father in London in 1696. Augustin Courtauld senior was described as 'of the parish of St Anne's Westminster Wine Cooper' (Courtauld, 72) on the apprenticeship of his son Augustin to another Huguenot, Simon Pantin, on 9 August 1701, and appeared in the Naturalization Act of 1709 as goldsmith, St Martin-in-the-Fields.

Augustin Courtauld was made free of the Goldsmiths' Company by service on 20 October 1708, when he registered his first mark. The following year he married Anne Bardin, with whom he had eight children. Of his three sons, only Samuel [i] followed his father's profession. The registers of the Goldsmiths' Company record Augustin as working as a largeworker at Church Court, St Martin's Lane, in 1708. Augustin's earliest known surviving work is a set of three casters, marked with the date letter for 1710. He supplied members of the London aristocracy and specialized in silver vessels for the fashionable new drinks—tea, coffee, and chocolate. He also developed an important line in two-handled cups. To judge by the many surviving examples bearing his mark, Augustin also specialized in trays and salvers, which, with their highly complex borders, called for the highest technical skill in their manufacture. By 1734 Augustin was probably running a sizeable workshop. All his recorded apprentices were of Huguenot descent: Edward Feline taken in 1709, Isaac Ribouleau in 1716, Lewis Ouvry in 1730, his son Samuel [i] in 1734, and his last recorded apprentice, Francis Quenouault, in 1739. Most of his wealth was channelled into his house and stock-in-trade, but he did invest £500 in East India stock from 1732 to 1739, and thereafter £1000. His prosperity was solid but modest. He was one of few goldsmiths in London to have his portrait painted, probably commissioned in 1730 from Hans Hysing. Though Augustin's mark appears on work until 1746, only one piece is made in the rococo fashion. It is probable that this was made by his son Samuel [i] who had joined him by the date it was made.

**Peter Courtauld** (1689/90–1729), Augustin's half-brother, was the only son of Augustin Courtauld senior and his second wife, Esther Potier (1656–1732), also a refugee from La Rochelle, whom he married in 1688 or 1689 at the French church in Glasshouse Street, London. Peter was born in London and in 1705 was apprenticed like Augustin to Simon Pantin. He broke his indentures in 1709 when he married Judith Pantin, daughter of Esau Pantin of St James's, Westminster, another goldsmith and a relative of his master. Though he was entered as a freeman of the Goldsmiths' Company in 1712, Peter Courtauld did not register his first mark until 1721, from an address in Litchfield Street, St John's, Westminster, presumably because he was still employed by Simon Pantin. His only recorded apprentice was Thomas Bonnet, whom he took in 1723. No piece of silver made by him has yet been identified. He was buried in St Martin-in-the-Fields in 1729.

Augustin Courtauld moved in 1729 to Chandos Street, where he died in 1751. He was buried on 14 April at St Luke's, Chelsea, leaving in his will 'the sum of four hundred pounds' (PRO, PROB 11/787/107) and all his utensils and patterns used in his trade to his son **Samuel** [i] **Courtauld** (1720–1765). Samuel [i] was apprenticed to his father in 1734, and made free of the Goldsmiths' Company in 1747, registering his first mark at the Rising Sun in Chandos Street in October 1746, the premises acquired by his father before 1739. It is probable that his trade card in the Heal

collection dates from this period. Samuel's work does not appear to have survived in any great quantity, and from the little that has there is no evidence that he was creative of new forms or decoration; he seems to have been content to follow prevailing designs and ornament. On his father's death in 1751 he moved to new premises at The Crown in Cornhill, facing the Royal Exchange, which attracted important City customers including the Clothworkers' Company. Only two apprentices taken by him are recorded in the Goldsmiths' Company registers, George Cowles in 1751 and Stephen Dupont in 1753. In August 1749 he married at St Luke's, Old Street, in Finsbury, Louisa Ogier [**Louisa Perina Courtauld** (1729–1807)], the youngest daughter of Peter Ogier [ii] (d. 1740), a silk weaver, and his wife, Catherine Rabaud, of Sigournay in Poitou. They had five sons, including Peter [iii] who carried on the family business in Spitalfields and was joint executor of Samuel [ii]'s will. Louisa is supposed to have been smuggled into England in a barrel of potatoes in 1729. Her father had come over earlier and set up as a silk weaver in Spitalfields.

It was probably Louisa's family connections with the City and the East End that contributed to Samuel [i]'s move. Their son George was apprenticed in 1761 to a Peter Merzeau, a silk throwster in Spitalfields, and began the family connection with the silk industry from which Courtaulds plc and Courtaulds Textiles plc ultimately grew. Her mother's will left money for her 'maintenance and education until she shall attain the age of 21 years' (Daily Mail Weekend, 12). Her father, despite his past as a refugee, left £2560 to her and to each of her siblings. Only two years after being made a liveryman of the Goldsmiths' Company, Samuel [i] died suddenly in February 1765 at the age of forty-five and was buried at Chelsea on 24 February. He left all his property to his wife, who succeeded as head of the business. She appears, from the presence of an unregistered joint mark of 1768, to have been in partnership with one of her husband's former apprentices, George Cowles (d. 1811), with whom she appears in the parliamentary report list of 1773. In the same year, 1768, George Cowles married Samuel [i] Courtauld's niece Judith Jacob. It was during this period that Louisa had her portrait painted, according to family tradition by Zoffany, a tenant of Augustin Jacobs, but more probably by Nathaniel Dance. The partnership, according to an advertisement in the Gloucester Journal of 29 September, was dissolved in 1777 when Cowles moved to Lombard Street. A printed billhead for Louisa Courtauld used for invoicing four second-hand dessert spoons in the 1760s is signed by her shop assistant Judith Touzeau, a fellow Huguenot and parishioner of her mistress.

Louisa's eldest and only other surviving son, **Samuel** [ii] **Courtauld** (1752–1821), was born on 20 October 1752 and baptized at Threadneedle Street Church on 25 October, and made free of the Goldsmiths' Company by patrimony in 1778. He entered a joint mark with his mother Louisa in 1777 from 21 Cornhill where they remained until 1780, when they were succeeded by John Henderson. Louisa retired to Clapton in Essex where she died on 12 January 1807 and was buried at Christ Church, Spitalfields. Samuel, according to the eldest daughter of his brother George, 'squandered his father's fortune in high living in France' and later settled in America as 'a kind of itinerant merchant' (Courtauld, 87). He married Sarah Miles Wharton (1772–1836), of Philadelphia. Samuel died in 1821 and was buried in the Old Swedes churchyard, Wilmington, Delaware. Thus, after more than seventy years, the connection of the Courtauld family with goldsmithing came to an end. HELEN CLIFFORD

Sources S. L. Courtauld, *The Huguenot family of Courtaulds* (1957) · V. L. Chester, *Early history of the family of Courtaulds* (1911) · E. A. Jones and S. A. Courtauld, *Some silver wrought by the Courtauld family of silversmiths* (1940) · T. Murdoch, 'The Courtaulds: silversmiths for three generations, 1708–1780', *Proceedings of the Society of Silver Collectors*, 2/4 (1984), 85–96 · A. G. Grimwade, *London goldsmiths, 1697–1837: their marks and lives, from the original registers at Goldsmiths' Hall*, 3rd edn (1990), 474–5, 742 · J. F. Hayward, *The Courtauld silver* (1975) · E. Wenham, 'The Courtauld family', *Antique Collector*, 16 (1945), 12 · D. C. Coleman, *Courtaulds: an economic and social history*, 1 (1969) · J. Banister, 'Three generations in silver', *Country Life*, 171 (1982), 1628–9 · C. Lever, 'The Courtauld family of goldsmiths', *Apollo*, 100 (1974), 138–41 · *The Courtauld family: Huguenot silversmiths*, ed. Worshipful Company of Goldsmiths (1985) [exhibition catalogue, Goldsmiths' Hall, London, 4 June – 12 July 1985] · P. Glanville and V. F. Goldsborough, *Women silversmiths, 1685–1845* (1990) · will, PRO, PROB 11/787/107 [Augustin Courtauld] · 'The life and loves of an early Essex girl', *Daily Mail Weekend* (27 Nov 1993), 12
Archives priv. coll., Courtauld family papers
Likenesses portrait, 1738 (Samuel [i] Courtauld, aged eighteen), priv. coll.; repro. in Courtauld, *Huguenot family* · portrait, 1758 (Samuel [i] Courtauld, aged thirty-eight), priv. coll.; repro. in Courtauld, *Huguenot family* · attrib. (separately) J. Zoffany, or N. Dance, oils (Louisa Courtauld), priv. coll.; repro. in Courtauld, *Huguenot family* · oils (Augustin Courtauld, with child), priv. coll.; repro. in Courtauld, *Huguenot family* · oils (Augustin Courtauld), priv. coll.; repro. in Courtauld, *Huguenot family*
Wealth at death £400 will to son; also all his utensils and patterns; Augustin Courtauld: will, PRO, PROB 11/787/107

**Courtauld, Augustin** (1685–1751). *See under* Courtauld family (*per.* 1708–1780).

**Courtauld, Augustine** (1904–1959), Arctic explorer, was born on 26 August 1904 at Bocking, Braintree, Essex, the eldest child of Samuel Augustine Courtauld (1865–1953), a director of the family textile firm, and his wife, Edith Anne (Edian) Lister (d. 1951), daughter of Walter Venning Lister. He had one brother and one sister and was a cousin of Samuel *Courtauld (1876–1947). August, as he was known, was educated at Charterhouse, which he disliked, and Trinity College, Cambridge, which he enjoyed and where he read engineering and geography and from where he graduated BA in 1926. In that year he joined James Wordie's summer expedition to east Greenland as photographer. The party spent the summer surveying the area between Pendulum Øer and Davy Sund. They also took gravity readings in the area. In the spring of 1927 Courtauld travelled with Francis Rodd and Peter Rodd to the mountains of Aïr in the southern Sahara. The party travelled to Kano, down the Niger to Timbuktu, thence to Dakar, and home in the spring of 1928. Little is known of this expedition as it was not written up by any member of the party.

After an unsuccessful attempt at a career with a firm of City stockbrokers, Courtauld returned to Greenland in the summer of 1929 on another expedition with Wordie. Courtauld was one of the party that reached the summit of Petermann Peak, then the highest known point in the Arctic, but which the party established was only 9300 feet high and not 14,000 feet as had previously been thought. In 1930 Courtauld met H. G. Watkins, who was planning an expedition to Greenland to explore the possibilities of an air route from the United Kingdom to western Canada over the ice cap. Courtauld secured substantial funds from his family for Watkins's British Arctic air route expedition. An essential part of the meteorological programme was the establishment of the ice-cap station some 140 miles north-west of the base camp and 8500 feet above sea level and its maintenance throughout the whole year by two men who would be relieved at approximately monthly intervals by dog sledge or aircraft. As winter approached weather conditions were so severe that a party, including Courtauld, took six weeks to reach the ice-cap station from the base camp and it became clear that it would be many months before it could be relieved again. It was also clear that there was not enough food for two men to be left safely at the camp. Courtauld persuaded the party to allow him to man the station alone and he was left there on 5 December 1930. A relief party reached the vicinity of the station in late March 1931 but in appalling weather conditions they were unable to find it. On the return of the party with this alarming news Watkins, with Frederick Spencer Chapman and another companion, left the base camp and on 5 May located the ice-cap station, though it was completely submerged in snow. Courtauld had spent five months alone, part of the time imprisoned beneath the snow and in darkness. His home was a tent 10 feet in diameter covered by a snow house. He was cheerful and unperturbed. He characteristically wrote of this episode that his main aim had been to 'dispel strange ideas of danger and risk in leaving a man in such a situation', though the main result of his action had in fact been that the meteorological readings which were the scientific goal of the party were maintained uninterrupted at least until April when he ran out of fuel. He later recounted his experiences in a series of articles for *The Times*. In 1932 he was awarded the polar medal by George V.

In 1932 Courtauld married Mollie, elder daughter of Frank Douglas Montgomerie, land agent. They had known each other since childhood and together had four sons and two daughters. In the year of his marriage Courtauld bought a 22-ton gaff-rigged yawl which he named *Duet* and he and his family and friends had much pleasure from it. He was a skilled and fearless seaman. In the summer of 1935 Courtauld organized an expedition with Lawrence (Bill) Wager to Knud Rasmussen Land to map and climb a range of mountains which had been distantly sighted and photographed from an aircraft by Watkins. These proved to be the highest in the Arctic (12,200 feet) and were named the Watkins Range. Before the Second World War Courtauld joined the organization which was to become the Special Operations Executive, and in the summer of 1939 was asked by naval intelligence to take *Duet* up the Norwegian coast from Bergen to Trondheim gathering as much intelligence as he could. Severe fog tested his skill as a navigator but he brought *Duet* safely home.

Courtauld served throughout the Second World War in the Royal Naval Volunteer Reserve as sub-lieutenant (1939) and lieutenant (1940–45). He was never promoted beyond the rank of lieutenant as he did not take kindly to rules and regulations. After the war he devoted himself to local government and community service. He served on Essex county council from 1945 to 1955, and became a JP and deputy lieutenant in 1946, and high sheriff of Essex in 1953. He was a governor of Felsted School, chairman of Essex Association of Boys' Clubs, and vice-president of the Royal National Lifeboat Institution (RNLI) (1957), and gave a lifeboat to the institution in memory of his mother. He served three times on the council of the Royal Geographical Society and was honorary secretary between 1948 and 1951. He also served on the committee of management of the Scott Polar Research Institute.

In 1953 Courtauld was found to be suffering from multiple sclerosis and he became increasingly incapacitated, though for a time he was able to attend official and social occasions in his wheelchair. His Christian faith which had brought him comfort during his time in isolation in the Arctic also sustained him through his final illness. His autobiography, *Man the Ropes* (1957), shows the signs of his illness, but his anthology of polar writings, *From the Ends of the Earth* (1958), is a well-chosen collection. He had little interest in the social advantages which his family wealth might have brought him and characteristically used his money to further exploration and local causes in which he was personally interested. James Wordie described him as a 'loveable and popular member of any party' (*Polar Record*, 610). In 1956 he set up the Augustine Courtauld Trust to help causes which 'wouldn't get much help otherwise'.

Courtauld died in hospital in London on 3 March 1959. He was buried at sea from the lifeboat which he had given to the RNLI. He was in turn memorialized by a lifeboat given to the RNLI by his brother, Peter, and named *Augustine Courtauld*. On 21 October 1959 his widow became the second wife of R. A. Butler (later Lord Butler of Saffron Walden). They were married in the presence of their ten children and the marriage was very happy.

F. S. CHAPMAN, *rev.* ELIZABETH BAIGENT

**Sources** F. S. Chapman, *Northern lights* (1932) · *Polar Record*, 9/63 (1959), 609–10 · Q. Riley, *GJ*, 125 (1959), 286–7 · *The Times* (4 March 1959) · *WWW*, see also Samuel Augustine Courtauld · A. Courtauld, *Man the ropes* (1957) · personal knowledge (1971) · www.augustinecourtauldtrust.org

**Archives** Scott Polar RI, journals, 1926–35

**Likenesses** photographs, repro. in www.augustinecourtauldtrust.org

**Courtauld, Louisa Perina** (1729–1807). *See under* Courtauld family (*per.* 1708–1780).

**Courtauld, Peter** (1689/90–1729). *See under* Courtauld family (*per.* 1708–1780).

**Courtauld, Samuel** (1720–1765). *See under* Courtauld family (*per.* 1708–1780).

**Courtauld, Samuel** (1752–1821). *See under* Courtauld family (*per.* 1708–1780).

**Courtauld, Samuel** (1793–1881), silk manufacturer, was born in Albany, New York, USA, on 1 June 1793, the eldest son of George Courtauld (1761–1823) and Ruth, daughter of Stephen Minton of Cork. The Courtaulds had come to England as Huguenot refugees at the end of the seventeenth century where for three generations they worked and prospered as silversmiths in London. George Courtauld was apprenticed to a Spitalfields silk weaver in 1775 and set up as a silk throwster. In 1785, however, he made the first of a number of trips to America where, in 1789, he married Ruth Minton. Shortly after Samuel's birth his parents returned to England and to the silk industry. For some years Samuel worked for his father, who had become an ardent Unitarian with politically radical sympathies, but who proved to be a remarkably incompetent businessman. By 1816 his position, and that of his family, was financially perilous. In that year, the ambitious Samuel, intent upon rescuing the family and restoring it to what he saw as its rightful social position, set up in business on his own account as a silk throwster in a small mill at Bocking, Essex. His father went back to America, where he died in 1823.

The family returned to England and became dependent upon Samuel Courtauld's success. After acquiring the lease of a larger water-powered mill at Bocking, he then converted an old corn mill in the neighbouring town of Halstead. In 1828 he established a long-enduring partnership with his younger brother George (1802–1861) and with his cousin and brother-in-law, Peter Alfred Taylor. In 1822 Courtauld had married Taylor's sister Ellen (1801–1872), daughter of William Taylor and Catherine Courtauld. This quintessentially family firm, by that time known as Samuel Courtauld & Co., then began a period of striking success. To silk throwing was added hand-loom weaving and, about 1830, the first foundation of the family's real wealth: the power-loom weaving, dyeing, and finishing of black silk mourning crape. A remarkable boom in black crape developed in Victorian England as the ancient ritual of mourning was formalized, publicized, and commercialized. Samuel Courtauld & Co. did very well out of it, becoming the country's biggest manufacturer of mourning crape. Until crape began to fall from fashion in the 1880s, the partners were regularly earning well over 30 per cent on their capital. During the last decade of his life Samuel, as the senior partner, was drawing an income from the business alone of about £46,000 per annum.

The partnership retained its family character as a new generation of Courtaulds and Taylors, together with members of related Unitarian families, came into the business after the mid-century. But family and firm alike were totally dominated by Samuel Courtauld. His prime contribution to the business consisted of his organizing ability and his driving ambition, allied to a shrewd practical intelligence and an immense capacity for hard work. A difficult colleague, his letters often reveal paranoid tendencies as he fluctuated between euphoria and highly autocratic behaviour on the one hand, and gloom and self-deprecation on the other. His attitude to his workers (over 3000 were employed by the firm in the 1880s) was characteristic of the day: a benevolent despotism informed by a profound belief in the merits of free enterprise; a concern to instil 'orderly and industrious habits' among the working poor by a system of fines and rewards; and a ruthless determination to stamp out incipient strikes or other symptoms of insubordination. The partners, aided by their wives, pursued an active local welfare policy, building workers' cottages, a coffee house, and a reading-room. In his younger days Samuel Courtauld had taken some part in local radical activities; and he later played an important role in the celebrated Braintree church rates case, which led ultimately to the abolition of church rates and was a notable victory for the principle of religious freedom. But his other attempts at political involvement bore little fruit. Stiff and domineering in manner, yet sensitive to insult, he lacked the resilience necessary for politics. As *The Times* observed in its obituary, 'had the death of Mr. Courtauld happened some 30 or 40 years ago a popular hero would have passed away' but he lived on 'to be almost forgotten' (24 March 1881, 10e).

In 1854 Courtauld bought the substantial mansion of Gosfield Hall, between Halstead and Bocking, in Essex, with 2000 acres, an estate augmented by further purchases. He had a London house and a yacht. At his death, on 21 March 1881, at Gosfield Hall, he was worth about £700,000. His wife had died in 1872; their only child died in infancy. Apart from legacies of between £30,000 and £35,000 apiece to two nephews, and sundry lesser bequests, he left the bulk of his estate to two adopted children.       D. C. COLEMAN

**Sources** D. C. Coleman, *Courtaulds: an economic and social history*, 3 vols. (1969–80) · S. L. Courtauld, *The Huguenot family of Courtauld*, 3 vols. (privately printed, London, 1957–67) · S. A. Courtauld, ed., *Courtauld family letters, 1782–1900*, 7 vols. (1916) · J. F. Hayward, *The Courtauld silver* (1975) · D. C. Coleman, 'Courtauld III, Samuel', *DBB* · *The Times* (24 March 1881)

**Archives** Essex RO, Chelmsford, early records of Courtaulds plc
**Likenesses** photographs, repro. in Coleman, *Courtaulds*, vol. 1 · photographs, repro. in Courtauld, *Huguenot family of Courtauld*, vol. 3
**Wealth at death** under £700,000: probate, 22 April 1881, *CGPLA Eng. & Wales*

**Courtauld, Samuel** (1876–1947), industrialist and patron of the arts, was born at Bocking, Essex, on 7 May 1876, the second son of Sydney Courtauld, a silk manufacturer, and his wife, Sarah Lucy, the daughter of William Sharp. The Courtaulds had arrived in England as Huguenot refugees at the end of the seventeenth century. Three generations of the family worked as London silversmiths. The silk firm

Samuel Courtauld (1876–1947), by Fayer, mid-1930s

was effectively founded in 1816 by Sydney's uncle, Samuel Courtauld (1793–1881). Samuel, the great-nephew of the founder, followed precedent and in 1898 joined the company. He had meanwhile been educated at Rugby School (1890–94) and was then sent to Krefeld and Lyons to learn the techniques of textile manufacture. In 1901—the year in which, on 20 June, he married Elizabeth Theresa Frances (*d.* 1931), the only daughter of Edward Kelsey—he became manager of the company's weaving mill at Halstead, and in 1908 he was appointed general manager of all the firm's textile mills. This promotion was not mere nepotism. He was the only member of the family in the business to have earned the approbation of H. G. Tetley, an outsider to the family but then the dominant power in the company and the architect of its move from silk into rayon. Courtauld, who proved himself an able and vigorous manager, joined the board of Courtaulds Ltd in 1915 and succeeded Tetley as joint managing director in 1917, when Tetley became chairman. On Tetley's death in 1921 the way was open for Courtauld to succeed as chairman of what had become a £12 million international concern. For the next quarter of a century he filled two roles in British public life: he was chairman of what was for most of that time the world's largest firm of rayon manufacturers, and he was one of Britain's best-known patrons of the arts.

The highly profitable company which Courtauld took over was just beginning to face competition as a big rayon boom got under way. His response to that boom exhibited certain central facets of his character. Clear, knowledgeable, and authoritative in his statements, he strove for conciliation and compromise, limits on competition, and ordered growth. Bold, aggressive, and risky business ventures of the sort which his great-uncle or Tetley had pursued were anathema to him. Many of the new rayon companies founded in the 1920s came crashing down in the 1930s depression. In 1931 Courtauld voiced his disapproval of what he called 'the senseless increase in production resulting from the orgy of company-promoting and speculation' and observed loftily that it was 'a discreditable chapter in industrial history' (Coleman, 2.219). Under his leadership the company which bore his family name became a highly respected industrial giant, a blue-chip security. It pursued a policy of financial conservatism, with large reserves and a cautious dividend policy.

Courtauld's own lengthy and forthright speeches at annual general meetings were something of an event in the business calendar. He became a public figure, yet he characteristically turned down the offer of a barony in 1937. His ideas on a variety of subjects were disseminated in numerous letters to *The Times* and, especially during the Second World War, by sundry pronouncements on industry and the state and on capital–labour relations. He sat on numerous committees concerned with such issues and was a visiting fellow and trustee of Nuffield College, Oxford. Some of his views—for example, his dislike of advertising and his advocacy of more government control of the economy and of a more sympathetic regard for the claims of labour to a share in management—did not go down well with some of his fellow businessmen. His dignified and respected leadership had costs as well as benefits for the company. It became complacent. Not until the end of 1938 did Courtauld tell his colleagues on the board that it had rested too much on its laurels, neglecting research. There was also a failure to understand the need for changes in organization, management, and personnel as the firm expanded. Too much power was left in the hands of unimaginative bosses whose rough and ready methods had worked in the past but who remained contemptuous of change. Again, it was not until the later 1930s, and then after the Second World War, that many necessary changes were brought about.

The fact that Courtauld was in many ways the antithesis of the adventurous entrepreneur owed much to his serious-minded upbringing. His parents retained longer than others of their generation a profound regard for the family Unitarianism. He inherited from his father both an interest in the technical side of the business and a regard for music; from his mother came an appreciation of art and literature. The latter found its outlet in his picture collecting and in his acquaintanceship with many prominent figures of the literary and artistic world, such as the Sitwells, Roger Fry, and Charles Morgan, as well as with Lydia Lopokova and John Maynard Keynes, who provided links between Bloomsbury and business. His collecting started before he became a very rich man and showed an adventurousness not evident in his business career, for it resulted in the building up of what became the finest collection of French Impressionist paintings in the country.

It contained many works by Degas, Renoir, Manet (including the famous *Bar at the Folies-Bergère*, for which he paid some £23,000 in 1926), Seurat, and especially Cézanne, whose cause he particularly championed. By far the greater part of the collecting was done in the 1920s; it virtually ended with the death of his wife on 25 December 1931. In 1923 he had given £50,000 to the Tate Gallery for the purchase of similar works.

On his wife's death Courtauld established and handsomely endowed the Courtauld Institute of Art in the University of London (which conferred on him an honorary DLitt), providing the new institute with the lease of his splendid Adam house, Home House, in Portman Square, and a substantial part of his own collection. He had strong emotional reactions to what these paintings revealed to him; and a sense of duty to make available to the public the civilizing influence of art. He was a trustee of the Tate Gallery from 1927 to 1937 and of the National Gallery from 1931 to 1947. He and his wife also gave financial support to music and concert-going in London. In the 1930s he became much enamoured of Christabel, Lady Aberconway; and his self-doubt and private quest for truth and beauty can be seen in many letters to her, letters often charged with a rather heavy sententiousness. It is perhaps hardly surprising that Edith Sitwell should have recorded, after conversation at a lunch party, that he made her feel 'unpardonably flippant' (Glendinning, 172).

In May 1946 Courtauld suffered a severe illness and in October resigned from the chairmanship. He remained on the board, but died on 1 December 1947, at his home, 12 North Audley Street, London. His will was proved at £1,030,126. After various legacies much of his property went to his only daughter, Sydney Elizabeth, and to her husband, Richard Austen Butler (later Lord Butler of Saffron Walden), whom she had married in 1926.

D. C. COLEMAN

**Sources** D. C. Coleman, *Courtaulds: an economic and social history*, 3 vols. (1969–80) • J. House, *Impressionism for England: Samuel Courtauld as patron and collector* (1994) • S. L. Courtauld, *The Huguenot family of Courtauld*, 3 vols. (privately printed, London, 1957–67) • C. Morgan, ed., *Ideals and industry* (1949) • V. Glendinning, *Edith Sitwell* (1981) • J. F. Hayward, *The Courtauld silver* (1975) • *DNB* • D. C. Coleman, 'Courtauld IV, Samuel', *DBB* • d. cert.
**Archives** Courtaulds plc, Coventry, company archives, business papers • Trinity Cam., corresp. and papers | BL, letters to Lady Aberconway, Add. MSS 52432–52435
**Likenesses** Fayer, photograph, 1933–7, repro. in Coleman, *Courtaulds*, 2 [*see illus.*] • R. de Maistre, oils, 1947, Courtaulds Ltd, London • B. Elkan, bronze head, Courtauld Inst. • A. Pann, oils, Courtaulds Ltd, London • painting, Courtaulds plc, Coventry • painting, priv. coll. • photographs, Courtaulds plc, Coventry; repro. in Coleman, *Courtaulds*, 2 • photographs, repro. in House, *Impressionism for England*
**Wealth at death** £1,030,126 7s. 3d.: probate, 8 Jan 1948, *CGPLA Eng. & Wales*

**Courten, Sir Peter**, baronet (d. 1624/5). *See under* Courten, Sir William (c.1568–1636).

**Courten, Sir William** (c.1568–1636), merchant and financier, was born in London, the son of William Courten, a merchant, and his wife, Margaret Casiere. His parents were religious refugees who fled from Leye in Flanders during 1568. His father set up a textile business in Abchurch Lane, London, then moved to Pudding Lane, where he traded in silk and linen cloth with Middelburg, Amsterdam, Flushing, and other ports in the Low Countries. On his death the bulk of his estate was divided between his wife and three surviving children, William, Peter, and Margaret, the widow of Mathias Bodean. Courten also made a number of charitable bequests to the Dutch church in London, of which he was a prominent member.

**Trading in Europe** The young William Courten was employed by his father as a factor in Haarlem, where he met and married his first wife, Margareta, the daughter of Peter Cromlyn, a wealthy merchant; the couple had a son, Peter [see below]. Courten's second wife was Hester Tryan, with whom he had four children: William [see below], who married Lady Katherine Egerton, daughter of John, first earl of Bridgewater; Hester, who married Sir Edward Littleton; Anne, who married Essex Devereux and then Richard Knightley; and Mary, who married Henry Grey, ninth earl of Kent. During a long career devoted mainly to overseas trade Courten developed one of the most extensive and, for a time, successful commercial businesses in London. In partnership with his brother, Peter, and brother-in-law, John Mounsey, he traded throughout Europe, creating an impressive Anglo-Dutch business empire with overlapping interests in shipping, finance, and colonization. He built more than twenty ships and employed between 4000 and 5000 mariners, providing some justification for his reputation as 'a memorable Merchant and good Comon wealth man' (Harlow, *Colonising Expeditions*, 29). As a young man Courten suffered a setback to his reputation when he was accused of illegally exporting gold coin in 1619. After legal proceedings in Star Chamber he was fined £20,000 and discharged with a general pardon. Though damaging, the case did not ruin his standing in the City or at court. Indeed, on 31 May 1622 he was knighted by the king; on 22 February 1624 his son received a similar honour.

**Transatlantic trading** During the early 1620s Courten became closely involved in Dutch transatlantic enterprise. He developed extensive interests in the Dutch tobacco colony on the River Essequibo in Guiana. In 1624 one of his ships, the *Olive*, under the command of captain John Powell, was involved in the capture of Bahia by a Dutch fleet. It was this ship which touched at the uninhabited island of Barbados on its return voyage the following year. Powell's report encouraged Courten to undertake the settlement of the island with a syndicate that included his brother and brother-in-law, as well as John Powell and Henry Powell. The outbreak of war with Spain in 1625 enabled the Courten syndicate to pursue their colonizing schemes in conjunction with privateering, though the first expedition to Barbados in 1626 was postponed by the seizure of a prize in the channel. The following year captain Henry Powell landed a group of eighty men and women on the island, and a similar number arrived in 1628. The settlers laid out estates and plantations on the island and elected John Powell the younger as governor. They were paid wages by the syndicate, but received no grant of land.

Courten played a leading role in the affairs of the syndicate. According to John Powell he was a 'verie worthye & vigorous imployer and provider Supplier and paymaster' (Harlow, *Colonising Expeditions*, 39). His personal investment in the enterprise is impossible to estimate, but it probably accounted for much of the 'prime Costs of planting', which were subsequently estimated to be about £12,000 (ibid., 29–32). Unfortunately Courten's title to Barbados was uncertain and open to challenge from rival groups. In July 1627 the king issued a grant to James Hay, first earl of Carlisle, of the Caribbee Islands, which included Barbados. Courten tried to protect his interests by relying on a powerful supporter at court, Philip Herbert, first earl of Montgomery and fourth earl of Pembroke, who was awarded a patent for the island in February 1628. Within a month Carlisle had acquired a second patent which made it clear that Barbados was included in his original grant. Although the legal confusion caused violent turmoil in Barbados, by the end of 1628 Carlisle had asserted his authority over the island; it remained in his hands, and those of his successors, until 1646. Later efforts by Courten's descendants to receive compensation for his losses were fruitless.

Despite the débâcle over Barbados, Courten's other commercial and financial interests continued to flourish. He lent £18,500 to James I in 1613 and 1614, and despite the usual delay in repayment he was ready to lend £13,500 to Charles I in July 1625. Indeed, he became an important moneylender in the City whose potential value to a government plagued by financial stringency was considerable. In July 1625 he was commended by the lord treasurer as someone who 'freely lends his money for supply of the King's instant occasions, and that without interest of the old debt' (*CSP dom.*, 1625–6, 74). The following year he was involved in discussions between the privy council and the 'merchant stranger' community in London concerning a proposal for a loan of £50,000 to the crown. In August 1626 he was unable or unwilling to lend £2000 to the king, claiming by way of justification to have paid £700 in customs duties since March. In 1628, however, he advanced £3000 to supply the king's needs. Courten's creditors later claimed that he lent £25,000 to Charles I, much of which remained unpaid at the time of his death. Courten also lent £4500 to the king's favourite, the duke of Buckingham, in 1627. His son later alleged that he advanced more than £3000 to the ill-fated Fishing Association of Britain and Ireland, in which he served as treasurer, though the loan was probably never repaid. Despite the scale of these financial dealings, Courten began to develop extensive landed interests during the 1620s and 1630s. In 1628 he acquired lands in Whittlewood Forest, Northamptonshire, valued at £5500. In 1630 he was involved in the purchase of drainable land in the manor of Hatfield, Yorkshire, from Sir Cornelius Vermuyden. He also acquired several manors in Kent. By 1633 his landed possessions were reportedly bringing him £6500 a year. In addition the king granted him various parcels of land in the fens in March 1635.

**Asia, the East India Company monopoly, and death** During the closing years of his life Courten became involved in an audaciously ambitious attempt to challenge the trading monopoly of the East India Company in Asia. His partners in this enterprise included Endymion Porter, an influential courtier who was groom of the bedchamber, Thomas Kynnaston, Samuel Bonnell, and others. Courten's involvement in the venture may be linked with overlapping ambitions to discover and colonize new lands in 'Terra Australis Incognita', which he laid out in an undated petition to the king (*CSP dom.*, *1625–6*, 206). The commission that he and his partners received from Charles I on 12 December 1635, authorizing a trading voyage to Goa, Malabar, China, and Japan, was justified by the East India Company's neglect of discovery and plantation in the East. The partnership also received a licence to export foreign gold and silver up to the value of £40,000.

The East India Company objected vociferously to Courten's commission. Charles I attempted to calm the company's fears, informing the governor, 'upon the word of a King and as hee is a Christian King', that no hindrance or damage was intended to the company's trade as the ships being prepared by Courten were for 'a voyage of discovery', and would not go where the company traded (Sainsbury, *Calendar …*, *1635–1639*, 157). Royal reassurances did little to allay the company's anxiety. On 8 March 1636 the governor presented the king with a petition against Courten's voyage. As the king was closely involved in the venture, to the extent that he invested £10,000 in the voyage, the company's objections fell on deaf ears. In any case its position was damaged by rumours that some of its own members were adventurers with Courten.

By April 1636 Courten and his partners had prepared a substantial fleet of six vessels under the command of captain John Weddell, an experienced seaman with long experience in the service of the East India Company. The charge of setting out the fleet amounted to £120,000, much of which was borrowed or came out of Courten's own pocket. At the king's persuasion, Sir Paul Pindar, a prominent city merchant and financier, apparently lent £36,000 to Courten. By any standards this was an enormous investment in a venture which was dangerously speculative. The strain on Courten soon began to show. According to Peter Mundy, who sailed with the fleet and kept a journal of its proceedings, Courten fell sick a little before the fleet's departure, 'questionlesse to see himselffe soe farre engaged uppon an uncertainety, And within 3 Monthes after our departure … he Departed allso this life. Without all Doubt the heavy Waightt of thatt businesse brake his heart' (Temple, 3.425). His death took place in London on 27 May 1636. It was perhaps fortunate that he did not live to witness the return of the fleet in December 1638. Though Weddell was able to carry on some trade at Goa and Macao, the voyage was marred by indiscriminate plunder and the sinking of two ships, whose loss was estimated at £150,000. Weddell was lost at sea on the return voyage. One ship, the *Sunne*, returned with a good lading of silks, sugar, gold, and other commodities. Even so, this was an 'unfortunate voyage', which deepened the problems inherited by Courten's son and heir (ibid., 3.427).

By the terms of his will Courten left the bulk of his estate to his son William, though provision was made for his three daughters, among whom Hester was left £4000, Mary £2000, and Anne £1000. Courten made many charitable bequests, leaving £100 to Christ Church Hospital and St Thomas's Hospital in London. In addition every captain and master of his ships was left a gold ring worth £3. As the greater part of his personal estate was overseas, and his estate in England was encumbered with debt, it is likely that few of these bequests were ever fulfilled. At the time of his death his estate in Holland was the subject of a complex legal dispute with his nephew, which was precipitated by the death of his brother in 1631 and his brother-in-law in 1632. His commercial and financial difficulties were discussed in several pamphlets published in the later seventeenth century by George Carew and other creditors on his estate. An extended profile of him was published by Andrew Kippis in his second edition of *Biographia Britannica* (1789), and several elegies appeared after his death, two of which survive in the Lansdowne manuscripts in the British Library. In his will he expressed a desire to be buried in the chancel of the parish church of St Andrew Hubbard, near Eastcheap, London, near his two wives.

**Other Courtens** **Sir Peter Courten**, baronet (*d.* 1624/5), of Pirton, Worcestershire, the eldest son of Sir William Courten and his first wife, married Jane, the daughter of Sir John Stanhope of Elvaston in Derbyshire. He deserted the commercial world of the City in favour of landed society in the provinces, and acquired lands in Worcestershire and Kent. He was made a baronet in 1622. He died childless, leaving the bulk of his estate to his wife, his half-brother, William, and his half-sisters, Hester, Mary, and Anne.

**William Courten** (*d.* 1655), the second son and the heir of Sir William Courten and the eldest child of his second wife, was a prominent merchant and shipowner in London. With his wife, Lady Katherine Egerton, he had at least two children, William *Courten and Katherine, though the son changed his name to Charleton following the bankruptcy and death of his father in 1655. Many of Courten's commercial interests were related to the East Indies venture initiated by his father. The partnership, since known as Courten's Association, was reorganized during 1637, when it received a new commission from the crown confirming all former grants and authorizing the partners to send out ships and goods to the East for five years 'without impeachment or denial of the East India Company or others' (Sainsbury, *Calendar …*, *1635–1639*, 276). From the start, however, Courten and the association were hindered by financial difficulties. Saddled with inherited debts, Courten apparently borrowed £80,000 to 'discharge his father's engagements' (*Portland MSS*, 8.7). When the king understood how hardly some of Sir William's creditors had dealt with his son, he instructed the farmers of the customs to supply him with money. Two years later, in December 1638, Charles I granted the office of surveyor of the petty customs in London to Courten and others, to be held for life after the death of Richard Carmarden.

The king's actions may have provided some relief for the pressing financial problems Courten inherited, but they did little to remove their cause. Although Courten and his partners continued to set out ships to the East, their efforts were dogged by misfortune and deepening hostility from the East India Company. Alarmed at Weddell's establishment of a trading factory at Bhatkal on the Malabar coast in 1637, the company bitterly objected to the setting up of another factory by Courten's men at Rajapur in 1639. In March 1640, however, the king indicated that he was prepared to leave the sole trade of the East Indies to the company. The following year Courten suggested that he might be willing to give up his trade if the company provided compensation. These negotiations, and other efforts to reach an accommodation in 1644, failed. In March 1647 a proposal put forward by the House of Commons, confirming the company's trading privileges, was rejected by the Lords. After failing to reach agreement with the company, Courten petitioned parliament in an attempt to gain compensation for the alleged injuries he had suffered as a result of the company's continuing opposition.

Ill luck contributed to Courten's mounting financial difficulties. The association lost two ships at sea during 1639. Worse followed in 1643, when a ship was captured by the Dutch in the Strait of Malacca; the loss to the association was estimated at £75,000, and seems to have been the primary cause of Courten's insolvency. Increasingly, the association's commercial operations were affected by want of money. In 1646 agents for the East India Company expressed surprise at the empty ships being sent out by Courten. Rumours circulated that he had set up a mint at his ill-fated settlement on Madagascar, established in 1645 but abandoned the following year, which was coining counterfeit gold and silver for use in his trade in India. With his personal affairs in a hopeless condition Courten fled overseas, leaving his wife and associates to salvage what they could from the wreckage of his financial collapse. The association struggled on under the management of new leadership, which included the radical merchant Maurice Thompson, but by 1649 it had been incorporated into the East India Company.

The Courten Association was a dramatic failure. It is difficult to disagree with the comment of one of Courten's servants, John Farren, that 'designes of that nature were most proper to a Company rather then a particular man' (Foster, *English Factories*, 8.39). In this sense the association was no match for the financial resources of the East India Company. Nevertheless its trading activities severely disrupted the company's trade in the east, causing damage later estimated at £100,000. Courten's close personal involvement in the association did much to antagonize

some of the most powerful merchants in the City of London, and may partly explain his complaints about being over-assessed for ship money in 1637; apparently he was assessed to pay £50 by the court of aldermen, whose own assessments were only £10.

Courten died bankrupt in Florence in 1655. The complex financial situation that he inherited from his father was compounded by his own personal misfortune. His descendants and creditors made repeated efforts to recover some of the Courten estate. In 1659 an attempt was made to acquire compensation, to the value of £200,000, for Sir William Courten's investment in the settlement of Barbados. The following year, to provide for the grandchildren, George Carew was appointed to receive money previously lent by Sir William. But these, and other efforts to gain compensation in Holland for the seizure of shipping in 1643, were unavailing. The creditors and administrators of the Courten estate were still demanding letters of reprisal against the Dutch East India Company in the early eighteenth century.                                  JOHN C. APPLEBY

**Sources** E. B. Sainsbury, ed., *A calendar of the court minutes … of the East India Company*, 11 vols. (1907–38), vols. 1–3, 6 [1635–49, 1660–63] · W. Foster, ed., *The English factories in India*, 13 vols. (1906–27), vols. 5–8 · *CSP dom.*, 1619–23; 1625–6; 1628–9; 1636–9; 1655; 1659–61 · *APC*, 1625–30 · W. L. Grant and J. F. Munro, eds., *Acts of the privy council of England: colonial series*, 1: 1613–80 (1908) · *The travels of Peter Mundy in Europe and Asia, 1608–1667*, ed. R. C. Temple and L. M. Anstey, 3/1, Hakluyt Society, 2nd ser., 45 (1919) · *The travels of Peter Mundy in Europe and Asia, 1608–1667*, ed. R. C. Temple and L. M. Anstey, 5, Hakluyt Society, 2nd ser., 78 (1936) · V. T. Harlow, ed., *Colonising expeditions to the West Indies and Guiana, 1623–1667*, Hakluyt Society, 2nd ser., 56 (1925) · *CSP col.*, vols. 1, 5–6, 8 · R. Ashton, *The crown and the money market, 1603–1640* (1960) · *Seventh report*, HMC, 6 (1879) · *The manuscripts of his grace the duke of Portland*, 10 vols., HMC, 29 (1891–1931), vol. 8 · R. Brenner, *Merchants and revolution: commercial change, political conflict, and London's overseas traders, 1550–1653* (1993) · K. R. Andrews, *Ships, money, and politics: seafaring and naval enterprise in the reign of Charles I* (1991) · V. T. Harlow, *A history of Barbados, 1625–1685* (1926) · N. Currer-Briggs, ed., *English adventurers and Virginian settlers: the co-ordinated use of seventeenth century British and American records by genealogists*, 3 vols. (1969) · H. B. Morse, *The chronicles of the East India Company trading to China, 1635–1834*, 1 (1926) · R. H. Schomburgk, *The history of Barbados* (1848) · R. Lockyer, *Buckingham: the life and political career of George Villiers, first duke of Buckingham, 1592–1628* (1981) · G. Puckrein, 'Did Sir William Courteen really own Barbados?', *Huntington Library Quarterly*, 44 (1980–81), 135–49 · A. Kippis and others, eds., *Biographia Britannica, or, The lives of the most eminent persons who have flourished in Great Britain and Ireland*, 2nd edn, 4 (1789) · *The visitation of London, anno Domini 1633, 1634, and 1635, made by Sir Henry St George*, 1, ed. J. J. Howard and J. L. Chester, Harleian Society, 15 (1880) · will, PRO, PROB 11/171, sig. 69 · *The obituary of Richard Smyth … being a catalogue of all such persons as he knew in their life*, ed. H. Ellis, CS, 44 (1849) · GEC, *Baronetage* · I. Scouloudi, *Returns of strangers in the metropolis, 1593, 1627, 1635, 1639: a study of an active minority*, Huguenot Society of London, 57 (1985) · will of Sir Peter Courten, PRO, PROB 11/149, sig. 82
**Archives** Bodl. Oxf., MS Rawl. A.299 | BL, Sloane MS 3515 · PRO, Exchequer, port books, E 190 · PRO, high court of admiralty examinations, HCA 13
**Wealth at death** little survived; many bequests, incl. £7000 between three daughters: will, PRO, PROB 11/171 · in debt to est. £146,300: Scouloudi, *Returns of strangers*

**Courten, William** (*d.* 1655). *See under* Courten, Sir William (*c.*1568–1636).

**Courten** [*alias* Charleton], **William** (1642–1702), naturalist and collector, was born in London on 28 March 1642, the son of William Courten, who died insolvent at Florence in 1655, and Lady Katherine Egerton, daughter of John, first earl of Bridgewater. Sir William *Courten (*c.*1568–1636), merchant, was his other grandfather. After a good education Courten travelled in France, meeting Hans Sloane and Tancred Robinson, with whom he became friends, in Paris, and Jacob Tournefort in Montpellier, where he began his botanical studies. In 1663 he returned home to attend to his private affairs, probably on attaining his majority. From his father Courten inherited extensive debts, and from his grandfather complicated claims to territory in England and the West Indies. From both, however, he derived specimens and probably the habit of collecting. In England he lived until 1670 with his aunt, Anne, Lady Knightley, at Fawsley Lodge, Northamptonshire. After this he went abroad again for fourteen years. Little is known of his movements, but he probably spent some of the time at Montpellier. He was a close friend of William Sherard; other friends were Martin Lister, Leonard Plukenet, and Edward Llwyd. Through them Courten was in touch with John Ray and other naturalists, and should be considered as a fully integrated member of European circles of natural historians. His collection, although in part inherited, was built up over several decades by purchase and commission. In 1667 he purchased specimens from Hester Tradescant, but he also commissioned merchants and seamen to collect for him during their voyages. For many years he lived under the assumed name of Charleton, perhaps as a protection from his inherited creditors. Always available to fellow naturalists—Lister used specimens from Courten's collection in his *Historia conchyliorum* (1685–92)—soon after his return to England about 1684 Courten established his museum in a suite of ten rooms in the Temple, London, and opened it to the public in an up-to-date presentation. Sloane succeeded to this splendid collection, which formed no small part of the original foundation of the British Museum. The dried plants remain at the Natural History Museum. Courten died at Kensington on 29 March 1702, and was buried there, with an epitaph written by Sir Hans Sloane. His name is perpetuated in *Courtenia*, a genus founded by Robert Brown upon a plant from Java.

B. D. JACKSON, rev. A. J. TURNER

**Sources** A. Kippis and others, eds., *Biographia Britannica, or, The lives of the most eminent persons who have flourished in Great Britain and Ireland*, 2nd edn, 4 (1789), 334–52 · BL, Sloane MSS, 2944, 3324, 3328, 3961, 3962, 3987, 3988, 3997, 4019, 4023, 4034, 4036, 4062, 4067 · *The diary of John Evelyn*, 16 Dec 1686, 11 May 1690 · J. Evelyn, *Numismata: a discourse of medals, antient and modern* (1697), 282 · R. T. Gunther, 'The biological collections', *Early science in Oxford, 3: The biological sciences* (1925), 105, 166 · A. MacGregor, ed., *Tradescant's rarities: essays on the foundations of the Ashmolean Museum* (1983), 85–6 · R. D. Altick, *The shows of London* (1978), 14–15 · *The correspondence of John Ray*, ed. E. Lankester, Ray Society, 14 (1848) · *Further correspondence of John Ray*, ed. R. W. T. Gunther, Ray Society, 114 (1928) · C. E. Raven, *John Ray, naturalist: his life and works*, 2nd edn (1950) · C. Gibson-Wood, 'Classification and value in a seventeenth-century museum: William Courten's collection', *Journal of the History of Collections*, 9 (1997), 61–77

**Archives** BL, Sloane MSS, corresp. and papers | Bodl. Oxf., letters to John Locke

**Likenesses** oils, BM

**Courtenay**. *See also* Courtney.

**Courtenay, Edward**, first earl of Devon (*d.* 1509), magnate, was the son and heir of Sir Hugh Courtenay of Boconnoc (*d.* 1471) and his wife, Margaret, daughter and heir of Thomas Carminow. His father was nephew to Edward Courtenay, earl of Devon (*c.*1357–1419), and shared the Lancastrian loyalties of his cousins the earls. Sir Hugh was executed after the battle of Tewkesbury, at which the last earl of the senior line also died, leaving Edward as heir male to the earldom. Edward received a general pardon on 6 September 1472 and served on various local commissions from 1473 to 1477, perhaps assisted by a connection with the duke of Clarence fostered by his marriage to Elizabeth, daughter of Clarence's follower Philip Courtenay of Powderham. After Clarence's fall he remained in eclipse until 1483, when, despite promotion to the Cornwall commission of the peace, he joined in revolt against Richard III. He fled to Brittany, was attainted in 1484, and returned with Henry Tudor, who knighted him on 7 August. He fought at Bosworth and was created earl of Devon on 26 October 1485. Four days later he carried the second sword at Henry's coronation.

For the rest of the reign Devon remained a loyal but generally inconspicuous nobleman. He sat in council occasionally and attended major court functions, fought at Stoke in 1487 and on the French campaign in 1492 with a retinue of ninety-nine men, and was elected a knight of the Garter by April 1494. The landholdings restored to him in 1485 were concentrated above all in Devon, with substantial holdings in Cornwall and a scattering of manors in other southern and western counties. In 1501–2 those in Cornwall, Devon, and Somerset produced cash liveries of roughly £1025. In the south-west he was an active JP, was granted the constableship of Restormel Castle in February 1487, and was in trouble over retaining in 1494. His great test came in 1497, when he faced two waves of Cornish uprising. He seems to have done little to inhibit the march of Michael Joseph and Lord Audley to Blackheath, but in September he gathered the gentry of Devon and east Cornwall to confront Perkin Warbeck and the resurgent Cornish rebels. Forced to withdraw into Exeter, he defended the city through two days of intense fighting, on the second of which he was wounded in the arm, leaving the rebel army to march away to dissolution. Devon made his will on 27 May 1509 and died next day. He was buried at Tiverton with his wife, who had predeceased him; their gilded alabaster effigies no longer survive, but his arms are still carved in the church.

Edward Courtenay left his lands to his son **William Courtenay**, first earl of Devon (*c.*1475–1511), on the condition that he obtain the king's pardon and keep his due allegiance to the king and his heirs thereafter. This provision was necessary because Courtenay had been in prison since April 1502 and under attainder since 1504, charged with treasonable dealings with Edmund de la Pole, earl of Suffolk (d. 1513). Until his arrest Courtenay's career had been highly successful. He was made a knight of the Bath at the coronation of Elizabeth of York in 1487, and accompanied his father on the campaign of 1492. In 1495 he married the queen's younger sister, *Katherine (1479–1527), sixth daughter of *Edward IV and Elizabeth, née Woodville. He fought alongside his father in 1497, attended the Calais meeting in 1500, jousted at court in 1501 and 1502, and was paid an annuity from March 1501 for his daily and diligent attendance on the king. After Courtenay's arrest Queen Elizabeth took care of Katherine and their children, Edward, Henry, and Margaret, but Edward died in July 1502 and was followed by the queen in 1503, when Katherine was chief mourner at her funeral. In October 1507 Courtenay was transferred from the Tower of London to Calais Castle and it was said he would be executed. He was excluded from Henry VIII's accession pardon and remained in custody at Calais until at least September 1509, but Katherine was granted a pension of 200 marks by Henry VIII in July of that year and in due course her husband was released.

Courtenay returned to court life, jousting in the great Westminster tournament of February 1511. By 12 April of that year Henry had agreed to give him his father's lands and title, provided Katherine renounced her claim to the estates of the earldom of March, and on 10 May he was created earl of Devon. But before he could be invested or his attainder reversed in parliament, he died of pleurisy at Greenwich on 9 June. At the king's command he was buried with the honours due to an earl, at the London Blackfriars on 12 June. His son Henry *Courtenay (1498/9–1538) succeeded him as second earl of Devon of this new creation, and was later confirmed as successor to the 1485 earldom. His daughter Margaret married Henry, Lord Herbert, son of the earl of Worcester, in 1514, but died between 1520 and 1526. Katherine took a vow of celibacy and retired to the restored Devon estates, where she lived with a substantial household at Tiverton Castle until her death on 15 November 1527. She was buried at Tiverton but her monument too is lost.                                           S. J. GUNN

**Sources** GEC, *Peerage*, new edn, 4.328–30 · J. A. F. Thomson, 'The Courtenay family in the Yorkist period', *BIHR*, 45 (1972), 230–46 · M. Westcott, 'Katherine Courtenay, countess of Devon, 1479–1527', *Tudor and Stuart Devon … essays presented to Joyce Youings*, ed. T. Gray, M. Rowe, and A. Erskine (1992), 13–38 · S. J. Gunn, 'The courtiers of Henry VII', *EngHR*, 108 (1993), 23–49 · C. G. Bayne and W. H. Dunham, eds., *Select cases in the council of Henry VII*, SeldS, 75 (1958) · will, PRO, PROB 11/16/15 [Edward Courtenay] · will, PRO, C54/396 m.22d [William Courtenay] · W. E. Hampton, *Memorials of the Wars of the Roses: a biographical guide* (1979) · I. Arthurson, *The Perkin Warbeck conspiracy, 1491–1499* (1994) · Rymer, *Foedera*, 3rd edn, 5/4.44 · J. G. Nichols, ed., *The chronicle of Calais*, CS, 35 (1846) · A. H. Thomas and I. D. Thornley, eds., *The great chronicle of London* (1938) · *LP Henry VIII*, vol. 1 · BL, Add. MS 45131, fol. 68v

**Archives** BL, accounts 1477–8, Add. roll 64325 · PRO, accounts 1501–2, SC6/Hen VII/1096 · PRO, accounts 1507–8, SC6/Hen VII/1099

**Wealth at death** assigned landed income from estates not part of earldom of Devon £133 6s. 8d.; Devon, Cornwall, and Somerset estates produced cash liveries of about £1025 in 1501–2: will, PRO,

PROB 11/16/15 · lands restored to son valued for livery in 1528 at £1547 12s. 8d. p.a.; William Courtenay: will, PRO, C54/396 m. 22d

**Courtenay, Edward, first earl of Devon** (1526–1556), nobleman, was the second but only surviving son of Henry *Courtenay, marquess of Exeter (1498/9–1538), nobleman and courtier, and his second wife, Gertrude *Courtenay (d. 1558), daughter of William Blount, fourth Baron Mountjoy. He was a great-grandson of Edward IV, whose daughter Katherine had married his grandfather William Courtenay, earl of Devon, in 1495. Some of his earliest years were spent in the household of Mary Tudor, dowager queen of France and duchess of Suffolk, but after her death in 1533 he returned to his own family; he received private tuition from Robert Taylor of Oxford. Although Exeter had been a close companion of Henry VIII in the 1520s, he fell under increasing suspicion after the divorce crisis because of his wife's continuing support for Katherine of Aragon and his association with the disaffected Poles and Nevilles. It is interesting, in the light of his son's future ambitions, that the marquess was suspected of plotting to marry his son to Princess Mary. When the blow fell in November 1538, the twelve-year-old Edward joined his mother and father in the Tower of London. His father was executed on 9 December 1538, and Edward was to remain a prisoner—his 'diet' a regular £4 per month, but with arrangements for his tuition—for nearly fifteen years. Regarded as a serious dynastic threat, he was specifically excluded from the pardon at the beginning of Edward VI's reign.

Although some historians have seen the remnants of the Courtenay affinity at work in the western rebellion of the summer of 1549, the failure of the rebels to request Courtenay's release makes this unlikely, and there is no sign of his involvement in dissident activity in this period. In late November 1549 it was rumoured that he was to be set free as the conservatives enjoyed a brief ascendancy in the council in the wake of Protector Somerset's fall; if so, he was doubtless the victim of the reversal of fortunes which brought Northumberland and his associates to power. There is evidence in the Edwardian period of his attempt to gain favour with the regime: he dedicated to the duchess of Somerset a translation of the *Tratatto utilissimo del beneficio di Giesu Cristo crocifisso verso i Cristiani* (MS, CUL). A collaborative venture in which Reginald Pole had been involved, the *Beneficio* (c.1542) was one of the most influential works of the *spirituali*, the evangelical reformers within the Catholic church, whose Christocentric piety and ambiguous position on justification rendered them suspect to the Catholic authorities. Courtenay's interest in this work perhaps helps explain later doubts about his Catholic orthodoxy.

As a member of a family that had suffered for its Aragonese sympathies and as a fellow victim of the Edwardian regime, Courtenay was assured a swift rehabilitation by Mary. He was released from the Tower immediately on Mary's entry to her capital on 3 August 1553, created earl of Devon on 3 September, and made a knight of the Bath on 29 September. He received a sizeable grant of lands (valued at £1242 6s. 8d. p.a.) restoring much of the Courtenay inheritance on 28 September, and there were rumours that he would be made duke of York. Considerable optimism was felt about his future role. He won plaudits for his civility and bearing, and there was much enthusiasm for his intellectual accomplishments and musical interests. Pole expressed joy at his restoration, hailing him as the 'flower of the English nobility' (*Correspondence of Reginald Pole*, no. 720); his popularity among the Londoners was such that he was able to help prevent a full-scale riot at Dr Bourne's Paul's Cross sermon on 13 August; and he bore the sword of state at the coronation on 1 October.

Devon's standing made him the obvious candidate for those who wished for the queen to marry within the realm. During his imprisonment he had befriended the new lord chancellor, Stephen Gardiner, referring to him as his father. Gardiner was careful to avoid promoting Devon's case directly, but he argued vehemently against foreign entanglements. In spite of sympathy for the earl among some of her closest household officials, such as Sir Francis Englefield, Sir Robert Rochester, and Sir Edward Waldegrave, and among the nobility, Mary had no intention of marrying him and she saw very little of him in the first few weeks of the reign. His behaviour did not help his cause. Mary harboured suspicions that he was consorting with loose women; the reversal of his fortunes had clearly gone to his head, as he conducted himself arrogantly; he was reported to have threatened Geoffrey Pole with death as the man whose confession had sent his father to the block. Mary had determined on a Habsburg match, and on 29 October she secretly pledged herself to Philip II. The proposal inevitably leaked and aroused considerable anxiety (possibly stirred up by Gardiner) in parliament, which on 16 November sent a delegation to beg the queen not to marry a foreigner. Mary's angry rebuff drove several gentlemen into plotting. Over the ensuing weeks Sir James Croft, Sir Peter Carew, Sir Thomas Wyatt, and the duke of Suffolk hatched a conspiracy for simultaneous risings against the marriage in the west country (Devon's sphere of influence), Herefordshire, the midlands, and Kent. The rebels probably intended the deposition of Mary and her replacement by Elizabeth, possibly married to Devon. The extent of his involvement is unclear, and his hesitations may well help explain the lack of clarity in the rebels' objectives. The idea of a marriage between the earl and Elizabeth had some supporters at court (including Paget), who saw it as a means of neutralizing opposition to the queen's marriage, but Gardiner counselled him that he should marry the vilest woman in England rather than the queen's heretical sister, and the emperor, Charles V, had in any case vetoed the scheme in early December. Devon was in touch with Carew, and Sir Edward Rogers acted as an intermediary between him and Wyatt, but Noailles, the French ambassador, warned that he was unstable and not to be trusted, and reported a desperate plan to flee overseas, having arranged for the murder of his political opponents, Arundel and Paget. His mother, the marchioness of Exeter, high in the queen's confidence, tried to provide a steadying hand, but Devon

had seriously compromised himself by his contacts with the dissidents.

The government got wind of the conspiracy and the rebels were forced to act prematurely. Gardiner, fearing that he might be implicated by the involvement of his protégé, confronted Devon on 21 January 1554 and forced him into revealing what he knew. In the event the activity in the west country, Herefordshire, and the midlands subsided, but Sir Thomas Wyatt briefly posed a serious threat to the capital. Wyatt's defeat put the earl in a highly exposed position once again. A man 'born … to spend his life in prison' (MacCulloch, 286), he returned to the Tower on 12 February. Asked by the lieutenant of the Tower the cause of his incarceration, he replied with injured innocence, 'Truly, I cannot tell except I should accuse myselfe; lett the worlde judge' (Nichols, 59). But the noose was tightening. The Spanish ambassador Renard had become convinced that Mary would not be safe until Devon and Elizabeth were removed. Wyatt had implicated the earl in a statement before the council (albeit possibly under torture and in hope of a pardon). Devon's fortunes changed on 11 April, the day of Wyatt's execution, when there was a curious exchange between the two men. What passed between them at this interview was disputed, but the sheriffs of London who were present asserted that Wyatt had asked Devon's forgiveness for falsely accusing him. On the scaffold Wyatt dramatically exonerated both Elizabeth and Devon, much to the government's embarrassment. The earl was probably also being shielded by Gardiner, who concealed crucial evidence of his dealings with the French ambassador. The acquittal of Sir Nicholas Throckmorton on 17 April revealed the legal difficulties of proceeding against accessories. Devon was moved from the Tower to Fotheringhay on 25 May.

The earl's second confinement lasted until 6 April 1555. The regime was more confident about the succession because of the queen's supposed pregnancy, but it was felt best to get him out of the way by sending him overseas. He was at Brussels from 17 May enjoying the emperor's hospitality, but he was anxious to move on to Venice. He may not have felt entirely secure in the claustrophobic atmosphere of the imperial court, and there were regular scuffles between Spaniards and members of his household such that he came to suspect that they had been encouraged by the authorities. These suspicions may not have been unfounded. By the time he received his licence to travel to Italy in October 1555 a plot had been hatched by Philip's adviser Ruy Gómez to have him assassinated once he got there. He left Brussels on 7 November, travelling to Italy by way of Louvain, Cologne, Spires, and Augsburg and reaching Padua early in the new year. The assassination plot failed as the hired assassin had defected to the Venetian authorities. While ostensibly in Italy to refine his courtly accomplishments and to study—he ostentatiously enrolled at the University of Padua—Devon continued to associate with the regime's opponents. In the Low Countries he had established contacts with Sir Philip Hoby, a key figure in the conspiracy being organized by Sir Henry Dudley. Dudley's scheme involved the robbing of the exchequer, the murder of the queen, and her replacement by Elizabeth and Devon. In March 1556 and again in May the earl visited the duke of Ferrara, who sought to persuade him to join the group around Dudley in France. He refused to commit himself openly, but his willingness to consort with such exiles as the earl of Bedford and Sir Henry Killigrew confirmed the government's suspicions. Henri II of France maintained the pressure on him to declare his hand, offering to arrange his marriage to Mary, queen of Scots. But before these plans could come to fruition Devon died at Padua on 18 September 1556 of a fever contracted three weeks previously when caught in a storm while hawking. He was buried in the church of Sant'Antonio in Padua. The existence of an earlier plot to have him assassinated and the undoubted convenience of his demise have led to suspicions that he was poisoned. He was unfortunate that his royal blood ensured that he was the focus of repeated plots against Mary, but his years of imprisonment had not equipped him for politics, and his attempts to play both sides led to his being widely distrusted and politically ineffective.                    IAN W. ARCHER

**Sources** *CSP Spain, 1553–8* · *CSP dom.*, rev. edn, *1553–8* · *CSP Venice, 1527–58* · J. G. Nichols, ed., *The chronicle of Queen Jane, and of two years of Queen Mary*, CS, old ser., 48 (1850) · D. MacCulloch, 'The *Vita Mariae Angliae Reginae* of Robert Wingfield of Brantham', *Camden miscellany, XXVIII*, CS, 4th ser., 29 (1984), 181–301 · R. A. de Vertot, *Ambassades de messieurs de Noailles en Angleterre*, 5 vols. (Leiden, 1763) · *LP Henry VIII* · S. Caponetto, ed., *Il 'Beneficio di Christo' con le versione del secolo XVI: documenti e testimonianze* (Florence and Chicago, 1972) [includes Courtenay's translation] · GEC, *Peerage* · K. R. Bartlett, '"The misfortune that is wished for him": the life and death of Edward Courtenay, earl of Devon', *Canadian Journal of History*, 12 (1979), 1–28 · D. Loades, *Two Tudor conspiracies*, 2nd edn (1992) · J. Youings, 'The south-western rebellion of 1549', *Southern History*, 1 (1979), 99–122 · T. F. Mayer, *Reginald Pole, prince and prophet* (2000) · *CPR, 1557–8* · *The correspondence of Reginald Pole*, ed. T. F. Mayer (2002)
**Likenesses** plaster cast of lead metal, 1556 (after P. de Pastorini), NPG · attrib. S. van der Meulen, oils, Woburn Abbey, Bedfordshire · oils, repro. in D. Loades, *Mary Tudor* (1989)
**Wealth at death** est. early in Elizabeth's reign that he had been endowed by Mary with lands worth £1242 6s. 8d. p.a.: PRO, SP 12/1/64

**Courtenay** [*née* Blount], **Gertrude, marchioness of Exeter** (*d.* 1558), noblewoman and courtier, was the daughter of William *Blount, fourth Baron Mountjoy (*d.* 1534), and his first wife, Elizabeth, daughter and coheir to Sir William Say. Mountjoy, who had been tutored by Erasmus, served as chamberlain to Queen Katherine between 1512 and 1533. He was also lieutenant of Hammes, a fortress in the Calais marches. On 25 October 1519 Gertrude married, as his second wife, Henry *Courtenay, earl of Devon (1498/9–1538). Clearly the Blounts were in high favour at court: Courtenay was Henry VIII's first cousin, and a rising star within the privy chamber. The match was perhaps influenced by the recent birth of Henry Fitzroy, Henry VIII's bastard son from his liaison with Elizabeth Blount, a kinswoman of Gertrude.

All began well for the Courtenays. As countess of Devon, Gertrude attended the queen at the Field of Cloth of Gold in 1520. In 1525 Devon was created marquess of Exeter in

the same ceremony that saw Fitzroy dubbed duke of Richmond, and so Gertrude became a marchioness. Soon afterwards was born a son and heir, Edward *Courtenay (1526–1556); Henry, an earlier son, died in infancy. Royal grants of land augmented the ancestral estates in Devon, and marquess and marchioness both made regular appearances in the new year's gift rolls. When the validity of the king's marriage to Katherine of Aragon came under intense scrutiny, Henry Courtenay signed the petition of the English nobility to the pope to grant an annulment. However, both he and his wife had considerable sympathy for Katherine's cause, and they opposed the evangelicalism of Cromwell and Cranmer. Together with such prominent religious conservatives as Sir Thomas More and the countess of Salisbury, the marchioness of Exeter took an interest in the prophetic visions of Elizabeth Barton, the Canterbury nun who dared to predict King Henry's death should he repudiate Queen Katherine. Gertrude travelled in disguise to meet this Nun of Kent, and brought her to the Courtenay house at West Horsley in Surrey, where Barton experienced a trance. It was a risky association; Barton was executed for treason in 1534, and the marchioness was cited in the subsequent investigation.

Gertrude was a close friend of Queen Katherine and her daughter, Princess Mary. She regularly sent presents to Katherine, and in September 1533 was described by the imperial ambassador, Eustache Chapuys, as 'the sole consolation of the Queen and Princess' (*LP Henry VIII*, vol. 6, no. 1125). Thus the choice of the marchioness to be one of the godmothers at the christening and confirmation of Princess Elizabeth on the 10th of that month represented an attempt by Henry VIII to compel the Courtenays into a display of allegiance to the new order. Nevertheless, she continued to correspond with Princess Mary, whose house she had often visited in happier times. The execution of Queen Anne in May 1536 appeared to revive the fortunes of the Aragonese faction, and the marchioness kept Chapuys informed of developments at court. But their hopes were dashed a month later when Princess Mary was forced to recognize the royal supremacy and her own illegitimacy. In October 1537 Queen Jane was delivered of a son, and Gertrude Courtenay carried the new-born Prince Edward at his christening.

In the closing months of 1538 Cromwell struck at the conservatives with whom he had allied against Anne Boleyn two years earlier. Henry Courtenay's dominance of the privy chamber was an obstacle in the way of the principal secretary. On 5 November the marchioness was sent to the Tower, where she was to remain for the next eighteen months. Young Edward Courtenay, arrested with her, did not emerge from prison until 1553. Gertrude was interrogated about the allegedly traitorous behaviour of the marquess and the Exeter circle. Her connections with the long-dead Nun of Kent now returned to haunt her. In a letter to the king dated 30 November, Gertrude denied that she had placed any faith in Barton's prophecies, and asked forgiveness on grounds of her sex: 'I am a woman whose fragylitee and brittelnes ys suche as moost facillie easelie and lightlie ys seduced and brought in to abusion and light beliefe' (BL, Cotton MS Cleopatra E IV, fol. 94). If Gertrude thus sought the king's mercy for her husband, she petitioned in vain; Henry Courtenay was beheaded nine days later. Her own attainder for treason, without trial, was decreed by parliament in July 1539.

The years following Gertrude's release from the Tower are obscure. They were certainly lean times for the sometime marchioness, since the Courtenay estates were forfeit to the crown. Princess Mary, however, did not forget what the family had suffered on her behalf. Following her accession in 1553, Mary summoned Gertrude to court, where she was described as the queen's 'bedfellow'. Her closeness to Mary is attested by a letter of Jane Dudley, duchess of Northumberland, to Anne Paget in the wake of the Lady Jane Grey coup of July 1553. The duchess was pleading for her husband's life, and hoped that the marchioness of Exeter might intercede with the queen. While the duke of Northumberland did suffer execution, it seems that Gertrude had a role in securing the life of William Parr, marquess of Northampton, who had been Dudley's ally. The episode offers a window on the political influence wielded by the women attending Queen Mary. Gertrude went on to enjoy an honoured place in November's coronation procession.

The great issue at court, meanwhile, was the queen's marriage. The only plausible English candidate was Gertrude's son Edward, now released from the Tower and restored as earl of Devon. Courtenay had his backers, his mother among them; Simon Renard, ambassador for Charles V, feared that Gertrude's position in the privy chamber might disrupt his own plans for a match with Philip of Spain. As it turned out, Mary herself was set on the Spaniard, prompting Edward Courtenay to flirt with treason. His involvement with the plot of Sir Thomas Wyatt, Sir Peter Carew, and others resulted in his return to the Tower in February 1554. The marchioness was cast out of the court, and regained admission only in summer 1555. By this time her son had been freed and was travelling in Europe, carrying a royal licence but shadowed by agents of the Marian regime. Five letters that the marchioness wrote to Edward that year survive in the state papers. Her maternal concern for her only son is patently clear. She warns him against sin and evil company, yearns for news of his health, and chides him for not writing to his mother by his own hand. The last of her letters, dated November 1555, complains of colic and the stone. Gertrude lived long enough, however, to mourn Edward's mysterious death in Padua in September 1556.

The marchioness of Exeter made her will on 25 September 1558. She directed that a dirige and a trental of masses be sung at her burial and year's mind, and that monies should be distributed among the poor to pray for her husband and her own soul. Such Catholic obsequies, revived under Queen Mary, were very soon to disappear with Elizabeth's accession. Gertrude died shortly thereafter, and was buried in Wimborne Minster in Dorset. Her sole executor was Anthony Harvey, her husband's old surveyor.

J. P. D. COOPER

**Sources** GEC, *Peerage* · BL, Cotton MS Cleopatra E IV, fols. 94–5 · *LP Henry VIII*, vols. 3–21 · *CSP dom.* · H. Miller, *Henry VIII and the English nobility* (1986) · D. Loades, *Mary Tudor: a life*, pbk edn (1992) · C. Merton, 'The women who served Queen Mary and Queen Elizabeth: ladies, gentlewomen and maids of the privy chamber, 1553–1603', PhD diss., U. Cam., 1992 · E. W. Ives, *Anne Boleyn* (1986) · B. A. Murphy, *Bastard prince: Henry VIII's lost son* (2001) · S. J. Gunn, 'A letter of Jane, duchess of Northumberland, in 1553', *EngHR*, 114 (1999), 1267–71 · will, PRO, PROB 11/40. sig. 1 · K. R. Bartlett, 'The misfortune that is wished for him: the exile and death of Edward Courtenay, earl of Devon', *Canadian Journal of History*, 14 (1979), 1–28
**Wealth at death** see will, PRO, PROB 11/40, sig. 1

**Courtenay, Henry**, marquess of Exeter (1498/9–1538), nobleman and courtier, was the eldest surviving son of William *Courtenay, earl of Devon (*c.*1475–1511) [*see under* Courtenay, Edward (*d.* 1509)], and *Katherine (1479–1527), sixth daughter of Edward IV and Elizabeth, *née* Woodville.

**Royal cousin** Courtenay's lineage proved to be both his blessing and his curse. His family had deep roots in Devon and Cornwall, but Henry's blood mingled the royal with the noble. His paternal grandfather Edward *Courtenay of Boconnoc (*d.* 1509) was created earl of Devon for his defection from Richard III and support of Henry of Richmond in 1485. Another mark of Tudor favour came in 1495 when Edward Courtenay's son William married Katherine, the younger sister of Henry VII's wife, Elizabeth. But William's period of attendance on the king and jousting at court came to an abrupt end in April 1502, when he was sent to the Tower for conspiring against Henry with his wife's cousin, the Yorkist pretender Edmund de la Pole, earl of Suffolk. Henry Courtenay's earliest memories would thus have been of his father in disgrace, attainted in 1504 and later imprisoned in Calais under threat of execution. The queen supported her close kin through these difficult days: her privy purse accounts for 1502/3 record the servants, nurses, food, and clothes provided for Henry and his sister Margaret. Courtenay appears to have received an education befitting his rank. He was tutored by Giles Duwes, who taught French to all Henry VII's children, and in Henry VIII's reign he was described as 'the king's neer kinsman, and hath been brought up of a childe with his grace in his chamber' (Miller, 85).

Having been released soon after Henry VIII's accession, William Courtenay died within a month of his creation as earl of Devon in 1511. Henry, the second earl, secured the reversal of his father's attainder the following year. His fortunes continued to improve as he grew older. He entered the ceremonial life of the court in 1514, when he was chosen by Louis XII of France to attend Queen Mary in the diplomatic negotiations of that year. Henry VIII plainly enjoyed the company of his younger kinsman, and Courtenay rose to a position of prominence among the king's gentle companions. By 1519 he was one of the select band afforded daily livery and apartments within the royal household, and his accounts record the winter sport of the court at Greenwich: indoor tennis and shuffleboard, and a snowball fight with the king. When not at play, Courtenay had his boatman ferry him upstream for dinner with Charles Brandon and confession at the Savoy Chapel. In 1520, as he came of age, his easy intimacy with his royal cousin was formalized when he became a gentleman of the privy chamber and was sworn of the council. Together with the duke of Suffolk and the marquess of Dorset, Courtenay excelled in feats of arms at the Field of Cloth of Gold in 1520, and the same trio led the jousts honouring the emperor Charles V's visit to England in 1522. In 1521 he was invested with the Garter, and he became constable of Windsor in 1525. Another demonstration of the king's friendship came at Corpus Christi the same year, when Courtenay was led into the royal presence by Suffolk and Dorset to be created marquess of Exeter. This was only the eighth marquessate to have existed in the English peerage, and was granted on the same occasion that Henry Fitzroy became duke of Richmond. When Wolsey sought to rein in the privy chamber by the Eltham ordinances of 1526, Exeter kept his position at the king's demand—the only point on which the cardinal did not have his own way.

Courtenay married twice. His first bride was Elizabeth, daughter of John Grey, second Viscount Lisle, and *suo jure* Baroness Lisle by the death of her father. Her wardship had initially been purchased by Charles Brandon, but was subsequently acquired by Katherine, countess of Devon, for £4000. Henry married Elizabeth some time after June 1515; she died in 1519, aged only about fourteen. On 25 October 1519 he married his second wife, Gertrude *Courtenay (d. 1558), daughter of William Blount, fourth Baron Mountjoy, lieutenant of Hammes and the queen's chamberlain. Gertrude's Catholic piety, which led her into a risky association with the Nun of Kent in 1533, echoed the religious conservatism of her husband. Their first son, Henry, died young, leaving their second son, Edward *Courtenay (1526–1556), heir to the title.

**West-country landowner** Although recognized as earl of Devon on his father's death, Henry Courtenay had to wait another fifteen years before receiving his full inheritance. The first earl was able to bequeath his son the Boconnoc lands, six manors in Cornwall and five in Devon, but the more substantial estates of the earldom of Devon were granted to Henry's mother for life in 1512. Katherine lived on until 1527, compelling him to rely on his cousin's princely generosity to support him in the life of a noble courtier. Like the lesser men around him, Courtenay had to play the patronage game, although his proximity to the king left him better placed than most. He had his first royal grant of land in 1521. The Cornish manor of Caliland and the keepership of Birling in Kent followed in 1522, and his marquessate was supported by the gift of Dartington in Devon and the constableship of Restormel in Cornwall. He also benefited from Buckingham's fall, taking over the duke's London houses in St Laurence Poultney and All Hallows. Nor did his traditional religion prevent Courtenay from accepting a favourable lease of the Augustinian priory of Breamore, Hampshire, on its dissolution in 1536.

With the death of his mother Courtenay, who was now in his twenty-ninth year, added thirty-four Devon manors and twelve in Cornwall to his Boconnoc inheritance, and another sixteen between Dorset and Hampshire. He had already become high steward of the duchy of Cornwall and lord warden of the stannaries in 1523; now he was a west-country landowner on the grand scale. Yet the local power of this ancient family had waned since the high days of the fourteenth century, when the Courtenays had nominated knights of the shire and commanded an impressive force of armed retainers. Like his father before him, the marquess of Exeter chose the life of a courtier over that of a provincial nobleman. He continued to maintain his Devon houses: Colcombe Castle near Colyton, Columbjohn in Broadclyst, and his fine residence at Tiverton, described in 1538 as 'the head and chief mansion house, moated, walled and embattled round like a castle, with all manner of houses of offices and lodgings within the same' (Westcott, 'Katherine Courtenay', 24). But from the early 1530s the Courtenays were resident at West Horsley, Surrey; this was the house that featured in the accusations that prompted the downfall of the Exeter circle. Although taking a personal interest in ecclesiastical patronage, the marquess generally delegated his affairs in Devon and Cornwall to a network of bailiffs, stewards, and client gentlemen. Such a man was Sir Thomas Denys, detailed by Courtenay to investigate the Exeter women who rioted in defence of St Nicholas's Priory in 1536. The marquess commanded great respect and deference in the western shires, but was not the resident magnate that his Courtenay grandfather had been. The survey of Tiverton Castle in 1528 significantly noted that the best of the plate and stable equipment was being transported to London for the marquess's use.

**Conspirator and Catholic** If the royal court provided the backdrop for Henry Courtenay's jousting triumphs, then it was also the scene of his downfall and the destruction of his house. His mistake was to enter a world of faction and politics in which he was outclassed by Thomas Cromwell: an *éminence grise* by Courtenay's reckoning, but no less deadly for that. The relationship between them, the one pre-eminent in the privy chamber and the other commanding the privy council, was sufficiently strained to set a rumour circulating in Somerset in 1537 that Courtenay had been sent to the Tower for stabbing Cromwell with a dagger. The two men co-operated in the successful plot against Anne Boleyn in 1536, but Cromwell was lighter on his feet than his temporary allies in the Aragonese faction, promptly accusing Courtenay and Sir Nicholas Carew of favouring Princess Mary as Henry VIII's successor. The king forced Exeter into a public display of loyalty by placing him in the cavalry vanguard sent against the northern insurgents later that year, to the intense distress of the marchioness. Yet the Courtenays had clearly returned to a position of trust by 1537: Prince Edward was carried to his Hampton Court baptism by the marchioness on 15 October, and her husband served as an attendant in the king's absence.

One year later the marquess of Exeter was suddenly arrested on a charge of treason. His alleged accomplices were his friends Sir Edward Neville and Henry Pole, Lord

Montague, whose brother Sir Geoffrey Pole was the principal informant against them. The three were charged with desiring the king's death and seeking to deprive him of his title as supreme head of the church. They were also accused of conspiring with Reginald Pole, the exiled brother of Henry and Geoffrey and the only English cardinal, whose dream it was to reclaim England for the Roman church. Multiple interrogations of the alleged traitors and their households during November 1538 focused on conversations held in private, admissible as evidence of traitorous intent since the Act of Treasons of 1534. Typical were the words reported to have been spoken by Exeter to Montague in August 1536: 'I trust ones to have a faire day upon these knaves which rule abowte the kyng; and I trust to se a mery woreld oone day' (PRO, KB 8/11/2). The interrogators made much of loose talk among Courtenay's affinity in Devon and Cornwall in 1531 that the marquess was heir apparent to the throne, a claim which had prompted the king briefly to eject him from the privy chamber in that year. This whiff of past treason was seized upon by Richard Morison, one of Cromwell's most favoured propagandists, when he came to chronicle the 'Exeter conspiracy' in his *An Invective Ayenste the Great and Detestable Vice, Treason* of 1539. Morison trumpeted the events of 1531 as proof that Exeter and his companions had been engaged in a Romish plot with Cardinal Pole in 1538. The truth behind the 1531 allegations is more prosaic: Exeter had been intervening in a private dispute on the part of his father-in-law, Lord Mountjoy, and was awarded huge damages in 1534 against a Cornishman who had accused him of unlawful retaining.

Its roots in Tudor royal propaganda, the claim that Courtenay was at the core of a 1538 conspiracy to overthrow Henry VIII was elaborated by the Victorian historian J. A. Froude, who wrote that the Courtenays were 'petty sovereigns in Devonshire and Cornwall', commanding a party that was 'on all grounds, religious, political, and historical, the most dangerous which could be formed' (Froude, 3.131). Yet there is no evidence that Courtenay contemplated armed insurrection, either in 1538 or earlier, even assuming that he was capable of mustering tenants and tinners from south-western estates where he had spent little enough time as lord. The marquess had benefited greatly from his proximity to his sovereign, to whom he almost certainly had a genuine sense of loyalty. This sense of allegiance did not extend to Cromwell, whose 1536 religious injunctions were inflicting severe damage upon a Catholic devotional world which Exeter, his friends, and his marchioness all held dear. This antipathy towards the lord privy seal, combined with a certain sympathy for Reginald Pole, left Exeter vulnerable to the unfounded accusations of treachery levelled against him in 1538. Cromwell chose the right moment to strike: Charles V and François I were considering cementing their truce of July 1538 with an invasion of heretic England, circumstances in which Exeter and especially Montague could plausibly be slandered as a potential fifth column.

The poison once administered, the end came quickly.

Having been indicted and found guilty by his peers in Westminster Hall on 3 December, Courtenay was beheaded with Montague on Tower Hill on 9 December 1538. The manner of his death befitted his noble status; some of his humble retainers were not so lucky, dispatched as common traitors. Within months Sir Nicholas Carew was also dead, arrested and executed on a charge of favouring the designs of the late marquess. Attainder in parliament was followed by the systematic dismantling of the house of Courtenay of Boconnoc. Exeter was formally degraded from the Garter, his arms 'throwne downe'. His lands, houses, and goods were carefully inventoried by the crown, right down to the insignia of the Garter and Edward Courtenay's little gilt sword contained in the inner wardrobe of the marquess's London house. Courtenay manors were assumed into the duchy of Cornwall or regranted to Henry VIII's new man in the west country, John, Lord Russell, who took his place as lord warden of the stannaries.

Careful record keeping on the part of the crown offers a window into the household of an earlier Tudor nobleman and courtier. Music had enjoyed a favoured place at the marquess's house at West Horsley, where there were a double virginal, three pairs of regals (a kind of small organ), and nine viols in 1538. Courtenay also kept hawks there. Among his 103 yeomen and grooms of the chamber were Roger Eleys, a stannary bailiff who shot well with a handgun; William Boothe, who could sing three-man songs; and William Tremayle, his fool. Several of them were good Cornish wrestlers. Like other senior peers, Courtenay patronized a troupe of players who performed at court. More sinister in the eyes of the crown was the manuscript copy of Thomas More's 'Richard III', a study in tyrannical kingship, in the possession of the Exeter circle.

The popular Catholic uprising in the south-west in 1549 offers an intriguing epilogue to Henry Courtenay's story, in that several of the gentlemen and clergy prominent in the rebellion had been members of the late marquess's affinity in Devon and Cornwall. The conservative cleric Richard Crispin, whose release from the Tower was demanded by the rebels, had been Courtenay's chaplain and was involved in the affair of the Nun of Kent. The rebel captain John Bury had also been in Exeter's service and was now a servant of Sir Thomas Denys. Denys himself, who was undoubtedly sympathetic to the rebels, had been loyal to the marquess; and another gentleman who attempted to parley with the rebels, Anthony Harvey, had been Courtenay's surveyor and would be the marchioness's sole executor. That the Devon uprising began in the village of Sampford Courtenay implies that the marquess of Exeter's stand for traditional religion was locally honoured a decade after his death. Although the attainder was reversed in Mary's reign to allow the Devon title to pass to Edward Courtenay, the earldom fell into abeyance after his death until the House of Lords finally declared it to rest in the Powderham branch of the Courtenay family in 1831. J. P. D. COOPER

**Sources** GEC, *Peerage*, 4.330–31 · king's bench, baga de secretis, PRO, KB 8/11/1–8/11/3 · state papers, general series, Henry VIII, PRO, SP 1/121/67; SP 1/140/3–1/140/4 · *LP Henry VIII*, vol. 13/2 · R. Morison, *An invective ayenste the great and detestable vice, treason* (1539) · J. A. Froude, *History of England*, 12 vols. (1856–70), vol. 3 · M. H. Dodds and R. Dodds, *The Pilgrimage of Grace, 1536–1537, and the Exeter conspiracy, 1538*, 2 (1915), 277–327 · H. Miller, *Henry VIII and the English nobility* (1986) · M. R. Westcott, 'The estates of the earls of Devon, 1485–1538', MA diss., Exeter University, 1958 · M. Westcott, 'Katherine Courtenay, countess of Devon, 1479–1527', *Tudor and Stuart Devon … essays presented to Joyce Youings*, ed. T. Gray, M. Rowe, and A. Erskine (1992), 13–38 · D. Starkey, *The English court* (1987) · J. Youings, 'The south-western rebellion of 1549', *Southern History*, 1 (1979), 99–122 · J. P. D. Cooper, 'Propaganda, allegiance and sedition in the Tudor south-west, *c.*1497–1570', DPhil diss., U. Oxf., 1999, 133–52

**Courtenay, Henry Reginald** (1741–1803), bishop of Exeter, was born in the parish of St James's, Piccadilly, London, on 27 November 1741, the eldest surviving son of Henry Reginald Courtenay (1714–1763), tory MP for Honiton from 1741 to 1747 and 1754 to 1763, and his wife, Catherine (*d.* 1783), daughter of Allen Bathurst, first Earl Bathurst. He was admitted to Westminster School in 1751, and was elected a king's scholar in 1755. He matriculated at Christ Church, Oxford, on 19 June 1759. He took the degrees of BA in 1763, MA in 1766, and DCL in 1774. He was a tutor at Christ Church from 1763 to 1768, but, having taken orders, some valuable preferment speedily came to him. He was rector of Sapperton, Gloucestershire, from 1768 to 1773, when he received the living of Lee in Kent and a prebendal stall in Rochester Cathedral. On 26 January 1774 he married Lady Elizabeth Howard (*d.* 1815), eldest daughter of Thomas Howard, second earl of Effingham; they had two sons and four daughters. Their eldest son, William, sometime clerk assistant to parliament, successfully claimed the sixteenth-century earldom of Devon in 1831 on behalf of a kinsman, and himself became tenth earl of Devon in 1835. A younger son was Thomas Peregrine *Courtenay.

Also in 1774 Courtenay was appointed to the valuable living of St George's, Hanover Square, and became a chaplain-in-ordinary to George III. He vacated his prebend at Rochester in 1774, but he held a prebendal stall at Exeter from 1772 to 1794, and another at Rochester from 1783 to 1797. In January 1794 Courtenay's word was cited in evidence during the privy council inquiry into the invalid marriage of Prince Augustus Frederick, son of George III, and Lady Augusta Murray, which had been solemnized at St George's, Hanover Square, by his curate, John Downes. No blame was attached to Courtenay, and later that year he was nominated to the diocese of Bristol, and was consecrated on 11 May. He moved to the more lucrative see of Exeter on 10 March 1797. He was at the same time archdeacon of Exeter and maintained his London rectory until his death.

Several of Courtenay's sermons for charities and on state occasions were printed between 1795 and 1802, notably his charge to the clergy of the diocese of Bristol on the visitation of 1795, which was a robust defence of established religion. There was a corresponding charge to the clergy of Exeter in 1799. He died at Lower Grosvenor

Henry Reginald Courtenay (1741–1803), by John Downman, 1801

Street, London, on 9 June 1803, and was buried in the cemetery of the Grosvenor Chapel.

Richard Polwhele includes a letter from the bishop in his memoirs and observes of him:

> once only he visited his clergy and in private companies, wherever he went, all was solemn silence; of this I was myself a witness at several houses. But in his letters he was perfectly unreserved. Hence it may be inferred that his disinclination to talk either with clergymen or laymen was attributable to indisposition, rather than the proud feeling of superiority. (Polwhele, 2.536–7)

W. P. COURTNEY, rev. ANDREW ROBINSON

**Sources** Nichols, *Lit. anecdotes*, 9.158, 184 · *Fasti Angl.* (Hardy), 1.221, 383, 397, 430, 432; 2.584, 586 · G. Oliver, *Lives of the bishops of Exeter, and a history of the cathedral* (1861), 165, 274 · *GM*, 1st ser., 73 (1803), 602 · Burke, *Peerage* (1999) · J. Welch, *The list of the queen's scholars of St Peter's College, Westminster*, ed. [C. B. Phillimore], new edn (1852), 362, 366, 372, 410 · R. Polwhele, *Traditions and recollections; domestic, clerical and literary*, 2 (1826), 536–7 · R. Hole, *Pulpit, politics and public order in England, 1760–1832* (1989), 126 · *The later correspondence of George III*, ed. A. Aspinall, 5 vols. (1962–70) · *Old Westminsters* · Foster, *Alum. Oxon.* · E. Cruickshanks, 'Courtenay, Henry Reginald', HoP, *Commons, 1715–54*

**Likenesses** J. Downman, drawing, 1801; Christies, 19 June 1979, lot 86 [*see illus.*]

**Courtenay, John** (1738–1816), politician, was born in Carlingford, co. Louth, Ireland, on 22 August 1738, the second son of Henry Courtney (1693–1772?), revenue officer, of Newry, co. Down, and Mary (*bap.* 1700), daughter of the Revd William Major, prebendary of Ballymore, co. Armagh, and Charity Leigh. He claimed descent from a member of the Courtenay family of Powderham, Devon, who had settled in Ireland in Elizabeth's reign. Having been educated at Dundalk grammar school from 1748 he entered the army at Waterford as ensign in the 29th foot in

1756, and was promoted lieutenant in 1759. Later he became a recruiting officer at Manchester and at Belfast. He sold out in 1765, was made a commissioner for Irish musters, and settled at Black Rock, near Dublin; about the same time he married Esther (d. 1795). Having won the approval of the viceroy, Viscount Townshend, with a pamphlet in defence of a court martial, he contributed essays to a government journal, *The Batchelor*, a selection of which were published in 1772. In 1769, needing money, he sold his commissionership for £2175. He was appointed barrack master of Kinsale in 1772, a post worth £400 a year, but left Ireland with Townshend in the same year and in 1773 became secretary to him in his role as master-general of the Ordnance. In 1774 he visited Paris. The author of *The Rape of Pomona*, an elegy in Augustan rhyming couplets, Courtenay frequented London literary society, attaching himself to James Boswell as a fellow admirer of Samuel Johnson, on whose character he later published *A Poetical Review* (1786).

In 1780 Courtenay was returned to parliament for Tamworth, on Townshend's interest, allegedly as a stopgap candidate. He supported Lord North's administration, which preserved his seat but cost him his office in 1782. After opposing Shelburne he supported the Fox–North coalition, which restored him briefly to the Ordnance, as surveyor-general and secretary to Townshend, in 1783; he then joined the opposition to Pitt the younger. In 1787 Townshend went over to Pitt but allowed the impoverished Courtenay to retain his seat. He joined Brooks's Club and the Whig Club in 1788 and attended the Commons regularly, ever keen to make the members laugh with his sharp wit. This was easy on non-political subjects but, over-egging the pudding in his attempts to ambush ministers, he was obliged to apologize to Pitt on 15 May 1787 for the intemperance of his speech against Warren Hastings, of whose impeachment he became a manager.

Courtenay reproached Pitt on 25 May 1792 for abandoning parliamentary reform but ten days later, influenced by Fox, he deserted the radical Friends of the People. However, he remained a Friend of the Liberty of the Press. As the author of *Philosophical reflections on the late revolution in France and the conduct of the dissenters in England* (1790), and as a visitor to Paris in the autumn of 1792, he assailed Edmund Burke both in the Commons on 15 December 1792, and in print, in his *Poetical and Philosophical Essay on the French Revolution* (1793). During the period 1793–7 he frequently criticized the war with revolutionary France, as well as religious bigotry and the suppression of civil liberty at home, although his tone of coarse levity sometimes misfired. He ridiculed nostalgia for the *ancien régime* in *The Present State of the Manners, Arts, and Politics of France and Italy* (1794) and was caricatured by Sayers and Gillray as a revolutionary. In 1795 his wife committed suicide; they had three sons and five daughters, as well as three children who died in infancy.

From 1796 Courtenay sat for Appleby as Lord Thanet's nominee. Having voted for parliamentary reform on 26 May 1797 he seceded with the Foxites but returned occasionally to oppose Pitt's taxes, to vote against his renewed suspension of habeas corpus, and to champion his friend Edward Despard, a political prisoner. In 1800 he published *The Campaign*, lampooning the Dutch expedition, and voted against the refusal to negotiate peace. A critic of the Irish Act of Union, he called for compensatory Catholic relief, on 16 March 1801. His political rancour was abated when Pitt was replaced by Addington but it was revived by William Windham's decision to revoke his gift to Courtenay of the qualification for a parliamentary seat. He was fortunate, however, in that the late duke of Bedford's contribution to him of £200 a year was continued by his successor, and Thanet supplied the deficit in his income. Furthermore he was not averse to asking for public recompense for his Ordnance services, in the debate on 15 December 1802; and his support for the debt-ridden prince of Wales secured his son Kenneth a chaplaincy. He joined Fox in deploring the resumption of war with France in 1803, voted steadily with the opposition that felled Addington in 1804, and opposed the restored Pitt. His political associates engineered an annual subscription for him in 1805, and his situation was alleviated when the Foxites came to power in 1806 and placed him on the Treasury board. He did not press for the Ordnance or, as feared, for a privy councillorship. In January 1807 he declined the Ordnance treasurership, pleading poverty, whereupon Lord Grenville promised him the equivalent of his Treasury salary. Courtenay probably encouraged Thanet to make difficulties about his re-election at Appleby to prevent his transfer from the Treasury board to the Ordnance. He forfeited office when the ministry fell in March 1807. His last speech, on 24 February, had been in favour of the abolition of the slave trade; on 9 April he voted against his colleagues' dismissal.

The dissolution of 1807 found Courtenay weary of parliament and in Scotland, seeking a place or pension, with his mother's Scots ancestry as pretext. He was recalled to Appleby, where the Thanet interest was threatened. In the event he was enabled to forgo the seat and pocket £4000 for its sale. He still received £300 a year from his friends' annuity of 1805. Even so, he remained needy. His *Characteristic sketches of some of the most distinguished speakers in the House of Commons since 1780* (1808), a potboiler, was followed by *Incidental Anecdotes and a Biographical Sketch* (1809) and *Verses* (1811), addressed to the prince regent in the hope of winning a pension. Thanet again returned him for Appleby in 1812, to stave off creditors, but the seat was soon wanted for the more eligible George Tierney. Courtenay resisted, while admitting to his chief that he was 'almost worn out', having been, at best 'only an occasional skirmishing Cossack' (Grey MSS, 5 Nov 1812). A compensatory subscription raised by aristocratic whigs winkled him out on 16 December. Having suffered an apoplectic stroke in 1813 he died in London on 24 March 1816. In his will, dated 16 May 1815, he acknowledged that its modest provisions could scarcely be met.

ROLAND THORNE

**Sources** J. Courtenay, *Incidental anecdotes and a biographical sketch* (1809) · M. M. Drummond, 'Courtenay, John', HoP, *Commons, 1754–90* · R. G. Thorne, 'Courtenay, John', HoP, *Commons, 1790–1820* · *GM,*

1st ser., 86/1 (1816), 467 · *The historical and the posthumous memoirs of Sir Nathaniel William Wraxall, 1772–1784*, ed. H. B. Wheatley, 5 vols. (1884), vol. 2, pp. 85, 312; vol. 3, p. 453 · Cobbett, *Parl. hist.* · *Hansard 1* · Farington, *Diary*, 2.466; 8.3058 · Walpole, *Corr.*, 29.34, 47, 94, 104, 116 · *The manuscripts of J. B. Fortescue*, 10 vols., HMC, 30 (1892–1927), vol. 5, p. 466; vol. 8, p. 115 · *The Creevey papers*, ed. H. Maxwell, 1 (1903), 184 · Boswell, *Life*, 1.62, 222–3, 479; 2.268; 4.465 · will, PRO, PROB 11/1582, sig. 353 · U. Durham L., archives and special collections, Grey of Howick collection
**Archives** BL, Fortescue MSS, letters to Lord Grenville · Blair Adam, Fife, Blair Adam MSS, letters to William Adam · NRA, priv. coll., corresp. with brother-in-law, Laurence Campbell, and verses on political events · U. Durham L., Grey MSS
**Likenesses** J. Sayers, caricature, etching, pubd 1786, NPG · J. Sayers, caricature, etching, pubd 1788, NPG · J. Sayers, caricature, etching, 1794, BM, NPG · J. Gillray, caricature, etching, pubd 1798, NPG · J. Sayers, caricature, etching (*The impeachment*), NPG
**Wealth at death** under £300: PRO, death duty registers, IR 26/670; will, PRO, PROB 11/1582, sig. 353

**Courtenay, Peter** (*c*.1432–1492), bishop of Winchester, was the third son of Sir Philip Courtenay of Powderham (*d*. 1463), the head of a junior branch of the family of the earls of Devon, and his wife, Elizabeth, daughter of Walter, first Baron Hungerford of Hungerford (*d*. 1449). Courtenay initially studied at Oxford, where he was admitted bachelor of civil law in 1457, having studied for three years in the arts and for three years and one term in civil law. In November 1457 he matriculated in the faculty of law in Cologne. By April 1461 he was studying law at Padua, where he was elected rector, and was able to put the financial affairs of the studium on a sound footing. There is no record of his admission to a doctorate of canon law, but he probably did take the degree since Oxford was to offer him incorporation as DCnL in October 1478.

Courtenay was already a considerable pluralist. In 1448 he became a prebendary of both Salisbury and Wells and was granted a papal dispensation to hold two incompatible benefices, notwithstanding that he was aged only about sixteen. In 1452 he became rector of Diptford, Devon, and in the following year was made rector of Moreton Hampstead and archdeacon of Exeter. Further appointments followed, including prebends at Lincoln (1463) and Beverley (*c*.1471). In 1464 he was appointed archdeacon of Wiltshire and provost of St Edmund's, Salisbury. In 1470 he became master of St Anthony's Hospital, London. He was dean of Exeter from October 1476 to March 1477, and in April 1477 became dean of Windsor. On 9 September 1478 he was provided by the pope to the see of Exeter, received his temporalities on 3 November, and on 8 November was consecrated by Bishop Thomas Kemp of London at St Stephen's Chapel, Westminster, where Courtenay had been dean since 1472.

Courtenay's ecclesiastical advancement accompanied a successful political career. The Powderham Courtenays, unlike the senior line, supported the house of York, and Peter Courtenay promptly entered the service of Edward IV. The last reference to him in Padua is in January 1462. In June 1462 he was back in England and was commissioned by the king to offer the Garter to the duke of Milan. By November 1463 he was acting as Edward's proctor in the papal curia. In the late 1460s he and his elder brother

Philip were associated with Edward's brother George, duke of Clarence (*d*. 1478), who held the estates in the south-west forfeited in 1461 by Thomas Courtenay, sixth earl of Devon. The two brothers followed Clarence into opposition in 1470. During the readeption of Henry VI Peter Courtenay became that king's secretary, but accompanied Clarence back into the Yorkist camp in 1471. By March 1472 he had become Edward's secretary, a post he still held in May 1474. He was described as a royal councillor in 1477–8.

After the death of Edward IV, Courtenay was initially seen as an ally by Richard, duke of Gloucester. In May 1483 he was commissioned to deliver Richard's niece, the young Anne of Exeter, to the custody of the duke of Buckingham, and on 27 June (the day after Richard's assumption of the throne) Courtenay was present when Richard gave the great seal to John Russell, bishop of Lincoln (*d*. 1494). He subsequently reconsidered his allegiance and, with his younger brother Walter and a number of his cathedral clergy, supported the rising of autumn 1483 in favour of Henry Tudor. When the rising collapsed he escaped to join Tudor in exile in Vannes, Brittany. He was attainted and his temporalities forfeited in Richard III's parliament of January 1484. Courtenay returned to England with Tudor and was welcomed back by Oxford University, who wrote rejoicing that he had weathered the storm. On 8 September he was appointed keeper of the privy seal. He was given a place of honour at Henry's coronation as one of the two bishops who supported the king throughout the ceremony. Courtenay was present at the first parliament of Henry VII, where the sentences against him and the other rebels of 1483 were reversed, on 7 November 1485, and where he served as trier of Gascon petitions. On 29 January 1487 he was provided to the see of Winchester following the death of William Waynflete, receiving the temporalities on 2 April. He had ceased to be keeper of the privy seal by the end of February, the office going to Richard Fox (*d*. 1528), who also succeeded him at Exeter.

The surviving evidence suggests that Courtenay was a conscientious diocesan at both Exeter and Winchester, who conducted ordinations in person where possible, and might secure the services of a temporary suffragan to confer orders in his absence. He seems to have co-operated with Bishop Thomas Langton of Salisbury (*d*. 1501) in the latter's pursuit of Lollards—the prosecution of Richard Pitfin in 1491, apparently initiated by Langton, was concluded by Pitfin's abjuring his errors before Courtenay. The fact that Courtenay employed no vicar-general as bishop of Winchester no doubt reflects the considerable amount of time he was resident in his diocese. Nevertheless he continued to play a role in court life. He was present at the ratification of the treaty with Spain on 23 September 1490, and was a witness to the creation of Arthur as prince of Wales on 29 November following. Courtenay died on 23 September 1492 and was buried in his cathedral at the east end of the crypt below the lady chapel, where his coffin was found during restoration work in the 1880s. Courtenay had remodelled the lady chapel, adding a new eastern bay. He had also undertaken rebuilding at Exeter, where he is traditionally credited with completing the north tower and installing the astronomical clock, which still survives, although much restored, in the north transept.                                         ROSEMARY HORROX

**Sources** *Chancery records* • *CEPR letters*, vols. 12–15 • Emden, *Oxf.* • J. Otway-Ruthven, *The king's secretary and the signet office in the XV century* (1939) • G. Pengo, ed., *Acta graduum academicorum gymnasii Patavini, 1461–1470*, Fonti per la storia dell'università di Padova, 13 (1992) • R. J. Mitchell, 'English students at Padua, 1460–75', *TRHS*, 4th ser., 19 (1936), 101–18 • C. L. Scofield, *The life and reign of Edward the Fourth*, 2 vols. (1923) • R. Horrox, *Richard III, a study of service*, Cambridge Studies in Medieval Life and Thought, 4th ser., 11 (1989) • R. A. Griffiths and R. S. Thomas, *The making of the Tudor dynasty* (1987) • H. Anstey, ed., *Epistolae academicae Oxon.*, 2, OHS, 36 (1898) • F. Bussby, *Winchester Cathedral, 1079–1979* (1979) • R. T. W. McDermid, *Beverley Minster fasti: being biographical notes on the provosts, prebendaries, officers and vicars in the church of Beverley prior to the dissolution*, Yorkshire Archaeological Society, 149 (1993) • J. A. F. Thomson, *The early Tudor church and society, 1485–1529* (1993) • J. A. F. Thomson, *The later Lollards, 1414–1520* (1965)
**Archives** Devon RO, register

**Courtenay, Richard** (*c.*1381–1415), bishop of Norwich, was probably born at Powderham Castle, Devon, the son of Sir Philip Courtenay of Powderham and his wife, Anne, daughter of Sir Thomas Wake of Blisworth, Northamptonshire. His father was one of the youngest of the seventeen children of Hugh Courtenay, earl of Devon (*d.* 1377) and Margaret de Bohun, granddaughter of *Edward I, who left Richard a silver vessel worth £100 in 1391. She was also great-aunt, and a rare surviving relative, of Henry IV's first wife, Mary de Bohun (*d.* 1394), the final coheir of their family and mother of *Henry V, a tie that may have proved very significant for her grandson. Courtenay's uncles included Archbishop William *Courtenay, who called him 'my dearest child and foster son' and left him a mitre in 1396 against his becoming a bishop (Dahmus, 269). One brother, William, died young and the other, Sir John, was possibly younger than himself. There were two sisters.

Courtenay became a prebendary in Wingham College, Kent, on 1 November 1392 by the gift of his uncle William at about the age of eleven, and dean of South Malling College, Sussex, by the same route on 23 February 1395. He had collected five more prebends by then, and yet on 29 April 1395 his uncle secured a papal dispensation for him to have two more benefices, which he duly obtained. At this time, it might be noted, his uncle was still not sure that Courtenay would confirm his proposed career in the church or even go to university. In the event, he took orders in his native diocese, as subdeacon on 15 May 1399 and as priest on 18 December 1400, with a papal dispensation for his youth. Not everyone was pleased with his swift progress. Bishop Robert Rede declared him contumacious for failing to appear either in person or by proctor for the visitation of Chichester Cathedral in June 1397, where he was now precentor (until May 1407). He did submit a proctor for the bishop's visitation in 1403, only to be ordered to repair the property of the precentorship or suffer sequestration. He became dean of St Asaph by royal grant on 16 May 1402, perhaps an early sign of his friendship with Prince Henry and arising from the latter's campaign to hold north Wales against Owain Glyn Dŵr. He had resigned by February 1404, however, the Welsh rebels having overrun the cathedral. On 1 June 1403 Courtenay was collated by Bishop Henry Beaufort, a mutual friend of himself and the prince at Oxford, to the archdeaconry of Northampton, a lucrative sinecure. He added the deanship of Wells by election on 26 May 1410, which he may at least have inspected occasionally while travelling to and from his family home in Devon.

Meanwhile, Courtenay had been taking academic study very seriously. He was BCL of Oxford by 1399, and licensed to study civil law for a further five years on 19 July 1400. It was very unusual for such a securely destined young aristocrat to study civil law, especially so assiduously; most of his kind preferred theology. He was renting rooms in Queen's College in 1402/3 and for some years after, although not a prompt payer. His ability and connections did not escape notice in the university. He was elected chancellor in June 1406 and was still in office in 1408 and (probably continuously, although he was preparing to travel abroad in 1409) to September 1411.

Then the king ordered Courtenay's resignation. Although he had attended a university convocation to condemn Wycliffite literature on 26 June 1407, and was on a commission to inquire into disorders in the town on 4 April 1411, with orders to arrest nine men and bring them before the king and council on 13 May, he then led the university's resistance to Archbishop Thomas Arundel's high-handed disregard for its jurisdiction in his determination to 'purge' the Wycliffism he suspected there. Courtenay was, however, restored as chancellor as quickly as November 1411: Arundel admitted that there was little heresy to be found in the university, and the king in effect apologized with a handsome benefaction to the university at Courtenay's behest. He probably remained as chancellor until Whitsun 1413. This brush with the archbishop and king will have done nothing to undermine Prince Henry's affection for him, because he too was at serious odds with them in these years. Courtenay's personal project, meanwhile, was the secure establishment of the university's library, using his connections to create a distinguished roll of sponsors and their gifts. On 20 November 1412 his project was duly enacted by the university, which awarded him user's rights for his life as a mark of gratitude.

Courtenay was termed 'king's clerk' on 4 March 1402 and 1 September 1407, but was not serving in any permanent capacity. In 1406 he accompanied Princess Philippa to Copenhagen for her marriage, and was abroad from August until about December. On 1 September 1407 he had a writ of aid for his journey into Wales on 'divers business' of the king, and once there he took an oath from the rebels in Lampeter Castle that they would surrender if not relieved within an agreed time. Such a mission will have furthered Courtenay's association with the future Henry V, who was still leading the repression of Glyn Dŵr. They were evidently already close friends. The prince, too, had been a student in Queen's College, apparently before or in 1398 (when he was about eleven), which predates Courtenay's own known time there, though the latter would already have been well established at Oxford as a law student of high birth and connection. It is no surprise that the two kinsmen should have been drawn to each other. On 10 February 1412 Courtenay was included, undoubtedly at the prince's request, in an embassy to treat for a marriage between Henry and a daughter of the duke of Burgundy. With the accession of the prince as Henry V on 20 March 1413, Courtenay's silver spoon was set to turn to gold.

Indeed, the major see of Norwich fell vacant within a month. The king made no secret on his accession that he would secure quick promotion for his limited circle of trusted associates. Courtenay was elected (the date is unknown) and papally provided on 28 June, with a licence to be consecrated by any bishop on the 29th, perhaps with a view to snubbing Archbishop Arundel. He received his temporalities on 11 September 1413. In the event, he made his profession to Arundel on 17 September, and was consecrated by him at Windsor, a very personal gesture from the king, that same day. He never entered his diocese, leaving its routine administration to a vicar-general, William Westacre. However, he and his chancellor, John Hody, did deal with a few major items of business personally, and the bishop even performed a quite extensive ordination ceremony at Tewkesbury on 7 April 1414.

The reason for the bishop's absence is simple. By 6 June 1413 he was keeper of the king's jewels and treasurer of the chamber (a single position), and was thereby close to the king at all times and with a key role to play in the event of any military campaign. On 22 November 1413 he was appointed to hear an appeal from a military court, a rare hint of the kind of work for which his education had trained him. On 8 January 1414 he moved in Henry V's company from Eltham to Westminster to pre-empt the revolt of Sir John Oldcastle. On 31 May 1414 he, Bishop Thomas Langley of Durham, and Thomas Montagu, earl of Salisbury, were appointed to lead an embassy of fundamental importance to determine peace or war with France. They left on 10 July and reached Paris on 8 August; they returned on 3 October 1414. The French made unexpectedly large offers. Therefore Courtenay and Langley were appointed on 5 December to resume talks, and were paid for their embassy from 2 December 1414 to 29 March 1415. By then Henry V had already decided that there would be no settlement, and indeed there was not. His demands were impossible. In late June and early July at Winchester, from where the king was preparing his expedition along the south coast, Courtenay met for the last time with French envoys, who remarked to each other on the marked decline in his personal appearance (especially that he was putting on weight) even as their peace offers were being rebuffed once and for all. Courtenay was 6 feet tall, with golden-brown hair, and presumably had been handsome even the year before.

On 24 July 1415 Courtenay was appointed as an executor of Henry V's will. He crossed with the army on 13 August to undertake the siege of Harfleur. Evidently not in the fittest of condition, he is presumed to have contracted dysentery, like so many others there. Henry V himself was with him when he died, at Harfleur, between 14 and 16 September, and personally closed the bishop's eyes. Unlike the king, Courtenay had not made a will. Henry had the body sent back to the chapel of Edward the Confessor in Westminster Abbey, where it was buried in the plot he had already designated for his own interment. There he remains, unobtrusively sharing the magnificent royal tomb. When Henry himself was buried on 8 November 1422, Courtenay's feet had to be amputated and placed neatly under his armpits to allow the king's body its exact space. He was not to be moved. There was not, and never has been, any suggestion that theirs was more than a deep friendship, or that the bishop was an unworthy associate of the young king. Courtenay's noble origins and precocious studies suggested a rich future anyway, but Henry V's friendship promised him a share of greatness. For neither would life prove long enough for this promise to be fulfilled.　　　　R. G. DAVIES

**Sources** R. G. Davies, 'The episcopate in England and Wales, 1375–1443', PhD diss., University of Manchester, 1974, 3.ci–iii · Emden, *Oxf.* · episcopal register, Norfolk RO, Reg/4/7, fols. 72r–104v · Westminster Abbey Muniment Room, London, WAM 65041A and B · LPL, MS 20 · J. H. Dahmus, *William Courtenay, archbishop of Canterbury, 1381–1396* (1966)
**Archives** Norfolk RO, Reg/4/7, fols. 72r–104v

**Courtenay, Thomas**, thirteenth earl of Devon (1414–1458), magnate, was the only surviving child and heir of Hugh Courtenay, twelfth earl of Devon (d. 1422), and Anne (d. 1441), daughter of Richard, Lord Talbot. He married Margaret, a daughter of John *Beaufort, marquess of Dorset and of Somerset (c.1371–1410), and had with her three sons: Thomas [see below], who succeeded as earl, and Henry and John, who both died unmarried.

At the time of the twelfth earl's death the earldom of Devon was the single largest secular estate in that county. With lands concentrated in the southern and central parts of Devon, but with significant outliers in neighbouring counties, the earls enjoyed an annual landed income of about £1500 net in the later middle ages. These extensive estates, together with the family's comital status—restored to the Courtenay family in 1335, and held in conjunction with the honours of Plympton and Okehampton—gave the earls considerable political authority in the region. On a national scale, however, the Courtenay earls of Devon were among the poorest families of their rank.

Thomas Courtenay's father had been one of Henry V's most active wartime commanders, and spent almost all his brief period as earl of Devon (1419–22) on service overseas. When Thomas, after a long minority, aged eighteen and already a father, was given leave to enter his estates in February 1433, they represented barely half the full resources of the earldom. Not only did his mother, Countess Anne, enjoy her customary dowager third of the estate, but Earl Hugh had also entailed various other lands upon her. She lived until 1441 and occupied the chief seat of the earldom—Tiverton Castle, Devon, recently renovated by Thomas's grandfather—forcing Thomas himself to dwell in a secondary seat not far away at Colcombe, near Colyton.

Longer-term factors also exacerbated the situation. A significant redistribution of landed wealth within the upper echelons of west-country society had taken place since the late fourteenth century, and this meant that by 1441 the earl of Devon no longer possessed the clear ascendancy enjoyed by his predecessors. He was now challenged as a local source of patronage by a number of ambitious gentry families who enjoyed estates comparable in value to his own. Some of these families were elevated to the peerage during the course of the fifteenth century, such as the Brookes (lords Cobham), the Dynhams, and, pre-eminent among them, the Bonvilles. This local background helps explain Earl Thomas's response to national political developments. Henry VI's rule in the 1440s and 1450s, marked by drift and factionalism, served in the west country as elsewhere to inflame already heightened regional tensions.

Despite these disadvantages, alliances forged earlier by his father served Devon well at first. It is probable that the eight-year-old Thomas had been placed in the care of his future wife's family, the Beauforts, in 1422. His career in the late 1420s and 1430s followed the conventional pattern for a young aristocrat of the period—knighted in November 1429, he received numerous grants, saw military service abroad, and was appointed to commissions of the peace in the west country.

As political life polarized in the late 1430s and 1440s, Devon's connection with the Beaufort clique began to pay dividends. More grants followed, and in May 1441 he was appointed steward of the duchy of Cornwall—a blunder on the part of the government, since Bonville had been granted an almost identical post some years earlier which he still held. Nor were the benefits Devon acquired exclusively local for, in May 1445, he was appointed steward of England at the coronation of Queen Margaret—a well-orchestrated demonstration of the Beaufort family's power at court.

But an attachment to the Beaufort faction also carried risks. As it began to lose ground at court in the face of the growing influence of the duke of Suffolk's circle (to which Bonville was connected), so Devon came to be excluded from access to royal patronage. He did not help himself: aided and abetted by his Beaufort kinsmen, his struggle with Bonville for the stewardship of the duchy of Cornwall had turned violent enough to alarm the government in 1441, and (unlike Bonville) Devon refused to serve abroad in March 1443, hoping rather to strengthen his position at home. He was later to see action at Pont-l'Évêque, Normandy, in 1446, however, and after the death of Cardinal Beaufort in the summer of 1447 he began to attend court more regularly. The government attempted to deal even-handedly with both Devon and Bonville, but the former continued to lose ground to his rival, who was elevated to the peerage at the parliament of

1449 when, significantly, Devon suffered the indignity of losing his claim of parliamentary precedence over the earl of Arundel.

Bonville's continued favour at court under Suffolk and, after the latter's death in 1450, the earl of Somerset, did not immediately undermine Devon's local power base in the south-west, and his control over the Devon electorate remained strong throughout 1449 and 1450. Devon's growing attachment to the duke of York enhanced his own authority; his and York's troops briefly controlled London in the last months of 1450, during York's display of strength on his return from Wales to challenge Henry VI's advisers, and Devon used his connection with York to challenge Bonville and his friends in the field. Most local gentry kept their heads down when events turned violent, but the forces mobilized by the earl of Devon in the west country, ostensibly in support of York, still contained a respectable gentry contingent. His military campaign against Bonville almost succeeded in catching his prey, but ultimately led to humiliation and temporary imprisonment following York's submission to Henry VI at Dartford (March 1452). The ensuing eighteen months of exclusion from court irreversibly undermined Devon's hold on power in the localities.

Bonville used the period to good effect, and the local parliamentary returns and appointments to commissions favoured his associates and sucked the life out of Devon's 'connection'. The uncertainties that resulted from Henry VI's sudden insanity in July 1453, and the political crisis that followed, prompted Bonville to strengthen his forces both on land and at sea, and helped bring about Devon's indictment on a charge of treason. His acquittal cleared the path for York's appointment as protector (March 1454), but Bonville had so effectively entrenched himself in the west country that York had little alternative but to retain his services there.

Although Earl Thomas attended a number of council meetings, his greatest energies were directed towards bolstering his position at home. Law and order in Devon deteriorated alarmingly, and reached their nadir late in 1455. In the short term the earl appears to have retained the confidence of the duke of York, who used him as an intermediary between himself and the king in a last-ditch effort to avert bloodshed on the eve of the first battle of St Albans, on 22 May 1455. He accompanied the captive king back to London after the battle as a member of York's entourage but, for reasons that remain unclear, Devon was unable or unwilling to exploit York's token of good will. York built up connections with a number of families, such as the extensive and powerful Neville clan, who were at the same time deepening or forging closer ties with Bonville. Feeling desperate and threatened, Devon and his sons resorted to extreme violence. The brutal murder by his retainers of Nicholas Radford, a greatly respected lawyer and councillor of Bonville, shocked even the hardened sensibilities of the age. A winter of widespread disorder led to a pitched battle between Devon and Bonville at Clyst Bridge, east of Exeter (15 December 1455). Indecisive though it was, the battle led to the earl's arrest and it was only Henry VI's intervention after his resumption of power that saved him from being tried for treason.

Exclusion from court patronage significantly undermined Devon's position at home. Far fewer Devon gentry had supported him at Clyst than in his earlier campaigns, and the situation was not redeemed despite strenuous efforts by the earl to capitalize on a new alliance—this time with the king and Queen Margaret. Pardoned for his offences, he was restored to the bench of JPs and granted the keeping of the park and forest of Clarendon (February 1457). Devon was believed by some to have attempted to bring about a reconciliation between York and King Henry, but he died suddenly (but probably naturally) at Abingdon Abbey on 3 February 1458.

Thomas Courtenay, earl of Devon, has achieved notoriety as one of the more unruly of the 'overmighty subjects' who destabilized political life in the middle years of the fifteenth century. The private wars in which he was engaged in the 1440s and 1450s briefly pushed him to the centre of the national stage, first as a supporter of Richard, duke of York, and second as the instigator of violence so severe as to predispose many lords towards the establishment of York's second protectorate (in November 1455). But violence was entered upon only as a last resort when peaceful channels seemed closed to him, and Devon's career illustrates as graphically as any during the period the effects on a landed aristocrat of long-term financial crisis and exclusion from power and influence at court.

The thirteenth earl's eldest son and successor, **Thomas Courtenay**, fourteenth earl of Devon (1432–1461), remained an unflinching supporter of the queen, whose cousin Marie, daughter of Charles, count of Maine, he had married during 1456–7, and he received a number of grants. The desperate consequences of uncontained conflict are graphically illustrated in Courtenay's brief career. Present at the battle of Wakefield (where both Bonville's son and grandson were killed), and the second battle of St Albans (following which Bonville himself was executed), he was injured at Towton and, unable 'to voyde a waye … was take and behedddyed' at York on 3 April 1461 (*The Historical Collections of a Citizen of London*, 216).

MARTIN CHERRY

**Sources** R. L. Storey, *The end of the house of Lancaster*, new edn (1986) · M. Cherry, 'The struggle for power in mid-fifteenth-century Devonshire', *Patronage, the crown and the provinces*, ed. R. A. Griffiths (1981), 123–44 · M. Cherry, 'The Courtenay earls of Devon: the formation and disintegration of a late medieval aristocratic affinity', *Southern History*, 1 (1979), 71–97 · R. A. Griffiths, *The reign of King Henry VI: the exercise of royal authority, 1422–1461* (1981) · P. A. Johnson, *Duke Richard of York, 1411–1460* (1988) · GEC, *Peerage*, new edn, 4.326–7 · king's bench ancient indictments, PRO, KB 9 · inquisitions post mortem, PRO, C 139 · additional charters, BL · court rolls, Devon RO, CR 621 · Exeter city receivers' accounts, Devon RO · exchequer, king's remembrancer, accounts various, PRO, E 101/410/9 · ministers' accounts, PRO, Special collections, SC 6/1118/7 · Chancery records · 'William Gregory's chronicle of London', *The historical collections of a citizen of London in the fifteenth century*, ed. J. Gairdner, CS, new ser., 17 (1876), 55–239 · 'John Benet's chronicle for the years 1400 to 1462', ed. G. L. Harriss, *Camden miscellany, XXIV*, CS, 4th ser., 9 (1972)
**Wealth at death** £1516—value of full estate (1422): PRO, SC 6/1118/7

**Courtenay, Thomas, fourteenth earl of Devon** (1432–1461). *See under* Courtenay, Thomas, thirteenth earl of Devon (1414–1458).

**Courtenay, Thomas Peregrine** (1782–1841), politician and author, youngest son of Henry Reginald *Courtenay, bishop of Exeter, and his wife, Lady Elizabeth Howard, daughter of Thomas, second earl of Effingham, was born on 31 May 1782. He was educated at Westminster School from 1796. He was a junior clerk in the Treasury, 1799–1802, and attached himself to the Pittites and especially to Charles Long, Pitt's manager of places. From Long he secured a series of offices including the cashier of the Stationery Office (1802–13), the Ceylon agency (1804–6), and the deputy paymastership of the forces (1807–11). He defended Pitt in his *Plain Answer* (1803).

Courtenay became dissatisfied with merely accumulating offices, and the death of the father of his friend W. Dacres Adams gave him the parliamentary seat of Totnes in 1811, which he retained until 1832. A staunch ministerialist, he gained further offices, including the agency to the Cape (1813–33) and the secretaryship of the Board of Control (1812–28), and he was a commissioner of that board from July 1828 to November 1830. He was also Wellington's vice-president of the Board of Trade from May 1828 to November 1830. Courtenay, though notorious as a placeman, was an efficient if officious administrator and avoided scandal. He voted regularly for Catholic relief and supported reform of the poor laws in two pamphlets published in 1818. His Friendly Societies Bill, encouraging their development, was eventually passed in 1819. He was sworn of the privy council in May 1828. In 1830 he retired from the Board of Trade with a pension of £1000 p.a. and did not stand for the reformed parliament of 1832.

Courtenay was a member of the Camden and Granger societies and wrote a *Memoir of … Sir William Temple, Bart.* (2 vols., 1836) and *Commentaries on the Historic Plays of Shakespeare* (1840) (articles reprinted from the *New Monthly Magazine*). On 5 April 1805 Courtenay married Anne, daughter of Mayow Wynell Mayow of Sydenham, Kent. They had eight sons and five daughters; Anne died in December 1860. His brother became earl of Devon in 1835 and Courtenay was raised to the rank of an earl's younger son. Courtenay drowned on 8 July 1841 while bathing at Torquay.

H. C. G. MATTHEW

**Sources** GM, 2nd ser., 16 (1841), 3, 16 · HoP, Commons · E. Lodge, *Peerage, baronetage, knightage and companionage of the British empire*, 81st edn, 3 vols. (1912)
**Archives** Powderham Castle, Exeter, corresp. and papers; diary | NRA, priv. coll., corresp. with W. D. Adams · NRA, priv. coll., letters to earl of Haddington
**Likenesses** W. Drummond, lithograph (after E. U. Eddis), BM, NPG; repro. in *Athenaeum Portraits*, 30 (1836)

**Courtenay, William** (1341/2–1396), archbishop of Canterbury, was born at Exminster, Devon, in 1341 or 1342, being in his twenty-eighth year in August 1369. The fourth son of

William Courtenay (1341/2–1396), tomb effigy

Hugh Courtenay, tenth earl of Devon (1303–1377), and Margaret de Bohun, daughter of Humphrey (VII) de *Bohun, fourth earl of Hereford (d. 1322), through her he was a great-grandson of *Edward I. His family were a major influence in the south-west; his brother Sir Philip Courtenay also had an active political career, and was the father of Richard *Courtenay, who became bishop of Norwich, and to whom his uncle bequeathed a mitre in his will, specifically in case he should become a bishop.

**Education and early advancement** Courtenay received his university education at Oxford, where he had lodgings in June 1363. Although often said to have links with Stapledon Hall (the precursor of Exeter College), this cannot be confirmed. He was identified as a master in 1362; by October 1366 was a licentiate in laws; and had attained the doctorate by July 1367. In that year, described as a master and professor of civil law, he was chosen chancellor of the university, perhaps in part because of his noble connections. His admission on 10 June followed disagreement with the bishop of Lincoln, who disputed the election as contravening his rights. An appeal to Pope Urban V secured a bull confirming Courtenay's appointment. He was still chancellor in October 1368, possibly continuing until about Easter 1369. This brought his first encounter with academic heresy, in the process concerning Uthred Boldon in 1367–8. Courtenay retained an interest in Oxford affairs throughout his career, becoming involved in the dispute between the faculties of arts and laws in 1376, in the dispute between the university and St Frideswide's Priory in 1382, and in the controversy over the appointment of a provost at Oriel College in 1386. Continuing intellectual interest is suggested by the bequest of Bishop John Grandison of Exeter in 1360, of a book of either theology or canon law, at the choice of the executors, and his own will mentions several books that he owned.

Noble connections gave Courtenay the entrée to an elevated ecclesiastical career; such was evidently intended from an early age. In 1355 a petition to the pope by his mother's kinsman the earl of Hereford sought a canonry for him at Salisbury or St Asaph. Although approved, it was unsuccessful. His first recorded admission to a benefice (but possibly not his first appointment) was to a prebend in St Mary's Chapel in Exeter Castle on 18 September

1359. He was certainly a pluralist by 1361, holding a portion at Crewkerne with the Exeter prebend. Although not identified as a priest until 1366, he was a deacon by July 1362, presumably taking orders almost as soon as canonically permitted. His return to the survey of pluralists in 1366 recorded benefices worth some £100, including cathedral prebends at Wells, York, and Exeter. In 1369, below the canonical age (and so requiring a papal dispensation), he was appointed bishop of Hereford by Pope Urban V, displacing Thomas Brantingham whom the chapter had earlier elected. His bull of provision was issued on 17 August 1369, but consecration was delayed until 17 March 1370. He received the temporalities on 19 March, and was enthroned on 15 September.

Courtenay's register as bishop at Hereford offers scant evidence on which to judge his episcopate. He was frequently absent from the see during his first year of tenure; until December 1371 he regularly celebrated ordinations at Tiverton church for Bishop Brantingham of Exeter. From 1373, however, his residence within the diocese is more fully attested, and rarely interrupted. Despite its seeming remoteness, Hereford was not to be a backwater, nor did Courtenay neglect his church's interests. In December 1373 there occurred the first of several dramatic scenes which punctuated his career and found their way into the chronicles. In convocation he bluntly refused assent to a grant of clerical taxation to Edward III, protesting that he would pay nothing until various injuries inflicted on himself and his church by the king and his ministers were satisfactorily resolved. These grievances were not identified, nor is there record of any settlement; but Courtenay had made his mark, gaining a reputation as a defender of ecclesiastical liberties.

**Bishop of London** In 1375 Simon Sudbury was appointed archbishop of Canterbury, very much as a court candidate. It has been suggested that Pope Gregory XI considered Courtenay a more congenial choice, but if so his claims were not strongly advanced: he replaced Sudbury at London instead. The bull of translation was issued on 12 September, temporalities being restored on 2 December, spiritualities on the following day. Again, Courtenay's main advantage was probably his noble birth; he may also have been seen as a politic balance to Sudbury's links with John of Gaunt, duke of Lancaster (although those links, and Courtenay's opposition to Gaunt, may both have been exaggerated). Within the city of London, if not the diocese, Courtenay was apparently a reasonably popular bishop. The Londoners were prepared both to riot against John of Gaunt in his favour, and to calm their riots at his behest. Unfortunately, no register survives to record his governance of the see. A lingering attachment to the city may be reflected in one contemporary's tale that he was influential in securing the restoration of London's liberties in September 1392, after Richard II had abolished them.

Courtenay's move to London came at a critical political juncture, with Edward III in decline, Edward, the Black Prince, nearing death, and John of Gaunt, the next senior prince, popularly mistrusted. At the Good Parliament of

October–November 1376, which sought change and curbs on governmental corruption, Courtenay was among the Commons' nominees to the reform committee. This may reflect a general perception of his opposition to the court, and possibly also his long-standing links with Edmund, third earl of March, who was prominent in the anti-court movement. Not much came of this; and attempts to maintain momentum after parliament was dissolved by establishing an afforced royal council (with Courtenay among the membership) proved abortive.

Courtenay's relations with Archbishop Sudbury had begun badly, with a jurisdictional dispute over the powers of the dean of arches within London diocese. This seems to have acquired a personal dimension. Henceforth Courtenay and Sudbury often appear to be on opposing sides, with Courtenay seemingly more active than his archbishop and particularly asserting ecclesiastical rights. This, however, may reflect the bias of chroniclers more than reality.

Early 1377 was the most dramatic period of the pontificate. In January Courtenay published in London Gregory XI's bull against the Florentines, excommunicated because of the war between Florence and the papacy. The resulting disorder in the city (where Florentine property was ransacked) led to a government-imposed retraction, albeit published by proxy. At parliament in February Courtenay demanded that the disgraced William Wykeham, whom he had already supported before the council in the previous year, be restored to his full episcopal rights; in the parallel convocation he apparently led demands for redress of ecclesiastical grievances (although those presented were relatively minor), and again demanded Wykeham's reinstatement, stalling a grant of clerical taxation until this was achieved. How much personal motivation drove these events is uncertain: Courtenay may merely have been acting as a mouthpiece, as president of the convocation, standing in for Sudbury, and dean of the province. Either personal friendship or an intense concern for church liberties could explain his staunch defence of William Wykeham. Besides supporting him in parliament and convocation, he sought aid for Wykeham from Simon Langham (formerly archbishop of Canterbury, and now a cardinal resident at the curia), and even from the pope.

**Clashes with John of Gaunt and Wyclif** The convocation of February 1377 also witnessed Courtenay's first encounter with John Wyclif, whose activities and adherents bulked large in his later career. Wyclif had been summoned before convocation at St Paul's, to defend himself against charges of heresy, and arrived there with John of Gaunt and Henry, Lord Percy. Their provocative behaviour produced confrontation, but Courtenay maintained the dignity and procedural regulations of the church against an obvious attempt at intimidation. Gaunt, infuriated, threatened to pull the bishop from his seat, warned him against presuming too much on his noble connections, and eventually withdrew, muttering imprecations. In the furore, Wyclif was almost forgotten. Courtenay also confronted Wyclif in the second, somewhat obscure and

inconclusive, process against him at Lambeth early in 1378, in response to prompting from Pope Gregory XI.

The prolonged exchange of insults between Courtenay and Gaunt in February 1377 clearly revealed a poor relationship between bishop and prince. The frayed tempers displayed then stimulated existing anti-Gaunt feelings in London. These turned to riot following rumours that Gaunt planned to deprive the city of its liberties, riots quelled only by the intervention of Courtenay and Princess Joan of Wales. However, the seeming hostility may not have been deeply engrained: there are signs of a *rapprochement* between archbishop and prince in 1378, with Gaunt in July including Courtenay among those who were to have charge of his estates in the year after his death. This reconciliation was perhaps impaired in August following the murder of Robert Hawley in sanctuary in Westminster Abbey, which set Gaunt and Courtenay on opposing sides as representatives respectively of secular and ecclesiastical jurisdictional claims.

Following Edward III's death in June 1377, Courtenay was appointed in the following month to the continual council which ruled on Richard II's behalf, remaining a member until October 1378. He also sat on the committee to examine royal finances in April–May 1379, along with other committees after he had become archbishop of Canterbury.

During these years there is a possibility that Courtenay was establishing his own links with the curia, while also exploiting his position as bishop of London (and provincial dean) to establish a broader power base within the English church. Sudbury's seeming inactivity, meanwhile, may indicate either approval of Courtenay's behaviour (although his suggested partisan links with John of Gaunt make this unlikely), or his inability to oppose him. That Courtenay was a reliable papal supporter was appreciated at Rome. In September 1378 Pope Urban VI offered him a cardinal's hat, but the offer was rejected, never to be repeated. The bishop of London (presumably duly prompted) wrote to the pope asking for the appointment to be rescinded; but exactly why Courtenay turned it down is unknown. Possibly the offer was just badly timed, occurring so soon after Richard II's accession, when Courtenay was needed too much in England. Possibly Courtenay himself did not wish to go to the curia and to the relative poverty of a cardinal's estate epitomized in the recent experience of Simon Langham.

**Primate and chancellor** In 1381 Courtenay was translated, again following in Sudbury's footsteps, to the archbishopric of Canterbury. He was elected on 30 July, Sudbury having been murdered on 14 June during the peasants' revolt. Royal confirmation was given on 5 August, the appropriate papal bull issued on 9 September, and temporalities were restored on 23 October. In January 1382, on publication of the papal bulls, he took up the governance of the see, but a delay in investiture with the pallium prevented the full exercise of metropolitan authority until 6 May 1382. Despite this he still insisted on officiating at the coronation of Queen Anne of Bohemia on 22 January 1382.

The oath of obedience to Urban VI included a formal rejection of the Avignon antipope, Clement VII, and his adherents, but Courtenay was not notably involved in the debates on the papal schism (which had erupted in September 1378). His only recorded participation appears to be a debate with William Buxton in November 1384, which was less a debate than a reaffirmation of his loyalty to Urban VI.

Courtenay retained Canterbury until his death. The promotion to archbishop coincided with Courtenay's only period of formal state office: he was appointed chancellor on 10 August 1381, though his tenure was brief. He still held the post when parliament assembled early in November, but by the 18th had been replaced by Richard, Lord Scrope. This short period of high office remains rather puzzling. The appointment followed uncertainty over naming a new chancellor to succeed the murdered Archbishop Sudbury. Courtenay's appointment has been interpreted both as signalling the start of a policy of repression in response to the peasants' revolt, and as reflecting the temporary success of an anti-Gaunt *putsch* within the government. Contemporaries, however, pass no comment to validate either interpretation.

Courtenay's resignation after three months presumably followed a Commons' petition calling for new appointments of leading state officials, but who was behind that, and whether it reflected actual dissatisfaction with Courtenay's tenure, is unclear. In any case, he did not withdraw from political life completely. In November 1381 he was appointed to a reform commission, and in February 1382 to a Lords' committee to negotiate with the Commons. He was to reappear with an active political role in the crises of the later 1380s.

**The problem of heresy** Courtenay's pontificate attracts most attention for his dealings with Wyclif and the early Lollards. Despite their earlier meetings, precisely what the newly appointed archbishop personally thought of Wyclif is not clear: his direct attacks on him sometimes appear almost half-hearted, though Courtenay was a forceful opponent of unorthodoxy more generally. This, nevertheless, did not save Courtenay from the pen of the martyrologist John Foxe, who portrayed him as the evil force pushing Richard II to persecute a forerunner of protestantism.

Courtenay's involvement in the assault on the unorthodoxy that some derived from Wyclif's thought in 1382 is well documented. The key event was the assembly of theologians that met at Blackfriars in London on 17–21 May with Courtenay in attendance, having been summoned by the new archbishop in response particularly to Wyclif's recent pronouncements on the eucharist. Twenty-four propositions were debated and condemned as either heretical or erroneous, although Wyclif was not named as their originator. Once the condemnation had been issued, Courtenay embarked on a purge of Wyclif's alleged adherents at Oxford. This perhaps fits as well into the struggles by archbishops to dominate the late medieval university as it does into the history of English heresy: Courtenay was merely one of several archbishops

who sought to curb Oxford's autonomy. The attack on Wycliffism was effective: Courtenay's victory was demonstrated by his holding convocation there in November 1382. Thereafter Oxford remained relatively quiescent, although the debates provoked by Wyclif were not totally ended.

Having purged Oxford, Courtenay had to deal with Wyclif's supposed adherents, as they appeared across the country. He personally dealt with cases in Peterborough Abbey and Leicester during his visitation of Lincoln diocese in 1389. In May 1392 he chaired the heresy process against Henry Crump at Stamford. (Crump was no Wycliffite, but some of his statements smacked of heresy, and all heresy was to be repressed.) Exactly how active Courtenay personally was against heresy cannot be properly judged: some records have probably been lost. Nevertheless, in the 1380s heresy was more a threat in imagination than reality; even though in 1395 the twelve conclusions setting out a Lollard programme were posted on the door of Westminster Hall while parliament was in session. Courtenay did not rely solely on the ecclesiastical law in his efforts against heretics. In June 1382 he gained royal support for his actions, with bishops being authorized to require the arrest of unlicensed wandering preachers. This was the first of a range of sanctions against heretics which developed through to the reign of Henry V.

**Politics and affairs of state** As archbishop, Courtenay continued his determined upholding of ecclesiastical privileges, especially with regard to taxation. On 17 December 1384 he protested in parliament against a Commons' proposal that their grant of two fifteenths be conditional on a clerical grant of two tenths. Courtenay seemingly did not object to the clerical taxation as such, but to the attempt to impose it as a precondition of a lay grant. His principled stands sometimes produced major rows, but rarely caused long-term animosity. In Lent 1385, for instance, he clashed dramatically with Richard II. Courtenay spoke for a group warning Richard against the influence of some of his courtiers, who had reportedly urged the king to arrange the murder of John of Gaunt. Richard reacted angrily, threatening to seize the archbishop's temporalities, and, when he encountered Courtenay on the Thames shortly after, threatened to run him through. The archbishop seems to have withdrawn from public life for a while: according to Adam Usk he fled in fear to Devon, disguised as a monk, and Courtenay was certainly down at Exeter early in April 1385. The split with Richard lasted some months, until a reconciliation was effected by Robert Braybrooke, bishop of London, a respected kinsman of the king through the king's mother Joan (Emden, *Oxf.*, 1.254).

Courtenay's position made political involvement unavoidable, but he did escape entanglement in the major court faction-fighting of the 1380s. His presence is recorded at every parliament held during his tenure of Canterbury (he had been equally assiduous as bishop of London), but he eschewed fierce controversy. Like his brother Philip, who did not hide his preferences, he probably supported Bishop Despenser's Flemish crusade in

1383, against John of Gaunt's projected Castilian expedition. This, again, would not have endeared him to the prince; but, despite the fireworks, there is no sign of a lasting hostility to the family from Gaunt. Although Courtenay was appointed to the commission that emerged from the Wonderful Parliament in October 1386 to administer the realm for a year from 20 November 1386 to 19 November 1387, in the face of the king's wishes, he was no opponent of Richard II. When political crisis loomed as the commission's year of governance neared its end, Courtenay tried to be a calming influence between the king and the group later identified as the lords appellant. As an intermediary between the parties at Waltham Cross on 14 November 1387, he heard the charges which became the basis for the formal appeal against Richard's leading advisers in parliament in February 1388. When matters worsened, Courtenay led the ecclesiastical peers in withdrawing from parliament, protesting that the clergy could not participate because they were canonically barred from involvement in judgments of blood. Eighteen months later, on 3 May 1389, Courtenay was among the councillors present when Richard II reclaimed his authority, and announced that henceforth he would govern in his own right.

**Archbishop of Canterbury** As archbishop, Courtenay very much stood on his dignity. Throughout his pontificate he sought to exercise his rights of visitation, although this was rarely welcomed by his brother bishops. On 22 November 1382 Urban VI had granted him special visitatorial privileges; but the bull expired after two years, before it was fully exploited. The privileges were renewed, without time limit, on 23 April 1386. Thomas Brantingham of Exeter resolutely opposed the projected visitation of his diocese in 1384, but this need not reflect real personal differences; in 1389 John Waltham of Salisbury sought papal aid to ensure that any archiepiscopal visitation should be delayed until Salisbury's proper turn came round. In both cases the opposition soon collapsed, and the visitations took place. Courtenay's proposed visitation of the Benedictines at Gloucester College in Oxford likewise caused comment, but he withdrew when the peculiarities of that house's status were made clear.

Courtenay's rule coincided not merely with the papal schism, but with a period of anti-papal legislation. At the end of February 1390 he led a clerical protestation against the new Statute of Provisors, on the principled ground that this must not be in derogation of any papal right. In contrast, and logically, in the parliament of January–February 1393 he spoke in favour of the royal rights over the church reflected in the Statute of *Praemunire*. It was only Henry VIII who was to demonstrate to what dimensions this acknowledgement of traditional royal right might extend.

Within Courtenay's diocese there is no sign of any significant difficulties. His relations with his cathedral convent seem to have been good: although he insisted on his right of visitation, there is no sign of opposition. Indeed, he was a substantial benefactor to the cathedral. He transferred Meopham church to the priory, and beyond that

contributed handsomely to new building work and decoration of the church, including a window honouring St Ælfheah, and an image of the Trinity with apostles. His munificence was rewarded on 1 November 1395 when the prior and convent established an obit and anniversary in gratitude, together with mention in the daily mass said by the masters of the infirmary. He also clarified the position of Canterbury College, Oxford, on 16 January 1384 by issuing new statutes (perhaps based on a recasting begun under Archbishop Sudbury) which asserted the monastic character of the foundation.

As archbishop, Courtenay also confronted the lingering economic and social after-effects on archiepiscopal resources of the black death and subsequent recurrences of plague. During his pontificate several archiepiscopal houses were abandoned as superfluous to requirements. He also oversaw the first stages of the transition of estate management from direct farming to renting. However, he was emphatically still a landlord, indeed a lord, and fully capable of asserting his rights over his tenants. In 1388 he used his ecclesiastical powers of excommunication and interdict to quash resistance to his lordship at Romney in Kent; two years later at Wingham he forced some of his tenants to undergo a quasi-penance when they failed to perform carrying services in an appropriate manner.

**Last years and death** In the 1390s Courtenay was less prominent, perhaps less active. He appears in the records primarily as an efficient ecclesiastical administrator and a landlord. The relative political stability of these years may explain his apparent retreat from national politics: where there was less discord, there was less need for his talents as an intermediary. Richard II sought his support for the canonization of Edward II; what Courtenay thought of that proposal is not recorded. In March 1392 he issued a strongly worded decree against 'chop-churches', the intermediaries who trafficked in benefices for clerics seeking posts. Despite its good intentions the decree was not notably successful. Courtenay also reaffirmed earlier statutes establishing rectors' authority over stipendiary priests operating within their parishes. His last year as archbishop was slightly marred by attempts to levy a subsidy intended for his own coffers from the clergy of Canterbury province. Although this had been approved by Pope Boniface IX, it was resented by those who were required to pay. Courtenay's death, however, terminated the collection process.

Courtenay's will, a lengthy and detailed document, is undated, but can be placed in the summer of 1395, with a single deathbed codicil. Increasingly reduced mobility, along with the lengthy gap between the preparation of his will and Courtenay's actual death, at Maidstone on 31 July 1396, suggests that he suffered from a lingering illness. Probate was granted on 15 September 1396, the executors being kept busy for some years thereafter. The will sought burial in Exeter Cathedral (which had been his intention since at least 1381), but a deathbed codicil changed the site to the churchyard at Maidstone. In fact, however, he was interred in Canterbury Cathedral, on 4 August 1396, in a ceremony attended by Richard II and numerous courtiers.

He lies in the alabaster tomb bearing his effigy, at the feet of the Black Prince, and close to the site of the shrine of St Thomas. His lasting memorial was to be a collegiate foundation at Maidstone, adjoining the archiepiscopal palace. The project received papal approval on 25 July 1395, and royal authorization on 8 August 1395. However, death prevented Courtenay from seeing it through: his executors and successor were left to implement the foundation, and carry out the extensive building works that it entailed. The matrix for a commemorative brass still lies in the chancel of the church; its effigy and epitaph survived to be recorded in 1630.

**Conclusion** Courtenay's episcopal career covered a tempestuous period in English history. He held Hereford during the dotage of Edward III, London during the minority of Richard II, and Canterbury during years that saw relations between the king and his subjects often tense, the English church threatened by heresy, and the wider church suffering from the great schism between Avignon and Rome. Had he moved to join Urban VI in Rome in 1378, his career might have involved him in wider international diplomatic activity. As it was, he avoided close involvement in the machinations surrounding the schism: having declared for Urban VI, there was nothing to be discussed. At Canterbury he was neither a great archbishop nor a prominent actor on the national stage (except in connection with his dealings with Wyclif). Yet he was certainly a conscientious prelate, and an ardent upholder of the rights and privileges of his sees.

Courtenay was clearly well aware of his noble status, and maintained close ties with his family, and with Exeter. He was probably involved in making the arrangements concerning his parents' chantry in Exeter Cathedral, established in 1382; he was among the beneficiaries of the commemorations. For Adam Usk, Courtenay was 'that most excellent man' (*Chronicle of Adam of Usk*, 18), because he defended the church. Although a keen defender of rights and privileges, he seems to have respected the limits to his prerogatives, and knew how to save face without overstepping them. R. N. SWANSON

**Sources** J. Dahmus, *William Courtenay, archbishop of Canterbury, 1381–1396* (1966) · *Registrum Willelmi de Courtenay, episcopi Herefordensis, AD MCCCLXX–MCCCLXXV*, ed. W. W. Capes, CYS, 15 (1914) · A. K. McHardy, ed., *The church in London, 1375–1392*, London RS, 13 (1977) · LPL, Reg. Sudbury · LPL, Reg. Courtenay · CPR · W. H. Bliss, ed., *Calendar of entries in the papal registers relating to Great Britain and Ireland: petitions to the pope* (1896) · *CEPR letters* · W. A. Pantin, *Canterbury College, Oxford*, 3–4, OHS, new ser., 8, 30 (1950–85) · W. L. Warren, 'A reappraisal of Simon of Sudbury, bishop of London (1361–75) and archbishop of Canterbury (1375–81)', *Journal of Ecclesiastical History*, 10 (1959), 139–52 · D. N. Lepine, 'The Courtenays and Exeter Cathedral in the later middle ages', *Report and Transactions of the Devonshire Association*, 124 (1992), 41–58 · R. G. Davies, 'The attendance of the episcopate in English parliaments, 1376–1461', *Proceedings of the American Philosophical Society*, 129 (1985), 30–81 · G. Holmes, *The Good Parliament* (1975) · M. Cherry, 'The Courtenay earls of Devon: the formation and disintegration of a late medieval aristocratic affinity', *Southern History*, 1 (1979), 71–97 · F. R. H. Du Boulay and C. M. Barron, eds., *The reign of Richard II: essays in honour of May McKisack* (1971) · F. R. H. Du Boulay, *The lordship of Canterbury: an essay on medieval society* (1966) · *The chronicle of Adam Usk,*

*1377–1421*, ed. and trans. C. Given-Wilson, OMT (1997) · Emden, *Oxf.*, 1.502–4 · J. H. Dahmus, ed., *The metropolitan visitations of William Courtenay, archbishop of Canterbury, 1381–1396*, Illinois Studies in the Social Sciences, 31, no. 2 (1950)
**Archives** LPL, register
**Likenesses** alabaster tomb effigy, Canterbury Cathedral [*see illus.*]

**Courtenay, William**, first earl of Devon (*c.*1475–1511). *See under* Courtenay, Edward, first earl of Devon (*d.* 1509).

**Courtenay, Sir William**. *See* Thom, John Nichols (*bap.* 1799, *d.* 1838).

**Courtenay, William Reginald**, eleventh earl of Devon (1807–1888), politician and philanthropist, eldest son of William Courtenay, tenth earl (*d.* 19 March 1859), and his first wife, Lady Harriet Leslie, daughter of Sir Lucas Pepys, bt, was born in Charlotte Street, Bedford Square, London, on 14 April 1807. He was admitted at Westminster School on 16 September 1818, and matriculated from Christ Church, Oxford, on 30 March 1824. He was president of the Oxford Union Society in 1827. He took a first class in *literae humaniores* in 1827 and graduated BA in 1828, and BCL in 1831. From 1828 to 1831 he was a fellow of All Souls. He was created DCL on 27 June 1838, and was elected a governor of Westminster School in 1869.

Courtenay was called to the bar at Lincoln's Inn on 27 January 1832, and, with three others, edited volume 6 of *Cases Decided in the House of Lords on Appeal from the Courts of Scotland* (1832–3). From July 1841 he sat in parliament for South Devon, first as a Conservative, and then as a Peelite, but retired in February 1849 on his appointment as a poor-law inspector. From 1850 to 1859 he was secretary to the poor-law board. Courtenay married, on 27 December 1830, Lady Elizabeth Fortescue (1801–1867), seventh daughter of Hugh, first Earl Fortescue, and his wife, Hester. They were not successful parents. Their profligate first son, William Reginald, squandered the family money, dying in 1853 aged twenty-one; the third son, Edward Baldwin Courtenay (1836–1891), went bankrupt twice (1870 and 1878), consequently resigning his seat in the Commons. They had one other son and a daughter. Lady Devon died on 27 January 1867.

From 1835 until he succeeded to the peerage in 1859, Courtenay was styled Lord Courtenay. At the time of his succession the family estates in Devon and Ireland were worth about £35,000 per annum, but they had been heavily mortgaged by his two predecessors. He at once set to work to free them from these encumbrances, and was fast realizing his wishes when the extravagance of his son Edward involved them in still greater liability. Before his succession, Devon had returned to the Conservative Party, and in the Derby ministry he became chancellor of the duchy of Lancaster, and was sworn of the privy council (July 1866). He remained in that office until May 1867, and from that month to December 1868 he was president of the poor-law board. After that date he ceased to take an active part in politics, but his statement in the House of

William Reginald Courtenay, eleventh earl of Devon (1807–1888), by George Richmond, 1874

Lords on 7 June 1869 in favour of reading the Irish Church Bill a second time produced much effect on public opinion. He was chairman in 1870 of the commission appointed to inquire into the treatment of Fenian prisoners in English convict prisons.

Devon was for many years the most influential man in his county, and was generally known as 'the good earl'. For fifty-two years he presided at quarter sessions, and he was a director, and then chairman, of the Bristol and Exeter Railway. He made extensive improvements at Powderham Castle, planted the famous cedar avenue in its grounds, and aided the charitable foundations of Devon. In 1859 he built and endowed the church of St Paul at Newton Abbot, where he was the chief landed proprietor. His portrait by George Richmond dates from 28 April 1874, the year being confirmed by Richmond's account books (though the drawing also bears the date 1875). A statue of him, by E. B. Stephens ARA, was placed, in 1880, by public subscription in the Bedford Circus at Exeter.

In 1877, while riding through the plantations at Powderham on his seventieth birthday, Lord Devon was thrown from his horse. Though he did not altogether recover from this accident, he was engaged in active life until a few weeks before his death. He died at Powderham Castle on 18 November 1888, and was buried in the family vault in the chancel of Powderham church on 24 November. He was succeeded in the title by his son Edward Baldwin Courtenay, who that year became a Roman Catholic.

W. P. COURTNEY, *rev.* H. C. G. MATTHEW

**Sources** GEC, *Peerage* · *The Times* (19 Nov 1888) · *Devon and Exeter Daily Gazette* (19–26 Nov 1888)
**Archives** BL, corresp. with W. E. Gladstone, Add. MSS 44358–44483 · Flintshire RO, Hawarden, letters to Sir Stephen Glynne · Lpool RO, letters to fourteenth earl of Derby · Northumbd RO, Newcastle upon Tyne, letters to J. A. Blackett-Ord
**Likenesses** H. T. Ryall, portrait, 1846, repro. in *Portraits of eminent conservatives and statesmen*, 2nd ser. · G. Richmond, drawing, 1874, priv. coll. [*see illus.*] · G. Richmond, oils, 1874, Powderham Castle, Exeter · E. B. Stephens, statue, 1880, Bedford Circus, Exeter · A. S. Wortley, oils, exh. RA 1889, Scottish Amicable Life Assurance Society · W. Holl, stipple (after G. Richmond), BM; repro. in *Portraits of members of Grillion's Club from 1813 to 1863*, 2 (privately printed, 1864) · carte-de-visite, NPG
**Wealth at death** £2598 16s. 1d.: probate, 11 Jan 1889, *CGPLA Eng. & Wales*

**Courteville, Raphael** (*fl. c.*1673–*c.*1735), organist and composer, was the son of Raphael Courteville, a gentleman of the Chapel Royal who sang at the coronation of Charles II in 1661 and died on 28 December 1675. The second Courteville was probably a chorister in the chapel, and seems to have studied with John Hingston, who bequeathed him some music books and an organ on his death in 1683. The publication of some of Courteville's songs in 1686 suggests a date of birth that can hardly be later than 1673 or so. On the recommendation of the earl of Burlington he was appointed the first organist of St James's, Piccadilly, on 7 September 1691 at a salary of £20 a year. He compiled *Select Psalms and Hymns for the Use of the Parish Church … of St James, Westminster* (1697), which contains his hymn tune 'St James'.

Many of Courteville's songs were printed in John Playford's song miscellanies, such as *Comes amoris* (1687–94), *Vinculum societatis* (1688–91), *Thesaurus musicus* (1693–5), and *Deliciae musicae* (1695–6). They show the influence of Henry Purcell and include songs for plays, including Tate's *A Duke and No Duke* (1684), Southerne's *Oroonoko* (1695), and D'Urfey's *Don Quixote*, part 3 (1695). Some songs attributed merely to 'Mr Courteville' may be by John Courteville, a brother probably, whose autograph songbook dated 1691 is in the British Library. Instrumental music by Raphael Courteville includes pieces in *The Self Instructor on the Violin* (1695), *The Second Book of the Harpsichord Master* (1700), and two sets of sonatas, the first for two flutes (*c.*1700), the second (now lost) for two violins. Other instrumental music survives in manuscript. The date of his death is uncertain, but it is usually said to have occurred about 1735. His widow, Mary Abbott, was buried at St James's in May of that year.

A third **Raphael Courteville** (*fl.* 1720–1772) was, according to Hawkins, his son. He is referred to as 'Courteville Junior' in connection with a benefit concert shared with his father at York Buildings on 1 April 1720. He was one of the original members of the Society of Musicians, founded in 1738. There appears to be no actual record of his taking over from his father at St James's, but the evidence suggests, nevertheless, that he did. In 1753 and 1754 he was warned by the church authorities to take his duties more seriously or face dismissal. He was still in post at the time of his death, though earlier he had been reprimanded for paying his assistant—a Mr Richardson, who succeeded him—only a quarter of his stipend instead of half.

Courteville's main interest, however, was political journalism. Referring to the period around 1734, J. H. Plumb described him as 'the principal hack journalist of the *Daily Courant*' (Plumb, 315); he seems to have been a busy pamphleteer and propagandist on behalf of Sir Robert Walpole. He was the reputed author of *The Gazetteer*, a paper written in defence of the government, and it was probably this that won him the nickname Court-evil from his opponents. More substantially, he published *Memoirs of the Life and Administration of William Cecil, Baron Burleigh* (1738) and about 1760 *Arguments Respecting Insolvency*. A spoof letter of 1742, purporting to be signed by him, describes him as 'Organ-blower, Essayist, and Historiographer' (*Westminster Journal*, no. 50, 4 Dec 1742). On 14 September 1735 he married Lucy Green, a lady possessed of a fortune of £25,000. He was buried at St James's, Piccadilly, on 10 June 1772.                                    IAN SPINK

Sources Highfill, Burnim & Langhans, *BDA* · J. Hawkins, *A general history of the science and practice of music*, new edn, 2 (1875), 768 · J. H. Plumb, *Sir Robert Walpole*, 2 (1960), 315 · I. Spink, 'Courteville, Raphael (i)', *New Grove* · I. Spink, 'Courteville, Raphael (ii)', *New Grove*
Archives BL, letters to the duke of Newcastle, Add. MSS 32724–32887, *passim*

**Courteville, Raphael** (*fl.* **1720–1772**). *See under* Courteville, Raphael (*fl. c.*1673–*c.*1735).

**Courthope** [Courthopp], **Nathaniel** (*d.* **1620**), merchant navy officer, was one of at least four brothers, whose parentage and early life are unknown, enlisted in the East India Company's service in November 1609. He left England in the *Darling*, one of Sir Henry Middleton's fleet, on the company's sixth voyage in 1610, and the following year he became purser of the *Trade's Increase*. With his commander and others he was taken prisoner by the Turks and kept in captivity at Aden and Mocha. On regaining his freedom he was appointed agent to the company's factory at Succedana (Borneo). In 1616 he was placed in command of two ships, the *Swan* and the *Defence*, which were sent from Bantam (Java) to the islands of the Banda group. This important mission was intended to secure confirmation of an earlier surrender of the islands, and to establish an English claim to the island of Pulo Run. Courthope was ordered to resist all attempts by the Dutch to take possession of Pulo Run for themselves. After a voyage of two months he arrived at Pulo Run, where the islanders readily agreed to surrender themselves as subjects of the king. Courthope, however, was unable to carry on his expedition further, being compelled to fortify and defend the island against the Dutch, who seized one of his ships and established an effective blockade, which prevented the arrival of any relief missions. With the exception of one or two flying visits to neighbouring islands, he remained at Pulo Run for four years, experiencing great hardship in very difficult conditions. In recognition of this devoted if ultimately futile service to the company,

the directors recommended in January 1620 that Courthope be granted an annuity of £100 a year as well as preferment. Eventually, in October 1620, he sailed to Lantore in pursuit of two Dutch ships which, he had been informed, had entered the harbour there. In the engagement that followed, Courthope received a shot in the chest, and after leaping overboard was never seen again. The same year the Dutch expelled the English from both Pulo Run and Lantore.                      ALSAGER VIAN, *rev.* H. V. BOWEN

Sources S. Purchas, *Purchas his pilgrimes*, 4 vols. (1625), vol. 1, pp. 664–779 · *The journal of John Jourdain, 1608–1617*, ed. W. Foster, Hakluyt Society, 2nd ser., 16 (1905) · F. C. Danvers and W. Foster, eds., *Letters received by the East India Company from its servants in the east*, 6 vols. (1896–1902), vols. 1–5 · *CSP col.*, vols. 2–3 · will, PRO, PROB 11/140, sig. 74
Archives BL, Egerton MS 2086, fols. 26, 44

**Courthope, William** (**1807–1866**), herald, was born on 20 May 1807 at Rotherhithe, Surrey, the fourth of eight children and only son of Thomas Courthope (1775–1849) of Rotherhithe and subsequently of Camberwell, citizen and shipwright of London, and his wife, Mary (1775–1861), daughter and sole heir of John Buxton, sometime of Rotherhithe. After apprenticeship to his uncle John Bryan Courthope, citizen and merchant taylor of London in 1822, he was engaged in 1824 as private clerk by Francis Townsend, Rouge Dragon, to assist him in the editing of both Debrett's *Peerage* and *Baronetage*.

On Townsend's death in 1833 Courthope was appointed clerk to the College of Arms and succeeded him as editor of Debrett's publications. Between 1833 and 1839 he edited three editions of Debrett's *Peerage* (1834, 1836, 1838) and one of Debrett's *Baronetage* (1835). *A Synopsis of the Extinct Baronetage of England* edited by him was also published in 1835 without Debrett's name on the title-page. On 10 May 1838 he married Frances Elizabeth (1811–1890), daughter of the Revd Frederic Gardiner, rector of Llanwythern, Monmouthshire. They had no children, and in 1851 Courthope adopted Florence Sophia Poussett, the daughter of his sister Martha. She took the name of Courthope in 1862. On appointment as Rouge Croix in 1839 he resigned his editorships and was succeeded as editor of Debrett's works by G. W. Collen, subsequently Portcullis, clerk to G. F. Beltz. Courthope was appointed Somerset herald in 1854 and registrar of the college in 1859, and retained both positions until his death. He was called to the bar at the Inner Temple in 1851 but did not practise.

Sir Charles George Young, on being appointed Garter king of arms in 1842, made Courthope secretary to Garter. Courthope went as secretary to Garter missions to Constantinople (1856), Lisbon (1858), Berlin (1861), Copenhagen (1865), Hesse (1865), and Brussels (1866) to present the Order of the Garter to the respective sovereigns. His Berlin diary was published in 1989.

William Courthope was an antiquary of some distinction, best remembered for his *Historic Peerage of England* (1857). He described this work as a new edition of Sir H. Nicolas's *Synopsis of the Peerage*, but it is a great improvement on the original, deriving information from the manuscript collections of Robert Glover, Augustine Vincent, Sir Edward Walker, John Anstis, Stephen Martin Leake, and Francis Townsend, all in the College of Arms. He also enlarged and improved the 'Dissertation on dignities' which is prefixed to the work. He was an assiduous worker and good genealogist and wrote a *Memoir of Daniel Chamier Minister of the Reformed Church with Notices of the Descendants* (1852), of whom he was one, contributed to periodicals, and wrote the introduction to the 1859 edition of the English (Yorkist) version of the Rous roll, published as *A Pictorial History of the Earls of Warwick in the Rows Role*. He died at 3 Robertson Terrace, Hastings, Sussex, on 13 May 1866, having had phthisis for fifteen months, and was buried at Wadhurst. The College of Arms purchased from his executors eighty-four volumes of pedigrees and evidences especially relating to Sussex, his correspondence as editor of Debrett's *Peerage*, and a history of his ancestral parishes of Mayfield and Wadhurst. His library was sold at Sothebys on 23 June 1867.      THOMAS WOODCOCK

**Sources** GM, 4th ser., 2 (1866), 111 · *Herald and Genealogist*, 4 (1867), 468 · *Miscellanea Genealogica et Heraldica*, new ser., 3 (1880), 327 · W. H. Godfrey, A. Wagner, and H. Stanford London, *The College of Arms, Queen Victoria Street* (1963), 163–4 · A. Wagner, *Heralds of England: a history of the office and College of Arms* (1967) · A. R. Wagner, *The records and collections of the College of Arms* (1952) · F. J. French, 'Debrett: book and man. A history of the peerage', *Debrett's Peerage* (1990) · Courthope pedigree, Coll. Arms, WC 15,95; Norfolk VII,146 · 'Garter mission to Berlin, 1861', *Coat of Arms*, new ser., 8 (1989), 87–95, 120–27 · d. cert. · CGPLA Eng. & Wales (1866)
**Archives** BL, illuminated pedigree roll 'The genealogy of British kings', Add. MS 43968 · Coll. Arms, corresp. as editor of *Debrett's peerage*, history of Mayfield and Wadhurst, pedigrees and evidences · NL Wales, pedigrees of De Rutzen family compiled by Courthope · Suffolk RO, Ipswich, pedigrees of Broke and related families completed by Courthope | BL, letters to Philip Bliss, Add. MSS 34572–34579 · Bodl. Oxf., MSS Phillipps-Robinson, corresp. with Sir Thomas Phillipps
**Likenesses** pastel?, Coll. Arms
**Wealth at death** under £6000: probate, 1 June 1866, *CGPLA Eng. & Wales*

**Courthope, William John** [ *pseud.* Novus Homo] (1842–1917), poet and literary scholar, the elder son of William Courthope, was born on 17 July 1842 at South Malling, near Lewes, Sussex, where his father was rector. His mother, Caroline Elizabeth Ryle, was the daughter of John Ryle, banker and MP for Macclesfield, and a sister of John Charles Ryle, first bishop of Liverpool. Courthope's father died in 1849 and the three children were brought up by their uncle, the head of this ancient Sussex family, at Whiligh, near Wadhurst.

Courthope was sent to Blackheath and then taught at Harrow School by C. J. Vaughan and (from 1859) H. Montagu Butler. In 1861 he matriculated at Corpus Christi College, Oxford, and in 1862 became an exhibitioner of New College where he was a pupil of Edward Charles Wickham and formed a close friendship with John Conington, then Corpus professor of Latin, which continued until Conington's death in 1869. In 1865 Courthope published his first volume of poetry, *Poems by Novus Homo*, and was awarded the Newdigate prize. He graduated BA with a double first in classics in 1866. In 1868 he won the chancellor's prize with an essay entitled *The Genius of Spenser*, which was subsequently published in two editions that year.

As Courthope had a legacy which made him ineligible for a fellowship, he was called to the bar, and in 1869 he entered the education office as an examiner. Later that year he co-founded the *National Review*, of which he was joint editor until 1887, and published *Ludibria lunae*, a satire on the 'woman question'. In 1870 he published a second collection of poems, *The Paradise of Birds*, and married Mary Scott, eldest daughter of John Scott, her majesty's inspector of hospitals at Bombay. The couple settled at Wadhurst, Sussex, and raised a family of four sons and two daughters.

While working at the education office, Courthope began to collaborate with Whitwell Elwin on the standard edition of Alexander Pope's works in ten volumes (1871–89). Five volumes, edited by Elwin, had appeared by 1872. In 1881 a sixth followed, bearing Courthope's name as joint editor, and indicating that he would be solely responsible for the remainder. He took much care over the text, which had previously followed that of Bishop Warburton (1751) without examination of his sources. Courthope closed the series in 1889 with an acclaimed biography of Pope. The *Saturday Review* remarked that he 'has endeavoured to imitate the excellent example of Johnson, and make the study of the writer's work his main business, in preference to moralising upon his defects as a man'.

While working on Pope, Courthope contributed a volume on Joseph Addison in 1884 to the English Men of Letters series, produced *The Liberal Movement in English Literature* in 1885, and was appointed civil service commissioner in 1887. Five years later he was promoted to first civil commissioner. In his *History of English Poetry* (1895–1910) he undertook a work which had been projected by Pope and passed on to Thomas Gray and Thomas Warton, but never carried out. The *History* traced through successive poets the continuity of English poetry, locating each poet within a historical context. It ended at the Romantic period and was completed in six volumes. In 1895 Courthope was elected unanimously to the chair of poetry at Oxford, and made a CB, and in the following year was made an honorary fellow of New College. In 1901 he published the lectures given in his five years as professor under the title *Life in Poetry, Law in Taste*.

Courthope was elected fellow of the British Academy in 1907, to which he contributed many papers. His last published work was a translation (1914) of a selection from the *Epigrams* of the Roman poet Martial. He died at his home, The Lodge, Wadhurst, Sussex, on 10 April 1917. A volume of selected poetry, *The Country Town and other Poems*, was published posthumously in 1920.

     A. O. PRICKARD, *rev.* KATHERINE MULLIN

**Sources** Allibone, *Dict.* · A. T. C. Pratt, ed., *People of the period: being a collection of the biographies of upwards of six thousand living celebrities*, 2 vols. (1897) · *Men and women of the time* (1899) · H. Cox, *Who's who in Kent, Surrey, Sussex* (1911) · J. W. Mackail, 'W. J. Courthope', *PBA*, [8] (1917–18), 581–90 · WWW · A. O. Prickard, 'Memoir', in 'The country

*town', and other poems by the late William John Courthope* (1920) • *CGPLA Eng. & Wales* (1917)
**Archives** NRA, corresp. • Trinity Cam. | BL, letters to Lord Carnarvon, Add. MS 60775 • Bodl. Oxf., letters to Alfred Austin • LUL, letters to Austin Dobson • U. Leeds, Brotherton L., letters to Edmund Gosse • U. Reading, letters to Macmillans
**Wealth at death** £22,097 12s. 11d.: probate, 2 July 1917, *CGPLA Eng. & Wales*

**Courthopp, Nathaniel**. *See* Courthope, Nathaniel (*d.* 1620).

**Courtier, Peter Lionel** (1776–1847), poet, was born on 29 February 1776 in London, the son of Jean Louis Le Couteur (1739–1803), a merchant who had emigrated from Guernsey, and his wife, Sarah Dutton. He was educated by the Revd Morgan Jones at the dissenting academy at Hammersmith, but abandoned his clerical ambitions to work as a clerk for the firm of Law, publishers of textbooks. He founded the School of Eloquence, a literary and debating society whose members included the antiquary John Britton and Richard Alfred Davenport, later editor of the *Poetical Register*.

Courtier's first literary endeavour, *Poems* (1796), was well received; it was followed by *Revolutions, a Poem* (1796), a religious prophecy endorsing democratic principles, and *The Warning Voice* (1798), excoriating France. In 1797 Courtier left clerking to superintend the *Monthly Visitor*, whose contributors included Davenport and Thomas Dibdin. *The Pleasures of Solitude*, a long work in Spenserian stanzas, was published in 1800 and expanded in further editions in 1802 and 1804. Its success owed much to the popularity of Samuel Rogers's *Pleasures of Memory* and Thomas Campbell's *Pleasures of Hope*. On 14 July 1800 Courtier married Sarah Rhodes (*d.* 1853), the Myrtilla of his poems. He edited *Verulamiana*, extracts from Francis Bacon (1803), and shortly afterwards became editor of the *Universal Magazine*.

In 1805 appeared a new volume of *Poems*, and in 1806 the *Lyre of Love*, a chronological arrangement of love poems with biographical introductions. Unable to meet his household expenses Courtier was confined for debt in 1804, and in 1807 was incarcerated in the Fleet prison, a circumstance leading to dismissal from the *Universal Magazine* and permanent estrangement from his family. In 1809 he embarked on a new career as a journalist under the patronage of Eugenius Roche, for whom he worked at *The Day*, the *National Register*, and the *New Times*, supplementing a tenuous income by superintending a revision of Brown's *Self-interpreting Bible* and occasional contributions from the Literary Fund. For the *National Register* he composed a series of biographical essays on popular preachers republished under the signature Onesimus as *The Pulpit* (1809, 1812, 1816). A volume of poems, *Last Lays*, was prepared for the press in 1827 but did not appear. Upon the death of Roche in 1829 Courtier was reduced to extreme poverty and distress, his work as a police reporter hampered by frequent illnesses. In 1837 he reminded the Literary Fund that he had been among their earliest contributors four decades earlier; in 1841 his final appeal was

rejected with the notation 'not justifying assistance'. The poet died on 8 May 1847, aged seventy-one, and was buried at St Andrew's Church, Holborn, four days later.

DAVID HILL RADCLIFFE

**Sources** P. L. Courtier, ed., *Lyre of love* (1806) • [J. Watkins and F. Shoberl], *A biographical dictionary of the living authors of Great Britain and Ireland* (1816) • J. Britton, *Autobiography* (1850) • *British Critic*, 9 (1797), 557 • *Critical Review*, 22 (1798), 231 • private information (2004) [D. B. Courtier] • d. cert. • parish register, St Peter Port, Guernsey, 18 May 1739 [baptism: Jean Louis Le Couteur, father] • petition for royal licence for Lionel Courtier, son of Sarah, to add surname Dutton to that of Courtier, granted 21 July 1824, Coll. Arms
**Archives** BL, corresp. with Royal Literary Fund, loan 96

**Courtneidge** [*married name* Hulbert], **Dame** (**Esmerelda**) **Cicely** (1893–1980), actress, was born on 1 April 1893 in Sydney, Australia, the second of the three children and elder daughter of Robert Courtneidge (1859–1939), actor and theatre manager, and his wife, Rosaline May Adams (*d.* 1914), whose stage name was Rosie Nott and who had three sisters on the stage, one of whom was Ada Reeve, well known in her day as principal boy in the Drury Lane pantomimes. Cicely Courtneidge had early aspirations towards a stage career, and her first appearance (with one line to speak) was as Peaseblossom in her father's production of *A Midsummer Night's Dream*; she was aged eight.

At the age of fifteen, after two years' schooling in Switzerland, Cicely Courtneidge returned to England more determined than ever to be 'a great actress', and in this ambition she was encouraged by her father; but neither father nor daughter as yet realized her true métier in the theatre—that of a comedienne. Until the outbreak of war in 1914 she was destined to play *ingénue* roles in her father's productions, and at any rate was accomplished enough to be allowed (at her urgent request) to succeed Phyllis Dare in a leading part in the immensely successful musical comedy *The Arcadians*, at the Shaftesbury Theatre in London.

At the same theatre, in September 1913, Cicely Courtneidge played the part of Lady Betty Biddulph (a typical example of musical comedy nomenclature of that time) in *The Pearl Girl*, and it was then that she first met and played opposite her future husband, John Norman (Jack) *Hulbert (1892–1978), a young graduate aged twenty-one, just down from Cambridge. In June 1914 they again played opposite each other in an adaptation (mainly contrived by Hulbert) from a German comic opera, whose English version was entitled *The Cinema Star*. It ran successfully at the Shaftesbury Theatre until the outbreak of war, when its Germanic origin deterred London audiences and the play was withdrawn prematurely.

There followed for Cicely Courtneidge a depressing period of frustration, involving fruitless applications to theatre agents for engagements. The agents were not only discouraging as to her future in the theatre but inclined to attribute her rather frail reputation as a musical comedy *ingénue* to the influence of her father.

None the less, encouraged by her husband—they had married on 14 February 1916—who wrote daily letters to

Dame (Esmerelda) **Cicely Courtneidge** (1893–1980), by Bassano, 1913

her from the army camp where he was stationed, and by her father, who had belatedly realized where her talent in the theatre could be put to the best advantage, in her own words Cicely Courtneidge 'took to the halls'. 'Make them cry—and then make them laugh' was the substance of the advice given by her husband, and she did so for the remainder of her long stage career.

A hard life then began for Cicely Courtneidge, from fit-ups and one-night stands to occasional engagements in the provincial towns which in those days almost invariably contained a Victorian or Edwardian music-hall, with shows twice, or even three times, nightly. Helped by her father, she commissioned popular lyric writers to provide her with songs and words. These included 'The Knut in the RAF', the first, and one of the most successful, of her many male impersonations in uniform. There was about her a buoyancy and gaiety, an indefinable zest, which held the attention. With her tuneful voice, forceful humour, and vital personality, no one knew better how to get the right song across to an audience. By the end of the war in 1918 she had firmly established herself as a music-hall artiste, both in the provinces and in London.

Although after the armistice Cicely Courtneidge continued to perform in music-halls, her prevailing desire was to rejoin her husband in the stage partnership which had proved promising in the immediate pre-war period. But both now realized that light-hearted humour and burlesque, in revue and musical comedy, should be the dominant theme in their stage careers, though until the end

Cicely Courtneidge retained a broader style—a foothold in the music-hall of an earlier day.

In September 1921 Cicely Courtneidge appeared in a revue with her husband at the Royalty Theatre in London, but it was not until 1923 that they established their triumphant partnership and joint management, which resulted in a series of uninterrupted successes throughout eight years, in which both partners had star parts. Each was produced and stage-managed by Hulbert. These 'milestones in their joint career' (as they were called by Hulbert) were *Little Revue Starts at Nine O'Clock* (Little Theatre, 1923), *By-the-Way* (Apollo and Gaiety theatres, 1925–6), *Lido Lady* (Gaiety, 1926–7), *Clowns in Clover* (Adelphi Theatre, 1927–9), *The House that Jack Built* (Adelphi Theatre, 1929–30), and *Folly to be Wise* (Piccadilly Theatre, 1931).

In 1931 there occurred a set-back to the partnership which came as a surprise to both partners. The business side of their theatrical ventures had been entirely entrusted to a financier, through whose speculations the partnership became heavily in debt and the business went into liquidation. Hulbert at once accepted responsibility for the debts and undertook to repay all creditors, an undertaking he was able to fulfil by abandoning his stage career and devoting the next eight years to acting in films, a period which happened to coincide with a boom in the British film industry engendered by the coming of sound to the cinema. Cicely Courtneidge co-starred in two of the succession of films in which her husband appeared. In Noel Gay's *Soldiers of the King* (1933) she sang one of the most popular songs of her career, 'There's something about a soldier'; and in *Jack's the Boy* (1932) she shared with her husband a memorable sequence acted in Madame Tussaud's, with its climax in the chamber of horrors.

It was not until November 1938 that Cicely Courtneidge reappeared with her husband in London in *Under your Hat*, a spy story (with music and burlesque) by Arthur Macrae, which they both regarded as the happiest engagement of their joint stage career. It ran at the Palace Theatre until 1940, with a short interruption at the beginning of the war. During 1941 she gave a nightly three-hour entertainment in aid of the armed services at home and abroad, and at the end of each performance she appealed on the stage and from the auditorium for contributions from the audience, a personal request which was never in vain. Later during the war she formed a small company and took it at her own expense to Gibraltar, Malta, north Africa, and Italy, playing nightly to hospitals and to the services.

Cicely Courtneidge returned to London after the war and in November 1945 played the star part in Arthur Macrae's *Under the Counter*, produced by her husband at the Phoenix Theatre, which made fun of wartime shortages and the measures (legal and illegal) taken by the public to overcome them. This topical sally at recent restrictions had a run for two years in London, but when the show was produced (by Hulbert) in New York it was taken off after three weeks: the American audience did not comprehend the allusions to distresses they had not themselves endured. The set-back, however, was followed by a successful tour of the piece in Australia and New Zealand.

A few lean years followed, but Cicely Courtneidge made a great West End success, which proved to be the climax of her career, in *Gay's the Word* (Saville, February 1951) in a part written and songs composed for her by Ivor Novello— a personal triumph marred during the early part of its long run by Novello's sudden death. In 1967 at the Haymarket Theatre she gave a sensitive and endearing performance as Dora Randolph (originally played by Marie Tempest) in a revival of Dodie Smith's *Dear Octopus*, in which Hulbert played as convincingly the part of Dora's husband. The revival ran for nearly a year. As late as 1971, the year in which she celebrated her seventieth year on the stage, she played a leading part in a farce entitled *Move over, Mrs Markham*, which ran for eighteen months in London.

Further evidence of Cicely Courtneidge's versatility was given in her final film, *The L-Shaped Room* (1962), in which she played, movingly and memorably, the part of an elderly spinster, a lodger in a squalid London flat, involuntarily involved in the intrigues of others and spending her lonely days in arranging Christmas cards for sending to friends who had forgotten her.

Cicely Courtneidge was appointed CBE in 1951 and DBE in 1972. She died on 26 April 1980 in the Cintra Nursing Home, 7 Gwendolen Avenue, Putney, London, and was survived by her only child, a daughter.

D. PEPYS-WHITELEY, *rev.*

**Sources** C. Courtneidge, *Cicely* (1953) · J. Hulbert, *The little woman's always right* (1975) · J. Parker, ed., *Who's who in the theatre*, 6th edn (1930) · I. Herbert, ed., *Who's who in the theatre*, 16th edn (1977) · *WWW* · personal knowledge (1986) · m. cert. · d. cert.
**Archives** FILM BFI NFTVA, documentary footage · BFI NFTVA, performance footage | SOUND BL NSA, performance recordings
**Likenesses** Bassano, photograph, 1913, NPG [*see illus.*] · photographs, 1916–64, Hult. Arch.
**Wealth at death** £81,952: probate, 5 Aug 1980, *CGPLA Eng. & Wales*

**Courtney**. *See also* Courtenay.

**Courtney** [*née* Potter], **Catherine** [Kate], **Lady Courtney of Penwith** (1847–1929), social worker and internationalist, was born on 4 April 1847 at Gayton Hall, Herefordshire, the second of nine daughters of Richard Potter (1817–1892), railway entrepreneur and speculator, and his wife, Lawrencina, *née* Heyworth (1821–1882), whose father, Lawrence Heyworth, was also a railway entrepreneur. Among her four talented sisters was (Martha) Beatrice *Webb. She was educated by tutors at home and, briefly during the 1860s, at a London boarding-school for young ladies. Between 'coming out' at eighteen in 1865 and finally insisting on leaving home at twenty-eight in 1875, Kate Potter acted as the unwilling but competent organizer of the family household, both during the London season and for their months in the country at Standish, Gloucestershire. She longed to stop being a social parasite, on offer each year in the fashionable marriage market, and begged her parents to allow her to make a life of independent thought and action for herself instead. 'After a particularly difficult year … I made up my mind to leave home and go to Miss Octavia Hill to be trained for her work in

Catherine Courtney, Lady Courtney of Penwith (1847–1929), by George James Coates

London' (K. Courtney, journal, first entry, 1875). Kate Potter began as a trainee worker for the Charity Organization Society in Whitechapel and as an organizer of East End boys' clubs. She then joined Samuel and Henrietta Barnett, founders of Toynbee Hall and promoters of London settlement work. So warm and obviously genuine was her personality, and so anxious was she not to offend, that she actually managed to humanize her unlovable role of rent collector. In 1880 she met the Liberal cabinet minister Leonard Henry *Courtney (1832–1918), who was attracted by her hearty laugh. On 15 March 1883, when she was thirty-six and he fifty-one, they married, cheered on lustily by her well-wishers from Whitechapel. Their marriage, which was childless, was to prove a partnership of true minds for nearly forty years. Kate Courtney followed her husband's lead in becoming a Liberal Unionist and a suffragist—indeed she became a leader of the Women's Liberal Unionist Association in the 1890s, until she became disillusioned by its social conservatism and imperialism. She resigned from the association's committee on 24 October 1900.

Both the Courtneys were deeply committed to international peace and their first testing time had come in October 1899 with the outbreak of the Second South African War. They both became notorious as alleged 'pro-Boers', receiving scores of anonymous threatening letters. Leonard Courtney was dropped as Liberal candidate for Penwith, and Kate Courtney joined Emily Hobhouse in April 1900 in founding a women's committee of the South Africa conciliation movement that urged a negotiated settlement of the war: 'We have substituted uncivilized for civilized methods of warfare', she argued (K. Courtney, letter to the *Westminster Review*). In December she supported Emily Hobhouse's fact-finding mission to the British concentration camps at Bloemfontein, and throughout 1901 she helped both to organize relief in South Africa and to inform the British public about the atrocities being perpetrated by Britain on Afrikaner and African women and children.

When the First World War broke out Kate Courtney (who, on her husband's elevation to the peerage in 1906, had become Lady Courtney of Penwith) persisted in her humane pacifism; she consistently refused to wage war in spirit, insisting instead on championing 'innocent enemies' (K. Courtney, *Extracts from a Diary during the War*, 30 March 1915). Thus she helped to found an emergency committee to relieve destitute German civilians who had been stranded in Britain at the outbreak of the war; she visited German prisoners of war in prison ships; she publicized the work of her German counterparts in Berlin who were overseeing the welfare of British civilians and prisoners; she tried to intercede with the Home Office on behalf of German civilians threatened with deportation; she supported the American progressive Jane Addams's frustrated attempts in 1915 to organize a negotiated end to the war brokered by neutral nations; and finally, in 1918, she sought a way for British Quakers to go over to defeated Germany and take relief supplies to the starving over there. The first meeting of the Fight the Famine Committee was held at Kate Courtney's Chelsea home, 15 Cheyne Walk, in January 1919, when she was seventy-one, and out of that committee developed the Save the Children Fund.

Both Kate Courtney's *Extracts from a Diary* (1927) and her reflective, impassioned letters to the press in 1919–20 testify to her prophetic insight into the fatal consequences of righteous hatred and militarism. The popular press, for example the *Daily Sketch*, July 1919, pilloried her as 'pro-Hun'. Kate Courtney's alternative principles were those of E. D. Morel and his Union for the Democratic Control of Foreign Policy, and she was also a founding spirit behind the British sections of the Women's International League for Peace and Freedom and the League of Nations Union. 'Somebody must begin to be good if the better world we were promised is ever to come' she wrote to the *Daily News* in January 1920. She died at 15 Cheyne Walk on 26 February 1929, and was buried at Chelsea Old Church.

Kate Courtney's brilliant and much more famous sister, Beatrice Webb, condescended to her all her life: 'Dear Kate is an incurable sentimentalist' (B. Webb, *The Diary of Beatrice Webb*, 1982). But after Kate Courtney died, she wrote: 'Kate was the most beneficent of my sisters. … She was in a sense faultless—she had no malice, no envy, little egotism' (ibid., 6 March 1929). Other tributes to Kate Courtney's radiant personality are found in G. P. Gooch's *Life of Lord Courtney* (1920), Stephen Hobhouse's *Margaret Hobhouse* (1934), and Elizabeth Fox Howard's *Our Lady of Chelsea*, but it is her own words and deeds that deserve to survive her.                                    SYBIL OLDFIELD

**Sources** K. Courtney, *Extracts from a diary during the war* (privately printed, London, 1927) · K. Courtney, journal, BLPES, Courtney

MSS · B. Caine, *Destined to be wives* (1986) · S. Oldfield, *Women against the iron fist* (1989) · G. P. Gooch, *Life of Lord Courtney* (1920) · *Manchester Guardian* (27 Feb 1929) · *Woman's Leader* (8 March 1929) · E. F. Howard, 'My lady of Chelsea: Kate Courtney of Penwith', *Friends' Quarterly Examiner*, 63 (1929), 171–6 · S. Hobhouse, *Margaret Hobhouse* (1934) · GEC, *Peerage*

**Archives** BLPES

**Likenesses** G. J. Coates, painting, NPG [*see illus.*] · photograph, NPG; repro. in Oldfield, *Women against the iron fist* · photographs, Hadspen House, Somerset, Hobhouse Coll.; repro. in Caine, *Destined to be wives*

**Wealth at death** £27,391 13*s.*: probate, 2 May 1929, *CGPLA Eng. & Wales*

**Courtney, Sir Christopher Lloyd** (1890–1976), air force officer, was born at Hampstead, London, on 27 June 1890, the fourth son and youngest of the seven children of the author and editor William Leonard *Courtney (1850–1928), of Oxford and London, and his wife, Cornelia Blanche, the daughter of Commander Lionel Place RN. He spent two years at Bradfield College, but left at the age of fourteen on his mother's wishes to compete for a naval cadetship. He secured entry to the Royal Naval College, Dartmouth, in 1905, and after some years' service in warships qualified as lieutenant in 1911.

By then Courtney had already developed wider interests. Having seen aeronautical displays he applied in 1910 for flying training. He obtained this at length in 1912, at Eastchurch, and quickly qualified as a pilot (Royal Aero Club certificate no. 328). Four months later he was a flight commander at Yarmouth and by the outbreak of war a squadron commander in the newly constituted Royal Naval Air Service.

After recruiting 4 (later 204) squadron on the Isle of Grain, Courtney was given command of all the air units at Dover. Command at Eastchurch with his squadron then followed, and thus he built up 4 wing. It then joined other Royal Naval Air Service units in the Dunkirk area, where he commanded it from May 1916 to November 1917. Its work in reconnaissance, supporting naval attacks on the Belgian coast and intercepting Zeppelins, quickly brought him recognition. He was mentioned in dispatches in May 1917 and in November of that year was appointed chevalier of the Légion d'honneur and DSO.

On the formation of the RAF Courtney opted to join the new service and was soon director of air equipment in the new Air Ministry. Early in November 1918 he was promoted acting brigadier-general and sent out to form and command a new brigade—the 11th—in the independent force RAF, which was then bombing Germany from Lorraine. The armistice supervened; Sir H. M. Trenchard, the force commander, returned home and Courtney succeeded him. He was still only twenty-eight.

Such rapid promotion, with appointment as CBE in 1919, marked Courtney out for the highest positions. Nevertheless, he had to revert to wing commander when he received his permanent RAF commission. During the next twenty years he filled with quiet distinction a large variety of posts. In 1920–23 he commanded 2 (Indian) wing at Ambala; later he graduated from the Staff College at Quetta and moved on to be an instructor at the RAF Staff

College, Andover (1925–8). In 1931 (having been promoted air commodore in January) he successfully organized operations against rebel forces in southern Kurdistan, and the following year was appointed CB for his work. He remained in Iraq as chief staff officer until 1933, then returned home to a succession of posts in the Air Ministry, culminating in that of deputy chief of the air staff (1935–6). In the years immediately before the Second World War he was air officer commanding British forces in Iraq (1937–8); he had talks with General Milch of the German air ministry in Germany (1937), represented the RAF in the investigation by Lord Chatfield into the defences of India (1938–9), and, with increasing emphasis on reserves, commanded no. 16 (reserve) group (1938) and finally the new RAF reserve command (March 1939). These further services were acknowledged by appointment as KCB (1939).

Courtney was now being considered for the topmost posts in the service. He had narrowly missed becoming chief of the air staff in 1937, when C. L. N. Newall was preferred; but he was still young enough to succeed Newall. Meanwhile, in July 1938, he was notified that he was to succeed Sir Hugh Dowding at Fighter Command on 1 September 1939. Intensified war preparations then caused Dowding to be retained at Fighter Command longer than planned, but in June 1939 Courtney (now an air marshal) was again told that he would be succeeding him—this time on 31 March 1940. But he never did. The outbreak of war brought Dowding further short extensions of command, and in 1939 Courtney was injured in an aircraft accident during bad weather. One of his kneecaps was badly fractured—his leg was still in plaster when he accompanied the mission of Lord Riverdale to Canada three months later—and there was a permanent loss of mobility.

The major post that Courtney finally obtained, in January 1940, was that of air member for supply and organization. This gave him a seat on the Air Council and put him in charge of a vast department responsible not only for service organization but also for the provision of virtually every item required except (after May 1940) aircraft. And from 1942 onwards his huge responsibilities were greatly increased by the arrival of the American air forces, for whom he provided airfields (more than a hundred of them), station buildings, and the like. Within the department there were directorates-general for organization, for equipment, for works, and for servicing and maintenance, and beneath these there were scores of directorates and deputy directorates: in the *Air Force List* of April 1945 the names of the principal officers in works alone occupy twenty-five printed pages.

Over this huge realm Courtney presided with impeccable efficiency throughout the rest of the war. He won golden tributes from the Americans and in general provided a magnificent service for the RAF. His final honours included promotion to air chief marshal (temporary from January 1943 and confirmed in June) and appointment as GBE (1945) and as commander in the American Legion of Merit (1946).

After his retirement in November 1945 Courtney developed business interests and also gave much time to charitable activities such as the Victory Club and the Star and Garter Home. He derived much pleasure from his honorary membership of the Vintners' Company and was its master in 1964–5.

Courtney married in 1926 Constance (Micky) May Rayson, the daughter of George Edward Greensill, an accountant. He had no children, but there was a stepdaughter from his wife's first marriage. In appearance he was tall, distinguished, and very dark—so dark as to acquire as a cadet the nickname Black Courtney, which stuck to him for the rest of his career. Among his characteristics were his intelligence, his powers of administration, his capacity for work, his modest demeanour, and his natural courtesy. He was greatly liked as well as admired. He died in London on 22 October 1976, two years after his wife.           DENIS RICHARDS, rev.

**Sources** interviews between Courtney and E. B. Haslam, MOD, London, air historical branch · RAF Museum, Hendon, Courtney MSS · private information (1986) · personal knowledge (1986) · *The Times* (25 Oct 1976) · *The Times* (2 Nov 1976) · WWW
**Archives** Royal Air Force Museum, Hendon, letters and papers | Bodl. Oxf., corresp. with Sir Aurel Stein | FILM IWM FVA, actuality footage
**Likenesses** C. Dobson, oils, Vintners' Company hall · photographs, Royal Air Force Museum, Hendon
**Wealth at death** £31,233: probate, 9 Dec 1976, CGPLA Eng. & Wales

**Courtney, Edward**. See Leedes, Edward (1599–1677).

**Courtney, Francis**. See Blyth, Francis (c.1705–1772).

**Courtney, Dame Kathleen D'Olier** (1878–1974), suffragist and peace campaigner, was born on 11 March 1878 at 1 York Terrace, Gillingham, Kent, the youngest of five daughters and fifth of seven children of Lieutenant (later Major) David Charles Courtney (1845–1909) of the Royal Engineers, and his wife, Alice Margaret Mann. Her parents were Anglo-Irish gentry with military connections on both sides. She attended the Anglo-French College in Kensington and the Manse boarding-school in Malvern before spending seven months in Dresden studying German. She went to Lady Margaret Hall, Oxford, in January 1897 to read modern languages (French and German). She was awarded second-class honours in the university examination for women in 1900. While at Oxford, she formed a lifelong friendship with Maude Royden, suffragist and campaigner for the ordination of women.

Independent means gave Kathleen Courtney the opportunity to devote her life to social causes and world peace. After a short period working with the Lambeth Constitutional Girls' Club (a Lady Margaret Hall settlement), she became involved in the non-militant suffrage movement. A constitutionalist, she believed in education, argument, and reason. After a spell in Manchester (1908–11) as secretary of the North of England Society for Women's Suffrage, she moved to London and was honorary secretary (1911–15) of the National Union of Women's Suffrage Societies (NUWSS), led by Millicent Fawcett.

Suffrage agitation was suspended with the outbreak of

Dame Kathleen D'Olier Courtney (1878–1974), by Godfrey Argent, 1970

the First World War. The executive of the NUWSS split with half, led by Mrs Fawcett, supporting the government's war effort, and the other half, including Kathleen Courtney, resigning in the belief that the most vital task was to promote permanent international peace. In 1915 Kathleen Courtney was one of only three British delegates to attend the international peace conference at The Hague, which she had helped to organize. She was active in the British Women's Peace Crusade, launched in 1916, and was honorary secretary in the 1920s and chairman in the 1930s. She was one of the founders of the Women's International League for Peace and Freedom, and for ten years was chairman of the British section. She resigned in 1933 partly because she believed that the league's pacifism, calling for complete disarmament, was unrealistic.

During and after the First World War, Kathleen Courtney became associated with the Friends' War Victims Relief Committee, although not a Quaker herself. She worked for the Serbian Relief Fund in Salonika, took charge of a temporary Serbian refugee colony in Bastia, Corsica, and was decorated by the Serbian government. Those who knew her during this period described her as full of life and fun and an exceptional administrator. She went on to work for the Friends' committee in France, Austria, Poland, Czechoslovakia, and Greece. She was in Vienna for three years where she was horrified by the post-war scenes of starvation, particularly among refugees.

Kathleen Courtney had not forgotten the importance of extending the vote, however, and was an active officer of the National Council for Adult Suffrage in 1917, lobbying MPs for extension of the franchise until the act was passed in 1918. She was vice-president of the National Union of Societies for Equal Citizenship (as the NUWSS was renamed in 1919) and became involved in the work of the family endowment committee introducing, with Eleanor Rathbone, the idea of family allowances.

Kathleen Courtney attended the fourth women's international congress, held in Zürich in 1919 at the same time as the Paris peace conference. Active involvement in the League of Nations Union followed and she became a member of its executive in 1928 and vice-chairman in 1939. She was adamant that women must know more about international affairs. An excellent speaker, she spoke at conferences on its behalf all over the UK, and wrote regularly for the press on international affairs as well as travelling extensively in the USA, Canada, New Zealand, and Australia during the 1930s to lecture. She spent much time in Geneva, working as first vice-president of the Peace and Disarmament Committee of Women's International Organizations which was preparing a petition for disarmament (8 million signatures were collected) prior to the Geneva disarmament conference of 1932. She was an observer on behalf of women's organizations for the duration of that conference. When Abyssinia was invaded by Italy, she mobilized British and European women's organizations in the vain hope of preventing civilian bombing.

Kathleen Courtney's knowledge of the USA was of great service to the Ministry of Information during the Second World War. She made two hazardous voyages to the USA to plead for a permanent international organization for collective security, disarmament, and positive relief measures. She was an observer at the San Francisco conference in 1945 and her speeches were influential in persuading Americans of the value of the United Nations.

In 1945 Kathleen Courtney became deputy chairman of the United Nations Association, a voluntary non-governmental organization formed to support and publicize the UN charter ideals by educating and campaigning. In 1949 she became chairman of its executive committee and joint president (with Gilbert Murray). She retired from the chairmanship in 1951 but remained active in the association into her nineties. She was appointed CBE in 1946 and DBE in 1952. In 1968 she made a speech in Westminster at the fiftieth anniversary celebrations of the granting of votes to women.

Dame Kathleen Courtney was a forceful personality who did not suffer fools gladly, but her sternness was accompanied by grace and Victorian courtesy. She made an admirable chairman, able to cut through confusion and muddle. Her unemotional manner could make her seem cold but she believed that the head must rule the heart. She was determined to do the best for her causes and was a tireless, thorough organizer. Strikingly beautiful in her youth, she remained handsome and well dressed in her old age. In 1972 she was awarded the UN peace medal. She died at her home, 3 Elm Tree Court, Elm

Tree Road, London, on 7 December 1974. A memorial service was held on 11 April 1975 at St Martin-in-the-Fields, London. JANET E. GRENIER

**Sources** E. M. Chilver, 'Kathleen D'Olier Courtney', *Brown Book* (1975), 27–30 · A. Wiltsher, *Most dangerous women: feminist peace campaigners of the First World War* (1985) · M. Quass, 'UNA's first lady', *New World* (March 1968), 5 [Journal of United Nations Association] · M. Stott, 'Happy at 90', *The Guardian* (11 March 1968) · *The Times* (10 Dec 1974) · G. Bussey and M. Tims, *Pioneers for peace: Women's International League for Peace and Freedom, 1915–1965*, [2nd edn] (1980) · J. Liddington, *The long road to Greenham: feminism and anti-militarism in Britain since 1820* (1989), 147–9 · S. S. Holton, *Feminism and democracy: women's suffrage and reform politics in Britain, 1900–1918* (1986), 67–8 · W. A. Foster, *UN News* (Sept–Oct 1951) · S. Fletcher, *Maude Royden: a life* (1989) · BLPES, WILPF MSS [Women's International League for Peace and Freedom] · b. cert. · d. cert.

**Archives** Cumbria AS, Carlisle, papers relating to female suffrage · People's History Museum, Manchester, corresp. · Women's Library, London, corresp. and papers | BL, corresp. with Lord Cecil, Add. MS 51141 · BLPES, Women's International League for Peace and Freedom archives · Bodl. Oxf., corresp. with Gilbert Murray · IWM, letters and diaries, Friends' Relief Service, Salonika and eastern Europe · TCD, letters to Mary Childers | SOUND Women's Library, London, Brian Harrison tape 56, interviewing the Rt. Hon. Philip Noel-Baker, 26 April 1977 · Women's Library, London, recording of UNA function, speech (U Thant) and vote of thanks, K. Courtney

**Likenesses** G. Argent, photograph, 1970, NPG [*see illus.*] · J. Pannett, chalk drawing, Women's Library, London · photographs, Women's Library, London · portrait, repro. in *Record of the Women's International Congress* (June 1915), 13

**Wealth at death** £17,786: probate, 7 March 1975, *CGPLA Eng. & Wales*

**Courtney, Leonard Henry**, Baron Courtney of Penwith (1832–1918), journalist and politician, eldest son of the nine children of John Sampson Courtney (*d.* 1881), banker, of Alfreston House, Penzance, and his wife, Sarah (*d.* 1859), daughter of John Mortimer, was born at Penzance on 6 July 1832 and was baptized on 3 October 1832. He attended a local school and then worked for six years in Bolitho's Bank at Penzance. A local doctor taught him classics and mathematics in the evenings and he won a sizarship at St John's College, Cambridge. Courtney's university career was distinguished: he became second wrangler (1855), Smith's prizeman, and fellow of his college. In 1857 he went to London and in 1858 was called to the bar at Lincoln's Inn. After six years as a briefless barrister and freelance journalist—the latter being his real interest—he became in 1865 a leader writer for *The Times*, where J. T. Delane was the editor. During the next sixteen years he wrote some three thousand articles for the paper, and helped it maintain a Liberal patina as it drifted towards Conservatism. Courtney also contributed sixteen articles for the *Fortnightly Review*, mostly on political and economic topics. He became a close friend of its editor, John Morley.

From 1872 to 1875 Courtney was professor of political economy at University College, London. His political economy was not that of a thoroughgoing Liberal, for in the 1890s he sympathized with bimetallism, but he was always a free-trader. In 1874 he stood unsuccessfully as parliamentary candidate for Liskeard, in opposition to E. Horsman, also standing as a Liberal, though with tory

Leonard Henry Courtney, Baron Courtney of Penwith (1832–1918), by T (Théobald Chartran), pubd 1880

support; Courtney lost in a vicious campaign by five votes. On Horsman's death in 1876, he won the by-election and held the seat until 1885. In the Commons he was attached to the radical group centred around Joseph Chamberlain and Sir Charles Dilke. In 1880 W. E. Gladstone made him under-secretary for the Home Office and in 1881 he succeeded Sir M. Grant-Duff as under-secretary for the colonies, an appointment made in the face of strong opposition from Queen Victoria, for Courtney already had a reputation as an anti-imperialist. In May 1882 his favour with Gladstone was confirmed by his appointment as financial secretary to the Treasury in succession to Lord Frederick Cavendish.

Courtney was thus quickly launched on a promising political career, but one which relied on executive ability, for he from the first often irritated the Commons by his portentous and long-winded speeches, which reflected the worst features of his experience as a leader writer and professor. On 15 March 1883, at St Jude's, Whitechapel, he married Catherine or Kate [*see* Courtney, Catherine (1847–1929)], daughter of Richard Potter, formerly chairman of the Great Western Railway, and his wife, Lawrencina, *née*

Heyworth. The Courtneys made a formidable couple, prominent in radical circles, but with Leonard, especially, seen initially as something of a bore: his wife's sister Beatrice Webb thought 'he had no subtlety, no originality—he thought in the grooves made by other minds and by minds of the plainer sort' (Hart, 124). There was some social prejudice against Courtney, and in 1883, when the speakership was vacant, Dilke thought that Courtney would be unsuitable because he dropped his aitches.

Courtney's career was not, however, to run in the grooves of Liberal executive politics, for in 1884 during the debates on the Representation of the People Bill, he made the inclusion in the bill of proportional representation—which he had advocated since the 1870s—a condition of his membership of the government, and had to resign. From the back benches Courtney and John Lubbock (1834–1913) pressed the cause of proportional representation, especially with respect to school boards, local government, and home rule for Ireland, with no effect except for the aborted Irish county council measure of 1892 (introduced by A. J. Balfour). Courtney was elected for Bodmin in 1885. He opposed Gladstone's home rule proposals in 1886, but Gladstone rescued Courtney from political sterility by proposing him as chairman of committees and deputy speaker, which offices he held from 1886 until 1892. In them he was described as being 'impartially unfair to both sides'. In 1892 the Liberals encouraged him to stand for the speakership, but he declined, as he feared it would muzzle him. He was sworn of the privy council on 29 January 1889.

Despite Courtney's unionism, he remained a passionate anti-imperialist. He especially opposed British expansion in Africa, and argued against the 'forward' policy in Egypt, the Sudan, and South Africa. He opposed the annexation of the Transvaal in 1877, denounced the Jameson raid of 1896, and attacked the policy which led to the outbreak of the Second South African War in 1899. During that conflict he was chairman of the South African conciliation committee, which opposed demands for annexation of the Boer states and unconditional surrender. Courtney had always been an improbable Unionist, and this led to his final severance from that party. He did not stand for re-election in 1900. For the next six years Courtney 'lived the life of a political sage in Chelsea', as F. W. Hirst put it in the *Dictionary of National Biography*. His eyesight had already partially failed, but he turned to authorship, publishing *The Working Constitution of the United Kingdom* in 1901 and, anonymously, *The Diary of a Churchgoer* in 1904. However, he declined requests from the Electoral Reform Society to revive the cause of proportional representation until the Unionist government announced in February 1905 that there would be a redistribution of parliamentary seats. With the encouragement of Leonard and Kate Courtney, the Proportional Representation Society was revived and steadily campaigned throughout the years of Liberal government from 1905 to 1914.

Courtney stood unsuccessfully as a Liberal for West Edinburgh in 1906 and was given a peerage by Sir Henry Campbell-Bannerman in July that year, when he became Baron Courtney of Penwith. He often spoke in the Lords, assisting the meagre Liberal group there, even on home rule. He became a strong critic of Sir Edward Grey's foreign policy and an advocate of armament reduction. He attacked the entente with France and advocated a similar, balancing, agreement with Germany. After 1914 he criticized what he saw as the failings of British diplomacy. During the war he defended freedom of speech and freedom of conscience, and in a speech on 8 November 1915 was the first parliamentarian to call for peace negotiations, a cause he advocated until his death, as the only means of ending the war. He worked with the Union of Democratic Control to pursue justice for conscientious objectors, and he gained the respect of many young radicals: C. R. Buxton recorded: 'I should have become quite outrageously cynical about old age, if it had not been for Lord Courtney' (Harvie, 241).

Courtney died at his home, 15 Cheyne Walk, Chelsea, London, on 11 May 1918, and was buried four days later at Chelsea Old Church, London. His wife survived him by eleven years. The couple having no children, the barony became extinct. In Courtney's later years what had earlier seemed social inadequacies became strengths, and he and his wife played an important social as well as political role in giving vigour and tone to radical circles. His readiness to put principle before office gained him a place in the radical pantheon. F. W. Hirst, a friend and disciple, noted: 'To a mathematical mind and a strong logical sense, which insisted on arguing out every question, he united a very warm and emotional disposition' (*DNB*).

H. C. G. MATTHEW

**Sources** G. P. Gooch, *Life of Lord Courtney* (1920) · *DNB* · J. Hart, *Proportional representation* (1992) · Gladstone, *Diaries* · C. Harvie, *The lights of liberalism* (1976) · GEC, *Peerage*
**Archives** Arthur McDougall Fund, London, papers · BLPES, corresp. and papers · Duke U., Perkins L., family corresp. | BL, corresp. with Sir Charles Dilke, Add. MSS 43909–43921 · BL, corresp. with W. E. Gladstone, Add. MSS 44197–44519 · Bodl. Oxf., corresp. with Lord Kimberley · Bodl. Oxf., letters to Herbert Asquith · JRL, letters to C. P. Scott · Man. CL, letters to Mrs Fawcett · NA Scot., corresp. with A. J. Balfour · News Int. RO, corresp. relating to *The Times* · Pembroke College, Oxford, letters to G. B. Hill · U. Birm. L., corresp. with Joseph Chamberlain
**Likenesses** A. Legros, pencil drawing, 1883, FM Cam. · B. Stone, photograph, 1898–9, NPG · W. & D. Downey, woodburytype photograph, NPG; repro. in W. Downey and D. Downey, *The cabinet portrait gallery*, 3 (1892), 73 · Elliott & Fry, photograph, NPG · S. P. Hall, pencil sketch, NPG · R. Josey, mezzotint (after W. Carter), BM, NPG · London Stereoscopic Co., photograph, NPG · T [T. Chartran], watercolour study, NPG; repro. in *VF* (25 Sept 1880) [*see illus.*]
**Wealth at death** £56,672 2s. 6d.: probate, 25 July 1918, *CGPLA Eng. & Wales*

**Courtney, William Leonard** (1850–1928), philosopher and journalist, was born at Poona, India, on 5 January 1850, the youngest in the family of three sons and three daughters of William Courtney, of the Indian Civil Service, and his wife, Ann Edwardes, daughter of Captain Edward Scott RN, of Hoegarden House, Plymouth; his early years were profoundly influenced by his eldest sister, Emily (Minnie), a remarkable woman. Educated at Somerset College, Bath, under the Revd Hay Sweet Escott, a stimulating teacher, he was elected scholar of University College, Oxford, the vigorous life of which he enjoyed from 1868 to 1872. After gaining first classes in classical moderations (1870) and *literae humaniores* (1872), he won a fellowship at Merton College in the latter year, and shared the society of Mandell Creighton, William Wallace, R. J. Wilson, Andrew Lang, and F. H. Bradley among the fellows. In 1873 Courtney was appointed headmaster of his old school, Somerset College, and in the following year married Cordelia Blanche, daughter of Commander Lionel Place, RN, with whom he had three daughters and four sons, the youngest of whom was Air Marshal Sir Christopher *Courtney (1890–1976).

Courtney returned to Oxford in 1876, having been elected to a fellowship and tutorship in philosophy at New College, where he remained until 1890. His lectures, especially those on Plato's *Republic*, were remarkable for their excellent form and clear presentation of philosophical problems, and many distinguished pupils acknowledged their debt to his teaching. It was the period when a social life for married dons was beginning at the university and the Courtneys played an active part in it. He wrote on philosophy and, with Benjamin Jowett's help, promoted the foundation of the New Theatre, and assisted in the production of *Agamemnon* in Balliol College hall in 1880 and of the early plays of the Oxford University Dramatic Society (founded 1884). In the last enterprise he was associated with amateurs who later achieved fame—Arthur Bourchier, Ernest Holman Clark, and Harry Irving, whose father, Henry Irving, Courtney brought to lecture in Oxford in 1886. He was treasurer of the University Boat Club, and a conspicuous figure on the tow-path. This versatility possibly stood in the way of his reputation as a philosopher.

Courtney was already writing for *The World*, and for the *Fortnightly Review* and *Edinburgh Review*, and in 1882 he became assistant to T. H. S. Escott (son of his former headmaster), who was then editing the *Fortnightly*. Divided between his devotion to philosophy and the call of a wider sphere, he accepted, in 1890, a post on the *Daily Telegraph*—by then a staunchly unionist and imperialist paper—where he joined a group of able journalists, including John Merry Le Sage, Henry Duff Traill, and Edward Levy-Lawson (afterwards Lord Burnham), from whom he learned much. He left many friends, not only in New College, which he served with distinction and where he retained his fellowship for life, but in Oxford generally, chief among them being Edward Armstrong and Thomas Case.

Courtney worked for thirty-eight years in Fleet Street, writing general articles, and becoming in the mid-nineties chief drama critic and literary editor of the *Daily Telegraph*, a post he held until 1925; he wrote the weekly 'Book of the day', and always kept in touch with dramatic, literary, and general society at the Garrick Club (joined 1891), the Beefsteak Club (joined 1896), and elsewhere. His scholarly training and dramatic experience, his wide interests and resource in emergency, made him a first-rate journalist. In 1890–91 he edited *Murray's Magazine*, but he found his great opportunity when he became editor of the *Fortnightly Review* in 1894. He kept it at a high level on both the literary and the political side to the end of his life, editing it with sympathy and judgement. He had an uncommon flair for choosing subjects and writers, and delighted in encouraging new talent. For many years he was chairman of the publishing firm of Chapman and Hall.

Courtney's first wife died in 1907, and in 1911 he married Janet Elizabeth *Hogarth, an old pupil and friend, daughter of the Revd George Hogarth, vicar of Barton upon Humber, Lincolnshire, and sister of David George Hogarth; she shared his life as editor and journalist, to the great happiness of both.

Although Courtney gave up writing on philosophy after leaving Oxford, philosophy and religion remained near to his heart, and most of his writing had a serious note, the outcome of a sane outlook and a high ideal. His influence did much to keep journalism steady at a time of shifting standards. His philosophical studies, *The Metaphysics of John Stuart Mill* (1879), *Studies in Philosophy* (1882), and *Constructive Ethics* (1886), were published in his Oxford period; these were significant contributions, though not at the highest level. Of his later books, collected from his articles or written as holiday studies, the most original was *The Feminine Note in Fiction* (1904). His plays had little success.

Courtney was a tall and striking figure, resembling a soldier more than a philosopher. A portrait of him by Sir Hubert von Herkomer at New College is like him, but hardly does justice to his force of character. He was always a genial companion and a loyal friend. He died from cerebral thrombosis and general arteriosclerosis at his home, 36 Westbourne Gardens, London, on 1 November 1928.

P. E. MATHESON, rev. H. C. G. MATTHEW

**Sources** *The Times* (2 Nov 1928) · J. Courtney, *The making of an editor: W. L. Courtney, 1850–1928* (1930) · W. L. Courtney, *The passing hour* (1925)
**Archives** University of Rochester, New York, Rush Rhees Library, corresp. and literary papers | BL OIOC, letters to Sir Alfred Lyall · Richmond Local Studies Library, London, corresp. with Douglas Sladen · Royal Literary Fund, London, letters to Royal Literary Fund · Royal Society of Literature, London, letters to Royal Society of Literature · UCL, letters to Karl Pearson
**Likenesses** H. Furniss, pen-and-ink sketch, NPG · H. von Herkomer, oils, New College, Oxford · J. Russell & Sons, photograph, NPG · wood-engraving, NPG; repro. in *ILN* (13 Oct 1894)
**Wealth at death** £7014 13s. 2d.: probate, 12 Dec 1928, *CGPLA Eng. & Wales*

**Couse, Kenton** (1721–1790), architect, was born in Bermondsey, London, on 1 March 1721, the eldest son and only surviving child of Josias Couse (1693?–1755), goldsmith and linen draper of Cheapside, London, and his wife, Margaret (*b*. 1698), daughter of Alexander Kenton, master mariner. On 11 March 1736 he was apprenticed (for £49) to Henry Flitcroft, clerk of the works at Whitehall, Westminster, and St James's, and he served as labourer-in-trust at the same palaces from 1746 onwards. An assiduous officer (on 22 March 1765 he stayed up all night making out an abstract of the 1763 accounts for the Treasury), he was steadily promoted: he was clerk of the works at the Royal Mews from 1750 to 1766, clerk to the comptroller

(Flitcroft) from 1762 to 1766, and clerk of works at St James's, Whitehall, and Westminster, from 1766 to 1775. From 1775 to 1782 he served as secretary to the board and clerk of works at Carlton House and Buckingham House (the royal residence, where he may have constructed the prince of Wales's apartments on the north side). Some of the official clerkships were said to be extremely lucrative, although the salary was small. Couse was responsible for designing and building new committee rooms and an entrance for the House of Commons in Margaret Street (1766, 1768–70), refacing 10 Downing Street (1774–5), completing the rebuilding of the king's bench prison (1775–80) after William Robinson's death, and urgently rebuilding that prison and the Fleet, at a cost of some £40,000 in 1780–81, after the destruction wrought by the Gordon riots. In the 1782 reordering of the board of works his record of hard work and integrity earned him the administrative post of examiner, third in the hierarchy, which he held until his death. He also acted in a confidential private capacity for Thomas Worsley, the surveyor-general from 1760 to 1778, and subsequently for Worsley's widow.

In 1754 Couse unsuccessfully sought election as surveyor to the Goldsmiths' Company, of which he became a freeman by patrimony in 1756 and liveryman in 1776. Elected surveyor in 1762 (having already given professional advice), he was active in surveys and repairs of the Goldsmiths' estates, drawing up new schemes for their City property. He rebuilt their almshouses at Woolwich (1771; dem.), and designed a new assay office and other premises adjoining Goldsmiths' Hall (1772, 1781–4; dem. 1829) and a new barge.

Outside his official duties Couse reconstructed the east end of St Margaret's Church, Westminster, in a showy Perpendicular style (1758; dem.) and built Normanton church, Rutland (1764, rebuilt 1911) for Sir Gilbert Heathcote, for whom he also enlarged Normanton Park (1763–7; dem. 1911) and 29 Grosvenor Square, London (1764; dem. 1957). In collaboration with his erstwhile works colleague James Paine he built Richmond Bridge (1774–7, £30,000) and rebuilt Chertsey Bridge in stone (1780–85). Near by, at Botleys (for Sir Joseph Mawbey, bt, 1765; altered 1839), he excelled Chambers. He began Colney House, Shenley, Hertfordshire, for P. C. Crespigny about 1770, and completed it about 1785 for Governor Bourchier; he altered Wimpole Hall, Cambridgeshire, for Lord Hardwicke (1777–8; remodelled), and designed the reconstruction of the west wing of the Queen's College, Oxford, in 1778 after a fire. His Holy Trinity Church, Clapham Common (1774–6; altered), is commonplace. A subscriber to the continuation by John Woolfe and James Gandon of *Vitruvius Britannicus* (1767, 1771), Couse followed Flitcroft's Palladian footsteps with elegance and a fine sense of proportion.

Described as 'Liberal, honourable and punctual in all his engagements', Couse 'deservedly gained numberless friends, and never lost one in the practice of his profession for nearly fifty years' (*GM*, 959). He married, on 23 June 1750, Sarah (1730–1782), daughter of Charles Hamilton of Stable Yard, St James's, porter-in-ordinary and table decker to the princesses; they had four sons and four daughters. Having suffered from gout for some years, Couse died in his official house in Scotland Yard, Westminster, on 10 October 1790. In his will he directed that his substantial estate should be divided equally among his children, only three of whom survived him, and that he should be buried in Lambeth churchyard, where he was interred on 18 October, near his parents. M. H. PORT

**Sources** Colvin, *Archs.* · H. M. Colvin and others, eds., *The history of the king's works*, 6 vols. (1963–82), vols. 5–6 · will, PRO, PROB 11/1196, fol. 458 · *GM*, 1st ser., 60 (1790), 959 · registers, St Mary at Lambeth, LMA [burial, 1755 and 1790] · register, Bermondsey St Mary Magdalen, 1721, LMA [baptism] · Goldsmiths' Company Records, Foster Lane, London · apprenticeships, Joiners' Company Records, GL, Guildhall MSS 3052/5, fol. 174*v* · registers, St Martin-in-the-Fields, 1751–64, City Westm. AC [baptism] · parish register, St Mary Woolnoth, 1750, GL [marriage] · PRO, work 4/15; work 4/16 · private information (2004)
**Archives** Goldsmiths' Hall, Foster Lane, London, Goldsmiths' Company records, survey plans · Hovingham Hall, Yorkshire, corresp. with Thomas Worsley
**Wealth at death** approx. £18,000; incl. £17,350 in Bank of England stock: private information

**Cousen, John** (1804–1880), engraver, was born at Miryshaw, near Bradford, in Yorkshire, on 19 February 1804. Nothing is known of his parents. From about 1818 he was a pupil of John Scott (1774–1828), the noted animal engraver, in London, but at an early stage he developed an inclination towards landscape engraving, a preference to which he devoted himself almost exclusively for the rest of his professional career. Though little known today he became one of the ablest landscape engravers in a period that coincided with the rising status of contemporary landscape painting.

Cousen specialized in book illustration, of which his earliest work, *Val d'Ossola*, after William Brockedon, published in *Illustrations of the Passes of the Alps* (1828–9), appeared at a time of intense interest in travel writing and tours. He engraved drawings of landscape views by J. M. W. Turner, who undertook special tours in order to fulfil publishers' commissions. One of the most celebrated of these projects is *The Rivers of France* (1833–5), a series of works depicting views along the Seine and the Loire, accompanying text by Leitch Ritchie. Cousen's first contribution to this series was in 1834 with three engravings, which included *Light Towers of the Hève*, a delicate vignette that formed the title-page. The following year he engraved the title-page of Ritchie's *Château Gaillard*. He also contributed a plate, *Babylon*, after Turner, to *Landscape Illustrations of the Bible* (1836), a major work for which Turner contributed thirty designs. Rawlinson, author of the catalogue raisonné of Turner's engraved work, considered Cousen's vignettes and smaller plates to be unsurpassable.

Cousen's involvement with the *Art Journal*, the leading and most popular fine art publication during the nineteenth century, represents a substantial body of work; from 1849 to 1866 he supplied thirty-two plates, most after works by his contemporaries. The journal provided surveys of important collections to which Cousen contributed; these included paintings in the Royal Collection and the National Gallery, specifically those bequeathed by

Robert Vernon and those in the Turner Bequest. It was while working for the *Art Journal* that he produced his only known works after Old Masters, including Hobbema's *The Old Mill* and Berchem's *Crossing the Ford*.

Cousen also produced large single-sheet engravings. Thirteen of these are known to have been published, mostly by leading publishers, including Thomas Agnew & Sons, London. The earliest was *Mercury and Hersé*, after Turner, published in 1842; Cousen worked almost exclusively with steel plates, and this print is the only known example of his work engraved on copper. Eleven of these prints were declared to the Printsellers' Association, the body that from its foundation in 1847 regulated the issue of proofs of the most important prints in Britain. Proof impressions of twelve of these, signed by Cousen, are in the department of prints and drawings at the British Museum, together with unique working proofs, touched proofs, and many books containing his prints—including, for example, Turner's personal copy of Ritchie's *Wanderings by the Seine*.

His contemporaries considered Cousen somewhat reserved and of a retiring disposition, but his generosity and genial humour endeared him to his circle of friends. Ill health forced his retirement about 1864. He seems to have taken up painting about this time, and exhibited two oils, *Hastings* and *Arundel Park*, at the Royal Academy in 1863 and 1864 respectively. He died on 26 December 1880, at his home in Holmesdale Road, South Norwood, Surrey, and was buried in nearby Croydon cemetery. He was survived by his younger brother Charles Cousen (1819–1889), who also was a noted engraver. One of his executors was the engraver Lumb Stocks.

R. E. GRAVES, rev. DONATO ESPOSITO

**Sources** B. Hunnisett, *An illustrated dictionary of British steel engravers*, new edn (1989) · W. G. Rawlinson, *The engraved work of J. M. W. Turner*, 2 vols. (1908–13) · *The Times* (29 Dec 1880) · *The Athenaeum* (1 Jan 1881) · *Art Journal* (Feb 1881), 63 · CGPLA Eng. & Wales (1881)
**Wealth at death** under £25,000: probate, 5 March 1881, *CGPLA Eng. & Wales*

**Cousin** [*née* Cundell], **Anne Ross** (1824–1906), poet and hymn writer, only child of David Ross Cundell, an assistant surgeon of the 33rd regiment at Waterloo, and his wife, Ann, was born in Hull on 27 April 1824. Her family moved soon after to Leith, Midlothian. Educated privately, she became an expert pianist under John Muir Wood. Although raised as an Episcopalian, she became a Presbyterian. In 1847 she married the evangelical minister William Cousin (who was born at Leith in 1812 and died at Edinburgh in 1883). Cousin was called from the Chelsea Presbyterian Church to the Free Church at Irvine, Ayrshire, in 1850, and in 1859 to Melrose. He retired to Edinburgh in 1878.

Described as 'a lady of scholarly tastes and artistic temperament' (*MT*, 30), Cousin began publishing anonymous poems in the *Christian Treasury* in 1845. The intensity of her poems reflects contemporary religious turbulence in Scotland. Her best-known work is the joyous, visionary hymn 'The sands of time are sinking' of 1854. 'I wrote it', she

said, 'as I sat at work one Saturday evening, and though I threw it off at that time, it was the result of long familiarity with the writings of Samuel Rutherford, especially his Letters'. It appeared first as 'The Last Words of Samuel Rutherford' in nineteen stanzas in the *Christian Treasury* in 1857. It did not become generally known until J. Hood Wilson (1829–1903) of the Barclay Church, Edinburgh, introduced a version of five verses (only the fourth and fifth of which correspond with the now popular version) into a hymnal, *Service of Praise*, in 1865. It achieved wide circulation by its inclusion in many hymnals, including the *Song-Book of the Salvation Army* (1953). In Britain it is usually set to the hymn tune 'Rutherford' by Chrétien Urhan (1790–1845), while in America it is sung to a setting by the American evangelist Ira D. Sankey (1840–1908).

Cousin wrote other popular hymns, including 'O Christ, what burdens bowed Thy head' (from the poem 'The Substitute') and 'King eternal! King immortal' (from 'Adoration'). 'To thee and to thy Christ, O God' (from 'To God and his Christ') was included in *Hymns Ancient and Modern* (1875).

The refrain of 'The Sands of Time' gave the title to Cousin's *Immanuel's Land and other Pieces* (1876; 2nd edn, 1896). In this volume of 107 poems she demonstrates her versatility and proficiency, ranging from early Christianity and Scottish history to the anguish of a child's death and other bereavements. *An Anthology of Scottish Women Poets* (ed. C. Kerrigan, 1991) includes 'Christ within the Veil' and 'The Double Search'. The future reputation of the 'Scottish Christina Rossetti, with a more pronounced theology' (Campbell, 147) may depend on compositions neither intended nor adapted for public worship, and Cousin may be appreciated at least as much for expressions of human suffering and aspiration as for celebrations of divine grace.

Anne Ross Cousin had four sons and two daughters. John William Cousin (*d.* December 1910) included his mother in his *Short Biographical Dictionary of English Literature* (1910). Twenty-three years a widow, she died in Edinburgh on 6 December 1906. In 1910 a memorial window to Cousin and her husband was placed in St Aidan's United Free Church, Melrose.

J. C. HADDEN, rev. BONNIE SHANNON MCMULLEN

**Sources** D. F. Wright, 'Cousin, Anne Ross', *DSCHT* · *MT*, 48 (1907), 30 · W. Ewing, ed., *Annals of the Free Church of Scotland, 1843–1900*, 2 vols. (1914) · J. W. Cousin, *A short biographical dictionary of English literature* (1910) · C. Kerrigan, ed., *An anthology of Scottish women poets* (1991) · J. Julian, ed., *A dictionary of hymnology*, rev. edn (1907); repr. in 2 vols. (1957) · J. M. Barkley, *Handbook to the church hymnary* (1979) · D. Campbell, *Hymns and hymn makers* (1898) · G. Claghorn, *Women composers and hymnists: a concise biographical dictionary* (1984) · L. F. Benson, *The English hymn: its development and use in worship* (1915) · J. Wells, *The life of James Hood Wilson* (1904) · private information (1912) [Anne P. Cousin]

**Cousins, Frank** (1904–1986), trade unionist, was born on 8 September 1904 at 28 Minerva Street, Bulwell, Nottinghamshire, the eldest son in a family of ten (five sons and five daughters) of Charles Fox Cousins, miner, and his wife, Hannah, *née* Smith, the daughter of a miner from

Bulwell. He was educated at Beckett Road School in Wheatley, Doncaster, and King Edward elementary school, Doncaster, which he left at the age of fourteen in 1918 shortly before the end of the First World War. He immediately started work alongside his father, as a trainee at Brodsworth colliery in Doncaster, where he worked underground and joined the mineworkers' union (then the Yorkshire Miners' Association, which was part of the Miners' Federation of Great Britain, the forerunner of the National Union of Mineworkers). After working in the colliery for more than five years Cousins left to become a truck driver, first delivering coal locally and then, in 1931, as a long-distance road haulage driver—by which time he had joined the Transport and General Workers' Union (TGWU), led by Ernest Bevin. Meanwhile, on 26 December 1930 he married Annie Elizabeth (Nance; b. 1907), daughter of Percy Judd, railway clerk, of Doncaster. There were two sons and two daughters of the marriage.

Cousins mostly ferried meat between Scotland and London until July 1938, when he became a full-time official of the TGWU, as an organizer in the Doncaster district. In one sense he was born into trade unionism as were so many of his generation—men of great natural ability but without extended education or social opportunities open to the more prosperous groups in society. Becoming a trade union activist was a calling, quite the equal of similarly dedicated work for a political party. At this time Cousins first met Ernest Bevin, clashing with him over organizing road haulage workers into the union. It was a brotherly clash, but one which both men remembered, and especially Cousins, since he felt it may have been a turning point in his own career, demonstrating as it did his characteristic style as a fearless, stubborn, awkward, and rebellious negotiator. His physical stature helped to accentuate these characteristics: he was 6 feet 4 inches tall, powerfully built, and immensely strong. He spoke with a sharp rasping tone, especially when excited by events. His loyalty to his principles and political beliefs was absolute.

Cousins's development as a full-time official for the TGWU took him from Doncaster to Sheffield during the Second World War. In 1944 he was appointed to his first national trade union post, as national officer for the road haulage section of the TGWU, based in London. In October 1948 he was appointed national secretary for the group, a substantial achievement in view of his difficult relationship with the TGWU general secretary, Arthur Deakin, with whom he had frequently clashed, on industrial as well as political policy. Deakin, a rock of the established right-wing authority of the trade union movement, sought to keep Cousins firmly under control and, where possible, deny him advancement in the union. But a series of remarkable circumstances thrust Cousins into the top ranks of the TGWU.

Deakin died in 1955 before he could secure his preferred successor. The job of general secretary of the TGWU, arguably the most important power-broking role in the British labour movement, then went to Deakin's number two,

Arthur Tiffin, and to everyone's surprise Cousins was appointed by the union's executive as Tiffin's deputy. Tiffin died unexpectedly within six months of taking over and on 2 January 1956 Cousins was appointed 'acting' general secretary. Later, on 11 May 1956, after a union ballot, he was confirmed as general secretary by 503,560 votes to 77,916—which was the largest ballot return in the history of any British trade union. At that time the union ran membership ballots only for the general secretary's post.

The whole affair was an extraordinary sequence of events, which was to have far-reaching consequences for the entire labour movement—especially for the Labour Party, then under the leadership of Hugh Gaitskell. The largest union in the country had a left-wing radical at the helm for the first time in its history. Cousins immediately made an impact on the industrial front, first in the motor industry, where he inherited a difficult and tense climate of industrial relations as automation was being introduced, and then in London buses, where he led a strike lasting nearly two months. At the same time he quickly sought to switch the TGWU's traditional political stance from staunchly pro-Gaitskell to the support of Aneurin Bevan and the Bevanite left. In fact he went beyond this and personally associated himself and his family with the Campaign for Nuclear Disarmament. In 1960 Cousins led the campaign to 'ban the bomb' at the Labour Party conference at which Gaitskell was defeated on defence policy. The defeat precipitated Gaitskell's famous 'fight and fight, and fight again' speech.

After Gaitskell's death in 1963 Cousins played a prominent part in helping to secure Harold Wilson as leader of the Labour Party. In October 1964, when Wilson won the general election, Cousins was invited into the Labour cabinet as the first minister of technology. At the same time he was sworn of the privy council. Yet the rebellious instinct refused to desert him even in the cabinet. He quickly found himself at odds with Wilson, as he opposed all moves by the Wilson government to establish a statutory incomes policy. When, in the end, he failed to persuade his cabinet colleagues, he resigned from the Wilson government in July 1966. Shortly afterwards he also resigned his parliamentary seat at Nuneaton—a seat that had been found for him in a by-election in 1964 and which he assumed in January 1965.

Cousins consistently resisted any form of state control over pay, carrying this opposition back with him to the TGWU where, after resigning from the government, he resumed as general secretary in 1966. Yet he never again quite recaptured the force of his earlier years. However, during the three years which remained before he retired from the TGWU in September 1969, he ensured the succession of his chosen 'crown prince', Jack Jones.

Cousins's final role was as the founding chairman of the Community Relations Commission, set up in 1968 by the Wilson government, and charged with improving race relations in Britain. It was a cause close to Cousins's heart—so much so that he remained in the post for a short while even after the election of a Conservative government under Edward Heath in 1970. Indeed, he was persuaded to do so by the home secretary, Reginald Maudling. In November 1970 he finally resigned his chairmanship of the commission and went into retirement in the village of Wrington near Bristol, curiously enough only a few miles from where the founder of the TGWU, Ernest Bevin, was born. He refused several invitations to return to public life and declined a seat in the House of Lords. He died at the Royal Hospital, Chesterfield, Derbyshire, on 11 June 1986, of heart failure. He was survived by his wife and four children. His ashes were scattered across moorland near Chesterfield, and a memorial service was held at St Martin-in-the-Fields on 9 July 1986.

Cousins was the most forceful of all trade union leaders to emerge in the post-war years: he had a remarkable and galvanizing effect on the rank and file of the entire labour movement. He shifted the Labour Party and the trade union movement to the left and turned the Transport and General Workers' Union—then the largest union in the country—from a pillar of the Labour right-wing establishment into a driving force for radical left-wing reform.

The reasons behind Cousins's remarkable, albeit temporary, success went beyond his own forceful, commanding personality—he emerged on the trade union and political scene at a psychologically important moment in the post-war development of organized labour. By the mid-1950s a good deal of disillusion had set in to dampen the idealism of the immediate post-war years. The Attlee government's loss of office in 1951 led to a widespread conflict of ideas as to what kind of socialist programme should be adopted to appeal to the British voters. The split inside the Labour Party between right and left wing was sharper than ever, with the Gaitskellites and the Bevanites engaged in ideological warfare. Before Cousins the trade union majority within the TUC was solidly Gaitskellite. Cousins changed that balance and in the process began an ideological debate within the entire labour movement about the direction of a future Labour government. His eventual alliance with Harold Wilson—whom he decisively helped into the leadership of the party—was expected to be similar to the kind of alliance that Bevin had with Attlee in the 1945 Labour government. But that did not happen. The realities were conditioned by Labour's extremely narrow majority in the 1964 election, by disagreement within the Wilson cabinet, and by Cousins's own impatience. He wanted to push ahead with radical policies, not only in his own new Ministry of Technology, but also for the government as a whole. One example was his deep disagreement with Wilson's foreign policy, especially Britain's political support for the Americans in Vietnam. These factors, along with his refusal to accept a policy of wage restraint, led to his resignation from the government.

As a cabinet minister, at the pioneering technology department, Cousins was a failure—like so many 'imports' from industry. He did succeed in launching a number of important developments at the new ministry but his style in the Commons was too abrasive. He privately confessed to feeling ill at ease in the parliamentary ambience. The launching and development of a completely new department of state is, by definition, a formidable task; it requires experienced political skills which Cousins, the combative trade union leader, did not possess. Nor did he get the response he had hoped for from his cabinet colleagues—some of whom still resented the thrust of his political ideas.          GEOFFREY GOODMAN

**Sources** G. Goodman, *The awkward warrior: Frank Cousins, his life and times*, 2nd edn (1984) · G. Goodman, *Brother Frank* (1969) · M. Stewart, *Frank Cousins* (1968) · J. Jones, *Union man* (1986) · *WWW*, 1981–90 · *The Times* (12 June 1986) · b. cert. · m. cert. · d. cert. · personal knowledge (2004)
**Archives** U. Warwick Mod. RC, papers
**Likenesses** Emwood [J. Musgrave-Wood], pen-and-ink cartoon, 1963, NPG · group portrait, photograph, 1969 (*TGWU leaders*), Hult. Arch. · photograph, 1972, Hult. Arch. · photograph, repro. in Goodman, *Awkward warrior* · photograph, repro. in Stewart, *Frank Cousins*
**Wealth at death** £29,542: probate, 13 Oct 1986, *CGPLA Eng. & Wales*

**Cousins, James Henry Sproull** (1873–1956), writer and educationist, was born on 22 July 1873 at 29 Cavour Street, Belfast, the son of James Cousins (*d.* 1920), a sailor, and his wife, Susan Davis (*d.* 1915). His parents were both Wesleyan Methodists; his father retired from a sailing career to work for the Belfast harbour commission, while his mother managed the home and family. Having finished his formal schooling at the age of twelve Cousins studied shorthand and typing in the Belfast Mercantile Academy and later became private secretary and speech-writer for the mayor of Belfast.

Inspired by the fiction of Samuel Ferguson, Cousins joined the Gaelic League in Belfast and began to write romantic Celtic poetry, publishing his first poem, *Ben Madighan*, in 1894. Attracted by the literary revival, Cousins moved in 1897 to Dublin, where he worked first as a clerk in a coal and shipping company and then as a teacher at the high school on Harcourt Street. On 9 April 1903 he married Margaret Elizabeth Gillespie (1878–1954) [*see* Cousins, Margaret Elizabeth] of Boyle, co. Roscommon. Raised in the Church of Ireland, Margaret Gillespie was a music student. Their marriage began a co-operative venture in a range of social reform activities such as vegetarianism, cycling, feminism, religious ecumenism, and the revival of folk art and music.

From 1901 to 1905 James Cousins was a catalyst to the formation of the Abbey Theatre and of the Irish National Theatre, formed in April 1902, which he provided with its first two plays, *The Sleep of the King* and *The Racing Lug*. Although Yeats initially encouraged him to contribute plays, by October of 1902 he had notoriously 'snuffed out' Cousins, calling his work 'vulgar rubbish'. It is not clear why Yeats manifested such a sudden aversion to Cousins's plays, although critics have both noted the similarity of Yeats's ideas to those of Cousins and speculated on the likelihood of a clash of egos.

Instead Cousins became increasingly immersed in the occult. A friend of the poet–artist–occultist George Russell

(AE), he attended séances with AE and W. B. Yeats while Margaret Cousins became a medium with the dead. In July 1907 the Cousinses attended the convention of the Theosophical Society in London, at which the president, Annie Besant, instructed Margaret Cousins to form a theosophical lodge in Dublin. The theosophical belief in an ancient wisdom which embraced all knowledge, science, magic, and religion framed the Cousinses' romantic universalism. Theosophy's theoretical inclusiveness and celebration of feminine intuition afforded platforms of cultural authority to intellectual women excluded from mainstream churches, and to the men who supported them. Much of James Cousins's energy from 1908 to 1913 was taken up as a stalwart suffragist supporter of the Irish Women's Franchise League (IWFL), co-founded in 1908 by his wife. James Cousins co-edited the weekly newspaper of the IWFL, the *Irish Citizen*.

When an effort to direct a co-operative bank resulted in James Cousins's bankruptcy, the Cousinses decided to take up another position, marketing vegetarian foods for a British company. After two years near Liverpool, disillusioned by industrial English culture and the outbreak of the war, James Cousins wrote to Annie Besant at the international headquarters of the Theosophical Society in Madras to offer his editorial services to her nationalist newspaper *New India*.

On 11 November 1915 the Cousinses arrived in Madras. Although they had their differences with Besant over the place of feminism in the national movement, they spent the next forty years working in theosophical schools. For the most part they were stationed in the inland town of Madanapalle. While Margaret Cousins became a nationally known figure for her leadership of the women's movement, James Cousins became known for his promotion of both folk and classical arts, crafts, literature, and music. In 1922 he established a school for the arts in Madras which would become the renowned Kalakeshetra and from 1934 was art adviser to the government of Travancore. In India he continued to publish poetry and politically engaged literary treatises critical of western cultural imperialism. Altogether he published more than fifty books and countless articles. Both of the Cousinses were prominent activists throughout the Indian freedom movement.

From 1943 until her death in 1954 James Cousins nursed his wife through a series of strokes. He died on 20 February 1956 in Madanapalle, where his body was cremated the following day.                    CATHERINE CANDY

**Sources** J. H. Cousins and M. E. Cousins, *We two together* (1950) • A. Denson, *James H. Cousins (1873–1956) and Margaret E. Cousins (1878–1954): a bio-bibliographical survey* (1967) • W. A. Dumbleton, *James Cousins* (1980) • C. Nash, 'Geo-centric education and anti-imperialism: theosophy, geography and citizenship in the writings of J. H. Cousins', *Journal of Historical Geography*, 22 (1996), 399–411 • C. Candy, 'The occult feminism of Margaret Cousins in modern Ireland and India, 1878–1954', PhD diss., Loyola University, 1996 • R. Hogan and J. Kilroy, *Lost plays of the Irish renaissance* (1970) • b. cert.
**Archives** Kalakeshetra, Besant Nagar, Madras, India, drawings and MSS • Theosophical Society, Adyar, Madras, files | NA Ire.,

general prisons board papers and suffragette files • NL Ire., Denson MSS • NL Ire., Sheehy Skeffington collection
**Likenesses** photograph, repro. in Cousins and Cousins, *We two together* • photographs, Theosophical Society, Adyar, Madras • portrait, Madanapalle Theosophical College, Madanapalle, India

**Cousins** [*née* Gillespie], **Margaret Elizabeth** (1878–1954), social reformer and women's activist, was born on 7 November 1878 at Boyle, co. Roscommon, Ireland, the first child of Margaret Shera and her husband, Joseph Gillespie (d. 1930). Her father was the clerk of petty sessions in the Boyle court house, a unionist, and a protestant. Her parents provided a materially and emotionally comfortable middle-class childhood. Margaret attended Victoria High School for Girls in Londonderry on a scholarship and matriculated with distinction in 1898. She then went to the Royal Irish Academy of Music in Dublin where she acquired academic and professional reinforcement for her lifelong interest in music and earned the bachelor's degree in music from the Royal University of Ireland in October 1902. In 1900 she met James Henry Sproull *Cousins (1873–1956), an aspiring poet and playwright who had come from Belfast to Dublin where he was active in the Celtic revival. They married on 9 April 1903; at their wedding banquet she announced her commitment to the vegetarianism which her husband practised.

During the early years of the twentieth century Margaret Cousins became involved in organizational activities related first to vegetarianism and then to women's suffrage. In her memoirs, written with her husband, Margaret linked an invitation to speak at a vegetarian conference in Manchester with her initial awareness of the women's suffragist movement after attending a meeting of the National Council of Women held simultaneously in December 1906 (Cousins and Cousins, 128–9). Subsequently she began to campaign with women suffragists in Ireland and in England. In November 1908 she joined Francis and Hannah Sheehy Skeffington to found the militant Irish Women's Franchise League, which sought the franchise for Irish women on the same basis as that granted for Irish men. For not subordinating female suffrage to Irish home rule, the league was criticized as unpatriotic and its members as selfish. Disillusioned by the lack of impact that outdoor meetings and written propaganda had during the league's initial years, Margaret took up the militant tactics of the suffragettes, breaking windows on Downing Street in November 1910 and then at Dublin Castle in January 1913, and serving a one-month sentence of imprisonment in each case. Although she became an ally of English suffragists such as the Pethick-Lawrences, Cousins was careful to articulate the need for Irish suffragists to formulate goals and tactics suitable in the Irish situation.

Intimately linked with this public, political activity was Cousins's exploration of the occult and of theosophy. From the early 1900s she deemed herself to be especially receptive to the world of spirits and able to communicate with the spirits of deceased friends. Theosophy was congenial to such communication and to some feminist values. Theosophical authors proclaimed that males and females were on equal planes and that intuition, usually viewed as more developed in women than in men, was a higher means of knowing the world of spirits. Theosophical thought also emphasized the underlying unity of diverse elements such as religions and ethnic groups. Theosophy provided both a propitious ideological base and the entry to India, where Cousins would work for the remaining four decades of her life.

In 1913 the Cousinses moved to Garston, near Liverpool, where James worked for a vegetarian food company. Since Margaret was unable to establish close ties with English women activists in the Liverpool area, she felt rudderless and was eager to move to India when her husband obtained a position as literary editor on *New India*, a newspaper launched by Annie Besant, then the president of the Theosophical Society, at Adyar in the suburbs of Madras. Soon after arriving in Madras in November 1915 James Cousins lost his editorial post. In late 1916 the couple moved to Madanapalle, in the hinterland of Madras, where both taught at a theosophical college. Here Margaret became involved with women's rights issues. In 1917, when constitutional reform was imminent, she organized a deputation of Indian women and drafted a petition asking Edwin S. Montagu, the secretary of state for India, and the viceroy, Lord Chelmsford, for female suffrage. From then until the late 1930s she worked behind the scenes to gain and extend women's suffrage in India: briefing Indian women who lobbied British officials in London, writing supportive articles for Indian newspapers, and organizing campaigns for Indian women candidates when they became eligible for election to provincial assemblies.

Although content to be in the shadow of Annie Besant, Margaret was an active propagandist for theosophy as well as for women's rights. In 1917 she helped Dorothy Jinarajadasa, a British theosophist, to organize the Women's India Association, and became the editor of its journal, *Stri Dharma*, which was published in English, Telugu, and Tamil versions. The association and its journal linked political and social programmes. In 1926 Cousins embarked on planning for the All India Women's Conference, which focused initially on developing women's education, then on broader social and legal issues such as age of marriage, birth control, and a uniform civil code, while trying to remain aloof from political objectives which were deemed potentially divisive. Margaret was a longtime member of the standing committee of the conference and its president in 1936–7. She was particularly active as a propagandist, publishing numerous articles and two books on Indian women, *The Awakening of Asian Womanhood* (1922) and *Indian Womanhood Today* (1941). In the early 1940s poor health and 'the feeling that direct participation by me was no longer required, or even desired, by the leaders of Indian womanhood who were now coming to the front' (Cousins and Cousins, 740) led to her withdrawal from public activity. In 1943 Margaret suffered the first in a series of debilitating strokes.

A feminist first and a nationalist second, whether in Ireland or in India, Cousins sought to reform patriarchal ideology, practices, and institutions to equalize educational, political, and economic opportunities for women. Her ideology of the 'femaculine' which strove for 'a synthesis of the virtues of the masculine and feminine in which the defects of each are balanced if not eliminated' (M. Cousins, *Irish Citizen*, 12 June 1912, 10) was both conservative and radical. It reflected a belief that men and women had inherent characteristics, and led her to extol women's distinctive qualities as both biological and social mothers. At the same time she sought to achieve transfigured gender relationships based on equality. In Ireland and England she focused on suffrage issues, while in India her purview expanded to include better educational opportunities, health care, and working conditions for women as well as suffrage. She also became a vocal proponent of Indian freedom and supporter of Mahatma Gandhi, and protested against a government ban on free speech in Madras in 1932 which earned her a year's imprisonment. Although she was articulate about the inequities of class divisions within Indian society, her reform programme was directed at the concerns of middle- and upper-class Indian women. Even so, Cousins worked tirelessly to identify with Indian women as a colleague, to develop organizational and propaganda infrastructures which Indian women could utilize to pursue their own agendas, and to foster contacts between Indian women and women activists around the world. A life of service was her ideal, and in India she sought to be a builder of bridges between women.

Margaret Cousins died on 11 March 1954 in Adyar, Madras. She was cremated according to Hindu practices, and her ashes were deposited in the Ganges River at Varanasi. The All India Women's Conference honoured her contribution by naming their library at their national headquarters in New Delhi after her.

BARBARA N. RAMUSACK

**Sources** J. H. Cousins and M. E. Cousins, *We two together* (1950) • A. Denson, *James H. Cousins (1873–1956) and Margaret E. Cousins (1878–1954): a bio-bibliographical survey* (1967) • [S. Muthulaksmi Reddi], *Mrs Margaret Cousins and her work in India* (1956) • C. Candy, 'The occult feminism of Margaret Cousins in modern Ireland and India, 1878–1954', PhD diss., Loyola University of Chicago, 1996 • B. N. Ramusack, 'Catalysts or helpers? British feminists, Indian women's rights, and Indian independence', *The extended family*, ed. G. Minault (1981), 109–150 • C. Candy, 'Relating feminism, nationalisms and imperialisms: Ireland, India and Margaret Cousins's sexual politics', *Women's History Review*, 3 (1994), 581–94 • B. N. Ramusack, 'Cultural missionaries, maternal imperialists, feminist allies: British women activists in India, 1865–1945', *Women's Studies International Forum*, 13 (1990), 309–21 • C. Murphy, *The women's suffrage movement and Irish society in the early twentieth century* (1989)

**Archives** Theosophical Society Library, Madras (Chennai), Tamilnadu, India, Margaret Cousins and James Cousins collection, archives | L. Cong., Margaret Sanger MSS • Nehru Museum, New Delhi, All India Women's Conference papers • NL Ire., annual reports of the Irish Women's Franchise League • NL Ire., Sheehy Skeffington collection • Smith College, Northampton, Massachusetts, Sophia Smith collection

**Likenesses** photograph, 1913, repro. in Cousins and Cousins, *We two together* • photograph, repro. in Reddi, *Mrs Margaret Cousins*

**Cousins, Samuel** (1801–1887), engraver, was born at Victoria Terrace, Exeter, on 9 May 1801 and baptized at St Mary Steps, Exeter, on 24 May, the son of John Cousens, tradesman, and his wife, Mary; he was the second eldest of five brothers and four sisters. He attended the episcopal school in Exeter, where he showed great proficiency in art. His talents were discovered when a visitor to Exeter by chance saw some of his drawings in a shop window, bought several, and subsequently sent the boy to the Society of Arts in London. He was not yet ten years of age. On 28 May 1811 he was awarded the silver palette of the society for a drawing, *The Good Shepherd*, after a print by James Heath after Murillo. In the following year he received the silver Isis medal for another drawing, *A Magdalen*. This was seen by the noted mezzotint engraver Samuel William Reynolds (1774–1835), who in the autumn of 1814 took Cousins on as an apprentice, without the usual premium. After he had finished his apprenticeship he was Reynolds's assistant for four years.

Many early prints executed by Cousins were published under Reynolds's name. Cousins contributed to his master's great project of prints after Sir Joshua Reynolds (1820–25), for which he executed about ninety plates. However, four prints—portraits of Sir J. Banks, the Revd T. Lupton, Viscount Sidmouth, and the Revd J. Mitchell—executed between 1822 and 1825 record both Reynolds and Cousins as printmaker, a sign of Cousins's growing stature. On 19 February 1824 Cousins wrote: 'I have been lately finishing a half-length plate from a picture by Sir William Beechy. It is a portrait of the Duchess of Gloucester, a tolerably good plate, and I am to have my name to it' (Pycroft, 11). Confident of his abilities, Cousins set up independently at 104 Great Russell Street, near the British Museum. In 1826 he published his first two plates: *Master Lambton* and *Lady Ackland and her Children*, both after Sir Thomas Lawrence.

Cousins's principal output was dominated by prints after the two most illustrious former presidents of the Royal Academy: Reynolds and Lawrence. Following the first exhibition of Old Masters at the academy, in 1870, which included work by both these artists, prints after their work were much in demand. In 1875 Cousins was able to remark that 'the engravings I have done from Sir Joshua Reynolds's pictures have had such a ready sale … one I finished about a month ago since seems to please the people uncommonly, for all the 300 artist's proofs [the most expensive impressions] are sold' (Pycroft, 21–2).

However, it was work after his contemporaries that produced Cousins's most commercially successful prints. There was great demand for prints after the most popular paintings of the day, and publishers were able to issue many more artist's proofs of such work than was usually the case. For example Henry Graves & Co. issued 675 artist's proofs of Cousins's engraving of Sir Edwin Landseer's *The Maid and the Magpie*, and the Fine Art Society issued 625 of his engraving of Sir John Everett Millais's *Princes in the Tower*; the average was 100 or 200. The cost of these artist's proofs also reflected publishers' confidence in Cousins's work; the proofs of *The Maid and the Magpie* cost 10 guineas,

Samuel Cousins (1801–1887), by James Leakey, 1843

whereas standard impressions would have cost 3 guineas.

Cousins's career was closely connected with the Royal Academy, the primary exhibiting space and art institution in nineteenth-century Britain; he was elected an associate engraver in November 1835 and began exhibiting his engravings at the academy's annual summer exhibition in 1837. In 1854 he exhibited three portrait drawings, the only works of his that were not prints. In February 1855 he had the distinction of being one of only two engravers to be elected Royal Academician (the other was Lumb Stocks). He was determined to retire in 1874 but did not finally give up working professionally until 1884, and continued to send examples of his work to the Royal Academy until 1880.

Cousins was employed by many of the leading print publishers in London; Henry Graves & Co., and Paul and Dominic Colnaghi (and their affiliations) account for over three-quarters of his published output. Conscious of his status as one of the leading reproductive printmakers of his time he deposited at the British Museum, in January and March 1872, an almost complete set of his work. The gift contained fine artist's proofs, many signed, and followed a previous gift, in 1866, of a drawing that he executed at the age of fourteen—evidence of his precocious talent. The later gift substantially augmented the collection of his work already held by the museum, which now also holds a steel plate worked by him. He gave a smaller sample of his work, now in the Royal Albert Memorial Museum, to his home town, Exeter. Cousins was also a competent miniaturist. His miniature of Alexandra Zica-liotti, executed in oil on ivory, is in the Victoria and Albert Museum, London.

Cousins's reputation was pre-eminent in the art world of his time, and he was showered with accolades. In 1854 he was commissioned to engrave Winterhalter's *Napoleon III*, and upon its completion he received the order of the Légion d'honneur and a gold medal as *graveur étranger*. He was included in the popular publication *Artists at Home* by Frederick George Stephens (1884), which provided pro-files, illustrated by whole-page photographs, of artists in their homes. He had numerous one-man shows at a time when this was relatively novel, even for painters. These included one held in Manchester in 1877 by Thomas Agnew & Son, and others in London, at the Fine Art Society in 1883 and at Henry Graves & Co. in 1887. He is one of only a few British nineteenth-century reproductive print-makers for whose work a catalogue raisonné exists.

Cousins never married and lived for most of his life with one of his sisters, who survived him. A younger brother, Henry Cousins, also became a noted engraver. On 7 May 1887 he died at the house that since 1857 had been his home: 24 Camden Square, London. He was buried in High-gate cemetery, and left an estate valued at over £113,000. Two of his executors were the engravers Edward Goodall and Thomas Goff Lupton.

L. A. FAGAN, rev. DONATO ESPOSITO

**Sources** A. Whitman, *Samuel Cousins* (1904) · G. Pycroft, *Memoirs of Samuel Cousins RA* (1887) · Graves, *RA exhibitors* · BM, department of prints and drawings · *CGPLA Eng. & Wales* (1887) · IGI · G. W. Friend, ed., *An alphabetical list of engravings declared at the office of the Printsellers' Association, London*, 2 vols. (1892)
**Archives** V&A NAL, letters to Thomas Oldham Barlow and Mr Ward relating to Chalcographic Society
**Likenesses** J. Leakey, oils, 1843, NPG [see illus.] · C. W. Cope, sketch, c.1862, NPG · F. Holl, drawing, 1879, NPG · F. Holl, oils, 1879, Tate collection · C. Waltner, etching, 1881 (after F. Holl), BM · E. Long, oils, 1882, Royal Albert Memorial Museum, Exeter · A. S. Cope, oils, 1883, Aberdeen Art Gallery, MacDonald collection · S. A. Hart, pencil drawing, NPG · F. Joubert, carte-de-visite, NPG
**Wealth at death** £113,123 12s. 7d.: resworn probate, Dec 1887, *CGPLA Eng. & Wales*

**Coutances, Walter de** (d. 1207), administrator and arch-bishop of Rouen, was a native of Cornwall, son of Reinfrid and Gonilla, and brother of the royal servant Roger fitz Reinfrid, who probably introduced him into the king's household. His family probably originated in Normandy. Coutances bore the title *magister*, which he most likely earned in the schools of Paris. His contemporary at the Angevins' court, Gerald of Wales (d. 1220x23), described him as devoted to letters, and accomplished in secular and courtly matters. Coutances was a canon of Rouen Cath-edral by 1169, and became treasurer there in 1177. In Eng-land he became archdeacon of Oxford in 1173 or 1174. A royal clerk by the former year, he became vice-chancellor when Ralph de Warneville took the chancery. He was a member of the household of Henry, the Young King, until the outbreak of the 1173–4 rebellion, when he returned to Henry II's household. In 1176 and 1177 he went on missions for the king to the courts of the count of Flanders and the French king, and subsequently held as royal custodies the vacant abbeys of Wilton and Ramsey and the honour of Arundel. On the resignation of Geoffrey Plantagenet as bishop of Lincoln, Walter de Coutances was elected to the see on 2 May 1183, favoured by Henry II over three other candidates. He was ordained priest on 11 June 1183 by the bishop of Évreux, consecrated bishop on 3 July at Angers by the archbishop of Canterbury, and enthroned at Lin-coln on 11 December. He occupied the see for only eigh-teen months, too short a time to make any impression upon it. Nevertheless, he took part as bishop in the coun-cil at Westminster in 1184 that elected Baldwin arch-bishop of Canterbury, and Gerald of Wales accused him of damaging his see by reducing its resources and leaving it in debt.

In the summer of 1184 Coutances was elected arch-bishop of Rouen after Henry II had rejected the chapter's nominees and named as his candidates three English bishops, indicating Coutances as his personal choice. The pope confirmed his election on 17 November 1184. The chronicler William of Newburgh wrote that Coutances hesitated some time before leaving Lincoln for Rouen, pondering whether to prefer 'a more esteemed but poorer position' to 'his less esteemed but richer office', but, 'ambition for a higher office triumphed over the love of a higher income' (William of Newburgh, *Historia rerum Anglicarum*, ed. R. Howlett, Rolls Series, 1884, 236–7). As archbishop he continued to serve the king, going to the French court as an ambassador in 1186. The next year the monastic chapter at Canterbury appealed to him against the archbishop of Canterbury's attempt to found a secular college of canons, and he served as an arbitrator in that long and complex conflict between the Canterbury monks and the archbishop. In January 1188 Coutances took the cross, along with the kings of England and France, and later that year he again went as an envoy to Philip Augustus to seek reparation for damage the latter had done in Normandy. In 1189 he was present with Henry II at La Ferté-Bernard for his conference with Philip and Richard, and was one of the papally appointed arbitrators to whom the two kings had promised to submit.

Following Henry II's death the archbishop absolved Richard at Sées for his conduct toward his father and invested him with the duchy of Normandy at Rouen. Then, crossing to England, Coutances took part in Richard's coronation at Westminster and accompanied the king on his return to Normandy. In fulfilment of his crusading vow he accompanied Richard to Sicily, and wit-nessed a number of royal charters. At Messina in October 1190 he acted as one of Richard I's representatives work-ing to make peace between the people of the city and the crusaders. Before Richard set sail from Sicily Coutances took part in the king's arrangements with Philip; he was one of Richard's guarantors for his peace with Tancred, king of Sicily (r. 1190–94), and he was also appointed one of the treasurers of the crusading army.

Coutances travelled no further than Messina, for troubles in England resulting from the treachery of the king's brother, John, count of Mortain, and the unpopularity of the justiciar William de Longchamp, led Richard I to send the archbishop to the kingdom as his agent. He received papal release from his crusading vow, and returned to England in the spring of 1191, accompanying Eleanor of Aquitaine, the queen mother. Two royal letters authorized him to share authority with William de Longchamp. In England, he found a confused situation, as Longchamp increasingly aroused the hostility of the baronage, while Count John sought to use the justiciar's unpopularity to secure supreme power for himself. The chronicler Richard of Devizes accuses Coutances of playing a double part, but the archbishop was seeking to stand apart from both factions in order to act in the king's best interest. Coutances sought to mediate between Longchamp and Count John, and at a council at Winchester on 28 July 1191, they reached agreement over control of castles. However, Longchamp overplayed his hand by having Geoffrey Plantagenet, archbishop-elect of York and the king's half-brother, seized when he landed at Dover in September 1191, on his way to take possession of his new archbishopric—an act of violence that led to his being stripped of his justiciarship. Coutances then took up the justiciar's duties, although he never used the title in official documents. Longchamp surrendered his castles in England and fled to Normandy, where the archbishop of Rouen had him excommunicated. Longchamp's complaints to king and pope led to further confusion, and ultimately to papal intervention, culminating in Normandy being placed under interdict when William Fitzralph, steward of Normandy, sought to prevent papal agents from entering the duchy. In the meantime Coutances and his associates had seized the lands of Longchamp's see of Ely.

Coutances made certain that he governed England 'by the will and consent of his associates and by the counsel of the barons of the exchequer' during the two and a half years that he held the justiciarship, from September 1191 until the end of 1193 (*Chronica … Hovedene*, 3.141). A second task that Richard had assigned to him was to supervise the election of a new archbishop of Canterbury, following the death of Archbishop Baldwin in 1190. Doubtless both he and Longchamp had their sights set on the see, and each viewed the other as a rival. The Canterbury monks refused to elect the royal nominee, Guglielmo, archbishop of Monreale in Sicily. Reginald, bishop of Bath, was elected in November 1191, but died a month after the election. The archbishop of Rouen had to supervise a second election on 22 May 1193, which resulted in the election of Hubert Walter, the king's new nominee. Early in 1193 news of King Richard's imprisonment in Germany reached England, and Coutances turned his attention to securing the king's release; he held a council at Oxford in February that sent the abbots of Boxley and Robertsbridge to Germany to make contact with the captive king. Richard commanded Coutances to come to him in Germany, accompanying Queen Eleanor, and his departure ended his justiciarship. On 2 February 1194 the archbishop was present at Mainz for a meeting to consider terms for Richard's release. Following the king's release he remained in Germany as one of the hostages for payment of the ransom. Because the king never paid a final instalment of 10,000 marks, Coutances had to pay it himself in order to win his freedom.

The archbishop returned to England in May 1194, before going to Normandy, where he soon found himself at odds with both Richard I and Philip Augustus, as they struggled for control of the duchy. Soon after his return Coutances's attempts to negotiate a truce managed to annoy both monarchs. In January 1196, as part of the treaty of Louviers, the two kings tried to curb Coutances's freedom of action by making his manor of Les Andelys, strategically located on the Seine above Rouen, neutral ground subject to neither ruler. They made Les Andelys collateral for the archbishop's good conduct, subject to forfeiture if he excommunicated them or their officials or placed interdicts on their territories. Coutances fled to Cambrai, and he did not return to Rouen until July. Another conflict with Richard I soon arose over Les Andelys, once the king began construction of Château Gaillard on the archbishop's manor. The archbishop placed Normandy under an interdict and left for Rome in November 1196. Pope Celestine III (*r.* 1191–8) issued a ruling on 20 April 1197 that since construction of the castle was essential for Normandy's security, Coutances should accept an exchange of land with the king. On 16 October, Richard and Coutances agreed to an exchange that gave the archbishop the port of Dieppe and other territories, producing an annual income of nearly 2000 angevin pounds. Settlement of the dispute over Les Andelys marked the end of Coutances's service to the Angevin kings. Disillusioned with Richard, he concluded that since the king could not protect the Norman church, he must concentrate on his responsibility as archbishop to safeguard its properties.

On Richard I's death Coutances invested John as duke of Normandy on 25 April 1199, and received his oath to protect the church and its dignities. John soon afterwards confirmed the exchange of Dieppe and other properties for Les Andelys, but he challenged the archbishop's right to secular jurisdiction over his church's lands, over forest privileges, and other rights. Coutances purchased a delay in the proceedings for a fine of 1500 angevin pounds, but had to offer an additional 600 pounds before winning most of the rights in question. The archbishop took part in the peace settlement of Le Goulet between John and the French monarch on 22 May 1200. But he played no part in John's failed defence of Normandy, and after 1204 readily transferred his allegiance to Philip, investing him with the duchy, just as he earlier had Richard I and John.

Although absent from his province for almost the entire period from 1190 to 1194, Coutances was none the less an active archbishop. He negotiated with the seneschal of Normandy in 1190 to confirm continued immunity for clerics from the secular courts of Normandy. He also made innovations in ecclesiastical administration: some time before 1200 he began keeping a register of his judgments, and he appointed the first *officialis* at Rouen. He supervised the reconstruction of Rouen Cathedral, begun in 1155 and restarted after a disastrous fire in 1200. Walter de Coutances died on 16 November 1207 and was buried in the cathedral. The canons of Rouen remembered him as 'a magnificent benefactor of the church of Rouen' (*Recueil des historiens des Gaules et de la France*, 23.369). His magnificence is also demonstrated by the inventory of his personal possessions made at the time of his death. It lists jewels, altar vessels, vestments, and an impressive library, mostly of scriptural texts and works of theology, but also including books of canon law, saints' lives, and the writings of Statius, Juvenal, and Ovid.

Among Coutances's relatives was a nephew, Master John de Coutances, bishop of Worcester (1196–8). Several canons at Lincoln, and later at Rouen, bearing the toponymic 'de Coutances' may have been relatives; one of them, Richard, archdeacon of Rouen, was Coutances's nephew.                                RALPH V. TURNER

**Sources** P. A. Poggioli, 'From politician to prelate: the career of Walter of Coutances, archbishop of Rouen, 1184–1207', PhD diss., Johns Hopkins University, 1984 · L. Delisle and others, eds., *Recueil des actes de Henri II, roi d'Angleterre et duc de Normandie, concernant les provinces françaises et les affaires de France*, 1 (Paris, 1909) · *Fasti Angl., 1066–1300*, [Lincoln] · D. S. Spear, 'Les chanoines de la cathédrale de Rouen pendant la période ducale', *Annales de Normandie*, 41 (1991), 135–76 · L. Landon, *The itinerary of King Richard I*, PRSoc., new ser., 13 (1935) · *Gir. Camb. opera*, vol. 7 · *Chronicon Richardi Divisensis / The Chronicle of Richard of Devizes*, ed. J. T. Appleby (1963) · *Radulfi de Diceto … opera historica*, ed. W. Stubbs, 2 vols., Rolls Series, 68 (1876) · *Chronica magistri Rogeri de Hovedene*, ed. W. Stubbs, 4 vols., Rolls Series, 51 (1868–71) · R. Howlett, ed., *Chronicles of the reigns of Stephen, Henry II, and Richard I*, 4 vols., Rolls Series, 82 (1884–9), vols. 1–2 · *The historical works of Gervase of Canterbury*, ed. W. Stubbs, 2 vols., Rolls Series, 73 (1879–80) · W. Stubbs, ed., *Chronicles and memorials of the reign of Richard I*, 2: *Epistolae Cantuarienses*, Rolls Series, 38 (1865) · T. Bonnin, ed., *Cartulaire de Louviers* (1870), 156–7
**Archives** Archives Départementales de la Seine-Maritime, Rouen

**Coutanche, Alexander Moncrieff**, Baron Coutanche (1892–1973), bailiff of Jersey, was born in St Saviour, Jersey, on 9 May 1892, the younger son and third child of Adolphus Arnold Coutanche (1856–1921), notary public and captain in the Royal Jersey militia, and his wife, Jane Alexandrina (Ina) Finlayson (*d.* 1909), second daughter and coheir of Alexander Finlayson of Glasgow. The Coutanches had been landowners in the parish of Trinity, Jersey, from at least the early sixteenth century, but Coutanche was baptized Alexander Moncrieff in recognition of his Scottish ancestry. After attending Jersey high school and Victoria College, the local public school for boys, he graduated from the University of Caen, at that time a popular training for the Jersey bar, and then attended Carlisle and Gregson's London Academy with the intention of entering the Indian Civil Service. To his chagrin, having passed the entry examination, he was rejected for service in India on health grounds, a systolic murmur of his heart having been discovered. As a second best Coutanche decided upon a legal career, joined the chambers of John Beaumont (later privy councillor), Middle Temple, in 1912, with a view to practising at the Chancery bar, and was called to the Jersey bar in 1913.

Upon the declaration of war in 1914 Coutanche enthusiastically anticipated active service with the Royal Jersey militia, but was ordered to serve instead as assistant to the government secretary in Jersey. A further attempt to join up in the 'Devil's Own' (Inns of Court) regiment was frustrated by his being graded C.3 at medical examination. Not to be outdone, he signed on as a labourer in a munitions factory, and rose rapidly through the grades of chargehand and foreman to become a draftsman and member of the management committee. Meanwhile he was called to the English bar in 1915. On hearing from a Jersey colleague of the work of the War Claims Commission in France, he volunteered for similar duties and, in 1917, was posted to Belgium, with the rank of lieutenant, where he won the Belgian Croix de Guerre and was appointed chevalier of the order of the Crown. He was demobilized in 1920 with the rank of captain.

After a brief return to his London chambers, Coutanche was summoned home owing to the illness of his father and resumed the practice of Jersey law. In 1922 he topped the poll in an election for deputies and represented the town of Saint Helier in the states of Jersey. On 23 August 1924 he married Ruth Sophia Joan Gore (1902–1973), only child of Leicester Gore (1868–1931), a descendant of the first earl of Arran, and his wife, Sophia Harris Mitchell (*d.* 1926). There was one son, John Alexander Gore Coutanche (*b.* 1925), later a lieutenant-commander in the Royal Naval Reserve and a jurat of the royal court.

In 1925 Coutanche was appointed by the crown as solicitor-general and soon revealed his acumen in negotiating the settlement of Jersey's imperial contribution to the war effort with Whitehall. He then reformed the department of the law officers and reorganized the *greffe* (secretariat) of the states legislative assembly, and separated it from that of the royal court and judiciary. Promoted attorney-general in 1931, he continued his reforming work, drafting new laws on workmen's compensation, air navigation, import duties, and the humane slaughter of cattle. While respecting the Jersey tradition which preserved French as the official language, he also realized the practical necessity to use English in the courts if clients were to understand the proceedings, and was the first attorney-general to prosecute in English.

In 1935 the then bailiff, Charles de Carteret, resigned owing to failing eyesight, and Coutanche was elevated to that office, which combined the roles of president of the states and judge of the royal court. Among his early achievements was the opening of Jersey airport in 1937.

The Second World War was to bring Coutanche his greatest challenge. In 1940, when the island was demilitarized by the British government and the lieutenant-governor and garrison were withdrawn, Coutanche was sworn in as civil governor as well as bailiff and instructed by George VI, with advice from the London government, to remain at his post in face of the advancing German forces. On 1 July 1940 he read in the Royal Square the ultimatum of surrender, instructed the population to fly white flags, and personally lowered the union flag from the signal post above the town of St Helier. In this unforeseen situation the bailiff continued to sit in his court, presided over the states, reorganized by him as a supreme council of eight departments covering the major aspects of government, and maintained a dignified formal relationship with the German commandants and senior officers with whom he had to deal. His actions preserved a civil government between the occupying forces and the local population, about 40,000 of whom had remained in the island. Asked later what his attitude had been, Coutanche summed it up in two words: 'I protested.'

Orders requiring the registration of Jews and the restriction of their commercial activities were registered by the royal court on a number of occasions from October 1940 onwards but, thanks to Coutanche's personal intervention with the occupying power, the requirement to wear a yellow star was not registered or enforced. In September 1942 an order was received from Berlin for the deportation to Germany of all British subjects not born in Jersey. Coutanche did everything in his power to prevent this, but to no avail, as the order was believed to come directly from Hitler. The whole superior council considered resignation but decided ultimately that their continuance in office would, on balance, be for the greater good. Subsequently, 1200 persons, including five or six Jews, were deported to internment camps in Germany. By 1944, particularly after the D-day landings, Jersey was totally isolated by the allied blockade, and the food shortage, which had worsened over the years of occupation, became so acute that the bailiff insisted on appealing for the assistance of the Red Cross, through Switzerland, and many lives were saved by the timely arrival, in January 1945, of Red Cross parcels and other essential supplies.

9 May 1945 was indeed a happy birthday for Coutanche, as on that day he announced, from the royal court building, that he had personally witnessed the signing of the German surrender and that the island was free. Amid tumultuous rejoicing and scenes of great emotion he hoisted the union flag again over the building; an act which was replicated in almost every Jersey home. During a visit by George VI and Queen Elizabeth to the island soon after the liberation, Coutanche's singular service was recognized by his being dubbed a knight bachelor.

The post-war period brought pressures for change, and Coutanche presided over the constitutional changes of 1947 and 1948 when the membership of the states assembly was reformed. He also pressed for the creation of a Channel Islands court of appeal. Realizing that the burden of duties imposed on the bailiff as president of the legislature and chief justice for Jersey was becoming impossibly onerous under the pressures of growing affluence and more open government, he moved for the creation of the office of deputy bailiff, to which C. S. Harrison was appointed in 1949.

The universal high esteem in which he was held was evident when Coutanche celebrated twenty-five years as bailiff in 1960, when tributes were paid to him in the states assembly and the royal court, and a life-size portrait, painted by James Gunn, was unveiled in the royal court.

He continued in office until 1961 and upon his retirement was made a life peer.

Coutanche died where he had lived in St Brelade, Jersey, on 18 December 1973, and was buried at St Brelade. He was survived by his son, his wife having died earlier in 1973.

F. L. M. CORBET

**Sources** personal knowledge (2004) · private information (2004) · *Evening Post* [Jersey] (27 Aug 1960) · *Jersey Evening Post* (19 Dec 1973) · *Jersey Evening Post* (21 April 1974) · *The memoirs of Lord Coutanche*, ed. H. R. S. Pocock (1975) · F. L. M. Corbet and others, *A biographical dictionary of Jersey*, [2] (1998) · F. E. Cohen, *The Jews in the Channel Islands during the German occupation, 1940–45* (1998) · Burke, *Peerage* · WWW · *The Times* (19 Dec 1973)
**Archives** Judicial Greffe, Jersey, records of judgments and archives of the royal court · States Greffe, Jersey, proceedings of the State of Jersey
**Likenesses** J. Gunn, oils, 1960, Royal Court Chamber, Jersey
**Wealth at death** £27,423—in England and Wales: administration, 22 May 1974, *CGPLA Eng. & Wales*

**Coutts, Angela Georgina Burdett-**, *suo jure* Baroness Burdett-Coutts (1814–1906), philanthropist, was born on 21 April 1814 at 80 Piccadilly, London, the youngest of the six children of Sir Francis *Burdett (1770–1844), politician, and his wife, Sophia (d. 1844), the youngest daughter of Thomas *Coutts (1735–1822), banker, and his first wife, Susannah Starkie (d. 1815).

**Early life and family background** Angela Burdett passed her childhood with her parents at her father's country residences—Ramsbury, Wiltshire, and Foremark, Derbyshire—with occasional visits to Bath. Later, when Sir Francis Burdett's radical politics led to a breach with his wealthy father-in-law, the family moved to a house in St James's Square. Here Angela met scientists, politicians, and men of letters, including Babbage and Faraday, Gladstone and Disraeli, Charles Dickens, Thomas Moore, and Samuel Rogers, all of whom became lifelong friends. At Bath she met Sir James 'Rajah' Brooke (1803–1868), later the first raja of Sarawak, with whom she likewise developed an enduring friendship. She inherited many of her father's humanitarian views and, among other qualities, his natural and persuasive power as a public speaker. With her mother she undertook a foreign tour lasting some three years, during which she studied under local tutors in each country where they made a stay. Her grandfather's Coutts banking connection facilitated her introduction to a wide circle of European royalty and nobility. In Paris she was introduced to the French royal family, notably the future king Louis-Philippe and his sister Adelaide, who were friends of her mother and grandfather, and so established a lifelong connection of her own with the Orléans family.

After the death of his first wife in 1815 Thomas Coutts had married Harriot Mellon [see Beauclerk, Harriot], an actress, to whom, at his death on 24 February 1822, he bequeathed his entire fortune, including his interest in the family banking firm. On 16 June 1822 she gained a title by her marriage to William Aubrey de Vere Beauclerk, ninth duke of St Albans, and took the responsibility of choosing her eventual successor seriously. After careful observation of each of her first husband's grandchildren

Angela Georgina Burdett-Coutts, *suo jure* Baroness Burdett-Coutts (1814–1906), by Sir William Charles Ross, *c.*1847

she chose Angela as heir to the residuary portion of the estate, which amounted to some £1.8 million. The duchess's will made the inheritance conditional on the heiress not marrying a foreign national, in which event it would pass to the next in line, and stipulated that her successors take the surname of Coutts; Angela Burdett did so, in addition to her own, though she was often known simply as Miss Coutts. The selection of Angela as heir, which was revealed only after the duchess's death on 6 August 1837, caused surprise—yet, by the use to which she put her good fortune, she became, in the words of Edward VII, 'after my mother the most remarkable woman in the country' (Healey, 11).

**The heiress; social circle and pursuits** In autumn 1837 Angela Burdett-Coutts moved from her father's house to 1 Stratton Street, Piccadilly, taking there as her companion Hannah Meredith, her former governess who, until her death in December 1878, remained her inseparable friend and exerted a strong evangelical influence. Hannah Meredith's husband, William Brown, whom she married in 1844, was Angela's resident doctor until his death on 23 October 1855. As 'the richest heiress in all England' Burdett-Coutts enjoyed almost instant celebrity (T. Raikes, *Journal*, 1856–8, 4.345). Her appearance at Queen Victoria's coronation in June 1838 excited enormous curiosity: in 'Mr Barney Maguire's account of the coronation', in his

*Ingoldsby Legends*, the humorist Richard Barham drew attention to the presence of 'that swate charmer, the famale heiress, Miss Anja-lay Coutts'. Suitors were soon numerous and speculation was rife on her likely choice of a husband. She received many proposals from men anxious to repair their family fortunes—including, it was rumoured, from Prince Louis Napoleon (later Emperor Napoleon III). But, devoted as she was to philanthropic work, she declined all offers: to relieve embarrassment, Hannah Brown was accustomed to retire to the next room when she detected that a proposal was in the offing, and would return on the signal of a cough from her mistress after the inevitable refusal had been delivered. Angela Burdett-Coutts was undoubtedly the model for Adriana in Disraeli's novel *Endymion*: 'the greatest heiress in England', and 'an angelic being', with 'a melodious voice, choice accomplishments and the sweetest temper in the world' (Healey, 60). But Disraeli's heroine was also remarkable for wearing 'a look of pensive resignation' in the London salons: 'Her books interested her, and a beautiful nature, but she liked to be alone or with her mother' (ibid.).

John Cam Hobhouse, Baron Broughton, left a vivid contemporary physical description of the real Miss Coutts: 'If her complexion were good she would have a pleasing face. Her figure, though not sufficiently full, is good. Her voice is melodious, her expression sweet and engaging' (*Recollections of a Long Life*, 1909, 6.149). In defiance of Disraeli's imputations, she enjoyed intelligent, stimulating company: to Stratton Street and to her later residence (from 1849) at Holly Lodge, Highgate, she welcomed a varied circle of friends, including politicians, artists, scientists, writers, bishops, and actresses. Liszt played for her; Hans Andersen stayed at both addresses; Thomas Moore, on a visit in 1845, was shown her famous collection of jewels, which included a tiara that had belonged to Marie Antoinette. Both the French king Louis Philippe and Emperor Napoleon III remained friends during their spells in power; later, during his English exile, she was one of the former emperor's weekend guests at his receptions in Compiègne. Queen Victoria and other members of the royal family—who were customers of Coutts & Co.—also visited her at home. The queen was grateful for the financial assistance rendered at the beginning of her reign; Angela Burdett-Coutts gave similar help to the impecunious Princess Mary, duchess of Teck, a cousin of the queen, and to her daughter Princess May (later Queen Mary). The duchess's son Prince Francis was her godson.

Burdett-Coutts was a keen collector of antiquarian books and paintings: she bought many at Samuel Rogers's important sale in 1855, and sent agents to the Middle East to buy old manuscripts. In 1864 her friend William Harness, the literary scholar, arranged the purchase of the finest known first folio edition of Shakespeare at the then record price of £716 2s. (now in the Folger Museum, Washington, DC). Queen Victoria sent her a piece of Herne's oak, felled in a storm at Windsor, to make a casket for it. Remembering that her benefactress had been on the stage, she was a generous supporter of actors and actresses, among them William Macready and later Henry Irving, to whom she made a gift of Garrick's ring. She and Hannah Brown saw all his stage appearances; in 1871 she took him on a yachting party to the Mediterranean, on which trip he spotted the model for his characterization of Shylock in *The Merchant of Venice*.

**Philanthropy: Dickens and Wellington** The greater part of Angela Burdett-Coutts's time, however, was spent not on leisure pursuits but in administering and disbursing her vast fortune, which was further augmented after her father and mother died within a few days of each other in January 1844. Bereft, she turned to the duke of Wellington, and for the last six years of his life they were very close; gossips predicted their marriage, despite the age difference: he was seventy-six and she was thirty. When, in February 1847, she—very much in defiance of convention—proposed to him, he gently refused, but he remained a close friend and adviser. He taught her self-confidence, and notably encouraged her to learn the business details of banking: she should, he recommended, 'go through the stationary accounts' (Healey, 87). But he did not share her progressive ideas: aid to Ireland would, he believed, encourage beggars, while shorter working hours for her clerks would lead only to 'idleness and vice' (ibid.).

At the same time Angela was working with Charles Dickens on other projects with which the duke would have had little sympathy. From 1840 until the break-up of his marriage in 1857 Dickens guided her charitable work, acting as her official almoner and helping to investigate the many thousands of begging letters she received. In 1847 they founded a home, Urania Cottage, in Shepherd's Bush, Middlesex, for homeless women, many of whom had been prostitutes. Dickens planned this project with her; he regularly attended meetings of its administrators and wrote about it in his journal *All the Year Round*. He gave advice on her scheme for improved sanitation in the slum areas of Westminster, and drew her attention and support to the ragged schools; their discussions on education are reflected in *Hard Times*, and *Martin Chuzzlewit* was dedicated to her. Overall he encouraged her towards the practical direction of aid to the causes of distress. He considered her 'very, very far removed from all the Givers in all the Court Guides' (Healey, 68) and 'the noblest spirit we can ever know' (ibid., 129). In return for his advice and assistance she paid for the education of his son Charley at Eton and later in Germany.

**Endowments of churches and schools in Britain and abroad; patron of the arts and sciences** Dickens's influence on the direction of Angela Burdett-Coutts's philanthropy was deep and lasting: without him she might have concentrated exclusively on the Church of England, to which, in any case, she gave vast sums of money. Writing in 1869, the social historian William Howitt asserted that no woman, apart from a queen regnant or consort, had done as much for the established church. She built and endowed the church of St Stephen in Rochester Row, Westminster, at a cost of more than £90,000 as a memorial

to her father, who had represented Westminster in parliament for thirty years. The foundation-stone was laid on 20 July 1847, and the building, designed by Benjamin Ferrey, was consecrated on 24 June 1850. With its attached schools and vicarage, it remains—in spite of bomb damage—a striking and important example of the Gothic revival. Besides building the church, the patronage of which she retained, she created a new and complete parochial organization, including guilds, working and friendly societies, temperance societies, Bible classes, soup kitchens, and self-help associations. Her aim was to create a city community along the lines of the rural ones she had known from around the country homes of her childhood.

Additionally, Angela Burdett-Coutts gave Charles James Blomfield, the bishop of London, £15,000 for churches to be built at his discretion. The fruits of this gift were St John's, Limehouse (1853), St James, Hatcham (1854), and St John's, Deptford (1855). In 1877 she joined with the Turners' Company in giving four of the peal of twelve bells to St Paul's Cathedral. Another church dedicated to St Stephen, in the poorest district of Carlisle, was built at her expense and consecrated on 31 May 1865. In 1872 she acquired the right of presentation to the vicarage of Ramsbury on her father's Wiltshire estate; she also held the living of the adjoining parish of Baydon, and paid for the repair and restoration of both churches.

Angela Burdett-Coutts's deep religious beliefs informed her early interest in colonial expansion. In 1847 she endowed the bishoprics of Cape Town, South Africa, and Adelaide, South Australia, both of which were strictly modelled on the English diocesan system. Ten years later she founded the bishopric of British Columbia, providing £25,000 for the endowment of the church, £15,000 for the bishopric, and £10,000 towards the maintenance of the clergy. She intended that her colonial bishoprics should remain dependent on the Anglican church in England. In 1866, however, Robert Gray, bishop of Cape Town, in the course of his dispute with Bishop Colenso of Natal, declared his see to be an independent South African church. Angela Burdett-Coutts petitioned Queen Victoria to maintain the existing link, but to no avail, and the colonial bishoprics became independent. Her will stipulated that all her Church of England endowments would be nullified in the event of its disestablishment.

Under the influence of Dickens, Angela Burdett-Coutts made elementary and technical education an important part of her church work. In 1849 she built and established the schools connected with St Stephen's, Westminster, and in 1876 she founded and endowed the Townshend School, also in Westminster, partly from her own resources and partly from a bequest left at her entire discretion by the poet Chauncy Hare Townshend. The two schools were amalgamated in 1901 as the Burdett-Coutts and Townshend foundation schools; as a state primary, the school flourishes a century later. To complete her educational scheme for the district she founded in 1893 the Westminster Technical Institute, which was handed over to London county council in 1901 and later became a part of Westminster Kingsway College. Always practical and forward-looking, she was among the first to introduce sewing and cooking into the curriculum of elementary schools. She took a personal interest in Whitelands Training College for teachers, a Church of England foundation dating from 1841, and offered prizes as an incentive for good work in the area of household economy. (This was an abiding interest: in 1886 she provided the introduction for a book on home bee-keeping by Charles Jenyns.) In 1865, while at Torquay (where she kept a winter residence from 1860 to 1877), she devised a scheme of grouping schools in the rural districts of Devon (with 'ambulatory schoolmasters') which was adopted by the authorities. She continued her father's interest in the Birkbeck Literary and Scientific Institute (later Birkbeck College). In 1879, in collaboration with Louisa Twining, she founded a home for female art students in Brunswick Square, the first of its kind in London.

As a patron of the arts, Angela Burdett-Coutts funded numerous scholarships and prizes; individual artists who benefited from her patronage included Marshall Claxton, James John Hill, Anna Mary Howitt, Mary Ann Criddle, Rebecca Soloman, and John James Masquerier, for whom she sat as a model. Her purchase of Howitt's *Margaret Returning from the Fountain* (1854) provided a notable link with her philanthropic work: the painting's subject was a 'fallen' woman. She contributed also to the advance of education in the sciences. In 1861 she endowed two Oxford scholarships in geology and related areas of natural science, accompanied by a gift to the university of the Pengelly collection of Devon fossils, purchased by her from the geologist William Pengelly, who had encouraged her scientific, archaeological, and geological interests during her residences in Torquay. For the Royal Horticultural Society's botanical collection at Kew Gardens she purchased the rare and extensive Griffith collection of seaweed and Wilhelm Philipp Schimper's great herbarium of mosses.

**Ragged schools, the East End, and the Royal Society for the Prevention of Cruelty to Animals**  Poor and neglected children were always a particular concern for Angela Burdett-Coutts. Dickens had encouraged her to subsidize the Ragged School Union, started in 1844, and took her to see for herself the squalid poverty of child waifs in London. She actively helped the 'shoeblack brigades', established about 1851 to provide employment, and in 1874 made a first contribution of £5000 for a scheme to train poor boys to be sailors. Aware that starving children could not learn or work properly, she became president of the Destitute Children's Dinner Society, founded in 1866. She was an early patron of the London Society for the Prevention of Cruelty to Children, founded in 1883, but withdrew from the organization when, as the National Society for the Prevention of Cruelty to Children (NSPCC), it extended its operations nationwide.

Taking her inspiration from *Oliver Twist*, Burdett-Coutts took a particular interest in the East End of London. She was one of the first to build model housing for workers in the poorer districts: on the site of Nova Scotia Gardens in Bethnal Green, an area notorious for crime and disease, she had erected (in 1872) four blocks of model tenements, affording accommodation for more than 1000 people. It was renamed Columbia Square, and its courtyard design (if not its high Gothic architecture) was an influence on similar projects that followed. She had acted on the advice of Dickens in building flats rather than a garden city, an idea that came to fruition, however, in the construction of Holly Village, Highgate. These detached houses, set around lawns and flower gardens, were first intended for workers on her Holly Lodge estate. In the twentieth century they came to be regarded as period pieces of the Gothic revival, and became much sought after.

In 1864, as a means of reducing the cost of food in the East End, Burdett-Coutts began work on a scheme for a London market for fish and vegetables that would be free of the tolls imposed by existing markets. This became Columbia market, built on a site adjoining Columbia Square after a private act of parliament was secured in 1866. Another example of fine Gothic design—the architect was Henry Ashley Darbishire and the total cost £200,000—the building was opened on 28 April 1869 (*The Times*, 29 April 1869). But the venture proved to be one of her few philanthropic failures, owing to the antagonism of the established markets and the preference of many stallholders for street-based trading. After vainly seeking to make the enterprise work as a wholesale fish store, she made it over to the corporation of London in November 1871; it enjoyed no better success, and transferred it back to her three years later. The market was reopened in 1875 under an arrangement with three of the largest railway companies, but opposition, notably from Billingsgate fish market, was again too strong. In the 1880s an effort was made to rescue the scheme as a railway market served by a fleet of fishing boats and steamships. A new act of parliament was obtained for the necessary railway extensions, but the scheme foundered amid further objections. The building was afterwards used for warehouses and small factory units, and was demolished in 1958. The various Columbia market schemes, though unsuccessful, did at least draw public attention to the disadvantages of the market monopolies then in force.

About 1860 Burdett-Coutts started a sewing school for adult women in Brown's Lane, Spitalfields. They were fed and housed, and an organization of seamstresses, able to fulfil large government contracts, was formed on her initiative. She engaged trained nurses to visit the sick poor of the district, and to alleviate the dangers of childbirth in poor homes. When the importation of cheaper French silks all but destroyed the indigenous textile industry, she founded the East End Weavers' Aid Association in 1860, to assist the operatives in finding alternative employment. Many were installed in small shops, or trained for domestic service; others, in 1863, were given the means to emigrate to Queensland or Nova Scotia. In 1869 she sent some 1200 similarly affected weavers from Girvan, Ayrshire, to Australia. She instituted the Flower Girls' Brigade for flower sellers between thirteen and fifteen (1879), and simultaneously established a factory in Clerkenwell to teach crippled girls the art of artificial flower-making and other skills. A night school established in Shoreditch in 1875 later became the Burdett-Coutts Club for working-class men and boys—one of the first of many similar London foundations—to which a gymnasium was added in 1891. At Bethnal Green she took a great interest in the welfare of the costermongers, providing stables for their donkeys in Columbia Square and offering incentives for humane treatment of the animals.

Burdett-Coutts's love of animals owed much to the influence of her father. As president of the ladies' committee of the Royal Society for the Prevention of Cruelty to Animals (RSPCA) she instituted and provided funds for a national prize essay contest, for which thousands of children competed annually. She spoke at RSPCA meetings in all parts of the country; 'life, whether in man or beast, is sacred' was one of her much repeated sayings (Healey, 172). She was also a tireless letter writer in the cause: one such eloquent indictment of cruelty concerned the ill treatment of Edinburgh tram-horses (*The Times*, 5 Dec 1873). By her munificence, in the same year there was unveiled a fountain and statue beside George IV Bridge in the same city, in memory of Greyfriars Bobby, the dog who refused to leave his master's grave. (The freedom of the city of Edinburgh was conferred on her in January 1874.) She provided other fountains and drinking troughs in metropolitan areas, of which the best-known are in Victoria Park, Hackney (erected at a cost of £5000 in 1862), at London zoo, in Regent's Park, and in Ancoats, Manchester. As part of her interest in promoting self-reliance and sound household economy among the disadvantaged, she encouraged (and practised) the keeping and breeding of goats, and became president of the British Goat Society.

The fame that Burdett-Coutts had achieved as a philanthropist was acknowledged when, on 19 June 1871, she was raised to the peerage in her own right as Baroness Burdett-Coutts of Highgate and Brookfield, Middlesex. Public recognition of her work in London came with the award of the freedom of the city on 18 July 1872, a unique distinction for a woman at that time. Several of the London livery companies paid her a similar tribute: the Turners (1872), the Clothworkers (1873), the Haberdashers (1880), and the Coachmakers (1894). The general feeling towards her among the recipients of her charity was undoubtedly one of gratitude, though this did not necessarily equate with deference. The writer Compton Mackenzie recalled a live rumour from his London childhood that she was herself a sufferer from lice (Healey, 272), and her name came to be used as Cockney rhyming slang for 'boots'.

**Philanthropy in Ireland and abroad** Burdett-Coutts's philanthropic efforts were not confined to England. In Ireland, another concern shared with her father, she characteristically sought to combine relief of the immediate symptoms of distress with measures to secure permanent improvement of living conditions by providing the basis for viable and stable local economic development. In 1862 she responded to an appeal from Father Davis, a parish priest in county Cork, for aid to a distressed district in the south-west coast of Ireland, which had never recovered from the great famine. She established large relief stores of essential provisions at Cape Clear and Sherkin, and paid for three parties of emigrants to go to Canada. She sought also to create a demand in England for Irish embroidery and other cottage industries. Her chief work, however, was in reviving the local fishing industry, for which she advanced loans for the purchase of modern boats, fittings, and equipment. She visited the district in 1884, and with the assistance of Sir Thomas Brady inaugurated a fishery training school for 400 boys at Baltimore, co. Cork. She opened the school, amid an enthusiastic reception, on 16 August 1887. In other distressed districts in the west of Ireland she also took a keen interest: in 1880 she offered to advance £250,000 to the authorities for the supply of seed potatoes; this had a galvanizing effect, and the government eventually took the matter up themselves. She also sponsored research into the causes of potato disease.

Burdett-Coutts's philanthropic efforts in the wider world included aid for the enterprise of her friend Sir James Brooke, who founded the kingdom of Sarawak, on the island of Borneo, in 1842. She long maintained a model farm there to train local people in agriculture, provided funds for the naval defence of the country, and underwrote a number of Brooke's speculative ventures. In gratitude he left her the kingdom in the first draft of his will, though this was later altered. She gave generous financial support to David Livingstone for his African explorations, and gave similar help to Henry Morton Stanley, the rescuer of Livingstone; she later became one of Stanley's most influential friends and apologists. She encouraged his controversial 1887 expedition in search of Emin Pasha, which led on to the establishment of British colonies in east Africa. Elsewhere in Africa, she paid for the introduction of cotton gins in Abeokuta, southern Nigeria, on learning that the local industry was retarded by lack of machinery. The result was a large increase in cotton manufactures and trade, both of which were mainly in the hands of indigenous people. Others among her foreign benefactions included the provision of lifeboats on the coast of Brittany, and funds for the ordnance survey of Jerusalem. Her offer to restore the aqueducts of Solomon, and so secure a regular water supply for the population of that city, was not accepted.

In 1877, during the Russo-Turkish War, Baroness Burdett-Coutts made strenuous efforts on behalf of the Turkish peasantry displaced from Roumelia and Bulgaria by the Russian advance. Her eloquent appeal in the *Daily Telegraph* (13 August 1877) led to the formation of the Turkish Compassionate Fund, to which she subscribed £2000; in total some £50,000 was raised, and the refugees resettled in Asia Minor. This generosity left a lasting impression on the Turkish people, and on the Muslim world in general. After the cessation of hostilities in March 1878, the sultan conferred on her several honours, including the diamond star and first class of the military and knightly order of the Mejidiye, a decoration bestowed on no other woman except Queen Victoria. In 1879, inspired by the work of her friend Florence Nightingale, she served as president of a ladies' committee to aid the casualties of the Anglo-Zulu War. She sent out hospital equipment and staff, among whom the presence of trained women nurses was a notable feature. The voluntary hospitals of the Second South African War of 1899–1902, in which women nurses served—with the reluctant sanction of the military authorities—were largely modelled on her earlier experiment.

**Marriage, death, and legacy** On 22 December 1878 Burdett-Coutts's devoted companion Hannah Brown died; she was buried beside her husband in one of the Burdett-Coutts churches, St Stephen's, Westminster. In her loneliness the baroness turned to William Lehman Ashmead Bartlett (1851–1921) [*see* Coutts, William Lehman Ashmead Bartlett Burdett-], whom she had first encountered as a child being cared for by his widowed mother in Torquay. She paid for his education and he later travelled to help administer her relief work in Ireland and in Turkey. Despite the age difference—she was sixty-six, he was twenty-nine—they were married on 12 February 1881 at Christ Church, Down Street, London. Unsurprisingly, the match was disapproved of by many of her friends, including Gladstone and Disraeli, and by the partners in the Coutts bank. Queen Victoria called it 'positively distressing and ridiculous' (*Letters of Queen Victoria*, ed. A. C. Benson and Lord Esher, and G. E. Buckle, 2nd ser., 1926–8, 3.134); Burdett-Coutts's deafness to all objections may be seen as indicating the social and emotional insulation that her vast fortune had inevitably conferred on her. As a result of the marriage, her husband being of American birth, the clause in her benefactress's will was invoked, and she forfeited three-fifths of her income to her sister Clara Money, who took the name of Coutts, thus bequeathing the appropriate name Money-Coutts to her son and his descendants. Bartlett meanwhile took the name of Burdett-Coutts, and in 1885 was elected Unionist MP for Westminster. In this capacity he secured on his wife's behalf the passage of the Hampstead Heath Act, which widened public access to include Parliament Hill and other areas. Their marriage was reportedly happy; she made him sole executor and beneficiary of her will, and he carried on much of her charitable work after her death, including the Burdett-Coutts Club in Shoreditch.

Baroness Burdett-Coutts was obliged to make some retrenchments in her philanthropic activities after her marriage, but continued to take an active interest in world affairs. She appealed for the rescue of General Gordon from Khartoum in a letter to *The Times* (10 May 1884); to the end he carried with him a gift from her of a letter case. In 1889 she opened a pleasure ground on the site of Old St Pancras cemetery, featuring a sundial inscribed with a record of the famous people there buried. Among them was the Corsican patriot and refugee Pascal Paoli; with the approval of the French government she paid to have his remains repatriated to the island.

For the Chicago exhibition of 1893 Baroness Burdett-Coutts compiled and edited a book entitled *Women's mission: a series of congress papers on the philanthropic work of women by eminent writers*. This collection of thirty-two papers included contributions from Louisa Hubbard, Emily Jones, Maude Stanley, and Jane Stuart-Wortley. At the same time the duchess of Teck arranged for the separate publication of a memoir: *Baroness Burdett-Coutts: a Sketch of her Public Life and Work*. In a preliminary note the duchess wrote warmly of the philanthropic example that her friend had set, adding that she had 'ever sought, also, to increase the usefulness of women in their homes, to extend their opportunities of self-improvement, and to deepen the sources of influence which they derive from moral worth and Christian life' (Healey, 219–20). Direct political influence via the ballot box was, however, a different matter: Burdett-Coutts was never an advocate of female suffrage, and told Millicent Fawcett (19 November 1885) that 'it would neither benefit man nor woman to hazard the quiet but potent influence of good she now exercises in daily life, and to transform her into a political agent' (Women's Library, London, 1A/6619). Lady St Helier later wrote that she assisted the later campaigns of the women's movement in spite of herself, 'for she showed how a capable woman could transact all the different affairs of life with as great ability as a man' (St Helier, 224).

Baroness Burdett-Coutts died on 30 December 1906 of acute bronchitis at 1 Stratton Street, her central London home. Her body lay there in state for two days; nearly 30,000 paid their respects to a woman who had become known as the 'Queen of the Poor' (Healey, 17). She was buried in Westminster Abbey on 5 January 1907 in the nave, near the west door. Her grave is marked by a plain stone, but the inscription on the nearby memorial to her friend Lord Shaftesbury could easily have been applied to her: 'A long life spent in the cause of the helpless and suffering. Love and serve' (ibid., 227–8). The funeral congregation included the king, the queen, and the prince and princess of Wales, as well as costermongers in pearly costumes and East End flower girls.

It has been estimated that during her life Burdett-Coutts gave away between £3 million and £4 million. She had set a new standard in philanthropy: prompt and practical, her charity was given with style and without condescension. In her time she was an honoured institution and most of her enterprises bore lasting fruit. Even her visionary schemes that did not survive—Columbia market and Columbia Square—served as models for the shopping precincts and housing estates of a later era. In the breadth and sincerity of her sympathies and in the variety of her social and intellectual interests she has had no rival among philanthropists before or since. Her example not only provided an immense stimulus to charitable work among the rich and fashionable but also suggested solutions to many social problems.                    EDNA HEALEY

**Sources** *Baroness Burdett-Coutts, prepared for the World Columbian Exposition, by command of the duchess of Teck* (Chicago, 1893) • C. Patterson, *Angela Burdett-Coutts* (1953) • M. W. Patterson, *Sir Francis Burdett and his times* (1931) • *Letters of Charles Dickens to the Baroness Burdett-Coutts*, ed. C. Osborne (1931) • *The letters of Charles Dickens*, ed. M. House, G. Storey, and others, 3–8 (1974–95) • *Wellington and his* friends: letters of the first duke of Wellington, ed. seventh duke of Wellington [G. Wellesley] (1965) • E. Johnson, *The heart of Charles Dickens* (New York, 1952) • O. Rutter, *Rajah Brooke and the Baroness Burdett Coutts* (1935) • E. Healey, *Lady unknown* (1978) • Lady St Helier, *Memories of 50 years* (1909) • J. Forster, *Life of Charles Dickens* • B. Stoker, *Personal reminiscences of Henry Irving*, 2 vols. (1906) • F. K. Prochaska, *Women and philanthropy in nineteenth-century England* (1980) • F. K. Prochaska, 'Burdett-Coutts, Angela Georgina', *Europa biographical dictionary of British women* (1983) • H. L. Farrah, *Life of Robert Gray*, 2 vols. (1876) • G. W. Cox, *The life of John William Colenso*, 2 vols. (1888) • D. Cherry, *Painting women* (1993) • R. Walton, English to slang dictionary: www.rickwalton.com/cockney/englisht.htm • will • *CGPLA Eng. & Wales* (1907) • *Debrett's Peerage*

**Archives** BL, corresp., Add. MS 63097 • Bodl. Oxf., Burdett Collection MSS • Coutts & Co., London, archives • Hunt. • LPL, letters and papers • priv. coll., family MSS • Stratfield Saye, Hampshire, Wellington archives • W. Sussex RO, letters | BL, corresp. with C. Babbage, Add. MSS 37191–37199 • BL, corresp. with Sir Charles A. J. Brooke, Add. MS 45283 • BL, corresp. with W. E. Gladstone, Add. MSS 44399–44466 • BL, letters to A. H. Layard, Add. MSS 39012–39033, *passim* • BL, collection of C. C. Osborne for his biography of Burdett-Coutts, Add. MSS 46402–46408 • BL, corresp. with Sir James Brooke, Add. MSS 45274–45282 • Bodl. Oxf., letters to Benjamin Disraeli • Bodl. Oxf., letters to Mrs Disraeli • Harrowby Manuscript Trust, Sandon Hall, Staffordshire, corresp. with Harrowby family, etc. • Hove Central Library, Sussex, letters to Viscount Wolseley and Lady Wolseley • LPL, letters to A. C. Tait • W. Sussex RO, Chichester, corresp., Add. MSS 22, 243–643

**Likenesses** oils, 1828 (after S. J. Stump), Coutts & Co., London • oils, *c.*1840, NPG • attrib. J. Jacob, oils, 1846, City of Edinburgh Museums and Art Galleries • W. C. Ross, miniature, *c.*1847, NPG [*see illus.*] • W. C. Ross, portrait, *c.*1847, NPG • P. H. Skeolan, carte-de-visite, 1861–9, NPG • J. R. Swinton, oils, 1863, Royal Marsden Hospital, London • G. C. Adams, marble bust, 1874 • W. Brodie, marble bust, 1874 • London Stereoscopic Co., carte-de-visite, before 1877, NPG • London Stereoscopic Co., print, before 1877, NPG • E. Long, oils, 1883 • T. Chartran, lithograph, NPG; repro. in *VF* (3 Nov 1883) • T. Chartran, watercolour caricature, Coutts & Co., London • J. Drummond, portrait (in Edinburgh, 1874) • A. P. Tilt, group portrait, oils, Wellcome L. • G. Zobel, mezzotint (attrib. Julius Jacob), City of Edinburgh Museums and Art Galleries • G. Zobel, mezzotint (after J. R. Swinton), BM, NPG • cartoon, repro. in *VF* • lithograph, NPG

**Wealth at death** £79,482 15s. 4d.: probate, 1907, *CGPLA Eng. & Wales*

**Coutts, Harriot**. *See* Beauclerk, Harriot (1777?–1837).

**Coutts, John** (1699–1750), merchant and banker, was born on 28 July 1699, probably in Edinburgh, the son of Patrick Coutts of Edinburgh and his wife, Jean, *née* Dunlop. His father's family had long been settled in Montrose, where his grandfather John was provost in 1677. His mother came from the Dunlops of Garnkirk and thus connected the Coutts family with later important tobacco merchant families in Glasgow. Patrick Coutts left Montrose for Edinburgh, where he was active as a merchant from at least 1696, but, before he could accumulate an impressive estate, died in 1704, leaving £2500. John and his younger brother James were sent back to Montrose for education at the Old Grammar School under the supervision of their uncle Provost James Coutts. John returned to Edinburgh for an apprenticeship during 1713–19, and subsequently went into business for himself there. He was referred to as a merchant when he was made burgess and guild brother of the town in 1721. His younger brother James followed a similar course in London, where he eventually became a partner in the merchant firm of Alexander and James Coutts of Oxford Court, Cannon Street.

John Coutts's business was that of a commission merchant and dealer in corn. To this he soon added the negotiation of bills of exchange; that is, he purchased bills of exchange (particularly on London and Amsterdam) from local traders who needed cash and sold bills on such places to others who desired to make remittances. Such activity has enabled later writers to describe him as the first private banker in Edinburgh. His local importance was recognized by the contract to remit excise receipts to London and by his election in 1742 as a director of the Royal Bank of Scotland, at a time when its board contained very few merchants. Active inevitably in the municipal life of Edinburgh, in due course he became a member of the town council (1730), a baillie (1731 and 1741), and lord provost (1742–4). On the death of his brother James in 1740 he inherited £20,000, and thus was able as lord provost to introduce a much higher standard of civic entertainment. His position was most delicate during the Jacobite occupation of Edinburgh in 1745–6. His own politics and business connections (especially in the Royal Bank) were definitely whiggish, but both he and his wife had family connections suspected of Jacobitism. He and his family left the town before the occupation and stayed with his wife's family at Allandale in Berwickshire. Despite an apparent record of loyalty, he was suspect and is reported to have needed the protection of the duke of Argyll and his family. More suspect was his aged uncle, Provost James Coutts of Montrose, who had remained at his post during the occupation. During the repression after Culloden, the elder James was removed from his office and imprisoned. His nephew John was one of those giving bonds to free the old man. In the years immediately following, John Coutts's own health failed and, seeking a more salubrious climate, he embarked in 1749 on a trip to Italy. He died at Nola, near Naples, on 23 March 1750, at the age of fifty-one.

On 10 April 1730 John Coutts had married Jean Stuart, the sister of Sir John Stuart of Allanbank. Before she died, in 1736, the couple had four sons who survived to manhood: Patrick (*b.* 1731), John (*b.* 1732), James (*b.* 1733), and Thomas *Coutts (1735–1822). During the minority of his sons the provost conducted his Edinburgh business— John Coutts & Co.—with a succession of partners. However, before departing for Italy in 1749 he reconstituted the firm (with £4000 capital) as a partnership between himself, his eldest son, Patrick, and Archibald Trotter, a first cousin of his wife. As he took Patrick with him to Italy, the firm was in fact then run by Trotter, helped by the younger sons James and Thomas. After the death of their father John Coutts's four sons broke with Trotter and decided to continue the firm as a partnership between themselves and John Stephen, the husband of their late father's sister Christian and formerly a merchant in Leith. In 1752 an affiliated house with the same partners (eventually styled Coutts Brothers and Stephen) was established in London, the partners active there being Patrick, the eldest brother, Thomas, the youngest, and Thomas Stephen, the son of their Edinburgh partner. The other two Coutts brothers, John and James, remained for the time being in the Edinburgh firm. However, in 1755 James Coutts married Polly Peagrim, the niece and heir of George Campbell, the proprietor of a long-established bank in the Strand, London. At his marriage James Coutts left his family's Edinburgh house and became a partner in George Campbell's 'West End' bank. When Campbell died, in 1760, James Coutts took his brother Thomas out of the family's London (Jeffreys Square) affiliate and made him a partner in the Strand bank, which has survived to the present as Coutts & Co. This left John Coutts alone in charge of his father's old Edinburgh firm and Patrick in charge of the City or Jeffreys Square offshoot. A crisis ensued in 1761 when John Coutts died and Patrick became insane. Since neither James nor Thomas Coutts wished to leave the Strand bank, new partners and managers for the Edinburgh end of the old business were found in the persons of two of their former clerks, Sir William Forbes bt, of Pitsligo and James Hunter, later Sir James Hunter Blair, bt, MP, and for the London end in the person of Robert Herries, a Scots merchant then in Barcelona. For a time the Edinburgh and London houses continued as a single partnership, with the Coutts family interest continued via the participation of the brothers' uncles, William Cochrane and John Stephen. When the latter two were pensioned off in 1766 and 1771 respectively, the Coutts family connection in the provost's old business ended.

JACOB M. PRICE

**Sources** E. Healey, *Coutts & Co., 1692–1992: the portrait of a private bank* (1992) · W. Forbes, *Memoirs of a banking-house*, ed. [R. Chambers], [2nd edn] (1860) · C. Rogers, *Genealogical memoirs of the families of Colt and Coutts* (1879) · J. G. Low, *Notes on the Coutts family* (1892) · R. Richardson, *Coutts & Co., bankers, Edinburgh and London* (1900) · HoP, *Commons* · E. H. Coleridge, *The life of Thomas Coutts, banker*, 2 vols. (1920) · J. M. Price, *France and the Chesapeake: a history of the French tobacco monopoly, 1674–1791*, 2 vols. (1973) · S. G. Checkland, *Scottish banking: a history, 1695–1973* (1975) · R. M. Robinson, *Coutts': the history of a banking house* (1929) · 'John Coutts, merchant and banker', *Three Banks Review*, 26 (1955) · *Scots Magazine*, 12 (1750), 205
**Archives** NL Scot., Sir William Forbes MSS · priv. coll., Hunter-Blair MSS
**Likenesses** J. Macardell, mezzotint (after portrait by A. Ramsay), BM, NPG; repro. in Richardson, *Coutts & Co.*, frontispiece · A. Ramsay, portrait, priv. coll.; copy, presented to City of Edinburgh · sketch (after portrait by A. Ramsay), repro. in Forbes, *Memoirs of a banking-house*

**Coutts, Thomas** (1735–1822), banker, was born on 7 September 1735 in Edinburgh, the fourth son of John *Coutts (1699–1750), merchant and banker, and his wife, Jean Stuart (*d.* 1736). Coutts was educated at Edinburgh high school, during the period of the Jacobite rebellion of 1745. His father was on the town council from 1730, served as lord provost from 1742 to 1744, and was closely involved in the siege of Edinburgh. John Coutts took care to keep on good terms with George II's ministers in Scotland, Lord Ilay and Lord Milton, because his father's family in Montrose had Jacobite leanings and his wife, Jean, daughter of Sir John Stuart and Margaret Kerr, had relatives who were similarly suspect. In later years Thomas wrote, in a letter

Thomas Coutts (1735–1822), by Sir William Beechey, 1817 [detail]

to Cardinal Henry Benedict, duke of York, of his attachment to the 'House of Stuart, who's blood, I believe, ran in the veins of my mother' (Healey, *Coutts & Co.*, 203). These early experiences encouraged his naturally cautious nature and gave him a readiness to hedge his bets.

At fifteen Thomas Coutts was sent to London with his eldest brother, Patrick, and for ten years worked in his father's import and export business in Jeffreys Square in the City of London, where he gained valuable commercial experience. On 1 January 1761 he joined his elder brother James at a banking house in the Strand, founded in 1692 by John Campbell, a goldsmith–banker under the patronage of the duke of Argyll. By 1775 James Coutts had married John Campbell's granddaughter, and after the death of her father in 1760 he inherited the bank, which in 1761 was styled James and Thomas Coutts. When James became MP for Edinburgh (1762–7), Thomas Coutts took most of the responsibility at the bank. Later his brother had a mental breakdown, and he died on 15 February 1778, after which Thomas took sole charge.

Coutts now needed partners and his choice was shrewd: Edmund Antrobus from April 1779, Coutts Trotter from 1793, and Edward Marjoribanks from 1798 became pillars of strength, especially during Coutts's last years. Together they turned the failing business of 1761 into the highly profitable and prestigious business of 1822, the year of Thomas's death. Thomas Coutts nevertheless insisted that he and his heirs should retain 'the supremacy … of the House as well as the half share in the Bank' (Healey, *Lady Unknown*, 21). The other half was to be split between the working partners. This 'supremacy' was:

> The disposal, which is to rest with me while I live and with my family at my death, on the share or shares of my partners who may die or retire. And that everything, on any partner quitting business, shall be left in the hands of the person holding the supremacy.   (Healey, *Lady Unknown*, 21)

Coutts owed his success as a banker to his discretion and his understanding of human nature, which inspired trust and affection; and to his organizing and punctilious business practices, which brought financial gain. He ran the bank with clockwork efficiency, devising a daily routine for every clerk. In a long memorandum of 1801 he conceded that even though, in formulating the rules, he had 'consulted individual convenience as far as Regard for the Business would admit', in return he expected it to be 'rigidly and punctually attended to' (Healey, *Lady Unknown*, 22). It was Thomas Coutts's own shrewd intelligence which also kept the bank steady through very turbulent years of revolution and international upheaval. 'A banker's bed is not a bed of roses … when the whole world is in a very alarming state of confusion and England beset with foreign and domestic enemies' (ibid., 21). Coutts kept closely in touch with public affairs at home and throughout the world, through leading politicians such as Chatham and by maintaining a close network of Scottish friends and relatives abroad. Lord Macartney brought him wallpaper from China and Lord Minto news from India.

Coutts was unusually forthright in his condemnation of the government's role in the American War of Independence. He knew Paris well and followed the French Revolution with a personal interest, establishing a lasting link between his bank and the French royal family. Louis Philippe kept in touch with him during his years of exile. Many refugees left their valuables with him. In 1796 Coutts's agents in Ireland warned him of the dangers of a French invasion. Yet although he was interested in politics, he refused offers of a seat in parliament.

Some of the most influential aristocrats were Coutts's customers, but his greatest pride was in royal patronage. George III became a customer of the Coutts brothers at the beginning of his reign, through the influence of his prime minister and keeper of the privy purse, the earl of Bute, who had known their father, Provost Coutts. So began the lasting connection between Coutts & Co. and the royal family. The king trusted the discretion of his banker and in November 1787 admitted him to the 'Place and Quality of Gentleman of his Majesty's Privy Chamber' (Healey, *Coutts & Co.*, 129). In 1790 Coutts, while with his family on the grand tour, visited the last of the Stuarts, Cardinal Henry Benedict, duke of York, at Frascati. On his return he reported to the king, who later gave the cardinal a pension which was paid through Coutts & Co. So was granted his 'only ambition', which was as he wrote on 20 June 1800 to the cardinal, 'to be the Hand by which the Benevolence of Britain from the *best of men*, shall be convey'd to the last of

that illustrious Royal line—The rightful former Sovereigns of Scotland England & Ireland' (ibid., 203).

Royal customers brought prestige to Coutts & Co., but the accounts of the king's spendthrift sons caused Thomas Coutts more headaches than profit. He aided them, especially the prince of Wales and the dukes of York and Kent, but he also rebuked them with paternal sternness. Coutts was equally direct with other illustrious but reckless customers, such as Georgiana, duchess of Devonshire, a hopeless gambler, and Charles James Fox, who cheerfully squandered a fortune. He generously helped artists including Henry Fuseli, Sir Joshua Reynolds, Sir Thomas Lawrence, and Benjamin Robert Haydon. In 1817 Coutts wrote to Haydon that 'experience almost blasts all hopes as I have assisted several in your line in the course of a long life & have never succeeded'. Haydon considered that his letter 'did honour to his House heart and head' (Healey, *Coutts & Co.*, 135).

Conscious that, unlike his three handsome brothers, he was undistinguished in appearance, Coutts refused to let his friends paint him until late in life, when Sir William Beechey persuaded him to sit for his portrait. There is, however, an early miniature by J. Meyer, set in diamonds, which shows a delicate youth with translucent skin, watchful eyes, and a humorous mouth. The simplicity, even shabbiness, of his dress led strangers to mistake him for a poor man. Unlike other great bankers Thomas Coutts built no great country house; and he was happier in London in his modest villa and lovely garden on Highgate Hill than in his large house, 1 Stratton Street, Piccadilly. He preferred, he claimed, to keep his fortune liquid so that he could help his friends. Modestly, Coutts always referred to his prestigious bank as 'my shop'. Outside of business he had a genuine love of the arts, and always carried a volume of Shakespeare in his pocket. A supporter of Drury Lane and Covent Garden theatres, he was a friend of Garrick and other actors.

The discretion Coutts showed in his dealings with customers was matched by the secretiveness with which he had concealed his first marriage, on 18 May 1763, to Susannah Starkie (*d.* 1815), a nursemaid to his brother James's daughter. Seven months later his friends were still unaware of the marriage. They had three daughters: Susan, who in 1796 married George, third earl of Guilford; Frances, who married in 1800 John Stuart, first marquess of Bute; and Sophia, who in 1793 married the radical MP for Westminster, Sir Francis *Burdett. This last was a connection that was to cause the king's banker much embarrassment.

Susannah Coutts died at the beginning of 1815 after some years of mental illness. Soon after, on 18 January 1815, Thomas secretly married Harriot Mellon (1777–1837), the actress [see Beauclerk, Harriot], with whom he had been deeply in love since 1805. When this clandestine marriage was publicly discovered, Coutts married her again, on 12 April 1815. A warm-hearted, flamboyant, somewhat absurd character, Harriot made him very happy.

During the last seven years of his life Thomas Coutts

was increasingly frail, leaving most of the responsibility of the bank to his partners. To show his respect for Harriot's good judgement he bequeathed to her the bulk of his property, and his half share in the bank; he also left to her the choice of his heir. Coutts died at 1 Stratton Street, Piccadilly, London, on 24 February 1822. He was buried in the family tomb of the earl of Guilford at Wroxton. William Cobbett wrote in his *Political Register* that 'A million or more of money got together during a marriage with one wife has been made to pass to a second' (Healey, *Coutts & Co.*, 260). In 1827 Harriot married the ninth duke of St Albans; she died in 1837. She bequeathed an immense fortune to the youngest of Coutts's grandchildren, the 23-year-old Angela Burdett [see Coutts, Angela Georgina Burdett-, Baroness Burdett-Coutts], one of the great female philanthropists of the nineteenth century.

EDNA HEALEY

**Sources** E. Healey, *Coutts & Co., 1692–1992: the portrait of a private bank* (1992) • E. H. Coleridge, *The life of Thomas Coutts, banker*, 2 vols. (1920) • F. G. Hilton Price, *A handbook of London bankers*, enl. edn (1890–91) • W. Forbes, *Memoirs of a banking-house*, ed. [R. Chambers], [2nd edn] (1860) • C. Rogers, *Genealogical memoirs of the families of Colt and Coutts* (1879) • R. Richardson, *Coutts & Co., bankers, Edinburgh and London* (1900) • *The correspondence of George, prince of Wales, 1770–1812*, ed. A. Aspinall, 8 vols. (1963–71) • R. M. Robinson, *Coutts': the history of a banking house* (1929) • S. G. Checkland, *Scottish banking: a history, 1695–1973* (1975) • *The journal of the Rev. William Bagshaw Stevens*, ed. G. Galbraith (1965) • Chambers, *Scots.* (1835) • *Memoires de Louis Philippe, duc d'Orleans: écrits par lui-même*, 2 vols. (Paris, 1973–4) • E. Healey, *Lady unknown: the life of Angela Burdett-Coutts* (1978) • Coutts & Co. archives, 440 The Strand, London

**Archives** Bodl. Oxf., corresp. and papers • Bodl. Oxf., family corresp. and papers • Coutts & Co., 440 Strand, London • Royal Arch. • Royal Bank of Scotland, London • Sandon Hall, Staffordshire, Harrowby Manuscript Trust, corresp. | BL, letters to C. Whitefoord, Add. MSS 36593–36595 • Bodl. Oxf., corresp. with Doyle family • Chatsworth House, Derbyshire, letters to dukes of Devonshire • NA Scot., letters to Patrick and George Home • NL Scot., letters to Sir William Forbes • NL Scot., corresp. and accounts with Robert Liston • NL Scot., letters to Lord Melville • NL Wales, letters to first Baron Newborough • NRA, priv. coll., letters to William Adam • NRA, priv. coll., letters to Lord Lansdowne • PRO, letters to Lord Chatham and Lady Chatham and William Pitt, 30/8 • PRO NIre., letters to Lord Macartney • RA, letters to Thomas Lawrence • U. Hull, Brynmor Jones L., letters to Sir Charles Hotham-Thompson • Yale U., Beinecke L., letters to W. Smith

**Likenesses** G. Cruikshank, coloured engraving, pubd 1812, BM • W. Beechey, portrait, 1817, Coutts Bank, London [see illus.] • R. W. Sievier, stipple, pubd 1822 (after W. Beechey), BM, NPG • F. Chantrey, statue, 1827, Coutts & Co., Strand, London • F. Chantrey, plaster seated statue, AM Oxf. • J. Meyer, miniature (as a young man) • J. Nollekens, bust

**Wealth at death** over £1,000,000: *Cobbett's Weekly Political Register* (30 March 1822)

## Coutts, William Lehman Ashmead Bartlett Burdett-

(1851–1921), philanthropist and politician, was born in Plymouth, Massachusetts, on 20 June 1851, the second son of Ellis Bartlett (*d*. 1852) and his wife, Sophia, daughter of John King Ashmead of Philadelphia. His grandparents on both sides of the parental line were British subjects. His mother was widowed in 1852 and she moved to England with her two sons, William (who was known as Ashmead for much of his life) and Ellis Ashmead *Bartlett (1849–

1902). She settled in Torquay and met one of its most distinguished residents, the wealthy philanthropist Angela Georgina (from 1871 Baroness) Burdett-*Coutts (1814–1906). Angela Burdett-Coutts was charmed by the intelligence and quick wit of the younger son, sympathized with Mrs Bartlett's predicament, and paid for William's education, privately in Torquay and later at Highgate School. In 1870 he entered Keble College, Oxford, recently founded to provide an inexpensive education on Anglican lines for men of limited means, and held the first scholarship to be endowed at the college. After graduating with third-class honours in modern history (1874), he read for the bar at the Inner Temple, but moved into the baroness's secretariat and became increasingly involved in her philanthropic activities. In 1877 she dispatched him as voluntary special commissioner to organize the Turkish Compassionate Fund, founded to provide relief to Turkish villagers displaced during the Russo-Turkish War. Even though Bartlett succumbed to typhus, these moneys were administered efficiently. In 1879–80 Bartlett, having recovered, travelled to Ireland to organize charitable relief among Irish fishermen.

The most important event of Bartlett's life was his marriage to his mentor, the baroness, at Christ Church, Down Street, London, on 12 February 1881. The marriage of a young impecunious American, not yet thirty years old, to a wealthy woman in her late sixties provoked much gossip casting doubt on the veracity of Bartlett's motives. Queen Victoria herself referred to 'the *mad* marriage' (Healey, 213) and tried to dissuade the baroness from plighting her troth. A Miss Shirley came forward and claimed that Bartlett had had an affair with her, but the baroness was not deflected. What Edith Wharton called in her novel *The Buccaneers* (1938) a 'feeling of affinity with this new band of marauders' (*The Buccaneers*, 103) renewed the baroness's philanthropic energies, and she gained much happiness from the marriage. Yet there can be little doubt that Bartlett gained most. Henceforth he assumed his wife's name by royal licence. In 1885 he was elected Unionist MP for Westminster. Acting on the baroness's behalf, he secured the passage of the Hampstead Heath Act, which added Parliament Hill and 300 acres to those areas granted public access. He was a competent back-bencher, who acted as his wife's political agent. But he also took part in reorganizing the City of Westminster under the Local Government Act of 1899.

That same year Burdett-Coutts travelled to South Africa as the *Times* correspondent concerned with inquiring into the conditions endured by the sick and wounded during the Second South African War. His graphic account of their suffering spurred the setting up in 1900 of a royal commission of inquiry (chaired by Sir Robert Romer), which resulted in the reform of the Army Medical Services.

The baroness's fortune was reduced by three-fifths as a result of the legal action taken by her sister when she married an alien. Nevertheless, Burdett-Coutts did not manage his wife's financial affairs with acumen. Her wealth enabled him to pursue expensive hobbies, such as racing and horse breeding, and he founded the Brookfield stud; this went out of business in 1910. The baroness died in 1906, but Burdett-Coutts continued much of her charitable work. He helped found, and then served as treasurer of, the Great Northern Central Hospital; he was twice master of the Turners' Company, and was a governor of Christ's Hospital. Burdett-Coutts also busied himself with railway reform, contributing to the passage of the Railway (Accounts and Returns) Act of 1910. During the debates on parliamentary reform in 1917–18 he founded the Anti-Proportional Representation Committee. At the 1918 general election he was elected unopposed for the Abbey Division of Westminster and was sworn of the privy council in April 1921, but died suddenly at his home, Holly Lodge, Highgate, Middlesex, on 28 July 1921. He was buried at Frant, Sussex.

BRIAN HOLDEN REID

**Sources** E. Healey, *Lady unknown: the life of Angela Burdett-Coutts* (1978) · *The Times* (29 July 1921) · *WWW, 1916–28* · *WWBMP*, vol. 3 · M. Pugh, *Electoral reform in war and peace, 1906–18* (1978) · Coutts's Bank Archive

**Likenesses** A. P. Tilt, group portrait, painting, 1882 (*A garden party at Holly Lodge*), Wellcome L. · Spy [L. Ward], caricature, repro. in *VF* (12 March 1881) · group portrait, drawing (*The marriage of Baroness Burdett-Coutts and Ashmead Bartlett at Christ Church, Down St, 1881*), Mansell collection, London

**Wealth at death** £505,057 18s. 9d.: probate, 20 Sept 1921, *CGPLA Eng. & Wales*

**Couvreur** [née Huybers; *other married name* Fraser], **Jessie Catherine** [*pseud.* Tasma] (1848–1897), author, was born on 28 October 1848 at Southwood Lodge, Highgate, Middlesex, the second child and eldest daughter in a family of five sons and three daughters. Her mother, Charlotte Sophia, née Ogleby (1817–1908), who had run a small boarding-school in England, placed great store on genealogy, emphasizing throughout her life the status derived from having a French mother, and connections with a titled family through her English father. Jessie's father, (James) Alfred Huybers (1811–1893), came from Flemish merchant stock, and it was his decision to set up as a wine trader in the Australian colonies that took the family in 1852 to Hobart in Van Diemen's Land—soon to be renamed Tasmania. When she embarked on her career as an author, Jessie's choice of Tasma as pen-name declared her pride in the formative influence of the place. She helped educate her younger brothers and sisters and, in addition to the love of languages and intellectual debate derived from her increasingly eccentric mother, developed also a passion for outdoor pursuits, notably sea-bathing and horse-riding.

However, following her early marriage to Charles Forbes Fraser (1841–1913), in Hobart on 6 June 1867, Jessie spent only short periods in Tasmania. Charles Fraser was employed on rural properties owned by his well-connected family in the Australian mainland state of Victoria, among which the couple moved until incompatibilities between Charles's sporting interests and Jessie's cultural ones, compounded by financial problems, brought about their separation in December 1872. In March 1873 Jessie set sail with her mother and siblings for London via Cape Horn, to spend over two years in Brussels and Paris. On her return to Melbourne in 1875 she was reunited with Charles, and in 1877 she began to publish articles and stories, mainly in the Melbourne newspaper *The Australasian*, where her work appeared regularly to the late 1880s.

The Fraser marriage broke down finally in 1878. In 1879 Jessie was back in Europe, where she joined her mother and four siblings in Paris. Here, as Madame Jessie Tasma, she embarked on a career as lecturer on Australian subjects, praised for the quality of her French as well as her beauty and animation, and recognized in the mid-1880s by the award of the French honour *Officier d'Académie* (rarely accorded to foreigners and even more rarely to women), for services to cultural education.

It was while Jessie was in Venice to lecture in 1881 that she met the distinguished Belgian liberal politician and journalist Auguste Pierre Louis Couvreur (1827–1894), recently widowed. They married in London on 7 August 1885 and took up residence in Brussels, Jessie having secured a divorce during her last visit to Australia in 1883–4. She now began to write longer fictional works which both reworked her life experiences, especially in the Fraser marriage, and also celebrated the energy and opportunities of Australia while respecting the cultural values of the Old World. She had significant success with *Uncle Piper of Piper's Hill*, serialized in *The Australasian* in 1888 and published in book form in London in 1889. This mellow comedy, set in the booming city of Melbourne in the 1860s, dwells on the egalitarian possibilities of life in Australia by its depiction of the family of Tom Piper, who has migrated from England in the gold rushes and made money as a butcher and in real estate. This novel was rapidly followed by a volume of stories, *A Sydney Sovereign* (1890), and five more novels, none of them acclaimed as *Uncle Piper* had been. Writing for her living, Jessie produced also a translation into French, and journalism in both French and English, publishing frequently in Edmund Yates's London newspaper, *The World*.

In 1892 Auguste Couvreur was appointed Brussels correspondent for *The Times*. When he died on 23 April 1894, Jessie indefatigably took over the role until her own death from coronary heart disease at her home, 161 chaussée de Vleurgat, Brussels, on 23 October 1897. In accordance with her long-held principles she was cremated, though this required that her body travel by rail to Paris (where she was cremated at Père Lachaise) as cremation was illegal in Belgium. Her mother and five siblings—for whom she had had significant financial responsibility—survived her. Obituaries identified her prominence in the London literary scene, and her distinctive role as a cultural ambassador for Australia.

MARGARET HARRIS

**Sources** P. Clarke, *Tasma: the life of Jessie Couvreur* (1994) · R. Beilby and C. Hadgraft, *Ada Cambridge, Tasma, and Rosa Praed* (1979) · D. Byrne, *Australian writers* (1896) · 'Some Australian women: part II—"Tasma"', *Illustrated Sydney News* (25 April 1891) [includes photograph] · '"Tasma" (Mme Auguste Couvreur)', *The Queen* (13 Jan 1894) · *The Times* (25 Oct 1897) · J. C. Couvreur, diary, 1889–91, Mitchell L., NSW [microfilm copy] · *Tasma's diaries: the diaries of Jessie Couvreur, with another by her young sister Edith Huybers*, ed. P. Clarke (Canberra, 1995)

**Archives** priv. coll., diary [microfilm in Mitchell L., NSW] · priv. coll., diary and other papers, incl. cuttings | Mitchell L., NSW, Edward Huybers MSS · University of Queensland, Brisbane, Fryer Library, Edward and Edith Huybers MSS
**Likenesses** photograph, 1889, Mitchell L., NSW · Philippson, oils, 1890, priv. coll. · J. Reverdy, bust, 1890, priv. coll.

**Cove, Morgan** (1753–1830), pamphleteer, was the son of a Church of England clergyman, also Morgan Cove. He entered Trinity Hall, Cambridge, as a sizar in November 1768 and was elected a scholar of the college two years later. Trinity Hall at this period was heavily orientated towards the law, and this was his initial choice of career. He took his LLB in 1776 but he then changed course and became ordained.

Cove was inducted into the vicarage of Sithney, Cornwall, in 1780. His fame dates from 1795, when he published *An Essay on the Revenues of the Church of England*. One of the first contributions to the late Georgian movement for church reform, this pamphlet was later much quoted by clerical controversialists. A second edition came out in 1797 and was followed by a third, much enlarged, edition in 1816. Cove's arguments in favour of tithes—he stresses biblical and Anglo-Saxon precedent—were conventional; what made an impact was his calculation of clerical incomes. Using a variety of sources he was able to show that the beneficed clergy had to be content with a 'very moderate competency', living off aggregate annual revenue of £1,543,000 (Cove, 185). These calculations attracted little notice in the 1790s because ecclesiastical reform was not yet a major political issue, but they became influential when anti-clericalism attained stridency in the late 1820s and early 1830s.

Cove's defence of the bulwarks of establishment was admired by the tory bishop of Hereford, John Butler, who in 1799 presented him to the rectory of Eaton Bishop in Herefordshire. More preferment was in store. In April 1800 Cove was appointed to the prebend of Withington Parva in Hereford cathedral, being translated to the more lucrative prebend of Gorwall and Overbury a year later. In the same year in which he became a cathedral dignitary Cove published *An Inquiry into the Necessity, Justice, and Policy of a Commutation of Tithes*. Pitt, in 1799, had approached the bishops with a proposal for a form of cash commutation but had received little support (Evans, 80). Cove's aim was to rally the clergy against reform. He argued—and in this he was prophetic—that commutation would be deleterious to the clergy's long-term financial interests. At the same time he wanted to take the sting out of tithe disputes, shrewdly proposing the adoption of an enabling act that would allow tithe-holders to lease their tithes at fixed annual rents for terms not exceeding twenty-one years. Cove obtained a further promotion towards the end of his life, being made chancellor of the choir in Hereford Cathedral in October 1828. He died at Hereford on 9 April 1830. PETER VIRGIN

**Sources** G. F. A. Best, *Temporal pillars: Queen Anne's bounty, the ecclesiastical commissioners, and the Church of England* (1964) · P. Virgin, *The church in an age of negligence: ecclesiastical structure and problems of church reform, 1700–1840* (1989) · E. J. Evans, *The contentious tithe*

(1976) · *DNB* · Venn, *Alum. Cant.* · M. Cove, *An essay on the revenues of the Church of England* (1795)

**Covel** [Colvill], **John** (1638–1722), college head, was born at Horningsheath, also known as Horringer, Suffolk, on 2 April 1638, the third and youngest son of William Covel (*d.* 1661) and Alice, *née* Cook, of Pakenham. He was educated at Bury St Edmunds grammar school before proceeding to Cambridge, where he was admitted as a sizar to Christ's College on 31 March 1654. He graduated BA in 1658, was elected a fellow of the college in 1659, and proceeded MA in 1661. Three of his Latin orations as an MA are preserved among his papers (BL, Add. MS 22910). According to William Cole, he studied medicine and was then ordained. On 17 March 1670 Sir Eliab Harvey wrote to him that he had 'gott [him] chosen to goe Chapline to Constantinople' (BL, Add. MS 22910, fol. 29), although it appears that what Covel had been hoping and negotiating for in the previous months was the post of secretary to the ambassador, Sir Daniel Harvey. He is described as BD in a letter from Thomas Leader to Dr Parker on 29 October 1669, but there is no record of this degree, and his ordination, albeit certain, cannot be traced.

Covel was careful to take legal advice and to secure a royal letter ensuring that his absence from Cambridge would not entail the lapse of his fellowship, and it appears that he did not leave for Constantinople until late in 1670. In 1672 Sir Daniel Harvey died, leaving Covel in sole charge of the embassy until the arrival of Harvey's successor, Sir John Finch, in 1674. In the course of his term of office at Constantinople, which lasted until 1677, Covel travelled widely in Asia Minor, compiling a series of diaries replete with illustrations of buildings, inscriptions, and plants (BL, Add. MSS 22912–22914). He was an avid collector of paintings, coins and medals, printed books, curiosities, and especially of manuscripts, and—at the prompting of Peter Gunning, bishop of Ely, John Pearson, bishop of Chester, and William Sancroft, soon to be archbishop of Canterbury—he made a particular study of the Greek church and of its stand on transubstantiation. He corresponded, in vernacular Greek, with numerous patriarchs and with other Western travellers in French and Italian. Towards the end of his time in the Levant he made the journey to Nicomedia and Nicaea. He was the first Westerner to leave a written account of Athos (Hasluck), and is credited with being among the first Englishmen to be admitted there.

On his leisurely return to England, via Italy, Savoy, and France, in 1679 Covel was appointed Lady Margaret preacher, and created DD by royal mandate, but he was disappointed in his hopes of the oratorship. He was presented by Bishop Gunning to the living of Littlebury, Essex, and in 1681 by Christ's College to Kegworth, Leicestershire. It is likely that neither of these livings saw much of him as, in 1681, he was appointed chaplain to the princess of Orange, and left for The Hague. However, his employment was very abruptly terminated in October 1685 when the prince of Orange intercepted a letter from Covel to the English ambassador criticizing the princess's treatment by her husband. Covel returned to England

and, in November 1687, was instituted chancellor of York by James II. The following year Ralph Cudworth, master of Christ's, died, and the fellows, under the threat of having a new master intruded by the crown, elected Covel instead, perhaps without positive enthusiasm. Covel in fact proved a conscientious master, although the fellows grumbled at his income from renting rooms in the lodge to fellow-commoners.

Within two years Covel was elected vice-chancellor and it fell to his lot to present the university's loyal address to the new king, lately the prince of Orange. Covel was overwhelmed with embarrassment at the prospect and wrote furiously to his connections at the court, among them Isaac Newton, then MP for the university, to ascertain whether the king would countenance his appearance, finally receiving an assurance from Sir Owen Wynne that the king was reported to have said:

> 'That if Dr Covel came with the body of the University he would be admitted to kiss their Majesties hand'—though my Lord says he did at the same time discover by the King that he spoke it so, as if he would have been content the complement were made by another. (BL, Add. MS 22910, fol. 275)

Covel was duly admitted, but realized that he could entertain no hopes of promotion in William's reign. Under Anne he had better hopes, but he indicated that they were thwarted by Archbishop John Tillotson.

The remainder of Covel's long life was spent at Christ's, where he continued to correspond not only with a wide range of English scholars, including Isaac Newton, John Locke, and John Mill, but also (in modern Greek, French, Italian, and Latin) with Greek and other European scholars, whom he delighted to entertain in Cambridge. In the last year of his life, long after the subject had ceased to attract interest, there finally appeared his *Some account of the Greek church, with reflections on their present doctrine and discipline, particularly on the eucharist, and the rest of their seven pretended sacraments, compared with Jac. Goar's notes on the Greek ritual, or Euchologion*. An earlier work composed in Holland, under the title *Synodus Bethlemitica*, was suppressed.

From 1719 Covel was in sometimes acrimonious correspondence with Humfrey Wanley concerning the sale of his manuscripts to Lord Harley, a sale finally concluded for £300. Some 43 of his manuscripts, ranging from the twelfth to the seventeenth century remain in the Harleian collection. Covel died in Cambridge on 19 December 1722 at Christ's College and was buried in the chapel, where there is an inscription to him (currently obscured). His printed books, numbering some 3000, were catalogued by Humfrey Wanley but were, in the event, sold publicly by his nephew and executor Henry Sorel in 1724. Land in Suffolk and small sums of money were divided among several beneficiaries, including other nephews.

ELISABETH LEEDHAM-GREEN

**Sources** commonplace book, Yale U., Beinecke L., b. 140 · Covel's journals and corresp., BL, Add. MSS 22910–22914 · natural history notebook and commonplace book, BL, Add. MS 57495 · Christ's College, Cambridge, MS 143 · Christ's College, Cambridge, Cole MS xx. 72 · *A catalogue of the entire library of that reverend and learned antiquary Dr John Covel* (1724) [sale catalogue, Christopher Cock, London, 9 March 1724] · J. T. Bent, ed., *Early voyages and travels to the Levant*, 2: *Extracts from the diaries of Dr John Covel, 1670–79*, Hakluyt Society, 87 (1893) · J. Covel, *Voyages en Turquie, 1675–77: texte établi, annoté et traduit par Jean-Pierre Grélot, avec une préface de Cyril Mango* (1998) · F. W. Hasluck, 'Notes on manuscripts in the British Museum relating to Levant geography and travel', *British School at Athens Annual*, 12 (1905–6), 210–11 · F. W. Hasluck, 'The first English traveller's account of Athos', *British School at Athens Annual*, 17 (1910–11), 103–31 [printing sels. from Covel's journal] · *Horringer parish registers: baptisms, marriages and burials … 1558–1850* (1900) · M. W. Hervey, *Annals of a Suffolk village* (1930) · J. Raby, 'A seventeenth-century description of Iznic-Nicaea', *Deutsches Archäologisches Institut Abteilung: Istanbul, Mitteilungen*, 28 (1976), 149–88 · *The correspondence of Henry Hyde, earl of Clarendon, and of his brother, Laurence Hyde, earl of Rochester*, ed. S. W. Singer, 1 (1828), 163–7 · Z. C. von Uffenbach, 'Diary of a visit to Cambridge in 1710', *Cambridge under Queen Anne*, ed. J. E. B. Mayor (1911) · *The diary of Humfrey Wanley, 1715–1726*, ed. C. E. Wright and R. C. Wright, 2 vols. (1966) · will, PRO, PROB 11/589, sig. 23

**Archives** BL, catalogue of library, Add. MS 70485 · BL, corresp., journals, and papers, Add. MSS 22909–22914, 57495; Lansdowne MS 355 · Yale U., commonplace book | Bodl. Oxf., corresp. with John Locke and Lady Masham

**Likenesses** C. Guynier, portrait, 1716, Christ's College, Cambridge · V. Ritz, portrait (in later life), Christ's College, Cambridge · oils, Christ's College, Cambridge

**Wealth at death** £300 in cash bequests; plus remittance of £100 debt from Christ's: will, PRO, PROB 11/589, sig. 23

**Covell, William** (*d.* 1613), writer and Church of England clergyman, was born at Chatterton, Lancashire. Having matriculated as a pensioner from Christ's College, Cambridge, at Lent 1581, he graduated BA in 1585 and proceeded MA in 1588. In 1595 he published *Polimanteia, or, The meanes lawfull and unlawfull, to judge of the fall of a commonwealth, against the frivolous and foolish conjectures of this age, whereunto is added, a letter from England to her three daughters, Cambridge, Oxford, innes of court, and to all the rest of her inhabitants: perswading them to a constant unitie of what religion soever they are, for the defence of our dread soveraigne, and native cuntry: most requisite for this time wherein wee now live*. Dedicated to the earl of Essex, *Polimanteia* was issued by the Cambridge University printer. Often attributed in the past to William Clerke, its interest to posterity lies primarily in its references to Nash, Harvey, 'divine Spenser', 'happie Daniell', and above all 'sweet Shakespeare'—one of the earliest printed references to the bard.

*Polimanteia* is a work of polemic. As a fellow of Queens' College, Cambridge, from 1589 to 1599, Covell also expressed some controversial ideas from the pulpit. Preaching in St Mary's Church in December 1595 on the text 'My house is the house of prayer: but ye have made it a den of thieves', he inveighed against those who grasped at the properties and revenues of the church. On 2 January 1596 Roger Goad, provost of King's and vice-chancellor of the university, reported to Lord Burghley and Archbishop Whitgift that Covell's remarks had been directed 'offensively and extraordinarily, to charge the noblemen of this realm especially; and in sort also the bishops' (Strype, *Whitgift*, 2.319–20). The furious archbishop sought to bring Covell before the ecclesiastical commissioners, but Goad, fearing that the college fellows would interpret this as a threat to their privileges, won Whitgift's consent to deal with the matter himself. Covell, however, was unimpressed by the rebukes of Goad and the other college heads, and seems to have refused to apologize or retract.

This brush with authority brought Covell's radical career to a close, and his relations with Whitgift became much more cordial. Having become doctor of divinity at Cambridge in 1601, he was collated by the archbishop on 27 January 1603 to the vicarage of Sittingbourne, Kent, holding it in plurality with the vicarage of Leaveland in the same county until his resignation in 1603. In that year he published *A Just and Temperate Defence of the Five Books of Ecclesiastical Policie by R. Hooker*, and in 1604 *A modest and reasonable examination, of some things in use in the church of England, sundrie times heretofore misliked*. It is likely that these books were written at Whitgift's prompting; both were directed against nonconformity and each contained a dedication to the archbishop. Unfortunately Whitgift died before the second work went to press, so Covell redirected his epistolary preamble to Richard Bancroft, bishop of London, signing this on 27 May 1604, but including the original preface as an appendix. Further anti-puritan writings followed, notably *A Briefe Answer* (1606), responding to the 'Apologie' which the Lincolnshire clergyman John Burgess had addressed to the bishop of Lincoln, justifying his agonized stance on church ceremonies.

On 11 September 1609 Covell was instituted as subdean of Lincoln on the presentation of Archbishop Bancroft. On 8 May 1610 he was one of the seventeen founding fellows of Chelsea College. On 8 September 1612 he was instituted to the Lincoln prebend of All Saints-in-Hungate and was installed in person three days later. From 1605 he had also been rector of Mersham in Kent, and it was there that he died, and where he was buried on 2 February 1613.

STEPHEN WRIGHT

**Sources** *Fasti Angl., 1541–1857*, [Lincoln] · J. Strype, *The life and acts of John Whitgift*, new edn, 3 vols. (1822), vol. 2 · Venn, *Alum. Cant.*, 1/1.406 · W. Cowell [W. Covell], *A just and temperate defence … Hooker* (1603) · W. Cowell [W. Covell], *A modest and reasonable examination* (1604) · J. Strype, *Annals of the Reformation and establishment of religion … during Queen Elizabeth's happy reign*, new edn, 4 (1824) · W. C. [W. Covell], *Polimanteia* (1595)

**Coventry, Andrew** (1764–1832), agriculturist, was born at Stichill, Roxburghshire, the eldest son of George Coventry, minister of the Relief Church at Stichill, and his wife, Elizabeth Horn. Through his mother he inherited the estate of Shanwell, near Kinross, and some other property in Perthshire. He was educated at the parish school and at the University of Edinburgh. On 15 December 1782 he was elected a member of the Medical Society of Edinburgh; in September 1783 he graduated MD for a thesis, 'De scarlatina cynanchica'. It is not clear whether he ever practised as a physician, but he appears to have specialized in sciences relevant to agriculture.

In 1790 Sir William Pulteney endowed a chair of agriculture at Edinburgh University, nominating Coventry to be the first professor. Up to this time occasional lectures on agriculture had been delivered by other professors, such as the professor of chemistry, Dr William Cullen. A much fuller course had also been given by John Walker, professor of natural history, in 1788. The foundation of the new chair caused a good deal of friction, and the fact that it was the first time that a chair in Edinburgh had been endowed by a private individual also aroused opposition.

In spite of these obstacles, on 17 November 1790 Coventry became the first professor of agriculture at Edinburgh University, and he held the post until 1831. The endowment of the chair amounted to only £50 a year but Coventry had other sources of income, and became the main authority on agriculture in Scotland. His writings included *Remarks on Live Stock and Relative Subjects* (1806), *Discourses explanatory of the object and plan of the course of lectures on agriculture and rural economy* (1808), and *Notes on the Culture and Cropping of Arable Land* (1811).

Coventry was often called on to arbitrate in land questions, and to give evidence before the court of session and before committees of the House of Commons. In 1830 Loch Leven was drained and the surrounding lands were reclaimed under Coventry's supervision. It was also he who introduced the cultivation of turnips to Scotland. Coventry gave evidence before the royal commission appointed in 1826 to investigate the condition of the universities and colleges of Scotland, and said that he had given thirty-two courses, some of them consisting of more than 140 lectures. Although it was not possible to graduate with a degree in agriculture, Coventry had attracted classes varying in number from thirty to seventy-eight. Towards the end of his tenure of office, however, he appears to have lectured only in alternate years. In 1830 the royal commission recommended that the chair of agriculture should be abolished, unless the subject could be taught regularly. Coventry therefore resigned.

Coventry died in 1832, leaving at least two sons, and was buried in Buccleuch churchyard, Edinburgh.

ERNEST CLARKE, *rev.* ANNE PIMLOTT BAKER

**Sources** A. Grant, *The story of the University of Edinburgh during its first three hundred years*, 2 vols. (1884), vol. 1, pp. 345–8; vol. 2, p. 456 · *Distinguished men of the county, or, Biographical annals of Kinross-shire* (1932)
**Archives** NL Scot., lecture notes | NRA, priv. coll., letters to William Adam
**Likenesses** J. Tassie, paste medallion, 1764, Scot. NPG

**Coventry** [*née* Somerset]**, Anne, countess of Coventry** (1673–1763), religious writer, was born on 22 July 1673, the daughter of Henry *Somerset, then third marquess of Worcester and later first duke of Beaufort (1629–1700), politician, and Mary Capel (*bap.* 1630, *d.* 1715), gardener and botanist [*see* Somerset, Mary, duchess of Beaufort]. On 4 May 1691 she married Thomas Coventry, second earl of Coventry (*c.*1662–1710). Her husband died in August 1710, leaving her with large debts, which she eventually succeeded in repaying before she died. Their longest surviving child, Thomas (1702–1712), succeeded as third earl but died, aged nine, at Eton College on 28 January 1712. In 1726 the countess moved to her country house at Snitterfield, Warwickshire.

The countess was renowned for her charity and piety. She was interested in female education, and in 1709 she was one of the main patrons of Mary Astell's Charity School for Girls in Chelsea, which was linked to the Society for Promoting Christian Knowledge. She was a good friend and patron of Astell and shared many of her political and theological views. The countess, like Astell, may have been involved in Jacobite activities, through her sister Mary, duchess of Ormond. There is some evidence that privately she held nonjuring beliefs but she made no explicit break with the Church of England and strongly affirmed her membership of the church in her will.

*The Right Honourable Anne, countess of Coventry's meditations and reflections, moral and divine* was published in 1707 and again in 1727. The countess, however, was not only an author but an enthusiastic collector of books. An early eighteenth-century catalogue of her impressive library includes a large number of devotional and theological texts. Pieces on female education and history are also listed, and the countess was one of the subscribers to George Ballard's 1752 *Memoirs of Several Ladies of Great Britain, who have been Celebrated for their Writings or Skill in the Learned Languages, Arts and Sciences*. The catalogue also, more surprisingly, shows her interest in contemporary drama; her large collection of plays, mostly comedies, includes some racy plays and shows a sophisticated broadmindedness that reflects her involvement with fashionable life. It also perhaps hints at the pleasure in life that prompted her to tease Astell about her tendency to gloom.

The countess of Coventry died at Snitterfield, Warwickshire, on 14 February 1763, after fifty-two years of widowhood. In her will she asked to be buried with her husband and son in the vault at Croome Court, Worcestershire, but she was probably buried at her parents' family vault at Badminton, Gloucestershire. Her will included many individual bequests to female Somerset relatives, and she left her estate to her grandnephew, godson, and executor, Henry Somerset, fifth duke of Beaufort. Her friend and vicar Richard Jago praises her in a memorial sermon, *The Nature, and Grounds, of a Christian's Happiness* (1763), as an exemplary member of the Church of England.

EMMA MAJOR

**Sources** R. Perry, *The celebrated Mary Astell* (1986), 7, 173, 175, 177, 247–57, 267–8, 339–54 · will, PRO, PROB 11/887, sig. 219 · GEC, *Peerage*, new edn · ESTC · R. Jago, *The nature, and grounds, of a Christian's happiness* (1763) · J. Pearson, 'Women reading, reading women', *Women and literature in Britain, 1500–1700*, ed. H. Wilcox (1996), 82–3 · *GM*, 1st ser., 33 (1763), 98 · *British Museum catalogue* (1967) · P. Springborg, introduction, in *Political writings: Astell* (1996), xii · B. Hill, introduction, in M. Astell, *The first English feminist: reflections upon marriage and other writings*, ed. B. Hill (1986), 10 · private information (2004) · DNB

**Likenesses** G. Kneller, portrait, c.1678–1680, repro. in Perry, *The celebrated Mary Astell*

**Wealth at death** over £1300; individual bequests of valuable jewellery: will, PRO, PROB 11/887, sig. 219

**Coventry** [*née* Master; *other married name* Pytts], **Anne**, **countess of Coventry** (**1691–1788**), plaintiff in a marriage settlement case, was born on 21 August 1691 and baptized on 23 August 1691 at St Andrew's, Holborn, Middlesex, the daughter of Sir Streynsham *Master (1640–1724), of Codnor Castle, Derbyshire, and his second wife, Elizabeth, daughter of Richard Legh, of Lyme, Cheshire. In 1715 her father negotiated her marriage to Gilbert Coventry, fourth earl of Coventry (c.1668–1719), as his second wife. On 24 June 1715 her father and Coventry agreed the terms of the marriage settlement; Master was to pay Coventry a dowry of £10,000, and Coventry guaranteed Anne a jointure of £500 p.a. in the event of his death. Anne married Coventry on 27 June 1715 at the Guildhall Chapel, London.

Under the terms of the entail executed by Thomas, first earl of Coventry, on 24 March 1698, the possessor of the Coventry estate was allowed to appoint part of the estate up to the value of £500 p.a. as a jointure for his wife. The arrangement should have been straightforward but the Coventry estates, mainly in Worcestershire and Middlesex, were in disarray. The only part of the estate that was not mortgaged, the manor of Woolvey, could only generate a maximum of £400 p.a., and it took time to negotiate the release of part of another manor, Woolston, from its mortgage so that it could be used to pay for Anne's jointure. The settlement had only just been written and engrossed when Coventry fell ill in 1719; he was unable to execute the conveyance before his death at his family home, Croome Dabitot, Worcestershire, on 27 October 1719. He had drawn up and signed his will, which left his widow £3000 in addition to the jointure in his marriage settlement.

According to the entail the estate passed to his third cousin once removed William Coventry, MP for Bridport, who also succeeded as fifth earl of Coventry. The new earl, presumably anxious to avoid the further diminution of his inheritance, withheld payment of the jointure. Left without her income Anne brought a case against the earl of Coventry, his brothers Henry and Thomas Coventry, her stepdaughter Lady Anne Carew, executor of the fourth earl's will, and Sir William Carew. The case was heard before the lord chancellor, Thomas Parker, first earl of Macclesfield, on 16 May 1724. Macclesfield and the three other judges present agreed that the fourth earl had been free to settle the jointure on Anne and that, as the earl's instructions had been engrossed and the lands to be drawn upon specified, the settlement should stand. The case set an important precedent in equity law; the account by Richard Francis in his *Maxims of Equity* (1727) was held to be definitive.

Little seems to be known of the remainder of Anne's life. On 15 December 1752 at Great Witley, Worcestershire, she married Edmund Pytts (1696?–1753) of Kyre, Worcestershire, tory MP for Worcestershire from 1741 to 1753. He died on 24 November 1753. Anne died childless at her home, Holt Castle, Worcestershire, on 21 March 1788; in her will she requested that she be buried in the churchyard at Holt alongside Pytts, and left various legacies to members of the Master and Pytts families.

MATTHEW KILBURN

**Sources** R. Francis, *Maxims of equity*, 4th edn (1812), 73–91 [published and bound with J. Fonblanque, *A treatise of equity*, 4th edn, 2

(1812), but paginated separately] · will, PRO, PROB 11/1164, sig. 180 · GEC, *Peerage* · *GM*, 1st ser., 58 (1788), 277 · *The manuscripts of the House of Lords*, new ser., 12 vols. (1900–77), vol. 10, p. 71 · [H. Ballow], *A treatise of equity*, ed. J. Fonblanque, 4th edn, 2 vols. (1812), vol. 1, pp. 298, 301, 367; vol. 2, p. 287 · *IGI* · *DNB* · R. S. Lea, 'Pytts, Edmund', HoP, *Commons, 1715–54* · Burke, *Gen. GB* (1937)
**Wealth at death** comfortable; £500 p.a. since 1724: will, PRO, PROB 11/1164, sig. 180

**Coventry, (William) Francis Walter** (1725–1753/4), author, was born about 15 July 1725 at Mill End, Buckinghamshire, and baptized at Hambleden parish church on 18 July. He was one of two sons and three daughters born to Thomas Coventry, Turkey merchant and younger brother of William, fifth earl of Coventry, and Thomas's second wife, Gratia-Anna-Maria Brown, daughter of the Revd Thomas Brown of Polston, Wiltshire. After briefly attending Eton College (1742–4), in 1744 he was admitted as a pensioner to Magdalene College, Cambridge, where his cousin Henry was a fellow; he graduated BA in 1749 and proceeded MA in 1752. He was established vicar of Edgware by the earl of Coventry in 1751.

Coventry declared gentlemanly literary ambitions in *Penshurst*, a topographical poem published anonymously by Robert Dodsley in 1750 and inscribed to William and Elizabeth Perry, his hosts in the celebrated country house associated with Philip Sidney, Ben Jonson, and Edmund Waller: 'A simple shepherd, yet unknown,' he concludes, 'Aspires to snatch an ivy crown.' His lively novel of fashionable life, *The History of Pompey the Little, or, The Life and Adventures of a Lap-Dog*, caused a stir when it was published anonymously by Dodsley in 1751. Following the fortunes of a lap-dog through various situations, it records the follies of London society so vividly that some fashionable readers recognized the originals of its satiric portraits. Favourably noticed (by John Cleland) in the *Monthly Review* (February 1751), commended to Samuel Richardson by Lady Bradshaigh, and admired by Lady Mary Wortley Montagu, it was variously attributed to Sir John Hill, the printer William Bowyer, and Henry Fielding. Thomas Gray recognized 'three characters, which once made part of a comedy that [Coventry] showed me of his own writing' (*Works*, 1.344). Having given 50 guineas for the copyright, Dodsley paid a further £30 for extensive revisions to the third edition of 1752 (*Correspondence of Robert Dodsley*, 513, 531); it was frequently reprinted.

Coventry's position as a clergyman may explain why he remained anonymous despite his worldly novel's success. With more dignity, he edited *Philemon to Hydaspes* (1736–44), his late cousin Henry's dialogues on pagan religious errors, defending Henry's orthodoxy and dedicating the volume (1753) to another cousin, George William, sixth earl since 1751. In an essay on excesses of modern gardening (*The World*, 15, 12 April 1753) he satirized upstart pretenders to taste. A poetical epistle, 'To a Friend in Wales' (identified later as Wilmot Vaughan, an Eton friend subsequently created earl of Lisburne), joined *Penshurst* in volume 4 of Dodsley's *Collection of Poems* (1755), both ascribed to 'the late Mr. F. Coventry', as was 'Ode to the Honourable * * * *', a poem to a young MP in volume 6 (1758). Although Coventry added a dedicatory epistle to Henry Fielding

when he revised *Pompey*, little supports the occasional attribution to him of *An Essay on the New Species of Writing Founded by Mr. Fielding* (1751), a pamphlet published by William Owen, not Dodsley. Coventry died at Whitchurch, Middlesex, of smallpox according to the *Gentleman's Magazine*, and was buried in St Lawrence's Church, Little Stanmore, on 9 January 1754. DAVID OAKLEAF

**Sources** F. Coventry, *The history of Pompey the Little, or, The life and adventures of a lap-dog*, ed. R. A. Day (1974), xxxiii–xxxvii · J. D. [J. Dodsley], letter, *GM*, 1st ser., 46 (1776), 64 · *The correspondence of Robert Dodsley, 1733–1764*, ed. J. E. Tierney (1988) · Nichols, *Lit. anecdotes*, 2.202–3; 5.564–9 · [R. Dodsley], ed., *A collection of poems*, 6 vols. (1748–58) · W. P. Courtney, *Dodsley's collection of poetry, its contents and contributors: ... the history of English literature in the eighteenth century* (privately printed, London, 1910) · J. B. Harley and D. Hodson, eds., *The royal English atlas: eighteenth-century county maps of England and Wales by Emanuel Bowen and Thomas Kitchin* (1971) · W. Scott, 'Francis Coventry's *Pompey the Little*, 1751 and 1752', *N&Q*, 213 (1968), 215–19 · *Correspondence of Thomas Gray*, ed. P. Toynbee and L. Whibley, 3 vols. (1935); repr. with additions by H. W. Starr (1971) · Venn, *Alum. Cant.*

**Coventry, Henry** (1617/18–1686), politician, was the fourth son of Thomas *Coventry, first Baron Coventry (1578–1640), being the third son born to his second wife, Elizabeth (1583–1653), daughter of John Aldersey, a London merchant, and the widow of William Pichford (d. 1609), a London grocer. Coventry matriculated from Queen's College, Oxford, on 20 April 1632, aged fourteen, and graduated BA in 1633. By 1634 he was a fellow of All Souls; he proceeded MA in 1636 and BCL in 1638. He had been admitted specially to the Inner Temple in October 1633, but his initial career prospects lay in the civil law. His father's influence procured for him the post of chancellor of Llandaff, possibly as early as 1638. Upon his father's death in January 1640 he was given leave in May to travel, initially for three years. He visited France, the Low Countries, and Italy, including a stay in 1643 at the University of Padua. Although he remained a fellow of All Souls until 1648 he did not return to England until shortly before the Restoration in 1660.

By 1654 Coventry was a captain in the Dutch army, but he was also in communication with the court of the exiled Charles II. His absence from England during the civil wars was seen as a particular advantage, the duke of Ormond proposing in February 1655 'can any use be made of Mr Henry Coventry, who has no dangerous marks upon him in England' (Clarendon, *Hist. rebellion*, 3.12). Coventry returned to England in April 1660 in advance of the Restoration with letters for several prominent presbyterian leaders, including Anthony Ashley Cooper, the future earl of Shaftesbury, whose first wife had been Coventry's sister, Margaret (d. 1649). Despite royalist attempts to obtain for him a seat in Cornwall, Coventry was not elected to the Convention in 1660. Following the Restoration he resumed his fellowship at All Souls and in June 1660 he was appointed to local office in Worcestershire. In April 1661 he was returned to parliament for his family's traditional stronghold of Droitwich, taking over a seat from his nephew, Thomas Coventry, and being joined by his younger brother, William *Coventry, MP for Great Yarmouth.

Coventry was an accomplished debater and he was soon being utilized by the earl of Clarendon as a member of his 'management committee' (Seaward, 235) of the House of Commons. He began to accrue other honours, being named a groom of the bedchamber in January 1662, and he served as a commissioner of the Irish land settlement in 1662–3. Despite a personal visit to Zeeland in 1663 he was unable to retain his Dutch military commission. In 1664 he was listed as a court dependant and supported the repeal of the Triennial Act. In August 1664 he was appointed ambassador-extraordinary to Sweden, returning home in the summer of 1666. From March to September 1667 he served as a plenipotentiary at the Congress of Breda, which concluded the Second Dutch War. In October 1667 he defended Clarendon in the Commons and sought to prevent further proceedings against the fallen minister. His support for redress of grievances over supply in the Commons in 1669 led to reports that Charles II had stripped him of his bedchamber post, but if this was the case he had been restored by February 1670. In August 1671 he embarked on a second stint as envoy-extraordinary to Sweden, successfully persuading that country's government to join an alliance against the Dutch. In July 1672 he succeeded Sir John Trevor as secretary of state for the northern department, not that his appointment prevented the loss of £3000 in the stop of the exchequer. By virtue of this promotion he lost his bedchamber post, but he also became a privy councillor and a commissioner of prizes.

As secretary Coventry played a major role in communicating information from Charles II to the Commons. He also undertook a heavy load in the management of the Commons when it met again in February 1673, for example in defending the king's declaration of indulgence of the previous year. He was well suited to this role, one commentator noting he 'had the nice step of the house, and withal was wonderfully witty and a man of great veracity' (R. North, The Lives of … Francis North … Dudley North … John North, ed. A. Jessop, 3 vols., 1890, 1.119). In July 1673 he became an Admiralty commissioner and also a commissioner for Tangier and in September 1674 he transferred to the secretaryship for the southern department. His role as a parliamentary manager increased over time particularly after 1674, and, although he was not close to the lord treasurer, Thomas Osborne, earl of Danby, he continued to be a noted leader of the court interest in debate. In February 1677, after Coventry had defended the long prorogation of parliament, Shaftesbury noticed this by marking Coventry as 'doubly vile'. However, Coventry's reputation as 'the only honest minister the king had since my Lord Clarendon' (Bishop Burnet's History, 1.488) shielded him from attack by the whig opposition. In turn he did not exert himself in defence of Danby when the latter faced impeachment in the autumn of 1678. As Coventry himself admitted he was 'neither of a temper or condition to dissemble' (Marshall, 69). After initial scepticism concerning the testimony of Titus Oates,

Coventry came to the conclusion 'if he be a liar … he is the greatest and adroitest I ever saw' (ibid.), and so he became convinced of the veracity of the Popish Plot. His response to the attendant crisis was to be an early and consistent advocate of the alternatives to exclusion proposed by the crown, speaking on 22 November 1678 in favour of a proposal that a popish successor to Charles II be deprived of the right to dispense with the penal laws against Catholics.

By now Coventry was increasingly afflicted with the gout which restricted his appearances in the Commons. Nevertheless he was elected to the first Exclusion Parliament in February 1679, voting against the Exclusion Bill. He was retained in office and on the privy council when Shaftesbury and his followers were admitted to office in April 1679, although he gave up his Admiralty post in May. Re-elected to the second Exclusion Parliament in September 1679, he was laid up with gout for most of the proceedings. In February 1680 Narcissus Luttrell reported that he had been allowed to retire from the secretaryship, selling the office for £6500 to his successor, Sir Leoline Jenkins, who was appointed in April. Coventry was elected for Droitwich for the last time in February 1681, duly attending the Oxford parliament and making a plea for expedients to safeguard the protestant religion, rather than pass another exclusion bill.

Coventry retired from politics, living mainly at his house on the north-east corner of the Haymarket. He died unmarried on 7 December 1686 and was buried in St Martin-in-the-Fields. His will made extensive provision for the erection of a workhouse in Droitwich, 'that the industry of the indigent persons therein placed might make this charity comfortable to themselves and acceptable to God' (Nash, 1.328). The chief beneficiaries of his estate were two nephews, Francis Coventry, son of his brother Francis, and Henry Frederick Thynne, younger son of his sister Mary.　　　　　　　　　　STUART HANDLEY

**Sources** E. Rowlands, 'Coventry, Henry', HoP, Commons, 1660–90 • P. Seaward, The Cavalier Parliament and the reconstruction of the old regime, 1661–1667 (1998) • GEC, Peerage • will, PRO, PROB 11/385, sig. 160 • Calendar of the Clarendon state papers preserved in the Bodleian Library, ed. O. Ogle and others, 5 vols. (1869–1970) • F. A. Inderwick and R. A. Roberts, eds., A calendar of the Inner Temple records, 2 (1898) • Bishop Burnet's History • CSP dom., 1640–70 • T. Nash, Collections for the history of Worcestershire, 2 vols. (1781), vol. 1, p. 328 • M. Knights, Politics and opinion in crisis, 1678–81 (1994) • A. Marshall, Intelligence and espionage in the reign of Charles II, 1660–1685 (1994) • D. T. Witcombe, Charles II and the cavalier House of Commons, 1663–1674 (1966) • G. M. Bell, A handlist of British diplomatic representatives, 1509–1688, Royal Historical Society Guides and Handbooks, 16 (1990) • DNB
**Archives** Alnwick Castle, Northumberland, letter-book as envoy to the Netherlands • BL, corresp. and papers • Longleat House, Wiltshire | BL, Add. MSS 25122–25125 • BL, corresp. with Sir R. Bulstrode • BL, corresp. with Francis Parry • NL Ire., corresp. with duke of Ormond • V&A NAL, corresp. with Sidney Godolphin • Yale U., Beinecke L., letters to the earl of Carlingford
**Likenesses** M. Beale, portrait, Longleat House, Wiltshire
**Wealth at death** wealthy

**Coventry, Henry** (c.1710–1752), religious writer, was born in Twickenham, Middlesex, the only son of the Hon. Henry C. Coventry, of Cowley, Middlesex, landowner, and

Ann Coles, of Oxford. His father was younger brother of William Coventry, fifth earl of Coventry. After schooling at Eton College (1725–6), Coventry was educated at Magdalene College, Cambridge, where he graduated BA in 1729, and was elected to a fellowship in 1730, proceeding MA in 1733. He was the author of *Philemon to Hydaspes, relating a conversation with Hortensius upon the subject of false religion*, in five parts (1736–44). William Warburton accused Coventry of making unfair use of information, confidentially communicated, which was about to be published in the second volume of his own *Divine Legation* (1741). A pamphlet entitled *Future Rewards and Punishments Believed by the Antients* (1740) has been attributed to Coventry, who was also one of the contributors to the *Athenian Letters*.

Coventry died on 29 December 1752, possibly of a brain tumour, and was buried with his father. The Cambridge antiquary William Cole, who had met him frequently in the society of Conyers Middleton and Horace Walpole, remarked: 'He used to dress remarkably gay, with much gold lace, had a most prominent Roman nose, and was much of a gentleman' (Cole MSS, BL). The five parts of *Philemon to Hydaspes* were republished in one volume by his cousin, Francis Coventry (*d.* 1759), author, in 1753.

[ANON.], *rev.* ADAM JACOB LEVIN

**Sources** Venn, *Alum. Cant.* · A. Collins, *The peerage of England: containing a genealogical and historical account of all the peers of England*, 4th edn (1768) · Nichols, *Lit. anecdotes*, 3.43; 5.564–71; 9.80 · R. A. Austen-Leigh, ed., *The Eton College register, 1698–1752* (1927) · Walpole, *Corr.*, 9.7, 79–80, 140 · *GM*, 1st ser., 23 (1753), 51 · Watt, *Bibl. Brit.*, 1.264 · will, PRO, PROB 11/799, sig. 7 · BL, Cole MSS
**Wealth at death** £2300 bequeathed to various persons; real estate: will, PRO, PROB 11/799, sig. 7, fols. 56–58; Nichols, *Lit. anecdotes*, 9.80

**Coventry, Sir John** (*c.*1636–1685), politician, was the eldest son of John Coventry (*d.* 1652) of Barton, Pitminster, Somerset, and Elizabeth, daughter of John Colles of Barton, widow of Herbert Dodington of Breamore, Hampshire. Between 1655 and 1659 Coventry travelled in France, Italy, Hungary, Germany, and the Low Countries with his tutor, the poet Edward Sherburne. Suspicions of Roman Catholic influences during this tour led to his being made a ward of his uncle Sir Anthony Ashley Cooper. In 1656 his estates in Staffordshire, Derbyshire, and Somerset were valued at £3000 per annum. Coventry matriculated at Queen's College, Oxford, on 26 October 1660. He was made a knight of the Bath on the coronation of Charles II in 1661.

In 1667 Coventry went to Breda with his uncle Henry Coventry, who, with Lord Holles, negotiated the treaty ending the Second Anglo-Dutch War. Sir John carried the treaty to the king in late July for ratification, returning to Breda with it shortly afterwards. He was elected MP for Weymouth at a by-election in 1667, with the backing of the court, and was chosen for that seat in the two elections in 1679 and again in 1681. During his parliamentary career he followed Ashley Cooper's politics and was a fairly active MP, sitting on a number of committees and making twenty-nine recorded speeches. He attracted most attention because of the consequences of a remark he made in

the House of Commons in December 1670, when he moved for a tax on theatres. Sir John Berkenhead's comment that the theatres had been of great service to the king prompted Coventry to ask him if he meant the men or women players. This was taken to be an offensive reference to the king's relations with Nell Gwyn and Moll Davies. That night Coventry and his young servant were waylaid on their way home to Suffolk Street, Westminster, by members of the duke of Monmouth's troop in the guards, led by Sir Thomas Sandys, and Coventry's nose was slit to the bone. The House of Commons was so affronted that early in 1671 an act was passed 'to prevent malicious maiming and wounding' (22 & 23 Chas. II, c.1). Known as the Coventry Act, this was only repealed in 1828. Coventry probably was the model for the character of Amnon in John Dryden's *Absalom and Achitophel* (1681), in which the vengeful assault leads to Amnon's death. In fact, Coventry recovered and the damage to his face was not permanent.

Coventry was a Roman Catholic and in his will, made in 1667, stated that he had been so for several years. In 1673 a plan to deprive him of his parliamentary seat by compelling him to take the new test came to nothing. His conversation and company continued to raise doubts about his religion and in 1675 Henry Coventry urged him to marry someone who was both a protestant, to allay such suspicions, and wealthy enough to help clear his debts, which by 1667 were at least £2000. Despite his Catholicism, during the exclusion crisis Coventry described the duke of York as a protector of papists and called for his removal from the king's presence and councils. Like his father, Coventry was a heavy drinker and in 1680, when inebriated at a coffee house in the city, he said that the duke was a papist and a traitor.

Coventry was appointed a commissioner for sewers in Somerset in 1660, served as a justice of the peace for Wiltshire (1667–1670) and Somerset (1668–1670), was deputy lieutenant of Wiltshire (1668–75), and was made a freeman of Lymington, Hampshire, in 1679. When he died, unmarried, on 14 November 1685, he had not replaced his will of 1667, in which he left bequests of £100 to the poor English nuns at Paris and the English College in Rome, and requested to be buried in one of the queen's chapels if he died in England and a Roman Catholic church if he died abroad. However, his final resting place is unknown.

STEPHEN PORTER

**Sources** J. P. Ferris, 'Coventry, Sir John', HoP, *Commons, 1660–90*, 2.154–6 · will, PRO, PROB 11/381, fol. 132 · *JHC*, 9 (1667–87), 188–9 · BL, Add. MS 32094, fols. 351–2 · *LondG* (25–9 July 1667) · *LondG* (8–12 Aug 1667) · R. M. Kidson, ed., *The gentry of Staffordshire, 1662–1663*, Staffordshire RS, 4th ser., 2 (1958), 8–9 · *CSP dom.*, 1667, 328, 344, 350; 1679–80, 409 · Foster, *Alum. Oxon.* · *Third report*, HMC, 2 (1872), 94 · *Calendar of the manuscripts of the marquess of Ormonde*, new ser., 8 vols., HMC, 36 (1902–20), vol. 5, pp. 281, 285 · O. Airy, ed., *Essex papers*, CS, new ser., 47 (1890), 131
**Likenesses** oils, *c.*1650, Longleat, Wiltshire
**Wealth at death** see will, PRO, PROB 11/381, fol. 132

**Coventry, John** (1735–1812), maker of scientific instruments, was born on 2 April 1735 in the parish of Christ

Church, Southwark, Surrey, the son of John and Mary Coventry. He married his first wife, Mary Lively, at the church of St George the Martyr, Southwark, on 17 February 1760; they had eleven children before Mary died in childbirth in 1780. Although he earned his living as a painter at the Royal Mint, Coventry devoted his spare time to scientific pursuits, and applied his natural mechanical genius and great patience to the perfection of precision instruments. He established a reputation as the inventor of several measuring devices which achieved a higher degree of accuracy than ever before, and which were recommended by eminent scholars of his day.

As a young man Coventry was interested in electricity, especially its medical applications. He was introduced to Benjamin Franklin and William Henley, and assisted them in their electrical experiments. In 1769 he made a 12 foot refracting telescope, with which he observed the transit of Venus across the sun. He was also the inventor of a new hygrometer, more accurate than any which had been previously in use. This instrument was very generally employed by the chemists and other scientific men of his day. One of these hygrometers was made by George Adams, the younger, for George III, and is now in the Science Museum, London. This instrument was especially useful for the speed with which it responded to changes in the amount of moisture in the atmosphere, though it had the disadvantage of being adversely affected by dust. Coventry also developed micrometers for use with the microscope, consisting of fine parallel lines drawn with a diamond on ivory, glass, or silver, so that minute organisms could be measured. These micrometers were recommended in several contemporary publications on microscopy, and a set with rulings ranging from one-tenth to one ten-thousandth of an inch has been preserved in the collection of the Royal Microscopical Society at the Museum of the History of Science, Oxford. Coventry's principal work in his later years was the development of more precise statical balances for assaying gold, which he claimed were accurate to one-thousandth of a grain. Several of these were bought by the East India Company.

On 23 March 1783 Coventry married his second wife, Alice Dawson, at St Bride's Church, Fleet Street. Two daughters were born of this marriage. The family was living at 33 Red Cross Street, Southwark, when Alice died in 1809. Coventry himself died in December 1812, probably on the 8th, the date of the final codicil to his will, and was buried on 11 December at St Saviour's, Southwark. He was survived by three sons and four daughters, to each of whom he left £1000 in Bank of England stock, a legacy which suggests that his achievements as an instrument maker secured him a financial return as well as the admiration of his contemporaries.                    GLORIA CLIFTON

**Sources** GM, 1st ser., 83/1 (1813), 180–81 · copy of will, PRO, PROB 11/1539, fols. 157–8 · baptism registers, Southwark, Christ Church, 1727–37, LMA, P92/CTC/3 [Greater London History Library, photocopy R1065C (original not available for consultation)] · parish register, Southwark, St George the Martyr, 1754–72, LMA, P92/GEO/171 [marriages], no. 243 · St Saviour, Southwark, registers of baptisms, 1757–90, LMA, P92/SAV/3008 [microfilm X70/1 (original not available for consultation)] · St Saviour, Southwark,

registers of burials, 1812, LMA, P92/SAV/3009 [microfilm X70/1 (original not available for consultation)] · St Bride, Fleet Street, London, register of marriages, 1775–94, GL, MS 6542/2 · G. L'E. Turner, *The great age of the microscope: the collection of the Royal Microscopical Society through 150 years* (1989), 342–3 · A. Q. Morton and J. A. Wess, *Public and private science: the King George III collection* (1993), 468 · D. Brewster, *A treatise on new philosophical instruments* (1813), 70–1 · 'Micrometer', A. Rees and others, *The cyclopaedia, or, Universal dictionary of arts, sciences, and literature*, 45 vols. (1819–20) · *Encyclopaedia Britannica*, 3rd edn, 11 (1797), 707–8 · G. Adams, *Essays on the microscope*, 2nd edn (1798), 59–60

**Archives** RS, 'Of hygrometers', letters and papers 6, vol. 57, no. 177 [incl. drawing] | MHS Oxf., Royal Microscopical Society collection, set of micrometers by Coventry, 432 (409) · Sci. Mus., George III collection, E113, hygrometer made to Coventry's design by George Adams, inventory no. 1927-1817

**Wealth at death** see will, PRO, PROB 11/1539, fols. 157–8 · PRO, death duty registers, IR 26/542, fols. 155v–156r

**Coventry** [née Gunning], **Maria, countess of Coventry** (*bap.* 1732, *d.* 1760), figure of scandal, was born at Hemingford Grey Manor House, Huntingdonshire, an estate owned by her aunt, and baptized there on 15 August 1732, the eldest of the four daughters of Colonel John Gunning of Castle Coote, co. Roscommon, and Bridget, the daughter of Theobald Bourke, sixth Viscount Mayo. Her childhood was spent in Ireland after her father succeeded to the family estates. Maria and her younger sister Elizabeth (1733–1790) [*see* Campbell, Elizabeth] arrived in London in June 1751 and aroused considerable interest in fashionable society; Henrietta Knight, Lady Luxborough, wrote to William Shenstone of 'the beauty of the two Irish women, Miss Gunnings'. It was rumoured that Maria intended to go on the stage because her family was so poor. Nicknamed the Beauties, the two Gunning sisters were admired by George II and, although impoverished, both quickly made very good matches: on 1 March 1752 at St George's, Hanover Square, London, Maria married George William Coventry, sixth earl of Coventry (1722–1809), the grandest landowner in Worcestershire, with an estate at Croome Court, then being improved by Lancelot Brown; her sister Elizabeth had secretly married the duke of Hamilton less than a month before. The earl of Coventry was lord of the bedchamber to both George II and George III. He and his wife had a London house at 29 Piccadilly and Maria was a constant topic of contemporary gossip; crowds assembled to watch her when she appeared in public. The first of her five children, a daughter, was born in 1753, and an heir, George William (1758–1831), five years later. However, the Coventrys were already quarrelling in public, notoriously on a visit to Paris shortly after their marriage. A year later Lady Coventry was reputed to be in love with Frederick St John, second Viscount Bolingbroke (1734–1787), with whom she secretly corresponded, and late in 1756 it was rumoured that Lord Coventry would seek a divorce.

Lady Coventry's activities were recorded in many contemporary diaries and letters, all noting her beauty, but some describing her immature behaviour. Horace Walpole seems to have been particularly intrigued by her, while Mrs Delany considered her to have 'a fine figure, and [to be] vastly handsome, notwithstanding a silly look

Maria Coventry [Gunning], **countess of Coventry** (*bap.* **1732,** *d.* **1760**), by Jean-Étienne Liotard, 1750–55

sometimes about her mouth; she has a thousand airs, but with a sort of innocence that diverts one' (*Autobiography … Mrs Delany*, 300). Her portrait was painted by several leading artists, including Francis Cotes and Gavin Hamilton. She was seen in public towards the end of her life, at the Worcester music festival in 1758, dining at Strawberry Hill in 1759, and at Lord Ferrers's trial for treason in April 1760; there were press reports of her death in June 1760, but she returned to Croome in late July and died there on 30 September 1760; she was buried at Pirton church, in the adjacent parish, on 10 October. At the time a new family church—St Mary Magdalene at Croome d'Abitot—was being built on the Croome estate and after it was completed Lady Coventry's body was disinterred and reburied there, although there is no monument to her there. The cause of her death at the age of twenty-eight was rumoured to be lead poisoning, from the fashionable white cosmetic, ceruse, she used on her face, which was said to be ravaged by its effects. However, tuberculosis has also been thought responsible. In London in the summer shortly before her death she had received from the apothecary Daniel Graham, almost daily, medicines consistent with treatment for consumption, and in the autumn was attended by William Russell, the senior surgeon at Worcester Infirmary. In his *Elegies* (1761) William Mason included one on Lady Coventry and the Worcestershire historian T. R. Nash, who knew her well, admired 'the sweetness of her disposition and the goodness of her heart'. Lord Coventry married again in 1764.

JOAN LANE

**Sources** Walpole, *Corr.*, vols. 9, 16, 20, 35, 37 • E. A. B. Barnard, 'The Coventrys of Croome', *Transactions of the Worcestershire Historical Society*, 20 (1943), 32–42 • J. Lane, 'The furniture at Croome Court: the patronage of George William, 6th earl of Coventry', *Apollo*, 145 (Jan 1997), 25–9 • GEC, *Peerage* • *The letters of William Shenstone*, ed. M. Williams (1939) • T. Nash, *Collections for the history of Worcestershire*, 1 (1781), 473–4 • parish register, London, St George's, Hanover Square, 1 March 1752 [marriage] • parish register, Pirton, Worcestershire, 10 Oct 1760 [burial] • *The letters written by the late Right Honourable Lady Luxborough to William Shenstone, esq.* (1775), 271 • *The autobiography and correspondence of Mary Granville, Mrs Delany*, ed. Lady Llanover, 1st ser., 3 (1861)

**Archives** priv. coll., family MSS

**Likenesses** J.-E. Liotard, pastel drawing, 1750–55, Rijksmuseum, Amsterdam [*see illus.*] • K. Read, pastel drawing, 1750–59, Inveraray Castle • F. Cotes, oils, 1751, NG Ire. • F. Cotes, pastel drawing, 1751, Inveraray Castle • J. Macardell, mezzotint, 1753 (after G. Hamilton), Royal Collection • R. Houston, group portrait, mezzotint, pubd 1756 (*The three Gunning sisters*), BM • P. Cotes, miniature, 1757, Wallace Collection, London • F. Cotes, portrait (of Maria Coventry?), priv. coll. • G. Hamilton, oils, Inveraray Castle • G. Hamilton, oils, Woburn Abbey, Bedfordshire • H. D. Hamilton, pastel drawing, Courtauld Inst. • G. Hamilton?, portraits, priv. coll. • J. Highmore, oils, Waddesdon Manor, Buckinghamshire • double portrait, conversation piece (with the earl of Coventry); Sothebys, 30 June 1948 • portrait (after Liotard), priv. coll.

**Coventry, Sir Thomas** (1547–1606), judge, was the younger son of Richard Coventry, later of Cassington, Oxfordshire; his mother's surname was Turner. He was reputedly a direct descendant of John Coventry, the fifteenth-century sheriff and mayor of London. Born and brought up at Bewdley in Worcestershire, he settled in the county after his marriage to Margaret Jefferies (*b. c.*1551) of Earl's Croome. He was educated at Balliol College, Oxford, where he graduated BA in 1565. He was elected a fellow of the college in 1566, and in 1568 entered the Inner Temple. He was created bencher of the inn in 1591 and elected reader in 1593, though an outbreak of plague in London meant that his reading had to be postponed until the following year. He read on the Statute of Reversions, 32 Hen. VIII c. 34, comparing favourably the learning exercises practised in the inns of court with those of the universities. He was made serjeant-at-law in 1603, king's serjeant in 1605, and justice of the court of common pleas in January 1606; he was knighted the same year. He was already unwell by this time, though, and his tenure in the court was very brief. He died on 12 December 1606, survived by his wife, and was buried at his family home, Croome d'Abitot in Worcestershire. Coventry was a capable lawyer, appearing as counsel with such leading advocates as Sir Edward Coke and Sir Lawrence Tanfield, but his profession did not bring him the spectacular wealth achieved by some of his contemporaries. His reputation has been somewhat overshadowed by that of his eldest son, Thomas *Coventry, first Baron Coventry, who became lord keeper in 1625.

DAVID IBBETSON

**Sources** *Collins peerage of England: genealogical, biographical and historical*, ed. E. Brydges, 9 vols. (1812), vol. 3, p. 745 • will, PRO, PROB 11/109, fol. 92 • W. R. Prest, *The rise of the barristers: a social history of the English bar, 1590–1640* (1986), 352 • T. Nash, *Collections for the history of Worcestershire*, 2 vols. (1781–2) • W. H. Cooke, ed., *Students admitted to the Inner Temple, 1547–1660* [1878] • F. A. Inderwick and R. A. Roberts, eds., *A calendar of the Inner Temple records*, 5 vols. (1896–

1936) • Baker, *Serjeants*, 506 • Sainty, *Judges*, 74 • *Reg. Oxf.*, 1.258 • Burke, *Peerage* • Longleat House, Wiltshire, MS 196

**Wealth at death**   see will, PRO, PROB 11/109, fol. 92

**Coventry, Thomas**, first Baron Coventry (1578–1640), lawyer, was the eldest son of Sir Thomas * Coventry (1547–1606) of Croome D'Abitot, Worcestershire, justice of common pleas, and his wife, Margaret (*b. c.*1551), daughter and heir of William Jefferies of Croome D'Abitot. He matriculated at Balliol College, Oxford, in 1592, entered the Inner Temple in 1594, and was called to the bar in 1603. He was appointed recorder of London in 1616, solicitor-general in 1617, attorney-general in 1621, and lord keeper in 1625.

**Ascent: London and the Villiers connection**   Coventry's father laid the foundation of the family's fortunes in Worcestershire, purchasing the manor of Croome D'Abitot in 1592. Thomas continued to purchase manors in the shire and served on the Worcestershire bench, from 1624 as *custos rotulorum*; but the main focal points of his career were London, the legal profession, and the royal court. After being called to the bar he progressed through the various offices of the Inner Temple, becoming auditor, bencher, reader, and finally treasurer (1617–25). This provided him with valuable contacts, not least Sir Edward Coke, who had also served as treasurer. Sir Francis Bacon later described Coventry as 'bred by Lord Coke and seasoned in his ways' (Spedding, 6.97) and Coventry acted as executor of Coke's estate. He also made important connections in the City of London. By 1606 he had married Sarah Sebright (*bap.* 1583), whose uncle, William Sebright, was town clerk of London and about the same time he began acting as counsel to the Skinners' Company and also obtained the reversion of the town clerkship and the judgeship of the sheriff's court. Following Sarah's death he married, on 20 April 1610, Elizabeth Pichford, *née* Aldersey (1583–1653), the widow of a wealthy London grocer, William Pichford (*d.* 1609); through her he became engaged as counsel to the Grocers' Company. In addition he assisted the City's recorder, Sir Henry Montagu, in an important action brought by a London merchant against the lieutenant of the Tower. These connections stood him in good stead when in 1616 Montagu was promoted to replace Coke as chief justice of the king's bench.

Coventry's appointment to the recordership of London on 16 November 1616 was the big breakthrough of his career, setting him on the ladder for preferment to the crown's senior legal offices. His advancement was opposed by Attorney-General Bacon and the king's nominee for the post was Sir Henry Yelverton. However, Yelverton refused it and in the delay which ensued the lord mayor and aldermen took the initiative and nominated Coventry. His years of patiently cultivating City contacts had, at last, paid off. To progress further, however, he needed support at court and, to this end, he appears to have sought out the rising star, George Villiers, later duke of Buckingham. When Yelverton's promotion to the attorney-generalship early the following year left a vacancy for solicitor-general, Coventry's candidature was again opposed by Bacon (now lord keeper). However, after

what was described as 'secret lobbying' by Villiers (*Hastings MSS*, 4.16), together with a large down payment, Coventry secured the post on 14 March 1617 and was knighted at the same time.

From this point onwards Coventry was established as a Villiers client. In September 1625, when he was about to become lord keeper, he wrote to him acknowledging that 'in this and all other occasions that have concerned me [you] have out of your noblenes interjected for me to his Majestie and his royal father' (BL, Harley MS 1581, fol. 328). Support from the favourite was the *sine qua non* for advancement to high office by the mid-1620s; however, it was not the sole reason for Coventry's preferment. He was also acknowledged to be a very talented and effective advocate, with what Clarendon described as 'a plain way of speaking and delivery, without much ornament of elocution', but with 'a strange power of making himself believed' (Clarendon, *Hist. rebellion*, 1.58). These qualities, as well as his loyalty to Villiers, were on display in October 1619 at the trial of the disgraced lord treasurer, the earl of Suffolk. Reports suggest that Coventry outshone Attorney-General Yelverton in presenting the crown's case, pressing home the charges with some pertinent asides on the iniquities of corruption in high places. His performance also helped to forge his own reputation for sturdy integrity, showing 'the world in how little esteem he held greatns that would justle and stand in competition with justice' (BL, Sloane MS 3075, fol. 5).

When Yelverton was suspended from the attorney-generalship in June 1620 Coventry stood in for him, and he was the obvious replacement when Yelverton was finally dismissed the following January. Coventry's appointment, on 11 January 1621, led to his removal from the House of Commons, where he had been elected to serve for Droitwich in 1620. As chief legal officer to the Lords, it was argued, he would not be able properly to discharge his duties as MP. None the less, Coventry did make some significant contributions during the parliament. He requested answers from Lord Keeper Bacon to the charges of corruption which were brought against him, and he was involved in the proceedings against Edward Floyd, the Roman Catholic who had allegedly rejoiced at the misfortunes of the elector palatine. His most important intervention, however, was on 14 May 1621 when he presented formal charges in the Lords which secured the punishment of Yelverton for having compared Buckingham to Edward II's favourite Hugh Despenser. In the process he appears to have helped head off an intended coup against his patron.

**Lord keeper and the politics of the 1620s**   Coventry's appointment as lord keeper on 1 November 1625—to replace John Williams, bishop of Lincoln, whom Buckingham suspected of scheming against him—came at a time when the crown was looking to signal its commitment to the protestant cause and to working with parliament. Originally Buckingham had offered the post to John Preston, master of Emmanuel College, Cambridge, and a renowned puritan preacher. But Preston refused and Coventry may well have appeared the safest alternative among the duke's clientele. As a friend of Preston and the London puritan William Gouge, he had strong protestant credentials; and his reputation for integrity and independence would commend him to parliament. Within a few months of Coventry taking office, however, crown policy altered and he found himself having to support Charles's resort to prerogative government and the forced loan. This was not an entirely comfortable experience, but he managed to adapt.

During the late 1620s Coventry repeatedly showed himself to be a reliable servant of the king. On 29 March 1626 he took on the difficult task of acting as Charles's mouthpiece when he lambasted the House of Commons for their disloyal attacks on Buckingham and threatened them with dismissal if they did not become more co-operative. And in the debates on the petition of right on 22 April 1628 he presented the king's view that he was fully entitled to imprison without showing cause. In each case he probably had misgivings about what he was being required to do, but he executed orders loyally and efficiently. Where he had scope to express his own opinions he tended to follow a more moderate, pro-parliament/pro-protestant line, and during the forced loan he emerged as the most prominent of a group of councillors who were seeking to temper the excessive use of the prerogative and talk the king into summoning another parliament. In March 1627, when the council was asked to consider hanging loan refusers who resisted the press, he spoke strongly against it, pointing out the blatant illegality of such a course of action. And the following January when there was an intensive debate in council about whether to resummon parliament he was one of those who pressed for a new meeting. His comments on the role of a parliament in his opening address to the two houses on 7 March 1628 summed up his political philosophy:

Consider ... the means by which his Majesty useth to attain these purposes. It is by parliament, a way most pleasing to the English which brings forth many pardons, and causes good kings to refrain their prerogatives, and this way best suits his Majesty's own disposition. (Johnson and others, 2.9–10)

Coventry's readiness to speak out on behalf of the subject's interests during this period earned him a considerable public reputation as a 'good patriot' and there were persistent rumours that he was about to be dismissed from office. However, as the earl of Clare, a shrewd commentator on the workings of the court, observed, there was unlikely to be much truth in these since Coventry 'sticks at nothing that the Mair du Palais [Buckingham] would have' (Holles, 2.345). In spite of his independent line, Coventry does appear to have remained high in the duke's favour, being granted a peerage—as Baron Coventry of Aylesborough—on 10 April 1628 and enjoying the honour of having Buckingham act as godparent to his grandson a few weeks earlier. However, the reason was probably not the sycophancy which Clare was seeking to imply, but rather Buckingham's awareness of the need to cultivate clients with a reputation for moderation in case there was a new shift in royal policy.

Coventry was at his most influential while his patron was still alive and he had licence to express his opinions. After Buckingham's death in August 1628 he took more of a back seat. During 1634—unusually for him—he became caught up in the faction politics of the court and joined in the attempt led by the queen and Laud to topple Lord Treasurer Weston on corruption charges. But the failure of this seems to have confirmed his instinct to concentrate on his immediate duties as lord keeper and he devoted most of his energies to the administration of justice and the supervision of the legal system.

But Coventry did not become entirely divorced from matters of high policy. He remained an insistent advocate of parliament, attempting to talk the king out of a dissolution in March 1629 and in late 1633 putting the case for a new assembly. But, on the latter occasion, it was said that 'the king so rattled [him] that he is now become the most pliable man in England' and he does not appear to have raised the issue again (*Earl of Strafforde's Letters and Dispatches*, 1.141). Coventry also continued to push for a moderate Calvinist approach to religion. Earlier in 1633 he was said to have refused to seal a pardon for the forfeitures of recusants, an act which so incensed Charles that he threatened him with dismissal. And he had little time for Archbishop Laud or his policies. When Henry Sherfield was put on trial in Star Chamber for breaking a stained-glass window Coventry urged leniency and took the opportunity to speak out against religious images. In other respects, however, he tended to avoid political controversy. As Clarendon noted, he rarely ventured to express any opinion on matters relating to foreign policy. And his annual charges to the assize judges in Star Chamber—which were an important platform for communicating the privy council's priorities during the 1630s—almost invariably concentrated on politically uncontroversial matters relating to the execution of justice and maintenance of order. The chief exception was the charge in 1635 when he delivered a forceful statement of support for ship money and urged the judges to inform their local audiences 'how just it is the king should take this way seeing all are concerned in it' (*CSP dom.*, 1635, 128). Aside from this, however, he took little part in discussions about the legality of the levy and refrained from becoming involved in Hampden's case.

Coventry's broadly detached approach enabled him to survive in a court which during the 1630s became increasingly pro-Spanish and hostile to parliament. Clarendon claimed that he was the first lord keeper to die in office for 'near forty years' (Clarendon, *Hist. rebellion*, 1.57). This was slightly misleading (because Ellesmere had never actually been dismissed) but it was testimony to the reputation Coventry acquired as a solid and trustworthy royal servant of unimpeachable integrity. He never aspired to a major role in policy making, but his readiness to take a stand in support of the subject's interests struck a chord with public opinion and helped keep alive the tradition of 'moderate counsels' within Charles's government. He died on 14 January 1640 at Durham House, Strand, London, and was buried at Croome D'Abitot, leaving Thomas, his son with his first wife, to succeed him as Baron Coventry. His younger children with his second wife included Henry *Coventry and Sir William *Coventry.

RICHARD CUST

**Sources** A. Thrush, HoP, *Commons* [draft] · MS life of Coventry, BL, Sloane MS 3075, fols. 1–8 [written soon after his death] · Clarendon, *Hist. rebellion* · R. P. Cust, *The forced loan and English politics, 1626–1628* (1987) · R. P. Cust, 'Charles I, the privy council and the parliament of 1628', *TRHS*, 6th ser., 2 (1992), 25–50 · K. Sharpe, *The personal rule of Charles I* (1992) · R. Lockyer, *Buckingham: the life and political career of George Villiers, first duke of Buckingham, 1592–1628* (1981) · I. Morgan, *Prince Charles's puritan chaplain* (1957) · will, PRO, PROB 11/182, fols. 1–4v · *State trials*, 3.562–3 · *The letters and life of Francis Bacon*, ed. J. Spedding, 7 vols. (1861–74), vol. 6, p. 97 · *Report on the manuscripts of the late Reginald Rawdon Hastings*, 4 vols., HMC, 78 (1928–47), vol. 4, p. 16 · BL, Harley MS 1581, fol. 328 · R. C. Johnson and others, eds., *Proceedings in parliament, 1628*, 6 vols. (1977–83), vol. 2, pp. 9–10 · G. Radcliffe, *The earl of Strafforde's letters and dispatches, with an essay towards his life*, ed. W. Knowler, 1 (1739), 141 · *Letters of John Holles, 1587–1637*, ed. P. R. Seddon, 2 (1983)
**Archives** Birm. CA, official and other papers · BL, papers, speeches, etc., Harley MSS · Bodl. Oxf., papers as treasurer of Inner Temple · Croome D'Abitot, Worcestershire, MSS · Croome Estate Trust, Severn Stoke, official and other papers | CKS, corresp. with Lionel Cranfield · U. Durham L., letters to bishop of Durham
**Likenesses** C. Johnson, oils, 1634, Longleat, Wiltshire · oils, c.1634 (after C. Johnson), NPG · C. Johnson, oils, 1639, NPG; copy, Charlecote Park, Warwickshire
**Wealth at death** considerable wealth; left portions of £4000 for each of three daughters: will, PRO, PROB 11/182, fols. 1–4v

**Coventry, Walter of** (*fl.* 1293), chronicler, is the name traditionally given to the historical compiler of the composite narrative found in Cambridge, Corpus Christi College, MS 175 which extends from the time of Brutus to the reign of Edward I. A note in that manuscript attributes the narrative to 'brother Walter of Coventry'. The note suggested to William Stubbs, when he edited the manuscript in 1872–3, that Walter of Coventry was a member of the religious orders, and on account of the numerous references to York belonged in all probability to the Benedictine community of St Mary's in York. If Walter of Coventry was a monk of St Mary's he may have been introduced into the abbey by Abbot Simon Warwick (1258–96), who was one of the great reforming abbots of the house. No Walter of Coventry, however, has been found in the St Mary's records. The York references in the text refer principally to the archbishops and officials of the minster, and the association of the chronicle with St Mary's cannot on the present evidence be regarded as certain.

As it is transcribed in the Corpus manuscript, the work, which appears to have been written during the latter part of Edward I's reign, is almost entirely compilation. An introductory section in the *Memoriale* deals with the history of the kings of Britain from Brutus to Edward I. It contains items relating to Scottish history, including official documents put out by Edward I. The latest event which can be dated in this section appears to refer to the Anglo-Scottish agreement of 1293. This section, which uses northern sources, was utilized in its turn by the compiler of the north-country chronicle found in BL, Harley MS 3860. There can be no doubt therefore of its northern associations.

The main section of the chronicle preserves an account of English history from 1002 to 1225. This part of the narrative relies upon such standard accounts as those by Marianus Scottus, John of Worcester, Benedict of Peterborough, and Roger of Howden. Among its sources the most valuable is the so-called Barnwell chronicle, which in the text of Walter of Coventry covers the years 1202–25. The Barnwell account, which also survives in London, College of Arms, MS 10, is an important source for the reign of John. How the chronicle found its way into the work of Walter of Coventry is not entirely clear. The Barnwell account was not transcribed directly into that narrative, but came through some intermediate source, probably a thirteenth-century compilation made either at Peterborough, with which the archbishops of York had early associations, or Crowland. Whatever the origin of this particular section of the compilation, there can be no doubt that the final version of the work credited to Walter of Coventry was written not far from the city of York, and probably within the city itself.

JOHN TAYLOR

**Sources** *Memoriale fratris Walteri de Coventria* / *The historical collections of Walter of Coventry*, ed. W. Stubbs, 2 vols., Rolls Series, 58 (1872–3) · A. Gransden, *Historical writing in England*, 1 (1974), 339–45 · J. Taylor, *English historical literature in the fourteenth century* (1987), 148–9
**Archives** CCC Cam., MS 175

**Coventry, William** [called Claudius Conversus] (*fl.* c.1340/1360), Carmelite friar and historian, must have been a lay brother of the order, since if he was lame, as the name Claudius indicates, he could not have been ordained. Three of Coventry's historical works, written either c.1340 or c.1360, survive in the form of fifteenth- and sixteenth-century transcripts (Bodl. Oxf., MSS Laud misc. 722, Selden supra 72). All are concerned with the fortunes of his order. The *Chronica brevis* is annalistic in form and largely reproduces information well known from other Carmelite sources. The *De duplici fuga* and the *De adventu Carmelitarum in Angliam* are alternative versions of chapters in the *Speculum* of the French Carmelite Jean de Cheminot (1337), dealing with the dispersal of the order in the West. William Coventry's main contribution to the historiography of the order was to establish that the settlement of the Carmelites in England predated that in France. According to John Bale (d. 1563), who transcribed these works from a fifteenth-century manuscript, he wrote a total of ten books.

ANDREW JOTISCHKY

**Sources** A. Staring, *Medieval Carmelite heritage* (1989) · Bale, *Cat.*
**Archives** Bodl. Oxf., MS Laud misc. 722 · Bodl. Oxf., MS Selden supra 72

**Coventry, Sir William** (*bap.* 1627, *d.* 1686), politician, was baptized on 4 October 1627, the fifth son of Thomas *Coventry, first Baron Coventry (1578–1640), politician, the fourth born to his second wife, Elizabeth Aldersey (1583–1653), widow of William Pichford. He became a gentleman commoner of Queen's College, Oxford, in 1642, but left the university without taking a degree. 'He was young', writes Clarendon in his autobiography:

whilst the war continued; yet he had put himself before the end of it into the army, and had the command of a foot company, and shortly after travelled into France, where he remained whilst there was any hope of getting another army for the king, or that either of the other crowns would engage in his quarrel. But when all thoughts of that were desperate, he returned into England, where he remained for many years without the least correspondence with any of his friends beyond the seas. (*Life of … Clarendon*, 2.348)

By the time he wrote his autobiography, in old age, Clarendon had reason enough to dislike Coventry, also claiming that while he had not actually betrayed the Stuart cause those most zealous for the restoration of Charles II, even those among his relatives, tended to conceal from Coventry their secret plotting to hasten the king's return. No doubt motivated by the bitterness which surrounded his ejection from government, in which Coventry played a significant role, Clarendon's suspicions were nevertheless long held and deep-seated. Coventry's endorsement of Sir Gilbert Talbot's proposal, made in 1649, for setting up a royalist council in England to oversee the exiled king's affairs, may have caused jealousy. Both the future lord chancellor and Sir Edward Nicholas were of the opinion by 1650 that Coventry had become 'Presbyterian', indicating that he had joined with those closest to the queen mother at the Louvre, such as Lord Jermyn, who favoured the policy of setting up Charles II as a covenanted king, an idea to which both Hyde and Secretary Nicholas were instinctively hostile.

In September 1652 the king sent Coventry into England, where he appears to have remained. Although arrested in the aftermath of Penruddock's failed revolt, Coventry lived quietly under successive interregnum regimes, having apparently reconciled himself to the revolutionary turn of events through the good offices of his brother-in-law, Sir Anthony Ashley Cooper, later first earl of Shaftesbury. In 1660 he appears to have returned the favour, giving Charles firm reassurances of Sir Anthony's loyalty which the king himself received in very good part. Clarendon later claimed that Coventry had thrown his support firmly behind the restoration of Charles II only after the king's succession had been proclaimed. It is certainly true that just before the Restoration he went to The Hague and visited the royal princes, to whom he was already personally known. To James, duke of York, he offered his services, and he was straightaway appointed the duke's private secretary, no doubt partly because of the high regard in which Coventry's brother, Henry, was held at the Stuart court.

On returning to England, Coventry had the great honour of leading the royal entry into the City of London on 29 May 1660. The following year he was elected to the Commons on the duke of York's Admiralty interest, entering Cavalier Parliament as MP for Great Yarmouth. Coventry became very deeply concerned in the administration of the navy, and in 1662 was appointed a commissioner at £300 a year. He thus came into business relations with Samuel Pepys, who quickly became warmly attached to him. One modern editor of Pepys has referred to Coventry

as 'the hero of the Diary'. On one occasion, Pepys remarked of Coventry's regime at the Navy Office that 'we all, particularly myself, are more afraid of him than the King' (Shelley, 1, 13). His master's integrity was not beyond reproach, however. Reports were soon disseminated that Coventry was 'feathering his nest' by a sale of offices, and quarrels with his fellow commissioner, Sir George Carteret, whose directions he claimed to have followed faithfully, were perpetual. He admitted subsequently that, like everybody else, he did make money by selling offices, estimating his income in the first four years of office at around £25,000.

In October 1662 Coventry was made a commissioner for the government of Tangier. He was created DCL at Oxford on 28 September 1663, together with Henry Bennet, earl of Arlington, and was knighted and sworn of the privy council on 26 June 1665, after seeing action at the battle of Lowestoft. The earl of Clarendon had opposed both honours. In the course of the Dutch war charges of corruption in connection with the commissariat were again brought against Coventry, rapidly becoming a feature of his growing conflict with Clarendon, whose dominance Coventry came increasingly to see as an obstacle to effective government.

Meanwhile Coventry was distinguishing himself as a speaker in the House of Commons. Gilbert Burnet describes him about 1665 as 'a man of great notions and eminent virtues, the best speaker in the house, and capable of bearing the chief ministry' (*Bishop Burnet's History*, ed. Burnet and Burnet, 1.170). He attached himself to Bennet and made very fierce attacks on Clarendon's administration. He denied any kind of responsibility for the declaration of war with the Dutch in February 1664–5, but during that and two following sessions he and his brother Henry *Coventry practically led the house. Andrew Marvell, in his 'Last Instructions to a Painter', says:

All the two Coventries their generals choose;
For one had much, the other nought to lose.
Not better choice all accidents could hit,
While hector Harry steers by Will the wit.
(Marvell, 163)

The brothers did not have it all their own way, and when William misguidedly sought to pin the blame for the Medway débâcle on the duke of Albemarle, the admiral's supporters in the Commons made common cause with the lord chancellor's men. Coventry came under intolerable pressure in connection with his performance of the office of navy commissioner, and was forced to lay it down in May 1667.

Coventry's speeches in the House of Commons immediately contributed to Clarendon's fall later that year, but when the change of government took place at the end of August, he remained in the subordinate office of a commissionership of the Treasury, to which he had been appointed in the preceding June. The duke of York resented Coventry's attitude to his father-in-law, Clarendon, and told him so. Three days later Coventry resolved to leave the duke's service. He declared that this step was nowise connected with his attitude to Clarendon. Coventry told Pepys at the time that he regarded Clarendon as an incapable minister, but that he had no wish to seek political advancement by identifying himself with any faction.

Coventry's frankness and independence had raised up many enemies while his association with the Second Dutch War and his engagement in the coup against Clarendon left him exposed and vulnerable. In March 1669 he was informed that the duke of Buckingham and Sir Robert Howard were contemplating a caricature of him on the stage. He duly appeared in the mocking guise of Sir Cautious Trouble-All, in the play *The Country Gentlemen* (1669). The name he was given was a jibe at the epithet already bestowed on Coventry by the king himself, who called him 'visionaire' in derision of his gloomy prognostications on state affairs. Coventry sent a challenge to the duke. As soon as the fact came to the king's knowledge Coventry was sent to the Tower. He was at the same time excluded from the privy council and the Treasury, but this indignity was doubtless cast upon him by the influence of his political rivals—'to make way for the lord Clifford's greatness and the designs of the cabal' (*Bishop Burnet's History*, ed. Burnet and Burnet, 1.265). His friends, including Burnet (with whom Coventry corresponded on Reformation history—see his *Letter Written to Dr. Burnet*, published in 1685) as well as Pepys, visited him in the Tower in large numbers. On 9 March he petitioned for the royal pardon, and on 20 March he was released.

Having fallen from grace Coventry abandoned the court entirely, not without relief at his disengagement, having no stomach for the pro-French diplomacy on which policy came increasingly to rely. Already an effective parliamentarian he now reached the height of his popularity in the Commons, garnering much credit for the not entirely undeserved reputation of having sacrificed an extremely promising career at court for the sake of principled opposition to the danger of selling Englishmen into the clutches of the French. Although personally disinclined to see the active persecution of protestant dissenters he twice opposed the crown's power to suspend the Act of Uniformity. A leading parliamentary opponent of the so-called 'cabal', he also played a leading role in the attack on Danby. Despite his protection of Pepys against the earl of Shaftesbury's allegations of popery in 1677, he remained high in his brother-in-law's estimation at least until he came out in opposition to exclusion, largely on the grounds that it made no sense to reduce the duke of York to such desperation that his only hope lay with France and the Scots.

Coventry had not sought election to the first Exclusion Parliament, and was chosen to sit for Great Yarmouth again despite his absence from the poll. After the dissolution in July 1679, he finally retired to a country house at Minster Lovell, near Witney, Oxfordshire, interesting himself in local affairs and entertaining friends from Oxford. He tried to reduce the expenses attaching to the office of sheriff of the county from £600 to £60, and drew up regulations for the purpose. No offer of posts at court

could draw him back to public life, although Temple and Burnet concur in stating that at one time almost any office was at his disposal. He died unmarried at Somerhill, near Tunbridge Wells, on 23 June 1686, and was buried at Penshurst. He bequeathed £2000 to French protestants expelled from France, and £3000 for the redemption of captives in Algiers. Burnet and Temple credit Coventry with the highest political ability, and Clarendon, who naturally writes of him with acerbity, does not deny it.

Coventry's political views are best known from their affectionate portrayal in *The Character of a Trimmer*, which came out in 1688 with a title-page ascribing it to 'the Honourable Sir W. C.'. It was printed from a copy found among Coventry's papers, but the author was George Savile, marquess of Halifax, Coventry's nephew. This is a vindication of the presence of a middle political party, unconnected with either of the two recognized parties in parliamentary warfare. During his life Coventry admitted himself to be a trimmer, a title which he defines as 'one who would sit upright and not overturn the boat by swaying too much on either side' (Foxcroft, 2.275).

SIDNEY LEE, *rev.* SEAN KELSEY

**Sources** Foster, *Alum. Oxon.*, 1500–1714, 1.337 · W. A. Shaw, *The knights of England*, 2 vols. (1906), vol. 2, p. 240 · *The Nicholas papers*, ed. G. F. Warner, 1, CS, new ser., 40 (1886), 154, 208, 221, 225, 297, 304, 309 · *The life of Edward, earl of Clarendon … written by himself*, 3 vols. (1759), vol. 2, pp. 348–50 · *Calendar of the Clarendon state papers preserved in the Bodleian Library*, ed. O. Ogle and others, 5 vols. (1869–1970), vol. 4, pp. 593, 603, 607; vol. 5, p. 212 · E. Cruickshanks, 'Coventry, Hon. William', HoP, *Commons, 1660–90*, 2.157–63 · R. J. A. Shelley, 'Sir William Coventry: a patron of Pepys', a paper read before the Literary and Philosophical Society of Liverpool on Monday, March 21st 1932, BL · B. Pool, 'Sir William Coventry: Pepys's mentor', *History Today*, 24 (1974), 104–11 · V. Vale, 'Clarendon, Coventry and the sale of naval offices, 1660–8', *Cambridge Historical Journal*, 12 (1956), 107–25 · P. Seaward, *The Cavalier Parliament and the reconstruction of the old regime, 1661–1667* (1989) · *Bishop Burnet's History of his own time*, 1, ed. G. Burnet and T. Burnet (1724), 170, 265, 306 · *The life and letters of Sir George Savile … first marquis of Halifax*, ed. H. C. Foxcroft, 2 vols. (1898) · will, PRO, PROB 11/384, fols. 13v–15r · A. Davies, *Dictionary of British portraiture*, 1 (1979), 28 · GEC, *Peerage*, new edn, 3.476–7 · A. Marvell, *The complete poems*, ed. E. S. Donno (1985), 163 · J. A. Thynne and M. L. Boyle, *Biographical catalogue of the portraits at Longleat in the county of Wilts, the seat of the marquis of Bath* (1881)

**Archives** BL, naval papers and papers, Add. MS 32094 · Longleat House, Wiltshire, Coventry papers [microfilm] | McGill University, Montreal, McLennan Library, appeal from the private caballe at Whitehall to the Greate Council of the Nation · NMM, letters to Sir William Penn · NRA, priv. coll., letters to marquesses of Halifax

**Likenesses** J. Riley, oils, c.1670, Longleat, Wiltshire

**Wealth at death** £4000 in legacies; £2000 bequeathed for assistance of French Protestants; £3000 bequeathed for redemption of Englishmen taken as slaves in Turkey and Barbary; East India Company stock; real estate at Bampton; the lease of Wiveliscombe, Somerset: will, PRO, PROB 11/384, fols. 13v–15r

**Coverdale, Miles** (1488–1569), Bible translator and bishop of Exeter, was born in York. No details are known of his parentage or early education. According to Tanner he was ordained priest in Norwich by John Underwood, bishop of Chalcedon *in partibus*, who was chancellor of that diocese and archdeacon of Norfolk. John Underwood was suffragan to the bishop of Norwich from 1505 to 1541, so Tanner's date for the ordination, 1594 in roman numerals, is an error for 1514, when Coverdale was twenty-six.

**Early life until 1528** Coverdale became an Augustinian friar and went to the house of his order at Cambridge. He was there when Robert Barnes returned from Louvain to become prior, about 1520. Coverdale, 'with divers others of the university', was greatly influenced by the innovations of Barnes, who 'caused the house shortly to flourish with good letters', a reference to such authors as Terence, Plautus, and Cicero. The prior's increasing sympathy with the movement for religious reform became evident when he went on to 'read openly in the house Paul's Epistles, and put by Duns and Dorbel'. Barnes was converted 'wholly unto Christ' by Thomas Bilney as Foxe records and 'the first sermon that ever he [Barnes] preached of this truth' was that on 24 December 1525 in St Edward's Church, Cambridge, in which he followed 'the Scripture and Luther's Postil' (*Acts and Monuments*, ed. Pratt, 5.415). This led to his immediate arrest as a heretic, and he was summoned to London to appear before Wolsey in February 1526. Coverdale, throughout this spiritual progress, was at his superior's side, and even accompanied him to London to help in preparing his defence.

Once back in Cambridge, Coverdale took his degree: BCL according to Cooper, BTh according to Foxe. Twenty years later, John Bale recalled Coverdale at this time. The sketch should stand as epigraph for his whole life:

> Under the mastership of Robert Barnes he drank in good learning with a burning thirst. He was a young man of friendly and upright nature and very gentle spirit, and when the church of England revived, he was one of the first to make a pure profession of Christ ... he gave himself wholly, to propagating the truth of Jesus Christ's gospel and manifesting his glory ... The spirit of God ... is in some a vehement wind, overturning mountains and rocks, but in him it is a still small voice comforting wavering hearts. His style is charming and gentle, flowing limpidly along: it moves and instructs and delights. (Bale, 721; trans. Mozley, 3)

Some time before 1527 Coverdale probably met Thomas Cromwell. In a letter to him, 'from the Augustines this May-day', 1531, Coverdale writes that he has begun to taste of holy scriptures, but requires books to help him to a knowledge of the doctors. He desires nothing but books, and will be guided by Cromwell as to his conduct and in the instruction of others (*LP Henry VIII*, vol. 5, no. 221). Coverdale continued to move towards reform. By Lent 1528 he had left the Augustinians and 'going in the habit of a secular priest' (*Acts and Monuments*, ed. Pratt, 5.40) he preached in Essex against transubstantiation, the worship of images, and confession to the ear. These were dangerous views, and being, as John Hooker put it, 'very straitly pursued by the bishops', towards the end of 1528 he fled overseas.

**First exile, 1528–1535** Coverdale's movements in the next seven years are uncertain. It is possible that he is referred to in Tyndale's account in his *Parable of the Wicked Mammon*

(1528) of the making of his first English translation of the New Testament three years before:

> While I abode a faithful companion, which now hath taken another voyage upon him, to preach Christ where I suppose he was never yet preached (God, which put in his heart thither to go, send his spirit with him, comfort him, and bring his purpose to good effect). (*Doctrinal treatises*, 37)

(William Roy offered his help instead, and was not wholly satisfactory.) The phrases 'now hath taken another voyage ... to preach Christ' would tally with Coverdale's preaching in Essex after Lent 1528. Although the identification is seductive, it is no more than speculation.

Foxe has Coverdale in Hamburg for most of 1529, invited by Tyndale to help him retranslate his Pentateuch. The two men worked, Foxe writes, 'on the whole five books of Moses, from Easter till December, in the house of a worshipful widow, Mistress Margaret Van Emmersen, A.D.1529; a great sweating sickness being at the same time in the town' (*Acts and Monuments*, ed. Pratt, 5.120). Foxe is attractively specific. Perhaps Coverdale was indeed there, yet the story Foxe tells has too much against it. It first appears in a few lines in his last, 1576, version of *Acts and Monuments*. There, Tyndale suddenly sails from Antwerp to Hamburg to print his Pentateuch, and loses everything in a shipwreck on the coast of Holland. He proceeds to Hamburg and meets Coverdale there by appointment. For Tyndale to go to Hamburg makes no sense. Antwerp in 1529 had many fine printers with established trade with Britain. Among them was the dependable Martin de Keyser, who as 'Hans Luft of Marlborow' (not now understood to be Hoochstraten) had already printed Tyndale's *Mammon* and *The Obedience of a Christian Man* the year before under that name. Keyser would go on to print his other books, including his revised New Testament of 1534.

Tyndale had no reason to commit to an unknown printer in Hamburg his second most precious work, the first translation ever made from Hebrew into English. Coverdale, admirable and educated Christian as he was, and no doubt enriching company, at that time knew little if any Hebrew or Greek and would have been of small use for work on the Pentateuch: comparison of their translations of those five Old Testament books shows the distance in method between the two men. Most significantly, though the prologue to the Pentateuch is where Tyndale tells most about himself, neither man ever mentions the shipwreck and loss; nor does anyone else at the time or later. Perhaps Foxe's steady bent in successive editions of his *Acts* to align events in Tyndale's life with the biblical book of Acts (the climactic event in which is Paul's near-calamitous shipwreck) helped him to feel free to elaborate, in the ancient tradition of writing the lives of saints.

Although he gave no authorities, in 1868 the German scholar, J. P. Gelbert claimed that Coverdale worked as 'corrector' (proof-reader) with Martin de Keyser at Antwerp. It is not at all unlikely. Native English readers would be scarce and in demand for the lively book trade with Britain. It is known that in 1534 and 1535 Coverdale was in Antwerp. Foxe writes that in that year John Rogers joined Tyndale and Coverdale there: independently, George Joye can only mean those three men in his tale of how in February 1535 he scorned in Antwerp Tyndale 'and his two disciples that gaped so long for their master's morsel' of Bible translations (Joye, 22). Rogers, chaplain to the Antwerp English House, would shortly assemble 'Thomas Matthew's' English Bible. In 1534 there came out in Antwerp an English translation of Campensis's 1532 Latin paraphrase on the psalms, the most likely author being Coverdale. More to the point, Coverdale had begun to translate the whole Bible.

In England the question of making an official English Bible had been discussed by an assembly of divines convened by the king. On 24 May 1530 Archbishop Warham issued a public instrument on the assembly's behalf declaring that it was unnecessary for a Christian man to have the vernacular scriptures, which could only do harm, and that the people had no right to make this demand. The king promised, however, to ensure that 'learned men' would 'faithfully and purely' translate the New Testament, being satisfied there was no heresy (Wilkins, 3.728–37). Nothing happened. The scriptures in English continued to be burnt. Cranmer tried again in the autumn of 1534, and the New Testament was divided among nine or ten of 'the best learned bishops and other learned men'. It is known that Stephen Gardiner, bishop of Winchester, 'corrected' with hostility the gospels of Luke and John, and that John Stokesley, bishop of London, the scourge of reformers, ignored the archbishop's request to work on Acts, among other reasons claiming that 'Christe had bequeth him nothing in his testament' and so he thought it 'mere madness to bestowe any labour … where no gayne was', disdaining to have anything to do with the acts of 'mere simple poor fellows' (Nichols, 277–8).

**Coverdale's Bible, 1535**  Miles Coverdale, working alone in Antwerp, was the first to translate and print the entire Bible in English. Coverdale's Bible, the printing of which was finished on 4 October 1535, is properly revered for the achievement it is. For this handsome volume, soon reprinted in England by James Nicolson in Southwark, he modified Tyndale's New Testaments. After Tyndale's Pentateuch of 1530, however, only a handful of individual Old Testament books had been printed in English: in 1530 Martin de Keyser had printed George Joye's translations of the Psalms from Bucer's Latin version, his Isaiah in 1531, and his Jeremiah and Lamentations in 1534; and in 1534 T. Godfray had printed Joye's Proverbs and Ecclesiastes; none were from the Hebrew. Admittedly Coverdale himself was not translating from the Hebrew, as he made clear on his title-page. Yet he gave the people of England what so many wanted: the whole Bible printed in their own language. All the reformers across Europe insisted that the scriptures had to be taken whole, not in measured droplets.

Much ink has been used propounding one or another far-flung European city as the place where this fine book was printed. In 1534 Coverdale was in Antwerp, and did his translating there, and had almost certainly worked for Martin de Keyser, who had published his Psalms and other

books. Coverdale may well have seen Tyndale's and Joye's Bible translations come from his presses. Printing a complete Bible was a very large undertaking, but something Antwerp printers were accustomed to do. It is a relief to find that Coverdale's own Bible was indeed printed there, by Martin de Keyser himself. The entire work was undertaken at the sponsorship of Jacob Van Meteren, an Antwerp merchant trading with England.

The text is well set out and illuminated: sixty-seven small woodcuts are so repeated to make over 150 illustrations. Coverdale and de Keyser were the first to print the books of the Apocrypha as an appendix to the Old Testament. Pages have a scattering of marginal alternative readings and many cross-references. The title-page of the first printing, which includes at the foot a picture of King Henry VIII distributing bibles, notes that it was 'faithfully and truly translated out of Douche [German] and Latin into English'. In his dedication to King Henry, Coverdale explains that he has 'with a clear conscience purely and faithfully translated this out of five sundry interpreters', by which he means Tyndale, Luther, the Vulgate, the Zürich Bible, and Pagninus's Latin translation of the Hebrew. C. S. Lewis remarked in 1950 that among the great scholar-translators of the sixteenth century Coverdale 'shows like a rowing boat among battleships. This gave him a kind of freedom'; that is, 'to select and combine by taste. Fortunately his taste was admirable' (Lewis, 11).

Imitating the Swiss and German Bibles, Coverdale coined many compounds, some of which survive, like 'winebibber' at Proverbs 23: 20; or do not, like 'unoutspeakable' at Romans 8: 26; or should have done, like 'wintercool' at Proverbs 25: 13. He has favourite forms, like 'tender mercies', 'lovingkindness', and the excellent 'saving health'. His love of variation he defended in his prologue to the reader as part of his pleasure in a variety of translations. He followed Tyndale in keeping firmly to 'congregation', 'elder', and 'love' and other central New Testament terms for which he had been so attacked, though he used 'penance' for 'repentance' occasionally, pointing out that the former does mean the turning of the whole being to God. His skill with synonyms was most helpful in the poetic and prophetic books of the second half of the Old Testament, untouched by Tyndale, where his grasp (it seems, intuitive) of the parallelism of Hebrew poetry, well ahead of other western translators, produced many splendid passages, such as 'Seek ye the Lord while he may be found, call upon him while he is nigh' (Isaiah 55: 6). To Coverdale's 1535 Bible are owed many unforgettable phrases: 'She brought forth butter in a lordly dish' (Judges 5: 25); 'By the waters of Babylon we sat down and wept when we remembered Sion' (Psalm 137: 1); 'enter thou into the joy of thy lord' (Matthew 25: 21, 23); 'the pride of life' (1 John 2: 16); and many more.

**In England, 1535–1539**  Coverdale returned to England later in 1535. Probably in that year he saw through a London press his *Goostly Psalmes and Spirituall Songs Drawen out of the Holy Scripture*, English versions of already widespread German hymns, and the first printed English book of those metrical psalms which so dominated European (and later American) protestant worship. Anticipating Sternhold's first volume of nineteen psalms by a dozen years, and the great French outpouring by three decades, Coverdale's small book makes him the father of such scriptural hymnody in English. Nine of the twenty-four hymns, with two canticles, are closely associated with Luther's hymnal from Wittenberg, as are eight of the fourteen psalms. Coverdale in his preface states that he wants to supply 'godly songs' to be sung by 'minstrels … our young men that have the gift of singing … and our women singing at the wheels', instead of 'hey nonny nonny, hey troly loly, and such like phantasies'; more significantly, he hoped to prepare the way for a reformed service book, parallel to continental practices.

In 1535 Thomas Gybson published a *Concordance of the New Testament*, based on Tyndale but showing knowledge of the 1535 Bible: it was said to be by Coverdale. *A Faythful and True Pronostication upon the Yeare MCCCCCxxxvi … (A Spiritual Almanacke)* followed, and, in 1537, his translation from the German, as the short *Message of the Emperoure and of the Bishoppe of Rome*, printed by James Nicolson in Southwark, who, more importantly, printed two fresh editions of his Bible. The point to be made here is that the properly high reputation of Coverdale as Bible translator should not obscure his importance as an active reformer, steadily bringing to the English public key German texts: his publications of all kinds number nearly forty.

The version of the whole Bible in English known from its title page as 'Thomas Matthew's Bible' arrived in England from the Low Countries early in August 1537. Tyndale had been executed as a heretic outside Brussels on 6 October 1536. When he was martyred he had in print only the first quarter of his Old Testament, the Pentateuch. On Tyndale's arrest, John Rogers had rescued his manuscript of the historical books, Joshua to 2 Chronicles, and printed it in a complete Bible; the second half of the Old Testament was Coverdale's version. The New Testament was a reprinting of Tyndale's revision of 1534. Since Tyndale's name could not be mentioned, the book was issued under the name of Thomas Matthew. It was printed in Antwerp for Richard Grafton and Edward Whitchurch.

On 4 August 1537 Archbishop Cranmer sent to Cromwell a copy of 'Matthew's' Bible which he had just received from Grafton. Cromwell, who supported scriptural translations, had in the previous year begun the process of setting up an English Bible in every parish church. 'Matthew's' had been promptly licensed by the king as a semi-official way of fulfilling this promise, and Latimer, for one, forcefully commanded his clergy to get and read the scriptures in English, complaining that local clergy were slow. Some distribution began, but there was immediately a dearth of copies. Only 1500 had been printed, and there were almost 8500 parishes. Reprinting 'Matthew's' would raise hostility, and Coverdale's 1535 Bible, not being from the original languages, was judged insufficiently scholarly. Cromwell therefore initiated, with Cranmer's encouragement, a revision of that 1537 Bible. Grafton and Whitchurch were to publish it. The printing

would be done on the presses, superior to any in England, of François Regnault in Paris, who had supplied all English service books from 1519 to 1534. Coverdale was to do the revising in Paris.

In May 1538 printing began. Coverdale and the English overseers were pleased with progress, and on 23 June sent Cromwell some finished sheets and an explanation of the principles of translating and editing. Grafton complained of the inhibiting hostility of the bishop of Winchester, Stephen Gardiner, who was ambassador to France. Costs were outrunning provision. Cromwell sent 600 marks of his own, persuaded the king to recall Gardiner, and nominated Edmund Bonner to be both bishop of Hereford and the new ambassador. Bonner was encouraging, and kept Cromwell informed of the good progress of the great project. On 12 September, Grafton and Coverdale wrote to Cromwell that the work would soon be finished. The English community under Coverdale in Paris was showing solidarity (*LP Henry VIII*, 13/2, 277). Cromwell issued his famous second injunctions, requiring that 'a bible of the largest volume in English' be set up in every parish by Christmas 1538 (Wilkins, 3.815).

Things began to go seriously wrong. In Paris one of the English team was accused of heresy, and Bonner reported that some English bishops were working with the French court to halt the printing. In London the king altered the terms of the royal warrant, unfavourably. Coverdale wrote from Paris on 13 December that some of the 2500 finished copies had been confiscated by the Inquisition. Finally the work was stopped and Grafton and Whitchurch fled to London, while what had been printed was seized for burning. In February 1539 the French, in exchange for a diplomatic favour, agreed to release paper, type, and printers, but not the books. Grafton and Whitchurch returned to Paris to look for the printed sheets. Foxe tells the story that a corrupt French official had sold everything seized, four vats full of unbound pages, to a haberdasher 'to lap hats in' (*Acts and Monuments*, ed. Pratt, 5.411). All bound copies had indeed been burnt. Grafton and Whitchurch returned to England with paper, type, craftsmen, and a few salvaged unbound bibles. The rescued sheets were of the Old Testament as far as Job, and the New Testament as far as 1 Peter. Early in April fresh printing began in the Grey Friars in London, then in Cromwell's hands. By the end of April 3000 copies of this new Great Bible were ready, but none were moved until November. The delay, despite the fact that Cromwell's hold on power was increasingly slippery, seems to have been because he was negotiating for the 2500 sets still in the hands of the French inquisitor-general. With these, and with a second London printing of 3000 copies in March or April 1540, the great injunctions were fulfilled.

**The Great Bible, 1539** The description 'Great Bible' is justified, since it measured 337 mm by 235 mm. The title-page now has a grand King Henry almost at the top, and the whole large picture demonstrates his largesse in giving English bibles to every rank. For the text, Coverdale heavily revised 'Matthew's' Bible, not his own original. Some of his changes were no doubt frequently diplomatic, as he pointed out when he went back towards the Vulgate, and he severely reduced the number of marginal notes. Most of the changes were made because he was now able to use the translation of the Hebrew into Latin by Sebastian Münster, Germany's leading Hebraist, printed in 1535. The steady current in the Old Testament is towards greater accuracy to the original, not to speak of intelligibility. For the New Testament he returned to Erasmus's Latin. Coverdale continued to revise in two of the six successive editions, in those of April 1540 (with Cranmer's preface for the first time) and of July 1540. The Psalms, however, received less revision from their 1535 version. Coverdale's Psalms went forward to become the liturgical psalms of the reformed English church.

While the printing of the Great Bible was being finished in London, Coverdale was in Newbury, whence he reported to Cromwell about breaches in the king's laws against papism, sought out churches in the district where the honour of Becket was still maintained, and prepared to make a bonfire of any primers and other church books which had not been altered to match the king's proceedings. He had in 1538 published his diglot of the New Testament: the Latin was Erasmus's text from his *Novum instrumentum*, the English adapted from his own 1535 translation, but tending more towards the Vulgate. It was reprinted three times in 1538. But now the conservatives, led by Stephen Gardiner, bishop of Winchester, were rapidly beginning to recover their power and oppose Cromwell. On 28 June 1539 the Act of Six Articles, which ended official tolerance of religious reform, became law. Coverdale, like many others, soon fled overseas again.

**Second exile, 1540–1547** Before leaving England, Coverdale had married Elizabeth Macheson (*d.* 1565), a Scotswoman of noble family. Her sister Agnes married John Macalpine, or McAlpine: all three had come to England as religious exiles from Scotland. Macalpine became a prebendary of Salisbury in July 1538. When Coverdale, with his wife, left England they apparently went straight to Strasbourg, where they were welcomed by the wife of Calvin: the latter had escaped dissension by moving to that city. John Macalpine and his wife went via Bremen to Wittenberg, where he became DTh. There Philip Melanchthon gave him the name of Maccabaeus (presumably a cognomen for him as an independence fighter, but perhaps also a joke on his Scottish name, as MacCabaeus). On the invitation of the king of Denmark, Macalpine became professor of divinity at Copenhagen, and presently one of the translators of the Danish Bible of 1550. Both he and the king of Denmark would play an important part in Coverdale's later life.

On 28 July 1540 Robert Barnes was burnt alive at Smithfield. Two days later Thomas Cromwell was sent to the block on Tower Hill. The English exiles could not consider returning for some time. Coverdale remained in Strasbourg for about three years. He translated books from Latin and German—two were by Bullinger—and wrote an important defence of his martyred friend Barnes. This, the theologically gritty *Confutation of that Treatise which one J. Standish Made*, expressing in print his own revulsion at

the death of Barnes alongside that of Bale, Joye, and others, is his most significant reforming statement outside his Bible prefaces. He received from Tübingen the degree of DTh at this time, and visited Denmark. He wrote a tract describing the order of the Lord's supper as he had seen it in Denmark, which was later burnt with other works at Paul's Cross. While in Strasbourg, Coverdale made an important friendship with Conrad Hubert, Martin Bucer's secretary, who was also preacher at the church of St Thomas. Hubert was a native of Bergzabern, a small town 40 miles north of Strasbourg, and on his recommendation in September 1543 Coverdale became assistant minister of Bergzabern and headmaster of the town school, posts he held for five years.

Doctor Coverdale was welcomed thankfully by his predecessor, Nicolaus Thomae, whose competence had been undermined by illness. On 27 April 1544 Thomae wrote to Conrad Hubert that the new headmaster was 'a man of singular piety and incomparable diligence, a watchful and scrupulous performer of every duty of religion. Alleluia' (Mozley, 322). Other letters from Thomae before his death in summer 1546 give glimpses of Coverdale. He is now apparently learning Hebrew with admirable diligence. He is shocked at Luther's violent attack late in 1544 on the sacramental views of fellow reformers, including Zwingli and Oecolampadius. He gives amused advice over the dilemma of an aged and widowed ministerial colleague who is marrying a young girl. Twenty-one letters to Hubert from Coverdale himself have survived, giving news of the school and its pupils, some of whom have gone on to Strasbourg. His duties as assistant minister give him insights into the state of the church: catechizing is producing good results, but heretical teaching is increasing. He is described by a correspondent to Bullinger in April 1545 as 'well loved and honoured by all the ministers of the word and the other learned men of this region' (ibid., 12). He had continued to publish translations of German tracts, and in that year, his fifty-eighth, he produced *The Defence of a Certayne Poore Christen Man*.

In England, meanwhile, as Coverdale noted, blasphemous tongues did not cease to rail against him and to slander him, even to the king, as a maker of revolution. In the proclamation of 8 July 1546 all his books were condemned, and about a dozen of them, including his Bible, were burnt at Paul's Cross on 26 September 1546 by Bonner, who was now bishop of London. King Henry died on 27 January 1547.

**Bishop of Exeter, 1551–1553** Although Henry's successor, Edward, loved reform, Coverdale stayed for a further year in Germany, apparently awaiting a summons to return home. From Frankfurt on 26 March 1548 he wrote to Calvin that he was going back by invitation after an exile of eight years. He enclosed with the letter his own Latin and German translations of the new English order of communion. In London on 24 June he preached the festival sermon for the Merchant Taylors at St Martin Outwich. He soon became almoner to Queen Katherine Parr, now remarried, and worked on her project for the English translation of Erasmus's paraphrases. He preached the sermon at her funeral in September 1548 at Sudeley Castle in Gloucestershire. In October he was at Windsor Castle as royal chaplain, and was probably consulted by Cranmer, along with other bishops and divines, about the making of the first Book of Common Prayer. From there, writing also on behalf of Cranmer, he invited Paul Fagius of Strasbourg to England to escape rising persecution in Germany. Coverdale preached at Paul's Cross on the second Sunday in Lent 1549, again on Low Sunday, and again on Whit Monday, the day after the 'handselling' (first using) of the English prayer book, when the aldermen assembled on foot in their scarlet robes.

On that same day, however, 10 June 1549, events began in the west country that affected Coverdale greatly. Rebellion broke out in Devon and Cornwall against the new English prayer book. Lord Russell was sent to put it down. Coverdale went with him as preacher. A later writer recalled that 'none of the clergy were ready to risk life with Russell's expedition but old Father Coverdale' (*A Brieff Discours*, 232). On the field at Woodbury Windmill, Coverdale preached 'and caused general thanksgiving to be made unto God' (Mozley, 15). The rebellion was put down by the end of August, but Coverdale stayed on for several months, helping to pacify the people. He was doing the work that properly belonged to the bishop of Exeter: but that prelate, John Vesey, now eighty-six years old, had not stirred from Sutton Coldfield in Warwickshire, his birthplace, for some time before, and had left the diocese to look after itself. That Coverdale was effectively bishop was recognized by Latimer, who in a Lenten sermon in 1550 insisted that though Vesey bore the title, Coverdale was doing the work. In a letter to Bullinger of 1 June 1550, Pietro Martire Vermigli, known as Peter Martyr (then living in Oxford and helping Cranmer with the revision of the prayer book) described Coverdale as 'a good man who in former years acted as parish minister in Germany' who now 'labours greatly in Devon in preaching and explaining the Scriptures'. He prophesies that Coverdale will become bishop of Exeter (ibid.).

Coverdale was active in various offices, particularly that of preacher. Just before Easter 1551 he spent some time with Peter Martyr at Magdalen College, Oxford, attending his lectures on the epistle to the Romans, and preaching to the people; Peter Martyr called him 'an active preacher, and one that has well served the cause of the gospel' (Mozley, 15). Coverdale was in demand. In the winter of 1550–51 he preached funeral sermons for Sir James Welford at St Bartholomew by the Exchange, London, and for Lord Wentworth at Westminster Abbey. He was a member of the commission appointed in January 1551 to deal with Anabaptism and other heresy. He sat as judge at the trial of George van Parris, a Flemish Anabaptist denounced for Arian views: he knew no English, so Coverdale acted as interpreter. Parris was burnt alive in April 1551.

On 14 August 1551 John Vesey was ejected from his see and Coverdale nominated in his place. Vesey had drained the finances, and the new bishop inherited large debts. Coverdale was poor. He had returned from Germany poor in worldly goods—'pauper in hoc mundo', as John Bale put it in 1548 (Bale, 141). He could not raise the £500 due as first fruits: the crown, on the plea of Cranmer, remitted it. The wider debts incurred by Vesey were written off, and the whole see was revalued for the future at less than a third of its former worth. Coverdale, vested in surplice and cope, was consecrated at Croydon on 30 August 1551, and enthroned on 11 September. A curiosity is that on the day before his enthronement he and his wife were given permanent permission to eat flesh and milk in Lent and other fast days, with not more than five or six guests, despite an act of parliament that ordained abstinence.

Coverdale was regular in attendance at the House of Lords, and he sat on the commission appointed on 12 February 1552 to reform the canon law. His chief labour, however, was in his diocese. In his *Description of the City of Exeter*, John Hooker, then in his household, gives an account of how he 'most worthily did perform the office committed unto him':

> he preached continually upon every holy day, and did read most commonly twice in the week in some one church or other within this city. He was, after the rate of his livings, a great keeper of hospitality, very sober in diet, godly in life, friendly to the godly, liberal to the poor, and courteous to all men, void of pride, full of humility, abhorring covetousness, and an enemy to all wickedness and wicked men, whose companies he shunned, and whom he would in no wise shroud [shelter] or have in his house and company. His wife a most sober, chaste and godly matron: his house and household another church, in which was exercised all godliness and virtue. No one person being in his house which did not from time to time give an account of his faith and religion, and also did live accordingly … Yet the common people, whose old bottles would receive no new wine, could not brook nor digest him, for no other cause but because he was a preacher of the gospel, an enemy to papistry, and a married man.

Hooker reports that he was the victim of false suggestions, open railings, false libels, and secret backbitings. At Totnes and at Bodmin there were apparently attempts to poison him. His enemies the archdeacon of Barnstaple, John Pollard, and the vicar of Ipplepen, Walter Hele, were forced by him to recant in the cathedral (Mozley, 16–17).

A little before this time (16 August 1549) the second volume of Erasmus's important and popular *Paraphrases on the New Testament* were published. Working with Leonard Cox and John Olde, Coverdale's share was almost certainly Romans, Corinthians, Galatians, and a preface, and he edited the whole volume. England was twenty years behind Germany, and seven behind France, in translating the *Paraphrases*. At much the same time Coverdale also edited a corrected edition of the Lollard tract, *Wiclif's Wicket*. In 1550 he published a version of Werdmüllers *Precious Pearl*, made at the request and expense of the duke of Somerset, and very popular. That year saw a new edition of his 1535 Bible, printed by Froschover in Zürich.

On 6 July 1553 King Edward died. On Queen Mary's accession, Coverdale found himself summoned almost immediately to appear before the privy council. There he was ordered, on 1 September, 'to attend until the lords' pleasures be further known' (Mozley, 17). This seems to have meant house arrest in Exeter. In November 1553 and

April 1554 both Peter Martyr and the king of Denmark refer to him as having been a prisoner. On 18 September 1553 Coverdale was ejected and Vesey, now ninety and still in Warwickshire, was reinstated.

**Third exile, 1553–1559** Coverdale was in danger. John Hooker records the certainty of his enemies in Devon that he, above all bishops, would be burnt. He saw clearly how vulnerable he was, but stated that in spite of rumours that he would recant, he was:

> steadfastly determined never to return unto Egypt, never to kiss the calf … never to refuse or recant the word of life … for the corn that the Lord hath appointed for his own barn shall be safe enough, and kept full well by the help of him that is owner thereof.   (Mozley, 18)

He wrote an answer to a sermon given at Paul's Cross by Dr Hugh Weston which contained the famous words 'you have the word and we have the sword' (ibid.). He added his name to a statement of belief by twelve of his fellow prisoners. Meanwhile, the king of Denmark, at the request of Coverdale's brother-in-law 'Maccabaeus' in Copenhagen, wrote to Queen Mary on 25 April 1554 requesting Coverdale's release on the grounds that he had committed no crime: he was imprisoned only through the troubles of the time. If his presence in England is undesirable, adds the king, he, and his, will be welcome in Denmark. Queen Mary's reply, which has not survived, assures her fellow monarch that the only cause of Coverdale's detention is a debt which he owes to the crown, and there is no need for anxiety on any other account. The king replied on 24 September 1554. He is full of pleasure at her gracious answer, and that his fears were groundless, and he has comforted the grief of 'Maccabaeus' and his wife. He raises one further small point: the debt was due from Coverdale as bishop of Exeter; but Coverdale is no longer bishop of Exeter. What he received from the see was very small. If there are small faults in the accounts, the king is sure that the queen will overlook them. He greatly looks forward to welcoming Coverdale to Denmark and hearing from his own lips the story of the royal clemency.

Queen Mary did not reply for five months. On 18 February 1555 she wrote to the king that she would permit Coverdale to go to Denmark, 'though he is not yet quit of the debt of money which he is bound by law to pay to our treasury', and on the following day the privy council issued a passport permitting Coverdale 'to pass from hence towards Denmark with two of his servants, his bags and baggages' (Mozley, 20). Since none of those phrases can, it is hoped, refer to Mrs Coverdale, it must be assumed that her presence was taken for granted. It is possible that there were already children. The party arrived in Denmark, and no doubt the king's wish was fulfilled to hear from Coverdale's own lips the story of exactly how clement his queen had been—even to the pursuit of debts which her treasury's creative accounting had landed on his shoulders, for moneys belonging to periods when Coverdale was not bishop. Foxe is undoubtedly right: debt was merely 'a colourable excuse for shifting off the matter' (*Acts and Monuments*, ed. Pratt, 6.706). Fellow bishops who

conformed and put away their wives found similar debts cancelled.

The Coverdales did not stay long in Denmark; probably only a few weeks. The University of Copenhagen honoured him with a present of wine and claret. The king apparently offered him a benefice, but Coverdale, not knowing the language, refused. He set off for Wesel, where he served as chaplain to a small community of English people for three or four months. Then an invitation came from the magistrates at Bergzabern, approved by the prince, for him to resume his old work there. Coverdale accepted and, by way of Frankfurt, he arrived on 20 September 1555. He stayed for two years. Nothing is known of this second period in the town. He arrived when he was sixty-seven and left aged sixty-nine.

In summer 1557 Coverdale moved to Aarau. The English community at Wesel had been banished for theological reasons, and made its way slowly to Switzerland, arriving at Aarau on 11 August 1557. Coverdale joined them. In contemporary documents he is described as born at York, having a wife and two children, and lodging in the Frauenkloster. Then, a little over a year later, on 24 October 1558, he received leave to settle in Geneva.

Queen Mary died on 17 November 1558. Coverdale did not hasten home. It is most likely that he had gone to Geneva to work on the English Bible. Whittingham's New Testament had appeared there in 1557, and the whole Geneva Bible would be published in April 1560. Although his Hebrew, and apparently also now his Greek, could not match the local scholars' skills, Coverdale would no doubt have special things to offer as one who nearly two dozen years before had first translated the whole Bible singlehanded, the only Englishman to have done so, and then revised it under royal authority for the successive editions of the Great Bible. A life of Whittingham written about 1603 states that 'the learned that were at Geneva, as Bishop Coverdale … did undertake the translation of the Geneva Bible' (*A Brieff Discours*, 3). Writing later from London to William Cole at Geneva on 22 February 1560, Coverdale would show a lively interest in the progress of the work (Mozley, 23).

On 29 November 1558 Coverdale stood godfather to John Knox's son. On 16 December he became an elder of the English church in Geneva, and in that same month he joined in the reconciling letter sent by the leaders of that church to the other English churches on the continent. He seems to have set off for England in August 1559. On the way a piece of his luggage went astray. In London he and his family were able to lodge with the duchess of Suffolk, whom he had known at Wesel; he was now apparently appointed as preacher and tutor to her children. His letter to William Cole at Geneva, as well as thankfully reporting the arrival of the missing trunk in December (thanks to a friend in Antwerp), describes the duchess as having 'like us, the greatest abhorrence of the ceremonies' (Mozley, 23), that is, the increasing use of vestments.

**London, 1559–1569** Coverdale did not resume the bishopric of Exeter, though John Hooker wrote that he was 'appoynted agayne bishop of Exeter, but he refused it and contented himself to be a preacher of the gospel' (BL, Harley MS 5827, fols. 46–7). Hooker could have been wrong; Coverdale's association with Knox might have stood in the way of a new preferment. If he was offered and refused, several possible reasons can be guessed. At seventy-two he may have felt unwilling to take on not only the strenuous life of a bishop if the work were to be done well, but also the sorting out of the acute problems in the see. It had no money; nor had Coverdale: once again he had returned from exile penniless. Dislike of the vestments may have been a reason. Officiating with three other bishops (though technically he was not a bishop) at the ceremony of the consecration of Archbishop Matthew Parker in the chapel of Lambeth Palace on 17 December 1559, Coverdale wore a black gown, though his colleagues were vested in copes.

Not far short of five years after his return to England, in January 1564, Coverdale accepted from Edmund Grindal, bishop of London, the living of St Magnus the Martyr by London Bridge. He was too poor to pay the first fruits, and they were forgiven him by the queen. In Grindal's letter to Cecil praying for this concession, he pointed out that since his bishopric was taken from him he, Coverdale, had had neither pension nor annuity. He had in the meantime been an active preacher. On 12 November 1559 he was preaching at Paul's Cross, and again on 28 April 1560, before the mayor, aldermen, and a great audience. In July 1562 he delivered a funeral sermon in St Alfege, London Wall, where twelve clerks sang the service for the widow of a doctor of physic. In 1563 he fell victim to plague, but recovered, subsequently delivering a funeral sermon at St Olave's, Southwark, for which he received 40s. At Cambridge that year he was installed DTh, by incorporation from Tübingen. In April 1564 he acted for the vice-chancellor of Cambridge in conferring the same degree on Grindal, who had done much to try to get a post for Coverdale: every offer had been declined. Grindal wrote to Cecil proposing 'father Coverdale' for the vacant see of Llandaff:

> Surely it is not well that he, *qui ante nos omnes fuit in Christo*, should be now in his age without stay of living. I cannot herein excuse us bishops. Somewhat I have to say for myself: for I have offered him divers things, which he thought not meet for him.   (Nicholson, 283)

It does not appear that Llandaff was ever offered to him. The important collection concerning the Marian persecution which was published that year as *Certain Most Godly, Fruitful and Comfortable Letters of such True Saintes and Holy Martyrs as in the Late Bloodye Persecution Gave their Lyves* appeared under the name of Coverdale, but was essentially the work of Henry Bull.

Elizabeth Coverdale died early in September 1565, and was buried in St Michael Paternoster Royal on the 8th. Her husband married his second wife, Katherine, on 7 April 1566 at the same church. He resigned from St Magnus the Martyr in summer 1566, after two and a half years. It is possible that he left the living on puritan grounds, as in March of that year Archbishop Parker had caused great consternation among many clergy by his edicts prescribing what was to be worn, and by his summoning the London clergy to Lambeth to require their compliance. Coverdale excused himself from attending. He could not travel, he said, and there were other reasons. No doubt the reasons were those appearing in the letters sent by him and others to the divines of Geneva and Zürich declaring the distress of the faithful in England and asking for guidance in this day of perplexity.

As long as his strength permitted (he was now nearly eighty) Coverdale preached in London, with a keen following in godly circles, though since he was apparently becoming fearful for his safety they could not always discover where he would preach next. In winter 1567–8 he preached a course of eleven sermons in Holy Trinity Minories. From January 1568 he and his wife had lived in a house belonging to the Merchant Taylors in the parish of St Benet Fink in Broad Street ward. In January 1569 he gave his last sermon, at a regular service he was attending at St Magnus the Martyr, when it was found that there was no preacher. John Hooker describes what happened:

> certain men of the parish came unto him, and earnestly entreated that considering the multitude was great, and that it was pity they should be disappointed of their expectation, that it would please him to take the place for that time. But he excused his age and the infirmities thereof, and that his memory failed him, his voice scarce to be heard, and he not able to do it, that they would hold him excused. Nevertheless such were their importunate requests that, would he nould he, he must and did yield unto their requests: and between two men he was carried up into the pulpit, where God did with his spirit so strengthen him, that he made his last and the best and the most godly sermon that ever he did in all his life. And very shortly after he died, being very honourably buried with the presence of the duchess of Suffolk, the earl of Bedford, and many others, honourable and worshipful personages.   (BL, Harley MS 5827, fols. 46–7)

Coverdale died on 20 January 1569, and two days later was buried in the chancel of St Bartholomew by the Exchange, under the communion table. The marble stone and brass inscription were destroyed in the great fire of 1666. Surviving copies show Latin elegiacs to the effect that he was of singular uprightness and lived for eighty-one years. St Bartholomew's Church was pulled down in 1840 to make room for the Royal Exchange. Coverdale's remains were removed to the Wren church of St Magnus the Martyr, where they now lie, with a tablet on the east wall, close to the altar, amid what T. S. Eliot in part 3 of *The Waste Land* celebrates as 'inexplicable splendour of Ionian white and gold'. He left no will. On 23 January letters of administration were granted to his wife, Katherine. It appears that he has no living descendants.

**Assessment** Miles Coverdale was a man who was loved all his life for that 'singular uprightness' recorded on his tomb. He was always in demand as a preacher of the gospel. He was an assiduous bishop. He pressed forward with great work in the face of the complexities and adversities produced by official policies. His gift to posterity has been from his scholarship as a translator; from his steadily developing sense of English rhythms, spoken and sung;

and from his incalculable shaping of the nation's moral and religious sense through the reading aloud in every parish from his 'bible of the largest size'.

DAVID DANIELL

**Sources** J. F. Mozley, *Coverdale and his bibles* (1953) · S. L. Greenslade, ed., *The Coverdale Bible, 1535* (1975) · C. Hughes, 'Coverdale's *alter ego*', *Bulletin of the John Rylands University Library*, 65 (1982–3), 100–24 · *Remains of Myles Coverdale, bishop of Exeter*, ed. G. Pearson, Parker Society (1846) · *The acts and monuments of John Foxe*, ed. J. Pratt, [new edn], 8 vols. (1877) · *LP Henry VIII* · J. Bale, *Illustrium Maioris Britanniae scriptorum … summarium* (1548) · Tanner, *Bibl. Brit.-Hib.* · J. Foxe, *Actes and monuments* (1563) · Cooper, *Ath. Cantab.*, 1.268–74 · *State papers published under … Henry VIII*, 11 vols. (1830–52), vol. 1 · R. Holinshed and others, eds., *The chronicles of England, Scotland and Ireland*, [new edn], 3, ed. J. Hooker (1587), 111, 1308 · W. J. Harte, ed., *Gleanings from the commonplace book of John Hooker* (1926) · BL, Harley MS 5827, fols. 46, 72 · D. Daniell, 'Tyndale and Foxe', *John Foxe: an historical perspective* [Oxford 1997], ed. D. Loades (1999), 26–8 · J. P. Gelbert, *Magister Johann Bader's Leben und Schriften, Nicolaus Thomae und seine Briefe* (1868) · G. Latré, 'The place of printing of the Coverdale Bible', *The Bible as book: the Reformation*, ed. O. O'Sullivan and E. N. Herron (2000), 89–102 · *An apology made by George Joye, to satisfy, if it may be, W. Tindale, 1535*, ed. E. Arber (1882) · G. Hammond, *The making of the English Bible* (1982) · D. Wilkins, ed., *Concilia Magnae Britanniae et Hiberniae*, 3 (1737) · J. G. Nichols, ed., *Narratives of the days of the Reformation*, CS, old ser., 77 (1859) · *Sermons by Hugh Latimer*, ed. G. E. Corrie, Parker Society, 16 (1844) · W. Nicholson, ed., *The remains of Edmund Grindal*, Parker Society, 9 (1843) · [W. Whittingham?], *A brieff discours off the troubles begonne at Franckford* [1574] · C. S. Lewis, *The literary impact of the Authorized Version* (1950) · J. K. McConica, *English humanists and Reformation politics under Henry VIII and Edward VI* (1965); repr. with corrections (1968) · B. F. Westcott, *A general view of the history of the English Bible*, 3rd edn, rev. W. A. Wright (1905) · A. J. Slavin, 'The Rochepot affair', *Sixteenth Century Journal*, 10 (1979), 3–20 · GL, MS 4374/1 · *Doctrinal treatises and introductions to different portions of the holy scriptures: by William Tyndale, martyr 1536*, ed. H. Walter, Parker Society, 42 (1848) · S. Wabuda, 'Henry Bull, Miles Coverdale, and the making of Foxe's *Book of martyrs*', *Martyrs and martyrologies*, ed. D. Wood, SCH, 30 (1993), 245–58 · C. J. Sisson, 'Grafton and the London Grey Friars', *The Library*, 4th ser., 11 (1930–31), 121–49
**Archives** LPL, letters to the ecclesiastical commissioners

**Cow, Peter Brusey** (1815–1890), rubber manufacturer, was probably born in Woolwich, the younger son of John Cow, a master boat builder at Woolwich Dockyard. In 1830, at the age of fifteen, he was apprenticed to Charles Gower Collins, a linen draper of Lower Sloane Street, Chelsea. After completing his apprenticeship in 1835 he stayed with Collins until 1837, when he worked for Gainsford and Goods for a year. In 1838 he went to Swan and Edgar at Waterloo House, where he lived in, but was meantime in touch with Samuel Matthews, superintendent of the three London branches of Charles Macintosh & Co., rubber manufacturers, at 46 Cheapside, 66 Broad Street, and 58 Charing Cross. The firm's main activity was the manufacture of waterproof garments made of double-texture cloth. In 1842 Cow opened his own shop in Bishopsgate, selling lace and baby linen.

Cow was made a member of the Loriners' Company in 1843, and on 11 November that year married Sarah Hatfull, a doctor's daughter from Deptford. Matthews had meanwhile bought the Charing Cross branch of Macintosh & Co. and in 1846 offered Cow a joint share in the Cheapside business with his son George, which he accepted. The

Cows lived at the Cheapside premises and their first son, Peter Brusey (II), was born there in 1847. A second son, Douglas, followed in 1849, and there were also three daughters of the marriage: Sarah Elizabeth, later wife of Edward Spencer Alexander, Mary Billing, who married Richard Osmond Hearson, and Kate.

In 1850 Matthews took George out of the business and sold his share to Cow for £4000. The firm was now styled P. B. Cow, Rubber Manufacturer. In 1851 a factory was opened at Deptford Creek, and the Cows moved there. That same year, when it was the first to introduce waterproof tweed commercially, the firm won an award at the Great Exhibition at the Crystal Palace.

In 1852, with William G. Forster, Cow founded the Lonestone Chemical Works at Streatham, and in 1857 moved the manufacturing activity from the Deptford factory, which had become too small, to a former crêpe factory at Streatham. The firm still traded as P. B. Cow, and retained this name in 1861 when Cow took a partner, John Hill, to help at the Cheapside premises. The renamed firm of Cow and Forster resulted when Cow took Thomas Forster as partner in 1863, but when the partnership was renewed in 1868 the old name was reintroduced, in the style P. B. Cow, Hill & Co.

Cow's elder son had now joined the Streatham side of the business and became partner there in 1871. In 1874 Cow senior purchased the Cheapside property and soon after acquired the adjacent premises at no. 47 for the expanding business. In 1874 Cow's grandson, Peter Brusey (III), was born, and that same year his second son, Douglas, became a partner, sharing the management of the Cheapside business with Hill. In 1881 the Cheapside premises were destroyed by fire, and a new building was erected on the site. When Hill retired in 1887, to be succeeded by James Crump, the firm's cashier, the firm once again became P. B. Cow & Co.

Cow senior retired in 1888, by which time his already indifferent health was fast deteriorating. A winter stay in Hastings from November 1889 had no beneficial effect, and he returned gravely ill to Streatham, where he died of heart failure at his home, 15 Streatham Common on 27 March 1890. Cow was actively involved in church work throughout his life, and was on the building committee of St James's, Hatcham. While at Streatham he was churchwarden of Emmanuel Church, Streatham Common, and he donated generously to the building of St Andrew's Church, Lower Streatham.

ADRIAN ROOM

**Sources** *The India Rubber and Gutta-Percha and Electrical Trades Journal* (8 April 1890) · A. Standring, *A century of rubber, a tale of five generations during six reigns: P. B. Cow & Company, Ltd.* (c.1935) · W. G., *Cow's of Cheapside* [1930] · private information (2004) · d. cert. · m. cert. · b. certs. [Peter Brusey Cow II and Peter Brusey Cow III] · CGPLA Eng. & Wales (1890)
**Wealth at death** £96,536 18s. 9d.: resworn probate, July 1890, CGPLA Eng. & Wales

**Cowan, Charles** (1801–1889), paper manufacturer and politician, born on 7 June 1801 at 12 or 14 Charlotte Street, Edinburgh (as he said in his *Reminiscences*), was the eldest of the eleven children of Alexander Cowan (*d.* 1859), owner of paper mills at Penicuik, near Edinburgh. His mother was Elizabeth (*d.* 1829), daughter of George Hall of Crail, Fife, a merchant, and his wife, Helen, *née* Nairne. Sir John *Cowan was his brother. He was educated at the parish school at Penicuik, until his family moved to Edinburgh in 1811. He then attended Edinburgh high school until 1814, and Edinburgh University for the next three years (from the age of thirteen). In 1817 he went to Geneva and attended lectures for a year at the auditoire there. He passed through the Jura region on his way, and during his sojourn visited some of the mountainous areas of Switzerland. On his travels he sometimes felt himself in peril for his life. Nevertheless he sustained a taste for travel, and later visited Italy, Norway, Sweden, Russia, and the United States. Thomas Chalmers, an admired friend, accompanied him on one of his continental journeys. After returning from Geneva, Cowan entered the family business. On 19 October 1824 he married Catharine Menzies (*d.* 1871), second daughter of the minister of Lanark. They had two sons and seven daughters, of whom all except three daughters survived their father.

While giving much of his time and energy to his business, Cowan was also very interested in religion, politics, and sport. He was an elder of the Church of Scotland from 1830 to 1843, when he 'went out' with Chalmers at the Disruption and became a stalwart of the new Free Church. He was an elder of that church until his death, and was one of the chief founders of its sustentation fund. He was unusual among early Free Churchmen in being fairly favourable to voluntaryism (opposition to the concept of an established church). In the mid-1840s he actively opposed the intention of Peel's government to abolish the duty on imported paper. Perhaps partly because of this, and certainly because he opposed the Maynooth Bill in 1845, he was persuaded to stand as a radical candidate for Edinburgh in opposition to the whig Thomas Babington Macaulay in the general election of 1847. Despite his stand over the paper duty, he declared himself, in his election address of 24 July, a supporter of free trade. He also supported a national education system, the gradual abolition of established churches (due regard being shown for existing interests), and reform of the game laws and the law of entail. He was returned at the head of the poll, and Macaulay lost his seat.

From 1847 to 1852 Cowan sat on various parliamentary committees, and persuaded the Commons to adopt a resolution against billeting soldiery on private households in Scotland. But in 1851 his bill to abolish Scottish university tests was defeated by one vote on its second reading. He was particularly active in opposing indirect taxation and was, from 1849, a leading supporter of the Association for the Repeal of Taxes on Knowledge. In July 1852 he was re-elected for Edinburgh in a complicated contest, though Macaulay was now head of the poll and Cowan came second. In February 1856 Adam Black, the publisher, joined him in the representation, Macaulay having retired. Cowan and Black were returned unopposed in March 1857, after they had (somewhat unusually for radicals)

supported Palmerston over his defence of the bombardment of Canton (Guangzhou). However, Cowan did not stand again at the election of 1859. Thereafter he played little part in public life, and concerned himself with his paper-manufacturing business (of which he became head on his father's death in 1859) and his church. He died at his home, Wester Lea, Murrayfield, Edinburgh, on 29 March 1889.

Cowan was generally regarded, and not only in his own church and his own political party, as high-principled and hard-working, generous and hospitable. Among his enthusiasms was the vigorous ice-sport of curling, in which he competed ardently and was 'skip of his rink' for many years. According to the Revd John Kerr, author of *The History of Curling* (1890), Cowan 'saw the beneficial moral effects of curling on the community, and became a keen curler, not so much because of any selfish delight to be had in it, but because it was social, manly and healthy' (p. 239). In 1838 Cowan was a founder of the Royal Caledonian curling club, which by 1875 had 432 clubs in Europe and America affiliated to it. He contributed articles to the club's *Annual*. By 1888 he was the sole surviving founder member, and, as he was unable to attend the jubilee dinner in that year, a special telegram of greeting was sent to him.

IAN MACHIN

**Sources** C. Cowan, *Reminiscences* (privately printed, Edinburgh, 1878) · G. I. T. Machin, *Politics and the churches in Great Britain, 1832 to 1868* (1977) · I. G. C. Hutchison, *A political history of Scotland, 1832–1924* (1986) · G. O. Trevelyan, *The life and letters of Lord Macaulay*, [rev. edn], 2 vols. (1908) · C. Cowan, *Address to the electors of the city of Edinburgh, 24 July 1847* (1847) · *City of Edinburgh election [1852]: meeting of Mr Cowan with the electors* (1852) · *Poll-book of the election for the city of Edinburgh, 1852* (1854) · *Memoirs of Adam Black*, ed. A. Nicolson (1885) · J. Kerr, *The history of curling: Scotland's 'ain game', and fifty years of the Royal Caledonian Club* (1890) · *The Scotsman* (30 March 1889), 9 · Boase, *Mod. Eng. biog.* · C. D. Collet, *History of the taxes on knowledge: their origin and repeal*, 2 vols. (1899)
**Archives** BLPES, business book · Edinburgh Central Reference Library, diaries
**Wealth at death** £85,344 10s.: confirmation, 4 July 1889, *CCI*

**Cowan, Sir John**, baronet (1814–1900), paper manufacturer and political organizer, was born at 5 St John's Street, Edinburgh, on 7 May 1814, one of the eight children to reach maturity of Alexander Cowan (*d.* 1859), also a paper manufacturer, of Edinburgh and Valleyfield, Penicuik, Midlothian, and his wife, Elizabeth Hall (*d.* 1829), daughter of George Hall of Crail, Fife, merchant. Two of his three brothers achieved prominence as Liberal politicians. His elder brother Charles *Cowan (1801–1889) defeated T. B. Macaulay at the general election of 1847 and went on to represent Edinburgh for the next twelve years. His younger brother James (1816–1895) likewise represented the city from 1874 to 1882.

In his youth Cowan established a reputation as a dedicated student. After attending Edinburgh high school (where he used to beg his father to let him start the day at 4.15 a.m.) he continued his education at the universities of Edinburgh and Bonn. He then joined his brothers in the Penicuik paper-making firm, the original mill of which

Sir John Cowan, baronet (1814–1900), by unknown engraver, pubd 1894 (after Thomas Fall)

his grandfather Charles had bought and renamed Valleyfield. In later life Cowan was to head this family business, by then operating under the name of Alexander Cowan & Sons.

Twice married—first, in 1847 or 1848, to Jane Menzies (1820–1854), daughter of Alexander Gillespie of Sunnyside, near Lanark, and second, in 1857 or 1858, to Jane Falconar (1826–1861), daughter of William Currie of Linthill, Roxburghshire—Cowan was from 1861 a widower. Three children died before reaching adulthood.

Cowan was chairman of the Midlothian Liberal Association when the constituency was thrust into national prominence by having W. E. Gladstone as its MP. Under the impetus and sponsorship of the fifth earl of Rosebery and the organizational supervision of W. P. Adam, the Liberal chief whip, Cowan chaired the meetings held in Midlothian to request Gladstone to stand and sent the formal invitation. Gladstone accepted in a public letter addressed to Cowan in late January 1879. In the August of that year it was Cowan who wrote to Gladstone suggesting that he come to the constituency to address the public meetings held in November 1879 which made up Gladstone's first campaign in Midlothian. Although illness prevented Cowan from chairing any of the campaign meetings, he had already played a significant part in the organization of Gladstone's triumphant, if not unexpected, return over Midlothian's sitting Conservative MP, the earl of Dalkeith, at the general election held in April 1880. The Midlothian campaign of late 1879 and its follow-up of March and April 1880 resulted in the establishment of Gladstonianism as the dominant force in Liberal politics.

Cowan was a similarly central figure in all of Gladstone's subsequent re-elections for the county. He was active in national politics also to the extent that he held office in the Scottish Liberal Association and the Scottish Liberal Club. The relationship between Cowan and Gladstone was one marked by great warmth on both sides. Gladstone visited his constituency chairman several times at Beeslack House, Cowan's family home near Penicuik.

Cowan remained loyal to Gladstone when the Liberal Party split over the latter's Irish home-rule policy in 1886. Cowan's record of service and loyalty was recognized when he was created a baronet in 1894. It was to him that Gladstone wrote announcing his intention to stand down as Midlothian's member at the dissolution of 1895.

Like his brothers, Cowan was a founder member of the Free Church of Scotland. The family was related through both his father and his mother to Thomas Chalmers, the Free Church's leading figure in the Disruption of 1843. Cowan was an elder at Penicuik Free Church from 1850. His charitable instinct led him to set up a fund through which a proportion of the family firm's profits were channelled into philanthropic works. During his time as head of the business the Cowan Institute was built as an educational and leisure facility for the people of Penicuik. Cowan was also active in foreign missions and contributed generously to the work of David Livingstone, whom he counted a personal friend.

Cowan died on 26 October 1900 after suffering a heart attack near Beeslack House and was buried on 4 November at Old Glencorse kirkyard, near Penicuik. He was survived by two daughters, the baronetcy becoming extinct on his death.                          GORDON F. MILLAR

**Sources** *The Scotsman* (27 Oct 1900) · *The Scotsman* (5 Nov 1900) · *The Times* (27 Oct 1900) · *The Times* (29 Oct 1900) · *Glasgow Herald* (27 Oct 1900) · M. Forsyth, *The Cowans at Moray House* (1932) · Gladstone, *Diaries* · J. Morley, *The life of William Ewart Gladstone*, 3 (1903), 517–35 · J. Bee, 'Report on the centenary of Penicuik town hall', *The Penicuik Advertiser* (5 Jan 1995) · *WWW* · C. Cowan, *Reminiscences* (privately printed, Edinburgh, 1878) · Burke, *Peerage* · private information (2004) · C. B. B. Watson, *Alexander Cowan of Moray House and Valleyfield*, 2 pts (privately printed, Perth, 1915–17)
**Archives** priv. coll., diaries | BL, corresp. with W. E. Gladstone, Add. MS 44137
**Likenesses** engraving (after T. Fall), repro. in *ILN*, 104 (1894), 363 [*see illus.*]
**Wealth at death** £118,252 13s. 8d.: confirmation, 1 Dec 1900, *CCI*

**Cowan, John Anthony** (1929–1979), photographer, was born on 22 April 1929 at Gillingham, Kent, the only child of Irving Cowan and his wife, Elizabeth Edith, *née* Cobley (1907–1999). He attended schools in Gillingham, Lincolnshire, Bournemouth, and Ramsgate but showed little interest in academic study. The appetite for adventure that shaped his life was evident in his early ambition to become a fighter pilot. He joined the RAF in 1945 but his career in uniform was short-lived, and until 1958 saw him involved in varied and largely unsatisfactory efforts to earn a living. He married Joyce Gordon (*b*. 1929), a nurse, in June 1950 at Bearstead, Kent. Their daughter Nicola was born on 13 July 1954. They divorced in the same year. Cowan's second marriage (19 September 1959), to Sydney Smith (*b*. 1934), was also brief; they separated in February 1963 and divorced on 4 July 1967. They had three daughters: Carolyn, born on 7 February 1960; Atalanta, born on 20 June 1962; and Justine, born on 31 July 1963.

Cowan took up photography to make on-site photographs while working in civil engineering. Attracted to the possibilities of the medium, ambitious, and hungry for independence, he left his employers in 1958 to work freelance in what he described as 'the precarious region of Society Photography'. He liked the challenge of working in difficult conditions and made a speciality of available

**John Anthony Cowan** (1929–1979), by Allan Ballard, 1960s [right, with Allan Ballard]

light photography, including portrait, documentary, and theatre work. In March 1959 he staged his first one-man exhibition: 'Through the Light Barrier', sponsored by Kodak. He set up a studio at 426 Fulham Road, London, in the same year, and in August worked for the first time with model Grace Coddington. He was finding his form as a photographer of beautiful girls, and fashion became the territory in which he chose to operate. In February 1962 he worked for the first time with Jill Kennington, who had just started modelling. He established a close personal and working relationship with her that generated a rich flow of pictures over the next few years. In Kennington he had found the model with the looks and the personality to match his ambitions as a photographer.

Cowan was by instinct a location rather than a studio photographer and would devise dramatic picture-story ideas that might involve dangerous settings or situations. He created a sense of excitement while shooting and succeeded in infusing his pictures with a dynamic, explosive energy. He worked to greatest effect in black and white, making high-contrast prints of images that were a forceful expression of the fashions and mood of the early sixties. In 1964, from 1 April, he presented a one-man exhibition, 'The Interpretation of Impact through Energy', at Gordon's Cameras, 45 Kensington High Street, London. The exhibition included many of his pictures of Jill Kennington, printed large for added dramatic effect. Cowan was working for numerous magazines and newspapers, including *Vogue*, *Queen*, *Harper's Bazaar*, and *Elle*, *The Observer*, the *Sunday Times*, the *Daily Express* and the *Sunday Express*, the *Daily Mail*, and the *Daily Mirror*. By 1965 he was established in the studio at 39 Prince's Place, London, that was to provide, the following year, the principal set for Antonioni's film *Blow-up*. His relationship with Kennington came to an end in 1966.

The reckless personality that lay behind Cowan's creativity ultimately betrayed him. Always as careless with his finances as he was with people's feelings, he was by the late sixties a man whose career was in trouble. He spent time in Milan in 1968, and in Paris the following year, before moving to New York in November with model and

partner Erica Creer. They returned to Britain in September 1970. The seventies were difficult years, with Cowan never able to recapture the position that he had enjoyed as a fashionable photographer in the sixties. He died of cancer on 26 September 1979 in East Hagbourne, Oxfordshire; his funeral was held in nearby Wallingford. His negatives and archive material were left to his partner Gunilla Mitchell. Cowan's work was largely forgotten for twenty years until the publication in 1999 of Philippe Garner's *John Cowan through the Light Barrier.*          PHILIPPE GARNER

**Sources**  notes from interviews with Jill Kennington, Erica Creer, Gunilla Mitchell, Joyce Gordon, Sydney Smith, Elizabeth Cowan, Philippe Garner archive, London • John Cowan archives, including negatives, contacts, daybooks, newspaper and magazine cuttings, manuscript and typescript material, Philippe Garner archive, London • P. Garner, *John Cowan through the light barrier* (1999)
**Archives**  Philippe Garner archive, London, documents [copies] • priv. coll., archive
**Likenesses**  A. Ballard, double portrait, photograph, 1960–69, NPG [*see illus.*] • J. Cowan, self-portraits, photographs, repro. in Garner, *John Cowan*, 21, 139, 155, 156–7 • photographs, repro. in Garner, *John Cowan*

**Cowan, Minna Galbraith** (1878–1951), social worker and educational administrator, was born at Belmont, Paisley, on 1 May 1878 into an eminent Edinburgh legal family. Her parents were Hugh Cowan (1833–1898), sheriff-substitute for Renfrewshire and legal author, and his wife, Williamina Galbraith (1838–1920) of Johnstone Castle, Renfrewshire. Her grandfather was Lord Cowan (1806–1858), solicitor-general in 1851 and High Court judge. She was educated at home by governesses and then spent two years at Highfield School, Hendon, and two terms at Glasgow University. In 1897 she went to Girton College, Cambridge, where she took a second in the medieval and modern languages tripos (French and German) in 1900. As Cambridge degrees remained closed to women she took her MA from Trinity College, Dublin. She also studied in Paris. Girton's feminist ethos made its mark; she left college 'imbued with a great desire to work for women' (*Edinburgh Evening News*, 4 Nov 1935).

After Girton, Cowan moved to Edinburgh, where she shared a home in the New Town with her brother, John Cowan (1869–1935), an advocate. In 1912 she undertook a study tour of India which resulted in *The Education of the Women of India*. This included vivid descriptive writing but depended primarily on a formidable grasp of the complexities of the education system in India drawn from government reports and information sought from officials. Its sense of social and spiritual complexity, she acknowledged, drew on long conversations with missionaries and Indian friends. The education of women in the East was a fashionable cause in the British women's movement and was of particular concern to women teachers and women missionaries. Cowan's book was an expression of the imperial feminism of the period, an approach to the 'white woman's burden' that saw empire-building as a Christian task but that also contributed significantly to Indian girls' and women's education and emancipation. She uncritically accepted colonial rule and a Western feminist view of progress, yet wanted to see solutions 'on Indian and womanly lines' (*The Education of the Women of India*, 222). She described her philosophy as 'constructive Christianity' but was also influenced by Sister Nivedita (Margaret Noble, the Irish disciple of Dwami Vivekananda and supporter of Indian nationalism), and she admired Pandita Ramabai's educational work with widows. She hoped that Indian women might enjoy college life as 'that joyous springtime of youth, friendship and unfettered delight of study and leisure which have hitherto been withheld from them' (ibid., 222)—an indication of what her university education had meant to her.

Cowan founded the Girls' Auxiliary (later Girls' Association) of the Church of Scotland, and her first public role was to act as its first president. If she was inspired by an ideal of work in India, her view of education as the root of all progress was enacted at home. In 1914 she was elected to the Edinburgh school board, joining a number of prominent women activists. During the early part of the First World War she was busy with school reorganization and child welfare. She was a principal in the WRNS for the latter part of the war. When the Edinburgh education authority took over the role of the board in 1919 she was first convener of the statutory local advisory council of the education authority, as a representative of women's societies. In 1920 she was one of the first eleven students to take the diploma in social science at the Edinburgh School of Social Study and Training, which opened that year under the auspices of Edinburgh University.

In 1921 Cowan was elected to the Edinburgh education authority; she served on the higher education committee, which managed all aspects of the city's nine secondary schools (the equivalent of English grammar schools) and had a role in teacher training. In 1923 she became its convener. She was also an active member of the continuation classes, juvenile employment, and after-care committee of the Edinburgh education authority. She undertook a lecture tour of the USA in 1924 for the Institute of International Education, lecturing on Scottish education and society. The period was one of rapid development and increasing spending on education in Edinburgh. The authority had considerable responsibilities for child welfare and health, areas of particular interest to her. She contributed the chapter on education in *A Social Survey of the City of Edinburgh* (1926), edited by Marjorie Rackstraw. Among her initiatives were making free school meals available in the holidays and establishing the first play-centres for primary-age children to keep them off the streets in winter. She argued that class sizes should be cut to fifty (this was achieved in 1928). She also made several attempts to limit the hours for which school children were permitted to be employed; her campaign was supported by three organizations in which she was actively involved, the Edinburgh Women Citizens' Association, the National Council of Women (NCW), and the Edinburgh Juvenile Organisations Committee. A restriction was incorporated into the Children and Young Persons (Scotland) Act 1932. Cowan had considerable expertise in

the legal aspects of child welfare and wrote an authoritative commentary on the act of 1932, which, she said, 'marks a great advance in the social conscience of the country regarding its children' (Children and Young Persons (Scotland) Act 1932, 5). When the education authority's powers were passed to the city council in 1930 she became a co-opted member of the education committee for three years, but her role was much diminished.

Minna Cowan told the *Edinburgh Evening News* (4 November 1935) that her party-political involvement grew from her 'social work for women', in which she found that 'women's influence was necessary to change the laws to obtain justice for them and for children'. She was one of four Conservative women who published the booklet *Political Idealism* in 1924. Her essay on foreign policy is interesting for emphasizing the internationalism that resulted from new communication technologies (telegraph, telephone, and wireless) and because it argued for a 'machinery of International Relationship' through the League of Nations by contrast with Labour's vision of 'a World State' (*Political Idealism*, 12). She was on the executive of the East of Scotland Unionist Association and stood unsuccessfully as Unionist candidate for Paisley in 1929 and, again unsuccessfully, as National Government candidate for Edinburgh East in 1935. She was active in the local and national women's movement, primarily through the NCW. She chaired its Edinburgh branch, was a member of its national education subcommittee, and was national president from 1946 to 1947 and afterwards international vice-president.

Cowan worked for the Ministry of Food from 1939 to 1943 as assistant divisional officer for rationing for southeast Scotland, and took a leading part in developing the British restaurants. In 1944 she wrote *Our Scottish Towns: Evacuation and the Social Future*. In 1946 she was an observer at the organization conference of the United Nations. After the war she made frequent visits to Germany, arguing strongly for genuine social reconstruction and against the 'glaring' differentials in the standard of living of conquered and conquerors that she observed in 1947. As NCW president she established links with the post-war German women's movement, seeing women's participation in public life as crucial to its democratic future. In 1948 she was a British delegate at the conference of the congress of Europe at The Hague. She also campaigned for refugees and for the rehabilitation of Greek villages; she attended an Athens conference on the issue shortly before her death in an Edinburgh nursing home on 8 July 1951.

Like many educated middle-class women of the period, Minna Cowan created a career in public life that was semi-professional, mixing elected office and committee appointments in the growing fields of educational administration and social work and writing on education and law. In 1935 she was recognized as 'one of Edinburgh's foremost women in public life' (*Edinburgh Evening News*, 4 Nov 1935). She was appointed OBE. An appreciation after her death spoke of her zeal and single-minded purpose, her vigour, sociability, and personal kindness. She was not readily discouraged and showed 'unflagging enthusiasm in causes that were often difficult to initiate and … to sustain' (*The Scotsman*, 10 July 1951). A memorial fund organized by the NCW was spent on furnishing the president's room in its new London headquarters and on sponsoring three refugees to come to Edinburgh. SUE INNES

**Sources** K. T. Butler and H. I. McMorran, eds., *Girton College register, 1869–1946* (1948) · *The Scotsman* (10 July 1951) · *Edinburgh Evening News* (10 July 1951) · *Evening Dispatch* [Edinburgh] (10 July 1951) · *Edinburgh Evening News* (4 Nov 1935) · *The Scotsman* (20 Sept 1951) · minutes of the Edinburgh education authority, 1919–1930; minutes of the Edinburgh corporation education committee, 1930–1934, Edinburgh City Archives · Faculty of Advocates, Edinburgh · *The lady's who's who: who's who for British women … 1938–9* (1939) · K. Jayawardena, *The white woman's other burden: Western women and south Asia during British colonial rule* (1995) · A. Seldon and S. Bell, eds., *Conservative century: the conservative party since 1906* (1994) · CCI (1951)
**Likenesses** photograph, repro. in *The Scotsman* (10 July 1951) · photograph, repro. in *Edinburgh Evening News* (10 July 1951) · photograph, repro. in *Evening Dispatch* [Edinburgh]
**Wealth at death** £28,674 3s. 8d.: confirmation, 10 Aug 1951, CCI

**Cowan, Sir Robert** (*d.* 1737), administrator in India, was the son of Alderman John Cowan (*d.* 1733) of Londonderry and his first wife, Elizabeth. John Cowan's family originated in Stirling, settling in Northern Ireland in the early seventeenth century. Robert Cowan's early activities are little known, but it is clear that he was involved in matters commercial. Some time around 1707 he set up as a merchant in Lisbon, becoming a partner in the firm Cowan and Lort, which went bankrupt because, according to Cowan, Lort made some poor decisions at a time when Cowan was visiting England. For the rest of his life Cowan tried to find a reasonable composition whereby he could repay at least some of his portion of the firm's debts. He left £10,000 in his will to be divided equally among the 'lawful creditors'.

In 1719 Cowan secured the East India Company's permission to go to Bombay as a freemerchant. The ship, *Cassandra*, carrying him to India was taken by George Taylor's pirates off Madagascar (7 August 1720). Cowan assisted Captain James Macrae to negotiate the freedom of the survivors and to get them to Bombay in the ex-pirate vessel *Fancy*. Macrae used his influence to gain Cowan the patronage of Charles Boone, the governor of Bombay, which saw Cowan immediately established in the Bombay community in a far more advantageous condition than he would have enjoyed as a freemerchant.

Cowan's knowledge of the Portuguese language and culture were of immediate value to the Bombay establishment, which sent him to Goa (25 December 1720). He was charged with negotiating a new and more co-operative relationship between the Portuguese and the British settlements along the west coast of India, both in matters of trade and communications, and in combined operations against the pirate Khanoji Angria. In August 1721 Cowan and the Portuguese viceroy reached agreement on the various points at issue. As a result, Cowan was appointed to the Bombay council.

In 1722 Cowan was sent to Surat to investigate affairs at the British factory. His role in sorting out a number of problems was commended by the company's management. However, it also laid the basis for the dislike of Cowan by the personnel who were disciplined, an antagonism which continued throughout his stay in Bombay.

Between 7 January 1724 and 16 August 1726 Cowan was the chief of the British settlement at Mocha, on the Red Sea, where he tried to reorganize the company's coffee trade. At the same time he managed a significant expansion of trade between Mocha and the west coast of India. His efforts resulted in his promotion to second in council at Bombay (January 1726). On 14 January 1728 he was nominated as president and governor of Bombay, a position he assumed when William Phipps departed (10 January 1729).

Cowan's government was characterized by a significant expansion and maintenance of British political influence and trade in western India and the Red Sea–Persian Gulf area. He concentrated much effort on improving the security of British activities, removing the threat of European and Indian piracy, and he consolidated the British position against other Europeans.

In September 1734 Cowan's term as president and governor ended, and although he was willing to stay on, at least until he could realize all his current investments in the country trade, the company appointed John Horne to take over immediately. Along with the usual envy of Cowan's evident success as a merchant, and the customary factional conflicts between resident Britons and between their patrons in London, Cowan's situation was exacerbated by clear evidence that he had, on occasion, gone beyond what was acceptable practice in the distinction between employees acting on the company's behalf and trading privately. These occasions, while defensible in terms of special circumstances in any given year throughout the trading networks, gave his detractors enough substance to be credible, and he was recalled.

In 1735 Cowan returned to England with hopes of enjoying a 'competency' thought to have been around £100,000. On 31 January 1736 he was created a knight bachelor and received his accolade at Whitehall. The following year he was elected to parliament, as a whig, for Tregony borough (9 February 1737). His success was short-lived; he died, unmarried, a few days later (21 February 1737), in London, of complications caused by quinsy.

Robert Cowan's will, probated in Bombay (7 December 1737), left most of his estate to his younger brother William (who died in India around the end of 1736), and after him to his younger half-sister Mary (1713–1788), who also inherited her father's and her brother William's small estates. Mary Cowan married (Dublin, 30 June 1737) her cousin Alexander Stewart (1700–1781). Their son Robert Stewart (1739–1821) became the first marquess of Londonderry. I. B. WATSON

**Sources** PRO NIre., Robert Cowan MSS, D 654/B1/1 · PRO NIre., D 1613/3 · H. M. Hyde, *The rise of Castlereagh* (1933) · H. M. Hyde, *The Londonderrys: a family portrait* (1979) · H. Furber, *Bombay presidency in the mid-eighteenth century* (1965) · A. Das Gupta, *Indian merchants and the decline of Surat, c. 1700–1750* (1979) · HoP, *Commons, 1715–54*
**Archives** PRO NIre., letter-books, corresp., and business papers, D/654/B1/1

**Wealth at death** approx. £100,000: PRO NIre., Stone MSS, D/1613/3

**Cowan, Sir Robert** (1932–1993), businessman and public servant, was born on 27 July 1932 at Inverleith, Edinburgh, the youngest child and only son of John McQueen Cowan (1892–1960) and his wife, Adeline May, *née* Organe (*d.* 1981). His father, a distinguished botanist on the staff of the Royal Botanic Garden, subsequently became curator of the National Trust for Scotland's famous garden at Inverewe in Wester Ross. His mother, also a keen botanist, described this remarkable garden in her book *Inverewe: a Garden in the North-West Highlands* (1964). Cowan was educated at Edinburgh Academy and Edinburgh University, where he graduated in economics. In 1959 he married Margaret Morton, *née* Dewar (*b.* 1933), also an Edinburgh graduate and a Scot from Ayrshire. They were to have two daughters. The marriage was to be a great source of strength throughout his career, especially in the highlands, where Margaret supported his work and became involved herself in a range of public activities.

After national service as a flying officer in the Royal Air Force, Cowan (known to his friends as Bob) worked for Fisons and for Wolsey before joining PA management consultants in 1965. He was with PA for seventeen years, first in Birmingham and later, from 1976, as head of the company's operation in Hong Kong. The experience he gained there of a wide range of industrial problems, and particularly the interest he developed in marketing, was to stand him in good stead for the rest of his career.

In 1982 Cowan was appointed by the secretary of state for Scotland, George Younger, chairman of the Highlands and Islands Development Board (HIDB), the public body charged with the improvement of economic and social conditions in the vast, sparsely populated area comprising nearly half of Scotland's land mass and stretching from the Mull of Kintyre to the northern tip of Shetland. The post was executive and full-time; Cowan was the board's fifth chairman and, as it was to turn out, also its last, the HIDB being reformed into Highlands and Islands Enterprise, of which he became the first non-executive chairman in his last year. He was the only chairman of the HIDB to serve two five-year terms and, surprisingly, the first to come to the job from a career in business.

Cowan's was a post with daunting requirements. It involved a major public role, and a strong commitment to the highlands and islands was essential. It required vision, ability to lead and manage a substantial organization, the confidence to back one's judgement in taking the risks that are essential to success, and a prudent concern for the use of public funds. But there were also special factors, and Cowan had the willingness to fight hard for the interests of the area in dealings with government, the private sector, and other organizations; and the ability to relate to the ordinary people of the area, whatever their background or occupation.

Cowan took over the job at a difficult time. The recession of the early 1980s had hit the highlands hard, already causing the closure of the pulp mill at Fort William and the large aluminium smelter at Invergordon. It did not help him that, after his years in England and abroad, he was not known in the area. (For a time, he was known disparagingly as Bob Kow Wan.) However, it was not long before the people of the highlands warmed to his genial personality, the depth of his experience, his genuine concern, and his commitment.

By its nature the bulk of the board's work was on small projects and it is therefore difficult to highlight those that were special achievements. But Cowan was associated particularly with the impetus he gave to marketing in the area; the developments in salmon farming and in skiing, especially at Aonach Mor near Fort William; the modernization of telecommunications, which put the highlands ahead of other rural areas, greatly to the benefit of local business; and his tireless campaign for the University of the Highlands and Islands, a project which, alas, he did not live to see come to fruition. His final task was to oversee the upheaval involved in the transition from the HIDB to the new and much more devolved structure of Highlands and Islands Enterprise, a change imposed by government and not one he would have chosen. That it was achieved successfully owed much to his leadership, his diplomacy, and the care he took to make the reorganization as smooth as possible.

Cowan's genial personality, his strong sense of humour, and his natural authority combined with a refreshing informality, were immense assets to him in the post. He received a knighthood in 1989; and he was given honorary degrees by Aberdeen University, of which he was a member of court, and the University of Stirling. He was a member of the board of the Scottish Development Agency, of the Post Office Board for Scotland, and of the BBC Broadcasting Council for Scotland. He led the successful appeal to provide a scanner for Raigmore Hospital, Inverness, which proved a bitter irony when his last years were clouded by a long struggle against cancer. In this, too, he earned widespread respect for his courage and determination to carry on to the end. Indeed one of his best speeches was given to an international conference shortly before he retired, when the effects of his illness could no longer be disguised. He died at Raigmore Hospital, Inverness, on 7 January 1993, and was cremated five days later. He was survived by his wife and two daughters.

GAVIN MCCRONE

**Sources** personal knowledge (2004) · private information (2004) [Lady Cowan] · *The Times* (19 Jan 1993) · *The Independent* (19 Jan 1993) · *WWW* · Burke, *Peerage*
**Likenesses** photograph, repro. in *The Times* · photograph, repro. in *The Independent*
**Wealth at death** £41,149.24: confirmation, 6 April 1993, NA Scot., SC/CO 658/93

**Cowan, Samuel Tertius** (1905–1976), bacteriologist, was born Samuel Cowan at 87 Monton Road, Eccles, Lancashire, on 24 September 1905, the only child of Samuel Cowan (1875–1941), a Manchester optician, and his wife, Emily Woods (1879–1964). The third in direct line to bear the name Samuel, Cowan's middle name, Tertius, was added in 1926. His early life was spent near Lytham St Anne's, and he was educated mainly at nearby Buxton College. After studying at a Manchester crammer, in 1924 he went to Manchester University to study medicine, qualifying MB ChB in 1930 and MRCS LRCP in 1931. Later he obtained an MD (1933) and DSc (1953) from Manchester and fellowship of the Royal Society of Pathologists (1963).

In 1931, Cowan became house physician to F. E. Tylecote, professor of systematic medicine at Manchester Royal Infirmary, but he had probably already found an interest in pathology because within the year he became assistant resident medical officer and resident clinical pathologist there. In 1932 he was awarded a Dickinson memorial research scholarship in the bacteriology department at the university, and it was during this period of research that his enthusiasm was fired for the first time. Following the expiration of his scholarship Cowan spent a few months in medical practice but soon realized that his real interest lay in medical bacteriology. He returned to Manchester University, obtaining the diploma in bacteriology in 1934; he was then appointed research assistant in bacteriology at the university. A year later he moved to Hammersmith to the British Postgraduate Medical School.

In 1936 Cowan's research abilities led to his appointment as junior Freedom research fellow at the London Hospital. In the same year, on 20 June, he married Nancy Lingard Heathcott (b. 1909/10) of Chapel-en-le-Frith, Derbyshire. They had three children, a boy and two girls. A strong family man he enjoyed a very happy marriage and family life. At the outbreak of the Second World War he was lecturer in bacteriology at Manchester, a position to which he returned after five years of military service. During the war he served in the Royal Army Medical Corps rising to the rank of major.

In 1947 Cowan was appointed curator of the National Collection of Type Cultures (NCTC) then housed at the Lister Institute at Elstree to where it had been hastily removed at the outbreak of war. Space was limited and the collection was in some disarray. In 1949, when the collection was moved to the Central Public Health Laboratory at Colindale, Cowan embarked on a major programme of reorganization and rationalization that was to make NCTC one of the foremost collections of human and animal pathogenic bacteria in the world. At the same time Cowan played a major advisory role in the development of a rational policy for other British culture collections and, with others, he co-ordinated the system of Commonwealth culture collections which formed a collaborative body in the post-war years; a precursor in many ways of the World Federation of Culture Collections. In addition to the curatorship of NCTC, a position he held until his retirement, Cowan also served as director of the Public Health Laboratory (1961–1964) and deputy director of the Public Health Laboratory Service (1964–7). In those latter roles he displayed, in the words of Sir James Howie, 'qualities of loyalty, perception and diplomacy which made him a wise and acceptable administrator' (*BMJ*, 9 Oct 1976, 888).

In addition to his scientific work in diagnostic and systematic bacteriology Cowan had a deep interest in the philosophy of science. He was a prolific writer with the ability to express his information and ideas clearly and logically and often, unusual in scientific literature, with humour. He had an international reputation for his book, with K. J. Steel, *Manual for the Identification of Medical Bacteria* (1965, 1974) and he wrote a unique volume, *A Dictionary of Microbial Taxonomic Usage* (1968). These works summarized many of his contributions to the philosophy of bacterial systematics—contributions that ensured him a place in the history of bacterial taxonomy.

A man of slender build and kindly demeanour with twinkling eyes, Cowan was an excellent lecturer and teacher. He was unfailingly helpful to those who sought his advice. His qualities of courtesy, diplomacy, and open mindedness together with his strict scientific standards made him a highly respected member of national and international organizations. Somewhat deaf, Cowan made good use of his hearing aid when discussions became repetitive or sterile. He held a number of offices in the Society for General Microbiology and was made an honorary member in 1971. With others he was involved in the preparation of the first international bacteriological code of nomenclature, approved at the Congress of Microbiology in 1947. He served in several capacities on the international committee on bacteriological nomenclature (now the international committee on systematic bacteriology) and was elected life member in 1966. A trustee and member of the editorial board of Bergey's Manual Trust he played a key role in the production of the eighth edition of the standard international compilation, *Bergey's Manual of Determinative Bacteriology* (1974). His last contribution to bacteriology was an objective account of the problems involved in such an international venture which was read by the president of the Society for General Microbiology in January 1977.

In 1967 Cowan retired to the quiet country village of Queen Camel, near Yeovil, Somerset, but he remained active in bacteriological affairs in a much valued advisory capacity and by his writing. A railway enthusiast since boyhood, his last appointment was as curator of the Somerset and Dorset Railway Museum. He died suddenly of a heart attack in Hereford General Hospital on 24 September 1976 while on a visit with his wife to the town. He was cremated on 1 October 1976 and his ashes were scattered in the garden of his beloved Peacock Cottage in Queen Camel.                                    DOROTHY JONES

**Sources** P. H. A. Sneath, *Journal of General Microbiology*, 103 (1977), 1–7 · R. E. Gordon, 'S. T. Cowan', *American Society for Microbiology News*, 43 (1977), 226–7 · *BMJ* (9 Oct 1976), 888 · *BMJ* (23 Oct 1976), 1021 · Society for General Microbiology, Reading, archives, Cowan MSS · private information (2004) · personal knowledge (2004) · b. cert. · m. cert. · d. cert.

**Archives** Society for General Microbiology, Reading, archives
**Likenesses** photograph, 1976, Society for General Microbiology, Reading, archives; repro. in Sneath, 'Samuel Tertius Cowan, 1905–1976', 3
**Wealth at death** £33,758: probate, 4 Nov 1976, *CGPLA Eng. & Wales*

**Cowan, Sir Walter Henry**, baronet (1871–1956), naval officer, was born on 11 June 1871 at Crickhowell, Brecknockshire, the eldest son of Walter Frederick James Cowan who settled after retirement from the Royal Welch Fusiliers with the rank of major at Alveston, Warwickshire. His mother was Frances Anne, daughter of Henry John Lucas, physician, of Crickhowell. Although he had never been to school, Cowan passed into the navy in 1884, in the same term as David Beatty, with whom, two years later, he joined the *Alexandra*, flagship in the Mediterranean of the duke of Edinburgh. Invalided after less than a year, he returned home, but eventually rejoined the *Alexandra*. She came home in 1889, and Cowan was appointed to the *Volage* in the training squadron where he was promoted sub-lieutenant in 1890. Appointed to the *Boadicea*, flagship on the East India station, he took passage in the *Plassy*, a gunboat which was being delivered to the Royal Indian Marine. The *Plassy* took four months to reach Bombay, being nearly lost in a Bay of Biscay storm. Promoted lieutenant in 1892, Cowan was appointed first lieutenant of the gunboat *Redbreast* whence, after about a year, he was invalided again, this time with dysentery. On recovery, he applied for the west coast of Africa, then a very unhealthy station but with the attraction for Cowan that it offered a better chance of active service in one or other of the many punitive expeditions.

Cowan was appointed in 1894 to the small cruiser *Barrosa*, in which he was to serve for three and a half years. He assisted in refloating the French gunboat *Ardent* which had grounded 170 miles up the Niger River and soon afterwards was landed with the punitive expedition against Nimbi. After three months at the Cape the *Barrosa* was due for a turn of duty on the east coast where Cowan at once came in for the Mwele expedition, followed by a number of smaller expeditions from individual ships. The *Barrosa*'s next visit to the west coast was just in time for the Benin expedition of 1897 in which Cowan had control of the carriers. For the third time he was awarded the general Africa medal, this time with the Benin clasp.

Cowan's next appointment was to the *Boxer*, destroyer in the Mediterranean, which he commanded for a bare six months before being transferred to Nile service, in which he commanded the river gunboat *Sultan*. In her he took part in the battle of Omdurman (1898), after which all the gunboats were ordered to Fashoda, where a French force under Marchand had arrived via central Africa. The task of dealing with the French devolved almost completely upon Cowan who had the satisfaction of seeing them depart for home via Abyssinia. Cowan was left in command of all the gunboats, all the other naval officers returning to England. He had over a year more in Egypt and was aide-de-camp to Sir Reginald Wingate in the pursuit of the Khalifa in 1899.

When Lord Kitchener left for South Africa, Cowan gained his permission to accompany him. His status was afterwards regularized by his appointment as Kitchener's aide-de-camp and the whole of 1900 was spent in the field. He returned to England with Lord Roberts, to whose staff

Sir Walter Henry Cowan, baronet (1871–1956), by Walter Stoneman, 1919

he had just transferred, to be greeted coldly at the Admiralty for having gone to South Africa without their lordships' permission and for having been over two years away from sea service. Yet he was appointed to the *Prince George* as first lieutenant and, in June 1901, promoted commander at the age of thirty, with only eight and a half years' service as lieutenant. Cowan married in that year Catherine Eleanor Millicent (*d.* 1934), daughter of Digby Cayley, of Brompton by Sawdon, Yorkshire; they had one daughter.

Cowan was next appointed to command the *Falcon*, destroyer, as second in command of the Devonport destroyers under Roger Keyes. He had several different ships in the next two years, at the end of which, having built up a great reputation as a destroyer officer, he moved up to succeed Keyes in command, transferring in 1905, at the end of his time, to the scout *Skirmisher*, in which he was promoted captain (1906). He was then appointed to the *Sapphire* (1907) and in 1908 took command of the destroyers attached to the Channel Fleet. Then, after a year in the Reserve Fleet, he took command of a new light cruiser, the *Gloucester* (1910), for two years, taking no leave at all in the first so that he might have plenty in the second—for hunting, always a passion with him. He got plenty of it in his next job, two years as chief of staff to John De Robeck, the admiral of patrols, who was just as keen.

When war broke out in 1914 Cowan was in command of the *Zealandia*, but he was not happy in a slow ship. In less than six months, however, he went to the *Princess Royal* as flag captain to Osmond Brock, an appointment after his own heart, for the battle cruisers were certain to be in the forefront of any action. Yet he had to wait for almost eighteen months before it came. In the battle of Jutland (31 May 1916), the *Princess Royal* was severely damaged and had over a hundred casualties. It took some two months to repair her, during which Cowan paid a visit to the British front in France. In June 1917 he was made commodore of the 1st light cruiser squadron. His ships were constantly at sea and Cowan with them, to his great delight, for if one were damaged and out of action he could always shift his flag to another. On one occasion they went right into the Heligoland bight in the attempt to join action with a German light cruiser squadron, chasing it to within sight of Heligoland. In 1918 he was promoted rear-admiral and remained in his command, but there was little more activity for the remainder of the war.

In January 1919 Cowan and his squadron were sent to the Baltic, where the situation was extraordinarily involved. His task, as soon appeared, was to hold the ring for Finland and the Baltic states against the Bolsheviks, while keeping the Germans, still armed, to the terms of the armistice. In this he was ably assisted on shore by Stephen Tallents. His command lasted until the end of 1919 and he left only when the Russians were sealed up in Kronstadt by ice. Six months later he returned for the plebiscite in Danzig and then relinquished his command.

In 1921 Cowan was appointed to command the battle-cruiser squadron, consisting only of the *Hood* and *Repulse*. The highlight of the period was a visit to Brazil in 1922 during the international exhibition, where they created a great impression, for the battle cruisers had never been smarter or more efficient. Two years' unemployment followed, in the course of which he was promoted vice-admiral (1923), and after which he held the Scottish command (1925–6). Before this was over he accepted with alacrity the America and West Indies command (1926–8). It was a peacetime cruise, with his flag first in the *Calcutta*, then in the *Despatch*, but it concluded with a characteristic success, the salving of the *Dauntless* which had grounded in the entrance to Halifax harbour. Cowan was promoted admiral in 1927, appointed first and principal naval aide-de-camp to the king in 1930, and retired from the active list in 1931.

Cowan then became assistant secretary to the Warwickshire hounds; but on the outbreak of war in 1939 it was more than he could bear not to be involved. Eventually he was allowed to serve in the rank of commander and was appointed to the commandos under his old friend and chief, Roger Keyes. In due course he found himself in Egypt and served with the commandos in their various activities in north Africa. Finally, when his unit was disbanded, he attached himself to the 18th King Edward VII's Own cavalry, an Indian regiment. He served with them in all their operations in the western desert until he was taken prisoner on 27 May 1942 at Bir Hakeim, fighting an Italian tank crew single-handed, armed only with a revolver. He was repatriated in 1943 and, reappointed to the commandos, headed for Italy, where he took part in many operations against the Dalmatian Islands. For these

services in 1944 he was awarded a bar to the DSO which he had won in 1898. By this time he was seventy-three and beginning to feel the strain. He returned to England, where an inspection of a Royal Marine commando about to go overseas was his last service. In 1945 he reverted to the retired list. One more distinction, a very welcome one, was his: on 22 November 1946 he was appointed honorary colonel, the 18th King Edward VII's Own cavalry, whom he visited in India in 1947. He retired once more to Kineton, and died in Warneford Hospital, Leamington Spa, on 14 February 1956. In spite of his unequalled record of active service he had never even been wounded. He was appointed MVO in 1904, CB in 1916, KCB in 1919, and created a baronet in 1921. H. G. THURSFIELD, *rev.*

**Sources** *The Times* (15 Feb 1956) · L. Dawson, *Sound of the guns* (1949) · private information (1971) · personal knowledge (1971) · *WWW* · *CGPLA Eng. & Wales* (1956)

**Archives** NMM, corresp. and papers | BL, corresp. with Viscount Cunningham, Add. MS 52562

**Likenesses** W. Stoneman, photograph, 1919, NPG [*see illus.*] · L. Campbell Taylor, oils, 1920, IWM · A. S. Cope, group portrait, oils, 1921 (*Naval officers of World War I, 1914–18*), NPG · W. Stoneman, photograph, 1931, NPG · R. Moynihan, oils, IWM

**Wealth at death** £33,604 13*s*. 5*d*.: probate, 1 June 1956, *CGPLA Eng. & Wales*

**Cowans, Sir John Steven** (1862–1921), army officer, was born on 11 March 1862, at Woodbank, St Cuthbert Without, Carlisle, the eldest son of John Cowans and his wife, Jeannie (*née* Steven). His father was a prominent civil engineer, who founded Cowans, Sheldon & Co., cranemakers, at Carlisle, before retiring to a mansion and parkland, Hartland, at Cranford, Middlesex. John, who was known to his family and friends as Jack, was sent to Dr Burney's academy at Gosport, to prepare for the entrance examination for the navy. In 1878 he failed and went instead to the Royal Military College, Sandhurst, where he passed out near the top of the list in 1880 and joined the rifle brigade. This was one of the most socially prestigious infantry regiments, and he joined it in the same year as Henry Wilson and Charles à Court Repington, the latter a lifelong friend who, as a journalist in the First World War, staunchly defended Cowans's career and reputation. In 1881 Cowans became an aide-de-camp to Sir John Ross, who commanded the Poona division of the Bombay army. On 14 February 1884 Cowans married Eva Mary (*b.* 1858/9), daughter of John Edward Coulson, vicar of Long Preston, Yorkshire. They had no children. Cowans passed the Staff College course with distinction in 1890.

**Early staff career** Shortly afterwards Cowans made an impact as an industrious staff captain at the newly created mobilization section, where the development of improved procedures for the dispatch of forces overseas remained at an elementary stage in the aftermath of the Khartoum fiasco of 1886. Despite earnestly volunteering for active service Cowans arrived in India shortly after the conclusion of the Burma campaign in 1890 and too soon for action on the north-west frontier in 1897. In 1898 he became deputy assistant quartermaster-general and supervised transport for the expedition to Egypt; he was promoted major in 1898 and lieutenant-colonel in 1900.

He remained on staff duties in London throughout the Second South African War and, afterwards, having been gazetted colonel in 1903, he reviewed the mobilization plans of the 2nd division at Aldershot. In 1906 he returned to India as director of military education, a post he held until 1907 and in which he investigated the professional education of the officer corps at Lord Kitchener's behest. He served in India as director of staff duties (1907–8) and commanded the Bengal presidency brigade (1908–10). In 1910 Cowans returned to the War Office in London as director-general of the Territorial Force, and his commitment to the strengthening of the reservists, in numbers and equipment, reinforced the important role which they were expected to play if a continental commitment became necessary. In 1912 his crucial role in the mobilization plans for the British expeditionary force was confirmed by his appointment as quartermaster-general. In this post he was the supreme administrator of the supply services of the army, including accommodation, food, horses, clothing, and equipment, with responsibility for liaising with the Admiralty for their transport to the operational theatre. On the outbreak of war in 1914 Cowans was, by virtue of this appointment, the third military member of the army council. Lord Kitchener, who recognized his growing reputation for administrative ability, forbade him to go to France, but Cowans's route to high office clearly offended some military commentators. He was created KCB in 1913.

**First World War** In August 1914 it soon became clear that the quartermaster-general's branch would have to enlarge its functions dramatically to cope with the supply implications of mass industrialized war. Cowans managed the expansion of his department's work through a mixture of judicious personal intervention, excellent appointments which facilitated substantial delegation, patience in the face of the unprecedented task, and, in the early years, the maximizing of voluntary patriotic activity. Billeting provides an example of the scale of Cowans's problems and a measure of his success. The pre-war capacity of barrack accommodation was 175,000 men, yet by January 1915, 1,185,000 men had enlisted. In harsh, wintry conditions, large hutted camps were rapidly constructed to billet the recruits, although much depended on local raisers of manpower, who funded and employed labour, to construct the camps. This decentralized process was not the answer to the provision of divisional training centres in 1915, and the delays which ensued were more problematic than Cowans suggested in his post-war report on the supply services. The arrival of Dominion and, later, American troops, the growth of the technical arms of the army, and the expected evacuation of many services from France in March 1918 ensured that the availability of military accommodation in the United Kingdom (which was serving 1,750,000 men and women in 1918) remained a problem that never went away.

The pre-war horse census that Cowans had conducted ensured their rapid mobilization in 1914. He was also alert to the relatively novel value of motor lorries for carrying food, ammunition, and stores; they were eventually co-ordinated by the establishment of the Mechanical Transport Board in 1917. In semi-official correspondence with Edith, marchioness of Londonderry, founder of the Women's Legion, he accepted the employment of uniformed women for military-related work, and was more sympathetic to the practice of releasing men for front-line service by employing women to fill their former positions than were most general officers. He appointed quartermaster inspectors to control waste and promote salvage in 1915, and had a high regard for the work of voluntary organizations, such as the YMCA, which provided rest and recreation facilities for the forces both in Britain and on the fighting fronts. Cowans was instrumental in making valuable resources available to the YMCA, and its director, Arthur Yapp, referred to him in thankful terms as a 'genial autocrat' (Chapman-Huston and Rutter, 250).

Unlike some military administrators who operated in tightly focused departments and thought in 'pennyworths', Cowans understood that civil and military responsibilities, if well defined, were complementary in conditions of total war, and he had the capacity of 'going large' (Chapman-Huston and Rutter, 310) to ensure the availability of sufficient quantities of materials, whether entrenching tools or frost-bite ointment. The efficiency of the army postal service, the army veterinary corps, and army clothing department all bore testimony to his willingness to use civilian improvisers, albeit in roles subordinate to the military chain of command. But for all his willingness to maintain a wider perspective and to employ outside experts, Cowans was not a modernizer. His department's vulnerability to political interference stemmed from his adherence to the social presuppositions of the old regular army, and, in November 1916, threatened to bring about his downfall. Under new statutory provisions a court of enquiry admonished his 'departure from official propriety' (*Reports*, 4.327, 16 Nov 1916). When Mrs Cornwallis-West (better known as the actress Mrs Patrick Campbell) pursued a grievance against a young subaltern, which resulted in his peremptory transfer and unfair treatment, Cowans lent her his support, agreeing to 'fight for her if he had time' (ibid.). His intervention conveyed the impression that upholding the interests of the privileged social élite remained paramount at the unreconstructed War Office. Furthermore, in a separate case, Mrs Cornwallis-West corresponded with Cowans to recommend for promotion an infantry colonel of her acquaintance, at the same time criticizing another officer, and the court of inquiry found that Cowans had intervened in an issue far beyond his department's jurisdiction. Apart from the question of 'petticoat influence' at the War Office, Lloyd George, then secretary of state for war, reflected unfavourably on the adverse effects of this interference for 'the man at the bottom' (Taylor, 125), and the king's intervention merely increased Lloyd George's resolve to remove Cowans from the War Office. He owed the retention of his office to the political crisis of December 1916. Prime minister Lloyd George decided that continuity of office was more important than a demonstration of his power over the generals by a round of dismissals. The government's displeasure with Cowans was stated in the House of Commons on 22 December 1916, but its impact was limited by Lloyd George's knowledge that significant improvements had taken place in the administration of supply services for the Mesopotamian campaign, which came under Cowans's direction after July 1916.

Unsurprisingly Cowans regarded Asquith's resignation as the greatest blow to the British war effort after the death of Kitchener. Cowans was a warm admirer of Asquith, and, unlike many of his colleagues at the War Office, in March 1914 had been intent on 'damage limitation' during the Curragh mutiny (Beckett, 23). In return Asquith had respected the soldier's quest for autonomy in strategic and supply policy formulation. After 1916 the necessity for more collaborative inter-allied schemes to conserve scarce manpower and resources worried Cowans. Along with the adjutant-general, General Sir Nevil Macready, he resisted the plans for a common pool of manpower and material resources on the western front in 1918 and opposed the principle of unity of stores as a corollary of unity of command. Throughout the war the quartermaster's branch (or Q) remained a lively intersection of civil–military relations. For example, the survey and expansion of military railways in all theatres of war that in 1917 came under the supervision of businessman Sir Eric Geddes provided a constant reminder that the Q side of the War Office would be 'civilianized'. Cowans's old friend and ally, Charles Repington, vociferously opposed such a scheme in the *Morning Post* in September 1918.

**Reputation** Remarkably, therefore, Cowans was the only military member of the army council to remain in place throughout the war. He was a successful administrator within a hierarchical decision-making process with well-defined functions. He worked hard and late into the night, but not to the exclusion of social lunches and dinners. He depended on six hours' sleep a night, but left London every weekend for country house parties or to play golf. He demonstrated unostentatious efficiency and much adaptability in an army which desperately needed such unfashionable skills. Although Cowans and Lloyd George were personally incompatible, in his *War Memoirs* (1938) Lloyd George commended Cowans as 'the most capable soldier thrown up by the War in our Army' (Lloyd George, 1.493), excluding him from his otherwise comprehensive condemnation of 'brass hats' in London and on the western front. Many tributes included in Chapman-Huston and Rutter's two-volume hagiography (1924) noted Cowans's good humour, hearty laugh, and lurid storytelling. Asquith and George V agreed that if victory was attributable to any individuals, it was to Cowans and Sir Maurice Hankey (Roskill, 1.631), but few subsequent studies of Britain's war effort have troubled to acknowledge or assess the significance of this pre-eminent military administrator.

**Retirement and death** Cowans finally reached the rank of general in 1919, and received the GCB. He abruptly left the War Office in March 1919 to accept an invitation from

Shell Transport and Trading Company to visit Mesopotamia and survey its progress in oil exploration prior to joining the company. He looked forward to inaugurating a business career which would bring new challenges and increased remuneration. Moreover, leaving the army gave him the freedom to express his disgust at the absence of any reference to the work of the administrative services of the army in parliament's expression of thanks to the armed forces in July 1919. His letter of protest to Lloyd George was followed by a speech accepting the freedom of his home city, Carlisle, on 18 September 1919, in which he informed his audience that the war was essentially a contest of administration, rather than strategy, and asserted that the Q department had succeeded in meeting all demands placed upon it.

In 1920 Cowans's health declined quickly. He had an operation for a kidney condition in November 1920, but died on 16 April 1921 at the Villa Louise, Garavan, Menton, in the south of France, where he had gone to convalesce. He had been received into the Roman Catholic church five days earlier. He lay in state in Westminster Cathedral, and his funeral procession, in which many battalions of infantry took part, on 25 April, followed the long route of 5 miles to Kensal Green cemetery. The sombre spectacle reflected the endeavour to come to terms with a new type of military leader, the great departmental chief who had little experience of the battlefield. Cowans had been extravagant in many ways, and debt consumed his estate. To the king's chagrin his widow declined a pension, and to his consternation Cowans's orders and decorations were put up for sale shortly after his death. They were bought privately by his service friends and were subsequently placed in the United Services Museum. Cowans survived the blandishments of Mrs Cornwallis-West with his reputation intact and accusations of jobbery unproven, but four years after his death 'his name was dragged into one of the most lurid court cases of the post-war period' (Grigg, 369). In the early stages of the *Dennistoun v. Dennistoun* (1925) case mention was made of 'General X' as the lover of Mrs Dorothy Dennistoun in the years 1916–1920. During this alimony case she revealed, in the witness box, that he was Cowans, which caused a sensation.

KEITH GRIEVES

**Sources** D. Chapman-Huston and O. Rutter, *General Sir John Cowans GCB GCMG: the quartermaster general of the Great War*, 2 vols. (1924) · C. À Court Repington, *The First World War*, 2 vols. (1920) · *The rasp of war: the letters of H. A. Gwynne to the Countess Bathurst, 1914–1918*, ed. K. Wilson (1988) · *The Times* (18 April 1921) · *Parliamentary debates, House of Commons, 1916*, vol. 88; 22 Dec 1916; cols. 1825–1827 [Official Report. fifth ser.; oral answer, Mr Macpherson] · *Reports of the courts of enquiry, Parl. papers* (1917–18), 4.327, Cd 8435 · minutes of meetings of the military members of the army council, 1912–18, PRO, WO 163X · Bodl. Oxf., MSS Asquith · N. Macready, *Annals of an active life*, 2 vols. [1924] · D. Lloyd George, *War memoirs*, new edn, 2 vols. (1938) · C. Falls, *War books: an annotated bibliography of books about the Great War* (1930) [repr. 1989] · F. Stevenson, *Lloyd George: a diary*, ed. A. J. P. Taylor (1971) · S. W. Roskill, *Hankey, man of secrets*, 1 (1970) · 'Extracts', *General Routine Orders: Quartermaster-General's Branch*, 2 (1918) · *DNB* · B. Bond, *The Victorian army and the Staff College, 1854–1914* (1972) · I. F. W. Beckett and K. Simpson, eds., *A nation in arms: a social study of the British army in the First World War* (1985) ·

I. F. W. Beckett, ed., *The army and the Curragh incident, 1914* (1986) • C. À Court Repington, *The Times* (5 Jan 1917) • b. cert. • m. cert. • *CGPLA Eng. & Wales* (1921) • J. Grigg, *Lloyd George: from peace to war, 1912–1916* (1985); pbk edn (1997) • *Lady Cynthia Asquith: diaries, 1915–1918* (1968); repr. (1987)
**Archives** IWM, letters, etc. | Bodl. Oxf., letters to Herbert Asquith • HLRO, Lloyd George MSS • IWM, corresp. with Sir Henry Wilson • NRA Scotland, priv. coll., corresp. with Sir John Ewart • PRO, minutes of meetings of military members of the army council, WO 163X • PRO, quartermaster-general's MSS, WO 107 • PRO NIre., seventh marchioness of Londonderry MSS, letters to Lady Londonderry | FILM BFI NFTVA, documentary footage • BFI NFTVA, news footage • IWM FVA, news footage
**Likenesses** F. Dodd, charcoal and watercolour drawing, 1917, IWM • W. Orpen, portrait, exh. RA 1917 • J. S. Sargent, group portrait, oils, 1922 (*General officers of World War I*), NPG
**Wealth at death** £8822 10*s*. 11*d*.: probate, 22 June 1921, *CGPLA Eng. & Wales*

**Coward, Sir Cecil Allen** (1845–1938), lawyer, was born on 27 December 1845 at 11 Minerva Terrace, Islington, London, the second child and only son of John William Smith Coward (1815–1888), surgeon, and his first wife, Anna Eliza, *née* Bemfield (*d*. 1847). John Coward was born in Canada where his father was serving with the British army and qualified as an apothecary in 1838, the year before he married. Three years after the death of his first wife John Coward married again.

In 1856 the Coward family—John and his second wife, Jane (*née* MacFarlane), Cecil and his sister Emily, and the three young daughters born to John and Jane since they married in 1850—left England for New Zealand. There, after a brief and unsuccessful foray into sheep farming, John Coward established himself as a medical practitioner in Christchurch. He later also became Christchurch's coroner and medical officer to the lunatic asylum, the gaol, and the police. Cecil, who was eleven years old when the family emigrated, was educated at Mrs Alabaster's school in Christchurch where he was coached by her husband, the Revd Charles Alabaster, a noted Latinist. Coward was then articled to his brother-in-law, W. H. Wynn-Williams, another emigrant from Britain who had recently established himself in practice in Christchurch.

In 1865 Cecil Coward left Christchurch for England and when he arrived in London he entered the Inner Temple to read for the bar. It was then customary for would-be barristers to spend some time in a solicitor's office to gain experience and accordingly Coward went to the City firm of Thomas and Hollams (better known in the twentieth century as Coward, Chance & Co. and, since 1987, Clifford Chance), whose offices were then in Mincing Lane. The work and the prospects there, it seems, attracted Coward more than the bar and although he was called in 1867, he applied immediately to be disbarred and took articles with Griffith Thomas, senior partner of Thomas and Hollams. In 1870 Coward was admitted a solicitor and in 1873 he became a partner in the firm.

In 1874 Coward married Catherine Thomas, then aged twenty-six, the younger daughter of his former principal who had been the firm's senior partner from 1862 to 1873 and who was now a director of the Central Bank, a long-

established client of the firm. Between 1875 and 1881 five children—four daughters and a son, Cecil Robert—were born to Cecil and Catherine Coward. The family lived in Kensington, where Coward's income from the firm's very profitable practice enabled them to enjoy a comfortable way of life: according to the census returns in 1881 they employed five servants.

The firm, which now became Hollams, Son, and Coward, had been established in the City in 1802 and had built up a large mercantile, shipping, banking, insurance, and corporate practice. John Hollams was its senior partner from 1873 until 1910 and both his own and the firm's name stood high in the profession and in the City. The firm's clients included the Midland Bank, the Commercial Union insurance company, and the Imperial Bank of Persia (later the British Bank of the Middle East). Coward's own work for banking and corporate clients as well as distinguished individuals such as James Bryce (1838–1922) soon brought him a reputation for professional ability and integrity, enhancing that of the firm. Coward was appointed to Lord Macnaughten's judicature committee in 1906, to the royal commission on delays in the King's Bench Division in 1913, and to the royal commission on the civil service in 1915.

In 1910 Coward succeeded Sir John Hollams as senior partner of the firm. Dignified and autocratic, Coward was, as senior partners usually then were, aloof and remote from the staff. A hard worker himself, he would tolerate 'neither laziness, shiftiness, nor incompetence in others' (*The Times*) and he was a stickler for punctuality. He was not without a sense of humour, however, and those who got to know him found him just and kind. It was Coward as senior partner who decided to offer a partnership to Crompton Llewelyn Davies, in whom were combined great intellectual brilliance and anarchic tendencies. Davies, a Cambridge Apostle and friend of Bertrand Russell, had been articled with the firm and in 1912 had been appointed solicitor to the Post Office. However, in 1920 when his support for his wife's involvement with Sinn Féin in Ireland and their friendship with Michael Collins were revealed, Davies was dismissed by the Post Office.

Over 6 foot tall, Coward had a fine physique. A keen sportsman all his life, he regularly rode to hounds. He was also a keen golfer and a member of Woking Golf Club. A contemporary recalled that when the train arrived at Woking Station, all that could be seen of Coward, moving at great speed onto the course, was his 'coat of indefinably horsy cut with voluminous tails … flying down the fairway to the first hole' (Darwin, 82–3).

Like Sir John Hollams, Coward was active in the Law Society, becoming a member of its council in 1910 and serving as president in 1927–8. In 1928 he was knighted, as was then customary for those holding the office. He was also a member of the Justinians, a legal dining club, and of the Reform Club. In 1928, at the age of eighty-two, Coward retired from the firm and from professional life. His son, Robert, who was then aged fifty and a bachelor still very much under his father's thumb, had been a partner in the firm since 1910 and retired at the same time. Cecil Coward died at his home, 10 Melbury Road, Kensington, London, on 27 July 1938, at the age of ninety-two.          JUDY SLINN

**Sources** *The Times* (29 July 1938) · J. Slinn, *Clifford Chance: its origins and development* (1993) · B. Darwin, *Green memories* (1928) · b. cert. · d. cert.
**Likenesses** photograph, repro. in Slinn, *Clifford Chance*
**Wealth at death** £172,783 9s. 11d.: resworn probate, 31 Aug 1938, *CGPLA Eng. & Wales*

**Coward, Sir Henry** (1849–1944), chorus master, was born at Liverpool on 26 November 1849, the only son of Henry Coward, a Sheffield-born cutler who became an innkeeper and black-face minstrel, and his wife, Harriet Carr, who was also a singer. A hard youth as a cutler's apprentice in Sheffield was followed from 1870 by seventeen years of schoolteaching, of which sixteen were spent as headmaster of various elementary schools, a considerable achievement given that he was self-educated and at the age of twenty-one could hardly write or spell. Coward developed an interest in music after joining a tonic sol-fa class; in 1876 he founded the Sheffield Tonic Sol-fa Association, later named the Sheffield Musical Union, and directed it for nearly sixty years (1876–1933).

In 1887 Coward left teaching and devoted himself to music. He obtained at Oxford the degrees of BMus in 1889 and DMus in 1894. From 1896 to 1908 he was chorus master of the Sheffield music festival, which quickly achieved worldwide fame by setting up and maintaining a new standard of choral excellence. In 1906 and 1910 he took a Yorkshire chorus to Germany. In 1908 he was training and conducting choral societies in Sheffield, Leeds, Huddersfield, Newcastle, and Glasgow. In that year he and his singers toured Canada and in 1911 they made a round-the-world tour of the empire. These years were the zenith of Coward's career, and he was much requested as an adjudicator at various music festivals and as teacher, lecturer, and examiner. He was a music master at the Sheffield Training College and lecturer in music at Sheffield University. In later years his effects were criticized as mere tricks, and unfortunately the scope of his musicianship was always limited by his inability to handle an orchestra. A valuable exposition of his methods is given in his *Choral Technique and Interpretation* (1914) and its supplement 'CTI', the Secret (1938).

Coward was somewhat formidable at a first encounter, but those who came to know him learned to admire his humanity and integrity. He was knighted in 1926, and was made an honorary freeman of the city of Sheffield and of the Cutlers' Company of Hallamshire. In 1933 he received the honorary degree of DMus from the University of Sheffield. He was a lifelong advocate of the tonic sol-fa system of sight-singing and was president of the Tonic Sol-fa College in London (1929–43).

Coward was married three times: first, in 1875, to Mary Eliza, daughter of Charles Best, a silversmith of Sheffield; secondly, in 1894, abroad, to Louisa Hannah Best, the sister of his first wife, who had died; and thirdly, after the death of his second wife, in 1911, to Semima Alice, the daughter of Simeon Dewsnap, a cabinet-case manufacturer of Sheffield. There were four sons and four daughters of the first marriage. Coward died, a wealthy man, at his home, 6 Kenwood Road, Sheffield, at the age of ninety-four, on 10 June 1944.          F. H. SHERA, *rev.* JAMES J. NOTT

**Sources** J. A. Rodgers, *Dr. Henry Coward: the pioneer chorus master* (1911) · H. Coward, *Reminiscences* (1919) · *MT*, 85 (1944), 217–8 · Grove, *Dict. mus.* · Brown & Stratton, *Brit. mus.* · private information (1959) · personal knowledge (1959)
**Archives** BL, autograph MS of Bethany, Add. MS 50766 · Sheff. Arch., reminiscences
**Likenesses** photographs, *c.*1870–*c.*1910, repro. in Rodgers, *Dr. Henry Coward* · J. Moore, portrait, Tonic Sol-fa College, London
**Wealth at death** £12,367 10s. 7d.: probate, 28 Sept 1944, *CGPLA Eng. & Wales*

**Coward, James** (1824–1880), organist, born in London on 25 January 1824, was admitted at an early age into the Westminster Abbey choir. Solos were frequently entrusted to him both in the abbey and in concerts, and on more than one occasion he sang with the celebrated soprano Maria Malibran. His first appointment as organist was at Lambeth parish church. On the opening of the Crystal Palace at Sydenham in 1857 he became the first organist there, filling the situation with credit until his death. Coward was organist to the Sacred Harmonic Society throughout this period, and established the connection between the Crystal Palace organists and the Handel festival.

Coward was conductor of the Abbey and City glee clubs, and from 1864 until 1872 was conductor of the Western Madrigal Society. In addition, he was organist to St George's Church, Bloomsbury (1866–9), and to the grand lodge of the freemasons. His last church appointment was to St Magnus the Martyr, London Bridge, which he held until his death. He died suddenly on 22 January 1880 at his home, 38 Lupus Street, Pimlico, and was survived by his wife, Janet Margaret Coward. His funeral, with music by the Westminster Abbey and Chapel Royal choirs, was held at St Saviour's, Pimlico, and he was buried at the West London cemetery, Brompton, on 28 January.

Coward's compositions were characterized by considerable musical knowledge and artistic refinement. He won as many as thirteen prizes for his glees between 1845 and 1867, and published two collections, *Ten Glees* (1857) and *Ten Glees and a Madrigal* (1871). Other notable compositions included the anthem 'O Lord, correct me', the canon 'Sing unto God' (4 in 2), and the partsong 'Take thy banner'. He was best known for his transcriptions for the organ of operatic melodies, marches, and other pieces. Coward had remarkable powers of improvisation, which critics regretted were frequently required for the accompaniment of acrobatic displays and similar exhibitions at the Crystal Palace.

J. A. F. MAITLAND, *rev.* NILANJANA BANERJI

**Sources** *The Norwood News: Crystal Palace Chronicle* (31 Jan 1880) · *Musical Standard* (14 Feb 1880) · J. A. F. Maitland, 'Coward, James', Grove, *Dict. mus.* (1904–10) · D. Baptie, *A handbook of musical biography* (1883) · Brown & Stratton, *Brit. mus.* · M. Musgrave, *The musical life of the Crystal Palace* (1995)

**Wealth at death** under £600: probate, 23 Feb 1880, *CGPLA Eng. & Wales*

**Coward, Sir Noël Peirce** (1899–1973), playwright and composer, was born at Helmsdale, 5 Waldegrave Road, Teddington, Middlesex, on 16 December 1899, the second in the family of three sons (the eldest of whom died at the age of six) of Arthur Sabin Coward (1856–1937), a clerk, and his wife, Violet Agnes (1863–1954), daughter of Henry Gordon Veitch, captain and surveyor in the Royal Navy.

**Childhood and upbringing, 1899–1910** Coward's antecedence directly affected both his upbringing and his expectations. On his father's side his grandfather James Coward was an organist, chorister, and composer who performed at the Crystal Palace; on his mother's there was a genealogical connection to border gentry (her grandfather Henry Veitch was consul-general to Madeira, and Field Marshal Earl Haig was a distant cousin) and even a vague link to royalty (her sister married Henry Bulteel, nephew of Sir Henry Ponsonby, private secretary to Queen Victoria). It is clear that Violet Coward saw in her son's emerging talent an opportunity to regain the lost social status of her own family.

Both parents were musical, and Violet was interested in the theatre, taking her son—all the more precious because his elder brother, Russell, had died in 1898—to his first pantomime, *Aladdin*, in Kingston at Christmas 1903. Throughout his childhood Coward's family—increasingly penurious after Arthur Coward lost his job as a piano salesman during the First World War—moved through London's transpontine suburbs, circling ever closer to the city where Coward would make his name; from Teddington via Sutton, Battersea, and Clapham, eventually to Ebury Street where Violet Coward acquired a boarding-house on the fringes of Belgravia.

Throughout these moves Coward experienced a distinct lack of formal education, marking his first visit to school in Sutton by biting the teacher's arm, 'an action which I have never for an instant regretted' (Coward, *Present Indicative*, 7). The erratic nature of his schooling stemmed mostly from his, and his mother's, pursuit of a stage career, prompted by an early discernment of theatrical and musical talent. In 1908–09 Coward attended the Chapel Royal School in Clapham, but was not accepted by the choir itself, preferring the lessons at Janet Thomas's Dancing Academy in Hanover Square.

**Early stage appearances and writing, 1911–1921** In 1911 Coward made his first professional appearance on stage, as Prince Mussel in *The Goldfish*, an Edwardian fairy transformation piece directed by Miss Lila Field. The experience led to an audition for *The Great Name* later that year, given to Charles Hawtrey, the great actor–manager whom Coward hero-worshipped. Coward's one-line performance led to Hawtrey's production of *Where the Rainbow Ends*, a children's classic to rival *Peter Pan*, staged at the Savoy over the winter of 1911–12. The play also introduced Coward to Esmé Wynne, who became his confidante and co-writer; together they wrote adolescent playlets, two of

Sir Noël Peirce Coward (1899–1973), by Dorothy Wilding, 1930

which—*Woman and Whisky* and *Ida collaborates*—were produced as 'curtain-raisers' under their joint sobriquet, Esnomel, in 1917.

In the meantime Italia Conti engaged Coward to appear in Gerhardt Hauptmann's *Hannele* at the Liverpool Repertory Theatre in 1913—the occasion for his meeting another important feminine influence and later interpreter of his work, the actress Gertrude Lawrence. After a brief stint that summer as a boy pilot in *War in the Air*—which ended with him crashing his aeroplane—Coward achieved the ambition of all child actors, appearing as Slightly in *Peter Pan* for two years running.

Coward was a precocious adolescent who seemed sure of what he wanted in life. At the age of fourteen he had already entered into what was probably his first serious sexual relationship with another man, the bohemian artist Philip Streatfeild, a stylistic pupil of Henry Scott Tuke who took the boy on a painting holiday to Cornwall in the summer of 1914. During the war itself Coward became an unofficial mascot to Streatfeild's regiment, the Sherwood Foresters.

For Coward war did not, as yet, severely limit his ambitions. In 1916 he toured England in *Charley's Aunt* with Esmé Wynne, and managed to avoid conscription (there is reason to suppose that he did so purposefully at medical boards) until the spring of 1918, when he was finally called up. His reaction to the army was psychosomatic, it seems: he suffered a breakdown, manifested in severe and debilitating headaches, and spent time in the First London General Hospital at Camberwell in a ward full of shell-shock victims.

Discharged on medical grounds, Coward returned gratefully to his theatre life and an accumulating series of appearances on the West End stage. *The Saving Grace* in 1917, 'the real start of my name being known' (Castle, 4), having been rudely interrupted, he appeared in no less than three productions during 1919: the musical *Oh! Joy*; the drama *Scandal*; and *The Knight of the Burning Pestle* 'by Messrs Beaumont and Fletcher, two of the dullest Elizabethan writers ever known' (Castle, 38).

Although Philip Streatfeild died in 1917 from tuberculosis (from which Coward had also suffered, in a minor form), his legacy to Coward was an introduction to high society in the portly shape of Mrs Astley Cooper, eccentric hostess of Hambleton Hall, Rutland. Here Coward not only read Saki for the first time—another literary influence—but he experienced country-house life in a manner which later informed his dramatic work, especially *Hay Fever* (written, 1924; performed, 1925), with its comedy of appalling manners and ignored house guests, inspired by the bohemian Hambleton household.

Through Mrs Astley Cooper's influence, Coward travelled to the Mediterranean, and met Gladys Calthrop, who later became his stage designer; but it was Coward's first trip to New York in 1921 that provided the crucial impetus to national, and international, success. Coward returned to inject the staid drawing-room dramas of the London West End with the speed of Broadway, in the process inventing his own style—a style already hinted at in the pre-New York *I'll Leave it to You* (1920), suggested by Hawtrey and produced by him in Manchester and London.

**The twenties: *The Young Idea* to *Bitter Sweet*, 1922–1929**  Coward's first real dramatic success, *The Young Idea* (tour, 1922; Savoy Theatre, 1923), showed the influence both of Broadway and of Shaw in a comic drama which, with its two teenage protagonists, epitomized the new youth culture of the 1920s. The *Evening Standard* reported of the first night:

> When some bright remark in the classic way of English comedy was made, somebody behind me said ecstatically 'Another Noelism'. After somebody else on stage had worn a jazz kind of scarf, a party of people in a box whose horn spectacles set off their youth, hung quantities of the same material over the ledge.   (*Evening Standard*, 2 Feb 1923)

By the time the sensational *The Vortex* appeared in 1924, Coward was already a star in the making, and London was ready to be shocked.

*The Vortex* did just that, with its tale of an older woman taking a younger lover, and her son taking cocaine (commentators have since seen the drug as a mask for homosexuality). Coward went along with the convenient myth of his overnight success in the play which quickly transferred from Hampstead to the West End (see his memoir *Present Indicative*); yet this was as much a construction as the idea that *The Vortex* was the first English production to deal with drug abuse (the story of Billie Carleton, the chorus girl who died apparently from a cocaine overdose in 1918 and whose fate inspired Coward's play, had sparked off at least three drug-themed productions in 1919).

Coward may have already invented himself, but it was the fact that *The Vortex* cited the post-war neuroses as exemplified by 'decadent' Mayfair society; that its creator played the role of Nicky Lancaster in a dressing-gown; and that its characters called each other 'darling' in a flippant manner which established the play and its author as a central text for 1920s popular culture. Quite self-consciously, Coward used the image of a languid decadent—he appeared on the front page of *The Sketch* 'in bed wearing a Chinese dressing gown and an expression of advanced degeneracy' (Hoare, 139)—to promote himself and his work simultaneously, all the while subverting such notions with an ironic wink. 'I am never out of opium dens, cocaine dens, and other evil places', he told the *Evening Standard* and a public which wanted to believe him. 'My mind is a mass of corruption' (Lahr, 2).

Words were Coward's ammunition, and they rattled off his tongue like bullets from a Gatling gun, enunciated in the inimitable tone which he made his own, and yet which was the product of an early attempt to overcome both his mother's deafness and his own susceptibility to lisp. His physical stance was equally forthright. Never dressed less than elegantly, his slim, tallish figure was cut perfectly to his age, and his name became synonymous with the aspirational sophistication of a new meritocracy. In his style summary of the decade, *The Glass of Fashion*, Cecil Beaton observed that:

> All sorts of men suddenly wanted to look like Noel Coward— sleek and satiny, clipped and well groomed, with a cigarette, a telephone, or a cocktail at hand … Coward's influence spread even to the outposts of Rickmansworth and Poona. Hearty naval commanders to jolly colonels acquired the 'camp' manners of calling everything from Joan of Arc to Merlin 'lots of fun', and the adjective 'terribly' peppered every sentence.   (p. 153)

Coward's irresistible rise to the serious stage was mirrored in his musical theatre career. He had already ventured into revue with the highly successful *London Calling!* (written in 1923 and sponsored by the avowedly dilettante figure of Lord Lathom), with its memorable 'Hernia Whittlebot' satire on the Sitwells' *Façade*, produced by André Charlot in 1924; he followed it with *This Year of Grace* in 1928, and with the more serious-minded *Words and Music* in 1932. These all-singing, all-dancing spectaculars, dressed in high fashion by artists such as Gladys Calthrop, Oliver Messel, and Doris Zinkeisen, showcased such hit songs as the jazz-influenced patter of 'Dance Little Lady' and 'Poor little rich girl'; the sentimental sweetness of 'A Room with a View'; and the perennial party-piece of 'Mad Dogs and Englishmen' which became Coward's most instantly recognizable contribution to twentieth-century culture—after his image itself.

The revue form perfectly suited Coward's polymath talents, combining his dramatic and musical abilities in comedy, satire, and romance. With the Cochran-produced romantic musical *Bitter Sweet* (1929) he astutely subverted expectation by abandoning jazz age freneticism for the waltzes of his parents' generation. Some critics were sceptical: for W. J. Turner of the *Evening Standard* it 'finally smashed' his 'hopes of Mr Coward, for a more inane and witless composition never left the pen of a distinguished author' (*Evening Standard*, 19 July 1929). 'It would be too bad', wrote Coward, 'if I were encouraged to believe that there was anything remarkable in writing, composing and producing a complete operetta' (Coward, *Present Indicative*, 353). Yet James Agate defended the piece as a 'thundering good job' (*Sunday Times*, 21 July 1929) and—perhaps most importantly—the public embraced it, and its wistfully resonant hit, 'I'll See you Again'. 'People are tired of speedier and speedier shows', Coward told an American reporter when the show opened on Broadway and stopped the traffic on Sixth Avenue. 'After all, a chorus girl can only wave her arms and legs about so much' (*Boston Transcript*, 29 Oct 1929).

Coward's own talents were certainly ambidextrous. His theatrical profile was sustained throughout the 1920s by *Hay Fever* (1925), *Fallen Angels* (1925), and *Easy Virtue* (1926)—plays which, with their apparently flippant approach to questions of morality, broadened Coward's appeal while seeming dangerously near the edge of what was allowable on the public stage. That was the delicious frisson that his public came to love.

Coward also turned his attentions to the United States, with productions of *The Vortex*, *Hay Fever*, and *Easy Virtue* (1925–6) confirming his arrival on Broadway as 'a violent and glittering success' (Coward, *Present Indicative*, 264). America also consolidated his relationship with John (Jack) C. Wilson (1899–1961), a Yale-educated stockbroker-cum-producer whom he had met in London in May 1925, and who had now become his manager and lover. The relationship lasted for more than a decade, eventually soured, not by Wilson's marriage to Princess Natasha Paley in 1937, but by his developing alcoholism and mismanagement of Coward's funds.

By the late 1920s Coward had achieved international recognition. His own plays were the vehicles for this fame, as were his select appearances in those of other dramatists, such as Margaret Kennedy's *The Constant Nymph* (1926) and S. N. Berman's *The Second Man* (1928)—the spectacular failures of his own *Home Chat* and *Sirocco* (both 1927) were left to appearances by his more handsome rival, Ivor Novello. Intimately intertwined with his public profile was his burgeoning social ascendancy; successful connections with aristocracy and royalty seemed at times to cast him as a court entertainer. Yet his manifest dissatisfactions with the restrictions of British life lent him the transgressive air of a modern artist, although in his case it was more a sense of personal affront and creative frustration than of radical zeal.

Shortly after the run of *The Vortex*, Coward had spent a night in police custody having been found 'throwing flower-boxes about in the streets of the West End'; he had then declared to a friend that 'England's played out' and that he intended to make his future life in America (Hoare, 149). Part of his dissatisfaction came from the censorship of his plays by the lord chamberlain, a running battle which culminated in 1926 when *This was a Man* had its licence withheld. 'Every character in this play, presumably ladies and gentlemen, leads an adulterous life and

glories in doing so', thundered Sir Douglas Dawson of the lord chamberlain's advisory board. 'I find no serious "purpose" in the play, unless it be misrepresentation. At a time like this what better propaganda could the Soviet instigate and finance?' (Hoare, 165–6). Coward had the ear of the middle classes: when he appeared to voice subversive dissent, the consequences were that much more feared. The play was never performed in Britain.

**The thirties: *Cavalcade* to *Present Laughter*, 1930–1939**  By the early thirties Coward's increasingly mature work and its critical and popular success had established him as probably the most important dramatist of his day. Such was his theatrical omnipotence—of those who took the credit for first calling him the Master (a nickname only half-ironic), his idiosyncratic secretary, Lorn Loraine, had the earliest claim—that even Bloomsbury took notice. Virginia Woolf, flattered by his attentions, professed to have fallen 'in love' with the playwright and his work, and encouraged him to write more adventurously (*Letters of Virginia Woolf*, 471). The openly gay *Semi monde* (1926) and the anti-war polemic of *Post-Mortem* (1930; neither performed in Coward's lifetime), written after his brief appearance in a Singapore production of *Journey's End*, appeared to be Coward's attempt to write up to these expectations, only to confound them with the patriotism of *Cavalcade* (1931), an innovative Drury Lane spectacular of historical set-pieces which delighted his public and enraged his former friends and critics, who publicly accused Coward of having broken faith with the common man.

'A play which makes me rage', said Ethel Mannin; 'a tawdry piece of work', wrote Sean O'Casey; 'the finest essay in betrayal since Judas Iscariot', complained Beverley Nichols (Hoare, 235–6). Coward ascribed as much seriousness to such opinions as he did to the right-wing press which lauded his blockbuster as confirmation of the coming sway of Conservative government. His opening night curtain call referenced the unironic patriotism of his lead character's line: 'In spite of the troublous times we are living in, it is still pretty exciting to be English' (Lesley, 144). It was an emotional, almost atavistic statement of faith, yet in the light of his past and future pronouncements on the English condition, even that appears equivocal.

Coward, whose Far Eastern trip also produced the classic *Private Lives* (1930), had reached a forked road in his career, in which he chose the path of popular culture and personal celebrity. The play, enormously successful on both sides of the Atlantic, saw Coward and Gertrude Lawrence define the quintessential and quotable Cowardian roles of Elyot and Amanda, a divorced couple who find that they can live neither apart nor together, and who, combined, epitomize Coward's slyly subversive persona via wry references to his own emotional dilemmas. 'I'm glad I'm normal', declares Amanda's bluff, hearty husband Victor, '… aren't you?' 'I think very few people are completely normal really, deep down in their private lives', replies Amanda (act I). Contemporary critics realized that the play was probably his best work: it prompted Arnold Bennett to call him 'the Congreve of our day' (Hoare, 520), while A. G. Macdonnell dissected the play's exposition of the Coward style: 'Mr Coward's plot is the contrast between brilliant cosmopolitanism and stodgy Anglo-Saxondom, his stand is Infidelity and his device of stage-craft is the Bicker' (ibid., 213).

*Private Lives* established Coward as one of the world's highest-earning authors, with an annual income from 1929 of £50,000. Yet money and fame did not appear to quell his worrisome soul. He bored easily—professing ennui as the reason for his announcement during *Private Lives* that he would never appear in one production for more than three months—and suffered precarious health, with a second breakdown precipitated in 1926 by the pressures of public fame and his own private life.

Coward's reaction to such pressures was to travel, often to exotic destinations. Now he sought to escape his native land, where his dramas were censored and his private life proscribed. In 1932 Coward declared defiantly that he would not subject his latest work, *Design for Living*, to the lord chamberlain's blue pencil—knowing that its trio of amoral meritocrats and a hint of cosmopolitan bisexuality would not be licensed there anyhow. It was produced in New York in 1933; in London, not until 1939.

With the onset of the more serious thirties and the drift to war, Coward sought to reposition himself. A series of inconstant love affairs (with the playwright Keith Winter and actors Louis Hayward and Alan Webb) and a sense of over-achievement—of having done it all—made him restless once more. The cycle of playlets that comprised *Tonight at 8.30* was an inspired and fruitful way of staving off boredom, while the introspection afforded by travel informed his entertaining and often revealing memoirs, *Present Indicative*, and the equally revealing autobiographical overtones of *Present Laughter* (1939), in which the successful playwright Garry Essendine complains: 'Everyone worships me, it's perfectly nauseating', to which his former wife replies 'There's hell to pay if they don't'— a not altogether inaccurate portrayal of Coward's own ego (act I). He also turned to fiction with a sequence of short stories (*To Step Aside*, 1939; *Star Quality*, 1951; and others) that reflected his own childhood, theatre, and travel experiences, and which reward re-reading as a neglected aspect of Coward's creative output; a later novel, *Pomp and Circumstance* (1960), drew on his Jamaican life in a Mitfordesque manner—Coward remarked that it was so light that his publishers would have difficulty capturing it between hard covers.

**The Second World War, 1939–1945** With the outbreak of war Coward, perhaps in an attempt to exorcise the guilt of having evaded the First World War, lobbied Churchill and others for useful employment. After an unsuccessful stint in the Paris office of the bureau of propaganda, he undertook still undefined work for the British secret service (for whom he had probably performed information-gathering duties in 1939) in the United States, talking up American support for the war while gathering intelligence. However, back in London parliamentary questions were asked as to his fitness as a representative of Britain, and a planned trip to South America was scotched, Coward alleged, by forces working against him. They were the

same forces, it was said, responsible for the 'sabotage' of his knighthood, which evidence suggests that Coward expected in 1943 (Lesley, 225). This, along with his prosecution for contravening currency regulations in 1941 (which he regarded as 'celebrity-baiting'), contributed to Coward's increasing sense of dissatisfaction with his homeland (Hoare, 330).

Paradoxically, the war both consolidated and threatened Coward's public and creative status. He produced, with David Lean, a series of defining wartime films: *In which we Serve* (1942), *This Happy Breed* (1943), *Brief Encounter* (originally 'Still Life' from the *Tonight at 8.30* sequence; 1945), and the film of his highly successful 1941 play, *Blithe Spirit*, written initially to fill a financial gap, yet one of the most satisfying (and most frequently performed) of Coward's high comedies. The 'Play Parade' nationwide tour of 1942–3, comprising *Blithe Spirit*, *This Happy Breed*, and *Present Laughter*, was a morale-raising venture which further underlined Coward's importance in the collective consciousness, a sense epitomized by perhaps his finest contribution to the Dunkirk spirit, the affecting emotion of the song 'London Pride'. The war put Coward 'on the highest wave of his career so far', wrote Beaton, then photographing the 'Play Parade' tour, '… but his hand twitches nervously for more triumphs—and the applause of the matinée audience does not satisfy him—he is waiting already for the evening audience to arrive' (Hoare, 334).

**Post-war career, 1945–1964** For a man who came to be seen as the very epitome of Englishness—who would announce, in his imperial post-war exile, 'I *am* England, and England is me'—it is telling that Coward spent much of the rest of his life abroad (*Sunday Express*, 23 May 1965). With the coming of the Labour government in 1945 and subsequent high rates of taxation, his became a self-imposed estrangement; a decision taken for political, professional, financial, and emotional reasons: after the death of his mother in 1954, Coward felt there was nothing left to keep him in the country. 'I think on the whole that I have not done badly by England and I also think that England has not done very well by me', he told the actress Joyce Carey, another of his female confidantes, in 1955 (Hoare, 418).

In the late 1940s Coward settled in Jamaica, at Ocho Rios, where he built two homes, the beachside Blue Harbour and Firefly, a hilltop retreat, and where he found contentment in writing and painting in the company of Graham Philip Payn (*b.* 1918), the young South African-born actor with whom he spent the rest of his life. But happiness in his private world seemed to demand the price of a fall in Coward's professional fortunes. He appeared to lose his sense of timing, with the disaster of *Peace in our Time* (1947) positing a Nazi-invaded Britain when the country was quickly trying to forget its recent past. It prompted the *Evening Standard*'s Beverley Baxter to write of a 'crisis for Coward', and to ask if the playwright had survived the war (Morley, 259).

The seemingly unstoppable dynamic of Coward's pre-war career had begun to falter: musicals such as *Pacific*

*1860* (1946) and *Ace of Clubs* (1950), which attempted to replicate the American successes of *Oklahoma* and *Pal Joey*, did not win approval. Sheridan Morley, who wrote the second biography of Coward, *A Talent to Amuse* (1969) (the first, Patrick Braybrooke's opportunistic *The Amazing Mr Coward*, had appeared in 1933), saw Coward's post-war career as 'one long conjuring trick' (private information).

Yet it was Coward's stalwart ability to rise above the cynics ('I can take any amount of criticism', he declared, 'so long as it is unqualified praise') and invent himself anew (UK press report, undated). He resumed an intermittent film career—which had begun in 1917 with a bit part in D. W. Griffith's *Hearts of the World* and peaked pre-war with the Brooks-Brothers-clad Lothario of *The Scoundrel* in 1935—with elegant, witty, and sometimes self-parodying cameos in films such as *Around the World in Eighty Days* (1955), *Our Man in Havana* (1960), and *The Italian Job* (1968), for which he did receive praise.

He was similarly and rightly lauded for his cabaret runs at London's Café de Paris and The Desert inn, Las Vegas (reprised on the iconic LP *Noel Coward Live in Las Vegas*, which extended the impact and reach of his post-war revival). Such performances artfully drew upon the unfaded glamour of Coward's own past and his talent for entertaining—a talent honed in high society and now delighting what he dubbed 'Nescafé society'—and represented him for the modern age. Coward's television show with Mary Martin, *Together with Music* (1955), is the only extant evidence of the seemingly effortless charisma of his extraordinary stage presence.

But the effort, with age and infirmity, was becoming harder. Further attempts to revive his career in musicals with *After the Ball* (1953) and *Sail Away* (1959–61) were less well received, and plays such as *Relative Values* (1951) and *Quadrille* (1952) were seen as old-fashioned in a period when the Bright Young People had been replaced by Angry Young Men. When his drama in a theatrical old folks' home, *Waiting in the Wings*, opened to abusive notices in 1960—T. C. Worsley of the *Financial Times* called it 'nauseating'—Coward seemed bowed at last, deeply upset by the virulence of the criticism (J. Russell, ed., *File on Coward*, 1987, 80). Retreating to Jamaica, or his newly acquired tax advantage eyrie above Lake Geneva, Coward directed his animus at the modern stage and the modern world. The collapse of the empire and its colonies distressed him—not least because he had made his home in one (a sense of post-war decadence and moral decay explored in the unpublished play 'Volcano', written in 1956). Coward thought the disintegration of the Old World no good thing, and found it difficult to come to terms with the new. In 1948 he wrote in his diary: 'Gandhi has been assassinated. In my humble opinion, a bloody good thing but far too late' (*Diaries*, 103). Yet prejudice offended him: in South Africa four years previously he had spoken out for 'Cape coloureds', an expression of his 'strong contempt for any sort of racial discrimination' (Hoare, 344). The post-war changes in theatre were equally distressing for an artist whose life was about control, and

who feared the lack of it. (Coward disliked drunkenness for that reason, and admitted to having taken recreational drugs once only, smoking a joint in New York. Having become nauseous, he summoned a doctor—who put his patient to bed and promptly finished off the rest of the cigarette.)

Coward, who believed no actor should attend a rehearsal in anything less than a lounge suit, railed against kitchen-sink drama in three lectures in the *Sunday Times* in January 1961. His attacks were precisely targeted and wittily couched in the form of one long finger-wag from the Master, but their reactionary, if well-intended, hauteur was ill received in some quarters. 'The bridge of a sinking ship, one feels, is scarcely the ideal place to deliver a lecture on the technique of keeping afloat', wrote Kenneth Tynan in the rival *Observer* (Hoare, 467). Yet John Osborne defended the playwright as 'his own creation and contribution to this century', adding: 'anyone who cannot see that should keep well away from the theatre' (Morley, 268); Kenneth Tynan compared Harold Pinter's 'elliptical patter' to Coward's stylized dialogue (Lahr, 8); and in 1964 Laurence Olivier invited Coward to direct *Hay Fever* at the National Theatre, the first living dramatist to be produced there.

**Revival and last works, 1965–1973** 'Dad's renaissance', as Coward dubbed it, peaked with his creative swansong, the triptych of short plays, *A Suite in Three Keys* (1965). In the most substantial piece, *A Song at Twilight*, an elderly writer (vaguely based on Somerset Maugham) is confronted with his own hypocritical and wounding behaviour regarding his covert homosexuality. It was a theme close to home but, to Coward's credit, a charge that could never be made against him. While sexually circumspect (having learned early from the example of Oscar Wilde, whom he called a 'silly artificial old queen') and disdaining the social overtness of modern homosexuality, Coward was personally affronted by intolerance of any kind (*Diaries*, 508). The fact that he was writing *A Song at Twilight* as the bill to decriminalize homosexual behaviour was being passed by the House of Lords made it all the more pertinent, both to himself and to his now grown-up public.

In 1969 came Coward's 'Holy Week', a series of celebrations for his seventieth birthday culminating in a 'Midnight Matinee' theatrical tribute and the long-delayed offer of a knighthood, which he accepted. On 26 March 1973 Coward died of heart failure at Firefly in Jamaica; three days later he was buried on the brow of Firefly Hill, overlooking the north coast of the island. On 28 March 1984 a memorial stone was unveiled by the queen mother in Poets' Corner, Westminster Abbey.

Morley's effective biography (1969) was necessarily limited by the fact that its subject was still alive. When Morley made tentative forays into a discussion of Coward's sexuality, it was vetoed on the grounds that it might disturb elderly ladies in the home counties who still held a torch for him. 'I can't afford to offend their prejudice', he told Morley, 'nor do I really wish to disturb them this late in their lives; if I had a very young audience, I might think differently' (Hoare, 509). In 1976 Coward's life was recalled by Cole Lesley's affectionate *The Life of Noel Coward* (*Remembered Laughter* in the USA), although the *New York Times* noted: 'Mr Lesley's massive, authorised biography takes its name from Coward's last poem, and the title is one indication of the book's shortcomings'. 'Mr Lesley is entirely too reticent about Coward's love life, and … too unrevealing about his artistic process' (Hoare, 520). Of the critical works on Coward that followed, the one which best corrected the latter was John Lahr's *Coward the Playwright* (1982), while the *Diaries* (1982), edited by Graham Payn and Sheridan Morley and covering the years 1941–61, shed some light on the former, although at the same time revealing the depths of Coward's bitterness at the uncertain trajectory of his post-war career. The present author's own *Noel Coward: a Biography*, approved but not authorized by the Noël Coward estate, appeared in 1995; 'A wholly plausible portrait', wrote Michael Billington (*Country Life*, November 1995).

Coward's work received a new appraisal in the 1990s and early 2000, partly because of its aptness for exploitation in modern gay cultural themes, and partly via radical revivals by directors such as Philip Prowse (*Cavalcade*, 1999; *Semi monde*, 2001); it was as though his remarks about a young audience—and his own sexuality—had come back to haunt him like Elvira's ghost. The 1998 three-and-a-half-hour BBC television documentary, directed by Adam Low, and an album of cover versions by Sir Elton John, Sir Paul McCartney, Marianne Faithfull, the Pet Shop Boys, and others indicated his continuing relevance, and the reason for his survival when theatre was seen to be in decline: transcending his chosen medium, Coward had become an icon of style to a new generation, just as he had been in his own youth. This sense of currency was consolidated in 1999 at the centenary of Coward's birth, with numerous revivals in London and New York, the first academic convention (at the University of Birmingham, to coincide with the announcement that archival material in possession of the Noël Coward estate—loyally administered after Coward's death by his companion Graham Payn—would be lodged with the university), and the installation of commemorative statues in London, New York, and Jamaica.

But of all the images of Coward, the life mask by Paul Harmann in the National Portrait Gallery, made during the London run of *Private Lives* in 1930, gives the most accurate sense of the man's physical presence at the height of his powers. His features are set magisterially: hair scraped back off a high forehead, a blunt nose, the tapering eyes which gave him an increasingly oriental look, and an almost non-existent, resolutely stiff upper lip. Yet deep lines already course his young face, prompting St John Ervine to note in 1937 that 'neurosis and incipient TB have helped give him that curious old look he has' (*The Observer*, 3 July 1937).

Even as a child Coward had seemed old beyond his years. A cartoon published around the time of *Cavalcade*'s enormous success depicted the infant Noël in his perambulator, making notes for his future epic. 'Whether by genetic luck or environmental good judgement, Noël Coward never suffered the imprisonment of maturity', wrote Kenneth Tynan (Hoare, 202). It is perhaps apposite to note that the deepest emotional attachment of Coward's life was to his mother. 'Forty years ago', wrote Tynan when Coward was fifty-three, 'Noël Coward was Slightly in *Peter Pan*, and you might say that he has been wholly in *Peter Pan* ever since' (Lahr, 161). Throughout a life lived in the glare of the spotlight, Coward never lost his enthusiasm for performance; his was more than just 'a talent to amuse' ('If Love were All', from *Bitter Sweet*), although entertainment was the determining factor in almost all he did. As an actor, director, composer, dramatist, and author, he was more than the sum of his parts; he existed beyond the stage and the piano as an inimitable image of his own creation. Coward's many achievements were presented as a glittering, and sometimes wilfully unserious, façade behind which the 'real' man could hide; but it was a façade backed by a steely commitment—to his public, to his art, and to himself.                    PHILIP HOARE

**Sources** MSS, priv. coll. [to be deposited at U. Birm.] · P. Hoare, *Noël Coward: a biography* (1995) · N. Coward, *Present indicative* (1937) · N. Coward, *Future indefinite* (1954) · N. Coward, *Past conditional* (1986) · C. Lesley, *The life of Noel Coward* (1976) · S. Morley, *A talent to amuse* (1969) · J. Lahr, *Coward the playwright* (1982) · *The Noël Coward diaries*, ed. G. Payn and S. Morley (1982) · R. Mander and J. Mitchenson, *Theatrical companion to Coward* (1957) · BL, lord chamberlain's MSS · V. Coward, memoir, unpubd MS, Noel Coward estate · Covent Garden, London, Theatre Museum Collection · Lincoln Center, New York, Billy Rose Theater Collection · C. Castle, *Noel* (1972) · E. Wynne Tyson, diaries and letters, priv. coll. · C. Beaton, diaries, unpubd MSS, Beaton estate · C. Beaton, *The glass of fashion* (1954) · *The letters of Virginia Woolf*, ed. N. Nicolson, 3 (1977) · M. Dean, ed., *A private life*, BBC television documentary, 1983 [Michael Dean, director] · A. Low, ed., *Arena*, Noel Coward trilogy, three films, BBC, 1998 [Adam Low, director] · b. cert. · b. certs. [father, mother] · m. cert. [parents] · d. certs. [father, mother] · private information (2004)

**Archives** NRA, corresp. and literary papers · priv. coll., MSS | BFI, corresp. with Joseph Losey · BL, corresp. with League of Dramatists, Add. MS 63370 · BL, lord chamberlain's MSS · JRL, corresp. with Basil Dean · Mander and Mitchenson Theatre Collection, London · Theatre Museum, London, collection · Theatre Museum, London, letters to Esmé Wynne |FILM BBC WAC · BFI NFTVA, *Omnibus*, BBC, 8 April 1973 · BFI NFTVA, 'Let's face the music', Yorkshire Television, 16 July 1984 · BFI NFTVA, *South Bank Show*, LWT, 1 March 1992 · BFI NFTVA, *Arena*, BBC2, 11 April 1998 · BFI NFTVA, news footage · BFI NFTVA, propaganda film footage · Mander and Mitchenson Theatre Collection, London · Museum of Moving Image, New York, *Together with music*, Mary Martin (presenter), CBS 1956 · Museum of Moving Image, New York · Noel Coward estate · NPG · NYPL for the Performing Arts, Billy Rose Theater collection · Theatre Museum, London |SOUND BL NSA, 'Noel Coward talks', P546WC1, P798WC1, P801WC1 · BL NSA, documentary recordings · BL NSA, oral history interview · BL NSA, recorded talk

**Likenesses** photographs, 1905–69, Hult. Arch. · P. Harmann, life mask, 1930, NPG · E. Kapp, chalk drawing, 1930, Barber Institute of Fine Arts, Birmingham · D. Wilding, photograph, 1930, NPG [*see illus.*] · C. Beaton, portraits, 1930–69; Sothebys · H. Coster, photographs, 1939, NPG · C. Beaton, photograph, 1942, NPG · C. Dane, bronze bust, after 1945, NPG · C. Dane, oils, *c.*1945, NPG · P. Tanqueray, photograph, 1952, NPG · G. Argent, photograph,

1968, NPG · E. Seago, oils, Garr. Club · D. Wilding, photographs, NPG

**Wealth at death** £20,000—in England and Wales: probate, 14 June 1973, *CGPLA Eng. & Wales*

**Coward, Thomas Alfred** (1867–1933), ornithologist and journalist, was born on 8 January 1867, at Higher Downs Road, Bowdon, Cheshire, the youngest of the four children of Thomas and Sarah Coward. His father, who was engaged in textile bleaching, was also a much respected Congregational minister at Rusholme Road Chapel. He was educated at a school in Sale, Cheshire, before entering the family firm of Melland and Coward, bleachers, where he worked for about nineteen years. When the firm was taken over by a larger enterprise he gave up the career of a businessman and devoted himself to natural history, supplementing his private income by writing articles for a variety of journals and newspapers. His interest in natural history had been encouraged by a neighbour, Joseph Sidebotham, a noted lepidopterist, and by his father, who had been a founder of the Manchester Natural History Society and had helped to establish its collection, later transferred to the Manchester Museum.

Coward's many writings on natural history appeared in magazines of general interest, such as *Chambers Journal*, *Nineteenth Century*, *The Field*, and *Country Life*; and in journals devoted to particular interests, such as *The Zoologist*, *Proceedings of the Zoological Society*, *British Birds*, and *Memoirs and Proceedings of the Manchester Literary and Philosophical Society*. He also wrote articles for newspapers, including the *Manchester Guardian*; later in his life he became a successful broadcaster. Coward's literary style was notably clear and his lectures had the same quality. His first book, *The Birds of Cheshire*, written in collaboration with a former schoolfellow, was published in 1900. *Vertebrate Fauna of Cheshire* came out in 1910. In 1912 he wrote *The Migration of Birds* for the Cambridge Manuals of Science and Literature (2nd edn, 1929). Best-known among his many works, however, is his *Birds of the British Isles and their Eggs*, in three volumes, which was first published in 1919. He also published works on local history, including *Picturesque Cheshire* (1903), and *Cheshire Traditions and History* (1932).

In 1904 Coward married his cousin, Mary Constance Milne; the two made frequent long journeys together in their studies of natural history. Coward was closely associated with the Manchester Museum. In 1913 he was on the museum committee, and from March 1916 to January 1919 he was acting keeper. In 1922 he was again acting keeper for a short time. Coward was long a member of the Manchester Literary and Philosophical Society, which he joined in 1906 and of which he was president in 1921–3. Coward was a gentle, friendly man, who abhorred cruelty in all its forms. He died following a heart attack on 29 January 1933 at his home, Brentwood, Grange Road, Lower Bowdon, Cheshire: his wife survived him. Two nature reserves, Cotterill Clough and Marbury reed-bed, are dedicated to his memory.                DONALD CARDWELL

**Sources** *Nature*, 131 (1933), 367 · *Nature*, 132 (1933), 437 · *North Western Naturalist* (March 1933) · W. H. Mullens and H. K. Swann, *A bibliography of British ornithology from the earliest times to the end of 1912*

(1917), 151–2 · *The Ibis*, 13th ser., 3 (1933), 355–6 · *British Birds*, 25 (1933), 300–04 · *Manchester Memoirs*, 77 (1932–3), iii · private information

**Archives** Manchester Museum · U. Oxf., Edward Grey Institute of Field Ornithology, ornithological papers and field notes · Warrington Library, list of mammals

**Likenesses** photographs, Manchester Museum; repro. in *British Birds*, 302

**Wealth at death** £10,929 3s. 11d.: probate, 14 March 1933, *CGPLA Eng. & Wales*

**Coward, William** (1647/8–1738), merchant and benefactor of the Coward Trust, was born to unknown parents. Little is known of his early life, but, after establishing himself in the City of London, on 8 May 1676 he married Mary Watson (*bap.* 1653), whose parents were dead, and moved to Jamaica. He acquired a plantation on the River Morant and was elected to the second session (1681) of the Jamaican Assembly as one of the representatives of Port Royal. On his second marriage, on 26 January 1685, to Anna Gould (*bap.* 1659, *d.* 1738), daughter of John Gould, another plantation owner, and his wife, Honoria Thompson of Clapham, Surrey, he left his Jamaican estate in the hands of factors and settled in Walthamstow, then a favourite retreat for wealthy London nonconformists. He built a large house and grounds and an Independent meeting-house facing Marsh Street.

Because of Coward's Jamaican and shipping interests, it is usually assumed that he was involved in the slave trade. Dissenting principles at the time would have been no bar, and he must be expected to have used slaves on his plantation. It appears, however, that he was involved in slaving voyages only through chartering one of his ships to the Royal African Company, and that this venture ended abruptly in litigation in 1704 after three voyages. Chartering was part of his business. At different times his ships carried supplies for the Admiralty and Lutheran refugees to New York. They were mainly engaged, however, on round trips to Jamaica, and Coward was prominent among West Indies merchants in petitioning the House of Lords on the inadequacies of the Royal Navy's convoy protection of this trade, and on the practice of press-ganging merchant crews in Caribbean ports.

Coward was an equally vigorous defender of the dissenting interest. He was probably the Coward who was a manager of the common fund of the 'Happy Union' of Congregationalists and Presbyterians from 1690 to 1691. Later, he funded three sets of public lectures in City meeting-houses designed to defend Calvinist principles against the Arminianism increasingly preached from Presbyterian pulpits. The lectures were at Little St Helen's in 1726, Paved Alley, Lime Street, in 1730, and Bury Street, St Mary Axe, in 1733. As Coward aged, and became more erratic and testy, Philip Doddridge and his correspondents feared that his favour, and his fortune, would go to the upholders of 'Bigotry' and that 'the Gentlemen that are the advocates of Moderation [would] sink in his esteem' (*Calendar*, ed. Nuttall, letters 465 and 467). Coward's open quarrel with Thomas Bradbury, whom he dismissed as one of his lecturers, boded ill for the moderate party in dissent.

In fact, Coward retained his high regard for Isaac Watts,

whom he made one of the trustees of his will, and for Philip Doddridge, even though Doddridge grievously disappointed him by declining the principalship of the academy he had proposed to establish in Walthamstow after his death. In its place, Coward's will set up a trust fund 'for the education and training up of young men … to qualify them for the ministry of the gospel among the Protestant Dissenters', thus continuing the financial support he had given to such students in his lifetime.

While the Calvinist principles in which the students were to be instructed were stated in the will, the trustees were quite unfettered in their other main duty of disbursing the residue of the trust income 'in the interest of the true religion of Christ amongst the Protestant Dissenters'. Nor did Coward seek to control the doctrinal affiliation of future trustees, and his trustees consistently declined to apply doctrinal tests on admitting students to the succession of dissenting academies they supported. The Coward academies became seats of liberal theology in the later eighteenth century, before returning in the nineteenth to conventional trinitarian teaching. The trust supported New College, London, between 1850 and 1977, and currently contributes to the ministerial training funds of the United Reformed church. The trust's charitable funds have largely been devoted to chapel building and repair, and to the welfare of ministers and their families.

Coward died at his home in Marsh Street, Walthamstow, on 28 April 1738, aged ninety, after a brief illness, and was buried in Bunhill Fields on 3 May 1738. His widow, Anna, followed him within a fortnight. She contrived in this short interval to make her own will, in which she renounced Coward's modest bequests to her and claimed the 'custom of London', that is, one half of her husband's personal estate as the widow of a freeman. In this way the trust lost about half the capital Coward had intended for it, though together with the sale of his real estate in England it received about £30,000 in the currency of the time. Coward's lands in Jamaica, his main asset, were bequeathed to another William Coward, a cousin, who was clerk to the Saddlers' Company. By a descendant of this cousin's daughter, Mary, the trustees in 1874 were given a portrait of Coward, painted when he was about fifty. It depicts a short, stout man, stiff and imperious. He is soberly but well dressed, full jowled, with sharp eyes and a stern mouth. The portrait is now at Dr Williams's Library, together with the past records of the trust and the magnificent collection of books it built up over the centuries, including many of Doddridge's own.

JOHN HANDBY THOMPSON

**Sources** J. H. Thompson, *A history of the Coward Trust: the first two hundred and fifty years, 1738–1988* (1998), 1–10 · *Calendar of the correspondence of Philip Doddridge*, ed. G. F. Nuttall, HMC, JP 26 (1979), nos. 405–07, 410, 413, 417–9, 435, 465, 467, 488, 499, 504 · H. D. Budden, *The story of Marsh Street Congregational Church, Walthamstow* (1923) · S. Hanson, A. D. Law, and W. G. S. Tonkin, *Marsh Street congregations* (1969) · T. W. Davids, *Annals of evangelical nonconformity in Essex* (1863), 624 · W. Wilson, *The history and antiquities of the dissenting churches and meeting houses in London, Westminster and Southwark*, 4 vols. (1808–14), vol. 1, pp. 212, 244, 253, 363, 484; vol. 3, p. 490 · D. Lysons, *The environs of London*, 4 (1796), 222 · A. Gordon, ed., *Freedom after ejection: a review (1690–1692) of presbyterian and congregational nonconformity in England and Wales* (1917), 243 · T. Belsham, *Memoirs of the late Reverend Theophilus Lindsey* (1812), 286 · J. Stoughton, *Philip Doddridge* (1852), 228–34 · *GM*, 1st ser., 8 (1738), 221 · will, DWL · Bunhill Fields burial register, PRO · *IGI* · marriage allegations in the registry of the vicar general of the archbishop of Canterbury, Harleian Society, 1890–92

**Archives** DWL, family MSS · DWL, Coward Trust MSS

**Likenesses** oils (aged about fifty), DWL; photographic negative, NPG · oils, New College, London

**Wealth at death** approx. £150,000, incl. £57,601 personal estate in England, and £4817 real estate in England: *GM*, 1st ser., 8

**Coward, William** (*b.* 1656/7, *d.* in or before 1725), physician and theological writer, was born at Winchester, Hampshire, the son of William Coward. His mother was the daughter of George Lamphire, an apothecary in Winchester, and sister of John *Lamphire, an eminent physician at Oxford, Camden professor of history, and principal of Hart Hall, whose property Coward apparently inherited (*Remarks*, 1.248). It is likely that Coward received his early education in his native town, at Wykeham's School. In 1674 he moved to Oxford and became a commoner of Hart Hall. The following year Coward was admitted as scholar of Wadham College, where he obtained his BA degree on 27 June 1677. In January 1680 he was chosen probationer fellow of Merton College and two years later he published a Latin version of Dryden's *Absalom and Achitophel* (1681) which was eclipsed by the contemporary and greatly superior version by Francis Atterbury. Having determined to apply himself to the practice of medicine, Coward became MA on 13 December 1683, BM on 23 June 1685, and eventually DM on 2 July 1687. After quitting Oxford he exercised his profession in Northampton, from where he moved in 1693 or 1694 'upon Acc$^t$ of some Criminal Commerce w$^{th}$ some Woman' (*Remarks*, 1.304). Coward then settled in Lombard Street, London. In 1695 he published a medical work entitled *De fermento volatili nutritio conjectura rationalis* which received an honourable approbation from the censors of the College of Physicians who soon welcomed him as a candidate of the college.

In 1702, under the pseudonym Estibius Psychalethes, Coward published a theological treatise entitled *Second Thoughts Concerning Human Soul*, criticizing the notion of the soul as a spiritual and immortal substance surviving the body after death. Relying on Overton's mortalism, Glisson's vitalism, Hobbes's materialism, and Locke's speculation on 'thinking matter', Coward assumes that the concept of the immortality of the soul is a 'heathenish invention' welcomed by the first Christian fathers and then promoted by the Roman church. He states that life and soul are the same thing, consisting in a sort of power inherent in the matter of the human body and as such destined to propagate and to die together with it. Using scriptural and rational arguments he assumes that human beings are a kind of mortal thinking matter who receive immortality from God only after the final resurrection of the dead.

Despite his fideistic assumptions and claims to scriptural orthodoxy, Coward was attacked by many writers who accused him of materialism and atheism. Between 1702 and 1703 at least seven controversialists, including John Turner, John Broughton, François Menard, and William Nichols, published polemics against Coward's *Second Thoughts*. He replied with *Farther Thoughts Concerning Human Soul* (1703) and *The Grand Essay, or, A Vindication of Reason, and Religion, Against Impostures of Philosophy* (1704); the latter was criticized even by Toland, Collins, and Locke. On 10 March 1704 a complaint was made in the House of Commons about *Second Thoughts* and *The Grand Essay*. A committee was appointed to examine both, and on 17 March 1704 Coward was called to the bar, where he pleaded that if there was 'any thing therein, against Religion, or Morality', he was 'heartily sorry' and 'ready to recant' (*JHC*, 14.373, 379–80). The house resolved that the books contained offensive doctrines and ordered them to be burnt by the common hangman. The sentence increased the notoriety of Coward's books. In the same year he published another edition of *Second Thoughts* and the medical work *Remediorum medicinalium tabula generalis*. In 1705 he devoted himself to poetry, publishing *Abramideis*, a heroic poem in Miltonic style.

In the catalogue of the fellows of the Royal College of Physicians for 1706 Coward, listed under the head of candidates, is for the first time mentioned as residing in the country. According to Hearne (1.305) he had moved somewhere in the diocese of Norwich after having left London, probably because of the judgment he had undergone. During the same year he published *Ophthalmiatria*, a medical work in which he ridicules the Cartesian notion of an immaterial soul residing in the pineal gland. From a letter of his, dated 26 May 1706 and addressed to his friend Sir Hans Sloane, it appears that Sloane corrected the proofs and suggested that Coward should alter his dangerous opinions about the soul. About 1707 Coward published *The Just Scrutiny*, joining the controversy on the mortality of the soul aroused by Dodwell's *An Epistolary Discourse* (1706).

Confuted at home by many pamphleteers and ridiculed by Swift, Coward became well known in Germany, the Netherlands, and France where some of his works were reviewed in a number of periodical journals, and his name was often mentioned in catalogues of heretics and polemical works.

Little is known about Coward's life after 1707. In those years, according to Masson (6.763), Coward married Martha, daughter of Charles Fleetwood of Northampton and widow of Milton's nephew. In 1709 Coward wrote *Licentia poetica*, a didactic poem with a political appendix added to it. From 1718 he apparently settled at Ipswich from where, in 1722, he wrote again to Sir Hans Sloane. The omission of his name, in 1725, in the list of candidates of the catalogue of the College of Physicians indicates that Coward must have been dead by that year.            DARIO PFANNER

**Sources** A. Kippis and others, eds., *Biographia Britannica, or, The lives of the most eminent persons who have flourished in Great Britain and Ireland*, 2nd edn, 4 (1789) · *DNB* · J. P. Lobies and D. Masson-Steinbart, eds., 'Coward William', *Index biobibliographicus notorum hominum* (1988) · *Remarks and collections of Thomas Hearne*, ed. C. E. Doble and others, 11 vols., OHS, 2, 7, 13, 34, 42–3, 48, 50, 65, 67, 72 (1885–1921) · *JHC*, 14 (1702–4), 373, 379–80 · Wood, *Ath. Oxon.*, new edn, 2.360, 401; 4.480 · Munk, *Roll* · *A catalogue of the fellows and other members of the Royal College of Physicians, London* (1688); (1693–5) · *A catalogue of the fellows, candidates, honorary fellows, and licentiates of the Royal College of Physicians* (1704–86) · D. Masson, *The life of John Milton*, 7 vols. (1859–94) · *GM*, 1st ser., 57 (1787), 100 · D. Berman, 'Die Debatte über die Seele', *Die Philosophie des 17. Jahrhunderts*, ed. J. P. Schobinger (Basel, 1988), 759–81 · P. Kail, 'Coward, William', *The dictionary of eighteenth-century British philosophers*, ed. J. W. Yolton, J. V. Price, and J. Stephens (1999)
**Archives** BL, letters, Sloane MSS 4040, fol. 171; 4046, fol. 281

**Cowdray.** For this title name *see* Pearson, Weetman Dickinson, first Viscount Cowdray (1856–1927); Pearson, Weetman John Churchill, third Viscount Cowdray (1910–1995).

**Cowdrey, (Michael) Colin, Baron Cowdrey of Tonbridge** (1932–2000), cricketer, was born on 24 December 1932 at Putumala, near Ootacamund in southern India, the only child of Ernest Arthur Cowdrey, a tea planter, and his wife, Kathleen Mary (Molly) Taylor. Accorded the initials M. C. C., the customary contraction of the Marylebone Cricket Club, perhaps in the hope that he might one day play the game with distinction, he duly spent a lifetime playing, administering, and promoting it with unwavering dedication and acclaimed success. 'I was born into a family whose love for cricket amounted to a passion', he wrote in his autobiography *M.C.C.: the Autobiography of a Cricketer*, and even by the time he sailed with his parents from India to Britain, for the second time, at the age of five and a half, he was seldom without a bat in his hand. His father had been a good enough cricketer to play for a European eleven against the MCC side that toured India in 1926–7.

With his parents back in India, Colin Cowdrey's talent and enthusiasm for the game were fostered during the Second World War at Homefield Preparatory School in Sutton, Surrey. The headmaster, Charles Walford, made sure Cowdrey was encouraged, even to the point of interesting the legendary England batsman J. B. Hobbs in his charge's exceptional promise. 'Dear Master Cowdrey, I shall watch your career with much interest, and I wish you the very best of health and fortune', wrote Hobbs in 1940, in a handwritten letter that Cowdrey always prized.

After going to Tonbridge School in 1945, Cowdrey had five years in the cricket eleven there, in the first of which he scored 75 and 44 and took eight wickets, bowling leg-breaks, in Tonbridge's annual fixture against Clifton, then played at Lord's. On the assumption that he would be known by the first of his Christian names, *Wisden* wrote, 'Reported to be the youngest player to appear in a match at Lord's, the 13-year-old Michael Cowdrey contributed largely to the success of his side'. Although he remained an effective bowler throughout his schooldays, that side of Cowdrey's game fell away as his batting matured. His last season at Tonbridge, 1950, came to a fitting climax with innings of 126 not out and 55 for the public schools against the combined services at Lord's and his introduction into county cricket: the first of his 402 appearances for Kent was against Derbyshire in August of that year.

(Michael) Colin Cowdrey, Baron Cowdrey of Tonbridge (1932–2000), by Mark Pepper, 1987

Awarded a Heath Harrison exhibition, the 'gamesplayers' scholarship', to Brasenose College, Oxford, Cowdrey took it up in October 1951, and read geography between winning blues for rackets as well as cricket. He added another 100 to his Lord's collection, this one against Cambridge in the university match of 1953, but his selection to go to Australia and New Zealand with the MCC side of 1954–5, while still up at Oxford, was as surprising as it proved inspired. Len Hutton, who captained the MCC side, was sufficiently sceptical to lobby successfully for an extra batsman to be added to the party.

But in only his third first-class match of the tour Cowdrey scored a century in each innings against New South Wales, sharing a partnership of 163 with his delighted captain during the first of them, and no innings in the test series had more to do with England retaining the Ashes than his 102 out of a total of 191 on the first day of the third test match in Melbourne a week after his twenty-second birthday. It was the first and arguably the best of his twenty-two test hundreds, with none of the inhibitions that, with time, crept into his game. Nothing summed up better or more succinctly the impact made by that Melbourne innings than the four-word cable it prompted from Sir Pelham Warner, one of the game's father figures: it read, simply, 'Cowdrey. Melbourne. Magnificent. Warner'.

The Australian tour over, Cowdrey decided not to go back to Oxford to take his degree. Instead, he did a spell of national service in the RAF, cut short when he was discovered to have some hereditary weakness to do with his toes, a turn of events that caused some to think he was dodging the column. The RAF was, in fact, seeking to avoid liability to pay a disability pension, though there were mutterings in parliament and elsewhere about an outstanding young games player being declared unfit to do his service. In the event, and for one reason and another, Cowdrey was available for only one of the five test matches against South Africa in 1955, when he scored 1 and 50 at Trent Bridge; but for most of the next fifteen years he was an automatic choice for England, as he was, of course, for Kent, whom he captained from 1957 until 1971.

Cowdrey married on 15 September 1956 Penelope Susan Chiesman (b. 1932/3), daughter of Stuart and Jane Chiesman. They had three sons and a daughter. Two of the sons, Christopher and Graham, played cricket for Kent, and Christopher also won six test caps, one of them as England's captain against West Indies at Headingley in 1988.

On his day, when the ball was coming readily on to the bat and he was at one with his timing, Cowdrey was as handsome a batsman, and could make the game look as simple as anyone in the second half of the twentieth century. Many a time he was described as being like a galleon in full sail. Not infrequently, however, he seemed to be held back by self-doubt, so that he became accustomed to reading that with a touch of arrogance he would have been an even more telling player than he was. Commanding one day, he could be positively pawky the next. For all that, he was one of the treasures of the game—ever courteous, widely popular (not least in Australia), unfailingly attentive, a great accumulator of runs, and a superb slip-catcher. Between 1950 and 1976, when he played his last innings, he amassed 42,719 first-class runs, 7624 of them for England.

Cowdrey became the first cricketer from any country to play in 100 test matches, and scored 104 in the hundredth of them, against Australia at Trent Bridge in 1968, when he was also captain. His 120 test catches were a record at the time, as was his fourth wicket partnership of 411 with Peter May against West Indies at Edgbaston in 1957, after the two of them had come together when England, 288 runs behind on first innings, were 113 for three in the second and seemingly heading for defeat. In 1950 he led Kent to their first county championship for fifty-seven years, a victory which, being achieved with a largely home-bred team, was a cause of much local rejoicing and crowned what was a particularly felicitous partnership between Cowdrey and Leslie Ames, in his time a dashing cricketer for Kent and England, and, hereabouts, the manager of both. One of England's very few successful test series in the Caribbean was achieved, in the winter of 1967–8, with Cowdrey and Ames as captain and manager respectively.

So how was it that Cowdrey never led England in Australia, the one big disappointment of his playing career? He made five full tours there, as well as part of a sixth when he was sent for, in 1974–5, at the instigation of the England players and at the age of forty-two, to confront Dennis Lillee and Jeff Thomson, bowling for Australia with unforeseen ferocity. On successive tours of Australia Cowdrey was vice-captain to May (1958–9), Ted Dexter (1962–3), M. J. K. Smith (1965–6), and Ray Illingworth (1970–71), despite being senior in experience to the last three. What told against him was a lack not of determination or ambition but of decisiveness. He would probably have taken the side in 1970–71, had he not torn an Achilles tendon in 1969, when he seemed securely installed in the job. Illingworth took the chance which that offered him, and Cowdrey was never reinstated. Against his better judgement he accepted the vice-captaincy to Illingworth and had an unhappy tour, losing his place in the test side and having to watch from the pavilion balcony at Sydney while England regained the Ashes.

Cowdrey's last chance of reminding the Australians of just how good he had been came at Canterbury in 1975 against Ian Chappell's side. Then, with a brilliant innings of 151 not out, during which he took heavy toll of both Lillee and Thomson, he led Kent to their first victory over an Australian side since 1899. It was the last but one of his 107 first-class hundreds, of which only three were over 200, the highest of them being his 307 for MCC against South Australia at Adelaide in 1963.

The only remotely full-time job Cowdrey ever had outside cricket was with Barclays Bank International, for whom he worked, after his retirement from playing, in a public relations capacity, focusing on countries where he had links through the game. This was initiated by Sir Anthony Tuke, the chairman of Barclays and, like Cowdrey, a future president of MCC. When he was not on tour with the England side Cowdrey had spent a number of winters working for his father-in-law, Stuart Chiesman, whose family owned a group of department stores in Kent, and for a while he was a non-executive director of the south-eastern branch of Whitbread Fremlins, the brewers. He gave his time increasingly to cricketing and charitable causes, always generously and voluntarily. There were few things he enjoyed more than being able to use his countless contacts to do someone a good turn, and he was much in demand as a highly effective speaker. All who met him were struck by his modesty, and he was a committed churchgoer. Cowdrey's first marriage was dissolved in 1985, and on 23 September that year he married Anne Elizabeth Fitzalan-Howard (b. 1938), eldest daughter of the sixteenth duke of Norfolk and in her own right Lady Herries of Terregles. The duke had managed the MCC side to Australia in 1962–3, of which Cowdrey was vice-captain. While Lady Herries trained racehorses, Cowdrey would pay daily visits to the vicinity of the gallops at their home, Angmering Park, near Arundel, in Sussex, without ever claiming to be anything of an aficionado or himself mounting a horse.

From 1959 until his death Cowdrey was closely involved in the counsels of MCC. Sadly, though, as an unusually young president of the club in 1986–7, its bicentenary year, he had a difficult and somewhat harrowing term of office. Inheriting an unhappy relationship between MCC and the Test and County Cricket Board, he acted with unwonted firmness in exacting the premature retirement of the secretary of the club, J. A. Bailey, a matter which prompted D. G. Clark, himself a former president, to resign as treasurer. As a way of showing their consequent disapproval, a group of the club's members caused the annual accounts to be rejected, although the stance of president and committee was vindicated by a majority of 88 per cent at the special general meeting which this required. By then Cowdrey was in hospital, having had a quadruple heart bypass, an emergency which prevented him from presiding at both the bicentenary dinner at Guildhall and at the celebratory match at Lord's between MCC and the rest of the world.

His health restored, Cowdrey became chairman of the International Cricket Council in 1989, a position he held for four years and in which he collaborated with John Major, then prime minister, to bring South Africa back into the fold after the end of apartheid and in time for them to play in the world cup in Australia and New Zealand in 1992. He was knighted for services to cricket in 1992. He also oversaw the introduction of an international panel of referees and umpires to stand in test matches and one-day internationals, and fought consistently and passionately against the persistent use of fast short-pitched bowling, which he believed to be against the spirit of the game and detrimental to it as a spectacle. In 1997 he was created a life peer, as Baron Cowdrey of Tonbridge; he went regularly and enthusiastically to the House of Lords, where he spoke to the subject of sport among young people on behalf of the Conservative Party. In 1999 he became president of Kent County Cricket Club, and, whether by coincidence or because he was more of a worrier than was generally apparent, his health gave way again, just as it had when he was president of MCC. This time, on the eve of the Canterbury week, the social highlight of Kent's year, he suffered the stroke from which he never really recovered. Among his many other appointments he had been president of the Lord's Taverners, master of the Worshipful Company of Skinners, and a member of the council of the Winston Churchill Memorial Trust and also of the Britain–Australia Society. He was made a freeman of the City of London in 1962.

Lord Cowdrey died at home of a heart attack on 4 December 2000, two days after attending a fund-raising dinner at King Edward VII Hospital, Midhurst, where he had spent three months following his stroke at the end of July and been a patient on and off since his heart bypass in 1987. His memorial service at Westminster Abbey on 30 March 2001 attracted the great and the good from all round the cricket world.    JOHN WOODCOCK

**Sources** C. Cowdrey, *M.C.C.: the autobiography of a cricketer* (1976) · *The Times* (6 Dec 2000) · *The Independent* (6 Dec 2000) · *Daily Telegraph* (6 Dec 2000) · *The Guardian* (6 Dec 2000) · *The Scotsman* (6 Dec 2000) · *Financial Times* (6 Dec 2000) · WWW · *Wisden* (2004) · private information (2004) · m. certs.
**Likenesses** photographs, 1954–74, Hult. Arch. · M. Pepper, photograph, 1987, News International Syndication, London [*see*

*illus.*] • B. Organ, acrylic, 1996, Marylebone Cricket Club • photograph, repro. in *The Independent* • photograph, repro. in *Daily Telegraph* • photograph, repro. in *The Guardian* • photograph, repro. in *The Scotsman* • photograph, repro. in *Financial Times*

**Wealth at death** £416,365—gross; £372,155—net: probate, 22 May 2001, *CGPLA Eng. & Wales*

**Cowdroy, William** (1752–1814), playwright and radical publisher, is of obscure origins; details of his parentage and upbringing are unknown. He was apprenticed to John Monk, the printer of the tory *Chester Courant*, on 6 June 1764, and enrolled on 21 June 1770. He became a freeman of the city on 24 July 1777. He was probably already on the staff of the *Chester Chronicle* when its editor, John Fletcher, was imprisoned for libelling the recorder of Chester in 1785. Cowdroy thereafter assumed the editorship. It is likely that his *Directory and Guide for the County and City of Chester* (1789) was published from the same offices.

As a young man Cowdroy had dabbled in amateur acting, and once apprenticed he gave comic lectures, using masks, such as 'Lectures on Heads' in the manner of George Alexander Stevens. He enjoyed some success as a playwright, publishing *The Vaporish Man, or, Hypocrisy Detected* (1782), performed at theatres in Chester and Manchester, and sold by booksellers as distant as Shrewsbury. This was followed by the comic opera *Love Conquers All, or, The Cheshire Knight Outwitted* (c.1786), which was managed by Joseph Munden in its first production at Chester.

Moving to Greengate, Salford, in 1794, Cowdroy became the partner of Thomas Boden, the Manchester bookseller and printer already noted for publishing the proceedings of the trial of the Manchester radical Thomas Walker (1794). Together they published Thomas Battye's *The Red Basil Book* (1797). While this pamphlet caused some embarrassment for the town's 'principal inhabitants', it was Cowdroy's association with Battye which was more revealing, especially as the Manchester cotton merchant and government spy, Robert Gray, was to describe Battye as a United Englishman and very dangerous, often heard damning the king.

Cowdroy, with Boden, already enjoyed some notoriety as publisher of the radical *Manchester Gazette and Weekly Advertiser*, a successor to Walker's *Manchester Herald* (1792–3), and one of a relatively small number of titles to appear after the Pitt administration's crackdown on the radical movement. The first issue of the *Gazette* appeared on 21 November 1795, bearing the motto: 'Be Temperate in Political Disquisition. Give Free Operation to Truth'. Its agenda included objecting to the war with France, to increased taxation, and to the repressive measures of the government. The newspaper boasted that it was 'extensively circulated' as far as Derbyshire, Yorkshire, and London.

In 1798 Cowdroy's son, also William, was incriminated on the evidence of Gray, who had acted as an *agent provocateur* by making a down payment at his publishing works for the printing of radical literature. Among the materials published were *Declarations, Resolutions, and Constitution of the Society of United Englishmen*, and *Loyalty and Reason*. Gray had also attempted to ensnare Cowdroy senior, whose name, with Boden's, appeared on a government list of

'three printers'. Gray paid him at least one visit, and asked for a subscription for the United Irishman James O'Coigley's passage to France. Cowdroy donated 2s. While this proved insufficient ground for prosecution, his republican leanings were not in doubt. In his conversations with Thomas Jowell, a United Englishman secretary, he expressed his belief that, if the minds of the people could be cultivated, they would revolutionize themselves. England was, for Cowdroy, a country where 'priestcraft' was suffered and the Christian religion frightened people into obedience. An apocryphal tale also related Cowdroy's insistence at his fourth son's baptism, that the child be named Citizen.

Cowdroy died in Manchester on 13 August 1814, and was buried in St Mark's churchyard, Cheetham Hill, Manchester. At that time his publishing business was sufficiently lucrative for him to leave an estate worth up to £600, out of which his wife Sarah (d. 1821), about whom further details are unknown, received an annuity of £150. He had parted company with Boden in August 1799, and been left in full control of the *Manchester Gazette*. Thereafter, Sarah, with William junior, assumed control of the newspaper, sales of which rallied until the 1820s with the arrival of the *Manchester Guardian*. Cowdroy and his wife had three other sons, Thomas, Benjamin, and Citizen Howard, all of whom became printers, and two daughters Mary Eliza and Caroline.

CRAIG HORNER

**Sources** PRO, PC 1/41/139; PC 1/42/140; HO 42/45 • will, Lancs. RO • *Cowdroy's Manchester Gazette and Weekly Advertiser* (1796–9) • D. Nuttall, *A history of printing in Chester* (1969) • J. H. Nodal, ed., *City news notes and queries*, 8 vols. (1878–91), vol. 2 (1879) • T. Swindells, *Manchester streets and Manchester men*, 5 vols. (1906–8), vol. 1 (1906) • C. H. Timperley, *A dictionary of printers and printing* (1839) • D. Nuttall, ed., *Book trade in the north west project* (1981) • R. W. Procter, *Literary reminiscences and gleanings* (1860) • J. Smith, 'English radical newspapers in the era of the French Revolution', PhD diss., U. Lond., 1979

**Wealth at death** under £600: will, Lancs. RO

**Cowell, Edward Byles** (1826–1903), orientalist, born in St Clement's Street, Ipswich, on 23 January 1826, was the eldest son (in a family of three sons and one daughter) of Charles Cowell (d. 1842), who had inherited a successful business of merchant and maltster, and as a cultured Liberal was active in local affairs. His mother was Marianne, elder daughter of Nathaniel Byles Byles of the Hill House, Ipswich, also a successful merchant of that town.

Cowell was precocious, attending Ipswich grammar school from his eighth year. In 1841 he compiled a few numbers of the *Ipswich Radical Magazine and Review*, in which he showed sympathy with his father's politics, combined with a singularly wide reading in classical literature. He was first drawn to oriental literature in 1841 after finding in the public library of Ipswich a copy of Sir William Jones's works, including the *Persian Grammar* and the translation of Kalidasa's 'Sakuntala'. In the same year his reading of Macaulay's essay on Warren Hastings made him aware of Horace Hayman Wilson's *Sanskrit Grammar*, a copy of which he promptly acquired. Meanwhile he took his first steps in Persian, at first by himself, but soon with the aid of a retired Bombay officer, Major Hockley, who probably also initiated him into Arabic. As early as 1842, while still at school, he contributed to the *Asiatic Journal* a number of verse renderings from the Persian.

On his father's death in 1842 Cowell was taken from school to be trained for the management of the family business. But during the next eight years, while engaged in commerce, he read in his spare time with extraordinary zeal and variety. Of his scholarship and breadth of knowledge he soon gave proof in a series of contributions to the *Westminster Review*, writing on oriental and Spanish literature. At the same time he formed the acquaintance of many who shared his interests, among them the Arabic and Persian scholar William Hook Morley and the Persian scholar Duncan Forbes, and he also called on Carlyle in London. In 1846 he sought an introduction to 'the great professor', Horace Hayman Wilson, and four years later he read in the East India Library and obtained a loan of a Prakrit manuscript (Vararuci's 'Prakrta-Prakaśa'), his edition of which (1854) was destined to establish his reputation as a Sanskrit scholar. Through John Charlesworth, rector of Flowton near Ipswich, whose daughter Elizabeth Susan (c.1812–1899) he married on 23 October 1847, he came to know the poet and translator Edward FitzGerald, the best-known of his many friends and correspondents. Their correspondence at first related chiefly to classical literature. It was Cowell who gave FitzGerald his first lesson in the Persian alphabet.

In 1850, the next brother being now of an age to carry on the Ipswich business, Cowell matriculated at Magdalen Hall, Oxford, going with his wife into lodgings. 'I went there [to Oxford]', he wrote later, 'a solitary student, mainly self-taught; and I learned there the method of study'. During the six years of his university life he greatly widened his social circle, receiving visits not only from FitzGerald, who read Persian with him, but from Tennyson and Thackeray, to whom FitzGerald introduced him. He saw much of Jowett, Morfill, Max Müller, and Theodor Aufrecht, and was greatly aided by the lectures and tuition of the Sanskrit professor, Horace Hayman Wilson. In 1854 he took a first class in *literae humaniores* and an honorary fourth in mathematics. While missing the scholarship in Hebrew, he was awarded a special prize of books. The next two years were spent in coaching, chiefly in Aristotle's *Ethics*. He also catalogued Persian and other oriental manuscripts for the Bodleian Library.

As an undergraduate Cowell had made a reputation by his oriental publications. A translation of Kalidasa's 'Vikramorvaśī', though finished earlier, was published in 1851. His admirable edition of Vararuci's 'Prakrta-Prakaśa' followed in 1854. On taking his degree he wrote on the Persian poets for *Fraser's Magazine*, besides contributing to *Oxford Essays* (1855) an essay on Persian literature.

**In India** In June 1856 Cowell was appointed professor of English history in the re-formed Presidency College, Calcutta. His post involved him in arduous work. He soon instituted an MA course in the Calcutta University, and extended the themes of his lectures to political economy and philosophy. In 1857 Cowell became secretary of the Vernacular Literature Society, founded with the object of providing Indian readers with translations of good English literature. At the same time he was increasingly attracted to missionary work. He held Bible readings in his house on Sundays, and a number of conversions resulted, not without some risk of offence to his Hindu connections. One of his chief Calcutta friends was William Kay, principal of Bishop's College. Meanwhile he pursued oriental studies untiringly. Persian continued to fascinate him. Of two copies which he procured of the manuscript of 'Umar Khayyam belonging to the Asiatic Society at Calcutta, he sent one to FitzGerald. His own important article on 'Umar Khayyam appeared in the *Calcutta Review* in March 1858.

Having passed the government examinations in Hindustani and Bengali, Cowell undertook in 1858 an additional office at Calcutta, that of principal of the Sanskrit College founded by Warren Hastings. Cowell's predecessor was a native Indian scholar. His relations with the pandits of the college were soon close and affectionate. By their aid he acquired a profound knowledge of the scholastic Sanskrit literature in rhetoric and philosophy, while he stimulated the pandits' scholarly activity, and often gratified them with a prepared speech in Bengali and a Sanskrit 'Śloka'. Many Indian editions of works on rhetoric and poetry which were published in the Bibliotheca Indica, a series issued by the Asiatic Society of Bengal, of which he became early in 1858 a joint philological secretary, express their indebtedness to Cowell. His own Sanskrit publications during this period also appeared chiefly in the Bibliotheca Indica. With Dr R. Roer he continued the edition of the *Black Yajur Veda* (vols. 1 and 2, 1858–64), which he afterwards carried on alone—it was ultimately finished by its fifth editor in 1899; and singly he edited two Upanisads, the 'Kaustaki' (1861) and the 'Maitri' (1863; translation added 1870). The most important of his works at this time was his edition and translation of the 'Kusumanjali' with the commentary of Haridasa (1864). The book, which in respect of difficulty might be compared with the *Metaphysics* of Aristotle, supplies a Hindu proof of the existence of God. Cowell read it with Maheśa Candra, whose name he associated with his own on the title-page, and the edition was dedicated to Max Müller. He made a close study of the 'Siddhanta-Muktavali', a philosophical work, which he used as a college manual and examination textbook, and of the 'Sarvadaraanasamgraha', of which he translated one chapter, relating to the Carvaka system (*Journal of the Asiatic Society of Bengal*, 1862). He contemplated full translations of both books.

One of Cowell's last official duties in India was to visit the Tols (Indian quasi-colleges) at Nadia, which were homes of pandit research and had last been inspected by Wilson in 1829. His report, published in the *Proceedings of the Asiatic Society of Bengal* for 1867, supplied interesting details concerning the teaching methods of these institutions, and has become one of the more important sources for the history of indigenous Indian Sanskrit education and philosophical discourse.

**Return to England** By the spring of 1864 the state of Cowell's health demanded a furlough. With his oriental scholarship immensely strengthened he revisited England. His original intention of returning to India was not realized. In the summer of 1865 he became examiner in oriental subjects to the civil service commission; in the same year he refused a curatorship at the Bodleian and in 1866 a similar position at the British Museum. Occupying himself in varied literary work, he recommenced his general reading and renewed his contact and correspondence with Fitz-Gerald.

In 1867 the University of Cambridge bestowed on Cowell the newly founded professorship of Sanskrit. Theodor Aufrecht was another candidate, but Cowell was warmly supported by Max Müller and many eminent scholars and friends. He was elected on a general vote of the university by ninety-six votes to thirty-seven. He published his inaugural lecture on the Sanskrit language and literature in 1867. The remainder of his life was spent happily at Cambridge. In 1874 he became a fellow of Corpus Christi College. He retained the professorship and the fellowship until his death in 1903. During those thirty-six years his time was unstintingly given to his duties. He announced each term a formidable list of lectures, generally delivered at his own house. At first he lectured not only on Sanskrit but also on comparative philology, and became one of the founders of the Cambridge Philological Society, with which he was connected as auditor until the close of his life, and he contributed to the early numbers of the *Journal of Philology* (from 1868). In 1884 a lecturer was appointed to take charge of the more elementary Sanskrit teaching. Nevertheless, the pupils who read with Cowell were of all grades of proficiency, ranging from undergraduates grappling with their first Sanskrit play to eminent scholars (both English and foreign) eager to elucidate the various Indian philosophies, the Vedic hymns, the 'Zendavesta', or the Pali 'Jataka'. Alone or with his pupils Cowell issued an imposing series of Sanskrit texts and translations, of which the most important are *The Sarva-Darśana-Saṃgraha* (translated with A. E. Gough, Oriental Series, 1882); *Divyavadana* (edited with R. A. Neil, 1886); *The Buddha Karita of Aśvaghosha* (Anecdota Oxoniensia, Aryan Series, 8, 1893), with translation in Sacred Books of the East, 49, 1894; *The Jataka*, translated under Cowell's editorship (6 vols., 1895); *The Harṣacarita of Bana* (translated with F. W. Thomas, Oriental Translation Fund, new ser., 1897). Many of these and his exegetical and secondary works have been of lasting value and are still used over a century later by students and scholars of classical Indian literatures and philosophies.

Outside Sanskrit, Cowell still pursued other interests. Persian he resumed as opportunity offered. Spanish he always kept up, reading *Don Quixote*, at first with FitzGerald, and after his death with other friends in Cambridge. His Hebrew notes were used by Dr Kay in 1869 for the second edition of a translation of the book of Psalms, and later he studied the Talmud. About 1877 he took up archaeology and architecture, a new study which led him to translate into English Michelangelo's sonnets, two of

which were published in George Cowell's *Life and Letters of Edward Byles Cowell*. Welsh poetry and the science of botany had been passing fancies of Cowell's youth. During 1870–80 they were cultivated simultaneously in vacations spent in Wales, sometimes in company with the Cambridge professor of botany, (Charles) Carsdale Babington. The Welsh studies, which were inspired by Borrow's *Wild Wales*, culminated in a masterly paper on the poet Dafydd ap Gwilym, read before the Cymmrodorion Society in 1878, and published in *Y Cymmrodor* (July 1878). Cowell's manuscript translation of this poet's work is in the university library at Cambridge. Botany remained one of the chief pleasures of his later life, and his scientific interests extended to geology. He collected a complete flora of Cambridgeshire, and gave expression to his botanical enthusiasm in some charming sonnets.

In 1892 Cowell was prevailed upon to accept the presidency of the Arian section of the International Congress of Orientalists held in London. His inaugural address (comparing rabbinical and Brahmanical learning) and his charming Sanskrit 'Sloka' made a very favourable impression. In 1895 he was made an honorary member of the German Oriental Society. In 1898 he was awarded the gold medal of the Royal Asiatic Society, then bestowed for the first time. Among Cowell's other distinctions were the honorary LLD of Edinburgh University in 1875 and the honorary DCL of Oxford in 1896. In 1902 he was chosen as one of the original members of the British Academy.

Cowell's last publication was a verse translation, revised after thirty years, of some episodes from an old Bengali poem, 'Candi', which he had read at Calcutta and subsequently with Bengali students at Cambridge (*Journal of the Asiatic Society of Bengal*, 1903). Although he continued to lecture, he had long been conscious of failing powers when he died at his residence, 10 Scroope Terrace, Cambridge, on 9 February 1903. He was buried at Bramford, near Ipswich, beside his wife, who had predeceased him on 29 September 1899. They had no children. His wife's sister was the author Maria Louisa Charlesworth.

During his lifetime Cowell founded a scholarship in Sanskrit at the Sanskrit College in Calcutta (1878), and endowed a prize for classics at his old school in Ipswich; by his will he devised to Corpus Christi College the sum of £1500 for a scholarship in classics or mathematics, besides leaving his library for distribution between that college, the university library, the Fitzwilliam Museum, and Girton College.

Cowell was remarkable for the versatility of his knowledge of language and literature and for the breadth of his scholarly interests. Primarily a modest, patient, and serious savant, he was at the same time an accomplished man of letters, who excelled as an essayist, a familiar correspondent, and someone who could write charming and thoughtful verse. An unusual tenacity and subtlety of intellect appear in his mastery of Sanskrit logic and metaphysics (Nyaya and Vedanta). A chronological list of his writings is appended to George Cowell's 1904 biography.

F. W. Thomas, *rev.* J. B. Katz

**Sources** G. Cowell, *Life and letters of Edward Byles Cowell* (1904) · T. Wright, *The life of Edward Fitzgerald* (1904), esp. 1.214–55; 2.197f. · F. Pollock, *The Pilot* (21 Feb 1903) · C. Bendall, *The Athenaeum* (14 Feb 1903); repr. *Journal of the Royal Asiatic Society of Great Britain and Ireland* (1903), 419–24 · T. W. R. Davids, 'Edward Byles Cowell', *PBA*, [1] (1903–4), 302–6 · m. cert. · d. cert.
**Archives** CUL, corresp. and papers · V&A, MSS | BL OIOC, letters to H. H. Wilson, MS Eur. E 301 · CUL, letters from Edward Fitzgerald
**Likenesses** C. E. Brock, oils, *c*.1896, CCC Cam. · A. H. Cade, photograph, repro. in Wright, *Life of Edward Fitzgerald* · oils (after photograph), Sanskrit College, Calcutta
**Wealth at death** £11,449 19s. 7d.: probate, 21 March 1903, *CGPLA Eng. & Wales*

**Cowell, Florence** (1852–1926). *See under* Cowell, Samuel Houghton (1820–1864).

**Cowell, Gervase** [Gerry] (1926–2000), intelligence officer, was born on 4 August 1926 at 44 Clarendon Crescent, Sale, Manchester, the second son and youngest of the three children of Frederick Arthur Cowell (1885–1969), precision engineer, and his wife, Alice Mary, *née* Raffo (1894–1987). He attended St Joseph's Roman Catholic Primary School, Sale, before obtaining a scholarship to St Bede's College, Manchester, where he gained nine distinctions in school certificate—a school record. At the age of seventeen this soft-spoken, modest young man unexpectedly announced that on the way home from school he had volunteered for the Royal Air Force, not prepared to await call-up. The RAF sent him on the Cambridge University services Russian course (1945–6) and thereafter to Government Communications Headquarters (GCHQ) to work on Soviet intercepts. On demobilization he entered St Catharine's College, Cambridge (1948–50), where he graduated with first-class honours in Russian and French.

From Cambridge, Cowell was recruited to the Secret Intelligence Service (SIS) where he was known to colleagues as Gerry rather than Gervase. He was posted in 1951, at the height of the cold war, to West Berlin, then a small tripartite island surrounded by Soviet-occupied territory. His language accomplishments, which included excellent German, and his cool head stood him in good stead. In Berlin he met Pamela Ellen Alger (1925–2000), an SIS secretary. They married on 15 October 1953. They had two sons, Adrian and Christopher, and two daughters, Rosamund and Julienne.

Cowell was a man of many talents. He was an artist, mainly self-taught, and during his next posting, to Amman (1958–60), he held the first of several exhibitions of his work. He was no mean poet and in his spare time he translated Russian authors into English, under the pseudonym David Alger; *Red and Black* by Ivan Valery, published in 1962, was followed by others over the years.

In 1962 the Cowells were sent to Moscow on a vitally important assignment. They replaced the SIS husband-and-wife team of Rauri and Janet Chisholm who had been 'running' the spy Colonel Oleg Penkovsky. The latter passed over microphotographs of information on Soviet nuclear capacity, and this later enabled President Kennedy to foil Khrushchov's attempt to install SS4 liquid-fuelled rockets in Cuba, which would have had Washington within range. The original plan was for Mrs Cowell, as with Mrs Chisholm before her, to have apparent chance encounters with Penkovsky when out with her children, and Penkovsky, while admiring the baby, would drop his packet into the pram. In the event a new method was chosen, but before this could be put into effect contact was lost. It transpired that Penkovsky had already come under suspicion and had been arrested on 22 October 1962. He confessed under interrogation. Cowell was declared *persona non grata* and expelled.

Cowell was next posted as first secretary to Bonn (1964–6) where alongside his professional duties his talent for devising theatrical entertainment enlivened the social life of the embassy. He returned for a longer spell at home (1966–72) which enabled his wife to concentrate on bringing up their four children. Four years in Paris (1972–6) were followed by a further four years as first secretary in Tel Aviv (1978–82). His response to the landscape, the history, and the archaeology of Israel proved a great artistic stimulus and led to a full-scale exhibition of his paintings and publication of his poetry in Jewish journals.

From 1988 until he retired in 1996 Cowell was custodian of the files, held by the Foreign and Commonwealth Office, of the wartime Special Operations Executive (SOE). His friendly collaboration with the media ensured accurate and widespread recognition of SOE's doings and also brought him into close contact with the Special Forces Club. In 1992 he also became chairman of the club's historical subcommittee, a job he relished until his death. It satisfied his passion for detailed research and he was tireless in his determination to build SOE records for posterity. He assembled a definitive SOE roll of honour, and designed and organized the SOE memorial in the north cloister of Westminster Abbey as well as the monument at the former Ravensbruck concentration camp in memory of SOE women murdered there. In 2000 he was appointed MBE for services to the Special Forces Club. Asked by the queen what he did, he replied: 'I help the old to remember and the young to understand' (private information). He died of heart failure on 3 May 2000 at the Old Manse, 19 Middleton Road, Pickering, Yorkshire, on a visit to a war museum, and was buried on 11 May at the church of St John the Baptist, Campsea Ashe, Suffolk. He was survived by his four children and for six months by his wife, who died on 1 November 2000.                    E. H. VAN MAURIK

**Sources** *The Times* (8–11 May 2000) · *The Guardian* (16 May 2000) · *The Independent* (19 May 2000) · private information (2004) [Rosamund Cowell-Webb, daughter] · personal knowledge (2004)
**Likenesses** photograph, repro. in *The Guardian* · photograph, repro. in *The Independent*
**Wealth at death** £507,357—gross; £503,820—net: probate, 2 Jan 2001, *CGPLA Eng. & Wales*

**Cowell, John** (1554–1611), civil lawyer, was born at Ernsborough in Swimbridge, Devon. His parents' names are unknown. He attended Eton College and in 1570 matriculated as a pensioner of King's College, Cambridge, where he became a fellow in 1573. After proceeding BA in 1575 and MA in 1578 he was persuaded by Richard Bancroft, then bishop of London, to devote himself to the study of the civil law. He received the degree of LLD in 1584 and was admitted as an advocate of the arches on 26 April 1589. The following year he became a member of Doctors' Commons, but he rarely practised in the ecclesiastical or admiralty courts and accepted only a few judicial assignments.

Cowell served as official principal of the archdeacon of Colchester from 1602 to 1609 and as vicar-general to Bancroft, now archbishop of Canterbury, from February 1609 until 1611. In these capacities Cowell was known for administering frequent sentences of excommunication. He also served as a member of the court of high commission from 1605 until 1611. He sat on a variety of commissions, including those concerning piracy in 1606 and 1609, and the admiralty, in 1610, was JP for Cambridge from 1606 to 1610, and investigated nonconformity at the university. Cowell devoted the great portion of his time to academic pursuits. He served as the regius professor of civil law at Cambridge from 1594 until 1611 and as master of Trinity Hall, the stronghold of civil law studies at Cambridge, from 1598 until 1611. He also served as vice-chancellor of Cambridge in 1603 and 1604. Cowell's main academic project was to illustrate the similarities between the civil law and English common law. His first published work, *Institutiones juris Anglicani* (1605), sought to give the common law an organizational structure by placing it within the framework of the civil law. The immediate purpose of the book was to prepare for a union of English law and Scots law after the union of the crowns in 1603. The civil law, which had already made its mark on Scots law, would provide both legal systems with a common rational order and thus help to bring them into conformity. This book did not achieve great commercial success, being reprinted only once in Latin in 1630 and translated into English in a single edition of 1651.

Cowell's more famous and controversial publication, *The Interpreter* (1607), was a law dictionary which provided definitions of English legal terms, while also giving similar terms from the civil law. The controversy arose from Cowell's definition of a few terms that reflected a theory of royal absolutism, which was at the time often associated with the civil law. Cowell defined a king as having absolute power above the law, with parliament serving the monarchy. The book caused an uproar in the parliament of 1610, which was marked by a general fear of royal absolutism. MPs complained that Cowell had drawn his arguments from the imperial laws of the Roman emperors and that his book 'was to take away the power and authority of the parliament' (Foster, 1966, 1.18). It also angered common lawyers, who objected to Cowell's defence of the jurisdiction of the ecclesiastical and admiralty courts. Sir Edward Coke, chief justice of the common pleas, who called Cowell 'Dr Cowheel', also resented his derogatory comments regarding Sir Thomas Littleton, whose work on tenures served as Coke's main authority for the first volume of his *Institutes*. The protests caused James I to summon Cowell before him in the privy council and suppress the book by proclamation, claiming that it

was 'in some points very derogatory to the supreme power of this crowne; in other cases mistaking the true state of the parliament of this kingdome ... and speaking unreverently of the common law of England' (J. F. Larkin and P. L. Hughes, eds., *Stuart Royal Proclamations*, 1973, 1.244). Although James was privately sympathetic to Cowell and agreed with most of his political ideas, he used his prerogative power to diffuse some of the fury in the Commons and to prevent any further discussion of the book. *The Interpreter* continued to cause controversy in the parliament of 1621. Despite its suppression, the book proved to have considerable utility and was reprinted eleven times during the seventeenth and early eighteenth centuries. Cowell was disgraced by the royal condemnation of his work and retired from public life, resigning as professor of civil law on 25 May 1611. He died at Cambridge on 11 October and was buried in Trinity Hall. Having never married, Cowell gave his lands in Devon to his brother and his nephew, John Allen and Simon Cowell, while he bequeathed his house at Cambridge to Trinity Hall to support a lecture in logic. His books on civil and canon law were given to Trinity Hall's library.    BRIAN P. LEVACK

**Sources** B. P. Levack, *The civil lawyers in England, 1603–1641* (1973) · G. D. Squibb, *Doctors' Commons: a history of the College of Advocates and Doctors of Law* (1977) · abstract of the will of William Carole (Cowle), 2 Dec 1584, Exeter City Library · D. R. Coquillette, 'Legal ideology and incorporation: the English civilian writers, 1523–1607', *Boston University Law Review*, 61 (1981), 1–89 · J. P. Sommerville, *Royalists and patriots: politics and ideology in England, 1603–1640* (1999) · E. R. Foster, ed., *Proceedings in parliament, 1610*, 2 vols. (1966) · R. G. Usher, *The reconstruction of the English church*, 2 vols. (New York, 1910) · S. B. Chrimes, 'The constitutional ideas of Dr John Cowell', *EngHR*, 64 (1949) · B. P. Levack, *The formation of the British state* (1987) · will, PRO, PROB 11/118, sig. 86 · Venn, *Alum. Cant.*

**Archives** St John Cam., autograph MS, 'The interpreter'
**Wealth at death** see will, PRO, PROB 11/118, sig. 86

**Cowell, Joseph** [*real name* Joseph Leathley Whitshed] (**1792–1863**), actor, was born near Torquay, Devon, on 7 August 1792. His real surname was Whitshed. He was the son of a colonel in the army and the cousin of Admiral James Hawkins *Whitshed (1762–1849), and had ample opportunities for mingling with seamen and of seeing Nelson and the earl of St Vincent. He entered the navy at the age of thirteen and served for three years as a midshipman. When he turned sixteen he had three weeks' leave of absence before starting on a twelve months' cruise to the West Indies. During this period, although he had been educated strictly in the Roman Catholic faith, curiosity led him into a protestant church in London, and he fell in love with a young girl called Anna Creek, with whom he regularly visited the theatre. He saw Charles Kemble as Romeo, Mary Ann Davenport as the Nurse, and Charles Murray as Friar Laurence, and was more than half 'engaged' before he rejoined his ship and went to the West Indies. In a quarrel, he struck a superior officer, thus rendering himself liable to a court martial, with the probability of being shot. On the voyage home, however, a French ship was met, and he begged to be allowed to lose his life honourably in action. He did his duty so bravely that on arriving at Plymouth the admiral obtained his ante-dated 'discharge by sick-list'.

Whitshed then changed his name to Cowell and took to painting portraits. In January 1812 he applied to George Sandford of New York, at the Plymouth Theatre, for employment as an actor, giving his name as Leathley Irving. He was kindly received, taught his business, and made his first appearance as Belcour in Richard Cumberland's *The West Indian* at the Plymouth. Although nervous at first, he achieved a brilliant success. He obtained a regular engagement, and soon acted alongside Charles Incledon, Joseph Munden, Dorothy Jordan, W. H. Betty, and Charles Young. He received offers from the elder Macready for Newcastle and from Kelly for Portsmouth, but preferred to accept an engagement from Beverley at Richmond.

By this time Cowell had married Maria Murray, the daughter of Charles *Murray and the sister of William Henry Murray and Harriet Murray. (Harriet Murray married Henry Siddons, the son of Sarah Siddons and the nephew of Stephen Kemble; thus Cowell became connected to the two great theatrical families of the day, the Siddons and the Kembles.) The Cowells had three children, Joseph, Maria, and Samuel *Cowell (1820–1864). Joseph died young, having just begun his career as a scene painter at Covent Garden, and Maria died at the age of five. Samuel, however, went on to become as famous an actor as his father.

Meanwhile, ambition drove Joseph Cowell to try his hand at all varieties of tragedy and comedy; he laboured hard, but appeared at his best in low comedy. At Woolwich he commenced scene painting, and he also worked at Covent Garden with the elder Grieve, under Phillips. At Brighton he received his highest salary in England as an actor and painter. Tempted by better business, he joined Faulkner at a lower salary on the northern circuit, and started for York, 'the stepping-stone to London'. There he appeared as Crack in Thomas Knight's *The Turnpike Gate*. At Wakefield he left the company and joined that of Thomas Robertson at Lincoln. Finally Stephen Kemble offered him an engagement at Drury Lane, and he opened as Samson Rawbold in Colman's *The Iron Chest* and Nicholas in *The Midnight Hour*. On the death of Queen Charlotte (12 November 1818) the theatres were closed. Drury Lane ended the season in a state of bankruptcy, so Cowell composed and commenced acting a three hours' olio called *Cowell Alone, or, A Trip to London* on the Lincoln circuit. He returned to London for the Adelphi, was taken on by R. W. Elliston at Drury Lane, where he opened as James in *Blue Devils*, but soon returned to the Adelphi on a three-year engagement.

While Cowell was drawing from memory a portrait of Charles Kemble as Romeo for his friend Oxberry, he was brought to the notice of the American manager Stephen Price, and arranged with him to sail for the United States. Having terminated his engagement at Astley's, where he had been appearing in *Gil Blas*, he sailed alone from the Downs in September 1821, and arrived at New York the following month to begin at the Park Theatre in *The Foundling*

*of the Forest* and as his ever-successful Crack. He took the audience by storm. From this date onwards his career was prosperous, and he was a favourite in all the chief cities of the United States, notably in Boston, Philadelphia, Baltimore, and Louisville. About 1822 he married his second wife, Frances Sheppard (d. c.1838). Their daughter Sidney Frances (1823–1881) later married the actor and theatre manager H. L. Bateman [see Bateman, Sidney Frances].

In July 1823 Cowell left the Park Theatre. Early in February 1826 he received the warmest welcome at Charleston, and in September 1827 he opened the Philadelphia Theatre at Wilmington, Delaware. In 1829 his son Samuel, aged nine, appeared at Boston and journeyed with him to Cincinnati, 8 miles northwest of which, in the Whitewater township of Hamilton, Ohio, Cowell later bought a farm of 100 acres. Cowell also toured in New Orleans, leased a theatre in Nashville, and, in 1844, published in New York a record of his theatrical life, entitled *Thirty Years Passed among the Players in England and America*. But he was growing weary of his profession and returned to England in 1846, hoping for a retired life in Putney. However, his plans changed. In 1848 in London he married his third wife, Harriet Burke. He travelled again to America in 1850, revisited London in 1854, and, after making his final appearance on the stage in New York as Crack, finally returned to England in 1863. He died in London on 14 November 1863 and was buried in Brompton cemetery, where a stone was erected by his son-in-law, H. L. Bateman. His widow, Harriet, died in 1886.

J. W. Ebsworth, *rev.* Nilanjana Banerji

**Sources** Adams, *Drama* · J. Cowell, *Thirty years passed among the players in England and America*, 2 pts (1844) · *The Era* (15 Nov 1863) · *The Era* (22 Nov 1863) · *Who was who in America: historical volume, 1607–1896* (1963) · *N&Q*, 156 (1929), 461–2 · *DNB*
**Likenesses** three prints, Harvard TC

**Cowell, Philip Herbert** (1870–1949), mathematician and astronomer, was born on 7 August 1870 at Calcutta, the second son of Herbert Cowell (b. 1837), a barrister, and his wife, Alice (b. 1842), the third daughter of Newson Garrett, a merchant, of Aldeburgh, Suffolk. He was educated at a private school at Stoke Poges and in 1883 went to Eton College as a king's scholar; there he gained the Tomline prize in mathematics and in 1889 an entrance scholarship to Trinity College, Cambridge. He graduated as senior wrangler in 1892 and then carried out an investigation of the motion of the moon. He was elected a fellow of his college in 1894, in which year he assisted E. W. Brown in the preparation of his volume *An Introductory Treatise on Lunar Theory*.

In April 1896 Cowell was appointed to the new post of second chief assistant to the astronomer royal, then Sir William H. M. Christie, at the Royal Observatory, Greenwich. His duties included general administration, the supervision of observational work, and the adjustment of instruments, but he showed neither interest in nor aptitude for such work. He did, however, use his mathematical talents to improve the methods of processing the observational data, especially of those for the moon.

Over the next eleven years Cowell's researches were concerned almost entirely with the analysis of the Greenwich observations of the position of the moon in order to improve the constants in the lunar theories of, first, Hansen, and then Brown. He also studied the records of ancient eclipses of the sun in order to determine the secular accelerations of the moon and of the sun. For this work he was elected a fellow of the Royal Society in 1906.

Cowell is, however, best-known for his work with Andrew *Crommelin on the orbit of Halley's comet. In 1907 they started to compute the orbit of the comet between 1759 and its expected return in 1910, taking into account the observations made at the previous return in 1835. In 1908, however, they turned their attention to the orbit of the newly discovered eighth satellite of Jupiter. Because of its distance from the planet, the perturbations of its orbit by the sun were so large that the elements of the ellipse that approximated to the orbit changed rapidly; as a consequence the methods of integration normally used were very tedious. Cowell found that the direct integration of the rectangular co-ordinates of the satellite was much more efficient, and he and Crommelin applied this method to Halley's comet. Their predicted date of the return of the comet to perihelion proved to be in error by less than three days. After they had completed the integration they developed a modified procedure that is even more efficient. This work was published as an appendix to *Greenwich Observations* for 1909. Years later this procedure proved to be particularly well adapted to use in automatic computers; it is generally known as Cowell's method. For this, and his earlier work on the lunar theory, Cowell was awarded, in 1911, the gold medal of the Royal Astronomical Society, which published some fifty of his papers in its *Monthly Notices*.

In 1910 Cowell was appointed superintendent of the nautical almanac office. Although unable to obtain the support of the Admiralty for his plan to make the office a centre for research in dynamical astronomy, he nevertheless improved the methods of computation used there, and he carried through the remodelling of the first part of the *Nautical Almanac* for 1914 and introduced the *Nautical Almanac, Abridged for the Use of Seamen*. He was unsuccessful in his applications for the Plumian and Lowndean professorships at Cambridge, even though in 1913 he had just given a course of lectures connected with the latter chair, and did little research thereafter. L. J. Comrie became his deputy in 1926 and introduced sweeping changes in the content of the *Nautical Almanac* for 1931 in order to make it more useful for astronomers; he also introduced new calculating machines and the use of punched-card machines for the computations. Cowell, on the other hand, never used a calculating machine, but did all his arithmetical work by hand. On retirement on his sixtieth birthday he is said to have cleared his desk and left at precisely the hour of his birth.

Cowell married Phyllis (d. 1924), the daughter of Holroyd Chaplin, a solicitor, on 24 June 1901. There were no children. After his retirement in 1930 Cowell lived quietly at Aldeburgh, Suffolk, and took no further part in scientific activities. He was keenly interested in bridge and played chess at county standard. He died at his home, 63 Crag Path, Aldeburgh, of cardiac asthma on 6 June 1949. In an obituary note considered at the time to be too frank to publish, J. G. Bullocke, an assistant professor at the Royal Naval College, who shared Cowell's home after the death of his wife, wrote, 'Cowell paid for his genius … by certain deficiencies in his make-up that gave him the air of a clever and loveable child who required careful and sympathetic handling' (CUL, RGO 9/645).

GEORGE A. WILKINS

**Sources** E. T. Whittaker, *Obits. FRS*, 6 (1948–9), 375–84 • J. Jackson, *Monthly Notices of the Royal Astronomical Society*, 110 (1950), 125–8 • m. cert. • d. cert. • CUL, RGO 9/645
**Likenesses** photograph, repro. in Whittaker, *Obits. FRS*
**Wealth at death** £42,667 9s. 10d.: probate, 22 March 1950, *CGPLA Eng. & Wales*

**Cowell, Samuel Houghton** (1820–1864), actor and comic singer, the son of Joseph *Cowell and his first wife, Maria Murray, was born in London on 5 April 1820. He was taken by his father to America in 1822, and educated in a military academy at Mount Airey, near Philadelphia, where he made great progress in his few years of steady education. In 1829, at the age of nine, he made his first appearance on the stage, at Boston, as Crack in Thomas Knight's *The Turnpike Gate*, singing with his father the duet 'When off in curricle we go'. From that time onwards he earned his own living and was hailed as 'the young American Roscius'. He acted in all the chief theatres of the United States, some of his characters being Chick, Matty Marvellous, Bombastes Furioso, and one of the Dromios in Shakespeare's *The Comedy of Errors*, his father playing the other.

Cowell went to Scotland, and appeared in Edinburgh at the Theatre Royal and the Adelphi, under the management of his uncle, W. H. Murray. He became an established favourite, not only as an actor, but as a comic singer between the acts. On 5 November 1842 he married Emilie Marguerite Ebsworth (1818–1899), the daughter of Joseph *Ebsworth, a highly esteemed dramatist and teacher of music, and the well-known actress Mary Emma *Ebsworth. They had nine children, of whom two daughters, **Sydney Cowell** (1846–1925) and **Florence Cowell** [*known as* Mrs Alfred B. Tapping] (1852–1926), and one of the six sons, Joseph, became successful professional actors. After remaining for four years in Edinburgh, Cowell went to London on an engagement for three years, with Benjamin Webster, at the Adelphi, but soon abandoned this, and appeared in July 1844 as Alessio in *La sonnambula* at the Surrey Theatre. Before 1848 he moved to the Olympic as a stock comedian under Bolton's management, then for two years he was at the Princess's, under James Maddox, playing second to Henry Compton. Next he went to Covent Garden, under Alfred Bunn, and afterwards to Glasgow, under his old friend Edmund Glover, though he took other engagements at Belfast and Dublin.

Everywhere a favourite, flattered and tempted towards conviviality, and naturally restless, Cowell grew tired of dramatic study, which was always arduous in the provinces, where a frequent change of performances was necessary, and he decided to devote himself to character singing. His 'Billy Barlow', 'The Ratcatcher's Daughter', 'Clara Cline' (considered one of the sweetest and best of his own compositions), 'Robinson Crusoe', and the burlesque ditties of 'Alonzo the Brave' and 'Richard the Third' were embodied with so much dramatic spirit, in appropriate costume, with his rich voice and power of mimicry, that he virtually founded a new class of drawing-room entertainment, and gave such satisfaction that 'Evans's' of Covent Garden ('Paddy Green's') and Charles Morton's Canterbury Hall owed their popularity chiefly to him. He was hailed as the virtual founder of music-hall entertainment. Collections of *Sam Cowell's Songs* and photographic portraits of him in character used to be both enormously numerous and popular. He joined Conquest at the Royal Grecian, where he enacted Nobody with a *buffo* song in E. Leman Blanchard's extravaganza *Nobody in London*, which playfully satirized the Great Exhibition excitement of 1851.

Cowell twice appeared at Windsor Castle before the queen at her court theatricals. In August 1852 he was at St James's Theatre. In 1860, after immense success in provincial towns, he went again to America. The vessel encountered such stormy weather that his health was permanently injured. He had been wonderfully robust, but consumption developed after his return to London in 1862. He was invited to Blandford, Dorset, by his friend Robert Eyers of the Crown Hotel, to recover his health if possible, but soon after moving there he died, on 11 March 1864. He was buried in the cemetery at Blandford on 15 March, and a monument was erected by his friends. His widow died at the age of eighty on 13 January 1899.

J. W. EBSWORTH, *rev.* NILANJANA BANERJI

**Sources** T. A. Brown, *History of the American stage* (1870) · *Era Almanack and Annual* (1900) · *The life and reminiscences of E. L. Blanchard, with notes from the diary of Wm. Blanchard*, ed. C. W. Scott and C. Howard, 2 vols. (1891) · Hall, *Dramatic ports.* · personal knowledge (1887)

**Likenesses** R. Alexander, oils, 1842 · monument, Blandford cemetery · portrait, repro. in *Theatrical Times* (29 July 1848) · portrait, repro. in *Frank Leslie's Weekly* (10 Dec 1859) · twenty-one prints, Harvard TC

**Cowell, Sydney** (1846–1925). *See under* Cowell, Samuel Houghton (1820–1864).

**Cowen, Sir Frederic Hymen** [Hyman Frederick] (1852–1935), conductor and composer, was born on 29 January 1852 in Kingston, Jamaica, the younger son of Frederick Augustus Cowen (*d.* 1876) and his wife, Emily, the second daughter of James Davis of Kingston. Back in England, his father's positions as private secretary to the earl of Dudley and treasurer of Her Majesty's Theatre gave him the entrée to concerts at Dudley House (where he himself gave performances) and to opera productions. Cowen was a child prodigy: two dances for piano were published by the time he was seven, and when he was eight an operetta, *Garibaldi* (whose libretto was by his sister Rosalind), was performed privately. He made his public début as a pianist

in 1863; in 1864 he was the soloist in a performance of Mendelssohn's D minor piano concerto, and in 1865 he performed his own piano trio with the illustrious violinist Joseph Joachim and the cellist Pezze. That year he was awarded the second Mendelssohn scholarship (the first had been awarded to Arthur Sullivan), but his parents refused to accept the terms of the scholarship and he attended the conservatory at Leipzig independently. Later he studied in Berlin. A concert held at St James's Hall, London, in 1869 included his first symphony and his piano concerto, in which the composer, all of seventeen, was the soloist.

From 1871 Cowen spent about seven years as accompanist in J. H. Mapleson's touring opera company and at Her Majesty's, under Sir Michael Costa. Finding his hopes of becoming an opera conductor frustrated, he turned to orchestral conducting, and in 1880 conducted the Promenade Concerts (then held in Covent Garden). He continued to compose. Concert tours in Scandinavia led to the composition of his third symphony, the 'Scandinavian', the première of which he directed in 1880. Noted for its orchestral effects, this work gained international attention, being conducted by Hans Richter in Vienna in 1882 and later by Cowen himself in Budapest, Stuttgart, Cologne, and Paris, and it was also performed in the United States. Cowen's orchestral compositions eventually included six symphonies and various lighter pieces: he was especially known for the latter, such as the suite *The Language of Flowers* (1880). He also developed a reputation as a composer of choral works for music festivals, then a staple part of British musical life, and, in time, of nearly three hundred songs. Some are in a Schumann-esque style, but the majority are sentimental ballads which enjoyed great popularity. By the mid-1880s Cowen was among the leading members of the burgeoning 'English musical renaissance'. In 1884 he was engaged as a choral conductor in Glasgow; in the Birmingham festival of 1885 his cantata *The Sleepers* was heard alongside works by Gounod and Dvořák; and in 1888 he succeeded Sullivan as conductor of the Philharmonic Society, where he improved the orchestral standards and broadened the concert repertories. Grieg and Tchaikovsky were among the musicians who performed with the society during his conductorship. Such was his standing that, also in 1888, he was engaged as the conductor of the Centennial Exhibition in Melbourne for the then extraordinary fee of £5000.

In 1892 a disagreement over rehearsal time led to Cowen's dismissal from the Philharmonic. He now gave renewed energy to opera. Neither his *Pauline* (1876) nor *Thorgrim* (1890) had achieved success. *Signa* was intended as one of a series of English operas initiated in 1891 by D'Oyly Carte. When this project collapsed Cowen managed to have the première given in Milan—a rare achievement for a British composer—in 1893. But here and later in London it failed, as did *Harold* (1895). Cowen blamed these failures on non-musical factors, and with some justification; nevertheless, for all their stylistic versatility, ranging from the Italianate *Signa* to the more Wagnerian vein of *Thorgrim* and *Harold* (which he considered his best), his operas lack sustained dramatic power. Henceforth it was as a conductor that Cowen was primarily known. In 1893 he was again engaged as conductor of the Promenade Concerts, and in 1896 he succeeded Hallé at Manchester. Engagements at Liverpool and Bradford followed. He bitterly resented being forced to relinquish the Hallé post to Richter in 1899, claiming prejudice against British musicians in favour of a foreign conductor—a frequent complaint. The following year, 1900, saw his return to the Philharmonic Society and an engagement with the Scottish Orchestra, positions which he held until 1907 and 1910 respectively. While continuing as conductor of the Liverpool Philharmonic and the Bradford Festival Choral Society, he took on the triennial Cardiff festival in 1902 and the Handel festival at the Crystal Palace in 1903. Honorary doctorates were awarded by Cambridge in 1900 and by Edinburgh in 1910. Two years earlier, on 23 June 1908, he had married the 26-year-old Frederica Gwendoline, the only daughter of Frederick Richardson, a leather merchant. They had no children. Cowen was knighted in 1911.

This was the pinnacle of Cowen's career. But he found the extensive travelling increasingly tiring and gradually reduced his engagements. By the end of the First World War he had largely retired. The Handel festival of 1923 saw his last major appearance as a conductor. Late in life he gave children's radio broadcasts, published in 1933. His compositions were by this time rarely performed. He died at his home, 105 Maida Vale, London, on 6 October 1935, and was buried in the Jewish cemetery at Golders Green.

In 1932 Elgar had described Cowen as 'a dominating factor in the musical life of this country since 1875' (*The Times*, 7 Oct 1935). That importance rested on his work as a conductor. As a composer he was overshadowed first by Sullivan and later by Elgar himself, and his compositions lack outstanding imaginative invention. His conducting drew mixed reactions: for Bernard Shaw it was lethargic, and Cowen was disconcerted when Elgar, in a controversial lecture, placed him no higher than among 'choral men' (Elgar, 129). Nevertheless, for more than forty years he was a focal point in this branch of the musical profession, establishing the status of the British conductor despite assumptions regarding foreign musical superiority.

GEORGE BIDDLECOMBE

**Sources** F. H. Cowen, *My art and my friends* (1913) · J. E. Potts, 'Sir Frederick H. Cowen (1852–1935)', *MT*, 94 (1953), 351–3 · *The Times* (7 Oct 1935) · *MT*, 76 (1935), 1008 · *MT*, 39 (1898), 713–19 · *DNB* · E. Elgar, *A future for English music, and other lectures*, ed. P. M. Young (1968), 129, 147 · C. Ehrlich, *First philharmonic: a history of the Royal Philharmonic Society* (1995), 145–55 · A. Jacobs, *Arthur Sullivan: a Victorian musician*, 2nd edn (1992), 388–9 · M. Kennedy, *The Hallé, 1858–1983: a history of the orchestra* (1982), 8 · R. W. Grieg, *The story of the Scottish Orchestra* (1945), 6, 9 · *The Bodley Head Bernard Shaw: Shaw's music*, ed. D. H. Laurence, 3 vols. (1981), vol. 2, p. 974 · M. Musgrave, *The musical life of the Crystal Palace* (1995), 54–5 · E. W. White, *A history of English opera* (1983), 336–9 · J. Spencer, 'Cowen, Sir Frederic Hymen', *New Grove* · m. cert.
**Archives** BL, autograph score of a comic opera, Add. MS 52426 | Elgar Birthplace Museum, Worcester, letters to Sir Edward Elgar · priv. coll., Elgar MSS

**Likenesses** photograph, 1901, Mitchell L., Glas. · photograph, repro. in Cowen, *My art and my friends*, frontispiece
**Wealth at death** £6746 15s. 1d.: probate, 22 Nov 1935, *CGPLA Eng. & Wales*

**Cowen, Sir Joseph** (1800–1873). *See under* Cowen, Joseph (1829–1900).

**Cowen, Joseph** (1829–1900), politician and journalist, was born at his parents' home, Stella Hall, Blaydon-on-Tyne, co. Durham, on 9 July 1829. He was eldest of the four sons and one daughter of **Sir Joseph Cowen** (1800–1873) and his wife, Mary (*d.* 1851), daughter of Anthony Newton of Winlaton, near Gateshead. Joseph Cowen senior was a coal owner and firebrick and clay retort manufacturer. He was a co. Durham JP and an alderman for Newcastle upon Tyne. A life member and chairman of the River Tyne improvement commission, he was knighted on 14 March 1872 for his services on the commission, which rendered the river navigable for sea-going ships. He was elected as a radical MP for Newcastle in July 1865, and retained his seat until his death at his residence, Stella Hall, on 19 December 1873. Cowen's ancestors came from Lindisfarne, and for three centuries they had lived, laboured, and died on Tyneside, many of them as employees at Winlaton in Sir Ambrose Crowley's factory for smith's wares. Cowen's grandfather was the last member of the Cowen family to have been employed at this factory and, when it closed in 1816, this grandfather established his own factory at Blaydon Burn which Sir Joseph Cowen inherited and greatly enlarged. The younger Cowen, who derived a very large income from the works, sold them shortly before his death.

Cowen was educated first at a private school in Ryton, and then at the University of Edinburgh. His university career was chiefly remarkable for his pre-eminence in the debating society. While a student he interested himself in the revolutionary movements on the continent in 1848, and made Mazzini's acquaintance by letter. He took no degree. After leaving the university Cowen joined his father in business. On 24 July 1854 he married Jane, daughter of John Thompson of Fatfield, Durham.

Cowen continued to promote revolution throughout Europe. His movements were closely watched by spies in the service of foreign police in order that they might discover how revolutionary documents were imported into their respective countries. These papers were really smuggled among the overseas shipments of firebricks from Blaydon Burn. Cowen numbered among his guests and friends: Mazzini, Kossuth, Louis Blanc, and Ledru-Rollin; Wysocki, who was a leader of the insurgent Hungarians; Mieroslawski and Worcell, who were Poles in revolt against Russia; and Herzen and Bakunin, who were Russians and the declared enemies of the Russian government. Without his aid the lot of many foreign refugees in England would have been far harder, since his purse was always open to help them, and his pen was always ready to advocate their cause and encourage their efforts. There is some evidence to suggest that Cowen was somehow implicated in Orsini's attempt on the life of Napoleon III in

Joseph Cowen (1829–1900), by Lock & Whitfield, pubd 1881

1858. At home Cowen sympathized with Chartists and strenuously laboured on their behalf. He was an active member of the Northern Reform League, which was founded on 3 January 1858 and existed until 1862. In 1866 it was reorganized, with Cowen as chairman.

Cowen wrote much for the public press, and was a contributor from boyhood to the *Newcastle Chronicle*, of which, in later life, he became proprietor and editor. He also established a monthly, the *Northern Tribune*. On his father's death in 1873 he succeeded him as Liberal member for Newcastle, with a majority of 1003. His election was the source of a long controversy on account of the deep divide within Newcastle Liberalism between Cowen's own radical faction and the moderate wing led by Thomas Headlam (until 1873 Newcastle's second MP). Cowen's inability to co-operate with (or indeed tolerate) Headlam cost the latter his seat, which went to the Conservative candidate Charles Hamond. Cowen's intransigence and lack of party spirit did not please either Gladstone or John Bright. The fact that he resented their criticism and was obviously unwilling to compromise his personal views for the sake of party discipline and unity further strained his relationship with the men he had been elected to support. Nevertheless, he was chosen again at the general election in 1874. His maiden speech was delivered in 1876 on the Royal Titles Bill, and it made a strong impression on the House of Commons: Disraeli sent his compliments. Cowen did not conceal his satisfaction that a political opponent should have done so, nor his chagrin that Gladstone, whom he supported, disparagingly referred to one of his speeches as smelling of the lamp. Indeed, all his speeches were carefully prepared and very rhetorical in form, as were his writings. It was obvious that he had adopted too many of the mannerisms of Macaulay. In the House of Commons his delivery was marred by a strong Northumbrian accent; but this was no defect when he addressed his constituents. Yet Cowen was much more than a provincial demagogue: it is more appropriate to describe him as a sort of wealthy precursor to Keir Hardie, with whom indeed he shared some personality traits, such as an exasperating spirit of independence, which brought him into collision first with the parliamentary leadership of the Liberal Party, then with the Newcastle caucus, and finally with the whole of the party. At the local level this escalation became even more dramatic when Cowen began to support working-class candidates with a view to dismantling the power of the caucus. Ironically, in the process he himself resorted to a sort of 'anti-caucus caucus', the Democratic Federation, which in 1882 was made up of radicals firmly hostile to Gladstone's Irish policy of coercion. His popularity was somewhat lessened by what was considered to be his erratic conduct, such as the support he gave to the tory government in the case of the Russo-Turkish War; but he always cherished his right to independence in judgement and action. A home-ruler before Gladstone took up the question, Cowen remained so to the end of his life, but he also remained an imperialist of a pronounced type. He provides a good illustration of the extent to which commitment to the principle of national self-government and passionate support for the British empire were perceived as being reciprocally compatible, even in the most advanced radical circles. He cultivated independence in all relations of life. Though this contributed to his charisma and personal ascendancy among Newcastle artisans, his crusade against the very principle of party discipline and mass organization was the futile last stand of a romantic supporter of the old 'direct democracy' style of popular politics, at a time when—especially in the north-east—Labour politicians were successfully extending trade-union discipline and organization into the realm of politics. Therefore it is no surprise that Cowen's insistence in his anti-party mood eventually caused the breakup of his relationship with the Durham Miners' Association, just as previously it had spoiled his long and close friendship with Thomas Burt, leader of the Northumberland miners. His customary dress was that of a Northumbrian miner on a Sunday, which was then a novelty in the House of Commons. He had an aversion to society, yet, being very rich, open-handed, and well read, he was a welcome guest everywhere.

When entering a public meeting of the electors of Newcastle on 18 March 1880 Cowen was crushed and injured internally, and he never wholly recovered from the effects. He was re-elected in 1880, but retired at the general election in 1886 and refused to be a candidate again. He continued in charge of the *Newcastle Chronicle* until his sudden death at Stella Hall on 18 February 1900. A son and daughter survived him.

W. F. RAE, *rev.* EUGENIO F. BIAGINI

**Sources** *Debrett's Illustrated House of Commons and the Judicial Bench* (1867), 51 · *Newcastle Weekly Chronicle* (19 Feb 1900) [suppl.] · The

*Times* (19 Feb 1900) • E. R. Jones, *Life and speeches of Joseph Cowen* (1886) • Boase, *Mod. Eng. biog.* • W. Duncan, *Life of Joseph Cowen MP* (1904) • P. Brock, 'Joseph Cowen and the Polish exiles', *Slavonic and East European Review*, 32 (1953–4), 52–69 • M. Partridge, 'Alexander Herzen and the younger Joseph Cowen', *Slavonic and East European Review*, 41 (1962–3) • *DLB* • J. Kelly, 'Cowen, Joseph', *BDMBR*, vol. 2 • N. Todd, *The militant democracy: Joseph Cowen and Victorian radicalism* (1991) • *DNB*

**Archives** Tyne and Wear Archives Service, Newcastle upon Tyne, corresp. and papers | Holyoake House, Manchester, Co-operative Union archive, letter to G. J. Holyoake • U. Newcastle, Robinson L., letters to R. S. Watson • UCL, corresp. with Sir Edwin Chadwick **Likenesses** E. A. Venturi, oils, 1857, U. Newcastle • S. or E. Sawyer, oils, 1864, U. Newcastle • Irving, oils, *c*.1880, U. Newcastle • J. Dickenson, oils, 1883, U. Newcastle • W. Irving, oils, 1891, U. Newcastle • Lock & Whitfield, woodburytype photograph, NPG; repro. in T. Cooper, *Men of mark: a gallery of contemporary portraits* (1881) [*see illus.*] • Spy [L. Ward], caricature, chromolithograph, NPG; repro. in *VF* (27 April 1878) • caricature, chromolithograph, NPG; repro. in *Monetary Gazette* (1 Sept 1877), suppl. • portrait (Joseph Cowen), repro. in *ILN*, 68 (1876), 35 • portraits (Joseph Cowen), repro. in *ILN*, 64 (1874), 22, 36 • wood-engraving (after photograph by W. & D. Downey), NPG; repro. in *ILN* (2 May 1874) **Wealth at death** £501,927 19*s*. 0*d*.: resworn probate, Feb 1901, *CGPLA Eng. & Wales* (1900)

**Cowen, William** (1791–1864), landscape painter and printmaker, was born in Rotherham, Yorkshire. He was initially educated for the church. After travelling a great deal, and making many sketches in Britain and Ireland in the process, he won the patronage of Earl Fitzwilliam, who paid for him to travel to Switzerland and Italy; the stock of landscape sketches which he made there formed the basis for his paintings throughout his long career as an artist. He exhibited at the British Institution (1811–60), the Royal Academy (1823–39), and the Society of British Artists (1824–45), principally showing landscapes and topographical views of Switzerland and Italy; he contributed to the Leeds exhibition of 1825, submitted *Kilchurn Castle, Loch Awe, Scotland* to the fresco competition in Westminster Hall, London (1844), and showed several landscapes at the Free Exhibition of Modern Art at Hyde Park Corner (1848–9). He was also a founder member of the New Society of Painters in Water Colours but resigned after its first exhibition in 1832. In 1840 he visited Corsica, then unexplored by artists, and made many sketches: subsequently he published a series of twelve etchings of the island in 1843, including scenes associated with the early life of Napoleon. These were very favourably received, and in 1848, with two additions, they formed the illustrations to his book, *Six Weeks in Corsica*, which contained an account of his adventures and translations of Corsican poetry.

Cowen also published an etching of a church (1817); *Six Views of Italian and Swiss Scenery* (1824); *A View of Rotherham*, published in Ebenezer Rhodes's *Yorkshire Scenery* (1826), which also contains two engravings of Roche Abbey from Cowen's drawings; *Six Views of Woodsome Hall* (lithographs, 1851); two large aquatints of Harrow on the Hill and Chatsworth; a lithograph of Kirkstall Abbey; and a lithographed portrait of the African chief Jan Tzatzoe. According to exhibition lists, Cowen was living in Rotherham between 1811 and 1821 and from 1825 to 1831. He otherwise resided

in London; on his return from Corsica he lived at Gibraltar Cottage, Thistle Grove, Old Brompton. He died in London in 1864. There are examples of his watercolours in the British Museum, the Victoria and Albert Museum, and Kensington and Chelsea Library, London.

DELIA GAZE

**Sources** D. Child, *Painters in the northern counties of England and Wales* (1994) • J. Guest, *Historic notices of Rotherham* (1879) • H. Turnbull, *Artists of Yorkshire: a short dictionary* (1976) • Mallalieu, *Watercolour artists*, vol. 2 • H. M. Cundall, *A history of British water colour painting*, 2nd edn (1929) • Wood, *Vic. painters*, 3rd edn • L. Lambourne and J. Hamilton, eds., *British watercolours in the Victoria and Albert Museum* (1980) • Graves, *Brit. Inst.* • Graves, *RA exhibitors* • J. Johnson, ed., *Works exhibited at the Royal Society of British Artists, 1824–1893, and the New English Art Club, 1888–1917*, 2 vols. (1975)

**Cowham** [*married name* Lander], **Hilda Gertrude** (1873–1964), illustrator, was born on 29 July 1873 at the Wesleyan Training College, Horseferry Road, Westminster, the daughter of Joseph Henry Cowham, a teacher, and his wife, Eliza Anna, formerly Butcher. After attending Wimbledon College she studied at Lambeth School of Art and at the Royal College of Art in London. She had won a competition in *The Studio* while still at school, and as an art student contributed cartoons to *Pick-Me-Up* and *The Sketch*, and this encouraged her to make her career as an illustrator. Her work appeared in many magazines, including *Girl's Realm*, *The Graphic*, *Little Folks*, *Pearson's*, *Printer's Pie*, *The Queen*, *The Tatler*, and the *Windsor Magazine*, and she was one of the first women artists to work for *Punch*. Her subjects were often children—she has been said to have popularized the drawing of children with thin black legs and she drew in a distinctive style, usually with a brush and ink rather than a pen. She was considered among the best female comic artists and had a particular success with her creation of 'the Cowham kid' in the pages of *Punch*.

Besides working for magazines Cowham illustrated several books for children with decorative and whimsical drawings in pen or pencil, and with delicate, more detailed watercolours (for instance Edric Vredenburg's *Curly Heads and Long Legs*, *c*.1913). She also wrote a few books that she illustrated, including *Peter Pickle and his Dog Fido* (1906). Her work in this area as a 'nursery artist' influenced that of her friend Mabel Lucie Attwell. She made dolls, produced postcards and posters, and, starting in 1924, worked for Shelley Potteries at the Foley China Works in Fenton, Staffordshire, where she designed at least two series of nursery ware meant for children's use, and other pieces; these have now become collectors' items. Attwell followed her to Shelleys in 1926.

Cowham was a member of the Society of Graphic Artists and continued throughout her life to paint watercolour landscapes and interiors and to make etchings, exhibiting in London at the Royal Academy and at the Royal Institute of Painters in Water Colours, and in Paris and the United States. She married a painter and printmaker, Edgar Lander (*b*. 1883), who predeceased her. She died on 28 September 1964, at Ashley House, Shalford, Surrey. Her body was cremated. Examples of her work are held in the Victoria and Albert Museum, London.

ALAN HORNE

**Sources** M. Bryant and S. Heneage, eds., *Dictionary of British cartoonists and caricaturists, 1730–1980* (1994) · *The Studio*, 3 (1894), xvii · D. Wootton, *The illustrators: the British art of illustration, 1800–1999* (1999) · 'Sweet Pea Antiques and Collectibles', www.tias.com/stores/sweetpea/chris.html [Chris Davenport on Shelley china], 21 April 2001 · 'Shelley', www.rickhubbard-artdeco.co.uk, 21 April 2001 · S. Hill, *The Shelley style* (1990) · b. cert. · S. Houfe, *The dictionary of 19th century British book illustrators and caricaturists*, rev. edn (1996) · d. cert.

**Cowherd, William** (1763–1816), a founder of the Bible Christians (Cowherdites) and vegetarian, was born in Carnforth, Lancashire. Little is known of his early life, although his parents were probably James and Elizabeth Cowherd, or Coward. He described himself as a 'classical teacher in Beverley College', an institution for the preparation of candidates for the Anglican ministry, and from there he went to Manchester as curate to John Clowes, the Swedenborgian rector of St John's. Leaving Clowes he preached in the New Church Temple in Peter Street for a short time before 1800, in which year he opened a chapel called Christ Church, built for himself in King Street, Salford. Here he founded a congregation on Swedenborgian principles. His preaching, into which he freely introduced radical politics, soon secured him a large popular following. Cowherd broke with the New Church after their conference at Birmingham in 1808, mainly on the ground of renewed attempts to establish what he called 'a Swedenborgian priesthood'. On 28 June 1809 a rival conference met in Cowherd's chapel, attended by four ministers, Joseph Wright of Keighley, George Senior of Dalton, near Huddersfield, Samuel Dean of Hulme, and Cowherd, with a considerable number of laymen, including Joseph Brotherton, later MP for Salford. This conference formulated a scheme of doctrine which had a strong Swedenborgian tinge. Vegetarianism and teetotalism were, however, the hallmarks of the new sect and King Street was dubbed the Pudding Eaters' chapel. The 'Cowherdites' took the name of Bible Christians, but should be sharply distinguished from the Methodist body of the same name.

Cowherd on 26 March 1810 opened a grammar school and academy of science which afforded an excellent practical education. He was the presiding genius of the whole Bible Christian body, which included five congregations, at Salford, Hulme, Ancoats (the Round House, Every Street), Stockport, and Philadelphia, USA, which was founded by a group of Salford emigrants just before his death. Besides being a keen astronomer (he had an observatory on the roof of his chapel) Cowherd was a practical chemist and he treated the ailments of the poor with remedies of his own, so that he was popularly known as Dr Cowherd. He also provided generous quantities of soup for the poor in times of dearth. In 1811 he had a project for a printing office to bring out cheap editions of Swedenborg's works. Robert Hindmarsh, the New Church leader, went to Manchester to assist the scheme, but he and Cowherd differed about abstinence and other matters and soon quarrelled. Seceders from Cowherd and from Clowes built in 1813 a mainstream New Jerusalem church for Hindmarsh in Irwell Street, Salford, promptly called

the Beefsteak Chapel (confusingly and insultingly the name Beefsteak was later transferred to King Street). Cowherd died, unmarried, in Salford on 24 March 1816. He was buried beside his chapel: inscribed upon his tomb is a brief epitaph, written by himself with the telling summary (adapted from Pope): 'All feared, none loved, few understood', an indication that he knew his character to be both singular and uncompromising. His creed was a variant of Swedenborgianism: he held that humanity was perfectible and that only the eating of animal flesh and the drinking of spirituous liquors prevented the advent of an ideal humanity. Most of his congregations died out in the generation after his death, but King Street (after 1868 Cross Lane) chapel, the members of which included Joseph Brotherton and W. E. A. Axon, the Manchester librarian and historian, survived until 1932. Cowherd published *Select Hymns for the Use of Bible Christians* which reached a seventh edition in 1841. Posthumous was *Facts Authentic in Science and Religion: Designed to Illustrate a New Translation of the Bible* (pt 1, 1818; pt 2, 1820).

ALEXANDER GORDON, rev. IAN SELLERS

**Sources** W. Cowherd, *Report of a conference* (1809) · W. E. A. Axon, *History of the Bible Christian church, Salford* (1909) · P. J. Lineham, 'The English Swedenborgians, 1770–1840: a study in the social dimensions of religious sectarianism', DPhil diss., U. Sussex, 1978 · R. R. Gladish, *A history of New Church education* (1968) · W. E. A. Axon, ed., *The annals of Manchester: a chronological record from the earliest times to the end of 1885* (1886)

**Cowie, Benjamin Morgan** (1816–1900), dean of Exeter, born in Bermondsey, London, on 8 June 1816, was the youngest son of Robert Cowie, a merchant and insurance agent, descended from a Cornish family long settled in London. When about eight years old he was placed at a *pensionnat* at Passy, near Paris, under an instructor named Savary, and was taught mathematics for four years by two Savoyards named Peix and Sardou. He was admitted to St John's College, Cambridge, as a sizar in July 1833, and as a pensioner on 12 October 1833. He graduated BA as senior wrangler in 1839, MA in 1842, BD in 1855, and DD in 1880. In 1839 he was chosen second Smith's prizeman, being placed below Percival Frost, who was second wrangler. Cowie was admitted a fellow of St John's College on 19 March. He was admitted a student of Lincoln's Inn on 8 November 1837, but gave up law and was ordained deacon in 1841 and priest in 1842 by Joseph Allen, bishop of Ely. He lived for some years in college, and during this period prepared his *Descriptive catalogue of the manuscripts and scarce books in the library of St John's College, Cambridge*, issued by the Cambridge Antiquarian Society in 1843. In that year he vacated his fellowship by his marriage on 10 August 1843 at Poughill, Cornwall, to his cousin, Gertrude Mary (d. 15 March 1860), second daughter of Thomas Carnsew of Flexbury Hall, Poughill. They had several children.

In 1843 Cowie became curate at St Paul's, Knightsbridge, under William James Early Bennett, with whose high-church views he was in sympathy. In 1844 he was appointed principal and senior mathematical lecturer of the recently founded College for Civil Engineers at Putney, and during his residence there he acted as honorary secretary to the committee of management of St Mark's College at Chelsea for training parochial schoolmasters, then under the principalship of Derwent Coleridge. When the college for civil engineers closed in 1851 he lived for four or five years at the Manor House, Stoke D'Abernon, Cobham, Surrey. In 1852 and again in 1856 he was chosen select preacher at Cambridge. His sermons preached at Great St Mary's, Cambridge, in 1856 were published as *On sacrifice: the atonement, vicarious oblation, and example of Christ, and the punishment of sin*. In 1853 and 1854 he was Hulsean lecturer, his lectures being published as *Scripture Difficulties* (2 vols., 1853–4). In 1855 he was appointed professor of geometry at Gresham College, London. On 28 November 1856 he was appointed fifth minor canon and succentor of St Paul's Cathedral, and on 17 March 1857 he was presented to the rectory of St Lawrence Jewry with St Mary Magdalen, Milk Street, by the dean and chapter of St Paul's. He showed his sympathy with high-church tendencies by developing an elaborate ritual but without showing any marked sympathy with Roman doctrine. He acted as government inspector of schools from 1857 to 1872, and on 14 January 1871 was appointed chaplain-in-ordinary to the queen. In 1866 he was Warburton lecturer on prophecy at Lincoln's Inn, publishing his lectures in 1872 as *The Voice of God*.

In October 1872 W. E. Gladstone nominated Cowie dean of Manchester, and in 1880 he was chosen prolocutor of the lower house of the convocation of York, an office which he filled for three years. As dean of Manchester Cowie was custodian of the collegiate church, and the restoration of Chetham Chapel was due to his efforts. He was of moderate Tractarian sympathies. During the Lambeth synod, he invited all bishops attending from the USA— both high and low church—to preach. He did good service in Manchester in the cause of education, acting as a governor of the grammar school and as a member of the council of Owens College, and playing an important part in the founding of Manchester High School for Girls. In 1879, after the death of Francis Robert Raines, he was elected a feoffee of Chetham College. Upon the death of Turner Crossley he undertook the completion of the supplementary catalogue of Chetham's Library. Cowie was active in setting up charities in Manchester but ran into difficulties, which in part account for his transfer to the post of dean of Exeter in 1883. He held the deanery until his death, on 3 May 1900, at 26 New Cavendish Street, London.

Besides the works already mentioned, Cowie was the author of numerous published sermons, letters, and addresses, and contributed an essay, 'Toleration', to the second series of the *Church and the Age* (1874), edited by Archibald Weir and William Dalrymple Maclagan.

E. I. CARLYLE, *rev.* H. C. G. MATTHEW

**Sources** *The Times* (4 May 1900) · *The Eagle*, 21 (1900), 342–8 · Crockford (1900) · A. Boutflower, *Personal reminiscences of Manchester Cathedral, 1854–1912* (1913) · M. Hennell, *The deans and canons of Manchester Cathedral, 1840–1948* [1988] · *CGPLA Eng. & Wales* (1900) · Venn, *Alum. Cant.*

**Likenesses** T. C. Wageman, watercolour drawing, Trinity Cam.
**Wealth at death** £5041 2s. 9d.: probate, 3 July 1900, *CGPLA Eng. & Wales*

**Cowie, James** (1886–1956), painter, was born on 16 May 1886 at Netherton of Dalgety, a small upland farm near the village of Cuminestown in Aberdeenshire, the second of three sons of Peter Smart Cowie (1858–1919) and his wife, Katherine Tennant (1859–1926). With many generations of nonconformist farming folk in his ancestry, James was expected to carry on the family tradition, but he had other ideas. A clever, indeed an intellectual, youth, he finished his years at the local village school as a pupil teacher before commencing (but for some reason never completing) a degree course in English at Aberdeen University. Instead he enrolled in 1906 at the United Free Church Training College in Aberdeen, where his talent as a visual artist was encouraged by the art teacher, James Hector. In 1909 Cowie accepted the post of art master at Fraserburgh Academy, but in 1912, having decided to become a painter, he enrolled at the Glasgow School of Art which was then, under its young English director, Francis Newbery, acknowledged as one of the leading art schools in Britain. Newbery recognized Cowie's ability and agreed to allow him to complete the diploma course in two years instead of the usual three. Because he gained his diploma in 1914 just as war with Germany was declared, Cowie's strict conscientious scruples led to four years of uncreative labour with a pioneer corps. Afterwards, from 1918 to 1935, he worked as art master in a small Lanarkshire mining town not far from Glasgow. It was there, at Bellshill Academy, that he began to develop his primary gift of expression through drawing, using the art room as though it were his own studio, working along with his pupils, drawing the children, singly and in groups as they themselves worked, studying and recording details of their physiognomy, clothes, and attitudes, and thus generating ideas which might be developed later in his Glasgow studio. In 1918 Cowie married Nancy Buchanan, who had been a fellow student; her death in 1923 left him with a baby daughter, Ruth. Three years later he married Alice Graham, a teacher; the couple had a daughter, Barbara.

All his life Cowie looked to the early Renaissance for stimulation. He tended to despise work painted *au premier coup* and his own major paintings were invariably created after many careful drawings and preliminary studies. In this he was out of step with most of the Scottish painting of his day. Yet he did not despise the activity, or the importance, of the Royal Scottish Academy of which he became an associate member in 1936, full academician in 1943, and honorary secretary in 1948.

Cowie was appointed head of drawing and painting at Gray's School of Art, Aberdeen, in 1935 but he found the restrictions of art school routine distasteful and after only one session resigned in order to accept the more congenial post of warden at the Hospitalfield College of Art in Arbroath, Angus. He remained at Arbroath from 1937 until 1948; this was his most productive period both as a painter and as a teacher. Hospitalfield was then a residential summer school for a limited number of post-diploma

James Cowie (1886–1956), self-portrait, *c.*1950 [*The Blue Shirt*]

students from the four Scottish art schools, and it was there, in the large mock-baronial mansion built in the early nineteenth century over a medieval original and set in rich farmlands near the wide River Tay, that Cowie's work as an artist came to full fruition. In his paintings of the schoolchildren at Bellshill he had succeeded in developing a kind of realism which, to the perceptive viewer, was beginning to be rich in suggestion of what seemed to the artist the pitiful brevity of youth. Even at that early stage in his career his drawings and paintings had been full of references to the inexorable passing of time and to the ephemerality of existence: his sketchbooks and notebooks contain several fragmentary jottings and half-finished poems on this theme. Later, at Hospitalfield, he began to explore and develop a kind of metaphysical still life in which elements with a personal appeal for him— tanagra figurines and classical statuettes, prints from the old masters, sea shells, a leaf, an apple—would be married with fragments of mirror-reflected landscape to offer a sometimes puzzling wealth of associative meaning. Cowie was not so much a realist as a surrealist, but in a delicate, subtle manner which had little in common with Dalí or even Magritte. His landscapes, too, were almost invariably charged with mystery: in *Evening Star* (1944, Aberdeen Art Gallery), for example, an ambitious, life-size painting, he placed three female nudes in the mouth of a cave in sandstone rocks, a natural setting conveying a sense of menace. Yet for all the evidence of preconception and extreme care in composition in his finished works, his notebooks occasionally contain direct sketches in watercolour, including attempts to capture fleeting effects of light.

Cowie was in no sense a professional portrait painter, but to the few he did paint, such as the official portrait of his friend Sir Frank Mears, president of the Royal Scottish Academy (1944, Royal Scottish Academy, Edinburgh), and the earlier full-length studies of his daughters Ruth Cowie (1933, priv. coll.) and Barbara Graham Cowie (1938, Royal Scottish Academy, Edinburgh), he brought unusual insight. When he retired in 1948 he moved permanently to Edinburgh, where in 1952 he was awarded the honorary degree of LLD at the university. Later that year he was disabled by a severe stroke. James Cowie died at his home, 11 Rothesay Place, Edinburgh, on 18 April 1956 and was buried on 20 April in the churchyard of Kirkton of Auchterless, Monquitter, Aberdeenshire, under a headstone which he himself had designed for his parents and elder brother. He was survived by his second wife. His profound knowledge and understanding of the Italian quattrocento (a period beloved by him), his wide reading, and, above all, his sensitive draughtsmanship (perhaps the finest in Scotland in his day) combined to make his work exceptional. Collections of Cowie's work are in the Aberdeen Art Gallery and the Scottish National Gallery of Modern Art, Edinburgh.                                        CORDELIA OLIVER

**Sources** personal knowledge (2004) · private information (2004) · D. P. Bliss, *James Cowie memorial exhibition* (1957) [exhibition catalogue, Scottish Arts Council] · J. Cowie, sketchbooks and notebooks, priv. coll. · *CGPLA Eng. & Wales* (1956) · *Glasgow Herald* (19 April 1956) · grave, Kirkton of Auchterless churchyard, Monquitter, Aberdeenshire, Scotland

**Likenesses** J. Cowie, self-portrait, pencil and chalk study, 1940–49, U. Aberdeen · J. Laurie, pastel drawing, 1947, Scot. NPG · J. Cowie, self-portrait, oils, *c.*1950, U. Edin. [*see illus.*] · portrait, Scot. NPG

**Wealth at death** £968 3*s.* 0*d.*: confirmation, 7 Dec 1956, *CCI*

**Cowie, Mervyn Hugh** (1909–1996), conservationist, was born on 13 April 1909 in Nairobi, Kenya, the younger son of Herbert Hugh Cowie, settler, and his wife, Ada, *née* Harries. His father was formerly the chief magistrate of Johannesburg, and his mother was a determined pioneering woman of considerable character and fortitude. After spending his childhood in Kenya, Mervyn was sent 'home' to England to complete his schooling at Brighton College, which he entered with his elder brother, Dudley, in 1922. From there he went in 1930 to Brasenose College, Oxford, to read law, but his university career was cut short by his father falling seriously ill, necessitating his return to Kenya. He then went back to England and studied chartered accountancy. In 1932 he once more sailed for Kenya where he began working as an accountant.

On his return to east Africa, Cowie was shocked at the degradation of both wildlife and habitats that had occurred during his years away, and he set about trying to force the government to address the situation. His pleas falling on deaf ears, he took a drastic and somewhat bizarre measure. Writing pseudonymously to the *East African Standard* and other newspapers, he suggested all wildlife be eradicated in order to improve the country's farming. The public outcry at this 'radicalism' jarred the authorities into action. Cowie was made an honorary game warden, and conservation became a major legislative concern. Throughout the 1930s he worked as an accountant, served as a district councillor in Nairobi, joined the King's African rifles reserve, hunted big game in his spare time, and founded the game policy committee to oversee wildlife concerns such as the control of hunting licences. In 1934 he married Erica Mary (Molly) Beaty, a former ballet dancer, with whom he had two sons and a daughter.

On the outbreak of the Second World War in 1939 Cowie was commissioned into the Kenya regiment, and he served in Abyssinia, Madagascar, and the Middle East, rising to the rank of lieutenant-colonel. With the cessation of hostilities he returned to civilian life, determined to do all he could for game conservation. In 1946 he was appointed the founder director of the Kenya national parks service and succeeded in establishing the country's first game reserve, the Nairobi National Park. This was not without considerable, often vituperative, opposition from both die-hard colonials and native herders who had to surrender their grazing to the project. Undeterred, Cowie went on to create many other game reserves, including the internationally famous Tsavo Park and Amboseli Maasai Game Reserve. At the same time he considerably scaled down his hunting activities. In 1951 he was appointed a member of the legislative council, the colonial parliament. From this position of authority he was able to guide the development of conservation and at the same time foster the increase of tourism. From 1953 to 1956 his plans were temporarily upset by the Mau Mau uprising, during which he became director of manpower. Once the revolt was over he greatly contributed to the development of the tourist industry until it became the country's biggest foreign currency earner after coffee. For sixteen years from 1950 he was vice-president of the East African Tourist Travel Association. He was appointed CBE in 1960. Following the death of his first wife, Molly, in 1956, he married in 1957 Valori Hare Duke, formerly his secretary, and they had a son and a daughter.

With Kenya gaining its independence in 1963, Cowie's position came under threat, and in 1966 he was summarily dismissed with one month's salary in lieu of notice and no pension entitlement. His high-profile job, he was told, was being 'Africanised'. For six years Cowie struggled to make a living as an accountant and as a senior consultant to the World Wildlife Fund, fundraising mostly in London. Finally, in 1972, he returned to Nairobi as financial director of the African Medical and Research Foundation, which operated Kenya's flying doctor service. He retired in 1979 and, after a brief flirtation with Britain, tried to live out his years in Kenya. However, the rapid increase in violent crime in Nairobi forced him finally to leave his beloved Kenya for good, in 1989, and he settled near Saxmundham, Suffolk.

Always keen to share his passion for African wildlife with others, Cowie presented a series of BBC television natural history programmes, and served in a number of wildlife organizations. He wrote three books, of which the most famous, *Fly, Vulture* (1961), arose from his involvement with the 1951 film *Where No Vultures Fly*; it concerned his lifelong fight to establish game parks and counter ivory poaching. Considered to have been one of the most important conservationists of the twentieth century, Cowie was working on a fourth book at the time of his death from a heart attack, at the Ipswich Hospital, Ipswich, Suffolk, on 19 July 1996. He was survived by his second wife, Valori, and his five children.

MARTIN BOOTH

**Sources** M. Cowie, *Fly, vulture* (1961) · *The Guardian* (30 July 1996) · *The Times* (5 Aug 1996) · *The Independent* (21 Aug 1996) · *WWW* · personal knowledge (2004) · private information (2004) [family]
**Archives** CUL, corresp. with Sir Peter Markham Scott
**Likenesses** photograph, 1952 (with Princess Elizabeth), repro. in *The Guardian* · photograph, repro. in *The Times* · photograph, repro. in *The Independent* · photographs, priv. coll.

**Cowie, Robert Isaac** (1842–1874), physician and author, was born at Lerwick, the capital of the Shetland Islands, where both his father and uncle were well-known medical practitioners. His father was John Cowie, and his mother Margaret Cowie (*née* Greig). He was educated partly at Aberdeen, where he took the degree of MA, and at Edinburgh, where he was a favourite student of Sir James Y. Simpson. On the death of his father he took up his medical practice, and was held in high esteem, both for his professional and general character. He died suddenly from peritonitis at Commercial Street, Lerwick, on 1 May 1874, in his thirty-third year, survived by his widow, Janet (*née* Smith), formerly married to George Gray. Cowie was an enthusiastic lover of his native islands, one proof of which was his selection of certain physical peculiarities of the Shetland people as the subject of his thesis when applying for the degree of MD at Edinburgh University in 1866. At a later period he contributed to the International Congress at Paris an article on health and longevity, on the longevity of the Shetlanders, which excited considerable notice. Cowie published it, together with other material, in *Shetland, Descriptive and Historical* (1871 and later editions), the latter part being a descriptive account of the several islands of the group. The book retains its importance as an account of the islands.

W. G. BLAIKIE, *rev.* H. C. G. MATTHEW

**Sources** Boase, *Mod. Eng. biog.* · *BMJ* (6 June 1874), 760 · *Shetland Times* (4 May 1874) · R. Cowie, *Shetland, descriptive and historical*, 2nd edn (1875?) [memoir] · d. cert.

**Cowie, William Garden** (1831–1902), bishop of Auckland, was born in London on 8 January 1831; he was the second son of Alexander Cowie of St John's Wood, London, formerly of Auchterless, Aberdeenshire, and his wife, Elizabeth, also from Aberdeenshire, who was the daughter of Alexander Garden. Cowie was admitted as a pensioner of Trinity Hall, Cambridge, on 20 May 1852 and elected scholar in the following October. He gained the second highest mark of his year in the law tripos of 1854 and also gained a first class mark in theology. He graduated BA in 1855, MA in 1865, and DD in 1869. Ordained deacon in 1854 and priest in 1855, he was curate of St Clement's, Cambridge, in 1854 and of Moulton in Suffolk from 1855 to 1857.

Appointed, in 1857, chaplain to the forces in India, Cowie was present at the capture of Lucknow (receiving medal and clasp) and at the battles of Aliganj, Ruyah, and Bareilly. He accompanied Sir Neville Chamberlain's column in the Afghan campaign of 1863–4 (medal and clasp), and in 1864 acted as domestic and examining chaplain to G. E. L. Cotton, bishop of Calcutta. In 1865 he was chaplain in Kashmir; he worked with Dr Elmslie at the Punjab missions, warmly supported the work of the Church Missionary Society at Srinagar, and wrote *Notes on the Temples of Cashmere*.

In 1867 Cowie returned to England and became rector of Stafford. In 1868 Bishop G. A. Selwyn, after moving from the see of New Zealand to that of Lichfield, was empowered by the diocesan synod of Auckland to choose a successor for that diocese. He nominated Cowie, who, in 1869, was consecrated bishop of Auckland in Westminster Abbey. In the same year he married Eliza Jane (d. 1902), eldest daughter of William Webber of Moulton, Suffolk, and granddaughter of Sir Thomas Preston, bt, of Beeston Hall, Norfolk. They had at least one son.

Cowie readily won the confidence of the settlers, diligently visiting all parts of his diocese. He found many of the Maori alienated by the war, but was able to encourage the native ministry to establish native church boards in his northern archdeaconries. He ordained three Maori deacons in 1872, and with the help of the Society for the Propagation of the Gospel established twelve Maori clergymen. He promoted the development of St John's College, Auckland (for ordination candidates), of which he was visitor and governor, and in 1880 was made a fellow of the University of New Zealand and the Auckland University Council, 1883. He supported the Sailor's Home, Institute for the Blind, and the Women's Home in Auckland.

Cowie returned to England for the Lambeth conference of 1888 and in the same year published an account of his diocese, *Our Last Year in New Zealand*. In 1895 he was made primate of New Zealand. He visited England again for the diamond jubilee of Queen Victoria and for the Lambeth conference of 1897, receiving in that year an honorary degree of DD from the University of Oxford. He resigned his see in 1902 because of poor health, and died shortly afterwards at Wellington, New Zealand, on 26 June. He was given a military funeral and buried at St Stephen's cemetery, Tararua, Parnell, on 29 June. He was survived by his wife and one son.

A. R. BUCKLAND, *rev.* LYNN MILNE

**Sources** *The Times* (27 June 1902) · *Manchester Guardian* (1 Oct 1902) · *DNZB*, vol. 2 · *New Zealand Herald* (27 June 1902) · *Classified digest of the records of the Society for the Propagation of the Gospel in Foreign Parts, 1701-1892* (1893)
**Archives** U. Birm. L., letters to Church Missionary Society
**Likenesses** photograph, NPG

**Cowles** [*married name* Crawley], **(Harriet) Virginia Spencer** [*pseud.* Nancy Swift] **(1910–1983)**, journalist and author, was born on 24 August 1910 in Brattleboro, Vermont, USA, the second of the two children of Edward Spencer Cowles (1878–1954), a New York psychiatrist, and his wife, Florence Wolcott Jaquith (1887–1932), a writer and social columnist. Virginia rarely mentioned her past. Her mother, after eloping aged nineteen, divorced and moved to Boston; she was twenty-seven, with two daughters. A court awarded $60 monthly maintenance, but this was bitterly contested, and never came. Her mother survived by writing social columns for the *Boston Herald*, hand-setting each letter, her ankles swollen from standing as a compositor. From the age of eleven Cowles boarded in Massachusetts at the Waltham School for Girls, where, without other academic distinction, she was voted by her peers as the 'girl most likely to succeed'.

In Manhattan, New York, during the depression, Cowles lived off earnings precariously eked from selling advertising copy and magazine subscriptions. Her mother's death in 1932 left a $2000 life insurance windfall which funded a tour of Egypt, Ceylon, Burma, Malaya, Siam, China, and Japan with her sister, Mary, in 1934. She wrote an account of these journeys for William Randolph Hearst's 'March of events' column, and later wrote *Men are so Friendly* (1938), a light-hearted Nancy Mitford-like romp under the pseudonym Nancy Swift.

During the period from 1932 to 1937 Cowles, usually 'immaculate in her American war correspondent's uniform' (Crawley, 207), which included high heels and make-up, reported from a number of front lines. Her columns appeared in Hearst's *Sunday Syndicate*, the *New York Times*, and also in the British *Sunday Times* and *Daily Telegraph*. The 1937 headline 'New York society girl sees Americans fighting in Madrid's front trenches' (Sebba, 97) conjured up a carefree, wealthy image; that its human cost was considerable never saw print. In 1935 she interviewed Mussolini in Rome, two weeks after the Abyssinian invasion. She covered both sides of the Spanish Civil War, alternately detained by a Russian general commanding republicans and arrested by Franco's nationalists. In London her dispatch (unsigned) was quoted by Lloyd George in the Commons and she met Churchill at Chartwell through her friendship with Randolph Churchill. Just returned from Prague, where she had witnessed the response to Chamberlain's Munich betrayal, she sat next to Chamberlain at dinner and answered his query, 'What was it like?' In 1939 Cowles toured Russia to review Red Army purges; by new year she had tracked its relentless progress through sub-zero Finland. In Berlin she scooped the last peacetime report: in Paris she recorded the day of German invasion. At the age of thirty-two, crammed hurriedly into a small Hudson aeroplane in London with a surprised Harold Macmillan, on special assignment to north Africa and in civilian dress, Virginia was denied access to the front line. She appealed to General Eisenhower, who promptly cabled back: 'Miss Cowles can go where she likes; she is to be given every possible assistance' (Sebba, 155).

According to Sir Fitzroy Maclean, reporting by Cowles 'had a light touch … She was very ambitious, that was one of her great gifts—and she was unstoppable' (Sebba, 119). Charting female journalism a decade after her death, Anne Sebba noted that for Cowles 'writing was a way of understanding … world events' (ibid., 103). In *Looking for Trouble* (1941), her autobiography twice reprinted in that war-torn year, Cowles wrote: 'I had no qualifications as a war correspondent except curiosity' and, 'I wrote about the things I had seen and heard but did not try to interpret them' (pp. 7, 61). In 1941 she rallied support for the allied cause in the USA; during 1942–3 she served as special assistant to the American ambassador to London, Gilbert Winant. Cowles wrote *How America is Governed* (1944) and then covered the Italian campaign, the liberation of Paris, and the allied invasion of Germany. Churchill, seeing her in rowdy Walthamstow stadium two days before polling day in 1945, exclaimed: 'What a bad omen! *You* only appear when the established regime is falling to the ground!' (Cowles, *Winston Churchill*, 335). Captain Nigel Nicolson, actively engaged in holding a pass in Tunisia in February 1943, later remarked: 'her appearance was doubly startling: that she should be there at all at so critical a moment; and that she was the most beautiful young woman on whom, until then, I had ever set my eyes' (Nicolson, *Long Life*, 82–3). She combined objectivity with feminine charm: 'Even Monty adored her, and that was saying quite something!' (Nicolson, Memorial address).

Virginia Cowles married Aidan Merivale *Crawley (1908–1993), son of Canon A. Stafford Crawley, on 30 July 1945. The couple had two sons and a daughter. By nature compassionate, Virginia was variously described as ferocious, very direct, and, according to Evelyn Waugh, unprincipled. Asked if he minded, Aidan Crawley said: 'One thing you must remember about Virginia. She isn't *boring*' (private information). Both of them took their work, but never themselves, seriously. The arrival of Virginia's appointment as OBE for brave conduct, made on 1 July 1947, went unremarked in Aidan Crawley's memoirs. Her play, *Love Goes to Press*, brightened 1946 London before chilling Manhattan in January 1947. Her work after the war included *No Cause for Alarm* (1949), answering American questions on the Labour government, and also a major biography, *Winston Churchill: the Era and the Man* (1953).

Virginia's regular attendance at children's cricket, active canvassing for Aidan Crawley's Labour and subsequently Conservative parliamentary seats, entertaining in Chester Square, London, and running an active farm did not impair her relentless writing schedule; nor did her research for her husband's BBC documentaries on India, the Middle East, and Africa. Eight more biographies appeared, notably *Edward VII and his Circle* (1956), *The Phantom Major* (1958), *The Kaiser* (1963), *The Romanovs* (1971), and *The Rothschilds* (1973). While Rothschilds and Churchills dined with the family, she also made lifelong friends, many obscure, and often changed their lives.

In 1947 Virginia Cowles stated that 'being on English soil has a magic of its own for me' (Crawley, 217); but by 1974 the magic had run out. While she was living in Italy, France, and Spain, three last biographies appeared. She

dropped her American citizenship and had no English home: allegiance to place had ended. Diagnosed with imminently terminal emphysema, Virginia was driven by her husband through the tortuous Spanish hills of her youth at her request. *En route* for Mouton on 16 September 1983, their car turned over on the flat road across Les Grandes Landes; she was killed instantly. Her husband, although seriously injured, survived. Her body was cremated in Archeron, France.      ANN DAVENPORT DIXON

**Sources** H. Macmillan, *The blast of war, 1939–1945* (1967), 219 [vol. 2 of autobiography] · V. Cowles, *Looking for trouble* (1941) · V. Cowles, *Winston Churchill: the era and the man* (1953) · A. Crawley, *Leap before you look* (1988) · N. Nicolson, memorial address, 10 Feb 1994, London · A. Sebba, *Battling for news: the rise of the woman reporter* (1994) · N. Nicolson, *Long life* (1997) · S. Spanier, 'Afterword', in V. Cowles and M. Gellhorn, *Love goes to press* (1995) · M. Gellhorn, 'Introduction', in V. Cowles and M. Gellhorn, *Love goes to press* (1995) · C. Ogden, *Life of the party* (1994), 100 · A. Beevor and A. Cooper, *Paris after the liberation* (1994) · *Letters of Evelyn Waugh*, ed. M. Amory (1980), 161 · Countess of Ranfurly, *To war with Whitaker* (1995), 215–22 · private information (2004) [family] · A. Leslie, *Cousin Randolph* (1985), 39–40
**Archives** priv. coll.
**Likenesses** A. McBean, photograph, priv. coll.
**Wealth at death** £13,066: probate, 23 Feb 1984, *CGPLA Eng. & Wales*

**Cowley**. For this title name *see* Wellesley, Henry, first Baron Cowley (1773–1847); Wellesley, Henry Richard Charles, first Earl Cowley (1804–1884).

**Cowley, Abraham** (1618–1667), poet, was born in London, the seventh and posthumous son of Thomas Cowley (*d.* 1618), a stationer, and his wife, Thomasine. His mother obtained his admission as a king's scholar to Westminster School, which then enjoyed a considerable reputation. By his own account, Cowley had been first captivated by poetry as a child when he happened upon a copy of Edmund Spenser's *Faerie Queene* in his mother's parlour. His own career as a published poet began extremely early: *Poetical blossoms*, a collection of five poems, appeared in 1633; a second edition, adding 'Sylva, or Dyvers Copies of Verses', in 1636; and a third edition in 1637. According to the preface, the narrative poems 'Pyramus and Thisbe' and 'Constantius and Philetus' had been composed at the ages of ten and twelve respectively.

Cowley was admitted to Trinity College, Cambridge, as a pensioner on 21 April 1636, and became a scholar on 14 June 1637. Here on 2 February 1638 his Latin comedy *Naufragium joculare* was acted by members of his college before a university audience, and published subsequently; the same year saw the publication of an English pastoral comedy, *Love's riddle*, apparently written at the age of sixteen. On the occasion of Prince Charles's passing through Cambridge, Cowley's comedy *The Guardian* was acted for his entertainment on 12 March 1642. It remained unpublished until 1650, by which time Cowley had left England. Some non-dramatic poems can also be traced to these years, notably the elegy on his friend William Harvey.

Cowley had graduated BA in the winter of 1639/40, probably at the customary time in January; he was elected a

Abraham Cowley (1618–1667), by Sir Peter Lely, c.1666–7

'minor fellow' of Trinity on 30 October 1640; and he proceeded MA in 1642. In 1643, however, in common with many Cambridge fellows of royalist sympathies, he was ejected, and retired to Oxford, where he resided in St John's College. According to different accounts it was through Harvey's brother John, or through Stephen Goffe, that he began his association with Henry Jermyn, Harvey's cousin, whose secretary he became. This year he published a vigorous couplet satire, *The puritan and the papist*, roundly attacking both religious extremes, but interestingly confessing that if forced to choose, it would be the latter. Another political satire dating from this period is 'The Puritans Lecture'. It appeared in print under the title *A satyre against separatists*, ascribed to A. C. Generosus, in late 1642, and was reprinted in 1648 with *The four ages of England, or, The iron age*, both attributed to Cowley. In the preface to *Poems* (1656) Cowley denied all authorship of the latter, but remained silent on the question of the former poem.

The other important political poem from this period is *The civil war*, an unfinished epic poem celebrating the royalist successes up to the battle of Newbury and the heroic death of Lucius Cary, Viscount Falkland, whom Cowley had come to know and admire at Oxford. Cowley speaks of such a poem in the 1656 preface as abandoned when overtaken by events. A substantial portion of what is now known to be book 1 was published as *A poem on the late civil war* in 1679, but a mainly autograph manuscript of the full text, together with a transcript, was discovered among the Cowper (Panshanger) manuscripts at Hertfordshire Record Office (Herts. ALS) and published in 1973. It is now clear that Cowley adapted passages from *The civil war* for

his biblical epic the *Davideis*, and also for the final book of the *Plantarum libri sex*.

Possibly as early as 1644, and certainly by the beginning of 1646, Cowley left England in Jermyn's service to follow Queen Henrietta Maria into France. He was employed in missions to Jersey, Scotland, and the Low Countries, and in conducting secret correspondence in cipher between members of the royalist party, including that which passed between the exiled queen and Charles I. During his absence from England his cycle of love poems *The mistress* was published in 1647. Two distinct editions of this work have now been identified. Its popularity is well attested by the frequency with which individual poems appear in contemporary manuscript miscellanies and commonplace books, and were set to music by some of the most eminent composers of the period.

**Cowley in the interregnum** In mid- to late 1654 Cowley returned to England. According to his earliest biographer, Thomas Sprat, who misdates his arrival 1656, this was apparently to feign compliance with the Cromwellian regime but really to act as a royalist agent. He was arrested on 12 April 1655, in the aftermath of the abortive royalist risings in Yorkshire and at Salisbury that March, though by accident; the authorities had actually been seeking another person. He was released on bail of £1000, for which Dr Thomas Scarborough stood security. While in prison Cowley had prepared a major collection of his verse for publication. *Poems* (1656) omits the juvenilia and the political poems, but reprints *The mistress*. It also includes *Miscellanies*, a gathering of occasional poems, among them the elegies on Harvey and Crashaw, and the *Anacreontics*, some innocently bacchanalian imitations of the *Anacreontea*, then thought to be authentic poems of Anacreon; four books of the *Davideis*, an unfinished epic on the early career of David; and the *Pindarique odes*, which include imitations of two of Pindar's odes and several original poems executed in the same semi-irregular strophaic form. Both the *Davideis* and *Pindarique odes* have copious notes which testify to Cowley's scholarship, but it was the latter which were to prove the most influential part of his oeuvre.

Unfortunately the preface to *Poems* contains a passage which Cowley would have cause to regret. Speaking of the omission of the political poems and the unfinished *Civil War*, Cowley observes that it is now time for the conquered to set such things aside, to abandon the cause for which they have so long contended, to acquiesce in the mercy accorded by the victorious side. Sprat omitted this when the preface was reprinted in *Works* (1668), and is at pains to defend it in his own 'Account of the life and writings': he asserts that on Cowley's return to England he had found the royalist party in a sorry plight, but still too eager for ill-advised and potentially disastrous ventures; furthermore that Cowley was obliged to profess a passive obedience to the régime to secure his release from custody and pursue the designs for which he had been sent. Certainly Cowley's preface suggests that at worst he had come to despair of the royalist cause, in which he was scarcely alone, and that, temperamentally unsuited for the role in which he had been cast, he desired only a quiet life. His behaviour was less ambivalent than that of many who would declare for the king at the Restoration, yet it does seem to have been held against him. One would really need to know more of his actual political activities after his release, and how far he was the victim of rivalries within the royalist camp itself, before passing judgment.

Ostensibly Cowley passed the last years of the protectorate in the study of botany and medicine at Oxford, and also spent some time in Kent collecting samples. He proceeded to the degree of doctor of physic in 1657, and at this time seems to have gathered the materials for his Latin didactic poem *Plantarum libri sex*. His exact movements following Cromwell's death are unclear, but he returned to France in 1659 to renew his contacts with the royalist party there, though he seems to have been coolly received. Back in London before the Restoration, he hailed that event with a long Pindaric, *Ode: upon the blessed restoration and returne of his sacred majestie Charls the Second*, in which the king is compared to David entering his kingdom after the death of Saul.

**After the Restoration** Following the Restoration, Cowley published an unfinished political tract which he had begun during the protectorate of Richard Cromwell. *The visions and prophecies concerning England, Scotland, and Ireland* is dated 1661 on the title-page, though it was entered in the Stationers' register for October 1660, and dated November 1660 in the Thomason Tracts. In its preface it purports to be the posthumous work of Ezekiel Grebner, grandson of the Paul Grebner who had presented a book of prophecies, still extant in the library of Trinity College, Cambridge, to Elizabeth I. The younger Grebner is a former parliamentarian of the kind that had fought to rid Charles I of his evil counsellors, but sworn to preserve his crown and dignity, and has recoiled in horror at his execution. The work was to have been in three parts, of which only one is given here. After witnessing Oliver Cromwell's funeral, the author experiences a dream in which he encounters Cromwell's evil guardian angel and debates with him the deceased's character; the diabolic angel turns threatening, only to be driven off by the appearance of St George, the true guardian saint of England. The tract was reissued in 1661 under the title *A vision, concerning his late pretended highness, Cromwell the wicked*, under Cowley's own name. In a shortened preface, Cowley explains the original scope of the work which has become superfluous with the change of political events. The use of the Grebner persona, which seems to have been intended to appeal to moderate parliamentarians, is dropped entirely.

Cowley's scientific interests found expression in a short prose pamphlet entitled *A proposition for the advancement of learning*, also published in 1661, and reissued the same year under the alternative title *A proposition for the advancement of experimental philosophy*. This is an appeal for the foundation of a college for the pursuit of experiments, to which is attached a school providing a scientifically orientated education for boys. It outlines the design of the buildings, expenditure and regulations, staffing and stipends, and the curriculum of the school. His own botanical studies

issued in the first two books of his Latin didactic poem, *Plantarum*, published in 1662. Contrary to what has been sometimes asserted, Cowley neither was a member of the Royal Society nor attended its meetings, but he was certainly highly sympathetic to its aims. In 1667, at the request of his friend John Evelyn, he contributed a prefatory ode 'To the Royal Society' to Thomas Sprat's *History of the Royal Society*; in this, the last poem published in his lifetime, and possibly the last which he wrote, Bacon is acclaimed as the Moses of the new science, who surveyed but never entered the promised land.

On 16 December 1661 a revised version of Cowley's comedy *The Guardian* was produced under the new title *Cutter of Coleman-Street* by Sir William Davenant's company at the Duke's Theatre, Lincoln's Inn Fields. According to Cowley's preface to the 1663 printing of the play, on the opening night it met a hostile reception from part of the audience, who affected to see a satire upon the cavaliers at large in the characters of Colonel Cutter and Captain Worm, who are in fact mere raffish hangers-on disgracing the cause. Nevertheless the play enjoyed a successful run of a full week, and was revived several times after Cowley's death, the last occasion being in 1723.

In 1663 there appeared in Dublin a miscellany entitled *Poems by several persons*, containing verse mainly by Cowley, together with poems by Roger Boyle, Lord Orrery, Katherine Philips, and Clement Paman. Just how a Dublin printer should have come by the texts of poems by Cowley, some of them previously unpublished, is not entirely clear, though it seems plausible that Orrery, as a sometime patron of Cowley's, may have been responsible. Be that as it may, Cowley and his new publisher, Henry Herringman, acted quickly to secure the English copyright and supply a more accurate version of the texts, *Verses, lately written upon several occasions*. This slim volume contains emended texts of Cowley's poems from the Dublin volume, a reprint of his Restoration ode, and a previously unpublished ode upon Dr William Hervey, discoverer of the circulation of the blood. That it was very much an interim publication is shown by the subsequent relocation of six of the poems within the posthumous *Essays in verse and prose*.

One of the poems in the 1663 volume, 'The Complaint', voices in general terms Cowley's discontent at not having received the rewards he felt due to him for his services to the royal party. In particular he felt aggrieved that the mastership of the Savoy, which he believed to have been promised to him by both Charles I and Charles II, had been given to Gilbert Sheldon in 1661, and then to Henry Killigrew in 1663. This verse appeal for patronage had no effect upon the king, who indeed was often regarded by old royalists as readier to secure the loyalty of former opponents than to reward the faithful. Cowley was, however, relieved by the generosity of Jermyn, now earl of St Albans, and George Villiers, second duke of Buckingham, who procured him a lease on some of the queen mother's lands in Surrey. He settled at Barns Elms, and after two years moved to the Porch House at Chertsey in April 1665. The life of a Horatian gentleman farmer did not prove quite as he expected; in a letter to Sprat of 21 May 1665 he complained that both his tenants and his neighbours' cattle were troublesome, and that he had injured his ribs in a fall. Ironically, bucolic retirement proved the death of him: according to Sprat, he caught a chill while supervising his labourers in the fields, and died at Chertsey after a fortnight on 28 July 1667. On hearing of his death, Charles II observed that he had not left a better man behind him in England. Cowley received the most lavish funeral which had ever been given to a mere man of letters in England; he was buried on 3 August in Westminster Abbey, next to Chaucer and Spenser. His monument, erected by Buckingham, proclaims him 'Anglorum Pindarus, Flaccus, Maro, Deliciae, Decus, Desiderium aevi sui' ('The Pindar, Horace, and Virgil of the English, the glory and favourite of his age').

**Posthumous reputation** Under Cowley's will, dated 28 September 1665, Sprat had been appointed his literary executor. Under his supervision, a folio edition of the *Works* appeared in 1668. This reprints the contents of *Poems* (1656), together with the two prose tracts of 1661, and the 1663 *Verses* with some additional poems, published and unpublished; the most significant new material is *Several discourses by way of essays in verse and prose*, a collection of prose essays interspersed and accompanied by poems, dealing with such topics as 'Of Liberty', 'Of Agriculture', 'The Garden' (addressed to Evelyn), and 'Of Myself'. Sprat also undertook the publication of *Poemata Latina*, which includes the complete text of the *Plantarum* in six books. Of these the last, 'Sylva', is of great interest, centring upon a meditation on the oak as the national tree of England, and, through the royal oak which concealed Charles II in his flight from the battle of Worcester, proceeds to Cowley's final reflections upon the civil war. The juvenilia and the university plays were reprinted as *The second part of the works* in 1681.

Cowley never married. According to a story retailed by Samuel Johnson among others, he was in love only once in his life and lacked the courage to declare himself. Alexander Pope gave a more elaborate version to Joseph Spence, claiming that the lady, who eventually married Sprat's brother, was the Helenora of the poem 'The Chronicle', and that in his later years Cowley showed an aversion to women's society (Spence, 1.192); as Nethercot points out, the former story is most unlikely given that Cowley was seventeen years Sprat's senior and the two men seem not to have met until the late 1650s (Nethercot, 103). The truth is that these statements belong to the realm of posthumous, unsubstantiated tradition.

Something of Cowley's high reputation among his contemporaries has already been suggested. Some fourteen printings of the *Works* can be identified between 1668 and 1721. His impact upon later seventeenth-century poetry was profound: he carried Caroline wit-writing into the early Restoration period, and he received the tributes of both imitation and avowed admiration from such important poets as the earl of Rochester, John Oldham, and John Dryden, to say nothing of minor period figures whose verse is permeated by Cowley's influence. By the mid-

eighteenth century, a taste for Cowley had come to seem old-fashioned, but he still found qualified praise from Pope, William Cowper, and Samuel Johnson. The latter's critical estimate is severely judicious, but recognizes that Cowley's 'volatility is not the flutter of a light, but the bound of an elastick mind' (Johnson, *Poets*, 1.37), and emphasizes his achievement in the ode and in the classical translation. If not the peer of Spenser and Milton which his own age thought him, Cowley remains a poet of varied and considerable gifts, and of great historical importance.

ALEXANDER LINDSAY

**Sources** T. Sprat, 'An account of the life and writing', in *The works of Mr Abraham Cowley* (1668) • A. Cowley, preface, *Poems* (1656) • A. Cowley, *Collected works*, ed. T. Calhoun and others, 6 vols. (Newark, NJ, 1989–) • M. R. Perkin, *Abraham Cowley: a bibliography* (1977) • S. Johnson, *Lives of the English poets*, ed. G. B. Hill, [new edn], 3 vols. (1905) • J. Loiseau, *Abraham Cowley: sa vie, son oeuvre* (Paris, 1931) • A. H. Nethercot, *Abraham Cowley: the muse's Hannibal* (1931) • Wood, *Ath. Oxon.*, 1st edn • J. Spence, *Observations, anecdotes, and characters, of books and men*, ed. J. M. Osborn, new edn, 2 vols. (1966) • *Brief lives, chiefly of contemporaries, set down by John Aubrey, between the years 1669 and 1696*, ed. A. Clark, 2 vols. (1898) • Pepys, *Diary* • T. Sprat, 'De vita et scriptis A. Couleii', *Poemata Latina* (1668)

**Archives** BL, letters • Harvard U., letters • Morgan L., letters • NRA, letters and literary MSS • Princeton University Library, New Jersey, letters | Bodl. Oxf., Clarendon and Carte MSS, letters • Herts. ALS, letters to Sir William Cowper and others • Yale U., Osborn collection, letters

**Likenesses** P. Lely, oils, 1646? (*Young man as a shepherd*), Dulwich College, London • oils, *c*.1660 (after P. Lely), NPG • P. Lely, oils, *c*.1666–1667, NPG [*see illus.*] • M. Beale, portrait, Merton Oxf. • M. Beale?, portraits, Bodl. Oxf., Merton Oxf. • W. Faithorne, line engraving (after lost portrait by P. Lely, *c*.1660), BM, NPG; repro. in *Works* (1668), frontispiece • J. Hall, engraving, repro. in *Select works of Mr. A. Cowley*, ed. R. Hurd, 2 vols. (1772) • crayon drawing, Trinity Cam. • mezzotint (after unknown artist), NPG • pen-and-ink drawing (after engraving by R. Vaughan), NPG • portraits (after W. Faithorne), Trinity Cam.

**Wealth at death** see will, 18 Sept 1665, printed in Nethercot, *Abraham Cowley*, 296–7

# Cowley, Sir Arthur Ernest

**Cowley, Sir Arthur Ernest** (1861–1931), orientalist and librarian, was born on 13 December 1861 at 3 South Hill, Forest Hill, Sydenham, the fourth son among the seventeen children of Frederick Thomas Cowley (1822–1881), customs house agent, and his wife, Louisa Emily, *née* Boddy (1830–1912). He was educated at St Paul's School, London (1872–9), then at Trinity College, Oxford (1879–83), where he was an exhibitioner. He showed early promise but ill health and increasing interest in oriental languages resulted in his graduating with a fourth class in *literae humaniores* in 1883. Cowley then spent two years at the *collège cantonal*, Lausanne, Switzerland, improving his French and German, before becoming master in modern languages successively at Sherborne School (1885–9), and Magdalen College School, Oxford (1890–95).

In 1890 Cowley had begun work on the Samaritan liturgy at the suggestion of Alfred Neubauer, sub-librarian in charge of the Bodleian Library's oriental collections, and spent his vacations working in British and continental libraries. In 1894 he and John Frederick Stenning examined Greek and Semitic manuscripts in the library of St Catherine's Monastery on Mount Sinai. He was appointed an assistant sub-librarian at the Bodleian in 1896 to help

Neubauer, with whom he published *The Original Hebrew of a Portion of Ecclesiasticus* (1897), followed by *Facsimiles of the Fragments Hitherto Recovered of the Book of Ecclesiasticus in Hebrew* (1901). In 1898 he produced a revised edition of G. W. Collins's translation of Gesenius's *Hebrew Grammar*, which became the standard work of reference for English students.

Cowley succeeded Neubauer as sub-librarian in December 1899, also taking on his teaching of rabbinical Hebrew literature. A fellowship at Magdalen College followed in 1902. At the Bodleian he worked on a catalogue of its Sanskrit materials which was completed in 1905. With Neubauer he edited the second volume of the *Catalogue of Hebrew Manuscripts in the Bodleian Library* (1906). For this and his work with A. H. Sayce on fifth-century BC Aramaic papyri, published as *Aramaic Papyri Discovered at Assuan* (1906), he was awarded a DLitt by the university in 1908. His early studies culminated in the appearance of *The Samaritan Liturgy* in two volumes in 1909. A second, revised, edition of Gesenius followed in 1910. He was elected Sandars reader in bibliography at Cambridge in 1912.

On 3 April 1913 at St Margaret's, Westminster, Cowley married Mabel Beatrice Watts (*d.* 1950), of St Osyth's Priory, Essex, the second daughter of William Longmore Watts, rector of Boxted, Essex. The couple had no children of their own but adopted two sons. The war found Cowley too old for active service but in 1917 he spent six months with a British ambulance unit in France. In December 1918 he delivered the Schweich lectures on biblical archaeology at the British Academy, published as *The Hittites* in 1920. He was elected a fellow of the British Academy in July 1919, and served on its council from 1922 until 1931.

In 1919 Cowley succeeded Falconer Madan as Bodley's librarian. He began by tackling the problem of the growth of the unwieldy transcribed catalogue of printed books. Attempts to publish it were abandoned on grounds of cost and Cowley inaugurated a new catalogue on printed slips for all books published after 1919. His time as librarian was, however, chiefly characterized by his desire to see a unified library management system in the university, to be achieved by staffing other institutions from the Bodleian, the principle of dependent libraries. The process began in 1923, when a Bodleian assistant took charge of a separate library for law students. In 1927 the Radcliffe Library of scientific and medical books and the Indian Institute Library were placed under Bodley's librarian. Finally in 1929 the Rhodes House Library for books on the British dominions and colonies, the United States, and Africa was set up. A third, pressing concern was the perennial one of storage space for the ever-growing collections. The transfer to the Ashmolean Museum of collections of coins and engraved portraits helped, but much more space was needed. As early as 1921 Cowley had maintained that the existing library buildings could not be abandoned. He favoured the retention of the old library and the construction of an extension on the other side of Broad Street. After a decade of argument and discussions this idea was the one largely adopted shortly before his retirement.

Cowley still found time to pursue his scholarly interests.

In 1923 he published *The Aramaic Papyri of the Fifth Century*, a revision of his 1906 work, incorporating the critical results of the best-known Semitic scholars, his original text largely unaltered. The publication of *A Concise Catalogue of the Hebrew Printed Books in the Bodleian Library*, the culmination of thirteen years' work, followed in 1929.

Cowley's strength as a scholar lay not so much in high originality as in a complete mastery of his chosen field, to which he brought a painstaking and thorough accuracy. His knowledge of Hebrew and Aramaic was exhaustive. Combined, they marked him out as one of the leading Semitic scholars of his day.

As Bodley's librarian Cowley became more and more taken up with congresses, conferences, and international boards. In 1926, the year he received a DLitt from Cambridge University, he was invited to serve on the International Committee of Bibliography, becoming its chairman. The following year he was elected a corresponding member of the Institut de France, and also appointed a member of the royal commission on national museums and galleries. In June 1931 his knighthood was announced.

By then Cowley was already too ill to perform his duties in the library. On 3 May he had undergone an operation for the removal of a malignant tumour. He remained in hospital until the beginning of August, and resigned as Bodley's librarian on 31 July. While recuperating in Eastbourne he suffered a stroke; after returning to Oxford he had a second stroke and died at his home at 1 Holywell in the early hours of 12 October 1931. He was cremated at Golders Green crematorium on 14 October. His estate was bequeathed in trust to the university for the benefit of the Bodleian Library, subject to certain annuities.

Cowley had a strong muscular frame and generally enjoyed good health, though he was not fond of exercise. He had a Roman nose, a dignified bearing, with a red complexion and fierce blue eyes, which belied his nature; he was cheerful, genial, and kind, and always ready with help and advice when asked. He had a remarkable capacity for friendship with young and old alike, and was quickly on easy terms with all. Immensely sociable, he was a member of several Oxford common rooms, various dining clubs, and two London clubs, the Athenaeum and the Union. He was an enthusiastic freemason and filled various high offices, including mastership of the university lodge.

STEVEN TOMLINSON

**Sources** T. W. Allen, 'Arthur Ernest Cowley, 1861–1931', *PBA*, 19 (1933), 351–9 • 'Cowleiana', Bodl. Oxf., Library Records c. 440 • *The Times* (13 Oct 1931) • *DNB* • *Bodleian Quarterly Record*, 1–6 (1914–31) • H. H. E. Craster, *History of the Bodleian Library, 1845–1945* (1952) • reminiscences of Strickland Gibson, Bodl. Oxf., MS Library Records d. 1754 • P. S. Allen, letters to Aurel Stein, 1931, Bodl. Oxf., MS Allen 210, fols. 125–77 • Cowley family pedigree, *c.*1920, Bodl. Oxf., MS Pedigree Rolls 37 • *Oxford Times* (16 Oct 1931) • *Oxford Magazine* (12 Nov 1931) • R. B. Gardiner, ed., *The admission registers of St Paul's School, from 1748 to 1876* (1884) • matriculation record, 1879, Oxf. UA, OUA/UR/1/1/13 • *CGPLA Eng. & Wales* (1932)

**Archives** Bodl. Oxf., papers, Eng. hist. MSS c. 1045–52 • Bodl. Oxf., papers, Polyglot d. 2

**Likenesses** H. Collison, oils, 1925, Bodl. Oxf.

**Wealth at death** £14,672 11s. 10d.: resworn administration with will, 6 Jan 1932, *CGPLA Eng. & Wales*

**Cowley** [*née* Parkhouse], **Hannah** (1743–1809), playwright and poet, was born on 14 March 1743 in Tiverton, Devon, the younger daughter of Philip Parkhouse (*c*.1712–1790) and Hannah (*née* Richards). A brilliant Blundell's scholar, her father, disappointed of a church living, became a bookseller in Fore Street. His election as a corporator (councillor) gave him a vote under Tiverton's charter of 1615 in electing the town's two members of parliament: this brought the friendship of Lord Harrowby MP who was to take a keen interest in Hannah's education and subsequent literary success.

In 1772 Hannah married Thomas Cowley (1744–1797), whose mother, Mary Cowley, was a bookseller in Cockermouth, Cumberland. At an indifferent play in London, Hannah assured her husband she could do better herself: she did. She sent *The Runaway* anonymously to the great actor–manager, Garrick, who immediately recognized its potential and put it on at Drury Lane, on 15 February 1776. With Sarah Siddons in the starring role, it was a 'smash hit', highlighting the injustice of arranged marriages by which a father or guardian could legally give away his daughter or ward to a totally unsuitable husband to gratify some personal ambition or mere whim. Particularly earnestly debated throughout London society was the outburst by a young female character regarding the marriage vow 'to love, honour and obey'; 'I won't hear of it, "love" one might manage that perhaps, but "honour, obey"!—, tis strange the ladies had never interest enough to get this ungallant form amended'. This was near-heresy at the time, but the wording of the marriage vow remained controversial throughout the twentieth century.

Hannah Cowley was never boring or over-earnest: she did not rage against the wrongs to which women were subject, her satire was much more subtle. Most of her plays are fast-moving comedies which were performed throughout England and Ireland well into the nineteenth century; they reached the continent via Germany and Austria. The hilarious short farce *Who's the Dupe?* (Drury Lane, 10 May 1779) is characteristic. It depicts the plight of another near-victim of an arranged marriage, this time revolving around the relative educational attainments of the heroine's suitors. At one point, exasperated with her father's choice of Gradus, a dry-as-dust product of 'Brazen-nose', Elizabeth protests 'The education given to women shuts us entirely from such refined acquaintance'.

Hannah Cowley suffered throughout her career from jealousy and ill-founded criticism: basking in the success of *The Rivals* (1775) Richard Sheridan was determined to halt the meteoric rise to fame of this new and wildly popular woman rival. Having bought into the management of the Drury Lane theatre, he 'shelf'd' *The Runaway* to prevent a new run and had an understanding with Mr Harris, manager of Covent Garden theatre, that neither would accept any piece which the other refused. Both turned down Hannah's first tragedy, *Albina*, dedicated to Lord Harrowby. A well-worked study of jealousy, it was staged in July 1779 at

the Haymarket, a theatre more used to comedy; it was not a success. A strikingly similar play was put on by Harris at Covent Garden: *Percy*, by an aspiring young Bristol playwright, Hannah More, who had the patronage and support of David Garrick. *Percy* was soon followed by another More play, *Fatal Falsehood*. Again there were 'wonderful resemblances' and since *Albina* had been with Garrick when More was at Hampton, the source of the similarity was clear. Luckily, although the charges of plagiarism against *Percy* were not proved, Hannah Cowley could prove that *Albina* was written well before More's plays, or she would have been accused of 'the grossest plagiarism' (preface to *Albina*). Cowley and More's literary quarrel was conducted in a series of letters to the editor of the *St James's Chronicle*, even though both women deplored the indelicacy of appearing in the public press. The letters were reprinted in the *Gentleman's Magazine* of August 1779.

Hannah Cowley received only £30 for *Albina* and her father wrote to Lord Harrowby asking if she could be awarded a pension or a better position be found for her husband still 'employed among footmen and grooms below stairs at the Stamp Ofice'. The MP arranged a posting as captain to the East India Company (Chalk, *N&Q*, 1936, 243).

Hannah Cowley's next play, *The Belle's Stratagem* (Covent Garden, 22 February 1780), dedicated to Queen Charlotte, again underlines the lack of wisdom of arranged marriages, in its tale of Letitia and her promised suitor, Doricourt, recently returned from the grand tour, and full of disdain for her lack of worldliness. The heroine's manner of winning his admiration through a series of misleading disguises and a final revelation of her grace and beauty at a masked ball made this play Hannah Cowley's masterpiece. It was immensely popular with actors and actresses: Doricourt was played by 'Gentleman' Lewis, Charles Kemble, and later Sir Henry Irving; Letitia by Miss Younge, Dorothy Jordan, and Ellen Terry. The future was now assured; almost all subsequent plays were readily accepted. *Which is the Man?* (Covent Garden, 1783) chronicles the comic reaction of Fitzherbert, guardian of Julia Manners who, from force of circumstance, has married without his consent. *A Bold Stroke for a Husband* (Covent Garden, 1783), set in Madrid, features a wife's rescue of her husband from his mistress by dressing as a man. *More Ways than one* (Covent Garden, 1784) depicts the outwitting of Dr Freelove's plan to sell his ward, Arabella, to a lawyer friend, Evergreen, for a fee of £15,000.

*A School for Greybeards* (Drury Lane, 1786) was loosely based on Aphra Behn's *The Lucky Chance* (1687) and encountered some critical opposition. Hostile reviewers condemned Hannah Cowley for indecent language and objected to the impropriety of snatching away a bride already promised to the bridegroom. Her next play, *The Fate of Sparta* (Drury Lane, 1788), took refuge in classical precedent, as it was based on Plutarch's *Life of Agis*. It features, however, a consistently strong heroine, who mediates between her husband, waging a siege on Sparta, and her ancient father ensconced within the city. Although it emerged relatively free of the criticism that had marred the reception of *A School for Greybeards*, this was not to be the case with *A Day in Turkey, or, The Russian Slaves* (Covent Garden, 1791). After its first performance, Hannah Cowley was accused of dabbling in politics because the Russian Count Orlov's French valet, A La Grecque, never misses a chance of asserting the superiority of the new spirit (*liberté, égalité, fraternité*) then sweeping France and making fun of all less enlightened nations. Francophobe critics were bent on attributing the comic and outrageous utterances to the playwright who, on losing the honour of a royal command performance, justly complained, 'It is A La Grecque who speaks, not I'.

The prologue to Hannah Cowley's last play, *The Town before you* (Covent Garden, 1794), registers her profound dismay at the slapstick and buffoonery which were taking over the role of playwright and actor in the theatre. Her fascinating picture of late eighteenth-century London depicts a snobbish ne'er-do-well aristocrat, a clever conman, an up-from-country social climber, and, most importantly, a much-maligned woman sculptor, Lady Horatia Horton, who has dared to found her own successful studio and whose statues are roundly condemned as unlifelike by a bogus connoisseur and denigrated by her fiancé's father. Hannah had met the prototype of Lady Horatia, the Hon. Anne Damer, at the sumptuous receptions given by another renowned Tivertonian, the miniaturist Richard Cosway, and his talented and vivacious wife, Maria. The lively and elegant Hannah Cowley was an honoured guest in their London salon, among such celebrities as the prince regent, the duchess of Devonshire, Angelica Kauffmann, and Horace Walpole.

Hannah Cowley was also a successful poet. Written under the pseudonym of Anna Matilda, her poetic bantering with Robert Merry in *The World* attracted a wide readership but was harshly condemned with the work of the rest of the 'Della Cruscans' by Robert Gifford, in *The Baviad*. In 1780 she published *The Maid of Arragon*, a tale of filial piety fittingly dedicated to her father who had recognized and supported her talent. Her second long poem, *The Scottish Village, or, Pitcairn Green* (1786), demonstrates her love of unspoiled nature. Heart-broken to learn that planners had chosen a lovely green-field site at Pitcairn Green in Scotland for an extensive 'New Town', she imagined what such development might do to her beloved Devon countryside.

> The verdant face of this once happy plain
> The sharp-tooth'd mattock shall deform, tear …
> The future Town, submissive to their will
> Rises from Earth and spreads its skirts around …

Throughout her life, Hannah Cowley combined her extensive writing with her roles as wife and mother. Her husband died in 1797, on a trip to India to visit their younger daughter, Frances, who had married the Revd David Brown, later provost of Fort William College, Calcutta. Their elder daughter, Mary Elizabeth, had died in 1789, and their son was a lawyer, working in Portugal.

It was only in the twentieth century, however, that Hannah Cowley's role in the fight for justice for women was recognized. Her contribution deserves credit, as she delivered her message in a powerful and accessible medium, the theatre. In an age when many people were unable to read and appreciate the arguments put forth in Mary Wollstonecraft's *Vindication of the Rights of Woman* (1792), her popular challenging of traditional roles was of overriding importance in the wider dissemination of feminist views.

Formerly a worshipper at the old established church, St Peter's (1073), Hannah Cowley had become more attuned to the evangelical church of St George (1733) in later life. She died at Tiverton on 11 March 1809, and was buried there in 1809. The broken fragment of her tombstone was removed from the churchyard during an extension and now rests at the Tiverton Museum.

MARY DE LA MAHOTIÈRE

**Sources** M. de la Mahotière, *Hannah Cowley, Tiverton's playwright and pioneer feminist* (1997) · *The plays of Hannah Cowley*, ed. F. M. Link, 2 vols. (1979) · J. Bourne, ed., *Georgian Tiverton* (1986) · Tiverton pocket borough correspondence, Harrowby Manuscript Trust, Sandon Hall, Stafford · G. Barnett, *Richard and Maria Cosway: a biography* (1995) · W. Harding, *The history of Tiverton*, 2 vols. (1845–7) · A. Kendall, *David Garrick: a biography* (1985) · H. Cowley, *The Scottish village, or, Pitcairn Green* (1786) · R. W. Uphaus and G. M. Foster, eds., *The other eighteenth century: English women of letters, 1660–1800* (1991) · *GM*, 1st ser., 49 (1779)
**Archives** Sandon Hall, Stafford, Harrowby Manuscript Trust, Tiverton pocket borough corresp.
**Likenesses** J. Heath, line engraving, pubd 1783 (after R. S. Cosway), BM, NPG · J. Fittler, stipple and line engraving, pubd 1785 (after R. Cosway), BM, NPG · R. Cosway, pencil drawing, Hunt. L. · J. Fittler, print, repro. in T. Davies, *Memoirs of the life of David Garrick*, 2 vols. (1808) · T. Holloway, line engraving, BM, NPG; repro. in *European Magazine and London Review*, 15 (1789), facing p. 427 · G. Murray, line engraving (after R. Cosway), BM; repro. in *Biographical Magazine*

**Cowley, Sir John Guise** (1905–1993), army officer, was born at Mussooree, in the foothills of the Himalayas, during an earthquake on 20 August 1905, the son of the Revd Henry Guise Beatson Cowley, army chaplain, and his wife, Ethel Florence (*née* Prowse). When the family returned to England by ship John won a contest for the ugliest baby on board. His early years were spent in a Dorset village, where his father was the rector and Thomas Hardy was a neighbour. He recalled Hardy as a sad, wizened old man who spoke seldom but who occasionally, though an atheist, attended church services, at which he always asked Cowley's father to read the same passage from the Bible—Elijah's vision of the earthquake.

Cowley was educated at Wellington College, Berkshire, and the Royal Military Academy at Woolwich, before being commissioned into the Royal Engineers in 1925. His first posting was to Aldershot, where he recalled that on route marches the cooker was pulled by a horse while the cook walked behind trying to prepare a meal for the company when it halted; the cook always arrived black in the face from the smoke. In the general strike of 1926 Cowley was sent with a platoon to guard the waterworks at Luton. Before leaving he was warned by his very serious company commander, 'If you have to shoot, shoot to kill'. Instead Cowley arranged a football match between his men and the strikers, whom he found 'an extremely pleasant and reasonable lot of men' (personal knowledge).

In 1932 Cowley was posted to the Madras sappers and miners, and later went on to Quetta, where he learned Urdu. In 1935 Quetta was devastated by an earthquake which killed 25,000 people and injured many more. The walls of the local civil hospital collapsed, bringing down the roof on the patients as they lay in their beds. Cowley arranged that the roof should be propped up enough to enable him to crawl under it and drag out the survivors, many of whom were suffering from contagious diseases to which he was fully exposed as he carried them in his arms, but his unflinching courage caused others to follow his example. The lepers were rescued by him personally. Cowley was awarded the Albert medal (in 1971 converted into the George Cross, the civilian equivalent of the VC).

In 1936 Cowley returned to become an instructor at Woolwich; three years later he became a student at the Staff College, Camberley. Before he had completed the Camberley course in 1939 he was posted to the War Office, where he organized the dispatch of the cavalry division, with 2000 horses, to Palestine (it was mechanized soon afterwards). In 1940 he was posted to the western desert army, where he recalled having to wake up General Wavell in the middle of the night and tell him the Australians had captured Sidi Barrani. Wavell then wrote a personal note to Churchill, but though Cowley was sitting within 4 feet of Wavell for half an hour, Wavell did not utter a word to him, not even 'Thank you' or 'Good night'. Wavell was noted for his extreme taciturnity. In 1941 Cowley was trapped in Tobruk by one of Rommel's sweeping counter-attacks but was evacuated by sea and then put in charge of the docks at Alexandria. He remembered being visited by a confident military police officer who told him he had come to stop pilfering in the docks. Cowley warned him that stopping this ancient and traditional practice might prove difficult. Six days later the officer reappeared, saying he could continue no longer as all his own equipment and stores had been stolen. Cowley was next appointed to the staff of 7th armoured division, and then to 30th corps, where he was made responsible for planning and supply arrangements. On 16 December 1941 he married (Irene) Sybil, daughter of Percy Dreville Millen, of Berkhamsted, Hertfordshire; they had a son and three daughters.

After the battle of El Alamein, Cowley was posted to Fort Leavenworth, Kansas, to lecture about the war. His next postings were to allied forces headquarters at Caserta, near Naples, and to Brussels on the staff of Twenty-First Army group, where his task was to help refugees and the homeless in Belgium and the Netherlands. Then came a move to Minden with a brief to restore the German economy. The Volkswagen factory lay in the British zone, and he recalled that as it had never functioned in peacetime it was inspected by various motoring experts who said it was inefficient, had no future, and that neither the works nor the designs should be acquired for British industry. Cowley subsequently spent a year at the Imperial Defence College, had a stint on the defence research policy staff,

and then became director of administrative planning at the War Office. From 1953 he was chief of staff, headquarters, eastern command, before returning to the War Office as vice-quartermaster-general in 1956, just in time for the Suez crisis. He thought Anthony Eden seemed exhausted and mentally ill: the army wanted to land at Alexandria but Eden insisted on Port Said, which proved a disaster.

In 1957 Cowley became controller of munitions at the War Office. In this post he clashed with Duncan Sandys, the minister of supply, who thought that money should be spent on nuclear weapons rather than soldiers. Cowley pointed out that if nuclear weapons were ever used it would be the end of civilization. Sandys asked Macmillan to sack Cowley, but the prime minister refused. When the row died down Cowley was made master-general of the ordnance. He retired from the army in 1962 and on the day he left he was appointed a director of British Oxygen and Bowmaker. He soon joined other companies, but found time for the presidency of the New Forest Preservation Society and chairmanship of the governors of Wellington College and several other schools.

As a young man Cowley had been an excellent games player, first-class at squash, and had a golf handicap of three. Later he became a skilful bridge and croquet player. He traced the history of snooker back to Woolwich, where the 'snookers' (as the junior cadets were called) were allowed to play with extra balls after their seniors had finished at billiards. Cowley was appointed OBE in 1943, CBE in 1946, CB in 1954, and KBE in 1958. He was mentioned in dispatches four times. He died of bronchopneumonia and ischaemic heart disease on 7 January 1993, at Woodpeckers, Sway Road, Brockenhurst, Hampshire. He was survived by his wife and four children.

PHILIP WARNER

**Sources** *The Times* (9 Jan 1993) · *WWW*, 1991–5 · personal knowledge (2004) · Brompton barracks, Chatham, Kent, Royal Engineers Library, archives of the royal engineers · Burke, *Peerage* · d. cert.
**Archives** CAC Cam., corresp. and papers incl. memoir of Suez operation · King's Lond., Liddell Hart C., papers · Royal Engineers, Brompton Barracks, Chatham, Kent
**Likenesses** photograph, repro. in *The Times*

**Cowley, Sir (William) Percy** (1886–1958), judge and politician, was born at The Mount, Ramsey, Isle of Man, on 26 July 1886, the son of Robert Cowley, timber merchant and member of the House of Keys, and his wife, Emma Baker. He was educated at Ramsey grammar school and took law for his profession rather than farming. (His father's family had farmed at Crammag in Sulby Glen since 1642.) He was admitted to the Manx bar in 1909. On 12 May 1914 he married Emily Alison Martin (1891–1927), daughter of John Martin of Galwally House, Belfast; they had a daughter and two sons. They lived in some style at Ballaughton, their country house in Braddan, and became well-known figures on the island in their chauffeur-driven Rolls-Royce.

A leg problem kept Cowley out of the army in 1914, but he served throughout the war as paymaster sub-lieutenant to the commander-in-chief of the Mediterranean Fleet. He returned to the Isle of Man and legal practice in 1919, and took an increasingly prominent part in the local affairs of Ramsey. He was elected to the town board and served as its chairman from 1920 to 1921. He subsequently moved to Douglas to become a partner at Ring, LaMothe, Farrant, and Cowley. He served as high bailiff of Douglas, Ramsey, and Peel from 1925 to 1931, and was appointed a JP in 1931. Following his wife's early death in 1927, he married Ethel Muriel Kissack (1888/9–1983) of Douglas in 1929. In 1934 he was appointed to the Manx High Court as second deemster (as its judges are termed), the second highest legal position in the island. His forceful personality, legal knowledge, and ability to identify the salient points of any argument enabled him to sway many debates in Tynwald, where as a deemster he was an automatic member of the legislative council. Though firm as a judge, he was sympathetic towards the accused and heartily disliked sending anyone to prison.

Percy Cowley never forgot his rural roots, and the farming community often regarded him as 'their man'; he had the common touch, and a marked ability for making the law intelligible to his fellow islanders. As a prominent local figure he took a leading role in many community enterprises and associations, including the freemasons, the Royal Manx Agricultural Society, the Manx Blind Welfare Society, the Manx Merchant Navy Help Society, and the Ramsey cottage hospital. He sat on the boards of several companies, including the Steam Packet, the Palace and Derby Castle group, and Ramsey Gas Light Company.

Cowley served as an intelligence officer in the Isle of Man battalion of the Home Guard when the Second World War broke out. He was soon appointed to chair the war committee of Tynwald (known locally as the war cabinet), and stayed in post for the duration of the war. In this position he was largely responsible for setting up the establishments of the armed forces and the internment camps on the island at very short notice. The war over, he was appointed first deemster and clerk of the rolls in 1947, thereby becoming deputy governor of the island. In July 1947 he was the leading negotiator with the Admiralty for the purchase of Ronaldsway airport, when it was offered to the Manx government for £1 million. In a masterpiece of negotiation, he not only persuaded the Manx government of the value of the purchase, but reduced the price to £200,000. Even this appeared a prodigious sum at the time, but subsequent development and use of the airport proved Cowley's foresight. He was appointed KCB in 1952, a highly unusual distinction for a Manxman at that time. In 1956 he was created the eighth honorary freeman of Douglas. His years of hard work took their toll on his health, and he died suddenly on 13 January 1958 at the Cumberland Hotel, Marylebone, while visiting London. His death was a tremendous shock to the whole island. He was buried in Lezayre churchyard; his obituarist described him as 'the ablest Manxman of his generation' (*Isle of Man Weekly Times*, 17 Jan 1958).

Sir Percy Cowley had helped to set up the Manx National Trust to protect and preserve the island's heritage, and left it 783 acres at the Sound, with views across to the Calf of Man.

HENLEY CROWE

**Sources** *Isle of Man Weekly Times* (17 Jan 1958) · *Ramsey Courier and Northern Advertiser* (1 March 1946) · *Ramsey Courier and Northern Advertiser* (17 Jan 1958) · private information (2004) [Henry Callow; Patrick Cowley; J. B. Mylchrees; Moira Roseveare] · *WWW* · d. cert. · Manx Museum and Manx National Heritage, Douglas, Isle of Man

**Archives** Manx Museum and Manx National Heritage, Douglas, Isle of Man

**Cowley, Richard** (*bap.* 1568?, *d.* 1619), actor, may be the Richard, son of Robert Coolie, who was baptized on 9 October 1568 at St Albans, Hertfordshire, married Elizabeth Davies on 28 January 1592 in Bromyard, Herefordshire, and had a kinsman named Cuthbert (*b.* 1570). The actor had a wife named Elizabeth and children named Robert, Cuthbert, Richard, and Elizabeth, and his name was spelled Coolye in 1598. However, a marriage in Herefordshire in 1592 is uncomfortably close to the start of the actor's London theatrical career, and the identification must remain speculative.

In any case, Richard Cowley first surfaces as an actor in the early 1590s as a member of Strange's Men. In July 1593 he delivered letters from London to Strange's Men in Bristol, where they were on tour; in a letter of 1 August Edward Alleyn tells his wife: 'I reseved your Letter att bristo by richard couley' (Rutter, 75). Presumably he followed others of Strange's Men into the Lord Chamberlain's Men when that company was formed in 1594. He appears in the 'plot' (a theatre document whose precise function is uncertain) of the play *Seven Deadly Sins* as 'R Cowly', playing several minor male parts: the Lieutenant of the Tower in the Induction, a soldier and a lord in Envy, Giraldus and a musician in Sloth, and a lord in Lechery. This 'plot', traditionally thought to belong to Strange's Men *c*.1590, probably belonged instead to the Lord Chamberlain's Men in 1597–8. The use of 'Cowley' in the speech prefixes of both the Quarto (1600) and Folio (1623) versions of Shakespeare's *Much Ado about Nothing* reveals that he played Verges alongside Will Kempe's Dogberry around 1598.

Meanwhile, Cowley and his wife, Elizabeth, had settled in Holywell Street, in the parish of St Leonard, Shoreditch, London. Four of their children were baptized there: Robert (8 March 1596; buried 20 March 1597), Cuthbert (8 May 1597), Richard (29 April 1598; buried 26 February 1603), and Elizabeth (2 February 1602). In 1598 Richard Coolye of Holywell Street was assessed on £3 of goods, a respectable sum (Eccles, 45). In 1597 his wife consulted with Simon Forman, the famous astrologer, and apparently had an affair with him. On 20 August 1597 Forman recorded in his diary that he could not decide whether or not to visit her, and when he finally did the assignation was foiled when her husband arrived home. Forman wrote: 'If I had gone presently, I had found her alone' (Cerasano, 157).

In 1601 Cowley appears for the only time as payee for the court performances of the Chamberlain's Men, along with John Heminges. In 1603 he appears last in a list of nine players in the licence which created the King's Men, and in 1604 he occupies the same position in a list of nine King's Men who received red cloth for King James's procession through London. His position in these lists, and the fact that he appears in none of the cast lists of King's Men in either the Ben Jonson or the Beaumont and Fletcher folios, suggests that he was not a leading member of the company. In 1605 he was a legatee in the will of King's Man Augustine Phillips, who left 20s. in gold 'To my Fellowe Richard Coweley' (Honigmann and Brock, 73).

Cowley's wife was buried on 28 September 1616 at St Leonard's, and he himself was buried there on 12 March 1619. Six weeks earlier, on 28 January, his daughter Elizabeth, not quite seventeen years old, had married George Birch of the King's Men. Cowley's nuncupative will, dated 13 January 1618, appoints his daughter executor; it was witnessed by three of the King's Men—John Heminges, Cuthbert Burbage, and John Shank—and Thomas Ravenscroft, possibly the madrigalist.　　　DAVID KATHMAN

**Sources** E. Nungezer, *A dictionary of actors* (1929), 105 • E. K. Chambers, *The Elizabethan stage*, 4 vols. (1923), vol. 2, p. 312 • G. E. Bentley, *The Jacobean and Caroline stage*, 7 vols. (1941–68), vol. 2, p. 414 • E. A. J. Honigmann and S. Brock, eds., *Playhouse wills, 1558–1642: an edition of wills by Shakespeare and his contemporaries in the London theatre* (1993), 112 • *IGI* • M. Eccles, 'Elizabethan actors, I: A–D', *N&Q*, 236 (1991), 38–49, esp. 45 • S. P. Cerasano, 'Philip Henslowe, Simon Forman, and the theatrical community of the 1590s', *Shakespeare Quarterly*, 44 (1993), 145–58 • C. C. Rutter, ed., *Documents of the Rose playhouse* (1984) • T. W. Baldwin, *The organization and personnel of the Shakespearean company* (1927)
**Wealth at death** see will, 13 Jan 1618, Honigmann and Brock, eds., *Playhouse wills*

**Cowlin, Sir Francis Nicholas** (1868–1945), building contractor, was born on 23 September 1868 in Bristol, the second eldest of ten children of William Henry Cowlin (1841–1890), building contractor, and Annie (*b.* 1844), said to be the daughter of a plumbing contractor. He was educated privately and at nineteen joined his father's firm. In 1889 he enrolled at University College, Bristol, while remaining in the firm. Upon William Cowlin's death in 1890, control of the firm passed to the sons, of whom the eldest died in 1896.

Frank Cowlin, as he was known, was the senior of two partners and brothers (a third joined later) running a substantial business. Under their management the firm, William Cowlin & Son, enhanced its local reputation for progressiveness, and it carried out a succession of prestigious works including the 1892 restoration of Bristol Cathedral. In 1889 Cowlin diversified by acquiring an estate agency. He became a member, and sometime chairman, of the local branch of the Building Employers' Federation. Despite the Edwardian building recession the firm expanded in 1906 and began building a series of technically innovative reinforced concrete buildings. Cowlin's liberal political outlook found expression in 1908 in founder membership of Bristol Garden Suburb Association, and again in 1910 in the instigation of a small pension fund for some employees. The following year he was appointed a director (later he became chairman) of what was to become the Bristol and West Building Society. He further extended his firm in 1915 with decorating and warehousing services.

Important building works included numerous churches and prominent public and commercial buildings, largely in the Bristol area. Overseas works included the treasury in Kingston, Jamaica (after earthquake damage), and buildings in Toronto, Moose Jaw, and Winnipeg, Canada, and in Brazil. From presidency of the local commercial rooms in 1917, Cowlin progressed to the local chamber of commerce and, in 1921, he became sheriff of Bristol. In 1924, following ventures in housebuilding and quarrying, his firm became a private limited company, with Cowlin as chairman of the board. During his lifetime he transformed the business—its working capital multiplied nearly sixfold between 1900 (£36,000) and 1946 (£212,000). He was also chairman of the Bristol Waterworks Company and in 1929 became a director of the local gas company. Widening business interests contrasted with more geographically confined building works, although their scale and diversity remained undiminished. With his career at its peak, he was knighted in 1935. He was elected to the board of Eagle Star Insurance in 1940. He was also elected a fellow of the Institute of Builders, and FRSA.

Cowlin contributed unstintingly to a great variety of local concerns in sport, philanthropy, and the arts. In 1904 he was granted honorary life membership of Bristol Rugby Football Club, and his generous patronage led to its presidency, and, late in life, recognition as the 'grand old man of Bristol rugby'. He acted as president of three local charities, chairman of the local branch of the National Playing Fields Association and the council of the Royal West of England Academy, was a director of the local YMCA, and served on two hospital boards. A contemporary caricature depicted him in his mid-fifties as a handsome, warm, and open-looking golf player with moustache and pipe. Although a widely popular character, flourishing in public and civic life, he appears to have disliked publicity. A rare trait was his balance of high business acumen, sociability, public spiritedness, and appreciation of the arts. For his last thirty-five years he lived at Rodborough House, Ivywell Road, Sneyd Park, Bristol. He died a bachelor, aged seventy-six, on 26 July 1945 at Park Cottage, Cleeve, Somerset, and his ashes were buried on 30 July at Stoke Bishop parish church, Bristol, after a funeral service in Bristol Cathedral.　　　CHRISTOPHER POWELL

**Sources** William Cowlin & Son Ltd, *A record of building* (1928) • *The Times* (28 July 1945) • *Western Daily Press* (27 July 1945) • *Bristol Evening Post* (27 July 1945) • M. Dresser, 'Cowlin, Sir Francis Nicholas', *DBB* • E. Liveing, 'William Cowlin & Son', *Bristol Times and Mirror* (22 March 1923) • 'William Cowlin & Son Ltd', *Histories of famous firms* (1959), 24–5 [Bristol survey, pt 1] • 'William Cowlin & Son Ltd', *Illustrated Bristol News*, 6 (1963), 34–5 • 'Ports of the Bristol Channel', *Progress and commerce* (1893) • 'Bristol personalities', *Bristol Times and Mirror* (4 Oct 1922) • census returns for Parish of St Paul's, Bristol, 1881 • Bristol and Clifton Directory • d. cert.
**Likenesses** G. T., pen-and-ink caricature, repro. in 'Bristol personalities'
**Wealth at death** £170,730 17s. 10d.: probate, 26 Oct 1945, *CGPLA Eng. & Wales*

**Cowling, Thomas George** (1906–1990), mathematician and astrophysicist, was born on 17 June 1906 at 3 Harrogate Road, South Hackney, London, the second of the four sons of George Cowling, Post Office engineer, and Edith Eliza Cowling, *née* Nicholls. Cowling was educated at Sir George Monoux Grammar School, Walthamstow, from where in 1924 he went on an open scholarship in mathematics to Brasenose College, Oxford, where he won the university junior mathematical exhibition in 1925 and the scholarship in 1926. With a first-class degree, he took a diploma in education, followed by a three-year postgraduate scholarship at Brasenose. His research supervisor was Edward A. Milne, the first incumbent of the Rouse Ball chair of mathematics.

Cowling's acumen was quickly recognized. After gaining his DPhil he was invited to join Sydney Chapman at Imperial College as demonstrator. Their collaboration converted Chapman's 'skeleton' of a book into a standard text, *The Mathematical Theory of non-Uniform Gases* (1939), which treats kinetic theory by a systematic attack on the classical Boltzmann equation. Cowling was subsequently assistant lecturer in mathematics at Swansea (1933–7), and lecturer at Dundee (1937–8) and at Manchester (1938–45). In 1945–8 he was professor of mathematics at Bangor, moving then to his last post, as professor of applied mathematics at Leeds, becoming emeritus professor in 1970.

Over the three decades from 1928 to 1958 Cowling made outstanding contributions to knowledge about stellar structure and developments in cosmical electrodynamics, kinetic theory, and plasma physics. His achievements were recognized by many honours and awards: the Johnson memorial prize at Oxford (1935), election to the Royal Society (1947), the gold medal of the Royal Astronomical Society (1956) and its presidency (1965–7), honorary fellowship of Brasenose (1966), the Bruce medal of the Astronomical Society of the Pacific (1985), and the Hughes medal of the Royal Society (1990). Cowling married Doris Marjorie Moffatt on 24 August 1935. They had three children: Margaret Ann Morrison, Elizabeth Mary Offord (*d.* 1994), and Michael John Cowling, and six grandchildren.

A few years before Cowling began working on stellar structure, Sir Arthur Eddington had published his celebrated *Internal Constitution of the Stars*, in which he pictured a homogeneous star as a self-gravitating gaseous sphere in radiative equilibrium, with its luminosity fixed by its mass and chemical composition. From comparison of his 'standard model' with the masses and radii of observed 'main-sequence' stars, Eddington inferred that the as yet unknown stellar energy sources must be highly temperature-sensitive. Cowling's careful analysis strengthened Eddington's case—against the criticisms of Sir James Jeans—by showing that the models would nevertheless almost certainly be vibrationally stable. In parallel with Ludwig Biermann, he also showed that stars would normally have turbulent domains with very efficient convective energy transport.

The 'Cowling model', with its convective core and radiative envelope, is a physically more realistic replacement of Eddington's standard model, effectively removing the

Thomas George Cowling (1906–1990), by Walter Bird

confusion surrounding Eddington's 'mass–luminosity' relation. Cowling's analysis of vibrational stability was done in the mid-1930s. Subsequent developments in nuclear physics by Hans Bethe and C.-F. von Weizsäcker showed the Cowling model to be a paradigm for stars somewhat more massive than the sun, for which energy release by fusion of hydrogen into helium takes place through a highly temperature-sensitive catalytic cycle involving carbon and nitrogen, so yielding a convective core.

In low-mass stars like the sun, hydrogen fusion occurs through a direct and less temperature-sensitive path. The energy-generating core is now radiative, but because of the low surface temperature there is a deep convective envelope, extending from just beneath the surface and driven by the latent heat associated with the ionization of hydrogen and helium. Cowling pointed out that the condition of radiative transport through the surface layers must still be satisfied. The profundity of this comment showed up many years later in studies of evolved, inhomogeneous red giant stars by Fred Hoyle and Martin Schwarzschild and of contracting pre-main sequence stars by Chushiro Hayashi. Earlier, Milne had argued that the luminosity of a star should be sensitive to conditions in the surface, rather than depending essentially on radiative transfer through the bulk of the star, as in Eddington's theory. Cowling's work vindicated Eddington's approach for main-sequence stars, while implicitly allowing for such sensitivity in stars with extensive sub-surface convective zones.

Cowling's other contributions to stellar structure

include an important paper on binary stars and two pioneering papers on non-radial stellar oscillations, foreshadowing later work in 'helioseismology'. Simultaneously he published a series of studies on cosmical magnetism and on plasma physics, culminating in his superbly succinct monograph *Magnetohydrodynamics* (1959, 1976). His famous 'anti-dynamo theorem' for axisymmetric magnetic fields is implicit in virtually all subsequent studies of cosmical dynamos. His 'fossil' fields remain relevant to the observed strongly magnetic stars. A lively correspondence with Biermann brought out the requirements of a theory of both the structure and the origin of sunspots. While recognizing the seminal contributions of Hannes Alfvén (1908–1995) to magnetohydrodynamics, he applied his critical faculties to Alfvén's theory of the sunspot cycle, and defended the Chapman-Ferraro theory of geomagnetic storms against what he regarded as unjust attacks. Together with Biermann, Arnulf Schlüter, and Lyman Spitzer jun., he did much to clarify the concept of 'conductivity' for both fully and partially ionized gases.

Surprisingly, Cowling spent most of the years of the Second World War just teaching at Manchester University and doing service as an air-raid warden. Although initially involved by invitation in some defence-orientated work, he was later puzzled to find himself excluded. After the war he learned that he was considered a security risk on what now seem the flimsy grounds that he had 'undesirable associates', to wit the communist physicist Janossy and a pacifist church minister.

In his autobiographical essay 'Astronomer by accident' (1985) Cowling remarks that he and his brothers inherited the 'Puritan work ethic' from their nonconformist parents. He remained an active, non-fundamentalist Baptist, though in his later years he confessed to doubts, speaking of 'getting closer to mysticism rather than to a religion of set creeds'. His puritanism perhaps showed itself in his very high academic standards, which he applied as much to his own work as to that of others, and earned him the nickname Doubting Thomas. Everyone knew him by sight—his red hair and his great height made him conspicuous—and also looked up to him metaphorically, because of his combination of kindliness and intellectual power. Though he never had the opportunity to build up a school (his one outstanding PhD student was Eric Priest, later professor at St Andrews), many younger workers, including Nigel Weiss at Cambridge and Roger Tayler and Leon Mestel at Sussex, remembered with warmth his generous encouragement.

Cowling's research activity in his later decades was severely hampered by recurring bouts of ill health, beginning with a duodenal ulcer in 1954. He died in Newton Green Hospital, Leeds, on 16 June 1990, and his remains were cremated in Lawnswood cemetery, Leeds, on the 22nd. His wife survived him.                    LEON MESTEL

**Sources** T. G. Cowling, 'Astronomer by accident', *Annual Review of Astronomy and Astrophysics*, 23 (1985), 1 · D. DeVorkin, 'Transcript of an interview with T. G. Cowling', *Sources for the history of modern astrophysics* (1978) · L. Mestel, *Memoirs FRS*, 37 (1991), 103–25 · personal knowledge (2004) · private information (2004) · b. cert. · d. cert.
**Archives** RS
**Likenesses** W. Bird and others, photographs, *c.*1967, repro. in Mestel, *Memoirs FRS* · W. Bird and others, photographs, *c.*1967, repro. in Cowling, 'Astronomer by accident', 1 · W. Bird, photograph, Royal Astronomical Society [*see illus.*]
**Wealth at death** £139,256: probate, 16 Nov 1990, *CGPLA Eng. & Wales*

**Cowper, Sir Charles** (1807–1875), politician in Australia, was born on 26 April 1807 at Dryford, Lancashire, the third son of William Cowper (1778–1858), curate, and his first wife, Hannah Horner, who died soon after. William remarried, and in 1809 sailed with his family for New South Wales to take up a Sydney chaplaincy. There he remained until his death forty-nine years later. William Cowper was responsible for the entire education of Charles who grew into a slight, delicate youth of bright face and pleasing manner, sharing his father's equable temperament, capacity for hard work, and fervent evangelical faith. As the son of an Anglican clergyman he joined the families of the greater landowners and government officials in the ranks of the colonial upper class but, reared in the complex society of his father's parish, he lacked the arrogant exclusiveness of his peers. His wide contacts among city men were to form a vital basis for his political career.

Cowper joined the commissariat department in 1825. In June 1826 his charm and church connections won him the lucrative post of secretary to the Clergy and School Lands Corporation, a body set up on Colonial Office instructions, to be endowed with one seventh of crown lands whose revenues would provide for the upkeep of the Anglican clergy and for all education in New South Wales. Cowper's work for this body, and the commission which succeeded it in 1828, earned him official commendation, but colonial opposition to church pretensions led the Colonial Office to close down the commission in 1833. By then, Cowper held land grants in the county of Argyle and had purchased allotments in Sydney. In 1831 he had married Eliza (*d.* in or after 1875), second daughter of Daniel Sutton, of Wivenhoe, near Colchester, Essex. The Cowpers settled into the life of country gentry, raising six children, one of whom died in infancy, and steadily extending the family land holdings. On his 900 acre estate at Cobbitty, near Camden, New South Wales, Cowper built the family home and named it Wivenhoe. Eliza Cowper seems to have been an ideal Victorian wife, loyal, self-effacing, and uncomplaining. There is no reason to doubt a contemporary assessment of Cowper as 'a dutiful son, a kind father [and] a good husband' (*Town and Country Journal*, 30 Oct 1875). Appointed a justice of the peace in 1839, his conduct on the bench was exemplary.

In 1843 elections took place for the newly created legislative council of New South Wales. Cowper narrowly lost a bitter contest for the Camden seat but soon after won in Cumberland. During the next seven years he displayed remarkable energy in council affairs, including membership of eighty-three select committees. While he gave some support to the interests of his landholding friends, he advocated and activated Anglican church privileges with such fervour that he became known as 'Member for the Church of England' (*Sydney Morning Herald*, 30 Oct 1849), while the influence of his city business and professional friends plus shrewd recognition of increasingly democratic trends in New South Wales politics led him towards leadership of liberal political forces. From 1846 until its final triumph in 1852, he led the popular movement against the resumption of convict transportation to Australia. Cowper opposed conservative views in the drafting of a new constitution and was instrumental in persuading the government to build railways in New South Wales.

By 1856, when New South Wales received responsible government, Cowper was the acknowledged liberal leader. He topped the poll for the City of Sydney at the elections for the new legislative assembly but conservative forces led by James Macarthur were still strong enough to induce the governor, Sir William Denison (1804–1871), to bypass Cowper in favour of the conservative merchant Stuart Donaldson as first premier of the self-governing New South Wales. The Donaldson ministry fell to Cowper in August 1856. From then until 1866 he was the pre-eminent political leader in New South Wales. In 1858 the second Cowper ministry introduced manhood suffrage, vote by ballot, and representation primarily by population. The Cowper–John Robertson ministry of 1860–63 simplified the land titles system, opened public lands to small farmers, and, against Cowper's own beliefs, abolished state grants for public worship. The political adroitness that earned him the nickname Slippery Charlie reached its height in 1861 with his reconstruction of the solidly conservative upper house, the legislative council, into a body of his own ministry's appointees, against the wish of the new governor, Sir John Young (1807–1876), who wanted to reappoint the old-guard conservatives, and the demands of his own supporters for an elected body. Thereafter, the conservatives were a spent force, but the liberals split into ever-changing factions headed by ambitious leaders. Incessant opposition from factions led by James Martin and Henry Parkes, men who had once been colleagues, wore Cowper down, and by 1865 long years of neglecting his own business interests had brought him to the verge of bankruptcy. Public subscription saved Wivenhoe for his family, but when Martin brought about the downfall of his fourth ministry in January 1866, Cowper retired to the back benches for a year, and then left politics for a business career.

Having been made a CMG and re-elected in 1869, Cowper rejoined his old friend John Robertson in power and replaced him as premier in January 1870. At the end of that year he exercised his political skills for the last time in arranging for the coalition of the Martin and Robertson factions and his own appointment to the post of New South Wales agent-general in London. He was made a KCMG in 1872.

Cowper's London sinecure seemed under threat when the Robertson–Martin ministry fell to Henry Parkes in 1872; but Parkes, recalling old friendship and Cowper's contribution to liberal politics in New South Wales, allowed him to remain even when chronic illness overtook him later in 1872. He died at Kensington, in London, on 19 October 1875 and was buried in Highgate cemetery. 'He was', said Henry Parkes when he heard of Cowper's death, 'as valuable a public servant as we ever had in this colony' (*Sydney Morning Herald*, 26 Nov 1875).

ALAN POWELL

**Sources** A. W. Powell, *Patrician democrat: the political life of Charles Cowper, 1843–1870* (1978) · *Sydney Morning Herald* (1831–75) [various issues] · *Town and Country Journal* [Sydney] (30 Oct 1875), 694 · *AusDB*
**Archives** Mitchell L., NSW, corresp. and papers | PRO NIre., letters to Lord Belmore · State Archives of New South Wales, Sydney, colonial secretary's department, corresp. · State Library of New South Wales, Sydney, Parkes MSS; Macarthur MSS
**Likenesses** R. Read, oils, 1832, priv. coll. · photograph, 1865, State Library of New South Wales, Australia

**Cowper, Douglas** (1817–1839), painter, was born at Gibraltar on 30 May 1817, the fourth son of William Cowper (1778/1781–1841), a Gibraltar-born merchant, and his English-born wife, Isabella, *née* Douglas (b. 1791). By September 1829 the family was in Guernsey and Cowper had started at Elizabeth College, where he stayed until 1832. At twelve he made a clever watercolour portrait and he started painting in oils when aged sixteen. In 1834 he travelled to London, where he studied in Henry Sass's drawing academy. He became a student at the Royal Academy on 2 January 1836. In December 1836 Cowper won an academy silver medal for the best copy of N. Poussin's *Rinaldo and Armida* in Dulwich Picture Gallery. He first exhibited at the Royal Academy in 1837. Between then and 1839, the year of his death, Cowper exhibited seventeen paintings at the academy, the British Institution, and the Society of British Artists. He specialized in literary, genre, and fancy subjects. The work which convinced all of his great promise as a painter was *Othello Relating his Adventures*, shown at the Royal Academy in 1839. It was engraved by Edward Finden for part 9 of *The Royal Gallery of British Art* published in March 1842.

The best contemporary account of Cowper comes from his close friend W. P. Frith, a colleague at Sass's and then the Royal Academy Schools from early 1835 onwards. Frith describes Cowper as a 'fair, handsome, delicate youth [with] matchless application' (Frith, 1.43), 'universally liked and respected by all, admired for his genius' (ibid., 3.68). He was 'acknowledged to be one of the best draughtsmen in the Royal Academy' (ibid., 3.68) and 'one of the cleverest pupils [Sass] ever had' (ibid., 3.71). Cowper's portrait of Frith (1837–8) is reproduced as the frontispiece to volume 3 of Frith's *Autobiography*. Cowper's letter to Frith of May 1838 in which he comments on the current Royal Academy exhibition demonstrates his passion for and perceptiveness about art. In particular, it gives an interesting insight into what a young tyro thought about many of his contemporaries, especially those masters who, judging by reviews of his pictures, he clearly sought to emulate, David Wilkie, C. R. Leslie, and Daniel Maclise (ibid., 3.79–84). A seemingly brilliant career was cut short by the onset of consumption and Cowper died at St James's Place, St Peter Port, Guernsey, on 28 November 1839 and was buried in Candie cemetery, St Peter Port, on 4 December.                     L. H. CUST, rev. ROBIN HAMLYN

Sources Art Union, 1 (1839), 69–70 · Art Union, 1 (1839), 183–4 · The exhibition of the Royal Academy (1837–9) [exhibition catalogues] · Catalogue of the works of British artists in the gallery of the British Institution (1837–9) [exhibition catalogues] · exhibition catalogues (1837–9) [Society of British Artists] · The Athenaeum (9 Feb 1839), 117 · The Athenaeum (25 May 1839), 397 · W. P. Frith, My autobiography and reminiscences, 3 vols. (1887–8) · Literary Gazette (17 Dec 1836), 811 · Literary Gazette (25 May 1839), 332 · Literary Gazette (23 April 1842), 282 · students' register, RA · C. J. Durand and E. C. Ozanne, eds., The Elizabeth College register, 1824–1873, with a record of some earlier students: a chapter of island history (1898) · DNB · Redgrave, Artists · church burial register for Candie cemetery, St Peter Port, Guernsey · census returns for St Jaques, St Peter Port, Guernsey, 1841 [William Cowper, father, and Isabella Cowper, mother] · Guernsey Star (2 Dec 1839)

**Cowper, Ebenezer** (1804–1880). See under Cowper, Edward Shickle (1790–1852).

**Cowper, Edward Alfred** (1819–1893), mechanical engineer, was born in London on 10 December 1819, the son of Ann Applegath and her husband, Professor Edward Shickle *Cowper (1790–1852), head of the department of engineering at King's College, London, who, with his brother-in-law Augustus Applegath, developed an improved newspaper printing press. At the age of fourteen in 1833, Cowper was apprenticed for seven years to John Braithwaite, an eminent locomotive and railway engineer in London, and while in Braithwaite's service he invented, in 1837, the detonating railway fog signal, first tried on the Croydon line and widely used thereafter as an emergency safety measure. In 1841 Cowper joined Fox and Henderson, structural and railway engineers, in Smethwick, near Birmingham, where, as chief draughtsman and designer, he devised an ingenious method of casting railway chairs, and also designed the wrought-iron roof of the New Street Station in Birmingham, which, with a span of 211 feet, was the largest iron roof at the time of its completion. In 1846–7 he took a leading part in the foundation of the Institution of Mechanical Engineers; in 1848 he was elected a member of its council, and in 1880–81 served as president. He was elected a member of the Institution of Civil Engineers in 1860, and was a member of council in 1879.

At the end of 1851, after supervising preparation of the contract drawings for the Great Exhibition building (the Crystal Palace), Cowper left Fox and Henderson to practise on his own account in London as a consulting engineer. One of his first commissions was to undertake the necessary redesign of the Crystal Palace prior to its re-erection in Sydenham in 1852–4. Developing the ideas of his friend C. W. Siemens, in 1857 he invented the regenerative hot blast stove known as the Cowper stove, which greatly improved the economy of the hot blast process (patented in 1828 by James B. Neilson) in the making of steel. The first of these stoves was constructed in 1859, and various

improvements were effected in the design up to 1887 both by Cowper and by his son, Charles Edward Cowper, whom he took into partnership shortly before his death. The principle of the regenerative stove is still in widespread use in the iron and steel, glass, and other industries.

Cowper was also greatly interested in the economy of the steam engine, becoming an ardent advocate of compounding and steam-jacketing. About the year 1858 he introduced the steam-jacketed receiver which was subsequently known in the navy as 'Cowper's hot-pot'. Among his many other inventions were a wire spoke suspension wheel with a rubber tyre (practically the modern bicycle wheel) and the writing telegraph, which was an electromechanical precursor of modern facsimile equipment. He published several papers in the Proceedings of the Institution of Mechanical Engineers, including 'An inverted arch suspension bridge' (1847), 'Blast engines for the East Indian Iron Company' (1855), and 'Regenerative hot-blast stoves working at a temperature of 1,300°F' (1860). Cowper died of pneumonia at his home, Rastricke, Pine Grove, Weybridge, Surrey, on 9 May 1893, leaving a widow, Juliana. Their date of marriage is unknown; they had at least one son.                                      RONALD M. BIRSE

Sources PICE, 114 (1892–3), 369–72 · Institution of Mechanical Engineers: Proceedings (1893), 203–5 · The Times (23 May 1893) · Engineering (19 May 1893), 712–13 · Journal of the Iron and Steel Institute, 43 (1893), 172–3 · CGPLA Eng. & Wales (1893)
Wealth at death £24,329 15s. 11d.: probate, 14 June 1893, CGPLA Eng. & Wales

**Cowper, Edward Shickle** (1790–1852), printing engineer and university teacher, was born on 25 February 1790 at Southwark, the son of Edward Cowper, tea dealer. He was apprenticed in 1804 to Benjamin Lepard, a wholesale stationer in Covent Garden, and subsequently concerned himself with the paper and printing trades. His first patent, filed in 1813, was for a paper-cutting machine. In the same year he became a partner with Augustus *Applegath and Henry Mitton, as stereotype founders and printers, at Nelson Square, Southwark. On 4 December 1818 he married Applegath's sister, Ann (d. 1836).

In 1816 Cowper filed a patent for curved stereotype plates, for printing rolls of paper for hangings and other purposes; he then worked to improve the ink distribution on such plates, and the method of conveying the paper through the printer. His success in this respect led the proprietors of The Times newspaper to invite the partners to modify the Koenig press installed at their premises. Applegath and Cowper moved to Duke Street, which crosses Stamford Street, in 1820, and shortly afterwards Cowper left the partnership and set up as a consulting engineer. During the years 1817 to 1821 he and his youngest brother, Ebenezer [see below], were engaged by the Bank of England to develop a system of printing banknotes that would be difficult to forge, but although they were successful technically, the bank, being once more permitted to issue coin, declined to adopt their proposal. In 1823 Cowper filed a patent for printing a web of paper or fabric, and in 1827 another for a method of printing music. Also in 1827, the brothers brought out for *The Times* a new steam-powered 'multiple' machine with four cylinders which delivered 4000 sheets per hour, the most rapid of all machines working flat formes. Versions of the machine to cut rolls of paper into sheets, which Cowper patented in 1828, were used by many country newspapers until the early twentieth century. Trading as E. and E. Cowper, Edward and his younger brother Ebenezer manufactured and installed printing machinery throughout Europe.

In 1839 Cowper was appointed as part-time lecturer in a newly established class of manufacturing art and machinery, in the civil engineering department of King's College, London. His duty was to explain the design and construction of machinery and to accompany his students to factories and public works where machines could be seen in action. His lectures at King's College and elsewhere were judged to be brilliantly successful, his custom being wherever possible to exhibit actual objects rather than to rely on drawings or models. The department flourished and expanded, and in 1848 he was appointed professor of manufacturing art and mechanics.

Cowper had been ailing for some time when he was taken ill in the early part of 1852. After several remissions and relapses, he died at his home, 9 Kensington Park Villas, on 17 October 1852. He was buried at St James's Church in Hampstead, alongside his wife and a daughter (d. 1846); two sons, including Edward Alfred *Cowper, mechanical engineer, and two daughters survived him. The business was continued by his brother.

**Ebenezer Cowper** (1804–1880), printing engineer, was born at Enfield on 17 September 1804, the youngest brother of Edward Shickle Cowper. He was articled to Lloyd, an engineer of Gravel Hill, Southwark, and spent all his working life manufacturing and installing letterpress printing machines, mostly designed by Applegath and Cowper, in Britain and on the continent. Initially he worked in partnership with his brother, later with the firm of Wren and Bennett in Birmingham. In 1837 he married Harriot Jane Harrison. He died at 97 Harborne Road, Edgbaston, on 14 September 1880.

ANITA McCONNELL

**Sources** private information (2004) · J. Moran, *Printing presses—history and development* (1973) · E. Cowper, file, King's Lond. · Ward, *Men of the reign* · C. Knight, ed., *The English cyclopaedia: biography*, 3 (1856) · *Engineering* (24 Sept 1880), 257 [Ebenezer Cowper] · d. cert. · m. cert. [Ebenezer Cowper] · d. cert. [Ebenezer Cowper]
**Wealth at death** under £4000—Ebenezer Cowper: will, 1881

**Cowper, Francis Thomas de Grey**, seventh Earl Cowper (**1834–1905**), politician and landowner, was born on 11 June 1834 in Berkeley Square, London. Styled Viscount Fordwich until he succeeded to his father's title, he was the eldest in the family of two sons and four daughters of George Augustus Frederick Cowper, sixth Earl Cowper (1806–1856), and his wife, Anne Florence (1806–1880), elder daughter and coheiress of Thomas Philip de *Grey,

Francis Thomas de Grey Cowper, seventh Earl Cowper (1834–1905), by unknown lithographer (after Violet Manners, duchess of Rutland, 1894)

second Earl De Grey and fifth Baron Lucas (1781–1859). Based at Panshanger in Hertfordshire, Cowper was born into a family of great wealth at the centre of the whig political, social, and familial cousinhood. His paternal grandmother had one prime minister, William, second Viscount Melbourne, for a brother and another, Viscount Palmerston, as her second husband. On her death in 1869, Cowper inherited the neighbouring Hertfordshire estate of Brocket, along with other properties in Derbyshire and Nottinghamshire. On his mother's death, he came into the house and estate of Wrest, near Ampthill in Bedfordshire, as well as property in Lancashire and London. In middle life, Cowper was one of the wealthiest landowners in England with four country houses and a town house in St James's Square. Local county responsibilities were discharged during the autumn along with the holding of large house parties at Panshanger or Wrest, the spring was usually spent in London or abroad, while the summer months were taken up from late July by long spells in the highlands, first at Cluny near Inverness, and later at Torloisk, Isle of Mull.

Cowper's father, the sixth earl, was whig MP for Canterbury (1830–34) and lord lieutenant for Kent from 1836 until his death. More influential on her son was Cowper's mother, a strong evangelical tory despite her marriage, who retained powerful personal links with all of her children, managing Cowper's life until his own marriage. Cowper was also close to his siblings, and all were painted by Leighton about 1861–2. On the death of both his sister and brother-in-law in 1870 he became effectively the adoptive father of Ethel (Ettie) Fane, later Grenfell (Lady Desborough).

**Education and early political career** Cowper was educated first at preparatory school in Bembridge, Isle of Wight, and from September 1847 at Harrow School, at which he was unhappy and from which he was withdrawn at Easter 1849. He continued his education privately, until 1851 when he went up to Christ Church, Oxford, where he enjoyed the life of the aristocratic undergraduate, making friends in particular with William, eighth marquess of Lothian, whose brother, Walter, later married Cowper's sister, Amabel (1846–1906), and William, Lord Valletort (later fourth earl of Mount Edgcumbe). He toured Italy from late 1854, acquiring an interest in Florentine and Venetian painting, before returning home and deciding to submit for a degree in law and history, securing first-class honours in 1855. He had little interest in games, although later acquired a passion for stalking and shooting. Reading was his favourite pastime.

Entry to the Commons was frustrated by the death of Cowper's father on 15 April 1856, which also prompted a mental breakdown. Cowper was always to regret that he was thereby denied the conventional political apprenticeship to a public career for a man in his position. This combined with an already discernible shyness, and a lack of motivating energy, confined Cowper to largely local affairs and social life for the next twenty years. An early enthusiast for the volunteer movement, he took a continuing interest in home defence. He became lord lieutenant for Bedfordshire in 1861, and was made a KG in 1865. At this time, in the words of his wife and later biographer, his friendship with Louise, duchess of Manchester (wife of William, seventh duke, and later on his death, duchess of Devonshire, wife of Spencer Compton, eighth duke), became 'a very intimate one'. On 25 October 1870 Cowper married Katrine Cecilia (1845–1913), eldest daughter of William Compton, fourth marquess of Northampton, and Eliza, third daughter of Admiral the Hon. Sir George Elliot. Family tradition has it that Cowper was speeded in his proposal of marriage by rumours of an arranged connection between himself and Princess Louise, fourth daughter of Queen Victoria. The marriage was a happy one, with Katrine, an energetically sporting and Christian woman with artistic and literary interests, providing much of the backbone to Cowper's political and social life, as well as supporting him during his periods of chronic illness. There were no children.

During this period, Cowper was taken up with the ornate restoration of Panshanger (badly damaged by fire in 1855), in what Pevsner later called 'a grand rather pompous Neo-Italian style', and with the custody of its large collection of English portraits, Italian old master paintings, furniture, and porcelain. He purchased a *Madonna and Child* by Titian in 1874 (now in the Thyssen collection), and was himself painted by Watts in 1872, while Katrine was painted first by Edward Clofford and later by Poynter. Between 1871 and 1873 he built an additional seat, Beauvale Lodge, on his Nottinghamshire property, with

Edward Godwin as architect. As the patron of eighteen livings, he supported the rebuilding of the churches at Hertingfordbury and at Hertford, and paid for a new church at Eastwood, near Beauvale. Although not sharing the intense evangelicalism of his mother or the religious commitments of his wife, Cowper was a responsible patron and continued to urge more effective episcopal disciplines upon indolent or incompetent clergy.

Throughout his life, Cowper was very conscious of his whig pedigree, and in 1866 in an anonymous letter to *The Times* reaffirmed the whig tradition as that of the aristocratic support for extended individual political rights and moderate institutional reform. Disparaging ideas of fusion with moderate toryism, he urged his colleagues to accept the future leadership of W. E. Gladstone, whose background and experience he saw as leading him not to take 'a merely utilitarian view of politics' (Cowper, 139). He was not given office by Gladstone in 1868, but in April 1871 became a captain of the gentleman-at-arms, a court post coupled with being government spokesman in the House of Lords on Board of Trade matters. It was not a successful appointment. Cowper found the parliamentary routine irksome and the officials uncooperative, and he resigned in August 1873 on not being promoted to under-secretary. Despite political ambition, Cowper did not anticipate any further political opportunities.

**Lord lieutenant of Ireland** With Gladstone's return to office in 1880, Cowper was surprised to be offered the lord lieutenancy of Ireland. Despite his being, in Lord Spencer's words, 'more indolent than most men of his ability' (Spencer to Gladstone, 18 Sept 1880, BL, Add. MS 44308, fol. 42), Katrine persuaded him to accept. Noted by Lord Derby as 'a respectable but rather weak selection' (Political journal of the fifteenth earl of Derby, 30 April 1880, Derby MSS, Lpool RO), Cowper was not Gladstone's first choice—Lord Carlingford refused the post when offered it, because it was not linked to a seat in the cabinet, a position already assigned to the incoming chief secretary, W. E. Forster. It was seen by the Cowpers as an important political opportunity. For Gladstone, already short of very wealthy whig peers to take on these viceregal roles, it promised a balanced executive in Dublin. Cowper was formally sworn in on 5 May.

Cowper's period of office lasted until late April 1882 and did not prove to be the first chapter of a serious political career. In later life, both Cowpers were inclined to attribute this to the exclusive dominance established by Forster over all aspects of Irish government in both London and Dublin, which left Cowper with little independent authority. In fact, the explanation was more complex, involving a combination of bad luck, the severe challenges posed by the government of Ireland, as well as the temperamental differences between the two men.

Cowper made his state entry into Dublin on 27 May 1880. In T. H. Burke, under-secretary, he found a powerful and experienced official, and by early July 1880 Cowper was already commenting on how little he had to do. From mid-July until 20 September 1880 he was out of Ireland, owing to the death of his mother. He expressed whiggish anxieties over the Compensation for Disturbance Bill, and did not regret its defeat in the House of Lords on 3 August.

During the following autumn, Cowper supported the coercion measures to deal with rural crime in Ireland, but was already regarded by some leading Liberals as a cipher. Spencer urged him to become more energetically involved in the work of Dublin Castle, especially while Forster was in London. Perhaps as a result, Cowper prepared a vigorous cabinet memorandum on 28 December, which urged the banning of the Land League in addition to the suspension of habeas corpus and arms control, advice which went beyond that recommended by Forster, and which was not followed by the cabinet in its decisions on 30 December 1880.

The early months of the new year were largely taken up by the Dublin season, a social routine which Cowper found tedious, making him homesick. In executive matters, he continued to follow Burke's advice, becoming frustrated at the government's caution over its arrest of suspects, notably Father Sheehy. He supported the government's Irish land legislation, but contributed little to the discussions which led to Parnell's arrest and the proclamation of the Land League in the autumn.

Cowper increasingly found his position untenable. Forster, whom he found overbearing, had tried unsuccessfully to secure his removal in the previous May, and the Cowpers were anticipating retirement from September 1881. Thereafter, they largely restricted themselves to ceremonial duties, making a tour of Ulster in November, although privately they encouraged the landlord class in their attempts to develop a self-defence organization. On 28 December 1881 Cowper suggested to Gladstone that he step down within a few months, adding that he would want to do this at a time which would 'not give the impression of deserting in the middle of a battle, or of having been asked to retire from incompetence' (Cowper, 545). Gladstone agreed to Cowper's request, and by early April 1882, Spencer was reluctantly anticipating a return to Dublin in his place. For a few days there was some doubt about the timing of the change, with Cowper commenting to his brother that he saw no immediate prospect of escaping from 'this vile place' (ibid., 565). Then, a few days later, a possibly designedly tactless suggestion from Forster—that Cowper might take 'long leave' (ibid., 566)—brought matters to a head. Cowper demanded Gladstone bring forward his retirement, a development quickly leaked to the press. He resigned in a letter to the queen on 28 April. Although formally still in office, Cowper was kept completely in the dark about the final stages of the negotiations with Parnell and his colleagues, and on 2 May he initially resisted signing the papers releasing the Kilmainham prisoners. He also made it clear that he disapproved of the engagement entered into with Parnell, largely on the same grounds as had forced Forster's own resignation. The Cowpers left Dublin on 4 May. Much later Lady Cowper claimed that their decision owed more to Forster's attitude than they had admitted at the time.

Their experience led Cowper to support the abolition of the viceroyalty in January 1886.

**The whig grandee** Cowper never again seriously sought political office, adopting for the rest of his life a senatorial role in national politics as a whig grandee. He contributed a number of articles to the *Nineteenth Century* at the request of James Knowles, the editor, during the years of political crisis of 1884–6. In these he urged what he regarded as the traditional virtues of whiggery, in its historic role as the moderating influence within the Liberal Party. As in 1866, he did not support fusion between moderate whigs and tories. Like his whig leader, Hartington, he rejected Gladstone's declaration for home rule, and presided at the first great unionist meeting at Her Majesty's Theatre on 14 April 1886. Despite the bitterness of the Liberal Party's divisions over home rule, Cowper only slowly accepted that they were likely to become permanent. Keen to preside over the royal commission on the 1881 and 1885 Irish land legislation, Cowper was disappointed that the second Salisbury government did not, at first, accept all of his report's conciliatory recommendations. Later, Liberal Unionist pressure during the debates on the 1887 Irish Land Bill resulted in the commission's recommendations on rent adjudication and the rights of leaseholders being accepted. Cowper continued to advocate a pragmatic approach to state interference on welfare questions, and remained a convinced free trader until the end of his life.

In the years after 1886, Cowper suffered from chronic ill health but continued to be modestly involved in public life. He presided over the Gresham commission in 1893 charged with drafting a new constitution for the University of London. He was an early member of the newly formed Hertfordshire county council, being its chairman from 1891 to 1899. A continuing enthusiast for home defence, he was president of the Naval Volunteer Defence Association, and later entered the debate over the value of rifle clubs. He was a keen supporter of the Sunday opening of national museums and galleries.

For the most part the Cowpers' routine was a social one, of some historical significance in its own right, as their house at Panshanger became one of the meeting grounds for the group known from the late 1880s as the Souls which included A. J. Balfour, George Wyndham, and the young Curzon among its men, and Margot Tennant, Mary Elcho, Evelyn de Vesci, and Cowper's own niece, Ettie Grenfell, among its women. Here in a self-consciously exclusive atmosphere of high living, fine sympathies, and cultivated conversation, relationships and liaisons were nurtured, and in ways thought less vulgarly physical than in the circle around the prince of Wales. Party political divisions were not critical in deciding who should receive the Cowpers' hospitality, and literary and artistic persons were also invited. The Cowpers' own artistic tastes were, like those of the Souls, not avant-garde; both rejected realism in art, drama, and literature, as represented by Millet, Zola, or Ibsen, with Cowper paying £2000 for Burne-Jones's *Aurora* in 1898. Similarly, they remained essentially mid-Victorian in their views about the roles of men and women, regretting the decline in 'reserve' among women and opposing their increasingly public role.

A handsome man 6 feet tall with a firm profile in adult life, Cowper was described by Edmund Gosse as

> The very type, and probably the last example, of the old class of sheltered, refined, exquisitely proud Whig noblemen, exalted by wealth and station above the faintest fear of rebuff, and happy to be a Liberal because he saw human nature through rose-coloured glasses from a great distance. (Ellernberger, 30)

In the last years of his life, Cowper was confined to a bath chair. On 25 June 1905 he was taken seriously ill with an abdominal abscess, and failing to recover from the necessary operation, he died at Panshanger on 19 July 1905. He was buried in Hertingfordbury churchyard and a recumbent effigy by Henry Poole was erected by his widow in 1909. She died at Cannes on 23 March 1913 and was buried beside him. Since he had no direct heir, Cowper's estates were divided at his death, the bulk, including Panshanger, going eventually to his niece, Ettie Desborough.　　ALLEN WARREN

**Sources** [K. Cowper], *Earl Cowper, K. G.: a memoir by his wife* (privately printed, 1913) · *Florence Arnold-Forster's Irish journal*, ed. T. W. Moody and others (1988) · M. L. Boyle, ed., *Biographical catalogue of the portraits at Panshanger, the seat of Earl Cowper* (1885) · N. Ellernberger, 'The Souls, high society and politics in late Victorian Britain', PhD diss., University of Oregon, 1982 · *Hansard* · Lpool RO, Derby papers · Gladstone, *Diaries* · A. Warren, 'Forster, the liberals and new directions in Irish policy, 1880–1882', *Parliamentary History*, 6 (1987), 95–126 · GEC, *Peerage* · *DNB*
**Archives** Beds. & Luton ARS, corresp. and papers as lord-lieutenant of Bedfordshire · Herts. ALS, lecture notes | BL, corresp. with W. E. Gladstone, Add. MS 56453 · Glos. RO, corresp. with Sir Michael Hicks Beach · Herts. ALS, letters to Lord Desborough and Lady Desborough; corresp. with Lady Adine Fane
**Likenesses** Lord Leighton, portrait, *c*.1861–1862 · G. F. Watts, portrait, 1872, Hatfield House, Hertfordshire · lithograph, 1894 (after Violet, duchess of Rutland, 1894), NPG [*see illus.*] · H. Poole, effigy, 1909, Hertingfordbury churchyard, Hertfordshire · H. Cook, print (after W. C. Ross), BM, NPG · V. Granby, portrait, repro. in *Portraits of men and women* (1900) · E. Roberts, portrait; known to be at Panshanger in 1912 · C. W. Walton, print, NPG · portraits, repro. in *VF* (5 June 1880), 541 · portraits, repro. in *ILN* (30 March 1889), 398
**Wealth at death** £1,179,714 9*s*. 7*d*.: probate, 1 Dec 1905, *CGPLA Eng. & Wales*

## Cowper, George Nassau Clavering, third Earl Cowper

(**1738–1789**), art collector and patron, was born on 26 August 1738 and baptized on 17 September at St George's, Hanover Square, London. He was the only son and second child of William, second Earl Cowper (1709–1764), and his first wife, Lady Henrietta Nassau d'Auverquerque (*c*.1713–1747), the younger daughter of Henry, earl of Grantham, and his wife, Henrietta Butler, the daughter of the earl of Ossory. Lord Fordwich, as he was styled, was educated at Eton College. To complete his education he left for the continent in 1757 with a tutor. They visited the Netherlands and Germany before studying for two years in Switzerland. By June 1759 they were in northern Italy and in the following month they were recorded in Florence, where Fordwich became enamoured of the Marchesa Corsi. In September he travelled to Naples and Rome, where he started to form his collection of paintings but, against the

George Nassau Clavering Cowper, third Earl Cowper (1738–1789), by Johan Zoffany, *c*.1773

wish of his tutor and his father, Fordwich returned to Florence. In December 1759, in an unsuccessful bid to make him desert Corsi and Italy, his father had him returned to represent Hertford in parliament.

A caricature by Thomas Patch shows Fordwich in Pola in 1760; two years later he met Anton Raphael Mengs, who was eventually commissioned to paint for him during his visits to Florence in 1769 and 1773–4. The title and property inherited from his father in 1764 helped Cowper gain a position of importance within Florentine society. Soon after he commissioned Francis Harwood to sculpt a monument to his father (at St Mary's, Hertingfordbury, Hertfordshire) and, partly to demonstrate his political standing, he commissioned Giuseppe Macpherson to paint miniature copies of the self-portraits in the grand duke's collection, which were eventually used to curry favour with George III. In 1766 he became a member of the Accademia delle arti del Disegno (known as the Florentine Academy) and two years later he was elected to the Accademia della Crusca. He had a number of Handel oratorios translated into Italian and performed at his own expense.

Cowper was quick to use Johan Zoffany's talents after he arrived in Florence in 1772. He commissioned portraits from him and by June 1774 Zoffany was supplying Cowper with paintings which included two Madonnas by Raphael. Cowper also commissioned portraits from Giuseppe Antonio Fabrini and landscapes from Francesco Zuccarelli, Jakob Philipp Hackert, John Parker, and Hugh Primrose Dean. Zoffany left Florence in 1778 and without his discernment the growth of the collection faltered. None the less Cowper added Fra Bartolommeo's *Holy Family* in 1779 and, during the 1780s, he patronized Joseph Plura, Innocenzo Spinazzi, Hugh Douglas Hamilton, and Jacob More.

Concurrently with his artistic ventures Cowper equipped a large laboratory and supported the work of Count Alessandro Volta and in 1777 he was made a fellow of the Royal Society. In the following year he was created a prince of the Holy Roman empire which encouraged him to look to England for similar recognition. He coveted Sir Horace Mann's position as British resident and, hoping to gain preferment, he visited the British court in 1786. Despite giving George III a Raphael self-portrait, Cowper returned to Florence politically frustrated and resumed his artistic interests, buying paintings by Carlo Dolci and Dirk Helmbrecker. On 2 June 1775 at Florence he married Hannah (*c*.1758–1826), the youngest daughter of Charles Gore and his wife, Mary Cockerill. The couple had three sons, George (1776–1799), who inherited the title from his father, Peter (1778–1837), later fifth Earl Cowper, and Edward Spencer (1779–1823). The third Earl Cowper died of dropsy in Florence on 22 December 1789 and was buried at Hertingfordbury.                          HUGH BELSEY

Henry Cowper (*c*.1753–1840), by Sir Francis Legatt Chantrey, 1828

**Sources** B. Moloney, *England and Italy* (1969), 169–90 · J. Ingamells, ed., *A dictionary of British and Irish travellers in Italy, 1701–1800* (1997), 245–7 · B. Rousseau, 'Lord Cowper e la sua collezione', *Gazzetta Antiquaria*, 22–3 (1994), 74–83 · D. Sutton, 'Paintings at Firle Place', *The Connoisseur*, 134 (1959), 166–7 · H. Belsey, 'Newly discovered work by Francesco Harwood', *Burlington Magazine*, 122 (1980), 65–6 · J. A. Rice, 'An early Handel revival in Florence', *Early Music*, 18 (1990), 62–71 · E. Gibson, 'Earl Cowper in Florence and his correspondence with the Italian opera in London', *Music and Letters*, 68 (1987), 235–52 · G. Dragoni, 'Vicende dimenticate del mecenatismo bolognese dell' ultimo '700: l'aquisto della collezione di strumentazioni scientifiche di Lord Cowper', *Il Carrobbio*, 11 (1985), 68–85 · T. C. W. Blanning, '"That horrid electorate" or "Ma patrie germanique"? George III, Hanover, and the *Fürstenbund* of 1785', *HJ*, 20 (1977), 311–44 · GEC, *Peerage* · L. B. Namier, 'Cowper, George Nassau Clavering', HoP, *Commons, 1754–90* · Herts. ALS · PRO, SP 98/80, fol. 78

**Archives** Herts. ALS, corresp. and papers; papers relating to his art collection in Florence

**Likenesses** T. Patch, oils, 1760 (*The punch party*), Dunham Massey, Great Manchester · T. Patch, oils, 1761 (*Golden asses*), Lewis Walpole Library, Farmington, Connecticut · T. Patch, oils, *c*.1761 (*Gathering of dilettanti*), Sir Brinsley Ford Collection, London · T. Patch, oils, *c*.1765 (*A gathering at Sir Horace Mann's house*), Lewis Walpole Library, Farmington, Connecticut · T. Patch, oils, *c*.1765 (*A party at Horace Mann's house*), Lewis Walpole Library, Farmington, Connecticut · A. R. Mengs, oils, 1769; formerly Principe Corsini, Florence · J. Zoffany, oils, *c*.1773, Firle Place, Sussex [*see illus.*] · A. R. Mengs, oils, 1773–4, priv. coll. · J. Zoffany, oils, 1773–7, Royal Collection · J. Zoffany, oils, *c*.1775, Yale U. CBA · G. Macpherson, oils, 1775–80, priv. coll. · G. Fabrini, oils, 1780, Accademia Etrusca, Cortona · H. D. Hamilton, pastel drawing, 1786; Christies, Oct 1953, lot 5 · J. Wedgwood, ceramic medallion, 1786 · I. Spinazzi, marble, 1787, Milan art market

**Cowper, Henry** (*c*.1753–1840), clerk assistant of the House of Lords, was the youngest of the three sons of Lieutenant-General Spencer Cowper (*c*.1724–1797) of Ham Common, Surrey, and his wife, Charlotte, daughter of John Baber. He matriculated at Exeter College, Oxford, on 4 January 1771 but took no degree. He entered the Middle Temple as a student on 7 February 1770 and was called to the bar on

26 May 1775, becoming a bencher on 25 January 1811. Between 1774 and 1778 he acted as reporter of cases decided by the king's bench. His work in that capacity enjoyed a high reputation and helped to establish the principles of modern law reporting. In 1783 he published *Reports of cases in the court of king's bench from Hilary term 14 George III to Trinity term 18 George III* (3 vols.; 2nd edn, 1800). He was a commissioner of bankrupts from 1776 to 1785.

In January 1785 Cowper was appointed clerk assistant of the House of Lords and deputy clerk of the parliaments. The office of clerk of the parliaments was held successively by his grandfather William (1716–40), and William's younger brother, Ashley (1740–88), the sons of the judge Spencer Cowper (1670–1728). During this period the clerk ceased to officiate in person and the duties devolved upon the deputy clerk or clerk assistant. He was continued in the post of clerk assistant by the succeeding clerks, George Rose (1788) and Sir George Henry Rose (1818). Cowper thus became in effect the principal officer of the House of Lords. In that capacity he played an important role in the trial of Warren Hastings before the House of Lords, which opened in Westminster Hall on 13 February 1788. It has been speculated that his 'emphatical and interesting delivery of the defence' (*GM*, 1788) attracted the enmity of Edmund Burke, who subsequently referred to him as that 'Rogue Cowper' (*Correspondence of Edmund Burke*, 8.113) and as one of 'the known partisans of the delinquent' (ibid., 114). However, there is no evidence that Cowper used his position to influence the Lords in favour of Hastings. In February 1826 he retired on pension, after forty-one years' service.

Cowper married on 9 September 1779 his first cousin Maria Judith (*c*.1752–1815), daughter of Major William Cowper of Hertingfordbury Park, Hertfordshire; they had no children. He was a man of charitable disposition and was described as 'the Father of the poor'. He died on 28

November 1840, aged eighty-seven, at Tewin Water, Hertfordshire, and was buried at Hertingfordbury ten days later.                                                            J. C. SAINTY

**Sources** D. Warrand, ed., *Hertfordshire families* (1907), 147–8 · M. F. Bond, 'Clerks of the parliaments, 1509–1953', *EngHR*, 73 (1958), 78–85 · J. E. Cussans, *History of Hertfordshire*, 2/2 (1874); facs. repr. (1972), 110, 114 · *Lords Journals*, 37.177 · *Lords Journals*, 58.18, 24, 31, 36 · *GM*, 1st ser., 49 (1779), 470 · *GM*, 1st ser., 58 (1788), 350 · *GM*, 1st ser., 67 (1797), 353 · *GM*, 2nd ser., 15 (1841), 107, 320 · H. A. C. Sturgess, ed., *Register of admissions to the Honourable Society of the Middle Temple, from the fifteenth century to the year 1944*, 1 (1949), 167 · Foster, *Alum. Oxon.* · Holdsworth, *Eng. law* · *The correspondence of Edmund Burke*, ed. T. W. Copeland and others, 10 vols. (1958–78)
**Archives** Cowper Memorial Library, Olney, Northamptonshire, corresp. and papers | BL, letters to Lord Camelford and Lady Camelford, Add. MS 69297 · BL, letters to Lord Grenville, Add. MS 58979 · Bodl. Oxf., Brooke MS
**Likenesses** G. Hayter, portrait, oils, 1820–23 (*The trial of Queen Caroline, 1820*), NPG · F. Chantrey, drawing, 1823, NPG · F. L. Chantrey, marble bust, 1828, V&A [*see illus.*] · J. Jackson, portrait, exh. RA 1829, House of Lords
**Wealth at death** average income from office was £3600 (1803–1810): Bond, 'Clerks', 80, n. 6 · granted an annuity for life of £1000 with £500 to widow by letters patent: 21 Nov 1797, PRO, C66/3943, no. 2 · evidently rich; able to indulge charitable proclivities

**Cowper, John** (d. 1603), Church of Scotland minister, was the son of John Cowper, burgess and tailor of Edinburgh—deacon of the tailors in 1574—and his wife, Marion Duncan; William *Cowper (1568–1619), bishop of Galloway, was his brother. John Cowper studied at St Mary's College, St Andrews, where he graduated BA in 1577. Prior to his appointment to a parish, on 3 February 1586, James VI commanded him to pray for Mary, queen of Scots, from the pulpit of St Giles, Edinburgh, something which most of the kirk's ministers had refused to do. When Cowper also refused, the king ordered him to vacate the pulpit in favour of Patrick Adamson, archbishop of St Andrews. Cowper appeared before the king and privy council that afternoon and was warded in Blackness Castle at his own expense. The town council supported him to the extent of granting him £40 Scots to meet the expenses which he incurred during his confinement. On 22 March a bond of caution for £500 Scots was provided by his father and Andrew Borthwick on his release, on the understanding that he would make satisfaction to the king for his offence and would not preach or administer the sacraments without the king's licence. The bond continued to be held by the privy council until the following year.

On 23 November 1586 Cowper was elected one of the ministers of Edinburgh. He did not serve for long, being translated and inducted to the collegiate charge of Glasgow on 28 February 1587. There is no record of his being further involved in public affairs, but at the general assembly of 1602 he was appointed to visit the churches of Lothian. He died in Glasgow on 25 December 1603. Cowper was married to Elizabeth, sister of John Livingston of Baldoran, who survived him. Their son John was bursar of the University of Glasgow in 1603, and in 1614 their daughter Janet married Joseph Laurie, successively minister of Kirkintilloch, Stirling, Longforgan, and finally Perth, where Laurie held the collegiate charge which had once

been his wife's uncle's (from 1635 to 1640). Objections to the marriage by Janet's curators, who revealingly included members of the influential Livingston and Fleming families, were not sustained by the presbytery of Glasgow.                                              DUNCAN SHAW

**Sources** *Fasti Scot.*, 1.53; 3.451, 460 · J. D. Marwick, ed., *Extracts from the records of the burgh of Edinburgh, AD 1573–1589*, [4], Scottish Burgh RS, 5 (1882), 4.24, 51, 57–8, 464, 476–7, 496, 498, 511–12, 528, 530 · D. Calderwood, *The history of the Kirk of Scotland*, ed. T. Thomson and D. Laing, 8 vols., Wodrow Society, 7 (1842–9), vol. 4, pp. 606, 623, 630; vol. 5, p. 616 · T. Thomson, ed., *Acts and proceedings of the general assemblies of the Kirk of Scotland*, 3 pts, Bannatyne Club, 81 (1839–45) · *Reg. PCS*, 1st ser., 4.142–4, 155, 891, 191

**Cowper** [*née* Clavering], **Mary, Countess Cowper** (1685–1724), courtier and diarist, was the elder of the two surviving children of John Clavering (*bap.* 1655, *d.* in or after 1702), landowner and mine owner, of Chopwell, co. Durham, and his first wife, Anne Thompson. John was descended from the junior branch of the Claverings of Axwell, co. Durham, a wealthy coalmining family. Nothing is known of Mary's childhood; in her later teens she lived in London with her aunt Grace, Lady Wood, widow of Sir Thomas Wood, bishop of Coventry. By the time she reached adulthood Mary was admired for her beauty and her exceptional talent as a harpsichordist.

In the summer of 1706 William *Cowper (1665–1723), lord keeper of the great seal, initiated a clandestine courtship, having met Mary when she consulted him on a legal matter three years previously. Twenty years her senior, William couched his proposal letter in rational terms: 'I have chosen this plain narrative how I came not so much to be madly in love as to love a settled opinion I think from cool reason and judgement' (Herts. ALS, Panshanger MSS, D/EP F193). He offered her an annuity of £300 per year as separate income while his wife and as her jointure in widowhood. For fear that his impending elevation to a barony might be impeded by a jealous female rival, Mary and William were secretly married on 18 September 1706. Despite the fact that William was made Baron Cowper in October 1706, the marriage was not publicly acknowledged until February 1707. Mysterious marital beginnings aside, William and Mary adored one another, as their intensely affectionate correspondence attests. They had four children: Sarah (1707–1758), William (1709–1764), Anne (1710–1750), and Spencer *Cowper (1713–1774).

The accession of George I offered the opportunity for the commencement of Mary's two careers. She began her diary in October of 1714 on the occasion of being named a lady of the bedchamber for Caroline, princess of Wales, with the stated aim of writing an accurate account of events at court, which she 'intended hereafter to revise and digest into a better method' (*Diary*, 1). Mary had cleverly laid the groundwork for obtaining the post by beginning a correspondence with Caroline four years previously, as well as establishing contact with Baron Bernstorff, George's principal adviser. Furthermore, on the occasion of her first meeting the new king, she apparently made a good impression by proffering elegant compliments in fluent French.

**Mary Cowper, Countess Cowper (1685–1724),** by Sir Godfrey Kneller, 1709

Mary immediately put her new-found access to court and her language skill to use in acting as a go-between for her husband, who after resigning in 1710 had received the seals again in September 1714. The first day she attended the princess she gave Bernstorff 'A Treatise on the State of Parties, which I had transcribed and translated for my Lord, in French and English, to give the King' (*Diary*, 7). William had written this treatise to intimate that George I should rely on the whigs as his natural supporters. Mary was thus instrumental in whig efforts to incline the new monarch to their policies.

Moreover Mary's court connections and influence with her husband rendered her an effective patronage broker. Via her friendship with Bernstorff she obtained the post of physician to the princess of Wales for Sir David Hamilton and positions in customs and chancery court for her own kin and friends. Mary's kin had even greater cause to thank her after the rising of 1715, when two of her Jacobite cousins who had been participants gained clemency through her influence.

Mary recorded these successes in her diary, alongside descriptions of daily life at court. Although she noted the health costs associated with her post, mentioning that after her week of waiting 'I was ill from standing so long upon my feet' (*Diary*, 21), she clearly relished the job and the opportunities it afforded. When William, ill and exhausted, was tempted to resign in February 1716, Mary affirmed her role as devoted wife, yet signalled the value of her own career when she wrote:

> I offered him, if it would be any pleasure done him, to retire with him into the country, and quit too, and what was more,

never to repine at doing so, though it was the greatest sacrifice that could be made him.  (ibid., 75)

Both Lord and Lady Cowper helped to effect a brief thawing of relations between George I and the prince of Wales in 1718. In that same year, however, perhaps as a result of intervening in such an acrimonious quarrel, William finally did resign. Remarkably enough, Mary stayed at court with her husband's blessing:

> I think 'tis but reasonable, that at least for variety of living, you should find something more satisfaction in a court, than you can in a retired minister (who you know is always a peevish creature) and so solitary a place.  (Herts. ALS, Panshanger MSS, D/EP F193)

William, now Earl Cowper, continued to be an active politician in the House of Lords. Mary consequently soon found herself in a fix when, despite William's public opposition to the South Sea Company, she secretly borrowed money to invest in the stock and lost several hundred pounds when the Bubble finally deflated. At the end of 1720 Mary was still trying to repay creditors while keeping the whole affair secret from her husband. In that year as well there was another reconciliation between the king and the prince of Wales, but this time not with the help of the Cowpers. Rather, this episode marks the beginning of Mary's increasing resentment at Robert Walpole's ascendancy and her diary reflects her feeling of being frozen out of the court network of information and influence. Worse still, in 1722, in the midst of the investigation of the Jacobite plot centred on Christopher Layer, William Cowper was erroneously named a conspirator. In alarm at the prospect of the house being searched, Mary burnt everything in her diary that pertained to the royal quarrel, thus undercutting her own intention of supplying an accurate account of court politics for posterity. Only the portions of the diary covering October 1714 to October 1716 and April and May 1720 survive.

William Cowper unexpectedly died after a brief illness in October 1723. Mary, who in 1719 had written to him, 'You are all that is worth living for' (Herts. ALS, Panshanger MSS, D/EP F59), proceeded to act accordingly. She wrote her will on 10 December 1723, specifying that: 'In case it please God to take me out of this world to my dearest best beloved and most tenderest loving husband', she wished to be buried in the same coffin with him. If she outlived him by more than a year, 'as I hope I shall not', she asked for her coffin to be placed next to his (ibid., D/EP T1147). Her daughter Sarah described Mary's last weeks:

> The latter end of December my mother grew much weaker and extremely ill; she lost her appetite entirely, and at times her memory, so that she would speak of my Father as if living, ask for him, and expect him home. When she recollected his death, it seemed with so lively a grief as if it had just then happened. In short, she really had what is often talked of, but seen in very few instances, a broken heart. (ibid., D/EP F233, fol. 259)

Mary died on 5 February 1724 at Cole Green, Hertfordshire, and was buried in St Mary's Hertingfordbury, Hertfordshire, on 15 February. Lady Cowper's diary, edited by Charles Spencer Cowper, was first published in 1864.

ANNE KUGLER

**Sources** *DNB* · *Diary of Mary, Countess Cowper*, ed. [S. Cowper] (1864); 2nd edn (1865) · M. Cowper, correspondence, Herts. ALS, Panshanger MSS, D/EP F59 · W. Cowper, correspondence, Herts. ALS, Panshanger MSS, D/EP F193 · S. Cowper, 'Family books', Herts. ALS, Panshanger MSS, D/EP F228–233 · will, Herts. ALS, Panshanger MS, D/EP T1147 · Mary Cowper's marriage articles, Herts. ALS, Panshanger MS, D/EP F13 · *VCH Hertfordshire*, suppl. · M. Cowper, correspondence, from family members, Herts. ALS, Panshanger MSS, D/EP F194 · M. Cowper, correspondence, from outside family, Herts. ALS, D/EP F200, 202 · M. Cowper, diary, Herts. ALS, Panshanger MS, D/EP F205 · *The correspondence of Sir James Clavering*, ed. H. T. Dickinson, SurtS, 178 (1967) · R. Surtees, *The history and antiquities of the county palatine of Durham*, 2 (1820) · *The diary of Sir David Hamilton, 1709–1714*, ed. P. Roberts (1975) · C. Jones, 'Jacobitism and the historian: the case of William, first Earl Cowper', *Albion*, 23 (1991), 681–97
**Archives** Herts. ALS, corresp., diaries, and MSS
**Likenesses** G. Kneller, oils, 1709, priv. coll. [*see illus.*] · engraving (after G. Kneller), repro. in *Diary of Mary*, ed. Cowper · stipple, NPG
**Wealth at death** £300 p.a. jointure, plus added £500 p.a. jointure; also jewellery, coach, and horses: will of William Cowper; will of Mary Cowper, Herts. ALS

**Cowper [Cooper], Robert** (*c.*1465–1539/40), composer, was apparently brought up in Sussex, but of his parentage and musical training nothing is known. From early 1493 until October 1496 he served as a lay clerk in the choir of King's College, Cambridge, and he was admitted by the university to the degree of bachelor of music on 13 June 1494. During 1501–2 he was licensed to proceed as doctor of music on the grounds that five years of study and five years of practical experience so qualified him, and he was eventually admitted during 1506–7. Described as 'of Chichester diocese', he was ordained priest on 31 March 1498, and by June 1504 he had been engaged as a singing-man and apparently master of the choristers of the household chapel of Lady Margaret Beaufort, mother of King Henry VII. In 1504 and 1509 he received rewards for composing music for performance by the chapel's personnel of some twenty singing-men and eight boys, and he travelled to recruit boys and to buy books for their Latin education.

Cowper's employment following Lady Margaret's death in 1509 is unknown. He does not occur as a gentleman of the Chapel Royal; however, the preservation of four secular songs and a sacred piece in two manuscripts compiled *c.*1515–1520 and associated with the royal court indicates that he had secured service in some great household that was in close contact with royalty. Very possibly he worked in the chapel of William Warham, archbishop of Canterbury, patron of several of the numerous benefices in south-eastern counties to which Cowper was presented between 1511 and 1526. Towards the end of his life his principal employment was in some capacity, probably as master of the lady chapel choir, at Bury St Edmunds Abbey. It may have been in consequence of its dissolution that on 25 September 1539 he offered himself, unsuccessfully, for appointment as a minor canon of St Paul's Cathedral, London. He had died by early January 1540.

In 1597 Thomas Morley listed Cowper among the composers whose works he had consulted when compiling his *Plaine and Easie Introduction to Practicall Musicke*, and in 1598

Francis Meeres, in *Palladis tamia*, named him as one of England's 'excellent musicians'. Typically for a composer whose working environments included the aristocratic household, his pieces are both secular and ecclesiastical. No larger-scale compositions are known to have survived, though in 1529 his four-part masses were known at King's College, Cambridge. Almost half of his works now extant are known only from single voices, among them three pieces issued in *XX Songes* (1530), the earliest such anthology printed in England. The three songs preserved complete in the so-called King Henry VIII's MS are all for three voices; they manifest the academic discipline of canon and some particularly effective ringing of the changes on the contemporary commonplaces of part-writing. Similar qualities of deft canonic and contrapuntal composition are exhibited by the church music.   ROGER BOWERS

**Sources** Emden, *Cam.*, 164–5 · F. Kisby, 'A mirror of monarchy: music and musicians in the household of the Lady Margaret Beaufort, mother of Henry VII', *Early Music History*, 16 (1997), 203–34 · *Music at the court of Henry VIII*, ed. J. Stevens, 2nd edn, Musica Britannica, 18 (1973), nos. 14, 62, 63 · King's Cam. · M. Bateson, ed., *Grace book B*, 1 (1903), 59, 61, 223 · W. G. Searle, ed., *Grace book Γ* (1908), 4, 38 · GL, St Paul's Cathedral MSS · *The autobiography of Thomas Whythorne*, ed. J. M. Osborn (1961) · T. Morley, *A plain and easy introduction to practical music*, ed. R. A. Harman (1952), 6, 123, 322 · *Robert Cooper: 'Gloria in excelsis Deo'*, ed. H. B. Collins (1925) · M. K. Jones and M. G. Underwood, *The king's mother: Lady Margaret Beaufort, countess of Richmond and Derby* (1992) · J. Stevens, *Music and poetry in the early Tudor court* (1961) · St John Cam., Archives of household of Lady Margaret Beaufort, countess of Richmond and Derby
**Archives** BL, Add. MSS 17802–17805, 31922 · King's Cam. | GL, archives of St Paul's Cathedral

**Cowper [*née* Holled], Sarah, Lady Cowper** (1644–1720), diarist, was born on 14 February 1644 in Eastcheap, London, the only child of Samuel Holled (*d.* 1661), merchant, and his wife, Anne (*d.* 1664). Samuel was originally from Northamptonshire, but nothing else is known of Sarah's parents or of her childhood and education. Sole heir to her parents' estate of roughly £1000, two months after the death of her mother, on 11 April 1664 Sarah married William Cowper (1639–1706), lawyer, who at the end of that same year inherited a baronetcy and houses in London and Kent from his grandfather. Four sons followed in quick succession: William *Cowper (1665–1723); Samuel (August–October 1666); John (1667–1686); and Spencer *Cowper (1670–1728).

In areas other than reproductive, however, the marriage was a catastrophe. As Lady Cowper put it in 1701, 'Never met two more averse than we in humour, passions, and affections; our reason and sense, religion or morals agree not' (Herts. ALS, Panshanger MSS, D/EP F29, 1.162). Control over the household was the main source of conflict, but finances, religion, sex, and relations with kin and friends were also at issue. From Lady Cowper's perspective, Sir William was a disorderly, irreligious, tyrannical fool and in turn Sir William seems to have regarded his wife as smugly pious—a characterization not without merit, as her self-righteous commentary in 1702 on her husband indicates: 'I have lived with Sir W[illiam] (upon Computation) almost 14000 daies, and from the bottom of my Soul do beleive I never past one without Something to be forgiven him' (ibid., 1.185).

Despite her seemingly permanent state of seething resentment, Lady Cowper's social fortunes improved considerably over the course of her life. She became the wife of an MP when Sir William Cowper sat as a whig for Hertford from 1679 to 1681 and again from 1688 to 1700, then the mother of the lord keeper of the great seal and lord chancellor when her son William was named to those offices in 1705 and 1707 respectively. Near the end of her life she became mother of the chief justice of Chester when her son Spencer was appointed in 1717, and mother of an earl when William was granted that title in 1718. Lady Cowper's financial situation, however, was strained most of the time. Sir William's income was inadequate for his rank, and so the couple maintained a modest rented house in Charterhouse Yard and then in Holborn in London, and their county seat was a small, run-down remnant of the royal castle in Hertford. This disparity between rank and wealth aggravated marital disputes, as well as reinforcing Lady Cowper's anxieties about living up to the elevated social position into which she married.

Lady Cowper reacted to her social and familial situation first by compiling eleven commonplace books between 1670 and 1700 into which she transcribed selections from her readings on history, religion, politics, and philosophy, saying in a retrospective preface, 'if in the dayes of my youth I had not diverted my thoughts with such stuff as this book contains; the unhappy accidents of my life had been more than enough to have made me mad' (Herts. ALS, Panshanger MSS, D/EP F37). Then in 1700, in response to the boredom of a summer in the country, continuing marital strife, and most importantly her social isolation because of her son Spencer's trial for murder in 1699, she began a diary that she continued for the next sixteen years, writing more than 2300 pages in all. Remarkable for its chronicle of family tensions and its commentary on politics, religion, and the later Stuart social scene, this diary is all the more notable because in it Lady Cowper seamlessly blended her own words with those of prescriptive authors in order to indict her husband and sons while valorizing her own performance of the roles of wife, mother, gentlewoman, and pious Anglican. In the process of validating her own behaviour, she subverted contemporary ideology regarding the place and proper duties of womankind.

Lady Cowper's social circle included eminent latitudinarian clergy, notably Simon Patrick, bishop of Ely, and Gilbert Burnet, bishop of Salisbury, and the influential wives and widows of leading whig politicians, especially Rachel, Lady Russell, and Margaret, Lady Shaftesbury. This alliance with pillars of the established church may well have been a conscious strategy of opposition to her husband, who generally relied on the dissenting community in Hertford for political support. Through her social connections she was instrumental in arranging her son William's appointment as king's counsel in 1689.

Sir William's death on 26 November 1706 opened a new chapter in Lady Cowper's life. As she observed in 1708 looking back on her first year as a widow, 'Methinks I taste and feel that liberty is sweet' (Herts. ALS, Panshanger MSS, D/EP F29–35, 290). Financially independent with a jointure of £400 per year, she embarked on a spending spree for charity, gratified by the attention she received from clergy soliciting her donations to the Society for the Propagation of the Gospel and to charity schools. Her relationship with her eldest son, particularly tense in 1705 because of his refusal to let her share in the patronage opportunities of his elevation to high office, improved distinctly with his marriage to his second wife, Mary Clavering, in 1706. A dutiful daughter-in-law, Mary Cowper (1685–1724) pleased Lady Cowper especially by naming their first child after her.

In the days of her widowhood, Lady Cowper's main aggravation was overseeing troublesome servants; otherwise, she spent her time reading, writing, visiting, and going to church. The event that exercised her most was the trial of Dr Sacheverell at which her son William presided. The trial's outcome drove the whigs, including William, from office in 1711, and thereafter, Lady Cowper observed events at an increasingly cynical and infirm remove. Unable to breathe easily and plagued by arthritis, palsy, and near-blindness, she finally gave up writing in September 1716. When she died on 3 February 1720, possibly in London, her sons at her direction had her buried on 10 February at St Mary's Church, Hertingfordbury, Hertfordshire, where they erected a monument praising her 'industry, virtue, wisdom, and piety'.  ANNE KUGLER

**Sources** S. Cowper, diary, 1700–16, Herts. ALS, Panshanger MS, D/EP F29–35 · W. Cowper, memorandum book, 1658–90, Herts. ALS, Panshanger MS, D/EP F25 · S. Cowper, 'The medley', 1673, Herts. ALS, Panshanger MSS, D/EP F37 · Cowper papers, Herts. ALS, Panshanger MSS, D/EP F23 · D. Warrand, ed., *Hertfordshire families* (1907) · will of Samuel Holled, PRO, PROB 11/305, sig. 125 · will of Anne Holled, PRO, PROB 11/314, sig. 68 · will of William Cowper, PRO, PROB 11/492, sig. 4 · *DNB* · A. Kugler, *Errant plagiary: the life and writing of Lady Sarah Cowper (1644–1720)* (2002)
**Archives** Herts. ALS, Panshanger MSS
**Likenesses** P. Lely, oils, priv. coll.
**Wealth at death** under £100; £400 p.a. jointure settlement; more than 100 books; also household furnishings: will [Sir William Cowper] PRO, PROB 11/492, sig. 4; catalogue of books in London, 1701, Panshanger MSS, D/EP F36, Herts. ALS

**Cowper, Spencer** (1670–1728), judge, was born on 23 February 1670, the second surviving son of Sir William Cowper, second baronet (1639–1706) and MP, of the Castle, Hertford, and his wife, Lady Sarah (1644–1720), daughter of Samuel Holled, a prominent London merchant [*see* Cowper, Sarah, Lady Cowper]. William *Cowper, first Earl Cowper (d. 1723), was his elder brother. He was educated at Westminster School and matriculated at Christ's College, Cambridge, in 1686 before following his brother to the Middle Temple, where he was admitted in May 1687. On 4 February 1688 he married Pennington Goodere (d. 1727); their children included Judith *Madan, gentlewoman and poet. Two years later family interest with the corporation of London secured him the position of comptroller (or

Spencer Cowper (1670–1728), by Sir Godfrey Kneller

steward) of the Bridge House estates in Southwark, and in 1693 he was called to the bar. He subsequently followed the home circuit, which enabled him to take advantage of his family's strong influence at Hertford, but at the spring assizes in 1699 his prospects were compromised by the mysterious death of Sarah Stout, the daughter of a local Quaker family who had supported the Cowper electoral interest.

It appears that Sarah Stout had fallen in love with Cowper, although he was married, and became melancholy when he avoided her company. Spencer Cowper had been at the woman's house late on the evening before she was found drowned in the river, and two attorneys and a scrivener of his acquaintance, who were also in Hertford that day, were said to have enquired after her particularly. Despite the absence of any positive evidence against them, and a verdict of suicide at the coroner's inquest, Cowper and the other three men were tried for murder at Hertford on 16 July 1699. Besides the circumstantial evidence, the prosecution relied chiefly on the theory that as the body had floated, it must have been put in the water after death, and to meet this argument Cowper called expert medical testimony, including the famous physicians Samuel Garth and Hans Sloane, together with the anatomist William Cowper (not related). Although the judge (Baron Hatsell) was hostile and gave a poor summing-up, all the defendants were acquitted. It was alleged by Cowper at the trial that the prosecutions were malicious, maintained by an alliance of the local tories, who saw an opportunity to disable the town's principal whig family, and the Quakers, who wanted to clear their society from the reproach of suicide. Certainly there were powerful interests at stake:

pamphlets were published on both sides, and unsuccessful attempts were made to renew the prosecution by appeal of murder.

Although his family temporarily lost control of Hertford politics, Cowper's career was not damaged permanently, and in 1705 he took over his brother's parliamentary seat at Bere Alston in the whig interest. He was re-elected at the 1708 election and served as one of the managers at the trial of Dr Henry Sacheverell in 1710, but lost his seat in the electoral reaction to that event. The Cowper fortunes revived again after 1714, with the accession of the Hanoverians, and Spencer shared in the largesse, becoming attorney-general to the prince of Wales and one of the king's counsel, and securing election on the government interest for Truro, which he represented until he was made a judge. His eldest son, William, was given the very lucrative office of clerk of the parliaments. Cowper was even talked of to succeed Nicholas Lechmere as solicitor-general in 1715, but was passed over because the lord chancellor wanted to avoid any charge of nepotism. In 1717 he secured a major consolation prize in the form of the chief justiceship of Chester, with a salary of £730, plus fees. Although he acknowledged a debt to his brother's influence, even in 1720, after Lord Cowper had resigned the great seal, Spencer Cowper remained one of the busiest counsels in the court of chancery and the House of Lords. A new burst of advancement occurred with the accession of the prince as George II in 1727, when Cowper was made attorney-general to the duchy of Lancaster, and then (24 October 1727) a puisne justice of common pleas. His first wife died in November 1727; in July 1728 he married Theodora Stepney, a widow, but he died four months later, on 10 December 1728, after only a year on the bench, and was buried at his seat of Hertingfordbury in Hertfordshire. His second son, John, was the father of William Cowper the poet.

DAVID LEMMINGS

**Sources** Herts. ALS, Panshanger MSS · E. Cruickshanks, 'Cowper, Spencer', HoP, Commons, 1715–54 · Sainty, King's counsel · Sainty, Judges · D. Lemmings, Gentlemen and barristers: the inns of court and the English bar, 1680–1730 (1990) · H. A. C. Sturgess, ed., Register of admissions to the Honourable Society of the Middle Temple, from the fifteenth century to the year 1944, 3 vols. (1949) · State trials, 13.1106–1250 · Venn, Alum. Cant. · DNB

**Archives** Herts. ALS, Panshanger MSS · Herts. ALS, letters to first Earl Cowper; papers relating to Stout case

**Likenesses** G. Kneller, oils, Oriel College, Oxford [see illus.] · L. F. Roubiliac, marble effigy on monument, St Mary's Church, Hertingfordbury, Hertfordshire

**Cowper, Spencer** (1713–1774), dean of Durham, was born in London, the youngest son of William *Cowper, first Earl Cowper (1665–1723), lord chancellor, and his second wife, Mary Clavering (1685–1724) [see Cowper, Mary, Countess Cowper] of Chopwell, co. Durham. His mother shortly thereafter became lady in waiting to the princess of Wales, later Queen Caroline. Although a somewhat sickly child, who was to develop in adult life a form of hypochondria inherited from his mother, Cowper survived a smallpox attack. On 16 May 1729 he matriculated at Exeter College, Oxford, where he graduated BA in 1732, proceeding MA in 1734 and BD and DD by diploma in 1746. After his ordination in 1738 he became rector of Fordwich, Kent.

Cowper's swift ecclesiastical career may have been helped by the connections which sprang from a strong family tradition of court service. Indeed the short coronation epigram 'On the Sceptre Borne by the Queen' that has been attributed to him (Nichols, *Lit. anecdotes*, 2.364–5) suggests that by 1727 he had become well versed in the art of flattering royalty. In 1742 he was presented with a stall in Canterbury, which he resigned on his promotion to the deanery of Durham, where he was installed on 21 July 1746. He was untiring in his efforts to make Durham a musical centre, and had a new organ built in the cathedral. However, the many consents to sealing preserved in the Durham archives show that he resided in his northern post as infrequently as he could, on medical grounds, and that he usually preferred to spend the autumn in Durham and the other nine months of the year in Hertfordshire and Grosvenor Square, London. In 1743 he married Dorothy, daughter of Charles Townshend, second Viscount Townshend.

Besides the speech he delivered at the enthronement of Bishop Trevor in 1753, Cowper published *The Blessedness of Charity* (1753). This was a charity sermon redolent of the prevailing stewardship doctrines of the time. To a later work, comprising a collection of *Eight Discourses* (1773), he appended *A Letter to a Young Lady on the Sacrament*. His *Dissertation on the Distinct Powers of Reason and Revelation* (1774) expounded both trinitarian principles and latitudinarian views on the supremacy of reason. Cowper also edited *A Treatise on the Parallactic Angle* (1766). An edition of Dean Cowper's hitherto unpublished letters appeared in 1956, edited by Edward Hughes.

Cowper died at his deanery at Durham on 25 March 1774, and was buried in the east transept of the cathedral where a monument was erected in his memory. He bequeathed over £1000 to his domestic servants and ecclesiastical acquaintances, for the payment of which he instructed his executors to sell his 'Furniture Plate Books and Mathematical Instruments' (PRO, PROB 11/996, fol. 321). He was survived by his wife, who died on 19 May 1779 (*GM*). FRANÇOISE DECONINCK-BROSSARD

**Sources** W. Hutchinson, *The history and antiquities of the county palatine of Durham*, 2 (1787), 169–70 · *Letters of Spencer Cowper, dean of Durham, 1746–74*, ed. E. Hughes, SurtS, 165 (1956) · Foster, *Alum. Oxon.* · Nichols, *Lit. anecdotes* · will, PRO, PROB 11/996, fols. 321 ff. · GEC, *Peerage* · A. Chalmers, ed., *The general biographical dictionary*, new edn, 32 vols. (1812–17) · M. L. Boyle, ed., *Biographical catalogue of the portraits at Panshanger, the seat of Earl Cowper* (1885) · *GM*, 1st ser., 49 (1779), 271

**Archives** Cowper Memorial Library, Olney, Northamptonshire, holograph sermons | BL, 'Minutes of the depositions of the dean of Durham', 22/2/1753 and 23/2/1753, Egerton MS 3440, fols. f. 47, 61 · BL, corresp., Add. MSS 35592, fol. 42; 32731, fols. 206–8 · Bodl. Oxf., corresp. with John Charles Brooke · Herts. ALS, letters to second Earl Cowper · U. Durham L., consents to sealing, dean and chapter of Durham loose papers

**Likenesses** oils, deanery, Durham; repro. in Hughes, ed., *Letters of Spencer Cowper*

**Wealth at death** over £1000 in bequests; also bequeathed South Sea annuities and bank stocks to family; residue in trust for godsons: will, PRO, PROB 11/996, fols. 321 ff.

**Cowper** [Couper], **William** (1568–1619), bishop of Galloway, was the son of John Cowper, a merchant tailor of Edinburgh, and Marion Duncan. John *Cowper (d. 1603) was his brother. According to his autobiography,

> in my younger yeares I was trained up with the wrestlings of God; from my youth I have borne his yoke, exercised with his terrours; yet, so that many a time his sweet consolations have refreshed my soule. (Cowper, *Workes*, 3)

This emotional puritanism defined his personal piety and public ministry. He attended grammar school in Dunbar and aged thirteen went to St Andrews University where he graduated MA in 1583. He returned to Edinburgh and resisted his parents' plans for his future, having determined upon some religious course. He then went to England for more than two years, teaching in Hoddesdon for nearly a year, then studying with the Hebraist Hugh Broughton.

Cowper was licensed in Edinburgh in 1588 and admitted to the charge of Bothkenner in Stirlingshire. He transferred to the second charge, Perth, on 5 October 1595, retaining the post until 26 April 1614. He married first Elizabeth Duncanson, then Grizel Anderson, daughter of Robert, merchant burgess of Perth.

Cowper wrote a number of treatises, generally of a homiletic nature. His *Workes*, first published in 1623, exceeds 1100 folio pages, and consists in the main of materials written during his pastoral career at Perth, published individually from 1606; *A Holy Alphabet* (1613) is a book of meditations spoken at evening prayers. He wrote as a puritan pastor, a physician of souls, aspiring to the conversion of sinners and aiding them to acquire a suitable sense of assurance of salvation. He was emphatic upon the doctrine of election and included in his *Heaven Opened* an explanation of the 'golden chain of salvation' (Cowper, *Workes*, 156). His pastoral focus on religious psychology and Christian pilgrimage did not preclude social comment, noting the needs of the poor along with the proud and self-righteous behaviour of some: 'no sort of men are further from the Kingdome of God then proud justiciars' (ibid., 597).

Cowper wrote extensively against Roman Catholics, including a treatise, *Seven Dayes Conference, betweene a Catholicke-Christian, and a Catholicke Romane* (1613). He criticized them for their treatment of the Bible, merits, prayers to saints, transubstantiation, and subversion of government, and also maintained the typical protestant identification of Rome as the whore of Babylon. However, if presbyterians had no reason to object to his anti-Romanism, his migration into episcopacy made him a prime target of their hostility in the years when James VI restored episcopacy (1610) and introduced (1617) the liturgical changes known as the five articles of Perth (approved by the general assembly in 1618).

Between 1596 and 1608 Cowper attended six general assemblies of the kirk, and on 1 July 1606 he subscribed to the protest against episcopacy, but over the next decade he, along with his co-signatories John Abernethy and Adam Bellenden, accepted consecration to the restored Scottish episcopate. Cowper was nominated to the see of Galloway on 31 July 1612 and was consecrated on 4 October; he also became dean of the Chapel Royal. He justified his acceptance of a bishopric on grounds that he had never affirmed the parity of ministers; rather it was 'the Mother of confusion' (Cowper, *Apologie*, A2r), though he was also heard to repudiate 'that romane Hierarchie, the tyrannie of Antichrist' (D. Calderwood, *A Re-Examination of the Five Articles*, 1636, 239). The resolution to the paradox might ultimately be found in his advocacy of a blended polity, including both bishops and the courts of the presbyterian system.

Among contemporary Scottish divines Cowper was one of those most warmly disposed to Christian antiquity, and this played an important role in his acceptance of James's changes in the church. Among contemporary historians of the Scottish church, his interpretation, the *Dikaiologie* (1614), was the first to be printed. In this reply to the presbyterian David Hume of Godscroft he wrote that 'no Church since the dayes of Christ unto our Fathers dayes, was without Episcopall Government, and Mr David cannot shew one instance to the contrarie' (Cowper, *Dikaiologie*, 129); he proceeded to argue that the superintendency instituted at the time of the Reformation was itself a species of episcopacy. He found his contemporary lodestar in James VI and I whom he cast as a new Constantine 'who would lead Jerusalem and the world against Antichrist' (Williamson, 34). Thus he advanced a 'British' understanding of the Apocalypse which embraced both England and Scotland.

Cowper was heavily involved in the production of a new Scottish liturgy in 1618–19; the manuscript contains the inscription 'B. of Galloway Cowpers form of service'. Cowper died, shortly after the liturgy was drafted and before it could be published, at Edinburgh on 15 February 1619. His presbyterian nemesis David Calderwood described him as 'a man filled with self-conceate, and impatient of anie contradiction' (Calderwood, *History*, 7.349). He claimed that Cowper had extracted a fortune from diocesan and other lands, but the bishop's complaints about his living quarters in Edinburgh make this highly improbable. Cowper's epigraph on the title page of his *Dikaiologie* might be taken as his own epitaph: 'O what a griefe; that having to doe with enemies, wee are forced to fight with friends!'

DAVID GEORGE MULLAN

**Sources** *Fasti Scot.*, new edn, 7.354–6 · D. G. Mullan, *Episcopacy in Scotland: the history of an idea, 1560–1608* (1986) · D. G. Mullan, *Scottish puritanism, 1590–1638* (2000) · A. H. Williamson, *Scottish national consciousness in the age of James VI: the Apocalypse, the union and the shaping of Scotland's public culture* (1979), chap. 1 · G. Donaldson, ed., 'A Scottish liturgy of the reign of James VI', *Miscellany … X*, Scottish History Society, 4th ser., 2 (1965), 87–117 · W. Cowper, *The bishop of Galloway his dikaiologie: contayning a defence of his Apologie* (1614) · W. Cowper, *The workes* (1623) · D. Calderwood, *The history of the Kirk of Scotland*, ed. T. Thomson and D. Laing, 8 vols., Wodrow Society, 7 (1842–9)

**Cowper, William**, first Earl Cowper (1665–1723), politician and lord chancellor, was the eldest son of Sir William Cowper, second baronet (1639–1706), a whig politician and ally of Anthony Ashley Cooper, first earl of Shaftesbury, and Sarah (1644–1720), the diarist, a daughter of Sir Samuel Holled, a London merchant [see Cowper, Sarah, Lady Cowper]. Neither the precise date nor place of Cowper's birth is known though his family was well established in Hertfordshire and Kent. His great-grandfather, also William, had earned a baronetcy, and subsequent imprisonment with his son John (Sir William's father), for his loyalty to Charles I.

**Education and early career** William's early years were spent at Hertford Castle, the imposing family seat and political base for his father as MP for Hertford in 1679–81 and 1689–1700. For some years, from 1673, he attended a private school in St Albans. Some surviving letters to his mother show precocious intelligence, an elegant hand, and the orotund turn of phrase that would characterize his mature style. While there is no official record of his having been subsequently at Westminster School under Richard Busby (records of town pupils being incomplete), a later note of his refers to a compendium 'By wch I learnd ye Syrian Dialect at Westmr Schoole'; there was also mention at the trial of his brother Spencer *Cowper of the brothers having been at school together. William's own second son was sent to Westminster. It is only certain that he entered the Middle Temple on 8 March 1682.

Another question about Cowper's youth became notorious in the hands of a popular romancer. The story that he seduced Elizabeth Culling of Hertingfordbury Park, Hertfordshire, tricking her by a sham marriage ceremony, and having two children with her, may have originated in village gossip but it gained interest through his subsequent fame. It inspired a story, 'Hernando and Louisa', in Delarivier Manley's *New Atlantis* (1709), and the charge of bigamy insinuated by Jonathan Swift in the *Examiner* periodical (nos. 17, 22). Voltaire took up the story with the fanciful embellishment that Cowper wrote a treatise in favour of polygamy ('Femme, Polygamie' in *Dictionnaire philosophique*) while in *Biographia Britannica*, Andrew Kippis states the relationship as a fact. True or false, the story seems to have done little harm to Cowper's career. The man portrayed as a libertine appears later to have been a devoted husband. The supposed deceiver became the politician most noted among contemporaries for his probity and respect for the rules.

There was a boldness about Cowper that denotes the natural leader. He was called to the bar on 25 May 1688. On 7 July, with little but talent and a pleasing manner to reassure her reluctant father, he married Judith (d. 1705), daughter of Sir Robert Booth, a London merchant. In November of the same year, following the landing of William of Orange, he led a party of volunteers to join the prince's army at Wallingford. Before the subsequent flight of James II made this a safer choice for an aspiring politician he thus committed himself to the principles which had led his father in 1679 to support James's exclusion

William Cowper, first Earl Cowper (1665–1723), by Sir Godfrey Kneller, 1722

while duke of York. Ever a man to seize his chance, Cowper staked his future on their adoption in what he would term 'this happy Revolution'.

Cowper soon built up a substantial practice on the home circuit and attracted admiring notice for his handsome presence and sharp intelligence. He had a head for the law and a silver-toned voice for the jury. In 1694 he was appointed king's counsel, then significant promotion, and recorder of Colchester. By his advocacy in the court of chancery he attracted the notice of Lord Somers, who advised him to find a seat in parliament. A leading figure among the junto whigs and esteemed as the finest lawyer of his time, Somers proved to be a wise mentor. Cowper could not have found a sounder patron or model. Men boasted of the rule of law and balanced constitution. But the great issues arising out of the Nine Years' War—a degree of Anglican zeal which tested the limits of religious tolerance, the succession to the crown, and the persisting Jacobite threat—ensured that politics was a rough, unscrupulous, often corrupt, sometimes dangerous trade. It tested the nerve of combatants. It also put a premium on legal skills. Like that of Somers, Cowper's career illustrates the symbiotic relationship of law and politics in an age of revolution when the persuasive force of argument from precedent, and the certainty offered by legal definition, lent unique authority to lawyers' pronouncements.

**Parliamentarian and lawyer** In 1695, and again in 1698, Cowper was returned to parliament, in tandem with his father, as member for Hertford. The local family interest was damaged when Cowper's younger brother, Spencer, was tried for murder. The charge was flimsy but the death of a young woman (probably suicide) aroused local sympathy. Cowper was denigrated when he successfully resisted an application for a re-trial. In 1701 he therefore found himself a new seat, at Beeralston in Devon. Meanwhile he had been in the forefront of legal encounters. In 1696 he played a leading part in the prosecution of the conspirators in the Fenwick conspiracy against the life of the king, and, less worthily, of the nonjuring clergymen who gave them absolution on the scaffold. He was active in the parliamentary proceedings which led to the attainder of Sir John Fenwick, giving his reasons in arguments so prolix that they suggest an effort to wrap judicial murder in a cloak of legality. The same year saw him engaged in the prosecution of Captain Vaughan for levying war against the king on the high seas. Though unsuccessful, his prosecution at the sensational trial of Lord Mohun for the murder of Richard Coote further raised his profile in the fashionable world.

By the end of William's reign Cowper was a leading player among the whigs. When he spoke against the impeachment of Lord Chancellor Somers in 1701 he was, in effect, endorsing the whigs' continental war policy, and defending the king. With the accession of Queen Anne, renewal of war, and ascendancy of John, duke of Marlborough, and of his formidable duchess, Sarah, Cowper stood well at court. She was his friend and active patron; he would repay the debt with steady loyalty to her and with spirited defence of the duke at his time of disgrace.

At times Cowper's political bias may have affected his legal judgment. In the important test case of *Ashby* v. *White*, an elector sued the returning officer for the borough of Aylesbury for damages for having refused to receive his vote at the general election of 1700. The House of Lords overruled a judgment of the queen's bench to the effect that no such action lay. The matter being made a question of privilege by the Commons, Cowper argued weightily, but unsuccessfully, that the jurisdiction of the house did not extend to the restraining of the action, yet seems to have weakened his case by admitting that the house was sole judge of the validity of election returns and of the right of the elector to vote. Also in 1704, reflecting the desire of tories to sniff out cases where ministers might be profiteering from war, an information was laid by the attorney-general, by order of the house, against the whig leader Lord Halifax for neglecting, as auditor of the exchequer, to transmit the imprest rolls to the king's remembrancer. Cowper was retained for Halifax's defence. The prosecution broke down owing to a piece of bad Latin in the information. An indignant house censured Cowper for his part in the affair.

On 11 October 1705 Cowper succeeded Sir Nathan Wright as lord keeper of the great seal. Favourable words from the duchess of Marlborough may have counted for more than the proven incompetence of Wright. Cowper was 'not only of the Whig party but of such abilities and integrity as brought new credit to it' (King, 104), and 'for many years considered as the man who spoke the best of any in the House of Commons' (*Bishop Burnet's History*, 5.220). He insisted, as condition of acceptance, that he should have £2000 equipage money, a salary of £4000, and be raised to the peerage. John Evelyn further states that he stipulated for a pension of £2000 a year in view of his loss of practice. Though it rings true, Evelyn's statement is not confirmed by Cowper's own diary (printed in 1833) which starts at this point and provides until 1714 (after a break between 11 February 1706 and January 1709) a pithy commentary on political life. Perhaps he wrote to solace personal grief, his wife, Judith, having died on 2 April 1705, as did their only son before October of that year. Did he reckon, in vulnerable mood that, with transparency in financial matters, he could ward off the accusations of corruption which were a staple of opposition politics? His first public act was to renounce, in advance, the customary new year's gifts from chancery officials and counsel. When they arrived none the less, he refused them admittance. It made no friends among senior lawyers but enhanced his political reputation as being 'unique in acceptance by both parties as an honest man' (Green, 144). Cowper also enjoyed a good reputation with the queen who, though reluctant to accept him as adviser on church patronage, knew him to be devout and found him to be fair.

**Lord chancellor** In April 1706 Cowper was placed on the commission for the treaty of union with Scotland. On 1 May 1707 the Act of Union came into operation. On 4 May Cowper was declared by the queen in council lord high chancellor of Great Britain. The new dignity sealed a political achievement of high importance, a triumph for common sense and realism over the historic enmities and prejudices. Alongside Lord Somers, Cowper had acted as an intermediary and thus achieved prominence in the negotiations preceding the union. Deliberations were kept secret but it may be surmised that the two men, political allies and friends, worked closely together. Cowper's acumen, patience, and good humour, capitalizing on strong political and economic arguments for union and the material inducements on offer, were exactly the qualities needed to bring about the union.

On 18 September 1706 Cowper married Mary (1685–1724), daughter of John Clavering of Chopwell, co. Durham, and his first wife, Anne Thompson [see Cowper, Mary, Countess Cowper]. The marriage was kept secret until the following February. Meanwhile, on 9 October 1706 he was raised to the peerage with the title of Baron Cowper of Wingham in Kent. In his first recorded speech in the Lords (5 December 1706) he conveyed to the duke of Marlborough the thanks of the house for the victory of Ramillies. It was gratifying to the whigs, co-operating with Lord Treasurer Godolphin, to see military triumph vindicate their support for Marlborough. By 1709, however, the lord chancellor shared the tories' growing opposition and concern about Marlborough's intentions. Claims that the duke was intriguing to obtain the appointment of commander-in-chief for life prompted Cowper to declare that such a commission was unconstitutional and that he would never put the seal on it. Likewise he also expressed misgivings about the whigs' peace demands: 'nothing but seeing such great men believe it could ever incline me to think France reduced so low as to accept such conditions' (*Private Diary*, 41).

From late February 1710 Cowper presided at the trial of the high-church clergyman Henry Sacheverell in Westminster Hall. An inflammatory sermon denouncing the whigs had provoked ministers (with the exception of Cowper) to impeach Sacheverell for high crimes and misdemeanours. The lord chief justice held that the omission to specify passages invalidated the proceedings. Cowper abstained from expressing an opinion, and on the strength of a precedent from the reign of Charles I it was held immaterial. Sacheverell was found guilty, but lightly sentenced, so was seen to be vindicated and treated as a public hero. Political misjudgement by an unpopular ministry was followed by electoral defeat. Seeking a broad political base, the incoming first minister, Robert Harley, tried frantically to persuade Cowper to stay in office. But on 23 September, deaf even to Anne's pleading, he resigned since 'to keep in when all my friends are out would be infamous' (*Private Diary*, 44).

With Somers infirm Cowper became the effective leader of opposition to the tories now bent on disgracing Marlborough. He responded to Henry St John's attack on the late ministry with a heavy letter in *The Tatler* accusing the tories of 'black hypocrisy and prevarication, the servile prostitution of all English principles, and malevolent ambition' (*Scarce and Valuable Tracts … Lord Somers*, 2nd edn, 13.71–85). The patriotic theme recurs, as his wife would later express it: 'he would live a freeman and an Englishman and let them [politicians] have no hold on him on any occasion' (*Diary of Mary, Countess Cowper*, 147). In January 1711 he defended past conduct of the war in Spain against the tory charge that the whigs, who had held out for 'No peace without Spain', had deprived the earl of Peterborough of the supplies he needed for a successful campaign. In the debate on the address (7 December 1711) he supported Lord Nottingham's amending clause: that 'no peace could be safe or honourable to Great Britain or Europe if Spain and the West Indies were allotted to any branch of the house of Bourbon'. In June 1712 during the debate on negotiations for the peace—he later called it 'disgraceful' (Campbell, 4.422)—the tories implied that the reluctance of the Dutch to treat was due to the intrigues of the duke of Marlborough. Cowper riposted: 'according to our laws it can never be suggested as a crime in the meanest subject, much less in a member of that august assembly, to hold correspondence with our allies'. It was chivalrous—but an unsound statement of constitutional law. On other issues from this period Cowper spoke for the duke of Wharton's motion, designed to embarrass the tories over the succession issue, that a reward should be proclaimed for the apprehension of the pretender 'dead or alive' (8 April 1714). He also led the unsuccessful opposition to the Schism Bill for suppressing dissenters' schools and failed to get it amended in committee. But there was evidently a limit to his idea of toleration. He was, for example, strongly opposed to relief for Roman Catholics and elsewhere equated black people with 'cattle or inanimate merchandise'.

**Hanoverian politician** Opposition had proved a thankless task during the tory ascendancy. However, with the death of Anne (1 August 1714) and the arrival of the elector of Hanover, the situation changed dramatically. Cowper was appointed one of the 'lords justices' in whom, by the terms of the Regency Act of 1706, supreme power was vested during the interregnum. He helped engineer the unceremonious exclusion from future office of Henry St John (now Viscount Bolingbroke). Naturally mild-mannered, Cowper could be ruthless in a crisis. On 21 September 1714 he was re-appointed lord chancellor at St James's and on 23 October he proceeded in state to Westminster Hall to take a second oath. It was a theatrical demonstration of the authority of his ancient office. George I treated Cowper with marked respect, the king claiming that he and the duke of Devonshire were 'the only two [honest and disinterested] I have found in the kingdom'. Cowper took seriously his duty to ensure that the Hanoverian king should be advised about constitutional forms and political realities. He assumed that George would favour the whigs but was obliged to reassure him on a crucial point: 'It is an old scandal now almost worn out … that they [the whigs] are against the prerogative of the crown'. While lord justice he had composed for George a short and lucid political paper, *An Impartial History of Parties* (first printed in Campbell, 4.424). Unusual among ministers, Cowper had no French, the language of communication with the king, so it was translated by his wife, Lady Mary, now enjoying influence as lady of the bedchamber to Caroline, princess of Wales. Cowper's recommendations, in which he urged George to avoid coalition ministries, reflected his experience of the previous reigns. Anne might have endorsed it. At the same time he suggested that the opposition should have its fair share of the subordinate places. The argument for a broad base reflects the looming Jacobite threat and the uncertain allegiance of some tories.

None the less, while Cowper might offer carrots, he also kept a stick in hand. It was by his advice, for example, that Lord Chief Justice Trevor was dismissed, in October 1714. On 21 March 1715 Cowper also read George's speech which provoked the tories by its confident expression that the king would 'recover the reputation of this kingdom in foreign parts'. When Bolingbroke objected to the implied slur on the former monarch, Cowper replied by making a distinction between the queen and her ministry. Reflecting the new balance of power in the Lords, the address was carried by sixty-six to thirty-three. Likewise in the debate (9 July 1715) on the articles of impeachment exhibited against Robert Harley (now earl of Oxford), he argued, mindful of earlier tory tactics and impeachments, that there was sufficient ground for a charge of high treason.

To some, Cowper's approach seemed vindictive, but to him it was a policy justified in the light of the landing in Scotland in September 1715 of James Edward Stuart, the Jacobite claimant to the throne. The ensuing crisis brought out the best in Cowper as he exerted himself to infuse the king and his own colleagues on the bench with his patriotic spirit. Consequently local officials were purged, habeas corpus was suspended, and the Riot Act re-enacted, reinforced, and made to be the lasting guarantee of public order. Cowper's was a high-risk strategy since such measures led to violent antagonism. None the less it was one that the events of late 1715 fully justified. Cowper appreciated that the Jacobite rising had the potential to produce civil war, and it failed in large part only because of the Old Pretender's lack of resolve. Afterwards in March 1716 Cowper presided, as lord high steward, at the trial of the Jacobite fifth earl of Winton, the only one of the rebel lords who did not plead guilty. Winton's complicity could be proved but he sought an adjournment on the grounds that he had not had time to bring up his most important witnesses. Playing on the common Scottish expression 'Cupar law', Winton affected to deplore his being subjected to 'Cowper law as we used to say in our country, hang a man first and then judge him'. Notwithstanding his complaint, Winton was found guilty and sentenced to death, before his escape to France.

In the following month Cowper argued in favour of the Septennial Bill (10 April), reviewing the corrupting and unsettling effect of the Triennial Act, and declaring that it was necessary 'for the safety of the state'. In the absence of an official record, only phrases remain from his speeches, with contemporary opinion to recall their power. One such, in February 1718, appears to have been his championship of the Mutiny Bill, which proposed a standing army of 16,000 men and earned him Oxford's strong criticism. To Lady Cowper it was her husband's reputation for 'honesty and plain dealing' which proved his dominant political characteristic, often indeed to the alarm of less scrupulous colleagues who feared exposure at his hand. Mary's diary portrays the most loving of wives: 'I would rather live with him all my life on Bread and Cheese, up three Pair of Stairs than be all the world can make me and at the same time see him suffer' (*Diary of Mary, Countess Cowper*, 76). But her support sometimes outran discretion and in 1718 her position drew Cowper into the feud between the king and his son. In January of that year Cowper had opposed a projected bill for providing the king with an annuity of £100,000 with discretion to provide such a part of it as he might think fitting to the maintenance of the prince. From 1714 Cowper had been out of sympathy with the whig chieftains, notably James Stanhope (now Earl Stanhope) and Charles, second Viscount Townshend, with their international ambitions and cutthroat politics. Lady Cowper saw their deteriorating relationships in personal terms: 'The Lords of Cabinet Council were jealous of his Great Reputation and had a mind to keep him out' (ibid., 55). Cowper was repelled by the court's conduct and dismayed by the opening it provided for factionalism and anti-Hanoverian sentiment. He had, he believed, 'more than ordinary reason to … be concerned … having served the crown in capital cases by which I shall be exposed to revenge in case of a re-Revolution'. His decision to resign from the lord chancellorship was not welcomed by the king, who held him in high regard and created him Viscount Fordwiche and Earl

Cowper on 18 March 1718. Nevertheless on 15 April he resigned office, ostensibly on the grounds of failing health, though his own declining opinion of the king, based on opposition to George's religious toleration and policy to the royal grandchildren, was probably a more prominent factor. Cowper now retired to his estate, Cole Green near Hertingfordbury, Hertfordshire, which, despite its charms, held little attraction for a man who had been at the centre of power. Cowper was soon to show himself vigorous in opposition.

**Critic in the Lords** In the Lords, Cowper voted with the tories in their successful opposition to the repeal of the act 'for the preserving of the Protestant religion' which imposed disabilities on Roman Catholics, and of the more severe clauses of the Test and Corporation Acts, proposed in December 1718 by Stanhope. In February of the following year he supported Robert Walpole in the Commons in his attack on the Peerage Bill, which proposed to fix a numerical limit to the House of Lords. Cowper failed to prevent the bill, when reintroduced, from passing in the Lords, though it was thrown out by the Commons. He also opposed the bill for enabling the South Sea Company ('contrived for treachery and destruction') to increase its capital. On 7 April 1720, however, it passed the Lords without a division. A question addressed by Cowper to the ministry concerning an absconding cashier of the company on 23 January 1721 is the earliest recorded instance of such a demand for information.

Vigilance, public spirit, and independence of judgement characterize Cowper's later parliamentary performances in these years. His critics might see a crusty veteran, piqued by exclusion from office, but to admirers he was the elder statesman, relishing the freedom to speak his mind. His scope was wide. On 13 December 1721 he moved the repeal of certain clauses of the Quarantine Act. On 11 January 1722 he called attention to 'the pernicious practice of building ships of force for the French' and moved that the judges be ordered to introduce a bill to bring this to an end. One incident, on 3 February 1722, reveals the proud temper of the Lords and of Cowper's role as leader, now with the duke of Wharton as his ally. The incumbent lord chancellor, arriving two hours late for the session in the Lords, then excused himself on the ground that he had been detained by the king in council. Reviving an old custom the Lords had printed a protest, signed by Cowper, in which they affirmed that their house was 'the greatest council in the kingdom, to which all other councils ought to give way'. On 26 October 1722 Cowper opposed the committal of the duke of Norfolk to the Tower on suspicion of treason, so prompting an innuendo that Cowper was sympathetic to Jacobitism. In the course of his examination before a committee of the House of Commons (January–February 1723) the Jacobite conspirator Christopher Layer said that he had been informed that Cowper was a member of a club of disaffected persons known as Burford's Club. Cowper felt that he had to refute Layer's suggestion publicly. He had no sympathy with Jacobitism, nor for those who used it to blacken their political enemies. Furthermore, renewed attempts within late twentieth-

century Jacobite historiography to claim Cowper for the cause have since been effectively undermined (see Jones, 'Jacobitism and the historian'). None the less, Cowper did oppose the bill of pains and penalties brought against Bishop Atterbury for his involvement in Jacobite plotting, and closed the debate with a protest against the exercise of judicial powers by parliament without formal proceeding by impeachment. In any case, 'to make or deprive bishops is no part of the business of the state'. Completing a record of spirited opposition to an over-confident executive, on 15 May 1723 Cowper opposed Walpole's bill for 'laying a tax on Papists'. No government, he held, 'ever got advantage by persecuting a portion of its subjects'.

On 5 October 1723 Cowper caught a severe cold while travelling from London to Cole Green and there, five days later, he died. His wife survived him by only four months, dying on 5 February 1724. With him she was buried in St Mary's church, Hertingfordbury. The couple were survived by their four children, William (1709–1764), who inherited his father's title, Spencer *Cowper (1713–1774), later dean of Durham, Sarah (1707–1758), and Anne (1710–1750).

During his lifetime Cowper was frequently the subject of praise as an example to other public figures. In the 1710s he had befriended the poet and librettist John Hughes, securing (1717) and later retaining for him the position of secretary to the commissions of the peace in the court of chancery. Hughes repaid Cowper's friendship with an ode in his honour. More impressive was the testimony provided in *The Spectator* essay attributed to Hughes (no. 467, 26 August 1712), in which Cowper, as Manilius, was singled out for his 'courtly manners' and 'the undesigning Honesty by which he attained the Honours he has enjoy'd'. This man would ever be 'the principal figure in the room', a good listener, one 'who knew how to appear free and open without Danger of Intrusion and to be cautious without seeming reserved' (*The Spectator*, ed. D. F. Bond, 5 vols., 1965, 4.151, 154). For Philip Dormer Stanhope, fourth earl of Chesterfield, he was a consummate orator, while Alexander Pope hit on what many may have recognized:

Twas 'Sir Your law'—'Sir, your eloquence'—
Yours *Cowper's* manner and yours *Talbot's* sense

with its implication that Cowper's presence and style were more notable than his grasp of law. It is possible to point to deficiencies there, camouflaged by skill and experience in advocacy. Rather impracticable as a colleague is possibly how ministers found him. Beyond argument he was an upright man, with a sense of responsibility for the good of the state that transcended party allegiance or personal advantage. That, with his prime role in great events, led Lord Campbell in his *Lives of the Lord Chancellors* (1845–69) to regret that he did not draw on his experience to write, like Gilbert Burnet, a history of his times. His obituary notice (*Historical Register*, 1723) referred thus to his resignation in 1718: 'By his wisdom and moderation he had gained abundance of friends to the king, kept steady many wavering minds, brought the clergy to a better temper and hindered some, hot over-zealous spirits from running things to dangerous extremes'. These words, in measure and tone so much of the temper of the calmer times he lived to see, may fairly serve as a summary of Cowper's place in history.

GEOFFREY TREASURE

**Sources** *The private diary of William, first Earl Cowper, lord chancellor of England*, ed. [E. C. Hawtrey], Roxburghe Club (1833) · *Diary of Mary, Countess Cowper*, ed. [S. Cowper] (1864) · N. Hooke, *Memoirs of Sarah, duchess of Marlborough*, ed. W. King (1930) · *Private correspondence of Sarah, duchess of Marlborough*, 2 vols. (1838) · *Bishop Burnet's History*, vol. 5 · *State trials*, vols. 12–13, 15 · J. Campbell, *Lives of the lord chancellors*, 8 vols. (1845–69), vol. 4 and appx · *Historical Register* (1723) · G. S. Holmes, *British politics in the age of Anne* (1967) · J. Hoppit, *A land of liberty? England, 1689–1727* (2000) · J. H. Plumb, *Sir Robert Walpole: the making of a statesman* (1956) · J. H. Plumb, *The growth of political stability in England, 1675–1725* (1967) · *The diary of Sir David Hamilton, 1709–1714*, ed. P. Roberts (1975) · D. Green, *Queen Anne* (1970) · C. B. Realey, *The early opposition to Robert Walpole, 1720–1727* (1931) · Evelyn, *Diary* · C. Jones, 'Jacobitism and the historian: the case of William, first Earl Cowper', *Albion*, 23 (1991), 681–96 · W. Scott, ed., *A collection of scarce and valuable tracts … Lord Somers*, 2nd edn, 13 (1815)

**Archives** BL, diary, Add. MS 9091 · BL, diary, Add. MS 35854 [copy] · Herts. ALS, corresp. and papers | Cowper Memorial Library, Olney, letters to John Hughes

**Likenesses** oils, *c*.1710 (after J. Richardson?), NPG · G. Kneller, oils, 1722, NPG [*see illus.*]

**Cowper** [Cooper], **William** (1666/7–1710), surgeon and anatomist, was the youngest son of Richard Cowper of Petersfield, Hampshire. He was apprenticed in London first to the surgeon William Bignall on 4 April 1681 and afterwards to John Fletcher. Cowper was admitted a freeman of the Company of Barber–Surgeons on 3 March 1691 and thereafter practised in London, living in houses in Boswell Court and Essex Street. He also owned property in Wormley, Hertfordshire.

**Early publications** Cowper's first major work appeared in 1694, the *Myotomia reformata, or, A new administration of all the muscles of humane bodies; wherein the true uses of the muscles are explained, the errors of former anatomists concerning them confuted, and several muscles not hitherto taken notice of described: to which are subjoin'd, a graphical description of the bones; and other anatomical observations; illustrated with figures after the life*. This octavo volume is illustrated with ten plates of anatomy after Cowper's own drawings of subjects which he felt had previously not been properly illustrated. In addition, there is an appendix describing the anatomy of the penis and the mechanism of erection. Among the dedicatees was Edward Tyson, the comparative anatomist with whom Cowper collaborated on various projects and who proposed Cowper for membership of the Royal Society on 28 December 1698; he was elected on 11 January 1699. Cowper provided the designs for the five folding plates to Humphrey Ridley's *Anatomy of the Brain* (1695). These plates were engraved after Cowper's drawings by the Antwerp born Michael Vandergucht, with whom Cowper often worked. No record of any formal training in art survives for Cowper, but he was one of the sixteen founding members in 1689 of the Virtuosi of St

William Cowper (1666/7–1710), by John Closterman, in or before 1698

Luke, an early art club devoted to the promotion of connoisseurship and to the collecting of art.

**The Bidloo affair** Cowper's critical history has been overshadowed by the controversy connected with *The anatomy of humane bodies … Illustrated with large explications, containing many new anatomical discoveries and chirurgical observations: to which is added an introduction explaining the animal oeconomy*, printed in Oxford by Samuel Smith and Benjamin Walford in 1698. In this work Cowper provided a commentary to the plates by Gerard de Lairesse, remarkable for their detail. These plates had previously been published by Govard Bidloo as illustrations to his *Anatomia humani corporis* (Amsterdam, 1685). Smith and Walford had purchased pulls of the plates of the Dutch 1690 edition from Bidloo's publishers. Cowper supplied a new text in English and an appendix of nine extra plates of subjects he felt were lacking or poorly delineated, such as the arterial system of a foetus. Cowper's text is more extensive than Bidloo's brief commentary to the plates, which at times is restricted to the simple naming of parts, and is critical of it in several places. In addition to anatomical descriptions, Cowper included observations derived from his surgical practice, experiments, wax preparations, and his research in comparative anatomy. Lettering in red ink was added to the plates to accommodate Cowper's added observations: 'above seven-hundred references' by his own count. Although Cowper acknowledged the previous publication by Bidloo of the de Lairesse plates in the 'Address to the reader', this was no mollification to Bidloo, who had learned of Cowper's project before publication and believed that Cowper was preparing a translation of his text. The critical tone of the finished work undoubtedly added insult to injury, and the notably querulous Bidloo published a complaint in 1700 addressed to the Royal Society accusing Cowper of plagiarism, *Gulielmus Cowper criminis literarii citatus, coram tribunali … societatis Britanno-regiae per Godefridum Bidloo*, which included copies of letters to Cowper, most of which had gone unanswered, correspondence with his publishers, and a list of errors. The Royal Society, with some discomfort, declined to adjudicate on the matter, although Cowper was questioned at a meeting of the society on 20 March 1700 with regard to the engraved title page, in which the title and Cowper's name is pasted over that of Bidloo's, to which he replied that the title page had been 'ordered by the bookseller, not by himself' (Royal Society, Journal Book Copy, 9, fol. 200).

In his article, 'An account of a polypus taken out of the vena pulmonalis, and of the structure of that vessel', published in the *Philosophical Transactions* (22, 1701, 797–8), Cowper alluded to a forthcoming critical reply to Bidloo, which eventually appeared as the ironically titled *Eucharistia* (1701), to which he appended a list of corrections to Bidloo. In it, Cowper remarks that the majority of the plates were so poorly described as to suggest that they were not done after Bidloo's preparations but were perhaps done for another, putting forward, without proof, the name of the late Dutch anatomist Jan Swammerdam. In his defence Cowper draws attention to the fact that Bidloo is named throughout and that the text is new. Although the work is not a true plagiarism, nor hardly the first example of the re-use of plates in the history of anatomy, the notoriety of this case has served to obscure a true appreciation of Cowper and of his many original contributions to anatomical illustration. The book itself became a standard work on anatomy of the period and was republished by C. B. Albinus in Leiden in 1737, in a Latin translation by William Dundass in the same city in 1739, with another Latin edition appearing in Utrecht in 1750. In the year following the *Eucharistia*, Bidloo and Cowper would have had the opportunity to trade further remarks, as they both were present at the autopsy of William III on 10 March 1702. The Bidloo affair seemed not to affect the standing of Cowper greatly, newly elected to the Royal Society, nor did it reflect ultimately upon his reputation among his contemporaries, however much it may have coloured it in later times.

**Later works** In the *Philosophical Transactions* of November 1699 (21, 364–9) Cowper described the urethral glands, which he termed *glandula mucosae*, that now bear his name. Although he believed he was the first to detect them the French surgeon Jean Méry had in fact noted them in 1684. These glands, in addition to a third, are the subject of Cowper's *Glandularum quarundam, nuper detectarum, ductuumque earum excretoriorum, descriptio, cum figuris* (1702). This work is illustrated with three plates (one previously published in the 1699 article) and is bound with and prefixes the *Eucharistia*.

To Edward Tyson's book on the chimpanzee published in 1699, *Orang-outang, sive homo sylvestris, or, The anatomy of a pygmie compared with that of a monkey, an ape, and a man*, Cowper had contributed a chapter on the muscles, comparing the anatomy of chimpanzee and man, with reference to that of apes and monkeys. Cowper also provided eight folding plates of figures, engraved by Michael Vandergucht, after the subject that he and Tyson had dissected. Five years later, in 1704, Cowper again published with Tyson when he provided a description of the generative organs of the male opossum in a joint paper for the *Philosophical Transactions* (24, 1704, 1565–90): 'Carigueya, seu, Marsupiale Americanum masculum', being a follow up to the first report of the anatomy of a female opossum by Tyson in 1698.

Cowper, along with a Dr Branthwait, was called upon by his friend, the physician James Drake, to assist in Drake's posthumously published *Anthropologia Nova, or, A New System of Anatomy* (2 vols., 1707, with a second edition, 1717). Cowper provided all but four of the twenty-seven in-text plates. These illustrations supplemented plates appended to the first volume which were crude copies after Blancard and not Drake's choice but rather the legacy of the original contract for the book by the publishers (Smith and Walford) with the late Clopton Havers. In addition, some chapters in the book were either written by Cowper ('Of the nose', 2.526–49) or based on his publications ('Of the penis', 1.247–76). Drake remarks in the preface that the resolution of questions of anatomy was facilitated through reference to the 'Numerous Collection of Preparations and Drawings, which Mr. Cowper keeps by him; the latter being all done by himself from the Life' (p. iv).

It was Cowper's habit to re-use plates published in his earlier works, and just as some plates from the first edition of the *Myotomia reformata* and from Ridley's *Anatomy of the Brain* were published in the appendix of the 1698 *Anatomy of Humane Bodies*, so too do some previously published plates by Cowper appear in Drake's *Anthropologia nova*, along with several new plates, such as the five muscle figures of the second volume (plates 23–27). These figures in bold poses, some with narrative-filled landscapes, are similar in style to the figures that would appear in the second edition of the *Myographia reformata* of 1724. Copies were published under the name of the sculptor Ercole Lelli in the late eighteenth century in Bologna as *Anatomia esterna del corpo umano, per uso de'pittori e scultori*.

Cowper was at work on the plates for a revised edition of the *Myotomia reformata* by 1705, when an illustration of the heart, intended for the new edition, appeared as one of the figures illustrating an article on arterial disease (*Philosophical Transactions*, 24, 1705, 1970–77). This article also includes an early description of an aberrant pulse, later described by Vieussens in 1715 and again by the nineteenth-century physician Dominic Corrigan, after whom it is named. The second edition of the *Myotomia reformata*, a lavishly illustrated folio, did not appear, however, until 1724—fourteen years after Cowper's death.

**Reputation and achievement** Cowper was held in great esteem by his contemporaries. A skilled surgeon and anatomist, he was noted also for his knowledge of comparative anatomy, his use of wax injections in anatomical preparations, and for his anatomical illustrations, which appeared in his own publications as well as those of his friends and collaborators. When called to give medical evidence at the celebrated trial of Spencer Cowper of 18 July 1699 on the appearance of bodies after death by drowning, after stating to the court that they were not related, Spencer Cowper, conducting his own defence, declared 'I should be proud to own him if he were so, he is a man of great Learning, and I believe most People admit him the best Anatomist in Europe' (*The Tryal of Spencer Cowper*, 24). James Douglas, in the preface to his *Myographiae comparatae* (1707), called Cowper that 'most accurate and indefatigable Improver of Anatomy', praising his description of muscles and noting his fame for 'his wonderful Dexterity in Dissecting, and great Skill in Designing' (p. xii). He is also frequently remembered as a teacher of William Cheselden, the surgeon. Cowper was married to Katherine Venables with whom he had two daughters, Katherine and Phillipa. In failing health, Cowper conveyed his papers into the care of Dr Richard Mead and retired to Hampshire. He died on 8 March 1710 at the age of forty-three and was buried in the church of St Nicholas in Bishops Sutton, near New Alresford. According to the memorial stone in the church set up by his widow, it was work on the second edition of the *Myotomia reformata* which hastened his death: 'with unremitting perseverance, anxious to complete his Treatise of Myotomy he ruin'd his Constitution by severe labour and watchings, seiz'd at the first with an Asthmatick complaint, and afterwards with the Dropsy'. Mead remarks in the preface of *Myotomia reformata* that at the time of his death Cowper had completed the plates, but the text remained unfinished. The integration of Cowper's revisions to his interleaved copy of the 1694 edition was undertaken by James Jurin, secretary of the Royal Society. The work is preceded by a lengthy introduction by Henry Pemberton on muscular motion.

The plates by Cowper are entirely new and are a landmark in anatomical illustration, bridging the classicism of Vesalius of the sixteenth century and the realism of John Bell of the late eighteenth century, with expressive, powerful chapter head and tailpieces of fighting and expiring *écorchés* and inventive initial letters that are worthy successors to those of Vesalius's *Fabrica* of 1543. Mead remarks that among Cowper's notes for the second edition were drafts on anatomy for artists, but that these were in too unfinished a state to publish. They probably would have elucidated the three plates described as being for the use of painters and sculptors (plates 11–13). Some indication of Cowper's thoughts in this direction are to be found in his earlier comments to the third plate in his *Anatomy* of 1698. The suitability of Cowper's plates for artistic anatomy is demonstrated by their use in anatomy books for artists such as that of Lelli's *Anatomia esterna* and John Tinney's *Compendium anatomicum* (1743).

Cowper was an active member of the Royal Society, particularly in his early years of membership, and was one of those members who were called upon to submit the results of experimental research. His publications, including his frequent contributions to the *Philosophical Transactions*, reflect both his investigative and experimental methods, his surgical practice, his interest in comparative anatomy, and his use of wax injection and microscopy, the latter particularly for the demonstration of capillary action of the blood. An early paper established, through controlled experiments, the caustic nature of Colbatch's styptic (18, 1694, 42–4). In another, Cowper recounted his successful surgery on a ruptured achilles tendon, then generally considered to be inoperable (21, 1699, 153–60). In 1702 Cowper published a description of the preserved venous and arterial systems which John Evelyn had acquired in Venice in 1646 and donated to the Royal Society in 1667 (*Philosophical Transactions*, 23, 1702, 1177–201). These were illustrated in plates by Cowper together with supplementary figures after his own wax preparations and of the circulation of blood in a living dog, as viewed through a microscope. Other papers are 'An account of chylification' (19, 1696, 231–8), 'An account of a very large diseased kidney' (19, 1696, 301–9), 'An account of five pair of muscles, which serve for different motions of the head' (21, 1699, 130–41), 'An answer to Dr Wright's letter, concerning the cure of an apostemation in the lungs' (23, 1703, 1386–93), and 'Of hydatides inclosed with a stony crust in the kidney of a sheep' (25, 1706, 2304–5). Two accounts of dissections, written as letters to Sir Hans Sloane, were published posthumously (27, 1712, 512–14, 534–5). He presented the mesentery of a dog, injected with wax and mercury, at a meeting of the Royal Society on 4 March 1702, and placed in the society's repository the diseased arteries of a leg, injected with red wax (*Philosophical Transactions*, 24, 1705, 1970–71). In a Royal Society meeting on 30 June 1708 Sir Hans Sloane related that he had seen 'Mr. Cowper preserve a Dead Body by Injecting Spiritt of Wine into the Arteries which preserved it very well'. A large collection of 135 of Cowper's specimens was acquired by Sloane for his museum. Cowper's notes, letters, accounts of dissections and surgical cases, often illustrated, and his botanical and anatomical drawings, many preparatory for his published illustrations, also came into the possession of Sloane, and were later deposited in the British Library. Further drawings and proof pulls were acquired by William Hunter from Richard Mead, into whose hands Cowper had given them. These were later deposited in the Hunterian Collection in Glasgow University Library.          MONIQUE KORNELL

**Sources** Barber Surgeons' Company, apprentice bindings, 1672–1707, MS 5666/2, fol. 133 · Barber Surgeons' Company, admissions to freedom, 1665–1704, MS 5265/2, fol. 89 · Royal Society of London, Journal Book Copy, vols. 9, 10 · Royal Society of London, Council minutes, 1682–1727, vol. 2 · PRO, PROB 10/1456 · A. von Haller, *Bibliotheca anatomica*, 2 vols. (Zürich, 1774–7), vol. 1, pp. 768–70 · R. F. Buckman jun. and J. W. Futrell, 'William Cowper', *Surgery*, 99/5 (1986), 582–90 · K. B. Roberts and J. D. W. Tomlinson, *The fabric of the body: European traditions of anatomical illustration* (1992) · K. Bryn Thomas, *James Douglas of the Pouch and his pupil William Hunter* (1964) [lists Cowper's MSS and drawings in the Hunterian Collection, Glasgow] · A. MacGregor, ed., *Sir Hans Sloane: collector, scientist, antiquary, founding father of the British Museum* (1994) · F. Beekman, 'Bidloo and Cowper, anatomists', *Annals of Medical History*, new ser., 7 (1935), 113–29 · M. Cazort, M. Kornell, and K. B.

Roberts, *The ingenious machine of nature: four centuries of art and anatomy* (1996), nos. 72–74.4 [exhibition catalogue, National Gallery of Canada, 31 Oct 1996 – 5 Jan 1997] · M. Kornell, 'Anatomical drawings by Battista Franco', *Bulletin of the Cleveland Museum of Art*, 76/9 (1989), 320 n. 3 · I. Bignamini, 'George Vertue, art historian, and art institutions in London, 1689–1768', *Walpole Society*, 54 (1988), 1–148, esp. 23, 34, 40 n. 17 · C. Gysel, 'L'*Anatomia* de Govert Bidloo (1685) et le plagiat de William Cowper (1698)', *Revue Belge de médecine dentaire*, 42 (1987), 96–101 · P. Dumaître, *La curieuse destinée des planches anatomiques de Gérard de Lairesse* (1982) · *The tryal of Spencer Cowper, Esq., John Marson, Ellis Stevens, and William Rogers, Gent. Upon an indictment for the murther of Mrs Sarah Stout, a quaker, before Mr Baron Hatsell, at Hertford assizes, July 18, 1699 of which they were acquitted. With the opinions of eminent physicians and chyrurgeons on both sides, concerning drowned bodies, delivered in the tryal and the several letters produced in court* (1699) · memorial stone, St Nicholas's Church, Bishops Sutton, Hampshire

**Archives** BL, letters and papers, Sloane MSS 3408, 3409 | BL, Add. MS 5259 · U. Glas. L., Hunterian collection

**Likenesses** J. Closterman, portrait, in or before 1698, RCS Eng. [*see illus.*] · J. Richardson?, oils, *c.*1710, NPG · G. Kneller, oils, 1722, NPG · J. Smith, mezzotint (after J. Closterman), repro. in W. Cowper, *The anatomy of humane bodies* (1698), frontispiece · photograph, Wellcome L.

**Cowper, William** (*bap.* 1701, *d.* 1767), physician and antiquary, was baptized at St Peter's, Chester, on 29 July 1701, the third child of the Revd John Cowper (1671–1718), of Overlegh, near Chester, vicar of Middlewich and fellow of Brasenose College, Oxford, and Catherine (*d.* 1727), daughter of William Sherwin, beadle of divinity and bailiff of the University of Oxford. Little is known of Cowper's early education until he matriculated from St Mary Hall, Oxford, on 24 October 1714. He subsequently attended Brasenose College, with which his family had a long association, as a resident commoner from January 1717 to December 1718, although a manuscript biography among his papers claims he studied at Brasenose for four years. After leaving Oxford he studied medicine in Paris and London. He was commonly referred to as Doctor Cowper by fellow antiquaries and it is very probable that he was awarded his medical degree in Paris.

After completing his education Cowper returned to Overlegh, the familial home, perhaps in 1722 when on 19 August he married Elizabeth Lonsdale (1703/4–1728), daughter of John Lonsdale of High Riley, Lancashire; they had no children. His principal occupation was as a doctor and he took on and trained a number of apprentices. His family had long-standing connections with Chester and had been prominent in its government; his ancestor John Cowper was mayor in 1561, and his great-grandfather, who was mayor in 1641, was a key member of the civic élite who aligned the city with the king during the civil war. Continuing this tradition William was elected a common councillor on 30 July 1725, first sheriff in 1743, alderman in 1749, and finally mayor in 1753. He was an active and partisan tory with close links to the Grosvenor family and was an assiduous defender of their interest in the city.

Cowper was an active antiquary, copying and collating a large number of manuscripts relating to Chester and writing extensively, in manuscript form, on Chester's history.

Richard Gough claimed Cowper's intention was to publish a history of the city but there is little evidence of any attempt to publish these very complete writings. He was, however, writing a 'History of the Isle of Man', and his fellow antiquaries aided this, sending him numerous references. It is this history of the Isle of Man, not the history of Chester, that remained unfinished at his death. In spite of having been elected a fellow of the Society of Antiquaries on 2 August 1744, he was rather modest about his abilities, acknowledging the limitations of his treatise on druids to a correspondent and disparaging his Chester collections in a letter to Charles Lyttelton. He undertook research for friends and fellow antiquaries, producing a genealogy for Sir Robert Grosvenor and helping Browne Willis with research into a Cestrian family. Cowper's reputation is not without blemish, as he is widely accredited as the author of *A Summary of the Life of St Werburgh* (1749), which George Ormerod tentatively suggested was plagiarized, an accusation put more forcefully by Alexander Chalmers and which seems subsequently to have stuck. Some local antiquaries disparaged Cowper's work, notably the Revd John Allen of Tarporley to whom Cowper's poem *Il Penseroso* (1767) was dedicated. Allen and his friend William Cole similarly mocked Cowper's literary pretensions as 'high Bombast and fustian' (Livesey, 301).

It is probable that Cowper's chief claim to fame is the vast manuscript collections he wrote and collected, upon which all subsequent histories of Chester and Cheshire have relied heavily. Without this rich legacy of antiquarian notes, copies of lost manuscripts, and such like, the history of both Chester and Cheshire would have been considerably impoverished. He died at Overlegh on 20 October 1767 and was buried at St Peter's, Chester.

PHIL KNOWLES

**Sources** Biography of William Cowper, Ches. & Chester ALSS, DCC/16/45 · G. Ormerod, *The history of the county palatine and city of Chester*, 3 vols. (1819); 2nd edn, ed. T. Helsby (1882) · historical collections, vol. 2, material relating to the Isle of Man, Ches. & Chester ALSS, DCC/10 · letters from William Cowper to Charles Lyttelton, BL, Stowe MS 754, fol. 215r · [R. Gough], *Anecdotes of British topography*, 2 vols. (1768) · *A sketch of the materials for a new history of Cheshire … in a letter to Thomas Falconer … from the late Dr Gower* (1771) · J. Livesey, 'Tarporley in 1755', *Transactions of the Historic Society of Lancashire and Cheshire*, 64 (1912), 292–308 · [C. B. Heberden], ed., *Brasenose College register, 1509–1909*, 1, OHS, 55 (1909) · Foster, *Alum. Oxon.* · A. Chalmers, ed., *The general biographical dictionary*, new edn, 32 vols. (1812–17) · J. H. E. Bennet, ed., *The rolls of the freemen of the city of Chester*, 2, Lancashire and Cheshire RS, 55 (1908) · W. Cowper, letter to R. Grosvenor, 9 May 1750, Ches. & Chester ALSS, Eaton MS 7/2/12 · *DNB*

**Archives** Ches. & Chester ALSS, corresp. and papers relating to Chester and Cheshire, DCC/1 to DCC/47 · Ches. & Chester ALSS, collections relating to the history of Chester · Chester City Archive, Collectanea Devana

**Cowper, William** (1731–1800), poet and letter-writer, was born on 15 November 1731 at the rectory, Berkhamsted, Hertfordshire, the fourth child of the Revd John Cowper (pronounced Cooper; 1694–1756), and his first wife, Ann (1703–1737), daughter of Roger Donne of Ludham Hall, Norfolk. His father, who held the rectory of Berkhamsted from 1722 until his death, was the son of Spencer *Cowper

William Cowper (1731–1800), by George Romney, 1792

(1670–1728), a lawyer and whig politician who rose to be a justice of the common pleas, and nephew of William, first Earl Cowper (1665–1723), twice lord chancellor. The Donnes, long established in Norfolk, claimed a remote ancestor in Henry III and a more immediate one in John Donne, the poet and dean of St Paul's (the latter, though cherished by William Cowper, was probably collateral).

**Early life and education, 1731–1748** Of the seven children of John and Ann Cowper, only two survived infancy, William and John, whose birth on 7 November 1737 proved fatal to Ann. His mother's death put an abrupt end to the idyllic childhood recalled by William more than half a century later in his poem 'On the Receipt of my Mother's Picture'. He celebrates her ability to console, and the 'constant flow of love that knew no fall' (l. 65). He remembers the tolling of her funeral bell and the hearse leaving the rectory, and the promises of the maids that his mother would return, attributing his lifelong servitude to false hopes to this early experience. The closest substitute for the loving care of his mother he found in holidays spent with her relatives in Norfolk, especially with her brother Roger, the rector of Catfield, whose wife Harriot gave William his first books, John Bunyan's *Pilgrim's Progress* and John Gay's *Fables*. William earned praise for his recitation of Gay's 'The Hare and many Friends', a story of delusive hopes and implacable hunters appropriate to the poet who would later figure himself as a stricken deer (Cowper, 'The Task', *Poems*, 3.108–13).

William's education began at a dame-school in Berkhamsted to which the gardener drew him in a miniature carriage. While his mother still lived, he was sent to school a few miles away, in the home of the Revd William Davis, rector of Aldbury. Some months later, his father sent him to a more formally organized school conducted by another clergyman friend, the Revd William Pittman, at Markyate Street in Bedfordshire. Here Cowper began the study of Latin. Here he was bullied by a boy of fifteen, who treated him so brutally that he was afraid to raise his eyes above his persecutor's knees: 'I knew him by his shoe buckles better than by any other part of his dress' (*Letters*, 1.5). Specks on his eyes raised concerns for his eyesight, and his father sent him at the age of eight to live with Mrs Disney, an oculist, where he stayed without much improvement until he entered Westminster School in April 1742. He credited an attack of smallpox three years later with removing the specks, but his eyes were susceptible to inflammation for the rest of his life.

Westminster School was then at the height of its eighteenth-century influence, its location in the shadow of Westminster Abbey adjacent to the old parliament buildings aptly symbolizing its pre-eminence. Under a great headmaster, John Nicoll, it drew the sons of the great whig families which dominated English political life; it drew also many able boys from lesser families. Curriculum and methods of instruction had changed little since the sixteenth century. The fourth form was instructed by Pierson Lloyd, father of Cowper's friend and contemporary the poet Robert Lloyd, remembered for his gentleness and kindness. The fifth form was entrusted to the Latin poet Vincent Bourne, another gentle soul, who was the victim of practical jokes and even physical abuse: Cowper remembered seeing the future duke of Richmond 'set fire to his greasy Locks, & box his Ears to put it out again' (*Letters*, 1.481, 482). Yet harsh living conditions and aristocratic horseplay did not prevent Cowper and others from reading and learning. With his friend Richard Sutton (1733–1802), Cowper read through the *Iliad* and the *Odyssey*, thus beginning a lifetime's study of the Homeric epics. He practised the composition of Latin verse sufficiently to be able to translate his own verses or those of others into Latin, a skill that never deserted him. His youthful enthusiasm for the metaphysical verse of Abraham Cowley, a predecessor at Westminster, was gradually supplanted by a more judicious admiration of Matthew Prior (another old Westminster), and above all of Milton and *Paradise Lost*. He seems to have been a lively and active boy. A number of the friendships he formed at Westminster, though broken off after 1763, were revived with warmth in his later years.

**Law, literature, and love, 1749–1763** The Cowpers were a professional rather than a landed family, looking to the law, the church, and the army for their livelihood. John Cowper decided to make a barrister of his elder son, and a clergyman of the younger. This disposition, natural as it doubtless appeared to the family, placed William in the unhappy and ultimately disastrous position of being obliged to practise a profession he quickly came to dislike, and for which, by reason of his morbid fear of public performance, he was quite unsuited. Unwilling to oppose his respected father, he followed the line of least resistance, to be increasingly caught in a conflict between family expectations he could not retreat from and professional requirements he could not meet—a pattern to be repeated in later years. As the first step in his legal career, Cowper was admitted to the Middle Temple (29 April 1748). A visit to Bath in 1748 provided the occasion for his earliest surviving poem: 'Verses … on Finding the Heel of a Shoe', a venture in the mock heroic manner of a perennial favourite, John Philips's *The Splendid Shilling*. His friends were for the most part proceeding to Oxford or Cambridge, so a lonely future impended.

Certainly Cowper was in no hurry to embrace the profession which had been chosen for him, for he remained at home for nine months after leaving Westminster. Early in 1750 he returned to London, to gain a general introduction to the law by staying in the home and articling in the office of a solicitor, Mr Chapman, in Greville Street. The three years he spent here effectively undermined his father's plan, since he contracted an acute dislike of the law and its practitioners, perhaps not surprising in one who had hitherto received the liberal education of a gentleman. To escape from this uncongenial office, he spent much time at 30 Southampton Row, the home of his uncle Ashley Cowper, who held the lucrative office of clerk of the parliaments. Southampton Row, just minutes' walk from Greville Street, then marked the limit of urban development. Here, looking across fields to the village of Hampstead, he enjoyed the company of his cousins, Ashley's three daughters: Harriot (1733–1807), Theodora Jane (1734?–1824), and Elizabeth Charlotte (d. 1805).

Two important friendships date from this period. In 1751 Cowper was joined at Chapman's by another articling clerk, Edward Thurlow (1731–1806), whose less fastidious and more forceful personality qualified him to serve as lord chancellor from 1778 to 1792. Joseph Hill (1733–1811) was the son of an attorney, and something of a protégé of Ashley Cowper's. He qualified as both attorney and solicitor, and developed a highly successful practice among the wealthy and powerful, recommended by a well-deserved reputation for discretion.

In 1753 Cowper left Chapman's and took up residence in the Middle Temple, and began to keep the terms required to qualify for the bar. Although he might dislike the law, there is evidence in the form of marginal annotations that he studied the subject, and he may have spent more time on it than he later wished to admit. He satisfied the bar requirements minimally, paying fines in lieu of keeping five terms of the eight specified, and further fines for failing to appear for various exercises. He was called to the utter bar in June 1754, and at that time purchased chambers in his own name. Three years of further keeping of terms, dining in hall on certain days, and attendance at exercises were required. He satisfied these requirements, but as soon as they were complete he transferred his membership to the more fashionable Inner Temple, where he purchased pleasant chambers overlooking Hare Court (June 1757).

Meanwhile, Cowper had fallen in love with his cousin Theodora, and she with him, probably on a summer holiday with his mother's relatives in Norfolk in 1752. For three years the relationship ran a sometimes stormy course, faintly traceable in the surviving poems of this period. Cowper suffered a period of depression in 1753, possibly caused by personal and professional stress. Poems of 1755 suggest that the cousins were once again intensely involved with each other. Then Ashley Cowper intervened, refusing his consent to his daughter's marriage because William could not support her. Ashley doubtless intended to stimulate his nephew to professional exertion. William did make some attempt to practise; for in 1791 he adjured the young barrister Samuel Rose 'you will not lose him as I lost a legion of Attorneys myself—by never doing the business they brought me' (*Letters*, 3.497). His real interest, however, was not law but literature. He wrote learned marginal comments in his uncle's copy of Richard Bentley's edition of *Paradise Lost*, and read through Homer once again, this time with a fellow Templar, William Alston (1728–1799). He contributed essays to various periodicals, including five in *The Connoisseur*, edited by George Colman and Bonnell Thornton, and joined with Colman, Thornton, Lloyd, James Bensley, Charles Churchill, and Chase Price, in an informal literary society of old Westminsters styled the Nonsense Club. The death of his father in 1756 severed his links with Berkhamsted, and left him with an inheritance which enabled his removal to the Inner Temple and deferred the necessity of earning a living. The surviving letters of the late 1750s show him as a lively young man about town. He fell in love at least once (ibid., 1.82). His literary work included renderings of two satires for an English edition of Horace (1759) compiled by John Duncombe, a friend of his family, and four books of the *Henriade* translated for Tobias Smollett's edition of Voltaire (1762).

**Collapse, conversion, and recovery, 1763–1764** Throughout this period Cowper had continued to visit Ashley's house and to spend summer holidays with his uncle and cousins. He and Theodora never met or saw each other, and neither was spoken of in the presence of the other. Theodora's devotion remained constant, however, and her health suffered from the separation. When an opportunity to make his daughter happy presented itself, Ashley took action. In April 1763 Francis Macklay, clerk of the journals of the House of Lords, died. The position was at the disposal of Ashley Cowper, as clerk of the parliaments; William, incapable of public performance, believed it was particularly suited to him, since its business was transacted in private. Two other offices, however, became vacant at the same time, those of reading clerk and clerk of the committees. Since these, regularly held as a pair, were more valuable, Ashley Cowper offered them first to William, who accepted them. Immediately he had second thoughts, knowing that that he would be unequal to the public appearances necessary to the business of these positions, and begged his uncle to nominate him to the clerkship of the journals. Ashley, foreseeing trouble, reluctantly complied. Macklay's son, who had a fair claim to succeed his father, fomented opposition, and Cowper was informed that he would have to be examined at the bar of the House of Lords to establish his credentials. Such an inquisition in public was terrifying to him, yet he could not withdraw without injuring his uncle. Miserable months ensued, in which Cowper tried hopelessly to master the business of the clerkship, little aided by the clerks, who took Macklay's part.

Seeking temporary relief, Cowper spent a late summer holiday with Ashley Cowper and his family at Margate, only to suffer a disastrous failure of nerve. Convinced that his dearest hopes were allowed him only to be dashed, he could not bring himself to propose marriage to Theodora when the opportunity was given him. When he returned to London the sense of doom returned, and he began to think of escape. At first he hoped to go mad, but as the dreaded date early in December drew nearer the more certainly effective release of suicide recommended itself. About a week before the examination he bought a half-ounce of laudanum. Unable to swallow the fatal dose, he prepared for flight to France, then decided to drown himself, then attempted to stab himself with his penknife (the blade broke), and finally hanged himself with a garter which snapped just as he lost consciousness. He collapsed in his bed, where Thurlow found him in a state which thirty years later that coarse spirit could not recall without emotion. The clerkship and Theadora were lost forever. A terrible period followed, of acute misery, fear of death and of damnation. Everywhere there seemed to be fingers pointing at him, holding him up to contempt. His brother John, recently elected fellow of Corpus Christi College, came from Cambridge, but his attempts at consolation were useless. At last Cowper thought of his cousin the Revd Martin Madan, whom he had hitherto looked down upon as a Methodistical enthusiast. Madan's exposition of original sin and salvation by grace calmed him at once, and he removed as quickly as possible to Knightsbridge, in order to take lodgings next door to Madan. When alone at night, however, he found his terrors returned, and the next morning finally achieved the alienation of mind that he had earlier hoped for in vain. After family consultations, it was decided to send him to St Albans, to be under the care of Dr Nathaniel Cotton, physician and poet, with whom Cowper was already slightly acquainted. Cotton kept a residence for patients known as his 'Collegium Insanorum' and here Cowper spent the next eighteen months.

For weeks Cowper lay in despair, attempting suicide on at least one occasion. A calmer mood ensued, but no fundamental improvement, until chance readings in the Bible and a visit from his brother began to loosen his conviction that he was 'devoted to destruction' by an angry God (*Letters*, 1.39). On 26 July 1764 he picked up a Bible from a window-seat and opened it at random, lighting on Romans 3: 25. At once he felt strength to believe in Jesus as the propitiation for his sins, and in a moment was lost in paroxysms of joy.

Cowper remained at Dr Cotton's establishment for nearly a year after this sudden conversion. Cotton was himself evangelically inclined, and they spoke often of the sweetness of the scriptures and salvation. Cowper was determined never to return to London, and resigned the only official position he held, a commissionership of bankrupts worth £60 a year. As a result, his means were reduced to a point where he could barely support himself, and several of his relatives agreed to contribute money annually to provide him with an annual income close to the gentry threshold of £100. Joseph Hill assumed responsibility for Cowper's affairs, frequently supplementing the sometimes reluctant contributions from relatives and rent from the chambers in the Inner Temple (nominally £20 a year) to enable his friend to live as a gentleman. John Cowper located lodgings in Huntingdon, 16 miles from Cambridge, which would suit. On 17 June 1765 Cowper set out from St Albans, accompanied by Samuel Roberts, a young servant who had arrived at Dr Cotton's about the same time as Cowper.

**The Unwins and the Newtons, 1765–1773** They brought with them a boy named Richard Coleman, about seven years of age, the son of a drunken cobbler of St Albans. Cowper's plan was to rescue the lad from a brutal father and bring him up to succeed Sam Roberts as his personal servant (he then expected Roberts to leave him after a year or two). The summer passed pleasantly, though housekeeping expenses quickly got out of hand. In September an increasingly lonely existence was transformed by acquaintance with the Unwin family. The Revd Morley Unwin, rector of Grimston in Norfolk, resided in Huntingdon, serving a local chaplaincy and preparing young men for admission to Cambridge University. He had married in 1742 Mary Cawthorne [see Unwin, Mary (*bap.* 1723, *d.* 1796)], the daughter of an Ely draper, a lady of intelligence and culture. Their son William Cawthorne Unwin had graduated BA of Cambridge in 1764, and was preparing to take holy orders. A friendship with the family quickly developed, and in November, worried by the costs of independent housekeeping, Cowper decided to lodge and board with the Unwins. Morley Unwin was a rationalist clergyman, influenced by the theology of Samuel Clarke, but Mrs Unwin and her children were of the evangelical persuasion, and Cowper spent much time in conversation on serious subjects.

Cowper's financial position remained precarious, and his affairs came to a crisis late in the summer of 1766. His uncle Ashley questioned his need to keep a manservant and a dependent boy, and hinted that his relatives might be unwilling to subsidize this manner of living. Mrs Unwin offered to halve the charge for board and lodging; his cousin Harriot, now married to Sir Thomas Hesketh, privately supported his conduct, and her husband made up the contribution which a cousin had withdrawn. The crisis passed, and Cowper continued his comfortable life of religious retirement until 29 June 1767, when Morley Unwin was thrown from his horse, fracturing his skull. He died four days later. Mrs Unwin promptly decided to move to some place where she could find 'an Abode under the Sound of the Gospel' (*Letters*, 1.170), and on 14 September she moved with her daughter Susanna to Olney in north Buckinghamshire. There the Revd John Newton served as curate (under the patronage of Cowper's schoolfellow the earl of Dartmouth). Olney, a small market town perpetually distressed by the failure of the domestic lace making industry, appeared to Cowper to be 'abounding with Palm Trees and Wells of Living Water' (ibid., 1.179). After five months in temporary quarters, he moved with the Unwins into their new home, a house called Orchard Side on the south side of the market square, with a pleasant garden abutting on the garden of the vicarage, allowing the two households to exchange visits without going out into the streets. Late in the year Mrs Unwin fell ill with a 'Nervous Atrophy' which even Dr Cotton could not cure. Cowper's state of mind is represented in the lines 'Oh for a closer walk with God', composed early one morning (ibid., 1.187–8). Prayer effected what medicine could not, and three months later Mrs Unwin was quite recovered. Meanwhile, doubtless under the influence of Newton, Cowper wrote an account of his own conversion. Newton drew Cowper into his campaign to evangelize the people of Olney, to which Cowper contributed most of the sixty-six devotional poems collected in Newton's *Olney Hymns* (1779).

Cowper had a candidate for conversion even closer to home, his own brother, John, now a coming man at Cambridge, a respected scholar and officer of his college, and minister of nearby Foxton. But John was a worldly clergyman, whose heart an evening prayer meeting at Olney vicarage could not touch; of his conversation Cowper remarked: 'So much said about nothing, and so little about Jesus, is very painfull to us' (*Letters*, 1.199). Then in the autumn of 1769 John suffered a haemorrhage; whatever the cause, it presaged a long period of 'inward Decay' (ibid., 1.211). William went to Cambridge to be with him as he weakened physically. Periods of delirium became more frequent. Then on 10 March John woke from a sleep with words of salvation on his lips, and the last ten days of his life were spent in joyous spiritual communication with his brother. He died on 20 March 1770. William returned sad but triumphant to Olney, where he composed a short memoir of his brother's illness and conversion, adding it to the longer one of his own life to form *Adelphi* ('The Brothers'). The augmented work circulated in manuscript among the converted.

**Second collapse, 1773–1774** The unregenerate townspeople of Olney gossiped about the Orchard Side household, suspecting scandal in the relationship of Cowper to Mrs Unwin. This was a sensitive topic: Cowper's first assertions that Mrs Unwin was to him as a mother to a son come in letters written soon after Morley Unwin's death had created a potentially awkward situation. So long as Susanna Unwin lived with her mother, respectability was officially maintained, but when she became engaged to the Revd Matthew Powley in 1772 something had to be done. Newton naturally recommended that Cowper should marry Mrs Unwin, and they became engaged. Cowper now found himself in an impossible situation. He and Theodora had promised never to marry if they did not marry each other, and likewise to keep this promise an inviolable secret. Cowper could not marry Mrs Unwin, and could not explain why. His desperate claim to be an androgyne

incapable of marriage carried no conviction and brought no relief from Newton's urgings. In January 1773, once again trapped between conflicting obligations, Cowper broke down under the strain. The symptoms, more violent than those of 1763, included repeated attempts at suicide. The climax came late in February, when he dreamed that a voice cried to him *Actum est de te, periisti* (*Letters*, 1.510), that is, 'Your case has been decided; you have perished'. These words he interpreted as God's judgment on him, importing the obliteration of his soul at the moment of his death, and God's command that he should put an end to himself at the earliest opportunity. It was a dream 'before the recollection of which, all consolation vanishes, and, as it seems to me, must always vanish' (ibid., 2.385). In a cruel parody of his former confidence in God's love and mercy, Cowper for the remainder of his life believed firmly that he was the unique object of God's utter and unqualified reprobation. He never prayed nor entered a church again; when grace was being said at table he sat down and picked up his knife and fork to demonstrate his conviction of absolute exclusion from the Christian community.

All thoughts of a marriage between Cowper and Mrs Unwin were now dropped. Whatever the world might suppose, the reality was that she was his keeper. In April 1773 Cowper was moved from Orchard Side to the vicarage to escape the noise of the annual spring fair in the market place, and stayed for thirteen months. Back at Orchard Side, he tried to find release in carpentry and drawing. His neighbours gave him three young hares, later celebrated in verse and prose as Puss, Tiney, and Bess, whose undemanding companionship supplied welcome diversion. The handful of poems written in 1774, especially 'Hatred and Vengeance, my Eternal Portion', reveal his misery and despair; in 'Heu quam remotus', written '*die ultimo* 1774', he shrouds in Latin verse his enduring devotion to the Theodora whom he had betrayed and lost: '*Te vinculo nostram jugali*' ('you who are mine in the nuptial bond').

**Partial recovery and first volume of poems, 1774–1781** Cowper had dabbled in gardening at Huntingdon, and he now took it up again. When the series of his surviving letters resumes in 1776, there are several references to his melons, and his hotbed was producing cucumbers by the end of March in 1777. He was in touch with the professional gardeners of the great estates within a 30 mile radius of Olney, obtaining from them both advice and seeds. He recovered his interest in reading, borrowing the accounts of Cook's voyages and other books from Lord Dartmouth's library. Newspapers too engaged his attention, as France and Spain came to the support of the American revolution. His patriotism produced a series of poems, culminating in a venomous epigram in Latin and English in which he accounts for the Gordon riots of June 1780 as a vile French plot. Verses addressed to the Newtons (now removed to London) and William Unwin, however, echo the gentle humour of his letters.

In the early months of 1780 the evangelical party was dismayed by the publication of a work called *Thelyphthora*, by the Revd Martin Madan, the cousin who had so crucially aided Cowper in the crisis of 1763. Madan's pastoral experience had persuaded him that only a return to the concept of marriage which he found in the Pentateuch, whereby a man who had once lain with a woman was her husband and responsible for her thereafter, could alleviate the evils of prostitution. His fellow evangelicals were dismayed to find themselves associated with a plea for polygamy. Cowper, a distant observer, penned several short poems on the subject (he had not read the book), which were circulated anonymously in manuscript by Newton. In the autumn a review by the dissenting minister Samuel Badcock was generally agreed to have prevailed against Madan's arguments. Cowper, encouraged by Mrs Unwin, composed a narrative poem in heroic couplets describing allegorically the defeat of a false knight, by Sir Marmadan, under the title *Antithelyphthora*. Newton hastened this 200-line tale to his publisher, the radical Joseph Johnson, who issued it in an anonymous and quickly forgotten quarto edition on 1 January 1781.

The clash between Cowper's horror at his cousin's theories and his sense of family and personal obligations to Madan unleashed a great burst of creative energy. In the four months from December 1780 to March 1781 Cowper composed 2700 lines of verse. First of these 'moral satires' in pentameter couplets (more reminiscent of Edward Young's satires than of Pope's) was 'The Progress of Error', a renewed attack on Madan, broadened to scourge other corrupters of the public mind. 'Truth' sets up by contrast the evangelically inspired standards to which society should aspire. In 'Table Talk', two interlocutors debate politics and poetry by way of providing an introduction to what Cowper was beginning to think of as a second, more deliberate publication. 'Expostulation' presents Cowper as a prophet upbraiding the English for their national apostasy. In April 1781, when spring renewed opportunities for walking and gardening, Cowper thought these four poems, with a selection of shorter ones which he had by him, would make a satisfactory volume. Joseph Johnson, however, delayed his decision, allowing Cowper to complete four more long poems between May and October 1781. The book appeared in the first week of March 1782, its title asserting the gentility and professional affiliation of its retired yet engaged author in his first acknowledged publication: *Poems by William Cowper, of the Inner Temple, Esq.*

**Lady Austen and *The Task*, 1781–1784** In the summer of 1781 Cowper became acquainted with one of the most powerful influences on his poetic career: Lady Austen, the widow of Sir Robert Austen, bt. In 1781 Lady Austen made an extended visit to her sister Mrs Jones, wife of the curate of the neighbouring village of Clifton Reynes. Soon Lady Austen was thinking of taking up permanent residence at Olney, in the eastern portion of the Orchard Side house (not used by Cowper and Mrs Unwin). At the end of the year, she returned to London, followed by a 'Poetic Epistle' celebrating her friendship with Cowper and Mrs Unwin in the words '"A three-fold cord is not soon broken"'. A few weeks later, however, Lady Austen objected to some

expressions in Cowper's prose letters to her (written at her request as from brother to sister), and the friendship came to an end.

Reviews of *Poems* were generally unfavourable, finding the moral satires dull and the humour of the shorter pieces merely passable. The wealthy merchant John Thornton sent a copy to Benjamin Franklin at Passy and received a complimentary acknowledgement, which he passed on to Cowper. A copy sent to Cowper's old friend Thurlow, now lord chancellor, produced no response whatever. Cowper began a poem in couplets on education, wrote 200 lines, then desisted. His career as a publishing poet, begun by accident, might have petered out in disappointment once the original motive for writing had faded. Late in the spring, however, messages from Lady Austen indicated a desire for reconciliation, which duly took place in June when she returned to Clifton Reynes for another extended visit. Cowper devoted much of summer 1782 to translating some of the *Poésies et cantiques spirituelles* of Madame J.-M. Bouvier de la Mothe Guyon (1648–1717), at the request of his friend the Revd William Bull, Independent minister of Newport Pagnell. He later gave the booklet containing his translations (some more were added in 1783) to Bull, to publish if he wished. Cowper's occasional poems of the summer of 1782 show Lady Austen's growing influence: they are addressed to her, or relate incidents in which she was involved, or provide lyrics to be sung to her favourite melodies. One autumn afternoon, Lady Austen, noticing that Cowper was sinking into a depressed state, told him a story which had delighted her as a child, the misadventures of a linen draper on his wedding anniversary. The tale caught Cowper's fancy; he composed a ballad version, and through William Unwin's agency *The Diverting History of John Gilpin* was published anonymously in the *Public Advertiser* on 14 November 1782. In March 1785 it was included in an evening of Lenten readings by the popular actor John Henderson, with instant and enormous success. Thanks to Lady Austen, Cowper had written the most popular poem of the decade.

Lady Austen had taken up residence in the capacious Olney vicarage, and the winter months were spent in a constant interchange of visits. Then in the summer of 1783 Lady Austen, trying once again to alleviate his melancholy, challenged Cowper to write a poem on the sofa. He embarked on a history of the sofa in blank verse, and these lines led to others, until he found that he was writing a long poem about his life of retirement, about Olney and its scenery, about contemporary England, about the primacy of spiritual religion; found, in fact, that he was preparing another volume. As he completed the first draft of his poem in the spring of 1784, his association with Lady Austen came to an end. Details are lacking, but there seems to have been no quarrel; rather, a mutual recognition that the threefold cord had frayed beyond repair. Lady Austen later returned to Clifton Reynes and lived there from 1785 to 1790, but never saw Cowper again.

During the summer of 1784 Cowper revised his 6000-line poem, named *The Task* from its origin. He sent the fair copy to William Unwin, who had persuaded

Joseph Johnson to publish it sight unseen, on 10 October. Immediately he took up his 200-line fragment on education, and, appalled by a report that Westminster School now kept a surgeon on retainer to treat boys for venereal disease, turned it into *Tirocinium*, a 900-line assault on the immorality and irreligion of great public schools dedicated to Unwin, who had decided to educate his sons at home. Early in November he sent to Unwin the fair copy of this poem, a complimentary epistle to Joseph Hill, and *John Gilpin*. *The Task*, accompanied by these three poems, was published early in August 1785. It was an immediate critical and popular success, and its popularity continued to grow. Its condemnation of slavery and advocacy of the humane treatment of animals were slightly in advance of changes in public opinion, so that the poem became more representative of its readers' views as time went by. Its attacks on aristocratic immorality and conspicuous consumption chimed in with William Wilberforce's campaign, initiated by the royal proclamation of 1787, to recall the upper classes to their social and religious responsibilities. Like its evangelical Christianity, its patriotic zeal against everything French gained fresh significance in the 1790s, when Britain went to war with the godless republicans of revolutionary France. Its evocations of landscape and the domestic life have proved permanently appealing. Above all, Cowper demonstrated in *The Task* that blank verse could render every topic from the most mundane aspects of gardening to the day of judgement—a lesson not lost on the next generation of poets.

**From Homer to Milton, 1784–1792** On 21 November 1784, the day after he dispatched the final copy of *The Task* volume to Unwin, Cowper began to translate Homer's *Iliad*. More than a year later, when he could no longer conceal from Newton the fact that he was devoting himself to a pagan author, he claimed that he started to translate the *Iliad* merely to divert himself in a period of misery. The misery was real enough, but there was purpose in the enterprise. As a young man in the Temple, Cowper had found Pope's Homer false to the original. Thirty years later he had read Pope's version to Lady Austen and Mrs Unwin, complaining of its inadequacy, whereupon Lady Austen urged him to make a better translation himself. Her challenge moved him to undertake the most prolonged literary endeavour of his life. Working steadily at forty lines a day, he completed a draft of the *Iliad* on 13 January 1786.

Meanwhile *The Task* had moved his cousin Lady Hesketh, now widowed, to write to him, renewing a connection that had lapsed nearly eighteen years earlier. A new friendship further enlivened what had been a limited and lonely existence for Cowper and Mrs Unwin. Weston Hall, a mile west of Olney in the village of Weston Underwood, belonged to the Throckmorton family, and served as the home of the heir to the baronetcy. In May 1784, at the height of the ballooning frenzy set off by the success of the Montgolfiers, the current occupant of the hall, John Courtenay Throckmorton invited Cowper and Mrs Unwin to observe a balloon launch in his grounds. The balloon failed to fly, but Throckmorton and his young wife Maria showed much attention to Cowper and Mrs Unwin, and

despite confessional differences (the Throckmortons were Roman Catholics) what had been barely formal acquaintance began to develop into warm friendship.

Lady Hesketh came to stay with her cousin in June 1786. Happily she accepted his unconventional relationship with Mrs Unwin, whose devoted knitting of his stockings she duly reported back to Theadora in London. Orchard Side she did object to, as cramped, dilapidated, and poorly located. The Throckmortons could offer a much better house in the village of Weston Underwood, and Lady Hesketh would pay the costs of removal and supply new furnishings, some purchased on behalf of 'Anonymous' (Theadora, who added £50 a year to Cowper's income). Reports that Cowper and Mrs Unwin were associating with papists and driving about in Lady Hesketh's carriage drew a stern letter of rebuke from John Newton. He was respectfully told to mind his own business. Lady Hesketh departed on 14 November, and the next day Cowper and Mrs Unwin moved to Weston Underwood.

Improvement was swiftly overshadowed by bereavement. On 29 November 1786 William Unwin died of typhus, aged forty-four. The loss was a heavy blow, and almost certainly provoked the 'nervous fever' of which Cowper complains in his letters to Lady Hesketh early in January 1787. On the 15th of that month he received a visit from a young man, Samuel Rose, who had been a student at the University of Glasgow, and who called to convey his professors' appreciation of Cowper's two volumes of poetry. Two or three days later Cowper lapsed into a severe depression lasting several months. By September, enlivened by the prospect of another visit by Lady Hesketh, he had resumed his daily stint of translation and his engagement with a now widening circle of correspondents. The publication of *Proposals* for the publication of the Homer translation by subscription (spring 1786) had given an opening to old friends, many from Westminster School days, to resume contact, while through Lady Hesketh, Cowper became reconnected with members of his father's family. The repeated visits of Samuel Rose linked Cowper to a younger generation of readers. In January 1790 a visit from a cousin, John Johnson, restored cordial relations with his mother's family in Norfolk. Soon afterwards, Johnson's aunt Mrs Bodham sent to Cowper the portrait miniature which moved him to write 'On the Receipt of my Mother's Picture' (March 1790).

After the interruption of 1787, work on the Homer translation proceeded steadily, though with many revisions, recopyings, and delays. The completed manuscript was delivered to Joseph Johnson early in September 1790. Correction of the proofs, in some places amounting to a further round of revision, continued into May of 1791. The last pages, comprising the final list of 498 subscribers, was sent to London on 12 June, and the two bulky quarto volumes were published on 1 July. Ten days later, Rose negotiated a financial agreement with Johnson which netted the poet £1000. Cowper declared himself satisfied. As recently as 23 June he and Mrs Unwin had been reduced to their last guinea. Reviews were mixed.

The question now arose of what Cowper should write

next. A translation of a portion of the eighth book of *Aeneid* suggests that he may have contemplated rendering Virgil too into the Miltonic blank verse of his Homer. In May 1791 the Revd John Buchanan, his neighbour in Weston Underwood, presented him with the outline of a poem to be called 'The Four Ages of Man', a moral theme suitable to Cowper's genius. Cowper obligingly set to work, but made little headway. The fragment 'Yardley Oak', also in blank verse, probably represents an attempt to work into Buchanan's topic without the strait-jacket of his outline. Cowper could settle to nothing, however, and in September he reluctantly accepted Joseph Johnson's invitation to edit the works of Milton for a sumptuous new illustrated edition. The only attractive element of this project was the translation of Milton's Latin and Italian poems, and to this Cowper applied himself in the autumn of 1791. On 17 December Mrs Unwin suffered a stroke. She recovered, but his anxiety seems to have led Cowper to rely increasingly on Samuel Teedon, the Olney schoolmaster, for spiritual advice. He had completed work on Milton's Latin poems by February 1792. John Throckmorton's brother George helped him with the poems in Italian, a language of which Cowper knew little.

**William Hayley and the visit to Eartham, 1792**   In mid-March Cowper received a letter from the popular poet and playwright William Hayley, who had undertaken to write a life of Milton for an edition of Milton's works projected by another London publisher. Having seen a newspaper paragraph which depicted himself and Cowper as rivals, Hayley assured Cowper that they were not hostile competitors. Two months later, on 15 May 1792, he arrived at Weston, fortunately being present to take charge when Mrs Unwin suffered a second stroke on 22 May. By the time Hayley left on 1 June, she was receiving regular treatment with an electrical machine, and showed signs of improvement. Cowper's gratitude was unstinting. As Cowper nursed his own 'faithful and affectionate nurse' (*Letters*, 3.599), Hayley's admiration and generosity sustained him. He laid aside his barely begun commentary on *Paradise Lost*, and advised Joseph Johnson that he might be unable to do further work on the Milton edition.

Hayley meanwhile was urging the therapeutic value of an excursion to his home at Eartham near Chichester, where the fresh air of the Sussex Downs would surely help Mrs Unwin. Astonishingly, considering that he had refused every invitation to leave home for quarter of a century, Cowper agreed, and on 1 August 1792 he and Mrs Unwin, accompanied by Sam Roberts and his wife, set off for Eartham, where John Johnson was to join them. At the end of a long third day they reached Eartham. Mrs Unwin sustained the journey better than could have been expected, and her health and appetite seemed quickly to improve. The two poets collaborated on a revision of Cowper's translations of Milton's Latin and Italian poems, and on a translation of G. B. Andreini's *Adamo*. Also visiting Hayley at this time were the novelist Charlotte Smith and

the painter George Romney, whose famous sketch of Cowper was done about the middle of August. On 17 September Cowper and Mrs Unwin set out for home; on the 20th they were safely back in Weston Underwood.

**Weston Underwood and Norfolk, 1792–1800**   Mrs Unwin's condition had improved during the visit to Sussex, but she was still unable to stand or walk without assistance, and as winter advanced it became increasingly clear that further recovery was unlikely. Cowper was incapable of proceeding with the Milton edition; Hayley's enthusiastic offers of help and schemes to improve the proposed edition exacerbated rather than relieved Cowper's sense of failure. Once again, he was trapped between obligations (to Joseph Johnson and Buchanan) and an inability to fulfil them; once again he was drifting, waiting for the situation to resolve itself. This time, fate was kind. In December 1793 Joseph Johnson decided the Milton project was impracticable under wartime conditions, and cancelled it.

As the French Revolution intensified political differences in England, Cowper found himself under pressure from Lady Hesketh to renounce his lifelong whiggism and become, as she had, a Pittite. This he refused to do, while at the same time assuring her that he, and Rose and Hayley and his other new friends were as opposed to revolutionary excesses as she could be. Cowper's young cousin John Johnson was ordained, and took up the curacy of East Dereham in Norfolk. Lady Hesketh, unable to visit Weston Underwood in the summer of 1793, suggested that Cowper should consider moving to Norfolk, where a network of relatives on his mother's side could provide support. Cowper preferred to stay in familiar surroundings with his friends the Throckmortons. He almost completed a revision of his translation of Homer. Mrs Unwin's health was slowly deteriorating, as the lines 'To Mary' poignantly register. The spectacle of her decline took a heavy toll, and in the middle of January 1794 Cowper lapsed into a deep melancholia from which he never recovered.

For many months Lady Hesketh stayed at Weston, caring for her hosts. Mrs Unwin, querulous and irrational, continued to rule an increasingly dysfunctional household. Hayley visited in April 1794, but neither his presence nor his success in securing for Cowper a royal pension of £300 a year could alleviate the poet's profound depression. Finally, Lady Hesketh began to fear for her own health. In 1795 it was agreed among Cowper's relatives that he and Mrs Unwin should be moved to Norfolk in the care of John Johnson. This was represented to Cowper as a summer expedition, but he divined that if he left Weston, it would be never to return. As the planned date in July approached, he attempted to take his own life. The move was delayed, but on 28 July 1795 inexorably took place.

Johnson conveyed the invalids first to the seaside town of Mundesley, then, in October, to his home at Dunham Lodge. Sam Roberts, parting after thirty years, returned to Weston Underwood. Cowper was overwhelmed with despair, and could think only that 'He who made me, regrets that he ever did' (*Letters*, 4.458). In September 1796 John Johnson moved his household to East Dereham, and there

Mrs Unwin died on 17 December. Cowper was now so despondent that he appeared indifferent even to this loss, never mentioning her name again. Encouraged by John Johnson, however, he did return to writing. He could not bear to resume work on the revision of his Homer that he had abandoned in 1793, but he began a new and more radical revision of the translation in 1797, completing it in March 1799. That month he wrote a Latin poem on icebergs, immediately translating it into English; this was followed in April by 'The Cast-Away', translated into Latin five months later. He went on to make English versions of Latin poems by his former schoolmaster Vincent Bourne, Greek epigrams, and other Latin poems. In December, he translated into Latin Gay's 'The Hare and many Friends', the poem he had recited as a child. A revision of a passage in the *Iliad* was his last composition (23 January 1800). His health failed, and he died of 'a worn-out constitution' (Hayley, *Memoirs*, 2.106) on 25 April 1800, aged sixty-eight. He was buried in St Edmund's Chapel in the church of St Nicholas, East Dereham, on 3 May, with a memorial inscription by William Hayley.

**Reputation** Cowper's hymns, published at the time when hymn singing was beginning to become more widely acceptable in Anglican services, contributed a number of popular favourites to many collections throughout the English-speaking world; 'Oh for a closer walk with God' and 'God moves in a mysterious way' were perhaps the most often reprinted. Their emphasis on personal devotion and uncompromising doctrinal statements make a poor fit with protestantism as it has evolved since 1960, however, and they appear less frequently in recent hymnals.

The volume of 1785 contained the works which made Cowper a widely read poet. The religious tone of *The Task*, its domesticity, and its treatment of such topics as slavery and consideration for animals, all anticipated themes associated with the evangelical revival which began in the late 1780s and peaked in the 1820s. Hayley's biography (1803) revealed the charm of Cowper's letters, and stimulated interest in his personal life. As reprints multiplied on both sides of the Atlantic, a division grew between evangelical readers who saw Cowper as tragically separated by mental illness from his saving faith, and those who thought him a sensitive soul driven mad by the grim theology of Calvin. The publication in the mid-1830s of two rival editions of his works illustrates the split: the eight-volume *Life and Works* edited by the Revd T. S. Grimshawe, with an inferior life and without the translation of the heathen Homer, was intended for a popular evangelical audience; whereas Robert Southey's more expensively produced fifteen-volume set, including the Homer, with an excellent biography and some judicious notes, was addressed to more sophisticated readers.

Numerous Victorian editions of the English poems attest Cowper's continuing popularity, as do many illustrated editions of 'John Gilpin', Randolph Caldecott's the most familiar. In the later nineteenth century portions of *The Task* were often chosen as set books for school examinations. The four-volume edition of the letters issued in 1904 by Thomas Wright, the schoolmaster who had established Cowper and Newton Museum in his native Olney in 1900, and the editions of the poems by John Bailey and Humphrey Milford published almost simultaneously in 1905, mark the zenith of Cowper's reputation.

The emergence of English as a university subject about this time, and the subsequent development of a historically representative canon of works suitable for teaching, coincided with the revival of interest in Donne and the metaphysical poets. The bounds of a teaching canon are fairly rigid, and the need to make room for poets of the early seventeenth century caused Cowper, already overshadowed in literary history by his successors Wordsworth and Coleridge, to be dropped from the list of major authors. Like his contemporary Burns, however, Cowper has never lacked an audience among those who read poetry for pleasure, and recently there have been signs, especially in England, of renewed critical interest in his writings.

JOHN D. BAIRD

**Sources** *The letters and prose writings of William Cowper*, ed. J. King and C. Ryskamp, 5 vols. (1979–86) · *The poems of William Cowper*, ed. J. D. Baird and C. Ryskamp, 3 vols. (1980–95) · J. King, *William Cowper: a biography* (1986) · C. Ryskamp, *William Cowper of the Inner Temple, esq.: a study of his life and works to the year 1768* (1959) · N. Russell, *A bibliography of William Cowper to 1837* (1963) · W. Hayley, *The life, and posthumous writings, of William Cowper, esq.*, 3 vols. (1803–4) · W. Hayley, *Memoirs of William Hayley*, ed. J. Johnson, 2 vols. (1823) · K. Povey, 'Cowper and Lady Austen', *Review of English Studies*, 10 (1934), 417–27 · K. Povey, 'The banishment of Lady Austen', *Review of English Studies*, 15 (1939), 392–400 · T. Wright, *The life of William Cowper* (1892) · H. P. Stokes, *Cowper memorials: records of the Rev. John Cowper, M.A.* (1904) · G. Keynes, 'The library of William Cowper', *Transactions of the Cambridge Bibliographical Society*, 3 (1959–63), 47–69, 167 · N. H. Russell, addenda to 'The library of William Cowper', *Transactions of the Cambridge Bibliographical Society*, 3 (1959–63), 225–31

**Archives** Birm. CA, MS copy of memoirs entitled 'A narrative of Cowper's experience written by himself' · BL, autograph drafts of final poems, Dep 9987 · Bodl. Oxf., letters · Bodl. Oxf., papers relating to his conversations and effects · Bucks. RLSS, corresp. and papers · Cowper Memorial Library, Olney, corresp. and verses · Herts. ALS, corresp. and papers; letters · Hunt. L., corresp. and verses · LPL, letters and verses · McMaster University, Hamilton, Ontario, corresp. and verses · NRA, priv. coll., letters · Princeton University library, corresp. and poems · Trinity Cam., literary papers, incl. MSS and annotated drafts of verse translation of Homer's *Iliad* and *Odyssey* | Beds. & Luton ARS, letters to Lady Hesketh · BL, corresp. with William Hayley, Add. MS 39673 · BL, letters to William Unwin and John Unwin, Add. MSS 24154–24155 · Bodl. Oxf., letters of John Johnson relating to Cowper · LPL, letters to William Bull · Morgan L., corresp. with Walter Bagot · V&A NAL, Forster collection, letters and a MS volume belonging to him · Warks. CRO, letters to Mrs Throckmorton with verses

**Likenesses** L. F. Abbott, oils, 1792, NPG · G. Romney, pastel drawing, 1792, NPG [*see illus.*] · T. Lawrence, pencil drawing, 1793, Cowper Museum, Olney, Buckinghamshire · T. Lawrence, pencil drawing, 1793, Yale U. · F. Bartolozzi, engraving, 1799–1805 (after T. Lawrence) · W. Blake, oils, *c*.1800, Man. City Gall. · W. Harvey, pencil drawing (after L. F. Abbott), NPG · J. Jackson, oils, Northampton Museum and Art Gallery · portraits, repro. in Russell, *Bibliography*

**Wealth at death** not great; chief asset was library; £300 to Mrs Unwin; returned to donors funds given by relatives for his support: PRO, PROB 11/1347, fol. 139

**Cowper, William** (1778–1858), Church of England clergyman, was born on 28 December 1778 at Whittington,

Lancashire, the son of a yeoman farmer. He was educated locally, and at the age of seventeen became tutor to a clergyman's family at Northallerton in Yorkshire. He then worked as a clerk in the Royal Engineers' department in Hull. It was through the influence of the Revd Thomas Dykes, a leader of the evangelical revival in Hull, that he was converted and eventually prepared for ordination. He was ordained deacon in March 1808 by the bishop of Winchester in the Chapel Royal, St James's Palace, and became curate of Rawdon, near Leeds. Almost immediately afterwards he was invited by the Revd Samuel Marsden to accept a post as an assistant chaplain in New South Wales, and landed at Port Jackson in August 1809. By this time he had lost his first wife, Hannah Horner (d. 1808), with whom he had a daughter and three sons, the youngest of whom was Sir Charles *Cowper, the Australian politician. Before leaving England Cowper had married Ann Barrell (d. 1831), with whom he had one son, the Revd William Macquarrie Cowper, later dean of Sydney.

Cowper took up his ministry at the new church of St Philip in an association which was to last for the rest of his life. Until 1819 he was the only clergyman permanently resident in Sydney; he was all too aware of the low moral character of much of the colony and gave his whole-hearted support to such measures as Governor Macquarrie's proclamation against concubinage. Though Cowper's evangelical views were not popular with the governor, Macquarrie had sufficient regard for him to act as godfather to his son William and later to provide a dowry for Cowper's eldest daughter, Mary. Cowper was also instrumental in founding schools and in organizing branches of the British and Foreign Bible Society, the Religious Tract and Book Society, the Society for Promoting Christian Knowledge, a district committee of the Society for the Propagation of the Gospel, and the Benevolent Society of New South Wales. He also played an active part in the Church Missionary Society as well as working with and for the Aborigines. The pressure of this work took an increasing toll on his health.

In 1831 Cowper's wife, Ann, died and on 1 March 1836 he married Harriette Swaine, with whom he had a son and a daughter. By 1842 the cataracts from which he had suffered for several years forced him to return to England for treatment, his expenses being defrayed by a gift of £780 from his parishioners and the people of Sydney. During his stay in England he received a Lambeth DD. In 1848 Bishop Broughton collated him to the archdeaconry of Cumberland and Camden, New South Wales, and in 1852 he was appointed bishop's commissary when Broughton returned to England. After the bishop's death in 1853, Cowper presided over the diocese until the arrival of Bishop Barker in May 1855. He died in Sydney on 6 July 1858 and was given a state funeral before his burial in the Devonshire Street cemetery. His remains were later reinterred in the family vault in the Randwick cemetery, Sydney.                     J. M. RIGG, rev. CLARE BROWN

**Sources** AusDB, 1.254–6 · W. M. Cowper, The autobiography and reminiscences of William Macquarrie Cowper, dean of Sydney (1902) · A. Houison, 'The venerable Archdeacon Cowper', Australian History

Society Journal and Proceedings, 3/7 (1916) · The Times (6 Sept 1858), 9c · J. H. Heaton, Australian dictionary of dates and men of the time (1879)

**Cowper, William Francis**. See Temple, William Francis Cowper-, Baron Mount-Temple (1811–1888).

**Cowton, Robert** (fl. 1300–1315), Franciscan friar and theologian, took his name from Cowton in the North Riding of Yorkshire; he entered the order before the age of fourteen, and by 1300 was studying at the Oxford convent. In July of that year he was among the friars who were denied a licence by the bishop of Lincoln to hear confessions. He commented on the Sentences, presumably at Oxford, some time between 1304 and 1311, since he cited the Ordinatio of Duns Scotus (also called the Opus Oxoniense) and the Sentences commentary of William Nottingham, and he was, in turn, cited by Robert Walsingham and in the Quodlibeta of Giacomo da Ascoli. Since Cowton's name does not appear among the Franciscan lectors at either Oxford or Cambridge as listed by Eccleston, he did not incept as regent master in England. According to Bale he became a master in theology at Paris. It is not known when he died.

Cowton's commentary on the Sentences, his only known surviving work, was frequently copied in England and on the continent, and an abbreviated redaction was made by Richard Snettisham at the beginning of the fifteenth century. Twenty manuscripts of Cowton's original redaction, and thirteen manuscripts of the abbreviated version, still exist. Another abbreviation of this work, known as Notabilia, survives in two manuscripts. Other writings attributed to Cowton by Doucet are, in the case of the Determinationes, only questions extracted from his commentary on the Sentences, and the collatio belongs rather to the Dominican Thomas Sutton, who attacked some of the positions maintained by Cowton. Cowton is also credited with quodlibetal questions (incipit 'An inquisitor huius scientiae'), Disputationes magistrales, and some sermons.

To the extent that his writings have been studied, Cowton joined his Franciscan contemporaries in defending the doctrine of the immaculate conception, but in most other respects he did not subscribe to the positions of Duns Scotus, whom he had probably heard lecture at Oxford. In general, Cowton is representative of a pre-Scotistic tradition in Franciscan theology that was dependent on the thought of Henri de Gand, as was the case with other Oxford Franciscans before 1315, such as Richard Conington and William Nottingham.

W. J. COURTENAY

**Sources** Fratris Thomae vulgo dicti de Eccleston tractatus de adventu Fratrum Minorum in Angliam, ed. A. G. Little (1951) · A. Wood, Survey of the antiquities of the city of Oxford, ed. A. Clark, 2, OHS, 17 (1890), 386 · W. Woodford, 'Defensorium paupertatis', Magd. Oxf., MS 75, chap. 62 · S. F. Brown, 'Robert Cowton O. F. M. and the analogy of the concept of being', Franciscan Studies, new ser., 31 (1971), 5–40 · W. Dettloff, Die Entwicklung der Akzeptations- und Verdienstlehre von Duns Scotus bis Luther (1963), 14–22 · V. Doucet, Commentaires sur les 'Sentences': supplément au répertoire de M. Frédéric Stegmueller (1954), 78–9 · Der Sentenzenkommentar Peters von Candia, ed. F. Ehrle (1925), 82 · De immaculata conceptione Beatae Mariae Virginis secundum Thomam de Sutton OP et Robertum de Cowton OFM, ed. B. Hechich (1958) · A. G. Little, The Grey friars in Oxford, OHS, 20 (1892), 222–3 · O. Lottin, 'Robert Cowton et Jean Duns Scot', Recherches de Théologie

*Ancienne et Médiévale*, 21 (1954), 281–94 • H. Schwamm, *Robert Cowton OFM über das göttliche Vorherwissen* (Innsbruck, 1931) • F. Pelster, 'Thomas von Sutton, OP, ein Oxforder Verteidiger der thomistischen Lehre', *Zeitschrift für Katholische Theologie*, 46 (1922), 218–23, 227, 247, 251, 392–6 • H. Theissing, *Glaube und Theologie bei Robert Cowton OFM* (Münster, 1970) • Emden, *Oxf.*, 1.507

**Cox, Captain, of Coventry** (*fl.* **1575**), collector of ballads and romances, is described by his contemporary Robert Laneham as 'an od man, I promiz yoo: by profession a mason, and that right skilfull, very cunning in fens, and hardy az Gawin; … great oversight hath he in matters of storie' (Furnivall, 28–9). Very little is known of Cox beyond the description provided by Laneham in his 1575 account of the festivities in honour of Queen Elizabeth at Kenilworth. Among the entertainments provided on this occasion was a burlesque imitation of a battle, from an old romance, and Cox took a leading part. Cox's performance is recalled in Ben Jonson's *Masque of Owls … Presented by the Ghost of Captain Cox*, which was performed at Kenilworth in 1624. If Jonson is to be believed, Cox had fought at Boulogne with Henry VIII in 1544 (*Ben Jonson: Complete Masques*, 426). Cox, however, is noteworthy primarily for his sizeable and rather curious library, described in detail by Laneham as comprising ballads and romances, as well as plays, almanacs, and works of philosophy, poetry, and medicine. This list of more than sixty works provides important insight into Elizabethan reading habits.

A. H. Bullen, *rev.* Elizabeth Goldring

**Sources** *Captain Cox, his ballads and books, or, Robert Laneham's letter*, ed. F. J. Furnivall (1871) • J. Nichols, *The progresses and public processions of Queen Elizabeth*, new edn, 3 vols. (1823) • F. L. Colvile, *The worthies of Warwickshire who lived between 1500 and 1800* [1870] • *Ben Jonson: the complete masques*, ed. S. Orgel (1975) • *Ben Jonson*, ed. C. H. Herford, P. Simpson, and E. M. Simpson, 11 vols. (1925–52) • M. Drabble, ed., *The Oxford companion to English literature*, 5th edn (1985) • W. Dugdale, *The antiquities of Warwick and Warwick Castle: extracted from … 'Antiquities of Warwickshire'* (1786) • T. F. Dibdin, *The bibliomania, or, Book madness*, another edn, 4 vols. (1903)

**Cox, Alfred** (1866–1954), medical administrator, was born on 5 May 1866 at Middlesbrough, the second son in the family of eight children of Thomas Benjamin Cox, a bridgeyard worker, and his wife, Dinah Sanderson Skilbeck, a blacksmith's daughter. He was an unhealthy child. Shortly after his birth the family moved to Darlington, where at the age of fourteen Cox was made a monitor of Albert Road board school as a step to becoming a pupil teacher. This was not a success, and at the age of seventeen he began to study for the civil service lower division, work he continued while staying in Carlisle as assistant to an insurance agent. It was there that a doctor visiting the house persuaded him to become a dispenser assistant; this provided a mode of entry to the medical profession later forbidden by the General Medical Council. Cox gained a good deal of experience in midwifery and moved first to Stockton-on-Tees and later to Haydon Bridge, where he had more time for study; finally he moved to Newcastle upon Tyne, where he received free board and lodging and £1 a month from the general practitioner for whom he worked.

Despite this somewhat precarious existence Cox managed to matriculate at Edinburgh and on his twenty-first birthday he entered the University of Durham College of Medicine at Newcastle—still earning his keep as a dispenser assistant. He qualified MB, BS in 1891 and, with a capital of £30, immediately entered general practice in Gateshead. In 1894 he married Florence Amelia (*d.* 1927), daughter of Thomas Cheesman, iron merchant, of Newcastle upon Tyne. The marriage was childless. Cox served as district medical officer to the Gateshead poor-law union. In this capacity he gave evidence to the royal commission on the poor laws and relief of distress (April 1907). Shortly before he left Gateshead, in 1908, he became a factory surgeon.

Cox's long years of penurious drudgery probably stimulated his interest in medical politics and the reform of his profession. He played an active part in local politics in Gateshead, and was elected to its municipal council. With the rector of Gateshead he joined forces in a campaign for slum clearance. He was also a justice of the peace. In 1898 Cox formed the Gateshead Medical Association, and tried to reform club practice and the methods used by friendly societies in appointing doctors for their members. He was active in forming in other towns in the north various medical societies for discussing medico-political and medico-ethical matters. These provided a focus for the expression of dissatisfaction with the British Medical Association (BMA), which Cox had joined in 1893. A conference held by the Medical Guild of Manchester in May 1900 brought this dissatisfaction into the open, and the possibility of forming a new organization was debated. It was Cox who carried the day with a motion which gave the BMA a chance to reform itself, and the result of this was the setting up in the same year of the committee which brought in the new constitution of the BMA, which to all intents and purposes remained unchanged until the reforms adopted in 1966. Cox was a member of the constitution committee from 1900 to 1902.

Sidney and Beatrice Webb described the new BMA constitution of 1903 as a model of democratic organization. The culminating structure of this was the representative body, which at the annual representative meeting laid down the policy of the BMA. Cox was a representative from the beginning and the first honorary secretary of the Gateshead division, which replaced the Gateshead Medical Association he had formed. He was also honorary secretary of the north of England branch between 1902 and 1908, and its president in 1908. When the appointment of medical secretary to the BMA was being considered Cox was canvassed as a likely candidate, but he withdrew in favour of James Smith Whitaker, who was appointed in 1902. In the same year Cox was elected a member of the BMA's council on which he served until 1903. Cox was also a member of the parliamentary bills (later medico-politico) committee between 1899 and 1903 and again in 1907–8. In 1908 Cox became deputy secretary of the BMA, at an initial salary of £500 p.a., and gave up medical practice. When Smith Whitaker took office as deputy chairman of the National Health Insurance Commission in

1911, Cox succeeded him, being formally appointed medical secretary of the BMA in 1912.

One of Cox's first tasks in his new position was to represent the association as a witness before the select committee on patent medicines between 1912 and 1914. The introduction of national health insurance by Lloyd George was accompanied by a bitter struggle between the BMA and the government, and Smith Whitaker's decision to leave the BMA at the height of this was the subject of much criticism. But Cox at the time, and in the years to come, never ceased to defend his action. During the crisis, especially after he succeeded Smith Whitaker, Cox took on arduous and anxious duties, not least in trying to maintain professional unity in an atmosphere of distrust and reproach. He also played an important role in negotiating the system of professional consultation which allowed the new scheme to function efficiently. Following its introduction Cox became an enthusiastic supporter of national health insurance.

During the First World War, Cox acted as joint secretary of the central medical war committee set up to organize the supply of doctors to the armed forces. For this he was appointed OBE in 1918. The war over, much of his work as secretary of the BMA was concerned with negotiations between the medical profession and the Ministry of Health, and with the administration of a professional organization which over the years grew in numbers and strength. He also conducted an investigation into practice conditions in Britain, the findings of which influenced the BMA's proposals for a general medical service for the nation. As ambassador for the BMA he was successful in securing the allegiance to the home organization of doctors in Canada, which he visited in 1924 and 1930, and in South Africa, which he visited in 1925. In both countries there had been branches of the BMA and separate medical associations as well. By the time Cox died in 1954, the Canadian Medical Association and the South African Medical Association had become affiliated to the BMA. Another successful attempt to cement friendship among doctors of different countries was the formation in 1925 of the Association Professionnelle Internationale des Médecins (APIM); Cox was a co-founder and also one of its most enthusiastic supporters. After the Second World War the APIM was merged into a bigger organization, the World Medical Association.

Cox devoted much of his life to the welfare and interests of his profession, and in the British Medical Association he found a powerful instrument to that end. He retired as medical secretary in 1932, the year of the BMA's centenary, having stayed in office a year beyond retirement age in order to oversee the celebrations. On retirement Cox received a cheque for £1000 along with a book containing the names of some 7000 subscribers to his testimonial fund. He was made vice-president of the association in 1933. After leaving the BMA, Cox occupied a variety of positions. He was part-time general secretary of the British Health Resorts Association (1933–8); chairman of the advisory council, medical section, British Industries House; part-time medical secretary of the London public

medical service; medical adviser to the Proprietary Association of Great Britain; and, until the age of eighty, acting secretary to the National Ophthalmic Treatment Board (1941–6).

Beneath a rather stern exterior Cox had a warm and generous heart which kept him free from the jealousies which so often beset professional life. He seldom missed an opportunity to encourage younger colleagues. He was a man of great integrity, and up to the end of his long life he kept his friendships in constant repair and his interests undimmed. Early in his career he was a member of the Independent Labour Party, being greatly influenced by Keir Hardie, whom he knew personally. But he later became disillusioned with socialism. 'The end of it all', he wrote in his autobiography, 'seems inevitably to be the authoritarian State' (Cox, 221). He was a vigorous opponent of Bevan's National Health Service Bill, suggesting that it was a step on the road to national socialism and to the transformation of the minister of health into a 'medical Fuehrer'.

Cox wrote numerous articles for the medical press. He received the honorary degrees of LLD, from the University of Manitoba in 1930, and MA, from Durham in 1921. The BMA awarded him its gold medal in 1931. After several years of poor health and failing eyesight, Cox died in a nursing home at 54 Marine Parade, Brighton on 31 August 1954. His body was cremated at Golders Green crematorium on 4 September, and there was a memorial service at St Pancras parish church on 16 September.

HUGH CLEGG, *rev.* P. W. J. BARTRIP

**Sources** A. Cox, *Among the doctors* (1950) · *BMJ* (4 Sept 1954), 597–9 · *BMJ* (11 Sept 1954), 648–9 · *BMJ* (18 Sept 1954), 706–7 · *The Lancet* (11 Sept 1954) · *The Times* (1 Sept 1954) · *WW* · *WWW* · E. M. Little, *History of the British Medical Association, 1832–1932* [1932] · *The Times* (2 May 1932) · *The Times* (18 July 1932) · *The Times* (20 July 1932) · *The Times* (25 July 1932) · *The Times* (30 Sept 1932) · 'Select committee on patent medicines', *Parl. papers* (1914), vol. 9, no. 414 · P. Vaughan, *Doctors' Commons: a short history of the British Medical Association* (1959) · 'The Health Service Bill', *BMJ* (6 April 1946), 541 · personal knowledge (1971)

**Archives** Bodl. Oxf., corresp. and papers relating to BMA campaign against health insurance · British Medical Association

**Likenesses** A. Cope, oils, 1932, British Medical Association House, Tavistock Square, London · photographs, British Medical Association House, Tavistock Square, London

**Wealth at death** £1206 2s. 7d.: probate, 22 Sept 1954, *CGPLA Eng. & Wales*

**Cox, Arthur Hawker** (1813–1903), manufacturing chemist and local politician, was born in the Haymarket, London, in November 1813, one of a family of ten children born to Edward Treslove Cox and his wife, Sarah, *née* Homersham. His father, a native of Northampton, was a cabinet-maker. Little is known of the family except that one brother, Edward Homersham Cox, became a successful barrister.

Arthur Cox was apprenticed as a chemist and druggist at the age of fifteen to his uncle, a Mr Perrin, in Northampton and afterwards worked as an assistant at Dinnefords in New Bond Street. The Apothecaries Act of 1815 had, *inter alia*, recognized the position of the chemist and druggist as a wholesale and retail supplier of medicines; there was no qualifying examination for the occupation, but a five-year apprenticeship was the norm. Cox's surviving notebook, perhaps dating from his apprenticeship years, indicates a wide range of remedies supplied, including recipes not only for cough linctus and purgatives but also for sheep wash, cold cream, mushroom ketchup, and furniture paste. Family tradition has it that it was during his apprenticeship that he became interested in the development of a coating for pills to disguise the unpleasant taste of the ingredients, but it was not until 1854 that he sought and was granted patent protection for his tasteless, non-metallic coating for pills. The success of the coating provided the basis for his expansion into manufacturing.

On 21 October 1837 Cox married Mary Anne Strudwick; the couple had a son and four daughters. In 1839 they left London for Brighton where, in June that year, Cox opened his own shop at 29 Ship Street. Despite the demands of business and family, Cox soon began to participate in local politics. In the early 1840s he campaigned, as the honorary secretary of the Sussex branch, for the Anti-Corn Law League. A lifelong supporter of the Liberal Party, he was involved in the fight for the incorporation of Brighton. He was elected as one of the first councillors in 1854 and made an alderman in 1859; he remained so for more than forty years, serving three terms as mayor, in 1869, in 1882, and in 1883. The many civic events over which he presided included the opening, in August 1883, of Magnus Volk's pioneering Brighton and Rottingdean seashore electric tramroad.

Cox's business continued to grow as an increasing and more affluent population demanded and could afford medication. In 1871 he split the business, handing over the shop, now at 32 Ship Street, to his son, Homersham Edward; the latter, more dedicated to sailing—also his father's hobby—than to pharmacy, ran it unenthusiastically until the 1880s. Cox senior, although approaching sixty, moved the manufacturing business to St Martin's Place. He bought a house backing on to the factory premises and, on 13 January 1870, after the death of his first wife, he married Elizabeth Frances Claxton (d. 1897); the marriage produced three sons and four daughters. In the late 1880s and early 1890s the two eldest sons of his second marriage took over management of the factory.

Cox died on 6 April 1903 at 35 Wellington Road, Brighton, and was buried in Brighton cemetery three days later. The kindly disposition and engaging personality of his public persona concealed, as with so many of his class and time, an autocrat within his family. His daughter Eliza had married against his wishes and was cut out of his will, which, more significantly, provided for the conversion of his business into a private company to be run by his sons and provide for his unmarried daughters. The pharmaceutical manufacturing business of A. H. Cox & Co. Ltd continued to be largely owned and managed by the three succeeding generations of the Cox family until the 1970s. In 1978 the company moved from Brighton to a new factory in Barnstaple, Devon, and in 1984 it was bought by Hoechst UK, the British subsidiary of the German chemicals and pharmaceuticals group.                  JUDY SLINN

**Sources** J. A. Slinn, *Pills and pharmaceuticals: A. H. Cox & Co. Ltd, 1839–1989* (privately printed, 1989) · *Brighton Herald* (11 April 1903) · 'The revolutions of a pill', *Chemist and Druggist* (27 July 1901), 154–6 · *CGPLA Eng. & Wales* (1903) · *The Times* (8 April 1903)

**Likenesses** oils, A. H. Cox & Co. Ltd, Whidden Valley, Barnstaple, Devon

**Wealth at death** £17,562 5s. 4d.: probate, 30 June 1903, *CGPLA Eng. & Wales*

**Cox** [Coxe], **Benjamin** (*bap.* 1595, *d.* in or after 1663?), Baptist preacher, was baptized at Benson, Oxfordshire, on 13 April 1595, the son of William Cox, a clergyman, and his wife, probably Elizabeth Younge. He matriculated from Christ Church, Oxford, on 29 April 1609, aged fourteen, graduated BA from Broadgates Hall on 17 June 1613, and proceeded MA on 30 June 1617. The following year he was a lecturer at All Hallows-the-Great in London, and preached against the Book of Sports at Paul's Cross. He was probably the Benjamin Coxe who married Margaret Garrett at the parish church of High Bickington, Devon, on 6 January 1619: James Cox, who as a son of Benjamin, clergyman of Crediton, matriculated at Oxford in July 1638 aged seventeen, was almost certainly their son. In 1620 Cox was engaged as a preacher 8 miles to the north of Barnstaple, on terms that suggest he lived some distance away. In 1625 he was appointed for three years to deliver a weekly lecture in the parish church, but he seems to have resigned when in 1627 he accepted the perpetual curacy of Sampford Peverill near Crediton. There he was said to be conformable, and according to Bishop Joseph Hall later, 'one of the first in my diocese who removed his table in an altarly situation' (*CSP dom.*, *1639–40*, 20). About September 1639, however, he preached against divine-right episcopacy, an uncomfortably topical subject given the conflict with the Scots. Hall, a man of moderate Calvinist sympathies, was unable to persuade Cox to recant his views, and felt obliged to report the matter to Archbishop Laud. The archbishop recorded that Cox eventually 'made a handsome retractation voluntarily of himself, and satisfied the people', although local histories claim that he was deprived of his living.

It is certain that in 1640 Cox returned to Barnstaple, where he developed new disagreements with the established church, notably over admission to holy communion. Cox published his concerns in *A Thesis or Position Concerning the Administring and Receiving of the Lord's Supper* (1642), signed from Barnstaple on 6 April 1642. By this time he had arrived at semi-separatist views: in a letter of 5 July the vicar, Martin Blake, referred to his 'disciples' and sermons before 'whole congregations' (Blake, preface), and stressed the full separatist logic of his opponent's position. Cox's views then rapidly evolved in that direction. It is possible that he was already in touch with the Baptists and had rejected infant baptism. He also came to reject the high Calvinist theology for which he had once been noted. He was impressed by *A Treatise of Particular Predestination* (1642) by the Baptist soap-boiler Thomas Lambe, which, while accepting the concept of particular election, laid heavy stress on the proposition that Christ had died for all men. Probably in the winter of 1642–3 Cox arrived in London, where he sought out Lambe and joined his congregation at Bell Alley. In 1643 he travelled as an emissary to the parliamentarian stronghold of Coventry, where the pre-war Baptist congregation seems to have gained new recruits in both the town and the garrison. Richard Baxter recorded that he had been 'sent from London to confirm them' (Baxter, *Scripture*, preface). The two men met and disputed at Coventry, both verbally and in writing, and Cox, his famous opponent conceded, was 'no contemptible scholar' (Baxter, *Reliquiae*, 46). The military authorities were unhappy at Cox's uncompromising speeches against the national ministry, and required him to leave. But he soon returned, as outspoken as ever, and by early July was imprisoned. At Coventry about this time he encountered the view that men enjoyed the free will to accept or reject sin and salvation, and rejected it in *Some Mistaken Scriptures* (issued later, in 1646).

On release Cox returned to London, and shared his theological doubts with others in the congregation. When Lambe set down propositions setting out the fundamentals of his stance, Cox replied in a printed work which appears not to have survived. Lambe's rejoinder, *Christ Crucified*, angrily charged Cox with 'withdrawing from the church of God' and 'raising a faction both in city and country' (Lambe, sigs. A2r–A3v). Some time in 1645 Cox joined one of the seven London Calvinistic (Particular) Baptist churches which had published the previous October a joint confession of faith. As a mature, ordained clergyman and Oxford MA, with some reputation as a scholar, Cox was quickly drawn into the leadership. In December 1645, together with William Kiffin and Hanserd Knollys, he signed a declaration about a dispute on infant baptism, which had originated as a private meeting in the house of Edmund Calamy, but which the authorities had banned when the organizers sought to reconvene in an open forum. When in January 1646 the London churches reissued their confession in a new edition, Cox signed on behalf of a congregation led by himself and its probable founder, Thomas Kilcop, and he helped Samuel Richardson to distribute copies to members of parliament. In May there appeared *God's Ordinance*, by another prominent Calvinistic Baptist, John Spilsbury; Cox co-wrote the second part, in which are rebutted the tenets of the General Baptists. The confession had also aroused controversy, and Cox was persuaded to write *An Appendix to a Confession of Faith*, issued in November, which expounded its meaning at greater length and urged a communion founded on particular election, closed to the unbaptized.

It has been suggested that Cox was in Barnstaple in 1647 or, alternatively, was active at Bedford, where in 1648 he applied for ordination as a preacher. On 4 September some London presbyterians (who knew him) demanded that the Bedford authorities (who evidently did not) be informed by letter of the 'many heterodox tenents held by Mr Benjamin Coxe' (Surman, 58). On 19 October the London Provincial Assembly agreed, over the protest of Cornelius Burgess, that 'he shall have his approbation when he brings his certificate of [having] taken the covenant' (Mitchell and Struthers, 533). It was almost certainly he

who, at St Paul's Church, Bedford, on 22 March 1649, baptized his son Nehemiah, presumably as a means to confirm his orthodoxy, though there is no evidence of his having taken up a salaried lectureship in the town. It seems possible that he was associated in this period with Edward Harrison, formerly vicar of Kensworth, Bedfordshire, who had recently become a Baptist. Cox next appears on 16–17 March 1653 as a representative of the church of Kensworth at the fourth general meeting, held at Tetsworth, of the Abingdon association of Particular Baptist churches.

At the tenth general meeting on 26–7 December 1654 Cox, now resident at Dunstable, 2 miles from Kensworth, and thus well placed geographically, was chosen, together with John Pendarves (d. 1656), to assist in the foundation of a new association in the west midlands (1655), to whose churches the agreement drafted by the Abingdon associates was sent as a model. Cox attended several subsequent midlands meetings, certainly with the knowledge and approval of the London leaders. At the association meeting at Moreton in Marsh on 8 April 1658 Cox, who had been delegated to deal with the matter, attacked a Baptist minister, Richard Harrison, for accepting 'tythes once belonging by man's antichristian laws to the dean and chapter' of Hereford, and for defending the practice, which amounted to a 'covenanted hire … to preach in the parish churches so called in Herefordshire'; the state salaries paid to Baptist regimental chaplains were irrelevant to the case (White, *Records*, 44, 50). In early 1658 Kensworth and three Hertfordshire churches, thus far Abingdon affiliates, founded a new association; the following March, when they gathered at Dunstable, probably at Cox's house, they had been joined by representatives from several congregations; he was undoubtedly the leading figure in the new association. He also continued to attend Abingdon meetings until 1660.

After the Restoration Cox may have been engaged by Sir John Hartopp (1637–1722), who recorded hearing twenty-eight sermons by a 'Mr Cox' between 22 April and 30 December 1660. In the Baptists' statement against Venner published on 28 January 1661, a 'John Cox' (first name almost certainly misprinted) appears alongside Edward Harrison. This may suggest that he had returned to the London church founded by Kilcop, of which Harrison had later become pastor, and which met at Petty France, near Moorfields. He was present on 15 June 1662, when the meeting-house was raided by soldiers, and one Cox was reported in 1663, by a government agent, to be a preacher in Thames Street, and to be associated with Samuel Tull, of Petty France. But there is no information as to his further activities, or his death.

Cox's son Nehemiah seems to have become a shoemaker. In 1669, during John Bunyan's imprisonment, Nehemiah Cox joined his congregation. On 15 May 1670, he was preaching before the church in the house of John Fenne when the meeting was raided. For outspokenly criticizing the Church of England, Cox was sent to join Bunyan in prison. In December 1671 he was called to the ministry by the Bedford congregation, and the following year his name appeared on an application for a licence for a meeting-place at Maulden, just south of the town. A request to be granted his services by the Hitchin church in 1673 seems to have given rise to resentment, and the following year, having admitted some responsibility in the matter, Cox resigned. On 21 September 1675 Nehemiah was ordained as joint pastor with William Collins of his father's former congregation at Petty France. Soon he was persuaded by the senior London leaders to publish a refutation, *Vindiciae veritatis* (1677), of the views of the dissident west-country Baptist Thomas Collier. Towards the end of the decade, however, Cox enrolled at the university of Utrecht, from where he graduated MD on 5 August 1684 on the basis of a thesis 'de arthritide' (Innes Smith, 55). On 5 July 1686 as a widower of St Mildred's Bread Street, London, and doctor of physick, he was licensed to marry Margaret Smith, widow, of Newington Green, Middlesex, aged thirty-three, the daughter of Edmond Portman, a London gentleman, at the church of St Giles Cripplegate, London; they had one son, Edmund, who died on 11 August 1688. Nehemiah Cox lived long enough to gain admission (22 December 1687) to the Royal College of Physicians. He died on 5 May 1689 and was buried at Bunhill Fields.                                STEPHEN WRIGHT

Sources  T. Lambe, *Christ crucified: a propitiation for the sins of all men* (1646) • Foster, *Alum. Oxon.* • J. Chanter, *Martin Blake* • B. R. White, ed., *Association records of the Particular Baptists of England, Wales and Ireland to 1660* (1971–4) • J. R. Chanter and T. Wainwright, eds., *Reprint of Barnstaple records*, 2 vols. (1900) • Wood, *Ath. Oxon.*, new edn • R. Baxter, *Plain scripture proof of infants church-membership and baptism* (1651) • W. T. Whitley, 'Benjamin Coxe', *Baptist Quarterly*, 6 (1932), 50–59 • M. Blake, *The great question … discourse of Mr. B. Coxe* [1645] • B. R. White, 'The organisation of the Particular Baptists, 1644–1660', *Journal of Ecclesiastical History*, 17 (1966), 209–26 • *Calendar of the correspondence of Richard Baxter*, ed. N. H. Keeble and G. F. Nuttall, 2 vols. (1991) • *Reliquiae Baxterianae, or, Mr Richard Baxter's narrative of the most memorable passages of his life and times*, ed. M. Sylvester, 1 vol. in 3 pts (1696) • A. Mitchell and J. Struthers, eds., *Minutes of the Westminster Assembly* (1874) • *CSP dom.*, 1639–40 • C. E. Surman, ed., *The register-booke of the fourth classis in the province of London, 1646–59*, 2 vols. in 1, Harleian Society, 82–3 (1953) • *The works of the most reverend father in God, William Laud*, 5, ed. J. Bliss (1853) • J. Ivimey, *A history of the English Baptists*, 4 vols. (1811–30), vol. 1 • B. Coxe, H. Knollys, and W. Kiffen, *A declaration concerning the public dispute which should have been in the publike meetng house of Aldermanbury, 3rd Dec 1645* [1645] • R. L. Greaves, *John Bunyan and English nonconformity* (1992) • R. Innes Smith, *Students of medicine at Leiden* (1932) • *Bunhill Fields burial ground: proceedings in reference to its preservation* (1867) • G. J. Armytage, ed., *Allegations for marriage licences issued by the vicar-general of the archbishop of Canterbury, July 1679 to June 1687*, Harleian Society, 30 (1890) • *IGI* [parish records of St Paul, Bedford] • Munk, *Roll* • R. Hayden, ed., *The records of a church in Christ in Bristol, 1640–1687*, Bristol RS, 27 (1974)

**Cox, Sir Christopher William Machell** (1899–1982), educationist, was born on 17 November 1899 at Hastings, Sussex, the eldest of three sons of Arthur Henry Machell Cox (1870–1947), a schoolmaster and later headmaster of Mount House School, Plymouth, and his wife, Dorothy Alice Wimbush (1876–1947). He was educated at Clifton College from 1913 to 1918, and, after a brief period in 1918 as a second lieutenant in the Royal Engineers, at Balliol College, Oxford, from 1919 to 1923, where he took firsts in classical moderations (1920) and *literae humaniores* (1923).

Sir Christopher William Machell Cox (1899–1982), by Lafayette, 1928

Then followed postgraduate research, including fieldwork in Turkey, which resulted eventually in his only major publication, *Monumenta Asiae Minoris antiqua*, volume 5 (with Archibald Cameron), in 1937. He was elected to a university Craven fellowship and to a senior demyship at Magdalen College in 1924. In 1926 he was elected a fellow and tutor of New College, Oxford, to teach ancient Greek history, thus initiating a close association with the college that lasted until his death.

Cox might well have lived out the rest of his life as a popular but essentially obscure don at Oxford had it not been for an early interest in the African colonies, stimulated by a lifelong friendship with C. H. Baynes, his contemporary at Balliol, and his decision to return overland after a visit to South Africa in 1929 as a member of the delegation of the British Association for the Advancement of Science. He visited Khartoum, where he met, and made many friendships with, local educators, and this led, in 1937, to a pressing but quite unforeseen invitation to spend two years in Sudan as director of education and principal of Gordon College. He leapt at the idea and so embarked on what was to prove to be the start of a second career and the two happiest years of his life. He made a lasting impression, especially for the assistance he rendered to Lord De La Warr's educational commission, which visited east Africa in 1937 to report on the future of higher education. In 1938 he declined the principalship of Makerere College in Uganda, and soon after his return to Oxford in 1939 he also decided not to accept the offer of the headship of Achimota College in the Gold Coast.

The decisive turning point in Cox's career came towards the end of 1939, when, as a consequence of Malcolm MacDonald's determination as colonial secretary to initiate a major shake-up in colonial policy in general, he was appointed to the newly created post of educational adviser to the Colonial Office. The appointment of an adviser was originally recommended by Lord Hailey, initially for three years or until the end of the war, but Cox was destined to serve in the post for thirty years and become a legend in his own lifetime.

No one, least of all Cox, could have foreseen the key role he was to assume in the post-war period as the colonial empire was dismantled and colonial education was transformed. His role as an adviser placed him in a unique position. He was not an administrator in the conventional sense, nor did he direct a Colonial Office department of education. Nevertheless, he rapidly established himself as perhaps the key figure in determining colonial education policy. He played a decisive behind-the-scenes role in the creation of the Asquith commission (1943), which was set up to examine how best to provide for the ever-increasing need for university education in the colonies. The commission addressed such questions as whether new universities should be established in the colonies, and, if so, where and when, and what form they should take, as well as whether they should be based on the Oxbridge model or be more in keeping with the local environment and future skilled manpower needs. Evidence from Cox, who was probably the most influential witness interviewed by the commission, was crucial in shaping the final report, which strongly endorsed the establishment of new universities, initially as at Ibadan, on the Oxbridge model.

Cox masterminded the expansion of colonial education at all levels in the immediate post-war years. Over time, partly through regular overseas travel and also through the team of very able assistant educational advisers that he assembled in Whitehall, he built up a remarkable network of contacts which enabled him to keep abreast of developments and problems even in the most remote corners of the empire. At home he knew everyone that mattered in the university world and in education generally. He was particularly adept at working behind the scenes to achieve successful outcomes, as illustrated by his determination to defeat a short-sighted Conservative Party move to establish a uniform colonial education policy in the late 1940s. Instead, he orchestrated the highly successful Cambridge education conference of 1952.

The high status accorded to the advisory committee on education in the colonies, especially just after the war, was largely attributable to Cox's masterly handling of its membership and ongoing activities. The Colonial Development and Welfare Acts of 1940 and 1945 ushered in a new era of planned social and economic development and the advisory committee was entrusted with the task of overseeing the educational components of numerous ten-year development plans. Cox likewise figured prominently in rebuilding the colonial education service after the deprivations of the war years. He was also a confidant and close friend of Arthur Creech Jones, the colonial secretary, and Sir Andrew Cohen, head of the Africa section at the Colonial Office, and consequently a party to the key in-house discussions which led to a major reshaping of colonial policy after 1945.

Throughout his life Cox was one of the most garrulous and untidy of men, although, ironically, he shied away from public speaking whenever possible. He never married, his handwriting was frequently illegible, he never threw anything away, and he suffered recurrent and often debilitating bouts of depression, or 'the fumes' as he called it, but he also loved watching cricket (he was a member of the MCC), dining at the Athenaeum, and

spending his weekends at New College. Preparations for his many overseas trips were a regular ordeal for his immediate staff. His departure for west Africa in 1947 was recorded for posterity by one of his Whitehall colleagues, who wrote that, although he was not associated with the preparations made by Stanley when he visited Africa or when Cook toured the Pacific, he was quite sure that their preparations were as those for a half-day excursion to Brighton when compared with Cox's. Cox had none of the routine qualities of a senior civil servant and probably no bureaucracy in the world save Britain could have deployed him to such effect, much less tolerated him. Colin Legum, the noted African correspondent, once described him as a large restless man for whom neatly docketed facts, tidy formulas, files, routine, and formal administrative work mattered as little as gnats to elephants. He had, said Legum, a bulging mind crammed with ideas that bubbled over and scattered themselves profusely in a way that made ordinary conversation dull and unprofitable (PRO, CO 1045/1404).

Cox's services to colonial education were duly recognized when he was appointed CMG in 1944, KCMG in 1950, and GCMG in 1970. He also received numerous honorary degrees from 'new' Commonwealth universities, but perhaps the academic distinction that pleased him most was the degree of DCL that Oxford conferred on him in 1965. Cox worked as educational adviser to the Colonial Office for twenty-one years (1940–61) before being transferred to the newly created department of technical co-operation (1961–4), and finally to the Ministry of Overseas Development (1964–70). When he did eventually retire, at the age of seventy-one, it was jokingly rumoured in the corridors of Whitehall that the government had been considering the passage of an act of parliament to remove him. He lived out his retirement at New College as a much respected honorary fellow, and died in an Oxford hospital on 6 July 1982; his ashes were interred in New College.

CLIVE WHITEHEAD

**Sources** DNB · PRO, CO 1045/1476, CO 1045/1404 · New College, Oxford, Cox MSS · *New College Record* (1982) · C. Whitehead, 'Sir Christopher Cox: an imperial patrician of a different kind', *Journal of Educational Administration and History*, 21 (1989) · WW

**Archives** New College, Oxford, academic corresp. and files · PRO, papers, CO 1045 · U. Durham L., corresp. and papers relating to education in the Sudan | Bodl. RH, corresp. with Margery Perham

**Likenesses** Lafayette, photograph, 1928, NPG [see illus.] · M. Noakes, drawing, 1972, New College, Oxford

**Wealth at death** £155,676: probate, 19 Oct 1982, CGPLA Eng. & Wales

**Cox, Daniel** (d. 1750?), physician, proceeded MD at St Andrews on 8 November 1742. He was admitted as a licentiate of the Royal College of Physicians, London, on 26 June 1749 and elected physician to the Middlesex Hospital on 16 October 1746. He resigned from the hospital on 23 May 1749. He wrote *Observations on the Epidemic Fever of 1741, … with Remarks on the Use of Cortex*, published anonymously in 1741; *with New Cases, and on the Benefit of the Cool Method* (1742); third edition, *with … the Benefit of Bleeding and Purging* (1742). Cox is said by Munk to have died in January

1750; if so, he cannot have written, as Munk says, *An Appeal to the Public on Behalf of Elizabeth Canning* (1753), the introduction to Lorenz Heister's *Medical, Chirurgical and Anatomical Cases* (1755), *A Letter from a Physician to a Friend in the Country on the Subject of Inoculation* (1756), nor *Observations on the Intermittent Pulse* (1758). Cox was wrongly thought to have written the *Family Medical Compendium*, an edition of which was published in 1808 under his name. The author proved to be a different D. Cox, a chemist and druggist of Gloucester, who had rewritten a much earlier work.

WILLIAM HUNT, *rev.* CLAIRE L. NUTT

**Sources** Munk, *Roll* · D. Cox, *New medical compendium* (1808) · S. C. Lawrence, *Charitable knowledge: hospital pupils and practitioners in eighteenth-century London* (1996)

**Cox, David** (1783–1859), landscape painter, was born on 29 April 1783 at Heath Mill Lane in Deritend, on the industrial edge of Birmingham. A drawing by Samuel Lines (Birmingham Museums and Art Gallery) depicts the birthplace as a humble timber-framed cottage, with an adjoining outhouse that may have served as his father Joseph's workshop. Joseph Cox (*d.* 1831) was a blacksmith and whitesmith; his origins remain obscure: it is known only that he died on 26 June 1831, aged between sixty-four and sixty-eight, and was buried at Aston parish church, Birmingham. David Cox's mother, Frances (1744–1811), also buried at Aston, was the seventh of the fourteen children of Aris Walford, a farmer and miller of Small Heath, a rural suburb of Birmingham. According to Cox's first biographer, 'she had had a better education than his father, and was a woman of superior intelligence and force of character' (Solly, 2). William Hall's biography states that following her death in 1811, Joseph Cox married again, but no records have been discovered. David had an elder sister, Mary Ann, born in 1781, who married Andrew Ward, a Manchester organist and music teacher; they had no children.

**Early life in Birmingham and London, to 1814** Little reliable information survives about Cox's early life, the anecdotal history being best refined in Nathaniel Neal Solly's *Memoir of the Life of David Cox* (1873), a good biography which has the disadvantage of having been written by one who apparently never met his subject. The young David is said to have attended a basic local day school, and to have first shown talent as an artist—while recuperating from a broken leg—by painting paper kites with a box of colours provided by a cousin, identified by Solly as probably the son of John Allport, a 'painter in general' of Bull Street, Birmingham.

Unsuited to work in his father's smithy, Cox was sent for tuition under the town's only professional drawing-master, Joseph Barber (1757–1811), before entering into apprenticeship, about 1798, with an unsuccessful miniature painter named Fieldler (whose hanged body Cox is supposed to have discovered). Perhaps again through Allport, Cox then obtained work as a scene painter at the Theatre Royal, Birmingham, where he met one of the London masters of that business, Joseph de Maria, and the actor–manager William Macready (the elder). He was

David Cox (1783–1859), by Sir John Watson-Gordon, 1855

engaged by Macready for provincial tours, where 'he enacted the role of clown in a small country town' (Solly, 10); he also painted miniature scenery for the manager's young son, later the celebrated actor William Charles Macready. Following an introduction to the circus proprietor Philip Astley, and the offer of a job as scene painter in his theatre at Lambeth, Cox left Birmingham for London in 1804.

Cox found work at the Surrey Theatre, but retained contact with Birmingham, where the artists' colourman Allen Everitt paid him for lessons for his son Edward. Cox also renewed his friendship with Joseph Barber's son Charles, who visited him in London; they toured north Wales together in 1805 and 1806. In travelling to Wales, Cox may have been inspired by John Varley, a founder member of the Society of Painters in Water Colours. Some of his earliest known works show Varley's influence, especially the small views of London, including scenes along the Thames, that he sold to dealers such as Palser and Simpson. Cox's first exhibits at the Royal Academy in 1805 signalled his decision to become a professional watercolourist. Among his most ambitious early works was a large watercolour of 1807, *In Windsor Park* (V&A), which has echoes of classical painters such as Gaspard Poussin, whose work Cox is known to have copied. Varley unselfishly helped Cox to obtain pupils, including many of rank, among them Lady Sophia Cecil, Lady Exeter, and Henry Windsor, the future eighth earl of Plymouth. His standing as a drawing-master was reinforced by the publication of a number of successful manuals, beginning with *Ackermann's New Drawing Book in Light and Shadow* in 1809:

although not credited to Cox, its range of subjects—Birmingham, Wales, and London—strongly suggests that he supplied the images, if not the text. This was soon followed by *A Series of Progressive Lessons Intended to Elucidate the Art of Painting in Water Colours*, a hugely popular step-by-step drawing manual which was first published in 1811, and reached its ninth edition in 1845. *A Treatise on Landscape Painting and Effect in Water Colours* (1813–14, reissued 1840) cemented Cox's reputation, and was followed by *The Young Artist's Companion* (1819–20, revised 1825). Among the most influential of all drawing books, they had the unforeseen consequence of training a whole generation of amateurs to imitate his style.

In 1808 Cox married Mary Agg (1770/71–1845), the daughter of his first landlady at 16 Bridge Row, Lambeth; they moved into a cottage on the edge of Dulwich Common, where their only child, also named David, was born on 9 July 1809. Cox joined the group known as the Associated Artists in Water Colours, becoming its president in 1810 but also having to bear some of its debts when it collapsed in 1812. The large watercolour *Old Westminster* of 1811 (Laing Art Gallery, Newcastle upon Tyne) may have been shown at one of their last exhibitions. Happily, the experience did not prevent his being elected an associate of the Society of Painters in Water Colours in the same year, and a member in 1813. Apart from 1815 and 1817 Cox was to exhibit with the society every year—sometimes as many as forty pictures—until his death, totalling some 849 works; only Copley Fielding, Henry Gastineau, and William Collingwood Smith (who all passed the thousand mark) showed more. In 1812, responding to a short-lived initiative by the society to promote the exhibition of oil paintings alongside watercolours, Cox took the family to Hastings, and made some striking experiments in oil, working with William Havell. A few of these survive (mostly in the Birmingham Museums and Art Gallery's collection), but they do not seem to have been exhibited, and Cox was not to return to the medium for nearly thirty years.

**Hereford, 1814–1827** Having previously managed to avoid conscription into the militia, Cox accepted a post as drawing-master at the military college at Farnham in 1813 (with the honorary title of captain). Finding the work irksome, he decided to leave London, answering an advertisement in *The Times* for an appointment as drawing-master to a girls' school in Hereford, run by a Miss Croucher in the Gate House, Widemarsh Street: he taught here until 1819. The handsome salary of £100 a year required only two days' attendance a week, leaving the rest of his time free to paint, while retaining the opportunity of additional private teaching; he also taught at Hereford grammar school from 1815. In Hereford he found his best pupil, Joseph Murray Ince. With the help of an advance of £40 from Lady Arden, one of his London pupils, he settled his family in a cottage at Lower Lyde late in 1814, before moving to George Cottage, All Saints, Hereford, in the following spring. They moved to another cottage in nearby Parry's Lane in 1817, and Cox finally built a new home, Ash Tree House, in 1824.

The Hereford years witnessed Cox's artistic maturity. His exhibits at the Society of Painters in Water Colours reflect the sketching trips he was able to make in Herefordshire, Wales, and the midlands. In the 1820s he responded to the society's call for 'premium' pictures—large watercolours to rival the Royal Academy's historical and landscape oils—with annual *tours de force*, beginning with *George IV Embarking for Scotland from Greenwich* (1823; Walker Art Gallery, Liverpool) and including *Carthage—Aeneas and Achates* (1825; Birmingham Museums and Art Gallery) and *Pirates' Isle*, inspired by Byron (1826; priv. coll.). These attempts to match the scale and ambition of the paintings of J. M. W. Turner and John Martin gained him an increased reputation as well as important patrons such as the wine merchant and collector John Allnutt. Cox knew Turner's work, having been a subscriber to the *Liber Studiorum*, and followed his example by taking commissions for engravings: he had already contributed to John Hassell's collection of aquatints *Aqua pictura* (1813–18) and produced a set of *Six Views of the City of Bath* (1820) before drawing subjects for *The Hereford Guide* (1827, wood-engravings by Hugh Hughes) and *Graphic Illustrations of Warwickshire* (1829, engravings by William Radclyffe), alongside J. D. Harding and Peter DeWint. Cox made his first trip to the continent in 1826, taking his son, David, on a trip to Belgium with his brother-in-law, a tour extended with friends into Holland.

**Second period in London, 1827–1841** In 1827 Cox brought his family back to London, settling at 9 Foxley Road, in the largely rural suburb of Kennington. The art market had picked up, and there was plenty of teaching to supplement the sale of exhibition watercolours. He also began to exhibit with the revived Birmingham Society of Artists in 1829. Although Cox was the epitome of the insular Englishman—one story has him helping a friend out by drawing an egg rather than attempt the word in French—two further trips to the continent took place. In 1829 an intended six-week tour of northern France began at Calais, where he visited Louis Francia (1772–1839), the hospitable pupil of Thomas Girtin and friend of Richard Parkes Bonington, and embraced Amiens, Beauvais, and Rouen, mostly on foot. Arriving in Paris, where he was welcomed by the engraver John Pye, Cox suffered a sprained ankle, which prevented anything more than painting views of the capital from a carriage—but he produced sparkling on-the-spot studies which have become some of his most admired works (for example *Near the Pont d'Arcole, Paris*; Tate collection). A tour in 1832, Cox's last abroad, was confined to Calais, Dieppe, and Boulogne, where he witnessed a review in honour of Louis-Philippe, but it yielded material for working up studio watercolours for many years: his last *Calais Pier* was exhibited at the Society of Painters in Water Colours in 1837. The most important watercolour to derive from these tours was *The Louvre and Tuileries, Paris* (1838; V&A).

More to Cox's liking was the north of England, which he first visited in 1830. He often used Haddon Hall, Derbyshire, the abandoned seat of the Manners family, as a setting for romantic costume subjects, in the manner of

Joseph Nash's *Mansions of England in the Olden Time* (1839). Cox also painted complementary scenes of Bolsover Castle, Chatsworth, and Hardwick Hall: a large watercolour, *The Portrait Gallery, Hardwick Hall* (priv. coll.), was probably the work exhibited at the Society of Painters in Water Colours in 1840. The great sweep of Morecambe Bay, which Cox first saw in 1834 in the company of the stockbroker and art collector William Stone Ellis, became a favourite place and spawned many images of the treacherous passage across the sands, including *Ulverston Sands* (1836; Birmingham Museums and Art Gallery) and *Lancaster Sands* (1844; Harris Museum and Art Gallery, Preston). In compiling the majority of illustrations (thirty-four in all) for Thomas Roscoe's *Wanderings and Excursions in North Wales* (1836) and *South Wales* (1837), engraved by his old Birmingham friend William Radclyffe, Cox was given the opportunity to travel the length and breadth of the principality. The original watercolours for these—such as *Rhaiadr Cwm* (BM) and *Vale of Festiniog* (AM Oxf.)—are no less impressive than Turner's comparable work of this type and date. Cox also painted vignettes for the annual gift books, including *The Keepsake* (1841–3) and *Heath's Book of Beauty* (1840–45), a type of work seamlessly continued by his son, David.

By now established as one of the most accomplished and successful watercolourists of his generation, Cox continued to look for challenges in the development of his technique. In 1836 he accidentally came across a heavy, fibrous wrapping paper which he realized was a perfect support for looser, more experimental work. Finding that it came from Dundee, he ordered a ream: on arrival, its weight (and cost of carriage) took him aback, but in later years he regretted not having bought more of this 'Scotch' paper, which became something of a hallmark. Asked how he coped with its very visible lumps of impurity, he is said to have replied, 'Oh, I just put wings to them, and then they fly away as birds' (Solly, 81). After his death, a proprietary 'Cox' paper, of a rather sanitized kind, was produced by Dixon & Co. of Liverpool.

In 1839 Cox was introduced, by their mutual artist friend George Fripp, to the gifted young painter William James Müller. Cox had revived thoughts of painting in oils, and took lessons from the younger man. Finding the medium to his liking, he decided to leave London; he wrote in 1840 to his friend William Roberts that 'I am making preparations to sketch in oil, and also to paint, and it is my intention to spend most of my time in Birmingham for the purpose of practice' (Solly, 91). It was sensible to do this out of the public eye, as it was generally regarded as impossible to succeed in both mediums (with the notable exception of Turner). Indeed no member of the Old Watercolour Society or Royal Academy was allowed to join the other body—and such experimentation could even have damaged Cox's reputation.

**Return to Birmingham and last years in Harborne, 1841–1859**
Leaving his son, David, now also a professional painter, to maintain the teaching practice in London, Cox and his wife (together with their servant Ann Fowler) moved to Birmingham in the summer of 1841: Greenfield House, Harborne, surrounded by fields and more than 2 miles from the industrial centre, would be their final home. Cox took pleasure in its garden, which boasted 'a large willow-bush, of which [he] was immensely proud, having been originally a cutting from *the* willow which grew over Napoleon's tomb at St Helena' (Solly, 108).

Cox visited Wales with his son in 1842, but fell ill in the following year, recuperating with his sister, then living at Sale. The volume of works he exhibited at the Society of Painters in Water Colours remained constant, but he worked in earnest in oils, even showing a few at the Society of British Artists (1841–2), the British Institution (1842–3), and the Royal Academy (1843–4). These achieved little success, however, and after the rejection of a painting at the British Institution in 1844, future sales of oils were mostly to collectors and friends in Birmingham, such as Roberts, Charles Birch (owner of nearby Metchley Abbey), and Edwin Bullock, of Hawthorn House, Handsworth. The extent of his work in oil painting is only now becoming clear: over 350 are known, ranging from jewel-like panels such as *Crossing the Sands* (1848; Birmingham Museums and Art Gallery) to large canvases like *The Vale of Clwyd* (versions of 1846; Towneley Hall Art Gallery, Burnley; and 1849; FM Cam.) and his masterpiece *Rhyl Sands* (1854–5; Birmingham Museums and Art Gallery). In the dual treatment of some of his best subjects, as in *The Skylark* and *Sun, Wind and Rain*, all of 1845 (Birmingham Museums and Art Gallery, except the oil of *Rain, Wind and Sunshine*; Aberdeen Art Gallery), it becomes evident that his energies were moving from watercolour to oil. 'Give me oil,' he wrote to his son on 2 April 1843; 'I only wish I had begun earlier in life; the pleasure in painting in oil is so very satisfactory' (Solly, 186).

From 1844 to 1856 Cox made annual trips to the small Caernarvonshire village of Betws-y-coed, probably on the recommendation of Müller, since the first visit in 1844 was with Müller's pupil Harry Johnson. Situated at the junction of three rivers—the Conwy, Lledr, and Llugwy—and surrounded by mountains, it afforded a perfect range of landscape for both oils and watercolours which were in general becoming less fixedly topographical than imaginative, though imbued with a strong sense of place. Cox initially stayed at The Swan inn, but in later years took to the Royal Oak Hotel, for which in 1847 he painted a new sign (still to be seen inside) depicting King Charles hiding in an oak. The landlord, Edward Roberts, became a friend, and it was on the death of a young girl from his family that Cox painted the evocative *Welsh Funeral* (oil, 1848; Birmingham Museums and Art Gallery). Views based on Betws and its surrounding villages, such as Llanrwst and Trefriw, appeared among all his annual exhibits at the Society of Painters in Water Colours and provided the setting for his celebrated late watercolour of a bull raging against the elements, now known as *The Challenge*, but shown in 1856 under the title *On the Moors, Near Betws-y-coed* (V&A). This typified his later preference for compositions in which the subject, as well as the vigour of handling, took precedence over the view. As he wrote to his son in 1853, responding to criticism of his work as 'too rough': 'They forget they are the work of the mind, which I consider very far before portraits of places' (Solly, 228). This was a rare comment from an artist not much given to theorizing, but serves as a reminder that Cox, like Turner and DeWint in his later work, was one of the few artists in the mid-century to regard the creation of a painting as more significant than the depiction of a view.

Mary Cox died on 23 November 1845, at the age of seventy-four, and was buried in Harborne churchyard. Her loss was a severe blow to Cox, but he resumed travel as usual from 1846, with friends such as Ellis, Roberts, and William Hall, to Derbyshire, Yorkshire (Bolton Abbey in that year), and Betws. Indeed, he became increasingly associated with the Welsh village: 'He was a sort of little king at Betws, was waited on, respected, and beloved by all who came into contact with him. Lord Willoughby might be owner of the soil, but David Cox was lord of the people's affections' (Hall, 94). The place eventually became so popular with artists, as a result of his work there, that Cox found himself obliged to transfer his lodgings across the road to a farmhouse belonging to the Royal Oak. This proved more convenient in the years after 1853, when he suffered a severe attack of bronchitis followed by a stroke, which left him weakened but still able to paint. His last visit was marked by an entry in the hotel visitors' book for 22 September 1856.

Although praised by Thackeray in *Sketches after English Landscape Painters* (1850), as his style broadened Cox's work began to receive adverse criticism. Initially commended by Ruskin (whose father was a patron) in the first volume of *Modern Painters* (1843), his work, together with Constable's, was later to be condemned in an Oxford Slade lecture as 'the mere blundering of clever peasants'. Cox was less intolerant, offering help to the young George Price Boyce at Betws-y-coed in 1851, and even joining the Hogarth Club, essentially a Pre-Raphaelite establishment, in 1858. In his 'Academy notes' for the mid-1850s, which covered the watercolour societies as well as the Royal Academy, Ruskin did grudgingly acknowledge Cox's standing as the last representative of the Society of Painters in Water Colours' formative years: of his 1857 exhibits Ruskin wrote that 'there is not any other landscape which comes near these works of David Cox in simplicity or seriousness' (J. Ruskin, 'Academy notes, 1857', *The Works of John Ruskin*, ed. E. T. Cook and A. Wedderburn, 39 vols., 1903–12, 14.123).

A group of Cox's friends and admirers (including Ruskin) raised a subscription for a portrait to be painted in 1855, and Cox travelled to Edinburgh to sit for Sir John Watson-Gordon: this provided the opportunity for his only visit to Scotland. The painting (Birmingham Museums and Art Gallery) was presented to Cox at Metchley Abbey on 19 November 1855 and shown at the Royal Academy in the following year; a mezzotint of it was made by Samuel Bellin. Gordon, who thought him one of his most successful subjects, remarked on a resemblance in the

head to Sir Walter Scott, and in the lower face to Lord Brougham.

Ironically, it was only in the last years of his life that Cox began to receive wider recognition. Late in 1858 a one-man exhibition was arranged by the painter Clarkson Stanfield and others at the Conversazione Society's rooms in Hampstead. This was followed in spring 1859 by a show of 169 works at the German Gallery, New Bond Street, eliciting fulsome reviews: 'We have sometimes heard people say they cannot understand Cox', the *Art Journal* mused:

> [and] pity that they could not inhale the sweet breath of his hayfields and purple heaths, nor see the rushing of his summer showers, nor repose with him under the shadows of his thick umbrageous elms and his graceful ash-trees. Not understand Cox!, why there is hardly a peasant in the land who goes to his daily toil by the hedgerows, or in the fields, who could not thoroughly *feel* the truth and beauty of his landscapes. (May 1859, 211)

Cox's health, including his eyesight, had deteriorated in 1857, and he made a will in August 1858. He would have taken pleasure in the notices of the German Gallery exhibition, which opened in April 1859, but he succumbed again to bronchitis at the beginning of June, and died at Greenfield House on the morning of 7 June, with his son at his bedside. He was buried beside Mary in Harborne churchyard, the funeral on 14 June being attended by a large crowd, including Frederick Tayler, president of the Society of Painters in Water Colours. A memorial stained-glass window by Hardman & Co. was placed in the east end of St Peter's Church, Harborne, in 1874.

The obituary in the *Birmingham Daily Post* of 8 June was the first of many which hailed Cox as 'the contemporary of Turner and Girtin, and one of that small band of artists who have made the English school of water-colour painters the finest in the world'. As the century progressed, his name was commonly linked with those of Turner and Constable, the popularity of his work being reflected in prices achieved on the art market. The 4500 guineas achieved by *The Vale of Clwyd* in 1892 marked the peak of interest in his work, and was a sum exceeded by only a few British paintings in the whole of the century.

A marble bust by the leading Birmingham sculptor Peter Hollins (Birmingham Museums and Art Gallery) was commissioned by subscribers in 1860, and shown in tribute at the Society of Painters in Water Colours exhibition of 1862. Retrospective exhibitions were held at the Burlington Fine Arts Club in 1873 (jointly with works by DeWint, from the collection of John Henderson), the Liverpool Art Club in 1875, and at Birmingham Museums and Art Gallery in 1890. This was the high point of his fame, which was to dwindle in the twentieth century, although recent reappraisal of Victorian art has seen Cox rightly restored to his position as one of the most loved and lasting of painters of the British landscape.

**David Cox junior** (1809–1885), watercolour painter, was born on 9 July 1809 at Dulwich, the only child of David and Mary Cox. He was educated at the grammar school in Hereford, where the family had moved in 1814, and was taught by his father to paint and draw. He first exhibited at the Royal Academy (*Cottage in Herefordshire*) in 1827, the year the family returned to London. In 1826 he accompanied his father on the trip to Belgium, and went with him again to France in 1829, but in later years he travelled alone or with other artists of his own age, such as Edward Webb, with whom he toured Scotland in 1834 and Wales in 1837 and 1840. In 1841 he took over his father's drawing-master practice after Cox senior returned to Birmingham.

Cox married Hannah Blunt (1809–1854) on 29 September 1836, and moved to 4 Cowley Terrace, London. Their four children were all girls: Frances (1837–1899), Hannah (1840–1909), Mary Catherine (1844–1868), and Emily (1846–1922), but after the suicide of their mother on 14 June 1854 they decided not to risk marriage and childbearing, 'fearing hereditary weakness' (note in family papers). Cox remarried on 25 April 1866, but without prospect of his second wife, Elizabeth (Eliza) Newton, producing a child, he adopted a cousin, Henry Gardner Hills, in 1870.

Cox was elected an associate member of the New Society of Painters in Water Colours in 1841, becoming a full member in 1845; he resigned in the following year, and was elected an associate of the Society of Painters in Water Colours in 1848, and exhibited annually almost up to his death, showing some 580 works. Inevitably his work carried many of the characteristics of his father's style, and some examples were easily slotted into later editions of his father's drawing books. In early years he specialized in costume pictures, such as *The Picnic* (1830; BM). In landscape he was more willing to adopt modern proprietary colours, and the use of a particular kind of acid green, especially in contrast with dashes of pink, became something of a hallmark. Careful not to trade on a confusion of the name, he was scrupulous about signing his work in full—David Cox Junior or Jun—and it is unfortunate that quantities of poor imitations and forgeries of his father's work have been unfairly attributed to him. There is no evidence that he experimented with oils.

David Cox junior was much interested in foreign travel, despite his father's reported comment to a friend suggesting a trip to Switzerland: 'Don't try to induce David to go on the Continent in search of scenery. Wales, Yorkshire, and Derbyshire have been good enough for me, and I quite believe they may yet do for him' (Solly, 72). He went to France in 1852, as far as Lyons, and in 1853 to Grenoble, while his most extensive tour took him in 1869 to Geneva and the Swiss Alps, briefly crossing into Italy. Almost every other summer saw trips further afield than his father, often to Wales, but also to Scotland (1855 and 1872), the Lake District (1875), and Devon (1877). One of his major large annual exhibits at the Old Watercolour Society, *In the Pass of Llanberis*, is now in the Victoria and Albert Museum.

By 1848 the family was living at 2 New Park Road, Brixton Hill; they moved in 1876 to Chester House, Mount Ephraim Road, Streatham, where Cox died on 6 December 1885; he was buried in the adjacent cemetery at Norwood. A studio sale was held at Christies on 14 and 15 April 1886, although many of his father's pictures, which he had

inherited, had been sold in the 1870s, chiefly in a sale at Christies on 3 and 5 May 1873. According to one obituarist, 'Art has lost in him a Landscape Painter of the good old school … The remark has been made that it was artistically his misfortune to have been the son of his father; yet none admired his work more than his father himself' (*Academy*, 12 Dec 1886, quoted in Cooke, 68).

STEPHEN WILDMAN

**Sources** N. N. Solly, *Memoir of the life of David Cox* (1873); facs. edn (1973) · *DNB* · S. Wildman, ed., *David Cox, 1783–1859* [introductory essays by R. Lockett and J. Murdoch; incl. bibliography; exhibition catalogue, Birmingham Museums and Art Gallery, 26 July – 14 Oct 1983, and V&A, 9 Nov 1983 – 8 Jan 1984] · S. Wilcox, 'David Cox: his development as a painter in watercolours', PhD diss., Yale U., 1984 [Ann Arbor, 1985; incl. bibliography] · W. Hall, *A biography of David Cox*, ed. J. T. Bunce (1881) [with additions by J. T. Bunce] · W. Wallis and A. B. Chamberlain, eds., *Catalogue of a special collection of works by David Cox* (1890) [exhibition catalogue, Birmingham City Museum and Art Gallery] · J. L. Roget, *A history of the 'Old Water-Colour' Society*, 2 vols. (1891) · B. S. Long, 'David Cox (1783–1859)', *Old Water-Colour Society's Club*, 10 (1932–3), 1–19 · F. G. Roe, *The life and art of David Cox* (1946) · T. Cox, *David Cox* (1947) · M. Rooker, 'Bibliography on David Cox, landscape painter, 1783–1859', DipLib diss., U. Lond., 1955 [typescript in Birmingham Reference Library] · F. C. Phillips, 'Rural solitude in the city: David Cox's early years in London, 1804–1815', *Country Life*, 174 (1983), 1318–19 · P. Lord, *Clarence Whaite and the Welsh art world: the Betws-y-Coed artists' colony, 1844–1914* (1998) · I. Cooke, 'David Cox Junior: an artist in the shadows', *Old Water-Colour Society's Club*, 60 (1985), 47–69 · *The Athenaeum* (12 Dec 1885) · *The Times* (14 Dec 1885) · private information (2004) · d. cert.
**Archives** Birm. CL, MSS · Birmingham Museums and Art Gallery, MSS · NL Wales, letters
**Likenesses** Cox, self-portrait?, oils, c.1820, Hereford City Museum and Art Gallery · W. Radclyffe, oils, 1830, NPG · H. Johnson, pencil and watercolour, 1845, Birmingham Museums and Art Gallery · J. Watson-Gordon, oils, 1855, Birmingham Museums and Art Gallery [see illus.] · pencil drawing, 1855, NPG · photograph, c.1855, Birmingham Museums and Art Gallery · W. Boxall, oils, 1856, NPG · P. Hollins, marble bust, 1860–62, Birmingham Museums and Art Gallery · photograph, after 1866 (David Cox), priv. coll. · W. H. Hunt, double portrait, pencil (with father, David Cox), Birmingham Museums and Art Gallery · G. Morgan, bronze medallion, NPG · J. Watkins, carte-de-visite, NPG
**Wealth at death** under £12,000: probate, 1859 · £37,204 17s. 6d.—David Cox junior: resworn probate, 1886, *CGPLA Eng. & Wales*

**Cox, David, junior** (1809–1885). *See under* Cox, David (1783–1859).

**Cox, Edward William** (1809–1879), lawyer and publisher, was born at Taunton, the eldest son of William Charles Cox, manufacturer, and Harriet, daughter of William Upcott of Exeter. He was educated at Taunton College. In 1836 he married Sophia, daughter of William Harris, surgeon in the Royal Artillery; on 14 August 1844, he married Rosalinda Alicia, only daughter of J. S. M. *Fonblanque, commissioner of bankruptcy. There was one son from each marriage: Edward Bainbridge Cox (1838–1922), barrister and Conservative MP for Harrow; and Harding Edward de Fonblanque Cox (1854–1944), who wrote extensively on sporting subjects.

Little is known about Cox's activities until he reached his thirties, but thereafter he pursued a number of roles with determination and a flair for gaining public attention. After practising as a solicitor in Taunton, he was called to the bar at the Middle Temple in 1843 and joined the western circuit, becoming recorder of Helston and Falmouth (1857–68) and Portsmouth (1868–79). In 1868 he became serjeant-at-law and thereafter was appointed chairman of the second court of Middlesex sessions (1870–79). On the effective dissolution of the order of serjeants in 1877 he used part of his considerable private wealth to purchase the site of Serjeants' Inn in Chancery Lane. On four occasions he contested parliamentary seats as a Conservative. After three defeats (Tewkesbury, 1852 and 1857, and Taunton, 1865) he won at Taunton in 1868 but was subsequently unseated on an appeal against the result by his chief opponent. Cox was also a believer in spiritualism and published his ideas in studies such as *What Am I?* (1873) and *A Monograph of Sleep and Dreams, their Physiology and Psychology* (1878). He established, and was the president of, the Psychological Society of Great Britain (22 February 1875). This collapsed on his death and was dissolved on 31 December 1879. Some of those who had belonged to it were among the founders in 1882 of the Society for Psychical Research.

Cox made his mark on Victorian society through a talent for publishing. In 1854 he purchased and revived *The Field: a Gentleman's Newspaper Devoted to Sport*, and in 1862 he became a proprietor of *The Queen: a Lady's Newspaper*. He established in 1873 *The Country: a Journal of Rural Pursuits*, *The Critic* (1843–63), and *The Royal Exchange* (1875–9). With John Crockford, Cox's publisher since 1843, he published the *Clerical Journal* in 1853, and its supplements were published in the form of a clerical directory. In 1860 the latter became *Crockford's Clerical Directory*. For the general public Cox established in 1868 *Exchange and Mart*, which was to become an enduring and popular weekly feature of the periodical press. The management of these publications was later taken over by Cox's nephew, Horace Cox (1844–1918).

Cox was a prolific publisher of legal texts. His editions of law reports included *Reports of Cases in Criminal Law Determined in All the Courts of England and Wales* (1846–78), which was well received at the time and was referred to on many occasions during the twentieth century. He wrote a book on *The Advocate, his Training, Practice, Rights, and Duties* (1852), in which he attempted to express the lessons of professional experience in written form. A considerable number of his works gave practical guidance on current legal problems. They included *The Law and Practice of Registration and Elections* (1847), *The Law and Practice of Joint-Stock Companies* (1855), *The Law Relating to Cattle Plague* (1866), and *A Digest of all the Laws decided by the Courts relating to Magistrates' Parochial and Criminal Law* (1870). No legal topic was above or below his interests.

Cox's national reputation was made as the founder and editor of the *Law Times*. After its first appearance in 1843 he devoted more effort to this weekly periodical than to anything else. Its pages provided a balanced mixture of information about decisions of the courts, new statutes, the proceedings of law societies, promotions for practising lawyers, and comments on political, literary, musical, and theological developments of current concern. For the

reader its pages gave an impression of numerous legal developments set against social events and public issues. Throughout, legal practice was understood and criticized in its social setting.

For Victorians the strength of the journal lay in the way Cox made it interesting and acceptable to provincial solicitors. The new railway networks made possible the journal's distribution to a large number of solicitors throughout the country and Cox exploited the opportunity to the full. For the legal profession the consequences were momentous: previous publications had been written primarily for metropolitan lawyers but, over the following decades, the lawyers of London (the most important of whom were barristers) found that their near monopoly of influence in professional matters was being challenged; even if London lawyers retained considerable power they had to do so at the cost of consulting those who worked elsewhere and who were increasingly well informed.

The bar in particular was now exposed to informed criticism and Cox, as a barrister, used his personal knowledge of the profession to good effect. The tone of his criticism was florid and typical of early Victorian professional debate. For instance, when considering the suffering of a litigant who, shortly before a hearing, had a case transferred from the barrister who had been briefed to a barrister the litigant had never previously met, the *Law Times* acknowledged that though the practice permitting this was well established there was no intrinsic justification for it: 'at this time, when the profession is making glorious efforts for its purification, and for the exaltation of its social position by proving itself worthy of public respect, it behoves us no more to shrink from the investigation of alleged grievances which have been established than from the exposure and redress of abuses not recognised' (*Law Times*, 1845, 4 346). To an audience increasingly familiar with the works of Charles Dickens, the public criticism of lawyers, including eminent barristers, was both congenial and convincing.

However, Cox was more successful in responding to public indignation than in achieving the substance of professional reforms. For example, the late return of briefs was still permitted by the bar over a hundred years after Cox had criticized the practice. Support from the *Law Times* for the reform of the system of assizes helped to produce significant changes in the working of the courts in the 1870s, but much still remained to be done before local needs were met in a satisfactory manner. Attempts to encourage compulsory legal education for barristers had succeeded by 1872 but the new examinations commanded little respect. By the time of Cox's death in 1879, the *Law Times* had achieved only a few reforms in professional practice; but, more forcefully than any other legal publication, it had placed the mid-Victorian bar in a defensive position in professional debates.

Cox received no honour for criticizing what was probably the most powerful professional organization of the day. He died at his residence, Moat Mount, Hendon, on 24 November 1879, and was buried in Great Northern London cemetery on 29 November. R. C. J. COCKS

**Sources** *The Times* (26 Nov 1879) • *Law Times* (29 Nov 1879) • Boase, *Mod. Eng. biog.* • R. Cocks, *Foundations of the modern bar* (1983), chap. 3 and pp. 85, 88, 103, 118, 132, 157, 191–2 • A. C. Doyle, *The history of spiritualism*, 1, 2 (1926), 1.252, 294, 296; 2.49, 56 • J. Oppenheim, *The other world: spiritualism and psychical research in England, 1850–1914* (1985), 18, 19, 29–33 • M. Williams, *Later leaves* (1893), 23–4 • C. C. Watkins, 'Edward William Cox and the rise of "class journalism"', *Victorian Periodicals Review*, 15 (1982), 87–93 • J. L. Altholz, 'Mister Serjeant Cox, John Crockford, and the origins of *Crockford's clerical directory'*, *Victorian Periodicals Review*, 17 (1984), 153–93 • C. R. Dod, *Electoral facts, from 1832 to 1853*, ed. H. J. Hanham (1972), 44–69 • *CGPLA Eng. & Wales* (1879)
**Likenesses** wood-engraving (after photograph by London Stereoscopic Co.), NPG; repro. in *ILN* (6 Dec 1879)
**Wealth at death** under £200,000: probate, 11 Dec 1879, *CGPLA Eng. & Wales*

**Cox, Elizabeth** (*fl.* **1671–1688**), actress, was possibly the spinster of twenty-two who married John Bateman of St Paul's, Covent Garden, on 30 November 1661. Nothing is known of the early life of Betty Cox, whose first recorded performance was Lydia in William Wycherley's *Love in a Wood*, for the King's Company in March 1671. Early in her career she was popular as chaste, but witty heroines in roles such as Palmyra in Dryden's *Marriage à la mode*, Violetta in his *The Assignation*, as well as Constantia in Thomas Duffet's farce *The Amorous Old Woman*. When the company moved into the larger Drury Lane Theatre, Cox appears to have broadened her range, playing Octavia in Nathaniel Lee's *Nero* in 1674. She became a respected player of tragic heroines such as Desdemona, Indamore in Dryden's *Aureng-Zebe*, and probably the title role in Lee's *Sophonisba*, to which she spoke the epilogue in performances at London and Oxford.

We have no record of Cox's London appearances between 1676 and October 1681, when the epilogue to Lee's *Mithridates*, which she spoke with Cardell Goodman, implies that this was her return to the stage and has her declare 'the Devil's in 't if I'me past my Prime'. The *Satire to Julian* (1683) and other scandal verses identify Goodman and Cox as lovers. However, there are no further recorded performances from Cox. On 7 April 1683 Charles Killigrew, manager of the new United Company, was ordered by the lord chamberlain to answer her petition, possibly an unsuccessful bid for entry to the new company. The latest mention of her is in the satiric *Session of the Ladies* as 'Lord Lumley's cast player the fam'd Mrs Cox' (1688).

J. MILLING

**Sources** Highfill, Burnim & Langhans, *BDA*

**Cox, Francis Augustus** (1783–1853), Baptist minister, was born on 7 March 1783 in Leighton Buzzard, where his grandfather was a wealthy and well-regarded local Baptist. An only son, and for many years an only child, Cox inherited a sizeable estate from his grandfather, and had a comfortable childhood. Little is known about the early religious influences on him, other than the impression made by *Pilgrim's Progress*. While at Mr Comfield's private academy in Northampton, however, Cox is said to have shown leanings for the ministry. Baptized at Leighton Buzzard just before his thirteenth birthday, he began to preach in his mid-teens, and in the summer of 1798 was set apart by the church for the ministry. In August 1798 he entered Bristol Baptist Academy, going from there in 1800 to Edinburgh University, where he took an MA in 1802. After a short time assisting Isaiah Birt at the Baptist church in Devonport he became pastor of the Clipston church, Northamptonshire. He served there for some time before being ordained on 4 April 1804.

In the summer of 1806 Cox moved to Cambridge where, after preaching temporarily, and on Robert Hall's recommendation, he was invited to succeed Hall as pastor of the St Andrew's Street Church. Cox agreed, but his preaching seems not to have matched expectations. Resigning in April 1808 he returned for a time to Clipston, but found he could not settle. With no permanent appointment, and no thought of seeking one, he agreed to fill the pulpit at Shore Place, Hackney, temporarily in February 1811, and stayed for over forty-two years. For the last nine years he was aided, first as assistant and then as co-pastor, by Daniel Katterns. Soon after Cox arrived in Hackney the church moved to new premises in Mare Street. This chapel was subsequently twice enlarged, and a branch church established at Shoreditch. During Cox's time as sole pastor the church's membership increased more than six-fold. His preaching attracted a large and distinguished congregation.

Cox, said one contemporary, was a 'fine courtly gentleman', tall, genial, cultured, and urbane. Suited for public life by his temperament, abilities, and convictions, he was a sought-after and enthusiastic advocate of many public causes. Often he served these as secretary. 'It would', said one obituarist, 'be difficult to enumerate all the secretaryships which he sustained, or all the societies existing or extinct in which he took an active part.' Within the denomination Cox was an early supporter of the Baptist Union, becoming president in 1834, 1835, and again in 1852. He was joint secretary from 1824 of the Baptist Home Missionary Society; a promoter of the Baptist Irish Society and the Bible Translation Society; secretary of the Baptist Continental Society for nearly five years from 1831; and chairman in 1838 of the Baptist board on colonial apprenticeships. He helped start the *Baptist Magazine* in 1809, putting up some of the capital, and later contributed articles. He was mathematics tutor and occasional examiner at Stepney College from 1813 to 1822, and wrote a jubilee history of the Baptist Missionary Society, on whose committee he sat for forty years. In 1835 he travelled to America with James Hoby as a deputation from the Baptist Union. The visit was thought by many to have done too little to promote the abolition of slavery, but Cox's *Suggestions Designed to Promote the Revival and Extension of Religion …*, based on his observations in America and published the following year, helped shape future home-mission policy. While he was in America the University of Waterville conferred on him an honorary DD.

Beyond the denomination Cox was secretary of the General Body of Dissenting Ministers of the Three Denominations for those residing in and near London and Westminster from 1838 to 1841, and an active campaigner for greater religious freedom. He helped orchestrate the final campaign for the repeal of the Test and Corporation Act in 1827–8; helped found *The Patriot* newspaper in 1832; and was associated with groups such as the Protestant Society for the Protection of Religious Liberty, the Society for Promoting Ecclesiastical Knowledge, the Evangelical Voluntary Association, and the Religious Freedom Society. In 1844 he helped found the Anti-State Church Association, becoming one of its first secretaries, and in 1845 he led the opposition to state support for the Catholic Maynooth College. In the mid-1820s he had been a prime mover in the scheme to found a London university, which culminated in the formation of University College. Ministers of religion were excluded from the college council, but Cox was initially librarian. The university project brought him into contact with Lord Brougham who, as lord rector of Glasgow University, had secured for Cox an honorary LLD in 1824.

In addition to his public and pastoral duties Cox also published several works, starting in 1806 with an *Essay on the Excellence of Christian Knowledge*. Subsequent works included *The Life of Philip Melancthon* (1815); *Female Scripture Biography* (1817); a pamphlet, *On Baptism* (1824), in response to attacks by prominent Congregationalists; his two-volume *History of the Baptist Missionary Society, from 1792 to 1842* (1842); and, with James Hoby, *The Baptists in America* (1836). In addition Cox contributed numerous articles to journals including the *Eclectic Review* and the *Journal of Sacred Literature*, and in 1849 he edited the *Missionary World*. His intellectual interests were wide, ranging from modern astronomy to literature.

Cox was married three times: firstly, in 1809, to Elizabeth King of Watford. After her death he married Sarah Savery in 1821. His third wife, whom he married on 5 October 1847, was the widowed Hephzibah Hannah Finch Jones. Four of his seven children died before him—one son, Frederick, while training for the ministry at Stepney. His three remaining children were all in, or on their way to, Australia for health reasons at the time of his death. Cox died at his home in King Edward's Road, South Hackney, on 5 September 1853 of cancer of the stomach. He was buried in the Mare Street Chapel graveyard.

ROSEMARY CHADWICK

**Sources** *Baptist manual* (1854), 47–8 · *Biographical Magazine*, 5 (1854), 44–8 · *The Patriot* (8 Sept 1853) · *The Patriot* (15 Sept 1853) · *GM*, 2nd ser., 41 (1854), 323 · *Baptist Magazine*, 17 (1825), 52 · 'Resolutions of the Baptist Board on colonial apprenticeship', *Baptist Magazine*, 30 (1838), 161 · *Baptist Reporter*, 20 (1846), 190, 206–9 · *Baptist Reporter*, 21 (1847), 451 · K. R. M. Short, 'English Baptists and American slavery', *Baptist Quarterly*, 20 (1963–4), 243–62 · R. Carwardine, 'The evangelist system: Charles Roe, Thomas Pulford and the Baptist Home Missionary Society', *Baptist Quarterly*, 28 (1979–80), 209–25 · G. F. Nuttall, 'Letters from Robert Hall to John Ryland, 1791–1824', *Baptist Quarterly*, 34 (1991–2), 127–31 · S. A. Swaine, *Faithful men; or, memorials of Bristol Baptist College, and some of its most distinguished alumni* (1884) · E. A. Payne and A. R. Allan, *Clipston Baptist Church: the record of one hundred and fifty years' witness* (1932) · R. Robinson, *Church book: St Andrew's Street Baptist Church, Cambridge, 1720–1832* (1991) · will, PRO, PROB 11/2179

**Archives** UCL, letters

**Likenesses** C. Penny, stipple, pubd 1820, NPG · B. R. Haydon, group portrait, oils, 1841 (*The Anti-Slavery Society convention, 1840*), NPG · C. Baugniet, lithograph, BM, NPG · H. Cook, stipple (after Cocklin), NPG

**Wealth at death** considerable property; house in King Edward's Road; holdings incl. several premises in Hackney, Blackfriars, and Stony Stratford, plus meadowland in Leighton Buzzard; had also lent money secured on property; cash bequests amounting to £1250: will, PRO, PROB 11/2179

**Cox, George Valentine** (1786–1875), author, the son of Charles Cox, was born in Oxford and educated as a chorister at Magdalen College School. He matriculated from New College in 1802, aged sixteen, and took his BA in 1806 (MA, 1808). In 1806 he also became master of New College School, where he served until 1857. He was chaplain of New College from 1812 to 1820. Having been appointed esquire bedel in law in May 1806, he progressed to the bedelship in arts and medicine in 1815. He continued in this ceremonial university office, which provided an income from degree fees, until he retired on a generous pension in 1866; the title was abolished in 1856, but Cox's vested interest had been recognized. He was also university coroner, singly but later jointly, from 1808.

Cox's literary work included an unmemorable three-volume novel, *Jeanette Isabelle*, published anonymously in London in 1837: it is a tale of English aristocrats in France, breathlessly written and including some Oxford anecdotes. A translation of Zeller's work on the philosophy of the Greeks, begun in 1851, survives in manuscript (Bodleian Library, MSS Germ. c.2–6) and indicates more serious literary concerns. Later, perhaps encouraged by the example of Henry Gunning, the Cambridge bedell whose *Reminiscences* had been published in 1854, Cox drew on his memory and on an intermittent diary to write *Recollections of Oxford* (1868, with a corrected and moderately expanded second edition in 1870). It is an engagingly eccentric book, conveying a minor functionary's exaggerated sense of the importance of antique ceremonial, with some interesting vignettes of professors and heads of houses and snatches of jocose academic verse. There are chapters on the Hampden controversy, and on the Tractarian movement (from a low-church point of view), useful for the incidentals of academical background but with little sense of the theological urgency or reforming movements of the early Victorian University of Oxford.

Cox was married, and lived in Merton Street, Oxford. He died at Cowley Lodge, Oxford, on 19 March 1875. One of his sons, George (who predeceased him), was a fellow of New College from 1828 to 1838; another, John Charles, became vicar of Felsted, Essex.

ALAN BELL

**Sources** G. V. Cox, *Recollections of Oxford*, 2nd edn (1870) · Foster, *Alum. Oxon.* · *Jackson's Oxford Journal* (March 1875)

**Wealth at death** under £7000: probate, 21 April 1875, *CGPLA Eng. & Wales*

**Cox, George William** (1827–1902), historian, born at Benares, India, on 10 January 1827, was the eldest son of the six children of Captain George Hamilton Cox (*d.* 1841), of the East India Company's service, and Eliza Kearton, daughter of John Horne, planter, of St Vincent in the West Indies. A brother, Colonel Edmund Henry Cox of the Royal Marine

Artillery, fired the first shot against Sevastopol in the Crimean War. Sent to England in 1836, Cox attended a preparatory school at Bath and Ilminster grammar school. In August 1842 he was admitted to Rugby under A. C. Tait. In 1843 Cox won the senior school scholarship at Rugby, and in 1845 he was elected scholar of Trinity College, Oxford. Although he obtained only a second class in the final classical school in 1848, his scholarship was commended by the examiners. He both graduated BA and proceeded MA in 1859.

The Oxford Movement gained Cox's sympathy, and in 1850 he was ordained by Samuel Wilberforce, bishop of Oxford. In that year he married Emily Maria, daughter of W. Stirling, a lieutenant-colonel in the East India Company's army. They had five sons and two daughters. After serving a curacy at Salcombe Regis, Cox resigned owing to ill health, and in 1851 accepted the post of English chaplain at Gibraltar. But Cox's high-church views, which coloured his *Life of Boniface* in 1853, met with the disapproval of his bishop, Dr Tomlinson, and he gladly embraced the opportunity of accompanying J. W. Colenso on his first visit to South Africa as bishop of Natal (1853–4). On his return to England, Cox became curate of St Paul's, Exeter, in 1854 and for a year (1860–61) he was a master at Cheltenham College.

Meanwhile Cox's religious views completely changed. An article in the *Edinburgh Review* (January 1858) on H. H. Milman's *History of Latin Christianity* illustrates the development of his views on broad-church lines. He ardently supported Bishop Colenso in his stand for liberal criticism of the scriptures and in his struggle over his episcopal status in South Africa. He defended Colenso in a long correspondence with F. D. Maurice and warmly supported the bishop during his visit to England (1863–5). Cox's association with Colenso and the active support of Mrs Colenso who supplied him with many letters and papers after the bishop's death, gave him abundant material for his life of the bishop, which he published in 1888. In the same year he issued a last vindication of Colenso, in *The Church of England and the Teaching of Bishop Colenso*, maintaining Colenso's loyalty to the church.

Throughout his life Cox was largely occupied by literary or historical work of varied kinds. His earliest volume, *Poems Legendary and Historical* (1850), was written in collaboration with his friend E. A. Freeman. From 1861 to 1885 he was literary adviser to Messrs Longmans & Co., and for many years he was engaged in writing historical works which were widely read and much admired at the time but were not of permanent scholarly significance. These included *The Great Persian War* (1861), *Latin and Teutonic Christendom* (1870), *The Greeks and the Persians* (1876), *History of the Establishment of British Rule in India* (1881), *Lives of Greek Statesmen* (2 vols., 1886), and *A Concise History of England* (1887). His most elaborate work was a well-written *History of Greece* (2 vols., 1874), largely a derivative from George Grote's work. He published also on mythology, where he followed Max Müller with some independence. His *Tales from Greek Mythology* (1861), *A Manual of Mythology* (1867), *The Mythology of the Aryan Nations* (1870; new edn, 1882), and *An Introduction to the Science of Comparative Mythology* (1881) all enjoyed a wide vogue, although they pressed to extravagant limits the solar and nebular theory of the origin of myths. He was a frequent contributor to the leading reviews, and joint editor with William Thomas Brande of the *Dictionary of Science, Literature, and Art* (3 vols., 1865–7; new edn, 1875).

In 1877 Cox claimed to succeed to the baronetcy of Cox of Dunmanway, which had been granted to Sir Richard Cox (1650–1733) in 1706. He believed himself to be the heir male of William, the eighth son of the first baronet. On the death in 1873 of a distant cousin, Sir Francis Hawtrey Cox, the twelfth baronet, the title had been treated by the Ulster office of arms as extinct. Nevertheless it was then assumed by Cox's uncle, Colonel Edmund Cox, on whose death in 1877 Cox adopted the titular prefix. His right to the dignity was doubtful because he was unable to produce any documentary evidence to prove that his ancestor, William Cox, was actually a son of the first baronet and not merely a young man for whose apprenticeship the baronet had paid the fee. The title was also assumed by Major-General John Cox who claimed descent from John Cox of Brandon, younger brother of the second baronet. George Cox's right to the dignity was disallowed after his death. On 9 November 1911 the baronetage committee of the privy council advised George V that the name of Edmund Charles Cox, his eldest surviving son and at that time district superintendent of police at Poona, should not be entered on the official roll of baronets.

In 1880 Cox was appointed vicar of Bekesbourne by A. C. Tait, archbishop of Canterbury, and from 1881 to 1897 he was rector of the crown living of Scrayingham, Yorkshire. After the death of Bishop Colenso in 1882, the church council of Natal, having failed in a petition to the crown to appoint a new bishop by letters patent and also in an attempt to persuade the English archbishops and four other bishops to choose one for them, proceeded in August 1886 to elect Cox as Colenso's successor. Archbishop Benson, however, refused to apply for a royal licence to consecrate Cox on the ground that Natal had been from the beginning a part of the province of South Africa and that that province would not recognize the election. In the following year an attempt to persuade the crown to compel the archbishop also failed.

On 18 May 1896 Cox received a civil-list pension of £120. He died at Ivy House, Walmer, Kent, on 9 February 1902. His ashes were buried after cremation at Long Cross, Chertsey, Surrey.          G. S. WOODS, *rev.* PETER HINCHLIFF

**Sources** *The Times* (11 Feb 1902) · *The life of Frederick Denison Maurice*, ed. F. Maurice, 2 (1884), 449 · A. C. Benson, *The life of Edward White Benson*, 2 (1899), 500 · W. R. W. Stephens, *The life and letters of Edward A. Freeman*, 2 vols. (1895), 84, 128 · C. Lewis and G. E. Edwards, *Historical records of the church of the province of South Africa* (1934), 347–9 · P. B. Hinchliff, *The Anglican church in South Africa* (1963), 106–9 · private information (1912) · *CGPLA Eng. & Wales* (1902)

**Archives** LPL, corresp. and papers relating to Natal | BL, corresp. with W. E. Gladstone, Add. MSS 44410–44469 · Bodl. RH, corresp. with Colenso family

**Wealth at death** £3448 14s. 5d.: administration, 7 May 1902, *CGPLA Eng. & Wales*

**Cox, Sir (Ernest) Gordon** (1906–1996), crystallographer and public servant, was born on 24 April 1906 at Pretoria House, Southdown, Twerton, Somerset, the son of Ernest Henry Cox (1884–1987), railway clerk and market gardener, and his wife, Rosina, *née* Ring (1872–1931), the daughter of a chef, who had worked on a farm in Canada before her marriage. He grew up in a rural atmosphere of flowers and vegetables, horses and greenhouses. At the age of eleven he won a scholarship to the City of Bath Boys' School from where, in 1924, he proceeded to Bristol University to read physics under Arthur Mannering Tyndall. Following graduation with first-class honours in 1927, he joined, on Tyndall's recommendation, Sir William Henry Bragg in the Davy–Faraday Laboratory of the Royal Institution in London as a research assistant. There he learned the techniques of X-ray crystallography from W. T. Astbury, under whom he determined the structure of aluminium acetylacetone. He also began to calculate correction factors for photographic measurement of intensities. It was Bragg who suggested that he should investigate the crystalline structure of benzene. In order to reduce the smudging effects of thermal vibrations of atoms he pioneered techniques for taking X-ray photographs at low-temperatures. Using a low-temperature camera of his own design he showed that the six carbon atoms in benzene formed a planar ring, confirming Kathleen Lonsdale's work (using hexamethylbenzene) that it was a regular hexagon.

On 2 April 1929 Cox married a school friend, Lucie Grace Baker (1906–1962), daughter of Alfred Charles Nelson Baker, cabinet maker of South Lynscombe, Bath; they had a son, Keith Gordon *Cox (1933–1998), and a daughter, Patricia Ann Cox (b. 1931), who forged distinguished careers in petrology and in the Scottish civil service respectively. In the same year Walter Norman Haworth appointed Cox an assistant lecturer (from 1931, lecturer) in the chemistry department at Birmingham University. During the next decade he used Fourier analysis to determine the structures of sugars (establishing the stereochemistry of their pyranose rings) and, in collaboration with William Wardlow, the structures of many co-ordination compounds. The highlight of the Birmingham period was the determination of the crystal structure of ascorbic acid, vitamin C, for which Haworth received the Nobel prize for chemistry in 1937. Cox obtained his DSc from Bristol in 1936 and was promoted to a readership in crystallography at Birmingham in 1940.

Cox joined the Territorial Army in 1936 and during the early war years he remained at Birmingham working on the chemical structures of explosives and the dangers arising from their static electrification. In 1942 he was appointed director of the Special Operations Executive's Frythe Laboratory at Welwyn, and during 1944–5 he was made a lieutenant-colonel assigned to special duties (sabotage) with the Twenty-First Army group following the allied invasion of Europe. He became a friend of Victor Rothschild, who was working for MI5 at this time.

In 1945 Cox returned to Birmingham but was almost immediately appointed professor of inorganic and structural chemistry at the University of Leeds, where he seized the opportunity for building a large school of structural studies. A stream of high-grade structure determinations and bond length calculations flowed from the team of researchers he assembled, who were inevitably nicknamed 'Cox's pippins'. At Leeds he pioneered the use of digital and analogue computers in calculations, and he was quick to see how nuclear magnetic resonance apparatus would transform crystallography. He took on a large number of administrative roles at Leeds, and it was said that he sat on every committee except the wives' club.

In 1957 Cox's wartime friend Lord Rothschild appointed him a member of the Agricultural Research Council, which had been established by the department of agriculture in 1931 to supervise civil research. Three years later, in June 1960, he abandoned crystallography and left Leeds to begin a new career in London in succession to Sir William Slater as secretary of the council. Few farmers had heard of him, but his proven qualities as a scientist and administrator and his knowledge and love of the countryside stood him in good stead. As chief executive he had a good deal of independence from government control. In partnership with various universities he established new research institutes for food research, nitrogen fixation, structural chemistry, and invertebrate chemistry and physiology. In the knowledge that the Science and Technology Act (1965) would reduce the council's independence Cox decided to retire in September 1971. This gave him the freedom to be highly critical of Lord Rothschild's proposals in November 1971 that scientific research should be driven by a customer–contractor relationship. Their friendship cooled markedly. In 1971 he also retired from the council for science policy, on which he had served since 1964. His first wife having died in 1962, on 28 May 1968 he married a colleague and former pupil, Mary Rosaleen Truter (b. 1925), daughter of Dr D. N. Jackman and former wife of Dr E. V. Truter, lecturer in textile chemistry at Leeds University. She was also a crystallographer of distinction, becoming reader in crystallography at Leeds in 1960 and deputy director of the Agricultural Research Council's unit for structural chemistry at University College, London, in 1966.

Cox remained active in retirement, cultivating his Hampstead garden with plants from all over the world and offering his administrative skills to the British Association for the Advancement of Science as general secretary and to the Royal Institution as honorary treasurer, both from 1971 to 1976. He retained his west country burr and measured pace of speech throughout his life, and was loved for his quizzical look, humanity, and sense of humour. He was elected FRS in 1954 and knighted in 1964. He was vice-president of the Institute of Physics, 1950–53, and president of the British Food Manufacturing Industrial Research Association, 1971–5. He received honorary degrees from the universities of Newcastle, Birmingham, Bristol, Bath, and East Anglia. He died at Edenhall, Marie Curie Centre, 11 Lyndhurst Gardens, Camden, London, of prostate cancer on 23 June 1996 and was cremated at Golders Green five days later. He was survived by his wife, Mary, his son, Keith, and his daughter, Patricia.

W. H. Brock

**Sources** D. W. J. Cruickshank, *Memoirs FRS*, 46 (2000) · D. W. J. Cruickshank, 'Gordon Cox', *Journal of Applied Crystallography*, 30 (1997), 208 · 'Profile: science at the service of agriculture', *New Scientist* (1 Dec 1960), 1454–5 · F. Dainton, 'Sir Gordon Cox, 1906–96', *Chemistry in Britain*, 32/11 (1996), 58 · *The Independent* (1 July 1996) · *The Independent* (8 July 1996) · *The Times* (9 July 1996) · *WWW* · G. W. Cooke, ed., *Agricultural research, 1931–1981: a history of the agricultural research council* (1981) · P. P. Ewald, *50 years of X-ray diffraction* (1962) · S. Reeve, *Memoirs FRS*, 39 (1994), 365–80 · J. Postgate, 'The origins of the unit of nitrogen fixation at the University of Sussex', *Notes and Records of the Royal Society*, 52 (1998), 355–62 · b. cert. · m. cert. [Ernest Gordon Cox and Lucie Grace Baker] · d. cert.

**Archives** U. Leeds, papers

**Likenesses** Elliott & Fry, photograph, RS; repro. in *Memoirs FRS* · photographs, priv. coll.

**Wealth at death** £46,938: probate, 5 Sept 1996, *CGPLA Eng. & Wales*

**Cox, Harold** (1859–1936), economist and journalist, was born at Wimbledon on 16 August 1859, the second son of Homersham *Cox (1821–1897), a county court judge, and his wife, Margaret Lucy Cox (*b.* 1832/3). He was educated at Tonbridge School, whence he obtained a mathematical scholarship at Jesus College, Cambridge. He was president of the union in 1881, and after graduating as a senior optime in the mathematical tripos of 1882, became a university extension lecturer in Yorkshire. After coming under the influence of Edward Carpenter, according to his own account he spent nearly a year working as an agricultural labourer in Kent and Sussex 'in order to gain an insight into the life of English labourers'. From 1885 to 1887 he taught mathematics in the Muhammadan Anglo-Oriental College at Aligarh in India.

On his return to England in 1887 Cox joined Gray's Inn and read for the bar, but, turning to politics, he was appointed secretary of the Cobden Club in 1899. In that position he took a prominent part in opposing the tariff-reform proposals of Joseph Chamberlain, and in maintaining the pure tradition of *laissez-faire* liberalism against Liberal as well as Unionist innovations. He resigned the secretaryship in 1904 and in recognition of his services to free trade he was adopted as candidate by the Liberal Party in Preston, and won the seat at the general election in 1906. Cox represented the old Liberalism of retrenchment, disliked old-age pensions and, even more, Lloyd George's budget of 1909. He began working with Unionist free-traders—he had a connection with St Loe Strachey and *The Spectator*—and at the general election of January 1910 stood for Preston as a free-trade Liberal (Sir John Gorst being the official Liberal candidate); he came bottom of the poll. In 1911 he stood for Cambridge University at a by-election, again as a free-trade Liberal, but again without success; that ended his parliamentary career.

After his retirement from politics Cox constantly spoke and wrote against the growth of public expenditure and of bureaucracy. Although in early life he had been friendly with Sidney Webb, and had collaborated with him in a

book, *Eight Hours Day* (1891), he was now an uncompromising opponent of socialism; his book *Economic Liberty* (1920) is a good exposition of old-style Liberal individualism. His public work included membership (1914–15) of the inquiry into alleged German atrocities in Belgium, held under the chairmanship of Lord Bryce, and of the committee on public retrenchment (1916). From 1910 to 1912 he was an alderman of the London county council, and in 1913 he was elected an honorary fellow of Jesus College. On the death of A. R. D. Elliot in 1912, he was appointed editor of the *Edinburgh Review*; he held the post until 1929, when the journal ceased to be published, Cox lamenting: 'the political views that it was intended to support have ceased to play any leading part in the national life' (*Edinburgh Review*, 250, Oct 1929, 193).

Cox married Helen Clegg; she died childless in 1930 after they had moved from Gray's Inn to Old Kennards, Leigh, near Tonbridge, where Cox also died, from broncho-pneumonia and myocardial degeneration, on 1 May 1936.

F. W. Hirst, rev. H. C. G. Matthew

**Sources** *The Times* (2 May 1936) · *Economic Journal*, 46 (Sept 1936) · private information (1949) · P. F. Clarke, *Lancashire and the new liberalism* (1971) · *IGI*

**Archives** CAC Cam., corresp. with Channel Tunnel Co. · HLRO, letters to Andrew Bonar Law; corresp. with J. St L. Strachey · JRL, letters to the *Manchester Guardian* · King's AC Cam., letters to Oscar Browning · U. Newcastle, Robinson L., corresp. with Walter Runciman

**Wealth at death** £12,471 14s. 8d.: probate, 1 May 1936, *CGPLA Eng. & Wales*

**Cox, Harry Fred** (1885–1971), farmworker and singer, was born on 27 March 1885 at Pennygate, Barton Turf, Norfolk, one of the thirteen children (nine of whom survived beyond infancy) of Robert Cox (1837–1929?), fisherman, wherryman, and farmworker, and his wife, Sarah Whittaker, known as Nobbs (1850–1946?), farmworker, of Smallburgh, Norfolk. The family struggled hard to manage on low wages, and young Harry had 'more dinner times than dinners' (Kennedy, 'Harry Cox', 143). He started school at the age of six, for which his parents paid 2*d.* a week; and having, in his own words, 'learnt nothing' (ibid.), he left at the age of twelve to work on farms for 2*s.* 6*d.* a week.

Cox spent the whole of his working life on the land, within a few miles of his birthplace, save for his time in the navy during the First World War. He volunteered in January 1917, served on the minelayer HMS *Blanche*, based at Scapa Flow, and also sailed out of Chatham and Rosyth. He was discharged in April 1919. The many skills he acquired included those of woodman, thatcher, reed cutter, scytheman, hedge layer, basket maker, and livestock manager. In the last capacity he sometimes went without a day off for as much as seven months at a stretch, and in 1923 he endured a spell of unpopularity with workmates for refusing to join a strike for better wages because he feared for the welfare of the animals in his charge. He was a freelance worker, with an entrepreneurial turn of mind, and soon after his marriage to Elsie Mary Amis (1892–1951), at Potter Heigham church on 1 January 1927, he was able to find £100 with which to buy three one-up-and-down cottages at Cockleshell Corner, Catfield. He knocked two of these together to make a house which he called Sunnyside, and kept the third for work and storage. He and his wife had three children, of whom two died in infancy; the third, Myrtle, was born in 1931 and died in 1998.

Harry Cox learned songs in the main from his grandfather and father, both noted singers, but also from his mother and other relatives. Indeed, he actively sought anyone likely to have an interesting song: he claimed to have walked up to 15 miles and paid 6*d.* to one person for his contribution. From the age of four he heard his father singing in public houses, and at 'about eleven' (Kennedy, *Harry Cox: English Folk Singer*, 16) made his own début at the Union tavern, Smallburgh. At about the same time he started to learn to play the fiddle, and he later added the melodeon and tin whistle. As an adult he regularly played and sang at informal sessions in public houses such as The Windmill inn at Sutton, 3 miles from Potter Heigham. In 1921 another of the Windmill singers, Bob Miller, introduced Cox to the song-collecting composer E. J. Moeran. Moeran, hugely impressed, took friends such as Philip Heseltine (Peter Warlock) and Augustus John down to the Windmill, where, the latter wrote, 'of a Saturday evening several local folk-singers were known to gather, chief among whom was one Harry Cox, a first-rate singer with a large repertoire of traditional songs' (John, 12). Moeran noted down at least ten of these, and included arrangements of two in his *Six Folk Songs from Norfolk* (1924). In 1934 he arranged for Cox to travel to London, met him at the railway station, and took him to the Decca studios, where he made a record for distribution to members of the English Folk Dance and Song Society.

In 1942 the BBC asked Francis Collinson, who was about to produce a new series of radio programmes (*Country Magazine*), to visit 'a gold-mine of folk song by the name of Harry Cox'. He found a 'tall, rather spare, extremely lithe and active looking' man, who preferred to sing in his 'woodshed' (in fact his workshop), rather than in his house (Collinson, 145); it seems that Cox's wife disliked visitors, whom she deemed to be picking his brains. Collinson noted down fourteen songs, and persuaded the BBC, three years later, to make some recordings of Cox's singing. In 1947 Moeran revisited the Windmill to record Cox and others for a broadcast in the BBC's Third Programme; and in 1953 Peter Kennedy began to make further recordings of Cox for a radio series on traditional singers, *As I Roved out*. Many other song collectors found their way to Sunnyside in the 1950s and 1960s, including Ewan MacColl, Charles Parker, Mervyn Plunkett, and Leslie Shepard.

In 1961 Cox contributed tracks to *The Folk Songs of Britain*, a series of ten long-playing records which came out in America. Solo LPs followed in America in 1964 and in England the following year. In the meantime, jointly with another Norfolk man, Sam Larner, Cox was the subject of a television film, *The Singer and the Song* (1964), directed by Charles Parker.

Untroubled and unaffected by his growing fame, Cox quietly continued on his normal round until his death from prostate and liver cancer at Sunnyside, Catfield, on 6 May 1971. He was buried later in 1971 in Potter Heigham churchyard next to his wife, who had died of dropsy in 1951, aged fifty-nine. Two days before his death, Cox entreated a visitor 'not to let the old songs die out' (Marsh, 28); yet his own influence—greater, perhaps than that of any other English traditional singer—helped to ensure the fulfilment of his wish. He is admired for the breadth and variety of his repertory, some 140 items ranging from rough bawdry to high balladry, but above all for his technique, based, according to the BBC producer Francis Dillon, on 'a carefully placed decoration, a beautifully judged phrasing, an exact control of highly complex rhythm and a singing tone which requires no accompaniment' (Dillon, 139). Some thirty years after his death he was featured not only in *The Voice of the People*, a major compilation of twenty compact discs issued in 1998, but also two years later on solo albums of one and two CDs respectively. E. J. Moeran's characterization of him as 'that prince of singers' (Palmer, 348) proved to be justified.

ROY PALMER

**Sources** P. Kennedy, 'Harry Cox: English folk singer', *Journal of the English Folk Dance and Song Society*, 8/3 (1958), 142–5 · P. Kennedy, disc notes, *Harry Cox: English folk singer*, English Folk Dance and Song Society, LP 1004 (1965) [LP record] · R. Palmer, 'Neglected pioneer: E. J. Moeran (1894–1950)', *Folk Music Journal*, 8 (2001–5), 345–61 · F. Collinson, 'A reminiscence', *Journal of the English Folk Dance and Song Society*, 8/3 (1958), 145–6 · A. John, foreword, in C. Gray, *Peter Warlock* (1934), 12–13 · P. Marsh, 'Harry Cox', *Harry Cox: the bonny labouring boy*, Topic Records, TSCD 512D (2000) [disc notes, 3–28] · F. Dillon, ed., *'Country magazine': book of the BBC programme* (1950) · [M. Plunkett], 'Harry Cox—the Catfield wonder', *Ethnic*, 1/1 (Jan 1959), 4–8 · P. Kennedy, *Folk Music Journal*, 2 (1970–74), 160–63 · *East Anglia sings*, Third Programme, BBC Radio, 19 Nov 1947 [radio; commentary by E. J. Moeran] · *Harry Cox: what will become of England?*, Rounder Records, MA, 11661-1839-2 (2000) [disc notes] · M. G. Myer and B. Thomson, 'A visit to Harry Cox', *Folk Review*, 2/4 (Feb 1973), 8–12 · *The folk songs of Britain*, 10 LPs, Caedmon Records, New York (1961), and Topic Records, London (1968) · *The voice of the people*, 20 CDs, Topic Records, TSCD 651–650 (1998) · CGPLA Eng. & Wales (1971)

**Likenesses** B. Shuel, photograph, repro. in B. Pegg, *Folk: a portrait of English traditional music, musicians and customs* (1976) · drawing on record sleeve, repro. in Kennedy, *Harry Cox* · photographs, repro. in Marsh, 'Harry Cox' · portrait, repro. in Myer and Thomson, 'A visit to Harry Cox' · portrait, repro. in Kennedy, *Harry Cox*

**Wealth at death** £4011: probate, 27 Aug 1971, CGPLA Eng. & Wales

**Cox, Homersham** (1821–1897), judge, mathematician, and author, was born on 19 June 1821 at Newington, Surrey. The fourth son of Edward Treslove Cox, he was educated at Tonbridge School (1830–39) and at Jesus College, Cambridge (1839–44), graduating with second-class honours in the mathematical tripos. He registered as a student of the Inner Temple on 2 May 1845, and was called to the bar on 13 June 1851.

Cox supplemented his income from his law practice by writing for the *Daily Telegraph* for a number of years. He was acknowledged as both a speedy and a brilliant writer of leaders. He also wrote books upon a remarkably diverse range of subjects: differential and integral calculus, the institutions of British government, the law of parliamentary elections. His best-known and most successful work was titled *The First Century of Christianity* (1886; rev. edn, 1892); his *History of the Reform Bills of 1866 and 1867* (1868) and his *Institutions of English Government* (1863) are probably those of enduring interest, the latter reflecting his whiggish historicism.

Cox was appointed a commissioner at the Beverley election inquiry in 1869, and two years later was made a county court judge to serve on circuit no. 24 in mid-Wales. Thirteen years later, in 1884, he transferred to Cardiff, but within months replaced Judge Lindsdale on the Mid Kent circuit, where he remained until his retirement in 1893. The townsfolk of Tonbridge evinced much pride and pleasure in the success of a local boy as judge, and were gratified that Cox was awarded 'the biggest pension that could be awarded him' (*Maidstone & Kentish Journal*).

Cox was married to Margaret Lucy (*b.* 1832/3), whose maiden name is not known. They had at least five daughters and four sons. His second son was the economist and journalist Harold *Cox. He died at his home, Marlfield House, Tonbridge, after a very short illness, on 10 March 1897, and was buried two days later at Tonbridge cemetery.                                                    A. J. A. MORRIS

**Sources** J. Foster, *Men-at-the-bar: a biographical hand-list of the members of the various inns of court*, 2nd edn (1885) • *Law Journal* (13 March 1897), 154 • H. E. Stead, ed., *Register of Tonbridge School, 1826–1910* (1911) • *The Tonbridgian* (April 1897), 1284 • *Maidstone & Kentish Journal* (18 March 1897) • Venn, *Alum. Cant.* • *IGI* • census returns, 1881
**Wealth at death** £15,366 11s. 11d.: resworn probate, Sept 1897, CGPLA Eng. & Wales

**Cox, James** (*c.*1723–1800), jeweller and entrepreneur, was born in London, the son of Henry Cox (*c.*1691–1746), tailor of Broad Street, and his wife, Frances, *née* Matthews. He was apprenticed in 1738 to Humphry Pugh, goldsmith of Fleet Street and freeman of the Haberdashers' Company. From his trade card Pugh seems to have been a toyman, so Cox was probably trained mainly in retail skills rather than as a working goldsmith, though he later registered a mark at Goldsmiths' Hall as a smallworker.

Once out of his apprenticeship in June 1745, Cox set up in London as a goldsmith, jeweller, and toyman at the sign of the Golden Urn in Racquet Court, Fleet Street. In December 1745 he married Elizabeth Liron (1723–1782), daughter of a Huguenot merchant. In 1756 Cox entered into partnership with Edward Grace and moved into larger premises at 103 Shoe Lane. The partnership continued in the Cox's existing business, but also had close links with Grace's brother John, a merchant who shared the premises. Two years later, in November 1758, both businesses became bankrupt, with Cox and Grace, 'merchants', owing John Grace over £9000.

Undeterred, Cox remained in Shoe Lane and, following his discharge from bankruptcy in July 1763, began preparations to produce the extravagant musical clocks and other articles for export to the Far East, for which he was to become famous. This required heavy investment in raw materials and the establishment of an extensive network of craftsmen and suppliers; indeed, Cox was to claim in 1773 that he had for the past seven years employed about 800–1000 workers. Since the returns from this enterprise, though potentially high, were likely to be slow and uncertain, Cox's ability to undertake it so soon after his bankruptcy suggests that he had powerful financial backing. He also had the Liégeois mechanician John Joseph Merlin (1735–1803) as his chief craftsman. Few of the grander objects made by Cox's workforce survive, but they include the magnificent *Swan* automaton now in the Bowes Museum, and probably the *Peacock* clock in the Hermitage Museum, St Petersburg. Fortunately, Cox's appetite for publicity meant that other major works were described in contemporary newspapers and pamphlets, while many smaller articles with his signature can be found in public collections.

For several years Cox enjoyed considerable success, with total sales to India and China exceeding £550,000, but a downturn in the market by 1772 left him facing serious problems in selling his goods, and interest charges of £9000 per year. He urgently needed to speed up his returns, and though much of his stock-in-trade could be sold at auction, the more extraordinary objects needed different treatment. The possibility of a lottery may already have been in Cox's mind in February 1772, when he opened his museum in the lavishly refurbished Great Exhibition room in Spring Gardens, Charing Cross, in central London. The museum had originally been planned as a way of publicizing articles destined for export, and was on a grand scale, including twenty-two spectacular automata ranging from 9 feet to 16 feet high.

In spite of the substantial entry fee of half a guinea, the museum immediately became one of London's fashionable sights. Dr Johnson recommended it to Boswell soon after it opened: 'For power of mechanism and splendour of show', Johnson told him, it 'was a very fine exhibition' (Altick, 69). Boswell agreed, though some visitors regretted the lack of 'utility': in *Evelina* (1778) Fanny Burney's heroine observed that the museum was 'very astonishing, and very superb; yet, it afforded me but little pleasure, for it is a mere show, though a wonderful one' (ibid., 70). In spite of its popular success the museum could not resolve Cox's financial difficulties and after a year he petitioned parliament for permission to dispose of its contents by lottery.

Legislation was passed on 10 May 1773 and plans were made to sell 120,000 tickets at a guinea each, with 404 prizes said to be worth £197,500 (though £63,000 of this was the value of admission to the museum provided by the tickets). Major exhibits were offered as 'collective' prizes. Cox mounted a battery of publicity for the lottery in the press, appealing to patriotism (one of his favourite themes in defending the utility of his products), as well as cupidity. A stirring song which he composed to the apposite tune of 'Roast Beef of Old England' had the final verse:

> Thus Britain's white sails shall be kept unfurl'd,
> And our commerce extend, as our thunders are hurl'd,
> Till the Empress of Science is Queen of the World,

If we haste to buy into the Lott'ry,
If we haste to buy tickets from Cox.
(Altick, 72)

Unsurprisingly this British patriotism was toned down in the 1774 catalogue for the temporary exhibition of part of the museum in Dublin.

In spite of strenuous efforts Cox had difficulty in selling enough tickets and the lottery was not drawn until May–June 1775, with the museum closing to the public on 30 December. Unfortunately, the proceeds failed to restore Cox's finances. He had already tried to diversify into other markets: buying the Chelsea porcelain factory from Nicholas Sprimont in September 1769 may have been one such attempt, though he soon resold it to the owners of the Derby factory. A more promising new market was Russia, which bought a number of Cox's articles, but overall the attempts at diversification were inadequate. In 1777 Cox's son, John Henry, sailed to India to realize his father's eastern assets, but he had little success. Cox's problems were now compounded by the general damage to trade caused by the American War of Independence and he was once more declared bankrupt in November 1778.

Less is known of the last phase of James Cox's career. In 1780 John Henry Cox again sailed for the Far East to collect money owing to his father's estate, and this time he had more success. Until his death in Canton (Guangzhou) in October 1791 he remitted considerable sums to his father's creditors, while also trading in his own right. He also acted as agent for the new partnership of James Cox & Son, set up by his father and brother following Cox's discharge from bankruptcy. This partnership exported to the Far East decorative watches and similar articles made largely by the independent suppliers like Swiss watchmakers Jaquet-Droz et Leschot. Although apparently avoiding the much grander and more expensive automata of his earlier career, Cox still became heavily indebted to his suppliers in the late 1780s; the death of H. L. Jaquet-Droz in 1791, followed by that of Cox's son in Canton, probably put an end to Cox's overseas activities. In February 1792 the remaining Canton stock from the 1778 bankruptcy was auctioned by Christies in London, fetching 12,000 guineas for the assignees.

Cox & Son continued trading as jewellers in Shoe Lane until 1797, when the premises were given up. James Cox died in February 1800 in Watford, Hertfordshire, from where his body was brought for burial on 25 February in the family vault in the dissenters' burial-ground at Bunhill Fields, London. His very modest estate was valued at under £100; and although he had been so famous, no obituary is known.                                              ROGER SMITH

**Sources** C. Le Corbeiller, 'James Cox: a biographical review', *Burlington Magazine*, 112 (1970), 351–6 • R. Smith, 'James Cox (c. 1723–1800): a revised biography', *Burlington Magazine*, 142 (2000), 353–61 • A. R. Williamson, 'John Henry Cox', *Eastern traders* (1975), 1–35 • East India Company records, BL OIOC • Bodl. Oxf., John Johnson collection • C. Pagani, 'The clocks of James Cox', *Apollo*, 141 (Jan 1995), 15–22 • A. Chapuis, *La montre chinoise* (1919), 28–30, 61–4 • R. D. Altick, *The shows of London* (1978), 69–72 • M. Wright, 'The ingenious mechanick', *John Joseph Merlin: the ingenious mechanick*, ed.
A. French (1985), 47–62 [exhibition catalogue, Iveagh Bequest, Kenwood, London, 19 July–26 Aug 1985] • A. French, 'James Cox and J. J. Merlin', *John Joseph Merlin: the ingenious mechanick*, ed. A. French (1985), 123–8 [exhibition catalogue, Iveagh Bequest, Kenwood, London, 19 July–26 Aug 1985] • records of the Haberdashers' Company, GL • A. Weaving, 'Clocks for the emperor', *Antiquarian Horology and the Proceedings of the Antiquarian Horological Society*, 19 (1990–91), 367–88 • PRO, RG4/3986, p. 22 [burial] • administration, 6 Dec 1800, LMA, Diocese of London Consistory Court, register of wills and administrations, 1799–1801, DL/C/372, p. 332
**Archives** Bowes Museum, co. Durham, automata and clocks • Hermitage, St Petersburg, automata and clocks • Metropolitan Museum of Art, New York, clocks • Palace Museum, Beijing, automata and clocks • V&A, clocks | BL OIOC, East India Company records • Bodl. Oxf., John Johnson collection (lotteries) • CLRO, MSS • GL, MSS • PRO, MSS
**Wealth at death** under £100: administration, LMA, Diocese of London Consistory Court, register of wills and administrations, 1799–1801, DL/C/372, p. 332

**Cox, James** (1858–1920), trade unionist, was born at North Street, Bedminster, near Bristol, on 3 October 1858, the son of George Thomas Cox, a coalminer, and his wife, Ann, *née* Servy. He went to school in the area until the age of eleven. His childhood friends included a girl named Alice Maude Smith, the daughter of William Charles Smith, an accountant, and they were married at the Wesleyan Ebenezer Chapel, Bedminster, on 31 March 1879. She proved to be a devoted wife and 'a constant helper to him in all his labours' (*Northern Echo*, 4 Dec 1920).

At fourteen Cox entered the iron industry, which at that time was organized round three processes. First, iron ore was converted into pig iron in the blast furnace; next, pig iron was made into malleable iron in the forge; finally, malleable iron was rolled into rods, bars, or sheets in the mill. His first job was in a forge in Tipton, south Staffordshire, where he worked alongside an uncle. He subsequently became a sheet roller, first in Bristol and then in Wolverhampton. While working in Wolverhampton he was elected to the workmen's panel of the south Staffordshire mill and forge wages board, which had been established in 1876 in succession to the south Staffordshire iron trade conciliation board of 1872 to 1875. On the original board the workmen had been represented by the National Association of Ironworkers, but the employers had refused to continue this arrangement with the new board; and union organization in south Staffordshire had collapsed shortly afterwards.

In an attempt to revive unionism in south Staffordshire and elsewhere the National Association was superseded by the Associated Iron and Steel Workers in 1887 and Cox was elected to its first executive council. Four years later he was appointed assistant secretary and went to live in Darlington, where the union had its head office. He spent the rest of his life there and became widely known and respected in the town. He was a leading figure in the East Road Wesleyan Methodist Church, where a memorial window was installed after his death, and in the Liberal Association, which he served as chairman of the executive committee and as a Durham county councillor. He maintained his connection with both organizations until his death and in 1917 his work for the Liberal Association was acknowledged by the presentation of a silver tea and coffee service. His standing in the wider community was recognized by his appointment as a borough magistrate in 1899.

In the same year Cox succeeded Edward Trow as general secretary of the Associated Iron and Steel Workers and held this position until 1917, when the union was absorbed into a new, more broadly based organization, the Iron and Steel Trades Confederation. He was the linchpin in the complex inter-union negotiations which paved the way for the merger and then became a divisional officer of the confederation. In addition to the usual work of a union official he served on a number of delegations which investigated working conditions in other countries, most notably the Mosely industrial commission, which visited the USA in 1902. He played no part in the affairs of the TUC other than attending its annual conference as a representative of his union: he felt strongly that it should not have become politicized, particularly as this involved associating with the Labour Party.

Cox led the Associated Iron and Steel Workers on the same moderate, pragmatic lines as Trow, which meant in practice continued co-operation with the employers in conciliation boards. He was chairman of the workmen's panel of the board of arbitration and conciliation for the manufactured iron trade of the north of England from 1891 to 1899, when he took over as the paid secretary. He also became the paid secretary to the workmen's panel of the midland iron and steel wages board, which had replaced the south Staffordshire mill and forge wages board, in 1915. This dual responsibility, coupled with the demands of a new position in a much larger and quite different union from 1917, eventually proved too onerous and he retired from work a sick man early in 1920.

Cox's health never recovered and he died on 3 December 1920 at his home, 5 Mount Pleasant, Darlington. His wife survived him. There were no children of the marriage. Cox was buried on 6 December 1920 at the west cemetery in Darlington, following a service in the cemetery chapel.                                              ERIC TAYLOR

**Sources** Ironworkers' Journal [also called Journal of the Iron and Steel Trades Confederation] (1887–1920) [esp. obit. Dec 1920] · Northern Echo (4 Dec 1920) · Northern Echo (7 Dec 1920) [funeral notice] · Labour Tribune (1887–94) · J. H. Porter, 'David Dale and conciliation in the northern manufactured iron trade, 1869–1914', Northern History, 5 (1970), 157–71 · E. Taylor, The better temper: a commemorative history of the midland iron and steel wages board, 1876–1976 (1976), chap. 2 · 'Special note on the Mosely industrial commission', DLB, 5.208–11 · A. Birch, The economic history of the British iron and steel industry, 1784–1879 (1967) · J. C. Carr and W. Taplin, History of the British steel industry (1962) · A. Pugh, Men of steel, by one of them: a chronicle of eighty-eight years of trade unionism in the British iron and steel industry (1951) · b. cert. · m. cert. · census returns, 1881
**Likenesses** bronze bust; formerly Iron and Steel Trades Confederation, London · pen drawing, repro. in Labour Tribune (11 Oct 1891)
**Wealth at death** £938 17s. 6d.: probate, 6 May 1921, CGPLA Eng. & Wales

**Cox** [Coxe], **John** (fl. 1565–1583), translator, received some of his education at Oxford University. It is not certain whether he was a member of Brasenose College from Michaelmas term 1546, or whether he was an undergraduate at Christ Church from 1555. He probably left Oxford without a degree. In later life, Cox translated a number of prominent Reformed tracts into English, most notably among them two works by Zwingli's successor at Zürich, Heinrich Bullinger (1504–1575). The first, Questions of Religion Cast Abroad in Helvetia by the Adversaries of the same (1572), is a central apologia for the Zwinglian Reformation; the second is a call to unity among the Swiss clergy, entitled Exhortation to the Ministers of God's Worde in the Church of Christ (1575). Cox was convinced that by translating the Latin texts into English he 'could do God no better service and no greater pleasure to my countreymen, than to make them partakers of suche a precious perle as this' (Bullinger, Questions of Religion, sig. *iijr).

Two further translations of Reformed classics make up Cox's remaining œuvre. He extracted an examination of the penitential Psalm 51 from the exegetical work of the Bern reformer Wolfgang Musculus (1497–1563), which he published in London in 1565 under the title The Commentarye or Exposition of W. Musculus upon the Li Psalme. A translation, Treatise on the Word of God (1583), from the polemical work by Antoine de la Roche Chandieu (1534–1591), Jean Calvin's successor at Paris, rounds off his work.                                              J. ANDREAS LÖWE

**Sources** H. Bullinger, Questions of religion cast abroad in Helvetia by adversaries of the same, trans. J. Cox (1572), iijr · H. Bullinger, Exhortation to the ministers of God's worde in the Church of Christ, trans. J. Cox (1575) · W. Musculus, The commentarye or exposition of W. Musculus upon the li psalme, trans. J. Cox (1565) · A. de la Roche Chandieu, A treatise on the word of God, by Anth. Sadull, written against the traditions of men, trans. J. Cox (1583), colophon · [C. B. Heberden], ed., Brasenose College register, 1509–1909, 1, OHS, 55 (1909), 11 · Foster, Alum. Oxon. · Wood, Ath. Oxon.: Fasti (1815), 123

**Cox, Sir John** (d. 1672), naval officer and administrator, may have been the Captain John Cox of the Employment, hired by the state during the First Anglo-Dutch War in 1653. During the protectorate he gained considerable experience and an unblemished reputation as a ship's master. Upon the Restoration, and following his receipt of a certificate of loyalty, he was appointed master attendant at Chatham Dockyard on 4 July 1660, taking responsibility for all ships held in harbour. Here he replaced Thomas Arkinstall, a man disliked by the new regime and described as an Anabaptist. The office was of considerable importance, Chatham being the largest naval dockyard in the country. However, Cox's expertise as a seagoing officer was not lost to the navy, as he was appointed sailing master to the duke of York's flagship Royal Charles in 1665. Present at the battle of Lowestoft (3 June 1665) during the Second Anglo-Dutch War, he was involved in the controversy that resulted from the Dutch fleet's escape when the English fleet slackened sail overnight. The duke was initially held responsible with Cox, the senior master of the fleet, believing the order to have come from him. A parliamentary inquiry discovered that Henry Brouncker, an officer in the duke of York's household, had given the order, wishing to protect the duke. Despite the episode, no discredit fell upon Cox and as a reward for his efforts in the battle he was raised to the rank of captain and given command of the 58-gun *Mary*.

In April 1666 Cox was appointed master attendant at Deptford and in June of that year he captained the *Sovereign* during the Four Days Battle (1–4 June). In 1668, with the prospect of war with France, he was recognized as the duke of York's first captain when given command of his flagship, the *Prince*. In 1669 he returned to Chatham as resident commissioner, replacing the discredited Peter Pett. Cox had already been at odds with this influential family, the Petts having a quasi-monopoly of dockyard offices at Deptford and Chatham. Due to the influence of the Petts, his efforts to end corruption at Chatham were a failure. Indeed Pepys had expressed concern at Cox's return to Chatham, suggesting that it would be better to appoint John Tippetts to Chatham and Cox to Portsmouth, allowing both the advantage of working where they had not once been equals. As commissioner Cox was successful in clearing the Medway of ships wrecked during the Dutch raid in 1667, a task previously hindered by the attitude of his predecessors. He was again on board the *Prince* in 1672 and was knighted on 27 April while she was anchored at the Great Nore. Only five weeks later he was 'slain with a great shot being close by the Duke on the poop' of the *Prince* at the battle of Solebay on 28 May 1672 (Dyer, 225). He left a wife, Rachel, and five children: John, Elizabeth, Sarah, Lewis, and Mary.

PHILIP MacDOUGALL

**Sources** J. Charnock, ed., *Biographia navalis*, 1 (1794) · Pepys, *Diary* · *Samuel Pepys and the Second Dutch War: Pepys's navy white book and Brooke House papers*, ed. R. Latham, Navy RS, 133 (1995) [transcribed by W. Matthews and C. Knighton] · F. E. Dyer, 'Captain John Narbrough and the battle of Solebay', *Mariner's Mirror*, 15 (1929), 222–31 · P. G. Rogers, *The Dutch in the Medway* (1970) · PRO, ADM 2/1725 · PRO, SP 18/36/22 · will of Dame Rachel Cox, PRO, PROB 11/353, fols. 296v–298v

**Cox, John Charles** (1843–1919), antiquary and ecclesiologist, was born on 29 March 1843 at Parwich, Derbyshire, the sixth of the seven children of Revd Edward Cox (1802–1869) and Anna Horsfall (1803/4–1888). He had two brothers and four sisters. In 1843 his father was vicar of Parwich and in 1849 the family moved to Luccombe, Somerset, where his father was initially curate, then rector from 1856. John attended Repton School briefly in 1858, and continued his education at Somersetshire College, Bath. He entered Queen's College, Oxford, in 1862, but left without graduating in 1864–5. In December 1865 he was admitted as a partner in the Wingerworth Coal Company, Derbyshire, through his uncle, Henry Cox. On 23 October 1867 he married a distant cousin, Marian Smith (*b*. 1840). They had seven sons and three daughters born between 1868 and 1885, and lived at Chevin House, Hazelwood, near Belper, Derbyshire, until 1879.

Cox remained a partner in the coal company until 1885 and also benefited sufficiently from a generous marriage settlement to be financially independent; he was described in the 1871 census as a county magistrate, landowner, and colliery proprietor. Between 1868 and 1875 he aroused controversy as a magistrate giving public support

to a number of radical causes. He wrote several political pamphlets at this time, the first being *On the Established Church of Ireland* (1868). He was one of the founder members of the Land Tenure Reform Association in 1869. His chairmanship of two riotous meetings in Derby in 1871 and 1873 to which he had invited Sir Charles Dilke led to the lord chancellor's being petitioned (unsuccessfully) to remove him as a JP. He was president of the National Reform Union between at least 1873 and 1874. He stood as a parliamentary candidate for the National Education League at the Bath by-election on 28 June 1873, but withdrew before the poll. He also stood for Dewsbury as a radical Liberal at the general election of February 1874, when he secured 47 per cent of the votes; a local song, *The Death of J. C. Cox* (1874), commemorated his failure. Much of his energy at this time was devoted towards helping agricultural labourers. He was the most active member of the consultative committee of middle-class supporters of the National Agricultural Labourers' Union, founded in 1872, and developed a close friendship with Joseph Arch, president of the union. With his brother Henry Fisher Cox, he wrote a series of articles for *The Examiner* on 'The rise of the farm labourer' (1872–3), and the two brothers financed Arch's newspaper, the *English Labourer*, first published in June 1875. His involvement as a JP with the union was raised in the House of Commons on 25 March 1873, and he was summoned before the Farringdon magistrates on 15 April 1873 for obstruction when chairing one of its meetings.

Despite his early enthusiasm for disestablishment, Cox considered himself a churchman. After attending Lichfield College in 1879, he was ordained deacon in the Church of England in 1880 and priest in 1881. He was appointed curate of Christ Church, Lichfield, in 1880, and of Enville, Staffordshire, in 1883. He became rector of Barton-le-Street, Yorkshire, in 1886 and then of Holdenby, Northamptonshire (1893–1900). Some of his sermons were published, but he was best known in this period for his writings as a local historian, particularly of Derbyshire. His most substantial work was his earliest, 'Notes on the churches of Derbyshire', based on articles published anonymously in the *Derbyshire Times* in 1871–3, but enlarged to four volumes between 1875 and 1879. Cox was a fellow of the Royal Historical Society by 1873; he was awarded the Lambeth degree of doctor of laws in 1885 for his work on the records of the dean and chapter of Lichfield, and was elected fellow of the Society of Antiquaries of London in 1887. He wrote more than thirty articles for the journal of the Derbyshire Archaeological Society, and was its editor from 1885 to 1891. He also edited two national journals, *The Reliquary* (1887–1909) and *The Antiquary* (1888–94). While in Yorkshire he helped found and was first president of the East Riding Antiquarian Society. In 1899, as chairman of the Brixworth Board of Guardians, he gave a paper in favour of old-age pensions—recalling his long interest in social issues—to the Annual Poor Law Conference.

In 1900 Cox moved to Sydenham, Kent, and concentrated on writing. His later works established him as the leading authority on the English medieval parish church, and he was highly regarded for the breadth of his knowledge and the thoroughness of his historical research. A lucid writer in the nineteenth-century discursive tradition, Cox was so prodigious in his output that some of his works are rightly criticized for lacking accuracy and finish. The British Library catalogue contains about eighty references under his name. He contributed to numerous magazines, newspapers, and local and national archaeological journals. He was on the advisory council for the Victoria History of the Counties of England and compiled the sections on religious houses, ecclesiastical history, and forestry in thirteen volumes (1903–8). He edited for Methuen the series of the Antiquary's Books (1904–11) and also wrote several of them, notably *Parish Registers of England* (1909). He was the author of nine of Methuen's Little Guides to English counties (1903–16), and five of the County Churches series published by George Allen (1910–13). Cox's *How to Write a History of a Parish* (1879) was one of his most popular works, and reached five editions by 1909. His *English Parish Church* (1914) was the recognized handbook on the subject for many years.

Cox loved ancient ritual and the medieval church, and was indignant about the iconoclasm of the Reformation. He caused a considerable stir when he was received into the Roman Catholic Church on 25 April 1917 in the church of St Benedict, Stratton on the Fosse, Somerset, by the Revd Ethelbert Horne, OSB, of Downside Abbey. He suffered a cerebral haemorrhage at his home, 13 Longton Avenue, Sydenham, in November 1918, and died in the Brooklyn Nursing Home, Beckenham, on 23 February 1919. He was buried from the church of Our Lady and St Philip Neri, Sydenham, at Elmers End cemetery, Beckenham, on 28 February 1919.                  BERNARD NURSE

**Sources** R. F. Wearmouth, *Some working-class movements of the nineteenth century* (1948) • *The Tablet* (1 March 1919) • *Universe* (28 Feb 1919) • *The Guardian* [Church of England] (27 Feb 1919) • *Derby Mercury* (28 Feb 1919) • *WWW* • W. Cox, *Pedigree of Cox of Derbyshire* (1889) • C. J. James, *M.P. for Dewsbury* (1970) • M. Abbott, 'A short life of J. Charles Cox', *Derbyshire Miscellany*, 15 (2000), 127–33 [see also note on p. 176] • *Derby Mercury* (1871–4) • *Derbyshire Times* (1871–4) • D. A. Hamer, *The politics of electoral pressure* (1977) • P. Horn, *Joseph Arch (1826–1919): the farm workers' leader* (1971) • Crockford • m. cert. • d. cert. • parish register (burial), Sydenham, church of Our Lady and St Philip Neri, 28 Feb 1919 • D. G. Edwards, 'J. Charles Cox—a note on his coal mining interests', *Derbyshire Miscellany*, 16/3 (spring 2002), 92–3

**Archives** Derby Local Studies Library, Derby

**Wealth at death** £3500 1s. 3d.: probate, 29 April 1919, *CGPLA Eng. & Wales*

**Cox, Joseph Mason** (1763–1818), physician and asylum keeper, was born on 31 August 1763 at Bristol, the son of John Cox (*d.* 1788), a grocer, and Elizabeth Mason. His maternal grandfather, Joseph Mason, was the proprietor of a madhouse at Fishponds, near Bristol. About 1778 Joseph Mason Cox was placed by his grandfather as apprentice to Ebenezer Ludlow, a surgeon–apothecary of Sodbury. From November 1783 until August 1784 he was pupil to James Padmore Noble, surgeon to the Bristol Infirmary. He then pursued further medical studies in London, and subsequently at Edinburgh, Paris, and Leiden. Cox gained his MD at Leiden in June 1787. His early interest in the treatment of mental disorder was displayed in the subject of his thesis, *De mania*.

After Joseph Mason's death in 1779 the Fishponds madhouse was managed first by his daughters, Sarah and Elizabeth. When Sarah died in 1781, it passed to Elizabeth and John Cox. Following the death of his father, in June 1788, Joseph Mason Cox took over the house. He succeeded in consolidating Fishponds as one of the most successful of provincial private asylums. It catered for up to seventy patients, received mainly from the western counties. Cox married the wealthy Sarah Snooke of Bourton on the Water on 18 June 1795. They subsequently took up residence at Overn Hill House, Downend, Bristol. Cox later acquired other properties, including the manor of Patchway, near Bristol.

In addition to treatment at Fishponds, Cox also offered private consultations. His reputation as a mad-doctor was enhanced considerably by the publication of *Practical Observations on Insanity* in 1804, generally acknowledged as one of the period's most significant treatises on mental disorder. An enlarged second edition was published in 1806, and a third in 1813. There was also an American edition, as well as translations into French and German. Cox adhered to the established view that, given the correct treatment, most cases of insanity were curable in the early stages. Most of the methods he advocated in *Practical Observations* were similar to those of other contemporary practitioners, and included the use of emetic and purgative medicines, blisters, limited bleeding, and cold and warm baths. Purging he considered generally indispensable, as maniacs 'are frequently and most uniformly costive'. Vomiting, he was convinced, 'takes the precedence of every other curative mean'.

Although Cox argued that kindness and tenderness should be utilized wherever possible, he also accepted the need for coercive or drastic methods in certain cases. His celebrity largely rests on one particular treatment, known as the rotating chair or the circular swing chair, which he adapted from the work of Erasmus Darwin. The patient would be tightly strapped into a suspended chair, and rotated by a keeper turning a lever. The intensity of the treatment would vary according to the velocity, the duration, and whether the patient was in a vertical or prone position. The physical effects of swinging ranged from sleep, through vertigo, to evacuation and vomiting, which Cox considered particularly beneficial. There were also 'moral' treatment benefits, arising from the discomfort and fear induced, which acted as a deterrent to the repetition of undesirable behaviours. The circular swing chair remained in vogue, in public and private lunatic asylums, until about 1830.

A contemporary wrote that Cox was 'a fair classical scholar, spoke French fluently, and was altogether an accomplished gentleman and a pleasant companion. He was passionately fond of music, and for many years belonged to a quartet party, of which Joe Sturge was the leader' (Smith, 166).

Cox's later years were marred by poor health. He gave up the management of Fishponds in 1817, passing it on to his nephew. He died at Downend on 11 July 1818, aged fifty-five, and was buried at Downend Baptist Church, Bristol. His wife, Sarah, survived until 1852. The *Gentleman's Magazine* noted 'his amiable manners, the accomplishments of his mind, and the numerous Christian virtues which adorned his character through life and supported him in a long and painful illness' (*GM*, 92).     LEONARD D. SMITH

**Sources** J. M. Cox, *Practical observations on insanity* (1804); 2nd edn (1806) · H. Temple Phillips, 'The history of the old private lunatic asylum at Fishponds, Bristol, 1740–1859', MSc diss., University of Bristol, 1973 · R. Hunter and I. Macalpine, *Three hundred years of psychiatry, 1535–1860* (1963) · R. Porter, *Mind forg'd manacles: a history of madness in England from the Restoration to the Regency* (1987) · W. L. Parry-Jones, *The trade in lunacy: a study of private madhouses in England in the eighteenth and nineteenth centuries* (1972) · *Gloucester Journal* (25 Aug 1788) · R. Smith jun., 'Bristol Infirmary biographical memoirs', Bristol Royal Infirmary, Board Room, vol. 4 · private information (2004) · *GM*, 1st ser., 88/2 (1818), 92

**Cox, Keith Gordon** (1933–1998), geologist, was born on 25 April 1933 at 19 Sherbourne Road, Acocks Green, Birmingham, the second child of (Ernest) Gordon *Cox (1906–1996) and his wife, Lucie Grace, *née* Baker (1906–1962), a former schoolteacher. At the time of Cox's birth his father was lecturer in chemistry at Birmingham University. Cox and his elder sister, Patricia Ann Cox, spent the war years as evacuees in Canada. Following his return to England in 1944 Cox attended King Edward's School in Edgbaston, moving to Leeds grammar school in 1947 after his father had been appointed professor of inorganic and physical chemistry at Leeds University. In 1950 Cox won a Hastings scholarship to the Queen's College, Oxford, but delayed taking up his place until October 1952, after completing his national service in the Royal Engineers serving mainly in Germany, and reaching the rank of second lieutenant.

Cox's notably successful undergraduate career at Oxford, where he took a double first in honour moderations in natural science (1954) and finals in geology (1956), was marred only by an accident on a field excursion in the Lake District in 1955, as a result of which he lost an eye. The taste for field geology and igneous petrology which he acquired at Oxford was further developed in the Research Institute for African Geology at Leeds University; there, in 1956, Cox became an Oppenheimer scholar, working for his PhD on the Masukwe Complex in the Nuanetsi region of Southern Rhodesia, which he completed successfully in 1960. He continued his African work as a postdoctoral Oppenheimer research fellow and on 22 July 1961 married Gillian Mary Palmer (b. 1939), a Bedford College graduate in biology, whom he had known since childhood. They had three children, James, William, and Emma, and enjoyed a lifelong close and happy marriage.

Cox's early African work first acquainted him with the flood basalts of the Karoo region, one example of the vast outpourings of basic and other lavas which punctuate the earth's geological history. Cox and other Leeds geologists detailed the causative relationship between tectonic and magmatic events in southern Africa during the Mesozoic era in a model termed the Karoo volcanic cycle, which in some ways foreshadowed the later plate tectonics theory.

In 1963 Cox became lecturer in petrology at Edinburgh University, where he extended his studies of flood basalts to the Deccan in India and southern Arabia. Basalts form by the partial melting of the earth's mantle and are often associated with other volcanic rocks of the same age. Cox accordingly studied kimberlites—the diamondiferous rocks which contain fragments of the mantle, and the lavas of the Aden volcano whose variations he attributed to crystal fractionation of a parental basalt magma.

After returning to Oxford in 1972 as university lecturer in geology Cox began work on other flood basalt provinces—including the Parana region in South America, the Hebrides, and Antarctica—eventually establishing himself as a world authority on these rocks. Critically combining the results of his own field work and microscope studies with data from experimental petrology, isotope geochemistry, and, later, palaeomagnetism, he achieved, probably better than anyone else in his time, a clear appreciation of the whole spectrum of basalt phenomena, from derivation of the magma to its final solidification, and the role of basalt genesis in the fragmentation of tectonic plates, especially the ancient supercontinent of Gondwanaland.

Honours and position deservedly came his way: senior research fellow and tutor at Jesus College, Oxford (1973); *ad hominem* reader in petrology (1988); FRS (1988); editorships of the *Journal of Petrology* (1971–83) and *Earth and Planetary Science Letters* (1981–5). His lectures were models of clarity and his supervision of research students exacting but inspirational. The flavour of his teaching may be found in two influential textbooks, *An Introduction to the Practical Study of Crystals, Minerals and Rocks* (1967), written with B. N. Price and B. Harte, and *The Interpretation of Igneous Rocks* (1979), written with J. D. Bell and R. J. Pankhurst.

Cultured, witty, and hospitable, a gifted musician, watercolourist, and gardener—Keith Cox was widely known and admired and not only for his science. His premature death, by drowning in a sailing accident at Erraid, off the coast of Mull in the Hebrides, on 27 August 1998, cruelly cut short a life which had much more to offer.

DAVID BELL

**Sources** *Memoirs FRS* [forthcoming] · private information (2004) [family and colleagues] · D. Bell, *The Independent* (9 Sept 1998) · *The Times* (30 Sept 1998) · b. cert. · m. cert. · d. cert.
**Archives** University Museum, Oxford, papers
**Likenesses** photograph, repro. in *Memoirs FRS* [forthcoming]
**Wealth at death** under £200,000: probate, 1999, *CGPLA Eng. & Wales*

**Cox, Leonard** (b. c.1495, d. in or after 1549), schoolmaster, was, according to Anthony Wood, the second son of Laurence Cox of Monmouth and his wife, Elizabeth, *née* Willey. Nothing is known of his early years. He must have spent some time in France, and may also have studied in Prague: John Leland, in a Latin poem celebrating Cox's achievements, states that his praises were sung by both Prague and Paris ('Praga tuas cecinit, cecinitque Lutetia laudes'; Leland, 50). Between June 1514 and March 1516 Cox attended the University of Tübingen in Germany, where one of his teachers was Philip Melanchthon. His next documented appearance is at Cracow, where he matriculated in September 1518 having already gained the title of *poeta laureatus*. At both Tübingen and Cracow his place of origin is given as Thame in Oxfordshire. On 6 December 1518 he delivered a Latin oration, *De laudibus celeberrimae Cracoviensis academiae*: this was printed before the end of the year.

In 1520, after lecturing at the University of Cracow for two years, Cox accepted an invitation to become headmaster of the school in Levoča, a royal free city which then lay at the crossing of major trade routes within the kingdom of Hungary. At the end of 1521 he transferred to a similar post at Košice, some 40 miles to the south-east. The friends who arranged these appointments, Johann Henckel and Jan Antonin, born in Levoča and Košice respectively, were members of a humanist circle in eastern Europe dedicated to promoting the ideals of Desiderius Erasmus. Cox also enjoyed the patronage of several prominent figures in the civil and ecclesiastical life of Poland, all of them connected with Erasmus: they included Justus Ludovicus Decius, the Polish royal secretary, Krzysztof Szydłowiecki, prefect of the Cracow region, Piotr Tomicki, bishop of Cracow, his nephew Andrzej Krzycki, and the younger Jan Łaski, later to become a leading reformer.

When Henckel left Košice in 1524 Cox returned to Cracow and resumed lecturing at the university. His experiences as a schoolmaster bore fruit, however, with the publication in 1526 of a treatise on education, *Libellus de erudienda juventute*, dedicated to Tomicki and modelled principally on Quintilian and the *De ratione studii* of Erasmus. During the same year he published another pedagogical work, *Methodus humaniorum studiorum*, but this has not survived. Between 1526 and 1529 he ran a school whose pupils included the relatives or protégés of several of his noble patrons. On 28 March 1527, at the prompting of Szydłowiecki, he addressed a letter to Erasmus. Erasmus' reply was printed in his *Opus epistolarum* of 1529.

Having returned to England during 1529 Cox gained appointment as master of the grammar school at Reading. In February 1530 he supplicated for the degree of MA at Oxford, citing twelve years of study as evidence of fitness. (The statement that he was admitted to Cambridge in 1526–7 is based on a confusion.) During the same year he contributed prefatory verses in Latin to John Palsgrave's *Lesclarcissement de la langue francoyse*. It was probably also in 1530 that Cox's most important work, *The Arte or Crafte of Rhethoryke*, was printed for the first time. This was the first rhetorical treatise to be published in the English language. A second, corrected, edition was dated 1532. In his preface of dedication to Hugh Faringdon, the abbot of Reading, Cox informs the reader that the work is 'partely traunslatyd out of a werke of Rhethoryke wrytten in the lattyn tongue, and partely compyled of myne owne' (Cox, *Rhethoryke*, 42). He never names the author or title of the Latin work he has used. In 1899 Frederic I. Carpenter revealed it to be Melanchthon's *Institutiones rhetoricae*, first published in 1521. The scope of Cox's treatise is limited to

the fundamental division of rhetoric known as invention, that is, the devising of matter, true or plausible, that would make a speaker's or writer's case convincing.

Cox's religious outlook may well have begun to move towards advocacy of reform during the 1520s. After his return to England he soon made clear where his sympathies lay. In 1531 or 1532 he came to the assistance of John Frith, who had been placed in the stocks at Reading. According to John Foxe, Frith:

> desired that the schoolmaster of the town might be brought to him, who at that time was one Leonard Cox, a man very well learned … [Cox,] being overcome with his eloquence, did not only take pity and compassion on him, but also began to love and embrace such an excellent wit and disposition unlooked for, especially in such a state and misery … whereupon the schoolmaster went with all speed unto the magistrates, grievously complaining of the injury which they did show unto so excellent and innocent a young man. Thus Frith, through the help of the schoolmaster, was freely dismissed out of the stocks, and set at liberty without punishment.   (*Acts and Monuments*, 5.5–6)

In 1534 Cox published an English version of Erasmus' paraphrase on the epistle to Titus. His prologue celebrates the 'gracyous matrymonye' of Henry VIII and Anne Boleyn, and asserts the divine election of the king 'to be hed of his Englishe flocke, as well in spirituall governaunce as in erthly domynyon' (Cox, *Paraphrase of Erasmus Roterdame*, sig. Aiiʳ, Aviiʳ). He sent his translation to the printer John Toy and asked him to show it to Thomas Cromwell, for whom he proposed to translate either Erasmus' *Modus orandi Deum* or his paraphrases on the epistles to Timothy, or any work that Cromwell should decide. He added: 'I am also a translating of a boke which Erasmus made of the bringing upp of children [*De pueris instituendis*, 1529], which I intend to dedicate to the saide Master Cromwell' (Cox, *Rhethoryke*, 13). None of these projected translations was ever printed.

During the first half of 1540 Cox addressed two letters to Cromwell. Accompanying the first he presented a copy of his edition of William Lily's *De octo orationis partium constructione libellus*, corrected by Erasmus; in the second, dated 23 May 1540 from Caerleon, he looked forward to dedicating to Cromwell a work 'uppon rhetorik, which I entende to entitle Erotemata rhetorica' (Cox, *Rhethoryke*, 15). This treatise was never published. In 1541, however, Cox received a royal patent confirming his post as master of the school at Reading, and granting him use of the schoolhouse and an annual salary of £10 from the revenues of Cholsey manor, formerly the property of Reading Abbey. He was replaced as schoolmaster at Reading in 1546.

Cox's translation of the paraphrase on the epistle to Titus was reissued in 1549 as part of the project to provide copies of all the New Testament paraphrases for every parish church in England. For the new edition Cox replaced his earlier prologue with a letter of dedication to John Hales, clerk of the hanaper to Edward VI and founder of the grammar school at Coventry. In it he mentions that he possessed a licence to preach. He goes on to inform his readers that he had decided to translate two works by the fifth-century Greek patristic writer Mark the Hermit, 'the one of the lawe of the spirite, and the other of them that thynke to be justifyed by their workes' (Cox, 'Letter', sig. EEEEiir). These translations have not survived, but they are mentioned by John Bale, who states that the first of them was from Greek into Latin.

No reliable evidence relating to Cox's life after 1549 can be found. According to Anthony Wood he had a son named Francis. A man of this name graduated BD at Oxford in 1576 'after seventeen years in Theology'. He gained a doctorate in divinity at Oxford in 1594, held prebends in the diocese of Chichester, and died as a residentiary canon of Chichester Cathedral in 1613.

S. F. RYLE

**Sources** Wood, *Ath. Oxon.*, new edn, 1.123–4 · L. Cox, *The arte or crafte of rhethoryke*, ed. F. I. Carpenter (1899) · *Opus epistolarum Des. Erasmi Roterodami*, ed. P. S. Allen and H. M. Allen, 7: *1527–1528* (1928), 2–5, 70–71 · S. F. Ryle, 'Leonard Cox', *British rhetoricians and logicians, 1500–1660: second series*, DLitB, 281 (2003), 58–67 · *DNB* · Emden, *Oxf.*, 4.145 · P. G. Bietenholz and T. B. Deutscher, eds., *Contemporaries of Erasmus: a biographical register*, 1 (1985), 353–4 · L. Cox, trans., *The paraphrase of Erasm[us] Roterdame upon ye epistle of Paule unto Titus* [1534] · L. Cox, 'Letter', in *The seconde tome or volume of the paraphrase of Erasmus upon the Newe Testament*, trans. M. Coverdale and J. Old (1549) · J. Leland, *Principum, ac illustrium aliquot et eruditorum in Anglia virorum* (1589), 50 · *The acts and monuments of John Foxe*, ed. S. R. Cattley, 8 vols. (1837–41), vol. 5, pp. 5–6 · Rymer, *Foedera*, 1st edn, 14.714–15 · A. Breeze, 'Leonard Cox, a Welsh humanist in Poland and Hungary', *National Library of Wales Journal*, 25 (1987–8), 399–410 · A. Breeze and J. Glomski, 'An early British treatise upon education: Leonard Cox's *De erudienda iuventute* (1526)', *Humanistica Lovaniensia*, 40 (1991), 112–67 · private information (2004) [Mrs I. L. Williams]

## Cox, Leslie Reginald

**Cox, Leslie Reginald** (1897–1965), palaeontologist and malacologist, was born on 22 November 1897 in Islington, north London, the son of Walter Cox, and his wife, Jessie Lucy (*née* Witte). Educated at South Harringay county school, he won a foundation scholarship to Owen's School, Islington, in 1909. In 1916 he won an open scholarship to Queens' College, Cambridge but war service delayed his entry to the university. He joined the Royal Naval Air Service, experimental section, and worked on smokescreens and flame-throwers. In April 1918 he took part and was wounded in the raid to block the German submarine base at Zeebrugge. In 1919 he finally went to Cambridge to read for part one of the natural science tripos, making geology his main subject. He attained a double first (1920 and 1921), and took his MA in 1926. (He obtained his ScD in 1937.)

Cox's 1920 reputation as a promising member of the university jazz band may have led him to attend the art student's dances at South Kensington, at which he met his wife, Hilda Cecilia Lewis, associate of the Royal College of Arts, daughter of the Revd William John Lewis of Mountsorrel, Leicestershire: they were married in September 1925. Both their son and their daughter eventually took degrees in geology at Cambridge.

As a child Cox spent his holidays with grandparents at Charmouth, Dorset, where fossil collecting became a hobby. While at Cambridge he applied for a vacancy in the department of geology at the British Museum (Natural History) and was appointed an assistant keeper (second class) in 1922, becoming responsible for fossil Mollusca (apart from the Ammonoidea). He engaged in research on post-Palaeozoic Mollusca, and his scientific contribution was such that it was thought to be too valuable for his promotion to an administrative position. However, in 1951 he was given a special merit promotion to senior principal scientific officer, following his election as a fellow of the Royal Society in 1950. In 1961 Cox surprisingly accepted the post of deputy keeper in the department of palaeontology, adding its responsibilities to the many he had already undertaken.

Many of Cox's early papers consisted of faunal descriptions of material collected by field geologists during exploration throughout the world. These enabled him to gain a wide understanding of the diverse morphology of the Mollusca and their distribution through time. He augmented this with examination of major collections in institutions and with field work in Britain and occasionally in Europe. Methodically he compiled a unique card-index system to the literature, together with a thematic reprint collection, both of which formed a reliable basis for his wide research and subsequent authoritative publications.

A cursory analysis of Cox's publications (more than 160) indicates that Mesozoic faunas (52), particularly those of the Jurassic (40), were his main interest and that among the Mollusca this was directed to the Bivalvia (69). His involvement with colonial geology is revealed by those on African (27) and Indian (10) faunas. Although Cox's systematic description of British (28) and foreign faunas was important, his career was punctuated by more significant contributions. His work on the evolutionary history of the rudists, an aberrant group of bivalves (1933), was the first of several major reviews of molluscan subjects that either summarized previous work, or stimulated research: for example, the *Thoughts on Classification* of the two classes (both 1960); *Progress in Fossil Malacology* (1943); and *British Palaeontology: a Retrospect and Survey* (1957). Cox's collaboration (1948–50) with William Joscelyn Arkell to revise John Morris and John Lycett's monograph, *Great Oolite Mollusca*, was equally important, while his monograph on *British Cretaceous Pleurotomariidae* (1960) revealed the value of this neglected field. An interest in past literature and its relevance to nomenclature led to his authoritative work on William Smith (1930, 1942, 1948) and a sequence of papers in preparation for his *Treatise on Invertebrate Paleontology* contributions (1960, 1969), together with papers on several early descriptive works by writers such as Richard Pulteney (1940) and Gérard-Paul Deshayes (1942).

Cox's thoroughness when dealing with any subject was typified by the records he made of every published molluscan classification, in order to establish the usage and priority of supra-generic names. Although he was not trained as a zoologist, his methodology and acumen enabled Cox to write extremely useful biological reviews of all the invertebrate classes he was involved with. He was astute enough to recognize molluscan body organs and structures on the rare occasions that these were preserved in fossil specimens (1960), or to describe the discovery of a bivalved gastropod (1960).

As one of the world's authorities on Mollusca, Cox devoted the last decade of his career to contributions to the *Treatise on Invertebrate Paleontology*. The magnitude of these contributions to the gastropod and bivalve parts of this work was emphasized when the editors, R. C. Moore and N. D. Newell, dedicated the *Bivalvia* volumes to him. Cox's continued efforts in persuading other researchers to contribute, and then giving them generous assistance, were vital to that enterprise. But his own authoritative and comprehensive introductions to both sections have to be recognized as the most valuable outcome of his devotion to Mollusca.

Cox was acknowledged to be essentially a quiet and modest man, who dealt with everything in a calm manner and was never known to become irate. He kept his scientific and private lives separate. At Cambridge he had enjoyed rowing and retained this sporting link by attending Henley Regatta whenever possible. He regularly cycled into the museum from Hendon, a dangerous journey in the 1960s.

Through his career Cox became involved with several scientific societies. He joined the Geological Society in 1922, was awarded the Murchison fund in 1929, the Lyell medal in 1956; he served twice on its council (1940–44, 1950–55), and was three times appointed vice-president (1952–4, 1957–61, 1962–5). From 1925 he was treasurer of the Malacological Society of London. He served as treasurer until 1951 (running the society throughout the Second World War), and was president in 1957–60. As a member of the Geologists' Association, he was made a vice-president in 1953 and became president in 1954–5. Inevitably he was one of the founder members of the Palaeontological Association, served as vice-president between 1958 and 1960, and was president at the time of his death. Cox was appointed OBE in 1958. He died suddenly at his home 30 Haslemere Avenue, Hendon, on 5 August 1965. His wife and two children survived him. His geological colleagues acknowledged the irreplaceable loss of his guidance, wisdom, balanced judgement, and quiet humour.                                R. J. CLEEVELY

**Sources** A. Rothstein, E. I. White, and C. P. Nuttall, *Memoirs FRS*, 12 (1966), 106–21 · *DNB* · R. C. Moore and N. D. Newell, dedication, in L. R. Cox and others, *Mollusca 6: Bivalvia*, 3 vols. (1969–71), pt N of *Treatise on invertebrate paleontology*, vol. 1, N1–N2 · F. E. Eames, 'L. R. Cox', *Proceedings of the Malacological Society of London*, 37 (1966), 129–35 [bibliography] · C. P. Nuttall, 'Leslie Reginald Cox', *Proceedings of the Geological Society of London*, no. 1636 (1965–6), 187–8 · *The Times* (12 Aug 1965), 10 · *WWW* · W. T. Stearn, *The Natural History Museum at South Kensington: a history of the British Museum (Natural History), 1753–1980* (1981), 242 · *CGPLA Eng. & Wales* (1965) · personal knowledge (2004)
**Archives** NHM | NHM, corresp. with Charles Maurice Yonge
**Likenesses** photograph, repro. in Rothstein, White, and Nuttall, *Memoirs FRS*
**Wealth at death** £5719: probate, 8 Nov 1965, *CGPLA Eng. & Wales*

**Cox** [*née* Cunningham], **Marie-Thérèse Henriette** [Molly, Mollie] **(1925–1991)**, television producer, was born in Constantinople on 18 October 1925, the fourth of six children of Arthur Joseph Cunningham and his wife, Aileen Turner. Her father was Lloyds agent in Constantinople, and when he became editor of the *Egyptian Gazette* the family moved to Alexandria. On their return to England, Molly was educated at the Convent of the Assumption in Kensington Square, London. When she was sixteen she left school and worked as a clerk at the music publishers Boosey and Hawkes before joining the BBC in 1942 in the information unit of the overseas service. After a sound engineering course (on which she was the only woman trainee) she became a junior programme engineer, creating sound effects for many popular programmes including the serial *Dick Barton*, which presented difficult technical problems, with complicated action and effects enacted live. On 28 June 1947 she married the head of the studio management department, Charles Terence (Terry) Cox (1912/13–1962), son of John Cox, an aircraft engineer. She left the BBC when her two sons, Dominic and Oliver, were born.

After her husband's death in 1962 Molly Cox returned to work at the BBC in order to support her sons, first in radio and then in television, where she went on attachment to *Blue Peter*. In 1964 she joined the team led by Joy Whitby which created *Play School*, the new daily programme for pre-school children made for the opening of BBC2. Together with Cynthia Felgate, Anna Home, and Daphne Jones, she became a pioneering and talented producer in the children's programmes department. Her experience of her own children was extended to a keen understanding of the varied television audience, and especially to those disadvantaged children for whom television was a comfort and an escape. She believed that television could be a powerful influence for good, which could expand horizons and educate in the widest sense. She wanted to bring children the best in literature, music, art, and entertainment. A strong visual sense and keen intellect informed all her work, and led to an exploration of different forms and techniques. She insisted that children, though less experienced, were as varied in personality and interests as adults, and deserved as wide a range of programmes.

Out of the *Play School* unit a new series of story-telling was developed and, with Anna Home, Cox encouraged the best actors, writers, and graphic artists to contribute to the daily *Jackanory*, which for over twenty-five years presented the best of children's literature, from Greek myths to contemporary fiction. A strong narrative was a characteristic of all Cox's productions, whether fiction or documentary, and she used striking images in a variety of visual styles. She made series on history (*The Story behind the Story* and *Unsolved Mysteries*), on archaeology (*The Story beneath the Sands*), on scientific discoveries (*Breakthrough*), on natural history (*Fabulous Animals*), and on explorers and plant hunters, as well as two distinguished Bible series, *In the Beginning* and *A New Beginning*. She had a strong Christian faith, and after much research she presented effective stories from the Bible with Ray Smith as narrator and specially commissioned illustrations by Graham McCallam and Paul Birkbeck. These were a labour of love, as were explorations of other major religions through the eyes of children of different faiths who took part in a series of film exchanges with British children, in *If you were me*. Her outlook was always international and inclusive and led her to film in many different countries and to make special programmes in Northern Ireland.

All Cox's programmes were stimulating and imaginative; they were also entertaining, and recognized children's need for fun, humour, and activity. *Zokko* was the first original television comic, and invited the audience to send in jokes from the playground. *We are the Champions* was presented by Ron Pickering as the first televised children's competition comprising outdoor games. Through all her innovations Cox's vivid personality, dark, elegant good looks, and independence of thought were combined with humour to inspire her colleagues, and these qualities made her a valued contributor at international television meetings. She was a tireless advocate for public service broadcasting and the independence of the BBC. Her determination to make programmes specially for a British audience caused her to oppose the purchase of the much admired American series *Sesame Street*, since its cost would have brought an end to *Play School* and other BBC commissions. She was a formidable debater and a strong influence on the policy of the children's programmes department.

Away from the BBC, Cox was a loving mother and grandmother. The Roman Catholic church was central to her life. She supported the charity Prisoners of Conscience and the Society of St Vincent de Paul. After her retirement in 1987 she became secretary of a trust funding charities which supported victims of torture and slavery. She died of cancer at the Royal Brompton and National Heart Hospital, Chelsea, London, on 3 November 1991, and was buried at the Roman Catholic church in Marlow, Buckinghamshire. Her life was celebrated at a requiem mass at Farm Street Church, Farm Street, London, on 10 January 1992. She was survived by her two sons.

MONICA SIMS

**Sources** *The Independent* (7 Nov 1991) · *The Times* (4 Dec 1991) · personal knowledge (2004) · private information (2004) [Mrs Gerry Elwes; BBC colleagues] · m. cert. · d. cert.

**Likenesses** photograph, repro. in *The Independent*

**Wealth at death** £224,990: probate, 27 Feb 1992, *CGPLA Eng. & Wales*

**Cox, Owen** (*d.* 1665), naval officer, came probably from a seafaring family in north-east England, though nothing certain is known of his origins. He first appears in 1646, commanding a small prize on the north-east station, where he continued in other hired merchantmen. Early in 1648 he was nominated to command the *Phoenix*, a fourth-rate vessel under construction, but the move was aborted when the squadron in the Downs mutinied in May 1648 and declared in favour of the king. His ship, the *Pelican*, was among those to defect, but he himself escaped and a few days later he and several other commanders declared their continued loyalty to parliament. He was given a new command, the *Recovery*, and sailed in autumn 1648 with the earl of Warwick's expedition to confront Rupert and the rebel fleet at Helvoetsluys. Thereafter he served in the North Sea until 1650, when he was promoted to the *Constant Warwick*, a powerful privateer part owned by Warwick and hired by the state, and sailed with Henry Appleton's squadron to protect English shipping in the straits. Cox proved a successful commander, capturing several prizes and achieving some notoriety. On the outbreak of the First Anglo-Dutch War in 1652 Appleton's squadron took refuge at Leghorn. Cox found himself with another squadron under Richard Badiley, trapped at Elba, but Badiley soon sent him back to Leghorn to Appleton and his colleagues, 'to put some life into them' (Badiley, 1), and he was appointed to command the *Bonadventure* there. But Appleton opposed Cox's plan to recapture the *Phoenix*, which had been captured by the Dutch in August and was now among their ships at Leghorn, and when Cox persisted Appleton tried to sack him to scupper the plan. Cox ignored him and Badiley, who had now received overall command from England, backed the project. On 20 November 1652 Cox led a party of volunteers in a daring dawn raid, boarding the *Phoenix* as she lay at anchor amid the Dutch fleet, and carried her away to Naples after fierce hand-to-hand fighting. The exploit was long remembered. At Naples he was briefly gaoled after clashing with the Spanish viceroy over the sale of a prize, and then rejoined Badiley at Elba. Together they mounted an operation to relieve Appleton's squadron, planning to approach Leghorn to draw out the Dutch, whereupon Appleton would follow and the two small English squadrons would engage the larger Dutch force simultaneously. In the action that followed, on 4 March 1653, Appleton's force came out prematurely and was totally destroyed before the other squadron was near enough to help. On his return to England, Appleton blamed the disaster on Badiley and Cox, who had led their own force safely home, but an official inquiry vindicated them, and in December Cox was awarded £500 as reward and compensation for his losses. Cox retained his command of the *Phoenix*, in 1653–4, and fought in the great actions against the Dutch off the Gabbard and Texel, of which he sent an account to Cromwell.

Following the peace of 1654 Cox withdrew or was dropped from naval service, but failing to prosper appealed in vain to Cromwell in January 1656 for relief and employment, pleading his six children, the costs of medical treatment for his earlier injuries, and £400 he had lost by the capture of the *Bonaventure* at Leghorn. He may have commanded a merchant vessel in the straits later that year, but in 1658 with Sir George Ayscue he entered the service of the king of Sweden, and the two commanders and 700 seamen crossed to Sweden in November that year with William Goodsonn's expeditionary force. Cox's pugnacious spirit served the Swedes well. Commanding a fleet of ten ships in July 1659 he encountered a Dutch-Danish squadron at Ebeltoft, seized the larger vessels, burnt thirty transports, and captured 1000 Brandenburg and Imperial troops they were carrying. After firing more ships at Arhausen he returned to Sweden in triumph. His exploits had ruined Danish and Dutch plans to invade Swedish territory, and he was ennobled by Charles X of Sweden, appointed vice-admiral, and 'vastly rewarded' (Manley, 57). Following Sweden's peace with Denmark he returned to England in the summer of 1661, commanding the Swedish ship *Raphael* (70 guns). Though ostensibly bound for Portugal, he lay in the Downs for four months, allegedly denouncing the Restoration, commending Venner's recent Fifth Monarchist rising and predicting the speedy destruction of Charles II. He was arrested and gaoled in the Gatehouse, and Lord Chief Justice Foster hoped to find a second witness so that he could be tried for treason. None materialized, and when the Second Anglo-Dutch War broke out Cox was granted letters of marque in February 1665 as commander of the frigate *Nathan*. Dissidents urged him to use it to bring back republican exiles from the continent, or free General Lambert from Jersey. Cox was in fact planning to sail for the Mediterranean, but the ship foundered in a storm in Yarmouth road on 14 August, with the loss of all hands. The astrologer John Gadbury claimed to have warned him that the stars foretold disaster. Cox was certainly a long-standing devotee of astrology, and a client of both John Booker and William Lilly, to whom he had brought a gold chain in 1658 from the king of Sweden, as a reward for Lilly's propagandist writings.

Though Cox's independent spirit and tendency to ignore orders barred him from the highest positions in the Commonwealth navy, he was among its most successful and enterprising commanders.     BERNARD CAPP

**Sources** *CSP dom.*, 1649–65 · J. R. Powell and E. K. Timings, eds., *Documents relating to the civil war, 1642–1648*, Navy RS, 105 (1963) · H. Appleton, *A remonstrance of the fight in Leghorn Road* (1653) · R. Badiley, *Capt. Badiley's reply to certaine declarations from Capt. Seamen* (1653) · T. A. Spalding, *A life of Richard Badiley, vice-admiral of the fleet* (1899) · S. R. Gardiner and C. T. Atkinson, eds., *Letters and papers relating to the First Dutch War, 1652–1654*, 1, Navy RS, 13 (1899) · B. Capp, *Cromwell's navy: the fleet and the English revolution, 1648–1660* (1989) · R. C. Anderson, 'Ayscue and Cox in Sweden', *Mariner's Mirror*, 47 (1961), 298–300 · R. Manley, *The history of the late warres in Denmark* (1670) · PRO, HCA 25/9 · J. Gadbury, *Nauticum astrologicum* (1691)

**Cox, Sir Percy Zachariah** (1864–1937), diplomatist and colonial administrator, was born on 20 November 1864 at Herongate, Essex, the youngest of the three sons of Arthur Zachariah Cox, formerly Button (*d.* 1870), of Harwood Hall, Essex, deputy lieutenant of the county, and his wife Julienne Emily, younger daughter of Richard Saunders of Largey, co. Cavan, and Hawley House, Kent. He was educated at Harrow School and the Royal Military College, Sandhurst. In 1884 he obtained a commission with the 2nd Cameronians, then stationed in India. In 1889 he joined the Indian Staff Corps, and on 14 November he married (Louisa) Belle, youngest daughter of Surgeon-General John Butler Hamilton. Soon afterwards he held minor appointments in the Maratha states of Kolhapur and Savantvadi.

In 1893 Cox left India for the protectorate of British Somaliland, at that time governed by the resident at Aden

Sir Percy Zachariah Cox (1864–1937), by Vandyk, 1918

as a dependency of the government of India, and after this his career progressed rapidly. He was appointed assistant political resident at Zeila, transferred to the principal port of Berbera in 1894, and in May 1895 was made captain of a punitive expedition against the Rer Hared clan, which had blocked trade routes and was raiding coastal groups. Despite having at his command only 52 trained Indian and Somali troops and 1500 untrained and inefficient irregulars, he defeated the Rer Hared in only six weeks. The expedition had not been officially approved from Aden, but its success established Cox's reputation for military acumen and general ability. Later that year he was promoted assistant to the viceroy's agent in Baroda.

The next turning point in Cox's career came in 1899. He was intending to join the American explorer A. Donaldson-Smith in an expedition to the regions between the River Nile and Lake Rudolf, when the new viceroy of India, Lord Curzon, offered him the chance to become political agent and consul at Muscat (in what became Oman). He took up the post in October 1899 and was to spend virtually the rest of his career in the Middle East. His immediate task required all his powers of tact. Britain and France had both recognized the independence of Muscat, but the British had signed a secret land convention with its ruler, Sultan Feisal, and regarded the area as part of their informal empire, while the French not only gave protection to the local trade in slaves but leased a coaling station from Feisal. As a result Feisal had been ordered to board the British ship *Eclipse*, whose guns were trained on his palace, reprimanded, and told that the subsidy from the government of India had been removed.

This was the tense situation which Cox inherited and which he had to try to assuage. He succeeded remarkably well, so that the subsidy was restored, French influence was curtailed, and Feisal even agreed to send his son to the Delhi Durbar of 1903. In the same year Curzon visited Muscat, judging that Cox virtually ran the place, and invested Feisal with the GCIE. Cox himself had become a CIE in 1902.

In 1904 Cox was promoted acting political resident in the Persian Gulf as well as consul-general for the Persian provinces of Fars, Lurestan, and Khuzestan. He became resident in 1909. He had responsibility for the defence of the region, no easy task after the Persian revolution of 1905–7 and one which twice necessitated the calling in of imperial forces, to Bushehr in 1909 and Shiraz in 1911. He had also to promote British interests generally. One means for achieving this was his support of Sheikh Khaz-aal of Muhammarah, bordering Turkey in the Euphrates delta: he promised British aid when Turkey threatened aggression, and in return Khazaal leased the Shatt al-ʿArab, on the Euphrates estuary, to the Anglo-Persian Oil Company for the construction of refineries and an oil pipeline. At Kuwait Cox improved relations with the local ruler, Mubarak, and opened negotiations with Ibn Saʿud, the Wahabi ruler of Nejd who was eventually to extend his territories to cover virtually the whole of modern-day Saudi Arabia. Also to Cox's credit stands his promotion of British trade in the gulf, which more than doubled in value from 1904 to 1914, the suppression of the arms trade, and improvements in communications. He was created KCIE in 1911.

Cox (Kokkus to the Arabs) was highly respected for several reasons. He was a quick, efficient, and tireless worker; he was incorruptible; he had a genuine interest in the local people; he was shrewd and patient; he had a fine command of Arabic; and he was conspicuously silent, a trait which impressed the Arabs. He was also a popular and easily recognisable figure—tall, thin, and with a crooked nose, the result of an injury received in a football match. He was to become more popular still from 1914, when Turkey's entry into the First World War led Britain to promote Arab nationalism in the Persian Gulf.

Cox became secretary to the government of India early in 1914, but the outbreak of war saw his dispatch back to the gulf as chief political officer with the Indian expeditionary force. He was promoted an honorary major-general in the course of the war, and saw some action with Major-General Charles Townshend, but his main role was administrative and political. He masterminded the army's political relations in Mesopotamia. Baghdad was taken in March 1917 and Jerusalem in December. Palestine and Syria fell the following year. Before this, however, the campaigns against the Turks were long and arduous, and allies were needed. Cox's main contribution was to encourage the resistance of Ibn Saʿud, who was also being wooed by Turkey. In December 1915 Ibn Saʿud and Cox met at the Hasa oasis and signed a treaty whereby Britain was to grant a subsidy of £5000 a month. On the other hand the Foreign Office was encouraging Ibn Saʿud's arch-rival Sherif Hussein as the spearhead of an Arab nationalism which would help defeat the Turks. Cox knew that his treaty with Ibn Saʿud and the championing of Hussein were incompatible. But there could be no thought of resigning during the war, and instead he had to pretend to the Wahabi ruler that Britain's championing of the Sherif was not as serious as it seemed. As a sop, Ibn Saʿud was knighted. Cox himself was made KCSI in 1915 and GCIE in 1917.

Britain's policy in the Middle East was in many ways Machiavellian. As well as encouraging local rulers, Britain and France, in the Sykes–Picot agreement, decided to divide the region into spheres of influence. This dual policy was apparent in Mesopotamia (soon to be called Iraq): Britain accepted a League of Nations mandate for the region and at the same time set up an Arab administration which it aimed to control.

After the armistice in November 1918 Cox became acting-minister in Tehran, where he negotiated a (largely ineffectual) Anglo-Persian treaty, but in June 1920 he was appointed KCMG and made high commissioner in Iraq, where during the previous month a widespread revolt had broken out, largely in protest at the power exercised by British officials. Having arrived in Baghdad on 11 October 1920 to replace Sir Arnold Wilson, he embarked on the most important work of his career. His first action was to set up a council of state under the venerable naqib of Baghdad. Policy was hammered out in detail at the Cairo conference, with colonial secretary Winston Churchill, in March 1921. Initially Churchill had been in favour of withdrawing from the region, which was proving a drain on the exchequer and over whose boundaries there were numerous disputes: he advised maintaining a presence only at the Basrah oilfields. But Cox, ably supported by Gertrude Bell, his oriental secretary, argued strongly in favour of remaining and of setting up an Arab regime under Feisal, son of Sherif Hussein. Cox had Feisal named king of Iraq in July 1921, after he had sent the main rival claimant to the throne into exile. His accession was confirmed by a referendum later that month. Soon there was not a single British officer with executive power, Cox's men having to exercise influence as unobtrusively as possible.

It was a situation fraught with difficulty. In particular there was agitation that the mandate, which local people thought signified a degrading tutelage, should be replaced by a treaty. Cox accepted this, with the proviso that Britain should still be the mandatory power for Iraq at the League of Nations; but negotiating its provisions proved problematic. Feisal wanted to retain good relations with Britain, but his standing with Iraqis depended on his being seen not to be a British puppet. The British wanted a malleable figurehead, but he aspired to be a sovereign monarch. He dismissed several ministers without consulting Cox and he was loath to sign a 20-year treaty which pledged his willingness to be guided by the high commissioner on key issues. Cox began to feel that Feisal had 'unmistakably displayed the cloven hoof … he is without doubt both crooked and insincere' (Pearce, 69), and he was considering exiling him. A crisis was reached in August 1922, when a demonstration against Cox took place in the grounds of the king's palace, and the high commissioner demanded an apology from Feisal for this insult. Feisal was saved by a convenient attack of appendicitis a few days later: he took to his bed on 24 August 1922 and the compliant naqib signed the treaty in his absence, while Cox had a number of leading anti-British critics arrested. Cox followed up this success by meeting Ibn Saʿud for a second time at ʿUqair on the shore of the Hasa. Not only did he persuade Ibn Saʿud to recognize the kingdom of Iraq but, for the first time, he secured his agreement to limit his territory: where he and Cox disagreed over the precise boundaries on the map, they accepted that there should be a neutral zone between the two frontier lines. Cox was appointed GCMG in 1922, and he left Iraq for retirement in Britain on 4 May 1923, when the omens for the future of the new state looked relatively auspicious. According to one expert, 'he had done more than any other man to establish the infant Iraq state on a foundation of something like security' (Coke, 308).

In retirement Cox received honorary degrees from the universities of Oxford (1925) and Manchester (1929). He was president of the Royal Geographical Society (1933–1936) and chairman of the Mount Everest committee. He died on 20 February 1937 while hunting at Melchbourne, near Bedford. His wife, who had spent long periods with Cox abroad and who was appointed DBE in 1923, survived him; his only son was killed in action in 1917 and his only daughter died at birth.                                    ROBERT PEARCE

**Sources** DNB · P. P. Graves, *The life of Sir Percy Cox* (1941) · D. Howarth, *The desert king: the life of Ibn Saud* (1965) · R. Pearce, *Sir Bernard Bourdillon* (1987) · R. Coke, *The heart of the Middle East* (1925) · J. Darwin, *Britain, Egypt and the Middle East* (1981) · *The Times* (22 Feb 1937) · BL OIOC, 10R N/1/210, 177 · Walford, *County families* (1898) · *CGPLA Eng. & Wales* (1937)

**Archives** RGS, travel journals in Somaliland and Persian Gulf | BL, corresp. with Sir Arnold Wilson, Add. MS 52455 · CUL, corresp. with Lord Hardinge · St Ant. Oxf., Middle East Centre, corresp. with Humphrey Bowman · St Ant. Oxf., Middle East Centre, corresp. with H. St J. B. Philby

**Likenesses** Vandyk, photograph, 1918, NPG [*see illus.*] · W. Stoneman, photograph, 1924, NPG · W. Stoneman, photograph, 1930, NPG · bronze plaster bust, RGS

**Wealth at death** £28,455 8s. 9d.—'save and except unsettled land': probate, 16 April 1937, *CGPLA Eng. & Wales*

**Cox, Richard** (c.1500–1581), bishop of Ely, and one of the most influential of the first generation of protestant reformers, was born at Whaddon in Buckinghamshire. Nothing conclusive is known about his parents, though the heralds record his father's name as Richard.

**Education and early career** The younger Richard Cox was educated at Eton. From Eton he followed the predictable path to King's College, Cambridge, arriving there in 1519, gaining a fellowship in 1522, and proceeding BA in 1524. The next year he was one of those invited by Wolsey to form part of the first foundation of Cardinal College at Oxford as a junior canon. His BA was incorporated on 7 December 1525, and he was created MA in the following

Richard Cox (c.1500–1581), by unknown artist, c.1570–80

July. Cox was part of the group who carried reforming ideas from Cambridge to Oxford, though as a minor figure he was punished only by deprivation of his canonry when the heresy was uncovered. According to Foxe he 'conveyed himself away towards the north' (*Acts and Monuments*, 5.4) and remained out of the eye of the government for several years. In 1529 he became headmaster at Eton. His innovatory syllabus at Eton was designed to train pupils in the latest humanist pedagogy, and included use of the grammar texts of Peter Mosellanus, a Leipzig academic whose work has been characterized as radical Erasmianism. Roger Ascham in *The Schoolmaster* put into the mouth of the greatest of Cox's pupils, Walter Haddon, a double-edged compliment, describing Cox as 'the best schoolmaster of our time' and 'the greatest beater' (Ascham, 6–7). Throughout his career Cox retained this combination of concern for good learning and the authoritarianism of the schoolmaster.

Cox returned to Cambridge in 1535, perhaps at the persuasion of Bishop Goodrich of Ely, to whom he was chaplain, and proceeded BTh the same year. His DTh followed in 1537. By 1540 he had emerged as one of the reforming theologians routinely consulted by the Henrician regime. He answered the questions on the mass that preceded the drafting of the King's Book (1543), and was on the commission to nullify Henry's marriage to Anne of Cleves. Cox delivered the opening sermon at the convocation of 1542, and was one of those to whom the abortive task of providing a new translation of the Bible was assigned. It is difficult to characterize his theology at this time with any precision, though he was already firmly identified with the Cranmerian group of reformers. Like his archbishop, Cox placed great emphasis on due obedience to the king as supreme head of the church. He participated in 1546 in the attempts to persuade Anne Askew to moderate her views on the eucharist, and vigorously criticized Edward Crome for failing to make a proper recantation of his heretical views. He also cultivated friendship among those less ideologically committed: William Paget was a confidant, and the recipient of some of his most interesting letters on the state of the church and the dangers of lay greed.

**Dean of Christ Church, Oxford** With responsibility came promotion: Cox had already received the rectory of Kelshall, Hertfordshire, in February 1533, and by 1540 he was chaplain to both Cranmer and the king. Foxe says that it was Goodrich who brought him to Henry's attention. This is consistent with his royal appointment as archdeacon of Ely in December 1540. In June 1542 he became a prebendary of Lincoln, and in 1544 was presented by Cranmer to the rich benefice of Harrow on the Hill. He resigned Kelshall in February 1544, and gained Hougham, Lincolnshire, in November 1545. But the significant rewards of the late Henrician years were his elevation as the first dean of Osney Cathedral, Oxford, later transferred to Christ Church, in January 1544, and his appointment as tutor, and subsequently almoner, to young Prince Edward. In the latter role, which he occupied actively between 1543 and Henry's death, Cox played a critical part in moulding Edward's intellectual and religious views. Much historiographical debate has been focused on Cox's appointment, and on that of his fellow tutor John Cheke, made his 'supplement' in 1544. Little is certain, though there is a likelihood that Henry's physician, William Butts, and Sir Anthony Denny were advocates for the evangelical teaching team. Edward's relationship with Cox is given formal expression in his letters displaying his Latinity. The prince is said to have remarked: 'I have two tutors, Diligence [Cheke] and Moderation [Cox]' (Nichols, 1.ccxxxvi).

The one prize that eluded Cox in Henry's reign, as in the next, was a bishopric. He was considered for the proposed see of Southwell, Nottinghamshire, in the earliest version of the new bishoprics scheme in 1541–2, but these plans were rejected as too extravagant for the royal purse. In 1550 Marten Micronius wrote optimistically to Bullinger that Cox would be given the see of Winchester after Gardiner's deprivation; it went to John Ponet instead. This may be because Cox was of more value to the Edwardian regime in Oxford, where Christ Church became his principal base from the beginning of 1547. Somerset's regime recognized the need for reforming effort at Oxford, and in May 1547 the new dean of Christ Church was chosen as chancellor of the university. He faced a daunting task, which he tackled with predictable vigour. He welcomed Peter Martyr Vermigli to Oxford early in 1548, and did everything in his power to encourage other continental reformers to join him. At least eleven Swiss students did so, providing Cox with a major personal link to their key

mentor, Heinrich Bullinger. Cox encouraged Martyr to lecture on Corinthians, and in 1549 was a sympathetic moderator in the latter's great disputation on the real presence in the eucharist. He was also the dominant figure among the royal visitors appointed by the crown in November 1548, though not active until May and June 1549. The visitors presented new statutes to the university covering many issues, above all the enforcement of protestant worship. They also gained permanent notoriety for an overly zealous attack on 'superstitious' books, which, according to Gerard Langbaine, writing almost a century later, left 'not one book in it [the University Library] of all those goodly Manuscripts' (Langbaine, preface). Cox has always been particularly blamed for this assault, though there is no conclusive contemporary evidence about his role.

**Protestant evangelist** The book burning crisis is in sharp contrast with the dean's care for learning in Christ Church itself, where he was almost certainly the author of the 1547 Edwardian statutes and developed a strategy for undergraduate education which provided a model for later Tudor Oxford. Even on his own territory, however, Cox faced constant opposition from conservative canons such as William Tresham, one of Martyr's opponents in the 1549 eucharistic debate. One cause of conflict was Cox's marriage, which probably took place in 1547, and was flaunted after 1549 when his wife publicly resided in Christ Church, later joined by Mrs Vermigli. Within the wider university the dean struggled, with limited success, to suppress Catholic disputants and to promote protestants to college headships. In 1551 he was part of a second unpopular royal visitation of the university. By 1552 he sought permission to resign the difficult chancellorship and this was approved by convocation on 19 July.

Cox continued to be active in national religious politics despite the demands of Oxford. He was royal almoner, and was sometimes called on for major sermons, as in July 1548 when he preached against Gardiner at Paul's Cross. In 1550 he was required by the council to use his preaching skills in Sussex to calm protests at the removal of stone altars. He was one of the eight man commission to whom the final drafting of the revision of the ecclesiastical law was entrusted in 1551. Above all he appears to have been involved in all stages of the revision of the liturgy, the issue that was to dominate his Marian exile. These efforts brought further rewards. He was made a canon of Windsor in April 1548, and from October 1549 onwards he had a London base as dean of Westminster. As at Eton and Christ Church, Cox sought to regularize the educational and organizational life of the abbey. Westminster also provided him with his second experience of lay pressures on ecclesiastical property. The first had come in 1547 when he had been permitted to alienate the manor of Harrow on the Hill to Edward North, chancellor of augmentations. At Westminster the dean and chapter were unable to resist demands for long leases on their lands, and Cox struggled ineffectually to retrieve property within the precincts taken over by courtiers and other public figures.

**Exile** On Mary's accession Cox was imprisoned in the Marshalsea for his part in the Jane Grey affair. But he was released to house arrest on 19 August 1553, and found it relatively easy to escape to the continent with Edwin Sandys the following May. They seem to have made for Strasbourg, to become part of the English congregation already well established in that city. There Cox might have remained had the new congregation at Frankfurt not unwisely sent out invitations to the other scattered churches to participate with them in a reformed worship unconstrained by the Edwardian pattern. The 'learned men of Strassburg', as they are called in the key narrative of these events, were sufficiently alarmed to send Cox to restore discipline (Arber, 31). He found a congregation led by John Knox already using a radically simplified liturgy, though against the wishes of a dissenting minority. All Cox's preaching and disciplinary skills were engaged, and within two weeks of his arrival in March 1555 he had outmanoeuvred Knox by revealing the latter's seditious political views to the Frankfurt magistrates, and had him expelled. He then proceeded to reconstitute the pattern of worship with an adapted version of the 1552 Book of Common Prayer. Calvin, in a reluctant acceptance of the compromise in the interest of unity, described Cox as 'more given and addicted to your country than reason would' (ibid., 78).

In two ways, however, the conformists were willing to depart from home precedent. First, a hierarchy of head pastor, ministers, seniors, and deacons was established that was not dissimilar to Genevan models, though without congregational election. Second, the congregation retained the practice of singing metrical psalms that had not been an established part of Edwardian worship. Cox's own commitment to congregational singing is indicated by his translations of some of the Lutheran hymns incorporated in the printed editions of metrical psalms under Elizabeth, and by his use of the psalms in household worship when he was bishop of Ely. He left Frankfurt, probably in November 1555, and seems to have gone to Zürich to build personal contacts with the Swiss reformers, especially Bullinger. In 1557 he returned briefly to Frankfurt to mediate in the dispute between Robert Horne and Thomas Ashley on church order, then travelled to Cologne and Worms, making new acquaintances, including the Catholic humanist Cassander. The diversity of his contacts in exile is reflected in the range of his continental correspondents after 1559.

**Bishop of Ely** Cox returned swiftly to England on Elizabeth's accession, and preached some of the important sermons of the early months of the reign, including an hour and a half's tirade on the need for reform at the opening of the 1559 parliament, 'the peers standing the whole time' (*CSP Venice, 1558–80*, 23). When eight protestant divines were chosen to debate with the Catholics in May 1559 he was inevitably among them, though Robert Horne was their principal spokesman. He was nominated first for the

bishopric of Norwich, with a *congé d'élire* issued on 5 June 1559, but the deprivation of Bishop Thirlby enabled him to negotiate a transfer to the far more lucrative see of Ely, to which he was nominated on 28 July. Elizabeth and Cecil may have acquiesced in the change because of Cox's long experience with the universities: he had been nominated as a visitor of Oxford again in June 1559, and at Ely he quickly became embroiled in disciplinary issues at Cambridge. The price of promotion for all the new bishops was the exchange with the crown of lands for appropriated rectories and other spiritual properties under the new legislation 1 Eliz. c. 19. The legislation and its consequences were vigorously opposed by the incomers, especially by Cox, who orchestrated the protests of his colleagues to the queen. Lands willed to the church, they argued, were of their nature sacrosanct and appropriations should not be traded since 'the parishes ought to enjoy them' (Inner Temple, Petyt MS 538/54, fol. 53). This latter view Cox had already expounded in his letters to Paget in 1546: he continued to regard impropriations with abhorrence and in his last years tried to persuade Whitgift to fight for their restitution. Cox was nevertheless forced to accept the unequal exchange offered to Ely, whereby the see lost most of its outlying manors in Norfolk, Suffolk, and Hertfordshire. During the first decade of Elizabeth's reign he proved a vigorous diocesan, trying to remedy what he called the 'miserable and deplorable' state of his see with good discipline (BL, Add. MS. 5813, fol. 78). He visited in person, enforced rigorous standards for clerical residence, kept thorough records of ordination examinations, and, as time went on, developed a reputation as a stern investigator of Catholic recusancy.

In these early Elizabethan years Cox also played a striking role at the heart of the ecclesiastical regime. He often expressed his opinions with surprising candour to the queen, most famously in his opposition to her use of the crucifix and candles in her private chapel. In 1561 he took up the defence of priests' marriage, lecturing Elizabeth on its scriptural foundations. He also often formed a triumvirate with Parker and Grindal in collective attempts to develop or modify policy. They worked together on the ecclesiastical commission from 1559 to the early 1570s; shared the preparation of the 1561 *Interpretations*, the first attempt to define the use of vestments; collectively urged the queen to marry; discussed and approved Jewel's defence of the English church, and drafted the 1566 *Advertisements* on clerical dress and conformity. It is likely that Cox also shared with his fellow bishops the attempt to engage in further reform of the church in the 1563 convocation. His views often appear close to those of Grindal: marked by a concern for unity among protestants and for the provision of a proper ministry for the church. But in his suspicion of Geneva and his anxieties about discipline his position was nearer to that of Parker. Fear of Genevan influence may lie behind his insistence, as early as 1564, that there should be a new translation of the Bible, since the present diversity made 'a fowle gere' (PRO, SP 12/34/2). His own contribution to this project, published in 1568 as the Bishops' Bible, was the translation of Acts and

Romans. His concern for order is seen in his acceptance of the queen's right to her chapel crucifix, despite his deep ideological misgivings.

Cox's first wife, known only by her first name of Jane, died in 1568. He was quickly remarried; his new wife, also called Jane, was the daughter of George Awder, alderman of Cambridge, and widow of William Turner, the radical dean of Wells. It joined him, he wrote defensively to Cecil, to a good Christian woman of suitable age. The queen was not amused and Cox probably never regained her full favour. His second decade as prelate was overshadowed by this, by his problems with the temporalities of his see and by growing conflict with the puritan clergy. The challenge the last posed to episcopal government through their demand for presbyterianism seems to have dissipated his last sympathies for further reform. In the Admonition crisis of 1572 Cox acted as the bishops' chief apologist to the Swiss reformers who might counteract the influence of Geneva, Bullinger, and Rodolph Gualter. The puritans, he wrote to the latter in 1573, had broken down 'the barriers of all the order of our church' (Robinson, *Zurich Letters*, 1.280). Swiss mediation served little purpose, but the bishop had the satisfaction of neutralizing Zürich's sympathy with the godly and retaining his own friendships.

**Last years** By the early 1570s Cox was less active in national affairs, though he maintained a barrage of correspondence to Cecil and Elizabeth. Between May and October 1571 John Leslie, bishop of Ross and agent for Mary, queen of Scots, was his prisoner in London and the country, and kept a diary which shows the bishop entertaining his unwanted guest with considerable courtesy. They hunted together in the Isle of Ely and discussed the possibility of another general council of the church. Cox's old interest in learning was displayed when he urged Leslie to hunt out and save the books being lost from the Scottish monasteries. However, Cox's last years were overshadowed by conflict about the possessions of his see. The key actors were Roger, Lord North, who sought via the queen a long lease of the prize manor of Somersham, Huntingdonshire, and Sir Christopher Hatton, who wanted Ely Place in London. The bishop initially resisted both, alleging his duty to defend the property he had inherited, though eventually he yielded to the Hatton demand in 1576. He defended Somersham more vigorously, provoking North into producing a great bill of complaints against the bishop at the end of 1575, alleging partiality to his family, mismanagement of the Ely estates, and deficiencies in his service of the crown. Cox was presented as imperious as well as greedy, characteristics shared by his second wife, whom one tenant referred to as 'Jezebel'. Some colour is lent to this partial narrative by the language of the bishop's own letters. In 1562 in a fen rights dispute he had referred to the tenants of Wisbech as a 'stout ... disordered ... and lawless people' (*Ninth Report*, HMC, appx 1, 296). Though the North dispute was eventually compromised others followed, and by 1579 Cox had decided to seek leave to retire. After difficult negotiations he was granted the manor of Doddington for life and a pension of £200, and should have resigned in

February 1580, in his eightieth year. The agreement was never ratified and he died, still bishop, at Downham, Cambridgeshire, on 22 July 1581, and was buried in Ely Cathedral.

Cox's will left most of his goods, valued at £1334, to his widow and seven surviving children. One of his daughters, Joan, had married Matthew Parker's son John; his oldest son Richard achieved knighthood and a position of some influence in the Isle of Ely. The bishop's interesting inventory gives full details of his library, which was dominated by the writings of the fathers and by the controversial literature of the Reformation. The works of his friends in Switzerland, especially Bullinger and Gualter, had a prominent place on his shelves. In contrast, his earlier interests in humanist writing and teaching are barely reflected in his books. Cox remained until his death a very internationally minded protestant, who was nevertheless fiercely defensive of the English church; a determined advocate of reform through the supreme governorship, who deeply mistrusted Elizabeth and looked back to her brother's regime with nostalgia; a sharp enemy of the zealous godly who fought with equal zeal for his own vision of protestantism. Calvin described him as proud, arrogant, and possessed of 'an immoderate fervour for meddling' (Gorham, 348). He may have deserved the first two of these negative epithets; the last also seems accurate enough, but explains much of the dynamism he brought to the task of constructing a national church.

FELICITY HEAL

**Sources** R. van der Molen, 'Richard Cox, bishop of Ely: an intellectual biography of a Renaissance and Reformation administrator', PhD diss., Michigan State University, 1969 · G. L. Blackman, 'The career and influence of Richard Cox, bishop of Ely', PhD diss., U. Cam., 1953 · F. Heal, 'The bishops of Ely and their diocese, c.1515–1600', PhD diss., U. Cam., 1972 · *Hist. U. Oxf.* 3: *Colleg. univ.* · [W. Whittingham?], *A brief discourse of the troubles at Frankfort*, ed. E. Arber (privately printed, London, 1907) · H. Robinson, ed. and trans., *Original letters relative to the English Reformation*, 1 vol. in 2, Parker Society, [26] (1846–7) · H. Robinson, ed. and trans., *The Zurich letters, comprising the correspondence of several English bishops and others with some of the Helvetian reformers, during the early part of the reign of Queen Elizabeth*, 2 vols., Parker Society, 7–8 (1842–5) · *Correspondence of Matthew Parker*, ed. J. Bruce and T. T. Perowne, Parker Society, 42 (1853) · *The acts and monuments of John Foxe*, ed. S. R. Cattley, 8 vols. (1837–41) · R. Ascham, *The schoolmaster*, ed. L. V. Ryan, [new edn] (1967) · *LP Henry VIII*, vol. 19/1 · *Literary remains of King Edward the Sixth*, ed. J. G. Nichols, 1, Roxburghe Club, 75 (1857) · G. Langbaine, ed., *J. Cheke's 'The true subject to the rebel'* (1641) · *CSP Venice, 1558–80* · Inner Temple Library, London, Petyt MS 538/54 · BL, Add. MS 5813 · 'The diary of John Lesley, bishop of Ross, April 11–October 16, 1571', *The Bannatyne miscellany*, ed. D. Laing, 3, Bannatyne Club, 19b (1855), 113–56 · *Ninth report*, 1, HMC, 8 (1883) [Wisbech] · G. C. Gorham, ed., *Gleaning of a few scattered ears during the period of the Reformation in England* (1857) · C. H. Garrett, *The Marian exiles: a study in the origins of Elizabethan puritanism* (1938) · A. F. Leach, *Educational charters and documents, 598 to 1909* (1911) · Emden, *Oxf.*, 4.146–7 · PRO, SP 12/34/2 · BL, Lansdowne MS 29 · R. Cox, diary, CCC Cam., MS 168 · Gon. & Caius Cam., MS 53/30 · PRO, PROB 11/63 · J. W. Clay, ed., *The visitation of Cambridge ... 1575 ... 1619*, Harleian Society, 41 (1897)

**Archives** LPL, corresp.

**Likenesses** oils, c.1570–1580, Trinity Hall, Cambridge [see illus.] · oils, second version, Trinity Cam. · portrait, King's Cam. · portrait (posthumous), bishop's palace, Ely

**Wealth at death** £1334: will, PRO, PROB 11/63; inventory, Gon. & Caius Cam., MS 53/30

**Cox, Sir Richard**, **first baronet** (1650–1733), lord chancellor of Ireland and author, was born at Bandon, co. Cork, on 25 March 1650, the only child of Captain Richard Cox (*d.* 1651), an officer in the royalist army during the confederate wars, and his wife, Katherine (*d.* 1652), daughter of the recorder of Clonakilty, Walter Bird, and formerly wife of Captain Thomas Batten. Although his grandfather Michael Cox (*d.* 1659) had owned substantial property near Kilworth, co. Cork, the family estate was much reduced by the rebellion of 1641 and subsequent warfare. The younger Richard Cox inherited from his grandfather 'an interest' near Kilworth, which he sold for £150; following the Restoration he received land in Galway worth £26 per annum in settlement of his father's arrears of army pay. He was brought up by his grandfather Michael Cox, and later by his uncle John Bird, attending a school at Bandon and then that kept by Thomas Barry at Clonakilty. After leaving school at fifteen he 'spent three years idly' (*Autobiography*, 9) before beginning to practise as an attorney in the manor courts of the earl of Burlington and Cork, where his uncle was a seneschal. In September 1671 he travelled to London with the earl of Burlington and Cork and entered Gray's Inn, where he was called to the bar on 9 August 1673. After returning to Ireland he spent seven years living quietly at Clonakilty before, by his own account, I 'roused myself from that lethargy' (*Autobiography*, 11) and moved to Cork city to develop his legal practice. He was elected recorder of Kinsale in 1680, built up a profitable practice, and bought land. In 1685 he wrote an optimistic account of conditions in co. Cork for the proposed volume of topographical surveys organized by William Molyneux, celebrating the pacification of the region and its social and economic progress.

In April 1687 Cox fled the Catholic dominated Ireland of Tyrconnell, where he claimed to be in danger on account of a charge he had given as chairman of the quarter sessions at Bandon in April 1679, upholding the claim of a popish plot. He settled at Bristol, where he practised law and completed his *Hibernia Anglicana, or, The history of Ireland from the conquest thereof by the English to this present time*. This appeared in two parts, in 1689 and 1690, the first part dedicated to William and Mary, the second to William. He was the probable anonymous author of *Aphorisms Relating to the Kingdom of Ireland* of January 1689, comprising twenty-eight propositions addressed to members of the convention in England and arguing the case for immediate and substantial military intervention. When Sir Robert Southwell, whom he had come to know at Bristol, was appointed King William's secretary of state, Cox accompanied him to Ireland as one of his secretaries. He was appointed recorder of Waterford and on 15 September 1690 was sworn in as second justice of the common pleas. On 1 May 1691 he was appointed governor of the county and city of Cork. In the months that followed he presided over a brutal local war, using a greatly expanded local militia to defend an 80 mile frontier and suppress Jacobite irregulars operating within his territory. By his own

Sir Richard Cox, first baronet (1650–1733), by unknown artist

account his men 'killed and hanged not less than 3,000 of them' (TCD, MS 1180, p. 159, Cox to —, 8 Oct 1691). Following the end of the war Cox was admitted to the privy council on 13 April 1692 and knighted on 5 November.

On 10 February 1694 Cox became one of the commissioners for the administration of forfeited lands. In June 1695 he was removed from the privy council, according to himself because of his anticipated opposition to the proposed enactment of a toleration bill for protestant dissenters. He became chief justice of the common pleas on 16 May 1701 and was restored to the privy council a few days later. In the intensifying party rivalry of Queen Anne's reign he emerged as a leading tory. Having initially sought the patronage of the Boyle family he now became closely associated with the second duke of Ormond, becoming one of the trustees for his estate. He travelled to London in April 1703 for consultations about the forthcoming meeting of parliament, returned to Ireland with Ormond, and was sworn in as lord chancellor on 6 August. He served as lord justice 1705–7 and was created a baronet on 21 November 1706. When the other lord justice, Baron Cutts, died in January 1707 Cox risked impeachment by refusing to issue writs for the election by the privy council of a new chief governor on the grounds that this would have conflicted with Ormond's patent as viceroy.

When Ormond was replaced by the earl of Pembroke in June 1707 Cox was removed from the lord chancellorship as one of a series of dismissals intended to facilitate the admission to office of some of the former whig opposition. He returned to office under the next tory ministry, but in the lesser position of chief justice of the queen's bench (5 July 1711). Following the accession of George I he was again removed, in September 1714, and was subsequently censured by the House of Commons for his role in two political trials: the proceedings against Dudley Moore, who had defiantly delivered a suppressed eulogy of William III during a theatrical performance, and against the corporation of Dublin, which had refused to accept a tory mayor. He spent the rest of his life in retirement on his property at Dunmanway.

Cox was an unwavering supporter of the revolution of 1688. *Hibernia Anglicana* dismissed as groundless the distinction between *de jure* and *de facto* monarchy. Later he unhesitatingly supported the Hanoverian succession. However, he derided the notion of 'Revolution principles' and described himself as 'an anti-Whig. I hate their canting, lying and hypocrisy and I know too many of them aim at mutiny and schism' (Cox to Edward Southwell, 13 Aug 1714, BL, Add. MS 38157, fol. 108). In the same way he saw Catholics as irreconcilable opponents of the English and protestant interest in Ireland, while at the same time refusing to overstate the threat they posed. He believed that former Jacobites were entitled to the concessions agreed in the treaty of Limerick, and complained that the willingness of the forfeiture commissioners to do common justice was misrepresented as partiality. Later, in the tense summer of 1714, he refused to join in the general panic over the activities of French recruiting agents. He was also firmly hostile to dissent. In 1695 he opposed a toleration bill for protestant dissenters 'by saying I was content every man should have liberty "of going to heaven", but I desired nobody might have liberty of coming into government, but those who would conform to it' (*Autobiography*, 15). Later he condemned whig attempts to promote the repeal of the sacramental test by talking up the Catholic threat, where in fact 'five in six of the Irish are poor insignificant slaves, fit for nothing but to hew wood and draw water', insisting at the same time that dissenters could never be admitted to power, 'because assuredly if they were in, they would put us out' (Cox to Southwell, 24 Oct 1706, BL, Add. MS 38154, fol. 86).

The other great tenet of Cox's political life was his commitment to the English interest in Ireland. His *Some thoughts on the bill … for prohibiting the exportation of the woollen manufactures of Ireland to foreign parts* (1698), addressed to the House of Lords, argued that the proposed legislation would damage England itself, as well as Irish protestants, who were 'Englishmen sent over to conquer Ireland, your countrymen, your brothers, your sons, your relations, your acquaintance' (17). In 1714 he referred to plans, apparently never realized, to write a reply to William Molyneux's statement of Irish constitutional rights. He was also prepared to make some distinction between Catholics of English and of Irish descent. His contribution to Irish history, *Hibernia Anglicana*, is generally dismissed as a hasty compilation. It depicts pre-conquest Ireland as a violent and underdeveloped society, and traces the history of succeeding centuries in terms of the opposition between English government and Irish barbarism and treachery, complicated from the sixteenth century by the conflict between popery and protestantism. However he did not dismiss the native Irish as racially inferior. His *An Essay for the Conversion of the Irish* (1698) argues that the Gaelic Irish were in fact of the same ethnic origin as the people of Great Britain, and offers an optimistic account of the virtues they might display once liberated from popery. The allegation that he had the Gaelic poet Hugh MacCurtin imprisoned for having criticized *Hibernia Anglicana* appears to have originated, in 1749, with Charles Lucas, then engaged in controversy with Cox's grandson, and is most probably unfounded.

Cox married Mary Bourne (c.1658–1715), the daughter of John Bourne, a minor landowner in co. Cork, on 26 February 1674. She died on 1 June 1715. Cox died at Dunmanway on 3 May 1733, following a fit of apoplexy some months earlier, and was buried there. In 1699 he had noted the birth of his twenty-first child. On his death, however, his successor was his grandson **Sir Richard Cox**, second baronet (1702–1766), born on 23 November 1702, the son of Cox's eldest son, Richard (c.1678–1725), MP for Tallow (1703–15) and Clonakilty (1717–25), and Susanna French (d. 1716). Cox matriculated at Oxford on 4 May 1720. As MP for Clonakilty (1727–66) he opposed the government in 1737 but subsequently took a leading part in the proceedings against Charles Lucas, for which he was rewarded in 1750 with the collectorship of customs for Cork. He was one of Henry Boyle's strongest supporters during the money bill dispute of 1753–6, and one of the last of the party to be reconciled with the castle. However his appointment in 1758 to a seat on the Irish revenue board confirmed his return to full favour.

Cox was an improving landlord, praised for promoting the manufacture of linen round Dunmanway. He published several works on economic development, including *A letter from Sir Richard Cox to Thomas Prior, esquire, showing from experience a sure method to establish the linen manufacture* (1749). Using the pseudonym Anthony Litten he also wrote a series of pamphlets attacking Lucas under the title *The Cork Surgeon's Antidote Against the Dublin Apothecary's Poison* (1749). Though mainly concerned to defend the existing Anglo-Irish connection as beneficial to both kingdoms, and to attack Lucas as an irresponsible rabble-rouser, these included an effective critique of Lucas's autodidactic obsession with ancient grants and charters, arguing that texts and precedents from the remote past must be read in their historical context. Cox married Catherine Evans, daughter of a co. Limerick landowner, on 13 September 1725, and died in February 1766.

S. J. CONNOLLY

**Sources** *The autobiography of the Rt. Hon. Sir Richard Cox bart. lord chancellor of Ireland*, ed. R. Caulfield (1860) · F. E. Ball, *The judges in Ireland, 1221–1921*, 2 vols. (1926) · J. R. O'Flanagan, *The lives of the lord chancellors and keepers of the great seal of Ireland*, 2 vols. (1870) · letters from Cox to Edward Southwell, 1687–1726, BL, Add. MSS 38153–38157 · R. E. Burns, *Irish parliamentary politics in the eighteenth century*, 2 vols. (1989–90) · GEC, *Baronetage*
**Archives** University College, Cork, entry book of grants | BL, letters to Lord Nottingham, Add. MSS 29588–29589 · BL, letters to

Sir Robert Southwell and Edward Southwell, Add. MSS 38153–38157 · Bristol RO, corresp. with Edward Southwell · NL Ire., corresp. with duke of Ormond · TCD, corresp. with George Clarke · TCD, corresp. with William King
**Likenesses** oils, NG Ire. [*see illus.*] · portrait; formerly at Royal Hospital, Kilmainham, 1887

**Cox, Sir Richard**, second baronet (**1702–1766**). *See under* Cox, Sir Richard, first baronet (1650–1733).

**Cox, Richard** (1718–1803), army agent, was born in February or early March 1718, probably at Stapleton, in Darrington, near Pontefract in the West Riding of Yorkshire, the son of Joshua Cox and his wife, Mary, daughter of James Greenwood of Stapleton Park and York. He had an elder sister, Frances. The Cox family lived at Ledston Hall, near Pontefract, and was prosperous and well-connected. They moved at some point to Holborn, London, from where Joshua Cox was auditor of the estates of Lord Weymouth. Joshua acquired much property in the metropolis and took a lease of the manor of Quarley in Hampshire. On his death in 1757, all this real estate passed to his son, Richard. In 1747 Richard Cox had married Caroline (*d.* 1793), daughter of Sir William Codrington, baronet, of Dodington, Gloucestershire. Cox was then living at Aspenden Hall in Hertfordshire. They had one son and two daughters.

Cox was forty years old before his career became important. From 1746 he was secretary to General (afterwards Field Marshal) Lord Ligonier, who appointed him agent for the 1st regiment of foot guards in 1758. When Ligonier was made master-general of the Board of Ordnance in 1759, he appointed Cox secretary to the board and agent to the Royal Regiment of Artillery. Cox was also banker to Ligonier and his dependants. As agencies multiplied, he went into partnership with Henry Drummond, and moved his office to Craig's Court, Whitehall, in 1765; he kept on his former office in Albemarle Street, as a town house.

When Drummond left to enter his family's bank, the partnership became Cox and Mair (1772–9), then Cox, Mair, and Cox. This later change reflected the admission to partnership, with limited responsibilities, of Cox's son, Richard Bethell Cox (1754–1832), who married Jane Diana, daughter of John Drummond of Stanmore. Bad feeling arose with Arthur Mair, caused by Richard Bethell Cox's unbusinesslike behaviour. In 1783, when Mair died intestate, his administrator sued to recover money allegedly owing from the agency. Charles Greenwood, a cousin of Cox, was brought into full partnership in 1783. Richard Bethell Cox, accused by his own father of dissipation and extravagance, was forced to resign in 1790. His son, Richard Henry Cox, joined the agency in 1795, aged sixteen, and the partnership became Cox, Greenwood, and Cox in 1801. By then it was handling fourteen regiments of cavalry, sixty-four of foot, and seventeen of militia, and it was employing around thirty-five clerks.

Dickey Coxe, as his musician friend Dr Charles Burney referred to him (*Memoirs of Doctor Burney*, 3.195), was a socialite, who entertained lavishly both at Quarley and in

London. Besides Burney, who spent a week or two at Quarley every summer, Cox's intimates included David Garrick, who called him 'my dear old Friend the Richard of all Richards' (Lloyds TSB Group Archives, A56f/11), and Gabriel Piozzi, whose wife, Hester, thought him 'Musick-mad … People call Cox Cantabile Dicky now' (Balderston, 1.455). Another good friend was Sir Robert Murray Keith, a fellow member of a monthly dining club called The Gang. For none of these people, however, did Cox act formally as a banker, and his own current account as well as the banking affairs of his army agency were conducted by Messrs Drummond. In 1795 Cox opened a bank account with Thomas Hammersley of Pall Mall, brother-in-law of Charles Greenwood.

A portrait of Cox by Sir William Beechey shows a relaxed, opulent man of medium build. He outlived his wife by some ten years, dying on 26 August 1803, aged eighty-five. He was buried on 3 September 1803 at Quarley church, where his son erected a memorial bearing a twenty-five-line inscription. His daughter Caroline married Sir Thomas Champneys of Orchardleigh, Somerset; she died in 1791. His other daughter, Mary, married Benjamin de la Fontaine, barrack-master at the Savoy Palace, London.

After Cox's death, the Greenwood name took precedence in the agency. Only in 1834 did the simple title Cox & Co. emerge, and this survived until 1923, when the firm (having briefly absorbed Henry S. King & Co.) was taken over by Lloyds Bank.                                  JOHN BOOKER

**Sources** K. R. Jones, 'The Cox's of Craig's Court and Hillingdon', typescript, 1969, Lloyds TSB Group Archives · K. R. Jones, 'Cox's 1758–1923: the story of an army agent', typescript, Lloyds TSB Group Archives · R. S. Sayers, *Lloyds Bank in the history of English banking* (1957) · J. R. Winton, *Lloyds Bank, 1918–1969* (1982) · R. Whitworth, *Field Marshal Lord Ligonier: a story of the British army, 1702–1770* (1958) · Madame D'Arblay [F. Burney], *Memoirs of Doctor Burney*, 3 vols. (1832) · R. Lonsdale, *Dr Charles Burney: a literary biography* (1965) · J. Hemlow, J. M. Burgess, and A. Douglas, *A catalogue of the Burney family correspondence, 1749–1878* (1971) · *Thraliana: the diary of Mrs. Hester Lynch Thrale (later Mrs. Piozzi), 1776–1809*, ed. K. C. Balderston, 1 (1942) · H. Bolitho and D. Peel, *The Drummonds of Charing Cross* (1967) · Lloyds TSB Group Archives, A546f/11
**Archives** Lloyds TSB, London, archives, Cox & Co. MS A56 | BL, letters to Sir R. M. Keith · PRO, Board of Ordnance MSS, official letters as secretary to the board · Yale U., Beinecke L., letters to Dr Charles Burney
**Likenesses** D. Morier, oils, *c.*1758, Adjutant General's Corps Mess, Worthy Down, Winchester, Hampshire · G. Engleheart, miniature, 1779, priv. coll. · W. Beechey, oils, *c.*1790; two versions, Lloyds TSB Group plc, Cox's & King's Branch
**Wealth at death** under £100,000: will, PRO, PROB 11/1398

**Cox, Richard** (*c.*1776–1845), gardener, is a figure about whose early life little is known. His first career as a brewer in Bermondsey came to an end when he retired about 1820 to a house then called Lawn Cottage (later Colnbrook Lawn), in Colnbrook, near Slough, Buckinghamshire. A 2 acre garden surrounded the house, and here Cox devoted his time to horticultural experiments, among them the one that produced the apple bearing his name, Cox's orange pippin. Two pips of a Ribston pippin, sown in a pot about 1830, grew into seedlings of two new and promising varieties, Cox's pomona and Cox's orange pippin, though the second soon eclipsed the first to become the most popular English dessert apple. The original tree survived until 1911, when it was blown down in a storm.

In 1836 grafts of both of Cox's new apple trees were given to E. Small & Son, nurserymen of Colnbrook, who began to sell young trees locally four years later. About 1850 trees of the orange pippin were given a wider distribution by Charles Turner, of the Royal Nurseries, Slough, and the fruit soon began to attract attention. Thomas Ingram, Queen Victoria's head gardener at Frogmore and Windsor, showed the apple to a meeting of the British Pomological Society in December 1856, when it was acclaimed as one of the best kinds for the table, 'sweet, aromatic and very tender, a fair sized and handsome fruit'. At the Grand Fruit Exhibition of the Horticultural Society on 24 October 1857, 'Cox's Orange Pippin, a medium-sized, warm-looking, brownish-red variety with a yellow crisp flesh of most exquisite flavour', won first prize (Simmonds, *A Horticultural Who Was Who*, 14). After that its popularity spread so rapidly that by 1883, the year of the National Apple Congress held at the society's garden in Chiswick, 183 out of 231 exhibitors included it among the varieties they showed. In spite of its brilliant career, the society's delay in giving it an award of merit and a first-class certificate indicates unusual prudence, for 'the Château Yquem of apples', as E. A. Bunyard described it in 1929, did not receive these confirmations of its quality until 1962. Bunyard's accolade referred to a perfectly ripe Cox, left on its tree until October and not snatched off before it is anywhere near maturity, as so many commercially grown apples were later treated. The tree bearing Cox's orange pippin is vigorous enough to be a favourite for orchards in Britain and several other countries with a similar climate, and it has also been used as a parent in breeding a number of other varieties which share some of its desirable characteristics.

Richard Cox did not live long enough to see the triumph of his apple, for he died in Colnbrook on 20 May 1845, eight years after his wife, Ann. Both were buried in the churchyard of St Mary's, Harmondsworth. There was no mention of any children in his will.

SANDRA RAPHAEL, *rev.*

**Sources** A. Simmonds, 'Mr Cox of Cox's orange pippin', *Journal of the Royal Horticultural Society*, 68 (1943), 347–9 · A. Simmonds, *A horticultural who was who* (1948), 11–16 · F. A. Roach, *Cultivated fruits of Britain* (1985)

**Cox, Robert** (1810–1872), anti-sabbatarian writer, the son of Robert Cox, leather-dresser of Gorgie Mill, near Edinburgh, and of Anne Combe, sister of George and Dr Andrew Combe, was born at Gorgie on 25 February 1810. He received his early education at a private school and at the high school of Edinburgh. Besides attending the classes of law and of general science at the University of Edinburgh, he also studied anatomy under the notorious Dr Robert Knox. For some years he worked in the legal office of his uncle George Combe, who thought so highly of his nephew that he invited him to become a partner, an

offer which Cox declined. He passed as a writer to the signet in 1832, but chose to limit his legal work to business pressed on him by his family and friends. The majority of his time was spent instead on scientific and literary matters, and on schemes for the general benefit of the community. He was the active editor of Combe's *Phrenological Journal* for part of the first series, to which he also contributed numerous articles. At about the age of twenty-five he accepted the secretaryship of a literary institution in Liverpool, but resigned it in 1839 and returned to Edinburgh. Soon after his return he undertook the compilation of the index to the seventh edition of the *Encyclopaedia Britannica*. In 1841 he resumed the editorship of the *Phrenological Journal*, a position which he held until the death of Andrew Combe in 1847, when publication ceased.

Cox's attention was first directed to the sabbath question by the decision of the Edinburgh and Glasgow Railway Company to withdraw a limited passenger service on Sundays. Having qualified as a shareholder, he attended two half-yearly meetings of the company in 1850, and on each occasion moved that passenger carriages should be attached to the mail trains that ran regularly on Sundays. He reproduced his arguments in a small pamphlet, addressed to the directors, entitled *A Plea for Sunday Trains*, a work which he later expanded into a more substantial volume, *Sabbath Laws and Sabbath Duties* (1853). Cox's fascination with the subject led to further publications, including *The Whole Doctrine of Calvin about the Sabbath* (1860), *What is Sabbath Breaking?* (1863), and a compendious two-volume study of *The Literature of the Sabbath Question* (1865). He also contributed the chief portion of the article entitled 'Sabbath' to *Chambers's Encyclopaedia*. In addition to this anti-sabbatarian literature, he assisted his brothers Abram Cox of Kingston and Sir James Cox, one of her majesty's commissioners in lunacy, in the revision and republication of Combe's popular physiological works, and those of George Combe's books specially dealing with the brain and nervous system.

Especially fond of hillwalking, Cox took an active part in the Right of Way Association. He was the conservator of the Phrenological Museum in Edinburgh, secretary to the city's Phrenological Society, a director and warm supporter of the United Industrial Schools, a director of the School of Arts, and an active promoter of university endowment and of schemes connected with the higher education of the country. He enjoyed a reputation as a liberal patron of art, and was a member of the Edinburgh Association for Promotion of the Fine Arts. Cox died, unmarried, on 3 February 1872 at his home, 25 Rutland Street, Edinburgh.

T. F. HENDERSON, *rev.* CHARLES BRAYNE

**Sources** *The Scotsman* (5 Feb 1872) · C. Gibbon, *The life of George Combe: author of 'The constitution of man'*, 2 vols. (1878) · *CGPLA Eng. & Wales* (1872)
**Archives** NL Scot., corresp. with George Combe · U. Newcastle, letters to Sir Walter Trevelyan
**Wealth at death** £24,683 19s. 11d.: resworn confirmation, 26 April 1872, NA Scot., SC 70/1/157/374–393

**Cox, (Harold) Roxbee**, Baron Kings Norton (1902–1997), aeronautical engineer, was born on 6 June 1902 at 3 York Road, Handsworth, Staffordshire, the only child of William John Roxbee Cox (1877–1932), jeweller, and his wife, Amelia (d. 1949), daughter of Harry Stern of Handsworth. From an early age he was fascinated by aeroplanes, and he was taken by his father to air shows at Edgbaston and Bourneville to watch the daring aerobatics of the pilots of the early flying machines. He left Kings Norton grammar school at sixteen to take up an engineering apprenticeship with the Austin Motor Company at Longbridge, where he worked in the aircraft design section on the design of a single-seater biplane, the Austin Whippet. At the same time he studied for a London University external BSc, and was awarded a first-class degree in 1922. When Austin closed its aircraft department in 1921 he spent a year in the motor works before leaving for the Imperial College of Science and Technology in 1922 to do research on the aerodynamics and instabilities of wings, for which he was awarded a PhD in 1926. On 12 July 1927 he married (Doris) Marjorie (1902/3–1980), eldest daughter of Ernest Edward Withers, electrical engineer, of Northwood, Middlesex; they had two sons, Christopher (b. 1928) and Jeremy (b. 1932).

When, in 1924, the Air Ministry decided to revive the airship programme suspended after the crash of the R38 in 1921 Cox was the first to be recruited to the team at the newly formed Royal Airship Works at Cardington, Bedfordshire. The Air Ministry put two projects in motion aimed at exploring the possibility of lighter-than-air transport on a commercial basis, giving the same specifications to the government team at Cardington and to a private company, the Airship Guarantee Company, part of Metropolitan-Vickers, working in competition with each other. For five years Cox worked as chief calculator on the design of the R101 airship, and was awarded the R38 memorial prize by the Royal Aeronautical Society in 1928 for his paper 'External forces on an airship structure'. After the design was completed in 1929 he was transferred to the aerodynamics department of the Royal Aircraft Establishment (RAE) at Farnborough, and missed the inaugural flight of the R101 on 4 October 1930, which was intended to fly to India by way of Egypt. The flight ended in tragedy when the airship crashed in bad weather over Beauvais in northern France, killing forty-eight crew and passengers, including the secretary of state for air, Lord Thomson. In 1931, shortly after Cox was moved back to Cardington as chief technical officer, the government decided to bring all work on airships to an end, and the rival airship, the R100, was disposed of.

Cox spent much of the rest of the 1930s at the RAE working on aeroplanes. He looked at the problem of wing flutter in aircraft structures, publishing a number of papers which made an important contribution to air safety, while also lecturing on aircraft structures at Imperial College from 1932 to 1938. He was promoted to principal scientific officer in the aerodynamics department of the RAE in 1935. As head of the air defence department of the RAE

from 1936 he and his team devised the kite barrage balloons which were used to bring down German V1 flying bombs during the Second World War. In 1938 he became the first chief technical officer to the new Air Registration Board, set up to regulate standards of civil aircraft, but with the outbreak of the Second World War in 1939 he moved back to Farnborough as superintendent of scientific research.

When the Ministry of Aircraft Production was formed in 1940 Cox was appointed deputy director of scientific research, in charge of the jet propulsion programme. He first met Frank Whittle, inventor of the jet engine, early in 1940, and he was one of very few officials at the Ministry of Aircraft Production to realize from the start the importance of Whittle's engine. He became closely involved in the development of Whittle's work, and championed Whittle throughout the war. Whittle had patented the gas turbine jet propulsion engine in 1930, and set up his own company, Power Jets, in 1935, in order to develop an aircraft jet engine, but it was not until the beginning of the war that the Ministry of Aircraft Production placed an order with the Gloster Aircraft Company for an aeroplane in which the engine could be tested, and the first jet powered Gloster flew in 1941. Meanwhile, in July 1941, as part of the technical co-operation agreement between the British and American governments, Cox and Air-Vice-Marshal Linnell met representatives of the American government, and handed over details of Whittle's engine with a full set of drawings. Shortly afterwards a prototype engine was flown to GEC in Detroit, where the Americans, who had no jet engine of their own, were able to embark on a jet engine programme. Cox was awarded the medal of freedom with silver palm by the American government in 1947 in recognition of the importance of his role in facilitating the exchange of information during the war.

In England, Sir Henry Tizard, adviser to the Ministry of Aircraft Production, encouraged the leading aircraft designers and engineers to work on jet propulsion, and by early 1942 there were eleven firms involved, including Rolls-Royce, De Havilland, Bristol, and Metropolitan-Vickers. This led Cox to set up the gas turbine collaboration committee, with representatives from all the aero-engine manufacturers as well as Power Jets, which he convened for the first time in November 1941. He wanted to ensure that all those working on jet engine projects would pool their research and experience, and share what would normally be regarded as trade secrets. Although Whittle wanted to be in charge of manufacturing his engine at Power Jets the ministry did not think that he had the facilities to produce it in sufficient quantity, and gave the contract to manufacture the W2-B engine for Gloster fighters to the Rover Motor Company. After two years of delay while Power Jets and Rover argued over changes to the design, Cox, at Whittle's suggestion, persuaded Rolls-Royce to take over the production of the Whittle engine from Rover in 1943, and the first Gloster Meteors entered service in 1944. Cox was promoted to director of special projects in 1943.

When Sir Stafford Cripps, minister of aircraft production, decided in 1944 to nationalize Power Jets and amalgamate it with the gas turbine division of the RAE at Pyestock, on the grounds that Power Jets was largely financed by public money already and that it was important to have a state owned gas turbine establishment, Cox became chairman and managing director of the new company, Power Jets (Research and Development) Ltd. The company was intended to continue research on gas turbine engines, to design and build them, and to manufacture and test prototype engines, making knowledge available to other firms. Nevertheless in 1945 Cox was unable to prevent the aero-engine manufacturers from persuading officials at the ministry to bar Power Jets from building a prototype engine to production standard, on the ground that this would be in direct competition with industry. The official view was that the other firms were now in a position to manufacture their own jet engines, and there was no longer a need for Power Jets to do this. Whittle resigned from the board, and Power Jets was wound up at the beginning of 1946. It was replaced by the National Gas Turbine Establishment (NGTE), a research establishment under direct government control, and Cox was appointed director. The NGTE did not confine itself to aero-engine research, but was intended to provide information on technology and design for all applications of the gas turbine. Cox felt that Whittle had been unfairly treated in being denied the opportunity to develop and manufacture his own invention, and he was instrumental in getting the award made to Whittle in 1948 by the Royal Commission on Awards to Inventors increased to £100,000.

Cox left the NGTE in 1948 to become chief scientist at the Ministry of Fuel and Power, with the rank of deputy secretary. He was knighted in 1953, but left the civil service in 1954 when he realized that it was unlikely that he would ever be made a permanent secretary, as there was only one permanent secretary with a scientific background. He took on several company directorships, and was chairman of the Metal Box Company from 1961 to 1967. In 1965 he was created a life peer, as Baron Kings Norton of Wotton Underwood.

In 1943, as a vice-president of the Royal Aeronautical Society, Cox had chaired a conference on the post-war education of aeronautical engineers and on how best to build on the expertise acquired during the war in order to produce the future leaders of the British aviation industry. This led to the creation in 1946 of the College of Aeronautics on the site of RAF Cranfield, in Bedfordshire, a postgraduate institution offering two-year courses. Cox was one of the original governors, becoming deputy chairman of the board of governors from 1954, and in 1962 he succeeded Sir Frederick Handley Page as chairman. After the 1957 defence white paper had painted a depressing picture of the future of the British aviation industry, indicating that the RAF would be unlikely to need any new fighters or bombers, he helped Cranfield to diversify into wider engineering and technological areas, while keeping the emphasis on aeronautics. In 1969, when the College of Aeronautics at Cranfield received its royal charter to become Cranfield Institute of Technology (it changed its name to Cranfield University in 1993), he was appointed its first chancellor. He lived to see it become the largest European centre for applied research, development, and design in aeronautical engineering.

Cox sat on many public bodies. He was chairman of the Council for Scientific and Industrial Research from 1961 to 1965, chairman of the Air Registration Board from 1966 to 1972, chairman of the Council for National Academic Awards from 1964 to 1971, and president of the Royal Institution from 1969 to 1976. He became a fellow of Imperial College in 1960, and was awarded honorary degrees by the universities of Birmingham and Warwick, Cranfield Institute of Technology, and Brunel University. He was invited to give lectures on many occasions, including the Handley Page memorial lecture in 1969, and the Trueman Wood lecture at the Royal Society of Arts in 1985. He was the editor of *Gas Turbine Principles and Practice* (1955), and the author of numerous papers in scientific journals.

With a lifelong enthusiasm for balloons Cox built up a large collection of balloon and airship prints and paintings, and he was first chairman of the British Balloon Museum and Library from 1980. After the death of his first wife in 1980, he married, on 21 September 1982, Joan Ruth Pascoe (*b.* 1923/4), a sales manager with British Rail, and daughter of William George Pack of Torquay, a police officer. Cox died on 21 December 1997 at the General Hospital, Cheltenham, Gloucestershire.

ANNE PIMLOTT BAKER

**Sources** M. M. Postan, D. Hay, and J. D. Scott, *Design and development of weapons*, History of the Second World War, United Kingdom Civil Series (1964) · J. Golley, *Genesis of the jet* (1996) · F. Whittle, *Jet: the story of a pioneer* (1953) · R. Barker, *Field of vision: the first fifty years of Cranfield University* (1996) · P. Masefield, *To ride the storm: the story of the airship R101* (1982) · M. J. B. Davy, *Aeronautics: lighter-than-air craft* (1950) · G. Jones, *The jet pioneers* (1989) · R. Dennis, *Farnborough's jets: an account of early jet engine research at the Royal Aircraft Establishment* (1999) · *The Times* (22 Dec 1997) · *The Guardian* (23 Dec 1997) · *The Independent* (5 Jan 1998) · Burke, *Peerage* · *WW* · b. cert. · m. certs. [Doris Marjorie Withers; Joan Ruth Pascoe] · d. cert. · *CGPLA Eng. & Wales* (1998)

**Likenesses** photograph, repro. in *The Independent* · photograph, repro. in *The Guardian* · photograph, repro. in *The Times*

**Wealth at death** £807,173: probate, 18 March 1998, *CGPLA Eng. & Wales*

**Cox, Samuel** (1826–1893), religious journalist and author, was born on 19 April 1826 near London, and educated at a school at Stoke Newington. At the age of fourteen he was apprenticed at the London docks, where his father was employed, but on the expiry of his indentures he resigned his position and entered Stepney College to prepare himself for the Baptist ministry. After passing the college course and matriculating at London University, Cox became in 1852 pastor of the Baptist chapel in St Paul's Square, Southsea. In 1854 he accepted an invitation to Ryde, Isle of Wight, where he remained until 1859. A disorder in the throat compelled him to cease preaching, and caused him to turn his attention seriously to literature. He wrote for *The Freeman*, the organ of the Baptists, and occasionally acted as editor, and became a contributor to *The Nonconformist*, the *Christian Spectator*, *The Quiver*, and other religious periodicals. In 1861 he was appointed secretary to the committee for arranging the bicentenary of the Ejection of 1662. But his throat problem proved less permanent than had been feared, so that in 1863 he accepted a call to become pastor of the Mansfield Road Baptist Chapel, Nottingham, a position he occupied successfully and happily until 1888, when failing health compelled his resignation. In 1873 he married Eliza Tebbutt of Bluntisham, Huntingdonshire. He retired to Hastings, where he died at his home, Holme, Godrich Road, on 27 March 1893. He was buried in the general cemetery at Nottingham. His wife survived him.

Although Cox's ministry was effective and zealous, his chief activity was as a writer. His resumption of ministerial work in 1863 did not interfere with his literary energy, and he became in 1875 editor of *The Expositor*. The conception of this monthly magazine was evolved by Cox from his own work as a preacher and writer on the Bible. He was editor until 1884, being responsible for the first twenty volumes, some of which he wrote almost entirely himself. But he gathered round him a distinguished staff, including authors from a variety of denominations, such as W. C. Magee, Marcus Dods, and William Robertson Smith. The journal had a powerful influence on the religious thought of the day. Its general tendency is perhaps best indicated by a sentence in Cox's own exposition of his aims in the first number:

> Our sole purpose is to expound the scriptures honestly and intelligently by permitting them to explain themselves; neither thrusting upon them miracles which they do not claim or dogmas to which they lend no support, nor venturing to question the doctrines they obviously teach or the miracles which they plainly affirm.

Cox's services to learning received the remarkable recognition of nearly simultaneous offers from Aberdeen, Edinburgh, and St Andrews universities of their degree of DD. Cox accepted in 1882 the offer of the last-named, but found himself compelled after 1884 to resign his editorship because the breadth of his views had become displeasing to the proprietors of the magazine. Cox stated that he was the writer of thirty volumes and the editor of twenty more. Most of these were biblical expositions. The most widely read and influential was *Salvator mundi, or, Is Christ the Saviour of All Men?* (1877), which was followed in 1883 by a sequel, *The Larger Hope*, in which Cox defined his position with regard to universalism, and answered some of his critics. Among counterblasts to Cox's teaching may be mentioned *The Doctrines of Annihilation and Universalism ... with Critical Notes and a Review of 'Salvator mundi'* (1881), by Thomas Wood. The postscript of this challenges Cox's impartiality as editor of *The Expositor*, and is an instance of the kind of complaints which brought about his resignation.          RONALD BAYNE, *rev.* H. C. G. MATTHEW

**Sources** E. Cox, 'Prefatory memoir', in S. Cox, *The Hebrew twins* (1894) · *The Freeman* (7 April 1893) · *Independent and Nonconformist* (6 April 1893) · *British Weekly* (30 March 1893) · *Christian World* (30 March 1893) · *CGPLA Eng. & Wales* (1893) · P. Schaff and S. M. Jackson, *Encyclopedia of living divines and Christian workers of all denominations in Europe and America: being a supplement to Schaff-Herzog encyclopedia of religious knowledge* (1887)

**Archives** U. Nott. L., notes and sermons
**Wealth at death** £445 1s. 2d.: probate, 7 June 1893, *CGPLA Eng. & Wales*

**Cox, Sarah.** *See* Cornforth, Fanny (1835–c.1906).

**Cox, Thomas** (1655/6–1734), topographer and historian, was born in Essex, probably near Bishop's Stortford, Hertfordshire, where he attended the free grammar school. At the age of sixteen he was admitted sizar at Queens' College, Cambridge, on 27 March 1672 and he matriculated in the same year, graduating BA in 1675 and proceeding MA in 1679. He was ordained deacon in London on 16 March 1679 and priest on 18 March, and became rector of Chignall Smealy, near Chelmsford, Essex, on 19 June 1680, before continuing there until 1704. He became rector of the neighbouring parish of Broomfield on 11 February 1685 and rector of nearby Stock Harvard on 24 February 1703, and he held both livings until his death. He married Love Manwood, fifth daughter of Thomas Manwood of Lincoln's Inn and Priors in Broomfield, descendant of a family of distinguished barristers and antiquaries of that name from the south-east of England. They had a son, also named Thomas.

Cox was drawn into the convocation controversy of 1697–1717, which not only comprised an essential element of the contentions of English political parties, but also provoked further historical research into medieval and ecclesiastical history, notably the early history, constitution, and authority of the Church of England. In 1694 he contributed to the debate by publishing anonymously the first of several translations from the works of Louis-Ellies Du Pin, including *De antiqua ecclesiae disciplina* (1691), which he entitled *The Evangelical History, with Additions* (1694); a third edition appeared in 1703–7. The second, a response to Du Pin's *Nouvelle bibliothèque des auteurs ecclésiastiques* (5 vols., 1690) and *Lettre sur l'ancienne discipline de l'église* (1708), he named *A Compendious History of the Church* (4 vols., 1715–16), a prelude to an intended reunion between Gallicanism and Anglicanism. He also published selections from Plutarch's *Moralia* in translation in 1707, as *Morals by Way of Abstract done from the Greek*, and his translation of *Rerum memorabilium libri duo, quorum prior deperditarum* (1612), by the Italian jurist and antiquary Guido Pancirolli, appeared as *The History of many Memorable Things Lost* (2 vols., 1715; new edn, 1727). Cox was a noted preacher, and published two sermons: *Learning a Necessary Accomplishment for All Men* (1709), preached at the parish church, Felsted, Essex, on 30 August 1709, in which he advocated God's 'revelation, and inspiration' over reason and study as the path to true knowledge, and *The Influence of Religion in the Administration of Justice* (1726), preached at Chelmsford assizes, on 21 July 1726. He was also, until his resignation in 1730, a lecturer at St Michael, Cornhill, London.

In the historical field Cox contributed the lives of Richard II, Henry IV, Henry V, and Henry VI to *A complete history of England: with the lives of all the kings and queens thereof ... to ... William III* (3 vols., 1706), of which White Kennett, the whig bishop of Peterborough, was the principal author. In topography Cox's best-known work was *Magna Britannia et*

*Hibernia, antiqua et nova*, an enlargement of the sixth edition of William Camden's *Britannia* (1607), which first appeared in monthly parts as a supplement to the *Atlas geographus* (5 vols., 1711–17) and was then published in six volumes (1720–31). It contains only the English counties, to each of which is prefixed a map by Robert Morden. The description of Berkshire and the introductory account of the ancient state of Britain, of 1730, generally considered models of their kind, were contributed by Dr Anthony Hall.

Cox died on 11 January 1734, having been rector of Stock Harvard for over thirty years and vicar of Broomfield for almost fifty years. His son Thomas followed closely in his footsteps, attending Bishop's Stortford grammar school, under Dr Thomas Took, and Cambridge University in 1703. On 26 August 1712 at Bishop's Stortford parish church he preached a sermon to the scholars of the school, entitled *The Necessity of a Right Understanding, in Order to True Wisdom* (1712). After being chaplain to the earl of Orkney, he was rector of Chignall Smealy (1714–35) and of nearby Ramsden Bellhouse from 1734 when he succeeded, through his father's bequest, to the rectorship of Stock Harvard. He died on 26 July 1763.

RICHARD RIDDELL

**Sources** DNB · Venn, *Alum. Cant.* · T. Cox, *Learning a necessary accomplishment for all men* (1709), 2 · J. Gorton, *A general biographical dictionary*, 3 vols. (1841) · *GM*, 1st ser., 4 (1734), 50 · *GM*, 1st ser., 33 (1763), 415 · P. Morant, *The history and antiquities of the county of Essex*, 1 (1768), 204; 2 (1768), 52, 77–8, 82 · F. W. Austen, *Rectors of two Essex parishes and their times* (1943), 202–6, 315–18 · E. P. Gibson, *The annals of Ramsden Bellhouse*, ed. F. W. Austen (1927)
**Archives** Bodl. Oxf., various parts of Cox's *Magna Britannia* with MS additions | BL, edition of *History of Sussex* with MS additions by Sir William Burrell, Add. MS 5708

**Cox, Sir (George) Trenchard** (1905–1995), museum director, was born on 31 July 1905 at 19 Craven Hill, London, the son of William Pallett Cox, barrister, and his wife, Marion, *née* Beverley. He was educated at Eton College and at King's College, Cambridge, where he was a prizeman; in 1926 he took a third in part one of the modern and medieval languages tripos, and in 1928 a first in part two of the modern languages certificate of competent knowledge. Away from his studies Cox developed an interest in the arts. He was encouraged in this by a family friend, Cecil Harcourt-Smith, the director of the Victoria and Albert Museum; and at Cambridge he was inspired by Sydney Cockerell, the director of the Fitzwilliam Museum, to pursue a career in museums. He embarked on this in the then usual way by working, from 1929 to 1932, as a volunteer at the National Gallery and in the department of prints and drawings at the British Museum. During that period he also spent a semester, in 1930, at Berlin University, studying art history under Adolph Goldschmidt. For the rest of his life he would recall Goldschmidt and Charles Holmes, who supervised him at the National Gallery, as his two most important mentors. A brief stay in Paris before returning home led to Cox's *Jehan Foucquet, Native of Tours* (1931), a study of the French Renaissance painter.

From the British Museum, Cox joined the staff of the Wallace Collection in 1932 as assistant to the keeper, Sir James Mann. Although Cox did not warm to Mann, he acquired a lasting interest in the decorative arts of eighteenth-century France. He contributed to the catalogue of the exhibition of French art at Burlington House in 1932, and later produced two short works about the Wallace Collection. His marriage, on 14 November 1935, to Mary Désirée (Maisie), the only daughter of Sir Hugh Kerr *Anderson, master of Gonville and Caius College, Cambridge, proved blissfully happy. They had no children, but remained a devoted couple until her death in 1973. In the summer of 1939 Cox had the task of organizing the evacuation of the Wallace Collection's holdings from Hertford House, after which he was seconded for wartime duties at the Home Office, as private secretary to Sir Alexander Maxwell, the permanent under-secretary.

In 1944, having proved himself a most efficient administrator, Cox was appointed director of the Birmingham City Museum and Art Gallery. The challenge at Birmingham was daunting: the museum's premises, mostly converted for use as council offices during the war, had to be recovered for museum use, and extensive repairs and refurbishment had to be accomplished on a slender budget. But with the help of Dr Mary Woodall, keeper of the department of art, Cox established excellent relations with the Birmingham city corporation and overcame all difficulties to re-establish and increase the museum's high standing. He was exceptionally supportive of the museum's staff, never failing to write a note of congratulation to those responsible for an exhibition or new display. He encouraged everyone under his supervision to fulfil their potential, and established one of the most successful museum friends organizations of the period. In 1947 he paid tribute to Birmingham's most famous painter with the publication of his book *David Cox*.

In 1955 the minister of education, David Eccles, offered Cox the post of director and secretary of the Victoria and Albert Museum. The retiring director, Sir Leigh Ashton, had lost his grip, and a new man was urgently needed to restore morale at the museum. Cox accepted the offer and, despite Eccles's explanation that he had been selected to keep the seat warm for John Pope-Hennessy, he stayed until 1966. The first task he undertook set the tone of fairness and kindness that was to characterize his directorship: with the help of his assistant Terence Hodgkinson, he learnt the names of all the museum's staff within three weeks. Thereafter he greeted everybody by name—and slipped up only once, when confusing the identities of two typists who had temporarily exchanged places. His directorship was also marked by the creation of the museum's education and conservation departments; the reorganization of the National Art Library; such important acquisitions as the jade wine cup of Shah Jahan; and a high standard of exhibitions, notably that devoted to *Opus Anglicanum* in 1963. On Cox's initiative a female research assistant was promoted to assistant keeper grade, and (another first) a black warder was promoted supervising warder.

Beyond the Victoria and Albert Museum, Cox took an

active interest in the Museums Association, of which he became president in 1963, and in the International Council of Museums. He was also president of the National Association of Decorative and Fine Art Societies; and a fellow of the Royal Society of Arts and of the Society of Antiquaries. He was a staunch supporter of the social welfare activities of St Martin-in-the-Fields, where in retirement he served as people's warden from 1968 to 1979. Tentative and fastidious in manner, he was free of prejudice and self-effacing to a fault. He had very poor eyesight and when talking animatedly would wave his arms about and sway. He always felt at home on the continent, especially in France. Cox was appointed CBE in 1954, knighted in 1961, and appointed a chevalier of the Légion d'honneur in 1967. He died of bronchopneumonia and cancer at his home, 33 Queen's Gate Gardens, London, on 21 December 1995. GEORGE IRELAND

Sources *The Independent* (23 Dec 1995) · *The Times* (23 Dec 1995) · *Daily Telegraph* (28 Dec 1995) · C. M. Kauffmann, *Burlington Magazine*, 138 (1996), 257–8 · *WWW* · J. J. Withers, *A register of admissions to King's College, Cambridge, 1797–1925* (1929) · private information (2004) · b. cert. · m. cert. · d. cert.
Archives Birmingham Museums and Art Gallery | BL, corresp. with Sir Sydney Cockerell, Add. MS 52710 · TCD, corresp. with Thomas Bodkin
Likenesses M. Ambler, photograph, V&A · W. Coldstream, oils, Birmingham Museums and Art Gallery · photograph, repro. in *The Times* · photograph, repro. in *The Independent* · photograph, repro. in *Daily Telegraph*
Wealth at death £638,790: probate, 1 Feb 1996, *CGPLA Eng. & Wales*

**Cox, Walter** (1770–1837), journalist, was the son of a Westmeath bricklayer who apprenticed him to a gunsmith in Dublin. For some time he carried on business as a gunsmith, and in 1797 started a popular radical newspaper called the *Union Star*, which advocated a policy of assassination of targeted loyalists. In 1804 he went to America, but returned to Ireland and founded in 1807 the *Irish Magazine and Monthly Asylum for Neglected Biography*. The seditious tone of this periodical provoked the government, and Cox was frequently prosecuted and spent much time in gaol. Nevertheless it continued to appear with regularity until 1815, when the government offered Cox a pension of £100 per annum and a bonus of £400, on condition that he should surrender all copies in his possession and emigrate to America. After arriving in New York in 1816, Cox founded a journal called *The Exile*, similar in its popular radical character to the *Irish Magazine*. In a pamphlet entitled *The Snuff Box* he expressed his dissatisfaction with American political structures. When *The Exile* failed in 1820, Cox crossed to France and subsequently returned to Ireland. In 1835 his presence was discovered by the authorities and he was forced to forfeit his pension. He died at Dublin on 17 January 1837 in poverty.

The publisher of *Freeman's Journal*, Francis Higgins, described Cox as having a 'mean and despicable appearance', but also noted that he was an 'astonishing autodidact' who taught Euclid to working-class scholars in Dublin. During his residence in that country he is said to have been successively pawnbroker, chandler, dairyman,

and whisky dealer. Typical in some ways of the artisanal radical attracted to the republican movement, but never fully absorbed into the United Irish organization, Cox was first brought to the castle's attention in 1795 as a member of the Huguenots, a 'new penny club' with advanced political principles. The Huguenots was just one among a number of working-class republican clubs which were proliferating in Dublin in the mid-1790s. In the following year Cox was described as a member of a seditious masonic lodge, a member of the radical Telegraph Club, and a man who possessed a private press. In 1795 Cox's father was imprisoned by Lord Carhampton, a fact which he later claimed accounted for the journalist's particular vendetta against the general in the pages of the *Union Star*. If and when he actually joined the United Irishmen is unclear, though Cox later boasted that he had drawn up the plans for defending Dublin streets during the insurrection that were found on Lord Edward Fitzgerald when he was arrested. Nineteenth-century historian W. J. Fitzpatrick claimed Cox was one of Lord Edward's bodyguards, though that may have also been the journalist's boast. Since many of the radical artisan clubs with which Cox was affiliated were either incorporated in, or at least associated with, the United Irish movement, Cox can fairly be considered a member, but it is unlikely that he ever advanced to significant office in the organization. He clearly launched the *Union Star* on his own initiative. When a reward was offered in 1798 for the apprehension of the editor of the *Union Star* (published anonymously), Cox discovered himself to the authorities at Dublin Castle, and offered the government his services as a pamphleteer, but his offer was declined. The United Irishmen suspected him of being a paid castle agent, an *agent provocateur*, whose *Union Star* was used to discredit the movement. It was also rumoured that he betrayed Lord Edward Fitzgerald. NANCY J. CURTIN

Sources N. J. Curtin, *The United Irishmen: popular politics in Ulster and Dublin, 1791–1798* (1994) · R. R. Madden, *The United Irishmen: their lives and times*, 2nd ser., 2 vols. (1843) · W. J. Fitzpatrick, *The Sham Squire and the informers of 1798*, 3rd edn (1866) · NA Ire., Rebellion MSS · BL, Pelham MSS · PRO, Home Office MSS relating to Ireland

**Cox, William Sands** (1802–1875), surgeon and a founder of Queen's College, Birmingham, was the eldest son of Edward Townsend Cox (1769–1863), a well-known Birmingham surgeon. After being educated locally at the King Edward VI Grammar School, he was articled to his father and began to study medicine at Birmingham General Hospital. He later studied at Guy's and St Thomas's Hospitals, London, from 1821 to 1823, and after being admitted MRCS in 1824 he spent twelve months at the École de Médecine, Paris.

Cox had the idea of establishing a school of medicine in Birmingham, on the model of his friend Edward Grainger's Webb Street school of anatomy in London, and he visited numerous schools and hospitals on the continent and in Britain. In 1825 he settled in Birmingham and was appointed surgeon to the General Dispensary, and he gave his first lecture on anatomy, with physiological and surgical observations, on 1 December, at Temple Row. He became surgeon to the town infirmary, jointly with his father, in 1827. In 1828, after a good deal of opposition, he, in conjunction with doctors Johnstone, Booth, and others, founded the Birmingham school of medicine, later called Queen's College; Cox himself lectured on anatomy at first, and afterwards on surgery. In 1834 he took an active part in the formation of the Provincial Medical and Surgical (later the British Medical) Association, becoming a member of its council. In 1836 he was elected FRS.

In 1840 Cox founded the Queen's Hospital, Birmingham, to serve as a clinical school for the college, and through his work alone it was opened free of debt in 1841; he was naturally appointed senior surgeon, and later became consulting surgeon. Having secured considerable funds from the Revd Dr Philip Warneford, he was able to enlarge the scope of the medical school to that of a college, with instruction instituted in arts (1847) and theology (1851), and he secured for it in 1843 a royal charter by the title of Queen's College. In 1857 a sum of £1050 was subscribed by the public as a testimonial to Cox, which he devoted to founding scholarships and to completing the museums of Queen's College. In 1858–9 he was principal of the college. Cox aimed at making the college the nucleus of a university of the midlands, but unfortunately there were problems:

> he was autocratic in his mode of conducting both institutions, and as his administrative faculty was by no means equal to his creative power, and to the readiness with which he gave and obtained money, the college and hospital both became involved in a succession of serious quarrels between the founder and his associates. (*Birmingham Daily Post*, 28 Dec 1875)

These disagreements greatly injured the reputation of the college; the buildings were ill-planned, and the students' rents and other expenses high. An inquiry by the charity commissioners in 1860 led to the separation of the college and the hospital, after which Cox was obliged to cease taking part in the work of either. He left Birmingham in 1863, on his father's death, and lived successively at Bole Hall, near Tamworth, and at Leamington Spa. Cox was married to Isabella, who survived him. He died at Glass House, Kenilworth, on 23 December 1875 and was buried at Aston church, Birmingham.

Contrary to expectation, Cox left nothing to the institutions he had founded, but bequeathed £3000, with his medical library and instruments, to the cottage hospital at Moreton in Marsh, together with £12,000 to establish and support dispensaries in several suburbs of Birmingham; he also left funds to build and endow a dispensary at Tamworth and Kenilworth of £3000 each, and further money was given to endow scholarships at King Edward's School, Birmingham, and Guy's Hospital, London, and to complete a church he had built in Birmingham. Cox was a strong Conservative and churchman, and this hindered his success in Birmingham. He was a skilful surgeon, but sacrificed much private practice to his public projects.

Nevertheless he published a number of articles and books on medical subjects including *A Synopsis of the Bones, Ligaments, and Muscles, Blood-Vessels, and Nerves of the Human Body* (1831) and *A Memoir on Amputation of the Thigh at the Hip Joint*, (1845). He was a magistrate and deputy lieutenant for Warwickshire. G. T. Bettany, *rev.* Patrick Wallis

**Sources** *BMJ* (1 Jan 1876), 29 · *The Lancet* (15 April 1876) · *Birmingham Daily Post* (28 Dec 1875) · V. Skipp, *The making of Victorian Birmingham* (1983) · 'William Sands Cox', *Annals of the Queen's College, Birmingham*, ed. W. S. Cox, 4 vols. (1873), 4.155–60 · J. T. J. Morrison, *William Sands Cox and the Birmingham medical school* (1926) · CGPLA Eng. & Wales (1876) · d. cert.
**Likenesses** H. T. Maguire, lithograph, 1854, Wellcome L. · photograph, repro. in *Annals of the Queen's College, Birmingham*, ed. Cox, vol. 4 · photograph, repro. in T. H. Barber, ed., *Photographs of eminent medical men of all countries, with brief analytical notices of their works*, 2 vols. (1867–8)
**Wealth at death** under £50,000: probate, 24 Feb 1876, *CGPLA Eng. & Wales*

**Coxe, Daniel** (1640–1730), physician, natural philosopher, and colonial adventurer, was the son of Daniel Coxe (*d.* 1686), gentleman, of Stoke Newington, Middlesex. He matriculated at Jesus College, Cambridge, in 1659, becoming a scholar in 1661. Coxe first came to the fore in the mid-1660s as an associate of Robert Boyle: an important series of letters from Coxe to Boyle, dating from between 1665 and 1667, survives among the Boyle letters at the Royal Society, in which Helmontian and other themes are discussed; twenty-five years later, in 1692, Coxe was one of three doctors appointed to examine Boyle's chemical papers after his death.

On 22 March 1665 Coxe was elected a fellow of the Royal Society, in which he played an active role for the rest of the 1660s and a slightly less active one in the 1670s. His interest was particularly in chemical investigations; he devoted special attention to the chemical analysis of vegetable substances, his findings on which were published in three articles in *Philosophical Transactions* in 1674. These studies were evidently intended to form part of a grandiose history of vegetables, of which he presented a prospectus to the society in 1668; this was a sequel to the 'Enquiries concerning vegetables' that he had presented in 1665. The history as a whole never materialized. His articles, however, were not without influence, being attacked by the Scottish apothecary, Matthew MacKaile, in a book published in 1683, and continuing to be cited after that date.

In the 1660s and 1670s Coxe established a successful medical practice in London. He was awarded the degree of MD *per literas regias* at Cambridge in 1669, and became an honorary fellow of the College of Physicians, London, in 1680. He also acted as physician-in-ordinary to Charles II. In 1669 he participated in the pamphlet war between physicians and apothecaries by publishing *A discourse, wherein the interest of the patient in reference to physick and physicians is soberly debated*; this combined an attack on the apothecaries with a vindication of the role of an experimentally active physician, which he exemplified. In 1671

Coxe married Rebecca, daughter of John Coldman, a London alderman. Their son Daniel Coxe (*bap.* 1673) emigrated to America at the age of twenty-eight and thereafter took a prominent role in the affairs of West New Jersey, the province in which his father had played so important a role a generation earlier.

Coxe's chief claim to retrospective fame was his activity as a colonial adventurer: indeed, Daniel Defoe in his *Essay on Projects* (1697) singled out Coxe, along with William Penn and Anthony Ashley Cooper, first earl of Shaftesbury, in this connection. In the mid-1680s Coxe began to acquire property in West New Jersey, and in 1687 he purchased the proprietary rights of the province from the heirs of Edward Byllynge. He later bought more land, his holding in the area ultimately totalling 1 million acres; he also invested large sums in developing local fisheries and industries; he was among those who promoted a company for naval stores to be produced in New England; and he also encouraged the exploration and exploitation of the hinterland towards the Great Lakes. In 1692, however, he sold the bulk of his holdings and the right of proprietorship to a syndicate of forty-eight London merchants, the West New Jersey Society, for £9800.

By this time Coxe had shifted his interests further south to the province of 'Carolana'—covering the present North and South Carolina, Georgia, Florida, and Louisiana—which had been granted by Charles I to Sir Robert Heath, attorney-general, in 1629. Coxe acquired the title in the 1690s, and at the end of that decade he attempted to orchestrate settlement in the area in opposition to the parallel activities of the French. In 1698 he equipped two ships to explore the Mississippi; he also tried to encourage a Huguenot settlement on the Gulf of Mexico, and to float a joint-stock company to exploit Florida. These various schemes proved problematic, however, and little came of Coxe's ambitions, though they were briefly the subject of government interest in 1719, when the question arose of the English title to this part of America.

Coxe has been described as a pioneer of the idea that 'the destiny of the English in America embraced more than the settlement and exploitation of the Atlantic seaboard' (Crane, 50). His role in exploiting this area was recounted—together with a topographical account of somewhat questionable reliability—in *A Description of the English Province of Carolana*, published in 1722 by his son. Coxe died on 19 January 1730 in possession of the title to Carolana, which his descendants surrendered to the British government in 1769, in return for land in the colony of New York.                                    MICHAEL HUNTER

**Sources** G. D. Scull, 'A biographical notice of Dr Daniel Coxe, of London', *Pennsylvania Magazine of History and Biography*, 7 (1883), 317–37 • D. Coxe, *A description of the English province of Carolana, by the Spaniards call'd Florida, and by the French, la Louisiane* (1722) • A. Clericuzio, 'From Van Helmont to Boyle: a study of the transmission of Helmontian chemical and medical theories in seventeenth-century England', *British Journal for the History of Science*, 26 (1993), 303–34, esp. 327 • R. E. W. Maddison, *The life of the Honourable Robert Boyle, FRS* (1969), 203 • M. Hunter, *The Royal Society and its fellows, 1660–1700: the morphology of an early scientific institution*, 2nd edn (1994), 172–3 • T. Birch, *The history of the Royal Society of London*, 4 vols.

(1756–7), esp. vol. 2, pp. 32–40, 292 • *CSP dom., addenda, 1660–70*, 730 • W. A. Shaw, ed., *Calendar of treasury books*, 6, PRO (1913), 232 • M. MacKaile, *The diversitie of salts and spirits maintained* (1683) • F. H. Ellis, 'The author of Wing C6727: Daniel Coxe, FRS, or Thomas Coxe, FRS', *Notes and Records of the Royal Society*, 18 (1963), 36–8 • D. Defoe, *An essay on projects* (1697), 29 • V. W. Crane, *The southern frontier, 1670–1732* (1928), chap. 3 • A. G. Zimmerman, 'Daniel Coxe and the New Mediterranean Sea Company', *Pennsylvania Magazine of History and Biography*, 76 (1952), 86–96 • J. E. Pomfret, *The province of West New Jersey, 1609–1702* (1956), chap. 9 • F. E. Melvin, 'Dr Daniel Coxe and Carolana', *Mississippi Valley Historical Review*, 1 (1914), 257–62 • W. A. Whitehead and others, eds., *Documents relating to the colonial, revolutionary and post-revolutionary history of the state of New Jersey*, 2 (1881), 41ff. • Venn, *Alum. Cant.*
**Archives** Bodl. Oxf., Rawl. MSS • RS, Boyle MSS

**Coxe, Francis** [Fraunces Cox] (*fl.* 1560–1575), astrologer and medical practitioner, is known by three ephemeral publications. Nothing is known of his life before his magical practices attracted attention in 1561, when he was summoned before the privy council on a charge of sorcery. He was severely punished and he made a public confession of his 'employment of certayne sinistral and divelysh artes' at the pillory in Cheapside on 25 June 1561. On 7 July John Awdeley issued a broadside entitled *The Unfained Retractation of Fraunces Cox*. Coxe himself subsequently published a grovelling and terror-stricken pamphlet entitled *A short treatise declaring the detestable wickednesse of magicall sciences, as necromancie, coniurations of spirits, curiouse astrologie, and such lyke* (1561). In the preface he notes his lack of learning and, as was common among opponents of astrology, he admits 'that I have myself been an offender in these most detestable sciences, against whome I have compilyd this worke'. This pamphlet contains little more than a recommendation of William Fulke's more thorough arguments against astrology in *Antiprognosticon* (1560).

Coxe's most significant publication, *A Treatise of the Making and Use of Diverse Oils, Unguents, Emplasters and Distilled Waters* (1575), is missing. The title indicates that this was one of the first pamphlets to mark the increasing appeal of chemical therapy in England. It is listed in Andrew Maunsell's *Catalogue of English Printed Bookes* (1595), and may have been available for sale by William Cooper a century later, though Cooper's catalogue entry may be copied from Maunsell's. This pamphlet is wrongly identified as a source for Simon Forman's chemical knowledge; he referred to the fifteenth-century Oxford medical master, Johanne Cockes, not his near contemporary medical maverick.

Coxe may have written an almanac (*Prognostication*, n.d.), a single copy of which survives on the back of a ballad in the British Library. The date of Coxe's death is unknown.
                              EDWARD HERON-ALLEN, *rev.* LAUREN KASSELL

**Sources** A. Maunsell, *The … catalogue of English printed bookes* (1595) [in 2 pts] • F. Coxe, *The unfained retractation of Fraunces Cox* (1561) • C. Webster, 'Alchemical and Paracelsian medicine', *Health, medicine and mortality in the sixteenth century*, ed. C. Webster (1979), 301–31 • D. C. Allen, *The star-crossed Renaissance: the quarrel about astrology and its influence in England* (1941) • M. Edmond, 'Simon Forman's vade-mecum', *Book Collector*, 26 (1977), 44–60 · W. Cooper, *A catalogue of chymicall books* (1675)

**Coxe, Henry Octavius** (1811–1881), librarian, was born on 20 September 1811 at Bucklebury vicarage, Berkshire, the youngest child and eighth son of the Revd Richard Coxe (1753–1819) and his second wife, Susan Smith, of Normanton Hall, Leicestershire. He was educated at Westminster School, and from 1825 by his half-brother Richard Charles *Coxe, then a curate at Dover, where Henry acquired a great love of the sea and of boats. He matriculated in 1829 at Worcester College, Oxford, where he excelled at rowing. After a severe fall, he abandoned the honours school, and took a pass degree in 1833. The same year he joined the manuscript department at the British Museum, where he developed considerable skill as a palaeographer. In January 1839 he began work as sub-librarian at the Bodleian Library, Oxford, to which he devoted the rest of his life. On 9 April that year he married Charlotte Esther (1804/5–1895), second daughter of General Sir Tomkyns Hilgrove *Turner, who bought them the house, 17 Beaumont Street, which was to be their home for forty years. They had five children, of whom only two survived them: a son, Hilgrove, and a daughter, Susan Esther, who in 1870 married John Wordsworth (1843–1911), later bishop of Salisbury.

Coxe was ordained in 1833 and while in London served as curate first to his brother at Archbishop Tenison's Chapel, Regent Street, then at St Matthew, Spring Gardens, a large and poor district in the parish of St Martin-in-the-Fields. His ready sympathy and conscientiousness were well suited to parish work. He held a succession of curacies in the Oxford district: Culham (1839–48), Tubney (1848–55), Yarnton (1855), and Wytham (1856–68). In 1868 he became rector of Wytham, Berkshire, where the parsonage provided a welcome country residence. He was select preacher in the university in 1842 and Whitehall preacher in 1868.

Coxe's early years in Oxford were spent working on manuscripts. The volumes he contributed to the series of Bodleian 'quarto' catalogues—college manuscripts (1852), Greek manuscripts (1853), Canonici Greek and Latin manuscripts (1854), and Laud Latin and miscellaneous manuscripts (1858)—are a lasting monument to his scholarship and palaeographical skill. In his leisure hours he edited for publication a variety of texts, including Roger of Wendover's *Flores historiarum* for the English Historical Society (5 vols., 1841–4) and, for the Roxburghe Club, *The Black Prince: an Historical Poem* (1842), Gower's *Vox clamantis* (1857), and *The Apocalypse of St. John the Divine* (1876). In 1857 he was sent by the government to visit libraries of the Levant and to report on any important Greek manuscripts they contained. His official report, which lists and indexes 600 manuscripts in 24 different institutions, was published the following year.

During the 1850s the elderly Bulkeley Bandinel was frequently absent from his post as Bodley's librarian, and the library's governing body of curators looked to Coxe to initiate a general overhaul of its management. Having been dispatched by the curators to review practice in other

**Henry Octavius Coxe** (1811–1881), by George Frederic Watts, 1876

major libraries, he produced reports which recommended significant changes to the systems of claiming publications under the copyright privilege, of cataloguing, and of arranging the books on the shelves. The production of a new general catalogue, adopting the British Museum's moveable slip method, began in 1859. Its completion was to be the major achievement of Coxe's time as Bodley's librarian, a post to which he was unanimously elected in November 1860, on Bandinel's resignation.

Bandinel had enormously expanded and enriched the library's collections for the benefit of established scholars. It fell to his successor, in keeping with the recommendations of the university commission of 1850, to devise means of making the library more generally accessible. The production of the single catalogue of printed books was a major step in this direction, as was the provision in 1862 of a second reading room. The loan of the Radcliffe Library to the university provided a spacious room close to the Bodleian in which, following the example of the British Museum, modern periodicals and reference works could be made immediately available. As it was lit by gas, it could remain open in the evenings for the benefit of college tutors and undergraduates. In 1858 Coxe had advocated the rearrangement of the majority of the collections by subject as another way of making them more useful. By 1865, when new accessions were thus arranged, and those most in demand placed on the shelves of the Radcliffe Camera, he had abandoned the idea of reclassifying earlier holdings. As an alternative to the physical rearrangement of the book stock, Coxe proposed a classified catalogue and had an extra copy made of every entry in the new author catalogue for this purpose. Insufficient staff and funding prevented any progress with this scheme.

Coxe was a chaplain of Corpus Christi College, a delegate of Oxford University Press, and curator of the university galleries. For most of his life he was physically robust, and an enthusiastic rider, but as he approached fifty-five his health began to fail. After an operation in the autumn of 1874, he frequently refers in his diary to his 'malady', a painful kidney disorder. At Michaelmas 1880 he was taken gravely ill and he died at his home, Northgate, St Giles', Oxford, on 8 July 1881. He was buried four days later at Wytham. J. W. Burgon described Coxe as, at the time of his death, 'perhaps the most generally known and universally beloved character in Oxford' (Burgon, 123). Contemporary accounts refer to his kindliness, courtesy, and charm, which inspired affection in everyone he met. His skill as a mimic and story-teller made him excellent company. Archdeacon Palmer's verdict was that Oxford would find it difficult 'to get so good a librarian as Coxe … as loveable a librarian it is out of the question to expect' (ibid., 134).                                        MARY CLAPINSON

**Sources** H. H. E. Craster, *History of the Bodleian Library, 1845–1945* (1952); repr. (1981) · J. W. Burgon, 'Henry Octavius Coxe: the large-hearted librarian', *Lives of twelve good men*, [new edn], 2 (1889), 123–48 · W. D. Macray, 'Mr. Coxe's work at the Bodleian', *Transactions and Proceedings of the 4th and 5th annual meetings of the Library Association* (1884), 13–16 · W. D. Macray, *Annals of the Bodleian Library, Oxford*, 2nd edn (1890) · *The Times* (9 July 1881) · Bodl. Oxf., Library records d.1745–6, e.609–10 [extracts from Coxe's diaries] · letters to Coxe, 1839–81, Bodl. Oxf., Library records d.250–62 · *DNB* · m. cert. · d. cert. · parish register (burial), 1881, Wytham
**Archives** Bodl. Oxf., corresp. · Bodl. Oxf., notes on Latin and Greek MSS | BL, letters to W. C. Hazlitt, Add. MSS 38899–38913 · BL, corresp. with Sir Frederick Madden, Egerton MSS 2842–2848 · Bodl. Oxf., corresp. with Sir Thomas Phillipps · U. Edin. L., corresp. with James Halliwell-Phillipps · U. Edin. L., letters to David Laing
**Likenesses** F. Tatham, watercolour drawing, 1833, Bodl. Oxf. · R. A. J. Tyrwhitt, two pencil drawings, c.1853, Worcester College, Oxford · Smith, watercolour drawing, 1870 (after photograph), Bodl. Oxf. · G. F. Watts, oils, 1876, Bodl. Oxf. [see illus.] · R. St John Tyrwhitt, sepia drawing, CCC Oxf.
**Wealth at death** £14,118 8s. 1d.: probate, 13 Oct 1881, *CGPLA Eng. & Wales*

**Coxe, John**. See Cox, John (*fl.* 1565–1583).

**Coxe, Peter** (1753?–1844), writer and poet, was the fourth son of Dr William Coxe (*c.*1710–1760), physician to the household of George II, and his wife, Martha, daughter of Paul D'Aranda. His elder brother, William *Coxe (1748–1828), was archdeacon of Wiltshire. Coxe entered Charterhouse School aged ten under royal patronage and left at thirteen, becoming a London auctioneer. In 1807 he published *Another Word or Two, or, Architectural Hints in Lines*. Two years later came *The Exposé, or, Napoleon Buonaparte Unmasked*. Both were anonymous, but acknowledged in *The Social Day* (1823), which included thirty-two engravings and took so long to produce that several among his list of

over 500 prestigious subscribers died before it was finished. (Lownder, quoted in Allibone, called it 'a poem of no merit'.)

Coxe never married. He died at his residence in Wilmot Street, Brunswick Square, London, on 22 January 1844.
                                        T. F. HENDERSON, *rev.* JESSICA HININGS

**Sources** *GM*, 2nd ser., 22 (1844), 652–3 · P. Coxe, *The social day* (1823) · Munk, *Roll* · R. A. Austen-Leigh, ed., *The Eton College register, 1753–1790* (1921) · Allibone, *Dict.* · will, PRO, PROB 11/1993, sig. 101
**Likenesses** E. Scriven, stipple (after A. Robertson), BM, NPG; repro. in Coxe, *The social day*
**Wealth at death** exact sum unknown: will, PRO, PROB 11/1993, fol. 9

**Coxe, Richard** (*d.* 1596), Church of England clergyman, is first recorded on 27 November 1578 when he matriculated as a pensioner at Christ's College, Cambridge. He graduated BA in 1582 and on 16 December 1583 was incorporated in that degree at Oxford University. As a student of St John's College he proceeded MA at Oxford in 1584, and was incorporated at Cambridge in that degree in 1586. On 17 May 1589, following the death of John Hilton, he was instituted to the rectory of Diss, Norfolk, thereby inaugurating a long legal wrangle. Coxe had been presented to the living by Henry Radcliffe, ninth earl of Sussex, whose rights were challenged by Countess Frances, the widow of the previous earl. Although the new earl denied her claim to the advowson, Lady Sussex's right to the manor in jointure was unassailable, and she presented her own candidate, John Reed. Initially she was successful and Coxe found himself ejected. He was reinstated in November 1591, but a further bout of litigation soon led to his second ejection. Then one William Goddard entered the fray as Lady Sussex's new candidate, but the authorities refused to institute him and the rectory remained vacant. In these circumstances the rights of presentation lapsed into the hands of the crown. Coxe was able to obtain Elizabeth's patent which rendered void all other claims to the advowson, and he secured his own reinstitution on 2 December 1593. Richard Coxe is also recorded as vicar of Hempnall, Norfolk, in February 1593. It is not known whether issues of religious principle underlay the long struggle over the rectory of Diss, though it is possible that Coxe's austere style, demonstrated in his posthumous work *A short catechism, very necessary, for the plaine understanding of the principall points of Christian religion* (1620) was not to Lady Sussex's taste. In any case he was able to remain in his hard-won living for the rest of his life, which had ended in 1596, before 12 November, when the rectory passed to John Taverner.                                        STEPHEN WRIGHT

**Sources** F. Blomefield and C. Parkin, *An essay towards a topographical history of the county of Norfolk*, [2nd edn], 11 vols. (1805–10), vol. 1 · Venn, *Alum. Cant.*, 1/1.408 · Cooper, *Ath. Cantab.*, 2.222 · *Reg. Oxf.*, 2/2.364 · *The papers of Nathaniel Bacon of Stiffkey*, ed. A. H. Smith and G. M. Baker, 3: 1586–1595, Norfolk RS, 53 (1990) · J. Peile, *Biographical register of Christ's College, 1505–1905, and of the earlier foundation, God's House, 1448–1505*, ed. [J. A. Venn], 1 (1910)

**Coxe, Richard Charles** (1800–1865), Church of England clergyman, was the son of Richard Coxe, a Church of England priest in Bucklebury, Berkshire. Henry Octavius *Coxe was his half-brother. He was educated at Norwich grammar school. He was elected scholar of Worcester College, Oxford, in 1818, and graduated BA in 1821 and MA in 1824. He was ordained deacon in 1823 and priest in the following year. After acting for some time as chaplain of Archbishop Tenison's chapel, Regent Street, London, he obtained in 1841 the vicarage of Newcastle upon Tyne. In 1843 he was appointed honorary canon of Durham. From 1845 until he left Newcastle he received an annual supplement of 500 guineas to his income, subscribed by his parishioners. In 1853 he obtained the archdeaconry of Lindisfarne with the vicarage of Eglingham annexed, and in 1857 he was appointed canon of Durham.

Coxe enjoyed a high reputation as an eloquent preacher, and was a strenuous opponent—from a high-church point of view—of latitudinarianism in doctrine and practice, as well as a strong upholder of the rights and privileges of the clergy. His energy is evidenced in his voluminous publications, the quantity of which probably depreciated their quality. Besides numerous single sermons and addresses his *Lectures on the Evidences from Miracles* (1832) and *Remorse: Remorse for Intellectual and Literary Offences: Retribution* (1864) are of particular interest. Coxe was also a poet, publishing several volumes of verse, including *Six Ballads* (1842), *The Mercy at Marsdon Rocks* (1844), *Poems, Scriptural, Classical, Miscellaneous* (1845), and *Leda Tanah, the Martyr's Child; Derwent Bank* (1851). He published a volume of sonnets in 1848 and translated ballads from Portuguese for John Adamson's *Lusitania illustrata* (1842). Coxe was married to Louisa Arabella, daughter of the Revd J. Maule of Dover. Coxe died at Eglingham vicarage on 25 August 1865, survived by his wife, a daughter, and two sons. H. C. G. MATTHEW

**Sources** GM, 3rd ser., 19 (1865), 513–14 · Foster, *Alum. Oxon.* · J. Latimer, *Local records, or, Historical register of remarkable events which have occurred in Northumberland and Durham … 1832–57* (1857) · *Men of the time* (1865) · *CGPLA Eng. & Wales* (1865)
**Archives** Durham Cath. CL, papers | U. Durham L., letters to Henry George, third Earl Grey
**Wealth at death** under £3000: probate, 14 Oct 1865, *CGPLA Eng. & Wales*

**Coxe, Thomas** (*c.*1615–1685), physician, the son of Thomas Coxe of Corston, Somerset, entered Emmanuel College, Cambridge, in 1632 and graduated BA in 1635 and MA in 1638. He proceeded MD at Padua in 1641. In June 1643 he was one of three physicians sent by the College of Physicians to the parliamentary army, on the recommendation of the army commander, the earl of Essex. About 1646 he treated one of the brothers of Thomas Sydenham, which led to a chance encounter at which Coxe advised Sydenham to enter the medical profession, where he became one of the greatest of English physicians.

Coxe became a licentiate of the College of Physicians on 13 June 1646, incorporated his MD degree at Oxford on 15 October, and was admitted a candidate of the college on 4 November. He became a fellow on 13 June 1649. During this period he was associated with Samuel Hartlib and was one of the trustees of his proposed 'office of address' for encouraging scientific communication. In 1653 he was

appointed master of St Katharine's Hospital, London, for life, but he was replaced at the Restoration.

Coxe was active in the affairs of the College of Physicians before and after the Restoration, both as an office-holder and as a member of various committees. He was one of the original fellows of the Royal Society, elected on 20 May 1663, and was appointed physician to Charles II in 1665.

At the college Coxe served as censor in 1652–3, 1667–8, 1671–2, and 1674–6; he was also elect from 1675 to 1684, treasurer from 1676 to 1682, consiliarius from 1679 to 1682 and in 1683–4, and president in 1682–3. He gave the Harveian oration in 1660, but it was not yet customary for these to be printed. In 1656 he was a member of a committee on empirics. In 1663 he served on a committee negotiating for a new charter for the college, but the bill lapsed after its first reading in the House of Commons in 1664. In 1668 Coxe served on a committee to choose a new site for the rebuilding of the college after the great fire of London. His presidency is said to have been terminated after a year because of his whig sympathies.

In 1684 Coxe was forced by debts to leave the country and in 1685 he died of apoplexy at Boulogne, where he was also buried. His son Thomas followed him into the medical profession, graduating MB at Cambridge in 1664. JOHN SYMONS

**Sources** G. G. Meynell, *Materials for a biography of Dr Thomas Sydenham* (1988), 27–8, 68–9 · Munk, *Roll* · H. J. Cook, *The decline of the old medical regime in Stuart London* (1986) · C. Jamison, *The history of the Royal Hospital of St Katharine by the Tower of London* (1952) · G. Clark and A. M. Cooke, *A history of the Royal College of Physicians of London*, 1 (1964) · Venn, *Alum. Cant.* · DNB
**Archives** BL

**Coxe, William** (1748–1828), historian and Church of England clergyman, was born on 6 March 1748 in Dover Street, Piccadilly, London, the eldest son of William Coxe (*c.*1710–1760), physician to the king's household, and his wife, Martha, daughter of Paul D'Aranda. His younger brother was the writer and poet Peter *Coxe (1753?–1844). William was educated at Marylebone grammar school (1753–4) and then at Eton College (1754–64). He matriculated at King's College, Cambridge, at Easter, 1765; and then proceeded BA (1769), and MA (1772). He was a fellow of the college, 1768–71. Ordained deacon in London on 21 December 1771 he was priested on 15 March 1772.

After a short curacy at Denham near Uxbridge, Coxe became tutor to Lord Blandford, the eldest son of the third duke of Marlborough, at Blenheim. From 1775 to 1779 he accompanied the future eleventh earl of Pembroke on a European tour. These travels formed the basis of his three-volume *Travels into Poland, Russia, Sweden and Denmark* (1784). Coxe resumed his travels in 1784, accompanying the young Samuel Whitbread (1764–1815). From 1786 he held the college living of Kingston upon Thames, but on his return from further travels with H. B. Portman in 1788, Lord Pembroke presented him with the rectory of Bemerton near Salisbury (George Herbert's old parish), where he lived for the rest of his life.

The steady output of books continued, with a three-volume account of Switzerland, and a pamphlet attacking the radical Dr Richard Price, both in 1789. He also wrote lives of the poet and playwright John Gay (1797) and Sir Robert Walpole (1798). In August 1798 Coxe was staying with his friend Sir Richard Colt *Hoare (1758–1838) at his country house, Stourhead. Hoare had been travelling in Wales since 1793 and the two men decided on the spur of the moment to make a tour of Monmouthshire. The late summer weather was fine, and Coxe and Colt Hoare were 'delighted with the beauties of the scenery … the picturesque ruins of ancient castles … and the ancient houses of the county' (Coxe, preface). While staying with Hoare's friend James Greene at Llansanffraid Court near Abergavenny, the three men devised the idea of a county history. Greene effected the necessary introductions to the county gentry and their archives, and Coxe and Colt Hoare drew up plans for the book. Two further tours of the county followed in 1799. *An Historical Tour in Monmouthshire* appeared in 1801. Dedicated to Colt Hoare, it had been, Coxe reminded him 'commenced in your Company, written at your suggestion and embellished by your Pencil' (Coxe, dedication). It was also, he might have added, funded by Hoare's considerable wealth. In addition to Colt Hoare's numerous drawings, the book contained a series of plans of ancient earthworks by the land surveyor Thomas Morrice of Cardiff, making it one of the first British books to be illustrated with professionally surveyed plans of archaeological sites. The best advice had been sought on such topics as Welsh place names and Roman Britain, and a new map of the county had been specially commissioned.

Colt Hoare planned to follow up their success with a history of Wiltshire, written by Coxe and illustrated by himself. The collection of material began, but the project ran into unexpected problems which were to have far-reaching consequences for British archaeology. Monmouthshire was not rich in prehistoric sites earlier than its Iron Age hill forts, and the latter were readily explicable by reference to classical authors like Tacitus, who had written of the Silures. In Wiltshire, however, Avebury, Stonehenge, and the rich Bronze Age barrow burials were less easily explained in such terms. Coxe was a classicist and historian rather than a field archaeologist, and as a Church of England clergyman he may also have felt constrained by the conventional biblical account of human origins. Late in 1800 he made a start on Roman Wiltshire with Thomas Leman, and made some exploratory excavations in prehistoric barrows with William Cunnington, a wool merchant from Heytesbury, whom he introduced to Colt Hoare in April 1801. Progress was slow, however.

In December 1802 Coxe married Eleonora, *née* Shairp (1759–1830), widow of Thomas Yeldham of the British Trade Factory at St Petersburg. Coxe still hoped to complete the history, but made little progress, and eventually Colt Hoare took over the writing and research. Cunnington's and Colt Hoare's excavations of prehistoric barrows 'in the hope of meeting something which might supersede conjecture' (W. Cunnington, 123) marked a decisive advance from antiquarianism to archaeology. Colt

Hoare's *The Ancient History of Wiltshire* finally appeared between 1812 and 1821. In 1803 Coxe became a canon residentiary of Salisbury Cathedral, and in 1805 archdeacon of Wiltshire. He held several other livings, including Stourton (the church of Stourhead), and was chaplain to the Tower of London. He was a fellow of the Society of Antiquaries and a member of learned societies in Copenhagen and St Petersburg.

In 1802 Coxe produced a life of Horace Walpole, matching his earlier memoir of his father, Sir Robert. His *History of the House of Austria* appeared in 1807, and *Memoirs of the Kings of Spain* in 1813. Later works included *Memoirs of John, Duke of Marlborough* (1818), based on the Blenheim archives, as well as a life of Walpole's supporter Henry Pelham (1829). These studies established his reputation as a historian, and a modern authority has bracketed him with T. B. Macaulay and Dr Johnson as one of the fathers of modern biography (Plumb, 284).

In person Coxe was of medium height, erect and active, and was known for his genial character. In later years he became stout, and his love of good food was well known among his friends. From about 1819 his sight began to fail, and he eventually became blind. Happily, he otherwise retained his health and faculties to the end. When he died at Bemerton on 8 June 1828, at the age of eighty, John Fisher wrote to the painter John Constable how he had 'died of old age, unable to contend with two helps of salmon in lobster sauce, washed down with large draughts of Perry', resulting in dysentery. According to Fisher,

> A more irreproachable friendly man did not exist. He was always benevolently employed, & at his funeral the congregation disturbed the service with sobs. After a great dinner, he used to steal into his kitchen, and give his cook a guinea. His domestics never left him, a strong but silent compliment.  (Beckett, 237)

He was buried in the chancel of his church at Bemerton.

JEREMY KNIGHT

**Sources** *GM*, 1st ser., 98/2 (1828), 86–9 • Venn, *Alum. Cant.* • J. K. Knight, introduction, in W. Coxe, *An historical tour in Monmouthshire*, facs. edn (1995), 9–24 [followed by bibliography of Coxe's works] • *DNB* • R. H. Cunnington, *From antiquary to archaeologist: a biography of William Cunnington*, ed. J. Dyer (1975) • K. Woodbridge, *Landscape and antiquity: aspects of English culture at Stourhead, 1718 to 1838* (1970) • *The Pembroke papers, 1734–1780: letters and diaries of Henry, tenth earl of Pembroke and his circle*, ed. S. Herbert, new edn (1942) • William Coxe to W. O. Pughe, NL Wales, MSS 13222C–13224C, 1799–1803 • *John Constable's correspondence*, ed. R. B. Beckett, 6, Suffolk RS, 12 (1968) • J. H. Plumb, 'Thomas Babington Macaulay', *Men and places* (1966) • W. Coxe, *An historical tour in Monmouthshire*, 2 vols. (1801) • C. R. J. Currie and C. P. Lewis, eds., *English county histories: a guide* (1994) • parish register, Bemerton, Wilts. & Swindon RO • *Salisbury and Winchester Journal* (25 Jan 1830) • W. Cunnington, 'Account of tumuli opened in Wiltshire', *Archaeologia*, 15 (1806), 122–9, esp. 123 • parish register, St George's, Hanover Square, Wilts. & Swindon RO • R. A. Austen-Leigh, ed., *The Eton College register, 1753–1790* (1921)

**Archives** BL, collections, corresp., papers, and travel notes, Add. MSS 9078–9283 | BL, letters to second earl of Chichester, Add. MS 33112 • BL, corresp. with Sir Robert Keith and earls of Hardwicke, Add. MSS 35515–35541, 35620–35749 • BL, corresp. and papers relating to an edition of the duke of Newcastle's corresp., Add. MSS 33198–33201 • BL, notes relating to his arrangement of Wolterton Hall MSS and annotations to the corresp. of Horatio Walpole and Sir Robert Walpole, Add. MSS 63749A, 63750 • Bodl.

Oxf., corresp. with Thomas Burgess · Bodl. Oxf., corresp. with publishers Cadell & Davis · Bodl. Oxf., letters to John Nichols and J. G. Nichols · Bodl. Oxf., corresp. with Thomas Phillipps · Devizes Museum, Wiltshire Archaeological and Natural History Society, letters to William Cunnington · Linn. Soc., corresp. with Richard Pulteney · NL Wales, corresp. with W. O. Pughe, MSS 13222C–13224C · U. Nott. L., corresp. with fourth duke of Newcastle · Wilts. & Swindon RO, corresp. with eleventh earl of Pembroke

**Likenesses** C. Grignion, oils, 1784–6 · T. Holloway, engraving, 1786 (after C. Grignion), repro. in *European Magazine* (Jan 1787) · Hopwood, engraving, 1804 (after C. Grignion) · W. Beechey, oils, 1805, King's Cam. · Dunkerton, mezzotint, 1805 (after W. Beechey), NPG · W. T. Fry, engraving, 1816 (after drawing by J. Jackson; after W. Beechey) · G. Garrard, model for a bust, exh. RA 1819 · watercolour drawing, *c*.1820, NPG · A. Robertson, miniature, exh. RA 1821 · W. Pether, mezzotint (after C. Grignion, *c*.1784–1786), BM, NPG · J. Young, mezzotint (after C. Grignion), BM, NPG · portrait, repro. in R. Nichols, ed., *Monmouthshire Medley*, 2 (1977)

**Coxere, Edward** (*bap.* 1633, *d.* 1694), sailor, was baptized on 16 June 1633 at St Mary's Church, Dover, the seventh (but second surviving) child of John Coxere (*d.* 1633), sailor, and his wife, Wealthan, *née* Peace. His mother, widowed when he was only five months old, quickly married a local cordwainer, Robert Hayward, and they were prosperous enough to send him in 1647 to spend a year with a French family at Le Havre to learn the language, to prepare him for a career in commerce. They next sent him to live with a wine-cooper at Middelburg, but Coxere found a passage home within a week. With no taste for trade, he resolved to try the sea. His first experience, sailing to Spain as a cabin-boy, was inauspicious, for he was terrified by his master and badly seasick. He then joined his elder brother in the *George*, flagship of the English navy, serving as cabin-boy to the lieutenant, a Dover neighbour; but the ship was badly damaged by fire in December 1649 and Coxere was lucky to survive. His fortunes then improved. After sailing to Spain in a Dutch vessel with an English commander, he was happy to remain on board when it was hired by the Spanish navy; he became fluent in Dutch and Spanish and secured some booty from prizes. Sailing home in 1652, shortly after war had broken out between the Dutch and English, Coxere's ship was captured by English warships in the channel. Paradoxically he had been abroad for so long that he was mistaken for a Fleming and contrived to escape, making his way home to Dover where his mother initially failed to recognize him. His main concern now was to avoid the press-gang. He took a voyage to Newfoundland and Malaga, serving as coxswain, but on his return was forced to live at home as a virtual prisoner, a situation which eventually drove him to enlist in a frigate, where he served for the remainder of the war. In 1655 Coxere married Mary (1622–1681), daughter of Richard Highway, another Dover mariner, though he left his bride seven weeks later to sail as gunner on a trading voyage to the straits. The voyage proved disastrous. The vessel was captured by Spaniards and Coxere, who had brought most of his savings to trade on a private account, lost almost his whole estate. With typical courage and ingenuity he contrived to escape at

Malaga and worked his passage home on a Dutch vessel via Amsterdam, to find himself a father.

Coxere became a prisoner a second time in 1657 when his ship was taken in the straits by a Moorish privateer under a renegade English commander, and its company were held in Tunis as slaves. Sent to work in the naval docks at Porto Farino, Coxere was valued for his technical and linguistic skills but was chained in a dungeon every night and flogged at least once. After five months' slavery he was redeemed with other English prisoners under a treaty concluded by John Stokes with the dey at Tunis in spring 1658. Serving now in Stokes's squadron as an able seaman in the *Kent*, Coxere resolved to repair his shattered fortunes by plunder, and joined every boarding party. The rewards proved small, however, and he was allowed to transfer to a merchantman bound for the Canaries, for higher wages. This, too, proved unlucky for in September 1658 his ship was captured by a Spanish man-of-war and carried to Cadiz. Once more he contrived to escape, helped by his proficiency in Spanish, and eventually found his way back to Dover, as penniless as when he had left. In 1659 Coxere borrowed £15 to buy books, equipment, and a trading venture, and sailed to Newfoundland as chief mate under his brother-in-law on a voyage to lade fish for Alicante. Both this voyage and a sequel proved safe and profitable. Back at Dover in 1661 Coxere encountered two Quaker evangelists, Edward Burrough and Samuel Fisher, whose teaching was to transform his life. As a Quaker and pacifist Coxere found himself almost unemployable. Though he finally secured a mate's place in a ship owned by the Quaker Francis Bellars, he and several companions were arrested at a conventicle in Yarmouth and held close prisoners for seven months. Facing starvation, Coxere taught himself shoemaking to earn a pittance for bread. On his eventual release he was made master and merchant of a small Quaker-owned vessel and later, on the outbreak of the Second Anglo-Dutch War, bought a small hoy for coastal trading. He traded with this hoy for many years, making short voyages to the Netherlands and France. Soon after his wife's death in July 1681, however, Coxere experienced further religious persecution. He was convicted and fined under the Conventicle Act in 1683, and imprisoned two weeks later for refusing the oath of allegiance. Worse was to follow: in March 1684 he and eight others were arrested at the Quaker meetinghouse in Dover and held close prisoners for almost a year. Coxere died on 8 August 1694 at Scarborough, where two of his daughters had settled. His picaresque narrative, written in or after 1685, is one of the most vivid accounts of seafaring life, revealing an intelligent, brave and quickwitted man, hardened by danger and adversity but retaining both humour and humanity. BERNARD CAPP

**Sources** E. H. W. Meyerstein, ed., *Adventures by sea of Edward Coxere* (1945) [incl. bibliography]

**Coxeter, Thomas** (1689–1747), literary scholar and editor, was born on 20 September 1689 at Lechlade in Gloucestershire, the son of George Coxeter (*d.* 1702), gentleman, and his wife, Elizabeth, *née* Bathurst. The Coxeters had been long established at Lechlade. Thomas received his grounding in grammar from the Revd Mr Collier in the nearby village of Great Coxwell, and then attended Magdalen College School, Oxford, under the Revd Thomas Collins. He entered Trinity College, Oxford, on 7 July 1705 as a commoner. He appears not to have taken a degree, and moved on to London with the intention of qualifying in civil law. He abandoned this scheme on the death of his patron, Sir John Cooke (1666–1710), dean of arches and vicar-general of the see of Canterbury. Coxeter was probably the author of an elegy on Cooke's death, 'Astraea lacrimans', published in 1710. Thereafter he gave himself over to literary enterprises of varying degrees of merit, ranging from hack work to serious editorial projects. He helped to prepare the indexes of Dr John Hudson's edition of Josephus (1720), and furnished material for Joseph Ames's *Typographical Antiquities* (1749). He developed a particular interest in old plays, and formed an important collection of early editions. He was able to help Lewis Theobald with his edition of Shakespeare (1734), and to furnish material relating to early printings to Robert Dodsley as he prepared his *Select Collection of Old Plays* (1744). He came to regard Dodsley as a rival in the publication of specimens of early drama, but Coxeter never managed to bring his projects to the press. He circulated proposals for an edition of the plays of Thomas May in 1744, but the work never materialized; nor did his intended edition of the works of Thomas Sackville ever appear.

Coxeter's only success with the editing of old plays was to be posthumous, for *The Dramatic Works of Mr Philip Massinger, Compleat* did not appear until 1759, some twelve years after his death. In four volumes, and dedicated to Garrick, it was reissued in 1761. Coxeter's edition of Massinger was by eighteenth-century standards highly competent: it noted variant readings from early printings, drew attention to parallel passages in the dramatist's work, and glossed obscure phrases and terms. The edition was slightingly dismissed by William Gifford in the introduction to his edition of Massinger published in 1805, but unjustly so, and the *Edinburgh Review* came to Coxeter's defence in an article of April 1808. The most recent editors of Massinger speak well of Coxeter, remarking that he 'set the canon for all succeeding editions' (Edwards and Gibson, li).

Another of Coxeter's schemes that failed to develop was a plan to make a collection of all the English poets who had published a volume of verse. Johnson and Boswell discussed this scheme on 18 September 1777, with Johnson recollecting that Coxeter had collected 'about five hundred volumes of poets whose works were little known; but upon his death Tom Osborne bought them, and they were dispersed, which he thought a pity, as it was curious to see any series complete' (Boswell, *Life*, 3.158). The *Lives of the Poets* (1753) compiled by Theophilus Cibber and Robert Shiels was heavily indebted to Coxeter's collection and his manuscript notes thereon.

In February 1747 Coxeter was appointed secretary to a newly established 'Society for the Encouragement of … a Complete English History', but he died at Bridewell Hospital of a fever on Easter day that year, 19 April 1747. He was buried in the churchyard of the hospital. He left a son, Thomas, who enlisted as a soldier with the East India Company, and a daughter, Elizabeth, whose indigent condition was relieved from time to time by Samuel Johnson. The plight of his children suggests that Coxeter's pursuit of a literary career led him from a gentleman's estate to the fringes of Grub Street.                    GRAHAM PARRY

**Sources** GM, 1st ser., 51 (1781), 173–4 · *The plays of Philip Massinger*, ed. W. Gifford, 4 vols. (1805), 1.lxxxix–xciii · Nichols, *Lit. anecdotes*, 2.512–13 · Boswell, *Life* · P. Edwards and C. Gibson, 'General introduction', *The plays and poems of Philip Massinger*, 1 (1976) · *VCH Gloucestershire*, 7.111–12 · *The letters of Samuel Johnson*, ed. B. Redford, 2 (1992) · DNB
**Wealth at death** virtually nothing: GM

**Coxon, Thomas** (1654–1735), Jesuit, was born on 20 March 1654, and came from co. Durham. He may have been the John Coxson, son of a George Coxson, recorded as baptized on 21 March 1655 at Lanchester, co. Durham. He entered the Society of Jesus on 7 September 1676 at Watten, in Flanders, was educated at the Jesuit college in Liège, was ordained priest in 1687, and finally professed in 1694. From 1694 to 1730 he served mostly in England, mainly in the south-east, and later (1733–5) acted as procurator of the English College, St Omer. He is said to have translated several books into English and edited the second edition of William Petre's 1669 translation of Ribadeneira, *The Lives of Saints* (1730). He died at St Omer on 6 or 7 May 1735.                    THOMPSON COOPER, *rev.* J. T. RHODES

**Sources** G. Holt, *The English Jesuits, 1650–1829: a biographical dictionary*, Catholic RS, 70 (1984), 72 · H. Foley, ed., *Records of the English province of the Society of Jesus*, 5 (1879), 532–3; 7 (1882–3), 179 · M. J. Walsh, 'An eighteenth-century Jesuit bibliography', *Heythrop Journal*, 20 (1979), 50 · *The letter book of Lewis Sabran*, ed. G. Holt, Catholic RS, 62 (1971) · F. Blom and others, *English Catholic books, 1701–1800: a bibliography* (1996), nos. 52, 54 · T. H. Clancy, *English Catholic books, 1641–1700: a bibliography*, rev. edn (1996), no. 832 · A. de Backer and others, *Bibliothèque de la Compagnie de Jésus*, new edn, 2, ed. C. Sommervogel (Brussels, 1891), 1374; 9 (Brussels, 1900), 1598 · IGI

**Coxwell, Henry Tracey** [ *pseud.* Henry Wells] (1819–1900), balloonist, was the youngest son of Commander Joseph Coxwell of the Royal Navy (1774?–1832) and of Ann Godfry (probably *née* Reeves) and was the grandson of the Revd Charles Coxwell of Ablington House, Gloucestershire. He was born at the parsonage at Wouldham, near Chatham, Kent, on 2 March 1819 and went to school at Chatham, where his family moved in 1822, and later at Woolwich Common. After a very brief and unsuccessful attempt at commercial training at Amsterdam, in 1836 he was apprenticed to a surgeon dentist (probably in London) and by 1840 had his own practice in Islington. However, his first sight of Charles Green's balloon in 1828 at Rochester proved fateful, although it was not until 19 August 1844, at Pentonville, that Coxwell had an opportunity of making an ascent. Unfortunately, he unwittingly offended his hero Green by accompanying George Gale and John Hampton. In the autumn of 1845 (under the name of Henry Wells) he projected and edited *The Balloon, or,*

*Aerostatic Magazine*, the first periodical publication in the country on the subject, of which about twelve numbers appeared at irregular intervals. On 6 July 1847, at Vauxhall, he ascended in Gypson's balloon in company with Albert Smith, during a heavy storm. An enormous tear was discovered in the balloon, and the lives of the passengers were saved only by Coxwell's readiness in converting the balloon, as far as possible, into a parachute by releasing its neck.

In 1848 Coxwell abandoned dentistry to take on the management of a balloon, the *Sylph*, in Brussels. Already the veteran of fifty ascents, as a professional he was allegedly to exceed 1000. For several years he toured the continent, especially Germany, demonstrating the ease with which 'aerial torpedoes' could be discharged. In attempting to land near Hamburg in 1849, he was greeted (as a presumed Danish spy) with a hail of bullets. After returning to England three years later, he established at Tottenham a base for balloon tours of the country, which he later extended to Belfast and Glasgow. These had their tribulations. In 1864 his *Britannia* balloon was destroyed by rioters at Leicester. A crash in Cheshire in 1861 left him on crutches, but gave him leisure to consider replacing Charles Green as balloonist to James Glaisher. On 5 September 1862 Coxwell and Glaisher attained the greatest height on record, allegedly between 36,000 and 37,000 feet, or 'fully seven miles'. The uniqueness of this claim at the time permitted its acceptance, but greater familiarity with the upper atmosphere since then has led to its rejection. Glaisher became unconscious and Coxwell lost all sensation in his hands, but managed just in time to pull the valve-cord with his teeth. A final descent was safely made near Ludlow (from Wolverhampton).

Coxwell made experiments in military ballooning at Aldershot in July 1862. In 1863, in company with Henry Negretti, he made the first aerial trip in England for purposes of photography. When the Franco-Prussian War broke out in 1870 he went to manage some war balloons for the Germans. He formed two companies, two officers, and forty-two men, at Cologne, and his assistant went on to Strasbourg, but the town surrendered while Coxwell was still struggling to get his balloons inflated. In a volte-face he offered to open communications with beleaguered Paris. He complained of the lack of British interest in military aeronautics and of the rejection of his plans to take balloons to the Asante kingdom in 1874 and to the Arctic in 1876. By the time of the Second South African War his ideas aroused slightly more retrospective interest—just as a more robust alternative was about to become available. On 17 June 1885 he made his last ascent in a large balloon, the *City of York*, at the eponymous city which had become one of his favourite display centres. He died at Sandford House, Blatchington, near Seaford, Sussex, on 5 January 1900, leaving a widow, Lydia Hannah, whom he had married in or before 1862. As a balloonist of renown but always with aspirations to 'practical utility' (*Aeronautical Journal*, 119), Coxwell was to have no successors. JULIAN LOCK

**Sources** *DNB* · J. E. Hodgson, *The history of aeronautics in Great Britain, from the earliest times to the latter half of the nineteenth century* (1924), 264–73 · H. T. Coxwell, *My life and balloon experiences*, 2 vols. (1887–9) · Boase, *Mod. Eng. biog.* · E. S. Bruce, 'The balloon work of the late Mr. Henry Coxwell', *Aeronautical Journal*, 4 (1900), 118–20 · *The Times* (11 Sept 1862) · *The Times* (6 Jan 1900) · *ILN* (13 Jan 1900), 43 · L. T. C. Rolt, *The aeronauts: a history of ballooning, 1783–1903* (1966) · D. D. Jackson, *The aeronauts* (1981) · J. Glaisher and others, *Travels in the air*, ed. J. Glaisher (1871) · *Men and women of the time* (1899) · C. H. Turnor, *Astra castra: experiments and adventures in the atmosphere* (1865) · *IGI* · *CGPLA Eng. & Wales* (1900)

**Likenesses** Negretti & Zambra, carte-de-visite, 1862 (with James Glaisher), NPG; *see illus. in* Glaisher, James (1809–1903) · photograph, in or before 1864, repro. in Turnor, *Astra castra*, following p. 462 · Negretti & Zambra, photograph, repro. in Hodgson, *History of aeronautics*, following p. 274 · portrait, repro. in Hodder, *Heroes of Britain* (1878), vol. 1, pp. 254–7 · portraits, repro. in *Strand Magazine*, 2 (1896), 122–31 · wood-engraving, NPG; repro. in *ILN* (20 Jan 1884)

**Wealth at death** £9029 3s. 6d.: probate, 5 Feb 1900, *CGPLA Eng. & Wales*

**Coyne, Joseph Stirling** (1803–1868), playwright and journalist, was born at Birr, King's county, Ireland, the son of Denis Coyne (d. c.1850), port surveyor of Waterford, and his wife, Bridget Cosgrave. He was educated at Dungannon School, Tyrone, and intended for the legal profession, but the favourable reception of early contributions to some Dublin periodicals convinced him to give up law in favour of literature and drama. His first play, the farce *The Phrenologist* (Dublin, June 1835), was well received, and two others in the same genre, *Honest Cheats* and *The Four Lovers*, followed in April 1836. Later that year Coyne went to London with a letter of introduction from William Carleton, a principal contributor to the *Dublin University Magazine*, to Crofton Croker, who put him in touch with the London journals, including, among others, *Bentley's Miscellany*, where three of his short stories were published in 1841–2. His first London farce, *The Queer Subject*, was performed at the Adelphi Theatre (November 1836), and a year later he joined the literary staff of the short-lived newspaper the *Morning Gazette*, which closed after two months, on 2 December 1837. He married, on 19 June 1840, Anne Comins (1811?–1880), widow of Matthew Comins and daughter of Wilkins and Margaret Simcockes of Galway. The couple had at least two children: J. Denis Coyne and Edmund Stirling Coyne (d. 1902).

Coyne was part of the group which planned the publication of *Punch*, first issued on 17 July 1841, and was originally, with Horace Mayhew and Mark Lemon, a co-editor. Soon afterwards he was edged out by Lemon for not pulling his weight and when he was caught plagiarizing from an Irish paper Lemon barred him from contributing any further. Elsewhere he was well established as a journalist and actively contributed to the newspaper press and other journals over this period and later, when he became the drama critic of the *Sunday Times*.

Coyne's early prose tended to reinforce Irish stereotypes, as his fiction for *Bentley's Miscellany* shows. His keen sense of situational and verbal fun spilled over into the plays written for the Olympic, the Haymarket, and the Adelphi. He ventured successfully into parody in *Box and Cox Married and Settled at Last!* (1852), but his greatest achievements were the one-act domestic farces. To some extent his success depended on the talents of the Adelphi's low comedian, Edward Wright, who proved a perfect interpreter of Coyne's farcical heroes. Funniest were the eponymous *Binks the Bagman* (1843); Chesterfield Honeybun, the bewildered lawyer's clerk in *Did you Ever Send your Wife to Camberwell?* (1846); and Whittington Widgetts, the terrified tailor in *How to Settle your Accounts with your Laundress* (1847). Of the last two plays, the latter was translated into French (as *Une femme dans ma fontaine* for the Vaudeville, Paris), and the former, as *Did you Ever Send your Wife to Brooklyn?*, was acted and published in the United States. (The plays were anthologized respectively in 1973 and 1996.) At the revival of *Everybody's Friend* (Haymarket, 1859), renamed *A Widow Hunt* (St James's, 1867), the leading roles of Felix Featherley and Major Wellington de Boots were taken by Henry Irving and John Sleeper Clarke. Outside his normal range, Coyne's depiction of Lola Montez, mistress of Ludwig I of Bavaria, in a drama of the same name (Haymarket, 1848) provoked the intervention of the censor on political grounds and the play was stopped after two nights. A revised version, with all royal allusions removed, was allowed under the title *Pas de fascination*. Coyne was joint author (with N. P. Willis) of *Scenery and Antiquities of Ireland* (2 vols., 1842), elaborately illustrated by W. H. Bartlett; *Pippins and Pies, or, Sketches out of School* (1855); and *Sam Spangle, or, The History of a Harlequin* (1866). He also contributed several pieces to compendium volumes such as Albert Smith's *Gavarni in London* (1848), his *Sketches of London* (1859), and to *Mixed sweets from 'Routledge's Annual'* (1867).

In 1856 Coyne was appointed secretary to the Dramatic Authors' Society, founded in 1833 in defence of dramatic copyright. Under his leadership the society established a fixed scale for performance fees and appointed agents in the provinces to ensure that country managers paid their dues to authors in line with the London theatres. He appeared as a witness on copyright at the 1866 parliamentary inquiry into theatrical licensing and continued in the duties of the post until a few days before his death. He lived for many years at 3 Wilmington Square, Clerkenwell, London, but then moved to 61 Talbot Road, Westbourne Park, where he died of cancer on 18 July 1868; his wife survived him. He was buried in Highgate cemetery, Middlesex, on 21 July. At his death he was at work on a play entitled *The Home Wreck*, which was completed by his son Denis (performed at the Surrey Theatre in February 1869 and published by Thomas Lacy).

His cultivated indifference to his personal appearance prompted Douglas Jerrold's quip: 'Stirling Coyne—I call him filthy lucre' (Jerrold, 38). Even less charitably, another observer described his 'portentous appearance', occasioned by his heavy black moustaches drooping over his mouth, contrasting not only with his mass of greying hair but with his unimpressiveness in conversation, in which he reportedly 'had little to say and what he did say he said badly' (*Mid-Victorian Pepys*, xx). None the less he was an industrious and prolific writer, having written over sixty plays, including a few in collaboration with H. C. Coape,

Francis Talfourd, or H. Hamilton. Shameless in his plundering of Parisian farce with the aid of a French dictionary, Coyne was in that respect no different from many journeyman contemporary playwrights who used their talent successfully to amuse theatre audiences, but he was at the same time, in apparent contradiction, a fierce promoter of British authors' rights.

JOHN RUSSELL STEPHENS

**Sources** DNB · *The Era* (26 July 1868) · GM, 5th ser., 1 (1868), 413–14 · *Illustrated Sporting News*, 252 (1866) · *Sunday Times* (26 July 1868) · private information (1887) [E. S. Coyne] · R. G. G. Price, *A history of Punch* (1957) · *A mid-Victorian Pepys: the letters and memoirs of Sir William Hardman*, ed. S. M. Ellis (1923) · W. Jerrold, *Douglas Jerrold and Punch* (1910) · J. R. Stephens, *The profession of the playwright: British theatre, 1800–1900* (1992) · J. R. Stephens, *The censorship of English drama, 1824–1901* (1980) · A. Nicoll, *Early nineteenth century drama, 1800–1850*, 2nd edn (1955), vol. 4 of *A history of English drama, 1660–1900* (1952–9), 284–5, 578 [bibliography and performance data] · A. Nicoll, *Late nineteenth century drama, 1850–1900*, 2nd edn (1959), vol. 5 of *A history of English drama, 1660–1900* (1952–9), 327–8 [bibliography and performance data] · J. Shattock, ed., *The Cambridge bibliography of English literature*, 3rd edn, 4 (1999) · *The Times* (27 Jan 1880) · m. cert. · d. cert.

**Likenesses** H. Watkins, print, c.1856–1859, NPG · bust (after photograph by J. Watkins) · woodcut

**Wealth at death** under £5000: probate, 8 Aug 1868, CGPLA Eng. & Wales

**Coyte, William Beeston** (1740–1810), physician and botanist, was born on 24 December 1740, at either Bentley or Ipswich, Suffolk, the son of William Coyte (1708–1775), physician and botanist, and his wife, Elizabeth Cobbald of Layham. He attended Ipswich School, c.1751–1758, entered Queens' College, Cambridge, in 1758, and graduated MB in 1763. He practised medicine at Ipswich, writing to the *Medical Transactions* (3, 1785, 30) on a cure for epilepsy, and interested himself in botany, being a member of the Linnean Society from 1794 until his death. Coyte's marriage to Sarah Rowning (c.1740–1776) was ended by her death at Great Yarmouth on 21 September 1776. His second wife, Hester (c.1739–1820), daughter of Samuel Ewer, soap-boiler, of London, survived him with their three daughters.

Coyte's garden at Ipswich had been founded by his great-uncle, William Beeston (1672–1732), an eminent physician and botanist. It was bequeathed to William Coyte, and came on his death into the care of Coyte, who extended the range of plants under cultivation from rare exotics to more common British species. He published an annotated catalogue of its contents, *Hortus botanicus Gippovicensis, or, A systematical enumeration of the plants cultivated in Dr Coyte's botanic garden at Ipswich*, in 1796, followed by the first and only volume of his *Index plantarum* (1807).

After prolonged illness, Coyte died at his home on 3 March 1810, and was buried in the church of St Nicholas, Ipswich, as were both his wives. His extensive library and many of his plants had been sold in June 1790. Coyte's younger brother James (1749–1812) graduated BA at Gonville and Caius College, Cambridge, in 1771, was rector of Cantley from 1779, and was perpetual curate of St Nicholas, Ipswich, from 1785 until 1812.

B. D. JACKSON, *rev.* ANITA MCCONNELL

**Sources** F. Simpson, 'Dr William Beeston Coyte FLS, of "Coyte's Gardens"', *Suffolk Natural History: the Transactions of the Suffolk Naturalists' Society*, 19 (1983), 393 · H. E. Wilton, 'Coyte's Gardens, Ipswich', *Suffolk Review*, 1 (1958), 201–3 · *Ipswich Journal* (12 March 1810) · *GM*, 1st ser., 80 (1810), 389 · Nichols, *Illustrations*, 6.877–8 · *Extracts from the literary and scientific correspondence of Richard Richardson*, ed. D. Turner (1835), 184–5 · will, PRO, PROB 11/1511, sig. 237 · *The East Anglian, or, Notes and Queries on Subjects Connected with the Counties of Suffolk, Cambridge, Essex and Norfolk*, new ser., 13 (1909–10), 138
**Archives** Linn. Soc., corresp. with Sir James Smith

**Cozens, Alexander** (1717–1786), landscape painter, was born in Russia, the eldest of six children of Richard Cozens (1674–1735), the English chief shipbuilder to Peter the Great, and his wife, Mary, the daughter of Robert Davenport, also a shipbuilder in the tsar's employ.

**Russia and Italy** Davenport had married Mary Dodd of Woolwich in St James's, Duke Street, London, in 1696 before moving to Russia but gaps in the register book of the British factory in Russia leave no firm date or place for the marriage of Richard Cozens and Mary Davenport or for the birth of their two eldest sons, Alexander and Peter, whose sponsors were Prince Aleksandr Menshikov, admiral of the Russian fleet, and the tsar, Peter the Great. Alexander Cozens wrote in a copy of one of his later publications to Catherine the Great that he had been 'né au milieu du vaste Empire que V.M. gouverne' (*Principles of Beauty*, 1778, copy in the Tate collection). The births of his younger siblings, Mary (1722), Margaretta Maria (1724), Richard (1726), and finally Sarah (1732), are all recorded in St Petersburg where the shipyards were finally established after years of temporary yards at Kazan on the Don and in Archangel.

In 1736, after her husband's death, Mary Cozens, then living in Archangel, petitioned the Russian admiralty for financial support. Her petition indicated that Alexander Cozens, now nineteen, and his brother Peter, sixteen, had been sent to England in 1727, where, she stated, Alexander was studying painting and his brother Peter Latin; Richard had been sent to join them later and her three daughters were still in her care.

In a special resolution dated February 1737 the Admiralty stated that in order for the widow to be eligible for a pension her sons must return to St Petersburg and take up their father's trade. Unfortunately, no documents survive to indicate when they returned to Russia. Nothing further is known of Peter, but Richard later ran a printing works in Krasnoe which Catherine the Great visited in 1764, and Alexander also returned some time before 1745.

Cozens's earliest surviving work is a worn English halfpenny etched with a landscape and inscribed 'A Cozens fecit 1733' on one side and a bust etched on the other (Museum of London). *East View of Eton College* from the river, engraved by John Pine after an original design by A. Cozens, was published in 1742, but two small imaginary landscapes in pen and ink or wash, dated 1736 (Tate collection) and 1743 (BM) might have been drawn anywhere in northern Europe. George Lambert is the artist whose style is most likely to have inspired or influenced Cozens's work during his time in London, but there is no evidence to connect them. When Cozens returned to Russia, he would have encountered similar work at the Academy of Sciences, where all students drew from nature three times a week.

Cozens's next dated works are views in Rome drawn in 1746. The date of his arrival and departure from Italy are not known, but later comments by his pupil William Beckford indicate that he sailed there on a Swedish ship directly from St Petersburg to Leghorn, passing Corsica and perhaps spending his quarantine in a lazaretto off Spezia on Elba, recorded in a series of drawings. They are part of a large group made during his two-year sojourn in Italy which were lost before his return to England, but amazingly were later recovered and returned to him by his son (BM).

The only surviving sketchbook from Cozens's Italian years (Yale U. CBA) contains his ambitious statement of intent:

> I will studdy the beauty of Form & injoy elegant Ideas set the Image of a charming face fore my mind feed on its lovely Innocence & by it flatter my longing Soul with Visions of happyness tho' but in Picture for I will immure myself in solitude & paint the Graces act Truth and contemplate virtue.

Never adept at drawing the human figure, Cozens possessed an eye for composing landscape that was soon inspired not only by the real landscape he found about him in Rome and the surrounding campagna, but also by the paintings and drawings he encountered in the studios and collections of the city. The sketch book provides evidence that he studied with Claude-Joseph Vernet and experimented widely: painting in oils, sketching in ink with dry or heavily loaded brushes, inventing a box for carrying colours to paint out of doors, drawing after antique sculpture and classical ruins, and practising etching. Lists of rules and methods are also scattered throughout the sketchbook. These are the first indication of Cozens's often remarked-upon passion for systems, which were, in effect, an organized way of putting methods into writing so that they might be more easily followed, modified and corrected in practice, and eventually published for the use of other artists and pupils.

**Early career in England** The date of Cozens's return to England is not known, but the next signed and dated work is a large oil of 1748, *A View of Blenheim* (priv. coll.), of the palace seen from the park, which combines classical compositional elements learned in Italy and a very pastoral English landscape with horses in a meadow and deer in the park by the palace. He continued to paint landscape views of particular places throughout the rest of his career, including a pair of large oil paintings of Matlock (1756; ex Sothebys 9 June 1998, lots 5, 6), a large panoramic *South View of London* (1763), a watercolour *Greenwich and London from Woolwich* (1766; priv. coll.), and finally, *View in North Wales Taken from Wynstay, the Seat of Sir Watkin Williams Wynn, Bart* (exh. RA, 1781); most of his œuvre, however, consisted of uninhabited imaginary landscape compositions.

Nevertheless, it was Cozens's topographical skills, particularly the 'many Coasting Prospects' he had taken at sea, which gained him his first salaried post as a drawing-master, filling the position left vacant at Christ's Hospital by the death of Edward Lens in 1750. Orphans of the city guilds were educated there for apprenticeship in trades or to be bound out to sea, and their drawing lessons were meant to be tailored to their future needs. The drawing book produced by Lens and his father, Bernard, who taught at Christ's Hospital before him, included drawings of the human figure as well as landscapes and coastal views, and Cozens continued to teach the same type of lessons, providing additional examples of his own for his pupils to copy. There were complaints about the results from the examiners at Trinity House, to which Cozens responded that the students were dull and indifferent; he resigned shortly afterwards, in May 1754.

No parish records have been found to provide the date of Cozens's marriage to the daughter of the engraver John *Pine, or the birth of their son, John Robert *Cozens (1752–1797), in 1752, or daughter, Juliet Ann, but at this time he had already been employed by William Hunter to provide one of the drawings for *The Anatomy of the Human Gravid Uterus* (1774). There is also evidence that Cozens was already giving private lessons to the children of Simon, first Earl Harcourt: the eldest, Viscount Nuneham, commented that of all his drawing-masters 'Cozens was the only one that had a taste or thoroughly understood the business he professed' (14 Sept 1755, Lee of Hartwell papers, Aylesbury RO). The two views *Matlock High Tor* and *Matlock Vale* of the following year, recorded hanging at Kedleston in 1789, were probably commissioned by Lord Scarsdale, who was also the patron of Joseph Wright of Derby during this decade.

**Cozens's new method**   Alexander Cozens's first drawing manual was published in 1759: *An Essay to Facilitate the Inventing of Landskips, Intended for Students in the Art* (Hermitage, St Petersburg). In the two-page explanatory essay he began with a passage from the 1724 English edition of Leonardo da Vinci's *Treatise on Painting*, which described how invention of composition might be assisted by looking at accidents of nature, such as old walls covered with dirt or streaked stones. Cozens explained that a happy accident with an adept pupil had led him to improve upon Leonardo by creating those imperfect forms on purpose with some degree of design, and then using them as the basis for landscape compositions. These 'rude black Sketches' or 'blots' were drawn swiftly with a brush dipped in indian ink, from which hints were taken for the outline of a landscape drawn on a clean piece of post paper laid on top. He provided eight pairs of blots and outline landscapes drawn from them as examples of the eight styles of composition, which he listed in the essay, and he intended to exhibit eight finished shaded examples with figures at the shops of the printsellers Boydell and Austin. He engraved the examples himself, employing a unique, very early form of aquatint for the blots.

During the next two decades Cozens took rooms at Eton during term in order to provide lessons to the young men whose parents wished them to be taught drawing and he also continued to teach individuals privately, visiting them on their estates as well as in London and Bath. He was described as a 'Landscape painter' in Mortimer's *London Directory* in 1763, when his address was opposite the Golden Lion, Tottenham Court Road. The following year he moved to 12 (or 4) Leicester Street, Leicester Fields, where he was to remain. He published *A Treatise on Perspective and Rules for Shading by Invention* in 1765 but no copy survives.

Cozens's pupils numbered in the hundreds. The names of many can be ascertained from the subscribers to his 1778 publication, *The Principles of Beauty*, and included the young William Beckford (with whom he formed a particularly close bond), the collector George Beaumont, Lady Amabel Polwarth, the children of Francis Greville, first earl of Warwick, the Grimston family and their large circle of friends around York, as well as Sir James Grant and his friends in Scotland, and the children of George III.

Throughout these decades Cozens planned a number of publications, although the only one he was able to see through to completion was the long essay accompanied by a series of outline profiles with interchangeable hairstyles that constituted the sixteen characters of beauty mentioned above. They ranged from 'The Majestic (denoting dignity, independence)' to 'The Innocent (void of harm, no suspicion)', and formed a parallel system to that of sixteen species of landscape compositions (from 'the edge of a hill' to 'a spacious, extensive landscape'), the contemplation of which was intended to arouse specific passions or feelings, such as 'attention, caution, awe', or 'greatness, surprize, danger'. The landscapes, together with lists of objects and circumstances of weather or seasons which might be used with them, were part of a much larger project which was never completed. Only two parts were published—a printed sheet of lists and sixteen outline etchings of landscapes, entitled *The Various Species of Landscape &c. in Nature*, which appeared some time in the mid-1770s. Only a handful of copies survive (one in the British Museum), but Sir George Beaumont was in possession of a set, now in the Tate collection, when John Constable visited him at Coleorton and copied them in 1823.

In 1771 Cozens published *The Shape, Skeleton and Foliage of Thirty-Two Species of Trees*, which was clearly intended to form part of his *Various Species*, along with the series of 'circumstances' of skies which he printed later (see below). This complicated publishing programme is best understood through the five surviving finished examples he made in oil on paper to illustrate what might be described as his system for inventing 'moral' landscapes. Two of the oils are in English public collections, *Before a Storm* (Tate collection) and *Setting Sun* (Whitworth Art Gallery, Manchester), which indicate that the species of composition could be used with certain objects, including trees, and with certain circumstances of sky or weather, to produce a landscape which evoked specific emotions, such as grandeur or simplicity, even freedom and liberty, and which might be employed for moral improvement.

Such ambitions were commensurate with those of a

number of his contemporaries who were attempting to raise the status of landscape painting in British art. Cozens was an early member of the Society for the Encouragement of Arts, Manufactures, and Commerce and exhibited twice with the Free Society of Artists (1761, 1762), regularly with the Society of Artists, and yearly at the Royal Academy from 1772 to 1781, failing twice to be elected an associate academician.

**Last years** Cozens was a friend of many artists, including Ozias Humphry, Gavin Hamilton, William and Sawrey Gilpin, Joseph Wright of Derby, and William Hoare. His pupils wrote of him with affection and admiration, and purchased extensively at the sale after his death and were generous with their financial assistance when his son fell ill at a relatively early age in 1794. Just before Alexander Cozens's death at his home in Leicester Street, on 23 April 1786, he saw the publication of the final completed version of the system for inventing landscapes on which he had been working throughout his career: *A New Method of Assisting the Invention in Drawing Original Compositions of Landscape* (1785–6). Prefaced by a 33-page text which included a repeat of his list of sixteen kinds of composition of landscape, the work included several new refinements, including wrinkling the blots before using them, as well as mezzotints of sixteen blots and examples of finished compositions and thirty-two outline studies of clouds. It is the work for which he is now most famous, although its apparent novelty, often anachronistically described as 'modern', has also led to two centuries of misunderstanding his intentions, most notably by Edward Dayes, who dubbed him 'Blotmaster-General to the town' (E. W. Brayley, ed., *The Works of the Late Edward Dayes Including Professional Sketches of Modern Artists*, 1805, 325).

Described as 'A widower, late of St Anne's, Westminster' (Oppé, *Alexander and John Robert Cozens*, 42), Cozens died intestate and was buried in St James's, Piccadilly, London, on 30 April 1786. His estate was administered by his son John Robert and daughter Juliet Ann, and they sold his remaining works at Christies on 31 March 1787 (149 lots). A number of works were bought in and were included in John Robert's sale at Greenwoods on 9–10 July 1794.

KIM SLOAN

**Sources** A. P. Oppé, *Alexander and John Robert Cozens* (1952) · K. Sloan, *Alexander and John Robert Cozens: the poetry of landscape* (1986) · K. Sloan, 'A new chronology for Alexander Cozens: part I, 1717–59', *Burlington Magazine*, 127 (1985), 70–75 · K. Sloan, 'A new chronology for Alexander Cozens: part II, 1759–86', *Burlington Magazine*, 127 (1985), 355–63 · A. P. Oppé, 'A Roman sketch-book by Alexander Cozens', *Walpole Society*, 16 (1927–8), 18–93 · A. Wilton, *The art of Alexander and John Robert Cozens* (1980) [exhibition catalogue, Yale U. CBA, 17 Sept 1980 – 16 Nov 1980] · A. S. Kantor-Gukovskaia, 'Aleksandr Kozens i ermitazhnie risunki, svyazannie s ego metodom peizazhnoi kompozitsii' [Alexander Cozens and Hermitage drawings connected with his method of composing landscapes], *Trudy Gosudarstvennogo Ermitazha* [St Petersburg], 22 (1982), 88–98 · P. Joyner and K. Sloan, 'A Cozens album in the National Library of Wales, Aberystwyth', *Walpole Society*, 57 (1993–4), 79–136, esp. 79–94 · C. A. Cramer, 'Alexander Cozens's *New method*: the blot and general nature', *Art Bulletin*, 79 (1997), 112–29 · J. C. Lebensztejn, *L'art de la tache* (Paris, 1990)

**Archives** Yale U. CBA, MSS | East Riding of Yorkshire Archives Service, Beverley, Grimston MSS, list of 'various species' · East Riding of Yorkshire Archives Service, Beverley, letters to John Grimston · NA Scot., Seafield MSS

**Wealth at death** administration of estate granted to children; drawings sold at Christies for £64 11s. on 31 March 1787 (149 lots): Christies' copy of catalogue

**Cozens, John Robert** (1752–1797), landscape watercolour painter, is presumed to have been born in London, the elder of two children of Alexander *Cozens (1717–1786), landscape artist, and his wife, the daughter of the engraver John *Pine, whose first name is unknown. No record has been found of the place and date of his parents' marriage or of his birth or that of his sister, Juliet Ann, but his father must have been resident in London at this time, as he was employed as drawing-master to Christ's Hospital from 1750 to 1754. Traditionally the year of John Robert's birth has been assumed from C. R. Leslie's record of an inscription giving his age as nine on a lost pen drawing of three figures dated 1761 (Leslie, *Handbook*, 263).

**Early career** Although no manuscripts or letters by Cozens survive, we must assume from references in his work to passages from Pope, Milton (*Satan Summoning his Legions*, Tate collection), Virgil (*The Burning River of Hell*, ex Sothebys 8 April 1998, lot 50), and other classical as well as contemporary authors, that he received a sound education in addition to lessons in drawing from his father. Cozens exhibited landscape drawings at the Society of Artists every year from 1767 until 1771, when his address indicated he was living with his father at 4 Leicester Street, Leicester Fields.

Although these exhibited drawings are presumed lost, a recently discovered album of drawings by Cozens (NL Wales) charts his progress in drawing and his movements around the country during this period. From July to August 1768 he visited his uncle, Horace Pine, in Nacton, Suffolk, drawing local buildings including Landguard Fort, and views on nearby estates including those of William Fellowes, Thomas Fonnereau, and Lord Orwell. Cozens returned to London on the sloop *Samuel and Mary*, departing from Ipswich on 25 August and arriving in Woolwich the following day, taking a series of coastal views *en route*. In September he studied the ancient oak and beech trees at The Oaks, near Epsom, the home of his father's acquaintance Colonel John Burgoyne, and explored Maze Hill and Greenwich in the company of 'Stubbs and Newton', possibly identifiable as the young artist Richard Stubbs and William Newton, clerk of the works at Greenwich Hospital, who lived on Maze Hill. A few drawings of Hyde Park, Hammersmith, Hampstead, and Greenwich trace his progress in landscape studies in the environs of London over the next three years until the end of May 1772, when he set out on a brief trip to Matlock in Derbyshire, taking in the ruins of Verulam on the way.

In 1756 Alexander Cozens had painted a pair of views, *Matlock High Tor* and *Matlock Vale*, and John Robert's visit sixteen years later may have been on the advice of his father to search out a type of scenery not available in the London area. Alexander's mountainous landscapes were largely imaginary compositions, while John Robert Cozens was already clearly an artist whose inspiration lay in sketching landscapes from nature. Studies of waterfalls, rocky outcrops, deep crevices, and cliffs, along with more panoramic views and others composed along the lines of his father's invented landscape compositions, were the subjects of the experimental and increasingly accomplished drawings he made in a variety of media in the Matlock area in June 1772.

The album in Aberystwyth also contains a number of small tracings and sketches taken from prints which form an artist's *vade mecum* of examples of ruins, plants, animals, boats, and ships. Several of them appear as staffage in Cozens's *Eight Views of Bath*, published in November 1773. Not strictly topographical, Cozens's own distinctive approach, which relied upon landscape composition and imaginative use of light and shade to evoke moods, is already evident in this early series, each set individually washed or coloured by Cozens himself. His views of Bath must have been drawn on a visit to or even brief residence with his maternal relatives in that city.

In 1775 Cozens drew two views of the castle on Lundy Island in the Bristol Channel which were engraved for volume 4 of Francis Grose's *Antiquities of England and Wales* (1773–87) and a year later saw the exhibition of his only submission to the Royal Academy, an oil painting titled *A landscape, with Hannibal in his march over the Alps, showing to his army the fertile plains of Italy*, a painting which 'astounded everyone' (Thomas Grimston to his father, 11 May 1776, Sloan, 109). Last seen in 1876, the painting may have been based on his father's system for inventing landscape compositions through loose sketches or 'blots'. The landscape may have had a mountainous 'blot beginning' consisting of a blot, possibly drawn by his father, which was overlain by a drawing squared for enlargement and depicting mountains, fir trees, marching armies, and falling elephants (drawing, V&A). C. R. Leslie claimed that Turner spoke of the painting as a work from which he had learned more than anything else he had then seen (Leslie, 263) and Turner's own *Snowstorm: Hannibal Crossing the Alps* (exh. RA, 1812; Tate collection) was undoubtedly inspired by it. The painting may also have been the factor which persuaded the young classical scholar and antiquarian Richard Payne Knight to take Cozens with him on his continental tour commencing in August 1776.

**Continental tours**  Cozens's earliest surviving finished watercolour landscapes were based on the views he made on their tour of the rivers, mountains, and glaciers of Savoy. A series of fifty-six watercolours, mainly executed in greys, blues, and browns with details picked out in brown or grey pen and ink, once belonged to Payne Knight (a number are now in the BM). They demonstrate imaginative new compositional techniques, such as disappearing horizons, close-up views of rock faces, and wide panoramas which record the awesome grandeur and sublimity of the mountains and evoke the roar of cataracts and waterfalls or the silence of the great river valleys, many of them seldom before visited by British travellers.

After their tour of Savoy, Cozens and Knight continued on through Interlaken and Lake Lucerne to the spectacular gorge at Via Mala and finally entered Italy through the Splüngen Pass. Travelling via Pisa and Florence, they arrived in Rome by 27 November; Cozens was one of a large party of artists, including his father's friend Ozias Humphry, Henry Fuseli, and William Pars that Thomas Jones met that day in the English Coffee House.

In Rome, Cozens and Payne Knight appear to have gone separate ways: Payne Knight visited Naples and then Sicily, returning with drawings by Philip Hackert and Charles Gore for Cozens and others to work up into finished watercolours, while Cozens sketched in Rome and the Campagna. In addition to popular views of Rome, he produced a series of dramatic and original watercolours of caves and grottos (V&A) and serene, classically inspired views of lakes Albano and Nemi in the Alban Hills. Jones recorded that Cozens was not in good health in June 1778 and was staying in a villa outside the Porta Pia for the benefit of the air. They explored and sketched in the surrounding countryside together, Jones on his pony and Cozens 'on a jackAss which he had purchased for that purpose' (Janes, 73). He received commissions for his Swiss and Italian views from other travellers while still in Italy and after his return to England: there are eight names recorded on the verso of a 1776 sketch of the Pays de Valais (Sir John Soane's Museum, London) and up to ten versions are known of some of his views of Albano and Nemi.

Jones recorded that 'Little Cousins set off' from Rome for England on 8 April 1779 (Janes, 87). He may have returned briefly to London, but the name John Cozens appears as a ratepayer in Bath for a residence in the Westgate Buildings, near his uncle Robert Edge Pine in Cross Bath, from 24 June 1779 until December 1782. Bath was also near the seats of several of his father's patrons and friends, including Sir Richard Colt Hoare and William Beckford, who appears to have commissioned a number of watercolours of Italy from John Robert before departing on his own first visit to that country. In 1780 Beckford wrote from Naples to Alexander Cozens, enquiring 'Does your son go on with my drawings? … he cannot make too many. Having seen Italy I value them more than ever if that be possible' (Sloan, 138). A number of watercolours signed and dated that year, including *The Lake of Vico* and *On the Lake of Nemi* (Yale U. CBA), bear similar mounts and must have been part of this group made for Beckford. Although Cozens's name appears in the rate books of Bath in December 1782, six months earlier he had been swept into the enormous entourage Beckford had put together for his second trip to Italy, and which had left Dover on 16 May, racing over the Alps and arriving in Verona by 10 June.

Much of their journey and Cozens's second stay in Italy is recorded in seven surviving sketchbooks which contain pencil sketches washed in grey and blue ink, each inscribed with the location and date (Whitworth Art Gallery, Manchester). Many were later worked up into finished watercolours for other patrons, but the sketches were drawn mainly in order to provide a series of nearly a hundred of the most magnificent and poetic watercolour landscapes ever painted, produced at a prodigious rate for Beckford, who eventually sold them all at Christies on 10 April 1805.

After passing swiftly through Venice, Padua, and Bologna, the Beckford party arrived in Rome at the height of the malarial season and left almost immediately for Naples, where Jones found Cozens ill with a fever a week after his arrival on 6 July. He did not recover until the beginning of August and shortly afterwards Beckford's music master and Lady Hamilton, the wife of his cousin Sir William, both died, driving the wealthy young man back to friends in Switzerland. Thus on 10 September Jones found Cozens 'once more a free Agent and loosed from the Shackles of fantastic folly and Caprice' (Janes, 114).

For the next three months Cozens drew in the area around Naples, making a short excursion down the coast to Salerno, Gaeta, and Paestum in early November. Sir William Hamilton kept an eye on Cozens's progress for Beckford, reporting 'the vermin plays a good stick on the violioncello' and 'has made some charming sketches but I see by his book that he is indolent as usual' (Oppé, 112). Cozens made several sketches from Hamilton's villas at Portici and on the beach at Posillipo which he later worked up into serene watercolours with sweeping views of the Bay of Naples and Vesuvius, but he also produced other works such as the striking *Castle of St Elmo* (BM), which were clearly not to Beckford's taste and were destined for other patrons.

Cozens returned to Rome in early December, and on the 11 December made the first of many visits to the apartments of the painter Allan Ramsay and his son John, where he later met the painters Angelica Kauffmann and his father's old Rome acquaintance Gavin Hamilton, as well as his father's former pupil at Eton, the collector and amateur artist Sir George Beaumont, with whom he appears to have sketched during 1783. Many of these artists and patrons were to own versions of Cozens's watercolours after the drawings he made in Rome and the surrounding area. The Roman sketchbooks are lost, but must have contained the drawings for *St Peter's from the Villa Borghese, Rome* (Whitworth Art Gallery, Manchester), which recorded the glowing heat of a Roman summer sunset, and *Sepulchres in the Campagna* (AM Oxf.), two of the most evocative and melancholy watercolours he painted for Beckford.

Cozens remained in Rome until 15 September 1783, and returned home via Florence, Bologna, and the Italian Lakes, crossing the Alps at Mt Cenis and travelling past the Grande Chartreuse, which he recorded in one of the most spectacular and sublime of all the Beckford watercolours, *Entrance to the Grande Chartreuse* (AM Oxf.). It has been argued that just as the art of Alexander Cozens influenced Beckford's early writings, especially *Dreams, Waking Thoughts and Imaginings* (1783), so there was a mutual exchange, almost collaboration, between Beckford and the younger Cozens in their respective arts. In several instances the poetic landscapes form remarkable parallels to passages of melancholic sensibility in Beckford's letters written on this tour, clearly composed with eventual publication in mind.

**Later career and illness** Young Cozens was met by Thomas Jones in London on 19 November 1783 and visited the older artist in his hotel in the same city in January; little else is known of his movements over the next decade. In 1789 he issued *Delineations of the General Character, Ramifications and Foliage of Forest Trees*, a set of fourteen trees in soft-ground etching with aquatint. His father had issued a series of thirty-two individual engravings of trees, four to a sheet, in 1771, but John Robert's trees, including oak, elm, beech, willow, and the more exotic palm and cedar, were each set in an appropriate landscape. He pulled some proofs in soft-ground outline alone, which he then hand-coloured with yellow or orange-red washes in order to alter the mood of each landscape. Some surviving sets of the aquatints were also individually hand-coloured, with the result that few of the skies are the same in any two sets. The proofs and some of the aquatinted set were trimmed and individually mounted on soft-ground borders with handwritten titles and etched signatures, but in the final edition the images and border were all in one plate with printed titles and a formally engraved signature. The copperplates were included in Cozens's sale in 1794 and thirteen of the prints were reissued by W. H. Pyne in 1814 with a publication line.

A handful of Cozens's watercolours are dated between 1789 and his last dated work, *A Mountainous Landscape with Beech Tree* (1792; V&A). A few were larger, loosely painted and mannered versions of his earlier Italian and Swiss compositions, two were views in Greece based on drawings by James 'Athenian' Stuart and engraved for his and Nicholas Revett's *Antiquities of Athens* (1794, 1816), and the remainder were English views. There are several versions of his *London from Greenwich* and one of *The Thames from Richmond* (Yale U. CBA), in addition to watercolours of the villages of Dedham and Langham painted for Sir George Beaumont. Others depict Windsor, Windermere, and Lodore Falls. He is said to have visited and taught the Lake District amateur Thomas Sunderland, but there is no evidence to support this.

On 26 January 1794 the diarist Joseph Farington heard from Sir George Beaumont that Cozens was 'paralytic to a degree that incapacitated him' (Farington, *Diary*, 1.148) and a month later that he was under the care of Dr Monro. In June Payne Knight and Beaumont raised a subscription in order to pay for his care, garnering support from numerous prominent patrons of the arts, many of them former pupils of his father. The same month Cozens's brother-in-law, Charles Roberts, obtained the signatures of the greatest artists of the day on his application for assistance from the Royal Academy; the president, Benjamin West, headed a list including Thomas Banks, James Northcote, Richard Cosway, and William Hodges. On 9 and 10 July Greenwood held a sale of Cozens's property, including the contents of his studio, library, and many of his father's oil paintings, as well as all of his own remaining works, including copperplates of their publications.

Earlier that month Farington recorded:

Cozens's disorder is described to be a total decay of the nervous system. He appeared formerly to be of a silent, hesitating disposition and of grave manners. Some time since a total change took place, he became childishly noisy and talkative on trifles. He is described to be in his present state very cheerful. (Farington, *Diary*, 1.208)

The private subscription continued after Cozens's death and through 1800 in order to assist the artist's widow (d. 1804), a bookseller's daughter whose later married name was Barker, to whom he may or may not have been married, and his daughter Sophia (b. 1790). The grant from the academy was repeated annually and included an increase after the artist's death, which occurred in December 1797 at Northampton House in St John Street, Smithfield, one of Dr Monro's establishments; Cozens was buried on 1 January 1798 in St James's Church, Clerkenwell, London.

During Cozens's illness, Dr Monro employed Girtin and Turner to make copies of Cozens sketches and watercolours which Monro owned and borrowed from fellow enthusiasts, including his neighbour John Henderson and friend Sir George Beaumont. A decade after his death Henry Fuseli wrote that, rather than creating landscapes out of his father's 'fortuitous dashes of spots and blotches', John Cozens 'followed the arrangements of nature, which he saw with an enchanted eye, and drew with an enchanted hand' (Oppé, 158). Clearly the younger Cozens learned much from his father about the effects on the sensibilities of the viewer that could be produced through the manipulation of the component parts of a landscape, but he brought to watercolour his own personal vision, famously characterized by Constable as 'all poetry' (Leslie, *Memoirs of John Constable*, 89). His description of John Robert Cozens as 'the greatest genius that ever touched landscape' (ibid., 263) has been repeated so often that its impact has been deadened, but the fundamental influence of Cozens's poetic vision upon the work of not only Constable, but also Girtin and Turner and innumerable others of their generation, is indisputable. The Tate collection, the British Museum and Victoria and Albert Museum, London, the Whitworth Art Gallery, Manchester, the National Gallery of Scotland, Edinburgh, and the Yale Center for British Art, New Haven, Connecticut, all have large collections of Cozens's works.

KIM SLOAN

**Sources** A. P. Oppé, *Alexander and John Robert Cozens* (1952) • K. Sloan, *Alexander and John Robert Cozens: the poetry of landscape* (1986) • C. F. Bell and T. Girtin, 'The drawings and sketches of John Robert Cozens: a catalogue with an historical introduction', *Walpole Society*, 23 (1934–5) • A. Wilton, *The art of Alexander and John Robert Cozens* (1980) [exhibition catalogue, Yale U. CBA, 17 Sept 1980 – 16 Nov 1980] • P. Joyner and K. Sloan, 'A Cozens album in the National Library of Wales, Aberystwyth', *Walpole Society*, 57 (1993–4), 79–136 • F. Hawcroft, introduction, *Watercolours by John Robert Cozens* (1971) [exhibition catalogue, Whitworth Art Gallery, Manchester, and V&A 1971] • A. P. Oppé, ed., 'Memoirs of Thomas Jones, Penkerrig, Radnorshire', *Walpole Society*, 32 (1946–8) [whole issue] • C. R. Leslie, *A handbook for young painters* (1855) • C. Stumpf, ed., *Richard Payne Knight: expedition into Sicily* (1986) • E. S. Shaffer, '"To remind us of China"—William Beckford, mental traveller on the grand tour: the construction of significance in landscape', *Transports: travel, pleasure and imaginative geography, 1600–1830*, ed. C. Chard and H. Langdon (1996), 207–42 • J. Ingamells, ed., *A dictionary of British and Irish travellers in Italy, 1701–1800* (1997) • M. Clarke and N. Penny, eds., *The arrogant connoisseur: Richard Payne Knight, 1751–1824* (1982) [exhibition catalogue, Whitworth Art Gallery, Manchester, 1982] • M. Pilkington, *A dictionary of painters: from the revival of the art to the present period*, ed. H. Fuseli, 4th edn (1810) • C. R. Leslie, *Memoirs of the life of John Constable* (1843); 2nd edn (1845) • Farington, *Diary*
**Archives** BM
**Likenesses** bust, 1883 (posthumous), Institute of Painters in Watercolours, London • photograph (after R. E. Pine, c.1773), V&A
**Wealth at death** £80 proceeds of 1794 sale paid to Dr Monro for care; subscription raised from private contributors and RA to support Cozens, and his wife and daughter after his death: Oppé, *Alexander and John Robert Cozens*, 118–22

**Cozens-Hardy**. For this title name *see* Hardy, Herbert Hardy Cozens-, first Baron Cozens-Hardy (1838–1920).

**Crab, John** (c.1280–c.1352), pirate and merchant, was probably born in Muiden in Flanders. Active as a pirate from at least 1306, he was the most notorious of the Flemish privateers who preyed on English shipping during the Scottish War of Independence. His nephew Crabbekyn served with him at sea. Crab's attacks on English shipping led to frequent complaints by Edward II to the count of Flanders. But the count usually turned a blind eye, even pardoning him for murder and, in 1315, encouraging his piracy to obtain food during a famine. After 1310 Crab apparently settled in Aberdeen; Scottish and Flemish allies sold his plunder in Flanders. When Scotland recovered Berwick in 1318, Crab moved there with his family. He organized its defences and also supplied provisions for the Scottish crown, which considered him valuable enough to compensate victims of his piracy. In 1331 he served as constable of Berwick.

On the invasion of Scotland by Edward Balliol (d. 1363) in 1332, Crab took ten ships to besiege him at Perth, but the fleet was burnt and Crab fled on foot, to be captured shortly afterwards. Although the English parliament demanded his punishment, Edward III saw his potential usefulness and paid his ransom in return for his service. In 1333 Crab helped to direct the English siege of Berwick, where his expert knowledge of the defences ensured English success. The Berwick townspeople killed his son; this action, and Crab's anger that the Scots had not ransomed him, led him to give his allegiance to Edward III. As a burgess of Berwick, he was granted valuable lands there by the king in 1334, but he sold them when he was made constable of Somerton Castle in Lincolnshire for life. He continued to help English forces in Scotland, providing ships, soldiers, and siege engines, and refortifying Berwick, while in 1339 he helped protect English wool ships going to the Low Countries. His last active military service was probably at the battle of Sluys in 1340. In his final years he worked in England on Edward's castles and war engines, and he carried out various missions for the king until his death c.1352. Crab is a good representative of those medieval merchants who drew little distinction between trade and privateering, and his career also shows how medieval rulers used such men for their own ends.

Another **John Crab** (*fl.* 1342–*c.*1385), burgess of Aberdeen, has sometimes been confused with the merchant pirate, to whom he may have been related. His father was probably John Crab, an Aberdeen landholder in the 1320s. A burgess by 1342, after 1357 Crab was one of the burgh representatives negotiating David II's ransom, and he combined mercantile activity with royal service. During the 1360s he traded with England, lent money to the king, and purchased munitions in Flanders for Edinburgh Castle. He attended a general council in 1365 and parliament in 1367.

Crab was prominent among those medieval burgesses who invested in both rural and urban property. Outside Aberdeen his estates included Murtle, Denburn, Kincorth, and Findon; within the town he represented a new breed of rentiers who bought town property for profit. Nevertheless he was a pious man, who from the 1350s onwards gave the rents from a number of his urban holdings to the Aberdeen Carmelites. He arranged masses for himself and his late wife, Elizabeth (*d.* before 1382), in Arbroath Abbey, Angus, in 1384 and died shortly afterwards. The Crabstone in Aberdeen is thought to have been named from him or his family.

ELIZABETH EWAN

**Sources** H. S. Lucas, 'John Crabbe, Flemish pirate, merchant and adventurer', *Speculum*, 20 (1945), 334–50 · E. W. M. Balfour-Melville, 'Two John Crabbs', *SHR*, 39 (1960), 31–4 · *CDS* · G. Burnett and others, eds., *The exchequer rolls of Scotland*, 1–2 (1878) · J. Stevenson, ed., *Chronicon de Lanercost, 1201–1346*, Bannatyne Club, 65 (1839), 270 · *Barbour's Bruce*, ed. M. P. McDiarmid and J. A. C. Stevenson, 3, STS, 13 (1981), 17 · *Chancery records* · *RotS* · Marischal College charters, U. Aberdeen, MS M.390, Mass 1–19 · J. M. Thomson and others, eds., *Registrum magni sigilli regum Scotorum / The register of the great seal of Scotland*, 11 vols. (1882–1914), vol. 1 · *Calendar of inquisitions miscellaneous (chancery)*, PRO, 2 (1916) · J. Raine, *The history and antiquities of north Durham* (1852), no. 433 · *Thomae Walsingham, quondam monachi S. Albani, historia Anglicana*, ed. H. T. Riley, 2 vols., pt 1 of *Chronica monasterii S. Albani*, Rolls Series, 28 (1863–4), vol. 1, p. 194 · C. Innes, ed., *Registrum episcopatus Aberdonensis*, 2 vols., Spalding Club, 13–14 (1845) · *APS*, 1124–1423 · P. J. Anderson, ed., *Aberdeen friars, Red, Black, White and Grey*, Aberdeen University Studies, 40 (1909)

**Crab, John** (*fl.* 1342–*c.*1385). *See under* Crab, John (*c.*1280–*c.*1352).

**Crab, Roger** (*c.***1616–1680**), hermit, appears by his own account to have been 'begotten, and brought forth in the South-West of *England*' (Crab, *Dagons-Downfall*, 1). The names of his parents are as yet unknown. He was baptized by a clergyman with the customary two godfathers and a godmother in attendance. Crab was to claim that 'had not my natural Mother had twenty pounds a yeer, my Father and his Parents had not swopt; neither would they have agreed that they should have come together for generation' (ibid., 2). Elsewhere, he depicted himself as one of 'the lowest sort, and unlearned, being amongst day-labourers and journeymen' (Crab, *English Hermite*, 6–7). It was to be said of Crab that he served parliament 'seven years' in the civil wars. During the fighting his skull was apparently 'cloven to the braine' (ibid., 4).

In 1646 Crab's activities came to the attention of the heresiographer Thomas Edwards, who revealed that Samuel Fulcher 'an Egge man', had been 're-baptized by one *Crab* a Felt-maker'. According to Edwards, Crab of '*Southwark side*' was:

a Dipper and a Preacher, who vents strange doctrines against the Immortality of the soul, & c. This man was complained of this summer to the Lord Major, for speaking words against the King, as that it was better to have a golden Calfe or an Asse set up. (Edwards, 2.9, 3.110)

For proclaiming these opinions Crab was bound over to answer at the quarter sessions. He was convicted by Justice Bacon 'for scandalous words against the Kinges Ma[jes]tie' and fined 100 marks. On 26 March 1647 at the assize held at Southwark, Crab was ordered to remain in prison at the White Lion until he paid his fine and found sureties for his good behaviour. Towards the end of July he was still in confinement, his fine unpaid. In September Sir Thomas Fairfax wrote to William Lenthall, speaker of the House of Commons, requesting 'some inlargement' for Crab and several others 'committed meerly for speaking words against the King in time of War' (*Humble Remonstrance*, 1). Crab, however, seems not to have obtained his freedom, for he was to write that he endured 'two years imprisonment' at the hands of parliament (Crab, *English Hermite*, 4). It is suggestive that Crab was reportedly an agitator, one of the representatives of the rank-and-file on the general council of the New Model Army. This may explain his subsequent assertion that he was sentenced 'to death in the Field by my Lord Protector'; perhaps Crab played a prominent role in the unrest that engulfed parts of England in the spring of 1649 (ibid.). If so, it is possible that he escaped execution (a military punishment usually meted out to the ringleaders of mutinies) by drawing lots or through an act of clemency. Thereafter, he may have been cashiered from the army.

Crab resurfaced as a civilian in Chesham, Buckinghamshire. Richard Baxter had earlier publicly disputed with 'some Sectaries of *Chesham*', recounting the 'abundance of Nonsense which they uttered that day' (*Reliquiae Baxterianiae*, ed. M. Sylvester, 1696, 1.56). In August 1652 a satirical letter purportedly written from Chesham related that: 'we have amongst us a Crabbed cavelling fellow, being both a Barber, Hors-Dr. and a Hat-maker, that disturbs and jeers at Ministers that come to preach with us' (*Mercurius Democritus*, 4–11 Aug 1652, 148–9). The allusion is unmistakably to Crab, who was to affirm that he had 'often disputed [with] all [sect and ministers] in most Counties of *England*' (Crab, *English Hermite*, 1). While at Chesham Crab was '*a Haberdasher of hats, and kept a shop*' (ibid., foreword). It may be at this time that Crab experienced what he recalled as a conversion from darkness into light through the grace of '*that light which enlightneth every man that cometh into the world*' [John 1: 9] (ibid., 1). Looking upon the transgressions of his former life—pride, drunkenness, and gluttony—Crab resolved to relinquish his trade and sell his estate, giving all to the poor save 'a small matter' (ibid., foreword). He left for Ickenham near Uxbridge, Middlesex, while Thomas Godbold, curate of Uxbridge and vicar of Chesham, informed his friends that he was 'a Witch, and was run away, and would never come againe' (ibid., 'Dedication').

At Ickenham Crab rented a 'small' rood of ground on which he built a 'mean' cottage. Adopting a 'Hermeticall kinde of life' he began to wage war on his 'Old man' (the body), for '*The law of the old man in my fleshly members rebelled against the law of my mind*' [Romans 7: 23–24] (Crab, *English Hermite*, foreword; p. 2). Crab now undertook something akin to a process of ritual purification, embarking on a programme of fasting and prayer in a manner consonant with scriptural practice. Depriving himself of beer, ale, or wine he drank only water and instead of roast mutton, rabbit, and 'other dainty dishes' he ate 'broth thicknd with bran, and pudding made with bran, & Turnep leaves chop't together, and grass'. This diet made him so sick and weak that he almost died. Yet Crab survived, his humbled body filled with the 'love' of God (ibid., 2). Thereafter he subsisted on the produce of his small patch of earth, surviving on a vegetarian diet of corn, bread, bran, herbs, roots, dock leaves, mallows, and grass. His apparel was likewise of a 'meane' condition, for he wore a 'sackcloth frock' out of 'conscience' (ibid., foreword). Regarding himself as new born 'through the power of the eternal Creator' and looking upon himself as 'living in the new Life', Crab imagined himself to be 'above' gospel ordinances (Crab, *Dagons-Downfall*, 29; Crab, *English Hermite*, foreword). He claimed that God had 'enlightned' his understanding and with his new powers of spiritual discernment Crab forbore from eating flesh believing it to be 'an absolute enemy to pure nature' (cf. 1 Timothy 4: 1–3) (Crab, *English Hermite*, 2, 4). He also inveighed against the 'sinne of drunkennesse', observing that in times of dearth the same bushel of barley that yielded drink could provide bread sufficient for the weekly needs of two ordinary families (ibid., 7). Crab, moreover, now apprehended that his body was 'governed by the inclination of my Constitution from the starry heavens'. This new-found knowledge enabled him to 'administer physick to others', so that he had 'a hundred or sixe-score Patients at once' (ibid., 4). Such was Crab's interest in astrology that he consulted William Lilly on two or more occasions. Evidently Crab's fame began to spread for he attracted a follower of note—Captain Robert Norwood (c.1610–1654), who was to die of starvation after unsuccessfully attempting to imitate his master's strict regimen.

On 19 January 1654 the protectorate issued an ordinance declaring it a treasonable offence to write, print, proclaim, preach, or teach that the authority of the lord protector and the people assembled in parliament was tyrannical, usurped, or unlawful. About a year later, in the aftermath of the discovery of several serious plots against the government, Roger Crab was taken to London and apparently committed to the New Prison at Clerkenwell while awaiting trial 'before the Magistracy of this Nation'. At his trial Crab 'insisted much upon the Freedome of the Creature, and cleered himself of that particular, wherein they charged him with a reflection upon the Government by notion of Tyrany' (*A Perfect Account*, no. 210, 10–16 Jan 1655, 1680). After his release Crab seems to have lodged at the Golden Anchor in Whitecross Street with one Mr Carter, a glover (perhaps Gregory Carter, glover of St Giles's Cripplegate who in January 1641 had stood bail for Thomas Lambe, soapboiler, and other indicted conventiclers). Crab by now was a figure of curiosity, 'a gazing stock to the Nation, & a wonderment to many friends' and to clear his name from malicious imputations—that he opposed civil magistracy, was a leveller, Quaker, shaker, or ranter—he penned an account of his principles and conduct (Crab, *English Hermite*, 1). Entitled *The English Hermite, or, Wonder of this Age*, the work was printed in January 1655 and issued by a publisher who may have sought to profit from Crab's notoriety (the publisher's name was prudently omitted from the title-page).

Crab returned to his cottage at Ickenham only to again be brought before the courts. By his own account he appeared several times before justices of the peace on the charge of sabbath breaking (twice in the country and twice at the general sessions held at Hicks Hall). Once, having been put in the stocks 'by the heels' outside Ickenham church, he was moved to write some verse:

> My body is but Serpents meat,
> And that thou wouldst destroy;
> Thy honour and glory's but a cheat,
> For all must vanish away.
> (Crab, *Dagons-Downfall*, 24, 25)

Afterwards Crab wrote a fuller vindication of his conduct—*Dagons-Downfall, or, The Great IDOL Digged up Root and Branch* (1657). Taking the Philistines' God as his provocative theme, Crab denounced the abominations committed upon the 'great' whore's 'Market-Day':

> Now all the Serpents children, and the Whores worshippers
> have joyned together to deceive the simple and persecute
> the Righteous for denying the deceitful wickedness on her
> Idol Market-Day, where her Juglers cheat the people by
> setting up the high terms upon her two Idols, by calling the
> Stone House a Church; and the first day a Sabbath.
> (ibid., 18)

In January 1659 the Quaker Thomas Curtis wrote to George Fox relating the events of a 'very great and precious' meeting at Kimble, Buckinghamshire. Present were 'fish of all sorts', 'many of the world, some baptized, and some of Crab's company' (RS Friends, Lond., Swarthmore MS III, 87: T. Curtis to G. Fox, Reading, 5 Jan 1659). Crab's company seems to have amounted to little more than a handful of followers. Even so, they had a name for themselves—the Rationals. In 1659 Crab printed the 'Substance of a *Letter* given forth by the *Rationals*, to the Despised Remnant, and Seed of GOD, in the People called Quakers' (Crab, *Tender Salutation*, title-page). His epistle provoked a response from George Salter of Hedgerley Dean, Buckinghamshire, who pronounced that it was 'not the word of the Lord', but rather that there was 'much confusion in it'; Crab he likened to a 'corrupt bulk of Fog, who art like a quagmire that sucks up them that comes upon thee' (G. Salter, *An Answer to Roger Crabs Printed Paper to the Quakers*, 1659, 2, 5). Crab retorted with a *Gentle Correction for the High-Flown Backslider* (1659). His doctrines, however, did not escape the censure of another Quaker writer, who also denounced his teachings.

On 21 December 1663 licence was obtained for Roger Crab of St Bride's, London, a bachelor aged forty-seven or thereabouts, to marry Amy Markham, widow of St Andrew's, Holborn. The couple were married the following day in the parish of St Gregory by Paul's, London. It does not appear that this union produced any children. Crab's will, drawn up on 4 September 1680, began in unorthodox fashion:

> A matter of Thirty and five yeares agoe I had like to I have departed this humane Life And according to Scripture I looked upon my Selfe to regenerated upon which account the Lord himselfe took my Soule into his custody Soe itt would bee ridiculous for me to pr[e]sume to take upon me to dispose of my Soule againe. (London, Guildhall, MS 9171/37, fols. 297v–298r)

'Roger Crabb of Bethnall green Gent.' was buried at the church of St Dunstan and All Saints, Stepney, on 14 September 1680, where his tomb was afterwards known to local people as that of 'the pilgrim'. The inscription read 'Here remains all that was mortal of Mr. Roger Crab, who entered into eternity the 11th day of Septemb. 1680, in the 60 year of his age' (Caulfield, 2.156). Strype added that 'This *Crab*, they say, was a *Philadelphian*, or *Sweet Singer*' (Strype, vol. 2, appx, 99). No evidence has been found connecting Crab with either John Pordage or any of his immediate associates. It is suggestive, however, that Jane Lead, who in the 1690s established the Philadelphian Society on the foundations of Pordage's Behmenist community, received poor relief 'privately' at the Lady Mico's College in Stepney. Crab was survived by his wife, Amy, who married Benjamin Sweet of St Margaret's, Westminster, by licence in 1688.                                                   ARIEL HESSAYON

**Sources** A. Hessayon, 'A crabbed cavelling fellow': Roger Crab, the English hermit [forthcoming] • R. Crab, *The English hermite, or, Wonder of this age* (1655) • R. Crab, *Dagons-Downfall* (1657) • R. Crab, *A tender salutation* (1659) • T. Edwards, *Gangraena*, 3 vols. (1646), vol. 2, p. 9; vol. 3, p. 110 • *A humble remonstrance from his excellency Sir Thomas Fairfax* (1647) • Surrey assize roll, March 1647, PRO, ASSI35/88/8 mem. 1 • will, GL, MS 9171/37, fols. 297v–298r • C. Hill, 'The mad hutter', *Puritanism and revolution* (1958), 314–22 • J. Caulfield, *Portraits, memoirs and characters of remarkable persons, from the reign of Edward the Third to the revolution*, new edn, 2 (1813), 156 • parish register, St Dunstan and All Saints, Stepney, LMA, P93/DUN/279, 14 Sept 1680 [burial] • D. Lysons, *The environs of London*, 4 vols. (1792–6), vol. 3, p. 454 • J. Stow, *A survey of the cities of London and Westminster and the borough of Southwark*, ed. J. Strype, new edn, 2 vols. (1720), vol. 2, appx 997 • R. Roach, 'Account of the size and progress of the Philadelphian Society', Bodl. Oxf., MS Rawl. D. 833, fol. 82v
**Likenesses** woodcut, 1655, BM, NPG; repro. in Crab, *The English hermite* • pen-and-ink drawing, NPG
**Wealth at death** see will, GL, MS 9171/37, fols. 297v–298r

**Crabb, George** (1778–1851), lawyer and writer, was born on 8 December 1778 at Palgrave, Suffolk, the son of Zechariah Crabb and his wife, Elizabeth, *née* Jolly. His parents then moved to Wattisfield, where he was baptized on 27 December 1778. He was educated at a school at Diss, Norfolk, and under a private tutor. He began the study of medicine, but being unable to endure the dissecting room, where he could not attend a simple bleeding without fainting, he resigned his medical studies to become assistant to a bookseller. He soon left this to study for the

ministry at Northampton, but a sudden change in his religious views made it necessary for him again to choose a new profession. In 1797 he went to London, and on 6 January 1798 he married Maria Southgate (*b.* 1771), a woman seven years his senior, who subsequently edited *Tales for Children from the German*. He then became classics master at Thorp Arch School, Yorkshire.

In order to acquire a mastery of the German language Crabb lived from 1801 to 1806 in Bremen, where he supported himself at the same time by teaching English. He published a *German Grammar for Englishmen* (1799), *An Easy and Entertaining Selection of German Prose and Poetry* (1800), and *German and English Conversations* (1804), all of which became very popular as instruction books and passed through many editions. He also wrote an *English Grammar for Germans*.

In 1814 Crabb entered Magdalen Hall, Oxford, as a gentleman commoner, and graduated BA in 1821 and MA in 1822, with mathematical honours. He was called to the bar at the Inner Temple in 1829, and adopted the practice of conveyancer and chamber counsel, but on account of his retiring manner was not very successful, although his ability as a lawyer is indicated by his various legal publications. These include a *History of English Law* (1829), founded on Reeves's *History of English Law*; *Digest and Index of All the Statutes at Large* (4 vols., 1841–7); *The Law of Real Property* (2 vols., 1846); and *The Conveyancer's Assistant, or, Series of Precedents in Conveyancing and Common and Commercial Forms* (1835, 3rd edn 1845).

Crabb was also the author of various dictionaries which obtained wide popularity and numerous reprints, including a *Dictionary of English Synonymes* (1816), a *Universal and Technological Dictionary* (1823), a *Universal Historical Dictionary* (2 vols., 1825), and *A Dictionary of General Knowledge* (1830). The *Dictionary of English Synonymes*, with citations based on an original examination of standard authors of the seventeenth and eighteenth centuries, is the most notable of these. It is 'the oldest synonymy in the world' (Hausmann and others, 2.1068), revised as *Crabb's English Synonyms* in 1916, and reprinted in 1966.

In 1840 Crabb published *The New Pantheon of Mythology of All Nations*. Crabb's later years were marked by disappointment and poverty, and were passed in eccentric seclusion. He died at Hammersmith, Middlesex, on 4 December 1851, leaving his wife in straitened circumstances.

T. F. HENDERSON, *rev.* JOHN D. HAIGH

**Sources** *GM*, 2nd ser., 37 (1852), 307–8 • *BL cat.*, 72.2–4 • F. J. Hausmann and others, eds., *Wörterbücher: ein internationales Handbuch zur Lexikographie / Dictionaries: an international encyclopedia of lexicography*, 2 (Berlin, 1989), 1068 • G. Crabb, 'Preface', *English synonymes explained* (1816) • Boase, *Mod. Eng. biog.*, 1.745 • [J. Watkins and F. Shoberl], *A biographical dictionary of the living authors of Great Britain and Ireland* (1816) • S. I. Landau, *Dictionaries: the art and craft of lexicography* (1984); repr. (1989), 104 • *IGI*
**Wealth at death** died in poverty, leaving his wife in straitened circumstances: *GM*

**Crabb, Habakkuk** (1750–1794), dissenting minister, was born at Wattisfield, Suffolk, and baptized there on 8 August 1750, the youngest but one of fifteen children of Denny Crabb and Elizabeth Harrison. His father, a deacon of the Independent church at Wattisfield, was a man of private property, but as his family grew in number he was obliged to farm one of his estates and produce malt for the London market. Crabb became a pupil of John Walker, Congregational minister at Framlingham, and in 1766 proceeded to Daventry Academy under Caleb Ashworth. There the pressures of long hours of study (up to twenty hours a day) led to a nervous breakdown which caused him to repeat one year of his studies and left him with a nervous disorder which persisted for the remainder of his life.

After leaving Daventry in 1772 Crabb became Presbyterian minister at Stowmarket, where he was ordained on 3 June of that year. In 1776 he moved to Cirencester, where he became minister at the Presbyterian chapel in Gosditch Street. He married Eliza Norman (d. 1792) of Stowmarket in 1778. In 1787, with a view to better providing for his children, he accepted the offer of his brother-in-law, John Ludd Fenner, to assist him in his school and pulpit at Devizes.

In January 1789 Crabb accepted an invitation to become pastor of the congregation of his native village of Wattisfield, but this was not a rewarding experience. His theology was too heterodox—he was probably an Arian by this time—for his congregation. He prudently decided to resign, and in July or August 1790 he became minister at John Street Chapel, Royston, where, once the orthodox portion of the congregation had seceded, he found a 'flock in harmony with his theology' (Murch, 32). He was not a prolific writer and is credited with only one publication, a collection of sermons entitled *Sermons on Practical Subjects*, published posthumously in 1796 for the benefit of his seven orphaned children, and which was described by Hugh Worthington, in a preface to this work, as 'a valuable addition to the stock of English discourses'.

Eliza Crabb died giving birth to their seventh child in 1792 and Crabb died after a short illness on Christmas day 1794 in Royston, where he was buried. His nephew was the diarist Henry Crabb *Robinson.

ALEXANDER GORDON, *rev.* M. J. MERCER

Sources C. Surman, index, DWL · J. Murch, *A history of the Presbyterian and General Baptist churches in the west of England* (1835) · G. E. Evans, *Vestiges of protestant dissent* (1897) · *GM*, 1st ser., 65 (1795), 167

Archives DWL, New College archives, essays, L12/4

Crabb, James (1774–1851), Wesleyan Methodist preacher, was born in Wilton, Wiltshire, on 13 April 1774, the third son of James Crabb, a cloth manufacturer. He began an apprenticeship in his father's trade but, determined to devote himself to serving God, he purchased his early release in April 1794. He was appointed itinerant preacher by the Wesleyan conference in February 1795, travelling extensively around the southern counties of England. Ill health forced him to return to live at his father's home in Wilton later that same year. Following marriage in April 1798 to Martha Raddon and the birth of his first son, he accepted his father's offer to become a partner in the family business. Bankruptcy, caused by the French wars and a change of fashion in the cloth trade, forced Crabb, his

wife, and their six children to move to Salisbury (c.1802–3), where he worked as a dyer and seller of broadcloths. Business difficulties led to a further move to Romsey and employment first as a commercial traveller and then as a teacher. He lived in Southampton for the last quarter-century of his life, where he served as pastor of a chapel 'unconnected with any body of Dissenters' (Rudall, 120).

Crabb was described by his biographer, John Rudall, as being 'endowed with an apostolic spirit, and a love which embraced the ends of the earth', and his main wish was that he might 'be enabled to preach the Gospel to every creature' (Rudall, 121). His personal mission of improving the physical, moral, and spiritual condition of the people of Southampton and district was duly recognized in the memorial raised by public subscription after his death. As a young man he combined his missionary labours with the treatment of the sick, having acquired his medical knowledge through books and advice from friends. Although the need to support his growing family forced Crabb to return temporarily to the world of commerce, he nevertheless continued with his religious work and activities. He raised the subscriptions for the construction of a Wesleyan Methodist chapel at Wilton (1798) and opened a new school for the instruction of boys shortly after his move to Romsey.

However, Crabb is best remembered for his labours among the most poor, destitute, and neglected inhabitants of Southampton. With the help of Dr Lindoe, a retired physician, and the Revd Robert Heath, curate of All Saints, a female penitentiary for the reform of prostitutes was opened in the town in 1823, which served as an inspiration for similar ventures in Portsmouth and Salisbury. In 1827 Crabb helped to establish a Sunday school in Kingsland, then described as one of the most depraved areas of Southampton, and regularly preached to dockyard and railway navvies and the Itchen ferry sailors and fishermen, described by John Rudall as a wicked clan 'wholly destitute of all spiritual instruction' (Rudall, 106). Crabb also obtained special permission to board the steamers belonging to the Peninsular and Oriental Navigation Company (P. & O.) in order to hold services while the ships were in berth. It was at this time that Crabb preached to sailors from the deck of a vessel called *Speedy*, commanded by Captain John Bazin, with whom Crabb also sailed to Jersey to preach on the island's shores and in its chapels. The work of Captain Bazin in the service of Christ is recalled in Crabb's *An Account of the Life and Experience of Captain John Bazin* (1838).

The work which brought Crabb the greatest public notice, though, was with the Gypsies. Crabb was drawn to the cause of a people seen as outcasts and aliens from society by the harsh treatment meted out to a Gypsy at the Winchester assizes for 1827. In November of that year Crabb formed a committee 'to take into serious consideration, without loss of time, the peculiar habits, character, and condition of the forlorn Gipseys; and to adopt such measures as might be considered best calculated to promote their general improvement' (*A summary account of the proceedings of a provisional committee associated at Southampton with a view to the consideration and improvement of the condition of the gipseys*, n.d. [c.1832], 2). He also sought to bring knowledge of the Gypsies to a wider audience through his publication *The Gypsies' advocate, or, Observations on the origin, character, manners and habits of the English Gipsies* (1831). This was republished in shorter form as *A Condensed History of the Gypsies* (1843). Crabb himself frequently visited the Gypsy camps in Hampshire offering advice, sympathy, practical help, and religious instruction. A free school was opened for Gypsy children and a mission hut was erected for the adult Gypsies and poor of the district. In 1828 the Southampton committee appointed two agents, Mr Cope and Mr Stanley, the latter a settled Christian Gypsy, to visit the camps on a regular basis and provide instruction on the word of God and the benefits of a settled life. In December 1829 the camp visits were supplemented by an annual festival held in fields near Crabb's house and attended both by Gypsies and the gentry of the neighbourhood. Crabb was forced to discontinue his activities and involvement in 1847 because of ill health. A final meeting, the nineteenth, was held in the grounds attached to the mansion of William Betts in December 1848. Crabb's short farewell address to the Gypsies was published the same year. Crabb died at Milbrook, Southampton, on 17 September 1851.

DAVID MAYALL

**Sources** J. Rudall, *A memoir of the Rev. James Crabb, late of Southampton* (1854) · *Southern Daily Echo* (Jan–March 1952) · *GM*, 2nd ser., 36 (1851), 659–60 · J. Crabb, *A farewell address to the Gipsies* [1848] · d. cert.

**Archives** U. Southampton L., Cope MSS

**Crabb, Lionel Kenneth Philip** (1909–1956), naval frogman, was born on 28 January 1909 at 4 Greyswood Street, Streatham, London, the son of Hugh Alexander Crabb, a commercial traveller for a firm of photographic merchants, and his wife, Beatrice Goodall. Crabb was described by contemporaries as a most courageous diver able to endure great discomfort, but technically inept and a man of action rather than a thinker: those assessments well summarize an overexciting career below the surface that extended from 1941 to a controversial end in 1956.

Little is known about Crabby or Buster Crabb's early life save that it was modestly commercial—unlike his diving career, which combined a fascination for ultra-secret missions with Edwardian flamboyancy. He was apt, as a commander, to carry a gold-topped cane and wear a vivid waistcoat under a naval monkey jacket; and he displayed an imperious manner which contrasted oddly with his habitual lopsided grin and 5-foot-and-a-bit stature. Crabb joined the Royal Naval Volunteer Reserve before the war, and in 1940 he volunteered for bomb disposal duties. Following attacks by Italian human torpedoes in the Mediterranean a call went out for shallow-water divers to help defend Gibraltar harbour against submerged predators. Crabb responded to join a small team charged with singularly forbidding responsibilities. These included combating Italian underwater saboteurs and disabling weapons attached to ships' hulls, removing depth charges from sunken aircraft, and recovering dead bodies from the sea.

After the Italian armistice in 1943 Crabb co-opted frogmen of the former enemy into a resolutely non-bureaucratic anti-German activity near Venice; and, when the war ended, he was seconded to the Ministry of Agriculture and Fisheries in a risky venture to help observe the behaviour of trawlers at close hand. In 1947 he was invested with the George Medal and the OBE. Crabb was first into the water, in a vain effort to assist, after HM submarine *Truculent* had sunk by accident in the Thames estuary in 1950. He was promoted to commander in 1952, and on 15 March that year he married Margaret Elaine, the daughter of Henry Charles Brackenbury Williamson and the former wife of Ernest Albert Player. The couple separated in 1953, and divorced about two years later.

Crabb retired in 1954 but reappeared at Portsmouth on 17 April 1956 with a relatively junior member of the Secret Intelligence Service (SIS) and booked a room at the Sally Port Hotel. He met senior police officers and then went to HMS *Vernon* (the torpedo, anti-submarine, and diving establishment), where Crabb persuaded a clearance diver to dress him for an important dive on the following day and take him by car to the dockyard where the Soviet cruiser *Ordzhonikidze*, bearing the Soviet leaders Bulganin and Khrushchov to Britain for a formal visit, would be lying alongside the premier berth.

Subsequent events, although still the subject of media speculation, are in no doubt. At 5.30 p.m. on 18 April 1956 Crabb, required by the SIS on behalf of naval intelligence to measure the Russian cruiser's propellors for the benefit of the north Atlantic sound surveillance system (SOSUS), entered the water at King's Stairs some 80 yards from his objective; but he became caught in dockside piling and aborted. Early the next morning Crabb tried again but had difficulty with his equipment and swam back to King's Stairs for a few minutes. He returned to the water but was never seen alive again, except briefly at 7.35 a.m. by a lookout on one of the Soviet cruiser's escorting destroyers. A body, without head or extremities but with every indication of being Crabb, was discovered in Chichester harbour, Sussex, on 9 June 1957, over a year later. Meanwhile, the British government was embarrassed by clumsy attempts to cover up Crabb's disappearance. The prime minister, Anthony Eden, had expressly forbidden any intelligence operation during the Russian visit, and he was furious when he learned of MI6's involvement in the escapade.

The facts were that Crabb was middle-aged and unfit for diving at the limits of safety for non-revealing apparatus: a colleague remarked that he trained on whisky. Oxygen and/or carbon dioxide poisoning was almost inevitable in the circumstances. Tidal streams and currents predictably carried the corpse 10 miles to where it was eventually found—marking the sadly fruitless demise of a brave man.

RICHARD COMPTON-HALL

**Sources** private information (2004) · N. Elliott, *With my little eye: observations along the way* (1993) · M. Evans, 'MI6 director lies low between the covers', *The Times* (23 Nov 1991) · L. Kennedy, 'Coffin down the Mersey', *Daily Telegraph* (4 Dec 1993) · T. Bower, *The perfect English spy: Sir Dick White and the secret war, 1935–90* (1995) · *CGPLA*

*Eng. & Wales* (1956) • b. cert. • d. cert. • E. N. Poland, *The torpedomen: HMS Vernon's story, 1872–1986* (1993) • T. J. Waldron, *The frogmen: the story of the war-time underwater operators* (1954) • A. Dalton, 'Navy papers shed light on the murky death of diving spy', *The Scotsman* (22 April 1998) • R. Norton-Taylor, 'Dark deeds: the cries over frogman Crabbe laid to rest', *The Guardian* (12 Jan 1994) • *Navy List* • m. cert.

**Archives** SOUND IWM SA, oral history interview
**Likenesses** photograph, 1950, Hult. Arch. • photographs, Gov. Art Coll.
**Wealth at death** £1205 9s. 9d.: administration, 10 July 1956, CGPLA Eng. & Wales

**Crabbe, George** (1754–1832), poet and Church of England clergyman, was born on 24 December 1754 in Aldeburgh, Suffolk, the first of six children of George Crabbe (1733–1786), collector of salt duties, and his wife, Mary Lodwick (1725–1780), widow of a publican. Before settling in Aldeburgh, Crabbe's father had been a schoolmaster and parish clerk in Norton, near Loddon, Norfolk.

**Early life and education, 1754–1775** Crabbe was born in a house on the south side of Aldeburgh near Slaughden Quay that was later demolished by the sea in a storm. Aldeburgh in the eighteenth century was a mere shadow of a once prosperous seaport. The sea had eroded the lower part of the town to a distance of more than a mile, so that the town hall, once in the centre of a market place, now sat on the beach. Crabbe grew up on this shingle beach and the narrow spit of land, Slaughden Quay, separating the sea from the River Alde, where the custom house was located in which he assisted his father. His father owned an interest in a fishing boat, on which his son accompanied him, as well as in a smaller boat for sailing on the river. Crabbe's earliest education was from his father, who was especially fond of mathematics. He subscribed to *Martin's Philosophical Magazine* and sent in solutions to problems. He gave the poetry sections printed at the end of each number to his son, who learned the poems by heart and imitated them. When he was about ten years old his father sent him to Mr Harvey's Grammar School at Bungay, where he continued for a year, and then to Richard Haddon's Grammar School at Stowmarket, where he stayed until the age of fourteen. He was then apprenticed to a Mr Smith, a farmer–apothecary at Wickhambrook, where he was treated more as a farm-hand than as an apprentice apothecary, and he eventually rebelled and refused to work on the farm. At his father's second visit to deal with his son's obstinacy, he removed him from the farmer and got back most of the apprentice fee. Crabbe returned to Aldeburgh where he worked in his father's warehouse for several months before being sent to John Page, a surgeon in Woodbridge, who employed him in filling prescriptions and compounding medicines. While Crabbe was at Woodbridge, he read novels and poetry, and began contributing pastorals and lyrics to J. Wheble's *Ladies Magazine*, to the rival *Ladies Magazine* printed for G. Robinson, and to *Town and Country Magazine*. He won a prize for a poem on the subject of hope in J. Wheble's *Ladies Magazine* in September 1772, and wrote his first long poem, *Inebrity*, a satirical pastiche of some fifty quarto pages imitated from Pope's *Dunciad* and *An Essay on Man*. It was published

George Crabbe (1754–1832), by Henry William Pickersgill, c.1818–19

in Ipswich in 1775. One of his friends, William Springall Levett, introduced him to his future wife, Sarah Elmy (1751–1813), the niece of a wealthy farmer at Parham. Her father, James Elmy, had been a tanner, but he went bankrupt in 1759, deserted his family, and died in Guadeloupe in 1772. Her mother, also Sarah, was John Tovell's sister and lived at Beccles with her three daughters and a son.

**Failed apothecary, 1775–1779** At the end of four years with John Page, Crabbe returned to Aldeburgh and after a time serving as his assistant, he took over the apothecary shop of James Maskill, who left Aldeburgh. Crabbe improved on his practical knowledge gained at Woodbridge by reading, study, and learning anatomy by dissecting dogs. After a year he placed his practice in the hands of a neighbouring surgeon and went to London to acquire medical knowledge. There he attended the lectures of the Scottish midwives Orme and Lowder, who followed in the obstetrical tradition of Dr William Smellie. When Crabbe returned to Aldeburgh, he found that the surgeon with whom he had entrusted his practice had entered into a confederacy with his rival, Dr Burham Raymond, and had lost Crabbe many of his patients. Most of his practice was now among the poor and he soon fell into debt. At some time during his three years as a practising apothecary at Aldeburgh, Crabbe became engaged to Sarah Elmy. She would not, however, marry him until he achieved an income sufficient to support a family. His many journeys from Aldeburgh to Beccles while courting her provided the material for 'The Lover's Journey', published in *Tales* (1812). At the end of 1779, following a year of illness and increasing poverty, Crabbe reached a decision to give up medicine and go to London to try his fortune as an author. He wrote the following dated 31 December 1779 in a notebook: 'A thousand years, most adored Creator, are, in thy sight, as one day. So contract, in my sight, my calamities!' (*Letters*, 42).

**London and Edmund Burke, 1780–1781** Crabbe obtained a loan of £5 from Dudley Long, a Suffolk philanthropist living at Saxmundham. Long subsequently inherited the estate of Little Glemham from his aunt, took the name of North, and became an MP and one of the close associates of Charles James Fox. After discharging his debts Crabbe sailed to London aboard the sloop *Unity*, taking with him a box of clothes, his surgical instruments, his manuscript poetry, and £3 remaining from the loan. From his arrival in London in April 1780 he kept a journal, which he dedicated to Mira, his poetic name for Sarah Elmy. He took lodgings with Mr Vickery, a hairdresser near the exchange. Vickery soon moved to Bishopsgate Street and Crabbe followed him there. He lodged with Vickery a little over a year, during which time, he later said 'his chief study was to improve in versification, to read all such books as he could command, and to take as full and particular a view of mankind, as his time and his finances enabled him to do' ('Memoir', 197). His first attempt at publishing in London was a poem called 'The Hero' on Prince William Henry, the youngest son of George III and a captain in the Royal Navy. He sent the poem to the publisher James Dodsley on 27 April 1780 and the following day received a note from Dodsley rejecting the piece. He sent a poem entitled 'Epistle from the Devil' and another epistle 'From the Author' along with a preface to the publisher Thomas Beckett, who rejected them. Finally, in July 1780 Crabbe paid John Nichols to print 250 copies of *The Candidate: a Poetical Epistle to the Authors of the Monthly Review*. In setting out his estimate of his genius and ability, Crabbe imitates Horace (*Odes*, 1.6, 31; *Epistles*, 1.20, 2.1) and Boileau (*Épître*, 10), and is indebted to Pope's *Epistle to Dr Arbuthnot* for the tone of moral imperative, relying on 'honest truth' to 'Join, as of old, the Prophet and the Bard' (1.189). The work received unfavourable reviews from the *Critical Review* (September) and the *Gentleman's Magazine* (September). The *Monthly Review* (October) was understandably more favourable, allowing the poem to have some merit.

Because of his father's slight acquaintance with Lord North, Crabbe applied to him for employment and was ultimately dismissed with severity after waiting three months following a first interview. Crabbe wrote next to Lord Shelburne, sending him a verse panegyric 'To the Right Honorable the Earl of Shelburne' and an account of Lord North's treatment, concluding with a request for 'patronage and bread' (*Letters*, 79). Receiving no encouragement from Shelburne, Crabbe turned to Lord Chancellor Thurlow, who sent him a note saying he had no time to read verses. Crabbe's quest for patronage was impeded by the Gordon riots of early June 1780. Crabbe witnessed much of the violence and wrote a vivid account of the burning of Newgate prison and the escape of the prisoners.

Crabbe's next project was to undertake the publication by subscription of a poetical miscellany, probably containing an early version of *The Library*. Sarah Elmy and her family at Beccles procured over 200 subscribers and Crabbe received permission from Lord Rochford to be the dedicatee. Unfortunately, the printer defaulted and Lord Rochford failed to reply when Crabbe begged him for a loan. To compound Crabbe's difficulties, his landlord, Vickery, threatened him with arrest for a debt of £14. In these desperate circumstances, Crabbe made a final plea for patronage by addressing Edmund Burke in a letter sent in February or March 1781, enclosing the prospectus for his aborted miscellany and poetry manuscripts. In it he asks, 'Can You Sir in any Degree aid me with Propriety?' He pleads with Burke to 'Let me if possible interest your Compassion'. He offers to call on Burke the next day and says, 'If I have not the Happiness to obtain Credit with You, I will submit to my Fate: My Existence is a Pain to me … I have only to hope a speedy End to a Life so unpromisingly begun' (*Letters*, 5).

This pathetic solicitation most certainly brought the suicide of Thomas Chatterton in 1770 to Burke's mind, especially since he was MP for Bristol. Burke answered Crabbe's letter and invited him to his house and after their first meeting he became Crabbe's patron. He discharged Crabbe's debts, gave him an apartment in his home at Beaconsfield, guided him in revising *The Library*, and introduced him to his circle of friends. He himself took the manuscript of *The Library* to Dodsley, who agreed to underwrite the cost of publication and give Crabbe all of the profit. Crabbe sent his 250 subscribers copies of *The Library* in lieu of the miscellany originally projected. The poem, organized by the subject classification of books in a library, is in the tradition of Juvenal's tenth satire and Johnson's *The Vanity of Human Wishes*. In the lines on botany (ll. 167–82), Crabbe's interest in Linnaean classification is seen and in the passage on romance Crabbe's famous lines on pastoral in *The Village* (1783) are foreshadowed:

My doughty Giants all are slain or fled,
And all my Knights, blue, green, and yellow, dead.
(ll. 494–5)

The edition sold out in ten weeks and received favourable notice in the reviews. Even the prosaic Lord Thurlow made Crabbe amends for refusing to read his verses by presenting him with a £100 note and promising future preferment. As a result of his own inclinations and Burke's advice, Crabbe decided on a career in the church. In August Crabbe went to Beccles to see Sarah Elmy and on the way visited Dudley Long and his brother Charles Long at Saxmundham. Long solicited Philip Yonge, bishop of Norwich, on Crabbe's behalf. Yonge admitted Crabbe to deacon's orders on 21 December 1781 and he was licensed curate to the Revd James Bennet, rector of Aldeburgh.

**Ducal chaplain, 1782–1783** Crabbe preached his first sermon as curate of Aldeburgh on 20 January 1782 on 1 Peter 2: 17, 'Honour all men. Love the brotherhood. Fear God. Honour the king', an appropriate text for the surly parishioners who resented the success of the young curate following his failure as an apothecary only two years earlier. His eldest son recounts asking him about his feelings when he entered the pulpit for the first time. Crabbe answered:

> I had been unkindly received in the place—I saw unfriendly countenances about me, and, I am sorry to say, I had too much indignation,—though mingled, I hope, with better feelings,—to care what they thought of me or my sermon. (*Letters*, 109–10)

Even before his ordination, Crabbe had expressed to Burke a desire for some situation other than curate at Aldeburgh. Burke recommended Crabbe to Charles Manners, who succeeded his grandfather as fourth duke of Rutland in 1779. The duke needed a chaplain and felt that a promising young clergyman–poet would be an interesting companion and valuable addition to his establishment at Belvoir Castle. On 12 May 1782 Crabbe was appointed domestic chaplain to the duke of Rutland and had moved to Belvoir Castle by 15 May. On 4 August he was ordained priest by the bishop of Norwich. Crabbe's best way of showing gratitude to the duke was to elegize his brother Lord Robert Manners, a captain in the Royal Navy, who died in April 1782 of wounds suffered in the battle of Dominica, where he was in command of the *Resolution*. At first a separate elegy, Crabbe's 'Verses on his Brother's Death' became lines 112–207 of the second book of *The Village*. Crabbe was at work revising the poem late in 1782 when he was in London with the duke. He met Samuel Johnson at the home of Sir Joshua Reynolds, where Crabbe was a frequent visitor, and Reynolds solicited Johnson's assistance in correcting the poem. Johnson's contribution of lines 15–20 of *The Village*, which set up an antithesis between the Virgilian pastoral and the poetic imagination, is well known. *The Village* was printed by John Nichols and published by James Dodsley on 23 May 1783. The poem was highly praised in the *Critical Review* (July) as well as the *British Magazine* (August), but the *Monthly Review* (November) found Crabbe's view of the misery of rustic life exaggerated and pointed out the inconsistency of the second book's argument that virtue and happiness do not depend on rank with the generalizations about the wretched life of the inhabitants in the first book. However, it was *The Village* that permanently secured Crabbe's reputation. While Crabbe was in London in the winter of 1783, Lord Chancellor Thurlow asked Crabbe to breakfast and presented him with the crown livings of Frome St Quintin and Evershot in Dorset, worth about £200 a year, telling Crabbe that he was 'as like Parson Adams as twelve to a dozen' (*Letters*, 123).

**Marriage and Vale of Belvoir parishes, 1783–1792** Now that Crabbe had secured preferment, he and Sarah Elmy (1751–1813) were married at Beccles on 15 December 1783 and in January they visited his Dorset livings for several months. The duke of Rutland went to Ireland in February 1784 as lord lieutenant but Crabbe and his wife remained at Belvoir Castle until May 1785 when Crabbe became curate of the parish of Stathern, about 2½ miles south-west of Belvoir Castle. While at Belvoir, they had a child who only lived a few hours. Crabbe occupied himself while at Belvoir by writing *The News-Paper*, his last separately published poem in the eighteenth century, published in

March 1785. The poem satirizes the popular press for its trivial and scandalous content in the tradition of Pope's *Dunciad*. The poem is the weakest of Crabbe's mature productions, lacking, as Crabbe acknowledges in his preface, 'union and coherence' (*Poetical Works*, 1.179). Although he had received every courtesy and consideration from the duke of Rutland, Crabbe and his wife felt out of place living in Belvoir Castle in the absence of the Rutland family and attended by their servants. Crabbe remained at Stathern for four years. Three of their children were born there: George *Crabbe (1785–1857), his eldest son and biographer, John Waldron (*bap*. 1787, *d*. 1840), and Sarah Suzanna (*bap*. 1789). On 24 October 1787 the duke of Rutland died in Ireland of a fever. His body was returned for burial at Bottesford, the ancestral burial place of the Manners family. Following the funeral at Bottesford church, Crabbe delivered a eulogy in the chapel of Belvoir Castle which was printed by order of the duchess of Rutland.

During the next year, the widowed duchess persuaded Lord Chancellor Thurlow to exchange Crabbe's small Dorset livings for two more valuable ones near Belvoir Castle. In order to hold them, Crabbe applied to the archbishop of Canterbury for the LLB degree, which he received by passing a two-hour examination in Latin. The degree was granted on 10 January 1789. The day before receiving the degree, Crabbe was inducted into the livings of Muston in Leicestershire and West Allington in Lincolnshire, neighbouring parishes near Belvoir Castle. Crabbe moved from Stathern to the rectory at Muston on 25 February 1789.

The following summer Crabbe was asked by John Nichols to assist in the compilation of his monumental *History and Antiquities of Leicestershire* (8 vols., 1795–1815), and Crabbe produced 'The natural history of the vale of Belvoir', first published in 1790 in Nichols's *Bibliotheca Topographica Britannica*. Crabbe also contributed extensively to other parts of Nichols's *History*. He wrote 'The present state of Belvoir Castle, 1792'; made contributions to the 'Natural history of Hinckley'; wrote many of the commentaries on the plates for the 'Natural history of Barrow upon Soar'; and supplied notes and information for many of the parishes in the Vale of Belvoir, including Barkestone, Croxton-Kerrial, Eastwell, Goadby Marwood, Harby, Muston, Plungar, Stathern, and Waltham on the Wolds. In addition to his correspondence with John Nichols, he maintained a correspondence with Edmund Cartwright jun., the son of the rector of Goadby Marwood, who invented the steam-driven loom and built a mill near Doncaster. His son was interested in botany and they corresponded about many botanical subjects. During Crabbe's residence at Muston his infant daughter died (buried 12 September 1789) and three more children were born: Edmund (*bap*. 1790), Sarah (*bap*. 1791), who also died in infancy, and William (*bap*. 1792).

Crabbe's wife's uncle John Tovell died at Parham, Suffolk, on 6 October 1789. Crabbe was one of his executors and his will divided his estate between his two sisters (Crabbe's wife's mother and Elizabeth Tovell of Parham) or their heirs. Crabbe had grown weary of Muston and had no contact with the fifth duke of Rutland, who was still a schoolboy. He therefore decided to place curates in his parishes and move to Parham and live in Tovell's house, Ducking Hall.

**Suffolk parishes, 1792–1805** Crabbe and his family arrived at Parham on 28 November 1792. In becoming a non-resident rector of his parishes, Crabbe committed what he himself came to recognize as a dereliction of responsibility to his parishioners, which resulted in the defection of substantial numbers to dissenting congregations. Crabbe's son writes that 'it was a step reluctantly taken, and, I believe, sincerely repented of' (*Letters*, 150). Not only did the Crabbes endure the wrath of Tovell's sister, and the sullenness of neighbours deprived of Tovell's hospitality, but they also suffered the death of two of their children: William, who was buried on 6 September 1793, and Edmund, buried on 11 March 1796. Crabbe became acquainted with the Revd Richard Turner, who held the neighbouring living of Sweffling, and became his curate there in 1794. In 1797 he also became curate of Great Glemham. Crabbe's old benefactor Dudley Long North had inherited the estate of Little Glemham from his aunt in 1789 and Crabbe was a frequent visitor at Little Glemham Hall, where he met his old acquaintances Charles James Fox and Roger Wilbraham.

After the deaths of three of her children at Parham, Sarah succumbed to what appears to have been an extreme manic-depressive illness that culminated in her death in 1813. In order to provide her with a change of surroundings, Crabbe leased Great Glemham Hall from Dudley North and rented out Ducking Hall in 1796. During their four years at Great Glemham Hall, Crabbe educated his two surviving sons for the university after the eldest left Ipswich grammar school in 1798. During Crabbe's residence in Suffolk he began taking opium, a habit continued for the rest of his life. It was first prescribed for attacks of vertigo, and he later continued it to suppress painful attacks of *tic douloureux* or facial neuralgia. He continued his work for Nichols on the Leicestershire *History* and also completed a treatise on botany which was about to be printed by James Dodsley when John Davies, the vice-master of Trinity College, Cambridge, told him that English was not a fit language for a scientific work. Crabbe unfortunately accepted Davies's advice and burnt his manuscript. He provided 'a catalogue of plants growing in and about the parish of Framlingham' as an appendix to Hawes and Lodor's *History of Framlingham* (1798) and many notes for Turner and Dilwyn's *The Botanist's Guide through England and Wales* (1805). In late 1801 Dudley North and his brother decided to sell the Great Glemham estate and Crabbe and his family moved to a house in the nearby village of Rendham. His son says that in the winters of 1801 and 1802 his father wrote three novels which he ultimately consigned to the fire, agreeing with his wife that he had done better work in verse. He began work on 'The Parish Register' in 1802. In 1801 he, along with all non-resident incumbents, was directed by the bishop of Lincoln to return to his parishes; he succeeded, however, in obtaining a four-year stay of the order. In October 1803 his

eldest son entered Trinity College, Cambridge. In 1805 Crabbe finally returned to the rectory at Muston.

**Return to Leicestershire and later poetical works, 1805–1814** When Crabbe returned to Muston in October 1805, he found that a Methodist missionary had established a thriving congregation. An even more provoking discovery was that two of his own servants had been recruited by a disciple of William Huntington. Crabbe consoled himself by working on 'The Parish Register' which he published along with 'Sir Eustace Grey', a revised version of *The Library*, reprints of *The Village* and *The News-Paper*, and some shorter poems, in a volume entitled *Poems* (1807). Crabbe sent the manuscript to Fox, who had it read to him on his deathbed by Lord Holland, Fox's nephew. 'The Parish Register', a poem of nearly 2400 lines, is the major work in the volume. Its frame device is the clergyman–narrator overlooking the registers of baptisms, marriages, and burials at the beginning of a new year. This frame allowed Crabbe to incorporate striking character sketches based on individuals he had known as a clergyman. The most memorable subjects among Crabbe's portraits of parishioners include: Lucy Collins, seduced by an ostentatious farmer; Catherine Lloyd, the lonely miser hoarding her treasures; Richard Monday, the orphan who revenges himself on the parish for maltreatment; Robin Dingly, driven into feverish exile by false promises of inherited wealth; and Roger Cuff, denied charity by his relations, who returns wealthy and in turn denies his heartless relatives. The volume appeared in October and was the occasion of an important review by Francis Jeffrey in the *Edinburgh Review* (April 1808), contrasting Crabbe's realism and appeal to human nature with the obscure subjects of the Lake poets.

Even before *Poems* (1807) was published, Crabbe had begun work on *The Borough*, although some of the character sketches had been written years earlier. Crabbe drew on the towns he had known for his subjects; Aldeburgh, Beccles, Woodbridge, and Ipswich all supplied details and names for various sections. *The Borough* is described in twenty-four verse letters written to a friend. The letters move through descriptions of the church, vicar, curate, religious sects, elections, professions, trades, amusements, inns, players, and charitable institutions, culminating in an attack on the workhouse as an institution. This is followed by extended characters of representative poor: Jachin, the parish clerk who steals from the collection basket; Ellen Orford, the blind former schoolmistress; Able Keene, the ruined merchant; and Peter Grimes, the notorious abuser of apprentice boys. The final letters describe prisons and schools. *The Borough* was published in 1810 with a dedication to the duke of Rutland and a second edition was called for in four months. In reviewing *The Borough* Jeffrey this time, along with other reviewers, criticized Crabbe's stern view of life and his depraved characters. Most reviewers also criticized *The Borough* for haphazard arrangement and lack of links between the letters.

Crabbe next turned his efforts to his *Tales*, published in September 1812 with a dedication to the dowager duchess of Rutland. In the preface to *Tales*, Crabbe replies to criticism of *The Borough*, arguing that even Chaucer was strained to provide unity and connecting links in the *Canterbury Tales*. Crabbe also counters criticism that he lacks poetic imagination although he concedes that his style is not the high form that, for example, Shakespeare uses in *Midsummer Night's Dream*, but rather the style of accurate realistic description of men and manners in the tradition of Chaucer, Dryden, Pope, and Dr Johnson. *Tales* consists of twenty-one discrete narratives. The characters are of higher social standing than many of those in *The Borough*, perhaps in response to criticism of the vile and low figures in that work. Several of Crabbe's favourite themes are explored in multiple tales: exile and return, radicals and libertines as forces of social destruction, social inequality, and love and courtship. It was Sir Walter Scott's receipt of a complimentary copy of *Tales* from John Hatchard, the publisher, that occasioned the beginning of his correspondence with Crabbe, culminating in Crabbe's visit to Edinburgh in 1822. In a letter of 29 June 1813 Crabbe explains to Scott his situation in relation to the duke of Rutland. He tells Scott that he is 'one of the *old Race*'—friends of the old duke who make way for those of the new duke, but 'keep up a sort of Connection' (*Letters*, 114–15).

On 21 September 1813 Crabbe's wife died at Muston. He wrote of it a month later in a letter to her long-time friend Alethea Brereton Lewis. Crabbe says, 'she has been dying these ten years: more I believe … with Respect to Intellect & the more enquiring & reasoning of the Faculties, she, dear Creature had lost those even years since' (*Letters*, 117–18). Crabbe himself suffered a severe illness, possibly acute cholera, when Sarah died and took several weeks to recover. Both of Crabbe's sons were with him, having curacies nearby. Following his wife's death Crabbe was indifferent about continuing in Muston and was grateful when the duke of Rutland proposed exchanging it and West Allington for the living of Trowbridge in Wiltshire, for which he was the patron. Because of differences regarding the respective value of the livings, negotiations continued until the end of February 1814 and ended with the duke agreeing to give Crabbe the living of Croxton-Kerrial in the Vale of Belvoir in addition to Trowbridge. During the negotiation, Crabbe attended the celebration at Belvoir Castle for the christening of the marquess of Granby. The prince regent and the archbishop of Canterbury were present for the celebration. Crabbe dined at Belvoir on 6 January 1814, the last full day of the event.

**Rector of Trowbridge and final years, 1814–1832** Crabbe was instituted to the living of Croxton-Kerrial on 16 March 1814 and to Trowbridge two days later. When Crabbe arrived in Trowbridge, he found that the renovations to the rectory begun by his predecessor, Gilbert Beresford, had been left incomplete—thus beginning a protracted dispute which finally ended when Beresford confessed himself unable to pay for the dilapidations. Crabbe was, however, successful in recovering tithe money that had been improperly paid to Beresford after he resigned the living. Crabbe preached his first sermon in Trowbridge on 5 June on 2 Timothy 4: 2.

In March 1813 Crabbe began a correspondence with Charlotte Campion Williams, the daughter of a mine owner in Cornwall. She had sent Crabbe a narrative about a romantic case of love and constancy among the miners. She was engaged and was shocked when in June 1814, nine months after his wife's death, Crabbe declared his love and proposed a visit. She asked her friend Charlotte Ridout to write to Crabbe and inform him of her engagement. Miss Ridout did so in such a kind and flattering way that Crabbe transferred his proposals to her, saying they were kindred spirits and since he had seen neither of them it would make no difference. Charlotte Ridout (*d.* 1831) was the daughter of John and Caroline Ridout of Baughurst, Hampshire. She astonished her family by accepting Crabbe's offer and appointing a meeting with him at the home of her aunt at Sidmouth. Crabbe proposed to her on 22 September 1814 and was accepted. A date was set for the marriage and Charlotte's preparations were well under way when Crabbe broke off the engagement and broke her heart. Crabbe returned her picture on 12 December. He probably ended the relationship because of the objections of his sons, his own recollection of his anger at his father's second marriage, and the realization that he was in no position to provide for the support of a young family after his death.

Although Crabbe never remarried he always enjoyed the company and correspondence of female friends. In Trowbridge his most intimate friend was Maria Waldron (1785–1872), the daughter of a clothier. For many years it was rumoured that they would marry, but she died a spinster. Crabbe carried on a ten-year correspondence with Elizabeth Charter (1782–1860) whom he met at Bath in 1815. In 1817 Crabbe met Sarah Hoare (1777–1850), the daughter of the London banker Samuel Hoare (1751–1825), and Crabbe visited the Hoares at their Hampstead home every year from 1817 to 1830. Unfortunately Sarah Hoare destroyed Crabbe's letters to her and those she wrote to him which were returned to her by John Crabbe after his father's death. Another female friend who corresponded with Crabbe was the Irish Quaker writer Mary Leadbeater (1758–1826), the daughter of Abraham Shackleton, Edmund Burke's schoolmaster. She met Crabbe in 1784 at Burke's London house in St James's Square, and began her long correspondence with Crabbe in 1816, writing to him ostensibly to enquire whether his characters were drawn from actual persons. Her correspondence with Crabbe elicits more information about his poetry and literature than any other source.

On 2 December 1816 Crabbe's younger son John married Anna Maria Crowfoot, daughter of the Beccles physician William C. Crowfoot. John and his wife moved to the rectory at Trowbridge and he became his father's curate, with special responsibilities for services at the Staverton Chapel attached to the parish of Trowbridge. The following year, Crabbe's eldest son married Caroline Matilda Timbrell (1797–1834), daughter of Thomas Timbrell (1760–1820), a Trowbridge banker and attorney. George Crabbe jun. became curate of Pucklechurch in Gloucestershire, less than 20 miles north-west of Trowbridge.

Crabbe met William Lisle Bowles, vicar of the nearby village of Bremhill, in February 1815. Bowles was responsible for Crabbe's introduction to Lord Lansdowne and also introduced Crabbe to Thomas Moore and Samuel Rogers. Beginning in 1817 Crabbe made annual visits to London of about a month during the social season. He kept a journal of his visit in 1817 from 23 June until 24 July, recording his meetings with Rogers, Moore, Lord and Lady Holland, Ugo Foscolo, Thomas Campbell, Henry Brougham, John Kemble, Thomas Grenville, and John Murray, among others. He also met Lady Caroline Lamb, who sought to make him her confidant and confessor, and he sat for his portrait by Thomas Phillips, commissioned by Murray. His meeting with Murray led to Murray's becoming Crabbe's publisher; on 8 December 1818 Murray agreed to pay Crabbe £3000 for all of his copyrights and his new manuscript *Tales of the Hall*, published on 3 July 1819. These twenty-two tales are organized around the frame device of two brothers reunited at the hall of the elder brother after many years of separation. They act as the narrators throughout a poignant collection of poems dealing with love and marriage among characters drawn from the gentry. A new element in the development of Crabbe's verse tales is the interaction between George and Richard, the two narrators, and the situations and characters in the poems, causing the brothers to gain insight into each other and themselves. Crabbe became a member of the Literary Society in 1819 and was admitted to the Athenaeum in 1824.

In August 1822 Crabbe accepted an invitation from Sir Walter Scott to visit Edinburgh. Crabbe's visit coincided with the first royal visit to Scotland since the Jacobite rising of 1745. Crabbe was lodged at Scott's house in Castle Street and was thrust into the middle of most of the celebration which was orchestrated by Scott. In 1826 he became a magistrate in Trowbridge, being urged to accept an appointment by Bowles and Lord Lansdowne. As a magistrate he supported Bowles, a fellow justice, who successfully petitioned the crown for leniency in the case of Catherine Cook, a servant who was sentenced to two years at hard labour for stealing eight cups and saucers.

In October 1831, close to the end of his life, Crabbe witnessed and described in several letters to his eldest son (*Letters*, 311–13) the riots in Bristol occasioned by the visit of Sir Charles Wetherell, the attorney-general and recorder of Bristol, who was a vociferous opponent of the Reform Bill. Wetherell's entrance into Bristol on Saturday 29 October to open the assizes caused violence resulting in nearly 100 dead, the destruction of the mansion house, bishop's palace, new gaol, Gloucester county prison, and the Excise Office. Crabbe was rather indifferent toward the Reform Bill, although he stood to lose his votes for Aldeburgh and the city of Cambridge. He had a franchise in both as a member of a closed corporation and the Reform Bill would disenfranchise non-resident members of such bodies. He felt that the bill would do little to improve the lives of the lower classes.

A few months after his return to Trowbridge, Crabbe fell ill, beginning with a severe cold and progressing to a fever

and profound weakness. Crabbe died at the rectory at 7 in the morning of Friday 3 February 1832. At his funeral a few days later, ninety-two of the principal inhabitants followed his coffin to his grave in the chancel of St James's in Trowbridge. In 1833 a monumental tablet by the sculptor Edward Baily paid for by a public subscription was placed on the wall near his grave.

During Crabbe's nineteen years at Trowbridge, he had come to be loved and respected by the inhabitants. He had abandoned the harsh views of dissenters formed during his second residence at Muston and worked with the dissenting clergy in Trowbridge for the common good. Crabbe was never an extemporaneous preacher, always reading his texts and repeating his sermons at intervals and in different churches. He emphasized common human decency and morality in his sermons as he did in his life.

As a poet Crabbe was most highly regarded in his own time for the psychological realism of his characters and for the accuracy and vividness of his descriptions. The subsequent decline of his reputation was the result of two factors: the Victorian reaction against the neo-classical poets of the previous century with whom Crabbe was linked because of his pervasive use of the closed heroic couplet; and the decline of the verse tale as a popular genre, evidenced by Sir Walter Scott's abandoning verse tales for the novel. In the twentieth century Crabbe's best-known poems were the frequently anthologized *The Village* and letter 22 of *The Borough*, the tale of Peter Grimes, the infamous child murderer, made famous by Benjamin Britten, who based his first opera on Grimes.

THOMAS C. FAULKNER

**Sources** *Selected letters and journals of George Crabbe*, ed. T. C. Faulkner (1985) • *The poetical works of … George Crabbe, with … his life*, ed. [G. Crabbe], 1 (1834) • [N. Dalrymple-Champneys], introduction and notes, in *George Crabbe: the complete poetical works*, ed. N. Dalrymple-Champneys and A. Pollard, 3 vols. (1988) • R. Huchon, *George Crabbe and his times*, trans. F. Clarke (1907) • A. M. Broadley and W. Jerrold, *The romance of an elderly poet* (1913) • *A selection from the MSS and correspondence of Mary Leadbeater*, 2 vols. (1862) • T. Bareham and S. Gatrell, *A bibliography of George Crabbe* (1978) • parish registers, Parham, Suffolk RO • parish registers, Aldeburgh, Suffolk RO • parish register, Stathern, Leics. RO • bishop's transcripts, Leics. RO • N. Blackburne, *The restless ocean: the story of George Crabbe, the Aldeburgh poet, 1754–1832* (1972) • 'Memoir of the Rev. George Crabbe', *European Magazine and London Review*, 76 (1819), 197–200

**Archives** Bodl. Oxf., letters • Bodl. Oxf., manual of natural history • CUL, notebooks • Hunt. L., letters, poem, and sermons • John Murray, London, archives • Trinity Cam., botanical notes • U. Leeds, Brotherton L., corresp., notebooks, poems, and sermons • University of Chicago Library, sermons • Yale U., Sterling Memorial Library, papers • Yale U., Beinecke L., papers | BL, corresp. with Mary Leadbeater, Egerton MS 3709 • Bodl. Oxf., letters to John Nichols • Sheff. Arch., corresp. with Edmund Burke • V&A NAL, letters to James Wenn, his Ipswich attorney, and MS of poems • Yale U., Hilles collection

**Likenesses** T. Phillips, oils, 1816, John Murray Publishers, London • H. W. Pickersgill, oils, *c.*1818–1819, NPG [*see illus.*] • F. Chantrey, pencil drawing, 1821, NPG • W. Holl, stipple, 1847 (after T. Phillips), BM, NPG; repro. in G. Crabbe, *Works* (1847) • T. Thurlow, bust on monument, 1847, St Peter and St Paul's Church, Aldeburgh •

R. Cooper, stipple, BM, NPG · R. Sharples, miniature, Bristol City Museum and Art Gallery
**Wealth at death** £200: J. W. Crabbe to George Crabbe, jun., Dec 1833, U. Leeds, Brotherton L.

**Crabbe, George** (1785–1857), Church of England clergyman and writer, was born in November 1785 in the rectory at Stathern, Leicestershire, and baptized by his father on 16 November 1785. He was the elder of two surviving children of George *Crabbe (1754–1832), poet and Church of England clergyman, and his wife, Sarah Elmy (1751–1813), daughter of James Elmy, a bankrupt Beccles tanner who had deserted his family, and his wife, Sarah Tovell, sister of a wealthy farmer of Parham, Suffolk. Crabbe was educated by his father, at Ipswich grammar school (1796–8), and at Trinity College, Cambridge (1803–1807), where he graduated BA in 1807 and MA in 1811. In 1808 he took deacon's orders and in 1809 priest's orders. In 1808 he was licensed to the curacy of West Allington, Lincolnshire, one of his father's parishes, 2 miles north-west of his father's rectory at Muston, Leicestershire. On his father becoming rector of Trowbridge, Wiltshire, in 1814, George Crabbe, along with his brother John Waldron Crabbe (*bap.* 1787, *d.* 1840), assisted his father for a few months and then he chiefly resided in London from 1815 until his marriage in 1817, taking extensive walking excursions throughout the country.

On 10 April 1817 Crabbe married Caroline Matilda Timbrell (1797–1834), daughter of Thomas Timbrell (1760–1820), a Trowbridge attorney and banker, and Sarah Selfe (*d.* 1819). Crabbe moved to Pucklechurch, Gloucestershire, a village of 500 people, where he was curate for eighteen years, beginning about the time of his marriage. Crabbe and his wife had three sons and four daughters: Carolina (*b.* 1818); George (*bap.* 1819); Thomas (*bap.* 1821); Katherine (*b.* 1824); Sophia (*bap.* 1826); John (*bap.* 1828); and Mary (*bap.* 1832). His father was a frequent visitor to the vicarage at Pucklechurch, some 17 miles north-west of Trowbridge. In November 1822 Crabbe also became curate of the nearby parish of Wick and Abson.

Following his father's death on 3 February 1832 Crabbe began intensive work on a projected biography, for which he had been gathering materials for some time. He sent the manuscript to Samuel Rogers, who undertook to sound out publishers regarding the life and unpublished poems. On the failure of negotiations with Longmans, Rogers sent the manuscripts of Crabbe's unpublished poems to John Murray in June 1832 for his opinion. Murray passed them to John Gibson Lockhart, who took them with him on his journey with Sir Walter Scott from London to Scotland. In late February 1833 Murray expressed interest in publishing a new collected edition of Crabbe including a life and the unpublished poems and asked George Crabbe to send him his manuscript of the *Life*. By early May 1833 Murray had received two chapters and passed them to Lockhart. During 1833, Crabbe was actively seeking reminiscences of his father's life to incorporate into the remaining chapters. In May 1833 he wrote to Elizabeth Leadbeater Cole, the daughter of the Irish Quaker author Mary Leadbeater (1758–1826) for permission to use portions of her mother's letters to his father and asking if any letters from him to her were extant. Crabbe wrote to Murray in July that he had 'received the most valuable letters from Ballitore, exceeding all my hopes—letters addressed to the late Mrs. Leadbeater in which my father *discribes himself & speaks of his writings*' (5 July 1833, Bodl. Oxf., MS Don. d. 16) His most bitter disappointment, however, was the refusal of Sarah Hoare, daughter of the banker Samuel Hoare and one of his father's closest friends, acting on the advice of William Wordsworth, to make available the letters Crabbe had written to her. This correspondence is lost and was probably destroyed by Sarah Hoare herself, along with the letters she had written to Crabbe, which were returned to her.

On 13 September 1833 Murray made a proposal to print 5000 copies of the edition which would yield a profit of £207 per volume. He further proposed to give Crabbe the whole profit of £414 for the volumes containing the *Life* and unpublished poems and two-thirds of the profit on each subsequent edition of these volumes. Crabbe accepted this offer and reluctantly agreed to turn over Crabbe's letters and all of his manuscript of the *Life* to Lockhart, whom Murray hired to 'rewrite the Life and superintend the Works generally' for £300 on publication and £200 additional on the sale of 10,000 copies (Murray to Lockhart, 16 Oct 1833, MS letter-book, John Murray Archives). By far the greatest alteration Lockhart made in the *Life* was radical condensation—about 50 per cent of what Crabbe had written. Besides regret at the abridgement, Crabbe had severe reservations about the propriety of taking credit for being the sole author of the *Life*. The edition was published one volume a month from February to September 1834.

As the publication of the edition was nearing completion, Crabbe's wife died at Pucklechurch, leaving him a widower with seven children. As a result of Lockhart's soliciting patronage for him, Lord Chancellor Lyndhurst presented Crabbe to the crown livings of Bredfield and Petistree in Suffolk, valued at £330 per annum. Crabbe moved to Bredfield in late June 1835, where he became friends with Bernard Barton, Edward Fitzgerald, and Thomas Churchyard. During his residence at Bredfield, Crabbe published two theological works: *An Outline of a System of Natural Theology* (1840) and *Short Conclusions from the Light of Nature* (1849). Both works rely on the arguments of design and plenitude to prove the existence and attributes of God. They tend toward deism in that ongoing divine intervention in the physical and moral world is denied. A future life of rewards and punishments is postulated as the answer to the existence of moral evil. Crabbe makes a purgatorial argument for a future state where moral development is continued and completed in those who are deficient. Crabbe died on 17 September 1857 at Bredfield parsonage of epileptic seizures. He was buried in the churchyard at Bredfield on 22 September.

THOMAS C. FAULKNER

**Sources** *Selected letters and journals of George Crabbe*, ed. T. C. Faulkner (1985) · T. C. Faulkner, 'George Crabbe: Murray's 1834 edition of the life and poems', *Studies in Bibliography*, 32 (1979), 241–52 · *The letters of Edward FitzGerald*, ed. A. M. Terhune and A. B. Terhune, 4 vols. (1980) · *The poetical works of … George Crabbe, with … his life*, ed. [G. Crabbe], 1 (1834) · d. cert. · bishop's transcripts of Stathern parish registers, Leics. RO · Venn, *Alum. Cant.*, 1/1 · G. Crabbe, *Life of the Rev. George Crabbe, by his son* (1834), vol 1 of *The poetical works of the Rev. George Crabbe* [E. Fitzgerald's annotated copy, Trinity College Library, Cambridge] · register, Trowbridge, Wilts. & Swindon RO [marriage] · Pucklechurch parish register, Bristol RO · Crabbe to Elizabeth Cole, 23 Oct 1834, MS Egerton 3709A · Lord Lyndhurst, letter to George Crabbe, 18 Feb 1835, U. Leeds, Brotherton L.
**Archives** Yale U., Beinecke L., papers | John Murray, London, MS letter-book · U. Leeds, Brotherton L., A. M. Broadley's grangerized copy of *The life of the Rev. George Crabbe, LL.B by his son* · Yale U., Osborn and Hilles collections

**Crabtree, Henry**. *See* Krabtree, Henry (1642/3?–*c*.1693).

**Crabtree, Shirley** [*performing name* Big Daddy] (1930–1997), wrestler, was born on 14 November 1930 at St Luke's Maternity Home, Halifax, one of at least three sons of Shirley Crabtree, a stonemason's labourer, and his wife, Marian (*née* Briggs). His father's mother was a music-hall actress and apparently named her child after the eponymous heroine of the Charlotte Brontë novel before knowing his sex. Shirley senior evidently found the name character-building, as he passed it on to his own son; he played rugby league for Halifax and was also a circus strongman and a professional wrestler. The three Crabtree brothers were taught to wrestle at an early age by their father and, despite the fact that he left their mother when Crabtree was just seven, the son managed to follow in his father's footsteps. Crabtree was grateful for his father's early advice, as he often had to defend himself from jokes about Shirley Temple during his time at Battinson Road primary school in Halifax. Brought up by his mother in near poverty after his father had left—she worked in a brickyard for a woman's half wages to support the family—Crabtree particularly disliked Christmas, as well-meaning charities would inevitably send him girls' toys.

At the age of fourteen Crabtree left school to work in a cotton mill, but left this job two years later to play rugby league for Bradford Northern. However, his temper often got the better of him, and he never played for the first team. He eventually became a lifeguard at Blackpool with his brothers Brian and Max, and all three brothers took up wrestling. Max later became a promoter, but Brian broke his leg and turned to refereeing. Crabtree used his own name at first, but was also billed as the Blond Adonis or Mr Universe. He was often on the same bills as Jimmy Savile. At this stage he was a middleweight, but he soon realized that the largest wrestlers attracted the most support, and he put on weight and eventually weighed over 25 stone. He was often cast as a villain, most notably as the Battling Guardsman, as he had briefly served in the Coldstream Guards. He was also in *The Guinness Book of Records* as the owner of the largest chest in England, at 64 inches.

In 1976 the persona emerged that made Crabtree famous across the land. His brother Max, by now one of the

Shirley Crabtree [Big Daddy] (1930–1997), by Fresco Monte, 1979

sport's leading promoters, thought up the name Big Daddy, which was taken from the character played by Burl Ives in the film *Cat on a Hot Tin Roof*. His second wife, Eunice, made him a leotard from the chintz covers of their sofa, and Crabtree reinvented himself as a good guy. By now wrestling had become little more than a stage show, with the stunts carefully choreographed, although Crabtree stoutly denied this, saying that most of his fellow combatants were not intelligent enough for such forward planning. However, its popularity was enormous, and on Saturday afternoons ITV's *World of Sport* attracted over 10 million viewers.

The spectators were attracted less by the athletic endeavours of its exponents than by the glitz and glamour of the rituals, from the opening announcement by the commentator, Kent Walton, of 'Greetings, grapple fans' to the climactic battle between, inevitably, Big Daddy and his current arch-rival. His enemies included such wrestling luminaries as Mick McManus, Giant Haystacks [*see* Ruane, Martin Austin] (once in *The Guinness Book of Records* as the heaviest man in the UK), and Dave 'Fit' Finlay. The ritual of these bouts would involve Big Daddy striding into the arena to his signature tune, 'We shall not be moved', and chants of 'Ea-sy, ea-sy!' from his fans. A bigger and stronger opponent would overcome his smaller tag-team partner at the start of the bout and then try to antagonize Big Daddy. On finally being tagged into the ring, Big Daddy would out-muscle his opponent and gradually wear him down before applying his special finishing manoeuvre, known as 'the splash'. This involved him climbing onto the top rope and flopping down to crush his fallen opponent with his vast belly.

In the middle of the 1980s professional wrestling began to fall from grace, as former wrestlers made allegations in the tabloid press that the bouts were rigged. The Crabtrees were also accused of making the 'sport' too predictable, as Big Daddy always won his bouts. However, the fact remained that wrestling was a dangerous activity, as evidenced on 23 August 1987 in Great Yarmouth, when Big Daddy's 'splash' went terribly wrong, and his opponent, Malcolm 'King Kong' Kirk, died from a heart attack. Although cleared by a coroner's inquest, Crabtree blamed himself for the tragedy and retired from professional wrestling. Soon afterwards, the sport, by now considered outdated, was removed from the ITV schedules.

Wrestling had made Big Daddy a household name, and even prime minister Margaret Thatcher confessed to being a fan. He had cameo roles on television, including a commercial for tomato ketchup, and was a subject of *This is your Life*. He was always the children's favourite and undertook much charity work: most notably he once delivered his weight in chocolate to the sick children in Great Ormond Street Hospital. After retirement he moved back to Blackpool. Having suffered a stroke in 1993, he died of a left hemiplegia and diabetes in the Halifax General Hospital on 2 December 1997. His second wife, two sons, and four daughters survived him.

MARTIN P. CHOW

**Sources** *Daily Telegraph* (6 Dec 1997) · P. Perrone, 'Big Daddy', *The Independent* (3 Dec 1997) · 'Big Daddy', *The Times* (3 Dec 1997) · 'Big Daddy', www.neowrestling.com/bios/daddy.shtml · b. cert. · d. cert.
**Archives** FILM BFI NFTVA, *This is your life*, Thames, 7 March 1979 · BFI NFTVA, sports footage
**Likenesses** F. Monte, photograph, 1979, Daily Record Picture Library, Glasgow [*see illus.*] · photograph, *c.*1987, Hult. Arch.

**Crabtree, William** (*bap.* 1610, *d.* 1644), astronomer, was the son of John Crabtree (*d.* 1635) of Broughton, near Manchester, and his wife, Isabel, *née* Pendleton (*d.* 1646). He was baptized at Manchester on 29 July 1610. His father's will, drawn up on 30 January 1633, shows that he was then the only surviving son, with two younger sisters. Their paternal grandfather is said to have been a weaver; their father classed himself as a husbandman but was also the proprietor of a 'Loome house' containing 'three paire of Loomes'.

Where Crabtree was educated is unknown, but it is likely that he was a pupil at Manchester grammar school. There is no record of his having attended a university. Instead he engaged in the cloth trade, as a clothier or chapman (a middleman selling on cloth supplied by weavers); others entrusted money to him for this purpose on some kind of joint-stock basis. It was later said that he had 'bought cloth and baises and sent them to Blackwell hall' (Royal Greenwich Observatory MSS, RGO 1/40, fol. 22), a London centre for marketing woollen cloth. He may also have been involved in local administration, though the evidence for this is uncertain.

Crabtree's mother and sisters continued to live at Broughton after his father's death. He is said to have had a house built there, perhaps at the time of his marriage to Elizabeth (1612?–1654), daughter of Henry Pendleton, which took place at Manchester on 14 September 1633. At least four children were born to them and baptized at Manchester: Ann (or Hannah, 3 August 1634), Mary (21 May 1637), William (25 January 1640), and Easter (or Esther, 2 December 1642). All outlived their father.

Crabtree's circumstances were comfortable enough to enable him consistently to pursue an interest in astronomy. He had access to books, including those of Kepler and Galileo; he acquired a telescope and an astronomers' cross-staff. No manuscript records of his observations survive except for a few leaves now preserved among Flamsteed's papers (in the archives of the Royal Greenwich Observatory at Cambridge University Library, RGO 1/69D, fols. 120–24). These include observations of a lunar eclipse (10 December 1638); they also describe procedures used to correct a clock and 'try whether the Semicircle stood right in the Meridian'. Crabtree's planetary observations made between August 1636 and September 1638 were printed in John Wallis's edition of *Jeremiae Horroccii … opera posthuma* (1673); however, Edward Sherburne, in the appendix to his *Sphere of Marcus Manilius* (1675), says that these were 'not the tenth part' of Crabtree's recorded observations.

In 1636 Crabtree became acquainted with the young Jeremiah Horrocks of Toxteth, near Liverpool. Sherburne's statement that Horrocks, Crabtree, William Gascoigne, and William Milburne were put in contact with one another by Christopher Towneley has not been corroborated, but however it came about there was an active correspondence between Crabtree and Horrocks that continued until Horrocks's sudden death at the start of 1641. Excerpts from their letters appeared (in Latin translation) in Horrocks's *Opera posthuma*. In 1640 Crabtree described Horrocks as 'my friend and second self' (*PTRS*, 27, 1711, 288); he shared or influenced his friend's views on several issues. For instance, he preferred Kepler's astronomical tables to Lansberg's, so 'turned the Rudolphine tables into degrees and millesmes, and altered them into a far more concise, ready, and easy form' (ibid., 289). He also, unusually, expressed approval of Kepler's theories of planetary motion.

On 26 October 1639 Horrocks wrote to Crabtree that, by his own calculations, a transit of Venus across the face of the sun would occur on 24 November following. This rare phenomenon had not previously been observed. Horrocks's account (published in 1662) describes how his own efforts succeeded while his friend's were hampered by clouds; when the clouds broke Crabtree was so amazed at what he saw that he failed to take any measurements. Still, he produced a sketch and an acceptable estimate of the planet's diameter.

In 1640 Crabtree visited Gascoigne at Middleton, near Leeds, and reported to Horrocks Gascoigne's invention of a micrometer, hence of effective telescopic sights. A 'constant intercourse of mathematicall dissertations betwixt Mr Crabtree and Gascoigne' (*Correspondence of John Flamsteed*, 103) was maintained at least from December

1638 until June 1642; excerpts from and summaries of these letters are preserved among Flamsteed's papers. Extracts concerning sunspots appeared in the *Philosophical Transactions* in 1711.

Crabtree died between 19 July and 1 August 1644, when, according to parish records, he was buried at Manchester. Doubt was cast on this date because of an unfounded rumour (passed on by Flamsteed) that Crabtree lived on until the early 1650s. In fact a will made by a William Crabtree on 19 July 1644 and proved on 22 September 1645 divides property between a wife and children with the same names as those of the astronomer's family. The cause of his death is not known, but his will states that he was already 'sick in body'.

A romanticized nineteenth-century depiction of Crabtree observing the transit of Venus is among historical paintings by Ford Madox Brown in Manchester town hall. In reality, Crabtree's importance lay less in his practical work in astronomy than in his role as a correspondent with, and the preserver of documents relating to, Horrocks and Gascoigne. Some of these papers were obtained from his heirs by Jonas Moore and Christopher Towneley, others were bought by Dr John Worthington. Wallis's edition of Horrocks's *Opera posthuma* was based upon Worthington's collection supplemented from elsewhere: most notably, the account it gives of Horrocks's lunar theory came from a letter written to Gascoigne by Crabtree on 21 June 1642. FRANCES WILLMOTH

Sources *The registers of the cathedral church of Manchester*, 1 (1908) [introduction by E. Axon] • will and inventory, 1633–5, Lancs. RO, Cheshire wills WCW John Crabtree • CUL, Royal Greenwich Observatory papers, RGO 1/9, fols. 3–7; RGO 1/40, fols. 9–22; RGO 1/65A, fol. 112; RGO 1/68I, fols. 362–364; RGO 1/69A, fols. 23–25 • will, PRO, PROB 11/194, sig. 111 • probate act for Elizabeth Crabtree, 1657, PRO, PROB 8/51, p. 72 • *Jeremiae Horroccii…opera posthuma*, ed. J. Wallis (1673) • J. Horrocks, *Venus in sole visa* (1662) • E. Sherburne, *The sphere of Marcus Manilius: made an English poem with annotations and an astronomical appendix* (1675) • *The correspondence of John Flamsteed, the first astronomer royal*, ed. E. G. Forbes and others, 1 (1995) • J. E. Bailey, 'Jeremiah Horrox and William Crabtree', *Palatine Note-Book*, 2 (1882), 253–66 • J. J. Roche, 'The radius astronomicus in England', *Annals of Science*, 38 (1981), 1–32

Crace family ( *per. c.*1725–*c.*1900), interior decorators, came to prominence with Edward Crace (1725–1799), who was born at 40 Rochester Row, London, the son of Thomas Crace (*c.*1690–1774), a coach-maker of yeoman descent who was trading from 40 Rochester Row by 1724, and his wife, Mary (*bap.* 14 Sept 1690), whom he had married in 1718. Mary was the daughter of Henry Gregory (1660–1725), surveyor to the fabric of Westminster Abbey, whose brother, John Gregory (*b.* 1655), was college carpenter. Edward Crace was apprenticed to William Atkinson, an artist in the Painter–Stainers' Company, in 1741. His two brothers, John [i] Crace (1728–1806) and Charles Crace (1727–1784), worked with him in the family business, although John [i] later owned a print shop in Drury Lane. Drawings in the Victoria and Albert Museum, London, and the Cooper-Hewitt Museum in New York attest to the facility with which Edward and Charles designed coach panels and ornament in the then-fashionable rococo style. On 13

October 1748 Edward Crace was given the freedom of the Painter–Stainers' Company, and on 4 October 1752 he was admitted to the livery. Charles Crace published a book of designs for coach bodies in 1750, a copy of which survives in the Metropolitan Museum of Art in New York. Edward Crace married in 1753 Anne (*c.*1733–1764), the daughter of an artist, James Munn of Greenwich. Of their three children, it was their eldest son, John [ii] Crace (1754–1819), who eventually became head of the family decorating business. With his second wife, Martha (*c.*1740–1770), the daughter of William Bent, whom he married in 1765, Edward had another son who died aged twenty-five in 1791. They lived at 40 Long Acre, Covent Garden, London.

In 1768 Edward Crace made the transition from coach decorating to house decorating, establishing a business that was to continue until 1899, when it was dissolved by his great-great-grandson. Crace's first, and ultimately most important, commission was for the decoration and furnishing of the Pantheon on Oxford Road, London, begun in 1770 (dem.). It was likewise the first important commission for the architect, James Wyatt, who created a landmark in neo-classical architecture. Crace responded with painted arabesques and cameo decoration which Horace Walpole likened to the work of Raphael.

George III was equally impressed by the scholarly quality of the scheme, and at some time in the 1770s he engaged Edward Crace, reputedly of a quiet and studious disposition, to be keeper of the collection of paintings in the various royal residences. This occupied Crace until his retirement in the 1790s. An undated manuscript catalogue by Crace for the pictures at Queen's House (now Buckingham Palace) and his published catalogue of the pictures at Kensington Palace, dated 1778, are in the Archive of Art and Design at the Victoria and Albert Museum. As well as cataloguing, Edward Crace's duties included cleaning, restoring, and varnishing the paintings of the Royal Collection. Towards the end of his life Crace became infirm and devoted much time to collecting prints and drawings. This collection was a source of delight to his grandson Frederick [i] Crace [*see* Crace, Frederick (1779–1859)] when the latter came to visit and may have inspired his Crace Collection, now in the British Museum (print room) and British Library (map room) and the Guildhall Library, London. Edward Crace died on 7 December 1799 and was buried in Chiswick.

John [ii] Crace was born on 1 November 1754 at Greenwich. He was apprenticed to his father on 26 November 1767, but owing to his elopement with his second cousin, Ann (1758–1778), the daughter of Edward Eastham of Long Acre, whom he married in January 1776, there was a complete break between father and eldest son for several years, and John [ii] Crace began his own decorating business in 1776. According to family tradition, Ann Eastham was an heiress, being the granddaughter of John Gregory (1694–1758), a wealthy builder and decorator of Half Moon Street, Piccadilly, and the son of Henry Gregory, surveyor to Westminster Abbey. However, she died on 12 May 1778, five days after the birth of their second child, and by the end of October that year, John [ii] Crace, now settled at 55

Great Queen Street, had married Catherine (1754–1809), the daughter of John Wigzell of Greenwich. The couple went on to have seven children, and their three sons all worked in the family decorating business, as did Catherine herself. On 2 March 1785 John [ii] Crace received the freedom of the Painter–Stainers' Company, and on 3 June 1789 he was admitted to the livery. A handful of bills dating from 1780 to 1804 (Archive of Art and Design, V&A) demonstrates the fairly routine house decorating sometimes carried out by John Crace.

By 1801 John [ii] Crace had joined the circle of Sir John Soane in his capacity as painter to the board of works. He worked in conjunction with John Robins, an upholder (or interior decorator and upholsterer) and auctioneer, collaborating on a number of decorating and furnishing commissions, including 12 Lincoln's Inn Fields (*c*.1794), Pitzhanger Manor, Ealing (*c*.1802)—Soane's town and country houses—as well as at the Bank of England (1794). The major commissions of Crace's career, however, came from the future prince regent. These were at Carlton House (*c*.1785–1795) and the Royal Pavilion, Brighton (*c*.1801–1804), both in conjunction with his talented eldest son, Frederick [i] Crace, who acted as principal designer. The former was decorated in a sumptuous brand of neoclassicism inspired by French sources, while the latter was decorated in a bold scheme of chinoiserie, mostly superseded by the later chinoiserie decoration of Frederick [i] (1815–*c*.1825). John [ii] Crace died at his home in Knightsbridge on 9 May 1819, and was buried at St Martin-in-the-Fields, London. He left a considerable collection of Chinese *objets d'art* and topographical books on China, some of which were passed on to Frederick [i], and which must have inspired the father and son in their work at Brighton.

To continue the family decorating business, a partnership was formed in 1806 between the brothers Frederick [i] Crace, Alfred Crace (1781–1847), and Henry Crace (*b*. 1790). They were assisted by a cousin, John [iii] Crace, the son of John [i] Crace, the coach-maker-turned-print dealer. (The younger John worked for the Crace decorating business during his entire career, eventually moving with Frederick [i] Crace to 14 Wigmore Street in 1827.) The partnership began trading at 34 Curzon Street, moving to 51 Great Queen Street in 1812, later also trading from 230 Regent Street, before being dissolved owing to financial disputes particularly involving Alfred Crace. In 1830 John Gregory *Crace (1809–1889) had been sent to Rouen by his father, Frederick [i], to settle the debts Alfred had incurred. After the death of his first wife, Sarah Trery, in 1836, Alfred emigrated to Upper Canada. About this time he married his second wife, Ellen Nash, and assumed the surname Crace-Calvert. He died in Canada in 1847, leaving five children. The Crace decorating business reached its apex during the second half of the nineteenth century under the able direction of John Gregory Crace, assisted by his artistically gifted eldest son, John Dibblee *Crace (1838–1919), who closed the business in 1899 but continued to work as a consultant until the First World War.

Moreover, various Crace family members had distinguished themselves in the textile and timber trades during the second half of the nineteenth century. Dr Frederick Crace-Calvert, the son of Alfred Crace, published a definitive book on calico dyeing in Manchester in 1876, while Everard Crace, the son of John Gregory Crace, was apprenticed to a silk weaver in Lyons and wrote a manuscript (*c*.1875) on the subject that is now in the Victoria and Albert Museum, London. Another relation, Charles Napoleon Crace, descended from John [i] Crace, was a leading London timber merchant during this period. There can be no doubt that the international fame and reputation garnered by the Craces, and their successful undertaking of large and complex schemes of architectural decoration for some of the most important buildings of their day, were possible owing to the remarkable legacy of professional expertise in the building and decorating trades that had been continuously developed by family members since the seventeenth century.                    MEGAN ALDRICH

**Sources** V&A, Crace MSS • M. Aldrich, ed., *The Craces: royal decorators, 1768–1899* (London, John Murray, 1990) • M. Aldrich, *The Craces: royal decorators, 1768–1899* (1990) [exhibition catalogue, Royal Pavilion Art Gallery and Museums, Brighton, 9 Oct – 30 Dec 1990] • Crace genealogy, priv. coll.
**Archives** V&A, archive | Cooper-Hewitt Museum, New York, drawings [John Crace (*b*. 1754) and Frederick Crace (*b*. 1779)] • V&A, book of designs [Edward and Charles Crace] • V&A NAL, *Calico dyeing and printing* (Manchester, 1876) [Frederick Crace-Calvert]
**Likenesses** oils, *c*.1753 (Edward Crace and Martha Crace) • J. Hoppner, portrait, oils, *c*.1795 (John Crace), Royal Pavilion, Brighton

**Crace, Edward** (1725–1799). *See under* Crace family (*per. c*.1725–*c*.1900).

**Crace, Frederick** (1779–1859), interior decorator and collector of maps and prints, was born on 3 June 1779 at Park Row, Greenwich, the eldest son of John *Crace (1754–1819) [*see under* Crace family (*per. c*.1725–*c*.1900)], interior decorator and cabinet-maker, and his second wife, Catherine (1754–1809), daughter of John Wigzell of East Lane, Greenwich. He had two older half siblings, both of whom died young, as well as two brothers and four sisters. He was said to have been born prematurely (he was born little more than seven months after his parents' wedding), but he grew to be tall, stout, and hearty. He attended a day school near Brook Green, London, where his parents had a country house, then a boarding-school kept by a Mrs Bradbury, and lastly Lullington's school at Hammersmith, where he remained until he was fourteen or fifteen. In December 1793 he was bound apprentice, apparently in the Stationers' Company, to Richard Holland, an eminent builder. His grandfather Edward *Crace (1725–1799) [*see under* Crace family (*per. c*.1725–*c*.1900)] and father were distinguished decorators. Frederick began work for his father soon after being bound apprentice and worked under him for the Hon. Wilbraham Tollemache at 148 Piccadilly, and for the duke of Bedford at Woburn Abbey, where he painted and gilded. He next superintended the decorative works then being carried out for the prince of Wales at Carlton House.

Frederick Crace (1779–1859), by Frederick Henry Crace, c.1830

Frederick was skilled in the currently fashionable techniques of graining and marbling, and in decorative painting, and his work was noticed by the prince of Wales, for whom he worked under his father between about 1801 and 1804 at the Brighton Pavilion.

On 29 or 31 October 1804 at Chelsea, Crace married Augusta Harrop (1783/4–1827), daughter of John Gregory of Cheyne Walk, Chelsea, magistrate and treasurer of the Whig Club, and his wife, Mary. The couple married with the blessing of Augusta's father and despite the opposition of Frederick's. Crace continued to work for his father but his £300 annual allowance soon proved inadequate and the couple moved into lodgings at Arundel Street, Strand, and, at the urging of his father-in-law, about 1806 Frederick established a new partnership with himself as senior partner and his brothers Henry (b. 1790) and Alfred (1781–1847) as, respectively, partner and associate. Their father retired.

Crace's most important work was done between 1815 and 1820 at the Brighton Pavilion, for which he decorated the downstairs corridor and the music room in the Chinese manner: for the latter he also designed furnishings and furniture. He did much work at Windsor Castle (principally 1827–34, but also 1854–5) and at Buckingham Palace (from 1834).

Crace's work for George IV consolidated his reputation but not his fortune, as the king was notorious for non-payment of debts. The business may also have suffered after 1818, when Crace began to devote much time to collecting maps and views of London and its inhabitants. A collection had been begun by his grandfather Edward, and Frederick and his father, who were both commissioners of sewers for Westminster (Frederick from at least 1813) realized the practical as well as the aesthetic value of maps. According to his son, Frederick's aim became to have a view of every major building then or formerly in existence. He supplemented his prints with watercolour views commissioned from Thomas Hosmer Shepherd, Paul and Thomas Sandby, and others. The collection eventually comprised some five to six thousand drawings and prints, chiefly of buildings but also depicting special events and the customs and habits of Londoners. It also included a series of maps showing the growth of London from 1560 to 1859. Most of the items were mounted by Crace.

On 19 July 1826 Frederick's partnership with Henry and association with Alfred was dissolved, because his brothers had taken far more than their share out of the accounts. Shortly before this Augusta Crace began to suffer from a spinal complaint which left her bedridden. At the end of 1826 Crace took the house at 14 (in 1859 renumbered 38) Wigmore Street and moved her there. The house remained the Crace showrooms (with lodgings above) until 1899. She died there on 6 February 1827 and was buried in the Gregory vault at Cranford church.

Frederick and his wife had four stillborn children before the birth of their two surviving sons, John Gregory *Crace (1809–1889) and Frederick Henry Crace, both of whom worked for their father. In 1830 the elder, John Gregory, came of age and into an inheritance from his mother, and became partner in the renamed firm Frederick Crace & Son. John Gregory Crace's son John Dibblee *Crace was apprenticed to his grandfather Frederick in 1852.

Crace died at his home, Vine Cottage, Blyth Lane, Hammersmith, on 18 September 1859, at work on his collection until the end. He was buried at Norwood cemetery. His will was proved at under £1000, which suggests that he had formally passed the business to his son, though, because of the latter's illness, he remained unexpectedly active in the firm. John Gregory, who inherited his father's collection, completed its arrangement and published a catalogue in 1878. Following his father's wish that the collection be deposited intact in a public institution, in 1879 John Gregory sold most of it to the British Museum for £3000, half the sum it might have made had the items been sold individually. The collection is now divided between the map room of the British Library and the print room of the British Museum. Frederick's plans and views of London churches, including drawings attributed to him, were kept back by his son, who added to them for his own interest. They are now in the Guildhall Library, London (property of St Paul's Cathedral Library). The completeness and quality of the collection make it a unique source for historians, especially as a record of buildings since destroyed.

In addition to these well-known maps and prints, Crace left a significant library of oriental books, particularly works on art. His books and his journeys to visit, note, and sketch leading decorative schemes of the day show him to have been a particularly scholarly member of the distinguished Crace family. His drawings and designs, as well as the decorative schemes themselves, show him also to have been one of the most talented.

ELIZABETH BAIGENT

**Sources** J. G. Crace, 'The early history of the Crace family', typescript with addendum by other family members, LMA, 61.9 CRA · M. Aldrich, ed., *The Craces: royal decorators, 1768–1899* (London, John Murray, 1990) · M. Aldrich, *The Craces: royal decorators, 1768–1899* (1990) [exhibition catalogue, Royal Pavilion Art Gallery and Museums, Brighton, 9 Oct – 30 Dec 1990] · P. Jeffery, 'The lost Crace: Frederick Crace's plans, elevations, and sections of the churches of London', *London Topographical Record*, 27 (1995), 119–34 [pubn no. 149] · *The Times* (28 Nov 1879) · *CGPLA Eng. & Wales* (1860) · *LondG* (25 July 1826), 1850 · private information (2004)
**Archives** Cooper-Hewitt Museum, New York | V&A, Mostyn-Crace MSS
**Likenesses** F. H. Crace, drawing, *c*.1830, priv. coll. [*see illus.*]
**Wealth at death** under £1000: probate, 25 April 1860, *CGPLA Eng. & Wales*

**Crace, John** (1754–1819). *See under* Crace family ( *per. c*.1725–*c*.1900).

**Crace, John Dibblee** (1838–1919), interior decorator and author, was born on 19 January 1838 at 14 (later renumbered 38) Wigmore Street, Cavendish Square, London, the eldest of eleven surviving children of John Gregory *Crace (1809–1889), interior decorator and author, and his wife, Sarah Jane Hine Langley (1815–1894), the daughter of John Inwood Langley (1790–1874) of Greenwich, a civil servant at the Royal Naval Hospital. His father was renowned as a decorator who was in partnership for eight years with A. W. N. Pugin, the eminent Gothic revival architect, and was head of a decorating firm founded in 1768 by his great-great-grandfather Edward *Crace [*see under* Crace family], a coach-decorator and keeper of the king's pictures.

Possessing a quiet, even reserved, personality, J. D. Crace was artistically gifted from an early age. He studied the classics at Romanoff House School in Tunbridge Wells, Kent, from 1848 to 1852, where he was tutored by Thomas Alifree, who had spent three years in Russia teaching the children of Tsar Nicholas I. Crace was apprenticed in 1852 to his grandfather Frederick Crace (1779–1859), renowned as the decorator of the Royal Pavilion, Brighton. From 1852 to 1854 he studied at King's College School, London, but was recalled from school in the autumn of 1854, when his father's health broke down in the midst of important commissions. This marked the end of his formal education, but he continued to study continental decorative art by means of study tours for the rest of his life.

At the age of seventeen, and aided by his 75-year-old grandfather, young Crace took over the running of the family decorating firm until his father's recovery in the spring of 1855. The principal work in hand was the preparation of rooms at Windsor Castle for the reception of the French Emperor Napoleon III and Empress Eugénie on the occasion of their first state visit to Britain, in April 1855. Two letters written by J. G. Crace from Spain to his eldest son, now in the Victoria and Albert Museum archive of art and design, testify to the close working relationship between the two men. In 1855 they travelled together to Paris for the Universal Exhibition, then on to Berlin for study.

In his memoirs, now in the Victoria and Albert Museum archive of art and design, J. D. Crace recalled having grown up in a house where Pugin and Sir Joseph Paxton, designer of the Crystal Palace, were frequent visitors. Despite this, he was never to become a leading practitioner of the Gothic revival style. In early life, and into adulthood, Crace was subject to bronchial infection, which occasioned his first trip to the Middle East—Egypt (partly in the company of Frederick Leighton)—in 1868, followed by a visit to Palestine in 1869. The result was a lifelong fascination for Islamic design and active membership of the Palestine Exploration Fund. This was second only to his fascination for the art of Renaissance Italy, the result of a study tour in 1859 on the advice of another family friend, Sir Matthew Digby Wyatt, a leading Victorian designer. Crace was to return to Italy frequently throughout the next forty years of his career, and his interpretation of the Renaissance style was to characterize his career.

In 1859 J. D. Crace had been granted the freedom and livery of the Painter–Stainers' Company, but he first came to public notice for his role in assisting his father at the 1862 exhibition in London, where he exhibited his own designs and assisted his father with the latter's difficult task of decorating the exhibition building in a very short time. In 1866 J. D. Crace was admitted as a contributing visitor to the RIBA, followed by his participation in the 1867 Universal Exhibition in Paris.

The 1870s and 1880s were busy decades for Crace, who increasingly took over the running of the firm, having become a full partner with his father in 1873 on the occasion of his marriage on 6 February that year to Caroline Elizabeth Foster (1845–1947), daughter of Richard Foster, banker, of Lostwithiel, Cornwall. Important commissions during this time include Knightshayes, Devon (1874–82), where Crace worked in a mixed Gothic–Islamic style after the dismissal of the architect William Burges, and the Pompeian Room at Ickworth in Suffolk (1879) in conjunction with the architect Francis Penrose, a personal friend. J. D. Crace later noted that the principal figurative paintings had been executed by Henry Scholtz, a decorative painter his father had engaged in Paris to work on the lower library of Chatsworth in Derbyshire (1840–44). Such continuity is typical of the Crace firm and ensured its recognizable decorative style throughout the nineteenth century.

The most important work of J. D. Crace's career was undoubtedly the series of state and private rooms in a rich Renaissance style at Longleat House, Wiltshire (1874–82), for the fourth marquess of Bath. In Lord Bath, Crace found a patron completely attuned to his own passion for Renaissance Italy, which resulted in Crace's publication of *The Art of Colour Decoration* in 1912. Major late commissions were the redecoration of Leeds town hall in 1894, replacing his father's scheme of 1857, and the redecoration of the Royal Pavilion, Brighton (1884–98), replacing the work of his grandfather (1815–22) and great-grandfather (1801–4). During the 1890s Crace worked extensively for W. W. Astor, designing in a rich 'François Ier' manner at Cliveden, Buckinghamshire, 18 Carlton House Terrace, London, and the Astor estate office in London.

In 1884 J. D. Crace was elected master of the Painter–Stainers' Company; in 1908 the eminent painter Sir Lawrence Alma-Tadema presented him with a gold medal on behalf of the Institute of British Decorators, of which he was a founder and first president. In addition he held memberships of the Society of Arts and the Architectural Association. In 1889 his father died, and, feeling the loss keenly, he closed the business ten years later and worked as a consultant from home. In 1916 he suddenly lost his eyesight, and the last of the Crace decorators died quietly at home at 15 Gloucester Place, London, on 18 November 1919, leaving his wife and two children. He was buried in Norwood cemetery, London. His son, John Foster Crace, had been apprenticed to his father in 1900 but instead became a classics master at Eton College. His daughter, Mabyn Crace Collingham, did much organizing of the family papers after her father's death. In his own lifetime J. D. Crace prepared large gifts of drawings to the Victoria and Albert Museum and the Royal Institute of British Architects, ensuring the legacy of this remarkable family of designers to future generations. MEGAN ALDRICH

**Sources** M. Aldrich, ed., *The Craces: royal decorators, 1768–1899* (London, John Murray, 1990) · M. Aldrich, *The Craces: royal decorators, 1768–1899* (1990) [exhibition catalogue, Royal Pavilion Art Gallery and Museums, Brighton, 9 Oct – 30 Dec 1990] · M. Aldrich, 'Fit for an emperor at Windsor', *Country Life* (8 Dec 1988), 56–9 · M. Aldrich, 'The marquess and the decorator', *Country Life* (7 Dec 1989), 162–7 · J. D. Crace, *On the art of colour decoration* (1912) · H. C. Corlette, 'Architecture and painting: a tradition', *Art Journal*, new ser., 26 (1906), 201–7 · 'Our presidents: 3: John Dibblee Crace', *Journal of Decorative Art*, 12 (Jan 1893), 11–13 · C. H. Townsend, 'The late John Dibblee Crace', *RIBA Journal*, 27 (1919–20), 63–5 · 'Family history', Cooper-Hewitt Museum, New York · *CGPLA Eng. & Wales* (1919) · m. cert. · *Windsor Times* (17 Jan 1947)

**Archives** Longleat House, Wiltshire, archives, corresp. · Metropolitan Museum of Art, New York · RIBA BAL, architectural sketchbooks and drawings · V&A

**Likenesses** J. G. Crace, photographs, *c*.1855, V&A, department of prints and drawings · oils, *c*.1880, priv. coll.

**Wealth at death** £55,529 1*s*. 5*d*.: probate, 20 Jan 1920, *CGPLA Eng. & Wales*

**Crace, John Gregory** (1809–1889), interior decorator and author, was born on 26 May 1809 at 34 Curzon Street, London, the elder of two surviving sons of Frederick *Crace (1779–1859), interior decorator and collector, and his wife, Augusta Harrop Gregory (1783/4–1827), the daughter of John Gregory of Cheyne Walk, Chelsea, magistrate and treasurer of the Whig Club, and his wife, Mary. His father was renowned as decorator to the prince regent, and was head of a decorating firm founded in 1768 by Frederick's grandfather, Edward *Crace [see under Crace family], a coach decorator and keeper of the king's pictures.

Crace was apparently sickly as a young boy but grew very tall (6 feet 1 inch) and was of generally robust health as an adult. He was educated first at Dr Crombie's school in Greenwich, and later at Mr Pollard's school in South Kensington. Although he was never formally apprenticed,

he was admitted to the freedom of the Painter–Stainers' Company in 1855 and, after a long and distinguished career, became master in 1879–80. He made his first trip abroad to Paris in 1825 in the company of his father, and returned there frequently during his life. In 1829 he made an extended study tour of France and Germany in the company of a family friend, Mr Buchan, returning to Paris and Rouen the following year to assist with a lawsuit brought against his uncle, Alfred Crace. He was in Paris during the revolution of July 1830, witnessed fighting on the streets, and he himself narrowly missed being shot in the place des Grèves while browsing at a bookstall.

Crace began his career in 1825 by working for his father, who was commissioned to execute decorative work at Windsor Castle and Buckingham Palace by George IV. He later recalled rising at 5.30 each morning to give the workmen their orders for the day. On attaining the age of twenty-one in 1830 he received property and £3200 in cash from his mother's estate. This inheritance enabled him to become a full partner in his father's business, which was known thereafter as Frederick Crace & Son until the former's death in 1859, when it became J. G. Crace & Son. A memorandum in J. G. Crace's hand, now in the Victoria and Albert Museum archives, suggests that this partnership came at a critical point for the firm, whose business had significantly fallen off owing to Frederick Crace's having devoted himself almost exclusively to commissions for George IV, notorious for his non-payment of debts.

A further sense of urgency was added by Crace's marriage, on 26 January 1833, to Sarah Jane Hine (1815–1894), the daughter of John Inwood Langley (1780–1874), a civil servant at the Royal Naval Hospital, Greenwich. Crace had become friendly with Mr Langley while undertaking decorative work on behalf of his father, who was painter to the board of works. Shortly afterwards Crace and his wife, to whom he remained happily married all his life, began what was to become a large family of twelve children, eleven of whom survived infancy. Crace was determined to improve his income and build up a larger client base for the firm. To do so, in 1837 he embarked on a study tour of interior decoration in Paris, returning to decorate a new showroom at the Crace premises in 14 Wigmore Street, Cavendish Square (occupied by Crace & Son from 1827 to 1899, and renumbered 38 Wigmore Street in 1859). Invitations were issued to prospective clients and country house owners to view the new decorations in the French Renaissance and other styles at a series of open-house evenings.

The open-house evenings at Wigmore Street proved to be an immediate success, and Crace quickly established himself as the leading London decorator. One of his most important clients was Andrew Spencer Cavendish, the sixth duke of Devonshire, a patron of the arts whom Crace described as the noblest gentleman he ever knew. Throughout the 1840s Crace worked extensively for the duke, most notably at Devonshire House, London, and Chatsworth, Derbyshire, where he created a remarkable private library in the 'old French style', including a suite of library furniture. At Hardwick Hall, another Devonshire property, Crace was involved in the care and conservation of the important collection of early textiles. In conjunction with the great Gothic revival architect, A. W. N. Pugin, with whom he formed a partnership in 1844, from 1849 to 1852 Crace decorated and produced furniture at Lismore Castle, the duke's summer retreat in Ireland.

Crace also came to the attention of the queen and prince consort. In 1841 he designed wall and ceiling decoration in a medievalizing style at Taymouth Castle, Perthshire, for the second marquess of Breadalbane, who engaged him to create a suite of state rooms in which to receive Queen Victoria and Prince Albert. Crace's duties included attendance at the evening reception for the queen and Prince Albert, complete with fireworks, bonfires, and dancing highlanders. Prince Albert later asked Crace to decorate a number of interiors at Windsor Castle, including the Waterloo chamber (1860–62).

By 1844 Crace's designs—notably the Gothic state rooms he created at Knebworth, Hertfordshire, for the novelist Sir Edward Bulwer-Lytton—were displaying the imprint of Pugin in certain details. Crace had travelled to Munich in 1843 to study the principal buildings of the new town, built under the supervision of the architect Leo von Klenze. He came away with a theory of using bold polychromatic decoration in architecture that was to support his work in the Gothic style, which continued for about a decade after the death of Pugin (in 1852). His principal commissions in the Gothic style included Chirk Castle, Wales (1846–8), Eastnor Castle, Herefordshire (1849–50), Abney Hall, Cheshire (1852–7), and the new palace of Westminster (1845–69), all begun in partnership with Pugin, with whom he formed a close friendship.

It was, however, at the international exhibitions of 1851 and 1862 in London, of 1855 and 1867 in Paris, and at the 1857 Art Treasures Exhibition in Manchester, that Crace achieved a wider fame, beyond royal and country house circles, resulting in an increasing number of civic and institutional commissions. In 1851 he was closely involved with Pugin in creating the Medieval Court, and in 1862 he took over the decoration of the entire controversial building at short notice, as well as acting as exhibitor and a principal juror. He was again a juror in 1867 in Paris, where he exhibited and received a medal from the Imperial Commission under Napoleon III.

In 1852 Crace became interested in wet process photography and became a founder member of the Photographic Society (later the Royal Photographic Society). In 1855, to recover from a breakdown in his health, Crace travelled to Moorish Spain and made the first photographs of the Alhambra at Granada, the Alcázar at Seville, and other monuments. After the 1862 exhibition, his eldest son, John Dibblee *Crace, increasingly took over the running of the firm, becoming a partner with his father in 1873. This left the elder Crace free to devote himself to travel and study. As well as lecturing to the Institute of British Architects (later the RIBA) and other learned bodies, which he had done since 1839, he published a number of articles on colour theory, decorative practices, and the first history of wallpaper. He continued a limited amount of professional work during the 1880s.

Crace lived at the Wigmore Street premises from 1833 to 1851, when he moved to 6 Grove End Road, St John's Wood, with a garden laid out by his friend, Sir Joseph Paxton, staying there until 1858. Thereafter he lived in a large Italianate house, called Springfield, in Half Moon Lane, Dulwich, where he died at the age of eighty on 13 August 1889. J. D. Crace observed that with his father he had lost his most valued friend and adviser. The historic Crace decorating firm outlived John Gregory Crace by only ten years: his son wound up the business in 1899 in order to devote himself to decorating and consulting work.

MEGAN ALDRICH

**Sources** M. Aldrich, ed., *The Craces: royal decorators, 1768–1899* (London, John Murray, 1990) · M. Aldrich, *The Craces: royal decorators, 1768–1899* (1990) [exhibition catalogue, Royal Pavilion Art Gallery and Museums, Brighton, 9 Oct – 30 Dec 1990] · M. Aldrich, 'Gothic interiors of the nineteenth century: John Gregory Grace at Abney Hall', *V&A Album*, 5 (1986), 76–84 · M. Aldrich, 'Fit for an emperor at Windsor', *Country Life* (8 Dec 1988), 56–9 · M. Aldrich, 'The furniture of J. G. Grace & Son', *Antiques*, 139 (June 1991), 1140–49 · J. G. Crace, 'On colour [pt 1]', *The Builder*, 25 (1867), 874–5 · J. G. Crace, 'On colour [pt 2]', *The Builder*, 25 (1867), 888–9 · J. G. Crace, 'On the decoration of the international exhibition building', *Journal of the Society of Arts*, 10 (1861–2), 339–45 · J. G. Crace, 'The decorations of Chirk Castle', *The Builder*, 13 (1855), 449 · J. G. Crace, 'On the decoration of some of the buildings at Munich', *Journal of Proceedings of the Royal Institute of British Architects* (1850–51), 1–11 · 'Early history', Cooper-Hewitt Museum, New York, Accessions file [typescript] · *CGPLA Eng. & Wales* (1889) · Boase, *Mod. Eng. biog.* · d. cert. · A. W. N. Pugin, letters to J. G. Grace, 1844–52, RIBA BAL
**Archives** V&A, Mostyn-Crace MSS | Metropolitan Museum of Art, New York · RIBA, drawings collection · V&A, department of prints and drawings
**Likenesses** J. D. Crace, oils, *c*.1879, Worshipful Company of Painter-Stainers, London
**Wealth at death** £84,050 0s. 4d.: probate, 10 Oct 1889, *CGPLA Eng. & Wales*

**Cracherode, Clayton Mordaunt** (1730–1799), collector of books and prints, was born at Taplow, Buckinghamshire, on 23 June 1730, the only son of Mordaunt Cracherode (d. 1773), landowner and colonel of marines, who in 1740–44 sailed round the world with George Anson, and Mary (d. 1784), daughter of Thomas Morice and sister of William Morice, high bailiff of Westminster. His father's family came from Essex, where they held Cust Hall, Toppesfield, until 1708. The Cracherodes' alliance with the Mordaunts of Turvey Hall, Bedfordshire, dated from the sixteenth century. The name Clayton may come from the Morices.

In 1742 Cracherode entered Westminster School, where his contemporaries included Richard Cumberland, the dramatist, and Warren Hastings. His character was then already established as studious and reserved, though he was urbane in manner. He evinced a strong loyalty to Westminster for the rest of his life, and his annotations to Joseph Welch's *Alumni Westmonasterienses*, first printed in 1788 as *A List of Scholars of St Peter's College, Westminster*, are at the heart of the second and standard edition of the work.

Cracherode went on to Christ Church, Oxford, in June 1746, having the second place in that election, and graduated BA in 1750 and MA in 1753. He remained a student of Christ Church for the rest of his life, and once he had retired to London he never travelled further afield than

Oxford. He took orders, and accepted a curacy at Binsey, Oxfordshire, in October 1762, but his temperament deterred him from a career in the church, and he subsequently refused all offers of preferment.

Cracherode's own compositions were elegant, but few: some verses in *Carmina quadragesimalia*, a Christ Church collection printed in 1748, and a dutiful contribution to the university's mourning volume for Frederick, prince of Wales, in 1751. That modest accomplishment, however, was a measure of diffidence rather than of capacity. He was a learned bibliophile, and an assiduous and discriminating collector of prints and drawings, as well as of coins, medals, and various *materia* of natural history, including fossils. He was a regular customer of Thomas Payne's bookshop at the Mewsgate, the Literary Gallery, even in the 1750s. When he succeeded to his father's estate in 1773 he had substantial sums to spend, and he spent them resolutely, though like other collectors he often looked back wistfully to the opportunities and the prices of his youth. After Anthony Askew's death, in 1774, he had no consistent rivals as a purposeful collector but William Hunter, who died in 1783, and George III's agents.

Cracherode was not a recluse, but his style was certainly reclusive. He enjoyed the company of his close friends in London and Oxford, but his clubs were the bookshops, Peter Elmsley's in the Strand, and especially Payne's, which was known as the literary coffee house. He was an active and conscientious trustee of the British Museum from 1784, and was elected a fellow of the Royal Society in 1785 and of the Society of Antiquaries in 1787. On the other hand he notoriously never rode a horse, and though he made regular excursions to Clapham he never visited his lands in Hertfordshire. He was the owner there of a famous chestnut tree, of which others talked and he had only seen a drawing. Something more than indifference kept him from it. His manor of Great Wymondley was held by a serjeantry which would have bound him to serve as the king's cup-bearer at a coronation. The thought of having to appear in Westminster Hall was deeply oppressive to him, and any report of George III's ill health blighted his spirits.

It is not surprising that some of Cracherode's more ebullient contemporaries underestimated him. Samuel Denne, the author of several historical works, and a vigorous correspondent, thought him merely a sleeping member of the Society of Antiquaries. His taste and acumen as a collector were known only to a small number of dealers, and to a circle of friends which was not much larger. What he had accomplished became apparent only on his death.

Cracherode died at his house in Queen Square, Westminster, on 5 April 1799, and was buried on 13 April in the east walk of Westminster Abbey cloister, near his mother's grave. He had made his will in 1792, and his sister Anne (1718–1802), his sole executor and residuary legatee, proved it on 19 April 1799. Anne inherited his real estate, which could well bear his legacies of £1000 each to Westminster School and Christ Church, some charitable bequests which continued his lifelong philanthropy, and small bequests to his friends Cyril and William Jackson,

dean of Christ Church and bishop of Oxford respectively. His collections, three striking and eloquent items apart, went entire to the British Museum. He asked for all his personal papers to be destroyed, which they were.

Cracherode had some 4500 books, the last of which, a Terence and the dialogue attributed to Cebes, he bought only a few days before he died. A small number of them were working copies, or casual acquisitions. The rest constituted what might be described not as a library but as a cabinet, a carefully assembled display. They provided an unmatched conspectus of early printing, of the leading editions of the Greek and Latin classics at large, and of the silver age of Latin, comprising authors of the period from Augustus to Hadrian, to whom Cracherode had given particular attention. Beyond that, they were consistently chosen for their fine condition and aesthetic qualities. They included the Mainz *Catholicon* (1460) and the first illustrated edition of Dante's *Divina commedia* (1481), but not, at their first coming to the museum, the two great prizes of the Complutensian polyglot Bible, edited by Cardinal Francesco Ximenes (1522), and the first printed Greek text of Homer, edited by Demetrius Chalcondylas and published in two volumes at Florence in 1488–9. Those were bequeathed separately: the Bible, together with the Aldine Septuagint and Greek New Testament (1518), to Shute Barrington, and the Homer to Cyril Jackson. These were old and trusted friends, and they probably read Cracherode's intentions aright in duly passing their munificent legacies on to the museum, Jackson on retiring from the deanery, and Barrington by bequest.

Cracherode's gift was a landmark in the development of the museum. Although they were greatly outnumbered by the advent of the King's Library in 1828, his books advanced the library to an eminence that it had not previously attained. They were kept together throughout the nineteenth century, and after Smirke's remodelling of the museum there was a Cracherode room, in which the trustees held their meetings until their own board-room was completed in the 1840s.

The seven portfolios of drawings and 100 portfolios of prints were of no less significance in the development of those collections. They included many engravings by Dürer and Rembrandt, and like Cracherode's books they provided a foundation upon which comprehensive schemes of acquisition could be based. Unusually Cracherode had bought all his prints through an agent, John Thane (1748–1818); likewise his considerable collection of shells was supplied by a dealer, George Humphrey (d. 1830). Contemporaries were adequately impressed by the coins, gems, and minerals, but the heart of Cracherode's benefaction was a great fund of scholarly material, assembled on critical principles that have given it an enduring value.

Cracherode's chief pleasure in his treasures was probably visual: the evenness of his attention to his prints and his books suggests it, as does his taste for elegant bindings. He commissioned much of Roger Payne's finest work, including the red morocco of Cicero's *De oratore* (1468) and an Aldine Virgil (of 1505) bound with cameos set in the covers, in place of Cracherode's armorial stamp. Later students may deplore the loss of the original covers, but it is clear that Cracherode also preserved old bindings for their own sake, as on his Aldine Aristotle. He liked the best things to look well.       G. H. MARTIN

**Sources** DNB · *GM*, 1st ser., 69 (1799), 354–6, 373, 395 · A. Esdaile, *The British Museum Library* (1946) · J. Welch, *Alumni Westmonasterienses*, 2nd edn (1852) · W. J. Pressey, 'Notes from an old churchwardens' account-book', *Essex Review*, 27 (1918), 128–34 · P. R. Harris, *A history of the British Museum Library* (1998) · *IGI* · A. Griffiths, 'The Revd C. M. Cracherode', *Landmarks in print collecting: connoisseurs and donors at the British Museum since 1753*, ed. A. Griffiths (British Museum Press, 1996), 43–64 [exhibition catalogue, Museum of Fine Arts, Houston, TX, 1996, and elsewhere] · A. Davis, 'Portrait of a bibliophile: C. M. Cracherode', *Book Collector*, 23 (1974), 339–54, 489–505 · G. L. Wilkins, 'The Cracherode shell collection', *Bulletin of the British Museum (Natural History)*, History Series 1 (1953)

**Archives** BL, notebook as trustee of British Museum, Add. MS 47611 · NHM, catalogues of collection of shells

**Likenesses** H. Edridge, pencil drawing, priv. coll. · W. H. Worthington, line engraving (after H. Edridge), BM, NPG; repro. in T. F. Dibdin, *Biographical decameron* (1817)

**Wealth at death** £800 p.a. in rents, plus over £100,000 in 3 per cent: *GM* · will, PRO

**Crackanthorpe** [*formerly* Cookson]**, Hubert Montague** (1870–1896), writer, was born Hubert Montague Cookson on 12 May 1870 in London to Montague Hughes Cookson, later *Crackanthorpe (1832–1913), and his wife, Blanche Althea Elizabeth, *née* Holt (*d*. 1928). He changed his name to Crackanthorpe in 1888 in order to facilitate his father's legacy. The eldest of three sons, Crackanthorpe grew up in a financially comfortable household that cultivated his artistic and intellectual pursuits. Crackanthorpe's parents were both published writers. Montague Cookson enjoyed a celebrated legal career, and Crackanthorpe's mother pursued an ambitious social life at various gatherings at Rutland Gate and Newbiggin Hall, the ancestral home of the Crackanthorpes and the Cooksons. Crackanthorpe's education included five years at Eton College between 1883 and 1888. After spending a year in France, he returned to England in 1889 to study art with Selwyn Image, the tutor who introduced him to the works of decadent writers such as Walter Pater.

Crackanthorpe's initial foray into the literary world began with his contributions between January and September 1892 to *The Albemarle*, a journal financed by his father. These included a review of Henry James's recent playwriting activities and an interview with Emile Zola, the doyen of naturalist fiction. Crackanthorpe also published his first works of fiction in *The Albemarle*, including 'He Wins who Loses' (March 1892). Remarkably Jamesian in their style and texture, the short stories produced by Crackanthorpe during his brief life demonstrate a Pre-Raphaelite influence. In addition to his own later attempts at writing plays, Crackanthorpe mined the depths of realism and decadence in his short stories, a tendency that has prompted critics to credit him as one of the progenitors of early modernism. His work is often grouped among the coterie of other talented writers from

**Hubert Montague Crackanthorpe (1870–1896)**, by Bassano, *c*.1890

the 1890s who died young, a roster that includes such figures as Francis Adams, Aubrey Beardsley, Ernest Dowson, Lionel Johnson, and H. D. Lowry. On 14 February 1893, Crackanthorpe married Leila Macdonald, a writer from an immensely wealthy background. Their initially happy marriage proved to be the defining event of Crackanthorpe's life. The young couple soon relocated to France, where they lived in the Villa Baron near Sallespisse.

Crackanthorpe's literary corpus includes three volumes of short fiction and criticism, several critical essays, an uncollected story, and *The Light Sovereign*, a play that he wrote with Henry Harland. In addition to *The Albemarle*, Crackanthorpe's stories appeared in the *Yellow Book*, and Heinemann published *Wreckage: Seven Studies*, Crackanthorpe's first volume of short fiction, in 1893. The collection enjoyed praise from such esteemed critics as William Archer and Arthur Waugh, who both contended that Crackanthorpe's stories resonated with images derived from the works of Guy de Maupassant. Crackanthorpe's second collection of short fiction, *Sentimental Studies and a Set of Village Tales* (1895), received a decidedly mixed critical response, although a number of reviewers lauded the writer's realist tendencies and innovative techniques of characterization. Reviewers also praised Crackanthorpe's efforts at crafting the 'dialogue story', a popular literary form during the 1890s practised by Anthony Hope, among others. *Vignettes: a Miniature Journal of Whim and Sentiment*

(1896), the final volume published by Crackanthorpe during his lifetime, collected the writer's non-fictional periodical essays which had originally appeared in such journals as *The Speaker* and the *Saturday Review*.

Crackanthorpe's marriage deteriorated rapidly after the publication of his last volume. In early 1896, Leila had a miscarriage because of a venereal infection, possibly contracted from Crackanthorpe, and she departed soon after for Italy. During her absence, Crackanthorpe began an affair with Sissie Welch, the sister of Richard Le Gallienne and the wife of James Welch, the English actor. In the autumn of 1896 Leila returned to Paris with a lover of her own, the Comte d'Artaux. For a brief period the two couples shared a hostile residence in Paris. On the advice of her solicitor Leila left Hubert on 4 November and returned to London. After visiting his mother that same evening, Crackanthorpe was never seen alive again. On 24 December Crackanthorpe's body was discovered in the Seine. Although the cause of his death has never been determined, his biographers believe that he either committed suicide or accidentally drowned in the river which was in a perilously high flood stage during the latter months of 1896. He was cremated at Woking on 1 January 1897.

Crackanthorpe's untimely and mysterious passing was the subject of a number of conspicuous obituary notices following the discovery of his body. Le Gallienne's obituary of 2 January 1897, for example, was featured on the front page of *The Star*. 'We ask no longer why and how he died', Le Gallienne wrote.

> That he has left us thus of his free will, without a word of adieu, without a wave of the hand, is hard to think … He loved life so well, and it was so good a sight to see him alive so eagerly, so passionately, and with so vast and sympathetic a humanity.

*Last Studies*, which included three new short stories by Crackanthorpe, was published posthumously in late 1897.                                    KENNETH WOMACK

**Sources** E. J. O'Brien, ed., *The great modern English stories: an anthology* (1919) • D. Crackanthorpe, *Hubert Crackanthorpe and English realism in the 1890s* (1977) • W. Harris, 'Hubert Crackanthorpe as realist', *English Literature in Transition, 1880–1920*, 6 (1963), 76–84 • R. Le Gallienne, 'Hubert Crackanthorpe: in memoriam', *The Star* (2 Jan 1897) • W. Peden, 'Hubert Crackanthorpe: forgotten pioneer', *Studies in Short Fiction*, 7 (1970), 539–48 • W. Harris, 'A bibliography of writings about Hubert Crackanthorpe', *English Literature in Transition, 1880–1920*, 6 (1963), 85–91 • *CGPLA Eng. & Wales* (1897)
**Likenesses** Bassano, photograph, *c*.1890, NPG [*see illus.*]
**Wealth at death** £1131 18*s*. 0*d*.: administration, 29 April 1897, *CGPLA Eng. & Wales*

**Crackanthorpe** [*formerly* Cookson], **Montague Hughes** (1832–1913), barrister and eugenicist, was born on 24 February 1832, the sixth son of Christopher Cookson (1791–1834), a cousin of William Wordsworth, of Nowers, near Wellington, Somerset, and Jane (*d*. 1871), daughter of John Strother Ancrum. He was educated at Merchant Taylors' School, London, where he obtained a scholarship to study at St John's College, Oxford. He had a brilliant academic career, securing a double first in classical moderations and mathematics in 1852 and again in final schools in

1854, and won two university scholarships. He was a fellow of his college from 1850 until his marriage in 1869.

In 1859 Cookson was called to the bar by Lincoln's Inn, and worked for a while with such future judicial luminaries as Farrer Herschell and Horace Davey. He attached himself to the equity court of Mr Justice Fry, where he acquired a leading position, before moving to the court of Mr Justice North. Towards the end of his life he mainly concentrated on cases coming before the House of Lords and the judicial committee. On 6 April 1869 Cookson married Blanche Althea Elizabeth (*d*. 4 June 1928), the younger daughter of the Revd Eardley Chauncy Holt, a cousin of the liberal politician Hugh Childers. The marriage produced three sons, the author Hubert Montague *Crackanthorpe (1870–1896), Dayrell Eardley Montague (1871–1950), who became a diplomat, and the youngest, Oliver Montague (1876–1934), who became an army officer.

Cookson became a QC in 1875, but promotion to the bench eluded him, somewhat to the surprise of those who had once assumed that so brilliant a man would reach the very top of his profession. His obituarist in *The Times* attributes this failure to the impression he gave of not taking the law with the wholehearted seriousness shown by some of his competitors, coupled with the distraction of his many outside interests. Nevertheless Cookson was a respected figure in the legal world. He joined the Council of Legal Education and served as chairman of the Council of Law Reporting. He represented the general council of the bar at the International Congress of Advocates at Brussels in 1897 and at the International Congress of the Society of Comparative Legislation in Paris in 1900, where he was nominated for membership of the International Commission on Criminal Sentences.

In 1888 Cookson assumed the name of Crackanthorpe by royal licence upon succeeding to the landed estate of his cousin William Crackanthorpe (1790–1888), who had died unmarried. This bequest brought him the ownership of some 6000 acres at Newbiggin in Westmorland, along with the patronage of its parish. Crackanthorpe enjoyed the traditional life of a landed squire, but on rainy days he would while away the hours wrestling with abstruse mathematical problems, in which he retained an abiding interest. He also kept abreast of contemporary scientific work, about which he was remarkably well informed. Above all, Crackanthorpe relished the role of critic and journalist. He frequently wrote letters on topics of public concern to *The Times* and placed a succession of articles in the *Nineteenth Century*, *Fortnightly Review*, and *Contemporary Review*, some of which were later brought together in a book entitled *Population and Progress* (1907).

Crackanthorpe's political interests led him to seek a seat in parliament. He stood unsuccessfully for Kensington South in the 1885 general election and for Brixton in the 1886 general election, on both occasions as a Gladstonian, before breaking decisively with the Liberals over the merits of Irish home rule. But Crackanthorpe had a cross-bench mentality which ill fitted him for conventional political life, as had become apparent as early as 1879, when, writing in the *Nineteenth Century*, he had advocated the formation of a national party, a theme to which he was to return in the late 1880s.

Crackanthorpe's main claim on posterity lies in his courageous—some contemporaries thought foolhardy—advocacy of the practice of family limitation. This was the theme of one of his most influential articles, 'The morality of married life', published in the *Fortnightly Review* in 1872, an article which earned him a reputation as a Malthusian and was later used against him by his political opponents. In retrospect the furore is difficult to understand, since Crackanthorpe always took care to put distance between himself and the controversial Malthusian League, and was simply presenting the case, humanitarian, social, and economic, for a restraint of population growth. In 'The morality of married life', and later, he confined practical information to the recommending of the rhythm method of contraception—in an obscurely worded footnote which cited the works of various medical experts, all of them written in German!

By the start of the twentieth century Crackanthorpe's involvement in population questions was further stimulated by his encounter with the researches of Jacques Bertillon, who had demonstrated that in the urban areas of several European cities a relationship existed between poverty and high fertility. Crackanthorpe concluded that contraception was what he called the 'D. E.', the determining element, in the falling birth-rate among the affluent. He also came under the influence of Sir Francis Galton, the founder of eugenics, who happened to be his London neighbour.

In 1907 the Eugenics Education Society was established, and, following the unexpected resignation in May 1909 of its first president, James Crichton-Browne, it was to Crackanthorpe that its council turned for a successor, in accordance with Galton's expressed wish. Crackanthorpe accepted the offer because he believed that eugenics should be taken out of the scientist's laboratory and publicized more widely, even at the risk of some trivialization. Galton thereupon agreed to associate himself with the society as an honorary president. However, Crackanthorpe was already seventy-seven years of age when he assumed the society's presidency, and he held the post only until 1911. In any case, he was never in the mainstream of Edwardian eugenics. Prior to 1914 most eugenicists rejected all forms of birth control, partly on traditional moral grounds but also out of a belief that restraint was already taking place at the 'wrong end of the social scale', a process which they assumed was leading to the 'multiplication of the unfit' and therefore to racial deterioration. Crackanthorpe shared many of these fears, but argued that if the educated classes set a sound example in the responsible control of their own fertility, their social inferiors would quickly follow suit. He also blamed population growth for many of the social problems of the day—overcrowding, unemployment, and the like—and explained Germany's restless ambition on the world stage as the result of its rapid demographic expansion.

Thus, though holding highly conservative views on most political issues, Crackanthorpe is often labelled a reform eugenicist, because he combined eugenic beliefs with a commitment to the traditional liberal causes of peace and progress. He even took a mildly progressive line on female emancipation: 'Woman is now wide awake, her long slumber ended; to put her to sleep again is beyond human power', he proclaimed in 1907 (*Population and Progress*, 114–15). Crackanthorpe died at home at 20 Rutland Gate, Knightsbridge, London, as a result of longstanding emphysema and chronic bronchitis on 16 November 1913, shortly before the outbreak of the major war whose advent he had so dreaded. He was buried at All Saints, Ennismore Gardens, London. A close friend described Crackanthorpe as 'a man of wide and varied culture and reading, and of a genial temperament', 'a pleasant companion and a most gracious host'. He was survived by his wife.　　　G. R. SEARLE

**Sources** *The Times* (17 Nov 1913) · R. A. Soloway, *Birth control and the population question in England, 1877–1930* (1982) · G. R. Searle, *Eugenics and politics in Britain, 1900–1914* (1976) · R. A. Soloway, *Demography and degeneration: eugenics and the declining birthrate in twentieth-century Britain* (1990) · Burke, *Gen. GB* · MSS of the Eugenics Society · K. Pearson, *The life of Francis Galton*, 3 vols. (1914–30) · F. D'Arcy, 'The Malthusian League and the resistance to birth-control propaganda in late Victorian Britain', *Population Studies*, 31 (1971), 429–48 · *Eugenics Review*, 5 (1914), 352–3 · m. cert. · d. cert. · S. Gill, *William Wordsworth* (1989) · J. Foster, *Oxford men and their colleges* (1893) · *WW*

**Archives** Eugenics Society Library, London, records of the Eugenics Society · UCL, corresp. with Francis Galton

**Craddock, Sir Reginald Henry** (1864–1937), administrator in India and Burma, was born at Dharmsala, Punjab, on 11 March 1864, the youngest son of Surgeon-Major William Craddock, of the Bengal medical service, and his wife, Mary Charlotte, daughter of Francis Spencer Hawkins. Craddock was sent to Britain for education at Wellington College. In 1882 he passed the open examination for the Indian Civil Service and in 1884, after two years' probation at Keble College, Oxford, was posted to the Central Provinces.

Craddock was initially based at Jubbulpore. In December 1888, shortly after his marriage on 6 March that year to Frances Henrietta (1863/4–1932), younger daughter of General Henry Ralph Browne, he was made assistant to the Nagpur commissioner of settlements and agriculture. From 1894 until 1901 he was intermittently seconded to the Central Provinces secretariat on revenue, agricultural, and famine duties, and in 1896–7, and again in 1899–1901, took charge of the province's famine operations. In May 1895 he became second secretary to the chief commissioner of the Central Provinces and, five years later, chief secretary. He attained the rank of commissioner in March 1902 and in May 1907 was appointed chief commissioner. He was made a CSI in 1902.

Throughout the Central Provinces Craddock was renowned for his devotion to duty. His command of the vernacular and understanding of agricultural life outstripped that of most of his colleagues, and to his junior officers he was the model of a paternalistic ruler: benign and pragmatic, but firm. A conservative, Craddock saw himself as the defender of the peasant's traditions and rights against a rising tide of self-interested, Western-style nationalist agitation.

In 1911 Craddock was appointed KCSI and in March 1912 he became home member of the government of India under Lord Hardinge. Confronted with terrorism in Bengal and the widespread home-rule agitation of the war years his conservatism became more marked. He recognized no distinctions between moderates and extremists, and classified all critics of the government as fundamentally disloyal. In opposition to the liberal counsels of Lord Carmichael, governor of Bengal, he advocated suppression of political dissent and, after the war, sought to have the repressive provisions of the Defence of India Act preserved in peacetime legislation. The draconian and inflammatory Rowlatt bills were the ideological hangover of his time as home member.

In 1917 Craddock was appointed lieutenant-governor of Burma, but he was appalled to discover that there too nationalism had taken root. In contrast to the government of India's softly-softly approach to Gandhi's non-co-operation movement of 1920–22, in Burma Craddock cracked down hard. Bowing to the inevitability of local self-government, he devised a scheme of political reform which, in its niggardliness, reflected his view of the Burmese as the 'spoilt children of the East'—charming but entirely unfit for government. To his dismay, his scheme was jettisoned in favour of a version of the diarchy introduced in India under the Montagu–Chelmsford reforms. Fortunately, perhaps, Craddock left Burma in 1922, just before the reforms came into force.

Craddock retired in 1923 and was appointed GCIE. Back in London he became chairman of the Indian Civil Service (Retired) Association and in 1923–4 served as a member of the royal commission into the superior civil services in India. In 1929, when the Montagu–Chelmsford reforms were due for review, he published *The Dilemma in India* in which he derided the notion of Indian nationality and advocated an extension of electoral constituencies based on class, religion, and profession rather than territory. In 1931 he entered parliament as a Conservative member for the Combined English Universities. An obvious choice to sit on the joint select committee on Indian reforms, he was an outspoken, although cordial, opponent of further moves towards self-government in India.

Craddock died on 10 February 1937 at the Empire Nursing Home in Westminster, where he had been recovering from an operation. On 13 February his remains were cremated at Golders Green crematorium. His wife, Frances, who was made a CBE in 1919, had died in 1932 and Craddock was survived by a son and two daughters.

KATHERINE PRIOR

Sources The Times (11 Feb 1937) · History of services of gazetted and other officers … in the Central Provinces (1913) · D. A. Low, '"Civil martial law": the government of India and the civil disobedience movements, 1930–34', Congress and the raj: facets of the Indian struggle, 1917–47, ed. D. A. Low (1977), 165–98 · Speeches by Sir Reginald Craddock … lieutenant-governor of Burma, 1917–1922, 1924 · R. H. Craddock, The dilemma in India, 2nd edn (1929) · BL OIOC, Merton MSS · BL OIOC, Chelmsford MSS, MS Eur. E. 264 · BL OIOC, Curzon MSS · ecclesiastical records, BL OIOC · F. G. Lawrence, ed., Wellington College Register, January, 1859–December, 1933 (1933) · WWW, 1929–40

Archives BL OIOC, Chelmsford MSS · BL OIOC, Indian Civil Service (Retired) Association MSS · BL OIOC, Merton MSS · CUL, corresp. with Lord Hardinge, etc.
Likenesses W. Stoneman, photograph, 1930, NPG · photograph, repro. in The Times
Wealth at death £53,203 11s. 9d.: probate, 23 March 1937, CGPLA Eng. & Wales

**Cradock, Sir Christopher George Francis Maurice** (1862–1914), naval officer, was born on 2 July 1862 at Hartforth, Richmond, Yorkshire, the fourth son of Christopher Cradock (d. 1896) and his wife, Georgina, daughter of Major Gordon Duff, 92nd highlanders. Cradock entered the navy via the Royal Naval College, Dartmouth, in 1875. In the long period of unchallenged British naval supremacy during the nineteenth century it is not surprising that it was in campaigning on land that Kit (as he was generally known) Cradock would acquire a reputation for great gallantry. The term 'knightly' was easily applied to this very model of a late Victorian naval officer who never married. Tall, alert, and always immaculately dressed with a neatly trimmed beard, the well-spoken Cradock had a reputation as a fine sportsman and seaman. As commander in the Royal Naval College Britannia in 1895 he reminded the future Admiral Andrew Cunningham of Sir Francis Drake. Cradock also published, notably *Sporting Notes in the Far East* (1889) followed by *Wrinkles in Seamanship* (1894). His best-known work was *Whispers from the Fleet* (1907), a series of anecdotes and maxims providing common-sense advice for young officers that would also be carefully examined by historians after his death for possible explanations of his motives.

In 1884 Cradock served with the naval brigade on garrison duties in Upper Egypt. In 1891 he was with the eastern Sudan field force as aide-de-camp to the governor-general of the Red Sea and was present at the battle of Tokar and occupation of Affafit. He was awarded the khedive's bronze star with clasp and appointed to the order of the Mejidiye (fourth class). He served in the royal yacht (1894–6) and was commander in Britannia, where he was also master of the Britannia beagles. Cradock was in Chinese waters as commander of the dispatch vessel Alacrity during the Boxer uprising in 1900. He distinguished himself leading the British naval contingent in the capture of the Taku (Dagu) forts on 17 July and later commanding the naval brigade in the relief of the Tientsin (Tianjin) settlement and Admiral Sir Edward Seymour's column at Siku. He was also with the naval brigade at the capture of Peiyang (Beiyang) arsenal, Tientsin. The future Admiral Roger Keyes wrote of Cradock's 'fiery, ardent spirit' in action (Keyes, 210). Cradock was mentioned in dispatches, won the China medal with clasps, promotion to captain in April 1901, and was made a CB in June 1902. He was an aide-de-camp to Edward VII (1909–10) and was promoted rear-admiral in August 1910. Cradock was rear-admiral in the Atlantic Fleet (1911–12), and in December 1911 played an important role in the operations that rescued the princess royal and her husband, the duke of Fife, after the

Sir Christopher George Francis Maurice Cradock (1862–1914),
by unknown photographer, 1914

P. & O. liner *Delhi* was wrecked on the Moroccan coast near Cape Spartel. He was awarded the Board of Trade silver medal for gallantry in saving life at sea and in 1912 was made KCVO by George V 'for personal services'. In February 1913 Cradock received command of the North America and West Indies station and was subsequently praised for his action in helping to save British and American life and property during this turbulent period in Mexican history.

When the First World War began Cradock's 4th cruiser squadron in the West Indies consisted of four old County-class armoured cruisers and a light cruiser. Cradock, flying his flag in the *Suffolk*, was initially concerned with the protection of British trade. There were only two German cruisers, *Dresden* and *Karlsruhe*, on the western side of the Atlantic, but the area to be covered and the volume of shipping was immense and it was generally expected that the Germans would convert some of their fast liners into armed merchant cruisers. The Germans eventually ordered the *Dresden* into the Pacific but the *Karlsruhe* managed to avoid British forces and caused considerable trouble and loss before she was destroyed by an internal explosion. The Admiralty in the meantime reinforced North American waters, especially to cover the important troop convoys from Canada. Cradock shifted his flag to one of the reinforcements, the armoured cruiser *Good*

*Hope*, and, with the northern waters secure, switched his attention to the south. He was slowly proceeding down the western coast of South America searching for German raiders and attacking German trade when a potential menace appeared from the other side of the world. The Germans had a powerful east Asiatic squadron including the armoured cruisers *Scharnhorst* and *Gneisenau* under Vice-Admiral Maximilian von Spee based at Tsingtao (Qingdao). Japan's entry into the war on the side of the entente doomed Tsingtao but Spee's squadron was able to get away and work its way eastward across the Pacific. The Admiralty found Cradock had the nearest British force once they had sufficient intelligence to indicate that the Germans were heading for the west coast of South America. On 14 September the Admiralty ordered Cradock to concentrate a squadron that would be strong enough to meet the *Scharnhorst* and *Gneisenau* and to keep the old battleship *Canopus* and at least one County-class cruiser with his flagship until reinforcements in the form of the armoured cruiser *Defence* arrived from the Mediterranean. Once he had superior force, Cradock was to proceed to the Strait of Magellan to search for the Germans, ready either to search the Chilean coast as far as Valparaiso or to return to the east coast to the area of the River Plate. Cradock was now standing into danger for he did not enjoy superior force. *Scharnhorst* and *Gneisenau* were armed with eight 8.2 inch and six 5.9 inch guns and had the reputation of being crack ships. *Good Hope* had two 9.2 inch and sixteen 6 inch guns and *Monmouth* sixteen 6 inch guns but neither could use them in their lower casements in a heavy sea. In contrast, the guns in the German ships were mounted higher above the water and less affected by heavy seas. Furthermore, *Monmouth* had been hastily pulled out of the dockyard and manned with a scratch crew of coastguardsmen and boys. *Canopus* was also manned by a scratch crew of naval reservists and coastguards and her old 12 inch guns were actually outranged by the German 8.2 inch guns. In addition her new crew had little opportunity for gunnery exercises and were probably at a low standard of efficiency. The biggest problem, however, was the low speed of *Canopus*. Cradock must have known there would be little chance of bringing the German cruisers to action if his squadron was tied to the best speed of this elderly battleship, although these defects were exaggerated by the engineer commander of the *Canopus* who had apparently broken down under the strain of war. Cradock also had a light cruiser, the *Glasgow*, and the armed merchant cruiser *Otranto*, but the latter was merely a converted liner not meant to engage in action with real warships. These ships were more than offset by Spee's potential three protected cruisers, the *Leipzig*, *Nürnberg*, and *Dresden*.

The responsibilities for what would happen have been debated and one will never know exactly what was in Cradock's mind, what he thought the Admiralty expected him to do, and what the first lord, Winston Churchill, and first sea lord, Prince Louis of Battenberg, assumed he would do. Churchill and Battenberg were aware of the disparity in strength and thought Cradock should merely detach the light cruiser *Glasgow* to search the west coast of

South America while keeping his squadron concentrated with *Canopus* at the Falklands until the *Defence*, unfortunately delayed, arrived. Apparently this was never made clear to Cradock, who had Admiralty orders 'to search and protect trade in combination' and interpreted his orders as implying the Admiralty considered his force adequate and that his primary objective was to engage the Germans, something clearly impossible if tied to the *Canopus*. There is nothing in Cradock's record of bold and gallant action in the Sudan and China to indicate he would have been inclined to protest against the odds and the Admiralty apparently—and despite Churchill's subsequent denial of responsibility—did nothing to discourage him in the belief the Germans were his primary objective. Furthermore, he had the recent example of the court martial of Rear-Admiral Troubridge for failing to engage the battle cruiser *Goeben* in the Mediterranean at the commencement of the war in the belief this constituted the 'superior force' with which the Admiralty had ordered him to avoid engagement. Cradock may also have sensed that regardless of the outcome of any action it would be the Germans who could not afford to sustain damage far from home and with little likelihood of replenishing any large calibre ammunition they might expend. Arthur Balfour, the first lord in 1916, stressed this point when a memorial to Cradock was unveiled in York Minster that year. The Admiralty on 3 November belatedly ordered Cradock to remain concentrated with *Canopus* until *Defence* arrived, but the signal was too late for by this time the battle with the Germans had already taken place and Cradock and over 1600 of his men were dead.

Cradock, acting on wireless intercepts from the *Leipzig*, had been searching for the single German cruiser near the Chilean port of Coronel when he encountered Spee's force late in the day on 1 November. The *Canopus* was approximately 300 miles astern, convoying Cradock's colliers. Cradock detached the *Otranto* which could do little and engaged with *Good Hope*, *Monmouth*, and *Glasgow*. The battle began as the sun was setting and Cradock tried to close and force the action while the Germans would have the setting sun in their eyes. It was a desperate and bold manoeuvre in keeping with Cradock's traditional actions, but Spee refused to be drawn and once the setting sun dropped below the horizon it would be the German ships who were largely obscured in the dusk while the British were silhouetted in the afterglow. The German superior gunnery quickly told and first *Good Hope* and then *Monmouth* were sunk with all hands. Only the *Glasgow* escaped to warn *Canopus*.

Coronel was the most serious British defeat in a naval action in over a century although in little over a month Cradock would be avenged and Spee's squadron virtually annihilated by Admiral Sturdee's battle cruisers at the Falklands on 8 December. The debate will continue as to whether Cradock was acting in a quixotic and unflinching but mindless manner in accepting a battle he knew he could not win or, on the other hand, was pushed into doing so by ambiguous Admiralty orders that in his mind at least left him little honourable choice. In this vein, as

Balfour later put it, his courageous unselfishness and neglect of personal interest and ambition had shown a wise judgement in the interests of his country and 'there never was a nobler act' (Bennett, 106). Churchill may have been aware of the dilemma when a few weeks after Coronel he advised Admiral Beatty: 'Steer midway between Troubridge & Cradock & all will be well. Cradock preferred' (Ranft, 1.166). PAUL G. HALPERN

**Sources** G. Bennett, *Coronel and the Falklands* (1962) · *The Royal Navy list, or, Who's who in the navy* (1915) · R. Keyes, *Adventures ashore and afloat* (1939) · J. S. Corbett, *Naval operations*, 1 (1920) · A. Cunningham [first Viscount Cunningham], *A sailor's odyssey: the autobiography of admiral of the fleet, Viscount Cunningham of Hyndhope* (1951) · *The Beatty papers: selections from the private and official correspondence of Admiral of the Fleet Earl Beatty*, ed. B. Ranft, 1, Navy RS, 128 (1989) · *The Times* (7 Nov 1914) · *The Times* (14 Nov 1914) · *The Times* (21 Nov 1914) · A. Gordon, *The rules of the game: Jutland and British naval command* (1996) · W. S. Chalmers, *The life and letters of David, Earl Beatty* (1951) · W. James, *The sky was always blue* (1951) · A. J. Marder, *From the Dreadnought to Scapa Flow: the Royal Navy in the Fisher era, 1904–1919*, 5 vols. (1961–70), vol. 2 · W. S. Churchill, *The world crisis*, [2nd edn], 1 (1923) · *WWW*, 1897–1915 · Burke, *Gen. GB* (1939) · *CGPLA Eng. & Wales* (1915)

**Archives** BL, corresp. with Lord Keyes | FILM BFI NFTVA, documentary footage

**Likenesses** photograph, 1914, Hult. Arch. [*see illus.*] · A. S. Cope, group portrait, oils, 1921 (*Naval officers of World War I, 1914–18*), NPG

**Wealth at death** £1055 4*s*. 11*d*.: administration with will, 13 April 1915, *CGPLA Eng. & Wales*

**Cradock, Edward.** *See* Cradocke, Edward (*fl.* 1552–1594).

**Cradock, Harriet** (1809–1884). *See under* Lister, Thomas Henry (1800–1842).

**Cradock, John** (1707/8–1778), Church of Ireland archbishop of Dublin, was born at Wolverhampton, the son of William Cradock or Craddocke, Church of England clergyman. Aged seventeen he was admitted to St John's College, Cambridge, on 29 April 1725. He graduated BA (1729) and MA (1732), and was elected to a fellowship of the college, which he held with the rectory of Dry Drayton, Cambridgeshire. Subsequently he became rector of St Paul's, Covent Garden, London, and chaplain to John, fourth duke of Bedford. The degree of BD was conferred on him in 1740 and that of DD in 1749. Having accompanied the duke to Ireland on his appointment to the office of lord lieutenant, Cradock was promoted, in November 1757, to the bishopric of Kilmore; he held that see for fourteen years and was then translated to the archbishopric of Dublin, by patent dated 5 March 1772. In 1777 he was the target of a bitter attack by Patrick Duigenan, who, in his *Lachrymae academicae*, censured Cradock's favourable comments on John Hely-Hutchinson, provost of Trinity College, Dublin, the principal target of Duigenan's book. Cradock's own publications include sermons delivered to members of Cambridge University (1739) and the House of Commons (1752), and *A Charge Delivered at his Primary Visitation in St Patrick's Cathedral, Dublin* (1772).

Cradock was married to Mary St George, *née* Blaydwin (d. 1819) of Boston, Lincolnshire; they had one son, John Francis (1762–1839) [*see* Caradoc, John], who was raised to the Irish peerage with the title Baron Howden in 1819. A liberal-minded man with a reputation for benevolence, John Cradock died at the archbishop's palace of St Sepulchre's, Dublin, on 10 December 1778, and was buried in the southern aisle of St Patrick's Cathedral, Dublin. He was survived by his wife who died aged eighty-nine on 15 December 1819 and was buried in the abbey church, Bath.    B. H. BLACKER, rev. PHILIP CARTER

**Sources** H. Cotton, *Fasti ecclesiae Hibernicae*, 1–2 (1845–8) · Venn, *Alum. Cant.* · GEC, *Peerage*

**Cradock, John Francis**. *See* Caradoc, John Francis, first Baron Howden (1762–1839).

**Cradock, John Hobart**. *See* Caradoc, John Hobart, second Baron Howden (1799–1873).

**Cradock, Joseph** (1742–1826), writer, was born on 9 January 1742 at Leicester, the only surviving son of Joseph Cradock (c.1689–1759), landowner, and his first wife, Mary, *née* Annice (c.1703–1749). After the death of his first wife, his father married Anne Ludlam (d. 1774), sister of two eminent mathematicians, William and Thomas Ludlam. Cradock was educated at the Leicester grammar school. His father died in 1759, and shortly afterwards he was sent to Emmanuel College, Cambridge, where Richard Farmer, his schoolfellow, was a tutor. He had already developed an interest in the stage and a liking for London society, and left Cambridge without taking a degree. However, he was subsequently awarded the royal degree of master of arts by the duke of Newcastle, chancellor of the University of Cambridge, in 1765. In the same year he married Anna Francesca (d. 1816), the third daughter of Francis Stratford of Merivale Hall, Warwickshire. He took a house in a fashionable part of London (Dean Street, Soho), was an enthusiastic playgoer, and became known to the literati; he became a friend of David Garrick, and in 1767, Richard Farmer dedicated to him his *Essay on the learning of Shakespeare*.

Cradock soon afterwards settled at a country house which he had built at Gumley, on a scale which was to lead to financial embarrassment. He was high sheriff of Leicestershire in 1767 and 1781, and in 1768 he was elected a fellow of the Society of Antiquaries. He gave private theatricals at Gumley; that he was at least a gifted amateur actor can be estimated by the contemporary anecdote that Garrick once proposed to play the Ghost to his Hamlet. In 1769 he assisted Garrick in the arrangements for the Stratford jubilee. Cradock collected a fine library, and took pleasure in landscape gardening. His views on the latter subject are included in his *Village Memoirs* (1774), a fictitious epistolary correspondence between a clergyman, his son, and daughter. His musical skill made him a welcome guest at Lord Sandwich's house at Hinchingbrooke, where Martha Ray sang in oratorios, while Lord Sandwich played the kettledrum. He was a patron of the music meetings at Leicester, originated in 1771 for the benefit of the infirmary. There was a great occasion in 1774, when an ode written by Cradock, set to music by Boyce, was performed; among the audience were Lord Sandwich and Omai, the celebrated native from the island of Tahiti.

In 1771 a tragedy by Cradock, called *Zobeide*, based on

Voltaire's *Les Scythes*, was performed at Covent Garden with success. Voltaire acknowledged the work in a note dated Ferney, 9 October 1773, in which he wrote:

> Thanks to your muse, a foreign copper shines,
> Turn'd into gold and coin'd in sterling lines.
> (Cradock, 4.215)

In 1773 he wrote a pamphlet called *The Life of John Wilkes, Esq., in the Manner of Plutarch*, a Wilkite mob having broken his windows in Dean Street. In 1777 he published *An Account of some of the most Romantic Parts of North Wales* (he had climbed Snowdon in 1774). From 1783 to 1786 he travelled through France and the Netherlands. After his return his health forced him to withdraw from society, although he took part in various local events. In 1815 he published *Four Dissertations, Moral and Religious*. His wife died on 25 December 1816. In his later years he was a close friend of John Nichols, the antiquary. In 1821 he published a short novel against gambling, called *Fidelia, or, The Prevalence of Fashion*.

In 1823 growing financial embarrassments induced Cradock to sell his estate and library. He retired to London on a small annuity. In 1824 he published his tragedy, *The Czar*, which had been rehearsed, but not performed, years before. Its reception was good enough to encourage him to publish in 1826 his *Literary and Miscellaneous Memoirs* in two volumes. He included many anecdotes about prominent figures of the eighteenth century; particularly interesting are those concerning Oliver Goldsmith and Samuel Johnson, with whom he was acquainted.

J. B. Nichols described Cradock as 'a twin brother' to Garrick, both in 'personal likeness' and 'mental powers' (Nichols, 'Brief memoirs', lvii). He had a talent for acting, and was known to be a lively, cultured, and volatile person, particularly remembered for his 'great fund of anecdote' (ibid., i, lix). His friend George Dyer spoke favourably of his generosity of character, and added that he was strictly temperate, living chiefly on turnips, roasted apples, and coffee, and rarely drinking wine. His peculiarity of constitution required him to undergo a 'constant cupping', or bloodletting, sometimes twice a day. Yet when free from pain, he was cheerful and communicative. Cradock died at home in his apartments in the Strand on 15 December 1826. He was buried on 23 December in the parish vault of St Mary-le-Strand.

LESLIE STEPHEN, rev. CATHERINE A. JONES

**Sources** J. B. Nichols, 'Brief memoirs of the author', in J. Cradock, *Literary and miscellaneous memoirs*, ed. J. B. Nichols, 1 (1828), v–lx · J. Cradock, *Literary and miscellaneous memoirs*, ed. J. B. Nichols, 4 vols. (1828) · R. Farmer, *An essay on the learning of Shakespeare: addressed to Joseph Craddock*, 2nd edn (1767) · *Boswell's Life of Johnson*, ed. H. Frowde, 2 vols. (1904) · Venn, *Alum. Cant.*, 2/2 · Nichols, *Illustrations* · A. Sherbo, *Richard Farmer, master of Emmanuel College, Cambridge: a forgotten Shakespearian* (1992)

**Archives** BL, corresp., Add. MSS 52285–52286 · Bodl. Oxf., corresp.

**Likenesses** P. Audinet, line engraving, 1827 (after silhouette by Miers and Field, 1826), BM, NPG; repro. in Cradock, *Literary and miscellaneous memoirs*, vol. 1, frontispiece · R. H. Dyer, stipple, pubd 1828 (after miniature in enamel by N. Hone, 1764), NPG; repro. in Cradock, *Literary and miscellaneous memoirs*, vol. 2, frontispiece

**Wealth at death** inherited estate from father; estate taken over by Edward Cradock Hartopp in 1823; possessed moderate annuity until death: Nichols, 'Brief memoirs'; Leics. RO

**Cradock, Marmaduke** (*c*.1660–1716), painter, incorrectly called Luke Craddock by George Vertue, an error later repeated by Horace Walpole, was, according to Vertue, born in Somerton, Somerset. Baptismal registers earlier than 1697 do not survive for the parish, but Cradock's will confirms that he was from Somerset. In it he mentions four brothers, Edward, John, Oliver (to whom he bequeaths his 'real Estate in the County of Somerset'), and William Overton Cradock; a sister, Grace Gaite; and a cousin, Andrews Overton. The name Overton possibly indicates a connection with the family of Overton of Babcary, a parish adjacent to Somerton. Vertue, whose brief account of the artist is the earliest source, says Cradock was sent to London, where he first served an apprenticeship to a house painter and later taught himself, becoming 'one of the best painters of birds Fowles &c. of all his contemporarys' (Vertue, *Note books*, 1.79–80).

After Francis Barlow, in whose manner he worked, Cradock is recognized as the most important native-born painter of birds and animals of his time. His animated images of poultry, waterfowl, and farmyard scenes, like those of Barlow, concentrate on native species or those easily available to sketch. He apparently eschewed the patronage of 'Noblemen or Quality, always supposing they wou'd confine his genius to their fancy', and preferred instead to work for those who paid him a daily rate or for dealers (Vertue, *Note books*, 1.80). He is said to have worked rapidly, in a 'broad strong stile' (ibid.), and numerous repetitions of favoured compositions exist. It is not known if he employed studio assistants, although the otherwise unknown bird painter Coniers is said to have received instruction from him. So far, only three signed works by Cradock are known: *Peacocks, Doves, Turkeys, Chickens, and Ducks by a Classical Ruin in a Landscape* (Yale U. CBA), *A Peacock and other Birds in a Landscape* (Tate collection), and *Two Muscovy Ducks, a Partridge, Pheasant, and Squirrel in a Clearing* (with Lane Fine Art, London, 1991), and their fine quality is significantly above that of the numerous works attributed to him at auction. Five engravings by Joseph Sympson after Cradock were published between 1740 and 1743 (impressions, British Museum), and three drawings by Cradock in the same collection, two of which are watercolour studies of waterfowl and poultry, are evidence that he sketched from life. Vertue noted several of Cradock's 'best pieces' (Vertue, *Note books*, 2.13) at Mr Halstead's sale of pictures in May 1726, and in 1739 saw three overdoors of 'fowles dead game &c.' by Jacob Bogdani and by Cradock in Sir Robert Walpole's bedchamber, Whitehall. Cradock presented a panel painting of dead game to the Painter–Stainers' Company (Painter's Hall, London), of which he was presumably a member, although there is no documentary evidence for this. At the time of his death Cradock was living in Colchester Street, in the parish of St Mary's, Whitechapel, where he was buried on 24 March 1716. In his will, proved on 1 April 1717, as well as the

bequest to his brother Oliver mentioned above, he left £46 to Hannah Dale, 'wife of Humphrey Dale, painter', and all his prints to Dale's sons, Robert and Humphrey.

TABITHA BARBER

**Sources** Vertue, *Note books*, 1.79–80; 2.13; 4.51; 5.126; 6.177 · H. Walpole, *Anecdotes of painting in England: with some account of the principal artists*, ed. R. N. Wornum, new edn, 3 vols. (1888), vol. 2, pp. 267–8 · E. Croft-Murray and P. H. Hulton, eds., *Catalogue of British drawings*, 1 (1960), 291–2 [incl. details from Cradock's will] · L. Stainton and C. White, *Drawing in England from Hilliard to Hogarth* (1987), 220 [exhibition catalogue, BM] · E. Croft-Murray, *Decorative painting in England, 1537–1837*, 2 vols. (1962–70), 218 · C. Jackson, *Dictionary of bird artists of the world* (1999), 208–9 [incl. list of the principal works given to Cradock appearing at auction, 1983–96] · W. Gilbey, *Animal painters of England*, 3 vols. (1900–11), 129 · J. Egerton, ed., *British sporting and animal paintings, 1655–1867* (1978), 28 · will, 1 April 1717, PRO, PROB 11/557, sig. 75

**Wealth at death** £46 to Hannah Dale; all prints to Dale's two sons: will, 1 April 1717, PRO, PROB 11/557, sig. 75

**Cradock, Matthew** (*c*.1590–1641), merchant and colonial investor, was the second son of Matthew Cradock, rector of Hasguard, Pembrokeshire, and his wife, Dorothy Greenway, of Berkshire. The Cradocks were a prominent Staffordshire family and had made their fortune in the wool trade, while Cradock's grandfather and other members of his family were returned to parliament for Stafford borough. With the assistance of an uncle who was William Cockayne's factor in Hamburg, Matthew and his brother Zachary (who died in 1621 before completing his term) were apprenticed to Cockayne in the London Skinners' Company. Matthew was bound apprentice on 13 February 1606 for ten years; by the time of his freedom he was already trading to France and Spain. On 10 December 1622 he married Damaris (*d*. 1623), daughter of Richard Wyn of Shrewsbury; their daughter, also Damaris (*bap*. 1623), married Thomas, son of Thomas Andrewes, a prominent London politician, and may later have remarried to the Cambridge philosopher Ralph Cudworth. After his wife's death Cradock married in or before 1628 Rebecca (*d*. in or after 1641), a widow and daughter of Thomas Jordan, a London merchant. Two sons, Matthew (*bap*. 1628) and Thomas (*bap*. 1634), and a daughter, Mary (*bap*. 1637), were born of this union.

Cradock pursued a blossoming merchant career, taking advantage of offices he held in several of the merchant companies and the City of London. He extended his interests to the Baltic through joining the Merchant Adventurers, Eastland, and Russia companies, and by 1628 had at least £2000 of stock in the East India Company. By this date he also sought to diversify his trading interests by looking to potential colonization of North America. When on 4 March 1629 the Massachusetts Bay Company received its royal charter, transforming an informal organization with a land grant to the Massachusetts Bay area into a corporation, Cradock was a founding member. Shortly afterwards he was chosen by the investors as the first governor and head of the company. His cousin's husband, John Endecott, was chosen to represent the company in New England, but was subordinate to Cradock. By July 1629, however, Cradock was doubting the long-term merits of this structure, and on 28 July proposed moving the company's headquarters to New England. This had the dual advantage of protecting the company from the royal interference of a king who might see its profitable potential and of encouraging investors to settle in the colony, thus increasing its chances of success. A group of the company leaders agreed to migrate themselves if they could take the charter with them. Following an investigation into the legality of the move, the general council of the company agreed to the proposal. Cradock, who decided against moving to New England himself, was replaced as governor by John Winthrop on 20 October 1629.

Although he never visited the colony, Cradock remained an active member of the Massachusetts Bay Company. Regularly sending his servants to New England, he secured a separate plantation for himself at Medford within the Massachusetts colony, and pledged money for the foundation of Harvard College. He continued to advise Winthrop and was an advocate for the company in England; in 1635 he helped secure the passage to Massachusetts of Sir Henry Vane the younger, who became governor in the following year. Having risen to be first warden of the Skinners' Company by 1640, he sat for London in the Short and Long parliaments that year. Already an outspoken critic of impositions and tonnage and poundage, he furthered his activism against royal authority by advocating root and branch reform and generating support within the City for the protestation. However, his career as an opposition MP was cut short by his death on 27 May 1641. He was survived by his wife and his daughter by his first marriage; after payment of his debts they inherited his estate, which included houses in London and Romford, and land in New England.      TROY O. BICKHAM

**Sources** D. M. Gardener, 'Cradock, Matthew', HoP, *Commons, 1640–60* [draft] · R. L. Greaves, 'Cradock, Mathew', Greaves & Zaller, *BDBR*, 1.186–7 · L. S. Mayo, *John Endecott* (1936) · F. Rose-Troup, *The Massachusetts Bay Company and its predecessors* (1930) · S. E. Morison, *Builders of the bay colony* (1930) · R. Brenner, *Merchants and revolution: commercial change, political conflict, and London's overseas traders, 1550–1653* (1993) · *DNB* · R. L. Greaves, 'Andrewes, Thomas', Greaves & Zaller, *BDBR*, 1.16
**Archives** Mass. Hist. Soc., Winthrop papers
**Wealth at death** left property, land in New England, and small bequests to family: Gardener, 'Cradock, Matthew'

**Cradock, Phyllis Nan Sortain** [Fanny] **(1909–1994)**, television chef, was born on 26 February 1909 at Apthorp, Fairlop Road, Leytonstone, Essex, the daughter of Archibald Thomas Pechey, corn merchant, and his wife, Bijou Sortain, *née* Hancock. By the time of her first marriage she was referring to her father as an 'author', although there is no evidence to support the claim; she also embellished her surname, giving it as 'Primrose-Pechey'. Little is known about her parents, but she often said that her father was a wealthy gambler in his thirties when he married her mother, then a flighty teenaged beauty. The parents spent the winter season in Nice, and while the father lost the family fortune in the casino, the mother was being wooed by admirers who would give the young Phyllis some money as a bribe to leave them alone. She would take herself into the hotel kitchen, where a kind member

**Phyllis Nan Sortain** [Fanny] **Cradock** (1909–1994), by unknown photographer [with her husband, John Cradock]

of the staff would seat her on a shelf while she watched them cooking and learned the craft herself. In an alternative version, the infant Fanny was abandoned by her mother and brought up by grandparents until the age of ten, when she was sent to boarding-school, from which she was expelled at fifteen for dabbling in the supernatural. Everything about Fanny Cradock was preposterous. She was one of the first television 'chefs', but was a poor cook. Though it was part of the act to abuse him, she was devoted to her husband Johnny; but they were only married when she was already sixty-eight, and she had at least one husband still living. She had been a double bigamist.

On 10 October 1926, aged seventeen (although she gave her age as twenty-one) Fanny married Sidney Arthur Vernon Evans (*b.* 1903/4), an RAF pilot, and son of Arthur Vernon Evans, physician. His plane crashed shortly after the wedding—'I married on Wednesday, settled his debts on Friday and he died on Sunday', she told friends afterwards (though in other accounts the crash was four months later) (*The Times*, 14 Oct 1998). In those few days she became pregnant with her first son, Peter. When he was a toddler she locked him in a room at home while she did her rounds as a door-to-door saleswoman of encyclopaedias and vacuum cleaners, and finally gave him to be adopted by his paternal grandparents on condition that she did not see him again until he was twenty-one.

The child was at most a year old when, on 23 July 1928, Fanny married again; her husband was Arthur William Chapman (*b.* 1905/6), a civil engineer, and son of Lieutenant Arthur Chapman, army officer. They had a son, Christopher, but when this second son was four months old, she abandoned them both. Now penniless, she ran a ladies' dressmaking shop; though she couldn't herself sew a button on, she had a knack for dressing her customers. On 26 September 1939 she married, apparently bigamously, her third husband, Gregory Leo Edmund Dye (or Holden-Dye; *b*. 1911/12), a speciality salesman and auxiliary fireman, and son of Leo Dye, of independent means. Within a few weeks she had left him for Major John Cradock (*b*. 1904/5), an officer in the Royal Artillery, and son of Henry Cradock, wholesale woollen merchant. Johnny, as he came to be called on the television, was married with four children, whom he abandoned for Fanny; they met on Hackney Marshes during a troop concert. It would have astonished and outraged their fans, but Fanny and Johnny were not married until 7 May 1977, when she was sixty-eight (though she gave her age on the marriage certificate as fifty-five, while he gave his as sixty-five), saying she was the widow of her second husband, though he was still alive.

Fanny called herself Frances Dale on the spine of the nine romantic novels she wrote, and in the by-line she enjoyed as fashion editor of the *Sunday Graphic*. On Fleet Street she offered herself 'as an expert on beauty, hair care, spiritualism and even the lost city of Atlantis' (*The Times*, 17 Oct 1998). She said she 'had applied to the *Daily Express* for 18 years and got no answer' (*The Independent*, 29 Dec 1994), but in 1948 she joined that paper. Soon after this she and Johnny joined the *Daily Telegraph* under the *nom de plume* Bon Viveur. The women's editor pointed out the solecism (it should have been Bon Vivant, gourmand), but Fanny's common touch paid off: in a later copyright dispute with the *Daily Telegraph* she was able to cite the earlier argument. As well as writing a cookery column, they became restaurant critics, after a fashion. When they interviewed the duchess of Windsor, they expressed surprise that the duchess did not mention a single one 'of France's 11 top-ranking three-star restaurants' (*The Independent*, 29 Dec 1994).

It was a natural progression to live cookery demonstrations for the Gas Council, stage shows, and (after Fanny had her nose bobbed by Archibald McIndoe), television, where, from 1952 until the 1970s, they developed Johnny's character as the subservient sidekick, good only for handing Fanny her frying pan and knowing which wine to serve. Fanny's trademark was food so over-decorated it was baroque. Her rudeness and churlishness were renowned, and led to her downfall, when she savaged an amateur cook on Esther Rantzen's *The Big Time*. She was never asked to appear on television again.

Following their initial success, the Cradocks lived in a house in Blackheath, in south London, which they encouraged gossip columnists to refer to as 'Hollywood-style'. Their lifestyle included lavish parties, a cabin cruiser moored near Cannes, and fines for careless driving of their Rolls-Royce. They lived for a time in the Channel Islands, briefly in the west country, and then at Little Benfleet, near Clacton, Essex, where in 1987, the year of Johnny's death from cancer, they were the victims of an

£80,000 robbery. Fanny appealed to an audience that disappeared with the food revolution of the 1980s, one that forgave her pretensions and snobbery, and even the abuse she heaped upon Johnny or anyone who dared to call her Fanny, rather than Mrs Cradock. She died in a nursing home, Ersham House, Ersham Road, Hailsham, Sussex, on 27 December 1994, of cerebrovascular atherosclerosis.

PAUL LEVY

**Sources** *The Times* (29 Dec 1994) · *The Independent* (29 Dec 1994) · R. Young, 'Johnny dear …', *The Times* (17 Oct 1998) · 'The real Fanny Cradock', TV documentary, transmitted on Channel 4, 17 Oct 1998 · b. cert. · m. certs. · d. cert.
**Likenesses** photograph, repro. in *The Times* · photograph (with Johnny Cradock), repro. in *The Independent* [*see illus.*]
**Wealth at death** £204,696: probate, 1995, *CGPLA Eng. & Wales*

**Cradock, Samuel** (1620/21–1706), nonconformist minister, was the eldest son of Samuel Cradock (1582/3–1653), Church of England clergyman, and his wife, Elizabeth (*d*. in or after 1652). His younger brother was Zachary *Cradock, provost of Eton College, and his uncle was Matthew Cradock, the first governor of the Massachusetts Company. Cradock was admitted to Emmanuel College, Cambridge, on 25 May 1637, graduated BA in 1641, and proceeded MA in 1644. The following year he became a fellow of Emmanuel, tutoring among others the future bishop Richard Kidder, who entered the college in 1649, and who later recorded that Cradock 'did not only direct me in my studies, but made me sensible of my obligation to lead a life of religion' (*Life of Richard Kidder*, 3–4).

Cradock was sequestered into the living of Little Berkhamsted, Hertfordshire, on 26 July 1645, but on 18 October he complained to the committee for plundered ministers that the sequestered rector had refused to surrender the parsonage. On 11 June 1646 he was ordered to show cause why he was not officiating there, and gave the reason that he had been appointed rector of Baughurst in Hampshire in December 1645. On 10 October 1649 he was incorporated MA at Oxford, and obtained his BD at Cambridge in 1651. He was presented on 18 March 1653 to the rectory of Worplesdon in Surrey.

Cradock resigned his fellowship at Emmanuel in 1656 and on 24 June that year married Honoria (*bap*. 1628, *d*. 1709), daughter of Charles Fleetwood of the Vache, Chalfont St Giles, Buckinghamshire, sister of the regicide George Fleetwood, and second cousin of General Charles Fleetwood. They had two sons and four daughters; one son, Samuel, and two daughters predeceased him. The marriage was no doubt made possible by Cradock's presentation in 1656 to the college living of North Cadbury, Somerset, worth £300 per annum. His material circumstances were made even more comfortable in 1657 when he inherited the estate at Geesings, Wickhambrook, Suffolk, which was bequeathed to him by his cousin Walter Cradock. In 1659 Cradock published *Knowledge and practice, or, A plain discourse of the chief things necessary to be known, believed and practised in order to salvation*, which was written for his congregation at North Cadbury and which contained a recommendatory epistle from Edward Reynolds, the future bishop of Norwich. This work went through several editions before his death. Following the Restoration, Cradock was presented by the crown to North Cadbury, but he was ejected by the Act of Uniformity in 1662, his successor being instituted in January 1663.

Cradock continued to preach and to write, publishing *A Catechism on the Principles of the Christian Faith* and *The Harmony of the Four Evangelists* in 1668, the latter somewhat fortuitously after John Tillotson had 'preserved it from the flames' during the great fire of London in 1666 (Birch, 363); it was reprinted four times before 1685. In 1669 he was noted as one of the nonconformists preaching at a conventicle held at 'widow Fleetwood's' (presumably his sister-in-law, the widow of George Fleetwood) at the Park in Chalfont St Giles. In 1672 he published *The Apostolical History* and on 2 April he obtained a licence for a presbyterian meeting at Geesings, where he continued to live and preach for the next twenty-four years while maintaining excellent relations with the Church of England vicar. He also opened a dissenting academy, charging £20 per annum, plus £2 for his assistant in 1674 when one of Lord Wharton's younger sons was a pupil. Edmund Calamy was a pupil in 1686–8, and was taught 'logic, natural and moral philosophy and metaphysics' by Cradock, of whom he wrote, 'he lived upon his own estate, kept a good house, and was much respected by the gentlemen all round the country' (*Calamy rev.*, 140–41). Calamy also thought Cradock 'a man of a serious spirit, of solid judgement, of digested thought, of a clear method, and an unaffected style' (*Nonconformist's Memorial*, 3.180). In 1679 Cradock published *A Serious Dissuasive from some of the Reigning and Customary Sins of the Times. The History of the Old Testament Methodised* followed in 1683. His final published work was *A Plain and Brief Exposition and Paraphrase on the Revelation* (1690).

Cradock remained at Geesings until 1696 when provision was made on an adjoining estate for the performance of dissenting worship. He then left for Bishop's Stortford, Hertfordshire, where he continued to preach and he became pastor of the congregational church in nearby Stansted-Mountfitchet, where a meeting-house was erected in 1698. He died, aged eighty-five, on 7 October 1706 and was buried on the 11th at Wickhambrook. Samuel Bury, a minister from Bury St Edmunds, preached a funeral sermon on 18 October. Cradock was succeeded by his son Walter who had been called to the bar of the Middle Temple in 1690.                    STUART HANDLEY

**Sources** Calamy rev., 140–41 • Venn, *Alum. Cant.* • Wood, *Ath. Oxon.*, new edn, 4.123–4 • *The nonconformist's memorial … originally written by … Edmund Calamy*, ed. S. Palmer, [3rd cdn], 3 (1803), 178–81 • H. I. Longden, *Northamptonshire and Rutland clergy from 1500*, ed. P. I. King and others, 16 vols. in 6, Northamptonshire RS (1938–52), vol. 3, p. 279 • Foster, *Alum. Oxon.* • T. Birch, *The life of the Most Reverend Dr John Tillotson, lord archbishop of Canterbury*, 2nd edn (1753), 363 • J. C. Whitebrook, 'Samuel Cradock, cleric and pietist (1620–1706)', *Congregational History Society Transactions*, 5, 3–13 • S. Bury, *A funeral sermon occasioned by the death of the late Reverend Samuel Cradock B. D.* (1707) • *The life of Richard Kidder, D. D., bishop of Bath and Wells written by himself*, ed. A. E. Robinson, Somerset RS, 37 (1922), 3–4 • E. Calamy, *An historical account of my own life, with some reflections on the times I have lived in, 1671–1731*, ed. J. T. Rutt, 2 vols. (1829), vol. 1, pp. 132–5 • will of Samuel Cradock, PRO, PROB 11/226, fol. 180v • will of Walter Cradock, PRO, PROB 11/263, fol. 248 • *Buckinghamshire dissent and parish life, 1669–1712*, ed. J. Broad, Buckinghamshire RS, 28 (1993), 9 • IGI
**Likenesses** R. White, line engraving (after oil painting by unknown artist), BM, NPG; repro. in S. Cradock, *Knowledge and practice*, 4th edn (1702) • oils, DWL • portrait, BL, Add. MS 32352, fol. 40

**Cradock, Walter** (c.1606–1659), Independent minister, was born at Trefela in the parish of Llan-gwm Uchaf, near Usk, Monmouthshire, the eldest son of William Cradock, from a family with an estate of about £60 a year. Suggestions that he attended Oxford University cannot be substantiated, but he was curate first at Peterston-super-Ely in Glamorgan, and subsequently at Cardiff, where he served under the radical vicar, William Erbury. In 1633 Cradock was suspended from preaching for refusing Charles I's Book of Sports and left Cardiff for Wrexham where he stayed for a year and converted Morgan Llwyd. He spent time in parishes in the marches of Wales, where he encountered Richard Baxter at Shrewsbury. On 8 May 1638 he was in London, where he worshipped illegally and was summoned before the court of high commission; he never appeared, having left for Llanfair Waterdine, Shropshire, where he joined a separatist group. Here he came to the not uncritical attention of Brilliana, Lady Harley, who thought that Cradock sometimes did 'not judge clearly of things' (*Letters*, 26), and Stanley Gower, who thought him a Brownist.

In November 1639 Cradock returned to his native county to play a leading part in the founding of the Independent church at Llanfaches, but was forced with other Welsh radical preachers, on the outbreak of civil war, to move first to Bristol, and then, after witnessing the siege of that city by the royalists in 1643, to London. There he became a state-supported lecturer at All Hallows-the-Great, Thames Street, where he remained until 1646. He had already, in June 1641, petitioned parliament to supply godly preachers for Wales, and in July 1646 preached to the House of Commons on the inadequacy of the Welsh ministry, particularly in the Welsh language. On 19 October of that year Cradock was licensed and financed by parliament to preach in Wales as an itinerant, and based himself in Monmouthshire. Shortly afterwards Thomas Edwards denounced him as an antinomian, because of his preaching on Christian liberty. In 1647 Cradock, possibly aided by Vavasor Powell, brought out a version of the Bible in Welsh, and in 1648 he was on hand to observe the fall of Chepstow to Oliver Cromwell at the end of the second civil war in Wales.

In February 1650 Cradock was the first-named minister among those listed as itinerant preachers under the Act for the Propagation of the Gospel in Wales. He was energetic in support of this scheme, and preached as far from his own territory as Presteigne, Radnorshire. Unlike his fellow itinerants Powell and Llwyd, Cradock was not attracted to millenarian notions; he differed from them also in his positive view of the state-funded ministry. After the propagation scheme had fizzled out Cradock was settled, on 25 March 1653, as the minister at Usk, and responded to

*A Word for God*, Powell's hostile petition against the protectorate, with *A Humble Representation and Address* which took a supportive line towards Cromwell's religious policies; this was signed by over 700 people and presented to Cromwell on 4 February 1656. At Usk, Cradock was disturbed by Quakers, who considered him 'the chiefest priest in South Wales' (Gawler, 26), and invoked the powers of local magistrates to be rid of them. Nevertheless, he advised the Broadmead church, Bristol, not to expel Quakers from their midst, and served on the commission invited to consider the readmission of Jews to England, evidence of his broad theological sympathies. Cradock's fame rested on his preaching, which emphasized the joy and liberty of the Christian life. His works published in the later 1640s and early 1650s were all sermons. His lack of enthusiasm for millenarianism and the support he lent those struggling to maintain a state church cost him the friendship of some leading Welsh radical ministers during his lifetime, while his continual concern to stress the freedom of Christians led Baxter to re-open Edwards's attack on Cradock as an antinomian long after the latter's death. Baxter may have been responding to Cradock's enduring reputation; nearly a century after his death Methodists in north Wales found themselves called 'Cradockites'.

Cradock had married Catherine Langford, one of the nine daughters of Richard and Elizabeth Langford of Trefalun, Wrexham. The couple had two daughters, Eunice, and Lois, who married Richard Creed, clerk to the south Wales commissioners for the propagation of the gospel. Cradock himself is described as having been 'tall, pitted with small-pox … very robust, capable of much hardship and fatigue … affectionate, yet warm and hasty' (Charles and Jones, 173). He died on 24 December 1659 at Llan-gwm, where he was then living and where he was buried in the chancel of the church. His executor was his son-in-law Richard Creed.                STEPHEN K. ROBERTS

**Sources** T. Richards, *A history of the puritan movement in Wales* (1920) · DWB · G. Parry, 'Richard Creed: Mab yng Nghyfraith Walter Cradoc', *National Library of Wales Journal*, 24 (1985–6), 392–4 · G. F. Nuttall, *The Welsh saints, 1640–1660* (1957) · T. Rees, *History of protestant nonconformity in Wales*, 2nd edn (1883) · NL Wales, Clenennau MS 630 · T. Edwards, *Gangraena, or, A catalogue and discovery of many of the errours, heresies, blasphemies and pernicious practices of the sectaries of this time*, 3 (1646), 163 · *Letters of the Lady Brilliana Harley*, ed. T. T. Lewis, CS, 58 (1854), 26, 77 · F. Gawler, *A record of some persecutions … in south Wales* (1659) · *Gweithiau Morgan Llywd o Wynedd*, 1–2, ed. T. E. Ellis and J. H. Davies (1899–1908) · R. Baxter, *Catholick communion defended*, 2 vols. (1684) · [T. Charles and T. Jones], *Trysorfa ysbrydol* (1799–1801) · Greaves & Zaller, BDBR, 187–90 · J. Ballinger, *The Bible in Wales: a study in the history of the Welsh people* (1906), 30

**Cradock, Zachary** (1632/3–1695), college head, was the second son of Samuel Cradock, vicar of Greetham, Rutland (*d.* 1653), and younger brother of Samuel *Cradock (1620/21–1706). He followed his elder brother to Emmanuel College, Cambridge, where he was admitted pensioner on 29 May 1647, matriculating in the same year. He graduated BA in 1651. In 1650 he became chaplain of King's, taking his MA as a member of that college in 1654.

On 2 August 1654 he was elected a fellow of Queens' College, Cambridge (which he remained until 1659). In October 1656 Ralph Cudworth recommended him to Secretary Thurloe for appointment as chaplain to the English merchant community in Lisbon, having 'assured and particular knowledge of his great worth, both for piety and learning' (Thurloe, 5.522). Cradock occurs in this post in October 1657.

Some time after the Restoration Cradock, who proceeded BD in 1661 and DD in 1666, was made a chaplain to Charles II and preacher to Gray's Inn. In 1670 the king nominated him during an episcopal vacancy to a residentiary canonry and the prebend of Firle in Chichester Cathedral, with dispensation from residence while again in Portugal on public service. He was admitted on 8 and 11 February and retained his stall to death. He was also rector of Pett, Sussex.

On 2 December 1671 Cradock was appointed a fellow of Eton College. He frequently deputized for Provost Allestree, and on 24 December 1681 was elected to succeed him. The provostship was 'tug'd hard for' by Edmund Waller (Wood, *Ath. Oxon.*, 3.1272), but the privy council (to whom the king had referred the fellows' objections) ruled that Waller, a layman, was ineligible. Etonians then and later scoffed at Cradock's lowly connections (his elder brother being a nonconformist minister and the younger a London grocer). As provost he most memorably took objection to the practice of gated scholars having wine hoisted up to them in baskets.

Cradock's wider repute rested on his oratory; he was 'esteemed the best preacher of his age' (Lansdowne MS 987, fol. 117). Archbishop Sharp of York said that he felt unworthy to follow Cradock into the same pulpit. John Evelyn heard him many times, and always found his sermons 'pious & cleare & very sound divinity' (Evelyn, 4.196). He spoke extempore, but would often don his spectacles and affect to read from what, in fact, were blank pages in front of him. A sermon before the king on 10 February 1678 'upon the providence of God in the government of the world' was well received, and was published five times in Cradock's lifetime. This he liked to call his 'Works', having printed nothing else. Despite his great fluency in discourse, he allegedly had no patience for writing. Another sermon, preached at Eton, was published after his death as [Charity] *The Great End and Design of Christianity* (1706 and 1740). Cradock may probably be identified as donor of Charles I's works to Lambeth Palace Library.

Cradock was offered, but declined, for reasons of health, the deanery of Lincoln following the death of Daniel Brevint in May 1695. Cradock himself died on 16 October 1695, aged sixty-two, and was buried in Eton College chapel. He had never married. He bequeathed £40 to the poor of Eton, and £50 to Chichester Cathedral for prospective repairs to the west end (probably meaning a scheme of Christopher Wren's which was never put into effect). Thomas Richardson, fellow of Eton, received Cradock's month clock and the best of his books. Among his family Cradock mentioned his married sisters Massey and

Brooke, and his nephews Samuel Jordan and Zachary and Walter Wells. His younger brother John, of Aldgate (the grocer), was his executor.    C. S. KNIGHTON

**Sources** Venn, *Alum. Cant.*, 1/1.411 • Wood, *Ath. Oxon.*, new edn, 3.1272 • Thurloe, *State papers*, 5.522–3 • Evelyn, *Diary*, 4.4, 196, 278 • *Private correspondence and miscellaneous papers of Samuel Pepys, 1679–1703*, ed. J. R. Tanner, 2 (1926), 77 • *CSP dom.*, 1657–8, 466; 1670, 48; 1671, 515, 520, 576; 1695, 58 • A. C. Benson, *Fasti Etonenses* (1899), 87–9 • W. Sterry, ed., *The Eton College register, 1441–1698* (1943), xxviii, xxxi • W. Sterry, *Annals of the King's College of Our Lady of Eton beside Windsor* (1898), 143, 152–3 • H. C. Maxwell Lyte, *A history of Eton College, 1440–1898*, 3rd edn (1899), 272, 275, 278–9, 285–6 • *Fasti Angl., 1541–1857*, [Chichester], 29, 77 • BL, Lansdowne MS 987, fol. 117 • M. Hobbs, ed., *Chichester Cathedral: an historical survey* (1994), 145 • PRO, PROB 11/428, fols. 52–52v
**Likenesses** attrib. J. Greenhill, oils, Eton; repro. in Benson, *Fasti Etonenses* • portrait, Eton, provost's lodge
**Wealth at death** £350—specific cash legacies; residue to executor: will, PRO, PROB 11/428, fols. 52–52v

**Cradocke, Edward** (*fl.* 1552–1594), theologian and alchemist, was born in Staffordshire but spent most of his life at Oxford. Having matriculated at Christ Church in 1552 at the age of sixteen, he completed the BA (11 January 1556) and MA (10 February 1560), and immediately entered holy orders. Under Queen Mary he had embraced Catholicism but he reverted to the reformed church after Elizabeth's accession. Anthony Wood implies that he was elected Lady Margaret professor of theology (24 October 1565; annual stipend £20) only 'upon a great scarcity of Protestant divines in the university' (Wood, 1.632), but Cradocke soon completed two degrees in divinity (BTh, 1565; DTh, 1566) and held the Lady Margaret chair for nearly thirty years, far longer than any other incumbent. Since the professorship was tenable only upon biennial election by the doctors, inceptors, and bachelors (that is, advanced students) of theology, Cradocke perhaps merited Wood's more generous claim that he was 'numbered among the learned men of his time' (Wood, 1.633). John Strype calls him 'eminently learned', noting that he was a member of the 1562 synod convened by Matthew Parker, archbishop of Canterbury, at which the Thirty-Nine Articles were revised, and that in 1570 Parker preferred him in two ways: on 7 April Cradocke received the rectorship of St Mary Aldermary, London; and on 4 August he was made 'one of the Preachers in the Cathedral Church of Canterbury' (Strype, 316). Cradocke held both the London benefice and the Oxford chair until he resigned them in 1594. It is not known where or when he died, but in 1599 Simon Forman reminded himself to 'write to doctor Cradok of oxford for his sonn' (Bodl. Oxf., MS Ashmole 219, fol. 182). The 'sonn' may be an alchemical or a biological son.

Aside from one unpublished sermon (BL, MS Sloane 2987, fols. 73–6; another is reported in Add. MS 38492, fol. 88), Cradocke's only known theological writing is a 469-page discourse on God's providence, *The Shippe of Assured Safetie* (1572). A dedicatory epistle (to Robert Dudley, earl of Leicester and chancellor of the university, signed 19 May 1572) and a preface tell circumstantially how the plague suspended public lectures and sent most Oxonians flying. Staying behind and inspired by 'Goddes

Prouident care' for himself, the queen, Leicester, and 'the whole state of this realme', he 'compyled' his book (Cradocke, *Shippe*, sigs. A2–A6) during this visitation. Though theologically moderate, the work occasionally hints at Cradocke's scientific interests: for example, providential order is seen in astral influences and in 'the Anatomie of mans bodie'; 'as the lighte of nature', natural philosophy 'is not to be despised' (Cradocke, *Shippe*, 21–46).

Cradocke's only other publications are two twelve-line Latin poems—a tribute to Bishop John Jewel in Lawrence Humphrey's *Joannis Juelli Angli* (1573) and commendatory verses in Robert Peterson's translation of Giovanni della Casa's *Galateo* (1576). In the preface to *The Shippe*, Cradocke refers cryptically to an unpublished book 'in the latine tong', ready for the press 'a fewe yeres ago', that might have brought him renown.

If theology was Cradocke's public profession, alchemy was his chief avocation, having 'addicted himself' to its pursuit for 'many years' (Wood, 1.632). He knew the alchemists John Dee, who visited him at Oxford for three days in 1581, and Simon Forman, and wrote three undated alchemical works—a brief Latin prose text, 'Lapis philosophicus est duarum materiarum' (Bodl. Oxf., MS Ashmole 1408), a lengthy Latin poem, 'Tractatus de lapide philosophico, latinus versibus conscriptus' (Bodl. Oxf., MS Ashmole 1415), and 'A Treatise in English Verse vpon the Philosopher's Stone' (in R. M. Schuler, ed., *Alchemical Poetry, 1575–1700*, 1995). Both poems are dedicated to Queen Elizabeth. The English work, a coherent compilation of late medieval alchemical theory and practice, sees the alchemist as God's agent through whom art perfects nature in producing gold, and as 'a special instrument' of the church who can materially aid the spread of the gospel. For Cradocke, alchemy, no less than theology, was a divine calling.    ROBERT M. SCHULER

**Sources** Wood, *Ath. Oxon.* • Tanner, *Bibl. Brit.-Hib.* • J. Strype, *The life and acts of Matthew Parker* (1711) • E. Cradocke, *The shippe of assured safetie, wherein wee may sayle without danger towards the land of the liuing, promised to the true Israelites* (1572) • E. Cradocke, 'A treatise touching the philosopher's stone', *Alchemical poetry 1575–1700, from previously unpublished manuscripts*, ed. R. M. Schuler (1995), 3–48 • G. D. Duncan, 'Public lectures and professorial chairs', *Hist. U. Oxf. 3: Colleg. univ.*, 335–61 • *The private diary of Dr John Dee*, ed. J. O. Halliwell, CS, 19 (1842) • A. L. Rowse, *Simon Forman: sex and society in Shakespeare's age* (1974) • W. H. Black, *A descriptive, analytical and critical catalogue of the manuscripts bequeathed unto the University of Oxford by Elias Ashmole*, 2 vols. (1845–66) • Bodl. Oxf., MS Ashmole 219, fol. 182
**Archives** BL, Lansdowne MSS • BL, Sloane MSS • Bodl. Oxf., Ashmole MSS

**Craft** [*née* Smith], **Ellen** (1825/6–1891), slavery abolitionist, was born into slavery in Clinton, Georgia, the daughter of Major James Smith and Maria, one of his slaves. In 1837, aged eleven, she was given to her mistress's daughter, Eliza, on her marriage to Dr Robert Collins of Macon, Georgia. As a favourite servant the conditions of her slavery were mild. In Macon she met William *Craft (c.1825–1900), a slave apprenticed as a carpenter, and they were married about 1847.

Afraid of being separated from one another or having

future children taken away to be sold, the Crafts devised a plan in late 1848 to escape to the north. Ellen, who could pass for white, disguised herself as a slave master travelling to Philadelphia for medical treatment while William, who was darker-skinned, acted as her servant. Ellen put her right hand in a sling to avoid having to write her name, and wrapped up her face to reduce the need to converse with strangers during the journey. With Christmas holiday passes from their masters the slave couple escaped without arousing suspicion. William had saved some money, as slave artisans sometimes could, which paid for Ellen's clothes and their fares, first on a train to Savannah and then by boat, train, and coach to Philadelphia. Four days after leaving Macon they were being hidden by a Quaker family outside Philadelphia. Three weeks later they moved on, no longer in disguise, to the safety of Boston.

For the next eighteen months the Crafts lived in Boston safe, they thought, from possible recapture. Ellen worked as a seamstress, William as a cabinet-maker. Befriended by William Wells Brown, an anti-slavery lecturer and himself an escaped slave, they recounted their stories at many anti-slavery meetings, becoming well known among Boston's 2000-strong black community, about 20 per cent of whom were also fugitive slaves. The Fugitive Slave Bill in September 1850 threatened their freedom; within three days of the bill's passage some forty fugitive slaves fled Boston for Canada. In October 1850 two agents of Ellen and William's Georgia masters arrived in Boston intent on seizing them, but through a combination of legal suits and public protests the agents were forced to leave Boston without them.

On 7 November 1850 Ellen and William were 'officially' married by Theodore Parker (their earlier 'slave' marriage not being legally recognized). Later the same month they left Boston for England, travelling via Maine, Nova Scotia, and New Brunswick, where they caught the steamer for Liverpool. England was the safest, most logical haven; it had harboured fugitive slaves from America for many years. The Crafts toured widely with William Wells Brown in Scotland and the north and west of England, publicizing the slavery issue at public meetings and talks. With help from English abolitionists they studied for several years in the early 1850s at a trade school for rural youth in Ockham, Surrey. Here they learned to read and write, and also taught some manual skills to their fellow pupils.

Ellen and William had five children, all born in England: Charles Estlin Phillips (b. 1852), William, Stephen Brougham Dennoce (known as Brougham), Alice Isabella Ellen (known as Ellen), and Alfred. Both Crafts continued to be involved in the anti-slavery movement. Ellen was adamant that she would not return to live under a regime which endorsed slavery: 'I had much rather starve in England, a free woman, than be a slave for the best man that ever breathed upon the American continent' (*Anti-Slavery Advocate*, December 1852). After leaving Ockham the Crafts settled in London. From 1857 to 1867 their home was 12 Cambridge Road (afterwards renamed 26 Cambridge Grove), Hammersmith. *Running a Thousand Miles for Freedom*, the story of their early life and escape written by William Craft, was published in London in 1860 and was an immediate success.

During the 1860s William made two visits to Dahomey (Benin), his aims including that of bringing an end to the slave trade there. Ellen, who remained in England with the children, was active in the British and Foreign Freed-Men's Aid Society, and also raised money for a boys' school in Dahomey which her husband had founded and a girls' school in Sierra Leone. Through the efforts of friends, in November 1865 Ellen's mother, Maria, was brought over to London to join the family.

In August 1869, American slavery now abolished, the family (except for William junior and Brougham, who remained in England to continue their education until 1873) returned on the *Siberia* to Boston, where they lived for a time before buying a plantation at Woodville, Ways Station, in Bryan county, Georgia. The plantation was run as a co-operative to allow freed slaves to escape contract labour. Ellen died in 1891, in Bryan county, and was buried at her request near a favourite oak tree on the plantation.

JEROME FARRELL

**Sources** W. Craft, *Running a thousand miles for freedom, or, The escape of William and Ellen Craft from slavery* (1860) · R. J. M. Blackett, 'The odyssey of William and Ellen Craft', *Beating against the barriers: biographical essays in nineteenth-century Afro-American history* (1986) · K. Coleman and C. S. Gurr, eds., *Dictionary of Georgia biography*, 2 vols. (Athens, GA, 1983) · L. Gara, *Notable American women, 1607–1950: a biographical dictionary*, ed. E. T. James (1971) [article on Ellen Craft] · *West London Observer* (13 Feb 1858) · *West London Observer* (18 Dec 1858) · parish baptismal registers, 1850–69, Ockham, Surrey · census returns for Hammersmith, 1861 · directories, Hammersmith, 1850–69 · rate books, Hammersmith, 1850–69, Hammersmith and Fulham Archives and Local History Centre, London · 'Letter from Ellen Craft', *Anti-Slavery Advocate*, 3 (Dec 1852), 22

**Archives** Bodl. Oxf. · Hammersmith and Fulham Archives and Local History Centre, London

**Likenesses** daguerreotype, repro. in Craft, *Running a thousand miles* · engraving?, repro. in Blackett, 'The odyssey of William and Ellen Croft', a, 86

**Craft, William** (c.1825–1900), slavery abolitionist, was born into slavery in Georgia, and apprenticed as a carpenter in Macon. His family was broken up when his parents, brother, and sister were sold separately to pay off their master's debts. At the age of sixteen William was mortgaged to the local bank to raise capital to speculate in the cotton boom, and was later sold to the bank cashier to meet his master's mortgage payments. His new master, Ira H. Taylor, sent him back to the cabinet shop where he had been apprenticed. He married another slave, Ellen *Craft, née Smith (1825/6–1891), about 1847, and in December 1848 the two made a daring escape to the north.

The Crafts spent about eighteen months in Boston, where William worked as a cabinet-maker. In September 1850 the Fugitive Slave Bill threatened their freedom, and two agents of their Georgia masters arrived in Boston intent on recapturing the couple, who were 'legally' married on 7 November 1850 and had their first child in 1852. The Crafts had by then established themselves as leading members of Boston's black community, William having given an anti-slavery lecture tour with another fugitive slave, William Wells Brown, in January 1849; the community rallied to their defence, and the agents were forced to leave without them. The Crafts left Boston late in 1850 and, like other American fugitive slaves, sought refuge in England.

In Britain the Crafts participated with William Wells Brown in immensely popular lecture tours on the evils of slavery, travelling widely throughout Scotland and the north and west of England. They then spent three years at an agricultural school in Ockham, Surrey, supported financially by Lady Byron and others, which was to be the model for the schools that Craft later founded in Dahomey and Georgia.

After leaving Ockham, Craft returned to lecturing, continuing to denounce slavery and also promoting the boycott of slave-grown produce. In May 1859 the London Emancipation Committee, which aimed to influence British opinion against American slavery, was formed; the Crafts were both executive committee members. They published the story of their escape in *Running a Thousand Miles for Freedom* in 1860. Craft afterwards turned his attention to Africa, and in 1862 visited Dahomey (Benin) in the hope of persuading the king to abandon human sacrifices, cease participating in the slave trade, and encourage the cultivation of cotton. Craft's first short visit to Dahomey was followed in 1863 by a three-year stay, during which he opened a school at Ouidah and acted as an agent for the Company of African Merchants.

After William's return to London, in 1867 the Crafts concentrated on raising money for their planned return to Georgia, where they hoped to run a co-operative plantation which would allow freed slaves to escape contract labour. Leaving England in 1869 they lived in Boston briefly before returning south, first to Hickory Hill, South Carolina, then to Woodville, an 1800 acre plantation at Ways Station in Bryan county, Georgia. Their egalitarian farming methods met with resistance from neighbouring planters and Craft was also accused of mismanaging funds collected for the Woodville Co-operative Farm School which he had opened for seventy-five boys and girls to attend free of charge. Severe financial problems dogged the latter years of his life. Craft died on 28 January 1900 at the Charleston house of his daughter Ellen and her husband Dr William Demos Crum, and was buried in the Humane Friendly burial-ground in that city.

The return of the Crafts to America after the civil war to work with freed slaves showed courage and a commitment to improving the lot of Georgia's black population. Craft's activities in Dahomey may also have contributed to ending the slave trade there. The couple's famous escape from slavery and their many public lectures undoubtedly did much to further the abolitionist cause in both Britain and America.                                         JEROME FARRELL

**Sources** W. Craft, *Running a thousand miles for freedom, or, The escape of William and Ellen Craft from slavery* (1860) · R. J. M. Blackett, 'The odyssey of William and Ellen Craft', *Beating against the barriers: biographical essays in nineteenth-century Afro-American history* (1986) · K. Coleman and C. S. Gurr, eds., *Dictionary of Georgia biography*, 2 vols. (Athens, GA, 1983) · *Savannah Tribune* (17 Feb 1900) [quotes obit. in *Charleston enquirer*] · *West London Observer* (13 Feb 1858) · *West London Observer* (18 Dec 1858) · *Aberdeen Journal* (12 Feb 1851) · *British Friend*, 28 (1870), 92–3
**Archives** Bodl. Oxf. | Hammersmith and Fulham Archives and Local History Centre, London, Charles Chapman collection
**Likenesses** engravings, repro. in Blackett, 'The odyssey of William and Ellen Craft', 86, 111
**Wealth at death** minimal; almost bankrupt

**Craft, William H.** (1730x35–1805/1811), enamel painter, was employed at the Battersea enamel works in London. He was probably a relation, perhaps a brother, of Thomas Craft, who was employed at the porcelain works at Bow, and who produced the bowl now in the British Museum to which he affixed an account of its production, rendering it one of the few authenticated pieces of Bow china. Some evidence is given by Foskett that Craft may be identified with a William Craft or Croft of Tottenham, born *c*.1730. It is believed that from 1768 Craft was working in partnership with David Rhodes for Wedgwood in London. An artist named William Craft, aged thirty-nine, is recorded entering the Royal Academy Schools on 4 November 1774.

A prolific artist, William Craft exhibited numerous enamels at the Royal Academy in the years 1774–81 and from 1794 to 1795 painted portraits and subject pieces in enamel, clock faces, and landscapes. About 1798 he completed a series of works commemorating the naval heroes of the period. These enamels depicting Earl Howe, Earl St Vincent, Viscount Duncan, and Baron Nelson featured the names and dates of their victories. Most examples painted before 1782 were signed W. Craft. Other portrait enamels include a miniature of Lavinia, Countess Spencer, after Reynolds, signed and dated 1787 (priv. coll.) and large enamel portraits of Sir William Hamilton, dated 1802, are in the British Museum and the Ashmolean Museum, Oxford. A number of examples of his work are in the National Gallery, Dublin, including a self-portrait dated 1780. Foskett notes two possible dates of death, 1805 and 1811 (Foskett, 519).          L. H. CUST, rev. MICHAEL MARKER

**Sources** D. Foskett, *A dictionary of British miniature painters*, 2 vols. (1972) · Redgrave, *Artists* · H. Blättel, *International dictionary miniature painters / Internationales Lexikon Miniatur-Maler* (1992) · W. Chaffers, *Marks and monograms on European and Oriental pottery and porcelain: the British section*, 15th rev. edn, ed. G. A. Godden (1965) · Bénézit, *Dict.*, 4th edn · private information (1887)
**Likenesses** W. Craft, self-portrait, enamel on copper, 1780, NG Ire.

**Cragg, Robert** (*fl.* 1682–1689), conspirator and rebel, made three journeys between London and the Netherlands, under the alias of John Smith, in March–April of 1685, carrying messages between the surviving whig opposition in England and the exiled duke of Monmouth, who was preparing his ill-fated rebellion of June–July 1685. These communications carried by Cragg had a material impact upon the form which the rebellion took, and upon its outcome. Cragg was well suited to the role of messenger because he was, at the time, a minor figure and completely unknown to the government and its agents. He was an associate of the radical printer William Disney from about 1682 and seems to have made at least part of his living by distributing subversive pamphlets. In 1684 he was spreading a pamphlet which alleged that the whig earl of Essex had not committed suicide in the Tower before his trial in 1683, but had been murdered by government order. In 1684 he also ferried materials for another pamphlet on this dangerous subject to Amsterdam, to the radical preacher Robert Ferguson, and this experience in smuggling subversive material also recommended him for his missions in 1685.

At the beginning of March 1685 Disney paid Cragg to take an oral message to the duke of Monmouth in Amsterdam asking whether he intended to participate in the earl of Argyll's planned rebellion in the highlands, word of which had reached the radicals in England. In his confession written after the rebellion Cragg claimed that he did no more than deliver this message to Ferguson (who was acting for Monmouth), and that he did not see the duke. Other accounts, also confessions written after the rebellion, assert that Cragg not only saw Monmouth but went well beyond his instructions, saying that there would be much support, in men and money, if Monmouth invaded England while Argyll raised Scotland. Possibly Ferguson (who strongly wanted a rebellion) conveyed a lying account of his interview with Cragg to the duke, who was still uncertain whether a rebellion should be attempted. In any case Cragg then made two further journeys between London and Amsterdam during March and April, each time now conveying negative messages from England that there was no money or support to be had there and that Monmouth would do better to join with Argyll's venture, and returning with angry demands from the duke for money, armed men, and co-ordinated action from his former supporters. Cragg gives a telling account of the fear, incompetence, and lack of trust which prevented many potential allies from supporting the 1685 rebellion, so contributing to its failure.

As the venture came to its end at Sedgemoor, Cragg experienced a personal tragedy with the death of his wife and child. He did not escape abroad and was arrested in December 1685. There were rumours that before his arrest he had blackmailed prominent whigs contacted before the rebellion, and one exile wished that Cragg had been killed to silence him. However, though Cragg was held in prison for nine months and put under considerable pressure, his confession failed directly to incriminate surviving whig grandees such as Lord Delamere and the earl of Macclesfield, as James II undoubtedly hoped it would. After the 1688 revolution he was questioned by the privy council as to whether he had, in fact, been suborned to testify against these men. At the same time he was applying for assistance to John Wildman, now postmaster-general and dispenser of much patronage, but to no effect, and after 1689 he is not heard of again.

ROBIN CLIFTON

**Sources** R. L. Greaves, *Secrets of the kingdom: British radicals from the Popish Plot to the revolution of 1688–89* (1992) · D. J. Milne, 'The Rye House plot with special reference to its place in the exclusion contest and its consequences till 1685', PhD diss., U. Lond., 1949 · *The manuscripts of the House of Lords*, 4 vols., HMC, 17 (1887–94), vol. 2, pp. 393–408 [Robert Cragg's confession, Dec 1685] · R. Clifton, *The last popular rebellion: the western rising of 1685* (1984) · *CSP dom.*, 1682–9 · J. Ferguson, *Robert Ferguson the plotter: the secret of the Rye-house conspiracy and the story of a strange career* (1887) · Ford, Lord Grey, *The secret history of the Rye-House plot: and of Monmouth's rebellion* (1754) · C. Price, *Cold Caleb* [1956] · M. Ashley, *John Wildman, plotter and postmaster: a study of the English republican movement in the seventeenth century* (1947)

**Craggs, James, the elder** (*bap.* 1657, *d.* 1721), politician and government official, was the eldest son of Anthony Craggs (*d.* 1680?) of Holbeck, in Wolsingham parish, Durham, and Anne (1628–1672), daughter of the Revd Ferdinando Morecroft, rector of Stanhope in Wardell, Durham, and prebendary of Durham. He was born at Wyserley and baptized at Wolsingham on 10 June 1657. He was educated at the free grammar school at Bishop Auckland. At twenty-one he joined with his father in cutting off the entail and selling the whole of the family property. Forced to make his own way in the world, he travelled to London in 1680. After serving the duke of York and the earl of Peterborough, he became steward to the latter's son-in-law, the duke of Norfolk, in 1684. He was evidently sufficiently established to marry on 3 January 1684 at London, St Benet Paul's Wharf, Elizabeth (*c.*1662–1712), daughter of Jacob Richards, a corn chandler of Westminster, who was reputedly a maidservant to Lady Marlborough. They had three sons, only one of whom, James *Craggs the younger (1686–1721), survived infancy, and three daughters. It was his connection with the Marlboroughs which saw Craggs prosper. Arthur Maynwaring was later to write to Lady Marlborough that he liked 'to dine with a man [Craggs] that always drinks your health first' (BL, Add. MS 61459, fol. 153). It may have been his financial acumen which recommended Craggs to Lady Marlborough in the first instance: by the 1690s he was acting as the earl of Marlborough's private secretary while branching out into army clothing contracts and financial brokerage, paying particular attention to the East India Company. His refusal to submit his clothing accounts to the parliamentary commissioners of public accounts saw him committed to the Tower on 7 March 1695 for obstructing their inquiries. While in the Tower it was revealed that Craggs had received the largest single payment disbursed by the governor of the East India Company, Sir Thomas Cooke, part of it for his own use in the campaign to maintain the company's monopoly. In 1700 he was appointed secretary to the commission for stating the debts due to the army, but also continued his involvement in the East India Company. He served as a director of the old company in 1700–01 and 1702–5, and having been involved in the negotiations between the old and new East India companies, in 1702–4 he was chosen as a manager of the united company.

The accession of Queen Anne increased Craggs's prospects of official employment, associated as he was with the Marlboroughs. He was elected to parliament for Grampound, a seat presumably made available to him because of his close links with Marlborough and Lord Godolphin. Marlborough was keen to accommodate Craggs with an office, writing in August 1702 that he should be kept in good humour 'for I shall be able to make more use of him,

James Craggs the elder (*bap.* 1657, *d.* 1721), attrib. John Closterman, *c.*1710

than of any ten others' (Snyder, 109). In December 1702 Craggs was appointed as secretary to the master-general of the ordnance, Marlborough, adding the place of clerk of the deliveries on 18 June 1703. He retained the latter until March 1711 and his secretaryship until Marlborough's dismissal at the end of that year. In parliament Craggs supported the ministry, being sure to attend regularly, but his real importance as a politician lay in his access to Marlborough and the way in which the duke used him as an intermediary with other political groups. His colleague at the ordnance, James Lowther, wrote in 1705, 'Mr Craggs … is a very notable man and is in the secrets of the Duke of Marlborough and the present ministry and has explained a great many useful things to me which I could not but guess at before' (Cumbria AS, Carlisle, Lonsdale MSS D/Lons/W2/2/8, Lowther to Sir John Lowther of Whitehaven, 1 May 1705). With the disintegration of the predominantly whig ministry led by Lord Godolphin in the summer of 1710 Craggs was employed as a go-between to the new ministers, chiefly, the duke of Shrewsbury and Robert Harley, and later Henry St John. He was also moving closer to the ousted whig leaders, especially the earl of Sunderland, Marlborough's son-in-law. In the parliamentary attack on Marlborough which followed the duke's dismissal at the end of 1711 Craggs defended his mentor, particularly over his claims to be captain-general for life. With Marlborough in exile from the end of 1712, Craggs continued to participate in the whig opposition to the tory ministry. However, he lost his seat at the 1713 election.

With the accession of George I, Craggs was soon re-instated as clerk of deliveries of the ordnance, being promoted in 1715 to joint postmaster-general. However, he failed to regain a seat in the Commons. He now worked for Sunderland, his activities centred on the ministry's relationship with the City's leading business interests. He was also forward in promoting the career of his son, James, who was rapidly gaining stature as a politician in his own right. As a leading proprietor of South Sea stock he was an obvious candidate to join with the chancellor of the exchequer, John Aislabie, in negotiating the scheme whereby the government's debt was to be converted into South Sea stock in 1719. When the share price of the company's stock began to fall dramatically in the autumn of 1720, he was at the centre of attempts to remedy the situation, hosting a series of discussions between the company, the government and the Bank of England. However, as a close associate of the company's chief cashier, Robert Knight, he was deeply implicated when the South Sea Bubble burst. The Commons inquiry into the company's finances reported in January 1721 that he had received £30,000 worth of stock for which he had not paid, plus £50,000 on behalf of Sunderland. The death of his son on 16 February 1721 seemed to destroy him and he died on 16 March of apoplexy, although there were reports that it was suicide. He was buried at Charlton in Kent on 28 March. His death provided a convenient scapegoat for the ministry and he was found to have encouraged the South Sea scheme for his own profit. His estate was forced to pay £68,920 in compensation, a relatively insignificant amount considering that his estate was valued at £1,500,000, or £14,000 per annum. The bulk of his property lay in the Lewisham and Greenwich area and was divided between his three daughters: Margaret, the wife of Samuel Trefusis MP, Elizabeth, the wife of Edward Eliot MP, and Anne, the wife of John Newsham MP.

STUART HANDLEY

**Sources** HoP, *Commons, 1690–1715* [draft] · *Miscellanea Genealogica et Heraldica*, 2 (1869–76), 34–9 · A. Boyer, *The political state of Great Britain*, 21 (1721), 312; 22 (1721), 442–4 · *Hasted's history of Kent: corrected, enlarged, and continued to the present time*, ed. H. H. Drake (1886), 132, 140, 143 · IGI [Durham, London] · *The Marlborough–Godolphin correspondence*, ed. H. L. Snyder, 3 vols. (1975) · BL, Add. MSS 61164, 61459 · James Lowther to Sir John Lowther, 2nd bt, 1 May 1705, Cumbria AS, Carlisle, Lonsdale papers, D/Lons/W2/2/8 · H. C. Tomlinson, *Guns and government: the ordnance office under the later Stuarts*, Royal Historical Society Studies in History, 15 (1979), 225–6
**Archives** BL, letters in the Blenheim papers, Add. MS 61135 · BL, letters to duchess of Marlborough, Add. MS 61351 · BL, letters to duke of Marlborough, Add. MSS 61164–61166 · BL, letters to duke and duchess of Marlborough, Stowe MS 751 · BL, letters to Sunderland, Add. MS 61577
**Likenesses** G. Kneller, portrait, 1709 · attrib. J. Closterman, oils, *c.*1710, NPG [*see illus.*] · M. Dahl, oils, *c.*1719–1721, General Post Office, London · G. Vertue, engraving, 1728 (after G. Kneller, 1709), BM, NPG · J. Thornhill, portrait, 1887, Port Eliot; in possession of the earl of St Germans, 1887
**Wealth at death** £1,500,000; £14,000 p.a. at death: Boyer, *Political state*

**Craggs, James, the younger** (1686–1721), diplomatist and politician, was born in Westminster, London, on 9 April 1686, the second but only surviving son of James *Craggs the elder (*bap.* 1657, *d.* 1721), postmaster-general, and his wife, Elizabeth (*d.* 1712), the daughter of Jacob Richards, a corn chandler of Westminster. He was sent to Monsieur le Fevre's school in Chelsea and completed his education by travelling extensively on the continent, initially under the supervision of a friend of his father, Richard Hill, who in 1703 was the envoy to Savoy. In 1704 he was ordered home by his father on account of his financial extravagance, but he went abroad again in 1706, this time to Germany. Most of his time was spent in Hanover, where he gained the favour of the elector's half-sister, the countess von Platen (and reputedly became her lover). In order to take advantage of the knowledge he had gained on his travels his father solicited a diplomatic posting, presumably using his influence with the duke of Marlborough, and on 8 April 1708 Craggs received his credentials as secretary to the envoy to Spain, James Stanhope. He arrived in Barcelona on 29 May. Back in London in September 1708 he lobbied Godolphin and Marlborough to be made resident minister in Spain because Stanhope was expected to be absent for long periods on campaign. On 29 September he duly received his credentials as resident. For the next few years he was deeply involved in the diplomatic network linking Stanhope, Marlborough, and the ministry in London, and consequently travelled much between Spain, Italy, the Dutch republic, and Germany. In October 1710 he was back in London. Although he was promoted to envoy in March 1711, he returned to Spain because his appointment was quickly superseded.

The disgrace of Marlborough at the end of 1711 saw his father dismissed from his employments and Craggs himself out of favour. A seat in parliament was found for him at Tregony in Cornwall at the 1713 election, presumably on the interest of Hugh Boscawen, later first Viscount Falmouth. Once in the Commons he joined the Hanover Club, a repository of whig sentiment, and was prominent in the defence of Richard Steele when the latter was expelled from the house on 18 March 1714. No doubt owing to his knowledge of Hanover, Craggs was chosen by the privy council on 31 July to convey to the elector the news that the queen was dying.

Under the new dynasty Craggs was rewarded with the place of cofferer to the prince of Wales, which may well have been promised him before the death of Queen Anne. Re-election for Tregony followed in 1715, and November of that year saw him in Lancashire following the defeat of the Jacobites at Preston. On 13 April 1717 he was promoted to the secretaryship of war, although the quarrel between the king and the prince of Wales led him to resign his household post in December of that year. On 15 March 1718 he was advanced to the secretaryship of state for the south, complete with a place on the privy council. John Oldmixon recounted that his predecessor as secretary, Joseph Addison, believed Craggs to be 'as fit a man for it as any in the kingdom; and that he never knew any man who had a greater genius for business, whether in parliament or out of parliament' (Oldmixon, 659). Craggs himself saw his new post as a stepping stone to greater things. In May 1718 he wrote: 'after I have continued some two or three

years more where I am … I should be glad to rise higher' (Carswell, 106–7).

As a leading member of the Stanhope–Sunderland ministry in the Commons, Craggs had to defend the government from the attacks of the tories and the dissident whigs under Robert Walpole. On one occasion, during a debate on half-pay officers on 22 January 1718, he responded to Walpole's jibes about his inexperience with the riposte that he would stick to his opinions and 'not imitate them who changed theirs, as they were in or out of place' (Cobbett, *Parl. hist.*, 7.534). Craggs was a notable defender of the Peerage Bill in 1719, even though it was reputed that he disliked the measure. In the company of the chancellor, John Aislabie, he was a manager of the legislation which converted the national debt into South Sea stock. Altogether he subscribed £11,000 to buy stock and managed lists of subscribers accounting for stock worth nearly £691,500. Although he himself was not a beneficiary of the free distribution of stock, he did arrange for the king's mistresses to benefit. His father and his patron, Sunderland, were also beneficiaries, so that when the bubble burst he found himself under pressure. On 4 January 1721 he replied to an attack by William Shippen on unnamed 'great men' who had perpetrated the fraud by proclaiming his readiness 'to give satisfaction to any man who should question him either in that house or out of it' (ibid., 7.694). After the uproar that followed he explained that he meant merely to clear his conduct. Ironically, Craggs died of smallpox on 16 February 1721, the very day in which the first report of the secret committee inquiring into the bubble was presented to the Commons. He was buried on 2 March in the north aisle of Henry VII's chapel in Westminster Abbey. The interment took place at night to avoid potential riots, although his distinguished pallbearers included Spencer Compton, then speaker of the Commons, and Henry Pelham.

Few contemporaries had a bad word for the amiable Craggs, who was always compared favourably to his father. Described in 1711 as 'a very silly vain young fellow' (*Portland MSS*, 7.30), he was more often portrayed as 'open, generous and well natured' (*Fourteenth Report*, HMC, 511). While doubts about his abilities were expressed, his performance in office overcame most of these. His friend Alexander Pope produced the verses for his tomb and wrote on another occasion: 'there never lived a more worthy nature, a more disinterested mind'. Le Neve contented himself with the thought: 'here lies the last that died before the first of the family' (Carswell, 193), a reference to Craggs's father, who survived him by only a month. Although unmarried at the time of his death, Craggs had a natural daughter, Harriot, with the actress Hester Santlow (*c.*1690–1773) [*see* Booth, Hester]. She married, on 4 March 1726, the politician Richard Eliot (1694–1748). Her eldest son was created Baron Eliot on 13 January 1784. Her second husband, the Hon. John Hamilton, brother of James, first Viscount Hamilton, drowned on 18 December 1755; the only child by this marriage succeeded as second Viscount Hamilton. STUART HANDLEY

**Sources** R. R. Sedgwick, 'Craggs, James', HoP, *Commons* · J. Carswell, *The South Sea Bubble*, rev. edn (1993) · BL, Add. MS 61147, fols. 165–235 · BL, Add. MS 61517, fols. 1–61 · P. G. M. Dickson, *The financial revolution in England: a study in the development of public credit, 1688–1756* (1967); repr. (1993) · *The Marlborough–Godolphin correspondence*, ed. H. L. Snyder, 3 vols. (1975) · H. J. Jackson, *Miscellanea Genealogica et Heraldica*, 2 (1869–76), 37–8 · J. Oldmixon, *The history of England, during the reigns of King William and Queen Mary, Queen Anne, King George I* (1735) · Cobbett, *Parl. hist.* · *The manuscripts of his grace the duke of Portland*, 10 vols., HMC, 29 (1891–1931), vol. 7 · *Fourteenth report*, HMC (1896)

**Archives** BL, corresp., Add. MSS 15867, 15936, 16481 · Devon RO, corresp. and papers · FM Cam., family corresp., incl. letters to his daughter, Ann Newsham | BL, letters to James Dayrolle, Add. MS 15867 · BL, corresp. with Charles Whitworth, Add. MSS 37368–37383 · BL, letters to H. Worsley, Add. MS 15936 · CAC Cam., corresp. with Thomas Earle · CKS, corresp. with Lord Stanhope · NA Scot., corresp. with Lord Polwarth · NRA, priv. coll., letters to Sir John Norris · NYPL, corresp. with Lord Stair

**Likenesses** studio of G. Kneller, oils, *c*.1708, NPG · J. Simon, mezzotint, 1720, NPG · G. Vertue, line engraving, 1720 (after oil painting by studio of G. Kneller, *c*.1708), NPG · G. B. Guelfi, marble statue on monument, Westminster Abbey, London · C. Knight, stipple (after G. Kneller), NPG

**Craghead, Robert** (*c*.1633–1711), minister of the Presbyterian General Synod of Ulster and author, was born in Scotland to unknown parents and graduated MA from the University of St Andrews in 1653. In 1658 he commenced his ministry in Donoughmore, co. Donegal. In 1661 he was one of thirty-six Presbyterian ministers in Ireland ejected from his parish for refusing to conform to the established church. He remained with his people and contrived to exercise an effective ministry among them. The troubles of 1689 drove him and his family into the besieged city of Londonderry, and from it to Glasgow, where for a time he ministered in a congregation.

On 1 July 1690 he was called to be minister of the Presbyterian congregation in Londonderry, and remained there until his death. The bishop of Derry from 1691 to 1702 was William King, afterwards archbishop of Dublin. King had already crossed swords with Joseph Boyse, minister of Wood Street congregation in Dublin, on the subject of Presbyterian worship, hoping to persuade his readers to follow his own pilgrimage from Presbyterianism to Anglicanism. His representations of Presbyterian practice were factually incorrect, and Craghead felt impelled to answer them in two pamphlets, *An Answer to a Late Book Intituled 'A Discourse Concerning the Inventions of Men in the Worship of God'* (1694) and *An Answer to the Bishop of Derry's Second Admonition to the Dissenting Inhabitants of his Diocese* (1697). Neither work reveals Craghead as a particularly effective controversialist. His replies to King are orderly, thorough, and factual. They contain a wealth of information about Presbyterian life and spirituality, and especially about Presbyterian public worship. They confirm the very large numbers attending Presbyterian services in north-west Ulster at this time. While Boyse and Craghead display common purpose in their defence of Presbyterian forms of worship, it is fascinating to discern contrasting views on points of detail. Boyse reflects the broader and more English practice of Dublin Presbyterianism, while the stricter Ulster-Scot ethos of northern congregations is

firmly embodied in Craghead's work. Craghead's pamphlets lack the grace of Boyse's writing, and the fire of good polemic, but are none the less an important contribution.

Craghead's other writings were of a devotional and practical kind. His *Advice for the Assurance of Salvation* (1702) and the posthumous *Walking with God* (1712) have both been lost to posterity. His *Advice to Communicants* was first published in Glasgow in 1695, and was reprinted several times. It was an attempt to deal with many of the problems and difficulties felt by the ordinary people with whom Craghead worked as a pastor. It is a rich treasure house of Christian devotion and evidences the scrupulous care given by Craghead and others of his generation to the doubts and questions of his people. Through all his writings runs a firm Calvinist theology. Craghead married Agnes, daughter of the Revd John Hart, minister of Taughboyne, and they had three sons: Thomas, Robert, and Samuel. Craghead died in Londonderry on 22 August 1711. His son **Robert Craghead** (1684–1738) received a classical education at local schools before studying philosophy at Glasgow (1700) and Edinburgh universities and divinity at Leiden, whence he graduated MA in 1702. Following his return to Ireland he was licensed by the Londonderry presbytery and ordained minister at Capel Street, Dublin, on 11 October 1709. He proved to be a popular preacher and served as moderator of the General Synod of Ulster in 1719. While orthodox in doctrine, he wrote in support of the non-subscribers in the controversy over subscription to the Westminster confession and attempted to reconcile the two parties. He remained minister at Capel Street until his death in Dublin on 31 July 1738. His elder brother, Thomas (*d*. 1739), became minister of Donegal and Ballyshannon on 6 July 1698. In 1714 he emigrated to Boston on the ship *Thomas and Jane* and ministered in New England until his death in Hopewell in April 1739.

A. W. GODFREY BROWN

**Sources** T. Witherow, *Historical and literary memorials of presbyterianism in Ireland, 1623–1731* (1879) · J. S. Reid and W. D. Killen, *History of the Presbyterian church in Ireland*, new edn, 3 vols. (1867) · A. W. G. Brown, 'Irish Presbyterian theology in the early eighteenth century', PhD diss., Queen's University of Belfast, 1977 · J. S. Reid, *History of congregations of the Presbyterian church in Ireland*, ed. W. D. Killen (1886) · J. McConnell and others, eds., *Fasti of the Irish Presbyterian church, 1613–1840*, rev. S. G. McConnell, 2 vols. in 12 pts (1935–51) · J. Abernethy, 'A short account of the author', preface, in R. Craghead, *The true terms of Christian and ministerial communion founded on scripture alone* (1739)

**Craghead, Robert** (1684–1738). *See under* Craghead, Robert (*c*.1633–1711).

**Craig** [Craige], **Alexander,** of Rosecraig (1567?–1627), poet, was born in Banff, the son probably of William Craig (*fl*. 1560–1600), also burgess of that town. He entered St Leonard's College, University of St Andrews, in 1582, and graduated MA in 1586. He became a notary in his home town, but it seems that he followed King James to London about 1603, for his first book of poems, *The Poeticall Essays of Alexander Craige, Scoto-Britane*, was published in London in 1604, with a complimentary sonnet by Robert Ayton

(1570–1638), his fellow student at St Andrews, then a courtier. He was a legal secretary in the service of George, earl of Dunbar, in 1606, and 'upon consideratioun of the gude, trew and thankfull service done to his hienes' (but not specified), a royal pension of £400 Scots for his lifetime was awarded to Craig on 9 December 1605 and ratified two years later, on 11 August 1607 (*APS*, 4.389). It was paid, sometimes irregularly, at least until 1623. His second volume of poems, *The Amorose Songes, Sonets, and Elegies of M Alexander Craige, Scoto-Britaine*, was also printed in London, in 1606. At this time, he returned, or perhaps retired, to his native Banff (one of the poems in the 1606 volume is signed 'A. C. Scoto-Banfa'). Before 1609 he married Isabel Chisholm, with whom he had at least one son, James, and he purchased a house and land at Mayen, 6 miles north of Huntly by the River Deveron, in 1609. He had already acquired his permanent home of Rosecraig in Banff, thought to have been a site in the grounds of the old castle, which he described in a Latin epigram as 'a small house with a decent garden, comfortably furnished, and a little slope that yields me masses of roses' (*Poeticall Recreations*, 1623, 35).

Notwithstanding the habitual flattery of his king and patrons in his verse, Craig appears to have sought only a quiet life in Banff: he published no more in England, and his third volume of verse, *The Poeticall Recreations of Mr Alexander Craig of Rosecraig*, was published by the king's printer, Thomas Finlason, in Edinburgh in 1609. In 1617, when King James was progressing through Scotland, Craig presented an address of welcome at Kinnaird Castle, near Perth, subsequently printed in *The Muses Welcome to the High and Mighty Prince James* (1618). In 1621 he was commissioner for the burgh of Banff in the Scots parliament, and in 1623 published his last volume of verse, rather strangely using the title of his 1609 volume for a different set of poems: *The Poeticall Recreations of Mr Alexander Craig of Rose-Craig, Scoto-Britan* (Aberdeen, 1623). 'Kind, cunning Craig', as his friend Alexander Gardyne called him (A. Gardyne, *A Garden of Grave and Godlie Flowers*, 1609), is thought to have died at Banff in 1627; his son, James, was served heir to him on 20 December 1627. His wife remarried almost immediately, and died after 1653.

After his death his Aberdeen printer, Edward Raban, published *The Pilgrime and Heremite, in Forme of a Dialogue, by Master Alexander Craig* (1631), a curious long alliterative poem of which only one printed copy survives, lacking one signature, now in the Huntington Library. A complete version, copied in 1631 from a somewhat different authorial manuscript, was incorporated about 1705 into the commonplace book of William Thoirs of Muiresk (NL Scot., Adv. MS 35.4.14). Craig's poetry is mostly miscellaneous short verse: epigrams, Petrarchan sonnets, couplet verse, epideictic and dedicatory poems, thoroughly conventional, sometimes light and pleasant, but in its ostentation of learning and alliterative phrasing old-fashioned, even when he first published in London. All his known poetry, including verses written for the books of friends such as Alexander Gardyne, Patrick Gordon, and Sir John Scot, was reprinted with a biographical introduction by David Laing for the Hunterian Club: *The Poetical Works of Alexander Craig of Rose-Craig* (1873). Prior to that his address of welcome to King James and some other verse appeared in *Various Pieces of Fugitive Scottish Poetry* (1st ser., 1825; 2nd ser., 1853). MICHAEL R. G. SPILLER

**Sources** The poetical works of Alexander Craig of Rose-Craig, ed. D. Laing (1873) · Reg. PCS, 1st ser. · J. M. Thomson and others, eds., Registrum magni sigilli regum Scotorum / The register of the great seal of Scotland, 11 vols. (1882–1914), vols. 1–9 · register of sasines for Banff, NA Scot. · APS, 1593–1625 · matriculation and graduation records, U. St Andr.
**Archives** NL Scot., Adv. MS 35.4.14
**Wealth at death** Rosecraig, land at Mayen near Rothiemay; plus several crofts at Banff

**Craig, Archibald Campbell** (1888–1985), Church of Scotland minister, was born on 3 December 1888 at the Free Church manse, Forestfield, Kelso, the youngest of eleven children of Alexander McRae Craig, Free Church minister, and his wife, Margaret (Maggie) Cathcart, *née* Forrest. The atmosphere of his father's manse was devout and loving, and instilled in him a zest for learning, a deep sense of Christian reverence, and an appreciation of moral integrity. After schooling at Kelso high school he studied arts and subsequently divinity (the latter interrupted by the First World War) at Edinburgh University. He was actively involved in the Student Christian Movement while a student and witnessed the historic 1910 World Missionary Conference. His distinguished intelligence work with the Royal Scots resulted in his being decorated with the MC, and his experience of the war, in which his brother Forrest died, both turned him into a pacifist and convinced him of the merits of the good soldier. After a year working in the slum areas of Edinburgh's Pleasance district under the tutelage of Dr Harry Millar, and lecturing part time for Norman Kemp-Smith at the University of Edinburgh in philosophy, Craig was inducted in 1921 to Erskine Free Church in Galston, Ayrshire; the economic and political conditions in this mining area made a lasting impact on his Christian sense of the church's social mission. His pastoral and preaching gifts were conspicuous, and resulted in a further call in 1926 to Hillhead United Free Church in Glasgow, a lively student-filled congregation.

From then on Craig's life was in many respects pioneering. In 1930 he was invited to become Glasgow University's first full-time chaplain, a position he relished and developed with vigour among staff and students alike. In 1938 he was awarded his first DD degree, from Edinburgh University. (Subsequent ones came in his moderatorial year, 1961–2, from Glasgow, and from Trinity College, Dublin.) He also visited the huge missionary conference at Tambaram, near Madras, south India, in 1938, reinforcing his awareness of the ecumenical movement.

Throughout the Second World War, Craig served as the first general secretary of the British Council of Churches, based in London. He created grass-roots ecumenical activity all around the country through a series of 'religion and life' weeks, and worked with many who were to be founding fathers of the World Council of Churches in 1948, including William Temple, Reinhold Niebuhr, and Pitney van Dusen. Absence from a meeting in 1945 meant that he avoided a flying bomb which killed and injured several colleagues. After returning to Scotland in 1946 he spent a year as deputy leader of the Iona community, sharing George MacLeod's vision of a church renewed by ecumenical, social, political, and liturgical integrity. Probably owing to his suspected pacifist leanings, Craig was passed over for a chair of practical theology at Edinburgh in 1946. He nevertheless became the first incumbent of a lectureship in biblical studies, a new position in Glasgow's arts faculty in the following year. His lively and vigorous teaching impressed a generation of students. He was also deeply involved in the Scottish Churches Council and various other networks, pursuing deeper sharing of interdenominational life and faith. In 1950 he married Mary (May) Isobel Laidlaw, whom he had met first in Kelso forty-four years earlier.

The inter-church relations committee of the Church of Scotland, which Craig chaired, was instructed in May 1953 to renew earlier conversations with the Church of England, the Scottish Episcopal church, and the English Presbyterian church. It led to four years of massive media controversy, nicknamed 'the bishops' debate', centred on the issue of whether the Church of Scotland should move towards some form of episcopacy. In the end this controversy prompted Craig's saddened resignation from the post. In spite of that, the church nominated him moderator in 1961, and he spent a lively year (aged seventy-three), including a first ever formal visit to the Vatican to meet Pope John XXIII.

Craig's subsequent 24-year retirement was packed with activity, lecturing, writing, preaching, gardening, and, latterly, devoting himself to tender caring for May, who began to suffer from senile dementia. His main published works were *University Sermons* (1938), *Preaching in a Scientific Age* (1954), *God Comes Four Times* (1956), *The Church in the World* (1961), and *Jesus* (1968). He retained a lifelong concern that Christian faith should engage in open conversation with every area of secular knowledge—science, history, literary scholarship, psychology—and deplored clericalism in the church and any form of intellectual or moral sloth in the Christian community.

A man of huge warmth and geniality, intellectual energy, courage, wit, and integrity, Craig maintained a lifelong and voluminous correspondence with friends dating back to his Galston days. His skills as preacher, broadcaster, and lecturer won huge appreciation, and his contribution to burgeoning ecumenical life in the UK and beyond was immense. Craig died, aged ninety-six, at St John's Muir Crescent, Doune, Perthshire, on 26 August 1985, the day of his wife's funeral.

ELIZABETH TEMPLETON

**Sources** U. Edin., New Coll. L., Craig MSS · E. Templeton, *God's February: a life of Archie Craig* (1991) · b. cert. · d. cert.
**Archives** NRA, priv. coll., corresp. and papers · U. Edin., New Coll. L., corresp. and papers
**Wealth at death** £165,595.11: confirmation, 8 Oct 1985, *CCI*

**Craig, Edith Ailsa Geraldine** (1869–1947), theatre director and costumier, was born on 9 December 1869 at Gusterwoods Common, Hertfordshire, the first of two children of the actress Dame Ellen Alice *Terry (1847–1928) and Edward William *Godwin (1833–1886), architect, with whom Terry had eloped in 1868. The family lived in Fallows Green, Harpenden, Hertfordshire, designed by Godwin, until 1874. After her separation from Godwin in 1875, Terry was primary carer (helped by housekeeper Mrs 'Boo' Rumball) for Edith Craig and her brother (Edward Henry) Gordon *Craig (1872–1966). Terry's second husband, Charles Wardell (whom she married in 1877), provided a parental figure for the children such that Edith took the name Wardell. However, Terry's third husband, James Carew (whom she married in 1907), met with Edith Craig's disapproval. Craig was educated at Mrs Cole's school, a co-educational institution in Foxton Road, Earls Court, London; the Royal Academy of Music; by Alexis Hollander in Berlin, Germany from 1887 to 1890; and intermittently by Elizabeth Malleson of Dixton Manor Hall, Winchcombe, Gloucestershire.

Craig worked for the Lyceum Theatre company, designing costumes and acting under the stage name of Ailsa Craig, touring America in 1895 and 1907. Craig appeared with Henry Irving in a number of plays, such as *The Bells* (1895) by Leopold Lewis. In 1895 her performances in Sir Arthur Wing Pinero's *Bygones* and Charles Reade's *The Lyons Mail* respectively were praised by George Bernard Shaw and Eleanora Duse. Craig acted in plays by G. B. Shaw and H. Ibsen, toured with Mrs Brown Potter and the Independent Theatre, and was stage director for her mother on tour after she left the Lyceum Theatre.

With financial backing from her mother Craig started a business, Edith Craig & Co., producing costumes for several London theatre productions. During Terry's lease of the Imperial Theatre, Edith Craig collaborated with her mother and brother on various productions. In 1902–3 she collaborated with the artist Pamela Colman Smith on the design of scenes for W. B. Yeats's *Where there is Nothing* and J. M. Synge's *The Well of the Saints*. Craig was an active member of several significant theatre societies which produced experimental drama in London; some of them directly challenged the lord chamberlain's regulation of the stage: the Independent Theatre; the Stage Society; the Masquers; the Pioneer Players; the Phoenix Society; and the Renaissance Theatre Society.

Craig was active in the women's suffrage movement, selling newspapers in the street and working at branch level for the Women's Freedom League after getting into conversation with a woman selling its paper in the street. A member of many suffrage organizations, she worked in a professional capacity for the Actresses' Franchise League and independently on numerous successful suffrage productions. Craig notably directed *A Pageant of Great Women*, a play she devised with the writer and actor Cicely Hamilton. This was performed nationwide with audiences in some cases of 2000.

Craig consolidated her work as a director with the Pioneer Players (1911–25), the London-based theatre society

**Edith Ailsa Geraldine Craig (1869–1947)**, by Alfred Ellis, pubd 1895

which she founded. Under Craig's leadership this society became internationally known for promoting women's work in the theatre. It performed significant plays by women such as Susan Glaspell (*Trifles*, 1919, and *The Verge*, 1925), 'Hrotsvit' (*Paphnutius*, 1914), and Christopher St John (*The First Actress*, 1911, and *Macrena*, 1912). It also became renowned for its support of progressive political campaigns and its production of a number of significant translated plays by dramatists such as Paul Claudel, Anton Chekhov, Nikolay Eveinov, and Saint-Georges de Bouhelier.

After the Pioneer Players was effectively wound up in 1920, Craig worked on several productions in London and the provinces. Notable productions included nativity plays in London and York; John Fletcher's *The Faithful Shepherdesse* (1923), formerly directed by Craig's father, Godwin; Hugo von Hofmannstahl's *The Great World Theatre* (1924); the first modern production of John Webster's *The White Devil* (1925); and George Bernard Shaw's *Back to Methuselah* (1930). In the 1920s work took Craig to Hampstead, where she directed plays for the Everyman Theatre, and to Yorkshire as art director for Leeds Art Theatre. Craig valued the traditions of stagecraft but she also welcomed innovations in the theatre and film. Her expertise in the latter medium was demonstrated by her performance in *Fires of Fate* (1923), a film adaptation of a story by Sir Arthur Conan Doyle.

After her mother died in 1928, Craig began her campaign for a fitting memorial. In 1929 the barn in the grounds of Ellen Terry's house in Smallhythe Place, Tenterden, Kent, was converted into a theatre where Craig directed performances on the anniversary of Ellen Terry's death. The Priest's House, next door to Ellen Terry's house, Craig's home, became a dynamic cultural centre, attracting Radclyffe Hall and her partner Una Troubridge, together with Vita Sackville West and Virginia Woolf.

Active in teaching and adjudicating amateur theatricals for the British Drama League, the Women's Institute, and the British Empire Shakespeare Society, Craig gave one of the prestigious Shute lectures at the University of Liverpool in 1935. She developed a national reputation for her pageant productions at Mount Grace Priory, Northallerton, Yorkshire (1927) and the Tenterden jubilee pageant (1935). The Chilham pageant (1946) was Craig's last work.

Craig lived with the writer Christabel Marshall (known as Christopher Marie *St John) from 1899, when the two women shared a flat at 7 Smith Square, London. They lived in a flat in Adelphi Terrace House from 1907 to 1909 before moving to 31 Bedford Street, Covent Garden, where they were joined in 1916 by Clare *Atwood (known as Tony) (1866–1962), the artist, forming a permanent *ménage à trois* about which George Bernard Shaw urged St John to write. Although Craig rarely wrote, she was involved in some publications relating to her mother and to Bernard Shaw which provoked a rift in the relationship with her brother. Edward Gordon Craig's *Ellen Terry and her Secret Self* (1931) explicitly objected to *Ellen Terry and Bernard Shaw: a Correspondence* (1931) edited by St John. In 1932 Craig co-edited with St John *Ellen Terry's Memoirs*, responding to her brother's representation of their mother. Craig had taken on other family responsibilities that year, having adopted Ruby Chelta Craig, daughter of Edward Gordon Craig's son. Craig was reconciled with her brother some time before her death.

Opinions differed about Craig's personality. Some found her domineering and difficult to work with, while others enthused about her professionalism and inspirational effect on newcomers to the profession. May Whitty remembered her as a 'magician'. Craig's friends claimed that she was denied opportunities to establish herself in a permanent theatre; Lilian Baylis is said to have excluded her from a post at the Old Vic. However, Craig worked successfully on several collaborations and was credited with numerous directorial achievements—so much so, that George Bernard Shaw claimed that 'Gordon Craig has made himself the most famous producer in Europe by dint of never producing anything, while Edith Craig remains the most obscure by dint of producing everything' (Holledge, 162). Craig's work in the theatre received national press coverage yet she has rarely featured in theatre histories or biographies or autobiographies of her contemporaries. Overshadowed by her mother and brother, Craig has received recent critical re-evaluation by feminist critics, particularly in the ground-breaking work on Edwardian actresses by Julie Holledge (1981) and Katharine Cockin (1998). Literary portraits of Edith Craig have been claimed for Virginia Woolf's pageant organizer, Miss La Trobe, in *Between the*

*Acts* (1941) and for Clemence Dane's possessive daughter, Blanche Carroll, in *Eighty in the Shade* (1958).

Rheumatism prevented Craig from pursuing a musical career as a pianist. Later in life she had restricted mobility although she was reluctant to allow this to affect her work. Craig died of coronary thrombosis and chronic myocarditis on 27 March 1947 at Priest's House, Smallhythe Place, Tenterden, Kent, and her body was cremated.					KATHARINE COCKIN

**Sources** K. Cockin, *Edith Craig (1869–1947): dramatic lives* (1998) · E. Adlard, ed., *Edy: recollections of Edith Craig* (1949) · *Ellen Terry's memoirs*, ed. E. Craig and C. St John, rev. edn (1933) [with notes and biographical chapters by eds.] · *Ellen Terry and Bernard Shaw: a correspondence*, ed. C. St John (1931) · E. Terry, *The story of my life* (1908) · J. Holledge, *Innocent flowers: women in the Edwardian theatre* (1981) · M. Webster, *The same only different: five generations of a great theatre family* (1969) · N. Auerbach, *Ellen Terry: player in her time* (1987) · J. Melville, *Ellen and Edy* (1987) · D. Sinden, *Laughter in the second act* (1985)

**Archives** BL · Ellen Terry Memorial Museum, Smallhythe, Kent, archive · Theatre Museum, London | FILM BFI NFTVA

**Likenesses** A. Ellis, photograph, pubd 1895, NPG [*see illus.*] · C. Atwood, oils, Ellen Terry Memorial Museum, Kent · L. Connell, photograph, Ellen Terry Memorial Museum, Kent · M. Leon, photograph, Ellen Terry Memorial Museum, Kent

**Wealth at death** £14,747 19s. 2d.: probate, 4 Sept 1947, *CGPLA Eng. & Wales*

**Craig, Edward Anthony** [Teddy; *pseud.* Edward Carrick] (1905–1998), film and stage designer and artist, was born on 3 January 1905 in London, the third child and first son of (Edward Henry) Gordon *Craig (1872–1966), the renowned theatrical designer, and Elena Fortuna Meo (1879–1957), a virtuoso violinist. Theatre and art were in his blood. His paternal grandparents were the actress Ellen *Terry (1847–1928) and the architect and designer Edward *Godwin (1833–1886); his maternal grandfather was the artist Gaetano Meo (1849–1925), whose commissions included mosaics in St Paul's and Westminster cathedrals and Ernest Debenham's London mansion.

Gordon Craig lived a turbulent, romantic existence, and was absent for most of Teddy's infant years, which were spent in Southminster, Essex. Teddy never had a formal education, instead living a bohemian life, travelling around Europe with his parents and sister Nelly; he had periods in London and Kent with Ellen Terry, but the family finally settled in Rapallo on the Italian riviera. At the age of twelve he became his father's pupil assistant. Craig was a temperamental and impatient taskmaster, who expected him to become a Renaissance man on the wing. Teddy mastered a vast range of crafts, becoming an expert draughtsman, model-maker, wood-engraver, printer, and photographer, helping his father to produce the journal *The Mask* and other publications.

By 1926 Teddy had become his father's indispensable helpmate and business manager, and seemed destined to spend his life in his father's shadow. But he was determined to become independent, taking the first steps in 1923 by adopting a pseudonym, 'E. Carrick', for his wood-engravings ('carrick' being the Irish equivalent of the Scottish 'craig'). When his father sent him to London in 1927 Teddy jumped at the opportunity to break free.

Edward Anthony Craig (1905–1998), by unknown photographer

Armed with charm, enthusiasm, and boundless talent, he kept himself afloat by designing book jackets, selling wood-engravings, and writing art criticism. But like his father he was a man of vision, and he saw cinema as the art of the future.

A chance meeting with his step-grandfather, the actor James Carew, led to Craig's first break into the film world. In 1927 Edward Carrick, as he was to be known professionally for the rest of his film career, began working for the enlightened film-maker George Pearson at the Welsh-Pearson-Elder company, at Stoll Studios, Cricklewood. His first film was directed by Theodore Komisarjevsky, and he was soon being touted in the press as the youngest art director in England. With the security of his new job Carrick married Helen Ruskin Godfrey (1899–1960), the sister of an architect, on 23 October 1928, at the Paddington register office, London. Their two children, John (b. 1931) and Helen (b. 1934), followed the family's artistic path, John as an illustrator, Helen as a photographer and an author–illustrator of children's books. Following the collapse of Pearson's Cricklewood operations owing to the advent of sound, Carrick earned a precarious freelance living. He persuaded the restaurateur Peppino Leoni to display art at his Quo Vadis restaurant in Soho, founding the 'Grubb Group' of artists, who held annual shows throughout the 1930s. Along with wood-engraving and book illustration, writing also kept Carrick busy: he became one of cinema's first practitioners to write extensively about design.

Carrick also painted murals on commission. One was for the stage director Basil Dean. About to go into film production, he invited Carrick to become the art director at his new studios in Ealing. Carrick worked there from 1931 to 1935, designing, among others, the screen version of John Galsworthy's *Loyalties* (1933), a trio of Gracie Fields musicals, *Lorna Doone* (1934), and *Midshipman Easy* (1935), for which he built an ingenious ship atop scaffolding on the studio lot. Carrick's attention to period detail for *Lorna Doone* was much admired, and several of his designs were acquired by the Victoria and Albert Museum. By now Carrick was in demand, and in 1935 he became art director for the short-lived Criterion Film Productions, founded by Douglas Fairbanks jun. and Marcel Hellman.

Carrick was always generous in sponsoring and nurturing new talent, and in 1937 he founded the first film school in England, the AAT (Associated Artist Technicians') School, at 14 Soho Square. After bomb damage caused its abrupt closure early in the war, Carrick continued to formulate his ideas, teaching and inspiring people through his groundbreaking textbook on art direction, *Designing for Moving Pictures* (1941; revised in 1949 as *Designing for Films*). Although film was Carrick's primary occupation, throughout the 1930s he was also busy designing London stage productions, including *Macbeth* at the Old Vic (1932), Emlyn Williams's psychological thriller *Night must Fall* (1935), and J. B. Priestley's allegory *Johnson over Jordan* (1939). During the war years Carrick's gift for scenic realism proved invaluable as art director for the Crown Film Unit and the various service documentary units. Working with directors like Humphrey Jennings, Harry Watt, and Pat Jackson on such classic documentaries as *Target for To-Night* (1941), *Fires were Started* (1943), and *Western Approaches* (1944), Carrick made a direct contribution to the war effort, coping all the while with budgetary and rationing restrictions and government red tape.

After the war Crown's output shifted to peacetime concerns. When Crown moved from its base at Pinewood Studios, Carrick stayed to become supervising art director for the Rank Organization. Here he gave many new talents their first film work, and proved a gifted administrator as executive art director for Rank's umbrella organization, Independent Producers. Always active in promoting film design as an art form, Carrick continued to write and lecture about film-making and design. He became one of the prime movers behind the first British film designers' guild, the Society of British Film Art Directors and Designers. He also organized the society's showcase exhibition 'British Film Art' at the Victoria and Albert Museum in 1948, and compiled an invaluable related catalogue, *Art and design in the British film: a pictorial directory of British art directors and their work* (1948).

Through all the vicissitudes of the industry in the 1950s and early 1960s Carrick continued to design films, primarily as a freelance, bending his talents to a range of material: wartime stories (*Gift Horse*, 1951), thrillers (*Tiger Bay*, 1959), romantic comedies, pop musicals, Hammer horror (*The Nanny*, 1965, starring Bette Davis). In 1960 he did his only designing for television, of *Macbeth* for America's prestigious series Hallmark Hall of Fame; filmed in colour on location in Scotland with Maurice Evans and Judith Anderson, it was a play he knew well, as he had designed productions at the Old Vic in 1932 and Stratford in 1949. In 1965 he retired from film design to concentrate on research, writing, and lecturing. He wrote a biography of his father, *Gordon Craig: the Story of his Life*, which was published in 1968 two years after Craig's death, and a book about baroque theatre construction, a subject dear to his heart.

Carrick and his first wife, Helen, had separated about 1940 and later divorced; on 15 December 1956 he married Patricia Craig, *née* Marchant, but this marriage collapsed in 1957. He married (Evelyn) Mary Timewell (*b*. 1922), a film production secretary, on 10 September 1960 at Aylesbury, and they settled into a long and happy marriage, living first at Cutler's Orchard, Bledlow, and then at Southcourt Cottage in Long Crendon, Buckinghamshire. Despite ill health in his final years, Teddy Craig remained enthusiastic, ebullient, and charming to the end. When he spoke about the past and his enthusiasms, the years would drop away. He died, survived by his wife, on 21 January 1998 at Victoria Cottage Hospital, East Street, Thame, Oxfordshire, and was cremated on 29 January at Oxford crematorium, Headington.

Thanks to Craig's passion for collecting and preserving things (his father sometimes referred to him as 'the Magpie'), there are Craig/Carrick collections at the Harry Ransom Humanities Research Center at the University of Texas at Austin, and the British Film Institute, London. His work is also in the collections of the British Museum, the Metropolitan Museum of Art, the Victoria and Albert Museum, and the Yale Center for British Art.

CATHERINE A. SUROWIEC

**Sources** personal knowledge (2004) · private information (2004) · E. A. Craig, *Gordon Craig: the story of his life* (1968) · M. Steen, *A pride of Terrys: family saga* (1962) · *WW* · *Who's who in art* (1934–) · *Who's who in the theatre*, 14th edn (1967); repr. (1970) · E. Carrick, *Art and design in the British film* (1948) · *The Independent* (23 Jan 1998) · *The Times* (29 Jan 1998) · d. cert. · m. certs.
**Archives** BFI, Carrick collection, designs, BFI stills and posters · Ransom HRC, Craig/Carrick collection, designs and papers | V&A, department of prints and drawings, designs for the film *Lorna Doone* (1934) | SOUND BFI, London, BFI National Library, taped interviews (30 Jan 1991 and 27 Feb 1991), BECTU Oral History Project
**Likenesses** B. Rubbra, oils, 1980–1989?, priv. coll. · H. Craig, photographs · photograph, repro. in *The Times* [*see illus.*] · photograph, repro. in *The Independent*

**Craig, Edward Hubert Cunningham-** (1874–1946), geologist, was born on 22 April 1874 in Edinburgh, shortly after the death of his father. He was the younger son of Edward Cunningham Craig (1848–1874), medical student, and his wife, Mary Elizabeth, *née* Pattison (*b*. 1843). He attended Trinity College, Glenalmond, and entered Clare College, Cambridge, as a scholar in 1892. He graduated BA with a first in natural sciences (part one) in 1895. In the following year he became a geologist with the geological survey in Scotland and was elected a fellow of the Geological Society. His work resulted in contributions to five Scottish

Sheet Memoirs (1905–14) and several papers, including ones on the Sgùrr of Eigg and metamorphism. He was much involved in debating the geological theories of George Barrow in 1903.

In 1903 Cunningham-Craig was lent for two years by the survey as government geologist of Trinidad and Tobago, at a salary of £700 a year. His post was extended to 1907, by which time he had contributed nine colonial reports. His recognition of Trinidad's petroleum potential, on which he reported in April 1907, presaged a change in direction in his geological researches. From late in 1907 to 1912 he was geologist to the Burmah Oil Company, one of the first companies to use geologists in the search for oil. Craig conducted geological surveys in Persia in support of G. B. Reynolds, and was much involved in the discovery of oil at Masjed-e-Suleiman from May 1908. Six of the first seven wells here were sited by Craig and all produced oil.

Cunningham-Craig worked in Burma, India (particularly the region of Baluchistan), and Barbados, where he was in the service of the colonial government from 1910 to 1912. In 1912 he prospected for oil in Venezuela, and in 1913 was employed on the same task by the union government in South Africa. Between 1907 and 1914 he worked in various provinces in Canada, for Alberta, prospecting for oil and coal, and in Manitoba and New Brunswick. His classic *Oil Finding* appeared in 1912, which the first American oil hunters in the Maracaibo basin of Venezuela found 'extremely helpful' (R. Arnold and others, *The First Big Oil Hunt: Venezuela, 1911–1916*, 1960, 247).

In 1910 Cunningham-Craig married Anna Irene (*née* Cleaver); they had no children. From 1912 he was a London-based consulting petroleum geologist and geological adviser to both the Burmah (1912–46) and Anglo-Persian (1912–26) oil companies. He was a founder member in 1913 of the Institution of Petroleum Technologists in London and was elected FRSE in 1916.

Cunningham-Craig was appointed, in 1916, the wartime representative of the director of the trench-warfare supply department at factories making poison gas. In 1917 he was appointed senior geologist in the petroleum research department under the Ministry of Munitions, and he was also made geological adviser to the petroleum executive (1917–18). In 1918 he was technical adviser to the committee on the production of oil from home-based materials like cannel coal and oil shale. He disputed with John Cadman over whether oil could be made available in sufficient quantities from such native sources, although Cadman was ultimately proved right. Craig wrongly believed that the origins of oil shale and petroleum were related.

With the ending of war, Cunningham-Craig resumed consulting in geology worldwide. In the 1920s and 1930s he conducted more investigations in Egypt, Ecuador, the East Indies, Hungary, Romania, Estonia, Yugoslavia, Java, the United States, and finally Turkey. His book *Oil Finding* reached a lengthened second edition in 1920 (and there was a Russian translation in 1923). This 'valuable' book reviewed 'the subject … in perhaps the most orderly, concise, and thorough manner of any book that has, as yet,

been published and is the best published contribution … on petroleum geology as it is known today' (White, 485). Cunningham-Craig was a member of the Imperial Mineral Resources Bureau (amalgamated with the Imperial Institute in 1925) and retained his membership of their consultative committee on coal and petroleum until his death, on 24 April 1946 at the Kinellan Nursing Home in Beaconsfield, Buckinghamshire. In his early Burmah years, 'he was outstanding among his colleagues, in respect of geological knowledge and experience, mental and physical energy and independence of judgement' (Dewhurst, 352).                        H. S. TORRENS

**Sources** J. J. Howard and F. A. Crisp, eds., *Visitation of England and Wales*, 21 vols. (privately printed, London, 1893–1921), vol. 6 · T. D[ewhurst], 'E. H. C. Craig', *Journal of the Institute of Petroleum*, 32 (1946), 351–4 · E. B. Bailey, 'E. H. Cunningham-Craig', *Year Book Royal Society of Edinburgh* [1945–6] (1947), 17–18 · 'E. H. Cunningham-Craig', *Bulletin of the Imperial Institute*, 44 (1946), 148 · A. Beeby-Thompson, *Oil pioneer* (1961) · T. A. B. Corley, *A history of the Burmah Oil Company*, 2 vols. (1983–8) · R. W. Ferrier, *The history of the British Petroleum Company*, 1: *The developing years, 1901–1932* (1982) · *WWW* · E. W. Owen, *Trek of the oil finders* (1975) · 'Mr E. H. Cunningham Craig', *VF* · K. D. White, 'Review of *Oil finding, 1920*', *Bulletin of the American Association of Petroleum Geologists*, 6 (1922), 485–8 · J. Rowland and B. Cadman, *Ambassador for oil* (1960) · J. A. Greene, *A treatise on British mineral oil* (1919)

**Archives** BGS, MSS

**Likenesses** Spy [L. Ward], cartoon (as oil hunter), repro. in *VF* (1920–22) · portrait, priv. coll.

**Wealth at death** £14,846 0s. 1d.: probate, 3 Aug 1946, *CGPLA Eng. & Wales*

**Craig, Edward Thomas** (1804–1894), communitarian and journalist, the son of Joseph Craig and his wife, Elizabeth, was born in Manchester on 4 August 1804 and was baptized at the Gravel Lane Wesleyan Methodist chapel, Salford, on 7 October that year. Following the death of his father, Craig, then aged four, was sent to live with his paternal grandparents at Lancaster. One of his earliest memories was of Luddite prisoners being delivered to Lancaster Castle. The death of his grandmother meant that in 1815 he returned to Manchester, to live at Hanover Square with his mother's family, who were strict Calvinists. He was present at the Peterloo massacre in 1819. Craig recalled that:

> My maternal grandparents were rigid Puritans, and looked upon scientific books as the instruments of Satan for the ruin of souls, so that I had to read them in secret and during the night … The result of reading this class of books was a spirit of scepticism and enquiry into everything pertaining to human nature, and the relations of capital and labour, and made me dissatisfied with both.  (Craig, *The First Example*, 18–19)

Craig joined the Manchester Mechanics' Institution in 1825 and was 'an eager reader of works bearing on the human mind and on political economy' (Craig, *The First Example*, 18). By now he was working in the fustian trade, and in 1828 founded a Fustian Manufacturing Society based upon profit-sharing principles. He then organized a co-operative society (the Utility Society) in Salford and began to promote co-operation throughout the industrial towns of Lancashire. The Utility Society met in rooms belonging to his future father-in-law (who has not been identified), whose daughter he married in July 1833; they had at least one son, Francis. As a result of the Utility Society's discussions the Salford Sunday School and Social Institute was formed. Influenced by William King's *Co-Operator* (1828–30) and William Thompson's *Inquiry into the Principles of the Distribution of Wealth most Conducive to Human Happiness* (1824), Craig became secretary of a co-operative society in Manchester and helped to organize the first Co-operative Congress in Manchester on 26 and 27 May 1831. He later became editor of one of the early northern co-operative journals, the *Lancashire Co-Operator* (later the *Lancashire and Yorkshire Co-Operator*).

Craig's most important involvement with co-operation came when he was invited by John Scott Vandaleur to run his estate at Ralahine near Limerick on co-operative principles, Vandaleur seeing this as the way of ending the outbreaks of peasant violence that had troubled the estate. By November 1831 Craig had formulated his plans for Ralahine, which he set out in *The First Example of Profit Sharing and Home Rule* (n.d.). There was no single governor, master, or steward, and the estate was to be managed by a committee elected by members of the community. Education was to be available to all (in a school run by Mrs Craig); all profits were to belong to the members, and labour notes were to be introduced. The aims of Ralahine were:

> the acquisition of common capital … the mutual assurance of members against the evils of poverty … the attainment of the greater share of the comforts of life than the working classes now possess … the mental and moral improvement of its adult members, and the education of their children.
> (p. 23)

Craig's early time in Ireland was uncomfortable: 'A stranger myself, and moreover a *sassenach*, I was on one occasion struck with a stone, and had an ominous letter, with a coffin crudely drawn on it, laid in my way' (ibid., 11). Nevertheless, the community had two successful years before its sudden collapse, after Vandaleur had gambled away the estate and disappeared. Craig published his account of his experience in *The Irish Land & Labour Question, Illustrated in the History of Ralahine and Co-operative Farming* (1882).

On leaving Ralahine, Craig was invited by Lady Noel Byron to organize an industrial school at Ealing Grove, Middlesex, 'where labour in the garden or workshop should alternate with intellectual culture' (*Phrenological Magazine*, 58). He remained there until the end of 1835. Craig next became assistant editor of the *Star in the East*, and at the same time ran, together with his wife, a successful infants' school. From 1840 until 1856 Craig lectured on co-operation, psychology, and phrenology, in which he had become interested after hearing J. G. Spurzheim lecture in 1827. Craig was also interested in animal magnetism and thought-reading. He occasionally conducted his own experiments and described them in his journal the *Annals of Mesmerism*. According to his own account, in 1843 he was earning £25–£30 a week from lecturing. But ill health forced him to give this up, and after a spell working in the Post Office in 1853 he became principal of the Rotherham and Mexborough Mechanics' Institute.

Craig spent most of his later life as a journalist and by 1878 had been editor of six newspapers including the *Brighton Times*, the *Leamington Advertiser*, and the *Oxford University Herald*. He was also something of an inventor and in 1873 won a silver medal at the Cambridge Exhibition of Arts, Industry, and Manufactures for the greatest number of inventions in the catalogue (twenty-seven). An advocate of fresh air, abstinence, and vegetarianism, he also published *The Science of Life* (n.d.) in which he extolled the benefits of massage. Craig's health began to fail in his later years, though this did not stop him from contributing papers to the *American Socialist*, or from being one of the nine members who in June 1884 inaugurated the Hammersmith branch of the Democratic Federation (afterwards the Social Democratic Federation). In February 1885 he published a reminiscence of Peterloo in *The Commonweal*. It appears that he suffered a stroke early that year, but, though frail, he was able to attend the 1893 Co-operative Congress in Bristol. Craig died at his home, Ralahine, 10 Andover Road, Hammersmith, London, on 15 December 1894. His son, Francis, was in attendance, and he was also survived by his wife.      MICHAEL BEVAN

**Sources** J. Saville, 'Craig, Edward Thomas', *DLB*, vol. 1 · *IGI* · E. T. Craig, *The first example of profit sharing and home rule* [1892] · *Phrenological Magazine*, 4 (1883), 56–61 · *Phrenological Annual and Record* (1888) · E. T. Craig, *The science of life* [n.d.] · E. T. Craig, *The Irish land & labour question, illustrated in the history of Ralahine and co-operative farming* (1882) · R. Cooter, *Phrenology in the British Isles: an annotated historical biobibliography and index* (1989) · d. cert.

**Craig, (Edward Henry) Gordon** (1872–1966), theatre director and designer and wood-engraver, was born on 16 January 1872 in Railway Street, Stevenage, Hertfordshire, the only son and second child of the architect and radical Edward William *Godwin (1833–1886) and the actress Ellen Alice *Terry (1847–1928), whose name appears on Craig's birth certificate as Eleanor Alice Godwin, formerly Watkins. His elder sister was Edith Ailsa Geraldine *Craig, who later achieved prominence as a theatre director and costumier. Their parents were unmarried; indeed throughout their relationship, which began in 1868 and ended when Godwin left Terry in 1875, Ellen Terry was already married to her first husband, the artist George Frederic Watts. She had married Watts as a sixteen-year-old in 1864 and, in 1877, she was divorced from Watts and married to the actor Charles Wardell (stage name Charles Kelly). She judicially separated from Wardell in 1881.

**Early years** From an early age Craig lacked a father, had a peripatetic mother, and had a further uncertainty about his surname. Born Edward Godwin, by the age of nine he had become Edward Wardell. At sixteen, this uncertainty was resolved when he was baptized Edward Henry Gordon (the latter two names after his godparents Henry Irving and Lady Gordon). At the age of twenty-one he took the surname Craig by deed poll, after the rocky Scottish island Ailsa Craig. His schooling, too, was imprecise—he attended Southfield Park preparatory school, near Tunbridge Wells, from 1883 to 1886, and after a brief interlude at Bradfield College, returned to Southfield, where the headmaster wrote of him as 'a good boy—Flighty, but good' (E. Craig, 62). He moved on to a school in Heidelberg,

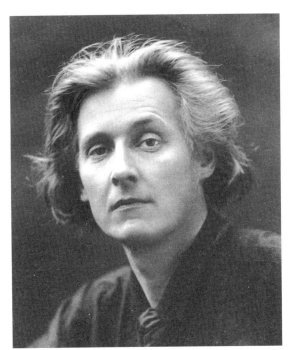

(Edward Henry) Gordon Craig (1872–1966), by George Charles Beresford, 1911

but in 1888 was expelled. Craig had had walk-on parts in the theatre from the age of six, and took his first speaking role in 1885 when he went to Chicago during the Christmas holidays to join his mother in Henry Irving's production of *Eugene Aram* by Edward Bulwer-Lytton. When his schooling was over he joined Irving's company at the Lyceum Theatre.

**Wood-engraving** Until 1897, when he ceased to act, Craig took roles including Hamlet (1894) and Macbeth (1896). He was hailed as the most promising young actor in England, and his mother observed 'I have never known anyone with so much natural gift' (*DNB*). On 27 March 1893 he married an actress, Helen Mary (May) Gibson (*b*. 1872/3), daughter of Robert Southam Gibson, with whom, by 1897, he had had four children. During this period, in which he was briefly an actor–manager (1897–9), his life took a new turn when he met the artists James Pryde and William Nicholson, who introduced him to woodcutting and engraving, and the making of plain black and white illustrations. Watching Nicholson at work put Craig under a spell of pleasure, and inspired him to take up this art. He had as natural a gift for wood-engraving as he had for acting, and in 1898 he launched a new magazine, *The Page*, largely written by him, albeit under inventive pseudonyms, and aimed at the worlds of theatre and the arts. It was illustrated with his own wood-engravings.

Craig's earliest wood-engraving was a portrait of the poet Walt Whitman (1893), taken from a photograph. This was a revolutionary work, one of the earliest 'white line' wood-engravings of the modern era, in which the image is made to emerge from the block, which prints black, by engraved lines which carry no ink and remain the colour

of the paper. Craig embraced wood-engraving wholeheartedly, with a boyish, breathless, energy, and by the end of 1899 had engraved nearly 200 blocks. This spontaneous, affectionate approach to creativity was an aspect of his character that articulated his entire life, embracing also the tone of his writing and his theatre design.

**Theatre design and direction** The marriage with May Gibson ended in 1898 after Craig had embarked on an affair with the actress Jess Dorynne, one of many liaisons that were to decorate his life. He continued to engrave wood, but, yearning again for the stage, was encouraged by the musician Martin Shaw to embark on stage design and direction. His first production, *Dido and Aeneas* (1900) for the Purcell Society at the Hampstead Conservatoire, was revolutionary. The restrictions of the building forced Craig to design his own stage, inspired by techniques pioneered by Hubert von Herkomer at Bushey, Hertfordshire, by creating an exceptionally low proscenium to hide the backcloth frames and lighting system. The effect was 'strikingly panoramic' (Innes, 38), and broke radically with the tradition of stage realism with the use of colour and light pouring in from above and evoking mood and movement. Harley Granville Barker articulated Craig's intentions by describing him as 'a supreme master of the theatre of the clouds' (*DNB*). This production was followed by Handel's *Acis and Galatea* (1902) at the Great Queen Street Theatre, where it was described by Granville Barker as 'an ever-shifting maze of colour, form, and motion' (ibid.). Haldane McFall observed to Craig that the colours in the first act were 'good enough to eat' (quoted E. Craig, 153).

By now Craig had shifted his affections once more, and was living with the 22-year-old violinist Elena Fortuna Meo (1879–1957), daughter of the Hampstead painter Gaetano Meo. He designed productions for his mother at the Imperial Theatre, Tothill Street, including Ibsen's *The Vikings at Helgeland* (1903) and Shakespeare's *Much Ado about Nothing* (1903). These drew yet more inventive lighting, staging, and costume effects from Craig—the church in *Much Ado*, act IV being evoked not so much by architecture but by diagonal streams of coloured light from an unseen stained-glass window illuminating a vast, partially obscured crucifix. The American theatre critic James Huneker wrote of *The Vikings at Helgeland*: 'Abolishing foot and border lights, sending shafts … from above, Mr Craig secures unexpected and bizarre effects' (J. Huneker, *Iconoclasts: a Book of Dramatists*, 1905, 32). Craig's theatre designs, which evoked the work of Edmund Dulac, Charles Ricketts, and Charles Shannon, appealed to artists rather more than to managers of the established theatre, and his productions had a high commercial failure rate. Through his inability to compromise, many projects were aborted or abandoned. Craig moved to Berlin in 1904, where he designed *Venice Preserv'd* by Otway at the Lessing Theatre (1905) and in the same year *The Tempest* by Shakespeare and Shaw's *Caesar and Cleopatra* for Max Reinhardt. He rarely returned to England—he and May had divorced in 1905, and by that same year he had had three children with Elena.

In 1905 also, Craig began his affair with the dancer Isadora Duncan (1878–1927), with whom he had two children. He and Duncan shared a passionate conviction for a unified theatre experience of dance, music, colour, and staging, which crossed national boundaries, under one controlling mastermind. They worked together on Craig's book *Isadora Duncan: Six Movement Designs* (1906), but in 1907 they parted, and Craig brought Elena and their children to live with him in Florence where he had settled. He designed a production of Ibsen's *Rosmersholm* (1907) which was staged at the Teatro della Pergola in Florence, where it was described by the Italian designer Enrico Corradini as 'a new architecture of great height, ranging in colour from green to blue …; it portrayed a *state of mind*' (E. Corradini, 'L'arte della scena', *Vita d'Arte*, 1908). His theatrical work took him to Moscow, where, in 1912, he designed a *Hamlet* for Konstantin Stanislavsky at the Art Theatre. This was a resounding success, especially its first court scene, with 'Claudius and Gertrude enthroned at the back of the stage in a glittering sea of gold, and Hamlet, a lonely black-clad figure, sitting far downstage, a silhouette under a great shadow' (*DNB*).

In Florence, Craig started his theatre magazine *The Mask*, which ran (with a break in the First World War) from 1908 until 1929, and he founded the School for the Art of the Theatre in 1913. His highly influential book *On the Art of the Theatre*, in which he expounded his visionary ideas, was published in 1911. For part of the First World War, Craig lived in Rome, where Elena and their children joined him, and in 1917 they moved to Rapallo where Craig wrote, drew, and engraved on wood, using cut wood blocks as figures for stage models. He was now an essentially European figure. His visits to England were brief, but nevertheless in his absence he had a continuing influence over the development of wood-engraving and the theatre in his native country. He became a leading, if distant, member of the Society of Wood Engravers, and contributed to their exhibitions. He wrote on both theatre (*The Theatre Advancing*, 1921) and wood-engraving (*Woodcuts, and some Words*, 1924), and made a final essay in theatre design in the production of Ibsen's *The Pretenders* in Copenhagen (1926). For this he received the Danish order of the knights of Dannebrøg (1930). His stage designs were published by Oxford University Press in 1930, and in 1937 he was appointed a royal designer for industry by the Royal Society of Arts. Throughout his life Craig could strike an elegant pose for the camera. Articulated by well-cut features and luxuriant hair, his style of dress seemed to linger in the early nineteenth century. Craig's small, sharp eyes and curved nose gave him a bird-like appearance into old age, but his was a garden bird rather than a raptor, quizzical and busy rather than aggressive.

Craig moved away from stage design in the 1930s, concentrating instead on writing and wood-engraving. His edition of *Hamlet*, published with his wood-engravings in 1929 by Count Kessler's Cranach Press in Weimar, became a classic of private-press book production. His biography of Henry Irving appeared in 1930, and that of his mother, *Ellen Terry and her Secret Self*, the following year. 'Still a

handsome amorist', as J. C. Trewin gently put it, Craig left Elena once again and went to Paris to live with his secretary, Daphne Woodward (1906–1965), and their daughter (*DNB*). This family was interned during the Second World War, but Craig continued his work on their release. After the war Craig travelled alone and settled in Vence, France, where he completed the memoir of his early life, *Index to the Story of my Days, 1872–1907*, published in 1957. Elena, who had retained a lifelong affection for him, died that same year.

Friends from the arts and the theatre made pilgrimages to visit Craig in his latter years. He was appointed Companion of Honour in 1958, and in 1964 he became the president of the Mermaid Theatre, London. His influence, taken up by Adolphe Appia and Max Reinhardt, passed on to younger generations of theatre directors including Tadeusz Kantor, Peter Brook, and Peter Hall. He died at Vence on 29 July 1966 after suffering two strokes. He was cremated in Marseilles on 1 August, and his ashes were buried in Elena's grave at Thame, Oxfordshire. Christopher Innes described Craig as 'passionate, improvident, mercurial, a self-taught genius who mastered almost everything except self-discipline and who scattered his energy among multitudinous projects; dogmatic yet secretly self-doubting, whimsical as well as visionary' (Innes, 8). Of his many children, one, Edward (Teddy) *Craig, his biographer, became a film designer and, under the pseudonym Edward Carrick, a distinguished wood-engraver.

JAMES HAMILTON

**Sources** E. Craig, *Gordon Craig: the story of his life* (1968) • C. Innes, *Edward Gordon Craig: a vision of the theatre* (1998) • G. Craig, *Index to the story of my days, 1872–1907* (1957) • T. Sidey, *Edward Gordon Craig* (1982) [exhibition catalogue, University of York] • H. MacFall, 'Concerning the woodcuts of Gordon Craig', *Print Collectors Quarterly*, 9 (Dec 1922), 407–32 • L. M. Newman, *Gordon Craig archives* (1976) • I. K. Fletcher and A. Rood, *Edward Gordon Craig: a bibliography*, London Society for Theatre Research (1967) • b. cert. • m. cert. [Helen Mary Gibson] • L. Lambourne, 'The genetic legacy', *E. W. Godwin: aesthetic movement architect and designer*, ed. S. W. Soros (1999), 353–8 [exhibition catalogue, Bard Graduate Center, New York, 17 Nov 1999–27 Feb 2000] • *DNB*

**Archives** Österreichische Nationalbibliothek, Vienna, designs, MSS, and papers • AM Oxf., designs, MSS, and papers • Bibliothèque de l'Arsenal, Paris, designs, MSS, and papers • Bibliothèque Nationale, Paris, MSS, designs, and papers • BM, designs, MSS, and papers • Claremont Colleges, California, Honnold/Mudd Library, designs, MSS, and papers • Hunterian Museum and Art Gallery, Glasgow, designs, MSS, and papers • NYPL, designs, MSS, and papers • NYPL for the Performing Arts, corresp., notebooks, and papers • Ransom HRC, designs, MSS, and papers • Theatre Museum, London, American tour journal • U. Cal., Los Angeles, designs, MSS, and papers • V&A, designs, MSS, and papers • Yale U., Beinecke L., designs, MSS, and papers | BL, corresp. with Society of Authors, Add. MSS 56684, 63227 • Ellen Terry Memorial Museum, Smallhythe, Kent, letters to James Carew • Ellen Terry Memorial Museum, Smallhythe, Kent, letters to Ellen Terry • Harvard U., Houghton L., letters to Virginia Clarke • Harvard U., Houghton L., letters to Thomas Moult • Harvard U., Houghton L., letters to William Rothenstein • Somerville College, Oxford, letters to Percy Withers and family • Tate collection, letters to Albert Rutherston • Theatre Museum, London, corresp. with Hal Burton; corresp. with Christopher Fry • U. Birm. L., letters to John Ramsay

Allardyce Nicoll and Josephine Nicoll |SOUND BL NSA, perform-
ance recordings; recorded talks

**Likenesses** G. C. Beresford, photograph, 1911, NPG [*see illus.*] ·
E. G. Craig, self-portrait, woodcut, 1919, U. Hull · W. Rothenstein,
sanguine drawing, 1922, Man. City Gall. · M. Beerbohm, watercolour caricature, 1924, V&A · B. Brandt, photograph, 1956, NPG ·
C. Beaton, photograph, 1962, NPG · R. S. Sherriffs, ink and pencil
caricature, NPG

**Craig, James** (1739–1795), architect, was born in Edinburgh, the eldest son of William Craig (1695–1762), merchant in Edinburgh, and Mary Thomson (1710–1790), sister
of the poet James Thomson (1700–1748), author of *The Seasons*. He was educated at George Watson's Hospital, Edinburgh, where he was admitted on 4 April 1748 by right of
his father and of his grandfather Robert Craig, a former
dean of guild. His date of birth was recorded here as 31
October 1739, which is almost certainly the correct date,
although it has previously been given as 31 October 1744
from a probably erroneous entry in the Edinburgh birth
register. Craig left Watson's Hospital on 2 May 1755 to
become apprentice to Patrick Jamieson, deacon of the
Incorporation of Wrights and Masons.

Craig is best-known as designer of the first New Town of
Edinburgh. His architectural début was in 1763, when he
submitted a proposal to build a bridge across the drained
north loch, to encourage development on the city's land
to the north. A plan of the proposed north bridge in the
*Scots Magazine* of July 1763 is signed 'James Craig Delint.',
although the actual design may be attributable to George
Fraser rather than Craig himself, and a different design
was adopted in 1765. However, Craig was awarded the
prize in August 1766 for the best of seven plans submitted
anonymously for the layout of the New Town itself.
Though judged as having 'the most merit' by the assessors, his plan was considered not good enough to be
immediately adopted. The scheme was then developed by
a group of advisers, including John Adam (1721–1792) and
William Mylne (d. 1790), and the final plan was approved
by the town council nearly a year later. Craig's prize plan
has not survived and it is unclear how much of his initial
design was incorporated but he remained closely involved
in drawing up the adopted plan, with related plans for
drainage and detailed feuing. He had, however, no responsibility for the architectural elevations of the houses in
the New Town, which initially had only to conform to
standard heights and building lines.

The nature of the site left little choice, as the principal
streets had to run east–west to make the most of the level
ground; but it has been suggested that Craig's original
scheme may have featured a central square with streets
radiating from it, which would have produced awkward
corners and unmanageable areas for development. The
principal reason for his success was his excellent use of
the site, by providing two outer streets with houses on one
side only, taking full advantage of the open views over gardens to north and south. The adopted scheme has two
squares linked by three wide streets and two minor
streets, with mews lanes to the rear for services. In 1768

Craig published an engraved version of this plan, dedicated to George III, and proudly surmounted by a quotation from Thomson's *Prospect of Britain*. A manuscript
drawing, now in the British Library, was presented to the
king in December 1767 for approval of the street names
and dedication.

Craig's best architectural work was the Physicians Hall,
George Street, Edinburgh (1773–9; dem. *c*.1843), a Palladian design for a public building in the centre of one of
the first blocks along the principal street of the otherwise
domestic New Town. In 1773 he was architect and planner
of St James's Square (dem. 1965), a private development at
the east end of Princes Street, the first terraced development to achieve a degree of unified architectural design in
Edinburgh. His unexecuted *Plan for Improving the City of
Edinburgh* (1786) shows a scheme stretching from Register
House to Nicolson Street, providing a crescent of houses
facing the university and Royal Infirmary, and an octagon
of tenements and shops round the Tron Kirk. This design
for the south bridge, an alternative to that proposed by
Robert Adam the previous year, was an imaginative town
planning scheme, but would have resulted in wholesale
demolition of parts of old Edinburgh.

Craig's professional life promised much but success
eluded him, owing partly to a lack of resources at the
beginning of his career, which would have allowed him to
travel, but partly also to his intransigent nature and excessive pride in his uncle James Thomson, whose posthumous patronage he frequently invoked. Though Thomson
was nearly always in debt, his sociability attracted friends
who later revered his memory, but his nephew lacked the
ability to take advantage of the help proffered. His energies were deployed in producing detailed drawings, usually large and coloured to impress his clients, neatly
drawn and minutely detailed. His later output ranged
from mundane building contracts to decorative drawings
for unexecuted monuments and surveys of country
houses for prestigious clients who did not adopt his
designs for alterations and extensions.

Craig died, unmarried, in the West Bow in Edinburgh on
23 June 1795, insolvent and unknown. His library can be
reconstructed from the inventory prepared by the Edinburgh auctioneer Cornelius Elliot: his books included a
number of publications covering not only the architectural orders and theory, building manuals, and pattern
books, but also books whose intellectual content would
inform a mind keen to play a part in Enlightenment Edinburgh. He had already pawned his New Town competition
gold medal and silver box containing the freedom of the
city to provide financial support for his elderly mother
and aunt. His debts amounted to about £250; his assets
were valued at £102 17s. 10d. He was buried on 26 June in
Greyfriars churchyard, his grave unmarked until 1967,
when a slab was placed on the site.

The New Town of Edinburgh went out of fashion in the
mid-nineteenth century until Robert Louis Stevenson,
who lived there, came to its defence, followed by Gerald
Baldwin Brown in the 1890s, who restored Craig's design
to a central position in the history of town planning. A

portrait of Craig by David Allan, painted about 1781, at the height of what success he had, is in the Scottish National Portrait Gallery: the unfinished plan with a proposed circus at the centre of the New Town on his lap, and his drawing for the Physicians Hall at his feet, indicate the importance he gave to these two examples of his work.

KITTY CRUFT and ANDREW FRASER

**Sources** K. Cruft and A. Fraser, eds., *James Craig, [1744]–1795: 'the ingenious architect of the New Town of Edinburgh'* (1995) · Colvin, *Archs.* · register of the names of boys elected and received into George Watson's Hospital from the commencement thereof at Whitsunday 1741, George Watson's College Library, Edinburgh, vol. 1, entry 44, 4 April 1748 · minutes of George Watson's Hospital, 19 Nov 1744–1756, George Watson's College Library, Edinburgh, petition for James Craig, 19 May 1755: indenture executed betwixt Pat. Jamieson and James Craig · Bridge Committee minutes, 1764–70, Edinburgh City Archives · NA Scot., Edinburgh Testaments, testament and probate inventory, CC8/10/51 A and B · A. J. Youngson, *The making of classical Edinburgh* (1966), 70–110 · G. B. Brown, 'The New Town of Edinburgh', *Transactions of the Edinburgh Architectural Association*, 1 (1891), 90–101 · F. C. Mears and J. Russell, 'The New Town of Edinburgh', *Book of the Old Edinburgh Club*, 22 (1938), 167–200; 23 (1940), 1–37 · M. K. Meade, 'Plans of the New Town of Edinburgh', *Architectural History*, 14 (1971), 40–52 · S. Harris, 'New light on the first New Town', *Book of the Old Edinburgh Club*, new ser., 2 (1992), 1–13 · K. Cruft, 'James Craig, 1739–1795: a correction of his date of birth', *Book of the Old Edinburgh Club*, new ser., 5 (2002), 103–5

**Archives** Royal College of Physicians of Edinburgh, corresp. | City of Edinburgh Museums and Galleries · NL Scot., MS 502/1–8 · Royal College of Physicians of Edinburgh

**Likenesses** D. Allan, oils, *c.*1781, Scot. NPG

**Wealth at death** debts of approx. £250; possessions valued at £102 17*s.* 10*d.* (furniture and household plenishings £51 3*s.* 10*d.*, books and pictures £51 14*s.* 0*d.*): NA Scot., Edinburgh testaments, CC8/10/51, A and B

**Craig, James**, first Viscount Craigavon (1871–1940), prime minister of Northern Ireland, was born on 8 January 1871 at The Hill, Sydenham, Belfast, one of the sons of James Craig (1828–1900), a whiskey distilling millionaire of Scottish origin. His father was a self-made man who had worked his way up from lowly positions in flour-mills, the linen bleaching business, and Dunville's Distillery, Belfast, and who made his fortune within twenty years. His mother, Eleanor Gilmore Browne (*b.* 1835), was the daughter of Robert Browne, a prosperous man who owned property in Belfast and a farm outside Lisburn, co. Antrim. They had eight sons and one daughter; James Craig was the seventh child and sixth son. He grew up in co. Down in Craigavon, a large house in grounds close to Belfast, and Tyrella, a house on Dundrum Bay. He was educated in a preparatory school near Craigavon, run by a Presbyterian minister, and in 1882 was sent to Merchiston Castle School, Edinburgh, a Church of Scotland public school; this enabled him to retain his Ulster accent, a valuable asset to his local political career. He left school at seventeen and worked in a firm of general agents and brokers in Belfast for thirty months, then in 1890 in a stockbroking firm in London, and then, after two years, he returned to Ulster and opened his own stockbroking firm, Craigs & Co., in Belfast.

James Craig, first Viscount Craigavon (1871–1940), by Olive Edis, *c.*1921

**Early career** Craig's background was typical of the middle-class business families who dominated Ulster politics, but his early instincts were for a life of action rather than business or politics. He was a restless, though successful, stockbroker, and he took his chance of leading a more physical life when he enlisted in the 3rd (militia) regiment of the Royal Irish Rifles on 11 January 1900 to serve in the Second South African War. Military life suited him well, but he became impatient with the lack of professionalism and efficiency in the British army in this its most severe test. He was seconded to the imperial yeomanry, becoming a lieutenant and then a captain, was taken prisoner in May 1900, but released by the Boers because of a perforated eardrum. On his recovery he became deputy assistant director of the Imperial Military Railways, showing the qualities of organization that were to mark his involvement in both British and Ulster politics. In June 1901 he was sent home suffering from dysentery, and by the time he was fit for service again the war was over. This experience was central to Craig's development. He revealed an easy-going style and an ability to get on with his men, but these qualities were combined with a certain resolution in his character. He was now familiar with imperialism and war, and he belonged to a younger generation of Unionists to whom the former was an essential part of their outlook, and the latter a possible means of defending their ideology.

Craig's father died in April 1900, leaving his son a legacy of £100,000. Craig now turned to the political life. He had acted for a brief period as honorary secretary to the Belfast

Conservative Association, and his interest in politics quickened when his brother Charles (who also served in the Second South African War) was elected Unionist MP for South Antrim in a by-election in February 1903. In March 1903 James Craig was selected to oppose a nationalist in North Fermanagh, mainly because he was able to finance his own campaign and did not need to draw on the slender funds of the local Unionist association. He was narrowly defeated, but on 11 November 1903 he was selected as candidate for East Down and won the seat in the general election of 1906, with a majority of 670. He held the seat in the two general elections of 1910, with increased majorities, and sat for East Down until the 1918 general election when following an increase in the number of co. Down constituencies, he was returned with a majority of 9932 for North Down, a seat which he held until 1921, after which he sat in the Northern Ireland parliament as one of the members for County Down. In appearance Craig was a large, strong-featured, red-faced man, easily open to caricature as a typical straight-talking Ulsterman or, alternatively, the bull-necked, inflexible Ulster Unionist. His wife, Cecil Mary Nowell Dering Tupper (d. 1960), whom he married on 22 March 1905 after a very brief courtship, was English, the daughter of Sir Daniel Tupper, assistant comptroller of the lord chamberlain's department of the king's household. They had twin sons and a daughter. She was obliged, as one of Craig's biographers put it, to make 'many abrupt and deep adjustments' to living in Ulster (Ervine, 109).

**The home rule crisis**  Craig was not an original thinker, nor even a very clever man; but he had the ability to win and keep the confidence of his constituents and his fellow Unionist MPs. He briefed himself well on other issues besides the Union. He spoke in favour of non-sectarian education, tariff reform, votes for women, and agricultural interests. He became one of the Unionist MPs who threw themselves into the campaign against the Liberal government's administration of Ireland, but he also took a keen interest in the reform of the British army, and he spoke for greater financial provision for Irish education, especially for teachers' salaries and the upkeep of the national schools. He quickly established his reputation as a promising back-bencher, displaying an even temper, and a careful mastery of detail. He was flung into prominence and even notoriety by the crisis over the third Home Rule Bill between 1912 and 1914.

Craig regarded it as axiomatic that a Dublin parliament, dominated by rural interests and the Roman Catholic church, would prove destructive to the interests of protestant and industrial north-east Ulster. He was a member of the Orange order, and grand master of a co. Down lodge, and though personally free from bigotry, he identified with the beliefs of the order and knew that it was central to the mobilization of Ulster Unionism. His grasp of grass-roots Ulster politics, and his genial personality, were vital in enabling him to maintain the unity of what was potentially a very divided movement. His organizational skills were also important as he and his fellow Unionists prepared to resist home rule by force of arms, using their

Ulster Volunteer Force (UVF), and to set up their own provisional government the day that home rule became law. He was willing to work behind the scenes, leaving the glory to Sir Edward Carson, a Dubliner and southern Unionist, whose leadership (Craig freely acknowledged) was indispensable in giving Unionism a powerful voice in Great Britain. Craig entered this dangerous period with his eyes open. He hoped to defeat home rule, but he prepared methodically for an armed clash which, following the Larne gun-running for the UVF in April 1914, seemed inevitable. The Liberal government, he declared, was a 'caucus, led by rebels' (Buckland, *Craig*, 32).

Craig's apparent imperturbability in the face of these developments never deserted him. The Liberals felt obliged to seek some kind of compromise on the Ulster issue, with perhaps four counties excluded from the operation of the Home Rule Bill for a period of time. Such suggestions failed to break the deadlock, but they posed difficulties for Craig and his colleagues: were they to abandon their solemn league and covenant of September 1912 which pledged them to oppose home rule for Ireland as a whole? This would be acceptable to most Ulster Unionists, but problematical for Unionists left outside the kind of 'excluded area' which the Liberals were discussing. The outbreak of the First World War in August 1914 postponed any decision on this matter, and the whole Irish question, though home rule was formally placed on the statute book in September. Craig used the opportunity to press home a propaganda advantage, placing the UVF at the disposal of the British government, and even ordering thousands of uniforms from Moss Brothers of London. The UVF was designated as the 36th (Ulster) division, and Craig became lieutenant-colonel and the division's assistant adjutant and quartermaster-general. His health prevented him from accompanying the division abroad, and in 1916 he reluctantly resigned his commission.

**Partition of Ireland**  Craig now resumed his political career, becoming a treasurer of his majesty's household and a Unionist whip. In 1917 he received a baronetcy in the new year honours list. When Sir Edward Carson resigned from the cabinet Craig followed him in January 1918, but he resumed his career a year later, becoming parliamentary secretary to the Ministry of Pensions. On 20 April 1920 he was given a promotion as financial secretary to the Admiralty under the former Unionist leader Walter Long. His steady, if unspectacular, rise in British politics was interrupted when the government introduced its Government of Ireland Bill in March 1920, giving home rule to 'southern' and 'northern' Ireland. Craig acted as a broker between the Ulster Unionists and the government in working out key details of this act, in particular the decision to make the second chamber of the Northern Ireland parliament a mere reflection of the Unionist majority in the lower house, with twenty-four of twenty-six members elected by the House of Commons, which produced an insignificant minority representation (only five nationalists in 1936). Craig also influenced the vital question of the area to be governed by the Northern Ireland parliament, which the British agreed to reduce from nine to six counties. However, Craig suggested that the problem of minorities in the border areas might be settled by a boundary commission:

> to examine the distribution of population along the borders of the Six Counties, and to take a vote in those districts on either side of and immediately adjoining that boundary in which there was a doubt as to whether they would prefer to be included in the Northern or the Southern Parliamentary area. (cabinet conclusions, 15 Dec 1919, CAB 23/18, PRO)

This suggestion was rejected by the government for fear of causing unease in those areas. Craig also used his influence to persuade the Unionists of co. Cavan, co. Monaghan, and co. Donegal to accept their severance from the new Northern Ireland state, arguing that it was necessary for the security of the state if Ulster Unionists were not soon to be outnumbered by a substantial, and growing, Catholic minority. Here Craig revealed a stern realism, and his determination to secure Ulster Unionism was seen also in his urging the cabinet, in July 1920, to push the Home Rule Bill quickly through parliament, and his defence of Unionists against the charge of using random violence against Catholics. He suggested that the UVF be reorganized as a separate unit to defend Northern Ireland against the IRA, and this led to the formation of the Ulster Special Constabulary in November 1920. When the Government of Ireland Act received the royal assent on 23 December 1920 Craig was, unsurprisingly, the chosen candidate for the job of making the state of Northern Ireland a reality, and he became leader of the Ulster Unionists and first prime minister of Northern Ireland, with the formal offer coming from the standing committee of the Ulster Unionist Council on 26 January 1921. He was sworn of the Irish privy council in 1921, and of the Northern Ireland privy council in 1922.

**Prime minister** The next four years were to be the most demanding of Craig's career. He had several tasks: to establish the state on firm foundations; to defend it against its enemies, within and without; to prevent its over-zealous supporters from taking the law into their own hands, thus destabilizing the state; and to keep a watchful eye on the British government which by the spring of 1921 was becoming increasingly anxious to reach a compromise with Sinn Féin. These were interrelated problems. From the start of serious negotiations with Sinn Féin the government was increasingly drawn into a strategy of accommodating Irish nationalism through the offer of dominion status, but with the question of partition regarded as central to the success of this policy. Tom Jones, assistant secretary to the cabinet, expressed the spirit of the government's approach when he declared that 'we are pledged not to coerce Ulster', adding that 'some would confine that to physical force' (Bew and others, 51). Lloyd George and his colleagues put pressure on Craig to place his parliament under Dublin rule as an enticement for Sinn Féin to accept dominion status, but in the end the difficulty was resolved by the very method that Craig had suggested earlier, that of a boundary commission, which should delimit the border if

Northern Ireland were to opt out of the Anglo-Irish treaty, which she duly did in December 1922. Meanwhile Craig wrestled with other problems.

In January 1922 Winston Churchill brought Craig and Michael Collins together in London to try to improve north–south relations and control the rising tide of violence in the north. Craig showed that he could make an effort to do business with the most unlikely of men. Both leaders agreed that they would make efforts to address the most troublesome problems, such as the southern boycott of northern business, and the expulsion of Roman Catholic workers from their employment in Belfast. But once again Craig confronted the difficulty that, however honest his intentions, he must, if he were to avoid dangerous criticism, stress to his Unionist followers those aspects of the pact that seemed most favourable to them. A second pact in March 1922 began, at Churchill's behest, with the words 'Peace is today declared'; but Collins remained actively hostile to the Northern Ireland state, and in any case Craig was obliged to pursue the implementation of those items most favourable to his less than secure fledgeling state. The whole affair demonstrated yet again that Craig was willing to take the wider view, both in Anglo-Irish relations and in relations between north and south; but also that he could never move too far ahead of his less sophisticated Unionist colleagues.

Craig's struggle with the British to give the new state a firm financial beginning was concluded successfully when a joint exchequer board was established to adjudicate disputes between the Northern Ireland government and the Treasury in June 1922 (much to Treasury officials' disgust). Craig resisted demands from the British government for a judicial inquiry into his government's security measures in May 1922, though he accepted an inquiry in secret. The inquiry was duly set up, but its head, S. G. Tallents, though no admirer of Craig and his colleagues, concluded that to push matters too far would be to endanger Craig's control of his Unionist followers, a pattern that was to be repeated in Craig's premiership.

These events revealed the successes and shortcomings of Craig's leadership. He was able to carry the British government with him in important respects because it did not want him to resign and place the responsibility of governing Northern Ireland directly on British shoulders. But all this was part of Craig's belief that his only political purpose must be to stand firm: 'no surrender' was the call. This did not deprive him of sympathy with the nationalist minority in his state, but it placed their welfare low in his order of priorities, and complaints about his abandonment of proportional representation for local elections in 1922, or his adoption of the special powers act in the same year, were ignored. He was often a voice for moderation, for example over the expulsion of Catholics from the Belfast shipyards in 1921–2, but his main concern was to maintain Unionist unity, and he did not want Catholics to see him as someone to whom they could 'come squealing' (Buckland, *Craig*, 87).

**Craig's government** Craig's premiership lasted another twenty years, but the pattern of his government was established in the climactic years of 1914–23. This was: a firm defence of the Ulster Unionist position; Unionist unity in the face of external and internal foes; and a cautiously worked out relationship with the British government. The heroic defiance of 1912–14, the demanding task of state construction between 1921 and 1925, were followed by a period marked by political stagnation and unimaginative leadership. This caution was reinforced, rather than challenged, by the devolutionary powers granted to Northern Ireland in 1921, which greatly restricted the role of the Northern Ireland parliament and executive, and left Northern Ireland, after 1927, dependent on subsidies from the British Treasury. The relationship between Stormont and the local authorities in Northern Ireland worked unsatisfactorily, with most services being administered by local authorities, which became a byword for patronage and deeply contested sectarian politics. Craig's state suffered from the decline of its heavy industries, and unemployment remained high, at an average figure of 26 per cent of the total workforce, and 30 per cent of the male workforce. Moreover, the local character of Northern Ireland politics in an area about the size of Yorkshire, and containing 1¼ million people, divided roughly into two-thirds protestant and the rest Catholic, rendered Craig vulnerable to pressure from local Unionists. Craig, often to the consternation of his more professionally minded colleagues, was inclined to respond to demands by handing out largesse that his government could hardly afford. He succumbed to pressure on the question of religious instruction in schools between 1923 and 1925. The Northern Ireland government sought to establish a non-sectarian and integrated educational system, but the Roman Catholic hierarchy rose up against any attempt to transfer its schools to state control, and protestant clergy agitated for Bible instruction in schools administered by local authorities, instruction which was protestant in content and doctrinally unacceptable to the Catholic minority. The result was that state schools became protestant schools, and again Craig revealed that visionary policies, or even just plain good intentions, were not in the gift of a leader of Ulster Unionists (or anybody else in Northern Ireland). Craig was in any event not a prime minister given to dragooning colleagues; indeed, he never dismissed a minister. His desire to maintain unity was seen in his emphasizing the threat from de Valera's government, with its constitutional claim to Northern Ireland and its irredentist rhetoric. Craig possessed no economic ideas, beyond leaving things to work out for themselves. Craig was made Viscount Craigavon of Stormont in 1927. He enjoyed being prime minister of Northern Ireland, with all the office's prestigious connotations. He received an honorary LLD from Queen's University, Belfast, in 1922 and a DCL from Oxford in 1926. His *Who's Who* entry proudly proclaimed him a knight of grace, order of St John, in 1937. His wife also enjoyed the perks of office, including using the cabinet secretary to telephone Fortnum and Mason in London to order marmalade. However, she also bore up well to the demands made on a prime minister in Northern Ireland, and when her husband was ill she would deputize for him at official functions.

Craig had made his career in British as well as Ulster politics; but his premiership showed little sign of his earlier close acquaintance with the British political world. He became intensely parochial, and suffered from his loss of intimacy with British politicians in 1938, when the British government concluded agreements with Dublin to end the 'economic war' between the two states, on terms highly unfavourable to Northern Ireland. He never tried to persuade Westminster to protect Northern Ireland's industries, especially the linen industry, which was central to its economy. He was anxious not to provoke Westminster, or draw too much attention to what was happening in Northern Ireland, especially in the treatment of the Catholic minority. His desire to retain the closest links with Great Britain was seen in April 1939, and again in May 1940, when he called for conscription to be applied in Northern Ireland (which the British government, fearing a nationalist backlash, refused). In February 1940 he declared in a radio broadcast that Ulstermen were 'King's men' (Ervine, 551). His indignation when Winston Churchill suggested to de Valera that partition might be re-examined if Éire would join the British war effort can be imagined.

**Death and assessment** James Craig died at his home, Glencraig, Craigavad, co. Down, on 24 November 1940, and was buried in the grounds of the Stormont parliament building. His wife survived him. He was succeeded as second viscount by his elder son, James (1906–1974). Inevitably, any assessment of his place in Irish, Ulster, and British politics is influenced by the history of Northern Ireland since his death, and especially by the 'troubles' that beset the state after 1968. Critics point to his failure to build bridges to the Catholic minority, but his statement in 1934 that he stood for 'a Protestant parliament and a Protestant state' must be seen in the context of de Valera's claim that 'we are a Catholic nation' (Buckland, *Factory of Grievances*, 72), and indeed Craig's whole career can be regarded as reactive, fashioned in opposition to the claims of Irish nationalism. Yet Craig was on good terms with individual nationalists, and he was punctilious in his dealings with the Roman Catholic hierarchy. But he did little to meet Catholic complaints about discrimination, and by the time of his death there were few Catholics in administrative posts, and fewer in the Royal Ulster Constabulary than there had been in 1922. He had no insight into, nor understanding of, the Roman Catholic mentality, and sought none. In 1938 he told the *Daily Express* that he was 'the one politician who can win an election without ever leaving his fireside' (Buckland, *Craig*, 122), which sums up both the limits of his ambition and the nature of his political power.                                          D. GEORGE BOYCE

**Sources** P. Buckland, *James Craig* (1980) · St J. Ervine, *Craigavon: Ulsterman* (1949) · P. Bew, P. Gibbon, and H. Patterson, *The state in Northern Ireland, 1921–1972* (1979) · P. Buckland, *The factory of grievances: devolved government in N. Ireland, 1921–1939* (1979) · A. T. Q. Stewart, *The Ulster crisis* (1967) · cabinet conclusions, 1919–22, PRO, CAB 23/18–30 · cabinet committee on Ireland, 1919–22, PRO, CAB

27/68 · P. Buckland, *Irish unionism, 2: Ulster unionism and the origins of Northern Ireland* (1973) · H. Shearman, *Not an inch: a study of Northern Ireland and Lord Craigavon* (1942) · M. A. Hopkinson, 'The Craig–Collins pacts of 1922: the attempted reforms of the Northern Ireland government', *Irish Historical Studies*, 27 (1990–91), 145–58 · *CGPLA NIre.* (1941)

**Archives** PRO NIre., corresp., T 3775 · PRO NIre., corresp., papers, and press cuttings vols., incl. papers of Lady Craigavon, D 1415/B 1–43, T 1908 | Bodl. Oxf., corresp. with H. A. Gwynne · HLRO, corresp. with Bonar Law · HLRO, letters to David Lloyd George · HLRO, corresp. with John St Loe Strachey · IWM, corresp. with Sir Henry Wilson · NL Ire., letters to John Redmond · PRO, British Cabinet MSS · PRO, corresp. with Ramsay Macdonald, PRO 30/69/1/191 · PRO NIre., corresp. with Edward Carson, D 1507 · PRO NIre., letters to Lady Londonderry, D 2846 · PRO NIre., letters to Lord Londonderry, D 3099 · PRO NIre., Northern Ireland Cabinet MSS | FILM BFI NFTVA, documentary footage · BFI NFTVA, news footage

**Likenesses** W. Stoneman, photograph, 1917, NPG · O. Edis, photograph, *c.*1921, NPG [*see illus.*] · J. Lavery, oils, 1923, Ulster Museum, Belfast · O. Edis, photographs, NPG · L. S. Merrifield, statue, Northern Ireland Houses of Parliament, Stormont · B. Partridge, pen-and-ink caricature (with Michael Collins), NPG; repro. in *Punch* (15 Feb 1922) · Who, caricature, Hentschel-colourtype, NPG; repro. in *VF* (19 July 1911) · photographs, repro. in Ervine, *Craigavon*

**Wealth at death** £3228 2*s.* 6*d.* effects in England: probate, 20 March 1941, *CGPLA NIre.* · £24,138 9*s.* 9*d.*: probate, 3 March 1941, *CGPLA NIre.*

**Craig, Sir James Gibson**, first baronet (1765–1850), lawyer and politician, was born on 11 October 1765 in St John Street, Edinburgh, the second son of the ten children of William Gibson (*d.* 1807), banker or merchant, and his wife, Mary Cecilia (*fl.* 1761–1772?), daughter of James Balfour of Pilrig. He was educated at the high school, Edinburgh, and in 1786 he was admitted as a writer to the signet. On 14 September 1796 he married Anne (*d.* 1837), the daughter of James Thomson, of Edinburgh; they had two sons and seven daughters. Their first son, William Gibson *Craig, became an MP and lord clerk register of Scotland, and their second son, James Thomson Gibson-*Craig, was a noted bibliophile.

In March 1823, following the death of his distant relative Robert Craig, James Gibson succeeded under an entail created by a deed of 1818 to the estate of Riccarton in Midlothian, and took the additional name of Craig. He remained an active member of his legal firm, Craig, Dalziel, and Brodie, all his life, and after his death the Society of Writers to the Signet paid special tribute to him as a leading member. He was also a director of various banks and public companies, and the deputy governor of the British Linen Company Bank. His professional advice was much sought after and respected even by his political opponents. It was for his political activities, however, that he was most noted by contemporaries.

James Gibson was a leading member of the Foxites or liberal whigs in Scotland. He first came to prominence during the 1790s, when he was active in advising, financing, and helping to organize the Scottish political reformers. Henry Cockburn expressed astonishment that Gibson was not prosecuted along with Thomas Muir and others in the treason trials of 1793–4 for his activities (Cockburn, *Life of Jeffrey*, 1.197). In his short memoir of his

friend John Allen (prefixed to the 1849 edition of the latter's *Inquiry into the Rise and Growth of the Royal Prerogative in England*), he gave an account of two political dinners he attended at the time of the revolution in France. One, organized by himself and Allen, was held at the Fortune tavern in Edinburgh in July 1791 to celebrate the fall of the Bastille; the other was given by Lord Daer at Hunter's Tavern, also in Edinburgh. On both occasions the proceedings were subject to close surveillance by the Edinburgh authorities. It was also said that Gibson used to stand at the head of Leith Walk in Edinburgh and mend the pens being used by signatories to petitions for reform.

During the short 'ministry of all the talents' of 1806–7, Gibson was given the posts of solicitor of stamps and deputy lieutenant of Edinburgh. He was particularly close to Francis Jeffrey, but he was also an associate of such men as Henry Erskine, John Clerk of Eldin, George Cranstoun, Henry Moncrieff Wellwood, and Henry Cockburn. In 1821 his professional reputation and personal honour were scurrilously attacked by the conservative *Beacon* newspaper, along with those of other leading whigs. He exposed the financial supporters of *The Beacon*, who included Walter Scott, and sued for defamation, for which he was awarded £500 in court. In a duel over the same affair, James Stuart of Dunearn fatally shot Sir Alexander Boswell, a contributor to the paper. Gibson challenged Scott, but he was pacified by an assurance from Scott's friends that Scott had not been directly involved and that the paper would fold immediately.

Craig, as he was now known, took a conspicuous role in the reform agitation of 1830–31, attending most if not all of the Edinburgh meetings and demonstrations, and appearing prominently in the celebration held after the passing of the act in 1832. Lord Grey created him a baronet of the United Kingdom on 30 September 1831 in recognition of his services to the whig party. In 1840 he campaigned vigorously on behalf of Adam Black for the position of mayor against the claim of Sir James Forrest, because Black supported civil equality for all religious denominations and Forrest did not. It is interesting, therefore, that he opposed the Disruption of the Church of Scotland in 1843, unlike many of his political associates; but he did so not because he supported the principle of patronage in the church, but rather because he opposed disestablishment, fearing that the 'spiritual independence' claimed by the Free Church party would be a danger to the state (*DNB*).

Large in person and in character, Craig was a well-known figure in early nineteenth-century Edinburgh. He was tall, athletic, and imposing in frame, and he was famous for his vigour, energy, and occasional wilfulness. He was also known for his integrity and kindness, however, and despite his earlier hostility to Scott, he took a leading part in ensuring that Scott was able to retain his library, furniture, and other personal possessions at Abbotsford after his bankruptcy in 1830.

Despite his familiarity to contemporaries and their estimation of his importance as a manager of the Scottish whigs or Liberals, Craig is rarely mentioned by historians of this period in Scottish political history or of the whig party, probably because he was not a public speaker, nor did he publish anything besides his short memoir of Allen and, it is said, a *Letter to the People of Scotland on the Jury Bill* (1815). Sir James Gibson Craig died on 6 March 1850, after suffering from an attack of bronchitis, at Riccarton House on his estate near Edinburgh (now the site of Heriot-Watt University), where he was also buried after a private funeral on 11 March.                    EMMA VINCENT MACLEOD

**Sources** old parish registers, NA Scot., 685.2/8 [birth], 685.1/52 [marriage], 685.2/16 [parents' marriage] · *Caledonian Mercury* (4 March 1850) · *Caledonian Mercury* (7 March 1850) · W. Anderson, *The Scottish nation*, 3 vols. in 9 (1875) · *GM*, 2nd ser., 33 (1850), 534 · J. G. Craig, 'Biographical sketch', in J. Allen, *Inquiry into the rise and growth of the royal prerogative in England*, ed. B. Thorpe, 2nd edn (1849), xi–xviii · H. Cockburn, *Life of Lord Jeffrey, with a selection from his correspondence*, 1 (1852), 197–8 · *The Scotsman* (6 March 1850) · *The Scotsman* (9 March 1850) · *The Scotsman* (13 March 1850) · 'Sir James Gibson Craig', *Encyclopaedia Britannica*, 8th edn (1853–60) · Irving, *Scots.* · J. G. Lockhart, *The life of Sir Walter Scott*, [new edn], 10 vols. (1902), vol. 3, pp. 158–65; vol. 10, p. 13 · *Memorials of his time, by Henry Cockburn*, new edn, ed. H. A. Cockburn (1909) · *DNB*

**Archives** Heriot-Watt University, corresp., mainly with his eldest son, William, on personal and family, estate, and political matters | NA Scot., letters to Sir John Dalrymple, eighth earl of Stair · NA Scot., letters to second Lord Panmure · NL Scot., corresp. with George Combe · NL Scot., corresp. with Archibald Constable · NL Scot., letters to Edward Ellice · NL Scot., account books as agent to Lord Tweeddale, MSS 14612–14613 · NRA Scotland, priv. coll., letters to Lord Moncreiff

**Likenesses** C. Smith, oils, *c*.1820, Signet Library, Edinburgh · T. Campbell, plaster bust, Scot. NPG · B. W. Crombie, pencil, ink, and watercolour studies, Scot. NPG · B. W. Crombie, repro. in *The modern Athenians* (1882), pl. 15 · H. Raeburn?, oils; copy, photograph, Scot. NPG

**Craig, Sir James Henry** (1748–1812), army officer and governor-in-chief of British North America, was born in Gibraltar of an eminent Scottish family, the son of Hew Craig, a judge at the British fortress of Gibraltar. He entered the army as an ensign in the 30th foot in 1763. After advanced military training, Craig returned to Gibraltar where, having the previous year been promoted as lieutenant of the 47th foot, he was appointed in 1770 as aide-de-camp to Colonel Robert Boyd, the lieutenant-governor. It was in the former capacity that he crossed the Atlantic in 1774 and participated gallantly in several of the early engagements of the American War of Independence. Craig suffered a severe wound at the battle of Bunker Hill in June 1775. In the following year, after transfer to Canada, he was instrumental in turning back the American invading force at Trois-Rivières, while in 1777 he was again twice wounded, once seriously, and made important contributions to engagements at Fort Ticonderoga, Hubbardton, and Freeman's Farm at Saratoga. Craig's exploits were recognized by Lieutenant-General John Burgoyne who raised him to the rank of major in the 82nd foot. From 1778 to 1781 Craig showed himself equally adept in dealing with assignments other than set pieces by his skilful reconnoitres both in Maine and North Carolina. His reward was to be promoted to lieutenant-colonel of the 16th regiment in 1781. At the conclusion of the

Sir James Henry Craig (1748–1812), attrib. Gerrit Schipper, 1807

American war he served for a time in Ireland where in 1790 he was promoted to the rank of colonel.

The outbreak of the revolutionary war with France once again set Craig upon his travels. In 1794 he first became adjutant-general, then major-general, in the duke of York's army in the Netherlands before participating during the following year in the capture of Cape Colony from the Dutch. His first gubernatorial experience was gained there while serving in Cape Town between 1795 and 1797. It is not implausible that the prevalent British condescension towards the perceived backwardness of Boer society might have led Craig to see similarities between it and the Canadian population which he was to encounter ten years later along the banks of the St Lawrence. It was at the conclusion of this term of office that he was, while briefly in England, invested with the Order of the Bath. He was now charged with another imperial duty as commander of a division of troops in Bengal where he showed firmness in dealing with disaffection in the ranks. Appointed lieutenant-general in January 1801, he returned to England a year later and took command of troops in the eastern district until March 1805. His final military assignment took him to Italy as a general where, due to Napoleon's success at the battles of Ulm and Austerlitz, he was frustrated in bringing pressure to bear upon the French flank by means of his 7000-strong army in northern Italy. Instead, early in the next year he relocated his troops to Sicily and proceeded to England where, on 29 August 1807, he was appointed captain-general and governor-in-chief of British North America, with special responsibility for administering Lower Canada.

Perhaps it was the gathering war clouds in North America, where problems of trade and frontiers plagued relations with the American republic, that accounted for Craig's appointment in such an important region. There was, however, a question mark concerning his health despite the fact that he had ostensibly recovered from very serious illness. Nor had his peripatetic and energetic mode of life led to tolerance of social and cultural difference; instead it merely confirmed him in the view that

Britain was the model society which provided the blueprint for universal improvement. In Lower Canada, however, he was faced with a mature nationalist movement among the otherwise socially conservative French political class. This development had been fuelled by the trauma of the conquest, overt exclusion from positions of power and privilege, and from more widespread fears regarding the loss of language and culture. Looked at from Craig's perspective, however, the chief difficulty arose from the fact that he had to operate within the confines of the system created by the Constitutional Act (1791) which had separated the old province of Quebec into the distinct provinces of Upper and Lower Canada with a representative assembly for each. To Craig this was akin to being handcuffed in the face of imminent danger. That William Pitt's government had seen fit to provide Lower Canada with a representative assembly seemed, with each passing year, to have been a misguided leap of faith. Certainly this viewpoint became orthodoxy among the influential British community which was based chiefly in the urban centres of Montreal and Quebec and made up slightly less than a quarter of the nearly 300,000 population of Lower Canada. The temporary alliance between British and French merchants, prior to the passing of the act, broke down shortly thereafter. During the course of the 1790s fears regarding the influence of French emissaries and American spies created an atmosphere of heightened fear and suspicion. One of the individuals most influential in raising this air of insecurity was the attorney-general Jonathan Sewell, who drafted legislation in 1797 which provided extensive powers to curtail rights of the individual and members of the assembly in any emergency. Another area of conflict, arising in part from the murky nature of its legal situation, was the Roman Catholic church. The British government had given some sustenance of hope to protestants when, in 1793, it appointed Jacob Mountain to the first bishopric in Lower Canada. The traditional role of the Roman Catholic church in educational matters also came under threat with the establishment of the Royal Institution for the Advancement of Learning in 1801.

On his arrival in October 1807 Craig therefore faced a position in which the main lines of conflict between the assembly under the control of the *parti canadien*, led by Pierre-Stanislas Bédard, and the 'château clique' which dominated the appointed legislative and executive councils were very well defined, and were vigorously promoted in rival newspapers, the *Quebec Mercury* (1804–) which spoke for the British community and *Le Canadien* (1806–) which supported the *parti canadien*. It was a situation to tax even the most judicious governor-in-chief. But it was not Craig's style to attempt to seek compromise. His instinct was to attack, and within several months of his arrival he had decided upon his strategy. Influenced by his civil secretary, Herman Witsius Ryland, Craig embraced almost completely the programme and outlook of the British party. In some areas of policy, such as the affairs of church and state, this analysis undoubtedly led Craig astray. As a first step towards making real what he took to be the legal

supremacy of the state over the church, he pressed for control over the right to make clerical appointments within the Roman Catholic church. Several long interviews with Joseph Octave Plessis, the Catholic archbishop of Quebec, proved desultory. Craig could not rid himself of suspicions that Plessis's church and clergy were in sympathy with the nationalists. In this regard he let his prejudices get the better of him. In fact Plessis's stance was more accommodating; he had, for example, chosen to describe as 'la conquête providentielle' what was to him Canada's ordained escape from the horrors of the French Revolution; in addition he showed himself willing, when necessary, to comply with the reading out of Craig's loyal proclamations within his churches.

In the more purely political sphere it is at least arguable that Craig's policies met with greater success. In his own mind action was necessary to draw the teeth of the nationalist party; otherwise the colony faced the risk of internal collapse in the event of confrontation with the American republic. Craig's strategy was defended by his civil secretary, Ryland, who had watched the former governor, Sir Guy Carleton, unreservedly but mistakenly put his faith in the French Canadian population's willingness to fight wholeheartedly for the British cause. Now Ryland and Craig watched with concern as the air of confrontation and resistance escalated. In the assembly Bédard and the *parti canadien* took provocative action to counter Craig's expressed wishes, prompting the governor-in-chief in May 1809 to enter the chamber, chastise the members, and prorogue the session, for which he was rebuked by the colonial secretary, Lord Castlereagh. New elections were held nearly a year later but did nothing to change the political complexion of the house. Faced with renewed resistance Craig once again terminated the session on 26 February 1810. This time, however, he decided to go several steps further. On 17 March he gave orders that the presses belonging to *Le Canadien* be seized and its backers imprisoned. At the same time Ryland was dispatched to London to try to ward off any criticism and to promote Craig's plans for reform. The new colonial secretary, Lord Liverpool, was willing to admit that the Constitutional Act had been a mistake but offered little more assistance. Gradually those connected with the newspaper were released although Bédard spent nearly a year in confinement. In some respects he was, upon release, a chastened man who never again enjoyed the same primacy of place. Whether or not Craig understood the dynamics of the *parti canadien* remains doubtful; he had, nevertheless, skilfully exploited divisions between Bédard and the more moderate elements from Montreal. Had he lived long enough Craig might have made the claim that his actions accounted for the loyal reaction of the population to the menace of American aggression in 1812–14. What he would have been less willing to acknowledge was how his strategy was used by Louis Joseph Papineau in the 1820s and 1830s to stimulate support for his own nationalist platform. In a manner typical of subsequent historiography, a late nineteenth-century biographer of Joseph

Octave Plessis was able to describe Craig as 'ce gouverneur de sinistre mémoire'.

As might have been expected, Craig's record in the matter of colonial defence was more impressive than his political performance. He applied himself to the need for the rebuilding of fortifications and was adept too in arguing the case for troop reinforcements. Fortunately the militia was not weakened despite his penchant for punishing any critic by removing his commission for however minor an indiscretion or baseless a suspicion of disloyalty. On the whole he also found the right people—such as Francis Gore in his capacity of lieutenant-governor of Upper Canada—to prevent the Shawnee Indians under Tecumseh from initiating armed conflict with the United States.

As it was, Craig's health was deteriorating rapidly and from 1810 he was seeking to be replaced as governor-in-chief. He finally left British North America in June 1811 and was to survive only a few months in London before his death on 12 January 1812. He may have been buried at St Anne's, Soho, according to the request made in his will. His record thus was a mixed one. Having never enjoyed an alternative environment provided by wife, family, or home, Craig's immersion in military and political life had been almost total. Indeed, he lived in a world where firmness of command and obedience to duty were the main priorities. Unfortunately, a lifetime's service to his country had not equipped him to meet the exacting challenges which faced him while in Lower Canada. That he terminated his contribution to the empire there has tended unfairly to overshadow the varied and distinguished military record he had compiled by 1807. It must be said, however, that he did himself few favours by the partisan role he chose to play within the increasingly polarized Lower Canadian society, thus gaining for himself the reputation among French Canadian nationalists of being an archetype of the Anglicizing instincts of British imperialism. Craig's will revealed that he had accumulated a sizeable fortune, held mainly in annuities and East India stock, which he distributed generously among friends in the military, political backers, and loyal adjutants and servants. Though unmarried, he also made financial provision for a natural daughter, Caroline Charlotte Craig, who in April of the year following her father's death married the Revd John Beerhaven.                JAMES STURGIS

**Sources** DNB • J.-P. Wallot, 'Craig, Sir James Henry', *DCB*, vol. 5 • J.-P. Wallot, *Un Québec qui bougeait* (Montreal, 1973) • H. T. Manning, *The revolt of French Canada, 1800–1835* (1961) • F. Ouellet, *Lower Canada, 1791–1840* (Toronto, 1980) • R. Christie, *A history of the late province of Canada*, 6 vols. (Montreal, 1866) • S. Gagnon, *Quebec and its historians* (Montreal, 1985) • J. Meisel, G. Rocher, and A. Silver, eds., *As I recall / Si je me souviens bien: historical perspectives* (1999) • B. Young and J. A. Dickinson, *A short history of Quebec: a socio-economic perspective* (Mississauga, 1988) • J. M. S. Careless, *Colonists and Canadiens, 1760–1867* (Toronto, 1971) • J. Sturgis, 'Anglicisation as a theme in Lower Canadian history, 1807–1843', *British Journal of Canadian Studies*, 3 (1988), 210–34 • D. Creighton, *The empire of the St Lawrence* (Toronto, 1956) • D. A. Muise, *A reader's guide to Canadian history*, 1 (Toronto, 1982) • will, PRO, PROB 11/1531, sig. 114
**Archives** Archives Nationales du Québec, private letters • BL, corresp., Add. MS 20176 [copies] • BL, corresp., Add. MSS 46702–46711, *passim* • Bodl. Oxf., orders [copies] • PAC Public Archives of Canada, J. Sewell collection, private letters • University of the Witwatersrand Library, Johannesburg, corresp. relating to Cape Colony [copies] • University of the Witwatersrand Library, Johannesburg, account of Cape of Good Hope [copy] | BL, corresp. with Sir J. Willoughby Gordon, Add. MS 49495, *passim* • BL, corresp. with second earl of Liverpool, Add. MSS 38243–38245, 38323, 38473, *passim* • BL, letters to A. Stewart, Add. MSS 40633–40634 • BL, letters to Lord Wellesley, Add. MS 13531 • Bucks. RLSS, letters to Lord Hobart • NAM, papers relating to Middlesex Regiment • NL Scot., corresp. with H. Elliot • PRO, Canadian career, CO 42 series • PRO NIre., letters to Henry Dundas and memoranda
**Likenesses** attrib. G. Schipper, pastel drawing, 1807, McGill University, Montreal, McCord Museum [*see illus.*] • portrait, National Archives, Ottawa, Canada
**Wealth at death** sizeable; est. £40,000–£50,000: will, PRO, PROB 11/1531, sig. 114

**Craig, James Thomson Gibson-** (1799–1886), writer to the signet and book collector, was born on 12 March 1799, the second son of Sir James Gibson *Craig (1765–1850), clerk of the signet, of Riccarton, Midlothian (who had in 1818 assumed the additional name and arms of Craig, and was created a baronet in 1831), and his wife, Anne (d. 1837), daughter of James Thomson, of Edinburgh. Sir William Gibson *Craig was his elder brother. He was educated at the high school and the university in Edinburgh, and was admitted writer to the signet in 1824. He practised as a partner in the firm J. T. Gibson-Craig, Dalziel, and Brodies. Politically a whig, like his father, and a man of cultivated taste, he moved in Edinburgh literary, antiquarian, and artistic circles, and he knew Scott and Macaulay, Cockburn and Jeffrey, Kirkpatrick Sharpe and David Laing, Raeburn and Fettes Douglas. He was an original member of the Bannatyne Club, to which he presented in 1828 an edition of *Papers relative to the marriage of King James VI of Scotland, with the Princess Anna of Denmark, 1589; and the form and manner of her majesty's coronation at Holyroodhouse, 1590*. In 1883 he sponsored a facsimile reprint of his ancestor John Craig's *Short Summe of the Whole Catechisme*, with a memoir of the author by Thomas Graves Law. Gibson-Craig assembled a very extensive library, the principal treasures of which were historic Scottish and French gold-tooled bookbindings, including volumes from the libraries of Mary, queen of Scots, and the earl of Bothwell. In 1882 he issued privately in an edition of only twenty-five copies a folio volume of *Fac-Similes of Old Bookbinding in the Collection of James Gibson Craig*.

Gibson-Craig married on 23 November 1841 Jane (d. 1863), second daughter of Sir John Peter Grant of Rothiemurchus and widow of Colonel Gervaise Pennington; they had no children. Gibson-Craig died in Edinburgh on 18 July 1886. His library was sold in London by Sotheby, Wilkinson, and Hodge over twenty-eight days between 27 June 1887 and 17 November 1888: 9674 lots produced a total of £15,509 4s. 6d. There was also a sale of his Scottish manuscripts by Dowells at Edinburgh in 1887, with interesting groups of Allan Ramsay and Robert Burns material, and pictures and objets d'art from Gibson-Craig's collection were included in three sales held by Christies in London in April 1887.                ALAN BELL

**Sources** *The Society of Writers to His Majesty's Signet with a list of the members* (1936) • J. M. Gray, *The Academy* (24 July 1886), 62 • *The Times*

(26 July 1886) · Sotheby, Wilkinson & Hodge (1887–8) [sales catalogues] · Burke, *Peerage*

**Archives** BL OIOC, letters from him and his wife to Sir J. P. Grant, MS Eur. 127 · NL Scot., letters to Liston family · U. Edin. L., special collections division, letters to David Laing

**Wealth at death** £68,789 5s. 7d.: confirmation, 12 Oct 1886, *CCI*

**Craig, John** (1512/13?–1600), Church of Scotland minister, came from a family of landed proprietors in Aberdeenshire. His father was killed at Flodden in 1513.

**Travels and teaching in Italy** A graduate of St Andrews University, Craig left for England and became tutor to Lord Dacre's children, a post he held for two years. On his return home he entered the Dominican order but was imprisoned on suspicion of heresy. After he was cleared of that charge he went back to England in the hope that Lord Dacre might secure for him a place at Cambridge, but when that failed left for France (about 1536) and then travelled to Rome, where he was encouraged by Cardinal Reginald Pole to enter the Dominican house at Bologna. There he was appointed to instruct the novices and subsequently was employed on Dominican business throughout Italy and went on a mission to the island of Chios in the Aegean Sea. Craig finally returned to Bologna, where he was appointed rector of the school, a position which gave him ready access to libraries, especially that of the Inquisition. There he read Calvin's *Institutes* and, having voiced his approval of Calvin and expressed his opinions too freely, was delated for heresy, sent to Rome for examination, and imprisoned for nine months. Condemned to death by the Inquisition, he was due to be burnt on 19 August 1559 but the preceding night Pope Paul IV died and a riot in the city resulted in the prisoners being freed. Craig made good his escape and headed for Milan. On the way, he met travellers bound for Vienna and accompanied them to Austria where he was brought to preach, it was said, before the emperor (presumably Ferdinand I, although John Spottiswoode has Maximilian II, emperor from 1564) who provided him with letters of safe conduct.

**Edinburgh ministry and opposition to Queen Mary** While travelling through Germany *en route* for England, Craig learned of the Reformation in Scotland and returned home to offer his services to the reformed church. His residence abroad for twenty-four years initially made him less useful than fellow reformers for preaching in the vernacular but for the more learned he preached in Latin in the Magdalen Chapel in Edinburgh. By 1561 he had sufficiently recovered his proficiency in Scots to enable him to become minister of Holyroodhouse or Canongate. That year, at the general assembly's request, Craig was one of those who authorized John Knox's form of excommunication and in June 1562 the assembly determined he should become Knox's colleague at St Giles's in Edinburgh. At some point he married Marion Smaill, about whom nothing else is known.

As minister in Edinburgh in 1564 Craig incurred the wrath of Queen Mary's secretary, William Maitland of Lethington, for a sermon in which he delivered a forthright denunciation of hypocrisy and corruption among nobles who diverted church revenues for their own use so that 'we cannot discern the Earle from the Abbot' (Knox, 4.375). In June that year, during a general assembly debate between courtiers and ministers on the powers of princes and subjects, Craig supported Knox's judgment against Lethington's by recounting the verdict he had heard at a disputation in the University of Bologna in 1553, namely that:

> all rulers, be they supreme or be they inferiour, may and ought to be reformed or deposed by them by whom they are chosin, confirmed, or admitted to their office, als oft as they breake that promise made by oath to their subjects. (Calderwood, 2.277)

When Knox was summoned before the privy council in August 1565 and ordered to abstain from preaching for fifteen or twenty days for offending Mary's husband, King Henry, Craig was invited to take his place. In December he and Knox were appointed by the general assembly to prepare for publication a form for fasting, to be printed by Lekprevik, which was incorporated in the Book of Common Order. In July 1568 he helped revise the form of excommunication.

Like Knox, Craig appears to have had foreknowledge of the murder of David Riccio, carried out in Mary's presence in March 1566. In that year, too, he presented a supplication to the queen for payment of ministers' stipends. When ordered by Mary to publish the banns of marriage between herself and the earl of Bothwell, Craig declared the marriage 'altogether unlawful' and voiced his objections both from the pulpit and before the council (Knox, 5.433). Following Knox's departure for England, Craig, left as the sole remaining minister of Edinburgh, sought the assistance of John Cairns as exhorter.

During the divisive civil war between the supporters of Queen Mary and those of her infant son, King James, Craig was suspected of remaining neutral. In his sermons he compared the state of the church in Edinburgh to the Jews oppressed by the Assyrians and the Egyptians. This offended many 'becaus he made the caus of both parteis alike' (Calderwood, 3.75–6). Despite the hostilities he remained in Edinburgh while others fled but he declined to preach to the nobles then assembled. Craig was elected moderator of the general assembly in March 1570 and, at its request, was one of those who sought an agreement between the king's men and the queen's supporters. Yet when challenged by Maitland of Lethington in 1571, he demonstrated his support for Mary's opponents in his retort that:

> seing there is a lawfull authoritie established in the persoun of the king and regent, throughout this realme, which ought to be obeyed by all the subjects therof, therefore our duetie is, as commissioners and members of the kirk, to admonishe everie one of your lordships to obey the same. (Calderwood, 3.80)

With other ministers, Craig seems to have refused to pray for the queen publicly when charged to do so by her supporters, although the *Diurnal of Remarkable Occurrents* indicates his opposition to the act of assembly in August 1571 prohibiting public prayers for Mary.

**Kirk, king, and further reformation** In 1572 Craig participated in the convention of Leith, called to secure a settlement on ecclesiastical endowment. That year the general assembly, of which he remained a regular attender, approved his transfer to a church in Montrose, but in 1573 he moved again to become minister of New Aberdeen, where he undertook some teaching in the university, again at the assembly's request. In March 1574 he was among those delegated by the assembly to investigate the behaviour of the chapter of Moray in admitting George Douglas to the bishopric. Reputed 'an eager opposer of Prelacie' (Row, 415), with Andrew Melville and James Lawson he opposed diocesan episcopacy in 1575. Again elected moderator of the assembly in October 1576, he was active in drafting the *Second Book of Discipline* (1578).

In 1579 Craig returned to Edinburgh to serve with John Duncanson as one of the king's ministers. By the time the general assembly met in the summer of 1580 alarm was growing among its members over the influence exercised over the young James VI by his cousin Esmé Stewart, recently arrived from France and newly granted the earldom of Lennox. In July, as Lennox was denounced as an agent of the counter-Reformation and a popish scare gathered pace, they censured Craig and Duncanson for not speaking out sufficiently against the Catholics in the earl's circle. In October Craig was involved in devising a strategy for establishing presbyteries to replace the oversight of bishops and visitors. While Lennox outmanoeuvred the earl of Morton and seized power in Scotland, Craig prepared a document firmly denouncing Catholicism and the papacy. On 28 January 1581 the king signed this negative confession, printed by royal command for distribution and subscription, and Lennox announced that he had become a protestant. In April the assembly organized distribution of the confession to churches, but its anxieties remained. When, following the death on 21 June of James Boyd, archbishop of Glasgow, Lennox advised the crown to prefer Robert Montgomerie as his successor, tensions erupted. Montgomerie was provided by the king on 3 October, but does not seem to have been consecrated. The assembly, convening again that month, elected Craig as its moderator for a third term, and he played a prominent part in its subsequent proceedings against the archbishop-in-waiting. He had enhanced his standing that July with the publication by the Edinburgh printer Henry Charteris of his *A Short Sum of the Whole Catechism*, written while he was at Aberdeen.

The palace revolution by the Ruthven raiders in August 1582 which ended Esmé Stewart's ascendancy was approved as 'the late actione of the Reformatione' by the general assembly. In the new political climate favourable to the presbyterians, the king found himself so sharply rebuked for backsliding by Craig in a sermon preached in his presence in September 1582 that he 'weeped, and said, he might have told him privatlie' (Calderwood, 3.674). But the tables were quickly turned in 1583 when the government of the Ruthven raiders gave way to the earl of Arran's conservative regime which legislated in 1584 against presbyteries and in favour of bishops and asserted

the crown's supremacy over the church. Craig denounced the Black Acts, proclaimed in May, and refused to obey the injunctions of the archbishop of St Andrews, Patrick Adamson. Summoned to appear before the king at Falkland, following parliamentary approval in August of subscription to the acts, he had heated exchanges with Adamson and Arran and was discharged from preaching and threatened with loss of stipend and banishment. With other ministers who refused to subscribe an oath of obedience to Adamson as their ordinary, Craig explained their scruples to the king, their antipathy to bishops, which would 'engender a new little Popedome in your Hienesse's realme', and the need for a meeting of the general assembly so 'that by commoun consent this caus concerning the whole policie and order of the kirk can be treatted and reasouned' (Calderwood, 4.211–18). By December 1584, however, Craig was induced to sign the subscription demanded by the crown. He did so only in so far as it was consistent with God's word and, as he explained, 'our subscriptioun was nather sought to be allowance, ather of the Acts of Parliament, nor of the state of the bishops, but to be a testimonie of our obedience to his Majestie' (Calderwood, 4.246). His example in acquiescing, which was thought to have 'done muche ill', accentuated divisions within the ministry and threatened to sow 'the seid of a feirfull schisme' (*Autobiography and Diary of … Melvill*, 229). In 1585 he preached a sermon to parliament on obedience to kings, criticizing the behaviour of the ministers who had fled to England.

**Last years** The fall of Arran's regime in November 1585 resulted in the formation of a coalition government which sought reconciliation with the church, and the general assembly, in which Craig continued to participate, was once more permitted to meet in 1586. In 1590 Craig officiated at Queen Anne's coronation and was active in producing for the general assembly a 'Form of Examination before Communion'. He rebuked the king to his face in a sermon preached in 1592, leading James to remark that had he known Craig might treat him so 'he would not have suffered him so long in his house' (Calderwood, 5.143). By 1595 the king drew the assembly's attention to how 'Mr Johne Craig is awaiting what houre it sall please God to call him, and is altogether unable to serve anie longer' (Calderwood, 5.368). Yet Craig survived until 1600, dying in Edinburgh on 12 October, reportedly in his eighty-eighth year. He left a son, William (d. 1616), who taught at Edinburgh and Saumur, and a daughter, Margaret, who in 1598 married an Edinburgh goldsmith, Robert Fairlie. Archbishop Spottiswoode considered that Craig 'was held in good esteem, a great divine and excellent preacher, of a grave behaviour, sincere, inclining to no faction, and, which increased his reputation, living honestly, without ostentation or desire of outward glory' (*History of the Church*, 3.91).

JAMES KIRK

**Sources** T. Thomson, ed., *Acts and proceedings of the general assemblies of the Kirk of Scotland*, 3 pts, Bannatyne Club, 81 (1839–45) · D. Calderwood, *The history of the Kirk of Scotland*, ed. T. Thomson and D. Laing, 8 vols., Wodrow Society, 7 (1842–9) · *CSP Scot.* · R. Bannatyne, *Memoriales of transactions* (1836) · T. Thomson, ed., *A diurnal of* remarkable occurrents that have passed within the country of Scotland, Bannatyne Club, 43 (1833) · The autobiography and diary of Mr James Melvill, ed. R. Pitcairn, Wodrow Society (1842) · J. Kirk, The Second Book of Discipline (1980) · J. Craig, Catechism, ed. T. G. Law (1885) · J. Kirk, Patterns of reform: continuity and change in the Reformation kirk (1989) · J. Row, The history of the Kirk of Scotland, from the year 1558 to August 1637, ed. D. Laing, Wodrow Society, 4 (1842) · J. Knox, The historie of the Reformation of the Church of Scotland (1644) · J. Spottiswood, The history of the Church of Scotland, ed. M. Napier and M. Russell, 3 vols., Bannatyne Club, 93 (1850) · A. R. MacDonald, The Jacobean kirk, 1567–1625: sovereignty, polity and liturgy (1998) · G. Donaldson, Scotland: James V to James VII (1965)

**Craig, John** (d. 1620?), physician, was probably born in Edinburgh, and has often been taken to be the third son of the eminent Scottish lawyer Thomas *Craig (1538?–1608), but he was in fact Thomas's younger brother (Dreyer, 516) and was thus the son of Robert Craig (d. 1575), merchant, of Edinburgh, and Katherine Bellenden (fl. 1528–1578), probably the daughter of Thomas Bellenden of Auchnoul. He matriculated at the University of Frankfurt an der Oder in 1573 and was already professor of mathematics and logic there when he graduated MD from the University of Basel in September 1580, having presented a thesis entitled Diexodus medica de hepatis dispositionibus. He left Frankfurt about 1582 to return to Edinburgh, where it is presumed that he concentrated on medical practice. On 3 January 1603 he was appointed principal mediciner, later termed principal or first physician, to James VI. He was, therefore, the first Scottish royal physician to be distinguished by this new title from the physicians-in-ordinary. He moved from Edinburgh to London shortly after this, when James acceded to the throne of England. He was elected to a fellowship of the College of Physicians, London, on 2 April 1604, and was promised admission on the first vacancy which should occur. He was, however, granted full privileges straight away. He was admitted officially as a fellow on 25 June 1604, on the death of Thomas Moffett, the famous entomologist. Some of the fellows apparently objected that his election was not lawful since he was not English, but after discussion it was unanimously decided that as the Scots lived on the same island as the English and were governed by the same king, they should not be excluded by the terms of a statute which was intended to keep out foreigners. Three years later, however, after a legal ruling which declared that Scots born before James's accession were not naturalized English, the college formally substituted 'British' for 'English' in the relevant statute. On 11 December 1605 Craig was named an elect of the college and was consiliarius in 1609 and 1617.

Craig has been identified as the father of the John Craig (d. 1655) who was also first physician to James VI and I. This is incorrect; the younger John Craig was the third son of Thomas Craig, and so was the elder John's nephew.

In his Athenae Oxonienses Anthony Wood repeats a story, allegedly from the mathematician William Oughtred, that Craig actually gave John Napier, inventor of logarithms, a crucial hint about how to develop this labour-saving mathematical technique. Returning from a trip to Denmark, Craig supposedly reported that a new method

devised by the astronomer Longomontanus (1562–1647), using 'proportional numbers', saved the tedious multiplication and division in astronomical calculations. Napier then determined to discover this method independently, and did so in a matter of weeks. There are a number of reasons why this story cannot be correct and it has usually been dismissed out of hand by historians. It now seems, however, that there may be a grain of truth in this account. While at Frankfurt an der Oder, about 1576, Craig met and received mathematical instruction from the gifted mathematical astronomer Paul Wittich (c.1546–c.1585). Wittich informed Craig of his new trigonometrical method for reducing the tedious labour of multiplying large numbers. Craig copied the details of this new method, known as 'prosthaphaeresis', into his own copy of Copernicus's De revolutionibus orbium coelestium (1543). It seems likely that Craig discussed this labour-saving mathematical technique with Napier on his return to Scotland. Craig's older brother, Thomas, was a legal colleague of Sir Archibald Napier, John Napier's father, and the two mathematicians had evidently become acquainted in their youth. It may well be, therefore, that William Oughtred, a shrewd mathematician himself, was correct to see a possible link between the technique of 'prosthaphaeresis' and Napier's invention of logarithms, although the details of this mathematical linkage remain obscure. Certainly Craig was among the first to know of Napier's new way of easing the burden of calculation by using logarithms and passed this information on to one of his correspondents, the famous Danish astronomer Tycho Brahe (1546–1601): thanks to a letter of Johannes Kepler (1571–1630), it is known that Craig wrote to Brahe in 1594 to tell him of the labour-saving tables on which Napier was engaged, and which he hoped would soon be completed.

Craig first became acquainted with Tycho Brahe in 1588, when he wrote a critique of Brahe's De mundi aetherei recentioribus phaenomenis (1588), a copy of which he probably received from the Scottish mathematician Duncan Liddel, who had been a student of Craig's at Frankfurt an der Oder from 1580 to 1582 and who knew Brahe. Although Craig's Capnuraniae restinctio, seu, Cometarum in aethera sublimationis refutatio thoroughly rejected Brahe's claim (based on careful attempts to establish the parallax of comets) that comets were not atmospheric phenomena but moved in the region of the planets, there followed a surprisingly respectful correspondence between the two men. Brahe even sent Craig a presentation copy of his book in 1588, and an 'apology' for it in 1589. Johannes Kepler and Longomontanus also began to write refutations of Craig's defence of Aristotelian cometary theory but neither completed the task. It is evident from one of Craig's letters to Brahe that Craig was not present on 20 March 1590 when James VI spent a day in Brahe's palace at Uraniborg on the island of Hven, off the coast of Denmark. A letter of 1594 to Brahe from Thomas Craig refers to John as his brother, so confirming that earlier biographical accounts, which refer to John as the third son of Thomas, are mistaken, and have confused this John Craig with his nephew, the John Craig who died in 1655.

Nothing is known of the circumstances or the precise date of Craig's death but John Argent (*d.* 1643) was made an elect of the College of Physicians in his place on 10 April 1620.                                          JOHN HENRY

**Sources** O. Gingerich and R. S. Westman, *The Wittich connection: conflict and priority in late sixteenth-century cosmology* (1988) · *Tychonis Brahe Dani opera omnia*, ed. J. L. E. Dreyer, 15 vols. (1913–29), vols. 5 and 7 · G. Molland, 'Scottish-continental intellectual relations as mirrored in the career of Duncan Liddel (1561–1613)', *The universities of Aberdeen and Europe: the first three centuries*, ed. P. Dukes (1995), 79–101 · G. Clark and A. M. Cooke, *A history of the Royal College of Physicians of London*, 1 (1964) · G. N. Clark, 'Royal physicians in Scotland, 1568–1853', *Medical History*, 11 (1967), 402–6 · M. Napier, *Memoirs of John Napier of Merchiston, his lineage, life, and times, with a history of the invention of logarithms* (1834) · Munk, *Roll* · J. L. E. Dreyer, *Tycho Brahe: a picture of scientific life and work in the sixteenth century* (1890)
**Archives** U. Edin. L., special collections division, Craig's copy of Copernicus's *De revolutionibus* with his marginalia

**Craig, John** (*d.* 1655), physician, was the third son of the eminent Scottish lawyer Sir Thomas *Craig (1538?–1608), and his wife, Helen Heriot of Lymphoy. He matriculated as a medical student at the University of Helmstedt on 21 July 1605, but he went on to Padua in 1607 when political troubles in Helmstedt resulted in the dispersal of the university. He rose to become one of the two first physicians to the English crown—the other being Theodore Turquet de Mayerne (1573–1655)—shortly before 3 December 1616, when he was elected as a fellow of the College of Physicians, London (although he was not admitted until June 1617, having to wait for a vacancy).

Craig attended James I during his final illness in 1625 but was ordered to leave the court as a result of his too vigorous denunciation of unorthodox treatments applied by the duke of Buckingham and his mother, the countess of Buckingham. The king's favourite had previously responded well to the treatments of a country practitioner by the name of John Remington, who lived at Dunmow in Essex. Accordingly, a messenger was dispatched and returned with a posset drink and a plaister to be applied to the king's stomach and wrists. These were evidently administered by Buckingham and his mother and were accompanied by a deterioration of James's condition. The regular physicians were highly indignant about this state of affairs, particularly as James had been refusing to submit to their prescriptions. Craig's language was so intemperate that Buckingham drove him from the sickroom, threatening to draw his sword, while Lady Buckingham knelt before the king's bed to plead for justice against accusations that she and her son had poisoned the king.

Craig had also served Prince Charles as physician, but on Charles's accession to the throne he was not appointed as first physician, possibly as a result of his earlier behaviour towards Buckingham. He was, however, appointed physician-in-ordinary in April 1635. In the records of the College of Physicians, Craig is listed among the *socii absentes* in 1630, but he had evidently returned to London by 1635. Otherwise nothing else is known of his life, except that he died in January 1655, and was buried in the church of St Martin-in-the-Fields.

Craig has usually been taken, erroneously, to be the son,

John Craig (*d.* 1655), by unknown artist

rather than the nephew, of the Scottish royal physician, John *Craig, who served James VI and I until his death in 1620. As if this were not confusing enough, Craig has also been confused with his supposed father in a significant number of the few accounts that exist of his life. His attendance at King James's deathbed is attributed to the older John Craig by Munk (*Roll*, 1.113), even though Munk had just pointed out that the senior Craig was 'certainly dead on the 10th of April, 1620' (ibid., 112). Gilbert Burnet, however, relates that the physician who was disgraced for saying that he believed the king had been poisoned (*History*, 29) was his mother's uncle. Bishop Burnet's mother, Rachel Johnston, was the daughter of Elizabeth Craig, who was one of the two daughters of Thomas Craig the lawyer. The identification of the younger John Craig as Rachel Johnston's uncle allows the conclusion, therefore, that he, rather than the older John Craig, was the third son of Thomas. If, as is often supposed, John Craig the elder were the son of Thomas, and John the younger were his son, Burnet would have said that it was his mother's cousin who claimed the king had been poisoned. No doubt the confusion has stemmed from the evident fact that both uncle and nephew were, from about 1616 to 1620, first physicians to James VI and I. The uncle was appointed to the Scottish crown, however, while the younger John Craig, although Scottish, was one of the separately appointed English first physicians.                     JOHN HENRY

**Sources** *Bishop Burnet's History of his own time: with the suppressed passages of the first volume*, ed. M. J. Routh, 6 vols. (1823) · Munk, *Roll* · G. Molland, 'Scottish-continental intellectual relations as mirrored in the career of Duncan Liddel (1561–1613)', *The universities of Aberdeen and Europe: the first three centuries*, ed. P. Dukes (1995), 79–101 · S. R. Gardiner, *History of England from the accession of James I to the outbreak of the civil war*, new edn, 5 (1886) · H. J. Cook, *The decline of*

the old medical regime in Stuart London* (1986) · *DNB* · will, PRO, PROB 11/247, sig. 244
**Likenesses** oils, Scot. NPG [*see illus.*]
**Wealth at death** substantial; left property and bequests: will, PRO, PROB 11/247, sig. 244

**Craig, John** (*c*.1663–1731), mathematician and Church of England clergyman, was the second son of James Craig (*c*.1632–1704), vicar of Hoddam in Dumfries, Scotland. In 1684 Craig matriculated at Edinburgh University, beginning his mathematical studies under David Gregory. In 1685 he travelled to Cambridge, where he published his first mathematical work, *Methodus figurarum lineis rectis & curvis comprehensarum quadraturas determinandi*. This was the first work published in England to use Leibniz's differential calculus (as opposed to Newton's fluxional calculus which was then still not in print). In 1687 Craig took his MA at Edinburgh University, and he moved to London in 1689. On 27 July 1693 he married Agnes Cleland (*c*.1669–1703) in the parish of St Martin-in-the-Fields; there were six children from the marriage.

Craig published two other major mathematical works, *Tractatus mathematicus de figurarum curvilinearum quadraturis et locis geometricis*, in 1693, and *De calculo fluentium, libri duo. Quibus subjunguntur libri duo de optica analytica* in 1718. In the first of these Leibniz's integral sign was used (for the first time in England), while in the second Craig used Newton's fluxional notation. In addition he published eight mathematical papers (chiefly on quadratures) in the *Philosophical Transactions* (1697–1710). He also contributed chapters to Cheyne's *Philosophical Principles* of 1715, and to Wotton's *Reflections* of 1694. The standard of his work was such that he was noted as a mathematician of the first order (he associated with Newton, Halley, and de Moivre), and the *Acta Eruditorum* of Leipzig ranked him among the originators of the calculus (after Leibniz, but before Newton). He was elected a fellow of the Royal Society on 30 November 1711.

In 1699 Craig published his *Theologiae Christianae principia mathematica*, a tract exhibiting the fusion of his mathematical and theological inclinations. This work has two main arguments. In the first two chapters Craig argues on probabilistic grounds that the evidence for any historical event (a) is weakened by the passage of time, the distance from the occurrence of the event, and the number of people by whom it is communicated, and (b) is strengthened by the number of witnesses and the number of independent communications. Moreover, oral and written testimony have different effects. Choosing the Newtonian fluxional calculus rather than a probabilistic one, Craig derives formulae for the calculation of the time at which the probability of an event will disappear, and applies them to the millennium. In the second part (chapters 3–6) of this tract, Craig gives a mathematical argument in support of Pascal's wager—that it is in one's self-interest to believe in God, since one who bets on believing is risking a finite happiness for a return of infinite heavenly happiness.

Later writers exhibited varying support for Craig's views. For example, David Hume ('Of miracles', *Enquiry*

*Concerning Human Understanding*, 1748, chap. 10) followed Craig in supposing that the evidence for the truth of Christianity would diminish with the passage of time, while David Hartley (*Observations on Man*, 1749) claimed that it would increase. Commentary on the *Theologiae* has, however, generally been adverse. One early writer viewed it as 'scandalous and prophane' (Edwards, 86), while in the *Penny Cyclopaedia* (3, 1837, 136) it is seen as 'a very silly attempt to apply numerical reasoning to historical evidence'. More sympathetically, Stigler finds in Craig's 'underappreciated book' (Stigler, 879) a formula tantamount to a logistic model for posterior odds: that is, Craig's probability should be understood as the logarithm of the ratio of the probability of the historical testimony as received at the present time, given the historical hypothesis in question, to the probability of the same testimony, given the negation of that hypothesis.

All Craig's ecclesiastical career was spent in the see of Salisbury. In 1692 he was collated vicar of Potterne, Wiltshire; in 1696 he became vicar of Gillingham Major; on 2 November 1708 he was collated in addition prebend of Durnford and canon of Salisbury Cathedral; and on 28 June 1726 he was collated prebend of Gillingham, a cure formerly held by his elder brother, William (*c*.1657–1721).

Craig died intestate at High Holborn, London, on 11 October 1731, and was buried three days later in the churchyard of St James's, Clerkenwell, London.

ANDREW I. DALE

**Sources** R. Nash, *John Craige's mathematical principles of Christian theology* (1991) · S. M. Stigler, 'John Craig and the probability of history: from the death of Christ to the birth of Laplace', *Journal of the American Statistical Association*, 81 (1986), 879–87 · N. Guicciardini, *The development of Newtonian calculus in Britain, 1700–1800* (1989) · J. Hutchins, *The history and antiquities of the county of Dorset*, 3rd edn, ed. W. Shipp and J. W. Hodson, 3 (1868) · K. Pearson, *The history of statistics in the 17th and 18th centuries* (1978) · *Fasti Angl.* (Hardy) · R. Hovenden, ed., *A true register of all the christenings, mariages, and burialles in the parishe of St James, Clerkenwell, from … 1551 (to 1754)*, 6, Harleian Society, register section, 20 (1894) · *The penny cyclopaedia of the Society for the Diffusion of Useful Knowledge*, 8 (1837), 134 · J. Edwards, *Some new discoveries of the uncertainty, deficiency, and corruptions of human knowledge and learning* (1714) · G. Cheyne, *Philosophical principles of religion: natural and revealed* (1715) · W. Wotton, *Reflections upon ancient and modern learning* (1694) · J. L. Chester and G. J. Armytage, eds., *Allegations for marriage licences issued by the bishop of London*, 2, Harleian Society, 26 (1887)
**Archives** Bodl. Oxf., Tanner MSS · U. Edin. L., Gregory MSS

**Craig, Sir John** (1874–1957), steel manufacturer, was born at Clydesdale, New Stevenston, Lanarkshire, on 11 December 1874, the fourth son of Thomas Craig, a furnaceman at David Colville's Dalzell ironworks, Motherwell, and his wife, Elizabeth Wilson. He was educated at Dalziel public school, Motherwell, and in 1888 went to work as an office boy with his father's employers. His energy and shrewdness soon marked him out for further promotion, and when John Colville entered parliament in 1895, Craig was entrusted with his duties at the Royal Exchange in Glasgow. In 1905 Craig was made ironworks salesman and five years later was invited by Archibald and David Colville jun. to join the board.

At this time Colvilles was expanding rapidly and by 1913

Sir John Craig (1874–1957), by Walter Stoneman, 1946

possessed an annual ingot capacity of over 350,000 tons, making it the second largest steel making firm in Britain. The demands of war accelerated this growth. Responding to appeals by the Ministry of Munitions to boost output, Colvilles purchased both the Clydebridge steelworks and the Glengarnock Iron and Steel Company. In order to safeguard fuel supplies, these acquisitions led to the purchase of the collieries of Archibald Russell Ltd. Craig played a major role in the exacting negotiations involved in the firm's expansion and, with the sudden deaths of David and Archibald Colville in 1916, he was elected to the chairmanship of the company. As such he was responsible for the further integration of the firm, forwards into the manufacture of sheets, alloy steel, and steel castings and backwards into limestone quarrying. Colvilles' most important product was ship plates and its largest customer was Harland and Wolff, and so when the shipbuilders attempted to secure their steel supplies by gaining control of the manufacturers, Craig welcomed the moves which led in 1920 to the sale of the majority of Colvilles' ordinary shares to the Belfast concern, part of the Royal Mail Group controlled by William, Viscount Pirrie (1847–1924). Although ultimate control of Colvilles thereby passed into the hands of Lord Pirrie, Craig's power within the firm was increased since Pirrie and his successor, Owen Philipps, Baron Kylsant, left the effective

direction of this part of their swollen empire to John Craig.

When the boom collapsed in 1921 Craig kept the works efficient, and embarked on protracted discussions with his fellow steelmakers both at home and abroad to try to reduce the severity of competition and with the government to obtain some degree of tariff protection. When these initiatives failed, he attempted to attain the more modest objective of strengthening Colvilles' position within Scotland. The first real breakthrough was the creation of Colvilles Ltd in 1931, the outcome of a merger of David Colville & Sons and the iron and steel making interests of Sir James *Lithgow (1883–1952) [see under Lithgow family]. Together Craig and Lithgow sought to build a modern iron and steel making group by the acquisition of the plate business of Stewarts and Lloyds, the Mossend works of William Beardmore & Co., the Steel Company of Scotland, and the Lanarkshire Steel Company. By 1936 Colvilles controlled 80 per cent of Scotland's ingot capacity.

It was one thing to control the industry, quite another fully to exploit the potential economies of scale offered by unified ownership. Financial constraints prevented what in retrospect is seen to have been the optimum solution, and Craig's own obduracy in refusing to close works at the cost of severe local unemployment inhibited the drive towards even greater productive efficiency. The Second World War and the ensuing post-war boom provided the opportunity for more radical reconstruction, but Craig's deeply felt social responsibility strengthened the more pragmatic calculations of his joint managing director, Sir Andrew McCance (1889–1983), in determining the policy of welding together Colvilles' collection of works. This policy eventually culminated in the creation of a fully integrated steelworks on a green-field site adjacent to the original Dalzell works: the Ravenscraig project.

The life of John Craig and the development of Colvilles are virtually synonymous. Aspects of his policies have been criticized. In seeking Colvilles' domination of a Scottish steel monopoly, his inflexibility of purpose may have retarded beneficial change, and his reluctance to close the least efficient works of the Colville group of companies undoubtedly constituted an obstacle to greater rationalization, but it is important to recognize that he strove always to preserve intact his inheritance from the Colville family and to care for the welfare of the labour force.

Craig's religious sincerity reflected itself in his whole life, according to a contemporary associate, and the eagerness with which he sought success for the works for which he was responsible, 'was not so much measured by shareholders' dividends as by the substance and security for the thousands of Scottish families whose breadwinners toiled at its furnaces and mills' (H. Douglass, *Colvilles Magazine*, spring 1957).

Craig married Jessie, daughter of John Sommerville, shovel plater, in 1901; they had three daughters and two sons, the elder of whom became the last chairman of the Colville group in 1964. Craig was appointed CBE in 1918 and knighted in 1943. The honorary degree of LLD was conferred upon him by Glasgow University in 1951. He retired from Colvilles in 1956, having been with the company for sixty-seven years.

During the time that he directed Colvilles, Craig also played a leading part in the affairs of the steel industry as a whole. He believed passionately in co-operation and threw himself into making a success of the National Federation of Iron and Steel Manufacturers, of which he was an original council member and, in 1922, third president. He was president of the Iron and Steel Institute in 1940–42, a member of the executive committee of the British Iron and Steel Federation, and a director of the British Iron and Steel Corporation. His only outside interests were his family, the Church of Scotland, and the YMCA, with which he had been actively associated at Motherwell since 1897, being the chairman of the Scottish National Council in 1927 and president in 1944. Sir John Craig died at his home, Cambusnethan Priory, Wishaw, Lanarkshire, on 1 February 1957. He was survived by his wife, and was buried at St Airbles cemetery, Motherwell, on 4 February.

WALTER TAPLIN, rev. PETER L. PAYNE

**Sources** P. L. Payne, *Colvilles and the Scottish steel industry* (1979) · S. Tolliday, *Business, banking and politics: the case of British steel, 1918–1939* (1987) · D. Murray, *Sir John Craig: sixty-seven years with Colvilles* [n.d., 1956?] · *Colvilles Magazine* (Aug 1920) · *Colvilles Magazine* (spring 1957) · C. A. Wurm, *Business, politics and international relations: steel, cotton and international cartels in British politics, 1924–1939*, trans. P. Salmon (1993) · J. C. Carr and W. Taplin, *History of the British steel industry* (1962) · P. L. Payne, 'Rationality and personality: a study of mergers in the Scottish iron and steel industry, 1916–1936', *Business History*, 19 (1977), 162–91 · R. H. Campbell, *The rise and fall of Scottish industry, 1707–1939* (1980) · *Glasgow Herald* (2 Feb 1957) · *The Scotsman* (2 Feb 1957) · *The Times* (2 Feb 1957) · *The Engineer* (8 Feb 1957) · d. cert. · *CGPLA Eng. & Wales* (1957)
**Archives** priv. coll. · U. Glas., Archives and Business Records Centre, corresp. and papers | Bank of England Archive, London, Bankers Industrial Development Co. and Securities Management Trust MSS · NA Scot., British Steel MS GD.464
**Likenesses** W. Stoneman, photograph, 1946, NPG [*see illus.*] · J. Epstein, bronze bust, priv. coll. · photograph, repro. in *Colvilles Magazine* (spring 1957) · photograph, repro. in Murray, *Sir John Craig* · photographs, priv. coll.; on loan to U. Aberdeen, King's College
**Wealth at death** £103,671 14s. 2d.: confirmation, 7 May 1957, *CCI*

**Craig, Sir Lewis, of Riccarton, Lord Wrightslands** (1569–1622), judge, was the eldest son of the lawyer and legal author Thomas *Craig (1538?–1608) of Riccarton, and his wife, Helen, daughter of Robert Heriot of Trabroun. He was educated at the University of Edinburgh, where he graduated MA in 1597. He studied civil law at Poitiers, was admitted advocate in 1600, was knighted and appointed an ordinary lord of session as Lord Wrightslands in 1604. After the death of his father he received a grant of the lands of Riccarton, near Edinburgh. He was admitted a member of the privy council on 9 June 1607, and continued to attend regularly until February 1610. He married Beatrice Chyrnesyde of East Nisbet, mother of his eldest son and heir, Thomas, to whom he resigned the lands of Riccarton in 1616. A daughter, Janet (b. 1614), married the politician George Pringle (1631–1689). He died on 6 February 1622.

J. M. RIGG, rev. SHARON ADAMS

**Sources** J. M. Thomson and others, eds., *Registrum magni sigilli regum Scotorum / The register of the great seal of Scotland*, 11 vols. (1882–1914), vol. 7 · *Reg. PCS*, 1st ser., vol. 7 · F. J. Grant, ed., *The Faculty of Advocates in Scotland, 1532–1943*, Scottish RS, 145 (1944) · D. Laing, ed., *A catalogue of the graduates … of the University of Edinburgh*, Bannatyne Club, 106 (1858) · G. Brunton and D. Haig, *An historical account of the senators of the college of justice, from its institution in MDXXXII* (1832)

**Craig, Maria** (1822–1905), Post Office official, was born in Dublin and was the wife, and almost certainly by 1853 the widow, of Robert Craig, a classical tutor, with whom she had at least two sons and two daughters. Her significance lies in her recruitment in 1853 as one of the first female employees of the private telegraph service and the General Post Office. In the middle of the nineteenth century there were few job opportunities for middle-class women; the professions were largely closed to women, and office work was still a male preserve. However, the newly established telegraph companies provided a new area of employment for women. By the 1850s a small number of private companies were providing the beginnings of a national telegraph system. Nationally, provision was decidedly patchy, but in London competition between the companies led to a considerable number of branch offices opening up. The Electric and International Telegraph Company was the largest of the companies and co-ordinated its London operations from Central Station, Moorgate. Central Station was organized on a scale which reflected its importance at the heart of the telegraph network: located on three floors, its instrument galleries serviced not only London's commercial, government, and private business, but also the provincial cities. Although male telegraphists, engineers, and boy messengers formed the core staff at Central Station, from the early 1850s the Electric began to recruit large numbers of female telegraphists. Women were found to be as good as men as manipulators of the Wheatstone needle instruments, while for lower wages a superior social class of women could be recruited. Like the other companies the Electric adopted a marriage bar, ensuring that, unlike male workers, women would not expect an accelerating pay scale. At Central Station the female staff was young, single, and respectable.

One of the first women to be recruited was Maria Craig, who started work at Central in 1853 and remained there for the rest of her working life. From the beginning she was employed in a key supervisory role. In 1855 she was the Electric's highest paid female employee, earning a fortnightly salary of £4 10s., compared to 10–14s. per week paid to the rest of the women. Unusually, she was married (but probably widowed), with at least one child, in a workforce otherwise composed of single women. The Scudamore report on the acquisition by the Post Office of the telegraph companies describes Mrs Craig as being employed as a 'matron' by the Electric in charge of the female telephonists at Central Station. Her marital status and relative maturity marked her off from the women in her charge.

Maria Craig's managerial role was a complex one, shaped partly by the nature of the work and partly by the youth and gender of the workers. Although telegraphy required a period of training, her main role does not appear to have been in this area. Rather, she was responsible for general supervision of the female staff, attending to their well-being and discipline. It was said she had a 'watchful eye'. Although only male telegraphists worked at night, the women were employed during a long day shift of up to ten hours, six days a week. Moreover, although the work was light, they were required to be in close attendance to their machines even when not directly involved in the transmission or receipt of messages. Close supervision was essential. While at work the women were not allowed to leave the station, but were granted certain privileges: the company set aside a kitchen and dining room for their use and provided tea and coffee, bread and butter, plus fuel, light, utensils, linen, and attendance.

The success of the Electric's system of female employment formed the basis for the further feminization of the workforce by the General Post Office, following the nationalization of the telegraphs in 1870. The Post Office expanded telegraphic communications, and embarked on an accelerated training programme and a big staff recruitment drive. Female employees had already proved to be cheaper and socially superior to men; they were also less militant at a time when male telegraphists were becoming unionized.

At Central Station the female workforce increased rapidly from 267 prior to transfer to 466 by September 1870. The Post Office fully exploited the maternal system of control already in place. Maria Craig continued in her role as matron. In the Scudamore report she was congratulated along with her staff for her forbearance during the stress of transfer. When Central was reorganized in 1870 she was given her own sitting room as part of the new female accommodation. Although there was a proliferation of female supervisors in the telegraph service in the 1870s, Maria Craig continued in her role as matron until her retirement in 1883. She was then earning £250 a year and, unusually for a woman, was provided with a pension. She died on Christmas eve 1905 at her home, 34 Harpenden Road, West Norwood, London, after an accidental fall.

Maria Craig's managerial role was not formally recognized by the Post Office. She was not mentioned in the Post Office establishment books, which were restricted to male officers at this time. Neither did she give evidence before either the Scudamore or Playfair inquiries of the 1870s. However, her importance in the management of women in a new area of technology cannot be underestimated. GREGORY ANDERSON

**Sources** treasury notes, pensions and gratuities, Post Office Heritage Services, London, pt 1, vol. 72 · F. I. Scudamore, *Report on the re-organization of the telegraph system of the United Kingdom* (1871) · J. Kieve, *The electric telegraph: a social and economic history* (1973) · Electric and International Telegraph Company, station staff book, BT Archives and Information Centre, London, part 81, vol. 65 · H. G. Swift, *A history of postal agitation*, rev. edn (1929) · 'Select committee on … the Post Office telegraph department', *Parl. papers* (1876), vol. 13, no. 357 · L. Holcombe, *Victorian ladies at work* (1973) · S. Cohn, *The process of occupational sex-typing* (1985) · *Once a Week* (2

March 1861) · *Once a Week* (16 March 1861) · d. cert. · *CGPLA Eng. & Wales* (1906) · census returns, 1881, 1901

**Archives** BT Archives and Information Centre, London, Electric and International Telegraph Company, station staff book, part 81, vol. 65 · Post Office Heritage Services, London, treasury notes, pensions and gratuities, part 1, vol. 72

**Wealth at death** £1214 4s. 4d.: resworn probate, 20 Feb 1906, *CGPLA Eng. & Wales*

**Craig, Robert** (*bap.* 1730, *d.* 1823), judge, was baptized on 3 May 1730 at Prestonkirk, Haddingtonshire, the second son of James Craig, professor of law in the University of Edinburgh, and his wife, Catherine, formerly Bathgate. He was admitted to the Scottish bar in 1754, and about 1756 was appointed one of the judges of the Edinburgh commissary court. This office he resigned in 1791. For many years he and his elder brother Thomas lived together, neither ever marrying. Craig and his brother were described as 'men of primitive habits', and their domestic life was of the utmost simplicity. Robert Craig's dress was recognized to be old-fashioned: 'He wore a plain coat, without any collar; a stock in place of a neckcloth; knee breeches; rough stockings; and shoes ornamented with massy buckles' (Paterson).

On his brother's death in 1814 Craig succeeded to the estate of Riccarton, being the last male heir in the descent of Thomas Craig (1538?–1608), writer on feudal law. He was a whig in politics. In 1795 he published an anonymous pamphlet, *An Inquiry into the Justice and Necessity of the Present War with France*, defending the right of nations to remodel their institutions without external interference. He died in Edinburgh on 13 February 1823.

J. M. SCOTT, rev. ANITA MCCONNELL

**Sources** Anderson, *Scot. nat.* · *Scots Magazine*, 12 (1730), 647 · J. Paterson, *Kay's Edinburgh portraits: a series of anecdotal biographies chiefly of Scotchmen*, ed. J. Maidment, 2 vols. (1885) · *IGI*

**Likenesses** A. van der Mijn, oils, 1765, Scot. NPG · J. Kay, caricature, etching, 1815, NPG · print, repro. in Paterson, *Kay's Edinburgh portraits*

**Craig, Robert** (1917–1995), Church of Scotland minister and theologian, was born in Markinch, Fife, on 22 March 1917, the son of John Craig (1886–1972), master mason, and his wife, Anne, *née* Peggie (*c.*1886–*c.*1926), a linen weaver. He was educated at the Bell-Baxter high school in Cupar and then at St Andrews University, where he graduated MA in 1938 and BD with distinction in systematic theology in 1941. After an assistantship at St John's Kirk, Perth, he was commissioned as chaplain to the forces. He was mentioned in dispatches for bravery during the Normandy landings. In 1945 he was posted with the 1st King's Own Scottish Borderers to Palestine and Egypt. In 1947 he took up the scholarship that had been waiting for him, to Union Theological Seminary, New York, where he studied under Reinhold Niebuhr and Paul Tillich, and graduated STM *magna cum laude* in 1948. His St Andrews PhD (1950) was the basis of his book *Social Concern in the Thought of William Temple* (1963). The Christian concern for social justice was to be his lasting theme.

From 1948 to 1950, while he was finishing his PhD, Craig was deputy leader of the Iona community under Dr George McLeod. They were two contrasting personalities whose friendship lasted until death. On 26 June 1950 Craig married Olga Wanda (*b*. 1920), daughter of Michael and Helena Strzelec. They had met in Palestine when she was serving as a staff sergeant with the Polish Auxiliary Women's Service; there was one son and one daughter. Later in 1950 they went to South Africa, where Craig became professor of divinity at Natal University. In 1957 he was appointed professor of religion at Smith College, Northampton, Massachusetts. In 1963 Craig returned to Africa, to Southern Rhodesia, as professor of theology in the University of Rhodesia. In 1980 he retired, having from 1969 been also principal and vice-chancellor of the university. In 1965 the party of Ian Smith had unilaterally declared independence, and intended to maintain white supremacy in Rhodesia. Liberal opinion across the world was against it, and even the Association of Commonwealth Universities threatened to boycott the University of Rhodesia. Friends advised Craig that he should not be there, but he felt that he was there for a purpose. The university was a multiracial institution (the only one in Rhodesia) and he intended to keep it that way. His sheer determination in defiance of the government succeeded, and in 1980 he was able to hand the multiracial University of Zimbabwe over to an African principal. He returned to Scotland having perforce left all his assets in Zimbabwe. An appointment to be minister of St Andrew's Memorial Church in Jerusalem took him back to familiar scenes and different political tensions. His gritty integrity and belief in the strength of ecumenical Christian fellowship made his leadership greatly valued, and he formed a close friendship with the mayor of Jerusalem, Teddy Kollek.

In 1985 Craig retired to the family home in Falkland, Fife, and to his surprise was called to be moderator of the general assembly of the Church of Scotland. He had never been to the general assembly before he took the chair in May 1986. His year as moderator showed the courage that characterized his whole life. He wore everywhere the eighteenth-century court-dress, lace, and tricorn hat of the moderator, but the message delivered in his gravelly Fife voice always addressed the contemporary world. On one occasion he alighted from a Lothian Region bus in full moderatorial dress at the front door of a social project he was due to visit, to be received by a slightly embarrassed civic delegation that had preceded him by limousine. His St Andrew's day sermon to the Scots MPs in Westminster did not endear him to the Conservative government of Margaret Thatcher:

> We are in serious danger of becoming again two nations—a few rich and many poor. We mobilized the best in human nature for justice and peace during the war. We are challenged to do the same for justice and peace today. (quoted in *The Independent*, 8 Feb 1995)

A similar furore arose when as moderator he paid an unscheduled visit to the peace camp at Faslane. He was no pacifist: indeed, as honorary chaplain to the forces he once conducted three Remembrance day services at different military cemeteries in Jerusalem. However, he respected the pacifist witness, and he could not see why those making that witness at the Trident base should be deemed unworthy of a moderatorial visit.

Those who met Craig in Falkland during his retirement may well have imagined that he had never left the place. His Fife accent, his innate courtesy, his stocky figure (with a cigarette never far from his lips), and his unpretentiousness betrayed nothing of a life of distinguished service overseas, or of the distinctions he had gained—a CBE (in 1981) and honorary degrees from St Andrews, Witwatersrand, Birmingham, Natal, and Zimbabwe. He was unawed by rank or labels, but treated everyone with the same courtesy and the same respect. As a father he encouraged and took pride in the achievements of his son and daughter, and in his final years enjoyed greatly the company and infant wisdom of his grandchildren. He died of a heart attack at his home, West Port, Falkland, Fife, on 30 January 1995 and was buried in Falkland. He was survived by his wife, children, and grandchildren.

JAMES A. WHYTE

**Sources** personal knowledge (2004) · private information (2004) [family] · *WWW* [forthcoming] · *Fasti Scot.*, new edn, vols. 9 and 10 · *The Scotsman* (1 Feb 1995) · *The Times* (8 Feb 1995) · *The Independent* (8 Feb 1995)
**Archives** NL Scot., papers, reports, and speeches as principal of the University of Rhodesia, Acc. 11220
**Likenesses** photograph, office of principal-clerk of general assembly, Edinburgh · photograph, repro. in *The Times* · photograph, repro. in *The Independent*
**Wealth at death** £68,731.31: confirmation, 3 May 1995, NA Scot., SC/CO 833/265

**Craig, Thomas** (1538?–1608), lawyer and jurist, was the eldest of the five sons of Robert Craig (*d*. 1575), merchant burgess of Edinburgh, and Katherine Bellenden (*fl.* 1528–1578), probably the daughter of Thomas Bellenden of Auchnoul, justice-clerk and senator of the college of justice. There was also at least one daughter, Jean. Of the other sons, John *Craig enjoyed a distinguished career as a physician, James became a merchant in Bordeaux, while Robert, a writer, married Elizabeth Drummond, daughter of the provost of Linlithgow. Robert Craig was a prosperous and well-connected merchant, who regularly supplied goods to the courts of Mary of Guise and her daughter; his wife also supplied the court with valuable decorative edgings for cloth, perhaps as part of her husband's business or perhaps independently. He was evidently close to Adam Bothwell, bishop of Orkney and commendator of Holyroodhouse, as indeed was his son. Craig's background was thus among the comfortable and well-connected merchants and professional class of Edinburgh and the lesser Scottish landowners.

In 1552, probably following study in the high school of Edinburgh, Thomas Craig matriculated as a student in St Leonard's College in St Andrews, graduating BA in 1555. He was probably then aged about seventeen. He did not stay to take his MA, but pursued his studies in France, at the University of Paris, and it was most likely there that he came under the influence of the neo-Thomist ideas of natural law that permeate his most important published work, *Jus feudale*. It also is probable that he studied law in

France, perhaps canon law at Paris and civil law elsewhere, as was normal for Scottish advocates of this era. His later writings certainly show him to have been very well acquainted with the works of contemporary French lawyers. On his return home, he probably attended the courts in the company of an experienced advocate to become familiar with 'practick', before admission as an advocate in February 1563.

**Patrons and promotions** Craig quickly acquired an important patron, being appointed a justice-depute by Archibald Campbell, fifth earl of Argyll, hereditary lord justice-general of Scotland. This appointment was doubtless secured by Craig's cousin Sir John Bellenden of Auchnoul, now justice-clerk. It was common for such posts to be held by relatively young advocates. In this capacity Craig presided over some notable political trials in the justice court at Edinburgh, for instance those in 1566 of Thomas Scott, sheriff-depute of Perth, and Henry Yaire, priest and servant of Lord Ruthven, for their part in the murder of David Riccio and treasonable seizure of the queen, and those of George Dalgleish, John Hay, and William Powrie in 1568 for the murder of Lord Darnley. This suggests that he was seen as trustworthy by those in power, although he did not preside over the 'fixed' trial that on 12 April 1567 acquitted Bothwell of Darnley's murder.

Craig's connections with the royal court and search for further patronage are reflected in his Latin verse. In 1565 he composed a Latin epithalamium for Queen Mary's marriage to Darnley. It is a typically humanistic effusion, full of elaborate classical allusion, with a strong patriotic theme. In 1567 he followed this with the *Genethliacon Jacobi principis Scotorum*, another poem with a strongly patriotic theme (it celebrates the birth of Prince James). Throughout his life Craig regularly produced patriotic and loyal Latin verses, many of them collected in Arthur Johnston's *Delitiae poetarum Scotorum hujus aevi illustrium* (1637).

In 1573, now enjoying the favour of the regime of Regent Morton, Craig was appointed sheriff-depute of Edinburgh, and must therefore have resigned his office of justice-depute. None the less, from 1576 onwards he is regularly recorded as pleading for the accused before the justice court, and did so for the rest of his life. He was also in regular practice before the privy council, which frequently dealt with sensitive cases concerning crime and public order, while the records of the court of session reveal his busy civil practice. His new appointment was a measure both of Craig's success at the bar and his ability to attract powerful patrons. Throughout his career he was rewarded with lucrative escheats. When justice-depute, he had acquired the specific escheats of various outlaws, and had also obtained the general gift of the unlaws of any six individuals outlawed. This must have been the foundation of his fortune. Such awards continued after he ceased to be a justice-depute, while in 1579 he was also appointed procurator for the collectory on a retainer of 200 merks per annum.

**Family affairs** By the 1570s Craig was well enough established to marry. His first wife was Helen Hamilton, the niece (or granddaughter) of Robert Richardson, commendator of St Mary's Isle. The marriage contract of October 1573 indicates that both families were able to settle substantial capital and lands on the couple. The marriage was short, however, as Helen had died by the end of 1575. It is likely that Craig's oldest son, Lewis, was born of this marriage. He had remarried by 1578, to Helen, daughter of Robert Heriot of Lymphoy (or Trabroun) and his wife, Helen Swinton (*d.* 1584), who made a subsequent marriage to Dr Edward Henryson, a noted humanist and scholar of Roman law. Thomas Henryson, Lord Chesters, the son of Edward Henryson and Helen Swinton, was thus the half-brother of Craig's second wife. As such he was one of Craig's many valuable connections.

Craig had a numerous and remarkable progeny. Lewis *Craig was admitted as an advocate in 1600 after study in Poitiers, before being knighted and appointed a lord of session as Lord Wrightslands in 1604; James, the second son, acquired estates in co. Cavan in Ireland (where he died in the wars in 1641) that he named Castle Craig and Craigston; John *Craig became a distinguished physician and was physician to James VI and Charles I; and Robert, the fourth son, was admitted as an advocate in 1620. Craig's daughter Margarita married Alexander Gibson of Durie, a senator of the college of justice; Elizabeth married James Johnston and was the mother of Archibald Johnston of Wariston, one of the drafters of the national covenant in 1638, and of Rachael, who married Robert Burnett of Crimond, also a senator of the college of justice, and was the mother of Gilbert Burnet, bishop of Salisbury; and Janet married Alexander Belsches of Tofts, an advocate.

Throughout his life Craig maintained close links with the centres of power and government in Scotland. Like many successful advocates, he lent substantial sums of money to noblemen and was involved in the complex networks of heritable bonds, wadsets, and loans that kept Scottish landowners solvent. Among the notables with whom he became financially involved were Bishop Bothwell of Orkney, his father's old acquaintance, to whose sons he acted as a curator after the bishop's death, Francis Stewart, fifth earl of Bothwell, on whose behalf he also acted before the justice court, and John Maitland of Thirlestane, successively royal secretary and chancellor. He also lent money to merchants and even to King James. It may have been his early links with the house of Argyll that led to his appearing before parliament in 1574 as advocate for the widow of Regent Moray (now countess of Argyll) and Moray's daughters. As befitted the son of a prominent burgess, Craig also often acted for the town of Edinburgh and served on a commission to select the master of the high school in 1562. His rewards included a special royal privilege relating to a tenement he built at the head of Craig's Close on Edinburgh's High Street in 1582, one which caused problems in the ambitious redevelopment of that part of the street in the 1690s.

**Legal writings** In 1578 Craig was appointed a commissioner to consider the laws and also to a committee to consider publication of acts of parliament. Throughout the sixteenth century concern was repeatedly expressed over the state of the law in Scotland, and various attempts were made to collect and publish texts of both customary laws and statutes. This was the context in which Craig's great work of legal history and exegesis, *Jus feudale*, was created; it also produced Sir John Skene's *Regiam majestatem* and Balfour's *Practicks*. He probably started work on *Jus feudale* in the late 1590s and there is considerable internal evidence to suggest that much of it was written in 1600. There was at least one revision, probably in 1606. The culmination of a lifetime's professional involvement in Scots law, it was enriched by frequent allusions to practice. Written in admirably clear Latin (which the poor English translation represents rather miserably), it is a typical humanistic work in its classical quotations and references and historical and philological discussions. That it originated in a patriotic concern for Scots law is revealed by Craig's stated Ciceronian aim of reducing that law to an ordered science, thereby making it easier for students to learn. He achieves this admirably, writing an accessible, learned, and well-structured work, in which he stresses the feudal origins of much Scots law (and English law too), and from that basis explains and expounds his subject in a logical fashion. He ultimately validates Scots law and its practices in the law of nature and nations in a way that to some extent anticipates Grotius. Craig gave full weight to the important late medieval commentators Bartolus and Baldus, but the principal intellectual influence on the work is French humanism, particularly the legal writings of the radical protestant François Hotman (with whose political views Craig will have disagreed strongly). Craig's systematic account of feudal land law and its principles influenced numerous later Scottish writers, and in particular Lord Stair in his *Institutions*, but also had an impact on English legal writers and on English understanding of the history of the common law.

It has been argued that Craig's concern with English law makes his work to some extent a unionist tract; but internal evidence suggests that his interest in English law only developed in the course of his research. More obviously linked with the approaching union of the crowns were two patriotic tracts which Craig had prepared for publication by 1602—*De jure successionis regni Angliae, libri Duo* (published in translation by James Gatherer in 1703 as *The Right of Succession to the Kingdom of England in Two Books*) and *De hominio disputatio adversus eos qui Scotiam feudum ligium Angliae, regemque Scotorum eo nomine hominium Anglo debere asserunt* (published in 1695 in translation by George Ridpath as *Scotland's Soveraignty Asserted*). In the first of these Craig argues strongly that kingship is not elective but dependent on hereditary right, and he attacks the notorious work of 'Doleman' (probably the Jesuit Robert Persons), composed in 1594 to impugn James's claim to succeed Elizabeth. In the second Craig argues for the ancient independence of the Scottish kingdom and refutes claims that Scottish kings had done homage for their kingdom. Both are linked with themes in *Jus feudale* and grew out of that work. In Craig's eyes the people had

irrevocably given up their natural liberties to the monarch, and while early kingship had been elective, it soon became hereditary to avoid dangerous disputes over succession; none the less he accepts a role for the people in law making.

**Last years** Craig continued to enjoy a successful career before the session, justice court, and privy council. In 1592 he was appointed with the king's advocate to reduce royal alienations during the king's minority. In 1603 he composed poems on the departure of King James and Prince Henry for England and he later composed a lengthy poem on James's coronation. In 1604 he was appointed one of the commissioners for the union of England and Scotland. He attended the sessions of that commission at Westminster, and as a result composed his *De unione regnorum Britanniae tractatus* of 1605 (not published until 1909). In this treatise he presents novel and essentially historical arguments concerning the possibility of a union of laws, claiming that it could be based on the feudal laws that were the common basis of both Scots and English law, or even on the civil law.

In 1604 Craig was nominated one of the advocates who could appear in the inner house, settling a problem that had emerged as Scottish procedure developed. A year later he was among the men named by the lords of session as most fitted to join their number. In 1606 he was appointed advocate for the church, and was one of the counsel for the six ministers accused of convoking the illegal general assembly held that year in Aberdeen, although he does not appear to have participated in their trial.

Craig died in Edinburgh on 26 February 1608. One of the clerks of the lords of session noted in the margin of the relevant page of the books of sederunt: 'Mr Thomas Craig deceissit the Friday about six houris in the morning' (NA Scot., CS 1/4², fol. 276r)—an unprecedented and unique addition to the formal court record, and one attesting the esteem in which Craig was held by those among whom he had passed a distinguished professional life. Within three weeks of his death the privy council wrote to the king requesting that he remember with liberality Craig's widow and children, particularly for his books on feudal law. Two years later the privy council recommended to the king the publication of Craig's manuscripts, once more singling out those on feudal law. A similar recommendation came from the estates in 1612, while in 1633 parliament granted a twenty-year privilege to Robert Craig for the publication of the *Jus feudale*. But although it evidently circulated widely in manuscript, it was not printed until 1655 in Edinburgh, in an edition by Lord Crimond, who was married to Craig's granddaughter. Craig left his family comfortably off and widely connected. In 1605 he paid £8000 Scots for sasine in the mains of Riccarton, so founding the estate associated with his name, though it was really built up and consolidated by his son Lewis, who acquired full rights in the estate. Despite the common attribution to Craig of a knighthood, he was never dubbed, but died as Mr Craig. JOHN W. CAIRNS

**Sources** register of deeds, NA Scot. · commissary court records, NA Scot. · J. Riddell, *Remarks upon Scotch peerage law* (1833) · J. M.

Anderson, ed., *Early records of the University of St Andrews*, Scottish History Society, 3rd ser., 8 (1926) · Gibson-Craig papers, Heriot-Watt University, Edinburgh · J. W. Cairns, T. D. Fergus, and H. L. MacQueen, 'Legal humanism and the history of Scots law: John Skene and Thomas Craig', *Humanism in Renaissance Scotland*, ed. J. MacQueen (1990), 48–74 · J. W. Cairns, 'The *Breve testatum* and Craig's *Ius feudale*', *Tijdschrift voor Rechtsgeschiedenis*, 56 (1988), 307–29 · D. B. Smith, 'Sir Thomas Craig, feudalist', *SHR*, 12 (1914–15), 271–302 · NA Scot., CC 8/8/45

**Archives** Heriot-Watt University, Edinburgh, archives, Gibson-Craig papers

**Likenesses** G. Vertue, line engraving, 1731, BM, NPG · etching, repro. in Craig, *Ius feudale*, ed. J. Baillie, 3rd edn (1721), prefix to

**Wealth at death** moveable £8324 [£18,000 Scots]: inventory, NA Scot., CC 8/8/45

**Craig, William** (1709–1784), Church of Scotland minister, was born in Glasgow in February 1709, the son of a city merchant. Educated at the University of Glasgow he graduated MA in 1736 and received a DD in 1764. As a young man he developed an enthusiasm for the moral writers of Greece and Rome, perhaps under the influence of his uncle Alexander Clark, a minister at Neilston in Renfrewshire. At Glasgow Craig was befriended by Francis Hutcheson, who arrived to teach moral philosophy in 1730 as Craig was completing his course of philosophical and theological studies. Hutcheson frequently attended services at which Craig preached and offered him advice on preaching 'to and from the heart' (Kippis, 414). Craig was licensed to preach in 1734 and ordained in 1737, settling in Cambusnethan in 1737 upon the presentation of Mr Lockhart. He was not warmly received, probably because of hostility to lay patronage and to his moderate preaching, with its emphasis upon moral principles and virtues rather than upon evangelical faith. Despite this reception, he refused two presentations in Ayrshire, one from the earl of Kilmarnock, before transferring in 1738 to the Wynd Church, Glasgow. There he developed a reputation as 'the George Wishart of Glasgow', in tribute to one of the kirk's greatest moral preachers.

In 1742 William Craig married Jean Anderson (d. 1758), the daughter of a wealthy Glasgow merchant; they had three children, including the judge William *Craig. In 1743 Craig and his friend William Leechman became candidates for the divinity chair at Glasgow University, but Craig soon withdrew from the competition, which Leechman narrowly won over the evangelical Glasgow minister John MacLauren. For the next nineteen years Craig continued preaching at the Wynd Church with moderate success, occasionally inspiring, always carefully avoiding speculative theology and warmly commending virtue as exemplified in the example of Jesus. Following the death of his wife, Jean, on 6 August 1758, he married in 1760 Rachel Kennedy, daughter of Gilbert Kennedy of Auchti-fardale.

When the seventh church in Glasgow, St Andrew's, was completed in 1762, Craig and his congregation removed to that elegant new building. Craig's affinity with the moral preaching associated with the moderate party is clearly demonstrated in two individual sermons published in Glasgow: 'The reverence which is due to the name of God' (1761) and 'The character and obligations of a minister of

the Gospel' (1764), as well as in a collection of sermons that he published in London: 'Twenty discourses on various subjects' (1775). In natural prose, trimmed of ornament and laboured imagery, Craig presents the fundamental doctrines of moderate theology: the existence and perfections of almighty God, his moral government of this world, and a future judgement. The most successful of his publications was 'An essay on the life of Jesus Christ', which was published by the Foulis brothers, first in 1767 and again in an enlarged edition of 1769; it was also translated into French.

Craig's final years were unhappy. His pleasant disposition was replaced by bitterness and deep melancholy as he reflected upon the death of his first wife and, with his health in decline, the death of his son, Alexander, a merchant who shared his love of the ancients, and then that of his second wife, who for years had been his comfort and solace. He died in Glasgow on 13 January 1784.

THOMAS DAVIDSON KENNEDY

**Sources** A. Kippis and others, eds., *Biographia Britannica, or, The lives of the most eminent persons who have flourished in Great Britain and Ireland*, 2nd edn, 5 vols. (1778–93) · *Fasti Scot.* · D. Runciman, *History of St Andrews Church for the last hundred years: a lecture, delivered in the corporation galleries, 1st March, 1860*, 2nd edn (1862) · W. I. Addison, ed., *The matriculation albums of the University of Glasgow from 1728 to 1858* (1913) · *Scotland and Scotsmen in the eighteenth century: from the MSS of John Ramsay, esq., of Ochtertyre*, ed. A. Allardyce, 2 vols. (1888)

**Craig, William**, Lord Craig (1745–1813), judge, was born in Glasgow, the son of William *Craig (1709–1784), a Church of Scotland minister in Glasgow, and subsequently dean of the faculties of the university. He studied at the University of Glasgow and possibly also at Edinburgh. He was admitted advocate at the Scottish bar in 1768. Politically an ally of Henry Dundas, Craig was appointed one of three depute advocates under Sir Ilay Campbell in 1784, alongside his friends Alexander Abercromby and Robert Blair. He held this office until 1787, when he was nominated sheriff-depute of Ayrshire. Following the death of David Dalrymple, Lord Hailes, Craig was raised to the court of session in December 1792 with the judicial title of Lord Craig. He won respect as a judge for his benevolent manner and the clarity of his rulings. In 1795 he was appointed to succeed Alexander Murray, Lord Henderland, as judge of the court of justiciary, an office he retained until 1812.

Throughout his career as a judge Craig combined his legal talents with literary pursuits. Along with the novelist and Edinburgh solicitor Henry Mackenzie and other advocates, he was a member of a convivial society at first called the Tabernacle. The club met once a week, sometimes in one tavern, sometimes in another, in order to conceal their proceedings from their acquaintances. Craig suggested that they launch a literary periodical from Edinburgh, on the model of *The Spectator*; *The Mirror*, edited by Mackenzie, first appeared on 23 January 1779. The club became known as the Mirror Club. *The Mirror* closed in 1780; its authors described the paper's origins as arising from 'a company of gentlemen, whom particular circumstances of connection brought frequently together … Cultivating letters in the midst of business, composition was to them an amusement only; that amusement was heightened by the audience which this society afforded' (*The Mirror*, 110, 27 May 1780). The same club also produced *The Lounger* (1785–7). Both titles ran into several collected editions in Edinburgh, London, and Dublin; after 1787 the authors publicly acknowledged their involvement. Craig's contributions, next to those of Mackenzie, were the most numerous, among them papers on Michael Bruce, the poet of Loch Leven (*The Mirror*, 36), and Shakespeare's dramatic character of Hamlet (*The Lounger*, 91). Craig was elected a literary fellow of the Royal Society of Edinburgh on 17 November 1783. He also served as rector of Glasgow University from 1801 to 1803.

Having retired from the court of justiciary through ill health, Craig died at his home at York Place, Edinburgh, on 8 July 1813. He never married. He was reported to have left an annuity to his first cousin Agnes M'Lehose, the Clarinda of Robert Burns. 　　　　H. W. DRESCHER

**Sources** Chambers, *Scots.* (1855) · H. W. Drescher, *Themen und Formen des periodischen Essays im späten 18. Jahrhundert* (Frankfurt am Main, [1971]) · *Literature and literati: the literary correspondence and notebooks of Henry Mackenzie*, ed. H. W. Drescher, 2 vols. (1989–99) · J. Kay, *A series of original portraits and caricature etchings … with biographical sketches and illustrative anecdotes*, ed. [H. Paton and others], new edn [2nd edn], 1 (1842), 302–4 · *The letters of Robert Burns*, ed. J. de Lancey Ferguson, 2nd edn, ed. G. Ross Roy, 2 vols. (1985) · *DNB* · J. Gary, *The Royal Society of Edinburgh: literary fellows, 1783–1812*, ed. S. Devlin-Thorp (1981), vol. 2 of *Scotland's cultural heritage* (1981–4), 19 · W. I. Addison, *A roll of graduates of the University of Glasgow from 31st December 1727 to 31st December 1897* (1898)
**Likenesses** J. Kay, caricature, etching, 1799, BM, NPG · G. Dawe, mezzotint (after A. Skirving), BM · H. Raeburn, oils, Parliament Hall, Edinburgh · A. Skirving, pastel drawing, Scot. NPG

**Craig, Sir William Gibson**, second baronet (1797–1878), politician and civil servant, was born on 2 August 1797. He was the eldest son in the family of two sons and seven daughters of Sir James Gibson, afterwards *Craig, first baronet (1765–1850), of Riccarton, Edinburgh, the whig politician, and his wife, Anne Thomson (d. 1837). The bibliophile James Thomson Gibson-*Craig was his younger brother. Educated at the high school of Edinburgh and a private school in Yorkshire, he was called to the Scottish bar in 1820. His connection with the bar was, however, merely nominal and, after devoting some time to foreign travel, on his return to Edinburgh he turned his attention to politics and other matters of public interest. In 1834 he served on the commission to inquire into church property in Ireland, and in the same year as a member of the general assembly of the Church of Scotland he gave his support to the Veto Act. He was elected MP for Midlothian in 1837, standing as a Liberal, and in 1841 exchanged that seat for that of the city of Edinburgh, for which he was elected with T. B. Macaulay. He retained the Edinburgh seat until 1852. On 29 August 1840 he married Elizabeth Sarah (d. 1895), daughter of John Henry Vivian, Liberal MP for Swansea.

Craig, who succeeded his father as second baronet on 6 March 1850, was from 1846 to 1852 a lord of the Treasury with responsibility for Scottish affairs. He took an active and prominent interest in the public affairs of Edinburgh.

He was one of the chief originators of the scheme for the water supply of the city, and through his suggestion a commission was in 1847 appointed to inquire into the whole subject of art in Scotland, the result of its deliberations being the erection of the National Gallery. In 1854 he was appointed to one of the unpaid seats at the Board of Supervision for the administration of the poor law in Scotland.

On 3 July 1862 Palmerston appointed Craig lord clerk register and keeper of the signet in Scotland, and on 8 December 1863 he was sworn of the privy council. A Treasury minute of March 1855 had suggested the abolition of the office of lord clerk register, which had become a sinecure. Craig practically revived its functions, and undertook the duties without payment while inquiries took place to decide the future of the office. He actively promoted reform of land registration in Scotland, culminating in the Land Registers (Scotland) Act, which extended the functions of the lord clerk register. In 1869 the salary of £1200 attached to the position was restored. It is owing to Craig's initiative that the documents of the register office, the privy council records, and the index volume to Thomson's *Acts of Parliament* were published.

Craig was a leading member of the Highland and Agricultural Society, of which he became treasurer in succession to Sir Thomas Dick Lauder. In 1848 he became deputy lieutenant of Midlothian. He was well known for his hospitality to men distinguished in politics and letters. Craig died at his home at Riccarton, on 12 March 1878. He was succeeded by his eldest son, James Henry Gibson-Craig (1841–1908), one of the family of three sons and three daughters. 　　T. F. HENDERSON, rev. H. C. G. MATTHEW

**Sources** *The Scotsman* (13 March 1878) · *Men of the time* (1875) · M. D. Young, '"A man of no common stamp" Sir William Gibson Craig of Riccarton, lord clerk register of Scotland, 1862–1878', *Miscellany Two*, ed. D. Sellar, Stair Society, 35 (1984), 295–315 · Burke, *Peerage* · Boase, *Mod. Eng. biog.* · *Proceedings of the Royal Society of Edinburgh*, 10 (1878–80), 24
**Archives** Heriot-Watt University, Edinburgh, Cameron Smail Library, corresp. and papers | Borth. Inst., letters to Lord Halifax · NL Scot., letters to Andrew Rutherford
**Likenesses** J. Watson-Gordon, oils, Scot. NPG
**Wealth at death** £62,830 2s. 9d.: probate, 10 June 1878, Edinburgh

**Craig, William James** (1843–1906), literary editor and university teacher, was born on 6 November 1843 at Camus-juxta-Bann, also known as Macosquin, co. Londonderry, the second son of George Craig (1800–1888) and his wife, Mary Catherine Sandys (1803–1879). His father was curate of Camus-juxta-Bann and later rector of Aghanloo, co. Londonderry. William Craig was educated at Portora School, Enniskillen, and admitted to Trinity College, Dublin, on 1 July 1861; he received his BA degree in 1865, with honours, and that of MA in 1870. At Trinity College he met and became the lifelong friend of Edward Dowden.

After a stint of tutoring in history and literature at Trinity, Craig migrated in 1874 to London, where he tutored for the army and civil service. Two years later he became professor of English language and literature at University College, Aberystwyth, where he organized a reading class in Shakespeare. He resigned from the position in 1879, but not without having instilled a love of literature in a number of his students. He returned to tutoring, eventually giving it up in 1898; some of those he tutored were later to become men of some prominence, for instance Lord Hugh Cecil, youngest son of the marquess of Salisbury, whom he taught in 1884. After retiring from teaching he devoted himself to reading, research, and publication in the area of Shakespeare studies. As early as 1883, however, he had published a collation of the folio texts of *Cymbeline* for the New Shakspere Society. Some ten years later, in 1894, he edited the complete works of Shakespeare in one volume with a brief glossary and an appended 'Index of characters' as well as an 'Index of first lines of songs, etc.'. As it was published by the Clarendon Press of Oxford, it became known as the Oxford Shakespeare.

The brief glossary appended to the Oxford Shakespeare was to be augmented by Craig into a comprehensive glossary, a project on which he was working when he died. Unfortunately, the materials which he left for this glossary were in such a state as to preclude posthumous publication. He did, however, edit the so-called 'Little Quarto Shakespeare' in forty volumes, completed two years before he died. The scholarly paraphernalia consists of an introduction to each of the plays and footnotes. For a brief period, from 1901 to his death five years later, he succeeded his friend Edward Dowden as general editor of the Arden Shakespeare, which also ran to forty volumes edited by various scholars. He himself edited *King Lear* and was at work editing *Coriolanus* at the time of his death, and the modern editor of the Arden *Coriolanus* (1976), Philip Brockbank, acknowledges having 'assimilated much from the 1922 Arden edition by W. J. Craig and R. H. Case' (Brockbank, ix). Dowden edited *Cymbeline*, making early reference to Craig's collation of the folio texts of the play and to his theories on the matter of possible sources of the story. Dowden also acknowledged that Craig 'With great generosity … placed a large body of his manuscript notes at my disposal, and gave me many later additions to this mass of annotations' (Dowden, xlii). A number of these are recorded in Dowden's own footnotes.

Contemporaries state that Craig was a tireless long-distance walker and a gregarious person. He died, a confirmed bachelor, in a nursing home at 12 Beaumont Street, London, on 12 December 1906 and was buried in Reigate churchyard. A number of volumes from his library are, fittingly, in the public library at Stratford upon Avon, donated by his sister Mrs Merrick Head.

ARTHUR SHERBO

**Sources** *DNB* · E. Dowden, 'Preface', *Cymbeline* (1903) · P. Brockbank, 'Preface', *Coriolanus* (1976) · *The Times* (18 Dec 1906) · *The Spectator* (5 Jan 1907) · d. cert. · *CGPLA Eng. & Wales* (1907)
**Wealth at death** £823 3s. 1d.: administration, 10 April 1907, *CGPLA Eng. & Wales*

**Craig, William Marshall** (d. 1827), painter, is 'said to have been the brother of James Craig, and Edinburgh architect' (Foskett, 519) [*see* Craig, James (1739–1795)], whose parents were William Craig (1695–1762), merchant in Edinburgh,

and Mary Thomson (1710–1790), sister of the poet James Thomson. After exhibiting at Liverpool in 1787, in 1788 he exhibited at the Royal Academy, being then resident at Manchester. In 1791, when he exhibited two figure subjects, he had settled in London. The following year he began as a miniature and portrait painter, varying this with occasional rustic figures and landscapes in watercolours in the manner of Richard Westall, and domestic scenes. Craig was drawing master to Princess Charlotte of Wales, miniature painter to the duke and duchess of York, and painter in watercolours to Queen Charlotte. He contributed little to Royal Academy exhibitions after 1821, and ceased to exhibit altogether in 1827. From 1808 to 1812 he also exhibited with the Associated Artists in Water-Colours, of which he became a member in 1810. In the first quarter of the century he shared with John Thurston the honour of being one of the principal designers on wood; and many of the popular engravers, including Thomas Bewick, Luke Clennell, and Charlton Nesbit, worked for a commonplace *Scripture Illustrated*, which he brought out in 1806. He also made most of the drawings for *The British Gallery of Pictures* of H. Tresham and W. Y. Ottley (1808). Mallalieu noted of these drawings that 'they are usually colourful and highly finished in a somewhat pointilliste fashion. They are also usually on a small scale' (Mallalieu, *Watercolour artists*, 72). He also contributed designs for the illustrations by J. S. Storer and others to E. W. Brayley's *Cowper, Illustrated by a Series of Views* (1813?); *An Essay on the Study of Nature in Drawing Landscape* (1793); *The Complete Instructor in Drawing* (1806); *The Sports of Love*, including six poems and six etchings (1818); *Lectures on Drawing, Painting, and Engraving*, delivered at the Royal Institution (1821); and *A Wreath for the Brow of Youth* (2nd edn, 1828), a book said to have been written for Princess Charlotte. He was a mediocre illustrator, but his watercolours are skilfully finished. One of them, *The Wounded Soldier*, was included in the William Smith gift to the South Kensington Museum (V&A). Other drawings by Craig are also in the Victoria and Albert Museum and in the British Museum, as well as numerous engravings after his portraits, some of which are mentioned in Richard Walker's catalogue of *Regency Portraits* (1985). The National Gallery of Scotland, Edinburgh, Newport Art Gallery, and the Castle Museum, Nottingham, also hold examples of his work. An advertisement in the *Manchester Chronicle* (18 February 1786) which reads: 'Mr Craig (Junior) Miniature Painting and Drawing. Instructed by his father & the ablest artist in London. Sets up in Manchester' presumably refers to Craig's son, W. Craig junior (Foskett, 519). J. K. Craig (*fl.* 1819–21), who exhibited at the Royal Academy 1819–1821 from W. M. Craig's address, 124 Oxford Street, London, was probably another son. Several artists called W. Craig who were all related exhibited from 88 Charlotte Street, Rathbone Place, London, Craig died in 1827. AUSTIN DOBSON, rev. ANNETTE PEACH

**Sources** D. Foskett, *Miniatures: dictionary and guide* (1987) · Mallalieu, *Watercolour artists* · Farington, *Diary* · R. Walker, *National Portrait Gallery: Regency portraits*, 2 vols. (1985) · R. K. Engen, *Dictionary of Victorian wood engravers* (1985) · S. Houfe, *The dictionary of British book* *illustrators and caricaturists, 1800–1914* (1978); rev. edn as *The dictionary of 19th century British book illustrators and caricaturists* (1996)

**Craigavon**. For this title name *see* Craig, James, first Viscount Craigavon (1871–1940).

**Craigen, Jessie Hannah** (1834/5–1899), public speaker, was the daughter of a Scottish sea captain and an Italian actress, names unknown. Though she once remarked that her childhood was spent in London, she also variously claimed roots in Scotland and the north of England.

Jessie Craigen began her working life at the age of four as a fairy in a pantomime, after her mother returned to the stage following the death of her father. As a young woman she abandoned the theatre, however, when 'religious scruples took hold of her' (Blackburn, *Englishwoman's Review*, 65). Instead, she adapted the skills learned there to public speaking, initially in the 1860s as an advocate of temperance. By 1871 she was also appearing on suffragist platforms in Scotland. In the early 1870s she helped establish a Dundee branch of the National Union of Women Workers, an affiliate of the Women's Protective and Provident Union.

Jessie Craigen's mode was to act as a freelance suffrage campaigner and speaker, travelling around the country accompanied only by Tiny, her dog, and holding impromptu outdoor meetings. Every so often members of the suffrage leadership would receive the petitions she had gathered in from her working-class audiences, 'very genuine and very dirty', together with requests for the odd £5 note to cover her expenses (Blackburn, *Englishwoman's Review*, 66). Her capacity to reach audiences beyond the town hall and the drawing-room brought her to the attention of the radical leadership of the Manchester Society for Women's Suffrage. She began to appear on the platform alongside national figures in 1879, at a series of major demonstrations in the larger provincial cities. On these occasions the beauty of her speaking voice and the power of her oratory were often recorded.

In other respects, some of her middle-class sponsors found her less satisfactory. She is described as a 'heavy, uncouth figure' by one of her closest colleagues at this time, Helen Blackburn, who also recorded that this 'strange, erratic genius' was of a wayward, temperamental character that could 'brook no constraint or control' (Blackburn, *Women's Suffrage*, 126; Blackburn, *Englishwoman's Review*, 66). She was generally either loved or loathed by those who came to know her. Her firmest supporters were among radical suffragists, including Anna Maria Priestman, Margaret Tanner, and Priscilla Bright McLaren. Through this network Jessie Craigen found additional employment with the Ladies National Association for the Repeal of the Contagious Diseases Acts (LNA) in the early 1880s. It was at this time also that she came to know Helen Taylor, daughter of Harriet Taylor and stepdaughter of John Stuart Mill, for whom she formed a passionate attachment.

Helen Taylor was by this time alienated from many in the suffrage leadership, and concentrating her political energies on the cause of the Irish Land League. Irish freedom was another question on which, like many radical suffragists, Jessie Craigen felt strongly. She was successfully wooed away from her women's movement activities to go to Ireland as a speaker for the Land League. There, however, she soon became disillusioned with Charles Stuart Parnell. Never one to keep any heartfelt conviction to herself, her attacks on Parnell appear to have caused a breach with Helen Taylor.

Jessie Craigen returned to England emotionally wounded and unemployed. Her friends set about finding her fresh work with the LNA and as a suffrage speaker. The failure to secure the inclusion of women in the 1884 Reform Act left the suffrage movement increasingly divided, and unable to raise sufficient resources to retain working women as speakers and organizers. In 1886 Anna Maria Priestman established a Jessie Craigen lecture fund which provided her friend with a yearly allowance for a few years more, in return for speaking and lecturing on a range of reform issues, including women's rights, Irish home rule, and anti-vivisection. Jessie Craigen's erratic behaviour and inability to live within her means tested her friendships to the full, and the lecture fund appears not to have continued after 1890. She died at her home, 2 Grove Villas, Ilford Lane, Ilford, on 5 October 1899.

SANDRA STANLEY HOLTON

**Sources** S. S. Holton, 'Silk dresses and lavender kid gloves: the wayward career of Jessie Craigen, working suffragist', *Women's History Review*, 5 (1996), 129–50 • S. S. Holton, *Suffrage days: stories from the women's suffrage movement* (1996) • *Englishwoman's Review*, 31 (1900), 65–6 • H. Blackburn, *Women's suffrage: a record of the women's suffrage movement in the British Isles* (1902) • P. T. Winskill, *Temperance standard bearers of the nineteenth century: a biographical and statistical temperance dictionary*, 2 vols. (1897–8) • *Zoophilist* (1 Nov 1899), 152 • S. Lewenhak, *Women and trade unions: an outline history of women in the British trade union movement* (1977) • *Women's Suffrage Journal* (1879–82) • d. cert.
**Archives** BLPES, Mill-Taylor collection, Helen Taylor corresp. • C. and J. Clark Ltd, Street, Millfield MSS, Anna Maria Priestman corresp. • U. Glas. L., special collections department, women's suffrage pamphlets
**Wealth at death** £73 0s. 6d.: probate, 26 Jan 1900, *CGPLA Eng. & Wales*

**Craighall**. For this title name *see* Hope, Sir John, Lord Craighall (1603×5–1654).

**Craigie, David** (1793–1866), physician, was born near Edinburgh in June 1793, took his medical degree in the university of that city in 1816, and in 1832 became a fellow of the Royal College of Physicians of Edinburgh. He was its president in 1861–3. His main claim to fame is as a medical writer. In 1828 he published a bulky *Elements of General and Pathological Anatomy*, of which a second edition appeared in 1848. It is the product of wide reading on morbid anatomy, and the facts drawn from the work of previous writers are often well arranged by Craigie. The part describing morbid changes in the pancreas is perhaps the best section of the book. Its defect is a lack of familiarity with diseased structures which can only be acquired in the postmortem room.

Craigie was physician to the Edinburgh Infirmary, but

was more of a writer than an observer. He became the owner of the *Edinburgh Medical and Surgical Journal*, and edited his periodical himself. He wrote *Elements of Anatomy, General, Special, and Comparative*, and in 1836 *Elements of the Practice of Physic*. He helped John Thomson in his *Account of the Life, Lectures, and Writings of William Cullen* (2 vols., 1859), and published thirty separate papers on medical subjects. They remain almost unread. After a long period of failing health Craigie died in September 1866. He left a number of books to the library of the Royal College of Physicians of Edinburgh.

NORMAN MOORE, *rev.* MICHAEL BEVAN

**Sources** *The Lancet* (8 Sept 1866) · W. S. Craig, *History of the Royal College of Physicians of Edinburgh* (1976)
**Archives** Royal College of Physicians of Edinburgh, notes

**Craigie** [*née* Richards], **Pearl** [*pseud.* John Oliver Hobbes] **(1867–1906)**, novelist and playwright, was born on 3 November 1867 at Chelsea, Massachusetts, the first of the five children of John Morgan Richards, merchant (1840/41–1918), and Laura Hortense, *née* Arnold (1846–1914). Both parents were from a long line of upper middle-class protestant Americans. Immediately after Pearl's birth her father settled in London in the patent medicine business, and from then on, her family resided there, spending summers in the Isle of Wight and frequently visiting the United States and travelling in Britain and Europe. Richards's business, which soon included American cigarettes, made him a millionaire. Pearl's parents were lively, hospitable, and close to their children—Laura religious, artistic, socially ambitious, and eccentric, John almost as passionately devoted to the theatre and journalism as to business. (He purchased *The Academy* in 1896 and in 1902 the London *Times* literature section, which he incorporated into *The Academy*.) Pearl and her siblings were always included in the Richardses' varied and interesting social circle.

A pretty, dark-haired, brown-eyed child, vivacious and precocious, Pearl was educated intermittently in a few day and boarding-schools, and at home with governesses and tutors, but mostly through voracious independent reading. From early childhood she scribbled letters, stories, and plays, which she 'produced' at home; she was a gifted, mischievous mimic. When she was nine years old, Dr Parker, family friend and preacher at the City Temple, published two of her stories in his newspaper, *The Fountain*. From her toddling days she was her father's constant companion.

In her teens, in England and Europe, Pearl continued to devour books, attend the theatre, write stories, and study music, becoming an accomplished pianist. She also frequented art museums, galleries, and concerts, and occasionally performed in amateur theatricals. In Paris from 1885 to 1886 she studied the French language, literature, and drama, and became quite Gallic in tastes and manners. She dressed fashionably and expensively, and in May 1886 she was presented at court. In some areas of her life, however, young Pearl was torn and unhappy. As the child of an American nonconformist who had made his money

**Pearl Craigie** (1867–1906), by George Charles Beresford, *c.*1903

in trade, she was hurt by fashionable society's snobbishness; she came to loathe the nonconformist spirit and recoiled from her mother's idiosyncrasies.

At the age of nineteen, on 16 February 1887, at Christ Church, Lancaster Gate, London, Pearl married Reginald Walpole Craigie (1860–1930), who was a handsome, popular man about town seven years her senior. He was a cashier at the Bank of England and a photographer, and his forebears included the duke of Marlborough and the earls of Orford and Cadogan. The marriage soon proved disastrous, 'a psychic earthquake whose repercussions would affect Pearl's whole life' (Harding, 53), as she found herself repelled by the fast society that Reginald enjoyed. She consequently immersed herself in University College classes in Greek and Latin language and literature, and at home closeted herself for hours, studying and writing. (In 1888 and 1889 she published a few journalistic pieces.) Reginald resented her literary pursuits and was madly jealous of her classics teacher. He also had at least one adulterous relationship, and drank excessively, becoming violent when drunk. Finding herself pregnant, an increasingly desperate Pearl rode her horse wildly in an attempt to abort the child, but on 15 August 1890 she gave birth to a son, John Churchill Craigie. After this she spent more and more time in her parents' home, and in May 1891, determined to prevent Craigie from having any access to the child, she went to live with her parents permanently. On 5 July 1892 she entered the Roman Catholic church, adopting the name Mary-Teresa; it was probably at this time that she took a vow of celibacy. On 4 July 1895, after a humiliating two-day hearing, she was granted a divorce on the grounds of Craigie's adultery and cruelty, and she was granted complete custody of her son.

The chief cause of the collapse of that marriage has only recently become known: not only did Reginald have syphilis; he gave at least a mild case of it to Pearl. That fact throws new light on many aspects of Pearl's life: the young couple's early return from their honeymoon in Cannes; Pearl's illness for the next six months and her temporary lameness; her attempt to abort her child; her subsequent erratic health, dependence on medical drugs, and early death; her vow of celibacy and strict keeping of it; and her frequent melancholy.

Re-established in her parents' luxurious homes in London and the Isle of Wight and from 1891 not only the 'brilliant Mrs Craigie' but the increasingly famous author John Oliver Hobbes, Pearl soon became one of society's most popular hostesses and guests. A fascinating conversationalist, she was also very attractive, petite, and elegant, with 'dark, brilliant eyes, restlessly intelligent and remotely tragic' (Harding, 97). For a brief term she was president of the Society of Women Journalists (1895–6) and the Ruskin Society (1903–4), and she supported many charitable causes, particularly for children. She travelled extensively in England, Scotland, and elsewhere in Europe and was royally entertained in the United States, once by President and Mrs Cleveland in the White House (1895). Early in 1903, as guest of the viceroy and vicereine, Lord and Lady Curzon, she attended Curzon's durbar in India. In the early 1900s she lectured widely in England and Scotland; on a hectic Lyceum tour in the winter of 1905–6 she was lionized in many cities in the United States.

In her character and personality, Pearl was a mass of contradictions. Indisputably brilliant, learned, witty, ambitious, self-dramatizing, moody, and extremely attractive to men, she seemed to some cold and self-aggrandizing, but to many more, warm, generous, and deeply religious, an ideal friend. Among the men with whom she had close platonic relationships were Walter Spindler, Alfred Goodwin (her classics teacher), George Moore, Owen Seaman, and—probably the most important romantic relationship in her life—George Nathaniel Curzon, Marquess Curzon of Kedleston. George Meredith, Edmund Gosse, William Archer, Thomas Hardy, Henry James, and Henry Irving all admired her, and her many clerical friends included the protestant Dr John Parker, the modernist Roman Catholic theologian the Revd George Tyrrell, and the Revd Mgr William Brown. Among her closest women friends were Zoë Procter (her secretary), Florence Henniker, Ellen Terry, Olga Nethersole, and, dearest of all, Mary Victoria *Curzon and Jennie Churchill, with whom Pearl helped to create the *Anglo-Saxon Review* (1899–1901) and with whom she played the piano in public concerts.

With *Some Emotions and a Moral* (1891), an ironic little love story, Pearl burst upon the literary scene as John Oliver Hobbes—John for her father and son, Oliver for Oliver Cromwell, Hobbes for Thomas Hobbes. (Pearl used a pseudonym mainly because her publisher, T. F. Unwin, wished to include the book in his new Pseudonym Library series.) That novella was immediately followed by three more (1892, 1893, 1894). Act I of a social comedy, 'The Fool's Hour' (in collaboration with George Moore, never completed), appeared in the first issue of the *Yellow Book* (April 1894); a one-act 'proverb', *Journeys End in Lovers' Meeting* (also in collaboration with Moore), was successfully produced at the Lyceum Theatre in 1895 with Ellen Terry in the lead.

From 1895 to 1906, in addition to short works, Pearl wrote nine full-length novels and several full-length plays, gaining a large following on both sides of the Atlantic. The most notable novels were: *The Gods, some Mortals, and Lord Wickenham* (1895), *The School for Saints* (1897), *Robert Orange* (1900), *Love and the Soul Hunters* (1902), *The Vineyard* (1904), and *The Dream and the Business* (1906). Her most successful play, a four-act comedy, *The Ambassadors*, was produced in 1898 at the Lyceum with George Alexander in the lead and enjoyed a long West End run. Her numerous essays are also noteworthy, especially 'George Eliot', 'George Sand', her many articles on the contemporary theatre, and *Dowries* (1904), a feminist pamphlet.

Those diverse works are linked by a strong family resemblance. Pearl's immediate *fin de siècle* world and her complex inner life are reflected throughout, but there are also consistent literary influences discernible throughout, spanning the classics of Western literature from the Bible and Homer to her own century and, in that century, particularly Thackeray, Ruskin, Newman, George Eliot, Meredith, Browning, Balzac, George Sand, and the contemporary French theatre. Certain themes resonated more and more firmly as their author matured: individual responsibility for one's fate; love as the primal force and the great educator; the importance of rational, unselfish love and the dangers of sentimentality, hypocrisy, and egotism; the inevitability of suffering; mankind's grounding in 'original ignorance' rather than 'original sin'; the necessity of renunciation, courage, and compassion; the strong vocational attractions of art and religion; and an unmilitant, apolitical feminism—a feminism based on a belief in women's worth, intelligence, and right to a good education and financial independence, but also on a conviction of women's essential psychological difference from men.

Opinions about Pearl Craigie's works have differed widely. While most readers would consider her novels 'good reads', her detractors have complained that her plots are often contrived, her wit and gem-like style chilling, and her characters unrealistic. Their appeal for others, however, lies in their lucid and graceful style, their fast-moving stories abounding in dramatic talk-filled scenes, their interesting characters, and their constant expression of their author's humour, rare psychological insight, and fine intelligence. Though the early novellas are probably the most charming, the mellow novels *Love and the Soul Hunters*, *The Vineyard*, and *The Dream and the Business* would probably appeal most to the modern reader. Her most impressive work, however, is the monumental two-volume novel comprising *The School for Saints* and its sequel *Robert Orange*. Set in Britain and Europe in the 1860s, the first volume is epic: a wide-ranging, political-religious-historical novel packed with adventure and intrigue, and also a romantic-psychological novel of Robert Orange's apprenticeship to life. The second volume is dramatic: more concentrated and more reliant upon theatrical episodes. The vast web of personal relationships in *The School* is complicated in *Robert Orange* by the addition of a third heroine. Throughout, politics, love, and religion vie for importance in Robert's life.

Pearl's life ended suddenly. Although she had remained active, her health had deteriorated under strains in her personal life—debts, her mother's idiosyncrasies, distress about Mary Curzon's long illness and death (18 July 1906), and the consequent revival of the old question as to whether Pearl and Curzon would marry. On 13 August 1906, she was found dead of heart failure in her bed at her London home, 56 Lancaster Gate. The literary world was stunned; more than 150 notices of her death appeared in the British press. Among the messages of condolence to her family were notes from the queen and the princess of Wales, and one from Reginald Craigie to his sixteen-year-old son. After a requiem mass at the Jesuit church in Farm Street, London, Pearl's body was buried on 17 August 1906 in Kensal Green Roman Catholic cemetery.

On 2 July 1908, thanks to the efforts of Jennie Churchill (Mrs George Cornwallis-West), Blanche Eliot, Zoë Procter, and many others, a memorial ceremony was held at University College, London, with Lord Curzon presiding. A plaque bearing a bronze portrait of Pearl Craigie, and £500 for a John Oliver Hobbes scholarship in English literature, were donated to University College. Simultaneously an identical plaque was donated to Barnard College, Columbia University, where Pearl had lectured.

MILDRED DAVIS HARDING

**Sources** M. D. Harding, *Air-bird in the water: the life and works of Pearl Craigie (John Oliver Hobbes)* (1996) • private information (2004) [family] • J. M. Richards, *Life of John Oliver Hobbes* (1911) • *The Times* (18 Feb 1887) • *The Times* (4 July 1895) • *The Times* (5 July 1895) • *The Times* (15 Aug 1906) • *The Times* (16 Aug 1906) • d. cert. [J. M. Richards] • d. cert. [R. W. Craigie] • *CGPLA Eng. & Wales* (1906) • J. M. Richards, *John Bull and Jonathan* (1905)

**Archives** New York University • NRA, priv. coll., family archives • Pearl Craigie Society, Gulfport, Florida • Penn State University, University Park, Pennsylvania • U. Reading L., letters; scrapbooks • University of Rochester, New York, Rush Rees Library, corresp. and papers | Ellen Terry Memorial Museum, Smallhythe, Kent, letters to Ellen Terry • NYPL, Berg collection • U. Leeds, Brotherton L., letters to Edmund Gosse

**Likenesses** L. Stacpoole, oils, 1885, repro. in Harding, *Air-bird* • photograph, 1892, repro. in Richards, *Life of John Oliver Hobbes* • W. Spindler, pen-and-ink sketch, 1895 • G. C. Beresford, photograph, c.1903, NPG [see illus.] • A. Drury, bronze bas-relief bust, c.1907–1908, UCL • London Stereoscopic Co., photograph on postcard, NPG • H. and S. Mendelssohn, photograph, repro. in Harding, *Air-bird* • W. Rothenstein, sketch, Penn State University Libraries, Pennsylvania • W. Spindler, oils, priv. coll. • bronze portrait plaque, UCL • photograph, repro. in Harding, *Air-bird*

**Wealth at death** £24,502 8s.: probate, 26 Sept 1906, *CGPLA Eng. & Wales*

**Craigie, Robert**, of Glendoick (*bap.* 1688, *d.* 1760), judge, was baptized on 4 March 1688 at Dunbarney, Perthshire, the second son of Lawrence Craigie of Kilgraston in Perthshire and his second wife, Katherine Colville, niece of Robert, second Lord Colville of Ochiltree. Through his mother he was related to prominent local Perthshire families, such as the Jacobite Oliphants of Gask. All his life he remained close to George Hay, eighth earl of Kinnoul, to whom (as Viscount Dupplin) he dedicated his theses for admission as an advocate. Dupplin and his father were both imprisoned on suspicion of Jacobitism in 1715. After studies at the University of St Andrews (MA, 1705) and a legal education (probably in the Netherlands), he was admitted to the Faculty of Advocates on 3 January 1710; his elder brother, Lawrence (*b.* 1686), followed him there in 1712.

While waiting for his practice at the bar to develop Craigie taught Roman law privately in Edinburgh between 1710 and 1714. In 1715 John Murray, first duke of Atholl, hereditary sheriff of Perthshire, appointed Craigie one of his sheriffs-depute, while despite Jacobite connections Craigie was also commissioned as one of the counsel to prosecute the rebels in 1716. In 1719 Robert Dundas, squadrone solicitor-general, appointed him as one of his deputes. With good family and Perthshire connections Craigie built up a successful practice and, particularly expert in feudal tenures, was considered 'an excellent civilian and feudalist' (Allardyce, 1.110). By 1742 he was described as 'the first lawyer at our Bar' (Yester Papers, NL Scot., MS 7046, fols. 72–3).

By the end of 1720 Craigie had married Barbara, daughter and heir of Charles Stewart of Carie, cloth merchant in Perth, and Isobel Craigie (probably a relation), enabling him in 1726 to purchase the estate of Glendoick on the Carse of Gowrie in Perthshire. The couple had at least eight children, Robert (*b.* 1725, died in infancy), Cecilia (*b.* 1727, who married Major Douglas of Strathnedry), Isobel (1728–1744), Robert (advocate, 1733–1756), Laurence (*b.* 1734, who died young), Charles (who inherited Glendoick but died childless in 1779), Anne (who married her first cousin John Craigie of Kilgraston in 1746), and John (who inherited Glendoick from his elder brother).

Links with the squadrone militated against political preferment during the long period of Argathelian domination of Scottish politics in the 1720s and 1730s, but Craigie preferred private practice and developing his estate. When Walpole's fall caused the earl of Ilay to lose his grip on Scottish management, Craigie, though his administrative abilities were questioned, was appointed lord advocate in 1742, John Hay, fourth marquess of Tweeddale being Scottish secretary; he was reluctant to accept, the salary of £1000 being significantly lower than his current earnings. He was put into parliament as MP for the Tain burghs, and stayed until 1747. Tweeddale's incompetent response to the Jacobite rising of 1745 led to the collapse of the squadrone's shaky control in Scotland, and in February 1746 Craigie, always a reluctant politician, lost office along with his master.

Considered for judicial appointment as an ordinary lord in 1746 and as lord president in 1747, Craigie continued practice as an advocate until, in 1754, he was appointed president of the court of session, by the influence of Philip Yorke, first Baron Hardwicke, who saw Craigie as a relatively independent figure, and Viscount Dupplin, closely associated with the duke of Newcastle. At the end of the next year, however, Archibald Campbell, third duke of Argyll, and Andrew Fletcher, Lord Milton, sought to win Craigie over with a lucrative appointment for his son-in-law, John Craigie of Kilgraston. Craigie held the office of lord president until his death in 1760, but 'proved to be a broken reed, bankrupt in leadership, organisation and energy' (Murdoch, 62), under whom business in the session became very delayed. He died in Edinburgh on 10 March 1760. The following generation, obsessed with 'politeness' and contemptuous of feudal learning, remembered him as a crabbed lawyer, lacking in the 'elegancies of life', 'deficient in point of breeding', and lacking 'exterior accomplishments' (Allardyce, 1.116–18), who was unsuited to head the bench, with an unsuitable wife 'neither [whose] birth nor manners gave her much inclination to go into polite society' (Tytler, 1.41–2).

JOHN W. CAIRNS

**Sources**  NA Scot., GD 1/609, GD 1/1167 · bap. reg. Scot., OPR index, ext. 950701 · G. W. T. Omond, *The lord advocates of Scotland from the close of the fifteenth century to the passing of the Reform Bill*, 2 vols. (1883) · A. Murdoch, *'The people above': politics and administration in mid-eighteenth-century Scotland* (1980) · J. S. Shaw, *The management of Scottish society, 1707–1764: power, nobles, lawyers, Edinburgh agents and English influences* (1983) · *Scotland and Scotsmen in the eighteenth century: from the MSS of John Ramsay, esq., of Ochtertyre*, ed. A. Allardyce, 2 vols. (1888) · A. F. Tytler, *Memoirs of the life and writings of the Honourable Henry Home of Kames*, 2 vols. (1807) · *Scots Courant* (1710–14) · J. M. Pinkerton, ed., *The minute book of the Faculty of Advocates*, 1: 1661–1712, Stair Society, 29 (1976)

**Archives**  NA Scot., Glendoick MSS, corresp.; corresp. and papers, GD 1/609 and GD 1/1167 · NL Scot., corresp. · West Highland Museum, Fort William, letters relating to the 'Forty-Five | NL Scot., corresp. with fourth marquess of Tweeddale

**Likenesses**  A. Ramsay, oils, 1740–49, Scot. NPG · A. Ramsay, oils, 1744, Scot. NPG

**Wealth at death**  Bank of Scotland stock worth £1000, six-tenths paid; estate of Glendoick; other moveable property: 5 July 1760, NA Scot., CC 8/8/118/2

Sir Robert Leslie Craigie (1883–1959), by unknown photographer

**Craigie, Sir Robert Leslie** (1883–1959), diplomatist, was born in Southsea on 6 December 1883, the elder child and only son of Commander (later Admiral) Robert William Craigie (1849–1911) and his wife, Henrietta Isabella Dinnis. He was educated at Heidelberg and entered the Foreign Office as a clerk in 1907. Promoted third secretary in 1908, he served as secretary to the international copyright conference at Berlin in 1908; secretary to the British delegation at the international sugar commission in Brussels from 1908 to 1913; secretary to the international conference for the protection of the elephant and rhinoceros in Africa, held in London in 1914; and secretary to the international conference relating to the New Hebrides, also held in London the same year. In 1916 he was promoted second secretary and posted to Bern as an additional commercial attaché, serving also as British representative on the inter-allied blockade committee. While in Switzerland he met Pleasant (d. 1956), daughter of Pleasant Alexander Stovall, a newspaper editor from Savannah, Georgia, who was then serving as United States minister in Bern. They married in 1918, and had one son.

Craigie remained in Bern until 1920, having been promoted first secretary in 1919. He then served briefly as acting high commissioner at Sofia, before being transferred to Washington, still as first secretary. In 1923 he returned to London, where he was employed by the department of overseas trade. He resumed his duties in the Foreign Office at the beginning of 1925.

In 1928 Craigie was promoted to counsellor, made head of the American department and designated the Foreign Office's chief negotiator in the area of naval arms limitation. In this capacity he was instrumental in negotiating the London naval treaties of 1930 and 1936 and the Anglo-German naval agreement of 1935. Craigie gained a reputation for being a meticulous and skilful diplomatist, winning praise from politicians such as Ramsay MacDonald and Sir John Simon. In recognition of his services he was made a CMG in 1929, a CB in 1930, and a KCMG in 1936, and promoted to assistant under-secretary of state in 1935.

On the basis of this reputation Craigie was appointed ambassador to Japan in 1937 and sworn of the privy council. This came as a surprise as he had not previously served in east Asia, but he did have some experience from the naval talks of negotiating with Japanese diplomats. His appointment was announced in the spring when there was a mood of renewed optimism about the chances of an Anglo-Japanese rapprochement. However, by the time he arrived in Japan in September 1937 the Sino-Japanese War had broken out and relations had deteriorated alarmingly.

Craigie saw his role in this new political situation as being to stop Japan from drifting further into the German orbit and thus threatening Britain with the possibility of a two-front war. Accordingly he argued that, as Britain was too weak to defend its interests in the region and as the United States was considered to be an unreliable potential ally, the best policy was to maintain an attitude of strict neutrality towards the war in China in order to avoid antagonizing Japan. He also contended that if Britain followed a conciliatory line it might well encourage moderates in the Japanese government to re-exert their influence. This view was opposed by the Foreign Office, which disparaged the idea that the moderates could exercise any power and felt that Britain should assist China in the hope that Japan would dissipate its energies in a prolonged war. In June 1939 the uncompromising attitude of the Foreign Office helped to contribute to a crisis in Anglo-Japanese relations over the status of the British concession at Tientsin (Tianjin) in north China. Craigie, who felt vindicated by the failure of Foreign Office policy, helped to resolve this crisis by exercising his astute diplomatic skills and again won high praise, this time from Chamberlain, who recommended his elevation to a GCMG, an award made in January 1941.

The start of the war in Europe did not lead to any substantial change in Craigie's interpretation of his role. He continued to argue the need for delicate handling of Japan and in February 1940 helped to neutralize another potentially dangerous crisis when HMS *Liverpool* intercepted a Japanese merchant vessel, the *Asama Maru*, just outside Japan's territorial waters. In addition, in June 1940 he was able, after months of laborious talks, to get a final solution to the Tientsin problem. However, just as he hoped that a corner had been turned another crisis rocked Anglo-Japanese relations.

In late June 1940 Japan demanded that Britain should close the Burma Road. This ultimatum arrived at Britain's lowest ebb in the war against Germany and, although the Foreign Office felt that Japan was bluffing, Winston Churchill's war cabinet decided to seek an acceptable compromise. Once again Craigie provided a diplomatic way out of the crisis, arranging a three-month closure of the Burma Road in return for a Japanese promise to seek a fair settlement of the war in China. Craigie hoped that this would lay the basis for better relations but he was to be sorely disabused. In late July 1940 the Konoe government came to office in Japan determined to take advantage of the opportunities offered by the apparent collapse of British power, and in the coming months signed the tripartite pact with Germany and Italy and occupied the northern part of French Indo-China. Craigie's hopes were dashed and in an attempt to contain Japan, Britain reacted by introducing a policy of economic sanctions, strengthening its military stance in the region, and developing a common front with the United States and the Netherlands.

Craigie broadly supported this idea of applying pressure on Japan but was disappointed that it was not accompanied by diplomatic incentives to change the nature of its foreign policy. In the autumn of 1941, fearful that war was imminent, he began to press the Foreign Office to become involved in the Japanese-American talks that were then taking place in Washington, and warned the foreign secretary, Anthony Eden, that Japan was prepared if necessary to fight. His advice was, however, ignored as Churchill and Eden believed that Japan was unappeasable and that the United States would not welcome British interference in the diplomatic process.

After the war in the Pacific began, Craigie was interned for seven months in the Tokyo embassy before being allowed to return to Britain. On his return he produced a controversial report in which he criticized the British government for not heeding his warnings in the autumn of 1941; Churchill was furious at his temerity and suppressed the report. Craigie also summarized his experiences in Japan in a more measured way in a book published in 1946, *Behind the Japanese Mask*.

Craigie retired from the Foreign Office in April 1944, but from 1945 to 1948 he was the British representative to the United Nations War Crimes Commission, and in 1949 he headed the British delegation to the Geneva conference for the protection of the victims of war. He died at The Day House, Sleepers Hill, Winchester, on 16 May 1959.

ANTONY BEST

**Sources** R. L. Craigie, *Behind the Japanese mask* (1946) · A. Best, *Britain, Japan and Pearl Harbor: avoiding war in East Asia, 1936–1941* (1995) · P. Lowe, *Great Britain and the origins of the Pacific war: a study of British policy in east Asia, 1937–1941* (1977) · *The Times* (18 May 1959) · R. J. Pritchard, *Far Eastern influences upon British strategy towards the great powers, 1937–1939* (1987) · D. C. Watt, *How war came: the immediate origins of the Second World War, 1938–1939* (1989) · B. A. Lee, *Britain and the Sino-Japanese War, 1937–1939* (1973) · F. S. G. Piggott, *Broken thread: an autobiography* (1950) · K. Sansom, ed., *Sir George Sansom and Japan* (1972) · *FO List* (1941) · S. O. Agbi, 'The Pacific war controversy in Britain: Sir Robert Craigie versus the foreign office', *Modern Asian Studies*, 17 (1983), 489–517 · *DNB* · A. Best, 'Sir Robert Craigie as ambassador to Japan, 1937–1941', *Britain and Japan: biographical portraits*, ed. I. Nish, 1 (1994), 238–51 · *CGPLA Eng. & Wales* (1959)

**Archives** Bodl. Oxf., Viscount Simon MSS · PRO, Ramsay MacDonald MSS, PRO 30/69 · PRO, Foreign Office general coresp., FO 371

**Likenesses** photograph, repro. in Craigie, *Behind the Japanese mask*, frontispiece [*see illus.*]

**Wealth at death** £4458 14s. 2d.: probate, 16 Sept 1959, *CGPLA Eng. & Wales*

**Craigie, Sir William Alexander** (1867–1957), lexicographer and philologist, was born in Dundee on 13 August 1867, the youngest son of James Craigie, jobbing gardener, and his wife, Christina Gow. His native speech was thus the lowland Scots of Forfarshire, and during his childhood he learned some Gaelic from his maternal grandfather and later his eldest brother. About the age of twelve he began reading the early Scottish writers. From the headmaster of his school—the West End Academy, Dundee—he gained a knowledge of phonetics. While attending St Andrews University, where he graduated with honours in classics and philosophy in 1888, he also found time to learn German and French, and began studying Danish and Icelandic. In his final session he carried out the research on the university library's manuscript of the early Scots Wyntoun's *Chronicle* which enabled him to demonstrate conclusively the relationships of the several versions of this work.

**Sir William Alexander Craigie (1867–1957),** by Harold Speed, 1949

With a Guthrie scholarship Craigie proceeded to Balliol College, Oxford, and thence, after one term, to Oriel College as a bible clerk. Apart from the work of his regular curriculum, which led to firsts in both honour moderations (1890) and *literae humaniores* (1892), he continued his private study of Scandinavian, attended lectures on Celtic, and began producing articles on these subjects for Scottish journals. The winter of 1892–3 he spent in Copenhagen, where he studied Icelandic manuscripts and learned modern Icelandic from Icelandic friends. From 1893 to 1897 he was assistant to the professor of Latin at St Andrews. In his spare time he continued his writing of articles, produced his valuable *Primer of Burns* (1896), and contributed translations from Icelandic and Danish to the fairy books and *Dreams and Ghosts* of Andrew Lang as well as his own *Scandinavian Folk-Lore* (1896).

On 28 June 1897 Craigie married Jessie Kinmond (1864/5–1947), daughter of William Hutchen, tailor and clothier, of Dundee; on her loving care and companionship he depended greatly. They had no children. Also in 1897 Craigie accepted an unexpected invitation to join the staff of the Philological Society's *New English Dictionary* in Oxford. He was appointed co-editor of the *New English Dictionary* with James A. H. Murray and Henry Bradley. Thereafter he continued to work on the dictionary until the completion of its supplement in 1933, producing the letters N, Q, R, U, and V, Si–Sq, and Wo–Wy, amounting to nearly a fifth of the main work, and about a third of the supplement.

Along with his daily stint of seven and a half hours of lexicography, which was far from using up all his energy

or exhausting his zest for work, Craigie kept alive all his old interests. In 1904 he was appointed Taylorian lecturer in the Scandinavian languages at Oxford, and in 1916 he became Rawlinson and Bosworth professor of Anglo-Saxon. In 1921 he began seriously to collect material for his projected dictionary of Older Scottish, and when in 1925 he moved to the University of Chicago, as professor of English, in order to edit a *Dictionary of American English*, he was for some years occupied simultaneously with three major dictionaries, yet still turning out a steady flow of other writings.

In 1936 Craigie resigned his Chicago chair and settled at Christmas Common, Watlington, Oxfordshire, on the Chiltern Hills. He now gave most of his time to the *Dictionary of the Older Scottish Tongue*, which he carried to the end of the letter I in 1955, when he was eighty-seven, before handing over to his successor. He had also continued to contribute to the American dictionary until its completion in 1944. After the war he produced his *Specimens of Icelandic Rímur* (3 vols., 1952), a masterly survey of a field of Icelandic literature in which his erudition and discernment were unrivalled, and a supplement (1957) to the *Icelandic Dictionary* of G. Vígfússon.

Craigie's remarkable knowledge of many languages was perfected, and friendships with the scholars of other countries cemented, in the course of the travels on which he and his wife spent all their vacations, visiting all the countries of northern Europe and in 1921 going round the world. In this way he became one of the most widely known of the scholars of his generation, and the quietly dignified, rather reserved, yet unfailingly kindly and companionable personality of this tiny Scotsman, with his modest tastes and tidy habits, and his fellow-feeling for simple folk and small nations, made him one of the best loved. His travels included four visits to Iceland, where he was revered by the whole nation.

Craigie was the ablest and most productive lexicographer of his time, and was universally recognized as the supreme master of the art and techniques of dictionary making. Yet in addition to his major works he contrived also to produce, almost entirely in his spare time, an astonishing number of other, smaller-scale but authoritative writings in many provinces of specialist philology, notably on Older Scottish and on English philology of every period. Over the whole extent of Icelandic literature, ancient and modern, he gained a greater mastery than perhaps any non-Icelander had ever done, and wrote valuably on skaldic verse and on the sagas as well as on his beloved *rímur*. These writings and others on Frisian and on Gaelic display his characteristic virtues of clarity, brevity, and directness, and his acute and perceptive observation of philological facts and details.

His published work was only part of the vast service Craigie rendered to scholarship. He gave a new impetus to Old Norse and Anglo-Saxon studies in Oxford and later in Chicago. Throughout his career he initiated and encouraged new scholarly enterprises. Out of his plan for 'completing the record of English' by means of the 'period dictionaries', which he launched in 1919, were born the great historical dictionaries which followed the *New English*, among them his own American and Scottish dictionaries. His lifelong interest in Frisian, and the enthusiastic support which he gave to the Frisian scholars in their attempt to re-establish their language, they recognized by making him one of the two original honorary members of the Frisian Academy on its foundation in 1938. His sponsorship, and the active leadership which he provided in partnership with Professor M. K. Pope, brought about the foundation in 1938 of the Anglo-Norman Text Society, and as its president he fostered this society's project (initiated in 1947) for an Anglo-Norman dictionary. His suggestion and encouragement led likewise to the founding of the Icelandic Rímur Society in 1947. He served for long periods as president or council member of a number of other famous learned societies in England and in Scotland. All his great academic prestige and his extensive range of contacts he placed at the service of these and other good causes of learning.

Craigie possessed an amazingly retentive memory and an ability to grasp at sight the essence of a problem and to marshal facts and arguments with great speed. Even so, his erudition, and his prodigious output, he achieved only by utilizing his time to the utmost, working methodically for most of each day and evening throughout his long life. Yet he was always accessible and ungrudging of his time to others. To the numerous authors of scholarly works who sought it he gave encouragement, fruitful advice, and abundant practical help.

The many honours awarded Craigie included honorary degrees from St Andrews (1907), Calcutta (1921), Oxford (1928), Cambridge (1928), Michigan (1929), Wisconsin (1932), and Iceland (1946); a knighthood in 1928 on completion of the *New English Dictionary*; an honorary fellowship of Oriel in the same year; and a fellowship of the British Academy in 1931. The Icelanders' appreciation of his friendship and his service to their literature was shown in many different ways, including a knighthood (1925) and a knight-commandership (1930) of the order of the Icelandic Falcon. In 1952 his eighty-fifth birthday was honoured by a gathering held at Oriel College, Oxford, when he was presented with a commemorative memoir and list of his publications, and his portrait by Harold Speed, which now hangs in the college. He died at Watlington on 2 September 1957.                    A. J. AITKEN, *rev.*

**Sources** J. M. Wyllie, *PBA*, 47 (1961), 273–91 · A memoir and a list of the published writings of Sir William A. Craigie (1952) · *SHR*, 32 (1953) · *The Times* (3 Sept 1957); (9 Sept 1957) · private information (1971) · personal knowledge (1971) · T. McArthur, ed., *The Oxford companion to the English language* (1992) · *CGPLA Eng. & Wales* (1958) · m. reg. Scot.

**Archives** NL Scot., corresp. · NL Scot., corresp. and papers | Orkney Archives, Kirkwall, letters to H. Marwick

**Likenesses** W. Stoneman, photograph, 1932, NPG · H. Speed, oils, 1949, Oriel College, Oxford [*see illus.*]

**Wealth at death** £4941 4s. 7d.: probate, 20 Jan 1958, *CGPLA Eng. & Wales*

**Craigmyle.** For this title name *see* Shaw, Thomas, first Baron Craigmyle (1850–1937).

**Craik** [*née* Mulock], **Dinah Maria** (1826–1887), writer, was born on 20 April 1826 at Longfield Cottage, Hartshill, near Stoke-on-Trent, Staffordshire, the eldest of three children of Thomas Samuel Mulock (c.1789–1869), who was then minister of an independent nonconformist chapel, and his wife, Dinah (1794–1845), a schoolmistress, the daughter of Thomas Mellard, a tanner, and his wife, Jane Bucknall. Thomas Mulock was a difficult and contentious man who unsuccessfully held several occupations; during part of his daughter's childhood he was confined to a lunatic asylum. Dinah Mulock had some early education at Brampton House Academy in Newcastle under Lyme, but by the age of thirteen she was helping her mother keep a private school. In 1839 the family moved to London, where Dinah Mulock learned languages and studied drawing at the School of Design, Somerset House. When his wife died in 1845, however, Thomas Mulock entirely deserted his children.

Although she had the training to become a governess, Dinah Mulock turned to writing as a profession. Her earliest work was in genres that could be quickly written and sold: poems and translations for *Chambers's Edinburgh Journal*, short moral tales for children, stories for monthlies such as *Bentley's Miscellany* and *Fraser's Magazine*. Her first novel, *The Ogilvies* (1849), drew attention for its emotional intensity. *Olive* (1850) was the wrenching story of a deformed girl who overcomes rejection, poverty, and loneliness to win success and love. *The Head of the Family* (1852) and *Agatha's Husband* (1853) consolidated Dinah Mulock's reputation as a popular writer who delineated complex emotional states with unusual power and understanding.

Her best-known novel, *John Halifax, Gentleman* (1856), is the archetypal story of a poor boy who makes good through honesty, initiative, and hard work. The events are precisely dated to provide an emblematic narrative of industrialization and the growing power of the middle classes. With appealing characters, the emotional attractions of love and pathos, and an overwhelming affirmation of its readers' values and beliefs, *John Halifax, Gentleman* became one of the nineteenth century's best-selling books. Although its very popularity damaged the author's reputation among intellectuals, it remains a readable story as well as a useful artefact of social history.

In *A Woman's Thoughts about Women* (published serially in *Chambers's Journal of Popular Literature, Science and Arts*, 1857), Dinah Mulock provided emotional support and confident advice for single women like herself. Strongly criticizing learned helplessness, she promoted self-sufficiency and cross-class sympathy. Yet she also acknowledged the pain and loneliness of single women's lives. Her two younger brothers were both dead by 1863. Tom (1827–1847), who had been articled to the master of a merchant ship, was killed in a shipboard accident and Benjamin (1829–1863) had drifted through various jobs, threatened suicide, and died of injuries after escaping from an asylum.

Dinah Mulock's novels in the decade after *A Woman's Thoughts about Women* worked out some of its themes. *A Life for a Life* (1859) promotes a single moral standard and demonstrates that women and men have similar strengths and emotions. *Mistress and Maid* (*Good Words*, 1862) emphasizes the common feelings that unite women despite class differences. 'Parson Garland's Daughter', one of two novellas published as *Two Marriages* (1867), tells the familiar story of a servant girl seduced by a gentleman's son but shows that effort, growth, and time can lead them to a happy ending. Most of her other novels and essays from the 1860s express the conflicts and ambiguities in women's situation.

On 29 April 1865, as she entered her fortieth year, Dinah Mulock was married to George Lillie Craik (1837–1905), a Glasgow-trained accountant who was the son of the Revd James Craik (1802–1870) and his wife, Margaret Grieve, and nephew of the author George Lillie Craik. This familial connection was to cause some professional confusion, as Georgiana Craik (1831–1895), daughter of the elder George Lillie Craik, was also a novelist and children's writer, and her books are sometimes confused with those of Dinah Craik. Soon after their marriage, the younger George Lillie Craik became a partner in Alexander Macmillan's publishing firm. There is, however, no evidence in Dinah Craik's bibliography that she ever considered abandoning her career; she published five novels during the next five years as well as working on essays, translations, and children's stories. Her earnings built a house (designed by the architect Norman Shaw) at Shortlands, near Bromley, Kent. Dinah Craik also chose to become a mother; in 1869 the Craiks took charge of a baby abandoned in their parish, named her Dorothy, and raised her as their own.

Although the overwhelming success of *John Halifax* was never repeated, *The Woman's Kingdom* (*Good Words*, 1868) provided a joyous solution to difficulties that haunted Dinah Craik's novels earlier in the decade. Echoing John Ruskin, the book affirms women's power to rule the moral realm. Yet, although she did not commit herself to the suffrage movement, Craik's last three full-length novels take up other women's issues: *A Brave Lady* (*Macmillan's Magazine*, 1869–70) is propaganda for the Married Women's Property Act; *Hannah* (*Saint Pauls*, 1871) is about marriage with a deceased wife's sister; and *Young Mrs. Jardine* (*Good Words*, 1879) suggests conditions that make it morally imperative for a good woman to separate from her husband.

In addition to novels and short fiction, Dinah Craik published essays, travel narratives, poetry, and translations. As an author for children, she wrote moral stories in her early years; a popular collection entitled *The Fairy Book* in 1863; and several later books for her daughter, Dorothy. The most enduring has been *The Little Lame Prince and his Travelling Cloak* (1875), a fantasy which teaches a lesson, allegorizes women's condition, and still exerts emotional power over some of its young readers.

Dinah Craik died suddenly of heart failure at her home, Corner House, Shortlands, near Bromley, Kent, on 12 October 1887, while preparing for Dorothy's wedding; she is buried in Keston churchyard, Kent. A tablet placed in the abbey at Tewkesbury recalled the site of *John Halifax, Gentleman* and the memory of its author. The evaluation provided by Richard Garnett in 1894 remains fitting:

> She was not a genius, and she does not express the ideals and aspirations of women of exceptional genius; but the tender and philanthropic, and at the same time energetic and practical womanhood of ordinary life has never had a more sufficient representative. (*DNB*)

SALLY MITCHELL

**Sources** A. L. Reade, *The Mellards and their descendants … with memoirs of Dinah Maria Mulock and Thomas Mellard Reade* (privately printed, London, 1915) · S. Mitchell, *Dinah Mulock Craik* (1983) [incl. bibliography of Craik's pubd work] · *DNB* · F. Martin, 'Mrs. Craik', *The Athenaeum* (22 Oct 1887), 539 · L. Parr, 'Dinah Mulock (Mrs Craik)', in Mrs Oliphant and others, *Women novelists of Queen Victoria's reign* (1897), 217–48 [repr. as *The author of 'John Halifax, gentleman': a memoir*, 1898] · S. Foster, 'Dinah Mulock Craik: ambivalent romanticism', *Victorian women's fiction: marriage, freedom and the individual* (1985) · S. M. Ellis, 'Dinah Maria Mulock (Mrs Craik)', *The Bookman*, 70 (1926), 1–5 · H. Keddie, *Three generations: the story of a middle-class Scottish family* (1911)
**Archives** BL, corresp., Add. MS 61896 · NL Scot., corresp. and literary MSS · Princeton University Library, corresp. and literary MSS · Tewkesbury Town Museum, letters · U. Cal., Los Angeles, corresp. · University of Iowa Libraries, Iowa City, corresp. | NL Scot., letters to William Blackwood & Sons · NL Scot., letters to Sir J. N. Paton · NYPL, Henry W. and Albert A. Berg Collection of English and American Literature, corresp.
**Likenesses** A. R. Hill, pencil drawing, 1845, NPG · H. von Herkomer, oils, 1887, NPG · H. H. Armstead, medallion on monument, Abbey church, Tewkesbury · B. Wollaston, photograph, photogravure, NPG · engraving (after photograph by H. S. Mendelssohn), repro. in *Harper's New Monthly Magazine* (June 1888), facing p. 3
**Wealth at death** £17,381 19s. 3d.: resworn probate, 1888, *CGPLA Eng. & Wales*

**Craik, George Lillie** (1798–1866), literary scholar, was born at Kennoway, Fife, on 18 April 1798. He was the son of the Revd William Craik, the schoolmaster of Kennoway, and his wife, Patterson Lilias. In 1812 Craik entered the University of St Andrews, where he studied philosophy, theology, and literature, winning prizes for his work in mathematics, grammar, theology, and Hebrew. He then taught in the grammar school at St Andrews (later Madras College), worked as a private tutor, and became the editor of a local newspaper, *The Star*. On 19 October 1826 he married Janet, the daughter of Cathcart Dempster of St Andrews. They had one son and three daughters, one of whom, Georgiana Marion, became a prolific novelist. Craik was strongly built, with brown hair and a red, freckled, bespectacled face. He was an ambitious man, determined to make his way in the world of learning and letters. Having first visited London in 1824, he decided to settle there in 1826. He gave lectures on poetry at Glasgow, Dublin, Belfast, and Liverpool on his journey southwards.

In London, Craik and his family lived in a modest house called Vine Cottage, in Cromwell Lane, Old Brompton. He wrote a good deal for Charles Knight, the publisher and popular educator. His first notable book for Knight was *The Pursuit of Knowledge under Difficulties* (2 vols., 1830–31), which was reprinted in various editions. Dickens, who possessed a copy, has Tony Weller allude to it in *Pickwick Papers* (ch. 33). Typical 'difficulties' that Craik discusses are humble station and obscure origin (as experienced by Haydn and Ben Jonson), the soldiering and sailing lives (Descartes and Captain Cook), extreme poverty (Erasmus), and exile and imprisonment (Ovid and Sir Walter Ralegh). Other works that Craik wrote for Knight's Library of Entertaining Knowledge were *The New Zealanders* (1830) and *Paris and its Historical Scenes* (1831). He was acquainted in London with Leigh Hunt, John Forster, and other writers, and from 1835 onwards he frequently visited the Carlyles at their house in Chelsea. Carlyle, who had read Craik's book on Paris, described him in a letter to John Stuart Mill as 'a man limited; but honest, and singularly *healthy*, and even robust, within his limits. He cannot be brilliant, but he can be decided, clear, and even emphatic' (*Collected Letters of Thomas and Jane Welsh Carlyle*, 8.312).

During the 1830s and 1840s Craik continued to write and edit for Charles Knight. With Charles MacFarlane and others, he produced *The Pictorial History of England* (originally published in parts, 1838–41, and then in other editions). *The History of British Commerce*, extracted from this, was published separately in 1844. He wrote *Sketches of the History of Literature and Learning in England* (6 vols., 1844–5; and subsequent editions), and thorough surveys of selected Renaissance authors, with *Spenser and his Poetry* (3 vols., 1845) and *Bacon: his Writings and his Philosophy* (3 vols., 1846–7). Craik also contributed to Knight's *Penny Magazine* and *Penny Cyclopaedia*.

A turning point in Craik's life was his appointment in 1849 as the professor of English literature and history at the newly established Queen's College, Belfast, where he was a popular and conscientious member of the academic staff. As well as teaching conventional university courses, Craik, like his colleagues, gave extramural classes, such as a course in 1852 for working men and townspeople on English writers. He was an examiner for the Indian Civil Service in 1859 and 1862. His publications at this period in his career included *The Romance of the Peerage* (4 vols., 1848–50), *Outlines of the History of the English Language* (1851), *The English of Shakespeare, Illustrated by a Philological Commentary on Julius Caesar* (1856), and the *Representation of Minorities* (1859). Above all, there was his *Manual of English Literature* (1862), which shows Craik's qualities at their best, as it systematically presents solid, clearly written information. It went through many editions, and its status as a standard history was confirmed by its inclusion in Everyman's Library in 1909.

Craik, whose wife had died in 1856, suffered a stroke in February 1866 while lecturing and died on 25 June 1866. He was buried at Holywood, near Belfast. A bust was placed in the entrance hall of Queen's College.

DONALD HAWES

**Sources** DNB · GM, 4th ser., 2 (1866), 265–6 · MS note by Lord Cockburn on copy of *Certificates in favour of Mr George L. Craik*, 1824, BL · *The collected letters of Thomas and Jane Welsh Carlyle*, ed. C. R. Sanders, K. J. Fielding, and others, [30 vols.] (1970– ) · T. W. Moody and J. C. Beckett, *Queen's, Belfast, 1845–1949: the history of a university*, 2 vols. (1959) · *The letters of Charles Dickens*, ed. M. House, G. Storey, and others, 1 (1965) · m. reg. Scot. · bap. reg. Scot. · bap. reg. Scot. [Lilias, Patterson]

**Archives** BL, letters to Leigh Hunt, Add. MSS 38110–38111, 3443–3449 · LUL, letters to Society for the Diffusion of Useful Knowledge · NL Scot., letters to J. S. Blackie · NL Scot., corresp. with Thomas Carlyle · U. Edin., New College, letters to Thomas Chalmers · U. Edin. L., letters to James Lorimer

**Likenesses** S. F. Lynn?, bust, Queen's University, Belfast

**Wealth at death** under £2000: administration, 11 Sept 1866, CGPLA Ire.

**Craik, Helen** (1751–1825), author, was born at Arbigland, Kirkbean, Dumfriesshire, the daughter of William Craik (1703–1798), agriculturist, justice of the peace, and inspector of customs, and Elizabeth (d. 1787), only daughter of William Stewart, of Shambellie, in Newabbey parish. She grew up at Arbigland, the manor house that her father had built in 1755. One of six legitimate children, she shared her birthplace with John Paul *Jones (1747–1792), the naval officer, son of John Paul, gardener at Arbigland, but rumoured to have been one of her father's illegitimate sons. Craik's powerful father was involved in local and national politics, and greatly increased the value of Arbigland through his agricultural innovation. He may also have been involved in the alleged murder (officially ruled a suicide) in 1792 of a man said to be Helen Craik's fiancé, a groom on her father's estate, whom local history sources suggest her family had killed because they disapproved of the relationship. The murder remains unverifiable, but Craik did leave Arbigland in 1792 for self-exile at her family's other estate: Flimby Hall, near Maryport, Cumberland. Though she was William Craik's sole surviving legitimate child, in 1792 he gave all his property to a distant relative, John Hamilton.

While still at Arbigland, Craik was a friend and correspondent of Robert Burns; he wrote to her in 1790 and 1792 of his admiration for her poem 'Helen' (lost), and she wrote the dedicatory poem on the title-page of his Glenriddell manuscript of poems. Most of her poetry is now lost; a few examples, published by her descendant George Neilson in the *Glasgow Herald* in 1919—such as her two poems to her friend Robert Riddell—survive. Neilson noted 'the recurrent Werterism of Miss Craik's poems', and that '[w]hether fostered by "Werter" or not, a kindred tragic sentimentality appears in Miss Craik's preference for suicidal and murderous subjects' (Neilson, 'The Maid of Enterkin: Burnsiana 1').

At Flimby between 1796 and 1805 Craik published five anonymous novels, all with William Lane's popular Minerva Press. Her first novel, *Julia de St. Pierre* (1796), in which she refers enigmatically to the 'peculiarly painful circumstances' in the life of the 'once persecuted Author' (vol. 1, p. 3), offers a sentimental portrait of a French emigrant woman as virtue in distress. This theme of persecuted, exiled women, often with murdered lovers or husbands and concerned with issues of justice, was one of Craik's favourites. Though published anonymously, like all her novels, *Julia* also included a long poem, 'The Maid of Enterkin'. Craik's descendant George Neilson referred to this poem in his article on her unpublished poetry in the *Glasgow Herald*, which also confirms her authorship of the five novels, previously attributed to her through a Minerva Press catalogue.

*Adelaide de Narbonne, with Memoirs of Charlotte de Cordet* (1800) is Craik's most innovative novel, one of the earliest historical novels, and possibly the first British fictional account of Charlotte Corday, who assassinated the Jacobin Marat in 1793. Craik allies her fictional heroine, Cordet, with the feminism of Mary Wollstonecraft, Mary Robinson, and Helen Maria Williams, the foremost British chronicler of the French Revolution. Drawing on the Gothic romances of Anne Radcliffe and Horace Walpole, Craik fashioned a unique hybrid of historical Gothic that addressed controversial recent events in France, particularly the destructive consequences of women's lack of political and economic rights. This concern with women's rights is also visible in *Stella of the North, or, The Foundling of the Ship* (1802) and in *The Nun and her Daughter, or, Memoirs of the Courville Family* (1805), the former set in Dumfriesshire. *Henry of Northumberland, or, The Hermit's Tale* (1800), based on the Hermit of Warkworth, is Craik's only known novel that is not set in her own day.

Craik outlived her relatives in Flimby, inheriting sums from them, and in 1807 gained half the proceeds of the sale of the family's Flimby estate (£16,504). She died at Flimby Hall, unmarried, on 11 June 1825. Her obituaries and her memorial in St Nicholas's Church, Flimby (where she was buried), remember her as a published author of works in English and French (now unknown), and as a dedicated philanthropist to the poor—a characteristic that she shares with her fictional heroines.

ADRIANA CRACIUN

**Sources** S. Arnott, 'The romance of Helen Craik of Arbigland', *Transactions of Dumfriesshire and Galloway Natural History and Antiquarian Society*, 11 (1923–4), 77–83 · G. Neilson, 'The maid of Enterkin: Burnsiana 1', *Glasgow Herald* (8 March 1919) · G. Neilson, 'The maid of Enterkin: poems by Helen Craik and Burnsiana', *Transactions and Journal Proceedings of the Dumfriesshire and Galloway Natural History and Antiquarian Society*, 3rd ser., 44 (1925), 64–76 · G. Neilson, 'The social and literary circle, 1790–1793: Burnsiana 2', *Glasgow Herald* (15 March 1919) · D. Blakey, *The Minerva Press, 1790–1820* (1939) · *The letters of Robert Burns*, ed. J. de Lancey Ferguson, 2nd edn, ed. G. Ross Roy, 2 vols. (1985) · [H. Craik], 'Letter, Miss Craik to James Grierson, esq., dated Flimby, 13th April, 1810', *Farmer's Magazine*, 46 (June 1811), 154–6 · [H. Craik], 'Letter, Miss Craik to James Grierson, esq., dated Flimby, May 1810', *Farmer's Magazine*, 46 (June 1811), 156–63 · *Dumfries Weekly Journal* (21 June 1825) · *Cumberland Pacquet* (14 June 1825) · A. Craciun, 'The new Cordays: Helen Craik and British representations of Charlotte Corday, 1793–1800', *Rebellious hearts: British women writers and the French Revolution*, ed. A. Craciun and K. Lokke (2001) · S. Arnott, 'Some Kirkbean folklore', *Transactions of Dumfriesshire and Galloway Natural History and Antiquarian Society*, 2nd ser., 11 (1894–5), 11–17 · R. Burns, *The Glenriddell manuscripts of Robert Burns* (1973)

**Craik, Sir Henry**, first baronet (1846–1927), civil servant and author, was born in Glasgow on 18 October 1846. He was the fifth son and the ninth of the ten children of the Revd James Craik DD, minister of St George's Church, Glasgow, and at one time moderator of the Church of Scotland, and his wife, Margaret, daughter of Walter Grieve, merchant, of Leith. From Glasgow high school he went, aged fourteen, to Glasgow University. In 1865 a Snell exhibition took him to Balliol College, Oxford, where he gained a first class in classical moderations (1867) and two

Sir Henry Craik, first baronet (1846–1927), by Sir Benjamin Stone, 1909

years later a second class in *literae humaniores* and a first class in law and modern history. In 1870 he was appointed a junior examiner in the education department, and became a senior examiner in 1878. He had married, on 17 December 1873, Fanny Esther (d. 13 Dec 1923), daughter of Charles Duffield of Manchester; they had three sons.

Craik's real opportunity came in 1885 when the Scotch education department (SED), a distinct entity since the Education (Scotland) Act of 1872, was transferred to the political control of the new Scottish Office. Craik was chosen as secretary of the autonomous department, and continued to occupy the post with great distinction until 1904. He was created a CB (1887) and then a KCB (1897). In 1906 he became Conservative member of parliament for the universities of Glasgow and Aberdeen. After the four Scottish universities were combined into a single constituency in 1918, he retained his seat as one of their three representatives until his death.

Perhaps inspired by his uncle George Lillie Craik, Craik combined a literary with an official career. He edited a series, the English Citizen, for Macmillan, which included his own *The State in its Relation to Education* (1884). He was a frequent contributor to the *Quarterly Review* and other periodicals; he published a *Life of Swift* (1882), *Selections from Swift* (1892), *English Prose Selections* (1893–6), and *A Century of Scottish History* (1901). Later publications included *Impressions of India* (1908) and a *Life of Edward, Earl of Clarendon* (1911).

Craik's conspicuous success as a civil servant was not

surprising, for he had a real aptitude for business and much practical sagacity, while his golden rule of 'look ahead' made him a master in the art of correspondence. Temperamentally irascible, he did not always find it easy to appreciate an opposite point of view. In his relations with his official chiefs he was a model of discretion and loyalty, and consequently his advice came to carry more and more weight with successive governments, whatever their political complexion; he was in especially close sympathy with Lord Balfour of Burleigh, Conservative secretary for Scotland from 1895 to 1903. By the end of Craik's period of office, many Scottish politicians and educationists were complaining of the 'despotic' methods of the SED, though his firm defence of Scottish interests was also widely appreciated.

As head of a small department, under a minister with many other interests, Craik was able to play a remarkably creative role. Although Treasury constraints meant that Scottish and English educational policy could not diverge very far, Craik used detailed amendments to the annual school code to bring about many significant changes. While a senior examiner, he had written a widely noted report on highland education, and as secretary he improved the financial condition of highland education and gave some recognition to the teaching of Gaelic. In elementary education, he gained much personal credit for ending the discredited system of 'payment by results', and for the abolition of fees, from 1890 onwards.

Perhaps Craik's most conspicuous achievement was the development of secondary education under the aegis of the state. The 1872 act had done little for secondary schools, but he successfully raised standards by bringing them under public inspection, by the creation of a leaving certificate linked to university entrance (1888), and by the department's control of state grants, which were extended to Scottish secondary education in 1892. Towards the end of his period of office, he also did much to encourage scientific, commercial, and technical education, though his personal preference was for the classics (he sent his own sons to Eton). He was a strong proponent of physical education and of military training for young men, and was a member of the royal commission on physical training in Scotland (1902). After leaving office, he abstained from direct criticism of his successors, but he opposed the public provision of school meals, which he thought undermined family responsibility, and remained attached to a rather narrow version of the Scottish tradition of the 'lad of parts', seeing educational opportunity as suited only to particularly able scholars. During the First World War, he chaired a committee on Scottish teachers' salaries which led to the introduction of a national scale in 1918.

As a politician, despite his well-stocked mind and his ripe experience, widened in later years by visits to South Africa (1903), Egypt and the Sudan (1907), India (1907–8), and Canada (1912), Craik never overcame the disability attaching to one who begins parliamentary life at sixty with no previous practice in public speaking. Moreover,

his relatively independent position as a university member induced a hardening of his innate conservatism. He sturdily refused to move with the times or to abate his dislike of new fangled devices from typewriters to cabinet secretariats. Nevertheless, he was popular in all quarters of the House of Commons, of which he ultimately became in years the oldest member. He was a man of exceptionally strong physique. His favourite recreation was hunting, and almost to the last he kept up the custom of taking morning exercise in the Row. On the outbreak of war in 1914, although then verging on seventy, he was one of the first to volunteer as a special constable.

Craik was sworn of the privy council in 1918 and created a baronet in January 1926. He died at his house, 5A Dean's Yard, Westminster, London, on 16 March 1927, and was buried in Highgate cemetery, Middlesex. He was succeeded as baronet by his elder son, George Lillie Craik (1874–1929), chief constable, Metropolitan Police (1910–14).

G. MACDONALD, rev. R. D. ANDERSON

**Sources** H. Craik, *Glasgow Herald* (April 1922–May 1925) [autobiographical articles] · private information (1937) · personal knowledge (1937) · A. Morgan, *Makers of Scottish education* (1929), 221–30 · d. cert. · *CGPLA Eng. & Wales* (1927) · Burke, *Peerage* (1939) · *WWW*, 1929–40 · *Glasgow Herald* (18–19 March 1927) · *Glasgow Herald* (21 March 1927)
**Archives** NL Scot. | BL, Blackwoods MSS · BL, corresp. with Macmillans, Add. MS 55045 · NA Scot., corresp. with G. W. Balfour · NA Scot., Lothian MSS · NL Scot., letters to Blackwoods · UCL, letters to Sir F. Galton
**Likenesses** B. Stone, photograph, 1909, NPG [*see illus.*] · Annan of Glasgow, photograph, Scot. NPG
**Wealth at death** £21,790 12s. 1d.: resworn probate, 21 July 1927, *CGPLA Eng. & Wales*

**Craik, Kenneth James William** (1914–1945), psychologist, was born on 29 March 1914 at 10 Trinity Road, Leith, Scotland, the son of James Bowstead Craik, writer to the signet, and his wife, Marie Sylvia, *née* Robson. Having studied psychology under James Drever sen. (and philosophy under Norman Kemp-Smith) at the University of Edinburgh, Craik moved to St John's College, Cambridge, and joined Frederic Bartlett's Cambridge Psychological Laboratory (Drever having warned Bartlett: 'Next term I am going to send you a genius'). Craik rapidly turned to research on hearing and perception, gaining a reputation for technical prowess in designing and making equipment as well as for intellectual liveliness and breadth of interest. After obtaining his PhD, with a thesis on visual adaptation (1940), he became a fellow of St John's (1941). With the onset of the Second World War the laboratory's work soon became oriented towards topics of military significance, particularly flying. Craik produced a steady stream of papers on such topics as visibility through fighter windscreens, instrument lighting, and differentiating muscular from mental fatigue, many involving an experimental cockpit he had designed. Most appeared as reports for the various official armed services committees on which he sat. Against this background of tackling practical problems of engineering and physiology Craik produced his only book, *The Nature of Explanation* (1943), a short but remarkably prescient work. After a brief, perspicuous, critique of traditional philosophical positions and an account of the modes of explanation emerging in such contemporary scientific developments as quantum physics, he turned to psychological explanation, and asked, 'What structure and process are required in a mechanical system to enable it to imitate correctly and to predict external processes or create new things?' At this point calculating machines came to the fore as centrally important models for psychological processes and Craik proceeded, speculatively, to explore their possible bearing on perception. '[T]he nervous system is viewed as a calculating machine capable of modelling or paralleling external events.' Craik rejected the symbolic logic and abstraction of contemporary logical positivism, viewing logical positivism's formal exercises as the last trace of a doomed *a priorism* 'fated to yield to an experimental approach'. Craik thus helped to initiate the information processing approach which was later to revolutionize post-war American psychology as 'cognitive psychology'. The posthumously published two-part paper 'Theory of the human operator in control systems' (*British Journal of Psychology*, 1948) developed his ideas further in relation to the new communication and control theory (renamed 'cybernetics' by Norbert Weiner in that year).

These two works aside, Craik's mature work remained largely inaccessible, much being officially restricted or for internal circulation in the applied psychology unit (of which he became the first director in 1944). Craik died in Addenbrooke's Hospital, Cambridge, on 7 May 1945 after being involved in an accident while cycling.

While Craik's reputation was maintained by his close colleagues, there was little visible basis for it available to outsiders. This was rectified in 1966 with the publication of *The Nature of Psychology*, an edited selection of unpublished papers, essays, and other writings (including the first description of what was later called the Craik–O'Brien–Cornsweet illusion). Evidence for the long-rumoured breadth and originality of Craik's interests and thought was at last available. Besides psychological theory and experimental work it included a variety of philosophical essays and pieces—some but fragments—on topics such as claustrophobia, Marxism, and science, and 'War as a part of life', plus a full, 80-item bibliography which included his wartime research. The tantalizing glimpses of Craik's unrealized potential contained in this volume reproduced on a wider scale the sense of loss which his Cambridge colleagues had always felt. In 1976 the Kenneth Craik Laboratory, Cambridge, was named in his honour. GRAHAM RICHARDS

**Sources** F. Bartlett, *British Journal of Psychology*, 36 (1945–6), 109–15 · d. cert. · b. cert. · private information (2004)
**Wealth at death** £5486 11s. 9d.: confirmation, 19 June 1945, *CCI*

**Crakanthorpe, Richard** (*bap.* 1568, *d.* 1624), Church of England clergyman and logician, was born at Little Strickland, Westmorland, and baptized on 25 January 1568 at Morland, the second son of John Crakanthorpe and Mabel Cowper. He matriculated at Queen's College, Oxford, on 13 December 1583, aged sixteen. According to Wood he was admitted as a 'poor serving child, then a tabardar' (Wood, *Ath. Oxon.*, 2.361). He graduated BA on 28 June 1587 and proceeded MA on 1 July 1590. At Queen's he came under the influence of the puritan John Reynolds, whom he later described as 'a walking library of all learning and all knowledge' (*Defensio ecclesia Anglicanae*, 494). He proceeded BTh on 12 July 1597 and became a fellow of Queen's in 1598. Anthony Wood says that Crakanthorpe 'being a noted preacher, and a profound disputant in divinity … was admired by all great men, and had in veneration, especially by the puritanical party, he being himself a zealot among them' (Wood, *Ath. Oxon.*, 2.361). Such was his reputation for preaching that he was selected in the notorious attempt to convert the Catholic prisoners of York Castle in 1600, and he had close links with Calvinist theologians such as Henry Airay, Robert Abbot, and Bodley's librarian Thomas James. He was also renowned as a teacher at Oxford, tutoring among others the Arminian Thomas Jackson, and was one of the few who left traces of their teaching methods (Queen's College, Oxford, library, MS 196).

With Thomas Morton, the future bishop of Chester and Durham, Crakanthorpe was chosen as chaplain to Lord Evers on his embassy to Germany in 1603. While abroad the two men 'did advantage themselves exceedingly by conversing with learned men of other persuasions, and by visiting several universities and libraries there' (Wood, *Ath. Oxon.*, 2.361). After his return Crakanthorpe was made chaplain to Thomas Ravis, the Calvinist bishop of London and chaplain-in-ordinary to the king. He was admitted to the rectory of Black Notley, near Braintree in Essex, on 21 January 1605, by favour of Sir John Leverson, who had had three sons at Queen's College. Crakanthorpe became DD on 17 July 1606. About this time he married Dorothy (*d.* in or after 1625); he was almost certainly the Richard Crakanthorpe who married Dorothy Kenne on 31 July 1606 at Goodnestone by Sandwich, Kent, for his will mentions two 'sons-in-law' (stepsons), George and Thomas Kenn. The Crakanthorpes had three children, John, Dorothy, and Elizabeth.

Crakanthorpe soon established himself as a religious controversialist. *A Sermon of Sanctification* (1608) was followed by *A sermon at the solemnizing of the happie inauguration of our most gracious and religious soveraigne King James* (1609), originally preached at Paul's Cross on 24 March 1608 as part of the propaganda campaign of the Virginia Company to establish an English colony in America. The sermon, based on texts from Kings and Micah, compared James to Solomon. Crakanthorpe violently denounced allegiance to the pope and strengthened arguments in favour of a divine mandate for civil power. The same theme underlay *Justinian the Emperor Defended, Against Cardinal Baronius* (1615).

On 4 May 1617 Crakanthorpe was presented by Bishop John King of London to the rectory of Paglesham, Essex, in succession to his friend John Barkham. Having maintained his links with Oxford through preaching and publication he evidently preserved an interest in teaching too. The latter of his two resulting textbooks, *Introductio in metaphysicam* (1619) and *Logicae libri quinque: de praedicabilibus* (1622), went through four editions by 1677. Though this was later criticized as symptomatic of the depths to which the quality of Oxford teaching had sunk, it remained popular throughout the seventeenth century. Within the conventional Aristotelian framework, Crakanthorpe introduced students to Tycho Brahe's work on the nova of 1572 and the comet of 1577 and gave them details of the telescopic discoveries of Galileo, from his *Sidereus nuncius* (1610). Crakanthorpe sought to revise the *Logicae*, to which end he sought the advice of Michael Honeywood, the president of Christ's College, Cambridge, but his death cut short the project. However, the work remained popular, appearing in student library catalogues in the 1680s. It also earned Crakanthorpe a satirical appearance in Thomas Randolph's comedy of 1630, *Aristippus, or, The Jovial Philosopher*, in which the author, with no taste for Oxford teachers, urged

Hang Brerewood and Carter,
in Crakenthorps garter
(*Poetical and Dramatic Works of Thomas Randolph*, ed. W. C. Hazlitt, vol. 1, 1875, 25)

Crakanthorpe remained a convinced Calvinist. The dedication of *A Sermon of Predestination, Preached at Oxford* (1620) to Sir Edward Barrett revealed that 'divers conferences' on the subject of election had taken place at Barrett's house (sig. A2r–v); in the sermon Crakanthorpe adhered strictly to Beza's doctrine of election. His two most important publications were both posthumous: *Defensio ecclesiae Anglicanae* (1625) and *Vigilius dormitans, Romes Seer Overseene* (1631). His aim in these works was to recapture the medieval church for the protestants, and his consistent argument was that the English Reformation did not establish a new church but purified a corrupt old one. In the *Defensio* Crakanthorpe took it upon himself to defend the Church of England against the apostate Marc'Antonio de Dominis, the infamous archbishop of Spalato. He refused to be drawn into disowning foreign churches and stressed how happy the English church was to help foreign protestants. He also rejected the view, held among others by the king, that Rome was the mother church. Wood described Crakanthorpe's work as 'the most exact piece for controversie since the time of the reformation' (Wood, *Ath. Oxon.*, 2.362). Crakanthorpe replied vituperatively against de Dominis, defending the views of his tutor Reynolds, whom de Dominis had attacked. The style was certainly hostile and Wood remarks that he was 'foul mouthed against the papists' (ibid.). It was a particularly vehement piece of anti-papal invective at a time when many were eager to play down differences between the Church of Rome and the Church of England. Richard Mountague, hinting of possible circulation in manuscript, wrote to John Cosin in January 1625, 'Dr Crakanthorp's booke I thought had ben out long since … I merveile the overseers lett it passe' (*Correspondence of John Cosin*, 1.44). In *Vigilius dormitans*, a vast vindication of the fifth general council, Crakanthorpe argued that papal infallibility began only at the council of Leo X. He argued that true doctrines in the Roman church were rendered invalid because they were held on the authority of the pope and not of God. Crakanthorpe's religious controversy expressed the division between the Church of England and that of Rome in absolute terms. His searching of medieval sources, for instance in *The Defence of Constantine* (1621), enabled later scholars to adhere more coherently to the idea that the English Reformation did not build a new church but cleansed an old one. He also wrote 'Popish falsifications' which was an answer to a work of the seminary priest Richard Broughton, and 'Animadversions on Cardinal Baronius his annals'; neither work has survived.

Crakanthorpe amassed considerable personal wealth. Bequests in his will, signed on 4 August 1624, included houses and lands from his livings and Colchester, and a library worth £230. He died later that year, survived by his wife, and was buried at Black Notley on 25 November; his funeral sermon was preached by his friend John Barkham, now dean of Bocking, Essex. James I said that he died for want of a bishopric. Mountague, on hearing of his death, wrote, 'I am sorry for it, because a good Archbishop might have made good use of him' (*Correspondence of John Cosin*, 1.44).

A. P. CAMBERS

**Sources** A. Milton, *Catholic and Reformed: the Roman and protestant churches in English protestant thought, 1600–1640* (1995) · *Hist. U. Oxf.*, vols. 3–4 · Wood, *Ath. Oxon.*, new edn · A. Fitzmaurice, '"Everey man, that prints, adventures": the rhetoric of the Virginia Company sermons', *The English sermon revisited*, ed. L. Ferrell and P. McCulloch (2000), 24–42 · N. Tyacke, *Anti-Calvinists: the rise of English Arminianism, c.1590–1640* (1987) · *The correspondence of John Cosin D.D., lord bishop of Durham*, ed. [G. Ornsby], 1, SurtS, 52 (1869) · Foster, *Alum. Oxon.* · J. Doelman, *King James and the religious culture of England* (2000) · will, LMA, DL/C/362, Richard Crakanthorpe, 1625, April; M/F x19/16, fols. 2r–3v · 'Narrative of the sermons in York Castle, 1600', BL, Add. MS 34250 · IGI [parish registers of Morland, Westmorland, and of Goodnestone by Sandwich, Kent] · J. Nicolson and R. Burn, *The history and antiquities of the counties of Westmorland and Cumberland*, 1 (1777), 448
**Archives** Queen's College, Oxford, MS 196 · Queen's College, Oxford, MS 224
**Wealth at death** disposed of £75 in will; plus library valued at £230; lands and houses in his livings and at Colchester: will, LMA, DL/C/362, Richard Crakanthorpe, 1625, April; M/F x19/16, fols. 2r–3v

**Crake, Augustine David** (1836–1890), religious writer and schoolmaster, the eldest son of Jesse Crake, was born on 1 October 1836 at Chalgrove, Oxfordshire, where his father kept a 'middle-class school'. He broke away from the strong Calvinistic surroundings amid which he had been brought up and was baptized into the Church of England in 1858. Having gained a position as a teacher, he was able to secure a degree at London University (matriculated 1862; BA 1864). He was ordained deacon by Bishop Samuel Wilberforce in 1865 and was appointed second master and chaplain of the Church of England middle-class school of All Saints, Bloxham, near Banbury, Oxfordshire, a position which he retained from 1865 to 1878. He was senior curate of St Michael's, Swanmore, on the Isle of Wight, in 1878–9 and vicar of St Peter's, Havenstreet, Isle of Wight, from 1879 to 1885, when he effected an exchange and became vicar of Cholsey, near Wallingford, Berkshire. In 1879 he married Annie Lucas, daughter of John Lucas of the Oxford observatory. He was also chaplain at Moulsford Asylum, Berkshire, in 1885–6.

Crake was the author of a long series of historical story-books, written to illustrate the trials and triumphs of the church in Britain; these stories, in which his topographical knowledge of Oxfordshire and Berkshire was used to advantage, were related orally in the first instance to the boys of the school at Bloxham. In 1873 he published a *History of the Church under the Roman Empire*, a more ambitious effort, which had a large circulation, being greatly in demand by students. Among his chief devotional books and stories were *Simple Prayers for School Boys* (1867, 1870); *Evanus: a Tale of the Days of Constantine the Great* (1872, 1885); *The Garden of Life* (1873), a devotional primer; *The Andreds-Weald* (1877), a tale of the Norman conquest; *Brian Fitz-Count, a Story of Wallingford Castle* (1887); *Yule Log Stories* (1887); and *Stories from Old English History* (1887). Crake edited *Offices for the hours of prime, sext, and compline; with special antiphons and chapters for the seasons of the church* in 1871 and was moreover joint editor with Joseph Oldknow of the *Priest's Book of Private Devotion* (1872). He died at Cholsey vicarage on 18 January 1890 at the age of fifty-three and was buried in Cholsey graveyard on 23 January.

THOMAS SECCOMBE, *rev.* NILANJANA BANERJI

**Sources** *The Guardian* (29 Jan 1890) • *Church Times* (24 Jan 1890) • Allibone, *Dict.* • *The Athenaeum* (1 Feb 1890), 150 • Crockford (1874) • *CGPLA Eng. & Wales* (1890)
**Wealth at death** £803 14s. 11d.: probate, 1 March 1890, *CGPLA Eng. & Wales*

**Crakelt, William** (1740/41–1812), classical scholar and lexicographer, was from about 1762 the curate at Northfleet in Kent, a role he fulfilled until his death. He was also master of the Northfleet grammar school, and was presented in 1774 to the vicarage of Chalk in Kent. In 1784 Crakelt published the first of what became various editions of John Entick's dictionaries: *Entick's New Spelling Dictionary, a New Ed., Enlarged by W. C.*; other editions were published in 1787, 1791, and in 1795. In 1786 there appeared *Entick's New Latin–English Dictionary, Augmented by W. C.*, followed by *Tyronis thesaurus, or, Entick's New Latin–English Dictionary: a New Edition Revised by W. C.* (1796). Crakelt also published a revised edition of Daniel Watson's English prose translation of Horace (1792) and translated Antoine René Mauduit's *New … Treatise of Spherical Trigonometry* (1768). Crakelt was intimate with the bookseller Charles Dilly, who, on his death in 1807, left a legacy to Crakelt's wife, Ann, and to her daughter, Mrs Eylard. Crakelt died at Northfleet on 22 August 1812, aged seventy-one, and was survived by his wife. Three further editions of Entick's dictionaries with Crakelt's additions were published posthumously.

W. W. WROTH, *rev.* PHILIP CARTER

**Sources** Nichols, *Lit. anecdotes*, 3.191–2; 8.438 • *GM*, 1st ser., 82/2 (1812), 298 • W. Crakelt, will, PRO, PROB 11/1545, fol. 101r–v

**Cramb** [Cram], **John Adam** (1861–1913), historian and defence publicist, was born at Denny in Stirlingshire on 4 May 1861, the fourth child and second son of David Cram,

John Adam Cramb (1861–1913), by unknown photographer, *c.*1911

who after failing in a photography and lithographic printing business worked as a carpenter, and of his wife, Elizabeth, *née* Marshall. The family moved to Bonnybridge, Stirlingshire, and after leaving school Cram worked in a pattern factory near his home, an unhappy episode he afterwards seldom mentioned. He read and was lastingly influenced by Carlyle. In October 1879 he went to Glasgow University to prepare for the ministry. He studied under Sir William Thomson (later Lord Kelvin) and others, went as a 'supply' preacher to various parishes, and changed the spelling of his name to Cramb. In 1886 he graduated with first-class honours in classics and was appointed Luke fellow in English literature. He studied in Bonn and attended lectures by Treitschke, whose Anglophobia and glorification of war made a lasting impression and led to Cramb's *Germany and England* (1914). He acquired a wide knowledge of German history and literature, and continued to be influenced by Treitschke, Nietzsche, and other German writers. Suffering religious doubts, he decided against entering the ministry.

Cramb worked unhappily as a schoolmaster at Melrose, then in 1887 travelled on the continent. On 4 October 1887 he married Lucy (*d.* 26 Sept 1918, aged seventy-two), third daughter of Edward W. Selby Lowndes, JP and deputy lieutenant, of Winslow House, Winslow, Buckinghamshire; they had one son, Meyrick. From 1887 to 1890 Cramb was lecturer in modern history at Queen Margaret College, Glasgow, a new women's college. In 1890, to advance his career, he moved to London, and from then on lived in the Notting Hill and Kensington area. He wrote for the press, including the *Daily News* and *St James's Gazette*, and contributed ten articles to the *Dictionary of National Biography*. From 1891 he was a modern history examiner for the civil service commissioners. From January 1892, after the committee's Cantabrigian first choice declined the post, Cramb was lecturer in modern history at Queen's College, Harley Street, London: a unique institution, never part of London University but providing university-style education to girls of senior secondary-school age and to adult lady part-time students. From May 1893 he was professor of modern history there. Walrus-moustached, multilingual, erudite, and enthusiastic, he was an ardent, judgemental, and wide-ranging lecturer, without notes. 'An arresting and dominating personality … with much of Thomas Carlyle's turn of phrase' (*Queen's College Magazine*, Dec 1913, 139), he much impressed his students. Katherine Mansfield wrote, 'Cramb, wonderful Cramb! … ageless and fiery … I couldn't write down Cramb's thunder. I simply wanted to sit and hear him' (*Journal*, 104). Another admiring student, Lilian M. Rigby (later Mrs C. E. B. Russell), daughter of Major-General C. P. Rigby (1820–1885), attended Cramb's lectures for ten years and later wrote his biography. He also gave short courses of lectures on history, literature, and philosophy at private houses. However he apparently did no primary research and he never published a work of academic history.

In 1903 Cramb met at the Queen's Hall, London, Lady Ottoline Morrell. In 1904 they had a close relationship, with Cramb apparently romantically besotted with her, but she ended it. He based his novel *Cuthbert Learmont* on it. After his death she wrote, 'He was as brilliant—& wonderful as anyone I ever met' (Darroch, 52).

In 1900, responding to the Second South African War, Cramb published his first book, *The Origins and Destiny of Imperial Britain*, originally lectures: fervent imperialist propaganda justifying the Second South African War, glorifying war and its sacrifice, and warning of the foreign, especially German, threat to Britain and the empire. The book's reception disappointed Cramb, not bringing the hoped-for recognition. In the book he favoured compulsory military training, and he supported the campaign by Lord Roberts and the revived National Service League. In 1906 he met Roberts, and in 1907 he lectured for the league. In 1910 Ian Hamilton's *Compulsory Service* attacked the compulsionist case. Roberts replied with *Fallacies and Facts* (1911). Cramb assisted Roberts in writing its first part, and himself wrote its anonymous third part, 'The argument from history': Lady Roberts wrote that the latter 'made mincemeat' of Hamilton's historical allusions. In the following years Cramb was Roberts's speech-writer for his 'national service' campaign. He was paid by Roberts from his private account. Through his friendship with Roberts and other officers Cramb became an occasional lecturer at the Staff College and military centres.

Cramb devoted much time to writing novels. He published, under the pseudonym J. A. Revermont, three: *Lucius Scarfield* (1908), *Cuthbert Learmont* (1910), and *The*

*Marrying of Hester Rainsbrook* (1913). According to his biographer 'none was a popular success … seeing that the mental effort required in reading them is greater than their entertainment value' (Russell, 157). Yet D. H. Lawrence considered *Hester Rainsbrook* 'rather good'. *Schönbrunn*, partly autobiographical but largely about Bonaparte, who fascinated Cramb, was published posthumously in 1918.

Himself German-influenced, Cramb in early 1913 delivered at Queen's College a series of lectures warning against German Anglophobia, aggression, and threat to Britain, asserting the 'ideal element' in war, and arguing against pacifism. They were published posthumously in June 1914 as *Germany and England*, which was extensively reprinted during the war. In the summer of 1913 Cramb's health much deteriorated, and he died of 'malignant disease of the duodenum' at his home, 55 Edith Road, West Kensington, on 7 October. His body was cremated at Golders Green, and the urn interred at Ightham churchyard, near Sevenoaks. Cramb contributed to shaping British attitudes before and during the First World War.

ROGER T. STEARN

**Sources** Mrs C. E. B. Russell, *John Adam Cramb* (1950) • R. T. Stearn, 'Lord Roberts' speech writer: Professor J. A. Cramb, 1861–1913', *Soldiers of the Queen*, 88 (1997) • S. J. Darroch, *Ottoline: the life of Lady Ottoline Morrell* (1976) • J. A. Cramb, letters to Lord Roberts, NAM, Roberts papers • Queen's College, London, minutes of committees, ledgers, and notebooks • *Queen's College Magazine* (1892–1913) • U. Glas., Archives and Business Records Centre • P. M. Kennedy, *The rise of the Anglo-German antagonism, 1860–1914* (1980) • R. G. Grylls, *Queen's College, 1848–1948* (1948) • E. Kaye, *A history of Queen's College, London, 1848–1972* (1972) • J. M. Murry, ed., *Journal of Katherine Mansfield* (1954) • D. James, *Lord Roberts* (1954) • A. J. A. Morris, *The scaremongers: the advocacy of war and rearmament, 1896–1914* (1984) • E. M. Spiers, *Haldane: an army reformer* (1980) • L. S. Amery, *My political life*, 1: *England before the storm* (1953) • M. J. Allison, 'The national service issue, 1899–1914', PhD diss., U. Lond., 1975 • *WWW* • M. Seymour, *Ottoline Morrell: life on the grand scale* (1992)
**Archives** Queen's College, London | NAM, Roberts MSS • Ransom HRC, Lady Ottoline Morrell MSS
**Likenesses** photographs, *c.*1893–*c.*1911, repro. in Russell, *John Adam Cramb*, frontispiece [*see illus.*]
**Wealth at death** £1114 6*s.* 3*d.*: administration, 6 Nov 1913, *CGPLA Eng. & Wales*

**Cramer, Franz** [François] **(1772–1848)**, violinist, the second son of Wilhelm *Cramer (*bap.* 1746, *d.* 1799), was born at Schwetzingen, near Mannheim, on 12 June 1772. He joined his father in London when very young. As a child he was so delicate that he was not allowed to study, but once his health improved he received violin lessons from his father, by whom he was placed in the opera orchestra without salary at the age of seventeen. He made his London début on 12 March 1792, joining his father in a Pleyel concerto for two violins. In 1794 he was elected a member of the Royal Society of Musicians, and three years later became a governor. On his father's death he succeeded to the latter's post as leader of the Ancient Concerts, and it is related that George III used to give him the right tempos when Handel's compositions were performed. He was soon recognized as one of London's foremost orchestral leaders, for example at the Philharmonic Society, and played at most of the provincial festivals and at the coronation of George IV. On the foundation of the Royal Academy of Music in 1822 he was appointed one of the first professors and in 1834 he succeeded Christian Kramer as master of the king's music.

With his wife, Anne (whom he had married by 1813), Cramer had at least four sons. Towards the end of his life he sustained a severe shock on the death of his second son, François, who died of consumption just after taking his degree at Oxford. He never recovered from this blow, though he continued working almost until his own death, which occurred at his residence in Westbourne Grove, London, on 25 July 1848.

Cramer was a respectable performer, but he excelled as a leader rather than as a soloist, and of his compositions only one violin capriccio survives. A kind-hearted and generous man, he was a much loved figure in London's music profession, although he was overshadowed by his more celebrated brother, Johann Baptist *Cramer.

W. B. SQUIRE, rev. SIMON MCVEIGH

**Sources** [J. S. Sainsbury], ed., *A dictionary of musicians*, 2 vols. (1824) · *Musical World* (5 Aug 1848) · *Annual Register* (1848) · J. E. Cox, *Musical recollections of the last half-century*, 2 vols. (1872) · *The Oracle* (12–13 March 1792) · Highfill, Burnim & Langhans, *BDA* · B. Matthews, ed., *The Royal Society of Musicians of Great Britain: list of members, 1738–1984* (1985) · C. F. Pohl, *Mozart und Haydn in London*, 2 vols. (Vienna, 1867) · F. Corder, *A history of the Royal Academy of Music from 1822 to 1922* (1922) · M. B. Foster, *History of the Philharmonic Society of London: 1813–1912* (1912)

**Likenesses** B. P. Gibbon, line engraving, pubd 1826 (after W. Watts), BM, NPG · I. W. Slater, lithograph, pubd 1832 (after J. Slater), BM · C. Moitte, lithograph (after Minasi), BM · attrib. J. Stephanoff, drawing, V&A

**Cramer, Johann Baptist** [John Baptist] (1771–1858), pianist and composer, was born on 24 February 1771 in Mannheim, the eldest son of the violinist Wilhelm *Cramer (bap. 1746, d. 1799) and his first wife. The details of his childhood remain unclear, but probably in 1774 he accompanied his mother to London, where his father was already firmly established as a leading violinist. The boy was also intended for the violin, but he secretly took every opportunity to practise on an old piano instead, showing such talent that his father agreed to entrust him to the pianist J. D. Benser. In 1780 he began to study with J. S. Schroeter, and made his London début on 5 April 1781 at his father's benefit concert. By 1783 he was already a concerto soloist of precocious brilliance, but he now turned for lessons to London's foremost virtuoso, and the founder of modern piano playing, Muzio Clementi. On 10 March 1784 they played a duet for two pianos at a Hanover Square concert, yet when Clementi abruptly left for the continent the association came to an end. Later in life Cramer played down the impact of Clementi's tuition; but whereas Schroeter stressed refinement and sensitivity, Clementi surely revealed to him the dramatic and expressive capabilities of the piano. Already Cramer's repertory extended beyond the *galanterie* of Schroeter and J. C. Bach to music by C. P. E. Bach, Scarlatti, Haydn, and Mozart, as well as Clementi himself. From 1785 to 1787 Cramer took counterpoint lessons with C. F. Abel, and around this time

**Johann Baptist Cramer (1771–1858),** by George Lethbridge Saunders, 1827

he became familiar with J. S. Bach's preludes and fugues, the beginning of a lifelong passion for the elder Bach's music.

After the 1788 season, during which his first piano sonatas and trios were published, Cramer embarked on a tour of Germany and France, staying for some time in revolutionary Paris. He returned to London in 1790, now recognized as a fully fledged piano virtuoso, and his career on London's concert platforms lasted for a further forty-five years. During the 1790s, following Clementi's retirement from the public stage, he vied with Jan Ladislav Dussek for the laurels, playing at the Professional Concert series, at concerts with Haydn, and so on. Many of Cramer's sonatas and his first concertos date from this lively period, when pianistic virtuosity was increasingly popular with concert audiences—thanks partly to technological developments by makers such as Broadwood.

In 1799 Cramer undertook a second continental tour, this time reaching as far as Vienna. Here he met Beethoven, who was later to describe him as the finest pianist of his day. Cramer was not always so complimentary about Beethoven's own music, though he did play a part in popularizing Beethoven's piano sonatas in England. After returning to London in 1800 he soon married, and (apart from one further tour in 1816–18) he settled in the capital for the rest of his performing career. On 24 January 1813 he attended the famous meeting that led to the foundation of the Philharmonic Society; during the first season he conducted from the piano in alternation with Clementi, and he appeared there most years until 1834. Cramer was revered and loved by London audiences as their 'glorious John', an honorary Englishman to be supported against foreign interlopers. Though he came to prefer salon concerts to public adulation, he regularly promoted benefit concerts, often with his brother Franz *Cramer. He was also a popular teacher with those able to afford his high fees, and in 1823 he joined the teaching staff of the new Royal Academy of Music.

Cramer's piano playing was renowned for its singing legato tone—it was probably this modern quality that particularly appealed to Beethoven. According to Ignaz Moscheles, 'those thin, well-shaped fingers are best suited for legato playing; they glide along imperceptibly from one key to the other, and whenever possible, avoid octave as well as staccato passages. Cramer sings on the piano in such a manner that he almost transforms a Mozart andante into a vocal piece' (*Aus Moscheles' Leben*, 1.51). He associated this legato directly with the heavier touch of the English piano. During the 1790s Cramer helped to develop other idiomatic techniques associated with the 'London pianoforte school': dramatic contrasts, rich chordal sonorities, fluid accompaniments, advanced pianistic figuration. Cramer's understanding of the piano is ably demonstrated in his most enduring monument, the eighty-four studies entitled *Studio per il pianoforte* (1804–8). Each study develops a single idea, occasionally acknowledging a debt to Bach or Handel, but always with the most imaginative pianism. Among the admirers of Cramer's collection were both Beethoven and Schumann.

Nevertheless Cramer could scarcely compete with the bravura and technical showmanship of the younger generation of Moscheles and Liszt. In 1833 a duet with Henri Herz provided a comical contrast between 'a young frisky colt' and 'a well-fed, cream-coloured state-horse' (*Life of Moscheles*, 1.293). Cramer began to cut a rather old-fashioned figure, regarded even as a bulwark against 'the inundation of bad taste by which we are threatened' (*Harmonicon*, 1823). He himself cultivated an image as a latter-day Mozartean. As a teenager he had been one of the earliest advocates of Mozart's piano concertos, and he performed them throughout his life, publishing some of his own cadenzas.

Cramer's own music also recalls Mozart in its graceful and elegant manner. Rarely profound or strikingly individual in melody, it is effective and well crafted rather than inspired, and certainly not on the level of Clementi or Dussek. Yet Cramer was at the forefront in developing idiomatic pianistic figurations and evocative textures, his poetic sonorities often anticipating Mendelssohn and the early Romantics. The studies apart, his most significant music is found in the sonatas, especially those of the 1800s. A few serious sonatas such as 'Le retour à Londres' date from after 1810, but Cramer's attention became directed increasingly towards the amateur market. For publication he produced innumerable rondos, variations, and fantasias on popular tunes and operatic melodies—so many, indeed, that his name eventually became a byword for musical baubles.

Partly this development reflected Cramer's own commercial interests. Like Clementi he went into music publishing, forming the partnership of Cramer and Keys in 1805, and five years later going into business with Samuel Chappell. In 1824 he joined forces with Addison and Beale, successfully specializing in the sale of piano music: the firm has survived to this day, under the name of J. B. Cramer & Co.

For all his benign image and high-minded commitment to his art, Cramer's nature could on occasion be barbed and even vindictive. Moscheles found him 'exceedingly intellectual and entertaining, he has a sharp satirical vein, and spares neither his own nor his neighbour's foibles' (*Life*, 1.51). His reputation for cleverness was not entirely complimentary, and some of his music displays a mischievous ear for parody. Perhaps as a consequence of the *Studio* (the idea and title of which Clementi claimed as his own), Cramer's relationship with his teacher remained uneasy: the tension was played out in their own publications, culminating in a vicious parody of Clementi's celebrated 'octave sonata'.

Cramer married for a second time in 1829, and in 1835 he retired from public life with a farewell concert on 19 May; his fellow pianists in turn honoured him with a musical banquet. The next ten years he spent mainly abroad, travelling to Munich and Vienna, and took up residence in Paris (although he did play a Mozart piano quartet at the Philharmonic Society in 1840). In 1845 he returned to England, and lived in retirement until his death, at his Kensington house, 9 The Terrace, on 16 April 1858. He was buried at Brompton cemetery on 22 April.

SIMON McVEIGH

**Sources** 'Memoir of John Baptist Cramer', *The Harmonicon*, 1 (1823), 179–81 • [J. S. Sainsbury], ed., *A dictionary of musicians*, 2 vols. (1824) • *Musical World* (24 April 1858), 264 • T. Schlesinger, *Johann Baptist Cramer und seine Klaviersonaten* (1928) • *Aus Moscheles' Leben: nach Briefen und Tagebüchern*, ed. [C. Moscheles], 2 vols. (Leipzig, 1872–3); trans. A. D. Coleridge, *Life of Moscheles: with selections from his diaries and correspondence* (1873) • T. B. Milligan, *Johann Baptist Cramer (1771–1858): a thematic catalogue of his works* (1994) • D. W. Krummel and S. Sadie, eds., *Music printing and publishing* (1990) • A. Tyson, 'A feud between Clementi and Cramer', *Music and Letters*, 54 (1973), 281–8 • N. Temperley, ed., *The London pianoforte school, 1766–1860*, 9–11 (1984) • F. Corder, *A history of the Royal Academy of Music from 1822 to 1922* (1922) • S. McVeigh, 'The Professional Concert and rival subscription series in London, 1783–1793', *Royal Musical Association Research Chronicle*, 22 (1989), 1–135 • J. Graue, 'The Clementi–Cramer dispute revisited', *Music and Letters*, 56 (1975), 47–54 • H. C. Robbins Landon, *Haydn in England: 1791–1795* (1976), vol. 3 of *Haydn: chronicle and works*

**Likenesses** G. H. Harlow, group portrait, oils, 1817 (*Court of the trial of Queen Catherine*), Royal Shakespeare Memorial Theatre Museum, Stratford upon Avon • E. Scriven, stipple, pubd 1819 (after J. Pocock), BM • Thomson, engraving, 1823 (after A. Wivell), repro. in *Harmonicon*, facing p. 179 • J. Thompson, stipple, pubd 1826 (after D. Barber), BM • G. L. Saunders, miniature, 1827, NPG [*see illus.*] • W. Sharp, lithograph, pubd 1830 (after W. Sharp), BM • B. Holl, stipple, pubd 1831 (after A. Wivell), BM • B. Wyon, bronze medal, 1845, NPG • A. B. Freebairn, engraving (after medal by B. Wyon), BM • G. H. Harlow, group portrait, oils (*Trial scene in Henry VIII*), probably Garr. Club • J. C. Horsley, oils, Broadwood & Sons • A. Le Moine, lithograph, Paris, France • Marlow, oils, Chappell & Co.

**Cramer, John Antony** (1793–1848), dean of Carlisle and historian, was born at Mittoden, Switzerland, the son of John Antony Cramer and his wife, Henrietta Courtet. He was a king's scholar at Westminster School from 1807 until 1811, when he was elected to a studentship at Christ Church, Oxford. One of the most distinguished undergraduates of his day and a pupil of Charles Lloyd, he repeated the feat of Robert Peel, later his patron, by gaining first-class honours in the university examinations for classics and mathematics. He graduated BA in 1814 and MA in 1817 before being ordained. He was tutor and rhetoric reader at Christ Church until 1824, when he vacated his studentship following his marriage in 1823 to Henrietta Ashton. In 1822 the dean and chapter of Christ Church presented him to the perpetual curacy of Binsey, Oxfordshire.

Cramer remained in Oxford with his family, taking private pupils, and was briefly (1823–5) vice-principal of St Alban Hall. He gained a reputation as an ancient historian, collaborating with his cousin Henry Lewis Wickham in publishing *A Dissertation of the Passage of Hannibal over the Alps* (1820; 2nd edn, 1828). On his own account he produced for the Clarendon Press a series of geographical and historical descriptions of Italy (1826), Greece (1828), and Asia Minor (1832) in classical antiquity. These were compilations from ancient writers, supplemented by the work of later travellers and German scholars. Although he was more widely travelled than most Oxford scholars of his time, his works were essentially the fruits of library study, though they suggested 'a new level of seriousness in the study of ancient texts' (Murray, 522–3), an objective which Cramer was also able to further as a university examiner between 1822 and 1824, and again in 1831. The university convocation elected him public orator in 1829, an office which involved delivering addresses on ceremonial occasions, including the installation of the duke of Wellington as chancellor of the university in 1834.

In 1831 Wellington's predecessor, Lord Grenville, appointed Cramer principal of New Inn Hall, Oxford, as part of his policy of reviving the halls under energetic heads. Cramer, who proceeded to the degree of DD on becoming principal, effectively restored the empty hall as a place of undergraduate education, plunging a large amount of his own money into rebuilding the premises. However, the halls were in terminal decline and student numbers remained small. His own scholarly work was directed towards editions of theological works, including a compilation of extracts on the New Testament from the Greek fathers (8 vols., 1838–44), though he also edited a collection of Greek manuscripts from the King's Library at Paris (4 vols., 1839–41). In 1841 he edited for the Camden Society the *Travels of Nicander Nucius of Corcyra in England in the Reign of Henry VIII*.

In August 1842 Cramer was appointed on the recommendation of Peel, who had consulted Archbishop Howley and Dean Gaisford, to the regius professorship of modern history at Oxford, made vacant by the death of Thomas Arnold. Though he was not a candidate for the chair, Cramer fulfilled the desirable criterion of being resident in Oxford. His moderate toryism also recommended him; in opposition to the Tractarians, he had supported the lifting of the university's censure upon the liberal theologian R. D. Hampden. He delivered his inaugural lecture on 2 March 1843. Modern history was still not a degree subject, so his lectures, which he organized as catechetical classes studying a set text in Latin or other foreign language, attracted only eight students on average. He was also interested in the study of modern European languages and in 1845 became one of the first curators of the Taylor Institution. In December 1844, again on Peel's recommendation, Cramer was appointed dean of Carlisle, though he continued to hold his Oxford chair. He died at Scarborough, Yorkshire, on 24 August 1848. His widow, three sons (the second of whom joined the service of the Austrian empire), and a daughter survived him.

M. C. CURTHOYS

**Sources** GM, 2nd ser., 30 (1848), 430 · Foster, *Alum. Oxon.* · *Old Westminsters*, 1.229 · E. G. W. Bill, *University reform in nineteenth-century Oxford: a study of Henry Halford Vaughan, 1811–1885* (1973) · O. Murray, 'The beginnings of Greats, 1800–1872: ancient history', *Hist. U. Oxf.* 6: *19th-cent. Oxf.*, 520–42
**Archives** BL, corresp. with Sir Robert Peel, Add. MSS 40498–40556, *passim*
**Likenesses** W. Brockedon, chalk drawing, 1834, NPG

**Cramer, Wilhelm** (*bap.* 1746, *d.* 1799), violinist, was born at Mannheim and baptized on 2 June 1746, the second son of the Mannheim violinist Jakob Cramer (1705–1770). He was a pupil of Johann Stamitz, Christian Cannabich, and Domenicus Basconi. He joined the Mannheim orchestra in around 1752 and when only seven years old played a concerto at a state concert. He quickly became regarded in Germany as an exceptional violinist, and in his sixteenth year went on a concert tour of the Netherlands, and on his return was appointed a member of the elector's band. He married at Mannheim, but around 1769 obtained leave to travel, the elector palatine allowing him £200 a year during his absence. He travelled through Germany (playing for the duke of Württemberg in Stuttgart), Italy, and France, where he performed at the Concert Spirituel in 1769–70. He retained his connection with Paris as much of his music was published there. On the invitation of Johann Christian Bach he went to London towards the end of 1772. He lived for a time with Bach, first at Queen Street, Golden Square, and then at Newman Street, and Bach is said to have corrected and tinkered with his compositions. An early appearance in London took place at a benefit concert under Bach and Abel (whose concerts he led up to 1781) in Hickford's Rooms on 22 March 1773. His success and the demand for him as a leader and soloist were so great that he overshadowed the previously dominant Felice Giardini and he resolved to settle in London (it is unclear whether he had resigned his post at Mannheim). He was followed in 1774 by his wife and eldest son, the renowned pianist and composer Johann Baptist *Cramer. His second son, the successful violinist Franz *Cramer, followed later. His wife appeared at a concert in 1774 as a singer, pianist, and harpist: Michael Kelly mentioned that she sang in Dublin in his youth and described her as 'a

Wilhelm Cramer (*bap.* 1746, *d.* 1799), by Thomas Hardy, 1794

beautiful woman' and 'a charming singer'. On 7 December 1777 Cramer became a member of the Society of Musicians. Around 1780 he succeeded Hay as leader at the Concert of Ancient Music and from 1785 he was leader at the Professional Concert, which he helped to organize. Other activities included performances at the Musical Fund concerts in 1787, and during the 1780s at the Nobility Concerts at the Anacreontic Society. As chamber musician to the king, he also directed the court concerts at Buckingham House and Windsor, and was leader, until Salomon's arrival, at the Pantheon in 1780–82, the Italian opera at the King's Theatre (most seasons from 1777 to 1796, before Viotti took over), and the Three Choirs festivals to great critical acclaim. He led at the Handel commemoration concerts in Westminster Abbey in 1784, 1787, 1791, and 1792, and at the concerts given in the Sheldonian Theatre on Haydn's visit to Oxford in 1791. Indeed, there is scarcely a musical performance at this time in which he did not appear, including as a soloist at charitable oratorio performances and Lenten series. He was also in demand at private concerts and frequently led at provincial festivals. He was removed from the leadership of the Italian opera in 1796 and replaced by Viotti, and in spite of his brilliant career, his later years were clouded with misfortune to the extent that a 'friendly commission of bankruptcy was obtained' (Bingley, 2.368–9) in order to extricate him from his difficulties. His last public appearance was at the Gloucester festival in 1799. After the death of his first wife Cramer married on 22 November 1780 Mary Madden, of Irish origin, with whom he had four children. The eldest of these, Charles, appeared as a violinist in 1792, when barely eight years old, at a benefit concert of his father's.

He was said to show great promise, but died in December 1799.

Cramer's playing at sight was celebrated, and the English critics, who often shunned virtuosity for its own sake, particularly appreciated the combination of rapid execution and facility with neatness, precision, and tasteful expression in his performance. The accuracy of his playing is reflected in the development of the pre-Tourte, 'Cramer' bow and springing bow stroke with which he is often associated. Until the arrival of Viotti and his new style, Cramer's versatility and accuracy helped him to retain his position as England's foremost violinist. His pupils included Samuel Wesley and Charles Weichsel, although his activities as a teacher were limited. He wrote around eleven violin concertos (no. 5 was published in London in 1783) and produced chamber works for violin and cello. He died in Charles Street, Marylebone, Middlesex, on 5 October 1799 and was buried on 11 October in a vault near the entrance to the old Marylebone burial-ground.　　　　W. B. SQUIRE, *rev.* DAVID J. GOLBY

**Sources** S. McVeigh, *The violinist in London's concert life, 1750–1784: Felice Giardini and his contemporaries* (1989) · J. C. Graue, 'Cramer, Wilhelm', *New Grove* · S. McVeigh, *Concert life in London from Mozart to Haydn* (1993) · W. Bingley, *Musical biography*, 2nd edn, 2 (1834), 368–9 · J. D. Brown, *Biographical dictionary of musicians: with a bibliography of English writings on music* (1886) · M. Kelly, *Reminiscences*, 1 (1826), 9–10 · *IGI*

**Likenesses** T. Hardy, oils, 1794, NPG [*see illus.*] · T. Hardy, stipple, pubd in or before 1794, BM, NPG · T. Bragg, portrait, 1803 (after G. Place), BM · J. Roberts, pencil sketch · J. F. Schröter (after photograph of T. Hardy portrait), Leipzig

**Cramond**. For this title name *see* Richardson, Elizabeth, *suo jure* baroness of Cramond (1576/7–1651).

**Cramp, Concemore Thomas Thwaites** [Charlie] (1876–1933), trade unionist, was born on 19 March 1876 at Staplehurst in Kent, the son of Cedelia Jane Cramp. No father is indicated on the birth certificate. At the age of twelve, after leaving Staplehurst board school, he went to work in the gardens of a local squire and subsequently was employed in London and near Portsmouth. He moved to the West Riding aged twenty and joined the Midland Railway, initially as a platform porter at Shipley and then at Rotherham. Subsequently he transferred to Sheffield and became a passenger guard. While in Sheffield he married, on 28 October 1900, Elizabeth Frances (*b.* 1876/7), daughter of James Baker, a farmer, of Staplehurst, Kent.

Charlie Cramp, as he was always known, joined the Amalgamated Society of Railway Servants (ASRS) at Rotherham, and became active in the 'all-grades campaign' of 1906–7. An interest in socialism was engendered by the writings of Edward Bellamy and by the influence, especially perhaps in Sheffield, of Edward Carpenter. His early attitudes were influenced by the Midland's policies. As with most railway companies, union recognition was opposed on principle. From 1906 the Midland modernized its operating methods and zealously pursued economies. Reforms were imposed through often autocratic local

Concemore Thomas Thwaites Cramp (1876–1933), by unknown photographer

supervisors. Cramp became recognized as an effective advocate of his colleagues' concerns.

Cramp's growing reputation led to his election to the ASRS executive for the three years beginning in 1911. He took a relatively militant position during the events surrounding the August 1911 strike. Under union rules his executive position was for one three-year term, but in 1913 the ASRS became the principal constituent of the National Union of Railwaymen (NUR). Cramp successfully argued that the NUR was a new union, and he could serve a second term. Subsequently, in 1917, he was elected for another three-year stint, this time as NUR president. The union's growth from 267,000 in 1913 to 481,000 in 1919 suggested a need for another full-time official. The general secretaryship, occupied since 1916 by J. H. Thomas, was divided. Thomas retained the political responsibilities and was recognized as the senior official; Cramp was elected as industrial general secretary. In some quarters he had a misleadingly radical reputation. During the 1919 railway strike Sir Maurice Hankey confided in his diary that Thomas's attempts to make a settlement had been thwarted: 'J. H. Thomas tried his utmost to effect a settlement, but since his trip to America he has been losing ground to his deputy Cramp, a sinister looking fellow reported to be a Bolshevist' (S. Roskill, *Hankey: Man of Secrets, Volume 2: 1919–1931*, 1972, 121).

Nothing could have been more inaccurate as a characterization of Cramp's subsequent career. During the 1914–18 war he had condemned unofficial strikes and had attempted to exploit the union's increased strength that had come with state control and rising membership, and was symbolized by company recognition. As a full-time official, he defended his members' war-time and immediate post-war advances in a difficult economic environment. The 1921 Railways Act codified an elaborate system of wage determination that placed a premium on pragmatism and presentation. Cramp proved a consummate advocate of his members' interests and, despite the intensification of road competition, he could claim a significant achievement. There was no reduction in railway workers' base rates until 1928. This record helps to explain Cramp's growing agnosticism about sympathetic strike action. In the 1921 mining crisis and in the 1926 general strike his first concern was to protect the achievements of the NUR. He was very much a member of the Trades Union Congress (TUC) establishment. A strong anti-communist, he insisted that a co-operative commonwealth could not be based on class antagonism.

Cramp's approach fitted well into the Labour Party of the 1920s. He served on the party's national executive from 1919 to 1929, and then swapped with Thomas, moving on to the TUC general council. When Thomas joined the National Government in August 1931 Cramp became head of the union, combining both industrial and political functions. He faced a discouraging prospect. The ending of his long and effective partnership with Thomas was followed rapidly by electoral disaster for the Labour Party; the railway companies demanded further wage cuts. Cramp's time as head of the union was tragically brief. On 13 July 1933 he collapsed while speaking to the NUR executive and died the following day, in a nursing home at 8 Beaumont Street, Marylebone, London. He was buried at Staplehurst parish church, survived by his wife and their daughter.

In many ways the antithesis of J. H. Thomas, Cramp was averse to sloganizing and theatricality. He had an unsentimental appreciation of what was feasible. The negotiating abilities that he had employed as a young guard confronting local officials were employed subsequently to protect railway workers, as road competition and economic depression threatened their familiar world.

DAVID HOWELL

**Sources** *Railway Review* (21 July 1933) · *Kentish Express* (21 July 1933) · P. S. Bagwell, *The railwaymen: the history of the National Union of Railwaymen*, [1] (1963) · D. Howell, *Respectable radicals: studies in the politics of railway trade unionism* (1999) · G. W. Alcock, *Fifty years of railway trade unionism* (1922) · H. A. Clegg, A. Fox, and A. F. Thompson, *A history of British trade unions since 1889*, 2 (1985) · G. A. Phillips, *The general strike: the politics of industrial conflict* (1976) · Labour party conference report, 1925 · b. cert. · m. cert. · d. cert.
**Archives** NA Scot., London and North Eastern railway collection, BR/LNE/8/779.Box18 · PRO, post general strike national negotiations material, Rail 786/6 · U. Warwick Mod. RC, corresp. as president of the ITWF · University of Warwick, National Union of Railwaymen collection, MS 127/NU/MUI/1/26, MS 127/NU/GA/3/98
**Likenesses** photograph, repro. in Bagwell, *The railwaymen* · photograph, People's History Museum, Manchester [see illus.] · photographs, University of Warwick, National Union of Railwaymen collection
**Wealth at death** £1304 17s. 8d.: probate, 11 Sept 1933, *CGPLA Eng. & Wales*

**Cramp, John Mockett** (1796–1881), Baptist minister and educationist, was the son of the Revd Thomas Cramp

(1768/9–1851) and his wife, Rebecca Gouger. He was born on 25 July 1796 at St Peter's, Isle of Thanet, and was educated from 1814 to 1817 at Stepney College, London. On 7 May 1818 he was ordained minister and became pastor of the Dean Street Baptist Chapel, Southwark. He was married first on 25 September 1820 to Maria Agate, who bore one daughter. After Maria's death he married, on 1 February 1826, Anne Burls, who bore eight children. In 1825 Cramp left the pastorate to enter the publishing trade. By 1827 the venture had proved unsuccessful and, on the death of his brother George, he returned to St Peter's to assist in his father's ministry. In 1841 he moved to Hastings to serve the Baptist church there. However, in 1844, at the request of the English Baptist Colonial Missionary Society, he left his church to become the president of the Canada Baptist College in Montreal.

Cramp's years in England included service at all levels of denominational affairs, including a period as president of the Baptist Union (1837–8). From 1825 to 1827 he was assistant editor of the *Baptist Magazine*. He was a founder member of the Society for Promoting General Knowledge (1825), the St Peter's and Broadstairs Christian Instruction Association (1825), and the Colonial Missionary Society (1830). As a political liberal he struggled for religious equality before the law and often wrote for the London *Patriot* on controversial issues such as church rates, tithes, education, and religious liberty.

During Cramp's presidency of the Canada Baptist College in Montreal (1844–9) he edited the *Montreal Register* and, after 1849, he edited the *Colonial Protestant*, the *Journal of Literature and Science*, and *The Pilot*. In 1851, by then a respected educationist and scholar among Canadian Baptists, he became president of the struggling Acadia College in Nova Scotia. Known as the 'second founder' of Acadia, he placed the institution on a solid financial footing and taught classical languages, history, philosophy, theology, logic, political economy, and geology. In 1853 Cramp assumed the newly created position of principal of the theological institute, but later resumed the college's presidency and laboured in that capacity until his retirement in 1869. As one of the most important Baptist authors of the nineteenth century, he brought to his Canadian co-religionists an educated perspective infused with a warm evangelical piety. Though not altogether comfortable with the radical evangelical revivalist spirituality of nineteenth-century Nova Scotia Baptists, Cramp remained sympathetic to his constituency.

During Cramp's tenure at Acadia he published at least twelve tracts and books, primarily in the area of church history. While theological works formed a significant part of his published work, he remains best-known for his *Baptist history: from the foundations of the Christian church to the close of the eighteenth century* (1868), which was still being reprinted in the late twentieth century. He also published in serialized form 'A history of the Baptists of Nova Scotia' in the *Christian Messenger*. Perhaps his most significant unpublished manuscript (preserved at Acadia University) is 'A system of Christian theology', which is a collection of his much revised classroom lecture notes. Cramp died at

Wolfville, Nova Scotia, on 6 December 1881, leaving behind a legacy of administrative prowess, educational expertise, and a considerable number of published works.                    G. A. RAWLYK

**Sources** T. A. Higgins, *Life of J. M. Cramp, D.D., 1796–1881* (1887) · W. M. Patterson, *Baptist successionism: a critical view* (1978) · R. S. Wilson, 'John Mockett Cramp as a church historian', *An abiding conviction: maritime baptists and their world*, ed. R. S. Wilson (1988) · B. M. Moody, 'Cramp, John Mockett', *DCB*, vol. 11 · E. C. Starr, ed., *A Baptist bibliography*, 5 (1957), 150
**Archives** Acadia University, Wolfville, Nova Scotia
**Likenesses** portrait, Acadia University, Wolfville, Nova Scotia

**Crampton, Sir John Fiennes Twisleton**, second baronet (1805–1886), diplomatist, born in Dawson Street, Dublin, on 12 August 1805, was the elder son of Sir Philip *Crampton MD FRS (1777–1858), surgeon-general to the forces. After education at Eton College and Trinity College, Dublin, he entered the diplomatic service as an unpaid attaché at Turin on 7 September 1826, and was transferred to St Petersburg on 30 September 1828. He became a paid attaché at Brussels on 16 November 1834, and at Vienna on 9 May 1839, and was promoted to be secretary of legation at Bern on 13 December 1844. He was then transferred, in the same capacity, on 3 July 1845, to Washington, where his most important diplomatic services were rendered. He served at first under Sir Richard Pakenham, and then under Sir Henry Lytton Bulwer, successive ministers plenipotentiary. He acted as chargé d'affaires from May 1847 to December 1849, and again from August 1850 until January 1852, when Bulwer left America after concluding the Clayton–Bulwer treaty, when he was himself appointed minister-plenipotentiary and envoy-extraordinary to the United States of America.

Crampton soon quarrelled with the Americans. During the Crimean War he actively recruited troops within the territories of the USA. By 1856, Lord Clarendon, the British foreign secretary, had made an apology, the Americans making Crampton's recall, with three British consuls, the price of concord. On 28 May 1856 President Pierce broke off relations with Crampton, who at once returned to Britain. Palmerston reinforced the North American squadron. Some expected war, but Palmerston accepted Crampton's recall. He rewarded him with a knighthood on 20 September 1856. On 2 March 1857 Crampton was appointed minister-plenipotentiary at Hanover, and on 31 March 1858 ambassador at St Petersburg.

On 10 June 1858 Crampton succeeded his father as second baronet and on 31 March 1860 he married Victoire (1837–1871) [*see* Balfe, Victoire], the singer, daughter of Michael *Balfe, the composer. She divorced him on the grounds of impotence in 1863. His last posting was on 11 December 1860, as minister-plenipotentiary and envoy-extraordinary at Madrid. He remained there until 1 July 1869, when he retired on a pension, after more than forty years' diplomatic service. He died, at the age of eighty-one, at his seat, Bushy Park, near Bray, co. Wicklow, on 5 December 1886.

H. M. STEPHENS, *rev.* H. C. G. MATTHEW

**Sources** *FO List* (1870)

**Archives** Bodl. Oxf., corresp. and papers · TCD, family corresp. and papers | BL, corresp. with Sir A. H. Layard · BL, letters to Sir J. G. Le Marchant · Bodl. Oxf., letters to fourth earl of Clarendon · Hants. RO, corresp. with Lord Malmesbury · Herts. ALS, letters to Lord Lytton · Notts. Arch., letters to John Savile · PRO, corresp. with Lord John Russell, PRO 30/22
**Wealth at death** £75,302 11s. 4d. in England: probate, 8 Jan 1887, CGPLA Ire.

**Crampton, Sir Philip**, first baronet (1777–1858), surgeon, was descended from a Nottinghamshire family that had settled in Ireland in the reign of Charles II, and was born in 16 William Street, Dublin, on 7 June 1777, the youngest of the three sons (there were also three daughters) of John Crampton (1732–1792), surgeon, and his wife, Anne Verner. Indentured to Solomon Richards in 1792 he studied at the Schools of Surgery. Passing for surgeon's mate early in 1798, he was briefly attached to the army of Sir John Moore. He took the LRCSI on 25 September 1798 and three days later was appointed surgeon to the Meath Hospital. He then studied in London, Edinburgh, and Glasgow, becoming MD at Glasgow in 1800 and MRCSI (equivalent to the later FRCSI) in 1801. Crampton married Selina Hamilton Cannon, third daughter of Patrick Hamilton Cannon, of Littleton, co. Westmeath, in 1802; they had two sons and four daughters. The elder son, John Fiennes Twisleton *Crampton, second baronet, husband of the singer Victoire Balfe, was named to commemorate the union of the Revd John Crampton (b. 1686), archdeacon of Tuam, and the Hon. Fiennes Twistleton, daughter of Lord Saye and Sele.

'Erinensis', *The Lancet*'s satirical Dublin correspondent, credited Crampton with 'much elegant mannerism combined with … much self-possession', but said he preferred 'the hunter's horn to the trump of fame … the saddle to the professor's chair' (Fallon, 157). Crampton nevertheless gave surgical lectures at the Meath and was one of the galaxy of stars that made the hospital a famous teaching centre. He was an excellent operator and his communications to the *Dublin Journal of Medical Science* included articles on head injuries, cleft palate, and dislocations. In Thomas Thomson's *Annals of Philosophy* (1813) he published a 'Description of an organ by which the eyes of birds are accommodated to different distances'. Crampton wrote no books, but under the pseudonym 'Physician' issued a pamphlet: *An attempt to explain on natural principles the cures, alleged to be miraculous, of Miss Lalor and Mrs Stuart* (1823). He also published *A Lecture Introductory to a Course of Clinical Instruction* (1835). He was a founder of the Royal Zoological Society of Ireland.

Crampton was elected FRS in 1812. In 1813 he was appointed surgeon-general to the forces in Ireland, and he was surgeon to the queen in Ireland, a member of the senate of the Queen's University of Ireland, and four times president of the Royal College of Surgeons in Ireland (in 1811, 1820, 1844, and 1855). In 1839 he was created baronet.

The Cramptons lived in Dublin at 14 Merrion Square, where a pear tree grew in the basement, a detail used by James Joyce in *Finnegans Wake*: 'so inseuladed as Crampton's peartree' (Joyce, 291). Crampton enjoyed, too, the amenities of his holiday home at St Valerie's, near Bray, co. Wicklow. When advanced in years, but physically vigorous, he boasted he could swim Lough Bray, ride into Dublin, and amputate a limb before breakfast. He died at his Dublin home on 10 June 1858, leaving instructions that his remains were to be encased in Roman cement before interment in Mount Jerome cemetery.                    J. B. LYONS

**Sources** C. A. Cameron, *History of the Royal College of Surgeons in Ireland*, 2nd edn (1916) · M. Fallon, ed., *The sketches of Erinensis: selections of Irish medical satire, 1824–1836* (1979) · J. Joyce, *Finnegans wake* (1939) · *Freeman's Journal* [Dublin] (11 June 1858) · *The Lancet* (19 June 1858), 618 · *BMJ* (26 June 1858) · Burke, *Peerage*
**Archives** BL, corresp. · TCD, corresp., papers, and wife's diaries | TCD, letters from Thomas More
**Likenesses** Count D'Orsay, lithograph, pubd 1841? (after his drawing, 1841), BM, NG Ire. · D. Lucas, mezzotint, pubd 1842 (after W. Stevenson), NG Ire., Wellcome L. · G. Sanders, mezzotint, pubd 1857 (after oil painting by S. C. Smith, 1850), NG Ire. · J. R. Kirk, marble bust, c.1859, Royal College of Surgeons of Ireland · J. R. Kirk, bust on monument, 1862, Dublin · C. Grey, pen drawing, NG Ire.; repro. in *Dublin University Magazine*, 15 (1840) · C. Robertson, miniature, NG Ire. · S. C. Smith, oils, NG Ire. · engraving, Royal College of Physicians of Ireland
**Wealth at death** under £7000: probate, 16 July 1858, CGPLA Eng. & Wales

**Crampton, Thomas Russell** (1816–1888), railway and civil engineer, was born on 6 August 1816, at Broadstairs, Kent, the son of John Crampton and his wife, Mary. He received his education at a private school. In 1831 he was articled to John Hague, engineer, of Cable Street, London. After serving his time, he acted, from 1839 to 1844, as assistant to Marc Brunel and subsequently to Daniel Gooch, under whose directions he prepared the drawings for the first locomotive for the Great Western Railway (GWR). Crampton then spent four years with John Rennie (1794–1874) and his brother, George Rennie, until in 1848 he commenced business on his own account.

In the meantime, George Stephenson and others had developed the steam locomotive into its characteristic form. Some engineers, however, were concerned that this placed limits on the diameter of the driving wheels, unless the centre of gravity was to be excessively high, so leading to instability. Following an idea originated by Baldwin, in the United States, Crampton sought to improve on Stephenson's basic arrangement by placing the driving axle behind the firebox, so enabling large-diameter driving wheels to be provided, but with the drawback of a low factor of adhesion. He took out a patent in 1843, and on 24 April 1849 expounded his ideas in a paper read before the Institution of Civil Engineers (*Proceedings*, 8, 1849, 233–61), which, however, drew considerable opposition from members.

In 1846 two locomotives to Crampton's designs were constructed for the Namur–Liège railway in Belgium. These were followed by others, notably, in 1848, one named *Liverpool*, for the London and North Western Railway (LNWR). Possessing 8 ft driving wheels, and weighing 35 tons, it was reputed to have been the most powerful locomotive of its day, achieving a speed of 62 m.p.h. while hauling a load of 180 tons. It gained a gold medal at the Great Exhibition of 1851, but its weight was too great for

**Thomas Russell Crampton** (1816–1888), by unknown engraver, 1860s

the permanent way of the period, and it was withdrawn in 1852.

Apart from *Liverpool*, and a small number of other isolated examples, Crampton's style of locomotive design did not receive recognition in Britain, but his ideas were taken up in France. During the latter part of the nineteenth century, many of the lighter express trains on the northern and eastern railways of France were hauled by 'la machine Crampton'. Altogether, some 320 locomotives of his design were said to have been built, including a number in Belgium and Germany.

Crampton, however, was much more than a locomotive engineer. In 1851 he played a leading part in laying the first successful submarine telegraph cable between Dover and Calais. Other important works with which he was associated were railway lines in Kent and Turkey, and, with Sir Charles Fox, the Berlin waterworks. He invented a rotary powdered-fuel furnace, brick-making machinery, and, with a channel tunnel in mind, a hydraulic tunnel-boring machine, which was described in a lecture given to the Institution of Mechanical Engineers in Leeds in 1882. He lived for many years in his native Broadstairs, where he was involved in the construction of the gasworks and waterworks, also presenting the parish church with its clock.

In 1862 Crampton had the misfortune to become involved with the controversial and insecure London, Chatham, and Dover Railway. He was one of the partners, along with the great public works contractors, Sir Samuel Morton *Peto and Edward Ladd *Betts, in a lump-sum contract (tendered at £5,979,000) to build the railway's metropolitan extension. As a result of Peto's ill-advised share dealings, the partners were declared bankrupt on 3 July 1867, owing over £1 million to secured and unsecured creditors. These liabilities were eventually discharged on 10 July 1868.

Crampton joined the Institution of Civil Engineers in 1846 as an associate, and became a member in 1854. He joined the Institution of Mechanical Engineers in 1847, the year of its formation, becoming a member of council in 1879 and a vice-president in 1883. He was also on the council of the Society of Telegraph Engineers. Napoleon III appointed him an officer of the Légion d'honneur, and he was also made an officer of the Prussian order of the Red Eagle.

Of a frank and genial manner, Crampton was twice married, and his second wife (who survived him) was listed on his death certificate as B. V. G. Crampton. There were six sons and a daughter. He died at his home, 19 Ashley Place, Victoria Street, Westminster, on 19 April 1888, and was buried in Kensal Green cemetery.

GEOFFREY HUGHES

**Sources** PICE, 94 (1887–8), 295–8 · *Institution of Mechanical Engineers: Proceedings* (1888), 437–9 · *The Times* (25 April 1888) · G. Glover, *British locomotive design, 1825–1960* (1967), 17 · G. F. Westcott, *The British railway locomotive, 1803–1853* (1958) · *The Locomotive* (March 1970), 67–70 · *Institution of Mechanical Engineers: Proceedings* (1876), 244–98 · *Institution of Mechanical Engineers: Proceedings* (1882), 440–50 · M. Sharman, *The Crampton locomotive* (1983) · d. cert. · *CGPLA Eng. & Wales* (1888) · Boase, *Mod. Eng. biog.* · H. Peto, *Sir Morton Peto: a memorial sketch* (1893) · J. L. Chown, *Sir Samuel Morton Peto: the man who built the houses of parliament* [1943]

**Likenesses** engraving, 1860–69, Sci. Mus. [*see illus.*]

**Wealth at death** £9449 14s. 5d.: probate, 6 June 1888, *CGPLA Eng. & Wales*

**Crampton, Victoire.** *See* Balfe, Victoire (1837–1871).

**Cranat ingen Buicín** (*fl.* 6th cent.). *See under* Munster, saints of (*act. c.*450–*c.*700).

**Cranbrook.** For this title name *see* Hardy, Gathorne Gathorne-, first earl of Cranbrook (1814–1906).

**Cranch, John** (1751–1821), genre painter, was born at Kingsbridge, Devon, on 12 October 1751. Little is known of his life prior to the exhibition of his first painting at the Society of Artists in 1791, *Burning of the Albion Mill*, when his address was given as 1 Old Broad Street, London. It seems that Cranch was largely self-taught, although he may have received some instruction from a Catholic priest while a clerk at Axminster. Cranch preferred rural genre themes, exemplified by *Monks with a Lantern in a Moonlit Landscape* (*c.*1795; Louvre, Paris), which combine the lighting effects of Joseph Wright of Derby with the sentimental rustic figures of George Morland. Cranch was a friend of J. T. 'Antiquary' Smith, and the two men played an influential role in the development of the young John Constable. In 1796 Cranch made a list of twelve books for Constable to read, and advised him to be wary of Sir Joshua Reynolds's *Discourses* in order that they not 'bias you against Familiar nature, life and manners which constitute as proper and as genuine a department of imitative art as *The Sublime* or *The Beautiful*' (Cormack, 43). Cranch exhibited only nine paintings during his lifetime, seven of which were shown at the 1808 British Institution exhibition; he was best-known for *Death of Chatterton*. Cranch also published two treatises: *On the Economy of Testaments* in 1794, and *Inducements to promote the fine arts of Great Britain by exciting native genius to independent effort and original design* in 1811. Cranch spent the final years of his life working in Bath, where he died in February 1821.

L. H. CUST, rev. DOUGLAS FORDHAM

**Sources** M. Cormack, *Constable* (1986) · Waterhouse, *18c painters* · Graves, *Soc. Artists* · Graves, *Brit. Inst.* · *GM*, 1st ser., 91/1 (1821)
**Archives** Boston PL, corresp. and papers · Museum National d'Histoire Naturelle, Paris, 'Remarks of animals, observed during a voyage of discovery' [photocopy, NHM]
**Likenesses** J. T. Smith, line and stipple engraving, pubd 1795, NPG

**Crandon, John** (*d.* 1654), religious controversialist, is an obscure figure. Little is known of his life, and what there is is compressed into his last year of life. Although he seems to have had a classical education, there is no record of his having attended either Oxford or Cambridge. In 1653, when he was rector of Fawley, he wrote his one book: *Mr Baxters Aphorismes Exorcised*. This assault on Richard Baxter's first published work thrust him into national prominence, and marks the beginning of a major doctrinal split within English protestantism. He was one of a pack of writers who claimed that Baxter was reneging on his Calvinist faith; what marked Crandon out from the others was not so much the content as the tone of his reply. Many of Baxter's correspondents pick up that point: 'ugly spirit' (Giles Firmin); 'rayling, scurrilous, bitter and ungrounded language' (William Duncombe); 'grosse slanders' (Peter Ince); 'Billingsgate language' (Henry Bartlett). As early as 21 June 1653 Bartlett had got wind of Crandon's manuscript in which Baxter was to be lampooned as a 'Papist Jesuit'. A few months later Bartlett wrote to Baxter to say that his efforts to dissuade Crandon from publication by a private conference with him had proved fruitless. Worse news was that Crandon was carrying opposition to the point of contacting eminent ministers in several counties to publicize his work (Keeble and Nuttall, 1.149, 155, 128, 111, 100). Thus, when the work was published, Baxter was well prepared. Even so, Baxter seemed winded by the savagery of the attack. Crandon accused him of wearing a presbyterian 'mask' to conceal his popery: what was to be a favourite taunt of Baxter against opponents later on would thus be first used against him. Moreover Crandon was the first to coin the phrase 'Baxterian Faith', which rapidly came into circulation to depict Baxter's efforts to dilute Calvinist doctrine. He noted a personality cult developing around Baxter: pilgrimages to Kidderminster to bless and be blessed by him as a 'matchlesse and supereminent Saint'; the popish scholasticism of his writings. He conjured up a network of Baxter's 'Circumsoraneous Legates' in the future linking up all over the county to propagate his false doctrine: all this well before Baxter's

ministerial associations had developed their own momentum (Crandon, dedicatory epistle).

Behind Crandon's abuse lay a profound theological difference. A metaphor summed it up. In his *Aphorismes* Baxter had a striking comparison to offer of the relation between Christ's universal righteousness and man's particular righteousness. A tenant, evicted for arrears in rent and consigned to prison, is redeemed by 'his Landlords son'. He acquires a new lease. All that he has to do in return is to pay 'but a pepper corn yearly to him' (Baxter, *Aphorismes*, 83–4). The point of the payment is the nugatory requirement. Baxter goes to great lengths to emphasize the subordinate character of the condition. But, subordinate or not, it is still a condition and, as such, it is unacceptable to a high Calvinist like Crandon: 'His one grain will sink us down to hell, so hot a poyson is Mr. Baxters pepper-corn' (Crandon, 1.xvi, 173–4). Baxter and Crandon were replaying an earlier debate between John Preston and John Saltmarsh on the same issue. Preston, like Baxter, emphasized 'so small a condition' but Saltmarsh argued back, like Crandon, that to attribute to man 'some small part in his salvation is really to put salvation in his power entirely' (Baxter, *Aphorismes*, 276). Crandon had to pay, in material terms, for his spiritual challenge. Henry Bartlett reported on 21 October 1653 that Crandon owed his printer £100 'and writes that he shall not be able to carry it through. But I find a generall disgust at such a mendicant way'. In March 1654 Peter Ince reports that Crandon's 'wife and children are impoverished by his printinge of the bookes and are now sending to friends to help them away with them wherein they will find somewhat to doe' (Keeble and Nuttall, 1.111, 128). By March 1654 Crandon had died, probably at Fawley, Hampshire. In his preface of 31 March, Baxter felt obliged to explain why he was publishing his reply even though Crandon had died since its composition. A month later letters of administration show that to his widow, Mary, has been consigned the task of discharging his debts.

In 1699 Samuel Young, whether or not in conscious homage to Crandon, named John Howe and William Bates as divines, 'who (if not *Baxterians*, are *Baxterianish*)'. His pamphlet was a tribute to 'the Sober, Pious Antinomians who disown the more Gross, and Damnable Doctrines before censur'd' and he there drew a distinction between Crandon and Tobias Crisp (a distinction not recognized by Baxter). He wanted proof of Crandon's claims of a Baxter spy network but concluded with this tribute to him: 'I think Mr. Crandon was a great Man, except in his own Eyes; as some Men never had so much Learning as they thought, said and printed, so he had not half so little as he thought' (Young, 7, 35, 38, 39). WILLIAM LAMONT

**Sources** *Calendar of the correspondence of Richard Baxter*, ed. N. H. Keeble and G. F. Nuttall, 2 vols. (1991) · Greaves & Zaller, *BDBR* · H. Boersma, *A hot pepper corn* (1993) · W. M. Lamont, *Richard Baxter and the millennium: protestant imperialism and the English revolution* (1979) · R. Baxter, *Aphorismes of justification* (1649) · J. Crandon, *Mr Baxters aphorismes exorcised* (1653) · *Richard Baxters apology* (1654) · [S. Young], *A new-years gift for the antinomians* (1699) · PROB 6/29, fol. 327

**Wealth at death** widow left to discharge debts: PRO, PROB 6/29, fol. 327; *Calendar*, ed., Keeble and Nuttall, 1.111, 128

**Crane, Sir Edmund Frank** (1886–1957), cycle manufacturer, was born on 21 November 1886 at 55 Cape Hill, Smethwick, Birmingham, the eldest of two sons in a family of six children of Edward John Crane, then a clerk, and his wife, Edith Maude Willmott. He was educated at Handsworth grammar school and soon after leaving became involved in the family's cycle business. The Petros Motor and Cycle Company Ltd, registered in his mother's name owing to his father's earlier bankruptcy, came to prominence in the early years of the century producing bicycles at prices well below those of the established manufacturers. This enterprise foundered in the face of hostility in the trade and went into liquidation in 1910. Crane, along with his father and brother Harry, only narrowly escaped imprisonment for alleged attempts to defraud the creditors of the business the following year, but their sentences were dismissed on their appeal.

In 1910 Crane and Harry went into partnership and founded the Hercules Cycle and Motor Company Ltd with £25 capital. Beginning with an output of twenty-five machines a week, assembled from bought-in components and targeted for sale in the Birmingham area, the company grew at a rapid rate. By 1922 output of cycles had reached 700 machines a week, and by 1928, 300,000 machines a year, of which over a third were exported. By 1933 the company had reached a total output of three million cycles, which it doubled by 1939, making it the largest cycle manufacturer in the world.

Crane's success lay in his commitment to produce a reliable and affordable bicycle, initially for lower-middle-class urban dwellers, and then for members of the working classes also. He placed great emphasis on the use of the bicycle for travelling to work rather than for weekend leisure usage, and the new inter-war housing estates, often ill served by public transport, provided a ready market. By a policy of scrupulously using the cheapest suppliers, and buying in bulk, the company drove down costs and where it was advantageous manufactured parts itself. Despite its name, the company remained highly specialized, did not enter the manufacture of motor vehicles, and did not contribute to innovations in bicycle design. In order to boost sales Crane spent considerable sums of money on advertising, particularly in newspapers, promoting cycling as a sport and in general, as well as making Hercules a household name. Crane married twice. His first marriage was on 22 May 1911 to a singer, Naomi, daughter of Samuel Tamkin, an artist from Edinburgh, with whom he had a daughter. The marriage was dissolved in 1938. His second marriage was on 10 August 1938 to Kathleen Margaret, daughter of Cecil Murray Wright, a soldier.

As a businessman Crane was single-minded and autocratic. This brought him into conflicts within the industry, where he was regarded as ruthless and unsympathetic to the trade's overall interest. Disagreements with the industry's trade association, the British Cycle and Motor Cycle Manufacturers' Trades Union Ltd, ultimately led to Crane withdrawing his company from it in 1933. In later years Crane delegated management of the works to trusted subordinates, while devoting more effort to strategic issues. He assumed complete financial control when he bought his brother Harry's share of the business following disagreements over the scale of the company's advertising. Although an attempt was made by Raleigh Cycle Holdings Ltd to effect a merger in 1935, with a highly advantageous offer alleged to have been £2.5 million along with a place on the board of the proposed new company, Crane declined it, probably because he would have found loss of overall control unpalatable. In 1946 he nevertheless sold his business for £3.25 million to Tube Investments. After only a few months on the board of that company Crane retired, initially to South Africa and later to Jersey, where he lived at Villa Millbrook, St Lawrence.

Crane's interests were golf and shooting and he was at one time a referee in amateur association football. His contributions to charitable works included donations towards the treatment of sufferers from tuberculosis. Although he did not enter political life at either local or national level, he made donations to the Conservative Party; for these public and political services, as well as for his company's export success, he received a knighthood in 1935. Crane died of heart failure on 18 September 1957 at Le Méridien, avenue Docteur Raymond Picaud, La Bocca, Cannes, in the south of France.

ANDREW MILLWARD

**Sources** WWW · *Future: the Magazine of Industry*, 5 (1947), 39–46 · *The Times* (19 Sept 1957) · *The Times* (4 Oct 1957) · *The Times* (7 Oct 1957) · *Birmingham Post* (3 Feb 1939) · *Motorcycle and Cycle Trader* (25 Jan 1929), 68 · *Hercules Cycle Magazine*, 1 (1934) · b. cert. · m. cert. · d. cert.
**Archives** Notts. Arch., Raleigh archives · U. Warwick Mod. RC, records of Bicycle Association, MSS 204
**Likenesses** photographs, 1928–46

**Crane, Edward** (1721–1749), Presbyterian minister, was born in Preston, the first or second son of Roger Crane (*d.* 1760), an ironmonger. He came from an old Lancashire family, attached to the parliamentary party and Presbyterian interest. From 1738 he studied for the nonconformist ministry at Caleb Rotheram's dissenting academy at Kendal with a grant from the Presbyterian Fund. He was minister at Ormskirk briefly between 1743 and 1744, then at Norwich from 1744. The Norwich Presbyterian congregation invited him to join the Hebraist John Taylor in assisting its aged minister, Peter Finch. In spring 1745, after discussing remuneration, he accepted. He found congenial lodgings with Thomas Mottram near the Presbyterian chapel (on the site of the Octagon Chapel, begun in 1754), but later moved out of the city with him. In 1747 the congregation desired Crane to settle in Norwich. This, he remarked, 'they thought could not be done any way so effectually and desirably as by matrimony' (Abram, 13). Once assured of an annual income of £80 he did as asked, on 4 August 1747 marrying Mary (Polly) Park of Ormskirk, who had long commanded his affections. Their daughter, Mary, was born in May 1748.

Crane was invited also to minister to the Dutch congregation in Norwich, which worshipped in the church now called Blackfriars Hall. He started learning Dutch, making progress despite eye strain. He was welcomed when visiting the Netherlands in 1748–9 to seek approbation from the church authorities, and was admitted as a theology student at Leiden in September 1748. On his return to Norwich he embarked on his new duties, preaching in Dutch as occasion required. While in Amsterdam conscientious scruples had, however, forbidden him to subscribe to the Heidelberg Confession. Consequently, when he suddenly died of a fever at the age of twenty-eight on 18 August 1749, his wife was not eligible for an annuity from a ministerial fund, even though a son, Edward, was born posthumously in 1749. Crane was commemorated in an elegy and an epitaph in the Dutch church in Norwich where he was buried; the anonymous verses lack the interest of his frank letters to relations that are published in *Memorials of an Old Preston Family* (1877). CHRISTOPHER SMITH

**Sources** W. A. Abram, ed., *Memorials of an old Preston family* (privately printed, Preston, 1877) · J. Browne, *A history of Congregationalism and memorials of the churches in Norfolk and Suffolk* (1877) · *DNB* · G. E. Evans, *Record of the provincial assembly of Lancashire and Cheshire* (1896), 146 · F. Nicholson and E. Axon, *The older nonconformity in Kendal* (1915), 617–18

**Crane, Elizabeth** (*d.* in or before **1606**), religious activist, was the eldest daughter of Sir Robert Hussey of Linwood, in Lincolnshire, who died in 1546, and his second wife, Dame Jane. Born towards the end of the reign of Henry VIII, she seems to have married Anthony Crane, a clerk controller in the royal household and resident of the parish of St Mary Aldermanbury, London, soon after Elizabeth's accession. On 8 April 1560 Anthony and Elizabeth Crane received a grant of the manor of Ockham, in Surrey, which Anthony gained permission to alienate six years later, before in 1571 obtaining a reversionary lease of the manor of East Molesey, also in Surrey, where since 1564 he had been a justice of the peace and member of the quorum. Anthony Crane was buried in the parish of St Martin-in-the-Fields on 18 August 1583, in his nuncupative will leaving all his goods to his wife and their daughter, Mary. About 1588 Mary Crane married an Aldermanbury merchant, Gerard Gore.

As early as 1572 Anthony Crane appears to have been associating with those forward protestants who, according to the hostile testimony of Richard Bancroft, erected a presbytery at Wandsworth, and his widow continued her connection with the reformers after her husband's death. On the destruction of his press in May 1588 for having printed Udall's treatise *The State of the Church of England Laid Open in a Conference*, usually known as *Diotrephes*, Robert Waldegrave and his wife brought the salvaged type to Elizabeth Crane's house in Aldermanbury. Robert Penry then procured a new press, and with her permission transferred the type to her country house at East Molesey. There that autumn Waldegrave printed John Udall's *Demonstration of Discipline*, together with *The Epistle to the Terrible Priests*, the first of the Martin Marprelate tracts, but his protector, who feared retaliation, dared not house the press any longer, and Penry had removed it to Northamptonshire by the end of October.

Late in 1588 or early in 1589 Elizabeth Crane married George *Carleton (1529–1590), the stepfather of Anthony Cope and friend of Sir Richard Knightley, to whose house at Fawsley Penry had taken the press. Suspected of complicity in the Marprelate tracts, in April 1589 Carleton was required to attend daily upon the privy council, while the following October his wife was imprisoned in the Fleet with the other harbourers of the press, Sir Richard Knightley, John Hales, and Roger Wigston and his wife. George Carleton died in January 1590, some months before his widow appeared in the Star Chamber on 17 May, when, having affirmed her loyalty to the queen and denied being a papist, Anabaptist, Brownist, or member of the Family of Love, she prayed 'that she mighte not be forced to be her owne Accuser, or els that shee mighte have her Articles and tyme for Counsell wherby shee mighte not hurte herself or Gode's people' (McCorkle, 279). She was fined 1000 marks for refusing the *ex officio* oath and a further £500 for sheltering the press, and was confined during the queen's pleasure, though the records do not reveal how long she remained in prison. She seems to have died before her daughter, who was buried in the parish of St Mary Aldermanbury on 1 March 1606. CLAIRE CROSS

**Sources** *CPR*, 1558–60, 456; 1563–6, nos. 137, 2457; 1569–72, no. 1349 · E. Arber, ed., *An introductory sketch to the Martin Marprelate controversy, 1588–1590* (1879) · J. N. McCorkle, 'A note concerning "Mistress Crane" and the Martin Marprelate controversy', *The Library*, 4th ser., 12 (1931–2), 276–83 · A. R. Maddison, ed., *Lincolnshire pedigrees*, 2, Harleian Society, 51 (1903), 528–9 · W. Pierce, *An historical introduction to the Marprelate tracts* (1908) · W. Pierce, *John Penry: his life, times and writings* (1923) · L. H. Carlson, *Martin Marprelate, gentleman: Master Job Throkmorton laid open in his colors* (1981) · P. Collinson, *The Elizabethan puritan movement* (1967) · P. Collinson, 'Carleton, George', *HoP, Commons, 1558–1603*

**Crane, Sir Francis** (*c.*1579–1636), courtier and tapestry manufacturer, is first recorded in 1606. His name does not appear in registers of admissions to Oxford, Cambridge, or the inns of court until 1619, when he was admitted to Gray's Inn. A memorial tablet in the church at Woodrising, Norfolk, provides an approximate date of birth, giving his age as 'about 57 years' in June 1636. Crane's parentage is unrecorded. His sisters, Joan and Edith, married into Cornish families, Bond and Arundell; but the *Visitation of Cornwall* mentions their brothers, not their father, making it unlikely that Francis was fifth in descent from the Cranes of Camborne, as stated by C. S. Gilbert (*An Historical Survey of the County of Cornwall*, 1817–20, vol 2., 88). British Library Harleian MS 1105, folios 7 and 11 shows the arms of Sir Francis and his brother Richard (with the additional canton of a baronet, 1643) to differ from those of the Cranes of Cornwall, of Chilton, Suffolk (wrongly ascribed to Sir Richard in Burke's *Extinct … Baronetcies* of 1866), and also from those of the Cranes of Loughton, Buckinghamshire, with whom their sisters' children intermarried. Estates left by the brothers were purchased, providing no evidence of family origins.

In April 1606 Francis Crane was granted reversion of the office of clerk of the parliament. He surrendered this in May 1613, becoming member of parliament for Penryn, 1614 and 1621, and for Launceston, 1624, with Prince

Charles's recommendation as duke of Cornwall. Crane served both Prince Henry and Charles, prince of Wales (whose secretaries were Adam Newton, Thomas Murray, and Francis Cottington, not Crane as previously stated in the *Dictionary of National Biography* and elsewhere). According to Crane's testimony, in 1611 he was in the service of the princes' kinsman Ludovick Stuart, duke of Lennox, who may have helped Crane to obtain the post of clerk of Prince Henry's council in July of that year. In May 1617 Crane was appointed auditor-general to Prince Charles, becoming a member of his council in 1623. On Charles's accession, Crane was among twenty commissioners chosen to manage duchy of Cornwall revenues to pay the king's debts. Described as 'gentleman' in 1611, 'esquire' in 1613, knighted on 4 September 1617, and granted arms in 1625, Crane was considered of sufficient social standing to become lay chancellor of the Order of the Garter in July 1626. He was proud of the honour, and had three portraits made wearing his badge of office. One portrait was reproduced in Mortlake tapestry.

Sir Francis Crane's fame rests on his establishment of the manufactory at Mortlake. Bearing his initials, the finest tapestries ever made in England are his lasting memorial. In 1618 James I's 'princely cogitation' led his privy council to enquire into certain possibilities of tapestry manufacture. Crane's proposals were accepted and, in August 1619, having been granted fees for the making of three baronets to offset initial costs, he acquired property at Mortlake for erecting workshops. These could accommodate eighteen looms, and by 1637 140 persons were dependent on the manufactory. During his lifetime, Crane's Flemish weavers, besides copying individual paintings, produced sets from seven major tapestry series. The earliest were based on sixteenth-century Brussels tapestries, *Vulcan and Venus*, *Solomon and Sheba*, and *The Months*; with new designs, *Hero and Leander*, *The Senses*, *The Horses*, following Francis Clein's installation as resident artist. Seven of Raphael's famous cartoons of *The Acts of the Apostles*, purchased in 1623 by Prince Charles, inspired Mortlake's greatest achievements. Recently discovered documents show Crane's efforts to secure two more cartoons from the original ten. His continuing involvement in the business lay in seeking 'patterns' for the weavers, obtaining customers—he even tried to find markets in Persia and India—and chasing bad debts. Drue Burton in 1630 accused Crane of overcharging, at £2000, for the first set of nine *Vulcan and Venus* tapestries, woven between September 1620 and June 1622; but Crane's appeal to James I in 1623, 'I am out already above 16000 l. in this busynes, and never made returne of more than 2500 l.' (*European Magazine*, Oct 1786, 285, *inter alia*), was probably true, given that Prince Charles owed him for three sets of gold tapestry in 1625, and Buckingham when assassinated still owed for two sets delivered in 1623. To settle his debts and encourage the manufactory, Charles I granted Crane in 1625 a ten-year annuity of £2000, half to terminate if debt and interest were paid.

His fortunes having revived, by 1629 Crane was contracting to lend the king £7500 (with another £5000 later) on the security of ten Northamptonshire manors, including Stoke Bruern and Grafton, where a second, abortive, tapestry manufactory was proposed. Crane was also granted the offices of master of game and high steward of the honour of Grafton; and, in 1633, park-keeper of Grafton and Pury. At Stoke Park, Crane built a new house, with decorations by Clein, and intended furnishing it with Mortlake tapestries which, the house being unfinished, were still not installed when he made his will in August 1635. Crane purchased more land in Northamptonshire, Ruthin in Denbighshire, and, aided by Henry Howard, Lord Maltravers, extensive estates of Sir Thomas Southwell in Norfolk. Sir Francis joined his patrons, the intermarried Stuarts and Howards, in monopolies for making farthing tokens granted to Crane together with Frances, duchess of Lennox and Richmond, in 1625, and with Lord Maltravers in 1636. Further business ventures included speculation in reclaiming East Anglian fens.

Income from offices, land, and enterprises was augmented by matrimony. Crane may have contracted to marry Sir Thomas Smith's widow, daughter of Lord Chandos, who was later accused by Lady Lake of paying Crane £4000 to release her to marry the earl of Exeter. In 1618 Sir Francis married Marie, *née* Le Maire (*d. c.*1642), 'the yong widow Swinnarton by whom he hath 400 li per annum … and 2000 li' (Brett to Trumbull, 1618, Downshire MSS Trumbull papers, 6.530). The bride came from two wealthy immigrant merchant families. Her mother was sister to Sir Samuel Tryon, for whom Crane obtained a baronetcy in 1620 in exchange for £2100 promised as his wife's portion. Her brother, Sir Peter Le Maire, dying in 1632, left his sister property. To Sir Francis, his executor, besides the residue of his estate, he left money to be used in charitable purposes. Crane in his will proposed founding 'dwellings of fyve poore knights' at Windsor, two from his brother-in-law, three at his own cost, and to provide £40 per annum for each knight's maintenance. He also left £500 towards repairing St Paul's Cathedral. Being childless, he divided his property between his wife and his brother Richard. Dame Marie received £800 per annum, plate, and household goods at Grafton, Mortlake, and London, and estates for life in Northamptonshire, including Stoke Park. Dying in Paris of gangrene, following an operation for the stone in April 1636, Sir Francis added a codicil asking to be buried at Woodrising, and begging his wife and brother to exchange the lands in Northamptonshire and Norfolk, so that his wife might live where her husband was buried. Crane died on 26 June in Paris, and was buried on 10 July at St Nicholas's Church, Woodrising; but, possibly through problems with the recent complex purchase of the Norfolk estates which led Richard Crane into chancery suits, the exchange did not occur, and Dame Marie remained in Northamptonshire. Richard Crane, inheriting all the buildings and tapestry stock at Mortlake, gave the works and sold the stock to the king in 1637. The manufactory survived the Commonwealth, but never attained the excellence of its early years and was officially closed in 1703.

Sir Francis, at his death, was reported by Lord Scudamore as 'like a stout and humble Christian and member of the Church of England' (Scudamore to Windebank, PRO SP 78/101, fol. 238 *v*). Sir Kenelm Digby described Crane as 'as generous a gentleman … as I have bin acquainted withall' (PRO SP 78/101, fols. 265–266v). Sir Francis himself once wrote: 'I … do holde reputacon to be a better parte of a mans fortune than wealth' (Crane to marquess of Buckingham 1623, BL, Harl. MS 1581, fol. 274).

WENDY HEFFORD

Sources  PRO, state papers, *passim* · PRO, Chancery suits, 'Crane' · PRO, wills, probate 11, 131, 161, 172, 246 · Duchy of Cornwall Office, patents [Prince Henry, Prince Charles] · acts of council, Duchy of Cornwall Office · miscellaneous, Duchy of Cornwall Office · BL, Downshire MSS in Trumbull papers [H.M.C. published to 1619] · L. Martin, 'Sir Francis Crane: director of the Mortlake tapestry factory and chancellor of the order of the Garter', *Apollo*, 113 (1981), 90–96 · W. G. Thomson, *Tapestry weaving in England* (1914) · *European Magazine and London Review*, 10 (1786), 285 · D. Howarth, 'William Trumbull and art collecting in Jacobean England', *British Library Journal*, 20 (1994), 140–62 · G. Baker, *The history and antiquities of the county of Northampton*, 2 vols. (1822–41) · J. Bridges, *The history and antiquities of Northamptonshire*, ed. P. Whalley, 2 vols. (1791) · F. Blomefield and C. Parkin, *An essay towards a topographical history of the county of Norfolk*, [2nd edn], 11 vols. (1805–10) · *CSP col.*, vols. 4, 6, 8 · C. S. Gilbert, *An historical survey of the county of Cornwall*, 2 (1820), 88 · memorial tablet, St Nicholas's Church, Woodrising, Norfolk · J. L. Vivian and H. H. Drake, eds., *The visitation of the county of Cornwall in the year 1620*, Harleian Society, 9 (1874)
Archives  Boughton House, Northamptonshire · Haddon Hall, Derbyshire · Lyme Park, Cheshire · Mobilier National, Paris · Royal Collection, Sweden · St James's Palace, London · St John's College, Oxford · V&A · Easton Neston, Northamptonshire | BL, Harley MS 1581, fols. 66, 118 · BL, Downshire MSS in Trumbull papers · PRO, state papers domestic, vol. ccxiv, no. 32
Likenesses  J. Fittler, engraving, 1820 (after chalk sketch by Vorsterman?), BM · L. Vorsterman, chalk drawing, BM · engraving (after G. Jameson?), BM · tapestry (*The Mortlake tapestry*; after Van Dyck?), priv. coll.
Wealth at death  lands and leases probably over £52,000; owed £2872 by king for tapestry: *CSP dom.*; Chancery dispatches

**Crane, John** (1570/71–1652), apothecary and benefactor, was born in Wisbech, Cambridgeshire. The details of his parents are unknown except that his father was born in Ipswich, Suffolk. The first evidence for him being in Cambridge occurs in 1599, when he was one of six people appointed to survey certain lands belonging to the parish of Great St Mary. There he became an eminent apothecary, and may have practised as a physician. On 30 September 1601 in Great St Mary's Church, Cambridge, he married Elizabeth (*bap.* 1581, *d.* 1661), the daughter of Peter Scarlett, an apothecary in that town. They shared the Scarlett family house in Trinity Street from 1607 to 1619, when they moved to where Senate House now stands, once the home of William *Butler (1535–1618), who had once lived in Crane's house and with whom he appears to have had a long-term sexual relationship. Butler left estate worth about £700 to Crane.

Edward Hyde, afterwards Lord Clarendon, when about twenty years old, was taken ill at Cambridge, and was attended by Crane. In his *Life* he calls him 'an eminent apothecary who had been bred up under Dr Butler, and was in much greater practice than any physician in the

university' (*GM*, 1st ser., 60, 1790, 509–10). Crane used to entertain openly all the Oxford scholars at the commencement, and to relieve privately all distressed royalists during the interregnum. He was lord of the manors of Kingston Wood and Kingston Saint George, Cambridgeshire, and in 1641 he served as high sheriff of that county. Crane died at Cambridge on 26 May 1652, aged eighty-one, and was buried on 1 June in Great St Mary's, in the chancel of which church there is a mural tablet with his arms, since disappeared, and a Latin inscription.

In his will dated 21 June 1651 Crane bequeathed to his widow £1000, the use of the Regent Walk house for life, and another house in Cambridge. He gave instructions that the house in which he lived, after the death of his widow (in 1661), was to be given to the regius professors of physic, to live in or to let. He also gave £100 to the university, 'to be lent gratis to an honest man, the better to enable him to buy good fish and fowl for the university, having observed much sickness occasioned by unwholesome food in that kind' (T. Fuller, *Worthies*, ed. J. Nichols, 1811, 1.166). The four towns of Wisbech, Cambridge, King's Lynn, and Ipswich received benefactions for setting up young men in business; his monetary legacies alone exceeded £6000 and the value of land and houses bequeathed to relatives was very great. He left legacies of £100 each and a ring of £5 value to Dr Wren, bishop of Ely, and Dr Brownrigg, bishop of Exeter, and he gave £100, but no ring, to Theophilus Buckworth, bishop of Dromore, Ireland.

THOMPSON COOPER, *rev.* JUANITA BURNBY

Sources  L. Martin, *John Crane, 1571–1652: the Cambridge apothecary and philanthropist; his biography and benefactions* (1977) · private information (1998) · will (copy), CUL, department of manuscripts and university archives, CUR 122(1) · parish register, Great St Mary, Cambs. AS, 30 Sept 1601 [marriage]
Wealth at death  very wealthy; bequests of over £6000

**Crane, Lucy** (1842–1882), author, was born on 22 September 1842 in Liverpool, the daughter of Thomas *Crane (1808–1859), portrait and miniature painter, and his wife, Marie Kearsley. Lucy's early years were spent in Torquay, where the family had moved in 1845, owing to Thomas Crane's ill health, and from here she went to school in London; in 1857 the family settled in west London. Her working life was spent as a governess, teaching children in private families; what little leisure time this left her was devoted to the study of music and literature.

Lucy Crane wrote both poetry and prose, examples of which were published in *The Argosy: a Magazine and Fireside Journal*, edited by C. W. Wood, as well as writing the original verses for several of the toy books whose wood-engraved illustrations were designed by her younger brother Walter *Crane (1845–1915) and printed in colours by Edmund Evans; these included *Annie and Jack in London* (1869), published by Routledge, and *How Jessie was Lost* (1868). She also selected and arranged the musical accompaniments to the nursery rhymes in the collections illustrated by her brother and published by Routledge as *The Baby's Opera: a Book of Old Rhymes with New Dresses* (1877) and *The Baby's Bouquet: a Fresh Bunch of Old Rhymes and Tunes* (1878). She translated from German a selection from the brothers Grimm's *Household Tales*, also illustrated by Walter Crane, which was published by Macmillan in 1882.

Lucy Crane's final years were spent writing a series of lectures on art, which she began delivering in London and Eastbourne; they earned her the distinction of being the only woman to be described as an art critic in the *Dictionary of National Biography*. She shared some of her brother's socialist beliefs about the function of art, and her writings were influenced by the ideas of Carlyle and Ruskin; she believed that 'art is not a thing having a separate existence; it is not merely a costly exotic, only cultivated by the wealthy few and intended to please a narrow circle of highly refined people' but 'a blossoming of the universal nature of man' (L. Crane, 291). She had just completed a lecture tour of the north of England when she was taken ill, and died suddenly at Bolton-le-Moors from a heart attack on 31 March 1882. She never married. Her lectures were published as *Art and the Formation of Taste*, with illustrations by Thomas and Walter Crane, who wrote, in the brief memorial to his sister with which the volume begins, that 'her health was never very strong, and her courage and energy were always greater than her powers of endurance' (Crane and Crane, xiii).          SARAH HYDE

**Sources** T. Crane and W. Crane, 'In memoriam', in L. Crane, *Art and the formation of taste: six lectures by Lucy Crane* (1882), ix–xiii · *DNB* · S. Hyde and G. Smith, eds., *Walter Crane: artist, designer and socialist* (1988) · I. Spencer, *Walter Crane* (1975) · W. Crane, *An artist's reminiscences* (1907) · C. C. Orr, ed., *Women in the Victorian art world* (1995) · *CGPLA Eng. & Wales* (1882)
**Archives** Kensington Central Library, London, Walter Crane archive
**Likenesses** W. Crane, portrait, repro. in Crane, *Art and the formation of taste*, frontispiece
**Wealth at death** £449 9s. 10d.: administration, 19 May 1882, *CGPLA Eng. & Wales*

**Crane, Nicholas** (*c*.1522–1588), Church of England clergyman, was born at Tannington, Suffolk. He was perhaps the man of these names who matriculated as a sizar at Gonville Hall, Cambridge, at Easter 1544, but Cooper's assertion that he was at Christ's College is not confirmed by the college records, while Crane himself stated in 1587 that before ordination he was a law student at the 'Inner Chauncery' (Carlson, 306).

On 25 April 1562, giving his age as forty, Crane was ordained priest by Edmund Grindal, bishop of London, as of the parish of St Peter Paul's Wharf, London, where he presumably served as curate. On 29 July he received letters patent from the lord keeper, Sir Nicholas Bacon, for the crown living of Deptford, Kent. Instituted by Edmund Guest, bishop of Rochester, on 16 September, he compounded twelve days later, with two parishioners of St Peter Paul's Wharf as sureties.

On 26 March 1566 Matthew Parker, archbishop of Canterbury, struck at clerical nonconformity in London by suspending thirty-seven ministers who refused to accept the canonical habits. Those continuing disobedient were liable to deprivation after three months. Since, on 24 June, Crane's successor received letters patent for Deptford at Guest's petition, Crane may, like Miles Coverdale, have

resigned rather than submit, or else Guest deprived him on his own authority in advance of Parker's deadline.

Like many ejected during 1566 Crane took to clandestine preaching on the outskirts of the city and engaged in semi-separatist activities. With about 100 followers, he and William Bonham were apprehended at Plumbers' Hall in June 1567. Yet Crane and Bonham apparently escaped imprisonment until the following spring, since in April 1569 they were stated to have been in prison 'one whole year'. Released at Grindal's intervention, on the grounds that clemency might persuade them to conform, Bonham was readmitted to preach in London on 1 May 1569 on signing a written promise of good behaviour; Crane only 'by word of mouth upon like promise' (Nicholson, 318).

In July 1569 Crane is recorded as administering communion (but not preaching) in the liberty of Holy Trinity Minories. Yet Grindal again committed both him and Bonham, probably in December, for 'disturbance of good order' (Nicholson, 318), and during the next three months the Minories churchwardens' accounts record money payments to both as 'preachers in prison'. To judge from these Bonham was released by midsummer 1570, Crane perhaps remaining incarcerated until November.

Out of nonconformist activities in the Minories after 1567 emerged the first known secret conference of nonconformist clergy. Led by John Field and Thomas Wilcox it began meeting in private houses in London, probably in 1570. From it developed the classical movement of the 1580s. According to Richard Bancroft in his biased exposé *Daungerous Positions and Proceedings* (1593) Crane and Bonham were founder members of the London conference.

Crane's precise whereabouts during his later years are unknown, although he continued to be associated with the Minories, being named with Wilcox and the churchwardens in the regulation of poor relief in December 1576. In 1583 he was one of many who signed the letter exhorting Thomas Cartwright to publish his confutation of the Reims New Testament. Thereafter he abandoned his would-be presbyterian colleagues, opting for outright separatism.

This decision may have been taken in 1583–4 when John Whitgift, archbishop of Canterbury, attempted to muzzle nonconformity by means of subscription to his three articles. At any rate, in *A Parte of a Register*, Field, or those who took the decision to publish it after his death, countenanced Crane's separatism to the extent of including in it his only surviving tract, the 'exceptions of Mai. Nicolas Crane, Preacher, against subscription, who died in Newgate, 1588'.

With John Greenwood and twenty of their congregation Crane was on 8 October 1587 arrested at a conventicle in the London parish of St Andrew by the Wardrobe, near Thomas Street. After examination he was imprisoned by Whitgift and John Aylmer, bishop of London. Further 'endighted', presumably by the high commission, he was sent to Newgate and died there 'of the infection' within months, aged sixty-six (Carlson, 315). Nothing is known of the wife and children mentioned in this report of his imprisonment and death.

Although Bancroft implicitly distinguished between them in *Daungerous Positions*, his bald references to 'Crane' and 'Crane of Roughampton' not unnaturally confused later writers. While there is no corroborating evidence for its existence, 'Crane of Roughampton' is stated by Bancroft to have been joint leader of a 'presbytery' in Wandsworth in 1572. If so he was probably Anthony Crane, master of the queen's household. He and his wife, Elizabeth, were correspondents of Thomas Wilcox. After his death Elizabeth Crane was involved with the secret Martin Marprelate press (1589–90) and married George Carleton, a leading Northamptonshire puritan. BRETT USHER

**Sources** P. Collinson, *The Elizabethan puritan movement* (1967) · P. Collinson, *Archbishop Grindal, 1519–1583: the struggle for a reformed church* (1979) · *A parte of a register* [1593] · A. Peel, ed., *The seconde parte of a register*, 2 vols. (1915) · A. F. S. Pearson, *Thomas Cartwright and Elizabethan puritanism, 1535–1603* (1925), 151, 201 · *CPR, 1560–63*, 415 · W. Nicholson, ed., *The remains of Edmund Grindal*, Parker Society, 9 (1843) · *The writings of John Greenwood, 1587–1590*, ed. L. H. Carlson (1962) · E. M. Tomlinson, *A history of the Minories, London*, 2nd edn (1922) · [R. Bancroft], *Daungerous positions and proceedings* (1593)
**Archives** BL, Harley MSS, reports about separatists · PRO, state papers, domestic

**Crane, Ralph** (*fl.* 1589–1632), poet and scribe, was the son of a freeman of the Merchant Taylors' Company. Although he may have been educated at the company's school his name is not recorded in its registers. The sources of Crane's biography are a rejoinder, dated 1623 (PRO, MS 1623, Requ. 2/393, no. 31), title-pages and dedications of his transcripts, indirect evidence of his connection with other datable texts, and the autobiographical preface to his only known published poetry. His *The Works of Mercy, both Corporal and Spiritual* (1621) was reissued as *The Pilgrim's New-Year's Gift, or, Fourteen Steps to the Throne of Glory*, probably in 1625, with the preface enlarged.

Having completed his formal education Crane travelled in England; then for seven years he clerked for Sir Anthony Ashley, who was clerk to the privy council from before 1588 to his resignation about 1609. In 1589 Thomas Lodge dedicated *Scilla's Metamorphosis* to his friend 'Sweet Master Crane', the only early reference to Crane in print. From about 1596 Crane served as an underwriter in the signet and privy seal office during the clerkship of Lewin Munck (the recipient of a dedicatory copy of *Works*); he also wrote for 'the Tribe of Levi' and in the inns of court.

Next, Crane wrote in his preface to his *Works*:

some imployment hath my usefull Pen
Had 'mongst those civill, well-deserving men,
That grace the Stage with honour and delight
… Under the Kingly Service they doe hold.
(R. Crane, *Works of Mercy*, 1621, sig. A6)

Crane's earliest surviving dramatic transcript, the unique copy of Ben Jonson's *Pleasure Reconciled to Virtue* (Chatsworth House, Chatsworth MSS), performed before King James on 6 January 1618, need not indicate a formal connection with the King's Company rather than the playwright. However, Crane's transcript of Fletcher's and

Massinger's heavily censored *Sir John Van Olden Barnavelt* (BL, Add. MS 18653), marked for performance by the company's bookkeeper, was written before the play was first presented in August 1619. In this instance Crane seems to have represented the playwrights as well as the company to the master of the revels, Sir George Buc (Howard-Hill, 'Buc') and possibly his work on the copy for Shakespeare's first folio (1623) started soon afterwards. When Crane's *Works of Mercy* was entered in the Stationers' register on 14 December 1620 he had had sufficient employment to compliment the company in the preface. Given the usual dating of Middleton's *Women Beware Women* as 1621, and its attribution to the King's Men, Crane must also have written the manuscript, from which Moseley's 1657 edition was printed, about this time.

Crane must have begun to transcribe copy for the first folio before February 1622, when composition and printing began (Hinman, 1.363–4), for the first play in the collection came from his pen. Besides *The Tempest*, the folio's *The Two Gentlemen of Verona*, *The Merry Wives of Windsor*, *Measure for Measure*, and *The Winter's Tale* derive, as first suggested by F. P. Wilson and confirmed by T. H. Howard-Hill (1972), from Crane's transcripts. In addition the copy for folio *Cymbeline* (Wells and others, 604) and *Othello* (Honigmann) are newly attributed to Crane. The earlier attribution of folio *2 Henry IV* to Crane's pen was revived by Honigmann (165–8). In April 1622 the first dated transcript, an informal copy of Thomas Middleton's invention for Edward Barkham's mayoral banquet, *A Song in Several Parts* (1622; PRO, MS SP Dom., v. 129, doc. 53) was apparently commissioned by Middleton. About that time, during the printing of the Shakespeare folio, Crane evidently copied a number of collaborative plays, all of which bear stage directions added by the King's Company bookkeeper (Bald, 104–9). They were Fletcher's and Massinger's *The Prophetess* (licensed for acting on 14 May 1622) and *The Spanish Curate* (acted on 24 October), and Fletcher's and Rowley's *The Maid in the Mill* (licensed on 29 August 1623). Henceforth Crane appears to have worked exclusively for individual playwrights.

Crane's transcript for John Webster's *The Duchess of Malfi* (1623), to which his patron Middleton contributed a commendatory poem, is overtly literary. As in *The Two Gentlemen of Verona*, *The Merry Wives of Windsor*, and *The Winter's Tale* Crane employed a characteristic style of massed entrances for stage directions, modelled on Jonson's neoclassical practice, and he distinguished sententious verses in italic script or with initial speech marks; the quarto bears such other common indications of his influence as characteristic spellings and elisions. Part of 1624 was spent in making copies of Middleton's notorious political play, *A Game at Chess*; the Archdall-Folger MS was dated 13 August. He also wrote BL, MS Lansdowne 690 and Bodl. Oxf., MS Malone 25, as well as the copy for the third edition and other manuscripts that did not survive. In the enlarged induction to *The Pilgrim's New-Year's Gift* (dated 1625 on account of its reference to the plague that raged in London) Crane complained that

now young ones raigne
Whil'st I (too old to cry about the street
Work for a Writer) no Imployment meet.
(Graves, 363)

Crane's undated transcript of Middleton's *The Witch* (Bodl. Oxf., MS Malone 12) was probably written after the Shakespeare folio copy but before *Demetrius and Enanthe*. After John Fletcher's death from plague in August 1625 Crane presented his transcript of Fletcher's *Demetrius and Enanthe* (NL Wales, MS Brogyntyn 42), the play published later as *The Humorous Lieutenant*, with his own dedication to Sir Kenelm Digby, dated 27 November 1625. This is his last known dramatic transcript; henceforth he transcribed only poetry and prose.

In 1626 Crane wrote the first (apparently) of many copies of Sir Henry Mainwaring's *Seaman's Glossary* (University of Illinois, MS q387.2 M 28b; Woudhuysen, 194–5). His first poetical collection (Bodl. Oxf., MS Rawl. poet. 61) consists of William Austin's *Hymns* and *Meditations* with Crane's dedication to his friend John Piers, dated 23 October 1626, followed by Crane's own *Summary and True Distinction between the Law and the Gospel*; then *Certain Selected Psalms of David*, largely by Francis Davison and Joseph Bryan, with others by Richard Gipps, Christopher Davison, William Bagnall, and Thomas Carey; and finally Philip Massinger's *London's Lamentable Estate* (*Plays and Poems*, 4.397–405). The prose work *The Faulty Favorite* (Hunt. L., EL 6870), possibly by William Austin and dedicated to John Egerton, earl of Bridgewater, is dated January 1631.

Another Crane transcript of Austin's meditations (Bodl. Oxf., MS Rawl. D. 301), dedicated to Lady Anne Cooper, may be dated about 1628 but BL, MS Harleian 6930, consisting only of the Psalms, must be placed early in the 1630s. Another collection of Davison's poems, dedicated to George Calvert, Lord Baltimore (BL, Add. MS 34752) must be dated before Baltimore's death on 15 April 1632 (Howard-Hill, 'Spelling', 27 bis). Crane's most lavishly presented collection, his *Handfull of Celestial Flowers* (BL, MS Harleian 3357), dedicated to Sir Francis Ashley in December 1632, is apparently his last transcript. It consists of Davison's poems together with the Psalms, other *Meditations on Job*, and Thomas Randolph's *A Divine Pastoral Eclogue*. It is not known when Crane died, but he was about 72 in 1632.

Crane is the most prominent literary scribe of the first part of the seventeenth century and was a significant agent in the transmission of plays written by several major Jacobean playwrights. His preparation of printer's copy for Shakespeare's first folio had profound textual consequences on the eight plays with which he has been associated.    T. H. HOWARD-HILL

**Sources** F. P. Wilson, 'Ralph Crane, scrivener to the king's players', *The Library*, 4th ser., 7 (1926–7), 194–215 · T. S. Graves, 'Ralph Crane and the king's players', *Studies in Philology*, 21 (1924), 362–6 · T. H. Howard-Hill, *Ralph Crane and some Shakespeare first folio comedies* (1972) · T. H. Howard-Hill, 'Spelling-analysis and Ralph Crane: a preparatory study of his life, spelling and scribal habits', PhD diss., Victoria University, Wellington, 1960 · R. C. Bald, *Bibliographical studies in the Beaumont & Fletcher folio of 1647* (1938) · J. R. Brown, 'The printing of John Webster's plays (III): *The duchess of Malfi*', *Studies in Bibliography*, 15 (1962), 57–69 · C. Hinman, *The printing and the proofreading of the first folio of Shakespeare*, 2 vols. (1963) · E. A. J. Honigmann, *The texts of 'Othello' and Shakespearian revision* (1996) · T. H. Howard-Hill, 'Buc and the censorship of *Sir John van Olden Barnavelt* in 1619', *Review of English Studies*, new ser., 39 (1988), 39–63 · T. H. Howard-Hill, *Middleton's 'vulgar pasquin': essays on 'A game at chess'* (1995) · *The plays and poems of Philip Massinger*, ed. P. Edwards and C. Gibson, 5 vols. (1976) · T. Middleton, *Women beware women*, ed. J. R. Mulryne (1975) · S. Wells and others, *William Shakespeare: a textual companion* (1987) · H. R. Woudhuysen, *Sir Philip Sidney and the circulation of manuscripts, 1558–1640* (1996)

**Crane, Stephen Townley** (1871–1900), writer, was born on 1 November 1871 at 14 Mulberry Place, Newark, New Jersey, USA, the last of the fourteen children of Jonathan Townley Crane DD (1819–1880), a Methodist minister, and Mary Helen Peck Crane (1827–1891), a doughty campaigner for the Women's Christian Temperance Union. Earlier Cranes fought in the American War of Independence and the Civil War; Stephen inherited, he said, a 'rage of conflict' he would put to good use. Writing too ran in the family: two brothers became professional journalists. After Jonathan Crane's death, the family moved to Asbury Park, New Jersey, where Stephen began to reject his religious upbringing. In 1888 he enrolled at the Hudson River Institute at Claverack, New York, and in 1890–91 started a brief ineffectual university education: one semester at Lafayette College, studying engineering, another at Syracuse University, where he won fame only on the baseball field. Yet he drafted his first book, *Maggie, a Girl of the Streets: a Story of New York*, a powerful short novel in the manner of Zola, a tale of New York tenement life and the tragic fate of a prostitute. In 1893 he published it at his own expense under the name Johnston Smith. It scarcely sold, but won the attention of the campaigners for the new realist movement, including Hamlin Garland and William Dean Howells.

Crane's life was brief, sickly (he suffered from tuberculosis), cosmopolitan, highly active, and eventful: an exemplary literary life of the 1890s, when all his work was done. To 'recover from college' (*Crane: Letters*, 109) he returned to Asbury Park and journalism, writing ironic newspaper sketches, and stories set in Sullivan County, New York. Developing his urban impressionism, he turned to New York's Bowery. Working in bohemian poverty, living off journalistic commissions in an artists' studio at 143 East 23rd Street (formerly the Art Students' League) and elsewhere, he gathered material for 'Bowery Tales', a sequence of 'experiments in misery', street-corner glimpses, impressions of poverty and inequality: a popular form of writing in a muck-raking age when city and ghetto were becoming great American subjects. In spring 1893 he began *The Red Badge of Courage: an Episode of the American Civil War*, a novella about a young soldier (the Youth) in an unnamed battle, evidently Chancellorsville (1863). Crane was not born when it occurred; the tale owes much to memoirs, earlier fiction, and, he said, the football field. What distinguishes it is its remarkable and tense immediacy, and its point of vision: all is seen as a sequence of impressions and emotions, images and fragmentary pictures of action.

The book appeared only as a newspaper serial, but led the syndicator Irving Bacheller to send Crane to the American West and Mexico as roving reporter in early 1895. This yielded many important experiences, leading to such fine stories as 'The Bride Comes to Yellow Sky' (1897) and 'The Blue Hotel' (1898). Returning to New York, Crane wrote the war stories of *The Little Regiment* (1896), and a novel of Manhattan bohemia, *The Third Violet* (1897). A volume of hard, irreligious, ironic poems, *The Black Riders and other Lines*, appeared in 1895. In September 1895 Appleton published *The Red Badge of Courage* in book form; in November it appeared in Britain, where it was a triumph. Crane found himself famous, hailed as a great naturalist and literary innovator. Coinciding with the rise of impressionist naturalism, the book became a classic, influencing many, including Joseph Conrad and Ernest Hemingway.

In 1896 Crane published a revised *Maggie*, and a companion piece, *George's Mother*. In September, investigating police corruption, he intervened to halt the arrest of a prostitute, Dora Clark. His court defence of her won much publicity, and the hostility of the New York police. It seemed prudent to take another Bacheller assignment, reporting impending American-Spanish conflict over Cuba. It was less prudent to sign on a ship, the *Commodore*, running guns to Cuban insurgents. When it sank off the Florida coast, Crane spent thirty nights in a drifting dinghy, leading to his most famous and perfect short story, 'The Open Boat' (1896). Less prudently still, Crane had fallen in love with Cora (Howorth) Taylor (1865–1910). Twice married, refused divorce by her British husband, Captain (later Sir) Donald William Stewart, she owned an upmarket brothel in Jacksonville, Florida, charmingly called the Hotel de Dream. In April 1897 they travelled to Greece to cover the Graeco-Turkish war, Cora writing as Imogene Carter, the first woman war correspondent. Returning in June, they chose to settle in Britain, where their liaison seemed less scandalous.

Crane and Cora rented Ravensbrook House, in Oxted, Surrey, and met Joseph Conrad, Ford Madox Hueffer, and Edward Garnett. Many American expatriate writers were settled in Britain, including Harold Frederic and Henry James; both became friends. 'Lean, blond, slow-speaking' said H. G. Wells, 'a rangy American who affected a western style and kept a six-gun' said Hueffer, Crane became figurehead of a remarkable literary scene: a 'ring of conspirators' conspiring to change and modernize literature, according to Wells. Heavily in debt, he wrote against the clock. In April 1898 he re-crossed the Atlantic to report the Spanish-American war, submitting forty reports from Cuba. He began *Active Service* (1899), about the Greek war, and the war-tales of *Wounds in the Rain* (1900). Back in England in January 1899, he rented the rambling, decaying, ancient manor of Brede Place, Northiam, near Rye, Sussex; James, Wells, Conrad, and Hueffer lived nearby. Living squirearchically, entertaining freely, he wrote furiously to stave off creditors: *War is Kind* (1899), poems; *The Monster and other Stories* (1899); *Whilomville Stories* (1900), based on his New Jersey childhood.

At a Christmas 1899 performance of a ghost story attended by many literary friends, Crane fell ill; in April 1900 he haemorrhaged again and was shipped to a sanatorium in the Black Forest: the Villa Eberhardt, Badenweiler. Here, on 5 June, he died of tuberculosis, only twenty-eight, owing $5,000, Cora correcting proofs at his bedside. It was, said James, 'an unmitigated unredeemed catastrophe' (James, 145)—though, on the basis of *The Red Badge*, some superb short stories, and his fundamental originality of technique, Crane's powerful influence on modern British and American fiction long survived. His body was returned to London, then shipped home to the family plot in Hillside, New Jersey. Cora secured publication of Crane's posthumous work, opened another Florida brothel, married a railroad-man who subsequently murdered one of her admirers, and died in Britain in 1910.

MALCOLM BRADBURY

**Sources** R. W. Stallman, *Stephen Crane: a biography* (1968) · *Stephen Crane: letters*, ed. R. W. Stallman and L. Gilkes (1960) · C. Benfey, *The double life of Stephen Crane* (1992) · *The works of Stephen Crane*, ed. F. Bowers, 10 vols. (1969–76) · E. Solomon, *Stephen Crane in England: a portrait of the artist* (1964) · L. Gilkes, *Cora Crane* (1960) · M. Seymour, *A ring of conspirators: Henry James and his literary circles, 1895–1915* (1988) · M. Bradbury, *Dangerous pilgrimages: trans-Atlantic mythologies and the novel* (1995) · J. B. Colvert, 'Stephen Crane', *American realists and naturalists*, ed. D. Pizer and E. N. Harbert, DLitB, 12 (1982), 100–24 · S. Wertheim, *A Stephen Crane encyclopedia* (1997) · *Henry James: letters*, ed. L. Edel, 4: *1895–1916* (1984)

**Archives** Col. U. · Syracuse Library, New York | NYPL, Berg collection · University of Virginia, Charlottesville, Alderman Library, Waller Barrett collection

**Likenesses** C. Knapp Linson, photograph, 1894 · photographs, repro. in Pizer and Harbert, eds., *American realists and naturalists*

**Wealth at death** £160: probate, 7 July 1900, CGPLA Eng. & Wales · $5000 in debt

**Crane, Thomas** (*bap.* **1631**, *d.* **1714**), Presbyterian minister, was baptized on 29 March 1631 at St Andrew's, Plymouth, the son of Thomas Crane, a merchant of the town. He matriculated from Exeter College, Oxford, in 1649 and graduated MA from Gloucester Hall, Oxford, in 1655. During his studies he received assistance from Richard Sherlock BD, a former chaplain of New College ejected in 1648, who held a rectory near the town. Crane was an assistant to Richard Alleine of Batcombe, Somerset, before he was admitted as rector of Rampisham, Dorset, in 1658. He married a daughter of William *Lyford, author and vicar of Sherborne. The couple had at least one son, Thomas (1661/2–1716), who matriculated at Exeter College, aged sixteen, in 1678.

After the Restoration, Crane was ejected from Rampisham in 1662 and moved to Beaminster, Dorset, where he was licensed as a Presbyterian on 8 May 1672. In that year he signed the letter from Dorset ministers thanking the king for his declaration of indulgence. A 'judicious constant Preacher to his Congregation at Beaminster', he was 'a great Observer of the Steps of Divine Providence … And so frequent was he in his Remarks thereon, that he was commonly called *Providence*' (*Calamy rev.*, 141). Indicted for non-attendance at church, Crane managed to escape prosecution because of a legal technicality; he was 'charg'd with *coming to Divine Service*, &c. instead of *not coming* to it' (ibid.). He was one of four ministers who at Lyme in Dorset on 25 August 1687 ordained several men to the Presbyterian ministry, including Thomas Hoare. In that year Hoare became his assistant and later succeeded him as pastor of his congregation. Crane died in August 1714 at Beaminster, where he was buried in the same month.

STEPHEN WRIGHT

**Sources** Calamy rev. · E. Calamy, *A continuation of the account of the ministers … who were ejected and silenced after the Restoration in 1660*, 2 vols. (1727) · A. Gordon, ed., *Freedom after ejection: a review (1690–1692) of presbyterian and congregational nonconformity in England and Wales* (1917) · W. Densham and J. Ogle, *The story of the Congregational churches of Dorset* (1899) · J. Hutchins, *The history and antiquities of the county of Dorset*, ed. W. Shipp and J. W. Hodson, 4 vols. (1861–70) · Foster, *Alum. Oxon.* · T. Crane, *Job's assurance of the resurrection* (1690) · R. Hine, *The history of Beaminster* (1914) · IGI

Thomas Crane
(1808–1859), self-
portrait, *c.*1840

**Crane, Thomas** (1808–1859), artist, was born at Chester, the son of Thomas Crane (*d.* 1836), a bookseller and newspaper editor in that town, and his wife (*d.* 1836), whose maiden name was Swinchatte. He had three brothers, William (*d.* 1843) and Philip, who later emigrated to Australia, and another brother, John. The Crane family had lived in Chester since the sixteenth century, attaining a prominent position in local society. Thomas's great-grandfather had been house surgeon to the Chester Infirmary in the middle of the eighteenth century, and his grandfather was a lieutenant in the Royal Navy. Showing considerable promise as an artist, Crane entered the Royal Academy Schools, in London, on 31 March 1825. This was made possible by the generosity of a patron, Edward Taylor, of Manchester. Two years later, at most, Crane returned to Chester to begin his professional career. His memorandum book showed that he soon received commissions to paint portrait miniatures of local figures, including the Stanleys of Alderley. He later received commissions for portraits from such Cheshire notables as George Harry Grey, sixth earl of Stamford and Warrington; Richard Grosvenor, second marquess of Westminster; and the Wilbrahams.

As well as working in both oil and watercolour, together with his three brothers, Crane ran a printing business from an outbuilding at their parents' home in Newgate Street. In 1829 the brothers designed tickets for a musical festival at Chester, and a portrait of the famous violinist Paganini was lithographed by William Crane. In 1832 Thomas and William illustrated the first edition of a book of hunting songs published by R. E. Egerton Warburton, a Cheshire resident. The illustrations included a portrait of the Cheshire huntsman Joe Maiden, twelve full-page scenes, and many vignettes. In 1836 the same two brothers illustrated a nursery tale, 'The Life and Adventures of Mr. Pig and Miss Crane', written by another local figure, Lady Delamere; the book was sold at a bazaar in the nearby village of Tarvin. Other prints produced by the Crane brothers included lithograph views of north Wales and portraits of well-known residents in the area, for instance, Sir Watkin Williams-Wynn and the reclusive 'Ladies of Llangollen' (Lady Eleanor Butler and Sarah Ponsonby). Crane first contributed to the exhibition of the Liverpool

Academy in 1832. In 1835 he was elected an associate, becoming a full member in 1838 and treasurer in 1841. Of the forty-seven works that he exhibited at the academy between 1832 and 1848 almost all were portraits. In 1839 he married Chester-born Marie Kearsley (*d.* after 1861) and went to live in London but, fearing the onset of tuberculosis, he moved away again, first to Leamington Spa and then, in 1841, to Maryland Street, Liverpool. Over the next four years his children Lucy, Thomas, and Walter were born.

Crane's worsening health led him to move to the Devon coast in October 1845. He and his family stayed there for the next twelve years, living at several addresses, including Laureston Villa, Upton, and 3 Park Place, Torquay. During these years Crane established an informal sketching club and made occasional visits to Manchester, Liverpool, Cheshire, and London. One such trip was to the Great Exhibition in Hyde Park, London, in 1851. With his health apparently restored, in 1857 the family moved to London with the hope that this would provide Crane with a greater number of clients. But after two years of gradually failing strength Crane died, at his house in Westbourne Park, in July 1859.

Crane's principal works, not to say principal source of income, were portraits in oil, watercolour, and crayon, but he also produced genre and landscape pictures when time permitted. He exhibited at the Royal Academy nine times, twelve times at the Royal Hibernian Academy, and three times each at the Society of British Artists and the British Institution. Among the paintings shown were *The Cobbler* (exh. RA, 1842); *The Legend of Beth-Gelert* (exh. Liverpool Academy, 1842; RHA, 1843); *The Old Romance* (exh. RA, 1843; Liverpool Academy, 1843; RHA, 1844); *Masquerading* (exh. RA, 1844); *The Deserted Village* (exh. British Institution, 1844); *The Waking Smile* (exh. Liverpool Academy, 1843; RHA, 1844); and *The Bay Window* (exh. RA, 1844; RHA, 1845). From these titles it appears that outside Liverpool, Crane preferred to exhibit his genre paintings. Of his portraits perhaps the best known is that of Mr Egerton Smith, publisher of the *Liverpool Mercury*, which was lithographed. Works in public collections include a topographical watercolour in the Grosvenor Museum, Chester, and prints in the British Museum. His son Walter *Crane (1845–1915) became a well-known artist and his daughter, Lucy *Crane (1842–1882), a respected art critic and children's author. ALBERT NICHOLSON, rev. MARY GUYATT

**Sources** W. Crane, *An artist's reminiscences* (1907) · E. Morris and E. Roberts, *The Liverpool Academy and other exhibitions of contemporary art in Liverpool, 1774–1867* (1998), 168 · H. C. Marillier, *The Liverpool school of painters: an account of the Liverpool Academy from 1810 to 1867, with memoirs of the principal artists* (1904), 92–4 · Redgrave, *Artists*, 105 · Bryan, *Painters* (1903–5), 1.350 · S. C. Hutchison, 'The Royal Academy Schools, 1768–1830', *Walpole Society*, 38 (1960–62), 123–91 · Graves, *Brit. Inst.*, 129 · A. M. Stewart and C. de Courcy, eds., *Royal Hibernian Academy of Arts: index of exhibitors and their works, 1826–1979*, 1 (1985), 173 · J. Johnson, ed., *Works exhibited at the Royal Society of British Artists, 1824–1893, and the New English Art Club, 1888–1917*, 2 vols. (1975), 111 · Graves, *RA exhibitors*, 2 (1905), 193–4
**Likenesses** T. Crane, self-portrait, *c*.1840, NPG [*see illus.*]

Walter Crane (1845–1915), by George Frederic Watts, 1891

**Crane, Walter** (1845–1915), illustrator, designer, and painter, was born on 15 August 1845 at 12 Maryland Street, Liverpool, the third child of Thomas *Crane (1808–1859), a portrait painter well established in the north-west of England, and his wife, Marie Kearsley. When he was three months old the family moved to Torquay because his father was thought to be consumptive, and Walter Crane spent a happy childhood there. His earliest memories included the ships in the harbour and the times the circus came to town. He was good at drawing but school brought on nervous attacks, so he stayed at home, learning from his father's work, stocking his mind from illustrated books, and sketching in the fields. Animals were his favourite subject. Thomas Crane's health improved in Torquay, and in 1857 he moved his family to London, hoping to get more work. Seeing a career in art for his son, he took him to the National Gallery and to the South Kensington Museum (now the Victoria and Albert). In January 1859 Walter Crane was apprenticed to the wood engraver W. J. Linton to learn the art of drawing on wood for illustration. He was thirteen. Six months later his father died.

Crane came thus abruptly out of childhood, walking from his mother's house in Notting Hill to Linton's workshop off the Strand each morning and back again in the evening. At the end of his three-year apprenticeship he could help to support his mother, sisters, and younger brother. But he had his own ambitions as well. He had entered a world of publishers, printers, artists, engravers, and journalists where art and commerce sat down together. This was the golden age of Victorian illustration, and he might one day shine alongside D. G. Rossetti and Charles Keene. He was reading Auguste Comte, J. S. Mill, Herbert Spencer, and Shelley and catching heady glimpses of how humanity, free of the old theologies, might take the future into its own hands. And he was painting on his own account, subjects from Keats and Tennyson. In 1862 his *Lady of Shalott* was hung at the Royal Academy. Though he was still in his teens and looking for work as a freelance illustrator, he seemed to have gone beyond his father.

In 1865 Crane was asked to contribute illustrations to a series of books for very young children, nursery rhymes and fairy tales, to be printed by Edmund Evans, the leading woodblock colour printer in London, and published by Routledge. Over the next ten years Crane illustrated thirty-seven of these Toy Books, as they were known. After the first nine his work began to emulate Japanese prints, with decorative compositions in flat, or very deep, perspective; and he began to furnish his pictures with the fashions and domestic bric-à-brac of the aesthetic movement, then on the rise in London—fans, blue-and-white china, and peacocks' feathers. Nursery rhymes and fairy tales are full of pigs going to market and dishes eloping with spoons. Crane had a taste for such fantasy, especially the anthropomorphic animals—was his name not a bird? His peculiar sensibility wedged animal lunacy up against high fashion. Picture books for children which did not moralize and colour printing from wood both flourished in the mid-Victorian period. Evans's skill and Crane's imagination raised them to new levels, and the Toy Books were an enormous success.

On 6 September 1871 Crane married Mary Frances Andrews (*c*.1846–1914), the daughter of a country gentleman from Essex, and they spent the next eighteen months in Italy. Crane worked at his book illustrations, painted in the landscape, and made portraits of his demure-looking wife. He was also working, in these years, on allegorical paintings with themes of human life and destiny inspired by the positivism of Auguste Comte and Herbert Spencer. He painted such allegories almost all his life, giving them such titles as *The Bridge of Life* and *The Roll of Fate*, and he valued them above his other work. It was his ambition to show them at the Royal Academy, but he showed there only once after 1862. Instead they appeared each year at the Dudley and the Grosvenor and other London galleries, never to any acclaim. That was hard to bear, and the success of his children's books put salt in the wound. The public acclaimed him as 'the academician of the nursery', but he wanted to be known as a distinguished allegorical painter. Much of his life was spent in pursuing this difficult ambition and, at the same time, in creating tolerable substitutes for it.

When the Cranes returned to London in 1873 they moved into a house in Wood Lane, Shepherd's Bush, then still on the edge of the city. Here, and later at Beaumont Lodge nearby, Crane lived and worked for almost twenty years. The couple entertained a lot and moved in the artistic and fashionable circles of Holland Park; George Howard, later twelfth earl of Carlisle, was a friend and patron, and so was Lord Leighton. Crane knew, and looked up to, William Morris and Edward Burne-Jones. At this time he widened the scope of his *œuvre*. He began to work as decorative artist, designing wallpapers, tiles, printed textiles, posters, stained glass, embroideries, decorative plasterwork. He was versatile and prolific. At first manufacturers wanted nursery tiles and nursery wallpapers, but he wanted to escape from the nursery. (Besides, he now had rivals there in Kate Greenaway and Randolph Caldecott.) He began to illustrate books for adults and works of literature. And in his decorative work he developed a versatile, linear style with scrollwork and emblematic, vaguely classical figures derived from his allegorical paintings. The aesthetic movement flourished in the 1870s, raising the status of decorative art, taking it seriously. That was what Crane wanted. It seemed as if decorative art might be a third way, between his success as an illustrator and his aspirations as a painter.

In 1884, after some friendly argument with William Morris, Crane became a socialist. He joined the Social Democratic Federation along with Morris, and as Morris changed allegiance Crane followed, joining the Socialist League later in 1884 and the Hammersmith Socialist Society in 1890. This was more a matter of personal loyalty than of shared beliefs, for the sources of Crane's socialism were different from Morris's: the radicalism of his master W. J. Linton, the positivist belief in progress, memories of the Paris commune of 1871. He became the artist of the cause, designing posters, trade-union banners, cartoons, and newspaper headings, adapting the emblematic figures of his paintings to socialist themes. His *The Triumph of Labour*, drawn for May day 1891 and reproduced in Crane's *Cartoons for the Cause, 1886–1896* (1896), is a Renaissance-style triumphal procession rendered in the gritty texture of wood-engraving and filled with sturdy workers, bullock carts, and banners. Morris said it was the best thing he had ever done.

In the 1880s Crane also became active in the politics of art. The arts and crafts movement championed the claims of decorative art in the 1880s, as the aesthetic movement had in the 1870s, but it had more intellectual weight, and it had its own organizations. The Art Workers' Guild, founded in 1884, brought architects and fine and decorative artists together under the banner of 'the unity of art'. Crane was a founder member. But the guild was a private club, not an exhibiting body, so Crane and the metalworker W. A. S. Benson led a movement to establish a separate exhibiting body for the decorative arts. The Arts and Crafts Exhibition Society, founded in 1888, held large and successful exhibitions in London, at first annually and then triennially. Crane was president from 1888 to 1893, William Morris from 1893 until his death in 1896, and Crane again until 1912. The society was a public platform for Crane, and after Morris's death he was probably the best-known decorative artist in Britain. This was the kind of prominence he had wished to enjoy as a successful painter.

In 1892 the Crane family moved from Shepherd's Bush to 13 Holland Street, off Kensington Church Street. They now had three children, Beatrice (*b.* 1873), Lionel (*b.* 1876), and Lancelot (*b.* 1880); two others did not survive their early years. Mary Crane was no longer the demure figure of the Italian portraits but a plump, slightly fantastic woman who drove herself alone round Kensington in a buggy, flouting propriety in a William Morris flower-patterned dress. They lived a life of self-conscious bohemianism. The house was full of pewter and china, carved figures, Indian idols, a live alligator, model ships, a marmoset that slept in the fireplace, Crane's unsold paintings, all higgledy-piggledy and gathering dust. Amid all this Crane played the part of the artist, a small, dapper man with carefully curled moustaches and a little beard, a flowing yellow silk tie, and a velvet coat. Colleagues were apt to laugh at him, and they mostly thought his earliest works, the Toy Books, were the best. But he was a lovable figure, and they indulged his staginess. Both he and Mary Crane loved dressing up and they threw enormous parties. For Lionel's twenty-first birthday they invited seven hundred people. Crane dressed up as a crane and Mary as an enormous sunflower.

In the 1890s and 1900s Crane enjoyed fame and public honours. In 1891–2 a major retrospective exhibition of his work toured the United States. In 1893 he was appointed director of design at Manchester School of Art. From 1893 to 1896 his exhibition toured Europe, and he was delighted to find that German collectors and museums bought his allegorical paintings, which chimed with German symbolist work. In 1898 he was appointed principal of the Royal College of Art. Three separate monographs were published on his work. A new and much larger retrospective opened in 1900 at the Applied Arts Museum in Budapest, where he and Mary Crane were fêted. It then toured Austria and Germany. At this point the Arts and Crafts Exhibition Society, of which he was still president, was invited to assemble the English contribution to the International Exhibition of Modern Decorative Art, due to open in Turin in 1902. Lacking financial resources, Crane and others simply moved his exhibition to Turin and added other arts and crafts exhibits. Crane was decorated by Victor Emmanuel III for his part in the exhibition, and from then on called himself Commendatore Crane.

In these decades Crane published an autobiography and a half-dozen books in which, among various technical subjects, he set out his conviction that decorative art had a distinguished history and wide intellectual scope; that it was the art of the people and would flourish only when the people were free; and that the arts and crafts movement was its modern champion against the threat of commercialism and the machine. These were typical arts and crafts arguments and were learned mostly from Morris, though they lacked Morris's passionate medievalism and mature socialism. Some of these books were translated into Dutch, German, and Hungarian. The boy who found school difficult, the young man who illustrated children's books, was now an authority, a writer on art.

Crane loved appearing on the public stage, but there were flaws in his performance. At Manchester he failed to steer the school towards a more practical, arts and crafts kind of teaching as was hoped, and he resigned after three years. At the Royal College he resigned after only one year. At Turin the English contribution was criticized in the press as old-fashioned, ill-displayed, and dominated by one man. The truth is that Crane was not a good chairman and that he hung on to the presidency of the Exhibition Society too long. Around 1910 the society was in trouble, losing money on exhibitions and shaken by the discontent of younger members. The arts and crafts architect C. R. Ashbee, who was younger than Crane but had been with the society since the beginning, wrote after Crane's death:

> He failed us in the crisis ... He could not give the younger men the lead they needed. That failure of his has I think destroyed the Society as a vital force ... Perhaps he was too gentle, too much a creature in a fairy story. (Ashbee, 266)

Ashbee was right. Crane's talent lay far from the public world, and by this time far in his past, with little children and domesticity. His best things were his lightest things. In the Beinecke Library at Yale University, and in the Houghton Library at Harvard University, are twenty-nine shiny black notebooks. These are some of the stories he made up for his own children at bedtime, telling them in pictures. They were known in the family as the black books. There is not much in his work that is finer than the visual wit and tenderness of these books, which were the work, Crane tells us, of the odd half-hours of winter evenings.

On 18 December 1914 Mary Crane was found dead on the railway line near Kingsnorth in Kent. The coroner's jury returned a verdict of suicide during temporary insanity. Walter Crane did not long outlive his wife: he died at Horsham Cottage Hospital, in Sussex, on 14 March 1915.

ALAN CRAWFORD

**Sources** W. Crane, *An artist's reminiscences* (1907) · I. Spencer, *Walter Crane* (1975) · G. Smith and S. Hyde, eds., *Walter Crane, 1845–1915: artist, designer and socialist* (1989) · W. Crane, *The work of Walter Crane, with notes by the artist* (1898) · P. G. Konody, *The art of Walter Crane* (1902) · A. Crane, 'My grandfather, Walter Crane', *Yale University Library Gazette*, 31/3 (1957), 97–109 · C. R. Ashbee, 'The Ashbee memoirs', 7 vols., 1938–40, V&A NAL, 7.265–8 · P. Stansky, *Redesigning the world: William Morris, the 1880s, and the arts and crafts* (1985) · C. Dakers, *The Holland Park circle* (1999) · *The Times* (21 Dec 1914), 5 · W. Rothenstein, *Men and memories: recollections of William Rothenstein*, 2 vols. (1931–2) · *CGPLA Eng. & Wales* (1915) · m. cert.
**Archives** Kensington Central Library, London, watercolours, drawings, designs, proofs, wallpapers, and corresp. · priv. coll., watercolours, drawings, designs, sketchbooks, family portraits, and corresp. · V&A, corresp. · Yale U., Beinecke L., letters and literary MSS | BL, corresp. with Macmillans, Add. MS 55232 · BL, corresp. with May Morris, William Morris, G. B. Shaw, and others, Add. MS 50531 · BLPES, corresp. with Fabian Society and independent labour party · Castle Howard, North Yorkshire, Howard papers, corresp. with George Howard, earl of Carlisle · Harvard U., Caroline Miller Parker collection, drawings, designs, sketchbooks, MSS, proofs, and corresp. · Harvard U., Houghton L., letters to James Stanley Little · JRL, letters to M. H. Spielmann · Ransom HRC, corresp. with John Lane · Richmond Local Studies Library, London, corresp. with Douglas Sladen · U. Glas. L., letters to D. S. MacColl · UCL, letters to Sir Francis Galton · V&A, Forster Library, papers of the Arts and Crafts Exhibition Society · Yale U., Catherine Tinker Patterson collection, drawings, designs, MSS, proofs, and corresp.
**Likenesses** Elliott & Fry, photograph, *c.*1875, NPG · G. Simonds, bronze bust, 1889, Art Workers' Guild, London · G. F. Watts, oils, 1891, NPG [*see illus.*] · T. A. Gotch, photograph, 1906, RIBA · photograph, *c.*1910, NPG · W. Crane, self-portrait, oils, 1912, Uffizi Gallery, Florence · Barraud, photograph, NPG; repro. in *Men and women of the day*, 4 (1891) · W. Crane, self-portrait, print (aged sixty), BM · W. Rothenstein, lithograph, BM, NPG
**Wealth at death** £3119 8*s.* 3*d.*: administration, 18 May 1915, *CGPLA Eng. & Wales*

**Crane, William** (*d.* 1545), musician and merchant, was of obscure origins, but by 1506 he had become a gentleman of the Chapel Royal, for in May of that year he performed at the entertainments given by Lady Margaret Beaufort for King Filippo of Castile at Croydon. According to the household ordinances of Edward IV, the gentlemen were to be 'men of worship endowed with vertuose, morall and speculatiif, as of theyre musike shewing in descant clene voysed, well relysed and pronouncyng eloquent in reading, sufficiaunt in organez playing' (Myers, 23). They sang the plainsong of the liturgy and its polyphony. Early in the reign of Henry VIII Crane played a key role in the 'disguisings', or court masques, and performed in *The Golldyn Arber in the Archeyrd of Pleyser* to celebrate the birth of Henry's son in February 1511, *Le fortresse dangerus* at new year 1512, and *The Pavillion in the Place Perilous* at new year 1515. He was also present at the Field of Cloth of Gold in 1520. No musical compositions by him are known. From Michaelmas 1523 Crane was fulfilling (in succession to William Cornish) the duties of the master of the choristers of the Chapel Royal, a post to which he was formally appointed on 12 May 1526, when he received the larger stipend of £40 per annum rather than the traditional 40 marks. From 1541 he enjoyed an additional annuity from the court of augmentations of £10 per annum. As master he was responsible for the twelve children of the Chapel Royal, for whom he received board wages of 26*s.* 8*d.* per month, and he continued to receive payments for entertainments performed by the children at Christmas. Henry VIII performed in disguisings himself; Crane seems to have been close to the king, and won £7 2*s.* 6*d.* in an archery contest with him in June 1532.

Henry's favour brought tangible rewards, as Crane was the recipient of a variety of royal patronage. He was granted the offices of waterbailiff of Dartmouth in June 1509 and of Bishop's Lynn in July 1535. From February 1514 until May 1530 he held the important post of comptroller of the tonnage and poundage of the petty custom in the port of London. He also received numerous import and export licences: to export 600 sacks of wool (1512), to export broadcloths and kerseys and import silk and wines (1514), to export broadcloths and kerseys (1515), to export and import French wine, woad, and hemp (1523), to import Gascon wine and woad (1527), and to export 400 tuns of double beer (1542). Crane was also active in supervising the repair and fitting out of the king's ships in the Woolwich Dockyards in 1513 and 1515. He acquired an impressive portfolio of property in the City and its environs. In 1511 he received from the king the lease of a tenement in Mark Lane in the parish of All Hallows Staining and a tenement belonging to the convent of St Mary Graces; in 1531 he acquired by royal grant the lease of Beaumont's Inn in Wood Street, and in 1540 ten tenements with gardens and three other rooms within the close of the recently dissolved priory of St Helen, Bishopsgate. From 1519 he leased from the Mercers' Company a prestigious property in Tower Street, where he lived during the 1520s; he held property on the royal manor of Havering atte Bower in Essex, of the park of which he was keeper in 1535; and his will shows him also to have owned a house in Greenwich.

Crane, who was resident successively in the London parishes of St Dunstan-in-the-East and in St Helen, Bishopsgate, was a very familiar figure in the City. The wool export licence of 1512 was held jointly with the executors of the prominent mercer Hugh Clopton, and the grant of property in Mark Lane of the same year was to be held jointly with Thomas Cremour, a London draper. He was drawn still further into the commercial world by his nomination by the king to the office of weigher of raw silks in February 1525. One of a number of royal initiatives in the 1520s which called into question the City's control over its own patronage, this action resulted in a tussle with the Mercers' Company, in whose gift the office traditionally lay. After litigation in Star Chamber it was agreed in May 1526 that Crane should hold the office, with the Mercers' nominee enjoying the deputyship. Crane, who had become a member of the company in 1525, cannot have been popular with the Mercers, for he was already heavily in arrears in the payment of the rent due from the Tower Street property. His connections with the royal household long protected Crane from the full force of the law, but in 1534 the Mercers transferred his interest to Sir Edmund Peckham, cofferer of the household, and induced Crane to stand to the arbitration of Thomas Cromwell. But he seems to have been well integrated into the framework of parochial religious life, and left a chalice of silver and gilt to the parish of St Helen, Bishopsgate, an act which bears out the conventionally conservative cast of the preamble to his will. His multifarious activities and enjoyment of royal favour made him a moderately prosperous man, who was assessed to the subsidy at £300 in goods in 1541. We do not know the identity of his wife, save that she was called Margaret. Apart from his religious bequests, she was the sole beneficiary of his will; there was a daughter (presumably dead by 1545), who in 1535 had apparently contracted herself to a rather dubious character by the name of Christopher Draper who had got himself nominated to a prebendal stall at York at the same time as he was pursuing the musician's daughter. Crane died on 7 July 1545 and was buried before the high altar of the church of St Helen, Bishopsgate.                    IAN W. ARCHER

**Sources** A. Ashbee, ed., *Records of English court music*, 9 vols. (1986–96) · F. L. Kisby, 'The royal household chapel in early Tudor London, 1485–1547', PhD diss., U. Lond., 1996 · will, PRO, PROB 11/31, sig. 7 · Mercers' Hall, London, Acts of Court · *LP Henry VIII* · A. R. Myers, ed., *The household of Edward IV: the black book and the ordinance of 1478* (1959)

# PICTURE CREDITS

Constable, John (1776–1837)—© National Portrait Gallery, London

Constable, William (1783–1861)—Philippe Garner collection

Constantine I (272/3–337)—photograph: AKG London

Constantine III (d. 411)—© Copyright The British Museum

Constantine, Learie Nicholas, Baron Constantine (1901–1971)—© National Portrait Gallery, London

Constantinidis, Joanna (1927–2000)—© Tim Macpherson / Ceramic Review; photograph National Portrait Gallery, London

Constantius I (250?–306)—© Copyright The British Museum

Conway, Henry Seymour (1719–1795)—from the collection belonging to the 13th Duke of Argyll

Conway, (William) Martin, Baron Conway of Allington (1856–1937)—© National Portrait Gallery, London

Conway, Moncure Daniel (1832–1907)—© National Portrait Gallery, London

Conyngham, Elizabeth, Marchioness Conyngham (1769–1861)—Birmingham Museums & Art Gallery

Cook, Arthur Bernard (1868–1952)—photograph reproduced by courtesy of The British Academy

Cook, Arthur James (1883–1931)—© reserved; collection Science & Society Picture Library; photograph National Portrait Gallery, London

Cook, Sir Edward Tyas (1857–1919)—© National Portrait Gallery, London

Cook, Eliza (1812–1889)—© National Portrait Gallery, London

Cook, Frederick Charles (1804–1889)—© National Portrait Gallery, London

Cook, George (1772–1845)—© National Portrait Gallery, London

Cook, James (1728–1779)—© National Maritime Museum, London, Greenwich Hospital Collection

Cook, Peter Edward (1937–1995)—© Cecil Beaton Archive, Sotheby's; collection National Portrait Gallery, London

Cook, Thomas (1808–1892)—Getty Images - Hulton Archive

Cooke, Alice Margaret (1867–1940)—© National Portrait Gallery, London

Cooke, Elisha (1678–1737)—photography courtesy Peabody Essex Museum

Cooke, George Frederick (1756?–1812)—Garrick Club / the art archive

Cooke, Henry (1788–1868)—photograph © Ulster Museum. Photograph reproduced with the kind permission of the Trustees of the National Museums & Galleries of Northern Ireland

Cooke, Thomas Potter (1786–1864)—photograph by courtesy Sotheby's Picture Library, London

Cooke, Thomas Simpson (1782–1848)—© National Portrait Gallery, London

Cooke, Sir William Fothergill (1806–1879)—Heritage Images Partnership

Cookson, Dame Catherine Ann (1906–1998)—© National Portrait Gallery, London

Cookson, Henry Wilkinson (1810–1876)—Master and Fellows of Peterhouse, Cambridge

Coomaraswamy, Ananda Kentish (1877–1947)—by permission of the Geological Society of London

Cooper, Anthony Ashley, first earl of Shaftesbury (1621–1683)—Collection Trustees of the Shaftesbury Estates; © reserved in the photograph

Cooper, Anthony Ashley, third earl of Shaftesbury (1671–1713)—© reserved

Cooper, Anthony Ashley-, seventh earl of Shaftesbury (1801–1885)—© National Portrait Gallery, London

Cooper, Sir Astley Paston, first baronet (1768–1841)—reproduced by kind permission of the President and Council of the Royal College of Surgeons of London

Cooper, Bryan Ricco (1884–1930)—© National Portrait Gallery, London

Cooper, Charles Henry (1808–1866)—Cambridgeshire Collection, Cambridge Central Library

Cooper, Diana Olivia Winifred Maud [Lady Diana Cooper], Viscountess Norwich (1892–1986)—by permission of the E. O. Hoppé Trust, Curatorial Assistance, Inc., Los Angeles; collection National Portrait Gallery, London

Cooper, (Alfred) Duff, first Viscount Norwich (1890–1954)—© Man Ray Trust / ADAGP, Paris, and DACS, London, 2004; collection National Portrait Gallery, London

Cooper, Edward (d. 1725)—© National Portrait Gallery, London

Cooper, Dame Gladys Constance (1888–1971)—© Tom Hustler / National Portrait Gallery, London

Cooper, Richard, the elder (bap. 1696?, d. 1764)—Scottish National Portrait Gallery

Cooper, Samuel (1607/8–1672)—The Royal Collection © 2004 HM Queen Elizabeth II

Cooper, Selina Jane (1864–1946)—The Women's Library, London Metropolitan University

Cooper, Susan Vera [Susie] (1902–1995)—© National Portrait Gallery, London

Cooper, Thomas (1759–1839)—© National Portrait Gallery, London

Cooper, Thomas Frederick [Tommy] (1921–1984)—© Michael Dyer; collection National Portrait Gallery, London

Coote, Sir Colin Reith (1893–1979)—© National Portrait Gallery, London

Coote, Sir Eyre (1726–1783)—© National Portrait Gallery, London

Cope, Charles West (1811–1890)—© National Portrait Gallery, London

Copeman, Sydney Arthur Monckton (1862–1947)—© National Portrait Gallery, London

Copleston, Edward (1776–1849)—courtesy of the Provost and Fellows of Oriel College, Oxford; photograph © Studio Edmark

Copleston, Frederick Charles (1907–1994)—photograph reproduced by courtesy of The British Academy

Copley, Esther (1786–1851)—© reserved

Copley, Sir Godfrey, second baronet (c.1653–1709)—© Copyright The British Museum

Copley, John Singleton (1738–1815)—National Portrait Gallery, Smithsonian Institution

Copley, John Singleton, Baron Lyndhurst (1772–1863)—© National Portrait Gallery, London

Coppin, George Selth (1819–1906)—La Trobe Picture Collection, State Library of Victoria

Coral, Joseph (1904–1996)—© News International Newspapers Ltd

Coram, Thomas (c.1668–1751)—Coram Foundation, Foundling Museum, London / Bridgeman Art Library

Corbet, Matthew Ridley (1850–1902)—© National Portrait Gallery, London

Corbett, Edward James (1875–1955)—The British Museum

Corbett, Harry (1918–1989)—© National Portrait Gallery, London

Corbett, Richard (1582–1635)—Christ Church, Oxford

Corbett, William (bap. 1680?, d. 1748)—© Copyright The British Museum

Corder, William (1804–1828)—© National Portrait Gallery, London

Core, Philip McCammon (1951–1989)—© reserved

Cornewall, Folliot Herbert Walker (bap. 1754, d. 1831)—© National Portrait Gallery, London

Cornewall, James (bap. 1698, d. 1744)—© National Portrait Gallery, London

Cornford, Frances Crofts (1886–1960)—© Estate of Sir William Rothenstein / National Portrait Gallery, London

Cornford, Francis Macdonald (1874–1943)—© courtesy the Artist's Estate / Bridgeman Art Library; the Master and Fellows, Trinity College, Cambridge

Cornford, (Rupert) John (1915–1936)—© National Portrait Gallery, London

Cornforth, Fanny [Sarah Cox] (1835–c.1906)—Ashmolean Museum, Oxford

Cornish, Sir Samuel, baronet (c.1715–1770)—in the collection of T. Fenton

Cornish, Vaughan (1862–1948)—The Royal Geographical Society, London

Cornwall, Sir James Handyside Marshall- (1887–1985)—© National Portrait Gallery, London

Cornwallis, Charles, first Marquess Cornwallis (1738–1805)—© National Portrait Gallery, London

Cornwallis, Frederick (1713–1783)—reproduced by kind permission of His Grace the Archbishop of Canterbury and the Church Commissioners: Photographic Survey, Courtauld Institute of Art, London

Cornwallis, Sir Thomas (1518/19–1604)—© Crown copyright / Photograph English Heritage Photo Library / NMR

Cornwallis, Sir William (1744–1819)—private collection. Photograph: Photographic Survey, Courtauld Institute of Art, London

Cornwell, John Travers (1900–1916)—The Imperial War Museum, London

Corry, Montagu William Lowry, Baron Rowton (1838–1903)—National Trust Photographic Library / John Hammond

Cory, William Johnson (1823–1892)—© National Portrait Gallery, London

Cosgrave, William Thomas (1880–1965)—by courtesy of Felix Rosenstiel's Widow & Son Ltd., London, on behalf of the Estate of Sir John Lavery; courtesy the Hugh Lane Municipal Gallery of Modern Art, Dublin

Cosin, John (1595–1672)—by kind permission of the Lord Bishop of Durham and the Church Commissioners of England. Photograph: Photographic Survey, Courtauld Institute of Art, London

Costa, Sir Michael Andrew Angus (1808–1884)—© National Portrait Gallery, London

Cosway, Baroness Maria Louisa Catherine Cecilia (1760–1838)—© National Portrait Gallery, London

Cosway, Richard (bap. 1742, d. 1821)—© National Portrait Gallery, London

Cotman, John Sell (1782–1842)—V&A Images, The Victoria and Albert Museum

Cotter, Patrick (1760/61–1806)—© National Portrait Gallery, London

Cottington, Francis, first Baron Cottington (1579?–1652)—© National Portrait Gallery, London

Cotton, Sir Arthur Thomas (1803–1899)—© National Portrait Gallery, London

Cotton, Charles (1630–1687)—® reserved

Cotton, Sir Charles, fifth baronet (1753–1812)—© Copyright The British Museum

Cotton, George Edward Lynch (1813–1866)—© National Portrait Gallery, London

Cotton, (Thomas) Henry (1907–1987)—© National Portrait Gallery, London

Cotton, Richard Lynch (1794–1880)—© National Portrait Gallery, London

Cotton, Sir Robert Bruce, first baronet (1571–1631)—© Copyright The British Museum

Cotton, Stapleton, first Viscount Combermere (1773–1865)—© National Portrait Gallery, London

Cotton, William Edward [Billy] (1899–1969)—Karsh / Camera Press

Couch, Sir Arthur Thomas Quiller- (1863–1944)—Collection Jesus College, Cambridge

Couch, Sir Richard (1817–1905)—© National Portrait Gallery, London

Coulshed, Dame (Mary) Frances (1904-1998)—© National Portrait Gallery, London

Coulson, Charles Alfred (1910–1974)—Godfrey Argent Studios / Royal Society

Coulton, George Gordon (1858–1947)—© National Portrait Gallery, London

Couper, Archibald Scott (1831–1892)—reproduced courtesy of the Library and Information Centre, Royal Society of Chemistry

Courtauld, Samuel (1876–1947)—© reserved; unknown collection; photograph National Portrait Gallery, London

Courtenay, Henry Reginald (1741–1803)—Christie's Images Ltd. (2004)

Courtenay, William (1341/2–1396)—by kind permission of the Dean and Chapter of Canterbury; photographer: Mrs Mary Tucker

Courtenay, William Reginald, eleventh earl of Devon (1807–1888)—private collection. Photograph: Photographic Survey, Courtauld Institute of Art, London

Courtneidge, Dame (Esmerelda) Cicely (1893–1980)—© National Portrait Gallery, London

Courtney, Catherine, Lady Courtney of Penwith (1847–1929)—© National Portrait Gallery, London

Courtney, Dame Kathleen D'Olier (1878–1974)—© National Portrait Gallery, London

Courtney, Leonard Henry, Baron Courtney of Penwith (1832–1918)—© National Portrait Gallery, London

Cousins, Samuel (1801–1887)—© National Portrait Gallery, London

Coutts, Angela Georgina Burdett-, *suo jure* Baroness Burdett-Coutts (1814–1906)—© National Portrait Gallery, London

Coutts, Thomas (1735–1822)—Coutts & Co.

Coventry [Gunning], Maria, countess of Coventry (*bap.* 1732, *d.* 1760)—Rijksprentenkabinet, Rijksmuseum, Amsterdam

Cowan, Sir John, baronet (1814–1900)—© National Portrait Gallery, London

Cowan, John Anthony (1929–1979)—© Allan Ballard / Scope Features; collection National Portrait Gallery, London

Cowan, Sir Walter Henry, baronet (1871–1956)—© National Portrait Gallery, London

Coward, Sir Noël Peirce (1899–1973)—© Tom Hustler / National Portrait Gallery, London

Cowdrey, (Michael) Colin, Baron Cowdrey of Tonbridge (1932–2000)—© News International Newspapers Ltd

Cowen, Joseph (1829–1900)—© National Portrait Gallery, London

Cowie, James (1886–1956)—© reserved; courtesy of the University of Edinburgh's Collections

Cowley, Abraham (1618–1667)—© National Portrait Gallery, London

Cowling, Thomas George (1906–1990)—© Royal Astronomical Society Library

Cowper, Francis Thomas de Grey, seventh Earl Cowper (1834–1905)—© National Portrait Gallery, London

Cowper, George Nassau Clavering, third Earl Cowper (1738–1789)—private collection. Photograph: The Paul Mellon Centre for Studies in British Art

Cowper, Henry (*c.*1753–1840)—V&A Images, The Victoria and Albert Museum

Cowper, Mary, Countess Cowper (1685–1724)—private collection. Photograph: The Paul Mellon Centre for Studies in British Art

Cowper, Spencer (1670–1728)—courtesy of the Provost and Fellows of Oriel College, Oxford

Cowper, William, first Earl Cowper (1665–1723)—© National Portrait Gallery, London

Cowper, William (1666/7–1710)—reproduced by kind permission of the President and Council of the Royal College of Surgeons of London

Cowper, William (1731–1800)—© National Portrait Gallery, London

Cox, Sir Christopher William Machell (1899–1982)—© National Portrait Gallery, London

Cox, David (1783–1859)—Birmingham Museums & Art Gallery

Cox, Sir Percy Zachariah (1864–1937)—© National Portrait Gallery, London

Cox, Richard (*c.*1500–1581)—Trinity Hall, Cambridge; photograph © National Portrait Gallery, London

Cox, Sir Richard, first baronet (1650–1733)—by courtesy of the National Gallery of Ireland

Coxe, Henry Octavius (1811–1881)—© National Portrait Gallery, London

Crabbe, George (1754–1832)—© National Portrait Gallery, London

Crabtree, Shirley [Big Daddy] (1930–1997)—Mirror Syndication International

Crace, Frederick (1779–1859)—private collection; © reserved in the photograph

Crackanthorpe, Hubert Montague (1870–1896)—© National Portrait Gallery, London

Cradock, Sir Christopher George Francis Maurice (1862–1914)—Getty Images – Hulton Archive

Cradock, Phyllis Nan Sortain [Fanny] (1909–1994)—© reserved; The Independent; photograph National Portrait Gallery, London

Craggs, James, the elder (*bap.* 1657, *d.* 1721)—© National Portrait Gallery, London

Craig, Edith Ailsa Geraldine (1869–1947)—© National Portrait Gallery, London

Craig, Edward Anthony (1905–1998)—© News International Newspapers Ltd

Craig, (Edward Henry) Gordon (1872–1966)—© National Portrait Gallery, London

Craig, James, first Viscount Craigavon (1871–1940)—© National Portrait Gallery, London

Craig, Sir James Henry (1748–1812)—McCord Museum of Canadian History, Montreal (M389)

Craig, John (*d.* 1655)—Scottish National Portrait Gallery

Craig, Sir John (1874–1957)—© National Portrait Gallery, London

Craigie, Pearl (1867–1906)—© National Portrait Gallery, London

Craigie, Sir Robert Leslie (1883–1959)—© reserved

Craigie, Sir William Alexander (1867–1957)—© Harold Speed / courtesy of the Provost and Fellows of Oriel College, Oxford; photograph © Studio Edmark

Craik, Sir Henry, first baronet (1846–1927)—© National Portrait Gallery, London

Cramb, John Adam (1861–1913)—A & C Black Ltd / © reserved

Cramer, Johann Baptist (1771–1858)—© National Portrait Gallery, London

Cramer, Wilhelm (*bap.* 1746, *d.* 1799)—© National Portrait Gallery, London

Cramp, Concemore Thomas Thwaites (1876–1933)—by permission of the People's History Museum

Crampton, Thomas Russell (1816–1888)—Heritage Images Partnership

Crane, Thomas (1808–1859)—© National Portrait Gallery, London

Crane, Walter (1845–1915)—© National Portrait Gallery, London